13632

13.00

Becky Walker
1021 Eigenmann
337-3038

2513

University Casebook Series

ACCOUNTING AND THE LAW, Third Edition (1964), with Problem Pamphlet

The late James L. Dohr, Director, Institute of Accounting, Columbia University,

Ellis L. Phillips, Jr., Professor of Law, Columbia University.

George C. Thompson, Professor, Columbia University Graduate School of Business, and

William C. Warren, Dean of the Law School, Columbia University.

ACCOUNTING, LAW AND (1949)

Donald Schapiro, Instructor in Law, Yale University, and

Ralph Wienshienk, Visiting Lecturer in Law, Yale University.

ACCOUNTING, MATERIALS ON, (1959), with 1968 Supplement

Robert Amory, Jr., Esq.,

W. Covington Hardee, Esq., Third Edition by

David R. Herwitz, Professor of Law, Harvard University, and

Donald T. Trautman, Professor of Law, Harvard University.

ADMINISTRATIVE LAW, Fourth Edition (1960), with Problems Supplement

Walter Gellhorn, Professor of Law, Columbia University, and

Clark Byse, Professor of Law, Harvard University.

ADMIRALTY (1969)

Jo Desha Lucas, Professor of Law, University of Chicago.

ADMIRALTY (1954)

The late Stanley Morrison, Professor of Law, Stanford University, and

The late George W. Stumberg, Professor of Law, University of Texas.

ADVOCACY, INTRODUCTION TO (1970)

Board of Student Advisers, Harvard Law School.

ANTITRUST LAW (1967), with 1969 Supplement

Harlan M. Blake, Professor of Law, Columbia University

Robert Pitofsky, Professor of Law, New York University.

ARBITRATION (1968)

Shelden D. Elliott, Professor of Law, New York University.

BANKRUPTCY ACT (Annotated) 1967 Edition

The late James Angell MacLachlan, Professor of Law Emeritus, Harvard University.

BIOGRAPHY OF A LEGAL DISPUTE, THE: An Introduction to American Civil Procedure (1968)

Marc A. Franklin, Professor of Law, Stanford University.

BUSINESS ORGANIZATION: EMPLOYMENT—AGENCY—PARTNERSHIP— ATTORNEYS, Third Edition (1965)

Alfred F. Conard, Professor of Law, University of Michigan, and

Robert L. Knauss, Associate Professor of Law, University of Michigan.

BUSINESS ORGANIZATION: CORPORATIONS (1948)

A. A. Berle, Jr., Professor of Law, Columbia University, and

William C. Warren, Dean of the Law School, Columbia University.

BUSINESS PLANNING (1966) with 1969 Problem Supplement

David R. Herwitz, Professor of Law, Harvard University.

CIVIL PROCEDURE, see Procedure

COMMERCIAL AND INVESTMENT PAPER, Third Edition (1964) with Statutory Materials

Roscoe T. Steffen, Professor of Law, University of California, Hastings College of the Law.

COMMERCIAL LAW, CASES & MATERIALS ON, Second Edition (1968) with Statutory Supplement

E. Allan Farnsworth, Professor of Law, Columbia University.

John Honnold, Professor of Law, University of Pennsylvania.

COMMERCIAL PAPER (1968), with Statutory Supplement

E. Allan Farnsworth, Professor of Law, Columbia University.

COMMERCIAL PAPER AND BANK DEPOSITS AND COLLECTIONS (1967) with Statutory Supplement

William D. Hawkland, Dean of the Law School, State University of New York at Buffalo.

COMMERCIAL TRANSACTIONS—Text, Cases and Problems, Fourth Edition (1968)

Robert Braucher, Professor of Law, Harvard University, and

Arthur E. Sutherland, Jr., Professor of Law, Harvard University.

COMPARATIVE LAW, Second Edition (1959)

Rudolf B. Schlesinger, Professor of Law, Cornell University.

CONFLICT OF LAWS, Fifth Edition (1970) with 1967 Supplement

Elliott E. Cheatham, Professor of Law, Vanderbilt University,

Erwin N. Griswold, Solicitor General of the United States,

Willis L. M. Reese, Professor of Law, Columbia University, and

Maurice Rosenberg, Professor of Law, Columbia University.

CONSTITUTIONAL LAW, Third Edition (1968) with Annual Supplement

Edward L. Barrett, Jr., Dean of the Law School, University of California at Davis,

Paul W. Bruton, Professor of Law, University of Pennsylvania, and

John O. Honnold, Professor of Law, University of Pennsylvania.

CONSTITUTIONAL LAW, Eighth Edition (1970)

Gerald Gunther, Professor of law, Stanford University.

Noel T. Dowling, late Professor of Law, Columbia University.

CONTRACT IN CONTEXT (1952)

Addison Mueller, Professor of Law, University of California at Los Angeles.

CONTRACTS, (1965) (Successor Volume to Patterson, Goble & Jones, Cases on Contracts) with Statutory Supplement

Harry W. Jones, Professor of Law, Columbia University.

E. Allan Farnsworth, Professor of Law, Columbia University.

William F. Young, Professor of Law, Columbia University.

CONTRACTS (1970)

Richard E. Speidel, Professor of Law, University of Virginia.

Edward J. Murphy, Professor of Law, University of Notre Dame.

CONTRACTS AND CONTRACT REMEDIES, Fourth Edition (1957)

Harold Shepherd, Professor of Law Emeritus, Stanford University, and

Harry H. Wellington, Professor of Law, Yale University.

CONTRACTS AND CONTRACT REMEDIES, Second Edition (1969)

John P. Dawson, Professor of Law, Harvard University, and

Wm. Burnett Harvey, Dean of the Law School, Indiana University.

CONVEYANCES, Second Edition (1941)

Marion R. Kirkwood, Professor of Law Emeritus, Stanford University.

COPYRIGHT, Unfair Competition, and Other Topics Bearing on the Protection of Literary, Musical, and Artistic Works (1960)

Benjamin Kaplan, Professor of Law, Harvard University, and

Ralph S. Brown, Jr., Professor of Law, Yale University.

CORPORATE REORGANIZATION, with Statutory Supplement (1950)

The late E. Merrick Dodd, Professor of Law, Harvard University, and

DeForest Billyou, Professor of Law, New York University.

CORPORATIONS, Fourth Edition—Unabridged, 1969

William L. Cary, Professor of Law, Columbia University.

CORPORATIONS, Fourth Edition—Abridged (1970)

William L. Cary, Professor of Law, Columbia University.

CREDITORS' RIGHTS, Fifth Edition (1957)

The late John Hanna, Professor of Law Emeritus, Columbia University, and The late James Angell MacLachlan, Professor of Law Emeritus, Harvard University.

CREDITORS' RIGHTS AND CORPORATE REORGANIZATION, Fifth Edition (1957)

The late John Hanna, Professor of Law Emeritus, Columbia University, and The late James Angell MacLachlan, Professor of Law Emeritus, Harvard University.

CREDITORS' RIGHTS AND SECURED TRANSACTIONS, 1967

William E. Hogan, Professor of Law, Cornell University.

William D. Warren, Professor of Law, University of California Los Angeles.

CRIMINAL JUSTICE, THE ADMINISTRATION OF, CASES AND MATERIALS ON, Second Edition (1969)

Francis C. Sullivan, Professor of Law, Louisiana State University.
Paul Hardin III, Professor of Law, Duke University.
John Huston, Professor of Law, University of Washington.
Frank R. Lacy, Professor of Law, University of Oregon.
Daniel E. Murray, Professor of Law, University of Miami.
George W. Pugh, Professor of Law, Louisiana State University.

CRIMINAL JUSTICE, Third Edition, 1968, two volumes: I. Criminal Law, II. Criminal Law Administration

Fred E. Inbau, Professor of Law, Northwestern University,
James R. Thompson, Professor of Law, Northwestern University, and
Claude R. Sowle, President, Ohio University.

CRIMINAL LAW (1969)

Lloyd L. Weinreb, Professor of Law, Harvard University.

CRIMINAL LAW AND ITS ADMINISTRATION (1940), with 1956 Supplement

The late Jerome Michael, Professor of Law, Columbia University, and Herbert Wechsler, Professor of Law, Columbia University.

CRIMINAL LAW AND PROCEDURE, Third Edition (1966)

Rollin M. Perkins, Professor of Law, University of California, Hastings College of the Law.

CRIMINAL PROCESS (1969)

Lloyd L. Weinreb, Professor of Law, Harvard University.

DAMAGES, Second Edition (1952)

The late Charles T. McCormick, Professor of Law, University of Texas, and William F. Fritz, Professor of Law, University of Texas.

DECEDENTS' ESTATES AND TRUSTS, Third Edition (1967)

John Ritchie III, Dean and Professor of Law, Northwestern University,
Neill H. Alford, Jr., Professor of Law, University of Virginia, and
Richard W. Effland, Professor of Law, Arizona State University.

DECEDENTS' ESTATES AND TRUSTS (1968)

Howard R. Williams, Professor of Law, Stanford University.

DOMESTIC RELATIONS, Fourth Edition (1961), with Statutory Supplement

Albert C. Jacobs, President, Trinity College, and
Julius Goebel, Jr., Professor of Law Emeritus, Columbia University.

DOMESTIC RELATIONS—Civil and Canon Law (1963)

Philip A. Ryan, Professor of Law, Georgetown University, and
Dom David Granfield, Associate Professor, Catholic University of America.

DYNAMICS OF AMERICAN LAW, THE: Courts, the Legal Process and Freedom of Expression (1968)

Marc A. Franklin, Professor of Law, Stanford University.

EQUITY, Fifth Edition (1967)
> The late Zechariah Chafee, Jr., Professor of Law, Harvard University, and Edward D. Re, Professor of Law, St. John's University.

EQUITY, RESTITUTION AND DAMAGES (1969)
> Robert Childres, Professor of Law, Northwestern University.

ETHICS, see Legal Profession

EVIDENCE (1968) with 1969 Supplement
> David W. Louisell, Professor of Law, University of California, Berkeley,
> John Kaplan, Professor of Law, Stanford University,
> Jon R. Waltz, Professor of Law, Northwestern University.

EVIDENCE, Fifth Edition (1965) with 1970 Supplement
> John M. Maguire, Professor of Law Emeritus, Harvard University.
> Jack B. Weinstein, Professor of Law, Columbia University.
> James H. Chadbourn, Professor of Law, Harvard University.
> John H. Mansfield, Professor of Law, Harvard University.

EVIDENCE (1968)
> Francis C. Sullivan, Professor of Law, Louisiana State University,
> Paul Hardin, III, Professor of Law, Duke University.

FEDERAL COURTS, Fifth Edition (1970)
> The late Charles T. McCormick, Professor of Law, University of Texas,
> James H. Chadbourn, Professor of Law, Harvard University, and
> Charles Alan Wright, Professor of Law, University of Texas.

FEDERAL COURTS AND THE FEDERAL SYSTEM (1953)
> The late Henry M. Hart, Jr., Professor of Law, Harvard University and
> Herbert Wechsler, Professor of Law, Columbia University.

FEDERAL RULES OF CIVIL PROCEDURE, 1968 Edition

FEDERAL TAXATION, see Taxation

FREE ENTERPRISE AND ECONOMIC ORGANIZATION, Third Edition (1966)
two volumes: I.   Concentration & Restrictive Practices, II.   Regulation of Entry, Rates and Discrimination
> Louis B. Schwartz, Professor of Law, University of Pennsylvania.

FUTURE INTERESTS AND ESTATE PLANNING (1961) with 1962 Supplement
> W. Barton Leach, Professor of Law, Harvard University, and
> James K. Logan, Dean of the Law School, University of Kansas.

FUTURE INTERESTS (1958)
> The late Philip Mechem, Professor of Law Emeritus, University of Pennsylvania.

INSURANCE, Fourth Edition (1961)
> The late Edwin W. Patterson, Professor of Law, Columbia University, and
> William F. Young, Professor of Law, Columbia University.

INTERNATIONAL LAW, See also Transnational Legal Problems and United Nations Law

INTERNATIONAL TRADE AND INVESTMENT, REGULATION OF (1970)
> Carl H. Fulda, Professor of Law, University of Texas,
> Warren F. Schwartz, Professor of Law, University of Texas.

INTERNATIONAL TRANSACTIONS AND RELATIONS (1960)
> Milton Katz, Professor of Law, Harvard University, and
> Kingman Brewster, Jr., President, Yale University.

INTRODUCTION TO THE STUDY OF LAW (1970)
> E. Wayne Thode, Professor of Law, University of Utah.
> J. Leon Lebowitz, Professor of Law, University of Texas.
> Lester J. Mazor, Professor of Law, University of Utah.

INTRODUCTION TO LAW, see also Legal Method, also On Law In Courts, also Dynamics of American Law

JUDICIAL CODE: Rules of Procedure in the Federal Courts with Excerpts from the Criminal Code, 1968 Edition

The late Henry M. Hart, Jr., Professor of Law, Harvard University, and Herbert Wechsler, Professor of Law, Columbia University.

JURISPRUDENCE (Temporary Edition Hard Bound) (1949)

Lon L. Fuller, Professor of Law, Harvard University.

JUVENILE COURTS (1967)

Hon. Orman W. Ketcham, Juvenile Court of the District of Columbia.
Monrad G. Paulsen, Dean of the Law School, University of Virginia.

LABOR LAW, Seventh Edition 1969 with Statutory Supplement

Archibald Cox, Professor of Law, Harvard University, and
Derek C. Bok, Dean of the Law School, Harvard University.

LABOR LAW (1968) with Statutory Supplement

Clyde W. Summers, Professor of Law, Yale University.
Harry H. Wellington, Professor of Law, Yale University.

LABOR RELATIONS (1949)

The late Harry Shulman, Dean of the Law School, Yale University, and
Neil Chamberlain, Professor of Economics, Columbia University.

LEGAL DRAFTING (1951)

Robert N. Cook, Professor of Law, University of Cincinnati.

LEGAL METHOD, Second Edition (1952)

Noel T. Dowling, late Professor of Law, Columbia University,
The late Edwin W. Patterson, Professor of Law, Columbia University, and
Richard R. B. Powell, Professor of Law, University of California, Hastings College of the Law.
Second Edition by Harry W. Jones, Professor of Law, Columbia University.

LEGAL METHODS (1969)

Robert N. Covington, Professor of Law, Vanderbilt University,
E. Blythe Stason, Professor of Law, Vanderbilt University,
John W. Wade, Dean of Law School, Vanderbilt University,
Elliott E. Cheatham, Professor of Law, Vanderbilt University,
Theodore A. Smedley, Professor of Law, Vanderbilt University.

LEGAL PROFESSION (1970)

Samuel D. Thurman, Dean of the College of Law, University of Utah.
Ellis L. Phillips, Jr., Professor of Law, Columbia University.
Elliott E. Cheatham, Professor of Law, Vanderbilt University.

LEGISLATION, Second Edition (1959)

Horace E. Read, Vice President, Dalhousie University.
John W. MacDonald, Professor of Law, Cornell Law School, and
Jefferson B. Fordham, Dean of the Law School, University of Pennsylvania.

LOCAL GOVERNMENT LAW (1949)

Jefferson B. Fordham, Dean of the Law School, University of Pennsylvania.

MODERN REAL ESTATE TRANSACTIONS, Second Edition (1958)

Allison Dunham, Professor of Law, University of Chicago.

MUNICIPAL CORPORATIONS, see Local Government Law

NEGOTIABLE INSTRUMENTS, see Commercial Paper

NEW YORK PRACTICE, Second Edition (1968)

Herbert Peterfreund, Professor of Law, New York University,
Joseph M. McLaughlin, Professor of Law, Fordham University.

OIL AND GAS, Second Edition (1964)

Howard R. Williams, Professor of Law, Stanford University,
Richard C. Maxwell, Dean of the Law School, University of California, Los Angeles, and
Charles J. Meyers, Professor of Law, Stanford University.

ON LAW IN COURTS (1965)

Paul J. Mishkin, Professor of Law, University of Pennsylvania.
Clarence Morris, Professor of Law, University of Pennsylvania.

OWNERSHIP AND DEVELOPMENT OF LAND (1965)
>Jan Krasnowiecki, Professor of Law, University of Pennsylvania.

PATENT, TRADEMARK AND COPYRIGHT LAW (1959)
>E. Ernest Goldstein, Professor of Law, University of Texas.

PLEADING & PROCEDURE: STATE AND FEDERAL, Second Edition (1968)
>David W. Louisell, Professor of Law, University of California, Berkeley, and
>Geoffrey C. Hazard, Jr., Professor of Law, University of Chicago.

PROCEDURE—Biography of a Legal Dispute (1968)
>Marc A. Franklin, Professor of Law, Stanford University.

PROCEDURE—CIVIL PROCEDURE (1961)
>James H. Chadbourn, Professor of Law, Harvard University, and
>A. Leo Levin, Professor of Law, University of Pennsylvania.

PROCEDURE—CIVIL PROCEDURE, Temporary Second Edition (1968)
>Richard H. Field, Professor of Law, Harvard University, and
>Benjamin Kaplan, Professor of Law, Harvard University.

PROCEDURE—CIVIL PROCEDURE, Second Edition (1970)
>Maurice Rosenberg, Professor of Law, Columbia University,
>Jack B. Weinstein, Professor of Law, Columbia University.
>Hans Smit, Professor of Law, Columbia University.

PROCEDURE—FEDERAL RULES OF CIVIL PROCEDURE, 1968 edition

PROCEDURE PORTFOLIO (1962)
>James H. Chadbourn, Professor of Law, Harvard University, and
>A. Leo Levin, Professor of Law, University of Pennsylvania.

PRODUCTS AND THE CONSUMER: Defective and Dangerous Products (1970)
>W. Page Keeton, Dean of the School of Law, University of Texas,
>Marshall S. Shapo, Professor of Law, University of Texas.

PROPERTY, Second Edition (1966)
>John E. Cribbet, Dean of the Law School, University of Illinois,
>William F. Fritz, Professor of Law, University of Texas, and
>Corwin W. Johnson, Professor of Law, University of Texas.

PROPERTY—PERSONAL (1953)
>The late S. Kenneth Skolfield, Professor of Law Emeritus, Boston University.

PROPERTY—PERSONAL, Third Edition (1954)
>Everett Fraser, Dean of the Law School Emeritus, University of Minnesota
>—Third Edition by
>Charles W. Taintor II, late Professor of Law, University of Pittsburgh.

PROPERTY—REAL—INTRODUCTION, Third Edition (1954)
>Everett Fraser, Dean of the Law School Emeritus, University of Minnesota.

PROPERTY—REAL PROPERTY AND CONVEYANCING (1954)
>Edward E. Bade, late Professor of Law, University of Minnesota.

PROPERTY, REAL, PROBLEMS IN (Pamphlet) (1969)
>Edward H. Rabin, Professor of Law, University of California, Davis

PUBLIC UTILITY LAW, see Free Enterprise, also Regulated Industries

RECEIVERSHIP AND CORPORATE REORGANIZATION, see Creditors' Rights

REGULATED INDUSTRIES (1967) with Statutory Supplement
>William K. Jones, Professor of Law, Columbia University.

RESTITUTION, Second Edition (1966)
>John W. Wade, Dean of the Law School, Vanderbilt University.

SALES AND SECURITY, Fourth Edition (1962), with Statutory Supplement
>George G. Bogert, James Parker Hall Professor of Law Emeritus, University of Chicago.
>The late William E. Britton, Professor of Law, University of California, Hastings College of the Law, and
>William D. Hawkland, Dean of the Law School, State University of New York at Buffalo.

SALES AND SALES FINANCING, Third Edition (1968) with Statutory Supplement

John Honnold, Professor of Law, University of Pennsylvania.

SECURITY, Third Edition (1959)

The late John Hanna, Professor of Law Emeritus, Columbia University.

SECURITIES REGULATION, Second Edition (1968) with 1969 Supplement

Richard W. Jennings, Professor of Law, University of California, Berkeley.
Harold Marsh, Jr., Professor of Law, University of California, Los Angeles.

TAXATION, FEDERAL, Sixth Edition (1966) with 1970 Supplement

Erwin N. Griswold, Solicitor General of the United States.

TAXATION, FEDERAL ESTATE AND GIFT, 1961 Edition with 1965 Supplement

William C. Warren, Dean of the Law School, Columbia University, and
Stanley S. Surrey, Professor of Law, Harvard University.

TAXATION, FEDERAL INCOME, 1960 Edition Integrated with 1961 Supplement and a 1964 Supplement

Stanley S. Surrey, Professor of Law, Harvard University, and
William C. Warren, Dean of the Law School, Columbia University.

TORTS, Second Edition (1952)

The late Harry Shulman, Dean of the Law School, Yale University, and
Fleming James, Jr., Professor of Law, Yale University.

TORTS, Fourth Edition (1967)

William L. Prosser, Professor of Law, University of California, Hastings College of the Law, and
The late Young B. Smith, Professor of Law, Columbia University.

TRADE REGULATION, Fourth Edition (1967) with 1970 Supplement

Milton Handler, Professor of Law, Columbia University.

TRADE REGULATION, see Free Enterprise

TRANSNATIONAL LEGAL PROBLEMS (1968) with Documentary Supplement

Henry J. Steiner, Professor of Law, Harvard University,
Detlev F. Vagts, Professor of Law, Harvard University.

TRIAL ADVOCACY (1968)

A. Leo Levin, Professor of Law, University of Pennsylvania,
Harold Cramer, Esq., Member of the Philadelphia Bar. (Maurice Rosenberg, Professor of Law, Columbia University, as consultant).

TRUSTS, Fourth Edition (1967)

George G. Bogert, James Parker Hall Professor of Law Emeritus, University of Chicago.
Dallin H. Oaks, Professor of Law, University of Chicago.

TRUSTS AND SUCCESSION, Second Edition (1968)

George E. Palmer, Professor of Law, University of Michigan.

UNITED NATIONS IN ACTION (1968)

Louis B. Sohn, Professor of Law, Harvard University.

UNITED NATIONS LAW, Second Edition (1967) with Documentary Supplement (1968)

Louis B. Sohn, Professor of Law, Harvard University.

WILLS AND ADMINISTRATION, 5th Edition (1961)

The late Philip Mechem, Professor of Law, University of Pennsylvania, and
The late Thomas E. Atkinson, Professor of Law, New York University.

WORLD LAW, see United Nations Law

University Casebook Series

EDITORIAL BOARD

CASES AND MATERIALS

ON

CONSTITUTIONAL LAW

By

GERALD GUNTHER
Professor of Law, Stanford University

and

NOEL T. DOWLING
Late Harlan Fiske Stone Professor Emeritus of Constitutional Law,
Columbia University

EIGHTH EDITION

Mineola, N. Y.
THE FOUNDATION PRESS, INC.
1970

To
B. G. and E. B. M. D.

PREFACE TO THE EIGHTH EDITION

This edition carries forward the substantial revision begun in the last. The updating of the casebook five years ago provided opportunity for the reshaping of several chapters. The portions relatively untouched then have now been thoroughly revised. Moreover, the rapid and important developments of the last five years have required reexamination as well as updating throughout the entire volume.

This edition includes materials through early April, 1970. The sheer volume of recent developments—reflected in the mounting size of annual supplements—made a new edition essential. And 1970 is an especially good time for new materials: the beginning of the Burger era is surely an apt vantage point to assess the Warren Court's major changes, to examine inchoate trends, and to identify frontier areas.

One of the major innovations of this edition, for example, is chapter 14, "Equal Protection, Old and New: The Expanding Contours of Constitutional Equality." Equal protection was one of the most vital and vigorous areas of Warren Court litigation. Probing of the potential reach of the emerging doctrines should be facilitated by the combining of major cases with extensive analytical notes, questions, and excerpts. Another new chapter, "Separation of Powers: The President, Congress, and the Court," brings together problems of interrelationships and conflicts that have reemerged—from Congressman Adam Clayton Powell's exclusion to the commitment of armed forces in Southeast Asia.

There are significant new departures in the presentation of the more traditional materials as well. The free speech materials, for example, have been expanded, supplemented with analytical notes, and regrouped into two chapters. Chapter 15 explores the core problems, from unlawful advocacy to street demonstrations and symbolic speech; chapter 16 applies those perceptions regarding the central thrust of the First Amendment to a series of additional problems.

Inclusion of the new developments and revision of the old unavoidably yielded a somewhat longer book. In attempting to keep it to manageable size, I have refused to permit editing of cases to degenerate into the gathering of skeletal segments of opinions. The Court's opinions must remain the major focus of constitutional law study, and a fair presentation of the richness and diversity of the Justices' thoughts in the major cases must guard against the misleading simplicity of brief quotations disclosing only a single theme in a prevailing opinion. This edition, moreover, devotes substantially increased space to legislative and historical materials and, especially, to analytical notes. I prefer text notes exploring the major problems (drawing on other scholars' studies where appropriate) to a potpourri of commentators' fragments.

"To the extent this revision promotes critical examination of constitutional problems, much of the credit belongs to Noel T. Dowling and Herbert Wechsler"—so I said in the preface to the last edition, and so I want to reiterate here. I have been much helped as well by valuable comments from some of those who have used the book at other schools, including William Cohen, John H. Ely, Andrew L. Kaufman, Louis Lusky, and especially Frank R. Strong, whose thoughtful, detailed book review of the seventh edition proved a rich source of suggestions in the preparation of the eighth. I have relied heavily on the extraordinary diligence and thoughtful criticisms of Robert L. Bouchier of the third-year class at Stanford. Second-year student Peter D. Bewley also gave valuable assistance. For secretarial aid, I am grateful to Anna Tower of the hospitable staff of the Center for Advanced Study in the Behavioral Sciences, and, above all, to my law school secretary, Bess Hitchcock, who as usual—and with her usual effectiveness—bore the major share of the burden.

GERALD GUNTHER

Stanford, California
May, 1970

PREFACE TO THE SEVENTH EDITION

There have been seven terms of the Supreme Court since the previous edition of this casebook. That is a long time, especially in constitutional law. The Court has never stood still; but, as the increasingly bulky annual supplements have shown, the recent pace has been remarkable even for an institution committed to change as well as continuity.

A new edition, then, has long been needed. My former colleague Herbert Wechsler and I, in consultation with Professor Dowling, began to plan a revision more than three years ago. Other commitments kept us from carrying through our plans. Last fall, I agreed to prepare an edition which would at least incorporate the recent developments and pave the way for the more substantial changes planned by us. Executing that undertaking, I found, provided the opportunity for substantial revision as well as updating.

I have tried to preserve the strengths which have gained the Dowling casebook such wide acceptance for three decades. At the same time, I have made changes in structure and content. Some of the changes carry forward in directions set by earlier editions; others draw upon the outline Herbert Wechsler and I prepared some years ago. Inevitably, I relied heavily upon my own experience with students at Columbia and Stanford and, above all, my own tastes: I have sought to compile the kind of volume I would most enjoy using in class.

The basic tripartite structure of the book—Judicial Function, Federal System and Individual Rights—remains intact. The Table of Contents reflects most of the revisions within that structure. For example, the materials on congressional protection of civil rights, traditionally found in the Individual Rights part, have been moved forward: they are now in the congressional powers chapter, for reasons set forth on page [447]. I have given greater emphasis to statutes and legislative history, as with the Civil Rights Act of 1964 and the Voting Rights Act of 1965. Moreover, I have continued developments begun in the sixth edition: the recasting and expansion of textual notes to provide background, sharpen focus, and promote analysis of a limited number of problems in depth; and the increased use of note headings to aid in the delineation of the issues. See, for example, Chapter [9], "State Taxation and Free Trade."

This edition presents an enlarged content without a substantial increase in pages. To achieve this, I have relied in part on techniques noted in Professor Dowling's preface to the previous edition: the book has been set in new type; the old materials have been thoroughly reexamined; the cases are newly edited; and the notes have been compiled "on a more selective basis" and rewritten "with less emphasis on cumulative illustrations." *

---

* I have been highly selective, too, with regard to bibliographical references. I frequently cite Selected Essays 1938–62 (1963); the reference is to Selected Essays on Constitutional Law 1938–1962 (1963), compiled and edited by a Committee of the Association of American Law Schools.

With the publisher's cooperation, I have been able to include all significant developments through the end of the 1964–65 Term of the Court. The cut-off date was June 15, 1965. Accordingly, it was possible to print not only the important end-of-term decisions but also, for example, the text of the Voting Rights Act of 1965 as adopted by the Senate. All in all, the volume contains 35 decisions of the most recent term: 11 as principal cases; substantial excerpts from 8 more; and discussions of an additional 16 in the notes.

But the expanded content is not solely attributable to recent developments. Throughout the volume, I have added principal cases, notes and historical sketches on earlier eras, in the belief that we must know more of the past to appreciate and evaluate where we are and, perhaps, where we are going. I have, in short, sought to sharpen awareness of historical contexts and developments within the organizational structure of topics.

To the extent this revision promotes critical examination of constitutional problems, much of the credit belongs to Noel T. Dowling and Herbert Wechsler; to the extent grasp falls short of reach, the responsibility is mine. I gratefully acknowledge the devoted and effective secretarial assistance of Mrs. Bess Hitchcock. And I am grateful, too, for the understanding forbearance of the Dean and the members of the faculty of Stanford Law School, who restrained their stimulating sociability and respected my cloistered existence while I was preparing this manuscript.

GERALD GUNTHER

Stanford, California
August, 1965

SUMMARY OF CONTENTS

PART I

THE JUDICIAL FUNCTION IN CONSTITUTIONAL CASES

PART II

THE STRUCTURE OF GOVERNMENT: NATION AND STATES IN THE FEDERAL SYSTEM

PART III

INDIVIDUAL RIGHTS

xix

SUMMARY OF CONTENTS

TABLE OF CONTENTS

PART I

THE JUDICIAL FUNCTION IN CONSTITUTIONAL CASES

CHAPTER 2.   SUPREME COURT REVIEW IN OPERATION—Cont'd

PART II

THE STRUCTURE OF GOVERNMENT: NATION AND STATES IN THE FEDERAL SYSTEM

TABLE OF CONTENTS

CHAPTER 4. THE COMMERCE POWER—Continued

TABLE OF CONTENTS

TABLE OF CONTENTS

TABLE OF CONTENTS

PART III

INDIVIDUAL RIGHTS

xliv

TABLE OF CONTENTS

TABLE OF CONTENTS

1

TABLE OF CONTENTS

TABLE OF CONTENTS

TABLE OF CONTENTS

•

TABLE OF CASES

The principal cases are in italic type.   Other cases discussed are in roman type.   References are to pages.

TABLE OF CASES

CASES AND MATERIALS ON
CONSTITUTIONAL LAW

Part I

THE JUDICIAL FUNCTION IN CONSTITUTIONAL CASES

Chapter 1

THE NATURE AND SOURCES OF THE SUPREME COURT'S AUTHORITY

Introduction. Constitutional law courses and materials emphasize Supreme Court decisions. But the Supreme Court is not the only court authorized to examine constitutional claims, and courts are not the only forums for significant constitutional debates. In the cases that follow, only a very few passages of the constitutional text get extensive scrutiny: the few words about judicial power in Article III; the allocations of legislative powers found especially in Article I, Section 8; the individual rights guarantees in the Bill of Rights and the post-Civil War Amendments. Yet many of the other provisions significantly affect the operations of constitutional government: those dealing with selection and structure of Presidency and Congress are obvious illustrations. And some provisions (that on impeachment, for instance) have given rise to major constitutional controversies that have not reached the courts.

Yet more than pedagogical tradition supports the emphasis on the Supreme Court. On those questions that do get to court, the Supreme Court's last word makes it obviously the most important judicial voice. And a remarkable range of constitutional questions *have* reached the Court: the 400 volumes of reports of a Court increasingly preoccupied with constitutional questions are no doubt the richest source of constitutional law.

It is traditional, too, to begin the examination of constitutional law problems with opinions from the Court presided over by Chief Justice John Marshall early in the Nineteenth Century. Thus Part I of this book begins with Marbury v. Madison and Martin v. Hunter's Lessee as principal cases; Part II, with McCulloch v. Maryland and Gibbons v. Ogden. Attention to Marshall Court cases is more than a ritualistic bow to historical landmarks: the reason is not simply that those cases were important in the development of judicial authority and federal power allocations; it is also that those cases of the early 1800s—much more so than many of the decisions of intervening years—are important *now*.

1

So it is with Marbury v. Madison. Some attention to it would be justified if it represented no more than the historical fact of the Court's first elaborate statement of its judicial review powers. But the extensive concern with Marbury here would not be warranted if it were merely a closed, albeit important, book. Instead, Marbury is very much alive: it rests on reasoning significant for the exercise of judicial power today.

To what extent, for example, is the authority asserted in Marbury simply an incidental by-product of the ordinary judicial function in deciding lawsuits: to look to the governing law, to consider the Constitution as one relevant source of law—and, in cases of conflicting legal statements, to give priority to the Constitution and to refuse enforcement of any contravening legal statement? To what extent does the Marbury authority rest instead on a claim that the Constitution thrust a more extraordinary mission upon the Supreme Court? Was the Court endowed with a roving commission to police the other branches—a charge to be the overseeing guardian of constitutional norms, to be the special enforcer of constitutional restrictions? In the proper reading of Marbury, in the answer to these questions, may lie answers to many of the questions of Part I of this book: May Congress curtail the Court's constitutional business? May the Court intervene in all constitutional disputes? Should it? Must it? When is resort to the Court appropriate? When permissible? Who may obtain answers to his constitutional questions from the Court? When? As to what questions?

Understanding the core reasoning of Marbury, then, is essential to thinking about Court power today. And appreciation of the Marbury reasoning in turn requires some attention to historical antecedents and context. The assertions of the power, and the justifications for it, did not spring full-blown in 1803: they reflected a variety of earlier developments, some directly relevant, some tangentially so. And it was only because a concrete dispute had been brought to the Court that John Marshall had an opportunity to speak about judicial power. To develop these themes of intellectual and political history, as well as to explore a number of issues opened up by Marbury, is the purpose of the materials that follow the case.

MARBURY v. MADISON

1 Cranch * 137, 2 L.Ed. 60 (1803).

On Petition for Mandamus.

[William Marbury was one of those named a justice of the peace for the District of Columbia at the very close of the Federalist Administration

---

* 1 Cranch was the first volume devoted wholly to the reports of cases in the Supreme Court, and it was not published until 1804. The 1790s cases were reported by A. J. Dallas in volumes which also covered Pennsylvania decisions. In 1816 Congress made provision for an official reporter. Henry Wheaton of New York was the first incumbent. He was succeeded in 1827 by Richard Peters, Jr., with whom he became involved in litigation, Wheaton v. Peters, 8 Pet. 591 (1834), on wheth-er a reporter "has or can have any copyright in the written opinions delivered by this Court." Wheaton lost. In 1884 it was announced (108 U.S. vi) that it "is the custom of the Court to cite decisions reported since Wallace only by the number in the official series, as '91 U.S.,' '92 U.S.,' &c." Up to 91 U.S. the reporters, and number of volumes for each, were as follows: Dallas, 4; Cranch, 9; Wheaton, 12; Peters, 16; Howard, 24; Black, 2; Wallace, 23.

of President John Adams, during that rash of last minute judicial appointments in March 1801 described in the historical note which follows this case. The incoming Jefferson Administration decided to disregard those appointments for which formal commissions had not been delivered before the end of Adams' term. Marbury and some disappointed colleagues then decided to go directly to the Supreme Court of the United States, in the December term 1801, to compel Jefferson's Secretary of State Madison to deliver their commissions. The Court was not able to decide on their 1801 request until February 1803. Before printing the opinion, the reporter summarized the earlier proceedings briefly. His paragraph is reprinted here both to clarify the technical posture of the case and to dramatize (by adding some proper names in brackets) the involvement of John Marshall in the underlying dispute.]

At the last term, viz., December term, 1801, William Marbury, Dennis Ramsay, Robert Townsend Hooe, and William Harper, by their counsel, Charles Lee, Esq., late attorney general of the United States, severally moved the court for a rule to James Madison, Secretary of State of the United States, to show cause why a mandamus should not issue commanding him to cause to be delivered to them respectively their several commissions as justices of the peace in the District of Columbia. This motion was supported by affidavits [including one by John Marshall's brother James] of the following facts: that notice of this motion had been given to Mr. Madison; that Mr. Adams, the late President of the United States, nominated the applicants to the senate for their advice and consent to be appointed justices of the peace of the District of Columbia; that the senate advised and consented to the appointments; that commissions in due form were signed by the said President appointing them justices, &c.; and that the seal of the United States was in due form affixed to the said commissions by the Secretary of State [John Marshall]; that the applicants have requested Mr. Madison to deliver them their said commissions, who has not complied with that request; and that said commissions are withheld from them . . .. Whereupon a rule was laid to show cause. . . .

Afterwards, on the 24th of February [1803], the following opinion of the Court was delivered by the Chief Justice [John Marshall]:

Opinion of the Court.

At the last term on the affidavits then read and filed with the clerk, a rule was granted in this case, requiring the Secretary of State to show cause why a mandamus should not issue, directing him to deliver to William Marbury his commission as a justice of the peace for the county of Washington, in the District of Columbia.

No cause has been shown, and the present motion is for a mandamus. The peculiar delicacy of this case, the novelty of some of its circumstances, and the real difficulty attending the points which occur in it, require a complete exposition of the principles on which the opinion to be given by the court is founded.

All of the principal cases in this volume, and most of those discussed in the notes, are decisions of the United States Supreme Court. Accordingly, the tribunal is not named in the materials below unless it is a court other than the Supreme Court.

These principles have been, on the side of the applicant, very ably argued at the bar. In rendering the opinion of the court, there will be some departure in form, though not in substance, from the points stated in that argument.

In the order in which the court has viewed this subject, the following questions have been considered and decided:

1st. Has the applicant a right to the commission he demands?

2d. If he has a right, and that right has been violated, do the laws of this country afford him a remedy?

3d. If they do afford him a remedy, is it a mandamus issuing from this court?

The first object of inquiry is—1st. Has the applicant a right to the commission he demands? . . .

It is . . . decidedly the opinion of the court, that when a commission has been signed by the president, the appointment is made; and that the commission is complete, when the seal of the United States has been affixed to it by the secretary of state. . . .

Mr. Marbury, then, since his commission was signed by the president, and sealed by the secretary of state, was appointed; and as the law creating the office, gave the officer a right to hold for five years, independent of the executive, the appointment was not revocable, but vested in the officer legal rights, which are protected by the laws of his country.

To withhold his commission, therefore, is an act deemed by the court not warranted by law, but violative of a vested legal right.

This brings us to the second inquiry; which is: 2dly. If he has a right, and that right has been violated, do the laws of his country afford him a remedy?

The very essence of civil liberty certainly consists in the right of every individual to claim the protection of the laws, whenever he receives an injury. One of the first duties of government is to afford that protection. . . .

The government of the United States has been emphatically termed a government of laws, and not of men. It will certainly cease to deserve this high appellation, if the laws furnish no remedy for the violation of a vested legal right.

If this obloquy is to be cast on the jurisprudence of our country, it must arise from the peculiar character of the case.

It behooves us, then, to inquire whether there be in its composition any ingredient which shall exempt it from legal investigation, or exclude the injured party from legal redress. . . .

Is it in the nature of the transaction? Is the act of delivering or withholding a commission to be considered as a mere political act, belonging to the executive department alone, for the performance of which entire confidence is placed by our constitution in the supreme executive; and for any misconduct respecting which, the injured individual has no remedy? That there may be such cases is not to be questioned; but that every act of duty, to be performed in any of the great departments of government, constitutes such a case, is not to be admitted. . . .

It follows, then, that the question, whether the legality of an act of the head of a department be examinable in a court of justice or not, must always depend on the nature of that act. . . .

By the constitution of the United States, the President is invested with certain important political powers, in the exercise of which he is to use his own discretion, and is accountable only to his country in his political character, and to his own conscience. To aid him in the performance of these duties, he is authorized to appoint certain officers, who act by his authority and in conformity with his orders.

In such cases, their acts are his acts; and whatever opinion may be entertained of the manner in which executive discretion may be used, still there exists, and can exist, no power to control that discretion. The subjects are political. They respect the nation, not individual rights, and being entrusted to the executive, the decision of the executive is conclusive. The application of this remark will be perceived by adverting to the act of congress for establishing the department of foreign affairs. This officer, as his duties were prescribed by that act, is to conform precisely to the will of the President. He is the mere organ by whom that will is communicated. The acts of such an officer, as an officer, can never be examinable by the courts.

But when the legislature proceeds to impose on that officer other duties; when he is directed peremptorily to perform certain acts; when the rights of individuals are dependent on the performance of those acts; he is so far the officer of the law; is amenable to the laws for his conduct; and cannot at his discretion sport away the vested rights of others.

The conclusion from this reasoning is, that where the heads of departments are the political or confidential agents of the executive, merely to execute the will of the President, or rather to act in cases in which the executive professes a constitutional or legal discretion, nothing can be more perfectly clear than that their acts are only politically examinable. But where a specific duty is assigned by law, and individual rights depend upon the performance of that duty, it seems equally clear that the individual who considers himself injured, has a right to resort to the laws of his country for a remedy. . . .

It is, then, the opinion of the Court [that Marbury has a] right to the commission; a refusal to deliver which is a plain violation of that right, for which the laws of his country afford him a remedy.

It remains to be inquired whether,

3dly. He is entitled to the remedy for which he applies?

This depends on—1st. The nature of the writ applied for; and 2dly. The power of this court.

1st. The nature of the writ. . . .

This writ, if awarded, would be directed to an officer of government, and its mandate to him would be, to use the words of Blackstone, "to do a particular thing therein specified, which appertains to his office and duty, and which the court has previously determined, or at least supposes, to be consonant to right and justice." Or, in the words of Lord MANSFIELD, the applicant, in this case, has a right to execute an office of public concern, and is kept out of possession of that right.

These circumstances certainly concur in this case.

Still, to render the mandamus a proper remedy, the officer to whom it is to be directed, must be one to whom, on legal principles, such writ may be directed; and the person applying for it must be without any other specific and legal remedy.

1st. With respect to the officer to whom it would be directed. The intimate political relation subsisting between the president of the United States and the heads of departments, necessarily renders any legal investigation of the acts of one of those high officers peculiarly irksome, as well as delicate; and excites some hesitation with respect to the propriety of entering into such investigation. Impressions are often received, without much reflection or examination, and it is not wonderful, that in such a case as this, the assertion, by an individual, of his legal claims in a court of justice, to which claims it is the duty of that court to attend, should at first view be considered by some, as an attempt to intrude into the cabinet, and to intermeddle with the prerogatives of the executive.

It is scarcely necessary for the court to disclaim all pretensions to such a jurisdiction. An extravagance, so absurd and excessive, could not have been entertained for a moment. The province of the court is, solely, to decide on the rights of individuals, not to enquire how the executive, or executive officers, perform duties in which they have a discretion. Questions, in their nature political, or which are, by the constitution and laws, submitted to the executive, can never be made in this court.

But, if this be not such a question; if so far from being an intrusion into the secrets of the cabinet, it respects a paper, which, according to law, is upon record, and to a copy of which the law gives a right, on the payment of ten cents; if it be no intermeddling with a subject, over which the executive can be considered as having exercised any control; what is there in the exalted station of the officer, which shall bar a citizen from asserting, in a court of justice, his legal rights, or shall forbid a court to listen to the claim; or to issue a mandamus, directing the performance of a duty, not depending on executive discretion, but on particular acts of congress and the general principles of law?

If one of the heads of departments commits any illegal act, under color of his office, by which an individual sustains an injury, it cannot be pretended that his office alone exempts him from being sued in the ordinary mode of proceeding, and being compelled to obey the judgment of the law. How then can his office exempt him from this particular mode of deciding on the legality of his conduct, if the case be such a case as would, were any other individual the party complained of, authorize the process?

It is not by the office of the person to whom the writ is directed, but the nature of the thing to be done that the propriety or impropriety of issuing a mandamus, is to be determined. Where the head of a department acts in a case, in which executive discretion is to be exercised; in which he is the mere organ of executive will; it is again repeated, that any application to a court to control, in any respect, his conduct, would be rejected without hesitation.

But where he is directed by law to do a certain act affecting the absolute rights of individuals, in the performance of which he is not placed under the particular direction of the President, and the performance of which, the President cannot lawfully forbid, and therefore is never presumed to have forbidden; as for example, to record a commission, or a patent for land, which has received all the legal solemnities; or to give a copy of such record; in such cases, it is not perceived on what ground the courts of the country are further excused from the duty of giving judgment, that right be done to an injured individual, than if the same services were to be performed by a person not the head of a department. . . .

This, then, is a plain case for a mandamus, either to deliver the commission, or a copy of it from the record; and it only remains to be enquired,

Whether it can issue from this court.

The act to establish the judicial courts of the United States authorizes the Supreme Court "to issue writs of mandamus in cases warranted by the principles and usages of law, to any courts appointed, or persons holding office, under the authority of the United States." *

The Secretary of State, being a person holding an office under the authority of the United States, is precisely within the letter of the description, and if this court is not authorized to issue a writ of mandamus to such an officer, it must be because the law is unconstitutional, and therefore absolutely incapable of conferring the authority, and assigning the duties which its words purport to confer and assign.

The constitution vests the whole judicial power of the United States in one Supreme Court, and such inferior courts as congress shall, from time to time, ordain and establish. This power is expressly extended to all cases arising under the laws of the United States; and, consequently, in some form, may be exercised over the present case; because the right claimed is given by a law of the United States.

In the distribution of this power it is declared that "the Supreme Court shall have original jurisdiction in all cases affecting ambassadors, other public ministers and consuls, and those in which a state shall be a party. In all other cases, the Supreme Court shall have appellate jurisdiction."

It has been insisted, at the bar, that as the original grant of jurisdiction, to the supreme and inferior courts, is general, and the clause, assigning original jurisdiction to the Supreme Court, contains no negative or restrictive words, the power remains to the legislature, to assign original jurisdiction to that court in other cases than those specified in the article which has

---

* The full text of Section 13 of the Judiciary Act of 1789, 1 Stat. 73: "*And be it further enacted*, That the Supreme Court shall have exclusive jurisdiction of all controversies of a civil nature, where a state is a party, except between a state and its citizens; and except also between a state and citizens of other states, or aliens, in which latter case it shall have original but not exclusive jurisdiction. And shall have exclusively all such jurisdiction of suits or proceedings against ambassadors or other public ministers, or their domestics, or domestic servants, as a court of law can have or exercise consistently with the law of nations; and original, but not exclusive jurisdiction of all suits brought by ambassadors or other public ministers, or in which a consul, or vice consul, shall be a party. And the trial of issues of fact in the Supreme Court in all actions at law against citizens of the United States shall be by jury. *The Supreme Court shall also have appellate jurisdiction from the circuit courts and courts of the several states in the cases hereinafter specially provided for; and shall have power to issue writs of prohibition to the district courts, when proceeding as courts of admiralty and maritime jurisdiction, and writs of mandamus, in cases warranted by the principles and usages of law, to any courts appointed, or persons holding office, under the authority of the United States.*" [Emphasis added.]

been recited; provided those cases belong to the judicial power of the United States.

If it had been intended to leave it in the discretion of the legislature to apportion the judicial power between the supreme and inferior courts according to the will of that body, it would certainly have been useless to have proceeded further than to have defined the judicial power, and the tribunals in which it should be vested. The subsequent part of the section is mere surplusage, is entirely without meaning, if such is to be the construction. If congress remains at liberty to give this court appellate jurisdiction, where the constitution has declared their jurisdiction shall be original; and original jurisdiction where the constitution has declared it shall be appellate; the distribution of jurisdiction, made in the constitution, is form without substance.

Affirmative words are often, in their operation, negative of other objects than those affirmed; and in this case, a negative or exclusive sense must be given to them, or they have no operation at all.

It cannot be presumed that any clause in the constitution is intended to be without effect; and, therefore, such a construction is inadmissible, unless the words require it.

If the solicitude of the convention, respecting our peace with foreign powers, induced a provision that the Supreme Court should take original jurisdiction in cases which might be supposed to affect them; yet the clause would have proceeded no further than to provide for such cases, if no further restriction on the powers of congress had been intended. That they should have appellate jurisdiction in all other cases, with such exceptions as congress might make, is no restriction; unless the words be deemed exclusive of original jurisdiction.

When an instrument organizing fundamentally a judicial system, divides it into one supreme, and so many inferior courts as the legislature may ordain and establish; then enumerates its powers, and proceeds so far to distribute them, as to define the jurisdiction of the Supreme Court by declaring the cases in which it shall take original jurisdiction, and that in others it shall take appellate jurisdiction; the plain import of the words seems to be, that in one class of cases its jurisdiction is original, and not appellate; in the other it is appellate, and not original. If any other construction would render the clause inoperative, that is an additional reason for rejecting such other construction, and for adhering to their obvious meaning.

To enable this court, then, to issue a mandamus, it must be shown to be an exercise of appellate jurisdiction, or to be necessary to enable them to exercise appellate jurisdiction.

It has been stated at the bar that the appellate jurisdiction may be exercised in a variety of forms, and that if it be the will of the legislature that a mandamus should be used for that purpose that will must be obeyed. This is true, yet the jurisdiction must be appellate, not original.

It is the essential criterion of appellate jurisdiction, that it revises and corrects the proceedings in a cause already instituted, and does not create that cause. Although, therefore, a mandamus may be directed to courts, yet to issue such a writ to an officer for the delivery of a paper, is in effect the same as to sustain an original action for that paper, and, therefore, seems not to belong to appellate, but to original jurisdiction. Neither is it necessary in such a case as this, to enable the court to exercise its appellate jurisdiction.

The authority, therefore, given to the Supreme Court, by the act establishing the judicial courts of the United States, to issue writs of mandamus to public officers, appears not to be warranted by the constitution; and it becomes necessary to inquire whether a jurisdiction so conferred can be exercised.

The question, whether an act, repugnant to the constitution, can become the law of the land, is a question deeply interesting to the United States; but, happily, not of an intricacy proportioned to its interest. It seems only necessary to recognize certain principles, supposed to have been long and well established, to decide it.

That the people have an original right to establish, for their future government, such principles, as, in their opinion, shall most conduce to their own happiness is the basis on which the whole American fabric has been erected. The exercise of this original right is a very great exertion; nor can it, nor ought it, to be frequently repeated. The principles, therefore, so established, are deemed fundamental. And as the authority from which they proceed is supreme, and can seldom act, they are designed to be permanent.

This original and supreme will organizes the government, and assigns to different departments their respective powers. It may either stop here, or establish certain limits not to be transcended by those departments.

The government of the United States is of the latter description. The powers of the legislature are defined and limited; and that those limits may not be mistaken, or forgotten, the constitution is written. To what purpose are powers limited, and to what purpose is that limitation committed to writing, if these limits may, at any time, be passed by those intended to be restrained? The distinction between a government with limited and unlimited powers is abolished, if those limits do not confine the persons on whom they are imposed, and if acts prohibited and acts allowed, are of equal obligation. It is a proposition too plain to be contested, that the constitution controls any legislative act repugnant to it; or, that the legislature may alter the constitution by an ordinary act.

Between these alternatives there is no middle ground. The constitution is either a superior paramount law, unchangeable by ordinary means, or it is on a level with ordinary legislative acts, and, like other acts, is alterable when the legislature shall please to alter it.

If the former part of the alternative be true, then a legislative act contrary to the constitution is not law: if the latter part be true, then written constitutions are absurd attempts, on the part of the people, to limit a power in is own nature illimitable.

Certainly all those who have framed written constitutions contemplate them as forming the fundamental and paramount law of the nation, and consequently, the theory of every such government must be that an act of the legislature, repugnant to the constitution, is void.

This theory is essentially attached to a written constitution, and is, consequently, to be considered, by this court, as one of the fundamental principles of our society. It is not therefore to be lost sight of in the further consideration of this subject.

If an act of the legislature, repugnant to the constitution, is void, does it, notwithstanding its invalidity, bind the courts, and oblige them to give it effect?   Or, in other words, though it be not law, does it constitute a rule as operative as if it was a law?   This would be to overthrow in fact what was established in theory;   and would seem, at first view, an absurdity too gross to be insisted on.   It shall, however, receive a more attentive consideration.

It is emphatically the province and duty of the judicial department to say what the law is.   Those who apply the rule to particular cases, must of necessity expound and interpret that rule.   If two laws conflict with each other, the courts must decide on the operation of each.

So if a law be in opposition to the constitution;   if both the law and the constitution apply to a particular case, so that the court must either decide that case conformably to the law, disregarding the constitution;   or conformably to the constitution, disregarding the law;   the court must determine which of these conflicting rules governs the case.   This is of the very essence of judicial duty.

If, then, the courts are to regard the constitution, and the constitution is superior to any ordinary act of the legislature, the constitution, and not such ordinary act, must govern the case to which they both apply.

Those, then, who controvert the principle that the constitution is to be considered, in court, as a paramount law, are reduced to the necessity of maintaining that courts must close their eyes on the constitution, and see only the law.

This doctrine would subvert the very foundation of all written constitutions.   It would declare that an act which, according to the principles and theory of our government, is entirely void, is yet, in practice, completely obligatory.   It would declare that if the legislature shall do what is expressly forbidden, such act, notwithstanding the express prohibition, is in reality effectual.   It would be giving to the legislature a practical and real omnipotence, with the same breath which professes to restrict their powers within narrow limits.   It is prescribing limits, and declaring that those limits may be passed at pleasure.

That it thus reduces to nothing what we have deemed the greatest improvement on political institutions—a written constitution—would of itself be sufficient, in America, where written constitutions have been viewed with so much reverence, for rejecting the construction.   But the peculiar expressions of the constitution of the United States furnish additional arguments in favour of its rejection.

The judicial power of the United States is extended to all cases arising under the constitution.

Could it be the intention of those who gave this power, to say that in using it the constitution should not be looked into?   That a case arising under the constitution should be decided without examining the instrument under which it arises?

This is too extravagant to be maintained.

In some cases, then, the constitution must be looked into by the judges. And if they can open it at all, what part of it are they forbidden to read or to obey?

There are many other parts of the constitution which serve to illustrate this subject.   It is declared, that "no tax or duty shall be laid on articles exported from any state." Suppose, a duty on the export of cotton, of tobacco or of flour; and a suit instituted to recover it. Ought judgment to be rendered in such a case? Ought the judges to close their eyes on the constitution, and only see the law?

The constitution declares "that no bill of attainder or ex post facto law shall be passed."

If, however, such a bill should be passed, and a person should be prosecuted under it; must the court condemn to death those victims whom the constitution endeavors to preserve?

"No person," says the constitution, "shall be convicted of treason unless on the testimony of two witnesses to the same overt act, or on confession in open court."

Here the language of the constitution is addressed especially to the courts. It prescribes, directly for them, a rule of evidence not to be departed from. If the legislature should change that rule, and declare *one* witness, or a confession *out* of court, sufficient for conviction, must the constitutional principle yield to the legislative act?

From these, and many other selections which might be made, it is apparent, that the framers of the constitution contemplated that instrument as a rule for the government of *courts,* as well as of the legislature.

Why otherwise does it direct the judges to take an oath to support it? This oath certainly applies in an especial manner, to their conduct in their official character. How immoral to impose it on them, if they were to be used as the instruments, and the knowing instruments, for violating what they swear to support!

Oath of office — Marshall claims supports concept of judicial review

The oath of office, too, imposed by the legislature, is completely demonstrative of the legislative opinion on this subject. It is in these words: "I do solemnly swear that I will administer justice without respect to persons, and do equal right to the poor and to the rich; and that I will faithfully and impartially discharge all the duties incumbent on me as ———, according to the best of my abilities and understanding agreeably to the *constitution* and laws of the United States."

Why does a judge swear to discharge his duties agreeably to the constitution of the United States, if that constitution forms no rule for his government? If it is closed upon him, and cannot be inspected by him?

If such be the real state of things, this is worse than solemn mockery. To prescribe, or to take this oath, becomes equally a crime.

It is also not entirely unworthy of observation, that in declaring what shall be the *supreme* law of the land, the *constitution* itself is first mentioned; and not the laws of the United States generally, but those only which shall be made in *pursuance* of the constitution, have that rank.

*Art VI *

Thus, the particular phraseology of the constitution of the United States confirms and strengthens the principle, supposed to be essential to all written constitutions, that a law repugnant to the constitution is void; and that *courts,* as well as other departments, are bound by that instrument.

The rule must be discharged.

THE HISTORICAL SETTING OF THE MARBURY CASE

1. *The political environment.* a. *Judicial "reform."* The Marbury case was an early manifestation of the clashes between the Jeffersonian Republicans and the Marshall Court. John Marshall, Secretary of State in the Cabinet of lame-duck President John Adams, was nominated as Chief Justice in January 1801 and took his oath of office on February 4, 1801. On February 17, the House of Representatives elected Thomas Jefferson as President. Marshall continued to act as Secretary of State through March 3, 1801, the end of Adams' term. Indeed, he may have stayed on somewhat longer: on March 4, 1801—the day Marshall as Chief Justice administered the oath of office to new President Jefferson—he agreed to comply with Jefferson's request "to perform the duties of Secretary of State until a successor be appointed." Oster, The Political and Economic Doctrines of John Marshall (1914), 182.

Four days before Jefferson's election, the Federalist Congress reorganized the federal judiciary. The Circuit Court Act of February 13, 1801, relieved the Justices of the Supreme Court of circuit-riding duty. In the past, Circuit Courts had been manned by District Court judges and Supreme Court Justices; the 1801 law established sixteen Circuit Court judgeships. The Jeffersonians were indignant: to them, the Circuit Court Act was the defeated Federalists' device to maintain control of one branch of the government. As expected, the new judgeships went to Federalists, for Adams hastily nominated his "midnight judges" during the last two weeks of his term. The Jeffersonian concern went beyond patronage: the partisan enforcement of the Alien and Sedition Laws had been a major target of their attacks in the political warfare that preceded the election of 1800.

Marbury and his co-petitioners were not among the "midnight judges" named pursuant to the Circuit Court Act. Their positions had been created even later: the Organic Act of the District of Columbia was passed on February 27, 1801, less than a week before the end of Adams' term. The Act authorized the President to name justices of the peace for the District. Adams named forty-two justices on March 2, 1801, and the Senate confirmations came on March 3, Adams' last day in office. The commissions of the petitioners in the Marbury case had been signed by Adams—as well as signed and sealed by Acting Secretary of State Marshall—but they had not been delivered by the end of the day; and the new President chose to treat them as a "nullity." As John Marshall wrote two weeks later, "I should . . . have sent out the commissions which had been signed & sealed but for the extreme hurry of the time."

Marshall was therefore intimately acquainted with the facts of the Marbury controversy. Yet the issue of the existence of the commissions was extensively considered in the Court hearing in the Marbury case. For example, an affidavit by James Marshall—John Marshall's brother—was introduced to prove the existence of some of the commissions. (James Marshall stated that he was to deliver a number of the commissions but that, "finding he could not conveniently carry the whole," he returned "several of them" to his brother's office. 1 Cranch, at 146.) In view of his involvement in the controversy, should Marshall have disqualified himself from participation in the decision? Compare Martin v. Hunter's Lessee, p. 32 below, where Mar-

[margin, handwritten:] Critics of Marshall's opinion argue that the weakness of his opinion is that he does not explain why the S Ct should be the body to exercise judicial review. Nowhere in the Constit. does it explicitly state the S Ct has this power. The best argument to be made for this however, was Marshall's Art III argument (P. 11)

shall did not sit because he and his brother James were interested property owners.

The Jeffersonians soon demonstrated that they would not complacently accept Federalist entrenchment in the judiciary: they made repeal of the Circuit Court Act of 1801 an early item of business in the new Congress. The 1801 Act was repealed on March 31, 1802, while the Marbury case was pending in the Supreme Court. The 1802 Act essentially reestablished the old Circuit Court system, with Supreme Court Justices and District Judges once again manning the Circuit Court benches. During these congressional debates, a few Jeffersonians for the first time questioned the Court's authority to consider the constitutionality of congressional acts. There was still another sign of the mounting hostility to the Court: Congress abolished the June and December Terms of the Supreme Court created by the 1801 Act and provided that there would be only one Term, in February. Accordingly, there was no Court session in 1802; the Court that had received Marbury's petition in December 1801 did not reconvene until February 1803.

b. *Impeachment.* The Jeffersonians soon unsheathed a still more potent weapon. Early in 1802, the House voted to impeach Federalist District Judge John Pickering of New Hampshire, and many feared that impeachment of Supreme Court Justices would follow. The choice of Pickering as the first target was a "tragic blunder," however. Pickering, an insane drunkard, was plainly incompetent to serve as a judge, but it took some stretching to convert this into "Treason, Bribery, or other High Crimes and Misdemeanors," as required by Article II, Section 4, of the Constitution. Nevertheless, the Senate voted to remove Pickering from office in March 1804. See Turner, "The Impeachment of John Pickering," 54 Am.Hist.Rev. 485 (1949).

On the day after Pickering's removal, Congress moved on to bigger game: the House impeached Supreme Court Justice Samuel Chase. To the Jeffersonians, Chase was a glaring example of Federalist abuse of judicial office: he had made electioneering statements from the bench in 1800, and he had conducted several vindictive sedition and treason trials. A few months after the Marbury decision, he provided the immediate provocation for his impeachment: in May 1803, in a partisan charge to the federal grand jury in Baltimore, he criticized the repeal of the 1801 Circuit Court Act and the activities of modern "reformers." The Senate trial of Chase was held early in 1805. Were judges impeachable for conduct that did not constitute an indictable offense? The debate was lengthy and important: if the case against Chase succeeded, it was widely expected, John Marshall and other federal judges would be next. But the Senate vote in March 1805 did not produce the constitutional majority necessary to convict Chase. The impeachment weapon was deflated—it was a "farce," "not even a scare-crow," as Jefferson reluctantly concluded. The Jefferson-Marshall dispute continued, but the Court had survived the most critical stage. [See generally I Warren, The Supreme Court in United States History (rev. ed. 1926), III Beveridge, The Life of John Marshall (1919), and Garraty, "The Case of the Missing Commissions," in Quarrels That Have Shaped the Constitution (Garraty ed. 1964).]

2. *Were there alternative grounds of decision?* Most contemporary commentary on the Marbury decision ignored the passages on the authority of

the courts to consider the constitutionality of congressional acts. Attention focused instead on the assertion of the right to examine some executive acts. Was Marshall's opinion a reflection of a "masterful sense of strategy," as is often alleged? Was it a shrewd scheme in which the denial of mandamus avoided an immediate confrontation with the executive and provided a shield for the Court's criticism of Jefferson's behavior—and for its assertion and exercise of judicial review over statutes? See, e. g., McCloskey, The American Supreme Court (1960), 40: "The decision is a masterwork of indirection, a brilliant example of Marshall's capacity to sidestep danger while seeming to court it, to advance in one direction while his opponents are looking in another."

Some critics of Marbury insist that, given Marshall's conclusion, the Court had no business saying any more than that it lacked jurisdiction. Were the opening parts of the opinion, on remedies against executive illegality, unnecessary or inappropriate? Jefferson insisted until the end of his life that most of the opinion was "merely an *obiter* dissertation of the Chief Justice." Jefferson to Justice William Johnson, June 12, 1823, I S. Car.His. & Gen.Mag. 1, 9–10 (1900). Compare the material on avoidance of constitutional questions, chap. 2, p. 159, below.

Other critics have insisted that Marshall could and should have made those important final pages on judicial review unnecessary by resolving the preliminary issues differently. For example, more than the signing and sealing might have been held necessary to complete the appointment, or greater presidential authority regarding appointees might have been recognized. See the material on the Presidential Removal Power, chap. 7, p. 572, below. And a position that mandamus was not available against Cabinet officials was possible. Note the further developments in Kendall v. United States, 12 Pet. 524 (1838), chap. 7, p. 575, below.

Moreover, the Court's interpretations of Section 13 and Article III have come under special attack. Though the specific Marbury holding has held up, Marshall's underlying conception of mutually exclusive categories of original and appellate jurisdiction has not prevailed. Congress may not add to the Court's original jurisdiction; but it may grant lower courts jurisdiction over cases within the constitutional description of Supreme Court original jurisdiction—and cases of that description may then come to the Supreme Court on appeal. For example, Section 13 itself recognized concurrent original jurisdiction in the lower courts, and several Supreme Court justices on circuit had sustained lower court jurisdiction in a foreign consul case as early as 1793, United States v. Ravara, 2 Dall. 297. Years later, the Supreme Court agreed. Bors v. Preston, 111 U.S. 252 (1884); see also Ames v. Kansas, 111 U.S. 449 (1884) (state against citizen of another state). And Marshall himself, in a rare admission, called some of the statements about Article III in Marbury unduly broad when he rejected Virginia's arguments against the Supreme Court's exercise of appellate jurisdiction in a case involving a state. See Cohens v. Virginia, 6 Wheat. 264 (1821), p. 46, below. See generally Powell, Vagaries and Varieties in Constitutional Interpretation (1956), 3–19, and Van Alstyne, "A Critical Guide to Marbury v. Madison," 1969 Duke L.J. 1.*

---

* A few years after Marbury, the Marshall Court also exercised the power   to hold a state statute unconstitutional. In Fletcher v. Peck, 6 Cranch 87

THE LEGITIMACY OF JUDICIAL REVIEW

Introduction. Was the judicial review authority asserted in Marbury v. Madison a usurpation? That question has long sparked controversy. See, e. g., the extensive attack on judicial review in Boudin, Government by Judiciary (1932). And the debate lives. See the elaborate defense of legitimacy in Berger, Congress v. the Supreme Court (1969).

The attackers say that Marshall's own opinion is question-begging and weak; that the Constitution does not explicitly authorize judicial review; that the Framers of the Constitution did not clearly intend to grant that extraordinary power; and that the pre-Convention theories and practices were not sufficiently clear and widespread to provide legitimation. The materials that follow reflect that ongoing debate, with particular emphasis on those aspects that bear on the contemporary justifications as well as historical legitimacy of judicial review. After a brief review of the historical roots of the authority and the Convention debates, there are longer excerpts from two significant early statements bearing on Marshall's reasoning: the most important anticipation of that reasoning, Alexander Hamilton's No. 78 of The Federalist; and the most important judicial attack on Marbury, the Gibson dissent in a Pennsylvania case, Eakin v. Raub. Professor Wechsler's debate with Judge Learned Hand illustrates the continuing controversy regarding the constitutional justification for Marbury—a controversy that bears immediately on contemporary evaluations and exercises of the Supreme Court's power.

1. *Historical antecedents.* Though Marshall's opinion in Marbury talked about general principles and constitutional text, not historical data, efforts to justify judicial review have often provoked explorations of historical roots. Some of the searches have been on rather remote and tangential byways. For example, there has been frequent mention of Lord Coke's famous statement in Dr. Bonham's Case, at 8 Rep. 118a (C.P. 1610), that "the common law will controul acts of Parliament and adjudge them to be utterly void" when the acts are "against common right and reason." But that was hardly descriptive of British practice in the Seventeenth century; by the Eighteenth, it was not even respectable dictum. More in point was the appellate jurisdiction of the Privy Council over colonial courts; but invalidation of legislation through that route was rare and unpopular. The practice of state courts in the years immediately following independence holds the greatest promise as a source of relevant information. But here, too, the examples are few and controversial; and there is doubt that many people at the Convention or in the early national period knew about the scattered actual or alleged examples of judicial invalidation of state legislation such as Holmes v. Walton, a New Jersey case of 1780. For an extensive selection of articles examining antecedents such as these, see Volume

(1810), a case from a lower federal court, a statute of Georgia was held to be in violation of the clause prohibiting the States from passing laws impairing the obligation of contracts. Clerke v. Harwood, 3 Dall. 342 (1797), appears to be the first case in which, on review of the judgment of a state court, a law of a state was held invalid, in that case as in conflict with a treaty; similar results had already been reached in cases from lower federal courts, e. g., Ware v. Hylton, 3 Dall. 199 (1796). Authority to review state court decisions was sustained against Virginia's challenge in Martin v. Hunter's Lessee, the next principal case.

I of Selected Essays on Constitutional Law (1938). See also Berger, Congress v. the Supreme Court (1969), which finds support for judicial review in these precedents even while recognizing their spottiness: he insists, at 46, that the argument does not "hinge upon whether there existed an established *practice* of judicial review, but rather on the Founders' *belief*" that precedents and statements like Coke's supported court enforcement of constitutional limits.

The general spread of ideas conducive to the acceptance of judicial review was in any event probably more important than the existence of specific precedents. A pervasive theme, and one reflected in Marshall's reasoning, was the development of written constitutions, with the assurance of limited government as a major purpose. Constitutionalism was hardly an American invention, but Americans had an unusually extensive experience with basic documents of government, from royal charters to state constitutions and the Articles of Confederation. Yet the constitutional historians who justify judicial review as a natural outgrowth of constitutionalism make an argument that is incomplete. It is possible to have a constitution without having judicial review. There is accordingly a large question-begging element in deriving judicial enforceability simply from the existence of written constitutions: to say that a government cannot exceed its constitutional powers does not demonstrate who is to decide whether there is conflict with the constitution. Viewing a constitution as a species of "law," then, becomes a vital link between constitutionalism and judicial competence to adjudicate constitutional issues. That link, hardly a prominent feature in the political theory of the Revolutionary era, is central in the Marbury opinion.

The background of practices and ideas amply demonstrates that the judicial review authority asserted in Marbury by Marshall was no sudden innovation or single-handed achievement. But the pre-Convention heritage hardly made the 1803 result inevitable. Nor does that heritage clearly tell us what was most important to Marshall when he wrote Marbury: was the emphasis on a Constitution-interpreting function of courts as incidental to their ordinary role, or was there reliance on a special Constitution-enforcing responsibility of courts as enforcers of limits on government? Was the main concern of Marbury the establishment of judicial *competence* to interpret the Constitution—because courts were in the business of deciding legal questions, because the Constitution was law, because Articles III and VI confirmed that the Constitution was a variety of law that might come before the courts? Or was Marshall more concerned with the broader theme of constitutions as an assurance of limited government—and with carving out for courts a role as special guardians of constitutional norms?

2. *The Constitutional Convention.* The Constitution does not explicitly grant the judicial review power asserted in Marbury. That silence has made the legitimacy debate possible. Did the Framers intend to grant the power? Some efforts to demonstrate an original understanding supporting judicial review have relied heavily on Framers' statements not made in Philadelphia in 1787. See Beard, The Supreme Court and the Constitution (1912). But the most persuasive data regarding Framers' intent are of course the Convention debates. See Farrand, The Records of the Federal Convention of 1787 (1911).

The Convention context in which the most important statements regarding judicial power were made was the discussion of the Council of Revision proposal—a proposal that judges join with the President in the veto process. That provision was rejected, partly on grounds supporting the legitimacy of judicial review. According to Madison's Notes, Luther Martin, for example, thought "the association of the Judges with the Executive" a "dangerous innovation": "A knowledge of mankind, and of Legislative Affairs cannot be presumed to belong in a higher degree to the Judges than to the Legislature. And as to the Constitutionality of laws, that point will come before the Judges in their proper official character. In this character they have a negative on the laws. Join them with the Executive in the Revision and they will have a double negative. It is necessary that the Supreme Judiciary should have the confidence of the people. This will soon be lost, if they are employed in the task of remonstrating agst. popular measures of the Legislature." See also Elbridge Gerry's argument that judges should not sit on the Council of Revision because "they will have a sufficient check agst. encroachments on their own department by their exposition of the laws, which involved a power of deciding on their Constitutionality. . . . It was quite foreign from the nature of ye. office to make them judges of the policy of public measures."

An incisive brief survey of the debates concludes: "The grant of judicial power was to include the power, where necessary in the decision of cases, to disregard state or federal statutes found to be unconstitutional. Despite the curiously persisting myth of usurpation, the Convention's understanding on this point emerges from its records with singular clarity." Hart and Wechsler, The Federal Courts and the Federal System (1953), 14. For an argument that courts were only to invalidate congressional acts interfering with judicial operations—and an attack on the accuracy of Madison's Notes—see Crosskey, Politics and the Constitution in the History of the United States (1953); for a criticism of Crosskey's "self-defense" theory, see Berger, Congress v. the Supreme Court (1969), 154–65.

Compare the survey of the historical data on legitimacy in Leonard W. Levy's excellent introduction to a paperback volume of selected essays edited by him, Judicial Review and the Supreme Court (1967). Levy quotes Edward S. Corwin's testimony on the 1937 Court-Packing Plan: "[I]n blunt language he declared, 'The people who say the framers intended [judicial review] are talking nonsense'—to which he hastily added, 'and the people who say they did not intend it are talking nonsense.'" Levy adds: "A close textual and contextual examination of the evidence will not result in an improvement on these propositions." Raoul Berger, however, found support for a more decisive stance: he thought it "reasonably plain" after an extensive review of the debates at the Convention, during ratification, and in the First Congress, that there was "an assumption by the leadership that judicial review would be available to keep Congress within Constitutional 'limits,'" and that "review was part of the Constitutional scheme"; he concluded that "criticism of conventional reliance on the Founders' statements" is "strained and insubstantial." Berger, Congress v. the Supreme Court (1969), 198, 335–36 and chaps. 3–5.

3. *The Federalist Papers.* Support of judicial review far more explicit than anything found in the Convention debates appears in The Federal-

ist. Hamilton, Jay and Madison wrote these newspaper essays in defense and explanation of the proposed Constitution as campaign documents in the ratification battle in New York. They have become the classic commentaries on the Constitution. The papers most directly concerned with the judiciary were five written by Alexander Hamilton, Nos. 78 to 82 of The Federalist. No. 82, for example, supports Supreme Court review of state court decisions, the issue considered in the next principal case. And the most famous, No. 78, contains some striking parallels to—as well as some provocative variations on—the Marbury v. Madison theme.

Hamilton, Federalist No. 78

. . . Whoever attentively considers the different departments of power must perceive, that in a government in which they are separated from each other, the judiciary, from the nature of its functions, will always be the least dangerous to the political rights of the constitution; because it will be least in a capacity to annoy or injure them. The executive not only dispenses the honors, but holds the sword of the community. The legislature not only commands the purse, but prescribes the rules by which the duties and rights of every citizen are to be regulated. The judiciary on the contrary has no influence over either the sword or the purse, no direction either of the strength or of the wealth of the society, and can take no active resolution whatever. It may truly be said to have neither Force nor Will, but merely judgment; and must ultimately depend upon the aid of the executive arm even for the efficacy of its judgments.

This simple view of the matter suggests several important consequences. It proves incontestibly that the judiciary is beyond comparison the weakest of the three departments of power; that it can never attack with success either of the other two; and that all possible care is requisite to enable it to defend itself against their attacks. . . . And it proves, in the last place, . . . that as from the natural feebleness of the judiciary, it is in continual jeopardy of being overpowered, awed or influenced by its coordinate branches; and that as nothing can contribute so much to its firmness and independence, as permanency in office, this quality may therefore be justly regarded as an indispensable ingredient in its constitution; and in a great measure as the citadel of the public justice and the public security.

The complete independence of the courts of justice is peculiarly essential in a limited constitution. By a limited constitution I understand one which contains certain specified exceptions to the legislative authority; such for instance as that it shall pass no bills of attainder, no ex post facto laws, and the like. Limitations of this kind can be preserved in practice no other way than through the medium of the courts of justice; whose duty it must be to declare all acts contrary to the manifest tenor of the constitution void. Without this, all the reservations of particular rights or privileges would amount to nothing.

Some perplexity respecting the right of the courts to pronounce legislative acts void, because contrary to the constitution, has arisen from an imagination that the doctrine would imply a superiority of the judiciary to the legislative power. It is urged that the authority which can declare the acts of another void, must necessarily be superior to the one whose acts may be declared void. As this doctrine is of great importance in all the American constitutions, a brief discussion of the grounds on which it rests cannot be unacceptable.

There is no position which depends on clearer principles, than that every act of a delegated authority, contrary to the tenor of the commission under which it is exercised, is void. No legislative act therefore contrary to the constitution can be valid. To deny this would be to affirm that the deputy is greater than his principal; that the servant is above his master; that the representatives of the people are superior to the people themselves; that men acting by virtue of powers may do not only what their powers do not authorise, but what they forbid.

If it be said that the legislative body are themselves the constitutional judges of their own powers, and that the construction they put upon them is conclusive upon the other departments, it may be answered, that this cannot be the natural presumption, where it is not to be collected from any particular provisions in the constitution. It is not otherwise to be supposed that the constitution could intend to enable the representatives of the people to substitute their *will* to that of their constituents. It is far more rational to suppose that the courts were designed to be an intermediate body between the people and the legislature, in order, among other things, to keep the latter within the limits assigned to their authority. The interpretation of the laws is the proper and peculiar province of the courts. A constitution is in fact, and must be, regarded by the judges as a fundamental law. It therefore belongs to them to ascertain its meaning as well as the meaning of any particular act proceeding from the legislative body. If there should happen to be an irreconcilable variance between the two, that which has the superior obligation and validity ought of course to be preferred; or in other words, the constitution ought to be preferred to the statute, the intention of the people to the intention of their agents.

Nor does this conclusion by any means suppose a superiority of the judicial to the legislative power. It only supposes that the power of the people is superior to both; and that where the will of the legislature declared in its statutes, stands in opposition to that of the people declared in the constitution, the judges ought to be governed by the latter, rather than the former. They ought to regulate their decisions by the fundamental laws, rather than by those which are not fundamental. . . .

It can be of no weight to say, that the courts on the pretence of a repugnancy, may substitute their own pleasure to the constitutional intentions of the legislature. This might as well happen in the case of two contradictory statutes; or it might as well happen in every adjudication upon any single statute. The courts must declare the sense of the law; and if they should be disposed to exercise *will* instead of *judgment*, the consequence would equally be the substitution of their pleasure to that of the legislative body. The observation, if it proved any thing, would prove that there ought to be no judges distinct from that body.

If then the courts of justice are to be considered as the bulwarks of a limited constitution against legislative encroachments, this consideration will afford a strong argument for the permanent tenure of judicial offices, since nothing will contribute so much as this to that independent spirit in the judges, which must be essential to the faithful performance of so arduous a duty.

This independence of the judges is equally requisite to guard the constitution and the rights of individuals from the effects of those ill humours which the arts of designing men, or the influence of particular conjunctures, sometimes disseminate among the people themselves, and which, though they speedily give place to better information and more deliberate reflection, have a tendency in the meantime to occasion dangerous innovations in the government, and serious oppressions of the minor party in the community. . . .

4. *Justice Gibson's dissent in Eakin v. Raub, 12 S. & R. 330 (Pa. 1825).* The following excerpts are from an opinion denying that the Pennsylvania Supreme Court is authorized to consider the constitutionality of acts of the state legislature. Five years after writing this dissent, Justice Gibson was a strong contender for a seat on the United States Supreme Court, but President Andrew Jackson ultimately named Gibson's fellow-Pennsylvanian, Henry Baldwin. Twenty years after Eakin v. Raub, when Gibson had become Pennsylvania's Chief Justice, he announced that he had changed his mind, both because an intervening state constitutional convention had silently "sanctioned the pretensions of the courts" and because of his "experience of the necessity of the case." Norris v. Clymer, 2 Pa. 277 (1845).

Gibson in Eakin v. Raub

I am aware, that a right to declare all unconstitutional acts void, without distinction as to either constitution, is generally held as a professional dogma; but I apprehend, rather as a matter of faith than of reason. . . . [I]t is not a little remarkable, that although the right in question has all along been claimed by the judiciary, no judge has ventured to discuss it, except Chief Justice Marshall . . . ; and if the argument of a jurist so distinguished for the strength of his ratiocinative powers be found inconclusive, it may fairly be set down to the weakness of the position which he attempts to defend. . . .

[T]he constitution is said to be a law of superior obligation; and consequently, that if it were to come into collision with an act of the legislature, the latter would have to give way; this is conceded. But it is a fallacy, to suppose, that they can come into collision *before the judiciary.* . . .

The constitution and the *right* of the legislature to pass the act, may be in collision; but is that a legitimate subject for judicial determination? If it be, the judiciary must be a peculiar organ, to revise the proceedings of the legislature, and to correct its mistakes; and in what part of the constitution are we to look for this proud preeminence? . . . [I]t is by no means clear, that to declare a law void, which has been enacted according to the forms prescribed in the constitution, is not a usurpation of legislative power. It is an act of sovereignty; and sovereignty and legislative power are said by Sir William *Blackstone* to be convertible terms. It is the business of the judiciary, to interpret the laws, not scan the authority of the lawgiver; and without the latter, it cannot take cognisance of a collision between a law and the constitution. So that, to affirm that the judiciary has a right to judge of the existence of such collision, is to take for granted the very thing to be proved . . . .

But it has been said to be emphatically the business of the judiciary, to ascertain and pronounce what the law is; and that this necessarily involves a consideration of the constitution. It does so: but how far? If the judiciary will inquire into anything beside the form of enactment, where shall it stop? There must be some point of limitation to such an inquiry; for no one will pretend, that a judge would be justifiable in calling for the election returns, or scrutinizing the qualifications of those who composed the legislature. . . .

[I]t will not be pretended, that the legislature has not, at least, an equal right with the judiciary to put a construction on the constitution; nor that either of them is infallible; nor that either ought to be required to surrender its judgment to the other. Suppose, then, they differ in opinion as to the constitutionality of a particular law; if the organ whose business it first is to decide on the subject, is not to have its judgment treated with respect, what shall prevent it from securing the preponderance of its opinion by the strong arm of power? . . . [T]he soundness of any construction which would bring one organ of the government into collision with another, is to be more than suspected; for where collision occurs, it is evident, the machine is working in a way the framers of it did not intend. . . .

But the judges are sworn to support the constitution, and are they not bound by it as the law of the land? . . . The oath to support the constitution is not peculiar to the judges, but is taken indiscriminately by every officer of the government, and is designed rather as a test of the political principles of the man, than to bind the officer in the discharge of his duty: otherwise, it were difficult to determine, what operation it is to have in the case of a recorder of deeds, for instance, who, in the execution of his office, has nothing to do with the constitution. But granting it to relate to the official conduct of the judge, as well as every other officer, and not to his political principles, still, it must be understood in reference to supporting the constitution, *only as far as that may be involved in his official duty;* and consequently, if his official duty does not comprehend an inquiry into the authority of the legislature, neither does his oath. . . .

But do not the judges do a *positive* act in violation of the constitution, when they give effect to an unconstitutional law? Not if the law has been passed according to the forms established in the constitution. The fallacy of the question is, in supposing that the judiciary adopts the acts of the legislature as its own; whereas, the enactment of a law and the interpretation of it are not concurrent acts, and as the judiciary is not required to concur in the enactment, neither is it in the breach of the constitution which may be the consequence of the enactment; the fault is imputable to the legislature, and on it the responsibility exclusively rests. . . .

But in regard to an act of assembly, which is found to be in collision with the constitution, laws or treaties of the *United States*, I take the duty of the judiciary to be exactly the reverse. By becoming parties to the federal constitution, the states have agreed to several limitations of their individual sovereignty, to enforce which, it was thought to be absolutely necessary, to prevent them from giving effect to laws in violation of those limitations, through the instrumentality of their own judges. . . .

5. *The Hand-Wechsler debate.* For an illuminating revival of the legitimacy debate, and sharp disagreement about the basis for judicial re-

view in the constitutional text, see Hand, The Bill of Rights (1958), 1–30, and Wechsler, "Toward Neutral Principles of Constitutional Law," in Principles, Politics, and Fundamental Law (1961), 4–10 [also printed in 73 Harv.L.Rev. 1 (1959) and Selected Essays 1938–62 (1963), 463]. Judge Learned Hand emphasized that there was "nothing in the United States Constitution that gave courts any authority to review the decisions of Congress," insisted that "it was a plausible—indeed to my mind an unanswerable—argument" that such an authority was inconsistent with separation of powers, and asserted that "when the Constitution emerged from the Convention in September, 1787, the structure of the proposed government, if one looked to the text, gave no ground for inferring that the decisions of the Supreme Court . . . were to be authoritative upon the Executive and the Legislature." Judge Hand found justification for the Supreme Court's assumption of judicial review authority solely in the practical need "to prevent the defeat of the venture at hand"—to keep the government from foundering. Professor Wechsler, relying on the Article VI Supremacy Clause and on Article III, replied: "I believe the power of the courts is grounded in the language of the Constitution and is not a mere interpolation."

The Hand-Wechsler debate of the mid-Twentieth Century illustrates how the legitimacy issue may influence views regarding the contemporary exercise of the power. Thus, Judge Hand concluded that "since this power is not a logical deduction from the structure of the Constitution but only a practical condition upon its successful operation, it need not be exercised whenever a court sees, or thinks that it sees, an invasion of the Constitution. It is always a preliminary question how importunately the occasion demands an answer." (Compare the materials on discretionary abstention, chap. 2, p. 142, below.) Professor Wechsler objected to so broad a discretion to decline to adjudicate a constitutional objection in a case properly before a court: "For me, as for anyone who finds the judicial power anchored in the Constitution, there is no such escape from the judicial obligations; the duty cannot be attenuated in this way." (The "duty," he added, was "not that of policing or advising Legislatures or Executives," but rather simply the duty "to decide the litigated case and to decide it in accordance with the law.")

The Hand-Wechsler debate illustrates, too, that evaluations of the content as well as timing of contemporary court decisions may evolve from discussions beginning with concern over legitimacy. Since Wechsler's defense of legitimacy is so closely tied to implications of the judicial function, he insisted that Constitution-interpreting courts must above all act like courts. Accordingly, he warned against "ad hoc evaluation" as "the deepest problem of our constitutionalism" and insisted that decisions must rest on "neutral principles": "the main constituent of the judicial process is precisely that it must be genuinely principled, resting with respect to every step that is involved in reaching judgment on analysis and reasons quite transcending the immediate result that is achieved." To Judge Hand, judicial review of legislative choices inevitably turned courts into "a third legislative chamber," adding: "For myself it would be most irksome to be ruled by a bevy of Platonic Guardians, even if I knew how to choose them, which I surely do not."

6. *Judicial review and democracy.* As the Hand-Wechsler debate illustrates, concern with the bases of judicial review in constitutional history and

text is often closely connected with explorations of the consistency between judicial review and democratic government. Views on that issue, too, may profoundly affect exercises and evaluations of the judicial power, as is amply revealed in many of the opinions in this volume. Anxiety about the undemocratic aspects of judicial review, for example, tends to support the judicial self-restraint stance long associated with Justice Frankfurter—the reluctance to intervene in the judgments of other branches of government.

Leonard W. Levy's paperback, Judicial Review and the Supreme Court (1967), is a useful selection of essays, and his Introduction includes a critical analysis of the major contending arguments regarding the propriety of judicial invalidation of legislative decisions. Classic statements seeing judicial review as undemocratic and as undercutting popular responsibility are Thayer, "The Origin and Scope of the American Doctrine of Constitutional Law," 7 Harv.L.Rev. 129 (1893), 1 Selected Essays 503 (1938), and Commager, Majority Rule and Minority Rights (1943). Important defenses of judicial intervention are Rostow, "The Democratic Character of Judicial Review," 66 Harv.L.Rev. 193 (1952), Selected Essays 1938–62 (1963), 1, and C. L. Black, Jr., The People and the Court: Judicial Review in a Democracy (1960). For provocative and sophisticated efforts during the sixties to justify judicial intervention while recognizing that it curbs representative government and majoritarian rule, see Bickel, The Least Dangerous Branch (1962), Shapiro, Law and Politics in the Supreme Court (1964), and Deutsch, "Neutrality, Legitimacy, and the Supreme Court: Some Intersections Between Law and Political Science," 20 Stan.L.Rev. 169 (1968). As noted, the issues in this debate are recurrent themes in judicial opinions and permeate any constitutional law course. The problems are best explored in the specific contexts of the cases below. See, e. g., the issues of judicial intervention and democratic processes raised by Justice Stone's Carolene Products case footnote, chap. 15, p. 1057, and by the opinions in Griswold v. Connecticut, chap. 11, p. 824.

7. *Judicial review abroad.* Since World War II, while Americans have continued to agonize over the justifiability of judicial review, more and more other nations have looked to courts to enforce constitutionalism. Judicial review has become especially important in Germany and Italy. Most judicial review mechanisms in civil law countries differ from the American in form: for example, creation of special Constitutional Courts has been the norm. But the American experience has been an important "persuasive authority" as to basic theory; and in practice there are signs of "a converging trend" in the exercise of judicial review in the American and civil law systems, as a sophisticated commentator suggests. Cappelletti, "The Significance of Judicial Review of Legislation in the Contemporary World," in Ius Privatum Gentium (Festschrift for Max Rheinstein, 1969), 147. See also Cappelletti and Adams, "Judicial Review: European Antecedents and Adaptations," 79 Harv.L.Rev. 1207 (1966).

THE AUTHORITATIVENESS OF THE COURT'S CONSTITUTIONAL INTERPRETATIONS

Introduction. Does it follow from Marshall's justification for judicial review that the Court's interpretations are binding on the other departments of government in the exercise of their official functions? May, or must, Congress and the President give independent consideration to the question of constitutionality in considering proposed legislation or executive action? See Congressional Deliberations on the Civil Rights Act of 1964, chap. 4, p. 327, below, and, generally, Morgan, Congress and the Constitution (1966).

Note that much of Marshall's argument is directed against contentions that courts lack *competence* or *authority* to consider constitutionality. Does it follow from this that the adjudication is a *final* decision of the issue and is *binding* on those not parties to the litigation? Does it follow that the judiciary is the *exclusive* source of constitutional interpretations? Note Marshall's statement that the Constitution is "a rule for the government of *courts,* as well as of the legislature" and his conclusion that "*courts*, as well as other departments, are bound by that instrument."

The materials which follow include some characteristic presidential assertions. Consider, with regard to each statement, whether anything in the President's position is inconsistent with Marshall's reasoning. Consider also whether any of the presidential positions is inconsistent with the view of judicial authority given in the 1958 decision in Cooper v. Aaron, the final excerpt, note 5a, below.

1. *Thomas Jefferson.* a. *Letter to Abigail Adams, Sept. 11, 1804* (VIII The Writings of Thomas Jefferson (Ford ed. 1897), 310):

". . . You seem to think it devolved on the judges to decide on the validity of the sedition law. But nothing in the Constitution has given them a right to decide for the Executive, more than to the Executive to decide for them. Both magistracies are equally independent in the sphere of action assigned to them. The judges, believing the law constitutional, had a right to pass a sentence of fine and imprisonment; because that power was placed in their hands by the Constitution. But the Executive, believing the law to be unconstitutional, was bound to remit the execution of it; because that power has been confided to him by the Constitution. That instrument meant that its co-ordinate branches should be checks on each other. But the opinion which gives to the judges the right to decide what laws are constitutional, and what not, not only for themselves in their own sphere of action, but for the Legislature & Executive also, in their spheres, would make the judiciary a despotic branch. Nor does the opinion of the unconstitutionality, & consequent nullity of that law, remove all restraint from the overwhelming torrent of slander, which is confounding all vice and virtue, all truth & falsehood, in the U. S. The power to do that is fully possessed by the several State Legislatures. . . . While we deny that Congress have a right to control the freedom of the press, we have ever asserted the right of the States, and their exclusive right, to do so. . . ."

b. *Letter to Judge Spencer Roane of Virginia, Sept. 6, 1819* (X The Writings of Thomas Jefferson (Ford ed. 1899), 140):

"In denying the right they usurp of exclusively explaining the constitution, I go further than you do, if I understand rightly your quotation from the Federalist, of an opinion that 'the judiciary is the last resort in relation *to the other departments* of the government, but not in relation to the rights of the parties to the compact under which the judiciary is derived.' If this opinion be sound, then indeed is our constitution a complete *felo de se.* For intending to establish three departments, co-ordinate and independent, that they might check and balance one another, it has given, according to this opinion, to one of them alone, the right to prescribe rules for the government of the others, and to that one too, which is unelected by, and independent of the nation.   .   .   .   My construction of the constitution is very different from that you quote.   It is that each department is truly independent of the others, and has an equal right to decide for itself what is the meaning of the constitution in the cases submitted to its action; and especially, where it is to act ultimately and without appeal.   .   .   .   ."

c.   *Letter to William C. Jarvis, Sept. 28, 1820* (X The Writings of Thomas Jefferson (Ford ed. 1899), 160):

".   .   .   You seem   .   .   .   to consider the judges as the ultimate arbiters of all constitutional questions; a very dangerous doctrine indeed, and one which would place us under the despotism of an oligarchy.
.   .   .   The constitution has erected no such single tribunal, knowing that to whatever hands confided, with the corruptions of time and party, its members would become despots.   It has more wisely made all the departments co-equal and co-sovereign within themselves.   If the legislature fails to pass laws for a census, for paying the judges and other officers of government, for establishing a militia, for naturalization as prescribed by the constitution, or if they fail to meet in congress, the judges cannot issue their mandamus to them; if the President fails to supply the place of a judge, to appoint other civil or military officers, to issue requisite commissions, the judges cannot force him.   .   .   .   The judges certainly have more frequent occasion to act on constitutional questions, because the laws of *meum* and *tuum* and of criminal action, forming the great mass of the system of law, constitute their particular department.   When the legislative or executive functionaries act unconstitutionally, they are responsible to the people in their elective capacity.   The exemption of the judges from that is quite dangerous enough.
.   .   .   ."

2.   *Andrew Jackson—Veto Message (on bill to recharter the Bank of the United States), July 10, 1832* (II Messages and Papers of the Presidents (Richardson ed. 1900), 576, 581–583):

".   .   .   It is maintained by the advocates of the bank that its constitutionality in all its features ought to be considered as settled by precedent and by the decision of the Supreme Court.   [McCulloch v. Maryland, 4 Wheat. 316 (1819), chap. 3, p. 201, infra.]   To this conclusion I can not assent.   Mere precedent is a dangerous source of authority, and should not be regarded as deciding questions of constitutional power except where the acquiescence of the people and the States can be considered as well settled.
.   .   .

"If the opinion of the Supreme Court covered the whole ground of this act, it ought not to control the coordinate authorities of this Government. The Congress, the Executive, and the Court must each for itself be guided by its own opinion of the Constitution.   Each public officer who takes an oath to support the Constitution swears that he will support it as he understands it, and not as it is understood by others.   It is as much the duty of the House of Representatives, of the Senate, and of the President to decide upon the constitutionality of any bill or resolution which may be presented to them for passage or approval as it is of the supreme judges when it may be brought before them for judicial decision.   The opinion of the judges has no more authority over Congress than the opinion of Congress has over the judges, and on that point the President is independent of both. The authority of the Supreme Court must not, therefore, be permitted to control the Congress or the Executive when acting in their legislative capacities, but to have only such influence as the force of their reasoning may deserve.

"But in the case relied upon the Supreme Court have not decided that all the features of this corporation are compatible with the Constitution. . . . Under the decision of the Supreme Court . . . it is the exclusive province of Congress and the President to decide whether the particular features of this act are *necessary* and *proper* in order to enable the bank to perform conveniently and efficiently the public duties assigned to it as a fiscal agent, and therefore constitutional, or *unnecessary* and *improper,* and therefore unconstitutional.

"Without commenting on the general principle affirmed by the Supreme Court, let us examine the details of this act in accordance with the rule of legislative action which they have laid down. It will be found that many of the powers and privileges conferred on it can not be supposed necessary for the purpose for which it is proposed to be created, and are not, therefore, means necessary to attain the end in view, and consequently not justified by the Constitution. . . . "

3. *Abraham Lincoln.* a. *Speeches during the Lincoln-Douglas Senatorial Campaign, July, October 1858.* (II The Collected Works of Abraham Lincoln (Basler ed. 1953), 494, 516; III id. 255):

[July 10, 1858:] "I have expressed heretofore, and I now repeat, my opposition to the Dred Scott Decision [Dred Scott v. Sandford, 19 How. 393 (1857)], but I should be allowed to state the nature of that opposition, and I ask your indulgence while I do so. What is fairly implied by the term Judge Douglas has used, 'resistance to the Decision?' I do not resist it. If I wanted to take Dred Scott from his master, I would be interfering with property, and that terrible difficulty that Judge Douglas speaks of, of interfering with property, would arise. But I am doing no such thing as that, but all that I am doing is refusing to obey it as a political rule. If I were in Congress, and a vote should come up on a question whether slavery should be prohibited in a new territory, in spite of that Dred Scott decision, I would vote that it should. . . . "

[July 17, 1858:] "Now, as to the Dred Scott decision; for upon that he makes his last point at me. He boldly takes ground in favor of that decision.

"This is one-half the onslaught, and one-third of the entire plan of the campaign. I am opposed to that decision in a certain sense, but not in the sense which he puts on it. I say that in so far as it decided in favor of Dred Scott's master and against Dred Scott and his family, I do not propose to disturb or resist the decision.

"I never have proposed to do any such thing. I think, that in respect for judicial authority, my humble history would not suffer in a comparison with that of Judge Douglas. He would have the citizen conform his vote to that decision; the Member of Congress, his; the President, his use of the veto power. He would make it a rule of political action for the people and all the departments of the government. I would not. By resisting it as a political rule, I disturb no right of property, create no disorder, excite no mobs. . . . "

[Oct. 13, 1858:] "We oppose the Dred Scott decision in a certain way, upon which I ought perhaps to address you a few words. We do not propose that when Dred Scott has been decided to be a slave by the court, we as a mob will decide him to be free. We do not propose that, when any other one, or one thousand, shall be decided by that court to be slaves, we will in any violent way disturb the rights of property thus settled; but we nevertheless do oppose that decision as a political rule which shall be binding on the voter, to vote for nobody who thinks it wrong, which shall be binding on the members of Congress or the President to favor no measure that does not actually concur with the principles of that decision. We do not propose to be bound by it as a political rule in that way, because we think it lays the foundation not merely of enlarging and spreading out what we consider an evil, but it lays the foundation for spreading that evil into the States themselves. We propose so resisting it as to have it reversed if we can, and a new judicial rule established upon this subject. . . . ."

b. *First Inaugural Address, March 4, 1861* (VI Messages and Papers of the Presidents (Richardson ed. 1900), 5, 9–10):

"I do not forget the position assumed by some that constitutional questions are to be decided by the Supreme Court, nor do I deny that such decisions must be binding in any case upon the parties to a suit as to the object of that suit, while they are also entitled to very high respect and consideration in all parallel cases by all other departments of the Government. And while it is obviously possible that such decision may be erroneous in any given case, still the evil effect following it, being limited to that particular case, with the chance that it may be overruled and never become a precedent for other cases, can better be borne than could the evils of a different practice. At the same time, the candid citizen must confess that if the policy of the Government upon vital questions affecting the whole people is to be irrevocably fixed by decisions of the Supreme Court, the instant they are made in ordinary litigation between parties in personal actions the people will have ceased to be their own rulers, having to that extent practically resigned their Government into the hands of that eminent tribunal. Nor is there in this view any assault upon the court or the judges. It is a duty from which they may not shrink to decide cases properly brought before them, and it is no fault of theirs if others seek to turn their decisions to political purposes. . . ."

4. *Franklin D. Roosevelt.* a. *Letter to Congressman Hill, July 6, 1935* (printed infra, chap. 4, p. 278).

b. *Proposed speech on the Gold Clause Cases, Feb. 1935:* (I F.D.R.— His Personal Letters, 1928–1945 (Elliott Roosevelt ed. 1950), 459–460) [from a draft speech President Roosevelt planned to deliver in the event the Court decided against the Government on the constitutionality of abrogating "gold clauses" in federal obligations—see Perry v. United States, 294 U.S. 330 (1935)]:

". . . I do not seek to enter into any controversy with the distinguished members of the Supreme Court of the United States who have participated in this . . . decision. They have decided these cases in accordance with the letter of the law as they read it. But it is appropriate to quote a sentence from the First Inaugural Address of President Lincoln: [quoting the "At the same time" sentence in note 3b, above] . . . .

"It is the duty of the Congress and the President to protect the people of the United States to the best of their ability. It is necessary to protect them from the unintended construction of voluntary acts, as well as from intolerable burdens involuntarily imposed. To stand idly by and to permit the decision of the Supreme Court to be carried through to its logical, inescapable conclusion would so imperil the economic and political security of this nation that the legislative and executive officers of the Government must look beyond the narrow letter of contractual obligations, so that they may sustain the substance of the promise originally made in accord with the actual intention of the parties. . . . I shall immediately take such steps as may be necessary, by proclamation and by message to the Congress of the United States."

5. *Cooper v. Aaron, criticism, and defiance: Are Court interpretations "the supreme law of the land"?* a. *The Cooper position.* Cooper v. Aaron, 358 U.S. 1 (1958), was the Little Rock, Arkansas, School Desegregation Case. The school board, seeking to desegregate the public schools pursuant to a plan approved by the lower federal courts, was blocked in its efforts by Governor Faubus' action in calling out the National Guard in September 1957. The Governor placed Little Rock Central High School "off limits" to Negro students. After a trial court injunction against the Governor, the troops were withdrawn. Thereafter Negro students were able to attend under the protection of federal Army and federalized National Guard troops. In February 1958, the School Board sought a two and one-half years postponement of the desegregation program in the U. S. District Court. The District Court granted relief in June 1958, after noting the "chaos, bedlam, and turmoil" and finding the situation "intolerable." The Court of Appeals reversed. The Supreme Court affirmed the Court of Appeals decision. The Court found that the school officials had acted in "entire good faith" but concluded that "the actions of the other state agencies responsible for those conditions compel us to reject the Board's legal position. . . . The constitutional rights of respondents are not to be sacrificed or yielded to the violence and disorder which have followed upon the actions of the Governor and legislature."

The Court's opinion bore an unusual designation: rather than being described as an opinion of the Court by a single named Justice, it was stated to be "by The Chief Justice (Warren), Mr. Justice Black, Mr. Justice Frankfurter, Mr. Justice Douglas, Mr. Justice Burton, Mr. Justice Clark, Mr. Justice Harlan, Mr. Justice Brennan, and Mr. Justice Whittaker." The problem of racial segregation culminating in the 1954 School Segregation Case, Brown v. Board of Education, 347 U.S. 483, is considered in chap. 18 below. The following excerpt from Cooper v. Aaron is at 358 U.S. 1, 17–19:

"What has been said, in the light of the facts developed, is enough to dispose of the case. However, we should answer the premise of the actions of the Governor and Legislature that they are not bound by our holding in the Brown case. It is necessary only to recall some basic constitutional propositions which are settled doctrine.

"Article VI of the Constitution makes the Constitution the 'supreme Law of the Land.' In 1803, Chief Justice Marshall, speaking for a unanimous Court, referring to the Constitution as 'the fundamental and paramount law of the nation,' declared in the notable case of Marbury v. Madison, 1

Cranch 137, 177, that 'It is emphatically the province and duty of the judicial department to say what the law is.'   This decision declared the basic principle that the federal judiciary is supreme in the exposition of the law of the Constitution, and that principle has ever since been respected by this Court and the Country as a permanent and indispensable feature of our constitutional system.   It follows that the interpretation of the Fourteenth Amendment enunciated by this Court in the Brown case is the supreme law of the land, and Art. VI of the Constitution makes it of binding effect on the States 'any Thing in the Constitution or Laws of any State to the Contrary notwithstanding.'   Every state legislator and executive and judicial officer is solemnly committed by oath taken pursuant to Art. VI, ¶3 'to support this Constitution.'   Chief Justice Taney, speaking for a unanimous Court in 1859, said that this requirement reflected the framers' 'anxiety to preserve it [the Constitution] in full force, in all its powers, and to guard against resistance to or evasion of its authority, on the part of a State. . . .'   Ableman v. Booth, 21 How. 506, 524.

"No state legislator or executive or judicial officer can war against the Constitution without violating his undertaking to support it.   Chief Justice Marshall spoke for a unanimous Court in saying that: 'If the legislatures of the several states may, at will, annul the judgments of the courts of the United States, and destroy the rights acquired under those judgments, the constitution itself becomes a solemn mockery . . . .'   United States v. Peters, 5 Cranch 115, 136.   A Governor who asserts a power to nullify a federal court order is similarly restrained.   If he had such power, said Chief Justice Hughes, in 1932, also for a unanimous Court, "it is manifest that the fiat of a state Governor, and not the Constitution of the United States, would be the supreme law of the land; that the restrictions of the Federal Constitution upon the exercise of state power would be but impotent phrases . . . .'   Sterling v. Constantin, 287 U.S. 378, 397–398 . . . . ."

Is the Court interpretation in Cooper v. Aaron a restatement of Marbury v. Madison—or is it a revision?   Does a Supreme Court interpretation bind state officials to a greater degree than federal officials?   Assuming that some of the presidential positions in notes 1–4 are consistent with Marbury, can they also be reconciled with Cooper v. Aaron?   Compare Gunther, "The Subtle Vices of the 'Passive Virtues'—A Comment on Principle and Expediency in Judicial Review," 64 Colum.L.Rev. 1–25 (1964):   "Bickel [Bickel, The Least Dangerous Branch (1962)] draws from Marbury v. Madison . . . the notion that the Court's 'doctrines are not to be questioned,' by citizens or by other departments of government. . . . That confuses Marshall's assertion of judicial authority to interpret the Constitution with judicial exclusiveness; that confuses Marbury v. Madison with statements in the Little Rock case, Cooper v. Aaron."   Note the suggestion of a "crucial difference" between Governor Faubus' stated opposition to the Brown decision and his efforts to block school board execution of a court-approved desegregation plan, in Horowitz and Karst, Law, Lawyers and Social Change (1969), 253.   Are the authors persuasive in their analogy— "it is the difference between arguing with the umpire and refusing to leave the base when you are called out"?

b. *Legitimate disagreement and improper defiance.* Is never-ending, chaotic questioning of Court interpretations inevitable if one takes a narrow view of authoritativeness pursuant to Marbury? Consider the solution advanced in Wechsler, "The Courts and the Constitution," 65 Colum.L.Rev. 1001, 1008 (1965), which draws on aspects of President Lincoln's position quoted in note 3b above. Lincoln spoke of the "chance" that the ruling "may be overruled and never become a precedent for other cases." Wechsler comments: "When that chance has been exploited and has run its course, with reaffirmation rather than reversal of decision, has not the time arrived when its acceptance is demanded, without insisting on repeated litigation? The answer here, it seems to me, must be affirmative, both as the necessary implication of our constitutional tradition and to avoid the greater evils that will otherwise ensue."

Does this position permit too broad a range of challenges to Court rulings, in theory or in practice? And is such criticism acceptable only so long as it is calm and rational? Note Professor Jaffe's observation that intense criticism is especially appropriate as well as probable in the area of constitutional adjudication: "There will be and there should be popular response to the Supreme Court's decision; not just the 'informed' criticism of law professors but the deep-felt, emotion-ladened, unsophisticated reaction of the laity. This is so because more than any court in the modern world the Supreme Court 'makes policy,' and is at the same time so little subject to formal democratic control. . . . Yet those who urge the Court on to political innovation are outraged when its decisions arouse, as they must, resentment and political attack." Jaffe, "Impromptu Remarks," 76 Harv.L.Rev. 1111 (1963).

6. *The legal consequences of judicial "invalidation."* Under the classic Marbury theory, a court confronted with an unconstitutional statute simply refuses enforcement to that law in the case before it. In civil law countries, by contrast, a court exercising judicial review issues a ruling of general invalidity binding on all, not just on the parties before it. But here, too, civil law and American law are closer in practice than in theory. Thus, it does not tell the whole story to say, as an American court has said, that a decision upon constitutionality "affects the parties only, for there is no judgment against a statute." Shephard v. Wheeling, 4 S.E. 635 (W.Va. 1887). For example, some practical reach of a court's ruling beyond the immediate parties is assured by the ordinary judicial adherence to stare decisis.

Yet to say that an invalidity ruling affects more than the parties is not to say that it is the same as wiping a statute off the books. It is as inaccurate to claim too broad an impact for a ruling as it is to state it too narrowly. The best-known example of overstatement is an assertion in Norton v. Shelby County, 118 U.S. 425 (1886), a statement that has required some important qualifications: "An unconstitutional statute is not a law; it confers no rights; it affords no protection; it creates no office; it is, in legal contemplation, as inoperative as though it had never been passed."

But a law held unconstitutional in an American court is by no means so wholly a nullity, as the Attorney General quite persuasively advised the President in 1937. The Supreme Court had held the District of Columbia minimum wage law unconstitutional in 1923, in the Adkins case; but in

1937, in sustaining a similar New York law in the West Coast Hotel Co. case, the Court formally overruled Adkins. (The cases are discussed in chap. 13, pp. 966 and 971, below.) The Attorney General advised that the 1923 ruling had simply "suspended" enforcement, and that the act was valid and enforceable after the 1937 decision, explaining: "The decisions are practically in accord in holding that the courts have no power to repeal or abolish a statute, and that notwithstanding a decision holding it unconstitutional a statute continues to remain on the statute books." 39 Ops.Atty.Gen. 22 (1937).

The Supreme Court itself has had occasion to warn that the problem is more subtle and complex than the Shelby County language suggested. In Chicot County Drainage District v. Baxter State Bank, 308 U.S. 371 (1940), the Court held that an unappealed decision applying a federal statute was res judicata despite a subsequent Supreme Court ruling in another case that the law was unconstitutional. Chief Justice Hughes stated:

"The courts below have proceeded on the theory that the Act of Congress having been found to be unconstitutional, was not a law; that it was inoperative, conferring no rights and imposing no duties, and hence affording no basis for the challenged decree. Norton v. Shelby County . . . . It is quite clear, however, that such broad statements as to the effect of a determination of unconstitutionality must be taken with qualifications. The actual existence of a statute, prior to such a determination, is an operative fact and may have consequences which cannot justly be ignored. The past cannot always be erased by a new judicial declaration. The effect of the subsequent ruling as to invalidity may have to be considered in various aspects, —with respect to particular relations, individual and corporate, and particular conduct, private and official. Questions of rights claimed to have become vested, of status, of prior determinations deemed to have finality and acted upon accordingly, of public policy in the light of the nature both of the statute and of its previous application, demand examination. These questions are among the most difficult of those which have engaged the attention of courts, state and federal, and it is manifest from numerous decisions that an all-inclusive statement of a principle of absolute retroactive invalidity cannot be justified." See generally Field, The Effect of an Unconstitutional Statute (1935).

Chief Justice Hughes stressed that "a principle of absolute retroactive invalidity" was unsupportable, while recognizing retroactivity as the normal consequence of judicial invalidation. More recently, attention has shifted from the scope of retroactivity to the permissibility of prospectivity. That problem has been raised by the Court's rapid expansion of federal constitutional rights in criminal proceedings. Could the Court announce new guarantees without permitting all those already convicted to benefit from those new rights? Beginning with Linkletter v. Walker, 381 U.S. 618 (1965), the Court decided that it could indeed withhold retroactive effect from its rulings. The Court found that "the Constitution neither prohibits nor requires retrospective effect," so that it was the Court's task to "weigh the merits and demerits" of retroactivity for the rule in question "by looking to the prior history," to the "purpose and effect" of the new constitutional rule, and to "whether retrospective operation will further or retard its operation." Determining which new rules should be limited to prospective effect under this approach—and deciding what "prospectivity" should mean—has given rise to repeated controversy since Linkletter, as the materials at chap. 12, p. 892, show. See generally Mishkin, "The High Court, the Great Writ, and the Due Process of Time and Law," 79 Harv.L.Rev. 56 (1965).

MARTIN v. HUNTER'S LESSEE

1 Wheat. 304, 4 L.Ed. 97 (1816).

This was an ejectment action involving about 800 acres of the "waste and ungranted land" of a 300,000-acre tract known as the Northern Neck of Virginia.[1] The Northern Neck had been owned by Thomas, Lord Fairfax, a citizen of Virginia, at his death in 1781. The suit was instituted in 1791 in the Superior Court at Winchester, Virginia. The plaintiff, David Hunter, claimed under a 1789 grant from the State of Virginia. The defendant, Denny Martin Fairfax, a British subject resident in England, claimed as the devisee of Lord Fairfax.

The original basis of Hunter's claim. Hunter's claim rested on a series of Virginia statutes relating to the forfeiture to the state of lands owned by British subjects. A 1779 law declared the escheat of property then belonging to British subjects and prescribed an inquest of office, a customary ritual by which title to a particular piece of land was formally vested in the state. Since the Northern Neck did not become the property of a British subject until the death of Lord Fairfax in 1781, additional legislation was necessary if these lands were to be forfeited to Virginia. Two laws enacted in 1782 dealt specifically with the Northern Neck. The first of these referred largely to persons who had in the past settled on unappropriated lands in the area subject to Lord Fairfax's proprietorship. It recited that the proprietorship had apparently "descended upon alien enemies," directed landholders to retain quit-rents then due, and ordered that future quit-rents be paid into the public treasury. The second law enacted in 1782 dealt with those who desired to settle upon still vacant and unappropriated lands in the Northern Neck. It provided as a temporary measure that formal entries for such lands might be made with the county surveyors in the area and that such entries were to be as valid as those formerly made under Lord Fairfax's direction. Land records, as in the past, were to be kept in an office established by Lord Fairfax.

More permanent arrangements as to the Northern Neck were made by a series of laws enacted three years later, in 1785. These directed that land records relating to the Neck be transferred to a central register's office in Richmond; exonerated landholders from quit-rents; provided for issuing formal grants in the name of the State to those who had previously made entries in the land records kept in Lord Fairfax's office; declared unappropriated lands in the district subject to grant in the same manner "as is by law

---

1. This statement of facts is based in part on Hart and Wechsler, The Federal Courts and the Federal System (1953), 403–07. Permission to use that statement is gratefully acknowledged. See also the accounts of the case in IV Beveridge, The Life of John Marshall (1919), 144–67; 1 Warren, The Supreme Court in United States History (rev. ed. 1926), 442–53; 2 Crosskey, Politics and the Constitution in the History of the United States (1953), 785–814; and Note, "Judge Spencer Roane of Virginia: Champion of States' Rights—Foe of John Marshall," 66 Harv.L.Rev. 1242, 1248–52 (1953).

escheat = reversion of property to the state in consequence of a want of any under, competent to inherit devisee = person to whom lands or other real property are devised or given by will.

directed in cases of other unappropriated lands belonging to this commonwealth"; and declared that general escheat laws of 1779, including the inquest requirement, were applicable to the Northern Neck.

Virginia's grant to David Hunter in 1789 rested on the authority conferred by the 1785 laws with respect to unappropriated lands. Hunter's land had not been the subject of any inquest or other proceeding for escheat.

The basis of the Martin claim. Denny Martin Fairfax's claim rested on the devise of his uncle, Lord Fairfax, whose name he had taken pursuant to a condition in the will. The claim was fortified by the Treaty of Peace with Great Britain of 1783, which provided that "no future confiscations shall be made." Moreover, the Jay Treaty of 1794—concluded after the ejectment action was instituted—stated that "British subjects who now hold lands in the territories of the United States . . . shall continue to hold them, according to the nature and tenure of their respective estates and titles therein; and may grant, sell or devise the same to whom they please, in like manner as if they were natives." The Martin view was that title to the land acquired under the will in 1781 had not vested in Virginia prior to 1783, and that it was thereafter protected by the treaty provisions.

The Marshall syndicate and the 1796 Act of Compromise. A series of events subsequent to the commencement of the ejectment action in 1791 also cast their shadow over the litigation. In 1793 or 1794, a syndicate including John Marshall and his brother James had contracted for the purchase of the main part of the Fairfax estate from Denny Martin Fairfax. Before the sale was consummated, a number of Northern Neck landholders who, like David Hunter, had received grants of "waste and unappropriated" Northern Neck lands from the state after 1785, petitioned the legislature for action to insure the validity of their claims. In 1796, the Virginia legislature accordingly passed a resolution proposing to relinquish "all claim to any lands specifically appropriated by . . . Lord Fairfax to his own use . . . if the devises [sic] of Lord Fairfax, or those claiming under them, will relinquish all claims to lands . . . which were waste and unappropriated at the time of the death of Lord Fairfax." John Marshall, describing himself as "one of the purchasers of the lands of Mr. Fairfax, and authorized to act for all of them," wrote to the Speaker of the Virginia House of Delegates that he had "determined to accede to the proposition." Thereafter, the compromise proposal was formally adopted by the legislature. On its face, the Act of Compromise appeared to add strength to the Hunter claim—if the courts were willing to consider the Act.

The progress of the litigation. The ejectment action, which had been initiated in 1791, was not submitted to the Superior Court for a decision until after the parties agreed to a statement of the facts, in 1793—before the Jay Treaty and the Act of Compromise. On the basis of the agreed statement, the Superior Court decided against Hunter in April 1794. An appeal to the Court of Appeals of Virginia was argued in May 1796. No decision had been rendered by 1803, when the appellee, Denny Martin Fairfax, died and the appeal accordingly abated. The appeal was not revived until 1808, against Philip Martin, Denny's heir and devisee.[2] The case was reargued before Judges Roane and Fleming in 1809.

2. Why, in view of the intervening Act of Compromise of 1796, was the appeal prosecuted? Compare IV Beveridge, op. cit. supra, 150 n. 4 (suggesting that

On the reargument, Hunter argued that Denny Martin Fairfax, as an alien, was incapable of holding land in Virginia; that title to the land had properly vested in Virginia pursuant to the legislation in the 1780's, which in effect had accomplished a valid escheat; and that the Act of Compromise in any event established his title. Philip Martin contended that Denny was capable of holding until his title was divested by an inquest or some equivalent act; that no vesting in the state took place before the protection of the 1783 Treaty of Peace took hold; and that the Act of Compromise could not be considered since it was not referred to in the agreed statement.

In 1810, the judgment of the Superior Court in favor of Martin was reversed. Judge Roane—Marshall's political enemy—held that Virginia law as to the incapacity of aliens to inherit land was not affected by any treaties; that, even if the treaties were applicable, Martin had acquired at best a defeasible title in 1781; that the laws of 1782, dealing with the Northern Neck, had in effect placed title in Virginia, and that the ordinary escheat proceedings were unnecessary where the legislature acted in this manner; that the 1785 laws merely reaffirmed the earlier taking of the property by Virginia; that Martin accordingly retained no property rights when the 1783 Treaty was adopted; and that, in any event, the Act of Compromise was binding, having been "intended to settle and determine this, among other suits." Judge Fleming disagreed as to the effect of the 1782 laws and believed that the 1783 treaty protected Martin's title. He concurred in Judge Roane's result solely on the basis of the Act of Compromise, which he held to be properly subject to judicial notice, although it had not been mentioned in the agreed statement of the case. Hunter v. Fairfax's Devisee, 15 Va. (1 Munf.) 218.

The United States Supreme Court on writ of error reversed the judgment by a three to one vote. Fairfax's Devisee v. Hunter's Lessee, 7 Cranch 603 (1813). Justice Story wrote the majority opinion. Justice Johnson dissented. Chief Justice Marshall did not participate. Justice Washington was absent on the argument, and Justice Todd on delivery of judgment.

Neither opinion in the Supreme Court mentioned the Act of Compromise, which had been the only common ground of decision in the Virginia court.[3] Justice Story held that an alien has the capacity to take title to land by descent, subject to divestiture by the sovereign; that none of the Virginia laws altered the common law requirement of inquest to vest title in the state,

---

the land claimed by Hunter was not in fact part of the syndicate purchase but was rather bought separately by James Marshall, and that the land was thus not included within the Compromise), with 2 Crosskey, op. cit. supra, 786–789 (claiming that the suit was a test case litigated merely for its value as a precedent in settling certain marginal rights relevant to the syndicate purchase but not covered by the Compromise, and that the action was an appropriate vehicle to determine such rights, even though the land involved was covered by the Compromise, in view of the Virginia practice in such cases, limiting the courts to the facts in the agreed statement). Note Judge Roane's comment in the first decision by the Virginia Court of Appeals, 15 Va. (1 Munf.) 218, 232, that Martin's objection to the consideration of the Compromise "cannot be justified on the principles of justice or good faith; and, I confess, I was not a little surprised that the objection should have been raised in the case before us."

3. Was there any justification for the Supreme Court's failure to mention the Act of Compromise? With Justice Story's explanation, in the opinion printed below, compare the views of Crosskey and Beveridge as to the bearing of the Compromise on this litigation, note 2 supra.

but at most proceeded on the erroneous belief that title had already vested in the commonwealth; and, therefore, that the Treaty of 1794 confirmed the undivested Martin title. Justice Johnson agreed that the Supreme Court could properly examine the title question for effective review on the treaty issue, but dissented on the ground that the state could dispense with the inquest requirement and had therefore properly taken title.

The Supreme Court mandate, directed to "the Honorable the Judges of the Court of Appeals in and for the Commonwealth of Virginia," stated that the "Court is of opinion that there is error in the judgment of the Court of Appeals," and "adjudged and ordered, that the judgment of the Court of Appeals . . . in this case be, and the same is hereby reversed and annulled, and that the judgment of the District Court of Winchester be affirmed, with costs; and it is further ordered, that the said cause be remanded to the said Court of Appeals . . . with instructions to enter judgment for the appellant." It ended with the formal provision: "You therefore are hereby commanded that such proceedings be had in said cause, as according to right and justice, and the laws of the United States, and agreeable to said judgment and instructions of said Supreme Court ought to be had, the said writ of error notwithstanding."

The question whether the Supreme Court's mandate should be obeyed "excited all that attention from the Bench and Bar which its great importance truly merited," and was argued at length before the Virginia Court of Appeals in 1814. A decision was not announced until well after a year later, in 1815; apparently, the Virginia court delayed publication in order to avoid encouraging the extreme secessionist feelings in New England based on opposition to the war with England. In 1815, the Court of Appeals (with four judges now sitting and delivering separate opinions) stated the joint conclusion—quoted at the beginning of the Supreme Court's opinion, infra—that Section 25 of the Judiciary Act of 1789 [4] was unconstitutional.

---

4. The text of section 25: "That a final judgment or decree in any suit, in the highest court of law or equity of a State in which a decision in the suit could be had, where is drawn in question the validity of a treaty or statute of, or an authority exercised under the United States, and the decision is against their validity; or where is drawn in question the validity of a statute of, or an authority exercised under any State, on the ground of their being repugnant to the constitution, treaties or laws of the United States, and the decision is in favour of such their validity, or where is drawn in question the construction of any clause of the constitution, or of a treaty, or statute of, or commission held under the United States, and the decision is against the title, right, privilege or exemption specially set up or claimed by either party, under such clause of the said Constitution, treaty, statute or commission, may be re-examined and reversed or affirmed in the Supreme Court of the United States upon a writ of error, the cita- tion being signed by the chief justice, or judge or chancellor of the court rendering or passing the judgment or decree complained of, or by a justice of the Supreme Court of the United States, in the same manner and under the same regulations, and the writ shall have the same effect, as if the judgment or decree complained of had been rendered or passed in a circuit court, and the proceeding upon the reversal shall also be the same, except that the Supreme Court, instead of remanding the cause for a final decision as before provided, may at their discretion, if the cause shall have been once remanded before, proceed to a final decision of the same, and award execution. But no other error shall be assigned or regarded as a ground of reversal in any such case as aforesaid, than such as appears on the face of the record, and immediately respects the before mentioned questions of validity or construction of the said constitution, treaties, statutes, commissions, or authorities in dispute."

The bases for this joint conclusion are indicated by the following extracts from the opinion of Judge Cabell: "The present government of the United States, grew out of the weakness and inefficacy of the confederation, and was intended to remedy its evils. Instead of a government of requisition, we have a government of power. But how does the power operate? On individuals in their individual capacity. No one presumes to contend, that the state governments can operate compulsively on the general government or any of its departments, even in cases of unquestionable encroachment on state authority. . . . Such encroachment of jurisdiction could neither be prevented nor redressed by the state government, or any of its departments, by any procedure acting on the Federal Courts. I can perceive nothing in the constitution which gives to the Federal Courts any stronger claim to prevent or redress, by any procedure acting on the state courts, an equally obvious encroachment on the Federal jurisdiction. The constitution of the United States contemplates the independence of both governments and regards the residuary sovereignty of the states, as not less inviolable, than the delegated sovereignty of the United States. It must have been foreseen that controversies would sometimes arise as to the boundaries of the two jurisdictions. Yet the constitution has provided no umpire, has erected no tribunal by which they shall be settled. The omission proceeded, probably, from the belief, that such a tribunal would produce evils greater than those of the occasional collisions which it would be designed to remedy. . . .

"If this Court should now proceed to enter a judgment in this case, according to instructions of the Supreme Court, the Judges of this Court, in doing so, must act either as Federal or as State Judges. But we cannot be made Federal Judges without our consent, and without commissions. Both these requisites being wanting, the act could not, therefore, be done by us, constitutionally, as Federal Judges. We must, then, in obeying this mandate, be considered still as State Judges. We are required, as State Judges to enter up a judgment, not our own, but dictated and prescribed to us by another Court. . . . But, before one Court can dictate to another, the judgment it shall pronounce, it must bear, to that other, the relation of an appellate Court. The term appellate, however, necessarily includes the idea of superiority. But one Court cannot be correctly said to be superior to another, unless both of them belong to the same sovereignty. It would be a misapplication of terms to say that a Court of Virginia is superior to a Court of Maryland, or vice versa. The Courts of the United States, therefore, belonging to one sovereignty, cannot be appellate Courts in relation to the State Courts, which belong to a different sovereignty—and, of course, their commands or instructions impose no obligation.

". . . But the act of Congress now under consideration, attempts, in fact, to make the State Courts Inferior Federal Courts, and to exercise through them, jurisdiction over the subjects of federal cognizance.

". . . [T]he appellate jurisdiction of the Supreme Court of the United States [under Article III of the Constitution], must have reference to the inferior Courts of the United States, and not to the State Courts. . . . It has been contended that the constitution contemplated only the objects of appeal, and not the tribunals from which the appeal is to be taken; and intended to give to the Supreme Court of the United States appellate jurisdiction in all the cases of federal cognizance. But this argument proves too much, and what is utterly inadmissible. It would give appellate jurisdiction, as well over the courts of England or France, as over the State courts; for, although I do not think the State Courts are foreign Courts in relation to the Federal Courts, yet I consider them not less independent than foreign Courts."

To the argument that without the appellate jurisdiction "there will be no other mode by which congress can extend the judicial power of the United States to the cases of federal cognizance; that there will, consequently be no uniformity of decision," Judge Cabell replied: "All the purposes of the constitution of the United States will be answered by the erection of Federal Courts, into which any party, plaintiff or defendant, concerned in a case of federal cognizance, may carry it for adjudication." Judges Roane and Fleming argued further that, even if Section 25 were constitutional, the case had not properly been before the Supreme Court, since the record did not show that the Virginia decision turned upon a treaty; and if the Supreme Court "had held itself at liberty, to go outside of the record, and resort to those reports, which are deemed authentic evidences of the decisions therein contained," the report would have shown "that the decision of this Court was rendered upon another, and ordinary ground of jurisdiction—the act of compromise."

With the Virginia court's refusal to obey the mandate, the stage was set for a second argument and decision in the United States Supreme Court:

STORY, J., delivered the opinion of the court.

This is a writ of error from the Court of Appeals of Virginia, founded upon the refusal of that court to obey the mandate of this court, requiring the judgment rendered in this very cause, at February term, 1813, to be carried into due execution. The following is the judgment of the Court of Appeals rendered on the mandate: "The Court is unanimously of opinion, that the appellate power of the Supreme Court of the United States does not extend to this court, under a sound construction of the constitution of the United States; that so much of the 25th section of the act of Congress to establish the judicial courts of the United States, as extends the appellate jurisdiction of the supreme court to this court, is not in pursuance of the constitution of the United States; that the writ of error, in this cause, was improvidently allowed, under the authority of that act; that the proceedings thereon in the Supreme Court were *coram non judice,* in relation to this court, and that obedience to its mandate be declined by the court."

The questions involved in this judgment are of great importance and delicacy. Perhaps it is not too much to affirm, that, upon their right decision, rest some of the most solid principles which have hitherto been supposed to sustain and protect the Constitution itself. . . .

The Constitution unavoidably deals in general language. It did not suit the purposes of the people, in framing this great charter of our liberties, to provide for minute specifications of its powers or to declare the means by which those powers should be carried into execution. It was foreseen that this would be a perilous and difficult, if not an impracticable, task. The instrument was not intended to provide merely for the exigencies of a few years, but was to endure through a long lapse of ages, the events of which were locked up in the inscrutable purposes of Providence. . . . Hence its powers are expressed in general terms, leaving to the legislature, from time to time, to adopt its own means to effectuate legitimate objects, and to mould and model the exercise of its powers, as its own wisdom, and the public interest, should require. . . .

The third article of the Constitution is that which must principally attract our attention. . . . The language of the article throughout is manifestly designed to be mandatory upon the legislature. Its obligatory force is so imperative, that Congress could not, without a violation of its duty, have refused to carry it into operation. The judicial power of the United States *shall be vested* (not may be vested) in one supreme court. and such inferior courts as Congress may, from time to time, ordain and establish. . . .

If, then, it is a duty of Congress to vest the judicial power of the United States, it is a duty to vest the *whole judicial power.* The language, if imperative as to one part, is imperative as to all. If it were otherwise, this anomaly would exist, that Congress might successively refuse to vest the jurisdiction in any one class of cases enumerated in the constitution, and thereby defeat the jurisdiction as to all; for the constitution has not singled out any class on which Congress are bound to act in preference to others.

The next consideration is as to the courts in which the judicial power shall be vested. It is manifested that a supreme court must be established; but whether it be equally obligatory to establish inferior courts, is a question of some difficulty. If congress may lawfully omit to establish inferior courts, it might follow, that in some of the enumerated cases the judicial power could nowhere exist. The supreme court can have original jurisdiction in two classes of cases only, viz., in cases affecting ambassadors, other public ministers and consuls, and in cases in which a state is a party. Congress cannot vest any portion of the judicial power of the United States, except in courts ordained and established by itself; and if in any of the cases enumerated in the constitution, the state courts did not then possess jurisdiction, the appellate jurisdiction of the supreme court (admitting that it could act on state courts) could not reach those cases, and consequently, the injunction of the constitution, that the judicial power *"shall be vested,"* would be disobeyed. It would seem, therefore, to follow, that congress are bound to create some inferior courts, in which to vest all that jurisdiction which, under the constitution, is *exclusively* vested in the United States, and of which the supreme court cannot take original cognizance. They might establish one or more inferior courts; they might parcel out the jurisdiction among such courts, from time to time, at their own pleasure. But the whole judicial power of the United States should be, at all times, vested either in an original or appellate form, in some courts created under its authority. . . .

It being, then, established that the language of this clause is imperative, the next question is as to the cases to which it shall apply. The answer is found in the constitution itself. The judicial power shall extend to all the cases enumerated in the constitution. As the mode is not limited, it may extend to all such cases, in any form, in which judicial power may be exercised. It may, therefore, extend to them in the shape of original or appellate jurisdiction, or both; for there is nothing in the nature of the cases which binds to the exercise of the one in preference to the other.* . . .

But, even admitting that the language of the constitution is not mandatory, and that congress may constitutionally omit to vest the judicial power in courts of the United States, it cannot be denied that when it is vested, it may be exercised to the utmost constitutional extent.

Shows that his 2nd argu. unnec. 4)

This leads us to the consideration of the great question as to the nature and extent of the appellate jurisdiction of the United States. We have already seen that appellate jurisdiction is given by the constitution to the supreme court in all cases where it has not original jurisdiction; subject, however, to such exceptions and regulations as congress may prescribe. It is, therefore, capable of embracing every case enumerated in the constitution, which is not exclusively to be decided by way of original jurisdiction. But the exercise of appellate jurisdiction is far from being limited by the terms of the constitution to the supreme court. There can be no doubt that congress may create a succession of inferior tribunals, in each of which it may vest appellate as well as original jurisdiction. The judicial power is delegated by the constitution in the most general terms, and may, therefore, be exercised by congress under every variety of form, of appellate or original jurisdiction. And as there is nothing in the constitution which restrains or limits this power, it must, therefore, in all other cases, subsist in the utmost latitude of which, in its own nature, it is susceptible.

As, then, by the terms of the constitution, the appellate jurisdiction is not limited as to the supreme court, and as to this court it may be exercised in all other cases than those of which it has original cognizance, what is there to restrain its exercise over state tribunals in the enumerated cases? The appellate power is not limited by the terms of the third article to any particular courts. The words are, "the judicial power (which includes appellate power) shall extend to *all cases*," &c., and "in all other cases before mentioned the supreme court shall have appellate jurisdiction." It is the *case*, then, and not *the court*, that gives the jurisdiction. If the judicial power extends to the case it will be in vain to search in the letter of the constitution for any qualification as to the tribunal where it depends. It is incumbent, then, upon those who assert such a qualification to show its existence by necessary implication. If the text be clear and distinct, no restriction upon its plain and obvious import ought to be admitted, unless the inference be irresistible.

It is the case, & not the ct. that gives juris.

If the constitution meant to limit the appellate jurisdiction to cases pending in the courts of the United States, it would necessarily follow that the jurisdiction of these courts would, in all the cases enumerated in the constitution, be exclusive of state tribunals. How otherwise could the jurisdiction extend to *all* cases arising under the constitution, laws, and treaties of the United States, or to *all* cases of admiralty and maritime jurisdiction? If some of these cases might be entertained by state tribunals, and no appellate jurisdiction as to them should exist, then the appellate power would not extend to *all*, but to *some*, cases. If state tribunals might exercise concurrent jurisdiction over all or some of the other classes of cases in the

Juris. extends to all cases

* Should these four paragraphs, on the "mandatory" nature of Article III, be taken literally? That question is considered further in a note near the end of this chapter, "Congress and the Lower Federal Courts," p. 57, below.

constitution without control then the appellate jurisdiction of the United States might, as to such cases, have no real existence, contrary to the manifest intent of the constitution. Under such circumstances, to give effect to the judicial power, it must be construed to be exclusive; and this not only when the *casus faederis* should arise directly, but when it should arise, incidentally, in cases pending in state courts. This construction would abridge the jurisdiction of such court far more than has been ever contemplated in any act of congress.

On the other hand, if, as has been contended, a discretion be vested in congress to establish, or not to establish, inferior courts at their own pleasure, and congress should not establish such courts, the appellate jurisdiction of the supreme court would have nothing to act upon, unless it could act upon cases pending in the state courts. Under such circumstances it must be held that the appellate power would extend to state courts; for the constitution is peremptory that it shall extend to certain enumerated cases, which cases could exist in no other courts. Any other construction, upon this supposition, would involve this strange contradiction, that a discretionary power vested in congress, and which they might rightfully omit to exercise, would defeat the absolute injunctions of the constitution in relation to the whole appellate power.

But it is plain that the framers of the constitution did contemplate that cases within the judicial cognizance of the United States not only might but would arise in the state courts, in the exercise of their ordinary jurisdiction. With this view the sixth article declares, that "this constitution, and the laws of the United States which shall be made in pursuance thereof, and all treaties made, or which shall be made, under the authority of the United States, shall be the supreme law of the land, and the judges in every state shall be bound thereby, any thing in the constitution or laws of any state to the contrary notwithstanding." It is obvious that this obligation is imperative upon the state judges in their official, and not merely in their private, capacities. From the very nature of their judicial duties they would be called upon to pronounce the law applicable to the case in judgment. They were not to decide merely according to the laws or constitution of the state, but according to the constitution, laws and treaties of the United States—"the supreme law of the land." . . .

It must, therefore, be conceded that the constitution not only contemplated, but meant to provide for cases within the scope of the judicial power of the United States, which might yet depend before state tribunals. It was foreseen that in the exercise of their ordinary jurisdiction, state courts would incidentally take cognizance of cases arising under the constitution, the laws, and treaties of the United States. Yet to all these cases the judicial power, by the very terms of the constitution, is to extend. It cannot extend by original jurisdiction if that was already rightfully and exclusively attached in the state courts, which (as has been already shown) may occur; it must, therefore, extend by appellate jurisdiction, or not at all. It would seem to follow that the appellate power of the United States must, in such cases, extend to state tribunals; and if in such cases, there is no reason why it should not equally attach upon all others within the purview of the constitution.

It has been argued that such an appellate jurisdiction over state courts is inconsistent with the genius of our governments, and the spirit of the constitution. That the latter was never designed to act upon state sovereignties, but only upon the people, and that if the power exists, it will materially impair the sovereignty of the states, and the independence of their courts. We cannot yield to the force of this reasoning; it assumes principles which we cannot admit, and draws conclusions to which we do not yield our assent.

[margin, handwritten: Argu. against suits of S.Ct. extending to state cts.]

[margin, handwritten: ↓ answer to above]

It is a mistake that the constitution was not designed to operate upon states, in their corporate capacities. It is crowded with provisions which restrain or annul the sovereignty of the states in some of the highest branches of their prerogatives. The tenth section of the first article contains a long list of disabilities and prohibitions imposed upon the states. Surely, when such essential portions of state sovereignty are taken away, or prohibited to be exercised, it cannot be correctly asserted that the constitution does not act upon the states. The language of the constitution is also imperative upon the states as to the performance of many duties. It is imperative upon the state legislatures to make laws prescribing the time, places, and manner of holding elections for senators and representatives, and for elections for senators and representatives, and for electors of president and vice-president. And in these, as well as some other cases, congress have a right to revise, amend, or supercede the laws which may be passed by state legislatures. When, therefore, the states are stripped of some of the highest attributes of sovereignty, and the same are given to the United States; when the legislatures of the states are, in some respects, under the control of congress, and in every case are under the constitution, bound by the paramount authority of the United States; it is certainly difficult to support the argument that the appellate power over the decisions of state courts is contrary to the genius of our institutions. The courts of the United States can, without question, revise the proceedings of the executive and legislative authorities of the states, and if they are found to be contrary to the constitution, may declare them to be of no legal validity. Surely the exercise of the same right over judicial tribunals is not a higher or more dangerous act of sovereign power.

Nor can such a right be deemed to impair the independence of state judges. It is assuming the very ground in controversy to assert that they possess an absolute independence of the United States. In respect to the powers granted to the United States, they are not independent; they are expressly bound to obedience by the letter of the constitution; and if they should unintentionally transcend their authority, or misconstrue the constitution, there is no more reason for giving their judgments an absolute and irresistible force, than for giving it to the acts of the other co-ordinate departments of state sovereignty. . . .

[margin, handwritten: Answer to claim that it would impair indep. of state judges.]

It is further argued, that no great public mischief can result from a construction which shall limit the appellate power of the United States to cases in their own courts: first, because state judges are bound by oath to support the constitution of the United States, and must be presumed to be men of learning and integrity; and, secondly, because congress must have an unquestionable right to remove all cases within the scope of the judicial power from the state courts to the courts of the United States, at any time before final judgment, though not after final judgment. As to the

[margin, handwritten: art VI]

first reason—admitting that the judges of the state courts are, and always will be, of as much learning, integrity, and wisdom, as those of the courts of the United States, (which we very cheerfully admit), it does not aid the argument. It is manifest that the constitution has proceeded upon a theory of its own, and given or withheld powers according to the judgment of the American people, by whom it was adopted. . . . .

This is not all. A motive of another kind, perfectly compatible with the most sincere respect for state tribunals, might induce the grant of appellate power over their decisions. That motive is the importance, and even necessity of *uniformity* of decisions throughout the whole United States, upon all subjects within the purview of the constitution. Judges of equal learning and integrity, in different states, might differently interpret a statute, or a treaty of the United States, or even the constitution itself: if there were no revising authority to control these jarring and discordant judgments, and harmonize them into uniformity, the laws, the treaties, and the constitution of the United States would be different in different states, and might, perhaps, never have precisely the same construction, obligation, or efficacy, in any two states. The public mischiefs that would attend such a state of things would be truly deplorable; and it cannot be believed that they could have escaped the enlightened convention which formed the constitution. What, indeed, might then have been only prophecy, has now become fact; and the appellate jurisdiction must continue to be the only adequate remedy for such evils.

There is an additional consideration, which is entitled to great weight. The constitution of the United States was designed for the common and equal benefit of all the people of the United States. The judicial power was granted for the same benign and salutary purposes. It was not to be exercised exclusively for the benefit of parties who might be plaintiffs, and would elect the national forum, but also for the protection of defendants who might be entitled to try their rights, or assert their privileges, before the same forum. Yet, if the construction contended for be correct, it will follow, that as the plaintiff may always elect the state court, the defendant may be deprived of all the security which the constitution intended in aid of his rights. Such a state of things can, in no respect, be considered as giving equal rights. To obviate this difficulty, we are referred to the power which it is admitted congress possess to remove suits from state courts to the national courts; and this forms the second ground upon which the argument we are considering has been attempted to be sustained.

This power of removal is not to be found in express terms in any part of the constitution; if it be given, it is only given by implication, as a power necessary and proper to carry into effect some express power. The power of removal is certainly not, in strictness of language, an exercise of original jurisdiction; it presupposes an exercise of original jurisdiction to have attached elsewhere. The existence of this power of removal is familiar in courts acting according to the course of the common law in criminal as well as civil cases, and it is exercised before as well as after judgment. But this is always deemed in both cases an exercise of appellate, and not of original jurisdiction. If, then, the right of removal be included in the appellate jurisdiction, it is only because it is one mode of exercising that power, and as congress is not limited by the constitution to any particular mode, or time of exercising it, it may authorize a removal either before or after judgment. The time, the process, and the manner, must be subject to its absolute legislative control. A writ of error is, indeed, but a process which removes the record of one court to the possession of another court, and enables the latter to inspect the proceedings, and give such judgment as its own opinion of the law and justice of the case may warrant. There is nothing in the nature of the process which forbids it from being applied by the legislature to interlocutory as well as final judgments. And if the right of removal from state courts exists before judgment, because it is included in the appellate power, it must, for the same reason, exist after judgment. And if the appellate power by the constitution does not include cases pending in state courts, the right of removal, which is but a mode of exercising that power, cannot be applied to them. Precisely the same objections, therefore, exist as to the right of removal before judgment, as after, and both must stand or fall together. Nor indeed, would the force of the arguments on either side materially vary, if the right of removal were an exercise of original jurisdiction. It would equally trench upon the jurisdiction and independence of state tribunals.

The remedy, too, of removal of suits would be utterly inadequate to the purposes of the constitution, if it could act only on the parties, and not upon the state courts. In respect to criminal prosecutions, the difficulty seems admitted to be insurmountable; and in respect to civil suits, there would, in many cases, be rights without corresponding remedies. If state courts should deny the constitutionality of the authority to remove suits from their cognizance, in what manner could they be compelled to relinquish the jurisdiction? In respect to criminal cases, there would at once be an end of all control, and the state decisions would be paramount to the constitution; and though in civil suits the courts of the United States might act upon the parties, yet the state courts might act in the same way; and this conflict of jurisdictions would not only jeopardize private rights, but bring into imminent peril the public interests.

On the whole, the court are of opinion, that the appellate power of the United States does extend to cases pending in the state courts; and that the 25th section of the judiciary act, which authorizes the exercise of this jurisdiction in the specified cases, by a writ of error, is supported by the letter and spirit of the constitution. We find no clause in that instrument which limits this power; and we dare not interpose a limitation where the people have not been disposed to create one.

Strong as this conclusion stands upon the general language of the constitution, it may still derive support from other sources. It is an historical fact, that this exposition of the constitution, extending its appellate power to state courts, was, previous to its adoption, uniformly and publicly avowed by its friends, and admitted by its enemies, as the basis of their respective reasonings, both in and out of the state conventions. It is an historical fact, that at the time when the judiciary act was submitted to the deliberations of the first congress, composed, as it was, not only of men of great learning and ability, but of men who had acted a principal part in framing, supporting, or opposing that constitution, the same exposition was explicitly declared and admitted by the friends and by the opponents of that system. It is an historical fact, that the supreme court of the United States have, from time to time, sustained this appellate jurisdiction in a great variety of cases, brought from the tribunals of many of the most important states in the union, and that no state tribunal has ever breathed a judicial doubt on the subject, or declined to obey the mandate of the supreme court, until the present occasion. This weight of contemporaneous exposition by all parties, this acquiescence of enlightened state courts, and these judicial decisions of the supreme court through so long a period, do, as we think, place the doctrine upon a foundation of authority which cannot be shaken, without delivering over the subject to perpetual and irremediable doubts.

The next question which has been argued, is whether the case at bar be within the purview of the 25th section of the judiciary act, so that this court may rightfully sustain the present writ of error? . . .

That the present writ of error is founded upon a judgment of the court below, which drew in question and denied the validity of a statute of the United States, is incontrovertible, for it is apparent upon the face of the record. That this judgment is final upon the rights of the parties, is equally true; for if well founded, the former judgment of that court was of conclusive authority, and the former judgment of this court utterly void. . . . The case, then, falls directly within the terms of the act. It is a final judgment in a suit in a state court, denying the validity of a statute of the United States; and unless a distinction can be made between proceedings under a mandate, and proceedings in an original suit, a writ of error is the proper remedy to revise that judgment. In our opinion, no legal distinction exists between the cases. . . .

But it is contended, that the former judgment of this court was rendered upon a case, not within the purview of this section of the judicial act, and that, as it was pronounced by an incompetent jurisdiction, it was utterly void, and cannot be a sufficient foundation to sustain any subsequent proceedings. To this argument, several answers may be given. In the first place, it is not admitted, that, upon this writ of error, the former record is before us. The error now assigned is not in the former proceedings, but in the judgment rendered upon the mandate issued after the former judgment. The question now litigated is not upon the construction of a treaty, but upon the constitutionality of a statute of the United States, which is clearly within our jurisdiction. In the next place, in ordinary cases, a second writ of error has never been supposed to draw in question the propriety of the first judgment, and it is difficult to perceive how such a proceeding could be sustained, upon principle. . . .

In this case, however, from motives of a public nature, we are entirely willing to waive all objections, and to go back and re-examine the question of jurisdiction, as it stood upon the record formerly in judgment. We have great confidence, that our jurisdiction will, on a careful examination, stand confirmed, as well upon principle as authority.* . . .

The objection urged at the bar is, that this court cannot inquire into the title, but simply into the correctness of the construction put upon the treaty by the court of appeals; and that their judgment is not re-examinable here, unless it appear on the face of the record, that some construction was put upon the treaty. If, therefore, that court might have decided the case upon the

---

* The remaining passages of the opinion raise in a preliminary way problems of adequate-state-grounds barriers to Supreme Court review—problems considered at greater length in chap. 2, sec. 3, p. 108, below.

invalidity of the title (and *non constat,* that they did not), independent of the treaty, there is an end of the appellate jurisdiction of this court.   In support of this objection, much stress is laid upon the last clause of the section, which declares, that no other cause shall be regarded as a ground of reversal than such as appears on the face of the record and immediately respects the construction of the treaty, &c., in dispute.

If this be the true construction of the section, it will be wholly inadequate for the purposes which it professes to have in view, and may be evaded at pleasure.   But we see no reason for adopting this narrow construction; and there are the strongest reasons against it, founded upon the words as well as the intent of the legislature.   What is the case for which the body of the section provides a remedy by writ of error?   The answer must be, in the words of the section, a suit where is drawn in question the construction of a treaty, and the decision is against the title set up by the party.   It is, therefore, the decision against the title set up, with reference to the treaty, and not the mere abstract construction of the treaty itself, upon which the statute intends to found the appellate jurisdiction.   How, indeed, can it be possible to decide, whether a title be within the protection of a treaty, until it is ascertained what that title is, and whether it have a legal validity?   From the very necessity of the case, there must be a preliminary inquiry into the existence and structure of the title, before the court can construe the treaty in reference to that title.   If the court below should decide, that the title was bad, and therefore, not protected by the treaty, must not this court have a power to decide the title to be good, and therefore, protected by the treaty?   Is not the treaty, in both instances, equally construed, and the title of the party in reference to the treaty, equally ascertained and decided?   .   .   .

It has been asserted at the bar, that, in point of fact, the court of appeals did not decide either upon the treaty, or the title apparent upon the record, but upon a compromise made under an act of the legislature of Virginia.   If it be true (as we are informed), that this was a private act, to take effect only upon a certain condition, viz., the execution of a deed of release of certain lands, which was matter *in pais,* it is somewhat difficult to understand, how the court could take judicial cognizance of the act, or of the performance of the condition, unless spread upon the record.   At all events, we are bound to consider, that the court did decide upon the facts actually before them.   The treaty of peace was not necessary to have been stated, for it was the supreme law of the land, of which all courts must take notice.   And at the time of the decision in the court of appeals, and in this court, another treaty had intervened, which attached itself to the title in controversy, and of course, must have been the supreme law to govern the decision, if it should be found applicable to the case.   It was in this view that this court did not deem it necessary to rest its former decision upon the treaty of peace, believing that the title of the defendant was, at all events, perfect, under the treaty of 1794.   .   .   .

We have thus gone over all the principal questions in the cause, and we deliver our judgment with entire confidence, that it is consistent with the constitution and laws of the land.   We have not thought it incumbent on us to give any opinion upon the question, whether this court have authority to issue a writ of *mandamus* to the court of appeals, to enforce the former judgments, as we did not think it necessarily involved in the decision of this cause.

It is the opinion of the whole court, that the judgment of the court of appeals of Virginia, rendered on the mandate in this cause, be reversed, and the judgment of the district court, held at Winchester, be, and the same is hereby affirmed.

JOHNSON, J. It will be observed, in this case, that the court disavows all intention to decide on the right to issue compulsory process to the state courts; thus leaving us, in my opinion, where the constitution and laws place us—supreme over persons and cases, so far as our judicial powers extend, but not asserting any compulsory control over the state tribunals. In this view, I acquiesce in their opinion, but not altogether in the reasoning or opinion of my brother who delivered it. . . .

SUPREME COURT AUTHORITY TO REVIEW STATE COURT JUDGMENTS

1. *The Cohens decision and state criminal cases.* Five years after Martin v. Hunter's Lessee, its principles were reaffirmed and extended in Cohens v. Virginia, 6 Wheat. 264 (1821). The Court held that Section 25 gave jurisdiction to review state court judgments in criminal proceedings as well. [Could an argument be made that Section 25 was limited to civil cases? See the text, quoted in footnote 4 to Martin, supra. At the time of Martin, Justice Story had unsuccessfully urged that Congress amend the Judicial Code to reach state criminal cases. As Story described the provision he drafted, it would give Supreme Court review in criminal cases "in the same manner as the existing law (Judicial Act 1789, s. 25) gives it in relation to *civil suits*." The statement was in a memorandum printed in part in I The Life and Letters of Joseph Story (W. W. Story ed. 1851), 293. Although counsel for Virginia in Cohens claimed that Section 25 did not cover the prosecution of the Cohens brothers for selling District of Columbia lottery tickets in Virginia, they did not argue that Section 25 was limited to civil cases. Chief Justice Marshall's opinion stated that Section 25 "comprehends expressly the case under consideration," but it is doubtful that he had in mind the civil-criminal distinction that had troubled Justice Story in 1816.]

In Cohens, Virginia moved to dismiss the writ of error to the Virginia court for want of jurisdiction, contending, inter alia, that the Constitution did not confer jurisdiction in controversies between a State and one of its own citizens, and that the grant of original jurisdiction in cases "in which a State shall be a party" excluded the exercise of appellate jurisdiction in such cases. The Court denied the motion and held that "the judicial power, as originally given, extends to all cases arising under the constitution or a law of the United States, whoever may be the parties."

Chief Justice Marshall's opinion pointed out that cases to which the jurisdiction of the federal courts may extend fall into two classes: "In the first, their jurisdiction depends on the character of the clause, whoever may be the parties. This class comprehends 'all cases in law and equity arising under this constitution, the laws of the United States, and treaties made, or which shall be made, under their authority.' This clause extends the jurisdiction of the Court to all the cases described, without making in its terms any exception whatever, and without any regard to the condition of the party. . . . In the second class, the jurisdiction depends entirely on the character of the parties. In this are comprehended 'controversies between two or more States, between a State and citizens of another State,' 'and between a State and foreign States, citizens or subjects.' If these be the parties, it is entirely unimportant what may be the subject of controversy. Be it what it may, these parties have a constitutional right to come into the Courts of the Union." [Marshall, who had not participated in Martin, also took the occasion to restate the defense of Section 25—an opportunity he had reached for as well two years earlier, in the concluding numbers of an anonymous series of newspaper replies to press attacks from Spencer Roane. See John Marshall's Defense of McCulloch v. Maryland (Gunther ed. 1969), 200–14.]

2. *State challenges to Supreme Court authority and authoritativeness.* A number of states other than Virginia challenged the right of the Supreme Court to review state court decisions in the period before the Civil War— often on grounds far broader than those advanced by Virginia in the Martin and Cohens cases. See generally Warren, "Legislative and Judicial Attacks on the Supreme Court of the United States—A History of the Twenty-Fifth Section of the Judiciary Act," 47 Am.L.Rev. 1, 161 (1913); Reference Note, "Interposition vs. Judicial Power—A Study of Ultimate Authority in Constitutional Questions," 1 Race Rel.L.Rep. 465 (1956). Warren's article describes challenges from the courts of seven states and mentions several attempts in Congress to repeal Section 25—the first major one in 1821, immediately after Cohens; the most serious one in 1831, see H.Rep.No. 43, 21st Cong., 2d Sess. (1831).

The position of Virginia in Martin should be distinguished from the more extreme positions denying the general authoritativeness—and occasionally the specific enforceability—of federal court decisions, on the ground of the states' right to "interpose" their own interpretations of the Constitution against federal action. These "interposition" statements ranged from the general protest of the Virginia and Kentucky Resolutions of 1798 to South Carolina's Nullification efforts in 1832 and the later Secession movement. Though these more extreme contentions tended to share common premises (e. g., the compact theory of the Union) and common language (e. g., "null and void" declarations), they, too, varied widely in operative consequences. An excellent sampling of the state resolutions appears in Ames, State Documents on Federal Relations (1906).

In examining the pre-Civil War state contentions, it is important to read the broad assertions in light of the specific remedial, operative portions of the state resolutions. As with the presidential statements quoted in the notes following Marbury v. Madison, supra, it is useful to distinguish between statements (a) denying that constitutional interpretations are exclusively the function of the federal courts or that federal interpretations bind the nation, and (b) asserting that federal court orders may be disobeyed. Compare, for example, Madison's 1800 Report on the Virginia Resolutions (see chap. 5, p. 420, infra) (denying that "the judicial authority is to be regarded as the sole expositor of the Constitution in the last resort" and urging congressional repeal of the Alien and Sedition Laws), with direct state defiance of federal court authority (e. g., the South Carolina Nullification Ordinance of 1832, making punishable as contempt the taking of certain appeals to the

United States Supreme Court, 1 South Carolina Statutes at Large 330 (1836); the act of December 1832, carrying the Ordinance into effect, providing in Section 6 that anyone arrested pursuant to a federal court order enforcing the tariff shall be entitled to habeas corpus and to damages for unlawful imprisonment, id. at 372; Georgia's defiance of the mandate in Worcester v. Georgia, 6 Pet. 515 (1832), see Burke, "The Cherokee Cases: A Study in Law, Politics, and Morality," 21 Stan.L.Rev. 500 (1969); and the bill passed by the Georgia House of Representatives in 1793, stating that "any Federal Marshal, or any other person" seeking to execute the mandate in Chisholm v. Georgia, 2 Dall. 419 (1793), shall be "guilty of felony, and shall suffer death, without the benefit of clergy, by being hanged," Ames, supra, 10.)

For more recent state "interposition" resolutions, reviving the pre-Civil War tradition, see, e. g., 1 Race Rel.L.Rep. 437–447 (1956) (1956 legislative resolutions of Alabama, Georgia, Mississippi, South Carolina, and Virginia). For Supreme Court replies, see Cooper v. Aaron, 358 U.S. 1 (1958), p. 28, supra, and Bush v. Orleans Parish School Board, 364 U.S. 500 (1960). In Bush, the Court, per curiam, denied motions for a stay of a three-judge District Court order enjoining the enforcement of Louisiana interposition laws directed at school desegregation. The Court quoted from the District Court decision, 188 F.Supp. 916, 926: "The conclusion is clear that interposition is not a *constitutional* doctrine. If taken seriously, it is illegal defiance of constitutional authority." The Supreme Court added: "The main basis for challenging this ruling is that the State of Louisiana 'has interposed itself in the field of public education over which it has exclusive control.' This objection is without substance, as we held, upon full consideration, in Cooper v. Aaron."

On the importance of Supreme Court review of cases challenging state laws, see, in addition to the principal case, Justice Holmes' well-known statement: "I do not think the United States would come to an end if we lost our power to declare an act of Congress void. I do think that the Union would be imperiled if we could not make that declaration as to the laws of the several states." Holmes, Collected Legal Papers (1920), 295.

3. *Enforcement of court mandates.* A Supreme Court reversal of a state court judgment may not be determinative of the outcome of the case. Ordinarily, the Supreme Court merely remands for "proceedings not inconsistent with the opinion of this Court." Under such a mandate, the state court is free to consider any undetermined questions or even to re-examine already decided matters of state law. If it is contended that the state court failed to follow the Supreme Court mandate, the appropriate remedy, when available, is to seek a new review of the judgment. In cases of state recalcitrance, the Supreme Court has at times entered judgment and awarded execution, or remanded with specific directions to enter judgment. On the availability of mandamus to compel obedience to a Supreme Court mandate where the state court decision on remand is nonfinal and accordingly not directly reviewable under the jurisdictional statutes, see Deen v. Hickman, 358 U.S. 57 (1958). See generally 28 U.S.C. §§ 2106 and 1651, and Stern and Gressman, Supreme Court Practice (4th ed. 1969), 87, 142.

A number of statutory provisions suggest specific remedies to overcome resistance to federal court orders: e. g., as to the powers and duties of

Habeas corpus—"produce body"

United States marshals in executing judgments, see 28 U.S.C. §§ 547, 549, 672; as to the use of the contempt power in the event of "disobedience or resistance," see 18 U.S.C. §§ 401, 402; as to the use of armed forces by the executive "to enforce the laws of the United States," see 10 U.S.C. §§ 332, 333, 15. See generally Reference Note, "Enforcement of Court Orders—Federal Contempt Proceedings and Prevention of Obstruction," 2 Race Rel.L.Rep. 1051 (1957), and Pollitt, "Presidential Use of Troops to Execute the Law," 36 N.C.L.Rev. 117 (1958).

Ex parte = by or for one party.

EX PARTE McCARDLE

7 Wall. 506, 19 L.Ed. 264 (1869).

Appeal from the Circuit Court for the Southern District of Mississippi.

[Under the post-Civil War Reconstruction Acts, Congress imposed military government on a large number of the former Confederate States. McCardle was a Mississippi newspaper editor in military custody on charges of publishing "incendiary and libelous articles." He brought this habeas corpus proceeding under an Act of Congress of February 5, 1867, which authorized federal courts to grant habeas corpus to anyone restrained "in violation of the Constitution" and which also authorized appeals to the Supreme Court. After the Circuit Court denied McCardle's habeas petition, he appealed to the Supreme Court. After the Supreme Court sustained jurisdiction of that appeal, 6 Wall. 318 (1868), and after argument was heard on the merits, Congress passed the Act of March 27, 1868. That law stated that so much of the 1867 Act "as authorized an appeal from the judgment of the Circuit Court to the Supreme Court of the United States, or the exercise of any such jurisdiction by said Supreme Court, on appeals which have been, or may hereafter be taken, be, and the same is hereby repealed." The historical context is developed further in note 1 following the opinion dismissing the appeal.]

The Chief Justice [CHASE] delivered the opinion of the Court.

The first question necessarily is that of jurisdiction; for, if the act of March, 1868, takes away the jurisdiction defined by the act of February, 1867, it is useless, if not improper, to enter into any discussion of other questions.

It is quite true, as was argued by the counsel for the petitioner, that the appellate jurisdiction of this Court is not derived from acts of Congress. It is, strictly speaking, conferred by the Constitution. But it is conferred "with such exceptions and under such regulations as Congress shall make."

It is unnecessary to consider whether, if Congress had made no exceptions and no regulations, this court might not have exercised general appellate jurisdiction under rules prescribed by itself. From among the earliest acts of the first Congress, at its first session, was the act of September 24th, 1789, to establish the judicial courts of the United States. That act provided for the organization of this court, and prescribed regulations for the exercise of its jurisdiction.

The source of that jurisdiction, and the limitations of it by the Constitution and by statute, have been on several occasions subjects of consideration here. In the case of Durousseau v. The United States [6 Cranch 307] particularly, the whole matter was carefully examined, and the court held, that while "the appellate powers of this court are not given by the judicial act, but are given by the Constitution," they are, nevertheless, "limited and regulated by that act, and by such other acts as have been passed on the subject." The court said, further, that the judicial act was an exercise of the power given by the Constitution to Congress "of making exceptions to the appellate jurisdiction of the Supreme Court." "They have described affirmatively," said the court, "its jurisdiction, and this affirmative description has been understood to imply a negation of the exercise of such appellate power as is not comprehended within it."

The principle that the affirmation of appellate jurisdiction implies the negation of all such jurisdiction not affirmed having been thus established, it was an almost necessary consequence that acts of Congress, providing for the exercise of jurisdiction, should come to be spoken of as acts granting jurisdiction and not as acts making exceptions to the constitutional grant of it.

The exception to appellate jurisdiction in the case before us, however, is not an inference from the affirmation of other appellate jurisdiction. It is made in terms. The provision of the act of 1867, affirming the appellate jurisdiction of this court in cases of habeas corpus is expressly repealed. It is hardly possible to imagine a plainer instance of positive exception.

We are not at liberty to inquire into the motives of the legislature. We can only examine into its power under the Constitution; and the power to make exceptions to the appellate jurisdiction of this court is given by express words.

What, then, is the effect of the repealing act upon the case before us? We cannot doubt as to this. Without jurisdiction the court cannot proceed at all in any cause. Jurisdiction is power to declare the law, and when it ceases to exist, the only function remaining to the court is that of announcing the fact and dismissing the cause. And this is not less clear upon authority than upon principle.

Several cases were cited by the counsel for the petitioner in support of the position that jurisdiction of this case is not affected by the repealing act. But none of them, in our judgment, afford any support to it. They are all cases of the exercise of judicial power by the legislature, or of legislative interference with courts in the exercising of continuing jurisdiction.

On the other hand, the general rule, supported by the best elementary writers, is, that "when an act of the legislature is repealed, it must be considered, except as to transactions past and closed, as if it never existed." And the effect of repealing acts upon suits under acts repealed, has been determined by the adjudications of this court. The subject was fully considered in Norris v. Crocker [13 How. 429] and more recently in Insurance Company v. Ritchie [5 Wall. 541]. In both of these cases it was held that no judgment could be rendered in a suit after the repeal of the act under which it was brought and prosecuted.

It is quite clear, therefore, that this court cannot proceed to pronounce judgment in this case, for it has no longer jurisdiction of the appeal; and judicial duty is not less fitly performed by declining ungranted jurisdiction than in exercising firmly that which the Constitution and the laws confer.

Counsel seem to have supposed, if effect be given to the repealing act in question, that the whole appellate power of the court, in cases of habeas corpus, is denied. But this is an error. The act of 1868 does not except from that jurisdiction any cases but appeals from Circuit Courts under the act of 1867. It does not affect the jurisdiction which was previously exercised.

The appeal of the petitioner in this case must be dismissed for want of jurisdiction.

CONGRESSIONAL CONTROL OF SUPREME COURT JURISDICTION

Introduction. Consider, in examining the principal case and the following notes: How far-reaching is the congressional power sustained in McCardle? Does the historical context of that case substantially weaken its force as precedent? Is it possible to state viable limits on the power of Congress to enact "Exceptions" and "Regulations" of the Supreme Court's appellate jurisdiction? Does Article III impose significant limits? Do other provisions of the Constitution—for example, the Fifth Amendment? Do basic constitutional assumptions about judicial review impose enforceable limits on the power of Congress? Is the Court really vulnerable to serious political reprisals from Congress unless limiting principles on McCardle can be stated? Or are there significant practical restraints on the jurisdiction-limiting weapon?

1. *McCardle in historical context.* Congressional policies after the Civil War produced sharp conflicts with the other branches. President Andrew Johnson opposed the Reconstruction Acts, for example; and there were repeated efforts to test their constitutionality in the courts. The McCardle case moved to a climax at the height of the tension between Congress and President and after two earlier efforts to elicit Supreme Court rulings had failed.

Soon after the basic provisions of reconstruction legislation had been passed over the President's veto, challenges in the courts were launched. Prospects for success seemed good if the Court reached the merits: the military government features looked vulnerable in view of a case decided by the Supreme Court just before the reconstruction laws were passed. Ex parte Milligan, 4 Wall. 2 (1867), chap. 7, p. 611, below. The first attack on the reconstruction laws in the Supreme Court came when the State of Mississippi challenged their constitutionality through an action to enjoin presidential enforcement. But in Mississippi v. Johnson, 4 Wall. 475 (1867), the Supreme Court concluded that it lacked power to issue such an order against the President. The State of Georgia immediately brought a similar action against the Secretary of War. Once again, the Court dismissed on jurisdictional grounds: it held in Georgia v. Stanton, 6 Wall. 50 (1868), that the suit raised nonjusticiable political questions. But then, while Congress was considering a variety of measures to curb the judicial threat to reconstruction, the Court took jurisdiction of McCardle's appeal.

With that constitutional challenge formally before the Court and with argument on the merits already concluded (but, as the official report noted, "before conference in regard to the decision proper to be made") Congress passed the 1868 law withdrawing appellate jurisdiction. By then, impeachment proceedings against President Johnson had begun. Nevertheless, he vetoed the law. With the Court standing by and withholding action on the case before it pending the outcome of the political battle, Congress overrode the veto. Argument on the jurisdiction-curtailing law was then sought in the Court. And, as one more manifestation of the political crisis hovering over the case, that argument had to be postponed because of (as the official report put it) "the Chief Justice being detained from his place here, by his duties in the Court of Impeachment."

There was one more effort to elicit a ruling on reconstruction after the dismissal of the McCardle appeal. In Ex parte Yerger, 8 Wall. 85 (1869), the Court took jurisdiction of a proceeding by another petitioner in military detention in Mississippi. Yerger, like McCardle, had unsuccessfully sought habeas in a lower federal court. But Yerger came to the Supreme Court by a route different from McCardle's: he did not invoke the appeal provision of the 1867 Act; accordingly, the Court found, the 1868 repeal did not apply. Yet a decision on the constitutionality of the Reconstruction Acts was once again averted: before the Court could rule on the merits, Yerger was released from military custody.

2. *The search for limits on congressional power.* Understandably, the congressional power to make exceptions to appellate jurisdiction proved tempting to some critics of Warren Court decisions. And their efforts to curtail Court jurisdiction in turn spurred the search for principles to blunt that weapon. A limit on Article III power articulated by Professor Henry M. Hart, Jr., has been widely resorted to by Court defenders in Congress and out. Hart urged that "the exceptions must not be such as will destroy the essential role of the Supreme Court in the constitutional plan." See Hart, "The Power of Congress to Limit the Jurisdiction of Federal Courts: An Exercise in Dialectic," 66 Harv.L.Rev. 1362, 1365 (1953). What is that "essential role"?

See also Ratner, "Congressional Power Over the Appellate Jurisdiction of the Supreme Court," 109 U.Pa.L.Rev. 157 (1960). Ratner would interpret the Article III congressional power as if it read: "With such exceptions and under such regulations as Congress may make, not inconsistent with the essential functions of the Supreme Court under this Constitution." He sees two such functions: to maintain the supremacy of federal law; and to provide "ultimate resolution of inconsistent or conflicting interpretations of federal law by state and federal courts." Would Section 25 of the 1789 Act have met that test? Would the present jurisdictional provisions, printed below, p. 59? Ratner would hold unconstitutional any effort to bar review "in every case involving a particular subject."

Compare Wechsler, "The Courts and the Constitution," 65 Colum.L. Rev. 1001 (1965), on constitutional arguments that would prohibit any alterations of appellate jurisdiction "motivated by hostility to the decisions of the Court": "I see no basis for this view and think it antithetical to the plan of the Constitution for the courts—which was quite simply that the Congress would decide from time to time how far the federal judicial institutions should be used within the limits of the federal judicial power."

Determining congressional power on the basis of the "constitutional plan" and the "essential functions" of the Supreme Court invites return to basic issues of Marbury v. Madison and judicial review. Thus, the Wechsler argument includes a reminder that federal courts do not pass on constitutional questions because of any "special function vested in them to enforce the Constitution or police the other agencies of government." And a lengthy defense of a broadly conceived view of judicial review is central in the most elaborate challenge to broad congressional power over appellate jurisdiction, Raoul Berger's book, Congress v. the Supreme Court (1969).

Berger concludes that "the express 'exceptions' power cannot bar access to judicial protection of constitutional rights." But only a small portion of his book-length attack on congressional power deals with the "exceptions" provision directly; most of the volume is a defense of the legitimacy of judicial review. Given the breadth of intended judicial power, he argues, it would be incongruous to authorize as much congressional control as the McCardle ruling and the Wechsler comment suggest: the Framers, he urges at 286, "were deeply concerned with, and in no little part designed judicial review as a restraint on, *Congressional* excesses. If the Court was intended to curb Congressional excesses in appropriately presented 'cases or controversies' and if an attempt to exercise that power might in turn be blocked by Congress as a judicial 'excess,' then the Convention was aimlessly going in circles." His narrow reading of the "exceptions" power is illustrated by his review, at 289, of the ratification debates: they "revolved almost exclusively about the retrial of facts found by a jury"; they contain "not the faintest intimation" that the "exceptions" clause "was designed to enable Congress to withdraw jurisdiction to declare an Act of Congress void." He agrees with Hart, moreover, that congressional power to regulate jurisdiction is subject to constitutional limits such as the Fifth Amendment. See Battaglia v. General Motors Corp., 169 F.2d 254, 257 (2d Cir. 1948).

Berger even invokes Franklin D. Roosevelt's resort to the Court-packing technique (see the note on the 1937 crisis in chap. 4, p. 285) to support his narrow reading of the "exceptions" power. The New Deal Administration would not have sought to increase the size of the Court if hostile decisions could have been blocked via the jurisdictional route: "All the hullabaloo about 'Court-packing' was so easily avoidable if this alternative is so legitimate and available." But are there not other explanations for that choice? For example, may not FDR's method of attacking the Court illustrate the severe practical limitation on the appellate-jurisdiction-curtailing technique? If Congress simply withdraws Supreme Court jurisdiction, inconsistent interpretations in lower courts are likely. Moreover, prior Supreme Court rulings would persist as precedents: "The jurisdiction of withdrawal thus might work to freeze the very doctrines that have prompted its enactment, placing an intolerable moral burden on the lower courts." Wechsler, "The Courts and the Constitution," 65 Colum.L.Rev. 1001, 1006 (1965). Would Berger's "constitutional plan" premise for a narrow reading of the "exceptions" power not also bar all other Court-curbing weapons of Congress (such as Court-packing), with the possible exception of impeachment?

3. *The vitality of McCardle and the Klein case.* Congress has not given the Court cause to reexamine McCardle directly, but Justice Douglas found occasion to call it in question in a footnote to a dissent a few years ago. "There is a serious question whether the McCardle case could command

a majority view today," he said in an opinion joined by Justice Black in Glidden Co. v. Zdanok, 370 U.S. 530, 605 (1962).

The Glidden case, with a majority opinion by Justice Harlan, dealt mainly with the distinction between Article I "legislative courts" and Article III courts. The context of Justice Douglas' remark about McCardle was as follows: "The opinion of my Brother Harlan stirs a host of problems that need not be opened. What is done will, I fear, plague us for years. First, that opinion cites with approval Ex parte McCardle, 7 Wall. 506, in which Congress withdraw jurisdiction of this Court to review a habeas corpus case that was *sub judice* and then apparently draws a distinction between that case and United States v. Klein, 13 Wall. 128, where such withdrawal was not permitted in a property claim. There is a serious question whether the McCardle case could command a majority view today. Certainly the distinction between liberty and property (which emanates from this portion of my Brother Harlan's opinion) has no vitality even in terms of the Due Process Clause."

Is that all there is to the Klein-McCardle distinction? Consider the fuller statement of Klein which follows. Does the Klein-McCardle difference reflect simply a preference of property over liberty? Or does the Klein case rest on a principle more acceptable today—a principle of continuing utility as a limit on congressional power over jurisdiction? Justice Harlan's reference to Klein came in the following passage in Glidden: "The authority [of Congress to control the jurisdiction of Article III courts] is not, of course, unlimited. In 1870, Congress purported to withdraw jurisdiction from the Court of Claims and from this Court on appeal over cases seeking indemnification for property captured during the Civil War, so far as eligibility therefor might be predicated upon an amnesty awarded by the President, as both courts had previously held that it might. Despite Ex parte McCardle, supra, the Court refused to apply the statute to a case in which the claimant had already been adjudgd to recover by the Court of Claims, calling it an unconstitutional attempt to invade the judicial province by prescribing a rule of decision in a pending case. United States v. Klein, 13 Wall. 128 [1872]."

In the Klein controversy, earlier rulings had held that a presidential pardon satisfied the requirement that a property claimant was not a supporter of the "rebellion." The new statute enacted while Klein's appeal was pending provided that a pardon was to be taken as showing quite the contrary, that the claimant had aided the rebellion, and went on to provide that the courts were to dismiss such claims for want of jurisdiction. The Court opinion holding the law unconstitutional stated that the Court would have upheld it as an exercise of the "exceptions" power if "it simply denied the right of appeal in a particular class of cases." But here the jurisdictional language was only "a means to an end": "to deny to pardons granted by the President the effect which this court had adjudged them to have." The Court concluded that dismissing the appeal would allow Congress to "prescribe rules of decision to the Judicial Department of the government in cases pending before it." There was a violation of separation of powers principles not only because of this legislative interference with judicial power but also because "impairing the effect of a pardon" infringed "the constitutional power of the Executive."

4. *Congressional control: contemporary concerns.* a. *The Roberts defense.* During the Warren years, most congressional interest in appellate jurisdiction was prompted by proposals for piecemeal withdrawals. Yet not long before, there was serious attention to suggestions to deprive Congress of that weapon. Former Justice Roberts, for example, proposed a constitutional amendment to assure the Court's appellate jurisdiction in all constitutional cases. "Now is the Time: Fortifying the Supreme Court's Independence," 35 A.B.A.J. 1 (1949). Senator John Marshall Butler of Maryland, with the support of several bar associations, introduced an amendment including such an assurance in 1953. S.J.Res. 44 83d Cong., 1st Sess. (1953). The Senate approved, but the House tabled. See 79 A.B.A.Rep. 242 (1954).

b. *The Jenner-Butler attack.* Within a few years, Congress became more concerned with curtailing jurisdiction than with safeguarding it. See, e. g., Senator Jenner's bill—provoked by several Warren Court decisions—eliminating appellate jurisdiction in cases involving, for example, the federal employees' security program, state subversive legislation, and state bar admissions. S. 2646, 85th Cong., 1st Sess. (1957). The rapid shift in political winds was symbolized by Senator John Marshall Butler: a sponsor of the pro-Court amendment in 1953, he now joined with Senator Jenner to sponsor a revised version of the Jenner proposal. The Jenner-Butler bill [S. 3386, 85th Cong., 2d Sess. (1958)] would have included the following provision—prompted by the 1957 decisions in Konigsberg v. State Bar, 353 U.S. 252, and Schware v. Board of Bar Examiners, 353 U.S. 252—: "Notwithstanding the provisions of sections 1253, 1254, and 1257 of [28 U.S.C.], the Supreme Court shall have no jurisdiction to review, either by appeal, writ of certiorari, or otherwise, any case where there is drawn into question the validity of any law, rule, or regulation of any State, or of any board of bar examiners, or similar body, or of any action or proceeding taken pursuant to any such law, rule, or regulation pertaining to the admission of persons to the practice of law within such State."

Would the Jenner-Butler provision have been constitutional? The bill was narrowly defeated. For the political struggle, see Murphy, Congress and the Court (1962), and Senate Judiciary Committee, Hearings on S. 2646, 85th Cong., Limitation of the Appellate Jurisdiction of the Supreme Court (1957–58). See generally Elliott, "Court-Curbing Proposals in Congress," 33 Notre Dame Law. 597 (1958).

Another provision in the Jenner-Butler omnibus proposal—in reaction to such cases as Watkins v. United States, 354 U.S. 178 (1957)—would have amended 2 U.S.C. § 192, the congressional contempt statute. That law states that anyone "who having being summoned as a witness" by any congressional committee and who wilfully "refuses to answer any question pertinent to the question under inquiry" shall be guilty of a misdemeanor. The Jenner-Butler bill would have added: "Provided, That for the purposes of this section any question shall be deemed pertinent unless timely objection is made thereto on the ground that such question lacks pertinency, or when such objection is made, if such question is ruled pertinent by the body conducting the hearing." Would this provision have been subject to substantial constitutional objections? Under McCardle? Under Klein?

c. *The Tuck and Dirksen bills.* Compare the unsuccessful congressional attempts in 1964 to curtail federal jurisdiction in legislative apportionment cases. The efforts were reactions to Baker v. Carr, 369 U.S. 186 (1962), and Reynolds v. Sims, 377 U.S. 533 (1964). The House adopted the Tuck bill, H.R. 11926, 88th Cong., 2d Sess.: "The Supreme Court shall not have the right to review the action of a Federal court or a State court of last resort concerning any action taken upon a petition or complaint seeking to apportion or reapportion any legislature of any State of the Union or any branch thereof. . . . The district courts shall not have jurisdiction to entertain any petition or complaint seeking to apportion or reapportion the legislature of any State of the Union or any branch thereof, nor shall any order or decree of any district or circuit court now pending and not finally disposed of by actual reapportionment be hereafter enforced."

In the Senate, Senator Dirksen proposed a bill, S. 3069, 88th Cong., 2d Sess., ultimately introduced as an amendment to a foreign aid bill. The Dirksen rider provided: "Upon application made by or on behalf of any State or by one or more citizens thereof in any action or proceeding in any court of the United States, or before any justice or judge of the United States, in which there is placed in question the validity of the composition of either house of the legislature of that State or the apportionment of the membership thereof, such action or proceeding shall be stayed until the end of the second regular session of the legislature of that State which begins after the date of enactment of this section." Debate on the proposal produced a "baby filibuster," various amendments, and finally Senate adoption of a "sense of Congress" bill stating that in any reapportionment suit the federal court order "could properly, in the absence of unusual circumstances," allow postponement for a limited time to enable the state legislature to reapportion itself. The differing House and Senate provisions on reapportionment were, in the end, eliminated by the conference committee. See McKay, "Court, Congress, and Reapportionment," 63 Mich.L.Rev. 255 (1964).

d. *The 1968 crime control bill and some questions.* The Senate Judiciary Committee's version of the 1968 crime control bill—provoked by decisions such as Miranda v. Arizona, 384 U.S. 436 (1966)—included a provision which stated that neither the Supreme Court nor any other Article III court "shall have jurisdiction to review or to reverse, vacate, modify, or disturb in any way, a ruling of any trial court of any State in any criminal prosecution admitting in evidence as voluntarily made an admission or confession of any accused." See Title II of the amended S. 917, 90th Cong., 2d Sess., in Sen.Rep.No.1097. That Report contains an elaborate defense of congressional power over jurisdiction, but all anti-Miranda provisions couched in jurisdictional terms were eliminated on the floor of the Senate prior to passage of the Omnibus Crime Control and Safe Streets Act of 1968.

Do any of these proposals raise constitutional questions? Under McCardle? Under Klein? Under Marbury v. Madison? Note the passage from Justice Rutledge's dissent in Yakus v. U. S., 321 U.S. 414, 468 (1944): "It is one thing for Congress to withhold jurisdiction. It is entirely another to confer it and direct that it be exercised in a manner inconsistent with constitutional requirements or, what in some instances may be the same thing, without regard to them. . . . Whenever the judicial power is called into play it is responsible directly to the fundamental law and no other authority can intervene to force or authorize the judicial body to disregard it."

Yakus involved the congressional effort in the Emergency Price Control Act of 1942 to restrict constitutional litigation to a single federal court. It provided that the validity of OPA regulations could be tested only in an administrative proceeding, subject to review by a specially constituted Emergency Court of Appeals and ultimately by the Supreme Court. The Yakus petitioners had not resorted to this exclusive statutory procedure and were not permitted to raise the defense of invalidity in a criminal prosecution for violation of an OPA regulation. The Supreme Court affirmed the convictions: "There is no constitutional requirement that that test [of the validity of a regulation] be made in one tribunal rather than in another, so long as there is an opportunity to be heard and for judicial review which satisfies the demands of due process, as is the case here." * For challenges to other congressional efforts to channel the place and timing of litigation in the federal courts, see South Carolina v. Katzenbach, 383 U.S. 301 (1966) (chap. 6, p. 534, below), sustaining a provision of the Voting Rights Act of 1965 limiting certain suits by states to courts in the District of Columbia, and Clark v. Gabriel, 393 U.S. 256 (1968), sustaining a ban on preinduction judicial review in the 1967 draft act (—but compare Oestereich v. Selective Service Board, 393 U.S. 233 (1968), finding that ban inapplicable to certain claims).

CONGRESS AND THE LOWER FEDERAL COURTS

1. *The Story position.* Recall Justice Story's statements regarding the "mandatory" nature of Article III, at the beginning of his opinion in Martin v. Hunter's Lessee, supra, suggesting that Congress must create lower federal courts and must vest full jurisdiction in them. Were his remarks intended to be legally binding on Congress—or were they merely a moral appeal to Congress? The latter explanation seems more consistent with Story's contemporaneous actions. In other cases, for example, he dismissed cases not within the jurisdictional statutes, on the ground that the lower court "has no jurisdiction which is not given by some statute." White v. Fenner, Fed. Cas. No. 17,547 (Cir.Ct.R.I.1818). Perhaps even more significant are his activities as legislative lobbyist at the time of Martin.

Story, who had seen state challenges to federal authority at close range in his New England circuit duties during the War of 1812, was particularly anxious to make use of the relative harmony at the end of the War to solidify national institutions. For several years, he wrote frequent letters to associates influential in Congress urging legislation and frequently enclosing drafts. In December 1815, for example, he asked the aid of the new Reporter, Henry Wheaton, in "vindicating the necessity of establishing other great national institutions: the extension of the jurisdiction of the courts of the U. S. over *the whole* extent contemplated in the Constitution; the appointment of national notaries public & national justices of the peace; national port wardens & pilots for all the ports of the U. S.; a national bank; & a national bankrupt law." I The Life and Letters of Joseph Story (W. W. Story ed. 1851), 271.

---

* The Act involved in Yakus also contained a ban on state court challenges. That provision was sustained in Bowles v. Willingham, 321 U.S. 503 (1944). May Congress compel state courts to entertain claims arising under federal statutes? May state courts enjoin illegal federal action? These problems are further considered in the materials on State Autonomy, chap. 10, sec. 2, infra.

One of his favorite projects was a comprehensive judicial code. In submitting one of his drafts, he made it clear that he did not think that Article III automatically created lower courts with full jurisdiction: "The object of this section is to give to the Circuit Court *original* jurisdiction of all cases intended by the Constitution to be confided to the judicial power of the United States, where that jurisdiction has not been already delegated by law. If it was proper in the Constitution to provide for such a jurisdiction, it is wholly irreconcilable with the sound policy or interests of the Government to suffer it to slumber. . . . It is truly surprising and mortifying to know how little effective power now exists in this department. . . . I will barely illustrate my positions by a reference to a single class of cases. No Court of the United States has any general delegation of authority 'in all cases in law and equity arising under the Constitution, the laws of the United States, and the treaties made, or to be made, under its authority.' The consequence is, that in thousands of instances arising under the laws of the United States, the parties are utterly without remedy, or with a very inadequate remedy." Id., 293–294.

The general "federal question" jurisdiction Story desired in 1816 was not in fact vested in the lower federal courts until 1875. Story's dicta in Martin were, apparently, an appeal to Congress—an appeal that failed. Moreover, the view that the creation and jurisdiction of lower federal courts was largely left to Congress is supported by the debates at the Constitutional Convention as well as by a number of court decisions.

At the Convention, the proposal for inferior federal courts was a major source of controversy. The relevant provisions of Article III reflect a compromise between opposing views: one insisting on the mandatory creation of lower federal courts; the other leaving initial application of federal law entirely to the state courts, with uniformity assured through Supreme Court review. And that compromise was reflected in the Judiciary Act of 1789 as well, creating some lower federal courts with some, but not nearly all, of the potential federal jurisdiction described in Article III.

2. *Sheldon v. Sill.* Among the most explicit Court decisions sustaining that view is Sheldon v. Sill, 8 How. 440 (1850), upholding the assignee clause of the 1789 Judiciary Act against a claim that the statute could not bar lower court jurisdiction of a case within the description of cases in Article III. Justice Grier's opinion explained:

"It must be admitted, that if the Constitution had ordained and established the inferior courts, and distributed to them their respective powers, they could not be restricted or divested by Congress. But as it has made no such distribution, one of two consequences must result,—either that each inferior court created by Congress must exercise all the judicial powers not given to the Supreme Court, or that Congress, having the power to establish the courts, must define their respective jurisdictions. The first of these inferences has never been asserted, and could not be defended with any show of reason, and if not, the latter would seem to follow as a necessary consequence. And it would seem to follow, also, that, having a right to prescribe, Congress may withhold from any court of its creation jurisdiction of any of the enumerated controversies. Courts created by statute can have no jurisdiction but such as the statute confers. No one of them can assert a just claim to jurisdiction exclusively conferred on another, or withheld from all.

"The Constitution has defined the limits of the judicial power of the United States, but has not prescribed how much of it shall be exercised by the Circuit Court; consequently, the statute which does prescribe the limits of their jurisdiction, cannot be in conflict with the Constitution, unless it confers powers not enumerated therein."

SUPREME COURT JURISDICTION: THE MODERN FRAME-WORK—CONSTITUTION, STATUTES, RULES

THE CONSTITUTION

Art. III, Sec. 1. The judicial Power of the United States, shall be vested in one supreme Court, and in such inferior Courts as the Congress may from time to time ordain and establish. . . .

Art. III, Sec. 2. The judicial Power shall extend to all Cases, in Law and Equity, arising under this Constitution, the Laws of the United States, and Treaties made, or which shall be made, under their Authority;—to all Cases affecting Ambassadors, other public Ministers and Consuls;—to all Cases of admiralty and maritime Jurisdiction;—to Controversies to which the United States shall be a Party;—to Controversies between two or more States;—between a State and Citizens of another State;—between Citizens of different States;—between Citizens of the same State claiming Lands under Grants of different States, and between a State, or the Citizens thereof, and foreign States, Citizens or Subjects.

In all Cases affecting Ambassadors, other public Ministers and Consuls, and those in which a State shall be a Party, the supreme Court shall have original Jurisdiction. In all the other Cases before mentioned, the supreme Court shall have appellate Jurisdiction, both as to Law and Fact, with such Exceptions, and under such Regulations as the Congress shall make. . . .

THE STATUTES

1. *Review of state court judgments. a. The modern provisions.* Review of state court proceedings is governed by Section 1257 of Title 28 of the United States Code:

"Final judgments or decrees rendered by the highest court of a State in which a decision could be had, may be reviewed by the Supreme Court as follows:

"(1) By appeal, where is drawn in question the validity of a treaty or statute of the United States and the decision is against its validity.

"(2) By appeal, where is drawn in question the validity of a statute of any state on the ground of its being repugnant to the Constitution, treaties or laws of the United States, and the decision is in favor of its validity.

"(3) By writ of certiorari, where the validity of a treaty or statute of the United States is drawn in question or where the validity of a State statute is drawn in question on the ground of its being repugnant to the Constitution, treaties or laws of the United States, or where any title, right, privilege or immunity is specially set up or claimed under the Constitution, treaties or statutes of, or commission held or authority exercised under, the United States."

b. *Assuring supremacy and uniformity.* Note the similarities and differences between Section 25 of the Judiciary Act of 1789 (quoted in a footnote to Martin v. Hunter's Lessee, above) and its modern counterpart, 28 U.S.C. § 1257. Thus, under Section 25 and well into the Twentieth Century, Supreme Court review was available only if the state court *denied* federal claims—for example, by sustaining a state statute or setting aside a federal law. Jurisdiction was broadened in 1914, when Supreme Court review was for the first time extended to cases in which the state court had *sustained* the federal claim. Assurance of greater uniformity in federal law interpretation, not simply assurance of federal supremacy, thus became a major goal of the review statute.

Is the uniformity need adequately met today? Not even the 1914 extension, now reflected in 28 U.S.C. § 1257(3), provides for the correction of all errors in state court interpretation of federal law. The decision which provoked the 1914 change illustrates the point. In Ives v. South Buffalo Ry. Co., 201 N.Y. 271 (1911), the state court had held New York's workmen's compensation law unconstitutional under the due process clauses of the federal as well as the state constitution. The New York court's interpretation of the federal due process clause was thought to be more restrictive than the Supreme Court's position, yet no review was possible under the old law. But under the 1914 expansion, ironically, review would also have been impossible— because of the "adequate state ground" limit on Supreme Court jurisdiction considered more fully in chap. 2, sec. 3, below.

c. *Appeals and certiorari.* Under section 25 and an expansion (enacted in 1867 and considered in Murdock v. City of Memphis, chap. 2, p. 109, below), all state cases within the statute could be taken to the Supreme Court as a matter of right, by writ of error. The 1914 expansion introduced review in the discretion of the Supreme Court in certain cases and that method was expanded by the Judges' Bill of 1925. Obligatory review is covered by the "appeal" sections of 28 U.S.C. § 1257; discretionary review by the "certiorari" provisions. The taking of an appeal in a case where certiorari is the appropriate mode of review is not ground for dismissal. Rather, 28 U.S.C. § 2103 requires that in such a case (whether from a state court or from a lower federal court) "the papers whereon the appeal was taken shall be regarded and acted on as a petition for writ of certiorari."

To a considerable extent, determination of whether appeal or certiorari is the appropriate channel of review of a state court decision lies within the discretion of counsel in framing his federal objection in the state court. That control by litigants rests largely on the interpretation of a predecessor to 28 U.S.C. § 1257 in Dahnke-Walker Milling Co. v. Bondurant, 257 U.S. 282 (1921). There, a Tennessee corporation brought a contract suit against a Kentucky resident in a Kentucky court. The defendant successfully contended in the state court that the contract was unenforceable because the corporation had not qualified to do business in Kentucky pursuant to a state statue. The plaintiff objected that the commerce clause of the United States Constitution prevented the application of the statute to an interstate commerce transaction. The state court conceded that the statute could not be applied to transactions in interstate commerce, but held that the transaction in question was "strictly intrastate." The Supreme Court decided that the case was properly before it on writ of error (now appeal), since the plaintiff "did not simply claim a right or immunity under the Constitution of the United States, but distinctly insisted that as to the transaction in question the Kentucky statute was void." When the state court nevertheless enforced the statute, its action constituted "an affirmation of its validity when so applied." Justice Brandeis, dissenting, insisted that "the validity of the statute was not actually drawn in question. Only the propriety of the application or use of the statute is questioned." He predicted: "If jurisdiction upon writ of error can be obtained by the mere claim in words that a state statute is invalid, if so construed as to 'apply' to a given state of facts, the right to a review will depend, in large classes of cases, not upon the nature of the constitutional question involved, but upon the skill of counsel." (Problems in the exercise of the appeal and certiorari jurisdictions are considered further with the Supreme Court Rules materials below and in chap. 2.)

2. *Review of judgments of federal courts.* The most commonly invoked provision as to lower federal court proceedings is 28 U.S.C. § 1254, which provides for Supreme Court review of cases in the Courts of Appeals:

"(1) By writ of certiorari granted upon the petition of any party to any civil or criminal case, before or after rendition of judgment or decree;

"(2) By appeal by a party relying on a State statute held by a court of appeals to be invalid as repugnant to the Constitution, treaties or laws of the United States, but such appeal shall preclude review by writ of certiorari at the instance of such appellant, and the review on appeal shall be restricted to the Federal questions presented;

"(3) By certification at any time by a court of appeals of any question of law in any civil or criminal case as to which instructions are desired, and upon such certification the Supreme Court may give binding instructions or require the entire record to be sent up for decision of the entire matter in controversy."

Review of cases in the Court of Claims and the Court of Customs and Patent Appeals is provided by 28 U.S.C. §§ 1255 and 1256. In a few cases, moreover, the Judicial Code provides for direct Supreme Court review of District Court decisions within the obligatory appeal jurisdiction. Thus, 28 U.S.C. § 1253 permits a direct appeal from an order granting or denying an injunction in any civil action required to be heard by three-judge District Courts. Three-judge District Courts are required, for example, in actions seeking to enjoin the enforcement of state and federal statutes upon constitutional grounds. See 28 U.S.C. §§ 2281 and 2282, and D. Currie, "The Three-Judge District Court in Constitutional Litigation," 32 U.Chi. L.Rev. 1 (1964). But three-judge courts are also required in cases of seemingly less importance. See 28 U.S.C. § 2325 (injunctions against ICC orders). Should the appeal-certiorari distinction be retained? Should review be a matter of Supreme Court discretion in all cases? Should there be fewer cases in the obligatory appeal category? Should there be different cases? See generally Strong, "The Time Has Come to Talk of Major Curtailment in the Supreme Court's Jurisdiction," 48 N.C.L.Rev. 1 (1969), urging that Supreme Court review be limited to constitutional cases and that a new court be established with final authority in nonconstitutional cases. [On the Supreme Court's original jurisdiction, see the Marbury v. Madison materials above and 28 U.S.C. § 1251.]

THE SUPREME COURT'S RULES

The Supreme Court's Rules were most recently revised in 1967 and are reported at 388 U.S. 933. The Rules include provisions governing review as of right (by appeal) and review at the discretion of the Court (by certiorari). See generally Stern and Gressman, Supreme Court Practice (4th ed. 1969).

1. *Appeal.* a. Review by appeal is initiated by filing a notice of appeal with the court from which the appeal is taken. The case is then docketed in the Supreme Court by filing the record, and the appeal is perfected by payment of the docket fee, entry of counsel's appearance, and filing of the Jurisdictional Statement. Typically, about 5 percent of the total cases disposed of in a Court Term are appeals. (The total caseload handled by the Court in recent Terms has been over 3000).

The contents of the Jurisdictional Statement are prescribed by Rule 15. The Statement must demonstrate the basis for the Court's jurisdiction. Rule 15(d), for example, provides in part: "If the appeal is from a state court, the statement of the case shall also specify the stage in the proceedings in the court of first instance, and in the appellate court, at which, and the manner in which, the federal questions sought to be reviewed were raised; the method of raising them (e. g., by a pleading, by request to charge and exceptions, by assignment of error); and the way in which they were passed upon by the court; with such pertinent quotations of specific portions of the record, or summary thereof, with specific reference to the places in the record where the matter appears (e. g., ruling on exception, portion of the court's charge and exception thereto, assignment of error) as will support the assertion that the rulings of the court were of a nature to bring the case within the statutory provision believed to confer jurisdiction on this court."

b. The Court does not hear oral argument in every appeal case which seems to satisfy the requirements apparent on the face of the jurisdictional statutes. To warrant oral argument, the questions in the case must be shown to be sufficiently substantial to require plenary consideration. If the questions are not so substantial, the Court will grant a motion to dismiss, in cases from state courts, or a motion to affirm, in cases from federal courts. One of the important purposes of the Jurisdictional Statement is, therefore, the weeding out of frivolous appeals. Thus Rule 15(e) requires in part: "If the appeal is from a state court, there shall be included a presentation of the grounds upon which it is contended that the federal questions are substantial (Zucht v. King, 260 U.S. 174, 176, 177), which . . . shall include the reasons why the questions presented are so substantial as to require plenary consideration, with briefs on the merits and oral argument, for their resolution." (Note that a dismissal for insubstantiality *does* express a view on the merits—see note d below.)

c. If a case meets all of the requirements of the obligatory jurisdiction, may the Court nevertheless refuse to consider the merits? May discretionary ingredients (appropriate on certiorari) properly enter the judgment on whether to adjudicate an appeal? That problem (of duty and discretion regarding adjudication) recurs throughout chap. 2. Note especially the handful of cases in which the Court has declined to decide on the merits cases apparently within the appeal jurisdiction, considered in chap. 2, sec. 4, "Discretionary Abstention from the Exercise of Jurisdiction."

d. Note the comments on the exercise of the appeal jurisdiction in *Ohio ex rel. Eaton v. Price*, 360 U.S. 246 (1959). "The Court's practice [said Justice Brennan, who voted to note probable jurisdiction], when considering a jurisdictional statement whereby a litigant attempts to invoke the Court's jurisdiction on appeal, is quite similar to its well-known one on applications for writs of certiorari. That is, if four Justices or more are of opinion that the questions presented by the appeal should be fully briefed and argued orally, an order noting probable jurisdiction or postponing further consideration of the jurisdictional questions to a hearing on the merits is entered. Even though this action is taken on the votes of only a minority of four of the Justices, the Court then approaches plenary consideration of the case anew as a Court; votes previously cast in Conference that the judgment of the Court appealed from be summarily affirmed, or that the appeal be dismissed for want of a substantial federal question, do not conclude the Justices casting them, and every member of the Court brings to the ultimate disposition of the case his judgment based on the full briefs and the oral arguments. Because of this, disagreeing Justices do not ordinarily make a public notation, when an order setting an appeal for argument is entered, that they would have summarily affirmed the judgment below, or have dismissed the appeal from it for want of a substantial federal question. Research has not disclosed any instance of such notations until today.

"The reasons for such forebearance are obvious. Votes to affirm summarily, and to dismiss for want of a substantial federal question, it hardly needs comment, are votes on the merits of a case, and public expression of views on the merits of a case by a Justice before argument and decision may well be misunderstood; the usual practice in judicial adjudication in this country, where hearings are held, is that judgment follow, and not precede them. Public respect for the judiciary might well suffer if any basis were given for an assumption, however wrong in fact, that this were not so. Thus, the practice of not noting dissents from such orders has been followed, regardless of how strongly Justices may have felt as to the merits of a case or how clearly they have thought decision in it controlled by past precedent. A precedent which appears to some Justices, upon the preliminary consideration given a jurisdictional statement, to be completely controlling may not appear to be so to other Justices. Plenary consideration can change views strongly held, and on close, reflective analysis precedents may appear inapplicable to varying fact situations. I believe that this approach will obtain in this case despite the unusual notation made today by four of my colleagues." [In the Eaton case, Justices Frankfurter, Clark, Harlan and Whittaker stated that they had voted against noting probable jurisdiction because they believed that the case should be affirmed on the authority of an earlier decision, *Frank v. Maryland*, 359 U.S. 360 (1959) (p. 891, infra). The Eaton case subsequently produced an affirmance by an equally divided Court. *Ohio ex rel. Eaton v. Price*, 364 U.S. 263 (1960).]

2. *Certiorari.* a. Review within the Court's discretionary jurisdiction is sought by filing a petition for writ of certiorari. The contents of the petition are prescribed by Rule 23. In cases from state courts, Rule 23(f), in language similar to that of Rule 15(d), quoted above, requires a detailed statement to "show that the federal question was timely and properly raised so as to give this court jurisdiction to review."

The votes of four Justices are sufficient for a grant of review on certiorari. The criteria governing the exercise of the Court's discretionary jurisdiction are stated in Rule 19, "Considerations Governing Review on Certiorari." Rule 19(1) provides: "A review on writ of certiorari is not a matter of right, but of sound judicial discretion, and will be granted only where there are special and important reasons therefor. The following, while neither controlling nor fully measuring the court's discretion, indicate the character of reasons which will be considered.

"(a) Where a state court has decided a federal question of substance not theretofore determined by this court, or has decided it in a way probably not in accord with applicable decisions of this court.

"(b) Where a court of appeals has rendered a decision in conflict with the decision of another court of appeals on the same matter; or has decided an important state or territorial question in a way in conflict with applicable state or territorial law; or has decided an important question of federal law which has not been, but should be, settled by this court; or has decided a federal question in a way in conflict with applicable decisions of this court; or has so far departed from the accepted and usual course of judicial proceedings, or so far sanctioned such a departure by a lower court, as to call for an exercise of this court's power of supervision."

b. How does the significance of a denial of a petition for writ of certiorari compare with that of a dismissal of an appeal? See the opinion of Justice Frankfurter "respecting the denial of the petition for writ of certiorari" in Maryland v. Baltimore Radio Show, 338 U.S. 912 (1950): "[A denial] simply means that fewer than four members of the Court deemed it desirable to review a decision of the lower court as a matter 'of sound judicial discretion.' . . . A variety of considerations underlie denials of the writ, and as to the same petition different reasons may lead different Justices to the same result. This is especially true of petitions for review on writ of certiorari to a State court. Narrowly technical reasons may lead to denials. Review may be sought too late; the judgment of the lower court may not be final; it may not be the judgment of a State court of last resort; the decision may be supportable as a matter of State law, not subject to review by this Court, even though the State court also passed on issues of federal law. A decision may satisfy all these technical requirements and yet may commend itself for review to fewer than four members of the Court. Pertinent considerations of judicial policy here come into play. A case may raise an important question but the record may be cloudy. It may be desirable to have different aspects of an issue further illumined by the lower courts. Wise adjudication has its own time for ripening.

"Since there are these conflicting and, to the uninformed, even confusing reasons for denying petitions for certiorari, it has been suggested from time to time that the Court indicate its reasons for denial. Practical considerations preclude. . . . If the Court is to do its work it would not be feasible to give reasons, however brief, for refusing to take these cases. The time that would be required is prohibitive, apart from the fact as already indicated that different reasons not infrequently move different members of the Court in concluding that a particular case at a particular time makes review undesirable. . . . Inasmuch, therefore, as all that a denial of a petition for a writ of certiorari means is that fewer than four members of the Court thought it should be granted, this Court has rigorously insisted that such a denial carries with it no implication whatever regarding the Court's views on the merits of a case which it has declined to review. The Court has said this again and again; again and again the admonition has to be repeated."

c.   Consideration of certiorari petitions clearly consumes a significant portion of the Court's time during the year. See the remarks of Chief Justice Vinson—typical of admonitions by Justices to members of the bar over the years—in an address to the American Bar Association in September, 1949 (69 S.Ct. v): "Throughout the year, in term time and vacation alike, each justice considers carefully every appeal and petition for certiorari or other relief filed with the Clerk. . . . Since the number of such applications has reached approximately fifteen hundred in each of the past several years, you can well understand the magnitude of the task. During the past term of Court, only about 15% of the petitions for certiorari were granted, and this figure itself is considerably higher than the average in recent years. While a great many of the 85% that were denied were far from frivolous, far too many reveal a serious misconception on the part of counsel concerning the role of the Supreme Court in our federal system. . . . Lawyers might be well advised, in preparing petitions for certiorari, to spend a little less time discussing the merits and a little more time demonstrating why it is important that the Court should hear them." For a similar appeal, see Justice Harlan's "Manning the Dikes," 13 Record N.Y.C. Bar Ass'n 541 (1958); for a different view, see Justice Douglas' "The Supreme Court and Its Case Load," 45 Corn.L.Q. 401 (1960). See also Prettyman, "Petitioning the United States Supreme Court—A Primer for Hopeful Neophytes," 51 Va.L.Rev. 582 (1965).

d.   The Court's recent workload is indicated by the following statistics summarizing the business of the October 1968 Term: 3117 cases finally disposed of, with 120 full opinions; 2749 certiorari petitions considered, of which 163 were granted. See "The Supreme Court, 1968 Term," 83 Harv. L.Rev. 7, 282 (1969), and generally Hart, "Foreword: The Time Chart of the Justices," 73 Harv.L.Rev. 84 (1959). Note especially among recent developments in the workload: the increase in the number of cases (compare, with the 3117 cases disposed of in the 1968 Term, 2401 cases disposed of in the 1963 Term, 1670 cases in the 1956 Term, and 1278 cases in the 1952 Term); the relative increase in the size of the Miscellaneous Docket as against the Appellate Docket; and the variations in the percentage of grants of certiorari petitions on the Miscellaneous Docket. The Miscellaneous Docket consists mainly of in forma pauperis petitions from prisoners. In the 1958 Term, for example, 15.3% of the certiorari petitions on the Appellate Docket were granted, as against 3.2% on the Miscellaneous Docket. By the 1962 Term, the figures were 14.3% on the Appellate Docket, 7.8% on the Miscellaneous Docket. By the 1968 Term, the Miscellaneous Docket had become much larger than the Appellate (1829 Miscellaneous cases disposed of, as against 1288 Appellate); and with that increase in absolute numbers, the relative percentage of Miscellaneous certiorari grants declined: 9.3% (101) of Appellate Docket petitions granted, as against 3.7% (62) on the Miscellaneous Docket.

e. In recent years, there has been considerable controversy—on and off the Court—regarding Supreme Court practice in handling certiorari cases. Among the areas of dispute: (a) grants of certiorari in employees' injury actions under federal statutes, on the issue of the adequacy of the evidence, see Note, "Certiorari Policy in Cases Arising Under the FELA," 69 Harv.L.Rev. 1441 (1956), Wilkerson v. McCarthy, 336 U.S. 53 (1949), Ferguson v. Moore-McCormack Lines, Inc., 352 U.S. 521 (1957); (b) the obligation of a Justice to vote on the merits after certiorari has been granted, see Rogers v. Missouri Pac. Ry. Co., 352 U.S. 500 (1957), and Leiman, "The Rule of Four," 57 Colum.L.Rev. 975 (1957); (c) the dismissal of certiorari as "improvidently granted" after argument on the merits, see Rice v. Sioux City Cemetery, 349 U.S. 70 (1955); (d) the summary disposition of cases on the merits, in brief per curiam memoranda, see Note, "Supreme Court Per Curiam Practice: A Critique," 69 Harv.L.Rev. 707 (1956), and Brown, "Foreword—The Supreme Court, 1957 Term," 72 Harv.L.Rev. 77 (1958).

Chapter 2

SUPREME COURT REVIEW IN OPERATION

An introductory note. Only the framework of constitutional adjudication is sketched in the preceding chapter. This chapter explores the process. The foundations of judicial authority considered above are essential but not adequate for an understanding of the institutional context of constitutional litigation. The "jurisdictional" and "procedural" materials which follow provide the minimal amplifications. The purpose of this chapter goes beyond the sharpening of professional skills in advancing constitutional claims for judicial consideration. The concern here is with court as well as with lawyer: under what circumstances is constitutional adjudication permissible and appropriate?

Some of the materials in this chapter will seem technical and esoteric. Yet these "technicalities," about when a court will speak and as to what issues, go to the heart of the Supreme Court's place in the federal system. The Court does not develop substantive doctrine at large or in a vacuum; it can interpret the Constitution only when it sits as a court deciding cases, as Marbury v. Madison made clear at the outset. This chapter, then, seeks to provide a minimum of "federal jurisdiction" material essential to an understanding of constitutional adjudication: What are the institutional limitations on the exercise of judicial review? What are the restrictions imposed by Constitution and Congress, and by the Court's own choices? And what, if any, institutional concerns justify these ground rules of constitutional litigation? *

Some pervasive questions. What are the bases for each of the limitations on the exercise of judicial power considered in this chapter? That is one of the recurrent questions to be kept in mind in examining these materials. Is the limitation compelled by Article III? By a jurisdictional statute? By a Court-made rule or policy? Though the cases in this area abound with obscurities and inconsistencies, an effort to make sense of them is worthwhile, if only because of the practical consequences. Thus, if a barrier to court access is derived from the "case or controversy" requirement of the Constitution, Congress cannot remove it; but if a court's refusal to decide rests simply on a self-imposed policy limitation, Congress can compel adjudication.

Most of the opinions speak about a number of separate prerequisites to the exercise of the federal judicial function—e. g., a concrete controversy (sec. 1, below); a litigant with standing to sue (sec. 2); no adequate state ground (sec. 3). But are these separately stated elements truly separable ones? Does each have a distinguishable content of its own? Are they requirements applicable to all litigation, whether of private law or public law?

---

* For further exploration of themes considered in this chapter, see generally Hart and Wechsler, The Federal Courts and the Federal System (1953); Wright, Federal Courts (1963); D. Currie, Federal Courts—Cases and Materials (1968); Stern and Gressman, Supreme Court Practice (4th ed. 1969); and Robertson and Kirkham, Jurisdiction of the Supreme Court of the United States (Wolfson and Kurland ed. 1951).

Or are they principled requirements relevant only to constitutional adjudication?

Are they perhaps not separable requirements at all, but rather merely illustrations of a single underlying institutional policy—e. g., of avoidance of constitutional questions unless absolutely necessary? That explanation is suggested especially by the materials in sec. 4. Is any such general policy compelled by the Constitution? Is it a permissible position? A principled one? Is the policy applicable to all courts? Just federal courts? Just the Supreme Court? Is it permissible in all Supreme Court cases, appeal as well as certiorari? Or is it mainly a discretionary policy of institutional prudence, a policy of ad hoc judgments about the political propriety of judicial intervention—judgments resting, e. g., on balancing the desirability of a decision against hostile repercussions and other institutional costs?

And are these limitations on adjudication—whether they are found to be separable or a single whole, whether externally imposed or court-made, whether principled or ad hoc—ultimately best understandable as disguised judgments on the merits? To what extent are the concerns of this chapter really not general institutional ones at all? These cases claim to worry about what courts are good for, and when. Are they really concerned with (or should they be more concerned about) how valuable the substantive claim is, and to whom? To what extent do (and to what degree should) decisions about the availability of a judicial forum turn on the merits of the constitutional claim?

SECTION 1. THE CONCRETE CONTROVERSY

Introduction. When is a dispute sufficiently real, far advanced, specific to justify court action? When will a federal court decide a dispute? Some contours of a model of a justiciable dispute emerge from the materials in this section. At one extreme lies the much-reiterated premise that the federal courts will not render "advisory opinions" on legal questions even though private citizens or public officials have intense curiosity about the answer. At the other end of the scale is the common situation of the defendant resisting enforcement of a criminal law against him: courts frequently adjudicate constitutional challenges raised in that context. Situations in between—between disputes not yet fully born or already dead and disputes as fully alive as they can be—give rise to most problems. How fully must a controversy have jelled to elicit a ruling? How eyeball-to-eyeball must the disputants' confrontation be? That problem arises most characteristically with requests for anticipatory relief—where a plaintiff, for example, is seeking a ruling on the legality of an action that he fears may be taken against him, rather than waiting to raise the issues as a defendant in an enforcement proceeding.

Among the frequently mentioned prerequisites in the materials below is the need for a concrete controversy, for a sufficiently non-hypothetical, non-abstract "ripe" dispute between truly "adverse" parties. What do these requirements mean? Are they the same for all litigation? Greater in private law disputes than in public law ones? Different in constitutional litigation?

And what justifies these requirements? Are they all derived from the principle that Article III courts may only exercise "judicial power" in situations identifiable as "Cases" or "Controversies"? Or are some of these limitations non-constitutional in origin? Based on the federal courts' authority to help shape the law of remedies in federal courts? Based on judicially developed policies responding to institutional self-defense perceptions—on prudential decisions to conserve the energies (and the political capital) of federal courts for a limited number of truly important constitutional causes?

NASHVILLE, C. & ST. L. RY. v. WALLACE

288 U.S. 249, 53 S.Ct. 345, 77 L.Ed. 730 (1933).

Appeal from the Supreme Court of Tennessee.

Mr. Justice STONE delivered the opinion of the Court.

Appellant brought suit in the Chancery Court of Davidson County, Tennessee, under the Uniform Declaratory Judgments Act of that state,[1] . . . to secure a judicial declaration that a state excise tax levied on the storage of gasoline . . . is, as applied to appellant, invalid under the commerce clause and the Fourteenth Amendment of the Federal Constitution. A decree for appellees was affirmed by the Supreme Court of the State, and the case comes here on appeal . . . ..

. . . [T]his Court, in ordering the cause set down for argument, invited the attention of counsel to the question "whether a case or controversy is presented in view of the nature of the proceedings in the state courts." This preliminary question, which has been elaborately briefed and argued, must first be considered, for the judicial power with which this Court is invested by Art. 3, § 1, of the Constitution, extends by Art. 3, § 2, only to "cases" and "controversies"; if no "case" or "controversy" is presented for decision, we are without power to review the decree of the court below. Muskrat v. United States, 219 U.S. 346.

In determining whether this litigation presents a case within the appellate jurisdiction of this Court, we are concerned, not with form, but with substance. See Fidelity National Bank v. Swope, 274 U.S. 123 . . . .. Hence, we look not to the label which the legislature has attached to the procedure followed in the state courts, or to the description of the judgment which is brought here for review, in popular parlance, as "declaratory," but to the nature of the proceeding which the statute authorizes, and the effect of the judgment rendered upon the rights which the appellant asserts.

Section 1 of the Tennessee Declaratory Judgments Act confers jurisdiction on courts of record "to declare rights . . . whether or not further

---

1. The procedure authorized by this Statute has been extensively adopted both in this country and abroad. It is said that the Uniform Act is in force in 16 of the States and Puerto Rico and that similar statutes have been enacted in 13 States, Hawaii and the Philippines. For a discussion of the history of this procedural device in France, Germany, Spain, Spanish America, Scotland, England and India, as well as in the United States, and the types of controversies in which it has been invoked, see Edwin M. Borchard, The Declaratory Judgment—A Needed Procedural Reform, 28 Yale L.J. 1, 105; Judicial Relief from Peril and Insecurity, 45 Harv.L.Rev. 793, 806; The Constitutionality of Declaratory Judgments, 31 Columbia L.Rev. 561. [Footnote by the Court.]

relief is or could be claimed" and provides that "no action or proceeding shall be open to objection on the ground that a declaratory judgment or decree is prayed for. The declaration may be either affirmative or negative in form and effect and such declaration shall have the force and effect of a final judgment or decree." By § 2 it is provided that "any person . . . whose rights, status or other legal relations are affected by a statute . . . may have determined any question of construction or validity arising under the . . . statute . . . and obtain a declaration of rights . . . thereunder."

Under § 6, the Court may refuse to render a declaratory judgment where, if rendered, it "would not terminate the uncertainty or controversy giving rise to the proceeding." Declaratory judgments may, in accordance with § 7, be reviewed as are other orders, judgments, or decrees, and under § 8 "further relief based on a declaratory judgment or decree may be granted whenever necessary or proper." Section 11 requires that "when declaratory relief is sought all persons shall be made parties who have or claim any interest which would be affected by the declaration, and no declaration shall prejudice the rights of persons not parties to the proceeding."

This statute has often been considered by the highest court of Tennessee, which has consistently held that its provisions may only be invoked when the complainant asserts rights which are challenged by the defendant, and presents for decision an actual controversy to which he is a party, capable of final adjudication by the judgment or decree to be rendered. . . . It has also held that no judgment or decree will be rendered when all the parties who will be adversely affected by it are not before the court. . . .

Proceeding in accordance with this statute, appellant filed its bill of complaint in the state Chancery Court, joining as defendants the appellees, the Attorney General and the state officials charged with the duty of collecting the gasoline privilege tax imposed by the Tennessee statute. The complaint alleged that appellant is engaged in purchasing gasoline outside the state, which it stores within the state pending its use within and without the state in the conduct of appellant's business as an interstate rail carrier; that appellees assert that the statute taxes the privilege of storing gasoline within the state and is applicable to appellant; that they have demanded payment of the tax in a specified amount and have determined to enforce their demand and that, under the circumstances alleged, the statute as applied to appellant is invalid under the commerce clause and the Fourteenth Amendment. The relief prayed was that the taxing act be declared unconstitutional as applied to appellant. The Chancery Court sustained the appellees' demurrer to the sufficiency in law of the allegations relied on to establish the unconstitutionality of the tax. Its final decree dismissing the bill on the merits has been affirmed by the highest court of the state.

That the issues thus raised and judicially determined would constitute a case or controversy if raised and decided in a suit brought by the taxpayer to enjoin collection of the tax cannot be questioned. . . . The proceeding terminating in the decree below, unlike that in . . . Muskrat v. United States, 219 U.S. 346, was between adverse parties, seeking a determination of their legal rights upon the facts alleged in the bill and admitted by the demurrer. Unlike Fairchild v. Hughes, 258 U.S. 126 [, and] Massachusetts v. Mellon, 262 U.S. 447 . . ., valuable legal rights asserted by the com-

plainant and threatened with imminent invasion by appellees, will be directly affected to a specific and substantial degree by the decision of the question
of law; and unlike Luther v. Borden, 7 How. 1; Field v. Clark, 143 U.S.
649; Pacific States Telephone & Telegraph Co. v. Oregon, 223 U.S. 118
. . . ., the question lends itself to judicial determination and is of the
kind which this court traditionally decides. The relief sought is a definitive
adjudication of the disputed constitutional right of the appellant, in the circumstances alleged, to be free from the tax . . .; and that adjudication is not, as in Gordon v. United States, 2 Wall. 561 . . ., subject to
revision by some other and more authoritative agency. Obviously the appellant whose duty to pay the tax will be determined by the decision of this
case, is not attempting to secure an abstract determination by the Court of the
validity of a statute, compare Muskrat v. United States, supra; . . . or
a decision advising what the law would be on an uncertain or hypothetical
state of facts, as was thought to be the case in Liberty Warehouse Co. v. Gran-
nis, 273 U.S. 70, and Willing v. Chicago Auditorium Ass'n, 277 U.S. 274
[see note 2 following this case]. Thus the narrow question presented for
determination is whether the controversy before us, which would be justiciable
in this Court if presented in a suit for injunction, is any the less so because
through a modified procedure appellant has been permitted to present it in the
state courts, without praying for an injunction or alleging that irreparable injury will result from the collection of the tax.

While the ordinary course of judicial procedure results in a judgment
requiring an award of process or execution to carry it into effect, such relief
is not an indispensable adjunct to the exercise of the judicial function.
. . . This Court has often exerted its judicial power to adjudicate boundaries between states, although it gave no injunction or other relief beyond
the determination of the legal rights which were the subject of controversy
between the parties, Louisiana v. Mississippi, 202 U.S. 1 . . ., and to review judgments of the Court of Claims, although no process issues against
the Government. United States v. Jones, 119 U.S. 477 . . .. As we
said in Fidelity National Bank & Trust Co. v. Swope, supra, "Naturalization
proceedings, Tutun v. United States, 270 U.S. 568; suits to determine a
matrimonial or other status; suits for instructions to a trustee or for the construction of a will, Traphagen v. Levy, 45 N.J.Eq. 448, 18 A. 222; bills of
interpleader so far as the stakeholder is concerned, Wakeman v. Kingsland,
46 N.J.Eq. 113, 18 A. 680; bills to quiet title where the plaintiff rests his
claim on adverse possession, Sharon v. Tucker, 144 U.S. 533; are familiar
examples of judicial proceedings which result in an adjudication of the
rights of litigants, although execution is not necessary to carry the judgment into effect, in the sense that damages are required to be paid or acts to
be performed by the parties." . . .

The issues raised here are the same as those which under old forms of
procedure could be raised only in a suit for an injunction or one to recover
the tax after its payment. But the Constitution does not require that the
case or controversy should be presented by traditional forms of procedure,
invoking only traditional remedies. The judiciary clause of the Constitution defined and limited judicial power, not the particular method by which
that power might be invoked. It did not crystallize into changeless form
the procedure of 1789 as the only possible means for presenting a case or

controversy otherwise cognizable by the federal courts. Whenever the judicial power is invoked to review a judgment of a state court, the ultimate constitutional purpose is the protection, by the exercise of the judicial function, of rights arising under the Constitution and laws of the United States. The states are left free to regulate their own judicial procedure. Hence, changes merely in the form or method of procedure by which federal rights are brought to final adjudication in the state courts are not enough to preclude review of the adjudication by this Court, so long as the case retains the essentials of an adversary proceeding, involving a real, not a hypothetical, controversy, which is finally determined by the judgment below. . . . As the prayer for relief by injunction is not a necessary prerequisite to the exercise of judicial power, allegations of threatened irreparable injury which are material only if an injunction is asked, may likewise be dispensed with if, in other respects, the controversy presented is, as in this case, real and substantial. . . . Accordingly, we must consider the constitutional questions raised by the appeal. [On the merits it was held that the tax did not constitute a forbidden burden on interstate commerce.]

Affirmed.

ADVISORY OPINIONS, DECLARATORY JUDGMENTS, AND THE "CASE OR CONTROVERSY" REQUIREMENT

1. *Advisory opinions.* a. *The 1793 refusal.* In 1793 President Washington sought the advice of the Justices of the Supreme Court on some perplexing legal questions then confronting him. The Justices declined to help. That refusal illustrates the most prominent, most continuously articulated boundary of justiciability: federal courts will not give "advisory opinions." What justifies that limitation? What are the objections to advisory opinions? What distinguishes forbidden "advice" from permissible adjudication?

George Washington's request to the Justices, forwarded by Secretary of State Jefferson, was understandable: the President genuinely needed legal assistance in dealing with a major national concern, America's neutrality toward the on-going war in Europe. Ships of the belligerents, especially French ships, were trying to use American ports. What were a neutral's rights and duties? The President would be "much relieved" if he could refer to the Justices the recurrent questions that seemed to fall within the range of judicial rather than executive expertise. The questions often arose "under circumstances which do not give a cognizance of them to the tribunals of the country," yet they were plainly legal questions: their solution, Washington's inquiry emphasized, depended "on the construction of our treaties, on the laws of nature and of nations, and on the laws of the land." The Justices' answers would "secure us against errors dangerous to the peace of the United States"; and the Justices' authority would "insure the respect of all parties." With this plea for help, the President submitted a long list of questions "which have already occurred, or may soon occur": for example, do our treaties with France permit the French "to fit out originally in and from the parts of the United States vessels armed for war"?

The questions seemed "legal"; the need for answers was real; nevertheless, Chief Justice John Jay and his brethren refused. They relied on the Constitution's separation of powers: the three branches "being in certain respects checks upon each other, and our being judges of a court in the last resort, are considerations which afford strong arguments against the propriety of our extra-judicially deciding the questions alluded to." [1]

b. *Some justifications for the refusal.* Is the ban on advisory opinions compelled by the language of Article III? [2] By the Framers' intent? Recall the rejection of Madison's proposal that judges sit on a Council of Revision, chap. 1, p. 17, above. Is the ban justified by institutional considerations? Because courts are less competent to give advice than to decide cases? Because courts would be too busy if they gave advice? Because courts would be more vulnerable to political attacks if they gave advice?

How persuasive are the arguments that the quality of the courts' work would suffer if advisory opinions were permitted? [3] Do courts need a concrete factual context to develop law with adequate focus and understanding? Do courts need adversary presentation to assure adequately reasoned development of law? Do these needs vary with the substantive issues presented? During the 1930's, the uncertainty regarding the constitutionality of New Deal laws gave rise to suggestions that the Supreme Court be authorized to issue advisory opinions. Were there stronger reasons against advisory opinions in the 1930's than in 1793?

Is the ban on advisory opinions necessary to conserve the Court's strength and energies? Would advisory opinions thrust courts into conflicts too early and too often? Is the ban on advisory opinions desirable because of the "value of having courts function as organs of the sober second thought of the community appraising action already taken, rather than as advisers at the front line of governmental action at the state of initial decision"? Hart and Wechsler, The Federal Courts and the Federal System (1953), 78.

1. See the documents reprinted in Hart and Wechsler, The Federal Courts and the Federal System (1953), 75–77. Note also the refusal by most of the Justices, sitting on circuit, to certify eligible pension claimants to the Secretary of War because the 1792 statute authorizing such proceedings improperly assigned duties "not of a judicial nature" to the courts (primarily because the court certifications were subject to executive revision). Hayburn's Case, 2 Dall. 409 (1796).

2. Note the discussion of Art. III judicial power in Muskrat v. United States, 219 U.S. 346 (1911): "'The power conferred on this court is exclusively judicial, and it cannot be required or authorized to exercise any other.' . . . 'Judicial power . . . is the power of a court to decide and pronounce a judgment and carry it into effect between persons and parties who bring a case before it for decision.' . . . By the express terms of the Constitution, the exercise of the judicial power is limited to 'cases' and 'controversies.' Beyond this it does not extend, and unless it is asserted in a case or controversy within the meaning of the Constitution, the power to exercise it is nowhere conferred. . . . 'The term "controversies," if distinguishable at all from "cases," is so in that it is less comprehensive than the latter, and includes only suits of a civil nature. . . . By cases and controversies are intended the claims of litigants brought before the courts for determination by such regular proceedings as are established by law or custom for the protection or enforcement of rights, or the prevention, redress, or punishment of wrongs'."

3. Note that advisory opinions on constitutional questions are authorized by the constitutions of several States (Massachusetts, New Hampshire, Maine, Rhode Island, Florida, Colorado, and South Dakota). See generally Field, "The Advisory Opinion—An Analysis," 24 Ind.L.J. 203 (1949), and Note, "Judicial Determinations in Nonadversary Proceedings," 72 Harv. L.Rev. 723 (1959).

c. *A modern justification: Flast v. Cohen.* Compare the Court's comments in Flast v. Cohen, 392 U.S. 83 (1968) (sec. 2, below): "[T]he implicit policies embodied in Article III, and not history alone, impose the rule against advisory opinions. [The rule] implements the separation of powers [and] also recognizes that such suits often 'are not pressed before the Court with that clear concreteness provided when a question emerges precisely framed and necessary for decision from a clash of adversary argument exploring every aspect of a multifaced situation embracing conflicting and demanding interests.' United States v. Fruehauf, 365 U.S. 146, 157 (1961). Consequently, the Article III prohibition against advisory opinions reflects the complementary constitutional considerations expressed by the justiciability doctrine: Federal judicial power is limited to those disputes which confine federal courts to a role consistent with a system of separated powers and which are traditionally thought to be capable of resolution through the judicial process."

2. *Declaratory judgments and the Willing case.* a. *The Willing problem.* Can the justifications for the advisory opinion prohibition support a general ban on declaratory judgments? It is difficult to see why any of the reasons against answering the President's questions in 1793, or the New Deal supporters' in the 1930's, should preclude adjudication of the Railroad's claim in the principal case. Yet at the time of that decision, serious doubts had been cast on the federal courts' ability to issue declaratory judgments by dicta in cases like Willing v. Chicago Auditorium Ass'n, 277 U.S. 274 (1928).

Willing was a suit in a lower federal court "in the nature of a bill to remove a cloud upon title." The Supreme Court held "that the proceeding does not present a case or controversy." Consider the facts: The Association held long-term leases on land and had constructed an auditorium. The building had become obsolete, and the Association desired to erect a new building. The lease did not explicitly authorize the Association to tear down the old building and erect a new one. There were some negotiations between the Association and Willing, one of the lessors. During "an informal, friendly, private conversation," Willing stated to an officer of the Association that he did not think the old building could be torn down without the consent of the lessors and the bondholders. The Association "never approached" most of the other lessors or the bondholders. A year after the talk with Willing, the Association brought this action against all the lessors and the trustee for the bondholders, to establish the right to tear down the old building.

Justice Brandeis' opinion for the Court stated that there was "neither hostile act nor a threat." Willing had merely expressed an informal, oral opinion. "What the plaintiff seeks is simply a declaratory judgment. To grant that relief is beyond the power of the federal judiciary." The proceeding "is not a case or controversy within the meaning of article 3 of the Constitution. The fact that plaintiff's desires are thwarted by its own doubts, or by the fears of others, does not confer a cause of action. No defendant has wronged the plaintiff or has threatened to do so."

Why was this not an Article III controversy? Because the plans of the parties had not sufficiently jelled? Because there were too many contingencies on both sides—uncertainty as to precisely what the plaintiff would do, uncertainty as to precisely what the defendants would do? Assuming *this* controversy was not within Article III, was Justice Brandeis' language too broad? Recall that he said: "To grant that [declaratory judgment] relief is beyond the power conferred upon the federal judiciary." Was that statement itself something of an advisory opinion?

b. *The Haworth response.* The decision in the principal case paved the way for the enactment of the Declaratory Judgment Act of 1934. That law, as amended (28 U.S.C. §§ 2201, 2202) provides: "In a case of actual controversy within its jurisdiction, except with respect to Federal taxes, any court of the United States . . ., upon the filing of an appropriate pleading, may declare the rights and other legal relations of any interested party seeking such declaration, whether or not further relief is or could be sought. Any such declaration shall have the force and effect of a final judgment or decree and shall be reviewable as such." The Act also makes provision for "further relief" whenever necessary or proper.

The Supreme Court sustained the constitutionality of the Act in Aetna Life Insurance Co. v. Haworth, 300 U.S. 227 (1937). Chief Justice Hughes explained: "The Declaratory Judgment Act of 1934, in its limitation to 'cases of actual controversy,' manifestly has regard to the constitutional provision and is operative only in respect to controversies which are such in the constitutional sense. The word 'actual' is one of emphasis rather than of definition. Thus the operation of the Declaratory Judgment Act is procedural only. In providing remedies and defining procedure in relation to cases and controversies in the constitutional sense the Congress is acting within its delegated power over the jurisdiction of the federal courts which the Congress is authorized to establish. . . . Exercising this control of practice and procedure the Congress is not confined to traditional forms or traditional remedies. . . . In dealing with methods within its sphere of remedial action the Congress may create and improve as well as abolish or restrict. The Declaratory Judgment Act must be deemed to fall within this ambit of congressional power, so far as it authorizes relief which is consonant with the exercise of the judicial function in the determination of controversies to which under the Constitution the judicial power extends.

"A 'controversy' in this sense must be one that is appropriate for judicial determination. . . . A justiciable controversy is thus distinguished from a difference or dispute of a hypothetical or abstract character; from one that is academic or moot. . . . The controversy must be definite and concrete, touching the legal relations of parties having adverse legal interests. . . . It must be a real and substantial controversy admitting of specific relief through a decree of a conclusive character, as distinguished from an opinion advising what the law would be upon a hypothetical state of facts. . . . Where there is such a concrete case admitting of an immediate and definitive determination of the legal rights of the parties in an adversary proceeding upon the facts alleged, the judicial function may be appropriately exercised although the adjudication of the rights of the litigants may not require the award of process or the payment of damages."

The statutory authorization of federal declaratory judgments has by no means ended controversy about the availability of the remedy. The relief can be granted only if there is a "case" in the Article III sense; and even when there is a "case," there is discretion to withhold relief. Should declaratory relief be denied unless the claimant could have resorted to a traditional remedy, as in the principal case? Even if a declaratory remedy should be available at an earlier point, should the remedy nevertheless be denied unless the dispute has jelled to some point beyond the minimum prerequisites of a "case"? See the "ripeness" problems in Mitchell and other cases, in the next group of notes.

3. *Moot and collusive cases.* To what extent do the policies against advisory opinions justify a refusal to decide cases that have become moot? Though the Court has consistently maintained that it is "without power to decide moot questions," St. Pierre v. United States, 319 U.S. 41 (1943), it has become more reluctant to find mootness, especially in criminal cases. The St. Pierre case was dismissed because the petitioner had completed serving his sentence; but, beginning with Fiswick v. United States, 392 U.S. 211 (1946), the Court reached the merits when it perceived significant collateral consequences from the conviction, though the sentence had been served. By 1968, in Sibron v. New York, 392 U.S. 40 (1968), the Court was compelled to recognize that the "collateral consequences" exception to St. Pierre had been expanded "to the point where it may realistically be said that inroads have been made upon the principle itself." Chief Justice Warren noted that the Court had "acknowledged the obvious fact of life that most criminal convictions do in fact entail adverse collateral consequences."

Should the Court hasten the decisional process or construe the mootness barrier narrowly in the interest of maximizing judicial protection of constitutional rights? In the Sibron case, the Court found a second exception to the St. Pierre mootness doctrine applicable: Sibron, unlike St. Pierre, had no way to bring his case to the Supreme Court before his sentence (six months) had expired. This exception recognized "the vital importance of keeping open avenues of judicial review of constitutional rights." Many constitutional problems are encountered primarily at a "low visibility" level, in prosecutions for "minor" offenses with short sentences. People "deprived of constitutional rights at this level" should not be "left utterly remediless and defenseless against repetitions of unconstitutional conduct." See Note, "Cases Moot on Appeal," 103 U.Pa.L.Rev. 772 (1955). For an illustration of the rarely invoked ban on deciding collusive suits, see United States v. Johnson, 319 U.S. 302 (1943), dismissing an action testing rent control because the nominal plaintiff, a tenant, had been procured by and at the expense of the defendant landlord. See also Lord v. Veazie, 8 How. 249 (1850).

RIPENESS

Introduction. Both Mitchell and Adler, the cases examined in the first two notes below, involved constitutional challenges to restrictions on the conduct of public employees. In Mitchell, the Court found most claims nonjusticiable; in Adler, by contrast, the Court reached the merits. Mitchell and Adler afford the opportunity to explore the nature and ingredients of ripeness: To what extent is ripeness derived from Article III? What factors go into the determination of ripeness? The more recent Food, Drug and Cosmetic Act cases in note 4, on the justiciability of nonconstitutional challenges to administrative regulations, probe additional variables that may be relevant to an assessment of ripeness.

1. *The Mitchell case.* United Public Workers v. Mitchell, 330 U.S. 75 (1947), was an attack on the political activities ban in the Hatch Act of 1940. Section 9(a) prohibits federal employees in the executive branch from taking "any active part in political management or in political campaigns." Several employees and their union brought suit to restrain the Civil Service Commission from enforcing section 9(a) against them, and for a declaratory judgment that the section is unconstitutional. The three-judge District Court dismissed the suit on the merits. The Supreme Court affirmed the judgment, but on other grounds as to most of the plaintiffs. Justice Reed's opinion for the Court contained the following passages:

"It is alleged that the individuals desire to engage in acts of political management and in political campaigns. Their purposes are as stated in the excerpt from the complaint set out in the margin.[1] . . .

"None of the appellants, except George P. Poole, has violated the provisions of the Hatch Act. They wish to act contrary to its provisions . . . and desire a declaration of the legally permissible limits of regulation. Defendants moved to dismiss the complaint for lack of a justiciable case or controversy. . . .

". . . At the threshold of consideration, we are called upon to decide whether the complaint states a controversy cognizable in this Court. We defer consideration of the cause of action of Mr. Poole . . . . The other individual employees have elaborated the grounds of their objection in individual affidavits for use in the hearing on the summary judgment. We select as an example one that contains the essential averments of all the others and print below the portions with significance in this suit.[2]

1. ". . . [T]he individual plaintiffs desire to engage in the following acts: write for publication letters and articles in support of candidates for office; be connected editorially with publications which are identified with the legislative program of UFWA [former name of the present union appellant] and candidates who support it; solicit votes, aid in getting out voters, act as accredited checker, watcher, or challenger; transport voters to and from the polls without compensation therefor; participate in and help in organizing political parades; initiate petitions, and canvass for the signatures of others on such petitions; serve as party ward committeeman or other party official; and perform any and all acts not prohibited by any provision of law other than [the Hatch Act]. . . ." [Footnote by the Court.]

2. ". . . I wish to engage in such activities on behalf of those candidates for public office who I believe will best serve the needs of this country and with the object of persuading others of the correctness of my judgments and of electing the candidates of my choice. This objective I wish to pursue by all proper means such as engaging in discussion, by speeches to conventions, rallies and other assemblages, by publicizing my views in letters and articles for publication in newspapers and other periodicals, by aiding in the campaign of candidates for political office by posting banners and posters in public places, by distributing leaflets, by 'ringing doorbells', by addressing campaign literature, and by doing any and all acts of like character reasonably designed to assist in the election of candidates I favor.

"I desire to engage in these activities freely, openly, and without concealment. However, I understand that the second sentence of Section 9(a) of the Hatch Act and the Rules of the C.S.C. provide that if I engage in this activity, the Civil Service Commission will order that I be dismissed from federal employment. Such deprivation of my job in the federal government would be a source of immediate and serious financial loss and other injury to me.

"At the last Congressional election I was very much interested in the outcome of the campaign and offered to help the party of my choice by being a watcher at the polls. I obtained a watcher's certificate but I was advised

Nothing similar to the fourth paragraph of the printed affidavit is contained in the other affidavits. The assumed controversy between affiant and the Civil Service Commission as to affiant's right to act as watcher at the polls on November 2, 1943, had long been moot when this complaint was filed. We do not therefore treat this allegation separately. The affidavits, it will be noticed, follow the generality of purpose expressed by the complaint. . . . They declare a desire to act contrary to the rule against political activity but not that the rule has been violated. In this respect, we think they differ from the type of threat adjudicated in Railway Mail Association v. Corsi, 326 U.S. 88. In that case, the refusal to admit an applicant to membership in a labor union on account of race was involved. Admission had been refused. . . . Definite action had also been taken in Hill v. Florida, 325 U.S. 538. In the Hill case an injunction had been sought and allowed against Hill and the union forbidding Hill from acting as the business agent of the union and the union from further functioning as a union until it complied with the state law. The threats which menaced the affiants of these affidavits in the case now being considered are closer to a general threat by officials to enforce those laws which they are charged to administer, compare Watson v. Buck, 313 U.S. 387, 400, than they are to the direct threat of punishment against a named organization for a completed act that made the Mail Association and the Hill cases justiciable.

"As is well known, the federal courts established pursuant to Article III of the Constitution do not render advisory opinions. For adjudication of constitutional issues, 'concrete legal issues, presented in actual cases, not abstractions,' are requisite. This is as true of declaratory judgments as any other field. These appellants seem clearly to seek advisory opinions upon broad claims of rights protected by the First, Fifth, Ninth and Tenth Amendments to the Constitution. As these appellants are classified employees, they have a right superior to the generality of citizens, . . . but the facts of their personal interest in their civil rights, of the general threat of possible interference with those rights by the Civil Service Commission under its rules, if specified things are done by appellants, does not make a justiciable case or controversy. Appellants want to engage in 'political management and political campaigns,' to persuade others to follow appellants' views by discussion, speeches, articles and other acts reasonably designed to secure the selection of appellants' political choices. Such generality of objection is really an attack on the political expediency of the Hatch Act, not the presentation of legal issues. It is beyond the competence of courts to render such a decision. . . .

"The power of courts, and ultimately of this Court, to pass upon the constitutionality of acts of Congress arises only when the interests of liti-

that there might be some question of my right to use the certificate and retain my federal employment. Therefore, on November 1, 1943, the day before election, I called the regional office of the Civil Service Commission in Philadelphia and spoke to a person who gave his name as . . . Mr. . . . . stated that if I used my watcher's certificate, the Civil Service Commission would see that I was dismissed from my job at the . . . for violation of the Hatch Act. I,

therefore, did not use the certificate as I had intended.
"I believe that Congress may not constitutionally abridge my right to engage in the political activities mentioned above. However, unless the courts prevent the Civil Service Commission from enforcing this unconstitutional law, I will be unable freely to exercise my rights as a citizen. (Identifying words omitted.)" [Footnote by the Court.]

gants require the use of this judicial authority for their protection against actual interference. A hypothetical threat is not enough. We can only speculate as to the kinds of political activity the appellants desire to engage in or as to the contents of their proposed public statements or the circumstances of their publication. It would not accord with judicial responsibility to adjudge, in a matter involving constitutionality, between the freedom of the individual and the requirements of public order except when definite rights appear upon the one side and definite prejudicial interferences upon the other.

"The Constitution allots the nation's judicial power to the federal courts. Unless these courts respect the limits of that unique authority, they intrude upon powers vested in the legislative or executive branches. . . . Should the courts seek to expand their power so as to bring under their jurisdiction ill-defined controversies over constitutional issues, they would become the organ of political theories. Such abuse of judicial power would properly meet rebuke and restriction from other branches. . . . No threat of interference by the Commission with rights of these appellants appears beyond that implied by the existence of the law and the regulations. . . . These reasons lead us to conclude that the determination of the trial court, that the individual appellants, other than Poole, could maintain this action, was erroneous.

". . . The appellant Poole does present by the complaint and affidavit matters appropriate for judicial determination. The affidavits filed by appellees confirm that Poole has been charged by the Commission with political activity and a proposed order for his removal from his position adopted subject to his right under Commission procedure to reply to the charges and to present further evidence in refutation. We proceed to consider the controversy over constitutional power at issue between Poole and the Commission as defined by the charge and preliminary finding upon one side and the admissions of Poole's affidavit upon the other. Our determination is limited to those facts. This proceeding so limited meets the requirements of defined rights and a definite threat to interfere with a possessor of the menaced rights by a penalty for an act done in violation of the claimed restraint." [Poole's constitutional challenge was rejected on the merits.]

Justice Rutledge dissented as to Poole and stated that he did not pass "upon the constitutional questions presented by the other appellants for the reason that he feels the controversy as to them is not yet appropriate for the discretionary exercise of declaratory judgment jurisdiction." Justice Frankfurter concurred in a separate opinion, and Justice Black dissented. Justice Douglas dissented in part. As to justiciability, he said:

"It is clear that the declaratory judgment procedure is available in the federal courts only in cases involving actual controversies and may not be used to obtain an advisory opinion in a controversy not yet arisen. Coffman v. Breeze Corporations, 323 U.S. 316, 324–325 and cases cited. The requirement of an 'actual controversy,' which is written into the statute . . . and has its roots in the Constitution . . . , seems to me to be fully met here.

"What these appellants propose to do is plain enough. If they do what they propose to do, it is clear that they will be discharged from their positions. . . . Their proposed conduct is sufficiently specific to show plainly that it will violate the Act. The policy of the Commission and the mandate of the Act leave no lingering doubt as to the consequences.[1]

". . . [T]o require these employees first to suffer the hardship of a discharge is not only to make them incur a penalty; it makes inadequate, if not wholly illusory, any legal remedy which they may have.[2] Men who must sacrifice their means of livelihood in order to test their rights to their jobs must either pursue prolonged and expensive litigation as unemployed persons or pull up their roots, change their life careers, and seek employment in other fields.

". . . Declaratory relief is the singular remedy available here to preserve the *status quo* while the constitutional rights of these appellants to make these utterances and to engage in these activities are determined. The threat against them is real not fanciful, immediate not remote. The case is therefore an actual not a hypothetical one. And the present case seems to me to be a good example of a situation where uncertainty, peril, and insecurity result from imminent and immediate threats to asserted rights. . . ."

2. *The Adler case.* Adler v. Board of Education, 342 U.S. 485 (1952), attacked New York's Feinberg Law of 1949, designed to eliminate "subversive persons from the public school system." The Act included provisions for the compilation of a list of subversive organizations by the school authorities; membership in any such organization constituted "prima facie evidence of disqualification" for any school position. The plaintiffs were taxpayers, parents of school children, and teachers. The appellate courts of the state rejected their constitutional challenges on the merits. On appeal, the Supreme Court affirmed, without discussing justiciability.

Justice Frankfurter's dissent, however, made it clear that the justiciability issue in Adler was a substantial one that called for discussion, especially in light of Mitchell. Justice Frankfurter argued that the case was not justiciable and that the Court should not decide the merits. With respect to the taxpayer and parent plaintiffs, he found lack of standing to sue. (Compare the dismissal on standing grounds in Doremus, sec. 2 below, decided on the same day as Adler.) His discussion of the ripeness-Mitchell problem came in the course of his insistence that the teacher plaintiffs, too, had failed to present a claim that could be adjudicated at this time:

"The allegations in the present action fall short of those found insufficient in the Mitchell case. These teachers do not allege that they have engaged in proscribed conduct or that they have any intention to do so. They do not suggest that they have been, or are, deterred from supporting causes or from joining organizations for fear of the Feinberg Law's interdict, except

1. The case is, therefore, unlike those situations where the Court refused to entertain actions for declaratory judgments, the state of facts being hypothetical in the sense that the challenge was to statutes which had not as yet been construed or their specific application known. See Electric Bond & S. Co. v. Securities and Exchange Commission, 303 U.S. 419, 443; Alabama State Federation of Labor v. McAdory, 325 U.S. 450. [Footnote by Justice Douglas.]

2. Where the legal remedy is adequate, it may be the more appropriate one. Thus in Coffman v. Breeze Corporations, supra, declaratory relief was denied a licensor of a patent who sued his licensee for an adjudication that the Royalty Adjustment Act was unconstitutional since it appeared that a suit to recover royalties was an adequate legal remedy and that the constitutional issues could be litigated there. [Footnote by Justice Douglas.]

to say generally that the system complained of will have this effect on teachers as a group. They do not assert that they are threatened with action under the law, or that steps are imminent whereby they would incur the hazard of punishment for conduct innocent at the time, or under standards too vague to satisfy due process of law. They merely allege that the statutes and Rules permit such action against some teachers. Since we rightly refused in the Mitchell case to hear government employees whose conduct was much more intimately affected by the law there attacked than are the claims of plaintiffs here, this suit is wanting in the necessary basis for our review.

"This case proves anew the wisdom of rigorous adherence to the prerequisites for pronouncement by this Court on matters of constitutional law. The absence in these plaintiffs of the immediacy and solidity of interest necessary to support jurisdiction is reflected in the atmosphere of abstraction and ambiguity in which the constitutional issues are presented."

Earlier in his dissent, Justice Frankfurter had noted that the case "comes here on the bare bones of the Feinberg Law only partly given flesh by the Regents' Rules." He stated further:

"We are asked to pass on a scheme to counteract what are currently called subversive influences in the public school system of New York. The scheme . . . is still an unfinished blueprint. We are asked to adjudicate claims against its constitutionality before the scheme has been put into operation, before the limits that it imposes upon free inquiry and association, the scope of scrutiny that it sanctions, and the procedural safeguards that will be found to be implied for its enforcement have been authoritatively defined. I think we should adhere to the teaching of this Court's history to avoid constitutional adjudications on merely abstract or speculative issues and to base them on the concreteness afforded by an actual, present, defined controversy, appropriate for judicial judgment, between adversaries immediately affected by it. In accordance with the settled limits upon our jurisdiction I would dismiss this appeal. An understanding of the statutory scheme and the action thus far taken under it is necessary to a proper consideration of the issues which for me control disposition of the case, namely, standing of the parties and ripeness of the constitutional question." [A renewed constitutional attack on the Feinberg Law, 15 years after Adler, proved more successful. Keyishian v. Board of Regents, 385 U.S. 589 (1967), chap. 15, p. 1133, below.]

3. *Some questions about Mitchell and Adler.* a. *The Art. III and the Supreme Court review dimensions: basis for reconciliation?* Mitchell and Adler raise questions on two levels—one involving the Article III contours themselves, the other pertaining to the additional problems of Supreme Court review of state adjudications. As to Article III: Does every dispute found not "ripe" fall short of being an Article III "case"? Or may some disputes be concrete enough to fall within Article III yet not ripe enough to warrant grant of a discretionary federal remedy? As to Supreme Court review: If a state court adjudicates a dispute concrete enough to be an Article III case, must not the Supreme Court decide the merits on appeal—even though federal declaratory or injunctive relief would have been denied on discretionary grounds if that case had started in a federal District Court? Are Mitchell and Adler reconcilable?

There is good reason to criticize the majority's failure even to mention the justiciability issue in Adler. But the result—the decision to adjudicate—may have been justifiable: there were reasons to reach the merits in Adler that were lacking in Mitchell. To be sure, Mitchell and Adler do not seem reconcilable if only the Article III dimension is considered: Mitchell seems hardly less ripe than Adler. But if the Supreme Court review dimension is also taken into account, Mitchell and Adler may be able to stand together: review of Adler may have been justified (despite the dismissal in Mitchell) because Adler originated in the state courts—and was not so unripe as to fall short of being an Article III case. These problems are explored further in the remainder of this note and in note 5, below.

b. *The minimal concreteness required for a ripe Art. III case; the greater concreteness required to exercise discretionary federal declaratory judgment jurisdiction.* To what extent is ripeness an aspect of the "case or controversy" requirement of Article III? To what extent is it a question of the law of remedies? What difference does it make? May a dispute fall so far short of ripeness that it does not present an Article III case? Was that the flaw in the Willing case, in the preceding notes? May a dispute be sufficiently concrete to meet the minimum requirements of Article III but nevertheless be sufficiently contingent to warrant dismissal on ripeness grounds in the exercise of a judicial discretion as to the federal declaratory judgments remedy? Was Mitchell such a case?

Can Mitchell and Adler be distinguished, then, because Mitchell was a federal suit and Adler an appeal from a state court decision? If Mitchell is viewed as a discretionary denial of a federal declaratory judgments remedy, as Justice Rutledge's separate opinion suggested, can it be authority for dismissing a state court appeal such as Adler—even if the dispute in Adler was at least as unripe as that in Mitchell, as Justice Frankfurter claimed? In reviewing a state court decision falling within the appeal jurisdiction of 28 U.S. C. § 1257(2), must not the Supreme Court decide the merits unless Article III is not satisfied? Is it accurate to say that the Court has no discretion to abstain from decision in such a case—unlike the discretion it may exercise over a federal court remedy like that sought in Mitchell? Is it accurate to say, in other words, that discretionary considerations appropriate in federal court litigation have no place in Supreme Court review of state cases within the appeal jurisdiction? Or does the law of remedies become "federalized" in all cases of Supreme Court review? Because of the overriding institutional need of the Supreme Court to avoid premature and excessive interventions? These problems recur in other contexts in the materials on standing and on discretionary abstention, secs. 2 and 4 below.

c. *The premature and the concrete in Adler and Mitchell.* Were the issues in Mitchell so abstract and premature as to ban all exercise of Article III power? Compare the questions in note 5 below. Are not the "unfit for adjudication" assertions of the majority more persuasive if they are read as going not to Article III power but merely to the issue of discretionary exercise of declaratory judgment discretion? In Adler, the state court thought some questions sufficiently "ripe" for adjudication. Was there not adequate ripeness to satisfy Article III policies at least as to some issues in Adler? Obviously, the teachers in Adler could not complain of specific actions taken against them—that challenge was indeed premature. But could they not properly argue that there could be *no* constitutional applications of the Feinberg Law? And if the state courts decided that claim, was not the Supreme Court compelled to review? What would have been the status of the state ruling if Justice Frankfurter's view had prevailed in the Supreme Court? Should the Supreme Court vacate the state court judgment when an appeal is dismissed on the "jurisdictional" ground of ripeness?

4. *The Food, Drug, and Cosmetic Act cases.* a. *The unripe case.* In a trio of 1967 cases, the Court pointed to the needs of the litigants and the shape of the legal issues as the governing criteria in determining whether a pre-enforcement nonconstitutional challenge to an administrative regulation is ripe for review. Justice Harlan, who wrote the majority opinions, stated that "a twofold inquiry must be made: first to determine whether the issues tendered are appropriate for judicial resolution, and second to assess the hardship to the parties if judicial relief is denied at that stage." Abbott Laboratories v. Gardner, 387 U.S. 136; Toilet Goods Ass'n v. Gardner, 387 U.S. 158; Gardner v. Toilet Goods Ass'n, 387 U.S. 167 (1967).

After finding no statutory bar to pre-enforcement suits challenging the agency's authority to issue the regulations, Justice Harlan's opinion in Abbott Laboratories noted that a "further inquiry" remained: "The injunctive and declaratory judgment remedies are discretionary, and courts traditionally have been reluctant to apply them to administrative determinations unless these arise in the context of a controversy 'ripe' for judicial resolution." Applying the dual criteria of "fitness of the issues" and "hardship to the parties," the Court found one of the three cases not ripe: Toilet Goods Ass'n v. Gardner.

In that case, cosmetics manufacturers attacked a regulation authorizing the agency to suspend certification service to those who refused administrative inspectors free access to manufacturing facilities and data. Although the petitioners had framed "a purely legal question: whether the regulation is totally beyond the agency's power under the statute," the Court found the first aspect of the ripeness inquiry unsatisfied—this legal issue was not one "appropriate for judicial resolution." Justice Harlan explained that the Court did not know "whether or when" an inspection would be ordered, and what reasons the administrator would give to justify his order. The validity of the challenged regulation ultimately turned on whether it was justified by "the statutory scheme as a whole," and that should not be decided at so early a stage:

"This will depend not merely on an inquiry into statutory purpose but concurrently on an understanding of what types of enforcement problems are encountered by the [agency], the need for various sorts of supervision in order to effectuate the goals of the Act, and the safeguards devised to protect legitimate trade secrets . . .. We believe that judicial appraisal of these factors is likely to stand on a much surer footing in the context of a specific application of this regulation than could be the case in the framework of the generalized challenge made here." Moreover, the second aspect of the ripeness inquiry justified postponement of adjudication, for the regulations would not immediately affect petitioners "in conducting their day-to-day affairs." And "no irremediable adverse consequences flow from requiring a later challenge to this regulation by a manufacturer who refuses to allow this type of inspection": the consequence of suspension of certification service pending review was relatively mild.

b. *The ripe cases.* The companion cases were found distinguishable on both criteria of ripeness. Abbott Laboratories involved a regulation requiring the "established name" of the drug to be used "every time" the proprietary name was employed. Gardner v. Toilet Goods Ass'n involved regulations expanding the definition of "color additives" subject to premarketing clearance. To the majority, answers to the legal questions in each of these cases seemed to turn less on factual context than in the "factory access" case. And the effect on the parties was greater: the regulations affected primary conduct, and withholding adjudication would subject the petitioners to the risk of "seizure of goods, heavy fines, adverse publicity," and "possible criminal liability."

c. *The dissent.* Justice Fortas, joined by Chief Justice Warren and Justice Clark, thought pre-enforcement review inappropriate in all three cases. The enforcement experience would bear on the legal issues in all three cases, not just one, he insisted; and compelling the petitioners to withhold court attacks "until enforcement is undertaken" was not unduly harsh: "The courts do not and should not pass on these complex problems in the abstract and the general—because these regulations peculiarly depend for their quality and substance upon the facts of particular situations. We should confine ourselves—as our jurisprudence dictates—to actual, specific, particularized cases and controversies, in substance as well as in technical analysis." Early in his opinion, Justice Fortas emphasized that his disagreement with the majority was "not with respect to the existence of jurisdiction to enjoin, but to the definition of occasions on which such jurisdiction may be invoked." Do Justice Fortas' closing remarks nevertheless cast doubt on "the existence of jurisdiction"? Near the end of his opinion, he referred to "this nonadjudicable mass assault" on the regulations and "this massive onslaught" which made "utterly impossible" "the kind of discrete judgments which are within judicial competence."

5. *Some further questions on ripeness.* a. *Parties' hardship, issues' shape, and Art. III.* The ripeness variables discussed in the food and drug cases purport to deal mainly with the question of whether a federal court should decide a case that falls within the boundaries of Article III and that is within its statutory jurisdiction. Are these variables relevant as well to determining whether there is a sufficiently ripe controversy to constitute an Article III "case"? May the legal issue be so intertwined with enforcement facts that pre-enforcement adjudication would violate Article III? May the hardship of delaying relief to the litigant be so minimal as to make pre-enforcement adjudication unconstitutional? Were the issues in Mitchell or Adler so "unfit" for adjudication under these criteria as to raise "case or controversy" doubts? Some issues only? Were the parties so unaffected by delay in Mitchell or Adler as to make present adjudication constitutionally improper? Or was the only proper concern in Mitchell and Adler the question of discretionary exercise of a jurisdiction well within the constitutional perimeter?

b. *The shape of the issues—and the merits.* In applying the "fitness of the issue" criterion in the food and drug cases, the Justices asked whether factual enforcement experience was necessary to decide the legal question. Does not that need for further facts itself depend on what legal question is asked? On how the judge views the substantive law? Some legal standards are less dependent on factual variations than others. And some judges are more inclined than others to formulate legal standards as questions of degree. May that explain the Frankfurter dissent in Adler?

c. *The hardship to the parties—and the merits.* To what extent should "hardship to the parties" affect ripeness? If ripeness is less of a barrier when delay in adjudication constitutes a hardship to one party, what of hardship to the other party (and to the public interest) from early adjudication? Should assessment of hardship vary with the nature of the legal claim? In the course of his dissent in the food and drug cases, Justice Fortas commented: "Where personal status or liberties are involved, the courts may well insist upon a considerable ease of challenging administrative orders." Should the First Amendment claim in Mitchell have lowered the ripeness barrier there? (Note the reliance on Mitchell in a 1969 case, Golden v. Zwickler, 394 U.S. 103, setting aside the District Court's declaratory relief against a ban on anonymous handbills in election campaigns because of a lack of "sufficient immediacy and reality" and emphasizing that the "constitutional question, First Amendment or otherwise, must be presented in the context of a specific live grievance.")

d. *Ripeness and the Court's needs.* Does the focus on parties' hardships unduly deemphasize the Court's institutional values, especially in constitutional litigation? Should ripeness be primarily concerned with protecting the Court from premature opinions—opinions with some of the defects of advisory ones, in quality and in vulnerability? Or should assessment of the parties' (and society's) need for a decision be the major ingredient of the ripeness determination?

SECTION 2. STANDING TO LITIGATE

Some introductory comments and questions. a. *The ingredients.* What is standing? How does it differ from ripeness and other ingredients of justiciability? The "gist of the question of standing," the Court said in Baker v. Carr, 369 U.S. 186 (1962) (sec. 5 below), is whether the litigant has "such a personal stake in the outcome of the controversy as to assure that concrete adverseness which sharpens the presentation of issues upon which the court so largely depends for illumination of difficult questions." Hart and Wechsler suggest that standing be viewed "as involving problems of the nature and sufficiency of the litigant's concern with the subject matter of the litigation as distinguished from problems of the justiciability—that is, the fitness for adjudication—of the legal questions which he tenders for decision." The Federal Courts and the Federal System (1953), 174. And note the statement in the 1969 ruling in Flast v. Cohen, the last principal case in this section: "The fundamental aspect of standing is that it focuses on the party . . . and not on the issues he wishes to have adjudicated. . . . [T]he question is whether the person whose standing is challenged is a proper party to request an adjudication of a particular issue and not whether the issue itself is justiciable."

b. *Who decides?* Some of the questions raised by these materials on standing resemble those on ripeness. For example, to what extent is standing an aspect of Article III? To what extent is it a discretionary judgment regarding federal court remedies? To the extent ingredients of standing are not compelled by Article III, institutions other than the Supreme Court (e. g., Congress and the states) will have a larger voice in shaping standing. Thus, cases such as Tileston and Doremus at the beginning of the section bear on the extent to which state court recognitions of standing must be given effect in Supreme Court review. And the notes accompanying Flast v. Cohen consider the scope of congressional control over standing.

c. *How decided?* How does the Court determine whether a litigant has a sufficiently distinctive personal interest to grant standing? Is the existence or threat of an actual substantial injury enough? Or must there be an invasion of "legal rights"? What is a "legal" injury? Does standing depend in part on the nature of the substantive claim being raised? Should there be no requirement of a distinctive individualized injury at all so long as a person genuinely wishes to litigate a claim in a concrete factual setting— i. e., are "public actions" by "mere" citizens permissible? Or do such "private attorneys general" suits raise too many of the dangers of advisory opinions? To what extent should a decision on standing turn on the needs of the parties and the society at large, to what extent on institutional values pertaining to the courts? Questions such as these run through all of the materials which follow and are raised in especially sharp form by Flast v. Cohen, the last principal case.

TILESTON v. ULLMAN

318 U.S. 44, 63 S.Ct. 493, 87 L.Ed. 603 (1943).

Appeal from the Supreme Court of Errors of Connecticut.

PER CURIAM. This case comes here on appeal to review a declaratory judgment of the Supreme Court of Errors of Connecticut that §§ 6246 and 6562 of the General Statutes of Connecticut of 1930—prohibiting the use of drugs or instruments to prevent conception, and the giving of assistance or counsel in their use—are applicable to appellant, a registered physician, and as applied to him are constitutional. 129 Conn. 84, 26 A.2d 582, 588.

The suit was tried and judgment rendered on the allegations of the complaint which are stipulated to be true. Appellant alleged that the statute, if applicable to him, would prevent his giving professional advice concerning the use of contraceptives to three patients whose condition of health was such that their lives would be endangered by child-bearing, and that appellees, law enforcement officers of the state, intend to prosecute any offense against the statute and "claim or may claim" that the proposed professional advice would constitute such an offense. The complaint set out in detail the danger to the lives of appellant's patients in the event that they should bear children, but contained no allegation asserting any claim under the Fourteenth Amendment of infringement of appellant's liberty or his property rights. The relief prayed was a declaratory judgment as to whether the statutes are applicable to appellant and if so whether they constitute a valid exercise of constitutional power "within the meaning and intent of Amendment XIV of the Constitution of the United States prohibiting a state from depriving any person of life without due process of law." On stipulation of the parties the state superior court ordered these questions of law reserved for the consideration and advice of the Supreme Court of Errors. That court, which assumed without deciding that the case was an appropriate one for a declaratory judgment, ruled that the statutes "'prohibit the action proposed to be done" by appellant and "are constitutional."

We are of the opinion that the proceedings in the state courts present no constitutional question which appellant has standing to assert.   The sole constitutional attack upon the statutes under the Fourteenth Amendment is confined to their deprivation of life—obviously not appellant's but his patients'.   There is no allegation or proof that appellant's life is in danger. His patients are not parties to this proceeding and there is no basis on which we can say that he has standing to secure an adjudication of his patients' constitutional right to life, which they do not assert in their own behalf. . . .   No question is raised in the record with respect to the deprivation of appellant's liberty or property in contravention of the Fourteenth Amendment, nor is there anything in the opinion or judgment of the Supreme Court of Errors which indicates or would support a decision of any question other than those raised in the superior court and reserved by it for decision of the Supreme Court of Errors.   That court's practice is to decline to answer questions not reserved. . . .

Since the appeal must be dismissed on the ground that appellant has no standing to litigate the constitutional question which the record presents, it is unnecessary to consider whether the record shows the existence of a genuine case or controversy essential to the exercise of the jurisdiction of this Court. Cf. Nashville, C. & St. L. Ry. Co. v. Wallace, 288 U.S. 249, 259.

Dismissed.

SOME PROBLEMS OF STANDING

1. *State-created standing and federal review—Tileston and Doremus.* a. *The source of the applicable law.* What justified the Supreme Court's dismissal in Tileston?   Did the Court find that there was no Article III "case"?   (Compare the last paragraph of Tileston with the explicit reliance on Article III in the Doremus dismissal, below.)   Did the Court find noncompliance with the statutory requirements of the obligatory appeal jurisdiction in 28 U.S.C. § 1257?   Is there any other source of Court discretion to decline adjudication in a case in which the state court decided the merits? Compare sec. 4, below.

Note the suggestion (Hart and Wechsler, The Federal Courts and the Federal System (1953), 174) that the question of standing "is the question whether the litigant has a sufficient personal interest in getting the relief he seeks, or is a sufficiently appropriate representative of other interested persons . . .. So viewed, the question is one of remedy, is it not, belonging to and dependent upon the applicable law of remedies?"   So viewed, why should not that applicable law be largely state rather than federal, in Supreme Court review of state decisions?   Why should not the Supreme Court review, so long as the state has chosen to adjudicate in a situation satisfying minimal Article III ingredients?   Does the Supreme Court's institutional interest in avoiding constitutional questions justify "federalizing" standing law in order to impose more rigid standing barriers than Article III and state law would require?

b. *State taxpayers.* Compare the handling of state court taxpayers' actions on Supreme Court review. During the period in which federal taxpayers wholly lacked standing to attack spending programs (see the Frothingham case, which follows), the Supreme Court repeatedly decided the merits in municipal taxpayers' suits challenging local action without even discussing the standing issue. See, e.g., Everson v. Board of Education, 330 U.S. 1 (1947) (local taxpayer challenging spending of public funds for transportation of parochial school students). But in Doremus v. Board of Education, 342 U.S. 429 (1952), the Court dismissed an appeal from a state court decision which had rejected an attack by taxpayers on the validity of Bible reading in the public schools:

"We do not undertake to say that a state court may not render an opinion on a federal constitutional question even under such circumstances that can be regarded only as advisory. But, because our own jurisdiction is cast in terms of 'case or controversy' we cannot accept as the basis for review, nor as the basis for conclusive disposition of federal law without review, any procedure which does not constitute such. The taxpayer's action can meet this test, but only when it is a good-faith pocketbook action. It is apparent that the grievance which it is sought to litigate here is not a direct dollars-and-cents injury but is a religious difference."

Justice Douglas, joined by Justices Reed and Burton, dissented: "If this were a suit to enjoin a federal law, it could not be maintained by reason of [the Frothingham case, below]. But New Jersey can fashion her own rules governing the institution of suits in her courts. If she wants to give these taxpayers status to sue . . ., I see nothing in the Constitution to prevent it. And where the clash of interests is as real and as strong as it is here, it is odd indeed to hold there is no case or controversy within the meaning of Art. III, § 2 of the Constitution." [1]

c. *Supreme Court rejection of individual interest recognized by the state.* Doremus and the principal case both indicate—though on different theories—that a state court finding of standing does not assure Supreme Court review. Note Justice Frankfurter's comments in Coleman v. Miller, 307 U.S. 433 (1939): "[T]he creation of a vast domain of legal interests is in the keeping of the states, and from time to time state courts and legislators give legal protection to new individual interests. Thus, while the ordinary taxpayers suit is not recognized in the federal courts, it affords adequate standing for review of state decisions when so recognized by state courts. . . . But it by no means follows that a state court ruling on the adequacy of legal interest is binding here." Why not, if Article III is satisfied? What if the state courts in Tileston and Doremus had decided for the plaintiffs? Would the Supreme Court have adhered to its position on

---

1. In 1963, the Court reached the substantive issue Doremus had sought to present and held that Bible reading in schools violated the Establishment Clause. See School District of Abington Township v. Schempp, 374 U.S. 203 (chap. 17 below), in which the majority found standing because the challengers were "school children and their parents directly affected" by the practices. The Court noted that the Doremus appeal was dismissed "upon the graduation of the school child involved and because of the appellants' failure to establish standing as taxpayers." (Compare Flast v. Cohen, below.) The Court also stated that "the requirements for standing to challenge state action under the Establishment Clause, unlike those relating to the Free Exercise Clause, do not include proof that particular religious freedoms are infringed."

standing? Would it have entered orders dismissing the appeals—and left intact the state injunctions based on federal substantive law?

d. *Standing and the Griswold case.* The Court reached the merits of the Connecticut birth control law 22 years after the Tileson dismissal. After once more avoiding decision in Poe v. Ullman, in 1962 (sec. 4 below), the Court held the law unconstitutional in Griswold v. Connecticut, in 1965 (chap. 11, p. 824, below). The appellants in Griswold had given birth control information at a clinic and were convicted as accessories to the violation of the "use" ban. The majority opinion noted: "We think that appellants have standing to raise the constitutional rights of the married people with whom they had a professional relationship. Tileston v. Ullman, 318 U.S. 44, is different, for there the plaintiff seeking to represent others asked for a declaratory judgment. In that situation we thought that the requirements of standing should be strict, lest the standards of 'case or controversy' in Article III of the Constitution become blurred. Here those doubts are removed by reason of a criminal conviction for serving married couples in violation of an aiding-and-abetting statute. Certainly the accessory should have standing to assert that the offense which he is charged with assisting is not, or cannot constitutionally be, a crime.

"This case is more akin to Truax v. Raich, 239 U.S. 33, where an employee was permitted to assert the rights of his employer; to Pierce v. Society of Sisters, 268 U.S. 510, where the owners of private schools were entitled to assert the rights of potential pupils and their parents; and to Barrows v. Jackson, 346 U.S. 249 [all in the next note]. The rights of husband and wife, pressed here, are likely to be diluted or adversely affected unless those rights are considered in a suit involving those who have this kind of confidential relation to them."

2. *Asserting the rights of others.* a. *The Pierce and NAACP exceptions.* Ordinarily, as Tileston emphasizes, one may not claim standing to vindicate the constitutional rights of someone else. But in Pierce v. Society of Sisters, 268 U.S. 510 (1925), where a parochial school challenged the constitutionality of a statute requiring parents to send children to public schools, the plaintiff in a federal court action was permitted to assert the rights of the parents in defending its own property rights. And in NAACP v. Alabama ex rel. Patterson, 357 U.S. 449 (1958), the NAACP—in resisting a state order to disclose its membership lists—was permitted to assert the rights of its members. The Court stated that the Association "argues more appropriately the rights of its members, and   . . .   its nexus with them is sufficient to permit that it act as their representative before this Court." Why could not Connecticut, in the Tileson case, find that the doctor's "nexus" with his patients was "sufficient" to permit him to "act as their representative"? Compare Griswold v. Connecticut, above, and see generally Sedler, "Standing to Assert Constitutional Jus Tertii in the Supreme Court," 71 Yale L.J. 599 (1962).

b. *Barrows v. Jackson, Art. III, and discretion.* One must usually be a member of the class discriminated against in order to have standing to attack a statute as denying the equal protection of the laws. Jeffrey Mfg. Co. v. Blagg, 235 U.S. 571 (1915). Compare Truax v. Raich, 239 U.S. 33 (1915), permitting an alien employee to enjoin the enforcement of a statute limiting the percentage of aliens on the employer's work force. In Barrows v. Jackson, 346 U.S. 249 (1953), a state court damage suit for breach of a racially restrictive covenant by selling real estate to a non-Caucasian, the defendant was permitted to challenge the enforcement of the covenant although he was not a member of the class discriminated against.

Justice Minton's majority opinion in Barrows v. Jackson suggested that the Article III requirements at the core of the law of standing were encased in discretionary, prudential considerations: "Ordinarily, one may not claim in this Court to vindicate the constitutional rights of some third party. . . . The requirement of standing is often used to describe the constitutional limitation of this Court to 'cases' and 'controversies.' . . . Apart from the jurisdictional requirement, this Court has developed a complementary rule of self-restraint for its own governance (not always clearly distinguished from the constitutional limitation) which ordinarily precludes a person from challenging the constitutionality by invoking the rights of others. . . . There are still other cases in which the Court has held that even though a party will suffer a direct substantial injury from application of a statute, he cannot challenge its constitutionality unless he can show that he is within the class whose constitutional rights are allegedly infringed." That was "salutary" as a general rule, but in this case "it would be difficult if not impossible for the persons whose rights are asserted to present their grievance before any court." Under these "peculiar circumstances," accordingly, "we believe the reasons which underlie our rule denying standing to raise another's rights, which is only a rule of practice, are outweighed by the need to protect the fundamental rights which would be denied by permitting the damage actions to be maintained."

c. *Defendants' standing and severability.* Compare the problems of defendants' standing and the severability of statutes illustrated by United States v. Raines, 362 U.S. 17 (1960), in which the trial court was reversed for invalidating a law on the basis of constitutional defects "in applications not before it." The United States had brought suit against certain voting registrars under the Civil Rights Act of 1957, which allowed the United States to act against "any person" depriving citizens of the right to vote on account of race or color. Although the complaint charged only official action, the District Court dismissed because the statute on its face applied to private action, supposedly beyond the constitutional scope of the 15th Amendment. Justice Brennan's majority opinion reversed on the basis of the general rule that "one to whom application of a statute is constitutional will not be heard to attack the statute on the ground that impliedly it might be taken as applying to other persons or other situations in which its application might be unconstitutional."

Justice Brennan found none of the exceptions to this rule applicable. Prominent among the "exceptions" noted by him were two instances of non-severable statutes: "[W]hen a state statute comes conclusively pronounced by a state court as having an otherwise valid provision or application inextricably tied up with an invalid one;" and "that rarest of cases where this Court can justifiably think itself able confidently to discern that Congress would not have desired its legislation to stand at all unless it could validly stand in its every application. Cf. . . . The Employers' Liability Cases, 207 U.S. 463, 501."[2]

2. Another "exception" noted by Justice Brennan raises quite different prob- lems and rests on substantive legal principles (especially regarding vague-

FEDERAL TAXPAYERS: THE FROTHINGHAM CASE

Mrs. Frothingham brought suit as a federal taxpayer in a District of Columbia court to restrain the Secretary of the Treasury from making expenditures under the Maternity Act of 1921, which provided for conditional financial grants to the states "to reduce maternal and infant mortality." She argued, inter alia, that the Act "is a usurpation of power not granted to Congress by the Constitution—an attempted exercise of the power of local self-government reserved to the States by the Tenth Amendment." The unanimous Supreme Court held that the suit "must be disposed for want of jurisdiction" because the plaintiff "has no such interest in the subject-matter, nor is such injury inflicted or threatened, as will enable her to sue." Frothingham v. Mellon, 262 U.S. 447 (1923).

Was the Court's decision based on Article III? Or did the Court rely on its authority to fashion federal equitable remedies? Did the grounds of decision preclude Congress from granting federal taxpayers standing to sue? Consider the Court's disposition of Mrs. Frothingham's claim; and compare the reasoning of Flast v. Cohen, the next principal case (and its impact on congressional power to lower standing barriers). The Court stated in Frothingham:

"[Plaintiff alleges] that she is a taxpayer of the United States; and her contention, though not clear, seems to be that the effect of the appropriations complained of will be to increase the burden of future taxation and thereby take her property without due process of law. The right of a taxpayer to enjoin the execution of a federal appropriation act, on the ground that it is invalid and will result in taxation for illegal purposes, has never been passed upon by this Court. In cases where it was presented, the question has either been allowed to pass sub silentio or the determination of it expressly withheld. Millard v. Roberts, 202 U.S. 429, 438; Wilson v. Shaw, 204 U.S. 24, 31; Bradfield v. Roberts, 175 U.S. 291, 295. The case last cited came here from the Court of Appeals of the District of Columbia, and that court sustained the right of the plaintiff to sue by treating the case as one directed against the District of Columbia, and therefore subject to the rule frequently stated by this Court, that resident taxpayers may sue to enjoin an illegal use of the moneys of a municipal corporation. Roberts v. Bradfield, 12 App.D.C. 453, 459–460. The interest of a taxpayer of a municipality in the application of its moneys is direct and immediate and the remedy by injunction to prevent their misuse is not inappropriate. It is upheld by a large number of state cases and is the rule of this Court. Crampton v. Zabriskie, 101 U.S. 601, 609. . . . The reasons which support the extension of the equitable remedy to

ness, overbroadness and the First Amendment) considered later in this volume: "This Court has indicated that where the application of these rules [barring a litigant from raising unconstitutional application of statutes to others and the 'closely related corollary that a litigant may only assert his own constitutional rights'] would itself have an inhibitory effect on freedom of speech, they may not be applied. See Smith v. California, 361 U.S. 147, 151; Thornhill v. Alabama, 310 U.S. 88, 97–98." Note a passage in Dombrowski v. Pfister, 380 U.S. 479 (1965) (sec. 4 below): "We have consistently allowed attacks on overly broad statutes with no requirement that the person making the attack demonstrate that his own conduct could not be regulated by a statute drawn with the requisite narrow specificity. [This exception to usual standing rules exists because of the] 'danger of tolerating, in the area of First Amendment freedoms, the existence of a penal statute susceptible of sweeping and improper application.'"

a single taxpayer in such cases are based upon the peculiar relation of the corporate taxpayer to the corporation, which is not without some resemblance to that subsisting between stockholder and private corporation. IV Dillon Municipal Corporations, 5th Ed., § 1580 et seq. But the relation of a taxpayer of the United States to the Federal Government is very different. His interest in the moneys of the Treasury—partly realized from taxation and partly from other sources—is shared with millions of others; is comparatively minute and indeterminable; and the effect upon future taxation, of any payment out of the funds, so remote, fluctuating and uncertain, that no basis is afforded for an appeal to the preventive powers of a court of equity.

"The administration of any statute, likely to produce additional taxation to be imposed upon a vast number of taxpayers, the extent of whose several liability is indefinite and constantly changing, is essentially a matter of public and not of individual concern. If one taxpayer may champion and litigate such a cause, then every other taxpayer may do the same, not only in respect of the statute here under review but also in respect of every other appropriation act and statute whose administration requires the outlay of public money, and whose validity may be questioned. The bare suggestion of such a result, with its attendant inconveniences, goes far to sustain the conclusion which we have reached, that a suit of this character cannot be maintained. It is of much significance that no precedent sustaining the right to maintain suits like this has been called to our attention, although, since the formation of the government, as an examination of the acts of Congress will disclose, a large number of statutes appropriating or involving the expenditure of moneys for nonfederal purposes have been enacted and carried into effect.

"The functions of government under our system are apportioned. To the legislative department has been committed the duty of making laws; to the executive the duty of executing them; and to the judiciary the duty of interpreting and applying them in cases properly brought before the courts. The general rule is that neither department may invade the province of the other and neither may control, direct or restrain the action of the other. We are not now speaking of the merely ministerial duties of officials. Gaines v. Thompson, 7 Wall. 347. We have no power per se to review and annul acts of Congress on the ground that they are unconstitutional. That question may be considered only when the justification for some direct injury suffered or threatened, presenting a justiciable issue, is made to rest upon such an act. Then the power exercised is that of ascertaining and declaring the law applicable to the controversy. It amounts to little more than the negative power to disregard an unconstitutional enactment, which otherwise would stand in the way of the enforcement of a legal right. The party who invokes the power must be able to show not only that the statute is invalid but that he has sustained or is immediately in danger of sustaining some direct injury as the result of its enforcement, and not merely that he suffers in some indefinite way in common with people generally. If a case for preventive relief be presented the court enjoins, in effect, not the execution of the statute, but the acts of the official, the statute notwithstanding. Here the . . . plaintiff [has] no such case. Looking through forms of words to the substance of [the] complaint, it is merely that officials of the executive department of the government are executing and will execute an act of Congress asserted to be unconstitutional; and this we are asked to prevent. To do so would be not to decide a judicial controversy, but to assume a position of authority over the governmental acts of another and coequal department, an authority which plainly we do not possess." *

FLAST v. COHEN

392 U.S. 83, 88 S.Ct. 1942, 20 L.Ed.2d 947 (1968).

Appeal from the United States District Court for the Southern District of New York.

Mr. Chief Justice WARREN delivered the opinion of the Court.

In Frothingham v. Mellon, 262 U.S. 447 (1923), this Court ruled that a federal taxpayer is without standing to challenge the constitutionality of a federal statute. That ruling has stood for 45 years as an impenetrable barrier to suits against acts of Congress brought by individuals who can assert only the interest of federal taxpayers. In this case, we must decide whether the Frothingham barrier should be lowered when a taxpayer attacks a federal statute on the ground that it violates the Establishment and Free Exercise Clauses of the First Amendment.

Appellants filed suit in the United States District Court for the Southern District of New York to enjoin the allegedly unconstitutional expenditure of federal funds under Titles I and II of the Elementary and Secondary Education Act of 1965 . . .. The complaint alleged that the seven appellants had as common attribute that "each pay income taxes of the United States," and it is clear from the complaint that the appellants were resting their standing to maintain the action solely on their status as federal taxpayers. The appellees, who are charged by Congress with administering the Elementary and Secondary Education Act of 1965, were sued in their official capacities.

The gravamen of the appellants' complaint was that federal funds appropriated under the Act were being used to finance instruction in reading, arithmetic and other subjects in religious schools, and to purchase textbooks and other instructional materials for use in such schools. . . . Such expenditures of federal tax funds, appellants alleged, violate the First Amendment because "they constitute a law respecting an establishment of religion" and because "they prohibit the free exercise of religion on the part of the [appellants] . . . by reason of the fact that they constitute compulsory taxation for religious purposes." The complaint asked for a declaration that appellees' actions in approving the expenditure of federal funds for the al-

---

* In a case decided in the same opinion as Mrs. Frothingham's, the State of Massachusetts proved no more successful in eliciting a constitutional ruling on the Maternity Act. Massachusetts v. Mellon, 262 U.S. 447 (1923). The Court held that the State "presents no justiciable controversy either in its own behalf or as the representative of its citizens." The complaint of invasion of states' rights was "political and not judicial in character." Nor could the State sue as representative of its citizens: "But the citizens of Massachusetts are also citizens of the United States. It cannot be conceded that a State, as parens patriae, may institute judicial proceedings to protect citizens of the United States from the operation of the statutes thereof." But a State was permitted to bring an original jurisdiction action as parens patriae in Georgia v. Pennsylvania R. R., 324 U.S. 439 (1945), an antitrust laws attack on rates as discriminatory. For cases (printed below) where state interests were found sufficient for standing to challenge the constitutionality of federal laws, see Missouri v. Holland, 252 U.S. 416 (1920) (protection of migratory birds) (chap. 5, p. 396), and South Carolina v. Katzenbach, 383 U.S. 301 (1966) (Voting Rights Act of 1965) (chap. 6, p. 534).

leged purposes were not authorized by the Act or, in the alternative, that if appellees' actions are deemed within the authority and intent of the Act, "the Act is to that extent unconstitutional and void." The complaint also prayed for an injunction to enjoin appellees from approving any expenditure of federal funds for the allegedly unconstitutional purposes. . . .

[The District Court] ruled on the authority of Frothingham that appellants lacked standing. . . . For reasons explained at length below, we hold that appellants do have standing as federal taxpayers to maintain this action, and the judgment below must be reversed. [Part I of the opinion, finding that a three-judge court was properly convened, is omitted.]

II.

[Frothingham v. Mellon] must be the starting point for analysis in this case. . . . Although the barrier Frothingham erected against federal taxpayer suits has never been breached, the decision has been the source of some confusion and the object of considerable criticism. The confusion has developed as commentators have tried to determine whether Frothingham establishes a constitutional bar to taxpayer suits or whether the Court was simply imposing a rule of self-restraint which was not constitutionally compelled.[1] . . . The opinion delivered in Frothingham can be read to support either position. . . . Whatever the merits of the current debate over Frothingham, its very existence suggests that we should undertake a fresh examination of the limitations upon standing to sue in a federal court and the application of those limitations to taxpayer suits.

III.

. . . [T]he judicial power of federal courts is constitutionally restricted to "cases" and "controversies." As is so often the situation in constitutional adjudication, those two words have an iceberg quality, containing beneath their surface simplicity submerged complexities which go to the very heart of our constitutional form of government. Embodied in the words "cases" and "controversies" are two complementary but somewhat different limitations. In part those words limit the business of federal courts to questions presented in an adversary context and in a form historically viewed as capable of resolution through the judicial process. And in part those words define the role assigned to the judiciary in a tripartite allocation of power to assure that the federal courts will not intrude into areas committed to the other branches of government. Justiciability is the term of art employed to give expression of this dual limitation placed upon federal courts by the case and controversy doctrine.

Justiciability is itself a concept of uncertain meaning and scope. . . . [T]hat doctrine has become a blend of constitutional requirements and policy

---

1. The prevailing view of the commentators is that Frothingham announced only a nonconstitutional rule of self-restraint. See, e. g., Jaffe, Standing to Secure Judicial Review: Private Actions, 75 Harv.L.Rev. 255, 302–303 (1961); Arthur Garfield Hays Civil Liberties Conference: Public Aid to Parochial Schools and Standing to Bring Suit, 12 Buffalo L.Rev. 35, 48–65 (1962); Davis, Standing to Challenge Governmental Action, 39 Minn. L.Rev. 353, 386–391 (1955). But see Hearings on S. 2097 before the Subcommittee on Constitutional Rights of the Senate Judiciary Committee, 89th Cong., 2d Sess., 465, 467–468 (1966) (statement of Prof. William D. Valente). The last-cited hearings contain the best collection of recent expression of views on this question. [Footnote by the Court.]

considerations. And a policy limitation is "not always clearly distinguished from the constitutional limitation." Barrows v. Jackson, 346 U.S. 249, 255 (1953). [See, for example, Justice Brandeis' concurring opinion in Ashwander v. Tennessee Valley Authority, considered in sec. 4, p. 142, below.]

. . . . [T]he Government's position is that the constitutional scheme of separation of powers, and the deference owed by the federal judiciary to the other two branches of government within that scheme, presents an absolute bar to taxpayer suits challenging the validity of federal spending programs. . . . An analysis of the function served by standing limitations compels a rejection of the Government's position.

Standing is an aspect of justiciability and, as such, the problem of standing is surrounded by the same complexities and vagaries that inhere in justiciability. . . . Some of the complexities peculiar to standing problems result because standing "serves, on occasion, as a shorthand expression for all the various elements of justiciability." In addition, there are at work in the standing doctrine the many subtle pressures which tend to cause policy considerations to blend into constitutional limitations.

Despite the complexities and uncertainties, some meaningful form can be given to the jurisdictional limitations placed on federal court power by the concept of standing. The fundamental aspect of standing is that it focuses on the party seeking to get his complaint before a federal court and not on the issues he wishes to have adjudicated. The "gist of the question of standing" is whether the party seeking relief has "alleged such a personal stake in the outcome of the controversy as to assure that concrete adverseness which sharpens the presentation of issues upon which the court so largely depends for illumination of difficult constitutional questions." Baker v. Carr, 369 U.S. 186, 204 (1962). In other words, when standing is placed in issue in a case, the question is whether the person whose standing is challenged is a proper party to request an adjudication of a particular issue and not whether the issue itself is justiciable. Thus, a party may have standing in a particular case, but the federal court may nevertheless decline to pass on the merits of the case because, for example, it presents a political question. A proper party is demanded so that federal courts will not be asked to decide "ill-defined controversies over constitutional issues," United Public Workers v. Mitchell, 330 U.S. 75, 90 (1947), or a case which is of "a hypothetical or abstract character." Aetna Life Insurance Co. v. Haworth, 300 U.S. 227, 240 (1937). So stated, the standing requirement is closely related to, although more general than, the rule that federal courts will not entertain friendly suits, . . . or those which are feigned or collusive in nature . . . .

When the emphasis in the standing problem is placed on whether the person invoking a federal court's jurisdiction is a proper party to maintain the action, the weakness of the Government's argument in this case becomes apparent. The question whether a particular person is a proper party to maintain the action does not, by its own force, raise separation of powers problems related to improper judicial interference in areas committed to other branches of the Federal Government. Such problems arise, if at all, only from the substantive issues the individual seeks to have adjudicated. Thus, in terms of Article III limitations on federal court jurisdiction, the question of standing is related only to whether the dispute sought to be adjudicated will be presented in an adversary context and in a form historically viewed as capable of judicial resolution. It is for that reason that the emphasis in standing problems is on whether the party invoking federal court jurisdiction has "a personal stake in the outcome of the controversy," Baker v. Carr, supra, at 204, and whether the dispute touches upon "the legal relations of parties having adverse legal interests." Aetna Life Insurance Co. v. Haworth, supra, at 241. A taxpayer may or may not have the requisite personal stake in the outcome, depending upon the circumstances of the particular case. Therefore, we find no absolute bar in Article III to suits by federal taxpayers challenging allegedly unconstitutional federal taxing and spending programs. There remains, however, the problem of determining the circumstances under which a federal taxpayer will be deemed to have the personal stake and interest that imparts the necessary concrete adverseness to such litigation so that standing can be conferred on the taxpayer *qua* taxpayer consistent with the constitutional limitations of Article III.

IV.

The various rules of standing applied by federal courts have not been developed in the abstract. Rather, they have been fashioned with specific reference to the status asserted by the party whose standing is challenged and to the type of question he wishes to have adjudicated. We have noted that, in deciding the question of standing, it is not relevant that the substantive issues in the litigation might be nonjusticiable. However, our decisions establish that, in ruling on standing, it is both appropriate and necessary to look to the substantive issues for another purpose, namely, to determine whether there is a logical nexus between the status asserted and the claim sought to be adjudicated. For example, standing requirements will vary in First Amendment religion cases depending upon whether the party raises an Establishment Clause claim or a claim under the Free Exercise Clause. See McGowan v. Maryland, 366 U.S. 420, 429–430 (1961). Such inquiries into the nexus between the status asserted by the litigant and the claim he presents are essential to assure that he is a proper and appropriate party to invoke federal judicial power. Thus, our point of reference in this case is the standing of individuals who assert only the status of federal taxpayers and who challenge the constitutionality of a federal spending program. Whether such individuals have standing to maintain that form of action turns on whether they can demonstrate the necessary stake as taxpayers in the outcome of the litigation to satisfy Article III requirements.

The nexus demanded of federal taxpayers has two aspects to it. First, the taxpayer must establish a logical link between that status and the type of legislative enactment attacked. Thus, a taxpayer will be a proper party to allege the unconstitutionality only of exercises of congressional power under the taxing and spending clause of Article I, § 8, of the Constitution. It will not be sufficient to allege an incidental expenditure of tax funds in the administration of an essentially regulatory statute. This requirement is consistent with the limitation imposed upon state taxpayer standing in federal courts in Doremus v. Board of Education, 342 U.S. 429 (1952). Secondly, the taxpayer must establish a nexus between that status and the precise nature of the constitutional infringement alleged. Under this requirement, the taxpayer must show that the challenged enactment exceeds specific constitutional limitations imposed upon the exercise of the congressional taxing and spending power and not simply that the enactment is generally beyond the powers delegated to Congress by Art. I, § 8. When both nexuses are established, the litigant will have shown a taxpayer's stake in the outcome of the controversy and will be a proper and appropriate party to invoke a federal court's jurisdiction.

The taxpayer-appellants in this case have satisfied both nexuses to support their claim of standing under the test we announce today. Their constitutional challenge is made to an exercise by Congress of its power under Art. I, § 8, to spend for the general welfare, and the challenged program involves a substantial expenditure of federal tax funds. In addition, appellants have alleged that the challenged expenditures violate the Establishment and Free Exercise Clauses of the First Amendment. Our history vividly illustrates that one of the specific evils feared by those who drafted the Establishment Clause and fought for its adoption was that the taxing and spending power would be used to favor one religion over another or to support religion in general. . . . [T]hat clause of the First Amendment [2] operates as a specific constitutional limitation upon the exercise by Congress of the taxing and spending power conferred by Art. I, § 8.

The allegations of the taxpayer in Frothingham v. Mellon, supra, were quite different from those made in this case, and the result in Frothingham is consistent with the test of taxpayer standing announced today. The taxpayer in Frothingham attacked a federal spending program and she, therefore, established the first nexus required. However, she lacked standing because her constitutional attack was not based on an allegation that Congress, in enacting the Maternity Act of 1921, had breached a specific limitation upon its taxing and spending power. The taxpayer in Frothingham alleged essentially that Congress, by enacting the challenged statute, had exceeded the general powers delegated to it by Art. I, § 8, and that Congress had thereby invaded the legislative province reserved to the States by the Tenth Amendment. To be sure, Mrs. Frothingham made the additional allegation that her tax liability would be increased as a result of the allegedly unconstitutional enactment, and she framed that allegation in terms of a deprivation of property without due process of law. However, the Due Process Clause of the Fifth Amendment does not protect taxpayers against increases in tax liability, and the taxpayer in Frothingham failed to make any additional claim that the harm she alleged resulted from a breach by Congress of the specific constitutional limitations imposed upon an exercise of the taxing and spending power. In essence, Mrs. Frothingham was attempting to assert the States' interest in their legislative prerogatives and not a federal taxpayer's interest in being free of taxing and spending in contravention of specific constitutional limitations imposed upon Congress' taxing and spending power.

2. Appellants have also alleged that the Elementary and Secondary Education Act of 1965 violates the Free Exercise Clause of the First Amendment. This Court has recognized that the taxing power can be used to infringe the free exercise of religion. Murdock v. Pennsylvania, 319 U.S. 105 (1943). Since we hold that appellants' Establishment Clause claim is sufficient to establish the nexus between their status and the precise nature of the constitutional infringement alleged, we need not decide whether the Free Exercise claim, standing alone, would be adequate to confer standing in this case. We do note, however, that the challenged tax in Murdock operated upon a particular class of taxpayers. When such exercises of the taxing power are challenged, the proper party emphasis in the federal standing doctrine would require that standing be limited to the taxpayers within the affected class. [Footnote by the Court.]

We have noted that the Establishment Clause of the First Amendment does specifically limit the taxing and spending power conferred by Art. I, § 8. Whether the Constitution contains other specific limitations can be determined only in the context of future cases. However, whenever such specific limitations are found, we believe a taxpayer will have a clear stake as a taxpayer in assuring that they are not breached by Congress. Consequently, we hold that a taxpayer will have standing consistent with Article III to invoke federal judicial power when he alleges that congressional action under the taxing and spending clause is in derogation of those constitutional provisions which operate to restrict the exercise of the taxing and spending power. The taxpayer's allegation in such cases would be that his tax money is being extracted and spent in violation of specific constitutional protections against such abuses of legislative power. Such an injury is appropriate for judicial redress, and the taxpayer has established the necessary nexus between his status and the nature of the allegedly unconstitutional action to support his claim of standing to secure judicial review. Under such circumstances, we feel confident that the questions will be framed with the necessary specificity, that the issues will be contested with the necessary adverseness and that the litigation will be pursued wih the necessary vigor to assure that the constitutional challenge will be made in a form traditionally thought to be capable of judicial resolution. We lack that confidence in cases such as Frothingham where a taxpayer seeks to employ a federal court as a forum in which to air his generalized grievances about the conduct of government or the allocation of power in the Federal System.

While we express no view at all on the merits of appellants' claims in this case, their complaint contains sufficient allegations under the criteria we have outlined to give them standing to invoke a federal court's jurisdiction for an adjudication on the merits.

Reversed.

Mr. Justice DOUGLAS, concurring.

While I have joined the opinion of the Court, I do not think that the test it lays down is a durable one for the reasons stated by my Brother HARLAN. I think, therefore, that it will suffer erosion and in time result in the demise of Frothingham v. Mellon, 262 U.S. 447. It would therefore be the part of wisdom, as I see the problem, to be rid of Frothingham here and now.

I do not view with alarm, as does my Brother HARLAN, the consequences of that course. Frothingham, decided in 1923, was in the heyday of substantive due process, when courts were sitting in judgment on the wisdom or reasonableness of legislation. . . . When the Court used substantive due process to determine the wisdom or reasonableness of legislation, it was indeed transforming itself into the Court of Revision which was rejected by the Constitutional Convention. It was that judicial attitude, not the theory of standing to sue rejected in Frothingham, that involved "important hazards for the continued effectiveness of the federal judiciary," to borrow a phrase from my Brother HARLAN. A contrary result in Frothingham in that setting might well have accentuated an ominous trend to judicial supremacy. But we no longer undertake to exercise that kind of power. Today's problem is in a different setting. Most laws passed by Congress do not contain even a ghost of a constitutional question. . . .

The States have experimented with taxpayers' suits and with only two exceptions now allow them. A few state decisions are frankly based on the theory that a taxpayer is a private attorney general seeking to vindicate the public interest. . . . Taxpayers can be vigilant private attorney generals. Their stake in the outcome of litigation may be *de minimis* by financial standards, yet very great when measured by a particular constitutional mandate. . . .

The judiciary is an indispensable part of the operation of our federal system. With the growing complexities of government it is often the one and only place where effective relief can be obtained. If the judiciary were to become a super-legislative group sitting in judgment on the affairs of people, the situation would be intolerable. But where wrongs to individuals are done by violation of specific guarantees, it is abdication for courts to close their doors. . . .

I would not be niggardly . . . in giving private attorneys general standing to sue. I would certainly not wait for Congress to give its blessing to our deciding cases clearly within our Article III jurisdiction. To wait for a sign from Congress is to allow important Constitutional questions to go undecided and personal liberty unprotected.

There need be no inundation of the federal courts if taxpayers' suits are allowed. There is a wise judicial discretion that usually can distinguish between the frivolous question and the substantial question, between cases ripe for decision and cases that need prior administrative processing, and the like. . . .

[T]he mounting federal aid to sectarian schools is notorious and the subterfuges numerous. I would be as liberal in allowing taxpayers standing to object to these violations of the First Amendment as I would in granting standing of people to complain of any invasion of their rights under the Fourth Amendment or the Fourteenth or under any other guarantee in the Constitution itself or in the Bill of Rights.

Mr. Justice STEWART, concurring.

I join the judgment and opinion of the Court, which I understand to hold only that a federal taxpayer has standing to assert that a specific expenditure of federal funds violates the Establishment Clause of the First Amendment. Because that clause plainly prohibits taxing and spending in aid of religion, every taxpayer can claim a personal constitutional right not to be taxed for the support of a religious institution. The present case is thus readily distinguishable from Frothingham v. Mellon, 262 U.S. 447, where the taxpayer relied not on an explicit constitutional prohibition but questioned instead the scope of the powers delegated to the national legislature by Article I of the Constitution. . . .

Mr. Justice FORTAS, concurring.

I would confine the ruling in this case to the proposition that a taxpayer may maintain a suit to challenge the validity of a federal expenditure on the ground that the expenditure violates the Establishment Clause. . . . There is no reason to suggest, and no basis in the logic of this decision for implying, that there may be other types of congressional expenditures which may be attacked by a litigant solely on the basis of his status as a taxpayer. . . .

Perhaps the vital interest of a citizen in the establishment issue, without reference to his taxpayer's status, would be acceptable as a basis for this challenge. We need not decide this. But certainly, I believe, we must recognize that our principle of judicial scrutiny of legislative acts which raise important constitutional questions requires that the issue here presented— the separation of state and church—which the Founding Fathers regarded as fundamental to our constitutional system—should be subjected to judicial testing. This is not a question which we, if we are to be faithful to our trust, should consign to limbo, unacknowledged, unresolved, and undecided. . . .

Mr. Justice HARLAN, dissenting. . . .

I.

It is desirable first to restate the basic issues in this case. The question here is not, as it was not in Frothingham, whether "a federal taxpayer is without standing to challenge the constitutionality of a federal statute." . . . It could hardly be disputed that federal taxpayers may, as taxpayers, contest the constitutionality of tax obligations imposed severally upon them by federal statute. . . .

The lawsuits here and in Frothingham are fundamentally different. They present the question whether federal taxpayers *qua* taxpayers may, in suits in which they do not contest the validity of their previous or existing tax obligations, challenge the constitutionality of the uses for which Congress has authorized the expenditure of public funds. These differences in the purposes of the cases are reflected in differences in the litigants' interests. An action brought to contest the validity of tax liabilities assessed to the plaintiff is designed to vindicate interests that are personal and proprietary. . . . I take it that the Court . . . believes that the interests of those who as taxpayers challenge the constitutionality of public expenditures may, at least in certain circumstances, be similar. Yet this assumption is surely mistaken.

The complaint in this case, unlike that in Frothingham, contains no allegation that the contested expenditures will in any fashion affect the amount of these taxpayers' own existing or foreseeable tax obligations. Even in cases in which such an allegation is made, the suit cannot result in an adjudication either of the plaintiff's tax liabilities or of the propriety of any particular level of taxation. The relief available to such a plaintiff consists entirely of the vindication of rights held in common by all citizens. . . .

Nor are taxpayers' interests in the expenditure of public funds differentiated from those of the general public because of any special rights retained by them in their tax payments. The simple fact is that no such rights can sensibly be said to exist. Taxes are ordinarily levied by the United States without limitations of purpose; absent such a limitation, [tax] payments received by the Treasury . . . become part of the Government's general funds. . . .

Surely it is plain that the rights and interests of taxpayers who contest the constitutionality of public expenditures are markedly different from those of "Hohfeldian" plaintiffs,[1] including those taxpayer-plaintiffs who

---

1. The phrase is Professor Jaffe's, adopted, of course, from W. Hohfeld, Fundamental Legal Conceptions (1923). I have here employed the phrases

challenge the validity of their own tax liabilities. We must recognize that these non-Hohfeldian plaintiffs complain, just as the petitioner in Frothingham sought to complain, not as taxpayers, but as "private attorneys-general." The interests they represent, and the rights they espouse, are bereft of any personal or proprietary coloration. They are, as litigants, indistinguishable from any group selected at random from among the general population, taxpayers and nontaxpayers alike. These are and must be, to adopt Professor Jaffe's useful phrase, "public actions" brought to vindicate public rights.[2]

It does not, however, follow that suits brought by non-Hohfeldian plaintiffs are excluded by the "case or controversy" clause of Article III of the Constitution from the jurisdiction of the federal courts. This and other federal courts have repeatedly held that individual litigants, acting as private attorneys-general, may have standing as "representatives of the public interest." Scripps-Howard Radio v. Comm'n, 316 U.S. 4, 15. See also Commission v. Sanders Radio Station, 309 U.S. 470, 477 . . . .. Compare Oklahoma v. Civil Service Comm'n, 330 U.S. 127, 137–139. . . . The various lines of authority are by no means free of difficulty, and certain of the cases may be explicable as involving a personal, if remote, economic interest, but I think that it is, nonetheless, clear that non-Hohfeldian plaintiffs as such are not *constitutionally* excluded from the federal courts. The problem ultimately presented by this case is, in my view, therefore to determine in what circumstances, consonant with the character and proper functioning of the federal courts, such suits should be permitted.[3] . . .

II.

As I understand it, the Court's position is that it is unnecessary to decide in what circumstances public actions should be permitted, for it is possible to identify situations in which taxpayers who contest the constitutionality of federal expenditures assert "personal" rights and interests, identical in principle to those asserted by Hohfeldian plaintiffs. This position, if supportable, would of course avoid many of the difficulties of this case . . . .. I believe that the Court's position is untenable.

The Court's analysis consists principally of the observation that the requirements of standing are met if a taxpayer has the "requisite personal interest in the outcome" of his suit. . . . This does not, of course, resolve the standing problem; it merely restates it. The Court implements this standard with the declaration that taxpayers will be "deemed" to have the

---

"Hohfeldian" and "non-Hohfeldian" plaintiffs to mark the distinction between the personal and proprietary interests of the traditional plaintiff, and the representative and public interests of the plaintiff in a public action. I am aware that we are confronted here by a spectrum of interests of varying intensities, but the distinction is sufficiently accurate, and convenient, to warrant its use at least for purposes of discussion. [Footnote by Justice Harlan.]

2. L. Jaffe, Judicial Control of Administrative Action 483 (1965). [Footnote by Justice Harlan.]

3. I agree that implicit in this question is the belief that the federal courts may decline to accept for adjudication cases or questions that, although otherwise within the perimeter of their constitutional jurisdiction, are appropriately thought to be unsuitable at least for immediate judicial resolution. Compare Ashwander v. Tennessee Valley Authority, 297 U.S. 288, 345–348; H. Wechsler, Principles, Politics, and Fundamental Law 9–15 (1961); and Bickel, Foreword: The Passive Virtues, 75 Harv.L.Rev. 40, 45–47. [Footnote by Justice Harlan.]

necessary personal interest if their suits satisfy two criteria: *first,* the challenged expenditure must form part of a federal spending program, and not merely be "incidental" to a regulatory program; and *second,* the constitutional provision under which the plaintiff claims must be a "specific limitation" upon Congress' spending powers. The difficulties with these criteria are many and severe, but it is enough for the moment to emphasize that they are not in any sense a measurement of any plaintiff's interest in the outcome of any suit. As even a cursory examination of the criteria will show, the Court's standard for the determination of standing and its criteria for the satisfaction of that standard are entirely unrelated.

It is surely clear that a plaintiff's interest in the outcome of a suit in which he challenges the constitutionality of a federal expenditure is not made greater or smaller by the unconnected fact that the expenditure is, or is not, "incidental" to an "essentially regulatory program." [4] . . . Presumably the Court does not believe that regulatory programs are necessarily less destructive of First Amendment rights, or that regulatory programs are necessarily less prodigal of public funds than are grants-in-aid, for both these general propositions are demonstrably false. . . . [An] interest as taxpayer arises, if at all, from the fact of an unlawful expenditure, and not as a consequence of the expenditure's form. Apparently the Court has repudiated the emphasis in Frothingham upon the amount of the plaintiff's tax bill, only to substitute an equally irrelevant emphasis upon the form of the challenged expenditure.

The Court's second criterion is similarly unrelated to its standard for the determination of standing. The intensity of a plaintiff's interest in a suit is not measured, even obliquely, by the fact that the constitutional provision under which he claims is, or is not, a "specific limitation" upon Congress' spending powers. Thus, among the claims in Frothingham was the assertion that the Maternity Act, 42 Stat. 224, deprived the petitioner of property without due process of law. The Court has evidently concluded that this claim did not confer standing because the Due Process Clause of the Fifth Amendment is not a specific limitation upon the spending powers. [5] Disregarding for the moment the formidable obscurity of the Court's categories, how can it be said that Mrs. Frothingham's interests in her suit were, as a consequence of her choice of a constitutional claim, necessarily less intense than those, for example, of the present appellants? I am quite unable to

4. I must note at the outset that I cannot determine with any certainty the Court's intentions with regard to this first criterion. Its use of Doremus v. Board of Education, 342 U.S. 429, as an analogue perhaps suggests that it intends to exclude only those cases in which there are virtually no public expenditures. . . . On the other hand, the Court also emphasizes that the contested programs may not be "essentially regulatory programs," and that the statute challenged here "involves a *substantial* expenditure of federal tax funds." . . . Presumably this means that the Court's standing doctrine also excludes any program in which the expenditures are "insubstantial" or which cannot be characterized as a "spending" program. [Footnote by Justice Harlan.]

5. It should be emphasized that the Court finds it unnecessary to examine the history of the Due Process Clause to determine whether it was intended as a "specific limitation" upon Congress' spending and taxing powers. Nor does the Court pause to examine the purposes of the Tenth Amendment, another of the premises of the constitutional claims in Frothingham. But see Gibbons v. Ogden, 9 Wheat. 1, 199; Veazie Bank v. Fenno, 8 Wall. 533, 541; United States v. Butler, 297 U.S. 1. And compare Everson v. Board of Education, 330 U.S. 1, 6. [Footnote by Justice Harlan.]

understand how, if a taxpayer believes that a given public expenditure is unconstitutional, and if he seeks to vindicate that belief in a federal court, his interest in the suit can be said necessarily to vary according to the constitutional provision under which he states his claim.

The absence of any connection between the Court's standard for the determination of standing and its criteria for the satisfaction of that standard is not merely a logical ellipsis. Instead, it follows quite relentlessly from the fact that, despite the Court's apparent belief, the plaintiffs in this and similar suits are non-Hohfeldian, and it is very nearly impossible to measure sensibly any differences in the intensity of their personal interests in their suits. The Court has thus been compelled simply to postulate situations in which such taxpayer-plaintiffs will be "deemed" to have the requisite "personal stake and interest." . . . The logical inadequacies of the Court's criteria are thus a reflection of the deficiencies of its entire position. These deficiencies will, however, appear more plainly from an examination of the Court's treatment of the Establishment Clause.

[T]he essence of its reasoning is evidently that a taxpayer's claim under the Establishment Clause is 'not merely one of ultra vires,' but instead asserts 'an abridgement [of individual rights].' . . . The Court's position is . . . that, because of the Establishment Clause's historical purposes, taxpayers retain rights under it quite different from those held by them under other constitutional provisions. . . . [G]iven the ultimate obscurity of the Establishment Clause's historical purposes, it is inappropriate for this Court to draw fundamental distinctions among the several constitutional commands upon the supposed authority of isolated dicta extracted from the clause's complex history. In particular, I have not found, and the opinion of the Court has not adduced, historical evidence that properly permits the Court to distinguish, as it has here, among the Establishment Clause, the Tenth Amendment and the Due Process Clause of the Fifth Amendment as limitations upon Congress' taxing and spending powers.[6]

The Court's position is equally precarious if it is assumed that its premise is that the Establishment Clause is in some uncertain fashion a more "specific" limitation upon Congress' powers than are the various other constitutional commands. It is obvious, first, that only in some Pickwickian sense are any of the provisions with which the Court is concerned "specific[ally]" limitations upon spending, for they contain nothing that is expressly directed at the expenditure of public funds. The specificity to which the Court repeatedly refers must therefore arise, not from the provisions' language, but from something implicit in their purposes. But this Court has often emphasized that Congress' powers to spend are coterminous with the purposes for which, and methods by which, it may act, and that the various constitutional commands applicable to the central government, including those

---

6. I will of course grant that claims under, for example, the Tenth Amendment may present "generalized grievances about the conduct of government or the allocation of power in the Federal System." . . . I will also grant that it would be well if such questions could be avoided by the federal courts. Unfortunately, I cannot see how these considerations are relevant under the Court's principal criterion, which I understand to be merely whether any given constitutional provision is, or is not, a limitation upon Congress' spending powers. It is difficult to see what there is in the fact that a constitutional provision is held to be such a limitation that could sensibly give the Court "confidence" about the fashion in which a given plaintiff will present a given issue. [Footnote by Justice Harlan.]

implicit both in the Tenth Amendment and in the General Welfare Clause, thus operate as limitations upon spending. . . . I can attach no constitutional significance to the various degrees of specificity with which these limitations appear in the terms or history of the Constitution. If the Court accepts the proposition, as I do, that the number and scope of public actions should be restricted, there are, as I shall show, methods more appropriate, and more nearly permanent, than the creation of an amorphous category of constitutional provisions that the Court has deemed, without adequate foundation, "specific limitations" upon Congress' spending powers.

Even if it is assumed that such distinctions may properly be drawn, it does not follow that federal taxpayers hold any "personal constitutional right" such that they may each contest the validity under the Establishment Clause of all federal expenditures. The difficulty, with which the Court never comes to grips, is that taxpayers' suits under the Establishment Clause are not in these circumstances meaningfully different from other public actions. . . . To describe taxpayers' rights and interests as personal, and to intimate that they are in some unspecified fashion to be differentiated from those of the general public, reduces constitutional standing to a word game played by secret rules.[7] . . .

III.

It seems to me clear that public actions, whatever the constitutional provisions on which they are premised, may involve important hazards for the continued effectiveness of the federal judiciary. Although I believe such actions to be within the jurisdiction conferred upon the federal courts by Article III of the Constitution, there surely can be little doubt that they strain the judicial function and press to the limit judicial authority. There is every reason to fear that unrestricted public actions might well alter the allocation of authority among the three branches of the Federal Government. It is not, I submit, enough to say that the present members of the Court would not seize these opportunities for abuse, for such actions would, even without conscious abuse, go far toward the final transformation of this Court into the Council of Revision which, despite Madison's support, was rejected by the Constitutional Convention. I do not doubt that there must be "some effectual power in the government to restrain or correct the infractions" of the Constitution's

---

7. I have equal difficulty with the argument that the religious clauses of the First Amendment create a "personal constitutional right," held by all *citizens,* such that any *citizen* may, under those clauses, contest the constitutionality of federal expenditures. The essence of the argument would presumably be that freedom from establishment is a right that inheres in every citizen, thus any citizen should be permitted to challenge any measure that conceivably involves establishment. Certain provisions of the Constitution, so the argument would run, create the basic structure of our society and of its government, and accordingly should be enforceable at the demand of every individual. Unlike the position taken today by the Court, such a doctrine of standing would at least be internally consistent, but it would also threaten the proper functioning both of the federal courts and of the principle of separation of powers. The Establishment Clause is, after all, only one of many provisions of the Constitution that might be characterized in this fashion. . . . [A]ny doctrine of standing premised upon the generality or relative importance of a constitutional command would, I think, very substantially increase the number of situations in which individual citizens could present for adjudication "generalized grievances about the conduct of government." I take it that the Court apart from my Brother DOUGLAS, and I are agreed that any such consequence would be exceedingly undesirable. [Footnote by Justice Harlan.]

several commands, but neither can I suppose that such power resides only in the federal courts. . . . The powers of the federal judiciary will be adequate for the great burdens placed upon them only if they are employed prudently, with recognition of the strengths as well as the hazards that go with our kind of representative government.

Presumably the Court recognizes at least certain of these hazards, else it would not have troubled to impose limitations upon the situations in which, and purposes for which, such suits may be brought. Nonetheless, the limitations adopted by the Court are, as I have endeavored to indicate, wholly untenable. This is the more unfortunate because there is available a resolution of this problem that entirely satisfies the demands of the principle of separation of powers. This Court has previously held that individual litigants have standing to represent the public interest, despite their lack of economic or other personal interests, if Congress has appropriately authorized such suits. See especially Oklahoma v. Civil Service Comm'n, supra, at 137–139. I would adhere to that principle.[8] Any hazards to the proper allocation of authority among the three branches of the Government would be substantially diminished if public actions had been pertinently authorized by Congress and the President. I appreciate that this Court does not ordinarily await the mandate of other branches of the Government, but it seems to me that the extraordinary character of public actions, and of the mischievous, if not dangerous, consequences they involve for the proper functioning of our constitutional system, and in particular of the federal courts, make such judicial forbearance the part of wisdom.[9] . . .

Such a rule could readily be applied to this case. Although various efforts have been made in Congress to authorize public actions to contest the validity of federal expenditures in aid of religiously affiliated schools and other institutions, no such authorization has yet been given.

8. My premise is, as I have suggested, that non-Hohfeldian plaintiffs as such are not excluded by Article III from the jurisdiction of the federal courts. The problem is therefore to determine in what situations their suits should be permitted, and not whether a "statute constitutionally could authorize a person who shows no case or controversy to call on the courts . . . ." Scripps-Howard Radio v. Comm'n, supra, at 21 (dissenting opinion). I do not, of course, suggest that Congress' power to authorize suits by specified classes of litigants is without constitutional limitation. This Court has recognized a panoply of restrictions upon the actions that may properly be brought in federal courts, or reviewed by this Court after decision in state courts. It is enough now to emphasize that I would not abrogate these restrictions in situations in which Congress has authorized a suit. The difficult case of Muskrat v. United States, 219 U.S. 346, does not require more. Whatever the other implications of that case, it is enough to note that there the United States, as statutory defendant, evidently had "no interest adverse to the claimants." . . . [Footnote by Justice Harlan.]

9. I am aware that there is a second category of cases in which the Court has entertained claims by non-Hohfeldian plaintiffs: suits brought by state or local taxpayers in state courts to vindicate federal constitutional claims. A certain anomaly may be thought to have resulted from the Court's consideration of such cases while it has refused similar suits brought by federal taxpayers in the federal courts. This anomaly, if such it is, will presumably continue even under the standing doctrine announced today, since we are not told that the standing rules will hereafter be identical for the two classes of taxpayers. Although these questions are not now before the Court, I think it appropriate to note that one possible solution would be to hold that standing to raise federal questions is itself a federal question. See Freund, in E. Cahn, Supreme Court and Supreme Law 35 (1954). This would demand partial reconsideration of, for example, Doremus v. Board of Education, supra. . . . [Footnote by Justice Harlan.]

This does not mean that we would, under such a rule, be enabled to avoid our constitutional responsibilities, or that we would confine to limbo the First Amendment or any other constitutional command. The question here is not, despite the Court's unarticulated premise, whether the religious clauses of the First Amendment are hereafter to be enforced by the federal courts; the issue is simply whether an *additional* category of plaintiffs, heretofore excluded from those courts, are to be permitted to maintain suits. The recent history of this Court is replete with illustrations . . . . that questions involving the religious clauses will not, if federal taxpayers are prevented from contesting federal expenditures, be left "unacknowledged, unresolved, and undecided." . . .

CONGRESSIONAL POWER AND THE INGREDIENTS OF STANDING

Introduction. May Congress confer standing after the Court has found a plaintiff's interest insufficient? That question was most frequently raised in the years between Frothingham and Flast in connection with legislative proposals to permit suits to challenge Establishment Clause violations. (See, e.g., the hearings cited in the first footnote to Flast.) The problem goes beyond taxpayers and religion, however. It invites further inquiry into the ingredients of standing: To what extent are standing barriers compelled by Article III? To what extent are they judicially created overlays that Congress may strip away?

1. *The injured competitor: TVA, Sanders, Hardin.* a. A series of cases involving competitors' standing to sue in federal courts bear on how courts answer standing issues on their own as well as on whether Congress may supply different answers. Do they suggest a two-layer view of standing: a minimal Article III requirement of a plaintiff specifically injured in fact; and a judicially-added requirement that the injury be of a certain legal variety?

Note, as a well-known example of an actual injury being insufficient for standing, Tennessee Electric Power Co. v. Tennessee Valley Authority, 306 U.S. 118 (1939). Private power companies sought to stop competition by the TVA on the ground that Congress lacked constitutional authority to establish the TVA. Though the plaintiffs' actual injury from competition was plain, they lacked standing—because theirs was not a "legal" injury, because there was no "legal right" to be free from lawful competition. What is a "legal right" for this purpose? Is this only a question-begging phrase? The Court suggested that the answer lay in examining analogous private litigation: Could plaintiffs have brought a legal action against a private defendant? Could plaintiffs have enjoined another company because its activities were unauthorized—because, as the Court put it, "its injurious competition is ultra vires"?

b. The standing barrier involved in the TVA litigation—requiring more than an actual injury for standing—may be modified by Congress. For example, in FCC v. Sanders Bros. Radio Station, 309 U.S. 470 (1940), a radio station sought judicial review of an FCC order granting a license to a new station in the same area. Sanders relied on a section of the Federal Communications Act allowing appeals from license orders not only by the applicant but also "by any other person aggrieved or whose interests are adversely affected by a decision of the Commission granting or refusing any such [license] application." See 47 U.S.C. § 402(b). The Court considered the Sanders appeal on the merits. Though stating the Act did not assure a licensee freedom from competition, the Court did not find that this deprived Sanders of standing: "Congress had some purpose in enacting § 402(b)(2). It may have been of opinion that one likely to be financially injured by the issue of a license would be the only person having a sufficient interest to bring to the attention of the appellate court errors of law. . . . It is within the power of Congress to confer such standing to prosecute an appeal."

See also Scripps-Howard Radio, Inc. v. FCC, 316 U.S. 4 (1942), where the Court stated that the Communications Act gave "these private litigants . . . standing only as representatives of the public interest." Justice Douglas, joined by Justice Murphy, dissented: if Congress did not give the appellant a substantive right to be free from competition, "I fail to see how an appeal statute constitutionally could authorize a person who shows no case or controversy to call on the courts to review an order of the Commission." What "case or controversy" difficulty troubled Justice Douglas here? Recall his dissent in Doremus, p. 88, supra. Before the passage from Doremus quoted above, he had said: "In the present case the issues are not feigned; the suit is not collusive; the mismanagement . . . that is alleged is clear and plain." Accordingly, he saw "nothing in the Constitution to prevent" New Jersey from giving the plaintiff in Doremus standing to sue. What, then, prevented Congress from giving standing in the FCC cases?

c. More recently, the Court has even permitted competitors to sue where the congressional removal of the standing barrier was at best implicit, rather than explicit as in the FCC cases. See Hardin v. Kentucky Utilities Co., 390 U.S. 1 (1968), recognizing a private utility's standing to challenge certain TVA power sales as violations of statutory restrictions on TVA territorial expansion. The Court emphasized that the cases which had rejected competitive injury as basis for standing (see note a) involved controversies in which "the statutory and constitutional requirements that the plaintiff sought to enforce were in no way concerned with protecting against competitive injury." In those situations, a competitor could not sue without an explicit statutory grant of standing. In Hardin, by contrast, the territorial limitation was designed to protect private utilities from TVA competition; the utility company, accordingly, had standing to sue as a member of the class intended to be protected by the provision; therefore, "no explicit statutory provision is necessary to confer standing."

d. The Court reexamined competitors' standing in Association of Data Processing Service Organizations v. Camp, 397 U.S. —— (1970). See also a companion case, Barlow v. Collins, 397 U.S. —— (1970). In finding standing in the Data Processing case, Justice Douglas emphasized two ingredients of standing: (1) the Art. III requirement that the challenged action caused the plaintiff "injury in fact"; and (2) "whether the interest sought to be protected by the complainant is arguably within the zone of interests to be protected or regulated by the statute or constitutional guarantee in question."

Justice Brennan's opinion concurring in the result, joined by Justice White, insisted that only inquiry (1) was relevant to standing. Requiring the second, "nonconstitutional step," he claimed, "comes very close to perpetuating the discredited requirement that conditioned standing on a showing by the plaintiff that the challenged governmental action invaded one of his legally protected interests." Examination of the statutory background goes only to the issue of reviewability of administrative action, not to the "constitutional requirement of standing," Justice Brennan emphasized. He stated: "When agency action is challenged, standing, reviewability, and the merits pose discrete, and often complicated, issues which can best be resolved by recognizing and treating them as such."

e. Note Justice Frankfurter's observation on standing ingredients in his concurrence in Joint Anti-Fascist Refugee Committee v. McGrath, 341 U.S. 123 (1951): "Adverse personal interest, even of such an indirect sort as arises from competition, is ordinarily sufficient to meet constitutional standards of justiciability. The courts may therefore by statute be given jurisdiction over claims based on such interests. . . . To require a court to intervene in the absence of a statute, however, . . . something more than adverse personal interest is needed. . . . A litigant ordinarily has standing to challenge governmental action of a sort that, if taken by a private person, would create a right of action cognizable by the courts. . . . Or standing may be based on an interest created by the Constitution or a statute."

2. *The concerned citizen.* In the competitors' standing cases, congressional lowerings of standing barriers were all on behalf of plaintiffs who were injured in actual, distinctive ways by the challenged governmental action. May Congress grant standing even where the plaintiff's grievance is indistinguishable from that of large numbers of people? May Congress authorize "any taxpayer" to bring suit against unconstitutional spending? May Congress authorize "any citizen" to bring suit against unconstitutional governmental action? Or would that be tantamount to directing advisory opinions in violation of Article III? Compare Bickel, "Foreword: The Passive Virtues," 75 Harv.L.Rev. 410 (1961), with Jaffe, "Standing to Secure Judicial Review: Public Actions," 74 Harv.L.Rev. 1265 (1961). See also Jaffe's conclusion in "Standing to Secure Judicial Review: Private Actions," 75 Harv.L.Rev. 255, 305 (1961): After noting the "potential correspondence between the lack of a conventional plaintiff and the lack of maturity," he adds: "I find it difficult to accept the conclusion . . . that an issue in every other respect apt for judicial determination should be nonjusticiable because there is no possibility of a conventional plaintiff—an issue in short in which everyone has a legitimate interest but only as a citizen."

_____

SECTION 3. ADEQUATE STATE GROUNDS AND SUPREME COURT REVIEW

_____

Introduction. a. *The problems.* When may the Supreme Court review state court decisions? What questions are reviewable in such cases? These problems (raised preliminarily in chap. 1 in the context of Martin v.

Hunter's Lessee and the statutory framework) are recurrent ones in the exercise of judicial review. They are especially troublesome when the state court ruling rests on a mixture of state and federal grounds, or when the state court fails to get to the federal issue because of an allegedly dispositive state 'ground. When do state law ingredients in a case preclude review of the federal law elements? When, and to what extent, may the Supreme Court reexamine the state law grounds of decision?

b. *The usual scope of review.* Ordinarily, only state court decisions resting on a dispositive federal ground are reviewable by the Supreme Court. And that review is ordinarily limited to the federal issue, as Murdock v. City of Memphis, the first case below, reaffirmed even after the nationalistic Congress of 1867 apparently broadened the scope of review under Section 25 of the Judiciary Act. Moreover, under the review practice that has evolved, the Supreme Court will dismiss for lack of jurisdiction appeals from decisions resting on "adequate" and "independent" state grounds.

c. *The substantive state ground.* State grounds of decision may be substantive or procedural. In both situations, assessing the "adequacy" and "independence" of the state ground may be difficult. Martin v. Hunter's Lessee and Murdock v. City of Memphis both involved state *substantive* grounds intertwined with federal ones. Minnesota v. National Tea Co., 309 U.S. 551 (1940) (p. 118 below), illustrates that mixture in a common modern setting: decisions referring to similar provisions in state and federal constitutions. There, a state tax was challenged not only under the equal protection clause of the 14th Amendment but also under a uniformity clause in the Minnesota Constitution. If the state court had construed the state provision independently of the federal one and had relied on both in invalidating the tax, the Supreme Court would have dismissed under the "familiar rule that where a judgment of a state court rests on two grounds, one involving a federal question and the other not, this Court will not take jurisdiction."

d. *The procedural state ground.* The most troublesome problems of "adequacy" have involved state procedural grounds of decision rather than substantive ones. When does non-compliance with state procedural requirements preclude Supreme Court review of a federal claim? That question, which has taken on special practical significance with the expansion of federal constitutional rights for state criminal defendants, is the major concern of this section. Henry v. Mississippi (p. 129 below), the material on procedural grounds that precede the Henry case, and the examination of the related problems of federal habeas corpus that follows Henry all bear on this area—one of the most sensitive regarding the allocation of functions among state and federal courts in the protection of federal rights.

MURDOCK v. CITY OF MEMPHIS

20 Wall. 590, 22 L.Ed. 429 (1875).

Error to the Supreme Court of Tennessee.

[In 1867, Congress enacted a number of amendments to Section 25 of the Judiciary Act of 1789. See the text of Section 25 in the footnote to Martin v. Hunter's Lessee, at p. 35, supra. The Murdock case considered the effect of the most important amendment—the elimination of the last sentence of Section 25: "But no other error shall be assigned or regarded as a ground for reversal in any such case as aforesaid, than such as appears on the face of the record, and immediately respects the before mentioned questions of validity or construction of the said constitution, treaties, statutes, commissions, or authorities in dispute." Did the excision of this sentence authorize or compel the Supreme Court to consider *every* question—state as well as federal—in a case coming from the state courts? That was the problem presented to the Court in 1875.

[Murdock sued Memphis to get back land which his executors had conveyed to the city. The city had conveyed the land to the United States; the United States later conveyed it back to the city. The state court decided against Murdock. The decision involved the general law of trusts as well as the federal statute reconveying the land. The facts were stated more fully by the Reporter as follows:]

In July, 1844,—Congress having just previously authorized the establishment of a naval depot in that city, and appropriated a considerable sum of money for the purpose—the ancestors of Murdock—by ordinary deed of bargain and sale, without any covenants or declaration of trust on which the land was to be held by the city, but referring to the fact of "the location of the naval depot lately established by the United States at said town"—conveyed to the city certain land described in and near its limits "for the location of the naval depot aforesaid."

By the same instrument (a quadrupartite one) both the grantors and the city conveyed the same land to one Wheatley, in fee, in trust for the grantors and their heirs, "in case the same shall not be appropriated by the United States for that purpose."

On the 14th of September, 1844, the city of Memphis, in consideration of the sum of $20,000 paid by the United States, conveyed the said land to the United States with covenant of general warranty; there being, however, in this deed to the United States no designation of any purpose to which the land was to be applied, nor any conditions precedent or subsequent, or of any kind whatsoever.

The United States took possession of the land for the purpose of the erection of a naval depot upon it, erected buildings, and made various expenditures and improvements for the said purpose; but in about ten years after, by an act of August 5th, 1854, transferred the land back to the city. The act was in these words:

"All the grounds and appurtenances thereunto belonging, known as the Memphis Navy Yard, in Shelby County, Tennessee, be, and the same is hereby, ceded to the mayor and aldermen of the city of Memphis, *for the use and benefit of said city.*"

[Murdock] charged that by the failure of the United States to appropriate the land for a naval depot, and the final abandonment by the United States of any intention to do so, the land came within the clause of the deed of July, 1844, conveying it to Wheatley in trust; or if not, that it was held by the city in trust for the original grantors, and the prayer sought to subject it to said trusts.

The answer, denying the construction put upon the deed of 1844, which established a trust, asserted that the land had been appropriated by the

United States as a naval depot within the meaning and intent of the deed of July, 1844, and that the subsequent perpetual occupation of it was not a condition subsequent; and consequently that the abandonment of it as a naval depot was not a breach of a condition such as divested the title so conveyed by the deed. It pleaded the statute of limitations. It also demurred to the bill as seeking to enforce a forfeiture for breach of condition subsequent.

The court sustained the demurrer, and also decreed that the city had a perfect title to the property against the complainants both under the act of Congress and the statute of limitations, and dismissed the bill. The Supreme Court of Tennessee affirmed this decree.

That court was also of opinion, and so declared itself to be, that the act of Congress "cedes the property in controversy in this cause to the mayor and aldermen of the city of Memphis, for the use of the city only, and not in trust for the complainant; and that the complainant takes no benefit under the said act."

The complainant thereupon sued out a writ of error to this court.

. . . .

Mr. Justice MILLER delivered the opinion of the court.

The proposition is that by a fair construction of the act of 1867 this court must, when it obtains jurisdiction of a case decided in a State court, by reason of one of the questions stated in the act, proceed to decide every other question which the case presents which may be found necessary to a final judgment on the whole merits. [The Court had asked counsel to argue whether that was a "true" construction of the 1867 act, and whether a statute so construed would be constitutional.]

There is . . . nothing in the language of the act, as far as we have criticized it, which in express terms defines the extent of the re-examination which this court shall give to such cases.

But we have not yet considered the most important part of the statute, namely, that which declares that it is only upon the existence of certain questions in the case that this court can entertain jurisdiction at all. Nor is the mere existence of such a question in the case sufficient to give jurisdiction—the question must have been *decided* in the State court. Nor is it sufficient that such a question was raised and was decided. It must have been decided in a certain way, that is, against the right set up under the Constitution, laws, treaties, or authority of the United States. The Federal question may have been erroneously decided. It may be quite apparent to this court that a wrong construction has been given to the Federal law, but if the right claimed under it by plaintiff in error has been conceded to him, this court cannot entertain jurisdiction of the case, so very careful is the statute, both of 1789 and of 1867, to narrow, to limit, and define the jurisdiction which this court exercises over the judgments of the State courts. Is it consistent with this extreme caution to suppose that Congress intended, when those cases came here, that this court should not only examine those questions, but all others found in the record?—questions of common law, of State statutes, of controverted facts, and conflicting evidence. Or is it the more reasonable inference that Congress intended that the case should be brought here that *those questions* might be decided and *finally* decided by the court established by the Constitution of the Union, and the court which has always been supposed to be not only the most appropriate but the only proper tribunal for their final decision? No such reason nor any necessity exists for the decision by this court of other questions in those cases. The jurisdiction has been exercised for nearly a century without serious inconvenience to the due administration of justice. The State courts are the appropriate tribunals, as this court has repeatedly held, for the decision of questions arising under their local law, whether statutory or otherwise. And it is not lightly to be presumed that Congress acted upon a principle which implies a distrust of their integrity or of their ability to construe those laws correctly.

. . . We are of opinion that upon a fair construction of the whole language of the section the jurisdiction conferred is limited to the decision of the questions mentioned in the statute, and, as a necessary consequence of this, to the exercise of such powers as may be necessary to cause the judgment in that decision to be respected. We will now advert to one or two considerations apart from the mere language of the statute, which seem to us to give additional force to this conclusion. . . .

The twenty-fifth section of the act of 1789 has been the subject of innumerable decisions, some of which are to be found in almost every volume of the reports from that year down to the present. These form a system of appellate jurisprudence relating to the exercise of the appellate power of this court over the courts of the States. That system has been based upon the fundamental principle that this jurisdiction was limited to the correction of errors relating solely to Federal law. And though it may be argued with some plausibility that the reason of this is to be found in the restrictive clause of the act of 1789, which is omitted in the act of 1867, yet an examination of the cases will show that it rested quite as much on the conviction of this court that without that clause and on general principles the jurisdiction extended no further. It requires a very bold reach of thought, and a readiness to impute to Congress a radical and hazardous change of a policy vital in its essential nature to the independence of the State courts, to believe that the body contemplated, or intended, what is claimed, by the mere omission of a clause in the substituted statute, which may well be held to have been superfluous, or nearly so, in the old one. . . .

There may be some plausibility in the argument that [federal] rights cannot be protected in all cases unless the Supreme Court has final control of the whole case. But the experience of eighty-five years of the administration of the law under the opposite theory would seem to be a satisfactory answer to the argument. It is not to be presumed that the State courts, where the rule is clearly laid down to them on the Federal question, and its influence on the case fully seen, will disregard or overlook it, and this is all that the rights of the party claiming under it require. . . .

This [statutory construction] renders unnecessary a decision of the question whether, if Congress had conferred such authority, the act would have been constitutional. It will be time enough for this court to inquire into the existence of such a power when that body has attempted to exercise it in language which makes such an intention so clear as to require it. . . .

It is proper, in this first attempt to construe this important statute as amended, to say a few words on another point. What shall be done by this court when the question has been found to exist in the record, and to have been decided against the plaintiff in error, and *rightfully* decided, we have already seen, and it presents no difficulties.

But when it appears that the Federal question was decided erroneously against the plaintiff in error, we must then reverse the case undoubtedly, if there are no other issues decided in it than that. It often has occurred, however, and will occur again, that there are other points in the case than those of Federal cognizance, on which the judgment of the court below may stand; those points being of themselves sufficient to control the case.

Or it may be, that there are other issues in the case, but they are not of such controlling influence on the whole case that they are alone sufficient to support the judgment.

It may also be found that notwithstanding there are many other questions in the record of the case, the issue raised by the Federal question is such that its decision must dispose of the whole case.

In the two latter instances there can be no doubt that the judgment of the State court must be reversed, and under the new act this court can either render the final judgment or decree here, or remand the case to the State court for that purpose.

But in the other cases supposed, why should a judgment be reversed for an error in deciding the Federal question, if the same judgment must be rendered on the other points in the case? And why should this court reverse a judgment which is right on the whole record presented to us; or where the same judgment will be rendered by the court below, after they have corrected the error in the Federal question?

We have already laid down the rule that we are not authorized to examine these other questions for the purpose of deciding whether the State court ruled correctly on them or not. We are of opinion that on these subjects not embraced in the class of questions stated in the statute, we must receive the decision of the State courts as conclusive.

But when we find that the State court has decided the Federal question erroneously, then to prevent a useless and profitless reversal, which can do the plaintiff in error no good, and can only embarrass and delay the defendant, we must so far look into the remainder of the record as to see whether the decision of the Federal question alone is sufficient to dispose of the case, or to require its reversal; or on the other hand, whether there exist other matters in the record actually decided by the State court which are sufficient to maintain the judgment of that court, notwithstanding the error in deciding the Federal question. In the latter case the court would not be justified in reversing the judgment of the State court.

But this examination into the points in the record other than the Federal question is not for the purpose of determining whether they were correctly or erroneously decided, but to ascertain if any such have been decided, and their sufficiency to maintain the final judgment, as decided by the State court.

Beyond this we are not at liberty to go, and we can only go this far to prevent the injustice of reversing a judgment which must in the end be reaffirmed, even in this court, if brought here again from the State court after it has corrected its error in the matter of Federal law.

Finally, we hold the following propositions on this subject as flowing from the statute as it now stands:

1.   That it is essential to the jurisdiction of this court over the judgment of a State court, that it shall appear that one of the questions mentioned in the act must have been raised, and presented to the State court.

2.   That it must have been decided by the State court, or that its decision was necessary to the judgment or decree, rendered in the case.

3.   That the decision must have been against the right claimed or asserted by plaintiff in error under the Constitution, treaties, laws, or authority of the United States.

4.   These things appearing, this court has jurisdiction and must examine the judgment so far as to enable it to decide whether this claim of right was correctly adjudicated by the State court.

5.   If it finds that it was rightly decided, the judgment must be affirmed.

6.   If it was erroneously decided against plaintiff in error, then this court must further inquire, whether there is any other matter or issue adjudged by the State court, which is sufficiently broad to maintain the judgment of that court, notwithstanding the error in deciding the issue raised by the Federal question.   If this is found to be the case, the judgment must be affirmed without inquiring into the soundness of the decision on such other matter or issue.

7.   But if it be found that the issue raised by the question of Federal law is of such controlling character that its correct decision is necessary to any final judgment in the case, or that there has been no decision by the State court of any other matter or issue which is sufficient to maintain the judgment of that court without regard to the Federal question, then this court will reverse the judgment of the State court, and will either render such judgment here as the State court should have rendered, or remand the case to that court, as the circumstances of the case may require.

Applying the principles here laid down to the case now before the court, we are of opinion that this court has jurisdiction, and that the judgment of the Supreme Court of Tennessee must be affirmed.   .   .   .

.   .   .   The complainants, in their bill, and throughout the case, insisted that the effect of the act of 1854 was to vest the title in the mayor or aldermen of the city in trust for them.

It may be very true that it is not easy to see anything in the deed by which the United States received the title from the city, or the act by which they ceded it back, which raises such a trust, but the complainants claimed a right under this act of the United States, which was decided against them by the Supreme Court of Tennessee, and this claim gives jurisdiction of that question to this court.

But we need not consume many words to prove that neither by the deed of the city to the United States, which is an ordinary deed of bargain and sale for a valuable consideration, nor from anything found in the act of 1854, is there any such trust to be inferred.   The act, so far from recognizing or implying any such trust, cedes the property to the mayor and aldermen *for the use of the city.*   We are, therefore, of opinion that this, the only Federal question in the case, was rightly decided by the Supreme Court of Tennessee.

But conceding this to be true, the plaintiffs in error have argued that the court having jurisdiction of the case must now examine it upon all the questions which affect its merits; and they insist that the conveyance by which the city of Memphis received the title previous to the deed from the city to the government, and the circumstances attending the making of the former deed are such, that when the title reverted to the city, a trust was raised for the benefit of plaintiffs.

After what has been said in the previous part of this opinion, we need discuss this matter no further. The claim of right here set up is one to be determined by the general principles of equity jurisprudence, and is unaffected by anything found in the Constitution, laws, or treaties of the United States. Whether decided well or otherwise by the State court, we have no authority to inquire. According to the principles we have laid down as applicable to this class of cases, the judgment of the Supreme Court of Tennessee must be

Affirmed.

Mr. Justice CLIFFORD, with whom concurred Mr. Justice SWAYNE, dissenting:

I dissent from so much of the opinion of the court as denies the jurisdiction of this court to determine the whole case, where it appears that the record presents a Federal question and that the Federal question was erroneously decided to the prejudice of the plaintiff in error. . . .

Mr. Justice BRADLEY, dissenting:

. . . I deem it very doubtful whether the court has any jurisdiction at all over this particular case. . . . Proving that the government did not appropriate the land for a navy yard is a very different thing from setting up a claim to the land under an act of Congress.

I think, therefore, that in this case there was no title or right claimed by the appellants under any statute of, or authority exercised under, the United States; and consequently that there was no decision against any such title; and, therefore, that this court has no jurisdiction.

But supposing, as the majority of the court holds, that it has jurisdiction, I cannot concur in the conclusion that we can only decide the Federal question raised by the record. If we have jurisdiction at all, in my judgment we have jurisdiction of the *case*, and not merely of a *question* in it. . . .

SUPREME COURT HANDLING OF CASES INVOLVING STATE SUBSTANTIVE GROUNDS OF DECISION

1. *The Murdock sequence and the modern practice.* The basic principle of Murdock—that Supreme Court review of state court decisions on federal issues does not extend to separable state law grounds of decisions—has generally been followed (and it applies to state procedural as well as substantive grounds). But the seven rules sequence described in the Murdock opinion no longer represents Supreme Court practice. Determining whether an adequate state ground exists now comes before, not after, assessing the

correctness of the federal ruling: if there is an adequate state ground, no concern with the merits of the federal issue is justified and dismissal follows. The modern approach is reflected in the following case:

In Fox Film Corp. v. Muller, 296 U.S. 207 (1935), a state court dismissed a contract suit on the grounds that (a) a concededly invalid arbitration clause in the contract was inseparable from the rest of the agreement and voided the entire contract; and (b) that the contract violated a federal antitrust statute. The Supreme Court "dismissed" the case "for want of jurisdiction." Justice Sutherland relied on the "settled rule" that "where the judgment of a state court rests upon two grounds, one of which is federal and the other nonfederal in character, our jurisdiction fails if the nonfederal ground is independent of the federal ground and adequate to support the judgment." He pointed out that the invalidity of the arbitration clause was "conceded" and that the question whether the provisions of a contract are nonseparable "is clearly a question of general and not of federal law." The state court ruling of nonseparability was "sufficient to conclude the case without regard to the determination . . . in respect of the federal question. It follows that the nonfederal ground is adequate to sustain the judgment."

2. *The state ground "adequate to support the judgment."* The fact that a state decision contains separable state and federal grounds does not without more produce the Fox Film-jurisdictional dismissal result. The posture of the case must be such that the state ground alone would support the result—i. e., that a different ruling on the federal law ground would not change the outcome. That is the Fox Film situation: a defendant raises state and federal defenses; sustaining the state defense disposes of plaintiff's claim no matter what the ruling on the federal defense; plaintiff would be no better off if the ruling sustaining the federal defense were set aside. Contrast another classic situation, where plaintiff relies on separable federal and state claims and loses on both in the state court. There, the state law ruling is not adequate to support the ruling against the plaintiff; a different view of the federal claim *would* change the outcome of the case; Supreme Court review of the federal issue is accordingly appropriate, because it *would* make a difference. That was the situation in Murdock, according to the majority's view of plaintiff's claim: he relied alternatively on state trust law and the federal statute.

Ives v. South Buffalo Ry. Co., 201 N.Y. 271 (1911) (noted in chap. 1, p. 60), was like the Fox Film model: the state court held a workmen's compensation law unconstitutional under the due process clauses of both state and federal constitutions; the law would have remained invalid even if the federal law ruling had been set aside. (Accordingly, though Ives provoked an expansion of the appeal statute, the case would have been nonreviewable even after the amendment.) Yet that model is a simple one only where it is clear that the state court truly rested on an independent reading of a parallel state provision. Compare the uncertainty about the ground of decision in Minnesota v. National Tea Co., note 5 below.

3. *The "independent" state ground and the scope of Supreme Court reexamination of the non-independent state issue.* In the Ives situation, there is no doubt that the state court is free to rely on the state ground if it wishes: once that reliance is clear, dismissal follows. A different and more complex problem of "adequacy" and "independence" of the state ground arises when there is reason to question the state's autonomy regarding the state ground.

The contract clause (Art. I, Sec. 10), for example, bars a state from impairing the obligation of contracts. If a litigant claims that a state law has unconstitutionally impaired his contract rights, is Supreme Court review precluded if a state court rules that (*a*) no contract was created under state contract law, and (*b*) even if there had been a valid contract, there was no unconstitutional impairment? Similarly, what of a claim that a state law constitutes deprivation of property without due process: is review barred of a ruling that (*a*) no property right existed under state law, and (*b*) even if there was property, there was no unconstitutional deprivation? Are grounds (*a*) in these examples truly separate state grounds, for autonomous state court disposition? Or may the Supreme Court review (*a*)—at least to a limited extent?

To what extent? Only to make certain that the state rulings (*a*) were not evasive ones, designed to defeat federal claims involved in (*b*)? Or do questions (*a*) become federalized because of the federal interest in (*b*)? This problem goes back at least as far as Story's opinion in Martin v. Hunter's Lessee, chap. 1, supra. Recall the closing passages: was there justification to set aside the state property ruling, on the title to the land [the question paralleling (*a*) above] in order to assure that federal treaty rights [the parallel to (*b*)] were secure? Concerned about evasion of federal guarantees, he insisted: "How, indeed, can it be possible to decide whether a title be within the protection of a treaty, until it is decided what that title is, and whether it have legal validity." That supported *some* reexamination of title (*a*) to safeguard treaty rights (*b*)—but did it justify reexamination as broad as Story's: "If the court below should decide, that the title was bad, and therefore not protected by the treaty, must not this court have a power to decide the title to be good, and therefore, protected by the treaty?" The permissible extent of Supreme Court reexamination of state grounds of decision challenged as not adequate is a recurrent question with respect to state procedural questions as well, and the problem is more fully pursued in that context, beginning with the next group of notes.

4. *The basis for the adequate state ground rule.* Is the "adequate state ground" rule a constitutional mandate, or is it simply a statutory command? Note the following recent statements:

a. Herb v. Pitcairn, 324 U.S. 117, 125–126 (1945): "The reason [for the adequate state ground rule] is so obvious that it has rarely been thought to warrant statement. It is found in the partitioning of power between the state and federal judicial systems and in the limitations of our own jurisdiction. Our only power over state judgments is to correct them to the extent that they incorrectly adjudge federal rights. And our power is to correct wrong judgments, not to revise opinions. We are not permitted to render an advisory opinion, and if the same judgment would be rendered by the state court after we corrected its views of federal laws, our review could amount to nothing more than an advisory opinion."

b. Fay v. Noia, 372 U.S. 391, 428–430 (1963): "It is a familiar principle that this Court will decline to review state court judgments which rest on independent and adequate state grounds, notwithstanding the co-presence of federal grounds. See, e. g., NAACP v. Alabama ex rel. Patterson, 357 U.S. 449; Fox Film Corp. v. Muller, 296 U.S. 207. . . . The deletion of the express restriction [in the last sentence of Sec. 25 of the 1789 Judiciary

Act] by the Judiciary Act of February 5, 1867 . . . did not enlarge this Court's power in that regard. Murdock v. City of Memphis, 20 Wall. 590. Murdock was a case involving state substantive grounds, but the principle is also applicable in cases involving procedural grounds. See, e. g., Herb v. Pitcairn, 324 U.S. 117, 125, 126; Davis v. Wechsler, 263 U.S. 22; Ward v. Board of County Com'rs, 253 U.S. 17. . . . Most of the opinion in the Murdock case is devoted to demonstrating the Court's lack of jurisdiction on direct review to decide questions of state law in cases also raising federal questions. It followed from this holding that if the state question was dispositive of the case, the Court could not decide the federal question. The federal question was moot; nothing turned on its resolution. And so we have held that the adequate state-ground rule is a consequence of the Court's obligation to refrain from rendering advisory opinions or passing upon moot questions."[1]

5. *Clarifying ambiguous state decisions.* A variety of approaches have been utilized by the Supreme Court when it is not clear whether the state court decision rested on state or federal grounds. In Minnesota v. National Tea Co., 309 U.S. 551 (1940), where the state court opinion had discussed the state as well as the federal constitution in invalidating a tax statute, the Supreme Court found "considerable uncertainty about the precise grounds for the decision. That is sufficient reason for us to decline at this time to review the federal question asserted to be presented. . . . But that does not mean that we should dismiss the petition." Instead, the Court vacated the judgment and remanded the case, "so that the federal question might be dissected out or the state and federal questions clearly separated." "It is fundamental that state courts be left free and unfettered by us in interpreting their state constitutions. But it is equally important that ambiguous or obscure adjudications by state courts do not stand as barriers to determination by this Court as to the validity under the federal constitution of state action. Intelligent exercise of our appellate powers compels us to ask for the elimination of the obscurities and ambiguities from the opinions in such cases." Chief Justice Hughes, joined by Justices Stone and Roberts, stated that the case should be dismissed as resting on an adequate nonfederal ground. For a more recent example of the Minnesota v. National Tea Co. clarification technique, see Department of Mental Hygiene v. Kirchner, 379 U.S. 985 (1965).

Ambiguities as to the grounds of decision may also be cured by a certificate from the state court stating that a federal question was presented and was necessarily passed upon. In Herb v. Pitcairn, 324 U.S. 117 (1945), where no such certificate had been obtained prior to argument, the Court continued the case "for such period as will enable counsel for petitioners with all convenient speed" to apply to the state court for such a certificate. Justice Jackson, writing for the Court, justified the procedure as follows: "But because we will not proceed with a review while our jurisdiction is con-

---

1. ". . . We need not decide whether the adequate state-ground rule is constitutionally compelled or merely a matter of the construction of the statutes defining this Court's appellate review. Murdock itself was predicated on statutory construction, and the present statute governing our review of state court decisions, 28 U.S.C. § 1257, limited as it is to '*judgments* or *decrees* rendered by the highest court of a State in which a decision could be had' (italics supplied), provides ample statutory warrant for our continued adherence to the principles laid down in Murdock." [Footnote by the Court.]

jectural it does not follow that we should not take steps to protect our jurisdiction when we are given reasonable grounds to believe it exists. We think the simplest procedure to do so, when the record is deficient, is to hold the case pending application to the state court for clarification or amendment." For an unsuccessful effort to obtain a certificate, see Dixon v. Duffy, 344 U.S. 143 (1952); for a certification that did not provide much clarification, see Covey v. Town of Somers, 351 U.S. 141 (1956). Note also the reliance on state statutory certification procedure in Dresner v. City of Tallahassee, 375 U.S. 136 (1963). See generally Comment, "Supreme Court Treatment of State Court Cases Exhibiting Ambiguous Grounds of Decision," 62 Colum. L.Rev. 822 (1962).

STATE PROCEDURAL GROUNDS

Introduction. a. *The model.* The posture of the typical state procedural grounds case differs from the state substantive grounds situations considered above. In the substantive grounds model, the state court discusses federal as well as state issues; the problem on Supreme Court review is to assess the significance and acceptability of the state ground in the state-federal mix. In the usual procedural grounds case, by contrast, the state court does not get to the federal claim at all; rather, the state decision relies solely on the state law ground and holds that noncompliance with the state procedural requirement precludes adjudication of the federal issue.

b. *Adequacy.* Yet the question on Supreme Court review is once again the "adequacy" of the state ground of decision. In the procedural grounds area, moreover, the problem of justifiable Supreme Court reexamination of the state ground emerges with especially sharp focus. How far, and on what bases, may the Supreme Court set aside the state procedural barrier to reaching the federal claim? When will and should the Supreme Court entertain a federal question despite a state court finding that it was not properly raised?

c. *State control.* From the beginning, as the Federalist Papers and the Supremacy Clause make clear, state courts have been looked to as a significant forum for the adjudication of federal claims. And from the beginning, a state's control of its judicial machinery has carried considerable autonomy in prescribing the processes for the raising of all claims (federal as well as state) in the state courts. Ordinarily, then, compliance with state procedural requirements as to the time and manner of raising and preserving federal questions is necessary in order to invoke Supreme Court review. What are the bases for the usual deference to state procedures? Does 28 U.S.C. § 1257 provide a sufficient explanation? Does the explanation lie in general rules of waiver? Is the deference a constitutional mandate?

d. *Supreme Court reexamination.* Deference to state procedures has never been total: precluding all Supreme Court review upon a state court's mere recital of a state procedural ground would endanger vindication of federal rights. What, then, are the governing considerations in determining whether the asserted state procedural ground is "adequate" to preclude review? The Supreme Court has often said that a state court's refusal to decide a federal question must rest on "fair" and "substantial" grounds. See, e. g., Lawrence v. State Tax Commission, 286 U.S. 276 (1932). What must be shown to establish unfairness or insubstantiality? How satisfactory is the following statement [Justice Clark, dissenting, in Williams v. Georgia, 349 U.S. 375, 399 (1955)]: "A purported state ground is not independent and adequate in two instances. *First,* where the circumstances give rise to an inference that the state court is guilty of an evasion—an interpretation of state law with the specific intent to deprive a litigant of a federal right. [A footnote at this point added: "This charge upon the integrity of a State Supreme Court is so serious that this Court has restricted such findings to cases where the state court decision lacked 'fair support' in the state law."] *Second,* where the state law, honestly applied though it may be, and even dictated by the precedents, throws such obstacles in the way of enforcement of federal rights that it must be struck down as unreasonably interfering with the vindication of such rights."

e. *The sources of the governing law.* What law governs Justice Clark's second ground: whether state law "unreasonably interferes with the vindication" of federal rights? Must the state rule—on its face or as applied—be in violation of a federal constitutional limitation such as the due process or equal protection clauses of the 14th Amendment in order to be "inadequate"? A procedural rule set aside for such reasons could not be applied to the assertion of *any* claims (state *or* federal) in the state courts. Or does the Supremacy Clause, Art. VI, Sec. 2, impose minimum federal requirements for state procedural mechanisms for the raising of federal claims? A state would be precluded from imposing that kind of procedural barrier only with respect to federal claims, not state ones. Or is there a "common law" of Supreme Court review that may supply the basis for finding the state ground "unreasonable" and hence "inadequate"? See generally Note, "The Untenable Nonfederal Ground in the Supreme Court," 74 Harv.L.Rev. 1376 (1961); Comment, "Supreme Court Treatment of State Procedural Grounds Relied on in State Courts to Preclude Decisions of Federal Questions," 61 Colum.L.Rev. 255 (1961).

The notes below examine the handling of a range of state procedural grounds by the Supreme Court. Consider especially the reasons put forth when procedural barriers have been set aside as inadequate. Henry v. Mississippi, which follows these notes, is a recent reexamination of the state procedural grounds problem. Does Henry offer new bases for attacking state barriers? See generally Hill, "The Inadequate State Ground," 65 Colum.L. Rev. 943 (1965); Sandalow, "Henry v. Mississippi and the Adequate State Ground: Proposals for a Revised Doctrine," 1965 Sup.Ct.Rev. 187. Does Henry suggest a "severe dilution" of the adequate state procedural ground, as Justice Harlan's dissent suggests? Should state procedural grounds be handled differently than substantive ones? Does the evolution of federal habeas corpus relief for state criminal defendants, traced in the notes following Henry, explain and justify the Henry approach?

1. *Stating the federal claim "with fair precision."* a. *The basic principle: Bryant and Ellis.* Bryant v. Zimmerman, 278 U.S. 63 (1928), stated the general rule: "There are various ways in which the validity of a state statute may be drawn in question on the ground that it is repugnant to the Constitution of the United States. No particular form of words or phrases is essential, but only that the claim of invalidity and the ground therefor be brought to the attention of the state court with fair precision and in due time. And if the record as a whole shows either expressly or by clear intendment that this was done, the claim is to be regarded as having

been adequately presented." In the trial court in that case, the petitioner had simply challenged a state statute as "unconstitutional," without any mention "of any constitutional provision, state or federal." The Supreme Court stated: "If this were all there plainly would be no basis for review in this Court." But there was "more": federal and state objections were raised more precisely on appeal in the state courts, and the state courts rejected the contentions. Accordingly, the Supreme Court passed on the merits of the federal claims.

The need for sufficiently precise pleadings is illustrated by Ellis v. Dixon, 349 U.S. 458 (1955). Petitioner claimed that the Yonkers Board of Education, in refusing the use of public school buildings to the Yonkers Committee for Peace for a forum on "peace and war," had discriminated against the Committee in violation of the equal protection guarantee. The Court emphasized that "petitioner has failed to allege in his pleading . . . . that other organizations of a similar character to the Committee for Peace have been allowed use of the Yonkers schools. The allegations of that pleading simply are that unnamed and undescribed 'organizations' have been allowed the use of Yonkers school buildings in the past 'for the purpose of public assembly and discussion.' Whether such organizations are in any way comparable to the Committee for Peace nowhere appears in the pleading. . . . What has been alleged is entirely too amorphous to permit adjudication of the constitutional issues asserted." The Court dismissed the writ of certiorari as improvidently granted, holding that it lacked jurisdiction because the highest state court's refusal to pass on the federal claim might have rested on an adequate nonfederal ground—the defectiveness of the pleading.

b. *Modern variations: Staub and NAACP.* Compare two recent cases in which the Court found authority to review despite noncompliance with state procedural rules: (i) In Staub v. City of Baxley, 355 U.S. 313 (1958), the Georgia Court of Appeals declined to consider a union organizer's federal objections against a licensing ordinance on the ground, inter alia, that the "attack should have been made against specific sections of the ordinance and not against the ordinance as a whole." Justice Whittaker's majority opinion rejected the claim that this constituted an adequate nonfederal ground: "We think this contention is 'without any fair or substantial support' (Ward v. Board of Comm'rs of Love County, [253 U.S. 17 (1920)]) and therefore does not present an *adequate* nonfederal ground of decision in the circumstances of this case. The several sections of the ordinance are interdependent in their application to one in appellant's position and constitute but one complete act for the licensing and taxing of her described activities. For that reason, no doubt, she challenged the constitutionality of the whole ordinance, and in her objections used language challenging the constitutional effect of all its sections. She did, thus, challenge all sections of the ordinance, though not by number. To require her, in these circumstances, to count off, one by one, the several sections of the ordinance would be to force resort to an arid ritual of meaningless form. Indeed, the Supreme Court of Georgia seems to have recognized the arbitrariness of such exaltation of form. Only four years ago that court recognized that an attack on such a statute was sufficient if 'the [statute] so challenged was invalid in every part for some reason alleged.' Flynn v. State, 209 Ga. 519, 522, 74 S.E.2d 461, 464 (1953). In enunciating that rule the court was following a long line of its own decisions." Why was the state ground "inadequate"? Because it departed from prior Georgia decisions and therefore was in effect an "evasion" of the federal claim? Or because the state rule independently violated federal law? What federal law? Due process? The Supremacy Clause? A "common law" of Supreme Court review?

Justice Frankfurter, joined by Justice Clark, dissented in Staub. He stated: "While the power to review the denial by a state court of a non-frivolous claim under the United States Constitution has been centered in this Court, carrying with it the responsibility to see that the opportunity to assert such a claim be not thwarted by any local procedural device, equally important is observance by this Court of the wide discretion in the States to formulate their own procedures for bringing issues appropriately to the attention of their local courts, either in shaping litigation or by appeal. Such methods and procedures may, when judged by the best standards of judicial administration, appear crude, awkward and even finicky or unnecessarily formal when judged in the light of modern emphasis on informality. But so long as the local procedure does not discriminate against the raising of federal claims and, in the particular case, has not been used to stifle a federal claim to prevent its eventual consideration here, this Court is powerless to deny to a State the right to have the kind of judicial system it chooses and to administer that system in its own way. It is of course for this Court to pass on the substantive sufficiency of a claim of federal right, . . . but if resort is had in the first instance to the state judiciary for the enforcement of a federal constitutional right, the State is not barred from subjecting the suit to the same procedures, *nisi prius* and appellate, that govern adjudication of all constitutional issues in that State. . . .

"[T]his Court has from the beginning demanded of litigants that they show in precisely what way and to what extent incursions have been made into their federally protected rights and rules have been developed designed to narrow as closely as possible the issues presented by such claims. Surely a state court is not to be denied the like right to protect itself from the necessity —sometimes even temptation—of adjudicating overly broad claims of unconstitutionality. . . . Of course, even if the Georgia rule is intrinsically reasonable and thus entitled to respect by this Court, we must be sure that it has not been applied arbitrarily in the case before us. . . . So long as a reasonable rule of state procedure is consistently applied, so long as it is not used as a means for evading vindication of federal rights, see Davis v. Wechsler, 263 U.S. 22, 24–25, it should not be refused applicability. . . . The record before us presents not the remotest basis for attributing to the Georgia court any desire to limit the appellant in the fullest opportunity to raise claims of federal right . . . . Consequently, this Court is left with no proper choice but to give effect to the rule of procedure on the basis of which this case was disposed of below."

(ii) For an extreme example of an asserted nonfederal ground of decision, see NAACP v. Alabama, 377 U.S. 288 (1964), one of several Court encounters with Alabama attempts to oust the organization from the state. In 1958, the Supreme Court set aside a contempt conviction in the case, 357 U.S. 449, p. 1316, infra. After two further Supreme Court decisions, a lower Alabama court finally reached the merits and permanently enjoined the NAACP from doing business in the state. The Supreme Court of Alabama affirmed that judgment without considering the merits. It relied entirely on the Alabama procedural rule "that where unrelated assignments of error are argued together and one is without merit, the others will not be considered." Proceeding to apply that rule to the Association's brief, the Alabama Supreme Court held that at least one of the assignments of error contained in each of the five numbered subdivisions of the Argument section of the NAACP brief was without merit, and that it would therefore not consider any of the other assignments.

Justice Harlan's opinion for a unanimous Court found "wholly unacceptable" the contention that this state ground was "adequate" to bar federal review. He thought it "crystal clear" that the Alabama rule "cannot reasonably be deemed applicable to this case." Consideration of federal rights, he stated, "may not be thwarted by simple recitation that there has not been observance of a procedural rule with which there has been compliance in both substance and form, in every real sense." He noted, moreover, that the Alabama courts had not "heretofore applied their rules respecting the preparation of briefs with the pointless severity shown here." The Court further rejected the suggestion that it remand the case for decision on the merits after finding the state ground inadequate: "While this might be well enough in other circumstances, in view of what has gone before, we reject that contention and proceed to the merits." The Court found none of the Alabama grounds for excluding the NAACP constitutionally justifiable.

The Court did not, however, grant the NAACP's request that it "formulate a decree for entry in the state courts which will assure the Association's right to conduct activities in Alabama without further delay." Justice Harlan stated that the Court "undoubtedly" had that power, citing Martin v. Hunter's Lessee, but stated that "we prefer to follow our usual practice and remand the case" for "prompt entry of a decree." He concluded: "Should we unhappily be mistaken in our belief that the Supreme Court of Alabama will promptly implement this disposition, leave is given the Association to apply to this Court for further appropriate relief." See also Wright v. Georgia, 373 U.S. 284 (1963).

2. *Raising the federal claim "in due time."* a. *The basic principle.* "No procedural principle is more familiar to this Court than that a constitutional right may be forfeited in criminal as well as civil cases by the failure to make timely assertion of the right before a tribunal having jurisdiction to determine it. . . . Courts may for that reason refuse to consider a constitutional objection even though a like objection had previously been sustained in a case in which it was properly taken. . . . While this Court in its discretion sometimes departs from this rule in cases from lower federal courts, it invariably adheres to it in cases from state courts." Chief Justice Stone in Yakus v. United States, 321 U.S. 414 (1944).

b. *Modern variations: Michel and Reece.* The "adequacy" of the state court's finding that the federal question was not presented in time may of course be challenged in the Supreme Court. Michel v. Louisiana, 350 U.S. 91 (1955), involved a Louisiana requirement that challenges to the composition of the grand juries must be made within three days after the expiration of the grand jury term. Three defendants claimed that Negroes had been systematically excluded from grand jury panels. The state courts found that the claims had been waived because they had not been presented within the statutory time limit. The Supreme Court majority found the time limit an adequate state ground on its face and as applied. The Court recognized that "in the circumstances of a particular case, the application of such a rule may not give a reasonable opportunity to raise the federal question," but found the opportunity adequate here—even as applied to a defendant who had been indicted by a grand jury whose term ended in March 1951, fled the state and was absent throughout the entire period in which, under state law, he could have raised the constitutional question.

Reece v. Georgia, 350 U.S. 85 (1955), decided on the same day as the Michel case, illustrates how the application of a state rule may be considered unreasonable because of "the circumstances of a particular case." The case involved a Georgia rule requiring that objections to the composition of a grand jury be made before indictment. The Supreme Court found that the rule "goes back to 1882 . . . and has been consistently followed in that State." The defendant, a "semi-illiterate Negro of low mentality," was arrested three days prior to the indictment. On the day after his indictment, counsel were appointed to represent him. Several days later, prior to the arraignment, a motion to quash the indictment on the ground that Negroes had been systematically excluded from grand jury service was rejected as too late. The Court unanimously reversed the rape conviction and remanded for a hearing on the constitutional claim. It found it unnecessary to consider whether, even with the assistance of counsel, the defendant would have had an opportunity to raise the objection under the Georgia rule, for "it is utterly unrealistic to say that he had such opportunity when counsel was not provided for him until the day after he was indicted."

3. *Preserving the federal claim in the state appellate channels.* The federal claim must be reasserted at every available opportunity in the state appellate courts to avoid a finding that it has been "waived." See, e. g., Dorrance v. Pennsylvania, 287 U.S. 660 (1932). Moreover, if a state court refuses to consider a federal claim because it is the wrong appellate court, that "wrong appellate procedure" reason would constitute "an adequate nonfederal ground, depriving this Court of jurisdiction." Ellis v. Dixon, 349 U.S. 458 (1955). For example, federal constitutional claims were "waived" because appeals were taken to the intermediate appellate court rather than directly to the Illinois Supreme Court in Central Union Tel. Co. v. Edwardsville, 269 U.S. 190 (1925), and Parker v. Illinois, 333 U.S. 571 (1948).*

---

* See also Gotthilf v. Sills, 375 U.S. 79 (1963), where the Court, per curiam, dismissed a writ of certiorari as improvidently granted because the judgment of the New York intermediate appellate court was not that of the "highest court of a State in which a decision could be had," within the meaning of 28 U.S.C. § 1257. Under New York law, the petitioner could have sought to appeal to the highest state court by obtaining the permission of the intermediate court; he did not seek such permission. The Court added: "Whether [under § 1257] that judgment is 'final', a question of purely federal law, involves entirely different considerations." Why is "finality" a question of "purely federal law"? Justice Douglas, joined by Chief Justice Warren and Justice Black, dissented. As to finality, he stated: "While 28 U.S.C. § 1257 . . . requires that judgments brought here for review be 'final,' we have recognized an exception—sometimes even to the point of reviewing interlocutory decrees—where the controversy has proceeded to a point where the 'losing party [will] be irreparably injured if review [is] unavailing.' Republic Natural Gas Co. v. Oklahoma, 334 U.S. 62, 68." Note also the division on the finality issue in Mills v. Alabama, 384 U.S. 214 (1966), and see generally Dyk, "Supreme Court Review of Interlocutory State-Court Decisions: 'The Twilight Zone of Finality'," 19 Stan.L.Rev. 907 (1967).

4. *Unanticipated state court rulings and the Herndon case.* a. *The general principle.* The Supreme Court may consider federal claims despite a state finding that they have not been properly presented when the federal question sought to be raised stems from an unanticipated state court ruling. In Missouri v. Gehner, 281 U.S. 313 (1930), the challenged construction of the state statute was not used until the case was decided by the highest state court. The federal objection was not raised until the petition for rehearing, and the state court refused to consider it. The Supreme Court, holding that the federal claim had been presented "at the first opportunity" and that the appellant was not "bound to anticipate such a construction," considered the claim on the merits and reversed. In Brinkerhoff-Faris Trust & Savings Co. v. Hill, 281 U.S. 673 (1930), the state court denied relief for failure to resort to an administrative remedy, although earlier decisions had held the administrative agency without authority to grant the relief. In both cases, the federal claim was presented to the highest state courts after the initial decisions there; in both the Supreme Court found the state courts' action a denial of the right to a hearing guaranteed by the due process clause and remanded for a hearing in the state courts.

b. *The Herndon application.* Compare the refusal to apply the "unanticipated state ruling" exception in Herndon v. Georgia, 295 U.S. 441 (1935). Appellant was convicted in a Georgia court of an attempt to incite insurrection. The Supreme Court dismissed his appeal for lack of jurisdiction because "no federal question was seasonably raised" below. Appellant claimed that his federal contention was timely though not raised until a petition for rehearing in the highest state court: his objection, he insisted, was to an unanticipated construction given to the statute by the highest state court's decision affirming his conviction. Justice Sutherland's majority opinion in Supreme Court found that "the ruling here assailed should have been anticipated" by the appellant.

Consider the context. What could and should appellant have done in the earlier stages of his case? The trial judge had construed the statute favorably to the appellant in his charge: the jury was told that the evidence must show that "immediate serious violence" against the state "was to be expected or was advocated." The highest state court relied on a different construction it had given the statute in another case (Carr v. State). Appellant's conviction was held justified under the Carr standard, which did not contain the immediacy ingredient in the trial court's construction: "it was sufficient if the defendant intended an insurrection to follow *at any time.*" It was that construction that appellant challenged under the federal "clear and present danger" approach. (See chap. 15, below.) Justice Sutherland found the attack too late: appellant could not plead ignorance of the Carr interpretation; he should have "preserve[d] his right to review here by appropriate action upon the original hearing in the court below."

How could the federal claim have been preserved? Note Justice Cardozo's comment in his dissent: "It is a novel doctrine that a defendant who has had the benefit of all he asks, and indeed a good deal more, must place a statement on the record that if some other court at some other time shall read the statute differently, there will be a denial of liberties that at the moment of the protest are unchallenged and intact. Defendants charged with crime are as slow as are men generally to borrow trouble for the future." The motion for rehearing was time enough to press the claim, under the doctrine of the Gehner and Brinkerhoff-Faris cases (note 4a above): "It is the doctrine that must prevail if the great securities of the Constitution are not to be lost in a web of procedural entanglements."

   c.   *Challenging a statute: "on its face"; "as construed"; "as applied."* Justice Cardozo's comment is persuasive with respect to the specific challenge here involved: to say that Herndon should have attacked the Carr standard construction of the statute at an earlier point was indeed burdensome. But were there not other constitutional objections Herndon could have raised at an earlier stage without undue practical difficulty? Herndon's situation reflects a pervasive problem of constitutional litigation: the implications of differing types of challenges to statutes. Distinguish, in the materials below, claims that a statute is invalid "on its face," invalid "as construed," and invalid "as applied." Cardozo's objection was to the majority's failure to find the "as construed" attack timely. Could Herndon have challenged the statute "on its face"—for example, as creating too vague a standard of criminal law? Should Herndon have objected to his conviction at the trial level on "as applied" grounds: for example, that the evidence introduced against him did not show that "clear and present danger" required by his view of the federal free speech guarantee; in other words, that his *conduct* as shown by the evidence (quite apart from the statutory rule involved) was protected by the Federal Constitution?

   [Herndon ultimately did prevail on the merits. After the dismissal in Herndon v. Georgia, he petitioned for a writ of habeas corpus in a state court, contending that the statute as construed and applied failed to set up an ascertainable standard of guilt and restrained his freedom of speech without due process of law. The state courts treated the proceeding as properly raising issues of federal constitutional law and rejected the contentions. In Herndon v. Lowry, 301 U.S. 242 (1937), the Supreme Court took jurisdiction on appeal and reversed on the merits. That decision is printed below, chap. 15, p. 1089.]

   5.   *"Important intervening circumstances" subsequent to a state court decision resting on local procedural grounds—the Patterson and Williams cases.* a.   *Patterson v. Alabama.* In certain exceptional circumstances, the Supreme Court may vacate a state court judgment and remand the case even though the asserted state procedural ground of decision is not found inadequate. In Patterson v. Alabama, 294 U.S. 600 (1935), the defendant, who had been sentenced to death after a rape conviction, claimed racial discrimination in jury selection. The highest state court declined to consider the objection on the ground that it had been raised too late. In a companion case, free of the procedural difficulty, the state court rejected the claim on the merits. The Supreme Court granted certiorari in both cases. In the companion case, Norris v. Alabama, 294 U.S. 587 (1935), the Court reversed on the merits. In the Patterson case, the state procedural ground was found supported by earlier state decisions. Nevertheless, the Court vacated the judgment and remanded the case. Believing that the state court might have viewed the procedural defect differently if it had known that the constitutional objection was valid, the Court concluded that "the state court should have an opportunity to examine its powers in the light of the situation which has now developed. . . . . In the exercise of our appellate jurisdiction we have power not only to correct error in the judgment under review but to make such disposition of the case as justice requires. . . .

We have said that to do this is not to review, in any proper sense of the term, the decision of the state court upon a nonfederal question but only to deal appropriately with a matter arising since its judgment and having a bearing upon the right disposition of the case."

b. *Williams v. Georgia.* Consider whether the Patterson principle was properly applied in Williams v. Georgia, 349 U.S. 375 (1955). There, petitioner claimed discrimination in jury selection through the use of a practice condemned by the Supreme Court in Avery v. Georgia, 345 U.S. 559 (1953), a case which arose in the same county as the Williams case. The Avery case was decided by the Supreme Court two months after the trial of Williams. Thereafter, Williams filed a motion for a new trial and appealed unsuccessfully to the highest state court without raising the discrimination objection. That claim was presented to the state courts for the first time in an extraordinary motion in the trial court subsequent to the state court's affirmance of the conviction and some six months after the Supreme Court's decision in Avery. The motion was denied and the Georgia Supreme Court affirmed, recognizing the validity of the constitutional claim under Avery, but holding that the claim could only be presented before trial and that, even if the motion were an appropriate remedy, the requirements for invoking that procedure had not been satisfied. The United States Supreme Court, after examining prior state cases, concluded that the state courts had power to consider the extraordinary motion. Although Justice Frankfurter's opinion for the Court stated that the "discretionary decision to deny the motion does not deprive this Court of jurisdiction to find that the substantive issue is properly before us," it chose not to exercise that jurisdiction. [On what theory could the state court's failure to exercise its discretion constitute an inadequate state ground? Justice Frankfurter did not explain this passing remark in Williams; but it has been relied on to support review in subsequent cases. See the footnote to Justice Black's concurrence in Henry, which follows.] Rather, relying on Patterson v. Alabama, and stressing that "the facts of this case are extraordinary" and that "life is at stake," the Williams Court remanded the case to the Georgia Supreme Court for reconsideration. As in Patterson, the Court found an "important factor which has intervened" since the state court's affirmance: here, the State Attorney General had conceded the merits of the constitutional claim in oral argument before the Supreme Court, although the County Solicitor General had urged in the state courts that no denial of equal protection was involved. Justices Clark, Reed and Minton dissented. Note also the 5:4 division on the applicability of the Patterson principle in Giles v. Maryland, 386 U.S. 66 (1967). Compare Henry v. Mississippi, the next principal case.

c. *The vitality of the general rule.* Although some of the cases in these notes and Henry v. Mississippi, below, represent inroads on the adequate state grounds barrier, the Court continues to insist that ordinarily it will not examine federal claims on review if they have not first been submitted to the state courts. Note Cardinale v. Louisiana, 394 U.S. 437 (1969), reiterating the general rule "that the Court will not decide federal constitutional issues raised here for the first time on review of state court decisions." Justice White's majority opinion ordered dismissal of the writ of certiorari "for want of jurisdiction"; Justices Black, Douglas and Fortas concurred in the dismissal of the writ, "believing it to have been improvidently granted." The majority stressed "petitioner's admitted failure to raise the issue he presents here in any way below, the failure of the state court to pass on this issue, the desirability of giving the State the first opportunity to apply its statute on an adequate record, and the fact that a federal habeas remedy may remain if no state procedure for raising the issue is available to petitioner."

6. *"Harmless error": state procedural rule or federal law?* In Chapman v. California, 386 U.S. 18 (1967), the prosecutor's argument to the jury had commented on petitioners' failure to testify at their trial. Shortly after the trial, the Supreme Court—in Griffin v. California, 380 U.S. 609 (1965) (chap. 12, p. 878, below)—held that the California rule permitting such comment violated the federal privilege against self-incrimination. The highest state court in Chapman recognized that petitioners had been denied a federal constitutional right but nevertheless affirmed their convictions, applying the state constitution's harmless error provision. The Supreme Court reversed in a majority opinion by Justice Black: federal rather than state law is determinative; the appropriate federal rule is that there can be harmless constitutional errors in some circumstances; but the error in this case was not harmless.

After stating that the "application of a state harmless-error rule is, of course, a state question where it involves only errors of state procedure or state law," the Court insisted that state law could not govern where the impact of federal constitutional violations had to be assessed: "[W]e cannot leave to the States the formulation of the authoritative laws, rules, and remedies designed to protect people from infractions by the States of federally guaranteed rights." In fashioning a federal harmless error rule, the Court recognized that prior cases—involving, for example, coerced confession and right to counsel claims—had indicated that "there are some constitutional rights so basic to a fair trial that their infraction can never be treated as harmless error." But, Justice Black concluded, "there may be some constitutional errors which in the setting of a particular case are so unimportant and insignificant that they may, consistent with the Federal Constitution, be deemed harmless, not resulting in the automatic reversal of the conviction." The applicable standard should be "that before a federal constitutional error can be held harmless, the court must be able to declare a belief that it was harmless beyond a reasonable doubt." Here, it had not been demonstrated "beyond a reasonable doubt" that the improper comments "did not contribute to petitioners' convictions." (Compare Harrington v. California, 395 U.S. 250 (1969), where three members of the Chapman majority dissented from an application of Chapman because, as they saw it, the majority had shifted the inquiry "from whether the constitutional error contributed to the conviction to whether the untainted evidence provided 'overwhelming' support for the conviction.")

In a lengthy dissent in Chapman, Justice Harlan concluded "that a state appellate court's reasonable application of a constitutionally proper state harmless-error rule to sustain a state conviction constitutes an independent and adequate state ground of judgment." The application of the state rule here had "no direct relation to federal constitutional provisions, rather it is an analysis of the question whether this admittedly improper comment had any significant impact on the outcome of the trial." Justice Harlan emphasized that any state harmless error rule that he would permit to be applied would itself have to meet federal constitutional standards. The state rule would have to survive two inquiries: "Is the California harmless-error provision consistent with the guarantee of fundamental fairness embodied in the Due Process Clause of the Fourteenth Amendment?" Was its application in this instance "a reasonable one or was the rule applied arbitrarily to evade the underlying constitutional mandate of fundamental fairness?"

HENRY v. MISSISSIPPI

379 U.S. 443, 85 S.Ct. 564, 13 L.Ed.2d 408 (1965).

Certiorari to the Supreme Court of Mississippi.

Mr. Justice BRENNAN delivered the opinion of the Court.

Petitioner was convicted of disturbing the peace, by indecent proposals to and offensive contact with an 18-year-old hitchhiker to whom he is said to have given a ride in his car. The trial judge charged the jury that "you cannot find the defendant guilty on the unsupported and uncorroborated testimony of the complainant alone." The petitioner's federal claim derives from the admission of a police officer's testimony, introduced to corroborate the hitchhiker's testimony. The Mississippi Supreme Court held that the officer's testimony was improperly admitted as the fruit of "an unlawful search . . . ." The tainted evidence tended to substantiate the hitchhiker's testimony by showing its accuracy in a detail which could have been seen only by one inside the car. In particular, it showed that the right-hand ashtray of the car in which the incident took place was full of Dentyne chewing gum wrappers, and that the cigarette lighter did not function. The police officer testified that after petitioner's arrest he had returned to the petitioner's house and obtained the permission of petitioner's wife to look in petitioner's car. The wife provided the officer with the keys, with which the officer opened the car. He testified that he tried the lighter and it would not work, and also that the ashtray "was filled with red dentyne chewing gum wrappers."

The Mississippi Supreme Court first filed an opinion which reversed petitioner's conviction and remanded for a new trial. The court held that the wife's consent to the search of the car did not waive petitioner's constitutional rights . . . . Acting in the belief that petitioner had been represented by nonresident counsel unfamiliar with local procedure, the court reversed despite petitioner's failure to comply with the Mississippi requirement that an objection to illegal evidence be made at the time it is introduced.
. . .

After the first opinion was handed down, the State filed a Suggestion of Error, pointing out that petitioner was in fact represented at his trial by competent local counsel, as well as by out-of-state lawyers. Thereupon the Mississippi Supreme Court withdrew its first opinion and filed a new opinion in support of a judgment affirming petitioner's conviction. The new opinion is identical with the first save for the result, the statement that petitioner had local counsel, and the discussion of the effect of failure for whatever reason to make timely objection to the evidence. "In such circumstances, even if honest mistakes of counsel in respect to policy or strategy or otherwise occur, they are binding upon the client as a part of the hazards of courtroom battle." . . . We vacate the judgment of conviction and remand for a hearing on the question whether the petitioner is to be deemed to have knowingly waived decision of his federal claim when timely objection was not made to the admission of the illegally seized evidence.

It is, of course, a familiar principle that this Court will decline to review state court judgments which rest on independent and adequate state grounds, even where those judgments also decide federal questions. The principle applies not only in cases involving state substantive grounds, Murdock v. City of Memphis, 20 Wall. 590, but aso in cases involving state procedural grounds. . . . But it is important to distinguish between state substantive grounds and state procedural grounds. Where the ground involved is substantive, the determination of the federal question cannot affect the disposition if the state court decision on the state law question is allowed to stand. Under the view taken in Murdock of the statutes conferring appellate jurisdiction on this Court, we have no power to revise judgments on questions of state law. Thus, the adequate nonfederal ground doctrine is necessary to avoid advisory opinions.

These justifications have no application where the state ground is purely procedural. A procedural default which is held to bar challenge to a conviction in state courts, even on federal constitutional grounds, prevents implementation of the federal right. Accordingly, we have consistently held that the question of when and how defaults in compliance with state procedural rules can preclude our consideration of a federal question is itself a federal question. . . . These cases settle the proposition that a litigant's procedural defaults in state proceedings do not prevent vindication of his federal rights unless the State's insistence on compliance with its procedural rule serves a legitimate state interest. In every case we must inquire whether the enforcement of a procedural forfeiture serves such a state interest. If it does not, the state procedural rule ought not be permitted to bar vindication of important federal rights.[1]

The Mississippi rule requiring contemporaneous objection to the introduction of illegal evidence clearly does serve a legitimate state interest. By immediately apprising the trial judge of the objection, counsel gives the court the opportunity to conduct the trial without using the tainted evidence. If the objection is well taken the fruits of the illegal search may be excluded from jury consideration, and a reversal and new trial avoided. But on the record before us it appears that this purpose of the contemporaneous-objection rule may have been substantially served by petitioner's motion at the close of the State's evidence asking for a directed verdict because of the erroneous admission of the officer's testimony. For at this stage the trial judge could have called for elaboration of the search and seizure argument and, if persuaded, could have stricken the tainted testimony or have taken other appropriate corrective action. . . . In these circumstances, the delay until the close of the State's case in presenting the objection cannot be said to have frustrated the State's interest in avoiding delay and waste of time in the disposition of the case. If this is so, and enforcement of the rule here would serve no substantial state interest, then settled principles would preclude treating the state ground as adequate; giving effect to the contemporaneous-

1. This will not lead inevitably to a plethora of attacks on the application of state procedural rules; where the state rule is a reasonable one and clearly announced to defendant and counsel, application of the waiver doctrine will yield the same result as that of the adequate, nonfederal ground doctrine in the vast majority of cases. [Footnote by the Court.]

objection rule for its own sake "would be to force resort to an arid ritual of meaningless form." Staub v. City of Baxley, 355 U.S. 313, 320 . . . .[2]

We have no reason, however, to decide that question now or to express any view on the merits of petitioner's substantial constitutional claim. For even assuming that the making of the objection on the motion for a directed verdict satisfied the state interest served by the contemporaneous-objection rule, the record suggests a possibility that petitioner's counsel deliberately bypassed the opportunity to make timely objection in the state court, and thus that the petitioner should be deemed to have forfeited his state court remedies. . . . [The record] is enough to justify an evidentiary hearing to determine whether petitioner "after consultation with competent counsel or otherwise, understandingly and knowingly forewent the privilege of seeking to vindicate his federal claims in the state courts, whether for strategic, tactical, or any other reasons that can fairly be described as the deliberate by-passing of state procedures . . . ." Fay v. Noia, 372 U.S. 391, 439. [Fay v. Noia is considered in the notes on federal habeas corpus which follow this case.]

The evidence suggests reasons for a strategic move. . . . Although trial strategy adopted by counsel without prior consultation with an accused will not, where the circumstances are exceptional, preclude the accused from asserting constitutional claims, see Whitus v. Balkcom, 333 F.2d 496 (C.A. 5th Cir. 1964), we think that the deliberate bypassing by counsel of the contemporaneous-objection rule as a part of trial strategy would have that effect in this case.

Only evidence extrinsic to the record before us can establish the fact of waiver, and the State should have an opportunity to establish that fact. In comparable cases arising in federal courts we have vacated the judgments of conviction and remanded for a hearing, suspending the determination of the validity of the conviction pending the outcome of the hearing. . . . We think a similar course is particularly desirable here, since a dismissal on the basis of an adequate state ground would not end this case; petitioner might still pursue vindication of his federal claim in a federal habeas corpus proceeding in which the procedural default will not alone preclude consideration of his claim, at least unless it is shown that petitioner deliberately bypassed the orderly procedure of the state courts. Fay v. Noia, supra, at 438.

Of course, in so remanding we neither hold nor even remotely imply that the State must forego insistence on its procedural requirements if it finds no waiver. Such a finding would only mean that petitioner could have a federal court apply settled principles to test the effectiveness of the procedural default to foreclose consideration of his constitutional claim. If it finds the procedural default ineffective, the federal court will itself decide the merits of his federal claim, at least so long as the state court does not wish to do so. By permitting the Mississippi courts to make an initial determination of waiver, we serve the causes of efficient administration of criminal justice, and of harmonious federal-state judicial relations. Such a disposition may make unnecessary the processing of the case through federal courts already

2. We do not rely on the principle that our review is not precluded when the state court has failed to exercise discretion to disregard the procedural default. See Williams v. Georgia, 349 U.S. 375. We read the second Mississippi Supreme Court opinion as holding that there is no such discretion where it appears that petitioner was represented by competent local counsel familiar with local procedure. [Footnote by the Court. On this "principle," see the footnote to Justice Black's concurring opinion, infra.]

laboring under congested dockets,[3] or it may make unnecessary the relitigation in a federal forum of certain issues. See Townsend v. Sain, 372 U.S. 293, 312–319 [also in the notes which follow]. The Court is not blind to the fact that the federal habeas corpus jurisdiction has been a source of irritation between the federal and state judiciaries. It has been suggested that this friction might be ameliorated if the States would look upon our decisions in Fay v. Noia, supra, and Townsend v. Sain, supra, as affording them an opportunity to provide state procedures, direct or collateral, for a full airing of federal claims.[4] That prospect is better served by a remand than by relegating petitioner to his federal habeas remedy. Therefore, the judgment is vacated and the case is remanded to the Mississippi Supreme Court for further proceedings not inconsistent with this opinion.

It is so ordered.

Mr. Justice BLACK, dissenting.

Petitioner contends that his conviction was based in part on evidence obtained by an allegedly unlawful search in violation of the United States Constitution. I would decide this federal question here and now. I do not believe that the Mississippi procedural trial rule relied on by the State can shut off this Court's review, nor do I find a particle of support for the Court's suggestion that petitioner knowingly waived his right to have this constitutional question decided by the state trial court. . . .

Nor do I believe that Mississippi's procedural rule concerning the stage of a trial at which constitutional objections should be made is the kind of rule that we should accept as an independent, adequate ground for the State Supreme Court's refusal to decide the constitutional question raised by petitioner. In Williams v. Georgia, 349 U.S. 375, this Court held that where a State allows constitutional questions "to be raised at a late stage and be determined by its courts as a matter of discretion, we are not concluded from assuming jurisdiction and deciding whether the state court action in the particular circumstances is, in effect, an avoidance of the federal right." *

3. Habeas corpus petitions filed by state prisoners in federal district courts increased from 1,903 to 3,531, or 85.5%, from the 1963 to the 1964 fiscal year. Annual Report of the Director, Administrative Office of the United States Courts, p. 46 (1964); our own Miscellaneous Docket, where cases of state prisoners are primarily listed, continues to show substantial increases. The number has increased from 878 for the 1956 Term to 1,532 for the 1963 Term. [Footnote by the Court.]

4. See Meador, Accommodating State Criminal Procedure and Federal Post-conviction Review, 50 A.B.A.J. 928 (October 1964). And see Brennan, Some Aspects of Federalism 19–21 (address to Conference of Chief Justices, Aug. 7, 1964). [Footnote by the Court.]

* Justice Black's position in this opinion —based on an unexplained remark in Williams v. Georgia, see note 5 preceding this case—became the basis for a Court exercise of review jurisdiction in Sullivan v. Little Hunting Park, Inc., 396 U.S. 229 (1969) (the community facilities discrimination case, chap. 6, p. 527 infra). What is the "unexercised discretion" basis for finding a state ground inadequate? Is it justifiable?

Note footnote 2 to the majority opinion, supra, disavowing reliance on the assumed Williams "principle" that "review is not precluded when the state court has failed to exercise discretion to disregard the procedural default." In the Sullivan case, the highest state court twice dismissed petitioner's appeal for failure to comply with the requirement that opposing counsel be given "reasonable written notice of the time and place of tendering the transcript and a reasonable opportunity" to examine it. Justice Douglas' majority opinion found this an inadequate state ground, with little explanation. He recognized that the state court had not "fashioned a novel

No Mississippi court opinions or state statutes have been called to our attention that I read as denying *power* of the State Supreme Court, should that court wish to do so, to consider and determine constitutional questions presented at the time this one was. In fact, as I understand counsel for the State, the Supreme Court of Mississippi does have power in its discretion to consider such questions regardless of when they are presented. . . . Yet this Court now apparently holds that the state court may, if it chooses to do so, depart from its prior cases and apply a new, stricter rule against this defendant and thereby prevent this Court from reviewing the case to see that his federal constitutional rights were safeguarded. I do not believe the cherished federal constitutional right of a defendant to object to unconstitutionally seized evidence offered against him can be cut off irrevocably by state-court discretionary rulings which might be different in particular undefined circumstances in other cases. I think such a procedural device for shutting off our review of questions involving constitutional rights is too dangerous to be tolerated. . . .

Mr. Justice HARLAN, with whom Mr. Justice CLARK and Mr. Justice STEWART join, dissenting.

Flying banners of federalism, the Court's opinion actually raises storm signals of a most disquieting nature. While purporting to recognize the traditional principle that an adequate procedural, as well as substantive, state ground of decision bars direct review here of any federal claim asserted in the state litigation, the Court, unless I wholly misconceive what is lurking in today's opinion, portends a severe dilution, if not complete abolition, of the concept of "adequacy" as pertaining to state procedural grounds.

In making these preliminary observations I do not believe I am seeing ghosts. For I cannot account for the remand of this case in the face of what is a demonstrably adequate state procedural ground of decision by the Mississippi Supreme Court except as an early step toward extending in one way or another the doctrine of Fay v. Noia, 372 U.S. 391, to direct review. In that case, decided only two Terms ago, the Court turned its back on history . . . and did away with the adequate state ground doctrine in federal habeas corpus proceedings.

procedural requirement for the first time in this case; cf. NAACP v. Alabama" (note 1b preceding this case). He asserted instead that past state decisions "do not enable us to say that Virginia has so consistently applied its notice requirement as to amount to a self-denial of the *power* to entertain the federal claim here presented if the Supreme Court of Appeals desires to do so. See Henry v. Mississippi, 379 U.S. 443, 455–457 (Black, J., dissenting). Such a rule, more properly deemed discretionary than jurisdictional, does not bar review here by certiorari."

Justice Harlan, joined by Chief Justice Burger and Justice White, would have found the state ground inadequate on the basis of the NAACP v. Alabama principle, but rejected the majority's reasons for the result as "unclear and confusing." He especially objected to the majority's "loose use of the word 'discretionary'," since it might suggest "that any decision made pursuant to a broad standard cannot provide an adequate state ground. Surely a state ground is no less adequate simply because it involves a standard which requires a judgment of what is reasonable, and because the result may turn on a close analysis of the facts of a particular case in light of competing policy considerations." Williams v. Georgia "does not in my view support the reasoning of the majority. I think the result in Williams rests upon a determination of inconsistency in the application of the State's procedural requirements for a new trial."

Believing that any step toward extending Noia to direct review should be flushed out and challenged at its earliest appearance in an opinion of this Court, I respectfully dissent.

I. The Mississippi Supreme Court did not base its ultimate decision upon petitioner's federal claim that his wife's consent could not validate an otherwise improper police search of the family car, but on the procedural ground that petitioner (who was represented by three experienced lawyers) had not objected at the time the fruits of this search were received in evidence. This Court now strongly implies, but does not decide (in view of its remand on the "waiver" issue) that enforcement of the State's "contemporaneous-objection" rule was inadequate as a state ground of decision because the petitioner's motion for a directed verdict of acquittal afforded the trial judge a satisfactory opportunity to take "appropriate corrective action" with reference to the allegedly inadmissible evidence. . . .

From the standpoint of the realities of the courtroom, I can only regard the Court's analysis as little short of fanciful. The petitioner's motion for a verdict could have provoked one of three courses of action by the trial judge, none of which can reasonably be considered as depriving the State's contemporaneous-objection rule of its capacity to serve as an adequate state ground.

1. The trial judge might have granted the directed verdict. But had this action been appropriate, the Supreme Court of Mississippi, in its first opinion, would have ordered the prosecution dismissed. Since it did not, and the matter is entirely one of state law, further speculation by this Court should be foreclosed.

2. The trial judge might have directed a mistrial. The State's interest in preventing mistrials through the contemporaneous-objection requirement is obvious.

3. The remaining course of action is the example given by the Court; the trial judge could have denied the motion for a directed verdict, but, *sua sponte*, called for elaboration of the argument, determined that the search of the automobile was unconstitutional, and given cautionary instructions to the jury to disregard the inadmissible evidence when the case was submitted to it.

The practical difficulties with this approach are manifestly sufficient to show a substantial state interest in their avoidance, and thus to show an "adequate" basis for the State's adherence to the contemporaneous-objection rule. . . .

As every trial lawyer of any experience knows, motions for directed verdicts are generally made as a matter of course at the close of the prosecution's case, and are generally denied without close consideration unless the case is clearly borderline. It is simply unrealistic in this context to have expected the trial judge to pick out the single vague sentence from the directed verdict motion and to have acted upon it with the refined imagination the Court would require of him. . . .

Thus the state interest which so powerfully supports the contemporaneous-objection rule is that of maximizing correct decisions and concomitantly minimizing errors requiring mistrials and retrials. The alternative for the State is to reverse a trial judge who, from a long motion, fails to pick out and act with remarkable imagination upon a single vague sentence relating to admissibility of evidence long since admitted. A trial judge is a decision-maker, not an advocate. To force him out of his proper role by requiring him to coax out the arguments and imaginatively reframe the requested remedies for the counsel before him is to place upon him more responsibility than a trial judge can be expected to discharge.

There was no "appropriate corrective action" that could have realistically satisfied the purposes of the contemporaneous-objection rule. Without question the State had an interest in maintaining the integrity of its procedure, and thus without doubt reliance on the rule in question is "adequate" to bar direct review of petitioner's federal claim by this Court.[1]

II. The real reason for remanding this case emerges only in the closing pages of the Court's opinion. It is pointed out that even were the contemporaneous-objection rule considered to be an adequate state ground, this would not, under Fay v. Noia, preclude consideration of Henry's federal claim in federal habeas corpus unless it were made to appear that Henry had deliberately waived his federal claim in the state proceedings. It is then said that in the interest of "efficient administration of criminal justice" and "harmonious" relations between the federal and state judiciaries the Mississippi courts should be given the opportunity to pass, in the first instance, on the waiver issue; the prospect is entertained that such action on the part of this Court will encourage the States to grasp the "opportunity" afforded by Fay v. Noia and Townsend v. Sain by providing "state procedures, direct or collateral, for a full airing of federal claims." It is "suggested" that were this to be done "irritation" and "friction" respecting the exercise of federal habeas corpus power *vis-à-vis* state convictions "might be ameliorated."

What does all this signify? The States are being invited to voluntarily obliterate all state procedures, however conducive they may be to the orderly conduct of litigation, which might thwart state-court consideration of federal claims. But what if the States do not accept the invitation? Despite the Court's soft-spoken assertion that "settled principles" will be applied in the future, I do not think the intimation will be missed by any discerning reader of the Court's opinion that at the least a substantial dilution of the adequate state-ground doctrine may be expected. A contrary prediction is belied by the implication of the opinion that under "settled principles," the contemporaneous-objection rule relied upon in this case could be declared inadequate.

To me this would not be a move toward "harmonious" federalism; any further disrespect for state procedures, no longer cognizable at all in federal habeas corpus, would be the very antithesis of it. While some may say that, given Fay v. Noia, what the Court is attempting to do is justifiable as a means of promoting "efficiency" in the administration of criminal justice, it is the sort of efficiency which, though perhaps appropriate in some watered-down form of federalism, is not congenial to the kind of federalism

---

1. As the first opinion by the Mississippi Supreme Court shows, there is discretion in certain circumstances to lower the procedural bar. It does not follow that this Court is completely free to exercise that discretion. Even in cases from lower federal courts we do so only if there has been an abuse. If, in order to insulate its decisions from reversal by this Court, a state court must strip itself of the discretionary power to differentiate between different sets of circumstances, the rule operates in a most perverse way. [Footnote by Justice Harlan.]

I had supposed was ours. I venture to say that to all who believe the federal system as we have known it to be a priceless aspect of our Constitutionalism, the spectre implicit in today's decision will be no less disturbing than what the Court has already done in Fay v. Noia.

Believing that the judgment below rests on an adequate independent state ground, I would dismiss the writ issued in this case as improvidently granted.

STATE PROCEEDINGS AND FEDERAL HABEAS CORPUS

Introduction. The dimensions of the state procedural grounds barrier to *direct* Supreme Court review may be affected by developments in another area in which state procedures bear on access to a federal forum—that of *collateral* federal relief for state prisoners, via habeas corpus. In lowering the state procedure barrier in Fay v. Noia, 372 U.S. 391 (1963) (note 2 below), the Court purported to deal solely with federal habeas and to leave direct review untouched. Yet, as Henry v. Mississippi shows, reducing the procedural obstacles on one of the roads to federal relief understandably has had repercussions on the other. These notes sketch the judicial and legislative developments in federal habeas before and after Fay v. Noia, not only because of their influence on Supreme Court review of state judgments (as in Henry) but also, more generally, because they provide another context in which to assess the appropriate extent of state control over its procedural mechanisms for asserting federal rights.

Is a state prisoner barred from federal collateral relief if his efforts to obtain a state hearing failed because of noncompliance with state procedures? Before Fay v. Noia, noncompliance was a bar to such habeas relief, much as it was to direct Supreme Court review. Was that because the adequate state grounds doctrine had equal applicability to collateral and direct federal review? Was it because of the special "exhaustion" provision in the jurisdictional statute (note 1 below)? During that period, the federal habeas remedy seemed to have a double-or-nothing aspect: if a state court had reached the merits of the prisoner's federal claim, the federal habeas court could also adjudicate it; if the state court had not reached the claim on procedural grounds, the federal court was also precluded. Fay v. Noia (note 2) ended that seeming anomaly: a federal habeas ruling became possible in both cases. And post-Noia amendments to the statute, in turn, have increased the restraints on federal relitigation of the merits already considered by a state court (note 3).

1. *State procedural barriers and federal habeas corpus before Fay v. Noia: Brown v. Allen and the "exhaustion" statute.* a. *The Brown v. Allen practice.* The almost total barrier which noncompliance with state procedures formerly imposed on federal habeas was illustrated in the Court's most important consideration of the problem prior to Noia, Daniels v. Allen, decided sub nom. Brown v. Allen, 344 U.S. 443 (1953). There the Court found federal habeas corpus unavailable to a petitioner who had perfected his appeal too late in the state courts. The state trial court had granted petitioner 60 days in which to serve a statement of the case on appeal. Counsel did not serve the statement until 61 days had expired, and the appeal was struck as out of time. Justice Reed's opinion for the Court

stated: "[W]here the state action was based on an adequate state ground, no further examination is required, unless no state remedy for the deprivation of federal constitutional rights ever existed. Mooney v. Holohan, 294 U.S. 103 [note 5 below]; Ex parte Hawk, 321 U.S. 114." He added: "Failure to appeal is much like a failure to raise a known and existing question of unconstitutional proceeding or action prior to conviction or commitment. . . . A failure to use a state's available remedy, in the absence of some interference or incapacity, bars federal habeas corpus. The statute requires that the applicant exhaust available state remedies."

Justice Frankfurter, who dissented because he found an arbitrary state failure to exercise discretion to extend the appeal time, nevertheless stated: "Of course, nothing we have said suggests that a federal habeas corpus jurisdiction can displace a State's procedural rule requiring that certain errors be raised on appeal. Normally rights under the Federal Constitution may be waived . . . . When a State insists that a defendant be held to his choice of trial strategy and not be allowed to try a different tack on State habeas corpus, he may be deemed to have waived his claim and thus have no right to assert on federal habeas corpus. . . . However, this does not touch one of those extraordinary cases in which a substantial claim goes to the very foundation of a proceeding, as in Moore v. Dempsey, 261 U.S. 86."

b. *The statute.* Was the practice during the Brown v. Allen period simply an application of the adequate state grounds doctrine to habeas? Did it rest on "waiver" principles? On the "exhaustion" language of the jurisdictional statute, which follows? Note the discussion in Noia and consider the opening provisions of 28 U.S.C. § 2254:

"(a) The Supreme Court, a Justice thereof, a circuit judge, or a district court shall entertain an application for a writ of habeas corpus in behalf of a person in custody pursuant to the judgment of a State court only on the ground that he is in custody in violation of the Constitution or laws or treaties of the United States.

"(b) An application for a writ of habeas corpus in behalf of a person in custody pursuant to the judgment of a State court shall not be granted unless it appears that the applicant has exhausted the remedies available in the courts of the State, or that there is either an absence of available State corrective process or the existence of circumstances rendering such process ineffective to protect the rights of the prisoner.

"(c) An applicant shall not be deemed to have exhausted the remedies available in the courts of the State, within the meaning of this section, if he has the right under the law of the State to raise, by any available procedure, the question presented."

[Sec. 2254(b) and (c), the exhaustion provisions, were 1948 codifications of judicially developed doctrines. See Young v. Ragen, 337 U.S. 235 (1949). Sec. 2254(a) was added in a 1966 revision. For another 1966, post-Noia addition, see § 2254(d), note 3 below.]

2. *The Fay v. Noia modification.* The Brown v. Allen approach was reexamined in Fay v. Noia, 372 U.S. 391 (1963). In 1942, Noia was convicted of felony murder in New York. His coerced confession claim was rejected at the trial and he did not appeal. His two co-defendants appealed their convictions in 1942, were unsuccessful, but were able to sustain their

coerced confession claims in collateral challenges to the convictions in 1955 and 1956. The Supreme Court held that Noia was entitled to federal habeas corpus relief despite his failure to seek direct review of his 1942 conviction. Justice Brennan summarized the majority's position as follows: "(1) Federal courts have *power* under the federal habeas statute to grant relief despite the applicant's failure to have pursued a state remedy not available to him at the time he applies; the doctrine under which state procedural defaults are held to constitute an adequate and independent state law ground barring direct Supreme Court review is not to be extended to limit the power granted the federal courts under the federal habeas statute. (2) Noia's failure to appeal was not a failure to exhaust 'the remedies available in the courts of the State' as required by § 2254; that requirement refers only to a failure to exhaust state remedies still open to the applicant at the time he files his application for habeas corpus in the federal court. (3) Noia's failure to appeal cannot under the circumstances be deemed an intelligent and understanding waiver of his right to appeal such as to justify the withholding of federal habeas corpus relief."

Though the Court stated "that the federal habeas judge may in his discretion deny relief to an applicant who has deliberately bypassed the orderly procedure of the state courts and in so doing has forfeited his state court remedies," it found no such "deliberate bypassing" in Noia's case: "For Noia to have appealed in 1942"—after he had been sentenced to life imprisonment—"would have been to run a substantial risk of electrocution. . . . He declined to play Russian roulette in this fashion. This was a choice by Noia not to appeal, but under the circumstances it cannot realistically be deemed . . . in any way a deliberate circumvention of state procedures." In the course of the opinion, the Court overruled the Darr v. Burford holding [339 U.S. 200 (1950)] "that a state prisoner must ordinarily seek certiorari in this Court as a precondition of applying for federal habeas corpus."

In explaining the conclusions regarding the federal habeas court's power, Justice Brennan distinguished the adequate state ground barrier on direct review of state judgments in the Supreme Court. In addition to the passage quoted above (in the notes following Murdock, at p. ——, supra), note the following comments: "Thus, a default such as Noia's, if deemed adequate and independent (a question on which we intimate no view), would cut off review by this Court of the state *coram nobis* proceeding in which the New York Court of Appeals refused him relief. It is contended that it follows from this that the remedy of federal habeas corpus is likewise cut off. The fatal weakness of this contention is its failure to recognize that the adequate state-ground rule is a function of the limitations of *appellate* review. But while our appellate function is concerned only with the judgments or decrees of state courts, the habeas corpus jurisdiction of the lower federal courts is not so confined. The jurisdictional prerequisite is not the judgment of a state court but detention *simpliciter*. . . .

"To be sure, this may not be the entire answer to the contention that the adequate state-ground principle should apply to the federal courts on habeas corpus as well as to the Supreme Court on direct review of state judgments. The Murdock decision may be supported not only by the factor of mootness, but in addition by certain characteristics of the federal system. . . . For the federal courts to refuse to give effect in habeas proceedings to state procedural defaults might conceivably have some effect upon the States' regulation of their criminal procedures. But the problem is crucially different from that posed in Murdock of the federal courts' deciding questions of substantive state law. In Noia's case the only relevant substantive law is federal—the Fourteenth Amendment. State law appears only in the procedural framework for adjudicating the substantive federal question. The paramount interest is federal. . . . That is not to say that the States have not a substantial interest in exacting compliance with their procedural rules from criminal defendants asserting federal defenses. Of course orderly criminal procedure is a desideratum, and of course there must be sanctions for the flouting of such procedure. . . .

"Surely this state interest in an airtight system of forfeitures is of a different order from that, vindicated in Murdock, in the autonomy of state law within the proper sphere of its substantive regulation. . . . Certainly this Court has differentiated the two situations in its application of the adequate state-ground rule. While it has deferred to state substantive grounds so long as they are not patently evasive of or discriminatory against federal rights, it has sometimes refused to defer to state procedural grounds only because they made burdensome the vindication of federal rights. That the Court nevertheless ordinarily gives effect to state procedural grounds may be attributed to considerations which are peculiar to the Court's role and function and have no relevance to habeas corpus proceedings in the Federal District Courts. . . .

"A practical appraisal of the state interest here involved plainly does not justify the federal courts' enforcing on habeas corpus a doctrine of forfeitures under the guise of applying the adequate state-ground rule. We fully grant . . . that the exigencies of federalism warrant a limitation whereby the federal judge has the discretion to deny relief to one who has deliberately sought to subvert or evade the orderly adjudication of his federal defenses in the state courts. Surely no stricter rule is a realistic necessity. . . . [W]e reject as unsound in principle, as well as not supported by authority, the suggestion that the federal courts are without power to grant habeas relief to an applicant whose federal claims would not be heard on direct review in this Court because of a procedural default furnishing an adequate and independent ground of state decision."

In a lengthy dissent, Justice Harlan, joined by Justices Clark and Stewart, set forth his reasons for thinking that the "decision, both in its abrupt break with the past and in its consequences for the future, is one of the most disquieting that the Court has rendered in a long time." He concluded that "the federal courts have no *power,* statutory or constitutional, to release the respondent Noia from state detention. This is because his custody by New York does not violate any federal right, since it is pursuant to a conviction whose validity rests upon an adequate and independent state ground which the federal courts are required to respect."

3. *Federal hearings after state court decisions on the merits: Townsend v. Sain and the 1966 statute.* a. *The Townsend guidelines.* Fay v. Noia opened the federal habeas door wider where the state court had *not* reached the merits. A companion case, Townsend v. Sain, 372 U.S. 293 (1963), sought to assure fuller federal hearings where the state court *had* ruled on the federal claim. The Court reviewed at length the problem of

"the power and duty of federal judges, on habeas corpus, to hold evidentiary hearings—that is, to try issues of fact anew." Chief Justice Warren summarized the new standards in the following passage:

"Where the facts are in dispute, . . . a federal evidentiary hearing is required unless the state-court trier of fact has after a full hearing reliably found the relevant facts. . . . We hold that a federal court must grant an evidentiary hearing to a habeas applicant under the following circumstances: If (1) the merits of the factual dispute were not resolved in the state hearing; (2) the state factual determination is not fairly supported by the record as a whole; (3) the fact finding procedure employed by the state court was not adequate to afford a full and fair hearing; (4) there is a substantial allegation of newly discovered evidence; (5) the material facts were not adequately developed at the state court hearing; or (6) for any reason it appears that the state trier of fact did not afford the habeas applicant a full and fair fact hearing."

Justice Stewart's dissent joined by Justices Clark, Harlan and White, questioned the wisdom of "attempting to erect detailed hearing standards for the myriad situations presented by federal habeas corpus applications." [In a third case (in addition to Noia and Townsend) in "the trilogy of 'guideline' decisions" for post-conviction proceedings, the Court dealt with the major collateral remedy for *federal* prisoners—28 U.S.C. § 2255, a remedy in the sentencing court enacted as a substitute for the habeas remedy in the district in which the prisoner is in custody. See Sanders v. United States, 373 U.S. 1 (1963).]

b. *The earlier legislative proposals.* The broader availability of habeas under Fay v. Noia and Townsend v. Sain gave new impetus to the demands for congressional curtailments of the habeas jurisdiction, to minimize federal court interference with state criminal law administration. The demands had been widespread in the pre-Noia years. See Pollak, "Proposals to Curtail Federal Habeas Corpus for State Prisoners: Collateral Attack on the Great Writ," 66 Yale L.J. 50 (1956). Among the most prestigious recommendations (repeatedly urged by the Judicial Conference of the United States) was that federal three-judge courts be convened before state prisoners could be released. But that proposal was withdrawn because of "serious problems of administration." As a House Report noted: "Following such decisions [as Fay v. Noia and Townsend v. Sain], the number of applications for writs of habeas corpus by State court prisoners has greatly increased. This vast increase . . . became a matter of concern to the Judicial Conference, and brought about a reexamination" of its three-judge court recommendation. H.R.Rep.No.1892, 89th Cong., 2d Sess. (1966).

c. *The 1966 revision.* The 1966 reexamination did produce other modifications in the habeas statute, however. See 80 Stat. 1104. According to the Chairman of the Judicial Conference's Habeas Corpus Committee, the changes sought "to prevent the abuse of the writ of habeas corpus" and "to expedite the disposition of nonmeritorious and repetitious applications" by state prisoners. These purposes were to be attained, he explained, "by provisions for a qualified application of the doctrine of res judicata in Federal court habeas corpus proceedings brought by State prisoners, by provisions according a presumption of correctness to factual determinations made at a hearing on the merits by State Courts and by provisions with respect to the burden of proof in Federal court proceedings for habeas corpus by state prisoners." Sen.Rep.No.1797, 89th Cong., 2d Sess. (1966).

The major addition to § 2254 is new subsection (d), recasting the Townsend v. Sain guidelines regarding the impact on federal habeas corpus proceedings of prior state court hearings on the merits. Sec. 2254(d) rephrases and elaborates the six numbered criteria in the Townsend opinion. In Townsend, however, those criteria appear in the context of a general requirement of a federal hearing *unless* the state has held a full hearing. In the statute, by contrast, the norm is that the state determinations "shall be presumed to be correct" *unless* specified defects in the state hearing are shown.

4. *Habeas corpus and the state courts' obligation to hear post-conviction claims.* a. *The principle.* In Mooney v. Holohan, 294 U.S. 103 (1935), the state prisoner alleged that he was confined in violation of due process because (a) he had been convicted on the basis of the prosecution's knowing use of perjured testimony, and (b) the state had failed "to provide any corrective judicial process by which a conviction so obtained may be set aside." The Court's per curiam opinion stated: "Reasoning from the premise that the petitioner has failed to show a denial of due process in the circumstances set forth in his petition, the Attorney General urges that the State was not required to afford any corrective judicial process to remedy the alleged wrong. The argument falls with the premise. Frank v. Mangum, 237 U.S. 309, 335; Moore v. Dempsey, 261 U.S. 86, 91." However, the Court denied habeas corpus relief because the petitioner had not yet invoked the state "corrective judicial process" and "it is not shown to be unavailable."

b. *The Illinois merry-go-round.* The duty of the states to provide, within the existing framework of their judicial systems, a post-conviction procedure for the vindication of federal rights, was central in a series of cases involving the "Illinois merry-go-round"—the uncertainties in state decisions regarding state remedies for federal rights. See, e. g., Young v. Ragen, 337 U.S. 235 (1949), where habeas corpus had been denied by the state courts on the ground that it was an "inappropriate remedy." The Supreme Court remanded: "We can recognize the difficulties with which the Illinois Supreme Court is faced in adapting available state procedure to the requirement that prisoners be given some clearly defined method by which they may raise claims of denial of federal rights. Nevertheless, that requirement must be met." Thereafter Illinois passed a new Post-Conviction Hearing Act. In Jennings v. Illinois, 342 U.S. 104 (1951), relief had been denied under that Act. The Supreme Court vacated the judgment and remanded the case: "On remand, petitioners should be advised whether their claims that constitutional rights were infringed at their trials may be determined under the Post-Conviction Hearing Act, or whether that Act does not provide an appropriate state remedy in these cases. . . . If Illinois does not provide an appropriate remedy for such a determination, petitioners may proceed without more in the United States District Court." Is a proceeding in a federal court the only possible sanction where the State fails in its duty to provide an adequate post-conviction remedy? See Note, "Effect of the Federal Constitution in Requiring State Post-Conviction Remedies," 53 Colum.L.Rev. 1143 (1953).

SECTION 4. DISCRETIONARY ABSTENTION FROM THE EXERCISE OF JURISDICTION

Introductory note. May the Supreme Court refuse to review a state court case for reasons other than those grounded in the requirements of Article III or the jurisdictional statute? That question was posed by some of the materials in earlier sections of this chapter; it is the central concern of this section. Consider, first, the statements by Chief Justice Marshall and by Justice Brandeis. Are they wholly inconsistent? Or can Marshall's emphasis on the duty to decide be reconciled with Brandeis' stress on avoidance of constitutional adjudication? Then consider the dismissals of the appeals in Rescue Army, Naim v. Naim, and Poe v. Ullman—rare instances of Court failures to decide on the merits cases apparently within the obligatory review jurisdiction under the statute. Did the Court give adequate justifications for not reaching the merits in these cases? Does the Court have discretion to avoid such decisions for institutional reasons? Are the specific ingredients of justiciability considered in the preceding sections merely illustrations of broad policy choices regarding avoidance and intervention that the Court may and should make, as the prevailing opinions in Rescue Army and Poe suggest?

MARSHALL AND BRANDEIS: CONFLICTING VIEWS

Chief Justice MARSHALL in COHENS v. VIRGINIA, 6 Wheat. 264, 404 (1821): "It is most true that this Court will not take jurisdiction if it should not: but it is equally true, that it must take jurisdicion if it should. The judiciary cannot, as the legislature may, avoid a measure because it approaches the confines of the constitution. We cannot pass it by because it is doubtful. With whatever doubts, with whatever difficulties, a case may be attended, we must decide it, if it be brought before us. We have no more right to decline the exercise of jurisdiction which is given, than to usurp that which is not given. The one or the other would be treason to the constitution. Questions may occur which we would gladly avoid; but we cannot avoid them. All we can do is, to exercise our best judgment, and conscientiously to perform our duty."

Justice BRANDEIS in ASHWANDER v. TVA, 297 U.S. 288, 346–348 (1936) (concurring opinion): "The Court developed, for its own governance in the cases confessedly within its jurisdiction, a series of rules under which it has avoided passing upon a large part of all the constitutional questions pressed upon it for decision. They are:

"1. The Court will not pass upon the constitutionality of legislation in a friendly, non-adversary, proceeding, declining because to decide such questions 'is legitimate only in the last resort, and as a necessity in the determination of real, earnest and vital controversy between individuals. It never was the thought that, by means of a friendly suit, a party beaten in the legislature could transfer to the courts an inquiry as to the constitutionality of the legis-

lative act.'   Chicago & Grand Trunk Ry. v. Wellman, 143 U.S. 339, 345.
. . . .

"2.   The Court will not 'anticipate a question of constitutional law in advance of the necessity of deciding it.'   Liverpool, N. Y. & P. S. S. Co. v. Emigration Commissioners, 113 U.S. 33, 39;   . . .   'It is not the habit of the Court to decide questions of a constitutional nature unless absolutely necessary to a decision of the case.'   Burton v. United States, 196 U.S. 283, 295.

"3.   The Court will not 'formulate a rule of constitutional law broader than is required by the precise facts to which it is to be applied.'   Liverpool, N. Y. & P. S. S. Co. v. Emigration Commissioners, supra.   . . .

"4.   The Court will not pass upon a constitutional question although properly presented by the record, if there is also present some other ground upon which the case may be disposed of.   This rule has found most varied application.   Thus, if a case can be decided on either of two grounds, one involving a constitutional question, the other a question of statutory construction or general law, the Court will decide only the latter.   Siler v. Louisville & Nashville R. Co., 213 U.S. 175, 191;   Light v. United States, 220 U.S. 523, 538.   Appeals from the highest court of a state challenging its decision of a question under the Federal Constitution are frequently dismissed because the judgment can be sustained on an independent state ground.   Berea College v. Kentucky, 211 U.S. 45, 53.

"5.   The Court will not pass upon the validity of a statute upon complaint of one who fails to show that he is injured by its operation.   Tyler v. The Judges, 179 U.S. 405;   Hendrick v. Maryland, 235 U.S. 610, 621. Among the many applications of this rule, none is more striking than the denial of the right of challenge to one who lacks a personal or property right. Thus, the challenge by a public official interested only in the performance of his official duty will not be entertained.   . . .   In Fairchild v. Hughes, 258 U.S. 126, the Court affirmed the dismissal of a suit brought by a citizen who sought to have the Nineteenth Amendment declared unconstitutional. In Massachusetts v. Mellon, 262 U.S. 447, the challenge of the federal Maternity Act was not entertained although made by the Commonwealth on behalf of all its citizens.

"6.   The Court will not pass upon the constitutionality of a statute at the instance of one who has availed himself of its benefits.   Great Falls Mfg. Co. v. Attorney General, 124 U.S. 581.   . . . .

"7.   'When the validity of an act of the Congress is drawn in question, and even if a serious doubt of constitutionality is raised, it is a cardinal principle that this Court will first ascertain whether a construction of the statute is fairly possible by which the question may be avoided.'   Crowell v. Benson, 285 U.S. 22, 62.''

ASHWANDER AND THE "NEO–BRANDEISIAN FALLACY"

Note the comments on the content and uses of the Ashwander rules in Gunther, "The Subtle Vices of the 'Passive Virtues'—A Comment on Principle and Expediency in Judicial Review," 64 Colum.L.Rev. 1 (1964): * "[J]uris-

* Reprinted with the permission of the publisher, © copyright 1964, The Directors of the Columbia Law Review Association, Inc.

diction under our system is rooted in Article III and congressional enactments, . . . it is not a domain solely within the Court's keeping." The view that the Court has a general discretion not to adjudicate "frequently professes to find support in the Brandeis opinion in the Ashwander case. Brandeis' statement regarding "cases confessedly within [the Court's] jurisdiction" is "sound and of principled content; it is not an assertion of a vague Court discretion to deny a decision on the merits in a case within the statutory and constitutional bounds of jurisdiction. The Brandeis rules are a far cry from the neo-Brandeisian fallacy that there is a general 'Power To Decline the Exercise of Jurisdiction Which Is Given,' that there is a general discretion not to adjudicate though statute, Constitution, and remedial law present a 'case' for decision and confer no discretion. [The 'Power to Decline' quotation is from Bickel, The Least Dangerous Branch (1962), 127.]

"Of course the Court often may and should avoid 'passing upon a large part of all of the constitutional questions pressed upon it for decision.' Four of the seven Brandeis rules involve well-known instances of such avoidance— avoidance only of some or all of the *constitutional* questions argued, *not* avoidance of all decision on the merits of the case. . . . The remaining rules given by Brandeis deal with situations in which there is no 'case' or 'controversy' in terms of the jurisdictional content of Article III—as with the 'nonadversary' proceeding of his first rule—or where there is a lack of what Bickel calls 'pure' standing in the constitutional sense, or where the state of the remedial law prevents a 'case' from arising. In these Brandeis categories, decision on the merits is precluded because the jurisdictional requirements of Article III are not met; in the earlier ones, the jurisdiction to decide the merits is in fact exercised and all that is avoided is decision on some or all of the constitutional issues presented.

"The only possible Brandeis contribution to the fallacy lies in his reference to all of the categories as 'cases confessedly within' the Court's jurisdiction. But that referred to the fact that all of the jurisdictional requirements added by the statute had been met; and adjudication on the merits did in fact result in all of his categories, except where a jurisdictional requirement originating in the Constitution had not been satisfied. There is a sad irony in the transformation of the Brandeis passage into a veritable *carte blanche* for Court discretion as to jurisdiction; and there is sad irony too in the invocation of Brandeis' principled concern with threshold questions by members and appraisers of the Court who would assert a virtually unlimited choice in deciding whether to decide. The neo-Brandeisian fallacy has fortunately not yet gained a firm, persistent foothold on the Court."

Note also the reference to the Ashwander rules in the majority opinion in Flast v. Cohen, sec. 2, p. 93, supra. Chief Justice Warren pointed to them as illustrations of "not always clearly distinguished" strands of policy considerations and constitutional limitations. The Flast opinion elaborated: "Because the rules operate in 'cases confessedly within [the Court's] jurisdiction,' they find their source in policy, rather than purely constitutional, considerations. However, several of the cases cited by Mr. Justice Brandeis . . . articulated purely constitutional grounds for decision. See, e. g., Massachusetts v. Mellon, 262 U.S. 447 (1923) . . . ."

RESCUE ARMY v. MUNICIPAL COURT OF LOS ANGELES

331 U.S. 549, 67 S.Ct. 1409, 91 L.Ed. 1666 (1947).

Appeal from the Supreme Court of California.

Mr. Justice RUTLEDGE delivered the opinion of the Court.

On the merits this appeal presents substantial questions concerning the constitutional validity of ordinances of the City of Los Angeles governing the solicitation of contributions for charity.   First and Fourteenth Amendment grounds are urged as nullifying them chiefly in the view that they impose prior restraints upon and unduly abridge appellants' rights in the free exercise of their religion.   Those rights, as claimed, are to engage in soliciting donations for charity as a part of their religion free from the ordinances' restrictions.

.   .   .

Similar, but also distinct, questions were involved in Gospel Army v. Los Angeles, dismissed today for jurisdictional reasons. 331 U.S. 543. This case, however, arose procedurally in a different fashion, so that it is not subject to the same jurisdictional defect.   And the procedural difference is important, not merely for our jurisdiction but also for determining the propriety of exercising it in the special circumstances presented by this appeal.

The California Supreme Court heard and determined the Gospel Army case several months in advance of this one.   It sustained the regulations in both instances .   . ..   But the attack upon the city ordinances in the Gospel Army case covered a much wider range than here, and the court's principal opinion was rendered in that cause.   Hence in this case it disposed of overlapping issues merely by references a fortiori to its "approval" of the challenged provisions in the Gospel Army opinion.   .   .   .

[Both cases involved a municipal ordinance of the city of Los Angeles which set out a comprehensive scheme for the regulation of all solicitations. Article 4 specifically governed charitable solicitations, and included a large number of closely interrelated sections and subdivisions.   The Rescue Army brought this action to prohibit continuation of criminal proceedings against one of its officers, Murdock.   Murdock had been twice convicted in Los Angeles Municipal Court of violations of specified sections of the ordinance. Both convictions were reversed by the state court, one for admission of incompetent evidence, one because the evidence was insufficient.   Fearing further prosecution, the Rescue Army sought a writ of prohibition directed to the Municipal Court, on the ground that the sections in question constituted an unconstitutional interference with freedom of religion.   The state supreme court denied the writ, citing its Gospel Army opinion.

[Because of the state court's "mode of treatment" of this case, the "interlacing relationships" between the provisions involved in the two cases, and the dismissal of the Gospel Army appeal, the U. S. Supreme Court faced "difficult problems in determining exactly how much of the regulatory scheme approved in the Gospel Army opinion, and hence also how much of that decision, must be taken as having been incorporated" in the state court's determination of this case.   The references to the indictments in the two prior trials did not make it clear what sections were the basis for the convictions.   A literal view would require the determination of the constitutionality of every section in the Article, which might prove to be unnecessary after a more definite state court interpretation.   In the event that some sections of Article 4 were found to be unconstitutional, there would still remain the question for state determination as to the severability of the invalid sections.   The Gospel Army case was dismissed because the state court judgment upholding the regulations had remanded for further proceedings and hence was "not final for the purposes of our jurisdiction on appeal," see 28 U.S.C. § 1257.   "On the other hand this particular appeal is not subject to that . . . infirmity," since the state court prohibition proceeding was an "independent suit, in relation to the criminal prosecution."   The Court proceeded:]

While therefore we are unable to conclude that there is no jurisdiction in this cause, nevertheless compelling reasons exist for not exercising it.

From Hayburn's Case, 2 Dall. 409, to . . . . the Hatch Act case decided this term [United Public Workers v. Mitchell, 330 U.S. 75, p. 77, supra], this Court has followed a policy of strict necessity in disposing of constitutional issues.   The earliest exemplifications, too well known for repeating the history here, arose in the Court's refusal to render advisory opinions and in applications of the related jurisdictional policy drawn from the case and controversy limitation.   U.S.Const., Art. III.   The same policy has been reflected continuously not only in decisions but also in rules of court and in statutes made applicable to jurisdictional matters, including the necessity for reasonable clarity and definiteness, as well as for timeliness, in raising and presenting constitutional questions.   Indeed perhaps the most effective implement for making the policy effective has been the certiorari jurisdiction conferred upon this Court by Congress. . . .

The policy, however, has not been limited to jurisdictional determinations.   For, in addition, "the Court [has] developed, for its own governance in the cases confessedly within its jurisdiction, a series of rules under which it has avoided passing upon a large part of all the constitutional questions pressed upon it for decision."   [Ashwander] . . .

Some, if not indeed all, of these rules [in the Ashwander opinion] have found "most varied applications."   And every application has been an instance of reluctance, indeed, of refusal, to undertake the most important and the most delicate of the Court's functions, notwithstanding conceded jurisdiction, until necessity compels it in the performance of constitutional duty.

Moreover the policy is neither merely procedural nor in its essence dependent for applicability upon the diversities of jurisdiction and procedure, whether of the state courts, the inferior federal courts, or this Court.   Rather it is one of substance, grounded in considerations which transcend all such particular limitations.   Like the case and controversy limitation itself and the policy against entertaining political questions, it is one of the rules basic to the federal system and this Court's appropriate place within that structure.

Indeed in origin and in practical effects, though not in technical function, it is a corollary offshoot of the case and controversy rule.   And often the line between applying the policy or the rule is very thin.[1]   They work, within their respective and technically distinct areas, to achieve the same practical

1. Indeed more than once the policy has been applied in order to avoid the necessity of deciding the "case or controversy" jurisdictional question, when constitutional issues were at stake on the merits, e. g., recently in declaratory judgment proceedings. See . . . United Public Workers v. Mitchell, 330 U.S. 75. . . . [Footnote by the Court.]

purposes for the process of constitutional adjudication, and upon closely related considerations.

The policy's ultimate foundations, some if not all of which also sustain the jurisdictional limitation, lie in all that goes to make up the unique place and character, in our scheme, of judicial review of governmental action for constitutionality. They are found in the delicacy of that function, particularly in view of possible consequences for others stemming also from constitutional roots; the comparative finality of those consequences; the consideration due to the judgment of other repositories of constitutional power concerning the scope of their authority; the necessity, if government is to function constitutionally, for each to keep within its power, including the courts; the inherent limitations of the judicial process, arising especially from its largely negative character and limited resources of enforcement; withal in the paramount importance of constitutional adjudication in our system.

All these considerations and perhaps others, transcending specific procedures, have united to form and sustain the policy. Its execution has involved a continuous choice between the obvious advantages it produces for the functioning of government in all its coordinate parts and the very real disadvantages, for the assurance of rights, which deferring decision very often entails. On the other hand it is not altogether speculative that a contrary policy, of accelerated decision, might do equal or greater harm for the security of private rights, without attaining any of the benefits of tolerance and harmony for the functioning of the various authorities in our scheme. For premature and relatively abstract decision, which such a policy would be most likely to promote, have their part too in rendering rights uncertain and insecure.

As with the case and controversy limitation, however, the choice has been made long since. Time and experience have given it sanction. They also have verified for both that the choice was wisely made. Any other indeed might have put an end to or seriously impaired the distinctively American institution of judicial review.[2] And on the whole, in spite of inevitable exceptions, the policy has worked not only for finding the appropriate place and function of the judicial institution in our governmental system, but also for the preservation of individual rights.

Most recently both phases of its operation have been exemplified in declaratory judgment proceedings. Despite some seemingly widespread misconceptions,[3] the general introduction of that procedure in both state and federal spheres has not reversed or modified the policy's general direction or effects.

2. It is not without significance for the policy's validity that the periods when the power has been exercised most readily and broadly have been the ones in which this Court and the institution of judicial review have had their stormiest experiences. See, e. g., Brant, Storm Over the Constitution (1936). [Footnote by the Court.]

3. . . . [T]he procedure has been utilized to bring for decision challenges to an entire array of statutory provisions alleged to violate rights secured by an almost equal array of constitutional provisions. The strategic conception seems to have been that the declaratory judgment suit furnishes a ready vehicle for presenting and securing decision of constitutional matters, solely upon the pleadings, in highly abstract or premature, if not hypothetical states of fact, and *en masse.* Such a notion of course is essentially contradictory of the policy and, if accepted, would go far toward nullifying it. [Footnote by the Court.]

One aspect of the policy's application, it has been noted, has been by virtue of the presence of other grounds for decision. But when such alternatives are absent, as in this case, application must rest upon considerations relative to the manner in which the constitutional issue itself is shaped and presented.

These cannot be reduced to any precise formula or complete catalogue. But in general, as we have said, they are of the same nature as those which make the case and controversy limitation applicable, differing only in degree. To the more usual considerations of timeliness and maturity, of concreteness, definiteness, certainty, and of adversity of interests affected, are to be added in cases coming from state courts involving state legislation those arising when questions of construction, essentially matters of state law, remain unresolved or highly ambiguous. They include, of course, questions of incorporation by reference and severability, such as this case involves. Necessarily whether decision of the constitutional issue will be made must depend upon the degree to which uncertainty exists in these respects. And this inevitably will vary with particular causes and their varying presentations.

Accordingly the policy's applicability can be determined only by an exercise of judgment relative to the particular presentation, though relative also to the policy generally and to the degree in which the specific factors rendering it applicable are exemplified in the particular case. It is largely a question of enough or not enough, the sort of thing precisionists abhor but constitutional adjudication nevertheless constantly requires. [F]or a variety of reasons the shape in which the underlying constitutional issues have reached this Court presents, we think, insuperable obstacles to any exercise of jurisdiction to determine them.

Those reasons comprise not only obstacles of prematurity and comparative abstractness arising from the nature of the proceeding in prohibition and the manner in which the parties have utilized it for presenting the constitutional questions. They also include related considerations growing out of uncertainties resulting from the volume of legislative provisions possibly involved, their intricate interlacing not only with each other on their face but also in the California Supreme Court's disposition of them, and especially from its treatment of this case by reference in considerable part to the Gospel Army case, difficulties all accentuated for us of course by the necessity for dismissal of that cause here. . . .

We are not unmindful that our ruling will subject the petitioner Murdock to the burden of undergoing a third trial or that this burden is substantial. Were the uncertainties confronting us in relation to this Court's historic policy less in number, and resolving them not so far from our appropriate function in cases coming from state courts, the inconvenience of undergoing trial another time might justify exercising jurisdiction in this cause. But, consistently with the policy, jurisdiction here should be exerted only when the jurisdictional question presented by the proceeding in prohibition tenders the underlying constitutional issues in clean-cut and concrete form, unclouded by any serious problem of construction relating either to the terms of the questioned legislation or to its interpretation by the state courts.

Our decision of course should be without prejudice to any rights which may arise upon final determination of the Municipal Court proceeding, relative to review in this Court of that determination. With that reservation we think the only course consistent, upon this record, at once with preservation of appellants' rights and with adherence to our long-observed policy, is to decline to exercise jurisdiction in this cause.

Accordingly, the appeal is dismissed, without prejudice to the determination in the future of any issues arising under the Federal Constitution from further proceedings in the Municipal Court.

Mr. Justice BLACK concurs in the result.

Mr. Justice MURPHY, with whom Mr. Justice DOUGLAS concurs, dissenting.

It is difficult for me to believe that the opinion of the Supreme Court of California is so ambiguous that the precise constitutional issues in this case have become too blurred for our powers of discernment. . . .

THE NAIM DISMISSAL

1. *The litigation.* Mrs. Ruby Elaine Naim sued Mr. Ham Say Naim for an annulment of their marriage "on the ground of their racial ineligibility to marry one another," in view of the Virginia miscegenation law. The parties left Virginia in 1952 to be married in North Carolina, concededly "for the purpose of evading the Virginia law which forbade their marriage." After the marriage, they "immediately returned to Norfolk, Virginia, where they lived together as husband and wife." The state trial court found the marriage void and granted the annulment. The Supreme Court of Appeals of Virginia affirmed. It considered the federal constitutional objections to the miscegenation law at length—and rejected them all. 197 Va. 80, 87 S.E.2d 749 (1955). The case was brought to the United States Supreme Court by appeal. The full opinion of that Court, Naim v. Naim, 350 U.S. 891 (1955), follows:

"Appeal from the Supreme Court of Appeals of Virginia. *Per Curiam:* The inadequacy of the record as to the relationship of the parties to the Commonwealth of Virginia at the time of the marriage in North Carolina and upon their return to Virginia, and the failure of the parties to bring here all questions relevant to the disposition of the case, prevents the constitutional issue of the validity of the Virginia statute on miscegenation tendered here being considered 'in clean-cut and concrete form, unclouded' by such problems. Rescue Army v. Municipal Court, 331 U.S. 549, 584. The judgment is vacated and the case remanded to the Supreme Court of Appeals in order that the case may be returned to the Circuit Court of the City of Portsmouth for action not inconsistent with this opinion."

On remand, the Supreme Court of Appeals of Virginia stated [197 Va. 734, 90 S.E.2d 849 (1956)]: ". . . [T]he material facts were not . . . in dispute. The record showed that the complainant in the suit, a white woman, was an actual bona fide resident of, and domiciled in, Virginia, and had been for more than a year next preceding the commencement of the suit; that the defendant was a Chinese and a non-resident of Virginia at the time of the institution of the suit; that they had gone to North Carolina to be married for the purpose of evading the Virginia law which forbade their marriage, were married in North Carolina and immediately returned to and lived in Virginia as husband and wife. . . .

"The record before the Circuit Court of the City of Portsmouth was adequate for a decision of the issues presented to it. The record before this court was adequate for deciding the issues on review. The decision of the Circuit Court adjudicated the issues presented to that court. The decision of this court adjudicated the issues presented to it. The decree of the trial court and the decree of this court affirming it have become final so far as these courts are concerned.

"We have no provision either under the rules of practice and procedure of this Court or under the statute law of this Commonwealth by which this court may send the cause back to the Circuit Court with directions to re-open the cause so decided, gather additional evidence and render a new decision. . . .

"We therefore adhere to our decision of the cause and to the decree of this court which affirmed the final decree of the Circuit Court of the City of Portsmouth holding that the marriage of the parties to this cause was void."

The case was once again taken to the United States Supreme Court. That Court's per curiam opinion on the second appeal, 350 U.S. 985 (1956), follows in full:

"Appeal from the Supreme Court of Appeals of Virginia. The motion to recall the mandate and to set the case down for oral argument upon the merits, or, in the alternative, to recall and amend the mandate is denied. The decision of the Supreme Court of Appeals of Virginia of January 18, 1956, 197 Va. 734, 90 S.E.2d 849, in response to our order of November 14, 1955, 350 U.S. 891, leaves the case devoid of a properly presented federal question."

2. *The justification.* Was there any justification for the Court's disposition of the Naim case? In law? In policy? Do you agree with the comment that the dismissal of the appeal rested "on procedural grounds that . . . are wholly without basis in the law"? Wechsler, "Toward Neutral Principles of Constitutional Law," 73 Harv.L.Rev. 1, 34 (1959). Note also the Bickel-Gunther differences on this issue reflected in Gunther, "The Subtle Vices of the 'Passive Virtues'—A Comment on Principle and Expediency in Judicial Review," 64 Colum.L.Rev. 1, 11–12 (1964): "Bickel's [Bickel, The Least Dangerous Branch (1962)] cavalier amalgamation of certiorari and appeal is a vast if not mischievous overstatement, in fact and in law. . . . [He states:] 'Thus a decision on the validity of anti-miscegenation statutes was avoided through the dismissal of an appeal, which is to be explained in terms of the discretionary considerations that go to determine the lack of ripeness.' . . . In an earlier chapter, Bickel praised that dismissal as an example of the operation of 'techniques that allow leeway to expediency without abandoning principle'; 'the Court found no insuperable difficulty,' he notes with admiration, 'in leaving open the question of the constitutionality of anti-miscegenation statutes, though it would surely seem to be governed by the principle of the Segregation Cases' decided two years earlier. I will withhold comment for the moment on Bickel's judgment that this achievement was possible without 'abandoning principle'; the immediate question is Bickel's reliance on this dismissal for descriptive and normative purposes in handling appeals generally.

"Where . . . is the legal basis for the discretion Bickel would condone and indeed advocate in this and similar cases within the appeal jurisdiction?   No doubt there were strong considerations of expediency against considering the constitutionality of anti-miscegenation statutes in 1956.   But does not the appeal jurisdiction, too, have a 'content of its own'? The content of this 'passive virtue' device is of course more than minimal: it derives from congressional regulation of the Supreme Court's appellate jurisdiction.   .   .   .   The Court, to be sure, has sometimes honored the appeal statute in the breach: the miscegenation case is on the books, and there are a very few dismissals similarly indefensible in law.   But these are still only aberrations, and surely more can be expected of Bickel than to exaggerate them to the level of the commonplace and to elevate them to the level of the desirable and the acceptable."   [Eleven years after Naim, the Court reached the merits of an appeal challenging the Virginia miscegenation statutes, in Loving v. Virginia, 388 U.S. 1 (1967), involving criminal convictions of a white man and his Negro wife who had returned to Virginia after marrying in the District of Columbia.   The laws were held unconstitutional.   See chap. 18, p. 1412, below.]

POE v. ULLMAN
367 U.S. 497, 81 S.Ct. 1752, 6 L.Ed.2d 989 (1961).

Appeal from the Supreme Court of Errors of Connecticut.[*]

Mr. Justice FRANKFURTER announced the judgment of the Court in an opinion which The Chief Justice [WARREN], Mr. Justice CLARK and Mr. Justice WHITTAKER join.

These appeals challenge the constitutionality, under the Fourteenth Amendment, of Connecticut statutes which, as authoritatively construed by the Connecticut Supreme Court of Errors, prohibit the use of contraceptive devices and the giving of medical advice in the use of such devices.   In proceedings seeking declarations of law, not on review of convictions for violation of the statutes, that court has ruled that these statutes would be applicable in the case of married couples and even under claim that conception would constitute a serious threat to the health or life of the female spouse.

No. 60 combines two actions brought in a Connecticut Superior Court for declaratory relief.   The complaint in the first alleges that the plaintiffs Paul and Pauline Poe are a husband and wife   .   .   .   .   Mrs. Poe has had three consecutive pregnancies terminating in infants with multiple congenital abnormalities from which each died shortly after birth.   Plaintiffs have consulted Dr. Buxton, an obstetrician and gynecologist of eminence   .   .   .   . In view of the great emotional stress already suffered by plaintiffs, the probable consequence of another pregnancy is psychological strain extremely disturbing to the physical and mental health of both husband and wife.   Plaintiffs know that it is Dr. Buxton's opinion that the best and safest medical treatment which could be prescribed for their situation is advice in methods of preventing conception.   Dr. Buxton knows of drugs, medicinal articles and instruments which can be safely used to effect contraception.   Medically, the use of these devices is indicated as the best and safest preventive measure

---

[*] Together with Buxton v. Ullman, also on appeal from the Supreme Court of Errors of Connecticut.

necessary for the protection of plaintiffs' health. Plaintiffs, however, have been unable to obtain this information for the sole reason that its delivery and use may or will be claimed by the defendant State's attorney (appellee in this Court) to constitute offenses at Connecticut law. The State's attorney intends to prosecute offenses against the State's laws, and claims that the giving of contraceptive advice and the use of contraceptive devices would be offenses forbidden by Conn.Gen.Stat.Rev., 1958, §§ 53–32 and 54–196. Alleging irreparable injury and a substantial uncertainty of legal relations (a local procedural requisite for a declaration), plaintiffs ask a declaratory judgment that §§ 53–32 and 54–196 are unconstitutional, in that they deprive the plaintiffs of life and liberty without due process of law.

The second action in No. 60 is brought by Jane Doe, a twenty-five year-old housewife. . . . Mrs. Doe recently underwent a pregnancy which induced in her a critical physical illness . . . . Another pregnancy would be exceedingly perilous to her life. She, too, has consulted Dr. Buxton, who believes that the best and safest treatment for her is contraceptive advice. The remaining allegations of Mrs. Doe's complaint, and the relief sought are similar to those in the case of Mr. and Mrs. Poe.

In No. 61, also a declaratory judgment action, Dr. Buxton is the plaintiff. Setting forth facts identical to those alleged by Jane Doe, he asks that the Connecticut statutes prohibiting his giving of contraceptive advice to Mrs. Doe be adjudged unconstitutional, as depriving him of liberty and property without due process. . . .

Appellants' complaints in these declaratory proceedings do not clearly, and certainly do not in terms, allege that appellee Ullman threatens to prosecute them for use of, or for giving advice concerning, contraceptive devices. The allegations are merely that, in the course of his public duty, he intends to prosecute any offenses against Connecticut law, and that he claims that use of and advice concerning contraceptives would constitute offenses. The lack of immediacy of the threat described by these allegations might alone raise serious questions of non-justiciability of appellants' claims. See United Public Workers v. Mitchell, 330 U.S. 75, 88. But even were we to read the allegations to convey a clear threat of imminent prosecutions, we are not bound to accept as true all that is alleged on the face of the complaint and admitted, technically, by demurrer, any more than the Court is bound by stipulation of the parties. Swift & Co. v. Hocking Valley R. Co., 243 U.S. 281, 289. Formal agreement between parties that collides with plausibility is too fragile a foundation for indulging in constitutional adjudication.

The Connecticut law prohibiting the use of contraceptives has been on the State's books since 1879. . . . During the more than three quarters of a century since its enactment, a prosecution for its violation seems never to have been initiated, save in State v. Nelson, 126 Conn. 412, 11 A.2d 856. The circumstances of that case, decided in 1940, only prove the abstract character of what is before us. There, a test case was brought to determine the constitutionality of the act as applied against two doctors and a nurse who had allegedly disseminated contraceptive information. After the Supreme Court of Errors sustained the legislation on appeal from a demurrer to the information, the State moved to dismiss the information. Neither counsel nor our own researches have discovered any other attempt to enforce the prohibition of distribution or use of contraceptive devices by criminal process. The unreality of these law suits is illumined by another circumstance. We were advised by counsel for appellant that contraceptives are commonly and notoriously sold in Connecticut drug stores. Yet no prosecutions are recorded; and certainly such ubiquitous, open, public sales would more quickly invite the attention of enforcement officials than the conduct in which the present appellants wish to engage—the giving of private medical advice by a doctor to his individual patients, and their private use of the devices prescribed. The undeviating policy of nullification by Connecticut of its anti-contraceptive laws throughout all the long years that they have been on the statute books bespeaks more than prosecutorial paralysis. . . .

The restriction of our jurisdiction to cases and controversies within the meaning of Article III of the Constitution . . . is not the sole limitation on the exercise of our appellate powers, especially in cases raising constitutional questions. The policy reflected in numerous cases and over a long period was thus summarized in the oft-quoted statement of Mr. Justice Brandeis: "The Court [has] developed, for its own governance in the cases confessedly within its jurisdiction, a series of rules under which it has avoided passing upon a large part of all the constitutional questions pressed upon it for decision." Ashwander v. Tennessee Valley Authority, 297 U.S. 288, 341, 346 (concurring opinion). In part the rules summarized in the Ashwander opinion have derived from the historically defined, limited nature and function of courts and from the recognition that, within the framework of our adversary system, the adjudicatory process is most securely founded when it exercised under the impact of a lively conflict between antagonistic demands, actively pressed, which make resolution of the controverted issue a practical necessity. . . .

These considerations press with special urgency in cases challenging legislative action or state judicial action as repugnant to the Constitution. . . . The various doctrines of "standing," "ripeness," and "mootness," which this Court has evolved with particular, though not exclusive, reference to such cases are but several manifestations—each having its own "varied application"—of the primary conception that federal judicial power is to be exercised to strike down legislation, whether state or federal, only at the instance of one who is himself immediately harmed, or immediately threatened with harm, by the challenged action. . . .

. . . The Court has been on the alert against use of the declaratory judgment device for avoiding the rigorous insistence on exigent adversity as a condition for evoking Court adjudication. This is as true of state court suits for declaratory judgment as of federal. By exercising their jurisdiction, state courts cannot determine the jurisdiction to be exercised by this Court. Tyler v. Judges of the Court of Registration, 179 U.S. 405; Doremus v. Board of Education, 342 U.S. 429. Although we have held that a state declaratory-judgment suit may constitute a case or controversy within our appellate jurisdiction, it is to be reviewed here only "so long as the case retains the essentials of an adversary proceeding, involving a real, not a hypothetical, controversy, which is finally determined by the judgment below." Nashville, C. & St. L. R. Co. v. Wallace, 288 U.S. 249, 264. . . . Indeed, we have recognized, in such cases, that ". . . the discretionary element characteristic of declaratory jurisdiction, and imported perhaps from equity jurisdiction and practice without the remedial phase, offers a convenient instrument for making . . . effective" the policy against premature constitutional decision. Rescue Army v. Municipal Court, 331 U.S. 549, 573, n. 41.

Insofar as appellants seek to justify the exercise of our declaratory power by the threat of prosecution, facts which they can no more negative by complaint and demurrer than they could by stipulation preclude our determining their appeals on the merits. . . . If the prosecutor expressly agrees not to prosecute, a suit against him for declaratory and injunctive relief is not such an adversary case as will be reviewed here. C. I. O. v. McAdory, 325 U.S. 472, 475. Eighty years of Connecticut history demonstrate a similar, albeit tacit agreement. The fact that Connecticut has not chosen to press the enforcement of this statute deprives these controversies of the immediacy which is an indispensable condition of constitutional adjudication. This Court cannot be umpire to debates concerning harmless, empty shadows. To find it necessary to pass on these statutes now, in order to protect appellants from the hazards of prosecution, would be to close our eyes to reality.

Nor does the allegation by appellants Poe and Doe that they are unable to obtain information concerning contraceptive devices from Dr. Buxton "for the sole reason that the delivery and use of such information and advice may or will be claimed by the defendant State's Attorney to constitute offenses," disclose a necessity for present constitutional decision. It is true that this Court has several times passed upon criminal statutes challenged by persons who claimed that the effects of the statutes were to deter others from maintaining profitable or advantageous relations with the complainants. See, e. g., Truax v. Raich, 239 U.S. 33; Pierce v. Society of Sisters, 268 U.S. 510. But in these cases the deterrent effect complained of was one which was grounded in a realistic fear of prosecution. We cannot agree that if Dr. Buxton's compliance with these statutes is uncoerced by the risk of their enforcement, his patients, are entitled to a declaratory judgment concerning the statutes' validity. And, with due regard to Dr. Buxton's standing as a physician and to his personal sensitiveness, we cannot accept, as the basis of constitutional adjudication, other than as chimerical the fear of enforcement of provisions that have during so many years gone uniformly and without exception unenforced.

Justiciability is of course not a legal concept with a fixed content or susceptible of scientific verification. Its utilization is the resultant of many subtle pressures, including the appropriateness of the issues for decision by this Court and the actual hardship to the litigants of denying them the relief sought. Both these factors justify withholding adjudication of the constitutional issue raised under the circumstances and in the manner in which they are now before the Court.

Dismissed.

Mr. Justice BLACK dissents because he believes that the constitutional questions should be reached and decided.

Mr. Justice BRENNAN, concurring in the judgment.

I agree that this appeal must be dismissed for failure to present a real and substantial controversy which unequivocally calls for adjudication of the rights claimed in advance of any attempt by the State to curtail them by criminal prosecution. I am not convinced, on this skimpy record, that these appellants as individuals are truly caught in an inescapable dilemma. The true controversy in this case is over the opening of birth-control clinics on a large scale; it is that which the State has prevented in the past, not the use of contraceptives by isolated and individual married couples. It will be time enough to decide the constitutional questions urged upon us when, if ever, that real controversy flares up again. Until it does, or until the State makes a definite and concrete threat to enforce these laws against individual married couples—a threat which it has never made in the past except under the provocation of litigation this Court may not be compelled to exercise its most delicate power of constitutional adjudication.*

Mr. Justice DOUGLAS, dissenting. . . .

These cases are dismissed because a majority of the members of this Court conclude, for varying reasons, that this controversy does not present a justiciable question. That conclusion is too transparent to require an extended reply. The device of the declaratory judgment is an honored one.

. . . .

What are these people—doctor and patients—to do? Flout the law and go to prison? Violate the law surreptitiously and hope they will not get caught? By today's decision we leave them no other alternatives. It is not the choice they need have under   . . .   our constitutional system. [The discussion of the merits in the dissents is omitted. See Griswold v. Connecticut, 381 U.S. 479 (1965) (chap. 11, p. 824, below)].

Mr. Justice HARLAN, dissenting.

. . . In my view the course which the Court has taken does violence to established concepts of "justiciability," and unjustifiably leaves these appellants under the threat of unconstitutional prosecution. . . .

[T]he fact that justiciability is not precisely definable does not make it ineffable. Although a large number of cases are brought to bear on the conclusion that is reached, I think it is fairly demonstrable that the authorities fall far short of compelling dismissal of these appeals. . . .

[T]he Court, in the course of its decisions on matters of justiciability, has developed and given expression to a number of important limitations on the exercises of its jurisdiction, the presence or absence of which here should determine the justiciability of these appeals. Since all of them are referred to here in one way or another, it is well to proceed to a disclosure of those which are *not* involved in the present appeals, thereby focusing attention on

* Shortly after the decision in the principal case, the Planned Parenthood League of Connecticut opened a birth control clinic in New Haven "to provide information, instruction and medical advice to married persons concerning various means of contraception," and to furnish patients with "various contraceptive devices, drugs or materials." The State promptly brought charges against the executive director of the league, Mrs. Estelle T. Griswold, and the medical director of the center, Dr. C. Lee Buxton (one of the appellants in the principal case). The defendants were convicted of aiding, abetting and counselling married women in the violation of Connecticut's ban against contraceptives. The Connecticut Supreme Court of Errors relied on its earlier decisions in rejecting the constitutional challenges and affirming the convictions. State v. Griswold, 151 Conn. 544, 200 A.2d 479 (1964). On appeal, the United States Supreme Court reached the constitutional merits at last and held the law unconstitutional. Griswold v. Connecticut, 381 U.S. 479 (1965) (chap. 11, p. 824, below). The Griswold Court's comments on standing are printed in the notes following Tileston v. Ullman, sec. 2, p. 86, above.

the one factor on which reliance appears to be placed by both the plurality and concurring opinions in this instance.

First: It should by now be abundantly clear that the fact that only Constitutional claims are presented in proceedings seeking *anticipatory* relief against state criminal statutes does not for that reason alone make the claims premature. . . .

Hence, any language in the cases where the Court has abstained from exercising its jurisdiction, to the effect that we should not "entertain Constitutional questions in advance of the strictest necessity" . . . is not at all apposite in the present cases. For these appeals come to us from the highest court of Connecticut, thus affording us—in company with previous State interpretations of the same statute—with a clear construction of the scope of the statute, thereby in effect assuring that our review constitutes no greater interference with state administration than the state procedures themselves allow.

Second: I do not think these appeals may be dismissed for want of "ripeness" as that concept has been understood in its "varied application." . . . Certainly the appellants have stated in their pleadings fully and unequivocally what it is that they intend to do; no clarifying or resolving contingency stands in their way before they may embark on that conduct. Thus there is no circumstance besides that of detection or prosecution to make remote the particular controversy. And it is clear beyond cavil that the mere fact that a controversy such as this is rendered still more unavoidable by an actual prosecution, is not *alone* sufficient to make the case too remote, not ideally enough "ripe" for adjudication, at the prior stage of anticipatory relief. . . .

Third: This is not a feigned, hypothetical, friendly or colorable suit such as discloses "a want of truly adversary contest." . . .

Indeed, as will be developed below, I think both the plurality and concurring opinions confuse on this score the predictive likelihood that, had they not brought themselves to appellee's attention, he would not enforce the statute against them, with some entirely suppositious "tacit agreement" not to prosecute, thereby ignoring the prosecutor's claim, asserted in these very proceedings, of a right, at his unbounded prosecutorial discretion to enforce the statute.

Fourth: The doctrine of the cases dealing with a litigant's lack of standing to raise a Constitutional claim is said to justify the dismissal of these appeals. . . . But this doctrine in turn needs further particularization lest it become a catch-all for an unarticulated discretion on the part of this Court to decline to adjudicate appeals involving Constitutional issues.

There is no question but that appellants here are asserting rights which are peculiarly their own, and which, if they are to be raised at all, may be raised most appropriately by them. Cf. Tileston v. Ullman, 318 U.S. 44. . . . Nor do I understand the argument to be that this is the sort of claim which is too remote ever to be pressed by anyone, because no one is ever sufficiently involved. Cf. Massachusetts v. Mellon, Frothingham v. Mellon, supra. Thus, in truth, it is not the parties pressing this claim but the occasion chosen for pressing it which is objected to. But as has been shown the fact that it is anticipatory relief which is asked cannot of itself make the occasion objectionable.

We are brought, then, to the precise failing in these proceedings which is said to justify refusal to exercise our mandatory appellate jurisdiction: that there has been but one recorded Connecticut case dealing with a *prosecution* under the statute. The significance of this lack of recorded evidence of prosecutions is said to make the presentation of appellants' rights too remote, too contingent, too hypothetical for adjudication in the light of the policies already considered. . . . In my view it is only as a result of misconceptions both about the purport of the record before us and about the nature of the rights appellants put forward that this conclusion can be reached.

As far as the record is concerned, I think it is pure conjecture, and indeed conjecture which to me seems contrary to realities, that an open violation of the statute by a doctor (or more obviously still by a birth control clinic) would not result in a substantial threat of prosecution. Crucial to the opposite conclusion is the description of the 1940 prosecution instituted in State v. Nelson, 126 Conn. 412, 11 A.2d 856, as a "test case" which, as it is viewed, scarcely even punctuates the uniform State practice of nonenforcement of this statute. I read the history of Connecticut enforcement in a very different light. . . .

. . . In short, I fear that the Court has indulged in a bit of slight-of-hand to be rid of the case. It has treated the significance of the absence of prosecutions during the twenty years since Nelson as identical with that of the absence of prosecutions during the years before Nelson. It has ignored the fact that the very purpose of the Nelson prosecution was to change defiance into compliance. It has ignored the very possibility that this purpose may have been successful.[1] The result is to postulate a security from prosecution for open defiance of the statute which I do not believe the record supports.

These considerations alone serve to bring appellants so squarely within the rule of Pierce v. Society of Sisters, 268 U.S. 510, and Truax v. Raich, 239 U.S. 33, that further demonstration would be pointless. . . .

The Court's disposition assumes that to decide the case now, in the absence of any consummated prosecutions, is unwise because it forces a difficult decision in advance of any exigent necessity therefor. . . . What is meant is simply that the appellants are more or less free to act without fear of prosecution because the prosecuting authorities of the State, in their discretion and at their whim, are, as a matter of prediction, unlikely to decide to prosecute.

Here is the core of my disagreement with the present disposition. As I will develop later in this opinion, the most substantial claim which these

---

[1] The concurring opinion concludes, apparently on the basis of the Nelson episode that the "true controversy in this case is over the opening of birth-control clinics on a large scale . . . ." It should be said at once that as to *these* appeals this is an entirely unwarranted assumption. . . .

In sum, the strong implication of the concurring opinion that a suit for anticipatory relief brought by a birth-control clinic (though it would raise no different issues and present a record no less "skimpy") would succeed in invoking our jurisdiction where these suits fail, exposes the fallacy underlying the Court's disposition: the unprecedented doctrine that a suit for anticipatory relief will be entertained at the instance of one who is forced to violate a statute flagrantly, but not at the urging of one who may violate it surreptitiously with a high probability of avoiding detection. [Footnote by Justice Harlan.]

married persons press is their right to enjoy the privacy of their marital relations free of the enquiry of the criminal law, whether it be in a prosecution of them or of a doctor whom they have consulted. And I cannot agree that their enjoyment of this privacy is not substantially impinged upon, when they are told that if they use contraceptives, indeed whether they do so or not, the only thing which stands between them and being forced to render criminal account of their marital privacy is the whim of the prosecutor.

· · ·

If we revert again to the reasons underlying our reluctance to exercise a jurisdiction which technically we possess, and the concrete expression of those underlying reasons in our cases,   .   .   .   then I think it must become clear that there is no justification for failing to decide these married persons' appeals.   .   .   .   It seems to me to destroy the whole purpose of anticipatory relief to consider the prosecutor's discretion, once all legal and administrative channels have been cleared, as in any way analogous to those other contingencies which make remote a controversy presenting Constitutional claims.   .   .   .

Mr. Justice STEWART [also noted a dissent from the dismissal of the appeals].

THE POE DISMISSAL

1. *The justification.* Poe v. Ullman, like Rescue Army and Naim, was a refusal to adjudicate a state court case apparently within the Court's obligatory appeal jurisdiction. Was the Poe dismissal any more justifiable? Note Gunther, "The Subtle Vices of the 'Passive Virtues'—A Comment on Principle and Expediency in Judicial Review," 64 Colum.L.Rev. 1, 12 (1964), commenting on Bickel, The Least Dangerous Branch (1962): "[Bickel states] that it was 'wise' and proper that the Court withheld decision [in Poe v. Ullman]. And nothing but a 'dictum in Cohens v. Virginia' stood in the way of the Court's refusal to adjudicate. Was that all that really stood in the way? John Marshall, in Cohens, uttered words which Bickel repeatedly undertakes to disparage, for they flatly contradict his notions of permissible Court abstention. 'We have no more right to decline the exercise of jurisdiction which is given,' Marshall said, 'than to usurp that which is not given.' But the only way in which this can be viewed as insignificant dictum is to argue that there are no adequate reference points for determination of the jurisdiction assigned to the Court. But there are: there is the Constitution; there is the statute. Under Bickel's analysis as well as the Court's, Poe v. Ullman was a 'case' within Article III; moreover, it was one of that small group of cases Congress has made it the Court's duty to decide." See also Note, "The Discretionary Power of the Supreme Court to Dismiss Appeals From State Courts," 63 Colum.L.Rev. 688 (1963), and Note, "Threat of Enforcement—Prerequisite of a Justiciable Controversy," 62 Colum.L.Rev. 106 (1962).

2. *The "monkey law" case: evolution in justiciability?* Compare the majority's summary disposition of the justiciability issue in Epperson v. Arkansas, 393 U.S. 97 (1968), a state court challenge to a 1928 law barring the teaching of evolution (the "monkey law" case noted further in chap. 17, p. 1372.) Justice Fortas' majority opinion simply noted: "There is no rec-

ord of any prosecutions in Arkansas under its statute. It is possible that the statute is presently more of a curiosity than a vital fact of life in [Arkansas, Mississippi, and Tennessee]. Nevertheless, the present case was brought, the appeal as of right is properly here, and it is our duty to decide the issues presented." Only Justice Black was troubled: "I am by no means sure that this case presents a genuinely justiciable case or controversy." Yet the Court "brushes aside these doubts and leaps headlong into the middle of the very broad problems involved," in the face of the state's "pallid, unenthusiastic, even apologetic defense of the Act," and merely because, nearly forty years "after the law has slumbered on the books as though dead, a teacher alleging fear that the State might arouse from its lethargy and try to punish her has asked for a declaratory judgment holding the law unconstitutional."

INTERPRETING STATUTES TO AVOID CONSTITUTIONAL QUESTIONS

1. *The policy and its risks.* a. *The principle.* "[I]t is a cardinal principle that this Court will first ascertain whether a construction of the statute is fairly possible by which the [constitutional] question may be avoided." So ended the last of Justice Brandeis' seven rules in the Ashwander case, above; and that statement echoes a principle enunciated by the Court from the beginning. Indeed, Chief Justice Marshall, in the very case juxtaposed with the Brandeis rules at the beginning of this section, decided the merits on the basis of statutory interpretation: where such a basis is available, he said, "it will be unnecessary, and consequently improper, to pursue any inquiries, which would then be merely speculative, respecting the power of Congress in the case." Cohens v. Virginia, 6 Wheat. 264, 441 (1821).

b. *Statutory distortion risks.* The principle has obvious limitations, however. See Chief Justice Vinson's warning in Shapiro v. United States, 335 U.S. 1, 31 (1948): "The canon of avoidance of constitutional doubts must, like the 'plain meaning' rule [in the interpretation of statutes], give way where its application would produce a futile result, or an unreasonable result 'plainly at variance with the policy of the legislation as a whole'." Note, in the materials that follow, the applications of the technique of avoidance through interpretations of statutes (or regulations). See, e. g., Watkins v. United States, 354 U.S. 178 (1957); Greene v. McElroy, 360 U.S. 474 (1959); Pennsylvania v. Nelson, 350 U.S. 497 (1956), all infra; cf. Note, "Pre-Emption as a Preferential Ground: A New Canon of Construction," 12 Stan.L.Rev. 208 (1959), Selected Essays 1938–62 (1963), 310, chap. 8, p. 671, infra. See generally, Note, "Supreme Court Interpretation of Statutes to Avoid Constitutional Decisions," 53 Colum.L.Rev. 633 (1953). Note the interpretation to avoid constitutional issues in Schneider v. Smith, 390 U.S. 17 (1968), finding lack of statutory authorization for the merchant seamen's security screening program; but compare the reliance on constitutional grounds (rather than on the statutory interpretation route taken by the lower court) in invalidating another internal security measure a month earlier, in United States v. Robel, 389 U.S. 258 (1967), see Gunther, "Reflections on Robel—It's Not What the Court Did, But the Way That It Did It," 20 Stan.L.Rev. 1140 (1968).

c. *Constitutional trial balloons.* This avoidance technique risks not only indefensible statutory interpretation but also irresponsible constitutional adjudication. There may be temptation to strain for a meaning in the statute beyond that "fairly possible" in order to avoid constitutional interpretation. Yet constitutional interpretation may not be wholly avoided: tentative interpretations may be ventured in the very process of stating *what* constitutional issues are being avoided; there may be temptation to launch constitutional trial balloons and indulge in free floating constitutional dicta without the restraints of fashioning constitutional law dispositive of the case. Do the following materials illustrate that risk?

2. *Kent v. Dulles and the remanding function.* Consider, with respect to these risks, the disposition in Kent v. Dulles, 357 U.S. 116 (1958). Were its constitutional statements akin to an advisory opinion? Is advice acceptable in this context because it is only tentative, because it serves to make Congress sensitive to constitutional issues, yet leaves to Congress opportunity to change the scope of the statute? Kent had been denied a passport pursuant to the Secretary of State's regulation requiring an applicant to submit an affidavit "as to whether he was then or ever had been a Communist." The statutory authority relied on was an act adopted in 1856, 22 U.S.C. § 211a: "The Secretary of State may grant and issue passports . . . under such rules as the President shall designate and prescribe for and on behalf of the United States, and no other person shall grant, issue, or verify such passports." In 1952, Congress adopted a law stating that, after a prescribed proclamation by the President, it is "unlawful for any citizen of the United States to depart from or enter, or attempt to depart from or enter, the United States unless he bears a valid passport." 8 U.S.C. § 1185. The Court "only conclude[d] that § 1185 and § 211a do not delegate to the Secretary the kind of authority exercised here," according to Justice Douglas' majority opinion. "Thus we do not reach the question of constitutionality," he asserted. Yet the opinion contained several passages elaborating the constitutional right underlying the statutory interpretation:

"The right to travel is a part of the 'liberty' of which the citizen cannot be deprived without the due process of law of the Fifth Amendment. So much is conceded by the Solicitor General . . . . Freedom of movement is basic in our scheme of values. . . . Freedom of movement also has large social values. . . . Freedom to travel is, indeed, an important aspect of the citizen's 'liberty.' We need not decide the extent to which it can be curtailed. . . . Since we start with an exercise by an American citizen of an activity included in constitutional protection, we will not readily infer that Congress gave the Secretary of State unbridled discretion to grant or withhold it. . . . [T]he right of exit is a personal right included within the word 'liberty' as used in the Fifth Amendment. If that 'liberty' is to be regulated, it must be pursuant to the lawmaking functions of the Congress. . . . And if that power is delegated, the standards must be adequate to pass scrutiny by the accepted tests. . . . Where activities or enjoyment, natural and often necessary to the well-being of an American citizen, such as travel, are involved, we will construe narrowly all delegated powers that curtail or dilute them. . . . We hesitate to find in this broad generalized power an authority to trench so heavily on the rights of the citizen. . . . To repeat, we deal here with a constitutional right of the citizen, a right which we must assume Congress will be faithful to respect. We would be faced with important constitutional questions were we to hold that Congress by § 1185 and § 211a had given the Secretary authority to withhold passports to citizens because of their beliefs or associations. Congress has made no such provision in explicit terms; and absent one, the Secretary may not employ that standard to restrict the citizens' right of free movement." *

Compare the advocacy of a Court "remanding" function—sending back to Congress "for a second reading" a statutory problem "the implications of which Congress failed to see"—in Bickel and Wellington, "Legislative Purpose and the Judicial Process: The Lincoln Mills Case," 71 Harv.L.Rev. 1 (1957). Was the Court exercising a "remanding" function in Kent v. Dulles? Cf. Bickel, "Foreword: The Passive Virtues," 75 Harv.L.Rev. 40 (1961), Selected Essays 1938–62 (1963), 24. Can the exercise of the "remanding" function be called "statutory interpretation"? Is the Court authorized to "remand" to Congress? Compare Justice Frankfurter's statement in Textile Workers Union v. Lincoln Mills, 353 U.S. 448, 460 (1957): "[T]his Court cannot do what a President sometimes does in returning a bill to Congress. We cannot return this provision [Section 301 of the Taft-Hartley Act] to Congress and respectfully request that body to face the responsibility placed upon it by the Constitution to define the jurisdiction of the lower courts with some particularity and not to leave these courts at large."

DISTRICT COURT ABSTENTION

Introduction. The Supreme Court is not the only tribunal that occasionally declines to adjudicate even though jurisdiction is granted by the Constitution and the statutes. The federal District Courts, too, have exercised a discretion to abstain, and more frequently than the Supreme Court. Is District Court abstention more justifiable? When should federal courts abstain so that state courts may decide?

Federal district court abstention has been especially important and controversial in suits challenging state action on federal grounds—suits made possible by a Supreme Court decision in 1908, Ex parte Young. Congress was asked to curtail the exercise of the Ex parte Young jurisdiction; but the legislative restrictions imposed were of limited scope (note 1 below). Since

---

* Note the subsequent fate of passport restrictions in the Court: In Aptheker v. Secretary of State, 378 U.S. 500 (1964) (p. 1121, infra) the Court held "unconstitutional on its face" § 6 of the Subversive Activities Control Act of 1950, making it a crime for members of certain Communist organizations to obtain or use passports. The Court found that the Section "too broadly and indiscriminately restricts the right to travel and thereby abridges the liberty guaranteed by the Fifth Amendment." But in Zemel v. Rusk, 381 U.S. 1 (1965), a divided Court sustained the State Department's author-

ity, under the broad statute involved in Kent v. Dulles, to refuse passports for travel to Cuba. In attempting to distinguish Kent, the majority noted that there had been an administrative practice of area restrictions on travel prior to Congress' reenactment of § 211(a) in 1926, and that the action here rested on "foreign policy considerations affecting all citizens," rather than "any characteristic peculiar to appellant." But the area restrictions sustained in Zemel are not criminally enforceable under the statutory provision requiring "a valid passport for travel." United States v. Laub, 385 U.S. 475 (1967).

1940, Court decisions have made significant additional inroads on federal jurisdiction (notes 2 and 3); and the judicially-developed doctrines regarding District Court abstention have produced much confusion and delay (note 4). The American Law Institute has recently suggested that abstention once again be placed entirely on statutory grounds: the ALI's recent proposals for revisions of Title 28 of the United States Code include a "rationalized and simplified" abstention section (note 5). The especially sharp controversy about the application of abstention and related doctrines in civil rights and liberties litigation is reflected in note 6 and in Dombrowski v. Pfister, the next principal case.

1. *Statutory restrictions and Ex parte Young.* Ex parte Young, 209 U.S. 123 (1908), made possible the broad and frequently invoked application of federal jurisdiction to state official action. A federal district court had ordered Young, a state attorney general, to cease enforcing a law regulating railroad rates, on the ground that it violated the Fourteenth Amendment. The Supreme Court held that the Eleventh Amendment assurance of state immunity from federal court suits did not bar the suit against the state official: "If the Act which the state Attorney General seeks to enforce be a violation of the Federal Constitution, the officer in proceeding under such enactment, comes into conflict with the superior authority of that Constitution, and he is in that case stripped of his official or representative character and is subjected in his person to the consequences of his individual conduct." [And two years later the Court found that such "individual conduct" not entitled to the Eleventh Amendment state immunity nevertheless constituted "state action" within the reach of the Fourteenth Amendment's restraints. Home Tel. and Tel. Co. v. Los Angeles, 227 U.S. 278 (1913).]

The pleas that Congress close the doors opened by Ex parte Young met only limited success: in 1910, a statute was enacted requiring that there be three-judge federal courts in most cases challenging state action (28 U.S.C. § 2281); the Johnson Act of 1934 (28 U.S.C. § 1342) prohibits most federal injunctions against state rate orders where "a plain, speedy and efficient remedy" in state courts is available; and a 1937 law (28 U.S.C. § 1341) similarly bars federal injunctions against state taxes. But Congress left many doors to the federal courts open. Thereafter, the Supreme Court undertook to close some of the doors Congress had not seen fit to shut. Why? How adequate were the justifications?

2. *The Pullman case.* Railroad Commission v. Pullman Co., 312 U.S. 496 (1941), launched the modern history of judicially-developed District Court abstention. There, a state agency's order was challenged as violating state law as well as the federal Constitution. Justice Frankfurter's opinion for a unanimous Court directed the District Court to "stay its hand": "to retain the bill pending a determination of proceedings, to be brought with reasonable promptness, in the state court." Adjudication of the unclear state law issue might make decision on the constitutional question unnecessary. A lower federal court's decision of the state issue "cannot escape being a forecast rather than a determination"; the "resources of equity are equal to an adjustment that will avoid the waste of a tentative decision as well as the friction of a premature constitutional adjudication." Justice Frankfurter spoke of "a doctrine of abstention appropriate to our federal system whereby the federal courts, 'exercising a wise discretion,' restrain their authority because of 'scrupulous regard for the rightful independence of the state governments' and for

the smooth working of the federal judiciary." And this judge-made doctrine was appropriate even though it went beyond the limitations Congress had seen fit to impose: "This use of equitable powers is a contribution of the courts in furthering the harmonious relation between state and federal authority without the need of rigorous congressional restriction of those powers."

3. *The Alabama Public Service case.* Compare Justice Frankfurter's separate opinion a decade later, in Alabama Public Service Commission v. Southern Ry., 341 U.S. 341 (1951). A railroad suit in a federal court challenged, under the Due Process Clause, a state order barring discontinuance of certain railroad passenger service. The Court found no unclear state statutory issue, as in Pullman, and no constitutional challenge to the state statute as such. Nor was federal action barred by the Johnson Act. Nevertheless, Chief Justice Vinson's majority opinion concluded that the federal court's jurisdiction "should not be exercised in this case as a matter of sound equitable discretion." He noted that "adequate state court review of an administrative order based upon predominantly local factors is available" and stated that the court should not act unless it "is convinced that the asserted federal right cannot be preserved except by granting" federal injunctive relief.

Justice Frankfurter's opinion concurring in the result, joined by Justice Jackson, protested that the Court's order directing the District Court to dismiss the suit rested on "a line of argument in plain disregard of congressional legislation." Was Justice Frankfurter's Pullman opinion, supra, subject to the same criticism? Compare also his opinion on Supreme Court discretion to abstain, in Poe v. Ullman, supra. In Alabama Public Service, Justice Frankfurter would have ordered dismissal because of the insubstantiality of the constitutional claim. But the majority's reasons, he insisted, flew in the face of the Court's "consistent" view "that it cannot overrule the determination of Congress as to whether federal courts should be allowed jurisdiction, concurrent with the State courts, even where the plaintiff seeks to restrain action of a state agency." He noted that the jurisdictional issue "has been continuously before Congress," and that "explicit and detailed legislation" controlled. He insisted that the "obligatory jurisdiction" Congress had left to the federal courts was "not to be denied because as a matter of policy it might be more desirable to raise such constitutional claims in the state courts." The Court, he argued, had in effect amended the federal question jurisdiction grant (28 U.S.C. § 1331), and it did not "change the significance of the Court's decision to coat it with the sugar of equity maxims. . . . By one fell swoop the Court now finds that Congress indulged in needless legislation in the Acts of 1910, 1913, 1925, 1934, and 1937." [See also the judicially-developed area of abstention recognized in Burford v. Sun Oil Co., 319 U.S. 315 (1943), where the Court stated that federal jurisdiction should have been "declined" in an action challenging a Texas oil proration order, because Texas courts were "working partners" with the state agency in developing the complex "regulatory system for the oil industry." The Court was divided, with Justice Frankfurter writing the dissenting opinion.]

4. *The consequences of abstention—confusion and delay.* Are the institutional values of abstention (such as avoidance of needless constitutional adjudication and of federal-state friction) worth the cost? Not only has there been uncertainty in determining when abstention is appropriate, but there has been confusion as well about what should happen when a federal court chooses to abstain: Is abstention merely a postponement of federal adjudication, or a

total relinquishment? Should the court stay or dismiss? Should the entire case go to the state courts, or only a portion? Should state adjudication (with the availability of Supreme Court review) end the litigation, or may the litigant return to the federal District Court?

The Court has repeatedly insisted, as in Harrison v. NAACP, 360 U.S. 167 (1959), that abstention does not "involve the abdication of federal jurisdiction but only the postponement of its exercise." Yet the federal as well as the state issues are often presented to the state court after the federal trial court abstains, and the state court's decision is often reviewable in the Supreme Court. Thus the case may never return to the federal trial court. Indeed, the Court has occasionally insisted that the federal as well as the state issue must be submitted to the state court. See Government Employees v. Windsor, 353 U.S. 364 (1957). But see the "clarification" in England v. Louisiana Medical Examiners, 375 U.S. 411 (1964): "The [Windsor] case does not mean that a party must litigate his federal claims in the state courts, but only that he must inform those courts what his federal claims are, so that the state statute may be construed 'in light of' those claims." What if the state courts then proceed to adjudicate the federal claim they have been "informed" about?

In England, the Court tried to clarify the procedure upon abstention: "It is true that, after a post-abstention determination . . . by the state courts, a litigant could seek direct review in this Court. . . . But such review . . . is an inadequate substitute for the initial District Court determination . . . to which the litigant is entitled in the federal courts. This is true as to issues of law; it is especially true as to issues of fact. . . . [A] party may elect to forgo that right. . . . But we see no reason why a party, after unreservedly litigating his federal claims in the state courts although not required to do so, should be allowed to ignore the adverse state decision and start all over again in the District Court." [Extensive delays may ensue while uncertainties such as these are resolved: five years of litigation in Windsor failed to produce a ruling on the merits; in England, a ruling on the merits came after nine years.]

5. *The ALI proposal.* The American Law Institute's proposals for revisions of Title 28 of the United States Code include a new § 1371 designed to set forth all of the circumstances in which a three-judge district court may abstain in favor of state adjudication. ALI, Study of the Division of Jurisdiction Between State and Federal Courts (1969), 48–50 (text), 282–98 (commentary). Subsections (a) and (b) of the proposed § 1371 are based on the Johnson Act and the tax injunction statute adopted in the 1930's (note 1 above). The ALI's effort to codify the desirable parts of the judicially-developed abstention doctrines are in subsection (c), quoted below. [Subsection (f) bars abstention beyond the circumstances set forth in the new statute: it prohibits additional "judge-made notions of abstention."] Subsection (d) clarifies the consequences of abstention: abstention produces a stay, not a dismissal; but ordinarily litigation through the state court route (with the possibility of Supreme Court review) ends the case. Subsection (g) excepts certain actions from the abstention authorization of § 1371: suits by the United States; and some civil rights actions (see note 6, below). The core abstention section, § 1371(c), would provide:

"A district court may stay an action, otherwise properly commenced in or removed to a district court under this title, on the ground that the action presents issues of State law that ought to be determined in a State proceeding, if the court finds: (1) that the issues of State law cannot be satisfactorily determined in the light of the State authorities; and (2) that abstention from the exercise of federal jurisdiction is warranted either by the likelihood that the necessity for deciding a substantial question of federal constitutional law may thereby be avoided, or by a serious danger of embarrassing the effectuation of State policies by a decision of State law at variance with the view that may be ultimately taken by the State court, or by other circumstances of like character; and (3) that a plain, speedy, and efficient remedy may be had in the courts of such State; and (4) that the parties' claims of federal right, if any, including any issues of fact material thereto, can be adequately protected by review of the State court decision by the Supreme Court of the United States."

The ALI concluded (at 285) that there was "no wholly satisfactory answer" in fashioning an acceptable abstention doctrine: "To litigate these cases entirely through the federal courts strains state-federal relations, may make necessary the premature decision of federal constitutional questions, and requires the federal court to pass on questions of state law in circumstances under which an erroneous decision may seriously interfere with state substantive policies. To litigate such cases entirely through the state courts, with review in the United States Supreme Court, deprives plaintiff of federal fact-finding, and of federal protection during the pendency of the state action. To shuttle the cases back and forth from state to federal court, as present doctrines permit, 'operates to require piecemeal adjudication in many courts.'"

The ALI decided against authorizing abstention "merely to avoid a federal constitutional question." The commentary explains, at 287: "The risk that the federal court will decide a constitutional question unnecessarily, because it has made an erroneous determination of some question of state law, does not seem sufficiently grave to justify imposing on litigants the delay and expense of abstention." Under the proposal, for example, presence of an avoidable constitutional issue [§ 1371(c) (2)] does not justify deferring to a state court "in a case where there are fact issues material to the federal claim of such importance as to preclude a stay under § 1371(c) (4)." [The federal court retaining jurisdiction in such cases may nevertheless be able to avoid constitutional rulings by deciding them on dispositive state grounds. See Siler v. Louisville & N. R. R., 213 U.S. 175 (1909).]

6. *Abstention and civil rights.* The propriety of abstention in suits to protect federal civil rights and liberties has long stirred controversy. The Court has rejected arguments that federal courts should *always* refuse to abstain in civil rights cases. See, e. g., the divided Court's ruling in Harrison v. NAACP, 360 U.S. 167 (1959). But cases such as Dombrowski v. Pfister, which follows, illustrate the powerful claim of certain constitutional rights to prompt federal adjudication. And the recent ALI proposal for a new 28 U.S.C. § 1371 goes a long way (though far from all the way) toward barring abstention in civil rights cases, because "of an especially strong national interest in a federal forum for such cases." § 1371(g) requires the district courts to adjudicate actions for denials of the right to vote or of equal protection, "if such denial is alleged to be on the basis of race, creed, color or national origin." [On abstention generally see, in addition to the ALI commentary, Wright, Federal Courts (1963), 157–77.]

DOMBROWSKI v. PFISTER

380 U.S. 479, 85 S.Ct. 1116, 14 L.Ed.2d 22 (1965).

Appeal from the United States District Court for the Eastern District of Louisiana.

Mr. Justice BRENNAN delivered the opinion of the Court.

Appellants filed a complaint in the District Court for the Eastern District of Louisiana, invoking the Civil Rights Act [42 U.S.C. § 1983] and seeking declaratory relief and an injunction restraining appellees—the Governor, police and law enforcement officers, and the Chairman of the Legislative Joint Committee on Un-American Activities in Louisiana—from prosecuting or threatening to prosecute appellants for alleged violations of the Louisiana Subversive Activities and Communist Control Law and the Communist Propaganda Control Law. Appellant Southern Conference Educational Fund, Inc. (SCEF), is active in fostering civil rights for Negroes in Louisiana and other States of the South. Appellant Dombrowski is its Executive Director; intervenor Smith, its Treasurer; and intervenor Waltzer, Smith's law partner and an attorney for SCEF. The complaint alleges that the statutes on their face violate the First and Fourteenth Amendment guarantees securing freedom of expression, because overbreadth makes them susceptible of sweeping and improper application abridging those rights. Supported by affidavits and a written offer of proof, the complaint further alleges that the threats to enforce the statutes against appellants are not made with any expectation of securing valid convictions, but rather are part of a plan to employ arrests, seizures, and threats of prosecution under color of the statutes to harass appellants and discourage them and their supporters from asserting and attempting to vindicate the constitutional rights of Negro citizens of Louisiana.

A three-judge district court . . . dismissed the complaint . . . . The majority were of the view that the allegations conceded to raise serious constitutional issues, did not present a case of threatened irreparable injury to federal rights which warranted cutting short the normal adjudication of constitutional defenses in the course of state criminal prosecutions; rather, the majority held, this was an appropriate case for abstention, since a possible narrowing construction by the state courts would avoid unnecessary decision of constitutional questions. . . .

We reverse.

In Ex parte Young, 209 U.S. 123, the fountainhead of federal injunctions against state prosecutions, the Court characterized the power and its proper exercise in broad terms: it would be justified where state officers ". . . threaten and are about to commence proceeding, either of a civil or criminal nature, to enforce against parties affected an unconstitutional act, violating the Federal Constitution . . ." 209 U.S., at 156. Since that decision, however, considerations of federalism have tempered the exercise of equitable power,[1] for the Court has recognized that federal interfer-

---

1. 28 U.S.C. § 2283 (1958 ed.) provides that:

"A court of the United States may not grant an injunction to stay proceedings in a State court except as expressly authorized by Act of Congress,

or where necessary in aid of its jurisdiction, or to protect or effectuate its judgments."

The District Court did not suggest that this statute denied power to issue the

ence with a State's good-faith administration of its criminal laws is peculiarly inconsistent with our federal framework. It is generally to be assumed that state courts and prosecutors will observe constitutional limitations as expounded by this Court, and that the mere possibility of erroneous initial application of constitutional standards will usually not amount to the irreparable injury necessary to justify a disruption of orderly state proceedings. In Douglas v. City of Jeannette, 319 U.S. 157, for example, the Court upheld a district court's refusal to enjoin application of a city ordinance to religious solicitation, even though the ordinance was that very day held unconstitutional as so applied on review of a criminal conviction under it. Murdock v. Pennsylvania, 319 U.S. 105. Since injunctive relief looks to the future, and it was not alleged that Pennsylvania courts and prosecutors would fail to respect the Murdock ruling, the Court found nothing to justify an injunction. And in a variety of other contexts the Court has found no special circumstances to warrant cutting short the normal adjudication of constitutional defenses in the course of a criminal prosecution.[2] In such cases it does not appear that the plaintiffs "have been threatened with any injury other than that incidental to every criminal proceeding brought lawfully and in good faith, or that a federal court of equity by withdrawing the determination of guilt from the state courts could rightly afford petitioners any protection which they could not secure by prompt trial and appeal pursued to this Court." . . .

But the allegations in this complaint depict a situation in which defense of the State's criminal prosecution will not assure adequate vindication of constitutional rights. They suggest that a substantial loss or impairment of freedoms of expression will occur if appellants must await the state court's disposition and ultimate review in this Court of any adverse determination. These allegations, if true, clearly show irreparable injury.

A criminal prosecution under a statute regulating expression usually involves imponderables and contingencies that themselves may inhibit the full exercise of First Amendment freedoms. . . . When the statutes also have an overbroad sweep, as is here alleged, the hazard of loss or substantial impairment of those precious rights may be critical. For in such cases, the statutes lend themselves too readily to denial of those rights. The as-

injunctions sought. This statute and its predecessors do not preclude injunctions against the institution of state court proceedings, but only bar stays of suits already instituted. See Ex parte Young, supra. See generally Warren, Federal and State Court Interference, 43 Harv.L.Rev. 345, 366–378 (1930); Note, Federal Power to Enjoin State Court Proceedings, 74 Harv. L.Rev. 726, 728–729 (1961). Since the grand jury was not convened and indictments were not obtained until after the filing of the complaint, which sought interlocutory as well as permanent relief, no state "proceedings" were pending within the intendment of § 2283. To hold otherwise would mean that any threat of prosecution sufficient to justify equitable intervention would also be a "proceeding" for § 2283. . . . We therefore find it unnecessary to resolve the question whether suits under 42 U.S.C. § 1983 (1958 ed.) come under the "expressly authorized" exception to § 2283. . . . [Footnote by the Court.]

2. See, e. g., Beal v. Missouri Pac. R. Co., 312 U.S. 45 (mere threat of single prosecution); Spielman Motor Sales Co., Inc. v. Dodge, 295 U.S. 89 (same); Watson v. Buck, 313 U.S. 387 (no irreparable injury or constitutional infirmity in statute); Fenner v. Boykin, 271 U.S. 240 (same). It is difficult to think of a case in which an accused could properly bring a state prosecution to a halt while a federal court decides his claim that certain evidence is rendered inadmissible by the Fourteenth Amendment. Cf. Cleary v. Bolger, 371 U.S. 392; Stefanelli v. Minard, 342 U.S. 117. [Footnote by the Court.]

sumption that defense of a criminal prosecution will generally assure ample vindication of constitutional rights is unfounded in such cases. See Baggett v. Bullitt, supra, at 379. For "[t]he threat of sanctions may deter . . . almost as potently as the actual application of sanctions. . . ." NAACP v. Button, 371 U.S. 415, 433. Because of the sensitive nature of constitutionally protected expression, we have not required that all of those subject to overbroad regulations risk prosecution to test their rights. For free expression—of transcendent value to all society, and not merely to those exercising their rights—might be the loser. If the rule were otherwise, the contours of regulation would have to be hammered out case by case—and tested only by those hardy enough to risk criminal prosecution to determine the proper scope of regulation. . . . By permitting determination of the invalidity of these statutes without regard to the permissibility of some regulation on the facts of particular cases, we have, in effect, avoided making vindication of freedom of expression await the outcome of protracted litigation. . . .

Appellants' allegations and offers of proof outline the chilling effect on free expression of prosecutions initiated and threatened in this case. Early in October 1963 appellant Dombrowski and intervenors Smith and Waltzer were arrested by Louisiana state and local police and charged with violations of the two statutes. Their offices were raided and their files and records seized. Later in October a state judge quashed the arrest warrants as not based on probable cause, and discharged the appellants. Subsequently, the court granted a motion to suppress the seized evidence on the ground that the raid was illegal. Louisiana officials continued, however, to threaten prosecution of the appellants, who thereupon filed this action in November. Shortly after the three-judge court was convened, a grand jury was summoned . . .. [After the federal court dismissed the complaint] the grand jury returned indictments under the Subversive Activities and Communist Control Law against the individual appellants.

These events, together with repeated announcements by appellees that the appellant organization is a subversive or Communist-front organization, whose members must register or be prosecuted under the Louisiana statutes, have, appellants allege, frightened off potential members and contributors. . . . Seizures of documents and records have paralyzed operations and threatened exposure of the identity of adherents to a locally unpopular cause. . . . Although the particular seizure has been quashed in the state courts, the continuing threat of prosecution portends further arrests and seizures, some of which may be upheld and all of which will cause the organization inconvenience or worse. . . . Not only does the complaint allege far more than an "injury other than that incidental to every criminal proceeding brought lawfully and in good faith," but appellants allege threats to enforce statutory provisions other than those under which indictments have been brought. Since there is no immediate prospect of a final state adjudication as to those other sections—if, indeed, there is any certainty that prosecution of the pending indictments will resolve all constitutional issues presented—a series of state criminal prosecutions will not provide satisfactory resolution of constitutional issues.

It follows that the District Court erred in holding that the complaint fails to allege sufficient irreparable injury to justify equitable relief.

The District Court also erred in holding that it should abstain pending authoritative interpretation of the statutes in the state courts, which might hold that they did not apply to SCEF, or that they were unconstitutional as applied to SCEF. We hold the abstention doctrine is inappropriate for cases such as the present one where, unlike Douglas v. City of Jeannette, statutes are justifiably attacked on their face as abridging free expression, or as applied for the purpose of discouraging protected activities.

First, appellants have attacked the good faith of the appellees in enforcing the statutes, claiming that they have invoked, and threaten to continue to invoke, criminal process without any hope of ultimate success, but only to discourage appellants' civil rights activities. If these allegations state a claim under the Civil Rights Act, 42 U.S.C. § 1983, as we believe they do, . . . the interpretation ultimately put on the statutes by the state courts is irrelevant. For an interpretation rendering the statute inapplicable to SCEF would merely mean that appellants might ultimately prevail in the state courts. It would not alter the impropriety of appellees' invoking the statute in bad faith to impose continuing harassment in order to discourage appellants' activities, as appellees allegedly are doing and plan to continue to do.

Second, appellants have challenged the statutes as overly broad and vague regulations of expression. We have already seen that where, as here, prosecutions are actually threatened, this challenge, if not clearly frivolous, will establish the threat of irreparable injury required by traditional doctrines of equity. We believe that in this case the same reasons preclude denial of equitable relief pending an acceptable narrowing construction. In considering where injunctive relief should be granted, a federal district court should consider a statute as of the time its jurisdiction is invoked, rather than some hypothetical future date. The area of proscribed conduct will be adequately defined and the deterrent effect of the statute contained within constitutional limits only by authoritative constructions sufficiently illuminating the contours of an otherwise vague prohibition. [T]his cannot be satisfactorily done through a series of criminal prosecutions, dealing as they inevitably must with only a narrow portion of the prohibition at any one time, and not contributing materially to articulation of the statutory standard. We believe that those affected by a statute are entitled to be free of the burdens of defending prosecutions, however expeditious, aimed at hammering out the structure of the statute piecemeal, with no likelihood of obviating similar uncertainty for others. Here, no readily apparent construction suggests itself as a vehicle for rehabilitating the statutes in a single prosecution, and appellants are entitled to an injunction. The State must, if it is to invoke the statutes after injunctive relief has been sought, assume the burden of obtaining a permissible narrow construction in a noncriminal proceeding before it may seek modification of the injunction to permit future prosecutions.

On this view of the "vagueness" doctrine, it is readily apparent that abstention serves no legitimate purpose where a statute regulating speech is properly attacked on its face, and where, as here, the conduct charged in the indictments is not within the reach of an acceptable limiting construction readily to be anticipated as the result of a single criminal prosecution and is not the sort of "hardcore" conduct that would obviously be prohibited under any construction. In these circumstances, to abstain is to subject those affected to the uncertainties and vagaries of criminal prosecution, whereas the reasons for the vagueness doctrine in the area of expression demand no less than freedom from prosecution prior to a construction adequate to save the statute. In such cases, abstention is at war with the purposes of the vagueness doctrine, which demands appropriate federal relief regardless of the prospects for expeditious determination of state criminal prosecutions. Our view of the proper operation of the vagueness doctrine does not preclude district courts from modifying injunctions to permit prosecutions in light of subsequent state court interpretation clarifying the application of a statute to particular conduct.

We conclude that on the allegations of the complaint, if true, abstention and the denial of injunctive relief may well result in the denial of any effective safeguards against the loss of protected freedoms of expression, and cannot be justified.

[The Court held two of the provisions unconstitutional on their face, reversed, and remanded. Justices Black and Stewart did not participate in the decision.]

It is so ordered.

Mr. Justice HARLAN, whom Mr. Justice CLARK joins, dissenting.

The basic holding in this case marks a significant departure from a wise procedural principle designed to spare our federal system from premature federal judicial interference with state statutes or proceedings challenged on federal constitutional grounds. This decision abolishes the doctrine of federal judicial abstention in all suits attacking state criminal statutes for vagueness on First-Fourteenth Amendment grounds. As one who considers that it is a prime responsibility of this Court to maintain federal-state court relationships in good working order, I cannot subscribe to a holding which displays such insensitivity to the legitimate demands of those relationships under our federal system. I see no such incompatibility between the abstention doctrine and the full vindication of constitutionally protected rights as the Court finds to exist in cases of this kind.

In practical effect the Court's decision means that a State may no longer carry on prosecutions under statutes challengeable for vagueness on "First Amendment" grounds without the prior approval of the federal courts. For if such a statute can be so questioned (and few, at least colorably, cannot) then a state prosecution, if instituted after the commencement of a federal action, must be halted until the prosecuting authorities obtain in some other state proceeding a narrowing construction, which in turn would presumably be subject to further monitoring by the federal courts before the state prosecution would be allowed to proceed.

For me such a paralyzing of state criminal processes cannot be justified by any of the considerations which the Court's opinion advances in its support. High as the premium placed on First Amendment rights may be, I do not think that the Federal Constitution prevents a State from testing their availability through the medium of criminal proceedings, subject of course to this Court's ultimate review.

Underlying the Court's major premise that criminal enforcement of an overly broad statute affecting rights of speech and association is in itself a deterrent to the free exercise thereof seems to be the unarticulated assumption that state courts will not be as prone as federal courts to vindicate constitutional rights promptly and effectively. Such an assumption should not be indulged in the absence of a showing that such is apt to be so in a given case. No showing of that kind has been made. On the contrary, the Louisiana courts in this very case have already refused to uphold the seizure of appellants' books. . . . We should not assume that those courts would not be equally diligent in construing the statutes here in question in accordance with the relevant decisions of this Court.

The Court suggests that "a substantial loss or impairment of freedoms of expression will occur if appellants must await the state court's disposition and ultimate review in this Court of any adverse determination." . . . But the possibility of such an impairment is not obviated by traveling the federal route approved here. Even in the federal courts the progress of litigation is not always as swift as one would like to see it. . . . [1]

Had this statute been a federal enactment and had this Court been willing to pass upon its validity in a declaratory judgment or injunction action, I can hardly believe that it would have stricken the statute without first exposing it to the process of narrowing construction in an effort to save as much of it as possible. See, e. g., Dennis v. United States, [341 U.S. 494]. Yet here the Court has not only made no effort to give this state statute a narrowing construction, but has also declined to give the Louisiana courts an opportunity to do so with respect to the acts charged in the pending prosecutions against these appellants. The statute thus pro tanto goes to its doom without either state or federal court interpretation, and despite the room which the statute clearly leaves for a narrowing constitutional construction. . . . This seems to me to be heavy-handed treatment of the first order. . . .

While I consider that abstention was called for, I think the District Court erred in dismissing the action. It should have retained jurisdiction for the purpose of affording appellants appropriate relief in the event that the state prosecution did not go forward in a prompt and bona fide manner. See Harrison v. NAACP, 360 U.S. 167.

FEDERAL RELIEF AGAINST STATE PROSECUTIONS

Introduction. Ordinarily, federal courts avoid pre-conviction intervention in state criminal proceedings; Supreme Court review of state convictions and habeas corpus relief in collateral post-conviction proceedings are the usual channels of federal relief. But these routes may not give adequate protection to federal rights, especially in civil rights cases. See generally Amsterdam, "Criminal Prosecutions Affecting Federally Guaranteed Civil Rights: Federal Removal and Habeas Corpus Jurisdiction to Abort State Court Trial," 113 U.Pa.L.Rev. 793 (1965). When is pre-conviction protection available? Is Dombrowski a readily invokable bar against threatened

---

1. In this case appellants are pursuing a consistent course of conduct, and the only question is whether the Louisiana statutes apply to such conduct. Thus, this case comes within the "bulk of abstention cases in this Court . . . [where] the unsettled issue of state law principally concerned the applicability of the challenged statute to a certain person or a defined course of conduct, whose resolution in a particular manner would eliminate the constitutional issue and terminate the litigation." Baggett v. Bullitt, [377 U.S. 360]. The present case is indistinguishable from Harrison v. NAACP, 360 U.S. 167 . . . . [Footnote by Justice Harlan.]

prosecution? What can be done about prosecutions already under way? When may a defendant remove a state prosecution to a federal court?

1. *Injunctive and declaratory relief against threatened prosecutions.* How far-reaching is the Dombrowski departure from the norm of federal nonintervention in threatened state prosecutions? The Court's elaborations suggest that the federal injunction remedy is indeed an exceptional one, but that the limitations on its use do not fully carry over to declaratory relief. Thus, Cameron v. Johnson, 390 U.S. 611 (1968), read the Dombrowski authorization narrowly, but Zwickler v. Koota, 389 U.S. 241 (1967), insisted that the inhibitions regarding injunctive remedies are inapplicable to declaratory relief: "A federal district court has the duty to decide the appropriateness and the merits of the declaratory request irrespective of its conclusion as to the propriety of the issuance of the injunction."

In Zwickler, the challenge was to a New York ban on distribution of anonymous handbills; the claim was that the statute was void on its face because of impermissible "overbreadth"; the relief requested was declaratory as well as injunctive. The District Court dismissed the case because of its view of Dombrowski: finding no "special circumstances" to overcome the normal ban on federal injunctive relief, it concluded that it was required to abstain from a declaratory judgment as well. The Supreme Court held this to be a mistake: the propriety of injunctive and of declaratory relief are separate issues. Abstention was not here justified as to declaratory relief: this was a challenge for overbreadth, not vagueness; there was no prospect of a state interpretation which would avoid the federal question. And abstention was especially inappropriate because this was a First Amendment challenge. [On remand, the District Court invalidated the handbill law on the merits. Once again, the Supreme Court reversed—this time because the lower court should have dismissed on ripeness grounds. Golden v. Zwickler, 394 U.S. 103 (1969)].

In Cameron, the challenge was to a Mississippi anti-picketing law and, as in Zwickler, the challengers combined requests for declaratory and injunctive relief. They sought a declaration that the law was overly broad and vague, and accordingly void on its face, and they requested an injunction alleging that the state was prosecuting them in bad faith for the purpose of discouraging their civil rights activities. Unlike the trial court in Zwickler, the District Court here gave a declaratory judgment (rejecting the constitutional attack) before denying the injunction request (for failure to show the "special circumstances" necessary under Dombrowski). The Supreme Court agreed with both aspects. Justice Brennan's majority opinion explained that the Dombrowski prosecutions under statutes "patently unconstitutional on their face" presented a situation of "bad faith" invocation of statutes "to impose continuing harassment in order to discourage appellants' activities." Here, on the other hand, "there was no harassment, intimidation, or oppression of these complainants in their efforts to exercise their constitutional rights." And mere failure to show that the statute was in fact violated did not justify federal injunctive relief: the question before the federal court was not guilt or innocence, but "whether the statute was enforced against them with no expectation of convictions but only to discourage exercise of protected rights." The "mere possibility of erroneous application of the statute" is not the kind of "irreparable injury" necessary under Dombrowski "to justify a disruption of orderly state proceedings."

2. *Relief against prosecutions under way: the ban on stays and the ALI proposal.* As the first footnote to Dombrowski shows, the injunction-ban of 28 U.S.C. § 2283 ordinarily bars stays of prosecutions that have been commenced. Dombrowski did not decide whether civil rights actions are within the statutory exception to that ban. Compare the more specific exception in the ALI's proposed revision of the federal judicial code. Its ban on federal injunctions on state court proceedings, § 1372, provides a number of exceptions, including an explicit one regarding civil rights if "(7) the injunction is to restrain a criminal prosecution that should not be permitted to continue either because the statute or other law that is the basis of the prosecution plainly cannot be constitutionally applied to the party seeking the injunction or the prosecution is so plainly discriminatory as to amount to a denial of equal protection of the laws." American Law Institute, Study of the Division of Jurisdiction Between State and Federal Courts (1969), 52 (text), 308–10 (commentary on clause 7).

3. *Relief against prosecutions under way: the civil rights removal statute and the 1966 cases.* When may a state court defendant transfer his case to a federal court? 28 U.S.C. § 1443, derived from the Civil Rights Act of 1866, authorizes removal of any criminal or civil case "(1) Against any person who is denied or cannot enforce in the court of such State a right under any law providing for equal civil rights . . .," and "(2) For any act under color of authority derived from any law providing for equal rights, or for refusing to do any act on the ground that it would be inconsistent with such law."

The most important provision, § 1343(1), received its first extensive consideration in 60 years—and a relatively narrow interpretation—in companion cases in 1966, Georgia v. Rachel, 384 U.S. 780, and City of Greenwood v. Peacock, 384 U.S. 808. The Court noted the sharp increase in attempts to remove criminal cases in the mid-1960's, especially in the Fifth Circuit. In examining § 1343(1), Justice Stewart's majority opinions stressed that it contained two requirements: defendants seeking to remove must show not only that they rely on a right under a law "providing for . . . equal civil rights," but also that they are "denied or cannot enforce" that right in the state courts. The Court interpreted both elements strictly. It concluded that the "equal civil rights law" description applies only to laws "providing for specific civil rights stated in terms of racial equality"; broad First Amendment or Due Process claims, accordingly, could not support removal under § 1443(1). And, in order to show that they are "denied or cannot enforce" these specific rights in state courts, defendants must be able to point to a "predicted denial" which appears "with relative clarity prior to trial." Ordinarily, the denial must be "manifest in a formal expression of state law"—a state law discriminatory on its face.

If petitioners were, as alleged, "being prosecuted on baseless charges solely because of their race," the Court recognized, there was indeed "an outrageous denial of their federal rights"; but removal was not an available remedy under the present statute. Other remedies were available: for example, direct review of state court judgments by the Supreme Court; injunction of state court proceedings where appropriate under Dombrowski v. Pfister; ultimate federal habeas corpus relief; and civil and criminal sanctions against state officials under federal civil rights laws. But the scope of § 1443 (1) removal was not to be expanded: after "an independent examination," the Court concluded that the late Nineteenth Century interpretations "were correct in their basic conclusion that the provisions of § 1443(1) do not operate to work a wholesale dislocation of the historic relationship between the state and federal courts in the administration of the criminal law." Justice Douglas, joined by Chief Justice Warren and Justices Brennan and Fortas, dissented, emphasizing that "the federal regime was designed from the beginning to afford some protection against local passions and prejudices by the important pretrial federal remedy of removal."

The ALI proposals on the federal judicial code do not urge broadening the civil rights removal authority recognized in 28 U.S.C. § 1343(1) and the 1966 cases. The commentary stresses general policy: "proper respect for the states suggests that they should be allowed to use their own courts for routine matters of law enforcement." With regard to the special risks in civil rights cases, the ALI finds it "preferable to permit injunctions against state proceedings in some such cases [see note 2, supra], rather than to broaden the special removal statute for such cases." American Law Institute, Study of the Division of Jurisdiction Between State and Federal Courts (1969), 27 (text of § 1312(c)), 205, 308. Why are injunctions preferable? Are they adequate?

SECTION 5. POLITICAL QUESTIONS

Introductory note. Not all constitutional questions that arise in the course of litigation are decided by the courts: the Court has held that certain issues—"political questions"—cannot be resolved by the judiciary. What distinguishes issues that are justiciable—despite the fact that adjudication may have significant political consequences—from issues that are nonjusticiable because "political"? Is the "political question" doctrine derived from the Constitution? From Article III? From other provisions of the Constitution? Is the doctrine a discretionary policy device for screening cases which the Court deems appropriate for decision by other departments? Consider, in examining the materials in this section, the merits of the conflicting views which follow.

CONFLICTING VIEWS: WECHSLER AND BICKEL

Wechsler, "Toward Neutral Principles of Constitutional Law," 73 Harv. L.Rev. 1, 7, 9, Selected Essays 1938–62 (1963), 463, 468: "The line [between political and justiciable questions] is thin, indeed, but I suggest that it is thinner than it needs to be or ought to be. . . . I submit that in [political question cases], the only proper judgment that may lead to an abstention from decision is that the Constitution has committed the determination of the issue to another agency of government than the courts. Difficult as it may be to make that judgment wisely, whatever factors may be rightly weighed in situations where the answer is not clear, what is involved is in itself an act of constitutional interpretation, to be made and judged by standards that should govern the interpretive process generally. That, I submit, is *toto caelo* different from a broad discretion to abstain or intervene."

Bickel, "Foreword: The Passive Virtues," 75 Harv.L.Rev. 40, 46, Selected Essays 1938–62 (1963), 24, 29: "[O]nly by means of a play on words can the broad discretion that the courts have in fact exercised be turned into an act of constitutional interpretation. The political-question doctrine simply resists being domesticated in this fashion. There is something different about it, in kind, not in degree, from the general 'interpretive process'; something greatly more flexible, something of prudence, not construction and principle."

THE CONTEXT OF BAKER v. CARR—JUSTICIABILITY AND DISTRICTING BEFORE 1962

Introduction. The most important decision on political questions is Baker v. Carr, 369 U.S. 186 (1962). That case arose in the context of a legislative districting controversy. These notes provide background for a consideration of Baker by sketching the Court's earlier encounters with apportionment and related disputes.

1. *Colegrove v. Green, 328 U.S. 549 (1946).* In Colegrove, the Court considered a federal court action to enjoin Illinois officials from proceeding with an election of Congressmen. Only seven Justices participated in the decision, because of the death of Chief Justice Stone and the absence of Justice Jackson. The appellants contended that the Illinois law apportioning congressional districts was unconstitutional because the districts were not of approximate equality in population. Justice Frankfurter announced the judgment of the Court affirming the dismissal of the complaint, but his opinion was joined only by Justices Reed and Burton. He stated: "We are of opinion that the petitioners ask of this Court what is beyond its competence to grant. This is one of those demands on judicial power which cannot be met by verbal fencing about 'jurisdiction.' . . . [E]ffective working of our government revealed this issue to be of a peculiarly political nature and therefore not meet for judicial determination. . . . The basis for the suit is not a private wrong, but a wrong suffered by Illinois as a polity. . . . [T]his controversy concerns matters that bring courts into immediate and active relations with party contests. From the determination of such issues this Court has traditionally remained aloof. It is hostile to a democratic system to involve the judiciary in the politics of the people. . . . [D]ue regard for the Constitution as a viable system precludes judicial correction. Authority for dealing with such problems resides elsewhere. Article I, § 4 of the Constitution. . . . The short of it is that the Constitution has conferred upon Congress exclusive authority to secure fair representation by the States in the popular House and left to that House determination whether States have fulfilled their responsibilities. . . . Whether Congress faithfully discharges its duty or not, the subject has been committed to the exclusive control of Congress. . . . Courts ought not to enter this political thicket. . . . The Constitution has many commands that are not enforceable by courts because they clearly fall outside the conditions and purposes that circumscribe judicial action."

The deciding vote was cast by Justice Rutledge, who concurred in the result. He thought the issue was justiciable, but concluded that the complaint should be dismissed for want of equity: "I think the cause is of so delicate a character . . . that the jurisdiction should be exercised only in the most compelling circumstances. . . . The right here is not absolute. And the cure sought may be worse than the disease. I think, therefore, the case is one in which the Court may properly, and should, decline to exercise its jurisdiction." Justice Black, joined by Justices Douglas and Murphy, dissented: "It is my judgment that the District Court had jurisdiction; that the complaint presented a justiciable case and controversy; and that petitioners had standing to sue, since the facts alleged show that they have been injured as individuals."

2. *MacDougall v. Green, 335 U.S. 281 (1948).* Two years after Colegrove, that dismissal was cited by the Court—but in a ruling on the merits. In MacDougall, a federal trial court had denied, for "want of jurisdiction," an injunction against the enforcement of an Illinois law requiring that nominating petitions for state-wide candidates of new parties include signatures from 200 voters from each of at least 50 of the State's 102 counties. The plaintiffs alleged that 52% of the state's voters resided "in Cook County alone," and that "only 13% reside in the 53 least populous counties." The Supreme Court affirmed the denial of relief: "To assume that political power is a function exclusively of numbers is to disregard the practicalities of government. Thus, the Constitution protects the interests of the smaller against the greater by giving in the Senate entirely unequal representation to populations. It would be strange indeed, and doctrinaire for this Court, applying such broad constitutional concepts as due process and equal protection of the laws, to deny a State the power to assure a proper diffusion of political initiative as between thinly populated counties and those having concentrated masses, in view of the fact that the latter have practical opportunities for exerting their political weight at the polls not available to the former. . . Colegrove v. Green." Justice Rutledge concurred separately; Justice Douglas, joined by Justices Black and Murphy, dissented. [MacDougall was overruled on the merits in Moore v. Ogilvie, 394 U.S. 814 (1969), p. 1451, infra.]

3. *South v. Peters, 339 U.S. 276 (1950).* Residents of the most populous county in Georgia sought to enjoin operation of a state statute which allegedly reduced the weight of plaintiffs' votes to one-tenth the weight of those in other counties by providing that all of a county's "unit votes" in a primary election would be awarded the candidate receiving the highest popular vote in the county. Counties were allocated from two to six unit votes, depending on population. The Supreme Court affirmed the lower court's dismissal of the petition: "Federal courts consistently refuse to exercise their equity powers in cases posing political issues arising from a state's geographical distribution of electoral strength among its political subdivisions." Justices Douglas and Black dissented on the ground that the county unit system violated "the right to have the vote counted at full value without dilution or discount." [The Georgia county unit system was held unconstitutional in Gray v. Sanders, 372 U.S. 368 (1963)—considered, together with other post-Baker v. Carr developments on reapportionment, in chap. 18, below.]

4. *Gomillion v. Lightfoot, 364 U.S. 339 (1960).* A 1957 Alabama statute redefining the city boundaries of Tuskegee was challenged as a device to disenfranchise Negroes. The statute, which altered "the shape of Tuskegee from a square to an uncouth twenty-eight-sided figure," was alleged to result in removing from the city "all save only four or five of its 400 Negro

voters while not removing a single white voter or resident." The District Court dismissed the complaint on the ground that it had "no control over, no supervision over, and no power to change any boundaries of municipal corporations." The Court of Appeals affirmed. On certiorari, the Supreme Court, in an opinion by Justice Frankfurter, reversed on the basis of the Fifteenth Amendment. The Court concluded that the complaint "amply alleges a claim of racial discrimination." The allegations, if proved, would "abundantly establish" that the 1957 law "was not an ordinary geographic redistricting measure even within familiar abuses of gerrymandering." If the allegations were supported at trial, "the conclusion would be irresistible, tantamount for all practical purposes to a mathematical demonstration, that the legislation is solely concerned with segregating white and colored voters by fencing Negro citizens out of town so as to deprive them of their pre-existing municipal vote."

The Court rejected arguments based on "seemingly unconfined dicta" regarding unlimited state control over its political subdivisions. The Court also found no barrier to trial in "political question" arguments drawn from Colegrove v. Green: "The appellants in Colegrove complained only of a dilution of the strength of their votes as a result of legislative inaction over a number of years. The petitioners here complain that affirmative legislative action deprives them of their votes" contrary to the Fifteenth Amendment. "While in form this is merely an act redefining metes and bounds, if the allegations are established, the inescapable human effect of this essay in geometry and geography is to despoil colored citizens, and only colored citizens, of their theretofore enjoyed voting rights. That was not Colegrove v. Green." Mr. Justice Douglas joined the Court's opinion but stated that he adhered to his dissents in Colegrove and in South v. Peters, supra. Mr. Justice Whittaker, concurring, thought that "the decision should be rested not on the Fifteenth Amendment, but rather on the Equal Protection Clause of the Fourteenth Amendment." [Compare Wright v. Rockefeller, 376 U.S. 52 (1964), rejecting a claim that congressional districts in Manhattan were racially gerrymandered: Appellants failed to prove that the legislature "was either motivated by racial considerations or in fact drew the districts on racial lines."]

BAKER v. CARR

369 U.S. 186, 82 S.Ct. 691, 7 L.Ed.2d 663 (1962).

Appeal from the District Court for the Middle District of Tennessee.

Mr. Justice BRENNAN delivered the opinion of the Court.

This civil action was brought under 42 U.S.C. §§ 1983 and 1988 to redress the alleged deprivation of federal constitutional rights. The complaint, alleging that by means of a 1901 statute of Tennessee apportioning the members of the General Assembly among the State's 95 counties, "these plaintiffs and others similarly situated, are denied the equal protection of the laws accorded them by the Fourteenth Amendment to the Constitution of the United States by virtue of the debasement of their votes," was dismissed by a three-judge court. . . . We hold that the dismissal was error, and remand the cause to the District Court for trial and further proceedings consistent with this opinion. . . .

. . . . Tennessee's standard for allocating legislative representation among her counties is the total number of qualified voters resident in the respective counties, subject only to minor qualifications. . . . . In 1901 the General Assembly . . . passed the Apportionment Act here in controversy. In the more than 60 years since that action, all proposals in both Houses of the General Assembly for reapportionment have failed to pass.

Between 1901 and 1961, Tennessee has experienced substantial growth and redistribution of her population. . . . . It is primarily the continued application of the 1901 Apportionment Act to this shifted and enlarged voting population which gives rise to the present controversy. . . . [The complaint alleges] that "because of the population changes since 1900, and the failure of the Legislature to reapportion itself since 1901," the 1901 statute became "unconstitutional and obsolete." Appellants also argue that, because of the composition of the legislature effected by the 1901 Apportionment Act, redress in the form of a state constitutional amendment to change the entire mechanism for reapportioning, or any other change short of that, is difficult or impossible. [Appellants] seek a declaration that the 1901 statute is unconstitutional and an injunction restraining the appellees from acting to conduct any further elections under it. They also pray that unless and until the General Assembly enacts a valid reapportionment, the District Court should either decree a reapportionment by mathematical application of the Tennessee constitutional formulae to the most recent Federal Census figures, or direct the appellees to conduct legislative elections, primary and general, at large. They also pray for such other and further relief as may be appropriate.

I. THE DISTRICT COURT'S OPINION AND ORDER OF DISMISSAL.

Because we deal with this case on appeal from an order of dismissal granted on appellees' motions, precise identification of the issues presently confronting us demands clear exposition of the grounds upon which the District Court rested in dismissing the case. The dismissal order recited that the court sustained the appellees' grounds "(1) that the Court lacks jurisdiction of the subject matter, and (2) that the complaint fails to state a claim upon which relief can be granted . . . .."

In the setting of a case such as this, the recited grounds embrace two possible reasons for dismissal:

First: That the facts and injury alleged, the legal bases invoked as creating the rights and duties relied upon, and the relief sought, fail to come within that language of Article III of the Constitution and of the jurisdictional statutes which define those matters concerning which United States District Courts are empowered to act;

Second: That, although the matter is cognizable and facts are alleged which establish infringement of appellants' rights as a result of state legislative action departing from a federal constitutional standard, the court will not proceed because the matter is considered unsuited to judicial inquiry or adjustment.

We treat the first ground of dismissal as "lack of jurisdiction of the subject matter." The second we consider to result in a failure to state a justiciable cause of action. . . .

. . . [W]e hold today only (a) that the court possessed jurisdiction of the subject matter; (b) that a justiciable cause of action is stated upon which appellants would be entitled to appropriate relief; and (c) because appellees raise the issue before this Court, that the appellants have standing to challenge the Tennessee apportionment statutes. Beyond noting that we have no cause at this stage to doubt the District Court will be able to fashion relief if violations of constitutional rights are found, it is improper now to consider what remedy would be most appropriate if appellants prevail at the trial.

II. JURISDICTION OF THE SUBJECT MATTER.

The District Court was uncertain whether our cases withholding federal judicial relief rested upon a lack of federal jurisdiction or upon the inappropriateness of the subject matter for judicial consideration—what we have designated "nonjusticiability." The distinction between the two grounds is significant. In the instance of nonjusticiability, consideration of the cause is not wholly and immediately foreclosed; rather, the Court's inquiry necessarily proceeds to the point of deciding whether the duty asserted can be judicially identified and its breach judicially determined, and whether protection for the right asserted can be judicially molded. In the instance of lack of jurisdiction the cause either does not "arise under" the Federal Constitution, laws or treaties (or fall within one of the other enumerated categories of Art. III, § 2), or is not a "case or controversy" within the meaning of that section; or the cause is not one described by any jurisdictional statute. Our conclusion [infra] that this cause presents no nonjusticiable "political question" settles the only possible doubt that it is a case or controversy. Under the present heading of "Jurisdiction of the Subject Matter" we hold only that the matter set forth in the complaint does arise under the Constitution and is within 28 U.S.C. § 1343.

. . . Since the District Court obviously and correctly did not deem the asserted federal constitutional claim unsubstantial and frivolous, it should not have dismissed the complaint for want of jurisdiction of the subject matter. And of course no further consideration of the merits of the claim is relevant to a determination of the court's jurisdiction of the subject matter.
. . . .

The appellees refer to Colegrove v. Green, 328 U.S. 549, as authority that the District Court lacked jurisdiction of the subject matter. Appellees misconceive the holding of that case. The holding was precisely contrary to their reading of it. . . . Several subsequent cases similar to Colegrove have been decided by the Court in summary per curiam statements. None was dismissed for want of jurisdiction of the subject matter. . . . Two cases decided with opinions after Colegrove likewise plainly imply that the subject matter of this suit is within District Court jurisdiction. [MacDougall v. Green, South v. Peters] . . .

III. STANDING. . . .

It would not be necessary to decide whether appellants' allegations of impairment of their votes by the 1901 apportionment will, ultimately, entitle them to any relief, in order to hold that they have standing to seek it. If such impairment does produce a legally cognizable injury, they are among those who have sustained it. They are asserting "a plain, direct and adequate interest in maintaining the effectiveness of their votes," Coleman v. Miller, 307 U.S. at 438, not merely a claim of "the right possessed by every citizen to require that the government be administered according to law" . . ..

IV. JUSTICIABILITY. . . .

Of course the mere fact that the suit seeks protection of a political right does not mean it presents a political question. Such an objection "is little more than a play upon words." Nixon v. Herndon, 273 U.S. 536, 540. Rather, it is argued that apportionment cases, whatever the actual wording of the complaint, can involve no federal constitutional right except one resting on the guaranty of a republican form of government [Art. IV, Sec. 4], and that complaints based on that clause have been held to present political questions which are nonjusticiable.

We hold that the claim pleaded here neither rests upon nor implicates the Guaranty Clause and that its justiciability is therefore not foreclosed by our decisions of cases involving that clause. . . . To show why we reject the argument based on the Guaranty Clause we must examine the authorities under it. But because there appears to be some uncertainty as to why those cases did present political questions, and specifically as to whether this apportionment case is like those cases, we deem it necessary first to consider the contours of the "political question" doctrine.

Our discussion, even at the price of extending this opinion, requires review of a number of political question cases, in order to expose the attributes of the doctrine—attributes which, in various settings, diverge, combine, appear, and disappear in seeming disorderliness. Since that review is undertaken solely to demonstrate that neither singly nor collectively do these cases support a conclusion that this apportionment case is nonjusticiable, we of course do not explore their implications in other contexts. That review reveals that in the Guaranty Clause cases and in the other "political question" cases, it is the relationship between the judiciary and the coordinate branches of the Federal Government, and not the federal judiciary's relationship to the States, which gives rise to the "political question."

We have said that "in determining whether a question falls within [the political question] category, the appropriateness under our system of government of attributing finality to the action of the political departments and also the lack of satisfactory criteria for a judicial determination are dominant considerations." Coleman v. Miller, 307 U.S. 433, 454–455. The nonjusticiability of a political question is primarily a function of the separation of powers. Much confusion results from the capacity of the "political question" label to obscure the need for case-by-case inquiry. Deciding whether a matter has in any measure been committed by the Constitution to another branch of government, or whether the action of that branch exceeds whatever authority has been committed, is itself a delicate exercise in constitutional interpretation, and is a responsibility of this Court as ultimate interpreter of the Constitution. To demonstrate this requires no less than to analyze representative cases and to infer from them the analytical threads that make up the political question doctrine. We shall then show that none of those threads catches this case.

Foreign relations: There are sweeping statements to the effect that all questions touching foreign relations are political questions. Not only does resolution of such issues frequently turn on standards that defy judicial application, or involve the exercise of a discretion demonstrably committed to the executive or legislature; but many such questions uniquely demand single-voiced statement of the Government's views. Yet it is error to suppose that every case or controversy which touches foreign relations lies beyond judicial cognizance. Our cases in this field seem invariably to show a discriminating analysis of the particular question posed, in terms of the history of its management by the political branches, of its susceptibility to judicial handling in the light of its nature and posture in the specific case, and of the possible consequences of judicial action. For example, though a court will not ordinarily inquire whether a treaty has been terminated, since on that question "governmental action . . . must be regarded as of controlling importance," if there has been no conclusive "governmental action" then a court can construe a treaty and may find it provides the answer. . . . Though a court will not undertake to construe a treaty in a manner inconsistent with a subsequent federal statute, no similar hesitancy obtains if the asserted clash is with state law. . . .

While recognition of foreign governments so strongly defies judicial treatment that without executive recognition a foreign state has been called "a republic of whose existence we know nothing," and the judiciary ordinarily follows the executive as to which nation has sovereignty over disputed territory, once sovereignty over an area is politically determined and declared, courts may examine the resulting status and decide independently whether a statute applies to that area. Similarly, recognition of belligerency abroad is an executive responsibility, but if the executive proclamations fall short of an explicit answer, a court may construe them seeking, for example, to determine whether the situation is such that statutes designed to assure American neutrality have become operative. . . .

Dates of duration of hostilities: Though it has been stated broadly that "the power which declared the necessity is the power to declare its cessation, and what the cessation requires," . . . here too analysis reveals isolable reasons for the presence of political questions, underlying this Court's refusal to review the political departments' determination of when or whether a war has ended. Dominant is the need for finality in the political determination, for emergency's nature demands "a prompt and unhesitating obedience," Martin v. Mott, 12 Wheat. 19, 30 (calling up of militia). . . . But deference rests on reason, not habit. The question in a particular case may not seriously implicate considerations of finality— e. g., a public program of importance (rent control) yet not central to the emergency effort. Further, clearly definable criteria for decision may be available. In such case the political question barrier falls away. . . . On the other hand, even in private litigation which directly implicates no feature of separation of powers, lack of judicially discoverable standards, and the drive for even-handed application, may impel reference to the political departments' determination of dates of hostilities' beginning and ending. . . .

Validity of enactments: In Coleman v. Miller, supra, this Court held that the questions of how long a proposed amendment to the Federal Constitution remained open to ratification, and what effect a prior rejection had on a subsequent ratification, were committed to congressional resolution and

involved criteria of decision that necessarily escaped the judicial
lar considerations apply to the enacting process: "the respect o
and independent departments," and the need for finality and c
the status of a statute contribute to judicial reluctance to inqui
passed, it complied with all requisite formalities. Field v. Cla
649. . . . But it is not true that courts will never delve i
ture's records upon such a quest: If the enrolled statute lacks
date, a court will not hesitate to seek it in the legislative journal
preserve the enactment. . . . The political question doctrin
maintenance of governmental order, will not be so applied as to
ly disorder.

    The status of Indian tribes: This Court's deference to the political de-
partments in determining whether Indians are recognized as a tribe, while
it reflects familiar attributes of political questions, . . . also has a
unique element in that "the relation of the Indians to the United States is
marked by peculiar and cardinal distinctions which exist no where else.
. . . [The Indians are] domestic dependent nations . . . in a state
of pupilage. Their relation to the United States resembles that of a ward to
his guardian." The Cherokee Nation v. Georgia, 5 Pet. 1, 16, 17 [1831].[1]

1. This case, so frequently cited for the
broad proposition that the status of
an Indian tribe is a matter for the
political departments, is in fact a noteworthy example of the limited and
precise impact of a political question.
The Cherokees brought an original suit
in this Court to enjoin Georgia's assertion of jurisdiction over Cherokee
territory and abolition of Cherokee
government and laws. Unquestionably
the case lay at the vortex of most
fiery political embroilment. See 1
Warren, The Supreme Court in United
States History (Rev. ed.), 729–779.
But in spite of some broader language
in separate opinions, all that the Court
held was that it possessed no original
jurisdiction over the suit: for the
Cherokees could in no view be considered either a State of this Union
or a "foreign state." Chief Justice
Marshall treated the question as one
of *de novo* interpretation of words in
the Constitution. The Chief Justice
did say that "The acts of our government plainly recognize the Cherokee
nation as a state, and the courts are
bound by those acts," but here he
referred to their existence "as a state,
as a distinct political society, separated from others . . . ." From
there he went to "A question of much
more difficulty . . . . Do the
Cherokees constitute a foreign state
in the sense of the constitution?" Id.,
at 16. Thus, while the Court referred
to "the political" for the decision
whether the tribe was an entity, a
separate polity, it held that whether
being an entity the tribe had such
status as to be entitled to sue origi-

nally was a judicially soluble issue:
criteria were discoverable in relevant
phrases of the Constitution and in the
common understanding of the times.
As to this issue, the Court was not
hampered by problems of the management of unusual evidence or of possible interference with a congressional
program. Moreover, Chief Justice Marshall's dictum that "It savours too
much of the exercise of political power to be within the proper province
of the judicial department," id., at 20,
was not addressed to the issue of the
Cherokees' status to sue, but rather
to the breadth of the claim asserted
and the impropriety of the relief
sought. Compare Georgia v. Stanton,
6 Wall. 50, 77. The Chief Justice
made clear that if the issue of the
Cherokees' rights arose in a customary
legal context, "a proper case with
proper parties," it would be justiciable.
Thus, when the same dispute produced
a case properly brought, in which the
right asserted was one of protection
under federal treaties and laws from
conflicting state law, and the relief
sought was the voiding of a conviction under that state law, the Court
did void the conviction. Worcester v.
Georgia, 6 Pet. 515 [1832]. There, the
fact that the tribe was a separate polity served as a datum contributing to
the result, and despite the consequences in a heated federal-state controversy and the opposition of the other branches of the National Government, the judicial power acted to reverse the State Supreme Court. An
example of similar isolation of a political question in the decision of a

Yet, here too, there is no blanket rule. While " 'It is for [Congress] . . . ., and not for the courts, to determine when the true interests of the Indian require his release from [the] condition of tutelage' . . . ., it is not meant by this that Congress may bring a community or body of people within the range of this power by arbitrarily calling them an Indian tribe" . . . .. Able to discern what is "distinctly Indian," the courts will strike down any heedless extension of that label. They will not stand impotent before an obvious instance of a manifestly unauthorized exercise of power.

It is apparent that several formulations which vary slightly according to the settings in which the questions arise may describe a political question, although each has one or more elements which identifies it as essentially a function of the separation of powers. Prominent on the surface of any case held to involve a political question is found a textually demonstrable constitutional commitment of the issue to a coordinate political department; or a lack of judicially discoverable and manageable standards for resolving it; or the impossibility of deciding without an initial policy determination of a kind clearly for nonjudicial discretion; or the impossibility of a court's undertaking independent resolution without expressing lack of the respect due coordinate branches of government; or an unusual need for unquestioning adherence to a political decision already made; or the potentiality of embarrassment from multifarious pronouncements by various departments on one question.

Unless one of these formulations is inextricable from the case at bar, there should be no dismissal for nonjusticiability on the ground of a political question's presence. The doctrine of which we treat is one of "political questions," not one of "political cases." The courts cannot reject as "no law suit" a bona fide controversy as to whether some action denominated "political" exceeds constitutional authority. The cases we have reviewed show the necessity for discriminating inquiry into the precise facts and posture of the particular case, and the impossibility of resolution by any semantic cataloguing.

But it is argued that this case shares the characteristics of decisions that constitute a category not yet considered, cases concerning the Constitution's guaranty, in Art. IV, § 4, of a republican form of government. A conclusion as to whether the case at bar does present a political question cannot be confidently reached until we have considered those cases with special care. We shall discover that Guaranty Clause claims involve those elements which define a "political question," and for that reason and no other, they are nonjusticiable. In particular, we shall discover that the nonjusticiability of such claims has nothing to do with their touching upon matters of state governmental organization.

Republican form of government: Luther v. Borden, 7 How. 1, though in form simply an action for damages for trespass was, as Daniel Webster said in opening the argument for the defense, "an unusual case." The defendants, admitting an otherwise tortious breaking and entering, sought to justify their action on the ground that they were agents of the established lawful government of Rhode Island, which State was then under

case is Luther v. Borden, 7 How. 1, see infra. [Footnote by the Court. See also Burke, "The Cherokee Cases: A Study in Law, Politics, and Morality," 21 Stan.L.Rev. 500 (1969).]

martial law to defend itself from active insurrection; that the plaintiff was engaged in that insurrection; and that they entered under orders to arrest the plaintiff. The case arose "out of the unfortunate political differences which agitated the people of Rhode Island in 1841 and 1842," 7 How., at 34, and which had resulted in a situation wherein two groups laid competing claims to recognition as the lawful government. The plaintiff's right to recover depended on which of the two groups was entitled to such recognition; but the lower court's refusal to receive evidence or hear argument on that issue, its charge to the jury that the earlier established or "charter" government was lawful, and the verdict for the defendants, were affirmed upon appeal to this Court. . . .

Clearly, several factors were thought by the Court in Luther to make the question there "political": the commitment to the other branches of the decision as to which is the lawful state government; the unambiguous action by the President, in recognizing the charter government as the lawful authority; the need for finality in the executive's decision; and the lack of criteria by which a court could determine which form of government was republican.

But the only significance that Luther could have for our immediate purposes is in its holding that the Guaranty Clause is not a repository of judicially manageable standards which a court could utilize independently in order to identify a State's lawful government. The Court has since refused to resort to the Guaranty Clause—which alone had been invoked for the purpose—as the source of a constitutional standard for invalidating state action. See . . . Pacific States Tel. Co. v. Oregon, 223 U.S. 118 (claim that initiative and referendum negated republican government held nonjusticiable); . . . Ohio ex rel. Bryant v. Akron Metropolitan Park District, 281 U.S. 74 (claim that rule requiring invalidation of statute by all but one justice of state court negated republican government held nonjusticiable); Highland Farms Dairy v. Agnew, 300 U.S. 608 (claim that delegation to agency of power to control milk prices violated republican government, rejected).

Just as the Court has consistently held that a challenge to state action based on the Guaranty Clause presents no justiciable question so has it held, and for the same reasons, that challenges to congressional action on the ground of inconsistency with that clause present no justiciable question. In Georgia v. Stanton, 6 Wall. 50, the State sought by an original bill to enjoin execution of the Reconstruction Acts . . . . It seemed to the Court that the only constitutional claim that could be presented was under the Guaranty Clause, and Congress having determined that the effects of the recent hostilities required extraordinary measures to restore governments of a republican form, this Court refused to interfere with Congress' action at the behest of a claimant relying on that very guaranty. . . .[2]

2. On the other hand, the implication of the Guaranty Clause in a case concerning congressional action does not always preclude judicial action. It has been held that the clause gives Congress no power to impose restrictions upon a State's admission which would undercut the constitutional mandate that the States be on an equal footing. Coyle v. Smith, 221 U.S. 559. And in Texas v. White, 7 Wall. 700, although Congress had determined that the State's government was not republican in form, the State's standing to bring an original action in this Court was sustained. [Footnote by the Court.]

We come, finally to the ultimate inquiry whether our precedents as to what constitutes a nonjusticiable "political question" bring the case before us under the umbrella of that doctrine. A natural beginning is to note whether any of the common characteristics which we have been able to identify and label descriptively are present. We find none: The question here is the consistency of state action with the Federal Constitution. We have no question decided, or to be decided, by a political branch of government co-equal with this Court. Nor do we risk embarrassment of our government abroad, or grave disturbance at home if we take issue with Tennessee as to the constitutionality of her action here challenged. Nor need the appellants, in order to succeed in this action, ask the Court to enter upon policy determinations for which judicially manageable standards are lacking. Judicial standards under the Equal Protection Clause are well developed and familiar, and it has been open to courts since the enactment of the Fourteenth Amendment to determine, if on the particular facts they must, that a discrimination reflects *no* policy, but simply arbitrary and capricious action.

This case does, in one sense, involve the allocation of political power within a State, and the appellants might conceivably have added a claim under the Guaranty Clause. Of course, as we have seen, any reliance on that clause would be futile. But because any reliance on the Guaranty Clause could not have succeeded it does not follow that appellants may not be heard on the equal protection claim which in fact they tender. . . .

We conclude then that the nonjusticiability of claims resting on the Guaranty Clause which arises from their embodiment of questions that were thought "political," can have no bearing upon the justiciability of the equal protection claim presented in this case. Finally, we emphasize that it is the involvement in Guaranty Clause claims of the elements thought to define "political questions," and no other feature, which could render them non-justiciable. Specifically, we have said that such claims are not held non-justiciable because they touch matters of state governmental organization. Brief examination of a few cases demonstrates this. [See, e. g., Gomillion v. Lightfoot, 364 U.S. 339 (1960) (p. 176, supra).]

We conclude that the complaint's allegations of a denial of equal protection present a justiciable constitutional cause of action upon which appellants are entitled to a trial and a decision. The right asserted is within the reach of judicial protection under the Fourteenth Amendment. . . .

Reversed and remanded.

Mr. Justice WHITTAKER did not participate in the decision of this case.

Mr. Justice DOUGLAS, concurring.

While I join the opinion of the Court and, like the Court, do not reach the merits, a word of explanation is necessary.[1] . . .

So far as voting rights are concerned, there are large gaps in the Constitution. Yet the right to vote is inherent in the republican form of govern-

1. I feel strongly that many of the cases cited by the Court and involving so-called "political" questions were wrongly decided. In joining the opinion, I do not approve those decisions but only construe the Court's opinion in this case as stating an accurate historical account of what the prior cases have held. [Footnote by Justice Douglas.]

ment envisaged by Article IV, Section 4 of the Constitution. . . . A "republican form" of government is guaranteed each State by Article IV, Section 4, and each is likewise promised protection against invasion.[2] That the States may specify the qualifications for voters is implicit in Article I, Section 2, Clause 1 . . . . It is, however, clear that by reason of the commands of the Constitution there are several qualifications that a State may not require. . . .

The traditional test under the Equal Protection Clause has been whether a State has made "an invidious discrimination," as it does when it selects "a particular race or nationality for oppressive treatment." . . . Universal equality is not the test; there is room for weighting. . . .

It is said that any decision in cases of this kind is beyond the competence of courts. Some make the same point as regards the problem of equal protection in cases involving racial segregation. Yet the legality of claims and conduct is a traditional subject for judicial determination. Adjudication is often perplexing and complicated. An example of the extreme complexity of the task can be seen in a decree apportioning water among the several States. Nebraska v. Wyoming, 325 U.S. 589, 665. The constitutional guide is often vague, as the decisions under the Due Process and Commerce Clauses show. The problem under the Equal Protection Clause is no more intricate. See Lewis, Legislative Apportionment and the Federal Courts, 71 Harv.L.Rev. 1057, 1083–1084.

There are, of course, some questions beyond judicial competence. Where the performance of a "duty" is left to the discretion and good judgment of an executive officer, the judiciary will not compel the exercise of his discretion one way or the other (Kentucky v. Dennison, 24 How. 66, 109), for to do so would be to take over the office. . . .

Where the Constitution assigns a particular function wholly and indivisibly [3] to another department, the federal judiciary does not intervene.

---

2. The statements in Luther v. Borden, 7 How. 1, 42, that this guaranty is enforceable only by Congress or the Chief Executive is not maintainable. Of course the Chief Executive, not the Court, determines how a State will be protected against invasion. Of course each House of Congress, not the Court, is "the Judge of the Elections, Returns, and Qualifications of its own Members." Article I, Section 5, Clause 1. But the abdication of all judicial functions respecting voting rights (7 How., at 41), however justified by the peculiarities of the charter form of government in Rhode Island at the time of Dorr's Rebellion, states no general principle. It indeed is contrary to the cases discussed in the body of this opinion—the modern decisions of the Court that give the full panoply of judicial protection to voting rights. . . .

Moreover, the Court's refusal to examine the legality of the regime of martial law which had been laid upon Rhode Island is indefensible, as Mr. Justice Woodbury maintained in his dissent. . . .

What he wrote was later to become the tradition, as expressed by Chief Justice Hughes in Sterling v. Constantin, 287 U.S. 378, 401: "What are the allowable limits of military discretion, and whether or not they have been overstepped in a particular case, are judicial questions." [Footnote by Justice Douglas.]

3. The category of the "political" question is, in my view, narrower than the decided cases indicate. . . .

In The Pocket Veto Case, 279 U.S. 655, the Court undertook a review of the veto provisions of the Constitution and concluded that the measure in litigation had not become a law. Cf. Coleman v. Miller, 307 U.S. 433.

Georgia v. Stanton, 6 Wall. 50, involved the application of the Reconstruction Acts to Georgia—laws which destroyed by force the internal regime of that State. Yet the Court refused to take

. . . . None of those cases is relevant here. There is no doubt that the federal courts have jurisdiction of controversies concerning voting rights. . . . .

The justiciability of the present claims being established, any relief accorded can be fashioned in the light of well-known principles of equity.[4]

Mr. Justice CLARK, concurring.

One emerging from the rash of opinions with their accompanying clashing of views may well find himself suffering a mental blindness. The Court holds that the appellants have alleged a cause of action. However, it refuses to award relief here—although the facts are undisputed—and fails to give the District Court any guidance whatever. One dissenting opinion, bursting with words that go through so much and conclude with so little, contemns the majority action as "a massive repudiation of the experience of our whole past." Another describes the complaint as merely asserting conclusory allegations that Tennessee's apportionment is "incorrect," "arbitrary," "obsolete," and "unconstitutional." I believe it can be shown that this case is distinguishable from earlier cases dealing with the distribution of political power by a State, that a patent violation of the Equal Protection Clause of the United States Constitution has been shown, and that an appropriate remedy may be formulated. . . .

. . . . Try as one may, Tennessee's apportionment just cannot be made to fit the pattern cut by its Constitution. . . . . An examination of Table I accompanying this opinion [omitted here] conclusively reveals that the apportionment picture in Tennessee is a topsy-turvical of gigantic proportions. This is not to say that some of the disparity cannot be explained, but when the entire Table is examined—comparing the voting strength of counties of like population as well as contrasting that of the smaller with the larger counties—it leaves but one conclusion, namely that Tennessee's apportionment is a crazy quilt without rational basis. . . .

Although I find the Tennessee apportionment statute offends the Equal Protection Clause, I would not consider intervention by this Court into so delicate a field if there were any other relief available to the people of Tennessee. But the majority of the people of Tennessee have no "practical

jurisdiction. That question was no more "political" than a host of others we have entertained. See, e. g., Pennsylvania v. West Virginia, 262 U.S. 553; Youngstown Sheet & Tube Co. v. Sawyer, 343 U.S. 579; Alabama v. Texas, 347 U.S. 272.

Today would this Court hold nonjusticiable or "political" a suit to enjoin a Governor who, like Fidel Castro, takes everything into his own hands and suspends all election laws?

Georgia v. Stanton, supra, expresses a philosophy at war with Ex parte Milligan, 4 Wall. 2, and Duncan v. Kahanamoku, 327 U.S. 304. The dominance of the civilian authority has been expressed from the beginning. See Wise v. Withers, 3 Cranch 331, 337; Sterling v. Constantin, supra, note 2. [Footnote by Justice Douglas.]

4. The recent ruling by the Iowa Supreme Court that a legislature, though elected under an unfair apportionment scheme, is nonetheless a legislature empowered to act . . . . is plainly correct.

There need be no fear of a more disastrous collision between federal and state agencies here than where a federal court enjoins gerrymandering based on racial lines. See Gomillion v. Lightfoot, supra.

The District Court need not undertake a complete reapportionment. It might possibly achieve the goal of substantial equality merely by directing respondent to eliminate the egregious injustices. Or its conclusion that reapportionment should be made may in itself stimulate legislative action. . . . [Footnote by Justice Douglas.]

opportunities for exerting their political weight at the polls" to correct the existing "invidious discrimination." Tennessee has no initiative and referendum. I have searched diligently for other "practical opportunities" present under the law. I find none other than through the federal courts. The majority of the voters have been caught up in a legislative straight jacket. Tennessee has an "informed, civically militant electorate" and "an aroused popular conscience," but it does not sear "the conscience of the people's representatives." This is because the legislative policy has riveted the present seats in the Assembly to their respective constituencies, and by the votes of their incumbents a reapportionment of any kind is prevented. The people have been rebuffed at the hands of the Assembly; they have tried the constitutional convention route, but since the call must originate in the Assembly it, too, has been fruitless. They have tried Tennessee courts with the same result, and Governors have fought the tide only to flounder. It is said that there is recourse in Congress and perhaps that may be, but from a practical standpoint this is without substance. To date Congress has never undertaken such a task in any State. We therefore must conclude that the people of Tennessee are stymied and without judicial intervention will be saddled with the present discrimination in the affairs of their state government.

Finally, we must consider if there are any appropriate modes of effective judicial relief. The federal courts are of course not forums for political debate, nor should they resolve themselves into state constitutional conventions or legislative assemblies. Nor should their jurisdiction be exercised in the hope that such a declaration as is made today may have the direct effect of bringing on legislative action and relieving the courts of the problem of fashioning relief. To my mind this would be nothing less than blackjacking the Assembly into reapportioning the State. If judicial competence were lacking to fashion an effective decree, I would dismiss this appeal. However, like the Solicitor General of the United States, I see no such difficulty in the position of this case. One plan might be to start with the existing assembly districts, consolidate some of them, and award the seats thus released to those counties suffering the most egregious discrimination. Other possibilities are present and might be more effective. But the plan here suggested would at least release the strangle hold now on the Assembly and permit it to redistrict itself. . . .

As John Rutledge (later Chief Justice) said 175 years ago in the course of the Constitutional Convention, a chief function of the Court is to secure the national rights. Its decision today supports the proposition for which our forebears fought and many died, namely, that to be fully conformable to the principle of right, the form of government must be representative. That is the keystone upon which our government was founded and lacking which no republic can survive. It is well for this Court to practice self-restraint and discipline in constitutional adjudication, but never in its history have those principles received sanction where the national rights of so many have been so clearly infringed for so long a time. National respect for the courts is more enhanced through the forthright enforcement of those rights rather than by rendering them nugatory through the interposition of subterfuges. In my view the ultimate decision today is in the greatest tradition of this Court.

Mr. Justice STEWART, concurring.

The separate writings of my dissenting and concurring brothers stray so far from the subject of today's decision as to convey, I think, a distressingly inaccurate impression of what the Court decides. For that reason, I think it appropriate, in joining the opinion of the Court, to emphasize in a few words what the opinion does and does not say. . . .

Contrary to the suggestion of my brother HARLAN, the Court does not say or imply that "state legislatures must be so structured as to reflect with approximate equality the voice of every voter." . . . The Court does not say or imply that there is anything in the Federal Constitution "to prevent a State, acting not irrationally, from choosing any electoral legislative structure it thinks best suited to the interests, temper, and customs of its people." . . . And contrary to the suggestion of my brother DOUGLAS, the Court most assuredly does not decide the question, "may a State weight the vote of one county or one district more heavily than it weights the vote in another?" . . .

. . . I repeat, the Court today decides only: (1) that the District Court possessed jurisdiction of the subject matter; (2) that the complaint presents a justiciable controversy; (3) that the appellants have standing. My brother CLARK has made a convincing prima facie showing that Tennessee's system of apportionment is in fact utterly arbitrary—without any possible justification in rationality. My brother HARLAN has, with imagination and ingenuity, hypothesized possibly rational bases for Tennessee's system. But the merits of this case are not before us now. . . .

Mr. Justice FRANKFURTER, whom Mr. Justice HARLAN joins, dissenting.

The Court today reverses a uniform course of decision established by a dozen cases, including one by which the very claim now sustained was unanimously rejected only five years ago. The impressive body of rulings thus cast aside reflected the equally uniform course of our political history regarding the relationship between population and legislative representation —a wholly different matter from denial of the franchise to individuals because of race, color, religion or sex. Such a massive repudiation of the experience of our whole past in asserting destructively novel judicial power demands a detailed analysis of the role of this Court in our constitutional scheme. Disregard of inherent limits in the effective exercise of the Court's "judicial Power" not only presages the futility of judicial intervention in the essentially political conflict of forces by which the relation between population and representation has time out of mind been and now is determined. It may well impair the Court's position as the ultimate organ of "the supreme Law of the Land" in that vast range of legal problems, often strongly entangled in popular feeling, on which this Court must pronounce. The Court's authority—possessed neither of the purse nor the sword—ultimately rests on sustained public confidence in its moral sanction. Such feeling must be nourished by the Court's complete detachment, in fact and in appearance, from political entanglements and by abstention from injecting itself into the clash of political forces in political settlements.

A hypothetical claim resting on abstract assumptions is now for the first time made the basis for affording illusory relief for a particular evil even though it foreshadows deeper and more pervasive difficulties in consequence. The claim is hypothetical and the assumptions are abstract because the Court does not vouchsafe the lower courts—state and federal—guidelines for formulating specific, definite, wholly unprecedented remedies for the inevitable litigations that today's umbrageous disposition is bound to stimulate in connection with politically motivated reapportionments in so many States. In such a setting, to promulgate jurisdiction in the abstract is meaningless. It is as devoid of reality as "a brooding omnipresence in the sky" for it conveys no intimation what relief, if any, a District Court is capable of affording that would not invite legislatures to play ducks and drakes with the judiciary. For this Court to direct the District Court to enforce a claim to which the Court has over the years consistently found itself required to deny legal enforcement and at the same time to find it necessary to withhold any guidance to the lower court how to enforce this turnabout, new legal claim, manifests an odd—indeed an esoteric—conception of judicial propriety. One of the Court's supporting opinions, as elucidated by commentary, unwittingly affords a disheartening preview of the mathematical quagmire (apart from divers judicially inappropriate and elusive determinants) into which this Court today catapults the lower courts of the country without so much as adumbrating the basis for a legal calculus as a means of extrication. Even assuming the indispensable intellectual disinterestedness on the part of judges in such matters, they do not have accepted legal standards or criteria or even reliable analogies to draw upon for making judicial judgments. To charge courts with the task of accommodating the incommensurable factors of policy that underlie these mathematical puzzles is to attribute, however flatteringly, omnicompetence to judges. . . .

Recent legislation, creating a district appropriately described as "an atrocity of ingenuity," is not unique. Considering the gross inequality among legislative electoral units within almost every State, the Court naturally shrinks from asserting that in districting at least substantial equality is a constitutional requirement enforceable by courts. Room continues to be allowed for weighting. This of course implies that geography, economics, urban-rural conflict, and all the other non-legal factors which have throughout our history entered into political districting are to some extent not to be ruled out in the undefined vista now opened up by review in the federal courts of state reapportionments. To some extent—aye, there's the rub. In effect, today's decision empowers the courts of the country to devise what should constitute the proper composition of the legislatures of the fifty States. If state courts should for one reason or another find themselves unable to discharge this task, the duty of doing so is put on the federal courts or on this Court, if State views do not satisfy this Court's notion of what is proper districting.

We were soothingly told at the bar of this Court that we need not worry about the kind of remedy a court could effectively fashion once the abstract constitutional right to have courts pass on a state-wide system of electoral districting is recognized as a matter of judicial rhetoric, because legislatures would heed the Court's admonition. This is not only a euphoric hope. It implies a sorry confession of judicial impotence in place of a frank acknowledgment that there is not under our Constitution a judicial remedy for every political mischief, for every undesirable exercise of legislative power. The Framers carefully and with deliberate forethought refused so to enthrone the judiciary. In this situation, as in others of like nature, appeal for relief does not belong here. Appeal must be to an informed, civically militant electorate. In a democratic society like ours, relief must come through an aroused popular conscience that sears the conscience of the people's representatives. In any event there is nothing judicially more unseemly nor more self-defeating than for this Court to make *in terrorem* pronouncements, to indulge in merely empty rhetoric, sounding a word of promise to the ear, sure to be disappointing to the hope. . . .

The Colegrove doctrine, in the form in which repeated decisions have settled it, was not an innovation. It represents long judicial thought and experience. From its earliest opinions this Court has consistently recognized a class of controversies which do not lend themselves to judicial standards and judicial remedies. To classify the various instances as "political questions" is rather a form of stating this conclusion than revealing of analysis. Some of the cases so labelled have no relevance here. But from others emerge unifying considerations that are compelling.

The cases concerning war or foreign affairs, for example, are usually explained by the necessity of the country's speaking with one voice in such matters. While this concern alone undoubtedly accounts for many of the decisions, others do not fit the pattern. . . . The dominant consideration is "the lack of satisfactory criteria for a judicial determination". . . .

This may be, like so many questions of law, a matter of degree. Questions have arisen under the Constitution to which adjudication gives answer although the criteria for decision are less than unwavering bright lines. Often in these cases illumination was found in the federal structures established by, or the underlying presuppositions of, the Constitution. . . . It is also true that even regarding the duration of war and the status of Indian tribes, referred to above as subjects ordinarily committed exclusively to the non-judicial branches, the Court has suggested that some limitations exist upon the range within which the decisions of those branches will be permitted to go unreviewed. . . . But this is merely to acknowledge that particular circumstances may differ so greatly in degree as to differ thereby in kind, and that, although within a certain range of cases on a continuum, no standard of distinction can be found to tell between them, other cases will fall above or below the range. The doctrine of political questions, like any other, is not to be applied beyond the limits of its own logic, with all the quiddities and abstract disharmonies it may manifest. See the disposition of contentions based on logically distorting views of Colegrove v. Green . . . in Gomillion v. Lightfoot, 364 U.S. 339.

The Court has been particularly unwilling to intervene in matters concerning the structure and organization of the political institutions of the States. . . . The cases involving Negro disfranchisement are no exception to the principle of avoiding federal judicial intervention into matters of state government in the absence of an explicit and clear constitutional imperative. For here the controlling command of Supreme Law is plain and unequivocal. . . .

The influence of these converging considerations—the caution not to undertake decision where standards meet for judicial judgment are lacking, the reluctance to interfere with matters of state government in the absence of an unquestionable and effectively enforceable mandate, the unwillingness

to make courts arbiters of the broad issues of political organization historically committed to other institutions and for whose adjustment the judicial
process is ill-adapted—has been decisive of the settled line of cases, reaching back more than a century, which holds that Art. IV, § 4, of the Constitution, guaranteeing to the States "a Republican Form of Government," is
not enforceable through the courts. . . .

The present case involves all of the elements that have made the Guarantee Clause cases non-justiciable. It is, in effect, a Guarantee Clause claim
masquerading under a different label. But it cannot make the case more fit
for judicial action that appellants invoke the Fourteenth Amendment rather
than Art. IV, § 4, where, in fact, the gist of their complaint is the same—
unless it can be found that the Fourteenth Amendment speaks with greater
particularity to their situation. . . . Art. IV, § 4, is not committed by
express constitutional terms to Congress. It is the nature of the controversies arising under it, nothing else, which has made it judicially unenforceable. . . .

At first blush, [appellants'] charge of discrimination based on legislative underrepresentation is given the appearance of a more private, less impersonal claim, than the assertion that the frame of government is askew.
. . . However, the discrimination relied on is the deprivation of what
appellants conceive to be their proportionate share of political influence.
This, of course, is the practical effect of any allocation of power within the
institutions of government. . . .

What, then, is this question of legislative apportionment? Appellants
invoke the right to vote and to have their votes counted. But they are permitted to vote and their votes are counted. They go to the polls, they cast
their ballots, they send their representatives to the state councils. Their
complaint is simply that the representatives are not sufficiently numerous or
powerful—in short, that Tennessee has adopted a basis of representation
with which they are dissatisfied. Talk of "debasement" or "dilution" is circular talk. One cannot speak of "debasement" or "dilution" of the value
of a vote until there is first defined a standard of reference as to what a
vote should be worth. What is actually asked of the Court in this case is
to choose among competing bases of representation—ultimately, really,
among competing theories of political philosophy—in order to establish an
appropriate frame of government for the State of Tennessee and thereby for
all the States of the Union.

In such a matter, abstract analogies which ignore the facts of history
deal in unrealities; they betray reason. This is not a case in which a State
has, through a device however oblique and sophisticated, denied Negroes or
Jews or redheaded persons a vote, or given them only a third or a sixth of
a vote. That was Gomillion v. Lightfoot, 364 U.S. 339. What Tennessee
illustrates is an old and still widespread method of representation—representation by local geographical division, only in part respective of population—in preference to others, others, forsooth, more appealing. Appellants contest this choice and seek to make this Court the arbiter of the
disagreement. They would make the Equal Protection Clause the charter
of adjudication, asserting that the equality which it guarantees comports,
if not the assurance of equal weight to every voter's vote, at least the basic
conception that representation ought to be proportionate to population, a

standard by reference to which the reasonableness of apportionment plans may be judged.

To find such a political conception legally enforceable in the broad and unspecific guarantee of equal protection is to rewrite the Constitution. See Luther v. Borden, supra. Certainly, "equal protection" is no more secure a foundation for judicial judgment of the permissibility of varying forms of representative government than is "Republican Form." Indeed since "equal protection of the laws" can only mean an equality of persons standing in the same relation to whatever governmental action is challenged, the determination whether treatment is equal presupposes a determination concerning the nature of the relationship. This, with respect to apportionment, means an inquiry into the theoretic base of representation in an acceptably republican state. For a court could not determine the equal-protection issue without in fact first determining the Republican-Form issue, simply because what is reasonable for equal protection purposes will depend upon what frame of government, basically, is allowed. To divorce "equal protection" from "Republican Form" is to talk about half a question.

The notion that representation proportioned to the geographic spread of population is so universally accepted as a necessary element of equality between man and man that it must be taken to be the standard of a political equality preserved by the Fourteenth Amendment—that it is, in appellants' words, "the basic principle of representative government"—is, to put it bluntly, not true. However desirable and however desired by some among the great political thinkers and framers of our government, it has never been generally practiced, today or in the past. It was not the English system, it was not the colonial system, it was not the system chosen for the national government by the Constitution, it was not the system exclusively or even predominantly practiced by the States at the time of adoption of the Fourteenth Amendment, it is not predominantly practiced by the States today. Unless judges, the judges of this Court, are to make their private views of political wisdom the measure of the Constitution—views which in all honesty cannot but give the appearance, if not reflect the reality, of involvement with the business of partisan politics so inescapably a part of apportionment controversies—the Fourteenth Amendment, "itself a historical product," . . . provides no guide for judicial oversight of the representation problem. . . .

Manifestly, the Equal Protection Clause supplies no clearer guide for judicial examination of apportionment methods than would the Guarantee Clause itself. Apportionment, by its character, is a subject of extraordinary complexity, involving—even after the fundamental theoretical issues concerning what is to be represented in a representative legislature have been fought out or compromised—considerations of geography, demography, electoral convenience, economic and social cohesions or divergencies among particular local groups, communications, the practical effects of political institutions like the lobby and the city machine, ancient traditions and ties of settled usage, respect for proven incumbents of long experience and senior status, mathematical mechanics, censuses compiling relevant data, and a host of others. . . . The practical significance of apportionment is that the next election results may differ because of it. Apportionment battles are overwhelmingly party or intra-party contests. It will add a virulent source of friction and tension in federal state relations to embroil the federal judiciary in them. . . .

Although the District Court had jurisdiction in the very restricted sense of power to determine whether it could adjudicate the claim, the case is of that class of political controversy which, by the nature of its subject, is unfit for federal judicial action. The judgment of the District Court, in dismissing the complaint for failure to state a claim on which relief can be granted, should therefore be affirmed.

Dissenting opinion of Mr. Justice HARLAN, whom Mr. Justice FRANKFURTER joins. . . .

Once one cuts through the thicket of discussion devoted to "jurisdiction," "standing," "justiciability," and "political question," there emerges a straight-forward issue which, in my view, is determinative of this case. Does the complaint disclose a violation of a federal constitutional right, in other words, a claim over which a United States District Court would have jurisdiction under 28 U.S.C. § 1343(3) and 42 U.S.C. § 1983? The majority opinion does not actually discuss this basic question, but, as one concurring Justice observes, seems to decide it *"sub silentio."* However, in my opinion, appellants' allegations, accepting all of them as true, do not, parsed down or as a whole, show an infringement by Tennessee of any rights assured by the Fourteenth Amendment. Accordingly, I believe the complaint should have been dismissed for "failure to state a claim upon which relief can be granted."

In short, there is nothing in the Federal Constitution to prevent a State, acting not irrationally, from choosing any electoral legislative structure it thinks best suited to the interests, temper, and customs of its people. I would have thought this proposition settled by MacDougall v. Green, 335 U.S. 281, at p. 283, in which the Court observed that to "assume that political power is a function exclusively of numbers is to disregard the practicalities of government"

The suggestion of my Brother FRANKFURTER that courts lack standards by which to decide such cases as this, is relevant not only to the question of "justiciability," but also, and perhaps more fundamentally, to the determination whether any cognizable constitutional claim has been asserted in this case. Courts are unable to decide when it is that an apportionment originally valid becomes void because the factors entering into such a decision are basically matters appropriate only for legislative judgment. And so long as there exists a possible rational legislative policy for retaining an existing apportionment, such a legislative decision cannot be said to breach the bulwark against arbitrariness and caprice that the Fourteenth Amendment affords. . . .

From a reading of the majority and concurring opinions one will not find it difficult to catch the premises that underlie this decision. The fact that the appellants have been unable to obtain political redress of their asserted grievances appears to be regarded as a matter which should lead the Court to stretch to find some basis for judicial intervention. While the Equal Protection Clause is invoked, the opinion for the Court notably eschews explaining how, consonant with past decisions, the undisputed facts in this case can be considered to show a violation of that constitutional provision. The majority seems to have accepted the argument, pressed at the bar, that if this Court merely asserts authority in this field, Tennessee and other "malapportioning" States will quickly respond with appropriate political action, so that this Court need not be greatly concerned about the federal courts becoming further involved in these matters. At the same time the majority has wholly failed to reckon with what the future may hold in store if this optimistic prediction is not fulfilled. Thus, what the Court is doing reflects more an adventure in judicial experimentation than a solid piece of constitutional adjudication.

. . . Those observers of the Court who see it primarily as the last refuge for the correction of all inequality or injustice, no matter what its nature or source, will no doubt applaud this decision and its break with the past. Those who consider that continuing national respect for the Court's authority depends in large measure upon its wise exercise of self-restraint and discipline in constitutional adjudication, will view the decision with deep concern.*

POLITICAL QUESTIONS AND JUSTICIABILITY

1. *Criteria of decision beyond the judicial grasp.* a. *The Coleman v. Miller formulation.* The Court's opinion in Baker v. Carr notes among the identifying features of a political question "a lack of judicially discoverable and manageable standards." To what extent is that lack an independent ground of nonjusticiability? Note a well-known passage in Coleman v. Miller, 307 U.S. 433 (1939), in the course of Chief Justice Hughes' explanation why courts could not decide whether the proposed Child Labor Amendment, proposed by Congress in 1924, had lost its vitality through lapse of time and accordingly could not be ratified by a state legislature in 1937:

"Where are to be found the criteria for such a judicial determination? None are to be found in Constitution or statute. In their endeavor to answer this question petitioners' counsel have suggested that at least two years should be allowed; that six years would not seem to be unreasonably long; that seven years had been used by the Congress as a reasonable period; that one year, six months and thirteen days was the average time used in passing upon amendments which have been ratified since the first ten amendments; that three years, six months and twenty-five days has been the longest time used in ratifying. To this list of variables, counsel add that 'the nature and extent of publicity and the activity of the public and of the legislatures of the several States in relation to any particular proposal should be taken into consideration.' That statement is pertinent, but there are additional matters to be examined and weighed. When a proposed amendment springs

---

* The cases after Baker v. Carr—developing the substantive constitutional standards applicable to legislative apportionment cases—are considered in chapter 18, below. See Reynolds v. Sims, the 1964 "one-man, one-vote" case, p. 1438, and the accompanying material. For a sampling of the extensive commentary on Baker v. Carr, see Neal, "Baker v. Carr: Politics in Search of Law," 1962 Supreme Court Rev. 252; McCloskey, "Foreword: The Reapportionment Case", 76 Harv. L.Rev. 54 (1962); Emerson, "Malapportionment and Judicial Power," 72 Yale L.J. 64 (1962); and McKay, "Political Thickets and Crazy Quilts: Reapportionment and Equal Protection," 61 Mich.L.Rev. 645 (1963).

from a conception of economic needs, it would be necessary, in determining whether a reasonable time had elapsed since its submission, to consider the economic conditions prevailing in the country, whether these had so far changed since the submission as to make the proposal no longer responsive to the conception which inspired it or whether conditions were such as to intensify the feeling of need and the appropriateness of the proposed remedial action. *In short, the question of a reasonable time in many cases would involve, as in this case it does involve, an appraisal of a great variety of relevant conditions, political, social and economic, which can hardly be said to be within the appropriate range of evidence receivable in a court of justice and as to which it would be an extravagant extension of judicial authority to assert judicial notice as the basis of deciding a controversy with respect to the validity of an amendment actually ratified.* On the other hand, these conditions are appropriate for the consideration of the political departments of the Government. The questions they involve are essentially political and not justiciable. They can be decided by the Congress with the full knowledge and appreciation ascribed to the national legislature of the political, social and economic conditions which have prevailed during the period since the submission of the amendment." (Emphasis added.)

b. *The adequacy of the formulation.* Does this formulation adequately distinguish the reasonable time question in Coleman from those issues courts have found justiciable? Did the Baker v. Carr claim involve more manageable criteria? Did Brown v. Board of Education, the 1954 School Segregation decision (chap. 18, p. 1422) call for appraisal of a narrower "variety of relevant conditions"? Compare the formulation in Scharpf, "Judicial Review and the Political Question: A Functional Analysis," 75 Yale L.J. 518, 587 (1966):

"[The Supreme Court may find a political question] when its access to relevant information is insufficient to assure the correct determination of particular issues, when the Court would have to question the position taken by the government in an international dispute, or when an independent determination by the Court would interfere with the specific responsibilities of another department for dealing with a wider context which itself would be beyond the Court's reach. But even though one or more of these factors may be present, the Court will not usually apply the doctrine to the constitutional guarantees of individual rights and to conflicts of competence among the departments of the federal government and between the federal government and the states."

c. *Complexity, justiciability, and the merits.* Were the questions in Baker v. Carr significantly more complex than in other areas of equal protection litigation (chap. 14 below) or in free speech controversies? Did concern over complexity in Baker simply reflect views on the merits? Compare Justice Frankfurter's exploration of multiple variables with the simple "one-man, one-vote" rule derived by the majority in subsequent apportionment cases, chap. 18 below. If the Baker question was truly complex, why should not the equal protection claim have been dismissed on the merits? Compare Justice Frankfurter's view with Justice Harlan's: What justification was there for finding Baker nonjusticiable, rather than ruling on the merits that the challenged action was not unconstitutional?

2. *Constitutional commitment of the issue to other organs.* a. *The Wechsler examples.* In the listing of identifying features of political ques-

tions in Baker v. Carr, the reference to lack of judicially manageable standards is preceded by mention of "a textually demonstrable commitment of the issue to a coordinate political department." What constitutional provisions can be interpreted as containing such a "commitment"? Herbert Wechsler's "Toward Neutral Principles of Constitutional Law" lecture, noted at the beginning of this section, finds such commitments "explicit" with respect to impeachments in Art. I, § 3 (Senate's "sole Power to try") and to the seating or expulsion of Congressmen in Art. I, § 5 (each House shall judge "Qualifications of its own Members" and may "expel a Member"). He suggests, moreover, that such commitments to other branches are "implicit" in other provisions—e. g., the "Republican Form of Government" clause.

b. *The Powell case.* What is necessary to demonstrate such textual commitments, explicit or implicit? In Powell v. McCormack, 395 U.S. 486 (1969), holding that Congressman Adam Clayton Powell, Jr., had been unlawfully excluded from the House, the Court, in the course of setting aside a number of political question objections, found that Art. I, § 5, did not constitute such a commitment: "[W]e have concluded that Art. I, § 5, is at most a 'textually demonstrable commitment' to Congress to judge only the qualifications expressly set forth in the Constitution." The Powell case is printed with other separation of powers materials in chap. 7, p. 577, below.

c. *The Guarantee Clause.* But the Republican Form of Government Guarantee continued to be found nonjusticiable in Baker v. Carr, as it had in the important earlier political question cases (both examined in the principal case), Luther v. Borden, 7 How. 1 (1849), and Pacific States Tel. & Tel. Co. v. Oregon, 223 U.S. 118 (1912). Was Baker nevertheless really "a Guarantee Clause claim masquerading under a different label," as Justice Frankfurter argued? Should the Clause be found justiciable? See Bonfield, "Baker v. Carr: New Light on the Constitutional Guarantee of Republican Government," 50 Calif.L.Rev. 245 (1962): "The clause is neither textually committed to the exclusive enforcement of another department, nor bare of judicially discoverable or manageable standards." See also Bonfield, "The Guarantee Clause of Article IV, Section 4: A Study in Constitutional Desuetude," 46 Minn.L.Rev. 513 (1962).

d. *The amendment process.* Are the constitutional amendment provisions in Art. V "textually demonstrable commitments"? In Coleman v. Miller, 307 U.S. 433 (1939), the Court—before turning to the "reasonable time" issue, note a above—disposed of the question whether a state legislature could ratify an amendment after a previous rejection: "[This question] should be regarded as a political question pertaining to the political departments, with the ultimate authority in the Congress in the exercise of its control over the promulgation of the adoption of the amendment." See also the concurring opinion by Justice Black, for four of the Justices, insisting that the Court had not made it clear enough that the Constitution "grants Congress exclusive power to control submission of constitutional amendments." He urged that courts should avoid any dicta regarding amendments, so that there would be no doubt at all that amendment process issues were wholly "political questions," entirely to be decided by Congress, the department "to which the Constitution has committed it." (See also the materials on the amendment process below, chap. 5, sec. 5, p. 407.)

3. *Controversy, enforceability, and justiciability.* a. *The relevance of remedies.* Should difficulty in formulating effective judicial remedies bar justiciability? Should risk of defiance to court orders? Should the Court invoke the political question doctrine to avoid excessively controversial adjudications? These factors do not appear in the list of identifying features of Baker v. Carr. Were they relevant to the justiciability issue there? In the School Segregation Cases? In Establishment Clause Cases?

b. *Enforcement and the Powell case.* Should enforcement problems play a larger role when the Court risks disobedience from President and Congress rather than from the states? These problems are considered further with the separation of powers materials in chap. 7, below. Thus, though a Cabinet member was the defendant, it was presidential action that was found illegal in the Steel Seizure Case, Youngstown Sheet & Tube Co. v. Sawyer, 343 U.S. 579 (1952) (p. 556 below). Compare ousted Congressman Powell's suit against Speaker McCormack and others, Powell v. McCormack, 395 U.S. 486 (1969), already noted and also printed in chap. 7 (p. 577). The Court dismissed the action against the named Congressmen, partly because of the Speech and Debate Clause, Art. I, § 6. Judicial review of the exclusion of Powell was achieved by proceeding with the action against those defendants who were House employees rather than legislators.

Among the political question arguments rejected in Powell was that adjudication would produce a "potentially embarrassing confrontation between coordinate branches." The Court noted: "The alleged conflict that such an adjudication may cause cannot justify the courts' avoiding their constitutional responsibility." And a footnote to that sentence added: "In fact, the Court has noted that it is an 'inadmissible suggestion' that action might be taken in disregard of a judicial determination. McPherson v. Blacker, 146 U.S. 1, 24 (1892)." The Powell decision also rejected the argument that the case was not justiciable because a court could not "mold effective relief." The Court did not reach the question whether the Speech and Debate Clause barred coercive relief, since plaintiff had also sought available declaratory relief.

c. *Justiciability and Vietnam.* Problems of complexity, controversiality, and enforceability are also suggested by the unsuccessful efforts to elicit an adjudication of the legality of American military involvement in Vietnam. See, for example, the dissents from the denial of certiorari in Mora v. McNamara, 389 U.S. 934 (1967) (p. 601, infra), especially Justice Stewart's reference to the "serious preliminary issues of justiciability" raised by the case. These questions, too, are considered further with the separation of powers discussion in chap. 7, below.

Part II

THE STRUCTURE OF GOVERNMENT: NATION AND STATES IN THE FEDERAL SYSTEM

Introduction. Stronger government was necessary, but government must not become too powerful: these were dominant concerns to the Framers, and the Constitution reflects their effort to accommodate these needs and risks. That document granted greater powers to the central government to cure some of the weaknesses under the Articles of Confederation; yet the Constitution also assured restraints on governmental power. To the drafters of 1787, protection against excessive concentrations of power lay less in explicit limits such as the "shall nots" of the Bill of Rights than in diffusions of power among a variety of governmental units. Thus, the Constitution allocates powers among nation and states: a federal division of powers is achieved by specifying (most notably in Art. I, Sec. 8) those powers Congress might exercise and by emphasizing (in the Tenth Amendment) that undelegated powers were "reserved to the States respectively, or to the people." Moreover, the less-than-total powers given to the national government are diffused among three separate branches, separately described in the first three Articles of the Constitution.

Part II of this casebook deals with these grants and dispersals of power. These chapters explore not only the governmental actions these grants justify but also the limits these grants imply. How can the scope of national authority be articulated with an adequate regard for the interest in local autonomy? That is the focus of chapters 3 through 6: they examine the extent and limits of authority when national power seeks to reach arguably local affairs. Chapter 7 turns from the nation-state dimension to examine the restraints imposed by the separation of powers within the national government—by the distribution of national powers among executive, legislative, and judicial branches. Chapters 8, 9, and 10 return to the federalism, nation-state dimension: they focus on states rather than national authority—and especially on the limits on state power imposed by national governmental concerns, particularly as reflected in the grant to Congress of the power to regulate interstate commerce.

Chapter 3

NATIONAL POWERS AND LOCAL ACTIVITIES: ORIGINS AND RECURRENT THEMES

Introduction: Federalism—Antiquarian Relic? Contemporary Value? Federalism is the major concern of Part II of this book. The first four chapters of Part II, on the scope of the powers granted to Congress by the Constitutional Convention, include the most controversial impacts of federalism on

American history.   Again and again in these pages, legislation enacted with great popular support is held unconstitutional by the Supreme Court.   And in a larger number of instances, states' rights arguments—some principled, some disingenuous—have defeated or delayed congressional action.   The materials that follow focus on federalism-related limits on national power: limits developed in the interest of curtailing national intrusion into intra-state affairs, as distinguished from restraints stemming from individual rights guarantees (considered in Part III of this book).

The controversial impacts of federalism-related limits suggest questions relevant to much of what follows: What were the historical justifications for American federalism?   How successfully has the Supreme Court applied those values to changing circumstances?   These questions in turn raise even more basic ones: Does federalism retain sufficient value in the modern context, or is it an obsolete obstruction to be dismissed with minimal lip service?   And should the Supreme Court be the predominant custodian of federalism?   Are substantial Court-imposed limits on congressional power unnecessary because local interests are adequately safeguarded by the political processes?   Even if Court restraint vis-a-vis Congress is appropriate, is the Court never-theless compelled to act as the interventionist umpire of the federal system vis-a-vis the states, by blocking state intrusions on national interest?   Re-call Justice Holmes' famous remark: "I do not think the United States would come to an end if we lost our power to declare an act of Congress void. I do think that the Union would be imperiled if we could not make that declaration as to the laws of the several states."   Holmes, Collected Legal Papers (1920), 295.   But so long as the power "to declare an act of Con-gress void" exists, is the Court justified in relinquishing it in part, or in adopting a greater "hands-off" attitude in some areas than in others?

The appropriate role of the Court in the evolution of federalism is an issue apparent on the face of many of the materials that follow.   Related, equally pervasive questions typically lurk beneath the surface: What are the values, historical and contemporary, of federalism?   Can it still be said that federalism increases liberty, encourages diversity, promotes creative experi-mentation and responsive self-government?   Or is it a legalistic obstruction, a harmful brake on governmental responses to pressing social issues, a shield for selfish vested interests?   Is federalism a theme that constitutional law must grapple with simply because it is *there,* in the Constitution?   Is the prime challenge it poses that of minimizing the obstacles that the complexities of federalism put in the way of meeting modern needs?   Or does federalism embody more appealing values that deserve some of the imaginative enthu-siasm with which modern constitutional law embraces the promotion of such values as equality and freedom of speech?

"Diversity, pluralism, experimentation, protection from arbitrary ma-joritarianism and over-centralization, and a greater degree of citizen partici-pation"—so a recent effort to articulate the values inherent in American fed-eralism puts it.   Advisory Commission on Intergovernmental Relations, Ur-ban America and the Federal System (1969), 105.   Yet, as that Report il-lustrates, those values will not be adequately realized unless the federal sys-tem can respond more effectively to such pressing modern problems as "the malaise of our metropolitan areas."   That Report urges "aggressive and imaginative" structural and fiscal assistance so that states—with boundaries reflecting history rather than current functional needs—may help cure the "illness" of "the problem of making metropolitan areas governable."

Federalism has not only been the American response for governing large geographical areas with diverse local needs. The federal model has also provided a mechanism for governments of other nations, as well as for international cooperation. See generally Wheare, Federal Government (3d ed. 1953); Macmahon (ed.), Federalism: Mature and Emergent (1955); Friedrich, Trends of Federalism in Theory and Practice (1968). The frictions and accommodations during 180 years of American experience, the concerns of the materials that follow, deserve consideration not only for their own sake but also for the light they shed on federalism's capacity to adapt to future needs, here and elsewhere.

Congressional powers should be broadly construed.

McCULLOCH v. MARYLAND

4 Wheat. 316, 4 L.Ed. 579 (1819).

Error to the Court of Appeals of the State of Maryland.

[A Maryland statute enacted in 1818 provided that no bank operating in Maryland "without authority from the state" could issue bank notes "except upon stamped paper" issued by the state. The act specified the "fees" payable for the stamped paper, ranging from ten cents for a five dollar note to twenty dollars for every thousand dollar note. Any bank subject to the requirement could, however, "relieve itself from the operation of the provisions aforesaid, by paying annually, in advance, . . . the sum of fifteen thousand dollars." The statute also provided for penalties for violators: for example, the president, cashier and all other officers of the bank were to "forfeit" five hundred dollars "for each and every offense." The penalties were enforceable by indictment or by "action of debt, in the county court . . ., one-half to the informer, and the other half to the use of the state."

[This action for the statutory penalty was brought in the County Court of Baltimore County by one John James, suing for himself and the State, against James McCulloch, the Cashier of the Baltimore branch of the Bank of the United States. It was admitted that the Bank was doing business without authority from the State and that McCulloch had issued bank notes without complying with the Maryland law. The case was decided against McCulloch on the basis of the agreed statement of facts, and the decision was affirmed by the Maryland Court of Appeals. From there, the case was taken by writ of error to the Supreme Court.* For the historical context of the dispute, see the materials following the Court's opinion.]

* The Official Reporter noted that "this case involving a constitutional question of great importance, and the sovereign rights of the United States and the State of Maryland, and the Government of the United States having directed their Attorney General to appear for the plaintiff in error, the Court dispensed with its general rule permitting only two counsel to argue for each party." Six counsel (United States Attorney General William Wirt, Daniel Webster and William Pinkney for the Bank; State Attorney General Luther Martin, Joseph Hopkinson and Walter Jones for Maryland) argued the case over a period of nine days. The opinion was delivered only three days after the arguments had been concluded.

Mr. Chief Justice MARSHALL delivered the opinion of the Court:

In the case now to be determined, the defendant, a sovereign State, denies the obligation of a law enacted by the legislature of the Union, and the plaintiff, on his part, contests the validity of an act which has been passed by the legislature of that State. The constitution of our country, in its most interesting and vital parts, is to be considered; the conflicting powers of the government of the Union and of its members, as marked in that constitution, are to be discussed; and an opinion given which may essentially influence the great operations of the government. No tribunal can approach such a question without a deep sense of its importance, and of the awful responsibility involved in its decision. But it must be decided peacefully, or remain a source of hostile legislation, perhaps of hostility of a still more serious nature; and if it is to be so decided by this tribunal alone can the decision be made. On the Supreme Court of the United States has the constitution of our country devolved this important duty.

The first question made in the cause is, has Congress power to incorporate a bank?

It has been truly said that this can scarcely be considered as an open question, entirely unprejudiced by the former proceedings of the nation respecting it. The principle now contested was introduced at a very early period of our history, has been recognized by many successive legislatures, and has been acted upon by the judicial department, in cases of peculiar delicacy, as a law of undoubted obligation.

It will not be denied, that a bold and daring usurpation might be resisted, after an acquiescence still longer and more complete than this. But it is conceived that a doubtful question, one on which human reason may pause, and the human judgment be suspended, in the decision of which the great principles of liberty are not concerned, but the respective powers of those who are equally the representatives of the people are to be adjusted; if not put at rest by the practice of the government, ought to receive a considerable impression from that practice. An exposition of the constitution, deliberately established by legislative acts, on the faith of which an immense property has been advanced, ought not to be lightly disregarded.

The power now contested was exercised by the first Congress elected under the present constitution. The bill for incorporating the bank of the United States did not steal upon an unsuspecting legislature, and pass unobserved. Its principle was completely understood, and was opposed with equal zeal and ability. After being resisted, first in the fair and open field of debate, and afterwards in the executive cabinet, with as much persevering talent as any measure has ever experienced, and being supported by arguments which convinced minds as pure and as intelligent as this country can boast, it became a law. The original act was permitted to expire; but a short experience of the embarrassments to which the refusal to revive it exposed the government, convinced those who were most prejudiced against the measure of its necessity and induced the passage of the present law. It would require no ordinary share of intrepidity to assert that a measure adopted under these circumstances was a bold and plain usurpation, to which the constitution gave no countenance.

These observations belong to the cause; but they are not made under the impression that, were the question entirely new, the law would be found irreconcilable with the constitution.

In discussing this question, the counsel for the State of Maryland have deemed it of some importance, in the construction of the constitution, to consider that instrument not as emanating from the people, but as the act of sovereign and independent States. The powers of the general government, it has been said, are delegated by the States, who alone are truly sovereign; and must be exercised in subordination to the States, who alone possess supreme dominion.

It would be difficult to sustain this proposition. The Convention which framed the constitution was indeed elected by the state legislatures. But the instrument, when it came from their hands, was a mere proposal, without obligation, or pretensions to it. It was reported to the then existing Congress of the United States, with a request that it might "be submitted to a convention of delegates, chosen in each State by the people thereof, under the recommendation of its legislature, for their assent and ratification." This mode of proceeding was adopted; and by the convention, by Congress, and by the state legislatures, the instrument was submitted to the people. They acted upon it in the only manner in which they can act safely, effectively, and wisely, on such a subject, by assembling in convention. It is true they assembled in their several States—and where else should they have assembled? No political dreamer was ever wild enough to think of breaking down the lines which separate the States, and of compounding the American people into one common mass. Of consequence, when they act, they act in their States. But the measures they adopt do not, on that account, cease to be the measures of the people themselves, or become the measures of the state governments.

From these conventions the constitution derives its whole authority. The government proceeds directly from the people; is "ordained and established" in the name of the people; and is declared to be ordained, "in order to form a more perfect union, establish justice, insure domestic tranquillity, and secure the blessings of liberty, to themselves and to their posterity." The assent of the States, in their sovereign capacity, is implied in calling a convention, and thus submitting that instrument to the people. But the people were at perfect liberty to accept or reject it; and their act was final. It required not the affirmance, and could not be negatived, by the state governments. The constitution, when thus adopted, was of complete obligation, and bound the state sovereignties. . . . .

The government of the Union, then, (whatever may be the influence of this fact on the case), is emphatically, and truly, a government of the people. In form and in substance it emanates from them. Its powers are granted by them, and are to be exercised directly on them, and for their benefit.

This government is acknowledged by all to be one of enumerated powers. The principle, that it can exercise only the powers granted to it, would seem too apparent to have required to be enforced by all those arguments which its enlightened friends, while it was depending before the people, found it necessary to urge. That principle is now universally admitted. But the question respecting the extent of the powers actually granted, is perpetually arising, and will probably continue to arise, as long as our system shall exist.

In discussing these questions, the conflicting powers of the general and state governments must be brought into view, and the supremacy of their respective laws, when they are in opposition, must be settled.

If any one proposition could command the universal assent of mankind, we might expect it would be this—that the government of the Union, though limited in its powers, is supreme within its sphere of action. This would seem to result necessarily from its nature. It is the government of all; its powers are delegated by all; it represents all, and acts for all. Though any one State may be willing to control its operations, no State is willing to allow others to control them. The nation, on those subjects on which it can act, must necessarily bind its component parts. But this question is not left to mere reason: the people have, in express terms, decided it, by saying, "this constitution, and the laws of the United States, which shall be made in pursuance thereof," "shall be the supreme law of the land," and by requiring that the members of the state legislatures, and the officers of the executive and judicial departments of the states shall take the oath of fidelity to it.

The government of the United States, then, though limited in its powers, is supreme; and its laws, when made in pursuance of the constitution, form the supreme law of the land, "any thing in the constitution or laws of any state to the contrary notwithstanding."

Among the enumerated powers, we do not find that of establishing a bank or creating a corporation. But there is no phrase in the instrument which, like the articles of confederation, excludes incidental or implied powers; and which requires that everything granted shall be expressly and minutely described. Even the 10th amendment, which was framed for the purpose of quieting the excessive jealousies which had been excited, omits the word "expressly," and declares only that the powers "not delegated to the United States, nor prohibited to the States, are reserved to the States or to the people"; thus leaving the question, whether the particular power which may become the subject of contest has been delegated to the one government, or prohibited to the other, to depend on a fair construction of the whole instrument. The men who drew and adopted this amendment had experienced the embarrassments resulting from the insertion of this word in the articles of confederation, and probably omitted it to avoid those embarrassments. A constitution, to contain an accurate detail of all the subdivisions of which its great powers will admit, and of all the means by which they may be carried into execution, would partake of the prolixity of a legal code, and could scarcely be embraced by the human mind. It would probably never be understood by the public. Its nature, therefore, requires, that only its great outlines should be marked, its important objects designated, and the minor ingredients which compose those objects be deduced from the nature of the objects themselves. That this idea was entertained by the framers of the American constitution, is not only to be inferred from the nature of the instrument, but from the language. Why else were some of the limitations, found in the ninth section of the 1st article, introduced? It is also, in some degree, warranted by their having omitted to use any restrictive term which might prevent its receiving a fair and just interpretation. In considering this question, then, we must never forget that it is *a constitution* we are expounding.

Although, among the enumerated powers of government, we do not find the word "bank" or "incorporation," we find the great powers to lay and collect taxes; to borrow money; to regulate commerce; to declare and conduct a war; and to raise and support armies and navies. The sword and the purse, all the external relations, and no inconsiderable portion of the industry of the nation, are entrusted to its government. It can never be pretended that these vast powers draw after them others of inferior importance, merely because they are inferior. Such an idea can never be advanced. But it may with great reason be contended, that a government, entrusted with such ample powers, on the due execution of which the happiness and prosperity of the nation so vitally depends, must also be entrusted with ample means for their execution. The power being given, it is the interest of the nation to facilitate its execution. It can never be their interest, and cannot be presumed to have been their intention, to clog and embarrass its execution by withholding the most appropriate means. Throughout this vast republic, from the St. Croix to the Gulph of Mexico, from the Atlantic to the Pacific, revenue is to be collected and expended, armies are to be marched and supported. The exigencies of the nation may require that the treasure raised in the north should be transported to the south, *that* raised in the east conveyed to the west, or that this order should be reversed. Is that construction of the constitution to be preferred which would render these operations difficult, hazardous, and expensive? Can we adopt that construction (unless the words imperiously require it), which would impute to the framers of that instrument, when granting these powers for the public good, the intention of impeding their exercise by withholding a choice of means? If, indeed, such be the mandate of the constitution, we have only to obey; but that instrument does not profess to enumerate the means by which the powers it confers may be executed; nor does it prohibit the creation of a corporation, if the existence of such a being be essential to the beneficial exercise of those powers. It is, then, the subject of fair inquiry, how far such means may be employed.

It is not denied, that the powers given to the government imply the ordinary means of execution. That, for example, of raising revenue, and applying it to national purposes, is admitted to imply the power of conveying money from place to place, as the exigencies of the nation may require, and of employing the usual means of conveyance. But it is denied that the government has its choice of means; or, that it may employ the most convenient means, if, to employ them, it be necessary to erect a corporation.

On what foundation does this argument rest? On this alone: The power of creating a corporation, is one appertaining to sovereignty, and is not expressly conferred on Congress. This is true. But all legislative powers appertain to sovereignty. The original power of giving the law on any subject whatever, is a sovereign power; and if the government of the Union is restrained from creating a corporation, as a means for performing its functions, on the single reason that the creation of a corporation is an act of sovereignty; if the sufficiency of this reason be acknowledged, there would be some difficulty in sustaining the authority of Congress to pass other laws for the accomplishment of the same objects.

The government which has a right to do an act, and has imposed on it the duty of performing that act, must, according to the dictates of reason, be allowed to select the means; and those who contend that it may not select any appropriate means, that one particular mode of effecting the object is excepted, take upon themselves the burden of establishing that exception. . . . The power of creating a corporation, though appertaining to sovereignty, is not, like the power of making war, or levying taxes, or of regulating commerce, a great substantive and independent power, which cannot be implied as incidental to other powers, or used as a means of executing them. It is never the end for which other powers are exercised, but a means by which other objects are accomplished. . . . The power of creating a corporation is never used for its own sake, but for the purpose of effecting something else. No sufficient reason is, therefore, perceived, why it may not pass as incidental to those powers which are expressly given, if it be a <u>direct mode of executing them.</u>

But the constitution of the United States has not left the right of Congress to employ the necessary means, for the execution of the powers conferred on the government, to general reasoning. To its enumeration of powers is added that of making "all laws which shall be necessary and proper, for carrying into execution the foregoing powers, and all other powers vested by this constitution, in the government of the United States, or in any department thereof."

The counsel for the State of Maryland have urged various arguments, to prove that this clause, though in terms a grant of power, is not so in effect; but is really restrictive of the general right, which might otherwise be implied, of selecting means for executing the enumerated powers.

In support of this proposition, they have found it necessary to contend, that this clause was inserted for the purpose of conferring on Congress the power of making laws. . . . That a legislature, endowed with legislative powers, can legislate, is a proposition too self-evident to have been questioned.

But the argument on which most reliance is placed, is drawn from the peculiar language of this clause. Congress is not empowered by it to make all laws, which may have relation to the powers conferred on the government, but such only as may be *"necessary and proper"* for carrying them into execution. The word *"necessary"* is considered as controlling the whole sentence, and as limiting the right to pass laws for the execution of the granted powers, to such as are indispensable, and without which the power would be nugatory. That it excludes the choice of means, and leaves to Congress, in each case, that only which is most direct and simple.

Is it true, that this is the sense in which the word "necessary" is always used? Does it always import an absolute physical necessity, so strong, that one thing, to which another may be termed necessary, cannot exist without that other? We think it does not. If reference be had to its use, in the common affairs of the world, or in approved authors, we find that it frequently imports no more than that one thing is convenient, or useful, or essential to another. To employ the means necessary to an end, is generally understood as employing any means calculated to produce the end, and not as being confined to those single means, without which the end would be entirely unattainable. Such is the character of human language, that no word conveys to the mind, in all situations, one single definite idea; and nothing is more common than to use words in a figurative sense. Almost all compositions contain words, which, taken in their rigorous sense, would convey a meaning different from that which is obviously intended. It is essential to just construction, that many words which import something excessive should be understood in a more mitigated sense—in that sense which common usage justifies. The word "necessary" is of this description. It has not a fixed character peculiar to itself. It admits of all degrees of comparison; and is often connected with other words which, increase or diminish the impression the mind receives of the urgency it imports. A thing may be necessary, very necessary, absolutely or indispensably necessary. To no mind would the same idea be conveyed by these several phrases. This comment on the word is well illustrated by the passage cited at the bar, from the 10th section of the 1st article of the constitution. It is, we think, impossible to compare the sentence which prohibits a State from laying "imposts or duties on imports or exports, except what may be *absolutely* necessary for executing its inspection laws," with that which authorizes Congress "to make all laws which shall be necessary and proper for carrying into execution" the powers of the general government, without feeling a conviction that the convention understood itself to change materially the meaning of the word "necessary," by prefixing the word "absolutely." This word, then, like others, is used in various senses; and, in its construction, the subject, the context, the intention of the person using them, are all to be taken into view.

Let this be done in the case under consideration. The subject is the execution of those great powers on which the welfare of a nation essentially depends. It must have been the intention of those who gave these powers, to insure, as far as human prudence could insure, their beneficial execution. This could not be done by confiding the choice of means to such narrow limits as not to leave it in the power of Congress to adopt any which might be appropriate, and which were conducive to the end. This provision is made in a constitution intended to endure for ages to come, and, consequently, to be adapted to the various *crises* of human affairs. To have prescribed the means by which government should, in all future time, execute its powers, would have been to change, entirely, the character of the instrument, and give it the properties of a legal code. It would have been an unwise attempt to provide, by immutable rules, for exigencies which, if foreseen at all, must have been seen dimly, and which can be best provided for as they occur. To have declared that the best means shall not be used, but those alone without which the power given would be nugatory, would have been to deprive the legislature of the capacity to avail itself of experience, to exercise its reason, and to accommodate its legislation to circumstances. If we apply this principle of construction to any of the powers of the government, we shall find it so pernicious in its operation that we shall be compelled to discard it. . . .

Take, for example, the power "to establish post offices and post roads." This power is executed by the single act of making the establishment. But, from this has been inferred the power and duty of carrying the mail along the post road, from one post office to another. And, from this implied power, has again been inferred the right to punish those who steal letters from the post office, or rob the mail. It may be said, with some plausibility, that the right to carry the mail, and to punish those who rob it, is not indispensably necessary to the establishment of a post office and post road. This right is indeed essential to the beneficial exercise of the power, but not indispensably necessary to its existence. So, of the punishment of the crimes of stealing or falsifying a record or process of a Court of the United States, or of perjury in such Court. To punish these offenses is certainly conducive to the due administration of justice. But courts may exist, and may decide the causes brought before them, though such crimes escape punishment.

The baneful influence of this narrow construction on all the operations of the government, and the absolute impracticability of maintaining it without rendering the government incompetent to its great objects, might be illustrated by numerous examples drawn from the constitution, and from our laws. The good sense of the public has pronounced, without hesitation, that the power of punishment appertains to sovereignty, and may be exercised whenever the sovereign has a right to act, as incidental to his constitutional powers. It is a means for carrying into execution all sovereign powers, and may be used, although not indispensably necessary. It is a right incidental to the power, and conducive to its beneficial exercise.

If this limited construction of the word "necessary" must be abandoned in order to punish, whence is derived the rule which would reinstate it, when the government would carry its powers into execution by means not vindictive in their nature? If the word "necessary" means "needful," "requisite," "essential," "conducive to," in order to let in the power of punishment for the infraction of law; why is it not equally comprehensive when required to authorize the use of means which facilitate the execution of the powers of government without the infliction of punishment?

In ascertaining the sense in which the word "necessary" is used in this clause of the constitution, we may derive some aid from that with which it is associated. Congress shall have power "to make all laws which shall be necessary and *proper* to carry into execution" the powers of the government. If the word "necessary" was used in that strict and rigorous sense for which the counsel for the State of Maryland contend, it would be an extraordinary departure from the usual course of the human mind, as exhibited in composition, to add a word, the only possible effect of which is to qualify that strict and rigorous meaning; to present to the mind the idea of some choice of means of legislation not straightened and compressed within the narrow limits for which gentlemen contend.

But the argument which most conclusively demonstrates the error of the construction contended for by the counsel for the State of Maryland, is founded on the contention of the convention, as manifested in the whole clause. To waste time and argument in proving that, without it, Congress might carry its powers into execution, would be not much less idle than to hold a lighted taper to the sun. As little can it be required to prove, that in the absence of this clause, Congress would have some choice of means. That it might employ those which, in its judgment, would most advantageously effect the object to be accomplished. That any means adapted to the end, any means which tended directly to the execution of the constitutional powers of the government, were in themselves constitutional. This clause, as construed by the State of Maryland, would abridge, and almost annihilate this useful and necessary right of the legislature to select the means. That this could not be intended, is, we should think, had it not been already controverted, too apparent for controversy. We think so for the following reasons:

1st. The clause is placed among the powers of Congress, not among the limitations on those powers.

2d. Its terms purport to enlarge, not to diminish the powers vested in the government. It purports to be an additional power, not a restriction on those already granted. . . . Had the intention been to make this clause restrictive, it would unquestionably have been so in form as well as in effect.

The result of the most careful and attentive consideration bestowed upon this clause, is, that if it does not enlarge, it cannot be construed to restrain the powers of Congress, or to impair the right of the legislature to exercise its best judgment in the selection of measures to carry into execution the constitutional powers of the government. If no other motive for its insertion can be suggested, a sufficient one is found in the desire to remove all doubts respecting the right to legislate on that vast mass of incidental powers which must be involved in the constitution, if that instrument be not a splendid bauble.

We admit, as all must admit, that the powers of the government are limited, and that its limits are not to be transcended. But we think the sound construction of the constitution must allow to the national legislature that discretion, with respect to the means by which the powers it confers are to be carried into execution, which will enable that body to perform the high duties assigned to it, in the manner most beneficial to the people. Let the end be legitimate, let it be within the scope of the constitution, and all means which are appropriate, which are plainly adapted to that end, which are not prohibited, but consistent with the letter and spirit of the constitution, are constitutional.

That a corporation must be considered as a means not less usual, not of higher dignity, not more requiring a particular specification than other means, has been sufficiently proved. If we look to the origin of corporations, to the manner in which they have been framed in that government from which we have derived most of our legal principles and ideas, or to the uses to which they have been applied, we find no reason to suppose that a constitution, omitting, and wisely omitting, to enumerate all the means for carrying into execution the great powers vested in government, ought to have specified this. Had it been intended to grant this power as one which should be distinct and independent, to be exercised in any case whatever, it would have found a place among the enumerated powers of the government. But being considered merely as a means, to be employed only for the purpose of carrying into execution the given powers, there could be no motive for particularly mentioning it. . . .

If a corporation may be employed indiscriminately with other means to carry into execution the powers of the government, no particular reason can be assigned for excluding the use of a bank, if required for its fiscal operations. To use one, must be within the discretion of Congress, if it be an appropriate mode of executing the powers of government. That it is a convenient, a useful, and essential instrument in the prosecution of its fiscal operations, is not now a subject of controversy. All those who have been concerned in the administration of our finances, have concurred in representing its importance and necessity; and so strongly have they been felt, that statesmen of the first class, whose previous opinions against it had been confirmed by every circumstance which can fix the human judgment, have yielded those opinions to the exigencies of the nation. . . . The time has passed away when it can be necessary to enter into any discussion in order to prove the importance of this instrument, as a means to effect the legitimate objects of the government.

But, were its necessity less apparent, none can deny its being an appropriate measure; and if it is, the degree of its necessity, as has been very justly observed, is to be discussed in another place. Should Congress, in the execution of its powers, adopt measures which are prohibited by the constitution; or should Congress, under the pretext of executing its powers, pass laws for the accomplishment of objects not entrusted to the government; it would become the painful duty of this tribunal, should a case requiring such a decision come before it, to say that such an act was not the law of the land. But where the law is not prohibited, and is really calculated to effect any of the objects entrusted to the government, to undertake here to inquire into the degree of its necessity, would be to pass the line which circumscribes the judicial department, and to tread on legislative ground. This court disclaims all pretensions to such a power.

After this declaration, it can scarcely be necessary to say that the existence of state banks can have no possible influence on the question. No trace is to be found in the constitution of an intention to create a dependence of the government of the Union on those of the states, for the execution of the great powers assigned to it. Its means are adequate to its ends; and on those means alone was it expected to rely for the accomplishment of its ends. To impose on it the necessity of resorting to means which it cannot control, which another government may furnish or withhold, would render its course precarious; the result of its measures uncertain, and create a dependence on other governments, which might disappoint its most important designs, and is incompatible with the language of the constitution. But were it otherwise, the choice of means implies a right to choose a national bank in preference to state banks, and Congress alone can make the election.

After the most deliberate consideration, it is the unanimous and decided opinion of this Court, that the act to incorporate the Bank of the United States is a law made in pursuance of the constitution, and is a part of the supreme law of the land.

The branches, proceeding from the same stock, and being conducive to the complete accomplishment of the object, are equally constitutional. It would have been unwise to locate them in the charter, and it would be unnecessarily inconvenient to employ the legislative power in making those subordinate arrangements. The great duties of the bank are prescribed; those duties require branches; and the bank itself may, we think, be safely trusted with the selection of places where those branches shall be fixed; reserving always to the government the right to require that a branch shall be located where it may be deemed necessary.

It being the opinion of the Court, that the act incorporating the bank is constitutional; and that the power of establishing a branch in the State of Maryland might be properly exercised by the bank itself, we proceed to inquire—

2. Whether the State of Maryland may, without violating the constitution, tax that branch?

That the power of taxation is one of vital importance; that it is retained by the States; that it is not abridged by the grant of a similar power to the government of the Union; that it is to be concurrently exercised by the two governments: are truths which have never been denied. But, such is the paramount character of the constitution that its capacity to withdraw any subject from the action of even this power, is admitted. The States are expressly forbidden to lay any duties on imports or exports, except what may be absolutely necessary for executing their inspection laws. If the obligation of this prohibition must be conceded—if it may restrain a State from the exercise of its taxing power on imports and exports; the same paramount character would seem to restrain, as it certainly may restrain, a State from such other exercise of this power, as is in its nature incompatible with, and repugnant to, the constitutional laws of the Union. A law, absolutely repugnant to another, as entirely repeals that other as if express terms of repeal were used.

On this ground the counsel for the bank place its claim to be exempted from the power of a State to tax its operations. There is no express provision for the case, but the claim has been sustained on a principle which so entirely pervades the constitution, is so intermixed with the materials which compose it, so interwoven with its web, so blended with its texture, as to be incapable of being separated from it, without rending it into shreds.

This great principle is, that the constitution and the laws made in pursuance thereof are supreme; that they control the constitution and laws of the respective States, and cannot be controlled by them. From this, which may be almost termed an axiom, other propositions are deduced as corollaries, on the truth or error of which, and on their application to this case, the cause has been supposed to depend. These are, 1st. that a power to create implies a power to preserve. 2nd. That a power to destroy, if wielded by a different hand, is hostile to, and incompatible with these powers to create and to preserve. 3d. That where this repugnancy exists, that authority which is supreme must control, not yield to that over which it is supreme.

. . .

That the power of taxing [the bank] by the States may be exercised so as to destroy it, is too obvious to be denied. But taxation is said to be an absolute power, which acknowledges no other limits than those expressly prescribed in the constitution, and like sovereign power of every other description, is trusted to the discretion of those who use it. But the very terms of this argument admit that the sovereignty of the State, in the article of taxation itself, is subordinate to, and may be controlled by the constitution of the United States. How far it has been controlled by that instrument must be a question of construction. In making this construction, no principle not declared, can be admissible, which would defeat the legitimate operations of a supreme government. It is of the very essence of supremacy to remove all obstacles to its action within its own sphere, and so to modify every power vested in subordinate governments, as to exempt its own operations from their own influence. This effect need not be stated in terms. It is so involved in the declaration of supremacy, so necessarily implied in it, that the expression of it could not make it more certain. We must, therefore, keep it in view while construing the constitution.

The argument on the part of the State of Maryland is, not that the States may directly resist a law of Congress, but that they may exercise their acknowledged powers upon it, and that the constitution leaves them this right in the confidence that they will not abuse it.

Before we proceed to examine this argument, and to subject it to the test of the constitution, we must be permitted to bestow a few considerations on the nature and extent of this original right of taxation, which is acknowledged to remain with the States. It is admitted that the power of taxing the people and their property is essential to the very existence of government, and may be legitimately exercised on the objects to which it is applicable, to the utmost extent to which the government may choose to carry it. The only security against the abuse of this power, is found in the structure of the government itself. In imposing a tax the legislature acts upon its constituents. This is in general a sufficient security against erroneous and oppressive taxation.

The people of a State, therefore, give to their government a right of taxing themselves and their property, and as the exigencies of government cannot be limited, they prescribe no limits to the exercise of this right, resting confidently on the interest of the legislator, and on the influence of the constituents over their representative, to guard them against its abuse. But the means employed by the government of the Union have no such security, nor is the right of a State to tax them sustained by the same theory. Those means are not given by the people of a particular State, not given by the constituents of the legislature, which claim the right to tax them, but by the people of all the States. They are given by all, for the benefit of all—and upon theory, should be subjected to that government only which belongs to all.

It may be objected to this definition, that the power of taxation is not confined to the people and property of a State. It may be exercised upon every object brought within its jurisdiction.

This is true. But to what source do we trace this right? It is obvious, that it is an incident of sovereignty, and is co-extensive with that to which it is an incident. All subjects over which the sovereign power of a State extends, are objects of taxation; but those over which it does not extend, are, upon the soundest principles, exempt from taxation. This proposition may almost be pronounced self-evident.

The sovereignty of a State extends to everything which exists by its own authority, or is introduced by its permission; but does it extend to those means which are employed by Congress to carry into execution powers conferred on that body by the people of the United States? We think it demonstrable that it does not. Those powers are not given by the people of a single State. They are given by the people of the United States, to a government whose laws, made in pursuance of the constitution, are declared to be supreme. Consequently, the people of a single State cannot confer a sovereignty which will extend over them.

If we measure the power of taxation residing in a State, by the extent of sovereignty which the people of a single State possess, and can confer on its government, we have an intelligible standard, applicable to every case to which the power may be applied. We have a principle which leaves the power of taxing the people and property of a state unimpaired; which leaves to a State the command of all its resources, and which places beyond its reach, all those powers which are conferred by the people of the United States on the government of the Union, and all those means which are given for the purpose of carrying those powers into execution. We have a principle which is safe for the States, and safe for the Union. We are relieved, as we ought to be, from clashing sovereignty; from interfering powers; from a repugnancy between a right in one government to pull down what there is an acknowledged right in another to build up; from the incompatibility of a right in one government to destroy what there is a right in another to preserve. We are not driven to the perplexing inquiry, so unfit for the judicial department, what degree of taxation is the legitimate use, and what degree may amount to the abuse of the power. The attempt to use it on the means employed by the government of the Union, in pursuance of the constitution, is itself an abuse, because it is the usurpation of a power which the people of a single State cannot give.

We find, then, on just theory, a total failure of this original right to tax the means employed by the government of the Union, for the execution of its powers. The right never existed, and the question whether it has been surrendered, cannot arise.

But, waiving this theory for the present, let us resume the inquiry, whether this power can be exercised by the respective States, consistently with a fair construction of the constitution.

That the power to tax involves the power to destroy; that the power to destroy may defeat and render useless the power to create; that there is a plain repugnance, in conferring on one government a power to control the constitutional measures of another, which other, with respect to those very measures, is declared to be supreme over that which exerts the control, are propositions not to be denied. But all inconsistencies are to be reconciled by the magic of the word CONFIDENCE. Taxation, it is said, does not necessarily and unavoidably destroy. To carry it to the excess of destruction would be an abuse, to presume which, would banish that confidence which is essential to all government.

But is this a case of confidence? Would the people of any one State trust those of another with a power to control the most insignificant operations of their State government? We know they would not. Why, then, should we suppose that the people of any one State should be willing to trust those of another with a power to control the operations of a government to which they have confided their most important and most valuable interests? In the legislature of the Union alone, are all represented. The legislature of the Union alone, therefore, can be trusted by the people with the power of controlling measures which concern all, in the confidence that it will not be abused. This, then, is not a case of confidence, and we must consider it as it really is.

If we apply the principle for which the State of Maryland contends, to the constitution generally, we shall find it capable of changing totally the character of that instrument. We shall find it capable of arresting all the measures of the government, and of prostrating it at the foot of the States. The American people have declared their constitution, and the laws made in pursuance thereof, to be supreme; but this principle would transfer the supremacy, in fact, to the States.

If the States may tax one instrument, employed by the government in the execution of its powers, they may tax any and every other instrument. They may tax the mail; they may tax the mint; they may tax patent rights; they may tax the papers of the custom-house; they may tax judicial process; they may tax all the means employed by the government, to an excess which would defeat all the ends of government. This was not intended by the American people. They did not design to make their government dependent on the States. . . .

. . . This is not all. If the controlling power of the States be established; if their supremacy as to taxation be acknowledged; what is to restrain their exercising this control in any shape they may please to give it? Their sovereignty is not confined to taxation. That is not the only mode in which it might be displayed. The question is, in truth, a question of supremacy;

and if the right of the States to tax the means employed by the general government be conceded, the declaration that the constitution, and the laws made in pursuance thereof, shall be the supreme law of the land, is empty and unmeaning declamation. . . .

It has also been insisted, that, as the power of taxation in the general and state governments is acknowledged to be concurrent, every argument which would sustain the right of the general government to tax banks chartered by the States, will equally sustain the right of the States to tax banks chartered by the general government.

But the two cases are not on the same reason. The people of all the States have created the general government, and have conferred upon it the general power of taxation. The people of all the States, and the States themselves, are represented in Congress, and, by their representatives, exercise this power. When they tax the chartered institutions of the States, they tax their constituents; and these taxes must be uniform. But, when a State taxes the operations of the government of the United States, it acts upon institutions created, not by their own constituents, but by people over whom they claim no control. It acts upon the measures of a government created by others as well as themselves, for the benefit of others in common with themselves. The difference is that which always exists, and always must exist, between the action of the whole on a part, and the action of a part on the whole—between the laws of a government declared to be supreme, and those of a government which, when in opposition to those laws, is not supreme.

But if the full application of this argument could be admitted, it might bring into question the right of Congress to tax the state banks, and could not prove the right of the States to tax the Bank of the United States.

The Court has bestowed on this subject its most deliberate consideration. The result is a conviction that the States have no power, by taxation or otherwise, to retard, impede, burden, or in any manner control, the operations of the constitutional laws enacted by Congress to carry into execution the powers vested in the general government. This is, we think, the unavoidable consequence of that supremacy which the constitution has declared.

We are unanimously of opinion, that the law passed by the legislature of Maryland, imposing a tax on the Bank of the United States, is unconstitutional and void.

This opinion does not deprive the States of any resources which they originally possessed. It does not extend to a tax paid by the real property of the bank, in common with the other real property within the State, nor to a tax imposed on the interest which the citizens of Maryland may hold in this institution, in common with other property of the same description throughout the State. But this is a tax on the operations of the bank, and is, consequently, a tax on the operation of an instrument employed by the government of the Union to carry its powers into execution. Such a tax must be unconstitutional.

[In the judgment appended to the opinion it was held that the Maryland statute "is contrary to the Constitution of the United States, and void." The judgment below was reversed and it was ordered that judgment be entered in the initial court for McCulloch.]

IMPLIED POWERS AND THE NECESSARY AND PROPER CLAUSE—THE HISTORICAL CONTEXT

Introduction. The nation was thirty years old when the Bank case came to the Supreme Court. The issues presented were not novel ones in 1819: both the specific question of the constitutionality of the Bank and the general one regarding the scope of national powers had been repeatedly debated since the beginning. These notes can only suggest some of the highlights of the contentions before 1819 and during the following decade. But the McCulloch decision, important as it is, was no more the end than the beginning of the debate. The scope of the national legislature's authority to reach local affairs is a characteristic, never-ending problem of our federal system. It continues to breed conflicts and to generate searches for new accommodations; and the next two chapters will trace some of these conflicts and accommodations from Marshall's day to ours.

1. *The allocation of powers in the Articles of Confederation and the Constitution.* a. *The Confederation.* The American federal structure allocates powers between nation and states by enumerating the powers delegated to the national government and acknowledging the retention by the states of the remainder. That allocation technique did not originate at the Constitutional Convention. The Articles of Confederation followed a similar scheme. What the Convention contributed was an expansion of enumerated national powers to remedy perceived weaknesses under the Articles. Thus, the most important enumeration of congressional powers in the Constitution, Art. I, Sec. 8, had a counterpart quite similar in form if not in scope in one of the Articles of Confederation:

"Article IX. The United States in Congress assembled, shall have the sole and exclusive right and power of determining on peace and war, . . . —of sending and receiving ambassadors—entering into treaties and alliances, provided that no treaty of commerce shall be made whereby the legislative power of the respective States shall be restrained from imposing such imposts and duties on foreigners, as their own people are subjected to, or from prohibiting the exportation or importation of any species of goods or commodities whatsoever—of establishing rules for deciding in all cases, what captures on land or water shall be legal, and in what manner prizes taken by land or naval forces in the service of the United States shall be divided or appropriated—of granting letters of marque and reprisal in times of peace—appointing courts for the trial of piracies and felonies committed on the high seas and establishing courts for receiving and determining finally appeals in all cases of captures. . . .

"The United States in Congress assembled shall also have the sole and exclusive right and power of regulating the alloy and value of coin struck by their own authority, or by that of the respective States—fixing the standard of weights and measures throughout the United States—regulating the trade and managing all affairs with the Indians, not members of any of the States, provided that the legislative right of any State within its own limits be not infringed or violated—establishing and regulating post-offices from one State to another, throughout all the United States, and exacting such postage on the papers passing thro' the same as may be requisite to defray the expenses of the said office—appointing all officers of the land forces, in the service of the United States, excepting regimental officers—appointing all the officers of the naval forces, and commissioning all officers whatever in the service of the United States—making rules for the government and regulation of the said land and naval forces, and directing their operations. . . . . ."

Note also the acknowledgment of power retained by the states in Art. IX of the Articles, asserting that each state retained "every power, jurisdiction and right, which is not by this confederation expressly delegated to the United States." That provision had its counterpart in the Tenth Amendment of the Constitution, which omits the adverb "expressly" in assuring that the "powers not delegated to the United States" nor prohibited to the States "are reserved to the States respectively, or to the people." The move from Articles to Constitution was not, then, one from a central government of no powers to one with all powers; rather, it was a shift from one with less powers to one with more powers (and with improved machinery to enforce those powers, through a separate national executive and judiciary). And the Tenth Amendment was designed to allay fears that were an understandable concomitant of greater powers, fears frequently expressed in the ratification debates: the fears of an excessively powerful, excessively centralized national government.

Note the differences between the congressional power grants in the two documents. The most important new specifications were the grants of the power to levy taxes and regulate interstate and foreign commerce. It was the lack of these powers (the Confederation's funds, for example, came from the states, who had the sole power to impose taxes) that had been most widely blamed for the failures of the Articles. It was failures like these that were central in the survey of the "insufficiency of the present confederation to the preservation of the Union" in the Federalist Papers, and that led Hamilton to ask in Federalist No. 15: "[W]hat indication is there of national disorder, poverty and insignificance that could befall a community so peculiarly blessed with natural advantages as we are, which does not form a part of the dark catalogue of our public misfortunes."

b. *The Constitutional Convention.* Consensus that the new Constitution should strengthen national powers did not inevitably mean that a more ample enumeration of powers would be the chosen technique. Rather than building on the enumeration format of the Articles, a simpler, more general, more inclusive statement of congressional powers was conceivable. That, indeed, was the approach the Convention adopted initially. Is it significant that the specification route was ultimately followed in Article I? At the Convention, the Virginia plan proposed "that the National Legislature ought to be empowered to enjoy the Legislative Rights vested in Congress by the Confederation; and moreover to legislate in all cases to which the separate States are incompetent, or in which the harmony of the United States may be interrupted by exercise of individual Legislation." And the Convention delegates, indeed, twice voted for formulations in similarly general terms. See I Farrand, Records of the Federal Convention of 1787 (1911) 47, 53; II id. 21. The ultimate scheme of Art. I, Sec. 8,—specifying the granted powers and ending with the Necessary and Proper Clause—originated in the Convention's Committee of Detail.

There was virtually no discussion of the Necessary and Proper Clause at the Convention. Many of the fears of a powerful central government during the ratification discussions focused on that Clause, however. Defenders of the Constitution—such as Hamilton and Madison—insisted that the Clause was "harmless" and that objections to it were a "pretext." As Madison explained in No. 44 of the Federalist Papers: "Had the Constitution been silent on this head there can be no doubt that all the particular powers, requisite as means of executing the general powers, would have resulted to the government, by unavoidable implication." Recall the McCulloch opinion.

2. *The Jefferson–Hamilton debate on the Bank in 1791.* With the establishment of the new government, agreement on the general formulations among the supporters of the new Constitution soon gave way to conflict on applications. The best known dispute in Washington's Administration warrants special attention: it was characteristic of the emerging conflicts between broad and narrow constructionists; and it focused on the very issue that ultimately came to the Court in McCulloch—and provided some of the ideological heritage that found its way into Marshall's opinion on the constitutionality of the Bank.

In December 1790, Alexander Hamilton, Washington's Secretary of the Treasury, sent to the House of Representatives a lengthy Report urging the incorporation of a national bank. He listed as among its principal advantages "the augmentation of the active or productive capital," a greater "facility to the government in obtaining pecuniary aids, especially in sudden emergencies," and the "facilitating of the payment of taxes." Less than two months later, Congress enacted a law creating the First Bank of the United States—a law much like the one passed in 1816 and sustained in McCulloch. While the bill was on Washington's desk, the President requested opinions on constitutionality from Attorney General Edmund Randolph, Secretary of State Thomas Jefferson, and Alexander Hamilton. Randolph's first response stated that the measure was unconstitutional. Jefferson's answer agreed with Randolph's result, but Hamilton insisted that his project was constitutional. The President followed his Treasury Secretary's advice. Excerpts from the Jefferson and Hamilton opinions follow.

Jefferson:

I consider the foundation of the Constitution as laid on this ground: That "all powers not delegated to the United States, by the Constitution, nor prohibited by it to the States, are reserved to the States or to the people." . . . To take a single step beyond the boundaries thus specially drawn around the powers of Congress, is to take possession of a boundless field of power, no longer susceptible of any definition.

The incorporation of a bank, and the powers assumed by this bill, have not, in my opinion, been delegated to the United States, by the Constitution.

I. They are not among the powers specially enumerated. . . .

II. Nor are they within either of the general phrases, which are the two following:—

1. To lay taxes to provide for the general welfare of the United States, that is to say, "to lay taxes for *the purpose* of providing for the general welfare." For the laying of taxes is the *power,* and the general welfare the *purpose* for which the power is to be exercised. They are not to lay taxes *ad libitum for any purpose they please*; but only *to pay the debts or provide*

for the welfare of the Union. In like manner, they are not *to do anything they please* to provide for the general welfare, but only to *lay taxes* for that purpose. To consider the latter phrase, not as describing the purpose of the first, but as giving a distinct and independent power to do any act they please, which might be for the good of the Union, would render all the preceding and subsequent enumerations of power completely useless.

It would reduce the whole instrument to a single phrase, that of instituting a Congress with power to do whatever would be for the good of the United States; and, as they would be the sole judges of the good or evil, it would be also a power to do whatever evil they please. . . .

. . . It is known that the very power now proposed *as a means* was rejected as *an end* by the Convention which formed the Constitution. A proposition was made to them to authorize Congress to open canals, and an amendatory one to empower them to incorporate. But the whole was rejected, and one of the reasons for rejection urged in debate was, that then they would have a power to erect a bank, which would render the great cities, where there were prejudices and jealousies on the subject, adverse to the reception of the Constitution.

2.   The second general phrase is, "to make all laws *necessary* and proper for carrying into execution the enumerated powers." But they can all be carried into execution without a bank. A bank therefore is not *necessary,* and consequently not authorized by this phrase.

It has been urged that a bank will give great facility or convenience in the collection of taxes. Suppose this were true: yet the Constitution allows only the means which are *"necessary,"* not those which are merely "convenient" for effecting the enumerated powers. If such a latitude of construction be allowed to this phrase as to give any non-enumerated power, it will go to every one, for there is not one which ingenuity may not torture into a *convenience* in some instance *or other,* to *some one* of so long a list of enumerated powers. It would swallow up all the delegated powers, and reduce the whole to one power, as before observed. Therefore it was that the Constitution restrained them to the *necessary* means, that is to say, to those means without which the grant of power would be nugatory. . . .

It may be said that a bank whose bills would have a currency all over the States, would be more convenient than one whose currency is limited to a single State. So it would be still more convenient that there should be a bank, whose bills should have a currency all over the world. But it does not follow from this superior conveniency, that there exists anywhere a power to establish such a bank; or that the world may not go on very well without it.

Can it be thought that the Constitution intended that for a shade or two of *convenience,* more or less, Congress should be authorized to break down the most ancient and fundamental laws of the several States; such as those against Mortmain, the laws of Alienage, the rules of descent, the acts of distribution, the laws of escheat and forfeiture, the laws of monopoly? Nothing but a necessity invincible by any other means, can justify such a prostitution of laws, which constitute the pillars of our whole system of jurisprudence. Will Congress be too straight-laced to carry the constitution into honest effect, unless they may pass over the foundation-laws of the State government for the slightest convenience of theirs?

The negative of the President is the shield provided by the constitution to protect against the invasions of the legislature: 1. The right of the Executive. 2. Of the Judiciary. 3. Of the States and State legislatures. The present is the case of a right remaining exclusively with the States, and consequently one of those intended by the Constitution to be placed under its protection.

It must be added, however, that unless the President's mind on a view of everything which is urged for and against this bill, is tolerably clear that it is unauthorised by the Constitution; if the pro and the con hang so even as to balance his judgment, a just respect for the wisdom of the legislature would naturally decide the balance in favor of their opinion. It is chiefly for cases where they are clearly misled by error, ambition, or interest, that the Constitution has placed a check in the negative of the President.

Hamilton: *In favor of estab. of bank.*

In entering upon the argument, it ought to be premised that the objections of the Secretary of State and the Attorney-General are founded on a general denial of the authority of the United States to erect corporations. The latter, indeed, expressly admits, that if there be anything in the bill which is not warranted by the Constitution, it is the clause of incorporation.

Now it appears to the Secretary of the Treasury that this *general principle* is *inherent* in the very *definition* of government, and *essential* to every step of the progress to be made by that of the United States, namely: That every power vested in a government is in its nature *sovereign,* and includes, by *force* of the *term,* a right to employ all the *means* requisite and fairly applicable to the attainment of the *ends* of such power, and which are not precluded by restrictions and exceptions specified in the Constitution, or not immoral, or not contrary to the *essential ends* of political society.

This principle, in its application to government in general, would be admitted as an axiom; and it will be incumbent upon those who may incline to deny it, to prove a distinction, and to show that a rule which, in the general system of things, is essential to the preservation of the social order, is inapplicable to the United States. . . .

. . . [I]t is unquestionably incident to *sovereign power* to erect corporations, and consequently to *that* of the United States, in *relation* to the *objects* intrusted to the management of the government. The difference is this: where the authority of the government is general, it can create corporations in *all cases;* where it is confined to certain branches of legislation, it can create corporations *only* in those cases. . . .

. . . It is conceded that *implied powers* are to be considered as delegated equally with *express ones.* Then it follows, that as a power of erecting a corporation may as well be *implied* as any other thing, it may as well be employed as an *instrument* or *means* of carrying into execution any of the specified powers, as any other *instrument* or *means* whatever. The only question must be in this, as in every other case, whether the means to be employed, or, in this instance, the corporation to be erected, has a natural relation to any of the acknowledged objects or lawful ends of the government. Thus a corporation may not be erected by Congress for superintending the police of the city of Philadelphia, because they are not authorized to *regulate* the *police* of that city.   But one may be erected in relation to the collection of taxes, or to the trade with foreign countries, or to the trade between the States, or with the Indian tribes;   because it is the province of the Federal Government to *regulate* those objects, and because it is incident to a general *sovereign* or *legislative* power to *regulate* a thing, to employ all the means which relate to its regulation to the best and greatest advantage.

A strange fallacy seems to have crept into the manner of thinking and reasoning upon this subject.   Imagination appears to have been unusually busy concerning it.   An incorporation seems to have been regarded as some *great independent substantive thing;* as a political end of peculiar magnitude and moment;   whereas it is truly to be considered as a *quality, capacity,* or *means* to an end.   .   .   .

.   .   .   [T]he Secretary of State maintains, that no means are to be considered *necessary* but those without which the grant of the power would be *nugatory*.   Nay, so far does he go in his restrictive interpretation of the *word*, as even to make the case of *necessity* which shall warrant the constitutional exercise of the power to depend on *casual* and *temporary* circumstances; an idea which alone refutes the construction.   The *expediency* of exercising a particular power, at a particular time, must, indeed, depend on circumstances;   but the constitutional right of exercising it must be uniform and invariable, the same today as tomorrow.

All the arguments, therefore, against the constitutionality of the bill derived from the accidental existence of certain State banks—institutions which happen to exist today, and, for aught that concerns the government of the United States, may disappear tomorrow—must not only be rejected as fallacious, but must be viewed as demonstrative that there is a *radical* source of error in the reasoning.

It is essential to the being of the national government, that so erroneous a conception of the meaning of the word *necessary* should be exploded.

It is certain, that neither the grammatical nor popular sense of the term requires that construction.   According to both, *necessary* often means no more than *needful, requisite, incidental, useful* or *conducive to*.   It is a common mode of expression to say, that it is *necessary* for a government or a person to do this or that thing, when nothing more is intended or understood, than that the interests of the government or person require, or will be promoted by, the doing of this or that thing.   The imagination can be at no loss for exemplifications of the use of the word in this sense.   And it is the true one in which it is to be understood as used in the Constitution.   The whole turn of the clause containing it indicates, that it was the intent of the Convention, by that clause, to give a liberal latitude to the exercise of the specified powers.   The expressions have peculiar comprehensiveness.   They are, "to make all *laws* necessary and proper for *carrying into execution* the *foregoing powers,* and *all other powers* vested by the Constitution in the *Government* of the United States, or in any *department* or *officer* thereof."

To understand the word as the Secretary of State does, would be to depart from its obvious and popular sense, and to give it a restrictive operation, an idea never before entertained.   It would be to give it the same force as if the word *absolutely* or *indispensably* had been prefixed to it.

Such a construction would beget endless uncertainty and embarrassment. The cases must be palpable and extreme, in which it could be pronounced, with certainty, that a measure was absolutely necessary, or one, without which the exercise of a given power would be nugatory.   There are few measures of any government which would stand so severe a test.   To insist upon it, would be to make the criterion of the exercise of any implied power, a *case of extreme necessity;* which is rather a rule to justify the overleaping of the bounds of constitutional authority, than to govern the ordinary exercise of it. . . .

The *degree* in which a measure is necessary can never be a *test* of the legal right to adopt it; that must be a matter of opinion, and can only be a *test* of expediency.   The *relation* between the *measure* and the *end;* between the *nature* of the *means* employed towards the execution of a power, and the object of that power, must be the criterion of constitutionality, not the more or less of *necessity* or *utility.* . . .

This restrictive interpretation of the word *necessary* is also contrary to this sound maxim of construction; namely, that the powers contained in a constitution of government, especially those which concern the general administration of the affairs of a country, its finances, trade, defence, etc., ought to be construed liberally in advancement of the public good. . . . . The means by which national exigencies are to be provided for, national inconveniences obviated, national prosperity promoted, are of such infinite variety, extent, and complexity, that there must of necessity be great latitude of discretion in the selection and application of those means.   Hence, consequently, the necessity and propriety of exercising the authorities intrusted to a government on principles of liberal construction. . . .

But while on the one hand the construction of the Secretary of State is deemed inadmissible, it will not be contended, on the other, that the clause in question gives any *new* or *independent* power.   But it gives an explicit sanction to the doctrine of *implied powers*, and is equivalent to an admission of the proposition that the government, as to its *specified powers* and *objects*, has plenary and sovereign authority, in some cases paramount to the States; in others, co-ordinate with it.   For such is the plain import of the declaration, that it may pass all *laws* necessary and proper to carry into execution those powers. . . .

. . . This criterion is the *end*, to which the measure relates as a *means*.   If the *end* be clearly comprehended within any of the specified powers, and if the measure have an obvious relation to that *end*, and is not forbidden by any particular provision of the Constitution, it may safely be deemed to come within the compass of the national authority.   There is also this further criterion, which may materially assist the decision: Does the proposed measure abridge a pre-existing right of any State or of any individual?   If it does not, there is a strong presumption in favor of its constitutionality, and slighter relations to any declared object of the Constitution may be permitted to turn the scale. . . .

Another argument made use of by the Secretary of State is, the rejection of a proposition by the Convention to empower Congress to make corporations, either generally, or for some special purpose.

What was the precise nature or extent of this proposition, or what the reasons for refusing it, is not ascertained by any authentic document, or even by accurate recollection. . . .

But whatever may have been the nature of the proposition, or the reasons for rejecting it, it includes nothing in respect to the real merits of the question.

The Secretary of State will not deny that, whatever may have been the intention of the framers of a constitution or of a law, that intention is to be sought for in the instrument itself, according to the usual and established rules of construction. Nothing is more common than for laws to *express* and *effect* more or less than was intended. If, then, a power to erect a corporation in any case be deducible, by fair inference, from the whole or any part of the numerous provisions of the Constitution of the United States, arguments drawn from extrinsic circumstances, regarding the intention of the Convention, must be rejected. . . .

It is presumed to have been satisfactorily shown in the course of the preceding observations:

1. That the power of the government, as to the objects intrusted to its management, is, in its nature, sovereign.

2. That the right of erecting corporations is one inherent in, and inseparable from, the idea of sovereign power.

3. That the position, that the government of the United States can exercise no power but such as is delegated to it by its Constitution, does not militate against this principle.

4. That the word *necessary*, in the general clause, can have no *restrictive* operation derogating from the force of this principle; indeed, that the degree in which a measure is or is not *necessary*, cannot be a *test* of *constitutional right*, but of *expediency only*.

5. That the power to erect corporations is not to be considered as an *independent* or *substantive* power, but as an *incidental* and *auxiliary* one, and was therefore more properly left to implication, than expressly granted.

6. That the principle in question does not extend the power of the government beyond the prescribed limits, because it only affirms a power to *incorporate* for purposes *within the sphere* of the *specified powers*.

And lastly, that the right to exercise such a power in certain cases is unequivocally granted in the most *positive* and *comprehensive* terms. . . .

. . . [I]t remains to show the relation of such an institution to one or more of the specified powers of the government. Accordingly it is affirmed that it has a relation, more or less direct, to the power of collecting taxes, to that of borrowing money, to that of regulating trade between the States, and to those of raising and maintaining fleets and armies. To the two former the relation may be said to be immediate; and in the last place it will be argued, that it is clearly within the provision which authorizes the making of all *needful rules and regulations* concerning the *property* of the United States, as the same has been practised upon by the government.

A bank relates to the collection of taxes in two ways—*indirectly*, by increasing the quantity of circulating medium and quickening circulation, which facilitates the means of paying directly, by creating a *convenient species* of medium in which they are to be paid. . . .

A bank has a direct relation to the power of borrowing money, because it is a usual, and in sudden emergencies an essential, instrument in the obtaining of loans to government. . . .

The institution of a bank has also a natural relation to the regulation of trade between the States, in so far as it is conducive to the creation of a convenient medium of *exchange* between them, and to the keeping up a full circulation, by preventing the frequent displacement of the metals in reciprocal remittances. . . .

A hope is entertained that it has, by this time, been made to appear, to the satisfaction of the President, that a bank has a natural relation to the power of collecting taxes—to that of regulating trade—to that of providing for the common defence—and that, as the bill under consideration contemplates the government in the light of a joint proprietor of the stock of the bank, it brings the case within the provision of the clause of the Constitution which immediately respects the property of the United States. . . .

3. *Broad and narrow construction: the Jeffersonian positions and the 1804 Marshall reply.* The fear of "consolidation" of powers in the national government did not end with the 1791 Bank controversy. Indeed, strict construction of congressional authority became a central plank in the opposition platform of the Jeffersonian Republicans later in the decade. When Jefferson drafted the Kentucky Resolutions, and Madison those of Virginia, in 1798, their protests against the Federalists' Alien and Sedition Laws were not simply defenses of First Amendment freedoms. The Resolutions also reflected an insistence on states' rights: a protest against the tendency of "the Federal Government to enlarge its powers by forced constructions" (Virginia Resolutions); a protest against the "construction applied by the General Government" to such provisions as the Necessary and Proper Clause, an assertion that "'words meant by [the Constitution] to be subsidiary only to the execution of the limited powers ought not to be so construed as themselves to give unlimited powers" (Kentucky Resolutions). (Compare "Has the Warren Court Repudiated Marshall's View of the Necessary and Proper Clause?" chap. 5, p. 420, below.)

After the Republicans assumed power in 1801, the responsibilities of their offices compelled Jefferson and Madison to depart from consistent adherence to the strict construction position. At times, it was left to such orthodox Republicans as John Randolph and John Taylor of Caroline and Spencer Roane to defend the traditional Jeffersonian creed. Yet, from a number of sources—and for a variety of motives, from philosophical conviction to temporary self-interest—the opposing positions on national powers were kept alive to and beyond the year McCulloch was decided.

The purity of Jefferson's constitutional principles was more apparent in the years before and after his presidential terms than while he was in office. President Jefferson found it possible, for example, to overcome his constitutional scruples regarding the purchase of Louisiana: though at first he thought it "important, in the present case, to set an example against broad construction," he ultimately dropped his plan to seek a constitutional amendment to ratify his actions: "If . . . our friends shall think differently, certainly I shall acquiesce with satisfaction; confiding, that the good sense of our country will correct the evil of construction when it shall produce ill effects." See VIII The Writings of Thomas Jefferson (Ford ed.), 248, 262; and, generally, Levy, Jefferson and Civil Liberties—The Darker Side (1963). Compare Jefferson's colorful articulation of strict constructionist fears when he commented, just before he was elected President, on a bill to grant a federal charter to a mining company: "Congress are authorized to defend the nation. Ships are necessary for defence; copper is necessary for ships; mines, necessary for copper; a company necessary to work the mines; and who can doubt this reasoning who has ever played at 'This is the

House that Jack Built'? Under such a process of filiation of necessities, the sweeping clause makes clean work." (Quoted in 1 Warren, The Supreme Court in United States History (rev. ed. 1926), 501.) (Note the manifestations of "House that Jack Built" arguments in the cases below.)

While Jefferson was in the White House, supporters of national legislation continued to maintain that congressional powers should be broadly construed. And an early opinion by Chief Justice Marshall gave support to that position, in a case anticipating the more elaborate discussion in McCulloch. In sustaining a law giving priority, in insolvency cases, to debts owing to the United States, Marshall said: "In construing [the Necessary and Proper Clause] it would be incorrect, and would produce endless difficulties, if the opinion should be maintained that no law was authorized which was not indispensably necessary to give effect to a specified power. Where various systems might be adopted for that purpose, it might be said with respect to each, that it was not necessary, because the end might be obtained by other means. Congress must possess the choice of means, and must be empowered to use any means which are in fact conducive to the exercise of a power granted by the constitution." United States v. Fisher, 2 Cranch 358, 396 (1805).

4. *National powers after the War of 1812.* The controversy over the scope of congressional powers intensified in the years immediately before the McCulloch decision. Before and during the War, more and more Federalists hostile to the Jefferson and Madison Administrations began to embrace strict construction theories. By the end of the War, that Party was in its death throes. But proposals for ambitious congressional programs now came from a new generation of Republicans, especially in the short period of nationalistic optimism that followed the end of the War of 1812. Compare the broad-scale national action advocated by Justice Story at the time of Martin v. Hunter's Lessee, as noted above, chap. 1, p. 32.

The drive to charter the Second Bank of the United States was only a small part of that wave of nationalism. In 1816, for example, John C. Calhoun was still more than a decade away from his role as chief theoretician of the Nullifiers; in 1816, Calhoun was the legislative leader who successfully steered the Bank bill through the House, supported the tariff, and proposed a national system of roads and canals. See generally 1 The Papers of John C. Calhoun (Meriwether ed. 1959). So with Henry Clay: as Speaker of the House early in 1817, he praised Calhoun's roads and canals bill and defended his American System—particularly those "most worthy" subjects, "Internal Improvements and Domestic Manufactures." 2 The Papers of Henry Clay (Hopkins ed. 1961), 308.

Yet each of these nationalistic proposals faced opponents—in Congress, where Daniel Webster was among the critics for a while, in the White House, and in the country at large. The opposition arguments, moreover, were frequently couched in constitutional terms. President Madison, for example, vetoed Calhoun's bill establishing an internal improvements fund from the bonus paid to the United States under the Bank charter. He found "insuperable difficulty in reconciling the bill with the Constitution," for authority for the congressional action was not "among the enumerated powers" and did not fall "by any just interpretation" within the Necessary and Proper Clause. (Compare the Butler case, chap. 5, p. 366, below.) Madison's conscience would not permit him to endorse such a "constructive extension of the powers of Congress," such an "inadmissible latitude of construction." I Messages and Papers of the Presidents (Richardson ed. 1900), 584.

McCulloch v. Maryland, then, was not an abstract or novel exercise in constitutional interpretation. The scope of congressional powers had been a continuous and controversial issue in American debates from the start. The McCulloch opinion added a weighty ingredient to the debate—but the debate continued. President Monroe, for example, vetoed the Cumberland Road Bill in 1822—though the Justices, unofficially, did not agree with his position. With President John Quincy Adams' election in 1825, a strong supporter of broad congressional powers at last came into office. Thus, Adams' proposals included not only internal improvements but national action in aid of education and science as well (see II id., 311). But by now Congress was reluctant, and the Adams Administration faced increasingly hostile constitutional and political criticism.

Much of the constitutional criticism in the 1820's came from the state legislatures. The resolutions adopted illustrate both the pervasiveness of the criticism and the challenges to McCulloch inherent in the attacks. See generally Ames, State Documents on Federal Relations (1906). Late in 1825, for example, the South Carolina legislature—still years away from Nullification but increasingly discontent with national action—asked a special committee to report on "the decisions of the Federal Judiciary, and the Acts of Congress contravening the letter and spirit of the Constitution." There was little doubt about the prime judicial target: as a similar committee reported two years later "with great pain," the "reasoning of the Court in the case of McCulloch v. the State of Maryland" was "founded on a misconstruction" of the Constitution. I Statutes at Large of South Carolina 231 (1836). That was the premise that underlay the action of the South Carolina legislature in December 1825, when it adopted the special committee's recommended Resolutions (id., 229):

"1. *Resolved*, That Congress does not possess the power, under the constitution, to adopt a general system of internal improvement as a national measure.

"2. *Resolved*, That a right to impose and collect taxes, does not authorize Congress to lay a tax for any other purposes than such as are necessarily embraced in the specific grants of power, and those necessarily implied therein.

"3. *Resolved*, That Congress ought not to exercise a power granted for particular objects, to effect other objects, the right to effect which has never been conceded.

"4. *Resolved*, That it is an unconstitutional exercise of power, on the part of Congress, to tax the citizens of one State to make roads and canals for the citizens of another State.

"5. *Resolved*, That it is an unconstitutional exercise of power, on the part of Congress, to lay duties to protect domestic manufacturers."

The impact of McCulloch v. Maryland extended far beyond the immediate issues of the case, far beyond its own day—not only to South Carolina in the 1820's, but also to the recurrent disputes about the scope of congressional power since. But it is not enough to view McCulloch in its larger setting; a word about the immediate context accordingly follows.

5. *The Bank controversy: politics and economics.* The expiration of
the charter of the First Bank of the United States in 1811 coincided with—
and to some extent contributed to—increasing national fiscal difficulties.
Financial problems were aggravated during the War of 1812, and demands
for a new national bank proliferated. By the end of the War, even President
Madison—who, in his 1800 Report on the Virginia Resolutions, had echoed
Jefferson's argument that the first Bank was unconstitutional—began to
urge consideration of a successor institution: in his Annual Message of December 1815, he advised Congress that "the probable operation of a national bank will merit consideration." I Messages and Papers of the Presidents (Richardson ed. 1900), 566.

The Republicans in Congress did not need that reminder. They had
approved a new bank charter almost a year earlier, but the President had
vetoed it in January 1815. But the Veto Message demonstrated that the
Administration's constitutional position had shifted: while disapproving the
details of the bill, President Madison had "waived" the question of congressional power to incorporate a bank, "as being precluded in my judgment
by repeated recognitions under varied circumstances of the validity of such
an institution in acts of the legislative, executive, and judicial branches of
the Government." Id., at 555. In 1816, Congress established a Second
Bank acceptable to Madison; and Marshall's 1819 opinion sustaining its
constitutionality took pains to remind the nation of Madison's "waiver".

The Bank got off to a flourishing start. In 1817 and for most of 1818,
few questions about constitutionality were raised: the country was in a post-
war economic boom, trade was active, prices were rising. And the Bank
of the United States, which could have exercised some of the regulatory functions of a modern central bank by controlling credit expansion, chose instead
to be "liberal" and to encourage the speculative boom. The harsh morning-
after was not far off, however: by the fall of 1818, a financial panic and
depression shook the economy. The Bank, short of specie reserves, called
in its excessive loans—and the debtors, state banks and private individuals,
reacted with understandable anger toward the central "monied power," the
"monster" Bank. In October 1818, a congressional investigation of the Bank
began, and there was considerable support for repeal of its charter. The January 1819 report of the investigating committee found that the Bank had indeed suffered from loose management under its first president, William
Jones. But the charter-repeal move failed in February 1819; instead, Jones
resigned and was succeeded by the far more competent Langdon Cheves.

When the McCulloch case came before the Court, then, the Bank was
the center of the most heated issue of the congressional session. Moreover,
by early 1819, the Baltimore branch of the Bank—one of eighteen branches
in existence at the time—was the most controversial of the Bank's operations,
for reasons going quite beyond Maryland's tax. As cashier, James McCulloch
was no minor functionary: in the Bank's structure, the branch cashiers were
the chief executive agents of the central management in Philadelphia. And
during the congressional investigation, McCulloch was the Bank's main legislative lobbyist in Washington. He was even more busy at home: the Baltimore branch was the most active of all, and McCulloch and his cohorts—
branch president Buchanan and director Williams—were systematically loot-
ing the Bank by instigating unsecured loans and by sanctioning unreported
overdrafts. Reports of Baltimore misconduct were circulating in Washington

by late 1818; by the time the case was argued in March 1819, there were rumors that McCulloch was heavily implicated. But there were also indignant denials of rumors, and widespread disbelief that McCulloch and his associates had acted improperly. Official charges of misconduct by McCulloch did not come until a month after the Court decision; and in May, Langdon Cheves ordered his removal from office. Criminal proceedings against McCulloch and his associates were brought by Maryland and continued for several years, with Bank counsel aiding the prosecution. But Maryland had no embezzlement statute as yet, and the difficult effort to obtain a common law conspiracy conviction failed.

The banner of national power and supremacy was carried by a most unsavory figure, a scoundrel whose schemes cost the Bank more than a million dollars. But the Bank controversy litigated in the McCulloch case was not merely a Baltimore matter. The hard times, and the antipathy of state banks under pressure from the Bank of the United States, were producing anti-Bank measures in a number of states. Indiana and Illinois flatly prohibited banks not chartered by the state. Tennessee, Georgia, North Carolina, Kentucky and Ohio—like Maryland—imposed taxes on "foreign" bank operations—taxes that were typically even more burdensome than Maryland's. Similar efforts in several other state legislatures failed by narrow margins. The Court's decision did not silence all of the attacks: in the face of the McCulloch decision in March, Ohio chose to collect its $50,000 per branch tax by force, in September 1819. It took another Court decision—Osborn v. Bank of the United States, 9 Wheat. 738 (1824)—to settle the Ohio dispute and validate the Bank's statutory authority to sue in the federal courts. By that time, the Bank's difficulties had eased: it was managed more competently—by Cheves' successor, Nicholas Biddle—and the nation had recovered from the depression. Not until the Jackson Administration did the Bank face another severe attack. And the Jackson challenge was fatal: the McCulloch decision was not an adequate shield against President Jackson's veto of the 1832 Bank recharter, and the Bank went out of existence in 1836. [For additional background on the Bank controversy, see Catterall, The Second Bank of the United States (1903), and Hammond, Banks and Politics in America—From the Revolution to the Civil War (1957).]

. 6. *The Bank controversy: the constitutional contentions and John Marshall's pseudonymous defense.* By contrast with the often bitter and sometimes bizarre political controversies that engulfed the Bank, the constitutional submissions in the McCulloch case were calm and predicatable. The arguments for the Bank, by Attorney General Wirt and William Pinkney and Daniel Webster—who had voted against the Bank bill as a Federalist Congressman three years earlier—are, to be sure, reflected in the Marshall opinion. But counsel's arguments were largely conduits for constitutional contentions that had become staples in debates during the preceding three decades. Though Daniel Webster's reputation was substantially enhanced by his Court arguments in 1819, it was William Pinkney who was the major orator in the McCulloch case. And neither Webster nor Pinkney considered the McCulloch argument the chief challenge of the 1819 Term: they were preoccupied with other cases, especially their possible encounter if the Dartmouth College Case were to be reargued. As Pinkney wrote Webster in December 1818, a preargument "interchange of Ideas" between co-counsel for the Bank was unnecessary, since the argument probably would involve "little else than the threadbare topics connected with the constitutionality of the establishment of the Bank."

The constitutional arguments were not novel, and the pro-Bank holding was no surprise. But to the far-sighted, the case signified more than the immediate result. For John Marshall and his Virginia states' rights critics, especially, what was truly at stake was McCulloch's impact on national programs other than the Bank and, above all, on the general scope of national powers. General principles of constitutional interpretation really mattered the most in the long run. And general principles were central in a fierce ideological newspaper debate that ensued—with Spencer Roane of Virginia as the chief pseudonymous critic in the Richmond Enquirer, and John Marshall himself, for the only time in his career, as chief pseudonymous newspaper defender of the Court.

Within weeks of the McCulloch decision, the Richmond Enquirer, the chief organ of Virginia states' rights leaders, began publishing elaborate attacks. Marshall saw in them a revival of the feared strict constructionist principles of 1798: if they prevailed, "the constitution would be converted into the old confederation." The Chief Justice, afraid that no one else would make an adequate defense, took to the newspapers himself. In April 1819, he wrote two essays for a Philadelphia paper. But then Judge Spencer Roane —the writer of the defiant state court judgment that was reversed in Martin v. Hunter's Lessee and a leading Virginia politician as well as ideologue—sharply attacked McCulloch in a series of essays signed "Hampden." Marshall, his letters reveal, found himself "more stimulated on this subject than on any other because I believe the design to be to injure the Judges & impair the constitution." Anxious and intense, he hastily wrote nine elaborate essays that were published in the Alexandria Gazette over the pseudonym "A Friend of the Constitution." [For these recently discovered essays and their background, see Gunther (ed.), John Marshall's Defense of McCulloch v. Maryland (1969).]

The Bank aspects of the case are hardly mentioned in this newspaper battle, either by the attackers or by Marshall. As Marshall realized, it was doctrine, not result, that troubled the Virginians: they would have preferred "an obsequious, silent opinion without reasons"; it was "our heretical reasoning" that was "pronounced most damnable." And it was that reasoning that concerned Marshall most: he defended it against charges that it legitimated unlimited congressional powers; he denied that McCulloch endorsed consolidation; he insisted that the decision struck a moderate balance between excessively broad and unduly narrow conceptions of national powers. (His elaborations are considered further in the next group of notes.)

7. *The national bank—a "private" or "public" institution?* a. *In 1819.* Note that Marshall in McCulloch said very little about the organization and operations of the Bank. Should he have said more? Recall also that the Bank's success was considerably greater during its prosperous first year than in the depression months immediately preceding the decision. Could the 1819 circumstances have been relied on to challenge the constitutionality of the Bank, if the 1816 context provided substantial basis for the congressional judgment to charter the Bank?

The Bank was manifestly not a purely governmental operation—not like a mint or an army fort. As long ago as 1790, Hamilton had argued, in proposing a national bank: "To attach full confidence to an institution of this nature, it appears to be an essential ingredient in its structure that it shall be under a *private* not a *public* direction—under the guidance of *individual* interest, not of *public policy*." Any suspicion that the nationally chartered bank was "too much influenced by public necessity," he asserted, would "be a canker that would continually corrode the vitals of the credit of the bank." He added: "The keen, steady, and, as it were, magnetic sense of their own interest as proprietors, in the directors of a bank, pointing invariably to its true pole—the prosperity of the institution,—is the only security that can always be relied on for a careful and prudent administration" and for "permanent confidence" in the bank. (Hamilton's Report to the House on a National Bank, December 13, 1790). Obviously, Hamilton and the proponents of the Second Bank of the United States expected substantial governmental benefits from a congressionally chartered bank, as a source of loans, as a depository and fiscal agent, and as a stabilizer of currency. But these benefits were to be by-products of the bank's operations as a largely private, profit-making, commercial institution.

The charter of the Second Bank, accordingly, provided that eighty percent of the stock ownership and of the directors were to be private; twenty percent of the stock was government-owned, and the President nominated only five of the twenty-five directors. Walter Jones and Joseph Hopkinson mentioned the "private" nature of the Bank in the course of their argument in McCulloch, though mainly on the question of the Bank's immunity from state taxation rather than its constitutionality under Article I. Were the "private" features relevant, on either question? Should Marshall have discussed them? Compare Plous and Baker, "McCulloch v. Maryland: Right Principle, Wrong Case," 9 Stan.L.Rev. 710 (1957). Should Marshall, moreover, have emphasized that the Maryland tax was discriminatory? The problem of governmental tax immunities is considered further in chap. 10, below.

b. *In 1968.* Note the recent comments on these aspects of McCulloch in First Agricultural Nat. Bank v. State Tax Comm'n, 392 U.S. 339 (1968) (see also chap. 10, p. 764, infra). The majority reaffirmed the immunity of national banks from state taxation on statutory grounds and accordingly did not directly confront the state court's position that "the status of national banks has been so changed by the establishment of the Federal Reserve System that they should no longer be considered nontaxable by the States as instrumentalities of the United States." But Justice Thurgood Marshall's dissent, joined by Justices Harlan and Stewart, was prepared to reach the constitutional issue: in light of "the present functions and role of national banks," they should not be considered "constitutionally immune from nondiscriminatory state taxation." McCulloch and other "hoary cases" could "and perhaps should" be read as banning only discriminatory taxes. A modern national bank, he explained, is "a privately owned corporation existing for the private profit of its shareholders. It performs no significant federal governmental function that is not performed equally by state-chartered banks." The Bank of the United States of the McCulloch case was quite different, he insisted: it "would clearly be a federal instrumentality under the Court's most recent discussions of the doctrine."

CONGRESSIONAL POWER, POLITICAL RESTRAINTS, AND THE JUDICIAL FUNCTION

1. *Restraints on congressional power: judicial limitations.* Consider, in examining the McCulloch opinion and the cases in the next two chapters, what principled limits courts can impose to guard against excessive intrusion of national authority into local affairs. Are courts capable of articulating effective federalism-related limits (as distinguished from limits designed to protect individual rights, considered in Part III below)? Or is the imposition of restraints best left to the political process, in view of the representation of local interests in the national government? Did Marshall's McCulloch opinion in effect legitimate an unlimited congressional discretion?

a. *Necessary and proper means to achieve enumerated ends.* Do Marshall's formulations regarding means-ends relationships constitute restraints on congressional choices that are judicially enforceable? Marshall spoke of means "which tended directly to the execution" of delegated powers, "means which are appropriate" and "plainly adapted" to achieving legitimate ends. What are the limits on the chains of inferences—on the "House that Jack Built" arguments that Jefferson feared (p. 223 above)—that may be put forth to justify a statute as a "necessary and proper" means to effectuate a granted power? Must that justification be considered by Congress, or may it be supplied subsequent to enactment, by counsel's argument or by the Court's speculation about the justifications reasonable legislatures *might* have relied on?

Marshall wrote his pseudonymous "Friend of the Constitution" essays to counter Spencer Roane's charges that McCulloch gave "a general letter of attorney to the future legislators of the union," that in fact "the court had granted to congress unlimited powers under the pretext of a discretion in selecting means." See Gunther (ed.), John Marshall's Defense of McCulloch v. Maryland (1969). Marshall insisted that the required means-ends relationship was a judicially enforceable one, and some of his essays try to restate and elaborate the requirement. For example, "neither a feigned convenience nor a strict necessity; but a reasonable convenience, and a qualified necessity" had to be shown to demonstrate that means were constitutional; means must have "a plain relation to the end," they must be "direct, natural and appropriate." McCulloch, he insisted, denied "the unlimited powers of Congress to adopt any means whatever."

Yet, in view of the exercises of national power sustained by the Court in the cases that follow, was not Roane right after all about the effective scope of congressional discretion after McCulloch? Was he not right about the effect of McCulloch, if not about Marshall's purpose? Was that because McCulloch did not seriously look for limits? Because the McCulloch limits were inadequate? Could better limits have been stated? Consider Gunther, supra, at 20: "The degree of centralization that has taken place [since McCulloch] may well have come about in the face of Marshall's intent rather than in accord with his expectation. That centralization may be the inevitable consequence of economic and social changes. And this development may suggest the impossibility of articulating general constitutional standards capable of limiting those centralizing forces, particularly through judicial action. But to say this is very different from saying that Marshall knew he was engaging in a hopeless task."

b. *"Pretext"—congressional purpose and abuse of power.* In articulating limits on congressional choices, Marshall spoke not only of the required means-ends relationships, but also of congressional purposes. Can courts effectively assure legislative good faith in exercising powers? Should courts scrutinize the purity of legislative motives? Marshall asserted in McCulloch—and emphatically reiterated in his newspaper replies to Roane—that the Court would invalidate laws "for the accomplishment of objects not intrusted to the government," laws enacted "under the pretext" of exercising granted powers. See, e. g., Gunther (ed.), supra, at 187; see also Marshall's statement at 173: "It is not pretended that this right of selection [of means] may be fraudulently used to the destruction of the fair land marks of the constitution. Congress certainly may not under the pretext of collecting taxes, or of guaranteeing to each state a republican form of government, alter the law of descents; but if the means have a plain relation to the end—if they be direct, natural and appropriate," they are constitutional.

Is the "pretext" limitation a viable one, capable of judicial enforcement? Does it require a judicial determination of the "true" object of the law—of congressional purposes and motives? Are otherwise constitutional laws invalidated by impermissible "pretext" statements by Congress? Do the Art. I, Sec. 8, powers of Congress specify the permissible *aims* of legislation, or simply the permissible, objectively determinable *areas* of national regulation? Does the commerce clause, for example, authorize legislative control for any purpose so long as the field regulated is that of interstate commerce"? May Congress seek "morality," "police" objectives—may it, e. g., legislate against prostitution or for racial justice or against rioters—so long as the sanction of the law takes hold on some commerce-connected activity? Or must the regulation be enacted with a primarily commercial purpose? Or must the evil being regulated at least have commercial dimensions? May Congress enact a conditional prohibition of interstate movement of goods and persons with a major collateral objective of regulating intrastate activities not directly reachable? These problems are examined further below: see, e. g., Hammer v. Dagenhart, p. 261, and related materials in chap. 4, secs. 3 and 4, infra.

2. *Restraints on congressional power: The Political Safeguards of Federalism.* Consider, in examining the Court's efforts to formulate limiting principles in the cases that follow, whether the need for judicial control is minimal in view of the representation of local interests in the political structure of the national government. Do these "political safeguards" operate with equal effectiveness with regard to all kinds of congressional action? As effectively in cases of morals regulation as in cases of economic regulation? As effectively in spending situations as with proposals for direct regulation? Consider the following excerpts from Wechsler, "The Political Safeguards of Federalism—The Role of the States in the Composition and Selection of the National Government," in Principles, Politics and Fundamental Law (1961), 49–82: *

"Our constitution makers established a central government authorized to act directly upon individuals through its own agencies—and thus they

* The excerpts are reprinted here with the permission of the publisher, © copyright 1961 by the President and Fellows of Harvard College. The substance of the essay also appears in 54 Colum.L.Rev. 543 (1954) and in Selected Essays 1938–62 (1963), 185.

formed a nation capable of function and of growth. To serve the ends of federalism they employed three main devices: (1) They preserved the states as separate sources of authority and organs of administration—a point on which they hardly had a choice. (2) They gave the states a role of great importance in the composition and selection of the central government. (3) They undertook to formulate a distribution of authority between the nation and the states, in terms which gave some scope at least to legal processes for its enforcement.

"Scholarship—not only legal scholarship—has given most attention to the last of these enumerated mechanisms, perhaps because it has been fascinated by the Supreme Court and its interpretations of the power distribution clauses of the Constitution. The continuous existence of the states as governmental entities and their strategic role in the selection of the Congress and the President are so immutable a feature of the system that their importance tends to be ignored. Of the framers' mechanisms, however, they have had and have today the larger influence upon the working balance of our federalism. The actual extent of central intervention in the governance of our affairs is determined far less by the formal power distribution than by the sheer existence of the states and their political power to influence the action of the national authority. . . .

"National action has . . . always been regarded as exceptional in our polity, an intrusion to be justified by some necessity, the special rather than the ordinary case. This point of view cuts even deeper than the concept of the central government as one of granted, limited authority, articulated in the tenth amendment. National power may be quite unquestioned in a given situation; those who would advocate its exercise must none the less answer the preliminary question why the matter should not be left to the states. Even when Congress acts, its tendency has been to frame enactments on an *ad hoc* basis to accomplish limited objectives, supplanting state-created norms only so far as may be necessary for the purpose. Indeed, with all the centralizing growth throughout the years, federal law is still a largely interstitial product, rarely occupying any field completely, building normally upon legal relationships established by the states. As Henry Hart and I have put it elsewhere: 'Congress acts . . . against the background of the total *corpus juris* of the states in much the way that a state legislature acts against the background of the common law, assumed to govern unless changed by legislation.' As a state legislature views the common law as something to be left alone unless a need for change has been established, so Congress has traditionally viewed the governance of matters by the states.

"The tradition plainly serves the values of our federalism in so far as it maintains a burden of persuasion on those favoring national intervention. . . .

"If I have drawn too much significance from the mere fact of the existence of the states, the error surely will be rectified by pointing also to their crucial role in the selection and the composition of the national authority. More is involved here than that aspect of the companies between the larger and the smaller states that yielded their equality of status in the Senate. Representatives no less than Senators are allotted by the Constitution to the states, although their number varies with state population as determined by the census. Though the House was meant to be the 'grand depository of the democratic principle of the government,' as distinguished from the Senate's function as the forum of the states, the people to be represented with due def-erence to their respective numbers were the *people of the states*. And with the President, as with Congress, the crucial instrument of the selection—whether through electors, or, in the event of failure of majority, by the House voting as state units—is again the states. The consequence, of course, is that the states are the strategic yardsticks for the measurement of interest and opinion, the special centers of political activity, the separate geographical determinants of national as well as local politics. . . .

"To the extent that federalist values have real significance they must give rise to local sensitivity to central intervention; to the extent that such a local sensitivity exists, it cannot fail to find reflection in the Congress. In-deed, the problem of the Congress is and always has been to attune itself to national opinion and produce majorities for action called for by the voice of the entire nation. It is remarkable that it should function thus as well as it does, given its intrinsic sensitivity to any insular opinion that is dominant in a substantial number of the states. . . .

"The President must be, as I have said above, the main repository of 'national spirit' in the central government. But both the mode of his selec-tion and the future of his party require that he also be responsive to local values that have large support within the states. And since his programs must, in any case, achieve support in Congress—in so far as they involve new action—he must surmount the greater local sensitivity of Congress be-fore anything is done. . . .

"If this analysis is correct, the national political process in the United States—and especially the role of the states in the composition and selec-tion of the central government—is intrinsically well adapted to retarding or restraining new instrusions by the center on the domain of the states. Far from a national authority that is expansionist by nature, the inherent tendency in our system is precisely the reverse, necessitating the widest support before intrusive measures of importance can receive significant consideration, react-ing readily to opposition grounded in resistance within the states. Nor is this tendency effectively denied by pointing to the size or scope of the existing national establishment. However useful it may be to explore possible con-tractions in specific areas, such evidence points mainly to the magnitude of unavoidable responsibility under the circumstances of our time.

"It is in light of this inherent tendency, reflected most importantly in Congress, that the governmental power distribution clauses of the Constitu-tion gain their largest meaning as an instrument for the protection of the states. Those clauses, as is well known, have served far more to qualify or stop intrusive legislative measures in the Congress than to invalidate enacted legislation in the Supreme Court.

"This does not differ from the expectation of the framers quite as mark-edly as might be thought. For the containment of the national authority Madison did not emphasize the function of the Court; he pointed to the composition of the Congress and to the political processes. . . .

"The prime function envisaged for judicial review—in relation to fed-eralism—was the maintenance of national supremacy against nullification or usurpation by the individual states, the national government having no part in their composition or their councils. This is made clear by the fact that reliance on the courts was substituted, apparently on Jefferson's suggestion, for the earlier proposal to give Congress a veto of state enactments deemed to trespass on the national domain. And except for the brief interlude that ended with the crisis of the thirties, it is mainly in the realm of such policing of the states that the Supreme Court has in fact participated in determining the balances of federalism.[1] This is not to say that the Court can decline to measure national enactments by the Constitution when it is called upon to face the question in the course of ordinary litigation; the supremacy clause governs there as well. It is rather to say that the Court is on weakest ground when it opposes its interpretation of the Constitution to that of Congress in the interest of the states, whose representatives control the legislative process and, by hypothesis, have broadly acquiesced in sanctioning the challenged Act of Congress.

"Federal intervention as against the states is thus primarily a matter for congressional determination in our system as it stands. So too, moreover, is the question whether state enactments shall be stricken down as an infringement on the national authority. For while the Court has an important function in this area, as I have noted, the crucial point is that its judgments here are subject to reversal by Congress, which can consent to action by the states that otherwise would be invalidated. The familiar illustrations in commerce and in state taxation of federal instrumentalities do not by any means exhaust the field. The Court makes the decisive judgment only when—and to the extent that—Congress has not laid down the resolving rule.

"To perceive that it is Congress rather than the Court that on the whole is vested with the ultimate authority for managing our federalism is not, of course, to depreciate the role played by the Court, subordinate though it may be. It is no accident that Congress has been slow to exercise its managerial authority, remitting to the Court so much of what it could determine by a legislative rule. The difficulties of reaching agreement on such matters, not to speak of drafting problems of immense complexity, lend obvious attractiveness to the *ad hoc* judicial method of adjustment. Whether Congress could contribute more effectively to the solution of these problems is a challenging and open question. The legislative possibilities within this area of our policy have hardly been explored."

1. Of the great controversies with respect to national power before the Civil War, only the Bank and slavery within the territories were carried to the Court and its participation with respect to slavery was probably its greatest failure. The question of internal improvements, for example, which raised the most acute problem of constitutional construction, was fought out politically and in Congress. After the War only the Civil Rights Cases and income tax decisions were important in setting limits on national power—until the Child Labor Case and the New Deal decisions. The recasting of constitutional positions since the crisis acknowledges much broader power in the Congress—as against the states—than it is likely soon or ever to employ. [Footnote by Professor Wechsler.]

Chapter 4

THE COMMERCE POWER

Introduction. The poor condition of American commerce and the proliferating trade rivalries between the states were the immediate provocations for the calling of the Constitutional Convention.   One of the new Constitution's major innovations was a response to these concerns: Congress was granted the power "To Regulate Commerce with foreign Nations, and among the Several States."   That grant was to suppress the "interfering and unneighbourly regulations of some States,"—regulations which, "if not restrained by a national controul," would prove to be even more "serious sources of animosity and discord."   (Hamilton's No. 22 of The Federalist.) The national commerce power, it was hoped, would put an end to hostile state restrictions, retaliatory trade regulations, protective tariffs on imports from other states.

That congressional power, designed to promote a national market and curb Balkanization of the economy, has been a subject of extensive and continuous consideration by the Court since Marshall's day.   The commerce power has had a two-fold impact: as a restraint on state action (considered in chaps. 8 and 9), and as a source of national authority (the concern of this chapter).   In the hundreds of cases in which state regulations and taxes have been challenged under the commerce clause, free trade is the national interest that claims protection, and the tie to the historical roots of the clause is plain.   In the cases in which the clause is invoked to justify congressional regulation, the nexus with historical purposes is often more tenuous.   But the modern pressures for national action on a widening range of problems have prompted increasingly intense searches for constitutional justifications among the enumerated powers.   And in these searches, the commerce clause has proved to be a frequently attractive and often hospitable base for the assertion of regulatory authority.

This chapter examines in some detail the Court's efforts to articulate the scope and limits of the commerce power.   That examination is worthwhile not only for its own sake—for the sake of tracing the contours of congressional authority—but also for its institutional aspects, for the light it sheds on the Court's general capacity to develop enforceable limits on governmental powers.   Many of the doctrines in these cases have proved ineffective as restraints;   some of them have been explicitly abandoned by the Court.   Did these limits fail because they were unjustifiable in content?   Because they were applied inconsistently and with result-oriented biases?   What principled limits were possible?   What limits remain?   Does the history of commerce clause litigation suggest that judicially-developed doctrines limiting government tend to be facades for the personal preferences of the judges? Are restraints designed to protect individual rights likely to be more principled than the federalism-related limits considered here?

These general problems underlie the recurrent questions of commerce clause doctrine which surface in many of the cases in this chapter.   Congress has frequently sought to deal with problems far removed from the evils that gave rise to the commerce clause.   Does the purpose of Congress determine the legitimacy of resort to the commerce power? Can a standard of constitutionality distinguish between "commercial" and "economic" legislation on the one hand and "moral," "police" regulation on the other? Can limits be stated that do not require an inquiry into congressional purpose? Does the commerce clause curtail excessive intrusion of national power into local affairs? Are there adequate constitutional standards to distinguish between local affairs remote from commerce and intrastate activities with a sufficiently close connection to interstate commerce?

SECTION 1.   THE MARSHALL COURT'S GROUNDWORK

GIBBONS v. OGDEN
9 Wheat. 1, 6 L.Ed. 23 (1824).

Appeal from the Court for the Trial of Impeachments and Correction of Errors of the State of New York.

[The New York legislature granted to Robert Livingston and Robert Fulton the exclusive right to operate steamboats in New York waters. By assignment from Livingston and Fulton, Aaron Ogden acquired monopoly rights to operate steamboats between New York and New Jersey. Thomas Gibbons, a former partner of Ogden, began operating two steamboats between New York and Elizabethtown, New Jersey, in violation of Ogden's monopoly. Gibbons' boats were enrolled and licensed as "vessels employed in the coasting trade" under a federal law of 1793 (1 Stat. 305). Ogden obtained an injunction from the New York Court of Chancery ordering Gibbons to stop operating his ferries in New York waters. 4 Johns.Ch. 150 (1819). The highest New York court affirmed. 17 Johns. 488 (1820). Only a part of Chief Justice Marshall's opinion sustaining Gibbons' appeal is printed here— that portion discussing the national commerce power. The rest of the Marshall opinion—the part dealing with the validity of the New York monopoly under the Constitution and the federal law—appears later, with other materials on limitations of state power in chap. 8, at p. 615.]

Mr. Chief Justice MARSHALL delivered the opinion of the Court . . . :

The appellant contends that this decree is erroneous, because the laws which purport to give the exclusive privilege it sustains, are repugnant to the constitution and laws of the United States.

They are said to be repugnant—

1st. To that clause in the constitution which authorizes Congress to regulate commerce. . . .

This [Constitution] contains an enumeration of powers expressly granted by the people to their government. It has been said, that these powers ought to be construed strictly. But why ought they to be so construed? Is there one sentence in the constitution which gives countenance to this rule? . . . What do gentlemen mean, by a strict construction? If they contend only against that enlarged construction, which would extend words beyond their natural and obvious import, we might question the application of the term, but should not controvert the principle. If they contend for that narrow construction which, in support of some theory not to be found in the constitution, would deny to the government those powers which the words of the grant, as usually understood, import, and which are consistent with the general views and objects of the instrument; for that narrow construction, which would cripple the government, and render it unequal to the objects for which it is declared to be instituted, and to which the powers given, as fairly understood, render it competent; then we cannot perceive the propriety of this strict construction, nor adopt it as the rule by which the constitution is to be expounded. . . . If, from the imperfection of human language, there should be serious doubts respecting the extent of any given power, it is a well settled rule, that the objects for which it was given, especially when those objects are expressed in the instrument itself, should have great influence in the construction. . .

The words are, "Congress shall have power to regulate commerce with foreign nations, and among the several States, and with the Indian tribes."

The subject to be regulated is commerce; and our constitution being, as was aptly said at the bar, one of enumeration, and not of definition, to ascertain the extent of the power, it becomes necessary to settle the meaning of the word. The counsel for the appellee would limit it to traffic, to buying and selling, or the interchange of commodities, and do not admit that it comprehends navigation. This would restrict a general term, applicable to many objects, to one of its significations. Commerce, undoubtedly, is traffic, but it is something more: it is intercourse. It describes the commercial intercourse between nations, and parts of nations, in all its branches, and is regulated by prescribing rules for carrying on that intercourse. The mind can scarcely conceive a system for regulating commerce between nations, which shall exclude all laws concerning navigation, which shall be silent on the admission of the vessels of the one nation into the ports of the other, and be confined to prescribing rules for the conduct of individuals, in the actual employment of buying and selling, or of barter.

If commerce does not include navigation, the government of the Union has no direct power over that subject, and can make no law prescribing what shall constitute American vessels, or requiring that they shall be navigated by American seamen. Yet this power has been exercised from the commencement of the government, has been exercised with the consent of all, and has been understood by all to be a commercial regulation. All America understands, and has uniformly understood, the word "commerce" to comprehend navigation. It was so understood, and must have been so understood, when the constitution was framed. The power over commerce, including navigation, was one of the primary objects for which the people of America adopted their government, and must have been contemplated in forming it. The convention must have used the word in that sense; because all have understood it in that sense, and the attempt to restrict it comes too late. . . .

The word used in the constitution, then, comprehends, and has been always understood to comprehend, navigation within its meaning; and a power to regulate navigation is as expressly granted as if that term had been added to the word "commerce."

To what commerce does this power extend? The constitution informs us, to commerce "with foreign nations, and among the several States, and with the Indian tribes."

It has, we believe, been universally admitted that these words comprehend every species of commercial intercourse between the United States and foreign nations. No sort of trade can be carried on between this country and any other, to which this power does not extend. It has been truly said, that commerce, as the word is used in the constitution, is a unit, every part of which is indicated by the term.

If this be the admitted meaning of the word, in its application to foreign nations, it must carry the same meaning throughout the sentence, and remain a unit, unless there be some plain intelligible cause which alters it.

The subject to which the power is next applied, is to commerce "among the several States." The word "among" means intermingled with. A thing which is among others, is intermingled with them. Commerce among the States cannot stop at the the external boundary line of each State, but may be introduced into the interior.

It is not intended to say that these words comprehend that commerce which is completely internal, which is carried on between man and man in a State, or between different parts of the same State, and which does not extend to or affect other States. Such a power would be inconvenient, and is certainly unnecessary.

Comprehensive as the word "among" is, it may very properly be restricted to that commerce which concerns more States than one. The phrase is not one which would probably have been selected to indicate the completely interior traffic of a State, because it is not an apt phrase for that purpose; and the enumeration of the particular classes of commerce to which the power was to be extended, would not have been made had the intention been to extend the power to every description. The enumeration presupposes something not enumerated; and that something, if we regard the language or the subject of the sentence, must be the exclusively internal commerce of a State. The genius and character of the whole government seem to be, that its action is to be applied to all the external concerns of the nation, and to those internal concerns which affect the States generally; but not to those which are completely within a particular State, which do not affect other States, and with which it is not necessary to interfere, for the purpose of executing some of the general powers of the government. The completely internal commerce of a State, then, may be considered as reserved for the State itself.

But, in regulating commerce with foreign nations, the power of Congress does not stop at the jurisdictional lines of the several States. It would be a very useless power if it could not pass those lines. The commerce of the United States with foreign nations, is that of the whole United States. Every district has a right to participate in it. The deep streams which penetrate our country in every direction, pass through the interior of almost every State in the Union, and furnish the means of exercising this right. If Congress has the power to regulate it, that power must be exercised whenever the subject exists. If it exists within the States, if a foreign voyage may commence or terminate at a port within a State, then the power of Congress may be exercised within a State.

3\ We are now arrived at the inquiry—What is this power?

It is the power to regulate; that is, to prescribe the rule by which commerce is to be governed. This power, like all others vested in Congress, is complete in itself, may be exercised to its utmost extent, and acknowledges no limitations, other than are prescribed in the constitution. These are expressed in plain terms, and do not affect the questions which arise in this case, or which have been discussed at the bar. If, as has always been understood, the sovereignty of Congress, though limited to specified objects, is plenary as to those objects, the power over commerce with foreign nations, and among the several States, is vested in Congress as absolutely as it would be in a single government, having in its constitution the same restrictions on the exercise of the power as are found in the constitution of the United States. The wisdom and the discretion of Congress, their identity with the people, and the influence which their constituents possess at elections, are, in this, as in many other instances, as that, for example, of declaring war, the sole restraints on which they have relied to secure them from its abuse. They are the restraints on which the people must often rely solely, in all representative governments.

The power of Congress, then, comprehends navigation, within the limits of every State in the Union; so far as that navigation may be, in any manner, connected with "commerce with foreign nations, or among the several States, or with the Indian tribes." It may, of consequence, pass the jurisdictional line of New York, and act upon the very waters to which the prohibition now under consideration applies. . . .

This principle is, if possible, still more clear, when applied to commerce "among the several States." They either join each other, in which case they are separated by a mathematical line, or they are remote from each other, in which case other States lie between them. What is commerce "among" them; and how is it to be conducted? Can a trading expedition between two adjoining States, commence and terminate outside of each? And if the trading intercourse be between two States remote from each other, must it not commence in one, terminate in the other, and probably pass through a third? Commerce among the States must, of necessity, be commerce with the States. In the regulation of trade with the Indian tribes, the action of the law, especially when the constitution was made, was chiefly within a State. The power of Congress, then, whatever it may be, must be exercised within the territorial jurisdiction of the several States. . . .

The Court is aware that, in stating the train of reasoning by which we have been conducted to this result, much time has been consumed in the attempt to demonstrate propositions which may have been thought axioms. It is felt that the tediousness inseparable from the endeavour to prove that which is already clear, is imputable to a considerable part of this opinion. But it was unavoidable. The conclusion to which we have come, depends on a chain of principles which it was necessary to preserve unbroken; and, although some of them were thought nearly self-evident, the magnitude of the question, the weight of character belonging to those from whose judgment we dissent, and the argument at the bar, demanded that we should assume nothing.

Powerful and ingenious minds, taking, as postulates, that the powers expressly granted to the government of the Union, are to be contracted by construction, into the narrowest possible compass, and that the original powers of the States are retained, if any possible construction will retain them, may, by a course of well digested, but refined and metaphysical reasoning, founded on these premises, explain away the constitution of our country, and leave it, a magnificent structure, indeed, to look at, but totally unfit for use. They may so entangle and perplex the understanding, as to obscure principles, which were before thought quite plain, and induce doubts where, if the mind were to pursue its own course, none would be perceived. In such a case, it is peculiarly necessary to recur to safe and fundamental principles to sustain those principles, and, when sustained, to make them the tests of the arguments to be examined. [Additional excerpts from Chief Justice Marshall's opinion invalidating the New York monopoly grant appear in chap. 8, p. 615, infra. Justice Johnson's concurring opinion is omitted.]

GIBBONS v. OGDEN—A DOCTRINE FOR ALL NEEDS?

Gibbons v. Ogden, like McCulloch v. Maryland, is prominently and frequently cited in modern decisions sustaining very extensive exercises of congressional powers. Is that modern reliance on Marshall justifiable? Consider Wickard v. Filburn, 317 U.S. 111 (1942) (p. 314, below), one of the most important discussions of the commerce power. Justice Jackson's majority opinion in Wickard stated: "At the beginning Chief Justice Marshall described the federal commerce power with a breadth never yet exceeded. Gibbons v. Ogden, 9 Wheat. 1, 194–195. He made emphatic the embracing and penetrating nature of this power by warning that effective restraints on its exercise must proceed from political rather than from judicial processes." Is that a fair statement? Does Gibbons in effect abandon judicial restraints? Does Wickard v. Filburn? After McCulloch, Marshall vehemently denied Spencer Roane's charge that his principles gave Congress unlimited authority. Did Gibbons give Congress the carte blanche denied by McCulloch? What judicial limits did Marshall assert?

SECTION 2. THE BEGINNING OF MODERN ECONOMIC REGU-LATION: ANTITRUST LAWS AND RAILROAD LEGISLATION

EARLY LAWS AND RECURRENT DOCTRINAL DIFFICULTIES

1. *Early commerce clause legislation.* During the first century under the Constitution, most of the Court's discussions of the scope of the commerce power arose—as in Gibbons v. Ogden—in cases dealing with state action affecting commerce. Most of those cases, moreover, did not involve any exercise of the power by Congress at all; state laws were challenged as barred by the "dormant," unexercised commerce power. See chaps. 8 and 9 below. Large-scale regulatory action by Congress began with the Interstate Commerce Act in 1887 and the Sherman Anti-Trust Law in 1890, and challenges to these statutes initiated the major "modern" confrontations between the Court and congressional authority regarding commerce. Even before 1887, however, congressional action under the commerce power occasionally came before the Court. There were, for example, attempts to improve water and land transportation, as in the creation of a corporation with authority to construct a bridge, Luxton v. North River Bridge Co., 153 U.S. 525 (1894). Similar action was taken in the building and maintenance of railroad facilities —e. g., California v. Central Pacific R. Co., 127 U.S. 1 (1888), chartering of interstate carrier; Roberts v. Northern Pacific R. Co., 158 U.S. 1 (1859), cre-

ation of corporation for purpose of building railroad; Dubuque and Sioux
City R. R. Co. v. Richmond, 19 Wall. 584 (1874), providing for construction
of connections and bridges to form continuous lines.   There was also some
commerce clause legislation of a "police" character—e.g., in United States v.
Marigold, 9 How. 560 (1850), prohibiting importation of counterfeit money;
United States v. 43 Gallons of Whiskey, 93 U.S. 188 (1876), prohibition of
whiskey trade with Indians;   United States v. Boston & A. R. Co., 15 Fed. 209
(D.C.Mass.1883), regulation as to care of animals in transit.

   2. *Emerging doctrinal difficulties: regulation of national economic
problems vs. regulation of "police" problems.*   The rapid Nineteenth Century developments in industrialization, transportation and communication
produced national economic problems and demands for congressional regulation.   Control of railroad rates and of restraints on competition—considered
in the Knight case and the Shreveport Rate Case below—were the early congressional responses to these demands.

   a. *Regulating intrastate activities because of their relationship to interstate commerce.*   It was in cases such as Shreveport and Knight that the Court
tried to state the extent to which Congress might regulate local activities because of their relationship with interstate commerce.   The doctrinal problems
of those cases foreshadow the difficulties encountered in subsequent efforts
at national economic regulation—especially the New Deal attempts considered
in the Schechter, Carter, Jones & Laughlin, Darby and Wickard v. Filburn
decisions below.   How far, and with what justification, may Congress go to
reach intrastate activities related to national economic concerns?   Can intrastate activities be regulated when they can be considered a part of interstate
commerce, within "the stream of commerce"?   Is the production of goods not
reachable by the commerce power, because production neither is commerce
nor has a "direct" effect on commerce?   Or can production and consumption
of goods be regulated because they "affect" commerce?

   b. *Police regulations: morality and the commerce power.*   As the
Lottery Case illustrates, increased congressional interest in police regulation
and mounting congressional concern with economic problems were substantially contemporaneous developments.   Were these two types of laws treated differently by the Court?   Should they have been?   Is it useful, or possible, to
distinguish national legislation dealing with "police" problems—directed at
"bad" local activities such as gambling, prostitution, theft—from national
laws concerned with national economic problems?   Is it constitutionally significant that police legislation usually invoked prohibition of interstate transportation—rather than direct control of local activities—as the regulatory
device, as in the Lottery Case and in Hammer v. Dagenhart?   Should the
Court consider the "ulterior purpose" of legislation, if its immediate focus is
on the movement of commerce across state boundaries?   Are laws directed at
police problems less justifiable invocations of the commerce power than regulations of economic problems?

   What if economic and "police" objectives both underlie legislation?   Can
a distinction between economic and "police" aims be applied, for example,
to the Wagner Act or the Fair Labor Standards Act?   Can the Court make
such a distinction, in terms of primary purposes?   Should a legislator be
troubled by attempts to use the commerce clause for social or moral objectives?
Questions such as these should be kept in mind in examining the following
cases tracing the development of the modern commerce power.   And the last

series of questions, in particular, should be considered in examining the materials in sec. 6 below, dealing with the public accommodations sections of the Civil Rights Act of 1964.

UNITED STATES v. E. C. KNIGHT CO.

156 U.S. 1, 15 S.Ct. 249, 39 L.Ed. 325 (1895).

Appeal from the Circuit Court of Appeals for the Third Circuit.

[An equity action by the United States sought to set aside the American Sugar Refining Company's acquisition of the stock of four other sugar refineries. The bill alleged that the four acquired companies had produced about 33% of all sugar refined in the United States, and that American's acquisition gave it control of all refineries except one, producing about 2% of the total sugar refined. The action was brought under the Sherman Anti-Trust Act of 1890. Section 1 prohibited any contract, combination or conspiracy "in restraint of trade or commerce among the several states." Section 2 provided penalties for any person "who shall monopolize, or combine or conspire . . . to monopolize any part of the trade or commerce among the several States."

[The trial court's findings supported these allegations, found that American's purpose in purchasing the other refineries "was to obtain a greater influence or more perfect control over the business of refining or selling sugar in this country," but concluded that the facts did not show a contract, combination or conspiracy to restrain or monopolize commerce. The dismissal of the bill was affirmed by the Circuit Court of Appeals.]

Mr. Chief Justice FULLER, after stating the case, delivered the opinion of the court.

The fundamental question is, whether conceding that the existence of a monopoly in manufacture is established by the evidence, that monopoly can be directly suppressed under the act of Congress in the mode attempted by this bill. . . .

The argument is that the power to control the manufacture of refined sugar is a monopoly over a necessary of life, to the enjoyment of which by a large part of the population of the United States interstate commerce is indispensable, and that, therefore, the general government in the exercise of the power to regulate commerce may repress such monopoly directly and set aside the instruments which have created it. But this argument cannot be confined to necessaries of life merely, and must include all articles of general consumption. Doubtless the power to control the manufacture of a given thing involves in a certain sense the control of its disposition, but this is a secondary and not the primary sense; and although the exercise of that power may result in bringing the operation of commerce into play, it does not control it, and affects it only incidentally and indirectly. Commerce succeeds to manufacture, and is not a part of it. The power to regulate commerce is the power to prescribe the rule by which commerce shall be governed, and is a power independent of the power to suppress monopoly. But it may operate in repression of monopoly whenever that comes within the rules by which commerce is governed or whenever the transaction is itself a monopoly of commerce.

It is vital that the independence of the commercial power and of the police power, and the delimitation between them, however sometimes perplexing, should always be recognized and observed, for while the one furnishes the strongest bond of union, the other is essential to the preservation of the autonomy of the States as required by our dual form of government; and acknowledged evils, however grave and urgent they may appear to be, had better be borne, than the risk be run, in the effort to suppress them, of more serious consequences by resort to expedients of even doubtful constitutionality.

It will be perceived how far-reaching the proposition is that the power of dealing with a monopoly directly may be exercised by the general government whenever interstate or international commerce may be ultimately affected. The regulation of commerce applies to the subjects of commerce and not to matters of internal police. Contracts to buy, sell, or exchange goods to be transported among the several States, the transportation and its instrumentalities, and articles bought, sold, or exchanged for the purposes of such transit among the States, or put in the way of transit, may be regulated, but this is because they form part of interstate trade or commerce. The fact that an article is manufactured for export to another State does not of itself make it an article of interstate commerce, and the intent of the manufacturer does not determine the time when the article or product passes from the control of the State and belongs to commerce. This was so ruled in Coe v. Errol, 116 U.S. 517, 525 in which the question before the court was whether certain logs cut at a place in New Hampshire and hauled to a river town for the purpose of transportation to the State of Maine were liable to be taxed like other property in the State of New Hampshire. . . .

And again, in Kidd v. Pearson, 128 U.S. 1, 20, where the question was discussed whether the right of a State to enact a statute prohibiting within its limits the manufacture of intoxicating liquors, except for certain purposes, could be overthrown by the fact that the manufacturer intended to export the liquors when made, it was held that the intent of the manufacturer did not determine the time when the article or product passed from the control of the State and belonged to commerce, and that, therefore, the statute, in omitting to except from its operation the manufacture of intoxicating liquors within the limits of the State for export, did not constitute an unauthorized interference with the right of Congress to regulate commerce. And Mr. Justice Lamar remarked: "No distinction is more popular to the common mind, or more clearly expressed in economic and political literature, than that between manufacture and commerce. Manufacture is transformation—the fashioning of raw materials into a change of form for use. The functions of commerce are different. The buying and selling and the transportation incidental thereto constitute commerce; and the regulation of commerce in the constitutional sense embraces the regulation at least of such transportation. . . . If it be held that the term includes the regulation of all such manufactures as are intended to be the subject of commercial transactions in the future, it is impossible to deny that it would also include all productive industries that contemplate the same thing. The result would be that Congress would be invested, to the exclusion of the States, with the power to regulate, not only manufactures, but also agriculture, horticulture, stock raising, domestic fisheries, mining—in short, every branch of human industry. For is there one of them that does not contemplate, more or less clearly, an interstate or foreign market? Does not the wheat grower of the Northwest or the cotton planter of the South, plant, cultivate, and harvest his crop with an eye on the prices at Liverpool, New York, and Chicago? The power being vested in Congress and denied to the States, it would follow as an inevitable result that the duty would devolve on Congress to regulate all of these delicate, multiform and vital interests—interests which in their nature are and must be local in all the details of their successful management." . . .

In Gibbons v. Ogden, Brown v. Maryland, and other cases often cited, the state laws, which were held inoperative, were instances of direct interference with, or regulations of, interstate or international commerce; yet in Kidd v. Pearson the refusal of a State to allow articles to be manufactured within her borders even for export was held not to directly affect external commerce, and state legislation which, in a great variety of ways, affected interstate commerce and persons engaged in it, has been frequently sustained because the interference was not direct.

Contracts, combinations, or conspiracies to control domestic enterprise in manufacture, agriculture, mining, production in all its forms, or to raise or lower prices or wages, might unquestionably tend to restrain external as well as domestic trade, but the restraint would be an indirect result, however inevitable and whatever its extent, and such result would not necessarily determine the object of the contract, combination, or conspiracy.

Again, all the authorities agree that in order to vitiate a contract or combination it is not essential that its result should be a complete monopoly; it is sufficient if it really tends to that end and to deprive the public of the advantages which flow from free competition. Slight reflection will show that if the national power extends to all contracts and combinations in manufacture, agriculture, mining, and other productive industries, whose ultimate result may affect external commerce, comparatively little of business operations and affairs would be left for state control.

It was in the light of well-settled principles that the act of July 2, 1890, was framed. . . . Aside from the provisions applicable where Congress might exercise municipal power, what the law struck at was combinations, contracts, and conspiracies to monopolize trade and commerce among the several States or with foreign nations; but the contracts and acts of the defendants related exclusively to the acquisition of the Philadelphia refineries and the business of sugar refining in Pennsylvania, and bore no direct relation to commerce between the States or with foreign nations. The object was manifestly private gain in the manufacture of the commodity, but not through the control of interstate or foreign commerce. It is true that the bill alleged that the products of these refineries were sold and distributed among the several States, and that all the companies were engaged in trade or commerce with the several States and with foreign nations; but this was no more than to say that trade and commerce served manufacture to fulfill its function. Sugar was refined for sale, and sales were probably made at Philadelphia for consumption, and undoubtedly for resale by the first purchasers throughout Pennsylvania and other States, and refined sugar was also forwarded by the companies to other States for sale. Nevertheless it does not follow that an attempt to monopolize, or the actual monopoly of, the manufacture was an attempt, whether executory or consummated, to monopolize commerce, even though, in order to dispose of the product, the instrumentality of commerce was necessarily invoked. . . .

Decree affirmed.

Mr. Justice HARLAN, dissenting. . . .

While the opinion of the court in this case does not declare the act of 1890 to be unconstitutional, it defeats the main object for which it was passed. For it is, in effect, held that the statute would be unconstitutional if interpreted as embracing such unlawful restraints upon the purchasing of goods in one State to be carried to another State as necessarily arise from the *existence* of combinations formed for the purpose and with the effect, not only of monopolizing the ownership of all such goods in every part of the country, but of controlling the prices for them in all the States. This view of the scope of the act leaves the public, so far as national power is concerned, entirely at the mercy of combinations which arbitrarily control the prices of articles purchased to be transported from one State to another State. I cannot assent to that view. In my judgment, the general government is not placed by the Constitution in such a condition of helplessness that it must fold its arms and remain inactive while capital combines, under the name of a corporation, to destroy competition, not in one State only, but throughout the entire country, in the buying and selling of articles—especially the necessaries of life—that go into commerce among the States. The doctrine of the autonomy of the States cannot properly be invoked to justify a denial of power in the national government to meet such an emergency, involving as it does that freedom of commercial intercourse among the States which the Constitution sought to attain. . . .

THE IMPACT OF THE KNIGHT CASE ON ANTITRUST ENFORCEMENT

Though the language in Knight was relied on in later cases taking a narrow view of the national commerce power—see especially the Schechter and Carter cases, sec. 4 below—it did not paralyze Sherman Act enforcement. In a number of cases soon after Knight, the Court sustained antitrust proceedings. Some examples follow:

a. In Addyston Pipe & Steel Co. v. United States, 175 U.S. 211 (1899), the Court sustained an action against six companies manufacturing iron pipe who had made agreements in restraint of competition. The Court found that "it was the purpose of the combination, to directly and by means of such combination increase the prices." This was held to be a "direct restraint upon interstate commerce."

b. In Northern Securities Co. v. United States, 193 U.S. 197 (1904), the Court, in a 5-to-4 decision, sustained an action to set aside the control acquired by Northern over two companies operating parallel railroad lines. Justice Holmes urged in dissent that the statute be construed in such a way as "not to raise grave doubts" about its constitutionality. Recalling the "indirect effect" language of Knight, he added: "Commerce depends upon population, but Congress could not, on that ground, undertake to regulate marriage and divorce. If the act before us is to be carried out according to what seems to be the logic of the argument for the Government, which I do not believe that it will be, I can see no part of the conduct of life with which on similar principles Congress might not interfere."

Could marriage and divorce be regulated under the theory of Justice Holmes' dissent in Hammer v. Dagenhart, p. 261, below?

c.   A year later, in Swift & Co. v. United States, 196 U.S. 375 (1905), Justice Holmes wrote for the Court in sustaining the application of the Sherman Act to a conspiracy to monopolize the supply and distribution of fresh meats throughout the United States. The bill charged "a combination of a dominant proportion of the dealers in fresh meat throughout the United States not to bid against each other in the livestock markets of the different States, to bid up prices for a few days in order to induce the cattle men to send their stock to the stock yards, to fix prices at which they will sell, and to that end to restrict shipments of meat when necessary, to establish a uniform rule of credit to dealers and to keep a black list, to make uniform and improper changes for cartage, and finally, to get less than lawful rates from the railroads to the exclusion of competitors." In answer to the objection that the bill "does not set forth a case of commerce among the States," Justice Holmes said: "[C]ommerce among the States is not a technical legal conception, but a practical one, drawn from the course of business." [The Swift case spoke of regulating activities in the "stream of commerce"—a view that was to provide important support for the expansive application of the commerce clause in other areas. See the notes following the next principal case.]

d.   Application of the Sherman Act to labor activities began with Loewe v. Lawlor, 208 U.S. 274 (1908). That case involved an attempt to organize workers on hats through a boycott of hat manufacturers' products shipped in commerce. Despite the attempt to prevent application of the antitrust laws to organizing activities by labor, in the Clayton Act of 1914, certain boycotts and strikes continued to be held illegal, as in Duplex Printing Press Co. v. Deering, 254 U.S. 443 (1921). In response, the Norris-LaGuardia Act of 1931 restricted federal injunctions in labor disputes.

It has been suggested that the Court's principles in these labor antitrust cases "were strikingly deficient in neutrality," especially in contrast with some of the cases—see sec. 4 below—in which Congress sought to aid labor. Wechsler, Principles, Politics & Fundamental Law (1961), 32. Were these Court principles also non-neutral in comparison with those found in antitrust suits against business activities?

e.   It has been said that "Congress wanted to go to the utmost extent of its constitutional power in restraining trust and monopoly agreements." United States v. South-Eastern Underwriters Ass'n, 322 U.S. 533, 558 (1944) (holding the business of insurance to be covered by the antitrust laws despite older rulings stating that insurance was not commerce). Nevertheless, some recent decisions find businesses outside antitrust coverage though within the reach of the commerce power. E. g., United States v. Yellow Cab Co., 332 U.S. 218 (1947). Perhaps the best-known example is professional baseball. In Toolsen v. New York Yankees, 346 U.S. 356 (1953), the Court found reserve clauses in players' contracts outside the antitrust laws. The Court pointed to a decision in 1922 in which Justice Holmes had stated for the Court that "personal effort, not related to production, is not a subject of commerce." Federal Baseball Clubs v. National League, 259 U.S. 200. In Toolsen, the Court stated: "The business has been left for thirty years to develop, on the understanding that it was not subject to existing antitrust legislation. . . . Without reexamination of the underlying issues, the judgments below are affirmed on the authority of Federal Baseball Clubs . . . ., so far as that decision determines that Congress had no intention of including the business of baseball within the scope of the federal antitrust laws." Other professional sports, however, have been held subject to the antitrust laws. United States v. International Boxing Club, 348 U.S. 236 (1955); Radovich v. National Football League, 352 U.S. 445 (1957).

HOUSTON, EAST & W. TEXAS RY. CO. v. UNITED STATES [THE SHREVEPORT RATE CASE]

234 U.S. 342, 34 S.Ct. 833, 58 L.Ed. 1341 (1914).

Appeals from the Commerce Court.

Mr. Justice HUGHES delivered the opinion of the court.

These suits were brought in the Commerce Court by the Houston, East & West Texas Railway Company and the Houston & Shreveport Railroad Company, and by the Texas & Pacific Railway Company, respectively, to set aside an order of the Interstate Commerce Commission, dated March 11, 1912, upon the ground that it exceeded the Commission's authority. . . . The petitions were dismissed. 205 F. 380.

The order of the Interstate Commerce Commission was made in a proceeding initiated in March, 1911, by the Railroad Commission of Louisiana. The complaint was that the appellants, and other interstate carriers, maintained unreasonable rates from Shreveport, Louisiana, to various points in Texas, and further, that these carriers, in the adjustment of rates over their respective lines, unjustly discriminated in favor of traffic within the state of Texas, and against similar traffic between Louisiana and Texas. . . .

The gravamen of the complaint, said the Interstate Commerce Commission, was that the carriers made rates out of Dallas and other Texas points into eastern Texas which were much lower than those which they extended into Texas from Shreveport. The situation may be briefly described: Shreveport, Louisiana, is about 40 miles from the Texas state line, and 231 miles from Houston, Texas, on the line of the Houston, East & West Texas and Houston & Shreveport Companies (which are affiliated in interest); it is 189 miles from Dallas, Texas, on the line of the Texas & Pacific. Shreveport competes with both cities for the trade of the intervening territory. The rates on these lines from Dallas and Houston, respectively, eastward to intermediate points in Texas, were much less, according to distance, than from Shreveport westward to the same points. It is undisputed that the difference was substantial, and injuriously affected the commerce of Shreveport. It appeared, for example, that a rate of 60 cents carried first-class traffic a distance of 160 miles to the eastward from Dallas, while the same rate would carry the same class of traffic only 55 miles into Texas from Shreveport. . . .

The Interstate Commerce Commission found that the interstate class rates out of Shreveport to named Texas points were unreasonable, and it established maximum class rates for this traffic. These rates, we understand, were substantially the same as the class rates fixed by the Railroad Commission of Texas, and charged by the carriers, for transportation for similar distances in that state. The Interstate Commerce Commission also found that the carriers maintained "higher rates from Shreveport to points in Texas" than were in force "from cities in Texas to such points under substantially similar conditions and circumstances," and that thereby "an unlawful and undue preference and advantage" was given to the Texas cities, and a "discrimination" that was "undue and unlawful" was effected against Shreveport. In order to correct this discrimination, the carriers were directed to desist from charging higher rates for the transportation of any commodity from Shreveport to Dallas and Houston, respectively, and intermediate points, than were contemporaneously charged for the carriage of such commodity from Dallas and Houston toward Shreveport for equal distances, as the Commission found that relation of rates to be reasonable. 23 I.C.C. 31, 46–48. . . . The report states that under this order it will be the duty of the companies "to duly and justly equalize the terms and conditions" upon which they will extend "transportation to traffic of a similar character, moving into Texas from Shreveport, with that moving wholly within Texas," but that, in effecting such equalization, the class scale rates as prescribed shall not be exceeded. . . .

The attack was . . . upon that portion of the order which prohibited the charge of higher rates for carrying articles from Shreveport into Texas than those charged for eastward traffic from Dallas and Houston, respectively, for equal distances. There are, it appears, commodity rates fixed by the Railroad Commission of Texas for intrastate hauls, which are substantially less than the class, or standard, rates prescribed by that Commission; and thus the commodity rates charged by the carriers from Dallas and Houston eastward to Texas points are less than the rates which they demand for the transportation of the same articles for like distances from Shreveport into Texas. The present controversy relates to these commodity rates.

The point of the objection to the order is that, as the discrimination found by the Commission to be unjust arises out of the relation of intrastate rates, maintained under state authority, to interstate rates that have been upheld as reasonable, its correction was beyond the Commission's power. Manifestly the order might be complied with, and the discrimination avoided, either by reducing the interstate rate from Shreveport to the level of the competing intrastate rates, or by raising these intrastate rates to the level of the interstate rates, or by such reduction in the one case and increase in the other as would result in equality. But it is urged that so far as the interstate rates were sustained by the Commission as reasonable, the Commission was without authority to compel their reduction in order to equalize them with the lower intrastate rates. The holding of the Commerce Court was that the order relieved the appellants from further obligation to observe the intrastate rates, and that they were at liberty to comply with the Commission's requirements by increasing these rates sufficiently to remove the forbidden discrimination. The invalidity of the order in this aspect is challenged upon two grounds:

(1) That Congress is impotent to control the intrastate charges of an interstate carrier even to the extent necessary to prevent injurious discrimination against interstate traffic; and

(2) That, if it be assumed that Congress has this power, still it has not been exercised and hence the action of the Commission exceeded the limits of the authority which has been conferred upon it.

First. It is unnecessary to repeat what has frequently been said by this court with respect to the complete and paramount character of the power confided to Congress to regulate commerce among the several states. It is of the essence of this power that, where it exists, it dominates. Interstate trade was not left to be destroyed or impeded by the rivalries of local government. The purpose was to make impossible the recurrence of the evils which had overwhelmed the Confederation, and to provide the necessary basis of national unity by insuring "uniformity of regulation against conflicting and discriminating state legislation." By virtue of the comprehensive terms of the grant, the authority of Congress is at all times adequate to meet the varying exigencies that arise, and to protect the national interest by securing the freedom of interstate commercial intercourse from local control. . . .

Congress is empowered to regulate,—that is, to provide the law for the government of interstate commerce; to enact "all appropriate legislation" for its "protection and advancement" (The Daniel Ball, 10 Wall. 557, 564); to adopt measures "to promote its growth and insure its safety" (Mobile County v. Kimball, [102 U.S. 691]); "to foster, protect, control, and restrain" (Second Employers' Liability Cases, [223 U.S. 1]). Its authority, extending to these interstate carriers as instruments of interstate commerce, necessarily embraces the right to control their operations in all matters having such a close and substantial relation to interstate traffic that the control is essential or appropriate to the security of that traffic, to the efficiency of the interstate service, and to the maintenance of conditions under which interstate commerce may be conducted upon fair terms and without molestation or hindrance. As it is competent for Congress to legislate to these ends, unquestionably it may seek their attainment by requiring that the agencies of interstate commerce shall not be used in such manner as to cripple, retard, or destroy it. The fact that carriers are instruments of intrastate commerce, as well as of interstate commerce, does not derogate from the complete and paramount authority of Congress over the latter, or preclude the Federal power from being exerted to prevent the intrastate operations of such carriers from being made a means of injury to that which has been confided to Federal care. Whenever the interstate and intrastate transactions of carriers are so related that the government of the one involves the control of the other, it is Congress, and not the State, that is entitled to prescribe the final and dominant rule, for otherwise Congress would be denied the exercise of its constitutional authority, and the State, and not the Nation, would be supreme within the national field. . . .

In Baltimore & Ohio Railroad Co. v. Interstate Commerce Commission [221 U.S. 612] the argument against the validity of the Hours of Service Act (March 4, 1907, c. 2939, 34 Stat. 1415) involved the consideration that the interstate and intrastate transactions of the carriers were so interwoven that it was utterly impracticable for them to divide their employés so that those who were engaged in interstate commerce should be confined to that commerce exclusively. Employés dealing with the movement of trains were employed in both sorts of commerce; but the court held that this fact did not preclude the exercise of Federal power. As Congress could limit the hours of labor of those engaged in interstate transportation, it necessarily followed that its will could not be frustrated by prolonging the period of service through other requirements of the carriers, or by the commingling of duties relating to interstate and intrastate operations. . . . So, in the Second Employers' Liability Cases [223 U.S. 1], it was insisted that while Congress had the authority to regulate the liability of a carrier for injuries sustained by one employee through the negligence of another, where all were engaged in interstate commerce, that power did not embrace instances where the negligent employee was engaged in intrastate commerce. The court said that this was a mistaken theory, as the causal negligence, when operating injuriously upon an employee engaged in interstate commerce, had the same effect with respect to that commerce as if the negligent employee were also engaged therein. . . . .

While these decisions sustaining the Federal power relate to measures adopted in the interest of the safety of persons and property, they illustrate the principle that Congress, in the exercise of its paramount power, may prevent the common instrumentalities of interstate and intrastate commercial intercourse from being used in their intrastate operations to the injury of interstate commerce. This is not to say that Congress possesses the authority to regulate the internal commerce of a State, as such, but that it does possess the power to foster and protect interstate commerce, and to take all measures necessary or appropriate to that end, although intrastate transactions of interstate carriers may thereby be controlled.

This principle is applicable here. We find no reason to doubt that Congress is entitled to keep the highways of interstate communication open to interstate traffic upon fair and equal terms. That an unjust discrimination in the rates of a common carrier, by which one person or locality is unduly favored as against another under substantially similar conditions of traffic, constitutes an evil, is undeniable; and where this evil consists in the action of an interstate carrier in unreasonably discriminating against interstate traffic over its line, the authority of Congress to prevent it is equally clear. It is immaterial, so far as the protecting power of Congress is concerned, that the discrimination arises from intrastate rates as compared with interstate rates. The use of the instrument of interstate commerce in a discriminatory manner so as to inflict injury upon that commerce, or some part thereof, furnishes abundant ground for Federal intervention. Nor can the attemped exercise of state authority alter the matter, where Congress has acted, for a State may not authorize the carrier to do that which Congress is entitled to forbid and has forbidden.

It is to be noted—as the government has well said in its argument in support of the Commission's order—that the power to deal with the relation between the two kinds of rates, as a relation, lies exclusively with Congress. It is manifest that the state cannot fix the relation of the carrier's interstate and intrastate charges without directly interfering with the former, unless it simply follows the standard set by Federal authority. . . . . It is for Congress to supply the needed correction where the relation between intrastate and interstate rates presents the evil to be corrected, and this it may do completely, by reason of its control over the interstate carrier in all matters having such a close and substantial relation to interstate commerce that it is necessary or appropriate to exercise the control for the effective government of that commerce.

It is also clear that, in removing the injurious discriminations against interstate traffic arising from the relation of intrastate to interstate rates, Congress is not bound to reduce the latter below what it may deem to be a proper standard, fair to the carrier and to the public. Otherwise, it could prevent the injury to interstate commerce only by the sacrifice of its judgment as to interstate rates. Congress is entitled to maintain its own standard as to these rates, and to forbid any discriminatory action by interstate carriers which will obstruct the freedom of movement of interstate traffic over their lines in accordance with the terms it establishes.

Having this power, Congress could provide for its execution through the aid of a subordinate body; and we conclude that the order of the Commission now in question cannot be held invalid upon the ground that it exceeded the authority which Congress could lawfully confer.

Second. The remaining question is with regard to the scope of the power which Congress has granted to the Commission. . . . [The Court found the order authorized by the statute.]

In conclusion: Reading the order in the light of the report of the Commission, it does not appear that the Commission attempted to require the carriers to reduce their interstate rates out of Shreveport below what was found to be a reasonable charge for that service. So far as these interstate rates conformed to what was found to be reasonable by the Commission, the carriers are entitled to maintain them, and they are free to comply with the order by so adjusting the other rates, to which the order relates, as to remove the forbidden discrimination. But this result they are required to accomplish.
. . . .

Affirmed.

Mr. Justice LURTON and Mr. Justice PITNEY dissent.

EARLY JUSTIFICATIONS FOR REGULATION OF INTRASTATE MATTERS: LOCAL ACTIVITIES "AFFECTING" INTERSTATE COMMERCE; ACTIVITIES IN THE "CURRENT OF COMMERCE"

1. *Railroad legislation: impacts of local matters on interstate commerce.* Most of the early congressional attempts to regulate the railroad industry withstood constitutional attack. The Court repeatedly sustained the laws under the commerce power because of the effect of the intrastate activities regulated on interstate commerce. These rationales were of special significance when constitutional support was sought for control of other economic problems in later years. See secs. 4 and 5 below.

a. *Economic impacts—rate regulations.* Regulations of local impacts of rate structures were found justified because the intrastate affairs cast economic burdens on interstate matters. See, in addition to the principal case, Railroad Commission of Wisconsin v. Chicago, B. & O. R. R., 257 U.S. 563 (1922). There, the Court sustained an ICC order requiring a blanket increase in all intrastate rates, even though state law prescribed a lower maximum. The justification for the order differed from that in the Shreveport Rate Case: it was based on the expansion of the ICC's authority in the Transportation Act of 1920. As the Court explained: "Theretofore the control which Congress through the Interstate Commerce Commission exercised was primarily for the purpose of preventing injustice by unreasonable or discriminatory rates against persons and localities, and the only provisions of the law that inured to the benefit of the carriers were the requirement that rates should be reasonable, in the sense of furnishing compensation for the particular service rendered and the abolition of rebates. The new measure imposed an affirmative duty on the Interstate Commerce Commission to fix rates and to take other important steps to maintain an adequate service for the people of the United States." See also Dayton-Goose Creek Ry. Co. v. United States, 263 U.S. 456, (1924), upholding the power to control railroad earnings—intrastate as well as interstate—above a fair return, under the "recapture clause" of the 1920 Act; and Colorado v. United States, 271 U.S. 153 (1926), sustaining the power to order abandonment of an intrastate branch of a railroad, because the deficit incurred in operating that branch burdened the railroad's interstate activities.

b. *Physical impacts—safety regulations.* Safety regulations presented more tangible manifestations of local activities burdening interstate commerce: the obstruction to interstate movement caused by local accidents was a visible, physical one. See, in addition to the safety law decisions described in the principal case, Southern Railway v. United States, 222 U.S. 20 (1911). That case involved the Safety Appliance Act of 1893 as amended in 1903. The Court sustained a penalty judgment imposed for operating railroad cars equipped with defective couplers. Three of the cars were used in moving intrastate traffic. The Act covered all cars "used on any railroad engaged in interstate commerce"; the Court found that this provision was satisfied because the cars were used "on a railroad which is a highway of interstate commerce," and that the law did not require that the cars be used "in moving interstate traffic." And application of the statute to vehicles used in moving intrastate traffic was found constitutional, "not because Congress possesses any power to regulate intrastate commerce as such, but because its power to regulate interstate commerce . . .   may be exerted to secure the safety of the persons and property transported therein and of those who are employed in such transportation, no matter what may be the source of the dangers which threaten it." [Note the reliance on a related rationale in sustaining national regulation of labor relations (to avert the obstruction of strikes) in the Jones & Laughlin case, sec. 5, p. 289, below.] The Court emphasized "practical considerations" that "are of common knowledge," including the fact that "the absence of appropriate safety appliances from any part of any train is a menace not only to that train, but to others."

2. *The "current of commerce" theory.* a. *The Swift case.* The "current of commerce" rationale offered an alternative basis for arguing that an intrastate matter should be reachable under the commerce power: the local aspect was controllable not because of its effect on commerce, but because it could be viewed as part of the "current" itself. In Swift & Co. v. United States, 196 U.S. 375 (1905) (cited in the notes before the Shreveport case), Justice Holmes' opinion—sustaining a Sherman Act injunction against price fixing by meat dealers—contained the following language: "When cattle are sent for sale from a place in one state, with the expectation that they will end their transit, after purchase, in another, and when in effect they do so, with only the interruption necessary to find a purchaser at the stockyards, and when this is a typical, constantly recurring course, the current

thus existing is a current of commerce among the states, and the purchase of cattle is a part and incident of such commerce."

b. *The congressional reliance.* Congress successfully drew on this "current of commerce" concept in drafting subsequent regulation of stockyard practices. The Packers and Stockyards Act of 1921 was aimed primarily at preventing "unfair, discriminatory, or deceptive practices" by meat packers in interstate commerce. One of the provisions of the Act stated that "for the purpose of this Act . . . a transaction in respect to any article shall be considered to be in commerce if such article is part of that current of commerce usual in the livestock and meat packing industry, whereby livestock [and its products] are sent from one State with the expectation that they will end their transit, after purchase, in another. . . . Articles normally in such current of commerce shall not be considered out of such current through resort being had to any means or device intended to remove transactions in respect thereto from the provisions of this Act."

c. *Stafford v. Wallace.* Commission men and dealers in stockyards, subject to Secretary of Agriculture regulation of their charges and practices under the Act, challenged its constitutionality. The Supreme Court rejected the attack in Stafford v. Wallace, 258 U.S. 495 (1922). Chief Justice Taft's opinion for the Court—with only Justice McReynolds dissenting—contained the following passages:

"The stockyards are not a place of rest or final destination. . . . The stockyards are but a throat through which the current flows, and the transactions which occur therein are only incident to this current from the West to the East, and from one State to another. Such transactions can not be separated from the movement to which they contribute and necessarily take on its character. The commission men are essential in making the sales without which the flow of the current would be obstructed, and this, whether they are made to packers or dealers. The dealers are essential to the sales to the stock farmers and feeders. The sales are not in this aspect merely local transactions. They create a local change of title, it is true, but they do not stop the flow; they merely change the private interests in the subject of the current, not interfering with, but, on the contrary, being indispensable to its continuity. The origin of the livestock is in the West, its ultimate destination known to, and intended by, all engaged in the business is in the Middle West and East either as meat products or stock for feeding and fattening. This is the definite and well-understood course of business. The stockyards and the sales are necessary factors in the middle of this current of commerce. . . .

"It is manifest that Congress framed the Packers and Stockyards Act in keeping with the principles announced and applied in the opinion in the Swift Case. . . . The act deals with the same current of business, and the same practical conception of interstate commerce. . . .

". . . The reasonable fear by Congress that such acts, usually lawful and affecting only intrastate commerce when considered alone, will probably and more or less constantly be used in conspiracies against interstate commerce or constitute a direct and undue burden on it, expressed in this remedial legislation, serves the same purpose as the intent charged in the Swift indictment to bring acts of a similar character into the current of interstate commerce for federal restraint. Whatever amounts to more or less constant practice, and threatens to obstruct or unduly to burden the freedom of interstate commerce is within the regulatory power of Congress under the commerce clause, and it is primarily for Congress to consider and decide the fact of the danger and meet it. This court will certainly not substitute its judgment for that of Congress in such a matter unless the relation of the subject to interstate commerce and its effect upon it are clearly non-existent. . . .

"As already noted, the word 'commerce' when used in the act is defined to be interstate and foreign commerce. Its provisions are carefully drawn to apply only to those practices and obstructions which in the judgment of Congress are likely to affect interstate commerce prejudically. Thus construed and applied, we think the act clearly within congressional power and valid. . . ."

Do the last two paragraphs here quoted suggest a different theory of justification than the "current of commerce" approach of the earlier passages? Is there a significant difference between the "affecting commerce" and the "current of commerce" rationales? Note the attempts to rely on these justifications in subsequent commerce clause litigation, especially that considered in secs. 4 and 5.

SECTION 3. NATIONAL POLICE REGULATION: PROHIBITION OF INTERSTATE COMMERCE AS A TOOL

CHAMPION v. AMES
[THE LOTTERY CASE]

188 U.S. 321, 23 S.Ct. 321, 47 L.Ed. 492 (1903).

Appeal from the Circuit Court of the United States for the Northern District of Illinois.

[Appellant was arrested in Chicago to assure his appearance in a Federal court in Texas, where he had been indicted for conspiracy to violate the Federal Lottery Act of 1895. The law prohibited importing, mailing, or transporting "from one State to another in the United States," any "ticket, chance, share or interest in or dependent upon the event of a lottery . . . offering prizes dependent upon lot or chance." The indictment charged shipment by Wells Fargo Express, from Texas to California, of a box containing Paraguayan lottery tickets. Appellant challenged the constitutionality of the Act by seeking release on habeas corpus in Chicago. The Circuit Court dismissed the writ.]

Mr. Justice HARLAN delivered the opinion of the Court. . . .

We are of opinion that lottery tickets are subjects of traffic and therefore are subjects of commerce, and the regulation of the carriage of such tickets from State to State, at least by independent carriers, is a regulation of commerce among the several States.

But it is said that the statute in question does not regulate the carrying of lottery tickets from State to State, but by punishing those who cause them to be so carried Congress in effect prohibits such carrying; that in respect of the carrying from one State to another of articles or things that are,

in fact, or according to usage in business, the subjects of commerce, the
authority given Congress was not to *prohibit,* but only to *regulate.*   .   .   .

.   .   .   Are we prepared to say that a provision which is, in effect, a
prohibition of the carriage of such articles from State to State is not a fit
or appropriate mode for the *regulation* of that particular kind of commerce?
If lottery traffic, *carried on through interstate commerce,* is a matter of which
Congress may take cognizance and over which its power may be exerted,
can it be possible that it must tolerate the traffic, and simply regulate the
manner in which it may be carried on?   Or may not Congress, for the protection of the people of all the States, and under the power to regulate interstate commerce, devise such means within the scope of the Constitution,
and not prohibited by it, as will drive that traffic out of commerce among
the States?

In determining whether regulation may not under some circumstances
properly take the form or have the effect of prohibition, the nature of the
interstate traffic which it was sought by the act of May 2, 1895, to suppress
cannot be overlooked.   When enacting that statute Congress no doubt shared
the views upon the subject of lotteries heretofore expressed by this court.
In Phalen v. Virginia, 8 How. 163, 168, after observing that the suppression of nuisances injurious to public health or morality is among the most
important duties of Government, this court said: "Experience has shown that
the common forms of gambling are comparatively innocuous when placed
in contrast with the widespread pestilence of lotteries.   The former are confined to a few persons and places, but the latter infests the whole community; it enters every dwelling; it reaches every class; it preys upon the
hard earnings of the poor; it plunders the ignorant and simple."   In other
cases we have adjudged that authority given by legislative enactment to
carry on a lottery, although based upon a consideration in money, was not
protected by the contract clause of the Constitution; this, for the reason that
no State may bargain away its power to protect the public morals, nor excuse
its failure to perform a public duty by saying that it had agreed, by legislative enactment, not to do so.   Stone v. Mississippi, 101 U.S. 814; Douglas
v. Kentucky, 168 U.S. 488.

If a State, when considering legislation for the suppression of lotteries
within its own limits, may properly take into view the evils that inhere in
the raising of money, in that mode, why may not Congress, invested with
the power to regulate commerce among the several States, provide that such
commerce shall not be polluted by the carrying of lottery tickets from one
State to another?   In this connection it must not be forgotten that the power
of Congress to regulate commerce among the States is plenary, is complete
in itself, and is subject to no limitations except such as may be found in
the Constitution.   .   .   .   [S]urely it will not be said to be a part of any
one's liberty, as recognized by the supreme law of the land, that he shall be
allowed to introduce into commerce among the States an element that will
be confessedly injurious to the public morals.

If it be said that the act of 1895 is inconsistent with the Tenth Amendment, reserving to the States respectively or to the people the powers not
delegated to the United States, the answer is that the power to regulate
commerce among the States has been expressly delegated to Congress.

Besides, Congress, by that act, does not assume to interfere with traffic or commerce in lottery tickets carried on exclusively within the limits

of any State, but has in view only commerce of that kind among the several States. It has not assumed to interfere with the completely internal affairs of any State, and has only legislated in respect of a matter which concerns the people of the United States. As a State may, for the purpose of guarding the morals of its own people, forbid all sales of lottery tickets within its limits, so Congress, for the purpose of guarding the people of the United States against the "widespread pestilence of lotteries" and to protect the commerce which concerns all the States, may prohibit the carrying of lottery tickets from one State to another. In legislating upon the subject of the traffic in lottery tickets, as carried on through interstate commerce, Congress only supplemented the action of those States—perhaps all of them—which, for the protection of the public morals, prohibit the drawing of lotteries, as well as the sale or circulation of lottery tickets, within their respective limits. It said, in effect, that it would not permit the declared policy of the States, which sought to protect their people against the mischiefs of the lottery business, to be overthrown or disregarded by the agency of interstate commerce. We should hesitate long before adjudging that an evil of such appalling character, carried on through interstate commerce, cannot be met and crushed by the only power competent to that end. . . .

It is said, however, that if, in order to suppress lotteries carried on through interstate commerce, Congress may exclude lottery tickets from such commerce, that principle leads necessarily to the conclusion that Congress may arbitrarily exclude from commerce among the States any article, commodity or thing, of whatever kind or nature, or however useful or valuable, which it may choose, no matter with what motive, to declare shall not be carried from one State to another. It will be time enough to consider the constitutionality of such legislation when we must do so. The present case does not require the court to declare the full extent of the power that Congress may exercise in the regulation of commerce among the States. We may, however, repeat, in this connection, what the court has heretofore said, that the power of Congress to regulate commerce among the States, although plenary, cannot be deemed arbitrary, since it is subject to such limitations or restrictions as are prescribed by the Constitution. This power, therefore, may not be exercised so as to infringe rights secured or protected by that instrument. It would not be difficult to imagine legislation that would be justly liable to such an objection as that stated, and be hostile to the objects for the accomplishment of which Congress was invested with the general power to regulate commerce among the several States. But, as often said, the possible abuse of a power is not an argument against its existence. There is probably no governmental power that may not be exerted to the injury of the public. If what is done by Congress is manifestly in excess of the powers granted to it, then upon the courts will rest the duty of adjudging that its action is neither legal nor binding upon the people. But if what Congress does is within the limits of its power, and is simply unwise or injurious, the remedy is that suggested by Chief Justice Marshall in Gibbons v. Ogden, when he said: "The wisdom and the discretion of Congress, their identity with the people, and the influence which their constituents possess at elections, are, in this, as in many other instances, as that, for example, of declaring war, the sole restraints on which they have relied, to secure them from its abuse. They are the restraints on which the people must often rely solely, in all representative governments." . . .

Affirmed.

Mr. Chief Justice FULLER, with whom concur Mr. Justice BREWER, Mr. Justice SHIRAS and Mr. Justice PECKHAM, dissenting. . . .

. . . . That the purpose of Congress in this enactment was the suppression of lotteries cannot reasonably be denied. That purpose is avowed in the title of the act, and is its natural and reasonable effect, and by that its validity must be tested. . . .

The power of the State to impose restraints and burdens on persons and property in conservation and promotion of the public health, good order and prosperity is a power originally and always belonging to the States, not surrendered by them to the General Government nor directly restrained by the Constitution of the United States, and essentially exclusive, and the suppression of lotteries as a harmful business falls within this power, commonly called of police. . . .

It is urged, however, that because Congress is empowered to regulate commerce between the several States, it, therefore, may suppress lotteries by prohibiting the carriage of lottery matter. Congress may indeed make all laws necessary and proper for carrying the powers granted to it into execution, and doubtless an act prohibiting the carriage of lottery matter would be necessary and proper to the execution of a power to suppress lotteries; but that power belongs to the States and not to Congress. To hold that Congress has general police power would be to hold that it may accomplish objects not entrusted to the General Government, and to defeat the operation of the Tenth Amendment . . ..

The ground on which prior acts forbidding the transmission of lottery matter by the mails was sustained, was that the power vested in Congress to establish post offices and post roads embraced the regulation of the entire postal system of the country, and that under that power Congress might designate what might be carried in the mails and what excluded. . . .

But apart from the question of *bona fides,* this act cannot be brought within the power to regulate commerce among the several States, unless lottery tickets are articles of commerce, and, therefore, when carried across state lines, of interstate commerce; or unless the power to regulate interstate commerce includes the absolute and exclusive power to prohibit the transportation of anything or anybody from one State to another. . . .

Is the carriage of lottery tickets from one State to another commercial intercourse?

The lottery ticket purports to create contractual relations and to furnish the means of enforcing a contract right.

This is true of insurance policies, and both are contingent in their nature. Yet this court has held that the issuing of fire, marine, and life insurance policies, in one State, and sending them to another, to be there delivered to the insured on payment of premium, is not interstate commerce. Paul v. Virginia, 8 Wall. 168 . . ..

If a lottery ticket is not an article of commerce, how can it become so when placed in an envelope or box or other covering, and transported by an express company? To say that the mere carrying of an article which is not an article of commerce in and of itself nevertheless becomes such the moment it is to be transported from one State to another, is to transform a noncommercial article into a commercial one simply because it is transported. I cannot conceive that any such result can properly follow.

It would be to say that everything is an article of commerce the moment it is taken to be transported from place to place, and of interstate commerce if from State to State.

An invitation to dine, or to take a drive, or a note of introduction, all become articles of commerce under the ruling in this case, by being deposited with an express company for transportation. This in effect breaks down all the differences between that which is, and that which is not, an article of commerce, and the necessary consequence is to take from the States all jurisdiction over the subject so far as interstate communication is concerned. It is a long step in the direction of wiping out all traces of state lines, and the creation of a centralized Government. . . .

It will not do to say—a suggestion which has heretofore been made in this case—that state laws have been found to be ineffective for the suppression of lotteries, and therefore Congress should interfere. The scope of the commerce clause of the Constitution cannot be enlarged because of present views of public interest.

In countries whose fundamental law is flexible it may be that the homely maxim, "to ease the shoe where it pinches," may be applied, but under the Constitution of the United States it cannot be availed of to justify action by Congress or by the courts. . . .

"Should Congress," said [Marshall] in McCulloch v. Maryland, 4 Wheat. 316, 423, "under the pretext of executing its powers, pass laws for the accomplishment of objects not entrusted to the Government; it would become the painful duty of this tribunal, should a case requiring such a decision come before it, to say that such an act was not the law of the land." . . . .

The power to prohibit the transportation of diseased animals and infected goods over railroads or on steamboats is an entirely different thing, for they would be in themselves injurious to the transaction of interstate commerce, and, moreover, are essentially commercial in their nature. And the exclusion of diseased persons rests on different ground, for nobody would pretend that persons could be kept off the trains because they were going from one State to another to engage in the lottery business. However enticing that business may be, we do not understand these pieces of paper themselves can communicate bad principles by contact. . . .

I regard this decision as inconsistent with the views of the framers of the Constitution, and of Marshall, its great expounder. Our form of government may remain notwithstanding legislation or decision, but, as long ago observed, it is with governments, as with religions, the form may survive the substance of the faith. . . .

SUCCESSFUL EARLY USES OF THE COMMERCE-PROHIBITING POWER

1. *The ghost of Marshall.* Note the competing uses of Marshall statements in the Harlan and Fuller opinions. Was the "wisdom and discretion of Congress" quotation from Gibbons v. Ogden, used by Harlan, apposite to the problem of the principal case? Did that make it unnecessary to consider the "pretext" statement in McCulloch v. Maryland, quoted by Fuller? Would it have been possible to sustain the statute on the assumption

that its true "objects" were the control of intrastate lottery-promoting activities? On the theory that these activities "affected" or "burdened" commerce? On the basis of the "current of commerce" theory? Should the Court have insisted on an adequate justification for reaching intrastate activities? Was the failure to require such a justification (and the acceptance of the "prohibition" rationale) fatal to the development of a commerce power rationale of sufficient integrity and viability? Note the questions following the Child Labor Case at the end of this section, and compare the later uses of the commerce-prohibiting power, sec. 5 below.

2. *The impact on Congress.* Early-twentieth century reformers seeking a constitutional basis for broader federal "police" measures quickly seized on the encouragement provided by the majority position in the Lottery Case. In 1906, for example, Senator Albert J. Beveridge—later John Marshall's biographer—successfully proposed a Meat Inspection Amendment to an appropriations bill. The Amendment, backed by President Theodore Roosevelt and by popular support generated by such exposés as Upton Sinclair's "The Jungle," became law: it prohibited interstate shipment of meats that had not been federally inspected. In the same session, Congress enacted the Pure Food and Drugs Act. Later that year, Senator Beveridge suggested a law excluding from commerce goods produced by child labor. He was confident that the Lottery Case "absolutely settled" the constitutionality of his proposal. But passage of a child labor law was a decade away—and the Court, in Hammer v. Dagenhart, infra, found the 1916 Child Labor Law unconstitutional after all. See Braeman, "Albert J. Beveridge and the First National Child Labor Bill," 60 Indiana Magazine of History 1 (1964), and Braeman, "The Square Deal in Action: A Case Study in the Growth of the 'National Police Power,' " in Braeman, Bremner and Walter, Change and Continuity in Twentieth Century America (1964), 35–80.

3. *Exclusion of "harmful" goods.* The Lottery Case precedent was, however, adequate to sustain a wide variety of early-twentieth century laws excluding objects deemed harmful from interstate commerce. See Cushman, "The National Police Power under the Commerce Clause of the Constitution," 3 Minn.L.Rev. 289, 381 (1919). Decisions sustaining the Pure Food and Drugs Act and the Mann (White Slave) Act were especially important in building the hopes that were crushed by Hammer v. Dagenhart:

a. *Impure foods.* In Hipolite Egg Co. v. United States, 220 U.S. 45 (1911), a shipment of adulterated preserved eggs had been confiscated under the Pure Food and Drugs Act of 1906. The action was challenged on the ground that "the shipment had passed out of interstate commerce before the seizure of the eggs." A unanimous Court rejected the attack. Justice McKenna emphasized that the case involved "illicit articles—articles which the law seeks to keep out of commerce, because they are debased by adulteration." There could therefore be no insistence that "the articles must be apprehended . . . before they have become a part of the general mass of property of the State." That argument, he claimed, "attempts to apply to articles of illegitimate commerce the rule which marks the line between the exercise of Federal power and state power over articles of legitimate commerce. [See chap. 8, infra.] The contention misses the question in the case. There is here no conflict of national and state jurisdictions over property legally articles of trade. The question here is whether articles which are outlaws of commerce may be seized wherever found, and it certainly will not be contended that they are outside of the jurisdiction of the National Government when they are within the borders of a State. The question in the case, therefore is, What power has Congress over such articles? Can they escape the consequences of their illegal transportation by being mingled at the place of destination with other property? To give them such immunity would defeat, in many cases, the provision for their confiscation, and their confiscation or destruction is the especial concern of the law. The power to do so is certainly appropriate to the right to bar them from interstate commerce, and completes its purpose, which is not to prevent merely the physical movement of adulterated articles, but the use of them, or rather to prevent trade in them between the States by denying to them the facilities of interstate commerce. And appropriate means to that end, which we have seen is legitimate, are the seizure and condemnation of the articles at their point of destination. . . . McCulloch v. Maryland, 4 Wheat. 316.''

How far-reaching is this application of McCulloch v. Maryland? Does it justify a direct ban on producing adulterated goods as a "means appropriate to the right to bar them from interstate commerce"? Only if the goods are intended for interstate shipment? Does it justify national marriage and divorce standards as an "appropriate means" to implement a ban on interstate movement of persons married or divorced in violation of national standards? Only if the persons getting married or divorced intend to travel interstate? Does it offer a bootstrap technique of reaching local affairs via the prohibition route: in order to regulate a local matter, simply prohibit interstate movements connected with it and then reach the local matter as an incidental means to implement the interstate prohibition? Compare the passages on local control as an incident of interstate commerce prohibition in the Fair Labor Standards Act case, United States v. Darby, sec. 5, p. 296, below.

b. *Immoral women.* The Mann Act, prohibiting the transportation of women in interstate commerce for immoral purposes, was upheld in Hoke v. United States, 227 U.S. 308 (1913). Again, Justice McKenna wrote for a unanimous Court. He cited, in addition to the Lottery Case, United States v. Popper, 98 Fed. 423 (N.D.Cal.1899), involving an 1897 law prohibiting the "carrying of obscene literature and articles designed for indecent and immoral use from one State to another."

The opinion in Hoke contained one of the broadest early statements of the power: "[I]t must be kept in mind that we are one people; and the powers reserved to the States and those conferred on the Nation are adapted to be exercised, whether independently or concurrently, to promote the general welfare, material and moral. This is the effect of the decisions, and surely if the facility of interstate transportation can be taken away from the demoralization of lotteries, the debasement of obscene literature, the contagion of diseased cattle or persons, the impurity of food and drugs, the like facility can be taken away from the systematic enticement to and the enslavement in prostitution and debauchery of women, and, more insistently, of girls. . . . The principle established by the cases is the simple one, when rid of confusing and distracting considerations, that Congress has power over transportation 'among the several States'; that the power is complete in itself, and that Congress, as an incident to it, may adopt not only means necessary but convenient to its exercise, and the means may have the quality of police regulations.''

Justice McKenna dissented, however, when the Court, in a 5 to 3 decision, found the Mann Act applicable to activities not constituting "commercialized vice." Caminetti v. United States, 242 U.S. 470 (1917). Justice Day wrote for the majority. The dissent argued that "everybody knows that there is a difference between the occasional immoralities of men and women and that systematized and mercenary immorality epitomized in the statute's graphic phrase 'White-slave traffic.' And it was such immorality that was in the legislative mind and not the other. The other is occasional, not habitual—inconspicuous—does not offensively obtrude upon public notice. Interstate commerce is not its instrument as it is of the other, nor is prostitution its object or its end. It may, indeed, in instances, find a convenience in crossing state lines, but this is its accident, not its aid."

Should this objection to the interpretation of the Act be a basis for a valid constitutional objection? One year after Caminetti, the Court held the Child Labor Law unconstitutional, in the case that follows. Note that Justice Day once again wrote the majority opinion—and that Justice McKenna was once again with the dissenters.

HAMMER v. DAGENHART
[THE CHILD LABOR CASE]

247 U.S. 251, 38 S.Ct. 529, 62 L.Ed. 1101 (1918).

Appeal from the District Court of the United States for the Western District of North Carolina.

Bill by Roland H. Dagenhart, and by Reuben Dagenhart and John Dagenhart, minors, by Roland H. Dagenhart, their next friend, against W. C. Hammer, United States Attorney for the Western District of North Carolina to enjoin the enforcement of Act Sept. 1, 1916, intended to prevent interstate commerce in the products of child labor. The manufacturing company by which the two minor sons were employed was also named as defendant and it was alleged that the company had notified the plaintiff of the impending discharge of his sons on the effective date of the Act. The company answered, admitting substantially all the allegations except that of unconstitutionality of the Act. The Government moved to dismiss, on the ground that the Act was valid. A hearing was had on a rule to show cause why an injunction should not issue, and at its conclusion a decree enjoining enforcement of the act was issued, from which this appeal was taken.[1]

---

1. The statement of the case has been slightly enlarged from the record, and the statement by the Court omitted. The argument before the Supreme Court included the following contentions:

In support of the statute: "The act is upon its face a regulation. . . . It sharply distinguishes between the manufacture which lies wholly within one State, and the interstate movement. . . . The legislation of the States on the subject was not uniform, and many States were without the provisions which came to be regarded as the standard necessary for the public protection. . . . In the day of steam and electricity the play of the forces of competition makes the cause operating in one State immediately felt in another. The slightest difference in the cost of production, or what amounts to the same thing, a belief on the part of manufactures in the existence of such difference, alters the development of an industry. As the conviction grew that the employment of child labor was morally repugnant and socially unwise, it came to be regarded also in the light of unfair competition in trade among the States. . . . Thus, if one State desired to

The material section of the Act provides: "That no producer, manufacturer, or dealer shall ship or deliver for shipment in interstate or foreign commerce any article or commodity the product of any mine or quarry, situ-

limit the employment of children, it was met with the objection that its manufactures could not compete with manufacturers of a neighboring State which imposed no such limitation. The shipment of goods in interstate commerce by the latter, therefore, operates to deter the former from enacting laws it would otherwise enact for the protection of its own children. . . . The effect of low child labor standards in one State upon health in competing States is due entirely to the interstate character of the commerce in question. Because this is so a State can not protect itself. . . . That the articles excluded are themselves innocuous is immaterial. . . . Discussion of the inherent badness of things is largely futile. How do we judge of goodness or badness except by their effect? Those things which work ill effects when transported across state lines are for that reason evil. The transportation of products of child labor, therefore, can not be classed as innocuous in fact. . . . Congress believed that it was exercising in this case its power to forbid competition deemed unfair. . . . The extension of the prohibition to all products of the factory in which the child labors is a reasonable provision for the due enforcement of the act. . . . To urge the reserved powers of the States is to beg the question. The reserved powers of the States do not begin until the power of Congress leaves off. . . . Congress was attempting to regulate commerce in good faith and not to do indirectly what it could not do directly. It sought only to prevent the evil resulting from the interstate transportation of child-made goods. The court is confined to the purpose as expressed in the act."

Against the statute: "Is the act a regulation of commerce in the constitutional sense? Or is it a regulation of some one of the many internal affairs of the States which Congress is not empowered to deal with? . . . . It appears from the act itself: (1) That the articles made by children are in no way different from articles made by others. (2) That the purpose and effect of the act is to prevent the employment of children, and not to safeguard or promote commerce or the interests of persons or communities in the States into which child-made goods might be sent. That such is the purpose and expected effect, was avowed in the debates upon the floor of Congress, and before the committees to which the bill was referred. . . . The conditions reached and controlled by this act are subject only to that attribute of sovereignty called the 'police power.' . . . The Obscene Literature Case, the Bad Egg Case, the White Slave Case . . . yield the principle that Congress may prevent the facility of interstate commerce from being made an instrument of evil, but in each of these cases, the subject of regulation retains, while moving in commerce, and at its journey's end, the inherent capacity to further the evil. The regulation did not reach back to the place of the creation of the subject as in the case at bar. . . . A product of a condition which exists only within the confines of a State, before it may be said to affect commerce in such a way as to justify Congress in regulating it, must be one which retards or injures commerce, or in some manner burdens that commerce itself or one which retains its capacity to further an evil while actually moving in commerce. . . . Investigation of whether Congress has done by indirection that which it can not do directly, is not foreclosed by the statement that courts do not pass on the motives of Congress. They do not pass upon them to see whether they are good or bad, but when power is called into play, not for the purpose for which it was given, but for a covert purpose, it becomes not an abuse of a power, but the exercise of an unconferred power, and the duty is incumbent upon the court to determine this matter, and legislation may properly be characterized as covert, though its purpose and effect is to cure what is admitted to be an evil. . . . Covert legislation is legislation whose constitutional support bears no sincere relation to the legislative and popular purpose sought to be attained. . . . The act reaches beyond the body of commerce itself, and legislates in the *form* of a regulation of commerce to promote what is deemed to be the welfare of the people. It does more than prohibit the transportation of articles of commerce. In effect it is a prohibition of their creation, unless the local conditions of manufacture conform to the congressional standard. . . . Has Congress absorbed the police power of the States? If Congress has the power here asserted, it is difficult to conceive what is left to the States." (247 U.S., at 252–268.)

ated in the United States, in which within thirty days prior to the time of the removal of such product therefrom children under the age of sixteen years have been employed or permitted to work, or any article or commodity the product of any mill, cannery, workshop, factory, or manufacturing establishment, situated in the United States, in which within thirty days prior to the removal of such product therefrom children under the age of fourteen years have been employed or permitted to work, or children between the ages of fourteen years and sixteen years have been employed or permitted to work more than eight hours in any day, or more than six days in any week, or after the hour of seven o'clock postmeridian, or before the hour of six o'clock antemeridian."

Mr. Justice DAY delivered the opinion of the Court. . . .

The attack upon the act rests upon three propositions: First: It is not a regulation of interstate and foreign commerce; second: It contravenes the Tenth Amendment to the Constitution; third: It conflicts with the Fifth Amendment to the Constitution.

The controlling question for decision is: Is it within the authority of Congress in regulating commerce among the States to prohibit the transportation in interstate commerce of manufactured goods, the product of a factory in which, within thirty days prior to their removal therefrom, children under the age of fourteen have been employed or permitted to work, or children between the ages of fourteen and sixteen years have been employed or permitted to work more than eight hours in any day, or more than six days in any week, or after the hour of seven o'clock P.M., or before the hour of 6 o'clock A.M.? . . .

. . . . [I]t is insisted that adjudged cases in this court establish the doctrine that the power to regulate given to Congress incidentally includes the authority to prohibit the movement of ordinary commodities and therefore that the subject is not open for discussion. The cases demonstrate the contrary. They rest upon the character of the particular subjects dealt with and the fact that the scope of governmental authority, state or national, possessed over them is such that the authority to prohibit is as to them but the exertion of the power to regulate. [After discussing the Lottery Case, Hipolite, Hoke and similar decisions, the Court proceeded:]

In each of these instances the use of interstate transportation was necessary to the accomplishment of harmful results. In other words, although the power over interstate transportation was to regulate, that could only be accomplished by prohibiting the use of the facilities of interstate commerce to effect the evil intended.

This element is wanting in the present case. The thing intended to be accomplished by this statute is the denial of the facilities of interstate commerce to those manufacturers in the States who employ children within the prohibited ages. The act in its effect does not regulate transportation among the states, but aims to standardize the ages at which children may be employed in mining and manufacturing within the states. The goods shipped are of themselves harmless. The act permits them to be freely shipped after thirty days from the time of their removal from the factory. When offered for shipment, and before transportation begins, the labor of their production is over, and the mere fact that they were intended for interstate commerce transportation does not make their production subject to federal control under the commerce power.

Commerce "consists of intercourse and traffic . . . and includes the transportation of persons and property, as well as the purchase, sale, and exchange of commodities." The making of goods and the mining of coal are not commerce, nor does the fact that these things are to be afterwards shipped, or used in interstate commerce, make their production a part thereof. Delaware, Lackawanna & Western R. R. Co. v. Yurkonis, 238 U.S. 439.

Over interstate transportation, or its incidents, the regulatory power of Congress is ample, but the production of articles, intended for interstate commerce, is a matter of local regulation. . . . If it were otherwise, all manufacture intended for interstate shipment would be brought under federal control to the practical exclusion of the authority of the States, a result certainly not contemplated by the framers of the Constitution when they vested in Congress the authority to regulate commerce among the States. Kidd v. Pearson, 128 U.S. 1, 21.

It is further contended that the authority of Congress may be exerted to control interstate commerce in the shipment of child-made goods because of the effect of the circulation of such goods in other States where the evil of this class of labor has been recognized by local legislation, and the right to thus employ child labor has been more rigorously restrained than in the State of production. In other words, that the unfair competition, thus engendered, may be controlled by closing the channels of interstate commerce to manufacturers in those States where the local laws do not meet what Congress deems to be the more just standard of other States.

There is no power vested in Congress to require the States to exercise their police power so as to prevent possible unfair competition. Many causes may co-operate to give one State, by reason of local laws or conditions, an economic advantage over others. The Commerce Clause was not intended to give to Congress a general authority to equalize such conditions. In some of the States laws have been passed fixing minimum wages for women, in others the local law regulates the hours of labor of women in various employments. Business done in such States may be at an economic disadvantage when compared with States which have no such regulations; surely, this fact does not give Congress the power to deny transportation in interstate commerce to those who carry on business where the hours of labor and the rate of compensation for women have not been fixed by a standard in use in other States and approved by Congress. . . .

That there should be limitations upon the right to employ children in mines and factories in the interest of their own and the public welfare, all will admit. That such employment is generally deemed to require regulation is shown by the fact that the brief of counsel states that every State in the Union has a law upon the subject, limiting the right to thus employ children. In North Carolina, the State wherein is located the factory in which the employment was had in the present case, no child under twelve years of age is permitted to work.

It may be desirable that such laws be uniform, but our Federal Government is one of enumerated powers; "this principle," declared Chief Justice Marshall in McCulloch v. Maryland, 4 Wheat. 316, "is universally admitted."

The maintenance of the authority of the States over matters purely local is as essential to the preservation of our institutions as is the conservation of the supremacy of the federal power in all matters entrusted to the Nation by the Federal Constitution. . . . To sustain this statute would not be in our judgment a recognition of the lawful exertion of congressional authority over interstate commerce, but would sanction an invasion by the federal power of the control of a matter purely local in its character, and over which no authority has been delegated to Congress in conferring the power to regulate commerce among the States.

We have neither authority nor disposition to question the motives of Congress in enacting this legislation. The purposes intended must be attained consistently with constitutional limitations and not by an invasion of the powers of the States. This court has no more important function than that which devolves upon it the obligation to preserve inviolate the constitutional limitations upon the exercise of authority federal and state to the end that each may continue to discharge harmoniously with the other, the duties entrusted to it by the Constitution.

In our view the necessary effect of this act is, by means of a prohibition against the movement in interstate commerce of ordinary commercial commodities, to regulate the hours of labor of children in factories and mines within the States, a purely state authority. Thus the act in a two-fold sense is repugnant to the Constitution. It not only transcends the authority delegated to Congress over commerce but also exerts a power as to a purely local matter to which the federal authority does not extend. The far reaching result of upholding the act cannot be more plainly indicated than by pointing out that if Congress can thus regulate matters entrusted to local authority by prohibition of the movement of commodities in interstate commerce, all freedom of commerce will be at an end, and the power of the States over local matters may be eliminated, and thus our system of government be practically destroyed.

For these reasons we hold that this law exceeds the constitutional authority of Congress. It follows that the decree of the District Court must be

Affirmed.

Mr. Justice HOLMES, dissenting.

. . . The objection urged against the power is that the States have exclusive control over their methods of production and that Congress cannot meddle with them, and taking the proposition in the sense of direct intermeddling I agree to it and suppose that no one denies it. But if an act is within the powers specifically conferred upon Congress, it seems to me that it is not made any less constitutional because of the indirect effects that it may have, however obvious it may be that it will have those effects, and that we are not at liberty upon such grounds to hold it void.

The first step in my argument is to make plain what no one is likely to dispute—that the statute in question is within the power expressly given to Congress if considered only as to its immediate effects and that if invalid it is so only upon some collateral ground. The statute confines itself to prohibiting the carriage of certain goods in interstate or foreign commerce. Congress is given power to regulate such commerce in unqualified terms. It would not be argued today that the power to regulate does not include the power to prohibit. Regulation means the prohibition of something, and when interstate commerce is the matter to be regulated I cannot doubt that the regulation may prohibit any part of such commerce that Congress sees fit to forbid. At all events it is established by the Lottery Case and others that have followed it that a law is not beyond the regulative power of Congress merely because it prohibits certain transportation out and out. Champion v. Ames, 188 U.S. 321, 355, 359, et seq. So I repeat that this statute in its immediate operation is clearly within the Congress's constitutional power.

The question then is narrowed to whether the exercise of its otherwise constitutional power by Congress can be pronounced unconstitutional because of its possible reaction upon the conduct of the States in a matter upon which I have admitted that they are free from direct control. I should have thought that that matter had been disposed of so fully as to leave no room for doubt. I should have thought that the most conspicuous decisions of this Court had made it clear that the power to regulate commerce and other constitutional powers could not be cut down or qualified by the fact that it might interfere with the carrying out of the domestic policy of any State.

The manufacture of oleomargarine is as much a matter of state regulation as the manufacture of cotton cloth. Congress levied a tax upon the compound when colored so as to resemble butter that was so great as obviously to prohibit the manufacture and sale. In a very elaborate discussion the present Chief Justice excluded any inquiry into the purpose of an act which apart from that purpose was within the power of Congress. McCray v. United States, 195 U.S. 27. . . . And to come to cases upon interstate commerce, notwithstanding United States v. E. C. Knight Co., 156 U.S. 1, the Sherman Act has been made an instrument for the breaking up of combinations in restraint of trade and monopolies, using the power to regulate commerce as a foothold, but not proceeding because that commerce was the end actually in mind. The objection that the control of the States over production was interfered with was urged again and again but always in vain. . . .

The Pure Food and Drug Act . . . applies not merely to articles that the changing opinions of the time condemn as intrinsically harmful but to others innocent in themselves, simply on the ground that the order for them was induced by a preliminary fraud. Weeks v. United States, 245 U.S. 618. It does not matter whether the supposed evil precedes or follows the transportation. It is enough that in the opinion of Congress the transportation encourages the evil. I may add that in the cases on the so-called White Slave Act it was established that the means adopted by Congress as convenient to the exercise of its power might have the character of police regulations. . . . .

The notion that prohibition is any less prohibition when applied to things now thought evil I do not understand. But if there is any matter upon which civilized countries have agreed—far more unanimously than they have with regard to intoxicants and some other matters over which this country is now emotionally aroused—it is the evil of premature and excessive child labor. I should have thought that if we were to introduce our own moral conceptions where in my opinion they do not belong, this was preëminently a case for upholding the exercise of all its powers by the United States.

But I had thought that the propriety of the exercise of a power admitted to exist in some cases was for the consideration of Congress alone and that this Court always had disavowed the right to intrude its judgment upon questions of policy or morals. It is not for this Court to pronounce when prohibition is necessary to regulation if it ever may be necessary—to say that it is permissible as against strong drink but not as against the product of ruined lives.

The act does not meddle with anything belonging to the States. They may regulate their internal affairs and their domestic commerce as they like. But when they seek to send their products across the state line they are no longer within their rights. If there were no Constitution and no Congress their power to cross the line would depend upon their neighbors. Under the Constitution such commerce belongs not to the States but to Congress to regulate. It may carry out its views of public policy whatever indirect effect they may have upon the activities of the States. Instead of being encountered by a prohibitive tariff at her boundaries the State encounters the public policy of the United States which it is for Congress to express. The public policy of the United States is shaped with a view to the benefit of the nation as a whole. If, as has been the case within the memory of men still living, a State should take a different view of the propriety of sustaining a lottery from that which generally prevails, I cannot believe that the fact would require a different decision from that reached in Champion v. Ames. Yet in that case it would be said with quite as much force as in this that Congress was attempting to intermeddle with the State's domestic affairs. The national welfare as understood by Congress may require a different attitude within its sphere from that of some self-seeking State. It seems to me entirely constitutional for Congress to enforce its understanding by all the means at its command.

Mr. Justice McKENNA, Mr. Justice BRANDEIS and Mr. Justice CLARKE concur in this opinion.

PROBLEMS AND CONSEQUENCES OF THE CHILD LABOR CASE

1. *Viable limits on the commerce power and the Holmes dissent.* Is the majority's distinction of earlier cases involving the commerce-prohibiting power persuasive? Is the dissent needlessly broad? Should Justice Holmes have paid greater attention to the "unfair competition" effects of interstate shipment of the goods? Are the evils produced by child labor-made goods more closely related to "commercial" concerns than the evils involved in the Mann Act decisions and Lottery Case? Is it possible to argue that the Child Labor Act was more "economic," "commercial" in purpose than most of the "police" regulations sustained in the cases between the Lottery Case and Hammer?

Recall that, in his Northern Securities dissent (noted after the Knight case, p. 245, above), Justice Holmes could see "no part of the conduct of life with which on similar principles Congress might not interfere," if the "logic of the argument for the Government" were accepted. Can not the same be said of the "logic of the argument" of the Holmes dissent in Hammer? Was Justice Holmes simply ceasing to argue restrictions on the commerce-prohibiting power because the Court had abandoned the opportunity to adhere to viable limitations in the cases beginning with the Lottery Case? Was it necessary to ignore the "collateral" effects, to limit judicial vision to the "immediate effects" of the statute, to justify the Child Labor Law? Would it not have been possible to concede that the law in effect regulated local production for interstate commerce, and yet sustain it because the conditions regulated "affected" commerce? Note that Holmes' dissent suggests that the states "are free from direct control" regarding child labor. If that is so, is his dissenting position not an endorsement of the "pretext" usage of power condemned by Marshall in McCulloch v. Maryland?

2. *Other efforts to control child labor.* After the Hammer decision, Congress sought to regulate child labor through the taxing power. That law was invalidated in Bailey v. Drexel Furniture Co. (The Child Labor Tax Case), 259 U.S. 20 (1922) (printed in the next chapter, p. 351). Justice Holmes was with the majority there. After the unsuccessful legislative efforts, Congress submitted a proposed constitutional amendment authorizing national child labor laws to the States. The amendment has not yet been ratified; but the need for ratification has largely disappeared in view of the Court's decision in United States v. Darby, 312 U.S. 100 (1941) (sec. 5, p. 296, below).

3. *Later uses of the prohibition technique.* The Hammer decision did not bar continued use of the Lottery Case principle in other areas of regulation. For example, Brooks v. United States, 267 U.S. 432 (1925), sustained the constitutionality of the National Motor Vehicle Theft Act of 1919. That law prohibited interstate transportation of "a motor vehicle, knowing the same to have been stolen," and also provided punishment for anyone who "shall receive, conceal, store, barter, sell, or dispose of any motor vehicle, moving as, or which is a part of, or which constitutes interstate or foreign commerce, knowing the same to have been stolen." A unanimous Court stated that the transportation was "a gross misuse of interstate commerce," and that the prohibition of transportation was constitutional "because of its harmful result and its defeat of the property rights of those whose machines against their will are taken into other jurisdictions." The prohibition of receipt and concealment, in turn, was sustained since it "merely makes more effective the regulation" of transportation. Given Justice Holmes' theory in the Hammer v. Dagenhart dissent, would a ban on local child-labor production of goods for interstate commerce be justifiable as a means to make "more effective" the ban on interstate shipment? (For more recent uses of the commerce-prohibiting device as a regulatory tool, see the notes at p. 302, following United States v. Darby, below.)

SECTION 4. THE COURT THREATENS THE NEW DEAL

Introductory note. President Franklin D. Roosevelt took office in the midst of a grave economic crisis and with a call for "action, and action now." Symptoms of the great depression were everywhere: sharp drops in employment, production, income; business failures and home mortgage foreclosures. The response was swift: an unprecedented flow of far-reaching measures came from Congress—torrentially during the dramatic "First Hundred Days," with more deliberate speed thereafter.

Many New Deal measures were based on the commerce power, for the "problems were economic, and the Commerce Clause was the enumerated power most directly concerned with business and economic, or commercial matters." Would the new regulatory measures survive judicial scrutiny? There could be no certainty, for "there was ample authority in the Supreme Court opinions looking both ways." Stern, "The Commerce Clause and the National Economy, 1933–1946," 59 Harv.L.Rev. 645, 646 (1946), Selected Essays 1938–1962 (1963) 218, 219.

The first signs from the Supreme Court were encouraging. Early in 1934, 5 to 4 decisions sustained state laws in the face of attacks that were clearly substantial under prior interpretations of the contract and due process clauses. [Home Building & Loan Ass'n v. Blaisdell, 290 U.S. 398 (1934) (mortgage moratorium law); Nebbia v. New York, 291 U.S. 502 (1934) (milk price regulation)—both considered in chap. 14, infra.] A few months later, however, in the first Court test of a major New Deal law, the National Industrial Recovery Act of 1933 was wounded, though the reach of the commerce clause was not discussed: in the "hot oil" case, the petroleum code under the NIRA was invalidated on the ground of excessive delegation of legislative power to the executive. Panama Refining Co. v. Ryan, 293 U.S. 388 (1935). But an important early New Deal measure—a 1933 Joint Resolution declaring "gold clauses" in private contracts to be "against public policy"—was held valid, Norman v. Baltimore & O. R. R. Co., 294 U.S. 240 (1935), though the Government won only a narrow victory in its attempt to avoid payment under gold clauses in public obligations, Perry v. United States, 294 U.S. 330 (1935).

There was still no ruling on New Deal regulation under the commerce clause, however. That did not come until later in 1935. In the first test, a measure not central to the New Deal program—the Railroad Retirement Act of 1934—was invalidated. Railroad Retirement Board v. Alton R. Co., 295 U.S. 330 (1935). The decision was an especially gloomy omen because, as has been seen, Congress had long regulated railroad matters and had seldom encountered constitutional obstacles. Attempts to justify more important New Deal laws under the commerce clause failed soon after: three weeks after Alton, the Government lost the "sick chicken" case under the National Industrial Recovery Act, Schechter Poultry Corp. v. United States, 295 U.S. 495—a decision that seemed a return to "the horse-and-buggy age" to President Roosevelt; and in the following year, the Bituminous Coal Conservation Act of 1935 was held unconstitutional, Carter v. Carter Coal Co., 298 U.S. 238 (1936).

Excerpts from Alton, Schechter and Carter follow. Consider, with regard to each case, whether the majority position is consistent with earlier commerce clause developments. Can any of the rulings be justified as "principled"—as a decision that rests on "reasons that in their generality and their neutrality transcend any immediate result that is involved"? Wechsler, "Toward Neutral Principles of Constitutional Law," 73 Harv.L.Rev. 1, 19, Selected Essays 1938–1962 (1963) 463, 475. Or were these decisions simply wilful fiats by a Supreme Court majority hostile to reform, as many New Deal critics of the Court insisted?

RAILROAD RETIREMENT BOARD v. ALTON RAILROAD CO.

295 U.S. 330, 55 S.Ct. 758, 79 L.Ed. 1468 (1935).

Certiorari to the United States Court of Appeals for the District of Columbia.

Mr. Justice ROBERTS delivered the opinion of the Court. . . .

[This was a suit for an injunction against the enforcement of the Railroad Retirement Act, passed by Congress in 1934, establishing a compulsory retirement and pension plan for all carriers subject to the Interstate Commerce Act. The broad question presented by the record, as stated by the Court, was "whether a statutory requirement that retired employees shall be paid pensions is regulation of commerce between the States within Article I, § 8." Before coming to that question the Court concluded that several provisions of the Act violated the due process clause of the Fifth Amendment, that they were inseparable from the remainder of the Act, and that they made the Act invalid as a whole. The Court continued:]

. . . We are of opinion that [the Act] is also bad for another reason which goes to the heart of the law, even if it could survive the loss of the unconstitutional features which we have discussed. The Act is not in purpose or effect a regulation of interstate commerce within the meaning of the Constitution.

Several purposes are expressed in § 2(a), amongst them: to provide "adequately for the satisfactory retirement of aged employees"; "to make possible greater employment opportunity and more rapid advancement"; to provide by the administration and construction of the Act "the greatest practicable amount of relief from unemployment and the greatest possible use of resources available for said purpose and for the payment of annuities for the relief of superannuated employees." The respondents assert and the petitioners admit that though these may in and of themselves be laudable objects, they have no reasonable relation to the business of interstate transportation. The clause, however, states a further purpose, the promotion of "efficiency and safety in interstate transportation" . . . .

In final analysis, the petitioners' sole reliance is the thesis that efficiency depends upon morale, and morale in turn upon assurance of security for the worker's old age. Thus pensions are sought to be related to efficiency of transportation, and brought within the commerce power. . . . The theory is that one who has an assurance against future dependency will do his work more cheerfully, and therefore more efficiently. The question at once presents itself whether the fostering of a contented mind on the part of an employee by legislation of this type, is in any just sense a regulation of interstate transportation. If that question be answered in the affirmative, obviously there is no limit to the field of so-called regulation. The catalogue of means and actions which might be imposed upon an employer in any business, tending to the satisfaction and comfort of his employees, seems endless. Provision for free medical attendance and nursing, for clothing, for food, for housing, for the education of children, and a hundred other matters, might with equal propriety be proposed as tending to relieve the employee of mental strain and worry. Can it fairly be said that the power of Congress to regulate interstate commerce extends to the prescription of any or all of these things? Is it not apparent that they are really and essentially related solely to the social welfare of the worker, and therefore remote from any regulation of commerce as such? We think the answer is plain. These matters obviously lie ouside the orbit of Congressional power. The answer of the petitioners is that not all such means of promoting contentment have such a close relation to interstate commerce as pensions. This is in truth no answer, for we must deal with the principle involved and not the means adopted. If contentment of the employee were an object for the attainment of which the regulatory power could be exerted, the courts could not question the wisdom of methods adopted for its advancement.

No support for a plan which pensions those who have retired from the service of the railroads can be drawn from the decisions of this court sustaining measures touching the relations of employer and employee in the carrier field in the interest of a more efficient system of transportation. The Safety Appliance Acts, the Employers' Liability Acts, hours-of-service laws, and others of analogous character, cited in support of this Act, have a direct and intimate connection with the actual operation of the railroads. . . . The railway labor act was upheld by this court upon the express ground that to facilitate the amicable settlement of disputes which threatened the service of the necessary agencies of interstate transportation tended to prevent interruptions of service and was therefore within the delegated power of regulation. . . . Texas & New Orleans R. Co. v. Railway Clerks, 281 U.S. 548, 570–1. . . .

Stress is laid upon the supposed analogy between workmen's compensation laws and the challenged statute. It is said that while Congress has not adopted a compulsory and exclusive system of workmen's compensation applicable to interstate carriers, no one doubts the power so to do; and the Retirement Act cannot in principle be distinguished. The contention overlooks fundamental differences. . . . The power to prescribe an uniform rule for the transportation industry throughout the country justifies the modification of common law rules by the Safety Appliance Acts and the Employers' Liability Acts applicable to interstate carriers, and would serve to sustain compensation acts of a broader scope, like those in force in many states. The collateral fact that such a law may produce contentment among employees,— an object which as a separate and independent matter is wholly beyond the power of Congress,—would not, of course, render the legislation unconstitutional. . . . Workmen's compensation laws deal with existing rights and liabilities by readjusting old benefits and burdens incident to the relation of employer and employee. Before their adoption the employer was bound to provide a fund to answer the lawful claims of his employees; the change is merely in the required disbursement of that fund in consequence of the recognition that the industry should compensate for injuries occurring with or without fault. The Act with which we are concerned seeks to attach to the relation of employer and employee a new incident, without reference to any existing obligation or legal liability, solely in the interest of the employee, with no regard to the conduct of the business, or its safety or efficiency, but purely for social ends.

The petitioners, in support of their argument as to morale, rely upon the voluntary systems adopted in past years by almost all the carriers, and now in operation. The argument runs that these voluntary plans were adopted in the industry for two principal reasons—the creation of loyalty and the encouragement of continuity in service. . . .

. . . The petitioners, in effect, say: the carriers with certain objects and purposes have adopted voluntary systems; this proves that pensions are germane to the railroad business; Congress may legislate on any subject germane to interstate transportation; therefore Congress may for any reason or with any motive impose any type of pension plan. The contention comes very near to this,—that whatever some carriers choose to do voluntarily in the management of their business, at once invests Congress with the power to compel all carriers to do. The fallacy is obvious. The meaning of the commerce and due process clauses of the Constitution is not so easily enlarged by the voluntary acts of individuals or corporations. . . .

. . . We think it cannot be denied, and, indeed, is in effect admitted, that the sole reliance of the petitioners is upon the theory that contentment and assurance of security are the major purposes of the Act. We cannot agree that these ends if dictated by statute, and not voluntarily extended by the employer, encourage loyalty and continuity of service. We feel bound to hold that a pension plan thus imposed is in no proper sense a regulation of the activity of interstate transportation. It is an attempt for social ends to impose by sheer fiat non-contractual incidents upon the relation of employer and employee, not as a rule or regulation of commerce and transportation between the States, but as a means of assuring a particular class of employees against old age dependency. This is neither a necessary nor an appropriate rule or regulation affecting the due fulfilment of the railroads' duty to serve the public in interstate transportation. . . .

Affirmed.

The Chief Justice [HUGHES], dissenting.

I am unable to concur in the decision of this case. The gravest aspect of the decision is that it does not rest simply upon a condemnation of particular features of the Railroad Retirement Act, but denies to Congress the power to pass any compulsory pension act for railroad employees. . . . I think that the conclusion thus reached is a departure from sound principles and places an unwarranted limitation upon the commerce clause of the Constitution. . . .

The argument that a pension measure, however sound and reasonable as such, is *per se* outside the pale of the regulation of interstate carriers, because such a plan could not possibly have a reasonable relation to the ends which Congress is entitled to serve, is largely answered by the practice of the carriers themselves. . . .

. . . I think that it is clear that the morale of railroad employees has an important bearing upon the efficiency of the transportation service, and that a reasonable pension plan by its assurance of security is an appropriate means to that end. Nor should such a plan be removed from the reach of constitutional power by classing it with a variety of conceivable benefits which have no such close and substantial relation to the terms and conditions of employment. The appropriate relation of the exercise of constitutional power to the legitimate objects of that power is always a subject of judicial scrutiny. With approximately 82 per cent of railroad employees, 90 per cent of those employed in cable, telephone and telegraph companies, and about one-half of those in the service of electric railways, light, heat and power companies under formal pension plans, with the extensive recognition by national, state and local governments of the benefit of retirement and pension systems for public employees in the interest of both efficiency and economy, it is evidence that there is a widespread conviction that the assurance of security through a pension plan for retired employees is closely and substantially related to the proper conduct of business enterprises. . . .

The argument in relation to voluntary plans discloses the fundamental contention on the question of constitutional authority. In substance, it is that the relation of the carriers and their employees is the subject of contract; that the contract prescribes the work and the compensation; and that a compulsory pension plan is an attempt for social ends to impose upon the relation non-contractual incidents in order to insure to employees protection in their old age. And this is said to lie outside the power of Congress in the government of interstate commerce. Congress may, indeed, it seems to be assumed, compel the elimination of aged employees. A retirement act for that purpose might be passed. But not a pension act. The government's power is conceived to be limited to a requirement that the railroads dismiss their superannuated employees, throwing them out helpless, without any reasonable provision for their protection.

The argument pays insufficient attention to the responsibilities which inhere in the carriers' enterprise. Those responsibilities, growing out of their relation to their employees, cannot be regarded as confined to the contractual engagement. The range of existing federal regulation of interstate carriers affords many illustrations of the imposition upon the employer-employee relation of noncontractual incidents for social ends. A close analogy to the provision of a pension plan is suggested by the familiar examples of compensation acts. . . . . A thorough examination of the question of constitutional authority to adopt such a compulsory measure was made some years ago by a commission constituted under a Joint Resolution of Congress, of which Senator Sutherland (now Mr. Justice Sutherland) was chairman. 36 Stat. 884. Its elaborate and unanimous report, transmitted to Congress by President Taft with his complete approval, considered the constitutional question in all aspects, upheld the congressional power and proposed its exercise. Sen.Doc.No.338, 62d Cong. 2d sess. Among the principles announced was that "If the proposed legislation effectuates any constitutional power, it is not rendered unconstitutional because to a greater or less extent it may accomplish or tend to accomplish some other result which, as a separate and independent matter, would be wholly beyond the power of Congress to deal with." Id., p. 26. The legislation was deemed to be a regulation of interstate commerce because, among other specified things, of its effect on the state of mind of the employee. . . .

The effort to dispose of the analogy serves only to make it the more impressive. Compensation acts are said to be a response to the demands which inhere in the development of industry, requiring new measures for the protection of employees. But pension measures are a similar response. If Congress may supply a uniform rule in the one case, why not in the other? If affording certainty of protection is deemed to be an aid to efficiency, why should that consideration be ruled out with respect to retirement allowances and be admitted to support compensation allowances for accidents which happen in the absence of fault? Compensation acts do not simply readjust old burdens and benefits. They add new ones, outside and beyond former burdens and benefits, and thus in truth add a new incident to the relation of employer and employee.

When we go to the heart of the subject, we find that compensation and pension measures for employees rest upon similar basic considerations. . . . What sound distinction, from a constitutional standpoint, is there between compelling reasonable compensation for those injured without any fault of the employer, and requiring a fair allowance for those who practically give their lives to the service and are incapacitated by the wear and tear of time, the attrition of the years? I perceive no constitutional ground upon which the one can be upheld and the other condemned.

The fundamental consideration which supports this type of legislation is that industry should take care of its human wastage, whether that is due to accident or age. That view cannot be dismissed as arbitrary or capricious. It is a reasoned conviction based upon abundant experience. The expression of that conviction in law is regulation. When expressed in the government of interstate carriers, with respect to their employees likewise engaged in interstate commerce, it is a regulation of that commerce. As such, so far as the subject matter is concerned, the commerce clause should be held applicable. . . .

I think the decree should be reversed.

I am authorized to state that Mr. Justice BRANDEIS, Mr. Justice STONE, and Mr. Justice CARDOZO join in this opinion.

SCHECHTER POULTRY CORP. v. UNITED STATES

295 U.S. 495, 55 S.Ct. 837, 79 L.Ed. 1570 (1935).

Certiorari to the Circuit Court of Appeals for the Second Circuit.

[Section 3 of the National Industrial Recovery Act of 1933 authorized the President—ordinarily upon application by a trade or industrial association—to promulgate "codes of fair competition for the trade or industry." Most codes contained provisions regarding unfair trade practices, minimum wages and prices, maximum hours and collective bargaining. Violation of any code provision "in any transaction in or affecting interstate commerce" was made punishable as a misdemeanor.

[This case involved convictions for violating the minimum wage, maximum hour and trade practice provisions of the "Code of Fair Competition for the Live Poultry Industry of the Metropolitan Area in and about the City of New York." New York City was the largest live poultry market in the United States. Ninety-six percent of the poultry marketed there came from other states. Schechter operated wholesale poultry slaughterhouse markets in Brooklyn, New York. Poultry was ordinarily purchased from commission men in New York City, trucked to the Brooklyn slaughterhouses, and sold there to retail poultry dealers. The Court of Appeals sustained convictions on most charges, but reversed those regarding wage and hour requirements, "as these were not deemed to be within the congressional power of regulation." The defendants and the Government sought certiorari. The Court granted the writs on April 15, 1935, two months before the Act was to expire. The decision came on May 27, 1935.]

Mr. Chief Justice HUGHES delivered the opinion of the Court.
. . . .

First. . . . We are told that the provision of the statute authorizing the adoption of codes must be viewed in the light of the grave national crisis with which Congress was confronted. Undoubtedly, the conditions to which power is addressed are always to be considered when the exercise of power is challenged. Extraordinary conditions may call for extraordinary remedies. But the argument necessarily stops short of an attempt to justify action which lies outside the sphere of constitutional authority. Extraordinary conditions do not create or enlarge constitutional power. . . . .

Second. The question of the delegation of legislative power. [The Court held the delegation unconstitutional. See chap. 7, p. 574, infra.]

Third. The question of the application of the provisions of the Live Poultry Code to intrastate transactions. . . . . This aspect of the case presents the question whether the particular provisions of the Live Poultry Code, which the defendants were convicted for violating and for having conspired to violate, were within the regulating power of Congress. . . . .

(1) Were these transactions *"in"* interstate commerce? Much is made of the fact that almost all the poultry coming to New York is sent there from other States. But the code provisions, as here applied, do not concern the transportation of the poultry from other States to New York, or the transactions of the commission men or others to whom it is consigned, or the sales made by such consignees to defendants. When defendants had made their purchases, whether at the West Washington Market in New York City or at the railroad terminals serving the City, or elsewhere, the poultry was trucked to their slaughterhouses in Brooklyn for local disposition. The interstate transactions in relation to that poultry then ended. Defendants held the poultry at their slaughterhouse markets for slaughter and local sale to retail dealers and butchers who in turn sold directly to consumers. Neither the slaughtering nor the sales by defendants were transactions in interstate commerce. . . . .

The undisputed facts thus afford no warrant for the argument that the poultry handled by defendants at their slaughterhouse markets was in a *"current"* or *"flow"* of interstate commerce and was thus subject to congressional regulation. The mere fact that there may be a constant flow of commodities into a State does not mean that the flow continues after the property has arrived and has become commingled with the mass of property within the State and is there held solely for local disposition and use. So far as the poultry here in question is concerned, the flow in interstate commerce had ceased. . . . .

(2) Did the defendants' transactions directly *"affect"* interstate commerce so as to be subject to federal regulation? The power of Congress extends not only to the regulation of transactions which are part of interstate commerce, but to the protection of that commerce from injury. It matters not that the injury may be due to the conduct of those engaged in intrastate operations. . . . .

In determining how far the federal government may go in controlling intrastate transactions upon the ground that they "affect" interstate commerce, there is a necessary and well-established distinction between direct and indirect effects. The precise line can be drawn only as individual cases arise, but the distinction is clear in principle. Direct effects are illustrated by the railroad cases we have cited, as, e. g., the effect of failure to use prescribed safety appliances on railroads which are the highways of both interstate and intrastate commerce, injury to an employee engaged in interstate transportation by the negligence of an employee engaged in an intrastate movement, the fixing of rates for intrastate transportation which unjustly discriminate against interstate commerce. But where the effect of intrastate transactions upon interstate commerce is merely indirect, such transactions remain within the domain of state power. If the commerce clause were construed to reach all enterprises and transactions which could be said to have an indirect effect upon interstate commerce, the federal authority would embrace practically all the activities of the people and the authority of the State over its domestic concerns would exist only by sufferance of the federal government. . . .

. . . The persons employed in slaughtering and selling in local trade are not employed in interstate commerce. Their hours and wages have no direct relation to interstate commerce. The question of how many hours these employees should work and what they should be paid differs in no essential respect from similar questions in other local businesses which handle commodities brought into a State and there dealt in as a part of its internal commerce. This appears from an examination of the considerations urged by the Government with respect to conditions in the poultry trade. Thus, the Government argues that hours and wages affect prices; that slaughterhouse men sell at a small margin above operating costs; that labor represents 50 to 60 per cent. of these costs; that a slaughterhouse operator paying lower wages or reducing his cost by exacting long hours of work, translates his saving into lower prices; that this results in demands for a cheaper grade of goods; and that the cutting of prices brings about a demoralization of the price structure. Similar conditions may be adduced in relation to other businesses. The argument of the Government proves too much. If the federal government may determine the wages and hours of employees in the internal commerce of a State, because of their relation to cost and prices and their indirect effect upon interstate commerce, it would seem that a similar control might be exerted over other elements of cost, also affecting prices, such as the number of employees, rents, advertising, methods of doing business, etc. All the processes of production and distribution that enter into cost could likewise be controlled. If the cost of doing an intrastate business is in itself the permitted object of federal control, the extent of the regulation of cost would be a question of discretion and not of power.

The Government also makes the point that efforts to enact state legislation establishing high labor standards have been impeded by the belief that unless similar action is taken generally, commerce will be diverted from the States adopting such standards, and that this fear of diversion has led to demands for federal legislation on the subject of wages and hours. The apparent implication is that the federal authority under the commerce clause should be deemed to extend to the establishment of rules to govern wages and hours in intrastate trade and industry generally throughout the country, thus overriding the authority of the States to deal with domestic problems arising from labor conditions in their internal commerce.

It is not the province of the Court to consider the economic advantages or disadvantages of such a centralized system. It is sufficient to say that the Federal Constitution does not provide for it. Our growth and development have called for wide use of the commerce power of the federal government in its control over the expanded activities of interstate commerce, and in protecting that commerce from burdens, interferences, and conspiracies to restrain and monopolize it. But the authority of the federal government may not be pushed to such an extreme as to destroy the distinction, which the commerce clause itself establishes, between commerce "among the several States" and the internal concerns of a State. The same answer must be made to the contention that is based upon the serious economic situation which led to the passage of the Recovery Act,—the fall in prices, the decline in wages and employment, and the curtailment of the market for commodities. Stress is laid upon the great importance of maintaining wage distributions which would provide the necessary stimulus in starting "the cumulative forces making for expanding commercial activity." Without in any way disparaging this motive, it is enough to say that the recuperative efforts of the federal government must be made in a manner consistent with the authority granted by the Constitution.

We are of the opinion that the attempt through the provisions of the Code to fix the hours and wages of employees of defendants in their intrastate business was not a valid exercise of federal power. . . .

Reversed.

Mr. Justice CARDOZO, concurring.

The delegated power of legislation which has found expression in this code is not canalized within banks that keep it from overflowing. . . . This is delegation run riot. . . .

But there is another objection, far-reaching and incurable, aside from any defect of unlawful delegation. . . .

I find no authority in [the commerce clause] for the regulation of wages and hours of labor in the intrastate transactions that make up the defendants' business. As to this feature of the case little can be added to the opinion of the court. There is a view of causation that would obliterate the distinction between what is national and what is local in the activities of commerce. Motion at the outer rim is communicated perceptibly, though minutely, to recording instruments at the center. A society such as ours "is an elastic medium which transmits all tremors throughout its territory; the only question is of their size." Per Learned Hand, J., in the court below. The law is not indifferent to considerations of degree. Activities local in their immediacy do not become interstate and national because of distant repercussions. What is near and what is distant may at times be uncertain. . . . There is no penumbra of uncertainty obscuring judgment here. To find immediacy or directness here is to find it almost everywhere. If centripetal forces are to be isolated to the exclusion of the forces that oppose and counteract them, there will be an end to our federal system. . . .

I am authorized to state that Mr. Justice STONE joins in this opinion.

FROM SCHECHTER TO CARTER

At a press conference soon after Schechter, President Roosevelt spoke at length about the decision. In addition to his "horse-and-buggy age" re-

mark, he said, for example, that the case raised "the big issue in the country.
.   .   .   Does this decision mean that the United States Government
has no control over any national economic problem?"   Later, he added that
the decision "—if you accept the obiter dicta and all the phraseology of it—
seems to be squarely on the side of restoring to the States forty-eight different
controls over national economic problems.   .   .   .   In some ways it may
be the best thing that has happened to the country for a long time that such
a decision has come from the Supreme Court, because it clarifies the issue."
4 The Public Papers and Addresses of Franklin D. Roosevelt (1938), 212,
218–19.

But the decision was not necessarily fatal to the New Deal cause, either
in practical or doctrinal terms.   Though the Act had proved an effective
emergency measure for a brief period, its enforcement had become "too
cumbersome and unworkable."   And, as to doctrine, the "very weakness
of the Schechter case, from the Government's viewpoint, was its saving
grace."   The Court had not yet passed on congressional power "to control
trade practices or labor relations   .   .   .   in any major industry, such as
petroleum, lumber, coal or steel."   In future litigation, "the case—and perhaps its language—could clearly be distinguished, when and if such regulation was attempted."   Stern, "The Commerce Clause and the National Economy, 1933–46," 59 Harv.L.Rev. 645, 662 (1946), Selected Essays 1938–
1962 (1963), 227.

The attempt was made immediately.   For example, the right of collective bargaining, recognized in the NIRA, was guaranteed in a more permanent statute: the National Labor Relations Act (Wagner Act) became law
on July 5, 1935.   And President Roosevelt urged Congress to enact a law
establishing an NIRA-like regulatory scheme for the bituminous coal industry.
While this bill—introduced by Senator Joseph Guffey—was pending in a
House subcommittee, President Roosevelt wrote a controversial letter to the
chairman, Congressman Samuel B. Hill.   The July 6, 1935, letter, after stating
the need for the law and noting that its constitutionality depended on "whether production conditions directly affect, promote or obstruct interstate commerce," concluded: "Manifestly, no one is in a position to give assurance
that the proposed act will withstand constitutional tests.   .   .   .   But the
situation is so urgent and the benefits of the legislation so evident that all
doubts should be resolved in favor of the bill, leaving to the courts, in an
orderly fashion, the ultimate question of constitutionality.   A decision by
the Supreme Court relative to this measure would be helpful as indicating,
with increasing clarity, the constitutional limits within which this Government must operate.   .   .   .   I hope your committee will not permit
doubts as to constitutionality, however reasonable, to block the suggested
legislation."   4 The Public Papers and Addresses of Franklin D. Roosevelt
(1938), 297–98.

Did the concluding sentence of the President's letter constitute improper defiance of the Court?   Recall chap. 1, supra.   The bill became law
a few weeks later, and a test suit to invalidate it was commenced one day
thereafter.   The Court's decision on the Bituminous Coal Act follows.

CARTER v. CARTER COAL CO.

298 U.S. 238, 56 S.Ct. 855, 80 L.Ed. 1160 (1936).

Certiorari to the United States Court of Appeals for the District of Columbia.

[The Bituminous Coal Conservation Act of 1935 imposed a 15 percent tax on the disposal of coal at the mine. Producers could receive a 90 percent reduction of the tax by accepting a code to be formulated by a National Bituminous Coal Commission, with the aid of district boards. Under part II, minimum prices were to be set for each area. Under part III, the labor provisions, code members were to recognize the employees' "right to organize and bargain collectively," and wage and hour agreements negotiated by a specified percentage of producers and workers' representatives were to be binding on all code members.

[Carter brought a stockholder's suit against his company to enjoin it from paying the tax and complying with the code. The Commissioner of Internal Revenue was joined as a defendant. The trial court sustained the Act and dismissed the suit. "Because of the importance of the question and the advantage of a speedy final determination thereof," the Supreme Court granted certiorari before argument or decision in the Court of Appeals.]

Mr. Justice SUTHERLAND delivered the opinion of the Court.

. . .

The questions involved will be considered under the following heads:

1. The right of stockholders to maintain suits of this character. [The Court found the stockholders entitled to sue.]

2. Whether the suits were prematurely brought. [The Court found that the suits were not premature.]

3. Whether the exaction of 15 *per centum* on the sale price of coal at the mine is a tax or a penalty.

4. The purposes of the act as set forth in § 1, and the authority vested in Congress by the Constitution to effectuate them.

5. Whether the labor provisions of the act can be upheld as an exercise of the power to regulate interstate commerce.

6. Whether subdivision (g) of Part III of the Code, is an unlawful delegation of power.

7. The constitutionality of the price-fixing provisions, and the question of severability—that is to say, whether if either the group of labor provisions or the group of price-fixing provisions be found constitutionally invalid, the other can stand as separable. . . .

Third. . . . . That the "tax" is in fact a penalty is not seriously in dispute. The position of the Government, as we understand it, is that the validity of the exaction does not rest upon the taxing power but upon the power of Congress to regulate interstate commerce; and that if the act in respect of the labor and price-fixing provisions be not upheld, the "tax" must fall with them. With that position we agree and confine our consideration accordingly.

Fourth. Certain recitals contained in the act plainly suggest that its makers were of opinion that its constitutionality could be sustained under some general federal power, thought to exist, apart from the specific grants of the Constitution. The fallacy of that view will be apparent when we recall fundamental principles which, although hitherto often expressed in varying forms of words, will bear repetition whenever their accuracy seems to be challenged. The recitals to which we refer are contained in § 1 (which is simply a preamble to the act), and, among others, are to the effect that the distribution of bituminous coal is of national interest, affecting the health and comfort of the people and the general welfare of the nation; that this circumstance, together with the necessity of maintaining just and rational relations between the public, owners, producers, and employees, and the right of the public to constant and adequate supplies at reasonable prices, require regulation of the industry as the act provides. These affirmations—and the further ones that the production and distribution of such coal "directly affect interstate commerce," because of which and of the waste of the national coal resources and other circumstances, the regulation is necessary for the protection of such commerce—do not constitute an exertion of the *will* of Congress which is legislation, but a recital of considerations which in the *opinion* of that body existed and justified the expression of its will in the present act. Nevertheless, this preamble may not be disregarded. On the contrary it is important, because it makes clear, except for the pure assumption that the conditions described "directly" affect interstate commerce, that the powers which Congress undertook to exercise are not specific but of the most general character—namely, to protect the general public interest and the health and comfort of the people, to conserve privately-owned coal, maintain just relations between producers and employees and others, and promote the general welfare, by controlling nation-wide production and distribution of coal. These, it may be conceded, are objects of great worth; but are they ends, the attainment of which has been committed by the Constitution to the federal government? This is a vital question; for nothing is more certain than that beneficent aims, however great or well directed, can never serve in lieu of constitutional power. . . .

The proposition, often advanced and as often discredited, that the power of the federal government inherently extends to purposes affecting the nation as a whole with which the states severally cannot deal or cannot adequately deal, and the related notion that Congress, entirely apart from those powers delegated by the Constitution, may enact laws to promote the general welfare, have never been accepted but always definitely rejected by this court. . . . In the Framers' Convention, the proposal to confer a general power akin to that just discussed was included in Mr. Randolph's resolutions, the sixth of which, among other things, declared that the National Legislature ought to enjoy the legislative rights vested in Congress by the Confederation, and "moreover to legislate in all cases to which the separate States are incompetent, or in which the harmony of the United States may be interrupted by the exercise of individual Legislation." The Convention, however, declined to confer upon Congress power in such general terms; instead of which it carefully limited the powers which it thought wise to entrust to Congress by specifying them, thereby denying all others not granted expressly or by necessary implication. It made no grant of authority to Congress to legislate substantively for the general welfare . . . ., and no such authority exists, save as the general welfare may be promoted by the exercise of the powers which are granted. . . .

There are many subjects in respect of which the several states have not legislated in harmony with one another, and in which their varying laws and the failure of some of them to act at all have resulted in injurious confusion and embarrassment. . . . The state laws with respect to marriage and divorce present a case in point; and the great necessity of national legislation on that subject has been from time to time vigorously urged. Other pertinent examples are laws with respect to negotiable instruments, desertion and non-support, certain phases of state taxation, and others which we do not pause to mention. In many of these fields of legislation, the necessity of bringing the applicable rules of law into general harmonious relation has been so great that a Commission on Uniform State Laws, composed of commissioners from every state in the Union, has for many years been industriously and successfully working to that end by preparing and securing the passage by the several states of uniform laws. If there be an easier and constitutional way to these desirable results through congressional action, it thus far has escaped discovery. . . .

. . . . [T]he general purposes which the act recites . . . are beyond the power of Congress except so far, and only so far, as they may be realized by an exercise of some specific power granted by the Constitution. Proceeding by a process of elimination, which it is not necessary to follow in detail, we shall find no grant of power which authorizes Congress to legislate in respect of these general purposes unless it be found in the commerce clause—and this we now consider.

Fifth. . . . In exercising the authority conferred by this clause of the Constitution, Congress is powerless to regulate anything which is not commerce, as it is powerless to do anything about commerce which is not regulation. . . .

. . . One who produces or manufactures a commodity, subsequently sold and shipped by him in interstate commerce, whether such sale and shipment were originally intended or not, has engaged in two distinct and separate activities. So far as he produces or manufactures a commodity, his business is purely local. So far as he sells and ships, or contracts to sell and ship, the commodity to customers in another state, he engages in interstate commerce. In respect of the former, he is subject only to regulation by the state; in respect of the latter, to regulation only by the federal government. . . . Production is not commerce; but a step in preparation for commerce. . . .

We have seen that the word "commerce" is the equivalent of the phrase "intercourse for the purposes of trade." Plainly, the incidents leading up to and culminating in the mining of coal do not constitute such intercourse. The employment of men, the fixing of their wages, hours of labor and working conditions, the bargaining in respect of these things—whether carried on separately or collectively—each and all constitute intercourse for the purposes of production, not of trade. The latter is a thing apart from the relation of employer and employee, which in all producing occupations is purely local in character. Extraction of coal from the mine is the aim and the completed result of local activities. Commerce in the coal mined is not brought into being by force of these activities, but by negotiations, agreements, and circumstances entirely apart from production. Mining brings the subject matter of commerce into existence. Commerce disposes of it.

A consideration of the foregoing . . . renders inescapable the conclusion that the effect of the labor provisions of the act, including those in respect of minimum wages, wage agreements, collective bargaining, and the Labor Board and its powers, primarily falls upon production and not upon commerce; and confirms the further resulting conclusion that production is a purely local activity. It follows that none of these essential antecedents of production constitutes a transaction in or forms any part of interstate commerce. Schechter Corp. v. United States, supra, p. 542 et seq. Everything which moves in interstate commerce has had a local origin. Without local production somewhere, interstate commerce, as now carried on, would practically disappear. Nevertheless, the local character of mining, of manufacturing and of crop growing is a fact, and remains a fact, whatever may be done with the products.

Certain decisions of this court, superficially considered, seem to lend support to the defense of the act now under review. But upon examination, they will be seen to be inapposite. Thus, Coronado Coal Co. v. United Mine Workers, 268 U.S. 295, 310, and kindred cases, involved conspiracies to restrain interstate commerce in violation of the Anti-trust laws. The acts of the persons involved were local in character but the intent was to restrain interstate commerce, and the means employed were calculated to carry that intent into effect. Interstate commerce was the direct object of attack; and the restraint of such commerce was the necessary consequence of the acts and the immediate end in view. . . .

Another group of cases, of which Swift & Co. v. United States, 196 U.S. 375, is an example, rest upon the circumstance that the acts in question constituted direct interferences with the "flow" of commerce among the states. . . . It was nowhere suggested in these cases that the interstate commerce power extended to the growth or production of the things which, after production, entered the flow. . . .

But § 1 (the preamble) of the act now under review declares that all production and distribution of bituminous coal "bear upon and directly affect its interstate commerce"; and that regulation thereof is imperative for the protection of such commerce. The contention of the government is that the labor provisions of the act may be sustained in that view.

That the production of every commodity intended for interstate sale and transportation has some effect upon interstate commerce may be, if it has not already been, freely granted; and we are brought to the final and decisive inquiry, whether here that effect is direct, as the "preamble" recites, or indirect. The distinction is not formal, but substantial in the highest degree, as we pointed out in the Schechter case. . . .

Whether the effect of a given activity or condition is direct or indirect is not always easy to determine. The word "direct" implies that the activity or condition invoked or blamed shall operate proximately—not mediately, remotely, or collaterally—to produce the effect. It connotes the absence of an efficient intervening agency or condition. And the extent of the effect bears no logical relation to its character. The distinction between a direct and an indirect effect turns, not upon the magnitude of either the cause or the effect, but entirely upon the manner in which the effect has been brought about. If the production by one man of a single ton of coal intended for interstate sale and shipment, and actually so sold and shipped, affects interstate commerce indirectly, the effect does not become direct by multiplying the tonnage, or increasing the number of men employed, or adding to the expense or complexities of the business, or by all combined. It is quite true that rules of law are sometimes qualified by considerations of degree, as the government argues. But the matter of degree has no bearing upon the question here, since that question is not—What is the *extent* of the local activity or condition, or the *extent* of the effect produced upon interstate commerce? but—What is the *relation* between the activity or condition and the effect?

Much stress is put upon the evils which come from the struggle between employers and employees over the matter of wages, working conditions, the right of collective bargaining, etc., and the resulting strikes, curtailment and irregularity of production and effect on prices; and it is insisted that interstate commerce is *greatly* affected thereby. But, in addition to what has just been said, the conclusive answer is that the evils are all local evils over which the federal government has no legislative control. The relation of employer and employee is a local relation. . . . And the controversies and evils, which it is the object of the act to regulate and minimize, are local controversies and evils affecting local work undertaken to accomplish that local result. Such effect as they may have upon commerce, however extensive it may be, is secondary and indirect. An increase in the greatness of the effect adds to its importance. It does not alter its character. . . .

. . . A reading of the entire opinion [in Schechter] makes clear, what we now declare, that the want of power on the part of the federal government is the same whether the wages, hours of service, and working conditions, and the bargaining about them, are related to production before interstate commerce has begun, or to sale and distribution after it has ended.

Sixth. . . . [The Act] delegates the power to fix maximum hours of labor to a part of the producers and the miners. . . .

. . . The delegation is so clearly arbitrary, and so clearly a denial of rights safeguarded by the due process clause of the Fifth Amendment, that it is unnecessary to do more than refer to decisions of this court which foreclose the question. Schechter Corp. v. United States . . . ..

Seventh. Finally, we are brought to the price-fixing provisions of the code. The necessity of considering the question of their constitutionality will depend upon whether they are separable from the labor provisions so that they can stand independently. . . .

. . . The conclusion is unavoidable that the price-fixing provisions of the code are so related to and dependent upon the labor provisions as conditions, considerations or compensations, as to make it clearly probable that the latter being held bad, the former would not have been passed. The fall of the latter, therefore, carries down with it the former. . . .

The price-fixing provisions of the code are thus disposed of without coming to the question of their constitutionality; but neither this disposition of the matter, nor anything we have said, is to be taken as indicating that the court is of opinion that these provisions, if separately enacted, could be sustained. . . .

Separate opinion of Mr. Chief Justice HUGHES. . . .

The power to regulate interstate commerce embraces the power to protect that commerce from injury, whatever may be the source of the dangers which threaten it, and to adopt any appropriate means to that end. . . .

Congress thus has adequate authority to maintain the orderly conduct of interstate commerce and to provide for the peaceful settlement of disputes which threaten it. . . . But Congress may not use this protective authority as a pretext for the exertion of power to regulate activities and relations within the States which affect interstate commerce only indirectly. Otherwise, in view of the multitude of indirect effects, Congress in its discretion could assume control of virtually all the activities of the people to the subversion of the fundamental principle of the Constitution. If the people desire to give Congress the power to regulate industries within the State, and the relations of employers and employees in those industries, they are at liberty to declare their will in the appropriate manner, but it is not for the Court to amend the Constitution by judicial decision. . . .

But [the] Act also provides for the regulation of the prices of bituminous coal sold in interstate commerce and prohibits unfair methods of competition in interstate commerce. Undoubtedly transactions in carrying on interstate commerce are subject to the federal power to regulate that commerce and the control of charges and the protection of fair competition in that commerce are familiar illustrations of the exercise of the power, as the Interstate Commerce Act, the Packers and Stockyards Act, and the Anti-Trust Acts abundantly show. The Court has repeatedly stated that the power to regulate interstate commerce among the several States is supreme and plenary. . . . . . . The marketing provisions in relation to interstate commerce can be carried out as provided in Part II without regard to the labor provisions contained in Part III. That fact, in the light of the congressional declaration of separability, should be considered of controlling importance.

In this view, the Act, and the Code for which it provides, may be sustained in relation to the provisions for marketing in interstate commerce, and the decisions of the courts below, so far as they accomplish that result, should be affirmed.

Mr. Justice CARDOZO (dissenting).

. . . I am satisfied that the Act is within the power of the central government in so far as it provides for minimum and maximum prices upon sales of bituminous coal in the transactions of interstate commerce and in those of intrastate commerce where interstate commerce is directly or intimately affected. Whether it is valid also in other provisions that have been considered and condemned in the opinion of the court, I do not find it necessary to determine at this time. Silence must not be taken as importing acquiescence. . . .

Regulation of prices being an exercise of the commerce power in respect of interstate transactions, the question remains whether it comes within that power as applied to intrastate sales where interstate prices are directly or intimately affected. Mining and agriculture and manufacture are not interstate commerce considered by themselves, yet their relation to that commerce may be such that for the protection of the one there is need to regulate the other. Schechter Poultry Corp. v. United States, 295 U.S. 495, 544, 545, 546. Sometimes it is said that the relation must be "direct" to bring that power into play. In many circumstances such a description will be sufficiently precise to meet the needs of the occasion. But a great principle of constitutional law is not susceptible of comprehensive statement in an adjective. The underlying thought is merely this, that "the law is not indifferent to considerations of degree." Schechter Poultry Corp. v. United States, supra, concurring opinion, p. 554. It cannot be indifferent to them without an expansion of the commerce clause that would absorb or imperil the reserved powers of the states. At times, as in the case cited, the waves of causation will have radiated so far that their undulatory motion, if discernible at all, will be too faint or obscure, too broken by cross-currents, to be heeded by the law. In such circumstances the holding is not directed at prices or wages considered in the abstract, but at prices or wages in particular conditions. The relation may be tenuous or the opposite according to the facts. Always the setting of the facts is to be viewed if one would know the closeness of the tie. Perhaps, if one group of adjectives is to be chosen in preference to another, "intimate" and "remote" will be found to be as good as any. At all events, "direct" and "indirect," even if accepted as sufficient, must not be read too narrowly. . . . A survey of the cases shows that the words have been interpreted with suppleness of adaptation and flexibility of meaning. The power is as broad as the need that evokes it.

One of the most common and typical instances of a relation characterized as direct has been that between interstate and intrastate rates for carriers by rail where the local rates are so low as to divert business unreasonably from interstate competitors. In such circumstances Congress has the power to protect the business of its carriers against disintegrating encroachments. . . . To be sure, the relation even then may be characterized as indirect if one is nice or over-literal in the choice of words. Strictly speaking, the intrastate rates have a primary effect upon the intrastate traffic and not upon any other, though the repercussions of the competitive system may lead to secondary consequences affecting interstate traffic also. . . . What the cases really mean is that the causal relation in such circumstances is so close and intimate and obvious as to permit it to be called direct without subjecting the word to an unfair or excessive strain. There is a like immediacy here. Within rulings the most orthodox, the prices for intrastate sales of coal have so inescapable a relation to those for interstate sales that a system of regulation for transactions of the one class is necessary to give adequate protection to the system of regulation adopted for the other. The argument is strongly pressed by intervening counsel that this may not be true in all communities or in exceptional conditions. If so, the operators unlawfully affected may show that the Act to that extent is invalid as to them. . . .

I am authorized to state that Mr. Justice BRANDEIS and Mr. Justice STONE join in this opinion.

THE COURT–PACKING PLAN

1. *The background and the fate of the plan.* The decisions of the 1934–1936 period—those mentioned above as well as several others, especially United States v. Butler, 297 U.S. 1 (1936) (p. 366 below), invalidating the Agricultural Adjustment Act—persuaded the Roosevelt Administration that strong measures were needed to save the New Deal. Several major New Deal laws had already been held unconstitutional; others —the National Labor Relations Act and the Social Security Act among them—might well meet a similar fate. President Roosevelt did not make Court reform an issue in the 1936 election, however. Rather, he waited

until February 1937 to propose changes, giving reasons that seemed disingenuous to many. A month later, in a radio address, he challenged the Court more directly and defended his plan on a more forthright basis. But the content of the plan and its original method of presentation provoked widespread opposition—including that of a number of New Deal supporters. After extensive hearings, the Senate Judiciary Committee rejected the proposal in June 1937. While the controversy was raging, the Court handed down a number of decisions sustaining regulatory statutes, and Justice Van Devanter retired. The final Senate debate was almost anti-climactic: proposed amendments by the proponents failed to save the heart of the plan, and in late July it was in effect killed. The following excerpts are from documents in the body or the appendixes of Sen.Rep. No. 711, 75th Cong., 1st Sess. (1937) (Reorganization of the Federal Judiciary—Adverse Report of the Committee on the Judiciary).

a. *The Proposed Bill:*

When any judge of a court of the United States, appointed to hold his office during good behavior, has heretofore or hereafter attained the age of seventy years and has held a commission or commissions as judge of any such court or courts at least ten years, continuously or otherwise, and within six months thereafter has neither resigned nor retired, the President, for each such judge who has not so resigned or retired, shall nominate, and by and with the advice and consent of the Senate, shall appoint one additional judge to the court to which the former is commissioned. . . . No more than fifty judges shall be appointed thereunder, nor shall any judge be so appointed if such appointment would result in (1) more than fifteen members of the Supreme Court of the United States . . . . [Six Justices were over seventy in 1937: Butler (71), Hughes (75), Sutherland (75), McReynolds (75), Van Devanter (78), and Brandeis (81).]

b. *The President's Message to Congress, Feb. 5, 1937:*

It is . . . one of the definite duties of the Congress constantly to maintain the effective functioning of the Federal judiciary. . . . The judiciary has often found itself handicapped by insufficient personnel with which to meet a growing and more complex business. . . . Even at the present time the Supreme Court is laboring under a heavy burden. . . . It seems clear . . . that the necessity of relieving present congestion extends to the enlargement of the capacity of all the Federal courts. A part of the problem of obtaining a sufficient number of judges to dispose of cases is the capacity of the judges themselves. This brings forward the question of aged or infirm judges—a subject of delicacy and yet one which requires frank discussion. . . . Modern complexities call also for a constant infusion of new blood in the courts, just as it is needed in executive functions of the Government and in private business. . . . I, therefore, earnestly recommend that the necessity of an increase in the number of judges be supplied by legislation providing for the appointment of additional judges in all Federal courts, without exception, where there are incumbent judges of retirement age who do not choose to retire or to resign. If an elder judge is not in fact incapacitated, only good can come from the presence of an additional judge in the crowded state of the dockets; if the capacity of an elder judge is in fact impaired, the appointment of an additional judge is indispensable. This seems to be a truth which cannot be contradicted. . . .

p 53-59

Amend. V : no person shall be deprived of life
liberty & pursuit of happiness w/o due
process of law.

5th Amend : limits power of Cong. to enact
exceptions & regulations of S Cts
appellate juris. because can not
~~sum to~~ encroach on anything depriving
one of due process of law

Cong
U.S v. Klein (was not allowed to w/draw
juris of SCt to review a property claim case)
— Contrary to Ex Parte McCardle?

Distinction : due process clause

Klein case : It would have upheld it as
exercise of "exceptions" power if it
simply denied rt of appeal in a particular
class of cases.
But here the ct said dismissal of appeal
would allow Cong to "prescribe rules of
decision to Judic Dept of govt in cases
pending before it.
There was a violation of sep of powers
not only because of legis. interference
w/ judicial power but also because)
impairing effect of a pardon infringed
constit power of Pres.

Jenner-Butler Attack

Jenner bill would elim. appell. juris
in certain cases — see p 55

Klein : Rutledge — "It is one thing for Cong. to
w/hold juris. It is entirely another to
confer it & direct that it be exercised
in a manner inconsistent w/ constit
requirements.
Whenever the judicial power is called
into play it is resp. directly to
fundamental law & no acting authority
can intervene to force or authorize
the judicial body to disregard it.

Justice Story — Cong. must create lower cts &
must vest full juris in them.

Sheldon v. Sill — upheld assignee clause of
1789 Judic Act against a claim that
statute could not bar lower ct juris of
a case w/in desc of cases in Art III

Cong., having power to estab cts, must define
their respective jurisdicts. Have a rt to
prescribe, Cong may w/hold from any ct of its
creation juris of any of enumerated controversies
cts created by statute can have no juris
but such as statute confers

c. *Letter of Chief Justice Charles Evans Hughes to Senator Burton K. Wheeler, March 21, 1937:*

"MY DEAR SENATOR WHEELER: In response to your inquiries, I have the honor to present the following statement with respect to the work of the Supreme Court:

"1. The Supreme Court is fully abreast of its work. . . .

"7. An increase in the number of Justices of the Supreme Court, apart from any question of policy, which I do not discuss, would not promote the efficiency of the Court. It is believed that it would impair that efficiency so long as the Court acts as a unit. There would be more judges to hear, more judges to confer, more judges to discuss, more judges to be convinced and to decide. The present number of Justices is thought to be large enough so far as the prompt, adequate, and efficient conduct of the work of the Court is concerned. As I have said, I do not speak of any other considerations in view of the appropriate attitude of the Court in relation to questions of policy. . . .

"On account of the shortness of time I have not been able to consult with the members of the Court generally with respect to the foregoing statement, but I am confident that it is in accord with the views of the Justices. I should say, however, that I have been able to consult with Mr. Justice Van Devanter and Mr. Justice Brandeis, and I am at liberty to say that the statement is approved by them. . . ."

d. *Radio Address by President Roosevelt, March 9, 1937:*

. . . The American people have learned from the depression. For in the last three national elections an overwhelming majority of them voted a mandate that the Congress and the President begin the task of providing that protection—not after long years of debate, but now.

The courts, however, have cast doubts on the ability of the elected Congress to protect us against catastrophe by meeting squarely our modern social and economic conditions. . . .

I want to talk with you very simply about the need for present action in this crisis—the need to meet the unanswered challenge of one-third of a nation ill-nourished, ill-clad, ill-housed. . . .

When the Congress has sought to stabilize national agriculture, to improve the conditions of labor, to safeguard business against unfair competition, to protect our national resources, and in many other ways to serve our clearly national needs, the majority of the Court has been assuming the power to pass on the wisdom of these acts of the Congress—and to approve or disapprove the public policy written into these laws.

That is not only my accusation. It is the accusation of most distinguished Justices of the present Supreme Court. I have not the time to quote to you all the language used by dissenting Justices in many of these cases. . . .

We have, therefore, reached the point as a Nation where we must take action to save the Constitution from the Court and the Court from itself. We must find a way to take an appeal from the Supreme Court to the Constitution itself. We want a Supreme Court which will do justice under the Constitution not over it. In our courts we want a government of laws and not of men.

I want—as all Americans want—an independent judiciary as proposed by the framers of the Constitution. That means a Supreme Court that will enforce the Constitution as written—that will refuse to amend the Constitution by the arbitrary exercise of judicial power—amendment by judicial say-so. It does not mean a judiciary so independent that it can deny the existence of facts universally recognized. . . .

[My] plan has two chief purposes: By bringing into the judicial system a steady and continuing stream of new and younger blood, I hope, first, to make the administration of all Federal justice speedier and therefore less costly; secondly, to bring to the decision of social and economic problems younger men who have had personal experience and contact with modern facts and circumstances under which average men have to live and work. This plan will save our National Constitution from hardening of the judicial arteries. . . .

If such a law as I propose is regarded as establishing a new precedent, is it not a most desirable precedent? . . .

We cannot rely on an amendment as the immediate or only answer to our present difficulties. . . . Even if an amendment were passed, and even if in the years to come it were to be ratified, its meaning would depend upon the kind of Justices who would be sitting on the Supreme Court bench. An amendment like the rest of the Constitution is what the Justices say it is rather than what its framers or you might hope it is. . . .

e. *Conclusion of Adverse Report of Senate Judiciary Committee, June 14, 1937:*

We recommend the rejection of this bill as a needless, futile, and utterly dangerous abandonment of constitutional principle.

It was presented to the Congress in a most intricate form and for reasons that obscured its real purpose.

It would not banish age from the bench nor abolish divided decisions. . . .

It is a proposal without precedent and without justification.

It would subjugate the courts to the will of Congress and the President and thereby destroy the independence of the judiciary, the only certain shield of individual rights. . . .

It points the way to the evasion of the Constitution and establishes the method whereby the people may be deprived of their right to pass upon all amendments of the fundamental law.

It stands now before the country, acknowledged by its proponents as a plan to force judicial interpretation of the Constitution, a proposal that violates every sacred tradition of American democracy.

Under the form of the Constitution it seeks to do that which is unconstitutional.

Its ultimate operation would be to make this Government one of men rather than one of law, and its practical operation would be to make the Constitution what the executive or legislative branches of the Government choose to say it is—an interpretation to be changed with each change of administration.

It is a measure which should be so emphatically rejected that its parallel will never again be presented to the free representatives of the free people of America.

2. *The impact of the plan.* Two years after the Court-packing debate, President Roosevelt claimed that he had lost the battle but won the war. Do the decisions from 1937 on support that estimate? The Jones & Laughlin case, which follows, was decided on April 12, 1937, while the controversy was still raging. Two weeks earlier, the Court had overruled prior decisions invalidating minimum wage laws as violative of due process. West Coast Hotel Co. v. Parish, 300 U.S. 379, p. 971, infra. West Coast Hotel, in particular, provoked the charge that Justice Roberts had changed his position in the face of the Roosevelt challenge—the "switch in time" that supposedly "saved the Nine." But, as a memorandum left by the Justice demonstrates, the Court voted in West Coast Hotel weeks before the judicial reorganization plan was announced. See Frankfurter, "Mr. Justice Roberts," 104 U.Pa.L.Rev. 311 (1955). Compare Justice Roberts' votes in Alton, Schechter and Carter, supra, with those in the commerce clause decisions which follow; and his position in United States v. Butler, p. 366 below, with that in Steward Machine Co. v. Davis, p. 378. Note the changes in Court personnel from 1937 through 1941: President Roosevelt made seven appointments—Justices Black, Reed, Frankfurter, Douglas, Murphy, Byrnes and Jackson.

The background and consequences of the Court-packing plan are discussed in Jackson, The Struggle for Judicial Supremacy (1941). For the political aspects of the controversy, see the useful contemporary account in Alsop and Catledge, The 168 Days (1938), the colorful modern review in Baker, Back to Back—The Duel Between FDR and the Supreme Court (1967), and the astute retrospective analysis in Chapter 15, "Court Packing: The Miscalculated Risk," Burns, Roosevelt: The Lion and the Fox (1956).

SECTION 5.   THE COMMERCE POWER SINCE 1937—CONSTITUTIONAL REVOLUTION OR CONTINUITY?

NATIONAL LABOR RELATIONS BOARD v. JONES & LAUGHLIN STEEL CORP.

301 U.S. 1, 57 S.Ct. 615, 81 L.Ed. 893 (1937).

Certiorari to the Circuit Court of Appeals for the Fifth Circuit.

Mr. Chief Justice HUGHES delivered the opinion of the Court.

In a proceeding under the National Labor Relations Act of 1935, the National Labor Relations Board found that the respondent, Jones & Laughlin Steel Corporation, had violated the Act by engaging in unfair labor practices affecting commerce. The proceeding was instituted by the Beaver Valley Lodge No. 200, affiliated with the Amalgamated Association of Iron, Steel and Tin Workers of America, a labor organization. The unfair labor practices charged were that the corporation was discriminating against members of the union with regard to hire and tenure of employment, and was coercing and intimidating its employees in order to interfere with their self-organization. The discriminatory and coercive action alleged was the discharge of certain employees.

The National Labor Relations Board, sustaining the charge, ordered the corporation to cease and desist from such discrimination and coercion, to offer reinstatement to ten of the employees named, to make good their losses in pay, and to post for thirty days notices that the corporation would not discharge or discriminate against members, or those desiring to become members, of the labor union. As the corporation failed to comply, the Board petitioned the Circuit Court of Appeals to enforce the order. The court denied the petition, holding that the order lay beyond the range of federal power. 83 F.(2d) 998. We granted certiorari.

The scheme of the National Labor Relations Act . . . may be briefly stated. The first section sets forth findings with respect to the injury to commerce resulting from the denial by employers of the right of employees to organize and from the refusal of employers to accept the procedure of collective bargaining. There follows a declaration that it is the policy of the United States to eliminate these causes of obstruction to the free flow of commerce. The Act then defines the terms it uses, including the terms "commerce" and "affecting commerce." § 2. It creates the National Labor Relations Board and prescribes its organization. §§ 3–6. It sets forth the right of employees to self-organization and to bargain collectively through representatives of their own choosing. § 7. It defines "unfair labor practices." § 8. It lays down rules as to the representation of employees for the purpose of collective bargaining. § 9. The Board is empowered to prevent the described unfair labor practices affecting commerce and the Act prescribes the procedure to that end. . . .

. . . [T]he respondent argues (1) that the Act is in reality a regulation of labor relations and not of interstate commerce; (2) that the Act can have no application to the respondent's relations with its production employees because they are not subject to regulation by the federal government; and (3) that the provisions of the Act violate § 2 of Article III and the Fifth and Seventh Amendments of the Constitution of the United States.

The facts as to the nature and scope of the business of the Jones & Laughlin Steel Corporation have been found by the Labor Board and, so far as they are essential to the determination of this controversy, they are not in dispute. The Labor Board has found: The corporation is organized under the laws of Pennsylvania and has its principal office at Pittsburgh. It is engaged in the business of manufacturing iron and steel in plants situated in Pittsburgh and nearby Aliquippa, Pennsylvania. It manufactures and distributes a widely diversified line of steel and pig iron, being the fourth largest producer of steel in the United States. With its subsidiaries—nineteen in number—it is a completely integrated enterprise, owning and operating ore, coal and limestone properties, lake and river transportation facilities and terminal railroads located at its manufacturing plants. It owns or controls mines in Michigan and Minnesota. It operates four ore steamships on the Great Lakes, used in the transportation of ore to its factories. It owns coal mines in Pennsylvania. It operates towboats and steam barges used in carrying coal to its factories. It owns limestone properties in various places in Pennsylvania and West Virginia. It owns the Monongahela connecting railroad which connects the plants of the Pittsburgh works and forms an interconnection with the Pennsylvania, New York Central and Baltimore and Ohio Railroad systems. It owns the Aliquippa and Southern Railroad Company which connects the Aliquippa works with the Pittsburgh and Lake Erie, part of the New York Central system. Much of its product is shipped to its warehouses in Chicago, Detroit, Cincinnati and Memphis,—to the last two places by means of its own barges and transportation equipment. In Long Island City, New York, and in New Orleans it operates structural steel fabricating shops in connection with the warehousing of semi-finished materials sent from its works. Through one of its wholly-owned subsidiaries it owns, leases and operates stores, warehouses and yards for the distribution of equipment and supplies for drilling and operating oil and gas wells and for pipe lines, refineries and pumping stations. It has sales offices in twenty cities in the United States and a wholly-owned subsidiary which is devoted exclusively to distributing its product in Canada. Approximately 75 per cent. of its product is shipped out of Pennsylvania.

Summarizing these operations, the Labor Board concluded that the works in Pittsburgh and Aliquippa "might be likened to the heart of a self-contained, highly integrated body. They draw in the raw materials from Michigan, Minnesota, West Virginia, Pennsylvania in part through arteries and by means controlled by the respondent; they transform the materials and then pump them out to all parts of the nation through the vast mechanism which the respondent has elaborated."

To carry on the activities of the entire steel industry, 33,000 men mine ore, 44,000 men mine coal, 4,000 men quarry limestone, 16,000 men manufacture coke, 343,000 men manufacture steel, and 83,000 men transport its product. Respondent has about 10,000 employees in its Aliquippa plant, which is located in a community of about 30,000 persons. . . .

. . . [T]he record presents no ground for setting aside the order of the Board so far as the facts pertaining to the circumstances and purpose of the discharge of the employees are concerned. . . . We turn to the questions of law which respondent urges in contesting the validity and application of the Act.

First. The scope of the Act.—The Act is challenged in its entirety as an attempt to regulate all industry, thus invading the reserved powers of the States over their local concerns. It is asserted that the references in the Act to interstate and foreign commerce are colorable at best; that the Act is not a true regulation of such commerce or of matters which directly affect it but on the contrary has the fundamental object of placing under the compulsory supervision of the federal government all industrial labor relations within the nation. . . .

We think it clear that the National Labor Relations Act may be construed so as to operate within the sphere of constitutional authority. The jurisdiction conferred upon the Board, and invoked in this instance, is found in § 10(a), which provides:

"Sec. 10(a). The Board is empowered, as hereinafter provided, to prevent any person from engaging in any unfair labor practice (listed in section 8) affecting commerce."

The critical words of this provision, prescribing the limits of the Board's authority in dealing with the labor practices, are "affecting commerce." The Act specifically defines the "commerce" to which it refers (§ 2(6)):

"The term 'commerce' means trade, traffic, commerce, transportation, or communication among the several States . . .."

There can be no question that the commerce thus contemplated by the Act . . . is interstate and foreign commerce in the constitutional sense. The Act also defines the term "affecting commerce" (§ 2(7)):

"The term 'affecting commerce' means in commerce, or burdening or obstructing commerce or the free flow of commerce, or having led or tending to lead to a labor dispute burdening or obstructing commerce or the free flow of commerce."

[The Act] purports to reach only what may be deemed to burden or obstruct that commerce and, thus qualified, it must be construed as contemplating the exercise of control within constitutional bounds. It is a familiar principle that acts which directly burden or obstruct interstate or foreign commerce, or its free flow, are within the reach of the congressional power. Acts having that effect are not rendered immune because they grow out of labor disputes. . . . It is the effect upon commerce, not the source of the injury, which is the criterion. . . . Whether or not particular action does affect commerce in such a close and intimate fashion as to be subject to federal control, and hence to lie within the authority conferred upon the Board, is left by the statute to be determined as individual cases arise. We are thus to inquire whether in the instant case the constitutional boundary has been passed.

Second. The unfair labor practices in question. . . .

. . . [I]n its present application, the statute goes no further than to safeguard the right of employees to self-organization and to select representatives of their own choosing for collective bargaining or other mutual protection without restraint or coercion by their employer.

That is a fundamental right. Employees have as clear a right to organize and select their representatives for lawful purposes as the respondent has to organize its business and select its own officers and agents. Discrimination and coercion to prevent the free exercise of the right of employees to self-organization and representation is a proper subject for condemnation by competent legislative authority. . . .

Third. The application of the Act employees engaged in production.— The principle involved.—Respondent says that whatever may be said of employees engaged in interstate commerce, the industrial relations and activities in the manufacturing department of respondent's enterprise are not subject to federal regulation. The argument rests upon the proposition that manufacturing in itself is not commerce. Kidd v. Pearson, 128 U.S. 1, 20, 21; Schechter Corp. v. United States, supra; Carter v. Carter Coal Co., 298 U.S. 238, 304, 317, 327.

The Government distinguishes these cases. The various parts of respondent's enterprise are described as interdependent and as thus involving "a great movement of iron ore, coal and limestone along well-defined paths to the steel mills, thence through them, and thence in the form of steel products into the consuming centers of the country—a definite and well-understood course of business." It is urged that these activities constitute a "stream" or "flow" of commerce, of which the Aliquippa manufacturing plant is the focal point, and that industrial strife at that point would cripple the entire movement. Reference is made to our decision sustaining the Packers and Stockyards Act. Stafford v. Wallace, 258 U.S. 495. . . .

Respondent contends that the instant case presents material distinctions. . . . . Hence respondent argues that "If importation and exportation in interstate commerce do not singly transfer purely local activities into the field of congressional regulation, it should follow that their combination would not alter the local situation." . . .

We do not find it necessary to determine whether these features of defendant's business dispose of the asserted analogy to the "stream of commerce" cases. The instances in which that metaphor has been used are but particular, and not exclusive, illustrations of the protective power which the Government invokes in support of the present Act. The congressional authority to protect interstate commerce from burdens and obstructions is not limited to transactions which can be deemed to be an essential part of a "flow" of interstate or foreign commerce. Burdens and obstructions may be due to injurious action springing from other sources. The fundamental principle is that the power to regulate commerce is the power to enact "all appropriate legislation" for "its protection and advancement" (The Daniel Ball, 10 Wall. 557, 564); to adopt measures "to promote its growth and insure its safety" (Mobile County v. Kimball, 102 U.S. 691, 696, 697); "to foster, protect, control and restrain." Second Employers' Liability Cases, supra, p. 47. . . . That power is plenary and may be exerted to protect interstate commerce "no matter what the source of the dangers which threaten it." Second Employers' Liability Cases, p. 51; Schechter Corp. v. United States, supra. Although activities may be intrastate in character when separately considered, if they have such a close and substantial relation to interstate commerce that their control is essential or appropriate to protect that commerce from burdens and obstructions, Congress cannot be denied the power to exercise that control. Schechter Corp. v. United States, supra. Undoubtedly the scope of this power must be considered in the light of our dual system of government and may not be extended so as to embrace effects upon interstate commerce so indirect and remote that to embrace them, in view of our complex society, would effectually obliterate the distinction between what is national and what is local and create a completely centralized government. Id. The question is necessarily one of degree. . . .

That intrastate activities, by reason of close and intimate relation to interstate commerce, may fall within federal control is demonstrated in the case of carriers who are engaged in both interstate and intrastate transportation. There federal control has been found essential to secure the freedom of interstate traffic from interference or unjust discrimination and to promote the efficiency of the interstate service. . . . It is manifest that intrastate rates deal *primarily* with a local activity. But in rate-making they bear such a close relation to interstate rates that effective control of the one must embrace some control over the other. . . . Other illustrations are found in the broad requirements of the Safety Appliance Act and the Hours of Service Act. Southern Railway Co. v. United States, 222 U.S. 20 . . . . It is said that this exercise of federal power has relation to the maintenance of adequate instrumentalities of interstate commerce. But the agency is not superior to the commerce which uses it. The protective power extends to the former because it exists as to the latter.

The close and intimate effect which brings the subject within the reach of federal power may be due to activities in relation to productive industry although the industry when separately viewed is local. This has been abundantly illustrated in the application of the federal Anti-Trust Act. . . .

It is thus apparent that the fact that the employees here concerned were engaged in production is not determinative. The question remains as to the effect upon interstate commerce of the labor practice involved. In the Schechter case, supra, we found that the effect there was so remote as to be beyond the federal power. To find "immediacy or directness" there was to find it "almost everywhere," a result inconsistent with the maintenance of our federal system. In the Carter case, supra, the Court was of the opinion that the provisions of the statute relating to production were invalid upon several grounds . . .. These cases are not controlling here.

Fourth. Effects of the unfair labor practice in respondent's enterprise. —Giving full weight to respondent's contention with respect to a break in the complete continuity of the "stream of commerce" by reason of respondent's manufacturing operations, the fact remains that the stoppage of those operations by industrial strife would have a most serious effect upon interstate commerce. In view of respondent's far-flung activities, it is idle to say that the effect would be indirect or remote. It is obvious that it would be immediate and might be catastrophic. We are asked to shut our eyes to the plainest facts of our national life and to deal with the question of direct and indirect effects in an intellectual vacuum. Because there may be but indirect and remote effects upon interstate commerce in connection with a host of local enterprises throughout the country, it does not follow that other industrial activities do not have such a close and intimate relation to interstate commerce as to make the presence of industrial strife a matter of the most urgent national concern. When industries organize themselves on a national scale, making their relation to interstate commerce the dominant factor in their activities, how can it be maintained that their industrial labor relations constitute a forbidden field into which Congress may not enter when it is necessary to protect interstate commerce from the paralyzing consequences of industrial war? We have often said that interstate commerce itself is a practical conception. It is equally true that interferences with that commerce must be appraised by a judgment that does not ignore actual experience.

Experience has abundantly demonstrated that the recognition of the right of employees to self-organization and to have representatives of their own choosing for the purpose of collective bargaining is often an essential condition of industrial peace. Refusal to confer and negotiate has been one of the most prolific causes of strife. This is such an outstanding fact in the history of labor disturbances that it is a proper subject of judicial notice and requires no citation of instances. . . .

These questions have frequently engaged the attention of Congress and have been the subject of many inquiries. The steel industry is one of the great basic industries of the United States, with ramifying activities affecting interstate commerce at every point. The Government aptly refers to the steel strike of 1919–1920 with its far-reaching consequences. The fact that there appears to have been no major disturbance in that industry in the more recent period did not dispose of the possibilities of future and like dangers to interstate commerce which Congress was entitled to foresee and to exercise its protective power to forestall. It is not necessary again to detail the facts as to respondent's enterprise. Instead of being beyond the pale, we think that it presents in a most striking way the close and intimate relation which a manufacturing industry may have to interstate commerce and we have no doubt that Congress had constitutional authority to safeguard the right of respondent's employees to self-organization and freedom in the choice of representatives for collective bargaining.

Fifth. The means which the Act employs.—Questions under the due process clause and other constitutional restrictions. [These objections were also rejected.]

Our conclusion is that the order of the Board was within its competency and that the Act is valid as here applied. . . .

Reversed.

Mr. Justice McREYNOLDS delivered the following dissenting opinion in the cases preceding. [The dissent was applicable to Jones & Laughlin and to two companion cases. NLRB v. Fruehauf Trailer Co., 301 U.S. 49, involved the largest trailer manufacturer in the United States, with sales offices in twelve states. NLRB v. Friedman-Harry Marks Clothing Co., 301 U.S. 58, involved a Virginia clothing manufacturer. The majority emphasized that over 99 percent of the raw materials came from other states and that over 80 percent of the products were sold to other states. The dissent pointed out that the company produced "less than one-half of one per cent of the men's clothing produced in the United States and employs 800 of the 150,000 workmen engaged therein."]

Mr. Justice VAN DEVANTER, Mr. Justice SUTHERLAND, Mr. Justice BUTLER and I are unable to agree with the decisions. . . .

The three respondents happen to be manufacturing concerns—one large, two relatively small. The Act is now applied to each upon grounds common to all. Obviously what is determined as to these concerns may gravely affect a multitude of employers who engage in a great variety of private enterprises—mercantile, manufacturing, publishing, stock-raising, mining, etc. It puts into the hands of a Board power of control over purely local industry beyond anything heretofore deemed permissible. . . .

Any effect on interstate commerce by the discharge of employees shown here, would be indirect and remote in the highest degree, as consideration of the facts will show. In [Jones & Laughlin] ten men out of ten thousand were discharged; in the other cases only a few. The immediate effect in the factory may be to create discontent among all those employed and a strike may follow, which, in turn, may result in reducing production, which ultimately may reduce the volume of goods moving in interstate commerce. By this chain of indirect and progressively remote events we finally reach the evil with which it is said the legislation under consideration undertakes to deal. A more remote and indirect interference with interstate commerce or a more definite invasion of the powers reserved to the states is difficult, if not impossible, to imagine. . . .

We are told that Congress may protect the "stream of commerce" and that one who buys raw material without the state, manufactures it therein, and ships the output to another state is in that stream. Therefore it is said he may be prevented from doing anything which may interfere with its flow.

This, too, goes beyond the constitutional limitations heretofore enforced. If a man raises cattle and regularly delivers them to a carrier for interstate shipment, may Congress prescribe the conditions under which he may employ or discharge helpers on the ranch? The products of a mine pass daily into interstate commerce; many things are brought to it from other states. Are the owners and the miners within the power of Congress in respect of the miners' tenure and discharge? May a mill owner be prohibited from closing his factory or discontinuing his business because so to do would stop the flow of products to and from his plant in interstate commerce? May employees in a factory be restrained from quitting work in a body because this will close the factory and thereby stop the flow of commerce? May arson of a factory be made a Federal offense whenever this would interfere with such flow? If the business cannot continue with the existing wage scale, may Congress command a reduction? If the ruling of the Court just announced is adhered to these questions suggest some of the problems certain to arise. . . .

There is no ground on which reasonably to hold that refusal by a manufacturer, whose raw materials come from states other than that of his factory and whose products are regularly carried to other states, to bargain collectively with employees in his manufacturing plant, directly affects interstate commerce. In such business, there is not one but two distinct movements or streams in interstate transportation. The first brings in raw material and there ends. Then follows manufacture, a separate and local activity. Upon completion of this, and not before, the second distinct movement or stream in interstate commerce begins and the products go to other states. Such is the common course for small as well as large industries. It is unreasonable and unprecedented to say the commerce clause confers upon Congress power to govern relations between employers and employees in these local activities. . . .

It is gravely stated that experience teaches that if an employer discourages membership in "any organization of any kind" "in which employees participate, and which exists for the purpose in whole or in part of dealing with employers concerning grievances, labor disputes, wages, rates of pay, hours of employment or conditions of work," discontent may follow and this in turn may lead to a strike, and as the outcome of the strike there may be a block in the stream of interstate commerce. Therefore Congress may inhibit the discharge! Whatever effect any cause of discontent may ultimately have upon commerce is far too indirect to justify Congressional regulation. Almost anything—marriage, birth, death—may in some fashion affect commerce. . . .

UNITED STATES v. DARBY

312 U.S. 100, 61 S.Ct. 451, 85 L.Ed. 609 (1941).

Appeal from the District Court of the United States for the Southern District of Georgia.

Mr. Justice STONE delivered the opinion of the Court.

The two principal questions raised by the record in this case are, *first,* whether Congress has constitutional power to prohibit the shipment in interstate commerce of lumber manufactured by employees whose wages are less than a prescribed minimum or whose weekly hours of labor at that wage are greater than a prescribed maximum, and, *second,* whether it has power to prohibit the employment of workmen in the production of goods "for interstate commerce" at other than prescribed wages and hours. A subsidiary question is whether in connection with such prohibitions Congress can require the employer subject to them to keep records showing the hours worked each day and week by each of his employees including those engaged "in the production and manufacture of goods to-wit, lumber, for 'interstate commerce.'"

Appellee demurred to an indictment found in the district court for southern Georgia charging him with violation of § 15(a) (1) (2) and (5) of the Fair Labor Standards Act of 1938 . . .. The district court sustained the demurrer and quashed the indictment and the case comes here on direct appeal under § 238 of the Judicial Code, as amended . . . which authorizes an appeal to this Court when the judgment sustaining the demurrer "is based on the invalidity or construction of the statute upon which the indictment is founded."

The Fair Labor Standards Act set up a comprehensive legislative scheme for preventing the shipment in interstate commerce of certain products and commodities produced in the United States under labor conditions as respects wages and hours which fail to conform to standards set up by the Act. Its purpose, as we judicially know from the declaration of policy in § 2(a) of the Act, and the reports of Congressional committees proposing the legislation, . . . is to exclude from interstate commerce goods produced for the commerce and to prevent their production for interstate commerce, under conditions detrimental to the maintenance of the minimum standards of living necessary for health and general well-being; and to prevent the use of interstate commerce as the means of competition in the distribution of goods so produced, and as the means of spreading and perpetuating such substandard labor conditions among the workers of the several states. The Act also sets up an administrative procedure whereby those standards may from time to time be modified generally as to industries subject to the Act or within an industry in accordance with specified standards, by an administrator acting in collaboration with "Industry Committees" appointed by him.

Section 15 of the statute prohibits certain specified acts and § 16(a) punishes willful violation of it by a fine of not more than $10,000 and punishes each conviction after the first by imprisonment of not more than six months or by the specified fine or both. Section 15(1) makes unlawful the shipment in interstate commerce of any goods "in the production of which any employee was employed in violation of section 6 or section 7," which provide, among other things, that during the first year of operation of the Act a minimum wage of 25 cents per hour shall be paid to employees "engaged in [interstate] commerce or the production of goods for [interstate] commerce," § 6, and that the maximum hours of employment for employees "engaged in commerce or the production of goods for commerce" without increased compensation for overtime, shall be forty-four hours a week. § 7.

§ 15(a) (2) makes it unlawful to violate the provisions of §§ 6 and 7 including the minimum wage and maximum hour requirements just mentioned for employees engaged in production of goods for commerce. § 15(a) (5) makes it unlawful for an employer subject to the Act to violate § 11(c) which requires him to keep such records of the persons employed by him and of their wages and hours of employment as the administrator shall prescribe by regulation or order.

The indictment charges that appellee is engaged, in the state of Georgia, in the business of acquiring raw materials, which he manufactures into finished lumber with the intent, when manufactured, to ship it in interstate commerce to customers outside the state, and that he does in fact so ship a large part of the lumber so produced. There are numerous counts charging appellee [with violations of the Act]. The district court quashed the indictment in its entirety upon the broad grounds that the Act, which it interpreted as a regulation of manufacture within the states, is unconstitutional. . . .

The prohibition of shipment of the proscribed goods in interstate commerce. § 15(a) (1) prohibits, and the indictment charges the shipment in interstate commerce, of goods produced for interstate commerce by employees whose wages and hours of employment do not conform to the requirements of the Act. [T]he only question arising under the commerce clause with respect to such shipments is whether Congress has the constitutional power to prohibit them.

While manufacture is not of itself interstate commerce the shipment of manufactured goods interstate is such commerce and the prohibition of such shipment by Congress is indubitably a regulation of the commerce. The power to regulate commerce is the power "to prescribe the rule by which commerce is governed." Gibbons v. Ogden, 9 Wheat. 1, 196. It extends not only to those regulations which aid, foster and protect the commerce, but embraces those which prohibit it. . . . It is conceded that the power of Congress to prohibit transportation in interstate commerce includes noxious articles, . . . stolen articles, . . . kidnapped persons, . . . and articles such as intoxicating liquor or convict made goods, traffic in which is forbidden or restricted by the laws of the state of destination. . . .

But it is said that the present prohibition falls within the scope of none of these categories; that while the prohibition is nominally a regulation of the commerce its motive or purpose is regulation of wages and hours of persons engaged in manufacture, the control of which has been reserved to the states and upon which Georgia and some of the states of destination have placed no restriction; that the effect of the present statute is not to exclude the prescribed articles from interstate commerce in aid of state regulation as in Kentucky Whip & Collar Co. v. Illinois Central R. R. Co. [299 U.S. 334], but instead, under the guise of a regulation of interstate commerce, it undertakes to regulate wages and hours within the state contrary to the policy of the state which has elected to leave them unregulated.

The power of Congress over interstate commerce "is complete in itself, may be exercised to its utmost extent, and acknowledges no limitations other than are prescribed by the Constitution." Gibbons v. Ogden, supra, 196. That power can neither be enlarged nor diminished by the exercise or non-exercise of state power. Kentucky Whip & Collar Co. v. Illinois Central R. R. Co., supra. Congress, following its own conception of public policy concerning the restrictions which may appropriately be imposed on interstate commerce, is free to exclude from the commerce articles whose use in the states for which they are destined it may conceive to be injurious to the public health, morals or welfare, even though the state has not sought to regulate their use. . . .

Such regulation is not a forbidden invasion of state power merely because either its motive or its consequence is to restrict the use of articles of commerce within the states of destination; and is not prohibited unless by other Constitutional provisions. It is no objection to the assertion of the power to regulate interstate commerce that its exercise is attended by the same incidents which attend the exercise of the police power of the states. . . .

The motive and purpose of the present regulation is plainly to make effective the Congressional conception of public policy that interstate commerce should not be made the instrument of competition in the distribution of goods produced under substandard labor conditions, which competition is injurious to the commerce and to the states from and to which the commerce flows. The motive and purpose of a regulation of interstate commerce are matters for the legislative judgment upon the exercise of which the Constitution places no restriction and over which the courts are given no control. McCray v. United States, 195 U.S. 27; Sonzinsky v. United States, 300 U.S. 506, 513, and cases cited. "The judicial cannot prescribe to the legislative department of the government limitations upon the exercise of its ackowledged power." Veazie Bank v. Fenno, 8 Wall. 533. Whatever their motive and purpose, regulations of commerce which do not infringe some constitutional prohibition are within the plenary power conferred on Congress by the Commerce Clause. Subject only to that limitation, presently to be considered, we conclude that the prohibition of the shipment interstate of goods produced under the forbidden substandard labor conditions is within the constitutional authority of Congress.

In the more than a century which has elapsed since the decision of Gibbons v. Ogden, these principles of constitutional interpretation have been so long and repeatedly recognized by this Court as applicable to the Commerce Clause, that there would be little occasion for repeating them now were it not for the decision of this Court twenty-two years ago in Hammer v. Dagenhart, 247 U.S. 251. In that case it was held by a bare majority of the Court over the powerful and now classic dissent of Mr. Justice Holmes setting forth the fundamental issues involved, that Congress was without power to exclude the products of child labor from interstate commerce. The reasoning and conclusion of the Court's opinion there cannot be reconciled with the conclusion which we have reached, that the power of Congress under the Commerce Clause is plenary to exclude any article from interstate commerce subject only to the specific prohibitions of the Constitution.

Hammer v. Dagenhart has not been followed. The distinction on which the decision was rested that Congressional power to prohibit interstate commerce is limited to articles which in themselves have some harmful or deleterious property—a distinction which was novel when made and unsupported by any provision of the Constitution—has long since been abandoned. . . . The thesis of the opinion that the motive of the prohibition or its effect to control in some measure the use or production within the states of the article thus excluded from the commerce can operate to deprive the regulation of its constitutional authority has long since ceased to have force. . . .

The conclusion is inescapable that Hammer v. Dagenhart was a departure from the principles which have prevailed in the interpretation of the Commerce Clause both before and since the decision and that such vitality, as a precedent, as it then had has long since been exhausted. It should be and now is overruled.

Validity of the wage and hour requirements. Section 15(a) (2) and §§ 6 and 7 require employers to conform to the wage and hour provisions with respect to all employees engaged in the production of goods for interstate commerce. As appellees' employees are not alleged to be "engaged in interstate commerce" the validity of the prohibition turns on the question whether the employment, under other than the prescribed labor standards, of employees engaged in the production of goods for interstate commerce is so related to the commerce and so affects it as to be within the reach of the power of Congress to regulate it. . . .

Without attempting to define the precise limits of the phrase ["production for commerce"], we think the acts alleged in the indictment are within the sweep of the statute. The obvious purpose of the Act was not only to prevent the interstate transportation of the proscribed product, but to stop the initial step toward transportation, production with the purpose of so transporting it. Congress was not unaware that most manufacturing businesses shipping their product in interstate commerce make it in their shops without reference to its ultimate destination and then after manufacture select some of it for shipment interstate and some intrastate according to the daily demands of their business, and that it would be practically impossible, without disrupting manufacturing businesses, to restrict the prohibited kind of production to the particular pieces of lumber, cloth, furniture or the like which later move in interstate rather than intrastate commerce. . . .

The recognized need of drafting a workable statute and the well known circumstances in which it was to be applied are persuasive of the conclusion, which the legislative history supports . . . that the "production for commerce" intended includes at least production of goods, which, at the time of production, the employer, according to the normal course of his business, intends or expects to move in interstate commerce although, through the exigencies of the business, all of the goods may not thereafter actually enter interstate commerce.

There remains the question whether such restriction on the production of goods for commerce is a permissible exercise of the commerce power. The power of Congress over interstate commerce is not confined to the regulation of commerce among the states. It extends to those activities intrastate which so affect interstate commerce or the exercise of the power of Congress over it as to make regulation of them appropriate means to the attainment of a legitimate end, the exercise of the granted power of Congress to regulate interstate commerce. . . .

A recent example is the National Labor Relations Act for the regulation of employer and employee relations in industries in which strikes, induced by unfair labor practices named in the Act, tend to disturb or obstruct interstate commerce. . . . But long before the adoption of the National Labor Relations Act this Court had many times held that the power of Congress to regulate interstate commerce extends to the regulation through legislative action of activities intrastate which have a substantial effect on the commerce or the exercise of the Congressional power over it. . . .

In such legislation Congress has sometimes left it to the courts to determine whether the intrastate activities have the prohibited effect on the commerce, as in the Sherman Act. It has sometimes left it to an administrative board or agency to determine whether the activities sought to be regulated or prohibited have such effect, as in the case of the Interstate Commerce Act, and the National Labor Relations Act, or whether they come within the statutory definition of the prohibited Act, as in the Federal Trade Commission Act. And sometimes Congress itself has said that a particular activity affects the commerce, as it did in the present Act, the Safety Appliance Act and the Railway Labor Act. In passing on the validity of legislation of the class last mentioned the only function of courts is to determine whether the particular activity regulated or prohibited is within the reach of the federal power. . . .

Congress, having by the present Act adopted the policy of excluding from interstate commerce all goods produced for the commerce which do not conform to the specified labor standards, it may choose the means reasonably adapted to the attainment of the permitted end, even though they involve control of intrastate activities. Such legislation has often been sustained with respect to powers, other than the commerce power granted to the national government, when the means chosen, although not themselves within the granted power, were nevertheless deemed appropriate aids to the accomplishment of some purpose within an admitted power of the national government. . . . A familiar like exercise of power is the regulation of intrastate transactions which are so commingled with or related to interstate commerce that all must be regulated if the interstate commerce is to be effectively controlled. Shreveport Case, 234 U.S. 342; Currin v. Wallace, 306 U.S. 1; Mulford v. Smith, supra. Similarly Congress may require inspection and preventive treatment of all cattle in a disease infected area in order to prevent shipment in interstate commerce of some of the cattle without the treatment. Thornton v. United States, 271 U.S. 414. It may prohibit the removal, at destination, of labels required by the Pure Food & Drugs Act to be affixed to articles transported in interstate commerce. McDermott v. Wisconsin, 228 U.S. 115. . . .

We think also that § 15(a) (2), now under consideration, is sustainable independently of § 15(a) (1), which prohibits shipment or transportation of the proscribed goods. As we have said the evils aimed at by the Act are the spread of substandard labor conditions through the use of the facilities of interstate commerce for competition by the goods so produced with those produced under the prescribed or better labor conditions; and the consequent dislocation of the commerce itself caused by the impairment or destruction of local businesses by competition made effective through interstate commerce. The Act is thus directed at the suppression of a method or kind of competition in interstate commerce which it has in effect condemned as "unfair," as the Clayton Act has condemned other "unfair methods of competition" made effective through interstate commerce. . . .

The means adopted by § 15(a) (2) for the protection of interstate commerce by the suppression of the production of the condemned goods for interstate commerce is so related to the commerce and so affects it as to be within the reach of the commerce power. . . . Congress, to attain its objective in the suppression of nationwide competition in interstate commerce by goods produced under substandard labor conditions, has made no distinction as to the volume or amount of shipments in the commerce or of production for commerce by any particular shipper or producer. It recognized that in present day industry, competition by a small part may affect the whole and that the total effect of the competition of many small producers may be great. See H.Rept.No. 2182, 75th Cong. 1st Sess., p. 7. The legislation aimed at a whole embraces all its parts. . . .

So far as Carter v. Carter Coal Co., 298 U.S. 238, is inconsistent with this conclusion, its doctrine is limited in principle by the decisions under the Sherman Act and the National Labor Relations Act, which we have cited and which we follow. . . .

Our conclusion is unaffected by the Tenth Amendment which provides: "The powers not delegated to the United States by the Constitution, nor prohibited by it to the States, are reserved to the States respectively, or to the people." The amendment states but a truism that all is retained which has not been surrendered. There is nothing in the history of its adoption to suggest that it was more than declaratory of the relationship between the national and state governments as it had been established by the Constitution before the amendment or that its purpose was other than to allay fears that the new national government might seek to exercise powers not granted, and that the states might not be able to exercise fully their reserved powers. . . .

From the beginning and for many years the amendment has been construed as not depriving the national government of authority to resort to all means for the exercise of a granted power which are appropriate and plainly adapted to the permitted end. . . . Whatever doubts may have arisen of the soundness of that conclusion, they have been put at rest by the decisions under the Sherman Act and the National Labor Relations Act which we have cited. . . .

Validity of the requirement of records of wages and hours. § 15(a) (5) and § 11(c). These requirements are incidental to those for the prescribed wages and hours, and hence validity of the former turns on validity of the latter. Since, as we have held, Congress may require production for interstate commerce to conform to those conditions, it may require the employer, as a means of enforcing the valid law, to keep a record showing whether he has in fact complied with it. The requirement for records even of the intrastate transaction is an appropriate means to the legitimate end. . . .

Validity of the wage and hour provisions under the Fifth Amendment. [The due process objections were rejected.]

Reversed.

IMPLICATIONS OF DARBY AND RECENT USES OF THE COMMERCE–PROHIBITING DEVICE AS A REGULATORY TOOL

1. *The search for limits.* a. Do the "prohibition of shipment" aspects of Darby leave any "local" activity outside of congressional power? Consider again the questions raised earlier, especially in sec. 3. Note that the Court disavows all control over the "motive and purpose" of such regulation—citing only tax cases as authority. Was such a broad disavowal necessary or justified? Consider, in examining cases involving the taxing power as a regulatory device in the next chapter, whether the Court has in fact disavowed all "motive and purpose" control in the tax area. Does the disavowal in Darby signify a final rejection of the "pretext" limitation in McCulloch v. Maryland, where Marshall stated that the Court would invalidate laws "for the accomplishment of objects not entrusted to the government"? Would and should the Court sustain, as commerce power-supported legisla-

tion, prohibitions of interstate movement of persons not educated, or married, in accordance with national standards? Could Congress at least prohibit interstate shipment of goods by such persons? What "objects" are "entrusted" to Congress by the commerce clause? Should the Court restrict Congress to "commercial," "economic" objects? Did the opportunity to impose such a limitation pass with the line of decisions traced in sec. 3, starting with the Lottery Case?

b. Note that the Darby opinion sustains the wage and hour regulations of intrastate production activities as "means reasonably adapted to the attainment of the permitted end" of "excluding from interstate commerce all goods produced" under non-conforming standards. After offering this justification, the Court also finds the production regulations "sustainable independently" because of the "effect" of the intrastate activities on interstate commerce. If no such "effect" had been found, would the regulations have been valid? If so, has all discussion of "affecting commerce" or "stream of commerce" justifications become unnecessary? May Congress regulate any intrastate activity through a two-step bootstrap device: (1) prohibiting interstate movement by goods or persons connected with that activity; and (2), as a "means reasonably adapted to the attainment of the permitted end," directly regulating the intrastate activity? (See also the questions at the end of sec. 3, above.) Would validation of this technique constitute a judicial confession of the bankruptcy of commerce power doctrine? Are the "political safeguards of federalism" adequate protection against abuses of this power? In the area of economic regulation? In other areas of regulation as well?

c. In his Holmes Lecture in 1959, Herbert Wechsler said: "One of the speculations that I must confess I find intriguing is upon the question whether there are any neutral principles that might have been employed to mark the limits of the commerce power of the Congress in terms more circumscribed than the virtual abandonment of limits in the principle that has prevailed." Wechsler, "Toward Neutral Principles of Constitutional Law," 73 Harv.L.Rev. 1, 23–24 (1959), Selected Essays 1938–1962 (1963), 463, 478, Principles, Politics and Fundamental Law (1961), 3, 33. In reflecting on the contents of this section, consider what limits might have been employed—and what limits exist. Do the Jackson and Clark opinions in the Gambling Devices case in 1953 (infra, following these notes) suggest limits on the broad implications of the Darby case? Is there need to fashion greater limits? Is it too late to do so? When did it become too late?

2. *Some recent police regulations.* As noted in sec. 3, above, regulation through prohibition of commerce did not come to a complete halt with the Child Labor Case. Some examples of the subsequent uses of the technique for "police" purposes follow:

a. *Convict-made goods.* Kentucky Whip & Collar Co. v. Illinois Central R. Co., 299 U.S. 334 (1937), sustained the Ashurst-Sumners Act which made it unlawful to transport convict-made goods into any state where the receipt, sale or possession of such goods violated state law. The Court said: "The Congress has not sought to exercise a power not granted or to usurp the police powers of the States. It has not acted on any assumption of a power enlarged by virtue of state action. The Congress has exercised its plenary power which is subject to no limitation other than that which is founded in the Constitution itself. The Congress has formulated its own policy and established its own rule. The fact that it has adopted its rule in order to aid the enforcement of valid state laws affords no ground for constitutional objection."

b. *Kidnaping.* The Federal Kidnaping Act provides that "whoever shall knowingly transport or cause to be transported, or aid or abet in transporting, in interstate or foreign commerce, any person who shall have been unlawfully seized, confined, inveigled, decoyed, kidnaped, abducted, or carried away by any means whatsoever and held for ransom or reward or otherwise . . . shall be punished . . . : Provided, That the failure to release such person within seven days after he shall have been unlawfully seized, confined, inveigled, decoyed, kidnaped, abducted, or carried away shall create a presumption that such person has been transported in interstate or foreign commerce, but such presumption shall not be conclusive." See Gooch v. United States, 297 U.S. 124 (1936).

c. *Fugitives.* The Fugitive Felon and Witness Act provides that "it shall be unlawful for any person to move or travel in interstate or foreign commerce from any State, Territory, or possession of the United States, or the District of Columbia, with intent either (1) to avoid prosecution for murder, kidnaping, burglary, robbery, mayhem, rape, assault with a dangerous weapon, or extortion accompanied by threats of violence, or attempt to commit any of the foregoing, under the laws of the place from which he flees, or (2) to avoid giving testimony in any criminal proceeding in such place in which the commission of a felony is charged. Any person who violates the provision of this Act shall, upon conviction thereof, be punished by a fine of not more than $5,000 or by imprisonment for not longer than five years, or by both such fine and imprisonment." See Hemans v. United States, 163 F. 2d 228 (6th Cir. 1947).

d. *Organized crime.* More recent uses of the technique have been especially concerned with combating organized crime. See, e.g., President Johnson's Message, Law Enforcement and Administration of Justice, H.Doc. No. 103, 89th Cong., 1st Sess. (1965). Consider the following section of 18 U.S.C., one of several anti-crime provisions enacted in response to Kennedy Administration proposals in 1961. Does it raise constitutional difficulties in any of its applications?

§ 1952. *"Interstate and foreign travel or transportation in aid of racketeering enterprises.*

"(a) Whoever travels in interstate or foreign commerce or uses any facility in interstate or foreign commerce, including the mail, with intent to—

"(1) distribute the proceeds of any unlawful activity; or

"(2) commit any crime of violence to further any unlawful activity; or

"(3) otherwise promote, manage, establish, carry on, or facilitate the promotion, management, or carrying on, of any unlawful activity, and thereafter performs or attempts to perform any of the acts specified in subparagraphs (1), (2), and (3), shall be fined not more than $10,000 or imprisoned for not more than five years, or both.

"(b) As used in this section "unlawful activity" means (1) any business enterprise involving gambling, liquor on which the Federal excise tax has not been paid, narcotics, or prostitution offenses in violation of the laws of the State in which they are committed or of the United States, or (2) extortion or bribery in violation of the laws of the State in which committed or of the United States. . . . ''

    e. *Riots and disorders.* The format of the Kennedy Administration's anti-racketeering law may have inspired the scheme of the anti-riot amendments to Title I of the Civil Rights Act of 1968 (the provisions that were the basis for the federal conspiracy prosecutions arising out of the demonstrations at the 1968 Democratic National Convention in Chicago). Note the close similarity to the pattern of 18 U.S.C. § 1952 above (the anti-racketeering law) in the 1968 anti-riot law, 18 U.S.C. § 2101:

    § 2101. *"Riots.*

    "(a) (1) Whoever travels in interstate or foreign commerce or uses any facility of interstate or foreign commerce, including, but not limited to, the mail, telegraph, telephone, radio, or television, with intent—

    "(A) to incite a riot; or

    "(B) to organize, promote, encourage, participate in, or carry on a riot; or

    "(C) to commit any act of violence in furtherance of a riot; or

    "(D) to aid or abet any person in inciting or participating in or carrying on a riot or committing any act of violence in furtherance of a riot;
and who either during the course of any such travel or use or thereafter performs or attempts to perform any other overt act for any purpose specified in subparagraph (A), (B), (C), or (D) of this paragraph—

    "Shall be fined not more than $10,000, or imprisoned not more than five years, or both.

    "(b) In any prosecution under this section, proof that a defendant engaged or attempted to engage in one or more of the overt acts described in subpargaraph (A), (B), (C), or (D) of paragraph (1) of subsection (a) and (1) have traveled in interstate or foreign commerce, or (2) has use of or used any facility of interstate or foreign commerce, including but not limited to, mail, telegraph, telephone, radio, or television, to communicate with or broadcast to any person or group of persons prior to such overt acts, such travel or use shall be admissible proof to establish that such defendant traveled in or used such facility of interstate or foreign commerce. . . . ''*

    Compare Title X of the 1968 Civil Rights Act—a Title called the "Civil Obedience Act of 1968." It includes the following addition to Title 18 of the United States Code:

    § 231. *"Civil disorders*

    "(a) (1) Whoever teaches or demonstrates to any other person the use, application, or making of any firearm or explosive or incendiary device, or technique capable of causing injury or death to persons, knowing or having

---

* Is there a protected interest in interstate movement of persons that limits congressional commerce restrictions on interstate travel? For a recent consideration, see the decision invalidating residence requirements in welfare laws (especially Chief Justice Warren's separate opinion) in Shapiro v. Thompson, 394 U.S. 618 (1969) (printed infra, chap. 14, p. 1036, below). Note also, among earlier cases examining asserted rights to travel interstate, Crandall v. Nevada, 6 Wall. 35 (1867), Edwards v. California, 314 U.S. 160 (1941), United States v. Guest, 383 U.S. 745 (1966) (all infra), and see especially the note on personal mobility and the Edwards case, chap. 8, p. 652, infra.

reason to know or intending that the same will be unlawfully employed for use in, or in furtherance of, a civil disorder which may in any way or degree obstruct, delay, or adversely affect commerce or the movement of any article or commodity in commerce or the conduct or performance of any federally protected function; or

"(2) Whoever transports or manufactures for transportation in commerce any firearm, or explosive or incendiary device, knowing or having reason to know or intending that the same will be used unlawfully in furtherance of a civil disorder; or

"(3) Whoever commits or attempts to commit any act to obstruct, impede, or interfere with any fireman or law enforcement officer lawfully engaged in the lawful performance of his official duties incident to and during the commission of a civil disorder which in any way or degree obstructs, delays, or adversely affects commerce or the movement of any article or commodity in commerce or the conduct or performance of any federally protected function—

"Shall be fined not more than $10,000 or imprisoned not more than five years, or both. . . ."

3. *The Sullivan case: control of acts performed after the interstate movement ends.* a. *The extent of the reach.* Consider the constitutional justification offered to sustain the application of the Federal Food, Drug and Cosmetic Act of 1938 in United States v. Sullivan, 332 U.S. 689 (1948). Respondent, a Columbus, Ga., druggist, had bought a properly labeled 1000-tablet bottle of sulfathiazole from an Atlanta, Ga., wholesaler. The bottle had been shipped to the Atlanta wholesaler by a Chicago supplier six months earlier. Three months after the purchase by the Columbus druggist, he made two retail sales of 12 tablets each. In each case, he removed the tablets from the bottle and placed them in pill boxes marked "sulfathiazole." The pill boxes did not have directions for use or warnings of danger. Section 301(k) of the Act prohibits doing an act with respect to a drug "if such act is done while such article is held for sale after shipment in interstate commerce and results in such article being misbranded." The retail druggist was charged with such misbranding because of the failure to place the directions and warnings on the pill boxes.

The Circuit Court of Appeals reversed respondent's conviction by concluding that Section 301(k) should be "held to apply only to the holding for the first sale by the importer after interstate shipment." The Circuit Court feared that a broader reading "would result in far-reaching inroads upon customary control by local authorities of traditionally local activities" and "would raise grave doubts as to the Act's constitutionality." The Supreme Court reversed, in an opinion by Justice Black. After finding the Act applicable, the Court disposed of the constitutional question in one paragraph:

"It is contended that the Act as we have construed it is beyond any authority granted Congress by the Constitution and that it invades the powers reserved to the States. A similar challenge was made against the Pure Food and Drugs Act of 1906, 34 Stat. 768, and rejected, in McDermott v. Wisconsin, 228 U.S. 115. That Act did not contain § 301(k), but it did prohibit misbranding and authorized seizure of misbranded articles after they were shipped from one State to another, so long as they remained 'unsold.' The authority of Congress to make this requirement was upheld as a proper exercise of its powers under the commerce clause. There are two variants between the circumstances of that case and this one. In the McDermott case the labels involved were on the original containers; here the labels are required to be put on other than the original containers—the boxes to which the tablets were transferred. Also, in the McDermott case the possessor of the labeled cans held for sale had himself received them by way of an interstate sale and shipment; here, while the petitioner had received the sulfathiazole by way of an intrastate sale and shipment, he bought it from a wholesaler who had received it as the direct consignee of an interstate shipment. These variants are not sufficient we think to detract from the applicability of the McDermott holding to the present decision. In both cases alike the question relates to the constitutional power of Congress under the commerce clause to regulate the branding of articles that have completed an interstate shipment and are being held for future sales in purely local or intrastate commerce. The reasons given for the McDermott holding therefore are equally applicable and persuasive here. And many cases decided since the McDermott decision lend support to the validity of § 301(k). See, e. g., . . . Wickard v. Filburn, 317 U.S. 111 . . . United States v. Darby, 312 U.S. 100 . . . ." [Justice Rutledge concurred; Justice Frankfurter, joined by Justices Reed and Jackson, dissented on the construction of the Act, without mentioning the constitutional issue.]

     b. *The adequacy of the justification.* What is the constitutional basis for this application of the Act? Use of "means reasonably adapted" to "implementing" the commerce-prohibiting provisions? (Section 301(c) forbids the "introduction . . . into interstate commerce" of misbranded drugs.) Control of local activities "affecting" commerce? Control of activities "in" commerce? Does the Court's opinion provide an adequate explanation? Do the citations of Darby and Wickard v. Filburn, p. 314, infra? Does the citation of McDermott v. Wisconsin, 228 U.S. 115 (1913)? (In McDermott, a grocer possessing cans labeled "corn syrup", as required by federal law, was convicted under a Wisconsin law requiring that such cans carry only a "glucose" label. The Court, in reversing the conviction, stated that "Congress may determine for itself the character of the means necessary to make its purpose effectual in preventing the shipment in interstate commerce of articles of a harmful character, and to this end may provide the means of inspection, examination and seizure necessary. . . . The real opportunity for Government inspection may only arise when, as in the present case, the goods as packed have been removed from the outside box in which they were shippd and remain, as the act provides, 'unsold'.")

     4. *Limitless power to regulate economic problems?—The Public Utility Holding Company Act litigation.* a. *Introduction.* The commerce-prohibiting power has also been used to regulate more clearly "economic" problems. Note especially the series of constitutional challenges to the Public Utility Holding Company Act of 1935. To what extent do these decisions rest on commerce-prohibiting techniques of the Lottery Case-Darby variety? To what extent are they independently justified, or justifiable, on "in" commerce or "affecting" commerce grounds? Do these decisions demonstrate that no doctrinal limits on the modern commerce power exist, at least when it is invoked to meet economic needs? (Note the question at the end of 4c and in 4e below).

b.   *Electric Bond & Share.* In Electric Bond & Share Co. v. SEC, 303 U.S. 419 (1938), the Court, with only Justice McReynolds dissenting, sustained provisions compelling registration of holding companies and prohibiting the use of the instrumentalities of commerce (and of the mails) by unregistered companies: "When Congress lays down a valid rule to govern those engaged in transactions in interstate commerce, Congress may deny to those who violate the rule the right to engage in such transactions. Champion v. Ames, 188 U.S. 321."

c.   *North American Co.* In North American Co. v. SEC, 327 U.S. 686 (1946), the Court unanimously sustained a provision authorizing the SEC to require each holding company engaged in commerce to limit its operations to a single integrated public utility system. Justice Murphy wrote: "This broad commerce clause does not operate so as to render the nation powerless to defend itself against economic forces that Congress decrees inimical or destructive to the national economy. Rather it is an affirmative power commensurate with the national needs. . . . It is sufficient to reiterate the well-settled principle that Congress may impose relevant conditions and requirements on those who use the channels of interstate commerce in order that those channels will not become the means of promoting or spreading evil, whether of a physical, moral or economic nature. Brooks v. United States, 267 U.S. 432, 436–437. *This power permits Congress to attack an evil directly at its source, provided that the evil bears a substantial relationship to interstate commerce.* Congress thus has power to make direct assault upon such economic evils as those relating to labor relations, Labor Board v. Jones & Laughlin Corp. . . . ; to wages and hours, United States v. Darby, supra; to market transactions, Stafford v. Wallace . . . ; and to monopolistic practices, Northern Securities Co. v. United States, supra. The fact that an evil may involve a corporation's financial practices, its business structure or its security portfolio does not detract from the power of Congress under the commerce clause to promulgate rules in order to destroy that evil. Once it is established that the evil concerns or affects commerce in more states than one, Congress may act. . . . Congress in . . . the Public Utility Holding Company Act was concerned with the economic evils resulting from uncoordinated and unintegrated public utility holding company systems. These evils were found to be polluting the channels of interstate commerce and to take the form of transactions occurring in and concerning more states than one. Congress also found that the national welfare was thereby harmed, as well as the interests of investors and consumers. These evils, moreover, were traceable in large part to the nature and extent of the securities owned by the holding companies. Congress therefore had power under the commerce clause to attempt to remove those evils by ordering the holding companies to divest themselves of the securities that made such evils possible." [Emphasis added.]

Is the justification offered surprisingly detailed, given the Darby rationale? Could the corporate structure be controlled simply as an implementation of the conditional ban on the use of commerce facilities? Note the italicized sentence. Does it suggest a greater limitation on congressional power than that indicated by the two alternative justifications given in Darby for the regulation of wages and hours in production activities?

d.   *American Power & Light.* Compare American Power & Light Co. v. SEC, 329 U.S. 90 (1946), involving the "death sentence" provision of the Act and sustaining an SEC order compelling the dissolution of the petitioning company because its corporate structure was "unduly and unnecessarily complicated" and "unfairly and inequitably distributed voting power among the security holders." Justice Murphy's opinion for the Court stated:

"The Bond and Share system, including American and Electric, possesses an undeniable interstate character which makes it properly subject, from the statutory standpoint, to the provisions of § 11(b) (2). This vast system embraces utility properties in no fewer than 32 states, from New Jersey to Oregon and from Minnesota to Florida, as well as 12 foreign countries. Bond and Share dominates and controls this system from its headquarters in New York City. As was the situation in the North American case, the proper control and functioning of such an extensive multi-state network of corporations necessitates continuous and substantial use of the mails and the instrumentalities of interstate commerce. . . . Congress, of course, has undoubted power under the commerce clause to impose relevant conditions and requirements on those who use the channels of interstate commerce so that those channels will not be conduits for promoting or perpetuating economic evils. . . . Thus to the extent that corporate business is transacted through such channels, affecting commerce in more states than one, Congress may act directly with respect to that business to protect what it conceives to be the national welfare. . . . To deny that Congress has power to eliminate evils connected with pyramided holding company systems, evils which have been found to be promoted and transmitted by means of interstate commerce, is to deny that Congress can effectively deal with problems concerning the welfare of the national economy. We cannot deny that power. Rather we reaffirm once more the constitutional authority resident in Congress by virtue of the commerce clause to undertake to solve national problems directly and realistically, giving due recognition to the scope of state power. That follows from the fact that the federal commerce power is as broad as the economic needs of the nation."

e. *Substantial limits on broad dicta?* The opinions in these Public Utility Holding Act cases are favorite sources for broad judicial phrases to support commentators' assertions that the modern commerce power is virtually limitless. Yet the limits may be somewhat more substantial than the broad phrases suggest, if the passages are read with a grain of salt and in context. If the commerce power is truly limitless, what explains the extensive Court justifications for uses of the power? Cases disposing of constitutional qualms as curtly as Sullivan (note 3) are rare. Note that even the generous language in the North American case (note 4c) repeatedly speaks of "*economic* evils" and states that the evil regulated must have a substantial relationship to commerce (not simply that the person or activity reached must have some nexus with commerce, whether or not the evil regulated relates to that nexus). Consider, as an example of this problem, the issue suggested by Katzenbach v. McClung, p. 340 below: May racial discrimination at a restaurant be prohibited simply because the restaurant has *some* nexus with commerce (e. g., it serves mustard produced out-of-state)? Or does the commerce clause require that it is *racial discrimination* (the evil regulated), not simply *any* aspect of the restaurant's operations, that must have a relationship to interstate commerce? Contrast the statements of Attorney General Kennedy and Assistant Attorney General Marshall in the Senate hearings on the 1964 Civil Rights Act, p. 328 below.

Problems of assessing broad technical phrases in particular contexts are raised by the remaining materials in this chapter as well. Wickard v. Filburn, sec. 5, p. 314, is another favorite citation to support assertions of a de facto unlimited commerce power. Yet the broad statements in that case appear in an opinion articulating at length the factual and theoretical underpinnings for the "affecting commerce" justification relied on there. Consider also the Five Gambling Devices case, which follows. It is a statutory interpretation case, to be sure. Yet if all earlier doctrinal dicta were to be taken at face value and for all that they might be worth, should not the Justices have accepted the Government's view of the reach of the statute without difficulty? Do the Justices' doubts suggest lingering constitutional limits on the commerce power? Note the statement on the scope of constitutional powers in the opinion by Justice Jackson (author of some of the broadest statements in Wickard v. Filburn, p. 314, 11 years earlier): "While general statements, out of these different contexts, might bear upon the subject one way or another, it is apparent that the precise question tendered to us now is not settled by any prior decision." And note his reliance on "the implications and limitations of our federal system" and his sensitivity to "affairs considered normally reserved to the states" when he turns to the statutory interpretation problem. (See also the material on statutory interpretation in the final note in this section, at p. 321).

UNITED STATES v. FIVE GAMBLING DEVICES

346 U.S. 441, 74 S.Ct. 190, 98 L.Ed. 179 (1953).

Appeal from the United States District Court for the Middle District of Tennessee.*

Mr. Justice JACKSON announced the judgment of the Court and an opinion in which Mr. Justice FRANKFURTER and Mr. Justice MINTON join.

These cases present unsuccessful attempts, by two different procedures, to enforce the view of the Department of Justice as to construction of the Act of January 2, 1951, which prohibits shipment of gambling machines in interstate commerce but includes incidental registration and reporting provisions. Two indictments charge Denmark and Braun severally with engaging in the business of dealing in gambling devices without registering with the Attorney General and reporting sales and deliveries. Both indictments were dismissed. The other proceeding is a libel to forfeit five gambling machines seized by Federal Bureau of Investigation agents from a country club in Tennessee. It also was dismissed.

The three cases, here on Government appeals, are similar in features which led to their dismissal and which raise constitutional issues. The indictments do not allege that the accused dealers, since the effective date of the Act or for that matter at any other time, have bought, sold or moved gambling devices in interstate commerce, or that the devices involved in their unreported sales have, since the effective date of the Act or at any other time, moved in interstate commerce or ever would do so. The libel does not

---

* Together with No. 40, United States v. Denmark, and No. 41, United States v. Braun, on appeals from the United States District Court for the Southern District of Georgia.

show that the country club's machines were at any time transported in or in any way affect interstate commerce.

Section 2 of the Act prohibits transportation of gambling devices in interstate commerce except to any state which exempts itself or its subdivision by state law. Section 3 requires every manufacturer and dealer in gambling devices annually to register his business and name and monthly to file detailed information as to each device sold and delivered during the preceding month.[1] Section 6 provides criminal penalties for failure to register or for violation of the transportation section, and § 7 authorizes forfeiture of devices sold in violation of the Act.

The information requirements are not expressly limited to persons engaged or transactions occurring in interstate commerce or conditioned on any connection therewith. Neither does the Act by any specific terms direct its application to transactions such as we have here.

Appellees contend, first, that the Act should not be construed to reach dealers, transactions or machines unless shown to have some relation to interstate commerce; second, construed otherwise, the Act exceeds the power delegated to Congress under the Commerce Clause of the Constitution . . . . .

The Government answers, first, that the statute, literally read, reaches all dealers and transactions and the possession of all unreported devices without reference to interstate commerce; second, to make effective the prohibition of transportation in interstate commerce, Congress may constitutionally require reporting of all intrastate transactions . . . . .

We do not intimate any ultimate answer to the appellees' constitutional questions other than to observe that they cannot be dismissed as frivolous, nor as unimportant to the nature of our federation. No precedent of this Court sustains the power of Congress to enact legislation penalizing failure to report information concerning acts not shown to be in, or mingled with, or found to affect commerce. The course of decision relied on by the Government on analysis falls short of the holding asked of us here. Indeed, we find no instance where Congress has attempted under the commerce power to impose reporting duties under penal sanction which would raise the question posed by these proceedings. It is apparent that the Government's pleadings raise, and no doubt were intended to raise, a far-reaching question as to the extent of congressional power over matters internal to the individual states.

Of course, Congress possesses not only power to regulate commerce among the several states but also an inexact power "to make all laws which shall be necessary and proper for carrying into execution" its enumerated powers. In some instances Congress has left to an administrative body, such as the Interstate Commerce Commission or the National Labor Relations Board, the power to decide on a case-to-case basis whether the particular intrastate activity affects interstate commerce so as to warrant exercise of the

---

1. "Upon first engaging in business, and thereafter on or before the 1st day of July of each year, every manufacturer of and dealer in gambling devices shall register with the Attorney General his name or trade name, the address of his principal place of business, and the addresses of his places of business in such district. On or before the last day of each month every manufacturer of and dealer in gambling devices shall file with the Attorney General an inventory and record of all sales and deliveries of gambling devices as of the close of the preceding calendar month for the place or places of business in the district. . . . ."

power to reach into intrastate affairs. Decisions under this type of legislation give the Government no support, for no such determination is required by this Act, and the Government asserts no such finding by anyone is necessary. In other statutes Congress has set up economic regulations which lay hold of activities in interstate commerce but also include intrastate activities so intermingled therewith that separation is impractical or impossible. Of course, decisions upholding legislation requiring information in aid of the taxing power afford no support here, because the taxing power penetrates and permeates every activity, intrastate or interstate, within the Nation. While general statements, out of these different contexts, might bear upon the subject one way or another, it is apparent that the precise question tendered to us now is not settled by any prior decision.

The principle is old and deeply imbedded in our jurisprudence that this Court will construe a statute in a manner that requires decision of serious constitutional questions only if the statutory language leaves no reasonable alternative. United States v. Rumely, 345 U.S. 41. This is not because we would avoid or postpone difficult decisions. The predominant consideration is that we should be sure Congress has intentionally put its power in issue by the legislation in question before we undertake a pronouncement which may have far-reaching consequences upon the powers of the Congress or the powers reserved to the several states. . . .

This Court does and should accord a strong presumption of constitutionality to Acts of Congress. . . . But the presumption can have little realism when responsible congressional committees and leaders, in managing a bill, have told Congress that the bill will not reach that which the Act is invoked in this Court to cover.

We do not question that literal language of this Act is capable of the broad, unlimited construction urged by the Government. Indeed, if it were enacted for a unitary system of government, no other construction would be appropriate. But we must assume that the implications and limitations of our federal system constitute a major premise of all congressional legislation, though not repeatedly recited therein. Against the background of our tradition and system of government, we cannot say that the lower courts, which have held as a matter of statutory construction that this Act does not reach purely intrastate matters, have not made a permissible interpretation. We find in the text no unmistakable intention of Congress to raise the constitutional questions implicit in the Government's effort to apply the Act in its most extreme impact upon affairs considered normally reserved to the states.

Judges differ as to the value of legislative history in statutory construction, but the Government often relies upon it to sustain its interpretation of statutes. However, in this case its reference to legislative history is conspicuously meager and unenlightening. On the other hand, for what it is worth, appellees point out much that was reported by responsible committees and said by proponents of this antigambling-device legislation to indicate that Congress did not intend to raise the issues here presented and was not aware it was doing so. For example, Senator Johnson, sponsor of the bill which eventually became this Act, declared that ". . . . it keeps the Federal Government out of State and local police powers; no Federal official is going to become an enforcement officer in any State or locality." The committee handling the bill reported: "On the other hand, the committee desires to emphasize that Federal law enforcement in the field of gambling cannot and should not be considered a substitute for State and local law enforcement in this field." But here it was the Federal Bureau of Investigation which entered a country club and seized slot machines not shown ever to have had any connection with interstate commerce in any manner whatever. If this is not substituting federal for state enforcement, it is difficult to know how it could be accomplished. A more local and detailed act of enforcement is hardly conceivable. These cases, if sustained, would substantially take unto the Federal Government the entire pursuit of the gambling device. . . .

As we have indicated, the present indictments and libel are so framed as to apply in extreme form the most expansive interpretation of this Act. All that we would decide at present is a question of statutory construction. We think the Act does not have the explicitness necessary to sustain the pleadings which the Government has drafted in these cases. On this ground alone, we would affirm the judgments below.

Judgments affirmed.

[Mr. Justice BLACK, joined by Justice DOUGLAS, concurred because of the vagueness of the reporting provision, without reaching the commerce clause question.]

Mr. Justice CLARK, with whom The Chief Justice [WARREN], Mr. Justice REED and Mr. Justice BURTON concur, dissenting. . . .

The ultimate question presented by these cases is whether Congress has exceeded its constitutional power. I think it has not.

It appears that Congress in this Act has embarked on what it deemed the most effective course of action possible to eliminate one of the major sources of income to organized crime, while at the same time yielding to the policy of Nevada and a few other states where slot machines are legal and the underworld's control and profit are correspondingly minimized. The Act prohibits shipment of gambling devices into any state except those which act to exempt themselves from the statute. Section 3, which sets up the registration and filing requirements here in issue, was designed to make effective and enforceable the interstate shipment ban. It was thought that a report on each transfer of each machine before and after interstate shipment would enable enforcement officials to ascertain who transported the machine across state lines and thereby violated the law. Unless all such local sales were reported, it was thought that it would be an easy matter to conceal the identity of the interstate transporter by resorting to straw-man transactions, coverup intrastate "sales" before and after interstate shipment, and the like. In view of the established tie-up between slot machines and "Nation-wide crime syndicates," more stringent methods of enforcement were deemed necessary to accomplish the ban on interstate transportation of the machines than would be needed to control an activity in which dealers and manufacturers could be presumed to be law-abiding citizens who kept accurate books and accounts. The net effect of these considerations is to clearly establish that the registration and filing requirements of the Act amount to reasonably necessary, appropriate, and probably essential means for enforcing the ban on interstate transportation of gambling devices.

The question presented, then, is whether Congress is empowered by the Constitution to require information, reasonably necessary and appropriate to make effective and enforceable a concededly valid ban on interstate transportation of gambling devices, from persons not shown to be themselves engaged in interstate activity. I think that an affirmative answer is not inevitably dictated by prior decisions of the Court; but, more important, no decision precludes an affirmative answer. The question has not been previously decided because the legislative scheme utilized here apparently has not been heretofore attempted. But its novelty should not suggest its unconstitutionality.

In the body of decisional law defining the scope of Congress' powers in regard to interstate commerce, it has been clearly established that activities local in nature may be *regulated* if they can fairly be said to "affect" commerce, or where local goods are commingled with goods destined for interstate commerce, or were previously in interstate commerce. For present purposes, these cases at least establish that activities or goods intrastate in nature are not immune from congressional control where they are sufficiently related to interstate activities or goods controlled by Congress.

The Court also has on several occasions stated that the commerce power "extends to those activities intrastate which so affect interstate commerce *or the exercise of the power of Congress over it* as to make regulation of them appropriate means to the attainment of a legitimate end, the exercise of the granted power of Congress to regulate interstate commerce." I think it may accurately be said that every sale of slot machines affects the exercise of the power of Congress over commerce, in view of the elusive nature of the object whose interstate shipment is being controlled. . . .

. . . The Act's requirements of registration and filing as to local transactions are certainly not a mere ruse designed to invade areas of control reserved to the states, but are "naturally and reasonably adapted to the effective exercise of" the commerce power.

If Congress by § 3 had sought to *regulate* local activity, its power would no doubt be less clear. But here there is no attempt to regulate; all that is required is information in aid of enforcement of the conceded power to ban interstate transportation. The distinction is substantial. . . .

In my view Congress has power to require the information described in § 3 of the Act since the requirement is a means reasonably necessary to effectuate the prohibition of transporting gambling devices interstate. If it be suggested that such a holding would open possibilities for widespread congressional encroachment upon local activities whose regulation has been reserved to the states, I would point out, first, that power of *regulation* heretofore exclusively vested in the states remains there; and second, that the situation here is unique: the commodity involved is peculiarly tied to organized interstate crime and is itself illegal in the great majority of the states, and the federal law in issue was actively sought by local and state law enforcement officials as a means to assist them, not supplant them, in local law enforcement. I would *reverse* the judgments.

WICKARD v. FILBURN

317 U.S. 111, 63 S.Ct. 82, 87 L.Ed. 122 (1942).

On appeal from the District Court of the United States for the Southern District of Ohio.

Mr. Justice JACKSON delivered the opinion of the Court.

The appellee filed his complaint against the Secretary of Agriculture of the United States, three members of the County Agricultural Conservation Committee for Montgomery County, Ohio, and a member of the State Agricultural Conservation Committee for Ohio. He sought to enjoin enforcement against himself of the marketing penalty imposed by the amendment of May 26, 1941, to the Agricultural Adjustment Act of 1938, upon that part of his 1941 wheat crop which was available for marketing in excess of the marketing quota established for his farm. He also sought a declaratory judgment that the wheat marketing quota provisions of the Act as amended and applicable to him were unconstitutional because not sustainable under the Commerce Clause or consistent with the Due Process Clause of the Fifth Amendment. . . .

The appellee for many years past has owned and operated a small farm in Montgomery County, Ohio, maintaining a herd of dairy cattle, selling milk, raising poultry, and selling poultry and eggs. It has been his practice to raise a small acreage of winter wheat, sown in the Fall and harvested in the following July; to sell a portion of the crop; to feed part to poultry and livestock on the farm, some of which is sold; to use some in making flour for home consumption; and to keep the rest for the following seeding. The intended disposition of the crop here involved has not been expressly stated.

In July of 1940, pursuant to the Agricultural Adjustment Act of 1938, as then amended, there was established for the appellee's 1941 crop a wheat acreage allotment of 11.1 acres and a normal yield of 20.1 bushels of wheat an acre. He was given notice of such allotment in July of 1940 before the Fall planting of his 1941 crop of wheat, and again in July of 1941, before it was harvested. He sowed, however, 23 acres, and harvested from his 11.9 acres of excess acreage 239 bushels, which under the terms of the Act as amended on May 26, 1941, constituted farm marketing excess, subject to a penalty of 49 cents a bushel, or $117.11 in all. The appellee has not paid the penalty and he has not postponed or avoided it by storing the excess under regulations of the Secretary of Agriculture, or by delivering it up to the Secretary. The Committee, therefore, refused him a marketing card, which was, under the terms of Regulations promulgated by the Secretary, necessary to protect a buyer from liability to the penalty and upon its protecting lien.

The general scheme of the Agricultural Adjustment Act of 1938 as related to wheat is to control the volume moving in interstate and foreign commerce in order to avoid surpluses and shortages and the consequent abnormally low or high wheat prices and obstructions to commerce. Within prescribed limits and by prescribed standards the Secretary of Agriculture is directed to ascertain and proclaim each year a national acreage allotment for the next crop of wheat, which is then apportioned to the states and their counties, and is eventually broken up into allotments for individual farms.

. . .

. . . [The judgment below] permanently enjoined appellants from collecting a marketing penalty of more than 15 cents a bushel on the farm marketing excess of appellee's 1941 wheat crop, from subjecting appellee's entire 1941 crop to a lien for the payment of the penalty, and from collecting a 15-cent penalty except in accordance with the provisions of § 339 of the Act as that section stood prior to the amendment of May 26, 1941. The Secretary and his co-defendants have appealed. . . .

It is urged that under the Commerce Clause of the Constitution, Article I, § 8, clause 3, Congress does not possess the power it has in this instance sought to exercise. The question would merit little consideration since our decision in United States v. Darby, . . . except for the fact that this Act extends federal regulation to production not intended in any part for commerce but wholly for consumption on the farm. The Act includes a definition of "market" and its derivatives so that as related to wheat in addition to its conventional meaning it also means to dispose of "by feeding (in any form) to poultry or livestock which, or the products of which, are sold, bartered, or exchanged, or to be so disposed of." Hence, marketing quotas not only embrace all that may be sold without penalty but also what may be consumed on the premises. Wheat produced on excess acreage is designated as "available for marketing" as so defined and the penalty is imposed thereon. Penalties do not depend upon whether any part of the wheat either within or without the quota is sold or intended to be sold. The sum of this is that the Federal Government fixes a quota including all that the farmer may harvest for sale or for his own farm needs, and declares that wheat produced on excess acreage may neither be disposed of nor used except upon payment of the penalty or except it is stored as required by the Act or delivered to the Secretary of Agriculture.

Appellee says that this is a regulation of production and consumption of wheat. Such activities are, he urges, beyond the reach of Congressional power under the Commerce Clause, since they are local in character, and their effects upon interstate commerce are at most "indirect." In answer the Government argues that the statute regulates neither production nor consumption but only marketing; and, in the alternative, that if the Act does go beyond the regulation of marketing it is sustainable as a "necessary and proper" implementation of the power of Congress over interstate commerce.

The Government's concern lest the Act be held to be a regulation of production or consumption rather than of marketing is attributable to a few dicta and decisions of this Court which might be understood to lay it down that activities such as "production," "manufacturing," and "mining" are strictly "local" and, except in special circumstances which are not present here, cannot be regulated under the commerce power because their effects upon interstate commerce are, as matter of law, only "indirect." Even today, when this power has been held to have great latitude, there is no decision of this Court that such activities may be regulated where no part of the product is intended for interstate commerce or intermingled with the subjects thereof. We believe that a review of the course of decision under the Commerce Clause will make plain, however, that questions of the power of Congress are not to be decided by reference to any formula which would give controlling force to nomenclature such as "production" and "indirect" and foreclose consideration of the actual effects of the activity in question upon interstate commerce.

At the beginning Chief Justice Marshall described the federal commerce power with a breadth never yet exceeded. Gibbons v. Ogden, 9 Wheat. 1, 194–195. He made emphatic the embracing and penetrating nature of this power by warning that effective restraints on its exercise must proceed from political rather than from judicial processes. Id. at 197.

For nearly a century, however, decisions of this Court under the Commerce Clause dealt rarely with questions of what Congress might do in the exercise of its granted power under the Clause and almost entirely with the permissibility of state activity which it was claimed discriminated against or burdened interstate commerce. During this period there was perhaps little occasion for the affirmative exercise of the commerce power, and the influence of the Clause on American life and law was a negative one, resulting almost wholly from its operation as a restraint upon the powers of the states. In discussion and decision the point of reference instead of being what was "necessary and proper" to the exercise by Congress of its granted power, was often some concept of sovereignty thought to be implicit in the status of statehood. Certain activities such as "production," "manufacturing," and "mining" were occasionally said to be within the province of state governments and beyond the power of Congress under the Commerce Clause.

It was not until 1887 with the enactment of the Interstate Commerce Act that the interstate commerce power began to exert positive influence in American law and life. This first important federal resort to the commerce power was followed in 1890 by the Sherman Anti-Trust Act and, thereafter, mainly after 1903, by many others. These statutes ushered in new phases of adjudication, which required the Court to approach the interpretation of the Commerce Clause in the light of an actual exercise by Congress of its power thereunder.

When it first dealt with this new legislation, the Court adhered to its earlier pronouncements, and allowed but little scope to the power of Congress. United States v. E. C. Knight Co., 156 U.S. 1. These earlier pronouncements also played an important part in several of the five cases in which this Court later held that Acts of Congress under the Commerce Clause were in excess of its power.[1]

Even while important opinions in this line of restrictive authority were being written, however, other cases called forth broader interpretations of the Commerce Clause destined to supersede the earlier ones, and to bring about a return to the principles first enunciated by Chief Justice Marshall in Gibbons v. Ogden, supra.

Not long after the decision of United States v. Knight Co., supra, Mr. Justice Holmes, in sustaining the exercise of national power over intrastate activity, stated for the Court that "commerce among the states is not a technical legal conception, but a practical one, drawn from the course of business." Swift & Co. v. United States, 196 U.S. 375, 398. It was soon demonstrated that the effects of many kinds of intrastate activity upon interstate commerce were such as to make them a proper subject of federal regulation. In some cases sustaining the exercise of federal power over intrastate matters the term "direct" was used for the purpose of stating, rather than of reaching, a result; in others it was treated as synonymous with "substantial" or "material"; and in others it was not used at all. Of late its use has been abandoned in cases dealing with questions of federal power under the Commerce Clause.
. . . .

1. Employers Liability Cases, 207 U.S. 463; Hammer v. Dagenhart, 247 U.S. 251; Railroad Retirement Board v. Alton R. Co., 295 U.S. 330; Schechter Corp. v. United States, 295 U.S. 495; Carter v. Carter Coal Co., 298 U.S. 238 . . . . [Footnote by the Court.]

The Court's recognition of the relevance of the economic effects in the application of the Commerce Clause . . . has made the mechanical application of legal formulas no longer feasible. Once an economic measure of the reach of the power granted to Congress in the Commerce Clause is accepted, questions of federal power cannot be decided simply by finding the activity in question to be "production" nor can consideration of its economic effects be foreclosed by calling them "indirect." . . .

Whether the subject of the regulation in question was "production," "consumption," or "marketing" is, therefore, not material for purposes of deciding the question of federal power before us. That an activity is of local character may help in a doubtful case to determine whether Congress intended to reach it. The same consideration might help in determining whether in the absence of Congressional action it would be permissible for the state to exert its power on the subject matter, even though in so doing it to some degree affected interstate commerce. But even if appellee's activity be local and though it may not be regarded as commerce, it may still, whatever its nature, be reached by Congress if it exerts a substantial economic effect on interstate commerce and this irrespective of whether such effect is what might at some earlier time have been defined as "direct" or "indirect."

The parties have stipulated a summary of the economics of the wheat industry. Commerce among the states in wheat is large and important. Although wheat is raised in every state but one, production in most states is not equal to consumption. . . .

The wheat industry has been a problem industry for some years. Largely as a result of increased foreign production and import restrictions, annual exports of wheat and flour from the United States during the ten-year period ending in 1940 averaged less than 10 per cent of total production, while during the 1920's they averaged more than 25 per cent. The decline in the export trade has left a large surplus in production which in connection with an abnormally large supply of wheat and other grains in recent years caused congestion in a number of markets; tied up railroad cars; and caused elevators in some instances to turn away grains, and railroads to institute embargoes to prevent further congestion. . . .

In the absence of regulation the price of wheat in the United States would be much affected by world conditions. During 1941 producers who cooperated with the Agricultural Adjustment program received an average price on the farm of about $1.16 a bushel as compared with the world market price of 40 cents a bushel.

Differences in farming conditions, however, make these benefits mean different things to different wheat growers. There are several large areas of specialization in wheat, and the concentration on this crop reaches 27 per cent of the crop land, and the average harvest runs as high as 155 acres. Except for some use of wheat as stock feed and for seed, the practice is to sell the crop for cash. Wheat from such areas constitutes the bulk of the interstate commerce therein.

On the other hand, in some New England states less than one per cent of the crop land is devoted to wheat, and the average harvest is less than five acres per farm. In 1940 the average percentage of the total wheat production that was sold in each state as measured by value ranged from 29 per cent thereof in Wisconsin to 90 per cent in Washington. Except in regions of large-scale production, wheat is usually grown in rotation with other crops; for a nurse crop for grass seeding; and as a cover crop to prevent soil erosion and leaching. Some is sold, some kept for seed, and a percentage of the total production much larger than in areas of specialization is consumed on the farm and grown for such purpose. Such farmers, while growing some wheat, may even find the balance of their interest on the consumer's side.

The effect of consumption of homegrown wheat on interstate commerce is due to the fact that it constitutes the most variable factor in the disappearance of the wheat crop. Consumption on the farm where grown appears to vary in an amount greater than 20 per cent of average production. The total amount of wheat consumed as food varies but relatively little, and use as seed is relatively constant.

The maintenance by government regulation of a price for wheat undoubtedly can be accomplished as effectively by sustaining or increasing the demand as by limiting the supply. The effect of the statute before us is to restrict the amount which may be produced for market and the extent as well to which one may forestall resort to the market by producing to meet his own needs. That appellee's own contribution to the demand for wheat may be trivial by itself is not enough to remove him from the scope of federal regulation where, as here, his contribution, taken together with that of many others similarly situated, is far from trivial. National Labor Relations Board v. Fainblatt, 306 U.S. 601, 606, et seq.; United States v. Darby, supra, at 123.

It is well established by decisions of this Court that the power to regulate commerce includes the power to regulate the prices at which commodities in that commerce are dealt in and practices affecting such prices. One of the primary purposes of the Act in question was to increase the market price of wheat and to that end to limit the volume thereof that could affect the market. It can hardly be denied that a factor of such volume and variability as home-consumed wheat would have a substantial influence on price and market conditions. This may arise because being in marketable condition such home-grown wheat overhangs the market and if induced by rising prices tends to flow into the market and check price increases. But if we assume that it is never marketed, it supplies a need of the man who grew it which would otherwise be reflected by purchases in the open market. Homegrown wheat in this sense competes with wheat in commerce. The stimulation of commerce is a use of the regulatory function quite as definitely as prohibitions or restrictions thereon. This record leaves us in no doubt that Congress may properly have considered that wheat consumed on the farm where grown, if wholly outside the scheme of regulation, would have a substantial effect in defeating and obstructing its purpose to stimulate trade therein at increased prices. . . .

[The statute was also challenged as "a deprivation of property without due process of law contrary to the Fifth Amendment, both because of its regulatory effect on the appellee and because of its alleged retroactive effect." The contentions were rejected.]

Reversed.

THE COMMERCE POWER AND THE NATIONAL MARKET

The concept of a national market in goods—a concept rooted in the historical origins of the commerce clause, sec. 1 above—has proved a useful source of constitutional justifications for congressional regulation of activities "in" or "affecting" commerce in a number of modern cases, both before Wickard v. Filburn and since. Some examples follow:

✳ a. *Mulford v. Smith.* After the Court invalidated the Agricultural Adjustment Act of 1933 in United States v. Butler, 297 U.S. 1 (1936) (p. 366, below), as an unconstitutional regulation of "local" production, Congress enacted the Agricultural Adjustment Act of 1938. The marketing quota provisions of the Act were sustained as a regulation of a channel of commerce. Mulford v. Smith, 307 U.S. 38 (1939). Penalties imposed by the Act were payments to the government of one-half the market price of all tobacco sold above quota, the fine to be paid by warehousemen and deducted by them from the purchase price paid to the farmer. The Court—three years after Butler—emphasized that the Act did not purport to control production and added: "It sets no limit upon the acreage which may be planted or produced and imposes no penalty for the planting and producing of tobacco in excess of the marketing quota. It purports to be solely a regulation of interstate commerce, which it reaches and affects at the throat where tobacco enters the stream of commerce—the marketing warehouse. . . . Any rule, such as that embodied in the Act, which is intended to foster, protect and conserve that commerce or to prevent the flow of commerce from working harm to the people of the nation, is within the competence of Congress."

Note Currin v. Wallace, 306 U.S. 1 (1939), sustaining the Tobacco Inspection Act of 1935, which authorized the Secretary of Agriculture to establish standards of tobacco and designate markets where tobacco moves in interstate and foreign commerce. After such designation, no tobacco might be sold at auction on such markets unless previously inspected and certified to be in accordance with established standards. See also the recognition of the power of Congress to fix prices of commodities or services involved in sales or transactions in or affecting interstate commerce in the following cases: United States v. Rock Royal Co-operative, 307 U.S. 533 (1939), as to milk; Sunshine Anthracite Coal Co. v. Adkins, 310 U.S. 381 (1940), as to coal; Federal Power Commission v. Natural Gas Pipeline Co., 315 U.S. 575 (1942), as to natural gas.

b. *Wrightwood Dairy.* United States v. Wrightwood Dairy Co., 315 U.S. 110 (1942), sustained the congressional power to regulate subjects in local areas because of their being interrelated with, or having an appreciable effect upon, interstate commerce. In particular the case was concerned with federal control of the handling of milk in the Chicago marketing area. After citing cases to show that wholly intrastate competitive practices may be reached by the Sherman Act, the Court added: "So too the marketing of a local product in competition with that of a like commodity moving interstate may so interfere with interstate commerce or its regulation as to afford a basis for Congressional regulation of the intrastate activity. It is the effect upon the interstate commerce or its regulation, regardless of the particular form which the competition may take, which is the test of federal power."

Compare Justice Rutledge's statement in Mandeville Island Farms v. American Crystal Sugar Co., 334 U.S. 219, 236 (1948): "Congress' power to keep the interstate market free of goods produced under conditions inimical to the general welfare, United States v. Darby, 312 U.S. 100, 115, may be exercised in individual cases without showing any specific effect upon interstate commerce, United States v. Walsh, 331 U.S. 432, 437–438; it is enough that the individual activity when multiplied into a general practice is subject to federal control, Wickard v. Filburn, supra, or that it contains a threat to the interstate economy that requires preventive regulation."

STATUTORY FORMULAS AND RECENT USES OF THE COMMERCE POWER

1. *Statutory coverage formulas and constitutional limits.* a. *Coverage short of the limits.* As the scope of the commerce power has expanded, the actual range of national control has increasingly come to turn on congressional choices rather than constitutional limitations. (Compare chap. 8, sec. 2, Congressional Ordering of Federal-State Relationships.) But the fact that Congress chooses not to go as far as the Constitution permits does not make constitutional doctrines irrelevant. Thus, as the Five Gambling Devices case illustrated, constitutional limits affect statutory interpretation. Moreover, just as Congress has not in fact entered all areas of potential control, it frequently does not go to the constitutional limit in the areas actually regulated. Accordingly, the statutory formula of coverage often presents the major operative issue in drafting and interpreting modern commerce clause regulations. Compare, for example, the "affecting commerce" formula in the National Labor Relations Act (in the Jones & Laughlin case) with the narrower scope of the Fair Labor Standards Act (in the Darby case) as to employees engaged "in the production of goods for commerce." See Kirschbaum Co. v. Walling, 316 U.S. 517 (1942). Must the employee's activities be "useful" to production, "necessary" to production, "directly essential" to production to establish coverage under the FLSA? See Mitchell v. H. B. Zachry Co., 362 U.S. 310 (1960), involving a 1949 amendment further narrowing the scope of coverage.

b. *The FLSA, the enterprise concept, and the limits of power.* However, subsequent amendments (in 1961 and 1966) extended rather than narrowed the coverage of the FLSA. In considering these amendments the Court not only interpreted statutory coverage provisions but also reexamined constitutional limits. Maryland v. Wirtz, 392 U.S. 183 (1968), sustained application of both amendments. The 1966 Amendment applied the Act to employees of state-operated schools and hospitals; it was upheld against charges of interference with the autonomy of the operations of state government. (That aspect of the case is considered further in chap. 10, p. 768.) The 1961 amendment dealt with the major traditional concern of the FLSA, employees in private industry. To replace the previous coverage provision limited to employees "engaged in commerce or in the production of goods for commerce," the 1966 expansion of coverage extended the Act to every employee who "is employed in an enterprise engaged in commerce or in the production of goods for commerce." In effect, that amendment extended protection "to the fellow employees of any employee who would have been protected by the original Act," but it did not enlarge the class of employers subject to the Act. Justice Harlan's majority opinion found this "enterprise concept" constitutionally justified on alternative grounds: either under the original "unfair competition" theory of Darby or on the Jones & Laughlin "labor dispute" theory. With regard to the competition analysis, Justice Harlan noted: "There was obviously a 'rational basis' for the logical inference that the pay and hours of production employees affect a company's competitive position. The logical inference does not stop with production employees. When a company does an interstate business, its competition with companies elsewhere is affected by all its significant labor costs, not merely by the wages and hours of those employees who have physical contact with the goods in question." With respect to the labor dispute analysis, he commented that "there is a basis in logic and experience for the conclusion that substandard labor conditions among any group of employees, whether or not they are personally engaged in commerce or production, may lead to strife disrupting an entire enterprise."

With regard to potential limits on the scope of the commerce power, a footnote to the majority opinion (replying to the dissent by Justice Douglas mainly concerned with the state autonomy issue, noted in chap. 10, p. 768, below) is of particular interest. Justice Harlan stated: "The dissent suggests that by use of an 'enterprise concept' such as that we have upheld here, Congress could under today's decision declare a whole State an 'enterprise' affecting commerce and take over its budgeting activities. This reflects, we think, a misreading of the Act, of Wickard v. Filburn, supra, and of our decision. We uphold the enterprise concept on the explicit premise that an 'enterprise' is a set of operations whose activities in commerce would all be expected to be affected by the wages and hours of any group of employees, which is what Congress obviously intended. So defined, the term is quite cognizant of limitations on the commerce power. Neither here nor in Wickard has the Court declared that Congress may use a relatively trivial impact on commerce as an excuse for broad general regulation of state or private activities. The Court has said only that where a general regulatory statute bears a substantial relation to commerce, the *de minimis* character of individual instances arising under that statute is of no consequence."

2. *Recent legislation not using the commerce-prohibiting technique—constitutional problems?* Do the following recent provisions (all but the last additions to 21 U.S.C.) press "affecting commerce" justifications too far, in view of the scope of the commerce power under Darby, Wickard v. Filburn, et al.?

a. *Drugs.* § 360 [added in 1962]. *"Registration of drug producers.*
. . .

"(b) On or before December 31 of each year every person who owns or operates any establishment in any State engaged in the manufacture, preparation, propagation, compounding, or processing of a drug or drugs shall register with the Secretary his name, places of business and all such establishments."

[Public Law 87–781, which included 21 U.S.C. § 360, contained the following statement as Section 301: "The Congress hereby finds and declares that in order to make regulation of interstate commerce in drugs effective, it is necessary to provide for registration and inspection of all establishments in which drugs are manufactured, prepared, propagated, compounded, or processed; that the products of all such establishments are likely to enter the channels of interstate commerce and directly affect such commerce; and that the regulation of interstate commerce in drugs without provision for registration and inspection of establishments that may be engaged only in intrastate commerce in such drugs would discriminate against and depress interstate commerce in such drugs, and adversely burden, obstruct, and affect such interstate commerce."]

b. *Oleomargarine.* § 347 [added in 1950]. *"Intrastate sales of colored oleomargarine—Law governing.*

"(a) Colored oleomargarine or colored margarine which is sold in the same State or Territory in which it is produced shall be subject in the same manner and to the same extent to the provisions of this chapter as if it had been introduced in interstate commerce.

"(b) No person shall sell, or offer for sale, colored oleomargarine or colored margarine unless—

"(1) such oleomargarine or margarine is packaged,

"(2) the net weight of the contents of any package sold in a retail establishment is one pound or less,

"(3) there appears on the label of the package (A) the word 'oleomargarine' or 'margarine' in type or lettering at least as large as any other type or lettering on such label, and (B) a full and accurate statement of all the ingredients contained in such oleomargarine or margarine, and

"(4) each part of the contents of the package is contained in a wrapper which bears the word 'oleomargarine' or 'margarine' in type or lettering not smaller than 20-point type. . . .

"(c) No person shall possess in a form ready for serving colored oleomargarine or colored margarine at a public eating place unless a notice that oleomargarine or margarine is served is displayed prominently and conspicuously in such place and in such manner as to render it likely to be read and understood by the ordinary individual being served in such eating place or is printed or is otherwise set forth on the menu in type or lettering not smaller than that normally used to designate the serving of other food items. No person shall serve colored oleomargarine or colored margarine at a public eating place, whether or not any charge is made therefor, unless (1) each separate serving bears or is accompanied by labeling identifying it as oleomargarine or margarine, or (2) each separate serving thereof is triangular in shape. . .

"(e) For the purpose of this section colored oleomargarine or colored margarine is oleomargarine or margarine having a tint or shade containing more than one and six-tenths degrees of yellow, or of yellow and red collectively, but with an excess of yellow over red, measured in terms of Lovibond tintometer scale or its equivalent."

§ 347a. *"Congressional declaration of policy regarding oleomargarine sales.*

"The Congress finds and declares that the sale, or the serving in public eating places, of colored oleomargarine or colored margarine without clear identification as such or which is otherwise adulterated or misbranded within the meaning of this chapter depresses the market in interstate commerce for butter and for oleomargarine or margarine clearly identified and neither adulterated nor misbranded, and constitutes a burden on interstate commerce in such articles. Such burden exists, irrespective of whether such oleomargarine or margarine originates from an interstate source or from the State in which it is sold."

c. *The significance of legislative findings.* What is the significance of congressional findings, such as those in Public Law 87–781 and in 21

U.S.C. § 347a above? Are they significant in congressional consideration? In constitutional litigation? Are they useful? Necessary? Determinative? Note the discussion and disposition of these problems in the consideration of Title II of the Civil Rights Act of 1964 (sec. 6, p. 327, below).

d. *Air pollution.* Does the commerce clause authorize comprehensive federal control of air pollution? See Edelman, "Federal Air and Water Control: The Application of the Commerce Power to Abate Interstate and Intrastate Pollution," 33 Geo.Wash.L.Rev. 1067 (1965). Do the abatement provisions of the Federal Clean Air Act, 42 U.S.C. § 1857 et seq., raise constitutional problems? The Act authorized the U. S. Attorney General to bring an abatement action on behalf of the United States if the pollution is "endangering the health or welfare of persons in a state other than that in which the discharge or discharges (causing or contributing to such pollution) originate." But in those situations in which the pollution endangers "persons only in the state in which the discharge or discharges originate," the Attorney General may sue only on request of a Governor. Is that difference in the scope of authority in the two situations required by the commerce clause? Note the congressional findings in the Act, 42 U.S.C. § 1857(a), which include the following:

"(1) that the predominant part of the Nation's population is located in its rapidly expanding metropolitan and other urban areas, which generally cross the boundary lines of local jurisdictions and often extend into two or more States;

"(2) that the growth in the amount and complexity of air pollution brought about by urbanization, industrial development, and the increasing use of motor vehicles, has resulted in mounting dangers to the public health and welfare, including injury to agricultural crops and livestock, damage to and the deterioration of property, and hazards to air and ground transportation;

"(3) that the prevention and control of air pollution at its source is the primary responsibility of States and local governments . . .."

SECTION 6. THE COMMERCE POWER AND RACIAL DISCRIMINATION: THE PUBLIC ACCOMMODATIONS TITLE OF THE CIVIL RIGHTS ACT OF 1964

Scope Note. Congressional action to protect civil rights has been sporadic. After a period of intensive activity during Reconstruction, from 1866 to 1875, Congress was virtually silent for over three-quarters of a century. A revival of legislative productivity began with the Civil Rights Act of 1957. Most federal laws have been based on the post-Civil War Amendments; Congressional authority under these is the focus of chapter 6 below. But, as the omnibus Civil Rights Act of 1964 illustrates, Art. I, Sec. 8, of the Constitution may also provide authority for legislation to protect civil rights. The title of the Act reflects not only the wide-ranging content of the legislation but also the varied sources of power invoked: the commerce and spending powers, for example, as well as the Fourteenth and Fifteenth Amendments.

The 1964 legislation is entitled: "An Act to enforce the constitutional right to vote, to confer jurisdiction upon the district courts of the United States to provide injunctive relief against discrimination in public accommodations, to authorize the Attorney General to institute suits to protect constitutional rights in public facilities and public education, to extend the Commission on Civil Rights, to prevent discrimination in federally assisted programs, to establish a Commission on Equal Employment Opportunity, and for other purposes." Pub.L. 88–352, 78 Stat. 241. It became law on July 2, 1964, more than a year after President Kennedy urged comprehensive civil rights legislation in a message to Congress. A substantially revised version of the Administration bill passed the House on February 10, 1964. The first successful cloture vote on a civil rights bill (71 to 29) came on June 10, 1964, after weeks of Senate debate. After amendments, the Senate approved the bill on June 19, 1964, by a vote of 73 to 27.

The materials in this section emphasize Title II, on public accommodations, since it involved the most controversial use of the commerce power. Excerpts from the hearings and the text of the Title precede the Court decisions on the constitutionality and scope of the law. These materials are offered for reasons going beyond their intrinsic importance: the legislative deliberations suggest some of the problems of selecting constitutional bases and drafting statutory coverage formulas; and the extensive debates illustrate that constitutional discussions are not an exclusive judicial function in our system of government.

A. THE COVERAGE OF THE STATUTE

Title II—Injunctive Relief Against Discrimination in Places of Public Accommodation *

Sec. 201. (a) All persons shall be entitled to the full and equal enjoyment of the goods, services, facilities, privileges, advantages, and accommodations of any place of public accommodation, as defined in this section, without discrimination or segregation on the ground of race, color, religion, or national origin.

(b) Each of the following establishments which serves the public is a place of public accommodation within the meaning of this title if its operations affect commerce, or if discrimination or segregation by it is supported by State action:

(1) any inn, hotel, motel, or other establishment which provides lodging to transient guests, other than an establishment located within a building which contains not more than five rooms for rent or hire and which is actually occupied by the proprietor of such establishment as his residence;

(2) any restaurant, cafeteria, lunchroom, lunch counter, soda fountain, or other facility principally engaged in selling food for consumption on the premises, including, but not limited to, any such facility located on the premises of any retail establishment; or any gasoline station;

---

* The text printed here follows the numbering in Pub.L. 88–352, 78 Stat. 241.   See also the renumbered version, 42 U.S.C.A. §§ 2000a–2000a–6.

(3) any motion picture house, theater, concert hall, sports arena, stadium or other place of exhibition or entertainment; and

(4) any establishment (A) (i) which is physically located within the premises of any establishment otherwise covered by this subsection, or (ii) within the premises of which is physically located any such covered establishment, and (B) which holds itself out as serving patrons of such covered establishment.

(c) The operations of an establishment affect commerce within the meaning of this title if (1) it is one of the establishments described in paragraph (1) of subsection (b); (2) in the case of an establishment described in paragraph (2) of subsection (b), it serves or offers to serve interstate travelers or a substantial portion of the food which it serves, or gasoline or other products which it sells, has moved in commerce; (3) in the case of an establishment described in paragraph (3) of subsection (b), it customarily presents films, performances, athletic teams, exhibitions, or other sources of entertainment which move in commerce; and (4) in the case of an establishment described in paragraph (4) of subsection (b), it is physically located within the premises of, or there is physically located within its premises, an establishment the operations of which affect commerce within the meaning of this subsection. For purposes of this section, "commerce" means travel, trade, traffic, commerce, transportation, or communication among the several States, or between the District of Columbia and any State, or between any foreign country or any territory or possession and any State or the District of Columbia, or between points in the same State but through any other State or the District of Columbia or a foreign country.

(d) Discrimination or segregation by an establishment is supported by State action within the meaning of this title if such discrimination or segregation (1) is carried on under color of any law, statute, ordinance, or regulation; or (2) is carried on under color of any custom or usage required or enforced by officials of the State or political subdivision thereof; or (3) is required by action of the State or political subdivision thereof.

(e) The provisions of this title shall not apply to a private club or other establishment not in fact open to the public, except to the extent that the facilities of such establishment are made available to the customers or patrons of an establishment within the scope of subsection (b).

Sec. 202. All persons shall be entitled to be free, at any establishment or place, from discrimination or segregation of any kind on the ground of race, color, religion, or national origin, if such discrimination or segregation is or purports to be required by any law, statute, ordinance, regulation, rule, or order of a State or any agency or political subdivision thereof.

Sec. 203. No person shall (a) withhold, deny, or attempt to withhold or deny, or deprive or attempt to deprive, any person of any right or privilege secured by section 201 or 202, or (b) intimidate, threaten, or coerce, or attempt to intimidate, threaten, or coerce any person with the purpose of interfering with any right or privilege secured by section 201 or 202, or (c) punish or attempt to punish any person for exercising or attempting to exercise any right or privilege secured by section 201 or 202. [Sec. 204 provides for private civil relief; Sec. 205, for civil actions by the Attorney General in certain cases.] . . . .

B. THE CONGRESSIONAL DELIBERATIONS

Introduction. Consideration of the proposals that became the 1964 Act produced extensive hearings before several committees, and lengthy debates on the floor of both houses of Congress. Constitutional issues were discussed exhaustively. The selections that follow are from hearings in the early stages of the process, before the Senate Commerce Committee in July and August 1963. Hearings Before the Senate Committee on Commerce on S. 1732, 88th Cong., 1st Sess., parts 1 and 2. The Committee had before it the Administration proposal on public accommodations. Before the Administration bill was submitted to Congress in late June, it was widely reported that it would rely solely on the commerce clause. As introduced, it included references to the Fourteenth Amendment as well, but the commerce power focus predominated: for example, the proposed title was "Interstate Public Accommodations Act"; the introductory series of findings dealt almost entirely with commerce; the commerce emphases, and the afterthought nature of the Fourteenth Amendment reliance, were highlighted by the final "finding" that the "burdens on and obstructions to commerce which are described above can best be removed by invoking the powers of Congress under the fourteenth amendment and the commerce clause of the Constitution"; and the coverage provisions were entirely in commerce terms. (Section 201 (d) of the Act, on discrimination "supported by State action," was added subsequently, during the congressional consideration of the bill.) Note the Gunther comments made when the proposal rested solely on the commerce power, printed at p. 335 below, after the excerpts from the hearings.

Examine the coverage provisions of Title II in light of the concerns expressed during the hearings. Note the reluctance of some Senators to utilize the commerce clause rather than the Fourteenth Amendment. Was there basis for that reluctance in the Constitution or in the Court's decisions? Should a Senator be concerned even if the Court's decisions left the matter doubtful—or should that issue be left to the Court? Suppose a legislator has no doubts that a commerce clause-based law would be sustained by the courts. May he nevertheless claim that it is his duty, or right, to consider questions of constitutional "propriety" in casting his vote? Compare President Jackson's Veto Message on the rechartering of the Bank of the United States, chap. 1, p. 25, supra, and President Roosevelt's letter on the Guffey Coal Act, sec. 4, p. 278, supra. See generally Morgan, Congress and the Constitution (1966). (For further examination of the constitutional difficulties in the Fourteenth Amendment approach, see chap. 6, p. 447, below.)

Note that the bill as enacted omitted the recital of findings. Were Senator Monroney's statements about the importance of findings (p. 331, infra) justified? Were there significant differences regarding the scope of the commerce power between the views of Attorney General Kennedy (p. 329) and of Assistant Attorney General Marshall (p. 332)? Was there merit in Senator Magnuson's position (at p. 329) on the role of Congress in determining the reach of the commerce clause? *

* For additional hearings and debates, see Hearings Before Subcommittee No. 5 of the House Committee on the Judiciary on Miscellaneous Proposals Regarding . . . Civil Rights; Hearings Before the House Committee on the Judiciary on H.R. 7152, as Amended—both 88th Cong., 1st Sess.

THE SENATE COMMITTEE HEARINGS, 1963

MR. [ROBERT F.] KENNEDY [ATTORNEY GENERAL]. . . . We base this on the commerce clause which I think makes it clearly constitutional. In my personal judgment, basing it on the 14th amendment would also be constitutional. . . . I think that there is argument about the 14th amendment basis—going back to the 1883 Supreme Court decision [Civil Rights Cases, 109 U.S. 3, chap. 6, p. 454], and the fact that this is not State action—that therefore Congress would not have the right under the 14th amendment to pass any legislation dealing with it. . . .

Senator, I think that there is an injustice that needs to be remedied. We have to find the tools with which to remedy that injustice.

There are perhaps three provisions of the Constitution that might be applicable; the 13th amendment, the 14th amendment, and the commerce clause. . . .

There cannot be any legitimate question about the commerce clause. That is clearly constitutional. We need to obtain a remedy. The commerce clause will obtain a remedy and there won't be a problem about the constitutionality. . . .

SENATOR MONRONEY [DEM., OKLA.] . . . Mr. Attorney General, I think most of the members of this committee are sincerely in agreement with your strong plea for the elimination of discrimination. I think most of them would like to have legislation that could achieve this end instantly and totally. But many of us are worried about the use the interstate commerce clause will have on matters which have been for more than 170 years thought to be within the realm of local control under our dual system of State and Federal Government, based on the doctrine that those powers which were not specifically granted to the Federal Government by the Constitution are reserved to the States.

Is the test whether the line of business has a substantial effect on interstate commerce? Lodgings are covered, if they are public, and transients are served. Does that mean that all lodging houses under your theory of the effect on interstate commerce would be under Federal regulation, regardless of whether the transients that were using the lodgings were intrastate or interstate?

MR. KENNEDY. That is correct. If it is a lodging, a motel, that opens its doors to the general public, invites the general public, then it would be covered. . . .

SENATOR MONRONEY. If we pass this bill, even though the end we seek is good, I wonder how far we are stretching the Constitution. . . .

MR. KENNEDY. The point I would make, Senator, is that we are not going beyond any principle of the use of the commerce clause that has not already been clearly established, which has been passed in this Congress, and which has been ruled on by the courts. We are not stretching the commerce clause. We are not adding anything to the commerce clause. This is just like laws that have been passed by the Senate of the United States and the House of Representatives, and passed by the courts of the United States. . .

(1963)—; Hearings Before the House Committee on Rules on H.R. 7152, 88th Cong., 2d Sess. (1964); H.R.Rep. 914, 88th Cong., 1st Sess. (1963); Sen.Rep. No. 872, 88th Cong., 2d Sess. (1964).

SENATOR MONRONEY. I grant you that I can see ample evidence under all the historic interpretations of the interstate commerce clause that the Hilton hotel chain is in interstate commerce, that your national food stores are in interstate commerce, that your variety stores which have lunch counters are in interstate commerce. Many motels which are national in their operations are in interstate commerce. I raise no question about that. I think it is true. I think Congress does have the right to regulate those businesses under the commerce clause, because they operate in many States.

But I find it rather difficult to stretch the clause to cover an eating place simply because some of its meat moves from one State into another; or because the vegetables they serve come from Florida; or the oranges come from California. . . .

MR. KENNEDY. What I am saying is that there is precedent for passing this kind of legislation. With these precedents and with the great need that exists, the legislation should be as inclusive as possible, as long as it doesn't affect a personal or social relationship. . . .

The need is there. So therefore I think it follows that we should have the law.

SENATOR MONRONEY. I strongly doubt that we can stretch the Interstate Commerce Clause that far. I recognize that we can cover those that are interstate in their chosen operations, and therefore I feel that 50- or 60-percent compliance by those firms will bring about voluntary compliance on the part of the intrastate operators.

. . . Under your summary of the court's actions, there would hardly be any field of business in any State that is exempt from Federal regulation under the interstate commerce clause.

MR. KENNEDY. No, I didn't say that, Senator. That is not my point. Excuse me.

SENATOR MONRONEY. I am trying to get it straight. I am not trying to misinterpret you. If the court decisions and all the precedents that you have mentioned are, or have been construed to mean that a business, no matter how intrastate in its nature, comes under the interstate commerce clause, then we can legislate for other businesses in other fields in addition to the discrimination legislation that is asked for here.

MR. KENNEDY. If the establishment is covered by the commerce clause, then you can regulate; that is correct * . . ..

THE CHAIRMAN [SENATOR MAGNUSON, DEM., WASH.]. I think we ought to get this in perspective. Congress doesn't determine what is under the interstate commerce clause. The Constitution and court decisions determine that. Since it is regulatory in nature in passing any one of these bills, Congress can determine how far it wants to use the interstate commerce

---

* Compare the testimony by Assistant Attorney General Marshall, p. 332, and the following paragraph in a memorandum on the constitutionality of Title II subsequently submitted by the Justice Department and printed in an appendix to the Hearings (part II, at p. 1296):

"Of course, there are limits on congressional power under the Commerce Clause. It may be conceded that Congress does not hold the power to regulate all of a man's conduct solely because he has relationship with interstate commerce. What is required is that there be a relationship between interstate commerce and the evil to be regulated. Over the course of the years, various tests have been established for determining whether this relationship exists. The proposed legislation clearly meets these tests."

clause, how far down it wants to go, what it wants to cover, what it doesn't want to cover. This has been the case in all of these bills that come under the umbrella of the interstate commerce clause.

We can't pass a bill saying what is under interstate commerce, because the Constitution provides that; that would require a constitutional amendment. We are talking about how far you want to go or what you want to do in a particular field with a bill, or a number of bills. Whether a business is in interstate commerce or not is a question of the interpretation of the Constitution and of the courts' rules in these matters. . . .

SENATOR THURMOND [DEM. (now REP.), S. C.] Mr. Attorney General, isn't it true that all of the acts of Congress based on the commerce clause which you have mentioned in your statement were primarily designed to regulate economic affairs of life and that the basic purpose of this bill is to regulate moral and social affairs?

MR. KENNEDY. Well Senator, let me say this: I think that the discrimination that is taking place at the present time is having a very adverse effect on our economy. So I think that it is quite clear that under the commerce clause even if it was just on that aspect and even if you get away from the moral aspect—I think it is quite clear that this kind of discrimination has an adverse effect on the economy. I think all you have to do is look at some of the southern communities at the present time and the difficult time that they are having.

SENATOR THURMOND. And you would base this bill on the economic features rather than the social and moral aspect?

MR. KENNEDY. I think the other is an extremely important aspect of it that we should keep in mind. . . .

SENATOR THURMOND. Now how could the denial of services to an individual who is a resident and has no intention of leaving that State be a burden on interstate commerce?

MR. KENNEDY. Because we are talking about a cumulative situation here, Senator. It is not just an individual. If this was just an individual situation and there was one restaurant or one motel or one hotel, we wouldn't all be sitting here today.

What this is is a general practice, and a practice that has existed for many, many, many years. What we are trying to do is to get at that general practice.

The cumulative effect of a number of establishments which take in transients, and some of which would be interstate, some of which would be intrastate—the cumulative effect of all these has a major effect on interstate commerce. That is the theory, and it is a theory that has been borne out in a number of decisions. And I suppose the best known is Wickard v. Filburn, where the man just ran his own wheat farm. . . .

SENATOR THURMOND. What does "substantial" mean when you say "substantial"? That is what I am trying to get at. . . .

MR. KENNEDY. I don't think you can have any mathematical precision and a cutoff line. There has been a good deal of legislation that has been passed by Congress, passed on by this committee where you have expressions such as this. What is "interstate commerce"? Even if you didn't have "substantial," Senator, how would you be able to define it? You can't define, with mathematical precision, "interstate commerce." You can't define, specifically and particularly, "due process of law" or "equal protection of the laws." These are terms that we use frequently in our legislation and in court decisions. So you can't do that. But I think you could work it out in the individual case. . . .

SENATOR THURMOND. I am just trying to find out what, so a fellow would know, for instance, if he got three-fourths of his business from interstate travelers, would he be covered by this bill?

MR. KENNEDY. I would think he would.

SENATOR THURMOND. And only 30 percent was interstate; would that be covered?

MR. KENNEDY. I think it probably would. But I think it would depend somewhat where the [business] was established and perhaps a number of other factors. . . .

SENATOR THURMOND. Twenty percent?

MR. KENNEDY. Again, I think it would depend on other factors.

SENATOR THURMOND. What other factors?

MR. KENNEDY. Was he near an airport, Senator? I don't know.

SENATOR THURMOND. What difference does it make whether he is near an airport or 10 miles from the airport if 20 percent of his business came from out of State? Would he have to serve them?

MR. KENNEDY. I think these other factors play a role in it, Senator —whether an establishment deals with those in interstate commerce. That would be a factor you would have to take into consideration. I would say that perhaps it very well might be covered. But I think that he could, he wouldn't have any problem if he wouldn't discriminate. It wouldn't be difficult for him. He would decide, "I am not going to discriminate." . . .

SENATOR MONRONEY. I would like to ask the Attorney General for the purpose of the record to give us the effect in law, if any, of section 2, on page 1 through page 4 [the "Findings"]. This is the ordinary preamble of the bill, is it not; and would not have any effect before the courts in determining the scope of the law?

MR. KENNEDY. This is the ordinary preamble giving the purposes of the law, Senator; that is correct.

SENATOR MONRONEY. There is no law actually involved in it?

MR. KENNEDY. No.

SENATOR MONRONEY. The Court, whatever it decided on the scope of the interstate commerce clause, . . . would base its decision on the other sections of the bill, and this is merely, I guess, what the Court would call obiter dicta.

MR. KENNEDY. That is correct. . . .

THE CHAIRMAN [MAGNUSON]. When you use the commerce clause for a social objective there is plenty of precedent for that, too. We did that in the Mann Act; we did that in the Pinball Act, and the gambling regulations for social reasons. We don't have to do this. It is a matter of public policy.

The commerce clause is there. We can't stretch it, restrict it, or do anything with it. It is there. The Constitution will not change unless we have a constitutional amendment. . . .

SENATOR COOPER [REP., KY.]. I do not suppose that anyone would seriously contend that the administration is proposing legislation, or the Congress is considering legislation, because it has suddenly determined, after all these years, that segregation is a burden on interstate commerce. We are considering legislation because we believe, as the great majority of the people in our country believe, that all citizens have an equal right to have access to goods, services, and facilities which are held out to be available for public use and patronage.

If there is a right to the equal use of accommodations held out to the public, it is a right of citizenship and a constitutional right under the 14th amendment. It has nothing to do with whether a business is in interstate commerce or whether discrimination against individuals places a burden on commerce. It does not depend upon the commerce clause and cannot be limited by that clause, in my opinion as the administration bill would do. . . .

If we are going to deal with this question of the use of public accommodations, I think it imperative that Congress should enact legislation which would meet it fully and squarely as a right under the 14th amendment, and not indirectly and partially as the administration's approach would do.

Rights under the Constitution apply to all citizens, and the integrity and dignity of the individual should not be placed on lesser grounds such as the commerce clause. . . .

MR. [BURKE] MARSHALL [ASSISTANT ATTORNEY GENERAL, CIVIL RIGHTS DIVISION]. Let me dispel at the outset a possible misconception concerning the scope of S. 1732. We do not propose to regulate the businesses covered merely because they are engaged in some phase of interstate commerce. Discrimination by the establishments covered in the bill should be prohibited because it is that discrimination itself which adversely affects interstate commerce.

Section 2 of the bill describes in detail the effect of racial discrimination on national commerce. Discrimination burdens Negro interstate travelers and thereby inhibits interstate travel. It artificially restricts the market available for interstate goods and services. It leads to the withholding of patronage by potential customers for such goods and services. It inhibits the holding of conventions and meetings in segregated cities. It interferes with businesses that wish to obtain the services of persons who do not choose to subject themselves to segregation and discrimination. And it restricts business enterprises in their choice of location for offices and plants, thus preventing the most effective allocation of national resources.

Clearly, all of these are burdens on interstate commerce and they may therefore be dealt with by the Congress. . . .

SENATOR LAUSCHE [DEM., OHIO]. What is your definition of "substantial degree"?

MR. MARSHALL. More than minimal, Senator. . . . . I think that by more than minimal or not insignificant, we mean something that is substantial; something, for example, which if done by a whole lot of businesses taken together, has a substantial impact on interstate commerce.

Now I think that is true of the activities that are proscribed by this bill. Taken together, without question they have a substantial impact on interstate commerce. . . .

SENATOR ENGLE [DEM., CALIF.]. Let me keep the record straight on this point. I would prefer to base this legislation on article 14, if we could get away with it. I will admit the bill introduced is the Administration bill, of which I am a coauthor, which ties in the commerce clause and thereby gives us some wiggling room, you might say. But Senator Cooper is here now and what I asked is this. If you take his bill [S. 1591, banning discrimination in any business "affecting the public which is conducted under a State license"] and put it on the floor, and vote it out squarely on the 14th amendment, where are you going to end up—flat on your face?

MR. MARSHALL. Senator, it is my opinion that the Supreme Court would uphold that bill. But I think that, as I say, many lawyers would disagree with that, and I might well be wrong about it. On the other hand the power of Congress to deal with this problem as a commerce problem, which is what it is, is perfectly clear cut. . . .

SENATOR PROUTY [REP., VT.]. Mr. Marshall, getting down to the fundamentals, is discrimination the basic evil we think it is, because of its effect on commerce or because of its effect on man and his dignity?

MR. MARSHALL. Senator, I think that discrimination is a basic evil because of its effect on people. But it also has an effect on commerce. And Congress has a clear power and responsibility to deal with that effect. . . .

SENATOR PASTORE [DEM., R. I.]. I am a little disturbed about the carefulness we are exercising on both sides here with relation to the inviolability of an opinion of the Supreme Court of 1883. I submit that until it is changed by another opinion of the Supreme Court, or by constitutional amendment, that it is the binding law of the land and we must preserve it.

But is there any constitutional prohibition about Congress taking a second bite at the cherry?

MR. MARSHALL. No, there isn't, Senator. . . .

SENATOR PASTORE. . . . I believe in this bill, because I believe in the dignity of man, not because it impedes our commerce. I don't think any man has the right to say to another man, You can't eat in my restaurant because you have a dark skin; no matter how clean you are, you can't eat at my restaurant

That deprives a man of his full stature as an American citizen. That shocks me. That hurts me. And that is the reason why I want to vote for this law.

Now, it might well be that I can effect the same remedy through the commerce clause. But I like to feel that what we are talking about is a moral issue, an issue that involves the morality of this great country of ours. And that morality, it seems to me, comes under the 14th amendment, where we speak about immunities and where we speak about equal protection of the law. I would like to feel that the Supreme Court of the United States is given another chance to review it, not under the commerce clause, but under the 14th amendment. . . . Do you see anything wrong in that?

MR. MARSHALL. Senator, I think it would be a mistake to rely solely on the 14th amendment. This bill, S. 1732, relies on the 14th amendment, and also relies on the commerce clause. I think it is plainly constitutional. I think if it relied solely on the 14th amendment, it might not be held constitutional. I think it would be a disservice to pass a bill that was later thrown out by the Supreme Court.

SENATOR PASTORE. I am not being critical of you. I am merely stating my own position. I am saying we are being a little too careful, cagey, and cautious, in debating this question of the 14th amendment. I realize you should bring all of the tools at your disposal and that is what you are doing. You are saying you are not only relying on the 14th amendment, you are relying on the commerce clause as well and you have every right to do that as a good lawyer. All I am saying here is that we have a perfect right to proceed under the 14th amendment and try it again.

MR. MARSHALL. Yes, Senator. . . .

MR. [JAMES J.] KILPATRICK, [EDITOR, RICHMOND NEWS-LEADER]. . . . [T]he language of this bill is based upon the theory that when my restaurant operator turns away this Negro customer, he has imposed this burden upon interstate commerce. I submit to your thought the interesting proposition that the whole thing can be reversed and turned around and the thrust sent backward.

Do you now lay the groundwork for a bill that compels me to patronize a particular place? If I withhold my patronage from Nick's Restaurant or Miller & Rhoads, or from a particular store, do I thereby impose a burden upon interstate commerce by not patronizing?

And if so, may you by Federal law reach out and compel me to trade? Is not the burden on interstate commerce the same in either case? It is an interesting question. . . .

THE CHAIRMAN [MAGNUSON]. There again, what is in interstate commerce? As a matter of public policy, we may all come to the conclusion you wouldn't want to put this under that authority. But there is no use of us here belaboring the point of what the interstate commerce clause includes, how far it may or may not extend, because it is written.

MR. KILPATRICK. If I can be serious for just a minute, sir, this is your primary obligation before it ever hits that court, to make that judgment, to bring to bear on it all the thought, power, energy, and intellect that you can to make the primary decision as to whether it is or is not constitutional. . . .

SENATOR PROUTY. Under the legislation presently before us, the concept of the commerce clause is paramount. Doesn't that suggest, in a sense, that Negroes, under the proposed legislation, will be treated as chattels, as goods in interstate commerce, rather than as American citizens?

MR. [ROY] WILKINS [NAACP]. Senator, I think that is, if you don't mind my saying so, an extreme interpretation. I think the commerce clause was drawn for the purpose of facilitating the conduct of business and the movement of people as well as goods in this country.

I don't see that there is anything in the basing of this on the interstate commerce clause that classifies Negroes as goods or chattels.

SENATOR PROUTY. That will be determined only because of its effect upon interstate commerce.

MR. WILKINS. Senator Prouty, I am trying to remember—I don't have to remember very hard. You recall the great difficulty we had as a nation in getting our hands on Al Capone. We had all the lawyers in the country, in and out of Congress, figuring out how to get hold of Capone, and nobody could arrive at anything except the income tax. They didn't hesitate to use the income tax to get hold of Al Capone just because they couldn't get hold of him for his obvious activities. They got him on a technicality. But they got him.

And as far as we are concerned, if we can get some of this under the commerce clause, we want it under the commerce clause, even though it may be, say, unorthodox. . . .

MR. [BRUCE] BROMLEY [N. Y. ATTORNEY; FORMER JUDGE, N. Y. COURT OF APPEALS] . . . Of course, I concede that Congress does not hold the power to regulate all of a man's conduct solely because he has at some time in the past imported goods in interstate commerce. And I not only concede, I assert there must be some connection between interstate commerce and the evil to be regulated. . . .

SENATOR MONRONEY. . . . I am still troubled on the interstate commerce clause. There are no restrictions on what we can rule to be in interstate commerce. Therefore, under the powers of the Federal Government is there any cutoff place—not just on bias, but on regulation, on policing powers of industry, corporate and otherwise—that the Federal Government would have?

I always presumed maybe it was just a tradition of the Government not to invade the States rights, but I also presumed there were certain definite limits beyond which we couldn't go in controlling matters which were intrastate in nature.

MR. BROMLEY. My dear Senator, I think there are plainly limits. Let's just take a very simple one.

You can't apply this law to a little barber shop whose activities have no substantial effect on interstate commerce. And you can't apply it in any area or any law under the commerce clause unless you are dealing with some activity which is either in the stream of commerce or has a substantial effect upon that flow in commerce.

I don't see, sir, why that worries you in the slightest. . . .

SOME COMMENTS FROM THE SIDELINES

a. *Gunther.* Consider the following excerpts from a letter by a Professor Gerald Gunther to the Department of Justice, dated June 5, 1963— several weeks before the Senate hearings printed above, two weeks before the submission of the Administration bill to Congress. Was there substance to the concerns expressed? Were all bases for concern removed by the testimony before Congress, as reflected in the Supreme Court opinions in Heart of Atlanta and McClung, infra?

"I was happy to note that the Administration has put off for a few days the submission of its new civil rights proposals to Congress. I hope that the additional time will permit the Justice Department to reexamine its reported decision to rely exclusively on the commerce clause. . . .

"My basic difficulties with the proposal in light of our constitutional structure may be briefly stated. If a federal ban on discrimination in such businesses as stores and restaurants is to be enacted, it should rest on the obviously most relevant source of national power, the Fourteenth Amendment, rather than the tenuously related commerce clause. The proposed end run by way of the commerce clause seems to me ill-advised in every respect. . . .

"Let me elaborate somewhat: I know of course that the commerce power is a temptingly broad one. But surely responsible statutory drafting should have a firmer basis than, for example, some of the loose talk in recent newspaper articles about the widely accepted, unrestricted availability of the commerce clause to achieve social ends. Some qualifications seem in order. Thus, most of the obviously 'social' laws, as with lottery and prostitution legislation, have their immediate impact on the interstate movement and rest on the power to prohibit that movement. Most 'social' laws are not directly aimed at intrastate affairs, are not attempts to regulate internal activities as such. Where immediate regulations of intrastate conduct have been imposed, a demonstrable economic effect on interstate commerce, business, trade has normally been required. That kind of showing has been made, for example, with regard to the control of 'local' affairs in the labor relations and agricultural production fields. The commerce clause 'hook' has been put to some rather strained uses in the past, I know; but the substantive content of the commerce clause would have to be drained beyond any point yet reached to justify the simplistic argument that all intrastate activity may be subjected to any kind of national regulation merely because some formal crossing of an interstate boundary once took place, without regard to the relationship between the aim of the regulation and interstate trade. The aim of the proposed anti-discrimination legislation, I take it, is quite unrelated to any concern with national commerce in any substantive sense.

"It would, I think, pervert the meaning and purpose of the commerce clause to invoke it as the basis for this legislation. And the strained use now suggested for the commerce power cannot even be justified by the argument that a national problem exists in an area to which the Constitution does not address itself. The Fourteenth Amendment, after all, . . . specifically focuses on the problem of racial discrimination; and the fifth section of the Amendment as well as the Necessary and Proper Clause speak to congressional power to enforce it. . . .

" . . . I would much prefer to see the Government channel its resources of ingenuity and advocacy into the development of a viable interpretation of the Fourteenth Amendment, the provision with a natural linkage to the race problem. That would seem to me a considerably less demeaning task than the construction of an artificial commerce facade; and it would carry the incidental benefit of giving the Department the opportunity to aid the Supreme Court in the fashioning of a more adequate rationale for the modern scope of the Fourteenth Amendment than is now apparent in this much criticized area of constitutional law. . . . "

b. *Wechsler.* Compare the July 18, 1963, letter by Professor Herbert Wechsler to the Chairman of the Senate Commerce Committee, Hearings on

S. 1732, 88th Cong., 1st Sess., part 2, 1193–94, which included the following paragraph:

"I should add that I see nothing fictive in the proposition that the practices to which the measure is directed may occur in or affect 'the commerce that concerns more States than one' or, even more plainly, may occur, as the Taft-Hartley Act requires, in an industry which affects such commerce. There are, in fact, effects upon such matters as the free movement of individuals and goods across State lines, the level of demand for products of the national market and the freedom of enterprises engaged in interstate commerce to abandon the restrictions that some of their local competitors may impose. To legislate within the area of such effects on commerce seems to me to fall within the great tradition of the Congress in the exercise of this explicit power."

c. *The lawyers' committee.* During the subsequent debates, a number of statements by constitutional law experts were introduced in support of the bill. An example is a March 30, 1964, letter by Harrison Tweed and Bernard G. Segal, for themselves and a number of other distinguished attorneys, to Senators Humphrey and Kuchel. Excerpts follow:

"With respect to title II, the congressional authority for its enactment is expressly stated in the bill to rest on the commerce clause of the Constitution and on the 14th amendment. The reliance upon both of these powers to accomplish the stated purpose of title II is sound. Discriminatory practices, though free from any State compulsion, support, or encouragement, may so burden the channels of interstate commerce as to justify, legally, congressional regulation under the commerce clause. . . .

"The grounding of the public accommodations title on the commerce clause is in keeping with a long tradition of Federal legislation, validated in many judicial decisions, and is not today open to substantial legal dispute. In exercising its power to regulate commerce among the States, Congress has enacted laws, encompassing the widest range of commercial transactions, similar to the regulatory scheme of title II of H.R. 7152."

C. THE COURT DECISIONS
HEART OF ATLANTA MOTEL v. UNITED STATES

379 U.S. 241, 85 S.Ct. 348, 13 L.Ed.2d 258 (1964).

Appeal from the United States District Court for the Northern District of Georgia.

Mr. Justice CLARK delivered the opinion of the Court.

This is a declaratory judgment action, 28 U.S.C. § 2201 and § 2202, attacking the constitutionality of Title II of the Civil Rights Act of 1964. . . . Appellant owns and operates the Heart of Atlanta Motel which has 216 rooms available to transient guests. The motel is located on Courtland Street, two blocks from downtown Peachtree Street. It is readily accessible to interstate highways 75 and 85 and state highways 23 and 41. Appellant solicits patronage from outside the State of Georgia through various national advertising media, including magazines of national circulation; it maintains over 50 billboards and highway signs within the State, soliciting patronage for the motel; it accepts convention trade from outside Georgia and approximately 75% of its registered guests are from out of State.   Prior to passage of the Act the motel had followed a practice of refusing to rent rooms to Negroes, and it alleged that it intended to continue to do so.   In an effort to perpetuate that policy this suit was filed.   .   .   .

It is admitted that the operation of the motel brings it within the provisions of § 201(a) of the Act and that appellant refused to provide lodging for transient Negroes because of their race or color and that it intends to continue that policy unless restrained.

The sole question posed is, therefore, the constitutionality of the Civil Rights Act of 1964 as applied to these facts.   The legislative history of the Act indicates that Congress based the Act on § 5 and the Equal Protection Clause of the Fourteenth Amendment as well as its power to regulate interstate commerce under Art. I, § 8, cl. 3 of the Constitution.

The Senate Commerce Committee made it quite clear that the fundamental object of Title II was to vindicate "the deprivation of personal dignity that surely accompanies denials of equal access to public establishments."   At the same time, however, it noted that such an objective has been and could be readily achieved "by congressional action based on the commerce power of the Constitution."   S.Rep.No. 872, at 16–17.   Our study of the legislative record, made in the light of prior cases, has brought us to the conclusion that Congress possessed ample power in this regard, and we have therefore not considered the other grounds relied upon.   This is not to say that the remaining authority upon which it acted was not adequate, a question upon which we do not pass, but merely that since the commerce power is sufficient for our decision here we have considered it alone.   Nor is § 201(d) or § 202, having to do with state action, involved here and we do not pass upon those sections.   .   .   .

While the Act as adopted carried no congressional findings the record of its passage through each house is replete with evidence of the burdens that discrimination by race or color places upon interstate commerce.   .   .   .   This testimony included the fact that our people have become increasingly mobile with millions of all races traveling from State to State;   that Negroes in particular have been the subject of discrimination in transient accommodations, having to travel great distances to secure the same;   that often they have been unable to obtain accommodations and have had to call upon friends to put them up overnight   .   .   . ;   and that these conditions had become so acute as to require the listing of available lodging for Negroes in a special guidebook which was itself "dramatic testimony of the difficulties" Negroes encounter in travel   .   .   ..   These exclusionary practices were found to be nationwide, the Under Secretary of Commerce testifying that there is "no question that this discrimination in the North still exists to a large degree" and in the West and Midwest as well.   .   .   .   This testimony indicated a qualitative as well as quantitative effect on interstate travel by Negroes. The former was the obvious impairment of the Negro traveler's pleasure and convenience that resulted when he continually was uncertain of finding lodging.   As for the latter, there was evidence that this uncertainty stemming from racial discrimination had the effect of discouraging travel on the part of a substantial portion of the Negro community.   .   .   .   We shall not burden this opinion with further details since the voluminous testimony presents overwhelming evidence that discrimination by hotels and motels impedes interstate travel.   .   .   .

The power of Congress to deal with these obstructions depends on the meaning of the Commerce Clause. Its meaning was first enunciated 140 years ago by the great Chief Justice John Marshall in Gibbons v. Ogden, 9 Wheat. 1 (1824). [Two pages of quotations are omitted.] In short, the determinative test of the exercise of power by the Congress under the Commerce Clause is simply whether the activity sought to be regulated is "commerce which concerns more than one state" and has a real and substantial relation to the national interest. Let us now turn to this facet of the problem.

That the "intercourse" of which the Chief Justice spoke included the movement of persons through more States than one was settled as early as 1849, in the Passenger Cases, 7 How. 283. [After quoting from Hoke and Caminetti, the Mann Act cases, the Court continued:] Nor does it make any difference whether the transportation is commercial in character. [Caminetti v. United States, 242 U.S. 470, at 484–486.] . . .

The same interest in protecting interstate commerce which led Congress to deal with segregation in interstate carriers and the white slave traffic has prompted it to extend the exercise of its power to gambling, Lottery Case, 188 U.S. 321 (1903); to criminal enterprises, Brooks v. United States, 267 U.S. 432 (1925); to deceptive practices in the sale of products, Federal Trade Comm'n v. Mandel Bros., Inc., 359 U.S. 385 (1959); to fraudulent security transactions, Securities & Exchange Comm'n v. Ralston Purina Co., 346 U.S. 119 (1953); to misbranding of drugs, Weeks v. United States, 245 U.S. 618 (1918); to wages and hours, United States v. Darby, 312 U.S. 100 (1941); to members of labor unions, Labor Board v. Jones & Laughlin Steel Corp., 301 U.S. 1 (1937); to crop control, Wickard v. Filburn, 317 U.S. 111 (1942); to discrimination against shippers, United States v. Baltimore & Ohio R. Co., 333 U.S. 169 (1948); to the protection of small business from injurious price cutting, Moore v. Mead's Fine Bread Co., 348 U.S. 115 (1954); to resale price maintenance, Hudson Distributors, Inc. v. Eli Lilly & Co., 377 U.S. 386 (1964); Schwegmann v. Calvert Distillers Corp., 341 U.S. 384 (1951); to professional football, Radovich v. National Football League, 352 U.S. 445 (1957); and to racial discrimination by owners and managers of terminal restaurants, Boynton v. Virginia, 364 U.S. 454 (1960).

That Congress was legislating against moral wrongs in many of these areas rendered its enactments no less valid. In framing Title II of this Act Congress was also dealing with what it considered a moral problem. But that fact does not detract from the overwhelming evidence of the disruptive effect that racial discrimination has had on commercial intercourse. It was this burden which empowered Congress to enact appropriate legislation, and, given this basis for the exercise of its power, Congress was not restricted by the fact that the particular obstruction to interstate commerce with which it was dealing was also deemed a moral and social wrong.

It is said that the operation of the motel here is of a purely local character. But, assuming this to be true, "if it is interstate commerce that feels the pinch, it does not matter how local the operation that applies the squeeze." United States v. Women's Sportswear Mfrs. Ass'n., 336 U.S. 460, 464 (1949). [A quotation from United States v. Darby, supra, is omitted.] Thus the power of Congress to promote interstate commerce also includes the power to regulate the local incidents thereof, including local activities in both the States of origin and destination, which might have a substantial and harmful effect upon that commerce. One need only examine the evidence which we have discussed above to see that Congress may—as it has—prohibit racial discrimination by motels serving travelers, however "local" their operations may appear.

Nor does the Act deprive appellant of liberty or property under the Fifth Amendment. The commerce power invoked here by the Congress is a specific and plenary one authorized by the Constitution itself. The only questions are: (1) whether Congress had a rational basis for finding that racial discrimination by motels affected commerce, and (2) if it had such a basis, whether the means it selected to eliminate that evil are reasonable and appropriate. If they are, appellant has no "right" to select its guests as it sees fit, free from governmental regulation. . . .

We, therefore, conclude that the action of the Congress in the adoption of the Act as applied here to a motel which concededly serves interstate travelers is within the power granted it by the Commerce Clause of the Constitution, as interpreted by this Court for 140 years. It may be argued that Congress could have pursued other methods to eliminate the obstructions it found in interstate commerce caused by racial discrimination. But this is a matter of policy that rests entirely with the Congress not with the courts. How obstructions in commerce may be removed—what means are to be employed—is within the sound and exclusive discretion of the Congress. It is subject only to one caveat—that the means chosen by it must be reasonably adapted to the end permitted by the Constitution. We cannot say that its choice here was not so adapted. The Constitution requires no more.

Affirmed.

[Excerpts from the concurring opinions of Justices Black, Douglas and Goldberg—applicable to this case and to McClung, which follows—appear after McClung.]

KATZENBACH v. McCLUNG

379 U.S. 294, 85 S.Ct. 377, 13 L.Ed.2d 290 (1964).

Appeal from the United States District Court for the Northern District of Alabama.

Mr. Justice CLARK delivered the opinion of the Court.

This case was argued with [Heart of Atlanta Motel, supra], decided this date, in which we upheld the constitutional validity of Title II of the Civil Rights Act of 1964 against an attack by hotels, motels, and like establishments. This complaint for injunctive relief against appellants attacks the constitutionality of the Act as applied to a restaurant. The case was heard by a three-judge United States District Court and an injunction was issued restraining appellants from enforcing the Act against the restaurant. . . . We now reverse the judgment. . . .

Ollie's Barbecue is a family-owned restaurant in Birmingham, Alabama, specializing in barbecued meats and homemade pies, with a seating capacity of 220 customers. It is located on a state highway 11 blocks from an interstate one and a somewhat greater distance from railroad and bus stations. The restaurant caters to a family and white-collar trade with a take-out service for Negroes. It employs 36 persons, two-thirds of whom are Negroes.

In the 12 months preceding the passage of the Act, the restaurant purchased locally approximately $150,000 worth of food, $69,783 or 46% of which was meat that it bought from a local supplier who had procured it from outside the State. The District Court expressly found that a substantial portion of the food served in the restaurant had moved in interstate commerce. The restaurant has refused to serve Negroes in its dining accommodations since its original opening in 1927, and since July 2, 1964, it has been operating in violation of the Act. The court below concluded that if it were required to serve Negroes it would lose a substantial amount of business.

. . .

[As to the commerce power, the District Court insisted that there must be] a close and substantial relation between local activities and interstate commerce which requires control of the former in the protection of the latter. The court concluded, however, that the Congress, rather than finding facts sufficient to meet this rule, had legislated a conclusive presumption that a restaurant affects interstate commerce if it serves or offers to serve interstate travelers or if a substantial portion of the food which it serves has moved in commerce. This, the court held, it could not do because there was no demonstrable connection between food purchased in interstate commerce and sold in a restaurant and the conclusion of Congress that discrimination in the restaurant would affect that commerce. . . .

. . . Sections 201(b)(2) and (c) place any "restaurant . . . principally engaged in selling food for consumption on the premises" under the Act "if . . . it serves or offers to serve interstate travelers or a substantial portion of the food which it serves . . . has moved in commerce."

Ollie's Barbecue admits that it is covered by these provisions of the Act. The Government makes no contention that the discrimination at the restaurant was supported by the State of Alabama. There is no claim that interstate travelers frequented the restaurant. The sole question, therefore, narrows down to whether Title II, as applied to a restaurant receiving about $70,000 worth of food which has moved in commerce, is a valid exercise of the power of Congress. The Government has contended that Congress had ample basis upon which to find that racial discrimination at restaurants which receive from out of state a substantial portion of the food served does, in fact, impose commercial burdens of national magnitude upon interstate commerce. The appellees' major argument is directed to this premise. They urge that no such basis existed. It is to that question that we now turn. . . .

As we noted in Heart of Atlanta Motel both Houses of Congress conducted prolonged hearings on the Act. And, as we said there, while no formal findings were made, which of course is not necessary, it is well that we make mention of the testimony at these hearings the better to understand the problem before Congress and determine whether the Act is a reasonable and appropriate means toward its solution. The record is replete with testimony of the burdens placed on interstate commerce by racial discrimination in restaurants. A comparison of per capita spending by Negroes in restaurants, theaters, and like establishments indicated less spending, after discounting income differences, in areas where discrimination is widely practiced. This condition, which was especially aggravated in the South, was attributed in the testimony of the Under Secretary of Commerce to racial segregation. . . . This diminutive spending springing from a refusal to serve Negroes and their total loss as customers has, regardless of the absence of direct evidence, a close connection to interstate commerce. The fewer customers a restaurant enjoys the less food it sells and consequently the less it buys. . . . In addition, the Attorney General testified that this type of discrimination imposed "an artificial restriction on the market" and interfered with the flow of merchandise. . . . In addition, there were many references to discriminatory situations causing wide unrest and having a depressant effect on general business conditions in the respective communities. . . .

Moreover there was an impressive array of testimony that discrimination in restaurants had a direct and highly restrictive effect upon interstate travel by Negroes. This resulted, it was said, because discrimination practices prevent Negroes from buying prepared food served on the premises while on a trip, except in isolated and unkempt restaurants and under most unsatisfactory and often unpleasant conditions. This obviously discourages travel and obstructs interstate commerce for one can hardly travel without eating. Likewise, it was said, that discrimination deterred professional, as well as skilled, people from moving into areas where such practices occurred and thereby caused industry to be reluctant to establish there. . . .

We believe that this testimony afforded ample basis for the conclusion that established restaurants in such areas sold less interstate goods because of the discrimination, that interstate travel was obstructed directly by it, that business in general suffered and that many new businesses refrained from establishing there as a result of it. Hence the District Court was in error in concluding that there was no connection between discrimination and the movement of interstate commerce. Rather than such connection being outside "common experience," as the court said, its conclusion flies in the face of stubborn fact.

It goes without saying that, viewed in isolation, the volume of food purchased by Ollie's Barbecue from sources supplied from out of state was insignificant when compared with the total foodstuffs moving in commerce. But, as our late Brother Jackson said for the Court in Wickard v. Filburn, 317 U.S. 111 (1942):

"That appellee's own contribution to the demand for wheat may be trivial by itself is not enough to remove him from the scope of federal regulation where, as here, his contribution, taken together with that of many others similarly situated, is far from trivial." At 127–128.

We noted in Heart of Atlanta Motel that a number of witnesses attested the fact that racial discrimination was not merely a state or regional problem but was one of nationwide scope. Against this background, we must conclude that while the focus of the legislation was on the individual restaurant's relation to interstate commerce, Congress appropriately considered the importance of that connection with the knowledge that the discrimination was but "representative of many others throughout the country, the total incidence of which if left unchecked may well become far-reaching in its harm to commerce." Polish Alliance v. Labor Board, 322 U.S. 643, 648 (1944).

With this situation spreading as the record shows, Congress was not required to await the total dislocation of commerce. . . .

. . . Much is said about a restaurant business being local but "even if appellee's activity be local and though it may not be regarded as commerce, it may still, whatever its nature, be reached by Congress if it exerts a substantial economic effect on interstate commerce . . . ." Wickard v. Filburn, supra, at 125. The activities that are beyond the reach of Congress are "those which are completely within a particular State, which do not affect other States, and with which it is not necessary to interfere, for the purpose of executing some of the general powers of the government." Gibbons v. Ogden, 9 Wheat. 1, 195 (1824). This rule is as good today as it was when Chief Justice Marshall laid it down almost a century and a half ago. . . .

The appellees contend that Congress has arbitrarily created a conclusive presumption that all restaurants meeting the criteria set out in the Act "affect commerce." Stated another way, they object to the omission of a provision for a case-by-case determination—judicial or administrative—that racial discrimination in a particular restaurant affects commerce.

But Congress' action in framing this Act was not unprecedented. In United States v. Darby, 312 U.S. 100 (1941), this Court held constitutional the Fair Labor Standards Act. . . .

Here, as there, Congress has determined for itself that refusals of service to Negroes have imposed burdens both upon the interstate flow of food and upon the movement of products generally. Of course, the mere fact that Congress has said when particular activity shall be deemed to affect commerce does not preclude further examination by this Court. But where we find that the legislators, in light of the facts and testimony before them, have a rational basis for finding a chosen regulatory scheme necessary to the protection of commerce, our investigation is at an end. The only remaining question—one answered in the affirmative by the court below—is whether the particular restaurant either serves or offers to serve interstate travelers or serves food a substantial portion of which has moved in interstate commerce.

The appellees urge that Congress, in passing the Fair Labor Standards Act and the National Labor Relations Act, made specific findings which were embodied in those statutes. Here, of course, Congress has included no formal findings. But their absence is not fatal to the validity of the statute, see United States v. Carolene Products Co., 304 U.S. 144, 152 (1938), for the evidence presented at the hearings fully indicated the nature and effect of the burdens on commerce which Congress meant to alleviate.

Confronted as we are with the facts laid before Congress, we must conclude that it had a rational basis for finding that racial discrimination in restaurants had a direct and adverse effect on the free flow of interstate commerce. . . . We think . . . that Congress acted well within its power to protect and foster commerce in extending the coverage of Title II only to those restaurants offering to serve interstate travelers or serving food, a substantial portion of which has moved in interstate commerce.

The absence of direct evidence connecting discriminatory restaurant service with the flow of interstate food, a factor on which the appellees place much reliance, is not, given the evidence as to the effect of such practices on other aspects of commerce, a crucial matter.

The power of Congress in this field is broad and sweeping; where it keeps within its sphere and violates no express constitutional limitation it has been the rule of this Court, going back almost to the founding days of the Republic, not to interfere. The Civil Rights Act of 1964, as here applied, we find to be plainly appropriate in the resolution of what the Congress found to be a national commercial problem of the first magnitude. We find it in no violation of any express limitations of the Constitution and we therefore declare it valid.

Reversed.

Mr. Justice BLACK, concurring. . . .

[Congress] described the nature and extent of operations which it wished to regulate, excluding some establishments from the Act either for reasons of policy or because it believed its powers to regulate and protect interstate commerce did not extend so far. There can be no doubt that the operations of both the motel and the restaurant here fall squarely within the measure Congress chose to adopt in the Act and deemed adequate to show a constitutionally prohibitable adverse effect on commerce. The choice of policy is of course within the exclusive power of Congress; but whether particular operations affect interstate commerce sufficiently to come under the constitutional power of Congress to regulate them is ultimately a judicial rather than a legislative question, and can be settled finally only by this Court. I agree that as applied to this motel and this restaurant the Act is a valid exercise of congressional power, in the case of the motel because the record amply demonstrates that its practice of discrimination tended directly to interfere with interstate travel, and in the case of the restaurant because Congress had ample basis for concluding that a widespread practice of racial discrimination by restaurants buying as substantial a quantity of goods shipped from other States as this restaurant buys could distort or impede interstate trade. . . .

I recognize that every remote, possible, speculative effect on commerce should not be accepted as an adequate constitutional ground to uproot and throw into the discard all our traditional distinctions between what is purely local, and therefore controlled by state laws, and what affects the national interest and is therefore subject to control by federal laws. I recognize too that some isolated and remote lunch room which sells only to local people and buys almost all its supplies in the locality may possibly be beyond the reach of the power of Congress to regulate commerce, just as such an establishment is not covered by the present Act. But in deciding the constitutional power of Congress in cases like the two before us we do not consider the effect on interstate commerce of only one isolated, individual, local event, without regard to the fact that this single local event when added to many others of a similar nature may impose a burden on interstate commerce by reducing its volume or distorting its flow. . . . Measuring, as this Court has so often held is required, by the aggregate effect of a great number of such acts of discrimination, I am of the opinion that Congress has constitutional power under the Commerce and Necessary and Proper Clauses to protect interstate commerce from the injuries bound to befall it from these discriminatory practices. . . .

. . . In view of the Commerce Clause it is not possible to deny that the aim of protecting interstate commerce from undue burdens is a legitimate end. In view of the Thirteenth, Fourteenth and Fifteenth Amendments, it is not possible to deny that the aim of protecting Negroes from discrimination is also a legitimate end.[1] The means adopted to achieve these

---

1. We have specifically upheld the power of Congress to use the commerce power to end racial discrimination. Boynton v. Virginia, 364 U.S.

ends are also appropriate, plainly adopted to achieve them and not prohibited by the Constitution but consistent with both its letter and spirit. . . .

. . . Because the Civil Rights Act of 1964 as applied here is wholly valid under the Commerce Clause and the Necessary and Proper Clause, there is no need to consider whether this Act is also constitutionally supportable under section 5 of the Fourteenth Amendment which grants Congress "power to enforce, by appropriate legislation, the provisions of this article."

Mr. Justice DOUGLAS, concurring. . . .

Though I join the Court's opinion, I am somewhat reluctant here, as I was in Edwards v. California, 314 U.S. 160, 177, to rest solely on the Commerce Clause. My reluctance is not due to any conviction that Congress lacks power to regulate commerce in the interests of human rights. It is rather my belief that the right of people to be free of state action that discriminates against them because of race, like the "right to persons to move freely from State to State" (Edwards v. California, supra, at 177), "occupies a more protected position in our constitutional system than does the movement of cattle, fruit, steel and coal across state lines." Ibid. [The] result reached by the Court is for me much more obvious as a protective measure under the Fourteenth Amendment than under the Commerce Clause. For the former deals with the constitutional status of the individual, not with the impact on commerce of local activities or vice versa. . . .

A decision based on the Fourteenth Amendment would have a more settling effect, making unnecessary litigation over whether a particular restaurant or inn is within the commerce definitions of the Act or whether a particular customer is an interstate traveler. Under my construction, the Act would apply to all customers in all the enumerated places of public accommodation. . . .

In determining the reach of an exertion of legislative power, it is customary to read various granted powers together. . . . The "means" used in the present Act are in my view "appropriate" and "plainly adapted" to the end of enforcing Fourteenth Amendment rights as well as protecting interstate commerce. . . .

Thus while I agree with the Court that Congress in fashioning the present Act used the Commerce Clause to regulate racial segregation, it also used (and properly so) some of its power under § 5 of the Fourteenth Amendment. [Our] decision should be based on the Fourteenth Amendment, thereby putting an end to all obstructionist strategies and allowing every person—whatever his race, creed, or color—to patronize all places of public accommodation without discrimination whether he travels interstate or intrastate.

454; Henderson v. United States, 339 U.S. 816; Mitchell v. United States, 313 U.S. 80; cf. Bailey v. Patterson, 369 U.S. 31; Morgan v. Virginia, 328 U.S. 373. Compare cases in which the commerce power has been used to advance other ends not entirely commercial: e. g., United States v. Darby, 312 U.S. 100 (Fair Labor Standards Act); United States v. Miller, 307 U.S. 174 (National Firearms Act); Gooch v. United States, 297 U.S. 124 (Federal Kidnaping Act); Brooks v. United States, 267 U.S. 432 (National Motor Vehicle Theft Act); United States v. Simpson, 252 U.S. 465 (Act forbidding shipment of liquor into a "dry" State); Caminetti v. United States, 242 U.S. 470 (White-Slave Traffic [Mann] Act); Hoke v. United States, 227 U.S. 308 (White-Slave Traffic [Mann] Act); Hipolite Egg Co. v. United States, 220 U.S. 45 (Pure Food and Drug Act); Lottery Case, 188 U.S. 321 (Act forbidding interstate shipment of lottery tickets). [Footnote by Justice Black.]

Mr. Justice GOLDBERG, concurring.

I join in the opinions and judgments of the Court .   .   .   .

The primary purpose of the Civil Rights Act of 1964, however, and as I would underscore, is the vindication of human dignity and not mere economics.   .   .   .   Congress clearly had authority both under § 5 of the Fourteenth Amendment and the Commerce Clause to enact the Civil Rights Act of 1964.

DANIEL v. PAUL

In a broad interpretation of the 1964 Act in Daniel v. Paul, 395 U.S. 298 (1969), a divided Court found the Lake Nixon Club, a recreational facility near Little Rock, Arkansas, to be a "public accommodation" whose operations "affect commerce." The Club is "a 232-acre amusement area with swimming, boating, sun bathing, picnicking, miniature golf, and dancing facilities and a snack bar." * Justice Brennan's majority opinion found Lake Nixon's snack bar to be a covered public accommodation under §§ 201(a) (2) and 201(c) (2); that status automatically brought the entire establishment within the Act, under §§ 201(b) (4) and 201(c) (4). The snack bar, he found, was covered under either criterion of § 201(c) (2): it offered "to serve interstate travelers"; and "a substantial portion of the food" served there "has moved in commerce."

With respect to the former standard, he noted that the owners' "choice of advertising media leaves no doubt" that they "were seeking broad-based patronage from an audience which they knew to include interstate travelers" in the Little Rock area. Moreover, "it would be unrealistic to assume that none of the 100,000 patrons actually served by the Club each season was an interstate traveler." And since the snack bar "was established to serve all patrons of the entire facility, we must conclude that the snack bar offered to serve and served out-of-state persons." With respect to the second criterion, Justice Brennan thought there could be "no serious doubt" that a "substantial portion of the food" had "moved in interstate commerce." Although he conceded that the record was "not as complete on this point as might be desired," he pointed to the "limited fare—hot dogs and hamburgers on buns, soft drinks, and milk"—served by the snack bar, and the trial court's judicial notice that some of the ingredients of the bread and of the soft drinks probably came from out-of-state sources. "Thus, at the very least," Justice Brennan stated, "three of the four food items sold at the snack bar contain ingredients originating outside of the State."

The Court also found the Club a covered public accommodation under § 201(b) (3) of the Act, as a "place of entertainment" whose operations "affect commerce" because, under § 201(c) (3), its customary "sources of entertainment . . . move in commerce." Justice Brennan rejected the argument that "place of entertainment" referred only to establishments where patrons were spectators rather than direct participants, even though most of the legis-

---

* There was no challenge in the Supreme Court to the lower courts' finding that the Club was not an exempt "private club" under § 201(e) of the Act: a 25-cent "membership fee" system was "no more than a subterfuge to avoid coverage of the 1964 Act"; the Club was "simply a business operated for a profit with none of the attributes of self-government and member-ownership traditionally associated with private clubs."

lative discussion admittedly "focused on places of spectator entertainment rather than recreational areas." And he was easily satisfied that the "sources of entertainment [here] move in commerce." He was able to state the supporting data in three sentences: "The Club leases 15 paddle boats on a royalty basis from an Oklahoma company. Another boat was purchased from the same company. The Club's juke box was manufactured outside Arkansas and plays records manufactured outside the State."

Justice Black's dissent stated that he would have agreed with the result if the public accommodations law had been based on § 5 of the Fourteenth Amendment. But instead Congress had "tied the Act and limited its protection" to the commerce power. That required a finding that the Club's operations "affect commerce" within the meaning of § 201(c), and the lower courts' findings did not support coverage: "My trouble with the Court's holding is that it runs rough-shod over District Court findings supported by the record and emphatically affirmed by the Court of Appeals." He concluded: "While it is the duty of courts to enforce this important Act, we are not called on, nor should we hold subject to that Act this country people's recreation center, lying in what may be, so far as we know, a little 'sleepy hollow' between Arkansas hills miles away from any interstate highway. This would be stretching the Commerce Clause so as to give the Federal Government complete control over every little remote country place of recreation in every nook and cranny of every precinct and county in every one of the 50 States. This goes too far for me."

OTHER CIVIL RIGHTS PROVISIONS BASED ON THE COMMERCE POWER—TRANSPORTATION, LABOR RELATIONS, HOUSING

1. *Discrimination in transportation.* In decisions prior to the 1964 Act, the Court had found that general provisions of the Interstate Commerce Act prohibited racial segregation by interstate carriers. The Act makes it unlawful for an interstate railroad "to subject any person . . . to any undue or unreasonable prejudice or disadvantage in any respect whatsoever." Henderson v. United States, 339 U.S. 816 (1950), held that this provision prohibited railroad rules providing for segregation of Negroes in interstate dining cars. See also Mitchell v. United States, 313 U.S. 80 (1941).

The sections of the Act governing interstate motor vehicle common carriers apply the same restrictions and add a ban on "any unjust discrimination." In Boynton v. Virginia, 364 U.S. 454 (1960), the Court reversed a Virginia trespass conviction of a Negro interstate bus passenger who had been refused service at a restaurant in a bus terminal because of his race. The certiorari petition raised only constitutional challenges, based on the commerce clause and the Fourteenth Amendment. The Court, in an opinion by Justice Black, relied solely on the Interstate Commerce Act. Though there was no record evidence that the terminal or the restaurant were owned or controlled by the carrier, the majority concluded that the Act applied because "the terminal and restaurant operate as an integral part of the bus carrier's transportation service for interstate passengers." For a critical analysis, see Pollak, "The Supreme Court and the States: Reflections on Boynton v. Virginia," 49 Calif.L.Rev. 15 (1961).

2. *Discrimination in labor relations and Title VII of the 1964 Act.* a. Though the National Labor Relations Act and the Railway Labor Act, like the Interstate Commerce Act, contain no provisions specifically addressed to racial discrimination, interpretations have made them applicable to the civil rights area as well. For example, Steele v. Louisville & N. R. R., 323 U.S. 192 (1944), held that a union's status as exclusive bargaining agent under the Railway Labor Act carried the implied duty to represent all employees in the bargaining unit without discrimination. This duty was found to be enforceable by civil action in a federal court. The Steele doctrine was carried over to the National Labor Relations Act in Syres v. Oil Workers, 350 U.S. 892 (1955). In 1962, the NLRB found that claims of unfair representation could be brought as unfair labor practice proceedings before the agency. Miranda Fuel Co., 140 N.L.R.B. 181 (1962), enforcement denied, 326 F. 2d 172 (2d Cir. 1963). On July 1, 1964, the day before the enactment of the Civil Rights Act of 1964, the Labor Board applied the Miranda ruling to a racial discrimination case for the first time, finding that union discrimination deprived the employees of the right to bargain collectively through representatives of their own choosing, under Section 7 of the Act. See Sovern, "The National Labor Relations Act and Racial Discrimination," 62 Colum.L.Rev. 563 (1962); Recent Case, 78 Harv.L.Rev. 679 (1965).

b. Did these NLRB rulings survive the enactment of Title VII, "Equal Employment Opportunity", of the Civil Rights Act of 1964? See Sherman, "The Union's Duty of Fair Representation and the Civil Rights Act of 1964," 49 Minn.L.Rev. 771 (1965). These provisions began to go into effect on July 2, 1965. In essence, the Title prohibits covered employers, employment agencies and labor unions from discriminating on the basis of race, color, religion, sex, or national origin. The administrative provisions rely heavily on conciliation, mediation and cooperation with state agencies—through a newly created U. S. Equal Employment Opportunity Commission—; direct federal enforcement is largely left to private actions in federal courts. (Title III of the Proposed Civil Rights Act of 1967 would have given enforcement powers to the U. S. Commission, but these provisions were not included when portions of the 1967 proposals were enacted as the Civil Rights Act of 1968. See chap. 6, below.)

Note the broad coverage provisions of Title VII. It applies, for example, to labor organizations "engaged in an industry affecting commerce" and to employers "engaged in an industry affecting commerce" who meet certain numerical standards with respect to the number of employees—100 at the outset, 25 after July 2, 1968. Section 701(h) defines "industry affecting commerce" as "any activity, business, or industry in commerce or in which a labor dispute would hinder or obstruct commerce or the free flow of commerce and includes any activity or industry 'affecting commerce' within the meaning of the Labor-Management Reporting and Disclosure Act of 1959." During the Senate debate, the Department of Labor submitted a memorandum stating that "it is now well settled that the constitutional power extends to activities affecting commerce in any amount or volume not so minimal or sporadic as to fall within the doctrine of *de minimis non curat lex.*"

3. *Discrimination in housing: The 1966 and 1967 proposals, Title VIII of the 1968 Civil Rights Act—and the discovery of the 1866 law.*

President Johnson's State of the Union Message of January 12, 1966, announced that he would request legislation, "resting on the fullest constitutional authority of the Federal Government, to prohibit discrimination in housing." The request came in a special Civil Rights Message of April 28, 1966: "I ask the Congress to enact the first effective Federal law against discrimination in the sale and rental of housing." An amended Administration proposal was adopted by the House on August 9, 1966, but it did not come to a vote on the merits in the Senate. There, motions to invoke cloture twice fell ten votes short of the required two-thirds majority. Early in 1967, the Administration renewed its call for civil rights legislation but this effort also failed.

The President's Civil Rights Message of January 24, 1968, renewed his call for open housing legislation, but there was then little hope that any would be enacted. But when the House-adopted H.R. 2516 came before the Senate early in February, housing amendments were offered. And on March 4, 1968, after several efforts to bring the six weeks debate to an end, a cloture motion was approved by exactly the required two-thirds vote. (Among the new supporters of cloture and the bill was Senator Dirksen, who had earlier opposed fair housing laws on constitutional grounds.) After anti-riot and Indian rights amendments were added to the bill, the Senate passed the amended H.R. 2516 on March 11. On April 10, 1968,—six days after the assassination of Dr. Martin Luther King, Jr.—the House rejected efforts to send the bill to conference and accepted the Senate amendments. The amended H.R. 2516—including Title VIII, the fair housing provision—became law on April 11, 1968. Public Law 90-284, 82 Stat. 73.

Two months after the enactment of the 1968 Civil Rights Act, Jones v. Alfred H. Mayer Co., 392 U.S. 409 (1968), found in an 1866 statute based on the Thirteenth Amendment a comprehensive ban against racial discrimination in housing. The Jones case, which considers the relationship between the 1866 and 1968 provisions on housing discrimination, and excerpts from Title VIII of the 1968 Act, are printed below, chap. 6, p. 525. The recent proposals for national open housing legislation raised renewed questions of constitutional justification: Were they sustainable under the commerce clause? Under other grants of congressional power in Art. I, Sec. 8? Under the Thirteenth or Fourteenth Amendments? Consider these questions in light of the Jones case, and a related, later decision, Sullivan v. Little Hunting Park, 396 U.S. 229 (1970) (chap. 6, p. 517, infra).

President Johnson's State of the Union Message of January 12, 1966, announced that he would request legislation. Ending on the fuller constitutional authority. The request came in his Special Message of April 28, 1966: "I ask the Congress to enact one that effective Federal law making discrimination in the sale and rental of housing". An amended Administra-

Chapter 5

OTHER NATIONAL POWERS IN THE 1787 CONSTITUTION

Scope Note. The commerce power has been the most widely litigated and most controversial source of national authority to deal with local activities; chapter 4 accordingly examined it at length. This chapter deals more briefly with other national powers granted by the Constitutional Convention which have also had significant impact on the allocation of authority within the federal system. The taxing and spending powers, secs. 1 and 2, are of special interest because of their close functional and doctrinal ties to the commerce power. The Constitution described the taxing and spending powers in the opening clause of Art. I, Sec. 8: "The Congress shall have Power To lay and collect Taxes, Duties, Imports and Excises, to pay the Debts and provide for the common Defence and general Welfare of the United States." The manner in which taxes are imposed and the way in which money is spent can have significant regulatory impacts. As with commerce laws, taxing and spending measures have been used to deal with "police" as well as economic problems. Not surprisingly, regulations through taxing and spending have been resorted to in periods, as in the 1930's, when the need for legislation seemed great and the direct regulatory authority through the commerce clause was under constitutional clouds. To what extent are the functions and limits pertaining to the taxing and spending powers similar to, to what extent different from, those considered in connection with the commerce power? That is the primary theme of sections 1 and 2.

Sections 3 and 4 briefly consider powers with impacts on federalism that are significant even though less frequently litigated: they deal with the national authority relating to war and foreign relations (especially through treaties). Section 5 seeks merely to call attention to a number of other sources of national authority: each of these powers involves special historical problems; most of the powers, however, are of less general significance than those examined in greater detail in these materials. Section 6, the final section of this chapter, opens up a distinctive additional dimension: typically, the exercises of national power considered in that section do not encounter the federalism-related limits characteristic of all of the preceding materials; rather, those legislative efforts are challenged because of individual rights (not local autonomy) concerns. That section not only gives a preliminary view of individual rights issues that are developed further in Part III. It also, and most importantly, raises the question whether the presence of an individual rights concern affects the legitimate scope of congressional discretion to select means as developed in the cases since McCulloch: does the interpretation of "necessary and proper" change when the opposing restraining interest is individual rights, not federalism?

One other significant source of powers must be considered for a comprehensive view of congressional powers with significant impact on the division of powers in the federal system. That additional source lies not in the 1787 document itself but in the post-Civil War changes. The 13th,

14th and 15th Amendments each contain specific authorizations empowering Congress "to enforce this article by appropriate legislation." That authority long lay dormant because of congressional inaction and restrictive judicial interpretation. But new laws and new interpretations of the 1960's, especially with respect to voting and housing, have dramatized the vast potential impact of these Amendments on federalism. The examination of the effect of the post-Civil War Amendments on congressional powers (chap. 6) follows the survey in this chapter of the remaining national powers in the 1787 document.

SECTION 1. THE TAXING POWER

Introduction. To what extent may the national taxing power be used as a means of regulation? * The materials in this section examine the Court's handling of this problem, and they are offered primarily for critical comparison with the preceding commerce power cases. A number of relationships between the two lines of cases have already been noted. For example, tax cases were relied on in the Hammer v. Dagenhart dissent and in Darby; and Congress has repeatedly invoked one of the powers when the other proved to be an inadequate basis for national regulation, as in the child labor area.

Consider, in examining these cases, the similarities and the differences in the development of limits on the commerce and taxing powers. Do the differences in doctrine reflect differences in the nature of the problems? Has the Court been more successful in curbing "abuses" of the taxing power than of the commerce power? Is it easier to detect an invocation of the power to tax as a "pretext"? In short, compare the search for "motive" and "purpose" in tax cases with that in commerce cases. Is it important to distinguish taxes whose regulatory impact depends on the immediate deterring effect on the taxed activity from those whose regulatory effect rests on collateral reporting and enforcement provisions of the tax statute?

CHILD LABOR TAX CASE
[BAILEY v. DREXEL FURNITURE CO.]
259 U.S. 20, 42 S.Ct. 449, 66 L.Ed. 817 (1922).

Error to the District Court of the United States for the Western District of North Carolina.

---

* It is not the purpose of this Section to open a discussion of questions concerning national taxation that is clearly for revenue purposes. However, note should be taken of the power of Congress to tax for those purposes. The power "is given in the Constitution, with only one exception and only two qualifications. Congress cannot tax exports, and it must impose direct taxes by the rule of apportionment, and indirect taxes by the rule of uniformity. Thus limited, and thus only, it reaches every subject, and may be exercised at discretion." Chief Justice Chase, in License Tax Cases, 5 Wall. 462, 471 (1867). Concerning direct taxes and the requirement that they be apportioned, see Hylton v. United States, 3 Dallas 171 (1796); Pollock v. Farmers' Loan & Trust Co., 157 U.S. 429 (1895). For the development of the doctrine that the uniformity of indirect taxes is "geographic, not intrinsic," see Knowlton v. Moore, 178 U.S. 41 (1900), and Bromley v. McCaughn, 280 U.S. 124 (1929).

Mr. Chief Justice TAFT delivered the opinion of the court.

This case presents the question of the constitutional validity of the Child Labor Tax Law. The plaintiff below, the Drexel Furniture Company, is engaged in the manufacture of furniture in the Western District of North Carolina. On September 20, 1921, it received a notice from Bailey, United States Collector of Internal Revenue for the District, that it had been assessed $6,312.79 for having during the taxable year 1919 employed and permitted to work in its factory a boy under fourteen years of age, thus incurring the tax of ten per cent. on its net profits for that year. The Company paid the tax under protest, and after rejection of its claim for a refund, brought this suit. On demurrer to an amended complaint, judgment was entered for the Company against the Collector for the full amount with interest. The writ of error is prosecuted by the Collector direct from the District Court under § 238 of the Judicial Code.

The Child Labor Tax Law is Title XII of an act entitled "An Act To provide revenue, and for other purposes," approved February 24, 1919, c. 18, 40 Stat. 1057, 1138. The heading of the title is "Tax on Employment of Child Labor." . . . Section 1200 is as follows:

"Sec. 1200. That every person . . . operating (a) any mine or quarry situated in the United States in which children under the age of sixteen years have been employed or permitted to work during any portion of the taxable year; or (b) any mill, cannery, workshop, factory, or manufacturing establishment situated in the United States in which children under the age of fourteen years have been employed or permitted to work, or children between the ages of fourteen and sixteen have been employed or permitted to work more than eight hours in any day or more than six days in any week, or after the hour of seven o'clock post meridian, or before the hour of six o'clock ante meridian, during any portion of the taxable year, shall pay for each taxable year, in addition to all other taxes imposed by law, an excise tax equivalent to 10 per centum of the entire net profits received or accrued for such year from the sale or disposition of the product of such mine, quarry, mill, cannery, workshop, factory, or manufacturing establishment."

Section 1203 relieves from liability to the tax any one who employs a child, believing him to be of proper age. . . .

Section 1206 gives authority to the Commissioner of Internal Revenue, or any other person authorized by him, "to enter and inspect at any time any mine, quarry, mill, cannery, workshop, factory, or manufacturing establishment." The Secretary of Labor, or any person whom he authorizes, is given like authority in order to comply with a request of the Commissioner to make such inspection and report the same. Any person who refuses entry or obstructs inspection is made subject to fine or imprisonment or both.

The law is attacked on the ground that it is a regulation of the employment of child labor in the States—an exclusively state function under the Federal Constitution and within the reservations of the Tenth Amendment. It is defended on the ground that it is a mere excise tax levied by the Congress of the United States under its broad power of taxation conferred by § 8, Article I, of the Federal Constitution. We must construe the law and interpret the intent and meaning of Congress from the language of the act. The words are to be given their ordinary meaning unless the context shows that they are differently used. Does this law impose a tax with only that incidental restraint and regulation which a tax must inevitably involve? Or does it regulate by the use of the so-called tax as a penalty? If a tax, it is clearly an excise. If it were an excise on a commodity or other thing of value we might not be permitted under previous decisions of this court to infer solely from its heavy burden that the act intends a prohibition instead of a tax. But this act is more. ①It provides a heavy exaction for a departure from a detailed and specified course of conduct in business. That course of business is that employers shall employ in mines and quarries, children of an age greater than sixteen years; in mills and factories, children of an age greater than fourteen years, and shall prevent children of less than sixteen years in mills and factories from working more than eight hours a day or six days in the week. If an employer departs from this prescribed course of business, he is to pay to the Government one-tenth of his entire net income in the business for a full year. ②The amount is not to be proportioned in any degree to the extent or frequency of the departures, but is to be paid by the employer in full measure whether he employs five hundred children for a year, or employs only one for a day.③Moreover, if he does not know the child is within the named age limit, he is not to pay; that is to say, it is only where he knowingly departs from the prescribed course that payment is to be exacted. Scienter is associated with penalties, not with taxes. ④The employer's factory is to be subject to inspection at any time not only by the taxing officers of the Treasury, the Department normally charged with the collection of taxes, but also by the Secretary of Labor and his subordinates whose normal function is the advancement and protection of the welfare of the workers. In the light of these features of the act, a court must be blind not to see that the so-called tax is imposed to stop the employment of children within the age limits prescribed. Its prohibitory and regulatory effect and purpose are palpable. All others can see and understand this. How can we properly shut our minds to it?

It is the high duty and function of this court in cases regularly brought to its bar to decline to recognize or enforce seeming laws of Congress, dealing with subjects not entrusted to Congress but left or committed by the supreme law of the land to the control of the States. We can not avoid the duty even though it require us to refuse to give effect to legislation designed to promote the highest good. The good sought in unconstitutional legislation is an insidious feature because it leads citizens and legislators of good purpose to promote it without thought of the serious breach it will make in the ark of our covenant or the harm which will come from breaking down recognized standards. In the maintenance of local self government, on the one hand, and the national power, on the other, our country has been able to endure and prosper for near a century and a half.

Out of a proper respect for the acts of a coordinate branch of the Government, this court has gone far to sustain taxing acts as such, even though there has been ground for suspecting from the weight of the tax it was intended to destroy its subject. But, in the act before us, the presumption of validity cannot prevail, because the proof of the contrary is found on the very face of its provisions. Grant the validity of this law, and all that Congress would need to do, hereafter, in seeking to take over to its control any one of the great number of subjects of public interest, jurisdiction of which the States have never parted with, and which are reserved to them by the Tenth Amendment, would be to enact a detailed measure of complete regulation of the subject and enforce it by a so-called tax upon departures from it.   To give such magic to the word "tax" would be to break down all constitutional limitation of the powers of Congress and completely wipe out the sovereignty of the States.

The difference between a tax and a penalty is sometimes difficult to define and yet the consequences of the distinction in the required method of their collection often are important.   Where the sovereign enacting the law has power to impose both tax and penalty the difference between revenue production and mere regulation may be immaterial, but not so when one sovereign can impose a tax only, and the power of regulation rests in another. Taxes are occasionally imposed in the discretion of the legislature on proper subjects with the primary motive of obtaining revenue from them and with the incidental motive of discouraging them by making their continuance onerous.   They do not lose their character as taxes because of the incidental motive.   But there comes a time in the extension of the penalizing features of the so-called tax when it loses its character as such and becomes a mere penalty with the characteristics of regulation and punishment.   Such is the case in the law before us.   Although Congress does not invalidate the contract of employment or expressly declare that the employment within the mentioned ages is illegal, it does exhibit its intent practically to achieve the latter result by adopting the criteria of wrongdoing and imposing its principal consequence on those who transgress its standard.   .   .   .

The analogy of [Hammer v. Dagenhart] is clear.   The congressional power over interstate commerce is, within its proper scope, just as complete and unlimited as the congressional power to tax, and the legislative motive in its exercise is just as free from judicial suspicion and inquiry.   Yet when Congress threatened to stop interstate commerce in ordinary and necessary commodities, unobjectionable as subjects of transportation, and to deny the same to the people of a State in order to coerce them into compliance with Congress's regulation of state concerns, the court said this was not in fact regulation of interstate commerce, but rather that of State concerns and was invalid.   So here the so-called tax is a penalty to coerce people of a State to act as Congress wishes them to act in respect of a matter completely the business of the state government under the Federal Constitution.   This case requires as did the Dagenhart Case the application of the principle announced by Chief Justice Marshall in McCulloch v. Maryland, 4 Wheat. 316, 423, in a much quoted passage:

"Should Congress, in the execution of its powers, adopt measures which are prohibited by the Constitution; or should Congress, under the pretext of executing its powers, pass laws for the accomplishment of objects not intrusted to the government; it would become the painful duty of this tribunal, should a case requiring such a decision come before it, to say, that such an act was not the law of the land."

But it is pressed upon us that this court has gone so far in sustaining taxing measures the effect or tendency of which was to accomplish purposes not directly within congressional power that we are bound by authority to maintain this law.

The first of these is Veazie Bank v. Fenno, 8 Wall. 533.   In that case, the validity of a law which increased a tax on the circulating notes of persons

and state banks from one per centum to ten per centum was in question.
.   .   .   The second objection was stated by the court:

"It is insisted, however, that the tax in the case before us is excessive, and so excessive as to indicate a purpose on the part of Congress to destroy the franchise of the bank, and is, therefore, beyond the constitutional power of Congress."

To this the court answered (p. 548):

"The first answer to this is that the judicial cannot prescribe to the legis-lative departments of the government limitations upon the exercise of its acknowledged powers.   The power to tax may be exercised oppressively upon persons, but the responsibility of the legislature is not to the courts, but to the people by whom its members are elected.   So if a particular tax bears heavily upon a corporation, or a class of corporations, it cannot, for that reason only, be pronounced contrary to the Constitution."

It will be observed that the sole objection to the tax there was its excessive character.   Nothing else appeared on the face of the act.   It was an increase of a tax admittedly legal to a higher rate and that was all.   There were no elaborate specifications on the face of the act, as here, indicating the purpose to regulate matters of state concern and jurisdiction through an exaction so applied as to give it the qualities of a penalty for violation of law rather than a tax. .   .   .

But more than this, what was charged to be the object of the excessive tax was within the congressional authority, as appears from the second answer which the court gave to the objection.   After having pointed out the legitimate means taken by Congress to secure a national medium or currency, the court said (p. 549):

"Having thus, in the exercise of undisputed constitutional powers, undertaken to provide a currency for the whole country, it cannot be questioned that Congress may, constitutionally, secure the benefit of it to the people by appropriate legislation.   To this end, .   .   .   Congress may restrain, by suitable enactments, the circulation as money of any notes not issued under its own authority. .   .   ."

The next case is that of McCray v. United States, 195 U.S. 27.   That, like the Veazie Bank Case, was the increase of an exise tax upon a subject properly taxable in which the taxpayers claimed that the tax had become invalid because the increase was excessive.   It was a tax on oleomargarine, a substitute for butter.   The tax on the white oleomargarine was one-quarter of a cent a pound, and on the yellow oleomargarine was first two cents and was then by the act in question increased to ten cents per pound.   This court held that the discretion of Congress in the exercise of its constitutional powers to levy excise taxes could not be controlled or limited by the courts because the latter might deem the incidence of the tax oppressive or even destructive. It was the same principle as that applied in the Veazie Bank Case.   This was that Congress in selecting its subjects for taxation might impose the burden where and as it would and that a motive disclosed in its selection to discourage sale or manufacture of an article by a higher tax than on some other did not invalidate the tax.   In neither of these cases did the law objected to show on its face as does the law before us the detailed specifications of a regulation of a state concern and business with a heavy exaction to promote the efficacy of such regulation. .   .   .

[After discussing Flint v. Stone Tracy Co., 220 U.S. 107, the Court continued:] The fourth case is United States v. Doremus, 249 U.S. 86. That involved the validity of the Narcotic Drug Act, 38 Stat. 785, which imposed a special tax on the manufacture, importation and sale or gift of opium or coca leaves or their compounds or derivatives. It required every person subject to the special tax to register with the Collector of Internal Revenue his name and place of business and forbade him to sell except upon the written order of the person to whom the sale was made on a form prescribed by the Commissioner of Internal Revenue. The vendor was required to keep the order for two years, and the purchaser to keep a duplicate for the same time and both were to be subject to official inspection. Similar requirements were made as to sales upon prescriptions of a physician and as to the dispensing of such drugs directly to a patient by a physician. The validity of a special tax in the nature of an excise tax on the manufacture, importation and sale of such drugs was, of course, unquestioned. The provisions for subjecting the sale and distribution of the drugs to official supervision and inspection were held to have a reasonable relation to the enforcement of the tax and were therefore held valid.

The court said that the act could not be declared invalid just because another motive than taxation, not shown on the face of the act, might have contributed to its passage. This case does not militate against the conclusion we have reached in respect of the law now before us. The court, there, made manifest its view that the provisions of the so-called taxing act must be naturally and reasonably adapted to the collection of the tax and not solely to the achievement of some other purpose plainly within state power.

For the reasons given, we must hold the Child Labor Tax Law invalid and the judgment of the District Court is

Affirmed.

Mr. Justice CLARKE dissents.

THE USE OF THE TAXING POWER FOR REGULATORY PURPOSES

1. *The prior decisions.* The important decisions before the Child Labor Tax Case—Veazie Bank v. Fenno, McCray v. United States, and United States v. Doremus—are described in the principal case. Are the early decisions distinguishable, or did the principal case manifest a significant shift in approach? Is the relationship of the principal case to these earlier decisions like that of Hammer v. Dagenhart to the earlier commerce-prohibiting cases (e. g., Lottery, Mann Act, Pure Food and Drug)? See chap. 4, sec. 3, p. 254, and note 2 below.

In connection with Doremus, see Nigro v. United States, 276 U.S. 332 (1928), where the Court noted that the Narcotic Drug Act had been amended to produce substantial revenue from the tax and added: "If there was doubt of the character of this act as an alleged subterfuge, it has been removed by the change whereby what was a nominal tax before was made a substantial one."

2. *Early 20th century commerce and tax cases: parallels and contrasts.*
a. Note that Justice Holmes was in the majority in the principal case—just

four years after his dissent in Hammer v. Dagenhart. In the principal case, he joined in looking beyond the congressional label to invalidate because of forbidden purpose and effect; in his dissent in Hammer v. Dagenhart, the Child Labor Case under the commerce power, he insisted that the Court could not look to purposes and obvious collateral effects and was bound to sustain a law because Congress had invoked the commerce-prohibiting technique. Are Holmes' positions in the two cases reconcilable?

In Hammer v. Dagenhart, moreover, Holmes had relied on McCray, the oleomargarine tax case, to show that judicial inquiry into congressional purpose was improper. And the McCray tax decision of 1904, in turn, had relied on the commerce power Lottery Case of 1903 in rejecting the notion "that the judiciary may restrain the exercise of lawful power on the assumption that a wrongful purpose or motive has caused the power to be exerted." At the time of Hammer v. Dagenhart in 1916, in short, Holmes was opposing judicial invalidation because of improper purpose in tax (McCray) as well as commerce (Lottery, Child Labor) cases. By 1920, in the principal case, had Holmes abandoned that position? In commerce as well as in tax cases? Because he was in the minority in Hammer? Only in tax cases? Only in some tax cases—because bad purpose was clearer in the principal case than in McCray? Compare Justice Frankfurter's "purpose" position in Kahriger, the next principal case, and note the questions on tax-commerce parallels and contrasts after the Kahriger case.

b. Hill v. Wallace, 259 U.S. 44 (1922), decided on the same day as— and with reliance on—the principal case, is another illustration of alternate uses of the taxing and commerce powers. In Hill, the Court invalidated the Futures Trading Act, under which a tax of twenty cents was imposed on every bushel of grain involved in a contract of sale for future delivery—except sales on boards of trade meeting the requirements of the Act. The Hill decision was urged upon the Court to show the invalidity of a subsequent commerce clause-based regulation of boards of trade, the 1922 Grain Future Trading Act. That Act was sustained in Chicago Board of Trade v. Olsen, 262 U.S. 1 (1923). For similar successive invocations of the fiscal and commerce powers, compare United States v. Butler, p. 366, below, with Mulford v. Smith, chap. 4, p. 320, above (agricultural production and marketing).

3. *From the Child Labor Tax Case to Kahriger.* a. In United States v. Constantine, 296 U.S. 287 (1935), defendant was convicted in a federal district court of conducting the business of retail dealer in malt liquor contrary to the law of Alabama without having paid the special excise tax of $1000 imposed by an Act of Congress. He had paid the normal tax of $25 for conducting the business, and the question presented was "whether the exaction of $1000 in addition, by reason solely of his violation of state law, is a tax or penalty." Justice Roberts' opinion for the Court concluded "that the indicia which the section exhibits of an intent to prohibit and to punish violations of state law as such are too strong to be disregarded, remove all semblance of a revenue act and stamp the sum it exacts as a penalty. In this view the statute is a clear invasion of the police power, inherent in the states, reserved from the grant of powers to the federal government by the Constitution. . . . Reference was made in the argument to decisions of this Court holding that where the power to tax is conceded the motive for the execution may not be questioned. . . . They are not authority where, as in the present instance, under the guise of a taxing act the purpose is to usurp

the police powers of the state." Justice Cardozo, joined by Justices Brandeis and Stone, dissented: "Thus the process of psychoanalysis has spread to unaccustomed fields."

b. Sonzinsky v. United States, 300 U.S. 506 (1937), sustained the National Firearms Act of 1934, which imposed a $200 annual license tax on dealers in firearms. Noting that the "tax is productive of some revenue," the Court said "we are not free to speculate as to the motives which moved Congress to impose it or as to the extent to which it may operate to restrict the activities taxed. As it is not attended by an offensive regulation and since it operates as a tax, it is within the national taxing power." United States v. Sanchez, 340 U.S. 42 (1950), upheld the Marihuana Tax Act of 1937 which placed a tax ($100 per ounce) on the transfer of marihuana to an unregistered person, liability for its payment resting on the transferor in the event the transferee failed to pay. The statute contained no regulations other than the registration provisions and had for its primary objective the restriction of the traffic to accepted industrial and medicinal channels, with only a secondary objective of raising revenue. The tax is "a legitimate exercise of the taxing power despite its collateral regulatory purpose and effect."

UNITED STATES v. KAHRIGER

345 U.S. 22, 73 S.Ct. 510, 97 L.Ed. 754 (1953).

Appeal from the United States District Court for the Eastern District of Pennsylvania.

Mr. Justice REED delivered the opinion of the Court.

The issue raised by this appeal is the constitutionality of the occupational tax provisions of the Revenue Act of 1951,[1] which levy a tax on persons engaged in the business of accepting wagers, and require such persons

---

1. 26 U.S.C. (Supp. V) § 3285:
"(a) Wagers.
"There shall be imposed on wagers . . . an excise tax equal to 10 per centum of the amount thereof. . . ."

26 U.S.C. (Supp. V) § 3290:
"A special tax of $50 per year shall be paid by each person who is liable for tax under subchapter A or who is engaged in receiving wagers for or on behalf of any person so liable."

26 U.S.C. (Supp. V) § 3291:
"(a) Each person required to pay a special tax under this subchapter shall register with the collector of the district—
"(1) his name and place of residence;
"(2) if he is liable for tax under subchapter A, each place of business where the activity which makes him so liable is carried on, and the name and place of residence of each person who is engaged in receiving wagers for him or on his behalf. . . ."
[Footnote by the Court.]
[The Court did note quote the following sections. Should it have? Com-

pare footnote 2 infra and see note 2 following this case.]

[§ 3292: "Sections . . . 3275 . . . shall . . . apply to the special tax imposed by this subchapter. . . ."

[§ 3275: "Each collector shall, under regulations of the Commissioner, place and keep conspicuously in his office, for public inspection, an alphabetical list of the names of all the persons who have paid special taxes in his district, and shall state thereon the time, place, and business for which such special taxes have been paid, and upon application of any prosecuting officer of any State, county, or municipality, he shall furnish a certified copy thereof, as of a public record, for which a fee of $1 for each one hundred words or fraction thereof in the copy or copies so requested, may be charged."

[By the Internal Revenue Code of 1954, the sections were revised and renumbered. See 26 U.S.C. § 4401 et seq.; 26 U.S.C. § 6107.]

to register with the Collector of Internal Revenue. The unconstitutionality of the tax is asserted on two grounds. First, it is said that Congress, under the pretense of exercising its power to tax has attempted to penalize illegal intrastate gambling through the regulatory features of the Act (26 U.S.C. (Supp. V) § 3291) and has thus infringed the police power which is reserved to the states. Secondly, it is urged that the registration provisions of the tax violate the privilege against self-incrimination and are arbitrary and vague, contrary to the guarantees of the Fifth Amendment. [The second contention was rejected. The discussion is omitted.]

The case comes here on appeal, in accordance with 18 U.S.C. § 3731, from the United States District Court for the Eastern District of Pennsylvania, where an information was filed against appellee alleging that he was in the business of accepting wagers and that he willfully failed to register for and pay the occupational tax in question. Appellee moved to dismiss on the ground that the sections upon which the information was based were unconstitutional. The District Court sustained the motion on the authority of our opinion in United States v. Constantine, 296 U.S. 287. The court reasoned that while "the subject matter of this legislation so far as revenue purposes is concerned is within the scope of Federal authorities," the tax was unconstitutional in that the information called for by the registration provisions was "peculiarly applicable to the applicant from the standpoint of law enforcement and vice control," and therefore the whole of the legislation was an infringement by the Federal Government on the police power reserved to the states by the Tenth Amendment. United States v. Kahriger, 105 F.Supp. 322, 323.

The result below is at odds with the position of the seven other district courts which have considered the matter, and, in our opinion, is erroneous.

In the term following the Constantine opinion, this Court pointed out in Sonzinsky v. United States, 300 U.S. 506, at 513 (a case involving a tax on a "limited class" of objectionable firearms alleged to be prohibitory in effect and "to disclose unmistakably the legislative purpose to regulate rather than to tax"), that the subject of the tax in Constantine was "described or treated as criminal by the taxing statute." The tax in the Constantine case was a special additional excise tax of $1,000, placed only on persons who carried on a liquor business in violation of state law. The wagering tax with which we are here concerned applies to all persons engaged in the business of receiving wagers, regardless of whether such activity violates state law.

The substance of respondent's position with respect to the Tenth Amendment is that Congress has chosen to tax a specified business which is not within its power to regulate. The precedents are many upholding taxes similar to this wagering tax as a proper exercise of the federal taxing power. . . .

Appellee would have us say that, because there is legislative history[2] in-

2. There are suggestions in the debates that Congress sought to hinder, if not prevent, the type of gambling taxed. See 97 Cong.Rec. 6892:
"Mr. HOFFMAN of Michigan. Then I will renew my observation that it might if properly construed be considered an additional penalty on the illegal activities.

"Mr. COOPER. Certainly, and we might indulge the hope that the imposition of this type of tax would eliminate that kind of activity." 97 Cong.Rec. 12236: "If the local official does not want to enforce the law and no one catches him winking at the law, he may keep on winking at it, but when the Federal Government identifies a

dicating a congressional motive to suppress wagering, this tax is not a proper exercise of such taxing power. In the License Tax Cases, supra, it was admitted that the federal license "discouraged" the activities. The intent to curtail and hinder, as well as tax, was also manifest in the following cases, and in each of them the tax was upheld: Veazie Bank v. Fenno, 8 Wall. 533 (tax on paper money issued by state banks); McCray v. United States, 195 U.S. 27, 59 (tax on colored oleomargarine); United States v. Doremus, 249 U.S. 86, and Nigro v. United States, 276 U.S. 332 (tax on narcotics); Sonzinsky v. United States, 300 U.S. 506 (tax on firearms); United States v. Sanchez, 340 U.S. 42 (tax on marihuana).

It is conceded that a federal excise tax does not cease to be valid merely because it discourages or deters the activities taxed. Nor is the tax invalid because the revenue obtained is negligible. Appellee, however, argues that the sole purpose of the statute is to penalize only illegal gambling in the states through the guise of a tax measure. As with the above excise taxes which we have held to be valid, the instant tax has a regulatory effect. But regardless of its regulatory effect, the wagering tax produces revenue. As such it surpasses both the narcotics and firearms taxes which we have found valid.[3]

It is axiomatic that the power of Congress to tax is extensive and sometimes falls with crushing effect on businesses deemed unessential or inimical to the public welfare, or where, as in dealing with narcotics, the collection of the tax also is difficult. As is well known, the constitutional restraints on taxing are few. . . . The difficulty of saying when the power to lay uniform taxes is curtailed, because its use brings a result beyond the direct legislative power of Congress, has given rise to diverse decisions. In that area of abstract ideas, a final definition of the line between state and federal power has baffled judges and legislators.

While the Court has never questioned the above-quoted statement of Mr. Chief Justice Marshall in the McCulloch case [the "pretext" statement], the application of the rule has brought varying holdings on constitutionality. Where federal legislation has rested on other congressional powers, such as the Necessary and Proper Clause or the Commerce Clause, this Court has generally sustained the statutes, despite their effect on matters ordinarily considered state concern. When federal power to regulate is found, its exercise is a matter for Congress. Where Congress has employed the taxing clause a greater variation in the decisions has resulted. The division in this Court has been more acute. Without any specific differentiation between the power to tax and other federal powers, the indirect results from the exercise of the power to tax have raised more doubts. . . . It is hard to understand

law violator, and the local newspaper gets hold of it, and the local church organizations get hold of it, and the people who do want the law enforced get hold of it, they say, 'Mr. Sheriff, what about it? We understand that there is a place down here licensed to sell liquor.' He says, 'Is that so? I will put him out of business.' " [Footnote by the Court.]

3. One of the indicia which appellee offers to support his contention that the wagering tax is not a proper revenue measure is that the tax amount collected under it was $4,371,869, as compared with an expected amount of $400,000,000 a year. The figure of $4,371,869, however, is relatively large when it is compared with the $3,501 collected under the tax on adulterated and process or renovated butter and filled cheese, the $914,910 collected under the tax on narcotics, including marihuana and special taxes, and the $28,911 collected under the tax on firearms, transfer and occupational taxes. (Summary of Internal Revenue Collections, released by Bureau of Internal Revenue, October 3, 1952.) [Footnote by the Court.]

why the power to tax should raise more doubts because of indirect effects than other federal powers.

Penalty provisions in tax statutes added for breach of a regulation concerning activities in themselves subject only to state regulation have caused this Court to declare the enactments invalid. Unless there are provisions extraneous to any tax need, courts are without authority to limit the exercise of the taxing power. All the provisions of this excise are adapted to the collection of a valid tax.

Nor do we find the registration requirements of the wagering tax offensive. All that is required is the filing of names, addresses, and places of business. This is quite general in tax returns. Such data are directly and intimately related to the collection of the tax and are "obviously supportable as in aid of a revenue purpose." Sonzinsky v. United States, 300 U.S. 506, at 513. The registration provisions make the tax simpler to collect. . . .

Reversed.

Mr. Justice JACKSON, concurring.

I concur in the judgment and opinion of the Court, but with such doubt that if the minority agreed upon an opinion which did not impair legitimate use of the taxing power I probably would join it. But we deal here with important and contrasting values in our scheme of government, and it is important that neither be allowed to destroy the other. . . .

Of course, all taxation has a tendency, proportioned to its burdensomeness, to discourage the activity taxed. One cannot formulate a revenue-raising plan that would not have economic and social consequences. Congress may and should place the burden of taxes where it will least handicap desirable activities and bear most heavily on useless or harmful ones. If Congress may tax one citizen to the point of discouragement for making an honest living, it is hard to say that it may not do the same to another just because he makes a sinister living. If the law-abiding must tell all to the tax collector, it is difficult to excuse one because his business is law-breaking. . . .

But here is a purported tax law which requires no reports and lays no tax except on specified gamblers whose calling in most states is illegal. It requires this group to step forward and identify themselves, not because they, like others, have income, but because of its source. This is difficult to regard as a rational or good-faith revenue measure, despite the deference that is due Congress. On the contrary, it seems to be a plan to tax out of existence the professional gambler whom it has been found impossible to prosecute out of existence. Few pursuits are entitled to less consideration at our hands than professional gambling, but the plain unwelcome fact is that it continues to survive because a large and influential part of our population patronizes and protects it.

The United States has a system of taxation by confession. That a people so numerous, scattered and individualistic annually assesses itself with a tax liability, often in highly burdensome amounts, is a reassuring sign of the stability and vitality of our system of self-government. What surprised me in once trying to help administer these laws was not to discover examples of recalcitrance, fraud or self-serving mistakes in reporting, but to discover that such derelictions were so few. It will be a sad day for the revenues if the good will of the people toward their taxing system is frittered away in efforts to accomplish by taxation moral reforms that cannot be accomplished by direct legislation. But the evil that can come from this statute will probably soon make itself manifest to Congress. The evil of a judicial decision impairing the legitimate taxing power by extreme constitutional interpretations might not be transient. Even though this statute approaches the fair limits of constitutionality, I join the decision of the Court.

Mr. Justice BLACK, with whom Mr. Justice DOUGLAS concurs, dissenting [solely on the basis of the self-incrimination provision of the Fifth Amendment]. . . .

Mr. Justice FRANKFURTER, dissenting.

The Court's opinion manifests a natural difficulty in reaching its conclusion. Constitutional issues are likely to arise whenever Congress draws on the taxing power not to raise revenue but to regulate conduct. This is so, of course, because of the distribution of legislative power as between the Congress and the State Legislatures in the regulation of conduct.

To review in detail the decisions of this Court, beginning with Veazie Bank v. Fenno, 8 Wall. 533, dealing with this ambivalent type of revenue enactment, would be to rehash the familiar. Two generalizations may, however, safely be drawn from this series of cases. Congress may make an oblique use of the taxing power in relation to activities with which Congress may deal directly, as for instance, commerce between the States. Thus, if the dissenting views of Mr. Justice Holmes in Hammer v. Dagenhart, 247 U.S. 251, 277, had been the decision of the Court, as they became in United States v. Darby, 312 U.S. 100, the effort to deal with the problem of child labor through an assertion of the taxing power in the statute considered in Child Labor Tax Case, 259 U.S. 20, would by the latter case have been sustained. However, when oblique use is made of the taxing power as to matters which substantively are not within the powers delegated to Congress, the Court cannot shut its eyes to what is obviously, because designedly, an attempt to control conduct which the Constitution left to the responsibility of the States, merely because Congress wrapped the legislation in the verbal cellophane of a revenue measure.

 Concededly the constitutional questions presented by such legislation are difficult. On the one hand, courts should scrupulously abstain from hobbling congressional choice of policies, particularly when the vast reach of the taxing power is concerned. On the other hand, to allow what otherwise is excluded from congressional authority to be brought within it by casting legislation in the form of a revenue measure could, as so significantly expounded in the Child Labor Tax Case, supra, offer an easy way for the legislative imagination to control "any one of the great number of subjects of public interest, jurisdiction of which the States have never parted with . . . ." Child Labor Tax Case, at 38. I say "significantly" because Mr. Justice Holmes and two of the Justices who had joined his dissent in Hammer v. Dagenhart, McKenna and Brandeis, JJ., agreed with the opinion in the Child Labor Tax Case. Issues of such gravity affecting the balance of powers within our federal system are not susceptible of comprehensive statement by smooth formulas such as that a tax is nonetheless a tax although it discourages the activities taxed, or that a tax may be imposed although it may effect ulterior ends. No such phrase, however fine and well-worn, enables one to decide the concrete case.

What is relevant to judgment here is that, even if the history of this legislation as it went through Congress did not give one the libretto to the song, the context of the circumstances which brought forth this enactment—sensationally exploited disclosures regarding gambling in big cities and small, the relation of this gambling to corrupt politics, the impatient public response to these disclosures, the feeling of ineptitude or paralysis on the part of local law-enforcing agencies—emphatically supports what was revealed on the floor of Congress, namely, that what was formally a means of raising revenue for the Federal Government was essentially an effort to check if not to stamp out professional gambling.

A nominal taxing measure must be found an inadmissible intrusion into a domain of legislation reserved for the States not merely when Congress requires that such a measure is to be enforced through a detailed scheme of administration beyond the obvious fiscal needs, as in the Child Labor Tax Case, supra. That is one ground for holding that Congress was constitutionally disrespectful of what is reserved to the States. Another basis for deeming such a formal revenue measure inadmissible is presented by this case. In addition to the fact that Congress was concerned with activity beyond the authority of the Federal Government, the enforcing provision of this enactment is designed for the systematic confession of crimes with a view to prosecution for such crimes under State law.

It is one thing to hold that the exception, which the Fifth Amendment makes to the duty of a witness to give his testimony when relevant to a proceeding in a federal court, does not include the potential danger to that witness of possible prosecution in a State court . . .. It is a wholly different thing to hold that Congress which cannot constitutionally grapple directly with gambling in the States, may compel self-incriminating disclosures for the enforcement of State gambling laws, merely because it does so under the guise of a revenue measure obviously passed not for revenue purposes. The motive of congressional legislation is not for our scrutiny, provided only that the ulterior purpose is not expressed in ways which negative what the revenue words on their face express and which do not seek enforcement of the formal revenue purpose through means that offend those standards of decency in our civilization against which due process is a barrier.

I would affirm this judgment.

Mr. Justice DOUGLAS, while not joining in the entire opinion, agrees with the views expressed herein that this tax is an attempt by the Congress to control conduct which the Constitution has left to the responsibility of the States.

THE TAXING POWER AFTER KAHRIGER

1. *The taxing and commerce powers: modern parallels and contrasts.* Do the modern cases suggest more effective doctrinal limits on regulatory taxes than on commerce legislation? Is greater judicial scrutiny of congressional action authorized by Kahriger than by Darby and Wickard v. Filburn? Recall the questions in note 2 after the Child Labor Tax Case. With respect to judicial inquiry into the purposes and collateral effects of the commerce-prohibiting technique, the majority view in Hammer v. Dagenhart was overruled in United States v. Darby. Has there been a parallel development re-

garding the taxing power? Does the majority approach in the Child Labor Tax Case retain any greater vitality today than the discredited Hammer v. Dagenhart position?

Note that Justice Stone's opinion in Darby relied on McCray and Veazie Bank (the early taxing power cases discussed in the opening opinion of this section) in support of his refusal to inquire into the motive and purpose of commerce regulation; and Stone's opinion was for a unanimous Court. In the commerce area, in short, the modern Court appeared to abandon all "pretext" control. Yet as to taxing, in Kahriger, there are several dissents on that abuse of power issue from members of the modern Court. Is the difference explainable? (See also the 1969 dissent on the taxing power in the Minor-Buie case, note 3 below.)

2. *The overruling of Kahriger.* Kahriger was overruled solely on Fifth Amendment self-incrimination grounds (but with some observations tangentially relevant to the taxing power issue) in Marchetti v. United States, 390 U.S. 39 (1968). Justice Harlan's majority opinion concluded that the wagering tax laws "may not be employed to punish criminally those persons who have defended a failure to comply with their requirements with a proper assertion of the privilege against self-incrimination." He insisted: "The issue before us is *not* whether the United States may tax activities which a State or Congress has declared unlawful. The Court has repeatedly indicated that the unlawfulness of an activity does not prevent its taxation, and nothing that follows is intended to limit or diminish the vitality of those cases." But here the methods violated the Fifth Amendment: "Information obtained as a consequence of the federal wagering tax laws is readily available to assist the efforts of state and federal authorities to enforce" anti-gambling laws. In the course of his opinion, Justice Harlan repeatedly referred to the section printed in the editorial addition to footnote 1 of the Kahriger case, but not mentioned by the Court in Kahriger. For example: "The terms of the wagering tax system make quite plain that Congress intended information obtained as a consequence of registration and payment of the occupational tax to be provided to interested prosecuting authorities. See 26 U.S.C. § 6107." See also the companion cases to Marchetti, Grosso v. U. S., 390 U.S. 62 (1968) (involving the excise tax on wagering), and Haynes v. U. S., 390 U.S. 85 (1968) (involving the registration requirements of the National Firearms Act, "an interrelated statutory system for the taxation of certain classes of firearms"), as well as Leary v. United States, 395 U.S. 6 (1969) (involving the order form requirements of the transfer tax provisions of the Marihuana Tax Act).

In a separate concurring opinion in Marchetti and Grosso, Justice Brennan noted: "Whatever else Congress may have meant to achieve, an obvious purpose was to coerce evidence from persons engaged in illegal activities for use in their prosecution." Chief Justice Warren dissented. He commented: "The congressional intent to assist law enforcement should not be the excuse for frustrating the revenue purpose of the statutes before the Court." He feared that the Court was "opening the door to a new wave of attacks on a number of federal registration statutes whenever the registration requirement touches upon allegedly illegal activities." He noted that "registration is a common feature attached to a number of special taxes imposed by Title 26." But see the Court's rejection of a constitutional challenge based on the Marchetti line of cases in Minor v. United States (and Buie v. United States), 396 U.S. 87 (1969), sustaining the statutory prohibitions on selling narcotic drugs and marijuana without the written order forms required by law. Justice White's majority opinion said of the Fifth Amendment claim: "There is no real and substantial possibility that [the order form] requirement will in any way incriminate sellers for the simple reason that sellers will seldom, if ever, be confronted with an unregistered purchaser who is willing and able to secure the order form." (See also the next note.)

3. *Taxing power disagreements in 1969: The Minor-Buie dissent.* The Art. I, Sec. 8, taxing power issue was raised in the Minor-Buie case noted above, by Justice Douglas' dissent, joined by Justice Black; they objected to the affirmance of Buie's conviction for selling heroin without an order form, and they relied on grounds of federalism rather than on individual rights guarantees. Petitioner had raised only the Fifth Amendment issue, but Justice Douglas insisted: "[T]hat is not the end of the matter for me." He noted that order forms to purchase heroin cannot be secured, quoting the Government's concession in oral argument: "The order forms may only be used to purchase a lawful drug for a lawful purpose. Heroin is an unlawful drug for which there is no lawful purpose." The dissent continued:

"The Federal Government does not have plenary power to define and punish criminal acts. Its power in this regard derives from other powers specifically delegated to it by the Constitution, as the Tenth Amendment provides. . . . Section 4705(a) derives from the power 'to lay and collect taxes.' Its constitutionality on this basis was sustained in United States v. Doremus, 249 U.S. 86—a five-to-four decision [discussed in the Child Labor Tax Case, above].

"As I view this case, the Government is punishing an individual for failing to do something that the Government has made it impossible for him to do—that is, obtain an order form from the prospective purchaser prior to making a sale of heroin. Petitioner did, of course, have the option not to sell the heroin, and in that sense his compliance with the statute was indeed quite possible. This argument, however, overlooks the fact that the statute does not simply outlaw all sales of heroin. The critical interest of the Government is necessarily in the collecting of the tax imposed by the Act, and it is the order form which provides the crucial link to this proper constitutional purpose. In Nigro v. United States, 276 U.S. 332, 341 [see note 1 after the Child Labor Tax Case], Chief Justice Taft, speaking for the Court, said: 'In interpreting the Act we must assume that it is a taxing measure, for otherwise it would be no law at all. If it is a mere act for the purpose of regulating and restraining the purchase of the opiate and other drugs, it is beyond the power of Congress and must be regarded as invalid.' Thus it is the order form—not the mere sale—that constitutes the heart of the offense for which this petitioner was convicted. I do not see how the Government can make a crime out of not receiving an order form and at the same time allow no order forms for this category of sales.

"Nor is it relevant to suggest, as does the majority opinion, that a statute imposing a flat ban on sales of heroin might be sustainable under the Commerce Clause. We are concerned in this case with what the Congress did, not with what it might have done or might yet do in the future. It is clear that what Congress did in § 4705(a) was to enact a taxing measure. And the crime charged was not selling heroin, but selling it 'not in pursuance of a written order form,' as prescribed in § 4705(a)."

The only majority response to the dissenters' Article I objection came in a footnote: "The dissent suggests that the courts should refuse to enforce § 4705(a) as part of a revenue measure. But these very order form provisions were upheld long ago as valid revenue laws even though they operated to prevent large classes of people from obtaining order forms—and hence from acquiring drugs—at all. United States v. Doremus . . .; see Nigro v. United States . . .. A statute does not cease to be a valid tax measurement because it deters the activity taxed, because the revenue obtained is negligible, or because the activity is otherwise illegal. See, e. g., [Marchetti v. United States, United States v. Kahriger]. Even viewing § 4705 (a) as little more than a flat ban on certain sales, it is sustainable under the powers granted Congress in Art. I, § 8. See Yee Hem v. United States, 268 U.S. 178, 183 (1925); Brolan v. United States, 236 U.S. 216, 222 (1915); cf. United States v. Sullivan, 332 U.S. 689 (1948); United States v. Darby, 312 U.S. 100 (1941)."

SECTION 2. THE SPENDING POWER

Introduction. The spending power, though hardly the most litigated, probably has the most important impact of all on the actual functioning of the federal system. Whether in the context of payments to individuals for particular purposes (as with old age support under social security) or of conditioned grants to states (as with education or highways) or of direct financing of federal entrepreneurial operations (as with the TVA), the national decisions about how money is to be spent involve pervasive policy choices and have significant regulatory consequences. Yet to a large extent, the constitutionality of federal spending programs has not been justiciable, as was illustrated by the lack of success of Mrs. Frothingham and the State of Massachusetts in getting an adjudication on the Federal Maternity Act (chap. 2, p. 91). But the constitutional questions are no less real for the sparsity of judicial decisions: as the discussion in the first principal case shows, the scope of the spending power has been a recurrent source of controversy.

What are the legitimate purposes of national spending? What is the proper role of courts in assessing legitimacy when justiciability restraints permit decisions on the merits? What conditions may Congress impose on spending programs? What is constitutionally required with respect to the relationship between the condition, the particular program, and the general spending power? These are the questions for major attention in examining these selections from the rare encounters of the Court with the spending power.

UNITED STATES v. BUTLER
297 U.S. 1, 56 S.Ct. 312, 80 L.Ed. 477 (1936).

Certiorari to the Circuit Court of Appeals for the First Circuit.

Mr. Justice ROBERTS delivered the opinion of the Court.

In this case we must determine whether certain provisions of the Agricultural Adjustment Act, 1933, conflict with the Federal Constitution.

Title I of the statute is captioned "Agricultural Adjustment." Section 1 recites that an economic emergency has arisen, due to disparity between the prices of agricultural and other commodities, with consequent destruction of farmers' purchasing power and breakdown in orderly exchange, which, in turn, have affected transactions in agricultural commodities with a national public interest and burdened and obstructed the normal currents of commerce, calling for the enactment of legislation.

§ 2 declares it to be the policy of Congress:

"To establish and maintain such balance between the production and consumption of agricultural commodities, and such marketing conditions therefor, as will reestablish prices to farmers at a level that will give agricultural commodities a purchasing power with respect to articles that farmers buy, equivalent to the purchasing power of agricultural commodities in the base period."

The base period, in the case of cotton, and all other commodities except tobacco, is designated as that between August, 1909, and July, 1914.

The further policies announced are an approach to the desired equality by gradual correction of present inequalities "at as rapid a rate as is deemed feasible in view of the current consumptive demand in domestic and foreign markets," and the protection of consumers' interest by readjusting farm production at such level as will not increase the percentage of the consumers' retail expenditures for agricultural commodities or products derived therefrom, which is returned to the farmer, above the percentage returned to him in the base period.

§ 8 provides, amongst other things, that, "In order to effectuate the declared policy," the Secretary of Agriculture shall have power

"(1) To provide for reduction in the acreage or reduction in the production for market, or both, of any basic agricultural commodity, through agreements with producers or by other voluntary methods, and to provide for rental or benefit payments in connection therewith or upon that part of the production of any basic agricultural commodity required for domestic consumption, in such amounts as the Secretary deems fair and reasonable to be paid out of any moneys available for such payments." . . .

§ 9(a) enacts:

"To obtain revenue for extraordinary expenses incurred by reason of the national economic emergency, there shall be levied processing taxes as hereinafter provided. When the Secretary of Agriculture determines that rental or benefit payments are to be made with respect to any basic agricultural commodity, he shall proclaim such determination, and a processing tax shall be in effect with respect to such commodity from the beginning of the marketing year therefor next following the date of such proclamation. The processing tax shall be levied, assessed, and collected upon the first domestic processing of the commodity, whether of domestic production or imported, and shall be paid by the processor." . . .

§ 9(b) fixes the tax "at such rate as equals the difference between the current average farm price for the commodity and the fair exchange value," with power in the Secretary, after investigation, notice, and hearing, to readjust the tax so as to prevent the accumulation of surplus stocks and depression of farm prices. . . .

§ 12(a) appropriates $100,000,000 "to be available to the Secretary of Agriculture for administrative expenses under this title and for rental and benefit payments . . .;" and § 12(b) appropriates the proceeds derived from all taxes imposed under the act "to be available to the Secretary of Agriculture for expansion of markets and removal of surplus agricultural products. . . . administrative expenses, rental and benefit payments, and refunds on taxes." . . .

On July 14, 1933, the Secretary of Agriculture, with the approval of the President, proclaimed that he had determined rental and benefit payments should be made with respect to cotton; that the marketing year for that commodity was to begin August 1, 1933; and calculated and fixed the rates of processing and floor taxes on cotton in accordance with the terms of the act.

The United States presented a claim to the respondents as receivers of the Hoosac Mills Corporation for processing and floor taxes on cotton levied under sections 9 and 16 of the act. The receivers recommended that the claim be disallowed. The District Court found the taxes valid and ordered them paid. Upon appeal the Circuit Court of Appeals reversed the order. . . .

First. At the outset the United States contends that the respondents have no standing to question the validity of the tax. The position is that the act is merely a revenue measure levying an excise upon the activity of processing cotton—a proper subject for the imposition of such tax—the proceeds of which go into the federal treasury and thus become available for appropriation for any purpose. It is said that what the respondents are endeavoring to do is to challenge the intended use of the money pursuant to Congressional appropriation when, by confession, that money will have become the property of the government and the taxpayer will no longer have any interest in it. Massachusetts v. Mellon, 262 U.S. 447, is claimed to foreclose litigation by the respondents or other taxpayers, as such, looking to restraint of the expenditure of government funds. That case might be an authority in the petitioners' favor if we were here concerned merely with a suit by a taxpayer to restrain the expenditure of the public moneys. . . .
But here the respondents who are called upon to pay moneys as taxes, resist the exaction as a step in an unauthorized plan. The circumstance clearly distinguishes the case. The government in substance and effect asks us to separate the Agricultural Adjustment Act into two statutes, the one levying an excise on processors of certain commodities; the other appropriating the public moneys independently of the first. Passing the novel suggestion that two statutes enacted as parts of a single scheme should be tested as if they were distinct and unrelated, we think the legislation now before us is not susceptible of such separation and treatment.

The tax can only be sustained by ignoring the avowed purpose and operation of the act, and holding it a measure merely laying an excise upon processors to raise revenue for the support of government. Beyond cavil the sole object of the legislation is to restore the purchasing power of agricultural products to a parity with that prevailing in an earlier day; to take money from the processor and bestow it upon farmers who will reduce their acreage for the accomplishment of the proposed end, and, meanwhile, to aid these farmers during the period required to bring the prices of their crops to the desired level.

The tax plays an indispensable part in the plan of regulation. . . . A tax automatically goes into effect for a commodity when the Secretary of

Agriculture determines that rental or benefit payments are to be made for reduction of production of that commodity. The tax is to cease when rental or benefit payments cease. The rate is fixed with the purpose of bringing about crop-reduction and price-raising. It is to equal the difference between the "current average farm price" and "fair exchange value." It may be altered to such amount as will prevent accumulation of surplus stocks. . . . The whole revenue from the levy is appropriated in aid of crop control; none of it is made available for general government use. . . .

The statute not only avows an aim foreign to the procurement of revenue for the support of government, but by its operation shows the exaction laid upon processors to be the necessary means for the intended control of agricultural production. . . .

It is inaccurate and misleading to speak of the exaction from processors prescribed by the challenged act as a tax, or to say that as a tax it is subject to no infirmity. A tax, in the general understanding of the term, and as used in the Constitution, signifies an exaction for the support of the Government. The word has never been thought to connote the expropriation of money from one group for the benefit of another. . . .

We conclude that the act is one regulating agricultural production; that the tax is a mere incident of such regulation; and that the respondents have standing to challenge the legality of the exaction. . . . .

2 . Second. The Government asserts that even if the respondents may question the propriety of the appropriation embodied in the statute their attack must fail because Article I, § 8 of the Constitution authorizes the contemplated expenditure of the funds raised by the tax. This contention presents the great and the controlling question in the case. We approach its decision with a sense of our grave responsibility to render judgment in accordance with the principles established for the governance of all three branches of the Government.

There should be no misunderstanding as to the function of this court in such a case. It is sometimes said that the court assumes a power to overrule or control the action of the people's representatives. This is a misconception. The Constitution is the supreme law of the land ordained and established by the people. All legislation must conform to the principles it lays down. When an act of Congress is appropriately challenged in the courts as not conforming to the constitutional mandate the judicial branch of the Government has only one duty,—to lay the article of the Constitution which is invoked beside the statute which is challenged and to decide whether the latter squares with the former. All the court does, or can do, is to announce its considered judgment upon the question. The only power it has, if such it may be called, is the power of judgment. This court neither approves nor condemns any legislative policy. Its delicate and difficult office is to ascertain and declare whether the legislation is in accordance with, or in contravention of, the provisions of the Constitution; and, having done that, its duty ends. . . . .

. . . . Despite a reference in its first section to a burden upon, and an obstruction of the normal currents of commerce, the act under review does not purport to regulate transactions in interstate or foreign commerce. Its stated purpose is the control of agricultural production, a purely local activity, in an effort to raise the prices paid the farmer. Indeed, the Government does not attempt to uphold the validity of the act on the basis of the commerce clause, which, for the purpose of the present case, may be put aside as irrelevant.

The clause thought to authorize the legislation . . . confers upon the Congress power "to lay and collect Taxes, Duties, Imposts and Excises, to pay the Debts and provide for the common Defence and general Welfare of the United States. . . ." It is not contended that this provision grants power to regulate agricultural production upon the theory that such legislation would promote the general welfare. The Government concedes that the phrase "to provide for the general welfare" qualifies the power "to lay and collect taxes." The view that the clause grants power to provide for the general welfare, independently of the taxing power, has never been authoritatively accepted. Mr. Justice Story points out that if it were adopted "it is obvious that under color of the generality of the words, to 'provide for the common defence and general welfare,' the government of the United States is in reality, a government of general and unlimited powers, notwithstanding the subsequent enumeration of specific powers." The true construction undoubtedly is that the only thing granted is the power to tax for the purpose of providing funds for payment of the nation's debts and making provision for the general welfare.

Nevertheless, the Government asserts that warrant is found in this clause for the adoption of the Agricultural Adjustment Act. The argument is that Congress may appropriate and authorize the spending of moneys for the "general welfare"; that the phrase should be liberally construed to cover anything conducive to national welfare; that decision as to what will promote such welfare rests with Congress alone, and the courts may not review its determination; and, finally, that the appropriation under attack was in fact for the general welfare of the United States. . . .

Since the foundation of the Nation, sharp differences of opinion have persisted as to the true interpretation of the phrase. Madison asserted it amounted to no more than a reference to the other powers enumerated in the subsequent clauses of the same section; that, as the United States is a government of limited and enumerated powers, the grant of power to tax and spend for the general national welfare must be confined to the enumerated legislative fields committed to the Congress. In this view the phrase is mere tautology, for taxation and appropriation are or may be necessary incidents of the exercise of any of the enumerated legislative powers. Hamilton, on the other hand, maintained the clause confers a power separate and distinct from those later enumerated, is not restricted in meaning by the grant of them, and Congress consequently has a substantive power to tax and to appropriate, limited only by the requirement that it shall be exercised to provide for the general welfare of the United States. Each contention has had the support of those whose views are entitled to weight. This court has noticed the question, but has never found it necessary to decide which is the true construction. Mr. Justice Story, in his Commentaries, espouses the Hamiltonian position. We shall not review the writings of public men and commentators or discuss the legislative practice. Study of all these leads us to conclude that the reading advocated by Mr. Justice Story is the correct one. While, therefore, the power to tax is not unlimited, its confines are set in the clause which confers it, and not in those of § 8 which bestow and define the legislative powers of the Congress. It results that the power of

Congress to authorize expenditure of public moneys for public purposes is not limited by the direct grants of legislative power found in the Constitution.

But the adoption of the broader construction leaves the power to spend subject to limitations. . . .

. . . Hamilton, in his well known Report on Manufactures, states that the purpose must be "general, and not local." Monroe, an advocate of Hamilton's doctrine, wrote: "Have Congress a right to raise and appropriate the money to any and to every purpose according to their will and pleasure? They certainly have not." Story says that if the tax be not proposed for the common defence or general welfare, but for other objects wholly extraneous, it would be wholly indefensible upon constitutional principles. And he makes it clear that the powers of taxation and appropriation extend only to matters of national, as distinguished from local welfare. . . .

We are not now required to ascertain the scope of the phrase "general welfare of the United States" or to determine whether an appropriation in aid of agriculture falls within it. Wholly apart from that question, another principle embedded in our Constitution prohibits the enforcement of the Agricultural Adjustment Act. The Act invades the reserved rights of the states. It is a statutory plan to regulate and control agricultural production, a matter beyond the powers delegated to the federal government. The tax, the appropriation of the funds raised, and the direction for their disbursement, are but parts of the plan. They are but means to an unconstitutional end. . . .

. . . These decisions [from the Child Labor Tax Case to U. S. v. Constantine, supra] demonstrate that Congress could not, under the pretext of raising revenue, lay a tax on processors who refuse to pay a certain price for cotton and exempt those who agree so to do, with the purpose of benefiting producers.

Third. If the taxing power may not be used as the instrument to enforce a regulation of matters of state concern with respect to which the Congress has no authority to interfere, may it, as in the present case, be employed to raise the money necessary to purchase a compliance which the Congress is powerless to command? The Government asserts that whatever might be said against the validity of the plan, if compulsory, it is constitutionally sound because the end is accomplished by voluntary co-operation. There are two sufficient answers to the contention. The regulation is not in fact voluntary. The farmer, of course, may refuse to comply, but the price of such refusal is the loss of benefits. The amount offered is intended to be sufficient to exert pressure on him to agree to the proposed regulation. The power to confer or withhold unlimited benefits is the power to coerce or destroy. If the cotton grower elects not to accept the benefits, he will receive less for his crops; those who receive payments will be able to undersell him. The result may well be financial ruin. . . .

But if the plan were one for purely voluntary co-operation it would stand no better so far as federal power is concerned. At best, it is a scheme for purchasing with federal funds submission to federal regulation of a subject reserved to the states.

It is said that Congress has the undoubted right to appropriate money to executive officers for expenditure under contracts between the government and individuals; that much of the total expenditures is so made. But appropriations and expenditures under contracts for proper governmental purposes cannot justify contracts which are not within federal power. And contracts for the reduction of acreage and the control of production are outside the range of that power. An appropriation to be expended by the United States under contracts calling for violation of a state law clearly would offend the Constitution. Is a statute less objectionable which authorizes expenditure of federal moneys to induce action in a field in which the United States has no power to intermeddle? The Congress cannot invade state jurisdiction to compel individual action; no more can it purchase such action.

We are referred to numerous types of federal appropriation which have been made in the past, and it is asserted no question has been raised as to their validity. We need not stop to examine or consider them. . . . [S]uch expenditures have not been challenged because no remedy was open for testing their constitutionality in the courts. [Massachusetts v. Mellon, 262 U.S. 447.]

We are not here concerned with a conditional appropriation of money, nor with a provision that if certain conditions are not complied with the appropriation shall no longer be available. By the Agricultural Adjustment Act the amount of the tax is appropriated to be expended only in payment under contracts whereby the parties bind themselves to regulation by the Federal Government. There is an obvious difference between a statute stating the conditions upon which moneys shall be expended and one effective only upon assumption of a contractual obligation to submit to a regulation which otherwise could not be enforced. Many examples pointing the distinction might be cited. We are referred to appropriations in aid of education, and it is said that no one has doubted the power of Congress to stipulate the sort of education for which money shall be expended. But an appropriation to an educational institution which by its terms is to become available only if the beneficiary enters into a contract to teach doctrines subversive of the Constitution is clearly bad. An affirmance of the authority of Congress so to condition the expenditure of an appropriation would tend to nullify all constitutional limitations upon legislative power.

But it is said that there is a wide difference in another respect, between compulsory regulation of the local affairs of a state's citizens and the mere making of a contract relating to their conduct; that, if any state objects, it may declare the contract void and thus prevent those under the state's jurisdiction from complying with its terms. The argument is plainly fallacious. The United States can make the contract only if the federal power to tax and to appropriate reaches the subject-matter of the contract. If this does reach the subject-matter, its exertion cannot be displaced by state action. . . .

Congress has no power to enforce its commands on the farmer to the ends sought by the Agricultural Adjustment Act. It must follow that it may not indirectly accomplish those ends by taxing and spending to purchase compliance. The Constitution and the entire plan of our government negative any such use of the power to tax and to spend as the act undertakes to authorize. It does not help to declare that local conditions throughout the nation have created a situation of national concern; for this is but to say that whenever there is a widespread similarity of local conditions, Congress may ignore constitutional limitations upon its own powers and usurp those reserved to the states. If, in lieu of compulsory regulation of subjects within the states' reserved jurisdiction, which is prohibited, the Congress could invoke the taxing and spending power as a means to accomplish the same end, clause 1 of § 8 of article I would become the instrument for total subversion of the governmental powers reserved to the individual states.

If the act before us is a proper exercise of the federal taxing power, evidently the regulation of all industry throughout the United States may be accomplished by similar exercises of the same power. It would be possible to exact money from one branch of an industry and pay it to another branch in every field of activity which lies within the province of the states. The mere threat of such a procedure might well induce the surrender of rights and the compliance with federal regulation as the price of continuance in business. A few instances will illustrate the thought.

Let us suppose Congress should determine that the farmer, the miner or some other producer of raw materials is receiving too much for his products, with consequent depression of the processing industry and idleness of its employes. Though, by confession, there is no power vested in Congress to compel by statute a lowering of the prices of the raw material, the same result might be accomplished, if the questioned act be valid, by taxing the producer upon his output and appropriating the proceeds to the processors, either with or without conditions imposed as the consideration for payment of the subsidy. . . .

Suppose that there are too many garment workers in the large cities; that this results in dislocation of the economic balance. Upon the principle contended for an excise might be laid on the manufacture of all garments manufactured and the proceeds paid to those manufacturers who agree to remove their plants to cities having not more than a hundred thousand population. Thus, through the asserted power of taxation, the federal government, against the will of individual states, might completely redistribute the industrial population. . . .

These illustrations are given, not to suggest that any of the purposes mentioned are unworthy, but to demonstrate the scope of the principle for which the Government contends; to test the principle by its applications; to point out that, by the exercise of the asserted power, Congress would, in effect, under the pretext of exercising the taxing power, in reality accomplish prohibited ends. It cannot be said that they envisage improbable legislation. The supposed cases are no more improbable than would the present act have been deemed a few years ago. . . .

Hamilton himself, the leading advocate of broad interpretation of the power to tax and to appropriate for the general welfare, never suggested that any power granted by the Constitution could be used for the destruction of local self-government in the states. Story countenances no such doctrine. It seems never to have occurred to them, or to those who have agreed with them, that the general welfare of the United States, (which has aptly been termed "an indestructible Union, composed of indestructible States,") might be served by obliterating the constituent members of the Union. But to this fatal conclusion the doctrine contended for would inevitably lead. And its sole premise is that, though the makers of the Constitution, in erecting the federal government, intended sedulously to limit and define its powers, so as to reserve to the states and the people sovereign power, to be wielded by the states and their citizens and not to be invaded by the United States, they nevertheless by a single clause gave power to the Congress to tear down the barriers, to invade the states' jurisdiction, and to become a parliament of the whole people, subject to no restrictions save such as are self-imposed.   The argument when seen in its true character and in the light of its inevitable results must be rejected.   .   .   .

Affirmed.

Mr. Justice STONE, dissenting.   .   .   .

1.   The power of courts to declare a statute unconstitutional is subject to two guiding principles of decision which ought never to be absent from judicial consciousness.   One is that courts are concerned only with the power to enact statutes, not with their wisdom.   The other is that while unconstitutional exercise of power by the executive and legislative branches of the government is subject to judicial restraint, the only check upon our own exercise of power is our own sense of self-restraint.   For the removal of unwise laws from the statute books appeal lies not to the courts but to the ballot and to the processes of democratic government.

2.   The constitutional power of Congress to levy an excise tax upon the processing of agricultural products is not questioned.   The present levy is held invalid, not for any want of power in Congress to lay such a tax to defray public expenditures, including those for the general welfare, but because the use to which its proceeds are put is disapproved.

3.   As the present depressed state of agriculture is nation wide in its extent and effects, there is no basis for saying that the expenditure of public money in aid of farmers is not within the specifically granted power of Congress to levy taxes to "provide for the   .   .   .   general welfare."   The opinion of the Court does not declare otherwise.   .   .   .

It is with these preliminary and hardly controverted matters in mind that we should direct our attention to the pivot on which the decision of the Court is made to turn.   It is that a levy unquestionably within the taxing power of Congress may be treated as invalid because it is a step in a plan to regulate agricultural production and is thus a forbidden infringement of state power.   The levy is not any the less an exercise of taxing power because it is intended to defray an expenditure for the general welfare rather than for some other support of government.   Nor is the levy and collection of the tax pointed to as effecting the regulation.   While all federal taxes inevitably have some influence on the internal economy of the states, it is not contended that the levy of a processing tax upon manufacturers using agricultural products as raw material has any perceptible regulatory effect upon either their production or manufacture.   The tax is unlike the penalties which were held invalid in [cases from the Child Labor Tax Case to U. S. v. Constantine, supra] because they were themselves the instruments of regulation by virtue of their coercive effect on matters left to the control of the states.   Here regulation, if any there be, is accomplished not by the tax but by the method by which its proceeds are expended, and would equally be accomplished by any like use of public funds, regardless of their source.

The method may be simply stated.   Out of the available fund payments are made to such farmers as are willing to curtail their productive acreage, who in fact do so and who in advance have filed their written undertaking to do so with the Secretary of Agriculture. In saying that this method of spending public moneys is an invasion of the reserved powers of the states, the Court does not assert that the expenditure of public funds to promote the general welfare is not a substantive power specifically delegated to the national government as Hamilton and Story pronounced it to be. It does not deny that the expenditure of funds for the benefit of farmers and in aid of a program of curtailment of production of agricultural products, and thus of a supposedly better ordered national economy, is within the specifically granted power. But it is declared that state power is nevertheless infringed by the expenditure of the proceeds of the tax to compensate farmers for the curtailment of their cotton acreage. Although the farmer is placed under no legal compulsion to reduce acreage, it is said that the mere offer of compensation for so doing is a species of economic coercion which operates with the same legal force and effect as though the curtailment were made mandatory by Act of Congress. In any event it is insisted that even though not coercive the expenditure of public funds to induce the recipients to curtail production is itself an infringement of state power, since the federal government cannot invade the domain of the states by the "purchase" of performance of acts which it has no power to compel.

Of the assertion that the payments to farmers are coercive, it is enough to say that no such contention is pressed by the taxpayer, and no such consequences were to be anticipated or appear to have resulted from the administration of the act. The suggestion of coercion finds no support in the record or in any data showing the actual operation of the act. Threat of loss, not hope of gain, is the essence of economic coercion. . . . The presumption of constitutionality of a statute is not to be overturned by an assertion of its coercive effect which rests on nothing more substantial than groundless speculation.

It is upon the contention that state power is infringed by purchased regulation of agricultural production that chief reliance is placed. It is insisted that, while the Constitution gives to Congress, in specific and unambiguous terms, the power to tax and spend, the power is subject to limitations which do not find their origin in any express provision of the Constitution and to which other expressly delegated powers are not subject.

The Constitution requires that public funds shall be spent for a defined purpose, the promotion of the general welfare. Their expenditure usually involves payment on terms which will insure use by the selected recipients within the limits of the constitutional purpose. Expenditures would fail of their purpose and thus lose their constitutional sanction if the terms of payment were not such that by their influence on the action of the recipients the permitted end would be attained. The power of Congress to spend is inseparable from persuasion to action over which Congress has no legislative control. Congress may not command that the science of agriculture be taught in state universities. But if it would aid the teaching of that science by grants to state institutions, it is appropriate, if not necessary, that the grant be on the condition, incorporated in the Morrill Act, 12 Stat. 503, 26 Stat. 417, that it be used for the intended purpose. Similarly it would seem to be compliance with the Constitution, not violation of of it, for the government to take and the university to give a contract that the grant would be so used. It makes no difference that there is a promise to do an act which the condition is calculated to induce. Condition and promise are alike valid since both are in furtherance of the national purpose for which the money is appropriated.

These effects upon individual action, which are but incidents of the authorized expenditure of government money, are pronounced to be themselves a limitation upon the granted power . . . ..

Such a limitation is contradictory and destructive of the power to appropriate for the public welfare, and is incapable of practical application. The spending power of Congress is in addition to the legislative power and not subordinate to it. This independent grant of the power of the purse, and its very nature, involving in its exercise the duty to insure expenditure within the granted power, presuppose freedom of selection among divers ends and aims, and the capacity to impose such conditions as will render the choice effective. It is a contradiction in terms to say that there is power to spend for the national welfare, while rejecting any power to impose conditions reasonably adapted to the attainment of the end which alone would justify the expenditure.

The limitation now sanctioned must lead to absurd consequences. The government may give seeds to farmers, but may not condition the gift upon their being planted in places where they are most needed or even planted at all. The government may give money to the unemployed, but may not ask that those who get it shall give labor in return, or even use it to support their families. It may give money to sufferers from earthquake, fire, tornado, pestilence, or flood, but may not impose conditions, health precautions designed to prevent the spread of disease, or induce the movement of population to safer or more sanitary areas. All that, because it is purchased regulation infringing state powers, must be left for the states, who are unable or unwilling to supply the necessary relief. The government may spend its money for vocational rehabilitations, 48 Stat. 389, but it may not, with the consent of all concerned, supervise the process which it undertakes to aid. It may spend its money for the suppression of the boll weevil, but may not compensate the farmers for suspending the growth of cotton in the infected areas. It may aid state reforestation and forest fire prevention agencies, 43 Stat. 653, but may not be permitted to supervise their conduct. It may support rural schools, 39 Stat. 929, 45 Stat. 1151, 48 Stat. 792, but may not condition its grant by the requirement that certain standards be maintained. It may appropriate moneys to be expended by the Reconstruction Finance Corporation "to aid in financing agriculture, commerce, and industry," and to facilitate "the exportation of agricultural and other products." Do all its activities collapse because, in order to effect the permissible purpose in myriad ways the money is paid out upon terms and conditions which influence action of the recipients within the states, which Congress cannot command? The answer would seem plain. If the expenditure is for a national public purpose, that purpose will not be thwarted because payment is on condition which will advance that purpose. The action which Congress induces by payments of money to promote the general welfare, but which it does not command or coerce, is but an incident to a specifically granted power, but a permissible means to a legitimate end. If appropriation in aid of a program of curtailment of agricultural production is constitutional, and it is not denied that it is, payment to farmers on condition that they reduce their crop acreage is constitutional. It is not any the less so because the farmer at his own option promises to fulfill the condition.

That the governmental power of the purse is a great one is not now for the first time announced. Every student of the history of government and economics is aware of its magnitude and of its existence in every civilized government. Both were well understood by the framers of the Constitution when they sanctioned the grant of the spending power to the federal government, and both were recognized by Hamilton and Story, whose views of the spending power as standing on a parity with the other powers specifically granted, have hitherto been generally accepted.

The suggestion that it must now be curtailed by judicial fiat because it may be abused by unwise use hardly rises to the dignity of argument. So may judicial power be abused. . . . The power to tax and spend is not without constitutional restraints. One restriction is that the purpose must be truly national. Another is that it may not be used to coerce action left to state control. Another is the conscience and patriotism of Congress and the Executive. "It must be remembered that legislators are the ultimate guardians of the liberties and welfare of the people in quite as great a degree as the courts." Justice Holmes, in Missouri, Kansas & Texas Ry. Co. v. May, 194 U.S. 267, 270.

A tortured construction of the Constitution is not to be justified by recourse to extreme examples of reckless congressional spending which might occur if courts could not prevent expenditures which, even if they could be thought to effect any national purpose, would be possible only by action of a legislature lost to all sense of public responsibility. Such suppositions are addressed to the mind accustomed to believe that it is the business of courts to sit in judgment on the wisdom of legislative action. [Courts are not the only agency of government that must be assumed to have capacity to govern. Congress and the courts both unhappily may falter or be mistaken in the performance of their constitutional duty.] But interpretation of our great charter of government which proceeds on any assumption that the responsibility for the preservation of our institutions is the exclusive concern of any one of the three branches of government, or that it alone can save them from destruction is far more likely, in the long run, "to obliterate the constituent members" of "an indestructible union of indestructible states" than the frank recognition that language, even of a constitution, may mean what it says: that the power to tax and spend includes the power to relieve a nationwide economic maladjustment by conditional gifts of money.

Mr. Justice BRANDEIS and Mr. Justice CARDOZO join in this opinion.

THE BUTLER CASE AND CONDITIONAL SPENDING

The Butler decision contributed importantly to the pressure that produced the Court-packing plan a few months later; and the dissent provided useful ammunition for opponents of the Court. See the note on the Court-Packing Plan, chap. 4, p. 285. What was the significance of the Butler majority's endorsement of the Hamilton-Story position on the spending power?

Was that endorsement consistent with the result? Can the result in Butler be reconciled with the social security cases (Steward Machine and Helvering v. Davis), which follow? What are the permissible purposes of spending? What conditions on spending are permissible under the majority view in Butler? Under the dissent? Is it enough that the conditions are relevant to the general welfare? Must the conditions be related to the particular purpose of the spending program? What criteria for judicial scrutiny of conditions remain after the social security cases, below? Compare Flemming v. Nestor, printed in sec. 6 at p. 437, of this chapter.

STEWARD MACHINE CO. v. DAVIS

301 U.S. 548, 57 S.Ct. 883, 81 L.Ed. 1279 (1937).

Certiorari to the Circuit Court of Appeals for the Fifth Circuit.

Mr. Justice CARDOZO delivered the opinion of the Court.

The validity of the tax imposed by the Social Security Act on employers of eight or more is here to be determined.

Petitioner, an Alabama corporation, paid a tax in accordance with the statute, filed a claim for refund with the Commissioner of Internal Revenue, and sued to recover the payment ($46.14), asserting a conflict between the statute and the Constitution of the United States. Upon demurrer the District Court gave judgment for the defendant dismissing the complaint, and the Circuit Court of Appeals for the Fifth Circuit affirmed. . . . An important question of constitutional law being involved, we granted certiorari.

The Social Security Act (Act of August 14, 1935, c. 531, 49 Stat. 620, 42 U.S.C. c. 7 (Supp.)), is divided into eleven separate titles, of which only Titles IX and III are so related to this case as to stand in need of summary.

The caption of Title IX is "Tax on Employers of Eight or More." Every employer (with stated exceptions) is to pay for each calendar year "an excise tax, with respect to having individuals in his employ," the tax to be measured by prescribed percentages of the total wages payable by the employer during the calendar year with respect to such employment. § 901. One is not, however, an "employer" within the meaning of the act unless he employs eight persons or more. § 907(a). There are also other limitations of minor importance. . . . The proceeds, when collected, go into the Treasury of the United States like internal-revenue collections generally. § 905(a). They are not earmarked in any way. In certain circumstances, however, credits are allowable. § 902. If the taxpayer has made contributions to an unemployment fund under a state law, he may credit such contributions against the federal tax, provided, however, that the total credit allowed to any taxpayer shall not exceed 90 per centum of the tax against which it is credited, and provided also that the state law shall have been certified to the Secretary of the Treasury by the Social Security Board as satisfying certain minimum criteria. § 902. . . . Some of the conditions thus attached to the allowance of a credit are designed to give assurance that the state unemployment compensation law shall be one in substance as well as name. Others are designed to give assurance that the contributions shall be protected against loss after payment to the state. To this last end there are provisions that before a state law shall have the approval of the Board it must direct that the contributions to the state fund be paid over immediately to the Secretary of the Treasury to the credit of the "Unemployment Trust Fund." . . . For the moment it is enough to say that the Fund is to be held by the Secretary of the Treasury, who is to invest in government securities any portion not required in his judgment to meet current withdrawals. He is authorized and directed to pay out of the Fund to any competent state agency such sums as it may duly requisition from the amount standing to its credit. § 904(f).

Title III, which is also challenged as invalid, has the caption "Grants to States for Unemployment Compensation Administration." Under this title, certain sums of money are "authorized to be appropriated" for the purpose of assisting the states in the administration of their unemployment compensation laws . . . . The appropriations when made were not specifically out of the proceeds of the employment tax but out of any moneys in the Treasury. Other sections of the title . . . . are designed to give assurance to the Federal Government that the moneys granted by it will not be expended for purposes alien to the grant, and will be used in the administration of genuine unemployment compensation laws.

The assault on the statute proceeds on an extended front. Its assailants take the ground that the tax is not an excise; that it is not uniform throughout the United States as excises are required to be; that its exceptions are so many and arbitrary as to violate the Fifth Amendment; that its purpose was not revenue, but an unlawful invasion of the reserved powers of the states; and that the states in submitting to it have yielded to coercion and have abandoned governmental functions which they are not permitted to surrender. . . .

First: The tax, which is described in the statute as an excise, is laid with uniformity throughout the United States as a duty, an impost or an excise upon the relation of employment. . . .

Second: The excise is not invalid under the provisions of the Fifth Amendment by force of its exemptions. . . .

Third: The excise is not void as involving the coercion of the States in contravention of the Tenth Amendment or of restrictions implicit in our federal form of government.

. . . The case for the petitioner is built on the contention that here an ulterior aim is wrought into the very structure of the act, and what is even more important that the aim is not only ulterior, but essentially unlawful. In particular, the 90 per cent credit is relied upon as supporting that conclusion. But before the statute succumbs to an assault upon these lines, two propositions must be made out by the assailant. . . . There must be a showing in the first place that separated from the credit the revenue provisions are incapable of standing by themselves. There must be a showing in the second place that the tax and the credit in combination are weapons of coercion, destroying or impairing the autonomy of the states. The truth of each proposition being essential to the success of the assault, we pass for convenience to a consideration of the second, without pausing to inquire whether there has been a demonstration of the first.

To draw the line intelligently between duress and inducement there is need to remind ourselves of facts as to the problem of unemployment that are now matters of common knowledge. West Coast Hotel Co. v. Parrish,

300 U.S. 379. The relevant statistics are gathered in the brief of counsel for the Government. Of the many available figures a few only will be mentioned. During the years 1929 to 1936, when the country was passing through a cyclical depression, the number of the unemployed mounted to unprecedented heights. Often the average was more than 10 million; at times a peak was attained of 16 million or more. Disaster to the breadwinner meant disaster to dependents. Accordingly the roll of the unemployed, itself formidable enough, was only a partial roll of the destitute or needy. The fact developed quickly that the states were unable to give the requisite relief. The problem had become national in area and dimensions. There was need of help from the nation if the people were not to starve. It is too late today for the argument to be heard that in a crisis so extreme the use of moneys of the nation to relieve the unemployed and their dependents is a use for any purpose narrower than the promotion of the general welfare. Cf. United States v. Butler, 297 U.S. 1, 65, 66. . . . .

In the presence of this urgent need for some remedial expedient, the question is to be answered whether the expedient adopted has overlept the bounds of power. The assailants of the statute say that its dominant end and aim is to drive the state legislatures under the whip of economic pressure into the enactment of unemployment compensation laws at the bidding of the central government. Supporters of the statute say that its operation is not constraint, but the creation of a larger freedom, the states and nation joining in a cooperative endeavor to avert a common evil. Before Congress acted, unemployment compensation insurance was still, for the most part, a project and no more. Wisconsin was the pioneer. Her statute was adopted in 1931. At times bills for such insurance were introduced elsewhere, but they did not reach the stage of law. In 1935, four states (California, Massachusetts, New Hampshire and New York) passed unemployment laws on the eve of the adoption of the Social Security Act, and two others did likewise after the federal act and later in the year. The statutes differed to some extent in type, but were directed to a common end. In 1936, twenty-eight other states fell in line, and eight more the present year. But if states had been holding back before the passage of the federal law, inaction was not owing, for the most part, to the lack of sympathetic interest. Many held back through alarm lest in laying such a toll upon their industries, they would place themselves in a position of economic disadvantage as compared with neighbors or competitors. . . . Two consequences ensued. One was that the freedom of a state to contribute its fair share to the solution of a national problem was paralyzed by fear. The other was that in so far as there was failure by the states to contribute relief according to the measure of their capacity, a disproportionate burden, and a mountainous one, was laid upon the resources of the Government of the nation.

The Social Security Act is an attempt to find a method by which all these public agencies may work together to a common end. Every dollar of the new taxes will continue in all likelihood to be used and needed by the nation as long as states are unwilling, whether through timidity or for other motives, to do what can be done at home. At least the inference is permissible that Congress so believed, though retaining undiminished freedom to spend the money as it pleased. On the other hand fulfilment of the home duty will be lightened and encouraged by crediting the taxpayer upon his account with the Treasury of the nation to the extent that his contributions under the laws of the locality have simplified or diminished the problem of relief and the probable demand upon the resources of the fisc. . . .

Who then is coerced through the operation of this statute? Not the taxpayer. He pays in fulfilment of the mandate of the local legislature. Not the state. Even now she does not offer a suggestion that in passing the unemployment law she was affected by duress. . . . We cannot say that she [Alabama] was acting, not of her unfettered will, but under the strain of a persuasion equivalent to undue influence, when she chose to have relief administered under laws of her own making, by agents of her own selection, instead of under federal laws, administered by federal officers, with all the ensuing evils, at least to many minds, of federal patronage and power. There would be a strange irony, indeed, if her choice were now to be annulled on the basis of an assumed duress in the enactment of a statute which her courts have accepted as a true expression of her will. . . .

In ruling as we do, we leave many questions open. We do not say that a tax is valid, when imposed by act of Congress, if it is laid upon the condition that a state may escape its operation through the adoption of a statute unrelated in subject matter to activities fairly within the scope of national policy and power. No such question is before us. In the tender of this credit Congress does not intrude upon fields foreign to its function. The purpose of its intervention, as we have shown, is to safeguard its own treasury and as an incident to that protection to place the states upon a footing of equal opportunity. Drains upon its own resources are to be checked; obstructions to the freedom of the states are to be leveled. It is one thing to impose a tax dependent upon the conduct of the taxpayers, or of the state in which they live, where the conduct to be stimulated or discouraged is unrelated to the fiscal need subserved by the tax in its normal operation, or to any other end legitimately national. The Child Labor Tax Case, 259 U.S. 20, and Hill v. Wallace, 259 U.S. 44, were decided in the belief that the statutes there condemned were exposed to that reproach. . . . It is quite another thing to say that a tax will be abated upon the doing of an act that will satisfy the fiscal need, the tax and the alternative being approximate equivalents. In such circumstances, if in no others, inducement or persuasion does not go beyond the bounds of power. We do not fix the outermost line. Enough for present purposes that wherever the line may be, this statute is within it. Definition more precise must abide the wisdom of the future. . . .

United States v. Butler, supra, is cited by petitioner as a decision to the contrary. . . . The decision was by a divided court, a minority taking the view that the objections were untenable. None of them is applicable to the situation here developed.

(a) The proceeds of the tax in controversy are not earmarked for a special group.

(b) The unemployment compensation law which is a condition of the credit has had the approval of the state and could not be a law without it.

(c) The condition is not linked to an irrevocable agreement, for the state at its pleasure may repeal its unemployment law (§ 903(a) (6)), terminate the credit, and place itself where it was before the credit was accepted.

(d) The condition is not directed to the attainment of an unlawful end, but to an end, the relief of unemployment, for which nation and state may lawfully cooperate.

Fourth: The statute does not call for a surrender by the states of powers essential to their quasi-sovereign existence. . . .

A credit to taxpayers for payments made to a State under a state unemployment law will be manifestly futile in the absence of some assurance that the law leading to the credit is in truth what it professes to be. An unemployment law framed in such a way that the unemployed who look to it will be deprived of reasonable protection is one in name and nothing more. What is basic and essential may be assured by suitable conditions. The terms embodied in these sections are directed to that end. A wide range of judgment is given to the several states as to the particular type of statute to be spread upon their books. . . . In determining essentials Congress must have the benefit of a fair margin of discretion. One cannot say with reason that this margin has been exceeded, or that the basic standards have been determined in any arbitrary fashion. . . .

. . . [A]bdication is supposed to follow from § 904 of the statute and the parts of § 903 that are complementary thereto. § 903(a) (3). By these the Secretary of the Treasury is authorized and directed to receive and hold in the Unemployment Trust Fund all moneys deposited therein by a state agency for a state unemployment fund and to invest in obligations of the United States such portion of the Fund as is not in his judgment required to meet current withdrawals. We are told that Alabama in consenting to that deposit has renounced the plentitude of power inherent in her statehood.

. . . All that the state has done is to say in effect through the enactment of a statute that her agents shall be authorized to deposit the unemployment tax receipts in the Treasury at Washington. Alabama Unemployment Act of September 14, 1935, section 10(i). The statute may be repealed. § 903(a) (6). The consent may be revoked. The deposits may be withdrawn. The moment the state commission gives notice to the depositary that it would like the moneys back, the Treasurer will return them. . . .

The inference of abdication thus dissolves in thinnest air when the deposit is conceived of as dependent upon a statutory consent, and not upon a contract effective to create a duty. By this we do not intimate that the conclusion would be different if a contract were discovered. Even sovereigns may contract without derogating from their sovereignty. . . .

Fifth: Title III of the act is separable from Title IX, and its validity is not at issue.

The essential provisions of that title have been stated in the opinion. As already pointed out, the title does not appropriate a dollar of the public moneys. It does no more than authorize appropriations to be made in the future for the purpose of assisting states in the administration of their laws, if Congress shall decide that appropriations are desirable. The title might be expunged, and Title IX would stand intact. . . .

Affirmed.*

---

* Another judgment, given the same day the principal case was decided, sustained the Unemployment Compensation Law enacted by Alabama to fit into the program of the Social Security Act. Carmichael v. Southern Coal & Coke Co., 301 U.S. 495 (1937). In a comprehensive opinion by Justice Stone the Court dealt with a series of objections which raised the questions whether the Alabama statute "infringes the due process and equal protection clauses of the Fourteenth Amendment, and whether it is invalid because its enactment was coerced by the action of the Federal Government

Separate opinion of Mr. Justice McREYNOLDS. . . .

The invalidity, also the destructive tendency, of legislation like the Act before us were forcefully pointed out by President Franklin Pierce in a veto message sent to the Senate May 3, 1854. . . . I venture to set out pertinent portions of it which must appeal to all who continue to respect both the letter and spirit of our great charter.

"To the Senate of the United States:

"The bill entitled 'An Act making a grant of public lands to the several States for the benefit of indigent insane persons,' which was presented to me on the 27th ultimo, has been maturely considered, and is returned to the Senate, the House in which it originated, with a statement of the objections which have required me to withhold from it my approval. . . .

"It can not be questioned that if Congress has power to make provision for the indigent insane without the limits of this District it has the same power to provide for the indigent who are not insane, and thus to transfer to the Federal Government the charge of all the poor in all the States. . . . The question presented, therefore, clearly is upon the constitutionality and propriety of the Federal Government assuming to enter into a novel and vast field of legislation, namely, that of providing for the care and support of all those among the people of the United States who by any form of calamity become fit objects of public philanthropy. . . .

"I can not but repeat what I have before expressed, that if the several States, many of which have already laid the foundation of munificent establishments of local beneficence, and nearly all of which are proceeding to establish them, shall be led to suppose, as, should this bill become a law, they will be, that Congress is to make provision for such objects, the fountains of charity will be dried up at home, and the several States, instead of bestowing their own means on the social wants of their own people, may themselves, through the strong temptation which appeals to states as to individuals, become humble suppliants for the bounty of the Federal Government, reversing their true relations to this Union. . . ." . . . .

Separate opinion of Mr. Justice SUTHERLAND. . . .

The precise question . . . which we are required to answer . . . is whether the congressional act contemplates a surrender by the state to the federal government, in whole or in part, of any state governmental power to administer its own unemployment law or the state payroll-tax funds which it has collected for the purposes of that law. An affirmative answer to this question, I think, must be made. . . . .

Mr. Justice VAN DEVANTER joins in this opinion.

Mr. Justice BUTLER, dissenting.

I think that the objections to the challenged enactment expressed in the separate opinions of Mr. Justice McReynolds and Mr. Justice Sutherland are

in adopting the Social Security Act, and because it involves an unconstitutional surrender to the National Government of the sovereign power of the State." The conclusion was that the statute, "on its face, and as applied to appellees, is subject to no constitutional infirmity." Justice Sutherland delivered a dissenting opinion in which Justices Van Devanter and Butler concurred. Justice McReynolds also dissented.

well taken. I am also of opinion that, in principle and as applied to bring about and to gain control over state unemployment compensation, the statutory scheme is repugnant to the Tenth Amendment . . . . The Constitution grants to the United States no power to pay unemployed persons or to require the States to enact laws or to raise or disburse money for that purpose. The provisions in question, if not amounting to coercion in a legal sense, are manifestly designed and intended directly to affect state action in the respects specified. And, if valid as so employed, this "tax and credit" device may be made effective to enable federal authorities to induce, if not indeed to compel, state enactments for any purpose within the realm of state power, and generally to control state administration of state laws. . . .

HELVERING v. DAVIS

301 U.S. 619, 57 S.Ct. 904, 81 L.Ed. 1307 (1937).

Certiorari to the Circuit Court of Appeals for the First Circuit.

Mr. Justice CARDOZO delivered the opinion of the Court.

The Social Security Act . . . is challenged once again.

In Steward Machine Co. v. Davis, decided this day, we have upheld the validity of Title IX of the act, imposing an excise upon employers of eight or more. In this case Titles VIII and II are the subject of attack. Title VIII lays another excise upon employers in addition to the one imposed by Title IX (though with different exemptions). It lays a special income tax upon employees to be deducted from their wages and paid by the employers. Title II provides for the payment of Old Age Benefits, and supplies the motive and occasion, in the view of the assailants of the statute, for the levy of the taxes imposed by Title VIII. . . . Title II has the caption "Federal Old-Age Benefits." The benefits are of two types, first, monthly pensions, and second, lump sum payments, the payments of the second class being relatively few and unimportant. . . .

The scheme of benefits created by the provisions of Title II is not in contravention of the limitations of the Tenth Amendment.

Congress may spend money in aid of the "general welfare." Constitution, Art. I, § 8; United States v. Butler, 297 U.S. 1, 65; Steward Machine Co. v. Davis, supra. There have been great statesmen in our history who have stood for other views. We will not resurrect the contest. It is now settled by decision. United States v. Butler, supra. The conception of the spending power advocated by Hamilton and strongly reinforced by Story has prevailed over that of Madison, which has not been lacking in adherents. Yet difficulties are left when the power is conceded. The line must still be drawn between one welfare and another, between particular and general. Where this shall be placed cannot be known through a formula in advance of the event. There is a middle ground or certainly a penumbra in which discretion is at large. The discretion, however, is not confided to the courts. The discretion belongs to Congress, unless the choice is clearly wrong, a display of arbitrary power, not an exercise of judgment. . . .

Congress did not improvise a judgment when it found that the award of old age benefits would be conducive to the general welfare. The President's

Committee on Economic Security made an investigation and report, aided by a research staff of Government officers and employees, and by an Advisory Council and seven other advisory groups. Extensive hearings followed before the House Committee on Ways and Means, and the Senate Committee on Finance. A great mass of evidence was brought together supporting the policy which finds expression in the act. Among the relevant facts are these: The number of persons in the United States 65 years of age or over is increasing proportionately as well as absolutely. What is even more important the number of such persons unable to take care of themselves is growing at a threatening pace. More and more our population is becoming urban and industrial instead of rural and agricultural. The evidence is impressive that among industrial workers the younger men and women are preferred over the older. In times of retrenchment the older are commonly the first to go, and even if retained, their wages are likely to be lowered. The plight of men and women at so low an age as 40 is hard, almost hopeless, when they are driven to seek for reemployment. Statistics are in the brief. . . .

The problem is plainly national in area and dimensions. Moreover, laws of the separate states cannot deal with it effectively. Congress, at least, had a basis for that belief. States and local governments are often lacking in the resources that are necessary to finance an adequate program of security for the aged. This is brought out with a wealth of illustration in recent studies of the problem. Apart from the failure of resources, states and local governments are at times reluctant to increase so heavily the burden of taxation to be borne by their residents for fear of placing themselves in a position of economic disadvantage as compared with neighbors or competitors. We have seen this in our study of the problem of unemployment compensation. Steward Machine Co. v. Davis, supra. A system of old-age pensions has special dangers of its own, if put in force in one state and rejected in another. The existence of such a system is a bait to the needy and dependent elsewhere, encouraging them to migrate and seek a haven of repose. Only a power that is national can serve the interests of all.

Whether wisdom or unwisdom resides in the scheme of benefits set forth in Title II, it is not for us to say. The answer to such inquiries must come from Congress, not the courts. Our concern here, as often, is with power, not with wisdom. Counsel for respondent has recalled to us the virtues of self-reliance and frugality. There is a possibility, he says, that aid from a paternal government may sap those sturdy virtues and breed a race of weaklings. If Massachusetts so believes and shapes her laws in that conviction, must her breed of sons be changed, he asks, because some other philosophy of government finds favor in the halls of Congress? But the answer is not doubtful. One might ask with equal reason whether the system of protective tariffs is to be set aside at will in one state or another whenever local policy prefers the rule of *laissez faire*. The issue is a closed one. It was fought out long ago. When money is spent to promote the general welfare, the concept of welfare or the opposite is shaped by Congress, not the states. So the concept be not arbitrary, the locality must yield. Constitution, Art. VI, Par. 2.

[The tax upon employers was held to be a "valid excise or duty upon the relation of employment," on the authority of Steward Machine Co. v. Davis, supra.]

Reversed.

Mr. Justice McREYNOLDS and Mr. Justice BUTLER are of opinion that the provisions of the Act here challenged are repugnant to the Tenth Amendment . . . .

FEDERAL GRANTS TO INDIVIDUALS AND STATES AND FEDERAL ENTREPRENEURIAL ACTIVITIES

1. *The social security cases and federal grants to individuals.* Do the social security cases leave any federalism-related limits on the spending power, for judicial application in situations where spending programs can be litigated? What constitutional criteria must conditional spending programs meet? Are the only practical controls political ones? Are they adequate? Are there greater judicial restrictions when conditions in spending programs are challenged as restricting individual rights? Compare a more recent case under the Social Security Act, Flemming v. Nestor, 363 U.S. 603 (1960): it is printed below (sec. 6, p. 437), but may usefully be consulted at this point.

2. *Federal grants-in-aid to states.* The traditional and pervasive nature of federal spending programs was recognized in the Butler opinions. Policy guidance via the spending power, especially through conditioned grants-in-aid to the states, goes back to the beginning of the nation, as the Butler opinions recognized. The programs have increased considerably over the years. For a survey and commentary on modern dimensions, see two 1955 publications by the Commission on Intergovernmental Relations, Twenty-Five Grant-in-Aid Programs and Report to the President. For a discussion of earlier practice, see Elazar, The American Partnership: Intergovernmental Co-operation in the Nineteenth Century United States (1962). See generally Intergovernmental Relations Subcommittee of the House Government Operations Committee, Intergovernmental Relations in the United States—A Selected Bibliography, 84th Cong., 2d Sess. (1956), part IV.

There has been increasing opposition to narrow categorical grants-in-aid and considerable advocacy of broader unrestricted bloc grants to states and local governments. See, e. g., the support of revenue-sharing proposals such as the Heller Plan in the drive for "no strings money" instead of "strings money." Note Advisory Commission on Intergovernmental Relations, Tenth Annual Report (1969), 6: "Unless State and local governments are permitted 'free,' albeit limited, access to the prime power source—the Federal income tax—their positions within our federal system are bound to deteriorate."

Examination of the impacts of national spending on the federal system is one of the major functions of a permanent agency established in 1959, the Advisory Commission on Intergovernmental Relations, 5 U.S.C. § 2371 et seq. Among its tasks, as stated in the statutory "Declaration of purpose," is to "provide a forum for discussing the administration and coordination of Federal grant and other programs requiring intergovernmental cooperation"; to "give critical attention to the conditions and controls involved in the administration of Federal grant programs"; and to "recommend, within the framework of the Constitution, the most desirable allocation of governmental functions, responsibilities and revenues among the several levels of government."

3. *Federal spending and state autonomy.* a. A Tenth Amendment challenge to the Hatch Act was summarily rejected in Oklahoma v. United

States Civil Service Commission, 330 U.S. 127 (1947). The Hatch Act states that no state official primarily employed in activities "financed in whole or in part" by federal funds shall "take any active part" in political activities. A member of the State Highway Commission was also the state chairman of the Democratic Party. The federal agency ordered the Commissioner's removal. This demand "foreshadowed" if the state failed to obey, a federal order cutting off highway grants "in an amount equal to two years compensation" of the Commissioner.

The Court after rejecting a First Amendment challenge to the Hatch Act in a companion case, United Public Workers v. Mitchell, 330 U.S. 75 (chap. 2, p. 77, supra), found no substance in Oklahoma's attack on the removal order: "While the United States is not concerned with, and has no power to regulate, local political activities as such of state officials, it does have power to fix the terms upon which its money allotments to states shall be disbursed. . . . We do not see any violation of the state's sovereignty in the hearing or order. Oklahoma adopted the 'simple expedient' of not yielding to what she urges is federal coercion." Justice Reed wrote the majority opinion. Justices Black and Rutledge dissented without opinion.

b. For a critical comment on the decision, see Linde, "Justice Douglas on Freedom in the Welfare State—Constitutional Rights in the Public Sector," 39 Wash.L.Rev. 4, 30 (1964): "State officers . . . increasingly administer programs aided by federal funds; may Congress constitutionally decide which may be elected, which others politically appointed, and which must be in a non-partisan career status? Surely a line may be perceived between such conditions and conditions that go to the substance of the federally supported projects. . . . " Professor Linde notes that the 1961 Governors' Conference deplored "the tendency of federal agencies to dictate the organizational form and structure through which the states carry out federally supported projects." See Council of State Governments, State Government Organization and Federal Grant-in-Aid Program Requirements (1962), and compare the materials on state autonomy in chap. 10, below.

4. *Spending programs and the Civil Rights Act of 1964.* Before 1964, nondiscrimination policies in a number of federal programs were adopted by executive action—e. g., as to housing, airports, and employment on federally assisted construction. In 1963, the Civil Rights Commission urged that the President be authorized to suspend federal financial assistance to states acting in violation of the Constitution. President Kennedy commented: "I don't have the power to cut off aid in a general way as was proposed by the Commission, and I would think it would probably be unwise to give the President . . . . that kind of power." Title VI of the 1964 Civil Rights Act authorized selective cut-off of funds. Section 601 states the general policy: "No person in the United States shall, on the ground of race, color, or national origin, be excluded from participation in, be denied the benefits of, or be subjected to discrimination under any program or activity receiving Federal financial assistance." Several federal statutes contain provisions contemplating financial assistance to "separate but equal" facilities. One of these— in the Hill-Burton (Hospital Construction) Act, 42 U.S.C. 291e(f)—was held unconstitutional in Simkins v. Cone Memorial Hospital, 323 F.2d 959 (4th Cir. 1963), cert. denied, 376 U.S. 938 (1964). Title VI of the 1964 Act overrides all such provisions.

5. *Federal entrepreneurial activities and the TVA litigation.* The spending power has provoked controversy not only in the context of conditioned grants to individuals and states but also with respect to the financing of federal activities resembling commercial operations. Challenges to federal business activities, especially public power projects have been frequent, but typically failed. Test cases have frequently encountered justiciability barriers; and when the merits have been reached, the courts have often found constitutional justification in a variety of sources other than the spending power. The attempts to test the constitutionality of the Tennessee Valley Authority, a flood control, navigation and hydro-electric project, illustrate both aspects of this pattern. On the litigation strategy, see Freund, On Understanding the Supreme Court (1949), chap. 3.

a. The first unsuccessful broadscale attack was in Ashwander v. TVA, 297 U.S. 288 (1936). Stockholders of the Alabama Power Company challenged a contract between the Company and the federal agency. The contract included provisions for TVA purchase of transmission lines and disposition of electric power. The plaintiffs sought to use this vehicle to obtain "a general declaratory decree with respect to the rights of the Authority in various relations." The Court narrowed the issue sharply: it found that all of the electric energy under the contract was available at Wilson Dam, a dam begun in 1917 and completed in 1926, before the TVA was established. The Court agreed with the Government argument that "Wilson Dam was constructed, and the power plant connected with it was installed, in the exercise by the Congress of its war and commerce powers, that is, for the purposes of national defense and the improvement of navigation." The Government, moreover, had the right to convert the water power into electric energy, and the "electric energy thus produced" constitutes "property belonging to the United States." And the property power, Art. IV, Sec. 3, gave authority "to dispose of property constitutionally acquired." (The case produced Justice Brandeis' well-known concurring opinion on justiciability, noted in chap. 2, p. 142, supra.)

b. A subsequent omnibus attack on the TVA failed largely on standing grounds. Tennessee Electric Power Co. v. TVA, 306 U.S. 118 (1939). Nineteen power companies operating in nine different States sought an injunction against the Authority to restrain it from generating and distributing electricity in competition with complainants. The Court held that the complainants had no standing to maintain the suit: no legal right was involved; damage consequent on competition in such circumstances was *damnum absque injuria.* See also Alabama Power Co. v. Ickes, 302 U.S. 464 (1938), where a private utility company sought to enjoin Public Works Administration financial assistance to municipalities for the construction of competing electricity distribution systems. The Court found that neither the federal taxpayer status nor the threat of competition gave standing to sue. (See the discussion of competitors' standing in chap. 2, p. 106, supra.)

c. For earlier examples of governmental activity with a commercial aspect, see: establishment of banks, McCulloch v. Maryland, supra; First National Bank v. Fellows, 244 U.S. 416 (1917); ownership and operation of merchant ships, King County v. United States Shipping Board Emergency Fleet Corp., 282 Fed. 950 (9th Cir. 1922); establishment of a federal housing corporation, New Brunswick v. United States, 276 U.S. 547 (1928); establishment and operation of the Panama Railroad, Wilson v. Shaw, 204

U.S. 24 (1907); establishment of parcel post in competition with private express companies, 37 Stat. 567; and postal savings system in competition with banks, 36 Stat. 815. On the use of the commerce power as a basis for modern multi-purpose water power projects, see United States v. Appalachian Electric Power Co., 311 U.S. 377 (1940), and Oklahoma v. Atkinson, 313 U.S. 508 (1941).

SECTION 3. THE WAR POWER

Scope Note. This section has a limited purpose: to give a brief view of the use of the war power as a justification for national regulation of areas traditionally left to local control in the federal system. Governmental action based on military needs more frequently gives rise to conflicts with individual rights or with principles of civil-military relations and the separation of powers. These problems are considered at later points: see, e. g., court-martial jurisdiction over civilians overseas (Reid v. Covert, sec. 6, p. 410, of this chapter); military power over civilians during the Civil War (Ex parte Milligan, chap. 7, p. 611,); Presidential authority to commit military forces in view of congressional war power (Mora v. McNamara, chap. 7, p. 601,); and alleged racial discrimination in the detention of civilians during war (Korematsu v. United States, chap. 18, p. 1402).

WOODS v. MILLER CO.
333 U.S. 138, 68 S.Ct. 421, 92 L.Ed. 596 (1948).

Appeal from the District Court of the United States for the Northern District of Ohio.

Mr. Justice DOUGLAS delivered the opinion of the Court.

The case is here on a direct appeal, Act of August 24, 1937, 50 Stat. 752, 28 U.S.C. § 349a, from a judgment of the District Court holding unconstitutional Title II of the Housing and Rent Act of 1947. 61 Stat. 193, 196.

The Act became effective on July 1, 1947, and the following day the appellee demanded of its tenants increases of 40% and 60% for rental accommodations in the Cleveland Defense-Rental Area, an admitted violation of the Act and regulations adopted pursuant thereto. Appellant thereupon instituted this proceeding under § 206(b) of the Act to enjoin the violations. A preliminary injunction issued. After a hearing it was dissolved and a permanent injunction denied.

The District Court was of the view that the authority of Congress to regulate rents by virtue of the war power (see Bowles v. Willingham, 321 U.S. 503) ended with the Presidential Proclamation terminating hostilities on December 31, 1946,[1] since that proclamation inaugurated "peace-in-fact" though it did not mark termination of the war. It also concluded that, even if the war power continues, Congress did not act under it because it did not say so,

---

1. Proclamation 2714, 12 Fed.Reg. 1. That proclamation recognized that "a state of war still exists." On July 25, 1947, on approving S.J.Res. 123 terminating certain war statutes, the President issued a statement in which he declared that "The emergencies declared by the President on Septem-

and only if Congress says so, or enacts provisions so implying, can it be held that Congress intended to exercise such power.   .   .   .

We conclude, in the first place, that the war power sustains this legislation. The Court said in Hamilton v. Kentucky Distilleries Co., 251 U.S. 146, 161, that the war power includes the power "to remedy the evils which have arisen from its rise and progress" and continues for the duration of that emergency. Whatever may be the consequences when war is officially terminated, the war power does not necessarily end with the cessation of hostilities. We recently held that it is adequate to support the preservation of rights created by wartime legislation, Fleming v. Mohawk Wrecking & Lumber Co., 331 U.S. 111. But it has a broader sweep. In Hamilton v. Kentucky Distilleries Co., supra, and Ruppert v. Caffey, 251 U.S. 264, prohibition laws which were enacted after the Armistice in World War I were sustained as exercises of the war power because they conserved manpower and increased efficiency of production in the critical days during the period of demobilization, and helped to husband the supply of grains and cereals depleted by the war effort. Those cases followed the reasoning of Stewart v. Kahn, 11 Wall. 493, which held that Congress had the power to toll the statute of limitations of the States during the period when the process of their courts was not available to litigants due to the conditions obtaining in the Civil War.

The constitutional validity of the present legislation follows *a fortiori* from those cases. The legislative history of the present Act makes abundantly clear that there has not yet been eliminated the deficit in housing which in considerable measure was caused by the heavy demobilization of veterans and by the cessation or reduction in residential construction during the period of hostilities due to the allocation of building materials to military projects. Since the war effort contributed heavily to that deficit, Congress has the power even after the cessation of hostilities to act to control the forces that a short supply of the needed article created. If that were not true, the Necessary and Proper Clause, Art. I, § 8, cl. 18, would be drastically limited in its application to the several war powers. The Court has declined to follow that course in the past.   .   .   .   We decline to take it today. The result would be paralyzing. It would render Congress powerless to remedy conditions the creation of which necessarily followed from the mobilization of men and materials for successful prosecution of the war. So to read the Constitution would be to make it self-defeating.

We recognize the force of the argument that the effects of war under modern conditions may be felt in the economy for years and years, and that if the war power can be used in days of peace to treat all the wounds which war inflicts on our society, it may not only swallow up all other powers of Congress but largely obliterate the Ninth and the Tenth Amendments as well. There are no such implications in today's decision. We deal here with the consequences of a housing deficit greatly intensified during the period of hostilities by the war effort. Any power, of course, can be abused. But we cannot assume that Congress is not alert to its constitutional responsibilities. And the question whether the war power has been properly employed in cases such as this is open to judicial inquiry. Hamilton v. Kentucky Distilleries Co., supra; Ruppert v. Caffey, supra.

ber 8, 1939, and May 27, 1941, and the state of war continue to exist, however, and it is not possible at this time to provide for terminating all war and emergency powers." [Footnote by the Court.]

The question of the constitutionality of action taken by Congress does not depend on recitals of the power which it undertakes to exercise. Here it is plain from the legislative history that Congress was invoking its war power to cope with a current condition of which the war was a direct and immediate cause. Its judgment on that score is entitled to the respect granted like legislation enacted pursuant to the police power. See Block v. Hirsh, 256 U.S. 135; Marcus Brown Co. v. Feldman, 256 U.S. 170; Chastleton Corp. v. Sinclair, 264 U.S. 543. [Cases dealing with World War I rent control in the District of Columbia and New York.] . . .

Reversed.

Mr. Justice FRANKFURTER concurs in this opinion because it decides no more than was decided in Hamilton v. Kentucky Distilleries Co., 251 U.S. 146, and Jacob Ruppert v. Caffey, 251 U.S. 264, and merely applies those decisions to the situation now before the Court.

Mr. Justice JACKSON, concurring.

I agree with the result in this case, but the arguments that have been addressed to us lead me to utter more explicit misgivings about war powers than the Court has done. The Government asserts no constitutional basis for this legislation other than this vague, undefined and undefinable "war power."

No one will question that this power is the most dangerous one to free government in the whole catalogue of powers. It usually is invoked in haste and excitement when calm legislative consideration of constitutional limitation is difficult. It is executed in a time of patriotic fervor that makes moderation unpopular. And, worst of all, it is interpreted by judges under the influence of the same passions and pressures. Always, as in this case, the Government urges hasty decision to forestall some emergency or serve some purpose and pleads that paralysis will result if its claims to power are denied or their confirmation delayed.

Particularly when the war power is invoked to do things to the liberties of people, or to their property or economy that only indirectly affect conduct of the war and do not relate to the management of the war itself, the constitutional basis should be scrutinized with care.

I think we can hardly deny that the war power is as valid a ground for federal rent control now as it has been at any time. We still are technically in a state of war. I would not be willing to hold that war powers may be indefinitely prolonged merely by keeping legally alive a state of war that had in fact ended. I cannot accept the argument that war powers last as long as the effects and consequences of war, for if so they are permanent—as permanent as the war debts. But I find no reason to conclude that we could find fairly that the present state of war is merely technical. We have armies abroad exercising our war power and have made no peace terms with our allies, not to mention our principal enemies. I think the conclusion that the war power has been applicable during the lifetime of this legislation is unavoidable.

THE WAR POWER AND DOMESTIC REGULATION

1. *War time control of the economy.* Economic controls during World War II, in the Emergency Price Control Act of 1942, were sustained in

Bowles v. Willingham, 321 U.S. 503 (1944) (rents), and Yakus v. United States, 321 U.S. 414 (1944) (prices). The Act severely restricted usual procedural channels to test the validity of governmental regulations. In rejecting a challenge to the Act's failure to provide for a hearing before the rent orders took effect, the Court stated in Bowles v. Willingham: "National security might not be able to afford the luxuries of litigation and the long delays which preliminary hearings traditionally have entailed. We fully recognize . . . that 'even the war power does not remove constitutional limitations safeguarding essential liberties.' . . . But where Congress has provided for judicial review after the regulations or orders have been made effective it has done all that due process under the war emergency requires." (See chap. 1, p. 56.) The validity of the wartime Renegotiation Act was sustained as an exercise of the war power in Lichter v. United States, 334 U.S. 742 (1948). The Act provided for recapture of excessive profits realized on war contracts where the ultimate source of payment was the United States Government. Note also Silesian-American Corp. v. Clark, 332 U.S. 469 (1947), which contains a broad discussion of the power to seize the property of aliens during wartime.

2. *The war power and "police" regulations.* As noted in the principal case, the war power was invoked in Hamilton v. Kentucky Distilleries Co., 251 U.S. 146 (1920), to sustain a general prohibition law (enacted prior to the adoption of the Eighteenth Amendment): "That the United States lacks the police power, and that this was reserved to the States by the Tenth Amendment, is true. But it is none the less true that when the United States exerts any of the powers conferred upon it by the Constitution, no valid objection can be based upon the fact that such exercise may be attended by the same incidents which attend the exercise by a State of its police power, or that it may tend to accomplish a similar purpose."

SECTION 4. TREATIES, FOREIGN AFFAIRS, AND FEDERALISM

Scope Note. To what extent does the national government's authority over foreign affairs authorize national action in an otherwise local area? Are the usual federalism-related restraints inapplicable when national action is concerned with the conduct of foreign relations? These are the sole concerns of this section. Other constitutional problems pertaining to international affairs are left to later sections of this book. See, e. g., chap. 7 (on separation of powers), for the distinction between executive agreements and treaties and the related problems of executive-legislative relations.

Most of the cases in this section involve national action resting on the treaty power; the final notes consider whether there is a foreign affairs power of Congress independent of authority derived from treaties. To what extent may a treaty—either as a basis for national legislation or in its self-executing effect—permit national action not possible under other grants of power? That is the central question in these materials.

HAUENSTEIN v. LYNHAM

100 U.S. 483, 25 L.Ed. 628 (1880).

Error to the Supreme Court of Appeals of Virginia.

Mr. Justice SWAYNE delivered the opinion of the court.

Solomon Hauenstein died in the City of Richmond in the year 1861 or 1862, intestate, unmarried and without children. The precise date of his death is not material. At that time he owned and held considerable real estate in the City of Richmond. An inquisition of escheat was prosecuted by the escheator for that district. A verdict and judgment were rendered in his favor. When he was about to sell the property, the plaintiffs in error, pursuant to a law of the State, filed their petition, setting forth that they were the heirs-at-law of the deceased, and praying that the proceeds of the sale of the property should be paid over to them. Testimony was taken to prove their heirship as alleged, but the court was of opinion that, conceding that fact to be established, they could have no valid claim, and dismissed the petition. They removed the case to the Court of Appeals. That court, entertaining the same views as the court below, affirmed the judgment. They thereupon sued out this writ of error.

The plaintiffs in error are all citizens of Switzerland. The deceased was also a citizen of that country, and removed thence to Virginia, where he lived and acquired the property to which this controversy relates, and where he died. The validity of his title is not questioned. There is no proof that he denationalized himself or ceased to be a citizen and subject of Switzerland. His original citizenship is, therefore, to be presumed to have continued. Best on Presumptions, 186. According to the record his domicile, not his citizenship, was changed. The testimony as to the heirship of the plaintiffs in error is entirely satisfactory. There was no controversy on this subject in the argument here. The parties were at one as to all the facts. Their controversy was rested entirely upon legal grounds.

[Under the statutes of Virginia real estate of aliens dying intestate escheated to the State. A treaty between the United States and Switzerland, 1850, as construed by the court, gave the heirs the right to dispose of the property and withdraw the proceeds thereof.]

It remains to consider the effect of the treaty thus construed upon the rights of the parties.

That the laws of the State, irrespective of the treaty, would put the fund into her coffers, is no objection to the right or the remedy claimed by the plaintiffs in error. . . .

In Chirac v. Chirac, 2 Wheat. 259, it was held by this court that a treaty with France gave to her citizens the right to purchase and hold land in the United States, removed the incapacity of alienage and placed them in precisely the same situation as if they had been citizens of this country. The State law was hardly adverted to, and seems not to have been considered a factor of any importance in this view of the case. The same doctrine was reaffirmed touching this treaty in Carneal v. Banks, 10 Wheat. 181, and with respect to the British treaty of 1794, in Hughes v. Edwards, 9 Wheat. 489. A treaty stipulation may be effectual to protect the land of an alien from forfeiture by escheat under the laws of a State. Orr v. Hodgson, 4 Wheat. 453.

By the British treaty of 1794, "all impediment of alienage was absolutely leveled with the ground despite the laws of the States. It is the direct constitutional question in its fullest conditions. Yet the Supreme Court held that the stipulation was within the constitutional powers of the Union. Fairfax's Devisee v. Hunter's Lessee, 7 Cranch 603, 627; see Ware v. Hylton, 3 Dall. 199, 242." 8 Op.Atty's Gen. 417. Mr. Calhoun, after laying down certain exceptions and qualifications which do not affect this case, says: "Within these limits all questions which may arise between us and other powers, be the subject matter what it may, fall within the treaty-making power and may be adjusted by it." Treat. on the Const. and Gov. of the U.S. 204.

If the national government has not the power to do what is done by such treaties, it cannot be done at all, for the States are expressly forbidden to "enter into any treaty, alliance, or confederation." Const. art. 1, sec. 10.

It must always be borne in mind that the Constitution, laws and treaties of the United States are as much a part of the law of every State as its own local laws and Constitution. This is a fundamental principle in our system of complex national polity. . . .

We have no doubt that this treaty is within the treaty-making power conferred by the Constitution. And it is our duty to give it full effect. We forbear to pursue the topic further. In the able argument before us, it was insisted upon one side, and not denied on the other, that, if the treaty applies, its efficacy must necessarily be complete. The only point of contention was one of construction. There are, doubtless, limitations of this power as there are of all others arising under such instruments; but this is not the proper occasion to consider the subject. It is not the habit of this court, in dealing with constitutional questions, to go beyond the limits of what is required by the exigencies of the case in hand. What we have said is sufficient for the purposes of this opinion. . . .

[Judgment reversed.]

THE TREATY POWER AND THE STATES

1. *Treaties and state law.* As the principal case notes, the doctrine that a valid treaty overrides a state law on matters otherwise within state control goes back to 1796. Ware v. Hylton, 3 Dall. 199. In that case, a British creditor brought suit in the Circuit Court for Virginia against the defendants, citizens of Virginia, on a bond given by them in 1774. The defendants sought a discharge by virtue of payment in 1780 to Virginia under a statute passed by the state in 1777 confiscating British property. In reply plaintiff asserted that the statute had been nullified by the Treaty of Peace between Great Britain and the United States which provided that British creditors "shall meet with no lawful impediment to the recovery . . . of all debts, heretofore contracted." The lower court decided for the Virginia defendants. The Supreme Court reversed: "If doubts could exist before the establishment of the present national government, they must be entirely removed by the 6th article of the Constitution. A treaty cannot be the Supreme law of the land, that is of all the United States, if any act of a State Legislature can stand in its way." (Recall also the conflict between the treaty and the escheat under state law in Martin v. Hunter's Lessee, chap. 1, p. 32, and compare Zschernig v. Miller, in the final note in this section.)

   2. *The subject-matter of treaties.* a.   Are there any judicially enforceable limits on the treaty power? Are there any limits on what subjects a treaty may deal with? Whenever Article I powers prove insufficient to reach a local subject, may the national government overcome that obstacle by making a treaty with a cooperative foreign government? Are there any traditionally local questions that cannot be "properly the subject of negotiation with a foreign country"? Does not the fact that a treaty exists, that the treaty about a particular matter *has* been negotiated, demonstrate that the matter *is* a proper subject for negotiation? Can the courts scrutinize the good faith of President and Senate in making the treaty?

   b.   The "properly the subject of negotiation" phrase comes from Geofroy v. Riggs, 133 U.S. 258 (1890). Can the statement be considered an effective limit on the treaty power? Justice Field stated: "The treaty power, as expressed in the Constitution, is in terms unlimited except by those restraints which are found in that instrument against the action of the government or of its departments, and those arising from the nature of the government itself and of that of the States. It would not be contended that it extends so far as to authorize what the Constitution forbids, or a change in the character of the government or in that of one of the States, or a cession of any portion of the territory of the latter, without its consent. Fort Leavenworth R. Co. v. Lowe, 114 U.S. 525, 541. But with these exceptions it is not perceived that there is any limit to the questions which can be adjusted touching any matter which is properly the subject of negotiation with a foreign country." If this is not an effective limitation, are there others?

   3. *Legislation conflicting with treaties.* a.   In terms of domestic effect, legislation is on a par with treaties, and a later law may supersede a treaty. See Chee Chan Ping v. United States (The Chinese Exclusion Case), 130 U.S. 581 (1889). After holding an Act of Congress was in contravention of a treaty, Justice Field stated for the Court: "But it is not on that account invalid or to be restricted in its enforcement. The treaties were of no greater legal obligation than the Act of Congress. By the Constitution, laws made in pursuance thereof and treaties made under the authority of the United States are both declared to be the supreme law of the land, and no paramount authority is given to one over the other. A treaty, it is true, is in its nature a contract between nations, and is often merely promissory in its character, requiring legislation to carry its stipulations into effect. Such legislation will be open to future repeal or amendment. If the treaty operates by its own force and relates to a subject within the power of Congress, it can be deemed in that particular only the equivalent of a legislative Act, to be repealed or modified at the pleasure of Congress. In either case the last expression of the sovereign will must control." Where treaties and statutes are involved "the courts will endeavor to construe them so as to give effect to both." See Whitney v. Robertson, 124 U.S. 190 (1888).

   b.   On the distinction between international consequences of treaties and their domestic impacts, see also Justice Miller's comments in Edye v. Robertson (The Head Money Cases), 112 U.S. 580: "A treaty is primarily a compact between independent nations. It depends for the enforcement of its provisions on the interest and the honor of the governments which are parties to it. If these fail, its infraction becomes the subject of international negotiations and reclamations, so far as the injured party chooses to seek redress, which may in the end be enforced by actual war. It is obvious that with all this, the judicial courts have nothing to do and can give no redress. But a treaty may also contain provisions which confer certain rights upon the citizens or subjects of one of the nations residing in the territorial limits of the other, which partake of the nature of municipal law, and which are capable of enforcement as between private parties in the courts of the country. An illustration of this character is found in treaties which regulate the mutual rights of citizens and subjects of the contracting nations in regard to rights of property by descent or inheritance, when the individuals concerned are aliens."

MISSOURI v. HOLLAND

252 U.S. 416, 40 S.Ct. 382, 64 L.Ed. 641 (1920).

Appeal from the District Court of the United States for the Western District of Missouri.

Mr. Justice HOLMES delivered the opinion of the court.

This is a bill in equity brought by the State of Missouri to prevent a game warden of the United States from attempting to enforce the Migratory Bird Treaty Act of July 3, 1918, c. 128, 40 Stat. 755, and the regulations made by the Secretary of Agriculture in pursuance of the same. The ground of the bill is that the statute is an unconstitutional interference with the rights reserved to the States by the Tenth Amendment, and that the acts of the defendant done and threatened under that authority invade the sovereign right of the State and contravene its will manifested in statutes. The State also alleges a pecuniary interest, as owner of the wild birds within its borders and otherwise, admitted by the Government to be sufficient, but it is enough that the bill is a reasonable and proper means to assert the alleged quasi sovereign rights of a State. . . . A motion to dismiss was sustained by the District Court on the ground that the act of Congress is constitutional. . . . The State appeals.

On December 8, 1916, a treaty between the United States and Great Britain was proclaimed by the President. It recited that many species of birds in their annual migrations traversed many parts of the United States and of Canada, that they were of great value as a source of food and in destroying insects injurious to vegetation, but were in danger of extermination through lack of adequate protection. It therefore provided for specified closed seasons and protection in other forms, and agreed that the two powers would take or propose to their lawmaking bodies the necessary measures for carrying the treaty out. 39 Stat. 1702. The above mentioned act of July 3, 1918, entitled an act to give effect to the convention, prohibited the killing, capturing or selling any of the migratory birds included in the terms of the treaty except as permitted by regulations compatible with those terms, to be made by the Secretary of Agriculture. Regulations were proclaimed on July 31, and October 25, 1918. 40 Stat. 1812, 1863. It is unnecessary to go into any details, because, as we have said, the question raised is the general one whether the treaty and statute are void as an interference with the rights reserved to the States.

To answer this question it is not enough to refer to the Tenth Amendment, reserving the powers not delegated to the United States, because by

Article II, § 2, the power to make treaties is delegated expressly, and by Article VI treaties made under the authority of the United States, along with the Constitution and laws of the United States made in pursuance thereof, are declared the supreme law of the land. If the treaty is valid there can be no dispute about the validity of the statute under Article I, § 8, as a necessary and proper means to execute the powers of the Government. The language of the Constitution as to the supremacy of treaties being general, the question before us is narrowed to an inquiry into the ground upon which the present supposed exception is placed.

It is said that a treaty cannot be valid if it infringes the Constitution, that there are limits, therefore, to the treaty-making power, and that one such limit is that what an act of Congress could not do unaided, in derogation of the powers reserved to the States, a treaty cannot do. An earlier act of Congress that attempted by itself and not in pursuance of a treaty to regulate the killing of migratory birds within the States had been held bad in the District Court. United States v. Shauver, 214 Fed. 154. United States v. McCullagh, 221 Fed. 288. Those decisions were supported by arguments that migratory birds were owned by the States in their sovereign capacity for the benefit of their people, and that under cases like Greer v. Connecticut, 161 U.S. 519, this control was one that Congress had no power to displace. The same argument is supposed to apply now with equal force.

Whether the two cases cited were decided rightly or not they cannot be accepted as a test of the treaty power. Acts of Congress are the supreme law of the land only when made in pursuance of the Constitution, while treaties are declared to be so when made under the authority of the United States. It is open to question whether the authority of the United States means more than the formal acts prescribed to make the convention. We do not mean to imply that there are no qualifications to the treaty-making power; but they must be ascertained in a different way. It is obvious that there may be matters of the sharpest exigency for the national well being that an act of Congress could not deal with but that a treaty followed by such an act could, and it is not lightly to be assumed that, in matters requiring national action, "a power which must belong to and somewhere reside in every civilized government" is not to be found. Andrews v. Andrews, 188 U.S. 14, 33. What was said in that case with regard to the powers of the States applies with equal force to the powers of the nation in cases where the States individually are incompetent to act. We are not yet discussing the particular case before us but only are considering the validity of the test proposed. With regard to that we may add that when we are dealing with words that also are a constituent act, like the Constitution of the United States, we must realize that they have called into life a being the development of which could not have been foreseen completely by the most gifted of its begetters. It was enough for them to realize or to hope that they had created an organism; it has taken a century and has cost their successors much sweat and blood to prove that they created a nation. The case before us must be considered in the light of our whole experience and not merely in that of what was said a hundred years ago. The treaty in question does not contravene any prohibitory words to be found in the Constitution. The only question is whether it is forbidden by some invisible radiation from the general terms of the Tenth Amendment. We must consider what this country has become in deciding what that Amendment has reserved.

The State as we have intimated founds its claim of exclusive authority upon an assertion of title to migratory birds, an assertion that is embodied in statute. No doubt it is true that as between a State and its inhabitants the State may regulate the killing and sale of such birds, but it does not follow that its authority is exclusive of paramount powers. To put the claim of the State upon title is to lean upon a slender reed. Wild birds are not in the possession of anyone; and possession is the beginning of ownership. The whole foundation of the State's rights is the presence within their jurisdiction of birds that yesterday had not arrived, tomorrow may be in another State and in a week a thousand miles away. If we are to be accurate we cannot put the case of the State upon higher ground than that the treaty deals with creatures that for the moment are within the state borders, that it must be carried out by officers of the United States within the same territory, and that but for the treaty the State would be free to regulate this subject itself.

As most of the laws of the United States are carried out within the States and as many of them deal with matters which in the silence of such laws the State might regulate, such general grounds are not enough to support Missouri's claim. Valid treaties of course "are as binding within the territorial limits of the States as they are elsewhere throughout the dominion of the United States." Baldwin v. Franks, 120 U.S. 678, 683. No doubt the great body of private relations usually fall within the control of the State, but a treaty may override its power. We do not have to invoke the later developments of constitutional law for this proposition; it was recognized as early as Hopkirk v. Bell, 3 Cranch 454, with regard to statutes of limitation, and even earlier, as to confiscation, in Ware v. Hylton, 3 Dall. 199. It was assumed by Chief Justice Marshall with regard to the escheat of land to the State in Chirac v. Chirac, 2 Wheat. 259, 275; Hauenstein v. Lynham, 100 U.S. 483; Geofroy v. Riggs, 133 U.S. 258 . . . .

Here a national interest of very nearly the first magnitude is involved. It can be protected only by national action in concert with that of another power. The subject matter is only transitorily within the State and has no permanent habitat therein. But for the treaty and the statute there soon might be no birds for any powers to deal with. We see nothing in the Constitution that compels the Government to sit by while a food supply is cut off and the protectors of our forests and our crops are destroyed. It is not sufficient to rely upon the States. The reliance is vain, and were it otherwise, the question is whether the United States is forbidden to act. We are of opinion that the treaty and statute must be upheld. . . .

Decree affirmed.

Mr. Justice VAN DEVANTER and Mr. Justice PITNEY dissent.

THE MODERN CONCERN OVER LIMITS ON THE TREATY POWER: THE BRICKER AMENDMENT CONTROVERSY AND THE REID v. COVERT REASSURANCE

1. *The Bricker Amendment controversy.* a. *The background.* In the early 1950's, widely voiced concern that the treaty power was the Achilles' heel of the Constitution—that any and all constitutional limitations could be overriden via the international agreement route—spurred efforts to amend the Constitution. The broad dicta of Missouri v. Holland proved popu-

lar sources for those anxious to demonstrate the substantiality of the threat to constitutional restrictions.

The fears that built popular support for the Bricker Amendment were also fed by occasional arguments made in American courts that relied on the United Nations Charter; the concern was that the UN Charter or resolutions by UN agencies (e. g., the Draft Covenant on Civil and Political Rights approved by the UN Commission on Human Rights) might undercut American constitutional guarantees. The UN Charter, Art. 55, states that "the United Nations shall promote . . . universal respect for, and observance of, human rights and fundamental freedoms for all without distinction as to race, sex, language, or religion." By Article 56, all members "pledge themselves to take joint and separate action in cooperation with the Organization for the achievement of the purposes set forth in Article 55." In Fujii v. State, 217 P.2d 481 (1950), a California District Court of Appeal held the state's land law invalid on the ground that the UN Charter was self-executing. The California Supreme Court, however, rested its affirmance of the result on the Fourteenth Amendment, 38 Cal.2d 718, 242 P.2d 617 (1952). The state Supreme Court stated that it is "clear that the provisions of . . . the charter which are claimed to be in conflict with the alien land law are not self-executing." But the Court went on to say that the "humane and enlightened objectives" of the Charter are "entitled to respectful consideration by the courts and legislatures of every member nation, since that document expresses the universal desire of thinking men for peace and for equality of rights and opportunities."

b. *The scope of the Bricker proposal.* In June 1953, the Senate Committee on the Judiciary recommended (Sen. Rep. No. 412, 83d Cong., 1st Sess.) the submission of an amendment relating to treaties and executive agreements. The principal provisions were as follows:

"Sec. 1. A provision of a treaty which conflicts with this Constitution shall not be of any force or effect.

"Sec. 2. A treaty shall become effective as internal law in the United States only through legislation which would be valid in the absence of treaty.

"Sec. 3. Congress shall have power to regulate all executive and other agreements with any foreign power or international organization. All such agreements shall be subject to the limitations imposed on treaties by this article."

The second section was designed to destroy the doctrine of the self-executing effect of treaties (see Hauenstein v. Lynham) as well as the doctrine of enlargement of congressional power through treaties (see Missouri v. Holland.) That Bricker proposal was the subject of extended debate in the Senate in January and February, 1954. (On the executive agreements problem reflected in the proposal, see chap. 7, on separation of powers, at p. 593.) It was soon evident that the proposal, taken as a whole, would not receive Senate approval. Various substitutes were offered. With special regard to section 2, Senator Bricker proposed the following:

"A treaty or other international agreement shall become effective as internal law in the United States only through legislation by the Congress unless in advising and consenting to a treaty the Senate, by a vote of two-thirds of the Senators present and voting, shall provide that such treaty may become effective as internal law without legislation by the Congress." The proposed substitute failed to get the necessary two-thirds vote (42 for and 50 against). Senator Walter F. George offered another substitute, which (including sections 1 and 3 as previously agreed to by the Senate) was as follows:

"Sec. 1.   A provision of a treaty or other international agreement which conflicts with this Constitution shall not be of any force or effect.

"Sec. 2.   An international agreement other than a treaty shall become effective as internal law in the United States only by an act of the Congress.

"Sec. 3.   On the question of advising and consenting to the ratification of a treaty the vote shall be determined by yeas and nays, and the names of the persons voting for and against shall be entered on the Journal of the Senate." The George substitute came to a vote in February 1954. It failed, 60 for to 31 against—just short of the required two-thirds. Similar proposals during the following three years also failed.

3. *The reassurance of Reid v. Covert.* A Supreme Court decision in 1957—Reid v. Covert, 354 U.S. 1, printed in sec. 6, below—contained a passage directly responsive to some of the concerns voiced by Bricker Amendment supporters. Did it give adequate assurance on all of their concerns? In Reid v. Covert, the Court held unconstitutional article 2(11) of the Uniform Code of Military Justice which had authorized court martial jurisdiction over civilian dependents of American servicemen overseas. The Court sustained the claim that the constitutional powers of Congress under Art. I of the Constitution, in light of individual rights guarantees, were inadequate to support the law. (See the excerpts at p. 410, below.) Moreover, in the passage relevant to the Bricker issue, the Court rejected an argument that the law might be supportable because of the existence of an international agreement. Part II of Justice Black's majority opinion responded as follows:

"At the time of Mrs. Covert's alleged offense, an executive agreement was in effect between the United States and Great Britain which permitted United States' military courts to exercise exclusive jurisdiction over offenses committed in Great Britain by American servicemen or their dependents.[1] For its part, the United States agreed that these military courts would be willing and able to try and to punish all offenses against the laws of Great Britain by such persons. In all material respects, the same situation existed in Japan when Mrs. Smith killed her husband. Even though a court-martial does not

---

1. "Executive Agreement of July 27, 1942, 57 Stat. 1193. The arrangement now in effect in Great Britain and the other North Atlantic Treaty Organization nations, as well as in Japan, is the NATO Status of Forces Agreement, 4 U. S. Treaties and Other International Agreements 1792, T.I.A.S. 2846, which by its terms gives the foreign nation primary jurisdiction to try dependents accompanying American servicemen for offenses which are violations of the law of both the foreign nation and the United States. Art. VII, §§ 1(b), 3(a). The foreign nation has exclusive criminal jurisdiction over dependents for offenses which only violate its laws. Art. VII, § 2(b). However, the Agreement contains provisions which require that the foreign nations provide procedural safeguards for our nationals tried under the terms of the Agreement in their courts. Art. VII, § 9. Generally, see Note, 70 Harv. L.Rev. 1043.

Apart from those persons subject to the Status of Forces and comparable agreements and certain other restricted classes of Americans, a foreign nation has plenary criminal jurisdiction, of course, over all Americans—tourists, residents, businessmen, government employees and so forth—who commit offenses against its laws within its territory." [Footnote by Justice Black.]

give an accused trial by jury and other Bill of Rights' protections, the Government contends that article 2(11) of UCMJ, insofar as it authorizes the military trial of dependents accompanying the armed forces in Great Britain and Japan, can be sustained as legislation which is necessary and proper to carry out the United States' obligations under the international agreements made with those countries. The obvious and decisive answer to this, of course, is that no agreement with a foreign nation can confer power on the Congress, or on any order branch of government, which is free from the restraints of the Constitution.

"Article VI, the Supremacy Clause of the Constitution, declares:

'This Constitution, and the Laws of the United States which shall be made in Pursuance thereof; and all Treaties made, or which shall be made, under the Authority of the United States, shall be the supreme Law of the Land; . . . .'

There is nothing in this language which intimates that treaties and laws enacted pursuant to them do not have to comply with the provisions of the Constitution. Nor is there anything in the debates which accompanied the drafting and ratification of the Constitution which even suggests such a result. These debates as well as the history that surrounds the adoption of the treaty provision in Article VI make it clear that the reason treaties were not limited to those made in 'pursuance' of the Constitution was so that agreements made by the United States under the Articles of Confederation, including the important peace treaties which concluded the Revolutionary War, would remain in effect. It would be manifestly contrary to the objectives of those who created the Constitution, as well as those who were responsible for the Bill of Rights—let alone alien to our entire constitutional history and tradition—to construe Article VI as permitting the United States to exercise power under an international agreement without observing constitutional prohibitions. In effect, such construction would permit amendment of that document in a manner not sanctioned by Article V. The prohibitions of the Constitution were designed to apply to all branches of the National Government and they cannot be nullified by the Executive or by the Executive and the Senate combined. . . .

"There is nothing in Missouri v. Holland, 252 U.S. 416, which is contrary to the position taken here. There the Court carefully noted that the treaty involved was not inconsistent with any specific provision of the Constitution. The Court was concerned with the Tenth Amendment which reserves to the States or the people all power not delegated to the National Government. To the extent that the United States can validly make treaties, the people and the States have delegated their power to the National Government and the Tenth Amendment is no barrier.

"In summary, we conclude that the Constitution in its entirety applied to the trials of Mrs. Smith and Mrs. Covert. Since their court-martial did not meet the requirements of Art. III, § 2, or the Fifth and Sixth Amendments we are compelled to determine if there is anything *within* the Constitution which authorizes the military trial of dependents accompanying the armed forces overseas."

THE FOREIGN AFFAIRS POWER OF CONGRESS

1. *The source and nature of the power.* The treaty power involved in most of the materials above, and shared by President and Senate, is specifically provided for in the Constitution. And a treaty, as Missouri v. Holland illustrates, may in effect augment congressional powers. Is there also a foreign affairs power of Congress independent of authority derived from treaties? Where in the Constitution is it found? Note the statement in Perez v. Brownell, 356 U.S. 44, 57 (1958) (sec. 6, p. 426, below), sustaining a provision regarding loss of citizenship:

"Although there is in the Constitution no specific grant to Congress of power to enact legislation for the effective regulation of foreign affairs, there can be no doubt of the existence of this power in the law-making organ of the Nation. See United States v. Curtiss-Wright Export Corp., 299 U.S. 304, 318; Mackenzie v. Hare, 239 U.S. 299, 311–312. The States that joined together to form a single Nation and to create, through the Constitution, a Federal Government to conduct the affairs of that Nation must be held to have granted that Government the powers indispensable to its functioning effectively in the company of sovereign nations. The Government must be able not only to deal affirmatively with foreign nations, as it does through the maintenance of diplomatic relations with them and the protection of American citizens sojourning within their territories. It must also be able to reduce to a minimum the frictions that are unavoidable in a world of sovereigns sensitive in matters touching their dignity and interests."

In the cited passage in Curtiss-Wright [see also chap. 7, p. 593], the Court commented on "the powers of the federal government in respect of foreign or external affairs and those in respect of domestic or internal affairs. That there are differences between them, and that these differences are fundamental, may not be doubted. The two classes of powers are different, both in respect of their origin and their nature. The broad statement that the federal government can exercise no powers except those specifically enumerated in the Constitution, and such implied powers as are necessary and proper to carry into effect the enumerated powers, is categorically true only in respect of our internal affairs. . . . The powers to declare and wage war, to conclude peace, to make treaties, to maintain diplomatic relations with other sovereignties, if they had never been mentioned in the Constitution, would have vested in the federal government as necessary concomitants of nationality."

How extensive is this power "to enact legislation for the effective regulation of foreign affairs"? Is it limited to matters that are genuinely the subject matter of foreign relations? Can the Court reexamine the good faith or substantial factual basis for a congressional assertion that a problem *is* a foreign affairs concern? Is this congressional power subject to any greater limits than the Geofroy v. Riggs "properly the subject of negotiation" criterion regarding treaties, noted earlier, p. 395, supra? See generally Henkin, "The Treaty Makers and the Law Makers: The Law of the Land and Foreign Relations," 107 U.Pa.L.Rev. 903 (1959).

2. *The impact of national control over foreign affairs on state authority.* The national concern with foreign affairs is a strong one even though its bases are not fully specified in the Constitution. Not only may the authority sup-

port congressional legislation; its mere existence, though unexercised, may preclude state action. (Compare the impact of the unexercised commerce power on state action, chaps. 8 and 9 below.) That impact of the national authority is illustrated by Zschernig v. Miller, 389 U.S. 429 (1968), where the Court barred application of a state alien inheritance statute because of conflict with the federal foreign relations power. The Oregon courts had held that an East German next of kin of an Oregon intestate could not take personalty because of a statute which provided for escheat unless the non-resident alien claimant established three conditions regarding reciprocity. The statute required that claimants show (a) a reciprocal right of Americans to inherit property in the alien's country, (b) a right of Americans to receive payments here of funds from estates in the alien's country, and (c) the right of foreign heirs to receive the proceeds of Oregon estates "without confiscation." Justice Douglas' majority opinion concluded "that the history and operation of this Oregon statute make clear that [it] is an intrusion by the State into the field of foreign affairs which the Constitution entrusts to the President and the Congress. See Hines v. Davidowitz, 312 U.S. 52, 63." He commented that "in this reciprocity area under inheritance statutes, the probate courts of various States have launched inquiries into the type of governments that obtain in a particular foreign nation . . . . . As one reads the Oregon decisions, it seems that foreign policy attitudes, the freezing or thawing of the 'cold war,' and the like are the real desiderata. Yet they of course are matters for the Federal Government, not for local probate courts." Justice Stewart, joined by Justice Brennan, submitted a concurring opinion; Justice White dissented. And Justice Harlan, in an opinion concurring in the result, objected to the majority's constitutional position at length, concluding: "Essentially, the Court's basis for decision appears to be that alien inheritance laws afford state court judges an opportunity to criticize in dictum the policies of foreign governments, and that these dicta may adversely affect our foreign relations. In addition to finding no evidence of adverse effect in the record, I believe this rationale to be untenable because logically it would apply to many other types of litigation which come before the state courts."

SECTION 5. MISCELLANEOUS POWERS WITH DOMESTIC REGULATORY CONSEQUENCES

As some of the earlier materials indicate, Congress may draw on a variety of other powers in the framing of legislation with economic and other regulatory impacts. A brief, selective survey, and a note on constitutional amendments, follow:

1. *Congress and the monetary system.* In one of the "gold clause" cases, Norman v. Baltimore & Ohio R. Co., 294 U.S. 240 (1935), supra, Chief Justice Hughes described the power as follows: "The Constitution grants to the Congress power 'to coin money, regulate the value thereof, and of foreign coin.' Art. I, § 8, par. 5. But the Court in the legal tender cases did not derive from that express grant alone the full authority of the Congress in relation to the currency. The Court found the source of that authority in all the related powers conferred upon the Congress and appropriate to

achieve 'the great objects for which the government was framed,'—'a national government, with sovereign powers.' McCulloch v. Maryland, 4 Wheat. 316, 404–407; Knox v. Lee [12 Wall. 457], 532, 536; Juilliard v. Greenman [110 U.S. 421], 438. The broad and comprehensive national authority over the subjects of revenue, finance and currency is derived from the aggregate of the powers granted to the Congress, embracing the powers to lay and collect taxes, to borrow money, to regulate commerce with foreign nations and among the several States, to coin money, regulate the value thereof, and of foreign coin, and fix the standards of weights and measures, and the added express power 'to make all laws which shall be necessary and proper for carrying into execution' the other enumerated powers. Juilliard v. Greenman, supra, pp. 439, 440.

"The Constitution 'was designed to provide the same currency, having a uniform legal value in all the States.' It was for that reason that the power to regulate the value of money was conferred upon the Federal government, while the same power, as well as the power to emit bills of credit, was withdrawn from the States. The States cannot declare what shall be money, or regulate its value. [Concerning the provision that no State shall "coin money; emit bills of credit; make anything but gold and silver coin a tender in payment of debts," see Poindexter v. Greenhow (Virginia Coupon Cases), 114 U.S. 270 (1885).] Whatever power there is over the currency is vested in the Congress. Knox v. Lee, supra, p. 545. Another postulate of the decision in that case is that the Congress has power 'to enact the government's promises to pay money shall be, for the time being, equivalent in value to the representative of value determined by the coinage acts, or to multiples thereof.' Id., p. 553. Or, as was stated in the Juilliard case, supra, p. 447, the Congress is empowered 'to issue the obligations of the United States in such form, and to impress upon them such qualities as currency for the purchase of merchandise and the payment of debts, as accord with the usage of sovereign governments.' The authority to impose requirements of uniformity and parity is an essential feature of this control of the currency. The Congress is authorized to provide 'a sound and uniform currency for the country,' and to 'secure the benefit of it to the people by appropriate legislation.' Veazie Bank v. Fenno, 8 Wall. 533, 549.

"Moreover, by virtue of this national power, there attach to the ownership of gold and silver those limitations which public policy may require by reason of their quality as legal tender and as a medium of exchange. Ling Su Fan v. United States, 218 U.S. 302, 310. Those limitations arise from the fact that the law 'gives to such coinage a value which does not attach as a mere consequence of intrinsic value.' Their quality as legal tender is attributed by the law, aside from their bullion value. Hence the power to coin money includes the power to forbid mutilation, melting and exportation of gold and silver coin,—'to prevent its outflow from the country of its origin.' "

2. *The Postal Power.* a. *The mail and "police" regulations.* In Electric Bond & Share Co. v. SEC, 303 U.S. 419 (1938) (p. 308 supra), sustaining the registration provision of the Public Utility Holding Company Act of 1935, the Court said: "And while Congress may not exercise its control over the mails to enforce a requirement which lies outside its constitutional province, when Congress lays down a valid regulation pertinent to the use of the mails, it may withdraw the privilege of that use from those who disobey." See Cushman, "National Police Power under the Postal Clause of the

Constitution," 4 Minn.L.Rev. 402 (1920). "The constitutional principles underlying the administration of the Postoffice Department were discussed in the opinion of the Court in Ex parte Jackson, 96 U.S. 727, in which we held that the power vested in Congress 'to establish postoffices and post roads' included the power to 'designate what might be carried in the mails and what excluded,' whether such exclusion arose from the objectionable character of the matter upon grounds of public policy or the danger created by such matter to postal employees or other mail. Congress may 'also classify the recipients of such matter, and forbid the delivery of letters to such persons or corporations as, in its judgment, are making use of the mails for the purpose of fraud or deception or the dissemination among its citizens of information of a character calculated to debauch the public morality.' " Public Clearing House v. Coyne, 194 U.S. 497 (1904).

　　b. *Restraints on the control of the mail.* But the power over the mails is not as discretionary and comprehensive as that language would indicate. Some of the mail-prohibiting statements are even broader than the commerce-prohibiting ones and raise similar "pretext"-abuse of power questions. See chap. 4 p. 302. But the postal power, like all others, is at least subject to individual rights guarantees. Thus, in Hannegan v. Esquire, 327 U.S. 146 (1946), the Court declared that the power to withhold the second-class mail privilege from a magazine because, in the judgment of the Postmaster General, its contents are "bad" for the public is "abhorrent to our traditions," and added: "Grave constitutional questions are immediately raised once it is said that the use of mails is a privilege which may be extended or withheld on any grounds whatsoever." The warning in the Hannegan case bore fruit in 1965, when the Court held unconstitutional a Post Office screening procedure regarding foreign "communist political propaganda." Lamont v. Postmaster General (decided together with Fixa v. Heilberg), 381 U.S. 301 (1965). Acting under a 1962 statute, the Post Office screened foreign unsealed mail, detained "communist political propaganda," and notified the addressee that the mail would be destroyed unless the addressee requested delivery by returning a reply card within 20 days. Justice Douglas' opinion held the statutory scheme unconstitutional "because it requires an official act (*viz.* returning the reply card) as a limitation on the unfettered exercise of the addressee's First Amendment rights." He stated that the addressee "carries an affirmative obligation which we do not think the Government may impose on him. This requirement is almost certain to have a deterrent effect." Justice Brennan's concurrence, joined by Justice Goldberg, emphasized that the "right to receive publications" is a "fundamental" right necessary to make First Amendment rights "fully meaningful." (See also the next section of this chapter and Part III of this volume.)

　　3. *Patents, copyrights and trademarks.* A patent is a statutory privilege granted for a public purpose, Mercoid Corp. v. Mid-Continent Investment Co., 320 U.S. 661 (1944), and Congress may attach specific conditions to the grant, Special Equipment Co. v. Coe, 324 U.S. 370 (1945). On the common-law background and federal statutory development regarding copyrights, see Wheaton v. Peters, 8 Pet. 591 (1834), Holmes v. Hurst, 174 U.S. 82 (1899), and Chafee, "Reflections on the Law of Copyright," 45 Colum.L.Rev. 503, 719 (1945). On the constitutional scope of the power of Congress, see Mazer v. Stein, 347 U.S. 201 (1954).

That congressional copyright legislation does not deprive the states of their power to regulate combinations of copyright owners in restraint of trade, see Watson v. Buck, 313 U.S. 387 (1941). Compare two more recent decisions, Sears, Roebuck & Co. v. Stiffel Co., 376 U.S. 225 (1964), and Compco Corp. v. Day-Brite Lighting, Inc., 376 U.S. 234 (1964), holding that state unfair competition law may not be applied to bar imitation of products unpatentable under the federal patent laws. (Compare the effect of the commerce power on state authority, chap. 8 below.) The Trade-Mark Cases, 100 U.S. 82 (1879), held that the grant of power to "promote the progress of science and useful arts" gave Congress no power to establish a system of trade-mark registration. Current trade-mark legislation—the Lanham Act of 1946, 15 U.S.C. § 1051 et seq.—rests on the commerce power.

4. *Maritime law.* Article III, Section 2, extends the federal judicial power to cases in admiralty and maritime jurisdiction, and this was early construed as a source of federal legislative power as well. See The Genesee Chief, 12 How. 443 (1851), and Note, "From Judicial Grant to Legislative Power: The Admiralty Clause in the Nineteenth Century." 67 Harv.L.Rev. 1214 (1954). In The Belfast, 7 Wall. 624, 640 (1869), the Court said: "Difficulties attend every attempt to define the exact limits of admiralty jurisdiction, but it cannot be made to depend upon the power of Congress to regulate commerce, as conferred in the Constitution. They are entirely distinct things, having no necessary connection with one another, and are conferred, in the Constitution, by separate and distinct grants." Legislation affecting maritime matters may of course be supportable on the basis of the power to regulate interstate and foreign commerce, see The Lottawanna, 21 Wall. 588 (1875); but the national power based on the admiralty clause of Art. III is not simply an alternative source of control but is in some respects a more extensive one. See, e. g., In re Garnett, 141 U.S. 1, 12 (1892): "It is unnecessary to invoke the power given to Congress to regulate commerce with foreign nations, and among the several states, in order to find authority to pass the law in question. The act of Congress which limits the liability of shipowners was passed in amendment of the maritime law of the country, and the power to make such amendments is co-extensive with that law. It is not confined to the boundaries or class of subjects which limit and characterize the power to regulate commerce; but in maritime matters, it extends to all matters and places to which the maritime law extends." See also Southern Pacific Co. v. Jensen, 244 U.S. 205, 215 (1917).

As to the extent of admiralty jurisdiction, the Supreme Court, following the English rule, at first confined it to tidal waters, The Thomas Jefferson, 10 Wheat. 428 (1825), but since this excluded important navigable waters the earlier cases were overruled and successive extensions were made to the Great Lakes, The Genesee Chief, 12 How. 443 (1851); to navigable rivers, The Belfast, 7 Wall. 624 (1869); to canals, Ex parte Boyer, 109 U.S. 629 (1884); and to other bodies of water, Wisconsin v. Illinois, 278 U.S. 367 (1929). In short, admiralty jurisdiction attaches whenever the water upon which the cause of action has arisen is in fact navigable. The Daniel Ball, 10 Wall. 557 (1871).

5. *Congressional investigations.* Most of the recent challenges to legislative investigations have rested on claimed infringements of civil liberties, and the subject is accordingly examined at length in chap. 16, sec. 7. At this point, it is sufficient to note the existence and scope of the power to

investigate in aid of legislative powers, as described in one of the major modern cases, Barenblatt v. United States, 360 U.S. 109, 113 (1959) (p. 1335, infra): "The power of inquiry has been employed by Congress throughout our history, over the whole range of the national interests concerning which Congress might legislate or decide upon due investigation not to legislate; it has similarly been utilized in determining what to appropriate from the national purse, or whether to appropriate. The scope of the power of inquiry, in short, is as penetrating and far-reaching as the potential power to enact and appropriate under the Constitution. Broad as it is, the power is not, however, without limitations. Since Congress may only investigate into those areas in which it may potentially legislate or appropriate, it cannot inquire into matters which are within the exclusive province of one of the other branches of the Government. [See chap. 7, below.] And the Congress, in common with all branches of the Government, must exercise its powers subject to the limitations placed by the Constitution on governmental action, more particularly in the context of this case the relevant limitations of the Bill of Rights." There is no congressional power "to expose for the sake of exposure," but so long as "Congress acts in pursuance of its constitutional power, the Judiciary lacks authority to intervene on the basis of the motives which spurred the exercise of that power."

6. *Amending the Constitution.* a. Congress plays an important role in the amendment process set forth in Article V of the Constitution. All of the amendments so far adopted have been proposed by Congress; in all cases but one, Congress has chosen the state legislature method of ratification. (The Twenty-first Amendment was ratified by the convention method.) The choice of ratification methods for amendments proposed by Congress "lies in the sole discretion of Congress." United States v. Sprague, 282 U.S. 716 (1931). The veto power of the President "has nothing to do with the proposition, or adoption, of amendments to the Constitution." Hollingsworth v. Virginia, 3 Dallas 378 (1798). The two-thirds vote in each house required in proposing an amendment "is a vote of two-thirds of the members present— assuming the presence of a quorum—and not a vote of two-thirds of the entire membership, present and absent," National Prohibition Cases, 253 U.S. 350 (1920). The function of a state in ratifying a proposed amendment, "like the function of Congress in proposing the amendment is a federal function derived from the Federal Constitution; and it transcends any limitations sought to be imposed by the people of a State," Leser v. Garnett, 258 U.S. 130, 137 (1922), sustaining the Nineteenth Amendment despite alleged procedural irregularities in the legislatures of two States. In proposing amendments, Congress may fix a time limit on ratification. Dillon v. Gloss, 256 U.S. 368 (1921). The effect of an attempted ratification after a previous rejection by a state legislature is a "political question," "within the ultimate authority in the Congress in the exercise of its control over the promulgation of the adoption of the amendment." Coleman v. Miller, 307 U.S. 433 (1939) (see chap. 2, p. 195, above).

b. The alternative method of initiating the amendment process—a congressional call for a "Convention for proposing Amendments," "on the Application of the legislatures of two thirds of the several States"—has never been successfully used. Can or must Congress limit the scope of such a Convention, pursuant to the "Application"? Must all of the "Applications" be identical? Can Congress be compelled to call the Convention? A major effort to use this method was initiated by the Council of State Governments in the 1960's; the aim was an amendment to curtail federal control of state legislative apportionment. (See Reynolds v. Sims, chap. 18, p. 1438, infra.) Does an "Application" by two-thirds of the states for a Convention to consider a *particular* amendment proposal satisfy Article V? Note that this alternate route contemplates a "Convention to propose Amendments." Does that exclude a Convention to consider an amendment proposed by the states in their "Application"?

c. In 1963, the Council of State Governments proposed—and several states supported—an amendment which would authorize an entirely new amendment route, a route virtually bypassing the traditional congressional role in the process. The proposed revision would amend Article V to read (new route in italics): "The Congress, whenever two-thirds of both Houses shall deem it necessary, or, on the application of the Legislatures of two-thirds of the several states, shall propose amendments to this Constitution, which shall be valid to all intents and purposes, as part of this Constitution, when ratified by the Legislatures of three-fourths of the several States. *Whenever applications from the Legislatures of two-thirds of the total number of states of the United States shall contain identical texts of an amendment to be proposed, the President of the Senate and the Speaker of the House of Representatives shall so certify, and the amendment as contained in the application shall be deemed to have been proposed without further action by Congress.* No State, without its consent, shall be deprived of its equal suffrage in the Senate." Can anything be said for the proposal? See "Amending the Constitution to Strengthen the States in the Federal System," 36 State Gov't 10 (1963). What are the objections to it? See C. L. Black, Jr., "The Proposed Amendment of Article V: A Threatened Disaster," 72 Yale L.J. 957 (1963).

d. Are there any limitations on the content of constitutional amendments? Note the concluding proviso in Article V. In the National Prohibition Cases, 253 U.S. 350 (1920), it was unsuccessfully contended that the subject matter (prohibition) of the Eighteenth Amendment put it beyond the amending process. In Leser v. Garnett, 258 U.S. 130 (1922), it was contended, also unsuccessfully, that extension of suffrage to women was so great an addition to the electorate that, absent the state's consent (Maryland had refused to ratify the Nineteenth Amendment), it would destroy the state's autonomy as a political body and hence did not lie within the amending power. See generally Orfield, Amending the Federal Constitution (1942).

SECTION 6. THE SCOPE OF NATIONAL POWERS IN THE CONTEXT OF INDIVIDUAL RIGHTS LIMITATIONS: A NARROWER CONGRESSIONAL DISCRETION TO SELECT MEANS?

Scope Note. The materials in the earlier sections of this chapter have focused on only one group of limitations on national powers: those derived from the nature of the federal system and accordingly concerned with the intrusion of national authority into local affairs. But, as the opinions above have occasionally mentioned, national action is subject to a variety of constitutional restraints. One purpose of this section is to assure that emphasis on federalism limitations does not convey the misleading impression that restrictions on national power are one-dimensional. In large part, examination of the content of other restrictions is postponed to Part III, Individual Rights. But (as indicated in the Scope Note at the beginning of this chapter) the presentation of some national power cases involving non-federalism restrictions at this point has more than a preview function.

The aim is to encourage critical analysis of some of the doctrinal tools occasionally employed in national powers vs. individual rights cases—doctrines that appear closely related to those found in national power cases involving only federalism limitations. In cases arising in the context of limitations rooted in federalism concerns, the Court has endorsed a broad range of congressional discretion to implement Article I powers. No doubt, additional considerations properly come into play when exercises of those powers impinge on individual rights guarantees. Some of the decisions reflect that added concern indirectly and obscurely, by promulgating principles stating the congressional discretion more narrowly than in most cases involving Article I powers. Is that technique unsatisfactory, both for failing to provide adequate doctrinal support for individual rights and for creating unduly confusing and broad doubts about congressional discretion? Should the individual rights concern be expressed more directly through judicial interpretations addressed not to recasting Article I powers but to elaborating explicitly the individual rights limitations in the Bill of Rights and elsewhere?

Does (and should) the meaning of the Necessary and Proper Clause change, for example, when the objection to the law rests on a non-federalism ground? Cases from McCulloch to Wickard v. Filburn and United States v. Darby, in chaps. 3 and 4, recognize a broad congressional discretion to select the means to effectuate a delegated power. Does the scope of that discretion have to be redefined when opposing interests other than those derived from the federal system come into play? Should restrictions on the choice of means rest directly on the constitutional provision that may prohibit one of the possible "reasonable" means—rather than holding the prohibited means "unreasonable" or "inappropriate"? Does it make any difference whether the reason for a ruling of unconstitutionality is (a) that the law is not reasonably related to the effectuation of a delegated power in Article I, or (b) that the law, though appropriate to the effectuation of a delegated power under Article I under the broad choice legitimated by McCulloch and its progeny, is barred by another provision of the Constitution—such as the First Amendment or Article III or the Fifth Amendment?

For example, should the existence of constitutional jury trial guarantees influence the decision whether Congress could properly conclude that subjecting civilian dependents of servicemen abroad was an appropriate means to implement the Art. I, Sec. 8, power to "make Rules for the Government and Regulation of the land and naval Forces" (see Reid v. Covert, below)? Or should the recognition of citizenship in the Fourteenth Amendment influence the determination whether Congress can deprive a wartime deserter of citizenship as an appropriate means to implement the war-related powers of Art. I, Sec. 8 (see Trop v. Dulles, below)? If any of these individual rights guarantees prohibit the enactment, should not that result rest directly on the limiting prohibitions, instead of being expressed as an application of a purportedly general principle regarding the execution of

Art. I powers? The court martial cases which follow present some of these problems forcefully. Note especially the applications of the Necessary and Proper Clause, and contrast them with the cases that have gone before. [Though the principal cases in this section have been chosen primarily because they illustrate those general problems of doctrine and technique, they also provide opportunity to explore their specific contexts: e. g., the problems of court martial jurisdiction over civilians, and of loss of citizenship.]

REID v. COVERT

354 U.S. 1, 77 S.Ct. 1222, 1 L.Ed.2d 1148 (1957).

On Appeal from the United States District Court for the District of Columbia.

On Rehearing.*

Mr. Justice BLACK announced the judgment of the Court and delivered an opinion, in which The Chief Justice [WARREN], Mr. Justice DOUGLAS, and Mr. Justice BRENNAN join.

These cases raise basic constitutional issues of the utmost concern. They call into question the role of the military under our system of government. They involve the power of Congress to expose civilians to trial by military tribunals, under military regulations and procedures, for offenses against the United States thereby depriving them of trial in civilian courts, under civilian laws and procedures and with all the safeguards of the Bill of Rights. These cases are particularly significant because for the first time since the adoption of the Constitution wives of soldiers have been denied trial by jury in a court of law and forced to trial before courts-martial.

In No. 701 Mrs. Clarice Covert killed her husband, a sergeant in the United States Air Force, at an airbase in England. Mrs. Covert, who was not a member of the armed services, was residing on the base with her husband at the time. She was tried by a court-martial for murder under Article 118 of the Uniform Code of Military Justice [UCMJ]. . . . The court-martial asserted jurisdiction over Mrs. Covert under Article 2(11) of the UCMJ, which provides:

"The following persons are subject to this code: . . .

"(11) Subject to the provisions of any treaty or agreement to which the United States is or may be a party or to any accepted rule of international law, all persons serving with, employed by, or accompanying the armed forces without the continental limits of the United States . . . ."

. . . . While Mrs. Covert was being held in this country pending a proposed retrial by court-martial in the District of Columbia, her counsel petitioned the District Court for a writ of habeas corpus to set her free on the ground that the Constitution forbade her trial by military authorities. . . .

In No. 713 Mrs. Dorothy Smith killed her husband, an Army officer, at a post in Japan where she was living with him. She was tried for murder by a court-martial and despite considerable evidence that she was insane was

---

* Together with Kinsella v. Krueger, on certiorari to the United States Court of Appeals for the Fourth Circuit.

found guilty and sentenced to life imprisonment. . . . Mrs. Smith was then confined in a federal penitentiary in West Virginia. Her father, respondent here, filed a petition for habeas corpus in a District Court for West Virginia. . . .

The two cases were consolidated and argued last Term and a majority of the Court, with three Justices dissenting and one reserving opinion held that military trial of Mrs. Smith and Mrs. Covert for their alleged offenses was constitutional. 351 U.S. 470, 487. The majority held that the provisions of Article III and the Fifth and Sixth Amendments which require that crimes be tried by a jury after indictment by a grand jury did not protect an American citizen when he was tried by the American Government in foreign lands for offenses committed there and that Congress could provide for the trial of such offenses in any manner it saw fit so long as the procedures established were reasonable and consonant with due process. The opinion then went on to express the view that military trials, as now practiced, were not unreasonable or arbitrary when applied to dependents accompanying members of the armed forces overseas. In reaching their conclusion the majority found it unnecessary to consider the power of Congress "To make Rules for the Government and Regulation of the land and naval Forces" under Article I, § 8, cl. 14 of the Constitution.

Subsequently, the Court granted a petition for rehearing, 352 U.S. 901. Now, after further argument and consideration, we conclude that the previous decisions cannot be permitted to stand. [As to the haste with which the first decision was reached, see "Time for deliberation and the Supreme Court," note 3, p. 425, infra.] We hold that Mrs. Smith and Mrs. Covert could not constitutionally be tried by military authorities.

I.

At the beginning we reject the idea that when the United States acts against citizens abroad it can do so free of the Bill of Rights. The United States is entirely a creature of the Constitution. Its power and authority have no other source. It can only act in accordance with all the limitations imposed by the Constitution. When the Government reaches out to punish a citizen who is abroad, the shield which the Bill of Rights and other parts of the Constitution provide to protect his life and liberty should not be stripped away just because he happens to be in another land. . . . Among those provisions, Art. III, § 2, and the Fifth and Sixth Amendments are directly relevant to these cases. . . .

This Court and other federal courts have held or asserted that various constitutional limitations apply to the Government when it acts outside the continental United States. While it has been suggested that only those constitutional rights which are "fundamental" protect Americans abroad, we can find no warrant, in logic or otherwise, for picking and choosing among the remarkable collection of "Thou shalt nots" which were explicitly fastened on all departments and agencies of the Federal Government by the Constitution and its Amendments. Moreover, in view of our heritage and the history of the adoption of the Constitution and the Bill of Rights, it seems peculiarly anomalous to say that trial before a civilian judge and by an independent jury picked from the common citizenry are not fundamental rights. . . .

II.

[T]he Government contends that article 2(11) of UCMJ . . . can be sustained as legislation which is necessary and proper to carry out the United States' obligations under the international agreements. [The Court's response to that contention is printed above, sec. 4, at p. 400, after Missouri v. Holland.]

In summary, we conclude that the Constitution in its entirety applied to the trials of Mrs. Smith and Mrs. Covert. Since their court-martial did not meet the requirements of Art. III, § 2, or the Fifth and Sixth Amendments we are compelled to determine if there is anything *within* the Constitution which authorizes the military trial of dependents accompanying the armed forces overseas.

III.

Article I, § 8, cl. 14, empowers Congress "To make Rules for the Government and Regulation of the land and naval Forces." It has been held that this creates an exception to the normal method of trial in civilian courts as provided by the Constitution and permits Congress to authorize military trial of members of the armed services without all the safeguards given an accused by Article III and the Bill of Rights. But if the language of Clause 14 is given its natural meaning, the power granted does not extend to civilians —even though they may be dependents living with servicemen on a military base. The term "land and naval Forces" refers to persons who are members of the armed services and not to their civilian wives, children and other dependents. It seems inconceivable that Mrs. Covert or Mrs. Smith could have been tried by military authorities as members of the "land and naval Forces" had they been living on a military post in this country. Yet this constitutional term surely has the same meaning everywhere. The wives of servicemen are no more members of the "land and naval Forces" when living at a military post in England or Japan than when living at a base in this country or in Hawaii or Alaska.

The Government argues that the Necessary and Proper Clause (18) when taken in conjunction with Clause 14 allows Congress to authorize the trial of Mrs. Smith and Mrs. Covert by military tribunals and under military law. The Government claims that the two clauses together constitute a broad grant of power "without limitation" authorizing Congress to subject all persons, civilians and soldiers alike, to military trial if "necessary and proper" to govern and regulate the land and naval forces. . . .

It is true that the Constitution expressly grants Congress power to make all rules necessary and proper to govern and regulate those persons who are serving in the "land and naval Forces." But the Necessary and Proper Clause cannot operate to extend military jurisdiction to any group of persons beyond that class described in Clause 14—"the land and naval Forces." Under the grand design of the Constitution civilian courts are the normal repositories of power to try persons charged with crimes against the United States. And to protect persons brought before these courts, Article III and the Fifth, Sixth, and Eighth Amendments establish the right to trial by jury, to indictment by a grand jury and a number of other specific safeguards. By way of contrast the jurisdiction of military tribunals is a very limited and extraordinary jurisdiction derived from the cryptic language in Art. I, § 8, and, at most, was intended to be only a narrow exception to the normal and preferred method of trial in courts of law. Every extension of military jurisdiction is an encroachment on the jurisdiction of the civil courts, and, more important, acts as a deprivation of the right to jury trial and of other treasured constitutional protections. . . . In the light of these as well as other constitutional provisions, and the historical background in which they were formed, military trial of civilians is inconsistent with both the "letter and spirit of the constitution."

Further light is reflected on the scope of Clause 14 by the Fifth Amendment. . . . Since the exception in this Amendment for "cases arising in the land or naval forces" was undoubtedly designed to correlate with the power granted Congress to provide for the "Government and Regulation" of the armed services, it is a persuasive and reliable indication that the authority conferred by Clause 14 does not encompass persons who can not fairly be said to be "in" the military service.

Even if it were possible, we need not attempt here to precisely define the boundary between "civilians" and members of the "land and naval Forces." We recognize that there might be circumstances where a person could be "in" the armed services for purposes of Clause 14 even though he had not formally been inducted into the military or did not wear a uniform. But the wives, children and other dependents of servicemen cannot be placed in that category, even though they may be accompanying a serviceman abroad at Government expense and receiving other benefits from the Government.

. . .

The tradition of keeping the military subordinate to civilian authority may not be so strong in the minds of this generation as it was in the minds of those who wrote the Constitution. The idea that the relatives of soldiers could be denied a jury trial in a court of law and instead be tried by court-martial under the guise of regulating the armed forces would have seemed incredible to those men, in whose lifetime the right of the military to try *soldiers* for any offenses in time of peace had only been grudgingly conceded. The Founders envisioned the Army as a necessary institution, but one dangerous to liberty if not confined within its essential bounds. Their fears were rooted in history. . . .

In light of this history, it seems clear that the Founders had no intention to permit the trial of civilians in military courts, where they would be denied jury trials and other constitutional protections, merely by giving Congress the power to make rules which were "necessary and proper" for the regulation of the "land and naval Forces." Such a latitudinarian interpretation of these clauses would be at war with the well-established purpose of the Founders to keep the military strictly within its proper sphere, subordinate to civil authority. The Constitution does not say that Congress can regulate "the land and naval Forces and all other persons whose regulation might have some relationship to maintenance of the land and naval Forces." There is no indication that the Founders contemplated setting up a rival system of military courts to compete with civilian courts for jurisdiction over civilians who might have some contact or relationship with the armed forces. Courts-martial were not to have concurrent jurisdiction with courts of law over nonmilitary America. . . .

As this Court stated in United States ex rel. Toth v. Quarles, 350 U.S. 11, the business of soldiers is to fight and prepare to fight wars, not to try civilians for their alleged crimes. Traditionally, military justice has been a rough form of justice emphasizing summary procedures, speedy convictions and stern penalties with a view to maintaining obedience and fighting fitness in the ranks. Because of its very nature and purpose the military must place great emphasis on discipline and efficiency. Correspondingly, there has always been less emphasis in the military on protecting the rights of the individual than in civilian society and in civilian courts.

Courts-martial are typically *ad hoc* bodies appointed by a military officer from among his subordinates. They have always been subject to varying degrees of "command influence." In essence, these tribunals are simply executive tribunals whose personnel are in the executive chain of command. Frequently, the members of the court-martial must look to the appointing officer for promotions, advantageous assignments and efficiency ratings—in short, for their future progress in the service. Conceding to military personnel that high degree of honesty and sense of justice which nearly all of them undoubtedly have, the members of a court-martial, in the nature of things, do not and cannot have the independence of jurors drawn from the general public or of civilian judges.

We recognize that a number of improvements have been made in military justice recently by engrafting more and more of the methods of civilian courts on courts-martial. In large part these ameliorations stem from the reaction of civilians, who were inducted during the two World Wars, to their experience with military justice. Notwithstanding the recent reforms, military trial does not give an accused the same protection which exists in the civil courts. Looming far above all other deficiencies of the military trial, of course, are the absence of trial by jury before an independent judge after an indictment by a grand jury. Moreover the reforms are merely statutory; Congress—and perhaps the President—can reinstate former practices, subject to any limitations imposed by the Constitution, whenever it desires. As yet it has not been clearly settled to what extent the Bill of Rights and other protective parts of the Constitution apply to military trials.[2] . . .

[In Reid v. Covert, the judgment of the District Court directing that Mrs. Covert be released from custody was affirmed; in Kinsella v. Krueger, the judgment of the District Court was reversed and the case remanded with instructions to order Mrs. Smith released from custody.]

Mr. Justice WHITTAKER took no part in the consideration or decision of these cases.

---

2. Cf. Burns v. Wilson, 346 U.S. 137, 146, 148, 150; Note, 70 Harv.L.Rev. 1043, 1050–1053. But see Jackson v. Taylor, 353 U.S. 569; In re Grimley, 137 U.S. 147, 150. The exception in the Fifth Amendment, of course, provides that grand jury indictment is not required in cases subject to military trial and this exception has been read over into the Sixth Amendment so that the requirements of jury trial are inapplicable. Ex parte Quirin, 317 U.S. 1, 40. In Swaim v. United States, 165 U.S. 553, this Court held that the President or commanding officer had power to return a case to a court-martial for an increase in sentence. If the double jeopardy provisions of the Fifth Amendment were applicable such a practice would be unconstitutional. Cf. Kepner v. United States, 195 U.S. 100. [Footnote by Justice Black.]

Mr. Justice FRANKFURTER, concurring in the result. . . .

. . . The cases cannot be decided simply by saying that, since these women were not in uniform, they were not "in the land and naval Forces." . . . [T]his Court, applying appropriate methods of constitutional interpretation, has long held, and in a variety of situations, that in the exercise of a power specifically granted to it, Congress may sweep in what may be necessary to make effective the explicitly worded power. . . . This is the significance of the Necessary and Proper Clause, which is not to be considered so much a separate clause in Art. I, § 8, as an integral part of each of the preceding 17 clauses. Only thus may be avoided a strangling literalness in construing a document that is not an enumeration of static rules but the living framework of government designed for an undefined future. M'Culloch v. Maryland, 4 Wheat. 316; Hurtado v. California, 110 U.S. 516, 530–531.

Everything that may be deemed, as the exercise of an allowable judgment by Congress, to fall fairly within the conception conveyed by the power given to Congress "To make Rules for the Government and Regulation of the land and naval Forces" is constitutionally within that legislative grant and not subject to revision by the independent judgment of the Court. To be sure, every event or transaction that bears some relation to "the land and naval Forces" does not *ipso facto* come within the tolerant conception of that legislative grant. The issue in these cases involves regard for considerations not dissimilar to those involved in a determination under the Due Process Clause. Obviously, the practical situations before us bear some relation to the military. Yet the question for this Court is not merely whether the relation of these women to the "land and naval Forces" is sufficiently close to preclude the necessity of finding that Congress has been arbitrary in its selection of a particular method of trial. For, although we must look to Art. I, § 8, cl. 14, as the immediate justifying power, it is not the only clause of the Constitution to be taken into account. The Constitution is an organic scheme of government to be dealt with as an entirety. A particular provision cannot be dissevered from the rest of the Constitution. Our conclusion in these cases therefore must take due account of Article III and the Fifth and Sixth Amendments. We must weigh all the factors involved in these cases in order to decide whether these women dependents are so closely related to what Congress may allowably deem essential for the effective "Government and Regulation of the land and naval Forces" that they may be subjected to court-martial jurisdiction in these capital cases, when the consequence is loss of the protections afforded by Article III and the Fifth and Sixth Amendments. . . .

The prosecution by court-martial for capital crimes committed by civilian dependents of members of the armed forces abroad is hardly to be deemed, under modern conditions, obviously appropriate to the effective exercise of the power to "make Rules for the Government and Regulation of the land and naval Forces" when it is a question of deciding what power is granted under Article I and therefore what restriction is made in Article III and the Fifth and Sixth Amendments. I do not think that the proximity, physical and social, of these women to the "land and naval Forces" is, with due regard to all that has been put before us, so clearly demanded by the effective "Government and Regulation" of those forces as reasonably to demon-

strate a justification for court-martial jurisdiction over capital offenses.
. . .

I therefore conclude that, in capital cases, the exercise of court-martial jurisdiction over civilian dependents in time of peace cannot be justified by Article I, considered in connection with the specific protections of Article III and the Fifth and Sixth Amendments.

Mr. Justice HARLAN [who was in the majority in the first decision in the case], concurring in the result.

I concur in the result, on the narrow ground that where the offense is capital, Article 2(11) cannot constitutionally be applied to the trial of civilian dependents of members of the armed forces overseas in times of peace.
. . .

. . . I cannot accept the implication of my brother Black's opinion that this Article I power was intended to be unmodified by the Necessary and Proper Clause of the Constitution, and that therefore this power is incapable of expansion under changing circumstances. . . .

No less an authority than Chief Justice Marshall, in McCullouch v. Maryland, 4 Wheat. 316, has taught us that the Necessary and Proper Clause is to be read with *all* the powers of Congress. . . .

For analytical purposes, I think it useful to break down the issue before us into two questions: First, is there a rational connection between the trial of these army wives by court-martial and the power of Congress to make rules for the governance of the land and naval forces; in other words, is there any initial power here at all? Second, if there is such a rational connection, to what extent does this statute, though reasonably calculated to subserve an enumerated power, collide with other express limitations on congressional power; in other words, can this statute, however appropriate to the Article I power looked at in isolation, survive against the requirements of Article III and the Fifth and Sixth Amendments? I recognize that these two questions are ultimately one and the same, since the scope of the Article I power is not separable from the limitations imposed by Article III and the Fifth and Sixth Amendments. Nevertheless I think it will make for clarity of analysis to consider them separately. . . .

. . . [V]iewing Art. I, § 8, cl. 14 in isolation, subjection of civilian dependents overseas to court-martial jurisdiction can in no wise be deemed unrelated to the power of Congress to make all necessary and proper laws to insure the effective governance of our overseas land and naval forces.
. . .

I turn now to the other side of the coin. For no matter how practical and how reasonable this jurisdiction might be, it still cannot be sustained if the Constitution guarantees to these army wives a trial in an Article III court, with indictment by grand jury and jury trial as provided by the Fifth and Sixth Amendments. . . .

. . . [E]xcept for capital offenses, such as we have here, to which, in my opinion, special considerations apply, I am by no means ready to say that Congress' power to provide for trial by court-martial of civilian dependents overseas is limited by Article III and the Fifth and Sixth Amendments. . . .

Mr. Justice CLARK, with whom Mr. Justice BURTON joins, dissenting. . . .

Mr. Justice Burton and I remain convinced that the former opinions
of the Court are correct and that they set forth valid constitutional doctrine
under the long-recognized cases of this Court. . . .

THE NECESSARY AND PROPER CLAUSE IN THE COURT-MAR-
TIAL CONTEXT: THE KINSELLA ELABORATION
OF REID v. COVERT

Three years after Reid v. Covert, its doctrine was extended: in Kinsella
v. United States ex rel. Singleton, 361 U.S. 234 (1960), the Court found
unconstitutional the application of UCMJ Article 2(11) as applied "in time
of peace to civilian dependents charged with noncapital offenses." Justice
Clark's majority opinion elaborated on the Necessary and Proper Clause
interpretation of Reid v. Covert in the following passage:

"We now reach the Government's suggestion that, in the light of the
noncapital nature of the offense here, as opposed to the capital one in the
Covert case, we should make a 'fresh evaluation and a new balancing.' But
the power to 'make Rules for the government and Regulation of the land
and naval Forces' bears no limitation as to offenses. The power there granted
includes not only the creation of offenses but the fixing of the punishment
therefor. If civilian dependents are included in the term 'land and naval
Forces' at all, they are subject to the full power granted the Congress therein
to create capital as well as noncapital offenses. This Court cannot diminish
and expand that power, either on a case-by-case basis or on a balancing of the
power there granted Congress against the safeguards of Article III and
the Fifth and Sixth Amendments. Due process cannot create or enlarge
power. . . . Nor do we believe that due process considerations bring
about an expansion of Clause 14 through the operation of the Necessary
and Proper Clause. If the exercise of the power is valid it is because it is
granted in Clause 14, not because of the Necessary and Proper Clause. That
clause is not itself a grant of power, but a *caveat* that the Congress possesses
all of the means necessary to carry out the specifically granted 'foregoing'
powers of § 8 'and all other Powers vested by this Constitution. . . .'
As James Madison explained, the Necessary and Proper Clause is 'but merely
a declaration, for the removal of all uncertainty, that the means of carrying
into execution those [powers] otherwise granted are included in the grant.'
VI Writings of James Madison, edited by Gaillard Hunt, 383. There can
be no question but that Clause 14 grants the Congress power to adopt the
Uniform Code of Military Justice. Our initial inquiry is whether Congress can include civilian dependents within the term 'land and naval Forces'
as a proper incident to this power and necessary to its execution. If answered in the affirmative then civilian dependents are amenable to the Code.
In the second Covert case, supra, it was held they were not so amenable as
to capital offenses. Our final inquiry, therefore, is narrowed to whether
Clause 14, which under the second Covert case has been held not to include
civilian dependents charged with capital offenses, may now be expanded to

include the same civilian dependents but who are charged with noncapital offenses. We again refer to James Madison:

> 'When the Constitution was under the discussions which preceded its ratification, it is well known that great apprehensions were expressed by many, lest the omission of some positive exception, from the powers delegated, of certain rights, . . . might expose them to the danger of being drawn, by construction, within some of the powers vested in Congress, more especially of the power to make all laws necessary and proper for carrying their other powers into execution. In reply to this objection, it was invariably urged to be a fundamental and characteristic principle of the Constitution, that all powers not given by it were reserved; that no powers were given beyond those enumerated in the Constitution, and such as were fairly incident to them; . . . .' Writings, supra, at 390.

We are therefore constrained to say that since this Court has said that the Necessary and Proper Clause cannot expand Clause 14 so as to include prosecution of civilian dependents for capital crimes, it cannot expand Clause 14 to include prosecution of them for noncapital offenses.

> "Neither our history nor our decisions furnish a foothold for the application of such due process concept as the Government projects. Its application today in the light of the irreversibility of the death penalty would free from military prosecution a civilian accompanying or employed by the armed services who committed a capital offense, while the same civilian could be prosecuted by the military for a noncapital crime. It is illogical to say that 'the power respecting the land and naval forces encompasses . . . all that Congress may appropriately deem "necessary" for their good order' and still deny to Congress the means to exercise such power through the infliction of the death penalty. But that is proposed here. In our view this would militate against our whole concept of power and jurisdiction. It would likewise be contrary to the entire history of the Articles of War."

———

Compare the contrasting views of the role of the Necessary and Proper Clause in the other opinions in the Kinsella case. A separate opinion by Justice Whittaker, joined by Justice Stewart, agreed that civilian dependents could not be subjected to court-martial jurisdiction for noncapital offenses. His opinion included the following statement: "The source of the power, if it exists, is Art. I, § 8, cl. 14, of the Constitution." At this point, he added a footnote: "This does not overlook the 'Necessary and Proper' Clause, Art. I, § 8, cl. 18, of the Constitution, but, in my view, that Clause, though applicable, adds nothing to Clause 14, because the latter Clause, empowering Congress 'To make Rules for the Government and Regulation of the land and naval Forces,' plainly means *all necessary and proper rules* for those purposes. Mr. Justice Stewart is of the view that Clause 14 must be read in connection with the 'Necessary and Proper' Clause, and agrees with the views expressed in Mr. Justice Harlan's separate opinion as to the applicability and effect of that clause." Justice Harlan, joined by Justice Frankfurter, dissented in the Kinsella case, with the following remarks on the Necessary and Proper Clause:

"The Court's view of the effect of Covert in these noncapital cases stems from the basic premise that only persons occupying a military 'status' are within the scope of the Art. I, § 8, cl. 14 power. . . .

"I think the 'status' premise on which the Court has proceeded is unsound. Article I, § 8, cl. 14, speaks not in narrow terms of soldiers and sailors, but broadly gives Congress power to prescribe 'Rules for the Government and Regulation of the land and naval Forces.' This power must be read in connection with Clause 18 of the same Article [the Necessary and Proper Clause]. . . . Thus read, the power respecting the land and naval forces encompasses, in my opinion, all that Congress may appropriately deem 'necessary' for their good order. It does not automatically exclude the regulation of nonmilitary personnel.

"I think it impermissible to conclude . . . that the Necessary and Proper Clause may not be resorted to in judging constitutionality in cases of this type. The clause, itself a part of Art. I, § 8, in which the power to regulate the armed forces is also found, applies no less to that power than it does to the other § 8 congressional powers, and indeed is to be read 'as an integral part of each' such power. . . .

"Of course, the Necessary and Proper Clause cannot be used to 'expand' powers which are otherwise constitutionally limited, but that is only to say that when an asserted power is not appropriate to the exercise of an express power, to which all 'necessary and proper' powers must relate, the asserted power is not a 'proper' one. But to say, as the Court does now, that the Necessary and Proper Clause 'is not itself a grant of power' is to disregard Clause 18 as one of the enumerated powers of § 8 of Art. I.

"Viewing Congress' power to provide for the governing of the armed forces in connection with the Necessary and Proper Clause, it becomes apparent, I believe, that a person's 'status' with reference to the military establishment is but one, and not alone the determinative, factor in judging the constitutionality of a particular exercise of that power. By the same token, the major premise on which the Court ascribes to Covert a controlling effect in these noncapital cases disappears. . . .

"It is one thing to hold that nonmilitary personnel situated at our foreign bases may be tried abroad by courts-martial in times of peace for noncapital offenses, but quite another to say that they may be so tried where life is at stake. In the latter situation I do not believe that the Necessary and Proper Clause, which alone in cases like this brings the exceptional Article I jurisdiction into play, can properly be taken as justifying the trial of nonmilitary personnel without the full protections of an Article III court. . . . Before the constitutional existence of such a power can be found, for me a much more persuasive showing would be required that Congress had good reason for concluding that such a course is necessary to the proper maintenance of our military establishment abroad than has been made in any of the cases of this kind which have thus far come before the Court.

". . . I believe that the true issue on this aspect of all such cases concerns the closeness or remoteness of the relationship between the person affected and the military establishment. Is that relationship close enough so that Congress may, in light of all the factors involved, appropriately deem it 'necessary' that the military be given jurisdiction to deal with offenses committed by such persons? . . ."

DID THE WARREN COURT REPUDIATE MARSHALL'S VIEW OF THE NECESSARY AND PROPER CLAUSE?

1. *A narrow reading of national powers?* Obviously, the arguments against constitutionality in the court-martial cases rest on different considerations than those encountered in cases such as McCulloch v. Maryland and Wickard v. Filburn. The limiting factors on congressional powers here arise from Article III, the Bill of Rights, and the history of American civil-military relations, not from the federal system. Is this sufficient justification for interpreting the Necessary and Proper Clause differently here? Would the prevailing opinions in Reid and Kinsella have been more viable if they had stated that military trial of civilians accompanying the armed forces *was,* in Article I terms, an appropriate means to effectuate the Clause 14 power—but a means precluded by other provisions of the Constitution? Regulation of intrastate commerce is not a delegated power, yet that regulation is permissible when it is "necessary and proper" for the regulation of interstate commerce. How can it be said, then, that the subject-matter of Clause 14 ("the land and naval Forces") defines the outermost reach of that power—that regulation reaching something other than "the land and naval Forces" can not be an appropriate means to effectuate the Clause 14 power? Does this amount to a general repudiation of the broad interpretations of national powers from McCulloch v. Maryland through Wickard v. Filburn? Or is this only a pro tanto repudiation—is the broad Marshall reading still valid when states rights objections are the only ones raised? Compare United States v. Oregon, note 3 below. What kind of limitations must be raised to invoke the Reid-Kinsella substitute for the Marshall approach to congressional powers?

2. *The Warren Court's preference in historical roots—the spirit of 1798, not 1819?* Are the foregoing questions based on an exaggerated view of the Necessary and Proper Clause interpretations of Justices Black and Clark? Can their reading of the Clause be reconciled with Marshall's position? A closer look at the source relied on in the Kinsella case suggests that, at this late date, the anti-Marshall position did indeed win a victory—at least in this context.

Justice Clark in Kinsella quotes twice from James Madison's Writings for his interpretation of the Necessary and Proper Clause. The James Madison relied on was not, however, the Madison of 1788, the nationalist writer of such essays as No. 44 of the Federalist Papers. It was not the Madison of 1816, the President who reluctantly chose not to veto the charter of the Second Bank of the United States. See chap. 3, supra. Rather, the Madison relied on was the Madison of 1800, the states' rights publicist. Both quotations used by Justice Clark are from the lengthy Report of a committee of the Virginia legislature [VI Writings of James Madison (Hunt ed. 1906), 341–406] drafted by Madison to explain and justify the Virginia Resolutions of 1798. These Resolutions, like those of Kentucky, had protested the Alien and Sedition Acts, but the protests had encountered a hostile reception in other state legislatures. On the issue of national powers and the Necessary and Proper Clause, it is plain, the Madison Report was in the mainstream of strict construction doctrine—the *losing* side in McCulloch v. Maryland.

The Report defended, for example, the 1798 Virginia statement (also drafted by Madison) that condemned the "spirit . . . manifested by the Federal Government to enlarge its powers by forced constructions of the constitutional charter" and the "design to expound certain general phrases . . . so as to destroy the meaning and effect of the particular enumeration which necessarily explains and limits the general phrases." In addition to much general discussion of a two-fold emphasis on the "necessary" as well as the "proper" ingredient of Clause 18, Madison's Report contained a few examples of the objectionable "forced constructions for enlarging the Federal powers." The first and major example—"omitting others which have less occupied public attention, or been less extensively regarded as *unconstitutional*"—: "the *Bank Law,* which, from the circumstances of its passage, as well as the latitude of construction on which it was founded, strikes the attention with singular force." Id., 352–353. (Emphasis added.)

In short, Madison's 1800 view of the Necessary and Proper Clause— relied on by Justice Clark in 1960—was a reiteration of the Jeffersonian position against the chartering of the First Bank of the United States in 1791. In 1791, it will be recalled, Hamilton's view on the constitutionality of the Bank prevailed over Jefferson's, see chap. 3, p. 217, supra; and Hamilton's view in turn was that of the Marshall Court, in the supposedly authoritative exposition of the Necessary and Proper Clause in McCulloch v. Maryland. The Kinsella interpretation in 1960, then, appears to be a belated, albeit limited, victory for the position repudiated by Marshall.

3. *The scope of the belated victory for Virginia states' rights ideology: The United States v. Oregon dissent—taking Reid-Kinsella at face value rather than unarticulated narrow intent?* How limited a victory is it? Presumably, the result of McCulloch v. Maryland, or of Wickard v. Filburn, is not impaired by Kinsella. But can the Necessary and Proper Clause interpretation of the court-martial cases be restricted to non-federalism issues? Justices Black and Clark appear to think so, for they were both in the majority in United States v. Oregon, infra; but Justice Douglas' dissent suggests that not all Justices are prepared to restrict application of the broadly stated Reid-Kinsella version of the 1800 position to the immediate context of the revival.

Justice Black wrote the majority opinion in United States v. Oregon, 366 U.S. 643 (1961). He stated the facts as follows: "Adam Warpouske, an Oregon resident, died in a United States Veterans' Administration Hospital in Oregon without a will or legal heirs, leaving a net estate composed of personal property worth about $13,000. Oregon law provides that such property shall escheat to the State. A United States statute, on the other hand, provides that when a veteran dies without a will or legal heirs in a veterans' hospital, his personal property 'shall immediately vest in and become the property of the United States as trustee for the sole use and benefit of the General Post Fund. . . .' [38 U.S.C. § 17.] In reliance upon these provisions of their respective statutes, both the State of Oregon and the Government of the United States filed claims for Warpouske's estate in the Oregon probate court having jurisdiction of the matter." The Supreme Court decided that the United States was entitled to the estate under the statute. Justice Black's opinion concluded: "We see no merit in the challenge to the constitutionality. . . . Congress undoubtedly has the power—under its constitutional powers to raise armies and navies and to conduct wars—to pay pensions, and to build hospitals and homes for veterans. We think it plain that the same sources of power authorize Congress to require that the personal property left by its wards when they die in government facilities shall be devoted to the comfort and recreation of other ex-service people who must depend upon the Government for care. The fact that this law pertains to the devolution of property does not render it invalid. Although it is true that this is an area normally left to the States, it is not immune under the Tenth Amendment from laws passed by the Federal Government which are, as is the law here, necessary and proper to the exercise of a delegated power."

Justice Douglas, joined by Justice Whittaker, dissented: "I do not see how this decedent's estate can constitutionally pass to the United States. The succession of real and personal property is traditionally a state matter under our federal system. . . . That tradition continues. . . .

"The power to build hospitals and homes for veterans and to pay them pensions is plainly necessary and proper to the powers to raise and support armies and navies and to conduct wars. The power to provide for the administration of the estates of veterans (which are not made up of federal funds owing the veterans) is to me a far cry from any such power. But the present Act is of that character. . . .

"Only recently we warned against an expansive construction of the Necessary and Proper Clause. We stated that it is 'not itself a grant of power but a caveat that the Congress possesses all the means to carry out' the powers specifically granted. Kinsella v. Singleton, 361 U.S. 234, 247. Powers not given 'were reserved,' as Madison said. . . .

"Veterans or anyone else may make the United States a beneficiary of their estate, absent a state law that precludes it. . . . But if it is 'fairly incident' to raising and supporting armies and navies and conducting wars for the United States to take over the administration of the personal property of veterans who die intestate, I see no reason why Congress cannot take over their real estate too. I see no reason why, if the United States can go as far as we allow it to go today, it cannot supersede any will a veteran makes and thus better provide for the comfort, care, and recreation of other ex-service men and women who are dependent on the United States for care. And the more money the Federal Government collects for veterans the better the care they will receive. No greater collision with state law would be present where Congress took realty or displaced an entire will than here . . . .

"The Tenth Amendment does not, of course, dilute any power delegated to the national government. . . . But when the Federal Government enters a field as historically local as the administration of decedent estates, some clear relation of the asserted power to one of the delegated powers should be shown. At times the exercise of a delegated power reaches deep into local problems. Wickard v. Filburn . . . .. But there is no semblance of likeness here. The need of the Government to enter upon the administration of veterans' estates—made up of funds not owing from the United States—is no crucial phase of the ability of the United States to care for ex-service men and women or to manage federal fiscal affairs.

"Today's decision does not square with our conception of federalism. There is nothing more deeply imbedded in the Tenth Amendment, as I read history, than the disposition of the estates of deceased people. I do not see how a scheme for administration of decedents' estates of the kind we have here can possibly be necessary and proper to any power delegated to Congress. . . ." [Emphasis added.]

4. *A polemic postscript.* The point of this Reid-Kinsella to Madison to Oregon exercise is of course not to suggest that Marshall's view has in fact been broadly repudiated, or that the Reid-Kinsella-Oregon decisions are necessarily unsound in result. It is to suggest the importance of the content of the Court's reasoned elaborations of principle; it is to suggest that it is not enough to recognize that the limiting principles on national authority in the court-martial cases differ from those in Oregon; it is to suggest that a Court must not only perceive but also adequately articulate the differences. By resting the explanation in part on a general Necessary and Proper Clause interpretation, the Reid and Kinsella opinions convey doctrines of probably unintended breadth and assume the risk of application of the doctrines in such settings as United States v. Oregon. Could adequate opinions have been written in the court-martial cases without giving a somewhat unusual meaning to the Necessary and Proper Clause? By emphasizing Article III and the Bill of Rights—rather than Article I—as the sole sources of the limitations? Detailed examination of the content of Bill of Rights limitations will have to await later chapters. The remaining principal cases in this section raise problems somewhat similar to those in the court-martial cases: in the conflicts presented between national powers and individual rights, did the opinions allow Congress a discretion as to means like that found, for example, in recent commerce clause cases, with limitations arising from sources outside of Article I; or did the approach to implied powers shift significantly from that in earlier cases? [Before turning to those principal cases, consider briefly the following notes, pursuing somewhat further the specific military jurisdiction problems of Reid and Kinsella.]

MILITARY TRIBUNALS, CIVILIANS, AND CIVILIAN OFFENSES

1. *Civilians and military tribunals: the companion cases to Kinsella.* a. Three additional court-martial cases under Article 2(11) of the Uniform Code of Military Justice were decided on the same day as Kinsella, supra. Grisham v. Hagan, 361 U.S. 278; McElroy v. United States ex rel. Guagliardo, and Wilson v. Bohlender, 361 U.S. 281 (1960). Grisham involved a civilian convicted of a capital offense while employed overseas by the Army. Guagliardo and Wilson involved noncapital offenses by civilian employees. All of the court-martial convictions were set aside on the authority of Reid v. Covert and Kinsella. Justice Harlan, joined by Justice Frankfurter, supported court-martial jurisdiction over employees as well as dependents in noncapital cases, but not in capital cases. Justice Whittaker, joined by Justice Stewart, found authority for military jurisdiction over employees but not over dependents; he rejected the capital-noncapital distinction. Justice Whittaker stated: "Viewed in the light of its birth and history, is it not reasonably clear that the grant of Clause 14 to make rules for the government and regulation of the land and naval forces, empowers Congress to govern and regulate all persons so closely related to and intertwined with those forces as to make their government essential to the government of those forces? Do not civilians employed by the armed forces at bases in foreign lands to do essential work for the military establishment . . . occupy that status and stand in that relationship to the armed forces for which they worked? . . . In the light of all the facts, it would seem clear enough that Congress could rationally find that those persons are 'in' those forces and, though there be no shoot-

ing war, that those forces, in turn, are 'in the field'; and hence Congress could and did constitutionally make those employees subject to the military power."

b.   See also United States ex rel. Toth v. Quarles, 350 U.S. 11 (1955), decided before Reid v. Covert.   Several months after having been honorably discharged from the Air Force, Toth was arrested in Pennsylvania and taken to Korea to be tried by a court-martial on a charge of murder committed while he was an airman in Korea.   On habeas corpus, brought in the District Court for the District of Columbia and pursued through the Court of Appeals to the Supreme Court, it was held that Congress cannot subject ex-servicemen like Toth to trial by court-martial.   "They, like other civilians, are entitled to have the benefits of safeguards afforded those tried in the regular courts authorized by Article III."   In answer to the argument that discharged soldiers might escape punishment altogether, the Court suggested that Congress could provide for federal district court trials for them.   Justice Reed, joined by Justices Burton and Minton, submitted a dissenting opinion; and Justice Minton, joined by Justice Burton, also delivered a dissenting opinion.   [On military control of civilians in earlier periods and the background of civil-military relations, see also chap. 7 below, especially Ex parte Milligan, p. 611.]

2.   *Military personnel and nonmilitary offenses: O'Callahan v. Parker.* In O'Callahan v. Parker, 395 U.S. 258 (1969), a divided Court held that petitioner, though a soldier, could not be tried by court-martial and was entitled to trial by the civilian courts because his crimes were not "service-connected." Petitioner, stationed in Hawaii, challenged a court-martial conviction for attempted rape and housebreaking committed off-post while on an evening pass.   The Government argued that prior cases such as Kinsella demonstrated that court-martial jurisdiction turned on "status"—was the accused in the "land and naval Forces."   Justice Douglas' majority opinion rejected that argument.   The earlier cases showed, to be sure, that court-martial jurisdiction of a civilian was impermissible, and that military "status" was necessary, "but it does not follow that ascertainment of 'status' completes the inquiry, regardless of the nature, time, and place of the offense."

After a brief review of British and American history, the Court concluded "that the crime to be under military jurisdiction must be service-connected, lest 'cases arising in the land and naval forces or in the militia, when in actual service in time of war or public danger,' as used in the Fifth Amendment, be expanded to deprive every member of the armed services of the benefits of an indictment by a grand jury and a trial by a jury of his peers. The power of Congress to make 'rules for the government and regulations of the land and naval forces,' Art. I, § 8, cl. 14, need not be sparingly read in order to preserve those two important constitutional guarantees.   For it is assumed that an express grant of general power to Congress is to be exercised in harmony with express guarantees of the Bill of Rights."   Justice Douglas noted that petitioner was on leave, that the civil courts were open, that the offenses did not involve "flouting of military authority," and that the case dealt "with peacetime offenses, not with authority stemming from the war power."

Justice Harlan's dissent, joined by Justices Stewart and White, objected to the majority's "one-sided discussion" of the competing interests and its reliance on "at best wholly inconclusive historical data" and concluded "that the Court has grasped for itself the making of a determination which the Constitution has placed in the hands of the Congress." The prior cases, he insisted, showed "that military 'status' is a necessary *and sufficient* condition for the exercise of court-martial jurisdiction. The Court has never previously questioned what the language of Clause 14 would seem to make plain—that, given the requisite military status, it is for Congress and not the Judiciary to determine the appropriate subject-matter jurisdiction of courts-martial." Moreover, there were "strong and legitimate governmental interests which support the exercise of court-martial jurisdiction even over 'non-military' crimes." For example: "The soldier who acts the part of Mr. Hyde while on leave is, at best, a precarious Dr. Jekyll when back on duty." He objected, finally, to the "demoralizing state of uncertainty" created by the Court's failure to state a "general standard" regarding the allowable scope of court-martial jurisdiction.

3. *Time for deliberation and the Supreme Court: the handling of Reid v. Covert and Wilson v. Girard.* a. Did undue haste contribute to the inadequate first disposition of Reid v. Covert, which led to the rehearing that produced the decision printed above? Consider the chronology: The case was originally argued on May 3, 1956. The decision sustaining the constitutionality of the law came just five weeks later, on June 11, 1956. 351 U.S. 487. Justice Clark delivered the opinion of the Court. Chief Justice Warren and Justices Black and Douglas filed a brief dissent noting the "far-reaching importance" of the decision and adding: "The questions raised are complex. . . . [W]e need more time than is available in these closing days of the Term in which to write our dissenting views. We will file our dissents during the next Term of Court."

Justice Frankfurter filed a longer separate opinion labeled "Reservation." In the course of it, he said: "Grave issues affecting the status of American civilians throughout the world are raised by these cases; they are made graver by the arguments on which the Court finds it necessary to rely in reaching its result. Doubtless because of the pressure under which the Court works during its closing weeks, these arguments have been merely adumbrated in its opinion. To deal adequately with them, however, demands of those to whom they are not persuasive more time than has been available to examine and to analyze in detail the historical underpinning and implication of the cases relied upon by the Court, as a preliminary to a searching critique of their relevance to the problems now before the Court. . . . Time is required not only for the primary task of analyzing in detail the materials on which the Court relies. It is equally required for adequate reflection upon the meaning of these materials and their bearing on the issues now before the Court. Reflection is a slow process. Wisdom, like good wine, requires maturing. Moreover, the judgments of this Court are collective judgments. They are neither solo performances nor debates between two sides, each of which has its mind quickly made up and then closed. The judgments of this Court presuppose full consideration and reconsideration by all of the reasoned views of each. Without adequate study there cannot be adequate reflection. Without adequate reflection there cannot be adequate deliberation and discussion. And without these, there cannot be that full interchange of minds which is indispensable to wise decision and its persuasive formulation. The circumstances being what they are, I am forced, deeply as I regret it, to reserve for a later date an expression of my views."

Early in the next Term, on November 5, 1956, the Court granted the petition for rehearing. 352 U.S. 901. Justices Reed, Burton and Clark dissented. Justice Brennan, who had just been appointed to the Court (upon Justice Minton's retirement), did not participate in the decision granting rehearing. The case was reargued on February 27, 1957, and decided, in the manner reported above, on June 10, 1957. (Justice Whittaker, who took his seat on March 25, 1957, to replace the retired Justice Reed, did not participate in the decision in Reid v. Covert.) On the question of adequate time for Court deliberation, compare generally Hart, "Foreword—The Time Chart of the Justices," 73 Harv.L.Rev. 84 (1959), with Arnold, "Professor Hart's Theology," 73 Harv.L.Rev. 1298 (1960).

b. Compare with the foregoing cases, Wilson v. Girard, 354 U.S. 524 (1957). Japan and the United States had entered into an Administrative Agreement, pursuant to a treaty, covering the matter of the jurisdiction of the United States over offenses committed in Japan by members of the United States armed forces and providing that jurisdiction in any case might be waived by the United States. A soldier of the United States, while on active duty in Japan, caused the death of a Japanese woman, and the United States waived its jurisdiction over him, thus permitting him to be tried by a Japanese court. On review of proceedings begun in the District Court for the District of Columbia in which Girard sought to prevent his delivery over to the Japanese authorities, the Supreme Court, in a brief per curiam decision, found "no constitutional or statutory barrier" to the federal officials' waiver of jurisdiction over Girard. "A sovereign nation has exclusive jurisdiction to punish offenses against its laws committed within its borders, unless it expressly or impliedly consents to surrender its jurisdiction. Schooner Exchange v. M'Faddon, 7 Cranch 116, 136. Japan's cession to the United States of jurisdiction to try American military personnel for conduct constituting an offense against the laws of both countries was conditioned" by a provision that the "Authorities of the State having the primary right shall give sympathetic consideration to a request from the authorities of the other State for a waiver of its right in cases where the other State considers such waiver to be of particular importance."

Certiorari was granted in Wilson v. Girard on June 21, 1957. The case was argued on July 8, 1957, and decided three days later, July 11, 1957. In view of the Court's concern about constitutional restrictions on military jurisdiction—manifested in the preceding few years in Toth and Reid v. Covert, supra—did Girard's claim receive adequate consideration by the Court? Would the Court's per curiam answer have been adequate if the case had arisen in a different country and the petitioner had alleged that he was about to be delivered to a foreign nation which adjudicated cases in secret sessions of political officials and which utilized torture and maiming as a form of punishment?

PEREZ v. BROWNELL

356 U.S. 44, 78 S.Ct. 568, 2 L.Ed.2d 603 (1958).

Certiorari to the United States Court of Appeals for the Ninth Circuit.

Mr. Justice FRANKFURTER delivered the opinion of the Court.

Petitioner, a national of the United States by birth, has been declared to have lost his American citizenship by operation of the Nationality Act of 1940, 54 Stat. 1137, as amended by the Act of September 27, 1944, 58 Stat. 746. Section 401 of that Act [incorporated into § 349 of the Immigration and Nationality Act of 1952] provided that

"A person who is a national of the United States, whether by birth or naturalization, shall lose his nationality by: . . .

"(e) Voting in a political election in a foreign state or participating in an election or plebiscite to determine the sovereignty over foreign territory; or . . .

"(j) Departing from or remaining outside of the jurisdiction of the United States in time of war or during a period declared by the President to be a period of national emergency for the purpose of evading or avoiding training and service in the land or naval forces of the United States."

He seeks a reversal of the judgment against him on the ground that these provisions were beyond the power of Congress to enact.

Petitioner was born in Texas in 1909. He resided in the United States until 1919 or 1920, when he moved with his parents to Mexico, where he lived, apparently without interruption, until 1943. In 1928 he was informed that he had been born in Texas. At the outbreak of World War II, petitioner knew of the duty of male United States citizens to register for the draft, but he failed to do so. In 1943 he applied for admission to the United States as an alien railroad laborer, stating that he was a native-born citizen of Mexico, and was granted permission to enter on a temporary basis. He returned to Mexico in 1944 and shortly thereafter applied for and was granted permission, again as a native-born Mexican citizen, to enter the United States temporarily to continue his employment as a railroad laborer. Later in 1944 he returned to Mexico once more. [In 1947, he] was ordered excluded on the ground that he had expatriated himself; this order was affirmed on appeal. In 1952 petitioner, claiming to be a native-born citizen of Mexico, was permitted to enter the United States as an alien agricultural laborer. [He] claimed the right to remain by virtue of his American citizenship [but] was ordered deported as an alien not in possession of a valid immigration visa . . . .

Petitioner brought suit in 1954 in a United States District Court for a judgment declaring him to be a national of the United States. The court [found] that petitioner had remained outside of the United States from November 1944 to July 1947 for the purpose of avoiding service in the armed forces of the United States and that he had voted in a "political election" in Mexico in 1946. The court, concluding that he had thereby expatriated himself, denied the relief sought by the petitioner. The United States Court of Appeals for the Ninth Circuit affirmed. . . .

The first step in our inquiry must be to answer the question: what is the source of power on which Congress must be assumed to have drawn? Although there is in the Constitution no specific grant to Congress of power to enact legislation for the effective regulation of foreign affairs, there can be no doubt of the existence of this power in the law-making organ of the Nation. [See the passage quoted supra, p. 402.] The Government must be able not only to deal affirmatively with foreign nations, as it does through the maintenance of diplomatic relations with them and the protection of American citizens sojourning within their territories. It must also be able to reduce to a minimum the frictions that are unavoidable in a world of sovereigns sensitive in matters touching their dignity and interests.

The inference is fairly to be drawn from the congressional history of the Nationality Act of 1940, read in light of the historical background of expatriation in this country, that, in making voting in foreign elections (among other behavior) an act of expatriation, Congress was seeking to effectuate its power to regulate foreign affairs. The legislators, counseled by those on whom they rightly relied for advice, were concerned about actions by citizens in foreign countries that create problems of protection and are inconsistent with American allegiance. . . .

Broad as the power in the National Government to regulate foreign affairs must necessarily be, it is not without limitation. The restrictions confining Congress in the exercise of any of the powers expressly delegated to it in the Constitution apply with equal vigor when that body seeks to regulate our relations with other nations. Since Congress may not act arbitrarily, a rational nexus must exist between the content of a specific power in Congress and the action of Congress in carrying that power into execution. More simply stated, the means—in this case, withdrawal of citizenship—must be reasonably related to the end—here, regulation of foreign affairs. The inquiry—and, in the case before us, the sole inquiry—into which this Court must enter is whether or not Congress may have concluded not unreasonably that there is a relevant connection between this fundamental source of power and the ultimate legislative action.[1]

Our starting point is to ascertain whether the power of Congress to deal with foreign relations may reasonably be deemed to include a power to deal generally with the active participation, by way of voting, of American citizens in foreign political elections. Experience amply attests that in this day of extensive international travel, rapid communication and widespread use of propaganda, the activities of the citizens of one nation when in another country can easily cause serious embarrassments to the government of their own country as well as to their fellow citizens. We cannot deny to Congress the reasonable belief that these difficulties might well become acute, to the point of jeopardizing the successful conduct of international relations, when the citizen of one country chooses to participate in the political or governmental affairs of another country. The citizen may by his action unwittingly promote or encourage a course of conduct contrary to the interests of his own government; moreover, the people or government of the

---

1. The provision of the Fourteenth Amendment that "All persons born or naturalized in the United States, and subject to the jurisdiction thereof, are citizens of the United States . . ." sets forth the two principal modes (but by no means the only ones) for acquiring citizenship. Thus, in United States v. Wong Kim Ark, 169 U.S. 649 (Chief Justice Fuller and Mr. Justice Harlan dissenting), it was held that a person of Chinese parentage born in this country was among "all persons born . . . in the United States" and therefore a citizen to whom the Chinese Exclusion Acts did not apply. But there is nothing in the terms, the context, the history or the manifest purpose of the Fourteenth Amendment to warrant drawing from it a restriction upon the power otherwise possessed by Congress to withdraw citizenship. The limit of the operation of that provision was clearly enunciated in Perkins v. Elg, 307 U.S. 325, 329: "As at birth she became a citizen of the United States, that citizenship must be deemed to continue unless she has been deprived of it through the operation of a treaty or congressional enactment or by her voluntary action in conformity with applicable legal principles." [Footnote by Justice Frankfurter.]

foreign country may regard his action to be the action of his government, or at least as a reflection if not an expression of its policy. . . .

It follows that such activity is regulable by Congress under its power to deal with foreign affairs. And it must be regulable on more than an *ad hoc* basis. The subtle influences and repercussions with which the government must deal make it reasonable for the generalized, although clearly limited, category of "political election" to be used in defining the area of regulation. That description carries with it the scope and meaning of its context and purpose; classes of elections—nonpolitical in the colloquial sense—as to which participation by Americans could not possibly have any effect on the relations of the United States with another country are excluded by any rational construction of the phrase. . . .

The question must finally be faced whether, given the power to attach some sort of consequence to voting in a foreign political election, Congress, acting under the Necessary and Proper Clause, Art. I, § 8, cl. 18, could attach loss of nationality to it. Is the means, withdrawal of citizenship, reasonably calculated to effect the end that is within the power of Congress to achieve, the avoidance of embarrassment in the conduct of our foreign relations attributable to voting by American citizens in foreign political elections? The importance and extreme delicacy of the matters here sought to be regulated demand that Congress be permitted ample scope in selecting appropriate modes for accomplishing its purpose. The critical connection between this conduct and loss of citizenship is the fact that it is the possession of American citizenship by a person committing the act that makes the act potentially embarrassing to the American Government and pregnant with the possibility of embroiling this country in disputes with other nations. The termination of citizenship terminates the problem. Moreover, the fact is not without significance that Congress has interpreted this conduct, not irrationally, as importing not only something less than complete and unswerving allegiance to the United States, but also elements of an allegiance to another country in some measure, at least, inconsistent with American citizenship. . . .

It cannot be said, then, that Congress acted without warrant when, pursuant to its power to regulate the relations of the United States with foreign countries, it provided that anyone who votes in a foreign election of significance politically in the life of another country shall lose his American citizenship. To deny the power of Congress to enact the legislation challenged here would be to disregard the constitutional allocation of governmental functions that it is this Court's solemn duty to guard.

Because of our view concerning the power of Congress with respect to § 401(e) of the Nationality Act of 1940, we find it unnecessary to consider—indeed, it would be improper for us to adjudicate—the constitutionality of § 401(j), and we expressly decline to rule on that important question at this time.

Judgment affirmed.

Mr. Chief Justice WARREN, with whom Mr. Justice BLACK and Mr. Justice DOUGLAS join, dissenting.

The Congress of the United States has decreed that a citizen of the United States shall lose his citizenship by performing certain designated acts. The petitioner in this case, a native-born American, is declared to have lost his citizenship by voting in a foreign election.[1] Whether this forfeiture of citizenship exceeds the bounds of the Constitution is the issue before us. . . . The initial question here is whether citizenship is subject to the exercise of these general powers of government. . . . I cannot believe that a government conceived in the spirit of ours was established with power to take from the people their most basic right.

Citizenship *is* man's basic right for it is nothing less than the right to have rights. Remove this priceless possession and there remains a stateless person, disgraced and degraded in the eyes of his countrymen. He has no lawful claim to protection from any nation, and no nation may assert rights on his behalf. His very existence is at the sufferance of the state within whose borders he happens to be. In this country the expatriate would presumably enjoy, at most, only the limited rights and privileges of aliens, and like the alien he might even be subject to deportation and thereby deprived of the right to assert any rights. This government was not established with power to decree this fate.

The people who created this government endowed it with broad powers. They created a sovereign state with power to function as a sovereignty. But the citizens themselves are sovereign, and their citizenship is not subject to the general powers of their government. Whatever may be the scope of its powers to regulate the conduct and affairs of all persons within its jurisdiction, a government *of* the people cannot take away their citizenship simply because one branch of that government can be said to have a conceivably rational basis for wanting to do so.

The basic Constitutional provision crystallizing the right of citizenship is the first sentence of section one of the Fourteenth Amendment. . . . The Constitution also provides that citizenship can be bestowed under a "uniform rule of naturalization," but there is no corresponding provision authorizing divestment. Of course, naturalization unlawfully procured can be set aside. But apart from this circumstance, the status of the naturalized citizen is secure. . . . Under our form of government, as established by the Constitution, the citizenship of the lawfully naturalized and the native-born cannot be taken from them. . . .

It has long been recognized that citizenship may not only be voluntarily renounced through exercise of the right of expatriation but also by other actions in derogation of undivided allegiance to this country. . . .

Twice before, this Court has recognized that certain voluntary conduct results in an impairment of the status of citizenship. In Savorgnan v. United States, 338 U.S. 491, an American citizen had renounced her citizenship and acquired that of a foreign state. This Court affirmed her loss of citizenship . . . . Mackenzie v. Hare, 239 U.S. 299, involved an American woman who had married a British national. That decision sustained an Act of Congress which provided that her citizenship was suspended for the duration of her marriage. . . . Mackenzie v. Hare should not be understood

---

[1] . . . . The fact that the statute speaks in terms of loss of nationality does not mean that it is not petitioner's citizenship that is being forfeited. He is a national by reason of his being a citizen, § 101(b), Nationality Act of 1940 . . . . . Hence he loses his citizenship when he loses his status as a national of the United States. In the context of this opinion, the terms nationality and citizenship can be used interchangeably. . . . [Footnote by Chief Justice Warren.]

to sanction a power to divest citizenship. Rather this case, like Savorgnan, simply acknowledges that United States citizenship can be abandoned, temporarily or permanently, by conduct showing a voluntary transfer of allegiance to another country. . . .

The precise issue posed by Section 401(e) is whether the conduct it describes invariably involves a dilution of undivided allegiance sufficient to show a voluntary abandonment of citizenship. Doubtless under some circumstances a vote in a foreign election would have this effect. For example, abandonment of citizenship might result if the person desiring to vote had to become a foreign national or represent himself to be one. . . . And even the situation that bothered Committee Chairman Dickstein—Americans voting in the Saar plebiscite [1935]—might under some circumstances disclose conduct tantamount to dividing allegiance. Congressman Dickstein expressed his concern as follows:

> "I know we have had a lot of Nazis, so-called American citizens, go to Europe who have voted in the Saar for the annexation of territory to Germany, and Germany says that they have the right to participate and to vote, and yet they are American citizens."

There might well be circumstances where an American shown to have voted at the behest of a foreign government to advance its territorial interests would compromise his native allegiance. . . .

The fatal defect in the statute before us is that its application is not limited to those situations that may rationally be said to constitute an abandonment of citizenship. In specifying that any act of voting in a foreign political election results in loss of citizenship, Congress has employed a classification so broad that it encompasses conduct that fails to show a voluntary abandonment of American citizenship. "The connection between the fact proved and that presumed is not sufficient." . . . Voting in a foreign election may be a most equivocal act, giving rise to no implication that allegiance has been compromised. . . .

My conclusions are as follows. The Government is without power to take citizenship away from a native-born or lawfully naturalized American. The Fourteenth Amendment recognizes that this priceless right is immune from the exercise of governmental powers. If the Government determines that certain conduct by United States citizens should be prohibited because of anticipated injurious consequences to the conduct of foreign affairs or to some other legitimate governmental interest, it may within the limits of the Constitution proscribe such activity and assess appropriate punishment. But every exercise of governmental power must find its source in the Constitution. The power to denationalize is not within the letter or the spirit of the powers with which our Government was endowed. The citizen may elect to renounce his citizenship, and under some circumstances he may be found to have abandoned his status by voluntarily performing acts that compromise his undivided allegiance to his country. The mere act of voting in a foreign election, however, without regard to the circumstances attending the participation, is not sufficient to show a voluntary abandonment of citizenship. The record in this case does not disclose any of the circumstances under which this petitioner voted. We know only the bare fact that he cast a ballot. The basic right of American citizenship has been too dearly won to be so lightly lost.

I fully recognize that only the most compelling considerations should lead to the invalidation of congressional action, and where legislative judgments are involved, this Court should not intervene. But the Court also has its duties, none of which demands more diligent performance than that of protecting the fundamental rights of individuals. That duty is imperative when the citizenship of an American is at stake—that status, which alone, assures him the full enjoyment of the precious rights conferred by our Constitution. As I see my duty in this case, I must dissent.

Mr. Justice DOUGLAS, with whom Mr. Justice BLACK concurs, dissenting. . . .

What the Constitution grants the Constitution can take away. But there is not a word in that document that covers expatriation. The numerous legislative powers granted by Art. I, § 8 do not mention it. I do not know of any legislative power large enough and powerful enough to modify or wipe out rights granted or created by Cl. 1, § 1 of the Fourteenth Amendment. . . .

. . . Citizenship, like freedom of speech, press, and religion, occupies a preferred position in our written Constitution, because it is a grant absolute in terms. The power of Congress to withhold it, modify it, or cancel it does not exist. One who is native-born may be a good citizen or a poor one. Whether his actions be criminal or charitable, he remains a citizen for better or for worse, except and unless he voluntarily relinquishes that status. While Congress can prescribe conditions for voluntary expatriation, Congress cannot turn white to black and make any act an act of expatriation. For then the right granted by the Fourteenth Amendment becomes subject to regulation by the legislative branch. But that right has no such infirmity. . . .

Memorandum of Mr. Justice WHITTAKER.

Though I agree with the major premise of the majority's opinion—that Congress may expatriate a citizen for an act which it may reasonably find to be fraught with danger of embroiling our Government in an international dispute or of embarrassing it in the conduct of foreign affairs—I cannot agree with the result reached, for it seems plain to me that § 401(e) is too broadly written to be sustained upon that ground. . . . Voting in a political election in a particular foreign state may be open to aliens under the law of that state, as it was in presidential elections in the United States until 1928 . . .. Where that is so—and this record fails to show that petitioner's act of voting in a political election in Mexico in 1946 was not entirely lawful under the law of that state—such legalized voting by an American citizen cannot reasonably be said to be fraught with danger of embroiling our Government in an international dispute or of embarrassing it in the conduct of foreign affairs, nor, I believe, can such an act—entirely legal under the law of the foreign state—be reasonably said to constitute an abandonment or any division or dilution of allegiance to the United States. Since these are my convictions, I dissent from the majority's opinion and join in so much of the dissenting opinion of The Chief Justice as expresses the view that the act of a citizen of the United States in voting in a foreign political election which is legally open to aliens under the law of that state cannot reasonably be said to constitute abandonment or any division or dilution of allegiance to the United States. . . .

PEREZ AND LOSS OF CITIZENSHIP

1. *The Perez approach and the Trop decision.* a. Does Perez involve a conflict between powers and limitations? Do any of the opinions recognize such a conflict? Assuming the existence of a foreign affairs power of Congress, is Justice Frankfurter's analysis in accord with earlier cases involving Congressional choice of means in executing national powers? Does the first sentence of the Fourteenth Amendment supply a limitation akin to the First Amendment? Does Chief Justice Warren agree that there is a foreign affairs power of Congress? Does his conclusion that there is no "power to denationalize" rest on a survey of national powers or on a reading of limitations on powers? Does Justice Whittaker's dissent rest on an interpretation of national powers, of due process, or of the Fourteenth Amendment? Compare Justice Brennan's concurrence in Trop v. Dulles, the companion case to Perez, which follows.

b. In Trop v. Dulles, 356 U.S. 86 (1958), the Court held unconstitutional Section 401(g) of the Nationality Act of 1940, providing for loss of citizenship upon conviction and dishonorable discharge for wartime desertion. The majority in this case was composed of the Perez dissenters and Justice Brennan. Chief Justice Warren's opinion, joined by Justices Black, Douglas and Whittaker, relied on a number of grounds. He found the provision invalid under his Perez position "that citizenship is not subject to the general powers of the National Government." Moreover, he insisted that Section 401(g) could not stand "even under the majority's decision in Perez." He concluded that denationalization may not be "inflicted as a punishment, even assuming that citizenship may be divested pursuant to some governmental power." Use of denationalization as a punishment, turning the citizen into a stateless person, was found barred by the Eighth Amendment's prohibition of "cruel and unusual punishment."

Justice Brennan's concurrence explained his "paradoxical" position of being with the majority in both Perez and Trop. Section 401(g), but not Section 401(e), "lies beyond Congress' power to enact." The standard, he insisted, was "whether there exists a relevant connection between the particular legislative enactment and the power granted to Congress by the Constitution." In Perez, Congress had validly provided for loss of citizenship simultaneously with the act of voting "because Congress might reasonably believe that . . . there is no acceptable alternative to expatriation as a means of avoiding possible embarrassments to our relations with foreign nations." In Trop, however, denationalization could not be accepted as "a means reasonably calculated to achieve . . . the ultimate congressional objective— the successful waging of war." In elaboration of this, he stated: "Admittedly Congress' belief that expatriation of the deserter might further the war effort may find some—though necessarily slender—support in reason. But here, any substantial achievement, by this device, of Congress' legitimate purposes under the war power seems fairly remote. It is at the same time abundantly clear that these ends could more fully be achieved by alternative methods not open to these objections. In the light of these factors, and conceding all that I possibly can in favor of the enactment, I can only conclude that the requisite rational relation between this statute and the war power does not appear—for in this relation the statute is not 'really calculated to ef-

fect any of the objects entrusted to the government . . .,' M'Culloch
v. Maryland, 4 Wheat. 316, 423—and therefore that § 401(g) falls beyond
the domain of Congress."

c. Note that Justice Brennan did not rely on any limitation arising
from the Eighth Amendment or the first sentence of the Fourteenth; he
purported to rest solely on the Article I war power. Is his concluding statement truly in accord with McCulloch v. Maryland and subsequent cases about
the congressional choice of means? If the congressional choice finds "some
. . . support in reason," can it be invalid under McCulloch because
"these ends could be more fully achieved by alternative methods not open to
these objections"? Is the crux of this position the "objections" to the chosen method? Earlier in his opinion, Justice Brennan had referred to the
"manifest severity" of denationalization and had asked whether "the nature
of the penalty is rationally directed to achieve the legitimate ends of punishment." Is the basis of his position, then, his views of penology—of "the
legitimate ends of punishment"—rather than his judgment on what is reasonably calculated to promote the "legitimate end" of conducting the war?
If so, can such an approach be said to rest on the application of McCulloch
to the war power, without resort to the Eighth Amendment or any other constitutional limitation? Would his position have been more viable if it had
rested on the Eighth Amendment?

d. Justice Frankfurter, joined by three other Justices who had supported the majority result in Perez—Justices Burton, Clark and Harlan—,
dissented in Trop v. Dulles: "Can it be said that there is no rational nexus
between refusal to perform this ultimate duty of American citizenship and
legislative withdrawal of that citizenship? Congress may well have thought
that making loss of citizenship a consequence of wartime desertion would affect the ability of the military authorities to control the forces with which
they were expected to fight and win a major world conflict. It is not for us
to deny that Congress might reasonably have believed the morale and fighting efficiency of our troops would be impaired if our soldiers knew that their
fellows who had abandoned them in their time of greatest need were to remain in the communion of our citizens." On the Eighth Amendment objection, he noted that wartime desertion had been a capital offense since
1776 and added: "Is constitutional dialectic so empty of reason that it can be
seriously urged that loss of citizenship is a fate worse than death?"

2. *The avoidance of Perez: Mendoza-Martinez.* In Kennedy v. Mendoza-Martinez and Rusk v. Cort, decided in a single opinion, 372 U.S. 144
(1963), the Supreme Court held unconstitutional provisions of the Nationality Act of 1940 and the Immigration and Nationality Act of 1952 imposing
loss of citizenship for "departing from or remaining outside of the jurisdiction of the United States in time of war or . . . national emergency for
the purpose of evading or avoiding training and service" in the armed forces.
The Court based its decision on a ground which, according to Justice Goldberg's majority opinion, was not available in Perez and Trop and which
"obviates a choice here between the powers of Congress and the constitutional
guarantee of citizenship." The constitutional flaw found by the Court was
that "Congress has plainly employed the sanction of deprivation of nationality
as a punishment . . . without affording the procedural safeguards
guaranteed by the Fifth and Sixth Amendments." Justices Douglas and

Black joined the opinion of the Court but stated their adherence to their dissents in Perez. Justice Brennan submitted a lengthy concurring opinion even though he did not find it necessary "to resolve some felt doubts of the correctness of Perez, which I joined." Justice Stewart's dissent, joined by Justice White, denied that the statutes imposed "punishment in the constitutional sense of that term" and insisted that the denationalization provision was "precisely the same kind of regulatory measure, rational and efficacious, which this Court upheld against similar objections" in Perez. Justices Harlan and Clark also dissented.

　　3. *The overruling of Perez: Afroyim v. Rusk.* In Afroyim v. Rusk, 387 U.S. 253 (1967), petitioner, who had become a naturalized American citizen in 1926, moved to Israel in 1950 and voted in an election for the Israeli legislature in 1951. In 1960, an American consulate in Israel refused to renew his passport on the ground that he had lost his citizenship because of the statutory provision regarding voting "in a political election in a foreign state"—the provision sustained in Perez v. Brownell. The Court's 5–4 decision overruled Perez; the opinions concentrated on the purpose of the first sentence of the Fourteenth Amendment.

　　Early in the majority opinion, Justice Black noted that "great doubt" had been cast upon the soundness of Perez by other cases which had "consistently invalidated," on "various grounds," various other involuntary expatriation provisions. He proceeded to reject the Perez "idea" that, "aside from the Fourteenth Amendment, Congress has any general power, express or implied, to take away an American citizen's citizenship without his assent. . . . The Constitution, of course, grants Congress no express power to strip people of their citizenship, whether in the exercise of the implied power to regulate foreign affairs or in the exercise of any specifically granted power."

　　After noting some pre-Civil War views that Congress lacked power "to determine what conduct should and should not result in the loss of citizenship," Justice Black stated that "any doubt as to whether prior to the passage of the Fourteenth Amendment Congress had the power to deprive a person against his will of citizenship once obtained should have been removed by the unequivocal terms of the Amendment itself. . . . [T]he Amendment can most reasonably be read as defining a citizenship which a citizen keeps unless he voluntarily relinquishes it. Once acquired, this Fourteenth Amendment citizenship was not to be shifted, canceled, or diluted at the will of the Federal Government, the States, or any other government unit. It is true that the chief interest of the people in giving permanence and security to citizenship in the Fourteenth Amendment was the desire to protect Negroes. . . . This undeniable purpose of the Fourteenth Amendment to make citizenship of Negroes permanent and secure would be frustrated by holding that the Government can rob a citizen of his citizenship without his consent by simply proceeding to act under an implied general power to regulate foreign affairs or some other power generally granted."

　　Justice Harlan's dissent, joined by Justices Clark, Stewart and White, found the Court's reasoning "a remarkable process of circumlocution." He noted that "the Court fails almost entirely to dispute the reasoning in Perez; it is essentially content with the conclusory and quite unsubstantiated assertion that Congress is without 'any general power, express or implied,' to expatriate a citizen 'without his assent.' " He limited himself to "supplementing" Perez with an examination of the "historical evidence": to him, it confirmed the "narrow, essentially definitional purpose of the Citizenship Clause" and, accordingly, "Perez' soundness."

4. *Citizenship by naturalization: acquisition and loss.* a. *Acquisition.* The Constitution "contemplates two sources of citizenship, and two only,— birth and naturalization. Citizenship by naturalization can only be acquired by naturalization under the authority and in the forms of law. But citizenship by birth is established by the mere fact of birth under the circumstances defined in the Constitution." United States v. Wong Kim Ark, 169 U.S. 649 (1898). The power to establish rules of naturalization belongs exclusively to Congress. Chirac v. Chirac, 2 Wheat. 259 (1817). In Holmgren v. United States, 217 U.S. 509 (1910), it was held that Congress could confer authority on state courts to entertain naturalization proceedings. United States v. Schwimmer, 279 U.S. 644 (1929), denied naturalization to a woman who indicated an unwillingness to take up arms in defense of the country; United States v. Macintosh, 283 U.S. 605 (1931), held that naturalization could be denied to a man who testified that he would have to believe that the war was morally justified before he would take up arms. The Schwimmer and Macintosh cases (both 5:4 decisions) were overruled in Girouard v. United States, 328 U.S. 61 (1946), holding that a Canadian Seventh Day Adventist who was willing to take the oath of allegiance and to serve in a non-combatant position in the Army, but not to bear arms, was entitled to be naturalized.

b. *Loss for fraud in acquiring citizenship.* Congress has made provision for the cancellation of illegally or fraudulently procured certificates of naturalization. In Baumgartner v. United States, 322 U.S. 665 (1944), proceedings were brought in 1942 to cancel a certificate issued in 1932. The charge was that the applicant had not truly and fully renounced allegiance to his former country and that he had not in fact intended to support the Constitution and laws of the United States and to give them true faith and allegiance. In reversing the judgment of cancellation by the lower courts, the Supreme Court emphasized that the proof requisite to denaturalize a citizen "must be clear and unequivocal." See also Schneiderman v. United States, 320 U.S. 118 (1943).

c. *Loss for acts after acquiring citizenship.* In Schneider v. Rusk, 377 U.S. 163 (1964), the Court significantly limited the power of Congress to expatriate naturalized citizens. The Immigration and Nationality Act of 1952 provided that a naturalized citizen would lose his citizenship by "having a continuous residence for three years in the territory of a foreign state of which he was formerly a national or in which the place of his birth is situated," with certain exceptions. The Court, in an opinion by Justice Douglas, held that the section "violates due process." The Government's argument had relied, as in Perez v. Brownell, on the congressional power over foreign relations, in view of the "special problems engendered when naturalized citizens return for a long period to the country of their former nationalities." The Court found that the special provision applicable to naturalized citizens constituted an unconstitutionally discriminatory means to exercise that power. Though citizenship through naturalization rests on statute rather than the Fourteenth Amendment, "the rights of citizenship of the native born and of the naturalized person are of the same dignity and are coextensive," except for the constitutional provision regarding eligibility for the Presidency.

The majority opinion concluded: "This statute proceeds on the impermissible assumption that naturalized citizens as a class are less reliable and bear less allegiance to this country than do the native born. This is an assumption that is impossible for us to make. Moreover, while the Fifth Amendment contains no equal protection clause, it does forbid discrimination that is 'so unjustifiable as to be violative of due process.' . . . The discrimination aimed at naturalized citizens drastically limits their rights to live and work abroad in a way that other citizens may. It creates indeed a second-class citizenship. [Living abroad] is no badge of lack of allegiance and in no way evidences a voluntary renunciation of nationality and allegiance." Justice Clark, joined by Justices Harlan and White, dissented: "All that Congress did was face up to problems of the highest national importance by authorizing expatriation, the only adequate remedy. Appellant, with her eyes open to the result, chose by her action to renounce her derivative citizenship. Our cases have so interpreted such action for half a century. Mackenzie v. Hare, 239 U.S. 299 (1915). . . . Here appellant has been away from the country for 10 years, has married a foreign citizen, [has] borne four sons who are German nationals, and admits that she has no intention to return to this country. She wishes to retain her citizenship on a standby basis for her own benefit in the event of trouble. There is no constitutional necessity for Congress to accede to her wish."

FLEMMING v. NESTOR

363 U.S. 603, 80 S.Ct. 1367, 4 L.Ed.2d 1435 (1960).

Appeal from the United States District Court for the District of Columbia.

Mr. Justice HARLAN delivered the opinion of the Court.

From a decision of the District Court for the District of Columbia holding § 202(n) of the Social Security Act (68 Stat. 1083, as amended, 42 U.S.C. § 402(n)) unconstitutional, the Secretary of Health, Education, and Welfare takes this direct appeal pursuant to 28 U.S.C. § 1252. The challenged section . . . provides for the termination of old-age, survivor, and disability insurance benefits payable to, or in certain cases in respect of, an alien individual who, after September 1, 1954 (the date of enactment of the section), is deported under § 241(a) of the Immigration and Nationality Act (8 U.S.C. § 1251(a)) on any one of certain grounds specified in § 202(n).

Appellee, an alien, immigrated to this country from Bulgaria in 1913, and became eligible for old-age benefits in November 1955. In July 1956 he was deported pursuant to § 241(a) (6) (C) (i) of the Immigration and Nationality Act for having been a member of the Communist Party from 1933 to 1939. This being one of the benefit-termination deportation grounds specified in § 202(n), appellee's benefits were terminated soon thereafter, and notice of the termination was given to his wife, who had remained in this country. Upon his failure to obtain administrative reversal of the decision, appellee commenced this action in the District Court, pursuant to

§ 205(g) of the Social Security Act . . . to secure judicial review. On cross-motions for summary judgment, the District Court ruled for appellee, holding § 202(n) unconstitutional under the Due Process Clause of the Fifth Amendment in that it deprived appellee of an accrued property right. . . .

I.

We think that the District Court erred in holding that § 202(n) deprived appellee of an "accrued property right." 169 F.Supp., at 934. Appellee's right to Social Security benefits cannot properly be considered to have been of that order. . . .

To engraft upon the Social Security system a concept of "accrued property rights" would deprive it of the flexibility and boldness in adjustment to ever-changing conditions which it demands. . . .

II.

This is not to say, however, that Congress may exercise its power to modify the statutory scheme free of all constitutional restraint. The interest of a covered employee under the Act is of sufficient substance to fall within the protection from arbitrary governmental action afforded by the Due Process Clause. In judging the permissibility of the cut-off provisions of § 202(n) from this standpoint, it is not within our authority to determine whether the Congressional judgment expressed in that section is sound or equitable, or whether it comports well or ill with the purposes of the Act. . . . Helvering v. Davis, supra, 301 U.S. at page 644. Particularly when we deal with a withholding of a noncontractual benefit under a social welfare program such as this, we must recognize that the Due Process Clause can be thought to interpose a bar only if the statute manifests a patently arbitrary classification, utterly lacking in rational justification.

Such is not the case here. The fact of a beneficiary's residence abroad —in the case of a deportee, a presumably permanent residence—can be of obvious relevance to the question of eligibility. One benefit which may be thought to accrue to the economy from the Social Security system is the increased over-all national purchasing power resulting from taxation of productive elements of the economy to provide payments to the retired and disabled, who might otherwise be destitute or nearly so, and who would generally spend a comparatively large percentage of their benefit payments. This advantage would be lost as to payments made to one residing abroad. For these purposes, it is, of course, constitutionally irrelevant whether this reasoning in fact underlay the legislative decision, as it is irrelevant that the section does not extend to all to whom the postulated rationale might in logic apply. See . . . Steward Machine Co. v. Davis, 301 U.S. 548, 584–585 . . . . . Nor, apart from this, can it be deemed irrational for Congress to have concluded that the public purse should not be utilized to contribute to the support of those deported on the grounds specified in the statute.

We need go no further to find support for our conclusion that this provision of the Act cannot be condemned as so lacking in rational justification as to offend due process.

III.

The remaining, and most insistently pressed, constitutional objections rest upon Art. I, § 9, cl. 3, and Art. III, § 2, cl. 3, of the Constitution, and the Sixth Amendment. It is said that the termination of appellee's benefits amounts to punishing him without a judicial trial, see Wong Wing v. United States, 163 U.S. 228; that the termination of benefits constitutes the imposition of punishment by legislative act, rendering § 202(n) a bill of attainder, see United States v. Lovett, 328 U.S. 303; Cummings v. Missouri, 4 Wall. 277 [see chap. 7, p. 536, infra]; and that the punishment exacted is imposed for past conduct not unlawful when engaged in, thereby violating the constitutional prohibition on *ex post facto* laws, see Ex parte Garland, 4 Wall. 333. Essential to the success of each of these contentions is the validity of characterizing as "punishment" in the constitutional sense the termination of benefits under § 202(n).

In determining whether legislation which bases a disqualification on the happening of a certain past event imposes a punishment, the Court has sought to discern the objects on which the enactment in question was focused. Where the source of legislative concern can be thought to be the activity or status from which the individual is barred, the disqualification is not punishment even though it may bear harshly upon one affected. The contrary is the case where the statute in question is evidently aimed at the person or class of persons disqualified. . . .

Turning, then, to the particular statutory provision before us, appellee cannot successfully contend that the language and structure of § 202(n), or the nature of the deprivation, requires us to recognize a punitive design. Cf. Wong Wing v. United States, supra (imprisonment, at hard labor up to one year, of person found to be unlawfully in the country). Here the sanction is the mere denial of a noncontractual governmental benefit. No affirmative disability or restraint is imposed, and certainly nothing approaching the "infamous punishment" of imprisonment, as in Wong Wing, on which great reliance is mistakenly placed. Moreover, . . . it cannot be said, as was said of the statute in Cummings v. Missouri, supra, at 319; see Dent v. West Virginia, 129 U.S. 114, 126, that the disqualification of certain deportees from receipt of Social Security benefits while they are not lawfully in this country bears no rational connection to the purposes of the legislation of which it is a part, and must without more therefore be taken as evidencing a Congressional desire to punish. Appellee argues, however, that the history and scope of § 202(n) prove that no such postulated purpose can be thought to have motivated the legislature, and that they persuasively show that a punitive purpose in fact lay behind the statute. We do not agree.

We observe initially that only the clearest proof could suffice to establish the unconstitutionality of a statute on such a ground. Judicial inquiries into Congressional motives are at best a hazardous matter, and when that inquiry seeks to go behind objective manifestations it becomes a dubious affair indeed. Moreover, the presumption of constitutionality with which this enactment, like any other, comes to us forbids us lightly to choose that reading of the statute's setting which will invalidate it over that which will save it. "[I]t is not on sight implication and vague conjecture that the legislature is to be pronounced to have transcended its powers, and its acts to be considered as void." Fletcher v. Peck, 6 Cranch 87, 128.

Section 202(n) was enacted as a small part of an extensive revision of the Social Security program. The provision originated in the House of Representatives. . . . The discussion in the House Committee Report . . . does not express the purpose of the statute. However, it does say that the termination of benefits would apply to those persons who were "deported from the United States because of illegal entry, conviction of a crime, or subversive activity . . .." It was evidently the thought that such was the scope of the statute resulting from its application to deportation under the 14 named paragraphs of § 241(a) of the Immigration and Nationality Act. . . .[1]

Appellee argues that this history demonstrates that Congress was not concerned with the *fact* of a beneficiary's deportation—which it is claimed alone would justify this legislation as being pursuant to a policy relevant to regulation of the Social Security system—but that it sought to reach certain *grounds* for deportation, thus evidencing a punitive intent.[2] It is impossible to find in this meagre history the unmistakable evidence of punitive intent which, under principles already discussed, is required before a Congressional enactment of this kind may be struck down. Even were that history to be taken as evidencing Congress' concern with the grounds, rather than the fact, of deportation, we do not think that this, standing alone, would suffice to establish a punitive purpose. This would still be a far cry from the situations . . . where the legislation was on its face aimed at particular individuals. The legislative record, however, falls short of any persuasive showing that Congress was in fact concerned alone with the grounds of deportation. To be sure Congress did not apply the termination provision to all deportees. However, it is evident that neither did it rest the operation of the statute on the occurrence of the underlying act. The fact of deportation itself remained an essential condition for loss of benefits. . . .

Moreover, the grounds for deportation referred to in the Committee Report embrace the great majority of those deported, as is evident from an examination of the four omitted grounds, summarized in the margin.[3] In-

1. Paragraphs (1), (2) and (10) of § 241 (a) relate to unlawful entry, or entry not complying with certain conditions; paragraphs (6) and (7) apply to "subversive" and related activities; the remainder of the included paragraphs are concerned with convictions of designated crimes, or the commission of acts related to them, such as narcotics addiction or prostitution. [Footnote by the Court.]

2. . . . In addition, reliance is placed on a letter written to the Senate Finance Committee by appellant's predecessor in office, opposing the enactment of what is now § 202(u) of the Act . . . on the ground that the section was "in the nature of a penalty and based on considerations foreign to the objectives" of the program. . . . The Secretary went on to say that "present law recognizes only three narrowly limited exceptions [of which § 202(n) is one] to the basic principle

that benefits are paid without regard to the attitudes, opinions, behavior, or personal characteristics of the individual . . ." It should be observed, however, that the Secretary did not speak of § 202(n) as a penalty, as he did of the proposed § 202(u). The latter provision is concededly penal, and applies only pursuant to a judgment of a court in a criminal case. [Footnote by the Court.]

3. They are: (1) persons institutionalized at public expense within five years after entry because of "mental disease, defect, or deficiency" not shown to have arisen subsequent to admission (§ 241(a) (3)); (2) persons becoming a public charge within five years after entry from causes not shown to have arisen subsequent to admission (§ 241 (a) (8)); (3) persons admitted as nonimmigrants . . . who fail to maintain, or comply with the conditions of, such status (§ 241(a) (9)); (4) persons

ferences drawn from the omission of those grounds cannot establish, to the degree of certainty required, that Congressional concern was wholly with the acts leading to deportation, and not with the fact of deportation.[4] To hold otherwise would be to rest on the "slight implication and vague conjecture" against which Chief Justice Marshall warned. Fletcher v. Peck, supra, at 128.

The same answer must be made to arguments drawn from the failure of Congress to apply § 202(n) to beneficiaries voluntarily residing abroad. . . . Congress may have failed to consider such persons; or it may have thought their number too slight, or the permanence of their voluntary residence abroad too uncertain, to warrant application of the statute to them, with its attendant administrative problems of supervision and enforcement. Again, we cannot with confidence reject all those alternatives which imaginativeness can bring to mind, save that one which might require the invalidation of the statute.

Reversed.

Mr. Justice BLACK, dissenting.

For the reasons stated here and in the dissents of Mr. Justice Douglas and Mr. Justice Brennan I agree with the District Court that the United States is depriving appellee, Ephram Nestor, of his statutory right to old-age benefits in violation of the United States Constitution. . . . This action, it seems to me, takes Nestor's insurance without just compensation and in violation of the Due Process Clause of the Fifth Amendment. Moreover, it imposes an *ex post facto* law and bill of attainder by stamping him, without a court trial, as unworthy to receive that for which he has paid and which the Government promised to pay him. The fact that the Court is sustaining this action indicates the extent to which people are willing to go these days to overlook violations of the Constitution perpetrated against anyone who has ever even innocently belonged to the Communist Party. . . .

Mr. Justice DOUGLAS, dissenting. . . .

Congress could provide that only people resident here could get Social Security benefits. Yet both the House and the Senate rejected any residence requirements. . . . Congress concededly might amend the program to meet new conditions. But may it take away Social Security benefits from one person or from a group of persons for vindictive reasons? Could Congress on deporting an alien for having been a Communist confiscate his home, appropriate his saving accounts and thus send him out of the country penniless? I think not. Any such Act would be a bill of attainder. The difference, as I see it, between that case and this is one merely of degree. Social Security benefits, made up in part of this alien's own earnings, are taken from him because he once was a Communist.

The view that § 202(n), with which we now deal, imposes a penalty was taken by Secretary Folsom, appellant's predecessor, when opposing en-

knowingly and for gain inducing or aiding, prior to or within five years after entry, any other alien to enter or attempt to enter unlawfully (§ 241 (a) (13)). [Footnote by the Court.]

4. Were we to engage in speculation, it would not be difficult to conjecture that Congress may have been led to exclude these four grounds of deportation out of compassionate or *de minimis* considerations. [Footnote by the Court.]

largement of the category of people to be denied benefits of Social Security, e. g., those convicted of treason and sedition. . . .

The Committee Reports, though meagre, support Secretary Folsom in that characterization of § 202(n). The House Report tersely stated that termination of the benefits would apply to those persons who were deported "because of illegal entry, conviction of a crime, or subversive activity." . . . The aim and purpose are clear—to take away from a person by legislative *fiat* property which he has accumulated because he has acted in a certain way or embraced a certain ideology. That is a modern version of the bill of attainder—as plain, as direct, as effective as those which religious passions once loosened in England and which later were employed against the Tories here. I would affirm this judgment.

Mr. Justice BRENNAN, with whom The Chief Justice [WARREN] and Mr. Justice DOUGLAS join, dissenting. . . .

However, the Court cannot rest a decision that § 202(n) does not impose punishment on Congress' power to regulate immigration. It escapes the common-sense conclusion that Congress has imposed punishment by finding the requisite rational nexus to a granted power in the supposed furtherance of the Social Security program "enacted pursuant to Congress' power to 'spend money in aid of the general welfare.' " I do not understand the Court to deny that but for that connection, § 202(n) would impose punishment and offend not only the constitutional prohibition on *ex post facto* laws but also violate the constitutional guarantees against imposition of punishment without a judicial trial.

The Court's test of the constitutionality of § 202(n) is whether the legislative concern underlying the statute was to regulate "the activity or status from which the individual is barred" or whether the statute "is evidently aimed at the person or class of persons disqualified." It rejects the inference that the statute is "aimed at the person or class of persons disqualified" by relying upon the presumption of constitutionality. This presumption might be a basis for sustaining the statute if in fact there were two opposing inferences which could reasonably be drawn from the legislation, one that it imposes punishment and the other that it is purposed to further the administration of the Social Security program. The Court, however, does not limit the presumption to that use. Rather the presumption becomes a complete substitute for any supportable finding of a rational connection of § 202(n) with the Social Security program. For me it is not enough to state the test and hold that the presumption alone satisfies it. I find it necessary to examine the Act and its consequences to ascertain whether there is ground for the inference of a congressional concern with the administration of the Social Security program. . . .

The Court seems to acknowledge that the statute bears harshly upon the individual disqualified, but states that this is permissible when a statute is enacted as a regulation of the activity. But surely the harshness of consequences is itself a relevant consideration to the inquiry into the congressional purpose.[5] . . .

5. The Court, recognizing that Cummings v. Missouri, 4 Wall. 277, and Ex parte Garland, 4 Wall. 333, strongly favor the conclusion that § 202(n) was enacted with punitive intent, rejects the force of those precedents as drawing "heavily on the Court's first-hand acquaintance with the events and the

It seems to me that the statute itself shows that the sole legislative concern was with "the person or class of persons disqualified." Congress did not disqualify for benefits all beneficiaries residing abroad or even all dependents residing abroad who are aliens. If that had been the case I might agree that Congress' concern would have been with "the activity or status" and not with the "person or class of persons disqualified." The scales would then be tipped toward the conclusion that Congress desired to limit benefit payments to beneficiaries residing in the United States so that the American economy would be aided by expenditure of benefits here. Indeed a proposal along those lines was submitted to Congress in 1954, at the same time § 202 (n) was proposed, and it was rejected.

Perhaps, the Court's conclusion that regulation of "the activity or status" was the congressional concern would be a fair appraisal of the statute if Congress had terminated the benefits of all alien beneficiaries who are deported. But that is not what Congress did. Section 202(n) applies only to aliens deported on one or more of 14 of the 18 grounds for which aliens may be deported.

H.R.Rep. No. 1698, 83d Cong., 2d Sess. 25, 77, cited by the Court, describes § 202(n) as including persons who were deported "because of unlawful entry, conviction of a crime, or subversive activity." The section, in addition, covers those deported for such socially condemned acts as narcotic addiction or prostitution. The common element of the 14 grounds is that the alien has been guilty of some blameworthy conduct. In other words Congress worked its will only on aliens deported for conduct displeasing to the lawmakers.

This is plainly demonstrated by the remaining four grounds of deportation, those which do not result in the cancellation of benefits. Two of those four grounds cover persons who become public charges within five years after entry for reasons which predated the entry. A third ground covers the alien who fails to maintain his nonimmigrant status. The fourth ground reaches the alien who, prior to or within five years after entry, aids other aliens to enter the country illegally.

Those who are deported for becoming public charges clearly have not, by modern standards, engaged in conduct worthy of censure. The Government's suggestion that the reason for their exclusion from § 202(n) was an unarticulated feeling of Congress that it would be unfair to the "other country to deport such destitute persons without letting them retain their modicum of social security benefits" appears at best fanciful, especially since, by hypothesis, they are deportable because the conditions which led to their becoming public charges existed prior to entry.

The exclusion from the operation of § 202(n) of aliens deported for failure to maintain nonimmigrant status rationally can be explained, in the context of the whole statute, only as evidencing that Congress considered that

mood of the then recent Civil War, and 'the fierce passions which that struggle aroused.' " This seems to me to say that the provision of § 202(n) which cuts off benefits from aliens deported for past Communist Party membership was not enacted in a similar atmosphere. Our judicial detachment from the realities of the national scene should not carry us so far. Our memory of the emotional climate stirred by the question of communism in the early 1950's cannot be so short. [Footnote by Justice Brennan. Compare United States v. Brown, the 1965 bill of attainder decision printed in chap. 7, at p. 587, infra.]

conduct less blameworthy. Certainly the Government's suggestion that Congress may have thought it unlikely that such persons would work sufficient time in covered employment to become eligible for Social Security benefits cannot be the reason for this exclusion. For frequently the very act which eventually results in the deportation of persons on that ground is the securing of private employment. Finally, it is impossible to reconcile the continuation of benefits to aliens who are deported for aiding other aliens to enter the country illegally, except upon the ground that Congress felt that their conduct was less reprehensible. Again the Government's suggestion that the reason might be Congress' belief that these aliens would not have worked in covered employment must be rejected. Five years after entry would be ample time within which to secure employment and qualify. Moreover the same five-year limitation applies to several of the 14 grounds of deportation for which aliens are cut off from benefits and the Government's argument would apply equally to them if that in fact was the congressional reason.

This appraisal of the distinctions drawn by Congress between various kinds of conduct impels the conclusion, beyond peradventure that the distinctions can be understood only if the purpose of Congress was to strike at "the person or class of persons disqualified." The Court inveighs against invalidating a statute on "implication and vague conjecture." Rather I think the Court has strained to sustain the statute on "implication and vague conjecture," in holding that the congressional concern was "the activity or status from which the individual is barred." Today's decision sanctions the use of the spending power not to further the legitimate objectives of the Social Security program but to inflict hurt upon those who by their conduct have incurred the displeasure of Congress. . . .

Section 202(n) imposes punishment in violation of the prohibition against *ex post facto* laws and without a judicial trial. I therefore dissent.

———

THE SCOPE OF JUDICIAL INQUIRY: PURPOSE, MOTIVE, AND RATIONALITY

1. *The scope of inquiry in Flemming v. Nestor.* Does Justice Harlan's inquiry apply the standards regarding permissible conditions on governmental spending programs as discussed in the spending power cases, sec. 2 above? The limitations urged here do not stem from considerations of state autonomy. Does that alter the scope of congressional discretion as to conditions? Is the due process limitation in Part II of Justice Harlan's opinion identical with the rational relationship standard under the Necessary and Proper Clause? Is it accurate to say that neither Justice Harlan nor Justice Brennan applies a standard of judicial scrutiny of congressional choices regarding means that is identical with the standard of McCulloch and its progeny? Is it accurate to say that Justice Harlan is even more tolerant of congressional means-ends judgments than the Article I-federalism cases? And that Justice Brennan is more skeptical of legislative choices than most earlier cases? Is either deviation from the Art. I-federalism norm (toward greater judicial acquiescence or greater reexamination of legislative premises) justifiable?

2. *The legislative judgment: congressional actuality or judicial imagination?* Why is it "constitutionally irrelevant whether this reasoning in fact underlay the legislative decision," as Justice Harlan states in Part II of his

opinion? Must the Court sustain legislation if a rational argument for the condition can be imagined, whether or not that argument was in fact considered by Congress? Compare the close of the majority opinion: "Again, we cannot . . . reject all those alternatives which imaginativeness can bring to mind." Do considerations of propriety or feasibility inhibit the Court from demanding an affirmative showing that the legislative deliberations—rather than the Court's or counsel's "imaginativeness"—supply the basis for a finding of rationality? Do these considerations bar the Court from considering evidence in the legislative history that improper grounds were relied on by Congress, even if rational grounds could have been given by a hypothetical legislature? Compare the due process cases in chap. 13, infra. And consider the national power cases in earlier sections of this chapter: to what extent was the need to reach local matters as a means of regulating interstate commerce, for example, justified by arguments in fact considered by Congress, rather than by imaginative afterthoughts by counsel and Court?

3. *Purpose, motive, and the draft card burning case.* Note the discussion of "purpose" and "motive" in Part III of Justice Harlan's opinion. Does the Court disavow all inquiry into these, as it did in the Darby case, chap. 4, for example? Is it enough that a rational legislator might have had a legitimate purpose? Or is the Court willing to consider the "purpose" manifested in the legislative history? Is it possible to examine "purpose" without improper psychological inquiries into legislative "motive"? Is Justice Brennan's dissent as to purpose based on inferences from the face of the statute, inferences from the effect of the statute, evidence drawn from the record of legislative deliberation, or guesses as to hidden motives of legislators? Would clear-cut statements in the legislative record evidencing an aim to punish those deported on the specified grounds affect Part II of the Court's opinion? Part III? See "The Mysteries of Motive," in Bickel, The Least Dangerous Branch (1962), 208–221.

Compare the Court's effort to articulate the permissible extent of judicial inquiry into legislative purpose and motive in United States v. O'Brien, 391 U.S. 367 (1968). In that case the Court rejected a number of constitutional challenges to a conviction under a 1965 amendment to the draft law which prohibited knowing destruction or mutilation of draft certificates. The Court's disposition of most of the First Amendment objections is considered below (chap. 15, p. 1189). The rejection of one of defendant's claims warrants noting here: it was that the amendment was unconstitutional because the "purpose" of Congress was "to suppress freedom of speech." The Court rejected that argument "because under settled principles the purpose of Congress, as O'Brien uses that term, is not a basis for declaring this legislation unconstitutional." Chief Justice Warren's majority opinion elaborated that conclusion as follows:

"Inquiries into congressional motives or purposes are a hazardous matter. When the issue is simply the interpretation of legislation, the Court will look to statements by legislators for guidance as to the purpose of the legislature,[1]

---

1. "The Court may make the same assumption in a very limited and well-defined class of cases where the very nature of the constitutional question requires an inquiry into legislative purpose. The principal class of cases is readily apparent—those in which stat-

utes have been challenged as bills of attainder. The inquiry into whether the challenged statute contains the necessary element of punishment has on occasion led the Court to examine the legislative motive in enacting the statute. See, e. g., United States v.

because the benefit to sound decision-making in this circumstance is thought sufficient to risk the possibility of misreading Congress' purpose. It is entirely a different matter when we are asked to void a statute that is, under well-settled criteria, constitutional on its face, on the basis of what fewer than a handful of Congressmen said about it. What motivates one legislator to make a speech about a statute is not necessarily what motivates scores of others to enact it, and the stakes are sufficiently high for us to eschew guesswork. We decline to void essentially on the ground that it is unwise [to void] legislation which Congress had the undoubted power to enact and which could be reenacted in its exact form if the same or another legislator made a 'wiser' speech about it.

"O'Brien's position . . . rests upon a misunderstanding of Grosjean v. American Press Co., 297 U.S. 233 (1936), and Gomillion v. Lightfoot, 364 U.S. 339 (1960). These cases stand not for the proposition that legislative motive is a proper basis for declaring a statute unconstitutional, but that the inevitable effect of a statute on its face may render it unconstitutional. In these cases, the purpose of the legislation was irrelevant, because the inevitable effect—the 'necessary scope and operations,' McCray v. United States, 195 U.S. 27, 59 (1904)—abridged constitutional rights. The statute attacked in the instant case has no such inevitable unconstitutional effect, since the destruction of Selective Service certificates is in no respect inevitably or necessarily expressive. Accordingly, the statute itself is constitutional.

"We think it not amiss, in passing, to comment upon O'Brien's legislative purpose argument. . . . It is principally on the basis of statements by . . . three Congressmen that O'Brien makes his congressional 'purpose' argument. We note that if we were to examine legislative purpose in the instant case, we would be obliged to consider not only these statements but also the more authoritative reports of the Senate and House Armed Services Committees. . . . While both reports make clear a concern with the 'defiant' destruction of so-called 'draft cards' and with 'open' encouragement to others to destroy their cards, both reports also indicate that this concern stemmed from an apprehension that unrestrained destruction of cards would disrupt the smooth functioning of the Selective Service System."

Was this adequate as a description of judicial practice? Was this persuasive as a statement of the proper scope of judicial scrutiny? Is greater Court examination of actual legislative purpose possible? Wise? Do (and should) the answers depend on the constitutional provision invoked?

Lovett, 328 U.S. 303 (1946). Two other decisions not involving a bill of attainder analysis contain an inquiry into legislative purpose or motive of the type that O'Brien suggests we engage in in this case. Kennedy v. Mendoza-Martinez, 372 U.S. 144, 169–184 (1963); Trop v. Dulles, 356 U.S. 86, 95–97 (1958). The inquiry into legislative purpose or motive in Kennedy and Trop, however, was for the same limited purpose as in the bill of attainder decisions—i. e., to determine whether the statutes under review were punitive in nature. We face no such inquiry in this case. The 1965 Amendment to § 462(b) was clearly penal in nature, designed to impose criminal punishment on designated acts." [Footnote by the Court.]

Chapter 6

CONGRESSIONAL PROTECTION OF CIVIL RIGHTS: "APPROPRIATE LEGISLATION" UNDER THE POST–CIVIL WAR AMENDMENTS

AN INTRODUCTORY OVERVIEW

Each of the three post-Civil War Amendments grants Congress authority to protect civil rights: the final sections of the 13th, 14th, and 15th Amendments give "power to enforce" each Amendment "by appropriate legislation." These are not the only sources of congressional power to enact civil rights laws: the commerce power as well as other grants in the 1787 document have been invoked on behalf of civil rights. (See, e. g., chap. 4, p. 324, supra). But the post-Civil War additions, unlike the original grants, were born of a special concern with racial discrimination; and the civil rights powers they confer are potentially the most far-reaching.

Attention to powers of such focus and scope is warranted here in order to complete the examination of the important congressional powers in the context of federal system. And the recent renaissance of congressional reliance on these powers makes it especially inappropriate to follow the traditional casebook pattern of leaving all consideration of these issues to the concluding, "individual rights" chapters.

Consideration of these congressional powers against a background of Article I powers and the Necessary and Proper Clause is of special value and interest because the post-Civil War Amendments have evoked a pattern of institutional interactions unlike any under the Article I powers. Congressional action stimulated Court responses which helped inhibit further legislative enforcement; subsequent Court elaborations of the self-executing aspects of the Amendments in turn influenced a new cycle of congressional action. Congressional action came only at the very beginning and very recently; for the near-century intervening, the Amendments were effectively in the Court's sole keeping. After a series of Civil Rights laws during Reconstruction, between 1866 and 1875 (many of which foundered in the courts), there was no further significant legislative action until 1957. In the interval, decisions about the Amendments consisted mainly of judicial delineations of their self-executing aspects. But the modern laws have provoked new, broader Court statements of congressional powers.

That historical sequence of Court-Congress interactions produced the institutional collaborations and tensions pursued in this chapter. How far-reaching is the power to enact "appropriate legislation" under the Amendments? Is congressional discretion to be interpreted in the same manner here as under Art. I, Sec. 8, powers? Do the Court interpretations of the self-executing impacts of the Amendments mark the outermost limits of the congressional power? Or may Congress extend the scope and content of the Amendment beyond the boundaries set in prior Court interpretations?

Two specific problems are examined here to focus on these questions. The first is that of congressional power to expand the scope of the Amendments, to reach private as well as state action; that inquiry culminates in the Guest case (sec. 3, p. 545, infra). The second is the problem of congressional power to alter the substantive content of the Amendments, to add rights beyond those found to exist through judicial interpretation; that inquiry culminates in the Morgan case (sec. 4, p. 505, infra). To lay the groundwork for these inquiries, some examination of the Court's independent elaborations of the Amendments (sec. 2, infra) is necessary.

The prohibitions of § 1 of the 14th Amendment begin with "No State shall"; that Amendment (like the 15th but unlike the 13th) has traditionally been interpreted to reach only "state action" and not wholly private acts. Most of these "state action" interpretations have come in cases involving only the impact of § 1 of the Amendment operating of its own force, without legislative implementation. To what extent may Congress extend that scope? May Congress under § 5 reach private individuals in order to "enforce" rights "by appropriate legislation"? That is the problem of the Guest case.

To provide the statutory background, sec. 1 of this chapter examines the post-Civil War laws and their modern counterparts (which were the bases of the criminal prosecutions in Guest). Sec. 2 examines the evolution of the "state action" concept in the Court's hands: sec. 2A contains the restrictive readings that blocked some of the legislation in the 19th century; sec. 2B considers the amorphously expanding modern readings, in cases involving the scope of the 14th Amendment when it operates of its own force. These materials set the stage for the examination, in sec. 3, of the modern efforts to apply the remnants of the post-Civil War laws to private action, especially in Guest. That section concludes with the late sixties' varieties of congressional action (prompted in part by suggestions in opinions in Guest), and with the rediscovery in the Jones case (p. 517) of the 13th Amendment (which is not saddled with the state action limitation) as a source of congressional power over private conduct.

Section 4, finally, focuses on the question of congressional power to add new "rights" to those previously unearthed by the Court in the opening sections of the Amendments. The context selected for that study is the Voting Rights Act of 1965, which goes beyond prior, Court-imposed restrictions on voting discrimination in several respects. Morgan (p. 545) is the central case: it permits Congress to abolish a voting qualification pursuant to § 5 of the 14th Amendment even though the Court had not found the restriction invalid under § 1. That reading of congressional power (to participate via § 5 in giving content to 14th Amendment rights) has a counterpart in an aspect of Jones, permitting Congress in effect to delineate the content of 13th Amendment rights. These broad uses of the enforcement sections of the Amendments are potentially even more far-reaching than the authority sustained in the Guest case; powers of such range are an essential ingredient and an appropriate close of this study of congressional powers in the federal system.*

---

* Examining congressional elaboration of the Amendments before fully exploring all of the judicial interpretations (the focus of Part III of this book) is not without difficulties. But the problems selected for this chapter stand on their own; they permit analysis without the background of Part III. If prior examination of other individual rights materials is desired, however, consideration of this chapter can readily be deferred, to be taken up, most feasibly, after chaps. 14 and 18.

SECTION 1. THE LEGISLATIVE FRAMEWORK

THE LAWS OF THE RECONSTRUCTION ERA

Introduction: The historical background and the Slaughter-House cases. There was an intimate interrelationship between the emancipation aspect of the Civil War, the adoption of the 13th, 14th, and 15th Amendments, and the enactment of the Civil Rights Acts of 1866, 1870, 1871, and 1875. The central purpose of the Amendments was articulated in the course of the Court's first encounter with them, in 1873. Justice Miller's majority opinion in the Slaughter-House Cases, 16 Wall. 36 (chap. 11, p. 787, infra), stated:

"The most cursory glance at these [three amendments] discloses a unity of purpose, when taken in connection with the history of the times, which cannot fail to have an important bearing on any question of doubt concerning their true meaning. Nor can such doubts, when any reasonably exist, be safely and rationally solved without a reference to that history . . . . Fortunately that history is fresh within the memory of us all . . . . [Whatever] auxiliary causes may have contributed to bring about [the "war of the rebellion"], undoubtedly the overshadowing and efficient cause was African slavery. In that struggle slavery, as a legalized social relation, perished. . . . The proclamation of President Lincoln expressed an accomplished fact as to a large portion of the insurrectionary districts, when he declared slavery abolished in them all. But the war being over, those who had succeeded in re-establishing the authority of the Federal government were not content to permit this great act of emancipation to rest on the actual results of the contest or the proclamation of the Executive, both of which might have been questioned in after times, and they determined to place this main and most valuable result in the Constitution of the restored Union as one of its fundamental articles. Hence the thirteenth article of amendment of that instrument. . . .

"The process of restoring to their proper relations with the Federal government and with the other States those which had sided with the rebellion . . . developed the fact that, notwithstanding the formal recognition by those States of the abolition of slavery, the condition of the slave race would, without further protection of the Federal government, be almost as bad as it was before. Among the first acts of legislation adopted by several of the States . . . were laws which imposed upon the colored race onerous disabilities and burdens, and curtailed their rights in the pursuit of life, liberty, and property to such an extent that their freedom was of little value, while they had lost the protection which they had received from their former owners from motives both of interest and humanity.

"They were in some States forbidden to appear in the towns in any other character than menial servants. They were required to reside on and cultivate the soil without the right to purchase or own it. They were excluded from many occupations of gain, and were not permitted to give testimony in the courts in any case where a white man was a party. It was said that their lives were at the mercy of bad men, either because the laws for their protection were insufficient or were not enforced.

"These circumstances, whatever of falsehood or misconception may have been mingled with their presentation, forced upon [statesmen] the conviction that something more was necessary in the way of constitutional protection to the unfortunate race who had suffered so much. They accordingly passed through Congress the proposition for the fourteenth amendment, and they declined to treat as restored to their full participation in the government of the Union the States which had been in insurrection, until they ratified that article by a formal vote of their legislative bodies.

". . . A few years' experience satisfied the thoughtful men who had been the authors of the other two amendments that . . . these were inadequate for the protection of life, liberty, and property, without which freedom to the slave was no boon. They were in all those States denied the right of suffrage. . . . Hence the fifteenth amendment . . . . The negro having, by the fourteenth amendment, been declared to be a citizen of the United States, is thus made a voter in every State of the Union.

"We repeat, then, in the light of this recapitulation of events, almost too recent to be called history, but which are familiar to us all; and on the most casual examination of the language of these amendments, no one can fail to be impressed with the one pervading purpose found in them all, lying at the foundation of each, and without which none of them would have been even suggested; we mean the freedom of the slave race, the security and firm establishment of that freedom, and the protection of the newly-made freeman and citizen from the oppressions of those who had formerly exercised unlimited dominion over him. It is true that only the fifteenth amendment, in terms, mentions the negro by speaking of his color and his slavery. But it is just as true that each of the other articles was addressed to the grievances of that race, and designed to remedy them as the fifteenth."

1. _The 1866 Act_. The 13th Amendment, in 1865, gave constitutional support to the wartime Emancipation Proclamation, as Justice Miller's review notes. Congress considered additional protection of the newly freed Negro necessary, however—especially in view of the "black codes" enacted in several states, imposing severe legal restrictions just short of formal slavery. The Civil Rights Act of 1866, 14 Stat. 27, sought to end these restrictions. Section 1 stated that all persons born in the United States were "citizens of the United States" and proceeded to list certain rights of "such citizens, of every race and color, without regard to any previous condition of slavery": they were to "have the same right . . . to make and enforce contracts, to sue, be parties, and give evidence, to inherit, purchase, lease, sell, hold, and convey real and personal property, and to full and equal benefit of all laws . . . for the security of persons and property, as is enjoyed by white citizens, and shall be subject to like punishment . . ., and to none other, any law, statute, ordinance, regulation, or custom, to the contrary notwithstanding." [See the modern counterparts, 42 U.S.C. §§ 1981, 1982. § 1982 was the basis for the Jones decision, p. 517 infra.]

The "declaration" of rights in Section 1 was followed by a criminal enforcement provision, Section 2: "That any person who, under color of any law, statute, ordinance, regulation or custom, shall subject or cause to be subjected any inhabitant of any State or Territory to the deprivation of any right secured or protected by this act, or to different punishment . . . on account of [former slavery] or by reason of his color or race, that is prescribed for punishment of white persons, shall be deemed guilty of a misdemeanor."

The punishment provided was a maximum fine of $1000, a one year sentence, or both. [For the current version of this provision, see 18 U.S.C. § 242, infra, considered in a companion case to Guest, the Price case, p. 504, among others.]

During the debates on the 1866 Act, constitutional doubts were raised about the adequacy of the 13th Amendment to support the constitutionality of the law. The doubts were reflected in President Johnson's veto: "[W]here can we find a Federal prohibition against the power of any State to discriminate . . . ?" Congress overrode the veto, but the amendment machinery was immediately put in motion, and the 14th Amendment—designed at least in part to validate the 1866 Act—was ratified in 1868.

2. *The 1870 Act.* In 1870, the 15th Amendment was ratified. It prohibited denial of the franchise "on account of race, color, or previous condition of servitude"; unlike the 14th Amendment, it spoke explicitly about the race-slavery problem which provoked all of the post-Civil War Amendments. Congress promptly passed enforcement legislation. The 1870 Enforcement Act, 16 Stat. 140, dealt primarily with denials of voting rights. [The development of voting rights laws is traced in sec. 4, infra.] Section 6, however, contained broader terms: it made it a felony "if two or more persons shall band or conspire together, or go in disguise upon the public highway, or upon the premises of another, with intent to violate any provision of this act, or to injure, oppress, threaten or intimidate any citizen with intent to prevent or hinder his free exercise and enjoyment of any right or privilege granted or secured to him by the Constitution or laws of the United States, or because of his having exercised the same." [For the current version of this provision, see 18 U.S.C. § 241, infra. It was the basis for the indictment in the Guest case, infra, p. 505].

3. *The 1871 and 1875 Acts.* In 1871, Congress not only made amendments (16 Stat. 433) to the 1870 law, but enacted a new law, the Civil Rights Act of 1871, 17 Stat. 13. The 1871 Act "to enforce . . . the Fourteenth Amendment," known as the Ku Klux Klan Act, was "among the last of the reconstruction legislation to be based on the 'conquered province' theory which prevailed in Congress for a period following the Civil War. This statute [established] civil liabilities, together with parallel criminal liabilities." Collins v. Hardyman, 341 U.S. 651, 656 (1951) (p. 499 infra). The substance of these civil provisions has been preserved; they now appear in 42 U.S.C. § 1983 and 28 U.S.C. § 1343(3), infra, creating a cause of action and conferring federal jurisdiction for civil actions for deprivations, under color of state law, of rights secured by the Constitution and federal laws.* The Civil Rights Act of 1875, 18 Stat. 335, contained, inter alia, "public accommodations" provisions. These and other sections of the 1875 Act are discussed in the opinions in the 1883 Civil Rights Cases (p. 454 infra), holding the provisions unconstitutional

---

* Another provision of the 1871 Act, subsequently repealed, dealt with private criminal conspiracies directed against government operations or intended to deprive persons of the equal protection of laws. The latter provision was found beyond the reach of the 14th Amendment in United States v. Harris, 106 U.S. 629 (1882).

For a useful brief review of the post-Civil War laws, and their fate, see Gressman, "The Unhappy History of Civil Rights Legislation," 50 Mich.L. Rev. 1323 (1952). See also Carr, Federal Protection of Civil Rights (1947).

THE SURVIVING REMNANTS OF THE POST–CIVIL WAR LAWS: THE MODERN COUNTERPARTS

1. Criminal provisions:

18 U.S.C. § 241.[1] *"Conspiracy against rights of citizens.* If two or more persons conspire to injure, oppress, threaten, or intimidate any citizen in the free exercise or enjoyment of any right or privilege secured to him by the Constitution or laws of the United States, or because of his having so exercised the same; or

"If two or more persons go in disguise on the highway, or on the premises of another, with intent to prevent or hinder his free exercise or enjoyment of any right or privilege so secured—

"They shall be fined not more than $10,000 or imprisoned not more than ten years, or both; and if death results, they shall be subject to imprisonment for any term of years or for life."

18 U.S.C. § 242.[2] *"Deprivation of rights under color of law.* Whoever, under color of any law, statute, ordinance, regulation, or custom, willfully subjects any inhabitant of any State, Territory, or District to the deprivation of any rights, privileges, or immunities secured or protected by the Constitution or laws of the United States, or to different punishments, pains, or penalties, on account of such inhabitant being an alien, or by reason of his color, or race, than are prescribed for the punishment of citizens, shall be fined not more than $1,000 or imprisoned not more than one year, or both; and if death results shall be subject to imprisonment for any term of years or for life."

2. Civil provisions:

42 U.S.C. § 1981.[3] *"Equal rights under the law.* All persons within the jurisdiction of the United States shall have the same right in every State and Territory to make and enforce contracts, to sue, be parties, give evidence, and to the full and equal benefit of all laws and proceedings for the security of persons and property as is enjoyed by white citizens, and shall be subject to like punishment, pains, penalties, taxes, licenses, and exactions of every kind, and to no other."

42 U.S.C. § 1982.[4] *"Property rights of citizens.* All citizens of the United States shall have the same right, in every State and Territory, as is en-

---

1. Derived from Section 6 of the 1870 Act, supra. Before being designated 18 U.S.C. § 241, it was § 5508 of Rev. Stats., 1874–78; § 19 of the Criminal Code of 1909; and § 51 of the 1946 edition of 18 U.S.C. It is referred to by the earlier designations in some of the cases below. The concluding portions of the penalty provisions in §§ 241 and 242 were added by the 1968 Civil Rights Act. For a modern application of § 241, see the Price case, p. 504, infra.

2. Derived from Section 2 of the 1866 Act, supra, as amended by § 17 of the 1870 Act. The section was § 5510 of Rev.Stats., 1874–78; § 20 of the 1909 Criminal Code; and § 52 of the 1946 edition of 18 U.S.C. The section is discussed and applied in the Guest case, p. 505, infra.

That case helped provoke the first criminal law to protect civil rights that departed from the post-Civil War models. See the new 18 U.S.C. § 245, "Federally protected activities," added by Title I of the Civil Rights Act of 1968. Excerpts are printed below, after the Guest case, at p. 505.

3. Derived from the 1866 and 1870 Acts. It was § 1977 of Rev.Stats., 1874–78.

4. Derived from the 1866 Act. It was § 1978 of Rev.Stats., 1874–78. This

"color of law" = the appearance or semblance w/o
the substance, of legal st.

Sec. 1   CONGRESSIONAL PROTECTION   453

joyed by white citizens thereof to inherit, purchase, lease, sell, hold, and convey real and personal property."

42 U.S.C. § 1983.[5] *"Civil action for deprivation of rights.* Every person who, under color of any statute, ordinance, regulation, custom, or usage, of any State or Territory, subjects, or causes to be subjected, any citizen of the United States or other persons within the jurisdiction thereof to the deprivation of any rights, privileges or immunities secured by the Constitution and laws, shall be liable to the person injured in an action of law, suit in equity, or other proper proceedings for redress."[6]

28 U.S.C. § 1343.[7] *"Civil rights and elective franchise.* The district courts shall have original jurisdiction of any civil action authorized by law to be commenced by any person . . ..

"(3) to redress the deprivation, under color of any State law, ordinance, regulation, custom or usage, of any right, privilege or immunity secured by the Constitution of the United States or by any Act of Congress providing for equal rights of citizens or of all persons within the jurisdiction of the United States . . .."[8]

CIVIL RIGHTS LEGISLATION SINCE 1957

The modern revival of congressional civil rights activity began with the Civil Rights Act of 1957; that law, like the Civil Rights Act of 1960, was primarily designed to improve remedies against racial discrimination in voting. Voting laws, including the 1965 Act, are considered further in sec. 4, infra. The 1960 Act also included a criminal prohibition of interstate travel to avoid state prosecution for "damaging or destroying by fire or explosive" any structure, including schools and churches. See 18 U.S.C. § 1074. Another provision, 18 U.S.C. § 837(b), prohibited interstate transportation of explosives with knowledge that they will be used to damage certain buildings.

The 1957 Act also established the Civil Rights Commission, whose studies have been important in the consideration of subsequent legislation, as well as in litigation. Title V of the 1964 Act expanded the duties and dealt with the procedures of the Civil Rights Commission. Those titles

section was found to have a broad sweep and a solid constitutional base in the Jones case, Jones v. Alfred H. Mayer Co., 392 U.S. 409 (1968) (p. 517, infra).

5. Derived from Section 1 of the Civil Rights Act of 1871, Rev.Stats. § 1979 (1875). See the discussion in Monroe v. Pape, p. 501, infra.

6. Note also the following, less frequently litigated provisions of 42 U.S.C. § 1985 (derived from the 1871 Act) (civil damages recovery for conspiracy, inter alia, to deprive persons of equal protection of laws or to prevent state authorities from giving equal protection); § 1986 (derived from the 1871 Act) (neglecting to prevent acts wrongful under § 1985). See also the anti-peonage

law of 1867, now 42 U.S.C. § 1994, with a criminal provision in 18 U.S.C. § 1581. The provisions specifically dealing with voting are considered in sec. 4, infra.

7. Derived from Civil Rights Act of 1871, Rev.Stats. § 628 (1875).

8. See also § 1343(1) and (2) (damages for violations of 42 U.S.C. §§ 1985 and 1986, footnote 6, supra). Moreover, an increasingly important provision, 28 U.S.C. § 1443, authorizes defendants to remove certain civil rights cases from state to federal courts. See the consideration of this provision and other sources of federal jurisdiction in civil rights litigation in chap. 2 supra, at p. 173.

of the 1964 Act based primarily on Art. I powers of Congress have been
described elsewhere.   (See, e.g., the Public Accommodations Title, based
mainly on the commerce clause, chap. 4, p. 325.)   In addition, the 1964
Act included several provisions more directly rooted in the post-Civil War
Amendments: Titles I and VIII contained new voting rights provisions;
Titles III and IV dealt with desegregation of schools and other public
facilities; Title X established a Community Relations Service; and Title IX
authorized United States intervention in suits claiming denial of equal
protection and made reviewable remand orders in cases removed under
28 U.S.C. § 1443.

After the adoption of the 1965 Voting Rights Act (sec. 4 infra),
Johnson Administration proposals for omnibus civil rights laws were
repeatedly blocked in the Senate.   In 1968, however—after the assassination of Dr. Martin Luther King—a new Civil Rights Act was adopted.
The provisions of the 1968 Act of special concern in this chapter are the
elaborate additions to federal criminal laws dealing with civil rights violence, especially the new 18 U.S.C. § 245 (p. 516, infra).   See also p.
525, infra, on Title VIII, the fair housing law.   The 1968 Act also contained extensive provisions on Indian rights (Titles II–VII), a "Civil
Obedience Act of 1968" (Title X), and provisions on rioting (Sec. 104 of
Title I).

SECTION 2.   THE PROBLEM OF STATE ACTION *

A.   STATE ACTION IN THE 19TH CENTURY: THE COLLAPSE
OF EARLY CONGRESSIONAL EFFORTS TO
REACH PRIVATE CONDUCT

CIVIL RIGHTS CASES

109 U.S. 3, 3 S.Ct. 18, 27 L.Ed. 835 (1883).

On certificates of division from and writs of error to various Circuit
Courts of the United States.

* The literature on this problem is extensive.   See generally Lewis, "The
Meaning of State Action," 60 Colum.
L.Rev. 1083 (1960), Selected Essays
1938–62 (1963), 915.   Compare Wechs-
ler, "Toward Neutral Principles of
Constitutional Law," 73 Harv.L.Rev.
1 (1959), Selected Essays 1938–62
(1963), 463, with Pollak, "Racial Discrimination and Judicial Integrity: A
Reply to Professor Wechsler," 108 U.
Pa.L.Rev. 1 (1959), Selected Essays
1938–62 (1963), 819.   See also, e. g.,
Williams, "The Twilight of State Action," 41 Texas L.Rev. 347 (1963); Van
Alstyne and Karst, "State Action," 14
Stan.L.Rev. 3 (1961); Horowitz, "The
Misleading Search for 'State Action'
Under the Fourteenth Amendment,"
30 So.Cal.L.Rev. 208 (1957); and Henkin, "Shelley v. Kraemer: Notes for a
Revised Opinion," 110 U.Pa.L.Rev. 473
(1962).   For a critical review of the
literature as well as of the entire state
action concept (urging that it go into
"honored retirement as an innocuous
truism"), see C. L. Black, Jr., "Foreword: 'State Action,' Equal Protection,
and California's Proposition 14," 81
Harv.L.Rev. 69 (1967).

Mr. Justice BRADLEY delivered the opinion of the Court.

These cases were all founded on the first and second sections of . . . the Civil Rights Act, passed March 1st, 1875, entitled "An Act . . . to protect all citizens in their civil and legal rights." Two of the cases [are] indictments for denying to persons of color the accommodations and privileges of an inn or hotel; two of them . . . for denying to individuals the privileges and accommodations of a theatre . . . . The case of Robinson and wife against the Memphis & Charleston R. R. Company was an action . . . to recover the penalty of five hundred dollars given by the second section of the act; and the gravamen was the refusal by the conductor of the railroad company to allow the wife to ride in the ladies' car [because] she was a person of African descent. . . .

It is obvious that the primary and important question in all the cases is the constitutionality of the law. [It provides:] *ISSUE*

"Sec. 1. That all persons within the jurisdiction of the United States shall be entitled to the full and equal enjoyment of the accommodations, advantages, facilities, and privileges of inns, public conveyances on land or water, theatres, and other places of public amusement; subject only to the conditions and limitations established by law, and applicable alike to citizens of every race and color, regardless of any previous condition of servitude.

"Sec. 2. That any person who shall violate the foregoing section . . . shall for every such offence forfeit and pay the sum of five hundred dollars to the person aggrieved thereby [and] be deemed guilty of a misdemeanor, and, upon conviction thereof, shall be fined not less than five hundred nor more than one thousand dollars, or shall be imprisoned not less than thirty days nor more than one year . . . ."

Has Congress constitutional power to make such a law? Of course, no one will contend that the power to pass it was contained in the Constitution before the adoption of the last three amendments. The power is sought, first, in the Fourteenth Amendment, and the views and arguments of distinguished Senators, advanced whilst the law was under consideration, claiming authority to pass it by virtue of that amendment, are the principal arguments adduced in favor of the power. . . .

The first section of the Fourteenth Amendment . . . is prohibitory in its character, and prohibitory upon the States. It declares that: "No State shall make or enforce any law which shall abridge the privileges or immunities of citizens of the United States; nor shall any State deprive any person of life, liberty, or property without due process of law; nor deny to any person within its jurisdiction the equal protection of the laws."

It is State action of a particular character that is prohibited. Individual *State action* invasion of individual rights is not the subject-matter of the amendment. *argument* It has a deeper and broader scope. It nullifies and makes void all State legislation, and State action of every kind, which impairs the privileges and immunities of citizens of the United States, or which injures them in life, liberty or property without due process of law, or which denies to any of them the equal protection of the laws. It not only does this, but, in order that the national will, thus declared, may not be a mere *brutum fulmen*, the *empty threat* last section of the amendments invests Congress with power to enforce it by appropriate legislation. To enforce what? To enforce the prohibition. To adopt appropriate legislation for correcting the effects of such prohibited

State laws and State acts, and thus to render them effectually null, void, and innocuous. This is the legislative power conferred upon Congress, and this is the whole of it. It does not invest Congress with power to legislate upon subjects which are within the domain of State legislation; but to provide modes of relief against State legislation, or State action, of the kind referred to. It does not authorize Congress to create a code of municipal law for the regulation of private rights, but to provide modes of redress against the operation of State laws, and the action of State officers executive or judicial, when these are subversive of the fundamental rights specified in the amendment. . . . A quite full discussion of this aspect of the amendment may be found in United States v. Cruikshank, 92 U.S. 542 [p. 463, infra].

. . . In fine, the legislation which Congress is authorized to adopt in this behalf is not general legislation upon the rights of the citizen, but corrective legislation, that is, such as may be necessary and proper for counteracting such laws as the States may adopt or enforce, and which, by the amendment, they are prohibited from making or enforcing, or such acts and proceedings as the States may commit or take, and which, by the amendment, they are prohibited from committing or taking. It is not necessary for us to state, if we could, what legislation would be proper for Congress to adopt. It is sufficient for us to examine whether the law in question is of that character.

An inspection of the law shows that it makes no reference whatever to any supposed or apprehended violation of the Fourteenth Amendment on the part of the States. It is not predicated on any such view. It proceeds *ex directo* to declare that certain acts committed by individuals shall be deemed offences, and shall be prosecuted and punished by proceedings in the courts of the United States. It does not profess to be corrective of any constitutional wrong committed by the States; it does not make its operation to depend upon any such wrong committed. It applies equally to cases arising in States which have the justest laws respecting the personal rights of citizens, and whose authorities are ever ready to enforce such laws, as to those which arise in States that may have violated the prohibition of the amendment. In other words, it steps into the domain of local jurisprudence, and lays down rules for the conduct of individuals in society towards each other, and imposes sanctions for the enforcement of those rules, without referring in any manner to any supposed action of the State or its authorities.

If this legislation is appropriate for enforcing the prohibitions of the amendment, it is difficult to see where it is to stop. Why may not Congress with equal show of authority enact a code of laws for the enforcement and vindication of all rights of life, liberty, and property? If it is supposable that the States may deprive persons of life, liberty, and property without due process of law (and the amendment itself does suppose this), why should not Congress proceed at once to prescribe due process of law for the protection of every one of these fundamental rights, in every possible case, as well as to prescribe equal privileges in inns, public conveyances, and theatres? . . .

We have not overlooked the fact that the fourth section of the act now under consideration has been held by this court to be constitutional. That section declares "that no citizen, possessing all other qualifications which are or may be prescribed by law, shall be disqualified for service as grand or petit juror in any court of the United States, or of any State, on account of race, color, or previous condition of servitude; and any officer or other person charged with any duty in the selection or summoning of jurors who shall exclude or fail to summon any citizen for the cause aforesaid, shall, on conviction thereof, be deemed guilty of a misdemeanor, and be fined not more than five thousand dollars." In Ex parte Virginia, 100 U.S. 339 [1880], it was held that an indictment against a State officer under this section for excluding persons of color from the jury list is sustainable. But a moment's attention to its terms will show that the section is entirely corrective in its character. Disqualifications for service on juries are only created by the law, and the first part of the section is aimed at certain disqualifying laws, namely, those which make mere race or color a disqualification; and the second clause is directed against those who, assuming to use the authority of the State government, carry into effect such a rule of disqualification. In the Virginia case, the State, through its officer, enforced a rule of disqualification which the law was intended to abrogate and counteract. Whether the statute book of the State actually laid down any such rule of disqualification, or not, the State, through its officer, enforced such a rule: and it is against such State action, through its officers and agents, that the last clause of the section is directed. . . .

[C]ivil rights, such as are guaranteed by the Constitution against State aggression, cannot be impaired by the wrongful acts of individuals, unsupported by State authority in the shape of laws, customs, or judicial or executive proceedings. The wrongful act of an individual, unsupported by any such authority, is simply a private wrong, or a crime of that individual; an invasion of the rights of the injured party, it is true, whether they affect his person, his property, or his reputation; but if not sanctioned in some way by the State, or not done under State authority, his rights remain in full force, and may presumably be vindicated by resort to the laws of the State for redress. An individual cannot deprive a man of his right to vote, to hold property, to buy and sell, to sue in the courts, or to be a witness or a juror; he may, by force or fraud, interfere with the enjoyment of the right in a particular case; he may commit an assault against the person, or commit murder, or use ruffian violence at the polls, or slander the good name of a fellow citizen; but, unless protected in these wrongful acts by some shield of State law or State authority, he cannot destroy or injure the right; he will only render himself amenable to satisfaction or punishment; and amenable therefor to the laws of the State where the wrongful acts are committed. . . .

Of course, these remarks do not apply to those cases in which Congress is clothed with direct and plenary powers of legislation over the whole subject, accompanied with an express or implied denial of such power to the States, as in the regulation of commerce . . ., the coining of money, the establishment of post offices and post roads, the declaring of war, etc. In these cases Congress has power to pass laws for regulating the subjects specified in every detail, and the conduct and transactions of individuals in respect thereof. . . . If the principles of interpretation which we have laid down are correct, as we deem them to be (and they are in accord with the principles laid down in the cases before referred to, as well as in the recent case of United States v. Harris, 106 U.S. 629) [p. 464, infra], it is clear that the law in question cannot be sustained by any grant of legislative power made to Congress by the Fourteenth Amendment. . . . This is not corrective legislation; it is primary and direct. [W]hether Congress, in the exercise of its power to regulate commerce amongst the several States, might or might not pass a law regulating rights in public conveyances passing from one State to another, [is] a question which is not now before us, as the sections in question are not conceived in any such view.

But the power . . . is sought, in the second place, from the Thirteenth Amendment, which . . . declares "that neither slavery, nor involuntary servitude, except as a punishment for crime, whereof the party shall have been duly convicted, shall exist within the United States, or any place subject to their jurisdiction;" and it gives Congress power to enforce the amendment by appropriate legislation. [S]uch legislation may be primary and direct in its character; for the amendment is not a mere prohibition of State laws establishing or upholding slavery, but an absolute declaration that slavery or involuntary servitude shall not exist in any part of the United States.

It is true, that slavery cannot exist without law, any more than property in lands and goods can exist without law. [I]t is assumed, that the power vested in Congress to enforce the article by appropriate legislation, clothes Congress with power to pass all laws necessary and proper for abolishing all badges and incidents of slavery in the United States: and upon this assumption it is claimed, that this is sufficient authority for declaring by law that all persons shall have equal accommodations and privileges in all inns, public conveyances, and places of amusement; the argument being, that the denial of such equal accommodations and privileges is, in itself, a subjection to a species of servitude within the meaning of the amendment. . . .

. . . Congress, as we have seen, by the Civil Rights Bill of 1866, passed in view of the Thirteenth Amendment, before the Fourteenth was adopted, undertook to wipe out these burdens and disabilities, the necessary incidents of slavery, constituting its substance and visible form. [See the Jones case, p. 517, infra]. Whether this legislation was fully authorized by the Thirteenth Amendment alone, without the support which it afterward received from the Fourteenth Amendment, after the adoption of which it was re-enacted with some additions, it is not necessary to inquire. It is referred to for the purpose of showing that at that time (in 1866) Congress did not assume, under the authority given by the Thirteenth Amendment, to adjust what may be called the social rights of men and races in the community; but only to declare and vindicate those fundamental rights which appertain to the essence of citizenship, and the enjoyment or deprivation of which constitutes the essential distinction between freedom and slavery.

The only question under the present head . . . is, whether the refusal to any persons of the accommodations of an inn, or a public conveyance, or a place of public amusement, by an individual, and without any sanction or support from any State law or regulation, does inflict upon such persons any manner of servitude, or form of slavery, as those terms are understood in this country? Many wrongs may be obnoxious to the prohibitions of the Fourteenth Amendment which are not, in any just sense, incidents or elements of slavery. Such, for example, would be the taking of private property without due process of law; or allowing persons who have committed certain crimes (horse stealing, for example) to be seized and hung by the *posse comitatus* without regular trial . . . . Can the act of a mere individual, . . . refusing the accommodation, be justly regarded as imposing any badge of slavery or servitude upon the applicant, or only as inflicting an ordinary civil injury, properly cognizable by the laws of the State, and presumably subject to redress by those laws until the contrary appears?

[W]e are forced to the conclusion that such an act of refusal has nothing to do with slavery or involuntary servitude, and that if it is violative of any right of the party, his redress is to be sought under the laws of the State; or if those laws are adverse to his rights and do not protect him, his remedy will be found in the corrective legislation which Congress has adopted, or may adopt, for counteracting the effect of State laws, or State action, prohibited by the Fourteenth Amendment. It would be running the slavery argument into the ground to make it apply to every act of discrimination which a person may see fit to make as to the guests he will entertain, or as to the people he will take into his coach or cab or car, or admit to his concert or theatre, or deal with in other matters of intercourse or business. Innkeepers and public carriers, by the laws of all the States, so far as we are aware, are bound, to the extent of their facilities, to furnish proper accommodation to all unobjectionable persons who in good faith apply for them. If the laws themselves make any unjust discrimination, amenable to the prohibitions of the Fourteenth Amendment, Congress has full power to afford a remedy under that amendment and in accordance with it.

When a man has emerged from slavery, and by the aid of beneficent legislation has shaken off the inseparable concomitants of that state, there must be some stage in the progress of his elevation when he takes the rank of a mere citizen, and ceases to be the special favorite of the law . . . . There were thousands of free colored people in this country before the abolition of slavery . . . . Mere discriminations on account of race or color were not regarded as badges of slavery. If, since that time, the enjoyment of equal rights in all these respects has become established by constitutional enactment, it is not by force of the Thirteenth Amendment (which merely abolishes slavery), but by force of the [Fourteenth] and Fifteenth Amendments.

On the whole we are of opinion, that no countenance of authority for the passage of the law in question can be found in either the Thirteenth or Fourteenth Amendment of the Constitution; and no other ground of authority for its passage being suggested, it must necessarily be declared void. [J]udgment should be rendered upon the several indictments in those cases accordingly.

And it is so ordered.

Mr. Justice HARLAN dissenting.

The opinion in these cases proceeds, it seems to me, upon grounds entirely too narrow and artificial. I cannot resist the conclusion that the substance and spirit of the recent amendments of the Constitution have been sacrificed by a subtle and ingenious verbal criticism. . . .

The Thirteenth Amendment, it is conceded, did something more than to prohibit slavery as an *institution*, resting upon distinctions of race, and upheld by positive law. My brethren admit that it established and decreed universal *civil freedom* throughout the United States. But did the freedom thus established involve nothing more than exemption from actual slavery? . . . . Were the States against whose protest the institution was destroyed, to be left free, so far as national interference was concerned, to make or allow discriminations against that race, as such, in the enjoyment of those fundamental rights which by universal concession, inhere in a state of freedom? . . .

I do not contend that the Thirteenth Amendment invests Congress with authority, by legislation, to define and regulate the entire body of the civil rights which citizens enjoy, or may enjoy, in the several States. But I hold that since slavery . . . was the moving or principal cause of the adoption of that amendment, and since that institution rested wholly upon the inferiority, as a race, of those held in bondage, their freedom necessarily involved immunity from, and protection against, all discrimination against them, because of their race, in respect of such civil rights as belong to freemen of other races. Congress, therefore, under its express power to enforce that amendment, by appropriate legislation, may enact laws to protect that people against the deprivation, *because of their race,* of any civil rights granted to other freemen in the same State; and such legislation may be of a direct and primary character operating upon States, their officers and agents, and, also, upon, at least, such individuals and corporations as exercise public functions and wield power and authority under the State. . . .

It remains now to inquire what are the legal rights of colored persons in respect of the accommodations, privileges and facilities of public conveyances, inns and places of public amusement?

First, as to public conveyances on land and water. In New Jersey Steam Navigation Co. v. Merchants' Bank, 6 How. 344, this court . . . said that a common carrier is "in the exercise of a sort of public office, and has public duties to perform, from which he should not be permitted to exonerate himself without the assent of the parties concerned." . . . In Olcott v. Supervisors, 16 Wall. 678, it was ruled that railroads are public highways, established by authority of the State for the public use; that they are none the less public highways, because controlled and owned by private corporations; that it is a part of the function of government to make and maintain highways for the convenience of the public; that no matter who is the agent, or what is the agency, the function performed is *that of the State;* that although the owners may be private companies, they may be compelled to permit the public to use these works in the manner in which they can be used; that, upon these grounds alone, have the courts sustained the investiture of railroad corporations with the State's right of eminent domain, or the right of municipal corporations, under legislative authority, to assess, levy and collect taxes to aid in the construction of railroads. . . . The sum of the adjudged cases is that a railroad corporation is a governmental agency, created primarily for public purposes, and subject to be controlled for the public benefit. . . . Such being the relations these corporations hold to the public, it would seem that the right of a colored person to use an improved public highway, upon the terms accorded to freemen of other races, is as fundamental, in the state of freedom established in this country, as are any of the rights which my brethren concede to be so far fundamental as to be deemed the essence of civil freedom. "Personal liberty consists," says Blackstone, "in the power of locomotion, of changing situation, or removing one's person to whatever places one's

own inclination may direct, without restraint, unless by due course of law."
But of what value is this right of locomotion, if it may be clogged by such
burdens as Congress intended by the act of 1875 to remove?   They are
burdens which lay at the very foundation of the institution of slavery as
it once existed. . . .   The Thirteenth Amendment alone obliterated
the race line, so far as all rights fundmental in a state of freedom are concerned.

    Second, as to inns.   The same general observations which have been
made as to railroads are applicable to inns. . . .   [A] keeper of an
inn is in the exercise of a quasi-public employment.   The law gives him
special privileges and he is charged with certain duties and responsibilities
to the public.   The public nature of his employment forbids him from
discriminating against any person asking admission as a guest on account of
the race or color of that person.

    Third.   As to places of public amusement.   [P]laces of public amuse-
ment, within the meaning of the act of 1875, are such as are established
and maintained under direct license of the law.   The authority to establish
and maintain them comes from the public.   The colored race is a part of
that public.   The local government granting the license represents them as
well as all other races within its jurisdiction.   A license from the public
to establish a place of public amusement, imports, in law, equality of right,
at such places, among all the members of that public. . . .

    I am of the opinion that [racial] discrimination practised by corpora-
tions and individuals in the exercise of their public or quasi-public functions
is a badge of servitude the imposition of which Congress may prevent under
its power, by appropriate legislation, to enforce the Thirteenth Amendment
. . . .   It remains now to consider these cases with reference to the
power Congress has possessed since the adoption of the Fourteenth Amendment.   Much that has been said as to the power of Congress under the
Thirteenth Amendment is applicable to this branch of the discussion, and
will not be repeated. . . .   Remembering that this court, in the
Slaughter-House Cases, declared . . .   that each [recent] amendment
was addressed primarily to the grievances of [the slave] race—let us
proceed to consider the language of the Fourteenth Amendment. . . .

    The assumption that this amendment consists wholly of prohibitions
upon State laws and State proceedings in hostility to its provisions, is unauthorized by its language.   The first clause of the first section—"All persons born or naturalized in the United States, and subject to the jurisdiction
thereof, are citizens of the United States, and of the State wherein they
reside"—is of a distinctly affirmative character.   In its application to the
colored race, previously liberated, it created and granted, as well citizenship
of the United States, as citizenship of the State in which they respectively
resided. . . .   Further, they were brought, by this supreme act of the
nation, within the direct operation of that provision of the Constitution which
declares that "the citizens of each State shall be entitled to all privileges
and immunities of citizens in the several States."   Art. 4, § 2.

    The citizenship thus acquired, by that race, in virtue of an affirmative
grant from the nation, may be protected, not alone by the judicial branch
of the government, but by congressional legislation of a primary direct
character; this, because the power of Congress is not restricted to the en-

forcement of prohibitions upon State laws or State action. It is [to] enforce "the *provisions of this article*" of amendment . . . *all* of the provisions—affirmative and prohibitive . . .. If any right was created by that amendment [there is congressional power] to guard, secure, and protect that right. . . .

But what was secured to colored citizens of the United States—as between them and their respective States—by the national grant to them of State citizenship? With what rights, privileges, or immunities did this grant invest them? There is one, if there be no other—exemption from race discrimination in respect of any civil right belonging to citizens of the white race in the same State. That, surely, is their constitutional privilege when within the jurisdiction of other States. And such must be their constitutional right, in their own State, unless the recent amendments be splendid baubles, thrown out to delude those who deserved fair and generous treatment at the hands of the nation. Citizenship in this country necessarily imports at least equality of civil rights among citizens of every race in the same State. . . .

But if it were conceded that the power of Congress could not be brought into activity until the rights specified in the act of 1875 had been abridged or denied by some State law or State action, I maintain that the decision of the court is erroneous. There has been adverse State action within the Fourteenth Amendment as heretofore interpreted by this court. . . .

In every material sense applicable to the practical enforcement of the Fourteenth Amendment, railroad corporations, keepers of inns, and managers of place of public amusement are agents or instrumentalities of the State, because they are charged with duties to the public, and are amenable, in respect of their duties and functions to governmental regulation. It seems to me that, within the principle settled in Ex parte Virginia, a denial, by these instrumentalities of the State, to the citizen, because of his race, of that equality of civil rights secured to him by law, is a denial by the State, within the meaning of the Fourteenth Amendment. If it be not, then that race is left, in respect of the civil rights in question, practically at the mercy of corporations and individuals wielding power under the States.

But the court says that Congress did not, in the act of 1866, assume, under the authority given by the Thirteenth Amendment, to adjust what may be called the social rights of men and races in the community. . . . I agree that if one citizen chooses not to hold social intercourse with another, he is not and cannot be made amenable to the law for his conduct in that regard; for even upon grounds of race, no legal right of a citizen is violated by the refusal of others to maintain merely social relations with him. What I affirm is that no State, nor the officers of any State, nor any corporation or individual wielding power under State authority for the public benefit or the public convenience, can, consistently either with the freedom established by the fundamental law, or with that equality of civil rights which now belongs to every citizen, discriminate against freemen or citizens, in those rights, because of their race, or because they once labored under the disabilities of slavery imposed upon them as a race. The rights which Congress, by the act of 1875, endeavored to secure and protect are legal, not social rights. . . .

. . . It is, I submit, scarcely just to say that the colored race has been the special favorite of the laws. The statute of 1875, now adjudged to be unconstitutional, is for the benefit of citizens of every race and color. . . . Today, it is the colored race which is denied, by corporations and individuals wielding public authority, rights fundmental in their freedom and citizenship. At some future time, it may be that some other race will fall under the ban of race discrimination. If the constitutional amendments be enforced, according to the intent with which, as I conceive, they were adopted, there cannot be, in this republic, any class of human beings in practical subjection to another class, with power in the latter to dole out to the former just such privileges as they may choose to grant. . . .

———

CONGRESSIONAL INCAPACITY TO REACH PRIVATE ACTS UNDER THE 14TH AMENDMENT: SOME ADDITIONAL EXAMPLES

1. *Cruikshank, the 14th Amendment limitation to state action— and the recognition of other rights against private action.* a. United States v. Cruikshank, 92 U.S. 542 (1875), involved an indictment under Section 6 of the 1870 Act, the predecessor of 18 U.S.C. § 241, p. 452 supra. Three persons were convicted of participating in a lynching of two Negroes, under charges of conspiring to interfere with rights and privileges "granted and secured" by the Constitution. One of the charges referred to the "right and privilege peaceably to assemble together." The Court affirmed the trial court's grant of a motion in arrest of judgment. Chief Justice Waite stated that the indictment would have been adequate if it had charged interference with the right to assemble "for the purpose of petitioning Congress for a redress of grievances," an "attribute of national citizenship"; but the charge was merely a conspiracy "to prevent a meeting for any lawful purpose whatever."

Another charge—depriving citizens of "lives and liberty of person without due process of law"—was found "even more objectionable": "It is no more the duty or within the power of the United States to punish for a conspiracy to falsely imprison or murder within a State, than it would be to punish for false imprisonment or murder itself. The fourteenth amendment prohibits a State from depriving any person of life, liberty, or property, without due process of law; but this adds nothing to the rights of one citizen as against another." A final charge—to "injure" for having voted at an election—was also insufficient: the elections might have been state elections, and there was no claim of a conspiracy based on race; the charge, then, "is really nothing more than a conspiracy to commit a breach of the peace within a State. Certainly it will not be claimed that the United States have the power or are required to do mere police duty in the States."

b. Note that, while Cruikshank was an early assertion that 14th Amendment rights can only be infringed by state action, it also recognizes that the predecessor to § 241 may include rights, derived from other constitutional sources, that may be protected against private interferences as well. That distinction remained an important one in the search for bases of federal action against private misconduct; and the effort to articulate other constitutional sources of rights of national citizenship not subject to the 14th Amendment state action limits has remained a difficult one. Note, e. g., the division in the Williams cases, p. 498, infra; and consider, in examining the rights recited in the 1968 Civil Rights Act (18 U.S.C. § 245, infra, p. 516), which ones are traceable to sources other than the 14th Amendment.

Note the recognition of non-14th Amendment constitutional rights against private action in an opinion by a Justice not inclined to assert such rights loosely—Justice Harlan's 1966 opinion in the Guest case (p. 505, infra): "As a general proposition it seems to me very dubious that the Constitution was intended to create certain rights of private individuals as against other private individuals. . . . It is true that there is a very narrow range of rights against individuals which have been read into the Constitution. In Ex parte Yarbrough, 110 U.S. 651 [1884], the Court held that implicit in the Constitution is the right of citizens to be free of private interference in federal elections. United States v. Classic, 313 U.S. 299 [1941], extended this coverage to primaries. Logan v. United States, 144 U.S. 263 [1892], applied the predecessor of § 241 to a conspiracy to injure someone in the custody of a United States marshal; the case has been read as dealing with a privilege and immunity of citizenship, but it would seem to have depended as well on extrapolations from statutory provisions providing for supervision of prisoners. The Court in In re Quarles, 158 U.S. 532 [1895], extending Logan, supra, declared that there was a right of federal citizenship to inform federal officials of violations of federal law. See also United States v. Cruikshank, 92 U.S. 542, 552 [supra], which announced in dicta a federal right to assemble to petition the Congress for a redress of grievances."

2. *Harris.* United States v. Harris, 106 U.S. 629 (1882), held unconstitutional a criminal provision of the 1875 Act prohibiting conspiracies to deprive any persons of "the equal protection of the laws or of equal privileges and immunities under the law." (Compare the civil counterpart, derived from the 1871 Act and still on the books, 42 U.S.C. § 1985(3), considered in Collins v. Hardyman, p. 499, infra.) Harris, a private person, was charged with participating in a lynching—killing one person as well as beating three others while they were in the custody of a Tennessee sheriff. The Supreme Court held the statute unconstitutional: "When the State has been guilty of no violation of its provisions; when it has not made or enforced any law abridging the privileges or immunities of citizens of the United States; when no one of its departments has deprived any person of life, liberty, or property without due process of law, or denied to any person within its jurisdiction the equal protection of the laws; when, on the contrary, the laws of the State, as enacted by its legislative, and construed by its judicial, and administered by its executive departments, recognize and protect the rights of all persons, the amendment imposes no duty and confers no power upon Congress. . . . As, therefore, the section of the law under consideration is directed exclusively against the action of private persons, without reference to the laws of the State or their administration by her officers, we are clear in the opinion that it is not warranted by any clause in the Fourteenth Amendment to the Constitution." See also Baldwin v. Franks, 120 U.S. 678 (1887). Compare the parallel difficulties in reaching private action under the 15th Amendment— e. g., James v. Bowman, 190 U.S. 127 (1903), sec. 4, p. 529, infra.

B. JUDICIAL EXPANSION OF STATE ACTION IN THE 20TH CENTURY—DURING THE YEARS OF CONGRESSIONAL INACTION

PUBLIC FUNCTION, PRIVATE POWER, AND STATE ACTION

Introduction. During the 1940's, while congressional power under the 14th Amendment continued to lie dormant (more for political reasons than because of constitutional obstacles), the Supreme Court began to expand the boundaries of the state action concept. The results were usually clearer than the content and limits of the principles. What was obvious was that, in the cases before the Court, arguably private conduct was being treated as state action and was being subjected to 14th Amendment restrictions. What was often obscure was the extent to which other seemingly private activities would be reachable on the basis of those cases. One of the earliest, most amorphous, and potentially most far-reaching themes in the expansion of the state action concept—and one that has proved difficult to articulate and confine over the years—is the view that certain "private" action may be subject to the 14th and 15th Amendments if it constitutes exercise of a "public function." Consider the support for (and reach of) such a principle in the following materials.

1. *Marsh v. Alabama and the early "public function" talk.* One of the major sources of "public function" talk as a basis for extending the state action concept was Justice Black's majority opinion in a 1946 case, Marsh v. Alabama, 326 U.S. 501. There, the Court reversed a state trespass conviction of a Jehovah's Witness who had distributed religious literature in a company-owned town contrary to the wishes of the town's management. Justice Black rejected the contention that the corporate owner's control of the town was "coextensive with the right of a homeowner to regulate the conduct of his guests." He stated: "Ownership does not always mean absolute dominion. The more an owner, for his advantage, opens up his property for use by the public in general, the more do his rights become circumscribed by the statutory and constitutional rights of those who use it. . . Thus, the owners of privately held bridges, ferries, turnpikes and railroads may not operate them as freely as a farmer does his farm. Since these facilities are built and operated primarily to benefit the public and *since their operation is essentially a public function,* it is subject to state regulation." [Emphasis added.]

He added: "Whether a corporation or a municipality owns or possesses the town, the public in either case has an identical interest in the functioning of the community in such manner that the channels of communication remain free. . . . The 'business block' serves as the community shopping center and is freely accessible and open to the people in the area and those passing through. The managers appointed by the corporation cannot curtail the liberty of press and religion of these people consistently with the purposes of the Constitutional guarantees, and a state statute, as the one here involved, which enforces such action by criminally punishing those who attempt to distribute religious literature clearly violates the First and Fourteenth Amendments to the Constitution." Justice Reed, joined by Chief Justice Vinson and

Justice Burton, dissented from the "novel Constitutional doctrine": "The rights of the owner, which the Constitution protects as well as the rights of free speech, are not outweighed by the interests of the trespasser, even though he trespasses in behalf of religion or free speech." To what extent was the nature of the private activity determinative here? Was the invocation of state trespass law important to the finding of state action? Should it have been? Cf. Shelley v. Kraemer, p. 471, infra.

2. *The Marsh problem revisited: the Logan Valley Plaza case.* More than 20 years later, the Court relied extensively on Marsh (over Justice Black's dissent) in sustaining constitutional objections to a state court injunction banning peaceful picketing of a store in a privately owned shopping center. Amalgamated Food Employees Union v. Logan Valley Plaza, 391 U.S. 308 (1968). Justice Marshall's majority opinion concluded that the injunction could not be justified on the ground that the picketing constituted an unconsented invasion of private property rights: "The shopping center here is clearly the functional equivalent to the business district of Chickasaw involved in Marsh. It is true that, unlike the corporation in Marsh the respondents here do not own the surrounding residential property and do not provide municipal services therefor. [U]nlike the situation in Marsh, there is no power on respondents' part to have petitioners totally denied access to the community for which the mall serves as a business district. This fact, however, is not determinative. . . . We see no reason why access to a business district in a company town for the purpose of exercising First Amendment rights should be constitutionally required, while access for the same purpose to property functioning as a business district should be limited simply because the property surrounding the 'business district' is not under the same ownership."

Since "the shopping center serves as the community business block," Justice Marshall explained, "the State may not delegate the power, through the use of its trespass laws, wholly to exclude those members of the public wishing to exercise their First Amendment rights on the premises in a manner and for a purpose generally consonant with the use to which the property is actually put." He noted that, "unlike a situation involving a person's home, no meaningful claim to protection of a right of privacy can be advanced by respondents here." He added: "The economic development of the United States in the last 20 years reinforces our opinion of the correctness of the approach taken in Marsh. The large-scale movement of this country's population from the cities to the suburbs has been accompanied by the advent of the suburban shopping center. [The data] illustrate the substantial consequences for workers seeking to challenge substandard working conditions, consumers protesting shoddy or overpriced merchandise, and minority groups seeking nondiscriminatory hiring policies that a contrary decision here would have. Business enterprises located in downtown areas would be subject to on-the-spot public criticism for their practices, but businesses situated in the suburbs could largerly immunize themselves from similar criticism by creating a *cordon sanitaire* of parking lots around their stores. Neither precedent nor policy compels a result so at variance with the goal of free expression and communication that is the heart of the First Amendment." Justice Douglas concurred.

The author of Marsh v. Alabama, Justice Black, dissented. The majority, he insisted, had misread Marsh: "The question is under what circumstances can private property be treated as though it were public? The answer that Marsh gives is when that property has taken on *all* the attributes of a town, i. e., 'residential buildings, streets, a system of sewers, a sewage disposal plant and a "business block" on which business places are situated.' 326 U.S., at 502. I can find nothing in Marsh which indicates that if one of these features is present, e. g., a business district, this is sufficient for the Court to confiscate a part of an owner's private property and give its use to people who want to picket on it." There were also dissenting opinions by Justices Harlan and White. [Note also the discussion of First Amendment aspects of the case in chap. 15, p. 1185, infra.]

3. *The search for "public functions": Evans v. Newton.* Efforts to rely at least in part on "public function" rationales in areas other than company towns and shopping centers have typically encountered greater difficulties. But that theme was suggested as an alternative ground in Justice Douglas' majority opinion in the Court's first of two encounters with Senator Bacon's will, Evans v. Newton, 382 U.S. 296 (1966). [See also Evans v. Abney, 396 U.S. 435 (1970) (p. 476, infra.)]

Evans v. Newton involved a park created in Macon, Ga., pursuant to a trust established in the 1911 will of Senator Bacon. The trust provided that the park, Baconsfield, be used by white people only. The city originally acted as trustee. In the Newton litigation, after the city had stated that it could no longer constitutionally enforce the racial restriction, the state courts accepted the city's resignation as trustee and appointed private trustees instead. The Supreme Court held that Baconsfield could nevertheless not be operated on a racially restrictive basis. In explaining why the 14th Amendment prohibition continued to apply to the park despite the substitution of private trustees, Justice Douglas' majority opinion in Evans v. Newton relied in part on the ground that, so far as the record showed, "there has been no change in municipal maintenance and concern over this facility. [W]here the tradition of municipal control had become firmly established, we cannot take judicial notice that the mere substitution of trustees instantly transferred this park from the public to the private sector." Holding

But Justice Douglas suggested a "public function" ground as additional support: "This conclusion is buttressed by the nature of the service rendered the community by a park. The service rendered even by a private park of this character is municipal in nature. It is open to every white person, there being no selective element other than race. Golf clubs, social centers, luncheon clubs, schools such as Tuskegee was at least in origin, and other like organizations in the private sector are often racially oriented. A park, on the other hand, is more like a fire department or police department that traditionally serves the community. Mass recreation through the use of parks is plainly in the public domain . . .; and state courts that aid private parties to perform that public function on a segregated basis implicate the State in conduct proscribed by the Fourteenth Amendment. Like the streets of the company town in Marsh v. Alabama, supra, the elective process of Terry v. Adams [p. 470, infra], and the transit system of Public Utilities Comm'n v. Pollak [343 U.S. 451, (1951)], the predominant character and purpose of this park are municipal."

That passage evoked special criticism in Justice Harlan's dissent, joined by Justice Stewart: "More serious than the absence of any firm doctrinal support for this theory of state action are its potentialities for the future. Its fail-

cf. parks to schools

ing as a principle of decision in the realm of Fourteenth Amendment concerns can be shown by comparing—among other examples that might be drawn from the still unfolding sweep of governmental functions—the 'public function' of privately established schools with that of privately owned parks. Like parks, the purpose schools serve is important to the public. Like parks, private control exists, but there is also a very strong tradition of public control in this field. Like parks, schools may be available to almost anyone of one race or religion but to no others. Like parks, there are normally alternatives for those shut out but there may also be inconveniences and disadvantages caused by the restriction. Like parks, the extent of school intimacy varies greatly depending on the size and character of the institution.

"For all the resemblance, the majority assumes that its decision leaves unaffected the traditional view that the Fourteenth Amendment does not compel private schools to adapt their admission policies to its requirements, but that such matters are left to the States acting within constitutional bounds. I find it difficult, however, to avoid the conclusion that this decision opens the door to reversal of these basic constitutional concepts, and, at least in logic, jeopardizes the existence of denominationally restricted schools while making of every college entrance rejection letter a potential Fourteenth Amendment question.

"While this process of analogy might be spun out to reach privately owned orphanages, libraries, garbage collection companies, detective agencies, and a host of other functions commonly regarded as nongovernmental though paralleling fields of governmental activity, the example of schools is, I think, sufficient to indicate the pervasive potentialities of this 'public function' theory of state action. It substitutes for the comparatively clear and concrete tests of state action a catch-phrase approach as vague and amorphous as it is far-reaching."

[After the reversal in Evans v. Newton, the state courts held that the trust had failed because the Senator's intention had become impossible to fulfill and that the property had accordingly reverted to the heirs. A divided Supreme Court (Justices Brennan and Douglas dissenting) affirmed that decision. Evans v. Abney, 396 U.S. 435 (1970) (see p. 476, infra.)]

4. *Public function and private power.* Does the 14th Amendment become applicable whenever private action has substantial impact on important interests of individuals? Does such "private government" satisfy the "state action" requirement? Is the requisite formal state involvement provided by the probability that the "private government" is chartered by the state, or is a state licensee—or is in any event tolerated by the state? (Recall the first Justice Harlan's dissent in the Civil Rights Cases, supra, and compare Shelley v. Kraemer, infra.) Would such an approach be inconsistent with any genuine effort to preserve a "state action"—"private action" or "public sector"—"private sector" distinction? Is any such effort necessary or worthwhile? See C. L. Black, Jr., "Foreword: 'State Action,' Equal Protection, and California's Proposition 14," 81 Harv.L.Rev. 69 (1967). Would expansion of a "public function" or "private government" approach unduly constitutionalize all operations of the "private" group found

subject to the Amendments? See Wellington, "The Constitution, the Labor Union, and 'Governmental Action,' " 70 Yale L.J. 345 (1961).*

Consider the assertion of an "emerging principle" in Berle, "Constitutional Limitations on Corporate Activity—Protection of Personal Rights from Invasion through Economic Power," 100 U.Pa.L.Rev. 933 (1952). Berle suggests that "principle" to be that a corporation may be "as subject to constitutional limitations as is the state itself." He notes two prerequisites, the "undeniable fact" of the state's action in chartering the corporation, and "the existence of sufficient economic power . . . to invade the constitutional rights of the individual to a material degree." Berle offers as one of the justifications the fact that the state relies upon "the corporate system to carry out functions for which in modern life by community demand the government is held ultimately responsible." See also Hale, "Force and the State: A Comparison of 'Political' and 'Economic' Compulsion," 35 Colum.L.Rev. 149 (1935).

THE WHITE PRIMARY CASES

The white primary cases were a series of decisions in the forties and fifties holding that the Democratic Party groups in southern one-party states could not exclude Negroes from the pre-general election candidate selection process, despite the repeated efforts to eliminate all formal indicia [signs] of state involvement in the primary schemes. To what extent did these white primary cases support a general "public function" theory? To what extent did those cases rest on their special context of voting and elections? To what extent were they supportable on the basis of the 15th rather than the 14th Amendment? To what extent were they explainable on the basis of the fact or tradition of state regulation of primaries?

The sequence began with Nixon v. Herndon, 273 U.S. 536 (1924), where the exclusion of Negroes from Democratic primaries was expressed on the face of a state law. That was held to be state racial discrimination in violation of the 14th Amendment. Thereafter, the Texas legislature gave the executive committee of a party the power to prescribe membership qualifications. A resultant racial exclusion was again found unconstitutional under the 14th Amendment, in Nixon v. Condon, 286 U.S. 73 (1932), on the ground that the committee operated as the representative of the state. A subsequent, third round of Texas racial exclusions stemmed from action of the state party convention. That exclusion survived constitutional attack in Grovey v. Town- — *overruled* send, 295 U.S. 45 (1935): the convention was found to be an organ of a voluntary, private group, not of the state.

* On the obligation of a union designated as exclusive bargaining representative under federal labor legislation to avoid racial discrimination, see, e. g., Steele v. Louisville & Nashville R. Co., 323 U.S. 192 (1944), and Oliphant v. Brotherhood of Locomotive Firemen, 262 F.2d 359 (6th Cir. 1958), cert. denied, 359 U.S. 935 (1959). In Steele, the Court stated: "We think that the Railway Labor Act imposes upon the statutory representatives of a craft at least as exacting a duty to protect equally the interests of the members of the craft as the Constitution imposes upon a legislature to give equal protection . . . . Congress has seen fit to clothe the bargaining representative with powers comparable to those possessed by a legislative body . . . but it has also imposed . . . . a corresponding duty." See generally Sovern, "The NLRA and Racial Discrimination," 62 Colum.L. Rev. 563 (1962).

But Grovey v. Townsend was overruled nine years later, in Smith v. Allwright, 321 U.S. 649 (1944). The Court pointed to an intervening decision, United States v. Classic, 313 U.S. 299 (1941), which held that Art. I, Sec. 4, of the Constitution authorized congressional control of primaries "where the primary is by law made part of the election machinery." The Smith Court found Classic relevant, according to Justice Reed's majority opinion, "not because exclusion of Negroes from primaries is any more or less state action by reason of the unitary character of the electoral process but because the recognition of the place of the primary in the electoral scheme makes clear that state delegation to a party of the power to fix the qualifications of primary elections is delegation of a state function that may make the party's action the action of the state. When Grovey v. Townsend was written, the Court looked upon the denial of a vote in a primary as a mere refusal by a party of party membership. [O]ur ruling in Classic as to the unitary character of the electorial process calls for a reexamination as to whether or not the exclusion of Negroes from a Texas party primary was state action." The Court examined the state laws, found that primaries were "conducted by the party under state statutory authority," and concluded: "We think that this statutory system for the selection of party nominees for inclusion on the general election ballot makes the party which is required to follow these legislative directions an agency of the State in so far as it determines the participants in a primary election. The party takes its character as a state agency from the duties imposed upon it by state statutes; the duties do not become matters of private law because they are performed by a political party."

After Smith v. Allwright several efforts to preserve "private" white primaries by abandoning much of the state statutory framework were thwarted in the lower courts. Note especially the language in Rice v. Ellmore, 165 F.2d 387 (4th Cir. 1947), cert. denied, 333 U.S. 875 (1948), where South Carolina had repealed all primary laws. The Court of Appeals concluded: "Having undertaken to perform an important function relating to the exercise of sovereignty by the people, [the Party] may not violate the fundamental principles laid down by the Constitution for its exercise". See also Baskin v. Brown, 174 F.2d 391 (4th Cir. 1949).

In 1953, the issue came to the Supreme Court for the last time, in its most extreme "private" form. Terry v. Adams, 345 U.S. 461, involved racial exclusion in the "pre-primary" elections of the Jaybird Democratic Association, a "voluntary club" of white Democrats. Candidates winning the Jaybird elections typically ran unopposed in the Democratic primaries. The trial court found a "complete absence" of state involvement in the Jaybirds' operations. The Supreme Court nevertheless found the 15th Amendment applicable. There was no opinion on which a majority could agree, but only one Justice dissented.

Justice Black, joined by Justice Douglas and Burton, found that, as in Rice and Baskin, supra, "the combined Jaybird-Democratic-general election machinery" was unconstitutional. He stated that though the Amendment "excludes social or business clubs," it "includes any election" in which public officials are elected. Any election machinery with the "purpose or effect" of denying "Negroes on account of their race an effective voice in governmental affairs" was barred: "For a State to permit such a duplication of its election processes" as the Jaybird pre-primary was unconstitutional. In a separate opinion, Justice Frankfurter stated that the "vital requirement is that somewhere, to some extent, there be an infusion by conduct of officials . . . into any scheme" denying the franchise because of race. Here, the county election officials were in effect "participants in the scheme." The state, through "the action and abdication" of its officials, has permitted a procedure "which predetermines the legally devised primary." Justice Clark, joined by Chief Justice Vinson and Justices Reed and Jackson, concurred on the ground that the Jaybirds operated "as an auxiliary" of the local Party, and that the Jaybirds were therefore subject to the principles of Smith v. Allwright. Justice Minton was the only dissenter. He found no "state action"; rather, the Jaybirds' activities, like those of other pressure groups, were "attempts to influence or obtain state action." The Jaybirds, like other groups, caucused and conducted a "straw vote" regarding primary endorsements: "I do not understand that concerted action . . . which is successful somehow becomes state action."

SHELLEY v. KRAEMER †

334 U.S. 1, 68 S.Ct. 836, 92 L.Ed. 1161 (1948).

Certiorari to the Supreme Court of Missouri.

Mr. Chief Justice VINSON delivered the opinion of the Court.

These cases present for our consideration questions relating to the validity of court enforcement of private agreements, generally described as restrictive covenants, which have as their purpose the exclusion of persons of designated race or color from the ownership or occupancy of real property.

. . .

The first of these cases comes to this Court on certiorari to the Supreme Court of Missouri. On February 16, 1911, thirty out of a total of thirty-nine owners of property fronting both sides of Labadie Avenue between Taylor Avenue and Cora Avenue in the city of St. Louis, signed an agreement, which was subsequently recorded, providing in part:

". . . the said property is hereby restricted to the use and occupancy for the term of Fifty (50) years from this date, so that it shall be a condition all the time and whether recited and referred to as [sic] not in subsequent conveyances and shall attach to the land as a condition precedent to the sale of the same, that hereafter no part of said property or any portion thereof shall be, for said term of Fifty-years, occupied by any person not of the Caucasian race, it being intended hereby to restrict the use of said property for said period of time against the occupancy as owners or tenants of any portion of said property for resident or other purpose by people of the Negro or Mongolian Race."

. . .

On August 11, 1945, pursuant to a contract of sale, petitioners Shelley, who are Negroes, for valuable consideration received from one Fitzgerald a warranty deed to the parcel in question. The trial court found that petitioners had no actual knowledge of the restrictive agreement at the time of the purchase.

On October 9, 1945, respondents, as owners of other property subject to the terms of the restrictive covenant, brought suit in the Circuit Court of

† Together with McGhee v. Sipes, on certiorari to the Supreme Court of Michigan.

the city of St. Louis praying that petitioners Shelley be restrained from taking possession of the property and that judgment be entered divesting title out of petitioners Shelley and revesting title in the immediate grantor or in such other person as the court should direct. . . . The Supreme Court of Missouri . . . directed the trial court to grant the relief for which respondents had prayed. . . .

The second of the cases under consideration comes to this Court from the Supreme Court of Michigan. The circumstances presented do not differ materially from the Missouri case. . . .

Whether the equal protection clause of the Fourteenth Amendment inhibits judicial enforcement by state courts of restrictive covenants based on race or color is a question which this Court has not heretofore been called upon to consider. . . .

It cannot be doubted that among the civil rights intended to be protected from discriminatory state action by the Fourteenth Amendment are the rights to acquire, enjoy, own and dispose of property. Equality in the enjoyment of property rights was regarded by the framers of that Amendment as an essential pre-condition to the realization of other basic civil rights and liberties which the Amendment was intended to guarantee. Thus, § 1978 of the Revised Statutes [now 42 U.S.C. § 1982], derived from § 1 of the Civil Rights Act of 1866 which was enacted by Congress while the Fourteenth Amendment was also under consideration, provides:

"All citizens of the United States shall have the same right, in every State and Territory, as is enjoyed by white citizens thereof to inherit, purchase, lease, sell, hold, and convey real and personal property." This Court has given specific recognition to the same principle. Buchanan v. Warley, 245 U.S. 60 (1917).[1]

It is likewise clear that restrictions on the right of occupancy of the sort sought to be created by the private agreements in these cases could not be squared with the requirements of the Fourteenth Amendment if imposed by state statute or local ordinance. . . .

But the present cases . . . do not involve action by state legislatures or city councils. Here the particular patterns of discrimination and the areas in which the restrictions are to operate, are determined, in the first instance, by the terms of agreements among private individuals. Participation of the State consists in the enforcement of the restrictions so defined. The crucial issue with which we are here confronted is whether this distinction removes these cases from the operation of the prohibitory provisions of the Fourteenth Amendment.

Since the decision of this Court in the Civil Rights Cases, 109 U.S. 3 (1883), the principle has become firmly embedded in our constitutional law that the action inhibited by the first section of the Fourteenth Amendment is only such action as may fairly be said to be that of the States. That Amend-

1. Buchanan v. Warley held unconstitutional a city ordinance making it unlawful for any colored person to move in and occupy a house on a block where the majority of residents were whites. The ordinance was held to violate due process of law as an interference with "the civil right of a white man to dispose of his property if he saw fit to do so to a person of color." The issue arose in an action for specific performance of a contract for the sale of land. The vendee set up as a defense that he was a colored person and that the purchase of the land would violate the ordinance.

ment erects no shield against merely private conduct, however discriminatory or wrongful.

We conclude, therefore, that the restrictive agreements standing alone cannot be regarded as violative of any rights guaranteed to petitioners by the Fourteenth Amendment. So long as the purposes of those agreements are effectuated by voluntary adherence to their terms, it would appear clear that there has been no action by the State and the provisions of the Amendment have not been violated. Cf. Corrigan v. Buckley, [271 U.S. 323 (1926)]. But here there was more. These are cases in which the purposes of the agreements were secured only by judicial enforcement by state courts of the restrictive terms of the agreements. The respondents urge that judicial enforcement of private agreements does not amount to state action; or, in any event, the participation of the State is so attenuated in character as not to amount to state action within the meaning of the Fourteenth Amendment. Finally, it is suggested, even if the States in these cases may be deemed to have acted in the constitutional sense, their action did not deprive petitioners of rights guaranteed by the Fourteenth Amendment. . . .

That the action of state courts and judicial officers in their official capacities is to be regarded as action of the State within the meaning of the Fourteenth Amendment, is a proposition which has long been established by decisions of this Court. . . .

[T]he examples of state judicial action which have been held by this Court to violate the Amendment's commands are not restricted to situations in which the judicial proceedings were found in some manner to be procedurally unfair. It has been recognized that the action of state courts in enforcing a substantive common-law rule formulated by those courts, may result in the denial of rights guaranteed by the Fourteenth Amendment, even though the judicial proceedings in such cases may have been in complete accord with the most rigorous conceptions of procedural due process. . . . In Cantwell v. Connecticut, 310 U.S. 296 (1940), a conviction in a state court of the common-law crime of breach of the peace was, under the circumstances of the case, found to be a violation of the Amendment's commands relating to freedom of religion. . . .

The short of the matter is that from the time of the adoption of the Fourteenth Amendment until the present, it has been the consistent ruling of this Court that the action of the States to which the Amendment has reference includes action of state courts and state judicial officials. Although, in construing the terms of the Fourteenth Amendment, differences have from time to time been expressed as to whether particular types of state action may be said to offend the Amendment's prohibitory provisions, it has never been suggested that state court action is immunized from the operation of those provisions simply because the act is that of the judicial branch of the state government.

Against this background of judicial construction, extending over a period of some three-quarters of a century, we are called upon to consider whether enforcement by state courts of the restrictive agreements in these cases may be deemed to be the acts of those States; and, if so, whether that action had denied these petitioners the equal protection of the laws which the Amendment was intended to insure.

We have no doubt that there has been state action in these cases in the full and complete sense of the phrase. The undisputed facts disclose that petitioners were willing purchasers of properties upon which they desired to establish homes. The owners of the properties were willing sellers; and contracts of sale were accordingly consummated. It is clear that but for the active intervention of the state courts, supported by the full panoply of state power, petitioners would have been free to occupy the properties in question without restraint.

Ct: This is not case where state merely abstains from action.

These are not cases, as has been suggested, in which the States have merely abstained from action, leaving private individuals free to impose such discriminations as they see fit. Rather, these are cases in which the States have made available to such individuals the full coercive power of government to deny to petitioners, on the grounds of race or color, the enjoyment of property rights in premises which petitioners are willing and financially able to acquire and which the grantors are willing to sell. The difference between judicial enforcement and non-enforcement of the restrictive covenants is the difference to petitioners between being denied rights of property available to other members of the community and being accorded full enjoyment of those rights on an equal footing.

The enforcement of the restrictive agreements by the state courts in these cases was directed pursuant to the common-law policy of the States as formulated by those courts in earlier decisions. [The] judicial action in each case bears the clear and unmistakable imprimatur of the State. We have noted that previous decisions of this Court have established the proposition that judicial action is not immunized from the operation of the Fourteenth Amendment simply because it is taken pursuant to the state's common-law policy. Nor is the Amendment ineffective simply because the particular pattern of discrimination, which the State has enforced, was defined initially by the terms of a private agreement. State action, as that phrase is understood for the purposes of the Fourteenth Amendment, refers to exertions of state power in all forms. And when the effect of that action is to deny rights subject to the protection of the Fourteenth Amendment, it is the obligation of this Court to enforce the constitutional commands.

We hold that in granting judicial enforcement of the restrictive agreements in these cases, the States have denied petitioners the equal protection of the laws and that, therefore, the action of the state courts cannot stand. We have noted that freedom from discrimination by the States in the enjoyment of property rights was among the basic objectives sought to be effectuated by the framers of the Fourteenth Amendment. That such discrimination has occurred in these cases is clear. Because of the race or color of these petitioners they have been denied rights of owership or occupancy enjoyed as a matter of course by other citizens of different race or color. . . .

Argu. of Respondents

→ Respondents urge, however, that since the state courts stand ready to enforce restrictive covenants excluding white persons from the ownership or occupancy of property covered by such agreements, enforcement of covenants excluding colored persons may not be deemed a denial of equal protection of the laws to the colored persons who are thereby affected. This contention does not bear scrutiny. The parties have directed our attention to no case in which a court, state or federal, has been called upon to enforce a covenant excluding members of the white majority from ownership or occupancy of real property on grounds of race or color. But there are more fundamental considerations. The rights created by the first section of the Fourteenth Amendment are, by its terms, guaranteed to the individual. The rights established are personal rights. It is, therefore, no answer to these petitioners to say that the courts may also be induced to deny white persons rights of ownership and occupancy on grounds of race or color. Equal protection of the laws is not achieved through indiscriminate imposition of inequalities.

Nor do we find merit in the suggestion that property owners who are parties to these agreements are denied equal protection of the laws if denied access to the courts to enforce the terms of restrictive covenants and to assert property rights which the state courts have held to be created by such agreements. The Constitution confers upon no individual the right to demand action by the State which results in the denial of equal protection of the laws to other individuals. And it would appear beyond question that the power of the State to create and enforce property interests must be exercised within the boundaries defined by the Fourteenth Amendment. Cf. Marsh v. Alabama, 326 U.S. 501 (1946). . . .

The historical context in which the Fourteenth Amendment became a part of the Constitution should not be forgotten. Whatever else the framers sought to achieve, it is clear that the matter of primary concern was the establishment of equality in the enjoyment of basic civil and political rights and the preservation of those rights from discriminatory action on the part of the States based on considerations of race or color. . . . Upon full consideration, we have concluded that in these cases the States have acted to deny petitioners the equal protection of the laws guaranteed by the Fourteenth Amendment. . . .

Reversed.*

Mr. Justice REED, Mr. Justice JACKSON, and Mr. Justice RUTLEDGE took no part in the consideration or decision of these cases.

SHELLEY v. KRAEMER: THE APPLICATIONS AND THE SEARCH FOR LIMITS

Introduction. Does Shelley make 14th Amendment restrictions applicable whenever private choices are enabled to be carried out because of the backing of the state? Even if the decision to discriminate originates wholly with the individual and the state aid is extended neutrally, to enforce whatever private choice is made? Is private action converted into state action whenever the individual seeks court or police aid to enforce contract or property rights? Is there state aid whenever the state fails to forbid an individual choice which it has power to control? Given the pervasive state regulatory power—indeed, the pervasiveness of law as an ultimate backstop that makes

---

* In a companion case to Shelley, Hurd v. Hodge, 334 U.S. 24 (1948), the Court held that courts in the District of Columbia could not enforce restrictive covenants even though the 14th Amendment was not applicable to the federal government. Chief Justice Vinson stated that such action would deny "rights . . . protected by the Civil Rights Act"; moreover, it would be contrary to the public policy of the United States to allow a federal court to enforce an agreement constitutionally unenforceable in state courts.

private choices possible—does so broad a reading not convert virtually all private decisions into state action and obliterate the state-private distinction?

If Shelley were read at its broadest, a simple citation of the case would have disposed of most subsequent state action controversies—and would have provided a simple answer to all of the problems in the preceding materials. But, as the cases that follow illustrate, the Court has rejected so embracive a reading and has taken seriously the Shelley assurance that, despite same of its language, a state-private distinction was to be retained. The efforts to find limiting principles on the broad implications of Shelley have produced extensive commentary on and off the Court.

1. *Restrictive covenants in contracts: Barrows v. Jackson.* Chief Justice Vinson, the author of the Shelley opinion, dissented five years later when the Court held the Shelley principle applicable to an enforcement of a restrictive covenant by a damage suit against a co-covenantor. Barrows v. Jackson, 346 U.S. 249 (1953). The Court stated that permitting damage judgments would induce prospective sellers of restricted land either to refuse to sell to non-Caucasians or to "require non-Caucasians to pay a higher price to meet the damages which the seller may incur." The Court "will not permit or require" the state "to coerce respondent to respond in damages for failure to observe a restrictive covenant that this Court would deny [the state] the right to enforce in equity."

Do Shelley and Barrows bar recognition of a restrictive covenant as a defense in actions for damages for breach of contract? See Rice v. Sioux City Memorial Park Cemetery, 245 Iowa 147, 60 N.W.2d 110 (1953), aff'd by an equally divided Court, 348 U.S. 880 (1954), vacated and cert. dismissed as improvidently granted, 349 U.S. 70 (1955). Cf. Black v. Cutter Laboratories, 351 U.S. 292 (1956).

2. *Reverter provisions in deeds: Evans v. Abney.* The Court's 5:2 decision in its second encounter with the litigation over Baconsfield park in Macon, Ga., illustrated that Shelley had not barred all state involvement in enforcing private restrictions on property. Senator Bacon's will had conveyed property in trust to the city for use as a park "for white people only." After Evans v. Newton, 382 U.S. 296 (1966) (p. 467, supra), had held that Baconsfield could not be operated on a racially discriminatory basis, the state court ruled that "Senator Bacon's intention to provide a park for whites only had become impossible to fulfill and that accordingly the trust had failed and the parkland and other trust property had reverted by operation of Georgia law to the heirs of the Senator." The Supreme Court, in a majority opinion by Justice Black, held that this ruling did not constitute state discrimination under the 14th Amendment. Evans v. Abney, 396 U.S. 435 (1970).

The state court had rejected arguments that it should save the trust by applying the *cy pres* doctrine to amend the will by striking the racial restriction. The state court "concluded, in effect, that Senator Bacon would have rather had the whole trust fail than have Baconsfield integrated." Justice Black concluded that the termination of the trust and the enforcement of the reverter violated no federal rights: "[A]ny harshness that may have resulted from the State court's decision can be attributed solely to its intention to effectuate as nearly as possible the explicit terms of Senator Bacon's will."

He rejected an effort to stress "the similarities between this case and the case in which a city holds an absolute fee simple title to public park and

[left margin handwritten note:] cy-pres = intention of the party is carried out as near as may be, when it would be impossible or illegal to give it literal effect

then closes that park of its own accord solely to avoid the effect of a prior court order directing that the park be integrated as the Fourteenth Amendment commands. [A]ssuming *arguendo* that the closing of the park would in those circumstances violate the Equal Protection Clause, that case would be clearly distinguishable from the case at bar because there it is the State and not a private party which is injecting the racially discriminatory motivation. In the case at bar there is not the slightest indication that any of the Georgia judges involved were motivated by racial animus or discriminatory intent of any sort in construing and enforcing Senator Bacon's will. . . . [T]he language of the Senator's will shows that the racial restrictions were solely the product of the testator's own full-blown social philosophy."

He added: "Similarly, the situation presented in this case is also easily distinguishable from that presented in Shelley v. Kraemer, 334 U.S. 1 (1948), where we held unconstitutional state judicial action which had affirmatively enforced a private scheme of discrimination against Negroes. Here the effect of the Georgia decision eliminated all discrimination against Negroes in the park by eliminating the park itself, and the termination of the park was a loss shared equally by the white and Negro citizens of Macon since both races would have enjoyed a constitutional right of equal access to the park's facilities had it continued."

Petitioners insisted, moreover, that the state court had not really given effect to a clear-cut private intent, but had exercised choice in interpreting that intent as requiring a reverter. Justice Black rejected "the idea that the Georgia courts had a constitutional obligation in this case to resolve any doubt about the testator's intent in favor of preserving the trust. [W]e see no merit in the argument. [T]he Constitution imposes no requirement upon the Georgia court to approach Bacon's will any differently than it would approach any will creating any charitable trust of any kind. Surely the Fourteenth Amendment is not violated where, as here, a state court operating in its judicial capacity fairly applies its normal principles of construction to determine the testator's true intent in establishing a charitable trust and then reaches a conclusion with regard to that intent which, because of the operation of neutral and non-discriminatory state trust laws, effectively denies everyone, whites as well as Negroes, the benefits of the trust."

There were dissents by Justices Douglas and Brennan; Justice Marshall did not participate. Only Justice Brennan's dissent mentioned Shelley v. Kraemer: "[Shelley] stands at least for the proposition that where parties of different races are willing to deal with one another a state court cannot keep them from doing so by enforcing a privately authored racial restriction. Nothing in the record suggests that after our decision in Evans v. Newton, supra, the City of Macon retracted its previous willingness to manage Baconsfield on a nonsegregated basis, or that the white beneficiaries of Senator Bacon's generosity were unwilling to share it with Negroes, rather than have the park revert to his heirs. . . . Thus, so far as the record shows, this is a case of a state court's enforcement of a racial restriction to prevent willing parties from dealing with one another. The decision of the Georgia courts thus, under Shelley v. Kraemer, constitutes state action denying equal protection."

Justice Brennan placed greater emphasis on other, albeit related, arguments: "The exculpation of the State and city from responsibility for the closing of the park is simply indefensible on this record. This discriminatory closing is permeated with state action: at the time Senator Bacon wrote his will Georgia statutes expressly authorized and supported the precise kind of discrimination provided for by him; in accepting title to the park, public officials of the City of Macon entered into an arrangement vesting in private persons the power to enforce a reversion if the city should ever incur a constitutional obligation to desegregate the park; it is a *public* park that is being closed for a discriminatory reason after having been operated for nearly half a century as a segregated *public* facility. . . .

"[T]here is state action whenever a State enters into an arrangement which creates a private right to compel or enforce the reversion of a public facility. Whether the right is a possibility of reverter, a right of entry, an executory interest, or a contractual right, it can be created only with the consent of a public body or official, for example the official action involved in Macon's acceptance of the gift of Baconsfield. The State's involvement in the creation of such a right is also involvement in its enforcement; the State's assent to the creation of the right necessarily contemplates that the State will enforce the right if called upon to do so. Where, as in this case, the State's enforcement role conflicts with its obligation to comply with the constitutional command against racial segregation the attempted enforcement must be declared repugnant to the Fourteenth Amendment.

"Moreover, a State cannot divest itself by contract of the power to perform essential governmental functions. Thus a State cannot bind itself not to operate a public park in accordance with the Equal Protection Clause upon pain of forfeiture of the park. The decision whether or not a public facility shall be operated in compliance with the Constitution is an essential *governmental* decision. An arrangement which purports to prevent a State from complying with the Constitution cannot be carried out. Evans v. Newton, supra; see Pennsylvania v. Board of Directors, 353 U.S. 230 (1957) [infra]. Nor can it be enforced by a reversion; a racial restriction is simply invalid when intended to bind a public body and cannot be given any effect whatever, cf. Pennsylvania v. Brown, 392 F.2d 120 (C.A.3d Cir.) [infra]."

3. *Other testamentary provisions: the Girard College litigation.* Does Evans v. Abney, note 2, end the two decades of speculation about the impact of Shelley on the enforcement of restrictive provisions in wills? For example, may a court enforce a testamentary provision to cut off a beneficiary if he marries someone of another religion or race? See Gordon v. Gordon, 332 Mass. 197, 124 N.E.2d 228, cert. denied, 349 U.S. 957 (1955). Does Evans v. Abney cast doubt on the ultimate outcome of the lengthy Girard College litigation, cited at the end of Justice Brennan's dissent, supra?

In Pennsylvania v. Board of Trusts, 353 U.S. 230 (1957), petitioners were denied admission to the school on the basis of race, pursuant to Stephen Girard's will, probated in 1831, setting up a trust for a school for "poor white male orphans." The will named the City of Philadelphia as trustee; subsequently, a "Board of Directors of City Trusts," composed of city officials and persons named by local courts, was established to administer the trust and the college. The state court refused to order admission. The Supreme Court reversed per curiam: "The Board which operates Girard College is an agency of the State. . . . Therefore, even though the Board was acting as trustee, its refusal to admit [petitioners] was discrimination by the State." After the Court's reversal, the state courts substituted private persons as trustees to carry out Girard's will. The Supreme Court denied certiorari. In re Girard College Trusteeship, 391 Pa. 434, 138 A.2d 844, cert. denied, 357 U.S. 570 (1958). Ten years after that denial of certiorari, however, the Court of Appeals for the Third Circuit held that the state courts' substitution of private trustees was unconstitutional state action. Brown v. Pennsylvania, 392 F.2d 120 (1968), cert. denied, 391 U.S. 921 (1968). See Clark, "Charitable Trusts, the Fourteenth Amendment and the Will of Stephen Girard," 66 Yale L.J. 979 (1957).

4. *Trespass actions and the sit-in cases.* Does Shelley v. Kraemer bar the enforcement of state trespass laws against persons excluded from private property on racial grounds? Is the state's enforcement of the property owner's restrictions sufficient state action to make the 14th Amendment applicable? That was the broadest issue inherent in a number of sit-in convictions of demonstrators who had protested discrimination by restaurants and other businesses prior to the enactment of the public accommodations provisions of the 1964 Civil Rights Act. In a series of decisions in the early sixties, the Court set aside all of the convictions—without reading the broad Shelley issue. The broadest reading of Shelley would have covered these cases with ease; the failure to rely on Shelley and the statements in some of the cases suggested that more state involvement than even-handed enforcement of private biases was necessary to find unconstitutional state action.

For example, in Peterson v. South Carolina, 373 U.S. 244 (1963)—one of five sit-in cases reversed at that time—the Court found official segregation policies in the background and refused to inquire whether the restaurant manager would have excluded the demonstrators if the state had been wholly silent: The unconstitutional ingredients "cannot be saved by attempting to separate the mental urges of the discriminators." Justice Harlan's separate opinion asserted that the "ultimate substantive question" was whether "the character of the State's involvement in an arbitrary discrimination is such that it should be held *responsible* for the discrimination."

Another group of five sit-in cases reached the Court in 1964. The trespass convictions were once again reversed on "narrow" grounds; but this time six of the Justices reached the broader issues—and divided 3 to 3. None took a "simple" view of Shelley. For example, Justice Douglas, joined by Justice Goldberg, emphasized that the refusal of service in the segregated restaurants "did not reflect 'personal' prejudices but business reasons." In urging reversal in Bell v. Maryland, 378 U.S. 226 (1964), he explained:

"The property involved is not . . . a man's home or his yard or even his fields. Private property is involved, but it is property that is serving the public. . . . The home of course is the essence of privacy, in no way dedicated to public use, in no way extending an invitation to the public. Some businesses, like the classical country store where the owner lives overhead or in the rear, make the store an extension, so to speak, of the home. But such is not this case. The facts of these sit-in cases have little resemblance to any institution of property which we customarily associate with privacy. [We should not] hold that property voluntarily serving the public can receive state protection when the owner refuses to serve some solely because they are colored. . . .

"The preferences involved in [Shelley v. Kraemer] were far more personal than the motivations of the corporate managers in the present case

. . . . Why should we refuse to let state courts enforce *apartheid* in residential areas of our cities but let state courts enforce *apartheid* in restaurants? If a court decree is state action in one case, it is in the other. Property rights, so heavily underscored, are equally invoved in each case.

"The customer in a restaurant is transitory; he comes and may never return. The colored family who buys the house next door is there for keeps —night and day. If 'personal prejudices' are not to be the criterion in one case they should not be in the other. We should put these restaurant cases in line with Shelley v. Kraemer, holding that what the Fourteenth Amendment requires in restrictive covenant cases it also requires from restaurants."

Justice Black's dissent, joined by Justices Harlan and White, included a narrow interpretation of Shelley v. Kraemer—and an important suggestion of a congressional power to reach further into the private sphere under § 5 of the 14th Amendment than the Court could properly go under § 1. The opinion included the following passages:

"Section 1 of the Fourteenth Amendment, . . . unlike other sections,[1] is a prohibition against certain conduct only when done by a State. [T]his section of the Amendment does not of itself, standing alone, in the absence of some cooperative state action or compulsion, forbid property holders, including restaurant owners, to ban people from entering or remaining upon their premises, even if the owners act out of racial prejudice. . . .

"[Petitioners] contend that their conviction for trespass under the state statute was by itself the kind of discriminatory state action forbidden by the Fourteenth Amendment. . . . But a mechanical application of the Fourteenth Amendment to this case cannot survive analysis. The Amendment does not forbid a State to prosecute for crimes committed against a person or his property, however prejudiced or narrow the victim's views may be. Nor can whatever prejudice and bigotry the victim of a crime may have be automatically attributed to the State that prosecutes. Such a doctrine would not only be based on a fiction; it would also severely handicap a State's efforts to maintain a peaceful and orderly society. . . . It would betray our whole plan for a tranquil and orderly society to say that a citizen, because of his personal prejudices, habits, attitudes, or beliefs, is cast outside the law's protection and cannot call for the aid of officers sworn to uphold the law and preserve the peace. . . . None of our past cases justifies reading the Fourteenth Amendment in a way that might well penalize citizens who are law-abiding enough to call upon the law and its officers for protection instead of using their own physical strength or dangerous weapons to preserve their rights.

"[P]etitioners rely chiefly on [Shelley v. Kraemer]. That reliance is misplaced. . . . It seems pretty clear that the reason judicial enforcement of the restrictive covenants in Shelley was deemed state action was, not merely the fact that a state court had acted, but rather that state enforcement of the covenants had the effect of denying to the parties their federally guaranteed right to own, occupy, enjoy, and use their property without regard to race or color. Thus, the line of cases from Buchanan through Shelley establishes these propositions: (1) When an owner of property is willing to sell and a would-be purchaser is willing to buy, then the Civil Rights Act of 1866, which

1. E. g., § 5: "The Congress shall have power to enforce, by appropriate legislation, the provisions of this article." [Footnote by Justice Black.]

gives all persons the same right to 'inherit, lease, sell, hold and convey' property, prohibits a State . . . from preventing the sale on the grounds of the race or color of one of the parties. . . . (2) Once a person has become a property owner, then he acquires all the rights that go with ownership: 'the free use, enjoyment, and disposal of a person's acquisitions without control or diminution save by the law of the land.' . . . This means that the property owner may, in the absence of a valid statute forbidding it, sell his property to whom he pleases and admit to that property whom he will; so long as *both* parties are willing parties, then the principles stated in Buchanan and Shelley protect this right. But equally, when one party is unwilling, as when the property owner chooses *not* to sell to a particular person or *not* to admit that person, then . . . he is entitled to rely on the guarantee of due process of law, that is, 'law of the land,' to protect his free use and enjoyment of property and to know that only by valid legislation, passed pursuant to some constitutional grant of power, can anyone disturb this free use. . . .

"We do not believe that section 1 of the Fourteenth Amendment was written or designed to interfere with a storekeeper's right to choose his customers or with a property owner's right to choose his social or business associates, so long as he does not run counter to valid state or federal regulation. . . . We express no views as to the power of Congress, acting under one or another provision of the Constitution, to prevent racial discrimination in the operation of privately owned businesses, nor upon any particular form of legislation to that end." *

5. *Limits and new directions.* Does Shelley make the "public function" analysis (p. 465, supra) unnecessary? Can that analysis be used to limit and explain Shelley? Was Shelley in effect a zoning case? Note Justice Douglas' concurring opinion in Reitman v. Mulkey, p. 485 infra: "Leaving the zoning function to groups [e. g., real estate brokers] which practice discrimination and are licensed by the States constitutes state action in the narrowest sense in which Shelley can be construed." What is the relevance of licensing? Is there state action any time the state can regulate and fails to bar discrimination? Note the Burton case, which follows, and cf. Henkin, "Shelley v. Kraemer: Notes for a Revised Opinion," 110 U.Pa.L.Rev. 473 (1962). Do the cases which follow, requiring state involvement to a "significant extent" to convert "private" action into unconstitutional discrimination, indicate additional limits on broad readings of Shelley and suggest different directions for delineating the scope of the state action concept?

BURTON v. WILMINGTON PARKING AUTHORITY

365 U.S. 715, 81 S.Ct. 856, 6 L.Ed.2d 45 (1961).

Certiorari to the Supreme Court of Delaware.

Mr. Justice CLARK delivered the opinion of the Court.

In this action for declaratory and injunctive relief it is admitted that the Eagle Coffee Shoppe, Inc., a restaurant located within an off-street automobile

[handwritten margin note: State involvement "to some significant extent"]

---

parking building in Wilmington, Delaware, has refused to serve appellant food or drink solely because he is a Negro. The parking building is owned and operated by the Wilmington Parking Authority, an agency of the State of Delaware, and the restaurant is the Authority's lessee. . . . The Supreme Court of Delaware has held that Eagle was acting in "a purely private capacity" under its lease; that its action was not that of the Authority and was not, therefore, state action . . . . It also held that under 24 Del.Code § 1501,[1] Eagle was a restaurant, not an inn, and that as such it "is not required [under Delaware law] to serve any and all persons entering its place of business." . . . On the merits we have concluded that the exclusion of appellant under the circumstances shown to be present here was discriminatory state action in violation of the Equal Protection Clause of the Fourteenth Amendment.

The Authority was created . . . to provide adequate parking facilities for the convenience of the public . . . . The first project undertaken by the Authority was the erection of a parking facility . . . . Before it began actual construction of the facility, the Authority was advised by its retained experts that the anticipated revenue from the parking of cars and proceeds from sale of its bonds would not be sufficient to finance the construction costs of the facility. Moreover, the bonds were not expected to be marketable if payable solely out of parking revenues. To secure additional capital needed for its "debt-service" requirements, . . . the Authority decided . . . to enter long-term leases with responsible tenants for commercial use of some of the space available in the projected "garage building." The public was invited to bid for these leases.

In April 1957 such a private lease, for 20 years . . ., was made with Eagle Coffee Shoppe, Inc., for use as a "restaurant." . . . [The] lease contains no requirement that its restaurant services be made available to the general public on a non-discriminatory basis, in spite of the fact that the Authority has power to adopt rules and regulations respecting the use of its facilities except any as would impair the security of its bondholders. . .

. . . . It is clear, as it always has been since the Civil Rights Cases, that private conduct abridging individual rights does no violence to the Equal Protection Clause unless to some significant extent the State in any of its manifestations has been found to have become involved in it. [T]o fashion and apply a precise formula for recognition of state responsibility under the Equal Protection Clause is "an impossible task" which "this Court has never attempted." . . . Only by sifting facts and weighing circumstances can the nonobvious involvement of the State in private conduct be attributed its true significance.

[T]he Delaware Supreme Court seems to have placed controlling emphasis on its conclusion, as to the accuracy of which there is doubt, that only some 15% of the total cost of the facility was "advanced" from public funds; . . . . that anticipated revenue from parking was only some 30.5% of the total income, the balance of which was expected to be earned by the leasing;

---

1. The statute provides that: "No keeper of an inn, tavern, hotel, or restaurant, or other place of public entertainment or refreshment of travelers, guests, or customers shall be obliged, by law, to furnish entertainment or refreshment to persons whose reception or entertainment by him would be offensive to the major part of his customers, and would injure his business. . . ." [Footnote by the Court.]

. . . . that Eagle expended considerable moneys on furnishings; that the restaurant's main and marked public entrance is on Ninth Street without any public entrance direct from the parking area; and that "the only connection Eagle has with the public facility . . . is the furnishing of the sum of $28,700 annually in the form of rent which is used by the Authority to defray a portion of the operating expense of an otherwise unprofitable enterprise." . . . . While these factual considerations are indeed validly accountable aspects of the enterprise upon which the State has embarked, we cannot say that they lead inescapably to the conclusion that state action is not present. Their persuasiveness is diminished when evaluated in the context of other factors which must be acknowledged.

The land and building were publicly owned. . . . The costs of land acquisition, construction, and maintenance are defrayed entirely from donations by the City of Wilmington, from loans and revenue bonds and from the proceeds of rentals and parking services out of which the loans and bonds were payable. Assuming that the distinction would be significant, cf. Derrington v. Plummer, 5 Cir., 240 F.2d 922, 925, the commercially leased areas were not surplus state property, but constituted a physically and financially integral and, indeed, indispensable part of the State's plan to operate its project as a self-sustaining unit. . . . It cannot be doubted that the peculiar relationship of the restaurant to the parking facility in which it is located confers on each an incidental variety of mutual benefits. . . . Neither can it be ignored, especially in view of Eagle's affirmative allegation that for it to serve Negroes would injure its business, that profits earned by discrimination not only contribute to, but are indispensable elements in the financial success of a governmental agency.

Addition of all these activities, obligations and responsibilities of the Authority, the benefits mutually conferred, together with the obvious fact that the restaurant is operated as an integral part of a public building devoted to a public parking service, indicates that degree of state participation and involvement in discriminatory action which it was the design of the Fourteenth Amendment to condemn. It is irony amounting to grave injustice that in one part of a single building, erected and maintained with public funds by an agency of the State to serve a public purpose, all persons have equal rights, while in another portion, also serving the public, a Negro is a second-class citizen. [I]n its lease with Eagle the Authority could have affirmatively required Eagle to discharge the responsibilities under the Fourteenth Amendment imposed upon the private enterprise as a consequence of state participation. But no State may effectively abdicate its responsibilities by either ignoring them or by merely failing to discharge them whatever the motive may be. It is of no consolation to an individual denied the equal protection of the laws that it was done in good faith. . . . By its inaction, the Authority, and through it the State, has not only made itself a party to the refusal of service, but has elected to place its power, property and prestige behind the admitted discrimination. The State has so far insinuated itself into a position of interdependence with Eagle that it must be recognized as a joint participant in the challenged activity, which, on that account, cannot be considered to have been so "purely private" as to fall without the scope of the Fourteenth Amendment.

Because readily applicable formulae may not be fashioned, the conclusions drawn from the facts and circumstances of this record are by no means declared as universal truths on the basis of which every state leasing agreement is to be tested. Owing to the very "largeness" of government, a multitude of relationships might appear to some to fall within the Amendment's embrace, but that, it must be remembered, can be determined only in the framework of the peculiar facts or circumstances present. Therefore respondents' prophecy of nigh universal application of a constitutional precept so peculiarly dependent for its invocation upon appropriate facts fails to take into account "Differences in circumstances [which] beget appropriate differences in law" . . . . Specifically defining the limits of our inquiry, what we hold today is that when a State leases public property in the manner and for the purpose shown to have been the case here, the proscriptions of the Fourteenth Amendment must be complied with by the lessee as certainly as though they were binding covenants written into the agreement iself. . . .

Reversed and remanded.

Mr. Justice STEWART, concurring.

I agree that the judgment must be reversed, but I reach that conclusion by a route much more direct that the one traveled by the Court. In upholding Eagle's right to deny service to the appellant solely because of his race, the Supreme Court of Delaware relied upon a statute of that State which permits the proprietor of a restaurant to refuse to serve "persons whose reception or entertainment by him would be offensive to the major part of his customers . . . ." There is no suggestion in the record that the appellant as an individual was such a person. The highest court of Delaware has thus construed this legislative enactment as authorizing discriminatory classification based exclusively on color. Such a law seems to me clearly violative of the Fourteenth Amendment. I think, therefore, . . . that the statute, as authoritatively construed . . ., is constitutionally invalid.

Mr. Justice HARLAN, whom Mr. Justice WHITTAKER joins, dissenting.

The Court's opinion, by a process of first undiscriminatingly throwing together various factual bits and pieces and then undermining the resulting structure by an equally vague disclaimer, seems to me to leave completely at sea just what it is in this record that satisfies the requirement of "state action."

I find it unnecessary, however, to inquire into the matter at this stage, for it seems to me apparent that before passing on the far-reaching constitutional questions that may, or may not, be lurking in this judgment, the case should first be sent back to the state court for clarification as to the precise basis of its decision. . . .

If . . . the Delaware court construed this state statute "as authorizing discriminatory classification based exclusively on color," I would certainly agree, without more, that the enactment is offensive to the Fourteenth Amendment. It would then be quite unnecessary to reach the much broader questions dealt with in the Court's opinion. If, on the other hand, the state court meant no more than that under the statute, as at common law, Eagle was free to serve only those whom it pleased, then, and only then, would the question of "state action" be presented in full-blown form. . . .

Mr. Justice FRANKFURTER, dissenting. . . .

I certainly do not find the clarity that my brother Stewart finds . . . . If I were forced to construe that court's construction, I should find the balance of considerations leading to the opposite conclusion from his, namely, that it was merely declaratory of the common law and did not give state sanction to refusing service to a person merely because he is colored. The Court takes no position regarding the statutory meaning which divides my brothers Harlan and Stewart. If it [took Justice Stewart's view], it would undoubtedly take his easy road to decision . . . . Since the pronouncement of the Supreme Court of Delaware thus lends itself to three views, none of which is patently irrational, why is not my brother Harlan's suggestion for solving this conflict the most appropriate solution? . . .

REITMAN v. MULKEY

387 U.S. 369, 87 S.Ct. 1627, 18 L.Ed.2d 830 (1967).

Certiorari to the Supreme Court of California.*

Mr. Justice WHITE delivered the opinion of the Court.

The question here is whether Art. I, § 26 of the California Constitution denies "to any person . . . the equal protection of the laws" within the meaning of the Fourteenth Amendment of the Constitution of the United States. Section 26 of Art. I, an initiated measure submitted to the people as Proposition 14 in a statewide ballot in 1964, provides in part as follows:

> "Neither the State nor any subdivision or agency thereof shall deny, limit or abridge, directly or indirectly, the right of any person, who is willing or desires to sell, lease or rent any part or all of his real property, to decline to sell, lease or rent such property to such person or persons as he, in his absolute discretion, chooses."

The real property covered by § 26 is limited to residential property and contains an exception for state-owned real estate.

[T]he Mulkeys, who are husband and wife and respondents here, sued under §§ 51 and 52 of the California Civil Code [1] alleging that petitioners had refused to rent them an apartment solely on account of their race. An injunction and damages were demanded. Petitioners moved for summary judgment on the ground that §§ 51 and 52, insofar as they were the basis for the Mulkeys' action, had been rendered null and void by the adoption of Proposition 14 after the filing of the complaint. The trial court granted the motion and respondents took the case to the California Supreme Court. . . . That court . . . held that Art. I, § 26, was invalid as denying the equal protection of the laws guaranteed by the Fourteenth Amendment. . . .

-----

* Together with Snyder v. Prendergast, on certiorari to the same court. The facts of that case are omitted here.

1. Cal.Civil Code §§ 51 and 52 provide in part as follows:
"All persons within the jurisdiction of this State are free and equal, and no matter what their race, color, religion, ancestry, or national origin are entitled to the full and equal accommodations, advantages, facilities, privileges, or services in all business establishments of every kind whatsoever. . . .

"Whosoever denies, or who aids, or incites such denial, or whoever makes any discrimination, distinction or restriction on account of color, race, religion, ancestry, or national origin, contrary to the provisions of Section 51 of this code, is liable for each and every such offense for the actual damages, and two hundred fifty dollars ($250) in addition thereto, suffered by any person denied the rights provided in Section 51 of this code." [Footnote by the Court.]

We affirm the judgment of the California Supreme Court. We first turn to the opinion of that court, which quite properly undertook to examine the constitutionality of § 26 in terms of its "immediate objective," its "ultimate effect" and its "historical context and the conditions existing prior to its enactment." Judgments such as these we have frequently undertaken ourselves. . . . But here the California Supreme Court has addressed itself to these matters and we should give careful consideration to its views because they concern the purpose, scope, and operative effect of a provision of the California Constitution.

First, the court considered whether § 26 was concerned at all with private discriminations in residential housing. This involved a review of past efforts by the California Legislature to regulate such discriminations. The Unruh Act, Civ.Code §§ 51–52, on which respondents based their cases, was passed in 1959. The Hawkins Act . . . followed and prohibited discriminations in publicly assisted housing. . . . Finally, in 1963, came the Rumford Fair Housing Act, . . . superseding the Hawkins Act and prohibiting racial discriminations in the sale or rental of any private dwelling containing more than four units. That act was enforceable by the State Fair Employment Practice Commission.

It was against this background that Proposition 14 was enacted. Its immediate design and intent, the California court said, was "to overturn state laws that bore on the right of private sellers and lessors to discriminate," . . . and "to forestall future state action that might circumscribe this right." This aim was successfully achieved . . . .

Second, the court conceded that the State was permitted a neutral position with respect to private racial discriminations and that the State was not bound by the Federal Constitution to forbid them. But . . . the court deemed it necessary to determine whether Proposition 14 invalidly involved the State in racial discriminations in the housing market. Its conclusion was that it did.

To reach this result, the state court examined certain prior decisions in this Court in which discriminatory state action was identified. Based on these cases, . . . it concluded that a prohibited state involvement could be found "even where the State can be charged only with encouraging, rather than commanding discrimination . . . ." Also of particular interest to the court was Mr. Justice Stewart's concurrence in Burton v. Wilmington Parking Authority, 365 U.S. 715, where it was said that the Delaware courts had construed an existing Delaware statute as "authorizing" racial discrimination in restaurants and that the statute was therefore invalid. To the California court "the instant case presents an undeniably analogous situation" wherein the State had taken affirmative action designed to make private discriminations legally possible. Section 26 was said to have changed the situation from one in which discriminatory practices were restricted "to one where it is encouraged, within the meaning of the cited decisions"; § 26 was legislative action "which authorized private discrimination" and made the State "at least a partner in the instant act of discrimination . . . ." The court could "conceive of no other purpose for an application of § 26 aside from authorizing the perpetration of a purported private discrimination . . . ." The judgment of the California court was that § 26 unconstitutionally involves the State in racial discriminations and is therefore invalid under the Fourteenth Amendment.

There is no sound reason for rejecting this judgment. Petitioners contend that the California court has misconstrued the Fourteenth Amendment since the repeal of any statute prohibiting racial discrimination, which is constitutionally permissible, may be said to "authorize" and "encourage" discrimination because it makes legally permissible that which was formerly proscribed. But as we understand the California court, it did not posit a constitutional violation on the mere repeal of the Unruh and Rumford Acts. It did not read either our cases or the Fourteenth Amendment as establishing an automatic constitutional barrier to the repeal of an existing law prohibiting racial discriminations in housing; nor did the court rule that a State may never put in statutory form an existing policy of neutrality with respect to private discriminations. What the court below did was first to reject the notion that the State was required to have a statute prohibiting racial discriminations in housing. Second, . . . the court dealt with § 26 as though it expressly authorized and constitutionalized the private right to discriminate. Third, the court assessed the ultimate impact of § 26 in the California environment and concluded that the section would encourage and significantly involve the State in private racial discrimination contrary to the Fourteenth Amendment.

The California court could very reasonably conclude that § 26 would and did have wider impact than a mere repeal of existing statutes. . . . Private discriminations in housing were now not only free from Rumford and Unruh but they also enjoyed a far different status than was true before the passage of those statutes. The right to discriminate, including the right to discriminate on racial grounds, was now embodied in the State's basic charter, immune from legislative, executive, or judicial regulation at any level of the state government. Those practicing racial discriminations need no longer rely solely on their personal choice. They could now invoke express constitutional authority, free from censure or interference of any kind from official sources. . . .

This Court has never attempted the "impossible task" of formulating an infallible test for determining whether the State "in any of its manifestations" has become significantly involved in private discriminations. . . . Here the California court, armed as it was with the knowledge of the facts and circumstances concerning the passage and potential impact of § 26, and familiar with the milieu in which that provision would operate, has determined that the provision would involve the State in private racial discriminations to an unconstitutional degree. We accept this holding of the California court.

The assessment of § 26 by the California court is similar to what this Court has done in appraising state statutes or other official actions in other contexts. . . .

None of these cases squarely controls the case we now have before us. But they do illustrate the range of situations in which discriminatory state action has been identified. They do exemplify the necessity for a court to assess the potential impact of official action in determining whether the State has significantly involved itself with invidious discriminations. Here we are dealing with a provision which does not just repeal an existing law forbidding private racial discriminations. Section 26 was intended to authorize, and does authorize, racial discrimination in the housing market. The right to discriminate is now one of the basic policies of the State. The California Supreme

Court believes that the section will significantly encourage and involve the State in private discriminations. We have been presented with no persuasive considerations indicating that this judgment should be overturned.

Affirmed.*

Mr. Justice DOUGLAS, concurring. . . .

Real estate brokers and mortgage lenders are largely dedicated to the maintenance of segregated communities. . . . Proposition 14 is a form of sophisticated discrimination whereby the people of California harness the energies of private groups to do indirectly what they cannot under our decisions allow their government to do. . . .

Zoning is a state and municipal function. . . . When the State leaves that function to private agencies or institutions which are licensees and who practice racial discrimination and zone our cities into white and black belts or white and black ghettoes, it suffers a governmental function to be performed under private auspices in a way the State itself may not act. The present case is therefore kin to [Terry v. Adams].

Leaving the zoning function to groups which practice discrimination and are licensed by the States constitutes State action in the narrowest sense in which [Shelley v. Kraemer] can be construed. . . .

If we were in a domain exclusively private, we would have different problems. But urban housing is in the public domain as evidenced not only by the zoning problems presented but by the vast schemes of public financing with which the States and the Nation have been extensively involved in recent years. Urban housing is clearly marked with the public interest. . . . Since the real estate brokerage business is one that can be and is state-regulated and since it is state-licensed, it must be dedicated, like the telephone companies and the carriers and the hotels and motels, to the requirements of service to all without discrimination—a standard that in its modern setting is conditioned by the demands of the Equal Protection Clause of the Fourteenth Amendment.

Mr. Justice HARLAN, whom Mr. Justice BLACK, Mr. Justice CLARK, and Mr. Justice STEWART join, dissenting. . . .

In the case at hand California, acting through the initiative and referendum, has decided to remain "neutral" in the realm of private discrimination affecting the sale or rental of private residential property; in such transactions private owners are now free to act in a discriminatory manner previously forbidden to them. In short, all that has happened is that California has effected a *pro tanto* repeal of its prior statutes forbidding private discrimina-

* Note also Hunter v. Erickson, 393 U.S. 385 (1969), invalidating a city charter amendment requiring that any city council ordinance regulating real property transactions "on the basis of race, color, religion, national origin or ancestry must first be approved by a majority of the electors voting on the question at a regular or general election before said ordinance shall be effective." That amendment superseded an earlier fair housing ordinance adopted by the city council. The city sought to distinguish Reitman v. Mulkey "in that here the city charter declares no right to discriminate in housing, authorizes and encourages no housing discrimination, and places no ban on the enactment of fair housing ordinances." Justice White did not pursue that argument: elaboration of Reitman was unnecessary here because in this case, unlike Reitman, "there was an explicitly racial classification treating racial housing matters differently from other racial and housing matters." The case is considered further infra, chap. 18, p. 1417.

tion. This runs no more afoul of the Fourteenth Amendment than would have California's failure to pass any such antidiscrimination statutes in the first instance. . . .

The Court attempts to fit § 26 within the coverage of the Equal Protection Clause by characterizing it as in effect an affirmative call to residents of California to discriminate. The main difficulty with this viewpoint is that it depends upon a characterization of § 26 that cannot fairly be made. The provision is neutral on its face, and it is only by in effect asserting that this requirement of passive official neutrality is camouflage that the Court is able to reach its conclusion. In depicting the provision as tantamount to active state encouragement of discrimination the Court essentially relies on the fact that the California Supreme Court so concluded. It is said that the findings of the highest court of California as to the meaning and impact of the enactment are entitled to great weight. I agree of course, that *findings of fact* by a state court should be given great weight, but this familiar proposition hardly aids the Court's holding in this case. . . .

. . . The only "factual" matter relied on by the majority of the California Supreme Court was the context in which Proposition 14 was adopted, namely, that several strong antidiscrimination acts had been passed by the legislature, and opposed by many of those who successfully led the movement for adoption of Proposition 14 by popular referendum. These circumstances, and these alone, the California court held, made § 26 unlawful under this Court's cases interpreting the Equal Protection Clause. This, of course, is nothing but a legal conclusion as to federal constitutional law, the California Supreme Court not having relied in any way upon the State Constitution. Accepting all the suppositions under which the state court acted, I cannot see that its conclusion is entitled to any special weight in the discharge of our own responsibilities. Put in another way, I cannot transform the California court's conclusion of law into a finding of fact that the State through the adoption of § 26 is actively promoting racial discrimination. It seems to me manifest that the state court decision rested entirely on what that court conceived to be the compulsion of the Fourteenth Amendment, not on any fact-finding by the state courts.

There is no question that the adoption of § 26, repealing the former state antidiscrimination laws and prohibiting the enactment of such state laws in the future, constituted "state action" within the meaning of the Fourteenth Amendment. The only issue is whether this provision impermissibly deprives any person of equal protection of the laws. . . . [T]he present case does not seem to me even to approach those peripheral situations in which the question of state involvement gives rise to difficulties. See, e. g., Evans v. Newton . . . . The core of the Court's opinion is that § 26 is offensive to the Fourteenth Amendment because it effectively *encourages* private discrimination. By focusing on "encouragement" the Court, I fear, is forging a slippery and unfortunate criterion by which to measure the constitutionality of a statute simply permissive in purpose and effect, and inoffensive on its face.

It is true that standards in this area have not been definitely formulated, and that acts of discrimination have been included within the compass of the Equal Protection Clause not merely when they were compelled by a state statute or other governmental pressures, but also when they were said to be "induced" or "authorized" by the State. Most of these cases, however, can be approached in terms of the impact and extent of affirmative state governmental activities, e. g., the action of a sheriff, Lombard v. Louisiana, supra; the official supervision over a park, Evans v. Newton, supra; a joint venture with a lessee in a municipally owned building, Burton v. Wilmington Parking Authority, supra. In situations such as these the focus has been on positive state cooperation or partnership in affirmatively promoted activities, an involvement that could have been avoided. Here, in contrast, we have only the straightforward adoption of a neutral provision restoring to the sphere of free choice, left untouched by the Fourteenth Amendment, private behavior within a limited area of the racial problem. The denial of equal protection emerges only from the conclusion reached by the Court that the implementation of a new policy of governmental neutrality, embodied in a constitutional provision and replacing a former policy of antidiscrimination, has the effect of lending encouragement to those who wish to discriminate. In the context of the actual facts of the case, this conclusion appears to me to state only a truism: people who want to discriminate but were previously forbidden to do so by state law are now left free because the State has chosen to have no law on the subject at all. Obviously whenever there is a change in the law it will have resulted from the concerted activity of those who desire the change, and its enactment will allow those supporting the legislation to pursue their private goals.

A moment of thought will reveal the far-reaching possibilities of the Court's new doctrine, which I am sure the Court does not intend. Every act of private discrimination is either forbidden by state law or permitted by it. There can be little doubt that such permissiveness—whether by express constitutional or statutory provision, or implicit in the common law—to some extent "encourages" those who wish to discriminate to do so. Under this theory "state action" in the form of laws that do nothing more than passively permit private discrimination could be said to tinge *all* private discrimination with the taint of unconstitutional state encouragement.

. . . . I believe the state action required to bring the Fourteenth Amendment into operation must be affirmative and purposeful, actively fostering discrimination. Only in such a case is ostensibly "private" action more properly labeled "official." I do not believe that the mere enactment of § 26, on the showing made here, falls within this class of cases.

I think that this decision is not only constitutionally unsound, but in its practical potentialities short-sighted. Opponents of state antidiscrimination statutes are now in a position to argue that such legislation should be defeated because, if enacted, it may be unrepealable. More fundamentally, the doctrine underlying this decision may hamper, if not preclude, attempts to deal with the delicate and troublesome problems of race relations through the legislative process. The lines that have been and must be drawn in this area, fraught as it is with human sensibilities and frailties of whatever race or creed, are difficult ones. The drawing of them requires understanding, patience, and compromise, and is best done by legislatures rather than by courts. When legislation in this field is unsuccessful there should be wide opportunities for legislative amendment, as well as for change through such processes as the popular initiative and referendum. This decision, I fear, may inhibit such flexibility. . . . .

STATE INVOLVEMENT IN PRIVATE ACTION—"TO SOME SIGNIFICANT EXTENT"

Does Burton retreat from the broadest implications of Shelley, by suggesting that finding some nexus of the state with the private discrimination is not enough and by insisting that the state must be involved "to some significant extent" to bring the private conduct under the 14th Amendment? What was "significant" in Burton? Does Burton give any guidance for evaluating "significance"? Cf. Lewis, "Burton v. Wilmington Parking Authority—A Case Without Precedent," 61 Colum.L.Rev. 1458 (1961).

Was Justice Stewart's ground in Burton the "more direct," "easy road to decision"? Would Justice Harlan's suggestion of a construction that the statute "authorized" discrimination be a narrower ground? Does "authorization" differ from failure to prohibit? Is "authorization" of unrestrained private choices, by statute or common law, "significant involvement" by the state? Cf. Williams, "The Twilight of State Action," 41 Tex.L.Rev. 347 (1963). Why was the enforcement of the reverter in the Baconsfield park litigation, p. 476, supra, not "authorization" in this sense? Does Reitman clarify Justice Clark's "significant extent" or Justice Stewart's "authorization" criteria?

Is the 1970 decision in the Baconsfield park litigation, Evans v. Abney, p. 476 supra, a retreat from Burton and Reitman? Were not the "significant" state involvements recited in Justice Brennan's dissent there as substantial as those in Burton and Reitman? Before that decision, some commentators, noting that no modern court decision had rejected a discrimination claim because of the state action barrier, had suggested that the concept was moribund. See, e. g., C. L. Black, Jr., "Foreword: 'State Action,' Equal Protection and California's Proposition 14," 81 Harv.L.Rev. 69 (1967); and, note Karst and Horowitz, "Reitman v. Mulkey; A Telophase of Substantive Equal Protection," 1967 Sup.Ct.Rev. 39. Does Evans v. Abney revive it?

Is the Court's unwillingness to intrude further into the private sphere under § 1 of the 14th Amendment related to the increasing scope and exercise of congressional power to reach private activities under § 5 of the 14th Amendment? How broad is that power? Why—and to what extent—may Congress under § 5 go beyond where the Court has gone under § 1? How far may Congress go under the 13th Amendment? * These are the concerns of the materials which follow.

---

* See the Jones case, p. 517, infra, and the community facilities discrimination case, Sullivan v. Little Hunting Park, Inc., 396 U.S. 229 (1969), both decided under the 13th Amendment-based 1866 Civil Rights Act, 42 U.S.C. § 1982, rather than on the basis of state action analysis.

SECTION 3. CONGRESSIONAL POWER TO REACH PRIVATE CONDUCT UNDER THE 14TH AND 13TH AMENDMENTS: THE MODERN SCOPE

A. FEDERAL LEGISLATION AND CIVIL RIGHTS VIOLENCE: THE CASES BEFORE GUEST

SCREWS v. UNITED STATES

325 U.S. 91, 65 S.Ct. 1031, 89 L.Ed. 1495 (1945).

Certiorari to the United States Circuit Court of Appeals for the Fifth Circuit.

Mr. Justice DOUGLAS announced the judgment of the Court and delivered the following opinion, in which the Chief Justice [STONE], Mr. Justice BLACK and Mr. Justice REED, concur.

This case involves a shocking and revolting episode in law enforcement. Petitioner Screws was sheriff of Baker County, Georgia. He enlisted the assistance of petitioner Jones, a policeman, and petitioner Kelley, a special deputy, in arresting Robert Hall, a citizen of the United States and of Georgia. The arrest was made late at night in Hall's home on a warrant charging Hall with theft of a tire. Hall, a young negro about thirty years of age, was handcuffed and taken by car to the court house. As Hall alighted from the car at the court house square, the three petitioners began beating him with their fists and with a solid-bar blackjack about eight inches long and weighing two pounds. They claimed Hall had reached for a gun and had used insulting language as he alighted from the car. But after Hall, still handcuffed, had been knocked to the ground they continued to beat him from fifteen to thirty minutes until he was unconscious. Hall was then dragged feet first through the court house yard into the jail and thrown upon the floor dying. An ambulance was called and Hall was removed to a hospital where he died within the hour and without regaining consciousness. There was evidence that Screws held a grudge against Hall and had threatened to "get" him.

An indictment was returned against petitioners—one count charging a violation of § 20 of the Criminal Code, 18 U.S.C. § 52, and another charging a conspiracy to violate § 20 contrary to § 37 of the Criminal Code, 18 U.S.C. § 88. Sec. 20 provides: [See the text of 18 U.S.C. § 242, p. 452, supra].

The indictment charged that petitioners, acting under color of the laws of Georgia, "willfully" caused Hall to be deprived of "rights, privileges, or immunities secured or protected" to him by the Fourteenth Amendment—the right not to be deprived of life without due process of law; the right to be tried, upon the charge on which he was arrested, by due process of law and if found guilty to be punished in accordance with the laws of Georgia; that is to say that petitioners "unlawfully and wrongfully did assault, strike and beat the said Robert Hall about the head with human fists and a blackjack causing injuries" to Hall "which were the proximate and immediate cause of his death." A like charge was made in the conspiracy count.

The case was tried to a jury. The court charged the jury that due process of law gave one charged with a crime the right to be tried by a jury and sentenced by a court. On the question of intent it charged that ". . . if these defendants, without its being necessary to make the arrest effectual or necessary to their own personal protection, beat this man, assaulted him or killed him while he was under arrest, then they would be acting illegally under color of law, as stated by this statute, and would be depriving the prisoner of certain constitutional rights guaranteed to him by the Constitution of the United States and consented to by the State of Georgia."

The jury returned a verdict of guilty and a fine and imprisonment on each count was imposed. The Circuit Court of Appeals affirmed the judgment of conviction, one judge dissenting. 140 F.2d 662. The case is here on a petition for a writ of certiorari which we granted because of the importance in the administration of the criminal laws of the questions presented.

I. We are met at the outset with the claim that § 20 is unconstitutional, in so far as it makes criminal acts in violation of the due process clause of the Fourteenth Amendment. The argument runs as follows: It is true that this Act as construed in United States v. Classic, 313 U.S. 299, 328 [1941], was upheld in its application to certain ballot box frauds committed by state officials. But in that case the constitutional rights protected were the rights to vote specifically guaranteed by Art. I, § 2 and § 4 of the Constitution. Here there is no ascertainable standard of guilt. There have been conflicting views in the Court as to the proper construction of the due process clause. The majority have quite consistently construed it in broad general terms.   . . .   It is said that the Act must be read as if it contained those broad and fluid definitions of due process and that if it is so read it provides no ascertainable standard of guilt.   . . .

The serious character of that challenge to the constitutionality of the Act is emphasized if the customary standard of guilt for statutory crimes is taken. As we shall see specific intent is at times required. . . . But the general rule was stated in Ellis v. United States, 206 U.S. 246, 257, as follows: "If a man intentionally adopts certain conduct in certain circumstances known to him, and that conduct is forbidden by the law under those circumstances, he intentionally breaks the law in the only sense in which the law ever considers intent."   . . .   Under that test a local law enforcement officer violates § 20 and commits a federal offense for which he can be sent to the penitentiary if he does an act which some court later holds deprives a person of due process of law. And he is a criminal though his motive was pure and though his purpose was unrelated to the disregard of any constitutional guarantee. The treacherous ground on which state officials— police, prosecutors, legislators, and judges—would walk is indicated by the character and closeness of decisions of this Court interpreting the due process clause of the Fourteenth Amendment. . . . [See, e. g., chaps. 11 and 12, infra.] . . . If such a construction is not necessary, it should be avoided. This Court has consistently favored that interpretation of legislation which supports its constitutionality. . . . [W]e are of the view that if § 20 is confined more narrowly than the lower courts confined it, it can be preserved as one of the sanctions to the great rights which the Fourteenth Amendment was designed to secure.

II. We recently pointed out that "willful" is a word "of many meanings, its construction often being influenced by its context." . . . At times, . . . the word denotes an act which is intentional rather than accidental. . . . But "when used in a criminal statute, it generally means an act done with a bad purpose." . . . In that event something more is required than the doing of the act proscribed by the statute. . . . An evil motive to accomplish that which the statute condemns becomes a constituent element of the crime. . . . And that issue must be submitted to the jury under appropriate instructions. . . .

[I]f we construe "willfully" in § 20 as connoting a purpose to deprive a person of a specific constitutional right, we would introduce no innovation. The Court, indeed, has recognized that the requirement of a specific intent to do a prohibited act may avoid those consequences to the accused which may otherwise render a vague or indefinite statute invalid. The constitutional vice in such a statute is the essential injustice to the accused of placing him on trial for an offense, the nature of which the statute does not define and hence of which it gives no warning. . . . But where the punishment imposed is only for an act knowingly done with the purpose of doing that which the statute prohibits, the accused cannot be said to suffer from lack of warning or knowledge that the act which he does is a violation of law. The requirement that the act must be willful or purposeful may not render certain, for all purposes, a statutory definition of the crime which is in some respects uncertain. But it does relieve the statute of the objection that it punishes without warning an offense of which the accused was unaware. . . . We repeat that the presence of a bad purpose or evil intent alone may not be sufficient. We do say that a requirement of a specific intent to deprive a person of a federal right made definite by decision or other rule of law saves the Act from any charge of unconstitutionality on the grounds of vagueness. . . .

It is said, however, that this construction of the Act will not save it from the infirmity of vagueness since neither a law enforcement official nor a trial judge can know with sufficient definiteness the range of rights that are constitutional. But that criticism is wide of the mark. For the specific intent required by the Act is an intent to deprive a person of a right which has been made specific either by the express terms of the Constitution or laws of the United States or by decisions interpreting them. Take the case of a local officer who persists in enforcing a type of ordinance which the Court has held invalid as violative of the guarantees of free speech or freedom of worship. Or a local official continues to select juries in a manner which flies in the teeth of decisions of the Court. If those acts are done willfully, how can the officer possibly claim that he had no fair warning that his acts were prohibited by the statute? He violates the statute not merely because he has a bad purpose but because he acts in defiance of announced rules of law. He who defies a decision interpreting the Constitution knows precisely what he is doing. If sane, he hardly may be heard to say that he knew not what he did. Of course, willful conduct cannot make definite that which is undefined. But willful violators of constitutional requirements, which have been defined, certainly are in no position to say that they had no adequate advance notice that they would be visited with punishment. When they act willfully in the sense in which we use the word, they act in open defiance or in reckless disregard of a constitutional requirement which has been made specific and definite. When they are convicted for so acting, they are not punished for violating an unknowable something. . . .

    . . . The fact that the defendants may not have been thinking in constitutional terms is not material where their aim was not to enforce local law but to deprive a citizen of a right and that right was protected by the Constitution. When they so act they at least act in reckless disregard of constitutional prohibitions or guarantees. Likewise, it is plain that basic to the concept of due process of law in a criminal case is a trial—a trial in a court of law, not a "trial by ordeal." . . . It could hardly be doubted that they who "under color of any law, statute, ordinance, regulation, or custom" act with that evil motive violate § 20. Those who decide to take the law into their own hands and act as prosecutor, jury, judge, and executioner plainly act to deprive a prisoner of the trial which due process of law guarantees him. And such a purpose need not be expressed; it may at times be reasonably inferred from all the circumstances attendant on the act. . . .

The difficulty here is that this question of intent was not submitted to the jury with the proper instructions. The court charged that petitioners acted illegally if they applied more force than was necessary to make the arrest effectual or to protect themselves from the prisoner's alleged assault. But in view of our construction of the word "willfully" the jury should have been further instructed that it was not sufficient that petitioners had a generally bad purpose. To convict it was necessary for them to find that petitioners had the purpose to deprive the prisoner of a constitutional right, e. g. the right to be tried by a court rather than by ordeal. And in determining whether that requisite bad purpose was present the jury would be entitled to consider all the attendant circumstances—the malice of petitioners, the weapons used in the assault, its character and duration, the provocation, if any, and the like. . . .

III. It is said, however, that petitioners did not act "under color of any law" within the meaning of § 20 of the Criminal Code. We disagree. We are of the view that petitioners acted under "color" of law in making the arrest of Robert Hall and in assaulting him. They were officers of the law who made the arrest. By their own admissions they assaulted Hall in order to protect themselves and to keep their prisoner from escaping. It was their duty under Georgia law to make the arrest effective. Hence, their conduct comes within the statute. [The Court relied on the interpretation in the Classic case: "Misuse of power, possessed by virtue of state law and made possible only because the wrongdoer is clothed with the authority of state law, is action taken 'under color of' state law."] The meaning which the Classic case gave to the phrase "under color of any law" involved only a construction of the statute. Hence if it states a rule undesirable in its consequences, Congress can change it. We add only to the instability and uncertainty of the law if we revise the meaning of § 20 to meet the exigencies of each case coming before us. . . .

Since there must be a new trial, the judgment below is reversed.

Mr. Justice RUTLEDGE, concurring in the result.

For the compelling reason stated at the end of this opinion I concur in reversing the judgment and remanding the cause for further proceedings. But for that reason, my views would require that my vote be cast to affirm the judgment, for the reasons stated by Mr. Justice Murphy and others I feel forced, in the peculiar situation, to state. . . .

To the Constitution state officials and the states themselves owe first obligation. The federal power lacks no strength to reach their malfeasance in office when it infringes constitutional rights. If that is a great power, it is one generated by the Constitution and the Amendments, to which the states have assented and their officials owe prime allegiance. The right not to be deprived of life or liberty by a state officer who takes it by abuse of his office and its power is such a right. To secure these rights is not beyond federal power. This Sections 19 and 20 have done, in a manner history long since has validated. Accordingly, I would affirm the judgment.

My convictions are as I have stated them. Were it possible for me to adhere to them in my vote, and for the Court at the same time to dispose of the cause, I would act accordingly. The Court, however, is divided in opinion. If each member accords his vote to his belief, the case cannot have disposition. Stalemate should not prevail for any reason, however compelling, in a criminal cause or, if avoidable, in any other. My views concerning appropriate disposition are more nearly in accord with those stated by Mr. Justice Douglas, in which three other members of the Court concur, than they are with the views of my dissenting brethen who favor outright reversal. Accordingly, in order that disposition may be made of this case, my vote has been cast to reverse the decision of the Court of Appeals and remand the cause to the District Court for further proceedings in accordance with the disposition required by the opinion of Mr. Justice Douglas.

Mr. Justice MURPHY, dissenting. . . .

It is axiomatic, of course, that a criminal statute must give a clear and unmistakable warning as to the acts which will subject one to criminal punishment. And courts are without power to supply that which Congress has left vague. But this salutary principle does not mean that if a statute is vague as to certain criminal acts but definite as to others the entire statute must fall. Nor does it mean that in the first case involving the statute to come before us we must delineate all the prohibited acts that are obscure and all those that are explicit.

Thus it is idle to speculate on other situations that might involve Section 20 which are not now before us. We are unconcerned here with state officials who have coerced a confession from a prisoner, denied counsel to a defendant or made a faulty tax assessment. Whatever doubt may exist in those or in other situations as to whether the state officials could reasonably anticipate and recognize the relevant constitutional rights is immaterial in this case. Our attention here is directed solely to three state officials who, in the course of their official duties, have unjustifiably beaten and crushed the body of a human being, thereby depriving him of trial by jury and of life itself. . . . Knowledge of a comprehensive law library is unnecessary for officers of the law to know that the right to murder individuals in the course of their duties is unrecognized in this nation. . . .

Mr. Justice ROBERTS, Mr. Justice FRANKFURTER and Mr. Justice JACKSON, dissenting. . . .

Of course the petitioners are punishable. The only issue is whether Georgia alone has the power and duty to punish, or whether this patently local crime can be made the basis of a federal prosecution. The practical question is whether the States should be relieved from responsibility to bring their law officers to book for homicide, by allowing prosecutions in the federal courts for a relatively minor offense carrying a short sentence. The legal question is whether, for the purpose of accomplishing this relaxation of State responsibility, hitherto settled principles for the protection of civil liberties shall be bent and tortured. . . . We are asked to construe legislation which was intended to effectuate prohibitions against States for defiance of the Constitution, to be equally applicable where a State duly obeys the Constitution, but an officer flouts State law and is unquestionably subject to punishment by the State for his disobedience. . . .

But assuming unreservedly that conduct such as that now before us, perpetrated by State officers in flagrant defiance of State law, may be attributed to the State under the Fourteenth Amendment, this does not make it action under "color of any law." Section 20 is much narrower than the power of Congress. Even though Congress might have swept within the federal criminal law any action that could be deemed within the vast reach of the Fourteenth Amendment, Congress did not do so. . . . In the absence of clear direction by Congress we should leave to the States the enforcement of their criminal law, and not relieve States of the responsibility for vindicating wrongdoing that is essentially local or weaken the habits of local law enforcement by tempting reliance on federal authority for an occasional unpleasant task of local enforcement. . . .

Since the majority of the Court do not share this conviction that the action of the Georgia peace officers was not perpetrated under color of law, we, too, must consider the constitutionality of § 20. . . .

This intrinsic vagueness of the terms of § 20 surely cannot be removed by making the statute applicable only where the defendant has the "requisite bad purpose". Does that not amount to saying that the black heart of the defendant enables him to know what are the constitutional rights deprivation of which the statute forbids, although we as judges are not able to define their classes or their limits, or, at least, are not prepared to state what they are unless it be to say that § 20 protects whatever rights the Constitution protects? . . . .

It is as novel as it is an inadmissible principle that a criminal statute of indefinite scope can be rendered definite by requiring that a person "willfully" commit what Congress has not defined but which, if Congress had defined, could constitutionally be outlawed. Of course Congress can prohibit the deprivation of enumerated constitutional rights. But if Congress makes it a crime to deprive another of any right protected by the Constitution—and that is what § 20 does—this Court cannot escape facing decisions as to what constitutional rights are covered by § 20 by saying that in any event, whatever they are, they must be taken away "willfully." . . . *

---

* At the second trial, Screws was acquitted. See also the 18 U.S.C. § 242 prosecutions in Koehler v. United States, 189 F.2d 711 (5th Cir.), cert. denied, 342 U.S. 852 (1951), and Crews v. United States, 160 F.2d 746 (5th Cir. 1947). See Alfange, "Under Color of Law—Classic and Screws Revisited," 47 Cornell L.Q. 395 (1962).

THE WILLIAMS CASES

1. The predecessor of 18 U.S.C. § 242 was again before the Court in Williams v. United States, 341 U.S. 97 (1951). Defendant, a private detective who had been issued a special police officer's badge, was employed by a lumber company to investigate thefts of its property. Flashing his badge and accompanied by a regular police officer detailed to assist him in the investigation, he took four suspects to a shack on the company's premises and beat them until they confessed to the thefts. Indicted for depriving his victims, under color of law, of the right to be tried by due process of law, he was found guilty by a jury under instructions which conformed to the rulings in the Screws case. The Court affirmed. Justice Douglas, writing the opinion of the Court, thought that the jury could find that defendant was acting "under color" of state law. Defendant was "no mere interloper but had a semblance of policeman's power," and "the manner of his conduct of the interrogations makes clear that he was asserting the authority granted him and not acting in the role of a private person." While the application of § 242 to less obvious methods of coercion might present doubts as to the adequacy of the standard of guilt, "where police take matters in their own hands, seize victims, beat and pound them until they confess, there cannot be the slightest doubt that the police have deprived the victim of a right under the Constitution." Defendant acted willfully and purposely; his aim was "precisely to deny the protection that the Constitution affords." Justices Frankfurter, Jackson and Minton dissented for the reasons set forth in the dissent in the Screws case. Justice Black also dissented.

2. In a companion case, United States v. Williams, 341 U.S. 70 (1951), the same defendant, two of his employees who participated in the beatings, and the police officer detailed to assist him, were convicted of conspiracy under the predecessor of 18 U.S.C. § 241, p. 452, supra. The Court affirmed the Court of Appeals judgment which had reversed the convictions. Justice Frankfurter's opinion announcing the judgment of the Court was joined by Chief Justice Vinson and Justices Jackson and Minton. He noted that § 241 reaches conspiracies by private persons without a requirement of state action and concluded that it was not applicable to the conspiracy to deny Fourteenth Amendment rights charged in the indictment. Tracing the history of §§ 241 and 242 he concluded that since § 242, in conjunction with the general conspiracy statute enacted in 1867 (now 18 U.S.C. § 371), was intended to deal fully with conspiracies under color of state law to deprive persons of rights guaranteed by the Fourteenth Amendment, § 241 should be construed as protecting only those rights "which Congress can beyond doubt constitutionally secure against interference by private individuals. Decisions of this Court have established that this category includes rights which arise from the relationship of the individual and the Federal Government,"—e. g., "the right of citizens to vote in congressional elections"—and not "those rights which the Constitution merely guarantees from interference by a State." [Recall the material on non-14th Amendment rights, in sec. 1 supra, at p. 463.]

Justice Black concurred in the result on the ground that a prior acquittal of three of the defendants barred the present prosecution. Justice Douglas, joined by Justices Reed, Burton and Clark, dissented. Finding no substantial difference between §§ 241 and 242, they thought it was "strange to hear it said that though [§ 242] extends to rights guaranteed against state action by the Fourteenth Amendment, [§ 241] is limited to rights which the Federal Government can secure against invasion by private persons." If Congress had desired to draw a distinction along that line "it is hard to imagine that it would not have made its purpose clear in the language used." Since § 241 is "broad enough to include all constitutional rights," it clearly applies to "state officers, or those acting under color of state law, who conspire to wring confessions from an accused by force and violence." [See the re-examination of these issues in the Price case, p. 504, infra.]

COLLINS v. HARDYMAN

Collins, 341 U.S. 651 (1951), was a civil damage action under the predecessor of 42 U.S.C. § 1985(3), p. 451, supra. The section is applicable to "two or more persons" who "conspire . . . for the purpose of depriving . . . any person . . . of the equal protection of the laws, or of equal privileges and immunities under the laws." The complaint alleged that defendants conspired to deprive plaintiffs of their rights as citizens of the United States peaceably to assemble for the purpose of discussing national issues and of their equal privileges and immunities. Plaintiffs, members of a political club, stated that defendants broke up their meeting—planned to adopt a resolution opposing the Marshall Plan—and thus interfered also with their rights to petition the Government for redress of grievances, and that defendants did not conspire to interfere with meetings of groups with whose opinions they agreed. There was no allegation that defendants acted under color of law. (Plaintiffs abandoned that part of their claim which had sought to invoke the "going in disguise upon the highway" provision of § 1985(3) by stating that defendant's disguise consisted of "the unlawful and unauthorized wearing of caps of the American Legion.")

Justice Jackson's opinion for the Court concluded that no cause of action under § 1985(3) had been stated. His opinion included the following passages: "This statutory provision has long been dormant. The Act [of 1871], popularly known as the Ku Klux Act, was passed by a partisan vote in a highly inflamed atmosphere. . . . Its defects were soon realized when its execution brought about a severe reaction. . . .

"The provision establishing criminal conspiracies in language indistinguishable from that used to describe civil conspiracies came to judgment in United States v. Harris, 106 U.S. 629. It was held unconstitutional. This decision was in harmony with that of other important decisions during that period [Slaughter-House Cases; United States v. Reese; United States v. Cruikshank; Civil Rights Cases] by a Court, every member of which had been appointed by Presidents Lincoln, Grant, Hayes, Garfield or Arthur—all indoctrinated in the cause which produced the Fourteenth Amendment, but convinced that it was not to be used to centralize power so as to upset the federal system.

"While we have not been in agreement as to the interpretation and application of some of the post-Civil War legislation, the Court recently unanimously declared . . . : '[T]he action inhibited by the first section of the Fourteenth Amendment is only such action as may fairly be said to be that of the States.' [Shelley v. Kraemer, 334 U.S. 1, 13.] . . .

"It is apparent that, if this complaint meets the requirements of this Act, it raises constitutional problems of the first magnitude that, in the light of history, are not without difficulty. These would include issues as to congressional power under and apart from the Fourteenth Amendment, the reserved power of the States, the content of rights derived from national as distinguished from state citizenship . . . . Before we embark upon such a constitutional inquiry, it is necessary to satisfy ourselves that the attempt to allege a cause of action within the purview of the statute has been successful. . . .

"Passing the argument, fully developed in the Civil Rights Cases, that an individual or group of individuals not in office cannot *deprive* anybody of constitutional rights, though they may invade or violate those rights, it is clear that this statute does not attempt to reach a conspiracy to deprive one of rights unless it is a deprivation of equality, of 'equal protection of the law,' or of 'equal privileges and immunities under the law.' That accords with the purpose of the Act to put the lately freed Negro on an equal footing before the law with his former master. The Act apparently deemed that adequate and went no further.

"What we have here is not a conspiracy to affect in any way these plaintiffs' equality of protection by the law, or their equality of privileges and immunities under the law. There is not the slightest allegation that defendants were conscious of or trying to influence the law, or were endeavoring to obstruct or interfere with it. The only inequality suggested is that the defendants broke up plaintiffs' meeting and did not break up meetings of others with whose sentiments they agreed. To be sure, this is not equal injury, but it is no more a deprivation of 'equal protection' or of 'equal privileges and immunities' than it would be for one to assault one neighbor without assaulting them all, or to libel some persons without mention of others. Such private discrimination is not inequality before the law unless there is some manipulation of the law or its agencies to give sanction or sanctuary for doing so. Plaintiffs' rights were certainly invaded, disregarded and lawlessly violated, but neither their rights nor their equality of rights under the law have been, or were intended to be, denied or impaired. Their rights *under the laws* and to *protection of the laws* remain untouched and equal to the rights of every other Californian, and may be vindicated in the same way and with the same effect as those of any other citizen who suffers violence at the hands of a mob.

"We do not say that no conspiracy by private individuals could be of such magnitude and effect as to work a deprivation of equal protection of the laws, or of equal privileges and immunities under laws. Indeed, the post-Civil War Ku Klux Klan, against which this Act was fashioned, may have, or may reasonably have been thought to have, done so. It is estimated to have had a membership of around 550,000, and thus to have included 'nearly the entire adult male white population of the South.' It may well be that a conspiracy, so far-flung and embracing such numbers, . . . was able effectively to deprive Negroes of their legal rights and to close all avenues of redress or vindication, in view of the then disparity of position, education and opportunity between them and those who made up the Ku Klux Klan. We do not know. But here nothing of that sort appears. We have a case of a lawless political brawl, precipitated by a handful of white citizens against other white citizens.   California courts are open to plaintiffs and its laws offer redress for their injury and vindication for their rights.

"We say nothing of the power of Congress to authorize such civil actions as respondents have commenced or otherwise to redress such grievances as they assert.   We think that Congress has not, in the narrow class of conspiracies defined by this statute, included the conspiracy charged here.   We therefore reach no constitutional questions.   The facts alleged fall short of a conspiracy to alter, impair or deny equality of rights under the law, though they do show a lawless invasion of rights for which there are remedies in the law of California.   It is not for this Court to compete with Congress or attempt to replace it as the Nation's law-making body."

Justice Burton, joined by Justices Black and Douglas, dissented: "The right alleged to have been violated is the right to petition the Federal Government for a redress of grievances.   This right is expressly recognized by the First Amendment and this Court has said that 'The very idea of a government, republican in form, implies a right on the part of its citizens to meet peaceably for consultation in respect to public affairs and to petition for a redress of grievances.'   United States v. Cruikshank, 92 U.S. 542, 552 .   .   . .   The source of the right in this case is not the Fourteenth Amendment.   The complaint alleges that petitioners 'knowingly' did not interfere with the 'many public meetings' whose objectives they agreed with, but that they did conspire to break up respondents' meeting because petitioners were opposed to respondents' views, which were expected to be there expressed. Such conduct does not differ materially from the specific conspiracies which the Court recognizes that the statute was intended to reach.   .   .   .

"Congress certainly has the power to create a federal cause of action in favor of persons injured by private individuals through the abridgment of federally created constitutional rights.   It seems to me that Congress has done just this in R.S. § 1980(3).   This is not inconsistent with the principle underlying the Fourteenth Amendment.   .   .   .   Cases holding that [it is] directed only at state action are not authority for the contention that Congress may not pass laws supporting rights which exist apart from the Fourteenth Amendment."

MONROE v. PAPE

In Monroe, 365 U.S. 167 (1961), in an extensive examination of the scope of another civil remedy provision, 42 U.S.C. § 1983, p. 453, supra, the Court sustained a complaint which alleged that Chicago police officers had invaded petitioners' home, searched without a warrant, and illegally arrested and detained a member of the family.   The lower federal courts dismissed the action against the City and the police officers.   The Supreme Court, in an opinion by Justice Douglas, affirmed the dismissal as to the City, holding that Congress "did not undertake to bring municipal corporations within" the statute.   The Court found, however, that the complaint against the police stated a cause of action: the claimed police action constituted a deprivation of "rights, privileges, or immunities secured by the Constitution" within the meaning of the statute.   Justice Douglas explained:

"It has been said that when 18 U.S.C. § 241 made criminal a conspiracy 'to injure, oppress, threaten, or intimidate any citizen in the free exercise or enjoyment of any right or privilege secured to him by the Constitution,' it embraced only rights that an individual has by reason of his relation to the central government, not to state governments. United States v. Williams, 341 U.S. 70 (p. 498, supra). Cf. United States v. Cruikshank, 92 U.S. 542 . . . . But the history of the section of the Civil Rights Act presently involved does not permit such a narrow interpretation. Section 1979 came onto the books as § 1 of the Ku Klux Act of April 20, 1871. 17 Stat. 13. It was one of the means whereby Congress exercised the power vested in it by § 5 of the Fourteenth Amendment to enforce the provisions of that Amendment. . . . Allegation of facts constituting a deprivation under color of state authority of a right guaranteed by the Fourteenth Amendment satisfies to that extent the requirement of R.S. § 1979. . . . So far petitioners are on solid ground. For the guarantee against unreasonable searches and seizures contained in the Fourth Amendment has been made applicable to the States by reason of the Due Process Clause of the Fourteenth Amendment."

Moreover, the Court rejected the contention that police action could not be "under color of" state law if it violated state law. "It is no answer that the State has a law which if enforced would give relief. The federal remedy is supplementary to the State. . . . We conclude that the meaning given 'under color of' law in the Classic case and in the Screws and Williams cases was the correct one; and we adhere to it." In a lengthy review of the legislative history of the 1871 Act, Justice Douglas noted: "While one main scourge of the evil—perhaps the leading one—was the Ku Klux Klan, the remedy created was not a remedy against it or its members but against those who representing a State in some capacity were *unable* or *unwilling* to enforce a state law. . . . The debates were long and extensive. It is abundantly clear that one reason the legislation was passed was to afford a federal right in federal courts because by reason of prejudice, passion, neglect, intolerance or otherwise, state laws might not be enforced and the claim of citizens to the enjoyment of rights, privileges, and immunity guaranteed by the Fourteenth Amendment might be denied by the state agencies."

With regard to the intent required to impose civil liability, the Court stated: "In the Screws case we dealt with a statute that imposed criminal penalties for acts 'wilfully' done. We construed that word in its setting to mean the doing of an act with 'a specific intent to deprive a person of a federal right.' . . . We do not think that gloss should be placed on § 1979 which we have here. The word 'wilfully' does not appear in § 1979. Moreover, § 1979 provides a civil remedy, while in the Screws case we dealt with a criminal law challenged on the ground of vagueness. Section 1979 should be read against the background of tort liability that makes a man responsible for the natural consequences of his actions." * Justices Harlan and Stewart concurred in a separate opinion.

---

* Compare Tenney v. Brandhove, 341 U.S. 367 (1951), a civil action under the Civil Rights Acts against members of a state legislative investigating committee. Plaintiff contended that the hearing at which he appeared was not for a legislative purpose, but designed to intimidate him. The Court affirmed the dismissal of the complaint: Congress did not intend to limit the "privilege of legislators to be free from . . . civil process for what they do or say in legislative proceedings." See Note, "The Proper Scope of the Civil Rights Acts," 66 Harv.L.Rev. 1285 (1953), and, generally, Klitgaard, "The

Justice Frankfurter dissented at length, except as to the action against the City. He urged that the statements in Classic, Screws, and Williams should not control: "Thus, although this court has three times found that conduct of state officials which is forbidden by state law may be 'under color' of state law for purposes of the Civil Rights Acts, it is accurate to say that that question has never received here the consideration which its importance merits." He concluded that "police intrusion in violation of state law is not a wrong remediable under R.S. § 1979."

B. FEDERAL CRIMINAL SANCTIONS AGAINST CIVIL RIGHTS VIOLENCE IN THE LATE SIXTIES: THE GUEST CASE AND THE 1968 CIVIL RIGHTS ACT

Introduction. The materials which follow reveal interaction between Court and Congress with special vividness.* During the late sixties, all branches of the national government were concerned with the problems of federal criminal legislation against civil rights violence. President Johnson's State of the Union Message in January 1966 contained a brief request for laws to strengthen the authority of federal courts "to try those who murder, attack, or intimidate either civil rights workers or others exercising federal rights." But there was a delay of several months before that general suggestion was supplemented by detailed Administration proposals—a delay in part explained by the fact that the Supreme Court had before it two major cases invoking the existing criminal remedies, 18 U.S.C. §§ 241 and 242.

The cases arose out of two widely publicized acts of violence in 1964: the killing of Schwerner, Chaney and Goodman near Philadelphia, Mississippi (United States v. Price), and the killing of Lemuel A. Penn near Athens, Georgia (United States v. Guest). United States v. Price, summarized below, produced nearly unanimous resolutions of the problems which had divided the Court in the Williams cases in 1951 (p. 498, supra). United States v. Guest, which follows Price below, produced several important opinions on the reach of congressional power over private civil rights violence.

The Price and Guest cases were decided on March 28, 1966. Exactly a month later, the President submitted a special Civil Rights Message to Congress. Identical bills containing the Administration's proposed Civil Rights Act of 1966—and listing the prescribing of "penalties for certain acts of violence or intimidation" as one of the purposes—were immediately introduced in Congress. The 1966 efforts ended in a Senate filibuster. A slightly revised version of the 1966 proposal was included in the Administration's

Civil Rights Act and Mr. Monroe," 49 Calif.L.Rev. 145 (1961), Selected Essays 1938–62 (1963), 949.

Note also Pierson v. Ray, 386 U.S. 547 (1967), which found two significant limitations on liability under 42 U.S.C. § 1983: by analogy to Tenney v. Brandhove, judges are absolutely immune; and, despite the broad language of Monroe v. Pape, police officers may assert "the defense of good faith and probable cause."

* Note also the different variety of interaction, in sec. 3c infra, at p. 517, between the fair housing provision of the 1968 Civil Rights Act (adopted while the Jones case was pending in the Court) and the Court's revival of the 1866 Act in the Jones decision soon after.

1967 civil rights bill. In August 1967, the House passed a substitute version. H.R. 2516, 90th Cong. That bill, as substantially amended by the Senate, became the Civil Rights Act of 1968, Pub. Law 90–284, 82 Stat. 73 (April 11, 1968). Excerpts from the civil rights violence provisions in Title I of the 1968 Act are printed at the end of this section, at p. 516.

THE PRICE CASE

The appellees in United States v. Price, 383 U.S. 787 (1966), were three Mississippi law enforcement officials (Deputy Sheriff Price of Neshoba County, the Sheriff, and a policeman) and fifteen private individuals, all allegedly involved in the killing of Schwerner, Chaney and Goodman. There were two indictments against the 18 defendants: one based on 18 U.S.C. § 242; the other on § 241. The alleged conspiracy involved releasing the victims from jail at night, intercepting and killing them, and disposing of their bodies—all with the purpose to "punish" the victims summarily and thus to deprive them of their 14th Amendment right "not to be summarily punished without due process of law by persons acting under color of the laws of the State of Mississippi." The District Court dismissed most of the charges. On direct appeal, the Supreme Court reversed all of the dismissals. Justice Fortas wrote for the Court, emphasizing that the case involved only issues "of construction, not of constitutional power."

a. The first indictment (compare United States v. Williams, note 1, p. 498, supra) charged substantive violations of 18 U.S.C. § 242 (the "color of law" provision) as well as a conspiracy to violate that Section. The District Court sustained the conspiracy count against all of the defendants: as to the private defendants, the lower court found it "immaterial" that they were "not acting under color of law" because the charge was "that they were conspiring with persons who were so acting." But the trial court sustained the substantive counts against the three official defendants only; it dismissed these counts against the private defendants since they were not "officers in fact."

The Supreme Court reversed the dismissal of the substantive charges against the nonofficial defendants. Though § 242 concededly required "under color" of law charges, that did not prevent reaching these private defendants: "Private persons, jointly engaged with state officials in the prohibited action, are acting 'under color' of law for purposes of the statute. To act 'under color' of law does not require that the accused be an officer of the State. It is enough that he is a willful participant in joint activity with the State or its agents. In the present case, according to the indictment, the brutal joint adventure was made possible by state detention and calculated release of the prisoners by an officer of the State. This action, clearly attributable to the State, was part of the monstrous design described by the indictment. State officers participated in every phase of the alleged venture: the release from jail, the interception, assault and murder. It was a joint activity, from start to finish. Those who took advantage of participation by state officers in accomplishment of the foul purpose alleged must suffer the consequences of that participation. In effect, if the allegations are true, they were participants in official lawlessness, acting in willful concert with state officers and hence under color of law."

b. The second indictment charged all 18 defendants with a conspiracy under 18 U.S.C. § 241. The District Court dismissed the indictment against all, holding that the Section did not apply to rights protected by the Fourteenth Amendment—in accordance with the Frankfurter opinion in United States v. Williams, 341 U.S. 70 (1951), p. 498, note 2, supra. The Supreme Court, noting that the 4:4 division on this issue in 1951 had left the construction of § 241 "an open question," adopted the Douglas position in that Williams case: "In view of the detailed opinions in [Williams], it would be supererogation to track the arguments in all of their intricacy. On the basis of an extensive re-examination of the question, we conclude that the District Court erred; that § 241 must be read as it is written—to reach conspiracies 'to injure . . . any citizen in the free exercise or enjoyment of any right or privilege secured to him by the Constitution or laws of the United States . . .'; that this language includes rights or privileges protected by the Fourteenth Amendment; that whatever the ultimate coverage of the section may be, it extends to conspiracies otherwise within the scope of the section, participated in by officials alone or in collaboration with private persons; and that the indictment . . . properly charges such a conspiracy in violation of § 241."

The Court had no doubt that the § 241 indictment set forth "a conspiracy within the ambit of the Fourteenth Amendment." Like the § 242 indictment, supra, it "alleges that the defendants acted 'under color of law' and that the conspiracy included action by the State through its law enforcement officers to punish the alleged victims without due process of law in violation of the Fourteenth Amendment's direct admonition to the States." Justice Fortas added: "The present application of the statutes at issue does not raise fundamental questions of federal-state relationships. We are here concerned with allegations which squarely and undisputably involve state action in direct violation of the mandate of the Fourteenth Amendment."

UNITED STATES v. GUEST

383 U.S. 745, 86 S.Ct. 1170, 16 L.Ed.2d 239 (1966).

Appeal from the United States District Court for the Middle District of Georgia.

Mr. Justice STEWART delivered the opinion of the Court.

The six defendants in this case were indicted by a United States grand jury in the Middle District of Georgia for criminal conspiracy in violation of 18 U.S.C. § 241 (1964 ed.). . . . In five numbered paragraphs, the indictment alleged a single conspiracy by the defendants to deprive Negro citizens of the free exercise and enjoyment of several specified rights secured by the Constitution and laws of the United States.[1] The defendants moved

1. The indictment, filed on October 16, 1964, was as follows:
"THE GRAND JURY CHARGES:
"Commencing on or about January 1, 1964, and continuing to the date of this indictment, HERBERT GUEST, JAMES SPERGEON LACKEY, CECIL WILLIAM MYERS, DENVER WILLIS PHILLIPS, JOSEPH HOWARD SIMS, and GEORGE HAMPTON TURNER, did, within the Middle District of Georgia, Athens Division, conspire together, with each other, and with other persons to the Grand Jury unknown, to injure, oppress, threaten, and intimidate Negro citizens of the United States in the vicinity of Athens, Georgia, in the free exercise and enjoyment by said Negro citi-

to dismiss the indictment on the ground that it did not charge an offense under the laws of the United States. The District Court sustained the motion . . . .

The United States appealed directly to this Court under the Criminal Appeals Act, 18 U.S.C. § 3731.[2] . . . . It is now apparent that this Court does not have jurisdiction to decide one of the issues sought to be raised on this direct appeal. As to the other issues, however, our appellate jurisdiction is clear, and for the reasons that follow, we reverse the judgment of the District Court. As in United States v. Price, [supra], decided today, we deal here with issues of statutory construction, not with issues of constitutional power.

I.

The first numbered paragraph of the indictment, reflecting a portion of the language of § 201(a) of the Civil Rights Act of 1964, . . . alleged that the defendants conspired to injure, oppress, threaten, and intimidate Negro citizens in the free exercise and enjoyment of:

"The right to the full and equal enjoyment of the goods, services, facilities, privileges, advantages, and accommodations of motion picture theaters, restaurants, and other places of public accommodation."

The District Court . . . found a fatal flaw in the failure of the paragraph to include an allegation that the acts of the defendants were motivated by racial discrimination, an allegation the court thought essential to charge

zens of the following rights and privileges secured to them by the Constitution and laws of the United States:

"1. The right to the full and equal enjoyment of the goods, services, facilities, privileges, advantages, and accommodations of motion picture theaters, restaurants, and other places of public accommodation;

"2. The right to the equal utilization, without discrimination upon the basis of race, of public facilities in the vicinity of Athens, Georgia, owned, operated or managed by or on behalf of the State of Georgia or any subdivision thereof;

"3. The right to the full and equal use on the same terms as white citizens of the public streets and highways in the vicinity of Athens, Georgia;

"4. The right to travel freely to and from the State of Georgia and to use highway facilities and other instrumentalities of interstate commerce within the State of Georgia;

"5. Other rights exercised and enjoyed by white citizens in the vicinity of Athens, Georgia.

"It was a part of the plan and purpose of the conspiracy that its objects be achieved by various means, including the following:

"1. By shooting Negroes;
"2. By beating Negroes;
"3. By killing Negroes;
"4. By damaging and destroying property of Negroes;

"5. By pursuing Negroes in automobiles and threatening them with guns;
"6. By making telephone calls to Negroes to threaten their lives, property, and persons, and by making such threats in person;
"7. By going in disguise on the highway and on the premises of other persons;
"8. By causing the arrest of Negroes by means of false reports that such Negroes had committed criminal acts; and
"9. By burning crosses at night in public view.

"All in violation of Section 241, Title 18, United States Code."

The only additional indication in the record concerning the factual details of the conduct with which the defendants were charged is the statement of the District Court that: "It is common knowledge that two of the defendants, Sims and Myers, have already been prosecuted in the Superior Court of Madison County, Georgia, for the murder of Lemuel A. Penn and by a jury found not guilty." 246 F.Supp. 475, 487. [All footnotes by the Court.]

2. This appeal concerns only the first four numbered paragraphs of the indictment. The Government conceded in the District Court that the fifth paragraph added nothing to the indictment, and no question is raised here as to the dismissal of that paragraph.

an interference with rights secured by Title II of the Civil Rights Act of 1964. [T]he District Court's judgment . . . was based, at least alternatively, upon its determination that this paragraph was defective as a matter of pleading; it was not based upon the "construction of the statute." Settled principles of review under the Criminal Appeals Act therefore preclude our review of the District Court's judgment on this branch of the indictment. . . .

II.

The second numbered paragraph of the indictment alleged that the defendants conspired to injure, oppress, threaten, and intimidate Negro citizens of the United States in the free exercise and enjoyment of:

> "The right to the equal utilization, without discrimination upon the basis of race, of public facilities in the vicinity of Athens, Georgia, owned, operated or managed by or on behalf of the State of Georgia or any subdivision thereof."

Correctly characterizing this paragraph as embracing rights protected by the Equal Protection Clause of the Fourteenth Amendment, the District Court held as a matter of statutory construction that 18 U.S.C. § 241 does not encompass any Fourteenth Amendment rights, and further held as a matter of constitutional law that "any broader construction of § 241 . . . would render it void for indefiniteness." 246 F.Supp., at 486. In so holding, the District Court was in error, as our opinion in United States v. Price, decided today, makes abundantly clear.

To be sure, Price involves rights under the Due Process Clause, whereas the present case involves rights under the Equal Protection Clause. But no possible reason suggests itself for concluding that § 241—if it protects Fourteenth Amendment rights—protects rights secured by the one Clause but not those secured by the other. . . .

Moreover, inclusion of Fourteenth Amendment rights within the compass of 18 U.S.C. § 241 does not render the statute unconstitutionally vague. Since the gravamen of the offense is conspiracy, the requirement that the offender must act with a specific intent to interfere with the federal rights in question is satisfied. Screws v. United States, 325 U.S. 91; United States v. Williams, 341 U.S. 70, 93–95 (dissenting opinion). And the rights under the Equal Protection Clause described by this paragraph of the indictment have been so firmly and precisely established by a consistent line of decisions in this Court, that the lack of specification of these rights in the language of § 241 itself can raise no serious constitutional question on the ground of vagueness or indefiniteness.

Unlike the indictment in Price, however, the indictment in the present case names no person alleged to have acted in any way under the color of state law. The argument is therefore made that, since there exist no Equal Protection Clause rights against wholly private action, the judgment of the District Court on this branch of the case must be affirmed. On its face, the argument is unexceptionable. The Equal Protection Clause speaks to the State or to those acting under the color of its authority.

In this connection, we emphasize that § 241 by its clear language incorporates no more than the Equal Protection Clause itself; the statute does not purport to give substantive, as opposed to remedial, implementation to any rights secured by that Clause. Since we therefore deal here only with the bare terms of the Equal Protection Clause itself, nothing said in this opinion goes to the question of what kinds of other and broader legislation Congress might constitutionally enact under § 5 of the Fourteenth Amendment to implement that Clause or any other provision of the Amendment.[3]

. . .

This case . . . requires no determination of the threshold level that state action must attain in order to create rights under the Equal Protection Clause. This is so because, contrary to the argument of the litigants, the indictment in fact contains an express allegation of state involvement sufficient at least to require the denial of a motion to dismiss. One of the means of accomplishing the object of the conspiracy, according to the indictment, was "By causing the arrest of Negroes by means of false reports that such Negroes had committed criminal acts." In Bell v. Maryland, 378 U.S. 226, three members of the Court expressed the view that a private businessman's invocation of state police and judicial action to carry out his own policy of racial discrimination was sufficient to create Equal Protection Clause rights in those against whom the racial discrimination was directed. Three other members of the Court strongly disagreed with that view, and three expressed no opinion on the question. The allegation of the extent of official involvement in the present case is not clear. It may charge no more than co-operative private and state action similar to that involved in Bell, but it may go considerably further. For example, the allegation is broad enough to cover a charge of active connivance by agents of the State in the making of the "false reports," or other conduct amounting to official discrimination clearly sufficient to constitute denial of rights protected by the Equal Protection Clause. Although it is possible that a bill of particulars, or the proof if the case goes to trial, would disclose no co-operative action of that kind by officials of the State, the allegation is enough to prevent dismissal of this branch of the indictment.

III.

The fourth numbered paragraph of the indictment alleged that the defendants conspired to injure, oppress, threaten, and intimidate Negro citizens of the United States in the free exercise and enjoyment of:

> "The right to travel freely to and from the State of Georgia and to use highway facilities and other instrumentalities of interstate commerce within the State of Georgia." [4]

---

3. Thus, contrary to the suggestion in Mr. Justice Brennan's separate opinion, nothing said in this opinion has the slightest bearing on the validity or construction of Title III or Title IV of the Civil Rights Act of 1964, 42 U.S.C. §§ 2000b, 2000c (1964 ed).

4. The third numbered paragraph alleged that the defendants conspired to injure, oppress, threaten, and intimidate Negro citizens of the United States in the free exercise and enjoyment of:
"The right to the full and equal use on the same terms as white citizens of the

public streets and highways in the vicinity of Athens, Georgia."

Insofar as the third paragraph refers to the use of local public facilities, it is covered by the discussion of the second numbered paragraph of the indictment in Part II of this opinion. Insofar as the third paragraph refers to the use of streets or highways in interstate commerce, it is covered by the present discussion of the fourth numbered paragraph of the indictment.

The District Court was in error in dismissing the indictment as to this paragraph. The constitutional right to travel from one State to another, and necessarily to use the highways and other instrumentalities of interstate commerce in doing so, occupies a position fundamental to the concept of our Federal Union. It is a right that has been firmly established and repeatedly recognized. [See Crandall v. Nevada, 6 Wall. 35, invalidating a Nevada tax on every person leaving the State by common carrier.]

Although the Articles of Confederation provided that "the people of each State shall have free ingress and regress to and from any other State," that right finds no explicit mention in the Constitution. The reason, it has been suggested, is that a right so elementary was conceived from the beginning to be a necessary concomitant of the stronger Union the Constitution created. In any event, freedom to travel throughout the United States has long been recognized as a basic right under the Constitution. . . .

In Edwards v. California, 314 U.S. 160, invalidating a California law which impeded the free interstate passage of the indigent, the Court based its reaffirmation of the federal right of interstate travel upon the Commerce Clause. . . . It is . . . well settled in our decisions that the federal commerce power authorizes Congress to legislate for the protection of individuals from violations of civil rights that impinge on their free movement in interstate commerce. . . .

Although there have been recurring differences in emphasis within the Court as to the source of the constitutional right of interstate travel, there is no need here to canvass those differences further.[5] All have agreed that the right exists. Its explicit recognition as one of the federal rights protected by what is now 18 U.S.C. § 241 goes back at least as far as 1904. United States v. Moore, 129 F. 630, 633. We reaffirm it now.[6]

5. The District Court relied heavily on United States v. Wheeler, 254 U.S. 281, in dismissing this branch of the indictment. That case involved an alleged conspiracy to compel residents of Arizona to move out of that State. The right of interstate travel was, therefore, not directly involved. Whatever continuing validity Wheeler may have as restricted to its own facts, the dicta in the Wheeler opinion relied on by the District Court in the present case have been discredited in subsequent decisions. Cf. Edwards v. California, 314 U.S. 160, 177, 180 (Douglas, J., concurring); United States v. Williams, 341 U.S. 70, 80.

6. As emphasized in Mr. Justice Harlan's separate opinion, § 241 protects only against interference with rights secured by other federal laws or by the Constitution itself. The right to interstate travel is a right that the Constitution itself guarantees, as the cases cited in the text make clear. Although these cases in fact involved governmental interference with the right of free interstate travel, their reasoning fully supports the conclusion that the constitutional right of interstate travel is a right secured against interference from any source whatever, whether governmental or private. In this connection, it is important to reiterate that the right to travel freely from State to State finds constitutional protection that is quite independent of the Fourteenth Amendment.

We are not concerned here with the extent to which interstate travel may be regulated or controlled by the exercise of a State's police power acting within the confines of the Fourteenth Amendment. See Edwards v. California, 314 U.S. 160, 184 (concurring opinion); New York v. O'Neill, 359 U.S. 1, 6–8. Nor is there any issue here as to the permissible extent of federal interference with the right within the confines of the Due Process Clause of the Fifth Amendment. Cf. Zemel v. Rusk, 381 U.S. 1; Aptheker v. Secretary of State, 378 U.S. 500; Kent v. Dulles, 357 U.S. 116. [Note the discussion of this problem—and the invalidation of restrictions on the right to travel—in Shapiro v. Thompson, 394 U.S. 618 (1969) (Chap. 14, p. 1036, infra).]

This does not mean, of course, that every criminal conspiracy affecting an individual's right of free interstate passage is within the sanction of 18 U.S.C. § 241. A specific intent to interfere with the federal right must be proved, and at a trial the defendants are entitled to a jury instruction phrased in those terms. Screws v. United States, 325 U.S. 91, 106–107. Thus, for example, a conspiracy to rob an interstate traveler would not, of itself, violate § 241. But if the predominant purpose of the conspiracy is to impede or prevent the exercise of the right of interstate travel, or to oppress a person because of his exercise of that right, then, whether or not motivated by racial discrimination, the conspiracy becomes a proper object of the federal law under which the indictment in this case was brought. Accordingly, it was error to grant the motion to dismiss on this branch of the indictment.

For these reasons, the judgment of the District Court is reversed and the case is remanded to that court for further proceedings consistent with this opinion.

It is so ordered.

Mr. Justice CLARK, with whom Mr. Justice BLACK and Mr. Justice FORTAS join, concurring.

I join the opinion of the Court in this case, but believe it worthwhile to comment on its Part II . . . . .

The Court carves out of its opinion the question of the power of Congress, under § 5 of the Fourteenth Amendment, to enact legislation implementing the Equal Protection Clause or any other provision of the Fourteenth Amendment. The Court's interpretation of the indictment clearly avoids the question whether Congress, by appropriate legislation, has the power to punish private conspiracies that interfere with Fourteenth Amendment rights, such as the right to utilize public facilities. My Brother Brennan, however, says that the Court's disposition constitutes an acceptance of appellees' aforesaid contention as to § 241. Some of his language further suggests that the Court indicates *sub silentio* that Congress does not have the power to outlaw such conspiracies. Although the Court specifically rejects any such connotation, . . . it is, I believe, both appropriate and necessary under the circumstances here to say that there now can be no doubt that the specific language of § 5 empowers the Congress to enact laws punishing all conspiracies —with or without state action—that interfere with Fourteenth Amendment rights.

Mr. Justice HARLAN, concurring in part and dissenting in part.

I join Parts I and II [1] of the Court's opinion, but I cannot subscribe to Part III in its full sweep. To the extent that it is there held that 18 U.S.C. § 241 (1964 ed.) reaches conspiracies, embracing only the action of private persons, to obstruct or otherwise interfere with the right of citizens freely to engage in interstate travel, I am constrained to dissent. On the other hand, I agree that § 241 does embrace state interference with such interstate travel, and I therefore consider that this aspect of the indictment is sustainable on the reasoning of Part II of the Court's opinion.

1. The action of three of the Justices who join the Court's opinion in nonetheless cursorily pronouncing themselves on the far-reaching constitutional questions deliberately not reached in Part II seems to me, to say the very least, extraordinary. [Footnote by Justice Harlan.]

This right to travel must be found in the Constitution itself. . . . My disagreement with this phase of the Court's opinion lies in this: While past cases do indeed establish that there is a constitutional "right to travel" between States free from unreasonable *governmental* interference, today's decision is the first to hold that such movement is also protected against *private* interference, and, depending on the constitutional source of the right, I think it either unwise or impermissible so to read the Constitution. . . . .

As a general proposition it seems to me very dubious that the Constitution was intended to create certain rights of private individuals as against other private individuals. The Constitutional Convention was called to establish a nation, not to reform the common law. . . . It is true that there is a very narrow range of rights against individuals which have been read into the Constitution. . . . [See the passage quoted sec. 1, supra, at p. 464.] [These cases] are narrow, and are essentially concerned with the vindication of important relationships with the Federal Government—voting in federal elections, involvement in federal law enforcement, communicating with the Federal Government. The present case stands on a considerably different footing.

It is arguable that the same considerations which led the Court on numerous occasions to find a right of free movement against oppressive state action now justify a similar result with respect to private impediments. . . . Although this argument is not without force, I do not think it is particularly persuasive. There is a difference in power between States and private groups so great that analogies between the two tend to be misleading. If the State obstructs free intercourse of goods, people, or ideas, the bonds of the union are threatened; if a private group effectively stops such communication, there is at most a temporary breakdown of law and order, to be remedied by the exercise of state authority or by appropriate federal legislation. . . .

I do not gainsay that the immunities and commerce provisions of the Constitution leave the way open for the finding of this "private" constitutional right, since they do not speak solely in terms of governmental action. Nevertheless, I think it wrong to sustain a criminal indictment on such an uncertain ground. To do so subjects § 241 to serious challenge on the score of vagueness and serves in effect to place this Court in the position of making criminal law under the name of constitutional interpretation. It is difficult to subdue misgivings about the potentialities of this decision. . . . .

Mr. Justice BRENNAN, with whom The Chief Justice [WARREN] and Mr. Justice DOUGLAS join, concurring in part and dissenting in part.

I join Part I of the Court's opinion. I reach the same result as the Court on that branch of the indictment discussed in Part III of its opinion but for other reasons. See footnote [1], infra. And I agree with so much of Part II as construes 18 U.S.C. § 241 (1964 ed.) to encompass conspiracies to injure, oppress, threaten or intimidate citizens in the free exercise or enjoyment of Fourteenth Amendment rights and holds that, as so construed, § 241 is not void for indefiniteness. I do not agree, however, with the remainder of Part II which holds, as I read the opinion, that a conspiracy to interfere with the exercise of the right to equal utilization of state facilities is not, within the meaning of § 241, a conspiracy to interfere with the exercise of a "right . . . secured . . . by the Constitution" unless discriminatory conduct by state officers is involved in the alleged conspiracy.

I. . . .

[W]hile the order dismissing the second numbered paragraph of the indictment is reversed, severe limitations on the prosecution of that branch of the indictment are implicitly imposed. These limitations could only stem from an acceptance of appellees' contention . . ..

. . . I am of the opinion that a conspiracy to interfere with the right to equal utilization of state facilities described in the second numbered paragraph of the indictment is a conspiracy to interfere with a "right . . . secured . . . by the Constitution" within the meaning of § 241—without regard to whether state officers participated in the alleged conspiracy. I believe that § 241 reaches such a private conspiracy not because the Fourteenth Amendment of its own force prohibits such a conspiracy but because § 241, as an exercise of congressional power under § 5 of that Amendment, prohibits *all* conspiracies to interfere with the exercise of a "right . . . secured . . . by the Constitution" and because the right to equal utilization of state facilities is a "right . . . secured . . . by the Constitution" within the meaning of that phrase as used in § 241.[1]

My difference with the Court stems from its construction of the term "secured" as used in § 241 in the phrase a "right . . . secured . . . by the Constitution or laws of the United States." The Court tacitly construes the term "secured" so as to restrict the coverage of § 241 to those rights that are "fully protected" by the Constitution or another federal law. Unless private interferences with the exercise of the right in question are prohibited by the Constitution itself or another federal law, the right cannot, in the Court's view, be deemed "secured . . . by the Constitution or laws of the United States" so as to make § 241 applicable to a private conspiracy to interfere with the exercise of that right. The Court then premises that neither the Fourteenth Amendment nor any other federal law prohibits private interferences with the exercise of the right to equal utilization of state facilities.

In my view, however, a right can be deemed "secured . . . by the Constitution or laws of the United States," within the meaning of § 241, even though only governmental interferences with the exercise of the right are prohibited by the Constitution itself (or another federal law). The term "secured" means "created by, arising under or dependent upon," Logan v. United States, 144 U.S. 263, 293, rather than "fully protected." A right is "secured . . . by the Constitution" within the meaning of § 241 if it emanates from the Constitution, if it finds its source in the Constitution. Section 241 must thus be viewed, in this context, as an exercise of congressional power to amplify prohibitions of the Constitution addressed, as is invariably the case, to government officers; contrary to the view of the Court, I think we are dealing here with a statute that seeks to implement the Constitution, not with the "bare terms" of the Constitution. Section 241 is not confined to protecting rights against private conspiracies that the Constitution or

---

1. Similarly, I believe that § 241 reaches a private conspiracy to interfere with the right to travel from State to State. I therefore need not reach the question whether the Constitution of its own force prohibits private interferences with that right; for I construe § 241 to prohibit such interferences, and as so construed I am of the opinion that § 241 is a valid exercise of congressional power. [Footnote by Justice Brennan.]

another federal law also protects against private interferences. No such duplicative function was envisioned in its enactment. . . . Nor has this Court construed § 241 in such a restrictive manner in other contexts. Many of the rights that have been held to be encompassed within § 241 are not additionally the subject of protection of specific federal legislation or of any provision of the Constitution addressed to private individuals. [See the cases cited p. 464, supra.] The full import of our decision in United States v. Price [p. 504, supra] regarding § 241 is to treat the rights purportedly arising from the Fourteenth Amendment in parity with those rights just enumerated, arising from other constitutional provisions. The reach of § 241 should not vary with the particular constitutional provision that is the source of the right. . . .

For me, the right to use state facilities without discrimination on the basis of race is, within the meaning of § 241, a right created by, arising under and dependent upon the Fourteenth Amendment and hence is a right "secured" by that Amendment. It finds its source in that Amendment. . . . The Fourteenth Amendment commands the State to provide the members of all races with equal access to the public facilities it owns or manages, and the right of a citizen to use those facilities without discrimination on the basis of race is a basic corollary of this command. Cf. Brewer v. Hoxie School District No. 46, 238 F.2d 91 (C.A.8th Cir. 1956). Whatever may be the status of the right to equal utilization of *privately owned facilities*, see generally Bell v. Maryland, 378 U.S. 226, it must be emphasized that we are here concerned with the right to equal utilization of *public facilities owned or operated by or on behalf of the State.* To deny the existence of this right or its constitutional stature is to deny the history of the last decade, or to ignore the role of federal power, predicated on the Fourteenth Amendment, in obtaining non-discriminatory access to such facilities. . . .

In reversing the District Court's dismissal of the second numbered paragraph, I would therefore hold that proof at the trial of the conspiracy charged to the defendants in that paragraph will establish a violation of § 241 without regard to whether there is also proof that state law enforcement officers actively connived in causing the arrests of Negroes by means of false reports.

II.

My view as to the scope of § 241 requires that I reach the question of constitutional power—whether § 241 or legislation indubitably designed to punish entirely private conspiracies to interfere with the exercise of Fourteenth Amendment rights constitutes a permissible exercise of the power granted to Congress by § 5 of the Fourteenth Amendment "to enforce by appropriate legislation, the provisions of" the Amendment.

A majority of the members of the Court[2] expresses the view today that § 5 empowers Congress to enact laws punishing *all* conspiracies to interfere with the exercise of Fourteenth Amendment rights, whether or not state officers or others acting under the color of state law are implicated in the con-

2. The majority consists of the Justices joining my Brother Clark's opinion and the Justices joining this opinion. The opinion of Mr. Justice Stewart construes § 241 as applied to the second numbered paragraph to require proof of active participation by state officers in the alleged conspiracy and that opinion does not purport to deal with this question. [Footnote by Justice Brennan.]

spiracy. Although the Fourteenth Amendment itself, according to established doctrine, "speaks to the State or to those acting under the color of its authority," legislation protecting rights created by that Amendment, such as the right to equal utilization of state facilities, need not be confined to punishing conspiracies in which state officers participate. Rather, § 5 authorizes Congress to make laws that it concludes are reasonably necessary to protect a right created by and arising under that Amendment; and Congress is thus fully empowered to determine that punishment of private conspiracies interfering with the exercise of such a right is necessary to its full protection. It made that determination in enacting § 241, . . . and, therefore § 241 is constitutional legislation as applied to reach the private conspiracy alleged in the second numbered paragraph of the indictment.

I acknowledge that some of the decisions of this Court, most notably an aspect of the Civil Rights Cases, 109 U.S. 3, 11, have declared that Congress' power under § 5 is confined to the adoption of "appropriate legislation for correcting the effects of . . . prohibited State laws and State acts, and thus to render them effectually null, void, and innocuous." I do not accept—and a majority of the Court today rejects—this interpretation of § 5. It reduces the legislative power to enforce the provisions of the Amendment to that of the judiciary; and it attributes a far too limited objective to the Amendment's sponsors. Moreover, the language of § 5 of the Fourteenth Amendment and § 2 of the Fifteenth Amendment are virtually the same, and we recently held in South Carolina v. Katzenbach [p. 534, infra] that "[t]he basic test to be applied in a case involving § 2 of the Fifteenth Amendment is the same as in all cases concerning the express powers of Congress with relation to the reserved powers of the States." The classic formulation of that test by Chief Justice Marshall in McCulloch v. Maryland, 4 Wheat. 316, 421, was there adopted . . . . It seems to me that this is also the standard that defines the scope of congressional authority under § 5 of the Fourteenth Amendment. . . .

Viewed in its proper perspective, § 5 of the Fourteenth Amendment appears as a positive grant of legislative power, authorizing Congress to exercise its discretion in fashioning remedies to achieve civil and political equality for all citizens. No one would deny that Congress could enact legislation directing state officials to provide Negroes with equal access to state schools, parks and other facilities owned or operated by the State. Nor could it be denied that Congress has the power to punish state officers who, in excess of their authority and in violation of state law, conspire to threaten, harass and murder Negroes for attempting to use these facilities. And I can find no principle of federalism nor word of the Constitution that denies Congress power to determine that in order adequately to protect the right to equal utilization of state facilities, it is also appropriate to punish other individuals—not state officers themselves and not acting in concert with state officers—who engage in the same brutal conduct for the same misguided purpose.

III.

Section 241 is certainly not model legislation for punishing private conspiracies to interfere with the exercise of the right of equal utilization of state facilities. It deals in only general language "with Federal rights and with all Federal rights" and protects them "in the lump" . . . . .

[A]s the Court holds, a stringent scienter requirement saves § 241 from condemnation as a criminal statute failing to provide adequate notice of the proscribed conduct. The gravamen of the offense is conspiracy, and therefore, like a statute making certain conduct criminal only if it is done "willfully," § 241 requires proof of a specific intent for conviction. We have construed § 241 to require proof that the persons charged conspired to act in defiance, or in reckless disregard, of an announced rule making the federal right specific and definite. . . . Since this case reaches us on the pleadings, there is no occasion to decide now whether the Government will be able on trial to sustain the burden of proving the requisite specific intent *vis-à-vis* the right to travel freely from State to State or the right to equal utilization of state facilities. . . . In any event, we may well agree that the necessity to discharge that burden can imperil the effectiveness of § 241 where, as is often the case, the pertinent constitutional right must be implied from a grant of congressional power or a prohibition upon the exercise of governmental power. But since the limitation on the statute's effectiveness derives from Congress' failure to define—with any measure of specificity—the rights encompassed, the remedy is for Congress to write a law without this defect. To paraphrase my Brother Douglas' observation in Screws v. United States, 325 U.S., at 105, addressed to a companion statute with the same shortcoming, if Congress desires to give the statute more definite scope it may find ways of doing so.

CONGRESSIONAL POWER, THE GUEST CASE, AND THE NEW LAW

How far-reaching is the 14th Amendment power suggested in Justice Brennan's opinion? Is it essential that the private actor interfere with a state-victim relationship? Is it essential that the defendant intend to interfere with the victim's access to State facilities? Is it enough that murder of the victim, for example, has the effect of interfering with the victim's use of state facilities? Is that a limitless concept?

Is the victim-state relationship an essential ingredient for invoking § 5? May Congress move directly to reach private interferences with, e. g., access to private housing, on the ground that it is appropriate legislation to protect access to public housing? (Cf. the regulation of intrastate commerce to protect interstate commerce.) See generally, Cox, "Foreword—Constitutional Adjudication and the Promotion of Human Rights," 80 Harv.L.Rev. 9 (1966), and the notes following the Morgan case, p. 552, infra.

Consider the specification of protected rights in the new statute, 18 U.S.C. § 245, which follows. To what extent is it traceable to Guest? Does the specification cure the vagueness concerns regarding 18 U.S.C. §§ 241 and 242? What explains the differences in intent requirements for (b) (1) violations and (b) (2) acts? What explains the grouping into two subsections of § 245(b)? What are the sources of the various rights named? Which are 14th Amendment rights? Which stem from other provisions? Does the provision raise any constitutional questions?

THE CRIMINAL PROVISIONS ADDED BY THE
CIVIL RIGHTS ACT OF 1968:
18 U.S.C. § 245

§ 245. *Federally protected activities.* . . .

(b) Whoever, whether or not acting under color of law, by force or threat of force willfully injures, intimidates or interferes with, or attempts to injure, intimidate or interfere with—

(1) any person because he is or has been, or in order to intimidate such person or any other person or any class of persons from—

(A) voting or qualifying to vote, qualifying or campaigning as a candidate for elective office, or qualifying or acting as a poll watcher, or any legally authorized election official, in any primary, special, or general election;

(B) participating in or enjoying any benefit, service, privilege, program, facility or activity provided or administered by the United States;

(C) applying for or enjoying employment, or any perquisite thereof, by any agency of the United States;

(D) serving, or attending upon any court in connection with possible service, as a grand or petit juror in any court of the United States;

(E) participating in or enjoying the benefits of any program or activity receiving Federal financial assistance; or

(2) any person because of his race, color, religion or national origin and because he is or has been—

(A) enrolling in or attending any public school or public college;

(B) participating in or enjoying any benefit, service, privilege, program, facility or activity provided or administered by any State or subdivision thereof;

(C) applying for or enjoying employment, or any perquisite thereof, by any private employer or any agency of any State or subdivision thereof, or joining or using the services or advantages of any labor organization, hiring hall, or employment agency;

(D) serving, or attending upon any court of any State in connection with possible service, as a grand or petit juror;

(E) traveling in or using any facility of interstate commerce, or using any vehicle, terminal, or facility of any common carrier by motor, rail, water, or air;

(F) enjoying the goods, services, facilities, privi___s, advantages, or accommodations of any inn, hotel, motel, or other establishment which provides lodging to transient guests, or of any restaurant, cafeteria, lunchroom, lunch counter, soda fountain, or other facility which serves the public and which is principally engaged in selling food or beverages for consumption on the premises, or of any gasoline station, or of any motion picture house, theater, concert hall, sports arena, stadium, or any other place of exhibition or entertainment which serves the public, or of any other establishment which serves the public and (i) which is located within the premises of any of the aforesaid establishments or within the premises of which is physically located any of the aforesaid establishments, and (ii) which holds itself out as serving patrons of such establishments; or

(3) during or incident to a riot or civil disorder, any person engaged in a business in commerce or affecting commerce, including, but not limited to, any person engaged in a business which sells or offers for sale to interstate travelers a substantial portion of the articles, commodities, or services which it sells or where a substantial portion of the articles or commodities which it sells or offers for sale have moved in commerce; or

(4) any person because he is or has been, or in order to intimidate such person or any other person or any class of persons from—

(A) participating, without discrimination on account of race, color, religion or national origin, in any of the benefits or activities described in subparagraphs (1) (A) through (1) (E) or subparagraphs (2) (A) through (2) (F); or

(B) affording another person or class of persons opportunity or protection to so participate; or

(5) any citizen because he is or has been, or in order to intimidate such citizen or any other citizen from lawfully aiding or encouraging other persons to participate, without discrimination on account of race, color, religion or national origin, in any of the benefits or activities described in subparagraphs (1) (A) through (1) (E) or subparagraphs (2) (A) through (2) (F), or participating lawfully in speech or peaceful assembly opposing any denial of the opportunity to so participate—

shall be fined not more than $1,000, or imprisoned not more than one year, or both; and if bodily injury results shall be fined not more than $10,000, or imprisoned not more than ten years, or both; and if death results shall be subject to imprisonment for any term of years or for life. As used in this section, the term "participating lawfully in speech or peaceful assembly" shall not mean the aiding, abetting, or inciting of other persons to riot . . . .

C. CONGRESS, THE 13TH AMENDMENT, AND PRIVATE CONDUCT

JONES v. ALFRED H. MAYER CO.

392 U.S. 409, 88 S.Ct. 2186, 20 L.Ed.2d 1189 (1968).

Certiorari to the United States Court of Appeals for the Eighth Circuit.

Mr. Justice STEWART delivered the opinion of the Court.

In this case we are called upon to determine the scope and the constitutionality of an Act of Congress, 42 U.S.C. § 1982, which provides that:

"All citizens of the United States shall have the same right, in every State and Territory, as is enjoyed by white citizens thereof to inherit, purchase, lease, sell, hold, and convey real and personal property."

On September 2, 1965, the petitioners filed a complaint in the District Court for the Eastern District of Missouri, alleging that the respondents had refused to sell them a home in the Paddock Woods community of St. Louis County for the sole reason that petitioner Joseph Lee Jones is a Negro. Relying in part upon § 1982, the petitioners sought injunctive and other relief. The District Court sustained the respondents' motion to dismiss the complaint, and the Court of Appeals for the Eighth Circuit affirmed, concluding that § 1982 applies only to state action and does not reach private refusals to sell. [W]e reverse the judgment of the Court of Appeals. We hold that § 1982 bars *all* racial discrimination, private as well as public, in the sale or rental of property, and that the statute, thus construed, is a valid exercise of the power of Congress to enforce the Thirteenth Amendment.[1]

I.

At the outset, it is important to make clear precisely what this case does *not* involve. Whatever else it may be, 42 U.S.C. § 1982 is not a comprehensive open housing law. In sharp contrast to the Fair Housing Title

---

1. Because we have concluded that the discrimination alleged in the petitioners' complaint violated a federal statute that Congress had the power to enact under the Thirteenth Amendment, we find it unnecessary to decide whether that discrimination also violated the Equal Protection Clause of the Fourteenth Amendment. [Footnote by the Court.]

(Title VIII) of the Civil Rights Act of 1968, Pub.L. 90–284, 82 Stat. 73 [see the excerpts following this case], the statute in this case deals only with racial discrimination and does not address itself to discrimination on grounds of religion or national origin. It does not deal specifically with discrimination in the provision of services or facilities in connection with the sale or rental of a dwelling. It does not prohibit advertising or other representations that indicate discriminatory preferences. It does not refer explicitly to discrimination in financing arrangements or in the provision of brokerage services.[2] It does not empower a federal administrative agency to assist aggrieved parties. It makes no provision for intervention by the Attorney General. And, although it can be enforced by injunction, it contains no provisions expressly authorizing a federal court to order the payment of damages.

Thus, although § 1982 contains none of the exemptions that Congress included in the Civil Rights Act of 1968, it would be a serious mistake to suppose that § 1982 in any way diminishes the significance of the law recently enacted by Congress. [Shortly after the pendency and possible significance of this case were called to its attention,] the House passed the Civil Rights Act of 1968. Its enactment had no effect upon § 1982 [3] and no effect upon this litigation,[4] but it underscored the vast differences between, on the one hand, a general statute applicable only to racial discrimination in the rental and sale of property and enforceable only by private parties acting on their own initiative, and, on the other hand, a detailed housing law, applicable to a broad range of discriminatory practices and enforceable by a complete arsenal

2. . . . In noting that 42 U.S.C. § 1982 differs from the Civil Rights Act of 1968 in not dealing explicitly and exhaustively with such matters _ _, we intimate no view upon the question whether ancillary services or facilities of this sort might in some situations constitute "property" as that term is employed in § 1982. Nor do we intimate any view upon the extent to which discrimination in the provision of such services might be barred by 42 U.S.C. § 1981. [Footnote by the Court.]

3. At oral argument, the Attorney General expressed the view that, if Congress should enact the pending bill, § 1982 would not be affected in any way but "would stand independently." That is, of course, correct. The Civil Rights Act of 1968 does not mention 42 U.S.C. § 1982, and we cannot assume that Congress intended to effect any change, either substantive or procedural, in the prior statute. . . . See also § 815 of the 1968 Act: "Nothing in this title shall be construed to invalidate or limit any law of . . . any . . . jurisdiction in which this title shall be effective, that grants, guarantees or protects the . . . rights . . . granted by this title . . . ." [Footnote by the Court. Sec. 815 was entitled "Effect on State Laws."]

4. On April 22, 1968, we requested the views of the parties as to what effect, if any, the enactment of the Civil Rights Act of 1968 had upon this litigation. The parties and the Attorney General, representing the United States as amicus curiae, have informed us that the respondents' housing development will not be covered by the 1968 Act until January 1, 1969; that, even then, the Act will have no application to cases where, as here, the alleged discrimination occurred prior to April 11, 1968, the date on which the Act became law; and that, if the Act were deemed applicable to such cases, the petitioners' claim under it would nonetheless be barred by the 180-day limitation period of §§ 810(b) and 812(a). Nor did the passage of the 1968 Act after oral argument in this case furnish a basis for dismissing the writ of certiorari as improvidently granted. Rice v. Sioux City Cemetery, 349 U.S. 70, relied upon in dissent, . . . was quite unlike this case, for the statute that belatedly came to the Court's attention in Rice reached precisely the same situations that would have been covered by a decision in this Court sustaining the petitioner's claim on the merits. The coverage of § 1982, however, is markedly different from that of the Civil Rights Act of 1968. [Footnote by the Court.]

of federal authority.   Having noted these differences, we turn to a consideration of § 1982 itself.

II.

This Court last had occasion to consider the scope of 42 U.S.C. § 1982 in 1948, in Hurd v. Hodge, 334 U.S. 24 [the District of Columbia restrictive covenant case decided on the same day as Shelley v. Kraemer, p. 471, supra.] It is true that a dictum in Hurd said that § 1982 was directed only toward "governmental action," . . . but neither Hurd nor any other case before or since has presented that precise issue for adjudication in this Court.[5] Today we face that issue for the first time.

III.

We begin with the language of the statute itself. In plain and unambiguous terms, § 1982 grants to all citizens, without regard to race or color, "the same right" to purchase and lease property "as is enjoyed by white citizens." As the Court of Appeals in this case evidently recognized, that right can be impaired as effectively by "those who place property on the market" as by the State itself. . . .

On its face, therefore, § 1982 appears to prohibit *all* discrimination against Negroes in the sale or rental of property—discrimination by private owners as well as discrimination by public authorities. [R]espondents argue that Congress cannot possibly have intended any such result. Our examination of the relevant history, however, persuades us that Congress meant exactly what it said.

IV.

In its original form, 42 U.S.C. § 1982 was part of § 1 of the Civil Rights Act of 1866. That section was cast in sweeping terms:

> "*Be it enacted by the Senate and House of Representatives of the United States of America in Congress assembled,* That all persons born in the United States and not subject to any foreign power, . . . are hereby declared to be citizens of the United States; and such citizens, of every race and color, without regard to any previous condition of slavery or involuntary servitude, . . . shall have the same right, in every State and Territory in the United States, to make and enforce contracts, to sue, be parties, and give evidence, to inherit, purchase, lease, sell, hold, and convey real and personal property, and to full and equal benefit of all laws and proceedings for the security of person and property, as is enjoyed by white citizens, and shall be subject to like punishment, pains, and penalties, and to none other, any law, statute, ordinance, regulation, or custom, to the contrary notwithstanding."

5. Two of this Court's early opinions contain dicta to the general effect that § 1982 is limited to state action. Virginia v. Rives, 100 U.S. 313, 317–318; Civil Rights Cases, 109 U.S. 3, 16–17.
. . .
It is true that a dictum in Hurd v. Hodge, 334 U.S. 24, 31, characterized Corrigan v. Buckley, 271 U.S. 323, as having "held" that "[t]he action toward which the provisions of the statute . . . [are] directed is governmental action." 334 U.S., at 31. But no such statement appears in the Corrigan opinion, and a careful examination of Corrigan reveals that it cannot be read as authority for the proposition attributed to it in Hurd. . . . [Footnote by the Court.]

The crucial language for our purposes was that which guaranteed all citizens "the same right, in every State and Territory in the United States, . . . to inherit, purchase, lease, sell, hold, and convey real and personal property . . . as is enjoyed by white citizens . . . ." To the Congress that passed the Civil Rights Act of 1866, it was clear that the right to do these things might be infringed not only by "State or local law" but also by "custom, or prejudice." Thus, when Congress provided in § 1 of the Civil Rights Act that the right to purchase and lease property was to be enjoyed equally throughout the United States by Negro and white citizens alike, it plainly meant to secure that right against interference from any source whatever, whether governmental or private.

Indeed, if § 1 had been intended to grant nothing more than an immunity from *governmental* interference, then much of § 2 would have made no sense at all.[6] For that section, which provided fines and prison terms for certain individuals who deprived others of rights "secured or protected" by § 1, was carefully drafted to exempt private violations of § 1 from the criminal sanctions it imposed. There would, of course, have been no private violations to exempt if the only "right" granted by § 1 had been a right to be free of discrimination by public officials. Hence the structure of the 1866 Act, as well as its language, points to the conclusion urged by the petitioners in this case—that § 1 was meant to prohibit *all* racially motivated deprivations of the rights enumerated in the statute, although only those deprivations perpetrated "under color of law" were to be criminally punishable under § 2.

In attempting to demonstrate the contrary, the respondents rely heavily upon the fact that the Congress which approved the 1866 statute wished to eradicate the recently enacted Black Codes . . . . . The respondents suggest that the only evil Congress sought to eliminate was that of racially discriminatory laws in the former Confederate States. But the Civil Rights Act was drafted to apply throughout the country, and its language was far broader than would have been necessary to strike down discriminatory statutes.

That broad language, we are asked to believe, was a mere slip of the legislative pen. We disagree. For the same Congress that wanted to do away with the Black Codes *also* had before it an imposing body of evidence pointing to the mistreatment of Negroes by private individuals and unofficial groups, mistreatment unrelated to any hostile state legislation. . . .

In light of the concerns that led Congress to adopt it and the contents of the debates that preceded its passage, it is clear that the Act was designed to do just what its terms suggest: to prohibit all racial discrimination, whether or not under color of law, with respect to the rights enumerated therein—including the right to purchase or lease property.

Nor was the scope of the 1866 Act altered when it was re-enacted in 1870, some two years after the ratification of the Fourteenth Amendment. It is quite true that some members of Congress supported the Fourteenth Amendment "in order to eliminate doubt as to the constitutional validity of the Civil

---

6. Section 2 provided:
"That any person who, *under color of any law, statute, ordinance, regulation, or custom,* shall subject, or cause to be subjected, any inhabitant of any State or Territory to the deprivation of any right secured or protected by this act . . . shall be deemed guilty of a misdemeanor . . . ." (Emphasis added.)

For the evolution of this provision into 18 U.S.C. § 242, see Screws v. United States, 325 U.S. 91, 98–99; United States v. Price, 383 U.S. 787, 804. [Footnote by the Court.]

Rights Act as applied to the States." Hurd v. Hodge, 334 U.S. 24, 32--33. But it certainly does not follow that the adoption of the Fourteenth Amendment or the subsequent readoption of the Civil Rights Act were meant somehow to *limit* its application to state action. The legislative history furnishes not the slightest factual basis for any such speculation, and the conditions prevailing in 1870 make it highly implausible. For by that time most, if not all, of the former Confederate States, then under the control of "reconstructed" legislatures, had formally repudiated racial discrimination, and the focus of congressional concern had clearly shifted from hostile statutes to the activities of groups like the Ku Klux Klan, operating wholly outside the law.

Against this background, it would obviously make no sense to assume, without any historical support whatever, that Congress made a silent decision in 1870 to exempt private discrimination from the operation of the Civil Rights Act of 1866.[7] . . . All Congress said in 1870 was that the 1866 law "is hereby re-enacted." That is all Congress meant. . . . "We are not at liberty to seek ingenious analytical instruments" . . . to carve from § 1982 an exception for private conduct—even though its application to such conduct in the present context is without established precedent. And, as the Attorney General of the United States said at the oral argument of this case, "The fact that the statute lay partially dormant for many years cannot be held to diminish its force today."

V.

The remaining question is whether Congress has power under the Constitution to do what § 1982 purports to do: to prohibit all racial discrimination, private and public, in the sale and rental of property. Our starting point is the Thirteenth Amendment, for it was pursuant to that constitutional provision that Congress originally enacted what is now § 1982. . . .

As its text reveals, the Thirteenth Amendment "is not a mere prohibition of State laws establishing or upholding slavery, but an absolute declaration that slavery or involuntary servitude shall not exist in any part of the United States." Civil Rights Cases, 109 U.S. 3, 20. It has never been doubted, therefore, "that the power vested in Congress to enforce the article by appropriate legislation," ibid., includes the power to enact laws "direct and primary, operating upon the acts of individuals, whether sanctioned by State legislation or not." Id., at 23.

Thus, the fact that § 1982 operates upon the unofficial acts of private individuals, whether or not sanctioned by state law, presents no constitutional problem. . . . The constitutional question in this case, therefore, comes to this: Does the authority of Congress to enforce the Thirteenth Amendment "by appropriate legislation" include the power to eliminate all racial barriers to the acquisition of real and personal property? We think the answer to that question is plainly yes.

---

7. The Court of Appeals in this case seems to have derived such an assumption from language in Virginia v. Rives, 100 U.S. 313, 317–318, and Hurd v. Hodge, 334 U.S. 24, 31. . . . Both of those opinions simply asserted that, at least after its re-enactment in 1870, the Civil Rights Act of 1866 was directed only at governmental action. Neither opinion explained why that was thought to be so, and in each case the statement was merely dictum. . . . [Footnote by the Court.]

"By its own unaided force and effect," the Thirteenth Amendment "abolished slavery, and established universal freedom." Civil Rights Cases, 109 U.S. 3, 20. Whether or not the Amendment *itself* did any more than that—a question not involved in this case—it is at least clear that the Enabling Clause of that Amendment empowered Congress to do much more. For that clause clothed "Congress with power to pass *all laws necessary and proper for abolishing all badges and incidents of slavery in the United States.*" Ibid. (Emphasis added.) . . .

. . . Surely Congress has the power under the Thirteenth Amendment rationally to determine what are the badges and the incidents of slavery, and the authority to translate that determination into effective legislation. Nor can we say that the determination Congress has made is an irrational one. For this Court recognized long ago that, whatever else they may have encompassed, the badges and incidents of slavery—its "burdens and disabilities"—included restraints upon "those fundamental rights which are the essence of civil freedom, namely, the same right . . . to inherit, purchase, lease, sell and convey property, as is enjoyed by white citizens." Civil Rights Cases, 109 U.S. 3, 22. Just as the Black Codes, enacted after the Civil War to restrict the free exercise of those rights, were substitutes for the slave system, so the exclusion of Negroes from white communities became a substitute for the Black Codes. And when racial discrimination herds men into ghettos and makes their ability to buy property turn on the color of their skin, then it too is a relic of slavery.

Negro citizens North and South, who saw in the Thirteenth Amendment a promise of freedom—freedom to "go and come at pleasure" and to "buy and sell when they please"—would be left with "a mere paper guarantee" if Congress were powerless to assure that a dollar in the hands of a Negro will purchase the same thing as a dollar in the hands of a white man. At the very least, the freedom that Congress is empowered to secure under the Thirteenth Amendment includes the freedom to buy whatever a white man can buy, the right to live wherever a white man can live. If Congress cannot say that being a free man means at least this much, then the Thirteenth Amendment made a promise the Nation cannot keep.

Representative Wilson of Iowa was the floor manager in the House for the Civil Rights Act of 1866. In urging that Congress had ample authority to pass the pending bill, he recalled the celebrated words of Chief Justice Marshall in McCulloch v. Maryland, 4 Wheat. 316, 421 . . . . "The end is legitimate," the Congressman said, "because it is defined by the Constitution itself. The end is the maintenance of freedom . . . . A man who enjoys the civil rights mentioned in this bill cannot be reduced to slavery. . . . This settles the appropriateness of this measure, and that settles its constitutionality."

We agree. The judgment is

Reversed.

Mr. Justice DOUGLAS, concurring. . . .

Enabling a Negro to buy and sell real and personal property is a removal of one of many badges of slavery.

[P]rejudices, once part and parcel of slavery, still persist. The men who sat in Congress in 1866 were trying to remove some of the badges or "customs" * of slavery when they enacted § 1982. . . .

Mr. Justice HARLAN, whom Mr. Justice WHITE joins, dissenting. . . .

. . . I believe that the Court's construction of § 1982 as applying to purely private action is almost surely wrong, and at the least is open to serious doubt. The issue of the constitutionality of § 1982, as construed by the Court, and of liability under the Fourteenth Amendment alone,[1] also present formidable difficulties. Moreover, the political processes of our own era have, since the date of oral argument in this case, given birth to a civil rights statute embodying "fair housing" provisions which would at the end of this year make available to others, though apparently not to the petitioners themselves, the type of relief which the petitioners now seek. It seems to me that this latter factor so diminishes the public importance of this case that by far the wisest course would be for this Court to refrain from decision and to dismiss the writ as improvidently granted. . . .

Like the Court, I begin analysis of § 1982 by examining its language. . . . The Court finds it "plain and unambiguous" . . . that this language forbids purely private as well as state-authorized discrimination. With all respect, I do not find it so. For me, there is an inherent ambiguity in the term "right," as used in § 1982. The "right" referred to may either be a right to equal status under the law, in which case the statute operates only against state-sanctioned discrimination, or it may be an "absolute" right enforceable against private individuals. To me, the words of the statute, taken alone, suggest the former interpretation, not the latter.[2]

---

* My Brother Harlan's listing of some of the "customs" prevailing in the North at the time § 1982 was first enacted . . . shows the extent of organized white discrimination against newly freed blacks. As he states, "[r]esidential segregation was the prevailing pattern almost everywhere in the North." . . . Certainly, then, it was "customary." To suggest, however, that there might be room for argument in this case (post, at n. [3]) that the discrimination against petitioners was not in some measure a part and product of this longstanding and widespread customary pattern is to pervert the problem by allowing the legal mind to draw lines and make distinctions that have no place in the jurisprudence of a nation striving to rejoin the human race. [Footnote by Justice Douglas.]

1. Justice Harlan noted, in a footnote at another point, that the "state action" argument emphasized "the respondent's role as a housing developer who exercised continuing authority over a suburban housing complex with about 1,000 inhabitants."

2. Despite the Court's view that this reading flies in the face of the "plain and unambiguous terms" of the statute, . . . it is not without precedent. In the Civil Rights Cases, 109 U.S. 3, the Court said of identical language in the predecessor statute to § 1982:

"[C]ivil rights, such as are guaranteed by the Constitution against State aggression, cannot be impaired by the wrongful acts of individuals, unsupported by State authority . . . . The wrongful act of an individual, unsupported by any such authority, is simply a private wrong, or a crime of that individual; an invasion of the rights of the injured party, it is true . . . ; but if not sanctioned in some way by the State, or not done under State authority, his rights remain in full force, and may presumably be vindicated by resort to the laws of the State for redress. An individual cannot deprive a man of his right . . . to hold property, to buy and sell . . . ; he may, by force or fraud, interfere with the enjoyment of the right in a particular case . . . ; but, unless protected

Further, since intervening revisions have not been meant to alter substance, the intended meaning of § 1982 must be drawn from the words in which it was originally enacted. Section 1982 originally was a part of § 1 of the Civil Rights Act of 1866, 14 Stat. 27. . . . It seems to me that this original wording indicates even more strongly than the present language that § 1 of the Act (as well as § 2, which is explicitly so limited) was intended to apply only to action taken pursuant to state or community authority, in the form of a "law, statute, ordinance, regulation, or custom." And with deference I suggest that the language of § 2, taken alone, no more implies that § 2 "was carefully drafted to exempt private violations of § 1 from the criminal sanctions it imposed," . . . than it does that § 2 was carefully drafted to enforce all of the rights secured by § 1. . . .

The Court rests its opinion chiefly upon the legislative history of the Civil Rights Act of 1866. I shall endeavor to show that those debates do not, as the Court would have it, overwhelmingly support the result reached by the Court, and in fact that a contrary conclusion may equally well be drawn.

. . . It should be remembered that racial prejudice was not uncommon in 1866, even outside the South. Residential segregation was the prevailing pattern almost everywhere in the North. There were no state "fair housing" laws in 1866, and it appears that none had ever been proposed. In this historical context, I cannot conceive that a bill thought to prohibit purely private discrimination not only in the sale or rental of housing but in *all* property transactions would not have received a great deal of criticism explicitly directed to this feature. The fact that the 1866 Act received *no* criticism of this kind is for me strong additional evidence that it was not regarded as extending so far.

In sum, the most which can be said with assurance about the intended impact of the 1866 Civil Rights Act upon purely private discrimination is that the Act probably was envisioned by most members of Congress as prohibiting official, community-sanctioned discrimination in the South, engaged in pursuant to local "customs" which in the recent time of slavery probably were embodied in laws or regulations.[3] Acts done under the color of such "customs" were, of course, said by the Court in the Civil Rights Cases, 109 U.S. 3, to constitute "state action" prohibited by the Fourteenth Amendment. . . . Adoption of a "state action" construction of the Civil Rights Act would therefore have the additional merit of bringing its interpretation into line with that of the Fourteenth Amendment, which this Court has consistently held to reach only "state action." This seems especially desirable in light of the wide agreement that a major purpose of the Fourteenth Amendment, at least in the minds of its congressional proponents, was to assure that the rights conferred by the then recently enacted Civil Rights Act could not be taken away by a subsequent Congress. . . .

. . . In holding that the Thirteenth Amendment is sufficient constitutional authority for § 1982 as interpreted, the Court also decides a question of great importance. Even contemporary supporters of the aims of the 1866 Civil Rights Act doubted that those goals could constitutionally be achieved

in these wrongful acts by some shield of State law or State authority, he cannot destroy or injure the right . . . ." 109 U.S., at 17. [Footnote by Justice Harlan.]

3. The petitioners do not argue, and the Court does not suggest, that the discrimination complained of in this case was the product of such a "custom." [Footnote by Justice Harlan.]

under the Thirteenth Amendment, and this Court has twice expressed similar doubts. See Hodges v. United States, 203 U.S. 1, 16–18; Corrigan v. Buckley, 271 U.S. 323, 330. But cf. Civil Rights Cases, 109 U.S. 3, 22. . . .

The fact that a case is "hard" does not, of course, relieve a judge of his duty to decide it. Since, the Court did vote to hear this case, I normally would consider myself obligated to decide [it]. After mature reflection, however, I have concluded that this is one of those rare instances in which an event which occurs after the hearing of argument so diminishes a case's public significance, when viewed in light of the difficulty of the questions presented, as to justify this Court in dismissing the writ as improvidently granted.

The occurrence to which I refer is the recent enactment of the Civil Rights Act of 1968 . . . . In these circumstances, it seems obvious that the case has lost most of its public importance . . . . I think it particularly unfortunate for the Court to persist in deciding this case on the basis of a highly questionable interpretation of a sweeping, century-old statute which, as the Court acknowledges, . . . contains none of the exemptions which the Congress of our own time found it necessary to include in a statute regulating relationships so personal in nature. In effect, this Court, by its construction of § 1982, has extended the coverage of federal "fair housing" laws far beyond that which Congress in its wisdom chose to provide in the Civil Rights Act of 1968. The political process now having taken hold again in this very field, I am at a loss to understand why the Court should have deemed it appropriate or, in the circumstances of this case, necessary to proceed with such precipitous and insecure strides. . . .

THE FAIR HOUSING PROVISIONS OF THE
1968 CIVIL RIGHTS ACT

Excerpts from the Coverage Provisions of Title VIII—Fair Housing—of the Civil Rights Act of 1968 (Pub.Law 90–284, 82 Stat. 73):

POLICY

Sec. 801. It is the policy of the United States to provide, within constitutional limitations, for fair housing throughout the United States. . . .

EFFECTIVE DATES OF CERTAIN PROHIBITIONS

Sec. 803. (a) Subject to the provisions of subsection (b) and section 807, the prohibitions against discrimination in the sale or rental of housing set forth in section 804 shall apply:

(1) Upon enactment of this title, to—

(A) dwellings owned or operated by the Federal Government;

(B) dwellings provided in whole or in part with the aid of loans, advances, grants, or contributions made by the Federal Government, under agreements entered into after November 20, 1962, unless payment due thereon has been made in full prior to the date of the enactment of this title;

(C) dwellings provided in whole or in part by loans insured, guaranteed, or otherwise secured by the credit of the Federal Government, under agreements entered into after November 20, 1962, unless payment thereon has been made in full prior to the date of enactment of this title: *Provided,* That nothing contained in subparagraphs (B) and (C) of this subsection shall be applicable to dwellings solely by virtue of the fact that they are subject to mortgages held by an FDIC or FSLIC institution; and

(D) dwellings provided by the development or the redevelopment of real property purchased, rented, or otherwise obtained from a State or local public agency, receiving Federal financial assistance for slum clearance or urban renewal with respect to such real property under loan or grant contracts entered into after November 20, 1962.

(2) After December 31, 1968, to all dwellings covered by paragraph (1) and to all other dwellings except as exempted by subsection (b).

(b) Nothing in section 804 (other than subsection (c)) shall apply to—

(1) any single-family house sold or rented by an owner: *Provided*, That such private individual owner does not own more than three such single-family houses at any one time: *Provided further*, That in the case of the sale of any such single-family house by a private individual owner not residing in such house at the time of such sale or who was not the most recent resident of such house prior to such sale, the exemption granted by this subsection shall apply only with respect to one such sale within any twenty-four month period: *Provided further*, That such bona fide private individual owner does not own any interest in, nor is there owned or reserved on his behalf, under any express or voluntary agreement, title to or any right to all or a portion of the proceeds from the sale or rental of, more than three such single-family houses at any one time: *Provided further*, That after December 31, 1969, the sale or rental of any such single-family house shall be excepted from the application of this title only if such house is sold or rented (A) without the use in any manner of the sales or rental facilities or the sales or rental services or any real estate broker, agent, or salesman, or of such facilities or services of any person in the business of selling or renting dwellings, or of any employee or agent of any such broker, agent, salesman, or person and (B) without the publication, posting or mailing, after notice, of any advertisement or written notice in violation of section 804(c) of this title; but nothing in this proviso shall prohibit the use of attorneys, escrow agents, abstractors, title companies, and other such professional assistance as necessary to perfect or transfer the title, or

(2) rooms or units in dwellings containing living quarters occupied or intended to be occupied by no more than four families living independently of each other, if the owner actually maintains and occupies one of such living quarters as his residence. . . .

DISCRIMINATION IN THE SALE OR RENTAL OF HOUSING

Sec. 804. As made applicable by section 803 and except as exempted by sections 803(b) and 807, it shall be unlawful—

(a) To refuse to sell or rent after the making of a bona fide offer, or to refuse to negotiate for the sale or rental of, or otherwise make unavailable or deny, a dwelling to any person because of race, color, religion, or national origin.

(b) To discriminate against any person in the terms, conditions, or privileges of sale or rental of a dwelling, or in the provision of services or facilities in connection therewith, because of race, color, religion, or national origin.

(c) To make, print or publish, or cause to be made, printed, or published any notice, statement, or advertisement, with respect to the sale or rental of a dwelling that indicates any preference, limitation, or discrimination based on race, color, religion, or national origin, or an intention to make any such preference, limitation, or discrimination.

(d) To represent to any person because of race, color, religion, or national origin that any dwelling is not available for inspection, sale, or rental when such dwelling is in fact so available.

(e) For profit, to induce or attempt to induce any person to sell or rent any dwelling by representations regarding the entry or prospective entry into the neighborhood of a person or persons of a particular race, color, religion, or national origin. . . .

[Secs. 805 and 806 cover discrimination in financing and in brokerage services.]

EXEMPTION

Sec. 807. Nothing in this title shall prohibit a religious organization, association, or society, or any nonprofit institution or organization operated, supervised or controlled by or in conjunction with a religious organization, association or society, from limiting the sale, rental or occupancy of dwellings which it owns or operates for other than a commercial purpose to persons of the same religion, or from giving preference to such persons, unless membership in such religion is restricted on account of race, color, or national origin. Nor shall anything in this title prohibit a private club not in fact open to the public, which as an incident to its primary purpose or purposes provides lodgings which it owns or operates for other than a commercial purpose, from limiting the rental or occupancy of such lodgings to its members or from giving preference to its members. . . .

THE 1866 ACT AND 13TH AMENDMENT POWERS

1. *Sullivan v. Little Hunting Park.* The Court applied the newly discovered 1866 Act—and expanded its broad interpretation—in Sullivan v. Little Hunting Park, Inc., 396 U.S. 229 (1969), involving the refusal by a corporation operating community recreational facilities to permit assignment of a membership share to a Negro. Justice Douglas' majority opinion reversing the state court's dismissal of the action found the corporation's refusal an interference with the right to "lease" within the terms of the 1866 Act.

Justice Harlan's dissent, joined by Chief Justice Burger and Justice White, urged that certiorari be dismissed as improvidently granted because of the "complexities" under the 1866 Act and the existence of the 1968 fair housing law. He noted that the Court had gone beyond the Jones case, supra, "(1) by implying a private right to damages for violations of § 1982; (2) by interpreting § 1982 to prohibit a community recreation association from withholding, on the basis of race, approval of an assignment of a membership that was transferred incident to a lease of real property; and (3) by deciding that a white person who is expelled from a recreation association 'for the advocacy of [a Negro's] cause' has 'standing' to maintain an action for relief under § 1982." He insisted that the majority was "even more unwise than it was in Jones, in precipitously breathing still more life into § 1982, which is both vague and open-ended, when Congress has provided this modern statute, containing various detailed remedial provisions."

2. *The scope of congressional power.* How far-reaching is the 13th Amendment power recognized by Jones? Is it an adequate constitutional basis for all conceivable civil rights legislation directed at private conduct? Is there any action against racial discrimination that Congress may not consider to be a remedy against the "badges of servitude"? Justice Harlan's dissent in Sullivan, note 1 supra, commented: "And lurking in the background are grave constitutional issues should § 1982 be extended too far into some types of private discrimination [citing the 1883 Civil Rights Cases, p. 454, supra]." What are the constitutional limits? Are the concerns of the Civil Rights Cases relevant to 13th Amendment legislation? Compare the notes following the Morgan case, p. 552, infra.

SECTION 4. CONGRESSIONAL POWER TO MODIFY THE CONTENT OF CONSTITUTIONAL RIGHTS: THE MORGAN CASE AND THE VOTING RIGHTS ACT OF 1965

PROTECTION OF VOTING RIGHTS BEFORE THE 1965 ACT

Introduction. Not only the general provisions of the 14th Amendment but also the focused prohibition of the 15th speak to the issue of voting rights.

Several of the laws of the post-Civil War years dealt with the voting, but most were repealed or invalidated in the courts. By 1957, only a brief general provision remained on the statute books—42 U.S.C. § 1971(a) (1), derived from the 1870 Act:

"All citizens of the United States who are otherwise qualified to vote at any election by the people in any State   .   .   .   shall be entitled and allowed to vote at all such elections, without distinction of race, color, or previous condition of servitude; any constitution, law, custom, usage or regulation of any State   .   .   ., or by or under its authority, to the contrary notwithstanding."

Administration of state voting qualifications could be challenged as discriminatory under this statutory counterpart of the 15th Amendment, but the litigation process was difficult and slow. Voting qualifications could be challenged under the equal protection clause 14th Amendment as well; but, until the late sixties, no such attack succeeded. The Lassiter case in 1959, p. 530 infra, rejecting an on the face attack on literacy tests, illustrates the traditional Court refusal to strike down qualifications unless discriminatory application was demonstrated.*

The difficulties of securing voting rights initiated the revival of congressional rights action in the 1950's. The Civil Rights Acts of 1957 and 1960 were mainly concerned with racial disenfranchisement. The inadequacies of the case-by-case process of eliminating voting barriers led to the Voting Rights Act of 1965. Its major provisions directed at racial discrimination were considered in South Carolina v. Katzenbach, p. 534, infra. A provision with a rather different thrust, aimed at English literacy tests not found to be unconstitutional by the Court itself and not shown to have been administered with bias, were examined in Katzenbach v. Morgan, the most important case in this section, p. 545 infra. These introductory materials sketch the factual and legal background of the cases of the late sixties.

HISTORICAL BACKGROUND . . . †

While these measures [of 1870 and 1871] were sweeping, their enforcement was ultimately ineffective, and by 1894 most of them had been repealed. Beginning in the early 1890's a number of States enacted legislation establishing new voting qualifications. Among them was the literacy test. Prior to 1890, apparently no Southern State required proof of literacy, understanding of constitutional provisions or of the obligations of citizenship, or good moral character, as prerequisites to voting. However,   .   .   . these tests and devices were soon to appear in most of the States with large Negro populations.   .   .   .

* Only in the late sixties did the Court begin to find significant restrictions on voting barriers in the equal protection clause. That development, from "old" equal protection to "new," is traced in chap. 14, infra. A full acquaintance with the details is not necessary for analysis of the problems of this section; a useful overview of the general equal protection background can be gained, however, by examining the brief introductory sketch in chap. 14, p. 983, infra.

† This excerpt is from one of the major documents in the legislative history of the 1965 Act, Sen.Rep.No.162, Part 3, 89th Cong., 1st Sess.—a "Joint Statement of Individual Views" submitted by 12 members of the Senate Judiciary Committee in support of "the adoption of S. 1564, the Voting Rights Act of 1965."

It is significant that in 1890, 69 percent or more of the adult Negroes in seven Southern States which adopted these tests were illiterate . . . . At the same time alternative provisions for qualifying to vote were adopted to assure that illiterate whites were not disfranchised. Thus, in Louisiana, North Carolina, and Oklahoma, white voters were exempted from the literacy test by a " 'voting' grandfather clause." . . .

The history of 15th amendment litigation in the Supreme Court—from the beginning (United States v. Reese, 92 U.S. 214 [1] . . .) through the "grandfather clause" (Guinn v. United States . . .) [2] and the "white primary" [p. 469, supra], the resort to procedural hurdles (Lane v. Wilson, 307 U.S. 268), . . . to improper challenges (United States v. Thomas, 362 U.S. 58) [3], and, finally, the discriminatory use of tests (Schnell v. Davis,

---

1. United States v. Reese, 92 U.S. 214 (1875), involved an indictment under Sections 3 and 4 of the Civil Rights Act of 1870. The indictment charged that two inspectors at a municipal election had refused to receive and count the vote of a Negro citizen. The Court held that a demurrer to the indictment should be sustained: though the charge fell within the Fifteenth Amendment, the statute was not so limited. Section 4, for example, generally prohibited any interference with voting "by force, bribery, threats, intimidation, or other unlawful means"; it, like Section 3, was not limited to denials of voting rights because of race. Chief Justice Waite emphasized: "Every man should be able to know with certainty when he is committing a crime." He noted that the Fifteenth Amendment "does not confer the right of suffrage upon anyone"; it only protects against "discrimination." Cf. United States v. Raines, note 3, infra.

See also James v. Bowman, 190 U.S. 127 (1903). It held unconstitutional R.S. 5507, formerly Sec. 5 of the 1870 Civil Rights Act. It applied to "every person who . . . hinders . . . or intimidates another from exercising . . . the right of suffrage, to whom that right is guaranteed by the Fifteenth Amendment . . ., by means of bribery or threats of depriving such person of employment . . . or by threats of refusing to renew leases or contracts for labor, or by threats of violence . . . ." Justice Brewer's opinion rested on the grounds that "a statute which purports to punish purely individual action" and an indictment "which charges no discrimination on account of race" are not sustainable under the scope of congressional power under the Fifteenth Amendment.

2. In Guinn v. United States, 238 U.S. 347 (1915), the Court held invalid an

amendment to the Constitution of Oklahoma establishing literacy requirements for electors coupled with a "grandfather clause" exempting from the literacy test all persons entitled to vote on Jan. 1, 1866, or those whose ancestors were then entitled to vote. That date was prior to the ratification of the 15th Amendment. Examining the effect of the standards established by the amendment, the Court could find no other purpose than to evade the commands of the 15th Amendment. After this decision, Oklahoma passed another statute in 1916 requiring (with certain exceptions) all citizens then qualified to vote but who had not voted in the election of 1914 to register within a twelve day period. Failure to register would result in disenfranchisement. The practical effect of this legislation was held by the Court "to accord to the members of the Negro race who had been discriminated against in the outlawed registration system of 1914, not more than 12 days within which to reassert constitutional rights which were found in the Guinn case to have been denied them." The Court concluded that the "means chosen as substitutes for the invalidated 'grandfather clause' were themselves invalid under the Fifteenth Amendment." Lane v. Wilson, 307 U.S. 268 (1939).

3. That decision was a per curiam disposition on the authority of United States v. Raines, 362 U.S. 17 (1960). In the Raines case, the United States brought suit against certain Georgia voting registrars under the Civil Rights Act of 1957, which allows the United States to act against "any person" depriving citizens of the right to vote on account of race or color. Although the complaint involved only official action, the District Court dismissed because the statute on its face applied to private action, beyond the constitutional scope of the Fifteenth

336 U.S. 933; Louisiana v. United States . . .)[4]—indicates both the variety of means employed to bar Negro voting and the durability of these discriminatory policies. The barring of one contrivance has too often caused no change in result, only in methods. . . . The 15th amendment was intended to nullify "sophisticated as well as simple-minded modes of discrimination," Lane v. Wilson, 307 U.S. 263, 275 (1939).

[Before turning to the congressional recital of dissatisfactions with the 1957 and 1960 Acts, note the Court's approach to literacy tests in this period, in the cases which follow.]

LASSITER v. NORTHAMPTON COUNTY BOARD OF ELECTIONS

360 U.S. 45, 79 S.Ct. 985, 3 L.Ed.2d 1072 (1959).

Appeal from the Supreme Court of North Carolina.

Mr. Justice DOUGLAS delivered the opinion of the Court.

. . . Appellant, a Negro citizen of North Carolina, sued to have the literacy test for voters prescribed by that State declared unconstitutional and void. [She had] applied for registration as a voter. Her registration was denied by the registrar because she refused to submit to a literacy test as required by the North Carolina statute.[1] . . .

We come then to the question whether a State may consistently with the Fourteenth and Seventeenth Amendments apply a literacy test to all voters irrespective of race or color. . . .

The States have long been held to have broad powers to determine the conditions under which the right of suffrage may be exercised, . . . absent of course the discrimination which the Constitution condemns. Article I, § 2 of the Constitution in its provision for the election of members of the House of Representatives and the Seventeenth Amendment in its provision for the election of Senators provide that officials will be chosen "by the People." Each provision goes on to state that "the Electors in each State shall have the Qualifications requisite for Electors of the most numerous Branch

Amendment. On direct appeal, the Supreme Court reversed, in an opinion by Justice Brennan. Justice Brennan relied on the general rule that "one to whom application of a statute is constitutional will not be heard to attack the statute on the ground that impliedly it might also be taken as applying to other persons or other situations in which its application might be unconstitutional." Justice Brennan distinguished U. S. v. Reese, footnote 1, supra, as a case where application of the "standing" rules would "necessitate such a revision of the [text of a criminal statute] as to create a situation in which the statute can no longer give an intelligible warning of the conduct it prohibited." In Raines, Justice Brennan emphasized, "the conduct charged —discrimination by state officials

. . . —is certainly, as 'state action' and the clearest form of it, subject to" the Fifteenth Amendment. [See also chap. 2, p. 90, supra.]

4. The Schnell case is discussed in the opinion in Lassiter v. Northampton County Board of Elections, 360 U.S. 45 (1959), which follows. The Louisiana case appears after Lassiter.

1. This Act, passed in 1957, provides in § 163–28 as follows:
"Every person presenting himself for registration shall be able to read and write any section of the Constitution of North Carolina in the English language. It shall be the duty of each registrar to administer the provisions of this section." . . . [Footnote by the Court.]

of the State Legislature." So while the right of suffrage is established and guaranteed by the Constitution . . . it is subject to the imposition of state standards which are not discriminatory and which do not contravene any restriction that Congress, acting pursuant to its constitutional powers, has imposed. . . . While § 2 of the Fourteenth Amendment, which provides for apportionment of Representatives among the States according to their respective numbers counting the whole number of persons in each State (except Indians not taxed), speaks of "the right to vote," the right protected "refers to the right to vote as established by the laws and constitution of the State." . . .

We do not suggest that any standards which a State desires to adopt may be required of voters. But there is wide scope for exercise of its jurisdiction. Residence requirements, age, previous criminal record . . . are obvious examples indicating factors which a State may take into consideration in determining the qualifications of voters. The ability to read and write likewise has some relation to standards designed to promote intelligent use of the ballot. Literacy and illiteracy are neutral on race, creed, color, and sex, as reports around the world show. Literacy and intelligence are obviously not synonymous. Illiterate people may be intelligent voters. Yet in our society where newspapers, periodicals, books, and other printed matter canvass and debate campaign issues, a State might conclude that only those who are literate should exercise the franchise. . . .[2] We do not sit in judgment on the wisdom of that policy. We cannot say, however, that it is not an allowable one measured by constitutional standards.

Of course a literacy test, fair on its face, may be employed to perpetuate that discrimination which the Fifteenth Amendment was designed to uproot. No such influence is charged here. On the other hand, a literacy test may be unconstitutional on its face. In Davis v. Schnell, 81 F.Supp. 872, aff'd 336 U.S. 933, the test was the citizen's ability to "understand and explain" an article of the Federal Constitution. The legislative setting of that provision and the great discretion it vested in the registrar made clear that a literacy requirement was merely a device to make racial discrimination easy. We cannot make the same inference here. [The North Carolina requirement] seems to us to be one fair way of determining whether a person is literate, not a calculated scheme to lay springes for the citizen. Certainly we cannot condemn it on its face as a device unrelated to the desire of North Carolina to raise the standards for people of all races who cast the ballot.

Affirmed.

LOUISIANA v. UNITED STATES

In Louisiana v. United States, 380 U.S. 145 (1965), the Court sustained an order enjoining the State of Louisiana and officials of the State Board of Registration from enforcing Louisiana's "interpretation" test for voter registration, as contrary to 42 U.S.C. § 1971(a) (p. 528, supra)

---

2. Nineteen States . . . have some
sort of literacy requirement . . . .
[Footnote by the Court.]

and the Fourteenth and Fifteenth Amendments. The state constitutional provision was adopted in 1921, after the "grandfather clause" had been held unconstitutional. It began to be used extensively in the 1950's, after the "white primary" had been held unconstitutional. In 1960, the state constitution was amended to require an applicant "to be able to understand" as well as "give a reasonable interpretation" of any section of the state or federal Constitution "when read to him by a registrar." Justice Black's opinion affirming the District Court's injunction stated:

"The applicant facing a registrar in Louisiana . . . has been compelled to leave his voting fate to that official's uncontrolled power to determine whether the applicant's understanding of the Federal or State Constitution is satisfactory. As the evidence showed, colored people, even some with the most advanced education and scholarship, were declared by voting registrars with less education to have an unsatisfactory understanding of the constitution of Louisiana or of the United States. This is not a test but a trap, sufficient to stop even the most brilliant man on his way to the voting booth. The cherished right of people in a country like ours to vote cannot be obliterated by the use of laws like this, which leave the voting fate of a citizen to the passing whim or impulse of an individual registrar. Many of our cases have pointed out the invalidity of laws so completely devoid of standards and restraints."

The Court also affirmed the District Court's "freezing relief" decree, patterned after a section (42 U.S.C. § 1971(e)) of the voting referee provisions of the Civil Rights Act of 1960, infra. Justice Black stated: "We bear in mind that the court has not merely the power but the duty to render a decree which will so far as possible eliminate the discriminatory effects of the past as well as bar like discrimination in the future. . . . Appellants' chief argument against the decree concerns the effect which should be given the new voter-qualification test adopted by the Board of Registration in August 1962 . . . after this suit had been filed. The new test, says the State, is a uniform, objective, standardized 'citizenship' test administered to all prospective voters alike. Under it, according to the State, an applicant is 'required to indiscriminately draw one of ten cards. Each card has six multiple choice questions, four of which the applicant must answer correctly.' . . . [T]he District Court did not pass upon the validity of the new test, but did take it into consideration in formulating the decree. The court found that past discrimination against Negro applicants in the 21 parishes where the interpretation test had been applied had greatly reduced the proportion of potential Negro voters who were registered as compared with the proportion of whites. Most if not all of those white voters had been permitted to register on far less rigorous terms than colored applicants whose applications were rejected. Since the new 'citizenship' test does not provide for a reregistration of voters already accepted by the registrars, it would affect only applicants not already registered, and would not disturb the eligibility of the white voters who had been allowed to register while discriminatory practices kept Negroes from doing so. In these 21 parishes, while the registration of white persons was increasing, the number of Negroes registered decreased from 25,361 to 10,351. Under these circumstances we think that the court was quite right to decree that as to persons who met age and residence requirements during the years in which the interpretation test was used, use of the new 'citizenship' test should be postponed in those 21 parishes where registrars used the old interpretation test until those parishes have ordered a complete reregistration of voters, so that the new test will apply alike to all or to none." [Compare the related problems of relief under the 1965 Act, in the Gaston County Case, p. 544, infra.]

RECENT CONGRESSIONAL EFFORTS TO ELIMINATE DISCRIMINATION [THE 1957, 1960, AND 1964 ACTS] *

In 1957, Congress enacted its first major civil rights statute since the Reconstruction era. The Civil Rights Act of 1957 authorized the Attorney General to bring civil actions for injunctive relief to redress denials of the right to vote on account of race or color. He was also authorized to seek injunctive relief against intimidation, threats, or coercion for the purpose of interfering with the right to vote in Federal elections. The 1957 act also created the Civil Rights Commission and charged it with investigating denials on the right to vote and other matters.

The act's impact on eliminating voting discrimination has been disappointing. The inability to gain access to voting records impeded effective enforcement of the act. . . .

The 1960 statute amended the 1957 act. [For example, it required election officials to preserve voting records.]

Additional modifications in the voting laws were made in the Civil Rights Act of 1964. Title I of that act provided for the expedition of voting suits and their trial before a three-judge district court with a direct appeal to the Supreme Court. The 1964 statute also prohibited, with respect to registration conducted under State law for elections held solely or in part for Federal offices, [e. g.], the use of literacy tests as a qualification for voting unless they are administered and conducted wholly in writing. The statute further established a rebuttable presumption of literacy flowing from the completion of six grades in any recognized school.

Experience has shown that the case-by-case litigation approach will not solve the voting discrimination problem. The statistics alone are conclusive. . . . In Mississippi approximately 6.4 percent of voting age Negroes were registered in 1964, compared to 4.4 percent 10 years earlier. . . .

The inadequacy of existing laws is attributable to both the intransigence of local officials and dilatory tactics, two factors which have largely neutralized years of litigating effort by the Department of Justice. . . .

There can be no doubt about the present need for Federal legislation to correct widespread violations of the 15th amendment. The prevailing conditions in those areas where the bill will operate offer ample justification for congressional action because there is little basis for supposing that absent action, the States and subdivisions affected will themselves remedy the present situation in view of the history of the adoption and administration of the several tests and devices reached by the bill. The choice of the means to solve a problem within the legitimate concern of the Congress is largely a legislative question. . . . In enforcing the 15th amendment Congress may forbid the use of voter qualification laws where necessary to meet the risk of continued or renewed violations of constitutional rights even though,

---

* From the 1965 Senate Report—See note
† , p. 528, supra.

in the absence of the course of illegal conduct predicated upon the use of such tests, the same State laws might be unobjectionable. . . .

SOUTH CAROLINA v. KATZENBACH

383 U.S. 301, 86 S.Ct. 803, 15 L.Ed.2d 769 (1966).

On Bill of Complaint.

Mr. Chief Justice WARREN delivered the opinion of the Court.

By leave of the Court, . . . South Carolina has filed a bill of complaint, seeing a declaration that selected provisions of the Voting Rights Act of 1965 violate the Federal Constitution, and asking for an injunction against enforcement of these provisions by the Attorney General. Original jurisdiction is founded on the presence of a controversy between a State and a citizen of another State under Art. III, § 2, of the Constitution. . . .

The Voting Rights Act was designed by Congress to banish the blight of racial discrimination in voting, which has infected the electoral process in parts of our country for nearly a century. The Act creates stringent new remedies for voting discrimination where it persists on a pervasive scale, and in addition the statute strengthens existing remedies for pockets of voting discrimination elsewhere in the country. Congress assumed the power to prescribe these remedies from § 2 of the Fifteenth Amendment, which authorizes the National Legislature to effectuate by "appropriate" measures the constitutional prohibition against racial discrimination in voting. We hold that the sections of the Act which are properly before us are an appropriate means for carrying out Congress' constitutional responsibilities and are consonant with all other provisions of the Constitution. We therefore deny South Carolina's request that enforcement of these sections of the Act be enjoined.

I.

The constitutional propriety of the Voting Rights Act of 1965 must be judged with reference to the historical experience which it reflects. Before enacting the measure, Congress explored with great care the problem of racial discrimination in voting. . . .

Two points emerge vividly from the voluminous legislative history of the Act contained in the committee hearings and floor debates. First: Congress felt itself confronted by an insidious and pervasive evil which had been perpetuated in certain parts of our country through unremitting and ingenious defiance of the Constitution. Second: Congress concluded that the unsuccessful remedies which it had prescribed in the past would have to be replaced by sterner and more elaborate measures in order to satisfy the clear commands of the Fifteenth Amendment. We pause here to summarize the majority reports of the House and Senate Committees, which document in considerable detail the factual basis for these reactions by Congress. [The Court's summaries of the committee reports are omitted here. See the excerpts from S. Rep.No. 162, supra.]

II.

The Voting Rights Act of 1965 reflects Congress' firm intention to rid the country of racial discrimination in voting. The heart of the Act is a

Bill of attainder = a legis. act, directed against a designated person (nominally treason) w/o trial or conviction (usually treason) w/o trial or conviction according to recog. rules of procedure & passing sentence of death & attainder upon him guilty of an alleged crime (nominally treason) w/o trial or conviction according to recog. rules of procedure & passing sentence of death & attainder upon him

complex scheme of stringent remedies aimed at areas where voting discrimination has been most flagrant. Section 4(a)–(d) lays down a formula defining the States and political subdivisions to which these new remedies apply. The first of the remedies, contained in § 4(a), is the suspension of literacy tests and similar voting qualifications for a period of five years from the last occurrence of substantial voting discrimination. Section 5 prescribes a second remedy, the suspension of all new voting regulations pending review by [the Attorney General or a three-judge court in the District of Columbia] to determine whether their use would perpetuate voting discrimination. The third remedy, covered in §§ 6(b), 7, 9, and 13(a), is the assignment of federal examiners on certification by the Attorney General to list qualified applicants who are thereafter entitled to vote in all elections.

Other provisions of the Act prescribe subsidiary cures for persistent voting discrimination. Section 8 authorizes the appointment of federal pollwatchers in places to which federal examiners have already been assigned. Section 10(d) excuses those made eligible to vote in sections of the country covered by § 4(b) of the Act from paying accumulated past poll taxes for state and local elections. Section 12(e) provides for balloting by persons denied access to the polls in areas where federal examiners have been appointed.

The remaining remedial portions of the Act are aimed at voting discrimination in any area of the country where it may occur. Section 2 broadly prohibits the use of voting rules to abridge exercise of the franchise on racial grounds. Sections 3, 6(a), and 13(b) strengthen existing procedures for attacking voting discrimination by means of litigation. Section 4(e) excuses citizens educated in American schools conducted in a foreign language from passing English-language literacy tests. Section 10(a)–(c) facilitates constitutional litigation challenging the imposition of all poll taxes for state and local elections. Sections 11 and 12(a)–(d) authorize civil and criminal sanctions against interference with the exercise of rights guaranteed by the Act.

At the outset, we emphasize that only some of the many portions of the Act are properly before us. South Carolina has not challenged §§ 2, 3, 4(e), 6(a), 8, 10, 12(d) and (e), 13(b), and other miscellaneous provisions having nothing to do with this lawsuit. Judicial review of these sections must await subsequent litigation. In addition, we find that South Carolina's attack on §§ 11 and 12(a)–(c) is premature. No person has yet been subjected to, or even threatened with, the criminal sanctions which these sections of the Act authorize. . . . Consequently, the only sections of the Act to be reviewed at this time are §§ 4(a)–(d), 5, 6(b), 7, 9, 13(a), and certain procedural portions of § 14, all of which are presently in actual operation in South Carolina. . . .

Coverage formula.

The remedial sections of the Act assailed by South Carolina automatically apply to any State, or to any separate political subdivision such as a county or parish, for which two findings have been made: (1) the Attorney General has determined that on November 1, 1964, it maintained a "test or device," and (2) the Director of the Census has determined that less than 50% of its voting-age residents were registered on November 1, 1964, or voted in the presidential election of November 1964. . . . . As used throughout the

Act, the phrase "test or device" means any requirement that a registrant or voter must "(1) demonstrate the ability to read, write, understand, or interpret any matter, (2) demonstrate any educational achievement or his knowledge of any particular subject, (3) possess good moral character, or (4) prove his qualifications by the voucher of registered voters or members of any other class." § 4(c).

Statutory coverage of a State or political subdivision under § 4(b) is terminated if the area obtains a declaratory judgment from the District Court for the District of Columbia, determining that tests and devices have not been used during the preceding five years to abridge the franchise on racial grounds. . . . [N]o area may obtain a declaratory judgment for five years after the final decision of a federal court (other than the denial of a judgment under this section of the Act), determining that discrimination through the use of tests or devices has occurred anywhere in the State or political subdivision. These declaratory judgment actions are to be heard by a three-judge panel, with direct appeal to this Court. § 4(a).

South Carolina was brought within the coverage formula of the Act on August 7, 1965, pursuant to appropriate administrative determinations which have not been challenged in this proceeding. On the same day, coverage was also extended to Alabama, Alaska, Georgia, Louisiana, Mississippi, Virginia, 26 counties in North Carolina, and one county in Arizona. Two more counties in Arizona, one county in Hawaii, and one county in Idaho were added to the list on November 19, 1965. Thus far Alaska, the three Arizona counties, and the single county in Idaho have asked the District Court for the District of Columbia to grant a declaratory judgment terminating statutory coverage.

Suspension of tests.

In a State or political subdivision covered by § 4(b) of the Act, no person may be denied the right to vote in any election because of his failure to comply with a "test or device." § 4(a). On account of this provision, South Carolina is temporarily barred from enforcing the portion of its voting laws which requires every applicant for registration to show that he: "Can both read and write any section of [the State] Constitution submitted to [him] by the registration officer or can show that he owns, and has paid all taxes collectible during the previous year on, property in this State assessed at three hundred dollars or more." The Attorney General has determined that the property qualification is inseparable from the literacy test, and South Carolina makes no objection to this finding. Similar tests and devices have been temporarily suspended in the other sections of the country listed above.

Review of new rules.

In a State or political subdivision covered by § 4(b) of the Act, no person may be denied the right to vote in any election because of his failure to comply with a voting qualification or procedure different from those in force on November 1, 1964. This suspension of new rules is terminated, however, under either of the following circumstances: (1) if the area has submitted the rules to the Attorney General, and he has not interposed an objection within 60 days, or (2) if the area has obtained a declaratory judgment from the District Court for the District of Columbia, determining that the rules will not abridge the franchise on racial grounds. . . .

Federal examiners.

In any political subdivision covered by § 4(b) of the Act, the Civil Service Commission shall appoint voting examiners whenever the Attorney General certifies either of the following facts: (1) that he has received meritorious written complaints from at least 20 residents alleging that they have been disenfranchised under color of law because of their race, or (2) that the appointment of examiners is otherwise necessary to effectuate the guarantees of the Fifteenth Amendment. In making the latter determination, the Attorney General must consider, among other factors, whether the registration ratio of non-whites to whites seems reasonably attributable to racial discrimination, or whether there is substantial evidence of good-faith efforts to comply with the Fifteenth Amendment. § 6(b). These certifications are not reviewable in any court . . ..

The examiners who have been appointed are to test the voting qualifications of applicants . . .. §§ 7(a) and 9(b). Any person who meets the voting requirements of state law, insofar as these have not been suspended by the Act, must promptly be placed on a list of eligible voters. . . . A person shall be removed from the voting list by an examiner if he has lost his eligibility under valid state law, or if he has been successfully challenged through the procedure prescribed in § 9(a) of the Act. § 7(d). . . .

The listing procedures in a political subdivision are terminated under either of the following circumstances: (1) if the Attorney General informs the Civil Service Commission that all persons listed by examiners have been placed on the official voting rolls, and that there is no longer reasonable cause to fear abridgment of the franchise on racial grounds, or (2) if the political subdivision has obtained a declaratory judgment from the District Court for the District of Columbia, ascertaining the same facts which govern termination by the Attorney General, and the Director of the Census has determined that more than 50% of the non-white residents of voting age are registered to vote. . . .

On October 30, 1965, the Attorney General certified the need for federal examiners in two South Carolina counties, and examiners appointed by the Civil Service Commission have been serving there since November 8, 1965. Examiners have also been assigned to 11 counties in Alabama, five parishes in Louisiana, and 19 counties in Mississippi. . . .

III.

These provisions of the Voting Rights Act of 1965 are challenged on the fundamental ground that they exceed the powers of Congress and encroach on an area reserved to the States by the Constitution. South Carolina and certain of the *amici curiae* also attack specific sections of the Act for more particular reasons. They argue that the coverage formula prescribed in § 4(a)–(d) violates the principle of the equality of States, denies due process by employing an invalid presumption and by barring judicial review of administrative findings, constitutes a forbidden bill of attainder, and impairs the separation of powers by adjudicating guilt through legislation. They claim that the review of new voting rules required in § 5 infringes Article III by directing the District Court to issue advisory opinions. They contend that the assignment of federal examiners authorized in § 6(b) abridges due process by precluding judicial review of administrative findings and impairs the separation of powers by giving the Attorney General judicial functions; also that the challenge procedure prescribed in § 9 denies due process on account of its speed. Finally, South Carolina and certain of the *amici curiae* maintain that §§ 4(a) and 5, buttressed by § 14(b) of the Act, abridge due process by limiting litigation to a distant forum.

Some of these contentions may be dismissed at the outset. The word "person" in the context of the Due Process Clause of the Fifth Amendment cannot, by any reasonable mode of interpretation, be expanded to encompass the States of the Union, and to our knowledge this has never been done by any court. . . . Likewise, courts have consistently regarded the Bill of Attainder Clause of Article I and the principle of the separation of powers only as protections for individual persons and private groups, those who are peculiarly vulnerable to nonjudicial determinations of guilt. See United States v. Brown, 381 U.S. 437; Ex parte Garland, 4 Wall. 333. Nor does a State have standing as the parent of its citizens to invoke these constitutional provisions against the Federal Government, the ultimate *parens patriae* of every American citizen. Massachusetts v. Mellon, 262 U.S. 447, 485–486 . . . . The objections to the Act which are raised under these provisions may therefore be considered only as additional aspects of the basic question presented by the case: Has Congress exercised its powers under the Fifteenth Amendment in an appropriate manner with relation to the States?

The ground rules for resolving this question are clear. The language and purpose of the Fifteenth Amendment, the prior decisions construing its several provisions, and the general doctrines of constitutional interpretation, all point to one fundamental principle. As against the reserved powers of the States, Congress may use any rational means to effectuate the constitutional prohibition of racial discrimination in voting. Cf. our rulings last Term, sustaining Title II of the Civil Rights Act of 1964 . . . . We turn now to a more detailed description of the standards which govern our review of the Act. . . .

The basic test to be applied in a case involving § 2 of the Fifteenth Amendment is the same as in all cases concerning the express powers of Congress with relation to the reserved powers of the States. Chief Justice Marshall laid down the classic formulation, 50 years before the Fifteenth Amendment was ratified . . . . The Court has subsequently echoed his language [in McCulloch v. Maryland] in describing each of the Civil War Amendments:

> "Whatever legislation is appropriate, that is, adapted to carry out the objects the amendments have in view, whatever tends to enforce submission to the prohibitions they contain, and to secure to all persons the enjoyment of perfect equality of civil rights and the equal protection of the laws against State denial or invasion, if not prohibited, is brought within the domain of congressional power." Ex parte Virginia, 100 U.S., at 345–346. . . .

We therefore reject South Carolina's argument that Congress may appropriately do no more than to forbid violations of the Fifteenth Amendment in general terms—that the task of fashioning specific remedies or of applying them to particular localities must necessarily be left entirely to the courts. Congress is not circumscribed by any such artificial rules under § 2 of the Fifteenth Amendment. In the oft-repeated words of Chief Justice

Marshall, referring to another specific legislative authorization in the Constitution, "This power, like all others vested in Congress, is complete in itself, may be exercised to its utmost extent, and acknowledges no limitations, other than are prescribed in the constitution." Gibbons v. Ogden, 9 Wheat. 1, 196.

IV.

Congress exercised its authority under the Fifteenth Amendment in an inventive manner when it enacted the Voting Rights Act of 1965. First: The measure prescribes remedies for voting discrimination which go into effect without any need for prior adjudication. This was clearly a legitimate response to the problem, for which there is ample precedent under other constitutional provisions. See Katzenbach v. McClung, 379 U.S. 294, 302–304; United States v. Darby, 312 U.S. 100, 120–121. Congress had found that case-by-case litigation was inadequate to combat widespread and persistent discrimination in voting, because of the inordinate amount of time and energy required to overcome the obstructionist tactics invariably encountered in these lawsuits. After enduring nearly a century of systematic resistance to the Fifteenth Amendment, Congress might well decide to shift the advantage of time and inertia from the perpetrators of the evil to its victims. The question remains, of course, whether the specific remedies prescribed in the Act were an appropriate means of combatting the evil, and to this question we shall presently address ourselves.

Second: The Act intentionally confines these remedies to a small number of States and political subdivisions which in most instances were familiar to Congress by name. This, too, was a permissible method of dealing with the problem. Congress had learned that substantial voting discrimination presently occurs in certain sections of the country, and it knew no way of accurately forecasting whether the evil might spread elsewhere in the future. In acceptable legislative fashion, Congress chose to limit its attention to the geographic areas where immediate action seemed necessary. . . .

We now consider the . . . question of whether the specific States and political subdivisions within § 4(b) of the Act were an appropriate target for the new remedies. South Carolina contends that the coverage formula is awkwardly designed in a number of respects and that it disregards various local conditions which have nothing to do with racial discrimination. These arguments, however, are largely beside the point. Congress began work with reliable evidence of actual voting discrimination in a great majority of the States and political subdivisions affected by the new remedies of the Act. The formula eventually evolved to describe these areas was relevant to the problem of voting discrimination, and Congress was therefore entitled to infer a significant danger of the evil in the few remaining States and political subdivisions covered by § 4(b) of the Act. . . .

To be specific, the new remedies of the Act are imposed on three States —Alabama, Louisiana, and Mississippi—in which federal courts have repeatedly found substantial voting discrimination. Section 4(b) of the Act also embraces two other States—Georgia and South Carolina—plus large portions of a third State—North Carolina—for which there was more fragmentary evidence of recent voting discrimination mainly adduced by the Justice Department and the Civil Rights Commission. All of these areas were appropriately subjected to the new remedies. In identifying past evils, Congress obviously may avail itself of information from any probative source. . . .

The areas listed above, for which there was evidence of actual voting discrimination, share two characteristics incorporated by Congress into the coverage formula: the use of tests and devices for voter registration, and a voting rate in the 1964 presidential election at least 12 points below the national average. Tests and devices are relevant to voting discrimination because of their long history as a tool for perpetrating the evil; a low voting rate is pertinent for the obvious reason that widespread disenfranchisement must inevitably affect the number of actual voters. Accordingly, the coverage formula is rational in both practice and theory. It was therefore permissible to impose the new remedies on the few remaining States and political subdivisions covered by the formula, at least in the absence of proof that they have been free of substantial voting discrimination in recent years. . . .

It is irrelevant that the coverage formula excludes certain localities which do not employ voting tests and devices but for which there is evidence of voting discrimination by other means. Congress had learned that widespread and persistent discrimination in voting during recent years has typically entailed the misuse of tests and devices, and this was the evil for which the new remedies were specifically designed. At the same time, through §§ 3, 6(a), and 13(b) of the Act, Congress strengthened existing remedies for voting discrimination in other areas of the country. Legislation need not deal with all phases of a problem in the same way, so long as the distinctions drawn have some basis in practical experience. See Williamson v. Lee Optical Co., [chap. 14, p. 997]; Railway Express Agency v. New York [chap. 14, p. 992]. There are no States or political subdivisions exempted from coverage under § 4(b) in which the record reveals recent racial discrimination involving tests and devices. This fact confirms the rationality of the formula.

Acknowledging the possibility of overbreadth, the Act provides for termination of special statutory coverage at the behest of States and political subdivisions in which the danger of substantial voting discrimination has not materialized during the preceding five years. Despite South Carolina's argument to the contrary, Congress might appropriately limit litigation under this provision to a single court in the District of Columbia pursuant to its constitutional power under Art. III, § 1, to "ordain and establish" inferior federal tribunals. . . .

South Carolina contends that these termination procedures are a nullity because they impose an impossible burden of proof upon States and political subdivisions entitled to relief. As the Attorney General pointed out during hearings on the Act, however, an area need do no more than to submit affidavits from voting officials, asserting that they have not been guilty of racial discrimination through the use of tests and devices during the past five years, and then to refute whatever evidence to the contrary may be adduced by the Federal Government. Section 4(d) further assures that an area need not disprove each isolated instance of voting discrimination in order to obtain relief in the termination proceedings. The burden of proof is therefore quite bearable, particularly since the relevant facts relating to the conduct of voting officials are peculiarly within the knowledge of the States and political subdivisions themselves. . . .

The Acts bars direct judicial review of the findings by the Attorney General and the Director of the Census which trigger application of the coverage formula. We reject the claim by Alabama as *amicus curiae* that this provision is invalid because it allows the new remedies of the Act to be imposed in an arbitrary way. The Court had already permitted Congress to withdraw judicial review of administrative determinations in numerous cases involving the statutory rights of private parties. . . . In this instance, the findings not subject to review consist of objective statistical determinations by the Census Bureau and a routine analysis of state statutes by the Justice Department. These functions are unlikely to arouse any plausible dispute, as South Carolina apparently concedes. In the event that the formula is improperly applied, the area affected can always go into court and obtain termination of coverage under § 4(b), provided of course that it has not been guilty of voting discrimination in recent years. This procedure serves as a partial substitute for direct judicial review.

. . . South Carolina assails the temporary suspension of existing voting qualifications, reciting the rule laid down by Lassiter v. Northampton County Bd. of Elections, 360 U.S. 45, that literacy tests and related devices are not in themselves contrary to the Fifteenth Amendment. . . . The record shows that in most of the States covered by the Act, including South Carolina, various tests and devices have been instituted with the purpose of disenfranchising Negroes, have been framed in such a way as to facilitate this aim, and have been administered in a discriminatory fashion for many years. Under these circumstances, the Fifteenth Amendment has clearly been violated. . . .

The Act suspends literacy tests and similar devices for a period of five years from the last occurrence of substantial voting discrimination. This was a legitimate response to the problem, for which there is ample precedent in Fifteenth Amendment cases. . . . Underlying the response was the feeling that States and political subdivisions which had been allowing white illiterates to vote for years could not sincerely complain about "dilution" of their electorates through the registration of Negro illiterates. Congress knew that continuance of the tests and devices in use at the present time, no matter how fairly administered in the future, would freeze the effect of past discrimination in favor of unqualified white registrants. Congress permissibly rejected the alternative of requiring a complete re-registration of all voters, believing that this would be too harsh on many whites who had enjoyed the franchise for their entire adult lives. . . .

The Act suspends new voting regulations pending scrutiny by federal authorities to determine whether their use would violate the Fifteenth Amendment. This may have been an uncommon exercise of congressional power, as South Carolina contends, but the Court has recognized that exceptional conditions can justify legislative measures not otherwise appropriate. See Home Bldg. & Loan Assn. v. Blaisdell, [chap. 13, p. 930]; Wilson v. New, 243 U.S. 332. Congress knew that some of the States covered by § 4(b) of the Act had resorted to the extraordinary stratagem of contriving new rules of various kinds for the sole purpose of perpetuating voting discrimination in the face of adverse federal court decrees. Congress had reason to suppose that these States might try similar maneuvers in the future in order to evade the remedies for voting discrimination contained in the Act itself. Under the compulsion of these unique circumstances, Congress responded in a permissibly decisive manner.

For reasons already stated, there was nothing inappropriate about limiting litigation under this provision to the District Court for the District of Columbia, and in putting the burden of proof on the areas seeking relief. Nor has Congress authorized the District Court to issue advisory opinions, in violation of the principles of Article III invoked by Georgia as *amicus curiae.* The Act automatically suspends the operation of voting regulations enacted after November 1, 1964, and furnishes mechanisms for enforcing the suspension. A State or political subdivision wishing to make use of a recent amendment to its voting laws therefore has a concrete and immediate "controversy" with the Federal Government. . . . An appropriate remedy is a judicial determination that continued suspension of the new rule is unnecessary to vindicate rights guaranteed by the Fifteenth Amendment. . . .

The Act authorizes the appointment of federal examiners to list qualified applicants who are thereafter entitled to vote, subject to an expeditious challenge procedure. This was clearly an appropriate response to the problem, closely related to remedies authorized in prior cases. . . . In many of the political subdivisions covered by § 4(b) of the Act, voting officials have persistently employed a variety of procedural tactics to deny Negroes the franchise, often in direct defiance or evasion of federal court decrees. Congress realized that merely to suspend voting rules which have been misused or are subject to misuse might leave this localized evil undisturbed. . . .

After enduring nearly a century of widespread resistance to the Fifteenth Amendment, Congress has marshalled an array of potent weapons against the evil, with authority in the Attorney General to employ them effectively. Many of the areas directly affected by this development have indicated their willingness to abide by any restraints legitimately imposed upon them. We here hold that the portions of the Voting Rights Act properly before us are a valid means for carrying out the commands of the Fifteenth Amendment. Hopefully, millions of non-white Americans will not be able to participate for the first time on an equal basis in the government under which they live. We may finally look forward to the day when truly "[t]he right of citizens of the United States to vote shall not be denied or abridged by the United States or by any State on account of race, color, or previous condition of servitude."

The bill of complaint is

Dismissed.

Mr. Justice BLACK, concurring and dissenting.

. . . I have no doubt whatever as to the power of Congress under § 2 to enact the provisions of the Voting Rights Act of 1965 dealing with the suspension of state voting tests that have been used as notorious means to deny and abridge voting rights on racial grounds. This same congressional power necessarily exists to authorize appointment of federal voting registrars. I also agree with the judgment of the Court upholding § 4(b) of the Act which sets out a formula for determining when and where the major remedial sections of the Act take effect. I reach this conclusion, however, for a somewhat different reason than that stated by the Court, which is that "the coverage formula is rational in both practice and theory." I do not base my conclusion on the fact that the formula is rational, for it is enough for me that Congress by creating this formula has merely exercised its hitherto unquestioned and undisputed power to decide when, where, and upon what conditions its laws shall go into effect. . . .

    . . . I dissent from [the] holding that every part of § 5 of the Act is constitutional. Section 4(a), to which § 5 is linked, suspends for five years all literacy tests and similar devices in those States coming within the formula of § 4(b). Section 5 goes on to provide that a State covered by § 4(b) can in no way amend its constitution or laws relating to voting without first trying to persuade the Attorney General of the United States or the Federal District Court for the District of Columbia that the new proposed laws do not have the purpose and will not have the effect of denying the right to vote to citizens on account of their race or color. I think this section is unconstitutional on at least two grounds.

    (a) [I]t is hard for me to believe that a justiciable controversy can arise in the constitutional sense from a desire by the United States Government or some of its officials to determine in advance what legislative provisions a State may enact or what constitutional amendments it may adopt. . . .

    (b) My second and more basic objection to § 5 is that Congress has here exercised its power under § 2 of the Fifteenth Amendment through the adoption of means that conflict with the most basic principles of the Constitution. . . . Section 5, by providing that some of the States cannot pass state laws or adopt state constitutional amendments without first being compelled to beg federal authorities to approve their policies, so distorts our constitutional structure of government as to render any distinction drawn in the Constitution between state and federal power almost meaningless. . . . Certainly if all the provisions of our Constitution which limit the power of the Federal Government and reserve other power to the States are to mean anything, they mean at least that the States have power to pass laws and amend their constitutions without first sending their officials hundreds of miles away to beg federal authorities to approve them. Moreover, it seems to me that § 5 which gives federal officials power to veto state laws they do not like is in direct conflict with the clear command of our Constitution that "The United States shall guarantee to every State in this Union a Republican Form of Government." I cannot help but believe that the inevitable effect of any such law which forces any one of the States to entreat federal authorities in far-away places for approval of local laws before they can become effective is to create the impression that the State or States treated in this way are little more than conquered provinces. . . . [T]he Federal Government has heretofore always been content to exercise this power to protect federal supremacy by authorizing its agents to bring lawsuits against state officials once an operative state law has created an actual case and controversy. A federal law which assumes the power to compel the States to submit in advance any proposed legislation they have for approval by federal agents approaches dangerously near to wiping the States out as useful and effective units in the government of our country. I cannot agree to any constitutional interpretation that leads inevitably to such a result. . . .

In this and other prior Acts Congress has quite properly vested the Attorney General with extremely broad power to protect voting rights of citizens against discrimination on account of race or color. Section 5 viewed in this context is of very minor importance and in my judgment is likely to serve more as an irritant to the States than as an aid to the enforcement of the Act. I would hold § 5 invalid for the reasons stated above with full confidence that the Attorney General has ample power to give vigorous, expeditious and effective protection to the voting rights of all citizens.

INTERPRETATIONS OF THE 1965 ACT—AND ITS FUTURE

1. Chief Justice Warren's majority opinion in Allen v. State Board of Elections, 393 U.S. 544 (1969), gave a broad reading to § 5 of the Act by holding that each of four challenged changes in state election provisions (three in Mississippi and one in Virginia) constituted a "voting qualification or prerequisite to voting, or standard, practice, or procedure with respect to voting different from that in force or effect on November 1, 1964," and was accordingly subject to the approval requirements of § 5. Under the Mississippi amendments, (1) county supervisors were to be elected at large rather than by districts, (2) superintendents of education in certain counties were made appointive instead of elective, and (3) ballot access requirements for independent candidates running in general elections were stiffened. Virginia adopted new procedures for casting write-in votes which had the effect of barring the use of printed labels by illiterate voters.

The Chief Justice concluded that § 5 reached "any state enactment which altered the election law of a covered State in even a minor way"—including "state rules relating to the qualification of candidates" and "state decisions as to which offices shall be elective." Justice Harlan urged that § 5 "should properly be read to require federal approval only of those state laws that change either voting qualifications or the manner in which elections are conducted." Section 4, he argued, dealt only with "techniques that prevented Negroes from voting at all" and "Congress did not attempt to restructure state governments." Section 5 was "designed simply to interlock" with § 4, yet the Court had now gone beyond by requiring determinations "whether various systems of representation favor or disfavor the Negro voter." The majority decided, however, to "give only prospective effect to our decision." That, Justice Harlan (joined on this point by Justices Marshall and Douglas) objected, "reduced [§ 5] to a dead letter in a very substantial number of situations." Justice Black also dissented. (See also Hadnott v. Amos, 394 U.S. 358 (1969), involving an Alabama ballot access barrier like Mississippi's.)

2. In Gaston County v. United States, 395 U.S. 285 (1969), the Court considered the bearing of past unequal educational opportunities on a § 4(a) proceeding to reinstate a literacy test automatically suspended pursuant to § 4. Justice Harlan wrote for the majority here, concluding that "it is appropriate for a court to consider whether a literacy or educational requirement has the 'effect of denying the right to vote on account of race or color' because the State or subdivision which seeks to impose the requirement has maintained separate and inferior schools for its Negro residents who are now of voting age." He emphasized that the trial court had disclaimed "any per se rule": it had relied not only on the county's prior dual school system,

but on government evidence in this case showing "that the Negro schools were of inferior quality in fact as well as in law." Accordingly, the record revealed "the sad truth that throughout the years, Gaston County systematically deprived its black citizens of the educational opportunities it granted to its white citizens. 'Impartial' administration of the literacy test today would serve only to perpetuate these inequities in a different form." Justice Black again dissented.

3. Note the Nixon Administration's proposals (The New York Times, June 27, 1969) for substantial changes in federal law, in the face of wide support for a simple 5-year extension of the 1965 Act. Attorney General Mitchell told the House Subcommittee: "I cannot support what amounts to regional legislation. While Congress may have had sufficient reason to pass regional legislation in the 1965 Act, I do not believe that this justification exists any longer." The Administration recommended elimination of the prior approval procedure considered in the Allen case, note 1 above. New voting provisions would become ineffective only if blocked by a federal court order —after an action brought in a local federal court, rather than in the District of Columbia. Moreover, the Administration urged a nationwide ban on literacy tests. (The Attorney General commented that the Gaston County case, note 2 above, would probably have that effect in any event, since there were enough Negroes in this situation who had migrated to the North to make tests invalid almost everywhere.) The Administration also suggested a ban on residency qualifications in Presidential elections. The Administration bill was passed by the House late in 1969.

The Senate, however, rejected the Administration proposal. In March 1970, it adopted instead a 5-year extension of the 1965 Act, with some modifications. (See The New York Times, March 14, 1970.) The major additions (noted further below, p. 553): suspending literacy tests throughout the nation; adopting a 30-day residency requirement for Presidential elections; and lowering the voting age to 18 years for all elections. The House was expected to accept the Senate decision regarding extension of the 1965 Act, but considerable opposition to the voting age provision was anticipated.

KATZENBACH v. MORGAN

384 U.S. 641, 86 S.Ct. 1717, 16 L.Ed.2d 828 (1966).

Appeal from the United States District Court for the District of Columbia.*

Mr. Justice BRENNAN delivered the opinion of the Court.

This case concerns the constitutionality of § 4(e) of the Voting Rights Act of 1965. That law, in the respects pertinent in this case, provides that no person who has successfully completed the sixth primary grade in a public school in, or a private school accredited by, the Commonwealth of Puerto Rico in which the language of instruction was other than English shall be denied the right to vote in any election because of his inability to read or write English. Appellees, registered voters in New York City, brought this suit

---

* Together with New York City Board
of Elections v. Morgan, on appeal from
the same court.

to challenge the constitutionality of § 4(e) insofar as it *pro tanto* prohibits the enforcement of the election laws of New York requiring an ability to read and write English as a condition of voting. Under these laws many of the several hundred thousand New York City residents who have migrated there from the Commonwealth of Puerto Rico had previously been denied the right to vote, and appellees attack § 4(e) insofar as it would enable many of these citizens to vote.[1] . . . We hold that, in the application challenged in this case, § 4(e) is a proper exercise of the powers granted to Congress by § 5 of the Fourteenth Amendment and that by force of the Supremacy Clause, Article VI, the New York English literacy requirement cannot be enforced to the extent that it is inconsistent with § 4(e). . . .

The Attorney General of the State of New York argues that an exercise of congressional power under § 5 of the Fourteenth Amendment that prohibits the enforcement of a state law can only be sustained if the judicial branch determines that the state law is prohibited by the provisions of the Amendment that Congress sought to enforce. More specifically, he urges that § 4(e) cannot be sustained as appropriate legislation to enforce the Equal Protection Clause unless the judiciary decides—even with the guidance of a congressional judgment—that the application of the English literacy requirement prohibited by § 4(e) is forbidden by the Equal Protection Clause itself. We disagree. Neither the language nor history of § 5 supports such a construction. . . . A construction of § 5 that would require a judicial determination that the enforcement of the state law precluded by Congress violated the Amendment, as a condition of sustaining the congressional enactment, would depreciate both congressional resourcefulness and congressional responsibility for implementing the Amendment. It would confine the legislative power in this context to the insignificant role of abrogating only those state laws that the judicial branch was prepared to adjudge unconstitutional, or of merely informing the judgment of the judiciary by particularizing the "majestic generalities" of § 1 of the Amendment. . . .

Thus our task in this case is not to determine whether the New York English literacy requirement as applied to deny the right to vote to a person who successfully completed the sixth grade in a Puerto Rican school violates the Equal Protection Clause. Accordingly, our decision in Lassiter v. Northampton Election Bd., 360 U.S. 45, . . . is inapposite. . . . Lassiter did not present the question before us here: Without regard to whether the judiciary would find that the Equal Protection Clause itself

---

1. This limitation on appellees' challenge to § 4(e), and thus on the scope of our inquiry, does not distort the primary intent of § 4(e). The measure was sponsored in the Senate by Senators Javits and Kennedy and in the House by Representatives Gilbert and Ryan, all of New York, for the explicit purpose of dealing with the disenfranchisement of larger segments of the Puerto Rican population in New York. Throughout the congressional debate it was repeatedly acknowledged that § 4(e) had particular reference to the Puerto Rican population in New York. That situation was the almost exclusive subject of discussion. . . .

The Solicitor General informs us in his brief to this Court, that in all probability the practical effect of § 4(e) will be limited to enfranchising those educated in Puerto Rican schools. He advises us that, aside from the schools in the Commonwealth of Puerto Rico, there are no public or parochial schools in the territorial limits of the United States in which the predominant language of instruction is other than English and which would have generally been attended by persons who are otherwise qualified to vote save for their lack of literacy in English. [Footnote by the Court.]

nullifies New York's English literacy requirement as so applied, could Congress prohibit the enforcement of the state law by legislating under § 5 of the Fourteenth Amendment? In answering this question, our task is limited to determining whether such legislation is, as required by § 5, appropriate legislation to enforce the Equal Protection Clause.

By including § 5 the draftsmen sought to grant to Congress, by a specific provision applicable to the Fourteenth Amendment, the same broad powers expressed in the Necessary and Proper Clause, Art. I, § 8, cl. 18. The classic formulation of the reach of those powers was established by Chief Justice Marshall in McCulloch v. Maryland . . .. Ex parte Virginia, 100 U.S., at 345–346, decided 12 years after the adoption of the Fourteenth Amendment, held that congressional power under § 5 had this same broad scope . . .. Correctly viewed, § 5 is a positive grant of legislative power authorizing Congress to exercise its discretion in determining whether and what legislation is needed to secure the guarantees of the Fourteenth Amendment.

We therefore proceed to the consideration whether § 4(e) is "appropriate legislation" to enforce the Equal Protection Clause, that is, under the McCulloch v. Maryland standard, whether § 4(e) may be regarded as an enactment to enforce the Equal Protection Clause, whether it is "plainly adapted to that end" and whether it is not prohibited by but is consistent with "the letter and spirit of the Constitution." [1]

There can be no doubt that § 4(e) may be regarded as an enactment to enforce the Equal Protection Clause. . . . More specifically, § 4 (e) may be viewed as a measure to secure for the Puerto Rican community residing in New York non-discriminatory treatment by government—both in the imposition of voting qualifications and the provision or administration of governmental services, such as public schools, public housing and law enforcement.

Section 4(e) may be readily seen as "plainly adapted" to furthering these aims of the Equal Protection Clause. The practical effect of § 4(e) is to prohibit New York from denying the right to vote to large segments of its Puerto Rican community. Congress has thus prohibited the State from denying to that community the right that "is preservative of all rights." . . . This enhanced political power will be helpful in gaining nondiscriminatory treatment in public services for the entire Puerto Rican community.[2] Section 4

1. Contrary to the suggestion of the dissent, . . . § 5 does not grant Congress power to exercise discretion in the other direction and to enact "statutes so as in effect to dilute equal protection and due process decisions of this Court." We emphasize that Congress' power under § 5 is limited to adopting measures to enforce the guarantees of the Amendment; § 5 grants Congress no power to restrict, abrogate, or dilute these guarantees. Thus, for example, an enactment authorizing the States to establish racially segregated systems of education would not be—as required by § 5—a measure "to enforce" the Equal Protection Clause since that clause of its own force prohibits such state laws. [Footnote by the Court. Note the disagreement regarding this footnote in Shapiro v. Thompson, 394 U.S. 618 (1969) (printed below, chap. 14, p. 1036).]

2 Cf. James Everards' Breweries v. Day [265 U.S. 545], which held that, under the Enforcement Clause of the Eighteenth Amendment, Congress could prohibit the prescription of intoxicating malt liquor for medicinal purposes even though the Amendment itself only prohibited the manufacture and sale of intoxicating liquors for beverage purposes. Cf. also the settled principle applied in the Shreveport Case (Houston, E. & W. T. R. Co. v. United

(e) thereby enables the Puerto Rican minority better to obtain "perfect equality of civil rights and equal protection of the laws." It was well within congressional authority to say that this need of the Puerto Rican minority for the vote warranted federal intrusion upon any state interests served by the English literacy requirement. It was for Congress, as the branch that made this judgment, to assess and weigh the various conflicting considerations—the risk or pervasiveness of the discrimination in governmental services, the effectiveness of eliminating the state restriction on the right to vote as a means of dealing with the evil, the adequacy or availability of alternative remedies, and the nature and significance of the state interest that would be affected by the nullification of the English literacy requirement as applied to residents who have successfully completed the sixth grade in a Puerto Rican school. It is not for us to review the congressional resolution of these factors. It is enough that we be able to perceive a basis upon which the Congress might resolve the conflict as it did. There plainly was such a basis to support § 4(e) in the application in question in this case. Any contrary conclusion would require us to be blind to the realities familiar to the legislators.

The result is no different if we confine our inquiry to the question whether § 4(e) was merely legislation aimed at the elimination of an invidious discrimination in establishing voter qualifications. We are told that New York's English literacy requirement originated in the desire to provide an incentive for non-English speaking immigrants to learn the English language and in order to assure the intelligent exercise of the franchise. Yet Congress might well have questioned, in light of the many exemptions provided, and some evidence suggesting that prejudice played a prominent role in the enactment of the requirement, whether these were actually the interests being served. Congress might have also questioned whether denial of a right deemed so precious and fundamental in our society was a necessary or appropriate means of encouraging persons to learn English, or of furthering the goal of an intelligent exercise of the franchise.[3] Finally, Congress might well have concluded that as a means of furthering the intelligent exercise of the franchise, an ability to read or understand Spanish is as effective as ability to read English for those to whom Spanish-language newspapers and Spanish-language radio and television programs are available to inform them of election issues and governmental affairs. . . . [I]t was

States, 234 U.S. 342), and expressed in United States v. Darby, 312 U.S. 100, 118, that the power of Congress to regulate interstate commerce "extends to those activities intrastate which so affect interstate commerce or the exercise of the power of Congress over it as to make regulation of them appropriate means to the attainment of a legitimate end . . . ." Accord, Atlanta Motel v. United States, 379 U.S. 241, 258. [Footnote by the Court.]

3. Other States have found ways of assuring an intelligent exercise of the franchise short of total disenfranchisement of persons not literate in English. For example, in Hawaii, where literacy in either English or Hawaiian suffices, candidates' names may be printed in both languages . . . . Section 4(e) does not preclude resort to these alternative methods of assuring the intelligent exercise of the franchise. True, the statute precludes, for a certain class, disenfranchisement and thus limits the States' choice of means of satisfying a purported state interest. But our cases have held that the States can be required to tailor carefully the means of satisfying a legitimate state interest when fundamental liberties and rights are threatened, see, e. g., . . . Carolene Products Co., 304 U.S. 144, 152–153, n. 4; . . . and Congress is free to apply the same principle in the exercise of its powers. [Footnote by the Court.]

Congress' prerogative to weigh these competing considerations.   Here again, it is enough that we perceive a basis upon which Congress might predicate a judgment that the application of New York's English literacy requirement . . . constitute an invidious discrimination in violation of the Equal Protection Clause.

There remains the question whether the congressional remedies adopted in § 4(e) constitute means which are not prohibited by, but are consistent "with the letter and spirit of the Constitution."   The only respect in which appellees contend that § 4(e) fails in this regard is that the section itself works an invidious discrimination in violation of the Fifth Amendment by prohibiting the enforcement of the English literacy requirement only for those educated in American-flag schools (schools located within United States jurisdiction) in which the language of instruction was other than English, and not for those educated in schools beyond the territorial limits of the United States in which the language of instruction was also other than English.   This is not a complaint that Congress, in enacting § 4(e), has unconstitutionally denied or diluted anyone's right to vote but rather that Congress violated the Constitution by not extending the relief effected in § 4(e) to those educated in non-American-flag schools.   We need not pause to determine whether appellees have a sufficient personal interest to have § 4 (e) invalidated on this ground, see generally United States v. Raines, 362 U.S. 17, since the argument, in our view, falls on the merits.

Section 4(e) does not restrict or deny the franchise but in effect extends the franchise to persons who otherwise would be denied it by state law. Thus we need not decide whether a state literacy law conditioning the right to vote on achieving a certain level of education in an American-flag school (regardless of the language of instruction) discriminates invidiously against those educated in non-American-flag schools.   We need only decide whether the challenged limitation on the relief effected in § 4(e) was permissible. In deciding that question, the principle that calls for the closest scrutiny of distinctions in laws *denying* fundamental rights . . . is inapplicable; for the distinction challenged by appellees is presented only as a limitation on a reform measure aimed at eliminating an existing barrier to the exercise of the franchise.   Rather, in deciding the constitutional propriety of the limitations in such a reform measure we are guided by the familiar principles that . . .   "reform may take one step at a time, addressing itself to the phase of the problem which seems most acute to the legislative mind," Williamson v. Lee Optical Co. [chap. 14, p. 997].

Guided by these principles, we are satisfied that appellees' challenge to this limitation in § 4(e) is without merit.   In the context of the case before us, the congressional choice to limit the relief effected in § 4(e) may, for example, reflect Congress' greater familiarity with the quality of instruction in American-flag schools, a recognition of the unique historic relationship beteween the Congress and the Commonwealth of Puerto Rico, an awareness of the Federal Government's acceptance of the desirability of the use of Spanish as the language of instruction in Commonwealth schools, and the fact that Congress has fostered policies encouraging migration from the Commonwealth to the States.   We have no occasion to determine in this case whether such factors would justify a similar distinction embodied in a voting-qualification law that denied the franchise to persons educated in non-

American-flag schools. We hold only that the limitation on relief effected in § 4(e) does not constitute a forbidden discrimination since these factors might well have been the basis for the decision of Congress to go "no further than it did." . . .

Reversed.

Mr. Justice DOUGLAS joins the Court's opinion except for the discussion . . . of the question whether the congressional remedies adopted in § 4(c) constitute means which are not prohibited by, but are consistent with "the letter and spirit of the Constitution." On that question, he reserves judgment until such time as it is presented by a member of the class against which that particular discrimination is directed.

[CARDONA v. POWER, 384 U.S. 672 (1966), argued together with and decided on the same day as Morgan, was an appeal from a state court challenge to the New York literacy requirement. The state courts, prior to the enactment of § 4(e) of the Voting Rights Act, had rejected an equal protection attack. Justice Brennan's majority opinion vacated the judgment and remanded the case to the highest state court: appellant might be covered by § 4(e), and this case "might therefore be moot"; even if appellant were not so covered, the state courts should determine whether, in light of § 4(e), those applications of the state requirement not specifically prohibited by the federal law "have continuing validity."

[Justice Douglas, joined by Justice Fortas, dissented, finding the New York statute unconstitutional as applied to a person literate in Spanish: "New York . . . registers those who have completed six years of school in a classroom where English is the medium of instruction and those who pass an English literacy test. In my view, there is no rational basis—considering the importance of the right at stake—for denying those with equivalent qualifications except that the language is Spanish." Justice Harlan, joined by Justice Stewart, also reached the constitutional issue, but found no flaw under the equal protection clause. (See generally chap. 14, infra.) Their views, in a dissent also addressed to the Morgan decision, follow:]

Mr. Justice HARLAN, whom Mr. Justice STEWART joins, dissenting [in Cardona v. Power as well as in the Morgan cases]. . . .

I. [The Cardona Case.]

The Equal Protection Clause of the Fourteenth Amendment, which alone concerns us here, forbids a State from arbitrarily discriminating among different classes of persons. . . . [A] state enactment or practice may be struck down under the clause only if it cannot be justified as founded upon a rational and permissible state policy. . . . It is suggested that a differen: and broader equal protection standard applies in cases where "fundamental liberties and rights are threatened," . . . which would require a State to show a need greater than mere rational policy to justify classifications in this area. No such dual-level test has ever been articulated by this Court, and I do not believe that any such approach is consistent with the purposes of the Equal Protection Clause, with the overwhelming weight of authority, or with well-established principles of federalism which underlie the Equal Protection Clause.

. . . Given the State's legitimate concern with promoting and safeguarding the intelligent use of the ballot, and given also New York's long experience with the process of integrating non-English speaking residents into the mainstream of American life, I do not see how it can be said that this qualification for suffrage is unconstitutional. . . .

II. [The Morgan Cases.]

The pivotal question in this instance is what effect the added factor of a congressional enactment has on the straight equal protection argument dealt with above. . . . I believe the Court has confused the issue of how much enforcement power Congress possesses under § 5 with the distinct issue of what questions are appropriate for congressional determination and what questions are essentially judicial in nature.

When recognized state violations of federal constitutional standards have occurred, Congress is of course empowered by § 5 to take appropriate remedial measures to redress and prevent the wrongs. . . . But it is a judicial question whether the condition with which Congress has thus sought to deal is in truth an infringement of the Constitution, something that is the necessary prerequisite to bringing the § 5 power into play at all. . . .

. . . . The question here is not whether the statute is appropriate remedial legislation to cure an established violation of a constitutional command, but whether there has in fact been an infringement of that constitutional command, that is, whether a particular state practice or, as here, a statute is so arbitrary or irrational as to offend the command of the Equal Protection Clause of the Fourteenth Amendment. That question is one for the judicial branch ultimately to determine. Were the rule otherwise, Congress would be able to qualify this Court's constitutional decisions under the Fourteenth and Fifteenth Amendments, let alone those under other provisions of the Constitution, by resorting to congressional power under the Necessary and Proper Clause. In view of this Court's holding in Lassiter, supra, that an English literacy test is a permissible exercise of state supervision over its franchise, I do not think it is open to Congress to limit the effect of that decision as it has undertaken to do by § 4(e). In effect the Court reads § 5 of the Fourteenth Amendment as giving Congress the power to define the *substantive* scope of the Amendment. If that indeed be the true reach of § 5, then I do not see why Congress should not be able as well to exercise its § 5 "discretion" by enacting statutes so as in effect to dilute equal protection and due process decisions of this Court. In all such cases there is room for reasonable men to differ as to whether or not a denial of equal protection or due process has occurred, and the final decision is one of judgment. Until today this judgment has always been one for the judiciary to resolve.

I do not mean to suggest in what has been said that a legislative judgment of the type incorporated in § 4(e) is without any force whatsoever. Decisions on questions of equal protection and due process are based not on abstract logic, but on empirical foundations. To the extent "legislative facts" are relevant to a judicial determination, Congress is well equipped to investigate them, and such determinations are of course entitled to due respect. In South Carolina v. Katzenbach, supra, such legislative findings were made to show that racial discrimination in voting was actually occurring. Similarly, in Heart of Atlanta Motel, Inc. v. United States, 379 U.S. 241, and Katzenbach v. McClung, 379 U.S. 294, . . . the congressional determination that racial discrimination in a clearly defined group of public accommodations did effectively impede interstate commerce was based on "voluminous testimony" . . . which had been put before the Congress and in the context of which it passed remedial legislation.

But no such factual data provide a legislative record supporting § 4(e) [1] by way of showing that Spanish-speaking citizens are fully as capable of making informed decisions in a New York election as are English-speaking citizens. Nor was there any showing whatever to support the Court's alternative argument that § 4(e) should be viewed as but a remedial measure designed to cure or assure against unconstitutional discrimination of other varieties, e. g., in "public schools, public housing and law enforcement," . . . to which Puerto Rican minorities might be subject in such communities as New York. There is simply no legislative record supporting such hypothesized discrimination of the sort we have hitherto insisted upon when congressional power is brought to bear on constitutionally reserved state concerns. . . .

Thus, we have here not a matter of giving deference to a congressional estimate, based on its determination of legislative facts, bearing upon the validity *vel non* of a statute, but rather what can at most be called a legislative announcement that Congress believes a state law to entail an unconstitutional deprivation of equal protection. . . . At least in the area of primary state concern a state statute that passes constitutional muster under the judicial standard of rationality should not be permitted to be set at naught by a mere contrary congressional pronouncement unsupported by a legislative record justifying that conclusion.

To deny the effectiveness of this congressional enactment is not of course to disparage Congress' exertion of authority in the field of civil rights; it is simply to recognize that the Legislative Branch like the other branches of federal authority is subject to the governmental boundaries set by the Constitution. To hold, on this record, that § 4(e) overrides the New York literacy requirement seems to me tantamount to allowing the Fourteenth Amendment to swallow the State's constitutionally ordained primary authority in this field. For if Congress by what, as here, amounts to mere *ipse dixit* can set that otherwise permissible requirement partially at naught I see no reason why it could not also substitute its judgment for that of the States in other fields of their exclusive primary competence as well. . . .

CONGRESSIONAL POWER AND THE MORGAN CASE

1. *The scope of the Morgan rationale.* a. How far-reaching is the § 5 power recognized in Morgan? Do you agree with the assessment in Burt, "Miranda and Title II: A Morganatic Marriage," 1969 Sup.Ct.Rev. 81: "In effect, the Court is saying that—at least in some circumstances—where Congress and the Court disagree about the meaning of the Fourteenth Amendment, the Court will defer to Congress' version. The Court is suggesting that, to some extent at least, § 5 exempts the Fourteenth Amendment from the principle of Court-Congress relationships expressed by Marbury v. Madi-

---

1. There were no committee hearings or reports referring to this section, which was introduced from the floor during debate on the full Voting Rights Act. . . . [Footnote by Justice Harlan.]

son, that the judiciary is the final arbiter of the meaning of the Constitution." To what "extent"? Under what "circumstances"?

b.   Which aspect of the Court's rationale is most far-reaching: that viewing the statute as a remedy against discrimination in voting, or that justifying it as a remedy against discrimination in governmental services? Did the Court apply an unduly permissive standard of review regarding the bases for the legislative judgments under § 5? Was the Court unduly lenient in rejecting the equal protection challenge to the narrowness of the statute? Cf. chap. 14, infra. Is the majority's footnote [1] a substantial and justifiable barrier to future invocations of the Morgan power? Is the risk that future invocations may be viewed as efforts to "restrict" rather than "reform" a substantial barrier?

c.   On the majority's footnote, consider Cox, "Foreword: Constitutional Adjudication and the Promotion of Human Rights," 80 Harv.L.Rev. 91, 106, n. 86: "It is hard to see how the Court can consistently give weight to the congressional judgment in expanding the definition of equal protection in the area of human rights but refuse to give it weight in narrowing the definition where the definition depends upon appraisal of facts. The footnote, therefore, may not be the end of the argument." Compare Burt, supra, at 118, suggesting that "the Court was wrong to erect its apparently rigid footnote [1] limitation on § 5 legislation." Burt finds in the logic of Morgan a "congressional revisory authority" that "would be 'around the edges' of the Court's proclaimed doctrine"—i. e., a congressional power to redefine doctrine, but not too much: "As in Morgan, the Court would independently characterize the measure as a 'reform' that it approved or a 'restriction' that it did not."

d.   What legislation may find support in Morgan? The civil rights violence provisions of the 1968 Act, p. 516, supra? The fair housing provisions, p. 525, supra? Voting legislation to eliminate literacy and residence requirements and lower age qualifications? See Cox, supra, at 107, and note 2 below. Barring de facto segregation in public education? See Cox, supra, at 108, and chap. 18, p. 1427, infra. Adopting "a comprehensive code of criminal procedure applicable to prosecutions in state courts"? Cox, ibid, and note 3, infra. Applying to private conduct all restrictions governing "state action" under § 1 of the 14th Amendment (see sec. 2 of this chapter)? Undertaking some variations in the "one man" - "one vote" theme of the Court's reapportionment decisions? See Burt, supra, at 119, and chap. 18, p. 1436, infra.

2.   *The Morgan power and the 18-year-old vote.* The voting rights bill adopted by the Senate in March 1970 eliminated literacy tests and lowered the voting age in all elections. Does Morgan support these provisions? The 18-year-old vote provision gave rise to an extensive constitutional debate. See, e. g., Congressional Record, March 11, 1970. The proponents relied heavily on a statement by Professor (former Solicitor General) Cox (Harvard), resting on Morgan for the proposition that "Congress has constitutional power to determine what the Equal Protection Clause requires," though cautioning that "some constitutional scholars would not share my view that Congress can reduce the voting age without a constitutional amendment. Possibly, my reasoning runs the logic of Katzenbach v. Morgan into the ground." Id., at S 3482–83. Opponents introduced a statement by Dean Pollak (Yale), noting that prior to Morgan, "I would have supposed that no

serious case could be made that such a statute would be constitutional," and adding that Morgan "provides the basis for a modestly plausible, but not for an ultimately persuasive, case for the constitutionality of the statute." He urged reduction of the voting age by constitutional amendment rather than statute. Id., at § 3511.

3. *The Morgan power and the Miranda requirements.* Title II of the Omnibus Crime Control Act of 1968, chap. 12, p. 871, infra, included a partial overturning of the Court's requirements of safeguards in the questioning of suspects. (See the Miranda case, p. 859, infra.) Is that legislation justifiable under Morgan? Or is it barred by footnote [1], or as a "restrictive" rather than a "reforming" measure? See Cox, supra, at 108: "Congress would seem to have the power, under the second branch of the Morgan decision, . . . to make its own findings of fact and evaluation of the competing considerations in determining what constitutes due process and what measures are necessary to secure it in practice." See also Burt, supra, at 132, finding justification for the statute because the differences between Miranda and Title II "are limited in scope, and do not entrench upon the basic purposes which the Court was pursuing." But note his warning about the "substantial risks for the Court" in the Morgan doctrine: though the Court "retains ample doctrinal handles to disapprove congressional action, nonetheless its presentational rhetoric—that Congress has, to whatever degree, an 'independent' role in interpreting the Constitution—is likely to remove an important restraint on Congress which has, in the past, counseled great wariness in trespassing on the Court's prerogatives."

Chapter 7

SEPARATION OF POWERS:
THE PRESIDENT, CONGRESS, AND THE COURT

Scope Note. The theme of the preceding four chapters was the scope of national powers as affected by concerns of state autonomy. State powers as limited by national interests are considered in the three chapters that follow this. This chapter is a brief departure from the federal-state dimension to examine some problems arising from the allocation of national powers among the three branches of the central government.

Some of the overlapping and conflicting concerns of President, Congress, and Court have emerged in earlier chapters—e. g., the materials on the congressional control of Court jurisdiction and on the binding effect of judicial interpretations of the Constitution on the other branches (in chap. 1). Recall, moreover, the prominence of separation of powers principles in the Court's discussion of standing (Flast v. Cohen, chap. 2, p. 93) and political questions (Baker v. Carr, chap. 2, p. 177). In this chapter, selected issues pertaining to the tripartite nature of the national government are considered more intensively.

Section 1 emphasizes domestic concerns—both the type illustrated by the Steel Seizure controversy (the competition between the branches for "lawmaking" authority in the regulation of private conduct) and the type illustrated by Congressman Adam Clayton Powell's judicial challenge to his exclusion by the House (the claim of each branch to be free from interference by the others in its "internal" matters). Section 2 turns to external affairs, with particular emphasis on the conflict of powers regarding the making of foreign policy and the use of military forces.

SECTION 1. DOMESTIC AFFAIRS

A. EXECUTIVE–LEGISLATIVE RELATIONS: REGULATING PRIVATE CONDUCT

PRESIDENTIAL LEADERSHIP AND CONGRESSIONAL LAWMAKING

Introduction. The actual influence of the President, as the elected official with a national constituency and as party leader, is obviously great. What of his legal authority to deal with domestic problems? Does the chief executive have residual emergency power to regulate private conduct? Or is he limited to the specific tasks assigned by Article II and to the execution of laws Congress enacts? The executive power to make "law" has evoked frequent and intense battles over abstractions, with Presidents as well as commentators on opposing sides. But the operative and most helpful answers may lie less in embracive absolutes than in discriminating distinctions and practical adjustments: compare, for example, the broad assertions of Justice Black with the more careful analysis of Justice Jackson in the Steel Seizure Case, below.

Presidents and Justices. Presidents, like Justices, have taken a variety of positions on the scope of the executive power. Compare, for example, the opposing views of Presidents Theodore Roosevelt and William Howard Taft with the range of positions in the Steel Seizure Case. Roosevelt said that it was not only the President's "right but his duty to do anything that the needs of the Nation demanded unless such action was forbidden by the Constitution or by the laws." Pursuant to that view he acts "for the common well-being of all our people, whenever and in whatever manner . . . necessary, unless prevented by direct constitutional or legislative prohibition."

On the other side, William Howard Taft wrote: "The true view of the Executive function is, as I conceive it, that the President can exercise no power which cannot be fairly and reasonably traced to some specific grant of power or justly implied and included within such express grant as proper and necessary to its exercise. Such specific grant must be either in the Federal Constitution or in an Act of Congress passed in pursuance thereof. There is no undefined residuum of power which he can exercise because it seems to him to be in the public interest. . . . The grants of Executive power are necessarily in general terms in order not to embarrass the Executive within the field of action plainly marked for him, but his jurisdiction must be justified and vindicated by affirmative constitutional or statutory provision, or it does not exist."

YOUNGSTOWN SHEET & TUBE CO. v. SAWYER
[THE STEEL SEIZURE CASE]

343 U.S. 579, 72 S.Ct. 863, 96 L.Ed. 1153 (1952).

Certiorari to the United States Court of Appeals for the District of Columbia Circuit.

Mr. Justice BLACK delivered the opinion of the Court.

We are asked to decide whether the President was acting within his constitutional power when he issued an order directing the Secretary of Commerce to take possession of and operate most of the Nation's steel mills. The mill owners argue that the President's order amounts to lawmaking, a legislative function which the Constitution has expressly confided to the Congress and not to the President. The Government's position is that the order was made on findings of the President that his action was necessary to avert a national catastrophe which would inevitably result from a stoppage of steel production, and that in meeting this grave emergency the President was acting within the aggregate of his constitutional powers as the Nation's Chief Executive and the Commander in Chief of the Armed Forces of the United States. The issue emerges here from the following series of events:

In the latter part of 1951, a dispute arose between the steel companies and their employees over terms and conditions that should be included in new collective bargaining agreements. Long-continued conferences failed to re-solve the dispute. On December 18, 1951, the employees' representative, United Steelworkers of America, C.I.O., gave notice of an intention to strike when the existing bargaining agreements expired on December 31. The Fed-eral Mediation and Conciliation Service then intervened in an effort to get labor and management to agree. This failing, the President on December 22, 1951, referred the dispute to the Federal Wage Stabilization Board to investigate and make recommendations for fair and equitable terms of settle-ment. This Board's report resulted in no settlement. On April 4, 1952, the Union gave notice of a nation-wide strike called to begin at 12:01 a. m. April 9. The indispensability of steel as a component of substantially all weapons and other war materials led the President to believe that the proposed work stoppage would immediately jeopardize our national defense and that gov-ernmental seizure of the steel mills was necessary in order to assure the con-tinued availability of steel. Reciting these considerations for his action, the President, a few hours before the strike was to begin, issued Executive Order 10340 . . .. The order directed the Secretary of Commerce to take pos-session of most of the steel mills and keep them running. The Secretary im-mediately issued his own possessory orders, calling upon the presidents of the various seized companies to serve as operating managers for the United States. They were directed to carry on their activities in accordance with regu-lations and directions of the Secretary. The next morning the President sent a message to Congress reporting his action. . . . Twelve days later he sent a second message. . . . Congress has taken no action.

Obeying the Secretary's orders under protest, the companies brought proceedings against him in the District Court. Their complaints charged that the seizure was not authorized by an act of Congress or by any consti-tutional provisions. The District Court was asked to declare the orders of the President and the Secretary invalid and to issue preliminary and perman-ent injunctions restraining their enforcement. Opposing the motion for pre-liminary injunction, the United States asserted that a strike disrupting steel production for even a brief period would so endanger the well-being and safety of the Nation that the President had "inherent power" to do what he had done—power "supported by the Constitution, by historical precedent, and by court decisions." The Government also contended that in any event no preliminary injunction should be issued because the companies had made no showing that their available legal remedies were inadequate or that their injuries from seizure would be irreparable. Holding against the Government on all points, the District Court on April 30 issued a preliminary injunction restraining the Secretary from "continuing the seizure and possession of the plant . . . and from acting under the purported authority of Executive Order No. 10340." 103 F.Supp. 569. On the same day the Court of Ap-peals stayed the District Court's injunction, 197 F.2d 582. Deeming it best that the issues raised be promptly decided by this Court, we granted certiorari on May 3 and set the cause for argument on May 12. 343 U.S. 937. [This decision was announced on June 2, 1952.]

Two crucial issues have developed: *First.* Should final determination of the constitutional validity of the President's order be made in this case which has proceeded no further than the preliminary injunction stage?

Second. If so, is the seizure order within the constitutional power of the President?

I.

It is urged that there were non-constitutional grounds upon which the District Court could have denied the preliminary injunction and thus have followed the customary judicial practice of declining to reach and decide constitutional questions until compelled to do so. On this basis it is argued that equity's extraordinary injunctive relief should have been denied because (a) seizure of the companies' properties did not inflict irreparable damages, and (b) there were available legal remedies adequate to afford compensation for any possible damages which they might suffer. . . . Arguments as to both rest in large part on the Government's claim that should the seizure ultimately be held unlawful, the companies could recover full compensation in the Court of Claims for the unlawful taking. Prior cases in this Court have cast doubt on the right to recover in the Court of Claims on account of properties unlawfully taken by government officials for public use as these properties were alleged to have been. See e. g., Hooe v. United States, 218 U.S. 322, 335–336; United States v. North American Co., 253 U.S. 330, 333. But see Larson v. Domestic & Foreign Corp., 337 U.S. 682, 701–702. Moreover, seizure and governmental operation of these going businesses were bound to result in many present and future damages of such nature as to be difficult, if not incapable, of measurement. Viewing the case this way, and in the light of the facts presented, the District Court saw no reason for delaying decision of the constitutional validity of the orders. We agree with the District Court . . . .

II.

The President's power, if any, to issue the order must stem either from an act of Congress or from the Constitution itself. There is no statute that expressly authorizes the President to take possession of property as he did here. Nor is there any act of Congress to which our attention has been directed from which such a power can fairly be implied. Indeed, we do not understand the Government to rely on statutory authorization for this seizure. There are two statutes which do authorize the President to take both personal and real property under certain conditions. [The Selective Service Act of 1948, 62 Stat. 604, 625–627, 50 U.S.C.App. (Supp. IV) § 468; the Defense Production Act of 1950, Tit. II, 64 Stat. 798, as amended, 65 Stat. 138.] However, the Government admits that these conditions were not met and that the President's order was not rooted in either of the statutes. The Government refers to the seizure provisions of one of these statutes (§ 201(b) of the Defense Production Act) as "much too cumbersome, involved, and time-consuming for the crisis which was at hand."

Moreover, the use of the seizure technique to solve labor disputes in order to prevent work stoppages was not only unauthorized by any congressional enactment; prior to this controversy, Congress had refused to adopt that method of settling labor disputes. When the Taft-Hartley Act was under consideration in 1947, Congress rejected an amendment which would have authorized such governmental seizures in cases of emergency. Apparently it was thought that the technique of seizure, like that of compulsory arbitration, would interfere with the process of collective bargaining. Consequently, the plan Congress adopted in that Act did not provide for seizure under any circumstances. Instead, the plan sought to bring about settlements by use of the customary devices of mediation, conciliation, investigation by boards of inquiry, and public reports. In some instances temporary injunctions were authorized to provide cooling-off periods. All this failing, the unions were left free to strike if the majority of the employees, by secret ballot, expressed a desire to do so.

It is clear that if the President had authority to issue the order he did, it must be found in some provisions of the Constitution. And it is not claimed that express constitutional language grants this power to the President. The contention is that presidential power should be implied from the aggregate of his powers under the Constitution. Particular reliance is placed on provisions in Article II which say that "the executive Power shall be vested in a President . . . ."; that "he shall take Care that the Laws be faithfully executed"; and that he "shall be Commander in Chief of the Army and Navy of the United States."

The order cannot properly be sustained as an exercise of the President's military power as Commander in Chief of the Armed Forces. The Government attempts to do so by citing a number of cases upholding broad powers in military commanders engaged in day-to-day fighting in a theater of war. Such cases need not concern us here. Even though "theater of war" be an expanding concept, we cannot with faithfulness to our constitutional system hold that the Commander in Chief of the Armed Forces has the ultimate power as such to take possession of private property in order to keep labor disputes from stopping production. This is a job for the Nation's lawmakers, not for its military authorities.

Nor can the seizure order be sustained because of the several constitutional provisions that grant executive power to the President. In the framework of our Constitution, the President's power to see that the laws are faithfully executed refutes the idea that he is to be a lawmaker. The Constitution limits his functions in the law-making process to the recommending of laws he thinks wise and the vetoing of laws he thinks bad. And the Constitution is neither silent nor equivocal about who shall make laws which the President is to execute. The first section of the first article says that "All legislative Powers herein granted shall be vested in a Congress of the United States. . . ." After granting many powers to the Congress, Article I goes on to provide that Congress may "make all Laws which shall be necessary and proper for carrying into Execution the foregoing Powers and all other Powers vested by this Constitution in the Government of the United States, or in any Department or Officer thereof."

The President's order does not direct that a congressional policy be executed in a manner prescribed by Congress—it directs that a presidential policy be executed in a manner prescribed by the President. The preamble of the order itself, like that of many statutes, sets out reasons why the President believes certain policies should be adopted, proclaims these policies as rules of conduct to be followed, and again, like a statute, authorizes a government official to promulgate additional rules and regulations consistent with the policy proclaimed and needed to carry that policy into execution. The power of Congress to adopt such public policies as those proclaimed by the order is beyond question. It can authorize the taking of private property for public use. It can make laws regulating the relationships between employers and employees, prescribing rules designed to settle labor disputes, and fixing wages and working conditions in certain fields of our economy. The Constitution does not subject this lawmaking power of Congress to presidential or military supervision or control.

It is said that other Presidents without congressional authority have taken possession of private business enterprises in order to settle labor disputes. But even if this be true, Congress has not thereby lost its exclusive constitutional authority to make laws necessary and proper to carry out the powers vested by the Constitution "in the Government of the United States, or any Department or Officer thereof."

The Founders of this Nation entrusted the lawmaking power to the Congress alone in both good and bad times. It would do no good to recall the historical events, the fears of power and the hopes for freedom that lay behind their choice. Such a review would but confirm our holding that this seizure order cannot stand.

The judgment of the District Court is

Affirmed.

Mr. Justice FRANKFURTER.

Although the considerations relevant to the legal enforcement of the principle of separation of powers seem to me more complicated and flexible than may appear from what Mr. Justice Black has written, I join his opinion because I thoroughly agree with the application of the principle to the circumstances of this case. Even though such differences in attitude toward this principle may be merely differences in emphasis and nuance, they can hardly be reflected by a single opinion for the Court. Individual expression of views in reaching a common result is therefore important.

Mr. Justice FRANKFURTER, concurring. . . .

The issue before us can be met, and therefore should be, without attempting to define the President's powers comprehensively. I shall not attempt to delineate what belongs to him by virtue of his office beyond the power even of Congress to contract; what authority belongs to him until Congress acts; what kind of problems may be dealt with either by the Congress or by the President or by both . . . ; what power must be exercised by the Congress and cannot be delegated to the President. . . .

We must therefore put to one side consideration of what powers the President would have had if there had been no legislation whatever bearing on the authority asserted by the seizure, or if the seizure had been only for a short, explicitly temporary period, to be determined automatically unless Congressional approval were given. These and other questions, like or unlike, are not now here. I would exceed my authority were I to say anything about them. . . .

It cannot be contended that the President would have had power to issue this order had Congress explicitly negated such authority in formal legislation. Congress has expressed its will to withhold this power from the President as though it had said so in so many words. . . .

. . . . It is an inadmissibly narrow conception of American constitutional law to confine it to the words of the Constitution and to disregard the gloss which life has written upon them. In short, a systematic, unbroken, executive practice, long pursued to the knowledge of the Congress and never before questioned, engaged in by Presidents who have also sworn to uphold the Constitution, making as it were such exercise of power part of the structure of our government, may be treated as a gloss on "executive Power" vested in the President by § 1 of Art. II. . . .

Down to the World War II period . . . the record is barren of instances comparable to the one before us. Of twelve seizures by President Roosevelt prior to the enactment of the War Labor Disputes Act in June, 1943, three were sanctioned by existing law, and six others were effected after Congress, on December 8, 1941, had declared the existence of a state of war. In this case, reliance on the powers that flow from declared war has been commendably disclaimed by the Solicitor General. Thus the list of executive assertions of the power of seizure in circumstances comparable to the present reduces to three in the six-month period from June to December of 1941. We need not split hairs in comparing those actions to the one before us, though much might be said by way of differentiation. Without passing on their validity, as we are not called upon to do, it suffices to say that these three isolated instances do not add up, either in number, scope, duration or contemporaneous legal justification, to the kind of executive construction of the Constitution revealed in the Midwest Oil case. Nor do they come to us sanctioned by long-continued acquiscence of Congress giving decisive weight to a construction by the Executive of its powers. . . .

Mr. Justice DOUGLAS, concurring.

. . . [T]he fact that it was necessary that measures be taken to keep steel in production does not mean that the President, rather than the Congress, had the constitutional authority to act. The Congress, as well as the President, is trustee of the national welfare. . . . The branch of Government that has the power to pay compensation for a seizure is the only one able to authorize a seizure or make lawful one that the President had effected. That seems to me to be the necessary result of the condemnation provision in the Fifth Amendment. It squares with the theory of checks and balances expounded by Mr. Justice Black in the opinion of the Court in which I join. . . .

Mr. Justice JACKSON, concurring in the judgment and opinion of the Court.

That comprehensive and undefined presidential powers hold both practical advantages and grave dangers for the country will impress anyone who has served as legal adviser to a President in time of transition and public anxiety. While an interval of detached reflection may temper teachings of that experience, they probably are a more realistic influence on my views than the conventional materials of judicial decision which seem unduly to accentuate doctrine and legal fiction. . . .

A judge, like an executive advisor, may be surprised at the poverty of really useful and unambiguous authority applicable to concrete problems of executive power as they actually present themselves. Just what our forefathers did envision, or would have envisioned had they foreseen modern conditions, must be divined from materials almost as enigmatic as the dreams Joseph was called upon to interpret for Pharaoh. A century and a half of partisan debate and scholarly speculation yields no net result but only supplies more or less apt quotations from respected resources on each side of any question. They largely cancel each other. And court decisions are indecisive because of the judicial practice of dealing with the largest questions in the most narrow way.

The actual art of governing under our Constitution does not and cannot conform to judicial definitions of the power of any of its branches based on isolated clauses or even single Articles torn from context. While the Constitution diffuses power the better to secure liberty, it also contemplates that practice will integrate the dispersed powers into a workable government. It enjoins upon its branches separateness but interdependence, autonomy but reciprocity. Presidential powers are not fixed but fluctuate, depending upon their disjunction or conjunction with those of Congress. We may well begin by a somewhat over-simplified grouping of practical situations in which a President may doubt, or others may challenge, his powers, and by distinguishing roughly the legal consequences of this factor of relativity.

1. When the President acts pursuant to an express or implied authorization of Congress, his authority is at its maximum, for it includes all that he possesses in his own right plus all that Congress can delegate.[1] In these circumstances, and in these only, may he be said (for what it may be worth) to personify the federal sovereignty. If his act is held unconstitutional under these circumstances, it usually means that the Federal Government as an undivided whole lacks power. A seizure executed by the President pursuant to an Act of Congress would be supported by the strongest of presumptions and the widest latitude of judicial interpretation, and the burden of persuasion would rest heavily upon any who might attack it.

2. When the President acts in absence of either a congressional grant or denial of authority, he can only rely upon his own independent powers, but there is a zone of twilight in which he and Congress may have concurrent authority, or in which its distribution is uncertain. Therefore, congressional inertia, indifference or quiescence may sometimes, at least as a practical matter, enable, if not invite, measures on independent presidential responsibility. In this area, any actual test of power is likely to depend on the imperatives of events and contemporary imponderables rather than on abstract theories of law.[2]

---

1. It is in this class of cases that we find the broadest recent statements of presidential power, including those relied on here. United States v. Curtiss-Wright Corp., 299 U.S. 304 [p. 593, infra], involved, not the question of the President's power to act without congressional authority, but the question of his right to act under and in accord with an Act of Congress. The constitutionality of the Act under which the President had proceeded was assailed on the ground that it delegated legislative powers to the President. Much of the Court's opinion is *dictum* . . . .

That case does not solve the present controversy. It recognized internal and external affairs as being in separate categories, and held that the strict limitation upon congressional delegations of power to the President over internal affairs does not apply with respect to delegations of power in external affairs. It was intimated that the President might act in external affairs without congressional authority, but not that he might act contrary to an Act of Congress. . . . [Footnote by Justice Jackson.]

2. Since the Constitution implies that the writ of habeas corpus may be suspended in certain circumstances but does not say by whom, President Lincoln asserted and maintained it as an executive function in the face of judicial challenge and doubt. Ex parte

3. When the President takes measures incompatible with the expressed or implied will of Congress, his power is at its lowest ebb, for then he can rely only upon his own constitutional powers minus any constitutional powers of Congress over the matter. Courts can sustain exclusive presidential control in such a case only by disabling the Congress from acting upon the subject.[3] Presidential claim to a power at once so conclusive and preclusive must be scrutinized with caution, for what is at stake is the equilibrium established by our constitutional system.

Into which of these classifications does this executive seizure of the steel industry fit? It is eliminated from the first by admission, for it is conceded that no congressional authorization exists for this seizure. That takes away also the support of the many precedents and declarations which were made in relation, and must be confined, to this category.

Can it then be defended under flexible tests available to the second category? It seems clearly eliminated from that class because Congress has not left seizure of private property an open field but has covered it by three statutory policies inconsistent with this seizure. . . . None of these were invoked. In choosing a different and inconsistent way of his own, the President cannot claim that it is necessitated or invited by failure of Congress to legislate upon the occasions, grounds and methods for seizure of industrial properties.

This leaves the current seizure to be justified only by the severe tests under the third grouping, where it can be supported only by any remainder of executive power after subtraction of such powers as Congress may have over the subject. In short, we can sustain the President only by holding that seizure of such strike-bound industries is within his domain and beyond control by Congress. Thus, this Court's first review of such seizures occurs under circumstances which leave Presidential power most vulnerable to attack and in the least favorable of possible constitutional postures. . . .

The Solicitor General seeks the power of seizure in three clauses of the Executive Article, the first reading, "The executive Power shall be vested in a President of the United States of America." . . . I cannot accept the view that this clause is a grant in bulk of all conceivable executive power but regard it as an allocation to the presidential office of the generic powers thereafter stated.

The clause on which the Government next relies is that "The President shall be Commander in Chief of the Army and Navy of the United States . . . ." These cryptic words have given rise to some of the most persistent controversies in our constitutional history. Of course, they imply something more than an empty title. But just what authority goes with the

---

Merryman, 17 Fed.Cas. 144; Ex parte Milligan, 4 Wall. 2, 125 [p. 611, infra] . . . . Congress eventually ratified his action. Habeas Corpus Act of March 3, 1863, 12 Stat. 755. . . . [Footnote by Justice Jackson.]

3. President Roosevelt's effort to remove a Federal Trade Commissioner was found to be contrary to the policy of Congress and impinging upon an area of congressional control, and so his re-

moval power was cut down accordingly. Humphrey's Executor v. United States, 295 U.S. 602 [p. 572, infra]. However, his exclusive power of removal in executive agencies, affirmed in Myers v. United States, 272 U.S. 52 [p. 572, infra], continued to be asserted and maintained. Morgan v. Tennessee Valley Authority, 115 F.2d 990, cert. denied 312 U.S. 701 . . . . [Footnote by Justice Jackson.]

name has plagued Presidential advisers who would not waive or narrow it by nonassertion yet cannot say where it begins or ends. It undoubtedly puts the Nation's armed forces under Presidential command. Hence, this loose appellation is sometimes advanced as support for any Presidential action, internal or external, involving use of force, the idea being that it vests power to do anything, anywhere, that can be done with an army or navy.

That seems to be the logic of an argument tendered at our bar—that the President having, on his own responsibility, sent American troops abroad derives from that act "affirmative power" to seize the means of producing a supply of steel for them. . . . But no doctrine that the Court could promulgate would seem to me more sinister and alarming than that a President whose conduct of foreign affairs is so largely uncontrolled, and often even is unknown, can vastly enlarge his mastery over the internal affairs of the country by his own commitment of the Nation's armed forces to some foreign venture. I do not, however, find it necessary or appropriate to consider the legal status of the Korean enterprise to discountenance argument based on it.

Assuming that we are in a war *de facto*, whether it is or is not a war *de jure*, does that empower the Commander-in-Chief to seize industries he thinks necessary to supply our army? The Constitution expressly places in Congress power "to raise and *support* Armies" and "to *provide* and *maintain* a Navy." (Emphasis supplied.) This certainly lays upon Congress primary responsibility for supplying the armed forces. Congress alone controls the raising of revenues and their appropriation and may determine in what manner and by what means they shall be spent for military and naval procurement. I suppose no one would doubt that Congress can take over war supply as a Government enterprise. . . .

The third clause in which the Solicitor General finds seizure powers is that "he shall take Care that the Laws be faithfully executed . . . ." That authority must be matched against words of the Fifth Amendment that "No person shall be . . . deprived of life, liberty or property, without due process of law . . . ." One gives a governmental authority that reaches so far as there is law, the other gives a private right that authority shall go no farther. . . .

The Solicitor General lastly grounds support of the seizure upon nebulous, inherent powers never expressly granted but said to have accrued to the office from the customs and claims of preceding administrations. The plea is for a resulting power to deal with a crisis or an emergency according to the necessities of the case, the unarticulated assumption being that necessity knows no law.

Loose and irresponsible use of adjectives colors all nonlegal and much legal discussion of presidential powers. "'Inherent" powers, "implied" powers, "incidental" powers, "plenary" powers, "war" powers and "emergency" powers are used, often interchangeably and without fixed or ascertainable meanings.

The vagueness and generality of the clauses that set forth presidential powers afford a plausible basis for pressures within and without an administration for presidential action beyond that supported by those whose responsibility it is to defend his actions in court. The claim of inherent and unrestricted presidential powers has long been a persuasive dialectical weapon in political controversy. While it is not surprising that counsel should grasp support from such unadjudicated claims of power, a judge cannot accept self-serving press statements of the attorney for one of the interested parties as authority in answering a constitutional question, even if the advocate was himself. But prudence has counseled that actual reliance on such nebulous claims stop short of provoking a judicial test.

In the practical working of our Government we already have evolved a technique within the framework of the Constitution by which normal executive powers may be considerably expanded to meet an emergency. Congress may and has granted extraordinary authorities which lie dormant in normal times but may be called into play by the Executive in war or upon proclamation of a national emergency. In 1939, upon congressional request, the Attorney General listed ninety-nine such separate statutory grants by Congress of emergency or wartime executive powers. They were invoked from time to time as need appeared. Under this procedure we retain Government by law—special, temporary law, perhaps, but law nonetheless. The public may know the extent and limitations of the powers that can be asserted, and persons affected may be informed from the statute of their rights and duties.

In view of the ease, expedition and safety with which Congress can grant and has granted large emergency powers, certainly ample to embrace this crisis, I am quite unimpressed with the argument that we should affirm possession of them without statute. Such power either has no beginning or it has no end. If it exists, it need submit to no legal restraint. I am not alarmed that it would plunge us straightway into dictatorship, but it is at least a step in that wrong direction.

As to whether there is imperative necessity for such powers, it is relevant to note the gap that exists between the President's paper powers and his real powers. The Constitution does not disclose the measure of the actual controls wielded by the modern presidential office. That instrument must be understood as an Eighteenth-Century sketch of a government hoped for, not as a blueprint of the Government that is. Vast accretions of federal power, eroded from that reserved by the States, have magnified the scope of presidential activity. Subtle shifts take place in the centers of real power that do not show on the face of the Constitution.

Executive power has the advantage of concentration in a single head in whose choice the whole Nation has a part, making him the focus of public hopes and exceptions. . . .

Moreover, rise of the party system has made a significant extraconstitutional supplement to real executive power. . . . Party loyalties and interests, sometimes more binding than law, extend his effective control into branches of government other than his own and he often may win, as a political leader, what he cannot command under the Constitution. . . . I cannot be brought to believe that this country will suffer if the Court refuses further to aggrandize the presidential office, already so potent and so relatively immune from judicial review, at the expense of Congress.

But I have no illusion that any decision by this Court can keep power in the hands of Congress if it is not wise and timely in meeting its problems. A crisis that challenges the President equally, or perhaps primarily, challenges Congress. If not good law, there was worldly wisdom in the maxim attributed to Napoleon that "The tools belong to the man who can use them."

We may say that power to legislate for emergencies belongs in the hands of Congress, but only Congress itself can prevent power from slipping through its fingers.

The essence of our free Government is "leave to live by no man's leave, underneath the law"—to be governed by those impersonal forces which we call law. Our Government is fashioned to fulfill this concept so far as humanly possible. The Executive, except for recommendation and veto, has no legislative power. The executive action we have here originates in the individual will of the President and represents an exercise of authority without law. No one, perhaps not even the President, knows the limits of the power he may seek to exert in this instance and the parties affected cannot learn the limit of their rights. We do not know today what powers over labor or property would be claimed to flow from Government possession if we should legalize it, what rights to compensation would be claimed or recognized, or on what contingency it would end. With all its defects, delays and inconveniences, men have discovered no technique for long preserving free government except that the Executive be under the law, and that the law be made by parliamentary deliberations.

Such institutions may be destined to pass away. But it is the duty of the Court to be last, not first, to give them up.

Mr. Justice BURTON, concurring in both the opinion and judgment of the Court. . . .

The controlling fact here is that Congress, within its constitutionally delegated power, has prescribed for the President specific procedures, exclusive of seizure, for his use in meeting the present type of emergency. . . . Under these circumstances, the President's order of April 8 invaded the jurisdiction of Congress. . . .

Mr. Justice CLARK, concurring in the judgment of the Court. . . . .

I conclude that where Congress has laid down specific procedures to deal with the type of crisis confronting the President, he must follow those procedures in meeting the crisis; but that in the absence of such action by Congress, the President's independent power to act depends upon the gravity of the situation confronting the nation. I cannot sustain the seizure in question because here . . . . Congress had prescribed methods to be followed by the President in meeting the emergency at hand. . . . .

Mr. Chief Justice VINSON, with whom Mr. Justice REED and Mr. Justice MINTON join, dissenting. . . .

I. . . .

One is not here called upon even to consider the possibility of executive seizure of a farm, a corner grocery store or even a single industrial plant. Such considerations arise only when one ignores the central fact of this case— that the Nation's entire basic steel production would have shut down completely if there had been no Government seizure. . . .

Accordingly, if the President has any power under the Constitution to meet a critical situation in the absence of express statutory authorization, there is no basis whatever for criticizing the exercise of such power in this case.

II. . . .

Under [the plaintiffs' and the District Judge's] view, the President is left powerless at the very moment when the need for action may be most pressing and when no one, other than he, is immediately capable of action. Under this view, he is left powerless because a power not expressly given to Congress is nevertheless found to rest exclusively with Congress.

. . . [T]he Presidency was deliberately fashioned as an office of power and independence. Of course, the Framers created no autocrat capable of arrogating any power unto himself at any time. But neither did they create an automaton impotent to exercise the powers of Government at a time when the survival of the Republic itself may be at stake.

. . . [W]e are not called upon today to expand the Constitution to meet a new situation. For, in this case, we need only look to history and time-honored principles of constitutional law—principles that have been applied consistently by all branches of the Government throughout our history. It is those who assert the invalidity of the Executive Order who seek to amend the Constitution in this case.

III.

A review of executive action demonstrates that our Presidents have on many occasions exhibited the leadership contemplated by the Framers when they made the President Commander in Chief, and imposed upon him the trust to "take Care that the Laws be faithfully executed." With or without explicit statutory authorization, Presidents have at such times dealt with national emergencies by acting promptly and resolutely to enforce legislative programs, at least to save those programs until Congress could act. Congress and the courts have responded to such executive initiative with consistent approval.

Our first President displayed at once the leadership contemplated by the Framers. When the national revenue laws were openly flouted in some sections of Pennsylvania, President Washington, without waiting for a call from the state government, summoned the militia and took decisive steps to secure the faithful execution of the laws. When international disputes engendered by the French revolution threatened to involve this country in war, and while congressional policy remained uncertain, Washington issued his Proclamation of Neutrality. . . .

Jefferson's initiative in the Louisiana Purchase, the Monroe Doctrine, and Jackson's removal of Government deposits from the Bank of the United States further serve to demonstrate by deed what the Framers described by word when they vested the whole of the executive power in the President.

Without declaration of war, President Lincoln took energetic action with the outbreak of the Civil War. He summoned troops and paid them out of the Treasury without appropriation therefor. He proclaimed a naval blockade of the Confederacy and seized ships violating that blockade. Congress, far from denying the validity of these acts, gave them express approval. The most striking action of President Lincoln was the Emancipation Proclamation, issued in aid of the successful prosecution of the Civil War, but wholly without statutory authority.

In an action furnishing a most apt precedent for this case, President Lincoln directed the seizure of rail and telegraph lines leading to Washington without statutory authority. Many months, later, Congress recognized and confirmed the power of the President to seize railroads and telegraph lines and provided criminal penalties for interference with Government operation. This Act did not confer on the President any additional powers of seizure. Congress plainly rejected the view that the President's acts had been without legal sanction until ratified by the legislature. . . .

President Hayes authorized the wide-spread use of federal troops during the Railroad Strike of 1877. President Cleveland also used the troops in the Pullman Strike of 1895 and his action is of special significance. No statute authorized this action. No call for help had issued from the Governor of Illinois; indeed Governor Altgeld disclaimed the need for supplemental forces. But the President's concern was that federal laws relating to the free flow of interstate commerce and the mails be continuously and faithfully executed without interruption. To further this aim his agents sought and obtained the injunction upheld by this Court in In re Debs, 158 U.S. 564 (1895). The Court scrutinized each of the steps taken by the President to insure execution of the "mass of legislation" dealing with commerce and the mails and gave his conduct full approval. Congress likewise took note of this use of Presidential power to forestall apparent obstacles to the faithful execution of the laws. By separate resolutions, both the Senate and the House commended the Executive's action. . . .

In 1909, President Taft was informed that government owned oil lands were being patented by private parties at such a rate that public oil lands would be depleted in a matter of months. Although Congress had explicitly provided that these lands were open to purchase by United States citizens, 29 Stat. 526 (1897), the President nevertheless ordered the lands wihdrawn from sale "[i]n aid of proposed legislation." In United States v. Midwest Oil Co., 236 U.S. 459 (1915), the President's action was sustained as consistent with executive practice throughout our history. . . .

During World War I, President Wilson established a War Labor Board without awaiting specific direction by Congress. . . . Effectiveness of War Labor Board decision was accomplished by Presidential action, including seizure of industrial plants. Seizure of the Nation's railroads was also ordered by President Wilson.

Beginning with the Bank Holiday Proclamation and continuing through World War II, executive leadership and initiative were characteristic of President Franklin D. Roosevelt's administration. In 1939, upon the outbreak of war in Europe, the President proclaimed a limited national emergency for the purpose of strengthening our national defense. By May of 1941, the danger from the Axis belligerents having become clear, the President proclaimed "an unlimited national emergency" calling for mobilization of the Nation's defenses to repel aggression. The President took the initiative in strengthening our defenses by acquiring rights from the British Government to establish air bases in exchange for overage destroyers.

In 1941, President Roosevelt acted to protect Iceland from attack by Axis powers when British forces were withdrawn by sending our forces to occupy Iceland. Congress was informed of this action on the same day that our forces reached Iceland. The occupation of Iceland was but one of "at least 125 incidents" in our history in which Presidents, "without Congressional authorization, and in the absence of a declaration of war, [have] ordered the Armed Forces to take action or maintain positions abroad."

Some six months before Pearl Harbor, a dispute at a single aviation plant [North American Aviation, Inc.] at Inglewood, California, interrupted a segment of the production of military aircraft. . . . President Roosevelt ordered the seizure of the plant "pursuant to the powers vested in [him] by the Constitution and laws of the United States, as President of the United States of America and Commander in Chief of the Army and Navy of the United States." The Attorney General (Jackson) vigorously proclaimed that the President had the moral duty to keep this Nation's defense effort a "going concern." His ringing moral justification was coupled with a legal justification equally well stated:

"The Presidential proclamation rests upon the aggregate of the Presidential powers derived from the Constitution itself and from statutes enacted by the Congress." . . .

Following passage of the Smith-Connally Act [1943], seizures to assure continued production on the basis of terms recommended by the War Labor Board were based upon that Act as well as upon the President's power under the Constitution and the laws generally. A question did arise as to whether the statutory language relating to "any plant, mine, or facility equipped for the manufacture, production, or mining of any articles or materials" authorized the seizure of properties of Montgomery Ward & Co., a retail department store and mail order concern. The Attorney General (Biddle) issued an opinion that the President possessed the power to seize Montgomery Ward properties to prevent a work stoppage whether or not the terms of the Smith-Connally Act authorized such a seizure. . . . Accordingly, the President ordered seizure of the Chicago properties of Montgomery Ward in April, 1944, when that company refused to obey a War Labor Board order concerning the bargaining representative of its employees in Chicago. In Congress, a Select Committee to Investigate Seizure of the Property of Montgomery Ward & Co., assuming that the terms of the Smith-Connally Act did not cover this seizure, concluded that the seizure "was not only within the Constitutional power but was the plain duty of the President." *

More recently, President Truman acted to repel aggression by employing our armed forces in Korea. Upon the intervention of the Chinese Com-

---

* The constitutional challenge to this seizure was not decided by the Supreme Court. The Government brought a declaratory judgment action to establish the legality of the seizure and to enjoin interference with the Government's possession. The theory of the Government's case, based on Attorney General Jackson's opinion, was that the President's action was justified under either the War Labor Disputes Act or the "aggregate" of his powers as Chief Executive and Commander-in-Chief. The trial court dismissed the suit, holding that the Government was not entitled to an injunction, that the seizure was not justified, and that possession of the property was unauthorized. 58 F.Supp. 408 (1945). The Court of Appeals reversed the order of the trial court "with directions to enter one granting the relief sought by the plaintiff." The conclusion was based on the "authority of the President as Commander-in-Chief in the light of the War Labor Disputes Act," without consideration of the constitutional question. 150 F.2d 369 (7th Cir. 1945). Certiorari was granted by the Supreme Court but, the Government having meanwhile returned the properties to the owners, the Court entered an order vacating the judgment of the Circuit Court of Appeals and remanding the cause to the District Court with directions to dismiss it as moot. Montgomery Ward & Co. v. United States, 326 U.S. 690 (1945).

munists, the President proclaimed the existence of an unlimited national emergency requiring the speedy build-up of our defense establishment. Congress responded by providing for increased manpower and weapons for our own armed forces, by increasing military aid under the Mutual Security Program and by enacting economic stabilization measures . . . .

This is but a cursory summary of executive leadership but it amply demonstrates that Presidents have taken prompt action to enforce the laws and protect the country whether or not Congress happened to provide in advance for the particular method of execution. . . .

IV.

Focusing now on the situation confronting the President on the night of April 8, 1952, we cannot but conclude that the President was performing his duty under the Constitution "to take care that the laws be faithfully executed" —a duty described by President Benjamin Harrison as "the central idea of the office." . . .

The absence of a specific statute authorizing seizure of the steel mills as a mode of executing the laws—both the military procurement program and the anti-inflation program—has not until today been thought to prevent the President from executing the laws. . . .

There is no statute prohibiting seizure as a method of enforcing legislative programs. Congress has in no wise indicated that its legislation is not to be executed by the taking of private property (subject of course to the payment of just compensation) if its legislation cannot otherwise be executed. . . . Where Congress authorizes seizure in instances not necessarily crucial to the defense program, it can hardly be said to have disclosed an intention to prohibit seizures where essential to the execution of that legislative program. . . .

V. . . .

When the President acted on April 8, he had exhausted the procedures for settlement available to him. Taft-Hartley was a route parallel to, not connected with, the WSB procedure. The strike had been delayed 99 days as contrasted with the maximum delay of 80 days under Taft-Hartley. There had been a hearing on the issues in dispute and bargaining which promised settlement up to the very hour before seizure had broken down. Faced with immediate national peril through stoppage in steel production on the one hand and faced with destruction of the wage and price legislative programs on the other, the President took temporary possession of the steel mills as the only course open to him consistent with his duty to take care that the laws be faithfully executed. . . .

VI.

The diversity of views expressed in the six opinions of the majority, the lack of reference to authoritative precedent, the repeated reliance upon prior dissenting opinions, the complete disregard of the uncontroverted facts showing the gravity of the emergency and the temporary nature of the taking all serve to demonstrate how far afield one must go to affirm the order of the District Court.

The broad executive power granted by Article II to an officer on duty 365 days a year cannot, it is said, be invoked to avert disaster. Instead, the President must confine himself to sending a message to Congress recommending action. Under this messenger-boy concept of the Office, the President cannot even act to preserve legislative programs from destruction so that Congress will have something left to act upon. . . .

THE BREADTH OF THE STEEL SEIZURE DECISION

1. *Dicta and holding.* Does Justice Black recognize *any* "emergency powers" of the President? Does the majority of the Court? Is Justice Black's opinion unduly broad? Does the holding go beyond situation 3 described by Justice Jackson? Does the case stand for any principle other than that the President may not undertake domestic regulation on the basis of a policy contrary to that adopted by Congress? Do the broader statements suggest that the Court was unwise to speak about the merits? Could the Court have avoided the constitutional decision because of failure to satisfy the preconditions to equitable relief? See Freund, "Foreword—The Year of the Steel Case," 66 Harv.L.Rev. 89 (1952). Should the Court have delayed decision for longer than the three weeks between argument and decision in this case? *

2. *The broad statements: provocation and impact.* Were Justice Black's broad statements provoked by the broad arguments of the Government? Compare the Government's arguments in the District Court hearing, printed in Westin, The Anatomy of a Constitutional Law Case (1958), 56–65. For example, note the interchange between District Judge Pine and Assistant Attorney General Baldridge, id. at 64: *"The Court:* So . . . the Constitution . . . limited the powers of the Congress and limited the powers of the judiciary, but did not limit the powers of the Executive. Is that what you say? *Mr. Baldridge:* That is the way we read Article II of the Constitution. *The Court:* I see . . . ." A few days after the argument, President Truman issued a statement: "The powers of the President are derived from the Constitution, and they are limited, of course, by the provisions of the Constitution. . . ." Moreover, the Government submitted a supplemental brief in the District Court because of the "misunderstandings which may have arisen during the course of the oral argument." For President Truman's subsequent reflections, see Truman, II Memoirs: Years of Trial and Hope (1956), 475–78, concluding: "Whatever the six justices of the Supreme Court meant by their differing opinions . . . ., [the President] must always act in a national emergency."

3. *Applicability to external affairs.* Can Justice Jackson's distinction among situations, and the holding of the principal case as narrowly conceived, be applied outside the domestic sphere? For example, may there be some Presidential authority to commit and send armed forces overseas—so long as

---

* For a sampling of the extensive commentary provoked by the principal case, see Kauper, "The Steel Seizure Case: Congress, the President, and the Supreme Court," 51 Mich.L.Rev. 141 (1952), Selected Essays 1938–62 (1963), 129, and Corwin, "The Steel Seizure Case: A Judicial Brick Without Straw," 53 Colum.L.Rev. 53 (1953). For a use of the injunction authority under the Taft-Hartley Act in a later steel strike, see United Steelworkers v. United States, 361 U.S. 39 (1959).

there is no contrary policy established by Congress under its war and foreign relations powers? Or is Presidential authority broader outside the domestic area? Or (in view of the congressional power to declare war) is it narrower, when war-like activities are involved? Compare the debate regarding "national commitments" and the Vietnam war, sec. 2, p. 599, infra.

B. LEGISLATIVE–EXECUTIVE RELATIONS: INTERVENTION IN THE AFFAIRS OF THE OTHER DEPARTMENT

1. *Congressional interference in the internal affairs of the executive branch.* Many of the clashes between President and Congress arise not from competition over the immediate governance of private conduct but from efforts of one branch to intervene in internal activities of the other. There have been frequent conflicts, for example, between legislative demands for information and executive officials' refusals to comply, on instructions from the President, on grounds of interference with privileged deliberations. The recurrent debate on this issue exemplifies one of the important areas of constitutional controversy that takes place outside of the courtroom. See Younger, "Congressional Investigations and Executive Secrecy: A Study in the Separation of Powers," 20 U.Pitt.L.Rev. 755 (1959), Bishop, "The Executive's Right of Privacy: An Unresolved Constitutional Question," 66 Yale L.J. 477 (1957), and Berger, "Executive Privilege v. Congressional Inquiry," 12 U.C.L.A.L.Rev. 1044 (1965). [See also, on a related problem, Ginnane, "Control of Federal Administration by Congressional Resolutions and Committees," 66 Harv.L.Rev. 569 (1953).] Similar conflicts have arisen over efforts to reach executive documents for use in court proceedings. See Hardin, "The Executive Privilege in the Federal Courts," 71 Yale L.J. 879 (1962).

2. *Removal: May Congress limit Presidential authority?* a. *Introduction.* One of the few constitutional controversies between President and Congress that has reached the courts is the scope of executive control over personnel. Congressional authority to impeach includes "all civil officers," Art. II, sec. 5. See Yankwich, "Impeachment of Civil Officers under the Federal Constitution," 26 Geo.L.J. 849 (1938). May Congress play a role in the removal of officials by any other route, or is any further control solely in Presidential hands under the appointments provision, Art. II, sec. 2? The first modern judicial answer seemed to be a broad endorsement of executive autonomy, but subsequent decisions have found considerable room for congressional participation. See generally Corwin, The President: Office and Powers (4th ed. 1957).

b. *Myers and Humphrey's Executor.* Myers v. United States, 72 U.S. 52 (1926), involved a legislative provision that certain postmasters could not be removed by the President without the consent of the Senate. Chief Justice Taft's opinion for the Court, resting on an expansive reading of executive powers under Art. II, held that the statute was an unconstitutional restriction on the President's control over executive personnel. The Myers decision was limited, however, in Humphrey's Executor v. United States, 295 U.S. 602 (1935), involving removal of a member of an independent regulatory commission.

Humphrey was appointed by the President, with the consent of the Senate, a member of the Federal Trade Commission for a term of seven years. His resignation was requested by the President, and refused; the President then removed him from office. His executor instituted this action to recover salaries claimed due from the date of purported removal to the date of the Commissioner's death. The Supreme Court held that the Federal Trade Commission Act allows removal of a Commissioner only for causes therein specified and that, since the Commission acts primarily as a quasi-legislative agency, Congress may limit the President's power of removal: "To the extent that, between the decision in the Myers case, which sustains the unrestrictable power of the President to remove purely executive officers, and our present decision that such power does not extend to an office such as that here involved, there shall remain a field of doubt, we leave such cases as may fall within it for future consideration and determination as they may arise."

c. *Wiener.* Wiener v. United States, 357 U.S. 349 (1958), presented a "variant of the constitutional issue decided in" Humphrey's Executor. In order to make way for "personnel of my own selection," the President removed a member of the War Claims Commission. The Commission was established by Congress with "jurisdiction to receive and adjudicate according to law" certain claims for damages suffered at the hands of the enemy in connection with World War II. The members were appointed by the President by and with the advice and consent of the Senate; Congress made no provision for removal. The Court took the "essence" of the Humphrey decision to be that it "drew a sharp line of cleavage between officials who were part of the Executive establishment and were thus removable by virtue of the President's constitutional powers, and those who are members of a body 'to exercise its judgment without the leave or hindrance of any other official or any department of the government,' 295 U.S. at 625–626, as to whom a power of removal exists only if Congress may fairly be said to have conferred it. This sharp differentiation derives from the difference in functions between those who are part of the Executive establishment and those whose tasks require absolute freedom from Executive interference." Here the function of the Commission was of an "intrinsic judicial character." The Court concluded that "no such power [as claimed by him] is given to the President directly by the Constitution, and none is impliedly conferred upon him by statute simply because Congress said nothing about it. The philosophy of Humphrey's Executor . . . precludes such a claim."

3. *The pardoning power.* The President's power to grant reprieves and pardons, Art. II, Sec. 2, "is unlimited, with the exception stated [impeachment]. It extends to every offence known to the law, and may be exercised at any time after its commission, either before legal proceedings are taken, or during their pendency, or after conviction and judgment. This power of the President is not subject to legislative control." Ex parte Garland, 4 Wall. 333 (1866). But the allocation of this power to the President "has never been held to take from Congress the power to pass acts of general amnesty. . . . The distinction between amnesty and pardon is of no practical importance" except that amnesty "is generally applied where pardon is extended to whole classes or communities, instead of individuals, the distinction between them is one rather of philological interest than of legal importance." Brown v. Walker, 161 U.S. 591, 601 (1896). Recall United States v. Klein, 13 Wall. 128 (1872), considered in connection with the McCardle case, chap.

1, p. 54: in Klein, the congressional act withdrawing jurisdiction was found unconstitutional because it violated separation of powers in two respects—it not only interfered with the judicial power, but also with Presidential power to pardon.

4. *Delegation of legislative powers to the executive.* Contrast with the instances of executive-legislative conflict in the preceding notes, the problem of delegation of legislative powers. Delegation problems typically arise not when President and Congress are in conflict but when, if anything, they are in excessive harmony: the charge of improper delegation asserts that the legislature has left too much discretion to the executive, that Congress has not set forth sufficient guidance to the administrator. In two cases during the early New Deal period, the Court invalidated two acts as granting excessively broad authority to the President. Panama Refining Co. v. Ryan, 293 U.S. (chap. 4, p. 274, supra). In subsequent cases of economic regulations, how-(chap. 4, p. ——, supra). In subsequent cases of economic regulations, however, the Court has normally upheld broad delegations. See, e. g., Yakus v. United States, 321 U.S. 414 (1944). The problem of delegation in the regulation of foreign relations is considered in the Curtiss-Wright case, sec. 2, p. 593, of this chapter. There the Court indicated that the separation of powers standards of delegation applied to domestic affairs in Panama Refining and Schechter do not apply in the foreign affairs sphere; yet in dicta (quoted infra) in Kent v. Dulles, the 1958 passport regulation case, the Court cited Panama Refining Co. and not Curtiss-Wright in a case where the foreign affairs power allegedly clashed with individual rights. See generally Jaffe, "An Essay on Delegation of Legislative Power," 47 Colum.L.Rev. 359, 561 (1947), Selected Essays 1938–62 (1963), 89.

C. JUDICIAL—EXECUTIVE RELATIONS

Introduction. To what extent do separation of powers principles restrain judicial review of executive action? That issue was first encountered as early as Marbury v. Madison, the first case in this volume; and it was a broad insistence on executive immunity that was the primary source of President Jefferson's indignation over that decision. But John Marshall's asides in Marbury have prevailed: the Court will not abstain from all review simply because it is executive action that is challenged. The Court has not subjected the President himself to Court orders, to be sure: recall Mississippi v. (President Andrew) Johnson, 4 Wall. 475 (1867) (noted after McCardle, chap. 1, p. 51). Yet, despite the President's immunity, his judgments have not escaped scrutiny: they have been reexamined via suits to enjoin his subordinates from following his orders.

Mississippi v. Johnson stated that the Court lacked power to enjoin either President or Congress: neither "can be restrained in its action by the judicial department; though the acts of both, when performed, are, in proper cases, subject to its cognizance." The Court emphasized enforcement problems: If the President disobeyed an injunction, "it is needless to observe that the court is without power to enforce its process. If, on the other hand, the President complies with the order of the court and refuses to execute the acts of Congress, is it not clear that a collision may occur between the executive and legislative departments of the government? May not the House of

Representatives impeach the President for such refusal?   And in that case could this court interfere, in behalf of the President? "

Are those problems significantly diminished when a Cabinet member rather than the President is the defendant, as in the Steel Seizure Case? Should Mississippi v. Johnson have been mentioned by the Court there? Compare the problems of congressional immunity in Powell v. [Speaker of the House] McCormack, infra.   The process by which jurisdiction over federal executive action has developed—building in part on Marbury dicta— is sketched briefly in the notes that follow.

1. *The Kendall case and judicial control of federal executive action.* Marshall's statements in Marbury v. Madison with respect to the availability of mandamus to compel performance of ministerial acts by executive officials bore fruit in Kendall v. United States on the Relation of Stokes, 12 Pet. 524 (1838).   Congress had enacted a statute which directed the Postmaster General to credit the petitioner, Stokes, with certain sums to be determined by the solicitor of the Treasury.   When Postmaster General Kendall refused to allow the entire amount, the petitioner obtained a writ of mandamus from the Circuit Court of the District of Columbia.   The Supreme Court held unanimously that the Postmaster General had violated a ministerial duty in refusing to allow the credits and that mandamus was an appropriate common law remedy to enforce the duty.   Moreover, by a four to three vote, the Court held that the District of Columbia court had jurisdiction to issue mandamus, although earlier decisions had held that other federal courts had not been granted such statutory jurisdiction.   In the course of his opinion for the Court, Justice Thompson rejected sweeping arguments for the Postmaster General that issuance of the writ would constitute improper judicial interference with the actions of the executive:

"We do not think the proceedings in this case interfere, in any respect whatever, with the rights or duties of the executive; or that it involves any conflict of powers between the executive and judicial departments of the government.   The mandamus does not seek to direct or control the postmaster general in the discharge of any official duty, partaking in any respect of an executive character; but to enforce the performance of a mere ministerial act, which neither he nor the President had any authority to deny or control. . . .

"It was urged at the bar, that the postmaster general was alone subject to the direction and control of the President, with respect to the execution of the duty imposed upon him by this law; and this right of the President is claimed, as growing out of the obligation imposed upon him by the constitution, to take care that the laws be faithfully executed.   This is a doctrine that cannot receive the sanction of this court.   It would be vesting in the President a dispensing power, which has no countenance for its support in any part of the constitution; and is asserting a principle, which, if carried out in its results, to all cases falling within it, would be clothing the President with a power entirely to control the legislation of congress, and paralyze the administration of justice.

"To contend that the obligation imposed on the President to see the laws faithfully executed, implies a power to forbid their execution, is a novel construction of the constitution, and entirely inadmissible.   But although the argument necessarily leads to such a result, we do not perceive from the case that any such power has been claimed by the President."

2. *Continuing problems of remedies against federal officials.* The holding of the Kendall case by no means assured access to courts in all cases of illegal action by members of the executive branch. Indeed, considerable difficulties still remain in asserting claims against the United States and its officials—difficulties particularly stemming from uncertainties in the law of remedies and the availability of the defense of sovereign immunity. Consider, for example, the bases for private assertions of judicially enforceable rights against governmental officials in such cases as the Steel Seizure Case, supra. For a survey of the evolution since the Marbury and Kendall cases, and an analysis of the continuing problems, see "Developments in the Law— Remedies Against the United States and its Officials," 70 Harv.L.Rev. 827 (1957). On the occasionally greater availability of federal remedies against action of state officials, see Ex parte Young, 209 U.S. 123 (1908), chap. 2, p. 162, supra.

As an example of the contemporary nature of the problem, note that mandamus was available in Kendall only because the suit was brought in the District of Columbia, where there were courts of general jurisdiction. Other federal courts did not have jurisdiction to issue that writ in 1838—and did not obtain it until 1962, when 28 U.S.C. § 1361 was enacted: "The district courts shall have original jurisdiction of any action in the nature of mandamus to compel an officer or employee of the United States or any agency thereof to perform a duty owed to the plaintiff."

For an example of the recent tendency of the courts to expand the availability of remedies against executive officials—and to do so with rather inadequate elaboration of the reasons—see Harmon v. Brucker, 355 U.S. 579 (1958). Compare the careful analysis in Jones, "Jurisdiction of the Federal Courts to Review the Character of Military Administrative Discharges," 57 Colum.L.Rev. 917 (1957). The problem of judicial reexamination of executive judgments pertaining to military affairs is examined further in sec. 2 of this chapter, in connection with Ex parte Milligan, p. 611, infra.

D. JUDICIAL—LEGISLATIVE RELATIONS

Introduction. a. *Court review of congressional affairs and the Powell case.* A threshold question of separation of powers underlies every case in which the constitutionality of a congressional act is challenged: Do courts have *any* authority to review congressional judgments? That broad question was decided by Marbury v. Madison. But judicial competence to examine constitutionality has not meant that every congressional action is reviewable; and separation of powers principles have influenced the determination of the extent of Court authority. For example, the modern decisions shaping doctrines of standing and political questions (see chap. 2, supra) rest in large part on separation of powers considerations. Those considerations are especially prominent when courts are asked to re-examine the "internal affairs" of Congress; it is to focus on that especially sensitive variety of judicial consideration of legislative matters that the controversy about the seating of Congressman Powell is examined here. (Compare Bond v. Floyd, 385 U.S. 116

(1966) (p. ——, infra) examining a state legislature's refusal to seat an elected representative.)

b. *Congressional interference with judicial matters and the bills of attainder guarantee.* But separation considerations affect judicial-legislative relations in another direction as well: not only as a potential restraint on judicial interference in legislative matters but also as a check on legislative usurpation of judicial matters. That has already been noted in the materials following McCardle, chap. 1, p. 51: Article III itself, in its assignment of judicial powers to courts, may inhibit legislative withdrawals of jurisdiction. And there is an explicit safeguard against congressional usurpation of some judicial powers elsewhere in the Constitution: the prohibition of bills of attainder, in Art. I, Sec. 9. United States v. Brown, the final principal case in this section, examines a controversial modern application of that guarantee. That case and the related materials, moreover, emphasize that the bill of attainder provision, though typically invoked as a protection of the individual rights of dissidents, rests primarily on separation of powers values.

POWELL v. McCORMACK
395 U.S. 486, 81 S.Ct. 1944, 23 L.Ed.2d 491 (1969).

Certiorari to the United States Court of Appeals for the District of Columbia Circuit.

Mr. Chief Justice WARREN delivered the opinion of the Court.

In November 1966, Petitioner Adam Clayton Powell, Jr., was duly elected from the 18th Congressional District of New York to serve in the United States House of Representatives for the 90th Congress. However, pursuant to a House resolution, he was not permitted to take his seat. Powell (and some of the voters of his district) then filed suit in Federal District Court, claiming that the House could exclude him only if it found he failed to meet the standing requirements of age, citizenship, and residence contained in Art. I, § 2, of the Constitution—requirements the House specifically found Powell met—and thus had excluded him unconstitutionally. The District Court dismissed petitioners' complaint "for want of jurisdiction of the subject matter." The Court of Appeals affirmed the dismissal, although on somewhat different grounds, each judge [Burger, McGowan and Leventhal—see 395 F.2d 577 (1968)] filing a separate opinion. We have determined that it was error to dismiss the complaint and that Petitioner Powell is entitled to a declaratory judgment that he was unlawfully excluded from the 90th Congress.

I.—FACTS. . . .

When the 90th Congress met to organize in January 1967, Powell was asked to step aside while the oath was administered to the other members-elect. [Subsequently,] the House discussed the procedure to be followed in determining whether Powell was eligible to take his seat. After some debate, by a vote of 364 to 64 the House adopted House Resolution 1, which provided that the Speaker appoint a Select Committee to determine Powell's eligibility. . . .

. . . [O]n February 23, 1967, the Committee issued its report, finding that Powell met the standing qualifications of Art. I, § 2. . . .

However, the Committee further reported that Powell had asserted an unwarranted privilege and immunity from the processes of the courts of New York; that he had wrongfully diverted House funds for the use of others and himself; and that he had made false reports on expenditures of foreign currency to the Committee on House Administration. . . . The Committee recommended that Powell be sworn and seated as a member of the 90th Congress but that he be censured by the House, fined $40,000 and be deprived of his seniority. . . .

The report was presented to the House on March 1, 1967, and the House debated the Select Committee's proposed resolution. At the conclusion of the debate, by a vote of 222 to 202 the House rejected a motion to bring the resolution to a vote. An amendment to the resolution was then offered; it called for the exclusion of Powell and a declaration that his seat was vacant. The Speaker ruled that a majority vote of the House would be sufficient to pass the resolution if it were so amended. . . . After further debate, the amendment was adopted by a vote of 248 to 176. Then the House adopted by a vote of 307 to 116 House Resolution No. 278 in its amended form, thereby excluding Powell and directing that the Speaker notify the Governor of New York that the seat was vacant.

Powell and 13 voters of the 18th Congressional District of New York subsequently instituted this suit in the United States District Court for the District of Columbia. Five members of the House of Representatives were named as defendants individually and "as representatives of a class of citizens who are presently serving . . . as members of the House of Representatives." John W. McCormack was named in his official capacity as Speaker, and the Clerk of the House of Representatives, the Sergeant-at-Arms and the Doorkeeper were named individually and in their official capacities. The Complaint alleged that House Resolution No. 278 violated the Constitution, specifically Art. I, § 2, cl. 1, because the resolution was inconsistent with the mandate that the members of the House shall be elected by the people of each State, and Art. I, § 2, cl. 2, which, petitioners alleged, sets forth the exclusive qualifications for membership. The Complaint further alleged that the Clerk of the House threatened to refuse to perform the service for Powell to which a duly-elected Congressman is entitled, that the Sergeant-at-Arms refused to pay Powell his salary, and that the Doorkeeper threatened to deny Powell admission to the House Chamber.

Petitioners . . . requested the District Court grant a permanent injunction restraining respondents from executing the House Resolution, and enjoining the Speaker from refusing to administer the oath, the Clerk from refusing to perform the duties due a Representative, the Sergeant-at-Arms from refusing to pay Powell his salary and the Doorkeeper from refusing to admit Powell to the Chamber.[1] The complaint also requested a declaratory judgment that Powell's exclusion was unconstitutional. . . . While the case was pending on our docket [on certiorari], the 90th Congress officially terminated and the 91st Congress was seated. In November 1968, Powell had again been elected as the representative of the 18th Congressional District of New York, and he was seated by the 91st Congress. The resolution seating Powell also fined him $25,000. . . .

1. Petitioners also requested that a writ   named officials perform the same acts.
   of mandamus issue ordering that the   [Footnote by the Court.]

Respondents press upon us a variety of arguments to support the court below; they will be considered in the following order. (1) Events occurring subsequent to the grant of certiorari have rendered this litigation moot. (2) The Speech or Debate Clause of the Constitution, Art. I, § 6, insulates respondents' action from judicial review. (3) The decision to exclude Petitioner Powell is supported by the power granted to the House of Representatives to expel a member. (4) This Court lacks subject matter jurisdiction over petitioners' action. (5) Even if subject matter jurisdiction is present, this litigation is not justiciable either under the general criteria established by this Court or because a political question is involved.

II.—Mootness.

. . . We conclude that Powell's claim for back salary remains viable even though he has been seated in the 91st Congress and thus find it unnecessary to determine whether the other issues have become moot.[2] . . .

III.—Speech or Debate Clause

Respondents assert that the Speech or Debate Clause of the Constitution, Art. I, § 6, is an absolute bar to petitioners' action. . . . Freedom of legislative activity and the purposes of the Speech or Debate Clause are fully protected if legislators are relieved of the burden of defending themselves. In [Kilbourn v. Thompson, 103 U.S. 168 (1880), and Dombrowski v. Eastland, 387 U.S. 82 (1967)] we thus dismissed the action against members of Congress but did not regard the Speech or Debate Clause as a bar to reviewing the merits of the challenged congressional action since congressional employees were also sued. Similarly, this action may be dismissed against the Congressmen since petitioners are entitled to maintain their action against House employees and to judicial review of the propriety of the decision to exclude Petitioner Powell.[3] . . .

IV.—Exclusion or Expulsion

The resolution excluding Petitioner Powell was adopted by a vote in excess of two-thirds of the 434 Members of Congress—307 to 116. . . Article I, § 5, grants the House authority to expel a member "with the Concurrence of two thirds."[4] Respondents assert that the House may expel a

---

2. Petitioners do not press their claim that respondent McCormack should be required to administer the oath to Powell, apparently conceding that the seating of Powell has rendered this specific claim moot. Where several forms of relief are requested and one of these requests subsequently becomes moot, the Court has still considered the remaining requests. . . . Respondents also argue that the seating of Petitioner Powell has mooted the claims of Powell's constituents. Since this case will be remanded, that issue as well as petitioners' other claims can be disposed of by the court below. [Footnote by the Court.]

3. Given our disposition of this issue, we need not decide whether under the Speech or Debate Clause petitioners would be entitled to maintain this action solely against members of Congress where no agents participated in the challenged action and no other remedy was available. Cf. Kilbourn v. Thompson, 103 U.S. 168, 204–205 (1880). [Footnote by the Court.]

4. Powell was "excluded" from the 90th Congress, i. e., he was not administered the oath of office and was prevented from taking his seat. If he had been allowed to take the oath and subsequently had been required to surrender his seat, the House's action would have constituted an "expulsion." Since we conclude that Powell was excluded from the 90th Congress, we express no view on what limitations

member for any reason whatsoever and that, since a two-thirds vote was obtained, the procedure by which Powell was denied his seat in the 90th Congress should be regarded as an expulsion not an exclusion. . . .

. . . The Speaker ruled that the House was voting to exclude Powell, and we will not speculate what the result might have been if Powell had been seated and expulsion proceedings subsequently instituted. Nor is the distinction between exclusion and expulsion merely one of form. The misconduct for which Powell was charged occurred prior to the convening of the 90th Congress. On several occasions the House has debated whether a member can be expelled for actions taken during a prior Congress . . . [W]e will not assume that two-thirds of its members would have expelled Powell for his prior conduct had the Speaker announced that House Resolution 278 was for expulsion rather than exclusion. . . .

V.—SUBJECT MATTER JURISDICTION

As we pointed out in Baker v. Carr [chap. 2, p. 177, supra], there is a significant difference between determining whether a federal court has "jurisdiction over the subject matter" and determining whether a cause over which a court has subject matter jurisdiction is "justiciable." The District Court determined that "to decide this case on the merits . . . would constitute a clear violation of the doctrine of separation of powers" and then dismissed the complaint "for want of jurisdiction of the subject matter." . . . However, as the Court of Appeals correctly recognized, the doctrine of separation of powers is more properly considered in determining whether the case is "justiciable." We agree with the unanimous conclusion of the Court of Appeals that the District Court had jurisdiction over the subject matter of this case. However, for reasons set forth in Part VI, infra, we disagree with the Court of Appeals' conclusion that this case is not justiciable. . . .

Respondents . . . contend that this is not a case "arising under" the Constitution within the meaning of Article III. They emphasize that Art. I, § 5, assigns to each house of Congress the power to judge the elections and qualifications of its own members and to punish its members for disorderly behavior. Respondents also note that under Art. I, § 3, the Senate has the "sole power" to try all impeachments. Respondents argue that these delegations (to "judge," to "punish," and to "try") to the Legislative Branch are explicit grants of "judicial power" to the Congress and constitute specific exceptions to the general mandate of Article III that the "judicial power" shall be vested in the federal courts. Thus, respondents maintain, the "power conferred on the courts by article III does not authorize this Court to do anything more than declare its lack of jurisdiction to proceed."

We reject this contention. . . . It has long been held that a suit "arises under" the Constitution if petitioners' claims "will be sustained if the Constitution . . . [is] given one construction and will be defeated if it [is] given another." . . . Thus, this case clearly is one "arising under" the Constitution as the Court has interpreted that phrase. Any bar to federal courts reviewing the judgments made by the House or Senate in excluding a

may exist on Congress' power to expel or otherwise punish a member once he has been seated. [Footnote by the Court.]

member arises from the allocation of powers between the two branches of the Federal Government (a question of justiciability), and not from the petitioners' failure to state a claim based on federal law. . . .

VI.—Justiciability

. . . Two determinations must be made in this regard. First, we must decide whether the claim presented and the relief sought are of the type which admit of judicial resolution. Second, we must determine whether the structure of the Federal Government renders the issue presented a "political question"—that is, a question which is not justiciable in federal court because of the separation of powers provided by the Constitution.

A. *General Considerations.*

. . . Respondents do not seriously contend that the duty asserted and its alleged breach cannot be judicially determined. . . . Respondents do maintain, however, that this case is not justiciable because, they assert, it is impossible for a federal court to "mold effective relief for resolving this case." Respondents emphasize that petitioners asked for coercive relief against the officers of the House, and, they contend, federal courts cannot issue mandamus or injunctions compelling officers or employees of the House to perform specific official acts. Respondents rely primarily on the Speech or Debate Clause to support this contention.

We need express no opinion about the appropriateness of coercive relief in this case, for petitioners sought a declaratory judgment, a form of relief the District Court could have issued. . . . [A] request for declaratory relief may be considered independently of whether other forms of relief are appropriate. . . . We thus conclude that in terms of the general criteria of justiciability, this case is justiciable.

B. *Political Question Doctrine.*
1. Textually Demonstrable Constitutional Commitment.

. . . Respondents' first contention is that this case presents a political question because under Art. I, § 5, there has been a "textually demonstrable constitutional commitment" to the House of the "adjudicatory power" to determine Powell's qualifications. Thus it is argued that the House, and the House alone, has power to determine who is qualified to be a member.

In order to determine whether there has been a textual commitment to a co-ordinate department of the Government, we must interpret the Constitution. In other words, we must first determine what power the Constitution confers upon the House through Art. I, § 5, before we can determine to what extent, if any, the exercise of that power is subject to judicial review. . . . If examination of § 5 disclosed that the Constitution gives the House judicially unreviewable power to set qualifications for membership and to judge whether prospective members meet those qualifications, further review of the House determination might well be barred by the political question doctrine. On the other hand, if the Constitution gives the House power to judge only whether elected members possess the three standing qualifications set forth in the Constitution, further consideration would be necessary to determine whether any of the other formulations of the political question doctrine are "inextricable from the case at bar." [5] Baker v. Carr . . . . .

In order to determine the scope of any "textual commitment" under Art. I, § 5, we necessarily must determine the meaning of the phrase to "judge the qualifications of its members." Petitioners argue that the records of the debates during the Constitutional Convention, available commentary from the post-Convention, pre-ratification period, and early congressional applications of Art. I, § 5, support their construction of the section. Respondents insist, however, that a careful examination of the pre-Convention practices of the English Parliament and American colonial assemblies demonstrates that by 1787, a legislature's power to judge the qualifications of its members was generally understood to encompass exclusion or expulsion on the ground that an individual's character or past conduct rendered him unfit to serve. When the Constitution and the debates over its adoption are thus viewed in historical perspective, argue respondents, it becomes clear that the "qualifications" expressly set forth in the Constitution were not meant to limit the long recognized legislative power to exclude or expel at will, but merely to establish "standing incapacities," which could be altered only by a constitutional amendment. Our examination of the relevant historical materials leads us to the conclusion that petitioners are correct and that the Constitution leaves the House without authority to *exclude* any person, duly elected by his constituents, who meets all the requirements for membership expressly prescribed in the Constitution. . . .

Had the intent of the Framers emerged from these materials with less clarity, we would nevertheless have been compelled to resolve any ambiguity in favor of a narrow construction of the scope of Congress' power to exclude members-elect. A fundamental principle of our representative democracy is, in Hamilton's words, "that the people should choose whom they please to govern them." 2 Elliot's Debates 257. As Madison pointed out at the Convention, this principle is undermined as much by limiting whom the people can select as by limiting the franchise itself. In apparent agreement with this basic philosophy, the Convention adopted his suggestion limiting the power to expel. To allow essentially that same power to be exercised under the guise of judging qualifications would be to ignore Madison's warning, borne out in the Wilkes case and some of Congress' own post-Civil War exclusion cases, against "vesting an improper & dangerous power in the Legislature." 2 Farrand 249. Moreover, it would effectively nullify the Convention's decision to require a two-third vote for expulsion. Unquestionably, Congress has an interest in preserving its institutional integrity, but in most cases that interest can be sufficiently safeguarded by the exercise of its power to punish its members for disorderly behavior and, in extreme cases, to expel a member with the concurrence of two-thirds. In short, both the intention of the Framers, to the extent it can be determined, and an examination of the basic principles of our democratic system persuade us that the Constitution does not vest in the Congress a discretionary power to deny membership by a majority vote.

5. Consistent with this interpretation, federal courts might still be barred by the political question doctrine from reviewing the House's factual determination that a member did not meet one of the standing qualifications. This is an issue not presented in this case and we express no view as to its resolution. [Footnote by the Court.]

For these reasons, we have concluded that Art. I, § 5, is at most a "textually demonstrable commitment" to Congress to judge only the qualifications expressly set forth in the Constitution.   Therefore, the "textual commitment" formulation of the political question doctrine does not bar federal courts from adjudicating petitioners' claims.

2.   Other Considerations.

Respondents' alternate contention is that the case presents a political question because judicial resolution of petitioners' claim would produce a "potentially embarrassing confrontation between coordinate branches" of the Federal Government.   But, as our interpretation of Art. I, § 5, discloses, a determination of Petitioner Powell's right to sit would require no more than an interpretation of the Constitution.   Such a determination falls within the traditional role accorded courts to interpret the law, and does not involve a "lack of respect due [a] coordinate branch of government," nor does it involve an "initial policy determination of a kind clearly for nonjudicial discretion."   Baker v. Carr, supra, at 217.   Our system of government requires that federal courts on occasion interpret the Constitution in a manner at variance with the construction given the document by another branch.   The alleged conflict [6] that such an adjudication may cause cannot justify the courts' avoiding their constitutional responsibility.   . . .

Nor are any of the other formulations of a political question "inextricable from the case at bar."   Baker v. Carr, supra, at 217.   Petitioners seek a determination that the House was without power to exclude Powell from the 90th Congress, which, we have seen, requires an interpretation of the Constitution—a determination for which clearly there are "judicially manageable standards."   Finally, a judicial resolution of petitioners' claim will not result in "multifarious pronouncements by various departments on one question." For, as we noted in Baker v. Carr, supra, at 211, it is the responsibility of this Court to act as the ultimate interpreter of the Constitution.   Marbury v. Madison, 1 Cranch 137 (1803).   Thus, we conclude that petitioners' claim is not barred by the political question doctrine, and having determined that the claim is otherwise generally justiciable, we hold that the case is justiciable.

VII.—CONCLUSION

To summarize, we have determined the following: (1) This case has not been mooted by Powell's seating in the 91st Congress.   (2) Although this action should be dismissed against respondent Congressmen, it may be sustained against their agents.   (3) The 90th Congress' denial of membership to Powell cannot be treated as an expulsion.   (4) We have jurisdiction over the subject matter of this controversy.   (5) The case is justiciable.

Further, analysis of the "textual commitment" under Art. I, § 5 (see Part VI, Section B(1)), has demonstrated that in judging the qualifications of its members Congress is limited to the standing qualifications prescribed in the Constitution.   Respondents concede that Powell met these.   Thus, there is no need to remand this case to determine whether he was entitled to be seated in the 90th Congress.   Therefore, we hold that, since Adam Clay-

---

6. In fact, the Court has noted that it is an "inadmissible suggestion" that action might be taken in disregard of a judicial determination.   McPherson v. Blacker, 146 U.S. 1, 24 (1892).   [Footnote by the Court.]

ton Powell, Jr., was duly elected by the voters of the 18th Congressional District of New York and was not ineligible to serve under any provision of the Constitution, the House was without power to exclude him from its membership.

Petitioners seek additional forms of equitable relief, including mandamus for the release of Petitioner Powell's back pay. The propriety of such remedies, however, is more appropriately considered in the first instance by the courts below. Therefore, as to Respondents McCormack, Albert, Ford, Celler, and Moore, the judgment of the Court of Appeals for the District of Columbia Circuit is affirmed. As to Respondents Jennings, Johnson, and Miller, the judgment of the Court of Appeals for the District of Columbia Circuit is reversed and the case is remanded to that court with instructions to enter a declaratory judgment and for further proceedings consistent with this opinion.

It is so ordered.

Mr. Justice DOUGLAS. [The concurring opinion, omitted here, included the statement: "If this were an expulsion case I would think that no justiciable controversy were presented, the vote of the House being two-thirds or more."]

Mr. Justice STEWART, dissenting.

I believe that events which have taken place since certiorari was granted in this case on November 18, 1968, have rendered it moot, and that the Court should therefore refrain from deciding the novel, difficult, and delicate constitutional questions which the case presented at its inception. . . .[1]

The passage of time and intervening events have . . . made it impossible to afford the petitioners the principal relief they sought in this case. If any aspect of the case remains alive, it is only Congressman Powell's individual claim for the salary of which he was deprived by his absence from the 90th Congress. But even if that claim can be said to prevent this controversy from being moot, which I doubt, there is no need to reach the fundamental constitutional issues that the Court today undertakes to decide.

[T]he availability of effective relief for that [salary] claim against any of the present respondents is far from certain. [T]he Sergeant-at-Arms of the House—an official newly elected by each Congress—is responsible for the retention and disbursement to Congressmen of the funds appropriated for their salaries. These funds are payable from the United States Treasury upon requisitions presented by the Sergeant-at-Arms, who is entrusted with keeping the books and accounts "for the compensation and mileage of Members." A Congressman who has presented his credentials and taken the oath of office is entitled to be paid monthly on the basis of certificates of the Clerk

1. . . . The petitioners' argument that the case is kept alive by Powell's loss of seniority . . . is founded on the mistaken assumption that the loss of seniority is attributable to the exclusion from the 90th Congress and that seniority would automatically be restored if that exclusion were declared unconstitutional. But the fact is that Powell was stripped of seniority by the action of the 91st Congress, action which is not involved in this case and which would not be affected by judicial review of the exclusion from the 90th Congress. Moreover, even if the conduct of the 91st Congress were challenged in this case, the Court would clearly have no power whatsoever to pass upon the propriety of such internal affairs of the House of Representatives. [Footnote by Justice Stewart.]

and Speaker of the House. Powell's prayer for a mandamus and an injunction against the Sergeant-at-Arms is presumably based on this statutory scheme.

Several important questions remain unanswered, however, on this record. [I]t is far from clear that Powell has an appropriate or adequate remedy against the remaining respondents. For if the Speaker does not issue the requisite certificates and Congress does not rescind Resolution 278, can the House agents be enjoined to act in direct contravention of the orders of their employers? Moreover, the office of Sergeant-at-Arms of the 90th Congress has now expired, and the present Sergeant-at-Arms serves the 91st Congress. If he were made a party in that capacity, would he have the authority—or could the 91st Congress confer the authority—to disburse money for a salary owed to a Representative in the previous Congress, particularly one who never took the oath of office? Presumably funds have not been appropriated to the 91st Congress or requisitioned by its Sergeant-at-Arms for the payment of salaries to members of prior Congresses. Nor is it ascertainable from this record whether money appropriated for Powell's salary by the 90th Congress, if any, remains at the disposal of the current House and its Sergeant-at-Arms.

There are, then, substantial questions as to whether, on his salary claim, Powell could obtain relief against any or all of these respondents. On the other hand, if he was entitled to salary as a member of the 90th Congress, he has a certain and completely satisfactory remedy in an action for a money judgment against the United States in the Court of Claims. . . . I would remit Congressman Powell to that remedy, and not simply because of the serious doubts about the availability of the one he now pursues. Even if the mandatory relief sought by Powell is appropriate and could be effective, the Court should insist that the salary claim be litigated in a context that would clearly obviate the need to decide some of the constitutional questions with which the Court grapples today, and might avoid them altogether.[2]

. . .

If this lawsuit is to be prolonged, I would at the very least not reach the merits without ascertaining that a decision can lead to some effective relief. The Court's remand for determination of that question implicitly recognizes that there may be no remaining controversy between the Petitioner Powell and any of these respondents redressable by a court, and that its opinion today may be wholly advisory. But I see no good reason for any court even to pass on the question of the availability of relief against any of these respondents. Because the essential purpose of the action against them is no longer attainable and Powell has a fully adequate and far more appropriate remedy for his incidental back pay claim, I would withhold the discretionary relief prayed for and terminate this lawsuit now. Powell's *claim* for salary may not be dead, but this *case* against all these respondents is truly moot. . . .

---

2. It is possible, for example, that the United States in such an action would not deny Powell's entitlement to the salary but would seek to offset that sum against the amounts which Powell was found by the House to have appropriated unlawfully from Government coffers to his own use. [Footnote by Justice Stewart.]

BILLS OF ATTAINDER BEFORE BROWN

1. *The post-Civil War oaths: Cummings and Garland.* The bar on legislative usurpation of judicial functions represented by the bill of attainder prohibition received its first major Supreme Court examination during the Reconstruction Era, in the context of state as well as federal legislative attempts to exclude former supporters of the Confederacy from certain professions. (There is a counterpart to the Art. I, Sec. 9, ban on congressional bills of attainder in Art. I, Sec. 10, applicable to the states.)

In Cummings v. Missouri, 4 Wall. 277 (1867), and Ex parte Garland, 4 Wall. 333 (1867), the Court found the challenged loyalty oath provisions to be bills of attainder. In Cummings, the Court gave the following definition: "A bill of attainder is a legislative act which inflicts punishment without a judicial trial. If the punishment be less than death, the act is termed a bill of pains and penalties. In these cases the legislative body, in addition to its legitimate functions, exercises the powers and office of judge; it assumes, in the language of the text-books, judicial magistracy; it pronounces upon the guilt of the party, without any of the forms or safeguards of trial; it determines the sufficiency of the proofs produced, whether conformable to the rules of evidence or otherwise; and it fixes the degree of punishment in accordance with its own notions of the enormity of the offence."

In the Cummings case, the Court held invalid a Missouri provision which required of all priests and clergymen—as well as teachers, lawyers, and corporate officials—as a condition to the continued practice of their professions, an oath that they had not given aid to the enemies of the United States. (The Court held, moreover, that the law violated another constitutional prohibition—one coupled with that on bills of attainder in Art. I: the law was found to be an ex post facto law because it imposed punishment for past acts.* The Court found no relevant connection between past sympathy for the Confederacy and present professional fitness and concluded that the oath was exacted "not from any notion that the several acts designated indicated unfitness for the callings, but because it was thought that the several acts deserved punishment." (Recall the discussion in Flemming v. Nestor, the loss-of-social-security-benefits case in chap. 5, p. 437, supra.) In a companion case, Ex parte Garland, 4 Wall. 333 (1867), the Court held invalid an Act of Congress of 1865 which prohibited practice in federal courts by any attorney or counsel unless he had taken an oath that he had never en-

---

* The prohibition against ex post facto laws operates as a restraint on legislative power; it does not apply to changes effected by judicial decision. Ross v. Oregon, 227 U.S. 150 (1913). It was settled early that the ban applied to criminal, not civil, legislation. Calder v. Bull, 3 Dall. 386 (1798). Compare Justice Johnson's regretful comments on that limitation to criminal cases, in the Appendix to 2 Pet., at 681 (1829). In Calder v. Bull, the Court said the clause applied to the following: "1st. Every law that makes an action done before the passing of the law, and which was innocent when done, criminal; and punishes such action. 2d. Every law that aggravates a crime, or makes it greater than it was, when committed. 3d. Every law that changes the punishment, and inflicts a greater punishment, than the law annexed to the crime, when committed. 4th. Every law that alters the legal rules of evidence, and receives less or different, testimony, than the law required at the time of the commission of the offence, in order to convict the offender."

gaged in hostility to the United States. [Compare the modern loyalty oath cases involving public employees, chap. 16, p. 1300, infra.]

2. *The Lovett Case.* Compare United States v. Lovett, 328 U.S. 303 (1946): An Act of Congress provided that after a certain date no compensation should be paid to certain designated government agency employees, whose conduct had been the subject of investigation by a Congressional Committee. Respondents continued to work after the prescribed time and sued in the Court of Claims for reimbursement. Affirming a judgment in their favor, the Supreme Court held that the provision violated the prohibition against bills of attainder. See generally Note, "The Bounds of Legislative Specification: A Suggested Approach to the Bill of Attainder Clause," 72 Yale L.J. 330 (1962), which the Court relied on in Brown, the next case.

UNITED STATES v. BROWN

381 U.S. 437, 85 S.Ct. 1707, 14 L.Ed.2d 484 (1965).

Certiorari to the Court of Appeals for the Ninth Circuit.

Mr. Chief Justice WARREN delivered the opinion of the Court.

In this case we review for the first time a conviction under § 504 of the Labor-Management Reporting and Disclosure Act of 1959, which makes it a crime for a member of the Communist Party to serve as an officer or (except in clerical or custodial positions) as an employee of a labor union. Section 504, the purpose of which is to protect the national economy by minimizing the danger of political strikes,[1] was enacted to replace § 9(h) of the Taft-Hartley Act, which conditioned a union's access to the National Labor Relations Board upon the filing of affidavits by all of the union's officers attesting that they were not members of or affiliated with the Communist Party.

Respondent has been a working longshoreman on the San Francisco docks, and an open and avowed Communist, for more than a quarter of a century. He was elected to the Executive Board of Local 10 of the International Longshoremen's and Warehousemen's Union for consecutive one-year terms in 1959, 1960, and 1961. On May 24, 1961, respondent was charged in a one-count indictment returned in the Northern District of California with "knowingly and wilfully serv[ing] as a member of an executive board of a labor organization . . . while a member of the Communist Party, in wilful violation of Title 29, United States Code, Section 504." It was neither charged nor proven that respondent at any time advocated or suggested illegal activity by the union, or proposed a political strike. The jury found respondent guilty, and he was sentenced to six months' imprisonment. The Court of Appeals for the Ninth Circuit, sitting *en banc,* reversed and remanded with instructions to set aside the conviction and dismiss the indictment, holding that § 504 violates the First and Fifth Amendments to the Constitution. We granted certiorari, 379 U.S. 899.

1. In American Communications Ass'n v. Douds, 339 U.S. 382, 388 [1950], this Court found that "the purpose of § 9(h) of the [Taft-Hartley] Act [was] to remove . . . the so-called 'political strike'." Section 504 was designed to accomplish the same purpose as § 9(h), but in a more direct and effective way. H.R.Rep.No.741, 86th Cong., 1st Sess., p. 33; H.R.Rep.No.1147, 86th Cong., 1st Sess., p. 36. [Numbered footnotes by the Court.]

Respondent urges—in addition to the grounds relied on by the court below—that the statute under which he was convicted is a bill of attainder, and therefore violates Art. I, § 9, of the Constitution. We agree that § 504 is void as a bill of attainder and affirm the decision of the Court of Appeals on that basis. We therefore find it unnecessary to consider the First and Fifth Amendment arguments.

The provisions outlawing bills of attainder were adopted by the Constitutional Convention unanimously, and without debate. . . . A logical starting place for an inquiry into the meaning of the prohibition is its historical background. The bill of attainder, a parliamentary act sentencing to death one or more specific persons, was a device often resorted to in sixteenth, seventeenth and eighteenth century England for dealing with persons who had attempted, or threatened to attempt, to overthrow the government. . . The "bill of pains and penalties" was identical to the bill of attainder, except that it prescribed a penalty short of death . . . . Most bills of attainder and bills of pains and penalties named the parties to whom they were to apply; a few, however, simply described them. While some left the designated parties a way of escaping the penalty, others did not. . . .

While history . . . provides some guidelines, the wide variation in form, purpose and effect of ante-constitutional bills of attainder indicates that the proper scope of the Bill of Attainder Clause, and its relevance to contemporary problems, must ultimately be sought by attempting to discern the reasons for its inclusion in the Constitution, and the evils it was designed to eliminate. The best available evidence, the writings of the architects of our constitutional system, indicates that the Bill of Attainder Clause was intended not as a narrow, technical (and therefore soon to be outmoded) prohibition, but rather as an implementation of the separation of powers, a general safeguard against legislative exercise of the judicial function, or more simply—trial by legislature. . . . [T]he Bill of Attainder Clause not only was intended as one implementation of the general principle of fractionalized power, but also reflected the Framers' belief that the Legislative Branch is not so well suited as politically independent judges and juries to the task of ruling upon the blameworthiness of, and levying appropriate punishment upon, specific persons. [The Court's discussion of the Cummings, Garland, and Lovett cases is omitted.]

Under the line of cases just outlined, § 504 plainly constitutes a bill of attainder. Congress undoubtedly possesses power under the Commerce Clause to enact legislation designed to keep from positions affecting interstate commerce persons who may use such positions to bring about political strikes. In § 504, however, Congress has exceeded the authority granted it by the Constitution. The statute does not set forth a generally applicable rule decreeing that any person who commits certain acts or possesses certain characteristics (acts and characteristics which, in Congress' view, make them likely to initiate political strikes) shall not hold union office, and leave to courts and juries the job of deciding what persons have committed the specified acts or possess the specified characteristics. Instead, it designates in no uncertain terms the persons who possess the feared characteristics and therefore cannot hold union office without incurring criminal liability—members of the Communist Party.[2] . . .

2. We of course take no position on whether or not members of the Com-

munist Party are in fact likely to incite political strikes. The point we

The Solicitor General points out that in Board of Governors v. Agnew, 320 U.S. 441, this Court applied § 32 of the Banking Act of 1933 . . . .*
He suggests that for purposes of the Bill of Attainder Clause, such conflict-of-interest laws are not meaningfully distinguishable from the statute before us. We find this argument without merit. First, we note that § 504, unlike § 32 of the Banking Act, inflicts its deprivation upon the members of a political group thought to present a threat to the national security. . . .
Second, § 32 incorporates no judgment censuring or condemning any man or group of men. In enacting it, Congress relied upon its general knowledge of human psychology, and concluded that the concurrent holding of the two designated positions would present a temptation to *any* man—not just certain men or members of a certain political party. Thus insofar as § 32 incorporates a condemnation, it condemns all men. Third, we cannot accept the suggestion that § 32 constitutes an exercise in specification rather than rule-making. It seems to us clear that § 32 establishes an objective standard of conduct. Congress determined that a person who both (a) held a position in a bank which could be used to influence the investment policies of the bank or its customers, and (b) was in a position to benefit financially from investment in the securities handled by a particular underwriting house, might well be tempted to "use his influence in the bank to involve it or its customers in securities which his underwriting house has in its portfolio or has committed itself to take." 329 U.S., at 447. In designating bank officers, directors and employees as those persons in position (a), and officers, directors, partners and employees of underwriting houses as those persons in position (b), Congress merely expressed the characteristics it was trying to reach in an alternative, shorthand way.[3] . . .

It is argued, however, that in § 504 Congress did no more than it did in enacting § 32: it promulgated a general rule to the effect that persons possessing characteristics which make them likely to incite political strikes should not hold union office, and simply inserted in place of a list of those characteristics an alternative, shorthand criterion—membership in the Communist Party. Again, we cannot agree. The designation of Communists as

make is rather that the Constitution forbids Congress from making such determinations. [Footnote by the Court.]

* Section 32 of the Banking Act provides: "No officer, director, or employee of any corporation or unincorporated association, no partner or employee of any partnership, and no individual, primarily engaged in the issue, flotation, underwriting, public sale, or distribution, at wholesale or retail, or through syndicate participation, of stocks, bonds, or other similar securities, shall serve the same time as an officer, director, or employee of any member bank except in limited classes of cases in which the Board of Governors of the Federal Reserve System may allow such service by general regulations when in the judgment of the said Board it would not unduly influence the investment policies of such member bank or the ad-

vice it gives its customers regarding investments."

3.   The command of the Bill of Attainder Clause—that a legislature can provide that persons possessing certain characteristics must abstain from certain activities, but must leave to other tribunals the task of deciding who possesses those characteristics—does not mean that a legislature cannot use a shorthand phrase to summarize the characteristics with which it is concerned. For example, a legislature might determine that persons afflicted with a certain disease which has as one of its symptoms a susceptibility to uncontrollable seizures should not be licensed to operate dangerous machinery. In enacting a statute to achieve this goal, the legislature could name the disease instead of listing the symptoms, for in doing so it would merely be substituting a shorthand phrase which conveys the same meaning.

those persons likely to cause political strikes is not the substitution of a semantically equivalent phrase; on the contrary, it rests, as the Court in Douds explicitly recognized, 339 U.S., at 389, upon an empirical investigation by Congress of the acts, characteristsics and propensities of Communist Party members. In a number of decisions, this Court has pointed out the fallacy of the suggestion that membership in the Communist Party, or any other political organization, can be regarded as an alternative, but equivalent, expression for a list of undesirable characteristics. [See the Communist Party and membership cases in chap. 15, infra.] These cases are relevant to the question before us. Even assuming that Congress had reason to conclude that some Communists would use union positions to bring about political strikes, "it cannot automatically be inferred that all members shar[e] their evil purposes or participat[e] in their illegal activities." Schware v. Board of Bar Examiners, 353 U.S. 232, 246. In utilizing the term "members of the Communist Party" to designate those persons who are likely to incite political strikes, it plainly is not the case that Congress has merely substituted a convenient shorthand term for a list of the characteristics it was trying to reach.

The Solicitor General argues that § 504 is not a bill of attainder because the prohibition it imposes does not constitute "punishment." In support of this conclusion, he urges that the statute was enacted for preventive rather than retributive reasons—that its aim is not to punish Communists for what they have done in the past, but rather to keep them from positions where they will in the future be able to bring about undesirable events. [It] clearly appears that § 504 inflicts "punishment" within the meaning of the Bill of Attainder Clause. It would be archaic to limit the definition of "punishment" to "retribution." Punishment serves several purposes: retributive, rehabilitative, deterrent—and preventive. One of the reasons society imprisons those convicted of crimes is to keep them from inflicting future harm, but that does not make imprisonment any the less punishment. . . .

The Solicitor General urges us to distinguish Lovett on the ground that the statute struck down there "singled out three identified individuals." It is of course true that § 504 does not contain the words "Archie Brown," and that it inflicts its deprivation upon more than three people. However, the decisions of this Court, as well as the historical background of the Bill of Attainder Clause, make it crystal clear that these are distinctions without a difference. . . . We cannot agree that the fact that § 504 inflicts its deprivation upon the membership of the Communist Party rather than upon a list of named individuals takes it out of the category of bills of attainder.

We do not hold today that Congress cannot weed dangerous persons out of the labor movement, any more than the Court held in Lovett that subversives must be permitted to hold sensitive government positions. Rather, we make again the point made in Lovett: that Congress must accomplish such results by rules of general applicability. It cannot specify the people upon whom the sanction it prescribes is to be levied. Under our Constitution, Congress possesses full legislative authority, but the task of adjudication must be left to other tribunals. . . .

Affirmed.

Mr. Justice WHITE, with whom Mr. Justice CLARK, Mr. Justice HARLAN, and Mr. Justice STEWART join, dissenting. . . .

It is not difficult to find some of the cases and statutes which the necessary implications of the Court's approach will overrule or invalidate. American Communications Assn. v. Douds, 339 U.S. 382, which upheld the predecessor statute to § 504, is obviously overruled. . . . Similarly invalidated are statutes denying positions of public importance to groups of persons identified by their business affiliations, commonly known as conflict-of-interest statutes. . . .

In terms of the Court's analysis of the Bill of Attainder Clause, no meaningful distinction may be drawn between § 32 of the Banking Act [footnote * supra] and § 504. . . . Other legislative enactments relevant here are those statutes disqualifying felons from occupying certain positions. The leading case is Hawker v. New York, 170 U.S. 189, which upheld a provision prohibiting convicted felons from practicing medicine . . .. Though the Court makes no attempt to distinguish the Hawker type laws it apparently would save them, . . . and with them the provision of the statute now before the Court which disqualifies felons from holding union office. . . . Examples of statutes that will now be suspect because of the Court's opinion but were, until today, unanimously accepted as legitimate exercises of legislative power could easily be multiplied. Such a catalogue in itself would lead one to inquire whether the Court's reasoning does not contain some flaw that explains such perverse results.

One might well begin by challenging the Court's premise that the Bill of Attainder Clause was intended to provide a general dividing line between legislative and judicial functions and thereby to operate as the chief means of implementing the separation of powers. . . . [T]here are substantial reasons for concluding that the Bill of Attainder Clause may not be regarded as enshrining any general rule distinguishing between the legislative and judicial functions. . . .

The basic flaw in the Court's reasoning, however, is its too narrow view of the legislative process. . . . Congress is held to have violated the Bill of Attainder Clause here because, on the one hand, § 504 does not encompass the whole class of persons having characteristics that would make them likely to call political strikes and, on the other hand, § 504 does single out a particular group, members of the Communist Party, not all of whom possess such characteristics. Because of this combination of underinclusiveness and overinclusiveness the Court concludes that Communist Party members were singled out for punishment, thus rejecting the Government's contention that § 504 has solely a regulatory aim.

The Court's conclusion that a statute which is both underinclusive and overinclusive must be deemed to have been adopted with a punitive purpose assumes that legislatures normally deal with broad categories and attack all of an evil at a time. Or if partial measures are undertaken, a legislature singles out a particular group for regulation only because the group label is a "shorthand phrase" for traits that are characteristic of the broader evil. But this Court has long recognized in equal protection cases that a legislature may prefer to deal with only part of an evil. [See chap. 14, infra.] And it is equally true that a group may be singled out for regulation without any punitive purpose even when not all members of the group would be likely to engage in the feared conduct. . . . That is, the focus of legislative attention may be the substantial greater likelihood that some members of the group would engage in the feared conduct compared to the likelihood that members of other groups would do so. This is true because legislators seldom deal with abstractions but with concrete situations and the regulation of specific abuses. Thus many regulatory measures are enacted after investigation into particular incidents or the practices of particular groups and after findings by the legislature that the practices disclosed are inimical to the public interest and should be prevented in the future. Not surprisingly, the resulting legislation may reflect in its specificity the specificity of the preceding legislative inquiry. . . . But the fact that it does should not be taken, in itself, to be conclusive that the legislature's purpose is punitive. Admittedly the degree of specificity is a relevant factor—as when individuals are singled out by name—but because in many instances specificity of the the degree here held impermissible may be wholly consistent with a regulatory, rather than a punitive purpose, the Court's *per se* approach cuts too broadly and invalidates legitimate legislative activity.

Putting aside the Court's *per se* approach based on the nature of the classification specified by the legislation, we must still test § 504 against the traditional definition of the bill of attainder as legislative punishment of particular individuals. In my view, § 504 does not impose punishment and is not a bill of attainder.

We have said that "only the clearest proof could suffice" to establish that Congress' purpose was punitive rather than regulatory. Flemming v. Nestor, 363 U.S. 603, 617. . . . Congress' concern with the possibility of political strikes is not simply a fictional concern advanced to mask a punitive purpose. Congress has sought to forestall political strikes since 1947, when it adopted § 9(h) of the Taft-Hartley Act, which was sustained as a reasonable regulation in American Communications Assn. v. Douds, 339 U.S. 382. Section 504 was adopted as a fairer and more effective method of dealing with the same evil. . . . Nor can it be denied that § 504 is reasonably related to a permissible legislative objective. . . . Without question the findings previously made by Congress and the Subversive Activities Control Board afforded a rational basis in 1959 for Congress to conclude that Communists were likely to call political strikes, and sufficiently more likely than others to do so that special measures could appropriately be enacted to deal with the particular threat posed.

In view of Congress' demonstrated concern in preventing future conduct—political strikes—and the reasonableness of the means adopted to that end, I cannot conclude that § 504 had a punitive purpose or that it constitutes a bill of attainder. . . .

SECTION 2. INTERNATIONAL AND MILITARY AFFAIRS

Scope Note. Are the separation of powers concerns considered in sec. 1—especially the limits on executive action—substantially attenuated when the context is foreign affairs? Curtiss-Wright, which follows, contains broad statements about the special responsibility of the President. Does that special role carry legal authority in addition to that stated in Art. II and that granted by Congress? What are the President's powers as chief executive and "Commander in Chief"? Is the inherent executive power denied by the Steel Seizure Case available to the President when the action is external rather than domestic? And are the limits on delegation of legislative powers inapplicable to the foreign sphere?

These questions, suggested by the Curtiss-Wright opinion, introduce the problems of executive-legislative competition in the materials that follow. Does the President have autonomous authority to make foreign policy via international agreements and by-pass the treaty power route in which the Senate participates? That was one of the two areas of risks that propelled the Bricker Amendment campaign: the other—the states' rights concern stemming from Missouri v. Holland—has already been considered (chap. 5, p. 396); the Belmont case and related materials below consider the fears that executive agreements may undercut the congressional role and the treaty method. More recently, warnings of those risks of congressional subservience to the President have come from different sources: many of those who deprecated the fears in opposing the Bricker Amendment in the 1950's have demanded, in the context of the controversy over Vietnam, that Congress assert control over the executive. Senator Fulbright's leadership in the Foreign Relations Committee and the Senate's adoption of the "national commitment" resolution in 1969 illustrate that tendency.

The Vietnam debate has also attracted special attention to the President's authority regarding the use of armed forces. Art. II designates the President as "Commander in Chief." Art. I grants Congress the authority to declare war. To what extent do these powers conflict? How can they be accommodated? To what extent may the President authorize use of military force without a formal declaration of war? To what extent must and can Congress participate in the decision-making process? Constitutional questions such as these have seldom come to the courts, though they were discussed in the Civil War Prize Cases and are involved in the efforts to mount court challenges to the constitutional basis for sending Americans to fight in Vietnam. This concern with military matters in the specific context of international conflicts suggests the more general, related concern with which this chapter closes: the tradition and impact of the civil-military distinction, especially with respect to the military control of civilians.

UNITED STATES v. CURTISS–WRIGHT EXPORT CORP.

299 U.S. 304, 57 S.Ct. 216, 81 L.Ed. 255 (1936).

Appeal from the United States District Court for the Southern District of New York.

Mr. Justice SUTHERLAND delivered the opinion of the Court.

[A Joint Resolution of Congress provided that "if the President finds that the prohibition of the sale of arms and munitions of war in the United States to those countries now engaged in armed conflict in the Chaco may contribute to the re-establishment of peace between those countries, and if . . . he makes proclamation to that effect," then it shall be unlawful to make such a sale "except under such limitations and exceptions as the President prescribes." Penalties were prescribed. Appellee was indicted for conspiracy to sell arms in violation of the Joint Resolution and Proclamation. The district court sustained appellee's demurrer on the ground that the Resolution contained an unconstitutional delegation of legislative power to the President. The case was taken to the Supreme Court on direct appeal.]

Whether, if the Joint Resolution had related solely to internal affairs, it would be open to the challenge that it constituted an unlawful delegation of legislative power to the Executive, we find it unnecessary to determine. The whole aim of the resolution is to affect a situation entirely external to the United States, and falling within the category of foreign affairs. The determination which we are called to make, therefore, is whether the Joint Resolution, as applied to that situation, is vulnerable to attack under the rule that forbids a delegation of the law-making power. In other words, assuming (but not deciding) that the challenged delegation, if it were confined to internal affairs, would be invalid, may it nevertheless be sustained on the ground that its exclusive aim is to afford a remedy for a hurtful condition within foreign territory?

It will contribute to the elucidation of the question if we first consider the differences between the powers of the federal government in respect of foreign or external affairs and those in respect of domestic or internal affairs. That there was differences between them, and that these differences are fundamental, may not be doubted.

The two classes of powers are different, both in respect of their origin and their nature. The broad statement that the federal government can exercise no powers except those specifically enumerated in the Constitution, and such implied powers as are necessary and proper to carry into effect the enumerated powers, is categorically true only in respect of our internal affairs. In that field, the primary purpose of the Constitution was to carve from the general mass of legislative powers *then possessed by the states* such portions as it was thought desirable to vest in the federal government, leaving those not included in the enumeration still in the states. . . . That this doctrine applies only to powers which the states had, is self evident. And since the states severally never possessed international powers, such powers could not have been carved from the mass of state powers but obviously were transmitted to the United States from some other source. . . .

As a result of the separation from Great Britain by the colonies acting as a unit, the powers of external sovereignty passed from the Crown not to the colonies severally, but to the colonies in their collective and corporate capacity as the United States of America. . . .

It results that the investment of the federal government with the powers of external sovereignty did not depend upon the affirmative grants of the Constitution. The powers to declare and wage war, to conclude peace, to make treaties, to maintain diplomatic relations with other sovereignties, if they had never been mentioned in the Constitution, would have vested in the federal government as necessary concomitants of nationality. Neither the Constitution nor the laws passed in pursuance of it have any force in foreign territory unless in respect of our own citizens . . . ; and operations of the nation in such territory must be governed by treaties, international understandings and compacts, and the principles of international law. As a member of the family of nations, the right and power of the United

States in that field are equal to the right and power of the other members of the international family. Otherwise, the United States is not completely sovereign. The power to acquire territory by discovery and occupation . . . , the power to expel undesirable aliens . . . , the power to make such international agreements as do not constitute treaties in the constitutional sense . . . , none of which is expressly affirmed by the Constitution, nevertheless exist as inherently inseparable from the conception of nationality. . . .

Not only, as we have shown, is the federal power over external affairs in origin and essential character different from that over internal affairs, but participation in the exercise of the power is significantly limited. In this vast external realm, with its important, complicated, delicate and manifold problems, the President alone has the power to speak or listen as a representative of the nation. He *makes* treaties with the advice and consent of the Senate; but he alone negotiates. Into the field of negotiation the Senate cannot intrude; and Congress itself is powerless to invade it. . . .

It is important to bear in mind that we are here dealing not alone with an authority vested in the President by an exertion of legislative power, but with such an authority plus the very delicate, plenary and exclusive power of the President as the sole organ of the federal government in the field of international relations—a power which does not require as a basis for its exercise an act of Congress, but which, of course, like every other governmental power, must be exercised in subordination to the applicable provisions of the Constitution. It is quite apparent that if, in the maintenance of our international relations, embarrassment—perhaps serious embarrassment—is to be avoided and success for our aims achieved, congressional legislation which is to be made effective through negotiation and inquiry within the international field must often accord to the President a degree of discretion and freedom from statutory restriction which would not be admissible were domestic affairs alone involved. Moreover, he, not Congress, has the better opportunity of knowing the conditions which prevail in foreign countries, and especially is this true in time of war. He has his confidential sources of information. He has his agents in the form of diplomatic, consular and other officials. Secrecy in respect of information gathered by them may be highly necessary, and the premature disclosure of it productive of harmful results. . . .

In the light of the foregoing observations, it is evident that this court should not be in haste to apply a general rule which will have the effect of condemning legislation like that under review as constituting an unlawful delegation of legislative power. The principles which justify such legislation find overwhelming support in the unbroken legislative practice which has prevailed almost from the inception of the national government to the present day. . . .

[After discussing a number of "embargo and kindred acts," beginning with an embargo law of 1794, the Court continued:] The result of holding that the joint resolution here under attack is void and unenforceable as constituting an unlawful delegation of legislative power would be to stamp this multitude of comparable acts and resolutions as likewise invalid. . . . [A]n impressive array of legislation such as we have just set forth . . . by nearly every Congress from the beginning of our national existence to the present day, must be given unusual weight in the process of reaching a correct determination of the problem. A legislative practice such as we have here   .   .   .   goes a long way in the direction of proving the presence of unassailable ground for the constitutionality of the practice, to be found in the origin and history of the power involved, or in its nature, or in both combined.   .   .   .

.   .   .   [B]oth upon principle and in accordance with precedent, we conclude there is sufficient warrant for the broad discretion vested in the President to determine whether the enforcement of the statute will have a beneficial effect upon the re-establishment of peace in the affected countries; whether he shall make proclamation to bring the resolution into operation; whether and when the resolution shall cease to operate and to make proclamation accordingly; and to prescribe limitations and exceptions to which the enforcement of the resolution shall be subject.   .   .   .

Reversed.

[Justice McReynolds dissented.]

CURTISS–WRIGHT AND THE DELEGATION OF POWERS IN FOREIGN AFFAIRS

Contrast, with the statements on delegation of legislative power in the principal case, the Court's statements in Kent v. Dulles, 357 U.S. 116 (1958), the passport case noted in the materials on Interpreting Statutes to Avoid Constitutional Questions, chap. 2, p. 160, supra. In the course of the Kent opinion, the Court stated that, if the "right to exit" is to be regulated, "it must be pursuant to the law-making functions of the Congress. Youngstown Sheet & Tube Co. v. Sawyer, supra. And if that power is delegated, the standards must be adequate to pass scrutiny by the accepted tests. See Panama Refining Co. v. Ryan, 293 U.S. 388, 420–430."

Was Panama Refining, the decision striking down an economic regulation, see sec. 1, p. 574, the appropriate source of the "accepted test" for a case on regulating travel abroad? Should Curtiss-Wright have been mentioned? (Compare, on the broad delegation permitted in tariff laws, Hampton & Co. v. United States, 276 U.S. 394 (1928).) Does the failure to mention Curtiss-Wright suggest that its statements about the inapplicability of delegation concerns in the foreign sphere were too broad? May Curtiss-Wright also contain excessively broad dicta regarding the extra-constitutional source of foreign affairs power (cf. the Reid v. Covert excerpts on the treaty power, chap. 5, p. 400, supra) and regarding the Presidential predominance in external relations (cf. the materials that follow)?

UNITED STATES v. BELMONT

301 U.S. 324, 57 S.Ct. 758, 81 L.Ed. 1134 (1937).

Certiorari to the United States Court of Appeals for the Second Circuit.

Mr. Justice SUTHERLAND delivered the opinion of the Court.   .   .   .

[The United States, by action of President Roosevelt, recognized the Soviet Union on November 16, 1933. At the same time, an exchange of diplomatic correspondence—between the President and Maxim Litvinov—

effected an assignment by the Soviet Union to the United States of all Soviet claims against Americans who held funds of Russian companies seized after the Revolution.

[This action was brought by the United States, on the basis of that assignment, to recover funds deposited by a Russian corporation with Belmont, a private New York banker. The lower courts dismissed on the ground that the situs of the bank deposit was in New York and that a judgment for the United States would be a recognition of confiscation "contrary to the controlling public policy of the State of New York."]

. . . We do not pause to inquire whether in fact there was any policy of the State of New York to be infringed, since we are of opinion that no state policy can prevail against the international compact here involved. . . .

We take judicial notice of the fact that coincident with the assignment set forth in the complaint, the President recognized the Soviet Government, and normal diplomatic relations were established between that government and the Government of the United States, followed by an exchange of ambassadors. The effect of this was to validate, so far as this country is concerned, all acts of the Soviet Government here involved from the commencement of its existence. The recognition, establishment of diplomatic relations, the assignment, and agreements with respect thereto, were all parts of one transaction, resulting in an international compact between the two governments. That the negotiations, acceptance of the assignment and agreements and understandings in respect thereof were within the competence of the President may not be doubted. Governmental power over internal affairs is distributed between the national government and the several states. Governmental power over external affairs is not distributed, but is vested exclusively in the national government. And in respect of what was done here, the Executive had authority to speak as the sole organ of that government. The assignment and the agreements in connection therewith did not, as in the case of treaties, as that term is used in the treaty making clause of the Constitution (Article II, § 2), require the advice and consent of the Senate.

A treaty signifies "a compact made between two or more independent nations, with a view to the public welfare." Altman & Co. v. United States, 224 U.S. 583, 600. But an international compact, as this was, is not always a treaty which requires the participation of the Senate. There are many such compacts, of which a protocol, a modus vivendi, a postal convention, and agreements like that now under consideration are illustrations. . . .

Plainly, the external powers of the United States are to be exercised without regard to state laws or policies. . . . And while this rule in respect of treaties is established by the express language of clause 2, Art. VI, of the Constitution, the same rule would result in the case of all international compacts and agreements from the very fact that complete power over international affairs is in the national government and is not and cannot be subject to any curtailment or interference on the part of the several states. Compare United States v. Curtiss-Wright Export Corporation, 299 U.S. 304, 316 et seq. In respect of all international negotiations and compacts, and in respect of our foreign relation generally, state lines disappear. . . .

Judgment reversed.

Mr. Justice STONE.

I agree with the result, but I am unable to follow the path by which it is reached. . . . We may, for present purposes, assume that the United States, by treaty with a foreign government with respect to a subject in which the foreign government has some interest or concern, could alter the policy which a state might otherwise adopt. It is unnecessary to consider whether the present agreement between the two governments can rightly be given the same effect as a treaty within this rule, for neither the allegations of the bill of complaint, nor the diplomatic exchanges, suggest that the United States has either recognized or declared that any state policy is to be overridden. . . .

As respondent debtor may not challenge the effect of the assignment to the United States, the judgment is rightly reversed. . . .

Mr. Justice BRANDEIS and Mr. Justice CARDOZO concur in this opinion.

THE PRESIDENT, CONGRESS, AND EXECUTIVE AGREEMENTS

Introduction. Executive agreements such as those enforced in the principal case roused fears that this vehicle might bypass treaty-making and supersede legislation. But the magnitude of those risks turns on when such agreements are constitutionally justified. Are they supportable simply on the basis of an inherent Presidential authority to conduct foreign affairs? Or must they be made in pursuance of a statute or as incidental to an Art. II power (as with the relationship of the Litvinov Assignment to the President's power to recognize foreign governments)? And may Congress bar or overturn executive agreements?

1. *Executive agreements as alternatives to treaties.* a. To what extent may the Senate's role in international relations be curtailed by using executive agreements rather than treaties? For contrasting views, compare Borchard, "Shall the Executive Agreement Replace the Treaty," 53 Yale L.J. 664 (1944), with McDougal and Lans, "Treaties and Congressional-Executive or Presidential Agreements: Interchangeable Instruments of National Policy," 54 Yale L.J. 181 (1945). See also Mathews, "The Constitutional Power of the President to Conclude International Agreements," 64 Yale L.J. 345 (1955). The Bricker Amendment proposals (noted supra, chap. 5, p. 398) sought to block the executive agreement bypass. For example, sec. 2 of the version that failed narrowly in 1954 stated: "An international agreement other than a treaty shall become effective as internal law in the United States only by an act of Congress."

2. *Conflicts between executive agreements and legislation.* Can an executive agreement prevail over a statute? In United States v. Capps, 204 F.2d 655 (1953), the Fourth Circuit held that an agreement with Canada regarding the importation of potatoes was invalid because it conflicted with a prior law enacted by Congress under its power over foreign commerce. The Supreme Court affirmed the judgment without reaching the important issue of the validity of the executive agreement. 348 U.S. 296 (1955). Does the Capps case suggest need for care in reading the broad approval of executive agreements in cases such as Belmont?

Is it important to note, for example, that Presidential authority to make the Litvinov Agreement could be justified as incident to the specific constitutional authority to recognize foreign governments, without need to resort to broad inherent powers of the executive such as those suggested in Curtiss-Wright? Is it important to note, moreover, that the argued limits on executive agreements that the Court would not accept in Belmont stemmed from conflicting policies of the state, not from inconsistent policies of the coordinate national legislature? On the problem of resolving executive-legislative conflicts in this area, is it useful to invoke the three-pronged analysis at the beginning of Justice Jackson's opinion in the Steel Seizure Case, supra? Note that direct confrontations with Congress do not arise when executive agreements are adopted pursuant to statutory authority and do not rely on any autonomous Presidential power. For an example of such congressionally granted authority, see the Trade Agreements Act, authorizing modification of tariffs through Presidential agreements.

3. *The Pink case and the land-lease agreement.* a. The Litvinov Assignment involved in the Belmont case came before the Court again in United States v. Pink, 315 U.S. 203 (1942). The United States brought suit in the state courts to recover the assets of a nationalized Russian insurance company. The United States claimed that its rights under the Assignment had priority over those of foreign creditors. The state courts dismissed the suit on the basis of New York's public policy. Once again, the Supreme Court reversed. Justice Douglas' opinion stated that the President "has the power to determine the policy . . . to govern the question of recognition" and that such "international compacts and agreements as the Litvinov Assignment have a similar dignity" as treaties under the Supremacy Clause. See Note, "United States v. Pink: A Reappraisal," 48 Colum.L.Rev. 890 (1948).

b. For another controversial executive agreement—but, unlike the Litvinov Assignment, one not giving rise to constitutional litigation—see the pre-World War II land-lease agreement. In September 1940, President Roosevelt announced the signing of an executive agreement between the United States and Great Britain, providing for the lease of certain air and naval bases to the United States in return for fifty destroyers turned over to Britain. The President accompanied his message to Congress with an opinion by Attorney General Jackson upholding the agreement and discussing two principal questions: first, whether such an arrangement could be concluded by the President under an executive agreement rather than in pursuance of a treaty; second, whether authority existed in the President to alienate title to such ships. 39 Op.A.G. 484 (1940). That agreement, unlike that in the Pink case, was plainly not incidental to Presidential authority to recognize foreign governments. What Presidential powers could it draw on?

————

THE PRESIDENT, CONGRESS, AND THE USE OF ARMED FORCE: THE VIETNAM DEBATE

1. *Background: the Prize Cases.* In the Prize Cases, 2 Black 635 (1863), ships carrying goods to the Confederate States were seized by Union ships, pursuant to President Lincoln's April 1861 order declaring a blockade

of southern ports. The ships were condemned by federal court order. Owners of the ships and cargo appealed. The Supreme Court sustained most of the seizures in a 5:4 decision. Justice Grier's majority opinion included the following passages in response to the question, "Had the President a right to institute a blockade of ports in possession of persons in armed rebellion against the Government?":

"This greatest of civil wars was not gradually developed by popular commotion, tumultuous assemblies, or local unorganized insurrections. However long may have been its previous conception, it nevertheless sprung forth suddenly from the parent brain, a Minerva in the full panoply of *war*. The President was bound to meet it in the shape it presented itself, without waiting for Congress to baptize it with a name; and no name given to it by him or them could change the fact. . . .

"Whether the President in fulfilling his duties, as Commander-in-chief, in suppressing an insurrection, has met with such armed hostile resistance, and a civil war of such alarming proportions as will compel him to accord to them the character of belligerents, is a question to be decided *by him,* and this Court must be governed by the decisions and acts of the political department of the Government to which this power was entrusted. 'He must determine what degree of force the crisis demands.' The proclamation of blockade is itself official and conclusive evidence to the Court that a state of war existed which demanded and authorized a recourse to such a measure, under the circumstances peculiar to the case. . . .

"If it were necessary to the technical existence of a war, that it should have a legislative sanction, we find it in almost every act passed at the extraordinary session of the Legislature of 1861, which was wholly employed in enacting laws to enable the Government to prosecute the war with vigor and efficiency. And finally, in 1861, we find Congress 'ex majore cautela' and in anticipation of such astute objections, passing an act 'approving, legalizing, and making valid all the acts, proclamations, and orders of the President, &c., as if they had been *issued and done under the previous express authority* and direction of the Congress of the United States.'

"Without admitting that such an act was necessary under the circumstances, it is plain that if the President had in any manner assumed powers which it was necessary should have the authority or sanction of Congress, that on the well known principle of law, 'omnis ratihabitio retrotrahitur et mandato equiparatur,' this ratification has operated to perfectly cure the defect. . .

"On this . . . question therefore we are of the opinion that the President had a right, *jure belli,* to institute a blockade of ports in possession of the States in rebellion, which neutrals are bound to regard.

"By the Constitution, Congress alone has the power to declare a national or foreign war. It cannot declare war against a State, or any number of States, by virtue of any clause in the Constitution. The Constitution confers on the President the whole Executive power. He is bound to take care that the laws be faithfully executed. He is Commander-in-chief of the Army and Navy of the United States, and of the militia of the several States when called into the actual service of the United States. He has no power to initiate or declare a war either against a foreign nation or a domestic State. But by the Acts of Congress of February 28th, 1795, and 3d of March, 1807, he is authorized to call out the militia and use the military and naval forces of the United States in case of invasion by foreign nations, and to suppress insurrection against the government of a State or of the United States.

"If a war be made by invasion of a foreign nation, the President is not only authorized but bound to resist force, by force. He does not initiate the war, but is bound to accept the challenge without waiting for any special legislative authority. And whether the hostile party be a foreign invader, or States organized in rebellion, it is none the less a war, although the declaration of it be '*unilateral*.' Lord Stowell (The Eliza Ann, 1 Dod., 247) observes, 'It is not the less a war on that account, for war may exist without declaration on either side. It is so laid down by the best writers on the law of nations. A declaration of war by one country only, is not a mere challenge to be accepted or refused at pleasure by the other.'

"The battles of Palo Alto and Resaca de la Palma had been fought before the passage of the Act of Congress of May 13th, 1846, . . . which recognized 'a state of war as existing by the Act of the Republic of Mexico.' This Act not only provided for the future prosecution of the war, but was itself a vindication and ratification of the Act of the President in accepting the challenge without a previous formal declaration of war by Congress."

Justice Nelson's dissent, joined by Chief Justice Taney and Justices Catron and Clifford, included the following passage:

"The Acts of 1795 and 1807 did not, and could not, under the Constitution, confer on the President the power of declaring war against a State of this Union, or of deciding that war existed, and upon that ground authorize the capture and confiscation of the property of every citizen of the State whenever it was found on the waters. The laws of war, whether the war be civil or *inter gentes,* as we have seen, convert every citizen of the hostile State into a public enemy, and treat him accordingly, whatever may have been his previous conduct. This great power over the business and property of the citizen is reserved to the Legislative Department by the express words of the Constitution. It cannot be delegated or surrendered to the Executive. Congress alone can determine whether war exists or should be declared, and until they have acted, no citizen of the State can be punished in his person or property, unless he has committed some offense against a law of Congress passed before the act was committed, which made it a crime and defined the punishment." [Congressional ratification of the seizures was found ineffective as an ex post facto law.]

2. *Vietnam and the Constitution: The efforts to go to court.* The American involvement in Vietnam has provoked extensive debate about the respective authority of President and Congress in the making of foreign policy and in committing armed forces abroad. The efforts to bring the controversy into the courts have been unsuccessful, however. The range of separation of powers issues raised is reflected in the opinion of Justice Stewart dissenting from the denial of certiorari in Mora v. McNamara, 389 U.S. 934 (1967), an action by three army privates to block orders for shipment to Vietnam. Justice Stewart noted a number of "large and deeply troubling questions" in the case, though he cautioned: "Whether the Court would ultimately reach them depends, of course, upon the resolution of

serious preliminary issues of justiciability." The "questions of great magnitude" he singled out for specific mention were:

"I. Is the present United States military activity in Vietnam a 'war' within the meaning of Article I, Section 8, Clause 11 of the Constitution?

"II. If so, may the Executive constitutionally order the petitioners to participate in that military activity, when no war has been declared by the Congress?

"III. Of what relevance to Question II are the present treaty obligations of the United States?

"IV. Of what relevance to Question II is the joint Congressional ('Tonkin Bay') Resolution of August 10, 1964?

"(a) Do present United States military operations fall within the terms of the Joint Resolution?

"(b) If the Joint Resolution purports to give the Chief Executive authority to commit United States forces to armed conflict limited in scope only by his own absolute discretion, is the Resolution a constitutionally impermissible delegation of all or part of Congress' power to declare war?"

Justice Douglas also dissented in Mora v. McNamara. On justiciability he concluded: "These petitioners should be told whether their case is beyond judicial cognizance. If it is not, we should then reach the merits of their claims." Note also his dissents from the denials of certiorari in subsequent cases, e. g., McArthur v. Clifford, 393 U.S. 1002 (1968)—including the comment that the ruling in the Prize Cases, note 1 supra, was a 5:4 decision and involved "an internal insurrection which would perhaps be analogous here if the Vietnamese were invading the United States": "Would [the decision] have been the same if Lincoln had had an expeditionary force fighting a 'war' overseas?"

For other unsuccessful efforts to elicit Court rulings, see the denials of certiorari in Hart v. United States, 391 U.S. 956 (1968), and Holmes v. United States, 391 U.S. 936 (1968), with Justice Douglas again dissenting. A memorandum by Justice Stewart in Holmes emphasized that these cases only involved the power of Congress to require compulsory military service in the absence of a declaration of war. He added that he, too, would have voted for certiorari if the power "to compel military service in armed international conflict overseas" had been involved. See also the Court's denial of certiorari in a case in which a law professor sought to assert citizen's and taxpayer's standing to challenge the constitutionality of the Vietnam war. Velvel v. Nixon, 396 U.S. 1042 (1970). For the Tenth Circuit's explanation why Flast v. Cohen, chap. 2, p. 93, supra, did not support standing here, see 38 U.S. Law Week 2134 (1969). Compare the plaintiff's article, Velvel, "The War in Viet Nam: Unconstitutional, Justiciable, and Jurisdictionally Attackable," 16 Kan.L.Rev. 449 (1968).   •

3. *Vietnam and the Constitution: The constitutional debate in the Senate hearings.* The ongoing constitutional debate, in Congress and out [see, e. g., Note, "Congress, the President, and the Power to Commit Forces to Combat," 81 Harv.L.Rev. 1771 (1968), and Symposium, "Legality of United States Participation in the Viet Nam Conflict," 75 Yale L.J. 1084 (1966)], was reflected in Justice Douglas' dissent in Mora v. McNamara,

supra, when he noted that the questions raised there covered "the wide range of problems which the Senate Committee on Foreign Relations recently explored [Hearings on S.Res. No. 151, 90th Cong., 1st Sess. (1967)], in connection with the SEATO Treaty of February 19, 1955, and the Tonkin Gulf Resolution [78 Stat. 384 (1964)]." Justice Douglas elaborated:

"Mr. Katzenbach, representing the Administration, testified [in the Senate Hearings] that he did not regard the Tonkin Gulf Resolution to be 'a declaration of war' and that while the Resolution was not 'constitutionally necessary' it was 'politically, from an international viewpoint and from a domestic viewpoint, extremely important.' He added:

'The use of the phrase "to declare war" as it was used in the Constitution of the United States had a particular meaning in terms of the events and the practices which existed at the time it was adopted . . .

'[I]t was recognized by the Founding Fathers that the President might have to take emergency action to protect the security of the United States, but that if there was going to be another use of the armed forces of the United States, that was a decision which Congress should check the Executive on, which Congress should support. It was for that reason that the phrase was inserted in the Constitution.

'Now, over a long period of time, . . . there have been many uses of the military forces of the United States for a variety of purposes without a congressional declaration of war. But it would be fair to say that most of these were relatively minor uses of force. . . .

'A declaration of war would not, I think, correctly reflect the very limited objectives of the United States with respect to Vietnam. It would not correctly reflect our efforts there, what we are trying to do, the reasons why we are there, to use an outmoded phraseology, to declare war.'

"The view that Congress was intended to play a more active role in the initiation and conduct of war than the above statements might suggest has been espoused by Senator Fulbright (Cong. Rec., Oct. 11, 1967, pp. 14683–14690) [see also note 4, infra], quoting Thomas Jefferson who said:

'We have already given in example one effectual check to the Dog of war by transferring the power of letting him loose from the Executive to the Legislative body, from those who are to spend to those who are to pay.' [1]

"These opposed views are reflected in the Prize Cases, 2 Black 635, a five-to-four decision rendered in 1863. . . . During all subsequent periods in our history—through the Spanish-American War, the Boxer Rebellion, two World Wars, Korea, and now Vietnam—the two points of view urged in the Prize Cases have continued to be voiced.

1. 15 Papers of Jefferson 397 (Boyd ed., Princeton 1955). In the Federalist No. 69, at 465 (Cooke ed. 1961), Hamilton stated:
"The President is to be Commander in Chief of the army and navy of the United States. In this respect his authority would be nominally the same with that of the King of Great Britain, but in substance much inferior to it. It would amount to nothing more than the supreme command and direction of the military and naval forces, as first General and Admiral of the Confederacy; while that of the British King extends to the *declaring* of war and to the *raising* and *regulating* of fleets and armies; all which by the Constitution under consideration would appertain to the Legislature." [Footnote by Justice Douglas.]

"A host of problems is raised. Does the President's authority to repel invasions and quiet insurrections, do his powers in foreign relations and his duty to execute faithfully the laws of the United States, including its treaties, justify what has been threatened of petitioners? What is the relevancy of the Gulf of Tonkin Resolution and the yearly appropriations in support of the Vietnam effort?

". . . There are sentences in our opinions which, detached from their context, indicate that what is happening is none of our business:

> 'Certainly it is not the function of the Judiciary to entertain private litigation—even by a citizen—which challenges the legality, the wisdom, or the propriety of the Commander-in-Chief in sending our armed forces abroad or to any particular region.' Johnson v. Eisentrager, 339 U.S. 763, 789.

"We do not, of course, sit as a committee of oversight or supervision. What resolutions the President asks and what the Congress provides are not our concern. With respect to the Federal Government, we sit only to decide actual cases or controversies within judicial cognizance that arise as a result of what the Congress or the President or a judge does or attempts to do to a person or his property.

"In Ex parte Milligan [which follows] the Court relieved a person of the death penalty imposed by a military tribunal. . . . The fact that the political branches are responsible for the threat to petitioners' liberty is not decisive. . . . These petitioners should be told whether their case is beyond judicial cognizance. . . ."

4. *Vietnam and the Constitution: The Senate Committee Report and the "national commitment" resolution.* a. *The Fulbright Committee, 1967.* The Senate Hearings before Senator Fulbright's Committee produced an extensive report on the historical and constitutional aspects of the conduct of American foreign policy. Sen.Rep.No.797, 90th Cong., 1st Sess. (1967). The Report included the following passages:

"[T]he executive has acquired virtual supremacy over the making as well as the conduct of the foreign relations of the United States. The principal cause of the constitutional imbalance has been the circumstance of American involvement and responsibility in a violent and unstable world. . . .

"[T]he committee believes that changed conditions, though the principal cause of the present constitutional imbalance, are not its sole cause. . . . Both the executive and the Congress have been periodically unmindful of constitutional requirements and proscriptions, the executive by its incursions upon Congressional prerogative at moments when action seemed more important than the means of its initiation, the Congress by its uncritical and sometimes unconscious acquiescence in these incursions. If blame is to be apportioned, the greater share probably belongs to the Congress. . . .

"The committee believes that the division of powers spelled out in the Constitution is in fact compatible with our country's role as a world power. The principal purpose of that division, as Justice Brandeis noted, is liberty rather than efficiency, but, unless speed is equated with efficiency and deliberation held to be an obstacle to it, there is no reason why we cannot have under our system of government a foreign policy which is efficient as well as democratically made. . . . The committee does not share Mr. Katzenbach's view that the demarcation of authority between President and Congress can and should be left to be settled 'by the instinct of the nation and its leaders for political responsibility.' The framers of the Constitution gave us more specific and reliable guidelines for drawing the line of demarcation, particularly as to treaty-making and the authority to commit the country to war. . . . Excepting only the necessary authority of the President to repel a sudden attack, the war power was vested in the Congress. Only in recent years has it passed to the executive, contributing to the dangerous tendency toward executive supremacy in foreign policy, a tendency which the committee hopes to see arrested and reversed.

"During the 19th century American armed forces were used by the President on his own authority for such purposes as suppressing piracy, suppressing the slave trade by American ships, 'hot pursuit' of criminals across frontiers, and protecting American lives and property in backward areas or areas where government had broken down. Such limited uses of force without authorization by Congress, not involving the initiation of hostilities against foreign governments, came to be accepted practice, sanctioned by usage though not explicity by the Constitution.

"The use of the armed forces against sovereign nations without authorization by Congress became common practice in the 20th century. President Theodore Roosevelt used the Navy to prevent Colombian forces from suppressing insurrection in their province of Panama and intervened militarily in Cuba and the Dominican Republic. Presidents Taft and Wilson also sent armed forces to the Caribbean and Central America without Congressional authorization. In Haiti, the Dominican Republic, and Nicaragua these interventions resulted in the establishment of American military governments.

"President Wilson seized the Mexican port of Vera Cruz in 1914 as an act of reprisal, in order, he said, to 'enforce respect' for the government of the United States. The two Houses of Congress adopted separate resolutions in support of President Wilson's action but the Senate did not complete action on its resolution until after the seizure of Vera Cruz. . . .

"The military powers which had been acquired by Presidents in the 19th century—for purposes of 'hot pursuit' and the protection of American lives and property, and under treaties which conferred rights and obligations on the United States—were not serious infringements on Congress' war power because they had been used for the most part against individuals or bands of pirates or bandits and not against sovereign states. Roosevelt, Taft, and Wilson used these powers to engage in military action against sovereign states, thereby greatly expanding the scope of executive power over the use of the armed forces and setting precedents for the greater expansions of executive power which were to follow. . . .

"President Franklin Roosevelt expanded executive power over the use of the armed forces to an unprecedented degree. The exchange of overaged American destroyers for British bases in the Western Hemisphere was accomplished by executive agreement [supra], in violation of the Senate's treaty power, and was also a violation of the international law of neutrality, giving Germany legal cause, had she chosen to take it, to declare war on the United States. . . .

"The trend initiated by Theodore Roosevelt, Taft, and Wilson, and accelerated by Franklin Roosevelt, continued at a rapid rate under Presidents Truman, Eisenhower, Kennedy, and Johnson, bringing the country to the point at which the real power to commit the country to war is now in the hands of the President. The trend which began in the early 20th century has been consummated and the intent of the framers of the Constitution as to the war power substantially negated.

"By the late 1940's there had developed a kind of ambivalence as to the war power in the minds of officials in the executive branch, Members of Congress and, presumably, the country at large. On the one hand, it was and still is said that Congress alone has the power to declare war; on the other hand it was widely believed, or at least conceded, that the President in his capacity as commander in chief had the authority to use the armed forces in any way he saw fit. . . .

" . . . Why has Congress agreed to this rearrangement of powers which is without constitutional justification, and at its own expense?

"To some degree, it seems to be the result of the unfamiliarity of the United States with its new role as a world power. . . . Another possible factor in Congressional passivity is that Congress may have permitted itself to be overawed by the cult of executive expertise. . . .

"It is significant that in the case of the Formosa resolution [1955] President Eisenhower asked for *authority* rather than mere approval or support and that under the resolution adopted by Congress the President was 'authorized to employ the Armed Forces,' upon his own finding of necessity, for the defense of Formosa and the Pescadores. The use of the word *authorize* by both President and Congress strongly implied recognition by both that the authority to commit the armed forces lay with the Congress, to grant or withhold. The committee emphasizes this point as one which may have significance in possible future Congressional action on resolutions pertaining to the use of the armed forces. Although the word *authorize* was used in the Formosa resolution, the authorization was an extremely broad one, empowering the President to employ the armed forces to defend Formosa and the Pescadores 'as he determines necessary.' It can be argued that an authorization so general and imprecise amounts to an unconstitutional alienation of its war power on the part of the Congress. . . .

"Subsequent resolutions involving the possible use of armed force abandoned the principle of *authorization,* demonstrating not only ambivalence as to extent of the President's authority but a lack of attention to the underlying constitutional question. The Middle East resolution of 1957, the Cuba resolution of 1962, and the Gulf of Tonkin resolution of 1964 dropped the vital concept of Congressional authorization and instead used terminology which, by failing to express a grant of power by Congress, implied acceptance of the view that the President already had the power to use the armed forces in the ways proposed and that, the resolutions were no more than expressions of Congressional support and national unity. The prevailing attitude in each instance seems to have been one of concern not with constitutional questions but with the problem at hand and with the need for a method of dealing with it, heightened in all three cases by a sense of urgency. Nonetheless, precedents were set. . . .

"The Gulf of Tonkin resolution * represents the extreme point in the

---

* The text of the Southeast Asia (Tonkin Bay) Resolution, H.J.Res. 1145, 73 Stat. 384 (1964):

Whereas naval units of the Communist regime in Vietnam, in violation of the principles of the Charter of the United

process of constitutional erosion that began in the first years of this century. Couched in broad terms, the resolution constitutes an acknowledgment of virtually unlimited Presidential control of the armed forces. [I]n the case of the Gulf of Tonkin resolution there was a discrepancy between the language of the resolution and the intent of Congress. Although the language of the resolution lends itself to the interpretation that Congress was consenting in advance to a full-scale war in Asia should the President think it necessary, that was not the expectation of Congress at the time. In adopting the resolution Congress was closer to believing that it was helping to *prevent* a large-scale war by taking a firm stand than that it was laying the legal basis for the conduct of such a war. . . . It is difficult, therefore, to credit Under Secretary of State Katzenbach's contention that the Gulf of Tonkin resolution, combined with the SEATO Treaty, was the 'functional equivalent' of a declaration of war. In adopting a resolution with such sweeping language, however, Congress committed the error of making a *personal* judgment as to how President Johnson would implement the resolution when it had a responsibility to make an *institutional* judgment, first, as to what *any* President would do with so great an acknowledgment of power, and, second, as to whether, under the Constitution, Congress had the right to grant or concede the authority in question. . . .

"[T]he committee is well aware that there have been, and may in the future again be, instances of great national emergency such as the Cuban missile crisis when prompt action is essential. In such instances consultation with the Congress is by no means out of the question; Congress has demonstrated on many occasions that it is capable of acting as speedily as the executive. Should the urgency or the need of secrecy be judged so great, however, as to preclude any form of consultation with Congress, the President, as we have noted, has unchallenged authority to respond to a sudden attack upon the

Nations and of international law, have deliberately and repeatedly attacked United States naval vessels lawfully present in international waters, and have thereby created a serious threat to international peace; and

Whereas these attacks are part of a deliberate and systematic campaign of aggression that the Communist regime in North Vietnam has been waging against its neighbors and the nations joined with them in the collective defense of their freedom; and

Whereas the United States is assisting the peoples of southeast Asia to protect their freedom and has no territorial, military or political ambitions in that area, but desires only that these peoples should be left in peace to work out their own destinies in their own way: Now, therefore, be it

Resolved by the Senate and House of Representatives of the United States of America in Congress assembled, That the Congress approves and supports the determination of the President, as Commander in Chief, to take all necessary measures to repel any armed attack against the forces of the United States and to prevent further aggression.

Sec. 2. The United States regards as vital to its national interest and to world peace the maintenance of international peace and security in southeast Asia. Consonant with the Constitution of the United States and the Charter of the United Nations and in accordance with its obligations under the Southeast Asia Collective Defense Treaty, the United States is, therefore, prepared, as the President determines, to take all necessary steps, including the use of armed force, to assist any member or protocol state of the Southeast Asia Collective Defense Treaty requesting assistance in defense of its freedom.

Sec. 3. This resolution shall expire when the President shall determine that the peace and security of the area is reasonably assured by international conditions created by action of the United Nations or otherwise, except that it may be terminated earlier by concurrent resolution of the Congress.

United States.   This authority is recognized as nothing less than a duty and it is inconceivable that the Congress would fail to support the President in response to a direct attack on the United States.   Finally, should the President find himself confronted with a situation of such complexity and ambiguity as to leave him without guidelines for constitutional action, it would be far better for him to take the action he saw fit without attempting to justify it in advance and leave it to Congress or the courts to evaluate his action in retrospect.   A single unconstitutional act, later explained or pronounced unconstitutional, is preferable to an act dressed up in some spurious, precedent-setting claim of legitimacy.   As a member of the Nation's First Congress, Alexander White, of Virginia, said:

> 'It would be better for the President to extend his powers on some extraordinary occasions, even where he is not strictly justified by the Constitution, than the legislature should grant an improper power to be exercised at all times   .   .   .   .'

"For all of the foregoing reasons the committee rejects the contention that the war powers as spelled out in the Constitution are obsolete and strongly recommends that the Congress reassert its constitutional authority over the use of the armed forces.   No constitutional amendment or legislative enactment is required for this purpose;   all that is required is the restoration of constitutional procedures which have been permitted to atrophy.   .   .   .

"The committee does not believe that formal declarations of war are the only available means by which Congress can authorize the President to initiate limited or general hostilities.   Joint resolutions such as those pertaining to Formosa, the Middle East, and the Gulf of Tonkin are a proper method of granting authority, provided that they are precise as to what is to be done and for what period of time, and provided that they do in fact *grant authority* and not merely express approval of undefined action to be taken by the President.   That distinction is of the greatest importance.   As used in the recent past, joint resolutions have been instruments of political control over the Congress in the hand of the President, enabling him to claim support for any action he may choose to take and so phrased as to express Congressional acquiescence in the constitutionally unsound contention that the President in his capacity as commander in chief has the authority to commit the country to war.

"The committee therefore recommends that, in considering future resolutions involving the use or possible use of the armed forces, Congress—

"(1)   debate the proposed resolution at sufficient length to establish a legislative record showing the intent of Congress;

"(2)   use the words *authorize* or *empower* or such other language as will leave no doubt that Congress alone has the right to authorize the initiation of war and that, in granting the President authority to use the armed forces, Congress is granting him power that he would not otherwise have;

"(3)   state in the resolution as explicitly as possible under the circumstances the kind of military action that is being authorized and the place and purpose of its use;   and

"(4)   put a time limit on the resolution, thereby assuring Congress the opportunity to review its decision and extend or terminate the President's authority to use military force.   .   .   ."

b. *The Fulbright lecture, 1961.* Contrast, as an illustration of the shift in views between the Bricker Amendment controversy in the 1950's and the Vietnam debate, Senator Fulbright's statements in a 1961 lecture (Fulbright, "American Foreign Policy in the 20th Century under an 18th-Century Constitution," 47 Cornell L.Q. 1 *):

"The President already enjoys far greater authority in foreign affairs than in domestic policy, but it is still authority that falls short of his responsibilities. . . . He controls the external aspects of the Nation's power, which can be moved by his will alone—the armed forces, the diplomatic corps, the Central Intelligence Agency, and all of the vast executive apparatus. As Commander-in-Chief of the armed forces, the President has full responsibility, which cannot be shared, for military decisions in a world in which the difference between safety and cataclysm can be a matter of hours or even minutes. . . .

"The overriding problem of inadequate Presidential authority in foreign affairs, however, derives not from the internal relationships within the executive branch, but from the 'checks and balances' of Congressional authority in foreign relations. While Congress has many powers under the Constitution, having to do with foreign affairs, these powers do not enable the Congress to initiate or shape foreign policy, but to implement, modify, or thwart the proposals of the President. These powers, moreover, are widely dispersed within Congress, distributed among autonomous committees each under a chairman who owes little if anything in the way of political obligation to the President. . . .

"The question I put, without presuming to offer solutions, is whether in the face of the harsh necessities of the 1960's we can afford the luxury of 18th century procedures of measured deliberation. It is highly unlikely that we can successfully execute a long-range program for the taming, or containing, of today's aggressive and revolutionary forces by continuing to leave vast and vital decision-making powers in the hands of a decentralized, independent-minded, and largely parochial-minded body of legislators. The Congress, as Woodrow Wilson put it, is a 'disintegrated ministry,' a jealous center of power with a built-in antagonism for the Executive. . . . I submit that the price of democratic survival in a world of aggressive totalitarianism is to give up some of the democratic luxuries of the past. We should do so with no illusions as to the reasons for its necessity. It is distasteful and dangerous to vest the Executive with powers unchecked and unbalanced. My question is whether we have any choice but to do so."

c. *The "national commitment" resolution, 1969, and the problems of congressional consent.* The "national commitment" resolution first considered in the 1967 Foreign Relations Committee hearings was finally adopted by the Senate in modified form in June 1969. S.Res. 85, as modified [see 115 Cong.Rec. S7153], provides:

"Whereas accurate definition of the term 'national commitment' in recent years has become obscured: Now, therefore, be it

"*Resolved*, That (1) a national commitment for the purpose of this resolution means the use of the armed forces of the United States on foreign

* Reprinted with the permission of the publisher, © copyright 1961 by Cornell University.

territory, or a promise to assist a foreign country, government or people by the use of the armed forces or financial resources of the United States, either immediately or upon the happening of certain events, and (2) it is the sense of the Senate that a national commitment by the United States results only from affirmative action taken by the executive and legislative branches of the United States Government by means of a treaty, statute, or concurrent resolution of both Houses of Congress specifically providing for such commitment."

Does this change constitutional doctrine? Does it alter actual practice? Are the constitutional issues of Vietnam susceptible to constitutional adjudication? To an opinion patterned on Justice Black's in the Steel Seizure Case? On Justice Jackson's? Are the problems susceptible to a solution via congressional policy resolutions? Note Senator Mansfield's January 1970 suggestion that all outstanding congressional resolutions acquiescing in Presidential use of force—such as the Gulf of Tonkin one—be repealed.

Compare the analysis in the Note, "Congress, the President, and the Power to Commit Forces to Combat," 81 Harv.L.Rev. 1771 (1968). That Note emphasizes that the problems have "largely been left to historical practice," that the courts have been reluctant to enter "this classic separation-of-powers debate," and that the answer to the constitutional issue "must come from the interpretations provided through history by the two concerned parties themselves—the President and Congress." The writer concludes: "[A]ny attempt to brand particular conflicts as constitutional or unconstitutional is likely to be of little consequence. The constitutional analysis is better viewed as yielding a working directive to the executive and legislative branches that the commitment of the country to war be accomplished only through the closest collaboration possible, rather than an automatic formula for condemning or approving particular presidential action. The question should be: what concrete steps should the two branches take to assure that the policies behind the constitutional scheme are served?"

Is that the proper question? How should it be answered? On the Vietnam dispute, the Note finds that the Gulf of Tonkin Resolution leaves the extent of congressional authorization of the war "unclear" and suggests that "the ambiguity is best resolved" not by relying on congressional failure to repeal but "by resubmitting for congressional approval a resolution specifically phrased to give consent to the war."

CIVIL–MILITARY RELATIONS

The traditional suspicion of military control over civilians has been noted earlier, especially in the decisions rejecting court-martial control over civilians and non-military crimes. Reid v. Covert and O'Callahan v. Parker, chap. 5, pp. 410 and 424. Ex parte Milligan, which follows, is a classic statement of that traditional separation of military and civil jurisdictions.

That tradition has not precluded considerable deference to military judgments and tribunals. See, e. g., Korematsu v. United States, chap. 18, p. ——, sustaining the World War II exclusion of Japanese-Americans against a racial discrimination charge. Note, moreover, the validation of the trial of Nazi saboteurs by a military commission. Ex parte Quirin, 317 U.S. 1 (1942). See also In re Yamashita, 327 U.S. 1 (1946). And Hirota v. MacArthur, 388 U.S. 197 (1948), involving the post-war trial of Japanese defendants before an International Military Tribunal, held that the Supreme Court lacked power to review the judgments of such tribunals. (Justice Douglas, concurring, stated that the judgments were unreviewable because the Tribunal was not a judicial body but one constituted by the executive branch as an instrument of political and military power.) On the uncertain and controversial scope of civilian courts' authority to reexamine judgments of military courts, see, in addition to the courts-martial cases in chap. 5, sec. 6, Burns v. Wilson, 346 U.S. 137 (1953) (where Chief Justice Vinson asserted that the scope of federal habeas corpus in military cases "has always been more narrow than in civil cases" and suggested that the habeas inquiry was limited to inquiring whether the "military decision has dealt fully and fairly" with the allegations raised). See Bishop, "Civilian Judges and Military Justice: Collateral Review of Court-Martial Convictions," 61 Colum.L.Rev. 40 (1961), and Note, "Servicemen in Civilian Courts," 76 Yale L.J. 380 (1966).

EX PARTE MILLIGAN

4 Wall. 2, 18 L.Ed. 281 (1866).

This case came before the court upon a certificate of division from the judges of the Circuit Court of Indiana, on a petition for discharge from unlawful imprisonment.

Mr. Justice DAVIS delivered the opinion of the court.

On the 10th day of May, 1865, Lambdin P. Milligan presented a petition to the Circuit Court of the United States for the District of Indiana, to be discharged from an alleged unlawful imprisonment. The case made by the petition is this: Milligan is a citizen of the United States; has lived for twenty years in Indiana; and at the time of the grievances complained of, was not, and never had been in the military or naval service of the United States. On the 5th day of October, 1864, while at home, he was arrested by order of General Alvin P. Hovey, commanding the military district of Indiana; and has ever since been kept in close confinement.

On the 21st day of October, 1864, he was brought before a military commission, convened at Indianapolis, by order of General Hovey, tried on certain charges and specifications; found guilty, and sentenced to be hanged; and the sentence ordered to be executed on Friday, the 19th day of May, 1865. . . .

The controlling question in the case is this: Upon the facts stated in Milligan's petition, and the exhibits filed, had the military commission mentioned in it jurisdiction, legally, to try and sentence him? . . .

No graver question was ever considered by this court, nor one which more nearly concerns the rights of the whole people; for it is the birthright of every American citizen when charged with crime, to be tried and punished according to law. The power of punishment is alone through the means which the laws have provided for that purpose, and if they are ineffectual, there is an immunity from punishment, no matter how great an offender the individual may be, or how much his crimes may have shocked the sense of justice of the country, or endangered its safety. By the protection of the law human rights are secured; withdraw that protection, and they are at the mercy of wicked rulers or the clamor of an excited people. If there was law to justify this military trial, it is not our province to interfere; if there was not, it is our duty to declare the nullity of the proceedings.

.   .   .   The Constitution of the United States is a law for rulers and people, equally in war and in peace, and covers with the shield of its protection all classes of men, at all times, and under all circumstances.   No doctrine, involving more pernicious consequences, was ever invented by the wit of man than that any of its provisions can be suspended during any of the great exigencies of government.

Every trial involves the exercise of judicial power; and from what source did the military commission that tried him derive their authority? Certainly no part of the judicial power of the country was conferred on them .   .   .   .

But it is said that the jurisdiction is complete under the "laws and usages of war."

It can serve no useful purpose to inquire what those laws and usages are, whence they originated, where found, and on whom they operate; they can never be applied to citizens in states which have upheld the authority of the government, and where the courts are open and their process unobstructed. This court has judicial knowledge that in Indiana the Federal authority was always unopposed, and its courts always open to hear criminal accusations and redress grievances; and no usage of war could sanction a military trial there for any offence whatever of a citizen in civil life, in nowise connected with the military service.   Congress could grant no such power; and to the honor of our national legislature be it said, it has never been provoked by the state of the country even to attempt its exercise.   One of the plainest constitutional provisions was, therefore, infringed when Milligan was tried by a court not ordained and established by Congress, and not composed of judges appointed during good behavior.   .   .   .

It is claimed   .   .   .   that in a time of war the commander of an armed force (if in his opinion the exigencies of the country demand it, and of which he is to judge), has the power, within the lines of his military district, to suspend all civil rights and their remedies and subject all citizens as well as soldiers to the rule of his will; and in the exercise of his lawful authority cannot be restrained, except by his superior officer or the President of the United States.   .   .   .

The statement of this proposition shows its importance; for, if true, republican government is a failure, and there is an end of liberty regulated by law.   Martial law, established on such a basis, destroys every guarantee of the Constitution, and effectually renders the "military independent of and superior to the civil power"—the attempt to do which by the King of Great Britain was deemed by our fathers such an offence, that they assigned it to the world as one of the causes which impelled them to declare their independence. Civil liberty and this kind of martial law cannot endure together; the antagonism is irreconcilable; and, in the conflict, one or the other must perish. .   .   .

It is essential to the safety of every government that, in a great crisis, like the one we have just passed through there should be a power somewhere of suspending the writ of habeas corpus.   In every war, there are men of previously good character, wicked enough to counsel their fellow-citizens to resist the measures deemed necessary by a good government to sustain its just authority and overthrow its enemies; and their influence may lead to dangerous combinations. In the emergency of the times, an immediate public investigation according to law may not be possible; and yet, the peril to the country may be too imminent to suffer such persons to go at large. Unquestionably, there is then an exigency which demands that the government, if it should see fit in the exercise of a proper discretion to make arrests, should not be required to produce the persons arrested in answer to a writ of habeas corpus. The Constitution goes no further. It does not say after a writ of habeas corpus is denied a citizen, that he shall be tried otherwise than by the course of the common law; if it had intended this result, it was easy by the use of direct words to have accomplished it. . . .

It follows, from what has been said on this subject, that there are occasions when martial rule can be properly applied. If, in foreign invasion or civil war, the courts are actually closed, and it is impossible to administer criminal justice according to law, then, on the theatre of active military operations, where war really prevails, there is a necessity to furnish a substitute for the civil authority, thus overthrown, to preserve the safety of the army and society; and as no power is left but the military, it is allowed to govern by martial rule until the laws can have their free course. As necessity creates the rule, so it limits its duration; for, if this government is continued after the courts are reinstated, it is a gross usurpation of power. Martial rule can never exist where the courts are open, and in the proper and unobstructed exercise of their jurisdiction. It is also confined to the locality of actual war.
. . .

. . . The suspension of the privilege of the writ of habeas corpus does not suspend the writ itself. The writ issues as a matter of course; and on the return made to it the court decides whether the party applying is denied the right of proceeding any further with it.

[Chief Justice Chase, joined by Justices Wayne, Swayne, and Miller, delivered a concurring opinion.]

Chapter 8

STATE REGULATION AND THE NATIONAL ECONOMY: CONSTITUTIONAL LIMITATIONS AND CONGRESSIONAL ORDERING

Scope Note. In accordance with the plan sketched at the outset of Part II, attention now returns to the division of powers between nation and state in the federal system. The first four chapters of this Part focused on the scope of national powers; these final three chapters concentrate on the states. The major concern of chapters 8 and 9 is the basis and extent to which the grants of enumerated powers to the national government, and the exercise of those powers, affect the powers of the states. These materials reflect problems arising from the commerce clause, though other national powers—e. g., bankruptcy, Sturges v. Crowninshield, 4 Wheat. 122 (1819), and foreign affairs, Zschernig v. Miller, 389 U.S. 429 (1968) (chap. 5, p. 403, above)—

give rise to similar questions. Chapter 8 deals with the effect of the commerce clause on state regulation; chapter 9, with the impact on state taxation.

The commerce barrier to state action arises in two situations. In the first, Congress has taken no action, express or implied, indicating a policy of its own on the given subject matter. There, the objection to state authority rests entirely on the "dormant" commerce clause—on the unexercised commerce power itself, and the free trade value it symbolizes. In the other situation, Congress has exercised the power, has indicated its policy, and the challenge emphasizes valid, "supreme" national legislation compelling state action to give way. These materials are intended to center attention on the appropriate, respective roles of Court and Congress in furthering commerce clause values; on the source and scope of the commerce barrier to state action; and on the extent to which Congress has power to remove Court-discovered obstacles to state action.

SECTION 1. STATE REGULATION AND THE COMMERCE CLAUSE

Introduction: The vision and the achievement. In the cases in this section (and in the next chapter), state legislation is challenged on the basis of the unexercised commerce power. How effectively has the Court adjudicated such challenges? Has its performance matched its aspirations? Justice Jackson articulated the "free trade" goals of the commerce clause frequently and unusually well; the passages which follow in this introduction are from his opinion in H. P. Hood & Sons v. DuMond, 336 U.S. 525 (1949) (p. 661, infra). Consider, in examining the materials below, whether Justice Jackson stated the values and the criteria adequately: how well do (and can) Court decisions "give reality" to this "vision of the Founders"?

"The Commerce Clause is one of the most prolific sources of national power and an equally prolific source of conflict with legislation of the state. While the Constitution vests in Congress the power to regulate commerce among the states, it does not say what the states may or may not do in the absence of congressional action, nor how to draw the line between what is and what is not commerce among the states. Perhaps even more than by interpretation of its written word, this Court has advanced the solidarity and prosperity of this Nation by the meaning it has given to these great silences of the Constitution. . . .

"When victory relieved the Colonies from the pressure for solidarity that war had exerted, a drift toward anarchy and commercial warfare between states began. . . . The desire of the Forefathers to federalize regulation of foreign and interstate commerce stands in sharp contrast to their jealous preservation of the state's power over its internal affairs. . . .

"[The] principle that our economic unit is the Nation, which alone has the gamut of powers necessary to control of the economy, including the vital power of erecting customs barriers against foreign competition, has as its corollary that the states are not separable economic units. . . . The material success that has come to inhabitants of the states which make up this federal free trade unit has been the most impressive in the history of commerce, but the established interdependence of the states only emphasizs the necessity of protecting interstate movement of goods against local burdens and repressions. . . .

"[The] distinction between the power of the State to shelter its people from menaces to their health or safety and from fraud, even when those dangers emanate from interstate commerce, and its lack of power to retard, burden or constrict the flow of such commerce for their economic advantage, is one deeply rooted in both our history and our law. . . . This Court consistently has rebuffed attempts of states to advance their own commercial interests by curtailing the movement of articles of commerce, either into or out of the state, while generally supporting their right to impose even burdensome regulations in the interest of local health and safety. . . .

"Our system, fostered by the Commerce Clause, is that every farmer and every craftsman shall be encouraged to produce by the certainty that he will have free access to every market in the Nation, that no home embargoes will withhold his exports, and no foreign state will by customs duties or regulations exclude them. Likewise, every consumer may look to the free competition from every producing area in the Nation to protect him from exploitation by any. Such was the vision of the Founders; such has been the doctrine of this Court which has given it reality. . . ."

A. EARLY DEVELOPMENTS

GIBBONS v. OGDEN

9 Wheat. 1, 6 L.Ed. 23 (1824).

[The first part of Chief Justice Marshall's opinion in this case, as well as the facts of the dispute—printed with the materials on the congressional commerce power, chap. 4, p. 236, supra—should be reexamined at this point. In the remaining portions of the opinion, printed here, Chief Justice Marshall considered the impact of the commerce clause, and of national legislation based upon it, on the power of the state.]

The power of Congress, then, comprehends navigation, within the limits of every State in the Union; so far as that navigation may be, in any manner, connected with "commerce with foreign nations, or among the several States, or with the Indian tribes." It may, of consequence, pass the jurisdictional line of New York, and act upon the very waters to which the prohibition now under consideration applies.

But it has been urged with great earnestness, that although the power of Congress to regulate commerce with foreign nations, and among the serveral States, be co-extensive with the subject itself, and have no other limits than are prescribed in the constitution, yet the States may severally exercise the same power within their respective jurisdictions. In support of this argument, it is said that they possessed it as an inseparable attribute of sovereignty, before the formation of the constitution, and still retain it, except so far as they have surrendered it by that instrument; that this principle results from the nature of the government, and is secured by the tenth amendment; that an affirmative grant of power is not exclusive, unless in its own nature it be such that the continued exercise of it by the former possessor is inconsistent with the grant, and that this is not of that description.

The appellant, conceding these postulates, except the last, contends that full power to regulate a particular subject, implies the whole power, and leaves no residuum; that a grant of the whole is incompatible with the existence of a right in another to any part of it. . . .

The grant of the power to lay and collect taxes, is like the power to regulate commerce, made in general terms, and has never been understood to interfere with the exercise of the same power by the States; and hence has been drawn an argument which has been applied to the question under consideration. But the two grants are not, it is conceived, similar in their terms or their nature. Although many of the powers formerly exercised by the States, are transferred to the government of the Union, yet the State governments remain, and constitute a most important part of our system. The power of taxation is indispensable to their existence, and is a power which, in its own nature, is capable of residing in, and being exercised by, different authorities at the same time. . . . When, then, each government exercises the power of taxation, neither is exercising the power of the other. But, when a state proceeds to regulate commerce with foreign nations, or among the several States, it is exercising the very power that is granted to Congress, and is doing the very thing which Congress is authorized to do. There is no analogy, then, between the power of taxation and the power of regulating commerce.

In discussing the question, whether this power is still in the States, in the case under consideration, we may dismiss from it the inquiry, whether it is surrendered by the mere grant to Congress, or is retained until Congress shall exercise the power. We may dismiss that inquiry, because it has been exercised, and the regulations which Congress deemed it proper to make, are now in full operation. The sole question is, can a State regulate commerce with foreign nations and among the States, while Congress is regulating it?

The counsel for the respondent answer this question in the affirmative, and rely very much on the restrictions in the 10th section, as supporting their opinion. They say, very truly, that limitations of a power furnish a strong argument in favor of the existence of that power, and that the section which prohibits the States from laying duties on imports or exports, proves that this power might have been exercised, had it not been expressly forbidden; and, consequently, that any other commercial regulation, not expressly forbidden, to which the original power of the state is competent may still be made.

That this restriction shows the opinion of the Convention, that a State might impose duties on exports and imports, if not expressly forbidden, will be conceded; but that it follows as a consequence, from this concession, that a State may regulate commerce, with foreign nations and among the States, cannot be admitted. . . . This prohibition . . . is an exception from the acknowledged power of the States to levy taxes, not from the questionable power to regulate commerce. . . .

But the inspection laws are said to be regulations of commerce, and are certainly recognized in the constitution, as being passed in the exercise of a power remaining with the States.

That inspection laws may have a remote and considerable influence on commerce, will not be denied; but that a power to regulate commerce is the source from which the right to pass them is derived, cannot be admitted. The objects of inspection laws is to improve the quality of articles produced by the labor of the country; to fit them for exportation; or it may be, for domestic use. They act upon the subject before it becomes an article of foreign commerce, or of commerce among the states, and prepared it for that purpose. They form a portion of that immense mass of legislation which embraces everything within the territory of a State not surrendered to the general government; all which can be most advantageously exercised by the States themselves. Inspection laws, quarantine laws, health laws of every description, as well as laws for regulating the internal commerce of a state, and those which respect turnpike-roads, ferries, etc., are component parts of this mass.

No direct general power over these objects is granted to Congress; and, consequently, they remain subject to State legislation. If the legislative power of the Union can reach them, it must be for national purposes; it must be where the power is expressly given for a special purpose, or is clearly incidental to some power which is expressly given. It is obvious, that the government of the Union, in the exercise of its express powers, that, for example, of regulating commerce with foreign nations and among the States, may use means that may also be employed by a State, in the exercise of its acknowledged powers; that, for example, of regulating commerce within the State. If Congress license vessels to sail from one port to another, in the same State, the act is supposed to be, necessarily, incidental to the power expressly granted to Congress, and implies no claim of a direct power to regulate the purely internal commerce of a State, or to act directly on its system of police. So, if a State, in passing laws on subjects acknowledged to be within its control, and with a view to those subjects, shall adopt a measure of the same character with one which Congress may adopt, it does not derive its authority from the particular power which has been granted, but from some other, which remains with the State, and may be executed by the same means. All experience shows that the same measures, or measures scarcely distinguishable from each other, may flow from distinct powers; but this does not prove that the powers themselves are identical. Although the means used in their execution may sometimes approach each other so nearly as to be confounded, there are other situations in which they are sufficiently distinct to establish their individuality.

In our complex system, presenting the rare and difficult scheme of one general government, whose action extends over the whole, but which possesses only certain enumerated powers; and of numerous State governments which retain and exercise all powers not delegated to the Union, contests respecting power must arise. Were it even otherwise, the measures taken by the respective governments to execute their acknowledged powers, would often be of the same description, and might sometimes, interfere. This, however, does not prove that the one is exercising, or has a right to exercise, the powers of the other. . . .

It has been contended by counsel for the appellant, that, as the word "to regulate" implies in its nature, full power over the thing to be regulated, it excludes, necessarily, the action of all others that would perform the same operation on the same thing. That regulation is designed for the entire result, applying in those parts which remain as they were, as well as to those which are altered. It produces a uniform whole, which is as much disturbed and deranged by changing what the regulating power designs to leave untouched, as that on which it has operated.

There is great force in this argument, and the Court is not satisfied that it has been refuted.

Since, however, in exercising the power of regulating their own purely internal affairs, whether of trading or police, the States may sometimes enact laws, the validity of which depends on their interfering with and being contrary to, an act of Congress passed in pursuant of the constitution, the court will enter upon the inquiry, whether the laws of New York, . . . have, in their application to this case, come into collision with an act of Congress, and deprived a citizen of a right to which that act entitles him. Should this collision exist, it will be immaterial whether those laws were passed in virtue of a concurrent power "to regulate commerce with foreign nations and among the several States," or in virtue of a power to regulate their domestic trade and police. In one case and the other, the acts of New York must yield to the law of Congress; and the decision sustaining the privilege they confer, against a right given by a law of the Union, must be erroneous.

[The laws of New York were found to be in conflict with the Act of Congress. The decree below was reversed, and the bill of Ogden was dismissed.]

[The concurring opinion of Justice Johnson is omitted.]

WILLSON v. THE BLACK BIRD CREEK MARSH CO.

2 Pet. 245, 7 L.Ed. 412 (1829).

Error to the High Court of Errors and Appeals of the State of Delaware.

[The Company was authorized by a Delaware law to build a dam in Black Bird Creek—which flowed into the Delaware River—and also to "bank" the adjoining "marsh and low ground." The dam obstructed navigation of the creek. Willson and others were owners of a sloop licensed under the federal navigation laws. The sloop "broke and injured" the Company's dam in order to pass through the creek. The Company successfully sued for damages; the state courts rejected Willson's defense that the law authorizing the dam violated the commerce clause.

[William Wirt—who, with Daniel Webster, had argued against New York's power to establish the steamboat monopoly in Gibbons v. Ogden—was counsel for the Company. He described the creek as "one of those sluggish reptile streams, that do not run but creep, and which, wherever it passes, spreads its venom, and destroys the health of all those who inhabit its marshes." (Wirt wrote poetry and novels as an avocation.) He argued: "[C]an it be asserted, that a law authorising the erection of a dam, and the formation of banks which will draw off the pestilence, and give to those who have before suffered from disease, health and vigour, is unconstitutional? The power given by the constitution to congress to regulate commerce, may not be exercised to prevent such measures; and there has been no legislation by congress under the constitution, with which the proceedings of the defendants under the law of Delaware have interfered."]

Mr. Chief Justice MARSHALL delivered the opinion of the Court.

. . .

The act of assembly by which the plaintiffs were authorized to construct their dam, shows plainly that this is one of those many creeks, passing through a deep level marsh adjoining the Delaware, up which the tide flows for some distance. The value of the property on its banks must be enhanced by excluding the water from the marsh, and the health of the inhabitants probably improved. Measures calculated to produce these objects, provided they do not come into collision with the powers of the general government, are undoubtedly within those which are reserved to the states. But the measure authorised by this act stops a navigable creek, and must be supposed to abridge the rights of those who have been accustomed to use it.

. . .

The counsel for the plaintiffs in error insist that it comes in conflict with the power of the United States "to regulate commerce with foreign nations and among the several states."

If Congress had passed any act which bore upon the case; any act in execution of the power to regulate commerce, the object of which was to control state legislation over those small navigable creeks into which the tide flows, and which abound throughout the lower country of the middle and southern states; we should feel not much difficulty in saying that a state law coming in conflict with such act would be void.. But Congress has passed no such act. The repugnancy of the law of Delaware to the constitution is placed entirely on its repugnancy to the power to regulate commerce with foreign nations and among the several states; a power which has not been so exercised as to affect the question.

We do not think that the act empowering the Black Bird Creek Marsh Company to place a dam across the creeks, can under all the circumstances of the case, be considered as repugnant to the power to regulate commerce in its dormant state, or as being in conflict with any law passed on the subject.

There is no error, and the judgment is affirmed.

FROM BLACK BIRD TO COOLEY

Introduction. a. The Black Bird case was Marshall's last opportunity to write a Supreme Court opinion regarding state power to affect commerce.[1] In examining the Taney Court's early attempts to formulate criteria in this area, in the cases in these notes, consider the soundness of Professor Frankfurter's observation that "minds less sophisticated, less sensitive to the practical exigencies of government" turned Marshall's "tentative ideas . . . into obscuring formulas."[2] Consider, moreover, in examining the subsequent materials, whether the Cooley case and such "modern" cases as South-

---

1. Between Gibbon v. Ogden and the Black Bird case, he wrote an extensive opinion on state power to tax foreign commerce. Brown v. Maryland, 12 Wheat. 419 (1827), chap. 9, p. 686, infra.

2. Frankfurter, The Commerce Clause Under Marshall, Taney and Waite (1937), 31.

ern Pacific Co. v. Arizona, infra, in fact substituted improved, more "realistic" standards for Marshall's "abstract criteria." In Gibbons, Marshall emphasized the purpose of state regulation in distinguishing permissible "police" regulations from impermissible "commerce" regulations. Is the "purpose" emphasis used—or useful—in the post-Marshall cases?

b. For a decade and a half after Marshall's death in 1835—during the first half of the tenure of Marshall's successor, Taney—the Court groped for formulations with little clarity or agreement. To some Justices, for example, state regulations of "commerce" were prohibited, but regulations of "police" were constitutional. To Chief Justice Taney, *no* implied prohibitions from the dormant commerce clause were acceptable. With the Cooley decision in 1851, a new majority approach evolved at last—an approach that the modern Court has frequently asserted to be the still governing one. These notes sample the search for standards in the years preceding Cooley.

1. *The Miln case.* In Mayor of The City of New York v. Miln, 11 Pet. 102 (1837), the Court sustained a New York statute requiring the master of a vessel arriving in the port of New York from any point out of the state to report the names, residences, etc., of the passengers. Being of the opinion that the act "is not a regulation of commerce, but of police," the Court found it unnecessary to enter into any examination of the question whether the power to regulate commerce "be or be not exclusive of the States." Justice Story delivered a dissenting opinion in which he declared the act of New York "unconstitutional and void," and added: "In this opinion I have the consolation to know that I had the entire concurrence, upon the same grounds, of that great constitutional jurist, the late Mr. Chief Justice Marshall. Having heard the former arguments, his deliberate opinion was that the act of New York was unconstitutional."

2. *The Passenger Cases.* The Passenger Cases, 7 How. 283 (1849), invalidated two state laws. A New York statute imposed on the masters of ships coming from foreign or other state ports a tax for each passenger, the revenue to be used to defray the costs of examination of passengers for contagious diseases and to maintain a hospital for the treatment of those found to be diseased. A similar tax was imposed by a Massachusetts statute applicable to aliens, with the further requirement that the master should post a bond in the amount of $1000 for each alien likely to become a public charge. Both statutes were held "repugnant to the Constitution and laws of the United States, and therefore void." Five Justices concurred in the result and four (including Chief Justice Taney) dissented. There was no opinion by the Court, but a series of individual opinions.[3]

3. *The License Cases.* In one of the three cases decided together as The License Cases, 5 How. 504 (1847), plaintiffs in error purchased gin in

3. Twenty odd years later the problem was again before the Court in Henderson v. Mayor of New York, 92 U.S. 259 (1875). The statute of New York had been changed so as to require a bond, conditioned to indemnify against expense for support of the persons named therein, with an option to the ship-owner to pay a fixed sum for each passenger. It was held invalid, Justice Miller writing for the Court: "We are of opinion that this whole subject has been confided to Congress by the Constitution; that Congress can more appropriately and with more acceptance exercise it than any other body known to our law, state or national; that by providing a system of laws in these matters, applicable to all ports and to all vessels, a serious question, which has long been matter of contest and complaint, may be effectually and satisfactorily settled."

Boston and sold it, in the original cask, in Dover, New Hampshire, in violation of a state law. On appeal from convictions in the state courts, the judgments were affirmed by a unanimous Court, but without a majority concurring in any of the six opinions. Chief Justice Taney announced the judgments and delivered an opinion in which he said: "It is well known that upon this subject a difference of opinion has existed, and still exists, among the members of this court. But with every respect for the opinion of my brethren with whom I do not agree, it appears to me to be very clear, that the mere grant of power to the general government cannot, upon any just principles of construction, be construed to be an absolute prohibition to the exercise of any power over the same subject by the States. The controlling and supreme power over commerce with foreign nations and the several States is undoubtedly conferred upon Congress. Yet, in my judgment, the State may nevertheless, for the safety or convenience of trade, or for the protection of the health of its citizens, make regulations of commerce for its own ports and harbours, and for its own territory; and such regulations are valid unless they come in conflict with a law of Congress."

COOLEY v. BOARD OF WARDENS OF THE PORT OF PHILADELPHIA

12 How. 299, 13 L.Ed. 996 (1851).

Error to the Supreme Court of Pennsylvania.

[A Pennsylvania law of 1803 required every ship entering or leaving the port of Philadelphia to engage a local pilot. For failure to do so, the law imposed a penalty of half the pilotage fee, payable to the Board for a fund for superannuated pilots and their dependents. Cooley was held liable for the penalty, as consignee of two ships which had left the port without a local pilot.]

Mr. Justice CURTIS delivered the opinion of the Court.   .   .   .

That the power to regulate commerce includes the regulation of navigation, we consider settled. And when we look to the nature of the service performed by pilots, to the relations which that service and its compensations bear to navigation between the several States, and between the ports of the United States and foreign countries, we are brought to the conclusion, that the regulation of the qualifications of pilots, of the modes and times of offering and rendering their services, of the responsibilities which shall rest upon them, of the powers they shall possess, of the compensation they may demand, and of the penalties by which their rights and duties may be enforced, do constitute regulations of navigation, and consequently of commerce, within the just meaning of this clause of the Constitution.   .   .   .

It becomes necessary, therefore, to consider whether this law of Pennsylvania, being a regulation of commerce, is valid.

The act of Congress of the 7th of August, 1789, sec. 4, is as follows:

"That all pilots in the bays, inlets, rivers, harbors, and ports of the United States shall continue to be regulated in conformity with the existing laws of the States, respectively, wherein such pilots may be, or with such laws as the States may respectively hereafter enact for the purpose, until further legislative provision shall be made by Congress."

If the law of Pennsylvania, now in question, had been in existence at the date of this Act of Congress, we might hold it to have been adopted by Congress, and thus made a law of the United States, and so valid. Because this Act does, in effect, give the force of an Act of Congress, to the then existing State laws on this subject, so long as they should continue unrepealed by the State which enacted them.

But the law on which these actions were founded was not enacted till 1803. What effect, then, can be attributed to so much of the Act of 1789 as declares that pilots shall continue to be regulated in conformity "with such laws as the States may respectively hereafter enact for the purpose, until further legislative provision shall be made by Congress"?

If the States were divested of the power to legislate on this subject by the grant of the commercial power to Congress, it is plain this Act could not confer upon them power thus to legislate. If the Constitution excluded the States from making any law regulating commerce, certainly Congress cannot regrant, or in any manner reconvey to the States that power.[1] And yet this Act of 1789 gives its sanction only to laws enacted by the States. This necessarily implies a constitutional power to legislate; for only a rule created by the sovereign power of a State acting in its legislative capacity, can be deemed a law, enacted by a State; and if the State has so limited its sovereign power that it no longer extends to a particular subject, manifestly it cannot, in any proper sense, be said to enact laws thereon. Entertaining these views we are brought directly and unavoidably to the consideration of the question, whether the grant of the commercial power to Congress, did *per se* deprive the States of all power to regulate pilots. This question has never been decided by this court, nor, in our judgment, has any case depending upon all the considerations which must govern this one, come before this court. The grant of commercial power to Congress does not contain any terms which expressly exclude the States from exercising an authority over its subject matter. If they are excluded it must be because the nature of the power, thus granted to Congress, requires that a similar authority should not exist in the States. If it were conceded on the one side, that the nature of this power, like that to legislate for the District of Columbia, is absolutely and totally repugnant to the existence of similar power in the States, probably no one would deny that the grant of power to Congress, as effectually and perfectly excludes the States from all future legislation on the subject, as if express words had been used to exclude them. And on the other hand, if it were admitted that the existence of this power in Congress, like the power of taxation, is compatible with the existence of a similar power in the States, then it would be in conformity with the contemporary exposition of the Constitution (Federalist, No. 32), and with the judicial construction, given from time to time by this court, after the most deliberate consideration, to hold that the mere grant of such a power to Congress, did not imply a prohibition on the States to exercise the same power; that it is not the mere existence of such a power, but its exercise by Congress, which may be incompatible with the exercise of the same power by the States, and that the States may legislate in the absence of congressional

1. For later considerations of the problem of congressional authority to consent to state legislation affecting commerce—though the legislation would otherwise be barred by the "dormant" commerce power—see sec. 2B, p. 678, of this chapter.

regulations. Sturges v. Crowinshield, 4 Wheat. 193; Moore v. Houston, 5 Wheat. 1; Willson v. Black Bird Creek Marsh Co., 2 Pet. 251.

The diversities of opinion, therefore, which have existed on this subject, have arisen from the different views taken of the nature of this power. But when the nature of a power like this is spoken of, when it is said that the nature of the power requires that it should be exercised exclusively by Congress, it must be intended to refer to the subjects of that power, and to say they are of such a nature as to require exclusive legislation by Congress. Now, the power to regulate commerce, embraces a vast field, containing not only many, but exceedingly various subjects, quite unlike in their nature; some imperatively demanding a single uniform rule, operating equally on the commerce of the United States in every port; and some, like the subject now in question, as imperatively demanding that diversity, which alone can meet the local necessities of navigation.

Either absolutely to affirm, or deny, that the nature of this power requires exclusive legislation by Congress, is to lose sight of the nature of the subjects of this power, and to assert concerning all of them, what is really applicable but to a part. Whatever subjects of this power are in their nature national, or admit only of one uniform system, or plan of regulation, may justly be said to be of such a nature as to require exclusive legislation by Congress. That this cannot be affirmed of laws for the regulation of pilots and pilotage is plain. The Act of 1789 contains a clear and authoritative declaration by the first Congress, that the nature of this subject is such, that until Congress should find it necessary to exert its power, it should be left to the legislation of the States; that it is local and not national; that it is likely to be the best provided for, not by one system, or plan of regulations, but by as many as the legislative discretion of the several States should deem applicable to the local peculiarities of the ports within their limits.

Viewed in this light, so much of this Act of 1789 as declares that pilots shall continue to be regulated "by such laws as the States may respectively hereafter enact for that purpose," instead of being held to be inoperative, as an attempt to confer on the States a power to legislate, of which the Constitution had deprived them, is allowed an appropriate and important signification. It manifests the understanding of Congress, at the outset of the government, that the nature of this subject is not such as to require its exclusive legislation. The practice of the States, and of the national government, has been in conformity with this declaration, from the origin of the national government to this time; and the nature of the subject, when examined, is such as to leave no doubt of the superior fitness and propriety, not to say the absolute necessity, of different systems of regulation, drawn from local knowledge and experience, and conformed to local wants. How, then, can we say, that by the mere grant of power to regulate commerce, the States are deprived of all the power to legislate on this subject, because from the nature of the power the legislation of Congress must be exclusive. . . . .

It is the opinion of a majority of the court that the mere grant to Congress of the power to regulate commerce, did not deprive the States of power to regulate pilots, and that although Congress has legislated on this subject, its legislation manifests an intention, with a single exception, not to regulate this subject, but to leave its regulation to the several States. To these precise questions, which are all we are called on to decide, this opinion must

be understood to be confined. It does not extend to the question what other subjects, under the commercial power, are within the exclusive control of Congress, or may be regulated by the States in the absence of all congressional legislation; nor to the general question how far any regulation of a subject by Congress may be deemed to operate as an exclusion of all legislation by the States upon the same subject. We decide the precise questions before us, upon what we deem sound principles, applicable to this particular subject in the state in which the legislation of Congress has left it. We go no further.
. . .

Judgment affirmed.

Mr. Justice McLEAN, [dissenting]. . . .

Congress adopted the pilot laws of the States because it was well understood, they could have had no force, as regulations of foreign commerce or of commerce among the States, if not so adopted. By their adoption they were made acts of Congress, and ever since they have been so considered and enforced. . . . Congress may adopt the laws of a State, but it cannot enable a State to legislate. . . .

That a State may regulate foreign commerce, or commerce among the States, is a doctrine which has been advanced by individual judges of this court; but never before, I believe, has such a power been sanctioned by the decision of this court. In this case, the power to regulate pilots is admitted to belong to the commercial power of Congress; and yet it is held, that a State, by virtue of its inherent power, may regulate the subject, until such regulation shall be annulled by Congress. This is the principle established by this decision. . . . [Mr. Justice Wayne also dissented.]

Mr. Justice DANIEL, [concurring in the result]. I agree with the majority in their decision, . . . though I cannot go with them in the process or argument by which their conclusion has been reached. The power and the practice of enacting pilot-laws which has been exercised by the States from the very origin of their existence, although it is one in some degree connected with commercial intercourse, does not come essentially and regularly within that power of commercial regulation vested by the Constitution in Congress, and which by the Constitution must, when exercised by Congress, be enforced with perfect equality, and without any kind of discrimination, local or otherwise, in its application. . . . The true question here is, whether the power to enact pilot laws is . . . most appropriate and necessary to the State or the federal governments. It being conceded that this power has been exercised by the States from their very dawn of existence; that it can be practically and beneficially applied by the local authorities only; it being conceded, as it must be, that the power to pass pilot laws, as such, has not been in any express terms delegated to Congress, and does not necessarily conflict with the right to establish commercial regulations, I am forced to conclude that this is an original and inherent power in the States, and not one to be merely tolerated, or held subject to the sanction of the federal government. . . .

———

COOLEY AND THE MODERN DOCTRINE

The Cooley doctrine is frequently relied on in the modern cases, in sec. 1B below. See, e. g., Southern Pacific Co. v. Arizona. What is the "subject" found to be "local and not national" in Cooley?   All pilotage regulation? Pilotage regulation with a certain purpose?   Pilotage regulation with a certain effect?   Pilotage regulation recognized by Congress to be "local"?   Does the "national subject"—"local subject" approach require that the entire field of railroad regulation, for example, be characterized as either "local" or "national"?   Or may some state regulations of railroads be permissible, while others are invalid?   What is the "subject" found to be "national" in the Southern Pacific variety, p. 634, supra?

Leading modern cases such as Southern Pacific insist that they are applying Cooley.   Does the process of distinguishing "local" and "national" subjects in the modern cases differ from the Cooley approach?   Are "local" and "national" in the modern cases only conclusional labels for judgments resting on considerations going far beyond the "subject" of the regulation?   Cooley purported to abandon the "purpose" inquiry of the earlier cases for a scrutiny of the area regulated and the effect of the regulation.   Should "purpose" have been rejected as a guide?   What was the "purpose" of the pilotage law— safety, or economic support of pilots, or both?   Is there room for a "purpose" inquiry in the modern manifestations of the "Cooley doctrine"?   Does Southern Pacific, while paying lip service to Cooley, really represent an amalgamation of the Cooley "effect" emphasis with the pre-Cooley "purpose" concern?

B.   TRANSPORTATION

REGULATION OF TRANSPORTATION—THE BACKGROUND

1.   *Railroad rates: the Wabash case.*   a.   The problems perceived with the development of a nationwide railroad system provoked varied demands for legislative action.   See chap. 4, sec. 2, p. 240, supra.   Would pre-Civil War commerce clause doctrine prove adequate when these pressures produced responses from state legislatures?   Gibbons v. Ogden and the Cooley case continued to be cited; but the results hardly squared with a simplistic application of the "national-local subject" approach of Cooley.   When states sought to regulate the rates of interstate railroads, for example, the Court interposed commerce clause objections; yet many safety regulations were sustained, see note 2, infra.

b.   In Wabash v. St. L. & P. Ry. Co. v. Illinois, 118 U.S. 557 (1886), the Court held that the state's ban on railroad rate discriminations against shippers could not be enforced with regard to interstate shipments.   Congress had not acted, but the Court, under the Cooley formula, found that such regulations were of a "national," not "local," character.   The Court's inquiry emphasized that there might be "oppressive embarrassments" of interstate transportation if each of the through-states "could fix its own rules for prices, for modes of transit, for times and modes of delivery, and all other incidents to which the word 'regulation' can be applied." [1]   A few

---

1.   The Wabash case did not, however, end state control of intrastate rates— even where the regulation was attacked as burdening interstate traffic —in the absence of federal regulation.

Minnesota Rate Cases, 230 U.S. 352 (1913); cf. The Shreveport Rate Cases, 234 U.S. 342 (1914), chap. 4, p. 247, supra.

months after the decision, earlier pressures on Congress bore fruit and the Interstate Commerce Act of 1887 was adopted.

2. *Railroad safety regulations and the evolving Cooley doctrine.* But the Wabash ruling did not cover *all* "incidents of transportation to which the word 'regulation' can be applied"; whatever the Cooley "subject" in Wabash, it was not all that broad. Two years after Wabash, for example, the Court sustained a state examination requirement applied to engineers on interstate trains: the regulation was justified by safety considerations, and the impact on commerce was dismissed as "indirect." Smith v. Alabama, 124 U.S. 465 (1888). Many other "safety" laws were similarly sustained; a number are reviewed—and distinguished—in Southern Pacific Co. v. Arizona, infra.

3. *The attack on "direct" and "indirect" burdens criteria: the DiSanto case.* Citations of Cooley in the railroad cases could not obscure the fact that more particularized analyses underlay the results: the Cooley "subject" apparently varied with the type, and impact, of the regulation challenged. Was the increasingly common talk about "direct" and "indirect" effects on commerce a more helpful tool of analysis?[2] Justice Stone did not think so: in DiSanto v. Pennsylvania, 273 U.S. 34 (1927), soon after his appointment to the Court, he began a long campaign for more adequate articulation of the applicable criteria. Compare the attack on "direct"-"indirect" distinctions ir the cases on the congressional commerce power, chap. 4, supra.

In DiSanto, a state statute required a license fee of fifty dollars to be paid by travel agents selling steamship tickets for foreign travel. The license was revocable for misbehavior and was granted only after proof of good character and fitness. A majority of the Court held the statute unconstitutional as a "direct burden" on foreign commerce. The "purpose" of the "direct" regulation was irrelevant. Justice Brandeis, in a dissent concurred in by Justice Holmes, stated that the statute "places no direct burden on such

---

2. Was understanding of either the "direct"-"indirect" approach or the Cooley "subject" approach aided by Justice Hughes' statement in Port Richmond & Bergen Point Ferry Co. v. Board, 234 U.S. 317 (1914): "Coming then to the question now presented—whether a State may fix reasonable rates for ferriage from its shore to the shore of another State,—regard must be had to the basic principle involved. That principle is, as repeatedly declared, that as to those subjects which require a general system or uniformity of regulation the power of Congress is exclusive; that, in other matters, admitting of diversity of treatment according to the special requirements of local conditions, the States may act within their respective jurisdictions until Congress sees fit to act; and that, when Congress does act, the exercise of its authority overrides all conflicting state legislation. Cooley v. Board of Wardens . . . .. It is this principle that is applied in holding that a State may not impose direct burdens upon interstate commerce, for this is to say that the States may

not directly regulate or restrain that which from its nature should be under the control of the one authority and be free from restriction save as it is governed by valid Federal rule. . . . It was this principle which governed the decision in Wabash &c. Railway Co. v. Illinois, 118 U.S. 557, as to interstate railroad rates." [The Court held that New Jersey's regulation of rates of a New Jersey-New York ferry was constitutional: ferries (not operated in connection with railroads) are "a subject of a different character" from railroads; they are "instruments of local convenience . . subject to local regulation," at least where the state regulations are not "burdensome" or "discriminatory"; New Jersey's rate regulations, like pilotage or quarantine laws, may have a "direct" impact on commerce, but they cannot be invalidated "without considering the nature of the regulation and the special subject to which it relates"; the situation is "essentially local," and there is no "inherent necessity" for national regulation.]

commerce." In a separate dissent (Justices Holmes and Brandeis concurring), Justice Stone questioned the standard employed in determining the constitutionality of the statute: "In this case the traditional test of the limit of state action by inquiring whether the interference with commerce is direct or indirect seems to me too mechanical, too uncertain in its application, and too remote from actualities, to be of value. In thus making use of the expressions, 'direct' and 'indirect interference' with commerce, we are doing little more than using labels to describe a result rather than any trustworthy formula by which it is reached." It seemed clear to him that those interferences with interstate commerce which are not deemed forbidden are to be sustained, not because the effect on commerce is nominally indirect, but because a consideration of all the facts and circumstances, such as the nature of the regulation, its function, the character of the business involved and the actual effect on the flow of commerce, lead to the conclusion that the regulation concerns interests peculiarly local and does not infringe the national interest in maintaining the freedom of commerce. [The DiSanto decision was overruled in California v. Thompson, 313 U.S. 109 (1941): a law requiring licensing and bonding of travel agents, designed to prevent "fraudulent and unconscionable conduct," was held to deal with a problem "peculiarly a subject of local concern."]

4. *The adequacy of the "direct"-"indirect" approach: the Georgia blow-post law cases.* a. Where the "direct"-"indirect" labels as "remote from actualities," as "mechanical," as Justice Stone insisted? Note that Smith v. Alabama, the railroad safety case in note 2 above, talked of realistic "embarrassments" while using the "indirect" language; and note that Justice Brandeis, who was always sensitive to economic "actualities," spoke of "direct" burdens in DiSanto—as he did frequently—though he also concurred in Justice Stone's dissent. In examining Justice Stone's later contributions in this area, consider whether his formulations are substantially more helpful than the earlier standards.

b. Litigation regarding a Georgia safety law illustrates the capacity of Justices using mere "labels" to respond to "actualities." The Georgia blow-post law required railroads to erect posts 400 yards from railroad crossings and directed locomotive engineers, when passing the posts, to blow the train whistles and to "simultaneously" check speed "so as to stop in time should any person . . . be crossing" the tracks at the road crossing. Suits for injuries in crossing accidents relied on noncompliance with the law in claiming negligence; the defendants insisted that the law violated the commerce clause. In Southern Railway Co. v. King, 217 U.S. 524 (1910), the Court affirmed a judgment against the railroad. The pleadings had alleged that the blow-post law imposed "a direct burden on" interstate traffic. The Court's affirmance noted that the pleadings "set forth no facts which would make the operation of the statute unconstitutional." (A trial offer of proof regarding the burden of the statute was held properly excluded because of the deficient pleadings.)

Contrast the handling of a second case challenging application of the Georgia law, Seaboard Airline R. Co. v. Blackwell, 244 U.S. 310 (1917). There, the railroad's answer alleged that along the 123 miles of its track from Atlanta to the Georgia-South Carolina border, there were 124 grade crossings; that compliance with the law would require "practically a full stop at each of the road crossings"; that each stop would take from three to five minutes; and that compliance by the train involved in the accident would have changed a scheduled $4\frac{1}{2}$ hours' run into one of more than $10\frac{1}{2}$ hours. The state courts held that these pleadings were an inadequate defense: the law was a valid police regulation; any burden on commerce was "indirect." The Supreme Court reversed: the case was distinguishable from the Southern Railway case, *supra*, for the facts that were missing there were alleged here; and the allegations "compel the conclusion that the statute is a direct burden upon interstate commerce, and being such, is unlawful."

5. *State licensing, interstate carriers, and the importance of "purpose": the Buck and Bradley cases.* Do the "direct"-"indirect" or Cooley standards in the foregoing cases articulate the determinative considerations in such cases as Buck v. Kuykendall, 267 U.S. 307 (1925), and Bradley v. Public Utilities Commission, 289 U.S. 92 (1933)? Each case involved a state denial of a certificate of convenience and necessity to an applicant seeking to use the highways as an interstate carrier; in each case, Justice Brandeis wrote the Court's opinion; but the denial was set aside in one case and sustained in the other.

a. Buck, a citizen of Oregon, wanted to operate an "auto stage line" between Portland and Seattle. Washington denied the certificate because the territory was "already being \adequately served" by other carriers. In reversing, Justice Brandeis said: "It may be assumed that . . . the state statute is consistent with the Fourteenth Amendment; and also, that appropriate state regulations adopted primarily to promote safety upon the highways and conservation in their use are not obnoxious to the Commerce Clause, where the indirect burden imposed upon interstate commerce is not unreasonable. . . . The provision here in question is of a different character. Its primary purpose is not regulation with a view to safety or to conservation of the highways, but the prohibition of competition. It determines not the manner of use, but the persons by whom the highways may be used. It prohibits such use to some persons, while permitting it to others for the same purpose and in the same manner. Moreover, it determines whether the prohibition shall be applied by resort, through state officials, to a test which is peculiarly within the province of federal action— the existence of adequate facilities for conducting interstate commerce. The vice of the legislation is dramatically exposed by the fact that the State of Oregon had issued its certificate which may be deemed equivalent to a legislative declaration that, despite existing facilities, public convenience and necessity required the establishment by Buck of the auto stage line between Seattle and Portland. Thus, the provision of the Washington statute is a regulation, not of the use of its own highways, but of interstate commerce. Its effect upon such commerce is not merely to burden, but to obstruct it. Such state action is forbidden by the Commerce Clause."

b. In the Bradley case, eight years later, Ohio denied a certificate to operate between Cleveland, Ohio, and Flint, Michigan, on the ground that the highway to be used "is so badly congested by established motor vehicle operations, that the addition of the applicant's proposed service would create and maintain an excessive and undue hazard to the safety and security of the traveling public, and the property upon such highway." In sustaining the denial, Justice Brandeis noted that in Buck, *supra*, "safety was doubtless promoted when the certificate was denied," but "promotion of safety was merely an incident of the denial" designed "to prevent competition." In Bradley, by contrast, "the purpose of the denial was to promote safety; and the test employed was congestion of the highway. The effect of the denial upon interstate commerce was merely an incident." [3]

SOUTH CAROLINA STATE HIGHWAY DEPT. v. BARNWELL BROS.

303 U.S. 177, 58 S.Ct. 510, 82 L.Ed. 734 (1938).

Appeal from the District Court for the Eastern District of South Carolina.

Mr. Justice STONE delivered the opinion of the Court.

Act No. 259 of the General Assembly of South Carolina, of April 28, 1933, . . . prohibits use on the state highways of motor trucks and "semi-trailer motor trucks" whose width exceeds 90 inches, and whose weight including load exceeds 20,000 pounds. . . .

[The three-judge District Court] enjoined the enforcement of the weight provision against interstate motor carriers on the specified highways, and also the width limitation of 90 inches, except in the case of vehicles exceeding 96 inches in width. It exempted from the operation of the decree, bridges on those highways "not constructed with sufficient strength to support the heavy trucks of modern traffic or too narrow to accommodate such traffic safely," provided the state highway department should place at each end of the bridge proper notices warning that the use of the bridge is forbidden by trucks exceeding the weight or width limits . . . . .

The trial court rested its decision that the statute unreasonably burdens interstate commerce, upon findings, not assailed here, that there is a large amount of motor truck traffic passing interstate in the southeastern part of the United States, which would normally pass over the highways of South Carolina, but which will be barred from the state by the challenged restrictions if enforced, and upon its conclusion that when viewed in the light of their effect upon interstate commerce, these restrictions are unreasonable.

To reach this conclusion the court weighed conflicting evidence and made its own determinations as to the weight and width of motor trucks commonly used in interstate traffic and the capacity of the specified highways of the state to accommodate such traffic without injury to them or danger to their users. It found that interstate carriage by motor trucks has become a national industry; that from 85 to 90% of the motor trucks used in inter-

---

3. Compare Fry Roofing Co. v. Wood, 344 U.S. 157 (1952); An Arkansas statute required all contract carriers to obtain a "permit" before using the state's highways. The law listed certain factors to be considered in decisions on permit applications, including the adequacy of transportation services already performed by "any railroad, street railway or contract carrier." A carrier sought to enjoin enforcement of the statute on commerce clause grounds. The Court, in a 5:4 decision, affirmed denial of the injunction: "Unlike the situation in the Buck case, Arkansas has not refused to grant a permit for interstate carriage of goods on state highways. It has asked these driver-owners to do nothing except apply for a permit . . . . . And the State Commission here expressly disclaims any 'discretionary right to refuse to grant a permit for contract carriage where that carriage is in interstate commerce.' . . . . At present we hold only that Arkansas is not powerless to require interstate motor carriers to identify themselves as users of that state's highways." Justice Douglas' dissent insisted that this was "precisely the kind of control which the State of Washington tried to exercise over motor carriers and which was denied her in Buck v. Kuykendall." Cf. Castle v. Hayes Freight Lines, 348 U.S. 61 (1954), p. 675, infra.

state transportation are 96 inches wide and of a gross weight, when loaded, of more than ten tons; that only four other states prescribe a gross load weight as low as 20,000 pounds   .   .   . .

It also found that the gross weight of vehicles is not a factor to be considered in the preservation of concrete highways, but that the appropriate factor to be considered is wheel or axle weight; that vehicles engaged in interstate commerce are so designed and the pressure of their weight is so distributed by their wheels and axles that gross loads of more than 20,000 pounds can be carried over concrete roads without damage to the surface; that a gross weight limitation of that amount, especially as applied to semi-trailer motor trucks, is unreasonable as a means of preserving the highways; that it has no reasonable relation to safety of the public using the highways; and that the width limitation of 90 inches is unreasonable when applied to standard concrete highways of the state, in view of the fact that all other states permit a width of 96 inches, which is the standard width of trucks engaged in interstate commerce.

In reaching these conclusions, and at the same time holding that the weight and width limitations do not infringe the Fourteenth Amendment, the court proceeded upon the assumption that the commerce clause imposes upon state regulations to secure the safe and economical use of highways a standard of reasonableness which is more exacting when applied to the interstate traffic than that required by the Fourteenth Amendment as to all traffic; that a standard of weight and width of motor vehicles which is an appropriate state regulation when applied to intrastate traffic may be prohibited because of its effect on interstate commerce, although the conditions attending the two classes of traffic with respect to safety and protection of the highways are the same.

South Carolina has built its highways and owns and maintains them. It has received from the federal government, in aid of its highway improvements, money grants   .   .   . . But appellees do not challenge here the ruling of the district court that Congress has not undertaken to regulate the weight and size of motor vehicles in interstate motor traffic   .   .   . .

While the constitutional grant to Congress of power to regulate interstate commerce has been held to operate of its own force to curtail state power in some measure,[1] it did not forestall all state action affecting interstate commerce. Ever since Willson v. Black Bird Creek Marsh Co., 2 Pet. 245, and Cooley v. Board of Port Wardens, 12 How. 299, it has been recognized that there are matters of local concern, the regulation of which unavoidably involves some regulation of interstate commerce but which, because of their local character and their number and diversity, may never be fully dealt with by Congress. Notwithstanding the commerce clause, such regula-

1. State regulations affecting interstate commerce, whose purpose or effect is to gain for those within the state an advantage at the expense of those without, or to burden those out of the state without any corresponding advantage to those within, have been thought to impinge upon the constitutional prohibition even though Congress has not acted. . . .

Underlying the stated rule has been the thought, often expressed in judicial opinion, that when the regulation is of such a character that its burden falls principally upon those without the state, legislative action is not likely to be subjected to those political restraints which are normally exerted on legislation where it affects adversely some interests within the state. . . . [Footnote by the Court.]

tion in the absence of Congressional action has for the most part been left to the states . . . .

The commerce clause, by its own force, prohibits discrimination against interstate commerce, whatever its form or method, and the decisions of this Court have recognized that there is scope for its like operation when state legislation nominally of local concern is in point of fact aimed at interstate commerce, or by its necessary operation is a means of gaining a local benefit by throwing the attendant burdens on those without the state. . . . It was to end these practices that the commerce clause was adopted. . . . The commerce clause has also been thought to set its own limitation upon state control of interstate rail carriers so as to preclude the subordination of the efficiency and convenience of interstate traffic to local service requirements.

But the present case affords no occasion for saying that the bare possession of power by Congress to regulate the interstate traffic forces the states to conform to standards which Congress might, but has not adopted, or curtails their power to take measures to insure the safety and conservation of their highways which may be applied to like traffic moving intrastate. Few subjects of state regulation are so peculiarly of local concern as is the use of state highways. There are few, local regulation of which is so inseparable from a substantial effect on interstate commerce. Unlike the railroads, local highways are built, owned and maintained by the state or its municipal subdivisions. The state has a primary and immediate concern in their safe and economical administration. The present regulations, or any others of like purpose, if they are to accomplish their end, must be applied alike to interstate and intrastate traffic both moving in large volume over the highways. The fact that they affect alike shippers in interstate and intrastate commerce in large number within as well as without the state is a safeguard against their abuse.

. . . With respect to the extent and nature of the local interests to be protected and the unavoidable effect upon interstate and intrastate commerce alike, regulations of the use of the highways are akin to local regulation of rivers, harbors, piers and docks, quarantine regulations, and game laws, which, Congress not acting, have been sustained even though they materially interfere with interstate commerce.[2]

---

2. Among the state regulations materially affecting interstate commerce which this Court has upheld, Congress not acting, are those which sanction obstructions in navigable rivers, Willson v. Black Bird Creek Marsh Co., 2 Pet. 245 . . . ; approve the erection of bridges over navigable streams, Gilman v. Philadelphia, 3 Wall. 713 . . . ; require payment of fees as an incident to use of harbors, Cooley v. Board of Port Wardens, 12 How. 299 . . . ; control the location of docks, Cummings v. Chicago, 188 U.S. 410; impose wharfage charges, Packet Co. v. Keokuk, 95 U.S. 80 . . . ; establish inspection and quarantine laws, Turner v. Maryland, 107 U.S. 38 . . . ; Patapsco Guano Co. v. North Carolina Board of Agriculture, 171 U.S. 345 . . . ; and regulate the taking or exportation of domestic game, Geer v. Connecticut, 161 U.S. 519 . . . ; cf. Foster-Fountain Packing Co. v. Haydel, 278 U.S. 1, 13, holding invalid a local regulation ostensibly designed to conserve a natural resource but whose purpose and effect were to benefit Louisiana enterprise at the expense of businesses outside the state. [Footnote by the Court.]

[On the questions of what constitutes an "inspection" law, and what is a permissible inspection fee, see the Patapsco Guano case, supra. On quarantine laws, see Morgan's S. S. Co. v. Louisiana Board of Health, 118 U.S. 455 (1886).]

. . . This Court has often sustained the exercise of [state power over its own highways] although it has burdened or impeded interstate commerce. It has upheld weight limitations lower than those presently imposed, applied alike to motor traffic moving interstate and intrastate. Morris v. Duby, supra; Sproles v. Binford, [298 U.S. 407]. Restrictions favoring passenger traffic over the carriage of interstate merchandise by truck have been similarly sustained. Sproles v. Binford, supra; Bradley v. Public Utilities Comm'n, 289 U.S. 92, as has the exaction of a reasonable fee for the use of the highways. . . . Kane v. New Jersey, 242 U.S. 160; Interstate Busses Corp. v. Blodgett, 276 U.S. 245 . . . . .[3]

In each of these cases regulation involves a burden on interstate commerce. But so long as the state action does not discriminate, the burden is one which the Constitution permits because it is an inseparable incident of the exercise of a legislative authority, which, under the Constitution, has been left to the states.

Congress, in the exercise of its plenary power to regulate interstate commerce, may determine whether the burdens imposed on it by state regulation, otherwise permissible, are too great, and may, by legislation designed to secure uniformity or in other respects to protect the national interest in the commerce, curtail to some extent the state's regulatory power. But that is a legislative, not a judicial function . . . .. In the absence of such legislation the judicial function, under the commerce clause as well as the Fourteenth Amendment, stops with the inquiry whether the state legislature in adopting regulations such as the present has acted within its province, and whether the means of regulation chosen are reasonably adapted to the end sought. . . .

Here the first inquiry has already been resolved by our decisions that a state may impose non-discriminatory restrictions with respect to the character of motor vehicles moving in interstate commerce as a safety measure and as a means of securing the economical use of its highways. In resolving the second, courts do not sit as legislatures, either state or national. . . . When the action of a legislature is within the scope of its power, fairly debatable questions as to its reasonableness, wisdom and propriety are not for the determination of courts, but for the legislative body . . . . . It is not any the less a legislative power committed to the states because it affects interstate commerce, and courts are not any the more entitled, because interstate commerce is affected, to substitute their own for the legislative judgment. . . .

Since the adoption of one weight or width regulation, rather than another, is a legislative not a judicial choice, its constitutionality is not to be determined by weighing in the judicial scales the merits of the legislative choice and rejecting it if the weight of evidence presented in court appears to favor a different standard. . . . Being a legislative judgment it is presumed to be supported by facts known to the legislature unless facts judicially known or proved preclude that possibility. Hence, in reviewing the present determination we examine the record, not to see whether the findings of the court below are supported by evidence, but to ascertain upon

---

3. On highway use fees and taxes on interstate motor carriers, see chap. 9, infra.

the whole record whether it is possible to say that the legislative choice is without rational basis. . . . Not only does the record fail to exclude that possibility, but it shows affirmatively that there is adequate support for the legislative judgment.

At the outset it should be noted that underlying much of the controversy is the relative merit of a gross weight limitation as against an axle or wheel weight limitation. . . . The choice of a weight limitation based on convenience of application and consequent lack of need for rigid supervisory enforcement is for the legislature, and we cannot say that its preference for the one over the other is in any sense arbitrary or unreasonable. . . .

There was testimony before the court to support its conclusion that the highways in question are capable of sustaining without injury a wheel load of 8,000 or 9,000 pounds . . . . Much of this testimony appears to have been based on theoretical strength of concrete highways laid under ideal conditions, and none of it was based on an actual study of the highways of South Carolina . . . . There is uncontradicted testimony that approximately 60% of the South Carolina standard paved highways in question were built without a longitudinal center joint which has since become standard practice . . . ; and that owing to the distribution of the stresses on concrete roads when in use, those without a center joint have a tendency to develop irregular longitudinal cracks. As the concrete in the center of such roads is thinner than that at the edges, the result is that the highway is split into two irregular segments, each with a weak inner edge which, according to the expert testimony, is not capable of supporting indefinitely wheel loads in excess of 4,200 pounds. . . .

These considerations, with the presumption of constitutionality, afford adequate support for the weight limitation without reference to other items of the testimony tending to support it. Furthermore, South Carolina's own experience is not to be ignored. . . . The present weight limitation was recommended . . . after a full consideration of relevant data including a report by the state engineer who had constructed the concrete highways of the state and who advised a somewhat lower limitation as necessary for their preservation. The fact that many states have adopted a different standard is not persuasive. The conditions under which highways must be built in the several states, their construction and the demands made upon them, are not uniform. . . The legislature, being free to exercise its own judgment, is not bound by that of other legislatures. It would hardly be contended that if all the states had adopted a single standard, none, in the light of its own experience and in the exercise of its judgment upon all the complex elements which enter into the problem, could change it.

Only a word need be said as to the width limitation. While a large part of the highways in question are from 18 to 20 feet in width, approximately 100 miles are only 16 feet wide. On all the use of a 96 inch truck leaves but a narrow margin for passing. On the road 16 feet wide it leaves none. The 90 inch limitation has been in force in South Carolina since 1920 and the concrete highways which it has built appear to be adapted to vehicles of that width. The record shows without contradiction that the use of heavy loaded trucks on the highways tends to force other traffic off the concrete surface onto the shoulders of the road adjoining its edges and to increase repair costs materially. It appears also that as the width of trucks is increased it obstructs the view of the highway, causing much inconvenience and increased hazard in its use. It plainly cannot be said that the width of trucks used on the highways in South Carolina is unrelated to their safety and cost of maintenance, or that a 90 inch width limitation adopted to safeguard the highways of the State, is not within the range of the permissible legislative choice.

The regulatory measures taken by South Carolina are within its legislative power. They do not infringe the Fourteenth Amendment, and the resulting burden on interstate commerce is not forbidden.

Reversed.

Mr. Justice CARDOZO and Mr. Justice REED took no part in the consideration or decision of this case.

SOUTHERN PACIFIC CO. v. ARIZONA

325 U.S. 761, 65 S.Ct. 1515, 89 L.Ed. 1915 (1945).

Appeal from the Supreme Court of Arizona.

Mr. Chief Justice STONE delivered the opinion of the Court.

The Arizona Train Limit Law of May 16, 1912, ... makes it unlawful for any person or corporation to operate within the state a railroad train of more than fourteen passenger or seventy freight cars, and authorizes the state to recover a money penalty for each violation of the Act. The questions for decision are whether Congress has, by legislative enactment, restricted the power of the states to regulate the length of interstate trains as a safety measure and, if not, whether the statute contravenes the commerce clause of the Federal Constitution.

In 1940 the State of Arizona brought suit in the Arizona Superior Court against appellant, the Southern Pacific Company, to recover the statutory penalties for operating within the state two interstate trains, one a passenger train of more than fourteen cars, and one a freight train of more than seventy cars. . . . After an extended trial, without a jury, the court made detailed findings of fact on the basis of which it gave judgment for the railroad company. The Supreme Court of Arizona reversed and directed judgment for the state. . . .

[The state supreme court] thought that a state statute, enacted in the exercise of the police power, and bearing some reasonable relation to the health, safety and well-being of the people of the state, of which the state legislature is the judge, was not to be judicially overturned, notwithstanding its admittedly adverse effect on the operation of interstate trains. . . .

[The Court rejected a contention that Congress, by authorizing the Commerce Commission to regulate train lengths, had superseded state power.] Congress, in enacting legislation within its constitutional authority over interstate commerce, will not be deemed to have intended to strike down a state statute designed to protect the health and safety of the public unless its purpose to do so is clearly manifested, . . . or unless the state law, in terms or in its practical administration, conflicts with the Act of Congress, or plainly and palpably infringes its policy. . . . Congress, although asked to do so, has declined to pass legislation specifically limiting trains to seventy cars.   We are therefore brought to appellant's principal contention, that the state statute contravenes the commerce clause of the Federal Constitution.

Although the commerce clause conferred on the national government power to regulate commerce, its possession of the power does not exclude all state power of regulation. . . .   But ever since Gibbons v. Ogden, 9 Wheat. 1, the states have not been deemed to have authority to impede substantially the free flow of commerce from state to state, or to regulate those phases of the national commerce which, because of the need of national uniformity, demand that their regulation, if any, be prescribed by a single authority.   Cooley v. Board of Wardens, supra . . . ..   Whether or not this long recognized distribution of power between the national and the state governments is predicated upon the implications of the commerce clause itself, . . .   or upon the presumed intention of Congress, where Congress has not spoken, . . .   Dowling, Interstate Commerce and State Power, 27 Va.Law Rev. 1, the result is the same.

In the application of these principles some enactments may be found to be plainly within and others plainly without state power.   But between these extremes lies the infinite variety of cases, in which regulation of local matters may also operate as a regulation of commerce, in which reconciliation of the conflicting claims of state and national power is to be attained only by some appraisal and accommodation of the competing demands of the state and national interests involved. . . .

Congress has undoubted power to redefine the distribution of power over interstate commerce.   It may either permit the states to regulate the commerce in a manner which would otherwise not be permissible, . . .   or exclude state regulation even of matters of peculiarly local concern which nevertheless affect interstate commerce.   [See sec. 2 of this chapter, infra.]

But in general Congress has left it to the courts to formulate the rules thus interpreting the commerce clause in its application, doubtless because it has appreciated the destructive consequences to the commerce of the nation if their protection were withdrawn . . ., and has been aware that in their application state laws will not be invalidated without the support of relevant factual material which will "afford a sure basis" for an informed judgment. . . .   Meanwhile, Congress has accommodated its legislation, as have the states, to these rules as an established feature of our constitutional system.   There has thus been left to the states wide scope for the regulation of matters of local state concern, even though it in some measure affects the commerce, provided it does not materially restrict the free flow of commerce across state lines, or interfere with it in matters with respect to which uniformity of regulation is of predominant national concern.

Hence the matters for ultimate determination here are the nature and extent of the burden which the state regulation of interstate trains, adopted as a safety measure, imposes on interstate commerce, and whether the relative weights of the state and national interests involved are such as to make inapplicable the rule, generally observed, that the free flow of interstate commerce and its freedom from local restraints in matters requiring uniformity of regulation are interests safeguarded by the commerce clause from state interference.

While this Court is not bound by the findings of the state court, and may determine for itself the facts of a case upon which an asserted federal right depends . . ., the facts found by the state trial court showing the nature of the interstate commerce involved, and the effect upon it of the train limit law, are not seriously questioned. Its findings with respect to the need for and effect of the statute as a safety measure, although challenged in some particulars which we do not regard as material to our decision, are likewise supported by evidence. Taken together the findings supply an adequate basis for decision of the constitutional issue.

The findings show that the operation of long trains, that is trains of more than fourteen passengers and more than seventy freight cars, is standard practice over the main lines of the railroads of the United States, and that, if the length of trains is to be regulated at all, national uniformity in the regulation adopted, such as only Congress can prescribe, is practically indispensable to the operation of an efficient and economical national railway system. On many railroads passenger trains of more than fourteen cars and freight trains of more than seventy cars are operated, and on some systems freight trains are run ranging from one hundred and twenty-five to one hundred and sixty cars in length. Outside of Arizona, where the length of trains is not restricted, appellant runs a substantial proportion of long trains. In 1939 on its comparable route for through traffic through Utah and Nevada from 66 to 85% of its freight trains were over 70 cars in length and over 43% of its passenger trains included more than fourteen passenger cars.

In Arizona, approximately 93% of the freight traffic and 95% of the passenger traffic is interstate. Because of the Train Limit Law appellant is required to haul over 30% more trains in Arizona than would otherwise have been necessary. The record shows a definite relationship between operating costs and the length of trains, the increase in length resulting in a reduction of operating costs per car. The additional cost of operation of trains complying with the Train Limit Law in Arizona amounts for the two railroads traversing that state to about $1,000,000 a year. The reduction in train lengths also impedes efficient operation. More locomotives and more manpower are required; the necessary conversion and reconversion of train lengths at terminals and the delay caused by breaking up and remaking long trains upon entering and leaving the state in order to comply with the law, delays the traffic and diminishes its volume moved in a given time, especially when traffic is heavy. . . .

The unchallenged findings leave no doubt that the Arizona Train Limit Law imposes a serious burden on the interstate commerce conducted by appellant. It materially impedes the movement of appellant's interstate trains through that state and interposes a substantial obstruction to the national policy proclaimed by Congress, to promote adequate, economical and efficient railway transportation service. . . . Enforcement of the law in Arizona, while train lengths remain unregulated or are regulated by varying standards in other states, must inevitably result in an impairment of uniformity of efficient railroad operation because the railroads are subjected to regulation which is not uniform in its application. Compliance with a state statute limiting train lengths requires interstate trains of a length lawful in other states to be broken up and reconstituted as they enter each state according as it may impose varying limitations upon train lengths. The alternative is for the carrier to conform to the lowest train limit restriction of any of the states through which its trains pass, whose laws thus control the carriers' operations both within and without the regulating state. . . .

At present the seventy freight car laws are enforced only in Arizona and Oklahoma, with a fourteen car passenger car limit in Arizona. The record here shows that the enforcement of the Arizona statute results in freight trains being broken up and reformed at the California border and in New Mexico, some distance from the Arizona line. Frequently it is not feasible to operate a newly assembled train from the New Mexico yard nearest to Arizona, with the result that the Arizona limitation governs the flow of traffic as far east as El Paso, Texas. For similar reasons the Arizona law often controls the length of passenger trains all the way from Los Angeles to El Paso.

If one state may regulate train lengths, so may all the others, and they need not prescribe the same maximum limitation. The practical effect of such regulation is to control train operations beyond the boundaries of the state exacting it because of the necessity of breaking up and reassembling long trains at the nearest terminal points before entering and after leaving the regulating state. The serious impediment to the free flow of commerce by the local regulation of train lengths and the practical necessity that such regulation, if any, must be prescribed by a single body having a nation-wide authority are apparent.

The trial court found that the Arizona law had no reasonable relation to safety, and made train operation more dangerous. Examination of the evidence and the detailed findings makes it clear that this conclusion was rested on facts found which indicate that such increased danger of accident and personal injury as may result from the greater length of trains is more than offset by the increase in the number of accidents resulting from the larger number of trains when train lengths are reduced. In considering the effect of the statute as a safety measure, therefore, the factor of controlling significance for present purposes is not whether there is basis for the conclusion of the Arizona Supreme Court . . . .. The decisive question is whether in the circumstances the total effect of the law as a safety measure in reducing accidents and casualties is so slight or problematical as not to outweigh the national interest in keeping interstate commerce free from interferences which seriously impede it and subject it to local regulation which does not have a uniform effect on the interstate train journey which it interrupts.

The principal source of danger of accident from increased length of trains is the resulting increase of "slack action" of the train. Slack action is the amount of free movement of one car before it transmits its motion to an adjoining coupled car. This free movement results from the fact that in railroad practice cars are loosely coupled, and the coupling is often combined with a shock-absorbing device, a "draft gear", which, under stress, substantially increases the free movement as the train is started or stopped. . . .

On comparison of the number of slack action accidents in Arizona with those in Nevada, where the length of trains is now unregulated the trial court found that with substantially the same amount of traffic in each state the number of accidents was relatively the same in long as in short train operations. . . . Nor does it appear that slack action accidents occurring on passenger trains whatever their length, are of sufficient severity to cause serious injury or damage.

As the trial court found, reduction of the length of trains also tends to increase the number of accidents because of the increase in the number of trains. The application of the Arizona law compelled appellant to operate 30.08%, or 4,304, more freight trains in 1938 than would otherwise have been necessary. And the record amply supports the trial court's conclusion that the frequency of accidents is closely related to the number of trains run. The number of accidents due to grade crossing collisions . . . and to collisions between trains, which are usually far more serious than those due to slack action, and accidents due to locomotive failures, in general vary with the number of trains. The accident rate in Arizona is much higher than on comparable lines elsewhere, where there is no regulation of length of trains. The record lends support to the trial court's conclusion that the train length limitation increased rather than diminished the number of accidents. . . .

We think, as the trial court found, that the Arizona Train Limit Law, viewed as a safety measure, affords at most slight and dubious advantage, if any, over unregulated train lengths . . . . Its undoubted effect on the commerce is the regulation, without securing uniformity of the length of trains operated in interstate commerce, which lack is itself a primary cause of preventing the free flow of commerce by delaying it and by substantially increasing its cost and impairing its efficiency. In these respects the case differs from those where a state, by regulatory measures affecting the commerce, has removed or reduced safety hazards without substantial interference with the interstate movement of trains. Such are measures abolishing the car stove, New York, N. H. & H. R. Co. v. New York, 165 U.S. 628; requiring locomotives to be supplied with electric headlights, Atlantic Coast Line R. Co. v. Georgia, 234 U.S. 280; providing for full train crews, Chicago, R. I. & P. Ry. Co. v. Arkansas, 219 U.S. 453; St. Louis, I. M. & S. R. Co. v. Arkansas, 240 U.S. 518; Missouri Pac. R. Co. v. Norwood, 283 US. 249; and for the equipment of freight trains with cabooses, Terminal Railroad Ass'n v. Brotherhood, supra.

The principle that, without controlling Congressional action, a state may not regulate interstate commerce so as substantially to affect its flow or deprive it of needed uniformity in its regulation is not to be avoided by "simply invoking the convenient apologetics of the police power" . . . . [Numerous cases in which the commerce clause was held to invalidate local "police power" enactments are omitted.]

Here we conclude that the state does go too far. Its regulation of train lengths, admittedly obstructive to interstate train operation, and having a seriously adverse effect on transportation efficiency and economy, passes beyond what is plainly essential for safety since it does not appear that it will lessen rather than increase the danger of accident. Its attempted regulation of the operation of interstate trains cannot establish nation-wide control such as is essential to the maintenance of an efficient transportation system, which Congress alone can prescribe. The state interest cannot be preserved at the expense of the national interest by an enactment which regulates interstate train lengths without securing such control, which is a matter of national concern. To this the interest of the state here asserted is subordinate.

Appellees especially rely on the full train crew cases, Chicago, R. I. & Pac. Ry. Co. v. Arkansas, supra . . ., and also on South Carolina Highway Dept. v. Barnwell Bros., supra, as supporting the state's authority to regulate the length of interstate trains. While the full train crew laws undoubtedly placed an added financial burden on the railroads in order to serve a local interest, they did not obstruct interstate transportation or seriously impede it. They had no effects outside the state beyond those of picking up and setting down the extra employees at the state boundaries; they involved no wasted use of facilities or serious impairment of transportation efficiency, which are among the factors of controlling weight here. . . .

South Carolina Highway Dept. v. Barnwell Bros., supra, was concerned with the power of the state to regulate the weight and width of motor cars passing interstate over its highways, a legislative field over which the state has a far more extensive control than over interstate railroads. In that case . . . we were at pains to point out that there are few subjects of state regulation affecting interstate commerce which are so peculiarly of local concern as is the use of the state's highways. . . .

The contrast between the present regulation and the full train crew laws in point of their effects on the commerce, and the like contrast with the highway safety regulations, in point of the nature of the subject of regulation and the state's interest in it, illustrate and emphasize the considerations which enter into a determination of the relative weights of state and national interests where state regulation affecting interstate commerce is attempted. Here examination of all the relevant factors makes it plain that the state interest is outweighed by the interest of the nation in an adequate, economical and efficient railway transportation service, which must prevail.

Reversed.

Mr. Justice RUTLEDGE concurs in the result.

Mr. Justice BLACK, dissenting. . . .

In the state court a rather extraordinary "trial" took place. Charged with violating the law, the railroad admitted the charge. It alleged that the law was unconstitutional, however, and sought a trial of facts on that issue.
. . . .

Before the state trial judge finally determined that the dangers found by the legislature in 1912 no longer existed, he heard evidence over a period of 5½ months which appears in about 3000 pages of the printed record before us. It then adopted findings of fact submitted to it by the railroad, which cover 148 printed pages, and conclusions of law which cover 5 pages.
. . . This new pattern of trial procedure makes it necessary for a judge to hear all the evidence offered as to why a legislature passed a law and to make findings of fact as to the validity of those reasons. If under today's ruling a court does make findings as to a danger contrary to the findings of the legislature, and the evidence heard "lends support" to those findings, a court can then invalidate the law. In this respect, the Arizona County Court acted, and this Court today is acting, as a "super-legislature." . . .

The Supreme Court of Arizona did not discuss the County Court's so-called findings of fact. It properly designated the Arizona statute as a safety measure, and finding that it bore a reasonable relation to its purpose declined to review the judgment of the legislature as to the necessity for the passage of the act. In so doing it was well fortified by a long line of decisions of this Court. Today's decision marks an abrupt departure from that line of cases. . . .

The history of congressional consideration of this problem leaves little if any room to doubt that the choice of Congress to leave the state free in this field was a deliberate choice, which was taken with a full knowledge of the complexities of the problems and the probable need for diverse regulations in different localities. I am therefore compelled to reach the conclusion that today's decision is the result of the belief of a majority of this Court that both the legislature of Arizona and the Congress made wrong policy decisions in permitting a law to stand which limits the length of railroad trains. . . .

When we finally get down to the gist of what the Court today actually decides, it is this: Even though more railroad employees will be injured by "slack action" movements on long trains than on short trains, there must be no regulation of this danger in the absence of "uniform regulations." . . . We are not left in doubt as to why, as against the potential peril of injuries to employees, the Court tips the scales on the side of "uniformity." For the evil it finds in a lack of uniformity is that it (1) delays interstate commerce, (2) increases its cost and (3) impairs its efficiency. All three of these boil down to the same thing, and that is that running shorter trains would increase the cost of railroad operations. . . . [T]he Court's action in requiring that money costs outweigh human values is sought to be buttressed by a reference to the express policy of Congress to promote an "economical national railroad system." I cannot believe that if Congress had defined what it meant by "economical," it would have required money to be saved at the expense of the personal safety of railway employees. . . .

This record in its entirety leaves me with no doubt whatever that many employees have been seriously injured and killed in the past, and that many more are likely to be so in the future, because of "slack movement" in trains. Everyday knowledge as well as direct evidence presented at the various hearings, substantiates the report of the Senate Committee that the danger from slack movement is greater in long trains than in short trains. It may be that offsetting dangers are possible in the operation of short trains. The balancing of these probabilities, however, is not in my judgment a matter for judicial determination, but one which calls for legislative consideration. . . .

Mr. Justice DOUGLAS, dissenting.

I have expressed my doubts whether the courts should intervene in situations like the present and strike down state legislation on the grounds that it burdens interstate commerce. McCarroll v. Dixie Greyhound Lines, 309 U.S. 176, 183–189. My view has been that the courts should intervene only where the state legislation discriminated against interstate commerce or was out of harmony with laws which Congress had enacted. . . . It seems to me particularly appropriate that that course be followed here. For Congress has given the Interstate Commerce Commission broad powers of regulation over interstate carriers. . . . It is the expert on this subject. . . . And if its powers prove inadequate for the task, Congress, which has paramount authority in this field, can implement them. . . .

STATE SAFETY LAWS, TRUCKS, AND RAILROADS—
BARNWELL, SOUTHERN PACIFIC, BIBB

1. *The changing criteria of judicial scrutiny.* a. Does Chief Justice Stone's opinion in Southern Pacific adequately distinguish the principal case that precedes it, Barnwell? Is the commerce clause barrier more substantial in the Southern Pacific case? Is there any justification for greater permissiveness toward state regulation of trucks than of railroads? In 1938? In 1945? Today? Does Bibb, the principal case that follows (a 1959 decision involving trucks) apply a judicial review standard closer to that of Southern Pacific (the 1945 railroad case) or to that of Barnwell (the 1938 truck case)? What explains the changes in approach? The relative degree of state and federal financing of highways in 1938 and in 1959? The change in the importance of trucking to national trade between 1938 and 1959? The relative economic conditions of the motor carrier and railroad industries in 1938 and 1959? The changes in federal regulation of trucks and railroads (see sec. 2A below)?

b. In the article cited by Chief Justice Stone in the principal case—and written between Barnwell Bros. and this case—Professor Dowling criticized the "direct"-"indirect" test as "far from satisfying" and derived another doctrine from the cases: that, in the absence of congressional consent, "a Congressional negative will be presumed" where state regulation produces an "unreasonable interference" with commerce. Adoption of that reasonableness standard, he explained, would involve "an avowal that the Court is deliberately balancing national and local interests." That, he added, would require "a policy judgment." But the test of "reasonableness" in commerce cases "is not the same as . . . in due process cases." The article has been reprinted since the Southern Pacific decision, see Dowling, "Interstate Commerce and State Power," 27 Va.L.Rev. 1 (1940), Selected Essays 1938–62 (1963), 280. See also Dowling, "Interstate Commerce and State Power—Revised Version," 47 Colum.L.Rev. 547 (1947).

Was the test of "reasonableness" in commerce cases "not the same" as in due process cases (see also chap. 13, below) in Barnwell? Was it "not the same" in Southern Pacific? Was it "not the same" in Bibb? Should there be a difference in standards under the commerce and due process clauses?

2. *State full crew laws after Southern Pacific.* In invalidating the train length law in Southern Pacific, Chief Justice Stone explicitly distinguished cases such as Missouri Pac. R. Co. v. Norwood, 283 U.S. 249 (1931), which had sustained state full train crew laws. Yet there was considerable doubt whether full crew laws could on reexamination survive the judicial rigid scrutiny authorized by Southern Pacific. Nevertheless, a renewed challenge to the Arkansas full train crew laws proved unsuccessful. In Engineers v. Chicago, R. I. & P. R. Co., 382 U.S. 423 (1966), the Court rejected a preemption claim resting on a 1963 congressional act compelling arbitration of certain crew disputes. On remand for consideration of the constitutional challenges, the District Court found after a full hearing that the crew laws had "no substantial effect on safety of operations," placed "substantial financial burdens" on the carriers, and interfered with the continuity of railroad op-

erations. Accordingly, the trial court held the laws unconstitutional, in part on the basis of the Southern Pacific approach.

The Supreme Court reversed. Firemen v. Chicago, R. I. & P. R. Co., 393 U.S. 129 (1968). Justice Black's majority opinion concluded: "We think it plain that in striking down the full-crew laws on this basis, the District Court indulged in a legislative judgment wholly beyond its limited authority to review state legislation under the Commerce Clause." For example, the evidence regarding the need for additional crewmen was "conflicting" and "inconclusive." Moreover, it was "difficult at best to say that financial losses should be balanced against the loss of lives and limbs of workers"; the Court "certainly cannot do so on this showing." Moreover, Justice Black found no unconstitutional discrimination in mileage exemptions in the laws that had the effect of freeing all of Arkansas' 17 intrastate railroads from coverage, while leaving most of the 11 interstate railroads subject to them. The Court found evidence in the record suggesting "a number of legitimate reasons for the mileage exemption"—e. g., the "apparent use of much slower trains over the short lines." Accordingly, "we see no reason to depart from this Court's previous decisions holding that the Arkansas full-crew laws do not unduly burden interstate commerce or otherwise violate the Constitution." Disputes about the laws "will continue to be worked out in the legislatures and in various forms of collective bargaining."

BIBB v. NAVAJO FREIGHT LINES, INC.

359 U.S. 520, 79 S.Ct. 962, 3 L.Ed.2d 988 (1959).

Appeal from the United States District Court for the Southern District of Illinois.

Mr. Justice DOUGLAS delivered the opinion of the Court.

We are asked in this case to hold that an Illinois statute requiring the use of a certain type of rear fender mudguard on trucks and trailers operated on the highways of that State conflicts with the Commerce Clause of the Constitution. The statutory specification for this type of mudguard provides that the guard shall contour the rear wheel, with the inside surface being relatively parallel to the top 90 degrees of the rear 180 degrees of the whole surface. The surface of the guard must extend downward to within 10 inches from the ground when the truck is loaded to its maximum legal capacity. The guards must be wide enough to cover the width of the protected tire, must be installed not more than 6 inches from the tire surface when the vehicle is loaded to maximum capacity, and must have a lip or flange on its outer edge of not less than 2 inches.

Appellees, interstate motor carriers holding certificates from the Interstate Commerce Commission, challenged the constitutionality of the Illinois Act. A specially constituted three-judge District Court concluded that it unduly and unreasonably burdened and obstructed interstate commerce, because it made the conventional or straight mudflap, which is legal in at least 45 States, illegal in Illinois, and because the statute, taken together with a Rule of the Arkansas Commerce Commission requiring straight mudflaps, rendered the use of the same motor vehicle equipment in both States impossible.

The statute was declared to be violative of the Commerce Clause and appellants were enjoined from enforcing it. . . .

The power of the State to regulate the use of its highways is broad and pervasive. We have recognized the peculiarly local nature of this subject of safety, and have upheld state statutes applicable alike to interstate and intrastate commerce, despite the fact that they may have an impact on interstate commerce. South Carolina Highway Dept. v. Barnwell Bros. . . .

These safety measures carry a strong presumption of validity when challenged in court. If there are alternative ways of solving a problem, we do not sit to determine which of them is best suited to achieve a valid state objective. Policy decisions are for the state legislature, absent federal entry into the field.[1] Unless we can conclude on the whole record that "the total effect of the law as a safety measure in reducing accidents and casualties is so slight or problematical as not to outweigh the national interest in keeping interstate commerce free from interferences which seriously impede it" (Southern Pacific Co. v. Arizona . . .) we must uphold the statute.

The District Court found that "since it is impossible for a carrier operating in interstate commerce to determine which of its equipment will be used in a particular area, or on a particular day, or days, carriers operating into or through Illinois . . . will be required to equip all of their trailers in accordance with the requirements of the Illinois Splash Guard statute." With two possible exceptions the mudflaps required in those States which have mudguard regulations would not meet the standards required by the Illinois statute. The cost of installing the contour mudguards is $30 or more per vehicle. The District Court found that the initial cost of installing those mudguards on all the trucks owned by the appellees ranged from $4,500 to $45,840. There was also evidence in the record to indicate that the cost of maintenance and replacement of these guards is substantial.

Illinois introduced evidence seeking to establish that contour mudguards had a decided safety factor in that they prevented the throwing of debris into the faces of drivers of passing cars and into the windshields of a following vehicle. But the District Court in its opinion stated that it was "conclusively shown that the contour mud flap possesses no advantages over the conventional or straight mud flap previously required in Illinois and presently required in most of the states," (159 F.Supp., at 388) and that "there is rather convincing testimony that use of the contour flap creates hazards previously unknown to those using the highways." Id., at 390. These hazards were found to be occasioned by the fact that this new type of mudguard tended to cause an accumulation of heat in the brake drum, thus decreasing the effectiveness of brakes, and by the fact that they were susceptible of being hit and bumped when the trucks were backed up and of falling off on the highway.

These findings on cost and on safety are not the end of our problem. Local regulation of the weight of trucks using the highways upheld in Sproles

1. It is not argued that there has been a pre-emption of the field by federal regulation. While the Interstate Commerce Commission has, pursuant to § 204(a) of the Interstate Commerce Act (49 U.S.C. § 304(a)), promulgated its Motor Carriers Safety Regulations to govern vehicles operating in interstate or foreign commerce (see 49 CFR, Pts. 190–197), it has expressly declined to establish any requirements concerning wheel flaps, and has disclaimed any intention to occupy the field or abrogate state regulations not inconsistent with its standards. 54 M.C.C. 337, 354, 358. [Footnote by the Court. Compare sec. 2A, below.]

v. Binford, [286 U.S. 374], also involved increased financial burdens for interstate carriers. State control of the width and weight of motor trucks and trailers sustained in South Carolina Highway Dept. v. Barnwell Bros., supra, involved nice questions of judgment concerning the need of those regulations so far as the issue of safety was concerned. That case also presented the problem whether interstate motor carriers, who were required to replace all equipment or keep out of the State, suffered an unconstitutional restraint on interstate commerce. The matter of safety was said to be one essentially for the legislative judgment; and the burden of redesigning or replacing equipment was said to be a proper price to exact from interstate and intrastate motor carriers alike. And the same conclusion was reached in Maurer v. Hamilton, [309 U.S. 598], where a state law prohibited any motor carrier from carrying any other vehicle above the cab of the carrier vehicle or over the head of the operator of that vehicle. Cost taken into consideration with other factors might be relevant in some cases to the issue of burden on commerce. But it has assumed no such proportions here. If we had here only a question whether the cost of adjusting an interstate operation to these new local safety regulations prescribed by Illinois unduly burdened interstate commerce, we would have to sustain the law under the authority of the Sproles, Barnwell, and Maurer cases. The same result would obtain if we had to resolve the much discussed issues of safety presented in this case.

This case presents a different issue. The equipment in the Sproles, Barnwell, and Maurer cases could pass muster in any State, so far as the records in those cases reveal. We were not faced there with the question whether one State could prescribe standards for interstate carriers that would conflict with the standards of another State, making it necessary, say, for an interstate carrier to shift its cargo to differently designed vehicles once another state line was reached. We had a related problem in Southern Pacific Co. v. Arizona, supra . . .. More closely in point is Morgan v. Virginia, 328 U.S. 375, where a local law required a reseating of passengers on interstate busses entering Virginia in order to comply with a local segregation law. Diverse seating arrangements for people of different races imposed by several States interfered, we concluded, with "the need for national uniformity in the regulations for interstate travel." Id., at 386.[2] Those cases indicate the dimensions of our present problem.

2. In the Morgan case, in 1946, the Court noted that "related statutes of other states are important to show whether there are cumulative effects which make local regulation impracticable." The Morgan case came one year after Southern Pacific, supra, where Justices Black and Douglas had opposed the majority's approach. Justice Douglas did not explain his vote with the majority in Morgan. In a concurrence, Justice Black recalled his protests against the "undue burdens" doctrine, stated that he still believed that it led the Court to act as a "super-legislature," but concluded that in view "of the Court's present disposition to apply that formula, I acquiesce." Morgan relied on Hall v. DeCuir, 95 U.S. 485 (1878), which had invalidated as an unconstitutional bur-

den on commerce a Louisiana anti-segregation law of 1869 as applied to steamboats. See chap. 4, supra, and chap. 18, infra, on the current impact of federal laws and the Fourteenth Amendment on segregation in transportation facilities.

Note the more recent cases involving application of state civil rights laws to transportation. in Bob-Lo Excursion Co. v. Michigan, 333 U.S. 28 (1948), the Court sustained a state law barring racial discrimination as applied to an amusement park company's vessel operating from Detroit to the park, on an island in the Detroit River in Canadian waters. Though the Court found that the state was regulating foreign commerce, it upheld the law because of the company's "highly localized business." And in Colorado

An order of the Arkansas Commerce Commission, already mentioned, requires that trailers operating in that State be equipped with straight or conventional mudflaps. Vehicles equipped to meet the standards of the Illinois statute would not comply with Arkansas standards, and vice versa. Thus if a trailer is to be operated in both States, mudguards would have to be interchanged, causing a significant delay in an operation where prompt movement may be of the essence. It was found that from two to four hours of labor are required to install or remove a contour mudguard. Moreover, the contour guard is attached to the trailer by welding and if the trailer is conveying a cargo of explosives (e. g., for the United States Government) it would be exceedingly dangerous to attempt to weld on a contour mudguard without unloading the trailer.

It was also found that the Illinois statute seriously interferes with the "interline" operations of motor carriers— that is to say, with the interchanging of trailers between an originating carrier and another carrier when the latter serves an area not served by the former. These "interline" operations provide a speedy through-service for the shipper. Interlining contemplates the physical transfer of the entire trailer; there is no unloading and reloading of the cargo. The interlining process is particularly vital in connection with shipment of perishables, which would spoil if unloaded before reaching their destination, or with the movement of explosives carried under seal. Of course, if the originating carrier never operated in Illinois, it would not be expected to equip its trailers with contour mudguards. Yet if an interchanged trailer of that carrier were hauled to or through Illinois, the statute would require that it contain contour guards. Since carriers which operate in and through Illinois cannot compel the originating carriers to equip their trailers with contour guards, they may be forced to cease interlining with those who do not meet the Illinois requirements. Over 60 percent of the business of 5 of the 6 plaintiffs is interline traffic. For the other it constitutes 30 percent. All of the plaintiffs operate extensively in interstate commerce, and the annual mileage in Illinois of none of them exceeds 7 percent of total mileage.

This in summary is the rather massive showing of burden on interstate commerce which appellees made at the hearing.

Appellants did not attempt to rebut the appellees' showing that the statute in question severely burdens interstate commerce. Appellants' showing was aimed at establishing that contour mudguards prevented the throwing of debris into the faces of drivers of passing cars and into the windshields of a following vehicle. They concluded that, because the Illinois statute is a reasonable exercise of the police power, a federal court is precluded from weighing the relative merits of the contour mudguard against any other kind of mudguard and must sustain the validity of the statute notwithstanding the extent of the burden it imposes on interstate commerce. They rely in the main on South Carolina Highway Dept. v. Barnwell Bros., supra. There is language in that opinion which, read in isolation from such later decisions as Southern Pacific Co. v. Arizona, supra, and Morgan v. Virginia, supra,

Anti-Discrimination Comm'n v. Continental Airlines, 372 U.S. 714 (1963), the Court reversed the state court's holding that the state civil rights law could not be applied to the hiring of flight personnel by an interstate air carrier. The Morgan-DeCuir kind of burden, Justice Black stated, "simply cannot exist here." Moreover, hiring of employees is "a much more localized matter" than transporting passengers.

would suggest that no showing of burden on interstate commerce is sufficient to invalidate local safety regulations in absence of some element of discrimination against interstate commerce.

The various exercises by the States of their police power stand, however, on an equal footing. All are entitled to the same presumption of validity when challenged under the Due Process Clause of the Fourteenth Amendment. . . . Similarly the various state regulatory statutes are of equal dignity when measured against the Commerce Clause. Local regulations which would pass muster under the Due Process Clause might nonetheless fail to survive other challenges to constitutionality that bring the Supremacy Clause into play. Like any local law that conflicts with federal regulatory measures . . . ., state regulations that run afoul of the policy of free trade reflected in the Commerce Clause must also bow.

This is one of those cases—few in number—where local safety measures that are nondiscriminatory place an unconstitutional burden on interstate commerce. This conclusion is especially underlined by the deleterious effect which the Illinois law will have on the "interline" operation of interstate motor carriers. The conflict between the Arkansas regulation and the Illinois regulation also suggests that this regulation of mudguards is not one of those matters "admitting of diversity of treatment, according to the special requirements of local conditions," to use the words of Chief Justice Hughes in Sproles v. Binford, supra, at 390. A State which insists on a design out of line with the requirements of almost all the other States may sometimes place a great burden of delay and inconvenience on those interstate motor carriers entering or crossing its territory. Such a new safety device—out of line with the requirements of the other States—may be so compelling that the innovating State need not be the one to give way. But the present showing— balanced against the clear burden on commerce—is far too inconclusive to make this mudguard meet that test.

We deal not with absolutes but with questions of degree. The state legislatures plainly have great leeway in providing safety regulations for all vehicles—interstate as well as local. Our decisions so hold. Yet the heavy burden which the Illinois mudguard law places on the interstate movement of trucks and trailers seems to us to pass the permissible limits even for safety regulations.

Affirmed.

Mr. Justice HARLAN, whom Mr. Justice STEWART joins, concurring.

The opinion of the Court clearly demonstrates the heavy burden, in terms of cost and interference with "interlining," which the Illinois statute here involved imposes on interstate commerce. In view of the findings of the District Court . . . to the effect that the contour mudflap "possesses no advantages" in terms of safety over the conventional flap permitted in all other States, and indeed creates certain safety hazards, this heavy burden cannot be justified on the theory that the Illinois statute is a necessary, appropriate, or helpful local safety measure. Accordingly, I concur in the judgment of the Court.

THE HURON PORTLAND CEMENT CASE: COMMERCE CLAUSE OBJECTIONS AGAINST A BACKGROUND OF CONGRESSIONAL POLICY

1. *The commerce clause criteria.* A year after the extensive attention to the commerce clause claim in Bibb, the Court disposed of a seemingly substantial commerce objection almost summarily. Is the apparent difference in treatment explainable? Justifiable? The post-Bibb case was Huron Portland Cement Co. v. City of Detroit, 362 U.S. 440 (1960). The Court held that Detroit's Smoke Abatement Code could constitutionally be applied to the company's ships. The ships' boilers emitted smoke exceeding Detroit's maximum standard; compliance would require structural alterations in the boilers. Most of the Court's discussion was devoted to the claim that federal laws had preempted the field (see sec. 2A, infra). The Court found no bar either in the "extensive and comprehensive" federal boiler inspection provisions or in the federal licensing of the vessels. The main purpose of federal inspection was to assure safety; the Detroit ordinance was solely directed at air pollution. And possession of the federal license "does not immunize a ship from the . . . local police power, not constituting a direct regulation of commerce." Justice Stewart's opinion for the Court relied heavily on evidence of "Congressional recognition that the problem of air pollution is peculiarly a matter of state and local concern."

Justice Stewart disposed of the commerce clause objection in two paragraphs: "The claim that the Detroit ordinance, quite apart from the effect of federal legislation, imposes as to the appellant's ships an undue burden on interstate commerce needs no extended discussion. State regulation, based on the police power, which does not discriminate against interstate commerce or operate to disrupt its required uniformity, may constitutionally stand. . . .*

"It has not been suggested that the local ordinance, applicable alike to 'any person, firm or corporation' within the city, discriminates against interstate commerce as such. It is a regulation of general application, designed to better the health and welfare of the community. And while the appellant argues that other local governments might impose differing requirements as to air pollution, it has pointed to none. The record contains nothing to suggest the existence of any such competing or conflicting local regulations. Cf. Bibb v. Navajo Freight Lines, Inc., 359 U.S. 520. We conclude that no impermissible burden on commerce has been shown." Justice Douglas,

---

* Note Justice Stewart's "rephrasing" of "the general rule," for a unanimous Court a decade after the Huron case, in Pike v. Bruce Church, Inc., 397 U.S. —— (1970) (noted further below, at p. 669):

"Where the statute regulates evenhandedly to effectuate a legitimate local public interest, and its effects on interstate commerce are only incidental, it will be upheld unless the burden imposed on such commerce is clearly excessive in relation to the putative local benefits. Huron Cement Co. v. Detroit, 362 U.S. 440, 443. If a legiti-

mate local purpose is found, then the question becomes one of degree. And the extent of the burden that will be tolerated will of course depend on the nature of the local interest involved, and on whether it could be promoted as well with a lesser impact on interstate activities. Occasionally the Court has candidly undertaken a balancing approach in resolving these issues, Southern Pacific Co. v. Arizona, 325 U.S. 761, but more frequently it has spoken in terms of 'direct' and 'indirect' effects and burdens."

joined by Justice Frankfurter, dissented on the ground of federal preemption.

2. *Multiple inconsistent burdens—actuality or risk?* Were the commerce clause criteria as stated in Huron consistent with those in Bibb? With Southern Pacific? Is the "burden" argument only maintainable on a showing of "competing and conflicting local regulations"? What about the *risk* that other cities *may* impose such regulations if Detroit's authority is recognized? Must there be existing conflicting regulations, as in Bibb, for a valid commerce clause claim? Or is the potential of multiple inconsistent burdens enough, as suggested in Southern Pacific: "If one state may regulate train lengths, so may all the others . . . ." Compare the "multiple burdens" analysis—and the ambivalence about identifying the *actuality* or the *risk* of multiple taxation as the evil—in the tax cases, chap. 9, sec. 4, infra. What if Chicago and Cleveland were in the future to impose "competing and conflicting" regulations on the Huron Company's ships? Would that cause Detroit's ordinance to fall? Chicago's and Cleveland's? All three? Compare the Bibb case, supra.

Was the real explanation of the curt treatment of the commerce clause in Huron the Court's belief regarding congressional "recognition" of air pollution as a "local" matter? Would the Court have examined the commerce clause claim more carefully if there had been no such congressional "recognition"? Should that congressional recognition have influenced the statement of applicable commerce clause doctrine? Would it have been preferable to explain the case as an example of congressional consent to what might otherwise be unconstitutionally burdensome local regulation (see sec. 2B of this chapter)? On the influence of congressional policy on the disposition of commerce clause objections, see also Parker v. Brown, noted at the beginning of sec. 1D, p. 660, infra.

C.　ACCESS OF FOREIGN SELLERS TO LOCAL MARKETS

Introduction. Most of the leading cases in this subsection and the next —Baldwin, Dean Milk, Eisenberg, Hood—involve regulations of the dairy industry. That is not the only context that has given rise to problems of state regulations of incoming or outgoing commerce; but the unity of context of these decisions aids analysis of the Court's efforts to articulate protected values and constitutional limitations. What national commerce concerns are protected? What state justifications are recognized as legitimate? How does the Court determine state purposes and commerce effects? What of mixed state purposes and uncertain commerce effects? Are the Court's perceptions adequate? Or are its attributions of motives and assertions of effects too often question-begging? These problems of local regulations affecting out-of-state sellers and buyers are closely related to those posed by the imposition of state taxes on interstate sales transactions (see chap. 9, sec. 4), as note 5 below illustrates.

BALDWIN v. SEELIG, HOSTILE ECONOMIC BARRIERS—
AND "CATCH WORDS AND LABELS"

1. *The Baldwin decision.* Baldwin v. G. A. F. Seelig, Inc., 294 U.S.
511 (1935), dealt with the impact on interstate commerce of a state effort
to regulate milk prices. The New York Milk Control Act of 1933 set the
minimum prices to be paid by dealers to producers. In Nebbia v. New York,
291 U.S. 502 (1934) (a major constitutional decision of the New Deal period, printed in chap. 13, p. 967, below), the Court sustained the law as applied to New York's domestic economy, against a challenge that price regulation constituted a deprivation of liberty and property without the due process
of law required by the 14th Amendment. The Baldwin case found a year
later, however, that the commerce clause prohibited some applications of
the law. Seelig, a New York milk dealer, bought milk in Vermont at
prices lower than the New York minimum. The 1933 Act prohibited New
York sales of out-of-state milk if the milk was purchased below the price
set for similar purchases within New York. New York refused to license
Seelig to sell milk unless there was an agreement to conform to the state's
price regulation regarding the sale of imported milk. Seelig sued to enjoin
enforcement of the Act. The Supreme Court unanimously held the application of the Act unconstitutional.

Justice Cardozo stated that New York's regulation "set a barrier to traffic between one state and another as effective as if customs duties, equal to
the price differential, had been laid upon the thing transported. . . .
Nice distinctions have been made at times between direct and indirect burdens. They are irrelevant when the avowed purpose of the obstruction, as
well as its necessary tendency, is to suppress or mitigate the consequences of
competition between the states. Such an obstruction is direct by the very
terms of the hypothesis. We are reminded in the opinion below that a chief
occasion of the commerce clause was 'the mutual jealousies and aggressions
of the States, taking form in customs barriers and other economic retaliation.'
. . . . If New York, in order to promote the economic welfare of her
farmers, may guard them against competition with the cheaper prices of Vermont, the door has been opened to rivalries and reprisals that were meant
to be averted by subjecting commerce between the states to the power of the
nation."

The Court rejected the argument that the Act was justified by the state's
aim to assure "a regular and adequate supply of pure and wholesome milk."
Supply was jeopardized, it was claimed, when farmers cannot earn a living
income: "the economic motive is secondary and subordinate; the state intervenes to make its inhabitants healthy, and not to make them rich." Justice
Cardozo stated that these contentions could not justify the Act as a valid
"police" measure with only "incidental" impact on commerce: "This would
be to eat up the rule under the guise of an exception. Economic welfare is
always related to health . . . . Let such an exception be admitted, and
all that a state will have to do in times of stress and strain is to say that its
farmers and merchants and workmen must be protected against competition
from without, lest they go upon the poor relief lists or perish altogether. To
give entrance to that excuse would be to invite a speedy end of our national
solidarity. The Constitution was framed under the dominion of a political

philosophy less parochial in range. It was framed upon the theory that the peoples of the several states must sink or swim together, and that in the long run prosperity and salvation are in union and not division. . . . The line of division between direct and indirect restraints of commerce involves in its marking a reference to considerations of degree. Even so the border-land is wide between the restraints upheld as incidental and those attempted here. Subject to the paramount power of the Congress, a state may regulate the importation of unhealthy swine or cattle (. . . Mintz v. Baldwin, [289 U.S. 346]) or decayed or noxious foods. . . . Savage v. Jones, 225 U.S. 501 . . . . . So a state may protect its inhabitants against the fraudulent substitution, by deceptive coloring or otherwise, of one article for another. Plumley v. Massachusetts, 155 U.S. 461. . . . It may give protection to travelers against the dangers of overcrowded highways . . . . None of these statutes—inspection laws, game laws, laws intended to curb fraud or exterminate disease—approaches in drastic quality the statute here in controversy which would neutralize the economic consequences of free trade among the states. . . . .

". . . Neither the power to tax nor the police power may be used by the state of destination with the aim and effect of establishing an economic barrier against competition with the products of another state . . . . Restrictions so contrived are an unreasonable clog on the mobility of Commerce. They set up what is the equivalent of a rampart of customs duties designed to neutralize advantages belonging to the place of origin. They are thus hostile in conception as well as burdensome in result." [For the Court's comments on the "original package" doctrine in Baldwin, see the notes following Brown v. Maryland, chap. 9, p. 690, below.]

2. *Economic barriers and judicial competence.* Are all state economic barriers affecting an out-of-state supplier unconstitutional? Only those with certain effects? Only those with certain purposes? The New York regulation did not discriminate against the Vermont producer in the sense of imposing a ban on imports or singling out that seller for regulations not imposed on local producers. Was the effect nevertheless excessively burdensome because it tended "to neutralize advantages belonging to the place of origin"? Does Baldwin condemn economic burdens too broadly? When are such burdens permitted? When they are very light? Is the Court competent to assess the relative economic impacts of various "burdens," from inspection fees and highway use taxes to general price regulations and explicitly discriminatory fees?

3. *State purpose and judicial "psychoanalysis."* Does the permissibility of an economic burden turn on the state's purpose? Is the Court more competent to assess purpose than economic effect? Is Justice Cardozo's emphasis on purpose reconcilable with his objection to purpose inquiries involving the federal taxing power? In 1935, the year of the Baldwin decisions, he dissented from a decision in which the Court struck down a federal tax because "the purpose is to usurp" state police powers. Justice Cardozo countered: "Thus the process of psychoanalysis has spread to unaccustomed fields." United States v. Constantine, 296 U.S. 287 (1935) (noted before the Kahriger case, chap. 5, p. 357, supra). Does inquiry into "purpose" when state laws are challenged under the commerce clause, as in Baldwin, involve less difficult "psychoanalysis"? Is "psychoanalysis" a more appropriate Court function there?

4. *State purpose and interstate commerce.* What was the forbidden purpose in Baldwin, and why was it forbidden? Was hostility to Vermont producers New York's primary concern? The Court recognized that some state laws with "pure" police purposes—e. g., bans on "noxious foods"—were permissible barriers to imports. At the other extreme, obviously discriminatory laws to protect the local producers against foreign competitors are illegitimate. Did Justice Cardozo deny New York's contention that its law in Baldwin lay between those extremes? Is his analysis adequate to deal with this gray borderline area? Would it have been better to articulate the values and conflicting indicia and engage in a form of "balancing" of the Southern Pacific case, p. 634, infra?

The genuineness of New York's concern with destructive competition and adequate supplies in the dairy industry had been emphasized by the Court a year earlier, in rejecting the Fourteenth Amendment attack in the Nebbia case (see note 1 above). New York's interest was not simple economic bias against out-of-state competitors; it dealt primarily with local economic well-being and health. Given so urgent a concern, does not the state have a plausible claim to protection from out-of-state competition that threatens a vital domestic regulatory scheme? If that state need is not sufficient justification, would it not be preferable to articulate the limiting contours of the commerce clause free market that outweigh that need, rather than portraying the state's concern so unsympathetically?

5. *Hostile "economic barriers" and benign "equalization": the relevance of Justice Cardozo's Silas Mason opinion.* Compare, with Justice Cardozo's broad-gauged condemnation of New York's economic barrier in Baldwin, his rejection of a similar attack, on a tax barrier, in Henneford v. Silas Mason Co., 300 U.S. 577 (1937) (chap. 9, p. 723, below). The state imposed a sales tax on goods bought within the state; the decision sustained a use tax on goods bought out-of-state that had not been subjected to a sales tax in the state of origin. The point of that scheme was clear to the Court: local retail sellers "will be helped to compete upon terms of equality with retail dealers in other states who are exempt from a sales tax"; local buyers will "no longer [be] tempted to place their orders in other states" to escape the local sales tax.

Nevertheless, this was not a forbidden economic barrier to Justice Cardozo: "Equality is the theme that runs through all sections of the statute." Nor were the reasons for the tax fatal: "These motives cause it to be stigmatized as equivalent to a protective tariff. But motives alone will seldom, if ever, invalidate a tax that apart from its motives would be recognized as lawful. . . . Least of all will they be permitted to accomplish that result when equality and not preference is the end to be achieved. Catch words and labels, such as the words protective tariff, are subject to the dangers that lurk in metaphors and symbols, and must be watched with circumspection lest they put us off our guard."

Are the results in Baldwin and Silas Mason reconcilable? Are the reasons? Was Justice Cardozo's characterization of the Baldwin regulation—as a hostile "customs barrier"—unduly harsh? Was his characterization of the Silas-Mason tax—as an "equality" measure—unduly benign? Was he, too, "put off [his] guard" by the "catch words and labels" he warned against? Do the cases that follow suggest more balanced approaches?

6. *The vitality of Baldwin: the Polar Ice Cream case.* In its most recent encounter with "the recurring question of the validity of a State's attempt to regulate the supply and distribution of milk," a unanimous Court relied on the dairy industry decisions in these materials, especially Baldwin, in invalidating a Florida regulatory scheme which had the effect of reserving to local producers "a substantial share of the Florida milk market." Polar Ice Cream & Creamery Co. v. Andrews, 375 U.S. 361 (1964). Florida attempted to compel a local distributor to accept his total supply of certain milk from designated local producers at a fixed price and obligated the distributor to take all milk which the local producers offered. Justice White stated: "The principles of Baldwin are as sound today as they were when announced. The exclusion of foreign milk from a major portion of the Florida market cannot be justified as an economic measure to protect the welfare of Florida dairy farmers or as a health measure designed to insure the existence of a wholesome supply of milk. This much Baldwin and Dean [which follows] made clear." Justice White distinguished cases such as Eisenberg, p. 659, infra, because they did not involve "any attempt to reserve a local market for local producers or to protect local producers from out-of-state competition by means of purchase and allocation requirements imposed upon milk distributors."

7. *Personal mobility, hostile state barriers, and the commerce clause: Edwards v. California.* a. *Edwards and commerce.* In most commerce clause cases, it is interstate businesses that seek protection against state action. But the commerce clause is also one of several constitutional provisions that have been invoked to safeguard the individual's ability to move from state to state. Baldwin v. Seelig was relied on for that purpose in Edwards v. California, 314 U.S. 160 (1941), which struck down a law making it a misdemeanor to bring into California "any indigent person who is not a resident of the State, knowing him to be an indigent person." Justice Byrnes' opinion found this to be an unconstitutional burden on commerce. He quoted the Baldwin v. Seelig statement that the Constitution "was framed upon the theory that the peoples of the several states must sink or swim together" and commented: "It is difficult to conceive of a statute more squarely in conflict with this theory [than the California 'Okie' law]." It might well be true, as the state asserted, that "the huge influx of migrants into California in recent years has resulted in problems of health, morals and especially finance, the proportions of which are staggering." But no state could "isolate itself from difficulties common to all of them by restraining the transportation of persons and property across its borders."

b. *The Edwards concurrence.* The commerce clause has not been the only source of increasingly frequent arguments to support a right of personal mobility. In Edwards itself, for example, four of the Justices concurred on the basis of the rarely invoked privileges and immunities clause of the 14th Amendment (see chap. 11, p. 786, infra). Note, e. g., the concurrence of Justice Jackson: "[T]he migrations of a human being . . . do not fit easily into my notions as to what is commerce. To hold that the measure of his rights is the commerce clause is likely to result eventually in distorting the commercial law or in denaturing human rights." (Recall the discussion of commerce clause as against 14th Amendment bases in the materials on the public accommodations title of the 1964 Civil Rights Act, p. 325, supra.)

c. *Other constitutional supports of mobility.* The privileges and immunities clause of the 14th Amendment refers to the privileges of national citizenship. Another privileges and immunities clause in the Constitution, that referring to state citizenship, in Article IV, may also support personal mobility arguments. See chap. 10, p. 771, infra. Moreover, a right to travel may be an aspect of the "liberty" protected by the due process clause of Kent v. Dulles, 357 U.S. 116 (1958) (passport restrictions; chap. 2, p. 160, supra), and has also been implied from the existence of a national government, see Crandall v. Nevada, 6 Wall. 35 (1868) (invalidating tax on passengers leaving state via common carriers, and noting the citizen's "right to come to the seat of the government"—see the discussion in the Slaughter-House Cases, chap. 11, p. 787, infra). There are extensive discussions of the sources and scope of the right to travel in two cases considered elsewhere: United States v. Guest, 383 U.S. 745 (1966), chap. 6, p. 505 (civil rights violence); and Shapiro v. Thompson, 394 U.S. 618 (1969), chap. 14, p. 1036 (residence requirements in welfare laws).

DEAN MILK CO. v. CITY OF MADISON

340 U.S. 349, 71 S.Ct. 295, 95 L.Ed. 329 (1951).

Appeal from the Supreme Court of Wisconsin.

Mr. Justice CLARK delivered the opinion of the Court.

This appeal challenges the constitutional validity of two sections of an ordinance of the City of Madison, Wisconsin, regulating the sale of milk and milk products within the municipality's jurisdiction. One section in issue makes it unlawful to sell any milk as pasteurized unless it has been processed and bottled at an approved pasteurization plant within a radius of five miles from the central square of Madison. Another section which prohibits the sale of milk . . . in Madison unless from a source of supply possessing a permit issued after inspection by Madison officials, is attacked insofar as it expressly relieves municipal authorities from any duty to inspect farms located beyond twenty-five miles from the center of the city.

Appellant is an Illinois corporation engaged in distributing milk and milk products in Illinois and Wisconsin. . . . The Supreme Court of Wisconsin upheld the five-mile limit on pasteurization. As to the twenty-five-mile limitation the court ordered the complaint dismissed for want of a justiciable controversy. . . .

The City of Madison is the county seat of Dane County. Within the county are some 5,600 dairy farms with total raw milk production in excess of 600,000,000 pounds annually and more than ten times the requirements of Madison. Aside from the milk supplied to Madison, fluid milk produced in the county moves in large quantities to Chicago and more distant consuming areas, and the remainder is used in making cheese, butter and other products. At the time of trial the Madison milkshed was not of "Grade A" quality by the standards recommended by the United States Public Health Service

The area defined by the ordinance with respect to milk sources encompasses practically all of Dane County and includes some 500 farms which supply milk for Madison. Within the five-mile area for pasteurization are plants of five processors, only three of which are engaged in the general wholesale and retail trade in Madison. Inspection of these farms and plants is scheduled once every thirty days and is performed by two municipal inspectors, one of whom is full-time. The courts below found that the ordinance in question promotes convenient, economical and efficient plant inspection.

Appellant purchases and gathers milk from approximately 950 farms in northern Illinois and southern Wisconsin, none being within twenty-five miles of Madison. Its pasteurization plants are located at Chemung and Huntley, Illinois, about 65 and 85 miles respectively from Madison. Appellant was denied a license to sell its products within Madison solely because its pasteurization plants were more than five miles away.

It is conceded that the milk which appellant seeks to sell in Madison is supplied from farms and processed in plants licensed and inspected by public health authorities of Chicago, and is labeled "Grade A" under the Chicago ordinance which adopts the rating standards recommended by the United States Public Health Service. . . . Madison contends and we assume that in some particulars its ordinance is more rigorous than that of Chicago. . . . [W]e agree with appellant that the ordinance imposes an undue burden on interstate commerce.

This is not an instance in which an enactment falls because of federal legislation . . . . There is no pertinent national regulation by the Congress . . . . Nor can there be objection to the avowed purpose of this enactment. We assume that difficulties in sanitary regulation of milk and milk products originating in remote areas may present a situation in which " . . . it appears that the matter is one which may appropriately be regulated in the interest of the safety, health and well-being of local communities" . . . .

But this regulation, like the provision invalidated in Baldwin v. Seelig, Inc., supra, in practical effect excludes from distribution in Madison wholesome milk produced and pasteurized in Illinois. "The importer . . . may keep his milk or drink it, but sell it he may not." Id., at 521. In thus erecting an economic barrier protecting a major local industry against competition from without the State, Madison plainly discriminates against interstate commerce.[1] This it cannot do, even in the exercise of its unquestioned power to protect the health and safety of its people, if reasonable nondiscriminatory alternatives, adequate to conserve legitimate local interests, are available. Cf. Baldwin v. G. A. F. Seelig, Inc., supra; Minnesota v. Barber . . . . A different view, that the ordinance is valid simply because it professes to be a health measure, would mean that the Commerce Clause of itself imposes no limitations on state action other than those laid down by the Due Process Clause, save for the rare instance where a state artlessly discloses an avowed purpose to discriminate against interstate goods. . . . Our issue then is whether the discrimination inherent in the Madison ordinance can be justified in view of the character of the local interest and the available methods of protecting them. . . .

It appears that reasonable and adequate alternatives are available. If the City of Madison prefers to rely upon its own officials for inspection of distant milk sources, such inspection is readily open to it without hardship for it could

---

1. It is immaterial that Wisconsin milk from outside the Madison area is subjected to the same proscription as that moving in interstate commerce. . . . [Footnote by the Court].

charge the actual and reasonable cost of such inspection to the importing producers and processors. . . .   Moreover, appellee Health Commissioner of Madison testified that as proponent of the local milk ordinance he had submitted the provisions here in controversy and an alternative proposal based on § 11 of the Model Milk Ordinance recommended by the United States Public Health Service. The model provision imposes no geographical limitation on location of milk sources and processing plans but excludes from the municipality milk not produced and pasteurized conformably to standards as high as those enforced by the receiving city. In implementnig such an ordinance, the importing city obtains milk ratings based on uniform standards and established by health authorities in the jurisdiction where production and processing occur. The receiving city may determine the extent of enforcement of sanitary standards in the exporting area by verifying the accuracy of safety ratings of specific plants or of the milkshed in the distant jurisdiction through the United States Public Health Service, which routinely and on request spot checks the local ratings. . . .

To permit Madison to adopt a regulation not essential for the protection of local health interests and placing a discriminatory burden on interstate commerce would invite a multiplication of preferential trade areas destructive of the very purpose of the Commerce Clause. Under the circumstances here presented, the regulation must yield to the principle that "one state in its dealings with another may not place itself in a position of economic isolation." Baldwin v. Seelig, Inc., supra, at 527.

For these reasons we conclude that the judgment below sustaining the five-mile provision as to pasteurization must be reversed.

The Supreme Court of Wisconsin thought it unnecessary to pass upon the validity of the twenty-five-mile limitation, apparently in part for the reason that this issue was made academic by its decision upholding the five-mile section. In view of our conclusion as to the latter provision, a determination of appellant's contention as to the other section is now necessary. As to this issue, therefore, we vacate the judgment below and remand for further proceedings not inconsistent with the principles announced in this opinion.

It is so ordered.

Mr. Justice BLACK, with whom Mr. Justice DOUGLAS and Mr. Justice MINTON concur, dissenting.

. . . I disagree with the Court's premises, reasoning, and judgment.

(1) This ordinance does not exclude wholesome milk coming from Illinois or anywhere else. It does require that all milk sold in Madison must be pasteurized within five miles of the center of the city. But there was no finding in the state courts [that] Dean Milk Company is unable to have its milk pasteurized within the defined geographical area. . . . Dean's personal preference to pasteurize in Illinois, not the ordinance, keeps Dean's milk out of Madison.

(2) Characterization of § 7.21 as a "discriminatory burden" on interstate commerce is merely a statement of the Court's result, which I think incorrect. . . . [T]he state courts below found that § 7.21 represents a good-faith attempt to safeguard public health by making adequate sanitation

inspections possible. While we are not bound by these findings, I do not understand the Court to overturn them. Therefore, the fact that § 7.21, like all health regulations, imposes some burden on trade, does not mean that it "discriminates" against interstate commerce.

(3) This health regulation should not be invalidated merely because the Court believes that alternative milk-inspection methods might insure the cleanliness and healthfulness of Dean's Illinois milk. I find it difficult to explain why the Court uses the "reasonable alternative" concept to protect trade when today it refuses to apply the same principle to protect freedom of speech. Feiner v. New York, 340 U.S. 315. [Chap. 16, p. 1156.] No case is cited, and I have found none, in which a bona fide health law was struck down on the ground that some other method of safeguarding health would be as good as, or better than, the one the Court was called on to review. . . .

If, however, the principle announced today is to be followed, the Court should not strike down local health regulations unless satisfied beyond a reasonable doubt that the substitutes it proposes would not lower health standards. I do not think that the Court can so satisfy itself on the basis of its judicial knowledge. And the evidence in the record leads me to the conclusion that the substitute health measures suggested by the Court do not insure milk as safe as the Madison ordinance requires.

One of the Court's proposals is that Madison require milk processors to pay reasonable inspection fees at the milk supply "sources." Experience shows, however, that the fee method gives rise to prolonged litigation over the calculation and collection of the charges. . . . Moreover, nothing in the record before us indicates that the fee system might not be as costly to Dean as having its milk pasteurized in Madison. . . .

The Court's second proposal is that Madison adopt § 11 of the "Model Milk Ordinance." . . . The evidence indicates to me that enforcement of the Madison law would assure a more healthful quality of milk than that which is entitled to use the label of "Grade A" under the Model Ordinance. . . . [M]oreover, Madison would be required to depend on the Chicago inspection system . . . . But there is direct and positive evidence in the record that milk produced under Chicago standards did not meet the Madison requirements.

Furthermore, the Model Ordinance would force the Madison health authorities to rely on "spot checks" by the United States Public Health Service to determine whether Chicago enforced its milk regulations. The evidence shows that these "spot checks" are based on random inspection of farms and pasteurization plants. . . . . There was evidence that neither the farms supplying Dean with milk nor Dean's pasteurization plants were necessarily inspected in the last "spot check" of the Chicago milkshed made two years before the present case was tried. . . . On this record I would uphold the Madison law. At the very least, however, I would not invalidate it without giving the parties a chance to present evidence and get findings on the ultimate issues the Court thinks crucial—namely, the relative merits of the Madison ordinance and the alternatives suggested by the Court today.

DEAN MILK, "DISCRIMINATION," AND LESS BURDENSOME ALTERNATIVES

1. *"Discrimination."* a. The Dean Milk opinion asserts that "Madison plainly discriminates against interstate commerce," and immediately adds (footnote 1, above) that it is "immaterial" that intrastate milk from outside the Madison area was subject to the same prohibition as that moving in interstate commercee. This "discrimination" characterization illustrates one of the varied uses of the label in contexts short of an explicit singling out of interstate commerce for hostile treatment; the materials in this chapter and the next contain other examples. See also Minnesota v. Barber, 136 U.S. 313 (1890), cited in Dean Milk: It invalidated a statute forbidding the sale of meat unless there had been an inspection by a Minnesota official within a day of slaughter. The Court held that the law could not be applied to meat from animals slaughtered in Illinois: "[T]he enactment of a similar statute by each one of the states . . . would result in the destruction of commerce among the states." The "obvious and necessary" result of the law was to create "discrimination against the products and business of other states."

b. What was the meaning of "discrimination" in Dean Milk? In Barber? Is it useful to invoke that label in situations where interstate commerce is not singled out on the face of the law or in its application? In talking of discrimination, is the Court characterizing legislative purpose? Is it talking about effect? Is it saying anything that could not be said more clearly by balancing legitimate local justifications such as health and the burdens on commerce—and including in that balancing, perhaps, the "alternatives" examination of Dean Milk? (Compare the varied uses of "discrimination" in the handling of state taxes affecting commerce, ch. 9, p. 692, below.)

2. *"Alternatives."* a. The Dean Milk inquiry into the availability of less "discriminatory" or burdensome alternatives—which part (3) of Justice Black's dissent objected to as extending greater protection to commerce than to speech—has become a prominent feature of individual rights litigation as well, as the materials in Part III will show. See, e. g., the citation of Dean Milk in the development of the important "overbreadth" concept: "[E]ven though the governmental purpose be legitimate and substantial, that purpose cannot be pursued by means that broadly stifle fundamental personal liberties, when the end can be more narrowly achieved." Shelton v. Tucker, 364 U.S. 479 (1960) (chap. 16, p. 1320, below).

b. Is concern with possible alternative methods of regulation within judicial competence? Is Justice Clark's suggestion of alternatives in Dean Milk a haphazard uninformed intrusion into legislative spheres? Courts avoid these inquiries where a "mere rationality" standard prevails—e. g., with respect to congressional implementation of Art. I, Sec. 8, powers (see Flemming v. Nestor, ch. 5, p. 437, above), or in modern applications of the 14th amendment's due process clause to state economic regulation (ch. 13, sec. 4, below). Is more intensive scrutiny, including consideration of "alternatives," necessary to protect commerce clause values? To protect civil liberties?

3. *Alternatives and the Breard case.* Should the Dean Milk "alternatives" approach have been determinative in a case decided late in the same

year, Breard v. City of Alexandria, 341 U.S. 622 (1951)? The ordinance there [a "Green River type of ordinance"] prohibited door-to-door solicitation of orders to sell goods unless there were requests by the occupants. The ban was challenged by an employee of a company selling subscriptions for national magazines. Justice Reed's majority opinion rejected all constitutional objections—under the First Amendment as well as the commerce clause. He stated that "opportunists, for private gain, cannot be permitted to arm themselves with an acceptable principle, such as that of a right to work, a privilege to engage in interstate commerce, or a free press, and proceed to use it as an iron standard to smooth their path by crushing the living rights of others to privacy and repose."

Appellant claimed that the ordinance imposed "an undue and discriminatory burden" on commerce and was "tantamount to a prohibition" of a large interstate business. He argued that obtaining the resident's consent would be "too costly and the results negligible." The Court noted his contention that Dean Milk showed "that this Court will not permit local interests to protect themselves against out-of-state competition by curtailing interstate business" but commented: "It was partly because the regulation in Dean Milk Co. discriminated against interstate commerce that it was struck down." Justice Reed added: "Nor does the clause as to alternatives [in Dean Milk] apply to the Alexandria ordinance. Interstate commerce itself knocks at the door. It is only by regulating that knock that the interests of the home may be protected. . . . When there is a reasonable basis for legislation to protect the social, as distinguished from the economic, welfare of the community, it is not for this Court because of the Commerce Clause to deny the exercise" of local control.

Chief Justice Vinson's dissent, joined by Justice Douglas, concluded: "I would apply to this case the principles so recently announced in Dean Milk." Were there less burdensome alternatives to achieve Alexandria's objectives? The majority did not pursue that inquiry; it did consider alternatives briefly in another sense, in assessing the burden on the interstate business (rather than in determining the weight of the justification for the ordinance): "[T]he usual methods of seeking business are left open by the ordinance. That such methods do not produce as much business as house-to-house canvassing is, constitutionally, immaterial."

Is it justifiable to dismiss as "constitutionally immaterial" the impact of the ban on solicitation—even if alternative ways of doing business are left open? In cases applying the commerce clause in state taxation contexts, by sharp contrast, the Court has been especially protective of solicitors for interstate businesses. See the consistent invalidation of flat-fee license taxes in line on the "long line of 'drummer' cases" considered in the materials on "discrimination" in state taxation, chap. 9, p. 693, below. Can the Breard Court's position regarding regulation of solicitors be reconciled with that applicable to taxation of solicitors?

D. ACCESS OF FOREIGN BUYERS TO LOCAL RESOURCES

THE EISENBERG AND PARKER CASES—LEGITIMATE ECONOMIC PURPOSES?

1. *Eisenberg*. In Milk Control Board v. Eisenberg Farm Products, 306 U.S. 346 (1939), a New York milk dealer who bought milk from Pennsylvania producers for shipment out-of-state challenged Pennsylvania's minimum price regulation. The dealer operated a milk receiving plant in Pennsylvania. The milk he bought from Pennsylvania farmers was cooled at the plant for less than 24 hours; then, all of it was shipped to New York. Pennsylvania law set the minimum price to be paid by dealers to milk producers and required dealers to obtain a license. The Pennsylvania Milk Control Act of 1935 was similar to the New York law involved in the Baldwin case, supra; Eisenberg claimed the application of the law to him similarly violated the commerce clause. The state courts agreed with him, but the Supreme Court reversed.

Justice Roberts' majority opinion explained: "The purpose of the statute under review obviously is to reach a domestic situation in the interest of the welfare of the producers and consumers of milk in Pennsylvania. Its provisions with respect to license, bond, and regulation of prices to be paid to producers are appropriate means to the ends in view. The question is whether the prescription of prices to be paid producers in the effort to accomplish these ends constitutes a prohibited burden on interstate commerce, or an incidental burden which is permissible until superseded by Congressional enactment. That question can be answered only by weighing the nature of the respondent's activities, and the propriety of local regulation of them as disclosed by the record."

He insisted that the state did not attempt to regulate shipment to or sale in New York. The "activity affected" was "essentially local in Pennsylvania." "If dealers conducting receiving stations in various localities in Pennsylvania were free to ignore the requirements of the statute on the ground that all or a part of the milk they purchase is destined to another state the uniform operation of the statute locally would be crippled and might be impracticable. Only a small fraction of the milk produced by farmers in Pennsylvania is shipped out of the Commonwealth. There is, therefore, a comparatively large field remotely affecting and wholly unrelated to interstate commerce within which the statute operates. [The opinion noted that, in 1934, "approximately 4,500,000,000 pounds of milk were produced in Pennsylvania of which approximately 470,000,000 pounds were shipped out of the state."] These considerations we think justify the conclusion that the effect of the law on interstate commerce is incidental and not forbidden by the Constitution, in the absence of regulation by Congress." Baldwin v. G. A. F. Seelig, Inc. was not controlling. According to Justice Roberts, that decision "condemned an enactment aimed solely at interstate commerce attempting to affect and regulate the price to be paid for milk in a sister state, and we indicated that the attempt amounted in effect to a tariff barrier set up against milk imported into the enacting state." Is Eisenberg consistent with the Baldwin case, above? With the Hood case, the next principal case? See the questions following Hood, at p. 661.

2. *Parker.* Note also the rejection of a commerce clause challenge to another law designed to promote a local economic concern, in Parker v. Brown, 317 U.S. 341 (1943). A California raisin producer attacked a marketing scheme established pursuant to the state Agricultural Prorate Act. That law compelled each producer to put most of his raisin crop under the marketing control of a program committee, for the purpose of eliminating price competition among producers. As the Court noted, "since 95 per cent of the crop is marketed in interstate commerce, the program may be taken to have a substantial effect on the commerce, in placing restrictions on the sale and marketing of a product to buyers who eventually sell and ship it in interstate commerce." Nevertheless, the Court sustained the program. Chief Justice Stone explained:

"Whether we resort to the mechanical test sometimes applied by this Court in determining when interstate commerce begins with respect to a commodity grown or manufactured within a state and then sold and shipped out of it—or whether we consider only the power of the state in the absence of Congressional action to regulate matters of local concern, even though the regulation affects or in some measure restricts the commerce—we think the present regulation is within state power.

"In applying the mechanical test to determine when interstate commerce begins and ends . . . no case has gone so far as to hold that a state could not license or otherwise regulate the sale of articles within the state because the buyer, after processing and packing them, will, in the normal course of business, sell and ship them in interstate commerce. . . . But courts are not confined to so mechanical a test. When Congress has not exerted its power under the Commerce Clause, and state regulation of matters of local concern is so related to interstate commerce that it also operates as a regulation of that commerce, the reconciliation of the power thus granted with that reserved to the state is to be attained by the accommodation of the competing demands of the state and national interests involved. See Di Santo v. Pennsylvania, 273 U.S. 34, 44 (with which compare California v. Thompson [p. 627, supra]); South Carolina Highway Dept. v. Barnwell Bros., supra; Milk Control Board v. Eisenberg Co., 306 U.S. 346 . . . .

"Such regulations by the state are to be sustained, not because they are 'indirect' rather than 'direct,' see Di Santo v. Pennsylvania, supra; cf. Wickard v. Filburn, ... But they are to be upheld because upon a consideration of all the relevant facts and circumstances it appears that the matter is one which may appropriately be regulated in the interest of the safety, health and well-being of local communities, and which, because of its local character, and the practical difficulties involved, may never be adequately dealt with by Congress. . . . There may also be, as in the present case, local regulations whose effect upon the national commerce is such as not to conflict but to coincide with a policy which Congress has established with respect to it.

"Examination of the evidence in this case and of available data of the raisin industry in California, of which we may take judicial notice, leaves no doubt that the evils attending the production and marketing of raisins in that state present a problem local in character and urgently demanding state action for the economic protection of those engaged in one of its important industries. . . . The history of the industry, at least since 1929, is a record of a continuous search for expedients which would stabilize the marketing of the raisin crop and maintain a price standard which would bring fair return to the producers. It is significant of the relation of the local interest in maintaining this program to the national interest in interstate commerce, that throughout the period from 1929 until the adoption of the prorate program for the 1940 raisin crop, the national government has contributed to these efforts either by its establishment of marketing programs pursuant to Act of Congress or by aiding programs sponsored by the state. . . .

"This history shows clearly enough that the adoption of legislative measures to prevent the demoralization of the industry by stabilizing the marketing of the raisin crop is a matter of state as well as national concern and, in the absence of inconsistent Congressional action, is a problem whose solution is peculiarly within the province of the state. . . . The program was not aimed at nor did it discriminate against interstate commerce, although it undoubtedly affected the commerce by increasing the interstate price of raisins and curtailing interstate shipments to some undetermined extent. The effect on the commerce is not greater, and in some instances was far less, than that which this Court has held not to afford a basis for denying to the states the right to pursue a legitimate state end. . . .

"In comparing the relative weights of the conflicting local and national interests involved, it is significant that Congress, by its agricultural legislation, has recognized the distressed condition of much of the agricultural production of the United States . . . . It thus appears that whatever effect the operation of the California program may have on interstate commerce, it is one which it has been the policy of Congress to aid and encourage through federal agencies in conformity to the Agricultural Marketing Agreement Act, and § 302 of the Agricultural Adjustment Act. Nor is the effect on the commerce greater than or substantially different in kind from that contemplated by the stabilization programs authorized by federal statutes. . . ."

H. P. HOOD & SONS v. DU MOND

336 U.S. 525, 69 S.Ct. 657, 93 L.Ed. 865 (1949).

Certiorari to the Supreme Court of New York, Albany County.

Mr. Justice JACKSON delivered the opinion of the Court. . . .

[Hood distributed milk in Boston. The city obtained 90% of its milk supply from outside of Massachusetts. Hood had long obtained milk from New York producers and had maintained three receiving depots there. Hood sought a New York license to establish a fourth depot in New York, in the area that had been developed as a source of milk for Boston. One of the conditions under the New York law was that the "issuance of the license will not tend to a destructive competition in a market already adequately served." The New York Commissioner of Agriculture and Markets denied a license for the fourth depot on the basis of this provision. Hood had complied with other conditions of the law.]

The Commissioner found that Hood, if licensed at Greenwich, would permit its present suppliers, at their option, to deliver at the new plant rather than the old ones and for a substantial number this would mean shorter hauls and savings in delivery costs. The new plant also would attract twenty to thirty producers, some of whose milk Hood anticipates will or may be diverted from other buyers. Other large milk distributors have plants within the general area and dealers serving Troy obtain milk in the locality. He found that Troy was inadequately supplied during the preceding short season.

In denying the application for expanded facilities, the Commissioner states his grounds as follows:

> "If applicant is permitted to equip and operate another milk plant in this territory, and to take on producers now delivering to plants other than those which it operates, it will tend to reduce the volume of milk received at the plants which lose those producers, and will tend to increase the cost of handling milk in those plants.

> "If applicant takes producers now delivering milk to local markets such as Troy, it will have a tendency to deprive such markets of a supply needed during the short season. . . .

> "The issuance of a license to applicant which would permit it to operate an additional plant, would tend to a destructive competition in a market already adequately served, and would not be in the public interest."

Denial of the license was sustained by the Court of Appeals over constitutional objections duly urged under the Commerce Clause . . . .

Production and distribution of milk are so intimately related to public health and welfare that the need for regulation to protect those interests has long been recognized and is, from a constitutional standpoint, hardly controversial. . . . As the states extended their efforts to control various phases of export and import also, questions were raised as to limitations on state power under the Commerce Clause of the Constitution. . . .

The present controversy begins where the Eisenberg decision [supra] left off. New York's regulations, designed to assure producers a fair price and a responsible purchaser, and consumers a sanitary and modernly equipped handler, are not challenged here but have been complied with. It is only additional restrictions, imposed for the avowed purpose and with the practical effect of curtailing the volume of interstate commerce to aid local economic interests, that are in question here, and no such measures were attempted or such ends sought to be served in the Act before the Court in the Eisenberg case.

Our decision in a milk litigation most relevant to the present controversy deals with the converse of the present situation. Baldwin v. Seelig [supra. The extensive discussion of the case is omitted.]

This distinction between the power of the State to shelter its people from menaces to their health or safety and from fraud, even when those dangers emanate from interstate commerce, and its lack of power to retard, burden or constrict the flow of such commerce for their economic advantage, is one deeply rooted in both our history and our law. [See the passages quoted at the beginning of this chapter, p. 614.]

Baldwin v. Seelig, 294 U.S. 511, is an explicit, impressive, recent and unanimous condemnation by this Court of economic restraints on interstate commerce for local economic advantage, but it does not stand alone. This Court consistently has rebuffed attempts of states to advance their own commercial interests by curtailing the movement of articles of commerce, either into or out of the state, while generally supporting their right to impose even burdensome regulations in the interest of local health and safety. As most states serve their own interests best by sending their produce to market, the cases in which this Court has been obliged to deal with prohibitions or limitations by states upon exports of articles of commerce are not numerous. However, in a leading case, Oklahoma v. Kansas Natural Gas Co., 221 U.S. 229, the Court denied constitutional validity to a statute by which Oklahoma, by regulation of gas companies and pipe lines, sought to restrict the export of natural gas. The Court held that when a state recognizes an article to be a subject of commerce, it cannot prohibit it from being a subject of interstate commerce . . . . [Justice Jackson also discussed Pennsylvania v. West Virginia and Foster Packing Co. v. Haydel, note 2c, p. 699, infra.]

The material success that has come to inhabitants of the states which make up this federal free trade unit has been the most impressive in the history of commerce, but the established interdependence of the states only emphasizes the necessity of protecting interstate movement of goods against local burdens and repressions. We need only consider the consequences if each of the few states that produce copper, lead, high-grade iron ore, timber, cotton, oil or gas should decree that industries located in that state shall have priority. What fantastic rivalries and dislocations and reprisals would ensue if such practices were begun! Or suppose that the field of discrimination and retaliation be industry. May Michigan provide that automobiles cannot be taken out of that State until local dealers' demands are fully met? Would she not have every argument in the favor of such a statute that can be offered in support of New York's limiting sales of milk for out-of-state shipment to protect the economic interests of her competing dealers and local consumers? Could Ohio then pounce upon the rubber-tire industry, on which she has a substantial grip, to retaliate for Michigan's auto monopoly?

Our system, fostered by the Commerce Clause, is that every farmer and every craftsman shall be encouraged to produce by the certainty that he will have free access to every market in the Nation, that no home embargoes will withhold his exports, and no foreign state will by customs duties or regulations exclude them. Likewise, every consumer may look to the free competition from every producing area in the Nation to protect him from exploitation by any. Such was the vision of the Founders; such has been the doctrine of this Court which has given it reality.

The State, however, insists that denial of the license for a new plant does not restrict or obstruct interstate commerce, because petitioner has been licensed at its other plants without condition or limitation as to the quantities it may purchase. Hence, it is said, all that has been denied petitioner is a local convenience—that of being able to buy and receive at Greenwich quantities of milk it is free to buy at Eagle Bridge and Salem. It suggests that, by increased efficiency or enlarged capacity at its other plants, petitioner might sufficiently increase its supply through those facilities.

The weakness of this contention is that a buyer has to buy where there is a willing seller, and the peculiarities of the milk business necessitate location of a receiving and cooling station for nearby producers. . . . But the argument also asks us to assume that the Commissioner's order will not operate in the way he found that it would as a reason for making it. He found that petitioner, at its new plant, would divert milk from the plants of some other large handlers in the vicinity, which plants "can handle more milk." In the face of affirmative findings that the proposed plant would increase petitioner's supply, we can hardly be asked to assume that denial of the license will not deny petitioner access to such added supplies. While the state power is applied in this case to limit expansion by a handler of milk who already has been allowed some purchasing facilities, the argument for doing so, if sustained, would be equally effective to exclude an entirely new foreign handler from coming into the State to purchase. . . .

Since the statute as applied violates the Commerce Clause and is not authorized by federal legislation pursuant to that Clause, it cannot stand. The judgment is reversed and the cause remanded for proceedings not inconsistent with this opinion.

It is so ordered.

Mr. Justice BLACK, dissenting.

In this case the Court sets up a new constitutional formula for invalidation of state laws regulating local phases of interstate commerce. I believe the New York law is invulnerable to constitutional attack under constitutional rules which the majority of this Court have long accepted. The new formula subjects state regulations of local business activities to greater constitutional hazards than they have ever had to meet before. . . .

Had a dealer supplying New York customers applied for a license to operate a new plant, the commissioner would have been compelled under the Act to protect petitioner's plants supplying Boston consumers in the same manner that this order would have protected New York consumers. . . . The commerce clause should not be stretched to forbid New York's fair attempt to protect the healthful milk supply of consumers, even though some of the consumers in this case happen to live in Troy, New York. . . .

The language of this state Act is not discriminatory, the legislative history shows it was not so intended, and the commissioner has not administered it with a hostile eye. The Act must stand or fall on this basis notwithstanding the overtones of the Court's opinion. If petitioner and other interstate milk dealers are to be placed above and beyond this law, it must be done solely on this Court's new constitutional formula which bars a state from protecting itself against local destructive competitive practices so far as they are indulged in by dealers who ship their milk into other states. . . .

. . . The basic principles of the Cooley rule have been entangled and sometimes obscured with much language. In the main, however, those principles have been the asserted grounds for determination of all commerce cases decided by this Court from 1852 until today. . . . Many of the cases have used the words "restraints," "obstructions," "in commerce," "on commerce," "burdens," "direct burdens," "undue burdens," "unreasonable burdens," "unfair burdens," "incidental burdens," etc., but such words have almost always been used, as the opinions reveal, to aid in application of the Cooley balance-of-interests rule. . . .

In this Court, challenges to the Cooley rule on the ground that the rule was an ineffective protector of interstate commerce from state regulations have been confined to dissents and concurring opinions. Duckworth v. Arkansas, 314 U.S. 390, 400–401 . . . . . In the Duckworth case [a] concurring opinion expressed the view that the Court's opinion written by Chief Justice Stone, rooted as it was in the Cooley principle, "let commerce struggle for Congressional action to make it free," and expressed the writer's unwillingness to follow the Court's "trend" beyond the "plain requirements" of existing cases, at p. 401.*

The Cooley balancing-of-interests principle which the Court accepted and applied in the Duckworth case is today supplanted by the philosophy of the Duckworth concurring opinion which though presented in the Duckworth case gained no adherents.   For the New York statute is killed by a mere automatic application of a new mechanistic formula.   The Court appraises nothing, unless its stretching of the old commerce clause interpretation results from a reappraisal of the power and duty of this Court under the commerce clause. . . .

It was because New York attempted to project its law into Vermont that even its admitted health purpose was insufficient to outweigh Vermont's interest in controlling its own local affairs [in Baldwin v. Seelig.]   Added to this was the Court's appraisal of the law as a plain discrimination against interstate commerce . . .. Quite differently here New York has not attempted to regulate the price of milk in Massachusetts . . .; its law is not hostile to interstate commerce in conception or operation . . .. The circumstances and conditions that brought about invalidation of the law considered in the Baldwin case are too different from those here considered to rest today's holding on the Baldwin decision. . . .   Milk Board v. Eisenberg Co., 306 U.S. 346, would control this case but for the Court's limiting that case to its precise facts. . . .   Pennsylvania imposed these burdens on interstate commerce to promote health and to protect its farmers from the consequences of destructive competition among dealers.   This New York law was designed to promote health and to protect New York farmers from destructive competition in New York.   It requires more than invocation of the spectre of "Balkanization" and eulogy of the Constitution's framers to prove that there is a gnat's heel difference in the burdens imposed on commerce by the two laws. . . .

The basic question here is not the greatness of the commerce clause concept, but whether all local phases of interstate business are to be judicially immunized from state laws against destructive competitive business practices such as those prohibited by New York's law. . . .   While I have doubt about the wisdom of this New York law, I do not conceive it to be the function of this Court to revise that state's economic judgments.   Any doubt I may have concerning the wisdom of New York's law is far less, however, than is my skepticism concerning the ability of the Federal Government to

---

* The reference is to the concurring opinion by Mr. Justice Jackson in Duckworth v. Arkansas, 314 U.S. 390 (1942). The case sustained a statute of Arkansas requiring a permit for the transportation of intoxicating liquor through the State (the object being merely to identify those engaged in such transportation, their routes and points of destination). Mr. Justice Jackson, agreeing with the result on the basis of the Twenty-First Amendment, urged that, absent that provision, the result should have been opposite. In his view the inertia of government makes it unlikely that Congress, hard-pressed with more urgent matters, will correct minor obstructions to interstate commerce. "The practical result is that in default of action by us, [the States] will go on suffocating and retarding and Balkanizing American commerce, trade and industry."

reach out and effectively regulate all the local business activities in the forty-eight states.

I would leave New York's law alone.

Mr. Justice MURPHY joins in this opinion.

Mr. Justice FRANKFURTER, with whom Mr. Justice RUTLEDGE joins, dissenting.

If the Court's opinion has meaning beyond deciding this case in isolation, its effect is to hold that no matter how important to the internal economy of a State may be the prevention of destructive competition, and no matter how unimportant the interstate commerce affected, a State cannot as a means of preventing such competition deny an applicant access to a market within the State if that applicant happens to intend the out-of-state shipment of the product that he buys. I feel constrained to dissent because I cannot agree in treating what is essentially a problem of striking a balance between competing interests as an exercise in absolutes. Nor does it seem to me that such a problem should be disposed of on a record from which we cannot tell what weights to put in which side of the scales. . . .

This case falls somewhere between [the] most nearly decisive authorities. It is closer to [Buck v. Kuykendall, supra, p. 628] than to the Eisenberg case in that the denial of a license to enter a market because the market is "adequately served" imposes a disqualification beyond the power of the applicant to remove. In that respect the effect upon the free flow of commerce is more enduring than is the case where all that is required is compliance with a local regulation. The State's interest in restricting competition, moreover, is less obvious than its interest in preserving health or insuring probity in business dealings. Yet the commerce involved [in Buck] was exclusively interstate. Here, however, it does not appear that any of Hood's competitors sent milk out of the State, and, in fact, only about 8% of New York's entire production of milk is sent out. In this respect the case resembles the Eisenberg case, in which it appeared that only slightly more than 10% of the milk produced in Pennsylvania was exported. . . . But comparison could be carried further and still the similarities and dissimilarities of the facts in the record before us to the Eisenberg case and [the Buck case] would be inconclusive. In an area where differences of degree depend on slight differences of fact, precedent alone is an inadequate guide.

It is argued, however, that New York can have no interest in the restriction of competition great enough to warrant shutting its doors to one who would buy its products for shipment to another State. This must mean that the protection of health and the promotion of fair dealing are of a different order, somehow, than the prevention of destructive competition. But the fixing of prices was a main object of the regulation upheld in the Eisenberg case, and it is obvious that one of the most effective ways of maintaining a price structure is to control competition. . . .

As matters now stand, however, it is impossible to say whether or not the restriction of competition among dealers in milk does in fact contribute to their economic well-being and, through them, to that of the entire industry. And if we assume that some contribution is made, we cannot guess how much. Why, when the State has fixed a minimum price for producers, does it take steps to keep competing dealers from increasing the price by bidding against each other for the existing supply?   Is it concerned with protecting consumers from excessive prices?   Or is it concerned with seeing that marginal dealers, forced by competition to pay more and charge less, are not driven either to cut corners in the maintenance of their plants or to close them down entirely? Might these consequences follow from operation at less than capacity?   What proportion of capacity is necessary to enable the marginal dealer to stay in business?   Could Hood's potential competitors in the Greenwich area maintain efficient and sanitary standards of operation on a lower margin of profit? How would their closing down affect producers?   Would the competition of Hood affect dealers other than those in that area?   How many of those dealers are also engaged in interstate commerce?   How much of a strain would be put on the price structure maintained by the State by a holding that it cannot regulate the competition of dealers buying for an out-of-state market? Is this a situation in which State regulation, by supplementing federal regulation, is of benefit to interstate as well as to intrastate commerce?

We should, I submit, have answers at least to some of these questions before we can say either how seriously interstate commerce is burdened by New York's licensing power or how necessary to New York is that power. . . .

Nor should we now dispose of the case upon the claim that New York cannot discriminate against interstate commerce by keeping its milk for absorption by "local markets such as Troy." . . .   [T]here is much force in the argument that if a State cannot keep for its own use a natural resource like gas, as it can keep its wild game, Geer v. Connecticut, 161 U.S. 519 . . ., then *a fortiori* it cannot prefer its own inhabitants in the consumption of a product that would not have come into existence but for its commercial value. . . .   Broadly stated, the question is whether a State can withhold from interstate commerce a product derived from local raw materials upon a determination by an administrative agency that there is a local need for it.   For me it has not been put to rest by Pennsylvania v. West Virginia, supra.   More narrowly, the question is whether the State can prefer the consumers of one community to consumers in other States as well as to consumers in other parts of its own territory.   It is arguable, moreover, that the Commissioner was actuated not by preference for New York consumers, but by the aim of stabilizing the supply of all the local markets, including Boston as well as Troy, served by the New York milkshed. . . .

My conclusion, accordingly, is that the case should be remanded to the Supreme Court of Albany County . . . .

HOOD, FORBIDDEN ECONOMIC PURPOSES, AND CONTROL OVER LOCAL RESOURCES

1. *Economic purposes and balancing*. a. Does Hood abandon the Cooley-Southern Pacific balancing approach to establish a per se rule when economic interests (rather than the interest in health and safety, for example) underlie the state regulation?   Or does Hood assert that balancing continues, but that economic purposes tend to tip the balancing scale toward invalidation? Does Hood bar all state economic concerns?   Does it bar primarily any state protectionist interest to shield local industry against competition, as was per-

ceived in Baldwin? Does it bar any state interest in encouraging local economic well-being? Even if economic well-being plainly affects health, safety, etc.? Can the Hood ban on "economic restraints" for "local economic advantage" be reconciled with the Eisenberg Court's characterization of the price regulation found valid there as one "in the interest of the welfare of the producers and consumers of milk in Pennsylvania"? Can it be reconciled with the Parker Court's statement that the local marketing regulation "for the economic protection" of the important California raisin industry served "a legitimate state end"? Was it critical that the local regulation in Parker was found "not to conflict but to coincide with" congressional policy? (Recall the materials on Huron Portland Cement, at the end of sec. 1B, p. 647, supra; but note that the United States argued as amicus curiae in Parker "that the state program, though not inconsistent with federal agricultural legislation, was invalid" under the Sherman Act as well as the commerce clause.)

b.   Hood reemphasizes the distinction between a state's power to protect its people against dangers to "health or safety and from fraud," even to the point of affecting commerce, and its lack of power to impede commerce for local "economic advantage." Was that distinction adequately applied in condemning the New York regulation because in purpose and effect it restrained commerce "to aid local economic interests"? Was economic self-interest all that supported the state regulation? Compare Justice Frankfurter's questions and Justice Black's reference to "New York's fair attempt to protect the healthful milk supply of consumers."

2.   *State control of local resources, export embargoes, and the Cities Service case.*   a.   *The Hood principle.*   The Hood opinion states that the commerce clause assures that every producer will have "free access to every market in the Nation, that no home embargoes will withhold his exports." Does Hood simply stand for a ban on such embargoes? Does the Hood decision prohibit preference to local consumers? Was there such preference in the Hood case? Can the natural resources cases, note 2c below, be reconciled with the asserted anti-embargo principle?

b.   *Cities Service.*   In Cities Service Co. v. Peerless Co., 340 U.S. 179 (1950), a year after Hood, the Court sustained a state regulation of natural gas prices to conserve local resources. Was that consistent with the broad statements in Hood? Can it be reconciled with a narrow reading of Hood? Cities Service involved an order of the Oklahoma Corporation Commission fixing a minimum wellhead price on all gas taken from a particular natural gas field was held not to be violative of the commerce clause. The Court agreed with the findings of the Commission "that the taking of gas at the prevailing prices resulted in both economic and physical waste of gas, . . . loss to the State in gross production taxes, inequitable taking of gas from the common source of supply, and discrimination among various producers in the field." The Court unanimously concluded that it was "clear" that a "legitimate local interest is at stake." Moreover, "in a field of this complexity, we cannot say that there is a clear national interest so harmed that the state price-fixing orders here employed fall within the ban of the Commerce Clause. . . . Milk Control Board v. Eisenberg Farm Products, supra." Note the Court's basis for saying that the Hood case was "not inconsistent" with this holding: "The vice in the regulation invalidated by Hood was solely that it denied facilities to a company in interstate commerce on the articulated ground that such facilities would divert milk supplies needed by local consumers; in other words, the regulation discriminated against interstate commerce. There is no such problem here. The price regulation applies to all gas taken from the field, whether destined for interstate or intrastate consumers." Was this an adequate basis for distinguishing Hood?

c. *Embargoes on natural resources.* Hood suggested that a state may not hold on to local economic resources to meet local needs. Does that bar state efforts to conserve natural resources? Most of the cases discussed in Justice Jackson's opinion in Hood invalidated the local restrictions: e. g., Pennsylvania v. West Virginia, 262 U.S. 553 (1923), where, in view of the limited supply, West Virginia had required that local consumer demands be met before out-of-state shipments could be made (Justice Holmes dissented, saying that he could "see nothing in the commerce clause to prevent a State from giving a preference to its inhabitants in the enjoyment of its natural advantages"); Foster Packing Co. v. Haydel, 278 U.S. 1 (1928), where Louisiana had prohibited the shipment of raw shrimp out-of-state until shells and heads supposedly needed for fertilizer were removed (the Court found that the real purpose was "to bring about the removal of the packing and canning industry from Mississippi to Louisiana"). [See also Toomer v. Witsell, 334 U.S. 385 (1948), chap. 10, p. 772, below.] But other cases have sustained local controls: e. g., Geer v. Connecticut, 161 U.S. 519 (1896), upholding a statute prohibiting the killing of certain game birds for the purpose of shipment out of the state, even though sale of the game birds within the state was permitted (the Court emphasized property rights: the birds were collectively owned by the people of the state); Hudson County Water Co. v. McCarter, 209 U.S. 349 (1908), sustaining a New Jersey law prohibiting the transportation of water from that state's rivers and lakes to any other state (the Court noted the state interest in maintaining local rivers "substantially undiminished"). Can the water case be reconciled with the West Virginia natural gas case? The game bird case with the shrimp case? Do the water and game bird cases survive the balancing analysis and the Hood case?

Note also the Court's unanimous invalidation of a state regulation in Pike v. Bruce Church, Inc., 397 U.S. —— (1970) (noted p. 647, supra). The state prohibited the company from shipping uncrated cantaloupes from its Arizona ranch to its nearby California packing plant. Compliance with the requirement that the cantaloupes be packed in Arizona would have required a capital outlay of $200,000 by the company. The cantaloupes were of very high quality; when packed in California, they were not identified as Arizona-grown. Justice Stewart noted that the state's purpose here was not to keep the reputation of its own growers unsullied, "but to enhance their reputation through the reflected goodwill of the company's superior product." That state interest was found "legitimate" but "tenuous" and inadequate to justify the state-imposed burden: "The nature of that burden is, constitutionally, more significant than its extent. For the Court has viewed with particular suspicion state statutes requiring business operations to be performed in the home State which could more efficiently be performed elsewhere. . . . If the Commerce Clause forbids a State to require work to be done within its jurisdiction to promote local employment, then surely it cannot permit a State to require a person to go into the local packing business solely for the sake of enhancing the reputation of other producers within its borders."

SECTION 2. CONGRESSIONAL ORDERING OF FEDERAL–STATE RELATIONSHIPS

————

Introduction. The materials in section 1 of this chapter emphasized limits on state power derived from the commerce clause itself. But in many cases the commerce clause is not entirely "dormant"; with increasing frequency, objections based on the *exercise* of the congressional power are joined with those resting on the constitutional *grant* of the power. That, indeed, was so as early as Gibbons v. Ogden, supra; it is even more common in the context of proliferating national legislation of the Twentieth Century. This section, then, briefly examines the impact of congressional exercises of power. The major concern is with federal legislation (a) imposing new limits on state action, and (b) removing pre-existing barriers to state control. Most of the materials continue to deal with commerce problems, but congressional action is of course significant with regard to a wide range of other delegated powers as well. Moreover, the techniques of imposing new and removing old obstacles to state legislation should be viewed in a broader context, as a small sampling of the wide variety of devices available in the congressional ordering of federal-state relations. See the concluding note in this section. This section, in short, seeks to highlight what has been a pervasive but somewhat obscured phenomenon in the earlier materials: that the Court in fact operates as an important but limited partner of Congress in articulating federalism limits on state power; that Congress may play a decisive role in determining the relations between state and federal power, and in defining the operative scope of state and federal substantive law; and that the interrelationships between state and federal law present problems of subtlety and complexity for Congress and Court.

————

A. PREEMPTION OF STATE AUTHORITY

————

Scope Note. When Congress exercises a granted power, the federal legislation may displace state law under the Supremacy Clause. But Congress does not typically act on a wholesale basis, and congressional entry into a field does not necessarily end all state authority. In considering the preemption cases, as with the entire area of congressional ordering, it is vital to bear in mind an observation in Hart and Wechsler, The Federal Courts and the Federal System (1953), 435: "Federal law is generally interstitial in nature. It rarely occupies a legal field completely . . .. Federal legislation, on the whole, has been conceived and drafted on an *ad hoc* basis to accomplish limited objectives. It builds upon legal relationships established by the states, altering or supplanting them only so far as necessary for the special purpose. Congress acts, in short, against the background of the total *corpus juris* of the states in much the way that a state legislature acts against the background of the common law, assumed to govern unless changed by legislation." See also Hart, "The Relations Between State and Federal Law," 54 Colum.L. Rev. 489 (1954), and the note on Political Safeguards of Federalism, chap. 3, p. 231, supra.

"Preemption as a preferential ground."   What, then, is the function of the Court in examining claims that federal legislation has displaced state authority?   In part, the problem is one of statutory interpretation, and the cases accordingly require a particularized examination of the specific regulatory scheme.   Space limitations make an examination of the varied statutory contexts impossible here.   The illustrations of preemption problems in this section are designed to suggest some general themes, to reveal some trends, and to examine some considerations (going beyond those of traditional statutory interpretation) that may enter the Court's decisions in preemption controversies.   Consider, in reviewing the preemption issues raised in section 1 and in examining the illustrations in this section, the validity of the observations in the following student note [Note, "Pre-emption as a Preferential Ground: A New Canon of Construction," 12 Stan.L.Rev. 208 (1959), Selected Essays 1938–62 (1963), 310]:*

"Many of the Supreme Court's recent pre-emption decisions have been condemned as . . . unwarranted substitution of judicial wisdom for that of Congress. [E. g., Pennsylvania v. Nelson, p. 678, infra.]   Much of the criticism appears to have been misdirected.   The critics have focused discussion on whether there was a specific congressional intent to supersede state law rather than whether the coexistence of state law is compatible with the general purpose of the federal legislation involved.   Moreover, the critics have failed to appreciate that in many instances the same results might easily have been reached on other constitutional grounds had the Court not chosen to articulate them in terms of pre-emption.

"By framing the pre-emption question in terms of specific congressional intent the Supreme Court has manufactured difficulties for itself.   Apart from the difficult problem of defining which Congress' and which congressman's intent is relevant, this manner of stating the issue suggests that the pre-emption question was consciously resolved and that only diligent effort is needed to reveal the intended solution.   But Congress, embroiled in controversy over policy issues, rarely anticipates the possibile ramifications of its acts upon state law.   [P]re-emption questions are implicit in many federal statutes but remain for the courts to answer. . . .

"In the great majority of cases the pre-emptive implications of the federal statute must be derived without the aid of specific legislative guidance, and even when such guidance is offered, it does not represent the whole solution in many instances.   Thus several writers have suggested that the proper approach is to determine whether the continued existence of the state law is consistent with the general purpose of the federal statute by seeking to define the evil Congress sought to remedy and the method chosen to effectuate its cure.   And, to understand the evil and the remedy the court should look to the entire text of the statute, to its history, and to administrative interpretations, when available.

"Most of the cases appear to have adopted this approach, although lip service is still paid to the specific intent inquiry.   In some cases, however, the Court has precluded state action despite the fact that none of the interpretative sources revealed a federal policy which required the invalidation of the state law in question.   Just as the Court construes a statute in such a way as to avoid a constitutional question whenever possible, it may be that the Court bases its decision on the pre-emption ground in order to avoid reaching some other constitutional question. . . . At times the Court has precluded state action despite the fact that the process of interpretation failed to reveal a conflict of the strength that appears to be required to invoke the supremacy clause. Rather than treat this group of cases merely as another example of 'judicial legislation,' these decisions will be examined for signs that the Court is in actuality implementing constitutional principles external to the supremacy clause, while nominally deciding the case on the pre-emption ground.

[After discussing Pennsylvania v. Nelson and Hines v. Davidowitz, infra, the Note continued:] "Recently . . . the Court has relied increasingly on the pre-emption doctrine in cases which would have been decided under the commerce clause only a short time ago. It is now frequently argued (1) that the states lack concurrent power under the doctrine of Cooley v. Board of Wardens, and (2) that if the states possess such power, the field has been pre-empted by federal legislation. Almost all of the cases so argued which result in the preclusion of state action have rested on the pre-emption ground without reaching the commerce clause issue. The Court, however, appears to use essentially the same reasoning process in a case nominally hinging on pre-emption as it has in past cases in which the question was whether the state law regulated or burdened interstate commerce. . . .

". . . [T]he Court has adopted the same weighing of interests approach in pre-emption cases that it uses to determine whether a state law unjustifiably burdens interstate commerce. In a number of situations the Court has invalidated statutes on the pre-emption ground when it appeared that the state laws sought to favor local economic interests at the expense of the interstate market. On the other hand, when the Court has been satisfied that valid local interests, such as those in safety or in the reputable operation of local business, outweigh the restrictive effect on interstate commerce, the Court has rejected the pre-emption argument and allowed state regulation to stand. . . .

"The critics of the Court have discerned correctly that the pre-emption decisions do not uniformly represent the product of sound statutory construction, much less a supportable finding of specific congressional intent. Pre-emption can never be the product of statutory construction alone, since the Court and only the Court can make the final judgment of incompatibility required by the supremacy clause.

"As a practical matter, it is understandable that the Court has relied increasingly upon the pre-emption ground. By so doing, the Court in some measure shifts to Congress the odium for invalidating state law. But when the discrepancy between the judicial finding of congressional intent and the known temper of the Congress on the subject becomes too great, this attempt to shift responsibility backfires upon the Court in the form of accusations of 'judicial legislation.' If the Court continues to rationalize its pre-emption decisions in terms of spurious specific intent, or even if it speaks in terms of congressional purpose when it is actually motivated by other constitutional considerations, the Court can only earn the disrespect of the legal profession and the public.

"In order to use pre-emption validly as a substitute ground the Court must both make clear that it is invoking an overriding principle of decision and justify the use of such a principle. That the Court can do this is demonstrated by its use of the policy of clear statement by which constitutional issues are avoided through statutory construction. . . .

"Flexibility is gained by deciding a case on the pre-emption ground rather than on some other constitutional basis because pre-emption decisions invite congressional reconsideration and adjustment. It might seem, however, that even if Congress subsequently enacts a statute to remove the pre-emption barrier, the Court will be forced to invalidate the state law when next it is challenged, since the premise for employing pre-emption was that the Court believed the state law to be invalid on substantive constitutional grounds. In those situations where the alternative constitutional ground is an independent standard, such as due process or equal protection, congressional approval of the state law is not likely to alter the Court's hostile view of the state law, and the only effect of relying preferentially on pre-emption would be to postpone the eventual showdown. [But cf. the Morgan case, chap. 6, p. 545, supra.] But when the question is one of the negative implications of some affirmative constitutional grant of power, such as that over commerce, the view Congress takes of the permissible limits of state action is of proper concern to the Court. Used as a method of allowing Congress a greater share in the elaboration of the areas constitutionally reserved for its own action, the pre-emption doctrine can thus become a valuable device in the give and take between branches of the government which is the ultimate guarantee of sound constitutional government."

PREEMPTION: A CHANGE IN JUDICIAL APPROACH?

Does the course of decisions suggest a growing tendency to find preemption? A sampling of cases of a generation ago, and a contrast with more recent decisions, may provide a clue—though it bears renewed warning that general statements may be less important than the specific statutory contexts in evaluating preemption decisions.

1. *The typical formulas: the Rice and Hines cases.* In modern cases, the Court has frequently recited the standards articulated a generation ago. Are the standards applied similarly, however? Probably the most widely quoted passages are from Rice v. Santa Fe Elevator Corp., 331 U.S. 218, 229–230 (1947), and Hines v. Davidowitz, 312 U.S. 52, 67 (1941.) [See, e. g., Pennsylvania v. Nelson, 350 U.S. 497 (1956), below, (where the Rice and Hines passages are quoted).] In Rice, Justice Douglas stated: "The question in each case is what the purpose of Congress was. . . . Such a purpose may be evidenced in several ways. The scheme of federal regulation may be so pervasive as to make reasonable the inference that Congress left no room for the State to supplement it. . . . Or the Act of Congress may touch a field in which the federal interest is so dominant that the federal system will be assumed to preclude enforcement of state laws on the same subject. . . . Likewise, the object sought to be obtained by the federal law and the character of obligations imposed by it may reveal the same purpose. . . . Or the state policy may produce a result inconsistent with the objective of the federal statute." Is this approach, or any part of it, similar to that used when state statutes are challenged as conflicting with the constitutional *grant* of power to Congress, rather than its *exercise*?

In the Hines case, Justice Black stated that, in considering the validity of state laws in the light of federal laws touching the same subject, the Court "has made use of the following expressions: conflicting; contrary to; occupying the field; repugnance; difference; irreconcilability; inconsistency; violation; curtailment; and interference. But none of these expressions provides an infallible constitutional test or an exclusive constitutional yardstick. In the final analysis, there can be no one crystal clear distinctly marked formula." [1]

2. *Preemption in last generation's commerce cases: Kelly, Maurer, and related decisions.* a. In Kelly v. Washington, 302 U.S. 1 (1937), the Court held that enforcement of a state law requiring safety inspections of tugs was not barred by enactment of the federal Motor Boat Act of 1910. Chief Justice Hughes' opinion was typical of preemption cases of the period: "States are thus enabled to deal with local exigencies and to exert in the absence of conflict with federal legislation an essential protective power [although interstate commerce may be affected]. And when Congress does exercise its paramount authority, it is obvious that Congress may determine how far its regulation shall go. There is no constitutional rule which compels Congress to occupy the whole field. Congress may circumscribe its regulation and occupy only a limited field. When it does so, state regulation outside that limited field and otherwise admissible is not forbidden or displaced. The principle is thoroughly established that the exercise by the State of its police power, which would be valid if not superseded by federal action, is superseded only where the repugnance or conflict is so 'direct and positive' that the two acts cannot 'be reconciled or consistently stand together.' A few illustrations will suffice. . . ."

Chief Justice Hughes' "illustrations" in Kelly were substantially repeated by Justice Black four years later, in a footnote to his opinion in Hines v. Davidowitz, supra. In the Hines text, Justice Black emphasized the "broad national authority" in the international field and stated that the preemption effect of a federal alien registration law, dealing with "the rights, liberties and freedoms of human beings," was in an "entirely different category" from "state pure food laws regulating the labels on cans." At this point, he added the following footnote: "It is true that where the Constitution does not of

---

1. In the Hines case, the Court held that enforcement of Pennsylvania's Alien Registration Act of 1939 was barred by the federal Alien Registration Act of 1940. Much of the opinion —characteristically (see the student Note quoted supra)—dealt with the broad national power over aliens, rather than its specific exercise. [A more recent case drew on the constitutional dicta in Hines to invalidate a state law regarding inheritance by aliens because of its intrusion into the federal foreign affairs domain. Zschernig v. Miller, 389 U.S. 429 (1968) (chap. 5, p. 403, above).] The Court concluded in Hines that, "whether or not registration of aliens is of such a nature that the Constitution permits only one uniform system," Congress had enacted a uniform system. Jus-

tice Stone's dissent concluded that a congressional ban on state registration laws was "not to be inferred from the silence of Congress [regarding state authority] in enacting a law which at no point conflicts with the state legislation and is harmonious with it." Note also an earlier statement in the dissent: "Little aid can be derived from the vague and illusory but often repeated formula that Congress 'by occupying the field' has excluded from it all state legislation. Every Act of Congress occupies some field, but we must know the boundaries of that field before we can say that it has precluded [state legislation]. To discover the boundaries we look to the federal statute itself, read in the light of its constitutional setting and its legislative history."

itself prohibit state action, as in matters related to interstate commerce, and where the Congress, while regulating related matters, has purposely left untouched a distinctive part of a subject which is peculiarly adapted to local regulation, the state may legislate concerning such local matters which Congress could have covered but did not. Kelly v. Washington . . .. And see Reid v. Colorado, 187 U.S. 137, 147 (prohibition on introduction of diseased cattle or horses); Savage v. Jones, 225 U.S. 501, 529, 532 (requirement that certain labels reveal package contents); Carey v. South Dakota, 250 U.S. 118, 121 (prohibition of shipment by carrier of wild ducks); Dickson v. Uhlmann Grain Co., 288 U.S. 188, 199 (prohibition of margin transactions in grain where there is no intent to deliver); Mintz v. Baldwin, 289 U.S. 346, 350–352 (inspection of cattle for infectious diseases); Maurer v. Hamilton, 309 U.S. 598, 604, 614 (prohibition of car-over-cab trucking)."

b. In Maurer v. Hamilton, 309 U.S. 598 (1940), Justice Stone's opinion for the Court sustained Pennsylvania's prohibition of trucks carrying any other vehicle "above the cab of the carrier vehicle." The ICC had issued safety regulations for interstate truckers under the Motor Carrier Act of 1935; the regulations contained no "over-the-cab" provisions. Justice Stone found that the statute, while giving the ICC authority to prescribe requirements as to "safety and operation of equipment," did not authorize Commission regulation of "sizes and weight of motor vehicles." The Court found that the purpose of the Pennsylvania requirement was to regulate "weight and size"; accordingly, the state requirement was not barred by federal law. Justice Stone emphasized that the federal law must be read "mindful of the peculiar conditions of the traffic and the problems of state regulation." Compare his opinion in South Carolina State Highway Dept. v. Barnwell Bros., p. 629, supra. Justice Stone in Maurer insisted, moreover, that "Congressional intention to displace local laws in the exercise of its commerce power is not, in general, to be inferred unless clearly indicated by those considerations which are persuasive of the statutory purpose. This is especially the case when public safety and health are concerned." [2]

3. *Unexercised statutory authority to regulate and the Castle case.* a. In Maurer, in the preceding note, Justice Stone was reluctant to find preemption—as he was later, in Southern Pacific Co. v. Arizona, see the beginning of his opinion, p. 634, supra. Did Castle v. Hayes Freight Lines, 348 U.S. 61 (1954), manifest a different attitude toward unexercised ICC authority? Compare footnote 1 to Bibb v. Navajo Freight Lines, section 1B, at p. 643, supra.

The Castle case involved an enforcement provision of Illinois' weight limitation on trucks. Repeated violations of the regulation were punishable

---

2. Compare Napier v. Atlantic Coast Line R. R., 272 U.S. 605 (1926): State statutes prescribing automatic firebox doors and cab curtains on railroads were held precluded by the federal Boiler Inspection Act of 1911. The Act authorized the ICC to prescribe safety devices for locomotives, but the agency had issued no orders requiring the equipment demanded by the state laws. Justice Brandeis stated that the federal and state laws "are directed to the same object" and "operate on the same subject." The fact that there was no inconsistency between state and federal regulations was "without legal significance." In view of the authority delegated to the ICC, the federal Act "was intended to occupy the field." Compare the failure to find preemption in Huron Portland Cement Co. v. City of Detroit, 362 U.S. 440 (1960), p. 647, supra, where the purposes of the federal and state ship boiler regulations were found to be different.

by suspension of the carrier's right to use Illinois highways for periods of ninety days (10 or more violations) and one year (10 or more subsequent violations). Hayes sought to enjoin a prosecution for repeated violations. The highest state court held that imposition of the suspension sanction on Hayes' interstate operations was barred by the Federal Motor Carrier Act. The Supreme Court affirmed.

Justice Black noted that Hayes operated under an ICC certificate of convenience and necessity, pursuant to the "comprehensive plan" of federal regulation. The ICC's suspension authority was limited: willful violations of the Act or regulations under it had to be shown, and a hearing was required. "Under these circumstances, it would be odd if a state could take action amounting to a suspension or revocation of an interstate carrier's commission-granted right to operate. . . . It cannot be doubted that suspension of this common carrier's right to use Illinois highways is the equivalent of a partial suspension of its federally granted certificate. . . . That Illinois seeks to punish Hayes for violations of its road regulations does not justify this disruption of federally authorized activities. A state's regulation of weight and distribution of loads carried in interstate trucks does not itself conflict with the Federal Act. The reason for this, as pointed out in Maurer v. Hamilton, 309 U.S. 598, is that the Federal Act has a provision designed to leave states free to regulate the sizes and weights of motor vehicles. But it would stretch this statutory provision too much to say that it also allowed states to revoke or suspend the right of interstate motor carriers for violation of state highway regulations.

"It is urged that without power to impose punishment by suspension states will be without appropriate remedies to enforce their laws against recalcitrant motor carriers. We are not persuaded, however, that the conventional forms of punishment are inadequate to protect states from overweighted or improperly loaded motor trucks. Moreover, a Commission regulation requires motor carriers to abide by valid state highway regulations. . . . If, therefore, motor carriers persistently and repeatedly violate the laws of a state, we know of no reason why the Commission may not protect the state's interest, either on the Commission's own initiative or on complaint of the state." In the argument of the Castle case, Illinois pointed out that the ICC had never exercised its authority to revoke certificates of carriers violating state weight regulations. Illinois argued, moreover, that its experience—and that of other states—showed that a number of truckers considered fines for exceeding weight limitations economically preferable to compliance with load limits, and that there was accordingly no practical alternative to the suspension sanction. Did the Court take adequate account of these arguments?

b. See California v. Zook, 336 U.S. 725 (1949), sustaining a California law penalizing interstate carriers operating without an ICC permit. The dissent stated that this was the first holding that "States can impose an additional punishment for a federal offense unless Congress in so many words forbids the State to do it." Compare Chicago v. Atchison, T. & S. F. R. Co., 357 U.S. 77 (1956), holding that federal law precluded Chicago from deciding (by a licensing requirement) whether a transfer company could provide motor vehicle service for the transfer of interstate passengers between Chicago railroad terminals. See also a sequel to that case, Railroad Transfer Service v. Chicago, 386 U.S. 351 (1967), invalidating an amended Chicago licensing scheme. Would the Castle and Chicago cases be decided differently under the commerce clause in the absence of a federal statute?   Cf. Buck v. Kuykendall, p. 628, supra.

4.   *Some modern preemption decisions: the Campbell and Florida Avocado cases.*   a.   In Campbell v. Hussey, 368 U.S. 297 (1961), the Court found provisions of the Georgia Tobacco Identification Act barred by the 1935 Federal Tobacco Inspection Act.   The Georgia law required that tobacco of a certain type—defined in accordance with federal standards—be marked with a white identifying tag when received in warehouses for sale. The Court, in an opinion by Justice Douglas, rejected the argument that the Georgia requirement was valid because it "merely supplements the federal regulation."   "We do not have here the question whether Georgia's law conflicts with the federal law.   Rather we have the question of pre-emption. . . .   Congress, in legislating concerning the types of tobacco sold at auction, preempted the field."   Under the federal program, "complementary state regulation is as fatal as state regulations which conflict with the federal scheme."   Justice Whittaker concurred in the result.

Justice Black's dissenting opinion, joined by Justices Frankfurter and Harlan, insisted that "the Court's opinion presents not so much as one fact which indicates that Congress actually intended . . .   to preclude the States from passing laws which require only that warehousemen place a label on each lot of tobacco offered for sale truthfully showing its official federal type. . . .   Instead, the Court proceeds from the bare fact of congressional legislation to the conclusion of federal pre-emption by application of a mechanistic formula which operates independently of congressional intent."

b.   Campbell v. Hussey was distinguished in Florida Lime and Avocado Growers, Inc. v. Paul, 373 U.S. 132 (1963), involving a California statute barring avocados which did not meet the State's minimum-oil-content standard of maturity.   Federal marketing orders issued pursuant to the Agricultural Adjustment Act gauge the maturity of Florida avocados by standards other than oil content.   The Court, in a five-to-four decision, held that the Supremacy Clause did not prohibit California from excluding Florida avocados certified as mature under the federal regulations but containing less than the minimum California oil content.   Justice Brennan's majority opinion concluded that "there is neither such actual conflict between the two schemes of regulation that both cannot stand in the same area, nor evidence of a congressional design to pre-empt the field."   He noted that there was no "physical impossibility" of complying with both standards and that the "maturity of avocados seems to be an inherently unlikely candidate for exclusive federal regulation. . . .   Federal regulation by means of minimum standards . . .   of agricultural commodities, however comprehensive *for those purposes* [of marketing] that regulation may be, does not of itself import displacement of state control over the distribution and retail sale of those commodities in the interests of the *consumers* of the commodities within the State."   Nor could the Court find "an unambiguous congressional mandate" to exclude state regulation.   The federal law here involved, unlike that in Campbell v. Hussey, concerned "minimum" rather than "uniform" standards.   The statutory scheme was "one of maturity regulations drafted and administered locally by the growers' own representatives, and designed to do no more than promote orderly competition among the South Florida growers." The Court did not pass on commerce clause objections because of an inadequate trial record and remanded the case.

Justice White's dissent, joined by Justices Black, Douglas and Clark, concluded that the Supremacy Clause barred the application of California's "inconsistent and conflicting" legislation. The dissenters saw the federal scheme as a "comprehensive regulatory program" and insisted that California's interest was identical to the federal one. "There is no health interest here. The question is . . . a purely economic one. . . . Despite the repeated suggestions to this effect in the Court's opinion, there is no indication that the state regulatory scheme has any purpose other than protecting the good will of the avocado industry—such as protecting health or preventing deception of the public—unless as a purely incidental byproduct."

c. Consider to what extent these modern decisions rest more on considerations like those articulated in the "dormant" commerce clause cases, sec. 1 above, than on detailed examination of congressional scheme and purpose. Note, e. g., the emphasis in the Florida Avocado dissent on the state interest: "no health interest"; "a purely economic one." Do differing perceptions about the true state purpose explain the division on the Court in that case?

5. *Congressional control of preemption standards.* Would it be useful, or feasible, for Congress to enact a general rule for adjudication of preemption claims? Or must decisions in this field inevitably turn on the particular statutory context and the specific field (and purpose) of regulation? After the decision in Pennsylvania v. Nelson, 350 U.S. 497 (1956), a proposal for a general statute was introduced in several Congresses by Congressman Smith of Virginia. The Nelson case, applying the standards of Rice v. Santa Fe Elevator Corp., note 1, supra, held that a conviction for "sedition against the United States" under the Pennsylvania Sedition Act was barred by the Smith Act and other federal laws. Cf. Uphaus v. Wyman, 364 U.S. 388 (1960), chap. 16, p. 1334. The Court concluded: "Since we find that Congress has occupied the field to the exclusion of parallel state legislation, that the dominant interest of the Federal Government precludes state intervention, and that administration of state Acts would conflict with the operation of the federal plan, we are convinced that the decision of the Supreme Court of Pennsylvania [reversing Nelson's conviction on the ground of 'supersession of the state law' by federal law] is unassailable."

Congressman Smith's proposal (see, e. g., H.R. 3, 85th Cong., 2d Sess. (1958), which was passed by the House) provided: "No Act of Congress shall be construed as indicating an intent on the part of Congress to occupy the field in which such Act operates, to the exclusion of all State laws on the same subject matter, unless such Act contains an express provision to that effect, or unless there is a direct and positive conflict between such Act and a State law so that the two cannot be reconciled or consistently stand together."

B. CONSENT TO STATE LAWS

Scope Note. May Congress, instead of precluding state action through preemption, validate state laws regulating commerce—laws which, in the absence of the federal consent, would violate the commerce clause? In the Cooley case, p. 621, supra, the Court indicated that Congress could not validate laws which were "unconstitutional" under the commerce clause; yet a century later, it seemed clear to Justice Stone in the Southern Pacific case, p. 634, supra, that the "undoubted" congressional "power to redefine the distribution of power over interstate commerce" included the authority "to permit the states to regulate the commerce in a manner which would otherwise not be permissible." What is the justification for that congressional authority? What is its scope? The examples of congressional "consent" in this section are designed to explore those problems.*

1. *The Wilson Act of 1890 and the Rahrer case.* a. In Leisy v. Hardin, 135 U.S. 100 (1890), the Court invalidated an Iowa law prohibiting the sale of intoxicating liquors as applied to beer brewed in Illinois and offered for sale in the "original package"—see chap. 9, p. 690, infra—in Iowa. Chief Justice Fuller, after reviewing the Cooley doctrine, tied it to congressional intent and stated that "inasmuch as interstate commerce, consisting in the transportation, purchase, sale, and exchange of commodities, is national in its character, and must be governed by a uniform system, so long as Congress does not pass any law to regulate it, or allowing the States so to do, it thereby indicates its will that such commerce shall be free and untrammeled." He insisted that Peirce v. New Hampshire (one of the License Cases, p. 620, supra) "in so far as it rests on the view that the law of New Hampshire was valid because Congress had made no regulation on the subject, must be regarded as having been distinctly overthrown by numerous cases." Accordingly, he concluded that Leisy "had the right to import this beer into that State, and . . . had the right to sell it, by which act alone it would become mingled in the common mass of property within the State. Up to that point of time, we hold that, *in the absence of congressional permission to do so,* the State had no power to interfere by seizure . . . ." [Emphasis added.] [1]

b. On August 8, 1890, only a few months after the decision in Leisy v. Hardin, Congress passed the Wilson Act which provided that "all . . . intoxicating liquors . . . transported into any state or territory, or remaining therein, for use, consumption, sale, or storage therein, shall upon arrival in such state or territory be subject to the operation and effect of the laws of such state or territory enacted in the exercise of its police powers, to the same extent and in the same manner as though such . . . liquors had been produced in such state or territory, and shall not be exempt therefrom by reason of being introduced therein in original packages or otherwise." Thereafter it was held that by virtue of this Act a state may apply its prohibi-

---

* On the problems of congressional "consent," see generally Biklé, "The Silence of Congress," 41 Harv.L.Rev. 200 (1927); Dowling, "Interstate Commerce and State Power," 27 Va.L.Rev. 1 (1940), Selected Essays 1938–62 (1963), 280, and "Interstate Commerce and State Power—Revised Version," 47 Colum.L.Rev. 547 (1947); and Note, "Congressional Consent to Discriminatory State Legislation," 45 Colum.L. Rev. 927 (1945). And on the chapter as a whole, see Freund, "Umpiring the Federal System," 54 Colum.L.Rev. 561

(1954), Selected Essays 1938–62 (1963), 203.

1. But see Plumley v. Massachusetts, decided four years after Leisy, 155 U.S. 461 (1894). The Plumley decision sustained application of a state ban on sale of oleomargarine colored to resemble butter, even though the oleo involved was imported from another state and sold in the original package. Cf. Crossman v. Lurman, 192 U.S. 189 (1904), and Schollenberger v. Pennsylvania, 171 U.S. 1 (1898).

tion laws to sales of intoxicating liquors in the original packages. In re Rahrer, 140 U.S. 545 (1891). In passing this law, "Congress has not attempted to delegate the power to regulate commerce, or to exercise any power reserved to the States, or to grant a power not possessed by the States, or to adopt state laws. . . . It imparted no power to the State not then possessed, but allowed imported property to fall at once upon arrival within the local jurisdiction." [2] More than that, the Court added: "No reason is perceived why, if Congress chooses to provide that certain designated subjects of interstate commerce shall be governed by a rule which divests them of that character at an earlier period of time than would otherwise be the case, it is not within its competency to do so."

2. *The Webb-Kenyon Act of 1913 and the Clark Distilling case.* On March 1, 1913, Congress passed (over a Presidential veto) the Webb-Kenyon Act, "An Act divesting intoxicating liquors of their interstate character in certain cases"—a reliance on the "divesting" language of In re Rahrer, supra. The 1913 law provided that "the shipment or transportation of any . . . intoxicating liquor of any kind, from one State . . . into any other State . . . which said . . . liquor is intended by any person interested therein, to be received, possessed, sold, or in any manner used, either in the original package or otherwise, in violation of any law of such State . . . is hereby prohibited." An action was begun in a federal court in Maryland to compel a railway to accept a consignment of liquor tendered for shipment to West Virginia. To the defense that such shipment was illegal under the Webb-Kenyon Act, because the laws of West Virginia barred shipments of liquor into the State, it was countered that the federal law was unconstitutional. The Supreme Court stated that "if the 1913 Act was within the power of Congress to adopt, there is no possible reason for holding that to enforce the prohibitions of the state law would conflict with the commerce clause." The Act was adjudged a valid exercise of the commerce power by Congress. Clark Distilling Co. v. Western Maryland R. Co., 242 U.S. 311 (1917).[3] On the constitutional point, the Court accepted the Webb-Kenyon Act as "but a larger degree of exertion of the identical power which was brought into play in the Wilson Act." [4]

2. On the basis of permissive legislation by Congress similar to the Wilson Act, the Court sustained the power of the States to prohibit the sale, whether in original packages or not, of convict-made goods brought in from other States. Whitfield v. Ohio, 297 U.S. 431 (1936).

3. For an account of the legislative history of the Webb-Kenyon Act, with a background of the legislative history of the Wilson Act, see Dowling and Hubbard, "Divesting an Article of Its Interstate Character," 5 Minn.L.Rev. 100, 253 (1921).

4. The substance and much of the language of the Webb-Kenyon Act was written into the Twenty-First Amendment, which also repealed the Eighteenth. Missouri passed a law which prohibited bringing into the state intoxicating liquors produced in states which discriminated against the alcoholic products of Missouri. Missouri was using its laws as an "economic weapon of retaliation" in its commercial relations. Summarily rejecting the contention that such legislation violated the commerce clause and was not authorized by the Twenty-First Amendment, Justice Brandeis, for a unanimous Court, said: "Since that Amendment, the right of a State to prohibit or regulate the importation of intoxicating liquor is not limited by the commerce clause." Finch Co. v. McKittrick, 305 U.S. 395 (1939). Duckworth v. Arkansas, 314 U.S. 390 (1941), and Carter v. Virginia, 321 U.S. 131 (1944), sustained state laws relative to transportation of intoxicating liquor through the State: each relied in part on the Twenty-First Amendment.

In two 1964 decisions, however, the Court held that the Twenty-First Amendment did not leave absolute con-

3. *The McCarran Act of 1945 and the Prudential case.* In 1944, the Supreme Court found that the Sherman Anti-Trust Act of 1890 applied to the insurance business, even though the Court had held in 1868 that insurance was not commerce. United States v. South-Eastern Underwriters Ass'n, 322 U.S. 533 (1944). The Court concluded that "a nationwide business" like insurance "is not deprived of its interstate character merely because it is based upon . . . contracts which are local in nature." In response, Congress enacted the McCarran Act of 1945, 59 Stat. 33, 15 U.S.C. § 1011 et seq., which not only deferred and limited the applicability of anti-trust laws to the business, but also sought to assure continued state authority over insurance. The Act contained a declaration "that the continued regulation and taxation by the several States of the business of insurance is in the public interest, and that silence on the part of the Congress shall not be construed to impose any barrier to the regulation or taxation of such business by the several States."

Section 2 of the law provided: "(a) The business of insurance . . . shall be subject to the laws of the several States which relate to the regulation or taxation of such business.   (b) No Act of Congress shall be construed to invalidate, impair, or supersede any law enacted by any State for the purpose of regulating the business of insurance, or which imposes a fee or tax upon such business, unless such Act specifically relates to the business of insurance . . . ."

In Prudential Insurance Co. v. Benjamin, 328 U.S. 408 (1946), the Company, a New Jersey corporation, objected to the continued collection of a long-standing tax of 3% of the premiums received from all business done in South Carolina. No similar tax was required of South Carolina corporations. The Court assumed that the tax was "discriminatory" and hence invalid under the Court's commerce clause decisions, see chap. 9, infra. Nevertheless the Court rejected the Company's challenge and held that the McCarran Act validated the tax. Justice Rutledge disagreed with the Company's contention that "Congress' declaration of policy adds nothing to the validity of what the states have done within the area covered by the declara-

trol of liquor traffic to the states. In each case, Justice Stewart wrote the majority opinion; Justice Black, joined by Justice Goldberg, dissented. In the first case, the Court held that the Export-Import Clause, see chap. 9, sec. 1, infra, barred a Kentucky tax on whisky imported from Scotland and held in the original package. Department of Revenue v. James B. Beam Distilling Co., 377 U.S. 341. In the second case, the Court described the basic issue as "whether the Twenty-first Amendment so far obliterates the Commerce Clause as to empower New York to prohibit absolutely the passage of liquor through its territory, under the supervision of the United States Bureau of Customs acting under federal law, for delivery to consumers in foreign countries." The Court held that New York could not prohibit the sale of tax-free liquors to departing international airline travelers for de-

livery upon arrival at foreign destinations. Hostetter v. Idlewild Bon Voyage Liquor Corp., 377 U.S 324.

Compare Seagram & Sons v. Hostetter, 384 U.S. 35 (1966), sustaining a 1964 amendment of New York's Alcoholic Beverage Control Law requiring that liquor prices to domestic wholesalers and retailers be "no higher than the lowest" prices offered elsewhere in the country. Justice Stewart emphasized that this case, unlike the Idlewild one, concerned liquor destined for use, distribution, or consumption in New York: "In that situation, the Twenty-first Amendment demands wide latitude for regulation by the State. We need not now decide whether the mode of liquor regulation chosen by a State in such circumstances could ever constitute so grave an interference with a company's operations elsewhere as to make the regulation invalid under the Commerce Clause."

tion." To accept the claim "would ignore the very basis on which the Clark Distilling case [has] set the pattern of the law for governing situations like that now presented." He explained:

"Not yet has this Court held such a disclaimer [of a commerce clause prohibition] invalid . . . . On the contrary, in each instance it has given effect to the Congressional judgment contradicting its own previous one. It is true that rationalizations have differed concerning those decisions . . . . But the results have been lasting and are at least as important, for the direction given to the process of accommodating federal and state authority, as the reasons stated for reaching them. . . . [A]part from [the] function of defining the outer boundary of its power, whenever Congress' judgment has been uttered affirmatively to contradict the Court's previously expressed view that specific action taken by the states in Congress' silence was forbidden by the commerce clause, this body has accommodated its previous judgment to Congress' expressed approval. Some part of this readjustment may be explained in ways acceptable on any theory of the commerce clause and the relations of Congress and the courts toward its functioning. Such explanations however, hardly go to the root of the matter. For the fact remain that, in these instances, the sustaining of Congress' overriding action has involved something beyond correction of erroneous factual judgment in deference to Congress' presumably better-informed view of the facts . . . .

"[W]e would be going very far to rule that South Carolina no longer may collect her tax. To do so would flout the expressly declared policies of both Congress and the state. Moreover it would establish a ruling never heretofore made and in doing this would depart from the whole trend of decision in a great variety of situations most analogous to the one now presented. . . . The power of Congress over commerce exercised entirely without reference to coordinated action of the states is not restricted, except as the Constitution expressly provides, by any limitation which forbids it to discriminate against interstate commerce and in favor of local trade. . . .

"This broad authority Congress may exercise alone, subject to those limitations, or in conjunction with coordinated action by the states, in which case limitations imposed for the preservation of their powers become inoperative and only those designed to forbid action altogether by any power or combination of powers in our governmental system remain effective. Here both Congress and South Carolina have acted, and in complete co-ordination, to sustain the tax. It is therefore reinforced by the exercise of all the power of government residing in our scheme. Clear and gross must be the evil which would nullify such an exertion, one which could arise only by exceeding beyond cavil some explicit and compelling limitation imposed by a constitutional provision or provisions designed and intended to outlaw the action taken entirely from our constitutional framework. . . ."

OTHER TECHNIQUES OF CONGRESSIONAL ORDERING

As noted at the outset, congressional preemption and consent are examples of a far wider range of techniques Congress may employ in the ordering of the complex relations between federal and state law. Additional devices illustrating the central role of Congress should be noted in other chapters of this volume. For example: the congressional role in determining the scope of intergovernmental immunities, chap. 10, sec. 1, infra; federal incorporation or adoption of state law—expressly, as in the Federal Assimilative Crimes Act, chap. 10, p. 765, infra, and in the Federal Tort Claims Act, or by implication, as in a wide area of tax, copyright and bankruptcy law; and state administration of federal law, as in the unemployment compensation scheme of the Social Security Act, chap. 5, p. 382, supra, or in the varied exercises of the federal spending power through conditioned grants-in-aid to the states, ibid, or in the utilization of state courts for federal law enforcement, cf. Testa v. Katt, in the note on State Autonomy, chap. 10, p. 769, infra. See generally Hart, "The Relations Between State and Federal Law," 54 Colum.L.Rev. 489 (1954).

Chapter 9

STATE TAXATION AND FREE TRADE

Introduction. In a broad sense, the problems of state taxation resemble those of state regulation: the tax area, too, demands accommodation of legitimate local interests and the demands of a free, national economy; with regard to taxes as well as regulations, the commerce clause "by its own force" creates "an area of trade free from interference by the States"—but "even interstate business must pay its way, by bearing its share of local tax burdens." Recurrent statements such as these may reflect the underlying tensions in this area, but they do not go far to promote solution of specific problems. A more particularistic analysis of state taxation is required, if only because of the great volume of litigation, the great variety of taxes, and the great range of activities subjected to taxation. The Court has struggled with the multifaceted issues in this field since Marshall's day, with considerable self-doubt and with occasional pleas for Congressional aid. Even at the risk of engendering undue pessimism regarding the possibility of adequate comprehension of the field, two characteristic passages are worth noting at the outset:

Justice Clark in Northwestern States Portland Cement Co. v. Minnesota, 358 U.S. 450 (1959) (see p. 741, infra): "That there is a 'need for clearing up the tangled underbrush of past cases' with reference to the taxing power of the States is a concomitant to the negative approach resulting from a case-by-case resolution of 'the extremely limited restrictions that the Constitution places upon the states.' . . . Commerce between the States having grown up like Topsy, the Congress meanwhile not having undertaken to regulate taxation of it, and the States having understandably persisted in their efforts to get some return for the substantial benefits they have afforded it, there is little wonder that there has been no end of cases testing out state tax levies. The resulting judicial application of constitutional principles to specific state statutes leaves much room for controversy and confusion and little in the way of precise guides to the States in the exercise of their indispensable power of taxation. This Court alone has handed down some three hundred full-dress opinions spread through slightly more than that number of our reports. As was said in Miller Bros. Co. v. State of Maryland, 347 U.S. 340, 344 (1954), the decisions have been 'not always clear . . . consistent or reconcilable. A few have been specifically overruled, while others no longer fully represent the present state of the law.' From the quagmire there emerge, however, some firm peaks of decision which remain unquestioned."

Justice Frankfurter had said thirteen years earlier, in Freeman v. Hewit, 329 U.S. 249 (1946) (see p. 728, infra): "The power of the States to tax and the limitations upon that power imposed by the Commerce Clause have necessitated a long, continuous process of judicial adjustment. The history of this problem is spread over hundreds of volumes of our Reports. To attempt to harmonize all that has been said in the past would neither clarify what has gone before nor guide the future. Suffice it to say that especially in this field opinions must be read in the setting of the particular cases and as the product of preoccupation with their special facts."

In the space available here, a comprehensive examination of the varied problems raised in the hundreds of cases is impossible. The materials which follow portray some of the "firm peaks of decision which remain unquestioned" and probe some of the depths of the surrounding "quagmire." They reflect, moreover, the changing fashions in judicial analysis. Section 1 considers the major tax decision of the Marshall Court and the special problem of foreign imports; the remaining sections emphasize interstate commerce problems. Section 2 illustrates some relatively "firm peaks of decision"—taxes consistently held valid, and taxes invalidated with equal consistency. Sections 3 and 4 sample two areas of the "quagmire" that have evoked numerous conflicts and notable changes in Court approaches over the years: the varied tax problems of interstate transportation and sales transactions.

In examining these materials, some recurrent problems should be considered: To what extent does constitutionality turn on the "subject" of the tax? To what extent on the "measure" of the tax? To what extent do the Court's standards rest on "formal" bases? To what extent do they reflect "economic realities," the "actual" extent of the tax burden? (Compare, for example, Justice Stone's efforts to move from "direct"-"indirect" labels to "burden" analyses in the tax area, with his contributions in the regulatory area, chap.. 8, sec. 1, supra.) To what extent do the decisions rest on the commerce clause? To what extent do due process limits on state jurisdiction join with—or become confused with—commerce clause restrictions?

Consider in examining the decisions which follow whether they justify the comment of last generation's most astute critic of state tax decisions: "Law, like politics, makes strange bedfellows. Among the queerest of such companions are the doctrine that the states cannot tax interstate commerce and the fact that they can. The truth is that there is a wrong way and a right way for the states to tax interstate commerce. When the wrong way is adopted, the doctrine maintains its supremacy. When the right way is chosen, the fact prevails. The doctrine then saves its face by the nominalistic legerdemain of asserting that what is being taxed is not interstate commerce, but something else." [Thomas Reed Powell, "State Income Taxes and the Commerce Clause", 31 Yale L.J. 799 (1922).] Do the decisions justify the comment of one of the most discerning commentators of this generation: "As explicit constitutional and legislative guides have been absent, judicially made . . . formulations have been inadequate. Differences in appraisal, and sharp ones, have arisen [on the Court]. But on the whole, these differences seem to have been less important than differences in perception. . . . [T]he decisions seem adequate, and even wise, to the extent that the particular interests at stake, long-range as well as short, have been perceived and understood." [Ernest Brown, "The Open Economy: Mr. Justice Frankfurter and the Position of the Judiciary," 67 Yale L.J. 219 (1957), Selected Essays 1938–62 (1963), 371.]*

---

* For other useful analyses of the problems of this chapter, see, e. g., Note, "Developments in the Law—Federal Limitations on State Taxation of Interstate Business," 75 Harv.L.Rev. 953 (1962); Barrett, "State Taxation of Interstate Commerce—'Direct Burdens,' 'Multiple Burdens' or What Have You?" 4 Vand.L.Rev. 496 (1951), Selected Essays 1938–62 (1963), 324; Hartman, State Taxation of Interstate Commerce (1953); and Comment, "State Taxation of Multistate Businesses," 74 Yale L.J. 1259 (1965).

SECTION 1. STATE TAXES AND FOREIGN COMMERCE

BROWN v. MARYLAND

12 Wheat. 419, 6 L.Ed. 678 (1827).

Error to the Court of Appeals of Maryland.

[A Maryland statute of 1821, entitled "An act supplementary to the act laying duties on licenses to retailers of dry goods," required all "importers of foreign articles . . . and others selling the same by wholesale" to "take out a license as by the original act is directed." The license fee was $50. Brown was prosecuted for importing and selling foreign goods without obtaining a license. The highest state court affirmed the judgment against Brown.]

Mr. Chief Justice MARSHALL delivered the opinion of the Court.

The plaintiffs in error . . . insist that the act . . . is repugnant to two provisions in the Constitution of the United States.

1. To that which declares that "no State shall, without the consent of Congress, lay any imposts, or duties on imports or exports, except what may be absolutely necessary for executing its inspection laws."

2. To that which declares that Congress shall have power "to regulate commerce with foreign nations, and among the several States, and with the Indian tribes."

1. The first inquiry is into the extent of the prohibition upon States "to lay any imposts or duties on imports or exports." The counsel for the State of Maryland would confine this prohibition to laws imposing duties on the act of importation or exportation. . . .

An impost, or duty on imports, is a custom or a tax levied on articles brought into a country, and is most usually secured before the importer is allowed to exercise his rights of ownership over them, because evasions of the law can be prevented more certainly by executing it while the articles are in its custody. It would not, however, be less an impost or duty on the articles, if it were to be levied on them after they were landed. . . . What . . . are "imports"? The lexicons inform us, they are "things imported." If we appeal to usage for the meaning of the word, we shall receive the same answer. They are the articles themselves which are brought into the country.[1] "A duty on imports," then, is not merely a duty on the act of importation, but is a duty on the thing imported. It is not, taken in its literal sense, confined to a duty levied while the article is entering the country, but extends to a duty levied after it has entered the country. . . .

From the vast inequality between the different States of the confederacy, as to commercial advantages, few subjects were viewed with deeper interest, or excited more irritation, than the manner in which the several States exercised, or seemed disposed to exercise, the power of laying duties

---

1. A shipment originating in another State was subsequently held not to be an "import." Woodruff v. Parham, 8 Wall. 123 (1868); Brown v. Houston, 114 U.S. 622 (1885).

on imports.   From motives which were deemed sufficient by the statesmen
of that day, the [states'] power of taxation   .   .   .   was so far abridged as
to forbid them to touch imports or exports, with the single exception which
has been noticed.   Why are they restrained from imposing these duties?
Plainly, because, in the general opinion, the interest of all would be best
promoted by placing that whole subject under the control of Congress.
.   .   .   [I]t is plain, that the object [of the prohibition] would be as completely defeated by a power to tax the article in the hands of the importer
the instant it was landed, as by a power to tax it while entering the port.
There is no difference, in effect, between a power to prohibit the sale of an
article, and a power to prohibit its introduction into the country.   The one
would be a necessary consequence of the other.   No goods would be imported if none could be sold.   No object of any description can be accomplished by laying a duty on importation, which may not be accomplished
with equal certainty by laying a duty on the thing imported in the hands of the
importer.   It is obvious, that the same power which imposes a light duty, can
impose a very heavy one, one which amounts to a prohibition.   Questions of
power do not depend on the degree to which it may be exercised.   If it may be
exercised at all, it must be exercised at the will of those in whose hands it is
placed.   If the tax may be levied in this form by a State, it may be levied
to an extent which will defeat the revenue by impost, so far as it is drawn
from importations into the particular State.   We are told, that such wild
and irrational abuse of power is not to be apprehended, and is not to be taken
into view when discussing its existence.   .   .   .

.   .   .   Conceding, to the full extent which is required, that every
State would, in its legislation on this subject, provide judiciously for its own
interests, it cannot be conceded, that each would respect the interests of others.   A duty on imports is a tax on the article, which is paid by the consumer.
The great importing states would thus levy a tax on the non-importing States.
.   .   .   This would necessarily produce countervailing measures on the
part of those States whose situation was less favorable to importation
.   .   .

It may be conceded, that the words of the prohibition ought not to be
pressed to their utmost extent; that in our complex system, the object of the
powers conferred on the government of the Union, and the nature of the
often conflicting powers which remain in the States, must always be taken
into view, and may aid in expounding the words of any particular clause.
But, while we admit   .   .   .   that there must be a point of time when the
prohibition ceases, and the power of the State to tax commences; we cannot
admit that this point of time is the instant that the articles enter the country.
It is, we think, obvious, that this construction would defeat the prohibition.

The constitutional prohibition on the States to lay a duty on imports
.   .   .   may certainly come in conflict with their acknowledged power to
tax persons and property within their territory.   The power, and the restriction on it, though quite distinguishable when they do not approach each other,
may yet, like the intervening colours between white and black, approach so
nearly as to perplex the understanding, as colours perplex the vision in marking the distinction between them.   Yet the distinction exists, and must be
marked as the cases arise.   Till they do arise, it might be premature to state
any rule as being universal in its application.   It is sufficient for the present
to say, generally, that when the importer has so acted upon the thing im-

ported, that it has become incorporated and mixed up with the mass of property in the country, it has perhaps, lost its distinctive character as an import, and has become subject to the taxing power of the State; but while remaining the property of the importer, in his warehouse, in the original form or package in which it was imported, a tax upon it is too plainly a duty on imports to escape the prohibition in the constitution. . . .

The principle . . . for which the plaintiffs in error contend, that the importer acquires a right, not only to bring the articles into the country, but to mix them with the common mass of property, does not interfere with the necessary power of taxation which is acknowledged to reside in the States, to that dangerous extent which the counsel for the defendants in error seem to apprehend. It carries the prohibition in the constitution no farther than to prevent the States from doing that which it was the great object of the constitution to prevent.

But if it should be proved, that a duty on the article itself would be repugnant to the constitution, it is still argued, that this is not a tax upon the article, but on the person. The State, it is said, may tax occupations, and this is nothing more.

It is impossible to conceal from ourselves, that this is varying the form, without varying the substance. It is treating a prohibition which is general, as if it were confined to a particular mode of doing the forbidden thing. All must perceive, that a tax on the sale of an article, imported only for sale, is a tax on the article itself. It is true, the State may tax occupations generally, but this tax must be paid by those who employ the individual, or is a tax on his business. The lawyer, the physician, or the mechanic, must either charge more on the article in which he deals, or the thing itself is taxed through his person. This the State has a right to do, because no constitutional prohibition extends to it. So, a tax on the occupation of an importer, is in like manner, a tax on importation. It must add to the price of the article, and be paid by the consumer, or by the importer himself, in like manner as a direct duty on the article itself would be made. This the State has not a right to do, because it is prohibited by the constitution. . . .

We think, then, that the act under which the plaintiffs in error were indicted, is repugnant to that article of the constitution which declares, that "no State shall lay any impost or duties on imports or exports." [2]

2. Is it also repugnant to that clause in the constitution which empowers "Congress to regulate commerce with foreign nations, and among the several States, and with the Indian tribes"? . . .

---

2. A related prohibition (not involved in the principal case) is that no State shall, without the consent of Congress, "lay any Duty of Tonnage." Clyde Mallory Lines v. Alabama, 296 U.S. 261 (1935), sustained a harbor fee exacted under state law for a "policing service rendered by the State in the aid of the safe and efficient use of its port." Writing for a unanimous Court, Justice Stone said: "It seems clear that the prohibition against the imposition of any duty of tonnage was due to the desire of the Framers to supplement Article I, Section 10, Clause 2, denying to the states power to lay duties on imports or exports, . . . by forbidding a corresponding tax on the privilege of access by vessel to the ports of a state, and to their doubts whether the commerce clause would accomplish that purpose. . . . And duties of tonnage and duties on imports were known to commerce as levies upon the privilege of access by vessels or goods to the ports or to the territorial limits of a state and were distinct from fees or charges by authority of a state for services facilitating commerce, such as pilotage, towage, charges for loading and unloading cargoes, wharfage, storage, and the like."

If this power reaches the interior of a State, and may be there exercised [see Gibbons v. Ogden, chap. 4, supra], it must be capable of authorizing the sale of those articles which it introduces. Commerce is intercourse: one of its most ordinary ingredients is traffic. It is inconceivable, that the power to authorize this traffic . . . should cease at the point when its continuance is indispensable to its value. To what purpose should the power to allow importation be given, unaccompanied with the power to authorize a sale of the thing imported? Sale is the object of importation, and is an essential ingredient of that intercourse, of which importation constitutes a part. It is as essential an ingredient, as indispensable to the existence of the entire thing, then, as importation itself. It must be considered as a component part of the power to regulate commerce. Congress has a right, not only to authorize importation, but to authorize the importer to sell. . . .

We think, then, that if the power to authorize a sale exists in Congress, the conclusion that the right to sell is connected with the law permitting importation, as an inseparable incident, is inevitable.

If the principles we have stated be correct, the result to which they conduct us cannot be mistaken. Any penalty inflicted on the importer for selling the article in his character of importer, must be in opposition to the act of Congress which authorizes importation. Any charge on the introduction and incorporation of the articles into and with the mass of property in the country, must be hostile to the power given to Congress to regulate commerce, since an essential part of that regulation, and principal object of it, is to prescribe the regular means for accomplishing that introduction and incorporation. . . .

It has been contended, that this construction of the power to regulate commerce, as was contended in construing the prohibition to lay duties on imports, would abridge the acknowledged power of a State to tax its own citizens, or their property within its territory.

We admit this power to be sacred; but cannot admit that it may be used so as to obstruct the free course of a power given to Congress. We cannot admit, that it may be used so as to obstruct or defeat the power to regulate commerce. It has been observed, that the powers remaining with the States may be so exercised as to come in conflict with those vested in Congress. When this happens, that which is not supreme must yield to that which is supreme. . . . If the States may tax all persons and property found on their territory, what shall restrain them from taxing goods in their transit through the State from one port to another, for the purpose of re-exportation? The laws of trade authorize this operation, and general convenience requires it. Or what should restrain a State from taxing any article passing through it from one State to another, for the purpose of traffic? Or from taxing the transportation of articles passing from the State itself to another State, for commercial purposes? These cases are all within the sovereign power of taxation, but would obviously derange the measures of Congress to regulate commerce, and affect materially the purpose for which that power was given. We deem it unnecessary to press this argument farther, or to give additional illustrations of it, because the subject was taken up, and considered with great attention, in McCulloch v. The State of Maryland (4 Wheat. 316), the decision in which case is, we think, entirely applicable to this.

It may be proper to add, that we suppose the principles laid down in this case, to apply equally to importations from a sister State. We do not mean to give any opinion on a tax discriminating between foreign and domestic articles. . . .

[Judgment reversed. Justice Thompson's dissenting opinion is omitted.]

SOME ASPECTS OF BROWN v. MARYLAND—ORIGINAL PACKAGES, IMPORTS, AND DISCRIMINATION

1. *The "original package" doctrine and interstate commerce.* a. *State taxation.* Chief Justice Marshall's suggestion that the original package doctrine might serve as a guide for taxation of interstate commerce was not accepted by later Courts. In Woodruff v. Parham, 8 Wall. 123 (1869), a local tax on an auction sale of out-of-state goods was sustained: the Imports-Exports Clause did not apply to interstate transactions, and the Commerce Clause did not bar nondiscriminatory taxes on "local" sales. See also Hinson v. Lott, 8 Wall. 148 (1869), and Brown v. Houston, 114 U.S. 662 (1885).

b. *State regulation and the Baldwin case.* The original package doctrine has had somewhat greater vitality as a limit on state regulation. See, e. g., Leisy v. Hardin, 135 U.S. 100 (1890), chap. 8, p. 679, supra, invalidating Iowa's ban on liquor sales as applied to beer in the "original package." But even in this area, the doctrine has been of limited use. In Baldwin v. Seelig, 294 U.S. 511 (1935) (barring the application of New York's price regulations to the sale of Vermont milk, chap. 8, p. 649, supra), Seelig sought to sell some of the milk he had purchased out-of-state in the "original package." Though the Court sustained Seelig's commerce clause claim, it did not distinguish between milk in the "original" 40-quart cans and milk bottled in New York. Justice Cardozo's opinion contained the following passage: "The test of the 'original package' . . . is not inflexible and final for the transactions of interstate commerce, whatever may be its validity for commerce with other countries. . . . There are purposes for which merchandise, transported from another state, will be treated as a part of the general mass of property at the state of destination though still in the original containers. This is so, for illustration, where merchandise so contained is subjected to a nondiscriminatory property tax which it bears equally with other merchandise produced within the state. Sonneborn Bros. v. Cureton, 262 U.S. 506. . . . There are other purposes for which the same merchandise will have the benefit of the protection appropriate to interstate commerce, though the original packages have been broken and the contents subdivided. . . . In brief, the test of the original package is not an ultimate principle. It is an illustration of a principle. . . . It marks a convenient boundary and one sufficiently precise save in exceptional conditions. What is ultimate is the principle that one state in its dealings with another may not place itself in a position of economic isolation. Formulas and catchwords are subordinate to this overmastering requirement. Neither the power to tax nor the police power may be used [to establish] an economic barrier against competition . . . . The form of the packages in such circumstances is immaterial, whether they are original or broken."

2. *Taxation of "imports."* The Brown case, including its original package doctrine, has continued to be important as to taxation of foreign im-

ports, in determining when "importation" ceases and the articles have lost their immunity. In Low v. Austin, 13 Wall. 29 (1872), a general ad valorem property tax was held invalid as applied to imported goods stored in their original packages pending sale. Cf. Woodruff v. Parham, note 1a supra. In Hooven & Allison Co. v. Evatt, 324 U.S. 652 (1945), the Court invalidated a property tax on imported hemp stored in petitioner's warehouse for three years pending use in manufacturing.[1] But in companion cases, Youngstown Sheet & Tube Co. v. Bowers and United States Plywood Corp. v. City of Algoma, 358 U.S. 534 (1959), the Court held that the Imports-Exports Clause did not bar taxation where the taxpayers "have so acted upon the materials which they have imported for use in their manufacturing operations as to cause them to lose their distinctive character as 'imports' . . . by irrevocably committing them, after their importation journeys have definitely ended, to 'use in manufacturing' at the plant and point of final destination." The majority opinion, by Justice Whittaker, distinguished Hooven & Allison because "these are not cases of the mere storage in a warehouse of imported materials intended for eventual use in manufacturing" but rather situations where the imported materials "were so essential to current manufacturing requirements that they must be said to have entered the process of manufacturing." Justice Frankfurter, joined by Justice Harlan, dissented, insisting that the Court "disregards" the "historic course of adjudication" since Brown v. Maryland, supra. He stated that the situation in Hooven & Allison "so precisely parallels the circumstances now before us as to control these cases, unless Hooven & Allison is to be overruled. . . . In effect, the result of today's decision means that if imported goods are needed, they are taxable. If useless, they retain their constitutional immunity."[2]

3. *Discrimination and the Brown case.* In Brown, the $50 license tax on importers and wholesalers was an amendment to a law imposing a tax on "retailers." Why did Marshall fail to rest on what is now widely recognized as an unconstitutional "vice of discrimination" in taxation? Recall that he concluded his opinion with the statement: "We do not give any opinion on a tax discriminating between foreign and domestic articles." Note the comment in Brown, "The Open Economy: Mr. Justice Frankfurter and the Position of the Judiciary," 67 Yale L.J. 219 (1957), Selected Essays 1938–62 (1963), 371: "It was apparently not a quirk in the Marshall mentality, nor a tactic in the long-range constitutional strategy sometimes attributed to him, that led the Chief Justice not to dwell upon discrimination in Brown v. Maryland any more than he had in McCulloch v. Maryland." Compare the state tax aspect

1. Compare Waring v. The Mayor, 8 Wall. 110 (1868), May v. New Orleans, 178 U.S. 496 (1900), and Note, "State Taxation of Imports—When Does an Import Cease to Be an Import?" 58 Harv.L.Rev. 858 (1945). See also Canton Railroad Co. v. Rogan, 340 U.S. 511 (1951), noted, with related cases, in sec. 3, p. 711, infra.

2. When do goods become exports and hence immune from state taxation under the "exports" aspect of the Imports-Exports Clause? See, e. g., Richfield Oil Corp. v. Board of Equalization, 329 U.S. 69 (1946) (general sales tax cannot be imposed on sale of oil to foreign navy; when oil pumped from seller's dockside tanks into ship's hold, export took place); Crew Levick Co. v. Pennsylvania, 245 U.S. 292 (1917) (license tax measured by wholesaler's gross receipts cannot be applied to receipts from exports); cf. Empresa Siderurgica v. Merced County, 337 U.S. 154 (1949) (sustaining personal property tax on cement plant dismantled for export: "It is the entrance of the articles into the export stream that marks the start of the process of exportation. . . . Nothing less will suffice."). See Note, "Taxation Under the Import-Export Clause," 47 Colum.L.Rev. 490 (1947).

of McCulloch, chap. 10, p. 752, infra. Professor Brown notes, moreover, that the original Maryland tax statute—before the addition of importer-wholesaler amendment, invalidated in Brown—defined "retailer" as one "engaged in the selling of any goods . . . except such as are the . . . manufacture of the United States." Yet Marshall indicated that the retailer of imports— the handler after the first sale and after the original package was broken— would have to pay the protectionist license fee, though clearly discriminatory against imports. The evolution of the doctrine banning discriminatory taxes is considered in the next section.

SECTION 2. THE EXTREMES ON THE STATE TAX SPECTRUM: UNCONSTITUTIONAL DISCRIMINATION AND CONSTITU- TIONAL PROPERTY TAXES

"DISCRIMINATION": THE UNCONSTITUTIONAL END OF THE STATE TAX SPECTRUM

Introduction. Though the doctrine was not self-evident to Marshall, it has long been held that state taxes discriminating against commerce are barred by the commerce clause. The prohibition of obviously preferential, discriminatory taxes is one of the few clear peaks observable in the morass of tax litigation. Yet the quagmire covers the lower slopes of that mountain as well: "discrimination" is not a self-defining term, and once the issue goes beyond the patently preferential tax, there is much room for dispute about hidden and potential discrimination. "Discrimination" has come to include, for example, taxes which place "a greater burden upon interstate commerce" than upon "competing intrastate commerce of like character," and some taxes are barred because they contain too great a "risk" of discrimination. Accordingly, as in the regulatory area—see, e. g., the notes following the Dean Milk case, chap. 8, p. 657, supra—the Justices have often disagreed in identifying discrimination. This note is largely limited to the extremes in the decisional spectrum, and accordingly focuses on taxes which have evoked a judicial consensus regarding discrimination. But in view of the potential breadth of the category, concern about "discrimination" marks a number of cases in subsequent sections as well.

1. *Discrimination on the face of the statute: Welton v. Missouri.* a. The agreement that patent state discrimination against interstate commerce is unconstitutional—an agreement joined even by those Justices who oppose most judicial control based on the "dormant" commerce clause—was not articulated until after the Civil War. Welton v. Missouri, 91 U.S. 283 (1876), involved a Missouri license requirement for peddlers—itinerant sellers. The statute applied only to peddlers of merchandise "not the growth, produce or manufacture of this State"; peddlers of Missouri goods did not need a license. Welton was convicted of peddling without a license and fined $50. The Supreme Court reversed. Justice Field stated that the "very object" of the commerce clause was to protect "against discriminating State legislation." He added: "There is difficulty, it is true, . . . in drawing the line precisely where the commercial power of Congress ends and the power of the State begins. A similar difficulty was felt . . . in Brown v. Maryland . . . . It is sufficient now to hold that the commercial power continues

until the commodity has ceased to be the subject of discriminating legislation by reason of its foreign character. That power protects it, even after it has entered the State, from any burdens imposed by reason of its foreign origin. The act of Missouri encroaches upon this power in this respect, and is therefore . . . unconstitutional and void. The fact that Congress has not seen fit to prescribe any specific rules . . . does not affect the question."

2. *Discrimination in effect: Best & Co. v. Maxwell.* Reasonably obvious discrimination has been consistently condemned—even where the Court had to probe a short distance beneath the face of the statute to expose the discrimination. For example, in Best & Co. v. Maxwell, 311 U.S. 454 (1940), North Carolina imposed an annual privilege tax of $250 on anyone "not a regular retail merchant in the state" who displayed samples in a hotel room rented for the purpose of securing retail orders. The tax was successfully challenged by a New York retailer who had rented a display room in a North Carolina hotel. The Court recognized that the tax nominally applied to all who were not regular retailers, residents as well as nonresidents. That did not save the law: "We must assume [that those residents] competing with appellant for the sale of similar merchandise will normally be regular retail merchants." The retail stores, "not those who sell only by sample," were the "natural outlets" for merchandise. The only corresponding fixed-sum license tax on Best's "real competitors" was an annual $1 tax for the privilege of doing business. The "actual effect" of the law was "to discriminate in favor of intrastate business, whatever may be the ostensible reach of the language." Commerce "can hardly survive in so hostile an atmosphere." And the commerce clause "forbids discrimination, whether forthright or ingenious." Consider in examining the subsequent sections, how successfully the Court has unearthed the various techniques of "ingenious" discrimination.

3. *Discrimination as a risk: the "long line of 'drummer' cases."* a. *The rationale.* The Court has consistently invalidated taxes on solicitors of orders for out-of-state sellers. The "discrimination" condemned in this situation is certainly less obvious than in Welton, and at least a shade less so than in Best. The line of decisions originated with Robbins v. Shelby County Taxing District, 120 U.S. 489 (1887). As the Court said in Memphis Steam Laundry Cleaner v. Stone, 342 U.S. 389 (1952): "In the long line of 'drummer' cases, beginning with Robbins . . ., this Court has held that a tax imposed upon the solicitation of interstate commerce is a tax upon interstate commerce itself. Whether or not solicitation of interstate business may be regarded as a local incident of interstate commerce, the Court has not permitted state taxation to carve out this incident from the integral economic process of interstate commerce." Note, however, the many "local incidents of interstate commerce" that the Court *has* permitted to be "carved out," especially those noted in sec. 4, infra. In the Best & Co. case, note 1, supra, the Court explained that "the long line of decisions following Robbins" rested on "the actual and potential discrimination inherent in certain fixed-sum license taxes."

In the Robbins case itself, the statute imposed a "privilege" tax of $10 a week or $25 a month on "all drummers, and all persons not having a regular licensed place of business . . . and offering for sale or selling goods . . . by sample." The Court invoked the common label of that day in cases invalidating taxes, concluding that this was "clearly a tax on interstate commerce itself." But the sensitivity to discrimination is apparent in the

Robbins opinion. The Court rejected the defense "that no discrimination is made between domestic and foreign drummers— . . . that all are taxed alike." For, despite the face of the statute, the tax seemed to the Court "discriminative against the merchants and manufacturers of other States. They can only sell their goods in Memphis by the employment of drummers and by means of samples; whilst the merchants and manufacturers of Memphis, having regular licensed houses of business there, have no occasion for such agents; and if they had, they are not subject to any tax therefor. They are taxed for their licensed houses, it is true; but so, it is presumable, are the merchants and manufacturers of other States in the places where they reside; and the tax on drummers operates greatly to their disadvantage in comparison with the merchants and manufacturers of Memphis. And such was undoubtedly one of its objects. This kind of taxation is usually imposed at the instance and solicitation of domestic dealers, as a means of protecting them from foreign competition."

Note also Justice Stone's discussion of this type of tax in McGoldrick v. Berwind-White Co., 309 U.S. 33 (1940), p. 719, infra: "In some instances the tax [invalidated under the Robbins principle] appeared aimed at suppression or placing at a disadvantage this type of business when brought into competition with competing intrastate sales. . . . .[1] In all, the statute, in its practical operation, was capable of use, through increase in the tax, and in fact operated to some extent to place the merchant thus doing business interstate at a disadvantage in competition with untaxed sales at retail stores within the state. . . . [T]he rule of Robbins . . . has been narrowly limited to fixed-sum license taxes imposed on the business of soliciting orders for the purchase of goods to be shipped interstate." Should the rule be so limited? Compare the taxes on interstate sellers whose activities extend somewhat beyond solicitation, in sec. 4, infra. And recall the Court's failure to invalidate a local regulation banning all door-to-door solicitation, in Breard v. City of Alexandria, 341 U.S. 622 (1951), chap. 8, p. 658, supra.

b. *Discrimination in fact? Against whom?* Is it demonstrable that the flat fee drummer tax is actually or potentially discriminatory? In Robbins, Chief Justice Waite's dissent insisted that the Tennessee tax did not discriminate against out-of-state merchants. Indeed, he argued that the Court's decision created a discrimination "in favor of" the foreign seller: "Merchants in Tennessee are by law required to pay taxes on the amount of their stocks on hand and a privilege tax besides. Under these circumstances it is easy to see that if a merchant from another State could carry on a business in the District by sending his agents there with samples . . ., he would enjoy a privilege of exemption from taxation which the local merchant would not have."

4. *Offsetting discriminatory risks by equivalent taxes on local competitors.* a. *The scope and limits of judicial inquiry.* Is the Court com-

---

1. "When the Robbins case was decided, sixteen states required the payment of license taxes by some kinds of drummers. For citations of the statutes, see, Lockhart, Sales Tax in Interstate Commerce, 52 Harv.L.Rev. 617, 621. More recently it has been estimated that almost 800 municipal ordinances directed at drummers were adopted for the purpose of embarrassing this competition with local merchants. Hemphill, The House to House Canvasser in Interstate Commerce, 60 Am. L.Rev. 641. The [Robbins] court was cognizant of this trend . . . . Following this decision 19 such taxes were declared invalid. . . ." [Footnote by the Court.]

petent to assess arguments that an apparently discriminatory tax on out-of-state sellers is offset by an allegedly equivalent tax on local competitors? Can the Court assess the impact of the total tax structure on the local merchant, and compare it with the varied burdens on the foreign seller? Usually, the Court's inquiry into equivalent taxes has been limited. For example, the Court, relying on Robbins, invalidated a fixed-fee tax on out-of-state trucks soliciting laundry business and picking up laundry in Mississippi, in the Memphis Steam Laundry case, supra. If the tax were viewed as one on soliciting, the Court held, Robbins compelled its condemnation even though there was an argument that local laundries were subject to municipal license taxes, which offset the burden of the state-wide tax on the Memphis company. What would be relevant to an adequate weighing of the impact of taxation on in-state and out-of-state businessmen? Would it be necessary to determine the precise area of competition? Would it involve an inquiry into the total tax structure of the state of the market? Of the foreign businessman's home state? Is such an inquiry judicially manageable?

b. *Validation because of local equivalents: Arctic Maid and Dunbar-Stanley.* For a relatively rare example of a rejection of a claim of discrimination because of the existence of an equivalent domestic tax, see Alaska v. Arctic Maid, 366 U.S. 199 (1961). An Alaska tax on out-of-state freezer ships (operating along Alaska's shore to take on and freeze salmon caught there) was attacked on the ground, inter alia, that there was no tax on salmon caught and frozen in Alaska if it was destined to be canned in Alaska. The Court stated that this did not make the tax discriminatory: the relevant competitive market was that of Alaskan canneries, and Alaskan canneries paid a 6% tax on the salmon obtained for canning, as compared with the 4% tax on salmon taken onto the freezer ships for out-of-state canning. But Alaskans who froze fish for the immediate consumer market paid only a 1% tax. This disparity was put aside because the "freezer ships do not compete with those who freeze fish for the retail market." What if the freezer ships' home states imposed a tax on canning operations there? Would that demonstrate that Alaska's tax was "discriminatory"?

See also Dunbar-Stanley Studios v. Alabama, 393 U.S. 537 (1969), sustaining a $5 per week per locality tax on "transient or traveling" photographers. Appellant, a North Carolina photography firm, periodically sent employees to Alabama to take children's portraits for local branches of a chain store, which handled all advertising and other arrangements. Justice Fortas stated that the general rule against flat sum privilege taxes on solicitors did not ban this tax: if it had been a license tax on soliciting orders or making deliveries, "conflict with the Commerce Clause would be evident because these are minimal activities within a State without which there can be no interstate commerce"; but here the taxpayer was "engaged in an essentially local activity: the business of providing photographers' services." Nor was there an adequate showing of discrimination: "On the record before us, there is no basis for concluding that the $5 per week tax on transient out-of-state photographers is so disproportionate to the tax imposed on photographers with a fixed location [$25 per year] as to bear unfairly on the former." For example, appellant had visited no Alabama city more than five times in the year—incurring a maximum tax of $25, equal in amount to that payable by a photographer permanently located there.

5. *The "drummer"-"peddler" distinction.* Note the additional facet of this problem raised by an alternative contention in the Memphis Steam Laundry case: It was possible to read the state court's construction of the tax as one not on soliciting but rather on the separable "local activity" of picking up and delivering laundry. Accordingly, Mississippi sought to justify the tax under another line of decisions, the "peddler" cases, starting with Emert v. Missouri, 156 U.S. 296 (1895). "Peddlers," who carry their goods with them (unlike "drummers," who solicit orders for shipments from out-of-state through use of samples), may be taxed: "[T]his Court has sustained state taxation upon itinerant hawkers and peddlers on the ground that the local sale and delivery of goods is an essentially intrastate process whether a retailer operates from a fixed location or a wagon." But the peddler cases did not help Mississippi: even if this were a tax on local activities, it was invalid because discriminatory: "The 'peddler' cases are inapposite" upon "a showing of discrimination." The "discrimination" conclusion was based on the fact that a tax of $50 per truck was payable by the Memphis company to do business in one city, while a competitor from another Mississippi city was subject to only an $8 per truck tax.

Is the general rule, that peddlers' taxes are constitutional, justified as applied to peddlers carrying only out-of-state goods with them? Do any of the justifications for banning drummers' taxes apply to peddlers' taxes?

6. *The continued vitality of the drummer cases.* a. *Nippert and discriminatory "probabilities."* In Nippert v. City of Richmond, 327 U.S. 416 (1946), the Court rejected the argument that its decisions sustaining certain taxes on interstate sales transactions—e. g., McGoldrick v. Berwind-White Co., 309 U.S. 33 (1940), p. 719, infra—had impaired the special immunity of interstate solicitors under the Robbins doctrine. Richmond imposed an annual license tax of $50 and ½% of gross commissions over $1000 on "solicitors." Nippert was convicted of soliciting orders for an out-of-state retailer without a license. The Court held the tax invalid as one tending to discriminate, especially because it was a municipal tax: "The cumulative effect, practically speaking, of flat municipal taxes laid in succession upon the itinerant merchant as he passes from town to town is obviously greater than that of any tax of state-wide application likely to be laid by the legislature."

The Court emphasized the inherent discriminatory "probabilities" of the tax: In view of facts of "common knowledge, we cannot be unmindful" of the favoring of local competitors by these taxes, "or that in fact this is often if not always the object of the local commercial influences which induce their adoption. Provincial interests and local political power are at their maximum weight in bringing about acceptance of this type of legislation. . . . The drummer is a figure representative of a by-gone day. But his modern prototype persists under more euphonious appellations. So endure the basic reasons which brought about his protection from [this] kind of local favoritism." The Court stated, moreover: "It is no answer . . . that the tax is neither prohibitive nor discriminatory on the face of the ordinance; or that it applies to all local distributors doing business as appellant has done. Not the tax in a vacuum of words, but its practical consequences . . . are our concern. . . . The tax . . . cannot be taken to apply generally to local distributors in the same manner and with like effects as in application to out-of-state distributors. The very difference in locations of their business headquarters, if any, and of their activities makes this impossible. This, of course, is but another way of saying that the very difference between interstate and local trade, taken in conjunction with the inherent character of the tax, makes equality of application as between those two classes of commerce, generally speaking, impossible. It is true that the tax may strike as heavily upon some Virginia solicitors, and even upon some who confine themselves to Richmond, as it does upon others who come periodically or otherwise from Washington, New York or Cedar Rapids. And it may bear upon a few of the former more heavily than upon most of the latter. But neither consequence is the more probable one for the larger number of cases. The strong likelihood is the other way." Justice Douglas' dissent, joined by Justice Murphy, emphasized that there was no proof of actual discrimination. Compare Chief Justice Waite's dissent in the Robbins case, note 3a, supra.

b. *West Point Grocery and "discrimination."* In a more recent application of the Robbins doctrine, West Point Wholesale Grocery Co. v. City of Opelika, 354 U.S. 390 (1957), the Court invalidated a "privilege tax" of $250 on wholesale grocers delivering groceries from outside of the city. The Court held that the tax, as applied to a Georgia wholesale grocer, fell "squarely within" the ban on flat-fee privilege taxes. The Court added: "This is particularly so in that Opelika places no comparable flat-sum tax on local merchants." Local competitors were, however, subject to a city tax based on gross receipts; but an Opelika wholesaler would have to gross $280,000 a year to reach "the flat $250 amount imposed on all foreign grocers before they may set foot in the city. The Commerce Clause forbids any such discrimination against the free flow of trade."

What if the competing Opelika wholesalers all grossed more than $280,000 a year? Would that fact preclude a "discrimination" label? Or would the tax still be invalid because of the risk that other cities might impose similar flat fee taxes if Opelika's authority were recognized? Would there be any valid objection to the tax if West Point's sales in Opelika alone amounted to more than $280,000 a year?

7. *The Court's limited perception of discriminatory risks: Independent Warehouses and the permissible selection of vulnerable tax subjects.* a. Should the concern about the inherent risk of discrimination be limited to the taxes on interstate solicitors? Is the reasoning applicable to other situations? The Court has not been as perceptive about "probabilities" and "practical consequences" in assessing taxes outside the Robbins line of cases. For example, states have been permitted to single out a particular type of business for taxation, even though most companies engaged in it are out-of-state ones. See, e. g., Independent Warehouses v. Scheele, 331 U.S. 70 (1947), sustaining a local annual license fee on "the business of the storage of personal property in a warehouse," as applied to a coal depot used mainly by out-of-state shippers of coal. The Court relied on cases such as Minnesota v. Blasius, p. 699, infra, sustaining property taxes on goods temporarily stored while in transit.

Justice Jackson's dissent in Scheele viewed the New Jersey city's tax as, in effect, on "transportation of New York's coal supply . . . . [T]he ultimate burden falls on consumers in New York . . . who have no representation in the government which lays the tax . . . . Here is a tax that falls immediately upon a single taxpayer, for it does not appear that any other is similarly affected. It is a tax that falls ultimately on the non-residents of the taxing authority. . . . The Constitution laid restraints upon each locality lest their local advantages be pursued at the cost of commerce on which the prosperity of all depends." Note the "probabilities" inherent in taxes on interstate transportation facilities, sec. 3, infra, including the risk of exploitation of geographical advantages.

      b. Is the underlying concern of Robbins also applicable to tax statutes which single out goods in competition with local products? Should a dairy state's tax on oleomargarine be sustained? Or do "common knowledge" and "probabilities" compel the same result as in Robbins and Nippert—and Welton? See A. Magnano Co. v. Hamilton, 292 U.S. 40 (1934). Is the dairy state tax saved by naming the disfavored spread "generically rather than geographically"? Cf. Lockhart, "State Tax Barriers to Interstate Trade," 53 Harv.L.Rev. 1253 (1940); and see Barrett, " 'Substance' vs. 'Form' in the Application of the Commerce Clause to State Taxation," 101 U.Pa.L.Rev. 740 (1953).[2]

AD VALOREM PROPERTY TAXES: THE CONSTITUTIONAL END OF THE STATE TAX SPECTRUM

    Introduction. The usual ad valorem tax on personal and real property is imposed annually and is measured by a percentage of the value of the property. Just as the patent discrimination of the Welton v. Missouri variety has consistently provoked rulings of unconstitutionality, applications of the typical ad valorem tax to property permanently located within the taxing state have consistently avoided constitutional difficulties—even where property is owned by an interstate company and is used in interstate commerce. The constitutional invulnerability of this type of tax does not necessarily indicate that it is incapable of burdening interstate commerce: by the classification of taxable property,[1] or the assessment of values, potential

2. One other type of tax on the "unconstitutional" end of the state tax spectrum is the tax on the "privilege" of doing interstate commerce. See, e. g., Spector Motor Service v. O'Connor, 340 U.S. 602 (1951). That tax will be considered infra, sec. 3: though it is one of the clear "peaks," because of the consistent rulings of unconstitutionality, the holdings rest on grounds other than "discrimination."

1. The equal protection clause, see chap. 14, infra, has at times been pressed into service as a restraint on discriminatory classifications in state property taxation. In Wheeling Steel Corp. v. Glander, 337 U.S. 562 (1949), Ohio assessed an ad valorem tax on accounts receivable of a foreign corporation qualified to do business in Ohio, the accounts resulting from out-of-state sales of goods shipped from its Ohio plants. Under the statute, similar accounts receivable of domestic

corporations were free from the tax. The Court held that the tax denied the foreign corporation equal protection of the laws in violation of the Fourteenth Amendment. Note the reliance on Wheeling in WHYY, Inc. v. Glassboro, 393 U.S. 117 (1968), holding unconstitutional New Jersey's denial to the appellant of a tax exemption which the state accorded to domestic nonprofit corporations, solely because of appellant's foreign incorporation.

The Wheeling case was found distinguishable, however, in Allied Stores v. Bowers, 358 U.S. 522 (1959). The Court rejected an Ohio resident's challenge to an Ohio ad valorem tax which exempted "merchandise or agricultural products belonging to a nonresident . . . if held in a storage warehouse for storage only." The opinion of the Court, by Justice Whittaker, concluded that here "the discrimination against and actual restraints on the free market may arise. Cf. Nashville, C. & St. L. Ry. v. Browning, 310 U.S. 362 (1940). But the Court's decisions offer little basis for challenging such property taxes, short of flagrantly discriminatory schemes.

1. *Property in transit and at rest: Minnesota v. Blasius.* a. There has been considerable litigation, however, regarding tangible property not permanently located in the taxing state. Goods in actual interstate transit are immune from state taxation. See Kelly v. Rhoads, 188 U.S. 1 (1903); Powell, "Taxation of Things in Transit," 7 Va.L.Rev. 167 (1920). Difficulties have arisen in distinguishing between property "in transit" and "at rest." Minnesota v. Blasius, 290 U.S. 1 (1933), provides an example. Blasius was a livestock trader at the St. Paul stockyards. He normally purchased cattle from commission men at the market, for resale to out-of-state buyers. On May 1, the "tax day" for assessment of Minnesota's personal property tax, he owned eleven head of cattle; by the next day, he had sold all of the cattle to out-of-state purchasers. They were assessed for taxation under the general tax law of the state. The Court rejected his challenge that the tax had improperly taxed goods in interstate commerce. Cf. Stafford v. Wallace, 258 U.S. 495 (1922) (sustaining the federal Packers and Stockyards Act of 1921 on the "current of commerce" theory, chap. 4, p. 253).

To Chief Justice Hughes, the Stafford holding was no bar to the state tax: "But because there is a flow of interstate commerce which is subject to the regulating power of the Congress, it does not necessarily follow that . . . a state may not lay a nondiscriminatory tax upon property which, although connected with that flow as a general course of business, has come to rest and has acquired a situs within the state. . . . Where property has come to rest within a state, being held there at the pleasure of the owner, for disposal or use, so that he may dispose of it either within the state, or for shipment elsewhere, as his interest dictates, it is deemed to be a part of the general mass of property within the state and is thus subject to its taxing power. Here . . . transportation had ceased, and the cattle were sold on that market to Blasius, who became absolute owner and was free to deal with them as he liked. He could sell the cattle within the state or for shipment outside the state. He placed them in pens and cared for them awaiting such disposition as he might see fit to make for his own profit. The tax was assessed on the regular tax day while Blasius thus owned and possessed them. The cattle were not . . . in transit. Their situs

residents is not invidious nor palpably arbitrary because . . . it rests not upon the 'different residence of the owner,' but upon a state of facts that reasonably can be conceived to constitute a distinction, or a difference in state policy"—for example, a legitimate state policy to encourage use of Ohio warehouses by nonresidents, "with the attendant benefits to the State's economy." Justice Brennan's concurrence, joined by Justice Harlan, stated that this was not an adequate distinction of Wheeling, since residence was determinative as to taxability in both cases. Distinguishing Wheeling was possible only by "viewing the Equal Protection Clause as an instrument of federalism." Justice Brennan added: "The proper analysis, it seems to me, is that Wheeling applied the Equal Protection Clause to give effect to its role to protect our federalism by denying Ohio the power constitutionally to discriminate in favor of its own residents. . . . [I]n the present case, Ohio's classification based on residence operates *against* Ohio residents and clearly presents no state action disruptive of the federal pattern."

was in Minnesota where they had come to rest. There was no federal right to immunity from the tax."

b. Despite its innocuous appearance, the property tax may endanger the national interest in commerce. Would Blasius have had a substantial commerce claim, for example, if he had taken the cattle to Chicago, if Chicago's tax day were May 10, and if he had been taxed on the same cattle there? Would he have a substantial claim if he showed that he normally shipped cattle from state to state, that for nine months of the year most of his cattle was in Chicago, but that during March, April, and May he maintained an unusual number in St. Paul? Cf. note 2, infra. On the problem of risks in these taxes, note, moreover, that the Blasius case was relied on to justify the tax on storing coal, in Independent Warehouses v. Scheele, 331 U.S. 70 (1947), supra, over a dissent emphasizing the commerce-retarding aspects of the tax.

2. *Equipment of interstate carriers.* The taxability of carriers' equipment has been a prolific source of litigation. Does the fact that the equipment is not permanently in one state bar all state property taxation? If every state in which the equipment is used imposes a tax, will there not be unconstitutional multiple taxation of the same equipment? May the corporate domicile tax all of the carrier's equipment? May each state in which the equipment is used tax a portion of the fleet, based on a rational apportionment formula? The Court has struggled with these problems by discussing both the due process and the commerce clauses—at times using the two interchangeably and confusingly. And the Court has occasionally suggested differing rules for different types of equipment. Some samples of the decisions follow:

a. *Barges and the railroad analogy: Ott and Standard Oil.* In Ott v. Mississippi Barge Line Co., 336 U.S. 169 (1949), Louisiana imposed an ad valorem tax on barges and tow boats of foreign interstate carriers operating within its waters, and apportioned the tax on a ratio between the number of miles of appellee's lines in Louisiana and the number of miles of the entire line. The Supreme Court sustained the tax against both commerce clause and due process objections. It accepted the analogy of travel on inland waterways to that of railroads, where fair mileage apportionment had long been recognized. See, e. g., Pullman's Palace Car Co. v. Pennsylvania, 141 U.S. 18 (1891), and American Refrigerator Transit Co. v. Hall, 174 U.S. 70 (1889); cf. Central R. Co. v. Pennsylvania, 370 U.S. 607 (1962), p. 702, infra.

In Standard Oil Co. v. Peck, 342 U.S. 382 (1952), Ohio levied an ad valorem tax on the full value of a fleet of oil tankers owned by appellant, an Ohio corporation, and registered in Ohio. The vessel spent most of the year on water routes and at port terminals outside of Ohio, their only contacts with Ohio being an occasional stop for repairs or refueling at Cincinnati and the traversing of a seventeen and a half mile stretch of the Ohio River which bordered on the State. The Supreme Court, finding that appellant's vessels, under the Ott doctrine, had acquired a taxing situs in the several States in which they operated most of the year, held the Ohio tax on the full value of the vessels invalid under the due process clause: "The rule which permits taxation by two or more States on an apportionment basis precludes taxation of all property by the State of the domicil. See Union

Transit Co. v. Kentucky, 199 U.S. 194. Otherwise there would be multiple taxation of interstate operations and the tax would have no relation to the opportunities, benefits, or protection which the taxing State gives those operations."

b. *Airplanes: Northwest Air Lines and Braniff.* Compare the developments regarding the taxability of airplanes: Northwest Air Lines v. Minnesota, 322 U.S. 292 (1944), sustained a Minnesota personal property tax on the full value of petitioner's (a Minnesota corporation) entire fleet of airplanes which were continuously engaged in operations among several States. Justice Frankfurter "announced the conclusion and judgment of the Court" and delivered an opinion finding that Minnesota, by virtue of its predominant contacts with the planes, i. e., as both domiciliary State and location of its main place of business, had the right to levy such a tax, none of the planes, due to their transitory nature, having acquired a permanent location elsewhere.[2]

Ten years later, Braniff Airways v. Nebraska Board, 347 U.S. 590 (1954), upheld Nebraska's apportioned ad valorem tax on the flight equipment of an interstate air carrier. The carrier was not incorporated in Nebraska, nor was its principal place of business or "home port" there. The flight equipment was employed as a part of a system of interstate air commerce operating over fixed routes and using airports within Nebraska on regular schedules (about 18 stops daily). The case was disposed of on due process grounds. (See sec. e of this note, infra.) The tax situs issue, said the majority, "devolves into the question of whether eighteen stops per day by appellant's aircraft is sufficient contact with Nebraska to sustain that State's power to levy an apportioned ad valorem tax on such aircraft." The Court found that Nebraska's contact was sufficient, "even though the same aircraft do not land every day and even though none of the aircraft is continuously within the State."

2.   See Powell, "Northwest Air Lines v. Minnesota—Herein Also of Ships and Sealing Wax and Railroad Cars," 57 Harv.L.Rev. 1097 (1944), Selected Essays 1938–62 (1963), 390.

On the relative competence of Congress and other institutions to devise solutions to these problems, see the proposed uniform state law, used by Nebraska in the Braniff case, infra, and note the aftermath of the Northwest case, as recounted by Justice Frankfurther in Northwestern States Portland Cement Co. v. Minnesota, 358 U.S. 450 (1959), p. 741, infra: "In Northwest we pointed to the desirability of congressional action to formulate uniform standards for state taxation of the rapidly expanding airline industry. Following our decision Congress directed the Civil Aeronautics Board to study and report to Congress methods of eliminating burdensome, multiple state taxation of airlines. See H.R. Doc. No. 141, 79th Cong., 1st Sess. This report of the Board was a 158-page document whose length and complex economic content in dealing with only a single subject of state taxation, illustrate the difficulties and nonjudicial nature of the problem. Following the presentation of this extensive report, several bills were introduced into Congress providing for a single uniform apportionment formula to be used by the States in taxing airlines. H.R. 1241, 80th Cong., 1st Sess.; S. 2453, 80th Cong., 2d Sess.; S. 420, 81st Cong., 1st Sess. None of these bills was enacted.

"Australia has resolved the problem of conflicting and burdensome state taxation of commerce by a national arrangement whereby taxes are collected by the Commonwealth and from those revenues appropriate allocations are made annually to the States through the mechanism of a Premiers' Conference—the Prime Minister of the Commonwealth and the Premiers of the several States." See also the more recent congressional consideration of state tax problems, noted at the end of sec. 4, p. 747, infra.

c. *Railroads and ad valorem property taxes: Allocation, multiple tax risks, and Central Railroad.* The Court returned to the problems of allocation and multiple taxation of railroad equipment in Central R. Co. v. Pennsylvania, 370 U.S. 607 (1962), a case once again presenting "the intricate problems of accommodating, under the Due Process and Commerce Clauses, the taxing powers of domiciliary and other States with respect to the instrumentalities of interstate commerce." The domiciliary state, Pennsylvania, sought to impose an annual property tax on the total value of freight cars owned by the railroad company. The company insisted on apportionment, since "a considerable number of such cars spend a substantial portion of the tax year on the lines of other railroads located outside the State." The Court, in an opinion by Justice Harlan, held that, as to most of the cars used outside Pennsylvania, the company had "failed to sustain its burden of proving that a tax situs had been acquired elsewhere." The majority opinion stated that the multiple taxation risk prevents the domiciliary state "from imposing an ad valorem tax on any property to the extent that it could be taxed by another State, not merely on such property as *is* subjected to tax elsewhere." The Court insisted, however, that it would be an "unsound rule" to bar a domiciliary state's tax on "a mere general showing of continuous use of movable property outside the domiciliary State." As to most of the cars, the Court found no evidence "of either regular routes through particular nondomiciliary States or habitual presence, though on irregular missions, in particular nondomiciliary States." Justice Black submitted a concurring opinion "to express my doubts about the use of the Due Process Clause to strike down state tax laws." Justices Frankfurter and White did not participate.

In a dissenting opinion, Justice Douglas, joined by Chief Justice Warren and Justice Stewart, insisted that "we cannot . . . allow Pennsylvania to lay this tax and adhere to our recent decisions. . . . As a result of the Ott, Peck and Braniff cases the average of 2189.30 freight cars that run regularly, habitually, and continuously on lines of other railroads outside Pennsylvania could be taxed by other States, even though no State can identify the precise cars within its borders and even though the complement of cars is constantly changing. . . . Whatever the average in any one State, the total outside Pennsylvania and taxable elsewhere is known and definite. Since that is true, we sanction double taxation when we sustain this tax. We would not allow it in case of any other interstate business; and as I read the Constitution no exception is made that puts the railroad business at a disadvantage."

d. *Ad valorem property taxes and Norfolk Railroad: Valid in formula, "gross overreaching" in application.* For a rare instance of a finding of constitutional invalidity despite the presence of a traditional variety of tax and of a widely accepted apportionment formula, see Norfolk & W. R. Co. v. Tax Comm'n, 390 U.S. 317 (1968). Missouri imposed an ad valorem property tax on railroad rolling stock; the apportionment basis was "the familiar mileage formula"; the constitutional vice lay in the application. Justice Fortas' majority opinion found that the taxpayers had shown "that application of the mileage method [here] has resulted in such gross overreaching, beyond the values represented by the intrastate assets purported to be taxed, as to violate the Due Process and Commerce Clauses of the Constitution" and that the State had made "no effort to offset the convincing case" the railroads had made.

The facts showed that the N & W Railway had taken over the Missouri rolling stock of the Wabash Railroad; that the rolling stock had been assessed to N & W at almost three times the assessment to Wabash in the preceding year; and that the mileage formula resulted in attributing more than 8% of the N & W's rolling stock to Missouri, even though only about 3% of the total N & W fleet was in fact usually employed in Missouri. The Court stated that "our cases certainly forbid an unexplained discrepancy as gross as that in this case." And there was inadequate support for the highest state court's claim that the take-over of the Wabash property by the N & W had "enhanced" the value of the rolling stock: here, the record was "totally barren of any evidence relating to enhancement or to going-concern or intangible value, or to any other factor which might offset the devastating effect of the demonstrated discrepancy."

Justice Black dissented: "Where I differ with the Court is that I believe the burden of proof is on the railroad to show that the tax is excessive under all considerations rather than on the Commission to show sufficient enhancement of value to justify the tax." Note especially the concluding sentence in this dissent written by the author of the 1950 opinion in the Capitol Greyhound case, the next principal case, in sec. 3: Justice Black emphasized that the taxpayer here "did not prove that the *enhanced value* of its rolling stock was less than the tax assessment, or that the State was imposing on it taxes that were exorbitant on the full value of all its property, cf. Capitol Greyhound Lines v. Brice."

e. *The commerce-due process mix in property tax cases.* Note the alternate reliances on the due process and commerce clause cases in these property tax cases. Do the clauses serve any distinguishable functions in these contexts? In Braniff, sec. b of this note, Justice Reed's majority opinion stated: "The argument upon which appellant depends ultimately . . . is that its aircraft never 'attained a taxable situs within Nebraska' from which it argues that the Nebraska tax imposes a burden on interstate commerce. In relying upon the Commerce Clause on this issue and in not specifically claiming protection under the Due Process Clause of the Fourteenth Amendment, appellant names the wrong constitutional clause to support its position. While the question of whether a commodity en route to market is sufficiently settled in a state for purpose of subjection to a property tax has been determined by this Court as a Commerce Clause question, the bare question whether an instrumentality of commerce has tax situs in a state for the purpose of subjection to a property tax is one of due process. . . . Though inexplicit, we consider the due process issue within the clear intendment of [Braniff's] contention and hold such issue sufficiently presented."

Does this "wrong constitutional clause" talk make any sense? Do the Court's own reasons in these cases sound different from those given in deciding commerce clause questions? Note the "multiple taxation" concern in Northwest Air Lines, sec. b, and Central Railroad, sec. c, supra. Compare Justice Frankfurter's dissent in Braniff: "It cannot be said that for airplanes, flying regularly scheduled fights, to alight, stop over for a short time and then take off is so tenuously related to Nebraska that it would deny due process for that State to seize on these short stopovers as the basis of an ad valorem tax. But the incidence of a tax may offend the Commerce Clause, even though it may satisfy the Due Process Clause."

f. *"Property" taxes measured by gross receipts.* Do the problems of taxing carriers' equipment take on a significant added dimension when the state's tax on personal property is measured not on an ad valorem basis but on the basis of a percentage of the carrier's gross receipts, allocated on the basis of the miles traveled in the taxing state? See, e. g., Illinois Central R. Co. v. Minnesota, 309 U.S. 149 (1940), where the Court sustained a "property tax" on railroads. The tax was measured by the gross earnings from all intrastate business, plus a proportion of earnings from interstate business passing through the State equal to the proportion which mileage within the State bore to total mileage over which such business was done. See also Railway Express Agency v. Virginia, 358 U.S. 434 (1959), p. 713, infra. Does the Illinois Central case present some of the problems of the gross receipts taxes on interstate transportation, sec. 3, infra?

SECTION 3.   STATE TAXES AND INTERSTATE TRANSPORTATION

TOLLGATE STATES AND EXPLOITATION OF STRATEGIC LOCATION

Introduction. The reports contain frequent reminders that a basic purpose of the commerce clause is to assure free trade within the national economy. But the Court has hesitated to implement that free trade policy fully, as some of the earlier materials indicate. Justice Jackson, who was especially insistent on removing state barriers, was concerned about the implications of the state tax on coal storage in Independent Warehouses, Inc. v. Scheele, p. 697, supra, for example, but he was in dissent.[1] The Court's drawing back from full-scale enforcement of free trade, in the face of insistent state revenue needs and uncertain economic gauges regarding tax impacts, is illustrated in the handling of taxes affecting transportation facilities. State export taxes are plainly invalid; and a state frankly demanding a toll on passage through it would encounter constitutional barriers. Yet states are permitted to collect revenues from carriers in a variety of ways, and there is considerable opportunity to exploit geographic location. Some examples have already been considered, in the preceding notes. The purpose of this section is to explore some additional facets of the problem: the permissibility and variety of taxes to compensate the state for use of its highways; the impacts of taxes on gross receipts from transportation and related services; and the forbidden tax on the "privilege" of engaging in interstate business.

1. See also his opinions in H. P. Hood & Sons v. Du Mond, 336 U.S. 525 (1949), chap. 8, p. 661, supra, and Duckworth v. Arkansas, 314 U.S. 390, 400 (1940); see generally Jaffe, "Mr. Justice Jackson," 68 Harv.L.Rev. 940 (1955). Cf. Haskins, "The Discriminatory Effect of Multiple State Taxation of Interstate Carriers," 5 J.Pub.L. 327 (1956), Selected Essays 1938–62 (1963), 356.

CAPITOL GREYHOUND LINES v. BRICE

339 U.S. 542, 70 S.Ct. 806, 94 L.Ed. 1053 (1950).

Appeal from the Court of Appeals of Maryland.

Mr. Justice BLACK delivered the opinion of the Court.

The basic question presented is whether one of two Maryland taxes imposed on all common carriers transporting passengers over Maryland roads can be exacted from interstate carriers consistently with the commerce clause of the Federal Constitution. A subsidiary contention impliedly raised by carrier appellants here is that the tax is invalid as applied to them. The Supreme Court of Maryland upheld the tax . . . .

. . . In the language of appellants [the challenged] section imposes "a tax of 2% upon the fair market value of motor vehicles used in interstate commerce as a condition precedent to the issuance of certificates of title thereto (the issuance of such certificates being a further condition precedent to the registration and operation of such vehicles in the State of Maryland) . . . ."*

First. Appellants do not contend that as interstate carriers they are wholly exempt from state taxation. This Court and others have consistently upheld taxes on interstate carriers to compensate a state fairly for the privilege of using its roads or for the cost of administering state traffic regulations. Courts have invoked the commerce clause to invalidate state taxes on interstate carriers only upon finding that : (1) the tax discriminated against interstate commerce in favor of intrastate commerce; (2) the tax was imposed on the privilege of doing an interstate business as distinguished from a tax exacting contributions for road construction and maintenance or for administration of road laws; or (3) the amount of tax exceeded fair compensation to the state. This Maryland tax applies to interstate and intrastate commerce without discrimination. The tax proceeds are used by Maryland wholly for road purposes, and the State Supreme Court held that the tax was imposed for the privilege of road use. And . . . appellants [have not] specifically charged that the amount of taxes imposed on carriers will always be in excess of fair compensation. Their challenge is leveled against the formula, not the amount.

The taxes upheld have taken many forms. Examples are taxes based on mileage, chassis weight, tonnage-capacity, or horsepower, singly or in combination—a list which does not begin to exhaust the innumerable factors bearing on the fairness of compensation by each carrier to a state. . . . [I]n rejecting contentions that the validity of taxes must be determined by formula rather than result, the Court held that a flat fee on the privilege of using state highways "is not a forbidden burden on interstate commerce" unless "unreasonable in amount." Morf v. Bingaman, 298 U.S. 407, 412. . . . Yet clearly a flat fee is not geared to mileage, weight or any other factor relevant in considering the fairness of compensation for road use. Thus, unless we are to depart from prior decisions, the Maryland tax based on the cost of the vehicles should be judged by its result, not its formula, and

---

* Maryland also imposes a tax for each passenger seat of one-thirtieth of a cent per mile traveled on Maryland roads. . . . [Footnote by the Court.]

must stand unless proven to be unreasonable in amount for the privilege granted.

. . . Appellants argue that a tax on vehicle value should be forbidden by the commerce clause because it varies for each carrier without relation to road use. . . . Each of the appellant carriers . . . bought a new passenger-carrying vehicle and declared a purpose to use its vehicle on one of its Maryland routes. The Maryland portions of these three routes are 9, 41 and 64 miles respectively. The state taxes computed on the fair market value of each vehicle are $505.17, $580 and $372.55, respectively. This showing does indicate that the title tax falls short of achieving uniformity among carriers in relation to road use. . . . [I]t should be noted that the total charge of Maryland for the privilege of using its roads will not show the same disparity among carriers. For Maryland also charges a mileage tax, and this tax added to the title tax is what Maryland actually charges for its road privileges. Thus the total charge as among carriers does vary substantially with the mileage traveled.

We recognize that in the absence of congressional action this Court has prescribed the rules which determine the power of states to tax interstate traffic, and therefore should alter these rules if necessary to protect interstate commerce from obstructive barriers. But with full appreciation of congenital infirmities of the Maryland formula—and indeed of any formula in this field— as well as of our present rules to test its validity, we are by no means sure that the remedy suggested by appellants would not bring about greater ills. Complete fairness would require that a state tax formula vary with every factor affecting appropriate compensation for road use. These factors, like those relevant in considering the constitutionality of other state taxes, are so countless that we must be content with "rough approximation rather than precision." . . . Each additional factor adds to administrative burdens of enforcement, which fall alike on taxpayers and government. We have recognized that such burdens may be sufficient to justify states in ignoring even such a key factor as mileage, although the result may be a tax which on its face appears to bear with unequal weight upon different carriers. Aero Transit Co. v. Georgia Comm'n, 295 U.S. 285, 289. Upon this type of reasoning rests our general rule that taxes like that of Maryland here are valid unless the amount is shown to be in excess of fair compensation for the privilege of using state roads.

Our adherence to existing rules does not mean that any group of carriers is remediless if the total Maryland taxes are out of line with fair compensation due to Maryland. . . . [S]uch carriers may challenge the taxes as applied, and upon proper proof obtain a judicial declaration of their invalidity as applied. Ingels v. Morf, 300 U.S. 290. . . .

If a new rule prohibiting taxes measured by vehicle value is to be declared, we think Congress should do it. . . .

Second. Little need be said as to the faint contention here that the taxes actually levied against appellants are in excess of a fair compensation for the privilege of using Maryland roads. . . . The burden of proof in this respect is on a carrier who challenges a state law. . . . We agree with the Supreme Court of Maryland that here there is a complete and utter lack of proof sufficient to invalidate the state law on this ground. . . .

Affirmed.

Mr. Justice FRANKFURTER, whom Mr. Justice JACKSON joins, dissenting. . . .

From [the] body of decisions, the Court now extracts the principle that, so long as a tax is levied for highway purposes and does not formally discriminate against interstate commerce, it cannot be attacked for its tax formula or classification, but only for "excessiveness" of amount. Such a view collides with the guiding limitation upon State power announced in Interstate Transit, Inc. v. Lindsey, 283 U.S. 183, 186, that a tax intended to compensate for road use "will be sustained unless the taxpayer shows that it bears no reasonable relation to the privilege of using the highways or is discriminatory." . . .

In no prior case has the Court upheld a tax formula bearing no reasonable relationship to the privilege of road use. No support to the result now reached is lent by the fact that State tax formulas need not be limited to factors reflecting actual road use, such as mileage, but may be measured by the privilege of highway use extended to all alike. . . .

Systems of taxation need not achieve the ideal. But the fact that the Constitution does not demand pure reason and is satisfied by practical reason does not justify unreason. Though a State may levy a tax based upon the privilege granted, as distinguished from its exercise, this does not sanction a tax the measure of which has no reasonable relation to the privilege. Reason precludes the notion that a tax for a privilege may disregard the absence of a *nexus* between privilege and tax. . . .

Maryland's titling tax fails to meet the justifications that sustain a State's power to levy a tax on what is exclusively the carrying on of interstate commerce. . . . [O]ne cannot find any fair relationship between the tax and actual road use or the privilege of such use. The value of a vehicle is not a practical function of what the State affords. It has at best a most tenuous relationship to the privilege of using the roads, since differences in value are due to a vehicle's appointments or its age or to other factors which have no bearing on highway use. . . .

. . . [Q]uite apart from its formula, there are serious questions relating to the amount of this tax which the Court disregards. There is a show of fairness in the Court's suggestion that the tax will be declared bad if the amount exacted exceeds "fair compensation" to the States. . . . Under the guise of a special compensatory tax, however, a State may not exact more than the value of the services to be compensated. There is no showing that the tax levied here is excessive in this sense.

But for the proper maintenance of our federal system, and more particularly for the rigorous safeguarding of the national interests in interstate commerce, it is not sufficient that a State exact no more than the value of what it gives—with all the elusiveness of determining such value. A State must not play favorites in the operation of its taxing system between business confined within its borders and the common interests of the nation expressed through business conducted across State lines. Such favoritism is barred whether it is overtly designed or results from the actual operation of a taxing scheme. The Maryland tax does not obviously discriminate against interstate commerce. But a tax for the privilege of road use may impose serious disadvantages upon that commerce.

So long as a State bases its tax on a relevant measure of actual road use, obviously both interstate and intrastate carriers pay according to the facilities in fact provided by the State. But a tax levied for the privilege of using roads, and not their actual use, may, in the normal course of operations and not as a fanciful hypothesis, involve an undue burden on interstate carriers. While the privilege extended by a State is unlimited in form, and thus theoretically the same for all vehicles, whether interstate or intrastate, the intrastate vehicle can and will exercise the privilege whenever it is in operation, while the interstate vehicle must necessarily forego the privilege some of the time simply because of its interstate character, i. e., because it operates in other States as well. In the general average of instances, the privilege is not as valuable to the interstate as to the intrastate carrier. And because it operates in other States there is danger—and not a fanciful danger—that the interstate carrier will be subject to the privilege taxes of several States, even though his entire use of the highways is not significantly greater than that of intrastate operators who are subject to only one privilege tax.*

When a privilege tax is relatively small in amount, and therefore to be treated as a rough equivalent for what the State may exact with due regard to administrative practicalities, the danger of an unfair burden falling upon interstate commerce remains correspondingly small. Cf. Union Brokerage Co. v. Jensen, 322 U.S. 202, 210–11. But a large privilege tax presents dangers not unlike those arising from unapportioned gross receipts taxes on interstate transportation beyond a State's power to impose. Cf. Central Greyhound Lines, Inc. v. Mealey, 334 U.S. 653. These practical considerations prevailed against a State in Sprout v. South Bend, 277 U.S. 163:

> "A flat tax, substantial in amount and the same for busses plying the streets continuously in local service and for busses making, as do many interstate busses, only a single trip daily, could hardly have been designed as a measure of the cost or value of the use of the highways." . . .†

The problem is inescapably one of determining how much is too much, in the total nature of the tax. Thus, it becomes important to see how the Maryland tax compares in amount with similar taxes in prior cases. This is done, not to test the tax as individually applied to appellants, but to determine whether general application of a tax of this magnitude may fairly be deemed to burden interstate commerce unduly. Examination of decided cases reveals that the largest flat tax heretofore sustained was $15 for six months or $30 per year, and the largest annual tax based upon size or weight was $75. . . . . The Maryland taxes on the three appellants amounted to $372, $505

---

* These dangers are heightened when the tax falls upon an interstate motor carrier authorized to operate only on a fixed route. Quite illustrative of the seriousness of the general problem are the facts concerning one of appellants here, Capitol Greyhound Lines, which is authorized by the I.C.C. to operate a bus line over a fixed route between Cincinnati, Ohio and Washington, D. C., a distance of about 496 miles, only nine of which are over Maryland's State roads. To say that Capitol has an unlimited privilege to use Maryland's roads and is therefore being treated on a par with intrastate carriers is to ignore the admonition that "Regulation and commerce among the States both are practical rather than technical conceptions." . . . [Footnote by Justice Frankfurter.]

† Mr. Justice Brandeis' reference to a flat tax was not intended to exclude size or weight taxes, for the Sprout case involved a tax based upon seating capacity. Rather, he was referring to privilege, as distinguished from mileage, taxes.

The potentiality of unfair burdens on interstate commerce was presented sharply in the Sprout case since the tax was levied by a municipality and there were 33 other cities along the route of the interstate carrier. . . . [Footnote by Justice Frankfurter.]

and $580, but since the Maryland tax is not annual, these amounts are not comparable to amounts previously sustained. In order to equate them, information is needed as to the number of years typical motor carriers are likely to operate such busses over Maryland roads. Even taking the assumption of the Maryland Court of Appeals . . . that five years was a fair estimate, the amounts are in excess of any sustained by this Court. Therefore, even if the Court were to accept the formula . . ., the case should be remanded for a finding of the anticipated period of use in order to have some basis of appraising the validity of the amount.

. . . The Court's failure to treat the danger that large privilege taxes will unduly burden interstate commerce—quite apart from excessiveness in terms of State costs—is not unlike its explicit rejection of the requirement that the taxing formula be reasonably related to the purpose which alone justifies the tax. . . . [T]he Court attempts to avoid difficulties through what seems to me to be an exercise in absolutes. These problems involve questions of reasonableness and degree but their determination affects the harmonious functioning of our federal system. I do not believe they can be solved by disregarding the national interest merely because a State tax levied in a particular case does not on its face appear monstrous in amount. . . .

REACHING THE INTERSTATE CARRIER

1. *Compensation for use of highways: potential discrimination, actual exploitation, and the Capitol Greyhound case.* Do the opinions in Capitol Greyhound take adequate account of the potential discrimination in the "compensating" tax? See Barrett, " 'Substance' and 'Form' in the Application of the Commerce Clause to State Taxation," 101 U.Pa.L.Rev. 740 (1953): "All taxes of this character discriminate in favor of the constant user of roads within the state and, in the generality of instances, against the interstate operator whose use of the local roads is apt to be less extensive." Is this problem adequately met by Justice Cardozo's statement in a case sustaining a "moderate" flat tax—quoted in the dissent in Capitol Greyhound—that one "who receives a privilege without limit is not wronged by his own refusal to enjoy it as freely as he may"? Aero Mayflower Transit Co. v. Georgia Public Service Comm'n, 295 U.S. 285 (1935). Compare Brown, "The Open Economy: Mr. Justice Frankfurter and the Position of the Judiciary," 67 Yale L.J. 219 (1957), Selected Essays 1938–62 (1963), 371: "Our own preconstitutional history discloses that the ports and the states astride the trade routes exploited their situation to the disadvantage and displeasure of their less strategically situated neighbors, and that recriminations and reprisals resulted. . . . As through traffic equals, exceeds or predominates over local in any jurisdiction . . . a tax on transport, apportioned with whatever show of fairness one desires, can clearly be imposed at diminishing relative cost to the local taxpayers and voters."

In view of Maryland's strategic location in East Coast traffic, are the Capitol Greyhound references to fair compensation for use of highways persuasive? Compare the reliance on "common knowledge" in perceiving discriminatory probabilities in the Nippert case, p. 696, supra. Is the sustaining of a wide variety of compensation fees, reflected in Capitol Greyhound, related to the Court's tolerance of state regulation of highway use? See South Carolina State Highway Dept. v. Barnwell Bros., chap. 8, p. 629, supra. Does the greater scrutiny in the more recent regulatory cases—as in Bibb v. Navajo Freight Lines, chap. 8, p. 642, supra—suggest the possibility of increased Court control of state fees and taxes on motor vehicles?

2. *Gross receipts taxes on interstate transportation and the Central Greyhound case—Is "fair apportionment" an adequate safeguard?* a. *The background: from permissiveness to prohibition.* In the post-Civil War period, the Court sustained gross receipts taxes on railroads, though the receipts included income from interstate transportation. See, e. g., State Tax on Railway Gross Receipts, 15 Wall. 284 (1873), sustaining a tax of Pennsylvania— a strategically located state—with the statement that, while "a tax upon interstate transportation is invalid," there was no reason to invalidate a tax on "the fruits of such transportation after they have become intermingled with the general property of the carrier." The reasoning of that case was repudiated a few years later, in Philadelphia & So. S. S. Co. v. Pennsylvania, 122 U.S. 326 (1887): looking at "the substance of things, and not mere forms," the Court found no difference between a concededly invalid tax "on transportation" and a tax on the "fares and freights received" therefrom.

b. *Apportioned gross receipts: acceptable compromise?* More recently, however, there have been indications that a tax on gross receipts from transportation, if apportioned to mileage in the state, is permissible, at least where it is part of a general gross receipts tax. For example, in Central Greyhound Lines v. Mealey, 334 U.S. 653 (1948), New York imposed a tax on the bus company's entire gross receipts from transportation between New York City and Buffalo, N.Y., over routes using the highways of New Jersey and Pennsylvania. In invalidating that unapportioned tax, Justice Frankfurter stated: "If New Jersey and Pennsylvania could claim their right to make appropriately apportioned claims against that substantial part of the business of the appellant to which they afford protection, we do not see how on principle and precedent such a claim could be denied. This being so, to allow New York to impose a tax on the gross receipts for the entire mileage—on the 57.47% within New York as well as the 42.53% without—would subject interstate commerce to [an] unfair burden. . . . [T]he tax may constitutionally be sustained on the receipts from the transportation apportioned to the mileage within the State. . . . There is no question as to the fairness" of such an apportionment.

Do you agree that there is "no question as to the fairness"? Could an argument be made for letting New York tax the entire proceeds of the trip between points in the state, and denying New Jersey and Pennsylvania any share in the proceeds? Compare Brown, note 1 supra: "[T]he hazard from even apportioned transportation taxes is that of exploiting geographic position at the cost of the outsider." And note Justice Miller's dissent in the 1873 case (note 2a, supra) that sustained an unapportioned gross receipts tax: "[T]he reluctance of the little state of Rhode Island to give up the tax which she [levied through imposts] on the commerce of her sister states through the harbor of Newport, then the largest importing place in the Union, was the reason that she refused for nearly two years to ratify that instrument. . . . If the state of Pennsylvania, availing herself of her central position across the great line of necessary commercial intercourse between the east and the west, and of the fact that all the ways of land and water carriage must go through her territory, is determined to support her government and pay off her debt by a tax on this commerce, it is of small moment that we say she cannot tax the goods so transported, but may tax every dollar paid for such transportation." The tax, he insisted, was in effect on transportation: "I lay down the broad proposition that by no device or evasion, by no form of statutory words, can a state compel citizens of other states to pay to it a tax, contribution, or toll, for the privilege of having their goods transported through that state by the ordinary channels of commerce."

c. *The Canton Railroad dissent: The inadequacy of apportionment.* See also Canton Railroad Co. v. Rogan, 340 U.S. 511 (1951): The company maintained a marine terminal in Baltimore and operated railroad lines connecting the terminal with major trunk-line railroads; its operating revenue was from switching freight cars from the piers to the railroads, and from storage, wharfage, and other services. Appellant challenged the tax under the Imports-Exports Clause (sec. 1, supra) "insofar as the gross income by which the tax is measured includes revenues derived from the handling of goods in foreign trade." The entire tax was sustained. Exporting and importing "begin and end at water's edge." The tax "is not on the *goods,* but on the *handling* of them at port." If the handling were part of the immune export process, "so would hauling them to or from distant points or perhaps mining them or manufacturing them"; this would "create a zone of tax immunity never before imagined." The Court also rejected a commerce clause claim: "Where transportation is concerned, an apportionment according to mileage within the state is an approved method. Central Greyhound Lines v. Mealey . . .."

Justice Jackson, joined by Justice Frankfurter, submitted an opinion "reserving judgment." He noted: "If the roads to the ports may be obstructed with local regulation and taxes, inland producers may be made to pay tribute to the seaboard for the privilege of exportation, and the longer the road to port, the more localities that may lay burdens on the passing traffic. The evident policy of the Constitution is to avoid these burdens and maintain free and equal access to foreign ports for the inland areas. If the constitutional policy can be avoided by shifting the tax from the exported article itself to some incident such as carriage, unavoidable in the process of exportation, then the policy is a practical nullity." See also Western Maryland Ry. Co. v. Rogan, 340 U.S. 520 (1951), sustaining a tax under the same law levied on an interstate carrier.

d. *The Carter & Weeks majority: Perceiving the risk of exploitation in apportionment?* Compare with Canton Railroad, Joseph v. Carter & Weeks Stevedoring Co., 330 U.S. 442 (1947), invalidating under the commerce clause a New York City excise tax on the gross receipts of the company, engaged wholly within the territorial limits of the city in loading and unloading vessels engaged in interstate and foreign commerce. The Court relied on the invalidation of a similar tax in Puget Sound Stevedoring Co. v. State Tax Commission, 302 U.S. 90 (1937), and stated: "Although state laws do not discriminate against interstate commerce or in actuality or by possibility subject it to the cumulative burden of multiple levies, those laws may be unconstitutional because they burden or interfere with commerce. . . . Stevedoring, we conclude, is essentially a part of the commerce itself and therefore a tax upon its gross receipts or upon the privilege of conducting the business of stevedoring for interstate and foreign commerce, measured by those gross receipts, is invalid. . . . Such a rule . . . has reason to support it in the likelihood that such legislation will flourish more luxuriantly where the

most revenue will come from foreign or interstate commerce. Thus in port
cities and transportation or handling centers, without discrimination against
outstate as compared with local business, larger proportions of necessary revenue could be obtained from the flow of commerce. The avoidance of such
a local toll on the passage of commerce through a locality was one of the
reasons for the adoption of the Commerce Clause." Justice Douglas, joined
by Justice Rutledge, dissented on the application of the commerce clause:
"No other State could tax the same activity. The tax therefore is in its application nothing more than a gross receipts tax apportioned to reach only income derived from activities within the taxing State."

Should the Court have voiced its Carter & Weeks concerns in the other,
"fairly apportioned" gross receipts cases? In the "compensation for highway use" cases, note 1, supra? In the case of the personal property tax measured by apportioned gross receipts, Illinois Central R. Co. v. Minnesota, p.
704, supra? Should it have been sensitive to the exploitation concern in Independent Warehouses, the ad valorem property tax case, sec. 2, p. 697? [1]

3. *The forbidden "privilege" tax and interstate transportation: The
Spector Motor case.* a. Despite the Court's occasional readiness to sustain apportioned gross receipts taxes on interstate carriers, it has invalidated an
economically less significant burden: a tax on an apportioned part of net income. The basis of the holding was a principle extending beyond transportation taxes: the selection of a prohibited "subject" for the tax, despite the
apparently acceptable "measure." Spector Motor Service v. O'Connor, 340
U.S. 602 (1951). Why should the Court enforce a threshold "subject" barrier if the "measure" is sound? Is the rule entirely "formalistic," or are there
substantial justifications for this consistently applied prohibition?

In Spector, an out-of-state trucker engaged exclusively in interstate business successfully challenged a Connecticut tax requiring companies "carrying
on business in this state" to pay an annual excise tax "for the privilege of
carrying on . . . business" within the state. The tax was computed
at a nondiscriminatory 2% rate on that part of Spector's net income attributable to its business activities within Connecticut. The highest state court explicitly stated that the tax did not "rest upon the use of highways"; rather,
the state court called the tax one "upon the franchise of corporations for the
privilege of carrying on or doing business in the state, whether they be domestic or foreign." That characterization was fatal.

Justice Burton's opinion stated: "The objection to its validity does not
rest on a claim that it places an unduly heavy burden on interstate commerce
. . . .. The tax is not levied as compensation for the use of highways or
collected in lieu of an ad valorem property tax. Those bases of taxation have
been disclaimed by the highest court of the taxing State. . . . It serves

---

1. Compare the risk of another variety
of potential exploitation of special
state advantages: severance or processing taxes by a state containing a
great concentration of particular natural resources. Though export taxes
would clearly be unconstitutional,
these processing taxes are typically
sustained, on the theory that the tax is
on production, remote from commerce.
See, e. g., Heisler v. Thomas Colliery
Co., 260 U.S. 245 (1922); and compare

Interstate Oil Pipe Line Co. v. Stone,
337 U.S. 662 (1949), with Michigan-
Wisconsin Pipe Line Co. v. Calvert, 347
U.S. 157 (1957). See also the discussion of "resource profiteers" in Note,
75 Harv.L.Rev. 953, 970 (1962), and
Control of Natural Resources, chap. 8,
p. ——, supra. Compare the problem
of taxes on manufacturing, in the consideration of taxation of sales transactions, p. ——, infra.

no purpose for the State . . . to suggest that, if there were some intra-state commerce involved or if an appropriate tax were imposed as compensation for petitioner's use of the highways, the same sum of money as is at issue here might be collected lawfully from petitioner. Even though the financial burden on interstate commerce might be the same, the question whether a state may validly make interstate commerce pay its way depends first of all upon the constitutional channel through which it attempts to do so. . . .

"The answer in the instant case has been made clear by the courts of Connecticut. It is not a matter of labels. The incidence of the tax provides the answer. . . . The State is not precluded from imposing taxes upon other activities or aspects of this business which, unlike the privilege of doing interstate business, are subject to the sovereign power of the State. Those taxes may be imposed although their payment may come out of the funds derived from petitioner's interstate business, provided the taxes are so imposed that their burden will be reasonably related to the powers of the State and non-discriminatory. . . . In this field there is not only reason but long-established precedent for keeping the federal privilege of carrying on exclusively interstate commerce free from state taxation. To do so gives lateral support to one of the cornerstones of our constitutional law—McCulloch v. Maryland, supra."

b.   Would the tax have been sustained if it had been an apportioned tax "on" net income from the interstate business? See the Northwestern States Portland Cement Co. case, p. 741, infra. Why should the "privilege" incidence invalidate this type of tax? Is it because the tax "subject" implies a state power to exclude from the state the company doing interstate business? Even though the state has not sought to enforce its tax law by any exclusion sanction? Cf. Castle v. Hayes Freight Lines, chap. 8, p. 675, supra. See Note, 75 Harv.L.Rev. 953, 1033 (1962), suggesting that the approval of such a state "privilege" tax "might have broad implications" for determining "the validity of entrance fees, licenses and other state regulations, such as denial of access to state courts." Cf. Western Union Telegraph Co. v. Kansas, 216 U.S. 1 (1910) (unsuccessful state attempt to oust company for failure to pay tax measured by total capital). And note Memphis Natural Gas Co. v. Stone, 335 U.S. 80 (1948), sustaining a "franchise tax" (but not on the "privilege" relied on in the Spector tax) on a company doing only interstate business, justified as compensation for the protection afforded local incidents of interstate commerce—though there was no obvious correlation between the "protection" and the tax amount.[2]

---

2. Compare Railway Express Agency v. Virginia, 347 U.S. 359 (1954), with Railway Express Agency v. Virginia, 358 U.S. 434 (1959). In the first case, the Court invalidated, as a privilege tax, an "annual license tax" imposed, in addition to certain property taxes, on the exclusively interstate business of the Agency. Thereafter, Virginia enacted a new "franchise" tax. In the second case, that tax was sustained: "The new tax is not denominated a license tax laid on the 'privilege of doing business in Virginia'; nor is it 'in addition to the property tax' levied against appellant, nor as a condition precedent to its engaging in interstate commerce in the Commonwealth. The General Assembly has made crystal-clear that the tax is now a franchise tax laid on the intangible property of appellant, and is levied 'in lieu of taxes upon all of its other intangible property and . . . rolling stock.' The measure of the tax is on gross receipts, fairly apportioned, and, as to appellant, is laid only on those 'derived from the transportation within this State of express transported through, into, or out of this State.'" Justice Harlan concurred: "I share the reservations of Mr. Justice Brennan as to the propriety of considering the tax . . . as a property tax.

SECTION 4.   STATE TAXES AND INTERSTATE SALES

GROSS RECEIPTS, SALES, USE, AND NET INCOME TAXES ON INTERSTATE SALES AND RELATED "LOCAL INCIDENTS"

Introduction.   No area of state taxation has provoked more litigation and greater difficulty than that of interstate sales.   Some of the materials in the earlier sections of this chapter have touched on this problem; this section focuses on it more fully.

For many years, the Court prohibited all taxes on gross receipts from interstate sales.   The ban emerged in cases considering taxation of gross receipts from transportation, see sec. 3, supra: as noted there, the Court, after adopting a permissive attitude in the immediate post-Civil War years, turned to condemnation of such levies as "direct burdens on interstate commerce." Philadelphia & So. S. S. Co. v. Pennsylvania, 112 U.S. 326 (1887), p. 710, supra.   That doctrine was applied to gross receipts from sales as well.

A major shift in approach began with Western Live Stock v. Bureau of Revenue, 303 U.S. 250 (1938), infra.   Justice Stone's re-analysis of the cases there was part of his broader campaign against the "direct" - "indirect" terminology.   [See the manifestations of that theme in his decisions in chapters 4 (commerce power), 8 (state regulation), and 10 (intergovernmental immunities).]   He emphasized the danger of multiple tax burdens on interstate businesses, cf. chap. 8, sec. 1, supra; that emphasis loosened the restrictions on gross receipts and other "direct" taxes on commerce, for it tended to sustain taxes which were properly apportioned.   But the "multiple burdens" approach has brought problems of its own, and the Court has not adhered to it consistently.

Consider the following problems, for example: Does the "multiple taxation" criterion refer to the *risk* of multiple burdens: the risk that state B may tax the transaction if state A's tax is sustained?   Or must the taxpayer show an *actual* multiple burden: that state B in fact taxes the transaction which state A is attempting to tax?   Cf., e.g., Central R. Co. v. Pennsylvania, p. 702, supra.   Moreover, is the claim of multiple taxation—actual or potential— avoidable by carving out separable "local incidents" of the interstate transaction?   Though state A and state B may not both impose a tax "on gross receipts" from a sales transaction, may they achieve a similar result through a tax on manufacturing (measured by gross receipts) in state A and a tax on delivery or use (measured by gross sales price) in state B?   And when apportionment is attempted, can the Court adequately supervise the "fairness" of the apportionment?   Though state A and state B both impose taxes which

I find myself unable, however, to distinguish in any constitutional sense the 'in lieu' tax here involved from similar levies the validity of which has been sustained as applied to interstate enterprises . . . ."   Justice Brennan also concurred: "I must admit to some reservations whether the tax at bar can fairly be thought of as a property tax. . . .   To me, the more realistic way of viewing the tax and evaluating its constitutional validity is to take it as what it is in substance, a levy on gross receipts fairly apportionable to the taxing State." Justice Whittaker, joined by Justice Stewart, dissented.

are apportioned, may multiple taxation nevertheless result because states A and B use different "fair" apportionment formulas?

In examining these problems in the materials which follow, consider also the policy underlying the "multiple burdens" approach. Is multiple taxation objectionable simply because local businesses are favored if the interstate business may be taxed more than once for a single transaction? Is the multiple burdens concern justified even where there are no local competitors who may receive preferential treatment? Is it justified, for example, because multiple taxation puts an economic premium on confining business activities to a single state and deters interstate operations in the "open economy"? And should Congress rather than the Court assess the economic impacts of these taxes, and undertake to prescribe a single apportionment formula?

WESTERN LIVE STOCK v. BUREAU OF REVENUE

303 U.S. 250, 58 S.Ct. 546, 82 L.Ed. 823 (1938).

Appeal from the Supreme Court of New Mexico.

Mr. Justice STONE delivered the opinion of the Court. . . .

[New Mexico imposed a 2% privilege tax upon the gross receipts of certain businesses. Newspapers and magazines were taxed on the basis of their sales of advertising space. Appellants published a monthly livestock trade journal in New Mexico. The journal had an interstate circulation, and some of the advertisements were by out-of-state advertisers. The state courts rejected commerce clause objections to the tax.]

. . . . [We] address ourselves to appellants' argument that the present tax infringes the commerce clause because it is measured by gross receipts which are to some extent augmented by appellants' maintenance of an interstate circulation of their magazine.

It was not the purpose of the commerce clause to relieve those engaged in interstate commerce from their just share of state tax burden even though it increases the cost of doing the business. "Even interstate business must pay its way," . . . . and the bare fact that one is carrying on interstate commerce does not relieve him from many forms of state taxation which add to the cost of his business. He is subject to a property tax on the instruments employed in the commerce . . . and if the property devoted to interstate transportation is used both within and without the state a tax fairly apportioned to its use within the state will be sustained. . . . . Net earnings from interstate commerce are subject to income tax, . . . and if the commerce is carried on by a corporation a franchise tax may be imposed, measured by the net income from business done within the state, including such portion of the income derived from interstate commerce as may be justly attributable to business done within the state by a fair method of apportionment. . . .

All of these taxes in one way or another add to the expense of carrying on interstate commerce, and in that sense burden it; but they are not for that reason prohibited. On the other hand, local taxes, measured by gross receipts from interstate commerce, have often been pronounced unconstitutional. The vice characteristic of those which have been held invalid is that they have placed on the commerce burdens of such a nature as to be capable, in point of substance, of being imposed . . . or added to . . . with equal right by every state which the commerce touches, merely because interstate commerce is being done, so that without the protection of the commerce clause it would bear cumulative burdens not imposed on local commerce. . . . The multiplication of state taxes measured by the gross receipts from interstate transactions would spell the destruction of interstate commerce and renew the barriers to interstate trade which it was the object of the commerce clause to remove. . . .

It is for these reasons that a state may not lay a tax measured by the amount of merchandise carried in interstate commerce, . . . or upon the freight earned by its carriage. . . . Taxation measured by gross receipts from interstate commerce has been sustained when fairly apportioned to the commerce carried on within the taxing state, . . . and in other cases has been rejected only because the apportionment was found to be inadequate or unfair. . . . Whether the tax was sustained as a fair means of measuring a local privilege or franchise, . . . or as a method of arriving at the fair measure of a tax substituted for local property taxes, . . . it is a practical way of laying upon the commerce its share of the local tax burden without subjecting it to multiple taxation not borne by local commerce and to which it would be subject if gross receipts, unapportioned, could be made the measure of a tax laid in every state where the commerce is carried on. A tax on gross receipts from tolls for the use by interstate trains of tracks lying wholly within the taxing state is valid, . . . although a like tax on gross receipts from the rental of railroad cars used in interstate commerce both within and without the taxing state is invalid. . . . In the one case the tax reaches only that part of the commerce carried on within the taxing state; in the other it extends to the commerce carried on without the state boundaries, and, if valid, could be similarly laid in every other state in which the business is conducted.

In the present case the tax is, in form and substance, an excise conditioned on the carrying on of a local business, that of providing and selling advertising space in a published journal, which is sold to and paid for by subscribers, some of whom receive it in interstate commerce. The price at which the advertising is sold is made the measure of the tax. This Court has sustained a similar tax said to be on the privilege of manufacturing, measured by the total gross receipts from sales of the manufactured goods both intrastate and interstate. American Manufacturing Co. v. St. Louis [250 U.S. 459 (1919)]. The actual sales prices which measured the tax were taken to be no more than the measure of the value of the goods manufactured, and so an appropriate measure of the value of the privilege, the taxation of which was deferred until the goods were sold. . . .

Viewed only as authority, American Manufacturing Co. v. St. Louis, supra, would seem decisive of the present case. But we think the tax assailed here finds support in reason, and in the practical needs of a taxing system which, under constitutional limitations, must accommodate itself to the double demand that interstate business shall pay its way, and that at the same time it shall not be burdened with cumulative exactions which are not similarly laid on local business.

. . . [T]he business of preparing, printing and publishing magazine advertising is peculiarly local and distinct from its circulation whether or not that circulation be interstate commerce. . . . No one would doubt that the tax on the privilege would be valid if it were measured by the amount of advertising space sold. . . . Selling price, taken as a measure of value whose accuracy appellants do not challenge, is for all practical purposes a convenient means of arriving at an equitable measure of the burden which may be imposed on an admittedly taxable subject matter. Unlike the measure of the tax sustained in American Manufacturing Co. v. St. Louis, supra, it does not embrace the purchase price (here the magazine subscription price) of the articles shipped in interstate commerce. So far as the advertising rates reflect a value attributable to the maintenance of a circulation of the magazine interstate, we think the burden on the interstate business is too remote and too attenuated to call for a rigidly logical application of the doctrine that gross receipts from interstate commerce may not be made the measure of a tax. . . . Practical rather than logical distinctions must be sought. . . .

Here it is perhaps enough that the privilege taxed is of a type which has been regarded as so separate and distinct from interstate transportation as to admit of different treatment for purposes of taxation, . . . and that the value of the privilege is fairly measured by the receipts. The tax is not invalid because the value is enhanced by appellant's circulation of their journal interstate any more than property taxes on railroads are invalid because property value is increased by the circumstance that the railroads do an interstate business.

But there is an added reason why we think the tax is not subject to the objection which has been leveled at taxes laid upon gross receipts derived from interstate communication or transportation of goods. So far as the value contributed to appellants' New Mexico business by circulation of the magazine interstate is taxed, it cannot again be taxed elsewhere any more than the value of railroad property taxed locally. The tax is not one which in form or substance can be repeated by other states in such manner as to lay an added burden on the interstate distribution of the magazine. . . . All the events upon which the tax is conditioned—the preparation, printing and publication of the advertising matter, and the receipt of the sums paid for it— occur in New Mexico and not elsewhere. All are beyond any control and taxing power which, without the commerce clause, those states could exert through its dominion over the distribution of the magazine or its subscribers. The dangers which may ensue from the imposition of a tax measured by gross receipts derived directly from interstate commerce are absent.

In this and other ways the case differs from Fisher's Blend Station v. State Tax Comm'n, [297 U.S. 650 (1936)], on which appellants rely. There the exaction was a privilege tax laid upon the occupation of broadcasting, . . . and was measured by the gross receipts derived from that commerce. If broadcasting could be taxed, so also could reception. . . . In that event a cumulative tax burden would be imposed on interstate communication such as might ensue if gross receipts from interstate transportation could be taxed. . . .

Affirmed.

Mr. Justice McREYNOLDS and Mr. Justice BUTLER are of opinion that the judgment should be reversed.

SOME EARLY APPLICATIONS OF THE MULTIPLE BURDENS APPROACH

1. *Adams Mfg. Co. v. Storen, 304 U.S. 307 (1938):* Shortly after Western Live Stock, the Court relied on it to invalidate a 1% Indiana tax on an Indiana manufacturer's gross receipts from products shipped on orders taken from buyers in other states and foreign countries, subject to approval at the Indiana factory. Justice Roberts found an unconstitutional "tax upon gross receipts from commerce. The vice . . . . is that the tax includes in its measure, without apportionment, receipts derived from activities in interstate commerce, and that the exaction is of such a character that if lawful it may in substance be laid to the fullest extent by states in which the goods are sold as well as those in which they are manufactured. Interstate commerce would thus be subjected to the risk of a double tax burden to which intrastate commerce is not exposed." The Court rejected the state's reliance on American Manufacturing Co. v. St. Louis, 250 U.S. 459 (1919), discussed in Western Live Stock, supra. That tax was "upon the privilege of manufacturing" and "it was permissible to measure the tax by the sales price of the goods produced." But that did not authorize a tax which "reaches indiscriminately and without apportionment the gross compensation for both interstate commerce and intrastate activities."

Justice Black's dissent objected to the suggestion that Indiana could impose an apportioned tax: "If such power of apportionment or allocation exists at all, . . . the only repository . . . is not Indiana, not the Judiciary—but the National Congress." Moreover, he objected to invalidation of the tax on the basis of *"merely possible future unfair burdens.* Here the record does not indicate any charge or proof of an existing extraordinary, unfair or multiple tax burden. . . . [A]n unjust and unfair burden is actually imposed upon intrastate business, because of an apprehension of possible future injury to interstate commerce." Is the tax approved in the American Manufacturing case, distinguished in the majority opinion, free from the "multiple burdens" risk?

2. *Gwin, White & Prince v. Henneford, 305 U.S. 434 (1939):* One year later, Justice Stone used the multiple burdens test to invalidate a Washington "business activities" tax of 1% of the gross income, as applied to a Washington company engaged in marketing, in other states, apples and pears grown in Washington and Oregon. Justice Stone rejected the claim that the tax was on the "local business" of appellant's Washington activities promoting interstate marketing: "Here the tax . . . . is not apportioned to its activities within the state. If Washington is free to exact such a tax, other states to which the commerce extends may, with equal right, lay a tax similarly measured for the privilege of conducting within their respective territorial limits the activities there which contribute to the service. The present tax, though nominally local, thus in its practical operation discriminates against interstate commerce, since it imposes upon it, merely because interstate commerce is being done, the risk of a multiple burden to which local commerce is not exposed. . . . Unlawfulness of the burden depends upon its nature measured in terms of its capacity to obstruct interstate commerce, and not on the contingency that some other state may first have subjected the commerce to a like burden."

Justice Black again objected to decisions based on "conjectured 'multiple taxation'." He added: "No other State in which appellant's agents perform sales services has imposed a similar tax upon appellant measured by any part of its gross receipts. Such an eventuality—if it should occur—is given the title of 'multiple taxation.' . . . Since multiple taxation can only result if another State passes a valid, non-discriminatory tax law, two non-discriminatory state laws when combined become invalid and discriminatory under the Commerce Clause, as a result of the judgment here. . . . Only a comprehensive survey and investigation of the entire national economy—which Congress alone has power and facilities to make—can indicate the need for, as well as justify, restricting the taxing power of a State so as to provide against conjectured taxation by more than one State on identical income. . . . Unless we presuppose that the conjectured tax on appellant's gross income by another State would be valid, appellant has not even shown a hypothetical possibility of injury. I would return to the rule that—except for state acts designed to impose discriminatory burdens on interstate commerce because it *is* interstate—Congress alone must determine how far [commerce] . . . shall be free and untrammelled, how far it shall be burdened by duties and imposts, and how far it shall be prohibited." [1]

3. *The multiple burdens test and sales taxes on consumers: McGoldrick v. Berwind-White Coal Mining Co., 309 U.S. 33 (1940): a. The Stone opinion.* Was the risk of multiple taxation adequately perceived by Justice Stone in this case—one year after Gwin, White, two years after Western Live Stock? New York City imposed a "tax upon purchasers for consumption of tangible personal property." The tax was 2% "upon the amount of the receipts from every sale" in the City; and "sale" was defined as "any transfer of title or possession." The law directed the seller to collect the tax to be paid over to the City. Berwind-White resisted collection of the tax on sales to New York City consumers of coal mined by it in Pennsylvania. The Company maintained a sales office in New York. The sales contracts were entered into there. Its coal moved by rail from the Pennsylvania mines to New Jersey docks, and from there by barge to the point of delivery in the City. Justice Stone noted that the "ultimate burden" of the tax was on the buyer, measured by sale price, and that the tax was "conditioned upon events occurring within" New York. He concluded that the tax was constitutional:

1. In McCarroll v. Dixie Greyhound Lines, 309 U.S. 176 (1940), holding invalid an Arkansas tax on gasoline in excess of a specified amount carried in motor vehicle tanks to be used as fuel by such vehicles, Justice Black voiced similar objections: "Judicial control of national commerce—unlike legislative regulation—must from inherent limitations of the judicial process treat the subject by the hit and miss method of deciding single local controversies upon evidence and information limited by the narrow rules of litigation. Spasmodic and unrelated instances of litigation cannot afford an adequate basis for the creation of integrated national rules which alone can afford that full protection for interstate commerce intended by the Constitution. We would, therefore, leave the questions raised by the Arkansas tax for consideration of Congress in a nation-wide survey of the constantly increasing barriers to trade among the States." Justices Frankfurter and Douglas joined in his dissent.

Compare the different conclusion drawn from similar premises in Justice Frankfurter's dissent in the Northwestern States Portland Cement case in 1959, infra. Assuming that Congress *is* more competent to assess the problem, what should the Court do in the absence of congressional guidance: let the challenged tax stand, or invalidate it?

"Forms of state taxation whose tendency is to prohibit the commerce or place it at a disadvantage as compared or in competition with intrastate commerce and any state tax which discriminates against the commerce, are familiar examples of the exercise of state taxing power in an unconstitutional manner, because of its obvious regulatory effect upon commerce between the states.*

"But it was not the purpose of the commerce clause to relieve those engaged in interstate commerce of their just share of state tax burdens, merely because an incidental or consequential effect of the tax is an increase in the cost of doing business, Western Live Stock v. Bureau, 303 U.S. 250, 254. Not all state taxation is to be condemned because, in some manner, it has an effect upon commerce between the states, and there are many forms of tax whose burdens, when distributed through the play of economic forces, affect interstate commerce, which nevertheless fall short of the regulation of the commerce which the Constitution leaves to Congress. . . .

"Certain types of tax may, if permitted at all, so readily be made the instrument of impeding or destroying interstate commerce as plainly to call for their condemnation as forbidden regulations. Such are the taxes already noted which are aimed at or discriminate against the commerce or impose a levy for the privilege of doing it, or tax interstate transportation or communication or their gross earnings, or levy an exaction on merchandise in the course of its interstate journey. . . .

"The present tax as applied to respondent is without the possibility of such consequences. Equality is its theme, cf. Henneford v. Silas Mason Co., 300 U.S. 577, 583. It does not aim at or discriminate against interstate commerce. It is laid upon every purchaser, within the state, of goods for consumption, regardless of whether they have been transported in interstate commerce. Its only relation to the commerce arises from the fact that immediately preceding transfer of possession to the purchaser within the state, which is the taxable event regardless of the time and place of passing title, the merchandise has been transported in interstate commerce and brought to its journey's end. Such a tax has no different effect upon interstate commerce than a tax on the 'use' of property which has just been moved in interstate commerce, . . . or the familiar property tax on goods by the state of destination at the conclusion of their interstate journey. . . .

"We are unable to say that the present tax, laid generally upon all sales to consumers within the state, subjects the commerce involved where the goods

* Despite mechanical or artificial distinctions sometimes taken between the taxes deemed permissible and those condemned, the decisions appear to be predicated on a practical judgment as to the likelihood of the tax being used to place interstate commerce at a competitive disadvantage. . . . Privilege taxes requiring a percentage of the gross receipts from interstate transportation or from other activities in carrying on the movement of that commerce, which if sustained, could be imposed wherever the interstate activity occurs, have been struck down for similar reasons. . . . Fixed-sum license fees, regardless of the amount, for the privilege of carrying on the commerce, have been thought likely to be used to overburden the interstate commerce . . . .. Taxation of articles in course of their movement in interstate commerce is similarly foreclosed. . . . Lying back of these decisions is the recognized danger that, to the extent that the burden falls on economic interests without the state, it is not likely to be alleviated by those political restraints which are normally exerted on legislation where it affects adversely interests within the state. . . ." [Footnote by Justice Stone. Cf. his footnote in the Barnwell Bros. case, chap. 8, p. 629, supra.]

sold are brought from other states, to any greater burden or affects it more, in any economic or practical way, whether the purchase order or contract precedes or follows the interstate shipment.   Since the tax applies only if a sale is made, and in either case the object of interstate shipment is a sale at destination, the deterrent effect of the tax would seem to be the same on both.   Restriction of the scope of the commerce clause so as to prevent recourse to it as a means of curtailing state taxing power seems as salutary in the one case as in the other.   .   .   .

"It is also urged that the conclusion which we reach is inconsistent with the long line of decisions of this Court following Robbins v. Shelby County Taxing District, 120 U.S. 489, which have held invalid license taxes to the extent that they have sought to tax the occupation of soliciting orders for the purchase of goods to be shipped into the taxing state.   .   .   .   It is enough for present purposes that the rule of Robbins v. Shelby County Taxing District, supra, has been narrowly limited to fixed-sum licenses taxes imposed on the business of soliciting orders for the purchase of goods to be shipped interstate,   .   .   .   and that the actual and potential effect on the commerce of such a tax is wholly wanting in the present case.

"Finally, it is said that the vice of the present tax is that it is measured by the gross receipts from interstate commerce and thus in effect reaches for taxation the commerce carried on both within and without the taxing state.   Adams Manufacturing Co. v. Storen, 304 U.S. 307; Gwin, White & Prince v. Henneford, [305 U.S. 434]; cf. Western Live Stock v. Bureau, [303 U.S. 250].   [Such a tax] if sustained would exact tribute for the commerce carried on beyond the boundaries of the taxing state, and would leave each state through which the commerce passes free to subject it to a like burden not borne by intrastate commerce.   .   .   .

"The rationale of the Adams Manufacturing Co. case does not call for condemnation of the present tax.   Here the tax is conditioned upon a local activity, delivery of goods within the state upon their purchase for consumption.   It is an activity which apart from its effect on the commerce, is subject to the state taxing power.   The effect of the tax, even though measured by the sales price, as has been shown, neither discriminates against nor obstructs interstate commerce more than numerous other state taxes which have repeatedly been sustained as involving no prohibited regulation of interstate commerce."

b.   *The adequacy of the Stone distinctions: The Hughes dissent.*   Do you agree with Justice Stone's reasons for distinguishing Adams Manufacturing and the other multiple burdens cases of 1938–1940, supra?   Compare the arguments in the dissenting opinion of Chief Justice Hughes, joined by Justices McReynolds and Roberts:

"The tax on the gross receipts of the seller from these sales was manifestly an imposition upon the sales themselves.   Whether the tax be small or large, it is plainly to the extent of it a burden upon interstate commerce; and as it is imposed immediately upon the gross receipts from that commerce, it is a direct burden.   .   .   .

"How then can the laying of such a burden upon interstate commerce be justified?   It is urged that there is a taxable event within the State.   [But] the delivery is but the necessary performance of the contract of sale.   Like the shipment from the mines, it is an integral part of the interstate transaction. It is said that title to the coal passes to the purchaser on delivery. But the place where the title passes has not been regarded as the test of the interstate character of a sale. . . . Moreover, even if it were possible to sustain a state tax by reason of such delivery within the State, there would still be no ground for sustaining a tax upon the whole of the interstate transaction of which the delivery is only a part, as in the case of a tax upon the entire gross receipts. . . .

"The ground most strongly asserted for sustaining the tax in the present case is that it is non-discriminatory. But does it follow that a State may lay a direct tax upon interstate commerce because it is free to tax its own commerce in a similar way? . . . It would seem to be extraordinary if a State could escape the restriction against direct impositions upon interstate commerce by first laying exactions upon its own trade and then insisting that in order to make its local policy completely effective it must be allowed to lay similar exactions upon interstate trade. . . . Moreover, it may or may not be in the interest of the State to promote domestic trade in a given commodity. The State may seek by its taxing scheme to restrict such trade and the mere equivalency of a tax upon domestic business would not prevent the injurious effect upon interstate transactions. . . .

"But petitioner has insisted that in the present case there is no danger of multiple taxation in that New York puts its tax upon an event which cannot occur in any other State. Of course the delivery of the coal in New York is an event which cannot occur in another State. Just as New York cannot tax the shipment of coal from the mines in Pennsylvania or the transshipment of the coal in New Jersey, so neither Pennsylvania nor New Jersey can tax the delivery in New York. Petitioner's argument misses the point as to the danger of multiple taxation in relation to interstate commerce. The shipment, the transshipment and the delivery of the coal are but parts of a unitary interstate transaction. They are integral parts of an interstate sale. If, because of the delivery in New York, that State can tax the gross receipts from the sale, why cannot Pennsylvania by reason of the shipment of the coal in that State tax the gross receipts there? That would not be difficult, as the seller in a Pennsylvania corporation and in fact in many, if not in most instances, the purchase price of the goods shipped to New York is there received. The point is not that delivery in New York is an event which cannot be taxed by other States, but that the authority of New York to impose a tax on that delivery cannot properly be recognized without also recognizing the authority of other States to tax the parts of the interstate transaction which take place within their borders. If New York can tax the delivery, Pennsylvania can tax the shipment, and New Jersey the transshipment. And the latter States, respectively, would be as much entitled to tax the gross receipts from the sales as would New York. Even if it were assumed that the gross receipts from the interstate sales could be apportioned so that each State could tax such portion of the receipts as could be deemed to relate to the part of the transaction within its territory, still this would not help New York here, as there has been no attempt at apportionment. The taxation of the gross receipts in New York, on any appropriate view of what pertains to the interstate sales, would seem clearly to involve the danger of multiple taxation to which we have adverted in recent decisions. . . .

"The tax as here applied is open to the same objections as a tariff upon the entrance of the coal into the State of New York, or a state tax upon the privilege of doing an interstate business, and in my view it cannot be sustained without abandoning principles long established and a host of precedents soundly based."

4. *Separable "local incidents" of interstate sales transactions after Berwind-White: McLeod v. Dilworth Co., 332 U.S. 327 (1944):* a. After Berwind-White, there were a number of unsuccessful attempts to extend its "local incident" rationale to other contexts. In the McLeod case, for example, Arkansas levied a tax on the sale of goods by a Tennessee corporation having no office, plant, or other place of business within Arkansas. Orders were telephoned by travelling salesmen in Arkansas to the home office in Tennessee, and all orders were accepted in Tennessee. On approval, all goods were shipped from Tennessee, title passing on delivery of the goods to the carrier in Memphis. The Court affirmed a judgment holding that the Commerce Clause precluded the imposition of a sales tax by the state of destination on such transactions. The Court distinguished Berwind-White on the ground that in that case the corporation maintained its sales offices in New York City, took its contracts there, and made actual delivery there, so that in law and fact the sale sought to be taxed took place in New York City. On the other hand, the sale sought to be taxed in the instant case was consummated without the taxing state, and "for Arkansas to impose a tax on such transactions would be to project its powers beyond its boundaries and to tax an interstate transaction."

Justice Douglas, joined by Justices Black and Murphy, dissented, insisting that the decision "marks a retreat from the philosophy of the Berwind-White case." There was "a taxable event" in Arkansas, and there was "no showing that Tennessee was exacting from these vendors a tax on these same transactions or that Arkansas discriminated against them."

b. Recall also that in Nippert v. Richmond, 327 U.S. 416 (1946), p. 696, supra, the Court rejected the contention that Berwind-White had in effect overruled the Robbins line of "drummer" cases. In Nippert, the Court invalidated a local tax on solicitors and explained that the "local incidents upon which the tax in the Berwind-White case was based" are important chiefly in a "due process" sense—i.e., whether enough takes place within a state to justify its jurisdiction to tax. "Local incidents," however, are not enough to determine the interstate commerce question: "For the situation is difficult to think of in which some incident of an interstate transaction taking place within a State could not be segregated by an act of mental gymnastics and made the fulcrum of the tax."

USE TAXES: "EQUALITY" OR "PROTECTIVE TARIFF"?

1. *The Silas Mason case and "labels."* a. In the Berwind-White case, Justice Stone's defense of the New York City consumers sales tax relied in part on the "equality" argument of Henneford v. Silas Mason Co., 300 U.S. 577 (1937). That case (noted briefly earlier, with the materials on Baldwin v. Seelig, chap. 8, p. 649) was decided a year before Western Live Stock, at a time when it was still assumed that the state of destination in an interstate sales transaction could not impose sales and gross receipts taxes. The validation of use taxes in that 1937 decision has been a lasting one, and use taxes are permissible in a number of situations in which the commerce

clause forbids a sales tax, e. g., McLeod v. Dilworth Co., supra.   Consider the justifications offered in Silas Mason; and consider the justifications for adhering to that result after Western Live Stock.

b.   The Silas Mason case sustained a state tax on "the use of chattels" as applied to goods purchased in other states and used in Washington.   The taxpayers were contractors building a dam; they were taxed on machinery and supplies bought at retail in other states.   A Washington law imposed a 2% tax on retail sales in Washington; another section imposed a "compensating tax" of 2% for the "privilege of using" in the state goods bought at retail, but the use tax was inapplicable to any article which had already been subjected to a sales or use tax of at least 2%.   (For articles previously taxed at less than 2%, there was a partial exemption from the use tax.)   Justice Cardozo's opinion sustaining the tax described it as follows:

"The plan embodied in these provisions is neither hidden nor uncertain. . . .   [A] use tax is always payable where the user has acquired property by retail purchase in or from another state, unless he has paid a sales or use tax elsewhere before bringing it to Washington. . . .   The practical effect of a system thus conditioned is readily perceived.   One of its effects must be that retail sellers in Washington will be helped to compete upon terms of equality with retail dealers in other states who are exempt from a sales tax or any corresponding burden.   Another effect, or at least another tendency, must be to avoid the likelihood of a drain upon the revenues of the state, buyers being no longer tempted to place their orders in other states in the effort to escape payment of the tax on local sales.   Do these consequences, which must have been foreseen, necessitate a holding that the tax upon the use is either a tax upon the operations of interstate commerce or a discrimination against such commerce obstructing or burdening it unlawfully?"

Justice Cardozo found no valid objection to the subject or the measure of the tax.   As to the subject, this was a tax "upon the privilege of use after commerce is at an end," not a tax on commerce itself.   He found a similarity to property taxes on articles brought into the state.   He noted, however, that "a use so closely connected with delivery as to be in substance a part thereof might be subject to the same objection that would be applicable to a tax upon the sale itself."   Nor was the measure of the tax such as "to hamper" or "discriminate against" interstate commerce: "Equality is the theme that runs through all sections of the statute. . . .   When the account is made up, the stranger from afar is subject to no greater burdens as a consequence of ownership than the dweller within the gates.   The one pays upon one activity or incident, and the other upon another, but the sum is the same when the reckoning is closed.   Equality exists when the chattel subjected to the use tax is bought in another state and then carried into Washington.   It exists when the imported chattel is shipped from the state of origin under an order received directly from the state of destination.   In each situation the burden borne by the owner is balanced by an equal burden where the sale is strictly local. . . .

"We are told that a tax upon the use, even though not unlawful by force of its effects alone, is vitiated by the motives that led to its adoption.   These motives cause it to be stigmatized as equivalent to a protective tariff.   But motives alone will seldom, if ever, invalidate a tax that apart from its motives would be recognized as lawful. . . .   Least of all will they be permitted to accomplish that result when equality and not preference is the end to be achieved.   Catch words and labels, such as the words protective tariff, are subject to the dangers that lurk in metaphors and symbols, and must be watched with circumspection lest they put us off our guard.   A tariff, whether protective or for revenue, burdens the very act of importation, and if laid by a state upon its commerce with another is equally unlawful whether protection or revenue is the motive back of it.   But a tax upon use, or, what is equivalent for present purposes, a tax upon property after importation is over, is not a clog upon the process of importation at all, any more than a tax upon the income or profits of a business.   .   .   .   Yet a word of caution should be added here to avoid the chance of misconception.   We have not meant to imply by anything said in this opinion that allowance of a credit for other taxes paid to Washington made it mandatory that there should be a like allowance for taxes paid to other states.   A state, for many purposes, is to be reckoned as a self-contained unit, which may frame its own system of burdens and exemptions without heeding systems elsewhere.   If there are limits to that power, there is no need to mark them now.   It will be time enough to mark them when a taxpayer paying in the state of origin is compelled to pay again in the state of destination." [1]

c.   Recall Justice Cardozo's opinion two years earlier, in Baldwin v. Seelig, 294 U.S. 511 (1935), chap. 8, p. 649, supra, invalidating New York's attempt to apply its milk price regulations to local sales of Vermont-produced milk.   Are the Baldwin and Silas Mason situations sufficiently different to justify the condemnation in Baldwin, as a "protective tariff," and the approval in Silas Mason, as "equality"?   Was Justice Cardozo's criticism of such "catch words and labels" applicable to his own opinions in these cases?   Recall the question raised about the Baldwin case, supra.   Are the cases sufficiently distinguishable because Washington's tax cancelled only the advantage the out-of-state seller had because he was not subject to a sales tax, while New York's scheme cancelled all of the advantages the Vermont seller had because of lower costs of production—taxes as well as all other costs?   Washington's plan, in other words, still permitted some price com-

---

1.   For a successful attack on a use tax scheme as discriminatory under the commerce clause, see Halliburton Oil Well Cementing Co. v. Reily, 373 U.S. 64 (1963).   The Court stated that the Silas Mason case compelled an "inescapable" conclusion: "equal treatment for in-state and out-of-state taxpayers similarly situated is the condition precedent for a valid use tax on goods imported from out-of-state."   In Halliburton, the Court perceived unequal tax bases for in-state and out-of-state manufacturers-users of oil well servicing equipment, under the Louisiana sales-use tax pattern: even though the inequality might have been "an accident of statutory drafting," the "economic effects" were unacceptable.   Justice Brennan, concurring, thought that the result did not "flow from any duty upon the States to ensure absolute equality of economic burden as between sales and use taxpayers."   Even in Silas Mason, he pointed out, "the out-of-state use taxpayer is likely ultimately to incur a heavier burden than his in-state counterpart, the sales taxpayer.   Such a disparity may result, though the rate of taxation upon the two is identical, because the in-state seller is somewhat likelier to absorb some part of the sales-tax burden than is the out-of-state seller to absorb the burden of the use tax which his customer eventually must pay.   .   .   .   And we have also intimated   .   .   .   that a State may not be constitutionally obliged to credit the amount of sales taxes paid in other States against the use tax it imposes.   .   .   .   Nevertheless, if the Constitution does not mandate absolute equality of treatment   .   .   ., it assuredly does forbid discriminatory treatment by the States."   Justice Clark, joined by Justice Black, dissented, insisting that all "persons and like property similarly situated are   .   .   .   given identical treatment."

petition; New York's did not. But is the free trade ideal—so eloquently described by Justice Cardozo in Baldwin—adequately satisfied by a finding that at least *some* price competition remains in the consuming market?

Would the Washington use tax be subject to a multiple burdens attack if it did not contain the credit for sales taxes paid elsewhere? Could the tax scheme in Silas Mason have been attacked on a showing that the state of origin, though lacking a sales tax, imposed equivalent taxes, under other labels, on manufacturers, sellers or buyers?

2. *The "distinction" between sales and use taxes.* In McLeod v. Dilworth, p. 723, supra, where the Court distinguished Berwind-White in invalidating an Arkansas sales tax, the state also argued that the tax should be sustained because "Arkansas could have levied a tax of the same amount on the use of these goods." The Court rejected that defense: Arkansas had levied a sales tax; though a sales tax and a use tax "in many instances may bring about the same result," they are "different in conception" and "may have to justify themselves on different constitutional grounds." The Arkansas sales tax, unlike a use tax, involved "an assumption of power . . . which the Commerce Clause was meant to end." The Court added: "Though sales and use taxes may secure the same revenues and serve complementary purposes, they are . . . taxes on different transactions and for different opportunities afforded by a State." The dissenters insisted that a use tax and a sales tax "applied at the very end of the transaction have precisely the same economic incidence. Their effect on interstate commerce is identical."

3. *Constitutional limits on the use tax device.* a. *The wider leeway to use taxes.* In a number of decisions, the Court has reaffirmed its readiness to give wider leeway to use than to sales taxes, and has permitted states to impose the collection duty on the out-of-state seller. See, e. g., Nelson v. Sears Roebuck & Co., 312 U.S. 359 (1941) (out-of-state company established local retail stores, where orders for mail order purchases were also accepted; company compelled to collect use taxes on all sales, including mail order ones, since taxing state might rightly assume that mail-order business was aided by retail business); General Trading Co. v. Tax Commission, 322 U.S. 335 (1944) (company had no place of business in taxing state; all orders solicited by travelling salesmen, with shipments from out-of-state; use tax collection obligation of seller nevertheless sustained: "To make the distributor the tax collector for the State is a familiar and sanctioned device."). See Powell, "Sales and Use Taxes: Collection from Absentee Vendors," 57 Harv. L.Rev. 1086 (1944).

b. *The emergence of limits.* But there are limitations—arising from the due process clause if not the commerce clause—on imposing the collection duty on the out-of-state seller.[2] In Miller Bros. v. Maryland, 347 U.S. 340 (1954), Maryland sought to compel a Wilmington, Delaware, store to collect the use tax on goods sold to Maryland customers. Miller only made sales at its store; it accepted no mail or telephone orders. Maryland customers took their purchases with them or had them delivered by truck. Maryland seized Miller's delivery truck for failure to collect the use tax (amounting to $240 in over four years). The Court reversed, in a 5 to 4 decision. The Court stated that "due process requires some definite link, some minimum connec-

---

2. See also the successful attack on a use-sales tax scheme as discriminatory under the commerce clause, in Halliburton Oil Well Cementing Co. v. Reily, 373 U.S. 64 (1963), footnote 1 supra.

tion, between a state and the person, property or transaction sought to be taxed." Justice Jackson noted that Miller could not have been subjected to a sales tax, in view of the Dilworth case, supra, and concluded that Maryland could not make the same sales a basis for imposing liability on the seller for the Maryland residents' use taxes: "It would be a strange law that would make [Miller] more vulnerable to liability for another's tax than to a tax on itself." (Is it so "strange," in view of the "distinction" explained in Dilworth, note 2, supra?)

Justice Jackson's opinion in Miller noted that he had dissented in General Trading, note 3a, supra. In any event, he insisted, General Trading was distinguishable: there had been "active and aggressive," "continuous" local solicitation of sales in that case, not simply Miller's "occasional deliveries," with "no invasion or exploitation of the Maryland consumer market." He concluded, without reaching the commerce issue, that the tax-collecting burden "cannot be shifted to a foreign merchant in the absence of some jurisdictional basis not present here." Justice Douglas, joined by Chief Justice Warren and Justices Black and Douglas, dissented, relying on "the general principles" of General Trading. Compare Scripto, Inc. v. Carson, 362 U.S. 207 (1960), sustaining a use tax collection obligation in reliance on General Trading though the out-of-state seller did not employ full-time local solicitors, and though the part-time salesmen were called "independent contractors." Justice Clark found a sufficient "nexus" to satisfy the Miller Bros. standard in the "continuous solicitation" by the ten part-time salesmen. Justice Whittaker dissented, relying on commerce as well as due process grounds and citing Dilworth as well as the Miller Bros. case.

c. *Limits and National Bellas Hess.* In National Bellas Hess v. Department of Revenue, 386 U.S. 753 (1967), a divided Court sustained due process and commerce clause objections to the application of the Illinois use tax to a Missouri mail order seller. All of the seller's contacts with Illinois were via the mail or common carrier. To sustain the imposition of the use tax collection duty in this situation, Justice Stewart's majority opinion insisted, the Court "would have to repudiate totally the sharp distinction" in past decisions "between mail order sellers with retail outlets, solicitors, or property within a State, and those who do no more than communicate with customers in the State by mail or common carrier as part of a general interstate business." This "basic distinction," he concluded, was "a valid one, and we decline to obliterate it." To uphold state power here, he commented, would produce impediments to interstate business "neither imaginary nor remote": "The many variations in rates of tax, in allowable exemptions, and in administrative and record-keeping requirements could entangle National's interstate business in a virtual welter of complicated obligations to local jurisdictions with no legitimate claim to impose 'a fair share of the cost of local government.' The very purpose of the Commerce Clause was to ensure a national economy free from such unjustifiable local entanglements."

Justice Fortas, joined by Justices Black and Douglas, dissented: "There should be no doubt that this large-scale, systematic, continuous solicitation and exploitation of the Illinois consumer market is a sufficient 'nexus' to require Bellas Hess to collect from Illinois customers and to remit the use tax, especially when coupled with the use of the credit resources of residents of Illinois, dependent as that mechanism is upon the State's banking and credit institutions. . . . To excuse Bellas Hess from this obligation is to burden and penalize retailers located in Illinois who must collect the sales tax from their customers." He did not think that the Scripto case was "meaningfully distinguishable." Nor did "the mechanics of compliance" impose an undue burden: the majority's fear that they would "entangle" a seller "vastly underestimates the skill of contemporary man and his machines."

FREEMAN v. HEWIT: TEMPORARY ABANDONMENT OF THE MULTIPLE BURDENS APPROACH?

After several years of adherence to the multiple burdens analysis—despite the differences as to application and the flourishing of the use tax device—the Court's opinion in Freeman v. Hewit, 329 U.S. 249 (1946), came as something of a surprise. The tax invalidated presumably would have fallen under the Western Live Stock-Adams Mfg. Co. standard; but the opinion talked in pre-1938 "direct burden" terms. The case did not, however, signify the end of multiple taxation talk; that language has continued to appear in the opinions. Freeman v. Hewit is worth noting before turning to the more recent gross receipts and sales tax cases, for it reveals the continued vitality of an older doctrinal strain—see, e. g., Justice Goldberg's dissent in the 1964 General Motors case, p. 733, infra—and it contained a provocative concurring opinion.

a. In Freeman, the Indiana Gross Income Tax Act, see Adams Mfg. Co. v. Storen, p. 718, supra, was applied to gross receipts from the sale of stock by an Indiana stockholder. The stock was sold through brokers, the sale was consummated on the New York Stock Exchange, and the proceeds were received in Indiana. Justice Frankfurter's majority opinion stated that burdens on commerce imposed by police regulations may survive more easily than a tax:

"[R]evenue serves as well no matter what its source. To deny to a State a particular source of income because it taxes the very process of interstate commerce does not impose a crippling limitation on a State's ability to carry on its local function. Moreover, the burden on interstate commerce involved in a direct tax upon it is inherently greater, certainly less uncertain in its consequences, than results from the usual police regulations. The power to tax is a dominant power over commerce. Because the greater or more threatening burden of a direct tax on commerce is coupled with the lesser need to a State of a particular source of revenue, attempts at such taxation have always been more carefully scrutinized and more consistently resisted than police power regulations of aspects of such commerce. . . .

"To extract a fair tithe from interstate commerce for the local protection afforded to it, a seller State need not impose the kind of tax which Indiana here levied. As a practical matter, it can make such commerce pay its way, as the phrase runs, apart from taxing the very sale. . . . And where, as in this case, the commodities subsequently sold interstate are securities, they can be reached by a property tax by the State of domicil of the owner. . . . While these permitted taxes may, in an ultimate sense, come out of interstate commerce, they are not, as would be a tax on gross receipts, a direct imposition on [the] very freedom of commercial flow . . . . .

"It is suggested, however, that the validity of a gross sales tax should depend on whether another State has also sought to impose its burden on the transactions. If another State has taxed the same interstate transaction, the burdensome consequences to interstate trade are undeniable. But that, for the time being, only one State has taxed is irrelevant to the kind of freedom of trade which the Commerce Clause generated. The immunities implicit in the Commerce Clause and the potential taxing power of a State can hardly be made to depend, in the world of practical affairs, on the shifting incidence of the varying tax laws of the various States at a particular moment. Courts are not possessed of instruments of determination so delicate as to enable them to weigh the various factors in a complicated economic setting which, as to an isolated application of a State tax, might mitigate the obvious burden generally created by a direct tax on commerce. Nor is there any warrant in the constitutional principles heretofore applied by this Court to support the notion that a State may be allowed one single-tax-worth of direct interference with the free flow of commerce. An exaction by a State from interstate commerce falls not because of a proven increase in the cost of the product. What makes the tax invalid is the fact that there is interference by a State with the freedom of interstate commerce."

b. Justice Rutledge's concurring opinion questioned the Court's departure from the approach of the Adams Mfg. case, p. 718, supra—and of other multiple burdens cases—and proceeded to challenge that approach from another direction. He noted that the majority opinion placed "no emphasis upon apportionment, the absence of which the Adams opinion held crucial. The Court also puts to one side as irrelevant the factor there most stressed, namely, the danger of multiple taxation." He continued:

"Unless we are to return to the formalism of another day, neither the 'directness' of the incidence of a tax 'upon the commerce itself' nor the fact that its incidence is manipulated to rest upon some 'local incident' of the interstate transaction can be used as a criterion .   . . . It is for this reason that increasingly with the years emphasis has been placed upon practical consequences and effects, either actual or threatened, of questioned legislation to block or impede interstate commerce or place it at practical disadvantage with the local trade. Formulae and adjectives have been retained at times in intermixture with the effective practical considerations. But proportionately the stress upon them has been greatly reduced, until the present decision; and the trend of recent decisions to sustain state taxes formerly regarded as invalid has been due in large part to this fact. .   .   . In this view it would seem clear that the validity of such a tax as Indiana's .   .   . should be determined .   .   . by whether those forbidden consequences would be produced, either through the actual incidence of multiple taxes laid by different states or by the threat of them, with resulting uncertainties producing the same impeding consequences.

"The Adams decision did not take account of any difference, as regards the risk of multiple state taxation, between situations where the multiple burden would actually or probably be incurred in fact and others in which no such risk would be involved. '[T]he risk of a double tax burden' on which the Court relied to invalidate the levy was not one actually, probably, or even doubtfully imposed in fact by another state. It rather was one which resulted only from an assumed, and an unexercised, power in that state to impose a similar tax. .   .   . The ultimate risk which the Court sought to avoid was the danger that gross income or gross receipts tax legislation, without apportionment, might be widely adopted if the door were once opened .   . ..

Rather than incur this risk, with the anticipated consequent widespread creation of multiple levies, the Court in effect forestalled them at the source. Its action was prophylactic and the prophylaxis was made absolute.

"By thus relieving interstate commerce from liability to pay taxes in either state, without any showing that both had laid them, the effect was, not simply to relieve that commerce from multiple burden, but to give it exemption from taxes all other trade must bear. Local trade was thus placed at disadvantage with interstate trade . . . . Less broad and absolute alternatives are available and are adequate for the purpose of protection without creating the evils of total exemption.

"The alternative methods available for avoiding the multiple state tax burden may now be stated. They are: (1) To apply the Adams ruling, stopping such taxes at the source, unless the tax is apportioned, thus eliminating the cumulative burdens; (2) To rule that either the state of origin or the state of market, but not both, can levy the exaction; (3) To determine factually in each case whether application of the tax can be made by one state without incurring actual danger of its being made in another or the risk of real uncertainty whether in fact it will be so made. . . . I think the solution most nearly in accord with the commerce clause, at once most consistent with its purpose and least objectionable for producing either evils it had no design to bring or practical difficulties in administration, would be to vest the power to tax in the state of the market, subject to power in the forwarding state also to tax by allowing credit to the full amount of any tax paid or due at the destination. . . ."

c. Why did Justice Frankfurter speak in terms of "direct" rather than "multiple" burdens? See Brown, "The Open Economy: Mr. Justice Frankfurter and the Position of the Judiciary," 67 Yale L.J. 219 (1957), Selected Essays 1938–62 (1963) 371. Note that, two years after Freeman v. Hewit, Justice Frankfurter wrote for the Court in Central Greyhound v. Mealey, p. 710, supra, suggesting that several states might tax a "fairly apportioned" part of the proceeds from bus routes traversing New Jersey and Pennsylvania as well as New York. Did the Mealey opinion use the "direct burden" or "multiple taxation" approach? Note a remark by Justice Frankfurter in the course of his Freeman v. Hewit opinion: "Language alters, and there is a fashion in judicial writing as in other things." Do Justice Rutledge's alternatives in Freeman v. Hewit offer more appropriate solutions than Justice Frankfurter's standard or the Western Live Stock-Adams Mfg. approach? Has the Court moved toward Justice Rutledge's suggested solution? Cf. the General Motors case, p. 733, infra.

MULTIPLE BURDENS IN THE 1950's AND 1960's: SALES, GROSS RECEIPTS, AND NET INCOME TAXES

Introduction. Consider the following examples of modern decisions on state taxes related to interstate sales transactions. The multiple taxation language is obviously still in fashion. But do the decisions suggest a change in content? Has the Court relaxed the restrictions on state power beyond the loosening marked by the Western Live Stock line of cases? Does the multiple taxation risk receive more than lip service? Or has the multiple burdens inquiry shifted from concern about risks to concern solely with actual double taxation? Or is the "multiple taxation" obstacle overcome by simply meeting the "nexus" prerequisites of due process? Cf. Justice Black's dissent in Western Live Stock, supra, and Justice Rutledge's concurrence in Freeman v. Hewit, supra.

Note that the first opinion below, in the Norton case, was written by Justice Jackson, one of the strongest proponents of the free trade philosophy. Was Justice Reed correct in claiming that some of the sales taxed in Norton were immune under Berwind-White, as interpreted in Dilworth? Was Norton a due process or a commerce clause case? Does the second case below, General Motors, in turn extend Norton? Note that Justice Clark relies on Norton in General Motors. Note, moreover, that Justice Clark, who dissented from the limited immunity recognized in Norton—and who also dissented in Spector as well as a number of other decisions of the early 1950's— wrote the Court's opinions in the two most recent major tax cases, General Motors and Northwestern States Portland Cement, infra.

NORTON CO. v. DEPARTMENT OF REVENUE
340 U.S. 534, 71 S.Ct. 377, 95 L.Ed. 517 (1951).

Certiorari to the Supreme Court of Illinois.

Mr. Justice JACKSON delivered the opinion of the Court.

Petitioner, a Massachusetts corporation, manufactures and sells abrasive machines and supplies. . . . [I]t operates a branch office and warehouse in Chicago from which it makes local sales at retail. These sales admittedly subject it to an Illinois Occupation Tax "upon persons engaged in the business of selling tangible personal property at retail in this State." The base for computation of the tax is gross receipts. . . .

Not all of petitioner's sales to Illinois customers are over-the-counter, but the State has collected, under protest, the tax on the entire gross income of this company from sales to its inhabitants. . . . [T]he question is whether the State has exceeded the constitutional range of its taxing power by taxing all of petitioner's Illinois derived income.

In Worcester, Massachusetts, petitioner manufactures some 225,000 items, 18,000 of which it usually carries in stock. There are its general management, accounting, and credit offices, where it accepts or rejects all direct mail orders and orders forwarded by its Chicago office. If an order calls for specially built machines, it is there studied and accepted or rejected. Orders are filled by shipment f. o. b. Worcester either directly to the customer or via the Chicago office.

The Chicago place of business performs several functions. It carries an inventory of about 3,000 most frequently purchased items. From these it serves cash customers and those whose credit the home office has approved, by consummating direct sales. Income from these sales petitioner admits to be constitutionally taxable. But this office also performs useful functions for other classes of customers. For those of no established credit, those who order items not in local stock, and those who want special equipment, it receives their order and forwards it to the home office for action there. For many of these Illinois customers it also acts as an intermediary to reduce freight charges.   Worcester packages and marks each customer's goods but accumulates them until a carload lot can be consigned to the Chicago office. Chicago breaks the carload and reconsigns the separate orders in their original package to customers.   The Chicago office thus intervenes between vendor and Illinois vendees and performs service helpful to petitioner's competition for that trade in all Illinois sales except when the buyer orders directly from Worcester, and the goods are shipped from there directly to the buyer.

The Illinois Supreme Court recognized that it was dealing with interstate commerce.   It reiterated its former holdings "that there could be no tax on solicitation of orders only" in the State.   But no solicitors work the territory out of either the home office or the Chicago branch   .   .   .   . The Illinois court held that the presence of petitioner's local retail outlet .   .   .   was sufficient to attribute all income derived from Illinois sales to that outlet and render it all taxable.

Where a corporation chooses to stay at home in all respects except to send abroad advertising or drummers to solicit orders which are sent directly to the home office for acceptance, filling, and delivery back to the buyer, it is obvious that the State of the buyer has no local grip on the seller.   Unless some local incident occurs sufficient to bring the transaction within its taxing power, the vendor is not taxable.   McLeod v. Dilworth Co., 322 U.S. 327. Of course, a state imposing a sales or use tax can more easily meet this burden, because the impact of those taxes is on the local buyer or user.   Cases involving them are not controlling here, for this tax falls on the vendor.

But when, as here, the corporation has gone into the State to do local business by state permission and has submitted itself to the taxing power of the State, it can avoid taxation on some Illinois sales only by showing that particular transactions are dissociated from the local business and interstate in nature.   The general rule, applicable here, is that a taxpayer claiming immunity from a tax has the burden of establishing his exemption.   .   .   .

This corporation has so mingled taxable business with that which it contends is not taxable that is requires administrative and judicial judgment to separate the two.   We conclude that, in the light of all the evidence, the judgment attributing to the Chicago branch income from all sales that utilized it either in receiving the orders or distributing the goods was within the realm of permissible judgment.   Petitioner has not established that such services as were rendered by the Chicago office were not decisive factors in establishing and holding this market.   .   .   .

This corporation could have approached the Illinois market through solicitors only and it would have been entitled to the immunity of interstate commerce as set out in the Dilworth case.   But, from a competitive point of view, that system has disadvantages.   The trade may view the seller as remote and inaccessible.   He cannot be reached with process of local courts for breach of contract, or for service if the goods are defective or in need of replacement.   Petitioner elected to localize itself in the Illinois market with the advantages of a retail outlet in the State   .   .   .   .   Although the concern does not, by engaging in business within the State, lose its right to do interstate business with tax immunity,   .   .   .   it cannot channel business through a local outlet to gain the advantage of a local business and also hold the immunities of an interstate business.

The only items that are so clearly interstate in character that the State could not reasonably attribute their proceeds to the local business are orders sent directly to Worcester by the customer and shipped directly to the customer from Worcester. Income from those we think was not subject to this tax.

The judgment below is vacated and the cause remanded for further proceedings not inconsistent herewith.

Mr. Justice REED concurs with the Court's opinion and judgment except as it permits Illinois to use as a base for the tax computation petitioner's sales, consummated in Massachusetts by the acceptance of orders forwarded to petitioner there by its Illinois branch office, filled in Massachusetts, and shipped from Massachusetts directly, and not by transshipment through the Illinois branch, to the buyer. In those sales title passes to buyer in Massachusetts. . . . The transactions described above are interstate business.

. . . [In the Dilworth case,] we made it clear that a tax cannot be collected by the buyer's state on orders solicited in one state, accepted in another, and shipped at the purchaser's risk. That later clarifying holding seems to me to state the true rule applicable here. I can see no difference, constitutionally, between solicitation by salesmen in a branch office or on the road. Such sales, consummated by direct shipment to Illinois buyers from out of the state are interstate business and free of the tax Illinois has levied. . . .

Mr. Justice CLARK, dissenting in part.

I believe the respondent reasonably attributed all of the proceeds of petitioner's sales in Illinois to the company's local activities. I therefore agree with the Illinois Supreme Court that under the circumstances shipments sent directly to Illinois customers on orders sent directly to Worcester were subject to the tax. . . . Surely the Court's conclusion, that "Petitioner has not established that such services as were rendered by the Chicago office were not decisive factors in establishing and holding this market," applies with equal validity to the direct sales.

In maintaining a local establishment of such magnitude, petitioner has adopted the label of a home-town merchant. After it has received the manifold advantages of that label, we should not give our sanction to its claim made at taxpaying time that with respect to direct sales it is only an itinerant drummer. . . .

Mr. Justice BLACK and Mr. Justice DOUGLAS join in this opinion.

GENERAL MOTORS CORP. v. WASHINGTON

377 U.S. 436, 84 S.Ct. 1564, 12 L.Ed.2d 430 (1964).

Appeal from the Supreme Court of Washington.

Mr. Justice CLARK delivered the opinion of the Court.

This appeal tests the constitutional validity, under the Commerce and Due Process Clauses, of Washington's tax imposed upon the privilege of engaging in business activities within the State. The tax is measured by the appellant's gross wholesale sales of motor vehicles, parts and accessories delivered in the State. Appellant claims that the tax is levied on unapportioned gross receipts from such sales and is, therefore, a tax on the privilege of engaging in interstate commerce; is inherently discriminatory; results in the imposition of a multiple tax burden; and is a deprivation of property without due process of law. . . . [T]he Supreme Court of Washington [held] that all of the appellant's transactions were subject to the tax on the ground that the tax bore a reasonable relation to the appellant's activities within the State. . . . We have concluded that the tax is levied on the incidents of a substantial local business in Washington and is constitutionally valid and, therefore, affirm the judgment.

I. We start with the proposition that "[i]t was not the purpose of the commerce clause to relieve those engaged in interstate commerce from their just share of state tax burden even though it increases the cost of doing the business." [Western Live Stock] . . .

However, local taxes measured by gross receipts from interstate commerce have not always fared as well. Because every State has equal rights when taxing the commerce it touches, there exists the danger that such taxes can impose cumulative burdens upon interstate transactions which are not presented to local commerce. . . . Such burdens would destroy interstate commerce and encourage the re-erection of those trade barriers which made the Commerce Clause necessary. . . . And in this connection, we have specifically held that interstate commerce cannot be subjected to the burden of "multiple taxation." . . . Nevertheless, . . . it is well established that taxation measured by gross receipts is constitutionally proper if it is fairly apportioned.

A careful analysis of the cases in this field teaches that the validity of the tax rests upon whether the State is exacting a constitutionally fair demand for that aspect of interstate commerce to which it bears a special relation. For our purposes the decisive issue turns on the operating incidence of the tax. In other words, the question is whether the State has exerted its power in proper proportion to appellant's activities within the State and to appellant's consequent enjoyment of the opportunities and protections which the State has afforded. Where, as in the instant case, the taxing State is not the domiciliary State, we look to the taxpayer's business activities within the State, i. e., the local incidents, to determine if the gross receipts from sales therein may be fairly related to those activities. . . . "[T]he simple but controlling question is whether the state has given anything for which it can ask return."

Here it is admitted that General Motors has entered the State and engaged in activities therein. [It] contests the validity of the tax levy on four of its Divisions, Chevrolet, Pontiac, Oldsmobile and General Motors Parts. Under these circumstances appellant has the burden of showing that the operations of these divisions in the State are "dissociated from the local business and interstate in nature. The general rule, applicable here, is that a taxpayer claiming immunity from a tax has the burden of establishing his exemption." Norton Co. v. Department of Revenue, 340 U.S. 534, 537 (1951). [Additional quotations from the Norton case are omitted.] With these principles in mind, we turn to the facts.

II. 1. GENERAL MOTORS' CORPORATE ORGANIZATION AND SALES OPERATION.

. . . Chevrolet, Pontiac, Oldsmobile and General Motors Parts are divisions of General Motors, but they operate substantially independently of each other. The corporation manufactures automobiles, trucks and other merchandise which are sold to dealers in Washington. However, all of these articles are manufactured in other States. In order to carry on the sale, in Washington, . . . the corporation maintains an organization of employees in each of these divisions on a national, regional and district level. . . . [E]ach division, except General Motors Parts, maintained a zone office at Portland, Oregon. . . . Chevrolet Division also maintained a branch office at Seattle which was under the jurisdiction of the Portland zone office . . . . The orders for these products were sent by the dealers to the zone office located at Portland. They were accepted or rejected there or at the factory and the sales were completed by shipments f.o.b. the factories.

2. PERSONNEL RESIDING WITHIN THE STATE AND THEIR ACTIVITIES.

The sales organizations of the Chevrolet, Pontiac and Oldsmobile Divisions were similar in most respects. The zone manager was located in Portland and had charge of the sales operation. . . . The district managers lived within the State of Washington and their jobs were "the maintenance of a quality organization—dealer organization . . . ." While he had no office within the State, the district manager operated from his home where he received mail and telephone calls and otherwise carried on the corporation's business. He called upon each dealer in his district on an average of at least once a month, and often saw the larger dealers weekly. . . .

In addition to the district manager, each of the Chevrolet, Pontiac and Oldsmobile Divisions also maintained service representatives who called on the dealers with regularity, assisting the service department in any troubles it experienced with General Motors products. . . . During the tax period involved here the Chevrolet, Oldsmobile and Pontiac Divisions had an average of about 20 employees resident or principally employed in Washington. General Motors Parts Division employed about 20 more.

The Chevrolet Division's branch office at Seattle consisted of one man and his secretary. That office performed the function of getting better service for Washington dealers on orders of Chevrolet Division products. The branch office had no jurisdiction over sales or over other Chevrolet personnel in the State. . . .

3. OUT-OF-STATE PERSONNEL, PERFORMING IN-STATE ACTIVITIES.

The zone manager . . . visited with each Washington dealer on the average of once each 60 days, the larger ones, each month. About one-half of these visits were staged at the dealer's place of business and the others were at Portland. . . . The zone parts and service manager held responsibility for the adequacy of the Washington dealer services to customers. He worked through the local Washington service representative, but also made personal visits to Washington dealers and conducted schools for the promotion of good service policies. . . .

4. ACTIVITIES OF GENERAL MOTORS PARTS DIVISION.

. . . [T]he General Motors Parts Division warehoused, sold and shipped parts and accessories to Washington dealers for Chevrolet, Pontiac and Oldsmobile vehicles. It maintained warehouses in Portland and Seattle.

No personnel of this division visited the dealers, but all of the Chevrolet, Pontiac and Oldsmobile dealers in Washington obtained their parts and accessories from these warehouses. . . . The Seattle warehouse, which carried the items most often called for in Washington, employed from 20 to 28 people during the taxing period. The Portland warehouse carried the less frequently needed parts. The tax on the orders filled at the Seattle warehouse was paid but the tax on the Portland shipments is being protested.

III. "[I]t is beyond dispute," we said in Northwestern States Portland Cement Co. v. Minnesota [p. 741, infra], "that a State may not lay a tax on the 'privilege' of engaging in interstate commerce." But that is not this case. To so contend here is to overlook a long line of cases of this Court holding that an in-state activity may be a sufficient local incident upon which a tax may be based. . . . [W]e cannot say that appellant has shown that its activities within the State are not such incidents as the State can reach. Norton . . .. Unlike Field Enterprises, Inc., v. Washington, 47 Wash.2d 852, 289 P.2d 1010, aff'd [per curiam], 352 U.S. 806 (1956), citing Norton, supra, the Pontiac and Oldsmobile Divisions of General Motors had no branch offices in Washington. But these divisions had district managers, service representatives and other employees who were residents of the State and who performed substantial services . . .. We place little weight on the fact that these divisions had no formal offices in the State, since in actuality the homes of these officials were used as corporate offices. Despite their label as "homes" they served the corporation just as effectively as "offices." In addition, the corporation had a Chevrolet branch office and a General Motors Parts Division warehouse in Seattle.

Thus, in the bundle of corporate activity, which is the test here, we see General Motors' activity so enmeshed in local connections that it voluntarily paid taxes on various of its operations but insists that it was not liable on others. Since General Motors elected to enter the State in this fashion, we cannot say that the Supreme Court of Washington erred in holding that these local incidents were sufficient to form the basis for the levy of a tax that would not run contrary to the Constitution. Norton . . ..

IV. The tax that Washington levied is measured by the wholesale sales of the respective General Motors divisions in the State. It is unapportioned and, as we have pointed out, is, therefore, suspect. We must determine whether it is so closely related to the local activities of the corporation as to form "some definite link, some minimum connection, between a state and the person, property or transaction it seeks to tax." Miller Bros. Co. v. Maryland, 347 U.S. 340, 344–345 (1954). On the basis of the facts found by the state court we are not prepared to say that its conclusion was constitutionally impermissible. Norton . . .. Although mere entry into a State does not take from a corporation the right to continue to do an interstate business with tax immunity, it does not follow that the corporation can channel its operations through such a maze of local connections as does General Motors, and take advantage of its gain on domesticity, and still maintain that same degree of immunity.

V. A more difficult question might arise from appellant's claim of multiple taxation. Gwin, White & Prince, Inc., v. Henneford, 305 U.S. 434, 440 (1939). General Motors claims that some of its products taxed by Washington are manufactured in St. Louis where a license tax, measured by sales before shipment, is levied. See American Mfg. Co. v. St. Louis, 250

U.S. 459 (1919). It is also urged that General Motors' Oregon-based activity which concerns Washington sales might afford sufficient incidents for a similar tax by Oregon. . . . [I]n Northwestern States Portland Cement Co. v. Minnesota, [infra], we held that "[i]n this type of case the taxpayers must show that the formula places a burden upon interstate commerce in a constitutional sense." Appellant has not done this. It has not demonstrated what definite burden, in a constitutional sense, the St. Louis tax places on the identical interstate shipments by which Washington measures its tax. . . . And further, it has not been shown that Oregon levies any tax on appellant's activity bearing on Washington sales. In such cases we have refrained from passing on the question of "multiple taxation," . . . and we adhere to that position.

Affirmed.

Mr. Justice BRENNAN, dissenting.

. . . [T]he Court has, in my judgment, confused two quite different issues raised by the case, and in doing so has ignored a fatal defect in the Washington statute.

In order to tax any transaction, the Due Process Clause requires that a State show a sufficient "nexus between such a tax and transactions within a state for which the tax is an exaction." . . . But the strictures of the Constitution on this power do not stop there. For in the case of a gross receipts tax imposed upon an interstate transaction, even though the taxing State can show "some minimum connection," . . . the Commerce Clause requires that "taxation measured by gross receipts from interstate commerce . . . [be] fairly apportioned to the commerce carried on within the taxing state." Western Live Stock v. Bureau of Revenue, 303 U.S. 250, 256. See J. D. Adams Mfg. Co. v. Storen, 304 U.S. 307.

. . . In concluding that the tax in this case includes a fair apportionment . . . the Court relies upon the fact that Washington has sufficient contacts with the sale to satisfy the Norton standard, which was formulated to meet the quite different problem of defining the requirements of the Due Process Clause. . . . Our prior decisions clearly indicate that a quite different scheme of apportionment is required. Of course, when a sale may be localized completely in one State, there is no danger of multiple taxation, and, as in the case of a retail sales tax, the State may use as its tax base the total gross receipts arising within its borders. See McGoldrick v. Berwind-White Coal Mining Co., 309 U.S. 33. But far more common in our complex economy is the kind of sale presented in this case, which exhibits significant contacts with more than one State. In such a situation, it is the commercial activity within the State, and not the sales volume, which determines the State's power to tax, and by which the tax must be apportioned. While the ratio of in-state to out-of-state sales is often taken into account as one factor among others in apportioning a firm's total net income, see e. g., the description of the "Massachusetts Formula" in Note, 75 Harv.L.Rev. 953, 1011 (1962), it nevertheless remains true that if commercial activity in more than one State results in a sale in one of them, that State may not claim as all its own the gross receipts to which the activity within its borders has contributed only a part. Such a tax must be apportioned to reflect the business activity within the taxing State. . . . Since the Washington tax on wholesales is, by its very terms, applied to the "gross proceeds of sales," . . . it cannot be sustained under the standards required by the Commerce Clause.

Mr. Justice GOLDBERG, with whom Mr. Justice STEWART and Mr. Justice WHITE join, dissenting.

The issue presented is whether the Commerce Clause permits a State to assess an unapportioned gross receipts tax on the interstate wholesale sales of automobiles delivered to dealers for resale in that State. . . . The Court concludes . . . that the validity of Washington's wholesale sales tax may be determined by asking " 'the simple but controlling question [of] whether the state has given anything for which it can ask return.' " . . . This elusively simple test and its application to this case represent an important departure from a fundamental purpose of the Commerce Clause and from an established principle which had heretofore provided guidance in an area otherwise fraught with complexities and inconsistencies. . . .

On these facts the Court holds that the activities of the sales representatives constitute "an in-state activity" forming "a sufficient local incident upon which a tax may be based." . . . This decision departs from Norton Co. v. Department of Revenue, 340 U.S. 534, and adopts a test there rejected. . . .

Although the opinion of the Court seems to imply that there still is some threshold requirement of in-state activity which must be found to exist before a "fairly apportioned" tax may be imposed on interstate sales, it is difficult to conceive of a state gross receipts tax on interstate commerce which could not be sustained under the rationale adopted today. Every interstate sale invariably involves some local incidents—some "in-state" activity. It is difficult, for example, to distinguish between the in-state activities of the representatives here involved and the in-state activities of solicitors or traveling salesmen—activities which this Court has held are insufficient to constitute a basis for imposing a tax on interstate sales. McLeod v. J. E. Dilworth Co., 322 U.S. 327 . . . .. Surely the distinction cannot rest on the fact that the solicitors or salesmen make hotels or motels their "offices" whereas in the present case the sales representatives made their homes their "offices." In this regard, the Norton decision rested solidly on the fact that the taxpayer had a branch office and warehouse making intrastate retail sales.

The opinion of the Court goes beyond a consideration of whether there has been in-state activity of appropriate character to satisfy a threshold requirement for imposing a tax on interstate sales. The Court asserts as a general principle that the validity of a tax on interstate commerce "rests upon whether the State is exacting a constitutionally fair demand for that aspect of interstate commerce to which it bears a special relation." What is "fair"? How are we to determine whether a State has exerted its power in "proper proportion to appellant's activities within the State"? . . . I submit, with due respect for the complexity of the problem, that the formulation suggested by the Court is unworkable. Constitutional adjudication under the Commerce Clause would find little guidance in a concept of state interstate sales taxation tested and limited by the tax's "fair" proportion or degree. The attempt to determine the "fairness" of an interstate sales tax of a given percentage imposed on given activities in one State would be almost as unseemly as an attempt to determine whether that same tax was "fairly" apportioned in the light of taxes levied on the same transaction by other States. The infinite variety of factual configurations would readily frustrate the usual process of clarification through judicial inclusion and exclusion. The only coherent pattern that could develop would, in reality, ultimately be based on a wholly permissive attitude toward state taxation of interstate commerce.

The dilemma inhering in the Court's formulation is revealed by its treatment of the "more difficult," but inextricably related, question arising from the alleged multiple taxation. . . . [1] These problems are engendered by the rule applied here and cannot be evaded. For if it is "fair" to subject the interstate sales to the Washington wholesale sales tax because of the activities of the sales representatives in Washington, then it would seem equally "fair" for Oregon, which is the site of the office directing and consummating these sales, to tax the same gross sales receipts. Moreover, it would seem "fairer" for California, Michigan or Missouri—States in which automobiles are manufactured, assembled or delivered—to impose a tax measured by, and effectively bearing upon, the same gross sales receipts. . . . Presumably, if there is to be a limitation on the taxing power of each of these States, that limitation surely cannot be on a first-come-first-tax basis. Alternatively, if diverse local incidents can afford bases for multi-state taxation of the same interstate sale, then the Court is left to determine, out of some hypothetical maximum taxable amount, which proportion is "fair" for each of the States having a sufficient "in-state" contact with the interstate transaction.

The burden on interstate commerce and the dangers of multiple taxation are made apparent by considering Washington's tax provisions. [Washington imposed both a wholesalers tax and a manufacturers tax, but exempted the manufacturer-wholesaler from the manufacturers tax to the extent that he was taxed under the wholesalers tax.]

[A]n out-of-state firm manufacturing goods in a State having the same taxation provisions as does Washington would be subjected to two taxes on interstate sales to Washington customers. The firm would pay the producing State a local manufacturing tax measured by sales receipts and would also pay Washington a tax on wholesale sales to Washington residents. Under such taxation programs, if an out-of-state manufacturer competes with a Washington manufacturer, the out-of-state manufacturer may be seriously disadvantaged by the duplicative taxation. Even if the out-of-state firm has no Washington competitors, the imposition of interstate sales taxes, which add to the cost of producing, may diminish the demand for the product in Washington and thus affect the allocation of resources in the national economy. Moreover, the threat of duplicative taxation, even where there is no competitor manufacturing in the consuming State, may compel the out-of-state producer to relocate his manufacturing operations to avoid multiple taxation. Thus taxes such as the one upheld today may discourage the development of multistate business operations and the most advantageous distribution of our national resources; the economic effect inhibits the realization of a free and open economy unencumbered by local tariffs and protective devices. . . .

It may be urged that the Washington tax should be upheld because it taxes in a nondiscriminatory fashion all wholesale sales, intrastate and interstate, to Washington purchasers. The Commerce Clause, however, was

---

1. With respect to the view that the application of the Commerce Clause depends upon the existence of actual, as distinguished from potential, multiple taxation, compare Freeman v. Hewit, 329 U.S. 249, 256 . . . . [Footnote by Justice Goldberg.]

designed, as Mr. Justice Jackson said in H. P. Hood & Sons, Inc., v. Du Mond, 336 U.S. 525, 538, to create a "federal free trade unit"—a common national market among the States; and the Constitution thereby precludes a State from defending a tax on interstate sales on the ground that the State taxes intrastate sales generally. Nondiscrimination alone is no basis for burdening the flow of interstate commerce. . . . Freeman v. Hewit . . . .. A State therefore should not be enabled to put out-of-state producers and merchants at a disadvantage by imposing a tax to "equalize" their costs with those of local businessmen who would otherwise suffer a competitive disadvantage because of the State's own taxation scheme. The disadvantage stemming from the wholesale sales tax was created by the State itself and therefore the fact that the State simultaneously imposes the same tax on interstate and intrastate transactions should not obscure the fact that interstate commerce is being burdened in order to protect the local market.[2]

In my view the rules set forth in Norton . . . reflect an attempt to adhere to the basic purposes of the Commerce Clause. Therefore, in dealing with unapportioned taxes on interstate sales, I would adhere to the Norton rules instead of departing from them by adopting a standard of "fairness." I would hold that a manufacturer or wholesaler making interstate sales is not subject to a state gross receipts tax merely because those sales were solicited or processed by agents living or traveling in the taxing State. As Norton recognized, a different rule may be applied to the taxation of sales substantially connected with an office or warehouse making intrastate sales. The test adopted by the Court today, if followed logically in future cases, would seem to mean that States will be permitted to tax wholly interstate sales by any company selling through local agents or traveling salesmen. Such a rule may leave only mail-order houses free from state taxes on interstate sales. With full sympathy for the revenue needs of States, I believe there are other legitimate means of raising state revenues without undermining the common national market created by the Commerce Clause. I therefore respectfully dissent.

NET INCOME TAXES

Introduction. As the next case shows, the Court has been far more lenient toward net income taxes than to gross receipts taxes. Is the distinction justifiable? Is the economic difference between gross and net income taxes sufficiently great to justify the difference in constitutional treatment? Note the following passage, from United States Glue Co. v. Town of Oak Creek, 247 U.S. 321 (1918): "The difference in effect between a tax measured by gross receipts and one measured by net income . . . is manifest and substantial, and it affords a convenient and workable basis of distinction between a direct and immediate burden upon the business affected and a charge that is only indirect and incidental. A tax upon gross receipts affects each transaction in proportion to its magnitude, and irrespective of whether it is profitable or otherwise. Conceivably it may be sufficient to make the difference between profit and loss, or to so diminish the profit as

---

2. Cf. Baldwin v. G. A. F. Seelig, Inc., 294 U.S. 511, 523 . . . .. [Footnote by Justice Goldberg.]

to impede or discourage the conduct of the commerce. A tax upon the net profits has not the same deterrent effect, since it does not arise at all unless a gain is shown over and above expenses and losses, and the tax cannot be heavy unless the profits are large. Such a tax, when imposed upon net income from whatever source arising, is but a method of distributing the cost of government like a tax on property."

NORTHWESTERN STATES PORTLAND CEMENT CO. v. MINNESOTA

358 U.S. 450, 79 S.Ct. 357, 3 L.Ed.2d 421 (1959).

Appeal from the Supreme Court of Minnesota.*

Mr. Justice CLARK delivered the opinion of the Court.

[In the Minnesota case—No. 12—the state courts sustained a general corporate net income tax as applied to an Iowa cement-manufacturing company which sold about 48% of its products in Minnesota. It maintained a sales office in Minnesota with a staff of two salesmen, a manager, and a secretary. Orders were solicited subject to acceptance in and delivery from Iowa. In determining the taxable portion of the company's net income, Minnesota used a three-factor ratio: Minnesota sales, tangible property and payroll to total sales, property and payroll.

[In the Georgia case—No. 33—the state courts invalidated a similar net income tax as applied to an Alabama manufacturer of valves and pipe fittings. The company maintained a sales-service office in Atlanta—one salesman and one secretary, serving a five-state area. The salesman devoted about one-third of his time to soliciting orders in Georgia. The orders were subject to acceptance in Alabama, and shipments were made directly from there. Georgia determined the portion of income taxable there by a three-factor formula, based on inventory, wages and gross receipts.]

These cases concern the constitutionality of state net income tax laws levying taxes on that portion of a foreign corporation's net income earned from and fairly apportioned to business activities within the taxing State when those activities are exclusively in the furtherance of interstate commerce. No question is raised in either case as to the reasonableness of the apportionment of net income under the State's formulas nor to the amount of the final assessment made. . . . The importance of the question in the field of state taxation is indicated by the fact that thirty-five States impose direct net income taxes on corporations. . . . It is contended that each of the state statutes, as applied, violates both the Due Process and the Commerce Clauses of the United States Constitution. We conclude that net income from the interstate operations of a foreign corporation may be subjected to state taxation provided the levy is not discriminatory and is properly apportioned to local activities within the taxing State, forming sufficient nexus to support the same. . . .

[A review of decisions not involving net income taxes is omitted. See the "quagmire" passage from this opinion quoted at the beginning of this chapter.] [I]t has been established since 1918 that a net income tax

---

* Together with No. 33, Williams v. Stockham Valves & Fittings, Inc., on certiorari to the Supreme Court of Georgia.

on revenues derived from interstate commerce does not offend constitutional limitations upon state interference with such commerce. The decision of Peck & Co. v. Lowe, 247 U.S. 165, pointed the way. There the Court held that . . . a net income tax on the profits derived from [exportation] was not "laid on articles in course of exportation . . . . At most, exportation is affected only indirectly and remotely." . . . The first case in this Court applying the doctrine to interstate commerce was that of United States Glue Co. v. Town of Oak Creek, 247 U.S. 321 (1918). There the Court distinguished between an invalid direct levy which placed a burden on interstate commerce and a charge by way of net income derived from profits from interstate commerce. This landmark case and those usually cited as upholding the doctrine there announced, i. e., Underwood Typewriter Co. v. Chamberlain, 254 U.S. 113 (1920), and Memphis Natural Gas Co. v. Beeler, 315 U.S. 649 (1942), dealt with corporations which were domestic to the taxing State . . . or which had "established a 'commercial domicile' " there . . . .

But that the presence of such a circumstance is not controlling is shown by the cases of Bass, Ratcliff & Gretton, Ltd. v. State Tax Commission, 266 U.S. 271 (1924), and Norfolk & W. R. Co. v. North Carolina, 297 U.S. 682 (1936). In neither of these cases was the taxpayer a domiciliary of the taxing State, incorporated or with its principal place of business there, though each carried on substantial local activities. . . . These cases stand for the doctrine that the entire net income of a corporation, generated by interstate as well as intrastate activities, may be fairly apportioned among the States for tax purposes by formulas utilizing in-state aspects of interstate affairs. . . .

Any doubt as to the validity of our position here was entirely dispelled four years after Beeler, in a unanimous *per curiam* in West Publishing Co. v. McColgan, 328 U.S. 823 . . . . The case involved the validity of California's tax on the apportioned net income of West Publishing Company, whose business was exclusively interstate. . . . While the statement of the facts in that opinion recites that "The employees were given space in the offices of attorneys in return for the use of plaintiff's books stored in such offices," [the] opinion was not grounded on the triviality that office space was given West's solicitors by attorneys in exchange for the chanceful use of what books they may have had on hand for their sales activities. Rather, it recognized that the income taxed arose from a purely interstate operation. . . .

We believe that the rationale of these cases, involving income levies by States, controls the issues here. The taxes are not regulations in any sense of that term. Admittedly they do not discriminate against nor subject either corporation to an undue burden. While it is true that a State may not erect a wall around its borders preventing commerce an entry, it is axiomatic that the founders did not intend to immunize such commerce from carrying its fair share of the costs of the state government . . . .. The levies are not privilege taxes based on the right to carry on business in the taxing State. The States are left to collect only through ordinary means. . . .

While the economic wisdom of state net income taxes is one of state policy not for our decision, one of the "realities" raised by the parties is the possibility of a multiple burden resulting from the exactions in question. The answer is that none is shown to exist here. This is not an unapportioned tax which by its very nature makes interstate commerce bear more than its fair share. . . . Logically it is impossible, when the tax is fairly apportioned, to have the same income taxed twice. In practical operation, however, apportionment formulas being what they are, the possibility of the contrary is not foreclosed, especially by levies in domiciliary States. But that question is not before us. . . . There is nothing to show that multiple taxation is present. We cannot deal in abstractions. In this type of case the taxpayers must show that the formula places a burden upon interstate commerce in a constitutional sense. This they have failed to do.

It is also contended that Spector Motor Service v. O'Connor, 340 U.S. 602 (1951), requires a contrary result. But there it was repeatedly emphasized that the tax was "imposed upon the franchise of a foreign corporation for the privilege of doing business within the State . . . ." Thus, it was invalid under a long line of precedents, some of which we have mentioned. It was not a levy on net income but an excise or tax placed on the franchise of a foreign corporation engaged "exclusively" in interstate operations. . . . The taxes here, like that in West Publishing Co. v McColgan, supra, are based only upon the net profits earned in the taxing State. That incidence of the tax affords a valid "constitutional channel" which the States have utilized to "make interstate commerce pay its way." In Spector the incidence was the privilege of doing business, and that avenue of approach had long been declared unavailable under the Commerce Clause. . . . .

Nor will the argument that the exactions contravene the Due Process Clause bear scrutiny. The taxes imposed are levied only on that portion of the taxpayer's net income which arises from its activities within the taxing State. These activities form a sufficient "nexus between such a tax and transactions within a state for which the tax is an exaction." It strains reality to say . . . that each of the corporations here was not sufficiently involved in local events to forge "some definite link, some minimum connection" sufficient to satisfy due process requirements. Miller Bros. Co. v. State of Maryland . . . . [B]oth corporations engage in substantial income-producing activities in the taxing States.

No. 12—Affirmed. No. 33—Reversed.

Mr. Justice HARLAN, concurring. . . . [I]n my view the past decisions of this Court clearly point to, if indeed they do not compel, the sustaining of these two state taxing measures. . . . As I read the cases the existence of some income from *intrastate* business on the part of the taxed corporation, while sometimes adverted to, has never been considered essential to the valid taxation of such "interstate" income. The cases upholding taxes of this kind cannot, in my opinion, properly be said to rest on the theory that the income earned from the carrying on of interstate commerce was not in fact being taxed, but rather was being utilized simply to measure the income derived from some separate, but unidentified, intrastate commerce, which income was in truth the subject of the tax. . . . .

It is said that the taxes presently at issue were "laid on income from [interstate commerce] because of its source." If this were so I should of course vote to strike down their application here as unconstitutionally discriminatory against interstate commerce. But this seems to me plainly not such a case. . . . [T]he Minnesota and Georgia taxes are each part of a general scheme of state income taxation, reaching all individual, corporate, and other net income. The taxing statutes are not sought to be applied to portions of the net income of Northwestern and Stockham *because* of the source of that income—interstate commerce—but rather *despite* that source. . . .

I think it no more a "regulation of," "burden on," or "interference with" interstate commerce to permit a State within whose borders a foreign corporation engages *solely* in activities in aid of that commerce to tax the net income derived therefrom on a properly apportioned basis than to permit the same State to impose a nondiscriminatory net income tax of general application on a corporation engaging in *both* interstate and intrastate commerce therein and to take into account income from both categories. Cf. Peck & Co. v. Lowe, 247 U.S. 165. In each case the amount of the tax will increase as the profitability of the interstate business done increases. This Court has consistently upheld state net income taxes of general application so applied as to reach that portion of the profits of interstate business enterprises fairly allocable to activities within the State's borders. We do no more today.

Mr. Justice WHITTAKER, with whom Mr. Justice FRANKFURTER and Mr. Justice STEWART join, dissenting. . . . Direct taxation of "exclusively interstate commerce" is a substantial regulation of it and, therefore, in the absence of congressional consent, the States may not directly tax it. This Court has so held every time the question has been presented here until today. . . .

Mr. Justice FRANKFURTER, dissenting. . . . .

I venture to say that every . . . . decision—I say decision, not talk or dicta—on which reliance is placed, presented a situation where conjoined with the interstate commerce was severable local state business on the basis of which the state taxing power became constitutionally operative. The difference between those situations and this, as a matter of economics, involves the distinction between taking into account the total activity of the enterprise as a going business in determining a fairly apportioned tax based on locally derived revenues, and taxing a portion of revenue concededly produced by exclusively interstate commerce. . . .

I do not think we should take this new step. My objection is the policy that underlies the Commerce Clause, namely, whatever disadvantages may accrue to the separate States from making of the United States a free-trade territory are far outweighed by the advantages not only to the United States as a Nation, but to the component States. I am assuming, of course, that today's decision will stimulate, if indeed it does not compel, every State of the Union, which has not already done so, to devise a formula of apportionment to tax the income of enterprises carrying on exclusively interstate commerce. As a result, interstate commerce will be burdened not hypothetically but practically, and we have been admonished again and again that taxation is a practical matter.

I think that interstate commerce will be not merely argumentatively but actively burdened for two reasons:

First. It will not, I believe, be gainsaid that there are thousands of relatively small or moderate size corporations doing exclusively interstate business spread over several States. To subject these corporations to a separate income tax in each of these States means that they will have to keep books, make returns, store records, and engage legal counsel, all to meet the divers and variegated tax laws of forty-nine States, with their different times for filing returns, different tax structures, different modes for determining "net income," and, different, often conflicting, formulas of apportionment. This will involve large increases in bookkeeping, accounting, and legal paraphernalia to meet these new demands. The cost of such a far-flung scheme for complying with the taxing requirements of the different States may well exceed the burden of the taxes themselves, especially in the case of small companies doing a small volume of business in several States.

Second. The extensive litigation in this Court which has challenged formulas of apportionment in the case of railroads and express companies— challenges addressed to the natural temptation of the States to absorb more than their fair share of interstate revenue—will be multiplied many times when such formulas are applied to the infinitely larger number of other businesses which are engaged in exclusively interstate commerce. . . .

These considerations do not at all lead to the conclusion that the vast amount of business carried on throughout all the States as part of what is exclusively interstate commerce should not be made to contribute to the cost of maintaining state governments .   .   .. The question is whether the answer to this problem rests with this Court or with Congress.

I am not unmindful of the extent to which federal taxes absorb the taxable resources of the Nation, while at the same time the fiscal demands of the States are on the increase. These conditions present far-reaching problems of accommodating federal-state fiscal policy. But a determination of who is to get how much out of the common fund can hardly be made wisely and smoothly through the adjudicatory process. In fact, relying on the courts to solve these problems only aggravates the difficulties and retards proper legislative solution.

At best, this Court can only act negatively; it can determine whether a specific state tax is imposed in violation of the Commerce Clause. Such decisions must necessarily depend on the application of rough and ready legal concepts. We cannot make a detailed inquiry into the incidence of diverse economic burdens in order to determine the extent to which such burdens conflict with the necessities of national economic life. Neither can we devise appropriate standards for dividing up national revenue on the basis of more or less abstract principles of constitutional law, which cannot be responsive to the subtleties of the interrelated economies of Nation and State.

The problem calls for solution by devising a congressional policy. Congress alone can provide for a full and thorough canvassing of the multitudinous and intricate factors which compose the problem of the taxing freedom of the States and the needed limits on such state taxing power. Congressional committees can make studies and give the claims of the individual States adequate hearing .   .   .. The solution to these problems ought not to rest on the self-serving determination of the States of what they are entitled to out of the Nation's resources. Congress alone can formulate policies founded upon economic realities, perhaps to be applied to the myriad situations involved by a properly constituted and duly informed administrative agency.

APPORTIONMENT FORMULAS, MULTIPLE TAX RISKS, AND THE D. C. GENERAL MOTORS CASE

Though the holding in General Motors Corp. v. District of Columbia, 381 U.S. 553 (1965), rested on statutory grounds, the Court's opinion contained one of the few modern discussions of apportionment formulas, and the constitutional dicta are worth noting. The District of Columbia Income and Franchise Tax Act imposed a franchise tax on all corporations engaging in business in the District. The statutory measure of the tax was "that portion of the net income . . . as is fairly attributable to any trade or business carried on" in the District. The District Tax Commissioners were authorized to adopt regulations governing the allocation of income. The regulations provided that income from sales was to be apportioned on the basis of the proportion of District sales to total sales of the taxpayer. General Motors, whose principal offices and manufacturing facilities are outside of the District, made substantial sales to District automobile dealers. It challenged the Commissioner's single-factor, sales formula on the ground that this method attributed an "unreasonably high proportion of its income" to the District and was accordingly invalid under the statute and the commerce and due process clauses.

Justice Stewart's majority opinion concluded that "this method of allocation is not authorized by the D.C.Code"; he did not reach the constitutional objections. But constitutional considerations influenced the decision: in explaining the Court's reasons for departing from its normal practice of not reexamining interpretations of District of Columbia statutes, for example, Justice Stewart noted that lower court approval of the regulations "lends sanction to an apportionment formula seriously at variance with those prevailing in the vast majority of States and creates substantial dangers of multiple taxation."

In the course of the opinion, the Court noted: "The great majority of States imposing corporate income taxes apportion the total income of a corporation by application of a three-factor formula which gives equal weight to the geographical distribution of plant, payroll, and sales.[1] The use of an apportionment formula based wholly on the sales factor, in the context of general use of the three-factor approach, will ordinarily result in multiple taxation of corporate net income; for the States in which the property and payroll of the corporation are located will allocate to themselves 67% of the corporation's income, whereas the jurisdictions in which the sales are made will allocate 100% of the income to themselves. Conversely, in some cases enterprises will have their payroll and plant located in the sales-factor juris-

---

[1] "Of the 38 States requiring payment of such taxes, 26 employ varieties of a three-factor formula which takes into account the geographical distribution of a corporation's payroll, property and sales, generally giving equal weight to each factor. Another three use substantially the same formula, replacing the payroll factor with the broader category of manufacturing costs. Yet another three make use of a formula which incorporates the sales and property factors. Only four taxing jurisdictions use formulae based solely on the geographic distribution of corporate sales. See H.R.Rep.No. 1480, 88th Cong., 2d Sess., at 119." [Footnote by the Court. See the following note.]

dictions and make their sales in the three-factor jurisdictions so that only 33% of their incomes will be subject to state taxation. In any case, the sheer inconsistency of the District formula with that generally prevailing may tend to result in the unhealthy fragmentation of enterprise and an uneconomic pattern of plant location, and so presents an added reason why this Court must give proper meaning to the relevant provisions of the District Code.

"Moreover, the result reached in this case is consistent with the concern which the Court has shown that state taxes imposed on income from interstate commerce be fairly apportioned. . . . While the Court has refrained from attempting to define any single appropriate method of apportionment, it has sought to ensure that the methods used display a modicum of reasonable relation to corporate activities within the State. The Court has approved formulae based on the geographical distribution of corporate property and those based on the standard three-factor formula. See, e. g., Underwood Typewriter Co. v. Chamberlain [254 U.S. 113]; Butler Bros. v. McColgan, 315 U.S. 501. The standard three-factor formula can be justified as a rough, practical approximation of the distribution of either a corporation's sources of income or the social costs which it generates. By contrast, the geographical distribution of a corporation's sales is, by itself, of dubious significance in indicating the locus of either factor. We of course do not mean to take any position on the constitutionality of a state income tax based on the sales factor alone. For the present purpose, it is sufficient to note that the factors alluded to by this Court in justifying apportionment measures constitutionally challenged in the past lend little support to the use of an exclusively sales-oriented approach. In construing the District Code to prohibit the use of a sales-factor formula, we sacrifice none of the values which our scrutiny of state apportionment measures has sought to protect. . . ." Justices Black and Douglas dissented, finding the formula authorized by the statute.

THE CONGRESSIONAL STUDY AND THE PROPOSED INTERSTATE TAXATION ACT

Introduction. Reaction to the Northwestern States decision provoked the first comprehensive effort to formulate guidelines for state taxation of interstate commerce through congressional legislation rather than constitutional adjudication. The fears of increased taxation led to a stop-gap law within a few months of Northwestern States; that law also initiated what became a general study of taxation by a House Subcommittee. That Subcommittee's Recommendations, even in diluted form, have encountered resistance, in Congress and out. Nevertheless, the proposals are worth noting, for their suggestions of alternatives to judicially developed solutions as well as for the light they cast on the relative capacity of Congress and Court to deal with state tax problems.

1. *The 1959 stop-gap statute.* The statute enacted soon after the decision included the "Minimal Standards" provisions noted in the margin.[1]

---

1. Title I, "Imposition of Minimal Standards," provided:

Sec. 101. (a) No State, or political subdivision thereof, shall have power to impose . . . a net income tax on the income derived within such State by any person from interstate commerce if the only business activities within such State by or on behalf of

Would those prohibitions bar taxation in the situations presented in the principal case? Did the companies there engage in no more than "the solicitation of orders"? Is there any doubt about the constitutionality of the statute?

2. *The congressional study:* a. *The scope.* As part of the same statute, Congress initiated a general study of state taxation problems. As subsequently broadened, Title II directed the House Judiciary Committee and the Senate Finance Committee, "acting separately or jointly," to make "full and complete studies" (and report "proposals for legislation") on "all matters pertaining to the taxation of interstate commerce by the States."

b. *The Subcommittee Report.* The first published results of the study directed by Title II—a comprehensive and provocative empirical study of income taxes—appeared in 1964. Report of a Special Subcommittee of the House Judiciary Committee, State Taxation of Interstate Commerce, H.R.Rep. No. 1480, 88th Cong., 2d Sess. The final segment of the Report (on sales and use, capital stock, and gross receipts taxes) was submitted a year later, in 1965. H.R.Rep. No. 565, 89th Cong., 1st Sess. The 1964 Report concluded: "The present system works badly for both business and the States. [It is] a system in which the States are reaching farther and farther to impose smaller and smaller liabilities on more and more companies. [It is] a system which calls upon tax administrators to enforce the unenforceable, and the taxpayer to comply with the uncompliable."

Some general observations in the final chapter of the 1964 Report are especially worth noting: "The problems of multistate income taxation today result from the attempt to apply a highly complex system to many companies which are simply unable to deal with it. Clearly, big business is in interstate commerce, but all interstate commerce is not big business. There are in the United States 120,000 companies, at the very least, which sell goods across State lines. Of these, a great many and probably most have annual sales volumes under $1 million . . .. For the vast number of small- and moderate-sized companies . . ., the system simply has no relation to their ability to cope with it. Viewed in these terms, the results of the situation become apparent. In broad areas the demands of the States upon interstate businesses are largely disregarded. . . . In spite of a legal system in which companies are often required to file returns in States in which they

such person during such taxable year are either, or both, of the following:

(1) the solicitation of orders by such person, or his representative in such State for sales of tangible personal property, which orders are sent outside the State for approval or rejection, and, if approved, are filled by shipment or delivery from a point outside the State; and

(2) the solicitation of orders by such person, or his representative, in such State in the name of or for the benefit of a prospective customer of such person, if orders by such customer to such person to enable such customer to fill orders resulting from such solicitation are orders described in paragraph (1).
. . . .

(c) For purposes of subsection (a), a person shall not be considered to have engaged in business activities within a State during any taxable year merely by reason of sales in such State, or the solicitation of orders for sales in such State, of tangible personal property on behalf of such person by one or more independent contractors, or by reason of the maintenance of an office in such State by one or more independent contractors whose activities on behalf of such person in such State consist solely of making sales, or soliciting orders for sales, of tangible personal property. . . .

Sec. 103. For purposes of this title, the term "net income tax" means any tax imposed on, or measured by, net income.

maintain sales offices, or inventories of goods, or are merely represented by itinerant employees, the typical interstate company pays income taxes only where it has a factory, an administrative office, or a warehouse. . . . Overall, in cost terms, it would seem that the major significance of the prevailing system is not that it produces expensive compliance, but that the cost of full compliance is a major cause of noncompliance." (Compare Justice Frankfurter's opinion in the Northwestern States case p. 744, supra.) [2]

3. *The fate of the Subcommittee Recommendations: The proposed Interstate Taxation Act.* In 1965, a few weeks after its concluding Report, the Subcommittee's proposals for legislative solution of the state tax problem were ready. (See H.R.Rep. No. 952, 89th Cong., 1st Sess., and note 4 below.) The efforts to enact the Recommendations have encountered serious obstacles, however. The House Judiciary Committee, to be sure, approved the Recommendations unanimously, a bill embodying them was soon introduced (H.R. 11798, 89th Cong., 1st Sess.), and committee hearings commenced early in 1966. But during the ensuing committee consideration, considerable opposition to some of the proposals was voiced, especially from a number of state tax officials. After the hearings, the Subcommittee "formulated a more limited program." See H.R. 16491, 89th Cong., 2d Sess. House approval of the revised bill, H.R. 2158, 90th Cong., 2d Sess., finally came in May, 1968, but the proposed Interstate Taxation Act died in the Senate. In May, 1969, the Subcommittee once again cleared a similar proposal, see H.R. 7906 and H.R.Rep. No. 279, 91st Cong., 1st Sess., but it was not brought to a floor vote during that session. See generally an article by House Judiciary Committee Chairman Celler, "The Development of a Congressional Program Dealing with State Taxation of Interstate Commerce," 36 Fordham L. Rev. 385 (1968).

4. *The content of the Subcommittee Recommendations.* Though they have been watered down during the congressional considerations, a sampling of the 1965 Recommendations is worthwhile, to compare legislative proposals and capacities with judicial gropings. Note, e. g., the limits on income taxes, the restriction of gross receipts taxes to the state of origin, and the emphasis on the state of destination for sales and use taxes. The excerpts which follow

2. One earlier chapter of the 1964 Report also deserves special mention. In Chapter 16, "Proposals for the Division of Income," the Report examines the "effects of alternative apportionment formulas." The conclusion: "In terms of revenue impact, the detailed analysis undertaken by the Subcommittee staff indicates that the importance of choice among division-of-income rules is very much smaller than has traditionally been thought to be the case. . . . Thus, if a choice were made among three possible uniform formulas —a two-factor formula containing only property and payroll factors, a three-factor formula in which a sales-origin factor is added, and a three-factor formula in which a sales-destination factor is added—it appears that for 26 of the income tax States less than one-half of 1 percent of total tax revenues would be involved in the choice . . . . No formula which has been seriously proposed as a basis for uniformity constitutes a serious threat to the treasury of any of the income tax States. . . . If a choice among uniform formulas is to be made, it can be made primarily on the basis of other considerations. One of these considerations is the effect of the formula upon the cost to taxpayers of remitting their State income tax payments. . . . [I]t must be concluded that the effect of cost considerations is to suggest the adoption of a formula which is consistent with a relatively narrow scope of State income tax liability." Compare the one-factor (sales) formula in General Motors Corp. v. District of Columbia, supra.

are from the Subcommittee's Summary of Recommendations, chap. 38, H.R. Rep. 952, 89th Cong., 1st Sess. (1965):

A.   Introduction

. . . [T]he present situation is characterized by a conflict between the diversity and multiplicity prescribed by the various State laws and the limited extent to which such a system can realistically be complied with or enforced.   In dealing with the problems which result, two approaches are possible.   Under one approach, jurisdiction to tax the interstate company would be extended to all States into which it sells. The resulting broad spread of tax obligations would be made compatible with a reasonable level of compliance by the formulation of uniform provisions on such matters as measurement of the tax base, exemptions, attribution rules, and reporting methods. Furthermore, to achieve an effective level of enforcement, a broad assumption of administrative and collection responsibilities by the Federal Government would be required.

The alternative is to restrict the spread of jurisdiction to tax to a degree which is consistent with both operational practicability and a continuation of diversity in important areas of State tax law.   This approach has been accepted as the basic framework for the Committee's recommendations.   It is the approach which is most consistent with the preservation of maximum freedom in State and local tax policy, produces the least departure from existing practices, and is an effective means of resolving the serious problems which now exist.   In the area of sales taxation, however, the logic of the tax has suggested the desirability of making available to the States the option of participation in a program of cooperative administration. . . .

In formulating its recommendations, the Committee has followed a number of principles with respect to all of the taxes involved:

First, while ease of compliance has not been the only consideration in formulating these recommendations, it has been an important factor.

Second,   . . .   so too has the effect of the proposals on State revenues been given substantial weight. . . .   Estimates indicate that under the recommended program no State stands to gain or lose a significant percentage of its tax revenue.   Furthermore, by broadening jurisdiction to collect sales taxes and strengthening enforcement against out-of-State sellers, the recommendations would tend to increase sales tax collections, particularly in destination-oriented States. . . .   Third, a single standard is prescribed for determining the circumstances in which a business is required to file returns and pay tax to a State.   The test selected makes liability depend on owning or leasing realty in the State or having an employee whose services are performed entirely in the State—basically a business-location standard.   This test conforms closely to the current general practice . . . .

Fourth, the recommended program provides the interstate company with a body of uniform rules for attributing tax bases to the States.   In the income tax and capital stock tax areas this uniformity is achieved through the use of a two-factor property-payroll apportionment formula.   In the gross receipts tax area it is achieved by a uniform rule that attributes gross receipts from the sale of goods to the State of origin.   Sales taxes, on the other hand, are to be collected for the State where the buyer is located.

Fifth, these proposals are designed to achieve congruence between jurisdiction and the attribution of tax bases. In short, whenever income, capital stock, sales, or gross receipts are attributed to a particular State by the uniform attribution rules, that State has jurisdiction to impose a tax. . . .

B.   The Recommendations

INCOME TAXES

Division of income.—All income is apportioned by a two-factor formula based on property and payroll. . . .

Jurisdiction.—Jurisdiction is congruent with the apportionment of income. A corporation is taxable if it: (1) owns or leases realty in the State or (2) has an employee whose services are performed entirely in the State.

. . .

SALES AND USE TAXES

Locating sales.—Under uniform rules applicable to all States, sales are taxable by the State in which the buyer first receives physical delivery of the goods. The State of consumption or use may also impose a tax, but must give a credit for prior taxes paid to other States, or a refund to the extent of taxes subsequently paid to the State of delivery. . . .

Jurisdiction.—A State may not require a seller to collect a sales or use tax unless the seller: (1) owns or leases realty in the State, (2) has an employee whose services are performed entirely in the State, or (3) regularly uses his own vehicles or a private parcel service to make deliveries to private residences in the State.

However, in States which participate in a system of cooperative administration by adopting a model sales tax law to be prescribed by Congress, any seller making sales into the State will be required to collect taxes in accordance with the uniform rules provided. Each State will determine its own rate and will administer the model law with respect to predominantly intrastate sales. Under the model law no collection is required if the seller: (1) does not offer to make sales other than by prepaid mail order, and (2) has no contacts with the State other than the dissemination of advertising. . . .

GROSS RECEIPTS TAXES

Gross receipts from the sale of tangible personalty may be taxed only by the State of origin. The jurisdictional rule for corporate income taxes also applies to determine the circumstances in which a person is liable for a gross receipts tax. . . .

Chapter 10

INTERGOVERNMENTAL IMMUNITIES AND INTERSTATE RELATIONSHIPS

SECTION 1. INTERGOVERNMENTAL IMMUNITIES— TAXATION AND REGULATION

McCULLOCH v. MARYLAND

4 Wheat. 316, 4 L.Ed. 579 (1819).

[This case—holding unconstitutional Maryland's tax on the operations of the Bank of the United States—is printed at p. 201, supra. See also the consideration of the tax immunity of modern national banks, with the majority resting the immunity on statutory grounds and the dissenters finding no constitutionally required immunity, in First Agric. Nat. Bank v. State Tax Comm'n, 392 U.S. 339 (1968), at p. 764, below.]

THE GROWTH OF TAX IMMUNITIES

Introduction. McCulloch v. Maryland invalidated a state tax on the operations of the federally incorporated Bank. Ten years later, the Marshall Court held unconstitutional the application of a city's general property tax on a taxpayer's federal bonds. Weston v. Charleston, 2 Pet. 449 (1829). From these beginnings, and for over a century, constitutional tax immunities expanded in a number of directions. For example, though Marshall had left the matter in considerable doubt, the Court later held that state activities enjoyed a reciprocal immunity from federal taxation. And the Court steadily expanded the circle of immunity from the governmental activity itself to third persons—employees, patentees, lessees—in some way related to governmental activities.

Since the late 1930's, that circle has contracted sharply.[1] Yet the governmental immunity doctrine continues to have vitality, through statutory recognition as well as by constitutional mandate. This section briefly traces the growth and shrinking of the immunities from Marshall's day to Stone's, and then samples some of the contemporary dimensions of the doctrine.

1. *State immunity from federal taxation: Justice Nelson in Collector v. Day.* In Collector v. Day, 11 Wall. 113 (1871), Court held the salary of a state judge immune from the national income tax. Justice Nelson noted that the Taney Court had held a state could not tax a federal officer's salary, in Dobbins v. Erie County, 16 Pet. 435 (1842), and rejected the suggestion in McCulloch that federal taxation might not be subject to a similar limitation.

---

1. See generally Powell, "The Waning of Intergovernmental Tax Immunities," 58 Harv.L.Rev. 633 (1945); Powell, "The Remnant of Intergovernmental Tax Immunities," 58 Harv.L.Rev. 757 (1945), Selected Essays 1938–62 (1963), 403; Konefsky, Chief Justice Stone and the Supreme Court (1945), chap. I; Powell, Vagaries and Varieties in Constitutional Interpretation (1956), chap. IV.

With regard to reserved powers, "the State is as sovereign and independent as the general government." And "if the means and instrumentalities employed by [the national] government to carry into operation the powers granted to it are, necessarily, and, for the sake of self-preservation, exempt from taxation by the States, why are not those of the States depending upon their reserved powers, for like reasons, equally exempt from Federal taxation?"

Justice Bradley's dissent insisted "that the general government has the same power of taxing the income of officers of the State governments as it has of taxing that of its own officers. . . . The taxation by the State governments of the instruments employed by the general government in the exercise of its powers, is a very different thing. Such taxation involves an interference with the powers of a government in which other States and their citizens are equally interested with the State which imposes the taxation. In my judgment, the limitation of the power of taxation in the general government which the present decision establishes, will be found very difficult of control."

2. *The expansion of intergovernmental immunities to private taxpayers: From Justice Nelson to Justice Stone.* In the last third of the Nineteenth century and the first third of the Twentieth, many cases sustained private taxpayers' claims that their relationship to government entitled them to tax immunity. For example, state sales taxes could not be applied to sales made to the federal government, Panhandle Oil Co. v. Mississippi, 277 U.S. 218 (1928), and a federal tax could not be collected on sales by a private business to a state, Indian Motorcycle Co. v. United States, 283 U.S. 570 (1931). On the same premises—that the tax burden on the individual would ultimately fall on government—a private lessee of state lands did not have to pay federal income tax on profits from the lease, Burnet v. Coronado Oil & Gas Co., 285 U.S. 393 (1932), reciprocating the immunity from state income taxes that had been granted to a lessee of Indian lands in Gillespie v. Oklahoma, 257 U.S. 501 (1922). And, for a few years, even patent royalties were free from state income taxes. Long v. Rockwood, 277 U.S. 142 (1928), overruled in a copyright royalties case four years later, Fox Film Corp. v. Doyal, 286 U.S. 123 (1932).[2]

By the late 1930's, the repeated protests by Justice Stone and others finally produced a halt—and, soon, a retreat—in the trend. In a 5:4 decision, the Court held that proceeds from a construction contract with the United States were subject to a state gross receipts tax. James v. Dravo Contracting Co., 302 U.S. 134 (1937). And in Helvering v. Mountain Producers Corp., 303 U.S. 376 (1938), the Burnet and Gillespie cases, supra, were overruled and a lessee of state lands was held subject to the federal income tax. Shortly thereafter, Justice Stone had the opportunity to reexamine the scope of tax immunities, in the two major opinions which follow. Was Stone's approach a return to Marshall's or a new one? Note Stone's statement of the holding of McCulloch, at the beginning of the next case. Is it an accurate statement? Was Marshall speaking of congressional intent?

2. Compare Metcalf & Eddy v. Mitchell, 269 U.S. 514 (1926) (sustaining a state tax on the net income received for engineering work for the federal government).

HELVERING v. GERHARDT

304 U.S. 405, 58 S.Ct. 969, 82 L.Ed. 1427 (1938).

Certiorari to the Circuit Court of Appeals for the Second Circuit.

Mr. Justice STONE delivered the opinion of the Court. . . .

[Employees of the Port of New York Authority resisted the federal income tax on their salaries, as an unconstitutional burden on New York and New Jersey. The Authority, a bi-state corporation, was created pursuant to an interstate compact, see sec. 2B, infra, to improve the port and operate bridges, tunnels, terminals and other facilities. The Court of Appeals held that the salaries were exempt from the federal tax.]

The Constitution contains no express limitation on the power of either a state or the national government to tax the other, or its instrumentalities. The doctrine that there is an implied limitation stems from McCulloch v. Maryland, 4 Wheat. 316, in which it was held that a state tax laid specifically upon the privilege of issuing bank notes, and in fact applicable alone to the notes of national banks, was invalid since it impeded the national government in the exercise of its power to establish and maintain a bank . . . . It was held that Congress, having power to establish a bank by laws which . . . are supreme, also had power to protect the bank by striking down state action impeding its operations; and it was thought that the state tax in question was so inconsistent with Congress's constitutional action in establishing the bank as to compel the conclusion that Congress intended to forbid application of the tax to the federal bank notes.[1]

In sustaining the immunity from state taxation, the opinion of the Court, by Chief Justice Marshall, recognized a clear distinction between the extent of the power of a state to tax national banks and that of the national government to tax state instrumentalities. . . . The exercise of the national taxing power is . . . subject to a safeguard which does not operate when a state undertakes to tax a national instrumentality. . . .

We need not stop to inquire how far, as indicated in McCulloch v. Maryland, supra, the immunity of federal instrumentalities from state taxation rests on a different basis from that of state instrumentalities; or whether or to what degree it is more extensive. . . . It is enough for present purposes that the state immunity from the national taxing power, when recognized in Collector v. Day, supra, was narrowly limited to a state judicial officer engaged in the performance of a function which pertained to state governments at the time the Constitution was adopted, without which no state "could long preserve its existence."

There are cogent reasons why any constitutional restriction upon the taxing power granted to Congress, so far as it can be properly raised by implication, should be narrowly limited. One, as was pointed out by Chief

---

1. It follows that in considering the immunity of federal instrumentalities from state taxation two factors may be of importance which are lacking in the case of a claimed immunity of state instrumentalities from federal taxation. Since the acts of Congress within its constitutional power are supreme, the validity of state taxation of federal instrumentalities must de-pend (a) on the power of Congress to create the instrumentality and (b) its intent to protect it from state taxation. Congress may curtail an immunity which might otherwise be implied, ... or enlarge it beyond the point where, Congress being silent, the Court would set its limits. . . . [Footnote by the Court.]

Justice Marshall . . ., is that the people of all the states have created the national government and are represented in Congress. Through that representation they exercise the national taxing power. The very fact that when they are exercising it they are taxing themselves serves to guard against its abuse through the possibility of resort to the usual processes of political action which provides a readier and more adaptable means than any which courts can afford, for securing accommodation of the competing demands for national revenue, on the one hand, and for reasonable scope for the independence of state action, on the other.[2]

Another reason rests upon the fact that any allowance of a tax immunity for the protection of state sovereignty is at the expense of the sovereign power of the nation to tax. Enlargement of the one involves diminution of the other. When enlargement proceeds beyond the necessity of protecting the state, the burden of the immunity is thrown upon the national government with benefit only to a privileged class of taxpayers. . . . Once impaired by the recognition of a state immunity found to be excessive, restoration of [the national taxing] power is not likely to be secured through the action of state legislatures; for they are without the inducements to act which have often persuaded Congress to waive immunities thought to be excessive. . . .

In a period marked by a constant expansion of government activities and the steady multiplication of the complexities of taxing systems, it is perhaps too much to expect that the judicial pronouncements marking the boundaries of state immunity should present a completely logical pattern. But they disclose no purposeful departure from, and indeed definitely establish, two guiding principles of limitation for holding the tax immunity of state instrumentalities to its proper function. The one, dependent upon the nature of the function being performed by the state or in its behalf, excludes from the immunity activities thought not to be essential to the preservation of state governments even though the tax be collected from the state treasury. The state itself was taxed for the privilege of carrying on the liquor business in South Carolina v. United States, [199 U.S. 437], and a tax on the income of a state officer engaged in the management of a state-owned corporation operating a street railroad was sustained in Helvering v. Powers, [293 U.S. 214], because it was thought that the functions discouraged by these taxes were not indispensable to the maintenance of a state government. The other principle, exemplified by those cases where the tax laid upon individuals affects the state only as the burden is passed onto it by the taxpayer, forbids recognition of the immunity when the burden on the state is so speculative and uncertain that if allowed it would restrict the federal taxing power without affording any corresponding tangible protection to the state government; even though the function be thought important enough to demand immunity from a tax upon the state itself, it is not necessarily protected from a tax which well may be substantially or entirely absorbed by private persons. Metcalf & Eddy v. Mitchell, supra . . . .

With these controlling principles in mind we turn to their application in the circumstances of the present case. The challenged taxes . . . are

---

2. Compare Justice Stone's emphasis on the operation of the political processes in two cases decided shortly before Gerhardt: South Carolina State High- way Department v. Barnwell, 303 U.S. 177 (1938), chap. 8, p. 629, and United States v. Carolene Products Co., 304 U.S. 144 (1938), chap. 15, p. 1051.

upon the net income of respondents, derived from their employment in common occupations not shown to be different in their methods or duties from those of similar employees in private industry. The taxpayers enjoy the benefits and protection of the laws of the United States. They are under a duty to support the government and are not beyond the reach of its taxing power. A non-discriminatory tax laid on their net income, in common with that of all other members of the community, could by no reasonable probability be considered to preclude the performance of the function which New York and New Jersey have undertaken, or to obstruct it more than like private enterprises are obstructed by our taxing system. Even though, to some unascertainable extent, the tax deprives the state of the advantage of paying less than the standard rate for the services which they engage, it does not curtail any of those functions which have been thought hitherto to be essential to their continued existence as states. At most it may be said to increase somewhat the cost of the state governments because, in an interdependent economic society, the taxation of income tends to raise (to some extent which economists are not able to measure . . .) the price of labor and materials. The effect of the immunity if allowed would be to relieve respondents of their duty of financial support to the national government, in order to secure to the state a theoretical advantage so speculative in its character and measurement as to be unsubstantial. A tax immunity devised for protection of the states as governmental entities cannot be pressed so far. . . .

The basis upon which constitutional tax immunity of a state has been supported is the protection which it affords to the continued existence of the state. To attain that end it is not ordinarily necessary to confer on the state a competitive advantage over private persons in carrying on the operations of its government. There is no such necessity here, and the resulting impairment of the federal power to tax argues against the advantage. The state and national governments must co-exist. Each must be supported by taxation of those who are citizens of both. The mere fact that the economic burden of such taxes may be passed on to a state government and thus increase to some extent, here wholly conjectural, the expense of its operation, infringes no constitutional immunity. Such burdens are but normal incidents of the organization within the same territory of two governments, each possessed of the taxing power. . . .

. . .   [T]here may be state agencies of such a character and so intimately associated with the performance of an indispensable function of state government that any taxation of them would threaten such interference with the functions of government itself as to be considered beyond the reach of the federal taxing power. If the tax considered in Collector v. Day, supra, upon the salary of an officer engaged in the performance of an indispensable function of the state which cannot be delegated to private individuals, may be regarded as such an instance, that is not the case presented here. . . .

Reversed.

Mr. Justice BLACK, concurring. . . . .

While I believe [the Court's reasons] are adequate to support the tax, I find it difficult to reconcile this result with the principle announced in

Collector v. Day, 11 Wall. 113, and later decisions applying that principle. This leads me to the conclusion that we should review and re-examine the rule based upon Collector v. Day. That course would logically require the entire subject of intergovernmental tax immunity to be reviewed in the light of the effect of the Sixteenth Amendment authorizing Congress to levy a tax on incomes "from whatever source derived"   .   .   ..

[The dissenting opinion by Mr. Justice BUTLER, concurred in by Mr. Justice McREYNOLDS, is omitted.]

GRAVES v. O'KEEFE—FEDERAL EMPLOYEES AND STATE TAXES

In a second major Stone decision, Graves v. New York ex rel. O'Keefe, 306 U.S. 466 (1939), an employee of the Home Owners' Loan Corporation —established by Congress as an "instrumentality of the United States" and wholly government-owned—resisted the New York income tax on his salary. The state courts sustained his claim, in reliance on New York ex rel. Rogers v. Graves, 299 U.S. 401 (1937), which held that New York could not tax the salary of an employee of the Panama Railroad Company, another wholly-owned corporate instrumentality of the United States. The Supreme Court, one year after Gerhardt, reversed, again in an opinion by Justice Stone:

"The conclusion reached in the Gerhardt case   .   .   .   makes it imperative that we should consider anew the immunity here claimed for the salary of an employee of a federal instrumentality.   .   .   .   [S]uch differences as there may be between the implied tax immunity of a state and the corresponding immunity of the national government and its instrumentalities may be traced to the fact that the national government is one of delegated powers, in the exercise of which it is supreme. Whatever scope this may give to the national government to claim immunity from state taxation of all instrumentalities which it may constitutionally create, and whatever authority Congress may possess as incidental to the exercise of its delegated powers to grant or withhold immunity from state taxation, Congress has not sought in this case to exercise such power. Hence these distinctions between the two types of immunity cannot affect the question with which we are now concerned. The burden on government of a non-discriminatory income tax applied to the salary of the employee of a government or its instrumentality is the same, whether a state or national government is concerned.   .   .   .

"Assuming, as we do, that the Home Owners' Loan Corporation is clothed with the same immunity from state taxation as the government itself, we cannot say that the present tax on the income of its employees lays any unconstitutional burden upon it. All the reasons for refusing to imply a constitutional prohibition of federal income taxation of salaries of state employees, stated at length in the Gerhardt case, are of equal force when immunity is claimed from state income tax on salaries paid by the national government or its agencies. In this respect we perceive no basis for a difference in result whether the taxed income be salary or some other form of compensation, or whether the taxpayer be an employee or an officer of either a state or the national government, or of its instrumentalities. In no case is there basis for the assumption that any such tangible or certain economic burden is imposed on the government concerned as would justify a court's declaring that the taxpayer is clothed with the implied constitutional tax immunity of the government by which he is employed. . . . Collector v. Day, supra, and New York ex rel. Rogers v. Graves, supra, are overruled so far as they recognize an implied constitutional immunity from income taxation of the salaries of officers or employees of the national or a state government or their instrumentalities. . . . " Chief Justice Hughes concurred in the result. Justice Frankfurter submitted a concurring opinion, and Justice Butler, joined by Justice McReynolds, dissented.

NEW YORK v. UNITED STATES

326 U.S. 572, 66 S.Ct. 310, 90 L.Ed. 326 (1946).

Certiorari to the Circuit Court of Appeals for the Second Circuit.

Mr. Justice FRANKFURTER announced the judgment of the Court and delivered an opinion in which Mr. Justice RUTLEDGE joined.

Section 615(a) of the 1932 Revenue Act imposed a tax on mineral waters. The United States brought this suit to recover taxes assessed against the State of New York on the sale of mineral waters taken from Saratoga Springs, New York. The State claims immunity from this tax on the ground that "in the bottling and sale of the said waters the defendant State of New York was engaged in the exercise of a usual, traditional and essential governmental function." [The lower federal courts rejected New York's claim.]

On the basis of authority the case is quickly disposed of. When States sought to control the liquor traffic by going into the liquor business, they were denied immunity from federal taxes upon the liquor business. South Carolina v. United States, 199 U.S. 437; Ohio v. Helvering, 292 U.S. 360. And in rejecting a claim of immunity from federal taxation when Massachusetts took over the street railways of Boston, this Court a decade ago said: "We see no reason for putting the operation of a street railway [by a State] in a different category from the sale of liquors." Helvering v. Powers, 293 U.S. 214, 227. We certainly see no reason for putting soft drinks in a different constitutional category from hard drinks. . . .

But the fear that one government may cripple or obstruct the operations of the other early led to the assumption that there was a reciprocal immunity of the instrumentalities of each from taxation by the other. . . . The considerations bearing upon taxation by the States of activities or agencies of the federal government are not correlative with the considerations bearing upon federal taxation of State agencies or activities. The federal government is the government of all the States, and all the States share in the legislative process by which a tax of general applicability is laid.

In the older cases, the emphasis was on immunity from taxation. The whole tendency of recent cases reveals a shift in emphasis to that of limitation upon immunity. They also indicate an awareness of the limited role of courts in assessing the relative weight of the factors upon which immunity is based. Any implied limitation upon the supremacy of the federal power to levy a tax like that now before us, in the absence of discrimination against State activities, brings fiscal and political factors into play. The problem cannot escape issues that do not lend themselves to judgment by criteria and methods of reasoning that are within the professional training and special competence of judges. Indeed the claim of implied immunity by States from federal taxation raises questions not wholly unlike provisions of the Constitution, such as that of Art. IV, § 4, guaranteeing States a republican form of government, . . . which this Court has deemed not within its duty to adjudicate.

We have already held that by engaging in the railroad business a State cannot withdraw the railroad from the power of the federal government to regulate commerce. United States v. California, 297 U.S. 175. . . . Surely the power of Congress to lay taxes has impliedly no less a reach than the power of Congress to regulate commerce. There are, of course, State activities and State-owned property that partake of uniqueness from the point of view of intergovernmental relations. These inherently constitute a class by themselves. Only a State can own a Statehouse; only a State can get income by taxing. These could not be included for purposes of federal taxation in any abstract category of taxpayers without taxing the State as a State. But so long as Congress generally taps a source of revenue by whomsoever earned and not uniquely capable of being earned only by a State, the Constitution of the United States does not forbid it merely because its incidence falls also on a State. . . .

The process of Constitutional adjudication does not thrive on conjuring up horrible possibilities that never happen in the real world and devising doctrines sufficiently comprehensive in detail to cover the remotest contingency. Nor need we go beyond what is required for a reasoned disposition of the kind of controversy now before the Court. . . . So we decide enough when we reject limitations upon the taxing power of Congress derived from such untenable criteria as "proprietary" against "governmental" activities of the States, or historically sanctioned activities of Government or activities conducted merely for profit, and find no restriction upon Congress to include the States in levying a tax exacted equally from private persons upon the same subject matter.

Judgment affirmed.*

Mr. Justice JACKSON took no part in the consideration or decision of this case. [A concurring opinion by Justice RUTLEDGE is omitted.]

Mr. Chief Justice STONE, [joined by Justices REED, MURPHY and BURTON, concurring in the result.] . . .

In view of our decisions . . . ., we would find it difficult not to sustain the tax in this case, even though we regard as untenable the distinction between "governmental" and "proprietary" interests on which those cases rest to some extent. But we are not prepared to say that the national government may constitutionally lay a nondiscriminatory tax on every class of property and activities of States and individuals alike.

Concededly a federal tax discriminating against a State would be an unconstitutional exertion of power over a coexisting sovereignty within the same framework of government. But our difficulty with the formula, now first

---

* May the United States impose a tax on fees charged for admission to bathing beaches operated by a subdivision (local park district) of a State? In sustaining such a tax, the Court rested its conclusion on the "second restrictive principle" of Helvering v. Gerhardt, supra, relating to the "speculative and uncertain" effect of the tax. Wilmette Park District v. Campbell, 338 U.S. 411 (1949).

suggested as offering a new solution for an old problem, is that a federal tax which is not discriminatory as to the subject matter may nevertheless so affect the State, merely because it is a State that is being taxed, as to interfere unduly with the State's performance of its sovereign functions of government. The counterpart of such undue interference has been recognized since Marshall's day as the implied immunity of each of the dual sovereignties of our constitutional system from taxation by the other. . . . We add nothing to this formula by saying, in a new form of words, that a tax which Congress applies generally to the property and activities of private citizens may not be in some instances constitutionally extended to the States merely because the States are included among those who pay taxes on a like subject of taxation.

. . . [I]t is plain that there may be non-discriminatory taxes which, when laid on a State, would nevertheless impair the sovereign status of the State quite as much as a like tax imposed by a State on property or activities of the national government. . . . This is not because the tax can be regarded as discriminatory but because a sovereign government is the taxpayer, and the tax, even though non-discriminatory, may be regarded as infringing its sovereignty.

It is enough for present purposes that the immunity of the State from federal taxation would, in this case, accomplish a withdrawal from the taxing power of the nation a subject of taxation of a nature which has been traditionally within that power from the beginning. Its exercise now, by a non-discriminatory tax, does not curtail the business of the state government more than it does the like business of the citizen. It gives merely an accustomed and reasonable scope to the federal taxing power. Such a withdrawal from a non-discriminatory federal tax, and one which does not bear on the State any differently than on the citizen, is itself an impairment of the taxing power of the national government, and the activity taxed is such that its taxation does not unduly impair the State's functions of government. . . .

Mr. Justice DOUGLAS, with whom Mr. Justice BLACK concurs, dissenting. . . .

I do not believe South Carolina v. United States states the correct rule. A State's project is as much a legitimate governmental activity whether it is traditional or akin to private enterprise, or conducted for profit. . . . A State may deem it as essential to its economy that it own and operate a railroad, a mill, or an irrigation system as it does to own and operate bridges, street lights, or a sewage disposal plant. What might have been viewed in an earlier day as an improvident or even dangerous extension of state activities may today be deemed indispensable. . . . Here a State is disposing of some of its natural resources. Tomorrow it may issue securities, sell power from its public power project, or manufacture fertilizer. Each is an exercise of its power of sovereignty. Must it pay the federal government for the privilege of exercising that inherent power? If the Constitution grants it immunity from a tax on the issuance of securities, on what grounds can it be forced to pay a tax when it sells power or disposes of other natural resources? . . .

. . . If the federal government can place the local governments on its tax collector's list, their capacity to serve the needs of their citizens is at once hampered or curtailed. . . . Many state activities are in marginal enterprises where private capital refuses to venture. Add to the cost of these projects a federal tax and the social program may be destroyed before it can be launched. . . . To say the present tax will be sustained because it does not impair the State's functions of government is to conclude either that the sale by the State of its mineral water is not a function of government or that the present tax is so slight as to be no burden. The former obviously is not true. The latter overlooks the fact that the power to tax lightly is the power to tax severely. The power to tax is indeed one of the most effective forms of regulation. And no more powerful instrument for centralization of government could be devised. For with the federal government immune and the States subject to tax, the economic ability of the federal government to expand its activities at the expense of the States is at once apparent. That is the result whether the rule of South Carolina v. United States be perpetuated or a new rule of discrimination be adopted

The notion that the sovereign position of the States must find its protection in the will of a transient majority of Congress is foreign to and a negation of our constitutional system. There will often be vital regional interests represented by no majority in Congress. The Constitution was designed to keep the balance between the States and the nation outside the field of legislative controversy.

The immunity of the States from federal taxation is no less clear because it is implied. . . . The Constitution is a compact between sovereigns. The power of one sovereign to tax another is an innovation so startling as to require explicit authority if it is to be allowed. If the power of the federal government to tax the States is conceded, the reserved power of the States guaranteed by the Tenth Amendment does not give them the independence which they have always been assumed to have. They have relegated to a more servile status. They become subject to interference and control both in the functions which they exercise and the methods which they employ. . . .

Of course, the levying of the present tax does not curtail the business of the state government more than it does the like business of the citizen. But the same might be true in the case of many state activities which have long been assumed to be immune from federal taxation. When a municipality acquires a water system or an electric power plant and transmission facilities, it withdraws projects from the field of private enterprise. Is the tax immunity to be denied because a tax on the municipality would not curtail the municipality more than it would the prior private owner? Is the municipality to be taxed whenever it engages in an activity which once was in the field of private enterprise and therefore was once taxable? Every expansion of state activity since the adoption of the Constitution limits the reach of federal taxation if state immunity is recognized. Yet none would concede that the sovereign powers of the States were limited to those which they exercised in 1787. . . . [T]he major objection to the suggested test is that it disregards the Tenth Amendment, places the sovereign States on the same plane as private citizens, and makes the sovereign States pay the federal government for the privilege of exercising the powers of sovereignty guaranteed them by the Constitution. . . .

There is no showing whatsoever that an expanding field of state activity even faintly promises to cripple the federal government in its search for needed revenues. If the truth were known, I suspect it would show that the activity of the States in the fields of housing, public power and the like have increased the level of income of the people and have raised the standards of marginal or sub-marginal groups. Such conditions affect favorably, not adversely, the tax potential of the federal government.

PROBLEMS OF TAX IMMUNITIES—SOME
MODERN DIMENSIONS

1. *Sales taxes on government contractors.* The argument that taxes on private activities impose immediate economic burdens on government is at its strongest where a contractor performs work for the government on a cost-plus-fixed-fee basis. Nevertheless, in Alabama v. King & Boozer, 314 U.S. 1 (1941), the Court sustained a sales tax on a contractor's purchases of materials to be used in constructing an army camp under such a contract. The Court noted that the Gerhardt and O'Keefe cases, supra, precluded any immunity argument based simply on the passing on of the economic burden to the Government. Moreover, the Court rejected the argument that, because the contractor "in a loose and general sense" acted for the Government, the "legal incidence" of the tax was on the United States. But Kern-Limerick v. Scurlock, 347 U.S. 110 (1954), invalidated a similar tax in a similar situation, where the contract specifically authorized the contractor to "act as the purchasing agent of the Government" and where the Government was directly liable to the seller. The Court recognized that the economic impact of the tax on the Government was the same here as in King & Boozer, but emphasized that the "legal incidence" differed. The "form of contracts . . . may determine" taxability, in view of the tradition of sovereign immunity, "for decisions consistently prohibit taxes levied on the property and purchases of the Government itself." Compare Esso Standard Oil Co. v. Evans, 345 U.S. 495 (1953).

2. *Taxes on users of government property.* United States v. Allegheny County, 322 U.S. 174 (1944), held invalid a state ad valorem property tax on a mill, where the valuation included machinery leased from the United States and used in performing a federal contract. Compare S. R. A. v. Minnesota, 327 U.S. 558 (1946), upholding a tax on realty where legal title was in the United States with possession in a private party holding under an executory sales contract. Taxes on users of government property came before the Court in three companion cases in 1958; in each, the state tax was sustained by a divided Court. United States v. City of Detroit, 355 U.S. 465; United States v. Township of Muskegon, 355 U.S. 484; City of Detroit v. Murray Corp., 355 U.S. 489.

In the first Detroit case, the taxpayer was lessee of a government-owned plant used in his private manufacturing business; the tax was based on the value of the leased property. The Supreme Court affirmed the Michigan judgment sustaining the tax as neither discriminatory nor on the property of the United States, but as on the lessee's privilege of using the property in a private business. In the Muskegon case, the same tax statute was sustained as applied to an industrial plant furnished by the Government to a contractor, rent-free, for use in performing federal contracts.

In the Murray Corporation case, the tax law provided that "owners or persons in possession of any personal property shall pay all taxes assessed thereon." The taxpayer was operating as a subcontractor on government contracts, title to all parts and materials being in the United States. Though the tax was "styled a personal property tax" by the statute, the Court considered it as imposing a "levy on a private party possessing government property which it was using or processing in the course of its own business." The Court saw no distinction in the practical operation and effect of the taxes on persons using exempt real property (as in the first two cases) and taxes on persons possessing exempt personal property. The opinion in each of the cases was delivered by Justice Black. Remarks in the opinion in the first Detroit case reflect the Court's approach: "Today the United States does business with a vast number of private parties. In this Court the trend has been to reject immunizing these private parties from non-discriminatory state taxes as a matter of constitutional law. . . . Of course this is not to say that Congress, acting within the proper scope of its power, cannot confer immunity by statute where it does not exist constitutionally. Wise and flexible adjustment of intergovernmental tax immunity calls for political and economic considerations of the greatest difficulty and delicacy. Such complex problems are ones which Congress is best qualified to resolve." See note 3, infra.

In the Muskegon case, four Justices dissented, finding the tax indistinguishable from the property tax invalidated in United States v. Allegheny County, supra. In the other two cases, the decisions were by 7 to 2 votes: Justices Frankfurter and Harlan, who dissented in Muskegon, concurred in these because there was precedent for a privilege tax on the use of property, as distinguished from a tax "on" property. Justices Whittaker and Burton dissented in all three cases. For an analysis of these cases, see Whelan, "Government Contract Privileges: A Fertile Ground for State Taxation," 44 Va.L.Rev. 1099 (1958), Selected Essays 1938–62 (1963), 436.

Compare Rohr Aircraft Corp. v. San Diego County, 362 U.S. 628 (1960), invalidating a real property tax on federal property leased to a private company. The lessee was obligated to pay all taxes. The Court was primarily concerned with interpreting the scope of a federal statute waiving immunity on certain federal property; there was no difficulty with the situation in the absence of a waiver: "[T]he general rule is 'that lands owned by the United States of America or its instruments are immune from state and local taxation.' We think that the land here was 'owned' by the United States." Justices Black and Douglas dissented. Did Rohr Aircraft repudiate Justice Black's approach in the three 1958 cases, supra?

3. *Congressional ordering and tax immunities.* a. As in the Rohr Aircraft case, the scope of federal immunities often turns on congressional statements recognizing or waiving immunities. See, e. g., the statutory recognition of the rule of Weston v. Charleston, 2 Pet. 449 (1829), supra, exempting federal obligations from local taxation. 31 U.S.C. § 742.[1]

---

1. Compare Society for Savings v. Bowers, 349 U.S. 143 (1955) (property tax on mutual savings bank invalid because federal bonds in bank portfolio included in tax base), with Werner Machine Co. v. Director of Taxation, 350 U.S. 492 (1956) (franchise tax on corporations measured by "net worth" valid, though net worth includes investments in federal bonds).

Pollock v. Farmers Loan & Trust Co., 157 U.S. 429 (1895), held income from state and local bonds constitutionally immune from Federal taxation. Does that case still represent valid constitutional doctrine? The Internal Rev-

See also the statutes granting immunities to federal instrumentalities, as in Pittman v. Home Owners Loan Corp., 308 U.S. 21 (1939), and Federal Land Bank v. Bismarck Lumber Co., 314 U.S. 95 (1941); cf. Carson v. Roane-Anderson Co., 342 U.S. 232 (1952) (managing town and producing materials for Atomic Energy Commission). Would some of these federal activities be subject to state taxation, cf. New York v. United States, supra, in the absence of the statutory immunities?

b. Note the emphasis on the statutory grant of immunity when a divided Court reaffirmed the immunity of national banks from state taxation in First Agric. Nat. Bank v. State Tax Comm'n, 392 U.S. 339 (1968). The highest Massachusetts court had sustained the application of state sales and use taxes to purchases of personal property by a national bank. The state court had thought that "the status of national banks has been so changed by the establishment of the Federal Reserve System that they should no longer be considered nontaxable by the States as instrumentalities of the United States." In the Supreme Court, Justice Black's majority opinion sustaining the tax immunity did not reach the constitutional question. It found that federal legislation—12 U.S.C. § 548, derived from an 1864 law—"was intended to prescribe the only ways in which the States can tax national banks"; that since the decision in Owensboro Nat. Bank v. Owensboro, 173 U.S. 664 (1899), it had been "abundantly clear" that this provision marked "the outer limit" of taxability; and that, accordingly, "if a change is to be made in state taxation of national banks, it must come from the Congress, which has established the present limits."

Justice Marshall, in an extensive dissent joined by Justices Harlan and Stewart, concluded: "I think that in light of the present functions and role of national banks that they should not in this day and age be considered constitutionally immune from nondiscriminatory state taxation, and that § 548 should not be construed as giving them a statutory immunity from the taxes here involved." He insisted that the "hoary cases"—McCulloch, Osborn and Owensboro—could be given a limited reading. (See the notes following McCulloch, chap. 3, p. 229.) That would "require a reevaluation of the validity of the doctrine of intergovernmental tax immunities—a doctrine which does not rest upon any specific provisions of the Constitution, but rather upon this Court's concepts of federalism." Since Congress may provide statutory immunities, "there is litle reason for this Court to cling to the view that the Constitution itself makes federal instrumentalities immune from state taxation in the absence of authorizing legislation. The disparate kinds of instrumentalities and forms of state taxation create difficulties for *ad hoc* resolution of the immunity issue by this Court based only upon abstract concepts of federalism."

Though the Court had not indicated "any great desire to reconsider *in toto*" the constitutional immunity, there had been a wise trend to restrict the scope of the tax immunity of "private persons seeking to clothe themselves with governmental character." In view of that trend, a modern national bank "cannot be considered a tax-immune federal instrumentality." Developments since the creation of the Federal Reserve System in 1913 had produced

enue Code specifically exempts interest from such bonds. There has been considerable controversy about this provision and tax reform advocates

unsuccessfully urged its repeal or modification in the major tax law revision of 1969.

radical changes. National banks no longer issue currency; the Federal Reserve banks and the System are now the monetary and fiscal agents of the United States. National banks, to be sure, are required to be members of the System. But that did not make them "sufficiently quasi-public to enjoy the tax-immune status of federal instrumentalities. If that alone were enough, then it would seem that state banks which elected to join the Federal Reserve System should also be tax-immune federal instrumentalities. In any event, there is very little difference today between a national bank and its state-chartered competitor." And in construing the statute, "the issue is who shall bear the burden of seeking congressional action. I would put the burden where it ought to be, namely, on the private profitmaking corporation that seeks exemption from nondiscriminatory state taxation."

c. On congressional responses to state tax losses due to federal immunities, see the survey of federal statutory devices for making contributions to localities containing United States property, in Study Committee Report for the Commission on Intergovernmental Relations, Payments in Lieu of Taxes and Shared Revenues (1955). The Report considers examples of revenue sharing provisions, payments in lieu of taxes, and consents to property tax liability. The Report recommended additional waivers of immunity and payments in lieu of taxes. See also the Kestnbaum Commission's subsequent report, Commission on Intergovernmental Relations, A Report to the President (1955).

INTERGOVERNMENTAL IMMUNITIES AND REGULATORY STATUTES

1. *State regulation of federal activities.* In Johnson v. Maryland, 254 U.S. 51 (1921), the driver of a United States mail truck was fined under a Maryland law for driving the truck, in the course of his employment, without having obtained a license from the State. The Court reversed in reliance upon the principle of McCulloch v. Maryland: "Such a [licensing] requirement does not merely touch the government servants remotely by a general rule of conduct; it lays hold of them in their specific attempt to obey orders, and requires qualifications in addition to those that the government has pronounced sufficient." Miller v. Arkansas, 352 U.S. 187 (1956), held invalid, as applied to a federal contractor, an Arkansas law which required contractors to obtain a license from the State. In a per curiam opinion, the Supreme Court said the case came within the rationale of Johnson v. Maryland, supra.

Similarly, Public Utilities Comm'n of California v. United States, 355 U.S. 534 (1958), denied to California the power to impose a requirement of her consent to arrangements between carriers and the United States fixing rates for the transportation of federal property. Justice Harlan, joined by Chief Justice Warren and Justice Burton, delivered a dissenting opinion. He thought the Court had moved with "unnecessary haste" in striking down the state statute without waiting for a "clarifying construction" as to its effect upon federal interests. Compare Paul v. United States, 371 U.S. 245 (1963), holding that California could not apply its minimum milk price regulations to sales to United States military posts: "The collision between the federal policy of negotiated prices [competitive bidding] and the state policy of regulated prices is as clear and acute here as was the conflict between federal negotiated rates and state regulated rates in Public Utilities Comm'n of California v. United States, supra."

2. *Congressional ordering, "static conformity" and "dynamic conformity": state law on federal enclaves.* a. *The inapplicability of state law by its own force.* Under Art. I, Sec. 8, clause 17, Congress has power of "exclusive legislation" not only over the District of Columbia but also "over all Places purchased by the Consent of the legislature of the State . . . for the Erection of Forts, Magazines, Arsenals, dock-Yards, and other needful Buildings." A California milk price regulation, like that involved in Paul v. United States, note 1, supra, was accordingly held inapplicable to sales on a military installation: even though there was no conflicting federal regulation, the constitutional grant of power barred state regulation. Pacific Coast Dairy v. Department of Agriculture, 318 U.S. 285 (1943). State law is effective of its own force on federal enclaves only when a state conditions its "Consent" on its retention of jurisdiction over land acquired by the United States.

b. *Static conformity.* But what law governs federal enclaves where the State has not reserved jurisdiction and Congress has not supplied legislation? Ordinarily, only state law existing at the time of the acquisition remains enforceable; laws enacted subsequently are not effective on the enclave. See Stewart & Co. v. Sadrakula, 309 U.S. 94 (1940), applying a pre-acquisition state law requiring certain safeguards for workers in the case of the death of a workman engaged in constructing a post office: "The Constitution does not command that every vestige of the laws of the former sovereignty must vanish. On the contrary its language has long been interpreted so as to permit the continuance until abrogated of those rules existing at the time of the surrender of sovereignty which govern the rights of the occupants of the territory transferred. This assures that no area however small will be left without a developed legal system for private rights."

Is a "developed legal system" adequate? Development of legal systems is a continuing process. The "static conformity" of the quoted passage may produce a federal enclave where the applicable law is that of another day, while the surrounding state land is governed by a less obsolescent legal system. Is congressional enactment of substantive federal law the only way to achieve law reform on the enclave? Or may Congress enact "dynamic conformity," making state law changes after acquisition enforceable on the enclave?

c. *Dynamic conformity and the Assimilative Crimes Act.* In the Assimilative Crimes Act of 1948, Congress provided for such "dynamic conformity" by making the changing body of state criminal law applicable to federal enclaves. In United States v. Sharpnack, 355 U.S. 286 (1958), the Court sustained the constitutionality of the Act. Cf. Wayman v. Southard, 10 Wheat. 1 (1825), and United States v. Paul, 6 Pet. 141 (1831). In Sharpnack, appellee was charged with a sex crime on an Air Force Base in Texas. The Texas criminal statute "assimilated" was enacted two years after the 1948 Act. Justice Burton's majority opinion reviewed the long congressional experience with "static conformity" in assimilative crime laws for federal enclaves, and noted a number of examples of "dynamic conformity" in other areas of federal regulation. The 1948 Act, Justice Burton stated, "thus at last provided that within each federal enclave, to the extent that offenses are not pre-empted by congressional enactments, there shall be complete current conformity with the criminal laws of the respective States in which the enclaves are situated." He added:

"Having the power to assimilate the state laws, Congress obviously has like power to renew such assimilation annually or daily in order to keep the laws in the enclaves current with those in the States. That being so, we conclude that Congress is within its constitutional powers and legislative discretion when, after 123 years of experience with the policy of conformity, it enacts that policy in its most complete and accurate form. Rather than being a delegation by Congress of its legislative authority to the States, it is a deliberate continuing adoption by Congress for federal enclaves of such unpre-empted offenses and punishments as shall have been already put in effect by the respective States for their own government. Congress retains power to exclude a particular state law from the assimilative effect of the Act. This procedure is a practical accommodation of the mechanics of the legislative functions of State and Nation in the field of police power where it is especially appropriate to make the federal regulation of local conduct conform to that already established by the State."

Justice Douglas, joined by Justice Black, dissented: "It is . . . . the Congress, and the Congress alone, that has the power to make rules governing federal enclaves. . . . The power to make laws under which men are punished for crimes calls for as serious a deliberation as the fashioning of rules for the seizure of the industrial plants involved in the Youngstown case. [The Steel Seizure Case, chap. 7, p. 556, supra.] Both call for the exercise of legislative judgment; and I do not see how that requirement can be satisfied by delegating the authority to the President, the Department of the Interior, or, as in this case, to the States. . . .

"Here it is a sex crime on which Congress has never legislated. Tomorrow it may be a blue law, a law governing usury, or even a law requiring segregation of the races on buses and in restaurants. It may be a law that could never command a majority in the Congress or that in no sense reflected its will. It is no answer to say that the citizen would have a defense under the Fifth and Sixth Amendments to unconstitutional applications of these federal laws . . . . He is entitled to the considered judgment of Congress whether the law applied to him fits the federal policy. That is what federal lawmaking is. It is that policy which has led the Court heretofore to limit these Assimilative Crimes Acts to those state laws in force at the time of enactment of the Federal Act. United States v. Paul, 6 Pet. 141."

3. *Federal regulation of state activities. a. United States v. California.* In United States v. California, 297 U.S. 175 (1936), California operated a state-owned railroad in interstate commerce. One of the cars was not equipped with the coupling apparatus required by the Federal Safety Appliance Act. In defense to a suit by the United States to recover the statutory penalty for violation of the Act, California urged that it could not be subjected to the Act since it was performing a public function in a sovereign capacity. The Court rejected the claim: "[W]e think it unimportant to say whether the state conducts its railroad in its 'sovereign' or in its 'private' capacity. That in operating its railroad it is acting within a power reserved to the states cannot be doubted. . . . The analogy of the constitutional immunity of state instrumentalities from federal taxation, on which respondent relies, is not illuminating. That immunity is implied from the nature of our federal system and the relationship within it of state and national governments, and is equally a restriction on taxation by either of the instrumentalities of the other. . . . But there is no such limitation upon the plenary power to regulate

commerce. The state can no more deny the power if its exercise has been authorized by Congress than can an individual."

b. *Maryland v. Wirtz.* In Maryland v. Wirtz, 392 U.S. 183 (1968), noted in chap. 4, p. 321, the majority relied on United States v. California in rejecting a challenge to the extension of the Fair Labor Standards Act to employees of state schools and hospitals. Justice Harlan found the argument that the Act interfered with "sovereign state functions" untenable. National actions under the commerce power "may override countervailing state interests whether these be described as 'governmental' or 'proprietary' in character." Justice Douglas' dissent, joined by Justice Stewart, insisted that intergovernmental tax immunities principles such as those in New York v. United States, supra, rather than standard commerce power analyses, should provide the guide. He thought the majority's position "unexceptionable" as "an exercise in semantics" if "congressional federalism is the standard," but insisted that "what is done here is nonetheless such a serious invasion of state sovereignty protected by the Tenth Amendment that it is in my view not consistent with our constitutional federalism."

In elaborating, Justice Douglas stated that these statutory provisions "disrupt the fiscal policy of the States and threaten their autonomy in the regulation of health and education." Cases like United States v. California were distinguishable: the federal regulation there did not "overwhelm state fiscal policy. It is one thing to force a State to purchase safety equipment for its railroad and another to force it either to spend several million more dollars on hospitals and schools or substantially reduce services in these areas." If state autonomy did not limit the commerce power, he asked, "could Congress compel the States to build super highways criss-crossing their territory in order to accommodate interstate vehicles, to provide inns and eating places for interstate travelers, to quadruple their police forces in order to prevent commerce-crippling riots, etc? Could the Congress virtually draw up each State's budget to avoid 'disruptive effect[s] on . . . commercial intercourse'?" He concluded: "In this case the State as a sovereign power is being seriously tampered with, potentially crippled." (Note also the unsuccessful effort to assert state autonomy barriers to the spending power, Oklahoma v. U. S. Civil Service Commission, 330 U.S. 127 (1947), in note 3 following the social security cases, chap. 5, p. 387, supra.)

STATE AUTONOMY

1. *Territorial integrity.* Cases such as New York v. United States, United States v. California, and Maryland v. Wirtz, supra—which recognize some federal authority to tax and regulate state activities—suggest a somewhat broader inquiry into the present status of state autonomy. The Constitution contains a number of safeguards. In addition to the implications from the allocation of power between nation and states and from the Tenth Amendment considered in earlier chapters, note especially the assurance of territorial integrity in Article IV, Section 3: "No new State shall be formed or erected within the Jurisdiction of any other State, nor any State be formed by the Junction of two or more States, or Parts of States, without the Consent of the Legislatures of the States concerned as well as of the Congress." Note also the restriction on the amending power in Article V: "no State, without its Consent, shall be deprived of its equal Suffrage in the Senate."

2. *Conditions on the admission of new states.* May Congress restrict state autonomy by conditioning the admission of a state into the Union? The problem has been a prolific source of controversy, especially in extrajudicial debates, as those from 1819 to 1821 regarding the Missouri Compromise. Coyle v. Smith, 221 U.S. 559 (1911), involved the federal law providing for the admission of Oklahoma. It stipulated that the state capital should be temporarily located at Guthrie and not changed prior to 1913, and that meanwhile no public money should be appropriated for building a capitol. In 1910 Oklahoma passed an act removing the capital to Oklahoma City and appropriating money for buildings. Affirming a judgment which sustained the state act, Justice Lurton said: "The power to locate its own seat of government, and to determine when and how it shall be changed from one place to another, and to appropriate its own public funds for that purpose, are essentially and peculiarly state powers. That one of the original thirteen States could now be shorn of such powers by an act of Congress would not be for a moment entertained. . . . [C]onstitutional equality of the States is essential to the harmonious operation of the scheme upon which the Republic was organized." See Hanna, "Equal Footing in the Admission of States," 3 Baylor L.Rev. 519 (1951).

3. *State courts and the enforcement of federal law.* It is part of the basic constitutional scheme that state courts are not only competent but obligated to consider federal claims raised there. See the Supremacy Clause, Art. VI, Sec. 2, and chaps. 1 and 2, supra. And Congress may give federal courts exclusive jurisdiction to hear federal claims. See chap. 1, supra. But may Congress create new statutory rights and compel the states to make their judicial machinery available for enforcement proceedings? The Emergency Price Control Act of 1942 permitted treble damage suits for violations of federal price regulations to be brought in state as well as federal courts. Rhode Island's highest court held that the Act was a "penal" statute of a foreign sovereign which the state courts would not enforce. In Testa v. Katt, 330 U.S. 386 (1947), the Court reversed: even assuming the statute was penal, the Supremacy Clause does not permit state courts to decline enforcement of federal statutory rights on local policy grounds—at least where the state courts "have jurisdiction adequate and appropriate under established local law to adjudicate this controversy." The qualifying phrase is, of course, significant, though much of Justice Black's opinion speaks more broadly than that. Compare Chief Justice Taney's language in Kentucky v. Dennison, 24 How. 66 (1861), in the note on Interstate Rendition, sec. 2A, infra. See Note, "Utilization of State Courts to Enforce Federal Penal and Criminal Statutes: Development in Judicial Federalism," 60 Harv.L.Rev. 966 (1947).

4. *State courts and "interference" with federal action.* a. Federal courts have broad authority to grant habeas corpus where persons are in state custody. See chap. 2, supra. Do state courts have any similar authority with regard to those in federal custody? In Tarble's Case, 13 Wall. 397 (1872), a Wisconsin court had issued habeas corpus to discharge a soldier from the custody of a federal recruiting officer, on the ground that the soldier had enlisted while under age and without parental consent. The Supreme Court held that the state lacked authority, relying heavily on broad language in Ableman v. Booth, 21 How. 506 (1858), where the Wisconsin courts had ordered release of a person held under a federal charge. In the Booth litigation, Chief Justice Taney had said that "no State can authorize one of

its judges . . . to exercise judicial power, by habeas corpus or otherwise, within the jurisdiction of another and independent government. . . . [T]he State of Wisconsin had no more power to authorize these proceedings of its judges and courts, than it would have had if the prisoner had been confined in Michigan, or in any other State of the Union, for an offence against the laws of the State in which he was imprisoned. . . . [A]fter the return is made, and the State judge or court judicially apprized that the party is in custody under the authority of the United States, they can proceed no further." Accordingly, in Tarble's Case, Justice Field stated: "Such being the distinct and independent character of the two governments . . ., it follows that neither can intrude with its judicial process into the domain of the other, except so far as such intrusion may be necessary on the part of the National Government to preserve its rightful supremacy in cases of conflict of authority."

   b. If the federal courts' statutory jurisdiction on habeas corpus for state prisoners were repealed, would these cases be decided the same way? Perhaps Tarble's Case can be justified as resting on an exclusive federal jurisdiction implied from acts of Congress, though ordinarily concurrent state jurisdiction is assumed unless exclusive jurisdiction is fairly clear in the federal statutes. See Claflin v. Houseman, 93 U.S. 130 (1876). Unless Tarble's Case is so limited, does it not undercut the role of the state courts "as the primary guarantors of constitutional rights, and in many cases"—in view of the congressional authority over the jurisdiction of federal courts—perhaps "the ultimate" guarantors? See Hart and Wechsler, The Federal Courts and the Federal System (1953), 339, 388; and note Warren, "Federal and State Court Interference," 43 Harv.L.Rev. 345 (1930). For an excellent analysis of the Tarble and Booth cases, as well as the power of state courts to entertain damage and injunction actions against federal officials, see Arnold, "The Power of State Courts to Enjoin Federal Officers," 73 Yale L.J. 1385 (1964).* Contrast with the authority of the state courts the broad and frequently exercised federal power to enjoin state official action, stemming from Ex parte Young, 209 U.S. 123 (1908), and considered in chap. 2, p. 162, supra.

SECTION 2.   INTERSTATE RELATIONSHIPS

A.   INTERSTATE OBLIGATIONS

   Scope Note. The major constitutional source of interstate obligations is Article IV. The most important and most litigated provision has been Section 1, the Full Faith and Credit Clause. Full Faith and Credit problems are usually considered in conflict of laws courses and are not developed here. Two additional limitations—both in Article IV, Section 2—warrant notice, how-

---

* Note also the statute permitting federal officials to remove to the federal courts any state court action against them "for any act under color of such office," 28 U.S.C. § 1442(a) (1), broadly interpreted in Willingham v. Morgan, 395 U.S. 402 (1969).

ever: the interstate privileges and immunities clause and the obligation regarding rendition of fugutives from justice.

THE PRIVILEGES AND IMMUNITIES CLAUSE
OF ARTICLE IV

The injunction that the "Citizens of each State shall be entitled to all
Privileges and Immunities of Citizens in the several States" was a briefer
version of—but had the same purpose as [1]—a similar provision in the Articles
of Confederation.   In the first significant judicial interpretation of the clause,
Corfield v. Coryell, 4 Wash.C.C. 371, Fed.Cas.No.3,230 (Cir.Ct.E.D.Pa.,
1823), Justice Bushrod Washington described the scope of the clause broadly.[2]
But in Corfield itself, a state statute was held not to violate Article IV, Section
2, and the clause has had a rather limited function over the years: it serves as a
barrier against certain state discriminations against citizens of other states.
See, e. g., Paul v. Virginia, 8 Wall. 168 (1869): "[I]t inhibits discriminating
legislation . . . .   Indeed, without some provision of the kind removing
from the citizens of each State the disabilities of alienage in other States, and
giving them equality of privilege with citizens of those States, the Republic
would have constituted little more than a league of States; it would not have
constituted the Union which now exists." [3]

Moreover, the functions of several other provisions of the Constitution
overlap those of the interstate privileges and immunities clause—as has already been seen with regard to the anti-discrimination, nationalizing impact of
the commerce clause, chapters 8 and 9, supra, and as will be seen in the interpretations of the equal protection clause of the Fourteenth Amendment,
chap. 14, infra.   (The Fourteenth Amendment contains a privileges and
immunities clause as well.   It prohibits state infringements on the privileges
of *national*, not state, citizenship, and the Court's interpretations have made it
the least significant of the protections in Section 1 of the Fourteenth Amendment.   See chap. 11, p. 795, infra.)

The next principal case illustrates one of the Court's rare recent reliances
on the interstate privileges and immunities clause.   It deals with a statute

---

1. See the discussion in Justice Miller's
opinion in the Slaughter-House Cases,
  16 Wall. 36 (1873), chap. 11, p. 787,
infra.

2. For excerpts from the Corfield opinion, see the Slaughter-House Cases,
p. 790, infra.

3. In Paul v. Virginia, a Virginia statute
required foreign—but not domestic—
insurance companies, as a condition
of doing business in the State, to deposit with the State Treasurer bonds
of a specified amount and character.
The agent of a New York corporation
unsuccessfully challenged the statute
under Art. IV, Sec. 2. The Court held
that a corporation is not a citizen for
purposes of the clause, and that a
State may therefore exclude it except
upon such conditions as it sees fit.

The presumption of comity upon which
the right of a corporation to make
contracts in another State was upheld
in Bank of Augusta v. Earle, 13 Pet.
519 (1839), was rebutted by the statute
in this case.
Other constitutional provisions, however,
limit the types of conditions a state
may impose.   For examples of "unconstitutional conditions," see, e. g.,
Western Union Telegraph Co. v. Kansas, 216 U.S. 1 (1910) (attempt to oust
foreign corporation for failure to pay
franchise tax measured by total capital; invalid under due process and
commerce clauses); Terral v. Burke
Construction Co., 257 U.S. 529 (1922)
(corporation cannot be compelled to
"waive" right to resort to federal
courts); and Hale, "Unconstitutional
Conditions and Constitutional Rights,"
35 Colum.L.Rev. 321 (1935).

somewhat similar to that sustained in the first judicial consideration of the Clause, Corfield v. Coryell, supra; and it raises questions related to some that have arisen under the commerce clause, see chap. 8, sec. 1D, supra. In Corfield, Justice Washington sustained a New Jersey law prohibiting non-residents from gathering clams, oysters or shells in the state's waters. The Circuit Court rejected the claim that Article IV, Section 2, compelled New Jersey, in "regulating the use of the common property" of its citizens, "to extend to the citizens of all the other states the same advantages as are secured to their own citizens." Compare the discussion in the case which follows

----

TOOMER v. WITSELL

334 U.S. 385, 68 S.Ct. 1156, 92 L.Ed. 1460 (1948).

Appeal from the District Court for the Eastern District of South Carolina.

Mr. Chief Justice VINSON delivered the opinion of the Court.

This is a suit to enjoin as unconstitutional the enforcement of several South Carolina statutes governing commercial shrimp fishing in the three-mile maritime belt off the coast of that State. Appellants, who initiated the action, are five individual fishermen, all citizens and residents of Georgia, and a non-profit fish dealers' organization incorporated in Florida. [The three-judge District Court upheld the statutes.]

[South Carolina's regulations applied to a part of a large shrimp fishery extending from North Carolina to Florida. The shrimp are migratory. There are no federal regulations and attempts at uniform legislation by the adjoining states failed. Commercial shrimpers wanted to start trawling off the Carolinas in the summer and follow the shrimp down to Florida. They encountered state restrictions—some based on a desire to channel business derived from local waters to local residents. "Restrictions on non-resident fishing in the marginal sea . . . invited retaliation to the point that the fishery [was] effectively partitioned at the state lines." One of the statutes challenged—Section 3379—imposed license fees on shrimp boats: $25 on those owned by residents, $2500 on those belonging to non-residents.]

. . . Appellants' most vigorous attack is directed at § 3379 which . . . requires non-residents of South Carolina to pay license fees one hundred times as great as those which residents must pay. The purpose and effect of this statute, they contend, is not to conserve shrimp, but to exclude non-residents and thereby create a commercial monopoly for South Carolina residents. As such, the statute is said to violate the privileges and immunities clause of Art. IV, § 2, of the Constitution . . . .

The primary purpose of this clause, like the clauses between which it is located—those relating to full faith and credit and to interstate extradition of fugitives from justice—was to help fuse into one Nation a collection of independent, sovereign States. It was designed to insure to a citizen of State A who ventures into State B the same privileges which the citizens of State B enjoy.[1] For protection of such equality the citizen of State A was not to

----

1. See Paul v. Virginia, 8 Wall. 168, 180– 81 (1868); Travis v. Yale & Towne Mfg. Co., 252 U.S. 60, 78 (1920). [Footnote by the Court.]

be restricted to the uncertain remedies afforded by diplomatic processes and official retaliation. . . .

In line with this underlying purpose, it was long ago decided that one of the privileges which the clause guarantees to citizens of State A is that of doing business in State B on terms of substantial equality with the citizens of that State.

Like many other constitutional provisions, the privileges and immunities clause is not an absolute. It does bar discrimination against citizens of other States where there is no substantial reason for the discrimination beyond the mere fact that they are citizens of other States. But it does not preclude disparity of treatment in the many situations where there are perfectly valid independent reasons for it. Thus the inquiry in each case must be concerned with whether such reasons do exist and whether the degree of discrimination bears a close relation to them. The inquiry must also, of course, be conducted with due regard for the principle that the States should have considerable leeway in analyzing local evils and in prescribing appropriate cures. . . .

By [§ 3379] South Carolina plainly and frankly discriminates against non-residents, and the record leaves little doubt but what the discrimination is so great that its practical effect is virtually exclusionary. . . .

As justification for the statute, appellees urge that the State's obvious purpose was to conserve its shrimp supply, and they suggest that it was designed to head off an impending threat of excessive trawling. The record casts some doubt on these statements. But in any event, appellees' argument assumes that any means adopted to attain valid objectives necessarily squares with the privileges and immunities clause. It overlooks the purpose of that clause, which . . . is to outlaw classifications based on the fact of non-citizenship unless there is something to indicate that non-citizens constitute a peculiar source of the evil at which the statute is aimed.

. . . Nothing in the record indicates that non-residents use larger boats or different fishing methods than residents, that the cost of enforcing the laws against them is appreciably greater, or that any substantial amount of the State's general funds is devoted to shrimp conservation. But assuming such were the facts, they would not necessarily support a remedy so drastic as to be a near equivalent of total exclusion. The State is not without power, for example, to restrict the type of equipment used in its fisheries, to graduate license fees according to the size of the boats, or even to charge non-residents a differential which would merely compensate the State for any added enforcement burden they may impose . . . . We would be closing our eyes to reality, we believe, if we concluded that there was a reasonable relationship between the danger represented by non-citizens, as a class, and the severe discrimination practiced upon them.

The Travis case invalidated a New York income tax law as applied to Connecticut and New Jersey residents employed in New York, because the law granted to residents exemptions denied to nonresidents. Under the law, nonresidents were allowed credits against the New York tax if their home state imposed an income tax and granted reciprocal credits to New Yorkers working there. Connecticut and New Jersey had no income tax. The Court found no "adequate ground for the discrimination" and rejected a defense based on the reciprocity provision: New York's discrimination "would not be cured" by "like discriminations" in adjoining states; nor can "discrimination be corrected by retaliation," for "to prevent this was one of the chief ends" of the Constitution.

Thus, § 3379 must be held unconstitutional unless commercial shrimp fishing in the maritime belt falls within some unexpressed exception to the privileges and immunities clause.

Appellees strenuously urge that there is such an exception. Their argument runs as follows: Ever since Roman times, animals *ferae naturae* [have been] subject to control by the sovereign or other governmental authority. More recently this thought has been expressed by saying that fish and game are the common property of all citizens of the governmental unit and that the government, as a sort of trustee, exercises this "ownership" for the benefit of its citizens. . . . Each government may, the argument continues, regulate the corpus of the trust in the way best suited to the interests of the beneficial owners, its citizens, and may discriminate as it sees fit against persons lacking any beneficial interest. . . .

Language frequently repeated by this Court appears to lend some support to this analysis.[2] [McCready v. Virginia, 94 U.S. 391 (1876)] . . .

The whole ownership theory, in fact, is now generally regarded as but a fiction expressive in legal shorthand of the importance to its people that a State have power to preserve and regulate the exploitation of an important resource. And there is no necessary conflict between that vital policy consideration and the constitutional command that the State exercise that power, like its other powers, so as not to discriminate without reason against citizens of other States.

These considerations lead us to the conclusion that the McCready exception to the privileges and immunities clause, if such it be, should not be expanded to cover this case.

Thus we hold that commercial shrimping in the marginal sea, like other common callings, is within the purview of the privileges and immunities clause. And since we have previously concluded that the reasons advanced in support of the statute do not bear a reasonable relationship to the high degree of discrimination practiced upon citizens of other States, it follows that § 3379 violates Art. IV, § 2, of the Constitution.

Appellants maintain that by a parity of reasoning the statute also contravenes the equal protection clause of the Fourteenth Amendment. That may well be true, but we do not pass on this argument since it is unnecessary to disposition of the present case. . . .

Reversed . . . .

Mr. Justice FRANKFURTER, whom Mr. Justice JACKSON joins, concurring.

. . . I think it is fair to summarize the decisions which have applied Art. IV, § 2, by saying that they bar a State from penalizing the citizens of other States by subjecting them to heavier taxation merely because they are such citizens or by discriminating against citizens of other States in the pursuit of ordinary livelihoods in competition with local citizens. It is not conceivable that the framers of the Constitution meant to obliterate all special relations between a State and its citizens. This Clause does not touch the right of a State to conserve or utilize its resources on behalf of its own

2. The most extended exposition appears in the majority opinion in Geer v. Connecticut, 161 U.S. 519 (1896). [Footnote by the Court. Cf. chap. 8, p. 669, supra.]

citizens, provided it uses these resources within the State and does not attempt a control of the resources as part of a regulation of commerce between the States. A State may care for its own in utilizing the bounties of nature within her borders because it has technical ownership of such bounties or, when ownership is in no one, because the State may for the common good exercise all the authority that technical ownership ordinarily confers. . . .

But a State cannot project its powers over its own resources by seeking to control the channels of commerce among the States. It is one thing to say that a food supply that may be reduced to control by a State for feeding its own people should be only locally consumed. The State has that power and the Privileges-and-Immunities Clause is no restriction upon its exercise. It is a wholly different thing for the State to provide that only its citizens shall be engaged in commerce among the States, even though based on a locally available food supply. That is not the exercise of the basic right of a State to feed and maintain and give enjoyment to its own people. When a State regulates the sending of products across State lines we have commerce among the States as to which State intervention is subordinate to the Commerce Clause. . . .

[A concurring opinion by Justice Rutledge is omitted.]

INTERSTATE RENDITION

a. The rendition clause of Article IV, Section 2, speaks in mandatory terms: a fugitive from justice "shall . . . be delivered up" on "demand of the executive Authority of the State from which he fled." And in 1793, Congress prescribed the procedure to be followed in making the "demand." But the duty is not enforceable against a governor: in Kentucky v. Dennison, 24 How. 66 (1861), the Court denied Kentucky's mandamus petition to compel the Governor of Ohio to deliver a fugitive. The Court held that it had original jurisdiction to consider the application under Article III —see New Jersey v. New York, 5 Pet. 284 (1831)—but refused to issue the writ. Chief Justice Taney stated: "[L]ooking to the subject-matter [of the 1793 law], and the relations which the United States and the several States bear to each other, the court is of opinion, the words 'it shall be the duty' were not used as mandatory and compulsory, but as declaratory of the moral duty [which the Constitution created]. [S]uch a power would place every State under the control and dominion of the General Government, even in . . . its internal concerns and reserved rights. And we think it clear that the Federal government . . . has no power to impose on a State officer, as such, any duty whatever, and compel him to perform it." Cf. Testa v. Katt, 330 U.S. 386 (1947), sec. 1, p. 769, supra.

b. In Sweeney v. Woodall, 344 U.S. 86 (1952), a fugitive from an Alabama prison was held in Ohio pursuant to Alabama's extradition request. He sought federal habeas corpus on the ground that Alabama would subject him to unconstitutional cruel and unusual punishment. The Supreme Court, per curiam, held that the federal court in Ohio should not examine the merits: "The scheme of interstate rendition, as set forth in both the Constitution and the statutes which Congress has enacted to implement the Constitution, contemplates the prompt return of a fugitive from justice as soon as the state from which he fled demands him; these provisions do not contemplate an appearance by Alabama in respondent's asylum to defend against the claimed abuses of its prison system. Considerations fundamental to our federal system require that the prisoner test the claimed unconstitutionality of his treatment by Alabama in the courts of that State."

c. Congress has enacted legislation under the commerce clause to deal with interstate fugitives from justice. See the Fugitive Felon and Witness Act of 1934, 18 U.S.C. § 1073. Moreover, many states have adopted the Uniform Law to Secure the Attendance of Witnesses from Within or Without a State in Criminal Proceedings. In New York v. O'Neill, 359 U.S. 1 (1959), a divided Court rejected a claim that the Act as adopted by Florida was unconstitutional. Respondent, a citizen of Illinois, was in Florida to attend a convention. Pursuant to the statute, a lower Florida court responded to a certificate executed by a New York judge by summoning respondent before it to determine "whether he was to be given into the custody of New York authorities to be transported to New York to testify in a grand jury proceeding in that State." The lower court refused to grant New York's request, and the Supreme Court of Florida affirmed, holding that the law violated the due process clause and the privileges and immunities clauses in Art. IV, § 2, and in the Fourteenth Amendment. On certiorari, the Supreme Court reversed, in an opinion by Justice Frankfurter.

The Court found no federal constitutional provision which "clearly prevents" the statute and added: "The absence of a provision in the United States Constitution specifically granting power to the States to legislate respecting interstate rendition of witnesses presents no bar. . . . The Constitution did not purport to exhaust imagination and resourcefulness in devising fruitful interstate relationships . . . A citizen cannot shirk his duty, no matter how inconvenienced thereby, to testify in criminal proceedings and grand jury investigations in a State where he is found. There is no constitutional provision granting him relief from this obligation to testify even though he must travel to another State to do so." Justice Douglas, joined by Justice Black, dissented: "Whatever may be the sources of this right of free movement . . . it is an incident of national citizenship. . . . We allow today only what a constitutional amendment could achieve. We in effect amend Art. IV, § 2 by construction to add 'witnesses' to the group now embraced in Art. IV, § 2."

B. INTERSTATE COLLABORATION

WEST VIRGINIA ex rel. DYER v. SIMS
341 U.S. 22, 71 S.Ct. 557, 95 L.Ed. 713 (1951).

Certiorari to the Supreme Court of Appeals of West Virginia.

Mr. Justice FRANKFURTER delivered the opinion of the Court.

After extended negotiations eight States entered into a Compact to control pollution in the Ohio River system. See Ohio River Valley Water Sanitation Compact, 54 Stat. 752. Illinois, Indiana, Kentucky, New York, Ohio, Pennsylvania, Virginia and West Virginia recognized that they were faced with one of the problems of government that are defined by natural rather than political boundaries. Accordingly, they pledged themselves to cooperate in maintaining waters in the Ohio River basin in a sanitary condition through the administrative mechanism of the Ohio River Valley Water Sanitation Commission, consisting of three members from each State and three representing the United States.

The heart of the Compact is Article VI. This provides that sewage discharged into boundary streams or streams flowing from one State into another "shall be so treated   .   .   .   as to provide for substantially complete removal of settleable solids, and the removal of not less than forty-five per cent (45%) of the total suspended solids .   .   ." Industrial wastes are to be treated "to such degree as may be determined to be necessary by the Commission after investigation, due notice and hearing." Sewage and industrial wastes discharged into streams located wholly within one State are to be treated "to that extent, if any, which may be necessary to maintain such waters in a sanitary and satisfactory condition at least equal to the condition of the waters of the interstate stream immediately above the confluence."

Article IX provides that the Commission may, after notice and hearing, issue orders for compliance enforceable in the State and federal courts. .   .   .

By Article X the States also agree "to appropriate for the salaries, office and other administrative expenses, their proper proportion of the annual budget as determined by the Commission and approved by the Governors of the signatory States .   .   .."

The present controversy arose because of conflicting views between officials of West Virginia regarding the responsibility of West Virginia under the Compact.

The Legislature of that State ratified and approved the Compact on March 11, 1939.   .   .   .   Congress gave its consent on July 11, 1940, .   .   . and upon adoption by all the signatory States the Compact was formally executed by the Governor of West Virginia on June 30, 1948. At its 1949 session the West Virginia Legislature appropriated $12,250 as the State's contribution to the expenses of the Commission for the fiscal year beginning July 1, 1949.   .   .   .   Respondent Sims, the auditor of the State, refused to issue a warrant upon its treasury for payment of this appropriation. To compel him to issue it, the West Virginia Commissioners to the Compact Commission and the members of the West Virginia State Water Commission instituted this original mandamus proceeding in the Supreme Court of Appeals of West Virginia. The court denied relief on the merits .   .   ., and we brought the case here, .   .   .   because questions of obviously important public interest are raised.

The West Virginia court found that the "sole question" before it was the validity of the Act of 1939 approving West Virginia's adherence to the Compact. It found that Act invalid in that .   .   .   the Compact was deemed to delegate West Virginia's police power to other States and to the Federal Government .   .   ..

Control of pollution in interstate streams might, on occasion, be an appropriate subject for national legislation. .   .   .   But, with prescience, the Framers left the States free to settle regional controversies in diverse ways. Solution of the problem underlying this case may be attempted directly by the affected States through contentious litigation before this Court. .   .   . Adjudication here of conflicting State interests affecting stream pollution does not rest upon the law of a particular State. This Court decides such controversies according to "principles it must have power to declare." . . . But the delicacy of interstate relationships and the inherent limitations upon this Court's ability to deal with multifarious local problems have naturally led to exacting standards of judicial intervention and have inhibited the formulation of a code for dealing with such controversies. . . .

Indeed, so awkward and unsatisfactory is the available litigious solution for these problems that this Court deemed it appropriate to emphasize the practical constitutional alternative provided by the Compact Clause. Experience led us to suggest that a problem such as that involved here is "more likely to be wisely solved by coöperative study and by conference and mutual concession on the part of representatives of the States so vitally interested in it than by proceedings in any court however constituted." New York v. New Jersey, [256 U.S. 296]. The suggestion has had fruitful response.

The growing interdependence of regional interests, calling for regional adjustments, has brought extensive use of compacts. A compact is more than a supple device for dealing with interests confined within a region. That it is also a means of safeguarding the national interest is well illustrated in the Compact now under review. Not only was congressional consent required, as for all compacts; direct participation by the Federal Government was provided in the President's appointment of three members of the Compact Commission. . . .

But a compact is after all a legal document. Though the circumstances of its drafting are likely to assure great care and deliberation, all avoidance of disputes as to scope and meaning is not within human gift. Just as this Court has power to settle disputes between States where there is no compact, it must have final power to pass upon the meaning and validity of compacts. It requires no elaborate argument to reject the suggestion that an agreement solemnly entered into between States by those who alone have political authority to speak for a State can be unilaterally nullified, or given final meaning by an organ of one of the contracting States. A State cannot be its own ultimate judge in a controversy with a sister State. To determine the nature and scope of obligations as between States, whether they arise through the legislative means of compact or the "federal common law" governing interstate controversies (Hinderlider v. La Plata Co., 304 U.S. 92, 110), is the function and duty of the Supreme Court of the Nation. Of course every deference will be shown to what the highest court of a State deems to be the law and policy of its State, particularly when recondite or unique features of local law are urged. Deference is one thing; submission to a State's own determination of whether it has undertaken an obligation, what that obligation is, and whether it conflicts with a disability of the State to undertake it is quite another.

The Supreme Court of Appeals of the State of West Virginia is, for exclusively State purposes, the ultimate tribunal in construing the meaning of her Constitution. [D]ecisions of this Court make clear, however, that we are free to examine determinations of law by State courts in the limited field where a compact brings in issue the rights of other States and the United States. . . .

That a legislature may delegate to an administrative body the power to make rules and decide particular cases is one of the axioms of modern government. The West Virginia court does not challenge the general proposition but objects to the delegation here involved because it is to a body outside the State and because its Legislature may not be free, at any time, to withdraw the power delegated. We are not here concerned, and so need not deal, with specific language in a State constitution requiring that the State settle its problems with other States without delegating power to an interstate agency. What is involved is the conventional grant of legislative power. We find nothing in that to indicate that West Virginia may not solve a problem such as the control of river pollution by compact and by the delegation, if such it be, necessary to effectuate such solution by compact. If this Court, in the exercise of its original jurisdiction, were to enter a decree requiring West Virginia to abate pollution of interstate streams, that decree would bind the State. The West Virginia Legislature would have no part in determining the State's obligation. The State Legislature could not alter it; it could not disregard it, as West Virginia on another occasion so creditably recognized.* The obligation would be fixed by this Court on the basis of a master's report. Here, the State has bound itself to control pollution by the more effective means of an agreement with other States. The Compact involves a reasonable and carefully limited delegation of power to an interstate agency. Nothing in its Constitution suggests that, in dealing with the problem dealt with by the Compact, West Virginia must wait for the answer to be dictated by this Court after harassing and unsatisfactory litigation. . . .

Reversed and remanded.

Mr. Justice BLACK concurs in the result.

Mr. Justice REED, concurring.

I concur in the judgment of the Court but disagree with the assertion of power by this Court to interpret the meaning of the West Virginia Constitution. This Court must accept the State court's interpretation of its own Constitution unless it is prepared to say that the interpretation is a palpable evasion to avoid a federal rule. . . .

Under the Compact Clause . . . the federal questions are the execution, validity and meaning of federally approved state compacts. The interpretation of the meaning of the compact controls over a state's application of its own law through the Supremacy Clause and not by any implied federal power to construe state law.

---

* Justice Frankfurter's reference was presumably to the extensive litigation between Virginia and West Virginia to enforce West Virginia's obligation to assume a share of Virginia's public debt, upon the separation of the two states. The Court handed down nine opinions or orders in the case, from Virginia v. West Virginia, 206 U.S. 290 (1907), to Virginia v. West Virginia, 246 U.S. 565 (1918). The litigation raised major issues about the enforceability of a money judgment against a state. In one of the opinions, Justice Holmes used a phrase that found its way into the implementation decision in the School Segregation Cases, Brown v. Board of Education, 349 U.S. 294 (1955), chap. 18, p. 1422, infra. Justice Holmes said, in Virginia v. West Virginia, 222 U.S. 17, 19–20 (1911): "A question like the present should be disposed of without undue delay. But a State cannot be expected to move with the celerity of a private business man: it is enough if it proceeds, in the language of the English chancery, *with all deliberate speed*." [Emphasis added.] The controversy was finally resolved in 1919, when West Virginia enacted a law providing for payment of the Supreme Court's judgment. See Powell, "Coercing a State to Pay a Judgment: Virginia v. West Virginia," **17 Mich.** L.Rev. 1 (1918).

I would uphold the validity of the compact and reverse the judgment of West Virginia refusing mandamus, .   .   .   with an opinion based upon the Supremacy Clause.

Mr. Justice JACKSON, concurring. .   .   .

West Virginia, for internal affairs, is free to interpret her own Constitution as she will. But if the compact system is to have vitality and integrity, she may not raise an issue of *ultra vires,* decide it, and release herself from an interstate obligation. The legal consequences which flow from the formal participation in a compact consented to by Congress is a federal question for this Court. .   .   .

Estoppel is not often to be invoked against a government. But West Virginia assumed a contractual obligation with equals by permission of another government that is sovereign in the field. After Congress and sister States had been induced to alter their positions and bind themselves to terms of a covenant, West Virginia should be estopped from repudiating her act. For this reason, I consider that whatever interpretation she may put on the generalities of her Constitution, she is bound by the Compact, and on that basis I concur in the judgment.

_____

COMPACTS AND OTHER METHODS OF INTERSTATE COLLABORATION

1. *The utility of compacts.* The interstate compact device, illustrated in the principal case, has been used to deal with a wide variety of interstate and regional problems, including boundaries, natural resources regulation and allocation, flood control, transportation, taxation, and crime control. Compacts, like other devices, are not always effective. Recall, for example, the shrimp fishery problem, Toomer v. Witsell, p. 772, supra, where the affected states engaged in retaliatory legislation despite the existence of a compact. In a footnote to its opinion, 334 U.S. 338, n. 5, the Court stated: "At least three of the States (Florida, Georgia, and South Carolina) belong to the Atlantic States Marine Fisheries Commission, one of the principal aims of which is to secure the enactment of uniform fisheries laws. The Commission was established pursuant to an interstate compact .   .   . . Its duties, however, are largely consultative and advisory, and to date its efforts have produced little in the way of concrete results insofar as the South Atlantic shrimp fishery is concerned." [1]

1. See generally Zimmerman and Wendell, The Interstate Compact Since 1925 (1951); Thursby, Interstate Cooperation—A Study of the Interstate Compact (1953); Comm'n on Intergovernmental Relations, A Report to the President (1955); Leach and Sugg, The Administration of Interstate Compacts (1959); and Frankfurter and Landis, "The Compact Clause of the Constitution—A Study in Interstate Adjustments," 34 Yale L.J. 685 (1925). See also Grad, "Federal-State Compact: A New Experiment in Co-Operative Federalism," 63 Colum.L.Rev. 825 (1963), a discussion of a novel device with full participation of the national government: the Delaware River Basin Compact, approved in 1961, with Delaware, New Jersey, New York, Pennsylvania and the United States as participants, and establishing a Delaware River Basin Commission. In this compact, the United States not only "consents to" but "joins in" the agreement. Compare the federal participation—by appointment of several Commission members—in the Ohio River Valley Compact involved in the principal case.

2. *Congressional consent.* Interstate compacts require the consent of Congress; they rest on the constitutional prohibition, Art. I, Sec. 10, of any state "Agreement or Compact" with other states or foreign nations "without the consent of Congress." Congress has at times encouraged compacts by giving advance consent, as with crime and flood control. Do all interstate agreements require congressional consent? See Virginia v. Tennessee, 148 U.S. 503 (1893), stating that the Clause "is directed to the formation of any combination tending to the increase of political power in the States, which may encroach upon . . . the just supremacy of the United States," and that there are "many matters upon which different States may agree that can in no respect concern the United States."

3. *Other techniques of collaboration.* Note the availability of the techniques of uniform and reciprocal legislation in developing interstate cooperation. See, e. g., the Uniform Law challenged in New York v. O'Neill, 359 U.S. 1 (1959), in the note on Interstate Rendition, p. 776, supra. See also Starr, "Reciprocal and Retaliatory Legislation in the American States," 21 Minn.L.Rev. 371 (1937); Brocklebank, "Is the Uniform Reciprocal Enforcement of Support Act Constitutional?", 31 Ore.L.Rev. 97 (1952); Faught, "Reciprocity in State Taxation . . .," 92 U.Pa.L.Rev. 258 (1944); and recall the varied methods of federal-state cooperation considered in the earlier materials, especially chaps. 4, 5, and 8, sec. 2.

Part III

INDIVIDUAL RIGHTS

Scope Note. The Federal Constitution's protections of individual freedoms—primarily against interferences by state and federal governments—are central in the final Part of this book. Individual rights concerns have occasionally surfaced earlier, especially in the materials on congressional enforcement of the post-Civil War Amendments (chap. 6) and on the impact of personal rights limitations on the interpretation of the Necessary and Proper Clause (chap. 5, sec. 6). In the remaining chapters, the guarantees of individual rights are at the forefront.

Chapter 11 provides groundwork: it sketches the relevant constitutional assurances; and it explores, via materials drawn from the Court's search for standards to give content to the vague due process clause of the 14th Amendment, the judicial function in the articulation and enforcement of individual rights. Are the Justices limited to those rights explicitly and specifically listed, or does the Constitution authorize Court elaboration of more general values of fundamental liberties? The tension between these positions, emphasized in chapter 11, echoes throughout the rest. That tension regarding the appropriate judicial function has been especially marked in the area surveyed in chapter 12—that of procedural guarantees, particularly in criminal law enforcement. Chapter 13 considers the protection of economic interests afforded by the contract and due process clauses. Chapter 14 turns to the rapidly evolving concept of equality. The equal protection clause of the 14th Amendment, long a basis for only marginal intervention by the courts in policy-making in most circumstances, has recently emerged as a source of wide and amorphous substantive personal interests. Chapter 14 traces that evolution of the "new" equal protection from the "old." (Chapter 18 returns to that clause to examine some areas—e. g., racial discrimination—where equal protection has had a special meaning and bite.) Chapters 15 and 16 emphasize the freedom of expression—the ingredients of liberty reflected in provisions such as the speech and press protections of the First Amendment. And Chapter 17 deals with that Amendment's religion clauses.

Chapter 11

THE CONSTITUTIONAL FRAMEWORK

SECTION 1. THE CONSTITUTION, THE BILL OF RIGHTS, AND THE POST-CIVIL WAR AMENDMENTS

The 1787 document. The original Constitution contained relatively few protections of individual rights, apart from those resulting from the diffusions of power in the federal system considered in Part II. The most important limitation—certainly in terms of litigation—was the contract clause, examined in chap. 13, sec. 1, infra. Moreover, restrictions on state bills of attainder and ex post facto laws were coupled with the contract clause in Art. I, Sec. 10. The limitations on the national government in Art. I, Sec. 9, contained several important safeguards: the "privilege of the Writ of Habeas Corpus" could not be "suspended"; ex post facto laws and bills of attainder were prohibited. Art. III defined treason narrowly and assured jury trials in criminal cases. And Art. IV, Sec. 2, announced that the "Citizens of each State shall be entitled to all Privileges and Immunities of Citizens in the Several States." (See chap. 10, p. 771, supra, and sec. 2A, p. 795, infra.)

   The Bill of Rights. The ratification debates in several states revealed, however, that there was considerable demand for additional constitutional protection of individual—as well as state—rights. In response to these pressures, Madison introduced proposals for constitutional amendments at the first session of Congress, and the Bill of Rights was ratified in 1791. The Court held that these amendments were only applicable to the national government and did not limit the states. See Barron v. The Mayor and City Council of Baltimore, which follows. There was relatively little occasion for Supreme Court interpretation of these guarantees before the Civil War—in part because federal criminal cases were not ordinarily appealable to the Supreme Court. But the extra-judicial debate about the First Amendment, during the controversy over the Alien and Sedition Acts of 1798, was of considerable importance in later litigation regarding freedom of expression. (See chap. 15, p. 1131, infra.)

BARRON v. THE MAYOR AND CITY COUNCIL OF BALTIMORE

7 Pet. 243, 8 L.Ed. 672 (1833).

Error to the Court of Appeals of Maryland.

[Barron sued the City for making his wharf in Baltimore harbor useless. He claimed that the City had diverted the flow of streams in the course of street construction work; that this diversion had deposited "large masses of sand and earth" near the wharf; and that the water had become too shallow for most vessels. The trial court awarded Barron $45,000, but the state appellate court reversed.]

Mr. Chief Justice MARSHALL delivered the opinion of the Court.

The judgment brought up by this writ of error having been rendered by the court of a state, this tribunal can exercise no jurisdiction over it, unless it be shown to come within the provisions of the twenty-fifth section of the judicial act.

The plaintiff in error contends that it comes within that clause in the fifth amendment to the constitution, which inhibits the taking of private property for public use, without just compensation. He insists that this amendment, being in favour of the liberty of the citizen, ought to be so construed as to restrain the legislative power of a state, as well as that of the United States. If this proposition be untrue, the court can take no jurisdiction of the cause.

The question thus presented is, we think, of great importance, but not of much difficulty.

The constitution was ordained and established by the people of the United States for themselves, for their own government, and not for the government of the individual states. Each state established a constitution for itself, and, in that constitution, provided such limitations and restrictions on the powers of its particular government as its judgment dictated. The people of the United States framed such a government for the United States as they supposed best adapted to their situation, and best calculated to promote their interests. The powers they conferred on this government were to be exercised by itself; and the limitations on power, if expressed in general terms, are naturally, and we think, necessarily applicable to the government created by the instrument. They are limitations of power granted in the instrument itself; not of distinct governments, framed by different persons and for different purposes.

If these propositions be correct, the fifth amendment must be understood as restraining the power of the general government, not as applicable to the states. In their several constitutions they have imposed such restrictions on their respective governments as their own wisdom suggested; such as they deemed most proper for themselves. It is a subject on which they judge exclusively, and with which others interfere no farther than they are supposed to have a common interest.

The counsel for the plaintiff in error insists that the constitution was intended to secure the people of the several states against the undue exercise of power by their respective state governments; as well as against that which might be attempted by their general government. In support of this argument he relies on the inhibitions contained in the tenth section of the first article.

We think that this section affords a strong if not a conclusive argument in support of the opinion already indicated by the court.

The preceding section contains restrictions which are obviously intended for the exclusive purpose of restraining the exercise of power by the departments of the general government. Some of them use language applicable only to congress: others are expressed in general terms. The third clause, for example, declares that "no bill of attainder or ex post facto law shall be passed." No language can be more general; yet the demonstration is complete that it applies solely to the government of the United States. In addition to the general arguments furnished by the instrument itself, some of which have been already suggested, the succeeding section, the avowed purpose of which is to restrain state legislation, contains in terms the very prohibition. It declares that "no state shall pass any bill of attainder or ex post facto law." This provision, then, of the ninth section, however comprehensive its language, contains no restriction on state legislation.

The ninth section having enumerated, in the nature of a bill of rights, the limitations intended to be imposed on the powers of the general government, the tenth proceeds to enumerate those which were to operate on the state legislatures. These restrictions are brought together in the same section, and are by express words applied to the states. "No state shall enter into any treaty," &c. Perceiving that in a constitution framed by the people of the United States for the government of all, no limitation of the action of government on the people would apply to the state government, unless expressed in terms; the restrictions contained in the tenth section are in direct words so applied to the states.

. . . It would be tedious to recapitulate the several limitations on the powers of the states which are contained in this section. They will be found, generally, to restrain state legislation on subjects entrusted to the government of the union, in which the citizens of all the states are interested. In these alone were the whole people concerned. The question of their application to states is not left to construction. It is averred in positive words.

If the original constitution, in the ninth and tenth sections of the first article, draws this plain and marked line of discrimination between the limitations it imposes on the powers of the general government, and on those of the states; if in every inhibition intended to act on state power, words are employed which directly express that intent; some strong reason must be assigned for departing from this safe and judicious course in framing the amendments, before that departure can be assumed.

We search in vain for that reason.

Had the people of the several states, or any of them, required changes in their constitutions; had they required additional safeguards to liberty from the apprehended encroachments of their particular governments: the remedy was in their own hands, and would have been applied by themselves. A convention would have been assembled by the discontented state, and the required improvements would have been made by itself. The unwieldy and cumbrous machinery of procuring a recommendation from two-thirds of congress, and the assent of three-fourths of their sister states, could never have occurred to any human being as a mode of doing that which might be effected by the state itself. Had the framers of these amendments intended them to be limitations on the powers of the state governments, they would have imitated the framers of the original constitution, and have expressed that intention. Had congress engaged in the extraordinary occupation of improving the constitutions of the several states by affording the people additional protection from the exercise of power by their own governments in matters which concerned themselves alone, they would have declared his purpose in plain and intelligible language.

But it is universally understood, it is a part of the history of the day, that the great revolution which established the constitution of the United States, was not effected without immense opposition. Serious fears were extensively entertained that those powers which the patriot statesmen, who then watched over the interests of our country, deemed essential to union, and to the attainment of those invaluable objects for which union was sought, might be exercised in a manner dangerous to liberty. In almost every convention by which the constitution was adopted, amendments to guard against the abuse of power were recommended. These amendments demanded security against the apprehended encroachments of the general government— not against those of the local governments.

In compliance with a sentiment thus generally expressed, to quiet fears thus extensively entertained, amendments were proposed by the required majority in congress, and adopted by the states. These amendments contain no expression indicating an intention to apply them to the state governments. This court cannot so apply them.

We are of opinion that the provision in the fifth amendment to the constitution, declaring that private property shall not be taken for public use without just compensation, is intended solely as a limitation on the exercise of power by the government of the United States, and is not applicable to the legislation of the states. We are therefore of opinion that there is no repugnancy between the several acts of the general assembly of Maryland, given in evidence by the defendants at the trial of this cause, in the court of that state, and the constitution of the United States. This court, therefore, has no jurisdiction of the cause; and it is dismissed.

SECTION 2.   THE CONTENT OF THE 14TH AMENDMENT: THE DEVELOPMENT OF STANDARDS

A.   THE PURPOSES OF THE AMENDMENT, THE SLAUGHTER-HOUSE CASES, AND "PRIVILEGES AND IMMUNITIES" OF NATIONAL CITIZENSHIP

The post-Civil War Amendments. The 13th Amendment, in 1865, gave constitutional sanction to President Lincoln's wartime Emancipation Proclamation. The rights of Negroes continued to be severely limited by the "black codes" of several states, however. (See chap. 6, p. 450, supra.) Congress accordingly adopted the Civil Rights Act of 1866—over President Andrew Johnson's veto, based on constitutional grounds—and immediately set the amendment process in motion to assure the constitutional validity of the Act. The 14th Amendment was ratified in 1868. But the Amendment used even more sweeping, general terms than the Act it was designed to sustain: the Amendment's language was not limited to discrimination based on race, color or previous condition of servitude. Two years later, in 1870, the 15th Amendment did speak specifically about racial discrimination, in voting.

Largely because of the breadth of its language, the 14th Amendment has been the most controversial and most litigated of the post-Civil War Amendments. The reasons for the adoption of these amendments are reviewed in Justice Miller's majority opinion in the Slaughter-House Cases, which follows. That decision marks the first of many Court encounters with the argument that the 14th Amendment is not limited to problems of ex-slaves and racial discrimination. The acceptance of that argument in decisions subsequent to the Slaughter-House Cases has made that Amendment far the most prolific source of limits on states. But (as has already been demonstrated in chap. 6) the other Amendments have also had significant impacts: the 15th in the specific area of voting; the 13th as the only post-Civil War Amendment not subject to the "state action" limit on coverage.

SLAUGHTER-HOUSE CASES

16 Wall. 36, 21 L.Ed. 394 (1873).

Error to the Supreme Court of Louisiana.

Mr. Justice MILLER . . . . delivered the opinion of the Court.

[A Louisiana law of 1869 chartered a corporation and granted to it a 25-year monopoly "to maintain slaughterhouses, landings for cattle and stockyards" in three parishes. The parishes covered an area of 1154 square miles with a population of over 200,000, including the city of New Orleans. The statute also prescribed the rates to be charged at the company's facilities. Butchers not included in the monopoly challenged the statute under the 13th and 14th Amendments. The Supreme Court of Louisiana sustained the law.]

[The police] power is, and must be from its very nature, incapable of any very exact definition or limitation. Upon it depends the security of social order, the life and health of the citizen, the comfort of an existence in a thickly populated community, the enjoyment of private and social life, and the beneficial use of property. . . . The regulation of the place and manner of conducting the slaughtering of animals, and the business of butchering within a city . . . are among the most necessary and frequent exercises of this power. . . .

It may . . . be considered as established, that the authority of the legislature of Louisiana to pass the present statute is ample, unless some restraint in the exercise of that power be found in the constitution of that State or in the [recent] amendments to the [U.S.] Constitution . . . .

The plaintiffs in error . . . allege that the statute is a violation of the Constitution of the United States in these several particulars:

That it creates an involuntary servitude forbidden by the thirteenth article of amendment;

That it abridges the privileges and immunities of citizens of the United States;

That it denies to the plaintiffs the equal protection of the laws; and,

That it deprives them of their property without due process of law; contrary to the provisions of the first section of the fourteenth article of amendment.

This court is thus called upon for the first time to give construction to these articles.

We do not conceal from ourselves the great responsibility which this duty devolves upon us. No questions so far-reaching and pervading in their consequences, so profoundly interesting to the people of this country, and so important in their bearing upon the relations of the United States, and of the several States to each other and to the citizens of the States and of the United States, have been before this court during the official life of any of its present members. . . . .

The most cursory glance at these [three amendments] discloses a unity of purpose, when taken in connection with the history of the times, which cannot fail to have an important bearing on any question of doubt concerning their true meaning. Nor can such doubts, when any reasonably exist, be safely and rationally solved without a reference to that history. [The portions of the opinion reviewing the history are printed above, chap. 6, p. 449.] . . ..

. . . The word servitude [in the Thirteenth Amendment] is of larger meaning than slavery, as the latter is popularly understood in this country, and the obvious purpose was to forbid all shades and conditions of African slavery. It was very well understood that in the form of apprenticeship for long terms, as it had been practiced in the West India Islands, on the abolition of slavery by the English government, or by reducing the slaves to the condition of serfs attached to the plantation, the purpose of the article might have been evaded, if only the word slavery had been used. . . . And it is all that we deem necessary to say on the application of that article to the statute of Louisiana, now under consideration.* . . .

We repeat, then in the light of this recapitulation of events, almost too recent to be called history, but which are familiar to us all; and on the most casual examination of the language of these amendments, no one can fail to be impressed with the one pervading purpose found in them all, lying at the foundation of each, and without which none of them would have been even suggested; we mean the freedom of the slave race, the security and firm establishment of that freedom, and the protection of the newly-made freeman and citizen from the oppressions of those who had formerly exercised unlimited dominion over him. It is true that only the fifteenth amendment, in terms, mentions the negro by speaking of his color and his slavery. But it is just as true that each of the other articles was addressed to the grievances of that race, and designed to remedy them as the fifteenth.

We do not say that no one else but the negro can share in this protection. Both the language and spirit of these articles are to have their fair and just weight in any question of construction. Undoubtedly while negro slavery alone was in the mind of the Congress which proposed the thirteenth article, it forbids any other kind of slavery, now or hereafter. If Mexican peonage or the Chinese coolie labor system shall develop slavery of the Mexican or Chinese race within our territory, this amendment may safely be trusted to make it void. And so if other rights are assailed by the States which properly and necessarily fall within the protection of these articles, that protection

* The scope of the 13th Amendment— especially as a source of congressional power "rationally to determine what are the badges and the incidents of slavery" and to "translate that determination into effective legislation," against private as well as state action—was examined in Jones v. Alfred H. Mayer Co., 392 U.S. 409 (1968), the housing discrimination case, chap. 6, p. 517, supra. For earlier Court encounters with applications of the 13th Amendment to problems other than slavery, see Bailey v. Alabama, 219 U.S. 219 (1911), invalidating state laws which sought "to compel . . . service of labor" under contracts "by making it a crime to refuse or fail to perform it." See also Pollock v. Williams, 322 U.S. 4 (1944). But the Amendment does not bar all compulsory service—e. g., by seamen, Robertson v. Baldwin, 165 U.S. 275 (1897), or by soldiers, Selective Service Draft Law Cases, 245 U.S. 366 (1918). See generally tenBroek, "Thirteenth Amendment . . .—Consummation to Abolition and Key to the Fourteenth Amendment," 39 Calif.L.Rev. 171 (1951); Brodie, "The Federally-Secured Right to be Free from Bondage," 40 Geo.L.J. 367 (1952); and, on the enforcement of federal anti-peonage statutes, Shapiro, "Involuntary Servitude: The Need for a More Flexible Approach," 19 Rutgers L.Rev. 65 (1964).

will apply, though the party interested may not be of African descent. But what we do say, and what we wish to be understood is, that in any fair and just construction of any section or phrase of these amendments, it is necessary to look to the purpose which we have said was the pervading spirit of them all, the evil which they were designed to remedy, and the process of continued addition to the Constitution, until that purpose was supposed to be accomplished, as far as constitutional law can accomplish it.

. . . [The first sentence of the Fourteenth Amendment] declares that persons may be citizens of the United States without regard to their citizenship of a particular State, and it overturns the Dred Scott decision by making *all persons* born within the United States and subject to its jurisdiction citizens of the United States. That its main purpose was to establish the citizenship of the negro can admit of no doubt. . . .

The next observation is more important in view of the arguments of counsel in the present case. It is, that the distinction between citizenship of the United States and citizenship of a State is clearly recognized and established. Not only may a man be a citizen of the United States without being a citizen of a State, but an important element is necessary to convert the former into the latter. He must reside within the State to make him a citizen of it, but it is only necessary that he should be born or naturalized in the United States to be a citizen of the Union.

It is quite clear, then that there is a citizenship of the United States, and a citizenship of a State, which are distinct from each other, and which depend upon different characteristics or circumstances in the individual.

We think this distinction and its explicit recognition in this amendment of great weight in this argument, because the next paragraph of this same section, which is the one mainly relied on by the plaintiffs in error, speaks only of privileges and immunities of citizens of the United States, and does not speak of those of citizens of the several States. The argument, however, in favor of the plaintiffs rests wholly on the assumption that the citizenship is the same, and the privileges and immunities guaranteed by the clause are the same.

The language is, "No State shall make or enforce any law which shall abridge the privileges or immunities of citizens of *the United States*." It is a little remarkable, if this clause was intended as a protection to the citizen of a State against the legislative power of his own State, that the word citizen of the State should be left out when it is so carefully used, and used in contradistinction to citizens of the United States, in the very sentence which precedes it. It is too clear for argument that the change in phraseology was adopted understandingly and with a purpose.

Of the privileges and immunities of the citizen of the United States, and of the privileges and immunities of the citizen of the State, and what they respectively are, we will presently consider; but we wish to state here that it is only the former which are placed by this clause under the protection of the Federal Constitution, and that the latter, whatever they may be, are not intended to have any additional protection by this paragraph of the amendment. . . .

In the Constitution of the United States, [Art. IV, Sec. 2, states]: "The citizens of each State shall be entitled to all the privileges and immunities of citizens of the several States." . . . Fortunately we are not without judicial construction of this clause of the Constitution. The first and the leading case on the subject is that of Corfield v. Coryell, decided by Mr. Justice Washington in the Circuit Court for the District of Pennsylvania in 1823. "The inquiry," he says, "is, what are the privileges and immunities of citizens of the several States? We feel no hesitation in confining these expressions to those privileges and immunities which are *fundamental*; which belong of right to the citizens of all free governments, and which have at all times been enjoyed by citizens of the several States which compose this Union, from the time of their becoming free, independent, and sovereign. What these fundamental principles are, it would be more tedious than difficult to enumerate. They may all, however, be comprehended under the following general heads: protection by the government, with the right to acquire and possess property of every kind, and to pursue and obtain happiness and safety, subject, nevertheless, to such restraints as the government may prescribe for the general good of the whole." *

. . . The description, when taken to include others not named, but which are of the same general character, embraces nearly every civil right for the establishment and protection of which organized government is instituted. They are, in the language of Judge Washington, those rights which are fundamental. Throughout his opinion, they are spoken of as rights belonging to the individual as a citizen of a State. They are so spoken of in the constitutional provision which he was construing. And they have always been held to be the class of rights which the State governments were created to establish and secure. . . .

[Article IV] did not create those rights, which it called privileges and immunities of citizens of the States. It threw around them in that clause no security for the citizen of the State in which they were claimed or exercised. Nor did it profess to control the power of the State governments over the rights of its own citizens. Its sole purpose was to declare to the several States, that whatever those rights, as you grant or establish them to your own citizens, or as you limit or qualify, or impose restrictions on their exercise, the same, neither more nor less, shall be the measure of the rights of citizens of other States within your jurisdiction.

It would be the vainest show of learning to attempt to prove by citations of authority, that up to the adoption of the recent amendments, no claim or pretence was set up that those rights depended on the Federal government for their existence or protection, beyond the very few express limitations which the Federal Constitution imposed upon the States—such, for instance, as the prohibition against ex post facto laws, bills of attainder, and laws impairing the obligation of contracts. But with the exception of these and a few other restrictions, the entire domain of the privileges and immunities of citizens of the States, as above defined, lay within the constitutional and legislative power of the States, and without that of the Federal government. Was it the

---

* In Corfield v. Coryell, 4 Wash.C.C. 371, Fed.Cas. No. 3,230 (C.C.Pa.1823), a Pennsylvanian's boat had been seized by New Jersey officials under a New Jersey law prohibiting non-residents to gather clams, oysters or shells in New Jersey waters. The Circuit Court rejected the claim that the privileges and immunities clause of Art. IV, Sec. 2, compelled New Jersey, in "regulating the use of the common property" of its citizens, "to extend to the citizens of all the other states the same advantages as are secured to their own citizens." Compare Toomer v. Witsell, 334 U.S. 385 (1948), chap. 10, p. 772, supra.

purpose of the fourteenth amendment, by the simple declaration that no State should make or enforce any law which shall abridge the privileges and immunities of *citizens of the United States*, to transfer the security and protection of all the civil rights which we have mentioned, from the States to the Federal government?   And where it is declared that Congress shall have the power to enforce that article, was it intended to bring within the power of Congress the entire domain of civil rights heretofore belonging exclusively to the States?

All this and more must follow, if the proposition of the plaintiffs in error be sound.   For not only are these rights subject to the control of Congress whenever in it discretion any of them are supposed to be abridged by State legislation, but that body may also pass laws in advance, limiting and restricting the exercise of legislative power by the States, in their most ordinary and usual functions, as in its judgment it may think proper on all such subjects.   And still further, such a construction . . . would constitute this court a perpetual censor upon all legislation of the States, on the civil rights of their own citizens, with authority to nullify such as it did not approve as consistent with those rights, as they existed at the time of the adoption of this amendment.   The argument we admit is not always the most conclusive which is drawn from the consequences urged against the adoption of a particular construction of an instrument.   But when, as in the case before us, these consequences are so serious, so far-reaching and pervading, so great a departure from the structure and spirit of our institutions; when the effect is to fetter and degrade the State governments by subjecting them to the control of Congress, in the exercise of powers heretofore universally conceded to them of the most ordinary and fundamental character; when in fact it radically changes the whole theory of the relations of the State and Federal governments to each other and of both these governments to the people; the argument has a force that is irresistible, in the absence of language which expresses such a purpose too clearly to admit of doubt.

We are convinced that no such results were intended by the Congress which proposed these amendments, nor by the legislatures of the States which ratified them. . . .

But lest it should be said that no such privileges and immunities are to be found if those we have been considering are excluded, we venture to suggest some which owe their existence to the Federal government, its National character, its Constitution, or its laws.

One of these is well described in the case of Crandall v. Nevada [6 Wall. 35 (1868), noted in chap. 6, p. 509, supra].   It is said to be the right of the citizen of this great country, protected by implied guarantees of its Constitution, "to come to the seat of government to assert any claim he may have upon the government, to transact any business he may have with it, to seek its protection, to share its offices, to engage in administering its functions. He has the right of free access to its seaports, through which all operations of foreign commerce are conducted, to the subtreasuries, land offices, and courts of justice in the several States." . . .

Another privilege of a citizen of the United States is to demand the care and protection of the Federal government over his life, liberty, and property when on the high seas or within the jurisdiction of a foreign government. . . .   The right to peaceably assemble and petition for redress of grievances, the privilege of the writ of *habeas corpus,* are rights of the citizen guaranteed by the Federal Constitution. The right to use the navigable waters of the United States, however they may penetrate the territory of the several States, all rights secured to our citizens by treaties with foreign nations, are dependent upon citizenship of the United States, and not citizenship of a State. One of these privileges is conferred by the very article under consideration. It is that a citizen of the United States can, of his own volition, become a citizen of any State of the Union by a *bona fide* residence therein, with the same rights as other citizens of that State. To these may be added the rights secured by the thirteenth and fifteenth articles of amendment, and by the other clause of the fourteenth, next to be considered.

But it is useless to pursue this branch of the inquiry, since we are of opinion that the rights claimed by these plaintiffs in error, if they have any existence, are not privileges and immunities of citizens of the United States within the meaning of the clause of the fourteenth amendment under consideration. . . .

The argument has not been much pressed in these cases that the defendant's charter deprives the plaintiffs of their property without due process of law, or that it denies to them the equal protection of the law. . . .

We are not without judicial interpretation, . . . both State and National, of the meaning of [the due process] clause. And it is sufficient to say that under no construction of that provision that we have ever seen, or any that we deem admissible, can the restraint imposed by the State of Louisiana upon the exercise of their trade by the butchers of New Orleans be held to be a deprivation of property within the meaning of that provision.

"Nor shall any State deny to any person within its jurisdiction the equal protection of the laws."

In the light of the history of these amendments, and the pervading purpose of them, which we have already discussed, it is not difficult to give a meaning to this clause. The existence of laws in the States where the newly emancipated negroes resided, which discriminated with gross injustice and hardship against them as a class, was the evil to be remedied by this clause, and by it such laws are forbidden.

If, however, the States did not conform their laws to its requirements, then by the fifth section of the article of amendment Congress was authorized to enforce it by suitable legislation. We doubt very much whether any action of a State not directed by way of discrimination against the negroes as a class, or on account of their race, will ever be held to come within the purview of this provision. It is so clearly a provision for that race and that emergency, that a strong case would be necessary for its application to any other. But as it is a State that is to be dealt with, and not alone the validity of its laws, we may safely leave that matter until Congress shall have exercised its power, or some case of State oppression, by denial of equal justice in its courts, shall have claimed a decision at our hands. We find no such case in the one before us, and do not deem it necessary to go over the argument again, as it may have relation to this particular clause of the amendment. . . .

The adoption of the first eleven amendments to the Constitution so soon after the original instrument was accepted, shows a prevailing sense of danger at that time from the Federal power. And it cannot be denied that such a jealousy continued to exist with many patriotic men until the breaking out of the late civil war. It was then discovered that the true danger to the perpetuity of the Union was in the capacity of the State organizations to combine and concentrate all the powers of the State, and of contiguous States, for a determined resistance to the General Government.

Unquestionably this has given great force to the argument, and added largely to the number of those who believe in the necessity of a strong National government.

But, however prevading this sentiment, and however it may have contributed to the adoption of the amendments we have been considering, we do not see in those amendments any purpose to destroy the main features of the general system. Under the pressure of all the excited feeling growing out of the war, our statesmen have still believed that the existence of the States with powers for domestic and local government, including the regulation of civil rights—the rights of person and of property—was essential to the perfect working of our complex form of government, though they have thought proper to impose additional limitations on the States, and to confer additional power on that of the Nation.

But whatever fluctuations may be seen in the history of public opinion on this subject during the period of our national existence, we think it will be found that this court, so far as its functions required, has always held with a steady and an even hand the balance between State and Federal power, and we trust that such may continue to be the history of its relation to that subject so long as it shall have duties to perform which demand of it a construction of the Constitution, or of any of its parts. . . .

Affirmed.

Mr. Justice FIELD, dissenting: . . .

It is not necessary . . . to rest my objections to the act in question upon the terms and meaning of the thirteenth amendment. The provisions of the fourteenth amendment, which is properly a supplement to the thirteenth, cover, in my judgment, the case before us, and inhibit any legislation which confers special and exclusive privileges like these under consideration. . .

What, then, are the privileges and immunities which are secured against abridgment by State legislation? . . .

. . . The privileges and immunities designated [in Corfield v. Coryell] are those *which of right belong to the citizens of all free governments.* Clearly among these must be placed the right to pursue a lawful employment in a lawful manner, without other restraint than such as equally affects all persons. In the discussions in Congress upon the passage of the Civil Rights Act [of 1866] repeated reference was made to this language of Mr. Justice Washington. . . .

What the clause in question did for the protection of the citizens of one State against hostile and discriminating legislation of other States, the fourteenth amendment does for the protection of every citizen of the United States against hostile and discriminating legislation against him in favor of others, whether they reside in the same or in different States. If under the fourth article of the Constitution equality of privileges and immunities is secured between citizens of different States, under the fourteenth amendment the same equality is secured between citizens of the United States.

. . . All monopolies in any known trade or manufacture are an invasion of these privileges, for they encroach upon the liberty of citizens to acquire property and pursue happiness . . . To [citizens of the United States], everywhere, all pursuits, all professions, all avocations are open without other restrictions than such as are imposed equally upon all others of the same age, sex and condition. . . .

I am authorized by the Chief Justice [CHASE], Mr. Justice SWAYNE, and Mr. Justice BRADLEY, to state that they concur with me in this dissenting opinion.

Mr. Justice BRADLEY, also dissenting: . . .

Admitting . . . that formerly the States were not prohibited from infringing any of the fundamental privileges and immunities of citizens of the United States, except in a few specified cases, that cannot be said now, since the adoption of the fourteenth amendment. In my judgment, it was the intention of the people of this country in adopting that amendment to provide National security against violation by the States of the fundamental rights of the citizen. . . .

. . . [A]ny law which establishes a sheer monopoly, depriving a large class of citizens of the privilege of pursuing a lawful employment, does abridge the privileges of those citizens.

The amendment also prohibits any State from depriving any person (citizen or otherwise) of life, liberty, or property, without due process of law.

In my view, a law which prohibits a large class of citizens from adopting a lawful employment, or from following a lawful employment previously adopted, does deprive them of liberty as well as property, without due process of law. Their right of choice is a portion of their liberty; their occupation is their property. Such a law also deprives those citizens of the equal protection of the laws, contrary to the last clause of the section. . . .

But great fears are expressed that this construction of the amendment will lead to enactments by Congress interfering with the internal affairs of the States, and establishing therein civil and criminal codes of law for the government of the citizens, and thus abolishing the State governments in everything but name; or else, that it will lead the Federal courts to draw to their cognizance the supervision of State tribunals on every subject of judicial inquiry . . . .

In my judgment no such practical inconveniences would arise. Very little, if any, legislation on the part of Congress would be required to carry the amendment into effect. Like the prohibition against passing a law impairing the obligation of a contract; it would execute itself. The point would be regularly raised, in a suit at law, and settled by final reference to the Federal court. As the privileges and immunities protected are only those fundamental ones which belong to every citizen, they would soon become so far defined as to cause but a slight accumulation of business in the Federal courts. Besides, the recognized existence of the law would prevent its frequent violation. But even if the business of the National court should be increased Congress could easily supply the remedy by increasing their number and efficiency. The great question is, What is the true construction of the amendment? When once we find that, we shall find the means of giving it effect. The argument from inconvenience ought not to have a very controlling influence in questions of this sort. The National will and National interest are of far greater importance. . . .

    Mr. Justice SWAYNE, dissenting: . . .

    . . . The construction adopted by the majority of my brethren is, in my judgment, much too narrow. It defeats, by a limitation not anticipated, the intent of those by whom the instrument was framed and of those by whom it was adopted. To the extent of that limitation it turns, as it were, what was meant for bread into a stone. By the Constitution, as it stood before the war, ample protection was given against oppression by the Union, but little was given against wrong and oppression by the States. That want was intended to be supplied by this amendment. . . . Nowhere, than in this court, ought the will of the nation, as thus expressed, to be more liberally construed or more cordially executed. This determination of the majority seems to me to lie far in the other direction.

    I earnestly hope that the consequences to follow may prove less serious and far-reaching than the minority fear they will be.

THE AFTERMATH OF THE SLAUGHTER–HOUSE CASES: SUBSTANTIVE DUE PROCESS; PRIVILEGES AND IMMUNITIES

    1. *Substantive due process.* The insistence of dissenting Justices Bradley and Swayne that the due process clause imposed substantive limits on state economic regulation was echoed by other dissenters for the next generation. By the end of the 19th century, a majority of the Court embraced the "substantive due process" concept. And in the first three decades of the 20th century, the Court applied that doctrine frequently. But since 1937 the Court has followed a "hands-off" policy toward state regulation of the economy. These developments are traced in chap. 13, secs. 3 and 4, infra.

    2. *"Privileges and immunities" and the 14th Amendment.* The framers of the 14th Amendment had great difficulty in articulating any specific content for the privileges and immunities clause.* The Justices of the Supreme Court have not been able to be much more concrete so far. There have been only sporadic attempts to give the clause a broader scope than that found by Justice Miller in 1873, and its development has been overshadowed by expanding views of due process and equal protection, as the remaining materials in this volume illustrate. In Colgate v. Harvey, 296 U.S. 404 (1935), involving a Vermont tax provision, the Court for the first time invalidated a state law under the privileges and immunities clause of the 14th Amendment. But this interpretation of the clause was short-lived: the Colgate case was overruled in Madden v. Kentucky, 309 U.S. 83 (1940).

    For examples of reliances on the clause by individual Justices, see Edwards v. California, 314 U.S. 160 (1941) (chap. 8, p. 652, supra) (concurring opinion of Justice Douglas joined by Justices Black and Murphy—

---

* See Fairman, "Does the Fourteenth Amendment Incorporate the Bill of Rights? The Original Understanding," 2 Stan.L.Rev. 5 (1949), including a contemporary recollection that the clause "came from [Congressman] Bingham of Ohio. Its euphony and indefiniteness of meaning were a charm to him." Compare Justice Black's comments on Fairman and on Bingham in Duncan v. Louisiana, sec. 2B, p. 812, infra.

"the right to move freely from state to state"); Hague v. CIO, 307 U.S. 496 (1939) (concurring opinion by Justice Roberts, joined by Justice Black— right to assemble and "discuss national legislation"). See also Twining v. New Jersey, 211 U.S. 78 (1908), listing national privileges and immunities and including the rights to travel from state to state, to petition Congress, to vote for national officers, to enter the public lands, the right to be "protected against violence while in the lawful custody of a United States marshal," and "the right to inform the United States authorities of violation of its laws." Was there no constitutional protection of these rights prior to the 14th Amendment? Cf. McCulloch v. Maryland, chaps. 3 and 10, supra. Compare the materials on the privileges and immunities clause of Art. IV, Sec. 2, chap. 10, p. 771, supra.

B. THE MEANING OF DUE PROCESS: "FUNDAMENTAL STANDARDS" AND "INCORPORATION"

Introduction. Though the Court has stated that it prefers to mark the boundaries of the due process clause "by the gradual process of judicial inclusion and exclusion," [1] the Justices have repeatedly attempted to articulate general guidelines for the process of sharpening the "vague contours" of the clause. One of the earliest attempts came before the adoption of the 14th Amendment. In considering the validity of a distress warrant procedure under the Fifth Amendment, in Murray's Lessee v. Hoboken Land & Improvement Co., 18 How. 272 (1856), Justice Curtis stated: "The words, 'due process of law,' were undoubtedly intended to convey the same meaning as the words, 'by the law of the land,' in Magna Charta. Lord Coke, in his commentary on those words, (2 Inst. 50) says they mean due process of law. . . . The constitution contains no description of those processes which it was intended to allow or forbid. It does not even declare what principles are to be applied to ascertain whether it be due process. It is manifest that it was not left to the legislative power to enact any process which might be devised. The article is a restraint on the legislative as well as on the executive and judicial powers of the government, and cannot be so construed as to leave congress free to make any process 'due process of law,' by its mere will. To what principles, then, are we to resort to ascertain whether this process, enacted by congress, is due process? To this the answer must be twofold. We must examine the constitution itself, to see whether this process be in conflict with any of its provisions. If not found to be so, we must look to those settled usages and modes of proceeding existing in the common and statute law of England, before the emigration of our ancestors, and which are shown not to have been unsuited to their civil and political condition by having been acted on by them after the settlement of this country. . . . [T]hough 'due process of law' generally implies and includes actor, reus, judex, regular allegations, opportunity to answer, and a trial according to some settled course of judicial proceedings, . . . yet, this is not universally true."

1. Davidson v. New Orleans, 96 U.S. 97 (1877).

1. *The utility of history.* The "settled usages and modes of proceeding" in English law may indeed be persuasive in some cases, as Ownbey v. Morgan, 256 U.S. 94 (1921), demonstrates. There the Court sustained the validity of a Delaware statute under which, in foreign attachment proceedings, special bail was required of defendant as a condition of being heard on the merits. To the objection that the statute impeded and (no bail having been supplied) actually denied the right to be heard, the Court replied that a "process of law is due process within the meaning of constitutional limitations if it can show the sanction of settled usage both in this country and in England." The statute in question had been modeled on the custom of London and had been on the statute books of Delaware from early colonial days. "Not lightly to be vacated is the verdict of quiescent years," is the way Judge Cardozo once put the matter, Coler v. Corn Exchange Bank, 250 N.Y. 136, 164 N.E. 882 (1928).

2. *The inadequacy of history.* But English legal history may be silent on many of the issues arising under due process; and even where it speaks, the Court is not compelled to listen. See, e. g., Powell v. Alabama, 287 U.S. 45 (1932) (chap. 12, p. 841), finding a limited right to counsel essential to due process despite the lack of a corresponding guarantee in England in the late 18th century. Moreover, while the historical approach has been useful in upholding challenged procedures, the Court has not attempted to tie American lawmakers to the models of English tradition. See, e. g., Hurtado v. California, 110 U.S. 516 (1884), sustaining a California statute which permitted criminal proceedings to be instituted by information rather than grand jury indictment: "There is nothing in Magna Carta . . . which ought to exclude the best ideas of all systems and of every age. . . . [A]ny legal proceeding enforced by public authority, whether sanctioned by age and custom, or newly devised in the discretion of the legislative power, in furtherance of the general public good, which regards and preserves . . . principles of liberty and justice, must be held to be due process of law."

3. *The 14th Amendment and the Bill of Rights.* The problems of defining due process have come into sharpest focus in the continuing controversy over the relationship between the Bill of Rights and the 14th Amendment. The Marshall Court held that the Bill of Rights restrained the national government only and was not directly applicable to the states. Did the adoption of the 14th Amendment change that rule of Barron v. Baltimore? Did the new due process clause "absorb" or "incorporate" the old limitations on Congress? Are at least some of the guarantees of the Bill of Rights applicable to the states as a result of the post-Civil War Amendments? If so, do they limit the states in precisely the same way that they restrain the national government?

Questions such as these have provoked especially heated controversy in cases involving 14th Amendment limitations on state administration of criminal justice. The first two principal cases in this section—the Palko decision in 1937 and the Adamson case in 1947—contain the best-known 20th century statements on these issues. The third—the 1968 decision in Duncan v. Louisiana—illustrates a very recent encounter with the problem; the opinions in Duncan review the evolution of "incorporation" in the two decades after Adamson and reflect the modern Court's divisions. But the examples are numerous, for the issue is pervasive. Virtually every area of criminal law administration considered in the next chapter, for example, has seen controversy over this issue; indeed, concern with the general question of national judicial responsibility to give content to the procedural guarantees of 14th Amendment may at times have produced inadequate attention to the particular controversy before the Court.[2] The first three cases below, then, introduce a problem that will recur in the chapter that follows. And the final case in the section, Griswold v. Connecticut, illustrates the search for 14th Amendment standards in a broader context. It involves substantive liberty rather than criminal procedure, and it reflects a variety of views regarding Court intervention and restraint, the articulation and ordering of constitutional values, and the choice among vague and specific guarantees of individual rights—all pervasive themes not only in the next chapter but in all others in Part III.

PALKO v. CONNECTICUT

302 U.S. 319, 58 S.Ct. 149, 82 L.Ed. 288 (1937).

Appeal from the Supreme Court of Errors of Connecticut.

Mr. Justice CARDOZO delivered the opinion of the Court. . . .

Appellant was indicted in Fairfield County, Connecticut, for the crime of murder in the first degree. A jury found him guilty of murder in the second degree, and he was sentenced to confinement in the state prison for life. Thereafter the State of Connecticut, with the permission of the judge presiding at the trial, gave notice of appeal to the Supreme Court of Errors. This it did pursuant to an act adopted in 1886 . . . . . [T]he Supreme Court of Errors reversed the judgment [because of errors of law] and ordered a new trial. . . .

. . . [D]efendant was brought to trial again. . . . [H]e made the objection that the effect of the new trial was to place him twice in jeopardy for the same offense, and in so doing to violate the Fourteenth Amendment of the Constitution of the United States. Upon the overruling of the objection the trial proceeded. The jury returned a verdict of murder in the first degree, and the court sentenced the defendant to the punishment of death. The Supreme Court of Errors affirmed. . . .

1. The execution of the sentence will not deprive appellant of his life without the process of law assured to him by the Fourteenth Amendment of the Federal Constitution.

Argument ✳

The argument for appellant is that whatever is forbidden by the Fifth Amendment is forbidden by the Fourteenth also. . . . To retry a defendant, though under one indictment and only one, subjects him, it is said, to double jeopardy in violation of the Fifth Amendment, if the prosecution is one on behalf of the United States. From this the consequence is said to follow that there is a denial of life or liberty without due process of law, if the prosecution is one on behalf of the People of a State. . . .

2. See, e. g., Bartkus v. Illinois, 359
U.S. 121 (1959) (ch. 12, p. 917, infra).

We do not find it profitable to mark the precise limits of the prohibition of double jeopardy in federal prosecutions. The subject was much considered in Kepner v. United States, 195 U.S. 100, decided in 1904 by a closely divided court. The view was there expressed for a majority of the court that the prohibition was not confined to jeopardy in a new and independent case. It forbade jeopardy in the same case if the new trial was at the instance of the government and not upon defendant's motion. . . . All this may be assumed for the purpose of the case at hand, though the dissenting opinions . . . show how much was to be said in favor of a different ruling. Right-minded men, as we learn from those opinions, could reasonably, even if mistakenly, believe that a second trial was lawful in prosecutions subject to the Fifth Amendment, if it was all in the same case. Even more plainly, right-minded men could reasonably believe that in espousing that conclusion they were not favoring a practice repugnant to the conscience of mankind. Is double jeopardy in such circumstances, if double jeopardy it must be called, a denial of due process forbidden to the states? The tyranny of labels . . . must not lead us to leap to a conclusion that a word which in one set of facts may stand for oppression or enormity is of like effect in every other.

We have said that in appellant's view the Fourteenth Amendment is to be taken as embodying the prohibitions of the Fifth. His thesis is even broader. Whatever would be a violation of the original bill of rights (Amendments I to VIII) if done by the federal government is now equally unlawful by force of the Fourteenth Amendment if done by a state. There is no such general rule.

The Fifth Amendment provides, among other things, that no person shall be held to answer for a capital or otherwise infamous crime unless on presentment or indictment of a grand jury. This court has held that, in prosecutions by a state, presentment or indictment by a grand jury may give way to informations at the instance of a public officer. Hurtado v. California, 110 U.S. 516 . . . . . The Fifth Amendment provides also that no person shall be compelled in any criminal case to be a witness against himself. This court has said that, in prosecutions by a state, the exemption will fail if the state elects to end it. Twining v. New Jersey, 211 U.S. 78, 106, 111, 112. . . . . The Sixth Amendment calls for a jury trial in criminal cases and the Seventh for a jury trial in civil cases at common law where the value in controversy shall exceed twenty dollars. This court has ruled that consistently with those amendments trial by jury may be modified by a state or abolished altogether. Walker v. Sauvinet, 92 U.S. 90; Maxwell v. Dow, 176 U.S. 581 . . . . . As to the Fourth Amendment, one should refer to Weeks v. United States, 232 U.S. 383, 398, and as to other provisions of the Sixth, to West v. Louisiana, 194 U.S. 258.

On the other hand, the due process clause of the Fourteenth Amendment may make it unlawful for a state to abridge by its statutes the freedom of speech which the First Amendment safeguards against encroachment by the Congress . . . . ; or the like freedom of the press . . . . ; or the free exercise of religion . . . . ; or the right of peaceable assembly, without which speech would be unduly trammeled . . . . ; or the right of one accused of crime to the benefit of counsel. Powell v. Alabama, 287 U.S. 45. In these and other situations immunities that are valid as against the federal government by force of the specific pledges of particular amendments have been found to be implicit in the concept of ordered liberty, and thus, through the Fourteenth Amendment, become valid as against the states.

The line of division may seem to be wavering and broken if there is a hasty catalogue of the cases on the one side and the other. Reflection and analysis will induce a different view. There emerges the perception of a rationalizing principle which gives to discrete instances a proper order and coherence. The right to trial by jury and the immunity from prosecution except as the result of an indictment may have value and importance. Even so, they are not of the very essence of a scheme of ordered liberty. To abolish them is not to violate a "principle of justice so rooted in the traditions and conscience of our people as to be ranked as fundamental." Snyder v. Massachusetts, [291 U.S. 97, 105]. Few would be so narrow or provincial as to maintain that a fair and enlightened system of justice would be impossible without them. What is true of jury trials and indictments is true also, as the cases show, of the immunity from compulsory self-incrimination. . . . This too might be lost, and justice still be done. Indeed, today as in the past there are students of our penal system who look upon the immunity as a mischief rather than a benefit, and who would limit its scope, or destroy it altogether. No doubt there would remain the need to give protection against torture, physical or mental. Brown v. Mississippi, [297 U.S. 278]. Justice, however, would not perish if the accused were subject to a duty to respond to orderly inquiry. The exclusion of these immunities and privileges from the privileges and immunities protected against the action of the states has not been arbitrary or casual. It has been dictated by a study and appreciation of the meaning, the essential implications, of liberty itself.

We reach a different plane of social and moral values when we pass to the privileges and immunities that have been taken over from the earlier articles of the federal bill of rights and brought within the Fourteenth Amendment by a process of absorption. These in their origin were effective against the federal government alone. If the Fourteenth Amendment has absorbed them, the process of absorption has had its source in the belief that neither liberty nor justice would exist if they were sacrificed. . . .[1] This is true, for illustration, of freedom of thought, and speech. Of that freedom one may say that it is the matrix, the indispensable condition, of nearly every other form of freedom. With rare aberrations a pervasive recognition of that truth can be traced in our history, political and legal. So it has come about that the domain of liberty, withdrawn by the Fourteenth Amendment from encroachment by the states, has been enlarged by latter-day judgments to include liberty of the mind as well as liberty of action. The extension became, indeed, a logical imperative when once it was recognized, as long ago it was, that liberty is something more than exemption from physical restraint, and that even in the field of substantive rights and duties the legislative judgment, if oppressive and arbitrary, may be over-

---

1. " . . . it is possible that some of the personal rights safeguarded by the first eight Amendments against National action may also be safeguarded against state action, because a denial of them would be a denial of due process of law, Chicago, Burlington & Quincy Railroad v. Chicago, 166 U.S. 226. If this is so, it is not because those rights are enumerated in the first eight Amendments, but because they are of such a nature that they are included in the conception of due process of law." [Footnote by the Court. The quotation is from Twining v. New Jersey, supra.]

ridden by the courts.[2] . . . Fundamental too in the concept of due process, and so in that of liberty, is the thought that condemnation shall be rendered only after trial. . . . The hearing, moreover, must be a real one, not a sham or a pretense. Moore v. Dempsey, 261 U.S. 86 . . . . For that reason, ignorant defendants in a capital case were held to have been condemned unlawfully when in truth, though not in form, they were refused the aid of counsel. . . . The decision did not turn upon the fact that the benefit of counsel would have been guaranteed to the defendants by the provisions of the Sixth Amendment if they had been prosecuted in a federal court. The decision turned upon the fact that in the particular situation laid before us in the evidence the benefit of counsel was essential to the substance of a hearing.

Our survey of the cases serves, we think, to justify the statement that the dividing line between them, if not unfaltering throughout its course, has been true for the most part to a unifying principle. On which side of the line the case made out by the appellant has appropriate location must be the next inquiry and the final one. Is that kind of double jeopardy to which the statute has subjected him a hardship so acute and shocking that our polity will not endure it? Does it violate those "fundamental principles of liberty and justice which lie at the base of all our civil and political institutions"? Hebert v. Louisiana, [272 U.S. 312]. The answer surely must be "no." What the answer would have to be if the state were permitted after a trial free from error to try the accused over again or to bring another case against him, we have no occasion to consider. We deal with the statute before us and no other. The state is not attempting to wear the accused out by a multitude of cases with accumulated trials. It asks no more than this, that the case against him shall go on until there shall be a trial free from the corrosion of substantial legal error. . . . This is not cruelty at all, nor even vexation in any immoderate degree. If the trial had been infected with error adverse to the accused, there might have been review at his instance, and as often as necessary to purge the vicious taint. A reciprocal privilege . . . has now been granted to the state. There is here no seismic innovation. The edifice of justice stands, its symmetry, to many, greater than before.

2. The conviction of appellant is not in derogation of any privileges or immunities that belong to him as a citizen of the United States. . . .

Affirmed.[3]

Mr. Justice BUTLER dissents.

2. The "absorption" of First Amendment liberties via the 14th is traced in chap. 15, infra. The development of "substantive due process" limits on economic regulation is considered in chap. 13, sec. 3, infra.

3. In Benton v. Maryland, 395 U.S. 784 (1969) (preceding the Duncan case,

at p. 811, infra), the Court found that the Fifth Amendment's double jeopardy guarantee "should apply to the States through the Fourteenth." The Court added: "Insofar as it is inconsistent with this holding, Palko v. Connecticut is overruled."

ADAMSON v. CALIFORNIA

332 U.S. 46, 67 S.Ct. 1672, 91 L.Ed. 1903 (1947).

Appeal from the Supreme Court of California.

Mr. Justice REED delivered the opinion of the Court.

The appellant, Adamson, a citizen of the United States, was convicted, without recommendation for mercy, by a jury in a Superior Court of the State of California of murder in the first degree. . . . [T]he sentence of death was affirmed by the Supreme Court of the state. The provisions of California law which were challenged in the state proceedings as invalid under the Fourteenth Amendment . . . permit the failure of a defendant to explain or to deny evidence against him to be commented upon by court and by counsel and to be considered by court and jury. . . .

[Appellant, in addition to the privileges and immunities clause,] relies upon the due process of law clause of the Fourteenth Amendment to invalidate the provisions of the California law . . . (a) because comment on failure to testify is permitted, (b) because appellant was forced to forego testimony in person because of danger of disclosure of his past convictions through cross-examination, and (c) because the presumption of innocence was infringed by the shifting of the burden of proof to appellant in permitting comment on his failure to testify.

We shall assume, but without any intention thereby of ruling upon the issue, that permission by law to the court, counsel and jury to comment upon and consider the failure of defendant "to explain or to deny by his testimony any evidence or facts in the case against him" would infringe defendant's privilege against self-incrimination under the Fifth Amendment if this were a trial in a court of the United States under a similar law. Such an assumption does not determine appellant's rights under the Fourteenth Amendment. [After rejecting the privileges and immunities claim, the Court continued:]

Appellant secondly contends that . . . the privilege against self-incrimination, . . . to its full scope under the Fifth Amendment, inheres in the right to a fair trial. A right to a fair trial is a right admittedly protected by the due process clause of the Fourteenth Amendment. . . . The due process clause of the Fourteenth Amendment, however, does not draw all the rights of the federal Bill of Rights under its protection. That contention was made and rejected in Palko v. Connecticut . . . . Nothing has been called to our attention that either the framers of the Fourteenth Amendment or the states that adopted intended its due process clause to draw within its scope the earlier amendments to the Constitution. Palko held that such provisions of the Bill of Rights as were "implicit in the concept of ordered liberty" . . . . became secure from state interference by the clause. But it held nothing more.

. . . For a state to require testimony from an accused is not necessarily a breach of a state's obligation to give a fair trial. Therefore, we must examine the effect of the California law applied in this trial to see whether the comment on failure to testify violates the protection against state action that the due process clause does grant to an accused. The due process clause forbids compulsion to testify by fear of hurt, torture or exhaustion.

It forbids any other type of coercion that falls within the scope of due process.
. . . So our inquiry is directed, not at the broad question of the constitutionality of compulsory testimony from the accused under the due process
clause, but to the constitutionality of the provision of the California law that
permits comment upon his failure to testify. . . .

It is true that if comment were forbidden, an accused in this situation
could remain silent and avoid evidence of former crimes and comment upon
his failure to testify. We are of the view, however, that a state may control
such a situation in accordance with its own ideas of the most efficient administration of criminal justice. The purpose of due process is not to protect
an accused against a proper conviction but against an unfair conviction.
When evidence is before a jury that threatens conviction, it does not seem
unfair to require him to choose between leaving the adverse evidence unexplained and subjecting himself to impeachment through disclosure of former crimes. . . .

Affirmed.

Mr. Justice FRANKFURTER, concurring. . . .

For historical reasons a limited immunity from the common duty to
testify was written into the Federal Bill of Rights, and I am prepared to
agree that, as part of that immunity, comment on the failure of an accused
to take the witness stand is forbidden in federal prosecutions. It is so, of
course, by explicit act of Congress. . . . But to suggest that such a
limitation can be drawn out of "due process" in its protection of ultimate
decency in a civilized society is to suggest that the Due Process Clause fastened
fetters of unreason upon the States. . . .

Between the incorporation of the Fourteenth Amendment into the
Constitution and the beginning of the present membership of the Court—a
period of seventy years—the scope of that Amendment was passed upon by
forty-three judges. Of all these judges, only one, who may respectfully be
called an eccentric exception, ever indicated the belief that the Fourteenth
Amendment was a shorthand summary of the first eight Amendments.
. . .

The short answer to the suggestion that the [due process clause] was a
way of saying that every State must thereafter initiate prosecutions through
indictment by a grand jury, must have a trial by a jury of twelve in criminal
cases, and must have trial by such a jury in common law suits where the
amount in controversy exceeds twenty dollars, is that it is a strange way of
saying it. It would be extraordinarily strange for a Constitution to convey
such specific commands in such a roundabout and inexplicit way. . . .
The notion that the Fourteenth Amendment was a covert way of imposing
upon the States all the rules which it seemed important to Eighteenth Century
statesmen to write into the Federal Amendments, was rejected by judges who
were themselves witnesses of the process by which the Fourteenth Amendment became part of the Constitution. . . . [A]t the time of the ratification of the Fourteenth Amendment the constitutions of nearly half of the
ratifying States did not have the rigorous requirements of the Fifth Amendment for instituting criminal proceedings through a grand jury. It could
hardly have occurred to these States that by ratifying the Amendment they
uprooted their established methods for prosecuting crime and fastened upon
themselves a new prosecutorial system.

Indeed, the suggestion that the Fourteenth Amendment incorporates the first eight Amendments as such is not unambiguously urged. . . . There is suggested merely a selective incorporation of the first eight Amendments into the Fourteenth Amendment. Some are in and some are out, but we are left in the dark as to which are in and which are out. Nor are we given the calculus for determining which go in and which stay out. If the basis of selection is merely that those provisions of the first eight Amendments are incorporated which commend themselves to individual justices as indispensable to the dignity and happiness of a free man, we are thrown back to a merely subjective test. . . . If all that is meant is that due process contains within itself certain minimal standards which are "of the very essence of a scheme of ordered liberty," Palko v. Connecticut . . ., putting upon this Court the duty of applying these standards from time to time, then we have merely arrived at the insight which our predecessors long ago expressed. . . .

. . . The Amendment neither comprehends the specific provisions by which the founders deemed it appropriate to restrict the federal government nor is it confined to them. The Due Process Clause of the Fourteenth Amendment has an independent potency, precisely as does the Due Process Clause of the Fifth Amendment in relation to the Federal Government. It ought not to require argument to reject the notion that due process of law meant one thing in the Fifth Amendment and another in the Fourteenth. . . . Are Madison and his contemporaries in the framing of the Bill of Rights to be charged with writing into it a meaningless clause? . . .

A construction which gives to due process no independent function but turns it into a summary of the specific provisions of the Bill of Rights would . . . assume that no other abuses would reveal themselves in the course of time than those which had become manifest in 1791. Such a view not only disregards the historic meaning of "due process." It leads inevitably to a warped construction of specific provisions of the Bill of Rights to bring within their scope conduct clearly condemned by due process but not easily fitting into the pigeon-holes of the specific provisions. It seems pretty late in the day to suggest that a phrase so laden with historic meaning should be given an improvised content consisting of some but not all of the provisions of the first eight Amendments, selected on an undefined basis, with improvisation of content for the provisions so selected.

And so, when, as in a case like the present, a conviction in a State court is here for review under a claim that a right protected by the Due Process Clause of the Fourteenth Amendment has been denied, the issue is not whether an infraction of one of the specific provisions of the first eight Amendments is disclosed by the record. The relevant question is whether the criminal proceedings which resulted in conviction deprived the accused of the due process of law to which the United States Constitution entitled him. Judicial review of that guaranty of the Fourteenth Amendment inescapably imposes upon this Court an exercise of judgment upon the whole course of the proceedings in order to ascertain whether they offend those canons of decency and fairness which express the notions of justice of English-speaking peoples even toward those charged with the most heinous offenses. These standards of justice are not authoritatively formulated anywhere as though they were prescriptions in a pharmacopoeia. But neither does the application of the Due Process Clause imply that judges are wholly at large. The judicial judgment in applying the Due Process Clause must move within the limits of accepted notions of justice and is not to be based upon the idiosyncrasies of a merely personal judgment. The fact that judges among themselves may differ whether in a particular case a trial offends accepted notions of justice is not disproof that general rather than idiosyncratic standards are applied. An important safeguard against such merely individual judgment is an alert deference to the judgment of the State court under review.

Mr. Justice BLACK, dissenting. . . .

This decision reasserts a constitutional theory spelled out in Twining v. New Jersey, 211 U.S. 78, that this Court is endowed by the Constitution with boundless power under "natural law" periodically to expand and contract constitutional standards to conform to the Court's conception of what at a particular time constitutes "civilized decency" and "fundamental liberty and justice." Invoking this Twining rule, the Court concludes that although comment upon testimony in a federal court would violate the Fifth Amendment, identical comment in a state court does not violate today's fashion in civilized decency and fundamentals and is therefore not prohibited by the Federal Constitution as amended.

. . . I would not reaffirm the Twining decision. I think that decision and the "natural law" theory of the Constitution upon which it relies degrade the constitutional safeguards of the Bill of Rights and simultaneously appropriate for this Court a broad power which we are not authorized by the Constitution to exercise. My reasons for believing that the Twining decision should not be revitalized can best be understood by reference to the constitutional, judicial, and general history that preceded and followed the case. . . .

. . . I am attaching to this dissent an appendix which contains a résumé, by no means complete, of the Amendment's history.* In my judgment that history conclusively demonstrates that the language of the first section of the Fourteenth Amendment, taken as a whole, was thought by those responsible for its submission to the people, and by those who opposed its submission, sufficiently explicit to guarantee that thereafter no state could deprive its citizens of the privileges and protections of the Bill of Rights. Whether this Court ever will, or whether it now should, in the light of past decisions, give full effect to what the Amendment was intended to accomplish is not necessarily essential to a decision here. However that may be, our prior decisions, including Twining, do not prevent our carrying out that purpose, at least to the extent of making applicable to the states, not a mere part, as the Court has, but the full protection of the Fifth Amendment's provision against compelling evidence from an accused to convict him of crime. And I further contend that the "natural law" formula which the Court uses to reach its conclusion in this case should be abandoned as an incongruous excrescence on our Constitution. . . .

. . . I fear to see the consequences of the Court's practice of substituting its own concepts of decency and fundamental justice for the language of the Bill of Rights as its point of departure in interpreting and en-

---

* The appendix is omitted. For an historical examination disagreeing with Justice Black's conclusion, see Fairman, "Does the Fourteenth Amendment Incorporate the Bill of Rights? The Original Understanding," 2 Stan. L.Rev. 5 (1949). For Justice Black's review of the historical dispute and reply to Fairman, see the 1968 decision in Duncan, p. 812, infra.

forcing that Bill of Rights. If the choice must be between the selective process of the Palko decision applying some of the Bill of Rights to the States, or the Twining rule applying none of them, I would choose the Palko selective process. But rather than accept either of these choices, I would follow what I believe was the original purpose of the Fourteenth Amendment—to extend to all the people of the nation the complete protection of the Bill of Rights. To hold that this Court can determine what, if any, provisions of the Bill of Rights will be enforced, and if so to what degree, is to frustrate the great design of a written Constitution.

It is an illusory apprehension that literal application of some or all of the provisions of the Bill of Rights to the States would unwisely increase the sum total of the powers of this Court to invalidate state legislation. . . . It must be conceded, of course, that the natural-law-due-process formula, which the Court today reaffirms, has been interpreted to limit substantially this Court's power to prevent state violations of the individual civil liberties guaranteed by the Bill of Rights. But this formula also has been used in the past, and can be used in the future, to license this Court in considering regulatory legislation, to roam at large in the broad expanses of policy and morals and to trespass, all too freely, on the legislative domain of the States as well as the Federal Government.

[S]ince words can have many meanings, interpretation obviously may result in contraction or extension of the original purpose of a constitutional provision, thereby affecting policy. But to pass upon the constitutionality of statutes by looking to the particular standards enumerated in the Bill of Rights and other parts of the Constitution is one thing; to invalidate statutes because of application of "natural law" deemed to be above and undefined by the Constitution is another. . . .

Mr. Justice DOUGLAS joins in this opinion.

Mr. Justice MURPHY, with whom Mr. Justice RUTLEDGE concurs, dissenting.

While in substantial agreement with the views of Mr. Justice BLACK, I have one reservation and one addition to make.

I agree that the specific guarantees of the Bill of Rights should be carried over intact into the first section of the Fourteenth Amendment. But I am not prepared to say that the latter is entirely and necessarily limited by the Bill of Rights. Occasions may arise where a proceeding falls so far short of conforming to fundamental standards of procedure as to warrant constitutional condemnation in terms of a lack of due process despite the absence of a specific provision in the Bill of Rights.

That point, however, need not be pursued here inasmuch as the Fifth Amendment . . . guarantee against self-incrimination has been violated in this case. . . *

---

* In Malloy v. Hogan, 378 U.S. 1 (1964), the Court held that the Fifth Amendment's privilege against self-incrimination was applicable to the states under the Fourteenth: "Decisions of the Court since Twining and Adamson have departed from the contrary view expressed in those cases." A year later, the Court overruled the specific holding in Adamson and found unconstitutional the California rule permitting comment on the defendant's failure to testify. Griffin v. California, 380 U.S. 609 (1965). See chap. 12, p. 878, infra. Note the discussion of "incorporation" developments from Adamson to 1968 in Duncan v. Louisiana, the next principal case.

A CASE STUDY IN DUE PROCESS METHODOLOGY: FOURTH AMENDMENT VIOLATIONS, "CONDUCT THAT SHOCKS THE CONSCIENCE," AND THE WOLF–ROCHIN–IRVINE SEQUENCE

Consider the process and problems of articulating due process criteria as reflected in the series of cases that follow. The majority in each case was committed to the Palko-Adamson approach. Does the course of the decisions suggest the inadequacy of that approach? Because it is too unpredictable? Because it is too idiosyncratic and personal? Were the failings—particularly of Justice Frankfurter—in the application rather than the statement of the approach? Should there have been greater emphasis on the facts—in Wolf, for example? But would not such greater emphasis have added to the unpredictability of the approach? Does the "incorporation" of "specific" rights approach offer more satisfactory analyses of these cases? How "specific" is the 4th Amendment? And what "specific" rights of the Bill of Rights are directly involved in stomach-pumping and blood-testing?

1. *Wolf.* In Wolf v. Colorado, 338 U.S. 25 (1949), the Court, in an opinion by Justice Frankfurter reaffirming the Palko approach, stated that the "security of one's privacy against arbitrary intrusion by the police—which is at the core of the Fourth Amendment—is basic to a free society. It is therefore implicit in 'the concept of ordered liberty' and as such enforceable against the States through the Due Process Clause." Accordingly, "were a State affirmatively to sanction such police incursion into privacy," it would violate the 14th Amendment. The Court added, however, that "the ways of enforcing such a basic right raise questions of a different order"; the problem of remedies was susceptible of "varying solutions." And the Court therefore concluded that the federal exclusionary rule—the rule that "the Fourth Amendment [bars] the use of evidence secured through illegal search and seizure" in federal prosecutions—was not applicable to the states by way of the 14th Amendment. Accordingly, the state court conviction under review was affirmed though it rested on evidence illegally obtained.

Justice Frankfurter once again insisted that defining due process was "a gradual and empiric process of 'inclusion and exclusion' "; yet his opinion in Wolf did not state the specific facts in the case. Rather, he described the question presented in the abstract. (From the state reports, it appears that the illegal police conduct consisted of seizing a doctor's records without a warrant, at the time of an arrest; there was no brutality.) Justice Black, adhering to his Adamson position, nevertheless concurred in the Wolf affirmance, on the ground that "the federal exclusionary rule is not a command of the Fourth Amendment but is a judicially created rule of evidence which Congress might negate." Justices Douglas, Murphy and Rutledge dissented, with Justice Murphy stating that the exclusionary rule was the only effective sanction for violations of the search and seizure guarantee: "[T]here is but one alternative to the rule of exclusion. That is no sanction at all."

2. *Rochin.* Three years after Wolf, the Court decided Rochin v. California, 342 U.S. 165 (1952). Justice Frankfurter again wrote the majority opinion. The Court reversed the state court conviction—without mentioning Wolf. In Rochin (unlike Wolf) Justice Frankfurter stated the facts in detail: three detectives broke into petitioner's room and saw two capsules on a

night table next to his bed; he put the capsules in his mouth; the detectives "jumped on him" to extract the capsules, were unsuccessful, and took him to a hospital; and in the hospital, a doctor, under police direction, "forced an emetic solution through a tube into Rochin's stomach." Petitioner vomited as a result of the "stomach-pumping"; the vomited matter contained two morphine capsules; and the capsules were used in evidence to convict Rochin.

Justice Frankfurter's opinion concluded "that the procedings by which this conviction was obtained do more than offend some fastidious squeamishness or private sentimentalism about combatting crime too energetically. This is conduct that shocks the conscience. Illegally breaking into the privacy of the petitioner, the struggle to open his mouth and remove what was there, the forcible extraction of his stomach's contents—this course of proceeding by agents of government to obtain evidence is bound to offend even hardened sensibilities. They are methods too close to the rack and the screw to permit of constitutional differentiation."

The Court relied in part on decisions reversing convictions based on coerced confessions; these showed, Justice Frankfurter insisted, that state law enforcement must "respect certain decencies of civilized conduct." Coerced confessions are constitutionally excluded from trials "not only because of their unreliability" but also because, even if independently verifiable, they "offend the community's sense of fair play and decency." Similarly, to permit admission of the capsules in Rochin's case "would be to afford brutality the cloak of law"; it would be "a stultification" of the Court's responsibility to hold "that in order to convict a man the police cannot extract by force what is in his mind but can extract what is in his stomach." Accordingly, "on the facts" here, petitioner had been convicted "by methods that offend the Due Process Clause."

In the course of his Rochin opinion, Justice Frankfurter once again defended the Palko-Adamson approach at length; and Justice Black, in dissent, once again attacked it. Justice Frankfurter stated: "The vague contours of the Due Process Clause do not leave judges at large. We may not draw on our merely personal and private notions and disregard the limits that bind judges in their judicial function. Even though the concept of due process of law is not final and fixed, these limits are derived from considerations that are fused in the whole nature of our judicial process. These are considerations deeply rooted in reason and in the compelling traditions of the legal profession. . . . Due process of law thus conceived is not to be derided as resort to a revival of 'natural law.' To believe that this judicial exercise of judgment could be avoided by freezing 'due process of law' at some fixed stage of time or thought is to suggest that the most important aspect of constitutional adjudication is a function for inanimate machines and not for judges . . . . Even cybernetics has not yet made that haughty claim. To practice the requisite detachment and to achieve sufficient objectivity no doubt demands of judges the habit of self-discipline and self-criticism, incertitude that one's own views are incontestable and alert tolerance toward views not shared. . . . The faculties of the Due Process Clause may be indefinite and vague, but the mode of their ascertainment is not self-willed. In each case 'due process of law' requires an evaluation based on a disinterested inquiry pursued in the spirit of science, on a balanced order of facts exactly and fairly stated, on the detached consideration of conflicting claims, on a judgment not *ad hoc* and episodic but duly mindful of reconciling the needs both of continuity and of change in a progressive society."

Justice Black retorted: "I believe that faithful adherence to the specific guarantees in the Bill of Rights insures a more permanent protection of individual liberty than that which can be afforded by the nebulous standards stated by the majority. What the majority hold is that the Due Process Clause empowers this Court to nullify any state law if its application 'shocks the conscience,' offends 'a sense of justice' or runs counter to the 'decencies of civilized conduct.' The majority emphasize that these statements do not refer to their own consciences or to their senses of justice and decency. . . . We are further admonished to measure the validity of state practices, not by our reason, or by the traditions of the legal profession, but by 'the community's sense of fair play and decency'; by the 'traditions and conscience of our people'; or by 'those canons of decency and fairness which express the notions of justice of English-speaking peoples.' . . .

"If the Due Process Clause does vest this Court with such unlimited power to invalidate laws, I am still in doubt as to why we should consider only the notions of English-speaking peoples to determine what are immutable and fundamental principles of justice. Moreover, one may well ask what avenues of investigation are open to discover 'canons' of conduct so universally favored that this Court should write them into the Constitution?

"Some constitutional provisions are stated in absolute and unqualified language such, for illustration, as the First Amendment stating that no law shall be passed prohibiting the free exercise of religion or abridging the freedom of speech or press. Other constitutional provisions do require courts to choose between competing policies, such as the Fourth Amendment which, by its terms, necessitates a judicial decision as to what is an 'unreasonable' search or seizure. There is, however, no express constitutional language granting judicial power to invalidate *every* state law of *every* kind deemed 'unreasonable' or contrary to the Court's notion of civilized decencies . . . . [Past cases] show the extent to which the evanescent standards of the majority's philosophy have been used to nullify state legislative programs passed to suppress evil economic practices. What paralyzing role this same philosophy will play in the future economic affairs of this country is impossible to predict. Of even graver concern, however, is the use of the philosophy to nullify the Bill of Rights. I long ago concluded that the accordion-like qualities of this philosophy must inevitably imperil all the individual liberty safeguards specifically enumerated in the Bill of Rights." (Justice Black—as did Justice Douglas—joined in the vote to reverse Rochin's conviction on the basis of the Adamson dissent, insisting that petitioner's Fifth Amendment privilege against self-incrimination had been violated.) [1]

---

1. The dissent by Justice Douglas stated that "words taken from [an accused's] lips, capsules taken from his stomach, blood taken from his veins are all inadmissible . . . because of the command of the Fifth Amendment," where the accused has not consented. He pointedly noted that evidence taken from Rochin's stomach would be admissible "in the majority of states where the question has been raised." [In Wolf, Justice Frankfurter (in arguing that the exclusionary rule was not required by the due process clause) had emphasized that "most of the English-speaking world"—including 30 states—did not regard the rule as "vital" to "the protection of the right of privacy."]

3. *Irvine.* Two years after Rochin and five years after Wolf, the Court was faced with the task of reconciling divergent implications of the decisions. In Irvine v. California, 347 U.S. 128 (1954), petitioner was convicted of gambling offenses in part on the basis of incriminating statements overheard by police officers by means of a listening apparatus installed in petitioner's home. While petitioner and his wife were absent from their home, the police arranged to have a locksmith make a door key. Two days later, officers used the key to enter the home and installed a concealed microphone in the hall. A hole was bored in the roof of the house to string wires to a neighboring garage containing a receiver. On two subsequent occasions, officers again used the key to enter the house and move the microphone to more favorable locations—first to the bedroom, then to the bedroom closet.

Justice Jackson announced the judgment of the Court affirming the conviction and delivered an opinion in which Chief Justice Warren and Justices Reed and Minton joined. He stated that each of the repeated entries of petitioner's home without a warrant was "a trespass, and probably a burglary"; that the police practices would be "almost incredible" if they had not been admitted; and that "few police measures have come to our attention that more flagrantly, deliberately and persistently violated the fundamental principle declared by the Fourth Amendment." But, he concluded, the holding of Wolf "would seem to control here." Moreover, he rejected petitioner's reliance on Rochin: "That case involved, among other things, an illegal search of the defendant's person. But it also presented an element totally lacking here—coercion . . ., applied by a physical assault. . . . This was the feature which led to a result in Rochin contrary to Wolf. Although Rochin raised the search-and-seizure question, this Court studiously avoided it and never once mentioned the Wolf case. . . . However obnoxious are the facts in the case before us, they do not involve coercion, violence or brutality to the person, but rather a trespass to property, plus eavesdropping." (Justice Jackson added a suggestion, for himself and the Chief Justice, that the police conduct might constitute a federal crime and that a copy of the record and the opinion should be forwarded "for attention of the Attorney General of the United States.") Justice Clark, concurring, said that he would have opposed the result in Wolf had he been on the Court then, but felt compelled to apply it here: "In light of the 'incredible' activity of the police here, it is with great reluctance that I follow Wolf. Perhaps strict adherence to the tenor of that decision may produce needed converts for its extinction."

Justice Frankfurter dissented, insisting that his opinions in Wolf and Rochin had been misunderstood by Justice Jackson here: "The comprehending principle of [Wolf and Rochin] is at the heart of 'due process.' The judicial enforcement of the Due Process Clause is the very antithesis of a Procrustean rule. . . . In the Wolf case, the Court rejected one absolute. In Rochin, it rejected another. . . . Wolf did not change prior applications of the requirements of due process, whereby this Court considered the whole course of events by which the conviction was obtained. . . . Neither of these concepts [search and seizure and self-incrimination] was invoked by the Court in Rochin, so of course the Wolf case was not mentioned. While there is in the case before us, as in Rochin, an element of unreasonable search and seizure, what is decisive here, as in Rochin, is additional aggravating conduct which the Court finds repulsive. . . . There was lacking here physical violence. . . . We have here, however, a more powerful and offensive control over the Irvines' life than a single, limited physical trespass. Certainly the conduct of the police here went far beyond a bare search and seizure."

Justice Burton joined Justice Frankfurter's dissent. Justices Black and Douglas also dissented, relying mainly on the asserted violation of the Fifth Amendment, made applicable to the states under their view in Adamson.

4. *The aftermath.* There have been several additional chapters in the doctrinal saga illustrated by the Wolf-Rochin-Irvine series.[2] The most important recent installment—Mapp v. Ohio, 367 U.S. 643 (1961) (overruling Wolf)—and related developments will be found in chap. 12, p. 878, infra.

"INCORPORATION" SINCE ADAMSON

a. The 1968 decision in Duncan v. Louisiana, which follows, reexamines the "incorporation" controversy two decades after Adamson and reviews the vast expansion of 14th Amendment procedural rights in the intervening years. The major modern decisions finding additional guarantees of the Bill of Rights applicable to the states are cited in footnotes 3 to 9 of Justice White's opinion; all are noted further in the next chapter.

The "incorporation" controversy has generated much commentary. In addition to the articles noted in Duncan, see especially Kadish, "Methodology and Criteria in Due Process Adjudication: A Survey and Criticism," 66 Yale L.J. 319 (1958), Selected Essays 1938–62 (1963), 522; Schaefer, "Federalism and State Criminal Procedures," 70 Harv.L.Rev. 1 (1956); Note, "The Adamson Case: A Study in Constitutional Technique," 58 Yale L.J. 268 (1949), Selected Essays 1938–62 (1963), 506; Israel, "Gideon v. Wainwright—The 'Art' of Overruling," 1963 Sup.Ct.Rev. 211; Allen, "Due Process and State Criminal Procedures: Another Look," 48 Nw.U.L. Rev. 16 (1953); and Henkin, " 'Selective Incorporation' in the Fourteenth Amendment," 73 Yale L.J. 74 (1963).

b. The process of "incorporation" has continued since Duncan. Benton v. Maryland, 395 U.S. 784 (1969), found "that the double jeopardy prohibition of the Fifth Amendment represents a fundamental ideal in our constitutional heritage, and that it should apply to the States through the Fourteenth Amendment." Justice Marshall's majority opinion added: "Insofar

2. See, e. g., Breithaupt v. Abram, 352 U.S. 432 (1957), where petitioner had been convicted of manslaughter in an auto accident. The state relied on a blood test taken in a hospital after the accident, while petitioner was unconscious. The test showed that he had been drinking. Justice Clark's opinion for the majority (which included Justice Frankfurter) rejected the illegal search claim on the basis of Wolf. Additional objections to the police conduct were also rejected· "We see nothing comparable here to the facts in Rochin"—"indiscriminate taking of blood" might violate due process, but this blood test, by a doctor, was not "offensive"; such tests have "become routine." Chief Justice Warren, joined by Justices Black and Douglas, urged reversal on the basis of Rochin: "Only personal reaction to the stomach pump and the blood test can distinguish them." Justice Douglas, joined by Justice Black, also submitted a separate dissenting opinion. See also Schmerber v. California, 384 U.S. 757 (1966), a 5:4 decision adhering to the Breithaupt result.

as it is inconsistent with this holding, Palko v. Connecticut is overruled."
He explained: "Our recent cases have thoroughly rejected the Palko notion
that basic constitutional rights can be denied by the States as long as the
totality of the circumstances do not disclose a denial of 'fundamental fairness.' Once it is decided that a particular Bill of Rights guarantee is 'fundamental to the American scheme of justice,' Duncan v. Louisiana [infra], the
same constitutional standards apply against both the State and federal Governments. Palko's roots had thus been cut away years ago. We today only
recognize the inevitable. . . . The validity of petitioner's larceny conviction must be judged not by the watered-down standard enunciated in
Palko, but under this Court's interpretations of the Fifth Amendment double
jeopardy provision."

Justice Harlan, joined by Justice Stewart, dissented from the reversal
of the conviction because he did not think that the Court should have "reached out" to decide the merits of the case. But if those were reached, he made
clear, he too would have been prepared to reverse on constitutional grounds
—but via the "traditional due process approach" of Palko rather than the
majority's route of "incorporating" all of the details of the federal double
jeopardy guarantee. [See also the renewal of the Duncan debate between
Justices Black and Harlan in In the Matter of Samuel Winship, 397 U.S. ——
(1970), on the "reasonable doubt" standard in juvenile proceedings, noted
infra, chap. 12, p. 915.]

DUNCAN v. LOUISIANA

391 U.S. 145, 88 S.Ct. 1444, 20 L.Ed.2d 491 (1968).

Appeal from the Supreme Court of Louisiana.

Mr. Justice WHITE delivered the opinion of the Court.

Appellant, Gary Duncan, was convicted of simple battery in the Twenty-
fifth Judicial District Court of Louisiana. Under Louisiana law simple battery is a misdemeanor, punishable by a maximum of two years' imprisonment
and a $300 fine. Appellant sought trial by jury, but because the Louisiana
Constitution grants jury trials only in cases in which capital punishment or
imprisonment at hard labor may be imposed, the trial judge denied the request. Appellant was convicted and sentenced to serve 60 days in the parish
prison and pay a fine of $150. Appellant [alleges] that the Sixth and
Fourteenth Amendments to the United States Constitution secure the right to
jury trial in state criminal prosecutions where a sentence as long as two years
may be imposed. . . .

. . . . In resolving conflicting claims concerning the meaning of this
spacious language [of due process], the Court has looked increasingly to the
Bill of Rights for guidance; many of the rights guaranteed by the first eight
Amendments to the Constitution have been held to be protected against state
action by the Due Process Clause of the Fourteenth Amendment. That clause
now protects the right to compensation for property taken by the State;[1]

---

1. Chicago, B. & Q. R. Co. v. Chicago,
166 U.S. 226 (1897). [All footnotes
to this opinion are by the Court.]

the rights of speech, press, and religion covered by the First Amendment; [2] the Fourth Amendment rights to be free from unreasonable searches and seizures and to have excluded from criminal trials any evidence illegally seized;[3] the right guaranteed by the Fifth Amendment to be free of compelled self-incrimination;[4] and the Sixth Amendment rights to counsel,[5] to a speedy [6] and public [7] trial, to confrontation of opposing witnesses,[8] and to compulsory process for obtaining witnesses.[9]

  The test for determining whether a right extended by the Fifth and Sixth Amendments with respect to federal criminal proceedings is also protected against state action by the Fourteenth Amendment has been phrased in a variety of ways in the opinions of this Court. The question has been asked whether a right is among those " 'fundamental principles of liberty and justice which lie at the base of all our civil and political institutions,' " Powell v. Alabama, 287 U.S. 45, 67 (1932); [10] whether it is "basic in our system of jurisprudence," In re Oliver, 333 U.S. 257, 273 (1948); and whether it is "a fundamental right, essential to a fair trial," Gideon v. Wainwright, 372 U.S. 335, 343–344 (1963); Malloy v. Hogan, 378 U.S. 1, 6 (1964); Pointer v. Texas, 380 U.S. 400, 403 (1965). [The majority opinions in Gideon and Pointer were written by Justice Black. Justice Brennan wrote Malloy.] The claim before us is that the right to trial by jury guaranteed by the Sixth Amendment meets these tests. The position of Louisiana, on the other hand, is that the Constitution imposes upon the States no duty to give a jury trial in any criminal case, regardless of the seriousness of the crime or the size of the punishment which may be imposed. Because we believe that trial by jury in criminal cases is fundamental to the American scheme of justice, we hold that the Fourteenth Amendment guarantees a right of jury trial in all criminal cases which—were they to be tried in a federal court—would come within the Sixth Amendment's guarantee.[11] Since

2. See, e. g., Fiske v. Kansas, 274 U.S. 380 (1927).

3. See Mapp v. Ohio, 367 U.S. 643 (1961).

4. Malloy v. Hogan, 378 U.S. 1 (1964).

5. Gideon v. Wainwright, 372 U.S. 335 (1963).

6. Klopfer v. North Carolina, 386 U.S. 213 (1967).

7. In re Oliver, 333 U.S. 257 (1948).

8. Pointer v. Texas, 380 U.S. 400 (1965).

9. Washington v. Texas, 388 U.S. 14 (1967).

10. Quoting from Hebert v. Louisiana, 272 U.S. 312, 316 (1926).

11. In one sense recent cases applying provisions of the first eight Amendments to the States represent a new approach to the "incorporation" debate. Earlier the Court can be seen as having asked, when inquiring into whether some particular procedural safeguard was required of a State, if a civilized system could be imagined that would not accord the particular protection. For example, Palko v. Connecticut, 302 U.S. 319, 325 (1937), stated: "The right to trial by jury and the immunity from prosecution except as the result of an indictment may have value and importance. Even so, they are not of the very essence of a scheme of ordered liberty . . . .. Few would be so narrow or provincial as to maintain that a fair and enlightened system of justice would be impossible without them." The recent cases, on the other hand, have proceeded upon the valid assumption that state criminal processes are not imaginary and theoretical schemes but actual systems bearing virtually every characteristic of the common-law system that has been developing contemporaneously in England and in this country. The question thus is whether given this kind of system a particular procedure is fundamental whether, that is, a procedure is necessary to an Anglo-American regime of ordered liberty. It is

we consider the appeal before us to be such a case, we hold that the Constitution was violated when appellant's demand for jury trial was refused.

The history of trial by jury in criminal cases has been frequently told. It is sufficient for present purposes to say that by the time our Constitution was written, jury trial in criminal cases had been in existence in England for several centuries and carried impressive credentials traced by many to Magna Carta. . . .

Jury trial continues to receive strong support. The laws of every State guarantee a right to jury trial in serious criminal cases; no State has dispensed with it; nor are there significant movements underway to do so. . . .

We are aware of prior cases in this Court in which the prevailing opinion contains statements contrary to our holding today that the right to jury trial in serious criminal cases is a fundamental right and hence must be recognized by the States as part of their obligation to extend due process of law to all persons within their jurisdiction. Louisiana relies especially on Maxwell v. Dow, 176 U.S. 581 (1900); Palko v. Connecticut, 302 U.S. 319 (1937); and Snyder v. Massachusetts, 291 U.S. 97 (1934). None of these cases, however, dealt with a State which had purported to dispense entirely with a jury trial in serious criminal cases. Maxwell held that no provision of the Bill of Rights applied to the States—a position long since repudiated—and that the Due Process Clause of the Fourteenth Amendment did not prevent a State from trying a defendant for a noncapital offense with fewer than 12 men on the jury. . . . Perhaps because the right to jury trial was not directly at stake, the Court's remarks about the jury in Palko and Snyder took no note of past or current developments regarding jury trials, did not consider its purposes and functions, attempted no inquiry into how well it was performing its job, and did not discuss possible distinctions between

this sort of inquiry that can justify the conclusions that state courts must exclude evidence seized in violation of the Fourth Amendment, Mapp v. Ohio, 367 U.S. 643 (1961); that state prosecutors may not comment on a defendant's failure to testify, Griffin v. California, 380 U.S. 609 (1965); and that criminal punishment may not be imposed for the status of narcotics addiction, Robinson v. California, 370 U.S. 660 (1962). Of immediate relevance for this case are the Court's holdings that the States must comply with certain provisions of the Sixth Amendment, specifically that the States may not refuse a speedy trial, confrontation of witnesses, and the assistance, at state expense if necessary, of counsel. See cases cited in nn. [5–9], supra. Of each of these determinations that a constitutional provision originally written to bind the Federal Government should bind the States as well it might be said that the limitation in question is not necessarily fundamental to fairness in every criminal system that might be imagined but is fundamental in the context of the criminal processes maintained by the American States.

When the inquiry is approached in this way the question whether the States can impose criminal punishment without granting a jury trial appears quite different from the way it appeared in the older cases opining that States might abolish jury trial. See, e. g., Maxwell v. Dow, 176 U.S. 581 (1900). A criminal process which was fair and equitable but used no juries is easy to imagine. It would make use of alternative guarantees and protections which would serve the purposes that the jury serves in the English and American systems. Yet no American State has undertaken to construct such a system. Instead, every American State, including Louisiana, uses the jury extensively, and imposes very serious punishments only after a trial at which the defendant has a right to a jury's verdict. In every State, including Louisiana, the structure and style of the criminal process—the supporting framework and the subsidiary procedures—are of the sort that naturally complement jury trial, and have developed in connection with and in reliance upon jury trial.

civil and criminal cases.   In Malloy v. Hogan, supra, the Court rejected Palko's discussion of the self-incrimination clause. Respectfully, we reject the prior dicta regarding jury trial in criminal cases.

The guarantees of jury trial in the Federal and State Constitutions reflect a profound judgment about the way in which law should be enforced and justice administered. A right to jury trial is granted to criminal defendants in order to prevent oppression by the Government. . . . Providing an accused with the right to be tried by a jury of his peers gave him an inestimable safeguard against the corrupt or overzealous prosecutor and against the compliant, biased, or eccentric judge. If the defendant preferred the common-sense judgment of a jury to the more tutored but perhaps less sympathetic reaction of the single judge, he was to have it. Beyond this, the jury trial provisions in the Federal and State Constitutions reflect a fundamental decision about the exercise of official power—a reluctance to entrust plenary powers over the life and liberty of the citizen to one judge or to a group of judges. . . . The deep commitment of the Nation to the right of jury trial in serious criminal cases as a defense against arbitrary law enforcement qualifies for protection under the Due Process Clause of the Fourteenth Amendment, and must therefore be respected by the States.

Of course jury trial has "its weaknesses and the potential for misuse," Singer v. United States, 380 U.S. 24, 35 (1965). We are aware of the long debate, especially in this century, among those who write about the administration of justice, as to the wisdom of permitting untrained laymen to determine the facts in civil and criminal proceedings. Although the debate has been intense, with powerful voices on either side, most of the controversy has centered on the jury in civil cases. . . . The State of Louisiana urges that holding that the Fourteenth Amendment assures a right to jury trial will cast doubt on the integrity of every trial conducted without a jury. Plainly, this is not the import of our holding. Our conclusion is that in the American States, as in the federal judicial system, a general grant of jury trial for serious offenses is a fundamental right, essential for preventing miscarriages of justice and for assuring that fair trials are provided for all defendants. We would not assert, however, that every criminal trial—or any particular trial—held before a judge alone is unfair or that a defendant may never be as fairly treated by a judge as he would be by a jury. Thus we hold no constitutional doubts about the practices, common in both federal and state courts, of accepting waivers of jury trial and prosecuting petty crimes without extending a right to jury trial. However, the fact is that in most places more trials for serious crimes are to juries than to a court alone; a great many defendants prefer the judgment of a jury to that of a court. Even where defendants are satisfied with bench trials, the right to a jury trial very likely serves its intended purpose of making judicial or prosecutorial unfairness less likely.[12]

12. Louisiana also asserts that if due process is deemed to include the right to jury trial, States will be obligated to comply with all past interpretations of the Sixth Amendment, an amendment which in its inception was designed to control only the federal courts and which throughout its history has operated in this limited environment where uniformity is a more obvious and immediate consideration. In particular, Louisiana objects to application of the decisions of this Court interpreting the Sixth Amendment as guaranteeing a 12-man jury in serious criminal cases, Thompson v. Utah, 170 U.S. 343 (1898); as requiring a unanimous verdict before guilt can be found, Maxwell v. Dow, 176 U.S. 581, 586 (1900); and as barring procedures

Louisiana's final argument (court does not agree)

Louisiana's final contention is that even if it must grant jury trials in serious criminal cases, the conviction before us is valid and constitutional because here the petitioner was tried for simple battery and was sentenced to only 60 days in the parish prison. We are not persuaded. It is doubtless true that there is a category of petty crimes or offenses which is not subject to the Sixth Amendment jury trial provision and should be not subject to the Fourteenth Amendment jury trial requirement here applied to the States. [See the jury trial materials in the next chapter, p. 899.] We need not, however, settle in this case the exact location of the line between petty offenses and serious crimes. It is sufficient for our purposes to hold that a crime punishable by two years in prison is, based on past and contemporary standards in this country, a serious crime and not a petty offense. Consequently, appellant was entitled to a jury trial and it was error to deny it.

The judgment below is reversed and the case is remanded for proceedings not inconsistent with this opinion.

Mr. Justice BLACK, with whom Mr. Justice DOUGLAS joins, concurring.

. . . I agree [with the holding] for reasons given by the Court. I also agree because of reasons given in my dissent in Adamson v. California, 332 U.S. 46, 68. . . . I am very happy to support this selective process through which our Court has since the Adamson case held most of the specific Bill of Rights' protections applicable to the States to the same extent they are applicable to the Federal Government. Among these are the right to trial by jury decided today, the right against compelled self-incrimination, the right to counsel, the right to compulsory process for witnesses, the right to confront witnesses, the right to a speedy and public trial, and the right to be free from unreasonable searches and seizures.

Twining held that none of the bill of rights were held enforceable against the states

All of these holdings making Bill of Rights' provisions applicable as such to the States mark, of course, a departure from the Twining doctrine holding that none of those provisions were enforceable as such against the States. The dissent in this case, however, makes a spirited and forceful defense of that now discredited doctrine. I do not believe that it is necessary for me to repeat the historical and logical reasons for my challenge to the Twining holding contained in my Adamson dissent and Appendix to it. What I wrote there in 1947 was the product of years of study and research. My appraisal of the legislative history followed 10 years of legislative ex-

by which crimes subject to the Sixth Amendment jury trial provision are tried in the first instance without a jury but at the first appellate stage by de novo trial with a jury, Callan v. Wilson, 127 U.S. 540, 557 (1888). It seems very unlikely to us that our decision today will require widespread changes in state criminal processes. First, our decisions interpreting the Sixth Amendment are always subject to reconsideration, a fact amply demonstrated by the instant decision. In addition, most of the States have provisions for jury trials equal in breadth to the Sixth Amendment, if that amendment is construed, as it has been, to permit the trial of petty crimes and offenses without a jury. Indeed, there appear to be only four States in which juries of fewer than 12 can be used without the defendant's consent for offenses carrying a maximum penalty of greater than one year. Only in Oregon and Louisiana can a less-than-unanimous jury convict for an offense with a maximum penalty greater than one year. However 10 States authorize first-stage trials without juries for crimes carrying lengthy penalties; these States give a convicted defendant the right to a de novo trial before a jury in a different court. The statutory provisions are listed in the briefs filed in this case.

perience as a Senator of the United States, not a bad way, I suspect, to learn the value of what is said in legislative debates, committee discussions, committee reports, and various other steps taken in the course of passage of bills, resolutions, and proposed constitutional amendments. My Brother Harlan's objections to my Adamson dissent history, like that of most of the objectors, relies most heavily on a criticism written by Professor Charles Fairman and published in the Stanford Law Review. 2 Stan.L.Rev. 5 (1949). I have read and studied this article extensively, including the historical references, but am compelled to add that in my view it has completely failed to refute the inferences and arguments that I suggested in my Adamson dissent. Professor Fairman's "history" relies very heavily on what was *not* said in the state legislatures that passed on the Fourteenth Amendment. Instead of relying on this kind of negative pregnant, my legislative experience has convinced me that it is far wiser to rely on what *was* said, and most importantly, said by the men who actually sponsored the Amendment in the Congress. I know from my years in the United States Senate that it is to men like Congressman Bingham, who steered the Amendment through the House, and Senator Howard, who introduced it in the Senate, that members of Congress look when they seek the real meaning of what is being offered. And they vote for or against a bill based on what the sponsors of that bill and those who oppose it tell them it means. The historical appendix to my Adamson dissent leaves no doubt in my mind that both its sponsors and those who opposed it believed the Fourteenth Amendment made the first eight Amendments of the Constitution (the Bill of Rights) applicable to the States.

In addition to the adoption of Professor Fairman's "history," the dissent states that "the great words of the four clauses of the first section of the Fourteenth Amendment would have been an exceedingly peculiar way to say that 'The rights heretofore guaranteed against federal intrusion by the first eight Amendments are henceforth guaranteed against state intrusion as well.' " In response to this I can say only that the words "No State shall make or enforce any law which shall abridge the privileges or immunities of citizens of the United States" seem to me an eminently reasonable way of expressing the idea that henceforth the Bill of Rights shall apply to the States.[1] What more precious "privilege" of American citizenship could there be than that privilege to claim the protections of our great Bill of Rights? I suggest that any reading of "privileges or immunities of citizens of the United States" which excludes the Bill of Rights' safeguards renders the words of this section of the Fourteenth Amendment meaningless. . . . [I]f anything, it is "exceedingly peculiar to read the Fourteenth Amendment differently from the way I do.

While I do not wish at this time to discuss at length my disagreement with Brother Harlan's forthright and frank restatement of the now discredited Twining doctrine, I do want to point out what appears to me to be the basic difference between us. [D]ue process, according to my Brother Harlan, is to be a phrase with no permanent meaning, but one which is found to shift from time to time in accordance with judges' predilections and understandings of what is best for the country. If due process means this,

---

1. My view has been and is that the Fourteenth Amendment, *as a whole*, makes the Bill of Rights applicable to the States. This would certainly include the language of the Privileges and Immunities Clause, as well as the Due Process Clause. [Footnote by Justice Black.]

the Fourteenth Amendment, in my opinion, might as well have been written that "no person shall be deprived of life, liberty or property except by laws that the judges of the United States Supreme Court shall find to be consistent with the immutable principles of free government." It is impossible for me to believe that such unconfined power is given to judges in our Constitution that is a written one in order to limit governmental power.

Another tenet of the Twining doctrine as restated by my Brother Harlan is that "due process of law requires only fundamental fairness." But the "fundamental fairness" test is one on a par with that of shocking the conscience of the Court. Each of such tests depends entirely on the particular judge's idea of ethics and morals instead of requiring him to depend on the boundaries fixed by the written words of the Constitution. Nothing in the history of the phrase "due process of law" suggests that constitutional controls are to depend on any particular judge's sense of values. . . . The due process of law standard for a trial is one in accordance with the Bill of Rights and laws passed pursuant to constitutional power, guaranteeing to all alike a trial under the general law of the land.

Finally I want to add that I am not bothered by the argument that applying the Bill of Rights to the States, "according to the same standards that protect those personal rights against federal encroachment," interferes with our concept of federalism in that it may prevent States from trying novel social and economic experiments. I have never believed that under the guise of federalism the States should be able to experiment with the protections afforded our citizens through the Bill of Rights. . . . No one is more concerned than I that the States be allowed to use the full scope of their powers as their citizens see fit. And that is why I have continually fought against the expansion of this Court's authority over the States through the use of a broad, general interpretation of due process that permits judges to strike down state laws they do not like.

In closing I want to emphasize that I believe as strongly as ever that the Fourteenth Amendment was intended to make the Bill of Rights applicable to the States. I have been willing to support the selective incorporation doctrine, however, as an alternative, although perhaps less historically supportable than complete incorporation. The selective incorporation process, if used properly, does limit the Supreme Court in the Fourteenth Amendment field to specific Bill of Rights' protections only and keeps judges from roaming at will in their own notions of what policies outside the Bill of Rights are desirable and what are not. And, most importantly for me, the selective incorporation process has the virtue of having already worked to make most of the Bill of Rights' protections applicable to the States.

Mr. Justice FORTAS, concurring [in an opinion also applicable to a companion case, Bloom v. Illinois, 391 U.S. 194 (1968)]. . . .

[A]lthough I agree with the decision of the Court, I cannot agree with the implication that the tail must go with the hide: that when we hold, influenced by the Sixth Amendment, that "due process" requires that the States accord the right of jury trial for all but petty offenses, we automatically import all of the ancillary rules which have been or may hereafter be developed incidental to the right to jury trial in the federal courts. I see no reason whatever, for example, to assume that our decision today should require us to impose federal requirements such as unanimous verdicts or a jury of 12 upon the

States. We may well conclude that these and other features of federal jury practice are by no means fundamental—that they are not essential to due process of law—and that they are not obligatory on the States.

I would make these points clear today. Neither logic nor history nor the intent of the draftsmen of the Fourteenth Amendment can possibly be said to require that the Sixth Amendment or its jury trial provision be applied to the States together with the total gloss that this Court's decisions have supplied. . . . To take this course, in my judgment, would be not only unnecessary but mischievous because it would inflict a serious blow upon the principle of federalism. . . . Our Constitution sets up a federal union, not a monolith.

This Court has heretofore held that various provisions of the Bill of Rights . . . . "are all to be enforced against the States under the Fourteenth Amendment according to the same standards that protect those rights against federal encroachment." Malloy v. Hogan, 378 U.S. 1. [U]nless one adheres slavishly to the incorporation theory, body and substance, the same conclusion need not be superimposed upon the jury trial right. I respectfully but urgently suggest that it should not be. . . .

Mr. Justice HARLAN, whom Mr. Justice STEWART joins, dissenting.

Every American jurisdiction provides for trial by jury in criminal cases. The question before us is not whether jury trial is an ancient institution, which it is; nor whether it plays a significant role in the administration of criminal justice, which it does; nor whether it will endure, which it shall. The queston in this case is whether the State of Louisiana, which provides trial by jury for all felonies, is prohibited by the Constitution from trying charges of simple battery to the court alone. In my view, the answer to that question, mandated alike by our constitutional history and by the longer history of trial by jury, is clearly "no."

. . . . The Due Process Clause of the Fourteenth Amendment requires that [state] procedures be fundamentally fair in all respects. It does not, in my view, impose or encourage nationwide uniformity for its own sake; it does not command adherence to forms that happen to be old; and it does not impose on the States the rules that may be in force in the federal courts except where such rules are also found to be essential to basic fairness.

The Court's approach to this case is an uneasy and illogical compromise among the views of various Justices on how the Due Process Clause should be interpreted. The Court does not say that those who framed the Fourteenth Amendment intended to make the Sixth Amendment applicable to the States. And the Court concedes that it finds nothing unfair about the procedure by which the present appellant was tried. Nevertheless, the Court reverses his conviction: it holds, for some reason not apparent to me, that the Due Process Clause incorporates the particular clause of the Sixth Amendment that requires trial by jury in federal criminal cases—including, as I read its opinion, the sometimes trivial accompanying baggage of judicial interpretation in federal contexts. I have raised my voice many times before against the Court's continuing undiscriminating insistence upon fastening on the States federal notions of criminal justice,[1] and I must do so again in

---

1. See, e. g., my opinions in Mapp v. Ohio, 367 U.S. 643, 672 (dissenting);   Ker v. California, 374 U.S. 23, 44 (concurring); Malloy v. Hogan, 378

this instance. With all respect, the Court's approach and its reading of history are altogether topsy-turvy. . . .

[The 14th Amendment's] restrictions are couched in very broad and general terms . . .. Consequently, for 100 years this Court has been engaged in the difficult process Professor Jaffe has well called "the search for intermediate premises." [2] The question has been, Where does the Court properly look to find the specific rules that define and give content to such terms as "life, liberty, or property" and "due process of law"?

A few members of the Court have taken the position that the intention of those who drafted the first section of the Fourteenth Amendment was simply, and exclusively, to make the provisions of the first eight Amendments applicable to state action.[3] This view has never been accepted by this Court. In my view, often expressed elsewhere, the first section of the Fourteenth Amendment was meant neither to incorporate, nor to be limited to, the specific guarantees of the first eight Amendments. The overwhelming historical evidence marshalled by Professor Fairman demonstrates, to me conclusively, that the Congressmen and state legislators who wrote, debated, and ratified the Fourteenth Amendment did not think they were "incorporating" the Bill of Rights [4] and the very breadth and generality of the Amendment's provisions suggest that its authors did not suppose that the Nation would always

U.S. 1, 14 (dissenting); Pointer v. Texas, 380 U.S. 400, 408 (concurring); Griffin v. California, 380 U.S. 609, 615 (concurring); Klopfer v. North Carolina, 386 U.S. 213, 226 (concurring). [All footnotes to this opinion are by Justice Harlan.]

2. Jaffe, Was Brandeis an Activist? The Search for Intermediate Premises, 80 Harv.L.Rev. 986 (1967).

3. See Adamson v. California, 332 U.S. 46, 71 (dissenting opinion of Black, J.); O'Neil v. Vermont, 144 U.S. 323, 366, 370 (dissenting opinion of Harlan, J.); (1892); H. Black, "Due Process of Law," in A Constitutional Faith 23 (1968).

4. Fairman, Does the Fourteenth Amendment Incorporate the Bill of Rights? The Original Understanding, 2 Stan.L.Rev. 5 (1949). Professor Fairman was not content to rest upon the overwhelming fact that the great words of the four clauses of the first section of the Fourteenth Amendment would have been an exceedingly peculiar way to say that "The rights heretofore guaranteed against federal intrusion by the first eight Amendments are henceforth guaranteed against state intrusion as well." He therefore sifted the mountain of material comprising the debates and committee reports relating to the Amendment in both Houses of Congress and in the state legislatures that passed upon it. He found that in the immense corpus of comments on the purpose and effects of the proposed amendment, and on its virtues and defects, there is almost no evidence whatever for "incorporation." The first eight Amendments are so much as mentioned by only two members of Congress, one of whom effectively demonstrated (a) that he did not understand Barron v. Baltimore, 7 Pet. 243, and therefore did not understand the question of incorporation, and (b) that he was not himself understood by his colleagues. One state legislative committee report, rejected by the legislature as a whole, found § 1 of the Fourteenth Amendment superfluous because it duplicated the Bill of Rights: the committee obviously did not understand Barron v. Baltimore either. That is all Professor Fairman could find, in hundreds of pages of legislative discussion prior to passage of the Amendment, that even suggests incorporation.

To this negative evidence the judicial history of the Amendment could be added. For example, it proved possible for a Court whose members had lived through Reconstruction to reiterate the doctrine of Barron v. Baltimore, that the Bill of Rights did not apply to the States, without so much as questioning whether the Fourteenth Amendment had any effect on the continued validity of that principle. E. g., Walker v. Sauvinet, 92 U.S. 90; see generally Morrison, Does the Fourteenth Amendment Incorporate the Bill of Rights? The Judicial Interpretation, 2 Stan.L.Rev. 140 (1949).

be limited to mid-19th century conceptions of "liberty" and "due process of law" but that the increasing experience and evolving conscience of the American people would add new "intermediate premises." In short, neither history, nor sense, supports using the Fourteenth Amendment to put the States in a constitutional straitjacket with respect to their own development in the administration of criminal or civil law.

Although I therefore fundamentally disagree with the total incorporation view of the Fourteenth Amendment, it seems to me that such a position does at least have the virtue, lacking in the Court's selective incorporation approach, of internal consistency: we look to the Bill of Rights, word for word, clause for clause, precedent for precedent because, it is said, the men who wrote the Amendment wanted it that way. For those who do not accept this "history," a different source of "intermediate premises" must be found. The Bill of Rights is not necessarily irrelevant to the search for guidance in interpreting the Fourteenth Amendment, but the reason for and the nature of its relevance must be articulated.

Apart from the approach taken by the absolute incorporationists, I can see only one method of analysis that has any internal logic. That is to start with the words "liberty" and "due process of law" and attempt to define them in a way that accords with American traditions and our system of government. This approach, involving a much more discriminating process of adjudication than does "incorporation," is, albeit difficult, the one that was followed throughout the 19th and most of the present century. It entails a "gradual process of judicial inclusion and exclusion," seeking, with due recognition of constitutional tolerance for state experimentation and disparity, to ascertain those "immutable principles . . . of free government which no member of the Union may disregard." Due process was not restricted to rules fixed in the past . . .. Nor did it impose nationwide uniformity in details . . ..

The relationship of the Bill of Rights to this "gradual process" seems to me to be twofold. In the first place it has long been clear that the Due Process Clause imposes some restrictions on state action that parallel Bill of Rights restrictions on federal action. Second, and more important than this accidental overlap, is the fact that the Bill of Rights is evidence, at various points, of the content Americans find in the term "liberty" and of American standards of fundamental fairness. . . .

Today's Court still remains unwilling to accept the total incorporationists' view of the history of the Fourteenth Amendment. This, if accepted, would afford a cogent reason for applying the Sixth Amendment to the States. The Court is also, apparently, unwilling to face the task of determining whether denial of trial by jury in the situation before us, or in other situations, is fundamentally unfair. Consequently, the Court has compromised on the ease of the incorporationist position, without its internal logic. It has simply assumed that the question before us is whether the Jury Trial Clause of the Sixth Amendment should be incorporated into the Fourteenth, jot-for-jot and case-for-case, or ignored. Then the Court merely declares that the clause in question is "in" rather than "out." [5]

5. The same illogical way of dealing with a Fourteenth Amendment problem was employed in Malloy v. Hogan, 378 U.S. 1, which held that the Due Process Clause guaranteed the protection of the Self-Incrimination Clause

The Court has justified neither its starting place nor its conclusion. If the problem is to discover and articulate the rules of fundamental fairness in criminal proceedings, there is no reason to assume that the whole body of rules developed in this Court constituting Sixth Amendment jury trial must be regarded as a unit. The requirement of trial by jury in federal criminal cases has given rise to numerous subsidiary questions respecting the exact scope and content of the right. It surely cannot be that every answer the Court has given, or will give, to such a question is attributable to the Founders; or even that every rule announced carries equal conviction of this Court; still less can it be that every such subprinciple is equally fundamental to ordered liberty.

Examples abound. I should suppose it obviously fundamental to fairness that a "jury" means an "impartial jury." I should think it equally obvious that the rule, imposed long ago in the federal courts, that "jury" means "jury of exactly twelve," is not fundamental to anything: there is no significance except to mystics in the number 12. Again, trial by jury has been held to require a unanimous verdict of jurors in the federal courts, although unanimity has not been found essential to liberty in Britain, where the requirement has been abandoned.

One further example is directly relevant here. The co-existence of a requirement of jury trial in federal criminal cases and a historic and universally recognized exception for "petty crimes" has compelled this Court, on occasion, to decide whether a particular crime is petty, or is included within the guarantee. Individual cases have been decided without great conviction and without reference to a guiding principle. The Court today holds, for no discernible reason, that if and when the line is drawn its exact location will be a matter of such fundamental importance that it will be uniformly imposed on the States. This Court is compelled to decide such obscure borderline questions in the course of administering federal law. This does not mean that its decisions are demonstrably sounder than those that would be reached by state courts and legislatures, let alone that they are of such importance that fairness demands their imposition throughout the Nation.

Even if I could agree that the question before us is whether Sixth Amendment jury trial is totally "in" or totally "out," I can find in the Court's opinion no real reasons for concluding that it should be "in." The basis for differentiating among clauses in the Bill of Rights cannot be that only some clauses are in the Bill of Rights, or that only some are old and much praised, or that only some have played an important role in the development of federal law. These things are true of all. The Court says that some clauses are more "fundamental" than others, but it turns out to be using this word in a sense that would have astonished Mr. Justice Cardozo and which, in addition, is of no help. The word does not mean "analytically critical to procedural fairness" for no real analysis of the role of the jury in making procedures fair is even attempted. Instead, the word turns out to mean "old," "much

of the Fifth Amendment against state action. I disagreed at that time both with the way the question was framed and with the result the Court reached. See my dissenting opinion, id., at 14. I consider myself bound by the Court's holding in Malloy with respect to self-incrimination. See my concur-

ring opinion in Griffin v. California, 380 U.S. 609, 615. I do not think that Malloy held, nor would I consider myself bound by a holding, that every question arising under the Due Process Clause shall be settled by an arbitrary decision whether a clause in the Bill of Rights is "in" or "out."

praised," and "found in the Bill of Rights." The definition of "fundamental" thus turns out to be circular. . . .

The argument that jury trial is not a requisite of due process is quite simple. . . . If due process of law requires only fundamental fairness, then the inquiry in each case must be whether a state trial process was a fair one. The Court has held, properly I think, that in an adversary process it is a requisite of fairness, for which there is no adequate substitute, that a criminal defendant be afforded a right to counsel and to cross-examine opposing witnesses. But it simply has not been demonstrated, nor, I think, can it be demonstrated, that trial by jury is the only fair means of resolving issues of fact.

The jury is of course not without virtues. . . . The jury system can also be said to have some inherent defects, which are multiplied by the emergence of the criminal law from the relative simplicity that existed when the jury system was devised. . . . That trial by jury is not the only fair way of adjudicating criminal guilt is well attested by the fact that it is not the prevailing way, either in England or in this country. . . .

In the United States, [two] experts have estimated that, of all prosecutions for crimes triable to a jury, 75% are settled by guilty plea and 40% of the remainder are tried to the court.[6] . . . [I] see no reason why this Court should reverse the conviction of appellant, absent any suggestion that his particular trial was in fact unfair, or compel the State of Louisiana to afford jury trial in an as yet unbounded category of cases that can, without unfairness, be tried to a court. . . .

In sum, there is a wide range of views on the desirability of trial by jury, and on the ways to make it most effective when it is used; there is also considerable variation from State to State in local conditions such as the size of the criminal caseload, the ease or difficulty of summoning jurors, and other trial conditions bearing on fairness. We have before us, therefore, an almost perfect example of a situation in which the celebrated dictum of Mr. Justice Brandeis should be invoked. It is, he said,

> "one of the happy incidents of the federal system that a single courageous State may, if its citizens choose, serve as a laboratory . . . .."
> New State Ice Co. v. Liebmann, 285 U.S. 262, 280, 311 (dissenting opinion).

This Court, other courts, and the political process are available to correct any experiments in criminal procedure that prove fundamentally unfair to defendants. That is not what is being done today: instead, and quite without reason, the Court has chosen to impose upon every State one means of trying criminal cases; it is a good means, but it is not the only fair means, and it is not demonstrably better than the alternatives States might devise.

I would affirm the judgment of the Supreme Court of Louisiana.

6. Kalven & Zeisel, [The American Jury,] at 12–32.

"INCORPORATION" TRIUMPHANT?

Reeaxamine the battle over due process criteria in light of Duncan. Does the "fundamental rights" approach persist in name only, with "incorporation" providing the spirit? And has "selective incorporation" proceeded so far as to "select" all of the Bill of Rights for "incorporation" in fact? Does the new approach afford defense against the charges of subjectiveness and idiosyncrasy and unpredictability long levied against the "fundamental rights" approach? Consider, in the fuller examination of rights of the accused in the next chapter, how predictable and coherent the interpretations of the "specific" rights of the Bill of Rights prove to be. Has the direction of the Court vindicated the warning that emphasis on "specific" rights produces distortion of those rights? What values are promoted by making all interpretations of the specific guarantees of the Bill of Rights applicable via the 14th Amendment, "bag and baggage"? Federalism? Defendants' rights? The economy of judicial labors? Predictability? Certainty?

GRISWOLD v. CONNECTICUT

381 U.S. 479, 85 S.Ct. 1678, 14 L.Ed.2d 510 (1965).

On appeal from the Supreme Court of Errors of Connecticut.

Mr. Justice DOUGLAS delivered the opinion of the Court.

Appellant Griswold is Executive Director of the Planned Parenthood League of Connecticut. Appellant Buxton is a licensed physician and a professor at the Yale Medical School who served as Medical Director for the League at its Center in New Haven—a center open and operating from November 1 to November 10, 1961, when appellants were arrested.*

They gave information, instruction, and medical advice to *married persons* as to the means of preventing conception. They examined the wife and prescribed the best contraceptive device or material for her use. Fees were usually charged, although some couples were serviced free.

The statutes whose constitutionality is involved in this appeal are §§ 53–32 and 54–196 of the General Statutes of Connecticut (1938). The former provides:

"Any person who uses any drug, medicinal article or instrument for the purpose of preventing conception shall be fined not less than fifty dollars or imprisoned not less than sixty days nor more than one year or be both fined and imprisoned."

Section 54–196 provides:

"Any person who assists, abets, counsels, causes, hires, or commands another to commit any offense may be prosecuted and punished as if he were the principal offender."

The appellants were found guilty as accessories and fined $100 each, against the claim that the accessory statute as so applied violated the Fourteenth Amendment. . . . The Court of Errors affirmed that judgment.

---

* See the materials on Poe v. Ullman, chap. 2, p. 151, supra.

[The Court's reasons for holding "that appellants have standing to raise the constitutional rights of the married people with whom they had a professional relationship" are stated after Tileston v. Ullman, chap. 2, at p. 86, supra.]

Coming to the merits, we are met with a wide range of questions that implicate the Due Process Clause of the Fourteenth Amendment. Overtones of some arguments suggest that Lochner v. New York, 198 U.S. 45, should be our guide. But we decline that invitation as we did in West Coast Hotel Co. v. Parrish, 300 U.S. 379; Olsen v. Nebraska, 313 U.S. 236; Lincoln Union v. Northwestern Co., 335 U.S. 525; Williamson v. Lee Optical Co., 348 U.S. 483; Giboney v. Empire Storage Co., 336 U.S. 490. [See the discussion of these cases, on the Court's modern "hands-off" attitude toward state economic regulation, in chap. 13, infra.] We do not sit as a super-legislature to determine the wisdom, need, and propriety of laws that touch economic problems, business affairs, or social conditions. This law, however, operates directly on an intimate relation of husband and wife and their physician's role in one aspect of that relation.

The association of people is not mentioned in the Constitution nor in the Bill of Rights. The right to educate a child in a school of the parents' choice—whether public or private or parochial—is also not mentioned. Nor is the right to study any particular subject or any foreign language. Yet the First Amendment has been construed to include certain of those rights.

By Pierce v. Society of Sisters [268 U.S. 510 (1925)], the right to educate one's children as one chooses is made applicable to the States by the force of the First and Fourteenth Amendments. By Meyer v. Nebraska [262 U.S. 390 (1923)], the same dignity is given the right to study the German language in a private school. In other words, the State may not, consistently with the spirit of the First Amendment, contract the spectrum of available knowledge. The right of freedom of speech and press includes not only the right to utter or to print, but the right to distribute, the right to receive, the right to read . . . and freedom of inquiry, freedom of thought, and freedom to teach . . . . Without those peripheral rights the specific rights would be less secure. And so we reaffirm the principle of the Pierce and the Meyer cases.

In NAACP v. Alabama, 357 U.S. 449, 462, we protected the "freedom to associate and privacy in one's association," noting that freedom of association was a peripheral First Amendment right. Disclosure of membership lists of a constitutionally valid association, we held, was invalid [p. 1316, infra]. In other words, the First Amendment has a penumbra where privacy is protected from governmental intrusion. In like context, we have protected forms of "association" that are not political in the customary sense but pertain to the social, legal, and economic benefit of the members. . . .

The foregoing cases suggest that specific guarantees in the Bill of Rights have penumbras, formed by emanations from those guarantees that help give them life and substance. See Poe v. Ullman, 367 U.S. 497, 516–522 (dissenting opinion). Various guarantees create zones of privacy. The right of association contained in the penumbra of the First Amendment is one, as we have seen. The Third Amendment in its prohibition against the quartering of soldiers "in any house" in time of peace without the consent of the owner is another facet of that privacy. The Fourth Amendment explicitly affirms the "right of the people to be secure in their persons, houses, papers, and effects against unreasonable searches and seizures." The Fifth Amendment in its Self-Incrimination Clause enables the citizen to create a zone of privacy which government may not force him to surrender to his detriment. The Ninth Amendment provides: "The enumeration in the Constitution, of certain rights, shall not be construed to deny or disparage others retained by the people." . . .

We have had many controversies over these penumbral rights of "privacy and repose." See, e. g., Breard v. Alexandria, 341 U.S. 622, 626, 644; Public Utilities Comm'n v. Pollak, 343 U.S. 451; Monroe v. Pape, 365 U.S. 167 . . . . These cases bear witness that the right of privacy which presses for recognition here is a legitimate one.

present case ✱   The present case, then, concerns a relationship lying within the zone of privacy created by several fundamental constitutional guarantees. And it concerns a law which, in forbidding the *use* of contraceptives rather than regulating their manufacture or sale, seeks to achieve its goals by means having a maximum destructive impact upon that relationship. Such a law cannot stand in light of the familiar principle, so often applied by this Court, that a "governmental purpose to control or prevent activities constitutionally subject to state regulation may not be achieved by means which sweep unnecessarily broadly and thereby invade the area of protected freedom." NAACP v. Alabama, 377 U.S. 288, 307. Would we allow the police to search the sacred precincts of marital bedrooms for telltale signs of the use of contraceptives? The very idea is repulsive to the notions of privacy surrounding the marriage relationship.

We deal with a right of privacy older than the Bill of Rights—older than our political parties, older than our school system. Marriage is a coming together for better or for worse, hopefully enduring, and intimate to the degree of being sacred. The association promotes a way of life, not causes; a harmony in living, not political faiths; a bilateral loyalty, not commercial or social projects. Yet it is an association for as noble a purpose as any involved in our prior decisions.

Reversed.

Mr. Justice HARLAN, concurring in the judgment.

I fully agree with the judgment of reversal, but find myself unable to join the Court's opinion. The reason is that it seems to me to evince an approach to this case very much like that taken by my Brothers Black and Stewart in dissent, namely: the Due Process Clause of the Fourteenth Amendment does not touch this Connecticut statute unless the enactment is found to violate some right assured by the letter or penumbra of the Bill of Rights.

In other words, what I find implicit in the Court's opinion is that the "incorporation" doctrine may be used to *restrict* the reach of Fourteenth Amendment Due Process. For me this is just as unacceptable constitutional doctrine as is the use of the "incorporation" approach to *impose* upon the States all the requirements of the Bill of Rights . . . .

In my view, the proper constitutional inquiry in this case is whether this Connecticut statute infringes the Due Process Clause of the Fourteenth Amendment because the enactment violates basic values "implicit in the concept of ordered liberty," Palko v. Connecticut, 302 U.S. 319, 325. For reasons stated at length in my dissenting opinion in Poe v. Ullman, supra, I believe that it does. While the relevant inquiry may be aided by resort to one or more of the provisions of the Bill of Rights, it is not dependent on them or any of their radiations. The Due Process Clause of the Fourteenth Amendment stands, in my opinion, on its own bottom. . . .

While I could not more heartily agree that judicial "self-restraint" is an indispensable ingredient of sound constitutional adjudication, I do submit that the formula suggested for achieving it is more hollow than real. "Specific" provisions of the Constitution, no less than "due process," lend themselves as readily to "personal" interpretations by judges whose constitutional outlook is simply to keep the Constitution in supposed "tune with the times" . . . . Need one go further than to call up last Term's reapportionment cases . . . .? [See chap. 18, p. 1438, infra.] . . . .

Mr. Justice GOLDBERG, whom The Chief Justice [WARREN] and Mr. Justice BRENNAN join, concurring.

I agree with the Court that Connecticut's birth control law unconstitutionally intrudes upon the right of marital privacy, and I join in its opinion and judgment. Although I have not accepted the view that "'due process' as used in the Fourteenth Amendment incorporates all of the first eight Amendments," . . . I do agree that the concept of liberty protects those personal rights that are fundamental, and is not confined to the specific terms of the Bill of Rights. My conclusion that the concept of liberty is not so restricted and that it embraces the right of marital privacy though that right is not mentioned explicitly in the Constitution is supported both by numerous decisions of this Court, referred to in the Court's opinion, and by the language and history of the Ninth Amendment. In reaching the conclusion that the right of marital privacy is protected, as being within the protected penumbra of specific guarantees of the Bill of Rights, the Court refers to the Ninth Amendment . . . . I add these words to emphasize the relevance of that Amendment to the Court's holding. . . .

This Court, in a series of decisions, has held that the Fourteenth Amendment absorbs and applies to the States those specifics of the first eight amendments which express fundamental personal rights. The language and history of the Ninth Amendment reveal that the Framers of the Constitution believed that there are additional fundamental rights, protected from governmental infringement, which exist alongside those fundamental rights specifically mentioned in the first eight constitutional amendments.

The Ninth Amendment reads, "The enumeration in the Constitution, of certain rights, shall not be construed to deny or disparage others retained by the people." The amendment is almost entirely the work of James Madison. It was introduced in Congress by him and passed the House and Senate with little or no debate and virtually no change in language. It was proffered to quiet expressed fears that a bill of specifically enumerated rights could not be sufficiently broad to cover all essential rights and that the specific mention of certain rights would be interpreted as a denial that others were protected. . . .

While this Court has had litle occasion to interpret the Ninth Amendment [1] "[i]t cannot be presumed that any clause in the constitution is in-

1. This Amendment has been referred to as "The Forgotten Ninth Amendment," in a book with that title by Bennet B. Patterson (1955). Other

tended to be without effect." Marbury v. Madison, 1 Cranch 137, 174. . . . The Ninth Amendment to the Constitution may be regarded by some as a recent discovery but since 1791 it has been a basic part of the Constitution which we are sworn to uphold. To hold that a right so basic and fundamental and so deep-rooted in our society as the right of privacy in marriage may be infringed because that right is not guaranteed in so many words by the first eight amendments to the Constitution is to ignore the Ninth Amendment and to give it no effect whatsoever. . . .

A dissenting opinion suggests that my interpretation of the Ninth Amendment somehow "broaden[s] the powers of this Court." . . . With all due respect, I believe that it misses the import of what I am saying. I do not take the position of my Brother Black in his dissent in Adamson v. California, 332 U.S. 46, 68, that the entire Bill of Rights is incorporated in the Fourteenth Amendment, and I do not mean to imply that the Ninth Amendment is applied against the States by the Fourteenth. Nor do I mean to state that the Ninth Amendment constitutes an independent source of rights protected from infringement by either the States or Federal Government. Rather, the Ninth Amendment shows a belief of the Constitution's authors that fundamental rights exist that are not expressly enumerated in the first eight amendments and an intent that the list of rights included there not be exhaustive. As any student of this Court's opinions knows, this Court has held, often unanimously, that the Fifth and Fourteenth Amendments protect certain fundamental personal liberties from abridgment by the Federal Government or the States. . . . The Ninth Amendment simply shows . . . the intent of the Constitution's authors that other fundamental personal rights should not be denied such protection or disparaged in any other way simply because they are not specifically listed in the first eight constitutional amendments. I do not see how this broadens the authority of the court; rather it serves to support what this Court has been doing in protecting fundamental rights.

Nor am I turning somersaults with history in arguing that the Ninth Amendment is relevant in a case dealing with a *State's* infringement of a fundamental right. While the Ninth Amendment—and indeed the entire Bill of Rights—originally concerned restrictions upon *federal* power, the subsequently enacted Fourteenth Amendment prohibits the States as well from abridging fundamental personal liberties. And, the Ninth Amendment,

---

commentary on the Ninth Amendment includes Redlich, Are There "Certain Rights . . . Retained by the People"? 37 N.Y.U.L.Rev. 787 (1962), and Kelsey, The Ninth Amendment of the Federal Constitution, 11 Ind.L.J. 309 (1936). As far as I am aware, until today this Court has referred to the Ninth Amendment only in United Public Workers v. Mitchell, 330 U.S. 75, 94–95; Tennessee Electric Power Co. v. TVA, 306 U.S. 118, 143–144; and Ashwander v. TVA, 297 U.S. 288, 330–331. See also Calder v. Bull, 3 Dall. 386, 388; Loan Assn. v. Topeka, 20 Wall. 655, 662–663.

In United Public Workers v. Mitchell, [chap. 2, p. 77, supra], the Court

stated: "We accept appellants' contention that the nature of political rights reserved to the people by the Ninth and Tenth Amendments are involved. The right claimed as inviolate may be stated as the right of a citizen to act as a party official or worker to further his own political views. Thus we have a measure of interference by the Hatch Act and the Rules with what otherwise would be the freedom of the civil servant under the First, Ninth and Tenth Amendments. And, if we look upon due process as a guarantee of freedom in those fields, there is a corresponding impairment of that right under the Fifth Amendment." [Footnote by Justice Goldberg.]

in indicating that not all such liberties are specifically mentioned in the first eight amendments, is surely relevant in showing the existence of other fundamental personal rights, now protected from state, as well as federal, infringement. In sum, the Ninth Amendment simply lends strong support to the view that the "liberty" protected by the Fifth and Fourteenth Amendments from infringement by the Federal Government or the States is not restricted to rights specifically mentioned in the first eight amendments. . . .

In determining which rights are fundamental, judges are not left at large to decide cases in light of their personal and private notions. Rather, they must look to the "traditions and [collective] conscience of our people" to determine whether a principle is "so rooted [there] . . . as to be ranked as fundamental." . . . I agree fully with the Court that, applying these tests, the right of privacy is a fundamental personal right, "emanating from the totality of the constitutional scheme under which we live." . . .

The entire fabric of the Constitution and the purposes that clearly underlie its specific guarantees demonstrate that the rights to marital privacy and to marry and raise a family are of similar order and magnitude as the fundamental rights specifically protected. . . .

The logic of the dissents would sanction federal or state legislation that seems to me even more plainly unconstitutional than the statute before us. Surely the Government, absent a showing of a compelling subordinate state interest, could not decree that all husbands and wives must be sterilized after two children have been born to them. Yet by their reasoning such an invasion of marital privacy would not be subject to constitutional challenge because, while it might be "silly," no provision of the Constitution specifically prevents the Government from curtailing the marital right to bear children and raise a family. While it may shock some of my Brethren that the Court today holds that the Constitution protects the right of marital privacy, in my view it is far more shocking to believe that the personal liberty guaranteed by the Constitution does not include protection against such totalitarian limitation of family size, which is at complete variance with our constitutional concepts. Yet, if upon a showing of a slender basis of rationality, a law outlawing voluntary birth control by married persons is valid, then, by the same reasoning, a law requiring compulsory birth control also would seem to be valid. In my view, however, both types of law would unjustifiably intrude upon rights of marital privacy which are constitutionally protected.

In a long series of cases this Court has held that where fundamental personal liberties are involved, they may not be abridged by the States simply on a showing that a regulatory statute has some rational relationship to the effectuation of a proper state purpose. . . . The State, at most, argues that there is some rational relation between this statute and what is admittedly a legitimate subject of state concern—the discouraging of extra-marital relations. . . . The rationality of this justification is dubious, particularly in light of the admitted widespread availability to all persons in the State of Connecticut, unmarried as well as married, of birth control devices for the prevention of disease, as distinguished from the prevention of conception . . . . But, in any event, it is clear that the State interest in safeguarding marital fidelity can be served by a more discriminately tailored statute, which does not, like the present one, sweep unnecessarily broadly, reaching far be-

Conn. statute is too broad

yond the evil sought to be dealt with and intruding upon the privacy of all married couples. . . .

Finally, it should be said of the Court's holding today that it in no way interferes with a State's proper regulation of sexual promiscuity or misconduct. As my Brother Harlan so well stated in his dissenting opinion in Poe v. Ullman, supra, at 553:

"Adultery, homosexuality and the like are sexual intimacies which the State forbids . . . but the intimacy of husband and wife is necessarily an essential and accepted feature of the institution of marriage, an institution which the State not only must allow, but which always and in every age it has fostered and protected. It is one thing when the State exerts its power either to forbid extra-marital sexuality . . . or to say who may marry, but it is quite another when, having acknowledged a marriage and the intimacies inherent in it, it undertakes to regulate by means of the criminal law the details of that intimacy."

In sum, I believe that the right of privacy in the marital relation is fundamental and basic—a personal right "retained by the people" within the meaning of the Ninth Amendment. Connecticut cannot constitutionally abridge this fundamental right, which is protected by the Fourteenth Amendment from infringement by the States. I agree with the Court that petitioners' convictions must therefore be reversed.

Mr. Justice WHITE, concurring.

In my view this Connecticut law as applied to married couples deprives them of "liberty" without due process of law, as that concept is used in the Fourteenth Amendment. I therefore concur in the judgment of the Court reversing these convictions under Connecticut's aiding and abetting statute. [T]he liberty entitled to protection under the Fourteenth Amendment includes the right "to marry, establish a home and bring up children." Meyer v. Nebraska, 262 U.S. 390, 399, and "the liberty . . . to direct the upbringing and education of children," Pierce v. Society of Sisters, 268 U.S. 510, 534–535 . . . . . Surely the right invoked in this case, to be free of regulation of the intimacies of the marriage relationship, "come[s] to this Court with a momentum for respect lacking when appeal is made to liberties which derive merely from shifting economic arrangements." Kovacs v. Cooper, 336 U.S. 77, 95 (opinion of Frankfurter, J.) [p. 1053, infra].

The Connecticut anti-contraceptive statute deals rather substantially with this relationship. . . . In my view, a statute with these effects bears a substantial burden of justification when attacked under the Fourteenth Amendment. . . .

An examination of the justification offered, however, cannot be avoided by saying that the Connecticut anti-use statute invades a protected area of privacy and association or that it demeans the marriage relationship. The nature of the right invaded is pertinent, to be sure, for statutes regulating sensitive areas of liberty do, under the cases of this Court, require "strict scrutiny," . . . . and "must be viewed in light of less drastic means for achieving the same basic purpose." . . . . But such statutes, if reasonably necessary for the effectuation of a legitimate and substantial state interest, and not arbitrary or capricious in application, are not invalid under the Due Process Clause. . . .

As I read the opinions of the Connecticut courts and the argument of Connecticut in this Court, the State claims but one justification for its anti-use statute. . . . There is no serious contention that Connecticut thinks the use of artificial or external methods of contraception immoral or unwise in itself, or that the anti-use statute is founded upon any policy of promoting population expansion. Rather, the statute is said to serve the State's policy against all forms of promiscuous or illicit sexual relationships, be they premarital or extramarital, concededly a permissible and legitimate legislative goal.

Without taking issue with the premise that the fear of conception operates as a deterrent to such relationships in addition to the criminal proscriptions Connecticut has against such conduct, I wholly fail to see how the ban on the use of contraceptives by married couples in any way reinforces the State's ban on illicit sexual relationships. . . .

. . . It is purely fanciful to believe that the broad proscription on use facilitates discovery of use by persons engaging in a prohibited relationship or for some other reason makes such use more unlikely and thus can be supported by any sort of administrative consideration. Perhaps the theory is that the flat ban on use prevents married people from possessing contraceptives and without the ready availability of such devices for use in the marital relationship, there will be no or less temptation to use them in extramarital ones. This reasoning rests on the premise that married people will comply with the anti-use ban in regard to their marital relationship, notwithstanding total nonenforcement in this context and apparent nonenforcibility, but will not comply with criminal statutes prohibiting extramarital affairs and the anti-use statute in respect to illicit sexual relationships, a premise whose validity has not been demonstrated and whose intrinsic validity is not very evident. At most the broad ban is of marginal utility to the declared objective. A statute limiting its prohibition on use to persons engaging in the prohibited relationship would serve the end posited by Connecticut in the same way, and with the same effectiveness, or ineffectiveness, as the broad anti-use statute under attack in this case. I find nothing in this record justifying the sweeping scope of this statute, with its telling effect on the freedoms of married persons, and therefore conclude that it deprives such persons of liberty without due process of law.

Mr. Justice BLACK, with whom Mr. Justice STEWART joins, dissenting.

I agree with my Brother Stewart's dissenting opinion. And like him I do not to any extent whatever base my view that this Connecticut law is constitutional on a belief that the law is wise or that its policy is a good one. [T]he law is every bit as offensive to me as it is to my Brethren . . . who, reciting reasons why it is offensive to them, hold it unconstitutional. There is no single one of the graphic and eloquent strictures and criticisms fired at the policy of this Connecticut law either by the Court's opinion or by those of my concurring Brethren to which I cannot subscribe—except their conclusion that the evil qualities they see in the law make it unconstitutional. . . . .

. . . . I get nowhere in this case by talk about a constitutional "right of privacy" as an emanation from one or more constitutional provisions.[1] I like my privacy as well as the next one, but I am nevertheless compelled to admit that government has a right to invade it unless prohibited by some specific constitutional provision. For these reasons I cannot agree with the Court's judgment and the reasons it gives for holding this Connecticut law unconstitutional.

This brings me to the arguments made by my Brothers Harlan, White and Goldberg for invalidating the Connecticut law. [P]roperly construed neither the Due Process Clause nor the Ninth Amendment, nor both together, could under any circumstances be a proper basis for invalidating the Connecticut law. I discuss the due process and Ninth Amendment arguments together because on analysis they turn out to be the same thing— merely using different words to confer on this Court and the federal judiciary the power to invalidate any legislative act which the judges find irrational, unreasonable or offensive.

The due process argument which my Brothers Harlan and White adopt here is based, as their opinions indicate, on the premise that this Court is vested with power to invalidate all state laws that it considers to be arbitrary, capricious, unreasonable, or oppressive, or because of this Court's belief that a particular state law under scrutiny has no "rational or justifying purpose," or is offensive to a "sense of fairness and justice." If these formulas based on "natural justice," or others which mean the same thing,[2]

---

1. The phrase "right to privacy" appears first to have gained currency from an article written by Messrs. Warren and (later Mr. Justice) Brandeis in 1890 which urged that States should give some form of tort relief to persons whose private affairs were exploited by others. The Right to Privacy, 4 Harv.L.Rev. 193. Largely as a result of this article, some States have passed statutes creating such a cause of action, and in others state courts have done the same thing by exercising their powers as courts of common law . . . Observing that "the right of privacy . . . presses for recognition here," today this Court, which I did not understand to have power to sit as a court of common law, now appears to be exalting a phrase which Warren and Brandeis used in discussing grounds for tort relief, to the level of a constitutional rule which prevents state legislatures from passing any law deemed by this Court to interfere with "privacy." [Footnote by Justice Black.]

2. A collection of the catchwords and catch phrases invoked by judges who would strike down under the Fourteenth Amendment laws which offend their notions of natural justice would fill many pages. Thus it has been said that this Court can forbid state action which "shocks the conscience," Rochin v. California, 342 U.S. 165, 172, sufficiently to "shock itself into the protective arms of the Constitution," Irvine v. California, 347 U.S. 128, 138 (concurring opinion). It has been urged that States may not run counter to the "decencies of civilized conduct," Rochin, supra, at 173, or "some principle of justice so rooted in the traditions and conscience of our people as to be ranked as fundamental," Snyder v. Massachusetts, 291 U. S. 97, 105, or to "those canons of decency and fairness which express the notions of justice of English-speaking peoples," Malinski v. New York, 324 U.S. 410, 416 (concurring opinion), or to "the community's sense of fair play and decency," Rochin, supra, at 173. It has been said that we must decide whether a state law is "fair, reasonable and appropriate," or is rather "an unreasonable, unnecessary and arbitrary interference with the rights of the individual to his personal liberty or to enter into . . . contracts," Lochner v. New York, 198 U.S. 45, 56. States, under this philosophy, cannot act "in conflict with deeply rooted feelings of the community," Haley v. Ohio, 332 U.S. 596, 604 (separate opinion), or with "fundamental notion of fairness and justice," id., 607. . . . [Footnote by Justice Black.]

are to prevail, they require judges to determine what is or is not constitutional on the basis of their own appraisal of what laws are unwise or unnecessary.[3] The power to make such decisions is of course that of a legislative body. Surely it has to be admitted that no provision of the Constitution specifically gives such blanket power to courts to exercise such a supervisory veto over the wisdom and value of legislative policies and to hold unconstitutional those laws which they believe unwise or dangerous. I readily admit that no legislative body, state or national, should pass laws that can justly be given any of the invidious labels invoked as constitutional excuses to strike down state laws. But perhaps it is not too much to say that no legislative body ever does pass laws without believing that they will accomplish a sane, rational, wise and justifiable purpose. While I completely subscribe to the holding of Marbury v. Madison, 1 Cranch 137, and subsequent cases, that our Court has constitutional power to strike down statutes, state or federal, that violate commands of the Federal Constitution, I do not believe that we are granted power by the Due Process Clause or any other constitutional provision or provisions to measure constitutionality by our belief that legislation is arbitrary, capricious or unreasonable, or accomplishes no justifiable purpose, or is offensive to our own notions of "civilized standards of conduct." Such an appraisal of the wisdom of legislation is an attribute of the power to make laws, not of the power to interpret them. The use by federal courts of such a formula or doctrine or whatnot to invalidate state laws simply takes away from Congress and States the power to make laws based on their own judgment of fairness and wisdom and transfers that power to this Court for ultimate determination.

Of the cases on which my Brothers White and Goldberg rely so heavily, undoubtedly the reasoning of two of them supports their result here —as would that of a number of others which they do not bother to name, e. g., Lochner v. New York, 198 U.S. 45, Coppage v. Kansas, 236 U.S. 1, Jay Burns Baking Co. v. Bryan, 264 U.S. 504, and Adkins v. Children's Hospital, 261 U.S. 525 [all decisions of the first three decades of the 20th century striking down economic regulations, see chap. 13, sec. 3, infra]. The two they do cite and quote from, Meyer v. Nebraska, 262 U.S. 390, and Pierce v. Society of Sisters, 268 U.S. 510, both were decided in opinions by Mr. Justice McReynolds which elaborated the same natural law due process philosophy found in Lochner v. New York, supra, one of the cases on which he relied in Meyer, along with such other long-discredited decisions as, e. g., Adams v. Tanner, 244 U.S. 590, and Adkins v. Children's Hospital, supra. Meyer held unconstitutional, as an "arbitrary" and unreasonable interference with the right of a teacher to carry on his occupation and of parents to hire him, a state law forbidding the teaching of modern foreign languages to young children in the schools.[4] And in Pierce, relying prin-

3. See Hand, The Bill of Rights (1958) 70:
"[J]udges are seldom content merely to annul the particular solution before them; they do not, indeed they may not, say that taking all things into consideration, the legislators' solution is too strong for the judicial stomach. On the contrary they wrap up their veto in a protective veil of adjectives such as 'arbitrary,' 'artificial,' 'normal,' 'reasonable,' 'inherent,' 'funda-

mental,' or 'essential,' whose office usually, though quite innocently, is to disguise what they are doing and impute to it a derivation far more impressive than their personal preferences, which are all that in fact lie behind the decision." . . . [Footnote by Justice Black.]

4. In Meyer, in the very same sentence quoted in part by my Brethren in which he asserted that the Due

cipally on Meyer, Mr. Justice McReynolds said that a state law requiring that all children attend public schools interfered unconstitutionally with the property rights of private school corporations because it was an "arbitrary, unreasonable and unlawful interference" which threatened "destruction of their business and property." 268 U.S. at 536. Without expressing an opinion as to whether either of those cases reached a correct result in light of our later decisions applying the First Amendment to the States through the Fourteenth, I merely point out that the reasoning stated in Meyer and Pierce was the same natural law due process philosophy which many later opinions repudiated, and which I cannot accept. . . . Brothers White and Goldberg now apparently would start from [the] requirement that laws be narrowly drafted so as not to curtail free speech and assembly, and extend it limitlessly to require States to justify any law restricting "liberty" as my Brethren define "liberty." This would mean at the very least, I suppose, that every state criminal statute—since it must inevitably curtail "liberty" to some extent—would be suspect, and would have to be justified to this Court.

My Brother Goldberg has adopted the recent discovery [5] that the Ninth Amendment as well as the Due Process Clause can be used by this Court as authority to strike down all state legislation which this Court thinks violates "fundamental principles of liberty and justice," or is contrary to the "traditions and collective conscience of our people." He also states, without proof satisfactory to me, that in making decisions on this basis judges will not consider "their personal and private notions." One may ask how they can avoid considering them. Our Court certainly has no machinery with which to take a Gallup Poll.[6] And the scientific miracles of this age

Process Clause gave an abstract and inviolable right "to marry, establish a home and bring up children," Mr. Justice McReynolds asserted also that the Due Process Clause prevented States from interfering with "the right of the individual to contract." 252 U.S., at 399. [Footnote by Justice Black.]

5. See Patterson, The Forgotten Ninth Amendment (1955). Mr. Patterson urges that the Ninth Amendment be used to protect unspecified "natural and inalienable rights." P. 4. The Introduction by Roscoe Pound states that "there is a marked revival of natural law ideas throughout the world. Interest in the Ninth Amendment is a symptom of that revival." p. iii.

In Redlich, Are There "Certain Rights . . . Retained by the People"?, 37 N.Y.U.L.Rev. 787, Professor Redlich, in advocating reliance on the Ninth and Tenth Amendments to invalidate the Connecticut law before us, frankly states:

"But for one who feels that the marriage relationship should be beyond the reach of a state law forbidding the use of contraceptives, the birth control case poses a troublesome and chal-

lenging problem of constitutional interpretation. He may find himself saying, 'The law is unconstitutional—but why?' There are two possible paths to travel in finding the answer. One is to revert to a frankly flexible due process concept even on matters that do not involve specific constitutional prohibitions. The other is to attemp to evolve a new constitutional framework within which to meet this and similar problems which are likely to arise." Id., at 798. [Footnote by Justice Black.]

6. Of course one cannot be oblivious to the fact that Mr. Gallup has already published the results of a poll which he says show that 46% of the people in this country believe schools should teach about birth control. Washington Post, May 21, 1965, p. 2, col. 1. I can hardly believe, however, that Brother Goldberg would view 46% of the persons polled as so overwhelming a proportion that this Court may now rely on it to declare that the Connecticut law infringes "fundamental" rights, and overrule the longstanding view of the people of Connecticut expressed through their elected representatives. [Footnote by Justice Black.]

have not yet produced a gadget which the Court can use to determine what traditions are rooted in the "collective conscience of our people." Moreover, one would certainly have to look far beyond the language of the Ninth Amendment to find that the Framers vested in this Court any such awesome veto powers over lawmaking, either by the States or by the Congress. Nor does anything in the history of the Amendment offer any support for such a shocking doctrine. The whole history of the adoption of the Constitution and Bill of Rights points the other way . . .. That Amendment was passed, not to broaden the powers of this Court or any other department of "the General Government," but, as every student of history knows, to assure the people that the Constitution in all its provisions was intended to limit the Federal Government to the powers granted expressly or by necessary implication. If any broad, unlimited power to hold laws unconstitutional because they offend what this Court conceives to be "the collective conscience of our people" is vested in this Court by the Ninth Amendment, the Fourteenth Amendment, or any other provision of the Constitution, it was not given by the Framers, but rather has been bestowed on the Court by the Court. This fact is perhaps responsible for the peculiar phenomenon that for a period of a century and a half no serious suggestion was ever made that the Ninth Amendment, enacted to protect State powers against federal invasion, could be used as a weapon of federal power to prevent state legislatures from passing laws they consider appropriate to govern local affairs. Use of any such broad, unbounded judicial authority would make of this Court's members a day-to-day constitutional convention.

. . . The adoption of . . . a loose, flexible, uncontrolled standard for holding laws unconstitutional, if ever it is achieved, will amount to a great unconstitutional shift of power to the courts which I believe and am constrained to say will be bad for the courts and worse for the country. Subjecting federal and state laws to such an unrestrained and unrestrainable judicial control as to the wisdom of legislative enactments would, I fear, jeopardize the separation of governmental powers that the Framers set up and at the same time threaten to take away much of the power of States to govern themselves which the Constitution plainly intended them to have.[7]

I realize that many good and able men have eloquently spoken and written, sometimes in rhapsodical strains, about the duty of this Court to keep the Constitution in tune with the times. The idea is that the Constitution

---

7. Justice Holmes in one of his last dissents, Baldwin v. Missouri, 281 U. S. 586, 595, warned:
"I have not yet adequately expressed the more than anxiety that I feel at the ever increasing scope given to the Fourteenth Amendment in cutting down what I believe to be the constitutional rights of the States. As the decisions now stand, I see hardly any limit but the sky to the invalidating of those rights if they happen to strike a majority of this Court as for any reason undesirable. I cannot believe that the Amendment was intended to give us *carte blanche* to embody our economic or moral beliefs in its prohibitions. Yet I can think of no narrower reason that seems to me to justify the present and the earlier decisions to which I have referred. Of course the words 'due process of law,' if taken in their literal meaning, have no application to this case; and while it is too late to deny that they have been given a much more extended and artificial signification, still we ought to remember the great caution shown by the Constitution in limiting the power of the States, and should be slow to construe the clause in the Fourteenth Amendment as committing to the Court, with no guide but the Court's own discretion, the validity of whatever laws the States may pass." [Footnote by Justice Black.]

must be changed from time to time and that this Court is charged with a duty to make those changes. For myself, I must with all deference reject that philosophy. The Constitution makers knew the need for change and provided for it. Amendments suggested by the people's elected representatives can be submitted to the people or their selected agents for ratification. That method of change was good for our Fathers, and being somewhat old-fashioned I must add it is good enough for me. And so, I cannot rely on the Due Process Clause or the Ninth Amendment or any mysterious and uncertain natural law concept as a reason for striking down this state law. The Due Process Clause with an "arbitrary and capricious" or "shocking to the conscience" formula was liberally used by this Court to strike down economic legislation in the early decades of this century, threatening, many people thought, the tranquility and stability of the Nation. See, e. g., Lochner v. New York, 198 U.S. 45. That formula, based on subjective considerations of "natural justice," is no less dangerous when used to enforce this Court's views about personal rights than those about economic rights. I had thought that we had laid that formula, as a means for striking down state legislation, to rest . . . . Apparently my Brethren have less quarrel with state economic regulations than former Justices of their persuasion had. But any limitation upon their using the natural law due process philosophy to strike down any state law, dealing with any activity whatever, will obviously be only self-imposed. . . .

. . . The late Judge Learned Hand, after emphasizing his view that judges should not use the due process formula suggested in the concurring opinions today or any other formula like it to invalidate legislation offensive to their "personal preferences," made the statement, with which I fully agree, that:

> "For myself it would be most irksome to be ruled by a bevy of Platonic Guardians, even if I knew how to choose them, which I assuredly do not." [8]

So far as I am concerned, Connecticut's law as applied here is not forbidden by any provision of the Federal Constitution as that Constitution was written, and I am therefore to affirm.

Mr. Justice STEWART, whom Mr. Justice BLACK joins, dissenting.

Since 1879 Connecticut has had on its books a law which forbids the use of contraceptives by anyone. I think this is an uncommonly silly law. As a practical matter, the law is obviously unenforceable, except in the oblique context of the present case. As a philosophical matter, I believe the use of contraceptives in the relationship of marriage should be left to personal and private choice, based upon each individual's moral, ethical, and religious beliefs. As a matter of social policy, I think professional counsel about methods of birth control should be available to all, so that each individual's choice can be meaningfully made. But we are not asked in this case to say whether

---

8. [Hand, The Bill of Rights (1958)], at 73. While Judge Hand condemned as unjustified the invalidation of state laws under the natural law due process formula, see id., at 35–45, he also expressed the view that this Court in a number of cases had gone too far in holding legislation to be in violation of specific guarantees of the Bill of Rights. Although I agree with his criticism of use of the due process formula, I do not agree with all the views he expressed about construing the specific guarantees of the Bill of Rights. [Footnote by Justice Black. See the comments on Justice Black's reliance on Judge Hand in the notes following this case.]

we think this law is unwise, or even asinine. We are asked to hold that it violates the United States Constitution. And that I cannot do.

In the course of its opinion the Court refers to no less than six Amendments to the Constitution: the First, the Third, the Fourth, the Fifth, the Ninth, and the Fourteenth. But the Court does not say which of these Amendments, if any, it thinks is infringed by this Connecticut law.

We *are* told that the Due Process Clause of the Fourteenth Amendment is not, as such, the "guide" in this case. With that much I agree. There is no claim that this law, duly enacted by the Connecticut Legislature, is unconstitutionally vague. There is no claim that the appellants were denied any of the elements of procedural due process at their trial, so as to make their convictions constitutionally invalid. And, as the Court says, the day has long passed since the Due Process Clause was regarded as a proper instrument for determining "the wisdom, need, and propriety" of state laws. . . .

As to the First, Third, Fourth, and Fifth Amendments, I can find nothing in any of them to invalidate this Connecticut law, even assuming that all those Amendments are fully applicable against the States. [T]o say that the Ninth Amendment has anything to do with this case is to turn somersaults with history. The Ninth Amendment, like its companion the Tenth, which this Court held "states but a truism that all is retained which has not been surrendered," United States v. Darby, 312 U.S. 100, 124, was framed by James Madison and adopted by the States simply to make clear that the adoption of the Bill of Rights did not alter the plan that the *Federal* Government was to be a government of express and limited powers, and that all rights and powers not delegated to it were retained by the people and the individual States. Until today no member of this Court has ever suggested that the Ninth Amendment meant anything else, and the idea that a federal court could ever use the Ninth Amendment to annul a law passed by the elected representatives of the people of the State of Connecticut would have caused James Madison no little wonder.

What provision of the Constitution, then, does make this state law invalid? The Court says it is the right of privacy "created by several fundamental constitutional guarantees." With all deference, I can find no such general right of privacy in the Bill of Rights, in any other part of the Constitution, or in any case ever before decided by this Court.[1]

At the oral argument in this case we were told that the Connecticut law does not "conform to current community standards." But it is not the function of this Court to decide cases on the basis of community standards. We are here to decide cases "agreeably to the Constitution and laws of the United States." It is the essence of judicial duty to subordinate our own personal views, our own ideas of what legislation is wise and what is not. If, as I should surely hope, the law before us does not reflect the standards of the people of Connecticut, the people of Connecticut can freely exercise their

---

1. . . . . The Court does not say how far the new constitutional right of privacy announced today extends. See, e. g., Mueller, Legal Regulation of Sexual Conduct, at 127; Ploscowe, Sex and the Law, at 189. I suppose, however, that even after today a State can constitutionally still punish at least some offenses which are not committed in public. [Footnote by Justice Stewart.]

true Ninth and Tenth Amendment rights to persuade their elected representatives to repeal it. That is the constitutional way to take this law off the books.[2]

GRISWOLD, PENUMBRAS, AND DOUBLE STANDARDS

Griswold is of considerable interest because of its specific holding and its perception of a right to marital privacy. To what extent, for example, does this constitutionally recognized interest in privacy cast doubt on other statutes affecting marriage and sexual behavior? Statutes affecting other areas of private conduct—e.g., possession of marijuana? Note the 1969 decision in Stanley v. Georgia, on possession of obscene materials, chap. 16, p. 1254, infra, and see generally the Symposium on the Griswold case, 64 Mich. L.Rev. 197 (1965).

But Griswold is of even greater interest because of the range of judicial techniques and substantive due process criteria it discloses. Is Justice Black right in charging that Griswold is of a piece with the freewheeling, subjective variety of substantive due process adjudication long discredited in the economic regulation area (see chap. 13, sec. 3, infra)? Or is Griswold distinguishable? How?

The problem of justifying judicial intervention on behalf of some parts of the "life, liberty and property" protected by the due process clause of the 14th Amendment while keeping "hands off" others has been a pervasive one, especially since the 1937 Court crisis. Even if the inquiry is limited to the protection of "liberty," how can judicial intervention on behalf of some liberties be justified without intervening on behalf of all? How can the Court exert itself on behalf of political liberty without also being concerned about economic liberty? As chap. 13, sec. 4, shows (and as Justice Black reminds), the "Old Court" is condemned for substituting its own values and acting like a super-legislature in blocking economic and social regulation. Since 1937, the Court has disavowed that kind of intervention, while steadily increasing its scrutiny of legislation in other areas. The justifiability of that "double standard"—of strict scrutiny in some situations, hands-off in others—is central in the chapters to come.

One of the most influential justifications for that double standard—Justice Stone's footnote in the Carolene Products case, quoted at the beginning of chap. 15, p. 1051, infra—suggests that greatest scrutiny is justified when legislation conflicts with values expressed in the "specific" prohibitions of the Constitution or when it "restricts" the "political processes." And Justice Black has been in the forefront in urging the exercise of judicial power to invalidate interferences with "specific" guarantees. The Carolene Products justification and others are controversial enough when, for example, First Amendment freedoms are involved. But the value protected in the Griswold decision does not fit most of these explanations: even the Justices to whom the hard rock at the core of the penumbra is most visible would not call marital privacy a "specific" guarantee, or one central to the "political processes."

---

2. See Reynolds v. Sims, 377 U.S. 533, 562. The Connecticut House of Representatives recently passed a bill (House Bill No. 2462) repealing the birth control law. The State Senate has apparently not yet acted on the measure, and today is relieved of that responsibility by the Court. New Haven Journal Courier, Wed., May 19, 1965, p. 1, col. 4 and p. 13, col. 7. [Footnote by Justice Stewart.]

Is there, then, nothing more to be said for the Griswold decision than could have been said for any of the old Court's invalidations of state laws? Is it possible to articulate any satisfactory standard that justifies greater judicial scrutiny and insists on stronger justification for legislative restriction on liberty when marital privacy rather than economic liberty is affected? Do any of the Justices in the majority offer an adequate explanation? Which are more adequate than others?

Justice Black in Griswold repeatedly quotes Judge Learned Hand. That is ironic: as Justice Black's footnote 8 hints, Judge Hand repudiated any double standard and was profoundly skeptical of the judicial enforceability of the due process clause in any context, whether of civil liberties or of economic regulation: he disapproved of Justice Black's variety of "absolute" free speech enforcement (see chap. 15, infra) as he did of the Lochner case which invalidated maximum hour legislation for bakers in 1908 (p. 956, infra)— and as he probably would have of the Griswold case. As he said of the shift in the Court after the 1937 Court crisis (in a passage more fully quoted at the beginning of chap. 15, p. 1052, below), "it began to seem as though, when 'personal rights' were an issue, something strangely akin to the discredited attitude toward the Bill of Rights of the old apostles of the institution of property was regaining recognition." Judge Hand apparently thought that this was "an opportunistic reversion." To him, the principle of non-intervention via substantive due process could not mean "that, when concerned with interests other than property, the courts should have a wider latitude for enforcing their own predilections."

Does Griswold, then, illustrate the validity of Hand's critique? Compare the questions at the end of chap. 13, p. 981, infra. Can a Court willing to invalidate in Griswold keep hands off economic regulations on any ground other than personal predilections? Does the "penumbras"-"emanations" approach of Justice Douglas' opinion avoid subjective, idiosyncratic adjudication more effectively than Justice Goldberg's Ninth Amendment emphasis? Does either of those approaches channel judicial power more rigorously than the "fundamental values" approach of Justices Harlan and White?

Even Justice Frankfurter, who spoke most frequently against the double standard on the modern Court, and was thus closest to Judge Learned Hand's position, found some values more important than others. As Justice White's quotation from Justice Frankfurter's opinion in Kovacs v. Cooper shows, Justice Frankfurter thought some rights "come to this Court with a momentum for respect lacking when appeal is made to liberties which derive merely from shifting economic arrangements." [See chap. 15, p. 1053, infra.] How then does the Court determine the proper place of a particular right on this scale of values? How does Justice White, for example, defend placing the right invoked in Griswold at a different place in the hierarchy of values than "mere" economic rights?

Are liberty of contract and the right to use property, the rights most often defended in the discredited economic regulation cases of the early 20th Century, distinguishable because those rights are not specifically mentioned in the Constitution (unlike, for example, speech)? But are they not as specific as the Griswold right, even under the Douglas penumbra rationale? Could not liberty of contract been seen as an emanation from the contracts clause—not to speak of the "liberty" specified in the 14th Amendment?

And could not the use of property be seen as a penumbra of the specific mention of property in the condemnation clause of the Fifth Amendment,—not to speak of the historical importance of property rights and the "specific" reference to property in the 14th Amendment itself? See Kauper, "Penumbras, Peripheries, and Emanations, Things Fundamental and Things Forgotten: The Griswold Case," 64 Mich.L.Rev. 235 (1965). The materials that follow repeatedly raise related questions regarding the scope of judicial inquiry, double standards, requisite legislative justifications for restrictions on liberty, and alternative judicial techniques.

Chapter 12

PROCEDURAL RIGHTS IN THE ADMINISTRATION OF CRIMINAL JUSTICE

Introduction. The constitutional rights of the accused have been a major source of judicial business—and of political controversy—for the modern Supreme Court. Exhaustive treatment of the proliferating guarantees is not possible in a constitutional law course; the doctrinal elaborations tend more and more to be the concern of courses in criminal law and procedure. But some attention in constitutional law courses remains appropriate. This chapter seeks to give an overview of the developments and to examine a selected number of problems more intensively. Some of the materials—e.g., the interrogation rules of Miranda (p. 859)—focus on the judicial elaboration of detailed guarantees in the special context of the criminal process; and the content of specific constitutional safeguards pertaining to criminal law enforcement is the major emphasis of this chapter. But many of the materials serve the important additional purpose of casting further light on problems that were introduced in the preceding chapter and that are of special relevance in this course: the problems of judicial technique, Supreme Court function, and constitutional doctrine involved in giving content to the fair trial aspect of due process. Several of the cases in this chapter—e. g., Gideon v. Wainwright on counsel (p. 846) and Mapp v. Ohio on search and seizure (p. 878)—accordingly develop the issues of incorporation, of specificity and vagueness, and of subjectivity and predictability raised in the Palko-Adamson-Rochin-Duncan sequence above (chap. 11, pp. 798–812).

SECTION 1. RIGHT TO COUNSEL

POWELL v. ALABAMA

287 U.S. 45, 53 S.Ct. 55, 77 L.Ed. 158 (1932).

Certiorari to the Supreme Court of Alabama.

Mr. Justice SUTHERLAND delivered the opinion of the Court.

The . . . defendants are negroes charged with the crime of rape, committed upon the persons of two white girls. The crime is said to have been committed on March 25, 1931. The indictment was returned in a state court of first instance on March 31, and the record recites that on the same day the defendants were arraigned and entered pleas of not guilty. There is a further recital to the effect that upon the arraignment they were represented by counsel. But no counsel had been employed, and aside from a statement made by the trial judge several days later during a colloquy immediately preceding the trial, the record does not disclose when, or under what circumstances, an appointment of counsel was made, or who was appointed.

During the colloquy referred to, the trial judge, in response to a question, said that he had appointed all the members of the bar for the purpose of arraigning the defendants and then of course anticipated that the members of the bar would continue to help the defendants if no counsel appeared. . .

. . . As each of the three cases was called for trial, each defendant was arraigned, and, having the indictment read to him, entered a plea of not guilty. Whether the original arraignment and pleas were regarded as ineffective is not shown. Each of the three trials was completed within a single day. . . . The juries found defendants guilty and imposed the death penalty upon all. . . . The judgments were affirmed by the state supreme court. . . .

The record shows that on the day when the offense is said to have been committed, these defendants, together with a number of other negroes, were upon a freight train on its way through Alabama. On the same train were seven white boys and two white girls. . . . The two girls testified that each of them was assaulted by six different negroes in turn, and they identified the seven defendants as having been among the number. . . . Before the train reached Scottsboro, Alabama, a sheriff's posse seized the defendants and two other negroes. Both girls and the negroes then were taken to Scottsboro, the county seat. . . . [T]hey were met at Scottsboro by a large crowd. . . . It is perfectly apparent that the proceedings, from beginning to end, took place in an atmosphere of tense, hostile, and excited public sentiment. . . . [T]he record clearly indicates that most, if not all of [the defendants] were youthful . . . . They were ignorant and illiterate. . .

. . . It was the duty of the court having their cases in charge to see that they were denied no necessary incident of a fair trial. . . . The sole inquiry which we are permitted to make is whether the federal Constitution was contravened . . . ; and as to that, we confine ourselves . . . to the inquiry whether the defendants were in substance denied the right of counsel, and if so, whether such denial infringes the due process clause of the Fourteenth Amendment.

First. . . . It is hardly necessary to say that, the right to counsel being conceded, a defendant should be afforded a fair opportunity to secure counsel of his own choice. Not only was that not done here, but such designation of counsel as was attempted was either so indefinite or so close upon the trial as to amount to a denial of effective and substantial aid in that regard. . . .

[U]ntil the very morning of the trial no lawyer had been named or definitely designated to represent the defendants. Prior to that time, the trial judge had "appointed all the members of the bar" for the limited "purpose of arraigning the defendants." Whether they would represent the defendants thereafter, if no counsel appeared in their behalf, was a matter of speculation only, or, as the judge indicated, of mere anticipation on the part of the court. Such a designation, even if made for all purposes, would, in our opinion, have fallen far short of meeting, in any proper sense, a requirement for the appointment of counsel. How many lawyers were members of the bar does not appear; but, in the very nature of things, whether many or few, they would not, thus collectively named, have been given that clear appreciation of responsibility or impressed with that individual sense of duty which should and naturally would accompany the appointment of a selected member of the bar, specifically named and assigned.

[D]uring perhaps the most critical period of the proceedings against these defendants, that is to say, from the time of their arraignment until the beginning of their trial, when consultation, thorough-going investigation and preparation were vitally important, the defendants did not have the aid of counsel in any real sense, although they were as much entitled to such aid during that period as at the trial itself. . . . .

Nor do we think the situation was helped by what occurred on the morning of the trial. At that time . . . . Mr. Roddy, [a Tennessee lawyer], stated to the court that he did not appear as counsel, but that he would like to appear along with counsel that the court might appoint; that he had not been given an opportunity to prepare the case; that he was not familiar with the procedure in Alabama, but merely came down as a friend of the people who were interested; that he thought the boys would be better off if he should step entirely out of the case. Mr. Moody, a member of the local bar, expressed a willingness to help Mr. Roddy in anything he could do under the circumstances. . . . . With this dubious understanding, the trials immediately proceeded. . . .

It is not enough to assume that counsel thus precipitated into the case thought there was no defense, and exercised their best judgment in proceeding to trial without preparation. Neither they nor the court could say what a prompt and thorough-going investigation might disclose as to the facts. No attempt was made to investigate. No opportunity to do so was given. Defendants were immediately hurried to trial. . . . . Under the circumstances disclosed, we hold that defendants were not accorded the right of counsel in any substantial sense. . . . . The prompt disposition of criminal cases is to be commended and encouraged. But in reaching that result a defendant, charged with a serious crime, must not be stripped of his right to have sufficient time to advise with counsel and prepare his defense. . . .

Second. . . . . The question . . . which it is our duty . . . . to decide, is whether the denial of the assistance of counsel contravenes the due process clause of the Fourteenth Amendment to the federal Constitution.

If recognition of the right of a defendant charged with a felony to have the aid of counsel depended upon the existence of a similar right at common law as it existed in England when our Constitution was adopted, there would be great difficulty in maintaining it as necessary to due process. Originally, in England, a person charged with treason or felony was denied the aid of counsel, except in respect of legal questions which the accused himself might suggest. At the same time parties in civil cases and persons accused of misdemeanors were entitled to the full assistance of counsel. After the revolution of 1688, the rule was abolished as to treason, but was otherwise steadily adhered to until 1836, when by act of Parliament the full right was granted in respect of felonies generally. . . . .

An affirmation of the right to the aid of counsel in petty offenses, and its denial in the case of crimes of the gravest character, where such aid is most needed, is so outrageous and so obviously a perversion of all sense of proportion that the rule was constantly, vigorously and sometimes passionately assailed by English statesmen and lawyers. . . . . One of the grounds upon which Lord Coke defended the rule was that in felonies the court itself was counsel for the prisoner . . . . But how can a judge, whose functions are purely judicial, effectively discharge the obligations of counsel for the accused? He can and should see to it that in the proceedings before the court the accused shall be dealt with justly and fairly. He cannot investigate the facts, advise and direct the defense, or participate in those necessary conferences between counsel and accused which sometimes partake of the inviolable character of the confessional.

The rule was rejected by the colonies. . . . [I]n at least twelve of the thirteen colonies the rule of the English common law, in the respect now under consideration, had been definitely rejected and the right to counsel fully recognized in all criminal prosecutions, save that in one or two instances the right was limited to capital offenses or to the more serious crimes . . . .

One test which has been applied to determine whether due process of law has been accorded in given instances is to ascertain what were the settled usages and modes of proceeding under the common and statute law of England before the Declaration of Independence, subject, however, to the qualification that they be shown not to have been unsuited to the civil and political conditions of our ancestors by having been followed in this country after it became a nation. . . . Plainly, as appears from the foregoing, this test, as thus qualified, has not been met in the present case. . . .

It never has been doubted by this court, or any other so far as we know, that notice and hearing are preliminary steps essential to the passing of an enforceable judgment, and that they, together with a legally competent tribunal having jurisdiction of the case, constitute basic elements of the constitutional requirement of due process of law. . . .

What, then, does a hearing include? Historically and in practice, in our own country at least, it has always included the right to the aid of counsel when desired and provided by the party asserting the right. The right to be heard would be, in many cases, of little avail if it did not comprehend the right to be heard by counsel. Even the intelligent and educated layman has small and sometimes no skill in the science of law. If charged with crime, he is incapable, generally, of determining for himself whether the indictment is good or bad. He is unfamiliar with the rules of evidence. Left without the aid of counsel he may be put on trial without a proper charge, and convicted upon incompetent evidence, or evidence irrelevant to the issue or otherwise inadmissible. He lacks both the skill and knowledge adequately to prepare his defense, even though he have a perfect one. He requires the guiding hand of counsel at every step in the proceedings against him. Without it, though he be not guilty, he faces the danger of conviction because he does not know how to establish his innocence. If that be true of men of intelligence, how much more true is it of the ignorant and illiterate, or those of feeble intellect. If in any case, civil or criminal, a state or federal court were arbitrarily to refuse to hear a party by counsel, employed by and appearing for him, it reasonably may not be doubted that such a refusal would be a denial of a hearing, and, therefore, of due process in the constitutional sense. . .

In the light of the facts outlined in the forepart of this opinion—the ignorance and illiteracy of the defendants, their youth, the circumstances of public hostility, the imprisonment and the close surveillance of the defendants by the military forces, the fact that their friends and families were all in other states and communication with them necessarily difficult, and above all that they stood in deadly peril of their lives—we think the failure of the trial court to give them reasonable time and opportunity to secure counsel was a clear denial of due process.

But passing that, and assuming their inability, even if opportunity had been given, to employ counsel, . . . we are of opinion that, under the circumstances just stated, the necessity of counsel was so vital and imperative that the failure of the trial court to make an effective appointment of counsel was likewise a denial of due process within the meaning of the Fourteenth Amendment. Whether this would be so in other criminal prosecutions, or under other circumstances, we need not determine. All that it is necessary now to decide, as we do decide, is that in a capital case, where the defendant is unable to employ counsel, and is incapable adequately of making his own defense because of ignorance, feeblemindedness, illiteracy, or the like, it is the duty of the court, whether requested or not, to assign counsel for him as a necessary requisite of due process of law; and that duty is not discharged by an assignment at such a time or under such circumstances as to preclude the giving of effective aid in the preparation and trial of the case.
. . . .

The United States by statute and every state in the Union by express provision of law, or by the determination of its courts, make it the duty of the trial judge, where the accused is unable to employ counsel, to appoint counsel for him. In most states the rule applies broadly to all criminal prosecutions, in others it is limited to the more serious crimes, and in a very limited number, to capital cases. A rule adopted with such unanimous accord reflects, if it does not establish, the inherent right to have counsel appointed, at least in cases like the present, and lends convincing support to the conclusion we have reached as to the fundamental nature of that right. . . .

Judgments reversed.

Mr. Justice BUTLER, dissenting. . . .

If correct, the ruling that the failure of the trial court to give petitioners time and opportunity to secure counsel was denial of due process is enough, and with this the opinion should end. But the Court goes on to declare that "the failure of the trial court to make an effective appointment of counsel was likewise a denial of due process within the meaning of the Fourteenth Amendment." This is an extension of federal authority into a field hitherto occupied exclusively by the several States. Nothing before the Court calls for a consideration of the point. It was not suggested below and petitioners do not ask for its decision here. The Court, without being called upon to consider it, adjudges without a hearing an important constitutional question concerning criminal procedure in state courts. . . .

The record wholly fails to reveal that petitioners have been deprived on any right guaranteed by the Federal Constitution. . . .

Mr. Justice McREYNOLDS concurs in this opinion.

GIDEON v. WAINWRIGHT

372 U.S. 335, 83 S.Ct. 792, 9 L.Ed.2d 799 (1963).

Certiorari to the Supreme Court of Florida.

Mr. Justice BLACK delivered the opinion of the Court.

Petitioner was charged in a Florida state court with having broken and entered a poolroom with intent to commit a misdemeanor. This offense is a felony under Florida law. Appearing in court without funds and without a lawyer, petitioner asked the court to appoint counsel for him, whereupon the following colloquy took place:

"The Court: Mr. Gideon, I am sorry, but I cannot appoint Counsel to represent you in this case. Under the laws of the State of Florida, the only time the Court can appoint Counsel to represent a Defendant is when that person is charged with a capital offense. I am sorry, but I will have to deny your request to appoint Counsel to defend you in this case.

"The Defendant: The United States Supreme Court says I am entitled to be represented by Counsel."

Put to trial before a jury, Gideon conducted his defense about as well as could be expected from a layman. . . . The jury returned a verdict of guilty, and petitioner was sentenced to serve five years in the state prison. Later, petitioner filed in the Florida Supreme Court this habeas corpus petition . . . on the ground that the trial court's refusal to appoint counsel for him denied him rights "guaranteed by the Constitution and the Bill of Rights by the United States Government." . . . [T]he State Supreme Court . . . denied all relief. Since 1942, when Betts v. Brady, 316 U.S. 455, was decided by a divided Court [see note 1 following this case], the problem of a defendant's federal constitutional right to counsel in a state court has been a continuing source of controversy and litigation in both state and federal courts. To give this problem another review here, we granted certiorari. . . . Since Gideon was proceeding *in forma pauperis,* we appointed counsel to represent him and requested both sides to discuss in their briefs and oral arguments the following: "Should this Court's holding in Betts v. Brady, 316 U.S. 455, be reconsidered?"

I.

The facts upon which Betts claimed that he had been unconstitutionally denied the right to have counsel appointed to assist him are strikingly like the facts upon which Gideon here bases his federal constitutional claim. . . . Like Gideon, Betts sought release by habeas corpus, alleging that he had been denied the right to assistance of counsel in violation of the Fourteenth Amendment. Betts was denied any relief, and on review this Court affirmed. It was held that a refusal to appoint counsel for an indigent defendant charged with a felony did not necessarily violate the Due Process Clause of the Fourteenth Amendment, which for reasons given the Court deemed to be the only applicable federal constitutional provision. The Court said:

"Asserted denial [of due process] is to be tested by an appraisal of the totality of facts in a given case. That which may, in one setting, constitute a denial of fundamental fairness, shocking to the universal sense of justice, may, in other circumstances, and in the light of other considerations, fall short of such denial." 316 U.S., at 462.

. . . . Since the facts and circumstances of the two cases are so nearly indistinguishable, we think the Betts v. Brady holding if left standing would require us to reject Gideon's claim that the Constitution guarantees him the assistance of counsel. Upon full reconsideration we conclude that Betts v. Brady should be overruled.

II.

We accept Betts v. Brady's assumption, based as it was on our prior cases, that a provision of the Bill of Rights which is "fundamental and essential to a fair trial" is made obligatory upon the States by the Fourteenth Amendment. We think the Court in Betts was wrong, however, in concluding that the Sixth Amendment's guarantee of counsel is not one of these fundamental rights. Ten years before Betts v. Brady, this Court, after full consideration of all the historical data examined in Betts, had unequivocally declared that "the right to the aid of counsel is of this fundamental character." Powell v. Alabama, 287 U.S. 45, 68 (1932). While the Court at the close of its Powell opinion did by its language, as this Court frequently does, limit its holding to the particular facts and circumstances of that case, its conclusions about the fundamental nature of the right to counsel are unmistakable. . . .

. . . . The fact is that in deciding as it did—that "appointment of counsel is not a fundamental right, essential to a fair trial"—the Court in Betts v. Brady made an abrupt break with its own well-considered precedents. In returning to these old precedents, sounder we believe than the new, we but restore constitutional principles established to achieve a fair system of justice. Not only these precedents but also reason and reflection require us to recognize that in our adversary system of criminal justice, any person haled into court, who is too poor to hire a lawyer, cannot be assured a fair trial unless counsel is provided for him. This seems to us to be an obvious truth. Governments, both state and federal, quite properly spend vast sums of money to establish machinery to try defendants accused of crime. Lawyers to prosecute are everywhere deemed essential to protect the public's interest in an orderly society. Similarly, there are few defendants charged with crime, few indeed, who fail to hire the best lawyers they can get to prepare and present their defenses. That government hires lawyers to prosecute and defendants who have the money hire lawyers to defend are the strongest indications of the widespread belief that lawyers in criminal courts are necessities, not luxuries. The right of one charged with crime to counsel may not be deemed fundamental and essential to fair trials in some countries, but it is in ours. From the very beginning, our state and national constitutions and laws have laid great emphasis on procedural and substantive safeguards designed to assure fair trials before impartial tribunals in which every defendant stands equal before the law. This noble ideal cannot be realized if the poor man charged with crime has to face his accusers without a lawyer to assist him. . . . .
The Court in Betts v. Brady departed from the sound wisdom upon which the Court's holding in Powell v. Alabama rested. Florida, supported by two other States, has asked that Betts v. Brady be left intact. Twenty-two States,

as friends of the Court, argue that Betts was "an anachronism when handed down" and that it should now be overruled. We agree. . . .

Reversed.*

Mr. Justice DOUGLAS [concurred. The opinion is omitted.]

Mr. Justice CLARK, concurring in the result. . . . I must conclude here, as in Kinsella, [361 U.S. 234, chap. 5, p. 417, supra], that the Constitution makes no distinction between capital and noncapital cases. . . .

Mr. Justice HARLAN, concurring.

I agree that Betts v. Brady should be overruled, but consider it entitled to a more respectful burial than has been accorded, at least on the part of those of us who were not on the Court when that case was decided.

I cannot subscribe to the view that Betts v. Brady represented "an abrupt break with its own well-considered precedents." . . . It is evident that [the] limiting facts [in Powell v. Alabama] were not added to the opinion as an afterthought; they were repeatedly emphasized . . . and were clearly regarded as important to the result. Thus when this Court, a decade later, decided Betts v. Brady, it did no more than to admit of the possible existence of special circumstances in noncapital as well as capital trials, while at the same time to insist that such circumstances be shown in order to establish a denial of due process. The right to appointed counsel had been recognized as being considerably broader in federal prosecutions, see Johnson v. Zerbst, 304 U.S. 458, but to have imposed these requirements on the States would indeed have been "an abrupt break" with the almost immediate past. The declaration that the right to appointed counsel in state prosecutions, as established in Powell v. Alabama, was not limited to capital cases was in truth not a departure from, but an extension of, existing precedent.

The principles declared in Powell and in Betts, however, had a troubled journey throughout the years that have followed first the one case and then the other. Even by the time of the Betts decision, dictum in at least one of the Court's opinions had indicated that there was an absolute right to the services of counsel in the trial of state capital cases. . . . In noncapital cases, the "special circumstances" rule has continued to exist in form while its substance has been substantially and steadily eroded. In the first decade after Betts, there were cases in which the Court found special circumstances to be lacking, but usually by a sharply divided vote. However, no such decision has been cited to us, and I have found none, after . . . 1950. At the same time, there have been not a few cases in which special circumstances were found in little or nothing more than the "complexity" of the legal questions presented, although those questions were often of only routine difficulty. The Court has come to recognize, in other words, that the mere existence of a serious criminal charge constituted in itself special circumstances requiring the services of counsel at trial. In truth the Betts v. Brady rule is no longer a reality.

This evolution, however, appears not to have been fully recognized by many state courts, in this instance charged with the front-line responsibility for the enforcement of constitutional rights. To continue a rule which is

---

* On remand, Gideon was retried and, with the assistance of appointed coun- sel, acquitted. See Lewis, Gideon's Trumpet (1964).

honored by this Court only with lip service is not a healthy thing and in the long run will do disservice to the federal system.

The special circumstances rule has been formally abandoned in capital cases, and the time has now come when it should be similarly abandoned in non-capital cases, at least as to offenses which, as the one involved here, carry the possibility of a substantial prison sentence. (Whether the rule should extend to *all* criminal cases need not now be decided.) This indeed does no more than to make explicit something that has long since been foreshadowed in our decisions. . . .*

SOME PROBLEMS OF THE COUNSEL GUARANTEE

1. *Gideon and the overruling of Betts v. Brady.* a. *The reasons for overruling.* Was Gideon compelled by Powell? Was Betts v. Brady "wrong" when decided—an "abrupt break," as Justice Black asserts? Or was the more persuasive justification for the overruling of Betts the experience during the years in which the Betts doctrine prevailed? Or the inconsistent decisions during those years? Should Justice Black have emphasized these justifications? Is his failure to do so attributable to his position on "incorporation" (see his opinions in Adamson and Duncan, chap. 11, pp. 802 and 812, supra), even though he relies on the "fundamental rights" standard in Gideon? See generally Israel, "Gideon v. Wainwright: The 'Art' of Overruling," 1963 Sup.Ct.Rev. 211.

b. *The Betts case.* Did Justice Black state the Betts doctrine adequately? See Betts v. Brady, 316 U.S. 455 (1942). Petitioner claimed that "in every case, whatever the circumstances, one charged with a crime, who is unable to obtain counsel, must be furnished counsel by the state." The Court found that in the great majority of the States "appointment of counsel is not a fundamental right, essential to a fair trial," and concluded that the furnishing of counsel in every criminal case should therefore not be required as a matter of due process. The Court recognized, however, that "want of counsel in a particular case may result in a conviction lacking in such fundamental fairness" as is required by the 14th Amendment. In a dissent, Justice Black, joined by Justices Douglas and Murphy, stated that "the Fourteenth Amendment made the Sixth applicable to the states." For a summary of the standards used in applying the Betts rule, see Uveges v. Pennsylvania, 335 U.S. 437 (1948), Beaney, The Right to Counsel (1955), and Kamisar, "Betts v. Brady Twenty Years Later: The Right to Counsel and Due Process Values," 61 Mich.L.Rev. 219 (1962).

---

* In Pickelsimer v. Wainwright, 375 U. S. 2 (1963), Justice Harlan dissented from Court orders summarily remanding ten Florida cases for reconsideration in light of the principal case. He argued that "the question whether the States are constitutionally required to apply the [Gideon] rule retrospectively" deserves "full-dress consideration." He added: "In the current swift pace of constitutional change, the time has come for the Court to deal with this important and far-reaching subject." The problem of retroactivity and prospectivity of newly announced procedural safeguards, a recurrent one in these materials, has received fuller attention from the Court in the years since. See Linkletter v. Walker and the related materials infra, sec. 4, p. 892. The Court has not yet resolved conflicting views regarding the applicability of Gideon to misdemeanor cases. See the dissents from the denials of certiorari in Winters v. Beck, 385 U.S. 907 (1966), and Heller v. Connecticut, 389 U.S. 902 (1967).

2. *Right to court-appointed counsel in federal prosecutions.* In the federal courts, the right to counsel rests on the specific language of the Sixth Amendment: "In all criminal prosecutions, the accused shall enjoy the right . . . to have the Assistance of Counsel for his defence." That right has been held to include a right to assigned counsel, not just to representation by defendant's retained counsel. In Johnson v. Zerbst, 304 U.S. 458 (1938), the Supreme Court stated that the Sixth Amendment bars a valid conviction and sentence if the accused is not represented by counsel and has not competently and intelligently waived his right. On waiver of counsel, see Carnley v. Cochran, 369 U.S. 506 (1962). Compare the requirement of an affirmative showing that a guilty plea is intelligent and voluntary, because it involves waiver of several rights. Boykin v. Alabama, 395 U.S. 238 (1969), and Halliday v. United States, 394 U.S. 831 (1969). On the right to counsel before and after trial, see notes 3 and 4 below. On the new federal statutory provisions implementing the Sixth Amendment, see the material on the Criminal Justice Act of 1964, p. 854, infra.

3. *The scope of the right: judicial proceedings before and after trial.* For recognition of right to counsel before trial in certain state judicial proceedings, see, e. g., Hamilton v. Alabama, 368 U.S. 52 (1961), where defendant in a capital case was without counsel at the time of arraignment. The Court reversed because in Alabama arraignment "is a critical stage in a criminal proceeding. . . . Available defenses may be irretrievably lost, if not then and there asserted . . .." Moreover, the Court did not "stop to determine whether prejudice resulted" from the lack of counsel, for "the degree of prejudice can never be known." Without counsel, the accused was unable "to plead intelligently." On right to counsel after trial, see Mempa v. Rhay, 389 U.S. 128 (1967), holding counsel required in a deferred sentencing-probation revocation proceeding on the basis of the general principle "that appointment of counsel for an indigent is required at every stage of the criminal proceeding where substantial rights of a criminal accused may be affected."

4. *The scope of the right: police interrogations and lineups.* a. *Interrogations.* In a series of decisions purporting to rest primarily on Sixth Amendment principles and culminating in Escobedo v. Illinois, 378 U.S. 478 (1964), the Court evolved a suspect's right to consult with his lawyer during the course of police interrogation. More recently, the Court's elaborations of guidelines for in-custody questioning—including the right to consult with an attorney—have relied on the Fifth Amendment's self-incrimination privilege rather than the Sixth Amendment as the major constitutional underpinning. See Miranda v. Arizona, 384 U.S. 436 (1966), sec. 2, p. 859, infra. The problem of counsel during pre-indictment questioning can be pursued in connection with that case. For the pre-Escobedo evolution, see Crooker v. California, 357 U.S. 433 (1958), Cicenia v. Lagay, 357 U.S. 504 (1958), and Massiah v. United States, 377 U.S. 201 (1964). [In Escobedo itself, the majority concluded that where "the investigation is no longer a general inquiry into an unsolved crime but has begun to focus on a particular suspect, the suspect has been taken into police custody, the police carry out a process of interrogations that lends itself to eliciting incriminating statements, the suspect has requested and been denied an opportunity to consult with his lawyer, and the police have not effectively warned him of his absolute constitutional right to remain silent, the accused has been denied

"the Assistance of Counsel"   .   .   ., and that no statement elicited by the police during the interrogation may be used against him at a criminal trial."]

b. *Lineups and identification evidence.*   In United States v. Wade, 388 U.S. 218 (1967), and Gilbert v. California, 388 U.S. 263 (1967), the Court held (on the basis of the Sixth rather than the Fifth Amendment) that an accused may not be exhibited to prosecution witnesses before trial in the absence of his counsel, and that identification evidence at the trial must be excluded if it is tainted by such a pretrial confrontation.   In Wade, Justice Brennan's characterization of the lineup as a "critical stage" rested on his analysis of the "potential substantial prejudice" inherent in it and of the ability of counsel to help avoid that prejudice.   Various other preparatory steps in the gathering of prosecution evidence—for example, "systematized or scientific analyses of the accused's fingerprints, blood sample, clothing, hair"—were not "critical stages" entitling accused to the presence of counsel. Pretrial confrontations, on the other hand, presented greater risks, including mistaken identification because of "the degree of suggestion inherent in the manner in which the prosecution presents the suspect to witnesses."   The presence of counsel might avert prejudice "which may not be capable of reconstruction at trial."   Justice White, joined by Justices Harlan and Stewart, insisted that the Court's exclusion of relevant evidence rested on "unsupported assumptions."

Although most earlier right to counsel holdings had been applied retroactively, the Court held that the new extensions of the Sixth Amendment in Wade and Gilbert "should not be made retroactive."   Stovall v. Denno, 388 U.S. 293 (1967).   The Court relied on the Linkletter v. Walker criteria, p. 893 infra;   emphasized that absence of counsel at the confrontation produced injustice with less "certainty and frequency" than lack of counsel at other stages;   and noted the reliance of law enforcement authorities on the "virtually unanimous weight of authority" now invalidated by rulings "not foreshadowed in our cases."   Extensive criticisms of Wade and Gilbert were voiced in Congress during the consideration of the Omnibus Crime Control and Safe Streets Act of 1968, but the only response in the version ultimately adopted lay in the addition of a new § 3502 to 18 U.S.C., providing that the "testimony of a witness that he saw the accused commit or participate in the commission of the crime   .   .   .   shall be admissible in evidence" in any federal criminal prosecution.

5.   *Competence of counsel.*   Does the competence of counsel raise a constitutional issue under the Sixth Amendment?   Powell v. Alabama spoke of the "effective aid" of counsel.   A number of lower federal court decisions indicate that the claim is a permissible one, but is difficult to substantiate.   See the discussion in Mitchell v. United States, 258 F.2d 435 (D.C. Cir.1958):   " 'Effective' assistance of counsel obviously means something other than successful assistance.   [But if the trial lawyer's] conduct is so incompetent as to deprive his client of a trial in any real sense—render the trial a mockery or a farce is one descriptive expression—, the accused must have another trial, or rather, more accurately, is still entitled to a trial." See Waltz, "Inadequacy of Trial Defense Representation as a Ground for Post-Conviction Relief in Criminal Cases," 59 Nw.L.Rev. 289 (1964). Consider the impact of the Griffin principle (in the next group of notes) on this problem.   As to other aspects of "effective" assistance, see Glasser v. United States, 315 U.S. 60 (1942) (defendant's counsel representing other

defendants with conflicting interests); Avery v. Alabama, 308 U.S. 444 (1940) (failure to grant continuance to prepare defense); Reynolds v. Cochran, 365 U.S. 525 (1961) (failure to grant continuance to permit consultation with counsel prior to pleading to second offender charge); cf. Ferguson v. Georgia, 365 U.S. 570 (1961).

6. *Representation by counsel in non-criminal proceedings.* The right to the assistance of counsel in a state administrative investigation was considered in In re Groban, 352 U.S. 330 (1957). After a fire on the premises owned by the appellants, the Ohio State Fire Marshal subpoenaed them to appear as witnesses in an investigation into the causes of the fire. The Fire Marshal refused to permit appellants' counsel to be present at the proceeding. Appellants refused to be sworn and to testify without the presence of their counsel. The Fire Marshal summarily committed appellants to jail until such time as they should be willing to testify. Appellants unsuccessfully sought habeas corpus in the state courts. On appeal, the Supreme Court affirmed. Justice Reed's opinion stated that a criminal defendant's unqualified right to be heard through counsel of his own choice, recognized in Chandler v. Fretag, 348 U.S. 3 (1954), did not apply to a party in an "administrative investigation of incidents damaging to the economy or dangerous to the public." Justice Black, joined by Chief Justice Warren and Justices Douglas and Brennan, dissented, concluding that "it violates the Due Process Clause to compel a person to answer questions at a secret interrogation where he is denied legal assistance and where he is subject to the uncontrolled and invisible exercise of power by government officials." See also Anonymous Nos. 6 and 7 v. Baker, 360 U.S. 287 (1959) (state judicial inquiry into improper conduct by attorneys), and Note, "Representation by Counsel in Administrative Proceedings," 58 Colum.L.Rev. 395 (1958).

EQUALITY, POVERTY, AND THE GRIFFIN v. ILLINOIS PRINCIPLE: THE IMPACT ON COUNSEL FOR INDIGENTS

1. *Equal protection and the Griffin case.* The expanding availability of counsel traced above stemmed from interpretations of the Sixth Amendment and the fair trial aspects of due process. Modern interpretations of the equal protection clause of the 14th Amendment have added yet another source of developments. The germinal principle comes from Griffin v. Illinois, 351 U.S. 12 (1956) (considered more fully in chap. 14, at p. 1019, infra), which involved a claim for a free trial transcript rather than counsel. The indigent petitioners stated that the transcript was necessary for state appellate review of alleged non-federal errors in their conviction.

Justice Black's opinion for four of the five Justices in the majority relied on the equal protection clause as well as due process in sustaining petitioners' claim: "Providing equal justice for poor and rich, weak and powerful alike is an age-old problem. . . . It is true that a State is not required by the Federal Constitution to provide appellate courts or a right to appellate review at all. See, e. g., McKane v. Durston, 153 U.S. 684, 687–688. But that is not to say that a State that does grant appellate review can do so in a way that discriminates against some convicted defendants on account of their poverty." The dissenters insisted: "Illinois is not bound to make the defendants economically equal before its bar of justice. . . . Some [defendants] can afford better lawyers and better investigations of their cases. Some can afford bail, some cannot."

2. *The application to counsel: Douglas v. California.* After the Griffin decision in 1956, there was some speculation that its equality theme rather than the Sixth Amendment right might supply the basis for overruling Betts v. Brady, on the ground that assigned counsel were unavailable to the poor in some cases in which wealthier defendants were permitted to have retained counsel. See, e. g., the concurring opinion by Justice Douglas, joined by Justice Brennan, in McNeal v. Culver, 365 U.S. 109 (1961). But Betts was overruled in 1963 in Gideon v. Wainwright, supra, without an explicit reference to the Griffin case. On the day of the Gideon decision, however, a divided Court, in Douglas v. California, 372 U.S. 353 (1963), found the Griffin principle applicable to appointment of counsel in indigents' appeals. [The case is printed below, chap. 14, p. 1021.]

3. *The scope of the Griffin principle in the criminal process.* How far must (and should) government go in removing the financial disadvantages of the accused? What of the quality of counsel? Investigative aides and expert witnesses? Note the 1964 federal statute, note 4, infra. Bail? Note the 1966 federal law in sec. 6, p. 924. The Court has stated the constitutional requirement in very broad terms. See, e. g., Roberts v. LaVallee, 389 U.S. 40 (1967) (involving a trial request for a transcript of a preliminary hearing): "Our decisions for more than a decade now have made clear that differences in access to the instruments needed to vindicate legal rights, when based upon the financial situation of the defendant, are repugnant to the Constitution."

But the post-Griffin decisions do not go much beyond the transcript and counsel contexts. See, e. g., the application of the principle to filing fees in Burns v. Ohio, 360 U.S. 252 (1959), and Smith v. Bennett, 365 U.S. 708 (1961) (collateral proceedings); and note Lane v. Brown, 372 U.S. 477 (1963) (Public Defender's "unreviewable discretion" regarding free transcripts impermissible), and Long v. District Court, 385 U.S. 192 (1966) (transcript of habeas corpus proceeding). See also the Court's guideline opinions in interpreting the statute (28 U.S.C. § 1915) governing in forma pauperis appeals from federal convictions, e. g., Coppedge v. United States, 369 U.S. 438 (1962). On executive and legislative responses to the problem, see the Report of the Attorney General's Committee on Poverty and the Administration of Federal Criminal Justice (the Allen Committee) (1963), and the materials on the Criminal Justice Act of 1964, which follow, and the Bail Reform Act of 1966, sec. 6, p. 924, below.

4. *The Criminal Justice Act of 1964.* Congress enacted the Criminal Justice Act of 1964, 18 U.S.C. § 3006A, to "promote criminal justice by providing for the representation of defendants who are financially unable to obtain an adequate defense in criminal cases" in federal courts. 18 U.S.C. § 3006A(b) and (c) of the Act state in part: "In every criminal case in which the defendant is charged with a felony or a misdemeanor, other than a petty offense, and appears without counsel, the United States commissioner or the court shall advise the defendant that he has the right to be represented by counsel and that counsel will be appointed to represent him if he is financially unable to obtain counsel. Unless the defendant waives the appointment

of counsel, the United States commissioner or the court, if satisfied after appropriate inquiry that the defendant is financially unable to obtain counsel, shall appoint counsel to represent him. . . . A defendant for whom counsel is appointed shall be represented at every stage of the proceedings from his initial appearance before the United States commissioner or court through appeal."

Though the scope of the Act is broad—from preliminary hearing through appeal—it does not apply to collateral challenges to convictions. The Act carefully avoids the use of the term "indigent": "financial inability" under the Act was intended to be broader than "indigency"; a defendant need not be destitute to have counsel appointed.[1] Moreover, the Act extends beyond attorney's services. Section 3006A(e) states: "Counsel for a defendant who is financially unable to obtain investigative, expert, or other services necessary to an adequate defense in his case may request them in an ex parte application."[2] Section 3006A(a) describes the implementation methods: "Each United States district court . . . shall place in operation throughout the district a plan for furnishing representation for defendants . . . . The provision for counsel under each plan shall conform to one of the following: (1) Representation by private attorneys; (2) Representation by attorneys furnished by a bar association or a legal agency; or (3) Representation according to a plan containing a combination of the foregoing." The Act also prescribes compensation for legal and other services rendered. The recommendations which prompted the Act had included "a full-time or part-time public defender" as an additional option.[3] That option was in the Senate version of the bill, but was eliminated at the insistence of the House of Representatives.

5. *Collateral proceedings and jailhouse lawyers.* The Court has shown increasing concern over the problem of providing adequate assistance to prisoners preparing applications for collateral post-conviction relief—a problem not reached by the 1964 Act or most state provisions. In Hackin v. Arizona, 389 U.S. 143 (1967), for example, Justice Douglas dissented from the dismissal of an appeal challenging a conviction for unauthorized practice of law by an individual who had appeared in a state court habeas corpus proceeding on behalf of an indigent prisoner: "[F]or the majority of indigents, who are not so fortunate to be served by neighborhood legal offices, lay assistance may be the only hope for achieving equal justice at this time." And in Johnson v. Avery, 393 U.S. 483 (1969), the majority gave qualified endorsement to "jailhouse lawyers" as a source of assistance. The Court found invalid, as a restriction on access to federal habeas corpus, a Tennessee prison regulation that barred inmates from assisting other prisoners in preparing "Writs or other legal matters." Justice Fortas recognized that "prison 'writ writers' like petitioner are sometimes a menace to prison discipline and that their petitions are often so unskillful as to be a burden on the courts which receive them." Yet the Tennessee rule effectively prevented poorly

1. See Carter and Hansen, "The Criminal Justice Act of 1964," 36 F.R.D. 67 (1964).

2. Does the Griffin principle compel states to provide similar services? Cf. Bush v. Texas, 372 U.S. 586 (1963).

3. For opposing views on the desirability of public defender systems, compare David, "Institutional and Private Counsel: A Judge's View of the Public Defender System," 45 Minn.L. Rev. 753 (1961), with Dimock, "The Public Defender: A Step Towards a Police State?", 42 A.B.A.J. 219 (1956).

educated prisoners from filing habeas petitions. Accordingly, it could not be enforced "unless and until the State provides some reasonable alternative to assist inmates in the preparation of petitions for post-conviction relief."

In a concurrence, Justice Douglas commented more generally on the increasing complexities of government that made it difficult "for a person to process a claim or even to make a complaint" and stated that there were not enough lawyers "to manage or supervise all of these affairs." He concluded: "The cooperation and help of laymen, as well as of lawyers, is necessary if the right of 'reasonable access to the courts' is to be available to the indigents among us." Justice White's dissent, joined by Justice Black, expressed doubt "that the problem of the indigent convict will be solved by subjecting him to the false hopes, dominance, and inept representation of the average unsupervised jailhouse lawyer." He concluded that "the better course is not in effect to sanction and encourage spontaneous jailhouse lawyer systems but to decide the matter directly in the case of a man who himself needs help and in that case to rule that the State must provide access to the courts by ensuring that those who cannot help themselves have reasonably adequate assistance in preparing their post-conviction papers."

SECTION 2. INTERROGATIONS, CONFESSIONS, AND SELF–INCRIMINATION

Introduction. For three decades, from Brown v. Mississippi, 297 U.S. 278 (1936), to Miranda v. Arizona, 384 U.S. 436 (1966), the Court's scrutiny of the use of confessions in state criminal cases focused on the issue of "voluntariness." The criteria for determining whether a confession was admissible as "voluntary" or barred by due process as "coerced" changed over the years, but the case-by-case process of articulating constitutional requirements for interrogations persisted throughout that period. Miranda was an effort to substitute for that judicial approach a set of detailed, specific, Fifth Amendment-derived guidelines for the questioning of suspects.

Why was the "coercion" focus thought unsatisfactory? Is the Miranda technique more satisfactory? Does it have stronger support in constitutional principle? This section sketches the changing meaning of "coercion" and some sources of dissatisfaction with the old approach; examines the self-incrimination background that was relied on in developing the new approach to interrogations; and concludes with an examination of the Miranda standards.

DETENTION AND INTERROGATION DURING THE "COERCION" ERA

1. *Physical coercion and the Brown case.* The Court's scrutiny of confessions began with Brown v. Mississippi, 297 U.S. 278 (1936), where murder convictions had been based solely on confessions obtained through beatings participated in by deputy sheriffs. Chief Justice Hughes made it clear that the unanimous Court relied not on any self-incrimination privilege

but on the violation of fundamental fairness in setting aside convictions based on these obviously unreliable confessions:

"[T]he question of the right of the State to withdraw the privilege against self-incrimination is not here involved. . . . Compulsion by torture to extort a confession is a different matter [from "compulsion of the processes of justice by which the accused may be called as a witness and required to testify"]. The State is free to regulate the procedure of its courts in accordance with its own conceptions of policy, unless in so doing it 'offends some principle of justice so rooted in the traditions and conscience of our people as to be ranked as fundamental.' . . . Because a State may dispense with a jury trial, it does not follow that it may substitute trial by ordeal. The rack and torture chamber may not be substituted for the witness stand. . . . It would be difficult to conceive of methods more revolting to the sense of justice than those taken to procure the confessions of these petitioners, and the use of the confessions thus obtained as the basis for conviction and sentence was a clear denial of due process."

2. *Psychological coercion.* The frequency of coerced confession claims increased with the recognition in the years after Brown that there could be unconstitutional coercion even in the absence of physical compulsion. Thus, although Lisenba v. California, 314 U.S. 219 (1941), did not find questioning for protracted periods per se a denial of due process, Ashcraft v. Tennessee, 322 U.S. 143 (1944), found coercion where the defendant was kept incommunicado for 36 hours after his arrest, without sleep or rest, and questioned without respite by "relays of officers, experienced investigators, and highly trained lawyers." "There is torture of mind as well as body; the will is as much affected by fear as by force. . . . A confession by which life becomes forfeit must be the expression of free choice." Watts v. Indiana, 338 U.S. 49 (1949).

3. *The uncertain focus of the "coercion" inquiry.* The proliferating psychological coercion cases laid bare a pervasive difficulty: What was the primary Court concern? Actual coercion of the particular accused? The probable coercive impacts of the interrogation methods on the typical accused? The acceptability of those interrogation methods as a matter of "fairness," whether or not they tended to "overcome the will"?

In Haley v. Ohio, 332 U.S. 596 (1948), Justice Frankfurter commented: "But whether a confession of a lad of fifteen is 'voluntary' and as such admissible, or 'coerced' and thus wanting in due process, is not a matter of mathematical determination. Essentially it invites psychological judgment—a psychological judgment that reflects deep, even if inarticulate, feelings of our society." But the opinions increasingly made it clear that the Court's concern was less with the psychological state of mind of the accused than with the decency of the police conduct. Justice Frankfurter's opinion in Rochin v. California, 342 U.S. 165 (1952), emphasized, for example, that interrogation methods, not reliability alone, were pivotal: "Use of involuntary verbal confessions in State criminal trials is constitutionally obnoxious not only because of their unreliability. They are inadmissible under the Due Process Clause even though statements contained in them may be independently established as true. Coerced confessions offend the community's sense of fair play and decency." Confusions generated about this issue by Stein v. New York, 346 U.S. 156 (1953), led to repeated efforts to clarify. See, e. g., Spano v. New York, 360 U.S. 315 (1959), where the Court rejected the state's argument, relying on Stein, that reversal of a conviction was improper because "there is sufficient other evidence in the record from which the jury might have found guilt." * See also Rogers v. Richmond, 365 U.S. 534 (1961), explaining why convictions had been set aside even though independent evidence showed the confessions to be truthful: "Despite such verification, confessions were found to be the product of constitutionally impermissible methods in their inducement." See also the Haynes case, note 6, infra.

4. *The difficulties of the case-by-case method.* Some of the Court's difficulties of assessing voluntariness on a case-by-case basis during this period are reflected in the discussion of the varied indicia of coercive methods in Thomas v. Arizona, 356 U.S. 390 (1958). Local ranchers twice lassoed Thomas on the day of his arrest, but the sheriff immediately removed the ropes. Thomas confessed the next day. Justice Clark's opinion for the Court found no coercion: "Deplorable as these ropings are to the spirit of a civilized administration of justice, the undisputed facts before us do not show that petitioner's oral statement was a product of fear engendered by them. . . . Coercion here is posited solely upon the roping incidents. There is no claim and no evidence of physical beating, as in Brown v. Mississippi, 297 U.S. 278; of continuous relay questioning, as in Watts v. Indiana, 338 U.S. 49; of incommunicado detention, as in Fikes v. Alabama, 352 U.S. 191; or of psychiatric inducement, as in Leyra v. Denno, 347 U.S. 556. Petitioner is neither of tender age, as was the accused in Haley v. Ohio, 332 U.S. 596, nor of subnormal intelligence, as was the defendant in Fikes v. Alabama, supra. Nor, in view of his extensive criminal record, can he be thought an impressionable stranger to the processes of law. . . . No threats were made, no promises offered, no force used, and no intimation of mob action existent. . . . His statement appears to be the spontaneous exclamation of a guilty conscience."

Among other difficulties during the era of the "coercion" standard, note the problems of the scope of Supreme Court review of facts, see Watts v. Indiana, 338 U.S. 49 (1949), and of the allocation of functions between judge and jury in determining voluntariness, see Jackson v. Denno, 378 U.S. 368 (1964). Note also Culombe v. Connecticut, 367 U.S. 568 (1961), where Justice Frankfurter sought to articulate the standards in an opinion of over 60 pages—and reached a result different from that reached by several Justices who concurred with his principles, yet the same as that reached by several other Justices who reasoned along another route.

5. *The McNabb-Mallory rule and federal law enforcement.* Concurrently with its elaborations of the voluntariness standards, the Court was engaged in formulating standards for federal law enforcement that were more rigid than the amorphous due process-coercion criteria applicable to state proceedings. In McNabb v. United States, 318 U.S. 332 (1943), Justice Frankfurter stated: "While the power of this Court to undo convictions in state courts is limited to the enforcement of . . . 'fundamental principles of liberty and justice' . . . , the scope of our reviewing power over convictions brought here from the federal courts is not confined to ascertain-

---

* Not all constitutional errors require reversal, however; some errors, unlike coerced confessions, may be found to be "harmless" in some circumstances. See the discussion in Chapman v. California, 386 U.S. 18 (1967), noted chap. p, p. 128, supra.

ment of constitutional validity. Judicial supervision of the administration of criminal justice in the federal courts implies the duty of establishing and maintaining civilized standards of procedure and evidence. Such standards are not satisfied merely by observance of those minimal historic safeguards for securing trial by reason which are summarized as 'due process of law' and below which we reach what is really trial by force."

In the exercise of this "supervisory power" regarding "the formulation and application of proper standards for the enforcement of the federal criminal law in the federal courts," the Court held in McNabb that "incriminating statements elicited from defendants during unlawful detention" by federal officials are inadmissible in federal courts—even though illegal detention does not by itself make the use of a resulting confession involuntary. The requirement was reiterated in Mallory v. United States, 354 U.S. 449 (1957). The Court now views the McNabb-Mallory exclusionary rule as a judicial sanction for violations of Rule 5(a) of the Federal Rules of Criminal Procedure, promulgated in 1946. Rule 5(a) requires that an arrested person be taken before a committing magistrate "without unnecessary delay." After the decision in McNabb, and again after Mallory, proposals were introduced in Congress to specify that a confession is not inadmissible solely because of delay in taking the defendant before a magistrate.

Note the congressional response to Mallory in Title II of the Omnibus Crime Control and Safe Streets Act of 1968. Under new 18 U.S.C. 3501(c), confessions are not to be excluded "solely because of delay" in arraignment, "if such confession was made or given by such person within six hours immediately following his arrest or other detention."

6. *The movement toward detailed guidelines for state interrogations.* In the years immediately preceding Miranda v. Arizona, infra, the Court moved slowly away from case-by-case analysis and toward increasingly rigid, per se constitutional requirements governing police conduct. See, e. g., Escobedo v. Illinois, 378 U.S. 478 (1964), resting on the right to counsel, p. 850 supra. That tendency was noticeable even in cases purporting to apply the traditional "coercion" criteria.

In Haynes v. Washington, 373 U.S. 503 (1963), for example, the petitioner did not claim that he was physically abused, deprived of food or rest, or subjected to uninterrupted questioning for prolonged periods. Instead, he asserted that, "during the approximately 16-hour period between the time of his arrest and the making and signing of the written confession" of robbery, "he several times asked police to call an attorney and to call his wife." In reversing the conviction, Justice Goldberg's opinion noted that Haynes was not advised of his right to remain silent and to consult with an attorney. Moreover, "the police continued the incommunicado detention" after the first confession, while trying to get another statement. This, the Court found, was "an atmosphere of substantial coercion and inducement," an "inherently coercive context." The Court concluded: "We cannot blind ourselves to what experience unmistakably teaches: that . . . the basic techniques present here . . . are devices adapted and used to extort confessions. . . . We do not mean to suggest that all interrogation . . . is impermissible. The line between proper and permissible police conduct . . . and methods offensive to due process is, at best, a difficult one to draw, particularly in cases such as this where it is necessary to make fine judgments as to the effect of psychologically coercive pressures and inducements on the mind and will of an accused." Justice Clark, joined by Justices Harlan, Stewart, and White dissented: "I find no support in any of the 33 cases decided on the question by the Court" for a conclusion that the confession was involuntary.

What was determinative in Haynes: the use of pressure "techniques," or their actual impact on Haynes' "mind and will"? Was Escobedo a more satisfactory way than Haynes to handle the detention-interrogation problem? Is Miranda v. Arizona? Miranda v. Arizona, which follows, rests on the self-incrimination privilege rather than general due process underpinnings. The background of that Fifth Amendment privilege is sketched in the notes following the Miranda case.

MIRANDA v. ARIZONA
384 U.S. 436, 86 S.Ct. 1602, 16 L.Ed.2d 694 (1966).
Certiorari to the Supreme Court of Arizona.*

Mr. Chief Justice WARREN delivered the opinion of the Court.

The cases before us raise questions which go to the roots of our concepts of American criminal jurisprudence: the restraints society must observe consistent with the Federal Constitution in prosecuting individuals for crime. More specifically, we deal with the admissibility of statements obtained from an individual who is subjected to custodial police interrogation and the necessity for procedures which assure that the individual is accorded his privilege under the Fifth Amendment to the Constitution not to be compelled to incriminate himself.

We dealt with certain phases of this problem recently in Escobedo v. Illinois, 378 U.S. 478 (1964). . . . We granted certiorari in these cases . . . . in order further to explore some facets of the problems, thus exposed, of applying the privilege against self-incrimination to in-custody interrogation, and to give concrete constitutional guidelines for law enforcement agencies and courts to follow.

We start here, as we did in Escobedo, with the premise that our holding is not an innovation in our jurisprudence, but is an application of principles long recognized and applied in other settings. We have undertaken a thorough re-examination of the Escobedo decision and the principles it announced, and we reaffirm it. That case was but an explication of basic rights that are enshrined in our Constitution—that "No person . . . shall be compelled in any criminal case to be a witness against himself," and that "the accused shall . . . have the Assistance of Counsel"—rights which were put in jeopardy in that case through official overbearing. . . .

Our holding will be spelled out with some specificity in the pages which follow but briefly stated it is this: the prosecution may not use statements, whether exculpatory or inculpatory, stemming from custodial interrogation of the defendant unless it demonstrates the use of procedural safe-

* Together with Vignera v. New York [No. 760], on certiorari to the Court of Appeals of New York; Westover v. United States [No. 761], on certiorari to the United States Court of Appeals for the Ninth Circuit; and California v. Stewart [No. 584], on certiorari to the Supreme Court of California. (The docket number of Miranda v. Arizona was 759).

guards effective to secure the privilege against self-incrimination. By custodial interrogation, we mean questioning initiated by law enforcement officers after a person has been taken into custody or otherwise deprived of his freedom of action in any significant way.[1] As for the procedural safeguards to be employed, unless other fully effective means are devised to inform accused persons of their right of silence and to assure a continuous opportunity to exercise it, the following measures are required. Prior to any questioning, the person must be warned that he has a right to remain silent, that any statement he does make may be used as evidence against him, and that he has a right to the presence of an attorney, either retained or appointed. The defendant may waive effectuation of these rights, provided the waiver is made voluntarily, knowingly and intelligently. If, however, he indicates in any manner and at any stage of the process that he wishes to consult with an attorney before speaking there can be no questioning. Likewise, if the individual is alone and indicates in any manner that he does not wish to be interrogated, the police may not question him. The mere fact that he may have answered some questions or volunteered some statements on his own does not deprive him of the right to refrain from answering any further inquiries until he has consulted with an attorney and thereafter consents to be questioned.

I.

The constitutional issue we decide in each of these cases is the admissibility of statements obtained from a defendant questioned while in custody and deprived of his freedom of action. In each, the defendant was questioned by police officers, detectives, or a prosecuting attorney in a room in which he was cut off from the outside world. In none of these cases was the defendant given a full and effective warning of his rights at the outset of the interrogation process. In all the cases, the questioning elicited oral admissions, and in three of them, signed statements as well which were admitted at their trials. They all thus share salient features—incommunicado interrogation of individuals in a police-dominated atmosphere, resulting in self-incriminating statements without full warnings of constitutional rights. [T]he modern practice of in-custody interrogation is psychologically rather than physically oriented. . . . Interrogation still takes place in privacy. Privacy results in secrecy and this in turn results in a gap in our knowledge as to what in fact goes on in the interrogation rooms. A valuable source of information about present police practices, however, may be found in various police manuals and texts which document procedures employed with success in the past, and which recommend various other effective tactics. These texts are used by law enforcement agencies themselves as guides.[2] . . . .

1. This is what we meant in Escobedo when we spoke of an investigation which had focused on an accused. [Footnote by the Court. For an illustration that questioning need not be at the station house to make Miranda applicable, see Orozco v. Texas, 394 U.S. 324 (1969).]

2. The methods described in Inbau and Reid, Criminal Interrogation and Confessions (1962), are a revision and enlargement of material presented in three prior editions of a predecessor text, Lie Detection and Criminal Interrogation (3d ed. 1953). The authors and their associates are officers of the Chicago Police Scientific Crime Detection Laboratory and have had extensive experience in writing, lecturing and speaking to law enforcement authorities over a 20-year period. They say that the techniques portrayed in their manuals reflect their experiences and are the most effective psychological stratagems to

From these representative samples of interrogation techniques, the setting prescribed by the manuals and observed in practice becomes clear. In essence, it is this: To be alone with the subject is essential to prevent distraction and to deprive him of any outside support. The aura of confidence in his guilt undermines his will to resist. He merely confirms the preconceived story the police seek to have him describe. Patience and persistence, at times relentless questioning, are employed. To obtain a confession, the interrogator must "patiently maneuver himself or his quarry into a position from which the desired object may be obtained." When normal procedures fail to produce the needed result, the police may resort to deceptive stratagems such as giving false legal advice. It is important to keep the subject off balance, for example, by trading on his insecurity about himself or his surroundings. The police then persuade, trick, or cajole him out of exercising his constitutional rights.

Even without employing brutality, the "third degree" or the specific stratagems described above, the very fact of custodial interrogation exacts a heavy toll on individual liberty and trades on the weakness of individuals. . . . In the cases before us today, given this background, we concern ourselves primarily with this interrogation atmosphere and the evils it can bring. . . .

In these cases, we might not find the defendants' statements to have been involuntary in traditional terms. Our concern for adequate safeguards to protect precious Fifth Amendment rights is, of course, not lessened in the slightest. In each of the cases, the defendant was thrust into an unfamiliar atmosphere and run through menacing police interrogation procedures. . . . To be sure, the records do not evince overt physical coercion or patent psychological ploys. The fact remains that in none of these cases did the officers undertake to afford appropriate safeguards at the outset of the interrogation to insure that the statements were truly the product of free choice.

. . . The current practice of incommunicado interrogation is at odds with one of our Nation's most cherished principles—that the individual may not be compelled to incriminate himself. Unless adequate protective devices are employed to dispel the compulsion inherent in custodial surroundings, no statement obtained from the defendant can truly be the product of his free choice. . . .

II.

We sometimes forget how long it has taken to establish the privilege against self-incrimination, the sources from which it came and the fervor with which it was defended. [T]he privilege is fulfilled only when the person is guaranteed the right "to remain silent unless he chooses to speak in the unfettered exercise of his own will." Malloy v. Hogan, 378 U.S. 1, 8 (1964) [in the notes following this case].

employ during interrogations. Similarly, the techniques described in O'Hara, Fundamentals of Criminal Investigation (1959), were gleaned from long service as observer, lecturer in police science, and work as a federal criminal investigator. All these texts have had rather extensive use among law enforcement agencies and among students of police science, with total sales and circulation of over 44,000. [Footnote by the Court.]

The question in these cases is whether the privilege is fully applicable during a period of custodial interrogation. . . . We are satisfied that all the principles embodied in the privilege apply to informal compulsion exerted by law-enforcement officers during in-custody questioning. . . . As a practical matter, the compulsion to speak in the isolated setting of the police station may well be greater than in courts or other official investigations, where there are often impartial observers to guard against intimidation or trickery. . . .

. . . In addition to the expansive historical development of the privilege and the sound policies which have nurtured its evolution, judicial precedent . . . clearly establishes its application to incommunicado interrogation. [T]he reasoning in [Malloy v. Hogan, 378 U.S. 1 (1964)] made clear what had already become apparent—that the substantive and procedural safeguards surrounding admissibility of confessions in state cases had become exceedingly exacting, reflecting all the policies embedded in the privilege . . . . . . The voluntariness doctrine in the state cases, as Malloy indicates, encompasses all interrogation practices which are likely to exert such pressure upon an individual as to disable him from making a free and rational choice. The implications of this proposition were elaborated in our decision in Escobedo . . . ., decided one week after Malloy applied the privilege to the States.

Our holding there stressed the fact that the police had not advised the defendant of his constitutional privilege to remain silent at the outset of the interrogation . . . .. This was no isolated factor, but an essential ingredient in our decision. The entire thrust of police interrogation there, as in all the cases today, was to put the defendant in such an emotional state as to impair his capacity for rational judgment. . . . . A different phase of the Escobedo decision was significant in its attention to the absence of counsel during the questioning. . . . The denial of the defendant's request for his attorney . . . undermined his ability to exercise the privilege—to remain silent if he chose or to speak without any intimidation, blatant or subtle.
. . .

III.

Today, then, there can be no doubt that the Fifth Amendment privilege is available outside of criminal court proceedings and serves to protect persons in all settings in which their freedom of action is curtailed from being compelled to incriminate themselves. We have concluded that without proper safeguards the process of in-custody interrogation of persons suspected or accused of crime contains inherently compelling pressures which work to undermine the individual's will to resist and to compel him to speak where he would not otherwise do so freely. In order to combat these pressures and to permit a full opportunity to exercise the privilege against self-incrimination, the accused must be adequately and effectively apprised of his rights and the exercise of those rights must be fully honored.

It is impossible for us to foresee the potential alternatives for protecting the privilege which might be devised by Congress or the States in the exercise of their creative rule-making capacities. Therefore we cannot say that the Constitution necessarily requires adherence to any particular solution for the inherent compulsions of the interrogation process as it is presently conducted. Our decision in no way creates a constitutional straitjacket which will handicap sound efforts at reform nor is it intended to have this effect. We encourage Congress and the States to continue their laudable search for increasingly effective ways of protecting the rights of the individual while promoting efficient enforcement of our criminal laws. However, unless we are shown other procedures which are at least as effective in apprising accused persons of their right of silence and in assuring a continuous opportunity to exercise it, the following safeguards must be observed.

At the outset, if a person in custody is to be subjected to interrogation, he must first be informed in clear and unequivocal terms that he has the right to remain silent. [W]e will not pause to inquire in individual cases whether the defendant was aware of his rights without a warning being given. . . .

The warning of the right to remain silent must be accompanied by the explanation that anything said can and will be used against the individual in court. This warning is needed in order to make him aware not only of the privilege, but also of the consequences of forgoing it. . . . Moreover, this warning may serve to make the individual more acutely aware that he is faced with a phase of the adversary system—that he is not in the presence of persons acting solely in his interest.

[T]he right to have counsel present at the interrogation is indispensable to the protection of the Fifth Amendment privilege under the system we delineate today. Our aim is to assure that the individual's right to choose between silence and speech remains unfettered throughout the interrogation process. A once-stated warning, delivered by those who will conduct the interrogation, cannot itself suffice to that end among those who most require knowledge of their rights. [T]he need for counsel to protect the Fifth Amendment privilege comprehends not merely a right to consult with counsel prior to questioning, but also to have counsel present during any questioning if the defendant so desires. . . .

An individual need not make a pre-interrogation request for a lawyer. While such request affirmatively secures his right to have one, his failure to ask for a lawyer does not constitute a waiver. No effective waiver of the right to counsel during interrogation can be recognized unless specifically made after the warnings we here delineate have been given. The accused who does not know his rights and therefore does not make a request may be the person who most needs counsel. . . .

In order fully to apprise a person interrogated of the extent of his rights under this system, it is necessary to warn him not only that he has the right to consult with an attorney, but also that if he is indigent a lawyer will be appointed to represent him. Without this additional warning, the admonition of the right to consult with counsel would often be understood as meaning only that he can consult with a lawyer if he has one or has the funds to obtain one. . . .

Once warnings have been given, the subsequent procedure is clear. If the individual indicates in any manner, at any time prior to or during questioning, that he wishes to remain silent, the interrogation must cease. . . . If the individual states that he wants an attorney, the interrogation must cease until an attorney is present. . . .

This does not mean, as some have suggested, that each police station must have a "station house lawyer" present at all times to advise prisoners. It does mean, however, that if police propose to interrogate a person they must make known to him that he is entitled to a lawyer and that if he cannot afford one, a lawyer will be provided for him prior to any interrogation. If authorities conclude that they will not provide counsel during a reasonable period of time in which investigation in the field is carried out, they may do so without violating the person's Fifth Amendment privilege so long as they do not question him during that time.

If the interrogation continues without the presence of an attorney and a statement is taken, a heavy burden rests on the Government to demonstrate that the defendant knowingly and intelligently waived his privilege against self-incrimination and his right to retained or appointed counsel. . . . An express statement that the individual is willing to make a statement and does not want an attorney followed closely by a statement could constitute a waiver. But a valid waiver will not be presumed simply from the silence of the accused after warnings are given or simply from the fact that a confession was in fact eventually obtained. . . . Moreover, where in-custody interrogation is involved, there is no room for the contention that the privilege is waived if the individual answers some questions or gives some information on his own prior to invoking his right to remain silent when interrogated. . . .

Our decision is not intended to hamper the traditional function of police officers in investigating crime. . . . When an individual is in custody on probable cause, the police may, of course, seek out evidence in the field to be used at trial against him. Such investigation may include inquiry of persons not under restraint. General on-the-scene questioning as to facts surrounding a crime or other general questioning of citizens in the fact-finding process is not affected by our holding. It is an act of responsible citizenship for individuals to give whatever information they may have to aid in law enforcement. In such situations the compelling atmosphere inherent in the process of in-custody interrogation is not necessarily present.

In dealing with statements obtained through interrogation, we do not purport to find all confessions inadmissible. Confessions remain a proper element in law enforcement. . . . The fundamental import of the privilege while an individual is in custody is not whether he is allowed to talk to the police without the benefit of warnings and counsel, but whether he can be interrogated. There is no requirement that police stop a person who enters a police station and states that he wishes to confess to a crime, or a person who calls the police to offer a confession or any other statement he desires to make. Volunteered statements of any kind are not barred by the Fifth Amendment and their admissibility is not affected by our holding today.

To summarize, we hold that when an individual is taken into custody or otherwise deprived of his freedom by the authorities and is subjected to questioning, the privilege against self-incrimination is jeopardized. Procedural safeguards must be employed to protect the privilege, and unless other fully effective means are adopted to notify the person of his right of silence and to assure that the exercise of the right will be scrupulously honored, the following measures are required. He must be warned prior to any questioning that he has the right to remain silent, that anything he says can be used against him in a court of law, that he has the right to the presence of an attorney, and that if he cannot afford an attorney one will be appointed for him prior to any questioning if he so desires. Opportunity to exercise these rights must be afforded to him throughout the interrogation. After such warnings have been given, and such opportunity afforded him, the individual may knowingly and intelligently waive these rights and agree to answer questions or make a statement. But unless and until such warnings and waiver are demonstrated by the prosecution at trial, no evidence obtained as a result of interrogation can be used against him.[3]

IV. . . . .

If the individual desires to exercise his privilege, he has the right to do so. This is not for the authorities to decide. An attorney may advise his client not to talk to police until he has had an opportunity to investigate the case, or he may wish to be present with his client during any police questioning. In doing so an attorney is merely exercising the good professional judgment he has been taught. This is not cause for considering the attorney a menace to law enforcement. . . . .

It is . . . urged upon us that we withhold decision on this issue, until state legislative bodies and advisory groups have had an opportunity to deal with these problems by rule making. . . . Congress and the States are free to develop their own safeguards for the privilege, so long as they are fully as effective as those described above in informing accused persons of their right of silence and in affording a continuous opportunity to exercise it. In any event, however, the issues presented are of constitutional dimensions and must be determined by the courts. . . . Where rights secured by the Constitution are involved, there can be no rule making or legislation which would abrogate them.

V.

Because of the nature of the problem and because of its recurrent significance in numerous cases, we have to this point discussed the relationship of the Fifth Amendment privilege to police interrogation without specific concentration on the facts of the cases before us. We turn now to these facts to consider the application to these cases of the constitutional principles discussed above. In each instance, we have concluded that statements were obtained from the defendant under circumstances that did not meet constitutional standards for protection of the privilege. . . .

Therefore, in accordance with the foregoing, the judgments of the Supreme Court of Arizona in No. 759, of the New York Court of Appeals in No. 760, and of the Court of Appeals for the Ninth Circuit in No. 761 are reversed. The judgment of the Supreme Court of California in No. 584 is affirmed. . . . .*

3. In accordance with our holdings today and in Escobedo v. Illinois, 378 U.S. 478, 492, Crooker v. California, 357 U.S. 433 (1958) and Cicenia v. Lagay, 357 U.S. 504 (1958) are not to be followed. [Footnote by the Court.]

* Johnson v. New Jersey, 384 U.S. 719 (1966), limited Miranda (as well as Escobedo) to almost purely prospective operation. Chief Justice Warren's majority decision held that Miranda "applies only to cases in which the trial began after the date of our decision one week ago"—i. e., June 13, 1966. The Court applied the general criteria of earlier nonretroactivity rulings (e. g., Linkletter v. Walker) but, unlike those cases, did not even apply the new constitutional standards to cases still pending on direct appeal. See the materials on Linkletter and prospectivity, sec. 4, p. 892, infra. In Jenkins v. Delaware, 395 U.S. 213 (1969), moreover, the

Mr. Justice CLARK, dissenting in Nos. 759, 760, and 761, and concurring in result in No. 584.

. . . I am unable to join the majority because its opinion goes too far on too little, while my dissenting brethren do not go quite far enough. . . . I would consider in each case whether the police officer prior to custodial interrogation added the warning that the suspect might have counsel present at the interrogation and, further, that a court would appoint one at his request if he was too poor to employ counsel. . . .

Mr. Justice HARLAN, whom Mr. Justice STEWART and Mr. Justice WHITE join, dissenting.

I. Introduction. . . .

. . . The new rules are not designed to guard against police brutality or other unmistakably banned forms of coercion. Those who use third-degree tactics and deny them in court are equally able and destined to lie as skillfully about warnings and waivers. Rather, the thrust of the new rules is to negate all pressures, to reinforce the nervous or ignorant suspect, and ultimately to discourage any confession at all. The aim in short is toward "voluntariness" in a utopian sense, or to view it from a different angle, voluntariness with a vengeance.

To incorporate this notion into the Constitution requires a strained reading of history and precedent and a disregard of the very pragmatic concerns that alone may on occasion justify such strains. I believe that reasoned examination will show that the Due Process Clauses provide an adequate tool for coping with confessions and that, even if the Fifth Amendment privilege against self-incrimination be invoked, its precedents taken as a whole do not sustain the present rules. Viewed as a choice based on pure policy, these new rules prove to be a highly debatable if not one-sided appraisal of the competing interests, imposed over widespread objection, at the very time when judicial restraint is most called for by the circumstances.

II. Constitutional Premises. . . .

I turn now to the Court's asserted reliance on the Fifth Amendment, an approach which I frankly regard as a *trompe l'oeil*. The Court's opinion in my view reveals no adequate basis for extending the Fifth Amendment's privilege against self-incrimination to the police station. Far more important, it fails to show that the Court's new rules are well supported, let alone compelled, by Fifth Amendment precedents. Instead, the new rules actually derive from quotation and analogy drawn from precedents under the Sixth Amendment, which should properly have no bearing on police interrogation.

Court held that Miranda did not apply to a retrial after June 13, 1966, since petitioner's original trial had begun before that cut-off point.

Because of the prospective-only effect of Miranda, cases arising prior to the cut-off date are handled under the old "voluntariness" standards. See, e. g., Davis v. North Carolina, 384 U.S. 737 (1966), decided a week after Miranda, setting aside a 1959 murder conviction on coerced confession grounds; and note Kamisar, "A Dissent from the Miranda Dissents: Some Comments on the 'New' Fifth Amendment and the 'Old' Voluntariness Test," 65 Mich.L.Rev. 59 (1966).

The Court's opening contention, that the Fifth Amendment governs police station confessions, is perhaps not an impermissible extension of the law but it has little to commend itself in the present circumstances. Historically, the privilege against self-incrimination did not bear at all on the use of extra-legal confessions, for which distinct standards evolved; indeed, "the *history* of the two principles is wide apart, differing by one hundred years in origin, and derived through separate lines of precedents . . . ." 8 Wigmore, Evidence § 2266, at 401 (McNaughton rev. 1961). Practice under the two doctrines has also differed in a number of important respects. Even those who would readily enlarge the privilege must concede some linguistic difficulties since the Fifth Amendment in terms proscribes only compelling any person "in any criminal case to be a witness against himself." . . .

Though weighty, I do not say these points and similar ones are conclusive, for as the Court reiterates the privilege embodies basic principles always capable of expansion. Certainly the privilege does represent a protective concern for the accused and an emphasis upon accusatorial rather than inquisitorial values in law enforcement . . . . Accusatorial values, however, have openly been absorbed into the due process standard governing confessions . . . . Since extension of the general principle has already occurred, to insist that the privilege applies as such serves only to carry over inapposite historical details and engaging rhetoric and to obscure the policy choices to be made in regulating confessions.

Having decided that the Fifth Amendment privilege does apply in the police station, the Court reveals that the privilege imposes more exacting restrictions than does the Fourteenth Amendment's voluntariness test. It then emerges from a discussion of Escobedo that the Fifth Amendment requires for an admissible confession that it be given by one distinctly aware of his right not to speak and shielded from "the compelling atmosphere" of interrogation. . . . From these key premises, the Court finally develops the safeguards of warning, counsel, and so forth. I do not believe these premises are sustained by precedents under the Fifth Amendment.[1]

The more important premise is that pressure on the suspect must be eliminated though it be only the subtle influence of the atmosphere and surroundings. The Fifth Amendment, however, has never been thought to forbid *all* pressure to incriminate one's self in the situations covered by it. . . .

A closing word must be said about the Assistance of Counsel Clause of the Sixth Amendment, which is never expressly relied on by the Court but whose judicial precedents turn out to be linchpins of the confession rules announced today. . . . All these cases imparting glosses to the Sixth Amendment concerned counsel at trial or on appeal. While the Court finds no pertinent difference between judicial proceedings and police interrogation, I believe the differences are so vast as to disqualify wholly the Sixth Amendment precedents as suitable analogies in the present cases.[2]

---

1. I lay aside Escobedo itself; it contains no reasoning or even general conclusions addressed to the Fifth Amendment and indeed its citation in this regard seems surprising in view of Escobedo's primary reliance on the Sixth Amendment. [Footnote by Justice Harlan.]

2. Since the Court conspicuously does not assert that the Sixth Amendment itself warrants its new police-inter-

The only attempt in this Court to carry the right to counsel into the station house occurred in Escobedo, the Court repeating several times that that stage was no less "critical" than trial itself. . . . The sound reason why this right is so freely extended for a criminal trial is the severe injustice risked by confronting an untrained defendant with a range of technical points of law, evidence, and tactics familiar to the prosecutor but not to himself. This danger shrinks markedly in the police station where indeed the lawyer in fulfilling his professional responsibilities of necessity may become an obstacle to truthfinding. . . . The Court's summary citation of the Sixth Amendment cases here seems to me best described as "the domino method of constitutional adjudication . . . wherein every explanatory statement in a previous opinion is made the basis for extension to a wholly different situation." Friendly, supra, n. [2], at 950.

III. POLICY CONSIDERATIONS.

Examined as an expression of public policy, the Court's new regime proves so dubious that there can be no due compensation for its weakness in constitutional law. . . .

The Court's new rules aim to offset [the] minor pressures and disadvantages intrinsic to any kind of police interrogation. The rules do not serve due process interests in preventing blatant coercion since, as I noted earlier, they do nothing to contain the policeman who is prepared to lie from the start. The rules work for reliability in confessions almost only in the Pickwickian sense that they can prevent some from being given at all. In short, the benefit of this new regime is simply to lessen or wipe out the inherent compulsion and inequalities to which the Court devotes some nine pages of description. . . .

What the Court largely ignores is that its rules impair, if they will not eventually serve wholly to frustrate, an instrument of law enforcement that has long and quite reasonably been thought worth the price paid for it. There can be little doubt that the Court's new code would markedly decrease the number of confessions. . . .

How much harm this decision will inflict on law enforcement cannot fairly be predicted with accuracy. Evidence on the role of confessions is notoriously incomplete . . . . We do know that some crimes cannot be solved without confessions, that ample expert testimony attests to their importance in crime control, and that the Court is taking a real risk with society's welfare in imposing its new regime on the country. The social costs of crime are too great to call the new rules anything but a hazardous experimentation. While passing over the costs and risks of its experiment, the Court portrays the evils of normal police questioning in terms which I think are exaggerated. . . . It is also instructive to compare the attitude in this case of those responsible for law enforcement with the official views that existed when the Court undertook three major revisions of prosecutorial practice prior to this case, Johnson v. Zerbst, 304 U.S. 458, Mapp v. Ohio, 367 U.S. 643, and Gideon v. Wainwright, 372 U.S. 335. . . . By contrast, in this case new restrictions on police questioning have been opposed

rogation rules, there is no reason now to draw out the extremely powerful historical and precedential evidence that the Amendment will bear no such meaning. See generally Friendly, The Bill of Rights as a Code of Criminal Procedure, 53 Calif.L.Rev. 929, 943–948 (1965). [Footnote by Justice Harlan.]

by the United States and in an amicus brief signed by 27 States and Commonwealths, not including the three other States who are parties. No State in the country has urged this Court to impose the newly announced rules, nor has any State chosen to go nearly so far on its own. . . .

In closing this necessarily truncated discussion of policy considerations attending the new confession rules, some reference must be made to their ironic untimeliness. There is now in progress in this country a massive re-examination of criminal law enforcement procedures on a scale never before witnessed. . . . Despite the Court's disclaimer, the practical effect of the decision made today must inevitably be to handicap seriously sound efforts at reform, not least by removing options necessary to a just compromise of competing interests. Of course legislative reform is rarely speedy or unanimous . . . . But the legislative reforms when they came would have the vast advantage of empirical data and comprehensive study, they would allow experimentation and use of solutions not open to the courts, and they would restore the initiative in criminal law reform to those forums where it truly belongs. . . .

Mr. Justice WHITE, with whom Mr. Justice HARLAN and Mr. Justice STEWART join, dissenting. . . .

That the Court's holding today is neither compelled nor even strongly suggested by the language of the Fifth Amendment, is at odds with American and English legal history, and involves a departure from a long line of precedent does not prove either that the Court has exceeded its powers or that the Court is wrong or unwise in its present reinterpretation of the Fifth Amendment. It does, however, underscore the obvious—that the Court has not discovered or found the law in making today's decision, nor has it derived it from some irrefutable sources; what it has done is to make new law and new public policy in much the same way that it has in the course of interpreting other great clauses of the Constitution. This is what the Court historically has done. Indeed, it is what it must do and will continue to do until and unless there is some fundamental change in the constitutional distribution of governmental powers.

But if the Court is here and now to announce new and fundamental policy to govern certain aspects of our affairs, it is wholly legitimate to examine the mode of this or any other constitutional decision in this Court and to inquire into the advisability of its end product in terms of the long-range interest of the country. At the very least the Court's text and reasoning should withstand analysis and be a fair exposition of the constitutional provision which its opinion interprets. Decisions like these cannot rest alone on syllogism, metaphysics or some ill-defined notions of natural justice, although each will perhaps play its part. In proceeding to such constructions as it now announces, the Court should also duly consider all the factors and interests bearing upon the cases, at least insofar as the relevant materials are available; and if the necessary considerations are not treated in the record or obtainable from some other reliable source, the Court should not proceed to formulate fundamental policies based on speculation alone. . . . .

First, we may inquire what are the textual and factual bases of this new fundamental rule. To reach the result announced on the grounds it does, the Court must stay within the confines of the Fifth Amendment, which forbids self-incrimination only if *compelled*. Hence the core of the Court's opinion is that because of the "compulsion inherent in custodial surroundings [certain statements cannot] truly be the product of free choice." [T]he Court concedes that it cannot truly know what occurs during custodial questioning, because of the innate secrecy of such proceedings. . . . Judged by any of the standards for empirical investigation utilized in the social sciences the factual basis for the Court's premise is patently inadequate. . . .

If the rule announced today were truly based on a conclusion that all confessions resulting from custodial interrogation are coerced, then it would simply have no rational foundation. Compare Tot v. United States, 319 U.S. 463, 466 . . . . Even if one were to postulate that the Court's concern is not that all confessions induced by police interrogation are coerced but rather that some such confessions are coerced and present judicial procedures are believed to the inadequate to identify the confessions that are coerced and those that are not, it would still not be essential to impose the rule that the Court has now fashioned. Transcripts or observers could be required, specific time limits, tailored to fit the cause, could be imposed, or other devices could be utilized to reduce the chances that otherwise indiscernible coercion will produce an inadmissible confession.

On the other hand, even if one assumed that there was an adequate factual basis for the conclusion that all confessions obtained during in-custody interrogation are the product of compulsion, the rule propounded by the Court would still be irrational, for, apparently, it is only if the accused is also warned of his right to counsel and waives both that right and the right against self-incrimination that the inherent compulsiveness of interrogation disappears. But if the defendant may not answer without a warning a question such as "Where were you last night?" without having his answer be a compelled one, how can the Court ever accept his negative answer to the question of whether he wants to consult his retained counsel or counsel whom the court will appoint? And why if counsel is present and the accused nevertheless confesses, or counsel tells the accused to tell the truth, and that is what the accused does, is the situation any less coercive insofar as the accused is concerned? . . .

All of this makes very little sense in terms of the compulsion which the Fifth Amendment proscribes. That amendment deals with compelling the accused himself. It is his free will that is involved. Confessions and incriminating admissions, as such, are not forbidden evidence; only those which are compelled are banned. I doubt that the Court observes these distinctions today. [T]he Court not only prevents the use of compelled confessions but for all practical purposes forbids interrogation except in the presence of counsel. That is, instead of confining itself to protection of the right against compelled self-incrimination the Court has created a limited Fifth Amendment right to counsel. . . .

Criticism of the Court's opinion, however, cannot stop at a demonstration that the factual and textual bases for the rule it propounds are, at best, less than compelling. Equally relevant is an assessment of the rule's consequences measured against community values. . . .

The obvious underpinning of the Court's decision is a deep-seated distrust of all confessions. . . . This is the not so subtle overtone of the opinion—that it is inherently wrong for the police to gather evidence from the accused himself. And this is precisely the **nub** of this dissent. I see nothing wrong or immoral, and certainly nothing unconstitutional, with the police asking a suspect whom they have reasonable cause to arrest whether or not he killed his wife or with confronting him with the evidence on which the arrest was based, at least where he has been plainly advised that he may remain completely silent . . . .

The most basic function of any government is to provide for the security of the individual and of his property. . . . These ends of society are served by the criminal laws which for the most part are aimed at the prevention of crime. Without the reasonably effective performance of the task of preventing private violence and retaliation, it is idle to talk about human dignity and civilized values. . . .

In some unknown number of cases the Court's rule will return a killer, a rapist or other criminal to the streets and to the environment which produced him, to repeat his crime whenever it pleases him. As a consequence, there will not be a gain, but a loss, in human dignity. The real concern is not the unfortunate consequences of this new decision on the criminal law as an abstract, disembodied series of authoritative proscriptions, but the impact on those who rely on the public authority for protection and who without it can only engage in violent self-help with guns, knives and the help of their neighbors similarly inclined. There is, of course, a saving factor: the next victims are uncertain, unnamed and unrepresented in this case. . . .

THE CONGRESSIONAL RESPONSE TO MIRANDA: TITLE II OF THE 1968 CRIME CONTROL ACT

The widespread criticism of the Miranda decision bore fruit in the congressional effort at partial reinstatement of the voluntariness approach in Title II of the Omnibus Crime Control and Safe Streets Act of 1968. That Title adds a new Section 3501 to 18 U.S.C., stating that in federal prosecutions a confession "shall be admissible in evidence if it is voluntarily given." Note especially § 3501(b): "(b) The trial judge in determining the issue of voluntariness shall take into consideration all the circumstances surrounding the giving of the confession, including (1) the time elapsing between arrest and arraignment of the defendant making the confession, if it was made after arrest and before arraignment, (2) whether such defendant knew the nature of the offense with which he was charged or of which he was suspected at the time of making the confession, (3) whether or not such defendant was advised or knew that he was not required to make any statement and that any such statement could be used against him, (4) whether or not such defendant had been advised prior to questioning of his right to the assistance of counsel; and (5) whether or not such defendant was without the assistance of counsel when questioned and when giving such confession. The presence or absence of any of the above-mentioned factors to be taken into consideration by the judge need not be conclusive on the issue of voluntariness of the confession."

Is the statute constitutional? The law applies only to federal prosecutions. Could Congress make these standards applicable to state trials as well, drawing on its power to "enforce" the due process clause under § 5 of the 14th Amendment? Would such a law be justifiable under the rationale regarding § 5 set forth in the Morgan case in chap. 6 [Katzenbach v. Morgan,

384 U.S. 641 (1966), p. 545, supra]? See Burt, "Miranda and Title II: A Morganatic Marriage," 1969 Sup.Ct.Rev. 81, on the implications of the Morgan suggestion that Congress has some independent authority to interpret the 14th Amendment, and recall the notes at p. 552, supra.

The Senate Judiciary Committee's version of the 1968 law (see Sen.Rep. No. 1097, 90th Cong., 2d Sess.) had also included provisions directed at the effect of Miranda in state courts. The Committee version curtailed the Supreme Court's appellate jurisdiction in state confession cases (see chap. 1, p. 567, supra) and restricted federal habeas corpus jurisdiction regarding applicants in state custody, but these provisions were eliminated on the floor of the Senate. Note President Johnson's comments in signing the bill: "Title II of the legislation deals with certain rules of evidence only in Federal criminal trials .   . .. The provisions of Title II, vague and ambiguous as they are, can, I am advised by the Attorney General, be interpreted in harmony with the Constitution, and Federal practices in this field will continue to conform to the Constitution." Note also the report that the Justice Department under Attorney General Mitchell was prepared to argue that a confession obtained without Miranda warnings was admissible "if a Federal official inadvertently fails to give a full warning," in contrast with former Attorney General Clark's instructions that federal prosecutors adhere to Miranda requirements despite Title II. See Burt, supra, 1969 Sup.Ct.Rev. 81, at 130, n. 170.

THE SCOPE OF THE FIFTH AMENDMENT PRIVILEGE AGAINST SELF–INCRIMINATION

1. *Where asserted?* Although the Fifth Amendment states that no person "shall be compelled *in any criminal case* to be a witness against himself," the privilege may be asserted in proceedings other than criminal trials. The privilege applies "alike to civil and criminal proceedings, wherever the answer might tend to subject to criminal responsibility him who gives it." McCarthy v. Arndstein, 266 U.S. 34, 40 (1924) (bankruptcy proceeding). Thus, it may be invoked in grand jury proceedings, Blau v. United States, 340 U.S. 159 (1950), and in congressional investigations, Quinn v. United States, 349 U.S. 155 (1955).

2. *How claimed?* The method of claiming the privilege was discussed in Quinn v. United States, supra. The Court reversed convictions for contempt of congress for refusing to answer questions before congressional committees; it found an adequate invocation of the privilege where the refusal to answer was based on "the first and fifth amendments," as well as "the first amendment to the Constitution, supplemented by the fifth amendment." Chief Justice Warren's opinion stated that the privilege must not be applied "narrowly or begrudgingly" and that a claim of the privilege "does not require any special combination of words."

3. *Risk of incrimination.* "The privilege afforded not only extends to answers that would in themselves support a conviction .   .   . but likewise embraces those which would furnish a link in the chain of evidence needed to prosecute the claimant .   .   .. But this protection must be confined to instances where the witness has reasonable cause to apprehend danger from a direct answer. .   .   . The witness is not exonerated from

answering merely because he declares that in so doing he would incriminate himself—his say-so does not of itself establish the hazard of incrimination. It is for the court to say whether his silence is justified . . .. However, if the witness . . . were required to prove the hazard in the sense in which a claim is usually required to be established in court, he would be compelled to surrender the very protection which the privilege is designed to guarantee. To sustain the privilege, it need only be evident from the implications of the question, in the setting in which it is asked, that a responsive answer to the question or an explanation of why it cannot be answered might be dangerous because injurious disclosure could result." Hoffman v. United States, 341 U.S. 479 (1951). See also Blau v. United States, 340 U.S. 159 (1950).

4. *The "personal" nature of the privilege and waiver.* In Rogers v. United States, 340 U.S. 367 (1951), the Court emphasized that a refusal to answer cannot be justified by a desire to protect others from punishment, much less to protect another from interrogation by a grand jury. On the availability of the privilege to a custodian of documents, compare United States v. White, 322 U.S. 694 (1944), with Curcio v. United States, 354 U.S. 118 (1957).

On waiver, see the Rogers case, supra, where the Court found a waiver when petitioner answered grand jury questions about her Communist Party connections but refused, on Fifth Amendment grounds, to identify the person to whom she had given certain Party records: "Where criminating facts have been voluntarily revealed, the privilege cannot be invoked to avoid disclosure of the details." Compare the Court's subsequent attitude, in Emspak v. United States, 349 U.S. 190 (1955), where the Court refused to interpret a response to a congressional committee as "sufficiently unambiguous to warrant finding a waiver here. To conclude otherwise would be to violate this Court's own oft-repeated admonition that the courts 'must indulge every reasonable presumption against waiver of fundamental constitutional rights.' " [1]

5. *"Testimonial" or "communicative" vs. "physical" evidence.* a. In rejecting constitutional challenges to compulsory blood tests in Schmerber v. California, 384 U.S. 757 (1966), the Court considered at length "whether the withdrawal of the blood and admission in evidence of the analysis" at a drunken driving trial violated petitioner's self-incrimination privilege. The Court concluded: "We hold that the privilege protects an accused only from being compelled to testify against himself, or otherwise provide the State with evidence of a testimonial or communicative nature, and that the withdrawal of blood and use of the analysis in question in this case did not involve compulsion to these ends." Justice Brennan's opinion for a majority of five stated that the privilege had "never been given the full scope which the values it helps to protect suggest. . . . The distinction which has emerged, often expressed in different ways, is that the privilege is a bar against compelling 'communications' or 'testimony,' but that compulsion which makes a suspect or accused the source of 'real or physical evidence' does not violate it. Although we agree that this distinction is a helpful

---

1. As to inferences which may rationally be drawn from the claim of the privilege, compare Griswold, The Fifth Amendment Today (1955), with Hook, Common Sense and the Fifth Amendment (1957). See also Slochower v. Board of Higher Education and related cases on public demands for information from employees, chap. 16, p. 1303, infra.

framework for analysis, we are not to be understood to agree with past applications in all instances. . . . Some tests seemingly directed to obtain 'physical evidence,' for example, lie detector tests measuring changes in body function during interrogation, may actually be directed to eliciting responses which are essentially testimonial." Chief Justice Warren and Justices Black, Douglas, and Fortas dissented.

b. In United States v. Wade, 388 U.S. 218 (1967) (noted supra at p. 851) the Court relied on Schmerber in holding that "compelling the accused merely to exhibit his person for observation by a prosecution witness" at a post-indictment lineup "involves no compulsion of the accused to give evidence having testimonial significance." Justice Brennan's majority opinion found no Fifth Amendment violation, moreover, in compelling the accused "to speak within hearing distance of the witnesses, even to utter words purportedly uttered by the robber": "he was required to use his voice as an identifying physical characteristic, not to speak his guilt." Justice Fortas' dissent, joined by Chief Justice Warren and Justice Douglas, insisted that Schmerber did not compel an accused "actively to cooperate—to accuse himself by a volitional act which differs only in degree from compelling him to act out the crime." Justice Black also dissented. See also a companion case, Gilbert v. California, 388 U.S. 263 (1967), sustaining the taking of a handwriting sample as an "identifying physical characteristic" of one accused of bank robbery.

6. *Federal immunity statutes and the Ullmann case.* In Ullmann v. United States, 350 U.S. 422 (1956), the Court sustained the constitutionality of the Immunity Act of 1950. The Court held that the immunity provided by the Act was "sufficiently broad to displace the protection afforded by the privilege against self-incrimination" and that Congress had power to, and did, grant immunity from state as well as federal prosecution. The Court rejected the claim that the Fifth Amendment prohibits compulsion of otherwise incriminating testimony no matter what the scope of the immunity statute. The law authorized the compulsion of testimony in certain national security cases, upon a court order sought by the Attorney General. The statute provided that no witness "shall be prosecuted or subjected to any penalty . . . for or on account of any transaction, matter or thing concerning which he is compelled, after having claimed his privilege against self-incrimination, to testify or produce evidence, nor shall testimony so compelled be used as evidence in any criminal proceeding [except perjury and contempt] against him in any court."

Justice Frankfurter's majority opinion recalled that a similar law of 1893 had been sustained in Brown v. Walker, 161 U.S. 591 (1896), involving an investigation of Interstate Commerce Act violations.[2] Ullmann had refused to answer grand jury questions about Communist activities, despite the immunity; he insisted that the 1896 case was distinguishable because "the impact of the disabilities imposed by federal and state authorities and the public in general," including loss of job, passport eligibility, and "general public opprobrium," was "so oppressive that the statute does not give him true immunity." The Court replied that the immunity need "only remove those sanctions which generate the fear justifying invocation of the privilege"—

---

2. Compare Counselman v. Hitchcock, 142 U.S. 547 (1892), where the Court invalidated a predecessor to the 1893 law because "the immunity granted was incomplete."

i. e., criminal sanctions. Moreover, the Court construed the 1950 Act to bar
state prosecution as well; and national power to forbid state prosecution
was found under the national defense power and the Necessary and Proper
Clause.[3] [Compare the materials on the privilege and the federal system,
which follow.] Justice Douglas, joined by Justice Black, dissented in Ullmann, insisting that the Act left the witness subject to "penalties affixed to
criminal acts," in the sense of Boyd v. United States, 116 U.S. 616 (1886), and
arguing alternatively that Brown v. Walker should be overruled: "The Fifth
Amendment was designed to protect the accused against infamy as well as
against prosecution . . . [and] places the right of silence *beyond the
reach of government.*"

THE FIFTH AMENDMENT PRIVILEGE AND THE FEDERAL
SYSTEM: THE IMPACT OF MALLOY v. HOGAN

Malloy v. Hogan, 378 U.S. 1 (1964), repeatedly relied on in the Miranda
opinion, supra, was a major step in the progress of the "incorporation"
movement: it held the Fifth Amendment privilege applicable to the states
via the due process clause of the 14th Amendment. In Malloy and a companion case (Murphy v. Waterfront Commission, 378 U.S. 52) the Court
discarded doctrines of five much-debated cases: Twining v. New Jersey, 211
U.S. 78 (1908);[1] Adamson v. California, 332 U.S. 46 (1947), chap. 11,
p. 802, supra; United States v. Murdock, 284 U.S. 141 (1931);[2] Feldman
v. United States, 322 U.S. 487 (1944);[3] and Knapp v. Schweitzer, 357 U.S.
371 (1958).[4]

3. Similar provisions in federal immunity statutes restricting state criminal law enforcement power were sustained in Brown v. Walker, supra
(national commerce power), Adams v.
Maryland, 347 U.S. 179 (1954) (congressional investigatory power), and
Reina v. United States, 364 U.S. 507
(1960) (power to enforce narcotics
laws, under commerce and taxing
powers—"the supersession of state
prosecution is no less valid because
the States have traditionally regulated the traffic in narcotics").

1. Twining, which was discussed and
relied on in Adamson v. California,
chap. 11, p. 802, supra, stated that
"exemption from compulsory self-incrimination in the courts of the State
is not secured by any part of the
Federal Constitution." The Twining
Court, with only the first Justice
Harlan dissenting, sustained a state
law authorizing instructions that permitted juries to draw unfavorable inferences against defendants from
their failure to testify. Cf. Griffin v.
California, note 3, infra.

2. In Murdock, the Court held unanimously that appellee could not refuse
to answer questions in a federal tax
investigation on the ground of possible
incrimination under state law. The
Court relied on the English rule that
the privilege "does not protect witnesses against disclosing offenses in
violation of laws of another country."

3. Feldman, a 4 to 3 decision, sustained
a federal mail fraud conviction based
in part on testimony compelled in the
state courts under a state immunity
statute.

4. Knapp sustained a state contempt
conviction for refusal to answer in a
grand jury investigation. Petitioner
relied on the Fifth, not the 14th,
Amendment, claiming that the answer
might subject him to prosecution under federal labor laws. Justice
Frankfurter's majority opinion held
that the Fifth Amendment did not
limit the states and found also that
there was no showing "that the State
was used as an instrument of Federal
prosecution or investigation." Chief
Justice Warren and Justices Black
and Douglas dissented. Justice Black
stated that, in view of Murdock, Feldman and this case, "a person can be
whipsawed into incriminating himself
under both state and federal law even
though there is a privilege against

1. *Malloy v. Hogan.* Petitioner had been held in contempt for refusing to answer questions in a Connecticut gambling inquiry. The highest state court had held that there was no federal privilege and that the state constitutional privilege had been improperly invoked. The Supreme Court reversed: "We hold that the Fourteenth Amendment guaranteed the petitioner the protection of the Fifth Amendment's privilege against self-incrimination, and that under the applicable federal standard, the Connecticut Supreme Court of Errors erred in holding that the privilege was not properly invoked." Justice Brennan's opinion for the majority reviewed—much in the manner of Duncan v. Louisiana, chap. 11, p. 812, supra—the progress of "incorporation" under the Palko approach and concluded: "Decisions of the Court since Twining and Adamson have departed from the contrary view expressed in those cases." He found support for that conclusion in the coerced confession cases and in Mapp v. Ohio, which follows. Justice Brennan rejected the argument that "the availability of the federal privilege to a witness in a state inquiry is to be determined according to a less stringent standard than is applicable in a federal proceeding." He insisted that it "would be incongruous to have different standards" apply.

Justice Harlan, joined by Justice Clark, submitted one of the two dissenting opinions. He stated that he would hold "that principles of justice to which due process gives expression" prohibit a state from imprisoning a person "*solely* because he refuses to give evidence which may incriminate him under the laws of the State," noting that cases such as Twining had not decided this precise question. He objected, however, to "incorporating into due process, without critical examination, the whole body of law which surrounds a specific prohibition directed against the Federal Government." Justice White's dissenting opinion, joined by Justice Stewart, argued that petitioner's refusals to answer were not privileged under the Fifth Amendment standard and concluded: "Adherence to the federal standard of incrimination . . . in form only, while its content is eroded in application, is hardly an auspicious beginning for application of the privilege to the States."

2. *Murphy v. Waterfront Commission.* This case presented an issue related to Malloy: "whether one jurisdiction within our federal structure may compel a witness, whom it has immunized from prosecution under its laws, to give testimony which might then be used to convict him of a crime against another such jurisdiction." Petitioners were granted immunity under New Jersey and New York laws at a hearing of the Waterfront Commission, a bistate body established under an interstate compact. Nevertheless, they refused to answer questions about a work stoppage because "the answers might tend to incriminate them under *federal* law, to which the grant of immunity did not purport to extend." New Jersey's highest court affirmed a civil contempt judgment against them.

self-incrimination in the Constitution of both. . . . I cannot agree that we must accept this intolerable state of affairs as a necessary part of our federal system of government." See also Cohen v. Hurley, 366 U.S. 117 (1961), once again rejecting, in a 5 to 4 decision, the claim of a "federal constitutional right," under the Fourteenth Amendment, against incrimination in a state proceeding. The Cohen decision was overruled in Spevack v. Klein, 385 U.S. 511 (1967) (chap. 16, p. 1313, infra). The Spevack Court stated that Cohen had not "survived" Malloy v. Hogan.

The Supreme Court, in an opinion by Justice Goldberg, rejected the contention "that we should adhere to the 'established rule' [of Knapp, Feldman, and Murdock]. Our decision today [in Malloy v. Hogan] necessitates a reconsideration of this rule. Our review of the pertinent cases in this Court and of their English antecedents reveals that Murdock did not adequately consider the relevant authorities and has been significantly weakened by subsequent decisions of this Court, and, further, that the legal premises underlying Feldman and Knapp have since been rejected."

After holding "that the constitutional privilege against self-incrimination protects a state witness against incrimination under federal as well as state law and a federal witness against incrimination under state as well as federal law," Justice Goldberg turned to the "effect this holding has on existing state immunity legislation." He concluded "that a state witness may not be compelled to give testimony which may be incriminating under federal law unless the compelled testimony and its fruits cannot be used in any manner by federal officials in connection with a criminal prosecution against him. We conclude, moreover, that in order to implement this constitutional rule and accommodate the interests of the State and Federal Governments in investigating and prosecuting crime, the Federal Government must be prohibited from making any such use of compelled testimony and its fruits. This exclusionary rule, while permitting the States to secure information necessary for effective law enforcement, leaves the witness and the Federal Government in substantially the same position as if the witness had claimed his privilege in the absence of a state grant of immunity." Petitioners, accordingly, "may now be compelled to answer the questions propounded to them." However, since petitioners' refusal to answer had rested on a "reasonable fear" based on the now overruled Feldman decision, the Court vacated the contempt judgment: "Fairness dictates that petitioners should now be afforded an opportunity . . . to answer the questions."

Justice White, joined by Justice Stewart, submitted a lengthy concurring opinion, primarily to emphasize that "the Court does not accept the far-reaching and in my view wholly unnecessary constitutional principle that the privilege requires not only complete protection against any use of compelled testimony in any manner in other jurisdictions but also absolute immunity in these jurisdictions from any prosecution pertaining to any of the testimony given." His opinion warned of the dangers that would ensue "if immunity from prosecution under federal law" were made "a constitutionally required condition to testimonial compulsion in state proceedings." Such a broad rule, in sum, "would invalidate the immunity statutes of the 50 States since the States are without authority to confer immunity from federal prosecutions. The Federal Government would become the only law enforcement agency with effective power to compel testimony in exchange for immunity from prosecution under federal and state law." He concluded: "I believe the State may compel testimony incriminating under federal law, but the Federal Government may not use such testimony or its fruits in a federal criminal proceeding. Immunity must be as broad as, but not harmfully and wastefully broader than, the privilege against self-incrimination." In another opinion, Justice Harlan, joined by Justice Clark, concurred in the judgment but opposed the overruling of the constitutional basis of Feldman: "I cannot accept the majority's conclusion that a rule prohibiting federal authorities from using . . . incriminating testimony compelled in state proceedings is constitutionally required. . . . I would, however, adopt such a rule in the exercise of our supervisory power over the administration of federal criminal justice. See McNabb v. United States [p. 857, supra]."

3. *Griffin v. California: Malloy applied.* A year after Malloy, the Court applied its principle to overrule the specific holding of Adamson v. California, chap. 11, p. 802, supra. Griffin v. California, 380 U.S. 609 (1965). The Court held that the California rule sustained in Adamson, permitting comment on the defendant's failure to testify, violated the privilege against self-incrimination. The Court explained: "Comment on the refusal to testify . . . is a penalty imposed by courts for exercising a constitutional privilege. It cuts down on the privilege by making its assertion costly. It is said, however, that the inference of guilt for failure to testify as to facts peculiarly within the accused's knowledge is in any event natural and irresistible, and that comment on the failure does not magnify that inference into a penalty for asserting a constitutional privilege. . . . What the jury may infer given no help from the court is one thing. What they may infer when the court solemnizes the silence of the accused into evidence against him is quite another. [T]he inference of guilt is not always so natural or irresistible." (Note the reliance on the "penalty for exercising a constitutional privilege" aspect of Griffin in the argument challenging the death penalty in Maxwell v. Bishop, p. 923, infra.) Tehan v. Shott, 382 U.S. 406 (1966) held that the Griffin ruling was not to be applied retroactively, under the prospectivity principles of Linkletter v. Walker, sec. 4, p. 892, infra.

SECTION 3.   SEARCH, SEIZURE, AND EAVESDROPPING

MAPP v. OHIO

367 U.S. 643, 81 S.Ct. 1684, 6 L.Ed.2d 1081 (1961).

Appeal from the Supreme Court of Ohio.

Mr. Justice CLARK delivered the opinion of the Court.

Appellant stands convicted of knowingly having had in her possession and under her control certain lewd and lascivious books, pictures, and photographs in violation of § 2905.34 of Ohio's Revised Code. . . . [T]he Supreme Court of Ohio found that her conviction was valid though "based primarily upon the introduction in evidence of lewd and lascivious books and pictures unlawfully seized during an unlawful search of defendant's home." . . .

The State says that even if the search were made without authority, or otherwise unreasonably, it is not prevented from using the unconstitutionally seized evidence at trial, citing Wolf v. Colorado, 338 U.S. 25 (1949). [See the discussion of Wolf and its progeny in the materials on due process methodology, chap. 11, p. 807, supra.] On this appeal . . . it is urged once again that we review that holding.[1]

---

1. Other issues have been raised on this appeal but, in the view we have taken of the case, they need not be decided. Although appellant chose to

I.

Seventy-five years ago, in Boyd v. United States, 116 U.S. 616, 630 (1886), considering the Fourth and Fifth Amendments as running "almost into each other" on the facts before it, this Court held that the doctrines of those Amendments "apply to all invasions on the part of the government and its employes of the sanctity of a man's home and the privacies of life." [I]n the year 1914, in [Weeks v. United States, 232 U.S. 383], this Court "for the first time" held that "in a federal prosecution the Fourth Amendment barred the use of evidence secured through an illegal search and seizure." . . . This Court has ever since required of federal law officers a strict adherence to that command which this Court has held to be a clear, specific, and constitutionally required—even if judicially implied—deterrent safeguard without insistence upon which the Fourth Amendment would have been reduced to "a form of words." . . .

[margin: ✗ 4ᵗʰ Amend.]

II. . . .

. . . The Court's reasons [in Wolf] for not considering essential to the right to privacy, as a curb imposed upon the States by the Due Process Clause, that which decades before had been posited as part and parcel of the Fourth Amendment's limitation upon federal encroachment of individual privacy, were bottomed on factual considerations.

While they are not basically relevant to a decision that the exclusionary rule is an essential ingredient of the Fourth Amendment as the right it embodies is vouchsafed against the States by the Due Process Clause, we will consider the current validity of the factual grounds upon which Wolf was based.

[margin: exclusionary rules bars evidence obtained illegally]

The Court in Wolf first stated that "[t]he contrariety of views of the States" on the adoption of the exclusionary rule of Weeks was "particularly impressive" . . . . While in 1949, prior to the Wolf case, almost two-thirds of the States were opposed to the use of the exclusionary rule, now, despite the Wolf case, more than half of those since passing upon it, by their own legislative or judicial decision, have wholly or partly adopted or adhered to the Weeks rule. See Elkins v. United States, 364 U.S. 206, Appendix, pp. 224–232 (1960). Significantly, among those now following the rule is California which, according to its highest court, was "compelled to reach that conclusion because other remedies have completely failed to secure compliance with the constitutional provisions . . . ." People v. Cahan, 44 Cal.2d 434, 445, 282 P.2d 905, 911 (1955). In connection with this California case, we note that the second basis elaborated in Wolf in support of its failure to enforce the exclusionary doctrine against the States was that "other means of protection" have been afforded "the right to privacy." . . . The experience of California that such other remedies have been worthless and futile is buttressed by the experience of other States.

[margin: Calif. reversed Wolf v. Col.]

. . . Likewise, time has set its face against what Wolf called the "weighty testimony" of People v. Defore, 242 N.Y. 13, 150 N.E. 585 (1926). There

urge what may have appeared to be the surer ground for favorable disposition and did not insist that Wolf be overruled, the *amicus curiae*, who was also permitted to participate in the oral argument, did urge the Court to overrule Wolf. [Footnote by the Court.]

Justice (then Judge) Cardozo, rejecting adoption of the Weeks exclusionary rule in New York, had said that "[t]he Federal rule as it stands is either too strict or too lax." . . . However, the force of that reasoning has been largely vitiated by later decisions of this Court. These include the recent discarding of the "silver platter" doctrine which allowed federal judicial use of evidence seized in violation of the Constitution by state agents, Elkins v. United States, supra;[2] . . . and, finally, the formulation of a method to prevent state use of evidence unconstitutionally seized by federal agents, Rea v. United States, 350 U.S. 214 (1956).[3] . . .

It, therefore, plainly appears that the factual considerations supporting the failure of the Wolf Court to include the Weeks exclusionary rule when it recognized the enforceability of the right to privacy against the States in 1949, while not basically relevant to the constitutional consideration, could not, in any analysis, now be deemed controlling.

III.

Some five years after Wolf, in answer to a plea made here Term after Term that we overturn [it], this Court indicated that such should not be done until the States had "adequate opportunity to adopt or reject the [Weeks] rule." Irvine v. California, [chap. 11, p. 811, supra]. Today we once again examine Wolf's constitutional documentation of the right to privacy free from unreasonable state intrusion, and, after its dozen years on our books, are led by it to close the only courtroom door remaining open to evidence secured by official lawlessness in flagrant abuse of that basic right, reserved to all persons as a specific guarantee against that very same unlawful conduct. We

2. Elkins v. United States, 364 U.S. 206 (1960), overruled the "silver platter" doctrine of Lustig v. United States, 338 U.S. 74 (1949). Under Lustig, evidence illegally seized by state officials was excluded from the federal courts only if federal officers participated in the search: "A search . . . is not a search by a federal official if evidence secured by state authorities is turned over to the federal authorities on a silver platter." In Elkins, the Court, in a 5 to 4 decision relying on its "supervisory power over the administration of criminal justice in the federal courts," found that the Wolf decision had removed "the doctrinal underpinning for the admissibility rule." Accordingly, federal courts were to exclude "evidence obtained by state officers during a search, which, if conducted by federal officers," would have violated the Fourth Amendment.

3. In the Rea case, a federal narcotics prosecution had failed because the evidence had been obtained under a defective search warrant. Petitioner was then indicted in a state court. The Court, in a 5 to 4 decision, enjoined the federal officer who had seized the evidence from testifying in the state court or permitting the evidence to be used there. The majority (which included Justice Frankfurter, who had written Wolf) insisted that the injunction did not "in any way . . . interfere" with state law enforcement; the decision rested simply on "our supervisory power over federal law enforcement agencies. Cf. McNabb v. United States, [p. 857, supra]." The dissent argued that McNabb only applied to standards in federal prosecutions, and that the result could not be squared with the policies of Wolf and Stefanelli v. Minard, footnote 5, infra. Compare Wilson v. Schnettler, 365 U.S. 381 (1961), discussed in the principal case, where a similar injunction was refused. The Court distinguished Rea partly because here no "proceedings were ever taken . . . in any federal court." See also Cleary v. Bolger, 371 U.S. 392 (1963), decided after Mapp, where a divided Court held that the District Court had erred in relying on Rea to issue an injunction against state officials. The state officers planned to use, in a state trial, evidence that had been obtained by federal officers in violation of the Federal Rules.

hold that all evidence obtained by searches and seizures in violation of the
Constitution is, by that same authority, inadmissible in a state court.

IV.

Since the Fourth Amendment's right of privacy has been declared enforceable against the States through the Due Process Clause of the Fourteenth,
it is enforceable against them by the same sanction of exclusion as is used
against the Federal Government. Were it otherwise, ... the freedom
from state invasions of privacy would be so ephemeral and so neatly severed
from its conceptual nexus with the freedom from all brutish means of
coercing evidence as not to merit this Court's high regard as a freedom "implicit
in the concept of ordered liberty." . . . . The right to privacy, when
conceded operatively enforceable against the States, was not susceptible of
destruction by avulsion of the sanction upon which its protection and enjoyment had always been deemed dependent [in the federal courts] under the
Boyd, Weeks and Silverthorne cases. Therefore, in extending the substantive
protections of due process to all constitutionally unreasonable searches—state
or federal—it was logically and constitutionally necessary that the exclusion
doctrine—an essential part of the right to privacy—be also insisted upon as
an essential ingredient of the right newly recognized by the Wolf case. In
short, the admission of the new constitutional right by Wolf could not consistently tolerate denial of its most important constitutional privilege, namely,
the exclusion of the evidence which an accused had been forced to give by
reason of the unlawful seizure. To hold otherwise is to grant the right but
in reality to withhold its privilege and enjoyment. . . .

Indeed, we are aware of no restraint, similar to that rejected today,
conditioning the enforcement of any other basic constitutional right. . . .
This Court has not hesitated to enforce as strictly against the States as it
does against the Federal Government the rights of free speech and of a
free press, the rights to notice and to a fair, public trial, including, as it
does, the right not to be convicted by use of a coerced confession, however
logically relevant it be, and without regard to its reliability. . . . And
nothing could be more certain than that when a coerced confession is involved, "the relevant rules of evidence" are overridden without regard to
"the incidence of such conduct by the police," slight or frequent. Why
should not the same rule apply to what is tantamount to coerced testimony
by way of unconstitutional seizure of goods, papers, effects, documents, etc?
We find that, as to the Federal Government, the Fourth and Fifth Amendments and, as to the States, the freedom from unconscionable invasions of
privacy and the freedom from convictions based upon coerced confessions
do enjoy an "intimate relation" in their perpetuation of "principles of humanity and civil liberty [secured] only after years of struggle," Bram v. United
States, 168 U.S. 532, 543–544 (1897). . . . . The philosophy of each
Amendment and of each freedom is complementary to, although not dependent
upon, that of the other in its sphere of influence—the very least that together
they assure in either sphere is that no man is to be convicted on unconstitutional evidence. . . .

V.

Moreover, our holding . . . . is not only the logical dictate of prior
cases, but it also makes very good sense. . . . . Presently, a federal

prosecutor may make no use of evidence illegally seized, but a State's attorney across the street may, although he supposedly is operating under the enforceable prohibitions of the same Amendment. Thus the State, by admitting evidence unlawfully seized, serves to encourage disobedience to the Federal Constitution which it is bound to uphold. Moreover, as was said in Elkins, "[t]he very essence of a healthy federalism depends upon the avoidance of needless conflict between state and federal courts." 364 U.S., at 221. Such a conflict, hereafter needless, arose this very Term, in Wilson v. Schnettler, 365 U.S. 381 (1961), in which and in spite of the promise made by Rea, we gave full recognition to our practice in this regard by refusing to restrain a federal officer from testifying in a state court as to evidence unconstitutionally seized by him in the performance of his duties. Yet the double standard recognized until today hardly put such a thesis into practice. In non-exclusionary States, federal officers, being human, were by it invited to and did, as our cases indicate, step across the street to the State's attorney with their unconstitutionally seized evidence. Prosecution on the basis of that evidence was then had in a state court in utter disregard of the enforceable Fourth Amendment. If the fruits of an unconstitutional search had been inadmissible in both state and federal courts, this inducement to evasion would have been sooner eliminated. There would be no need to reconcile such cases as Rea and Schnettler, each pointing up the hazardous uncertainties of our heretofore ambivalent approach.

Federal-state cooperation in the solution of crime under constitutional standards will be promoted, if only by recognition of their now mutual obligation to respect the same fundamental criteria in their approaches. . . . Denying shortcuts to only one of two cooperating law enforcement agencies tends naturally to breed legitimate suspicion of "working arrangements" whose results are equally tainted. . . .

There are those who say, as did Justice (then Judge) Cardozo, that under our constitutional exclusionary doctrine "[t]he criminal is to go free because the constable has blundered." People v. Defore, 242 N.Y., at 21, 150 N.E., at 587. In some cases this will undoubtedly be the result.[4] But, as was said in Elkins, "there is another consideration—the imperative of judicial integrity." . . . Nor can it lightly be assumed that, as a practical matter, adoption of the exclusionary rule fetters law enforcement. . . .

The ignoble shortcut to conviction left open to the State tends to destroy the entire system of constitutional restraints on which the liberties of the people rest. Having once recognized that the right to privacy embodied in the Fourth Amendment is enforceable against the States, . . . we can no longer permit that right to remain an empty promise. Because it is enforceable in the same manner and to like effect as other basic rights secured by the Due Process Clause, we can no longer permit it to be revocable at the whim of any police officer who, in the name of law enforcement itself, chooses to suspend its enjoyment. Our decision, founded on rea-

---

4. As is always the case, however, state procedural requirements governing assertion and pursuance of direct and collateral constitutional challenges to criminal prosecutions must be respected. We note, moreover, that the class of state convictions possibly affected by this decision is of relatively narrow compass . . . . In any case, further delay in reaching the present result could have no effect other than to compound the difficulties. [Footnote by the Court. On the retroactivity problem in the Mapp context, see Linkletter v. Walker, p. 893, infra.]

son and truth, gives to the individual no more than that which the Constitution guarantees him, to the police officer no less than that to which honest law enforcement is entitled, and, to the courts, that judicial integrity so necessary in the true administration of justice. . . .

Reversed and remanded.

Mr. Justice BLACK, concurring. . . .

I am still not persuaded that the Fourth Amendment, standing alone, would be enough to bar the introduction into evidence against an accused of papers and effects seized from him in violation of its commands. . . . Reflection on the problem, however, in the light of cases coming before the Court since Wolf, has led me to conclude that when the Fourth Amendment's ban against unreasonable searches and seizures is considered together with the Fifth Amendment's ban against compelled self-incrimination, a constitutional basis emerges which not only justifies but actually requires the exclusionary rule.

. . . As I understand the Court's opinion in this case, we again reject the confusing "shock-the-conscience" standard of the Wolf and Rochin cases and, instead, set aside this state conviction in reliance upon the precise, intelligible and more predictable constitutional doctrine enunciated in the Boyd case. . . . The Court's opinion, in my judgment, dissipates the doubt and uncertainty in this field of constitutional law and I am persuaded . . . to depart from my prior views, to accept the Boyd doctrine as controlling in this state case and to join the Court's judgment and opinion which are in accordance with that constitutional doctrine.

Mr. Justice DOUGLAS, concurring. . . .

. . . I believe that this is an appropriate case in which to put an end to the asymmetry which Wolf imported into the law. See Stefanelli v. Minard, 342 U.S. 117; [5] Rea v. United States, 350 U.S. 214 . . . .

Memorandum of Mr. Justice STEWART.

. . . I express no view as to the merits of the constitutional issue which the Court today decides. I would, however, reverse the judgment in this case, because I am persuaded that [the Ohio obscenity law is unconstitutional].

Mr. Justice HARLAN, whom Mr. Justice FRANKFURTER and Mr. Justice WHITTAKER join, dissenting. . . .

[Although the Wolf issue] was indeed raised here and below among appellant's subordinate points, the new and pivotal issue brought to the Court by this appeal is whether [the Ohio obscenity law is constitutional]. That was the principal issue which was decided by the Ohio Supreme Court, which was tendered by appellant's Jurisdictional Statement, and which was briefed and argued in this Court. In this posture of things, I think it fair to

5. In Stefanelli v. Minard, 343 U.S. 117 (1951), the Court held that a federal court could not enjoin a state officer from using in a state prosecution evidence seized in violation of the "right" recognized in Wolf. Justice Frankfurter claimed that no "irreparable injury" justifying equitable relief was threatened: "At worst," petitioners might be convicted; but that, under Wolf, "would not deprive them of due process of law." See also Cleary v. Bolger, footnote 3, supra.

say that five members of this Court have simply "reached out" to overrule Wolf. . . .

I would not impose upon the States this federal exclusionary remedy. The reasons given by the majority for now suddenly turning its back on Wolf seem to me notably unconvincing.

First, it is said that "the factual grounds upon which Wolf was based" have since changed, in that more States now follow the Weeks exclusionary rule than was so at the time Wolf was decided. While that is true, a recent survey indicates that at present one half of the States still adhere to the common-law non-exclusionary rule . . . . But in any case surely all this is beside the point, as the majority itself indeed seems to recognize. . . . Moreover, the very fact on which the majority relies, instead of lending support to what is now being done, points away from the need of replacing voluntary state action with federal compulsion. . . .

. . . I do not see how it can be said that a trial becomes unfair simply because a State determines that evidence may be considered by the trier of fact, regardless of how it was obtained, if it is relevant to the one issue with which the trial is concerned, the guilt or innocence of the accused. Of course, a court may use its procedures as an incidental means of pursuing other ends than the correct resolution of the controversies before it. Such indeed is the Weeks rule, but if a State does not choose to use its courts in this way, I do not believe that this Court is empowered to impose this much-debated procedure on local courts . . . .

Finally, it is said that the overruling of Wolf is supported by the established doctrine that the admission in evidence of an involuntary confession renders a state conviction constitutionally invalid. . . . I believe this analogy is not a true one. The "coerced confession" rule is certainly not a rule that any illegally obtained statements may not be used in evidence. I would suppose that a statement which is procured during a period of illegal detention, McNabb v. United States, 318 U.S. 332, is, as much as unlawfully seized evidence, illegally obtained, but this Court has consistently refused to reverse state convictions resting on the use of such statements. . . .

The point, then, must be that in requiring exclusion of an involuntary statement of an accused, we are concerned not with an appropriate remedy for what the police have done, but with something which is regarded as going to the heart of our concepts of fairness in judicial procedure. . . . The pressures brought to bear against an accused leading to a confession, unlike an unconstitutional violation of privacy, do not, apart from the use of the confession at trial, necessarily involve independent Constitutional violations. What is crucial is that the trial defense to which an accused is entitled should not be rendered an empty formality by reason of statements wrung from him . . . . . That this is a *procedural right*, and that its violation occurs at the time his improperly obtained statement is admitted at trial, is manifest. . . .

This, and not the disciplining of the police, as with illegally seized evidence, is surely the true basis for excluding a statement of the accused which was unconstitutionally obtained. In sum, I think the coerced confession analogy works strongly *against* what the Court does today. . . .

SOME PROBLEMS OF SEARCH, SEIZURE, AND ELECTRONIC EAVESDROPPING

Introduction. Since 1961, when Mapp brought the arrest and search practices of state law enforcement officials under Supreme Court scrutiny, detailed elaboration of Fourth Amendment requirements has been an increasingly prominent part of the Court's criminal procedure business. Extensive treatment of the details in a constitutional law course is not feasible. These materials seek only to sketch some characteristic problems and to note the especially important and controversial developments.

1. *The search for standards: Ker and Aguilar.* a. Ker v. California, 374 U.S. 23 (1963), the Court's first "suitable opportunity for further explication" of Mapp, illustrates a recurrent source of difficulty: though the Court decided that the constitutional limits imposed on the states by Mapp were identical with those the Fourth Amendment placed on federal law enforcement, that "uniformity" ruling did not make all preexisting federal search and seizure law available to guide state officers; rather, since prior federal law rested in part on rules and statutes instead of the Constitution itself, it is necessary to determine whether a particular federal requirement is compelled by the Fourth Amendment before it can be imposed on the states via Mapp.

In the Ker case, for example, Justice Clark's discussion of "the standard by which State searches" must be evaluated had the support of all but Justice Harlan. But the eight Justices agreeing on the "standard" divided 4 to 4 on its application. Thus, Justice Harlan's vote, based on a different standard, was necessary for the 5 to 4 affirmance of the convictions. On the general standard, Justice Clark emphasized that "reasonableness is the same under the Fourth and Fourteenth Amendments," but he added that "the demands of our federal system compel us to distinguish between evidence held inadmissible because of our supervisory powers over federal courts and that held inadmissible because prohibited by the United States Constitution." Justice Harlan objected to the application of the "same constitutional standards" to federal and state searches and seizures; he thought that searches should be subject to "the more flexible concept of 'fundamental' fairness."

The division among the eight Justices who agreed on the general standard turned mainly on the question whether the police officers' unannounced entry into the petitioners' dwelling was unlawful. Justice Clark concluded that "the officers' method of entry was not unreasonable under the standards of the Fourth Amendment." Only one Supreme Court decision, Miller v. United States, 357 U.S. 301 (1958), had found a search by federal officers after an unannounced entry unlawful. Justice Brennan, for the four dissenting Justices, conceded that the Miller decision "did not rest upon constitutional doctrine but rather upon an exercise of this Court's supervisory powers." He went on to say, however: "Nothing we said in Miller so much as intimated that . . . the Fourth Amendment would not have required the same result." [Note the congressional consideration, early in 1970, of legislation to authorize "no knock" entries in narcotics laws enforcement.]

b. Note also the division on the Court in Aguilar v. Texas, 378 U.S. 108 (1964). The majority found that a Texas search warrant had been improperly issued "because the affidavit did not provide a sufficient basis for finding of probable cause," under the standard of Giordenello v. United States, 357 U.S. 480 (1958). Though Giordenello had construed the "probable cause" requirement of Rule 4 of the Federal Rules of Criminal Procedure, the Court found that the principles there derived from the Fourth Amendment, "not from our supervisory power." Justice Clark's dissent, joined by Justices Black and Stewart, insisted that Giordenello rested on the Court's supervisory powers, not the Constitution.

    2. *Searches without a warrant and the Chimel case.* Not every search without a warrant is invalid under the Fourth Amendment. Thus, a moving vehicle may be searched without a warrant, if probable cause for the search exists. See Carroll v. United States, 267 U.S. 132 (1925); Brinegar v. United States, 338 U.S. 160 (1949); Henry v. United States, 361 U.S. 98 (1959). Moreover, a limited search incident to a valid arrest is permissible, though the proper scope of such a search has presented much difficulty. Trupiano v. United States, 334 U.S. 699 (1948), held a seizure unconstitutional though there had been a valid arrest and stated that "law enforcement agents must secure and use search warrants whenever reasonably practicable." The broad language of Trupiano was short-lived, however. In United States v. Rabinowitz, 339 U.S. 56 (1950), the Court announced: "To the extent that Trupiano . . . requires a search warrant solely on the basis of the practicability of procuring it rather than upon the reasonableness of the search after a lawful arrest, that case is overruled."

    In 1969, in a major reexamination of the "search incident to arrest" problem, the Court once again changed course. Chimel v. California, 395 U.S. 752. The state courts had upheld the search of petitioner's entire three-bedroom house on the basis of the proposition for which Rabinowitz had been cited for nearly two decades: "That a warrantless search 'incident to a lawful arrest' may generally extend to the area that is considered to be in the 'possession' or under the 'control' of the person arrested." Justice Stewart's majority opinion concluded that that broad doctrine "can withstand neither historical nor rational analysis." The legitimate scope of the "search incident to arrest" was narrower: It was reasonable "to search the person arrested in order to remove any weapons." It was reasonable, moreover, to "seize any evidence on the arrestee's person in order to prevent its concealment or destruction." Moreover, there was justification "for a search of the arrestee's person and the area 'within his immediate control'—construing that phrase to mean the area from within which he might gain possession of a weapon or destructible evidence." But that marks the outer limit under the new Chimel standard: "There is no comparable justification . . . for routinely searching rooms other than that in which an arrest occurs—or, for that matter, for searching through all the desk drawers or other clothes or concealed areas in that room itself." Rabinowitz, "the subject of critical commentary for many years," was "no longer to be followed." Justice White, joined by Justice Black, dissented.

    3. *"Stop and frisk" practices and the Terry case.* In its first direct encounter with the "difficult and troublesome issues" raised by the police on-the-street "stop" of suspicious persons and the accompanying "frisk" for weapons, in Terry v. Ohio, 392 U.S. 1 (1968), the Court found a limited constitutional authority for the practice. Even though there was no "probable cause," no formal arrest, and no warrant, the practice was not necessarily

an "unreasonable search and seizure," and the resulting evidence need not be excluded from trial. Chief Justice Warren's careful phrasing of the majority holding stated that "where a police officer observes unusual conduct which leads him reasonably to conclude in light of his experience that criminal activity may be afoot and that the persons with whom he is dealing may be armed and presently dangerous; where in the course of investigating this behavior he identifies himself as a policeman and makes reasonable inquiries; and where nothing in the initial stages of the encounter serves to dispel his reasonable fear for his own or others' safety, he is entitled for the protection of himself and others in the area to conduct a carefully limited search of the outer clothing of such persons in an attempt to discover weapons which might be used to assault him. Such a search is a reasonable search under the Fourth Amendment, and any weapons seized may properly be introduced in evidence against the person from whom they were taken." Accordingly, petitioner's conviction for carrying a concealed weapon was affirmed.

The trial court, in holding the seized weapons admissible, had relied on the distinction between an investigatory "stop" and an arrest, and between a "frisk" for weapons and a full-blown search for evidence of crime. The Court rejected the argument "that the Fourth Amendment does not come into play at all as a limitation upon police conduct if the officers stop short of something called a 'technical arrest' or a 'full-blown search.'" Rather, the Amendment should be viewed as governing all intrusions "upon personal security, and to make the scope of the particular intrusion, in light of all the exigencies of the case, a central element in the analysis of reasonableness." Accordingly, reasonableness depended on "whether the officer's action was justified at its inception, and whether it was reasonably related in scope to the circumstances which justified the interference in the first place." The usual warrant procedure was not applicable, however. A limited "protective seizure and search for weapons" was justified even in the absence of "probable cause" for arrest, if "a reasonably prudent man" in the circumstances of the policeman "would be warranted in the belief that his safety or that of others was in danger."

In the course of his opinion, the Chief Justice commented that the exclusionary rule had "its limitations . . . as a tool of judicial control." For example, "in some contexts the rule is ineffective as a deterrent," given the wide diversity in street encounters between citizens and police: "[I]t is powerless to deter invasions of constitutionally guaranteed rights where the police either have no interest in prosecuting or are willing to forego successful prosecution in the interest of serving some other goal. . . . The wholesale harassment by certain elements of the police community, of which minority groups, particularly Negroes, frequently complain, will not be stopped by the exclusion of any evidence from any criminal trial. Yet a rigid and unthinking application of the exclusionary rule, in futile protest against practices which it can never be used effectively to control, may exact a high toll in human injury and frustration of efforts to prevent crime." Justices Harlan and White joined the opinion with separate memoranda. There was also a concurring memorandum by Justice Black. Justice Douglas dissented.

Two companion cases to Terry, Sibron v. New York and Peters v. New York—decided together at 392 U.S. 40 (1968)—arose in the context of the State's "stop and frisk" law, but the Court decided the cases without engaging in "the abstract and unproductive exercise" of ruling on the law's constitutionality "on its face." The statute authorizes police officers to "stop" people, "demand" explanations of them, and "search [them] for dangerous weapon[s]" in certain circumstances upon "reasonable suspicion" that they are engaged in criminal activity and that they represent a danger to the policeman. The Court affirmed the conviction in Peters on the ground that there had been "probable cause" for an arrest but reversed in Sibron because the policeman there did not have information to justify a self-protective search for weapons. There were separate concurring opinions by Justices Douglas, Harlan, White and Fortas, and an opinion by Justice Black dissenting in Sibron.

4. *The prerequisites of warrants and "probable cause."* Much search and seizure litigation does not deal directly with the Fourth Amendment's general ban on "unreasonable searches and seizures" but rather with the more specific requirement that warrants shall not issue "but upon probable cause" and with particular descriptions. See, e. g., Aguilar v. Texas, 378 U.S. 108 (1964), holding a state search warrant invalid on the ground that it was based on an affidavit that recited "mere conclusions" and therefore did not provide an adequate basis for a finding of probable cause. For a review of the criteria governing the issuance of hearsay warrants, see Spinelli v. United States, 393 U.S. 410 (1969). The majority found the FBI affidavit did not afford probable cause for issuance of a warrant because it failed to satisfy the "two-pronged test" of the Aguilar case: the magistrate must be given adequate information to demonstrate that (1) the informant's past record showed him to be "reliable," and (2) the "underlying circumstances" supported the informant's tip in the present case.* Note also the probable cause requirement to justify an arrest without a warrant. See Draper v. United States, 358 U.S. 307 (1959).

5. *The "fruit of the poisonous tree."* The ban of the Fourth Amendment extends to leads furnished by illegally seized evidence, as well as the use of the evidence itself. In Silverthorne Lumber Co. v. United States, 251 U.S. 385, (1920), books and documents illegally seized by federal agents had been returned by court order. Subsequently, petitioners were subpoenaed to produce the books and documents before a grand jury, refused, and were punished for contempt. The Supreme Court, in an opinion by Justice Holmes, reversed and rejected the claim that the Government may "use knowledge that it has gained" from the illegal seizure "to call upon the owners in a more regular form to produce them. The essence of a provision forbidding the acquisition of evidence in a certain way is that not merely evidence so acquired shall not be used before the Court but that it

---

* Note also United States v. Ventresca, 380 U.S. 102 (1965), where the Court sought to clarify "the standards by which a reviewing court should approach the interpretation of affidavits supporting warrants which have been duly issued by examining magistrates." The majority stated that affidavits must be tested "in a common-sense and realistic fashion. They are normally drafted by nonlawyers in the midst and haste of a criminal investigation." Compare Stanford v. Texas, 379 U.S. 476 (1965), holding that a broadly worded warrant—under which copies of approximately 300 books were seized pursuant to a Texas anti-subversion law—constituted an invalid "general warrant." The Court noted that the requirement that warrants must particularly describe the "things to be seized" is to be "accorded the most scrupulous exactitude when the 'things' are books." See Marcus v. Search Warrants, 367 U.S. 717 (1961), chap. 16, p. 1274, infra.

shall not be used at all." The Silverthorne "fruit of the poisonous tree" doctrine is not limited to physical, tangible evidence. In Wong Sun v. United States, 371 U.S. 471 (1963), Justice Brennan's opinion for the Court stated that "verbal evidence which derives so immediately from an unlawful entry and an unauthorized arrest as the officers' action in the present case is no less the 'fruit' of official illegality than the more common tangible fruits of the unwarranted intrusion." See Note, "Fruit of the Poisonous Tree—A Plea for Relevant Criteria," 115 U.Pa.L.Rev. 1136 (1967).

6. *Wire-tapping and electronic eavesdropping: From Olmstead to Katz and the 1968 Act.* a. *Olmstead and constitutional permission.* In Olmstead v. United States, 277 U.S. 438 (1928), the Court held that wire-tapping does not violate the Fourth of Fifth Amendments. Chief Justice Taft's majority opinion concluded: "[Liberal construction of the Fourth Amendment] can not justify enlargement of the language employed beyond the possible practical meaning of houses, persons, papers and effects, or so to apply the words search and seizure as to forbid hearing and sight." Justices Holmes, Brandeis, Butler and Stone each wrote a dissenting opinion. In Goldman v. United States, 316 U.S. 129 (1942), involving use of a detectaphone on a wall adjoining defendant's office, as well as in several other reexaminations of Olmstead, the Court refused to distinguish or overrule that 1928 decision; Olmstead and Goldman were not overruled in effect until 1967, in the Katz case, note 6d infra.

b. *The statutory ban.* Soon after the Olmstead ruling that wire-tapping did not constitute a violation of the Fourth Amendment, evidence so obtained was held inadmissible in the federal courts because of an exclusionary rule implied from Section 605 of the Federal Communications Act. Section 605 provides in part that "no person not being authorized by the sender shall intercept any communication and divulge or publish the [contents] of such intercepted communication to any person." See Nardone v. United States, 302 U.S. 379 (1937), and Nardone v. United States, 308 U.S. 338 (1939). The effect of that statutory wire-tapping ban on federal-state relations caused considerable controversy. In Schwartz v. Texas, 344 U.S. 199 (1952), the Court held that wire-tap evidence was admissible in state courts, despite the possible violation of federal law. Benanti v. United States, 355 U.S. 96 (1957), which involved evidence obtained pursuant to a state court order authorizing a wire-tap, stated that "evidence obtained by means forbidden by Section 605, whether by state or federal agents, is inadmissible in federal court."

Schwartz v. Texas was overruled in Lee v. Florida, 391 U.S. 378 (1968), which held inadmissible in a state trial evidence obtained by state police in violation of Section 605. Justice Stewart's majority opinion noted that Schwartz "was decided in the shadow of" Wolf and before Mapp and concluded: "In view of the Nardone and Benanti decisions, the doctrine of Schwartz v. Texas cannot survive the demise of Wolf v. Colorado." Justices Black, Harlan, and White dissented. In Fuller v. Alaska, 393 U.S. 80 (1968), the new rule was held applicable "only to trials in which the evidence is sought to be introduced after the date of our decision in Lee."

c. *Berger.* Berger v. New York, 388 U.S. 41 (1967), invalidated a New York statute authorizing official electronic eavesdropping ("bugging") pursuant to court order. A sharply divided Court concluded "that the language of New York's [permissive eavesdrop] statute is too broad in its sweep resulting in a trespassory intrusion into a constitutionally protected area" and held it "deficient on its face." Justice Clark's majority opinion concluded that the statute did not provide for "adequate judicial supervision or protective procedures." The Fourth Amendment's "particularity" requirements were not met: the eavesdrop order procedure failed to require identification of the conversations to be "seized" or of the specific crimes involved. Moreover, authorization of eavesdropping for up to two months involved too long a period. Finally, the statute—"necessarily because its success depends on secrecy"—authorized unconsented entry to place the recording device; it did not require "notice as do conventional warrants," nor any showing of "exigency" to avoid notice.

d. *Katz and the constitutional barrier.* Less than a year after Berger, in Katz v. United States, 389 U.S. 347 (1967), the Court in effect overruled Olmstead and Goldman, clearly held electronic surveillance subject to the Fourth Amendment without regard to physical trespass, but also provided new guidelines indicating the kind of judicial supervision that would make "bugging" constitutionally acceptable. As Justice Black's dissent in Katz put it: "The Berger case [set up] what appeared to be insuperable obstacles to the valid passage of . . . wiretapping laws by States. The Court's opinion in this case, however, removes the doubts about state power in this field and abates to a large extent the confusion and near paralyzing effect of the Berger holding."

In Katz, the Court set aside a conviction for transmitting wagering information where evidence had been obtained by FBI agents who had attached an electronic listening device to the outside of a telephone booth. Justice Stewart's majority opinion stated that "a person in a telephone booth may rely upon the protection of the Fourth Amendment." Nor did it make any difference that there had been no physical penetration of the booth: "We conclude that the underpinnings of Olmstead and Goldman have been so eroded by our subsequent decisions that the 'trespass' doctrine there enunciated can no longer be regarded as controlling." [In Desist v. United States, 394 U.S. 244 (1969), a divided Court found nonretroactivity appropriate for the Katz rule.]

But holding the Fourth Amendment applicable, the Court went on to emphasize, would not make all "bugging" impermissible. An appropriate judicial order could authorize "the carefully limited use of electronic surveillance." Indeed, the surveillance described by the Government here "was so narrowly circumscribed that a duly authorized magistrate, properly notified of the need for such investigation, specifically informed of the basis on which it was to proceed, and clearly apprised of the precise intrusion it would entail, could constitutionally have authorized, with appropriate safeguards, the very limited search and seizure that the Government asserts in fact took place." [As described by the Government, surveillance had not begun until there had been a showing of "a strong probability" of federal law violation, and "the surveillance was limited, both in scope and in duration."]

In a separate concurring opinion, Justice Douglas, joined by Justice Brennan, objected to a suggestion in Justice White's concurrence "as a wholly unwarranted green light for the Executive Branch to resort to electronic eavesdropping without a warrant in cases which the Executive Branch itself labels 'national security' matters." There was also a concurrence by Justice Harlan. Justice Black dissented at length. He insisted that the Fourth Amendment was limited to the protection of "tangible things," denied that conversations can be "seized," and concluded: "Rather than using language in a completely artificial way, I must conclude that the Fourth Amendment simply does not apply to eavesdropping." *

e. *The 1968 Act.* Note the relevant provisions in the Omnibus Crime Control and Safe Streets Act of 1968. Title III, "Wiretapping and Electronic Surveillance," permits court-approved interceptions by federal and state law enforcement officials in the investigation of a large number of listed crimes. See, e. g., Section 2516(2) regarding state officials and listing "murder, kidnapping, gambling, robbery, bribery, extortion, or dealing in narcotic drugs, marihuana or other dangerous drugs, or other crime dangerous to life, limb, or property, and punishable by imprisonment for more than one year, designated in any applicable State statute authorizing such interception, or any conspiracy to commit any of the foregoing offenses." Title III was one of the provisions President Johnson objected to when he signed the bill. He stated that he would continue in force his Administration's policy of confining "wire-tapping and eavesdropping to national security cases only—and then only with the approval of the Attorney General." Is Title III constitutional?

7. *The Fourth Amendment and intrusions into the body.* In Schmerber v. California, 384 U.S. 757 (1966), the Court—after finding no merit in due process and self-incrimination objections (see p. 873, supra)—also rejected the search and seizure challenge to a compulsory blood test. Justice Brennan's majority opinion noted: "Because we are dealing with intrusions into the human body rather than with state interferences with property relationships or private papers—'houses, papers, and effects'—we write on a clean slate." He stated that "once the privilege against self-incrimination has been found not to bar compelled intrusions into the body for blood to be analyzed for alcohol content, the Fourth Amendment's proper function is to constrain, not against all intrusions as such, but against intrusions which are not justified in the circumstances, or which are made in an improper manner." He concluded that "the police were justified in requiring petitioner to submit to the blood test" and that "the means and procedures employed in taking his blood respected relevant Fourth Amendment standards of reasonableness."

8. *Administrative inspections.* In Frank v. Maryland, 359 U.S. 360 (1959), a Baltimore Health Department inspector, claiming that he had found evidence of rodent infestation in back of appellant's house, sought permission to inspect the basement without a warrant. Appellant refused and was convicted of barring the inspection. In a 5:4 decision, the Court held that the

* On the type of hearing to be afforded to determine whether illegal electronic surveillance tainted the evidence against an accused, see Alderman v. United States, 394 U.S. 165 (1969), providing for broad access by the defense to the records of the overheard conversations and rejecting, even in national security cases, the government's suggestion of *in camera* screening by the trial judge. Note, however, Justice Stewart's concurrence in Giordano v. United States, 394 U.S. 310 (1969), insisting that "the constitutionality of electronic surveillance relating to the gathering of foreign intelligence information" remains an open question. And see the report (The New York Times, June 14, 1969) of a Justice Department claim that electronic surveillance without judicial approval is constitutional not only in foreign intelligence but also in domestic subversion situations.

conviction did not violate the "constitutional right of privacy" recognized in Wolf: "[I]nspection without a warrant, as an adjunct to a regulatory scheme for the general welfare of the community and not as a means of enforcing the criminal law, has antecedents deep in our history." But the upholding of warrantless administrative searches in municipal fire, health and housing inspection programs came to an end when Frank v. Maryland was overruled in Camara v. Municipal Court, 387 U.S. 523 (1967).

Camara held that the Fourth Amendment prevents prosecution for refusal to permit a warrantless code enforcement inspection of a personal residence. And a companion case, See v. Seattle, 387 U.S. 541 (1967), held Camara applicable to inspections of commercial premises. But the "probable cause" prerequisite for the issuance of warrants was found to be a less formidable requirement in the new administrative context than it has been in the traditional criminal one. Justice White's majority opinion in Camara concluded that "probable cause" to issue a warrant to inspect could exist "if reasonable legislative or administrative standards for conducting an area inspection are satisfied with respect to a particular dwelling." Those standards, he pointed out, would "not necessarily depend upon specific knowledge of the condition of the particular dwelling." Justice Clark's dissent, joined by Justices Harlan and Stewart, insisted that the Court's approach not only unjustifiably overruled Frank but "prostitutes" the "probable cause" requirement and established "a newfangled 'warrant' system that is entirely foreign to Fourth Amendment standards." See LaFave, "Administrative Searches and the Fourth Amendment: The Camara and See Cases," 1967 Sup.Ct.Rev. 1.

SECTION 4. THE RETROACTIVE EFFECT OF NEW CONSTITUTIONAL RULINGS

LINKLETTER AND THE CHANGING CONTOURS OF PROSPECTIVE OVERRULING

Introduction. The confusion in the lower courts about the retroactivity of the ruling in Mapp v. Ohio, p. 871, supra, prompted the Supreme Court to take its first detailed look (in 1965, in Linkletter v. Walker, note 1 infra) at a problem that had become more and more pressing as announcements of new constitutional rights proliferated.

Ordinarily, new judicial interpretations are retroactive. But as early as 1956, in Griffin v. Illinois (sec. 1, p. 852, supra), Justice Frankfurter urged the Court to give only prospective effect to the new Griffin requirements: "We must be mindful of the fact that there are undoubtedly convicts under confinement in Illinois prisons, in numbers unknown to us and under unappealed sentences imposed years ago, who will find justification in this opinion, unless properly qualified, for proceedings both in the state and the federal courts upon claims that they are under illegal detention. . . . It would be an easy answer that a claim that was not duly asserted—as was the timely claim by these petitioners—cannot be asserted now. The answer is too easy. Candor compels acknowledgment that the decision rendered today is a new ruling. . . . The judicial choice is not limited to a new ruling necessarily retrospective, or to rejection of what the requirements of legal protection, as now perceived, require. For sound reasons, law generally speaks prospectively. . . . We should not indulge in the fiction that the law now announced has always been the law and, therefore, that those who did not avail themselves of it waived their rights. It is much more conducive to law's self-respect to recognize candidly the considerations that give prospective content to a new pronouncement of law. . . . The rule of law announced this day should be delimited as indicated."

Suggestions such as these were made for the next decade but elicited no response from the majority. See, e. g., Justice Harlan's plea (in a footnote at p. 849, supra) that the Court give "full-dress consideration" to the retroactivity of the new counsel requirement announced by Gideon v. Wainwright. That "full-dress consideration" of the retroactivity problem came soon after, because of the uncertainty about the effect of the search and seizure decision in Mapp: after that 1961 decision, the lower federal courts split on the retroactivity of the ruling; most state courts held it not retroactive. In Linkletter v. Walker, 381 U.S. 618 (1965) (note 1 below), the Court at last confronted what had "become a most troublesome question in the administration of justice" and concluded in a 7:2 decision that retroactivity was not mandatory for all new constitutional rulings and that some could properly be limited to prospective effect.

But Linkletter did not end the retroactivity controversy; rather, it moved it into new directions. Cases since have not only produced divisions on the question whether prospectivity is proper for a particular newly announced right. There has been even greater controversy about the contours of prospectivity—the appropriate cut-off time once it is decided that full retroactivity is not warranted. The materials below illustrate both aspects of the controversy: note 2 reviews the process of determining whether a new guarantee should be denied retroactive effect in view of the Linkletter criteria; note 3 deals with the even more unstable and controversial area of selecting the proper cut-off point for "prospective only" rulings.

1. *The Linkletter case.* Justice Clark's majority opinion in Linkletter noted that "heretofore, without discussion, we have applied new constitutional rules to cases finalized before the promulgation of the rule"—citing applications of Griffin v. Illinois, Gideon v. Wainwright, and evolving standards regarding coerced confessions. The prior cases did not, however, demonstrate "an absolute rule of retroaction . . . in the area of constitutional adjudication." Rather, Justice Clark concluded, "the Constitution neither prohibits nor requires retrospective effect." The proper approach was to "weigh the merits and demerits" of retroactivity in each case "by looking to the prior history of the rule in question, its purpose and effect, and whether retrospective operation will further or retard its operation."

Accordingly, the Court examined "the purpose of the Mapp rule; the reliance placed upon the Wolf doctrine; and the effect on the administration of justice of a retroactive application of Mapp." Justice Clark emphasized that "all of the cases since Wolf requiring the exclusion of illegal evidence have been based on the necessity for an effective deterrent to illegal police action. . . . We cannot say that this purpose would be advanced by making the rule retrospective. . . . Nor would it add harmony to the delicate state-federal relationship . . . . Finally, the ruptured privacy of the victims' homes and effects cannot be restored. Reparation comes too late." Moreover, the deterrence purpose of Mapp "will not at this late date be served by the wholesale release of the guilty victims." Justice Clark added that retroactive application of Mapp "would tax the administration of justice to the utmost. Hearings would have to be held on the excludability of evidence long since destroyed, misplaced or deteriorated. If it is excluded, the witnesses available at the time of the original trial will not be available or if located their memory will be dimmed. To thus legitimate such an extraordinary procedural weapon that has no bearing on guilt would seriously disrupt the administration of justice."

Justice Clark rejected the argument that the same considerations were applicable to other areas—especially coerced confessions—where the Court had applied new rulings retrospectively. He noted that "there is no likelihood of unreliability or coercion present in a search and seizure case." Moreover, "in each of the three areas in which we have applied our rule retrospectively the principle that we applied went to the fairness of the trial—the very integrity of the fact-finding process. Here, . . . the fairness of the trial is not under attack. All that petitioner attacks is the admissibility of evidence, the reliability and relevancy of which is not questioned, and which may well have had no effect on the outcome."

The Court accordingly concluded that the exclusionary rule of Mapp should not apply to "state court convictions which had become final before rendition" of the Mapp decision.* Linkletter's burglary conviction had been affirmed by the Louisiana Supreme Court before Mapp; but the seizure of the evidence used in Linkletter's trial had taken place after the seizure in Mapp. Linkletter accordingly argued that the Mapp rule should at least date from the day of the seizure there, rather than that of the Supreme Court's decision. The Court, however, rejected the date of the seizure in Mapp as of "no legal significance. It was the judgment of this Court that changed the rule and the date of that opinion is the crucial date. [T]his is the better cut-off time." The Court accordingly concluded "that though the error complained of might be fundamental it is not of the nature requiring us to overturn all final convictions based upon it." [Note the subsequent developments as to cut-off time, note 3, infra.]

Justice Black, joined by Justice Douglas, dissented. He noted: "Linkletter must stay in jail; Miss Mapp, whose offense was committed before Linkletter's, is free. This different treatment of Miss Mapp and Linkletter points up at once the arbitrary and discriminatory nature of the judicial contrivance utilized here to break the promise of Mapp by keeping all people in jail who are unfortunate enough to have had their unconstitutional convictions affirmed before June 19, 1961." He stated that he "would follow this Court's usual practice and apply the Mapp rule to unconstitutional convictions which have resulted in persons being presently in prison. . . . I am at a loss to understand why those who suffer from the use of evidence secured by a search and seizure in violation of the Fourth Amendment should be treated differently from those who have been denied other guarantees of the Bill of Rights." The Mapp rule "should be given like dignity and effect as the coerced confession exclusionary rule."

---

* In a footnote, the Court explained: "By final we mean where the judgment of conviction was rendered, the availability of appeal exhausted, and the time for petition for certiorari had elapsed before our decision in Mapp v. Ohio."

Justice Black objected, moreover, to the Court's emphasis on the deterrence purpose of the Mapp rule: "I would say that if that is the sole purpose, reason, object and effect of the law, or of the rule, the Court's action in adopting it sounds more like law-making than construing the Constitution. . . . If the exclusionary rule has the high place in our constitutional plan of 'ordered liberty,' which this Court in Mapp and other cases has so frequently said that it does have, what possible valid reason can justify keeping people in jail under convictions obtained by wanton disregard of a constitutional protection which the Court itself in Mapp treated as being one of the 'constitutional rights of the accused'?" He concluded: "Careful analysis of the Court's opinion shows that it rests on the premise that the State's assumed interest in the old, repudiated rule outweighs the interests of the States and of the people convicted in having wrongful convictions set aside. It certainly offends my sense of justice to say that a State holding in jail people who were convicted by unconstitutional methods has a vested interest in keeping them there that outweighs the right of persons adjudged guilty of crime to challenge their unconstitutional convictions at any time."

Is the Court's denial of retroactivity too much like "law-making"? Are the different treatments of Linkletter and Miss Mapp "arbitrary and discriminatory"? Do the later developments (especially about cut-off time, note 3, infra) make "law-making" and "arbitrariness" attacks on the Court's approach less forceful? See generally Mishkin, "The High Court, the Great Writ, and the Due Process of Time and Law," 79 Harv.L.Rev. 56 (1965), and Schwartz, "Retroactivity, Reliability, and Due Process: A Reply to Professor Mishkin," 33 U.Chi.L.Rev. 719 (1966).

2. *Denials of retroactivity: some applications of Linkletter.* In Stovall v. Denno, 388 U.S. 293 (1967), the Court summarized the Linkletter factors regarding the basic choice between retroactivity and nonretroactivity as follows: "The criteria guiding resolution of the question implicate (a) the purpose to be served by the new standards, (b) the extent of the reliance by law enforcement authorities on the old standards, and (c) the effect on the administration of justice of a retroactive application of the new standards." That applications of these criteria have produced some controversy is illustrated in the following excerpt from Justice Harlan's dissent in Desist v. United States, 394 U.S. 244 (1969):

"Although it has more than once been said that 'new' rules affecting 'the very integrity of the fact-finding process' are to be retroactively applied, . . . this requirement was eroded to some extent in Johnson v. New Jersey [384 U.S. 719 (1966), on the Escobedo and Miranda rules] and yet further in Stovall v. Denno [the 1967 ruling, supra, on the Wade and Gilbert requirements as to lineup identification]; see also DeStefano v. Woods, 392 U.S. 631 (1968) [jury trial requirements nonretroactive]. Again, although it has been said that a decision will be retroactively applied when it has been 'clearly foreshadowed' in our prior case law, . . . the Court today rejects such a contention [by denying retroactive effect to the new rule regarding electronic surveillance announced in Katz v. United States, 389 U.S. 347 (1967)]."

3. *Cut-off time and the contours of prospectivity: the departures from Linkletter.* The Court has had even greater difficulties in choosing the cut-off point once some prospectivity has been found appropriate under the criteria

considered in notes 1 and 2, supra. The divisiveness of the date selection problem was reflected in Chief Justice Warren's last Term: the issue split the Court in five major cases. As the retiring Chief Justice put it (rather mildly) in one of the cases: "Our initial approach to prospective decision-making has undergone some modification." Jenkins v. Delaware, 395 U.S. 213 (1969).

In the early decisions rejecting retroactivity, the Court did not require "pure prospectivity": the new constitutional requirements there were applied to all cases still pending on direct review at the time they were announced. See Linkletter, note 1, supra (search and seizure), and Tehan v. Shott, 382 U.S. 406 (on the self-incrimination rule of Griffin v. California, sec. 2, p. 878, supra). But the Court began a new course with Johnson v. New Jersey, 384 U.S. 719 (1966) (on Escobedo and Miranda): it departed from Linkletter and Tehan and came closer to "pure prospectivity" by refusing to permit cases still pending on direct review to benefit from the new interrogation requirements. Thus, except for the parties in Escobedo and Miranda, those new rulings applied only to cases in which trial began after the date of the Supreme Court decisions in Escobedo and Miranda. As Chief Justice Warren commented in reviewing the developments in Jenkins v. Delaware: "With Johnson we began placing increasing emphasis upon the point at which law enforcement officials relied upon practices not yet proscribed."

Given that reliance emphasis, the trial date cut-off point of Johnson v. New Jersey could not last. "More recently," Chief Justice Warren continued in Jenkins, "we have selected the point of initial reliance." That development began with Stovall v. Denno, 388 U.S. 293 (1967) (on the Wade and Gilbert line-up requirements). Those new rulings were held applicable only in the immediate cases "and all future cases which involve confrontation for identification purposes conducted in the absence of counsel after" the dates of Wade and Gilbert. The fact that Wade and Gilbert were thus the only beneficiaries of the new rules was described as "an unavoidable consequence of the necessity that constitutional adjudications not stand as mere dictum."

Chief Justice Warren's attempt to state the justifications for the newer varieties of prospectivity emphasized "the problem inherent in prospective decision-making" generally: "some defendants benefit from the new rule while others do not, solely because of the fortuities that determine the progress of their cases from initial investigation and arrest to final judgment. The resulting incongruities must be balanced against the impetus the technique [of prospective overruling] provides for the implementation of long overdue reforms, which otherwise could not be practicably effected. Thus, raising the specter of potential anomalies does not further the difficult decision of selecting the precise event that should determine the prospective application of a newly formulated constitutional principle." He recognized "a large measure of judicial discretion" in selecting the proper time. "In our more recent decisions in this area, we have regarded as determinative the moment at which the discarded standards were first relied upon. See, e. g., Desist v. United States [in note 2, supra—on the electronic eavesdropping rules of Katz]; Stovall v. Denno, supra. The point of reliance is critical, not because of any constitutional compulsion, but because it determines the impact that newly articulated constitutional principles will have upon convictions obtained pursuant to investigatory and prosecutorial practices not previously proscribed."

In Jenkins v. Delaware itself, the Court held that the Miranda requirements did not apply to a retrial after June 13, 1966—the cut-off point set for the Miranda requirements by Johnson v. New Jersey—because Jenkins' original trial had begun before that cut-off point.   Justice Harlan dissented, urging that the Court reject "the *ad hoc* approach that has so far characterized our decisions in the retroactivity field."   See also his lengthy dissent in Desist, note 2, supra: "I can no longer . . . remain content with the doctrinal confusion that has characterized our efforts to apply the basic Linkletter principle.   'Retroactivity' must be rethought."   He objected to the reaffirmance of the Stovall v. Denno (nearly pure prospectivity) practice and concluded "that Linkletter was right" in insisting that all new requirements "must, at a minimum, be applied to all those cases which are still subject to direct review by this Court at the time the 'new' decision is handed down."   Justices Black and Douglas have also frequently dissented from pure prospectivity rulings, reiterating their Linkletter dissent.

SECTION 5.   FAIR TRIBUNAL AND FAIR HEARING

A.   THE IMPARTIAL JUDGE

1. *The basic principle: the Tumey case.*   Tumey v. Ohio, 273 U.S. 510 (1927), involved an Ohio law under which mayors had jurisdiction to try bootlegging cases anywhere in the county.   Half of the fines collected went to the municipal treasury.   A village ordinance provided that its mayor would receive the costs paid by defendants in cases of conviction.   At the trial, Tumey unsuccessfully objected that the mayor was disqualified by his financial interest.   The Supreme Court, in an opinion by Chief Justice Taft, reversed the conviction: "All questions of judicial qualification may not involve constitutional validity.   Thus matters of kinship, personal bias, state policy, remoteness of interest would seem generally to be matters merely of legislative discretion. . . .   But it certainly violates the Fourteenth Amendment and deprives a defendant in a criminal case of due process of law to subject his liberty or property to the judgment of a court, the judge of which has a direct, personal, substantial pecuniary interest in reaching a conclusion against him in his case. . . .

"From this review [of English common law] we conclude, that a system by which an inferior judge is paid for his service only when he convicts the defendant has not become so embedded by custom in the general practice either at common law or in this country that it can be regarded as due process of law, unless the costs usually imposed are so small that they may be properly ignored as within the maxim *de minimis non curat lex.*

"The Mayor received for his fees and costs in the present case $12, and from such costs under the Prohibition Act for seven months he made about $100 a month, in addition to his salary.   We can not regard the prospect of receipt or loss of such an emolument in each case as a minute, remote, trifling or insignificant interest.   It is certainly not fair to each defendant, brought before the Mayor for the careful and judicial consideration of his guilt or innocence, that the prospect of such a loss by the Mayor should weigh against his acquittal."

2. *Contempt proceedings.* a. The judge's impartiality is frequently challenged where the judge punishes alleged misconduct committed before him as contempt. In re Murchison, 349 U.S. 133 (1955), involved criminal contempt convictions of two witnesses by a judge before whom the witnesses had appeared in a previous "one-man grand jury" investigation. Michigan law permits state judges to conduct such "one-man grand jury" investigations about suspected crimes. The Supreme Court, in a 5 to 4 decision, held that the contempt proceedings violated due process: "A fair trial in a fair tribunal is a basic requirement of due process. Fairness of course requires an absence of actual bias in the trial of cases. But our system of law has always endeavored to prevent even the probability of unfairness. . . . It would be very strange if our system of law permitted a judge to act as a grand jury and then try the very persons accused as a result of his investigations. . . . It is true that contempt committed in a trial courtroom can under some circumstances be punished summarily by the trial judge. . . . But adjudication by a trial judge of contempt committed in his immediate presence in open court cannot be likened to the proceedings here."

b. The Supreme Court's supervisory power over federal judges punishing summarily for criminal contempt under Rule 42(a) of the Federal Rules of Criminal Procedure, for conduct "committed in the actual presence of the court," is illustrated by Offutt v. United States, 348 U.S. 11 (1954). There, the Court reversed a conviction of defense counsel for "contumacious and unethical conduct in open court": the judge had "become personally embroiled" and his behavior "precluded the atmosphere which should especially dominate a criminal trial." The Court concluded that, under the rule of Cooke v. United States, 267 U.S. 517 (1924), the trial judge should have requested the assignment of another judge to sit in the hearing on the contempt charge. Compare Sacher v. United States, 343 U.S. 1 (1952). See generally Frank, "Disqualification of Judges," 56 Yale L.J. 605 (1947). For a Court endorsement of contempt as a (but not the exclusive) means for controlling unruly defendants, see Illinois v. Allen, 397 U.S. —— (1970), noted below, p. 909.

———————————

B. THE PROSECUTOR AND THE GRAND JURY

1. *The prosecutor.* In Mooney v. Holohan, 294 U.S. 103 (1935), petitioner claimed that "the 'knowing use' by the State of perjured testimony to obtain the conviction and the deliberate suppression of evidence . . . constituted a denial of due process of law." In a per curiam decision, the Court, inter alia, rejected the State's contention "that the acts or omissions of a prosecuting attorney" can never "in and by themselves, amount . . . to a denial of due process of law." Due process is not satisfied "if a State has contrived a conviction through the pretense of a trial which in truth is but used as a means of depriving a defendant of liberty through a deliberate deception of court and jury by testimony known to be perjured." See also Miller v. Pate, 386 U.S. 1 (1967).

In the course of the majority opinion in Brady v. Maryland, 373 U.S. 83 (1963), Justice Douglas extended the Mooney principle as follows: "We now hold that the suppression by the prosecution of evidence favorable to an accused upon request violates due process where the evidence is material either to guilt or to punishment, irrespective of the good faith or bad faith of the prosecution." He added: "The principle of Mooney v. Holohan is not punishment of society for misdeeds of a prosecutor but avoidance of an unfair trial to the accused." Compare the uncertainty about the scope of the prosecution's duty to disclose in Giles v. Maryland, 386 U.S. 66 (1967).*

2. *The grand jury.* a. In federal prosecutions, the Fifth Amendment requires grand jury indictments in cases of "capital, or otherwise infamous" crimes. A federal crime is considered "infamous" if it is punishable by imprisonment at hard labor, whether or not in a penitentiary. United States v. Moreland, 258 U.S. 433 (1922). Hurtado v. California, 110 U.S. 516 (1884), held that the 14th Amendment did not prohibit a state from initiating criminal prosecutions by an information rather than by a grand jury indictment. In Costello v. United States, 350 U.S. 359 (1956), the Court held that a federal indictment was not invalidated by the fact that "only hearsay evidence was presented to the grand jury": "[I]n this country as in England of old the grand jury has convened as a body of laymen, free from technical rules, acting in secret, pledged to indict no one because of prejudice and to free no one because of special favor. [I]f indictments were to be held open to challenge on the ground that there was inadequate or incompetent evidence before the grand jury, the resulting delay would be great indeed." Moreover, the Court declined to establish a rule against the sufficiency of such evidence in exercise of its supervisory power over federal courts. See also the materials on discrimination in jury selection, p. 903, infra.

C. JURY TRIAL

1. *The constitutional guarantees.* The right to trial by jury in criminal cases in the federal courts is provided by Art. III, Sec. 3, and the Sixth Amendment of the Constitution. The right is to "a trial by jury as understood and applied at common law, and includes all the essential elements as they were recognized in this country and England when the Constitution was adopted. . . . Those elements were (1) that the jury should consist of twelve men, neither more nor less; (2) that the jury should be in the presence or under the superintendence of a judge having power to instruct them as to the law and advise them in respect of the facts; and (3) that the verdict should be unanimous." Patton v. United States, 281 U.S. 276

---

* In review of federal criminal convictions, the Supreme Court may reverse where the federal prosecutor oversteps "the bounds of that propriety and fairness which should characterize the conduct of such an officer." The interest of the United States "in a criminal prosecution is not that it shall win a case, but that justice shall be done." Though the prosecutor "may strike hard blows, he is not at liberty to strike foul ones. It is as much his duty to refrain from improper methods calculated to produce a wrongful conviction as it is to use every legitimate means to bring about a just one. It is fair to say that the average jury . . . has confidence that these obligations . . . will be faithfully observed. Consequently, improper suggestions, insinuations and, especially, assertions of personal knowledge are apt to carry much weight against the accused when they should properly carry none." Berger v. United States, 295 U.S. 78 (1935).

(1930).[1] The Sixth Amendment jury trial guarantee was held applicable to the states under the 14th, in Duncan v. Louisiana, 391 U.S. 145 (1968), printed in chap. 11, p. 812, above. Note also the Seventh Amendment right to a jury trial in certain federal civil cases (worth over twenty dollars). Should that right be "incorporated" into the 14th Amendment? See Walker v. Sauvinet, 92 U.S. 90 (1875), refusing to do so a century ago.

2. *Contempt cases and "petty" offenses.* The right to jury trial in contempt cases has been a fertile source of litigation in recent years; and the claims have produced a wavering, complex course of decisions. In Green v. United States, 356 U.S. 165 (1958), for example, the Court reaffirmed the traditional view that the Constitution does not require jury trial in contempt of court cases. But in United States v. Barnett, 376 U.S. 681 (1964) the majority opinion warned: "Some members of the Court are of the view that, without regard to the seriousness of the offense, punishment by summary trial without a jury would be constitutionally limited to that penalty provided for petty offenses." For a reflection of the Court's continuing divisions regarding criminal contempt—and for a review of the evolving standards for identifying the "petty offenses" exception to the jury trial guarantee—see Frank v. United States, 395 U.S. 147 (1969).

In the course of his majority opinion in Frank, Justice Marshall recalled: "For purposes of the right to trial by jury, criminal contempt is treated just like all other criminal offenses. The defendant is entitled to a jury trial unless the particular offense can be classified as 'petty.' Dyke v. Taylor Implement Mfg. Co., 391 U.S. 216 (1968); Bloom v. Illinois, 391 U.S. 194 (1968); Cheff v. Schnackenberg, 384 U.S. 373 (1966)." Criminal contempt differs from other crimes, however, in the standard applied to determine whether the offense is "petty." With regard to crimes generally, the Court finds "the severity of the penalty authorized" by the legislature to be the "most relevant indication of the seriousness of an offense." [Duncan v. Louisiana, 391 U.S. 145 (1968), p. 812, supra, for example, held a jury trial required in a state prosecution for simple battery resulting in a sixty days prison term, because the offense carried the maximum prison sentence of two years.] But the usual standard looking to "the severity of the penalty authorized, not the penalty actually imposed," is inapplicable in contempt: a person may be found in contempt "for a great many different types" of activities; Congress has not imposed limits on judicial discretion in imposing

---

1. Note United States v. Jackson, 390 U.S. 570 (1968), invalidating a provision of the Federal Kidnaping Act which authorized capital punishment only if "the jury shall so recommend." Justice Stewart's majority opinion held that this death penalty provision imposed "an impermissible burden" on the exercise of constitutional rights: "The inevitable effect of any such provision is . . . to discourage assertion of the Fifth Amendment right not to plead guilty and to deter exercise of the Sixth Amendment right to demand a jury trial." Congress was of course authorized "to mitigate the severity of capital punishment": limiting the death penalty to cases in which a jury recommended it was an entirely legitimate goal. But that could not save the provision: legitimate objectives "cannot be pursued by means that needlessly chill the exercise of basic constitutional rights." Justice White's dissent, joined by Justice Black, urged that it was adequate to scrutinize individual guilty pleas and jury trial waivers "in order to make sure that they have been neither coerced nor encouraged by the death penalty power in the jury." Accordingly, "I would not take the first step toward invalidation of statutes on their face because they arguably burden the right to jury trial." (Note the material on other challenges to capital punishment procedures, p. 922, infra.)

penalties. "Accordingly, this Court has held that in prosecutions for criminal contempt where no maximum penalty is authorized, the severity of the penalty actually imposed is the best indication of the seriousness of the particular offense." Accordingly, no jury trial is required for criminal contempt sentences up to six months.

D. TRIAL BY NEWS MEDIA

1. *Irvin v. Dowd.* In Irvin v. Dowd, 366 U.S. 717 (1961), the Court for the first time set aside a state conviction because newspaper publicity prevented a fair trial. Charges that petitioner had confessed to six murders had been widely publicized. He was indicted for one murder and convicted. The Court reversed: "It is not required . . . that the jurors be totally ignorant of the facts. . . . It is sufficient if the juror can lay aside his impression or opinion and render a verdict based on the evidence presented in court. . . . No doubt each juror was sincere when he said he would be fair and impartial to petitioner, but the psychological impact requiring such a declaration is often its father. . . . With his life at stake, it is not requiring too much that petitioner be tried in an atmosphere undisturbed by so huge a wave of public passion and by a jury other than one in which two-thirds of the members admit, before hearing any testimony, to possessing a belief in his guilt." Justice Clark dissented, however, when the Court reversed a murder conviction because of pre-trial publicity in Rideau v. Louisiana, 373 U.S. 723 (1963). He saw no "substantial nexus between the televised "interview" and petitioner's trial, which occurred almost two months later." [1]

2. *Estes v. Texas and television.* In Estes v. Texas, 381 U.S. 532 (1965), a divided Court produced a number of lengthy opinions on the issue of televising criminal trials. In proceedings against Billie Sol Estes on swindling charges, a two-day pretrial hearing had been considerably disrupted by the presence of personnel and equipment used for live televising. At the subsequent trial, television equipment was "relatively unobtrusive": it was restricted to a specially built booth at the rear of the courtroom, and live telecasting was prohibited during most of the trial. Portions of the trial were telecast by videotape. Justice Clark's "opinion of the Court" was fully joined only by Chief Justice Warren and Justices Douglas and Goldberg. Justice Harlan, whose vote was necessary for the judgment of reversal, joined with "reservations." Justices White, Stewart, Black and Brennan dissented.

Justice Clark noted that "one cannot put his finger on [the] specific mischief and prove with particularity wherein he was prejudiced." Nevertheless, the "untoward circumstances" were found "inherently bad" and "prejudice to the accused was assumed." He stated that the use of television "amounts to the injection of an irrelevant factor into court proceedings." He

---

1. For other examples of "outside unauthorized intrusions" into jury deliberations, see Remmer v. United States, 347 U.S. 227 (1954); id., 350 U.S. 377 (1956) (outsider approach to juror); and Gold v. United States, 352 U.S. 985 (1957) (reversal because of "unintentional official intrusion into the privacy of the jury"). See also the material on mob domination, infra, and note Turner v. Louisiana, 379 U.S. 466 (1965) ("continuous and intimate association" with jury during trial, by two deputy sheriffs who were prosecution witnesses, violates 14th Amendment).

noted, moreover, the "potential impact of television on the jurors," the possible impairment of the "quality of the testimony," the "additional responsibilities the presence of television places on the judge," and "the impact of courtroom television on the defendant." Justice Clark concluded: "[W]e cannot afford the luxury of saying that, because these factors are difficult of ascertainment in particular cases, they must be ignored. Nor are they 'purely hypothetical.' They are no more hypothetical than were the considerations deemed controlling in Tumey, Murchison, Rideau and Turner. They are real enough to have convinced the Judicial Conference of the United States, this Court and the Congress that television should be barred in federal trials by the Federal Rules of Criminal Procedure; in addition they have persuaded all but two of our States to prohibit television in the courtroom. They are effects that may, and in some combination almost certainly will, exist in any case in which television is injected into the trial process."

In an extensive, illustrated concurring opinion, Chief Justice Warren, joined by Justices Douglas and Goldberg, explained that he agreed "that the televising of criminal trials is inherently a denial of due process" but that he wished "to express additional views on why this is so." He concluded "(1) that the televising of trials diverts the trial from its proper purpose in that it has an inevitable impact on all the trial participants; (2) that it gives the public the wrong impression about the purpose of trials, thereby detracting from the dignity of court proceedings and lessening the reliability of trials; and (3) that it singles out certain defendants and subjects them to trials under prejudicial conditions not experienced by others." Justice Harlan's concurrence was based on the ground "that what was done in this case infringed the fundamental right to a fair trial."

Justice Stewart's dissent, joined by Justices Black, Brennan and White, stated: "I think that the introduction of television into a courtroom is, at least in the present state of the art, an extremely unwise policy. It invites many constitutional risks, and it detracts from the inherent dignity of a courtroom. But I am unable to escalate this personal view into a per se constitutional rule. And I am unable to find, on the specific record of this case, that the circumstances attending the limited televising of the petitioner's trial resulted in the denial of any right guaranteed to him by the United States Constitution. . . . There is no claim here based upon any right guaranteed by the First Amendment. But it is important to remember that we move in an area touching the realm of free communication, and for that reason, if for no other, I would be wary of imposing any per se rule, which, in the light of future technology, might serve to stifle or abridge true First Amendment rights."

3. *Sheppard v. Maxwell and control of newspaper publicity.* Justice Clark once again wrote for the majority in the Court's subsequent encounter with the "trial by news media" problem. Unlike the divisions in Estes, however, the Court was virtually unanimous in holding that Dr. Samuel H. Sheppard had been deprived of a fair trial in his 1954 Ohio conviction for the second degree murder of his wife "because of the trial judge's failure to protect Sheppard sufficiently from the massive, pervasive and prejudicial publicity that attended his prosecution." Only Justice Black dissented (without opinion) from the Court's holding that petitioner was entitled to federal habeas corpus relief. Sheppard v. Maxwell, 384 U.S. 333 (1966). Justice Clark's opinion described the "Roman holiday" atmosphere in detail, criticized

the trial judge's errors at length, and concluded with some general guidelines to minimize prejudicial news comment.

In commenting on the trial judge's conduct, the Court especially criticized his assumption that he lacked power to control the publicity: "Bearing in mind the massive pretrial publicity, the judge should have adopted stricter rules governing the use of the courtroom by newsmen . . . . Secondly, the court should have insulated the witnesses. . . . Thirdly, the court should have made some effort to control the release of leads, information, and gossip to the press by police officers, witnesses, and the counsel for both sides. . . . Had the judge, the other officers of the court, and the police placed the interest of justice first, the news media would have soon learned to be content with the task of reporting the case as it unfolded in the courtroom—not pieced together from extra-judicial statements."

More generally, the Court concluded: "From the cases coming here we note that unfair and prejudicial news comment on pending trials has become increasingly prevalent. . . . Of course, there is nothing that proscribes the press from reporting events that transpire in the courtroom. But where there is a reasonable likelihood that prejudicial news prior to trial will prevent a fair trial, the judge should continue the case until the threat abates, or transfer it to another county not so permeated with publicity. In addition, sequestration of the jury was something the judge should have raised *sua sponte* with counsel. If publicity during the proceedings threatens the fairness of the trial, a new trial should be ordered. But we must remember that reversals are but palliatives; the cure lies in those remedial measures that will prevent the prejudice at its inception. The courts must take such steps by rule and regulation that will protect their processes from prejudicial outside interferences. Neither prosecutors, counsel for defense, the accused, witnesses, court staff nor enforcement officers coming under the jurisdiction of the court should be permitted to frustrate its function. Collaboration between counsel and the press as to information affecting the fairness of a criminal trial is not only subject to regulation, but is highly censurable and worthy of disciplinary measures." [2]

E. DISCRIMINATION IN JURY SELECTION

1. *Racial discrimination in state jury selection.* a. Constitutional requirements regarding the selection of the panel come into play when the state provides juries. Racial discrimination in jury selection, in violation of the equal protection clause (see chap. 18, p. 1401, infra), has been the most commonly litigated claim.[1] In one of the earliest equal protection cases,

---

2. Compare the problems of reconciling free press and fair trial guarantees reflected in Craig v. Harney and Wood v. Georgia, chap. 16, pp. 1276 and 1279, infra, involving First Amendment challenges to contempt actions based on newspaper publicity during judicial proceedings. Note also the proposals of the Reardon Committee: ABA Project on Minimum Standards for Criminal Justice, Standards Relating to Fair Trial and Free Press (1966); and see Friendly and Goldfarb,

Crime and Publicity—The Impact of News on the Administration of Justice (1967).

1. For unsuccessful constitutional challenges not based on racial discrimination, see Fay v. New York, 332 U.S. 261 (1947) (New York "blue ribbon" juries; claim that workers and women were excluded), and Hoyt v. Florida, 368 U.S. 57 (1961) (all-male jury had convicted woman of murder of her husband; under Florida law,

Strauder v. West Virginia, 100 U.S. 303 (1880) (chap. 18, p. 1399) the Court reversed the murder conviction of a Negro because West Virginia legislation expressly limited jury service to whites. The cases since Strauder have typically involved claims of discrimination in the administration of the jury system, rather than racial exclusion on the face of the statute.

b. The Court has frequently emphasized that "proportional representation of races on a jury is not a constitutional requisite." The Constitution "requires only a fair jury selected without regard to race." Cassell v. Texas, 339 U.S. 282 (1950). But statistics may lay the basis for a discrimination claim. See, e. g., Avery v. Georgia, 345 U.S. 559 (1953), which upset a conviction where the scheme for drawing jurors put the names of white persons on white tickets and the names of Negroes on yellow tickets. Negroes were available for jury service but none was drawn in a panel of 60. The Court concluded that petitioner had established a prima facie case of discrimination and that the state had not overcome it. See also Whitus v. Georgia, 385 U.S. 545 (1967) (reliance on tax records maintained on a racially segregated basis). The Johnson Administration's civil rights proposals of 1967 urged congressional action applicable to state as well as federal jury selection, but only the federal court provisions were enacted (in 1968). See note 2, infra.

c. Compare, with the Avery case in note 1b above, Swain v. Alabama, 380 U.S. 202 (1965), where the quantitative case proved insufficient. The evidence showed "that while Negro males over 21 constitute 26% of all males in the county in this age group, only 10 to 15% of the grand and petit jury panels drawn from the jury box since 1953 have been Negroes. . . . There were four or five Negroes on the grand jury panel of about 33 in this case, out of which two served on the grand jury which indicted petitioner. Although there have been an average of six to seven Negroes on petit jury venires in criminal cases, no Negro has actually served on a petit jury from about 1950. In this case there were eight Negroes on the petit jury venire but none actually served, two being exempt and six being struck by the prosecutor in the process of selecting the jury." Justice White's majority opinion stated that an average of six to eight Negroes on the panels showed neither total exclusion nor "forbidden token inclusion" of Negroes. He concluded: "We cannot say that purposeful discrimination based on race alone is satisfactorily proved by showing that an identifiable group in a community is under-represented by as much as 10%." He noted that there had been no "meaningful attempt to demonstrate that the same proportion of Negroes" as whites "qualified under the standards being administered by the commissioners."

d. The Swain case also included a more unusual challenge: that the prosecutor had exercised "peremptory challenges to exclude Negroes" from serving on the jury in this case. Here, "the six Negroes available for jury service were struck [from the petit jury venire] by the prosecutor in the process of selecting the jury." The Court concluded that petitioner's challenge to "the alleged purposeful striking of Negroes from the jury" was "properly denied" by the state courts. Justice White stated: "Alabama con-

women were not called unless they registered for jury service). Compare note 3, infra, on federal juries, and see Witherspoon v. Illinois, 391 U.S.   510 (1968), noted infra, p. 921 (exclusion from jury simply because of general scruples against death penalty).

tends that its system of peremptory strikes—challenges without cause, without explanation and without judicial scrutiny—affords a suitable and necessary method of securing juries which in fact and in the opinion of the parties are fair and impartial. . . . Based on the history of this system and its actual use and operation in this country, we think there is merit in this position."

Swain also made a "broader claim" about peremptory challenges: not only that Negroes had been removed in his case, but also that there had never been a Negro on a petit jury in the county in either a civil or criminal case, and that "prosecutors have consistently and systematically exercised their strikes to prevent any and all Negroes on petit jury venires from serving on the petit jury itself." The Court agreed that this raised "a different issue." If there were proof of such a practice, the Court concluded, it "might support a reasonable inference that . . . the peremptory system is being used to deny the Negro the same right and opportunity to participate in the administration of justice enjoyed by the white population. These ends the peremptory challenge is not designed to facilitate or justify." In Swain's case, however, the Court found it unnecessary to pursue the matter, for the record did not clearly show "when, how often, and under what circumstances the prosecutor alone [rather than defense counsel as well] has been responsible for striking those Negroes who have appeared on petit jury panels." See Note, "Swain v. Alabama: A Constitutional Blueprint for the Perpetuation of the All-White Jury," 52 Va.L.Rev. 1157 (1966).

d.   Carter v. Jury Commission of Green County, 396 U.S. 320 (1970), was an unsuccessful effort to obtain a ruling that the Alabama jury selection process was unconstitutional on its face. The statute requires jury commissioners to select for jury service those persons who are "generally reputed to be honest and intelligent" and "esteemed in the community for their integrity, good character and sound judgment." Though there was "force" in the argument that these broad criteria provide state officials the opportunity to discriminate, the Court could not agree that the section "is irredeemably invalid on its face." Though there had been discrimination in the administration of the law, it was not "necessarily and under all circumstances invalid. The provision is devoid of any mention of race. Its antecedents are of ancient vintage, and there is no suggestion that the law was originally adopted or subsequently carried forward for the purpose of fostering racial discrimination. The federal courts are not incompetent to fashion detailed and stringent injunctive relief that will remedy any discriminatory application of the statute at the hands of the officials empowered to administer it."

See also the companion case, Turner v. Fouche, 396 U.S. 346 (1970), rejecting an on the face attack on the Georgia jury selection system, but finding a prima facie showing of discrimination in application. In Turner, appellants were also unsuccessful in obtaining an order directing that Negroes be appointed to the jury commission. Justice Douglas dissented on this claim: where the challenged state agency has a record of racial discrimination, he insisted, "the corrective remedy is proportional representation."

The form of the lawsuit in Turner was unusual. The appellants were Negroes who claimed that the state had refused to consider them for jury service. The Court noted: "This is the first case to reach the Court in which an attack upon alleged racial discrimination in choosing juries has been made by plaintiffs seeking affirmative relief, rather than by defendants challenging judgments of criminal conviction on the ground of systematic exclusion of Negroes from the grand juries that indicted them, the trial juries that found them guilty, or both. The District Court found no barrier to such a suit, and neither do we. Defendants in criminal proceedings do not have the only cognizable legal interest in nondiscriminatory jury selection. People excluded from juries because of their race are as much aggrieved as those indicted and tried by juries chosen under a system of racial exclusion."

2. *Jury selection in federal courts and the 1968 Act.* The Court's supervisory power over lower federal courts—as well as the Sixth Amendment's "impartial jury" guarantee—permits the Court to scrutinize federal jury composition "with greater freedom to reflect on notions of good policy than we may constitutionally exert over proceedings in state courts." Fay v. New York, 332 U.S. 261 (1947). Thus, in Thiel v. Southern Pacific Co., 328 U.S. 217 (1946), a civil action, the Court, relying on its "supervisory power", reversed a judgment for the defendant on the ground that daily wage earners were "deliberately and intentionally" excluded from the jury lists because of past experience that such persons were generally excused from jury duty in view of economic hardships.[2] Note the enactment in 1968 of the Jury Selection and Service Act, 82 Stat. 53. The Act states a policy "that all litigants in Federal courts entitled to trial by jury shall have the right to grand and petit juries selected at random from a fair cross section of the community in the district or division wherein the court convenes"; provides that no citizen shall be excluded from jury service "in the district courts of the United States on account of race, color, religion, sex, national origin, or economic status"; and provides guidelines for plans to assure "random selection of grand and petit jurors."

F. SOME ASPECTS OF A FULL AND FAIR HEARING

1. *Mob domination.* In Moore v. Dempsey, 261 U.S. 86 (1923), the Court, in an opinion by Justice Holmes, held that a federal habeas corpus hearing was required in view of the claim that the whole state proceeding was a "mask,—that counsel, jury, and judge were swept to the fatal end by an irresistible wave of public passion, and that the State Courts failed to correct the wrong." In such a case, "neither perfection in the machinery for the correction nor the possibility that the trial court and counsel saw no other way of avoiding the outbreak of the mob can prevent this Court from securing to the petitioners their constitutional rights." Accordingly, the federal District Judge was directed to examine the facts "for himself," for if true, they made the trial "absolutely void."

2. See also Ballard v. United States, 329 U.S. 187 (1946) (women improperly excluded from jury panel); Frazier v. United States, 335 U.S. 497 (1948) (narcotics conviction by District of Columbia jury composed entirely of Federal employees not a violation of "impartial jury" provision of Sixth Amendment); Dennis v. United States, 339 U.S. 162 (1950) (Communist Party official convicted for contempt of Congress; rejection of challenges to government employees on jury, on basis of "aura of surveillance and intimidation" allegedly caused by "Loyalty Order," not a violation of "impartial jury" guarantee). See generally Scott, "The Supreme Court's Control over State and Federal Criminal Juries," 34 Iowa L.Rev. 577 (1949).

2. *Public and speedy trial.* Does due process require that state court trials be public? In re Oliver, 333 U.S. 257 (1948), involved a "one-man grand jury" investigation which state judges are authorized to conduct under Michigan law. In the course of an investigation, petitioner was convicted in a secret hearing of contempt for allegedly evasive answers. In reversing the denial of habeas corpus by the state courts, Justice Black's opinion stated: "In view of this nation's historic distrust of secret proceedings, their inherent dangers to freedom, and the universal requirement of our federal and state governments that criminal trials be public, the Fourteenth Amendment's guarantee that no one shall be deprived of his liberty without due process of law means at least that an accused cannot be thus sentenced to prison."

On the "public trial" guarantee of the Sixth Amendment, see United States v. Kobli, 172 F.2d 919 (3d Cir. 1949). On the Sixth Amendment's "speedy trial" guarantee, see Pollard v. United States, 352 U.S. 354 (1957). The speedy trial guarantee was held applicable to the states in Klopfer v. North Carolina, 386 U.S. 213 (1967). In Smith v. Hooey, 393 U.S. 374 (1969), the Court considered the application of the guarantee "when the person under the state criminal charge is serving a prison sentence imposed by another jurisdiction." Petitioner, a federal prisoner, had made repeated requests that he be brought to trial on a 1960 Texas indictment. The Texas courts, emphasizing that "two separate sovereignties" were involved, insisted they were under no duty to honor his requests. The Supreme Court noted the federal policy of making its prisoners available in response to state requests and concluded that "Texas had a constitutional duty to make a diligent, good-faith effort to bring" petitioner to trial. [See also the note on the unruly defendants, p. 909, infra.]

3. *Confrontation and cross-examination. a. The Sixth Amendment right and the states.* The Sixth Amendment right of the accused to be "confronted with the witnesses against him" was primarily designed "to prevent depositions or *ex parte* affidavits . . . being used against the prisoner in lieu of a personal examination and cross-examination of the witness, in which the accused has an opportunity, not only of testing the recollection and sifting the conscience of the witness, but of compelling him to stand face to face with the jury in order that they may look at him, and judge by his demeanor upon the stand and the manner in which he gives his testimony whether he is worthy of belief." Mattox v. United States, 156 U.S. 237 (1895). In Snyder v. Massachusetts, 291 U.S. 97 (1934), Justice Cardozo said: "For present purposes we assume that the privilege [to confront one's accusers and cross-examine them] is reinforced by the Fourteenth Amendment, though this has not been squarely held." The "square holding" came 31 years later: Pointer v. Texas, 380 U.S. 400 (1965), held the Confrontation Clause of the Sixth Amendment applicable to the states. See also a companion case, Douglas v. Alabama, 380 U.S. 415 (1965).[1]

b. *Cross-examination and administrative hearings.* The Court has had several occasions to consider the right to cross-examination in administrative hearings. In Greene v. McElroy, 360 U.S. 474 (1959), petitioner's security

1. On confrontation in the context of sentencing procedures, see Williams v. New York, 337 U.S. 241 (1949), where petitioner unsuccessfully claimed that the judge's consideration of a pre-sentencing report violated due process. The Court cited "historical" and "practical" reasons for different evidentiary rules in trial and sentencing procedures.

clearance was revoked and he lost his job with a defense contractor. The Court held that the Defense Department was not authorized by statute or regulation to operate an industrial security clearance program which denied "the traditional procedural safeguards of confrontation and cross examination." Thus, though the Court spoke broadly about the importance of the claimed constitutional rights, the decision rested on "the absence of explicit authorization" for the administrative procedure.

An attempt to invoke Greene v. McElroy to invalidate certain rules of the U. S. Civil Rights Commission proved unsuccessful in Hannah v. Larche and Hannah v. Slawson, 363 U.S. 420 (1960). The challengers were witnesses—voting registrars as well as private citizens—summoned to appear at a Commission investigation of alleged Negro voting deprivations in Louisiana. They objected to rules providing "that the identity of persons submitting complaints to the Commission need not be disclosed, and that those summoned to testify before the Commission . . . may not cross-examine other witnesses." Chief Justice Warren emphasized that the Commission's function "is purely investigative and fact-finding. It does not adjudicate." He concluded that "the purely investigative nature of the Commission's proceedings, the burden that the claimed rights would place upon those proceedings, and the traditional procedure of investigating agencies in general, leads us to conclude that the Commission's Rules of Procedure comport with the requirements of due process." His majority opinion distinguished Greene v. McElroy as follows: "The governmental action there reviewed was certainly of a judicial nature. . . . By contrast, the Civil Rights Commission does not make any binding orders or issue 'clearances' or licenses having legal effect. Rather, it investigates and reports, leaving affirmative action, if there is to be any, to other governmental agencies where there must be action de novo."[2] (Compare the consideration of procedural due process in bar admission hearings, in Willner v. Committee on Character and Fitness, 373 U.S. 96 (1963), finding confrontation a requirement of due process in the particular circumstances. Note also In re Ruffalo, 390 U.S. 544 (1968), where Justice Douglas' majority opinion referred to disbarment proceedings as "adversary proceedings of a quasi-criminal nature," characterized disbarment as "a punishment or penalty imposed on the lawyer," and stated that the lawyer "is accordingly entitled to procedural due process, which includes fair notice of the charge." Compare the hearing requirements in welfare termination proceedings, note 12, p. 915, infra.)

2. Compare Cafeteria Workers v. McElroy, 366 U.S. 956 (1961). Petitioner Brawner, a short-order cook at a cafeteria privately operated on the premises of the Naval Gun Factory in Washington, D.C., was barred after the commanding officer withdrew her identification badge because "she had failed to meet the security requirements of the installation." The Court upheld the official action. Justice Stewart found, in legislative and executive provisions, the "explicit authorization found wanting in Greene." Nor was there any violation of due process: "We may assume that Rachel Brawner could not constitutionally have been excluded from the Gun Factory if the announced grounds for her exclusion had been patently arbitrary or discriminatory—that she could not have been kept out because she was a Democrat or a Methodist. It does not follow, however, that she was entitled to notice and a hearing when the reason advanced for her exclusion was, as here, entirely rational." He emphasized that "this is not a case where government action operated to bestow a badge of disloyalty or infamy, with an attendant foreclosure from other employment opportunity." Justice Brennan, joined by Chief Justice Warren and Justices Black and Douglas, dissented on the due process issue.

Hannah v. Larche was found distinguishable in Justice Marshall's opinion announcing the judgment of the Court in Jenkins v. McKeithen, 395 U. S. 411 (1969), that appellant had stated a cause of action in his federal court complaint challenging the procedures set forth in a 1967 Louisiana law establishing a Labor-Management Commission of Inquiry. The function of the Louisiana investigating agency was to determine whether there was probable cause to believe violations of criminal laws had occurred. Justice Marshall noted that the statute had been "drafted with Hannah in mind" and that the Commission's "structure and powers" were similar to those of the Civil Rights Commission. Nevertheless, he found "crucial differences"—though the state Commission did not "conduct, strictly speaking, a criminal proceeding," it "exercises a function very much akin to an official adjudication of criminal culpability." In his view, the Commission was "concerned only with exposing" criminal violations and with exercising "an accusatory function." Accordingly, its procedures were deficient: for example, it "severely limits the right of a person being investigated to confront and cross-examine the witnesses against him."

Only Chief Justice Warren and Justice Brennan joined Justice Marshall's opinion, however. The 5:3 majority for the result included also Justices Douglas and Black, who relied on their dissents in Hannah v. Larche. And the minority—Justice Harlan, joined by Justices Stewart and White—found Hannah v. Larche indistinguishable. They insisted that the state Commission was not primarily an "exposure" agency, but rather one engaged in preliminary investigations, with a "close resemblance to certain federal administrative agencies"—the FTC and SEC as well as the Civil Rights Commission—"and to the offices of prosecuting attorneys."

c. *Unruly defendants and the confrontation guarantee.* Though the Confrontation Clause ordinarily guarantees the accused's right to be present in the courtroom at every stage of his trial, that right may be lost by disruptive behavior. In Allen v. Illinois, 397 U.S. —— (1970), Justice Black's opinion for the Court held "that a defendant can lose his right to be present at trial if, after he has been warned by the judge that he will be removed if he continues his disruptive behavior, he nevertheless insists on conducting himself in a manner so disorderly, disruptive, and disrespectful of the court that his trial cannot be carried on with him in the courtroom. Once lost, the right to be present can, of course, be reclaimed as soon as the defendant is willing to conduct himself consistently with the decorum and respect inherent in the concept of courts and judicial proceedings."

The Court commented on alternative methods of control as well: "We believe trial judges confronted with disruptive, contumacious, stubbornly defiant defendants must be given sufficient discretion to meet the circumstances of each case. No one formula for maintaining the appropriate courtroom atmosphere will be best in all situations. We think there are at least three constitutionally permissible ways for a trial judge to handle an obstreperous defendant like Allen: (1) bind and gag him, thereby keeping him present; (2) cite him for contempt; (3) take him out of the courtroom until he promises to conduct himself properly." Justice Black concluded: "Being manned by humans, the courts are not perfect and are bound to make some errors. But, if our courts are to remain what the Founders intended, the citadels of justice, their proceedings cannot and must not be infected with the sort of scurrilous, abusive language and conduct paraded before the Illinois trial judge in this case."

Justice Brennan submitted a concurring opinion. A separate opinion by Justice Douglas, while agreeing with the Court's "basic hypothesis," thought this case a poor one in which to establish "appropriate guidelines for judicial control." This was a "classical criminal case" involving a sick and possibly insane defendant, "without any political or subversive overtones." The "real problems" lay in other kinds of trials: "political trials"; and "trials used by minorities to destroy the existing constitutional system and bring on repressive measures."

4. *The right to present defense witnesses.* In Washington v. Texas, 388 U.S. 14 (1967), Chief Justice Warren stated for the majority that the accused's right to have compulsory process for obtaining witnesses in his favor "stands on no lesser footing than the other Sixth Amendment rights" previously held applicable to the states, and that it "is so fundamental and essential to a fair trial that it is incorporated" in the 14th Amendment. The Court found that right violated by a state statue barring persons charged as co-participants in the same crime from testifying for one another—though they were not disqualified from testifying for the prosecution. Here, the witness' testimony had been blocked by that inadmissibility rule rather than by any state refusal to compel his attendance; but the Sixth Amendment right, examined in its common law context, was found broad enough to include the right to put the witness on the stand.

5. *Reasonable notice.* a. In reversing the summary contempt conviction in the "one-man grand jury" investigation in In re Oliver, 333 U.S. 257 (1948) (note 2, supra) the Supreme Court relied also on the "failure to afford the petitioner a reasonable opportunity to defend himself." The Court stated: "A person's right to reasonable notice of a charge against him, and an opportunity to be heard in his defense—a right to his day in court— are basic in our system of jurisprudence." The right to reasonable notice of the charges is illustrated by Cole v. Arkansas, 333 U.S. 196 (1948). Petitioners were convicted of violating a section of a statute making it an offense to promote an unlawful assemblage. The state supreme court affirmed on the ground that petitioners had violated another section of the statute, which proscribed the use of force and violence. The Supreme Court unanimously reversed: "It is as much a violation of due process to send an accused to prison following conviction of a charge on which he was never tried as it would be to convict him upon a charge that was never made." In the state supreme court, due process entitled petitioners "to have the validity of their conviction appraised on a consideration of the case as it was tried and as the issues were determined in the trial court."

Compare the unusual application of the "notice" requirement in Lambert v. California, 355 U.S. 225 (1957), involving an ordinance requiring anyone who had been convicted of a felony to register with the police chief. The Court, in a 5 to 4 decision, held that "actual knowledge of the duty to register or proof of the probability of such knowledge" was necessary to convict a person "wholly passive and unaware of any wrongdoing under this ordinance." Justice Frankfurter's dissent predicted that the decision would "turn out to be an isolated deviation . . . —a derelict on the waters of the law." On notice requirements in civil litigation—relied on as relevant analogies in Lambert—see, e. g., Walker v. City of Hutchinson, 352 U.S. 112 (1956), and the note which follows.

b. The Court relied on procedural due process criteria regarding civil litigation in invalidating Wisconsin's garnishment procedure in Sniadach v. Family Finance Corp., 395 U.S. 337 (1969). Justice Douglas' majority opinion sustained the claim that the procedure violated due process "in that notice and an opportunity to be heard are not given before the *in rem* seizure of the wages." Under state law, wages were frozen when the creditor obtained a summons and served it on the garnishee. Though the wages would be unfrozen if the wage earner won the main suit on the merits, "in the interim the wage earner is deprived of his enjoyment of earned wages without any opportunity to be heard or to tender any defense he may have." While a summary procedure might satisfy due process in extraordinary situations, "no situation requiring special protection to a state or creditor interest" was found here. Accordingly, the "interim freezing of the wages without a chance to be heard violates procedural due process."

The Court emphasized: "We deal here with wages—a specialized type of property presenting distinct problems in our economic system." Justice Douglas noted: "A prejudgment garnishment of the Wisconsin type is a taking which may impose tremendous hardship on wage earners with families to support"—it may "as a practical matter drive a wage earning family to the wall." He concluded: "Where the taking of one's property is so obvious, it needs no extended argument to conclude that absent notice and a prior hearing," the procedure "violates the fundamental principles of due process." Justice Harlan concurred in a separate opinion. Justice Black dissented at length: "The Court thus steps back into the due process philosophy which brought on President Roosevelt's Court fight. . . . This holding savors too much of the 'Natural Law,' 'Due Process,' 'Shock-the-conscience' test of what is constitutional for me to agree to the decision."

6. *Vagueness.* Compare the due process requirement of a minimum degree of definiteness in the statutory prescription of standards. See Note, "Due Process Requirements of Definiteness in Statutes," 62 Harv.L.Rev. 77 (1948). In Jordan v. DeGeorge, 341 U.S. 223 (1951), the Court stated, in a characteristic comment on "the 'void for vagueness' doctrine": "Impossible standards of specificity are not required. . . . The test is whether the language conveys sufficiently definite warning as to the prescribed conduct when measured by common understanding and practices." [3]

The "void for vagueness" doctrine is a multi-faceted one, and applications will recur in the chapters that follow—especially in the freedom of expression materials, chaps. 15 and 16. As the most astute commentator on "vagueness" has remarked, the doctrine "is most frequently employed as an implement for curbing legislative invasion of constitutional rights *other* than that of fair notice," though there is "an actual vagueness component in the vagueness decisions." Amsterdam, "The Void for Vagueness Doctrine in the Supreme Court," 109 U.Pa.L.Rev. 67 (1960), Selected Essays 1938–62 (1963), 560. (Emphasis added). The use of the vagueness doctrine as a

3. Compare United States v. National Dairy Products Corp., 372 U.S. 29 (1963), involving Section 3 of the Robinson-Patman Act which makes it a crime to sell goods at "unreasonably low prices for the purpose of destroying competition or eliminating a competitor." A divided Court rejected a challenge that the provision was unconstitutionally vague and indefinite.

tool to protect free speech illustrates a modern role of several of the "procedural" guarantees noted here: as later chapters will show, there has been a growing Court practice to protect highly valued substantive rights via the oblique technique of tailoring (and sometimes distorting) procedural safeguards. See, as additional examples of this trend, the procedural doctrines in the following note.

7. *Minimal evidentiary support: the Thompson v. Louisville principle.* In the Police Court of Louisville, Ky., petitioner was convicted of two offenses—loitering and disorderly conduct—and fined $10 on each. At the trial petitioner moved to dismiss the charges on the ground that conviction on the evidence offered would deprive him of liberty and property without due process of law. Under the law of Kentucky a police court fine of less than $20 on a single charge is not appealable or otherwise reviewable in any other Kentucky court. On certiorari to the Police Court, the Supreme Court reversed and remanded. Thompson v. Louisville, 362 U.S. 199 (1960). Justice Black stated: "The ultimate question presented to us is whether the charges against petitioner were so totally devoid of evidentiary support as to render his conviction unconstitutional under the Due Process Clause of the Fourteenth Amendment. Decision of this question turns not on the sufficiency of the evidence, but on whether this conviction rests upon any evidence at all." The Court concluded: "We find no evidence whatever in the record to support these convictions. Just as 'Conviction upon a charge not made would be sheer denial of due process,' so is it a violation of due process to convict and punish a man without evidence of his guilt."

Thompson v. Louisville has been applied in a variety of contexts, especially as a procedural technique for the indirect protection of substantive rights. See, e. g., the sit-in cases, chap. 6, p. 479, and the disturbance of the peace cases, chap. 15, p. 1137. In an application of the principle in a civil rights context, the Court stated that the "proposition for which [Thompson] stands is simple and clear. It has nothing to do with concepts relating to the weight or sufficiency of the evidence in any particular case. It goes, rather, to the most basic concepts of due process of law. Its application in Thompson's case turned . . . 'not on the sufficiency of the evidence, but on whether this conviction rests upon any evidence at all.'" Shuttlesworth v. Birmingham, 382 U.S. 87 (1965) (p. 1187, infra). Shuttlesworth's conviction rested in part on an ordinance prohibiting the failure to "comply with any lawful order . . . of a police officer." The state court construed the law to apply only to orders of police officers directing vehicular traffic. The Supreme Court found no evidence that the police officer was directing such traffic when he asked petitioner to move on, and no evidence that petitioner was "in, on, or around any vehicle at the time he was directed to move on." Accordingly, Justice Stewart concluded, it "was a violation of due process to convict and punish him without evidence of his guilt." See also the reliance on Thompson in Gregory v. Chicago, 394 U.S. 111 (1969). (p. 1160, infra).

8. *Statutory presumptions.* Note also the important function of due process as a limitation upon the creation of statutory presumptions; and consider the relationship of that function to the Thompson principle, note 7, supra. "Under our decisions a statutory presumption cannot be sustained if there be no rational connection between the fact proved and the ultimate fact presumed, if the inference of the one from proof of the other is arbitrary

because of lack of connection between the two in common experience." Tot v. United States, 319 U.S. 463 (1943). Note the application of the principle in United States v. Romano, 382 U.S. 136 (1965), where respondent's conviction for possession of an illegal still rested in part on a federal statutory presumption that presence at the site of an illegal still "shall be deemed sufficient evidence to authorize conviction, unless the defendant explains such presence to the jury." The Supreme Court held the conviction unconstitutional. Justice White explained: "It may be, of course, that Congress has the power to make presence at an illegal still a punishable crime, but we find no clear indication that it intended to so exercise this power. The crime remains possession, not presence, and, with all due deference to the judgment of Congress, the former may not constitutionally be inferred from the latter."

See also Leary v. United States, 395 U.S. 6 (1969), holding unconstitutional a provision deeming possession of marijuana sufficient evidence that the marijuana was illegally imported and that the defendant knew of the illegal importation, "unless the defendant explains his possession to the satisfaction of the jury." Justice Harlan stated for the Court: "The upshot of Tot, Gainey [United States v. Gainey, 380 U.S. 63 (1965)] and Romano is, we think, that a criminal statutory presumption must be regarded as 'irrational' or 'arbitrary' and hence unconstitutional, unless it can at least be said with substantial assurance that the presumed fact is more likely than not to flow from the proved fact on which it is made to depend." Under that standard, the "knowledge" part of the presumption violated due process: after an elaborate review of the data, the Court could not find "that a majority of marijuana possessors either are cognizant of the apparently high rate of importation or otherwise have become aware that *their* marijuana was grown abroad."

But a year later a divided Court sustained a similar statutory presumption dealing with heroin rather than marijuana. Turner v. United States, 396 U.S. 398 (1970). In Turner, the Court found it permissible to infer from the possession of heroin that the heroin was illegally imported; it refused to sustain such a presumption as applied to cocaine. Justice White emphasized that there was "no reasonable doubt that at the present time heroin is not produced in this country and that therefore the heroin Turner had was smuggled heroin." Justice Black, joined by Justice Douglas, submitted a vigorous dissent. See Note, "The Unconstitutionality of Statutory Criminal Presumptions," 22 Stan.L.Rev. 341 (1970).

9. *Hearings on the issue of sanity.* a. United States ex rel. Smith v. Baldi, 344 U.S. 561 (1953), rejected the claim of the petitioner, who had been convicted of murder, that it was a denial of due process for the trial court to refuse to appoint a psychiatrist to make a pre-trial examination. The majority of the Court found no constitutional mandate for such an appointment: the issue of defendant's sanity was heard by the trial court, and psychiatrists testified there. The dissenters insisted that the defendant had been denied a fair opportunity to establish the defense of insanity. Compare Massey v. Moore, 348 U.S. 105 (1954).

b. Is there a right to a formal hearing on claims that an accused has become insane after sentencing and prior to execution, as there is as to allegations of insanity at the time the crime was committed and at the time of trial? In Solesbee v. Balkcom, 339 U.S. 9 (1950), petitioner, under sentence of death after a state court conviction of murder, asked the Governor to post-pone his execution on the ground that he had become insane since the trial. Under authority of a state statute, the Governor appointed three physicians who examined petitioner and declared him sane. Petitioner contended that due process required that his sanity be determined by a formal judicial or administrative tribunal. The Court rejected the claim: "Postponement of execution because of insanity bears a close affinity not to trial for a crime but rather to reprieves of sentences in general. . . . Seldom, if ever, has this power of executive clemency been subjected to review by the courts."[4]

c.   For a consideration of the trial court's obligation to conduct, on its own initiative, a hearing on the defendant's competence to stand trial, where evidence of incompetence becomes manifest during a trial, see Pate v. Robinson, 383 U.S. 375 (1966). Is there a separate right to a hearing on defendant's competence to waive assistance of counsel, where defendant has already received a hearing on the issue of competence to stand trial? See Westbrook v. Arizona, 384 U.S. 150 (1966). Note also Baxstrom v. Herold, 383 U.S. 107 (1966), involving a prisoner who had been found insane while serving a sentence. The Court found constitutional defects in the statutory procedures for the civil commitment of prisoners at the expiration of their criminal sentences. On the increasing concern with standards in civil commitment proceedings, see, e. g., Note, "Due Process for All—Constitutional Standards for Involuntary Civil Commitment and Release," 34 U.Chi. L.Rev. 633 (1967).

10.   *Fairness and recidivist proceedings.* In Spencer v. Texas, 385 U.S. 554 (1967), the Court, in a 5:4 decision, rejected an attack on a habitual criminal statute. The "essence" of the challenged procedure, as described by the Court, was that, "through allegations in the indictment and the introduction of proof respecting a defendant's past convictions, the trial jury in the pending charge was fully informed of such previous derelictions, but was also charged by the court that such matters were not to be taken into account in assessing the defendant's guilt or innocence under the current indictment." Justice Harlan's majority opinion rejected the claim that this use of prior convictions was "so egregiously unfair upon the issue of guilt or innocence" as to violate due process. Though the Court "might well agree" that a two-stage jury trial was "probably the fairest" procedure "were the matter before us in a legislative or rule-making context," that was "a far cry from a constitutional determination that this method of handling the problem is compelled by the Fourteenth Amendment." The dissenters—Chief Justice Warren and Justices Fortas, Brennan and Douglas—agreed about the uncon-

---

4. The Solesbee ruling was extended, in a per curiam decision merely citing that case, in Caritativo v. California, 357 U.S. 549 (1958). The case involved a challenge to the California statutory procedure as to claims of insanity prior to execution, under which primary responsibility is vested in the prison warden rather than the governor. The warden's ex parte determination is ordinarily based on reports from prison psychiatrists. The Court found no due process violation. Justice Frankfurter, joined by Justices Douglas and Brennan, dissented. He objected to the summary extension of the "disturbing decision" in Solesbee and stated that there "can hardly be a comparable situation under our constitutional scheme of things in which an interest so great, that an insane man not be executed, is given such flimsy procedural protection, and where one asserting a claim is denied the rudimentary right of having his side submitted to the one who sits in judgment."

stitutionality of the challenged procedure, but divided about the retroactivity of such a rule.   Note Burgett v. Texas, 389 U.S. 109 (1967), where the result was praised in Chief Justice Warren's concurrence as "a needed limitation on the Spencer rule," though the Chief Justice added that "nothing except an outright rejection" of Spencer "would truly serve the cause of justice."   Burgett held inadmissible in a recidivist proceeding a prior conviction that was presumptively void under Gideon v. Wainwright.

11.   *Fairness and juvenile court proceedings.*   a.   A "narrow" decision in the spring of 1966, in Kent v. United States, 383 U.S. 541, suggested the imminence of careful Supreme Court scrutiny of juvenile court procedures. That warning bore fruit a year later: In re Gault, 387 U.S. 1 (1967), produced an elaborate discussion of constitutional requirements.   Gault was an appeal from the denial of state habeas corpus relief: petitioners had sought release of their 15-year-old son who had been found to be a delinquent by a juvenile court pursuant to the Arizona Juvenile Code and who had been committed to the State Industrial School "for the period of his minority [that is, until 21], unless sooner discharged by due process of law."   Petitioners argued that the state proceedings violated due process because they denied "the following basic rights": "1.   Notice of the charges; 2.   Right to counsel; 3.   Right to confrontation and cross-examination; 4.   Privilege against self-incrimination; 5.   Right to a transcript of the proceedings; and 6.   Right to appellate review."   The Court agreed with the first four of these objections and did not reach the last two.

Justice Fortas' majority opinion explored the gaps between "theoretical purpose" and "actual performance" in juvenile courts.   His critical examination of the juvenile court process noted claims that were "more rhetoric than reality," raised questions "as to whether fact and pretension . . . coincide," and warned against the obscuring effect of "sentiment" and "folklore."   And, whatever the advantages of the informal process, "the condition of being a boy does not justify a kangaroo court. . . . So wide a gulf between the State's treatment of the adult and of the child requires a bridge sturdier than mere verbiage, and reasons more persuasive than cliché can provide."   There were four additional opinions, but only Justice Stewart dissented from the judgment of reversal.

b.   In the Matter of Samuel Winship, 397 U.S. —— (1970), held that a state could not apply a "preponderance of the evidence" standard in a juvenile proceeding: "the constitutional safeguard of proof beyond a reasonable doubt is as much required during the adjudicatory stage of a delinquency proceeding as are those constitutional safeguards applied in Gault."   In reaching that result, Justice Brennan's majority opinion stated: "Lest there remain any doubt about the constitutional stature of the reasonable-doubt standard, we explicitly hold that the Due Process Clause protects the accused against conviction except upon proof beyond a reasonable doubt of every fact necessary to constitute the crime with which he is charged." Justice Black's dissent from that holding rested on his view of the 14th Amendment: the "reasonable doubt" standard is not specifically guaranteed by the Bill of Rights.   Justice Harlan submitted a concurring opinion.

12.   *Fairness and welfare recipients.*   A 5:3 decision in March 1970 held that due process requires that a welfare recipient be afforded an evidentiary hearing before the termination of benefits.   Goldberg v. Kelly,

—— U.S. —— (1970). Justice Brennan's majority opinion stated that "the crucial factor in this context—a factor not present in the case of the black-listed government contractor, the discharged government employee, the tax-payer denied a tax exemption, or virtually anyone else whose government largesse is ended—is that termination of aid pending resolution of a controversy over eligibility may deprive an *eligible* recipient of the very means by which to live while he waits." He insisted that "the interest of the eligible recipient in uninterrupted receipt of public assistance, coupled with the State's interest that his payments not be erroneously terminated, clearly outweighs the State's competing concern to prevent any increase in its fiscal and administrative burdens."

A "quasi-judicial trial" was not required, however; pre-termination hearings with "minimum procedural safeguards" satisfied the new constitutional obligation. A welfare recipient must have "timely and adequate notice detailing the reasons for the proposed termination, and an effective opportunity to defend by confronting any adverse witnesses and by presenting his own arguments and evidence orally." Though the Court did not hold that counsel must be provided, it found that "the recipient must be allowed to retain an attorney if he so desires." Moreover, stated reasons by an impartial decision maker were "essential."

There were dissents by Justice Black, Justice Stewart, and Chief Justice Burger (joined by Justice Black). Justice Black objected to the renewed invocation of "fairness" requirements of due process as a source of "judicial power for legislative purposes." Chief Justice Burger noted that HEW regulations which were about to go into effect would assure pre-termination hearings (including the right to appointed counsel) and added: "Against this background I am baffled as to why we should engage in 'legislating' via constitutional fiat." He commented, moreover: "The Court's action today seems another manifestation of the now familiar constitutionalizing syndrome: once some presumed flaw is observed, the Court then eagerly accepts the invitation to find a constitutionally 'rooted' remedy. If no provision is explicit on the point, it is then seen as 'implicit' or commanded by the vague and nebulous concept of 'fairness.' " In addition, he was concerned about the implications of the ruling: "For example, does the Court's holding embrace welfare reductions or denials of increases as opposed to terminations, or decisions concerning initial applications or requests for special assistance"? (Compare the Court's reliance on equal protection in scrutinizing conditions on welfare benefits, chap. 14, p. 1036, infra.)

———————

SECTION 6. OTHER PROBLEMS: DOUBLE JEOPARDY; PUNISHMENT; BAIL

A. DOUBLE JEOPARDY

1. *Successive prosecutions by the state.* In 1937, Palko v. Connecticut, chap. 11, p. 798, refused to "incorporate" the Fifth Amendment's double jeopardy guarantee into the 14th, and two decades later Hoag v. New Jersey, 356 U.S. 464 (1958), adhered to that ruling. But in 1969 Palko v. Connec-

ticut was overruled and the double jeopardy prohibition was held applicable to the states. Benton v. Maryland, 395 U.S. 784. Benton's first trial was for burglary and larceny, charged in a single indictment. He was acquitted of larceny but convicted of burglary. On appeal, the indictment was set aside because of a defect in the selection of the grand jurors. He was reindicted on both counts. At the second trial, he was convicted of both offenses. The Supreme Court found the larceny conviction unconstitutional.

2. *Successive state-federal prosecutions: the Bartkus and Abbate cases.* a. Petitioner in Bartkus v. Illinois, 359 U.S. 121 (1959), was acquitted in a federal trial for robbery of a federally insured savings and loan association. Thereafter he was convicted in an Illinois court for the same robbery, and sentenced to life imprisonment. The Supreme Court, in an extensive opinion by Justice Frankfurter largely devoted to another attack on the "incorporation" theory,[1] upheld the conviction. He noted "that state and federal courts had for years refused to bar a second trial even though there had been a prior trial by another government for a similar offense." Justice Black, joined by Chief Justice Warren and Justice Douglas, dissented: "If double punishment is what is feared, it hurts no less for two 'sovereigns' to inflict it than for one. [The Court] justifies the practice here in the name of 'federalism.' This, it seems to me, is a misuse and desecration of the concept."

In a separate dissent, Justice Brennan suggested that the opinions of Justices Frankfurter and Black had not focused adequately on the determinative question: "how much the federal authorities must participate in a state prosecution before it so infects the conviction that we must set it aside." Justice Frankfurter had noted that the federal investigator had turned over all of the evidence he had gathered against Bartkus to the Illinois prosecuting officials—including some evidence gathered after the federal acquittal. The majority opinion had also mentioned "a suggestion that the federal sentencing of the accomplices who testified against petitioner in both trials was purposely continued by the federal court until after they testified in the state trial." But to the majority the record showed merely "that federal officials acted in cooperation with state authorities, as is the conventional practice. . . . . It does not sustain the conclusion that the state prosecution was a sham and a cover for a federal prosecution, and thereby in essential fact another federal prosecution." In Justice Brennan's view, however, "highly displeased" federal authorities had "solicited the state indictment" and in general had so "prepared and guided the state prosecution" that "this particular state trial was in actuality a second federal prosecution" in violation of the Fifth Amendment. Chief Justice Warren and Justice Douglas supported Justice Brennan's dissent.

1. See the materials on the "incorporation" controversy, chap. 11, sec. 2B, supra. See also Frankfurter, "Memorandum on 'Incorporation' of the Bill of Rights Into the Due Process Clause of the Fourteenth Amendment," 78 Harv.L.Rev. 746 (1965), published shortly before the Justice's death. The memorandum includes a collection of cases rejecting "incorporation," as well as a "continuation" of the appendix to the Bartkus opinion, reviewing state law relating to guarantees similar to those in the Fifth, Sixth and Seventh Amendments. The memorandum was prepared before Justice Frankfurter's retirement: "I was only waiting for the opportunity to append the memorandum to an opinion in an appropriate case. Unfortunately, I was stricken before such an opportunity came."

b.   A companion case to Bartkus, Abbate v. United States, 359 U.S. 187 (1959), held that the Fifth Amendment's double jeopardy ban was not violated by "a federal prosecution of defendants already prosecuted for the same acts by a State." Justice Brennan stated that the Court did not "write on a clean slate in deciding this question" and reviewed the discussions of punishment by separate sovereignties from Houston v. Moore, 5 Wheat. 1 (1820), to United States v. Lanza, 260 U.S. 377 (1922) (federal prohibition law prosecution after state liquor law conviction; Fifth Amendment merely bars a second federal prosecution "after a first trial for the same offense, under the same authority"). The Court declined to overrule the "firmly established principle" of Lanza. Justice Black, joined by Chief Justice Warren and Justice Douglas, dissented.

3.   *Double jeopardy and the Fifth Amendment.* a. Does the Fifth Amendment prohibit the imposition of multiple punishments on the basis of a single transaction? In Blockburger v. United States, 284 U.S. 299 (1932), the Court found as a matter of statutory construction that a single sale of narcotics may violate two distinct provisions of the federal narcotics laws and upheld imposition of consecutive terms of imprisonment: "The applicable rule is that where the same act or transaction constitutes a violation of two distinct statutory provisions, the test to be applied to determine whether there are two offenses or only one, is whether each provision requires proof of a fact which the other does not." The Court reexamined the Blockburger rule and adhered to it in the face of a constitutional challenge in a 5:4 decision in Gore v. United States, 357 U.S. 386 (1958) (single sale of narcotics violates three provisions of narcotics laws and authorizes consecutive sentences).

b.   When does jeopardy attach? United States v. Perez, 9 Wheat. 579 (1824), held that retrial of a defendant, after the first trial had resulted in a "hung" jury, does not constitute double jeopardy. A prosecutor or judge may not discontinue the trial "when it appears that the jury might not convict"; but a second trial is not barred where "unforeseeable circumstances"—such as the failure of the jury to agree on a verdict—make completion of the first trial "impossible." See Wade v. Hunter, 336 U.S. 684 (1949). In Downum v. United States, 372 U.S. 734 (1963), on the prosecution's motion, the first jury was discharged after being sworn, because a key witness was absent. Petitioner was placed on trial before a second jury two days later. The Court's 5:4 decision found a violation of the double jeopardy guarantee, because, unlike the "hung" jury situation, there was no "imperious necessity" for the second jury. The dissenters emphasized that the first jury "had never begun to act" and that the prosecutor's "harmless oversight" should not bar the calling of a second jury.

c.   May a defendant claim double jeopardy to bar a new trial after his successful appeal from a conviction? Ordinarily, a new trial is permitted. Compare the discussion of appeals by the government, in the Palko case, p. 798, supra. A second trial after the defendant's appeal has been justified on the grounds that the accused "waived" his plea of former jeopardy or that the second trial "continues" the same jeopardy. But in the circumstances of Green v. United States, 355 U.S. 184 (1957), the Court, in a 5:4 decision, held a new trial barred after a successful appeal. At the first trial, Green was charged with first and second degree murder. He was found guilty of second degree murder. At the second trial, after his successful appeal, he was convicted of first degree murder. The first verdict, the Court concluded, was "an implicit acquittal" on the first degree charge. Moreover, "Green's jeopardy for first degree murder came to an end when the [first] jury was discharged." The Court rejected arguments that Green had "waived" the defense or that his appeal "continued" the jeopardy to the first degree charge. See generally Mayers and Yarborough, "Bis Vexari, New Trials and Successive Prosecutions," 74 Harv.L.Rev. 1 (1960).

d. In North Carolina v. Pearce (decided together with Simpson v. Rice), 395 U.S. 711 (1969), the Court considered the constitutional limitations on the length of sentences imposed after retrial of defendants who had successfully appealed their convictions. The Court had little difficulty answering the "more limited aspect" of the problem: "We hold that the constitutional guarantee against multiple punishments for the same offense absolutely requires that punishment already exacted must be fully 'credited' in imposing sentence upon a new conviction for the same offense." But on "the broader question"—"what constitutional limitations there may be upon the general power of a judge to impose upon reconviction a longer prison sentence than the defendant originally received"—there was a variety of views among the Justices. The double jeopardy guarantee, the Court concluded, "imposes no restrictions upon the length of a sentence imposed upon reconviction," other than the "credit" requirement. The ultimate rationale found adequate by a majority was "the premise that the original conviction has, at the defendant's behest, been wholly nullified and the slate wiped clean."

But the Court found a substantial limitation elsewhere in the Fourteenth Amendment: the Due Process Clause "requires that vindictiveness against a defendant for having successfully attacked his first conviction must play no part in the sentence he receives after a new trial. And since the fear of such vindictiveness may unconstitutionally deter a defendant's exercise of the right to appeal or collaterally attack his first conviction, due process also requires that a defendant be freed of apprehension of such a retaliatory motivation on the part of the sentencing judge." Accordingly, "whenever a judge imposes a more severe sentence upon a defendant after a new trial, the reasons for his doing so must affirmatively appear."

B. CRUEL AND UNUSUAL PUNISHMENT

1. *The Willie Francis case.* Petitioner was convicted of murder and sentenced to death. Electrocution was attempted but, because of mechanical difficulty with the chair, death did not result. Petitioner contended a second attempt at execution would constitute cruel and unusual punishment. The Court rejected the claim. Justice Reed's opinion, joined by Chief Justice Vinson and Justices Black and Jackson, assumed that the cruel and unusual punishment prohibition of the Eighth Amendment applied to the states under the 14th, but found no violation: the ban applies to "cruelty inherent in the method of punishment," not to an "unforeseeable accident." Justice Frankfurter delivered a concurring opinion. Justice Burton's dissent, joined by Justices Douglas, Murphy and Rutledge, objected to "death by installments" and argued that the impact on the petitioner, not the intent of the execution, should be determinative. Louisiana ex rel. Francis v. Resweber, 329 U.S. 459 (1947).

2. *Trop v. Dulles and the vague content of the specific Eighth Amendment guarantee.* Recall Trop v. Dulles, 356 U.S. 86 (1958), chap. 5, sec. 6,

p. 433, supra, holding unconstitutional a statute imposing loss of citizenship after dishonorable discharge for wartime desertion from the armed forces. In an opinion by Chief Justice Warren, four of the Justices found the provision a "penalty" subjecting the individual "to a fate forbidden by the principle of civilized treatment guaranteed by the Eighth Amendment." The opinion recognized that the "penalty" of denationalization was not "excessive in relation to the gravity of the crime," since wartime desertion is punishable by death. But the power of punishment must be exercised "within the limits of civilized standards"; the Eighth Amendment "must draw its meaning from the evolving standards of decency that mark the progress of a maturing society." Justice Frankfurter's dissent stated that "to insist that denationalization is 'cruel and unusual punishment' is to stretch that concept beyond the breaking point."

Recall the dispute about substituting the "specific" guarantees of the Bill of Rights for "vague" due process concepts in interpreting the 14th Amendment, in such cases as Adamson v. California and Rochin v. California, chap. 11, sec. 2B, supra. Is the Eighth Amendment as interpreted in Trop a "specific" or a "vague" guarantee?

3. *Narcotics addiction and criminality: Robinson v. California.* In Robinson v. California, 370 U.S. 660 (1962), the Court invalidated a California statute construed as making it a criminal offense to "be addicted to the use of narcotics." Justice Stewart's opinion for the Court concluded: "In the Court counsel for the State recognized that narcotic addiction is an illness. . . . We hold that a state law which imprisons a person thus afflicted as a criminal, even though he has never touched any narcotic drug within the State or been guilty of any irregular behavior there, inflicts a cruel and unusual punishment in violation of the Fourteenth Amendment. To be sure, imprisonment for ninety days is not, in the abstract, a punishment which is either cruel and unusual. But the question cannot be considered in the abstract. Even one day in prison would be a cruel and unusual punishment for the 'crime' of having a common cold." Justice Douglas concurred: "We would forget the teachings of the Eighth Amendment if we allowed sickness to be made a crime." Justice Harlan also concurred.

Justice White, dissenting, thought that the statute could have been construed to save its constitutionality: "I do not consider appellant's conviction to be a punishment for having an illness . . . , but rather a conviction for the regular, repeated or habitual use of narcotics immediately prior to his arrest and in violation of the California law." And in a concluding paragraph, he objected to the Court's constitutional ground: "Finally, I deem this application of 'cruel and unusual punishment' so novel that I suspect the Court was hard put to find a way to ascribe to the Framers of the Constitution the result reached today rather than to its own notions of ordered liberty. If this case involved economic regulation, the present Court's allergy to substantive due process would surely save the statute and prevent the Court from imposing its own philosophical predilections upon state legislatures or Congress. [See chap. 13, sec. 4, infra.] I fail to see why the Court deems it more appropriate to write into the Constitution its own abstract notions of how best to handle the narcotics problem, for it obviously cannot match either the States or Congress in expert understanding." Justice Clark also dissented. On the general problem of using the Eighth Amendment to limit what may be made criminal, see also the next note; Packer, "Making the Punishment Fit the Crime," 77

Harv.L.Rev. 1071 (1964); and Note, "Revival of the Eighth Amendment: Development of Cruel-Punishment Doctrine by the Supreme Court," 16 Stan.L.Rev. 996 (1964).

4. *Alcoholism and criminalty: Powell v. Texas.* May Robinson v. California be invoked as a bar to the conviction of a chronic alcoholic for drunkenness? That question sharply divided the Court in Powell v. Texas, 392 U.S. 514 (1968). The operative answer that emerged from the 4:1:4 split was: "Sometimes." Justice Marshall's opinion announcing the judgment affirming the conviction was a general rejection of the Eighth Amendment defense in alcoholism cases; but that opinion was joined by only three other Justices, Chief Justice Warren and Justices Black and Harlan. Justice White, whose concurring vote was necessary to the result, delineated circumstances in which the principles of Robinson would provide a defense. And the dissenters—Justice Fortas, joined by Justices Douglas, Brennan and Stewart—found a valid cruel and unusual punishment claim.

Appellant—after approximately 100 prior convictions for public intoxication—was convicted under a Texas statute making it a crime to be "found in a state of intoxication in any public place." The trial court ruled that "chronic alcoholism" was not a defense, but entered a number of "findings of fact" favorable to the appellant. For example, it found appellant to be "a chronic alcoholic who was afflicted with a disease of chronic alcoholism," and it stated that a "chronic alcoholic does not appear in public by his own volition but under a compulsion symptomatic of the disease of chronic alcoholism." Justice Marshall's opinion described these "findings" as "premises of a syllogism transparently designed to bring this case within the scope" of Robinson. He refused to build on these "findings," as he accused the dissent of doing, to conclude that "a person may not be punished if the condition essential to constitute the defined crime is part of the pattern of his disease and is occasioned by a compulsion symptomatic of the disease." That position, he insisted, "goes much too far on the basis of too little knowledge." Doctors did not agree as to the nature of "alcoholism" as a "disease"; there was no generally effective method of treatment; treatment facilities were inadequate. Accordingly, "to do otherwise than affirm might subject indigent alcoholics to the risk that they may be locked up for an indefinite period of time under the same conditions as before." Against this background, Justice Marshall concluded: "Faced with this unpleasant reality, we are unable to assert that the use of the criminal process as a means of dealing with the public aspects of problem drinking can never be defended as rational."

Justice Marshall urged that Robinson v. California not be extended. Appellant was convicted, "not for being a chronic alcoholic, but for being in public while drunk on a particular occasion." And unless Robinson is viewed narrowly, "it is difficult to see any limiting principle that would serve to prevent this Court from becoming, under the aegis of the Cruel and Unusual Punishment Clause, the ultimate arbiter of the standards of criminal responsibility, in diverse areas of the criminal law, throughout the country." He accordingly rejected the dissenters' insistence that Robinson meant that criminal penalties "may not be inflicted on a person for being in a condition he is powerless to change." That position would logically carry the Court too far into the area of substantive criminal law: "Nothing could be less fruitful than for this Court to be impelled into defining some sort of insanity test in constitutional terms. Yet, that task would seem to follow inexorably from an extension of Robinson in this case." Formulating a constitutional rule would "freeze the developing productive dialogue between law and psychiatry into a rigid constitutional mold. It is simply not yet the time to write into the Constitution formulas cast in terms whose meaning, let alone relevance, are not yet clear either to doctors or to lawyers." Justice Black, joined by Justice Harlan, joined the opinion in a separate concurrence.

Justice White, however, concurred only in the result: The "chronic alcoholic with an irresistible uge to consume alcohol should not be punishable for drinking or for being drunk." But appellant was convicted for a different crime, for being drunk in a public place. And there was no persuasive showing that appellant's alcoholism compelled him not only to drink but also to be in a public place. Justice Fortas' opinion for the four dissenters, disagreeing with Justice White's view of the facts, insisted that the findings demonstrated that appellant was not only incapable of resisting intoxication but also "could not prevent himself from appearing in public places" once intoxicated. Robinson, he insisted, stood for a central principle: "Criminal penalties may not be inflicted upon a person for being in a condition he is powerless to change." Here, the findings "read against the background of the medical and sociological data" showed that the conviction violated the Eighth Amendment: a person "may not be punished if the condition essential to constitute the defined crime is part of the pattern of his disease and is occasioned by a compulsion symptomatic of the disease."

5. *The constitutional attack on capital punishment and the Eighth Amendment.* There have been suggestions that the death penalty might be vulnerable to a frontal attack under the Eighth Amendment (see 5a infra), but most challenges have relied on other constitutional grounds (see 5b and 5c infra).

a. *The Rudolph v. Alabama suggestion.* In dissenting from the denial of certiorari in the Rudolph case, 375 U.S. 889 (1963), Justice Goldberg, joined by Justices Douglas and Brennan, urged that review be granted "to consider whether the Eighth and Fourteenth Amendments . . . permit the imposition of the death penalty on a convicted rapist who has neither taken nor endangered human life." He stated a number of questions he deemed "relevant and worthy of argument and consideration," including: "Is the taking of human life to protect a value other than human life consistent with the constitutional proscription against 'punishments which by their excessive . . . severity are greatly disproportioned to the offenses charged'? Can the permissible aims of punishment (e. g., deterrence, isolation, rehabilitation) be achieved as effectively by punishing rape less severely than by death . . . ?" Note also Boykin v. Alabama, 395 U.S. 238 (1969), where the Court reversed a conviction without reaching petitioner's claim that imposition of the death penalty for common law robbery violated the Eighth Amendment.

b. *The Witherspoon and Jackson decisions.* Two 1968 decisions, though not challenging the legality of capital punishment per se, found procedures for imposing it unconstitutional. United States v. Jackson, 390 U.S. 570, on the death penalty clause of the Federal Kidnaping Act, is noted above, at p. 900. And Witherspoon v. Illinois, 391 U.S. 510, held that a death sentence cannot be carried out "if the jury that imposed or recommended it was chosen by excluding veniremen for cause simply because they voiced general objections to the death penalty or expressed conscientious or religious scruples against the infliction." A jury so selected could not be expected to choose impartially between imprisonment or death. Justice Stewart's majority opinion concluded: "Whatever else might be said of capital punishment, it is at least clear that its imposition by a hanging jury cannot be squared with the Constitution. The State of Illinois has stacked the deck against the petitioner."

Justice Black's dissent, joined by Justices Harlan and White, objected to the "hanging jury" and "stacked the deck" charges against Illinois: "With all due deference it seems to me that one might much more appropriately charge that this Court has today written the law in such a way that the States are being forced to try their murder cases with biased juries. If this Court is to hold capital punishment unconstitutional, I think it should do so forthrightly, not by making it impossible for States to get juries that will enforce the death penalty." Compare Bumper v. North Carolina, 391 U.S. 543, decided on the same day as Witherspoon, where the Court affirmed a conviction for rape, an offense punishable by death unless the jury recommends life imprisonment. Petitioner was sentenced to life imprisonment; Witherspoon accordingly did not require reversal.

c. *The Maxwell v. Bishop argument.* In Maxwell v. Bishop, 393 U.S. 997 (1968), the Court granted certiorari on the following questions:

"Whether Arkansas' practice of permitting the trial jury absolute discretion, uncontrolled by standards or directions of any kind, to impose the death penalty violates the Due Process Clause of the Fourteenth Amendment?" [See Giaccio v. Pennsylvania, 382 U.S. 399 (1966).]

"Whether Arkansas' single-verdict procedure, which requires the jury to determine guilt and punishment simultaneously and a defendant to choose between presenting mitigating evidence on the punishment issue or maintaining his privilege against self-incrimination on the guilt issue, violates the Fifth and Fourteenth Amendments?" [See Griffin v. California, 380 U.S. 609 (1965), p. 878, supra.]

In May 1969, the Court set the Maxwell case for reargument in the fall of 1969; that fall, reargument was postponed, presumably to await a full Court.

_____

C. BAIL

1. *"Excessive bail" and the Eighth Amendment.* In Carlson v. Landon, 342 U.S. 524 (1952), aliens challenged the denial of bail pending determination of their deportability. Petitioners claimed a violation of the Eighth Amendment's provision that "excessive bail shall not be required." The Court rejected the claim: "The bail clause was lifted with slight changes from the English Bill of Rights Act. In England that clause has never been thought to accord a right to bail in all cases, but merely to provide that bail shall not be excessive in those cases where it is proper to grant bail. When this clause was carried over into our Bill of Rights, nothing was said that indicated any different concept. The Eighth Amendment has not prevented Congress from defining the classes of cases in which bail shall be allowed in this country. Thus in criminal cases bail is not compulsory where the punishment may be death. Indeed, the very language of the Amendment

fails to say all arrests must be bailable. We think, clearly, here that the Eighth Amendment does not require that bail be allowed under the circumstances of these cases." Justice Black, dissenting thought that "the Court now adds the right to bail to the list of other Bill of Rights guarantees that have recently been weakened to expand governmental powers at the expense of individual freedom." Justices Frankfurter, Douglas and Burton also dissented.[1]

2. *The indigent accused and bail reform.* What is the impact of the principle of Griffin v. Illinois, sec. 1, p. 852, supra, on bail practices? See Foote, "The Coming Constitutional Crisis in Bail," 113 U.Pa.L.Rev. 1125 (1965), and Packer, "Two Models of the Criminal Process," 113 U.Pa.L.Rev. 1 (1964). A number of recent studies and experiments have been concerned with inequalities in the administration of bail and with possible substitutes for the bail system. See, e. g., Ares, Rankin, and Sturz, "The Manhattan Bail Project: An Interim Report on the Use of Pre-Trial Parole," 38 N.Y. U.L.Rev. 67 (1963). And the Report of the Attorney General's Committee on Poverty and the Administration of Federal Criminal Justice (1963) contained proposals for bail reform and pre-trial release, in addition to the counsel recommendations noted earlier, p. 853. Among the conclusions: "Release of the accused on his own recognizance without additional financial securities, in proper cases, contributes importantly to solution of the problems of pre-trial release. The use of this procedure should be enlarged in the federal district courts. . . . It is vital to the development of a sound policy of pre-trial release in the federal courts that a system of nonpecuniary inducements to appearance of the accused at the trial be devised."

Partially in response to these recommendations, the Bail Reform Act of 1966 was adopted. Its major provisions add new §§ 3146–3152 to 18 U.S. C.; its stated purpose is "to revise the practices relating to bail to assure that all persons, regardless of their financial status, shall not needlessly be detained pending their appearance to answer charges, to testify, or pending appeal, when detention serves neither the ends of justice nor the public interest." Compare the Nixon Administration's controversial "preventive detention" proposal pending in Congress early in 1970.

---

1. Compare Stack v. Boyle, 342 U.S. 1 (1951), where the Court sustained a challenge to the District Court's fixing at $50,000 bail for each of several Smith Act defendants: "[T]he fixing of bail before trial in these cases cannot be squared with the statutory and constitutional standards." Since the function of bail is limited to assuring the presence of the accused to stand trial, "the fixing of bail for any individual defendant must be based upon standards relevant to the purpose." Discussions of bail standards also appear in opinions by individual Justices, sitting as Circuit Justices. These opinions are not officially reported. See, e. g., Rehman v. California, 85 S.Ct. 8 (1964).

Chapter 13

LIMITS ON THE REGULATION OF ECONOMIC AFFAIRS AND PROPERTY RIGHTS: SUBSTANTIVE DUE PROCESS AND THE CONTRACT CLAUSE

Introduction. The substantive impact of due process on economic regulation is the major concern of this chapter. The due process materials are preceded by a brief consideration of the contract clause, the major federal constitutional restraint on state economic regulation prior to the adoption of the 14th Amendment. Neither the contract clause nor due process impose substantial obstacles to economic regulation today. Yet the rise and decline of substantive due process, especially, is of major contemporary interest. The economic and property rights problems considered below, particularly in secs. 3 and 4, bear directly on the judicial function in the protection of those individual liberties that receive greater attention from the present Court. The "liberty" protected by the due process clauses of the Fifth and 14th Amendments was the source of the Court's now discredited intervention in economic legislation (see sec. 3); yet that same "liberty" language is the major basis for the Court's active enforcement of personal rights today. During the last generation, judicial protection of some varieties of "liberty" has declined sharply; with respect to other kinds of "liberty," there has been an equally dramatic rise in judicial intervention. The problems of theory and practice inherent in those tendencies have occasionally emerged earlier (see, e. g., the divisions on the Court in the 1965 birth control case, Griswold v. Connecticut, chap. 11, p. 824, supra); they are pursued further below (see, e. g., the introduction to chap. 15, p. 1050, infra). The Court's encounters with economic due process examined here not only influence its responses to personal rights claims, but provide essential background for a critical assessment of those responses.

SECTION 1. THE CONTRACT CLAUSE

THE CONTRACT CLAUSE IN THE 19TH CENTURY

During the first century of government under the Constitution, the prohibition of any state "Law impairing the Obligation of Contracts," Art. I, Sec. 10, was the major restraint on state economic regulation. Since the late 19th Century, when the Court began to interpret the due process clause of the 14th Amendment as a limitation on the content of state legislation, see sec. 3, infra, the contract clause has played a less prominent role in constitutional litigation. And as substantive due process restrictions on the police power diminished, as they have most markedly since the 1930's, contract clause barriers were lowered as well. Indeed, it has been suggested that interpretations of the contract and due process clauses have merged to such an extent that the "results might be the same if the contract clause were dropped out of the Constitution, and the challenged statutes all judged as reasonable or unreasonable deprivations of property" under the due process clause. Hale, "The Supreme Court and the Contract Clause," 57 Harv.L.Rev. 852, 890 (1944). Yet the contract clause has an importance of its own, in present-day as well as in historical terms. See, e. g., El Paso v. Simmons, 379 U.S. 497 (1965) (at the end of this section, at p. 935). In view of the independent significance of the contract clause, a brief examination of developments is appropriate before turning to the evolution of substantive due process.

The major purpose of the contract clause was to restrain state laws affecting private contracts. It was aimed mainly at debtor relief laws—for example, laws staying or postponing payments of debts and laws authorizing payments in installments or in commodities. Yet the Court first interpreted the contract clause in cases involving public grants rather than private contracts. Fletcher v. Peck, 6 Cranch 87 (1810); [1] New Jersey v. Wilson, 7 Cranch 164 (1812); [2] Dartmouth College v. Woodward, 4 Wheat. 518 (1819). As Marshall said in Dartmouth College—in holding that New Hampshire could not "pack" the College board of trustees by legislation increasing the size of the board, since the 1769 royal charter of the College had given the trustees the right to fill all vacancies on the board—: "It is more than possible that the preservation of rights of this description was not particularly in the view of the framers of the Constitution . . .. It is probable that interferences of more frequent recurrence, . . . of which the mischief was more extensive, constituted the great motive for imposing this restriction on the State legislatures." But that was no reason for limiting the scope of the clause.[3] A state grants of lands had already been held to be a contract in Fletcher v. Peck: "A contract executed is one in which the object of the contract is performed; and this, says Blackstone, differs in nothing from a grant. The contract between Georgia and the purchasers [of the Yazoo lands] was executed by the grants. A contract executed, as well as one which is executory, contains obligations binding on the parties." And the fact that a state was a party to the contract made no difference: "[If] grants are comprehended under the term contracts, is a grant from the state excluded . . . ? Is the clause to be considered as inhibiting the state from impairing the obligation of contracts between two individuals, but as excluding from that inhibition contracts made

---

1. In 1795, several companies had obtained a huge grant of land from the Georgia legislature. There were charges of bribery, and a new legislature annulled the grant. The grantees had in the meanwhile sold their lands to investors. The Court held the 1796 law invalid: "When . . . a law is in its nature a contract, when absolute rights have vested under that contract, a repeal of the law cannot devest those rights." Rights of innocent purchasers could not be affected by any "secret fraud" as to the original grant. The Court concluded that the law was barred "either by general principles which are common to our free institutions, or by the particular provisions" of the Constitution. On the background of the controversy, see Magrath, Yazoo: Law and Politics in the New Republic (1966).

2. The Court invalidated a New Jersey law of 1804 repealing a tax exemption which the colonial legislature had given for certain lands in 1758.

3. According to the Court, the royal charter was "a contract to which the donors, the trustees, and the crown (to whose rights and obligations New Hampshire succeeded) were the original parties." The 1816 New Hampshire law expanding the board of trustees took control of the College from "private literary men" and gave it to a group "entirely subservient to the will of the government." This was "subversive of that contract on the faith of which [the donors'] property was given." For a succinct analysis of this much-discussed case, see Baxter, Daniel Webster & the Supreme Court (1966).

with itself? The words . . . are applicable to contracts of every description."

A few weeks after the Dartmouth College decision, the Marshall Court applied the contract clause to a law closer to the "mischief" which supplied the Framers with the "great motive for imposing this restriction on the State legislatures": in Sturges v. Crowninshield, 4 Wheat. 122 (1819), the Court held unconstitutional a New York insolvency law discharging debtors of their obligations upon surrender of their property. And in Green v. Biddle, 8 Wheat. 1 (1823), the Court invalidated Kentucky's Occupying Claimants Law, designed to make it more difficult for landowners to eject those who in good faith had settled and made improvements on Western lands.

Historians have probably exaggerated the impact of the early contract clause decisions on American economic and legal developments. The cases did indeed restrict; but they did not compel legislative paralysis, they were not the keystone of American corporate development, they did not establish an inflexible safeguard for all vested rights.[4] The lack of statutory restrictions on corporations in the 19th century, for example, was probably more attributable to the legislators' unwillingness to enact them than to any constitutionally imposed incapacities. Indeed, in the Dartmouth College Case itself, Justice Story's concurring opinion had pointed out what the political leaders in New Hampshire and elsewhere already well knew: "If the legislature mean to claim such an authority" to alter or amend corporate charters, "it must be reserved in the grant. The charter of Dartmouth College contains no such reservation . . . ." After the Dartmouth decision, the Court later said, "many a State of the Union . . . inserted, either in its statutes or in its constitutions, a provision that charters thenceforth granted should be subject to alteration, amendment or repeal at the pleasure of the legislature."[5] Indeed, some legislatures had done so before the Dartmouth College decision. But many states gave special corporate privileges and failed to include adequate reservations of amending powers in corporate charters even after the Dartmouth decision. The relatively protected position of corporations later in the 19th Century, in short, was due less to any shield supplied by the Court than it was to the legislatures' own unwillingness to impose restraints—an unwillingness reflecting the laissez-faire philosophy of the day.

Moreover, the Court's interpretations from the beginning assured that the contract clause would not be an inflexible barrier to public regulation. Space does not permit a detailed charting of the doctrinal developments; only a few of the bases for sustaining legislative authority can be noted here. See also the opinion in Home Building & Loan Ass'n v. Blaisdell, 290 U.S. 398 (1934) (the next principal case); Hale, "The Supreme Court and the Contract

---

4. For an extreme example of the recurrent hyperbole in comments on the early cases, see Sir Henry Maine's statement that the contract clause "secured full play to the economical forces by which the achievement of cultivating the soil of the American continent has been performed; it is the bulwark of American individualism against democratic impatience and socialistic fantasy." Popular Government (1885), 247–48.

5. Looker v. Maynard, 179 U.S. 46 (1900), sustaining a stockholders' cumulative voting statute enacted pursuant to a reserved power clause in the Michigan constitution. In its opinion, the Court said that such a clause gave "at least" the power to make "any alteration . . . which will not defeat or substantially impair the object of the grant."

Clause," 57 Harv.L.Rev. 512, 621, 852 (1944); and Wright, The Contract Clause of the Constitution (1938).

The Dartmouth College Case, as noted, recognized the legislature's authority to reserve the power to amend corporate charters. A few years later, a closely divided Court—with Marshall in dissent—stated that the contract clause did not prohibit all state insolvency laws. Ogden v. Saunders, 12 Wheat. 212 (1827), held that such laws could be validly applied to contracts made after the law was enacted; the earlier decision in Sturges v. Crowninshield, supra, the Court made clear, applied only to retroactive insolvency laws.[6] Moreover, the Court soon elaborated on a distinction stated in Sturges and other early cases: that the constitutional ban on the impairment of contract "obligations" did not prohibit legislative changes in "remedies": "The distinction between the obligation . . . and the remedy . . . exists in the nature of things. Without impairing the obligation of the contract, the remedy may certainly be modified as the wisdom of the nation shall direct," the Court had said in Sturges. And in Bronson v. Kinzie, 1 How. 311 (1843), the Court stated that the permissible scope of remedial changes depended on their "reasonableness," provided "no substantial right" was impaired.[7] Justice Cardozo was guilty of something of an understatement when he said that the "dividing line" between remedy and obligation "is at times obscure." Worthen Co. v. Kavanaugh, 295 U.S. 56 (1935).[8] Yet the allowance of remedial changes provided some flexibility: it authorized extensions of time, for example—so long as extensions were not "so piled up as to make the remedy a shadow," as Cardozo put it.

The early Court safeguarded against excessively broad interpretations of publicly granted privileges as well. In Dartmouth College, the Marshall Court had to strain somewhat to find in the royal charter an implied inviolability of the trustees' rights. In later years, the Court tended to be less charitable in construing the grantees' privileges. In Providence Bank v. Billings, 4 Pet. 514 (1830), for example, Marshall refused to read an implied immunity from taxation into a bank's charter: state power was the norm; corporate privileges the exception; and special charter immunities had to be stated with some explicitness to be recognized by the Court. Roger Brooke Taney, Marshall's successor, quickly developed the Providence Bank approach, in the better-known Charles River Bridge Case in 1837.[9] The Charles River Bridge Company's charter to operate a toll bridge did not prevent the state from authorizing the construction of the competing, free Warren Bridge: "[T]he rule of construction . . . is now fully established to be this—that any ambiguity in the terms of the contract, must operate against the adventurers and in favor of the public, and the plaintiffs can claim nothing that is not clearly given them by the Act."

---

6. In Ogden, the Court justified the prospective operation of the insolvency law on the ground that laws in existence at the time of the making of a contract "enter into and form a part of" the contract.

7. In Bronson, the Court invalidated a state law restricting the mortgagee's rights on foreclosure. See also Von Hoffman v. City of Quincy, 4 Wall.

535 (1867): where a city is authorized to tax to meet its bond obligations, the state cannot withdraw the taxing authority "until the contract is satisfied."

8. See "Contract Clause Cases after Blaisdell," p. 934, **infra.**

9. Charles River Bridge v. Warren Bridge, 11 Pet. 420 (1837).

Moreover, the states were not left entirely powerless even where they had failed to reserve authority to amend charters and where strict construction of corporate privileges found a granted immunity. Certain powers of the state were held to be inalienable. No legislative assurance that the power of eminent domain would not be exercised could prevent subsequent action taking corporate property upon the payment of just compensation.[10] So, still more important, with at least some exercises of the police power: A Mississippi grant of a charter to operate a lottery did not bar the application of a later law prohibiting lotteries. "All agree that the legislature can not bargain away the police power," Chief Justice Waite said in Stone v. Mississippi, 101 U.S. 814 (1880).[11] "No legislature can bargain away the public health or the public morals." But, he added, "we have held, not, however, without strong opposition at times, that [the contract clause] protected a corporation in its charter exemptions from taxation." [12] As a later Court put it broadly: "It is settled that neither the 'contract' clause nor the 'due process' clause has the effect of overriding the power of the State to establish all regulations that are reasonably necessary to secure the health, safety, good order, comfort, or general welfare of the community; that this power can neither be abdicated nor bargained away, and is inalienable even by express grant; and all contract and property rights are held subject to its fair exercise." [13] And so with private contracts: "[P]arties by entering into contracts may not estop the legislature from enacting laws intended for the public good." [14]

In the late 19th century, the Court used broad language of that sort primarily in cases involving prohibitions of matters widely regarded as "evil": for example, lotteries and intoxicating beverages.[15] Compare the early development of the congressional commerce-prohibiting power, in the Lottery Case and related decisions, chap. 4, p. 254, supra. Would the Court also sustain legislation provoked by 20th century economic crises—the modern versions of the debtor relief laws that had motivated the adoption of the contract clause in 1787? The materials that follow focus on the interpretations of the contract clause in the contemporary economic context.

10. See, e. g., West River Bridge Co. v. Dix, 6 How. 507 (1848), and Pennsylvania Hospital v. Philadelphia, 245 U.S. 20 (1918).

11. Compare New Orleans Gas Co. v. Louisiana Light Co., 115 U.S. 650 (1885), holding that the police power argument did not justify elimination of the gas company's 50-year exclusive franchise by a subsequent anti-monopoly amendment to the state constitution. The Court added: "The right and franchises . . . can be taken by the public, upon just compensation to the company." See sec. 2, infra.

12. For recent litigation on 19th century state grants of tax exemptions to railroads, see Georgia R. Co. v. Redwine, 342 U.S. 299 (1952), and Atlantic Coast Line R. Co. v. Phillips, 332 U.S. 168 (1947).

13. Atlantic Coast Line R. Co. v. Goldsboro, 232 U.S. 548 (1914).

14. Manigault v. Springs, 199 U.S. 473 (1905).

15. See, e. g., Stone v. Mississippi, 101 U.S. 814 (1880); Beer Co. v. Massachusetts, 97 U.S. 25 (1878). During the same period, it should be noted, Court invalidation of state laws impairing corporate charter privileges reached its highest frequency in our history. Between 1865 and 1888, there were 49 cases in which state laws were held invalid under the contract clause—and 36 of these involved public grants rather than contracts between private parties. The Constitution of the United States of America (Gov't Printing Off., 1964 ed.), 409–10.

HOME BUILDING & LOAN ASS'N v. BLAISDELL

290 U.S. 398, 54 S.Ct. 231, 78 L.Ed. 413 (1934).

Appeal from the Supreme Court of Minnesota.

[Action by John H. Blaisdell and wife against the Home Building & Loan Association to secure an order extending the period of redemption from a foreclosure and sale of real property under a power of sale mortgage. Judgment for plaintiffs was affirmed by the state Supreme Court.]

Mr. Chief Justice HUGHES delivered the opinion of the Court.

Appellant contests the validity of Chapter 339 of the Laws of Minnesota of 1933, ... called the Minnesota Mortgage Moratorium Law, as being repugnant to the contract clause (Art. 1, § 10) and the due process and equal protection clauses of the Fourteenth Amendment of the Federal Constitution. . . . . .

The Act provides that during the emergency declared to exist, relief may be had through authorized judicial proceedings with respect to foreclosures of mortgages, and execution sales, of real estate; that sales may be postponed and periods of redemption may be extended. . . .

. . . We are here concerned with the provisions of Part One, § 4, authorizing the District Court of the county to extend the period of redemption from foreclosure sales "for such additional time as the court may deem just and equitable, [but not extending beyond May 1, 1935.]" The extension is to be made upon application to the court, on notice, for an order determining the reasonable value of the income on the property involved in the sale, or, if it has no income, then the reasonable rental value of the property, and directing the mortgagor "to pay all or a reasonable part of such income or rental value, in or toward the payment of taxes, insurance, interest, mortgage . . . indebtedness at such times and in such manner" as shall be determined by the court. . . . By another provision of the Act, no action, prior to May 1, 1935, may be maintained for a deficiency judgment until the period of redemption as allowed by existing law or as extended under the provisions of the act has expired. . . .

The [trial] court entered its judgment extending the period of redemption [from May 2, 1933] to May 1, 1935, subject to the condition that the appellees should pay to the appellant $40 a month through the extended period . . ., all these amounts to go to the payment of taxes, insurance, interest, and mortgage indebtedness. It is this judgment, sustained by the Supreme Court of the State . . ., which is here under review. . . .

We approach the questions thus presented upon the assumption made below . . . . that, during the period thus extended, ... the mortgagee-purchaser will be unable to obtain possession, or to obtain or convey title in fee, as he would have been able to do had the statute not been enacted. . . . Aside from the extension of time, the other conditions of redemption are unaltered. . . .

In determining whether the provisions for this temporary and conditional relief exceeds the power of the State by reason of the [contract clause], we must consider the relation of emergency to constitutional power, the historical setting of the contract clause, the development of the jurisprudence of this

Court in the construction of that clause, and the principles of construction which we may consider to be established.

Emergency does not create power. Emergency does not increase granted power or remove or diminish the restrictions imposed upon power granted or reserved. The Constitution was adopted in a period of grave emergency. Its grants of power to the Federal Government and its limitations of the power of the States were determined in the light of emergency, and they are not altered by emergency. . . .

While emergency does not create power, emergency may furnish the occasion for the exercise of power. . . . The constitutional question presented in the light of an emergency is whether the power possessed embraces the particular exercise of it in response to particular conditions. . . .

. . . [T]he reasons which led to the adoption of that clause . . . have frequently been described with eloquent emphasis. The widespread distress following the revolutionary period, and the plight of debtors had called forth in the States an ignoble array of legislative schemes for the defeat of creditors and the invasion of contractual obligations. Legislative interferences had been so numerous and extreme that the confidence essential to prosperous trade had been undermined and the utter destruction of credit was threatened. . . . It was necessary to interpose the restraining power of a central authority in order to secure the foundations even of "private faith." . . .

. . . To ascertain the scope of the constitutional prohibition we examine the course of judicial decisions in its application. These put it beyond question that the prohibition is not an absolute one and is not to be read with literal exactness like a mathematical formula. . . . The inescapable problems of construction have been: What is a contract? What are the obligations of contracts? What constitutes impairment of these obligations? What residuum of power is there still in the States, in relation to the operation of contracts, to protect the vital interests of the community? . . .

Not only is the [contract clause] qualified by the measure of control which the State retains over remedial processes, but the State also continues to possess authority to safeguard the vital interests of its people. . . . Not only are existing laws read into contracts in order to fix obligations as between the parties, but the reservation of essential attributes of sovereign power is also read into contracts as a postulate of the legal order. The policy of protecting contracts against impairment presupposes the maintenance of a government by virtue of which contractual relations are worth while,—a government which retains adequate authority to secure the peace and good order of society. This principle of harmonizing the constitutional prohibition with the necessary residuum of state power has had progressive recognition in the decisions of this Court. . . . The States retain adequate power to protect the public health against the maintenance of nuisances despite insistence upon existing contracts. . . .

Whatever doubt there may have been that the protective power of the State, its police power, may be exercised—without violating the true intent of the provision of the Federal Constitution—in directly preventing the immediate and literal enforcement of contractual obligations by a temporary and conditional restraint, where vital public interests would otherwise suffer, was removed by our decisions relating to the enforcement of provisions of leases during a period of scarcity of housing. . . . Marcus Brown Holding Co. v. Feldman, 256 U.S. 170; Edgar A. Levy Leasing Co. v. Siegel, 258 U.S. 242. . . . [In these cases, the] statutes of New York, declaring that a public emergency existed, directly interfered with the enforcement of covenants for the surrender of the possession of premises on the expiration of leases. Within the City of New York and contiguous counties, the owners of dwellings . . . were wholly deprived until November 1, 1922, of all possessory remedies for the purpose of removing from their premises the tenants or occupants in possession . . ., providing the tenants or occupants were ready, able, and willing to pay a reasonable rent. . . .

In these cases of leases, it will be observed that the relief afforded was temporary and conditional; that it was sustained because of the emergency due to scarcity of housing; and that provision was made for reasonable compensation to the landlord during the period he was prevented from regaining possession. . . . It is always open to judicial inquiry whether the exigency still exists upon which the continued operation of the law depends. Chastleton Corp. v. Sinclair, 264 U.S. 543, 547, 548. . . .

It is manifest from this review of our decisions that there has been a growing appreciation of public needs and of the necessity of finding ground for a rational compromise between individual rights and public welfare. The settlement and consequent contraction of the public domain, the pressure of a constantly increasing density of population, the interrelation of the activities of our people and the complexity of our economic interests, have inevitably led to an increased use of the organization of society in order to protect the very bases of individual opportunity. . . . [T]he question is no longer merely that of one party to a contract as against another, but of the use of reasonable means to safeguard the economic structure upon which the good of all depends.

It is no answer to say that this public need was not apprehended a century ago, or to insist that what the provision of the Constitution meant to the vision of that day it must mean to the vision of our time. If by the statement that what the Constitution meant at the time of its adoption it means today, it is intended to say that the great clauses of the Constitution must be confined to the interpretation which the framers, with the conditions and outlook of their time, would have placed upon them, the statement carries its own refutation. It was to guard against such a narrow conception that Chief Justice Marshall uttered the memorable warning—"We must never forget, that it is *a constitution* we are expounding" . . . .

. . . When we consider the contract clause and the decisions which have expounded it in harmony with the essential reserved power of the States to protect the security of their peoples, we find no warrant for the conclusion that the clause has been warped by these decisions from its proper significance . . . . With a growing recognition of public needs and the relation of individual right to public security, the Court has sought to prevent the perversion of the clause through its use as an instrument to throttle the capacity of the States to protect their fundamental interests. This development is a growth from the seeds which the fathers planted. . . . The principle of this development is, as we have seen, that the reservation of the reasonable exercise of the protective power of the State is read into all contracts, and there is no greater reason for refusing to apply this principle to Minnesota mortgages than to New York leases.

Applying the criteria established by our decisions, we conclude:

1.   An emergency existed in Minnesota which furnished a proper occasion for the exercise of the reserved power of the State to protect the vital interests of the community.   .   .   .

2.   The legislation was addressed to a legitimate end; that is, the legislation was not for the mere advantage of particular individuals but for the protection of a basic interest of society.

3.   In view of the nature of the contracts in question—mortgages of unquestionable validity—the relief afforded and justified by the emergency, in order not to contravene the constitutional provision, could only be of a character appropriate to that emergency, and could be granted only upon reasonable conditions.

4.   The conditions upon which the period of redemption is extended do not appear to be unreasonable.   .   .   .   As already noted, the integrity of the mortgage indebtedness is not impaired; interest continues to run; the validity of the sale and the right of a mortgagee-purchaser to title or to obtain a deficiency judgment, if the mortgagor fails to redeem within the extended period, are maintained; and the conditions of redemption, if redemption there be, stand as they were under the prior law.   The mortgagor during the extended period is not ousted from possession, but he must pay the rental value of the premises as ascertained in judicial proceedings and this amount is applied to the carrying of the property and to interest upon the indebtedness.   The mortgagee-purchaser during the time that he cannot obtain possession thus is not left without compensation for the withholding of possession.   .   .   . If it be determined, as it must be, that the contract clause is not an absolute and utterly unqualified restriction of the State's protective power, this legislation is clearly so reasonable as to be within the legislative competency.

5.   The legislation is temporary in operation.   It is limited to the exigency which called it forth.   .   .   .   [T]he operation of the statute itself could not validly outlast the emergency or be so extended as virtually to destroy the contracts.

We are of the opinion that the Minnesota statute as here applied does not violate the contract clause of the Federal Constitution.   Whether the legislation is wise or unwise as a matter of policy is a question with which we are not concerned.   What has been said on that point is also applicable to the contention presented under the due process clause.

Judgment affirmed.

Mr. Justice SUTHERLAND, dissenting.   .   .   .

If it be possible by resort to the testimony of history to put any question of constitutional intent beyond the domain of uncertainty, the foregoing leaves no reasonable ground upon which to base a denial that the clause of the Constitution now under consideration was meant to foreclose state action impairing the obligation of contracts *primarily and especially* in respect of such action aimed at giving relief to debtors *in time of emergency*.   And if further proof be required to strengthen what already is inexpungable, such proof will be found in the previous decisions of this court.   .   .   .

The Minnesota statute either impairs the obligation of contracts or it does not. If it does not, the occasion to which it relates becomes immaterial, since then the passage of the statute is the exercise of a normal, unrestricted, state power and requires no special occasion to render it effective. If it does, the emergency no more furnishes a proper occasion for its exercise than if the emergency were nonexistent. . . .

A statute which materially delays enforcement of the mortgagee's contractual right of ownership and possession does not modify the remedy merely; it destroys, for the period of delay, *all* remedy so far as the enforcement of that right is concerned. The phrase "obligation of a contract" in the constitutional sense imports a legal duty to perform the specified obligation of *that* contract, not to substitute and perform, against the will of one of the parties, a different, albeit equally valuable, obligation. And a state, under the contract impairment clause, has no more power to accomplish such a substitution than has one of the parties to the contract against the will of the other. It cannot do so either by acting directly upon the contract or by bringing about the result under the guise of a statute in form acting only upon the remedy.

I am authorized to say that Mr. Justice VAN DEVANTER, Mr. Justice McREYNOLDS, and Mr. Justice BUTLER concur in this opinion.

CONTRACT CLAUSE CASES AFTER BLAISDELL

The major modern decisions sustaining state laws against contract clause challenges are described in Justice Black's dissent in El Paso v. Simmons, the next principal case. But Blaisdell did not assure the validity of all state laws affecting contracts. State laws were held to violate the contract clause in the following cases:

a. Worthen Co. v. Thomas, 292 U.S. 426 (1934): An Arkansas law exempted payments on life insurance policies from garnishment. Though an emergency existed, the law was invalid, according to the opinion by Chief Justice Hughes, because it contained no time limitation and because the amount of exemption was not limited to the necessities of the particular case.

b. Worthen Co. v. Kavanaugh, 295 U.S. 56 (1935): A Municipal Improvement District issued bonds and pledged benefit assessments as security. A subsequent Arkansas law changed the procedures for enforcing the payment of benefit assessments, to protect property owners. Justice Cardozo's opinion for the Court concluded that the procedural changes were "an oppressive and unnecessary destruction of nearly all the incidents that give attractiveness and value to collateral security. . . . Not even changes of the remedy may be pressed so far as to cut down the security of a mortgage without moderation or reason."

c. Wood v. Lovett, 313 U.S. 362 (1941): In 1937, Arkansas repealed a 1935 law protecting purchasers at state tax sales from state attempts to set aside the transaction on the basis of certain irregularities. The Court held that the 1937 repeal could not be applied to a 1936 sale; under the contract clause, the purchaser in 1936 was entitled to rely on the 1935 law designed to make "the land saleable." Justice Black, joined by Justices Douglas and Murphy dissented, insisting that, under Blaisdell, Arkansas had not acted "unreasonably, unjustly, oppressively, or counter to sound policy." Compare Justice Black's comment on this dissent in his 1965 dissent in El Paso v. Simmons, which follows.

EL PASO v. SIMMONS

379 U.S. 497, 85 S.Ct. 577, 13 L.Ed.2d 446 (1965).

Appeal from the Court of Appeals for the Fifth Circuit.*

Mr. Justice WHITE delivered the opinion of the Court.

[In 1910, Texas sold some public land by contract calling for a small down payment. State law provided for forfeiture of the purchaser's rights for nonpayment of interest; but, in case of forfeiture, the purchaser or his vendee could reinstate his claim at any time upon payment of delinquent interest, provided no rights of third parties had intervened. In 1941, Texas amended its laws to limit this reinstatement right to five years from the forfeiture date.

[The land contracts in issue in this case were declared forfeited for nonpayment of interest in 1947—37 years after the contracts were made. Subsequently, Simmons purchased the contract rights to the land. In 1952, five years and two days after the forfeiture, Simmons tendered payment of back interest and filed for reinstatement. The State, relying on the 5-year limitation enacted in 1941, refused to reinstate the claims. In 1955, the State sold the land to the City of El Paso. Simmons, a citizen of Kentucky, brought a federal court action against the City to determine title to the land. The District Court granted the City's motion for summary judgment on the basis of the 1941 law. The Court of Appeals reversed, holding the 1941 law unconstitutional: the 1910 reinstatement provision conferred a vested contractual right; the 1941 statute "was not a mere modification of remedy but a change in the obligation of a contract." The Court of Appeals remanded for a trial on the City's additional defenses of laches and adverse possession. The Supreme Court reversed:]

We do not pause . . . to chart again the dividing line . . . between "remedy" and "obligation" . . . . For it is not every modification of a contractual promise that impairs the obligation of contract under federal law, any more than it is every alteration of existing remedies that violates the Contract Clause. . . . Assuming the provision for reinstatement after default to be part of the State's obligation, we do not think its modification by a five-year statute of repose contravenes the Contract Clause.

The decisions "put it beyond question that the prohibition is not an absolute one . . . ," as Chief Justice Hughes said in Home Building & Loan Assn. v. Blaisdell . . . . The Blaisdell opinion . . . makes it quite clear that "the State . . . continues to possess authority to safeguard the vital interests of its people. . . ."

Of course, the power of a State to modify or affect the obligation of contract is not without limit. . . . But we think the objects of the Texas

---

* The Court held that the appeal was improperly brought under 28 U.S.C. § 1254(2), because the judgment below was not final. Treating the appeal papers as a petition for certiorari pursuant to 28 U.S.C. § 2103, see chap. 1, p. 60, supra, the Court dismissed the appeal and granted certiorari.

statute make abundantly clear that it impairs no protected right under the Contract Clause. . . .

Texas, upon entering the Union, reserved its entire public domain, one-half of which was set aside under the 1876 Constitution to finance a universal system of free public education. These lands, over 42,000,000, acres, were to be sold as quickly as practicable in order to provide revenues for the public school system and to encourage the settlement of the vast public domain. The terms of sale were undemanding and designed to accomplish the widespread sale and development of the public domain. . . . The terms were frequently modified in favor of purchasers. . . . But eventually the evolution of a frontier society to a modern State, attended by the discovery of oil and gas deposits which led to speculation and exploitation of the changes in the use and value of the lands, called forth amendments to the Texas land laws modifying the conditions of sale in favor of the State. . . .

. . . The general purpose of the legislation enacted in 1941 was to restore confidence in the stability and integrity of land titles and to enable the State to protect and administer its property in a businesslike manner. "[T]he records [of the land office] show that through the years many thousands of purchase contracts . . . have been forfeited by failure of the purchasers to meet the small annual interest payments requisite to the maintenance of the contracts." . . . This state of affairs was principally attributable to the opportunity for speculation to which unlimited reinstatement rights gave rise. Forfeited purchaser contracts which had remained dormant for years could be reinstated if and when the land became potentially productive of gas and oil. . . .

No less significant was the imbroglio over land titles in Texas. The long shadow cast by perpetual reinstatement gave rise to a spate of litigation between forfeiting purchasers and the State or between one or more forfeiting purchasers and other forfeiting purchasers. . . . Where the same land had been sold and contracts forfeited several times, as was frequently the case, the right to reinstate could be exercised by any one of the forfeiting purchasers or his vendees. [I]t is in light of this situation that we judge the validity of the [1941] amendment.

The Contract Clause of the Constitution does not render Texas powerless to take effective and necessary measures to deal with the above. We note at the outset that the promise of reinstatement . . . was not the central undertaking of the seller nor the primary consideration for the buyer's undertaking. [T]he right of reinstatement [was] conditioned on the State's refusal or failure to dispose of the land by sale or lease. . . . We do not believe that it can seriously be contended that the buyer was substantially induced to enter into these contracts on the basis of a defeasible right to reinstatement in case of his failure to perform, or that he interpreted that right to be of everlasting effect. . . .

The State's policy of quick resale of forfeited lands did not prove entirely successful . . . . These developments, hardly to be expected or foreseen, operated to confer considerable advantages on the purchaser and his successors and a costly and difficult burden on the State. . . . Laws which restrict a party to those gains reasonably to be expected from the contract are not subject to attack under the Contract Clause, notwithstanding that they technically alter an obligation of a contract. . . .

. . . . The measure taken to induce defaulting purchasers to comply with their contracts, requiring payment of interest in arrears within five years, was a mild one indeed, hardly burdensome to the purchaser who wanted to adhere to his contract of purchase, but nonetheless an important one to the State's interest. The Contract Clause does not forbid such a measure.

Reversed.

Mr. Justice BLACK, dissenting.

I have previously had a number of occasions to dissent from judgments of this Court balancing away the First Amendment's unequivocally guaranteed rights of free speech, press, assembly and petition [see chap. 15, infra]. In this case I am compelled to dissent from the Court's balancing away the plain guarantee of [the contract clause], a balancing which results in the State of Texas' taking a man's private property for public use without compensation. . . . .

. . . . If the hope and realization of profit to a contract breaker are hereafter to be given either partial or sufficient weight to cancel out the unequivocal constitutional command against impairing the obligations of contracts, that command will be nullified by what is the most common cause for breaking contracts. I cannot subscribe to such a devitalizing constitutional doctrine.

. . . . The Court carefully does not deny that this promise by Texas is the kind of "obligation" which the Contract Clause was written to protect. The Court does not [treat] this as a mere change in court remedies for enforcement. Instead of relying on such grounds, the Court says that since the State acts out of what this Court thinks are good motives, and has not repudiated its contract except in a way which this Court thinks is "reasonable," therefore the State will be allowed to ignore the Contract Clause of the Constitution. There follow citation of one or two dicta from past cases, a bit of skillful "balancing," and the Court arrives at its conclusion: although the obligation of the contract has been impaired here, this impairment does not seem to the Court to be very serious or evil, and so therefore "the Contract Clause does not forbid such a measure." . . . .

[T]he Court's discussion of the Contract Clause and this Court's past decisions applying it is brief. [T]he first thing it is important to point out is that there is no support whatever in history or in this Court's prior holdings for the decision reached in this case. . . . The first great case construing the Contract Clause involved, much like the present case, an attempt by a State to relieve itself of the duty of honoring land grants which it regretted having made. [Fletcher v. Peck, p. 926, supra.] . . .

The Court does not purport to overrule any of these past cases, but I think unless overruled they require a holding that the Texas statute violates the Contract Clause. It is therefore at least a little surprising that the Court does not find it necessary to discuss them. Instead the Court quotes a few abstract statements from some other cases, hardly a solid and persuasive basis for devitalizing one of the few provisions which the Framers deemed of sufficient importance to place in the original Constitution . . .

The cases the Court mentions do not support its reasoning. [Blaisdell], which the Court seems to think practically read the Contract Clause out of the Constitution, actually did no such thing, as the Blaisdell opinion read in its entirety shows and as subsequent decisions of this Court were careful to point out. [T]he Blaisdell Court relied on [the] established distinction between an invalid impairment of a contract's obligation and a valid change in the remedy to enforce it. . . . Other state laws which did not meet the constitutional standard applied in Blaisdell were subsequently struck down. . . .[1]

None of the other cases which the Court quotes or mentions in passing altered in any way the rule established in Fletcher v. Peck, supra, and adhered to in Blaisdell and thereafter, that a State may not pass a law repudiating contractual obligations without compensating the injured parties.[2] Especially should this be true when . . . the contractual obligation repudiated is the State's own. . . .

[According to the Court,] a person can make a good deal with a State but if it turns out to be a very good deal for him or a very bad deal for the State, the State is free to renege at any time. And whether gains can "reasonably be expected from the contract" is of course, in the Court's view, for this Court to decide. . . .

. . . . On the side of the purchasers the Court finds nothing that weighs much . . . . The Court tries to downgrade the importance of the reinstatement obligation in the contract by volunteering the opinion that this obligation "was not the central undertaking of the seller [Texas] nor the primary consideration for the buyer's undertaking." Why the Court guesses this we are not told. My guess is different. . . . To my way of thinking it demonstrates a striking lack of knowledge of credit buying and selling even to imply that these express contractual provisions safeguarding credit purchasers

1. I dissented in Wood v. Lovett, [see p. 934, supra], because . . . I believed that the state law in that case, which protected purchasers of land against loss even though their titles were based only on quitclaim deeds, should have been upheld under Blaisdell. Even had my dissent prevailed, however, that case would not have supported the Court's holding in the case before us. [Footnote by Justice Black.]

2. None of the cases mentioned by the Court involved legislation by which a State attempted to repudiate its own contractual obligation without giving compensation, nor did any of them come near suggesting or implying that a State might do so. Honeyman v. Jacobs, 306 U.S. 539, . . . upheld a state statute providing that a mortgagee who bid at a foreclosure sale could not obtain a deficiency judgment if the value of the property equaled or exceeded the amount of the debt plus costs and interest; the Court said that the mortgagee under this law received all the compensation to which his contract entitled him, and that the statute "merely restricted the exercise of the contractual remedy." . . . Veix v. Sixth Ward Building & Loan Assn.,

310 U.S. 32, held only that by issuing shares of stock at a time when state law permitted shareholders to withdraw their shares in exchange for a cash refund a private company regulated by the State could not prevent the State from applying later general legislation forbidding shareholders to sue for the withdrawal value; this rule of course had been recognized in Blaisdell . . . . Gelfert v. National City Bank, 313 U.S. 221, upheld a New York law which redefined fair market value of property purchased by mortgagees at foreclosure sales; . . . the Court held that this law was merely a regulation of the remedy, and did not affect any substantial right given by the contract . . . Faitoute Iron & Steel Co. v. City of Asbury Park, 316 U.S. 502, which upheld a law binding all the creditors of a municipal corporation to an adjustment of claims if 85% of them agreed, said simply that as a practical matter the law rather than impairing the creditors' contracts was necessary to keep them from becoming worthless. East New York Savings Bank v. Hahn, 326 U.S. 230, upheld a mortgage moratorium law much like that in Blaisdell . . . . [Footnote by Justice Black.]

against forfeitures were not one of the greatest, if not the greatest, selling arguments Texas had to promote purchase of its great surfeit of lands. The Court's factual inference is all the more puzzling since its opinion emphasizes that many people entered these contracts for speculative purposes which without the redemption provision would not have been nearly so attractive.
. . .

Let us now look at some of the weights the Court throws on the scales on the side of Texas. . . . I do not believe that any or all of the things . . . on which the Court relies are reasons for relieving Texas of the unconditional duty of keeping its contractual obligations. . . . It is a commonplace that land values steadily rise when population increases and rise sharply when valuable minerals are discovered, and that many sellers would be much richer and happier if when lands go up in value they were able to welch on their sales. No plethora of words about state school funds can conceal the fact that to get money easily without having to tax the whole public Texas took the easy way out and violated the Contract Clause of the Constitution as written and as applied up to now. . . .

All this for me is just another example of the delusiveness of calling "balancing" a "test." With its deprecatory view of the equities on the side of Simmons and other claimants and its remarkable sympathy for the State, the Court through its balancing process states the case in a way inevitably destined to bypass the Contract Clause and let Texas break its solemn obligation. . . . James Madison said that the Contract Clause was intended to protect people from the "fluctuating policy" of the legislature. The Federalist, No. 44 . . . . Today's majority holds that people are not protected from the fluctuating policy of the legislature so long as the legislature acts in accordance with the fluctuating policy of this Court. . . .

[T]he real issue in this case is not whether Texas has constitutional power to pass legislation to correct these problems, by limiting reinstatements to five years following forfeiture. I think that there was and is a constitutional way for Texas to do this. But I think the Fifth Amendment forbids Texas to do so without compensating the holders of contractual rights for the interests it wants to destroy. Contractual rights, this Court has held, are property . . . . Our Constitution provides that property needed for public use, whether for schools or highways or any other public purpose, shall be paid for out of tax-raised funds fairly contributed by all the taxpayers, not just by a few purchasers of land who trusted the State not wisely but too well. It is not the happiest of days for me when one of our wealthiest States is permitted to enforce a law that breaks faith with those who contracted with it. . . .

RETROACTIVITY AND FEDERAL LEGISLATION

The contract clause applies only to state legislation. Congressional power to impair contracts and vested rights is similarly restricted, by the due process clause. In Lynch v. United States, 292 U.S. 571 (1934), the Court held that Congress could not cancel government war risk life insurance, as it had attempted to do in 1933. Justice Brandeis said: "Valid contracts are property, whether the obligor be a private individual, a municipality, a state, or the United States. Rights against the United States arising out of contract with it are protected by the Fifth Amendment. . . . When the United States enters into contract relations, its rights and duties therein are governed generally by the law applicable to contracts between private individuals. That the contracts of war risk insurance were valid when made is not questioned. As Congress had the power to authorize the Bureau of War Risk Insurance to issue them, the due process clause prohibits the United States from annulling them, unless, indeed, the action taken falls within the federal police power or some other paramount power." [1]

For an example of a retroactive change in United States obligations "within the federal police power or some other paramount power," see Lichter v. United States, 334 U.S. 742 (1948) (renegotiation and recapture of excess profits on government contracts). Cf. FHA v. Darlington, 358 U.S. 84 (1958) (sustaining 1954 "clarifying" amendment restricting use of housing constructed under FHA-insured mortgage in 1949; Justices Harlan, Frankfurter and Whittaker dissented on the basis of Lynch); and note Flemming v. Nestor, on termination of social security benefits, chap. 5, p. 437, supra. See also Battaglia v. General Motors, 169 F.2d 254 (2d Cir.), cert. denied, 335 U.S. 887 (1948), sustaining the Portal-to-Portal Pay Act of 1947, which had relieved employers of overtime pay liability created by an unanticipated Supreme Court interpretation of the Fair Labor Standards Act. On due process challenges to retroactive state legislation, see, e. g., Chase Securities Corp. v. Donaldson, 325 U.S. 304 (1945), upholding a Minnesota law which lifted the bar of the statute of limitations in pending suits. See generally Slawson, "Constitutional and Legislative Considerations in Retroactive Lawmaking," 48 Calif.L.Rev. 216 (1960), and Hochman, "The Supreme Court and the Constitutionality of Retroactive Legislation," 73 Harv.L.Rev. 692 (1960).

SECTION 2. REGULATION VS. TAKING: THE "PETTY LARCENY OF THE POLICE POWER" * AND JUST COMPENSATION

Introduction. The Fifth Amendment states that private property shall not "be taken for public use, without just compensation." The 14th Amendment has been interpreted to impose the same obligation on the states. Chicago, B. & Q. R. R. v. Chicago, 166 U.S. 226 (1897). Accordingly, when government seeks to "take" private land for a new schoolhouse or a park or an airfield, it resorts to the power of eminent domain: the property is taken through condemnation, and the owner is entitled to "just compensation." Under the police power and other regulatory powers, however, government may impose restrictions on property that produce a substantial diminution in its value; and

---

1. See also Perry v. United States, 294 U.S. 330 (1935) (one of the "gold clause" cases), and Louisville Joint Stock Land Bank v. Radford, 295 U.S. 555 (1935) (federal moratorium law for farmer-mortgagors).

* The phrase was used by Justice Holmes in a draft opinion he prepared in a case, Jackman v. Rosen-baum Co., 260 U.S. 22 (1922), decided shortly before the Pennsylvania Coal case, infra. He deleted the phrase in the final version: "my brethren, as usual and as I expected, corrected my taste . . .. It is done—our effort is to please." Holmes to Laski, October 22, 1922, I Holmes-Laski Letters (Howe ed. 1953), 456.

the Court has held that government need not compensate the owner for losses that are incidental consequences of valid regulations. When does government action give rise to a duty to compensate? When may government cause property losses without compensation, through "the petty larceny of the police power"? This section deals mainly with the problems of distinguishing compensable and non-compensable impositions of property losses by government. Do the cases suggest adequate criteria for making the distinction? Can the Court do better than Justice Holmes' effort in the Pennsylvania Coal Case, infra? For valiant modern efforts to articulate standards, see Michelman, "Property, Utility, and Fairness: Comments on the Ethical Foundations of 'Just Compensation' Law," 80 Harv.L.Rev. 1165 (1967), and Sax, "Takings and the Police Power," 74 Yale L.J. 36 (1964).

MILLER v. SCHOENE

276 U.S. 272, 48 S.Ct. 246, 72 L.Ed. 568 (1928).

Error to the Supreme Court of Appeals of Virginia.

Mr. Justice STONE delivered the opinion of the Court.

Acting under the Cedar Rust Act of Virginia . . . ., defendant in error, the state entomologist, ordered the plaintiffs in error to cut down a large number of ornamental red cedar trees growing on their property, as a means of preventing the communication of a rust or plant disease with which they were infected to the apple orchards in the vicinity. The plaintiffs in error appealed from the order to the circuit court of Shenandoah county which, after a hearing and a consideration of evidence, affirmed the order and allowed to plaintiffs in error $100 to cover the expense of removal of the cedars. Neither the judgment of the court nor the statute as interpreted allows compensation for the value of the standing cedars or the decrease in the market value of the realty caused by their destruction whether considered as ornamental trees or otherwise. But they save to plaintiffs in error the privilege of using the trees when felled. [The statute was challenged under the due process clause of the 14th Amendment.]

The Virginia statute presents a comprehensive scheme for the condemnation and destruction of red cedar trees infected by cedar rust. By § 1 it is declared to be unlawful for any person to "own, plant or keep alive and standing" on his premises any red cedar tree which is or may be the source or "host plant" of the communicable plant disease known as cedar rust, and any such tree growing within a certain radius of any apple orchard is declared to be a public nuisance, subject to destruction. Section 2 makes it the duty of the state entomologist " . . . to ascertain if any cedar tree or trees . . . constitute a menace to the health of any apple orchard in said locality . . . ." If affirmative findings are so made, he is required to direct the owner in writing to destroy the trees . . . . Section 5 authorizes the state entomologist to destroy the trees if the owner, after being notified, fails to do so. . . .

As shown by the evidence . . . ., cedar rust is an infectious plant disease in the form of a fungoid organism which is destructive of the fruit and foliage of the apple, but without effect on the value of the cedar. Its life cycle has two phases which are passed alternately as a growth on red cedar and on apple trees. It is communicated by spores from one to the other over a radius of at least two miles. It appears not to be communicable between trees of the same species, but only from one species to the other, and other plants seem not to be appreciably affected by it. The only practicable method of controlling the disease and protecting apple trees from its ravages is the destruction of all red cedar trees, subject to the infection, located within two miles of apple orchards.

The red cedar, aside from its ornamental use, has occasional use and value as lumber. It is indigenous to Virginia, is not cultivated or dealt in commercially on any substantial scale, and its value throughout the state is shown to be small as compared with that of the apple orchards of the state. Apple growing is one of the principal agricultural pursuits in Virginia. The apple is used there and exported in large quantities. Many millions of dollars are invested in the orchards, which furnish employment for a large portion of the population, and have induced the development of attendant railroad and cold storage facilities.

On the evidence we may accept the conclusion of the Supreme Court of Appeals that the state was under the necessity of making a choice between the preservation of one class of property and that of the other wherever both existed in dangerous proximity. It would have been none the less a choice if, instead of enacting the present statute, the state, by doing nothing, had permitted serious injury to the apple orchards within its borders to go on unchecked. When forced to such a choice the state does not exceed its constitutional powers by deciding upon the destruction of one class of property in order to save another which, in the judgment of the legislature, is of greater value to the public. It will not do to say that the case is merely one of a conflict of two private interests and that the misfortune of apple growers may not be shifted to cedar owners by ordering the destruction of their property; for it is obvious that there may be, and that here there is, a preponderant public concern in the preservation of the one interest over the other. . . . And where the public interest is involved preferment of that interest over the property interest of the individual, to the extent even of its destruction, is one of the distinguishing characteristics of every exercise of the police power which affects property. . . .

We need not weigh with nicety the question whether the infected cedars constitute a nuisance according to the common law; or whether they may be so declared by statute. . . . For where, as here, the choice is unavoidable, we cannot say that its exercise, controlled by considerations of social policy which are not unreasonable, involves any denial of due process. . . .

Affirmed.

PENNSYLVANIA COAL CO. v. MAHON

260 U.S. 393, 43 S.Ct. 158, 67 L.Ed. 322 (1922).

Error to the Supreme Court of Pennsylvania.

Mr. Justice HOLMES delivered the opinion of the Court.

This is a bill in equity brought by the defendants in error to prevent the Pennsylvania Coal Company from mining under their property in such way as to remove the supports and cause a subsidence of the surface and of their house. The bill sets out a deed executed by the Coal Company in 1878, under which the plaintiffs claim. The deed conveys the surface, but in express terms reserves the right to remove all the coal under the same, and the grantee takes the premises with the risk, and waives all claim for damages that may arise from mining out the coal. But the plaintiffs say that whatever may have been the Coal Company's rights, they were taken away by an Act of Pennsylvania, approved May 27, 1921, . . . commonly known there as the Kohler Act. The Court of Common Pleas . . . denied an injunction, holding that the statute if applied to this case would be unconstitutional.[1] On appeal the Supreme Court of the State . . . held that the statute was a legitimate exercise of the police power and directed a decree for the plaintiffs. . . .

The statute forbids the mining of anthracite coal in such way as to cause the subsidence of, among other things, any structure used as a human habitation with certain exceptions, including among them land where the surface is owned by the owner of the underlying coal and is distant more than one hundred and fifty feet from any improved property belonging to any other person. As applied to this case the statute is admitted to destroy previously existing rights of property and contract. The question is whether the police power can be stretched so far.

Government hardly could go on if to some extent values incident to property could not be diminished without paying for every such change in the general law. As long recognized some values are enjoyed under an implied limitation and must yield to the police power. But obviously the implied limitation must have its limits or the contract and due process clauses are gone. One fact for consideration in determining such limits is the extent of the diminution. When it reaches a certain magnitude, in most if not in all cases there must be an exercise of eminent domain and compensation to sustain the act. So the question depends upon the particular facts. The greatest weight is given to the judgment of the legislature but it always is open to interested parties to contend that the legislature had gone beyond its constitutional power.

This is the case of a single private house. No doubt there is a public interest even in this, as there is in every purchase and sale and in all that happens within the commonwealth. Some existing rights may be modified even in such a case. . . . But usually in ordinary private affairs the public interest does not warrant much of this kind of interference. A source of damage to such a house is not a public nuisance even if similar damage is inflicted on others in different places. The damage is not common or public. . . . The extent of the public interest is shown by the statute to be limited, since the statute ordinarily does not apply to land when the surface is owned by the owner of the coal. Furthermore, it is not justified as a protection of personal safety. That could be provided for by notice. Indeed the very foundation of this bill is that the defendant gave timely notice of its intent to mine under the house. On the other hand the extent of the taking is great. It purports to abolish what is recognized in Pennsylvania as an estate in land —a very valuable estate—and what is declared by the Court below to be a con-

---

1. The briefs and arguments showed that under Pennsylvania law as developed prior to the statute there were three distinct estates in mining property, namely (a) use of the surface, (b) ownership of subjacent minerals, and (c) right to have the surface supported. And it was contended by the company that surface support could be constitutionally acquired for public use only by eminent domain.

tract hitherto binding the plaintiffs. If we were called upon to deal with the plaintiffs' position alone we should think it clear that the statute does not disclose a public interest sufficient to warrant so extensive a destruction of the defendant's constitutionally protected rights.

But the case has been treated as one in which the general validity of the act should be discussed. . . . It seems, therefore, to be our duty to go farther in the statement of our opinion, in order that it may be known at once, and that further suits should not be brought in vain.

It is our opinion that the act cannot be sustained as an exercise of the police power, so far as it affects the mining of coal under streets or cities in places where the right to mine such coal has been reserved. As said in a Pennsylvania case, "For practical purposes, the right to coal consists in the right to mine it." Commonwealth v. Clearview Coal Co., 256 Pa. 328, 331. What makes the right to mine coal valuable is that it can be exercised with profit. To make it commercially impracticable to mine certain coal has very nearly the same effect for constitutional purposes as appropriating or destroying it. This we think that we are warranted in assuming that the statute does.

It is true that in Plymouth Coal Co. v. Pennsylvania, 232 U.S. 531, it was held competent for the legislature to require a pillar of coal to be left along the line of adjoining property, that with the pillar on the other side of the line would be a barrier sufficient for the safety of the employees of either mine in case the other should be abandoned and allowed to fill with water. But that was a requirement for the safety of employees invited into the mine, and secured an average reciprocity of advantage that has been recognized as a justification of various laws.

The rights of the public in a street purchased or laid out by eminent domain are those that it has paid for. If in any case its representatives have been so short sighted as to acquire only surface rights without the right of support we see no more authority for supplying the latter without compensation than there was for taking the right of way in the first place and refusing to pay for it because the public wanted it very much. The protection of private property in the Fifth Amendment presupposes that it is wanted for public use, but provides that it shall not be taken for such use without compensation. A similar assumption is made in the decisions upon the Fourteenth Amendment. . . . When this seemingly absolute protection is found to be qualified by the police power, the natural tendency of human nature is to extend the qualification more and more until at last private property disappears. But that cannot be accomplished in this way under the Constitution of the United States.

The general rule at least is that while property may be regulated to a certain extent, if regulation goes too far it will be recognized as a taking. It may be doubted how far exceptional cases, like the blowing up of a house to stop a conflagration, go—and if they go beyond the general rule, whether they do not stand as much upon tradition as upon principle. Bowditch v. Boston, 101 U.S. 16. In general it is not plain that a man's misfortunes or necessities will justify his shifting the damages to his neighbor's shoulders. . . . We are in danger of forgetting that a strong public desire to improve the public condition is not enough to warrant achieving the desire by a shorter cut than the constitutional way of paying for the change. As we already have said this is a question of degree—and therefore cannot be disposed of by general propositions. But we regard this as going beyond any of the cases decided by this Court. . . .

We assume, of course, that the statute was passed upon the conviction that an exigency existed that would warrant it, and we assume that an exigency exists that would warrant the exercise of eminent domain. But the question at bottom is upon whom the loss of the changes desired should fall. So far as private persons or communities have seen fit to take the risk of acquiring only surface rights, we cannot see that the fact that their risk has become a danger warrants the giving to them greater rights than they bought.

Decree reversed.

Mr. Justice BRANDEIS, dissenting. . . . .

Every restriction upon the use of property imposed in the exercise of the police power deprives the owner of some right theretofore enjoyed, and is, in that sense, an abridgment by the State of rights in property without making compensation. But restriction imposed to protect the public health, safety or morals from dangers threatened is not a taking. The restriction here in question is merely the prohibition of a noxious use. The property so restricted remains in the possession of its owner. The State does not appropriate it or make any use of it. The State merely prevents the owner from making a use which interferes with paramount rights of the public. Whenever the use prohibited ceases to be noxious,—as it may because of further change in local or social conditions,—the restriction will have to be removed and the owner will again be free to enjoy his property as heretofore.

The restriction upon the use of this property can not, of course, be lawfully imposed, unless its purpose is to protect the public. But the purpose of a restriction does not cease to be public, because incidentally some private persons may thereby receive gratuitously valuable special benefits. Thus, owners of low buidings may obtain, through statutory restrictions upon the height of neighboring structures, benefits equivalent to an easement of light and air. . . .   Furthermore, a restriction, though imposed for a public purpose, will not be lawful, unless the restriction is an appropriate means to the public end. But to keep coal in place is surely an appropriate means of preventing subsidence of the surface; and ordinarily it is the only available means. Restriction upon use does not become inappropriate as a means, merely because it deprives the owner of the only use to which the property can then be profitably put. The liquor and the oleomargarine cases settled that. Mugler v. Kansas, 123 U. S. 623, 668, 669; Powell v. Pennsylvania, 127 U. S. 678, 682. . . .   Nor is a restriction imposed through exercise of the police power inappropriate as a means, merely because the same end might be effected through exercise of the power of eminent domain, or otherwise at public expense. Every restriction upon the height of buildings might be secured through acquiring by eminent domain the right of each owner to build above the limiting height; but it is settled that the State need not resort to that power. . . .

It is said that one fact for consideration in determining whether the limits of the police power have been exceeded is the extent of the resulting diminution in value; and that here the restriction destroys existing rights of property and contract. But values are relative. If we are to consider the value of the coal kept in place by the restriction, we should compare it with the value of all other parts of the land. . . .   For aught that appears the value of the coal kept in place by the restriction may be negligible as compared with the value of the whole property, or even as compared with that part of it which is represented by the coal remaining in place and which may be extracted despite the statute. . . . .

It is said that . . . . the restriction upon mining cannot be justified as a protection of personal safety, since that could be provided for by notice. The propriety of deferring a good deal to tribunals on the spot has been repeatedly recognized. . . . . May we say that notice would afford adequate protection of the public safety where the legislature and the highest court of the State, with greater knowledge of local conditions, have declared, in effect, that it would not? If public safety is imperiled, surely neither grant, nor contract, can prevail against the exercise of the police power. . . .

. . . . [I]t is said that these provisions . . . . cannot be sustained as an exercise of the police power where the right to mine such coal has been reserved. The conclusion seems to rest upon the assumption that in order to justify such exercise of the police power there must be "an average reciprocity of advantage" as between the owner of the property restricted and the rest of the community; and that here such reciprocity is absent. Reciprocity of advantage is an important consideration, and may even be essential, where the State's power is exercised for the purpose of conferring benefits upon the property of a neighborhood, as in drainage projects, Wurts v. Hoagland, 114 U.S. 606; . . . . or upon adjoining owners, as by party wall provisions, Jackman v. Rosenbaum Co., [260 U.S. 22]. But where the police power is exercised, not to confer benefits upon property owners but to protect the public from detriment and danger, there is in my opinion, no room for considering reciprocity of advantage. There was no reciprocal advantage to the owner prohibited from using his oil tanks, in [Pierce Oil Corp. v. City of Hope,] 248 U.S. 498; his brickyard, in [Hadacheck v. Sebastian,] 239 U.S. 394; his livery stable, in [Reinman v. City of Little Rock,] 237 U.S. 171; his billiard hall, in [Murphy v. California,] 225 U.S. 623; his oleomargarine factory, in [Powell v. Pennsylvania,] 127 U.S. 678; his brewery, in [Mugler v. Kansas,] 123 U.S. 623; unless it be the advantage of living and doing business in a civilized community. That reciprocal advantage is given by the act to the coal operators.

SOME PROBLEMS OF THE "TAKING"-"REGULATION" DISTINCTION

1. *"Taking" by low-flying airplanes.* a. *Causby and Griggs.* In United States v. Causby, 328 U.S. 256 (1946), the Court held that respondents' property had been "taken" within the meaning of the Fifth Amendment "by frequent and regular flights of army and navy aircraft over respondents' land at low altitudes." Respondents owned 2.8 acres of land adjacent to a military airport in North Carolina; it had on it a house and various "outbuildings" used for raising chickens. The CAA-approved flight path passed 83 feet over the property—"which is 67 feet above the house, 63 feet above the barn and 18 feet above the highest tree." The Court of Claims found that, as a result of the noise of the planes, "respondents had to give up their chicken business. As many as six to ten chickens were killed in one day by flying into the walls from fright. . . . . Production also fell off. The result was the de-

struction of the use of the property as a commercial chicken farm. Respondents are frequently deprived of their sleep and the family has become nervous and frightened." The Court of Claims held that the United States had in effect taken an easement over the property and that respondents' property loss amounted to $2,000. The Supreme Court affirmed.

The Government relied on the fact that the flights were within the minimum safe altitudes prescribed pursuant to the Civil Aeronautics Act of 1938. The Act recognized "a public right of freedom of transit in air commerce through the navigable airspace of the United States." The Government insisted that "when flights are made within the navigable airspace without any physical invasion of the property of the landowners, there has been no taking of property; . . . that at most there was merely incidental damage occurring as a consequence of authorized air navigation." It also argued that "the landowner does not own superadjacent airspace which he has not subjected to possession by the erection of structures or other occupancy" and that "even if the United States took airspace owned by respondents, no compensable damage was shown." Any damages were claimed to be "merely consequential for which no compensation may be obtained under the Fifth Amendment."

The majority opinion, by Justice Douglas, agreed that "the air is a public highway"; but he insisted that this principle did not control the case: "For the United States conceded on oral argument that if the flights over respondents' property rendered it uninhabitable, there would be a taking compensable under the Fifth Amendment. It is the owner's loss, not the taker's gain, which is the measure of the value of the property taken. . . . If, by reason of the frequency and altitude of the flights, respondents could not use this land for any purpose, their loss would be complete. It would be as complete as if the United States had entered upon the surface of the land and taken exclusive possession of it. We agree that in those circumstances there would be a taking. Though it would be only an easement of flight which was taken, that easement, if permanent and not merely temporary, normally would be the equivalent of a fee interest. . . . The owner's right to possess and exploit the land—that is to say, his beneficial ownership of it—would be destroyed. It would not be a case of incidental damages arising from a legalized nuisance such as was involved in Richards v. Washington Terminal Co., 233 U.S. 546. In that case property owners whose lands adjoined a railroad line were denied recovery for damages resulting from the noise, vibrations, smoke and the like, incidental to the operations of the trains. In the supposed case the line of flight is over the land. And the land is appropriated as directly and completely as if it were used for the runways themselves.

"There is no material difference between the supposed case and the present one, except that here enjoyment and use of the land are not completely destroyed. But that does not seem to us to be controlling. The path of glide for airplanes might reduce a valuable factory site to grazing land, an orchard to a vegetable patch, a residential section to a wheat field. Some value would remain. But the use of the airspace immediately above the land would limit the utility of the land and cause a diminution in its value. . . . .

"We have said that the airspace is a public highway. Yet it is obvious that if the landowner is to have full enjoyment of the land, he must have exclusive control of the immediate reaches of the enveloping atmosphere.

. . . . The landowner owns at least as much of the space above the ground as he can occupy or use in connection with the land. . . . The fact that he does not occupy it in a physical sense—by the erection of buildings and the like—is not material. [T]he flight of airplanes, which skim the surface but do not touch it, is as much an appropriation of the use of the land as a more conventional entry upon it. . . .

"Flights over private land are not a taking, unless they are so low and so frequent as to be a direct and immediate interference with the enjoyment and use of the land. [T]he findings of the Court of Claims plainly establish that there was a diminution in value of the property and that the frequent, low-level flights were the direct and immediate cause. We agree with the Court of Claims that a servitude has been imposed upon the land."

Justice Black, joined by Justice Burton, dissented because "the effect of the Court's decision is to limit, by the imposition of relatively absolute constitutional barriers, possible future adjustments through legislation and regulation which might become necessary with the growth of air transportation, and [because] the Constitution does not contain such barriers. . . . Today's opinion is, I fear, an opening wedge for an unwarranted judicial interference with the power of Congress to develop solutions for new and vital and national problems. In my opinion this case should be reversed on the ground that there has been no 'taking' in the Constitutional sense."

See also Griggs v. County of Allegheny, 369 U.S. 84 (1962): The County, owner of the Greater Pittsburgh Airport, was held liable for the "taking" of an air easement over petitioner's property. The Court found that take-offs and landings at the nearby airport had so interfered with the use of petitioner's residence as to require compensation under the Causby holding. Justice Black, joined by Justice Frankfurter, dissented. He reviewed the "comprehensive plan for national and international air commerce" enacted by Congress and concluded that the United States, not the County, "owes just compensation." See Dunham, "Griggs v. Allegheny County in Perspective: Thirty Years of Supreme Court Expropriation Law," 1962 Sup.Ct.Rev. 63.

   b. *Railroads and airplanes.* What distinguished the Causby claim from that of the landowners adjacent to the railroad, the "case of incidental damages arising from a legalized nuisance," mentioned by Justice Douglas? Should the result in Causby have been different if the planes had inflicted the same damage without passing directly over respondents' property? [1]

   2. *Private property losses and war.* In the Causby case, note 1a supra, the airplanes were engaged in wartime flights from a military base, yet the losses were found compensable. In the cases that follow, the Court held that wartime losses were not compensable. Are the differences in result justifiable? Compare the riot problem, note 3 below.

   a. *Caltex.* In United States v. Caltex, 344 U.S. 149 (1952), the Court held that the owners of certain oil facilities in Manila were not entitled to compensation for the "requisition" and demolition of their property by the Army to prevent its imminent capture by the attacking Japanese. (The Army had

---

1. Compare also Panhandle Co. v. State Highway Commission, 294 U.S. 613 (1935) (holding a pipe line company not liable for the cost of moving its lines to permit building of a highway), with a long line of cases requiring railroads, at their own expense, to eliminate highway grade crossings, e. g., Atchison, T. & S. F. Ry. v. PUC, 346 U.S. 346 (1953).

paid for supplies used by it.) "The terse language of the Fifth Amendment is no comprehensive promise that the United States will make whole all who suffer from every ravage and burden of war. This Court has long recognized that in wartime many losses must be attributed solely to the fortunes of war, and not to the sovereign. No rigid rules can be laid down to distinguish compensable losses from non-compensable losses. Each case must be judged on its own facts." Justice Douglas, joined by Justice Black, dissented.

b. *Eureka.* In 1942, the War Production Board ordered the closing of gold mines, "to conserve the limited supply of equipment used by the mines" and to "divert available miners to more essential work." The Court held that there had been no "taking"; rather, "the damage to the mine owners was incidental to the Government's lawful regulation." United States v. Central Eureka Mining Co., 357 U.S. 155 (1958). Justice Burton stated that "the particular circumstances of each case" determined "whether a particular governmental restriction amounted to a . . . . taking." He recognized that "action in the form of regulation can so diminish the value of property as to constitute a taking," but added: "In the context of war, we have been reluctant to find that degree of regulation which . . . requires compensation to be paid." War, he noted, "makes demands which otherwise would be insufferable. But wartime economic restrictions, temporary in character, are insignificant when compared to the widespread uncompensated loss of life and freedom of action which war traditionally demands."

Justice Harlan, dissenting, insisted that the holding "is plainly outside the run of past decisions. . . . Where the Government proceeds by indirection, and accomplishes by regulation what is the equivalent of outright physical seizure of the property, courts should guard themselves against permitting formalities to obscure actualities." Justice Frankfurter also dissented.[2]

3. *Compensation and riots.* In National Board of YMCA v. United States, 395 U.S. 85 (1969), petitioners sued the Government for property damage inflicted by rioters after troops retreated into their buildings during the 1964 Panama disturbances. Justice Brennan's majority opinion found no compensable "taking." He insisted that "the troops were acting primarily in defense of petitioners' buildings," not "as part of a general defense of the Zone as a whole." Accordingly, "where, as here, the private party is the particular intended beneficiary of the governmental activity, 'fairness and justice' do not require that losses which may result from that activity 'be borne by the public as a whole,' even though the activity may also be intended incidentally to benefit the public."

The majority held, moreover, that the claim failed for lack of an adequate causal relationship between the Government action and the loss. This was one

2. Compare the doctrine that a landowner is not entitled to the dam site value of his land when the Government takes it to build a hydroelectric project. To compensate the owner for that ingredient of the value would supposedly allow him to profit improperly from the Government's "navigation servitude" in the stream. See, e. g., the 5:4 decision in United States v. Twin City Power Co., 350 U.S. 222 (1956). Note also United States v. Rands, 389 U.S. 121 (1967), holding that the Twin City principle of no compensation applies to port site value as well as to power site value of riparian land. For an effort to make sense of this principle in the general context of "just compensation" requirements, see Morreale, "Federal Powers in Western Waters: The Navigation Power and the Rule of No Compensation," 3 Nat.Res.J. 1 (1963).

of those unusual situations—like "the entry by firemen upon burning premises"—where "governmental occupation does not deprive the private owner of any use of his property." Here, the buildings were already under attack by rioters when the troops entered. The "temporary, unplanned occupation of petitioners' buildings in the course of battle" therefore did not constitute "direct and substantial enough government involvement to warrant compensation under the Fifth Amendment."

Justice Harlan's concurrence urged that "in deciding this particular case we should spare no effort to search for principles that seem best calculated to fit others that may arise before American democracy once again regains its equilibrium." He proposed that, "in riot control situations, the Just Compensation Clause may only be properly invoked when the military had reason to believe that its action placed the property in question in greater peril than if *no* form of protection had been provided at all." Here, the military action did not foreseeably increase the risk of damage; rather, the military reasonably believed their action would improve protection and there could accordingly be no compensation on the ground that the protection was "inadequate." Justice Harlan disagreed, however, with the majority's causation analysis. He noted the special benefit received here by the Government: "the troops retreated into the buildings to protect themselves from sniper fire." Justice Stewart also wrote a concurrence; Justice Black, joined by Justice Douglas, dissented.

4. *Zoning laws.* The leading case is Euclid v. Ambler Realty Co., 272 U.S. 365 (1926), where a closely divided Court sustained a typical zoning ordinance as a valid "police regulation." There, the Court faced for the first time "what is really the crux of the more recent zoning legislation, namely, the creation and maintenance of residential districts, from which business and trade . . . are excluded." An injunction against the ordinance was sought on the "broad ground that the . . . threatened enforcement of the ordinance, by materially and adversely affecting values and curtailing the opportunities of market, constitute a present and irreparable injury." The Court, in an opinion by Justice Sutherland, concluded that "the ordinance in its general scope and dominant features" was valid; it emphasized that it was not passing on complaints about specific applications of the ordinance.[3] After reviewing the history of zoning laws and the "comprehensive reports" of "commissions and experts," the Court found that it could not say that such ordinances "are clearly arbitrary and unreasonable, having no substantial relation to the public health, safety, morals, or general welfare." The constitutionality of particular applications, the Court noted, would depend on "the circumstances and the locality": "A nuisance may be merely a right thing in the wrong place —like a pig in the parlor instead of a barnyard." Justices Van Devanter, McReynolds and Butler dissented.

3. The plaintiff had alleged that he had held a vacant piece of property for industrial purposes and that the ordinance, by limiting the land to residential uses, would reduce the value of his land from $10,000 per acre to about $2,500 per acre. The Court limited itself to plaintiff's general challenge that the ordinance violated his property rights "by attempting regulations under the guise of the police power, which are unreasonable and confiscatory." Compare the invalidation of a specific application of a zoning law two years later, in Nectow v. Cambridge, 277 U.S. 183 (1928), and note the symposium on legal problems in zoning, in 20 Law & Contemp. Prob. (1955). Compare Goldblatt v. Town of Hempstead and Berman v. Parker, both infra.

Compare Goldblatt v. Hempstead, the next case, where, after a state court blocked an effort to reach a local problem via zoning, the town resorted to a "safety regulation"—and prevailed in the Supreme Court. Should the Court have scrutinized the regulation more carefully, as the dissenters in the highest state court had? (See the footnote at the end of the next case.) Was the Supreme Court's "hands off" attitude justified because appellants asserted merely a property right? The right not to have property "taken" without "just compensation" is a "specific" guarantee of the Bill of Rights applicable to the states through the 14th Amendment, is it not? Compare Griswold v. Connecticut, chap. 11, p. 824, and the notes at the end of this chapter, p. 981.

GOLDBLATT v. HEMPSTEAD

369 U.S. 590, 82 S.Ct. 987, 8 L.Ed.2d 130 (1962).

Appeal from the Court of Appeals of New York.

Mr. Justice CLARK delivered the opinion of the Court.

The Town of Hempstead has enacted an ordinance regulating dredging and pit excavating on property within its limits. Appellants . . . claim that it in effect prevents them from continuing their business and therefore takes their property without due process of law in violation of the Fourteenth Amendment. The trial court held that the ordinance was a valid exercise of the town's police power . . . . The New York Court of Appeals in a divided opinion affirmed. [W]e now affirm the judgment.

Appellant Goldblatt owns a 38-acre tract within the Town of Hempstead. [A]ppellant Builders Sand and Gravel Corporation was mining sand and gravel on this lot, a use to which the lot had been put continuously since 1927. Before the end of the first year the excavation had reached the water table leaving a water-filled crater which has been widened and deepened to the point that it is now a 20-acre lake with an average depth of 25 feet. The town has expanded around this excavation, and today within a radius of 3,500 feet there are more than 2,200 homes and four public schools with a combined enrollment of 4,500 pupils.

The present action is but one of a series of steps undertaken by the town in an effort to regulate mining excavations within its limits. A 1945 ordinance, No. 16, provided that such pits must be enclosed by a wire fence and comply with certain berm and slope requirements. Although appellants complied with this ordinance, the town sought an injunction against further excavation as being violative of a zoning ordinance. This failed [in 1956] because appellants were found to be "conducting a prior non-conforming use on the premises . . . ." The town did not appeal.

In 1958 the town amended Ordinance No. 16 to prohibit any excavating below the water table and to impose an affirmative duty to refill any excavation presently below that level. . . . In 1959 the town brought the present action to enjoin further mining by the appellants on the grounds that they had not complied with the ordinance, as amended . . . .

Concededly the ordinance completely prohibits a beneficial use to which the property has previously been devoted. However, such a characterization does not tell us whether or not the ordinance is unconstitutional. It is an oft-repeated truism that every regulation necessarily speaks as a prohibition.

If this ordinance is otherwise a valid exercise of the town's police powers, the fact that it deprives the property of its most beneficial use does not render it unconstitutional. . . .

This is not to say, however, that governmental action in the form of regulation cannot be so onerous as to constitute a taking which constitutionally requires compensation. Pennsylvania Coal Co. v. Mahon, 260 U.S. 393 (1922) . . . . There is no set formula to determine where regulation ends and taking begins. Although a comparison of values before and after is relevant . . . it is by no means conclusive . . . . How far regulation may go before it becomes a taking we need not now decide, for there is no evidence in the present record which even remotely suggests that prohibition of further mining will reduce the value of the lot in question. Indulging in the usual presumption of constitutionality, . . . we find no indication that the prohibitory effect of Ordinance No. 16 is sufficient to render it an unconstitutional taking if it is otherwise a valid police regulation. . . .

The ordinance in question was passed as a safety measure, and the town is attempting to uphold it on that basis. To evaluate its reasonableness we therefore need to know such things as the nature of the menace against which it will protect, the availability and effectiveness of other less drastic protective steps, and the loss which appellants will suffer from the imposition of the ordinance.

A careful examination of the record reveals a dearth of relevant evidence on these points. . . . [T]here was no indication whether the lake as it stood was an actual danger to the public or whether deepening the lake would increase the danger. [T]here was no showing how much, if anything, the imposition of the ordinance would cost the appellants. In short, the evidence produced is clearly indecisive on the reasonableness of prohibiting further excavation below the water table.

Although one could imagine that preventing further deepening of a pond already 25 feet deep would have a *de minimis* effect on public safety, we cannot say that such a conclusion is compelled by facts of which we can take notice. Even if we could draw such a conclusion, we would be unable to say the ordinance is unreasonable; for all we know, the ordinance may have a *de minimis* effect on appellants. Our past cases leave no doubt that appellants had the burden on "reasonableness." . . . This burden not having been met, the prohibition of excavation on the 20-acre-lake tract must stand as a valid police regulation. . . .

Appellants also [object to] such affirmative duties as refilling the existing excavation. . . . Since enforcement of these provisions was not sought in the present litigation, this Court . . . will not at this time undertake to decide their constitutionality. . . .

. . . . The claim that rights acquired in previous litigation are being undermined is completely unfounded. . . . The first suit was brought to enforce a zoning ordinance, while the present one is to enforce a safety ordinance. . . .

Affirmed.*

---

* Compare the statements of the dissenters in the 4 to 3 decision of the New York Court of Appeals in this case: "[T]he record here indicates a systematic attempt to force the defendants out of business. . . . A condition of continuing the business requires defendants to fill the existing excavation at a cost in excess of $1,-000,000. . . . [The 1958 amend-

EMINENT DOMAIN PROCEEDINGS AND JUDICIAL
SCRUTINY

1. *Public use.* a. To what extent is it a judicial question whether a taking is for a "public use"? In United States ex rel. TVA v. Welch, 327 U.S. 546 (1946), Justice Black's opinion stated: "We think that it is the function of Congress to decide what type of taking is for a public use and that the agency authorized to do the taking may do so to the full extent of its statutory authority. . . . It is true that this Court did say in City of Cincinnati v. Vester, 281 U.S. 439, 446, that 'It is well established that in considering the application of the Fourteenth Amendment the question what is a public use is a judicial one.' But . . . in Hairston v. Danville & Western R. Co., 208 U.S. 598, 607, this Court . . . said that 'No case is recalled where this court has condemned as a violation of the Fourteenth Amendment a taking upheld by the state court as a taking for public uses in conformity with its laws.' But whatever may be the scope of the judicial power to determine what is a 'public use' in Fourteenth Amendment controversies, this Court has said that when Congress has spoken on this subject 'Its decision is entitled to deference until it is shown to involve an impossibility.' Old Dominion Land Co. v. United States, 269 U.S. 55, 66. Any departure from this judicial restraint would result in courts deciding on what is and is not a governmental function and in their invalidating legislation on the basis of their view on that question at the moment of decision, a practice which has proved impracticable in other fields."

b. In Berman v. Parker, 348 U.S. 26 (1954), the constitutionality of the District of Columbia Redevelopment Act was challenged by the owners of a department store in the project area. They objected to condemnation because the property was in good condition and because, after the taking, the property would be under private management, to be redeveloped for private use. The Court rejected the challenge. Justice Douglas spoke first about the police power: "An attempt to . . . trace its outer limits is fruitless . . . . The definition is essentially the product of legislative determinations addressed to the purposes of government, purposes neither abstractly nor historically capable of complete definition. Subject to specific constitutional limitations, when the legislature has spoken, the public interest has been declared in terms well-nigh conclusive."

He then turned more specifically to the condemnation issue: "This principle admits of no exception merely because the power of eminent domain is involved. The role of the judiciary in determining whether that power is being exercised for a public purpose is an extremely narrow one. . . . The concept of the public welfare is broad and inclusive. . . . The values it represents are spiritual as well as physical, aesthetic as well as monetary. It is within the power of the legislature to determine that the community should be beautiful as well as healthy, spacious as well as clean, well-balanced as well as carefully patrolled.

ment] was directed at this single operation and designed to accomplish what the 1956 lawsuit had failed to do, viz., to destroy a lawful pre-existing use under the Town Zoning Ordinance. The object is not to promote public health and safety, but to end the operation of this business under the guise of regulation." Town of Hempstead v. Goldblatt, 9 N.Y.2d 101, 172 N.E.2d 562 (1961).

"[T]he power of eminent domain is merely the means to the end. . . . Once the object is within the authority of Congress, the means by which it will be attained is also for Congress to determine. Here one of the means chosen is the use of private enterprise for redevelopment of the area. Appellants argue that this makes the project a taking from one businessman for the benefit of another businessman. But the means of executing the project are for Congress and Congress alone to determine, once the public purpose has been established. . . . We cannot say that public ownership is the sole method of promoting the public purposes of community redevelopment projects. . . . The rights of these property owners are satisfied when they receive that just compensation which the Fifth Amendment exacts as the price of the taking."

    2. *Just compensation.* The "right to determine what shall be the measure of compensation . . . is a judicial and not a legislative question." Monongahela Navigation Co. v. United States, 148 U.S. 312, 327 (1893). The general measure of just compensation is the market value at the time of the taking; "the question is what has the owner lost, not what has the taker gained." See United States v. Miller, 317 U.S. 369 (1943). Among the problems of determining just compensation in particular circumstances, note: valuation of dam sites, United States v. Twin City Power Co., 350 U.S. 222 (1956) (supra); compensability of removal costs in taking of leasehold interests, United States v. General Motors Corp., 323 U.S. 373 (1945), and United States v. Westinghouse, 339 U.S. 261 (1950); impact of government price controls, United States v. Commodities Trading Corp., 339 U.S. 121 (1950) (OPA ceiling price constitutes "just compensation", though below the company's cost).

SECTION 3. SUBSTANTIVE DUE PROCESS AND ECONOMIC REGULATION: THE RISE OF JUDICIAL INTERVENTION

    Introduction. a. *From procedure to substance.* Although there had been a few intimations before the Civil War that the concept of "due process of law" imposed substantive restraints on the content of legislation,[1] the Court's early interpretations of the 14th Amendment refused to read it as a substantive safeguard of property and business activities. See the Slaughter-House Cases, 16 Wall. 36 (873), chap. 11, p. 781, supra. For some years, due process remained simply an assurance of fair procedures.[2] In the three decades following the Civil War, the contract clause continued to be the major barrier to state eco-

1. See Wynehamer v. People, 13 N.Y. 358 (1856); Dred Scott v. Sandford, 19 How. 393, 450 (1857); Corwin, "The Doctrine of Due Process before the Civil War," 24 Harv.L.Rev. 366, 460 (1911); Corwin, Liberty Against Government (1948).

2. See Den ex dem. Murray v. Hoboken Land & Improvement Co., 18 How. 272 (1855). Note also Munn v. Illinois, 94 U.S. 113 (1877), sustaining

an Illinois law regulating maximum charges of grain warehousemen, as businesses "affected with the public interest" (see Nebbia v. New York, p. 967, infra); Davidson v. New Orleans, 96 U.S. 97 (1878), sustaining a special assessment statute against property owners and objecting to the "strange misconception" that the due process clause was a "means" to challenge "the merits of the legislation."

nomic legislation. Toward the close of the century, however, there were increasing pressures—off the Court [3] as well as on it—to broaden the meaning of due process. In Santa Clara County v. Southern Pac. R. R., 118 U.S. 394 (1886), the Court held, without discussion, that corporations were "persons" within the meaning of the 14th Amendment.[4] And in Mugler v. Kansas, 123 U.S. 623 (1887), the Court, though sustaining a law prohibiting intoxicating beverages, announced that it was prepared to examine the substantive reasonableness of state legislation. Justice Harlan stated that not "every statute enacted ostensibly for the promotion" of "the public morals, the public health, or the public safety" would be accepted "as a legitimate exertion of the police powers of the State." The courts would not be "misled by mere pretenses": they were obligated, he insisted, "to look at the substance of things." Accordingly, if a purported exercise of the police powers "has no real or substantial relation to those objects, or is a palpable invasion of rights secured by the fundamental law, it is the duty of the courts to so adjudge." And facts "within the knowledge of all" would be relied on in making that determination. Ten years later, in the Allgeyer case, the Court for the first time invalidated a state statute on substantive due process grounds [5]—a judgment that was to be frequently repeated in the first three decades of the 20th century.

b. *Allgeyer and liberty of contract.* Allgeyer v. Louisiana, 165 U.S. 578 (1897), involved a Louisiana statute prohibiting anyone from doing any act in the State to effect insurance on any Louisiana property "from any marine insurance company which has not complied in all respects" with Louisiana law. Allgeyer was convicted for mailing a letter advising an insurance company in New York of the shipment of goods, in accordance with a marine policy. The company was not licensed to do business in Louisiana. The Supreme Court reversed, holding the statute violated the 14th Amendment "in that it deprives the defendants of their liberty without due process of law."

Justice Peckham's opinion contained an extended discussion of the power of the state in respect of foreign corporations and emphasized the fact that the insurance contract was made outside Louisiana. But it was the Court's articulation of the liberty of contract that gave the case its special significance in the development of substantive due process: "The liberty mentioned in that amendment means not only the right of the citizen to be free from the mere physical restraint of his person, as by incarceration, but the term is deemed to embrace the right of the citizen to be free in the enjoyment of all his faculties; to be free to use them in all lawful ways; to live and work where he will; to

---

3. See Twiss, Lawyers and the Constitution (1942).

4. See Graham, " 'The Conspiracy Theory' of the Fourteenth Amendment," 47 Yale L.J. 371 and 48 Yale L.J. 171 (1938). Justices Black and Douglas have objected to this interpretation. See the dissents in Connecticut General Life Ins. Co. v. Johnson, 303 U.S. 77 (1938), and Wheeling Steel Corp. v. Glander, 337 U.S. 562 (1944).

5. See also Chicago, M. & St. P. R. Co. v. Minnesota, 134 U.S. 418 (1890), invalidating a state law authorizing railroad rate regulation without providing for judicial review. The railroad was entitled to a judicial determination of the reasonableness of the rates; depriving the railroad of the power to charge reasonable rates by administrative order would be, "in substance and effect," a deprivation of property without due process of law. The long line of cases which tried to articulate the criteria for determining reasonableness in rate regulation began with Smyth v. Ames, 169 U.S. 466 (1898). For a review of the rate regulation developments after the 1890's, see FPC v. Hope Natural Gas Co., 320 U.S. 591 (1944), especially the separate opinions of Justices Black and Frankfurter.

earn his livelihood by any lawful calling; to pursue any livelihood or avocation,
and for that purpose to enter into all contracts which may be proper, necessary
and essential to his carrying out to a successful conclusion the purposes above
mentioned. . . .   When we speak of the liberty to contract for insurance
. . ., we refer to and have in mind the facts of this case . . .. The
act done within the limits of the State . . . we hold a proper act, one
which the defendants were at liberty to perform and which the state legislature
had no right to prevent, at least with reference to the Federal Constitution.
. . .

"In the privilege of pursuing an ordinary calling or trade and of acquiring, holding and selling property must be embraced the right to make all proper contracts in relation thereto, and although it may be conceded that this right
to contract in relation to persons or property or to do business within the jurisdiction of the State may be regulated and sometimes prohibited when the contracts or business conflict with the policy of the State as contained in its statutes, yet the power does not and cannot extend to prohibiting a citizen from
making contracts of the nature involved in this case outside of the limits and
jurisdiction of the State, and which are also to be performed outside of such
jurisdiction."

Allgeyer involved insurance regulation.   Soon after the turn of the century, its expansive conception of "liberty" bore fruit in more controversial contexts, exemplified by the Lochner case, which follows.   When the modern
Court looks back to the discredited "Allgeyer-Lochner-Adair-Coppage constitutional doctrine" (the phrase is from the Lincoln Federal Labor Union case in
1949, sec. 4, p. 974, infra), the Allgeyer reference is not to its specific setting
but to its significance in opening the door to substitution of the Justices' notions of public policy for legislative choices regarding economic and social regulation, as assertedly took place in Lochner.   Is that what happened in Lochner?   Has that due process philosophy been wholly rejected by the modern
Court?

LOCHNER v. NEW YORK

198 U.S. 45, 25 S.Ct. 539, 49 L.Ed. 937 (1905).

Error to the County Court of Oneida County, State of New York.

Mr. Justice PECKHAM . . . delivered the opinion of the
Court. . . .

[Lochner was convicted of violating the New York labor law, which prohibited employment in bakeries for more than 60 hours a week or more than
10 hours a day. Lochner was fined for permitting an employee to work in his
Utica, N. Y., bakery for more than 60 hours in one week.]

. . .   The employé may desire to earn the extra money, which
would arise from his working more than the prescribed time, but this statute
forbids the employer from permitting the employé to earn it. . . .
The statute necessarily interferes with the right of contract between the employer and employés . . . ..   The general rights to make a contract in
relation to his business is part of the liberty of the individual protected by the
Fourteenth Amendment of the Federal Constitution. Allgeyer v. Louisiana,

165 U.S. 578. . . . The right to purchase or to sell labor is part of the liberty protected by this amendment, unless there are circumstances which exclude the right. There are, however, certain powers, existing in the sovereignty of each State in the Union, somewhat vaguely termed police powers, the exact description and limitation of which have not been attempted by the courts. Those powers, broadly stated and without, at present, any attempt at a more specific limitation, relate to the safety, health, morals and general welfare of the public. Both property and liberty are held on such reasonable conditions as may be imposed by the governing power of the State in the exercise of those powers, and with such conditions the Fourteenth Amendment was not designed to interfere. . . .

. . . If the contract be one which the State, in the legitimate exercise of its police power, has the right to prohibit, it is not prevented from prohibiting it by the Fourteenth Amendment. Contracts in violation of a statute, either of the Federal or state government, or a contract to let one's property for immoral purposes, or to do any other unlawful act, could obtain no protection from the Federal Constitution, as coming under the liberty of person or of free contract. Therefore, when the State, by its legislature, in the assumed exercise of its police powers, has passed an act which seriously limits the right to labor or the right of contract in regard to their means of livelihood between persons who are *sui juris* (both employer and employé), it becomes of great importance to determine which shall prevail—the right of the individual to labor for such time as he may choose, or the right of the State . . . . .

This court has recognized the existence and upheld the exercise of the police powers of the States in many cases which might fairly be considered as border ones, and it has . . . been guided by rules of a very liberal nature, the application of which has resulted, in numerous instances, in upholding the validity of state statutes thus assailed. Among the later cases where the state law has been upheld by this court is that of Holden v. Hardy, 169 U.S. 366.* . . .

It must, of course, be conceded that there is a limit to the valid exercise of the police power by the State. . . . Otherwise the Fourteenth Amendment would have no efficacy and the legislatures of the States would have unbounded power, and it would be enough to say that any piece of legislation was enacted to conserve the morals, the health or the safety of the people . . . . The claim of the police power would be a mere pretext—become another and delusive name for the supreme sovereignty of the State to be exercised free from constitutional restraint. . . . In every case that comes before this court, therefore, where legislation of this character is concerned . . ., the question necessarily arises: Is this a fair, reasonable and appropriate exercise of the police power of the State, or is it an unreasonable, unnecessary and arbitrary interference with the right of the individual to his personal liberty or to enter into those contracts in relation to labor which may seem to him appropriate or necessary for the support of himself and his family? Of course the liberty of contract relating to labor includes both parties to it. The one has as much right to purchase as the other to sell labor.

This is not a question of substituting the judgment of the court for that of the legislature. If the act be within the power of the State it is valid, although

---

* Holden v. Hardy was decided in 1898, in the period between Allgeyer and Lochner. It sustained a Utah law limiting the employment of "workmen in all underground mines" to eight hours per day.

the judgment of the court might be totally opposed to the enactment of such a law. . . .

The question whether this act is valid as a labor law, pure and simple, may be dismissed in a few words. There is no reasonable ground for interfering with the liberty of person or the right of free contract, by determining the hours of labor, in the occupation of a baker. There is no contention that bakers as a class are not equal in intelligence and capacity to men in other trades or manual occupations . . . . They are in no sense wards of the State. Viewed in the light of a purely labor law, with no reference whatever to the question of health, we think that a law like the one before us involves neither the safety, the morals nor the welfare of the public, and that the interest of the public is not in the slightest degree affected by such an act. The law must be upheld, if at all, as a law pertaining to the health of the individual engaged in the occupation of a baker. It does not affect any other portion of the public than those who are engaged in that occupation. Clean and wholesome bread does not depend upon whether the baker works but ten hours per day or only sixty hours a week. The limitation of the hours of labor does not come within the police power on that ground.

. . . The mere assertion that the subject relates though but in a remote degree to the public health does not necessarily render the enactment valid. The act must have a more direct relation, as a means to an end, and the end itself must be appropriate and legitimate, before an act can be held to be valid which interferes with the general right of an individual to be free in his person and in his power to contract in relation to his own labor. . . .

We think the limit of the police power has been reached and passed in this case. There is, in our judgment, no reasonable foundation for holding this to be necessary or appropriate as a health law to safeguard the public health or the health of the individuals who are following the trade of a baker. If this statute be valid, . . . there would seem to be no length to which legislation of this nature might not go. . . .

We think that there can be no fair doubt that the trade of a baker, in and of itself, is not an unhealthy one to that degree which would authorize the legislature to interfere with the right to labor, and with the right of free contract . . . . In looking through statistics regarding all trades and occupations, it may be true that the trade of a baker does not appear to be as healthy as some other trades, and is also vastly more healthy than still others. To the common understanding the trade of a baker has never been regarded as an unhealthy one. Very likely physicians would not recommend the exercise of that or of any other trade as a remedy for ill health. Some occupations are more healthy than others, but we think there are none which might not come under the power of the legislature to supervise and control the hours of working therein, if the mere fact that the occupation is not absolutely and perfectly healthy is to confer that right upon the legislative department of the Government. . . . There must be more than the mere fact of the possible existence of some small amount of unhealthiness to warrant legislative interference with liberty. It is unfortunately true that labor, even in any department, may possibly carry with it the seeds of unhealthiness. But are we all, on that account, at the mercy of legislative majorities? . . . No trade, no occupation, no mode of earning one's living, could escape this all-pervading power . . . . In our large cities there are many buildings into which the sun penetrates for but a short time in each day, and these buildings are occupied by people carrying on the business of bankers, brokers, lawyers, real estate, and many other kinds of business . . .. Upon the assumption of the validity of this act under review, it is not possible to say that an act, prohibiting lawyers' or bank clerks, or others, from contracting to labor for their employers more than eight hours a day, would be invalid. . . .

It is also urged . . . that it is to the interest of the State that its population should be strong and robust, and therefore any legislation which may be said to tend to make people healthy must be valid as health laws, enacted under the police power. If this be a valid argument and a justification for this kind of legislation, it follows that the protection of the Federal Constitution from undue interference with liberty of person and freedom of contract is visionary, wherever the law is sought to be justified as a valid exercise of the police power. . . . Not only the hours of employés, but the hours of employers, could be regulated, and doctors, lawyers, scientists, all professional men, as well as athletes and artisans, could be forbidden to fatigue their brains and bodies by prolonged hours of exercise, lest the fighting strength of the State be impaired. We mention these extreme cases because the contention is extreme. We do not believe in the soundness of the views which uphold this law. On the contrary, we think that such a law as this, although passed in the assumed exercise of the police power, and as relating to the public health, or the health of the employés named, is not within that power, and is invalid. The act is not, within any fair meaning of the term, a health law, but is an illegal interference with the rights of individuals, both employers and employés, to make contracts regarding labor upon such terms as they may think best, or which they may agree upon with the other parties to such contracts. Statutes of the nature of that under review, limiting the hours in which grown and intelligent men may labor to earn their living, are mere meddlesome interferences with the rights of the individual, and they are not saved from condemnation by the claim that they are passed in the exercise of the police power . . . ., unless there be some fair ground, reasonable in and of itself, to say that there is material danger to the public health or to the health of the employés, if the hours of labor are not curtailed. All that [the State] could properly do has been done by it with regard to the conduct of bakeries, as provided for in the other sections of the act, [which] provide for the inspection of the premises where the bakery is carried on, with regard to furnishing proper wash-rooms and water-closets, apart from the bake-room, also with regard to providing proper drainage, plumbing and painting . . . and for other things of that nature . . . .

It was further urged on the argument that restricting the hours of labor in the case of bakers was valid because it tended to cleanliness on the part of the workers . . . . In our judgment it is not possible in fact to discover the connection between the number of hours a baker may work in the bakery and the healthful quality of the bread made by the workman. The connection, if any exists, is too shadowy and thin to build any argument for the interference of the legislature. . . . When assertions such as we have adverted to become necessary in order to give, if possible, a plausible foundation for the contention that the law is a "health law," it gives rise to at least a suspicion that there was some other motive dominating the legislature than the purpose to subserve the public health or welfare.

This interference on the part of the legislatures of the several States with the ordinary trades and occupations of the people seems to be on the increase. . . . . .

It is impossible for us to shut our eyes to the fact that many of the laws of this character, while passed under what is claimed to be the police power for the purpose of protecting the public health or welfare, are, in reality, passed from other motives. . . . .

It seems to us that the real object and purpose [of the New York law] were simply to regulate the hours of labor between the master and his employés (all being men, *sui juris*), in a private business, not dangerous in any degree to morals or in any real and substantial degree, to the health of the employés. Under such circumstances the freedom of master and employé to contract with each other in relation to their employment, and in defining the same, cannot be prohibited or interfered with, without violating the Federal Constitution. . . . .

Reversed.

Mr. Justice HARLAN, with whom Mr. Justice WHITE and Mr. Justice DAY concurred, dissenting. . . . .

It is plain that this statute was enacted in order to protect the physical well-being of those who work in bakery and confectionery establishments. It may be that the statute had its origin, in part, in the belief that employers and employés in such establishments were not upon an equal footing, and that the necessities of the latter often compelled them to submit to such exactions as unduly taxed their strength. Be this as it may, the statute must be taken as expressing the belief of the people of New York that, as a general rule, and in the case of the average man, labor in excess of sixty hours during a week in such establishments may endanger the health of those who thus labor. Whether or not this be wise legislation, it is not the province of the court to inquire. . . . I find it impossible, in view of common experience, to say that there is here no real or substantial relation between the means employed by the State and the end sought to be accomplished by its legislation. . . . I submit that this court will transcend its functions if it assumes to annul the statute of New York. It must be remembered that this statute does not apply to all kinds of business. It applies only to work in bakery and confectionery establishments, in which, as all know, the air constantly breathed by workmen is not as pure and healthful as that to be found in some other establishments or out of doors. . . . .

Statistics show that the average daily working time among workingmen in different countries is, in Australia, 8 hours; in Great Britain, 9; in the United States, 9¾; in Denmark, 9¾; in Norway, 10; Sweden, France and Switzerland, 10½; Germany, 10¼; Belgium, Italy and Austria, 11; and in Russia, 12 hours.

We judicially know that the question of the number of hours during which a workman should continuously labor has been, for a long period, and is yet, a subject of serious consideration among civilized peoples, and by those having special knowledge of the laws of health. . . . .

I do not stop to consider whether any particular view of this economic question presents the sounder theory. What the precise facts are it may be difficult to say. It is enough for the determination of this case, and it is enough for this court to know, that the question is one about which there is room for debate and for an honest difference of opinion. .   .   .

I take leave to say that the New York statute, in the particulars here involved, cannot be held to be in conflict with the Fourteenth Amendment, without enlarging the scope of the Amendment far beyond its original purpose and without bringing under the supervision of this court matters which have been supposed to belong exclusively to the legislative departments of the several States when exerting their conceded power to guard the health and safety of their citizens by such regulations as they in their wisdom deem best.   .   .   . A decision that the New York statute is void under the Fourteenth Amendment will, in my opinion, involve consequences of a far-reaching and mischievous character; for such a decision would seriously cripple the inherent power of the States to care for the lives, health and well-being of their citizens. Those are matters which can be best controlled by the States.   .   .   .

Mr. Justice HOLMES, dissenting.   .   .   .

This case is decided upon an economic theory which a large part of the country does not entertain. If it were a question whether I agreed with that theory, I should desire to study it further and long before making up my mind. But I do not conceive that to be my duty, because I strongly believe that my agreement or disagreement has nothing to do with the right of a majority to embody their opinions in law. It is settled by various decisions of this court that state constitutions and state laws may regulate life in many ways which we as legislators might think as injudicious or if you like as tyrannical as this, and which equally with this interfere with the liberty to contract. Sunday laws and usury laws are ancient examples. A more modern one is the prohibition of lotteries. The liberty of the citizen to do as he likes so long as he does not interfere with the liberty of others to do the same, which has been a shibboleth for some well-known writers, is interfered with by school laws, by the Post Office, by every state or municipal institution which takes his money for purposes thought desirable, whether he likes it or not. The Fourteenth Amendment does not enact Mr. Herbert Spencer's Social Statics. The other day we sustained the Massachusetts vaccination law. Jacobson v. Massachusetts, 197 U.S. 11. United States and state statutes and decisions cutting down the liberty to contract by way of combination are familiar to this court. Northern Securities Co. v. United States, 193 U.S. 197. Two years ago we upheld the prohibition of sales of stock on margins or for future delivery in the constitution of California. Otis v. Parker, 187 U.S. 606. The decision sustaining an eight hour law for miners is still recent. Holden v. Hardy, 169 U.S. 366. Some of these laws embody convictions or prejudices which judges are likely to share. Some may not. But a constitution is not intended to embody a particular economic theory, whether of paternalism and the organic relation of the citizen to the State or of *laissez faire*. It is made for people of fundamentally differing views, and the accident of our finding certain opinions natural and familiar or novel and even shocking ought not to conclude our judgment upon the question whether statutes embodying them conflict with the Constitution of the United States.

General propositions do not decide concrete cases. The decision will depend on a judgment or intuition more subtle than any articulate major premise. But I think that the proposition just stated, if it is accepted, will carry us far toward the end. Every opinion tends to become a law. I think that the word liberty in the Fourteenth Amendment is perverted when it is held to prevent the natural outcome of a dominant opinion, unless it can be said that a rational and fair man necessarily would admit that the statute proposed would infringe fundamental principles as they have been understood by the traditions of our people and our law. It does not need research to show that no such sweeping condemnation can be passed upon the statute before us. A reasonable man might think it a proper measure on the score of health. Men whom I certainly could not pronounce unreasonable would uphold it as a first instalment of a general regulation of the hours of work. Whether in the latter aspect it would be open to the charge of inequality I think it unnecessary to discuss.

LOCHNER AND THE DISCREDITED PERIOD OF JUDICIAL INTERVENTION

1. *What was wrong with the Lochner philosophy?* From the Lochner decision in 1905 to the 1930's, the Court invalidated a considerable number of laws on substantive due process grounds. Regulation of wages, prices, and employment relations were especially vulnerable: as the Court recalled in the Lincoln Federal Labor Union case, sec. 4, p. 974, infra, the Allgeyer-Lochner doctrine "was used to strike down laws fixing minimum wages and maximum hours in employment, laws fixing prices, and laws regulating business activities." Typically, as in Lochner, the decisions striking down such laws carried dissents, most often by Holmes and, later, Brandeis, Stone and Cardozo. The modern Court, see sec. 4, infra, has repeatedly insisted that it has turned its back on the evils of the Lochner philosophy.

What were those evils? The giving of substantive content to due process? The expansive view of liberty to include values not specifically stated in the Bill of Rights? The selection of the "wrong" values for protection? The failure to state general standards? The inadequacy of the general standards stated? The failure to apply the general standards with adequate receptiveness to factual data? The failure to apply the general standards with adequate consistency and neutrality?

Examining the cases in this section in light of questions such as these is of more than historical interest. Rejection of the Lochner heritage is a common starting point for modern Justices; reaction against the excessive intervention of the "Old Men" of the pre-1937 Court has strongly influenced the judicial philosophies of the successors. The modern Court has not drawn from Lochner the lesson that *all* judicial intervention via substantive due process is improper. Rather, it has withdrawn from careful scrutiny in most economic areas but has maintained and increased intervention with respect to a variety of non-economic liberties. Identifying the evils of the Lochner period is especially relevant, then, to determine (a) whether the modern Court's interventions avoid those evils, and (b) whether those evils warranted as substantial a withdrawal from the economic area as has taken place.

2. *The Lochner philosophy, non-economic rights, and civil liberties.* Not only economic regulations fell victim to substantive due process attacks in the 30 years beginning with Lochner. That period, it is often forgotten, also saw the early development of 14th Amendment protection of civil liberties (and of the rights of the accused). Thus, the Allgeyer-Lochner philosophy formed the basis for absorbing rights such as those in the First Amendment

into the 14th Amendment concept of liberty, as chap. 15 shows.   Justice Brandeis' eloquent defense of free speech in Whitney v. California, 274 U.S. 355 (1927) (p. 1080, infra), included a reluctant acceptance of the triumph of substantive due process—a triumph that supported the speech protection he advocated there: "Despite arguments to the contrary which had seemed to me persuasive, it is settled that the due process clause of the Fourteenth Amendment applies to matters of substantive law as well as to matters of procedure."

Moreover, the Allgeyer-Lochner philosophy helped justify intervention on behalf of non-economic rights other than those that had counterparts in the First Amendment.   Note, for example, the non-economic personal liberties recognized in Meyer v. Nebraska, 262 U.S. 390 (1923), involving a conviction of a parochial school teacher under a law prohibiting teaching "in any language other than English."   The Court reversed: "His right to teach (in German), and the rights of parents to engage him so to instruct their children, we think, are within the liberty of the Amendment."   Justice McReynolds added that "liberty" denotes "not merely freedom from bodily restraint but also the right of the individual to contract, to engage in any of the common occupations of life, to acquire useful knowledge, to marry, establish a home and bring up children, to worship God according to the dictates of his own conscience, and generally to enjoy those privileges long recognized at common law as essential to the orderly pursuit of happiness by free men."   See Warren, "The New Liberty under the Fourteenth Amendment," 39 Harv.L.Rev. 431 (1926).   Recall the reliance on the Meyer language in the 1965 decision on the Connecticut birth-control law, Griswold v. Connecticut, chap. 11, p. 824, supra.   Recall also Justice Black's rejection of the Meyer language, as a product of the Lochner philosophy, in his dissent in Griswold; and note the questions following that dissent, at p. 837.

3.   *Valid economic regulations during the Lochner period.*   Freewheeling judicial invalidation of economic regulations is the characteristic most commonly associated with the Lochner era.   Yet even during that period, most challenges to economic regulations were rejected: for example, as the footnote to Lochner shows, the Court had sustained a miners' hours law shortly before that decision; and it sustained a maximum hours law for women only three years later in Muller v. Oregon, which follows.   See also the Nebbia and West Coast Hotel opinions, sec. 4, infra, for a review of laws held constitutional during the Lochner era.   For a summary of the laws invalidated during this period, see The Constitution of the United States (Gov't Printing Office, 1964 ed.), 1431–85; for a survey of the laws sustained, see id., 973–85 (federal laws and due process), 1093–1146 (state laws and due process), 1284–1300 (state economic regulation and equal protection).   On the role of the 14th Amendment's equal protection clause as a source of limits on economic regulation—a role which paralleled but was less significant than that of substantive due process during this period—see chap. 14, sec. 1, infra.

JUDICIAL SCRUTINY OF ECONOMIC REGULATIONS DURING THE LOCHNER ERA—SOME EXAMPLES

1.   *Muller, Bunting, maximum hours, and the Brandeis brief.*   a.   Muller v. Oregon, 208 U.S. 412 (1908), sustained an Oregon law of 1903 which provided that "no female" shall be employed in any factory or laundry "more than ten hours during any one day."   The conviction of Muller, a laundry oper-

ator, was affirmed by the Supreme Court, "without questioning in any respect the decision" in Lochner. Justice Brewer's opinion emphasized that the liberty of contract "is not absolute," that it was obvious that "woman's physical structure" placed her "at a disadvantage in the struggle for subsistence," and that, "as healthy mothers are essential to vigorous offspring, the physical well-being of woman becomes an object of public interest." Moreover, "woman has always been dependent upon man." Legislation to protect women "seems necessary to secure a real equality of right"; and such protective legislation is valid, "even when like legislation is not necessary for men, and could not be sustained." The "inherent differences between the two sexes" justified "a difference in legislation" and "upholds that which is designed to compensate for some of the burdens which rest upon her."

b.   At the beginning of the Muller opinion, the Court made these observations: "In patent cases counsel are apt to open the argument with a discussion of the state of the art. It may not be amiss, in the present case, before examining the constitutional question, to notice the course of legislation, as well as expressions of opinion from other than judicial sources. In the brief filed by Mr. Louis D. Brandeis for the defendant in error is a very copious collection of all these matters, an epitome of which is found in the margin. . . .

"The legislation and opinions referred to in the margin may not be, technically speaking, authorities, and in them is little or no discussion of the constitutional question presented to us for determination, yet they are significant of a widespread belief that woman's physical structure, and the functions she performs in consequence thereof, justify special legislation . . .. Constitutional questions, it is true, are not settled by even a consensus of present public opinion, for it is the peculiar value of a written constitution that it places in unchanging form limitations upon legislative action . . .. At the same time, when a question of fact is debated and debatable, and the extent to which a special constitutional limitation goes is affected by the truth in respect to that fact, a widespread and long-continued belief concerning it is worthy of consideration. We take judicial cognizance of all matters of general knowledge."

c.   Louis D. Brandeis, with the assistance of Felix Frankfurter, prepared a similar brief in the litigation which led to the decision in Bunting v. Oregon, 243 U.S. 426 (1917). Brandeis was appointed to the Court before the argument, and Mr. Frankfurter submitted the brief. A divided Court—with Justice Brandeis not participating—sustained a law establishing a 10-hour day for manufacturing work, but permitting up to three hours overtime at a time-and-a-half rate. The conviction was for not paying the overtime rate in a flour mill. The Court did not mention the Lochner decision.

Is the "Brandeis brief" technique as useful in attacking legislation as in sustaining it? See Freund, On Understanding the Supreme Court (1949), 86–91, and Karst, "Legislative Facts in Constitutional Adjudication," 1960 Supreme Court Review 75. On the utility of the "Brandeis brief" and the presentation of "constitutional facts," see also Biklé, "Judicial Determination of Questions of Fact Affecting the Constitutional Validity of Legislative Action," 38 Harv.L.Rev. 6 (1924).

2.   *"Yellow dog" contracts, Coppage, and Adair.*   a.   The modern Court has referred to the discredited line of cases of the Lochner era as "the

Allgeyer-Lochner-Adair-Coppage constitutional doctrine." (See p. 975 infra.) The first two are noted above. Coppage and Adair involved laws protecting employees' rights to organize unions. In Coppage v. Kansas, 236 U.S. 1 (1915), Coppage had been convicted under a Kansas law of 1903 directed against "yellow dog" contracts: it prohibited employers from requiring that employees agree as a condition of employment "not to join or become or remain a member of any labor organization." The Supreme Court, in an opinion by Justice Pitney, held the law unconstitutional under the due process clause: "Included in the right of personal liberty and the right of private property . . . is the right to make contracts . . .. An interference with this liberty so serious as that now under consideration, and so disturbing of equality of right, must be deemed to be arbitrary, unless it be supportable as a reasonable exercise of the police power of the State. But, notwithstanding the strong general presumption in favor of the validity of state laws, we do not think the statute in question . . . can be sustained as a legitimate exercise of that power. . . .

"Of course we do not intend to say, nor to intimate, anything inconsistent with the right of individuals to join labor unions, nor do we question the legitimacy of such organizations so long as they conform to the laws of the land as others are required to do. Conceding the full right of the individual to join the union, he has no inherent right to do this and still remain in the employ of one who is unwilling to employ a union man, any more than the same individual has a right to join the union without the consent of that organization. . . .

"[I]t is said by the [state court] to be a matter of common knowledge that 'employees, as a rule, are not financially able to be as independent in making contracts for the sale of their labor as are employers in making contracts of purchase thereof.' No doubt, wherever the right of private property exists, there must and will be inequalities of fortune; and thus it naturally happens that parties negotiating about a contract are not equally unhampered by circumstances. This applies to all contracts and not merely to that between employer and employee. [I]t is from the nature of things impossible to uphold freedom of contract and the right of private property without at the same time recognizing as legitimate those inequalities of fortune that are the necessary result of the exercise of those rights. But the Fourteenth Amendment . . . recognizes 'liberty' and 'property' as coexistent human rights, and debars the States from any unwarranted interference with either.

"And since a State may not strike them down directly it is clear that it may not do so indirectly, as by declaring in effect that the public good requires the removal of those inequalities that are but the normal and inevitable result of their exercise, and then invoking the police power in order to remove the inequalities, without other object in view. The police power is broad, and not easily defined, but it cannot be given the wide scope that is here asserted for it, without in effect nullifying the constitutional guaranty."

Justice Day, joined by Justice Hughes, dissented. In another dissenting opinion, Justice Holmes stated: "In present conditions a workman not unnaturally may believe that only by belonging to a union can he secure a contract that shall be fair to him. . . . If that belief, whether right or wrong, may be held by a reasonable man, it seems to me that it may be enforced by law in order to establish the equality of position between the parties in which liberty of contract begins. Whether in the long run it is wise for the workingmen to enact legislation of this sort is not my concern, but I am strongly of opinion that there is nothing in the Constitution of the United States to prevent it . . .."

b. The Court in Coppage relied on <u>Adair v. United States,</u> 208 U.S. 161 (1908), which had held unconstitutional, under the due process clause of the Fifth Amendment, a federal law against "yellow dog" contracts on interstate railroads. The opinion in Adair was written by Justice Harlan, one of the dissenters in Lochner. Justice Harlan stated that "it is not within the function of government . . . to compel any person in the course of his business . . . to retain the personal services of another . . .. The right of a person to sell his labor upon such terms as he deems proper is . . . the same as the right of the purchaser of labor to prescribe the conditions. [T]he employer and the employee have equality of right, and any legislation which disturbs that equality is an arbitrary interference with the liberty of contract." What about the "disturbing of equality" in Muller v. Oregon, note 1, supra, decided in the same year as Adair? Compare the Adkins case in 1923, note 3, infra. Justices Holmes and McKenna dissented in Adair. Note the repudiation of Coppage and Adair, in Lincoln Federal Labor Union v. Northwestern Iron and Metal Co., 335 U.S. 525 (1949), sec. 4, p. 974, infra.

3. *Minimum wages and the Adkins case.* Though Bunting v. Oregon in 1917, note 1, supra, had sustained regulation of hours—including a requirement of overtime wages—(and though Muller v. Oregon in 1908, also in note 1, had sustained regulation of women's working hours), the Court held in 1923 that the District of Columbia law prescribing minimum wages for women was unconstitutional under the due process clause of the Fifth Amendment. <u>Adkins v. Children's Hospital</u>, 261 U.S. 525. Justice Sutherland emphasized that freedom of contract was "the general rule, and restraint the exception." Since Muller, he noted, the 19th Amendment had been adopted, and the civil inferiority of women was almost at a "vanishing point." Hence, the liberty of contract could not be subjected to greater restriction in the case of women than of men. The chief objection was that the law compelled payment of wages without regard to the employment contract, the business involved, or the work done: this was "a naked, arbitrary exercise" of legislative power. Chief Justice Taft and Justice Sanford dissented; Justice Brandeis did not participate.

In another dissent, Justice Holmes stated: "I confess that I do not understand the principle on which the power to fix a minimum for the wages of women can be denied by those who admit the power to fix a maximum for their hours of work. . . . The bargain is equally affected whichever half you regulate. . . . It will need more than the Nineteenth Amendment to convince me that there are no differences between men and women, and that legislation cannot take those differences into account." [The Adkins decision was adhered to in Morehead v. New York ex rel. Tipaldo, 298 U.S. 587 (1936) (involving a New York law invalidated under the 14th Amendment), but was overruled in West Coast Hotel Co. v. Parrish, 300 U.S. 379 (1937), sec. 4, p. 971, infra.]

4. *Price regulations.* The Court stated the general rule applied during this period to price (as well as wage) regulations as follows: "[A] state legislature is without constitutional power to fix prices at which commodities may be sold, services rendered, or property used, unless the business or property

involved is 'affected with the public interest.' "   Williams v. Standard Oil Co.,
278 U.S. 235 (1929).   See the discussion of price regulation in Nebbia v.
New York, 291 U.S. 502 (1934), which follows.   The Williams case involved gasoline prices;   see also Tyson & Brother v. Banton, 273 U.S. 418
(1927) (resale price of theatre tickets);   Ribnik v. McBride, 277 U.S. 350
(1928) (employment agency fees).   [The Tyson decision was explicitly overruled (in a per curiam decision, without argument, in Gold v. DiCarlo, 380
U.S. 520 (1965).   Ribnik had been overruled earlier, in Olsen v. Nebraska,
313 U.S. 236 (1941) (p. 978, infra).]

5.   *Restrictions on business entry and other economic regulations.*   a.
In New State Ice Co. v. Liebmann, 285 U.S. 262 (1932), the Court invalidated an Oklahoma law which treated the manufacture of ice like a public
utility, requiring a certificate of convenience and necessity as a condition of
entering the business.   Justice Brandeis' dissent contained an extensive discussion of the history and development of the certificate of convenience and
necessity.   See also Adams v. Tanner, 244 U.S. 590 (1917), holding unconstitutional a law prohibiting employment agencies which collected fees from
workers.   Justice McReynolds for the majority called the law an "arbitrary
and oppressive" ban on a "useful business";   Justice Brandeis dissented at
length.   Cf. Olsen v. Nebraska, p. 978, infra.

b.   Compare Weaver v. Palmer Bros., 270 U.S. 402 (1926), invalidating
a law prohibiting the use of shoddy in manufacturing bedding: "Here it is
established that sterilization eliminates the dangers, if any, from the use of
shoddy."   Nor was there greater basis for concern with public deception than
for the health argument: for other articles, the law required inspection and a
tag showing the materials used.   "Obviously, these regulations or others that
are adequate may be effectively applied to shoddy-filled articles."   The Court
concluded that the "absolute prohibition of the use of shoddy in comfortables
is purely arbitrary."   Justice Holmes, joined by Justices Brandeis and Stone,
dissented.   Would the ban on shoddy be sustainable under the principles of
the more recent decisions, sec. 4, infra?   Would it be sustained in fact, in view
of the summary way the Court has applied those principles?

SECTION 4.   SUBSTANTIVE DUE PROCESS AND ECONOMIC REGULATION: THE DECLINE OF JUDICIAL INTERVENTION

NEBBIA v. NEW YORK

291 U.S. 502, 54 S.Ct. 505, 78 L.Ed. 940 (1934).

Appeal from the County Court of Monroe County, New York.

Mr. Justice ROBERTS delivered the opinion of the Court.

The Legislature of New York established [in 1933] a Milk Control
Board with power   .   .   .   to "fix minimum and maximum   .   .   .   retail prices to be charged by   .   .   .   stores to consumers for consumption
off the premises where sold."   The Board fixed nine cents as the price to be

charged by a store for a quart of milk. Nebbia, the proprietor of a grocery store in Rochester, sold two quarts and a five cent loaf of bread for eighteen cents; and was convicted for violating the Board's order. . . . The question for decision is whether the Federal Constitution prohibits a state from so fixing the selling price of milk. We first inquire as to the occasion for the legislation and its history.

During 1932 the prices received by farmers for milk were much below the cost of production. . . . The situation of the families of dairy producers had become desperate and called for state aid similar to that afforded the unemployed, if conditions should not improve.

On March 10, 1932, the senate and assembly resolved "That a joint legislative committee is hereby created . . . to investigate the causes of the decline of the price of milk to producers and the resultant effect of the low prices upon the dairy industry and the future supply of milk to the cities of the State. . . .' " [The legislative committee's findings included the following:] Milk is an essential item of diet. . . . Failure of producers to receive a reasonable return . . . threatens a relaxation of vigilance against contamination. The production and distribution of milk is a paramount industry of the state, and largely affects the health and prosperity of its people. . . . The fluid milk industry is affected by factors of [price] instability peculiar to itself which call for special methods of control. . . .

The legislature adopted [this law] as a method of correcting the evils, which the report of the committee showed could not be expected to right themselves through the ordinary play of the forces of supply and demand, owing to the peculiar and uncontrollable factors affecting the industry. . . . [The Court then turned to the due process objection:]

Under our form of government the use of property and the making of contracts are normally matters of private and not a public concern. The general rule is that both shall be free of governmental interference. But neither property rights nor contract rights are absolute; for government cannot exist if the citizen may at will use his property to the detriment of his fellows, or exercise his freedom of contract to work them harm. Equally fundamental with the private right is that of the public to regulate it in the common interest. . . .

The Fifth Amendment, in the field of federal activity, and the Fourteenth, as respects state action, do not prohibit governmental regulation for the public welfare. They merely condition the exertion of the admitted power, by securing that the end shall be accomplished by methods consistent with due process. And the guaranty of due process, as has often been held, demands only that the law shall not be unreasonable, arbitrary or capricious, and that the means selected shall have a real and substantial relation to the object sought to be attained. It results that a regulation valid for one sort of business, or in given circumstances, may be invalid for another sort, or for the same business under other circumstances, because the reasonabless of each regulation depends upon the relevant fact. . . .

Legislation concerning sales of goods, and incidentally affecting prices, has repeatedly been held valid. In this class fall laws forbidding unfair competition by the charging of lower prices in one locality than those exacted in another, by giving trade inducements to purchasers, and by other forms of price discrimination. The public policy with respect to free competition has engendered state and federal statutes prohibiting monopolies, which have been upheld.   On the other hand, where the policy of the state dictated that a monopoly should be granted, statutes having that effect have been held inoffensive to the constitutional guarantees.   . . .

But we are told that because the law essays to control prices it denied due process.   Notwithstanding the admitted power to correct existing economic ills by appropriate regulation of business, ...   the appellant urges that the direct fixation of prices is a type of regulation absolutely forbidden.   . . .   But if, as must be conceded, the industry is subject to regulation in the public interest, what constitutional principle bars the state from correcting existing maladjustments by legislation touching prices?   We think there is no such principle.   The due process clause makes no mention of sales or of prices any more than it speaks of business or contracts or buildings or other incidents of property.   The thought seems nevertheless to have persisted that there is something peculiarly sacrosanct about the price one may charge for what he makes or sells, and that however able to regulate other elements of manufacture or trade, with incidental effect upon price, the state is incapable of directly controlling the price itself.   This view was negatived many years ago.   Munn v. Illinois, 94 U.S. 113 [1877].   [A]ppellant's claim is, however, that this court, in there sustaining a statutory prescription of charges for storage by the proprietors of a grain elevator, limited permissible legislation of that type to businesses affected with a public interest, and he says no business is so affected except it have one or more of the characteristics he enumerates [—primarily businesses that are public utilities or monopolies].   But this is a misconception.   . . .   It is true that the court [in Munn] cited a statement from Lord Hale's De Portibus Maris, to the effect that when private property is "affected with a public interest, it ceases to be juris privati only," but the court proceeded at once to define what it understood by the expression, saying: "Property does become clothed with a public interest when used in a manner to make it of public consequence, and affect the community at large"   . . . ..   Thus understood, "affected with a public interest" is the equivalent of "subject to the exercise of the police power"   . . . ..

It is clear that there is no closed class or category of businesses affected with a public interest, and the function of courts in the application of the Fifth and Fourteenth Amendments is to determine in each case whether circumstances vindicate the challenged regulation as a reasonable exertion of governmental authority or condemn it as arbitrary or discriminatory.   . . .   The phrase "affected with a public interest" can, in the nature of things, mean no more than that an industry, for adequate reason, is subject to control for the public good.   [T]here can be doubt that upon proper occasion and by appropriate measures the state may regulate a business in any of its aspects, including the prices to be charged for the products or commodities it sells.

So far as the requirement of due process is concerned, and in the absence of other constitutional restriction, a state is free to adopt whatever economic policy may reasonably be deemed to promote public welfare, and to enforce that policy by legislation adapted to its purpose.   The courts are without authority either to declare such policy, or, when it is declared by the legislative arm, to override it.   If the laws passed are seen to have a reasonable relation to a proper legislative purpose, and are neither arbitrary nor discriminatory, the requirements of due process are satisfied, and judicial determination to that effect renders a court functus officio.   . . .   Price control, like any other form of regulation, is unconstitutional only if arbitrary, discriminatory, or demonstrably irrelevant to the policy the legislature is free to adopt, and hence an unnecessary and unwarranted interference with individual liberty.

Tested by these considerations we find no basis in the due process clause of the Fourteenth Amendment for condemning the provisions of the Agriculture and Markets Law here drawn into question. [Recall the upholding of a commerce clause challenge to an application of the law a year after Nebbia, in Baldwin v. Seelig, chap. 8, p. 649, supra.]

The judgment is affirmed.

Separate opinion of Mr. Justice McREYNOLDS [dissenting]. . . .

Regulation to prevent recognized evils in business has long been upheld as permissible legislative action. But fixation of the price at which "A," engaged in an ordinary business, may sell, in order to enable "B," a producer, to improve his condition, has not been regarded as within legislative power. This is not regulation, but management, control, dictation . . . . The argument advanced here would support general prescription of prices for farm products, groceries, shoes, clothing, all the necessities of modern civilization, as well as labor, when some legislature finds and declares such action advisable and for the public good. This Court has declared that State may not by legislative fiat convert a private business into a public utility. . . . And if it be now ruled that one dedicates his property to public use whenever he embarks on an enterprise which the Legislature may think it desirable to bring under control, this is but to declare that rights guaranteed by the Constitution exist only so long as supposed public interest does not require their extinction. To adopt such a view, of course, would put an end to liberty under the Constitution. . . . Here, we find direct interference with guaranteed rights defended upon the ground that the purpose was to promote the public welfare by increasing milk prices at the farm. Unless we can affirm that the end proposed is proper and the means adopted have reasonable relation to it this action is unjustifiable. . . . The Legislative Committee pointed out as the obvious cause of decreased consumption notwithstanding low prices, the consumers' reduced buying power. Higher store prices will not enlarge this power; nor will they decrease production. . . . It is not true as stated that "the State seeks to protect the producer by fixing a minimum price for his milk." She carefully refrained from doing this; but did undertake to fix the price after the milk had passed to other owners. Assuming that the views and facts reported by the Legislative Committee are correct, it appears to me wholly unreasonable to expect this legislation to accomplish the proposed end—increase of prices at the farm. . . . Not only does the statute interfere arbitrarily with the rights of the little grocer to conduct his business according to standards long accepted . . .; but it takes away the liberty of twelve million consumers to buy a necessity of life in an open market. . . .

Mr. Justice VAN DEVANTER, Mr. Justice SUTHERLAND and Mr. Justice BUTLER authorize me to say that they concur in this opinion.*

---

* See also Anthracite Coal Co. v. Adkins, 310 U.S. 381 (1940), rejecting, inter alia, a Fifth Amendment challenge to the price-fixing provisions of the Bituminous Coal Act of 1937: "Price control is one of the means available . . . for the protection and promotion of the welfare of the economy."

WEST COAST HOTEL CO. v. PARRISH

300 U.S. 379, 57 S.Ct. 578, 81 L.Ed. 703 (1937).

Appeal from the Supreme Court of Washington.

Mr. Chief Justice HUGHES delivered the opinion of the Court.

This case presents the question of the constitutional validity of the minimum wage law of the State of Washington. . . .   *Issue*

The appellant conducts a hotel. The appellee Elsie Parrish was employed as a chambermaid and (with her husband) brought this suit to recover the difference between the wages paid her and the minimum wage fixed pursuant to   *Facts* the state law. The minimum wage was $14.50 per week of 48 hours. The appellant challenged the act as repugnant to the due process clause of the Fourteenth Amendment of the Constitution of the United States. . . .   The appellant relies upon the decision of this Court in Adkins v. Children's Hospital, 261 U.S. 525 [p. 966, supra].

The recent case of Morehead v. New York ex rel. Tipaldo, 298 U.S. 587 [1936], came here on certiorari to the New York court which had held the New York minimum wage act for women to be invalid. . . .   [This Court affirmed because it] considered that the only question before it was whether the Adkins case was distinguishable and that reconsideration of that decision had not been sought. . . .[1]

We think that the question which was not deemed to be open in the Morehead case is open and is necessarily presented here. . . .

The principle which must control our decision is not in doubt. The constitutional provision invoked is the due process clause of the Fourteenth Amendment governing the States, as the due process clause invoked in the Adkins case governed Congress. In each case the violation alleged by those attacking minimum wage regulation for women is deprivation of freedom of contract. What is this freedom? The Constitution does not speak of freedom of contract. It speaks of liberty and prohibits the deprivation of liberty without due process of law. In prohibiting that deprivation the Constitution does not recognize an absolute and uncontrollable liberty. . . .   [T]he liberty safeguarded is liberty in a social organization which requires the protection of law against the evils which menace the health, safety, morals and welfare of the people. Liberty under the Constitution is thus necessarily subject to the restraints of due process, and regulation which is reasonable in relation to its subject and is adopted in the interests of the community is due process. This essential limitation of liberty in general governs freedom of contract in particular. . . .

This power under the Constitution to restrict freedom of contract has had many illustrations. That it may be exercised in the public interest with respect to contracts between employer and employee is undeniable. Thus statutes have

---

1. Recall the explanation by Justice Roberts, in the memorandum left with Justice Frankfurter, of his votes in Morehead and West Coast Hotel, noted in the materials on the Court-Packing Plan, chap. 4, p. 289, supra. Justice Roberts was with the majority in each case. His memorandum sought to explain why these votes were not inconsistent. Some contemporary comment had viewed Justice Roberts' West Coast Hotel vote as "the switch in time that saved the Nine" from the Court-Packing Plan that failed in the Senate soon after.

been sustained limiting employment in underground mines and smelters to eight hours a day (Holden v. Hardy, 169 U.S. 366); in requiring redemption in cash of store orders or other evidences of indebtedness issued in the payment of wages (Knoxville Iron Co. v. Harbison, 183 U.S. 13); in forbidding the payment of seamen's wages in advance (Patterson v. Bark Eudora, 190 U.S. 169); in making it unlawful to contract to pay miners employed at quantity rates upon the basis of screened coal instead of the weight of the coal as originally produced in the mine (McLean v. Arkansas, 211 U.S. 539); in prohibiting contracts limiting liability for injuries to employees (Chicago, B. & Q. R. Co. v. McGuire, 219 U.S. 549); in limiting hours of work of employees in manufacturing establishments (Bunting v. Oregon, 243 U.S. 426); and in maintaining workmen's compensation laws (New York Central R. Co. v. White, 243 U.S. 188). . . .

We think that the .   .   . decision in the Adkins case was a departure from the true application of the principles governing the regulation by the State of the relation of employer and employed. .   .   . What can be closer to the public interest than the health of women and their protection from unscrupulous and overreaching employers? And if the protection of women is a legitimate end of the exercise of state power, how can it be said that the requirement of the payment of a minimum wage fairly fixed in order to meet the very necessities of existence is not an admissible means to that end? The legislature of the State was clearly entitled to consider the situation of women in employment, the fact that they are in the class receiving the least pay, that their bargaining power is relatively weak, and that they are the ready victims of those who would take advantage of their necessitous circumstances. The legislature was entitled to adopt measures to reduce the evils of the "sweating system," the exploiting of workers at wages so low as to be insufficient to meet the bare cost of living thus making their very helplessness the occasion of a most injurious competition. The legislature had the right to consider that its minimum wage requirements would be an important aid in carrying out its policy of protection. The adoption of similar requirements by many States evidences a deep-seated conviction both as to the presence of the evil and as to the means adapted to check it. Legislative response to that conviction cannot be regarded as arbitrary or capricious and that is all we have to decide. Even if the wisdom of the policy be regarded as debatable and its effects uncertain, still the legislature is entitled to its judgment.

There is an additional and compelling consideration which recent economic experience has brought into a strong light. The exploitation of a class of workers who are in an unequal position with respect to bargaining power and are thus relatively defenceless against the denial of a living wage is not only detrimental to their health and well being but casts a direct burden for their support upon the community. What these workers lose in wages the taxpayers are called upon to pay. The bare cost of living must be met. We may take judicial notice of the unparalleled demands for relief which arose during the recent period of depression and still continue to an alarming extent despite the degree of economic recovery which has been achieved. It is unnecessary to cite official statistics to establish what is of common knowledge through the length and breadth of the land. While in the instant case no factual brief has been presented, there is no reason to doubt that the State of Washington has encountered the same social problem that is present elsewhere. The community is not bound to provide what is in effect a subsidy for unconscionable employers. The community may direct its law-making power to correct the abuse which springs from their selfish disregard of the public interest. . . .

Our conclusion is that the case of Adkins v. Children's Hospital, supra, should be, and it is, overruled. The judgment of the Supreme Court of the State of Washington is

Affirmed.[2]

Mr. Justice SUTHERLAND.—Mr. Justice VAN DEVANTER, Mr. Justice McREYNOLDS, Mr. Justice BUTLER and I think the judgment of the court below should be reversed.

[T]he meaning of the Constitution does not change with the ebb and flow of economic events. . . . Neither the statute involved in the Adkins case nor the Washington statute . . . has the slightest relation to the capacity or earning power of the employee, to the number of hours which constitute the day's work, the character of the place where the work is to be done, or the circumstances or surroundings of the employment. The sole basis upon which the question of validity rests is the assumption that the employee is entitled to receive a sum of money sufficient to provide a living for her, keep her in health and preserve her morals. And as we pointed out at some length in [Adkins], . . . the question thus presented . . . can not be solved by any general formula prescribed by a statutory bureau, since it is not a composite but an individual question to be answered for each individual, considered by herself. What we said further in that case . . . is equally applicable here:

"The law takes account of the necessities of only one party to the contract. It ignores the necessities of the employer by compelling him to pay not less than a certain sum, not only whether the employee is capable of earning it, but irrespective of the ability of his business to sustain the burden, generously leaving him, of course, the privilege of abandoning his business as an alternative for going on at a loss. . . . To the extent that the sum fixed exceeds the fair value of the services rendered, it amounts to a compulsory exaction from the employer for the support of a partially indigent person, for whose condition there rests upon him no peculiar responsibility, and therefore . . . arbitrarily shifts to his shoulders a burden which, if it belongs to anybody, belongs to society as a whole. . . ."

Finally, it may be said that a statute absolutely fixing wages in the various industries at definite sums and forbidding employers and employees from contracting for any other than those designated, would probably not be thought to be constitutional. It is hard to see why the power to fix minimum wages does not connote a like power in respect of maximum wages. And yet, if both powers be exercised in such a way that the minimum and the maximum so nearly approach each other as to become substantially the same, the right to make any contract in respect of wages will have been completely abrogated. . . .

2. The Nebbia and West Coast Hotel decisions were relied on after 1937 to dispose of due process objections in a number of cases challenging commerce clause regulations, see chap. 4, sec. 5, supra. Note, e. g., the reliance on West Coast Hotel in sustaining federal minimum wage legislation in U. S. v. Darby, p. 296, supra.

THE NEW ERA: REDUCED JUDICIAL SCRUTINY OR ABDICATION?

The 1930's decisions printed above curtailed judicial intervention in economic regulation. Do the decisions since the 1940's, which follow, simply apply the Nebbia and West Coast Hotel approach? Or do they carry the rejection of the Lochner philosophy ever further, to an even greater "hands off" position? Compare the Court's elaborate explanation of the background and rationale for the legislation sustained in the 1930's cases with the curt statement (or assumption) of legislative justifications in the decisions below. Were the justifications so obvious, the relationships between means and ends so plainly rational in the Lincoln Federal Labor Union case (below) so that no more detailed statement was needed? Were the justifications equally obvious in Williamson v. Lee Optical Co. (p. 976)? And was the Day-Brite case (p. 979) so similar to plainly valid regulations of working conditions as to warrant so brief a judicial examination? In Day-Brite, the Court stated: "We could strike down this law only if we returned to the philosophy of the Lochner, Coppage and Adkins cases." Was there truly no middle ground? Or was greater scrutiny in some of these cases possible (and desirable) without risking the evils of the excessive judicial intervention of the Lochner era? (Note also the questions at the end of this chapter, at p. 981.)

LINCOLN FEDERAL LABOR UNION v. NORTHWESTERN IRON & METAL CO.*

335 U.S. 525, 69 S.Ct. 251, 93 L.Ed. 212 (1949).

Appeal from the Supreme Court of Nebraska.

Mr. Justice BLACK delivered the opinion of the Court.

Under employment practices in the United States, employers have sometimes limited work opportunities to members of unions, sometimes to nonunion members, and at other times have employed and kept their workers without regard to whether they were or were not members of a union. Employers are commanded to follow this latter employment practice in the states of North Carolina and Nebraska. A North Carolina statute and a Nebraska constitutional amendment provide that no person in those states shall be denied an opportunity to obtain or retain employment because he is or is not a member of a labor organization. To enforce this policy North Carolina and Nebraska employers are also forbidden to enter into contracts or agreements obligating themselves to exclude persons from employment because they are or are not labor union members. . . .

[Contentions that the laws impaired the obligation of contracts, violated First Amendment rights, and denied equal protection of the laws were found to have no merit.]

. . . It is contended that these state laws deprive appellants of their liberty without due process of law in violation of the Fourteenth Amendment.

---

* Together with Whitaker v. North Carolina, on appeal from the Supreme Court of North Carolina.

Appellants argue that the laws are specifically designed to deprive all persons within the two states of "liberty" (1) to refuse to hire or retain any person in employment because he is or is not a union member, and (2) to make a contract or agreement to engage in such employment discrimination against union or non-union members. . . .

Many cases are cited by appellants in which this Court has said that in some instances the due process clause protects the liberty of persons to make contracts. But none of these cases . . . ever went so far as to indicate that the due process clause bars a state from prohibiting contracts to engage in conduct banned by a valid state law. So here, if the provisions in the state laws against employer discrimination are valid, it follows that the contract prohibition also is valid. . . . We therefore turn to the decisive question under the due process contention, which is: Does the due process clause forbid a state to pass laws clearly designed to safeguard the opportunity of non-union workers to get and hold jobs, free from discrimination against them because they are non-union workers?

There was a period in which labor union members who wanted to get and hold jobs were the victims of widespread employer discrimination practices. Contracts between employers and their employees were used by employers to accomplish this anti-union employment discrimination. Before hiring workers, employers required them to sign agreements stating that the workers were not and would not become labor union members. Such anti-union practices were so obnoxious to workers that they gave these required agreements the name of "yellow dog contracts." This hostility of workers also prompted passage of state and federal laws to ban employer discrimination against union members and to outlaw yellow dog contracts. [After reviewing the Coppage and Adair cases, p. 964, supra, the Court continued:]

The Allgeyer-Lochner-Adair-Coppage constitutional doctrine was for some years followed by this Court. It was used to strike down laws fixing minimum wages and maximum hours in employment, laws fixing prices, and laws regulating business activities. . . .

This Court beginning at least as early as 1934, when the Nebbia case was decided, has steadily rejected the due process philosophy enunciated in the Adair-Coppage line of cases. In doing so it has consciously returned closer and closer to the earlier constitutional principle that states have power to legislate against what are found to be injurious practices in their internal commercial and business affairs, so long as their laws do not run afoul of some specific federal constitutional prohibition, or of some valid federal law. . . . Under this constitutional doctrine the due process clause is no longer to be so broadly construed that the Congress and state legislatures are put in a strait jacket when they attempt to suppress business and industrial conditions which they regard as offensive to the public welfare.

Appellants now ask us to return, at least in part, to the due process philosophy that has been deliberately discarded. Claiming that the Federal Constitution itself affords protection for union members against discrimination, they nevertheless assert that the same Constitution forbids a state from providing the same protection for non-union members. Just as we have held that the due process clause erects no obstacle to block legislative protection of union members, we now hold that legislative protection can be afforded non-union workers.

Affirmed.

[Justices FRANKFURTER, RUTLEDGE, and MURPHY concurred in separate opinions.]

WILLIAMSON v. LEE OPTICAL CO.
348 U.S. 483, 75 S.Ct. 461, 99 L.Ed. 563 (1955).

Appeal from the District Court for the Western District of Oklahoma.

Mr. Justice DOUGLAS delivered the opinion of the Court. . . .

The District Court held unconstitutional portions of three sections of [an Oklahoma law of 1953]. First, it held invalid under the Due Process Clause of the Fourteenth Amendment the portions of § 2 which make it unlawful for any person not a licensed optometrist or ophthalmologist to fit lenses to a face or to duplicate or replace into frames lenses or other optical appliances, except upon written prescriptive authority of an Oklahoma licensed ophthalmologist or optometrist.

An ophthalmologist is a duly licensed physician who specializes in the care of the eyes. An optometrist examines eyes for refractive error, recognizes (but does not treat) diseases of the eye, and fills prescriptions for eyeglasses. The optician is an artisan qualified to grind lenses, fill prescriptions, and fit frames.

The effect of § 2 is to forbid the optician from fitting or duplicating lenses without a prescription from an ophthalmologist or optometrist. In practical effect, it means that no optician can fit old glasses into new frames or supply a lens, whether it be a new lens or one to duplicate a lost or broken lens, without a prescription. The District Court . . . rebelled at the notion that a State could require a prescription . . . "to take old lenses and place them in new frames and then fit the completed spectacles to the *face* of the eyeglass wearer." . . . The court found that through mechanical devices and ordinary skills the optician could take a broken lens or a fragment thereof, measure its power, and reduce it to prescriptive terms. The court held that "Although on this precise issue of duplication, the legislature . . . was dealing with a matter of public interest, the particular means chosen are neither reasonably necessary nor reasonably related to the end sought to be achieved." . . . It was, accordingly, of the opinion that this provision of the law violated the Due Process Clause by arbitrarily interfering with the optician's right to do business. . . .

The Oklahoma law may exact a needless, wasteful requirement in many cases. But it is for the legislature, not the courts, to balance the advantages and disadvantages of the new requirement. It appears that in many cases the optician can easily supply the new frames or new lenses without reference to the old written prescription. It also appears that many written prescriptions contain no directive data in regard to fitting spectacles to the face. But in some cases the directions contained in the prescription are essential, if the glasses are to be fitted so as to correct the particular defects of vision or alleviate the eye condition. The legislature might have concluded that the frequency of occasions when a prescription is necessary was sufficient to justify this regulation of the fitting of eyeglasses. Likewise, when it is necessary to duplicate a lens, a written prescription may or may not be necessary. But the legislature might have concluded that one was needed often enough to require one in every case.   .   .   .

The day is gone when this Court uses the Due Process Clause of the Fourteenth Amendment to strike down state laws, regulatory of business and industrial conditions, because they may be unwise, improvident, or out of harmony with a particular school of thought.   .   .   .   We emphasize again what Chief Justice Waite said in Munn v. Illinois, 94 U.S. 113, 134, "For protection against abuses by legislatures the people must resort to the polls, not to the courts."

Secondly, the District Court held that it violated the Equal Protection Clause of the Fourteenth Amendment to subject opticians to this regulatory system and to exempt, as § 3 of the Act, does, all sellers of ready-to-wear glasses. The problem of legislative classification is a perennial one, admitting of no doctrinaire definition.   .   .   .   The prohibition of the Equal Protection Clause goes no further than the invidious discrimination. We cannot say that that point has been reached here. For all this record shows, the ready-to-wear branch of this business may not loom large in Oklahoma or may present problems of regulation distinct from the other branch. [See also the excerpt from this passage infra, chap. 14, p. 997.]

Third, the District Court held unconstitutional, as violative of the Due Process Clause   .   .   ., that portion of § 3 which makes it unlawful "to solicit the sale of   .   .   .   frames, mountings,   .   .   .   or any other optical appliances."   .   .   .   An eyeglass frame, considered in isolation, is only a piece of merchandise. But an eyeglass frame is not used in isolation   .   .   .   .; it is used with lenses; and lenses, pertaining as they do to the human eye, enter the field of health. Therefore, the legislature might conclude that to regulate one effectively it would have to regulate the other. Or it might conclude that both the sellers of frames and the sellers of lenses were in a business where advertising should be limited or even abolished in the public interest.   .   .   .

Fourth, the District Court held unconstitutional, as violative of the Due Process Clause of the Fourteenth Amendment, the provision of § 4 of the Oklahoma Act which reads as follows:

> "No person, firm, or corporation engaged in the business of retailing merchandise to the general public shall rent space, sublease departments, or otherwise permit any person purporting to do eye examination or visual care to occupy space in such retail store."

It seems to us that this regulation is on the same constitutional footing as the denial to corporations of the right to practice dentistry. Semler v. Dental Examiners [294 U.S. 608]. It is an attempt to free the profession, to as great an extent as possible, from all taints of commercialism. It certainly might be easy for an optometrist with space in a retail store to be merely a front for the retail establishment. In any case, the opportunity for that nexus may be too great for safety, if the eye doctor is allowed inside the retail store. Moreover, it may be deemed important to effective regulation that the eye doctor be restricted to geographical locations that reduce the temptations of commercialism. Geographical location may be an important consideration in a legislative program which aims to raise the treatment of the human eye to a strictly professional level. We cannot say that the regulation has no rational relation to that objective and therefore is beyond constitutional bounds.

What we have said is sufficient to dispose of the appeal . . . from the conclusion of the District Court that that portion of § 3 which makes it unlawful to solicit the sale of spectacles, eyeglasses, lenses, and prisms by the use of advertising media is constitutional. . . .

Affirmed in part and reversed in part.

OTHER EXAMPLES OF THE MODERN APPROACH

1. *Olsen v. Nebraska.* An early example of the "hands off" attitude was Olsen v. Nebraska, 313 U.S. 236 (1941), where the state courts had held unconstitutional a law fixing maximum employment agency fees, in reliance on Ribnik v. McBride, 277 U.S. 350 (1928), p. 967, supra. The Supreme Court unanimously reversed: "The drift away from [Ribnik] has been so great that it can no longer be deemed controlling authority. . . . In final analysis, the only constitutional prohibitions or restraints which respondents have suggested for the invalidation of this legislation are those notions of public policy embedded in earlier decisions of this Court but which, as Mr. Justice Holmes long admonished, should not be read into the Constitution. . . . Since they do not find expression in the Constitution, we cannot give them continuing vitality as standards by which the constitutionality of the economic and social programs of the states is to be determined."

2. *Ferguson v. Skrupa.* A more recent example of the deference to legislative judgments is Ferguson v. Skrupa, 372 U.S. 726 (1963), which reversed a three-judge court decision that had invalidated a Kansas statute regulating "the business of debt-adjusting." The lower court had relied on cases such as Adams v. Tanner, note 5, p. 967, supra. The law prohibited engaging in that business except as an incident to the practice of law. Justice Black stated for the Court: "In the face of our abandonment of the use of the 'vague contours' of the Due Process Clause to nullify laws which a majority of the Court believed to be economically unwise, reliance on Adams v. Tanner is as mistaken as would be adherence to Adkins v. Children's Hospital . . . .. Unquestionably, there are arguments showing that the business of debt adjusting has social utility, but such arguments are properly addressed to the legislature, not to us. We refuse to sit as a superlegislature to weigh the wisdom of legislation. . . . Whether the legislature takes for its textbook Adam Smith, Herbert Spencer, Lord Keynes, or some other is no concern of ours."

Justice Harlan concurred "on the ground that this state measure bears a rational relation to a constitutionally permissible objective. See Williamson v. Lee Optical Co. . . . ." Does Justice Harlan's statement suggest greater scrutiny than Justice Black's? More focused scrutiny? [Recall also Goldblatt v. Hempstead and Berman v. Parker, sec. 2, pp. 951 and 953, supra.]

DAY-BRITE LIGHTING, INC. v. MISSOURI

342 U.S. 421, 72 S.Ct. 405, 96 L.Ed. 469 (1952).

Appeal from the Supreme Court of Missouri.

Mr. Justice DOUGLAS delivered the opinion of the Court.

Missouri has a statute, . . . first enacted in 1897, which was designed to end the coercion of employees by employers in the exercise of the franchise. It provides that an employee may absent himself from his employment for four hours between the opening and closing of the polls without penalty, and that any employer who among other things deducts wages for that absence is guilty of a misdemeanor.

. . . November 5, 1946, was a day for general elections in Missouri, the polls being open from 6 A.M. to 7 P.M. One Grotemeyer, an employee of appellant, was on a shift that worked from 8 A.M. to 4:30 P.M. each day, with thirty minutes for lunch. His rate of pay was $1.60 an hour. He requested four hours from the scheduled work day to vote on November 5, 1946. That request was refused; but Grotemeyer and all other employees on his shift were allowed to leave at 3 P.M. that day, which gave them four consecutive hours to vote before the polls closed.

Grotemeyer left his work at 3 P.M. in order to vote and did not return to work that day. He was not paid for the hour and a half between 3 P.M. and 4:30 P.M. Appellant was found guilty and fined for penalizing Grotemeyer in violation of the statute. [The state courts rejected due process and equal protection challenges.]

The liberty of contract argument pressed on us is reminiscent of the philosophy of [Lochner, Coppage, and Adkins, supra] and others of that vintage. Our recent decisions make plain that we do not sit as a super-legislature to weigh the wisdom of legislation . . .. [T]he state legislatures have constitutional authority to experiment with new techniques; . . . they may within extremely broad limits control practices in the business-labor field . . ..

West Coast Hotel . . ., overruling Adkins . . ., held constitutional a state law fixing minimum wages for women. The present statute contains in form a minimum wage requirement. There is a difference in the purpose of the legislation. Here it is not the protection of the health and morals of the citizen. Missouri by this legislation has sought to safeguard the right of suffrage by taking from employers the incentive and power to use their leverage over employees to influence the vote. But the police power is not confined to a narrow category . . .. The protection of the right of suffrage under our scheme of things is basic and fundamental.

The only semblance of substance in the constitutional objection to Missouri's law is that the employer must pay wages for a period in which the employee performs no services. . . . Most regulations of business necessarily impose financial burdens on the enterprise for which no compensation is paid. Those are part of the costs of our civilization. Extreme cases are conjured up where an employer is required to pay wages for a period that has no relation to the legitimate end. Those cases can await decision as and when they arise. The present law has no such infirmity. It is designed to eliminate any penalty for exercising the right of suffrage and to remove a practical obstacle to getting out the vote. The public welfare is a broad and inclusive concept. . . . The judgment of the legislature that time out for voting should cost the employee nothing may be a debatable one. . . . But if our recent cases mean anything, they leave debatable issues as respects business, economic, and social affairs to legislative decision. We could strike down this law only if we return to the philosophy of the Lochner, Coppage, and Adkins cases.

The classification of voters so as to free employees from the domination of employers is an attempt to deal with an evil to which the one group has been exposed. The need for that classification is a matter for legislative judgment . . . ., and does not amount to a denial of equal protection under the laws.

Affirmed.

Mr. Justice FRANKFURTER concurs in the result.

Mr. Justice JACKSON, dissenting.

The constitutional issue in this case, if not very vital in its present application, surely is a debatable one. Two state courts of last resort, the only ones to consider similar legislation, have held it unconstitutional. Only unreviewed decisions of intermediate courts can be cited in support of the Court's holding.

. . . [Grotemeyer] demanded a four-hour leave of absence, with full pay, on election day to do campaigning and to get out the vote. It is stipulated that his residence was 200 feet from the polling place and that it actually took him about five minutes to vote. . . . For failure to pay something less than $3 for this hour and a half which Grotemeyer did not work and for which his contract did not provide that he should be paid, the employer is convicted of crime . . . ..

To sustain this statute by resort to the analogy of minimum wage laws seems so farfetched and unconvincing as to demonstrate its weakness rather than its strength. Because a State may require payment of a minimum wage for hours that are worked it does not follow that it may compel payment for time that is not worked. To overlook a distinction so fundamental is to confuse the point in issue.

The Court, by speaking of the statute as though it applies only to industry, sinister and big, further obscures the real principle involved. The statute plainly requires farmers, small service enterprises, professional offices, housewives with domestic help, and all other employers, not only to allow their employees time to vote, but to pay them for time to do so. It does not, however, require the employee to use any part of such time for that purpose. Such legislation stands in a class by itself and should not be uncritically commended as a mere regulation of "practices in the business-labor field." . . .

. . . [T]here must be some limit to the power to shift the whole voting burden from the voter to someone else who happens to stand in some economic relationship to him. Getting out the vote is not the business of employers; indeed, I have regarded it as a political abuse when employers concerned themselves with their employees' voting. It is either the voter's own business or the State's business. . . . [D]oes the success of an enticement to vote justify putting its cost on some other citizen?

The discriminatory character of this statute is flagrant. It is obvious that not everybody will be paid for voting and the "rational basis" on which the State has ordered that some be paid while others are not eludes me. If there is

a need for a subsidy to get out the vote, no reason is apparent to me why it should go to one who lives 200 feet from his polling place but not to a self-employed farmer . . .. Perhaps some plan will be forthcoming to pay the farmer by requiring his mortgagee to rebate some proportion of the interest on the farm mortgage if he will vote. It would not differ in principle. But no way occurs to me by which the doctor can charge some patient or the lawyer some client for the call he could not receive while he was voting. . . .
[A] constitutional philosophy which sanctions intervention by the State to fix terms of pay without work may be available tomorrow to give constitutional sanction to state-imposed terms of employment less benevolent.

THE "HANDS-OFF" APPROACH TO ECONOMIC LEGISLATION: PRINCIPLED OR AD HOC WITHDRAWAL? PERMANENT OR TEMPORARY DOUBLE STANDARD?

Introduction. The modern Court has handled challenges to economic regulation with a broad "hands-off" approach. No such statute has been invalidated on substantive due process grounds since 1937. Only one law has been held to violate equal protection standards—Morey v. Doud in 1957, below, chap. 14, p. 999. Indeed, opinions from the Court are rare, for most appeals raising substantive due process challenges are dismissed for want of a substantial federal question and argument is ordinarily heard only where a lower court has enjoined enforcement of a statute. Yet some Justices have occasionally expressed doubts about the extreme abstention from judicial intervention.

1. *Economic rights and the contrast with First Amendment liberties.* Has the Court gone too far in this area? Are the summary dispositions consistent with the minimal requirements of due process as articulated by the Court? In the First Amendment liberties area, substantive due process imposes greater restraints than ever. See chaps. 15 and 16, infra (especially the introductory materials on the double standard question, at p. 1051.) Is the distinction between "economic" and "civil liberties" cases sufficiently clear to justify the differences in judicial scrutiny? Is the "liberty" of the individual who is denied a master electrician's license under a guild-type state law all that different from the kind of "liberty" protected in the free speech cases? [1] Is it to be expected that a Court engaged in invalidating a considerable number of laws in the civil liberties area will be able to adhere consistently, and to quite the present extent, to non-intervention in the economic and social sphere? Is there any constitutional justification for the present degree of difference in judicial scrutiny of the two types of legislation? [2] See generally McCloskey, "Economic Due Process and the Supreme Court: An Exhumation and Reburi-

---

1. See, e. g., chap. 3, "The Right to Make a Living," in Gellhorn, Individual Freedom and Governmental Restraints (1956), 105–151, on "the significant interference with the traditional freedom to work" by "the occupational license."

2. Some state courts, applying state constitutional provisions similar to due process, scrutinize legislation in this area with greater care and invalidate laws more frequently. See Hetherington, "State Economic Regulation and Substantive Due Process of Law," 53 Nw.U.L.Rev. 13, 226 (1958), Selected Essays 1938–62 (1963), 487; Paulsen, "The Persistence of Substantive Due Process in the States," 34 Minn.L.Rev. 91 (1950); and the Struve article cited at the end of this paragraph of the text.

al," 1962 Sup.Ct.Rev. 34, and Struve, "The Less-Restrictive-Alternative Principle and Economic Due Process," 80 Harv.L.Rev. 1463 (1967).

2. *The contrast with unspecified non-economic liberties and the Griswold Case.* Does a decision like Griswold v. Connecticut (the 1965 Connecticut birth-control case, chap. 11, p. 824, supra) make the Court's "hands-off" stance in these economic regulation cases substantially more untenable? Recall Justice Black's dissent and the questions following that case. If personal liberties other than those listed in the Bill of Rights can claim substantive due process protection, can the modern Court summarily reject economic claims? Can the "hands-off" attitude be justified in principle? Can it be expected to be adhered to in practice by the present Court (and future Justices) when sufficiently harsh, unjust, albeit "economic" regulations are challenged? If the Court were to order values explicitly, economic liberties would presumably rank low in the hierarchy, compared with speech and marital privacy. But would economic liberties rank so low as to warrant the minimal judicial scrutiny of these post-Lochner era cases?

3. *The contrast with the "new" equal protection.* Does the "hands-off" attitude become even more untenable in principle and even more impermanent in practice in view of the recent rise of "substantive" equal protection, traced in the next chapter? Is the economic-personal rights distinction (double standard, if you will) breaking down in the equal protection area? And will that make it even more difficult to maintain it with respect to substantive due process, at least at the level of the extremes of difference in judicial attitudes revealed when the cases in this section are compared with the interventionist ones in the following chapters? Recent equal protection cases—emphasizing "equality" rather than the "liberty" theme of the 14th Amendment—have focused on poverty. In that context, the Court has recently found state justifications inadequate for "economic" legislation—see, Shapiro v. Thompson, a 1969 decision on conditions in welfare assistance, p. 1036, infra. The Court has similarly found legislative justification in "social" legislation insufficient to warrant intrusion into a protected constitutional area—see Levy v. Louisiana, p. 1033, infra, a 1969 challenge by illegitimate children to a state survival statute. The dissents in those cases insisted that the Court had applied far more than the minimal scrutiny supposedly appropriate in the economic-social regulation area. See Karst, "Invidious Discrimination: Justice Douglas and the Return of the 'Natural-Law-Due-Process Formula'," 16 U.C.L.A.L. Rev. 716 (1969). Consider, in examining those cases, whether the expanding scrutiny under equal protection may (and should) affect the Court's attitude in economic due process situations such as those considered above.

Chapter 14

EQUAL PROTECTION, OLD AND NEW: THE EXPANDING CONTOURS OF CONSTITUTIONAL EQUALITY

FROM MARGINAL INTERVENTION TO MAJOR CUTTING EDGE: AN INTRODUCTORY OVERVIEW

The equal protection clause of the 14th Amendment is undergoing a rapid and dramatic transformation: traditionally, it supported only minimal judicial intervention in most contexts; in the hands of the Warren Court, and especially during the late sixties, it became the favorite and most far-reaching tool for judicial protection of "fundamental" rights not specified in the Constitution. That transformation is the focus of this chapter: What are the ingredients, the justifications, and the limits of the new equal protection? How does it differ from the old? When is the judicial scrutiny of the new equal protection appropriate? Under what circumstances does the permissive "hands off" attitude of the old remain appropriate?

For many years, the impact of the equal protection clause was a very limited one, both in frequency of invocation and in scope of intervention. During the decades of extensive Court interference with state economic legislation under the 14th Amendment, it was usually substantive due process, not equal protection, that provided the cutting edge. (Recall the due process cases of those years, chap. 13, sec. 3, supra, and compare the occasions for invalidation via equal protection during that period reviewed in Morey v. Doud, sec. 1, p. 999, infra.) At the height of the Lochner era, for example, Justice Holmes could refer to equal protection as "the usual last resort of constitutional arguments." Buck v. Bell, 274 U.S. 200 (1927). And Justice Jackson's comment in the Railway Express case, 336 U.S. 106 (1949) (sec. 1, p. 992, infra), reflects the relatively narrow intrusion into the legislative domain associated with the traditional equal protection: "Invalidation of a statute or an ordinance on due process grounds leaves ungoverned and ungovernable conduct which many people find objectionable. Invocation of the equal protection clause, on the other hand, does not disable any governmental body from dealing with the subject at hand. It merely means that the prohibition on regulation must have a broader impact."

Only in special, limited contexts was equal protection found to have a deeper bite—most notably in racial discrimination cases, as suggested by the historical background of the 14th Amendment and as anticipated by the Slaughter-House Cases (chap. 11, p. 787, supra). But ordinarily the command of equal protection was only that government must not impose differences in treatment "except upon some reasonable differentiation fairly related to the object of regulation," as Justice Jackson put it in Railway Express, supra; and that rational classification requirement was usually satisfied easily, with courts extremely deferential to legislative judgments and easily satisfied that the means used might rationally relate to plausible ends.

When the Court abandoned the Lochner variety of substantive due process scrutiny in the thirties, in cases such as Nebbia and West Coast Hotel (chap. 13, sec. 4, supra), there were occasional exhortations that the Justices at least exercise a limited control over economic legislation through the less fatal review standards of equal protection. But—with the exception of Morey v. Doud, p. 999, infra—"economic" regulations survived Court scrutiny as unscathed under the traditional equal protection as under the deferential due process criteria, as the materials in sec. 1 illustrate.

Yet, as has already been noted in other chapters, the Court's conversion to non-interventionism since the thirties has not been an across-the-board phenomenon: intense review in Lochner situations has receded; but there has been active Court intervention indeed in other areas—those areas deemed more important, more fundamental. The double standards charge provoked by this development was noted in the concluding comments in the previous chapter (p. 981); it is the theme of the introduction to the next chapter, on First Amendment freedoms, as well (p. 1051).

When First Amendment rights are asserted, the Court has been able to find a variety of justifications for an interventionist rather than deferential approach—including the "specific" nature of the rights (see Justice Stone's Carolene Products footnote, p. 1051, infra). But what of fundamental rights not so clearly designated by constitutional text and history? To go back to substantive due process criteria risks accusations of reviving the discredited Lochner philosophy, as the debate about marital privacy in Griswold v. Connecticut demonstrated (p. 824, supra). The increasing popularity of equal protection as a widely available substantive restraint on legislation may be partly explainable by a desire of some Justices to protect values perceived as basic without appearing to embrace Lochner era approaches. (And the extent to which reliance on the new equal protection is not mere facade and truly avoids the pitfalls of the old substantive due process is one of the underlying problems posed by the materials that follow.)

Consider a comment in a comprehensive survey, "Developments in the Law—Equal Protection," 82 Harv.L.Rev. 1065, 1131 (1969): "The resurrection of a wider-ranging review when fundamental personal interests are at stake has come under the guise of equal protection rather than substantive due process. This development is not surprising in light of the discredit which had attached to the use of substantive due process in the field of business regulation. That activist Justices have not been hampered by the unavailability of substantive due process is shown by Mr. Justice Douglas' treatment of fundamental personal rights in Griswold v. Connecticut [p. 824, supra]. When equal protection is available as a *ratio decidendi*, due process may be abandoned with even less hesitation than when the alternative is a penumbra theory." To what extent is the new equal protection less amorphous, more solidly rooted and justifiable than the positions of those in the Griswold majority? The new equal protection materials below seek to aid evaluation as well as understanding of the evolving doctrines.

———

Scope Note. The aim of this chapter is to look at the roots, contents and implications of the new equal protection—to see how we got here, where we are, and where we are going. Section 1 examines the traditional equal protection criteria in the context of modern social and business regulation; the two following sections consider areas where the more rigorous judicial scrutiny of the new equal protection have gained a fairly tenacious and well-defined foothold—voting qualifications and related problems (sec. 2) and the criminal process (sec. 3); and the final section moves to the most amorphous and open-ended manifestations of the new equality, especially in the area of social welfare legislation (sec. 4).* But before engaging in this process of examining the evolution—from the old (sec. 1) to the reasonably well developed new (secs. 2 and 3) and to the most fluid, expanding elements of the new (sec. 4) —a preliminary look at two expansive descriptions of the scope of the new equal protection will provide a useful framework for assessing the intermediate stages of movement from old to new. The first statement is from a Justice critical of the development, the second from observers sympathetic to the evolving new equality.

A CRITICAL JUSTICE'S OVERVIEW: JUSTICE HARLAN IN SHAPIRO v. THOMPSON

The critical Justice is Justice Harlan, and his summary is from his dissent in Shapiro v. Thompson, 394 U.S. 618 (1969) (sec. 4, p. 1036, infra), holding residence requirements in welfare laws unconstitutional, a decision from Chief Justice Warren's final Term and one marking the culmination of the Warren Court's new equal protection.† Justice Harlan objected to the "expansion of the comparatively new constitutional doctrine that some state statutes will be deemed to deny equal protection of the laws unless justified by a 'compelling' governmental interest":

"In upholding the equal protection argument, the Court has applied an equal protection doctrine of relatively recent vintage: the rule that statutory classifications which either are based upon certain 'suspect' criteria or affect 'fundamental rights' will be held to deny equal protection unless justified by a 'compelling' governmental interest.

"The 'compelling interest' doctrine, which today is articulated more explicitly than ever before, constitutes an increasingly significant exception to the long-established rule that a statute does not deny equal protection if it is rationally related to a legitimate governmental objective. The 'compelling interest' doctrine has two branches. The branch which requires that classifications based upon 'suspect' criteria be supported by a compelling interest apparently had its genesis in cases involving racial classifications, which have at least since Korematsu v. United States, 323 U.S. 214, 216 (1944) [chap. 18, p. 1402, infra], been regarded as inherently 'suspect.' The criterion of 'wealth' apparently was added to the list of 'suspects' as an alternative justification for the rationale in Harper v. Virginia Bd. of Elections, 383 U.S. 663,

---

* Two special problems of equal protection, though touched on in this chapter, are deferred for fuller consideration to chap. 18, infra: the problems of racial discrimination and of legislative reapportionment. Racial discrimination was a central concern to the framers of the 14th Amendment, and racial classifications have evoked careful scrutiny over the years. Legislative apportionment, a far more recent concern, has become a major area of litigation. The "suspect" nature of racial criteria and the "fundamental interest" in voting recognized in the reapportionment cases form part of the backdrop for the developments traced in this chapter; but race and reapportionment have provoked elaborations of sufficient distinctiveness and complexity to warrant detailed treatment in a separate chapter, permitting this chapter to concentrate on the evolutions from old to new at the core of equal protection.

† Chief Justice Warren himself, however, dissented in Shapiro v. Thompson—though not because of disagreement with the criteria of the new equal protection. His dissent is at p. ——, below.

668 (1966) [sec. 2, p. 1005, infra], in which Virginia's poll tax was struck down. The criterion of political allegiance may have been added in Williams v. Rhodes, 393 U.S. 23 (1968) [sec. 2, p. 1016, infra]. Today the list apparently has been further enlarged to include classifications based upon recent interstate movement, and perhaps those based upon the exercise of *any* constitutional right, for the Court states:

> 'The waiting-period provision denies welfare benefits to otherwise eligible applicants solely because they have recently moved into the jurisdiction. But in moving . . . appellees were exercising a constitutional right, and any classification which serves to penalize the exercise of that right, unless shown to be necessary to promote a *compelling* governmental interest, is unconstitutional.'

"I think that this branch of the 'compelling interest' doctrine is sound when applied to racial classifications, for historically the Equal Protection Clause was largely a product of the desire to eradicate legal distinctions founded upon race. However, I believe that the more recent extensions have been unwise. For the reasons stated in my dissenting opinion in [Harper, p. 1005, infra], I do not consider wealth a 'suspect' statutory criterion. And when, as in [Williams v. Rhodes, p. 1016, infra] and the present case, a classification is based upon the exercise of rights guaranteed against state infringement by the Federal Constitution, then there is no need for any resort to the Equal Protection Clause; in such instances, this Court may properly and straightforwardly invalidate any undue burden upon those rights under the Fourteenth Amendment's Due Process Clause. . . .

"The second branch of the 'compelling interest' principle is even more troublesome. For it has been held that a statutory classification is subject to the 'compelling interest' test if the result of the classification may be to affect a 'fundamental right,' regardless of the basis of the classification. This rule was foreshadowed in Skinner v. Oklahoma, 316 U.S. 535, 541 (1942) [sec. 4, p. 1028, infra] in which an Oklahoma statute providing for compulsory sterilization of 'habitual criminals' was held subject to 'strict scrutiny' mainly because it affected 'one of the basic civil rights.' After a long hiatus, the principle reemerged in Reynolds v. Sims, 377 U.S. 533, 561–562 (1964) [chap. 18, p. 1438, infra] in which state apportionment statutes were subjected to an unusually stringent test because 'any alleged infringement of the right of citizens to vote must be carefully and meticulously scrutinized.' The rule appeared again in Carrington v. Rash, 380 U.S. 89, 96 (1965) [sec. 2, p. 1013, infra], in which, as I now see that case, the Court applied an abnormally severe equal protection standard to a Texas statute denying certain servicemen the right to vote, without indicating that the statutory distinction between servicemen and civilians was generally 'suspect.' This branch of the doctrine was also an alternate ground in Harper v. Virginia Bd. of Elections, supra, and apparently was a basis for the holding in Williams v. Rhodes, supra.[1] It has reappeared today in the Court's cryptic

---

1. "Analysis is complicated when the statutory classification is grounded upon the exercise of a 'fundamental' right. For then the statute may come within the first branch of the 'compelling interest' doctrine because exercise of the right is deemed a 'suspect' criterion and also within the second because the statute is considered to affect the right by deterring its exercise. Williams v. Rhodes, supra, is such a case insofar as the statutes involved both inhibited exercise of the right of political association and drew distinctions based upon the way the right was exercised.

suggestion that the 'compelling interest' test is applicable merely because the result of the classification may be to deny the appellees 'food, shelter, and other necessities of life,' as well as in the Court's statement, that '[s]ince the classification here touches on the fundamental right of interstate movement, its constitutionality must be judged by the stricter standard of whether it promotes a *compelling* state interest.'

"I think this branch of the 'compelling interest' doctrine particularly unfortunate and unnecessary. It is unfortunate because it creates an exception which threatens to swallow the standard equal protection rule. Virtually every state statute affects important rights. This Court has repeatedly held, for example, that the traditional equal protection standard is applicable to statutory classifications affecting such fundamental matters as the right to pursue a particular occupation,[2] the right to receive greater or smaller wages[3] or to work more or less hours,[4] and the right to inherit property.[5] Rights such as these are in principle indistinguishable from those involved here, and to extend the 'compelling interest' rule to all cases in which such rights are affected would go far toward making this Court a 'super-legislature.' This branch of the doctrine is also unnecessary. When the right affected is one assured by the Federal Constitution, any infringement can be dealt with under the Due Process Clause. But when a statute affects only matters not mentioned in the Federal Constitution and is not arbitrary or irrational, I must reiterate that I know of nothing which entitles this Court to pick out particular human activities, characterize them as 'fundamental,' and give them added protection under an unusually stringent equal protection test. . . . "

ANOTHER OVERVIEW, BY SYMPATHETIC OBSERVERS

Compare with this description of the new equality by a critic the sketch by two friendly academic observers who see substantive equal protection as "a result of the 'egalitarian revolution' to which the Warren Court has given crucial support" (Karst and Horowitz, "Reitman v. Mulkey: A Telophase of Substantive Equal Protection," 1967 Sup.Ct.Rev. 39, 57): "There are some 'classifications that are far from irrational, but that are nonetheless unconstitutional because they produce inequities that are unacceptable in this generation's idealization of America. In giving effect to the principle of substantive equal protection, sometimes the Court will state that a classification, even though rational, bears a heavier burden of justification than mere rationality. Sometimes the Court will state that the classification is impermissible, without any analysis of the degree of rationality or degree of justification. And sometimes the Court will apply the principle of the

---

The present case is another instance, insofar as welfare residence statutes both deter interstate movement and distinguish among welfare applicants on the basis of such movement. Consequently, I have not attempted to specify the branch of the doctrine upon which these decisions rest." [All footnotes by Justice Harlan.]

2. See, e. g., Williamson v. Lee Optical Co., 348 U.S. 483 (1955); Kotch v. Board of River Pilot Comm'rs, 330 U.S. 552 (1947) [both in sec. 1, infra, at p. 996].

3. See, e. g., Bunting v. Oregon, 243 U.S. 426 (1917) [chap. 13, p. 963, supra].

4. See, e. g., Miller v. Wilson, 236 U.S. 373 (1915).

5. See, e. g., Ferry v. Spokane, P. & S. R. Co., 258 U.S. 314 (1922).

'least onerous alternative' and hold a rational classification to be impermissible because the state has available to it a means of achieving its objective that will have less onerous effect upon interests protected by the Equal Protection Clause. The unconstitutional inequities may arise from the impact of a classification by government that fails to compensate for significant differences in classes that are not themselves the direct product of governmental action— that is, a state can deny equal protection of the laws by treating unequals equally. There may, in fact, have been no formal governmental classification in the traditional sense at all, but only a toleration by government of private conduct that has produced the inequality. To rectify these denials of equal protection the state may be required, if one wishes to put it this way, to perform an 'affirmative duty.' Since total equality as a governmental goal is both impossible and undesirable, some selection must be made of the areas in which equality is to be imposed by the judiciary in the name of the Constitution. The selection to date has been largely based on the Supreme Court's identification of fundamental interests, interests that carry relatively high priorities for the development of the nation's underdeveloped sectors."

[One of the authors of that sketch, Kenneth Karst, returned to the subject two years later—while "the law of substantive equal protection continues to grow"—and once again praised the trend, and especially Justice Douglas' contributions. Professor Karst's title is not intended as criticism: "Invidious Discrimination: Justice Douglas and the Return of the 'Natural Law-Due Process Formula,' " 16 U.C.L.A.L.Rev. 716 (1969). As he notes in his praise of the trend, with special relevance to this introductory overview: "Despite Justice Douglas' protestations to the contrary, this process of growth has been and properly continues to be a process in which the present generation of Justices has sought to fill the 'moral adjurations' of due process and equal protection from their own collective bosom. The doctrine of invidious discrimination [as used in the new equal protection cases] does not permit an escape from the problems associated with substantive due process."] *

As late as 1966, Justice Harlan could still insist that there was no "dual-level test" of equal protection: "It is suggested that a different and broader equal protection standard applies in cases where 'fundamental liberties and rights are threatened,' which would require a State to show a need greater than mere rational policy to justify classifications in this area. No such dual-level test has ever been articulated by this Court, and I do not believe any such ap-

---

* The similarity of the new equal protection to the old due process is frequently denied or obscured in the opinions below and is most often asserted by commentators less enthusiastic about the Court's performance than Karst. See, e. g., Michelman, "Foreword: On Protecting the Poor Through the Fourteenth Amendment," 83 Harv.L. Rev. 7, 17 (and n. 25) (1969): "[P]ossibly because of unhappy connotations associated with 'substantive due process' as well as because equal protection remains an empty conundrum without some frank infusion of judicially 'sculpted' values, the Court seems currently more comfortable in staking out and valuing 'fundamental' interests under the aegis of equal protection than it could well feel under due process. . . . If any doubts remain that the 'new' equal protection method—that of demanding a compelling state interest to justify measures which are 'invidious' and/or which encroach upon 'fundamental' interests —involves the Court in a sculpting and ranking of values not essentially different from what occurs under 'substantive due process,' it is the purpose of this Foreword to dispel such doubts."

proach [justified]." (Dissenting opinion to Cardona v. Power [sec. 3, p. 1013 infra], 384 U.S., at 659.) By 1969, in his Shapiro v. Thompson dissent, above, Justice Harlan was compelled to recognize that a new equal protection, demanding stricter scrutiny in some situations, had arrived. The existence of a dual-level test is a premise of these materials: the focus here is not on "whether" there is a new equal protection as well as an old, but "when," "how," and "why." The next section accordingly examines the range of operation of the "mere rationality," permissive, traditional judicial attitude; the subsequent sections explore contexts where the "strict scrutiny" aspect of the "dual-level test" of equal protection has been applied.

SECTION 1. THE OLD EQUAL PROTECTION: LIMITED JUDICIAL SCRUTINY UNDER THE TRADITIONAL STANDARDS

REASONABLENESS AND CLASSIFICATIONS WHICH ARE "UNDERINCLUSIVE" OR "OVERINCLUSIVE"

The traditional equal protection criteria do not place tight reins on the legislature. A much-quoted statement from the twenties—when substantive due process control of economic regulation was in vogue—conveys the permissiveness of the old standard: "[T]he classification must be reasonable, not arbitrary, and must rest upon some ground of difference having a fair and substantial relation to the object of the legislation, so that all persons similarly circumstanced shall be treated alike" * That approach is echoed in the modern equal protection cases in this section, which portray the clause as a not significantly greater restraint on legislation than contemporary economic due process (chap. 13, sec. 4, supra).

That traditional, limited judicial scrutiny approach was described by Professors Tussman and tenBroek in their classic analysis, "The Equal Protection of the Laws," 37 Calif.L.Rev. 341 (1949), Selected Essays 1938–62 (1963), 789 †:

"The equal protection of the laws is a 'pledge of the protection of equal laws.' But laws may classify. And 'the very idea of classification is that of inequality.' In tackling this paradox the Court has neither abandoned the demand for equality nor denied the legislative right to classify. It has taken a middle course. It has resolved the contradictory demands of legislative specialization and constitutional generality by a doctrine of reasonable classification.

"The essence of that doctrine can be stated with deceptive simplicity. The Constitution does not require that things different in fact be treated in law as though they were the same. But it does require, in its concern for equality, that those who are similarly situated be similarly treated. The measure of the reasonableness of a classification is the degree of its success in treating similarly those similarly situated.

* F. S. Royster Guano Co. v. Virginia, 253 U.S. 412, 415 (1920).

† Reprinted with the permission of the publisher, © 1949, California Law Review, Inc.

"[W]here are we to look for the test of similarity of situation which determines the reasonableness of a classification? The inescapable answer is that we must look beyond the classification to the purpose of the law. A reasonable classification is one which includes all persons who are similarly situated with respect to the purpose of the law.

"The purpose of a law may be either the elimination of a public 'mischief' or the achievement of some positive public good. To simplify the discussion we shall refer to the purpose of a law in terms of the elimination of mischief, since the same argument holds in either case. We shall speak of the defining character of characteristics of the legislative classification as the trait. We can thus speak of the relation of the classification to the purpose of the law as the relation of the Trait to the Mischief.

"[In the usual problem,] we are really dealing with the relation of two classes to each other. The first class consists of all individuals possessing the defining Trait; the second class consists of all individuals possessing, or rather, tainted by, the Mischief at which the law aims. The former is the legislative classification; the latter is the class of those similarly situated with respect to the purpose of the law. We shall refer to these two classes as T and M respectively.

"Now, since the reasonableness of any class T depends entirely upon its relation to a class M, it is obvious that it is impossible to pass judgment on the reasonableness of a classification without taking into consideration, or identifying, the purpose of the law. . . .

"There are five possible relationships between the class defined by the Trait and the class defined by the Mischief. These relationships can be indicated by the following diagrams:

(1)	(MT)	: All T's are M's and all M's are T's
(2)	(T)(M)	: No T's are M's
(3)	(M over T)	: All T's are M's but some M's are not T's
(4)	(T over M)	: All M's are T's but some T's are not M's
(5)	(T⌒M)	: Some T's are M's; some T's are not M's; and some M's are not T's

One of these five relationships holds in fact in any case of legislative classification, and we will consider each from the point of view of its 'reasonableness.'

"The first two situations represent respectively the ideal limits of reasonableness and unreasonableness. . . .

"Classification of the third type may be called 'under-inclusive.' All who are included in the class are tainted with the mischief, but there are others also tainted whom the classification does not include. Since the classification does not include all who are similarly situated with respect to the purpose of the law, there is a prima facie violation of the equal protection requirement of reasonable classification.

"But the Court has recognized the very real difficulties under which legislatures operate—difficulties arising out of both the nature of the legislative process and of the society which legislation attempts perennially to reshape— and it has refused to strike down indiscriminately all legislation embodying the classificatory inequality here under consideration.

"In justifying this refusal, the Court has defended under-inclusive classifications on such grounds as: the legislature may attack a general problem in a piecemeal fashion; 'some play must be allowed for the joints of the machine'; . . . 'the law does all that is needed when it does all that it can' . . .

"The fourth type of classification imposes a burden upon a wider range of individuals than are included in the class of those tainted with the mischief at which the law aims. It can thus be called 'over-inclusive.' . . . It is exemplified by the quarantine and the dragnet. The wartime treatment of American citizens of Japanese ancestry is a striking recent instance of the imposition of burdens upon a large class of individuals because some of them were believed to be disloyal. . . .

"The final situation to be considered is one in which the previously discussed factors of under-inclusiveness and over-inclusiveness are both present. While it may seem paradoxical to assert that a classification can be at once over-inclusive and under-inclusive, many classifications do, in fact, fall into this category, that is, they can be challenged separately on both grounds.

"For example, in the Hirabayashi case [Hirabayashi v. United States, 320 U.S. 81 (1943)] the classification of 'American citizens of Japanese ancestry' for the purpose of meeting the dangers of sabotage can be challenged both on the grounds that it is under-inclusive, since others—American citizens of German or Italian ancestry—are equally under the strain of divided loyalties, and that it is over-inclusive, since it is not supposed that all American citizens of Japanese ancestry are disloyal. The sustaining of this classification, therefore, requires both the finding of sufficient emergency to justify the imposition of a burden upon a larger class than is believed tainted with the Mischief and the establishment of 'fair reasons' for failure to extend the operation of the law to a wider class of potential saboteurs. . . . . "

In considering the applications of the traditional approach in the cases in this section, consider the observation that typical formulations—e. g., a classification must include "all [and only those] persons who are similarly situated with respect to the purpose of the law"—are "outwardly simple" but entail "some complex judgments": "First, how is the purpose of the law to be determined with respect to each separate statutory classification? Second, what does similarly situated mean and to what extent will the state be allowed to group together persons who are not quite similarly situated? The decisions dealing with economic regulation indicate that in this context the courts have used concepts of purpose and similar situation which give considerable leeway to the legislature. However, when suspect classifications or fundamental interests are involved, this leeway has been severely narrowed." "Developments in the Law—Equal Protection," 82 Harv.L.Rev. 1065, 1076 (1969).

To what extent were the classifications involved in the cases which follow in this section "overinclusive" or "underinclusive"? Should they have survived scrutiny under the traditional criteria? Should stricter scrutiny and heavier burdens of justification have been imposed?

RAILWAY EXPRESS AGENCY v. NEW YORK

336 U.S. 106, 69 S.Ct. 463, 93 L.Ed. 533 (1949).

Appeal from the Court of Appeals of New York.

Mr. Justice DOUGLAS delivered the opinion of the Court.

Section 124 of the Traffic Regulations of the City of New York promulgated by the Police Commissioner provides:

> "No person shall operate, or cause to be operated, in or upon any street an advertising vehicle; provided that nothing herein contained shall prevent the putting of business notices upon business delivery vehicles, so long as such vehicles are engaged in the usual business or regular work of the owner and not used merely or mainly for advertising."

Appellant is engaged in a nation-wide express business. It operates about 1,900 trucks in New York City and sells the space on the exterior sides of these trucks for advertising. That advertising is for the most part unconnected with its own business. It was convicted in the magistrate's court and fined. . . . .

The Court of Special Sessions concluded that advertising on vehicles using the streets of New York City constitutes a distraction to vehicle drivers and to pedestrians alike and therefore affects the safety of the public in the use of the streets. We do not sit to weigh evidence on the due process issue in order to determine whether the regulation is sound or appropriate; nor is it our function to pass judgment on its wisdom. See Olsen v. Nebraska, 313 U.S. 236. We would be trespassing on one of the most intensely local and specialized of all municipal problems if we held that this regulation had no relation to the traffic problem of New York City. It is the judgment of the local authorities that it does have such a relation. And nothing has been advanced which shows that to be palpably false.

The question of equal protection of the laws is pressed more strenuously on us. It is pointed out that the regulation draws the line between advertisements of products sold by the owner of the truck and general advertisements. It is argued that unequal treatment on the basis of such a distinction is not justified by the aim and purpose of the regulation. It is said, for example, that one of appellant's trucks carrying the advertisement of a commercial house would not cause any greater distraction of pedestrians and vehicle drivers than if the commercial house carried the same advertisement on its own truck. Yet the regulation allows the latter to do what the former is forbidden from doing. It is therefore contended that the classification which the regulation makes has no relation to the traffic problem since a violation turns not on what kind of advertisements are carried on trucks but on whose trucks they are carried.

That, however, is a superficial way of analyzing the problem . . . . . The local authorities may well have concluded that those who advertise their own wares on their trucks do not present the same traffic problem in view of the nature or extent of the advertising which they use. It would take a degree of omniscience which we lack to say that such is not the case. If that judgment is correct, the advertising displays that are exempt have less incidence on traffic than those of appellants.

We cannot say that that judgment is not an allowable one. Yet if it is, the classification has relation to the purpose for which it is made and does not contain the kind of discrimination against which the Equal Protection Clause affords protection.   It is by such practical considerations based on experience rather than by theoretical inconsistencies that the question of equal protection is to be answered.   .   .   .   And the fact that New York City sees fit to eliminate from traffic this kind of distraction but does not touch what may be even greater ones in a different category, such as the vivid displays on Times Square, is immaterial.   It is no requirement of equal protection that all evils of the same genus be eradicated or none at all.   .   .   .

Affirmed.

Mr. Justice RUTLEDGE acquiesces in the Court's opinion and judgment, *dubitante* on the question of equal protection of the laws.

Mr. Justice JACKSON, concurring.   .   .   .   .

My philosophy as to the relative readiness with which we should resort to [the due process and equal protection] clauses is almost diametrically opposed to the philosophy which prevails on this Court.   While claims of denial of equal protection are frequently asserted, they are rarely sustained.   But the Court frequently uses the due process clause to strike down measures taken by municipalities to deal with activities in their streets and public places which the local authorities consider as creating hazards, annoyances or discomforts to their inhabitants.   And I have frequently dissented when I thought local power was improperly denied.   See, for example [Saia v. New York, chap. 15, p. 1150, infra].

The burden should rest heavily upon one who would persuade us to use the due process clause to strike down a substantive law or ordinance.   Even its provident use against municipal regulations frequently disables all government —state, municipal and federal—from dealing with the conduct in question because the requirement of due process is also applicable to State and Federal Governments.   Invalidation of a statute or an ordinance on due process grounds leaves ungoverned and ungovernable conduct which many people find objectionable.

Invocation of the equal protection clause, on the other hand, does not disable any governmental body from dealing with the subject at hand.   It merely means that the prohibition or regulation must have a broader impact.   I regard it as a salutary doctrine that cities, states and the Federal Government must exercise their powers so as not to discriminate between their inhabitants except upon some reasonable differentiation fairly related to the object of regulation. [T]here is no more effective practical guaranty against arbitrary and unreasonable government than to require that the principles of law which officials would impose upon a minority must be imposed generally.   .   .   .   Courts can take no better measure to assure that laws will be just than to require that laws be equal in operation.

This case affords an illustration.   Even casual observations from the sidewalks of New York will show that an ordinance which would forbid all advertising on vehicles would run into conflict with many interests, including some, if not all, of the great metropolitan newspapers, which use that advertising extensively.   .   .   .   But any regulation applicable to all such advertising would require much clearer justification in local conditions to enable its enactment than does some regulation applicable to a few.   I do not mention this to criticize the motives of those who enacted this ordinance, but it dramatizes the point that we are much more likely to find arbitrariness in the regulation of the few than of the many. Hence, for my part, I am more receptive to attack on local ordinances for denial of equal protection than for denial of due process, while the Court has more often used the latter clause.

In this case, if the City of New York should assume that display of any advertising on vehicles tends and intends to distract the attention of persons using the highways and to increase the dangers of its traffic, I should think it fully within its constitutional powers to forbid it all. . . . Instead of such general regulation of advertising, however, the City seeks to reduce the hazard only by saying that while some may, others may not exhibit such appeals. The same display, for example, advertising cigarettes, which this appellant is forbidden to carry on its trucks, may be carried on the trucks of a cigarette dealer and might on the trucks of this appellant if it dealt in cigarettes. . . .

The City urges that this applies equally to all persons of a permissible classification, because, [while it] does not eliminate vehicular advertising, it does eliminate such advertising for hire and to this extent cuts down the hazard sought to be controlled.

. . . There is not even a pretense here that the traffic hazard created by the advertising which is forbidden is in any manner or degree more hazardous than that which is permitted. It is urged with considerable force that this local regulation does not comply with the equal protection clause because it applies unequally upon classes whose differentiation is in no way relevant to the objects of the regulation.

As a matter of principle and in view of my attitude toward the equal protection clause, I do not think differences of treatment under law should be approved on classification because of differences unrelated to the legislative purpose. The equal protection clause ceases to assure either equality or protection if it is avoided by any conceivable difference that can be pointed out between those bound and those left free. This Court has often announced the principle that the differentiation must have an appropriate relation to the object of the legislation or ordinance. . . .

The question in my mind comes to this. Where individuals contribute to an evil or danger in the same way and to the same degree, may those who do so for hire be prohibited, while those who do so for their own commercial ends but not for hire be allowed to continue? I think the answer has to be that the hireling may be put in a class by himself and may be dealt with differently than those who act on their own. But this is not merely because such a discrimination will enable the lawmaker to diminish the evil. That might be done by many classifications, which I should think wholly unsustainable. It is rather because there is a real difference between doing in self-interest and doing for hire, so that it is one thing to tolerate action from those who act on their own and it is another thing to permit the same action to be promoted for a price. . . .

Of course, this appellant did not hold itself out to carry or display everybody's advertising, and its rental of space on the sides of its trucks was only incidental to the main business which brought its trucks into the streets. But it is not difficult to see that, in a day of extravagant advertising more or less subsidized by tax deduction, the rental of truck space could become an obnoxious enterprise. While I do not think highly of this type of regulation, that is not my business, and in view of the control I would concede to cities to protect citizens in quiet and orderly use for their proper purposes of the highways and public places   .   .   ., I think the judgment below must be affirmed.

THE TRADITIONAL APPROACH IN OPERATION: RESTRICTIONS ON BUSINESS ENTRY

Some introductory questions. In the cases that follow, the Court rejected equal protection challenges to statutes charged with being "underinclusive" protections of a favored interest group. Were these situations in which Justice Jackson's Railway Express suggestion should have been heeded: Should the Court have insisted that the regulations "must have a broader impact," to safeguard against arbitrary action? Should the Court have demanded closer relationships between classifications and purposes? Should the Court have used less imaginativeness to think of conceivable rationales that *might* have influenced a hypothetical legislature? Should it have probed further to assess "real" purposes and motives? Could greater scrutiny of rationality of means or actuality of purposes be defended in these cases without abandoning the modern deferential stance toward most economic regulations challenged under substantive due process or equal protection? Note that in most of these cases several modern Justices did dissent—unlike the usually unanimous non-interventionist position in the substantive due process cases. (See also the comments in note 5, infra.) Should some of the interests affected in these cases have been considered "fundamental," warranting the exercise of the stricter judicial scrutiny characteristic of the cases in the subsequent sections of this chapter?

1. *Goesaert and women bartenders.* Goesaert v. Cleary, 335 U.S. 464 (1948), sustained a Michigan statute which provided that no woman could obtain a bartender's license unless she was "the wife or daughter of the male owner" of a licensed liquor establishment. In rejecting the equal protection challenge, Justice Frankfurter stated: "While Michigan may deny to all women opportunities for bartending, Michigan cannot play favorites among women without rhyme or reason. . . . Since bartending by women may, in the allowable legislative judgment, give rise to moral and social problems against which it may devise preventive measures, the legislature need not go to the full length of the prohibition if it believes that as to a defined group of females other factors are operating which either eliminate or reduce the moral and social problems otherwise calling for prohibition. Michigan evidently believes that the oversight assured through ownership of a bar by a barmaid's husband or father minimizes hazards that may confront a barmaid without such protecting oversight. This Court is certainly not in a position to gainsay such belief by the Michigan legislature. If it is entertainable, as we think it is, Michigan has not violated its duty to afford equal protection of its laws. We cannot cross-examine either actually or argumentatively the mind of Michigan legislators nor question their motives. Since the line they have drawn is not without a basis in reason, we cannot give ear to the suggestion that the real impulse behind this legislation was an unchivalrous desire of male bartenders to try to monopolize the calling."

Justice Rutledge, joined by Justices Douglas and Murphy, dissented: "While the equal protection clause does not require a legislature to achieve 'abstract symmetry' or to classify with 'mathematical nicety,' that clause does require lawmakers to refrain from invidious distinctions of the sort drawn by the statute challenged in this case. The statute arbitrarily discriminates between male and female owners of liquor establishments. A male owner although he himself is always absent from his bar, may employ his wife and daughter as barmaids. A female owner may neither work as a barmaid herself nor employ her daughter in that position, even if a man is always present in the establishment to keep order. This inevitable result of the classification belies the assumption that the statute was motivated by a legislative solicitude for the moral and physical well-being of women who, but for the law, would be employed as barmaids. Since there could be no other conceivable justification for such discrimination against women owners of liquor establishments, the statute should be held invalid as a denial of equal protection."

2. *Daniel and funeral insurance.* In Daniel v. Family Sec. Life Ins. Co., 336 U.S. 220 (1949), a South Carolina statute provided that life insurance companies and their agents may not operate an undertaking business, and undertakers may not serve as agents for life insurance companies. The appellee was the only company selling "funeral insurance" in South Carolina; most of its agents were undertakers. A three-judge district court held that the law violated the due process and equal protection clauses. The Supreme Court unanimously reversed.

Justice Murphy's opinion noted that the state might well have been concerned about "the beneficiary's tendency to deliver the policy's proceeds to the agent-undertaker for whatever funeral the money will buy, whether or not an expensive ceremony is consistent with the needs of the survivors." The Court summarily rejected the argument "that the 'insurance lobby' obtained this statute" from the legislature: The Court "must judge by results . . . . We cannot undertake a search for motive in testing constitutionality." On the claim that there was "no evil to be corrected" by the legislation, the Court replied: "We are not equipped to decide desirability; a court cannot eliminate measures which do not happen to suit its tastes if it seeks to maintain a democratic system. . . . We cannot say that South Carolina is not entitled to call the funeral insurance business an evil. Nor can we say that the statute has no relation to the elimination of those evils. There our inquiry must stop."

3. *Kotch and river pilots.* In Kotch v. Board of River Port Pilot Comm'rs, 330 U.S. 552 (1947), Louisiana's pilotage laws required that state pilots guide all ships going through the Mississippi River approaches to New Orleans. New pilots were appointed by the governor upon certification of names by a board composed of pilots. Only those with six months apprenticeship under an incumbent pilot were eligible for certification. Administration of the system was attacked on the ground that the board certified only relatives and friends of the incumbents.

The Supreme Court, in a 5:4 decision, rejected the equal protection challenge. Justice Black relied on the "entirely unique" nature of pilotage "in the light of its history in Louisiana": The object of the system "is to secure . . . the safest and most efficiently operated pilotage system practicable. We cannot say that the method adopted . . . is unrelated to this objective." He mentioned "the benefits to morale and esprit de corps which family and neighborly tradition might contribute" as one of the useful functions "a closely knit pilotage system may serve." Justice Rutledge, joined by Justices Reed, Douglas and Murphy, dissented: "Blood is, in effect, made the crux of selection." Even if the classification was related to the purpose of the system—even if family ties made the system more efficient—a standard of "race or consanguinity" was impermissible. Accordingly, the system was invalid for "unconstitutional administration," though valid on its face. (On racial classifications, see chap. 18, p. 1399, infra.)

4. *Lee Optical and opticians.* Recall that in Williamson v. Lee Optical Co., 348 U.S. 483 (1955) (printed in chap. 13, p. 976, supra), one of the challenges rested on equal protection rather than due process—and was as easily rejected by the Court. The lower court had held that Oklahoma's regulations regarding the handling of optical appliances, violated equal protection in subjecting opticians to the statute while exempting all sellers of ready-to-wear glasses. Justice Douglas' perfunctory reply, for the unanimous Court, was:

"The problem of legislative classification is a perennial one, admitting of no doctrinaire definition. Evils in the same field may be of different dimensions and proportions, requiring different remedies. Or so the legislature may think. Or the reform may take one step at a time, addressing itself to the phase of the problem which seems most acute to the legislative mind. The legislature may select one phase of one field and apply a remedy there, neglecting the others. The prohibition of the Equal Protection Clause goes no further than the invidious discrimination. We cannot say that that point has been reached here. For all this record shows, the ready-to-wear branch of this business may not loom large in Oklahoma or may present problems of regulation distinct from the other branch."

5. *Some concluding comments, on Morey, "selective intervention," and McGowan.* a. *Morey.* Compare with the rejection of the challenges in the preceding case the 1957 decision in Morey v. Doud, infra—the only regulation of business activities invalidated under the 14th Amendment since the abandonment of the Lochner approach in the thirties. Was there greater justification for invalidating in Morey than in the previous cases? Is the departure from permissiveness and the return to occasional intervention in Morey limited to closed, named class situations as in the American Express exemption in Morey? Should it be? (Recall the questions at the end of chap. 13, p. 981, supra.)

b. *"Selective intervention."* Note the effort to explain Justice Douglas' move "from abdication to selective intervention" by voting to invalidate several economic regulations, including Goesaert and Kotch, supra, and Morey, infra, in Karst, "Invidious Discrimination: Justice Douglas and the Return of the 'Natural-Law-Due-Process Formula,'" 16 U.C.L.A. Law Rev. 716 (1969). Karst notes that in each case the state was perpetuating "economic advantages for a favored group, at the expense of those who claimed to be relatively disadvantaged. The appeal of such an argument to a Justice with strong egalitarian views is great, great enough in these cases to overcome the inclination to keep the judiciary aloof from decisions about economic regulation."

But what about Justice Douglas' opinion in Lee Optical? That, Karst suggests, is distinguishable because there "the losers in the legislature were not permanently disadvantaged minorities. The opticians might well have anticipated new legislative alliances" [though, he concedes in a footnote, "the opticians are still looking for such an alliance"]. There were no such legislative alliance prospects for the excluded groups in Kotch and Goesaert, according to Karst. (But on that criterion, he adds, the "unfortunate" vote in Morey "is out of line.") In short, "consciously or not," the Douglas record accords with "a principle of activism in the cause of economic opportunity"—a principle which is "the equal protection analogue of the double standard of judicial review under the due process clauses, enunciated in Justice Stone's footnote 4 [chap. 15, p. 1051, infra], which made the legitimacy of judicial protection of the losers in the legislative process turn on the losers' long-term chances of becoming winners."

See the comments at p. 1052, infra, on the "protecting losing minorities" aspect of Justice Stone's Carolene Products footnote. Does application of that "losing minorities" rationale to losing *economic* (in addition to racial and religious) minorities abandon any effort to justify different levels of scrutiny in "economic" and "personal rights" litigation and substitute a single "standard" of intervening whenever an injustice is sufficiently blatant in the eyes of the Court? Is such a view in effect an acknowledgment that what was wrong with the Lochner era "superlegislature" Court was not its role but its composition? Cf. Karst, supra, at 746: "Perhaps . . . activism offers no particular risk to the judiciary's independence unless it is directed at the wrong substantive ends." (See also the additional comments on Karst infra, at p. 1046.)

c. *McGowan.* In a group of cases in 1961, state Sunday closing laws were sustained against challenges based on the two religion clauses of the First Amendment (see chap. 17, p. 1371, infra) as well as on equal protection. The Court rejected the latter attack by applying traditional, permissive standards. Why, in the context of First Amendment claims, was not a stricter judicial scrutiny appropriate, akin to that in the "fundamental interests" areas in the later sections of this chapter? In McGowan v. Maryland, 366 U.S. 420 (1961), for example, Chief Justice Warren spoke for a unanimous Court in rejecting the claim that the exemptions in the Maryland law violated equal protection. One of the provisions, for example, banned the Sunday sale of all merchandise "except the retail sale of tobacco products, confectioneries, milk, bread, fruits, gasoline, greases, drugs and medicines, and newspapers and periodicals." Chief Justice Warren stated:

"Although no precise formula has been developed, the Court has held that the Fourteenth Amendment permits the States a wide scope of discretion in enacting laws which affect some groups of citizens differently than others. The constitutional safeguard is offended only if the classification rests on grounds wholly irrelevant to the achievement of the State's objective. State legislatures are presumed to have acted within their constitutional power despite the fact that, in practice, their laws result in some inequality. A statutory discrimination will not be set aside if any state of facts reasonably may be conceived to justify it. . . . *

---

* See also the extremely permissive restatement of the traditional criteria by Chief Justice Warren in McDonald v. Board of Election, 394 U.S. 802 (1969) (after articulating the "exacting approach" of the new equal protection in the passage noted infra, p. 1012).

The "traditional" criteria included the following: "Legislatures are presumed to have acted constitutionally even if source materials normally resorted to for ascertaining their grounds for action are otherwise silent, and their statutory classifications will be set

"It would seem that a legislature could reasonably find that the Sunday sale of the exempted commodities was necessary either for the health of the populace or for the enhancement of the recreational atmosphere of the day . . .. The record is barren of any indication that this apparently reasonable basis does not exist, that the statutory distinctions are invidious, that local tradition and custom might not rationally call for this legislative treatment."

MOREY v. DOUD

354 U.S. 457, 77 S.Ct. 1344, 1 L.Ed.2d 1485 (1957).

Appeal from the United States District Court for the Northern District of Illinois.

Mr. Justice BURTON delivered the opinion of the Court.

This case concerns the validity of a provision in the Illinois Community Currency Exchanges Act, as amended, excepting money orders of the American Express Company from the requirement that any firm selling or issuing money orders in the State must secure a license and submit to state regulation. The objection raised is that this exception results in a denial of equal protection of the laws . . . to those who are subjected to the requirements of the Act. For the reasons hereafter stated, we hold that the Act is invalid as applied to others because of this discriminatory exception.

The appellees in this case are Doud, McDonald and Carlson, partners doing business as Bondified Systems, and Derrick, their agent. The partnership has an exclusive right to sell "Bondified" money orders in Illinois, directly or through agents. It contemplates selling these money orders in Illinois through agents principally engaged in operating retail drug or grocery stores. Derrick is the proprietor of a drug store in Illinois and operates a "Bondified" agency in that store. [The three-judge district court enjoined enforcement of the Act.][1] . . .

During the early 1930's, the closing of many banks in the Chicago area led to the development of simple banking facilities called currency exchanges. The principal activities of these exchanges were the cashing of checks for a fee and the selling of money orders. The fact that many of these exchanges went into business without adequate capital and without sufficient safeguards to protect the public resulted in the enactment of the Illinois Community Currency Exchanges Act in 1943. . . .

The following definition of a "community currency exchange" is crucial to this case:

" 'Community currency exchange' means any person, firm, . . . or corporation . . ., *engaged in the business of selling or issuing money orders under his or their or its name, or any other money orders (other than* United States Post Office money orders, *American Express Company money order[s]*, Postal Telegraph Company money orders, or

---

aside only if no grounds can be conceived to justify them." Does even a basic stance of permissiveness require leaning over backwards to quite that degree?

[1.] In so holding, the District Court declined to follow the Supreme Court of Illinois in sustaining the Act against a similar attack. . . . [Footnote by the Court.]

Western Union Telegraph Company money orders) . . .." (Emphasis supplied.) . . .[2]

[S]ince the Act bars the sale of money orders as a part of another business, the partnership is precluded from establishing outlets for the sale of "Bondified" money orders in drug and grocery stores, and Derrick is unable to secure a license for the sale of those money orders in his store. . . . Even if the partnership establishes outlets which are not a part of other businesses, those outlets will be licensed to sell "Bondified" money orders only if they show that the "convenience and advantage of the community" . . . will be promoted by the issuance of licenses to them. . . . Finally, any "Bondified" outlets will each . . . have to secure the required surety bond and insurance policy.

The American Express Company, on the other hand, because its money orders are excepted, is relieved of these licensing and regulatory requirements, and appears to be exempt from any regulation in Illinois. The American Express Company [organized in 1868] conducts a world-wide business which includes the sale of money orders. It sells money orders in Illinois in substantially the same manner as is contemplated by the "Bondified" partnership, through authorized agents located in drug and grocery stores. Since American Express money orders are not subject to the Act, they are sold legally in those stores as a part of their business. American Express outlets may be established without regard to the "convenience and advantage" of the community in which they operate. Finally, those outlets need not pay licensing and inspection fees nor file surety bonds and insurance policies with the State.

In determining the constitutionality of the Act's application to appellees in the light of its exception of American Express money orders, we start with the established proposition that the "prohibition of the Equal Protection Clause goes no further than the invidious discrimination." Williamson v. Lee Optical Co., 348 U.S. 483, 489. The rules for testing a discrimination have been summarized as follows:

> "1. The equal protection clause of the Fourteenth Amendment does not take from the State the power to classify in the adoption of police laws, but admits of the exercise of a wide scope of discretion in that regard, and avoids what is done only when it is without any reasonable basis and therefore is purely arbitrary. 2. A classification having some reasonable basis does not offend against that clause merely because it is not made with mathematical nicety or because in practice it results in some inequality. 3. When the classification in such a law is called in question, if any state of facts reasonably can be conceived that would sustain it, the existence of that state of facts at the time the law was enacted must be assumed. 4. One who assails the classification in such a law must carry the burden of showing that it does not rest upon any reason-

---

2. Appellees do not question the exception from the Act of the money orders of the United States Post Office, the Postal Telegraph Company and the Western Union Telegraph Company. In Currency Services, Inc. v. Matthews, 90 F.Supp. 40, 43, a three-judge District Court upheld the exception of these money orders from a similar Wisconsin statute. The court concluded that the State was without authority to regulate the sale of the United States Post Office money orders, and that the exception of Western Union money orders was reasonable since that company was regulated both by the Federal Communications Commission and by a state commission. It noted that the Postal Telegraph Company has merged with the Western Union Telegraph Company. [Footnote by the Court.]

able basis, but is essentially arbitrary."   Lindsley v. Natural Carbonic Gas Co., 220 U.S. 61, 78–79 [1911].

To these rules we add the caution that "Discriminations of an unusual character especially suggest careful consideration to determine whether they are obnoxious to the constitutional provision."   Louisville Gas Co. v. Coleman, 277 U.S. 32, 37–38 [1928]   . . ..

. . . If the exception [of American Express] is to be upheld, it must be on the basis on which it is cast—an exception of a particular business entity and not of a generic category.   The purpose of the Act's licensing and regulatory provisions clearly is to protect the public when dealing with currency exchanges.   Because the American Express Company is a world-wide enterprise of unquestioned solvency and high financial standing, the State argues that the legislative classification is reasonable.   . . . .

That the Equal Protection Clause does not require that every state regulatory statute apply to all in the same business is a truism.   For example, where size is an index to the evil at which the law is directed, discriminations between the large and the small are permissible.[3]   Moreover, we have repeatedly recognized that "reform may take one step at a time, addressing itself to the phase of the problem which seems most acute to the legislative mind."   Williamson v. Lee Optical Co., 348 U.S. 483, 489.   On the other hand, a statutory discrimination must be based on differences that are reasonably related to the purposes of the Act in which it is found.   Smith v. Cahoon, 283 U.S. 553 [1931], involved a state statute which required motor vehicles, operating on local highways as carriers for hire, to furnish bonds or insurance policies for the protection of the public against injuries received through negligence in these operations.   The Act excepted motor vehicles carrying specified products.   This Court held that the exception violated the Equal Protection Clause since the statutory purpose of protecting the public could not reasonably support a discrimination between the carrying of exempt products like farm produce and of regulated products like groceries.   " 'Such a classification is not based on anything having relation to the purpose for which it is made.' "   Id., at 567.

Of course, distinctions in the treatment of business entities engaged in the same business activity may be justified by genuinely different characteristics of the business involved.[4]   This is so even where the discrimination is by name.[5] But distinctions cannot be so justified if the "discrimination has no reasonable relation to these differences."   Hartford Co. v. Harrison, 301 U.S. 459, 463

---

3.   See Engel v. O'Malley, 219 U.S. 128, 138 (exception of businesses in which the average sum received for safekeeping or transmission was more than $500 from licensing requirements intended to protect the small depositor); see also, New York, N. H. & H. R. Co. v. New York, 165 U.S. 628 (exception of railroads less than 50 miles in length from a statute regulating the heating of railroad passenger cars and the placing of guards and guard posts on railroad bridges); Miller v. Strahl, 239 U.S. 426 (exception of hotels with less than 50 rooms from a statute requiring hotelkeepers to take certain fire precautions). [Footnote by the Court.]

4.   See German Alliance Ins. Co. v. Lewis, 233 U.S. 389 (exception of farmers' mutual insurance companies doing only farm business from a statute establishing rate regulation for fire insurance companies); Hoopeston Canning Co. v. Cullen, 318 U.S. 313 (different regulatory requirements for reciprocals and mutual companies). [Footnote by the Court.]

5.   See Erb v. Morasch, 177 U.S. 584 (exception of a named railroad from an ordinance limiting the speed of trains in a city) . . . .. [Footnote by the Court.]

[1937]. In that case, this Court held that a state statute which permitted mutual insurance companies to act through salaried resident employees, but which excluded stock insurance companies from the same privilege, violated the Equal Protection Clause.

The principles controlling in the Smith and Hartford Co. cases, supra, are applicable here. The provisions in the Illinois Act, such as those requiring an annual inspection of licensed community currency exchanges by the State Auditor, make it clear that the statute was intended to afford the public *continuing* protection. The discrimination in favor of the American Express Company does not conform to this purpose. The exception of its money orders apparently rests on the legislative hypothesis that the characteristics of the American Express Company make it unnecessary to regulate their sales. Yet these sales, by virtue of the exception, will continue to be unregulated whether or not the American Express Company retains its present characteristics. On the other hand, sellers of competing money orders are subject to the Act even though their characteristics are, or become, substantially identical with those the American Express Company now has. Moreover, the Act's blanket exception takes no account of the characteristics of the local outlets that sell American Express money orders, and the distinct possibility that they in themselves may afford less protection to the public than do the retail establishments that sell competing money orders. That the American Express Company is a responsible institution operating on a world-wide basis does not minimize the fact that when the public buys American Express money orders in local drug and grocery stores it relies in part on the reliability of the selling agents.

The effect of the discrimination is to create a closed class by singling out American Express money orders. The singling out of the money orders of one company is in a sense the converse of a case like Cotting v. Kansas City Stock Yards Co., 183 U.S. 79, 114–115 [1901]. . . . In the Cotting case this Court held that a regulatory statute that in fact applied to only one stockyard in a State violated the Equal Protection Clause. Although statutory discriminations creating a closed class have been upheld,[6] a statute which established a closed class was held to violate the Equal Protection Clause where, on its face, it was "an attempt to give an economic advantage to those engaged in a given business at an arbitrary date as against all those who enter the industry after that date." Mayflower Farms, Inc. v. Ten Eyck, 297 U.S. 266, 274 [1936]. The statute involved in that case granted a differential from the regulated price at which dealers could sell milk to those dealers in a specified class who were in business before April 10, 1933.

Unlike the American Express Company, appellees and others are barred from selling money orders in retail establishments. Even if competing outlets can successfully be established as separate businesses, their ability to secure licenses depends upon a showing of "convenience and advantage." Perhaps such a showing could not be made because the unregulated American Express Company had already established outlets in the community. And even if licenses were secured, the licensees would be required to pay licensing and investigatory fees and purchase surety bonds and insurance policies—costs that the American Express Company and its agents are not required to bear. The fact

---

6. See Watson v. Maryland, 218 U.S. 173 (exception of physicians who practiced prior to a specified date and treated at least 12 persons within a   year prior thereto from examination and certificate requirements). . . . [Footnote by the Court.]

that the activities of the American Express Company are far-flung does not minimize the impact on local affairs and on competitors of its sale of money orders in Illinois. This is not a case in which the Fourteenth Amendment is being invoked to protect a business from the general hazards of competition. The hazards here have their roots in the statutory discrimination.

Taking all of these factors in conjunction—the remote relationship of the statutory classification to the Act's purpose or to business characteristics, and the creation of a closed class by the singling out of the money orders of a named company, with accompanying economic advantages—we hold that the application of the Act to appellees deprives them of equal protection of the laws. . . .

Affirmed.

Mr. Justice BLACK, dissenting. . . .

[W]hatever one may think of the merits of this legislation, its exemption of a company of known solvency from a solvency test applied to others of unknown financial responsibility can hardly be called "invidious." Unless state legislatures have power to make distinctions that are not plainly unreasonable, then the ability of the States to protect their citizens by regulating business within their boundaries can be seriously impaired. I feel it necessary to express once again my objection to the use of general provisions of the Constitution to restrict narrowly state power over state domestic economic affairs.
. . .

Mr. Justice FRANKFURTER, whom Mr. Justice HARLAN joins, dissenting.

. . . As is usually true of questions arising under the Equal Protection Clause, the answer will turn on the way in which that clause is conceived. It is because of differences in judicial approach that the divisions in the Court in applying the clause have been frequent and marked. It is, I believe, accurate to summarize the matter by saying that the great divide in the decisions lies in the difference between emphasizing the actualities or the abstractions of legislation.

. . . Legislation is essentially empiric. It addresses itself to the more or less crude outside world and not to the neat, logical models of the mind. Classification is inherent in legislation; the Equal Protection Clause has not forbidden it. To recognize marked differences that exist in fact is living law; to disregard practical differences and concentrate on some abstract identities is lifeless logic.

The controlling importance of the differences in approach to a problem arising under the Equal Protection Clause is sharply illustrated by one's view of the decisions in cases like Louisville Gas Co. v. Coleman, 277 U.S. 32, and Hartford Co. v. Harrison, 301 U.S. 459. The Court relies on them. For me they are false leads. Both these decisions prevailed by the narrowest margin; both evoked powerful dissents; both manifest the requirement of nondiscriminatory classification as an exercise in logical abstractions. . . .

I regretfully find myself unable to appreciate why the State . . . may not choose to allow small units to carry on a business so fraught with public interest under the regulations devised by the statute under review, while at the same time it finds such measures of control needless in a case of "a worldwide enterprise of unquestioned solvency and high financial standing." The rational differentiation is of course that the latter enterprise contains within itself, in the judgment of Illinois, the necessary safeguards for solvency and reliability in issuing money orders and redeeming them. Surely this is a distinction of significance in fact that the law cannot view with a glass eye.

But it is suggested that the American Express Co. may not continue to retain "its present characteristics," while sellers of competing money orders may continue to be subject to the Act, even though their characteristics become "substantially identical with those the American Express Co. now has." What is this but to deny a State the right to legislate on the basis of circumstances that exist because a State may not under speculatively different circumstances that may never come to pass have such right. Surely there is time enough to strike down legislation when its constitutional justification is gone. Invalidating legislation is serious business and it ought not to be indulged in because in a situation not now before the Court, nor even remotely probable, a valid statute may lose its foundation. The Court has had occasion to deal with such contingency more than once. Regulatory measures have been sustained that later, in changed circumstances, were found to be unconstitutional. Compare . . . Block v. Hirsh, 256 U.S. 135, with Chastleton Corp. v. Sinclair, 264 U.S. 543.

. . . Neither the record nor our own judicial information affords any basis for concluding that Illinois may not put the United States Post Office, the Western Union Co., and the American Express Co. in one class and all the other money order issuers in another. . . . The vital fact is that the American Express Co. is decisely different from those money order issuers that are within the regulatory scheme. . . . Sociologically one may think what one may of the State's recognition of the special financial position obviously enjoyed by the American Express Co. Whatever one may think is none of this Court's business. In applying the Equal Protection Clause, we must be fastidiously careful to observe the admonition of Mr. Justice Brandeis, Mr. Justice Stone, and Mr. Justice Cardozo that we do not "sit as a super-legislature." . . .

SECTION 2. VOTING QUALIFICATIONS, ACCESS TO THE BALLOT, AND THE NEW EQUAL PROTECTION

BREEDLOVE v. SUTTLES

302 U.S. 277, 58 S.Ct. 205, 82 L.Ed. 252 (1937).

Appeal from the Supreme Court of Georgia.

Mr. Justice BUTLER delivered the opinion of the Court.

A Georgia statute provides that there shall be levied and collected each year from every inhabitant of the State between the ages of 21 and 60 a poll tax of one dollar, but that the tax shall not be demanded from the blind or from females who do not register for voting. . . . The state constitution declares that to entitle a person to register and vote at any election he shall have paid all poll taxes that he may have had opportunity to pay agreeably to law. . . . March 16, 1936, appellant, a white male citizen 28 years old, applied to appellee to register him for voting for federal and state officers at primary and general elections. He informed appellee he had [not] paid any poll taxes . . . .

[Appellant] asserts that the law offends the rule of equality in that it extends only to persons between the ages of 21 and 60 and to women only if they register for voting and in that it makes payment a prerequisite to registration. He does not suggest that exemption of the blind is unreasonable.

Levy by the poll has long been a familiar form of taxation, much used in some countries and to a considerable extent here, at first in the Colonies and later in the States. To prevent burdens deemed grievous and oppressive, the constitutions of some States prohibit or limit poll taxes. That of Georgia prevents more than a dollar a year. . . . Poll taxes are laid upon persons without regard to their occupations or property to raise money for the support of government or some more specific end. The equal protection clause does not require absolute equality. . . . Collection from all would be impossible for always there are many too poor to pay. Attempt equally to enforce such a measure would justify condemnation of the tax as harsh and unjust.

. . .

. . . The burden laid upon appellant is precisely that put upon other men. The rate is a dollar a year, commencing at 21 and ending at 60 years of age. The tax being upon persons, women may be exempted on the basis of special considerations to which they are naturally entitled. . . .

Payment as a prerequisite is not required for the purpose of denying or abridging the privilege of voting. It does not limit the tax to electors; aliens are not there permitted to vote, but the tax is laid upon them, if within the defined class. It is not laid upon persons 60 or more years old, whether electors or not. Exaction of payment before registration undoubledly serves to aid collection from electors desiring to vote, but that use of the State's power is not prevented by the Federal Constitution. . . .

Affirmed.

HARPER v. VIRGINIA BOARD OF ELECTIONS

383 U.S. 663, 86 S.Ct. 1079, 16 L.Ed.2d 169 (1966).

Appeal from the United States District Court for the Eastern District of Virginia.*

Mr. Justice DOUGLAS delivered the opinion of the Court.

These are suits by Virginia residents to have declared unconstitutional Virginia's poll tax. The three-judge District Court, feeling bound by our decision in [Breedlove, supra] dismissed the complaint. . . .

While the right to vote in federal elections is conferred by Art. I, § 2, of the Constitution . . ., the right to vote in state elections is nowhere expressly mentioned. It is argued that the right to vote in state elections is implicit, particularly by reason of the First Amendment, and that it may not constitutionally be conditioned upon the payment of a tax or fee. . . . We do not stop to canvass the relation between voting and political expression.

---

* Together with Butts v. Harrison, on appeal from the same court.

For it is enough to say that once the franchise is granted to the electorate, lines may not be drawn which are inconsistent with the Equal Protection Clause of the Fourteenth Amendment. That is to say, the right of suffrage "is subject to the imposition of state standards which are not discriminatory and which do not contravene any restriction that Congress, acting pursuant to its constitutional powers, has imposed." Lassiter v. Northampton Election Board, 360 U.S. 45, 51 [See chap. 6, p. 530, supra.] We were speaking there of a state literacy test which we sustained, warning that the result would be different if a literacy test, fair on its face, were used to discriminate against a class.[1] But the Lassiter case does not govern the result here, because, unlike a poll tax, the "ability to read and write . . . has some relation to standards designed to promote intelligent use of the ballot." . . .

We conclude that a State violates the Equal Protection Clause of the Fourteenth Amendment whenever it makes the affluence of the voter or payment of any fee an electoral standard. Voter qualifications have no relation to wealth nor to paying or not paying this or any other tax. Our cases demonstrate that the Equal Protection Clause of the Fourteenth Amendment restrains the States from fixing voter qualifications which invidiously discriminate. Thus without questioning the power of a State to impose reasonable residence restrictions on the availability of the ballot (see Pope v. Williams, 193 U.S. 621), we held in Carrington v. Rash, 380 U.S. 89, that a State may not deny the opportunity to vote to a bona fide resident merely because he is a member of the armed services. "By forbidding a soldier ever to controvert the presumption of non-residence, the Texas Constitution imposes an invidious discrimination in violation of the Fourteenth Amendment." . . . Previously we had said that neither homesite nor occupation "affords a permissible basis for distinguishing between qualified voters within the State." Gray v. Sanders, 372 U.S. 368, 380. We think the same must be true of requirements of wealth or affluence or payment of a fee.

Long ago in Yick Wo v. Hopkins, 118 U.S. 356, 370, the Court referred to "the political franchise of voting" as a "fundamental political right, because preservative of all rights." Recently in Reynolds v. Sims, 377 U.S. 533, 561–562 [chap. 18, p. 1438, infra], we said, "Undoubtedly, the right of suffrage is a fundamental matter in a free and democratic society. Especially since the right to exercise the franchise in a free and unimpaired manner is preservative of other basic civil and political rights, any alleged infringement of the right of citizens to vote must be carefully and meticulously scrutinized." There we were considering charges that voters in one part of the State had greater representation per person in the State Legislature than voters in another part of the State. We concluded:

"A citizen, a qualified voter, is no more nor no less so because he lives in the city or on the farm. This is the clear and strong command of our Constitution's Equal Protection Clause. This is an essential part of the concept of a government of laws and not men. This is at the heart of Lincoln's vision of 'government of the people, by the people, [and] for the people.' The Equal Protection Clause demands no less

1. . . . While the "Virginia poll tax was born of a desire to disenfranchise the Negro" (Harman v. Forssenius, 380 U.S. 528, 543) we do not stop to determine whether on this record the Virginia tax in its modern setting serves the same end. [Footnote by the Court.]

than substantially equal state legislative representation for all citizens, of all places as well as of all races."

We say the same whether the citizen, otherwise qualified to vote, has $1.50 in his pocket or nothing at all, pays the fee or fails to pay it. The principle that denies the State the right to dilute a citizen's vote on account of his economic status or other such factors by analogy bars a system which excludes those unable to pay a fee to vote or who fail to pay.

It is argued that a State may exact fees from citizens for many different kinds of licenses; that if it can demand from all an equal fee for a driver's license,[2] it can demand from all an equal poll tax for voting. But we must remember that the interest of the State, when it comes to voting, is limited to the power to fix qualifications. Wealth, like race, creed, or color, is not germane to one's ability to participate intelligently in the electoral process. Lines drawn on the basis of wealth or property, like those of race (Korematsu v. United States, 323 U.S. 214, 216) (chap. 18, p. 1402, infra), are traditionally disfavored. Griffin v. Illinois, 351 U.S. 12; Douglas v. California, 372 U.S. 353 [both sec. 3, p. 1018, infra]. To introduce wealth or payment of a fee as a measure of a voter's qualifications is to introduce a capricious or irrelevant factor. The degree of the discrimination is irrelevant. In this context—that is, as a condition of obtaining a ballot—the requirement of fee paying causes an "invidious" discrimination (Skinner v. Oklahoma, 316 U.S. 535, 541) [sec. 4, p. 1028, infra], that runs afoul of the Equal Protection Clause. Levy "by the poll," as stated in Breedlove v. Suttles, is an old familiar form of taxation; and we say nothing to impair its validity so long as it is not made a condition to the exercise of the franchise. Breedlove v. Suttles sanctioned its use as "a prerequisite of voting." To that extent the Breedlove case is overruled.

We agree, of course, with Mr. Justice Holmes that the Due Process Clause of the Fourteenth Amendment "does not enact Mr. Herbert Spencer's Social Statics" (Lochner v. New York, 198 U.S. 45, 75). Likewise, the Equal Protection Clause is not shackled to the political theory of a particular era. In determining what lines are unconstitutionally discriminatory, we have never been confined to historic notions of equality, any more than we have restricted due process to a fixed catalogue of what was at a given time deemed to be the limits of fundamental rights. See Malloy v. Hogan, 378 U.S. 1, 5–6. Notions of what constitutes equal treatment for purposes of the Equal Protection Clause *do* change. [When, in 1954,] we repudiated the "separate-but-equal" doctrine of Plessy as respects public education we stated: "In approaching this problem, we cannot turn the clock back to 1868 when the Amendment was adopted, or even to 1896 when Plessy v. Ferguson was written." Brown v. Board of Education, 347 U.S. 483, 492 [chap. 18, p. 1422, infra.]

In a recent searching re-examination of the Equal Protection Clause, we held, as already noted, that "the opportunity for equal participation by all voters in the election of state legislators" is required. [Reynolds v. Sims.] We decline to qualify that principle by sustaining this poll tax. Our conclusion, like that in Reynolds v. Sims, is founded not on what we think governmental policy should be, but on what the Equal Protection Clause requires.

---

2. Maine has a poll tax . . . which is not made a condition of voting; instead, its payment is a condition of obtaining a motor vehicle license or a motor vehicle operator's license. [Footnote by the Court.]

We have long been mindful that where fundamental rights and liberties are asserted under the Equal Protection Clause, classifications which might invade or restrain them must be closely scrutinized and carefully confined. See, e. g., [Skinner v. Oklahoma; Reynolds v. Sims; Carrington v. Rash . . . .]

Those principles apply here. For to repeat, wealth or fee paying has, in our view, no relation to voting qualifications; the right to vote is too precious, too fundamental to be so burdened or conditioned.

Reversed.

Mr. Justice BLACK, dissenting. . . .

I think the interpretation that this Court gave the Equal Protection Clause in Breedlove was correct. The mere fact that a law results in treating some groups differently from others does not, of course, automatically amount to a violation of the Equal Protection Clause. . . .

A study of our cases shows that this Court has refused to use the general language of the Equal Protection Clause as though it provided a handy instrument to strike down state laws which the Court feels are based on bad governmental policy. The equal protection cases carefully analyzed boil down to the principle that distinctions drawn and even discriminations imposed by state laws do not violate the Equal Protection Clause so long as these distinctions and discriminations are not "irrational," "irrelevant," "unreasonable," "arbitrary," or "invidious." The restrictive connotations of these terms . . . are a plain recognition of the fact that under a proper interpretation of the Equal Protection Clause States are to have the broadest kind of leeway in areas where they have a general constitutional competence to act. [I]t would be difficult to say that the poll tax requirement is "irrational" or "arbitrary" or works "invidious discriminations." State poll tax legislation can "reasonably," "rationally" and without an "invidious" or evil purpose to injure anyone be found to rest on a number of state policies including (1) the State's desire to collect its revenue, and (2) its belief that voters who pay a poll tax will be interested in furthering the State's welfare when they vote. Certainly it is rational to believe that people may be more likely to pay taxes if payment is a prerequisite to voting. And [whatever] may be our personal opinion, history is on the side of "rationality" of the State's poll tax policy. . . .

Another reason for my dissent from the Court's judgment and opinion is that it seems to be using the old "natural-law-due-process formula" to justify striking down state laws as violations of the Equal Protection Clause. . . . If basic changes as to the respective powers of the state and national governments are needed, I prefer to let those changes be made by amendment as Article V of the Constitution provides. . . .

. . . Moreover, the people, in § 5 of the Fourteenth Amendment, designated the governmental tribunal they wanted to provide additional rules to enforce the guarantees of that Amendment. The branch of Government they chose was not the Judicial Branch but the Legislative. I have no doubt at all that Congress has the power under § 5 to pass legislation to abolish the poll tax in order to protect the citizens of this country if it believes that the poll tax is being used as a device to deny voters equal protection of the law. . . . But this legislative power which was granted to Congress by

§ 5 of the Fourteenth Amendment is limited to Congress.* [F]or us to undertake in the guise of constitutional interpretation to decide the constitutional policy question of this case amounts, in my judgment, to a plain exercise of power which the Constitution has denied us but has specifically granted to Congress. . . .

Mr. Justice HARLAN, whom Mr. Justice STEWART joins, dissenting.

The final demise of state poll taxes, already totally proscribed by the Twenty-Fourth Amendment with respect to federal elections and abolished by the States themselves in all but four States with respect to state elections, is perhaps in itself not of great moment. But the fact that the *coup de grace* has been administered by this Court instead of being left to the affected States or to the federal political process [1] should be a matter of continuing concern to all interested in maintaining the proper role of this tribunal under our scheme of government. . . . My disagreement with the present decision is that in holding the Virginia poll tax violative of the Equal Protection Clause the Court has departed from long-established standards governing the application of that clause.

The Equal Protection Clause prevents States from arbitrarily treating people differently under their laws. Whether any such differing treatment is to be deemed arbitrary depends on whether or not it reflects an appropriate differentiating classification among those affected; the clause has never been thought to require equal treatment of all persons despite differing circumstances. The test evolved by this Court for determining whether an asserted justifying classification exists is whether such a classification can be deemed to be founded on some rational and otherwise constitutionally permissible state policy. . . . This standard reduces to a minimum the likelihood that the federal judiciary will judge state policies in terms of the individual notions and predilections of its own members, and until recently it has been followed in all kinds of "equal protection" cases.[2]

---

* But § 1 of the Fourteenth Amendment itself outlaws any state law which either as written or as applied discriminates against voters on account of race. Such a law can never be rational. "States may do a good deal of classifying that it is difficult to believe rational, but there are limits, and it is too clear for extended argument that color cannot be made the basis of a statutory classification affecting the right [to vote] set up in this case." Nixon v. Herndon, 273 U.S. 536, 541 (Holmes, J.). [Footnote by Justice Black.]

1. In the Senate hearings leading to the passage of the Voting Rights Act of 1965, some doubt was expressed whether state poll taxes could be validly abolished through the exercise of Congress' legislative power under § 5 of the Fourteenth Amendment. . . . I intimate no view on that question. [Footnote by Justice Harlan.]

2. I think the somewhat different application of the Equal Protection Clause to racial discrimination cases finds justification in the fact that insofar as that clause may embody a particular value in addition to rationality, the historical origins of the Civil War Amendments might attribute to racial equality this special status. See, e. g., Yick Wo v. Hopkins, 118 U.S. 356; Shelley v. Kraemer, 334 U.S. 1; Takahashi v. Fish & Game Comm'n, 334 U.S. 410; Brown v. Board of Education, 347 U.S. 483; Evans v. Newton, 382 U.S. 296; cf. Korematsu v. United States, 323 U.S. 214, 216. See Tussman & tenBroek, The Equal Protection of the Laws, 37 Calif.L.Rev. 341 (1949); Wechsler, Toward Neutral Principles of Constitutional Law, 73 Harv.L.Rev. 1, 33 (1959).

A similar characterization of indigency as a "neutral fact," irrelevant or suspect for purposes of legislative classification, has never been accepted by this Court. See Edwards v. Califor-

Reynolds v. Sims, supra, among its other breaks with the past, also marked a departure from these traditional and wise principles. . . . [Today] the Court reverts to the highly subjective judicial approach manifested by Reynolds. In substance the Court's analysis of the equal protection issue goes no further than to say that the electoral franchise is "precious" and "fundamental," and to conclude that "[t]o introduce wealth or payment of a fee as a measure of a voter's qualifications is to introduce a capricious or irrelevant factor." These are of course captivating phrases, but they are wholly inadequate to satisfy the standard governing adjudication of the equal protection issue: Is there a rational basis for Virginia's poll tax as a voting qualification? I think the answer to that question is undoubtedly "yes."

Property qualifications and poll taxes have been a traditional part of our political structure. [W]ith property qualifications, it is only by fiat that it can be said, especially in the context of American history, that there can be no rational debate as to their advisability. Most of the early Colonies had them; many of the States have had them during much of their histories; and, whether one agrees or not, arguments have been and still can be made in favor of them. For example, it is certainly a rational argument that payment of some minimal poll tax promotes civic responsibility, weeding out those who do not care enough about public affairs to pay $1.50 or thereabouts a year for the exercise of the franchise. It is also arguable, indeed it was probably accepted as sound political theory by a large percentage of Americans through most of our history, that people with some property have a deeper stake in community affairs, and are consequently more responsible, more educated, more knowledgeable, more worthy of confidence, than those without means, and that the community and Nation would be better managed if the franchise were restricted to such citizens. Nondiscriminatory and fairly applied literacy tests, upheld by this Court in [Lassiter], find justification on very similar grounds.

These viewpoints, to be sure, ring hollow on most contemporary ears. Their lack of acceptance today is evidenced by the fact that nearly all of the States, left to their own devices, have eliminated property or poll-tax qualifications; by the cognate fact that Congress and three-quarters of the States quickly ratified the Twenty-Fourth Amendment . . .. Property and poll-tax qualifications, very simply, are not in accord with current egalitarian notions of how a modern democracy should be organized. It is of course entirely fitting that legislatures should modify the law to reflect such changes in popular attitudes. However, it is all wrong, in my view, for the Court to adopt the political doctrines popularly accepted at a particular moment of our history and to declare all others to be irrational and invidious, barring them from the range of choice by reasonably minded people acting through the political process. It was not too long ago that Mr. Justice Holmes felt im-

nia, 314 U.S. 160, 184–185 (Jackson, J., concurring). Griffin v. Illinois, 351 U.S. 12, requiring free trial transcripts for indigent appellants, and Douglas v. California, 372 U.S. 353, requiring the appointment of counsel for such appellants, cannot fairly be so interpreted for although reference was made indiscriminately to both equal protection and due process the analysis was cast primarily in terms of the latter.

More explicit attempts to infuse "Equal Protection" with specific values have been unavailing. See, e. g., Patsone v. Pennsylvania, 232 U.S. 138 (alienage); West Coast Hotel Co. v. Parrish, 300 U.S. 379 (sex); Kotch v. Board of River Port Pilot Comm'rs, 330 U.S. 552, 564 (Rutledge, J., dissenting) (consanguinity). [Footnote by Justice Harlan.]

pelled to remind the Court that the Due Process Clause of the Fourteenth Amendment does not enact the *laissez-faire* theory of society, Lochner v. New York, 198 U.S. 45, 75–76. The times have changed, and perhaps it is appropriate to observe that neither does the Equal Protection Clause of that Amendment rigidly impose upon America an ideology of unrestrained egalitarianism.

. . . .

HARPER: A VOTING CASE? A POVERTY CASE?

Introduction. Are the justifications offered for the poll tax sufficient to survive the traditional "mere rationality" test? Or has the law "no relation" to any permissible state objective? If, as the dissenters argue, the classification is not wholly "irrational" in traditional terms, what explains the decision?

Harper appears to be a greater intervention than courts undertake pursuant to the old equal protection. Is that because "fundamental rights" of voting are affected—that state restrictions on voting carry an especially heavy burden of justification? Is it because of the classification criterion rather than the activity affected—because "lines drawn on the basis of wealth or property, like those of race," are "traditionally disfavored"? Were both features—effect on "fundamental rights" *and* classification by wealth—necessary to justify the high level of judicial scrutiny?

1. *Economic classifications.* Are wealth lines as traditionally disfavored as racial lines (see chap. 18, infra)? Are wealth classifications "suspect"—i. e., valid only if necessary to some compelling state interest (rather than valid so long as they are "rationally related" to some "permissible" governmental objective)? (See Michelman, "Foreword: On Protecting the Poor Through the Fourteenth Amendment," 83 Harv.L.Rev. 7 (1969).) Is the special scrutiny justified only when the formal classification is in terms of wealth? In Harper, the criterion was payment of a real tax, legally payable whether or not the taxpayer wished to vote. Was that nevertheless sufficiently close to a de jure wealth classification to warrant similar treatment?

What of a de facto wealth "classification"? Does the Harper suspiciousness of wealth lines apply to laws which bear unequally simply because of the unequal economic circumstances of the persons affected? That question is pursued further in connection with the criminal law administration cases, Griffin and Douglas, sec. 3, infra. Does the Harper attitude apply to all situations in which the state imposes fee requirements—e. g., university tuition or drivers' licenses? Or is the wealth factor important only when "fundamental" matters are affected by economic status?

Should Harper be viewed as a decision "about the interest in voting" rather than "as a statement about poverty and special judicial protection linked with that status," as suggested in Michelman, supra, at 23? Compare the voting interest developments in the cases below. The voting cases obviously form a significant part of the Harper context. Yet Harper *does* have the language about wealth, and that aspect as well receives mention in the cases. See the strong statement in McDonald v. Board of Election Commissioners, 394 U.S. 802 (1969) (note 3 infra), which sees "wealth" lines as an independent ground (apart from impact on "fundamental rights") for strict scrutiny.

2. *"Fundamental interests" and voting.* The voting context of Harper was obviously of significance to the Court, whatever the contribution of the wealth concern. How did voting become "fundamental" for federal constitutional purposes, when voting qualifications are ordinarily left to the States? A series of cases before and after Harper attest to the special scrutiny evoked by equal protection challenges in the voting context (see the next group of notes). A case of central importance in that development was the basic legislative reapportionment case, Reynolds v. Sims, 377 U.S. 533 (1964). For example, the Reynolds statement that "the right of suffrage is a fundamental matter in a free and democratic society" is quoted in Harper. (The special problems of the scope and implementation of the "one man-one vote" rule of Reynolds are traced below, chap. 18, p. 1438.)

3. *The combination of "suspect" wealth lines and "fundamental" rights.* Consider the subsequent references to Harper below in evaluating the significance of the presence of wealth criteria *and* voting rights in that case. Were both important? Were both necessary? Consider, for example, the Court's description of the new equal protection criteria in McDonald v. Board of Election Commissioners, 394 U.S. 802 (1969). Chief Justice Warren stated:

"Before confronting appellants' challenge to Illinois' absentee provisions, we must determine initially how stringent a standard to use in evaluating the classifications made thereunder and whether the distinctions must be justified by a compelling state interest; for, appellants assert that we are dealing generally with an alleged infringement of a basic, fundamental right. See, e. g. [Reynolds v. Sims; Harper]. Thus, while the "States have long been held to have broad powers to determine the conditions under which the right of suffrage may be exercised" [Lassiter], we have held that once the States grant the franchise, they must not do so in a discriminatory manner. See [Carrington v. Rash]. More importantly, however, we have held that because of the overriding importance of voting rights, classifications "which might invade or restrain them must be closely scrutinized and carefully confined" where those rights are asserted under the Equal Protection Clause [Harper]. And a careful examination on our part is especially warranted where lines are drawn on the basis of wealth or race [Harper], two factors which would independently render a classification highly suspect and thereby demand a more exacting judicial scrutiny. Douglas v. California, 372 U.S. 353 (1963) [sec. 3, p. 1021, infra.]; McLaughlin v. Florida, 379 U.S. 184, 192 (1964) [cf. Loving v. Virginia, chap. 18, p. 1412, infra.]"

[Note that not all voting litigation evokes that "exacting approach" of the new equal protection. In McDonald itself, after describing it, the Chief Justice found it "not necessary" to apply strict scrutiny to the challenged absentee ballot law—because the provisions were "not drawn on the basis of wealth or race," and because it had not been shown that they impaired "the fundamental right to vote." It was the right to receive absentee ballots, not the right to vote, that was at stake. In those circumstances, it was appropriate to apply "the more traditional standards" of equal protection, involving "wide leeway" to the states and "the presumption of statutory validity."]

VOTING RESTRICTIONS AND EQUAL PROTECTION—
BEFORE HARPER, AND SINCE

1. *Lassiter, Cardona, Carrington.*   a.   In 1959, as the Harper opinion recalls, the Court rejected an equal protection challenge to literacy tests, in Lassiter v. Northampton County Board of Elections, 360 U.S. 45.   (See chap. 6, p. 530, supra).   Justice Douglas wrote for a unanimous Court that "residence requirements, age, previous criminal record" were "obvious examples" of valid state voting qualifications.   Literacy had "some relation to standards designed to promote intelligent use of the ballot" and was "neutral on race, creed, color and sex."   He added: "Of course, a literacy test, fair on its face, may be employed" unconstitutionally.

b.   Six years later, in § 4(e) of the Voting Rights Act of 1965, Congress prohibited application of English literacy tests to those educated in Spanish language schools in Puerto Rico.   In Katzenbach v. Morgan, 384 U.S. 641 (1966), the Court sustained that exercise of congressional power. (See chap. 6, p. 545, supra, where the scope of congressional power to change the judicially determined contours of equal protection is considered.)   On the day of the Morgan decision, the Court remanded a case involving an equal protection challenge to New York's English literacy requirement that had been launched before § 4(e) was enacted.   Cardona v. Power, 384 U.S. 672 (1966).   Four of the Justices, however, reached the constitutional merits in Cardona—two sustaining the challenge, two rejecting it.

Justice Douglas, joined by Justice Fortas, found "no rational basis— considering the importance of the right at stake" for denying the vote to persons literate in Spanish.   Justice Harlan, joined by Justice Stewart, insisted that no "dual-level test" of equal protection was defensible (see the passage quoted in the introduction to this chapter, p. 985, supra) and concluded that the English literacy requirement satisfied the "mere rational policy" standard.

c.   A year before Cardona and Harper, however, the equal protection clause had been applied for the first time to invalidate a state voting qualification.   Carrington v. Rash, 380 U.S. 89 (1965), involved a Texas constitutional provision prohibiting any member of the armed forces who had moved to Texas during his military service from voting in any election "so long as he . . . is a member of the Armed Forces."   The Court concluded: "By forbidding a soldier ever to controvert the presumption of non-residence, the Texas Constitution imposes an invidious discrimination."   In the course of his opinion, Justice Stewart noted: "Texas has unquestioned power to impose reasonable residence restrictions of the availability of the ballot. [T]he privilege to vote in a state is within the jurisdiction of the state itself, to be exercised as the state may direct, and upon such terms as to it may seem proper, provided, of course, no discrimination is made between individuals, in violation of the Federal Constitution.   Pope v. Williams, [193 U.S. 621]."

Justice Harlan dissented in Carrington, insisting that the equal protection clause was "not intended to touch state electoral matters" and that the Texas provision was in any event "a rational classification."   [Note that Carrington is relied on in Harper; and note Justice Harlan's comment four years later (in a footnote to his dissent in Shapiro v. Thompson, 394 U.S. (1969) (p. 1044, infra)): "I recognize that in my dissenting opinion in [Harper] I characterized the test applied in Carrington as the traditional equal protection standard. I am now satisfied that this was too generous a reading of the Court's opinion."]

Would residence qualifications for voting survive the new equal protection scrutiny of Harper? The standards of Shapiro v. Thompson (sec. 4, p. 1036, infra, invalidating residence requirements in welfare laws)? Challenges to state residence requirements as applied to Presidential elections were pending before Congress and in the courts in 1970.*

2. *Kramer and Cipriano: limited purpose elections and the new equal protection.* a. The Court explained and applied the "rigid scrutiny" requirement of Harper in Kramer v. Union Free School District No. 15, 395 U.S. 621 (1969), which held that a state may not exclude otherwise qualified voters from limited purpose elections unless "the exclusions are necessary to promote a compelling state interest." The New York statute at issue could not meet that high burden of justification. It provided that residents of certain school districts could vote in school board elections only if "they (1) owned (or leased) taxable real property within the district, or (2) are parents (or have custody) of children enrolled in the local public schools." Chief Justice Warren's majority opinion emphasized that the law was subject to "a close and exacting examination" because "statutes distributing the franchise constitute the foundation of our representative society."

In a passage attempting to articulate the special requirements of equal protection in the voting rights area more carefully than in the Harper case, Chief Justice Warren continued: "Thus, state apportionment statutes, which may *dilute* the effectiveness of some citizens' votes, receive close scrutiny from this Court. [Reynolds v. Sims.] No less rigid an examination is applicable to statutes denying the franchise to citizens who are otherwise qualified by residence and age. Statutes granting the franchise to residents on a selective basis always pose the danger of *denying* some citizens any effective voice in the governmental affairs which substantially affect their lives. Therefore, if a challenged state statute grants the right to vote to some bona fide residents of requisite age and citizenship and denies the franchise to others, the Court must determine whether the exclusions are necessary to promote a compelling state interest. . . . Accordingly, when we are reviewing statutes which deny some residents the right to vote, the general presumption of constitutionality afforded state statutes and the traditional approval given state classifications if the Court can conceive of a 'rational basis' for the distinctions made are not applicable. See [Harper]. The presumption of constitutionality and the approval given 'rational' classifications in other types of enactments are based on an assumption that the institutions of state government are structured so as to represent fairly all the people. However, when the challenge to the

---

* Compare the attacks on poll taxes in other forums shortly before the 1966 decision in Harper. The 24th Amendment, ratified in 1964, eliminated the poll tax in federal elections. See Harman v. Forssenius, 380 U.S. 528 (1965), for an expansive reading of that Amendment.

Elimination of the few remaining poll tax provisions became a major political and constitutional issue in the debates on the Voting Rights Act of 1965. Section 9 of the Act was a compromise between those who wanted a flat congressional ban on poll taxes and those who wanted to leave the issue to the courts. The compromise consisted of a congressional "declaration" of unconstitutionality, joined with a direction to the Attorney General to institute court action against the poll tax.

statute is in effect a challenge of this basic assumption, the assumption can no longer serve as the basis for presuming constitutionality."

In applying this approach here, the Court found it unnecessary to decide "whether the State in some circumstances might limit the exercise of the franchise to those 'primarily interested' or 'primarily affected'" and "whether these particular elections are of the type in which the franchise may be so limited." For, even if that were so, "close scrutiny" of the classifications here "demonstrates that they do not accomplish this purpose with sufficient precision to justify" the restrictions. Here, the classifications "permit inclusion of many persons who have, at best, a remote and indirect interest in school affairs and on the other hand, exclude others who have a distinct and direct interest in the school meeting decisions." And validity of restrictions such as these depends in part "on whether all those excluded are in fact substantially less interested or affected than those the statute includes." (See the comment in note c, infra.)

Justice Stewart, joined by Justices Black and Harlan, insisted that a more lenient standard should apply. Under the "traditional," "familiar" equal protection test, there was no unconstitutional discrimination: "a legislative classification is invalid only 'if it rest[s] on grounds wholly irrelevant to achievement of the regulation's objectives.' [Kotch]." Justice Stewart insisted that the voting qualifications here were constitutionally indistinguishable from concededly valid requirements relating to residence, literacy, and age. Discrepancies in particular applications were "the inevitable concomitant of the line-drawing that is essential to lawmaking."

b.   In another special purpose election case decided on the same day, however, the Court was unanimous in invalidating the restriction. Cipriano v. City of Houma, 395 U.S. 701 (1969), held unconstitutional provisions of Louisiana law granting only property taxpayers the right to vote in elections called to approve the issuance of revenue bonds by a municipal utility. A per curiam opinion noted that revenue bonds to be financed from the operations of the utilities, not from property taxes, were involved and concluded: "The challenged statute contains a classification which excludes otherwise qualified voters who are as substantially affected and directly interested in the matter voted upon as are those who are permitted to vote." In a concurring notation, Justices Black and Stewart stated that this case, unlike Kramer, "involves a voting classification 'wholly irrelevant to achievement' of the State's objective. [Kotch]." (The Court held, however, that the decision should be applied prospectively only because "significant hardships" would result for those connected with municipal utilities if the ruling "were given full retroactive effect.")

c.   Can the literacy test sustained in Lassiter survive the new strict scrutiny of Harper and Kramer? Can age and durational residency requirements? Especially given the "exacting standard of precision" of Kramer, can it not be said, e. g., that age requirements permit some less mature persons to vote and exclude some more mature? [Cf. chap. 6, p. 553, supra.]

3.   *McDonald: absentee ballots and the old equal protection.* Contrast the rejection by a unanimous Court, in an opinion by Chief Justice Warren, of the challenge to the Illinois absentee voting ballot in McDonald v. Board of Election Commissioners, 394 U.S. 802 (1969). As noted earlier (p. 1012, supra), the Court stated the new equal protection criteria

in broad terms, but decided that the old, permissive rather than the new standards were appropriate for this voting case. County jail inmates awaiting trial had objected because Illinois had failed to include them among those entitled to vote absentee. Appellants claimed that the distinction "between those medically incapacitated and those 'judicially' incapacitated bears no reasonable relationship to any legitimate state objective." Moreover, they noted that Illinois provided absentee ballots for those "absent from the county for any reason," including pretrial detainees outside the county; they accordingly argued that it was "arbitrary to deny the absentee ballot to other unsentenced inmates simply because they happened to be incarcerated within their own resident counties." And they argued that special scrutiny of the classifications was justified because "voting rights are involved."

But the Court insisted that the "exacting approach" of the new equal protection was not the proper one, since the right to vote was not necessarily involved. The record did not show that Illinois might not find other ways to permit appellants to vote. (For example, the state might let prisoners vote in jail.) Accordingly, "the more traditional standards for evaluating" equal protection claims were appropriate. And the statute easily passed muster under those standards. The Court concluded that it was "not an arbitrary scheme or plan but, rather, the very opposite— a consistent and laudable state policy of adding, over a 50-year period, groups to the absentee coverage as their existence comes to the attention of the legislature." (Moreover, in articulating the "exacting standard" once again in the Kramer case, above, Chief Justice Warren reemphasized that McDonald was "different": Kramer was "an absolute denial of the franchise"; McDonald simply a law which made casting a ballot "easier for some who are unable to come to the polls." Recall the distinction between remedial and restrictive legislation in Katzenbach v. Morgan, chap. 6, p. 545, supra).

WILLIAMS v. RHODES—ACCESS TO THE BALLOT AND THE NEW EQUAL PROTECTION

1. *The decision.* In a hastily reached, divided, and potentially far-reaching decision, the Court held that Ohio's election laws imposed unduly burdensome obstacles on third parties in Presidential elections. Williams v. Rhodes (decided together with Socialist Labor Party v. Rhodes), 393 U.S. 23 (1968). Under Ohio law, the established major parties retained their positions on the ballot simply by obtaining 10% of the votes in the last gubernatorial election. Other parties, by contrast, were required to obtain signatures totaling 15% of the number of ballots cast in the last gubernatorial election and were compelled to file the petitions by early in February of the Presidential election year. These and "substantial additional burdens"—such as elaborate primary and party organization provisions— "made it virtually impossible for a new political party, even though it has hundreds of thousands of members, or an old party, which has a very small number of members, to be placed on the state ballots" for Presidential elections. In Williams, George Wallace supporters had formed a new party in January 1968 and had obtained more than 450,000 signatures (more than the required 15%) in the following six months, but their candidate

was denied a position on the ballot because the February deadline had passed. In the companion case, the Socialist Labor Party, an old party with a small membership, could not meet the 15% requirement. Justice Black's majority opinion found that both groups had stated valid equal protection claims.

The majority opinion held that the high justification standard of the new equal protection applied because the specially valuable rights to vote and to associate were involved, and it concluded that the state had "failed to show any 'compelling interest" which justifies imposing such heavy burdens" on these rights. Justice Black explained: "In determining whether or not a state law violates the Equal Protection Clause, we must consider the facts and circumstances behind the law, the interests which the State claims to be protecting, and interests of those who are disadvantaged by the classification. In the present situation the state laws place burdens on two different, although overlapping, kinds of rights—the right of individuals to associate for the advancement of political beliefs, and the right of qualified voters, regardless of their political persuasion, to cast their votes effectively. Both of these rights, of course, rank among our most precious freedoms." Here, it was plain that the Ohio laws "give the two old, established parties a decided advantage over any new parties struggling for existence and thus place substantially unequal burdens on both the right to vote and the right to associate." And a state could not "place such unequal burdens on minority groups where rights of this kind are at stake" without a showing of "a compelling state interest."

None of the state interests suggested here was found adequate to justify the "very restricted election laws." Encouraging a two party system to promote compromise and political stability could not support giving to particular parties a permanent monopoly. The interest in assuring majority rather than plurality winners did not justify stifling the growth of all new parties. And the aim of preventing voter confusion because of a very large number of parties could not support the crippling restrictions here —that was too remote a danger; and the experience of other states showed "that no more than a handful of parties attempts to qualify for ballot positions even when a very low number of signatures, such as 1% of the electorate, is required." Accordingly, "the totality of the Ohio restrictive laws taken as a whole imposes a burden on voting and associational rights which we hold is an invidious discrimination, in violation of the Equal Protection Clause."

Justice Douglas concurred in the majority opinion but stated that he would give more emphasis to the First Amendment. Similarly Justice Harlan, who concurred only in the result, stated that he "would rest this decision entirely" on "the basic rights of political association assured by the First Amendment" and insisted that it was "unnecessary to draw upon the Equal Protection Clause."

There were separate dissenting opinions by Justices Stewart and White and Chief Justice Warren. Justice Stewart would have applied the traditional, "mere rationality" standard of Equal Protection. Justice White emphasized that neither party had complied with Ohio's reasonable primary election requirements. Chief Justice Warren objected to the haste in deciding so major a case: "The ramifications of our decision today may be comparable to those of Baker v. Carr," yet the impending Presidential election of 1968 had permitted only seven days' deliberation. He noted, moreover, that the Court had left "unresolved what restrictions, if any, a State can impose"—though he found "intimations that a State can by reasonable regulation condition ballot position upon at least three considerations—a substantial showing of voter interest in the candidate seeking a place on the ballot, a requirement that this interest be evidenced sometime prior to the election, and a party structure demonstrating some degree of political organization."

[Note that Williams v. Rhodes was not relied on in several ballot access cases decided later in that final Term of Chief Justice Warren's tenure. Several were based on the Voting Rights Act of 1965 (e. g., Allen v. State Board of Elections, 393 U.S. 544 (1969) (chap. 6, p. 544, supra); and Moore v. Ogilvie, 394 U.S. 814 (1969) (chap. 18, p. 1451, infra) invalidated requirements of geographical distribution of support for new party candidates on the basis of the one man-one vote principle of Reynolds v. Sims without mentioning Williams v. Rhodes.]

2. *The implications.* How far-reaching is Williams v. Rhodes? What was the "voting" interest protected: not access to the ballot box, not equality of weight, but the right to "vote effectively"—i. e., for a particular candidate? Does that suggest a constitutional "right to write-in space," see "The Supreme Court, 1968 Term," 83 Harv.L.Rev. 96 (1969)? Is the basic concern in Williams with *groups* (i. e., minority positions) or with *individuals*? Should the elaborations of the new principles move in the direction of encouraging third parties (as in Williams itself)? Or should they move in the direction of encouraging the major parties to represent divergent viewpoints more effectively? See generally Barton," The General-Election Ballot: More Nominees or More Representative Nominee?," 22 Stan.L.Rev. 165 (1970), urging that the ambiguities of Williams be resolved by emphasizing reform of the party nominating processes while leaving the states considerable freedom to restrict the number of candidates on the final election ballot.

SECTION 3. POVERTY AND THE CRIMINAL PROCESS: AFFIRMATIVE DUTY TO ELIMINATE ECONOMIC HANDICAPS?

Introduction. To what extent is the new equal protection applicable to economic inequalities? Are formal classifications based on wealth "suspect"? Is "strict scrutiny" required when the "discrimination" is merely de facto rather than de jure? To what extent does equal protection guard against the differential impacts of general state activities on persons in unequal economic circumstances? To what extent is the state under an obligation to remove the obstacles which arise from economic inequalities? Is there a constitutional duty to eliminate poverty?

Questions such as these were suggested by language in Harper, the poll tax case (see note 1 after Harper, p. 1011, supra). In the development of the new equal protection, similar questions were raised even earlier—and have been raised more continuously—in connection with challenges to de facto barriers to indigents in the criminal process. Griffin v. Illinois in 1956, which follows, involved the availability of a trial transcript necessary to appellate review; post-Griffin cases have barred a variety of fee requirements when they denied to poor defendants hearings available to those able to pay (see chap. 12, p. 852, supra). And Douglas v. California in 1963 (printed below) relied on Griffin to impose an affirmative duty to provide appellate counsel in certain circumstances.

To what extent are Griffin and Douglas cases about "fundamental" criminal process rights? To what extent are they "poverty" cases? These questions, paralleling those raised about Harper (see p. 1011, supra), are explored here: Griffin and Douglas serve not only to pursue the constitutional dimensions of economic inequalities in the well-established voting and criminal process areas, but also to investigate the implications for other activities.

If the principles of Harper, Griffin, and Douglas were "extended indiscriminately," it has been suggested, "the states might one day find that the Constitution forbids them to impose upon the poor any fee, whether for tuition, roads, or licenses, and to furnish the poor many other services in areas in which there is significant state activity." Note, "Discriminations Against the Poor and the Fourteenth Amendment," 81 Harv.L.Rev. 435 (1967). Is that a fair statement? Are limits necessary to guard against extending the new principles of economic "discrimination" "indiscriminately"? Is it useful to speak of "discrimination"? Are these inequalities of constitutional significance only in matters of "fundamental" importance? Consider these questions in the light of Griffin, Douglas, and the materials following those cases.

THE GRIFFIN CASE

Illinois law provided appellate review in criminal cases as a matter of right; but to obtain review, defendants were required "to furnish the appellate court with a bill of exceptions or report of proceedings at the trial certified by the trial judge." A stenographic transcript of the trial was sometimes necessary to prepare the required documents. The indigent petitioners, in order to obtain review of alleged nonfederal errors in their armed robbery convictions, sought a free transcript; their request was denied on the ground that Illinois provided free transcripts only to indigent defendants sentenced to death. In this separate proceeding, petitioners claimed that the failure to provide the transcript, and the resulting "refusal to afford appellate review solely because of poverty," was a denial of due process and equal protection. The Supreme Court sustained their claim. Griffin v. Illinois, 351 U.S. 12 (1956).

Justice Black's opinion, joined by Chief Justice Warren, Justice Douglas, and Justice Clark, stated: "Providing equal justice for poor and rich, weak and powerful alike is an age-old problem. People have never ceased to hope and strive to move closer to that goal. . . . Surely no one would contend that either a State or the Federal Government could constitutionally provide that defendants unable to pay court costs in advance should be denied the right to plead not guilty or to defend themselves in court. . . . In criminal trials a State can no more discriminate on account of poverty than on account of religion, race, or color. Plainly the ability to pay costs in advance bears no rational relationship to a defendant's guilt or innocence and could not be used as an excuse to deprive a defendant of a fair trial. . . .

"There is no meaningful distinction between a rule which would deny the poor the right to defend themselves in a trial court and one which effectively denies the poor an adequate appellate review accorded to all who have money enough to pay the costs in advance. It is true that a State is not required by the Federal Constitution to provide appellate courts or a right to appellate review at all. See, e. g., McKane v. Durston, 153 U.S. 684, 687–688. But that is not to say that a State that does grant appellate review can do so in a way that discriminates against some convicted defendants on account of their poverty. . . . We do not hold, however, that Illinois must purchase a stenographer's transcript in every case where a defendant cannot buy it. The [Illinois] Supreme Court may find other means of affording adequate and effective appellate review to indigent defendants. For example, it may be that bystanders' bills of exceptions or other methods of reporting trial proceedings could be used in some cases."

Justice Frankfurter concurred in the judgment: "[N]either the fact that a State may deny the right of appeal altogether nor the right of a State to make an appropriate classification, based on differences in crimes and their punishment, nor the right of a State to lay down conditions it deems appropriate for criminal appeals, sanctions differentiations by a State that have no relation to a rational policy of criminal appeal or authorize the imposition of conditions that offend the deepest presuppositions of our society. . . . But when a State deems it wise and just that convictions be susceptible to review by an appellate court, it cannot by force of its exactions draw a line which precludes convicted indigent persons, forsooth erroneously convicted, from securing such a review merely by disabling them from bringing to the notice of an appellate tribunal errors of the trial court which would upset the conviction."

Justices Burton and Minton, joined by Justices Reed and Harlan, dissented: "We think the distinction [made by Illinois] between capital cases and noncapital cases is a reasonable and valid one. Illinois is not bound to make the defendants economically equal before its bar of justice. . . . Persons charged with crime stand before the law with varying degrees of economic and social advantage. Some can afford better lawyers and better investigations of their cases. Some can afford bail, some cannot. Why fix bail at any reasonable sum if a poor man can't make it?"

Justice Harlan also submitted a separate dissent. On the equal protection problem, he stated: "[N]o economic burden attendant upon the exercise of a privilege bears equally upon all, and in other circumstances the resulting differentiation is not treated as an invidious classification by the State, even though discrimination against 'indigents' by name would be unconstitutional. Thus, while the exclusion of 'indigents' from a free state university would deny them equal protection, requiring the payment of tuition fees surely would not, despite the resulting exclusion of those who could not afford to pay the fees. And if imposing a condition of payment is not the equivalent of a classification by the State in one case, I fail to see why it should be so regarded in another. . . . That is, the issue here is not the typical equal protection question of the reasonableness of a 'classification' on the basis of which the State has imposed legal disabilities, but rather the reasonableness of the State's failure to remove natural disabilities. I submit that the basis for [the] holding is simply an unarticulated conclusion that it violates 'fundamental fairness' for a State which provides for appellate review not to see to it that such appeals are in fact available to those it would imprison for serious crimes. . . . I see no reason to import new substance into the concept of equal protection to dispose of the case . . . ."

He then turned to the due process issue: "Illinois has steadily expanded the protection afforded defendants in criminal cases, and in recent years has made substantial strides towards alleviating the natural disadvantages of indigents. Can it be that, while it was not unconstitutional for Illinois to afford no appeals, its steady progress in increasing the safeguards against erroneous convictions has resulted in a constitutional decline? The due process challenge must . . . be directed to the basic step of permitting appeals at all without also providing an *in forma pauperis* procedure. But whatever else may be said of Illinois' reluctance to expend public funds in perfecting appeals for indigents, it can hardly be said to be arbitrary. A policy of economy may be unenlightened, but it is certainly not capricious. . . . I can find nothing in the past decisions of this Court justifying a holding that the Fourteenth Amendment confines the States to a choice between allowing no appeals at all or undertaking to bear the cost of appeals for indigents, which is what the Court in effect now holds."

DOUGLAS v. CALIFORNIA

372 U.S. 353, 83 S.Ct. 814, 9 L.Ed.2d 811 (1963).

Certiorari to the District Court of Appeal of California, Second Appellate District.

Mr. Justice DOUGLAS delivered the opinion of the Court.

. . . The record shows that petitioners requested, and were denied, the assistance of counsel on appeal, even though it plainly appeared they were indigents. In denying petitioners' requests, the California District Court of Appeal stated that it had "gone through" the record and had come to the conclusion that "no good whatever could be served by appointment of counsel." The District Court of Appeal was acting in accordance with a California rule of criminal procedure which provides that state appellate courts, upon the request of an indigent for counsel, may make "an independent investigation of the record and determine whether it would be of advantage to the defendant or helpful to the appellate court to have counsel appointed. . . . After such investigation, appellate courts should appoint counsel if in their opinion it would be helpful to the defendant or the court, and should deny the appointment of counsel only if in their judgment such appointment would be of no value to either the defendant or the court." People v. Hyde, 51 Cal.2d 152, 154, 331 P.2d 42, 43.

We agree, however, with Justice Traynor of the California Supreme Court, who said that the "[d]enial of counsel on appeal [to an indigent] would seem to be a discrimination at least as invidious as that condemned in Griffin v. Illinois . . . .." [In Griffin], the right to a free transcript on appeal was in issue. Here the issue is whether or not an indigent shall be denied the assistance of counsel on appeal. In either case the evil is the same: discrimination against the indigent. For there can be no equal justice where the kind of an appeal a man enjoys "depends on the amount of money he has." [Griffin.]

In spite of California's forward treatment of indigents, under its present practice the type of an appeal a person is afforded in the District Court of Appeal hinges upon whether or not he can pay for the assistance of counsel. If he can the appellate court passes on the merits of his case only after having the full benefit of written briefs and oral argument by counsel. If he cannot the appellate court is forced to prejudge the merits before it can even determine whether counsel should be provided. At this stage in the proceedings only the barren record speaks for the indigent, and, unless the printed pages show that an injustice has been committed, he is forced to go without a champion on appeal. Any real chance he may have had of showing that his appeal has hidden merit is deprived him when the court decides on an ex parte examination of the record that the assistance of counsel is not required.

We are not here concerned with problems that might arise from the denial of counsel for the preparation of a petition for discretionary or mandatory review beyond the stage in the appellate process at which the claims have once been presented by a lawyer and passed upon by an appellate court. We are dealing only with the *first appeal*, granted as a matter of right to rich and poor alike [Cal. Penal Code] from a criminal conviction. We need not now decide whether California would have to provide counsel for an indigent seeking a discretionary hearing from the California Supreme Court after the District Court of Appeal had sustained his conviction, or whether counsel must be appointed for an indigent seeking review of an appellate affirmance of his conviction in this Court by appeal as of right or by petition for a writ of certiorari which lies within the Court's discretion. But it is appropriate to observe that a State can, consistently with the Fourteenth Amendment, provide for differences so long as the result does not amount to a denial of due process or an "invidious discrimination." Williamson v. Lee Optical Co., 348 U.S. 483, 489; Griffin v. Illinois, supra, p. 18. Absolute equality is not required; lines can be and are drawn and we often sustain them. See . . . Goesaert v. Cleary, 335 U.S. 464. But where the merits of the one and only appeal an indigent has as of right are decided without benefit of counsel, we think an unconstitutional line has been drawn between rich and poor.

When an indigent is forced to run this gantlet of a preliminary showing of merit, the right to appeal does not comport with fair procedure. . . . The present case, where counsel was denied petitioners on appeal, shows that the discrimination is not between "possibly good and obviously bad cases," but between cases where the rich man can require the court to listen to argument of counsel before deciding on the merits, but a poor man cannot. There is lacking that equality demanded by the Fourteenth Amendment where the rich man, who appeals as of right, enjoys the benefit of counsel's examination into the record, research of the law, and marshalling of arguments on his behalf, while the indigent, already burdened by a preliminary determination that his case is without merit, is forced to shift for himself. The indigent, where the record is unclear or the errors are hidden, has only the right to a meaningless ritual, while the rich man has a meaningful appeal.

Reversed and remanded.

Mr. Justice CLARK, dissenting.

I adhere to my vote in Griffin v. Illinois, 351 U.S. 12 (1956), but, as I have always understood that case, it does not control here. . . . In my view neither the Equal Protection Clause nor the Due Process Clause requires more [than the California procedure.]

With this new fetish for indigency the Court piles an intolerable burden on the State's judicial machinery. Indeed, if the Court is correct it may be that we should first clean up our own house. We have afforded indigent litigants much less protection than has California. Last Term we received over 1,200 in forma pauperis applications in none of which had we appointed attorneys or required a record. Some were appeals of right. Still we denied the petitions or dismissed the appeals on the moving papers alone. At the same time we had hundreds of paid cases in which we permitted petitions or appeals to be filed with not only records but briefs by counsel, after which they were disposed of in due course. On the other hand, California furnishes the indigent a complete record and if counsel is requested requires its appellate courts either to (1) appoint counsel or (2) make an independent investigation of that record and determine whether it would be of advantage to the defendant or helpful to the court to have counsel appointed. . . .

There is an old adage which my good Mother used to quote to me, *i. e.*, "People who live in glass houses had best not throw stones." I dissent.

Mr. Justice HARLAN, whom Mr. Justice STEWART joins, dissenting.

In holding that an indigent has an absolute right to appointed counsel on appeal of a state criminal conviction, the Court appears to rely both on the Equal Protection Clause and on the guarantees of fair procedure inherent in the Due Process Clause of the Fourteenth Amendment, with obvious emphasis on "equal protection." In my view the Equal Protection Clause is not apposite — suitable, and its application to cases like the present one can lead only to mischievous results. This case should be judged solely under the Due Process Clause, and I do not believe that the California procedure violates that provision.

EQUAL PROTECTION.

To approach the present problem in terms of the Equal Protection Clause is, I submit, but to substitute resounding phrases for analysis. I dissented from this approach in [Griffin v. Illinois] [1] and I am constrained to dissent from the implicit extension of the equal protection approach here—to a case in which the State denies no one an appeal, but seeks only to keep within reasonable bounds the instances in which appellate counsel will be assigned to indigents.

The States, of course, are prohibited by the Equal Protection Clause from discriminating between "rich" and "poor" *as such* in the formulation and application of their laws. But it is a far different thing to suggest that this provision prevents the State from adopting a law of general applicability that may affect the poor more harshly than it does the rich, or, on the other hand, from making some effort to redress economic imbalances while not eliminating them entirely.

Every financial exaction which the State imposes on a uniform basis is more easily satisfied by the well-to-do than by the indigent. Yet I take it that no one would dispute the constitutional power of the State to levy a uniform sales tax, to charge tuition at a state university, to fix rates for the purchase of water from a municipal corporation, to impose a standard fine for criminal vio-

1. The majority in Griffin appeared to rely, as here, on a blend of the Equal Protection and Due Process Clauses in arriving at the result. So far as the result in that case rested on due process grounds, I fully accept the authority of Griffin. [Footnote by Justice Harlan.]

lations, or to establish minimum bail for various categories of offenses. Nor could it be contended that the State may not classify as crimes acts which the poor are more likely to commit than are the rich. And surely, there would be no basis for attacking a state law which provided benefits for the needy simply because those benefits fell short of the goods or services that others could purchase for themselves.

Laws such as these do not deny equal protection to the less fortunate for one essential reason: the Equal Protection Clause does not impose on the States "an affirmative duty to lift the handicaps flowing from differences in economic circumstances." To so construe it would be to read into the Constitution a philosophy of leveling that would be foreign to many of our basic concepts of the proper relations between government and society. The State may have a moral obligation to eliminate the evils of poverty, but it is not required by the Equal Protection Clause to give to some whatever others can afford.

Thus it should be apparent that the present case . . . is not one properly regarded as arising under this clause. California does not discriminate between rich and poor in having a uniform policy permitting everyone to appeal and to retain counsel, and in having a separate rule dealing *only* with the standards for the appointment of counsel for those unable to retain their own attorneys. The sole classification established by this rule is between those cases that are believed to have merit and those regarded as frivolous. And, of course, no matter how far the state rule might go in providing counsel for indigents, it could never be expected to satisfy an affirmative duty—if one existed —to place the poor on the same level as those who can afford the best legal talent available. . . .

The real question in this case, I submit, and the only one that permits of satisfactory analysis, is whether or not the state rule, as applied in this case, is consistent with the requirements of fair procedure guaranteed by the Due Process Clause. Of course, in considering this question, it must not be lost sight of that the State's responsibility under the Due Process Clause is to provide justice for all. Refusal to furnish criminal indigents with some things that others can afford may fall short of constitutional standards of fairness. The problem before us is whether this is such a case.

Due Process. . . .

[T]he appellate procedures involved here stand on an entirely different constitutional footing [than the right to counsel at trial. The question is] the narrow one whether the State's rules with respect to the appointment of counsel are so arbitrary or unreasonable, *in the context of the particular appellate procedure that it has established,* as to require their invalidation. . . .

What the Court finds constitutionally offensive in California's procedure bears a striking resemblance to the rules of this Court and many state courts of last resort on petitions for certiorari or for leave to appeal filed by indigent defendants pro se. . . . [A]s conscientiously committed as this Court is to the great principle of "Equal Justice Under Law," it has never deemed itself constitutionally required to appoint counsel to assist in the preparation of each of the more than 1,000 pro se petitions for certiorari currently being filed each Term. We should know from our own experience that appellate courts generally go out of their way to give fair consideration to those who are unrepresented.

The Court distinguishes our review from the present case on the grounds that the California rule relates to "the *first appeal,* granted as a matter of right." But I fail to see the significance of this difference. Surely, it cannot be contended that the requirements of fair procedure are exhausted once an indigent has been given one appellate review. Nor can it well be suggested that having appointed counsel is more necessary to the fair administration of justice in an initial appeal taken as a matter of right, which the reviewing court on the full record has already determined to be frivolous, than in a petition asking a higher appellate court to exercise its discretion to consider what may be a substantial constitutional claim. . . .

I cannot agree that the Constitution prohibits a State, in seeking to redress economic imbalances at its bar of justice and to provide indigents with full review, from taking reasonable steps to guard against needless expense. This is all that California has done. . . .

"DISCRIMINATION" AGAINST THE POOR AND THE SCOPE OF THE DUTY TO REMEDY ECONOMIC INEQUALITIES AND DEPRIVATIONS

Introduction. To what extent do the Griffin-Douglas principles prevent the state "from adopting a law of general applicability that may affect the poor more harshly than it does the rich," as Justice Harlan put it? Can these unequal effects be called "invidious discriminations" in the constitutional sense without implying an across-the-board state obligation to redress economic inequalities? Are all payment requirements "suspect," albeit de facto, discriminations based on wealth, giving rise to the new equal protection level of scrutiny? Recall Chief Justice Warren's 1969 summary of the situations in which the new equal protection standards are applicable: in the McDonald case, 394 U.S. 802 (p. 1012, supra), he stated that careful review "is especially warranted where lines are drawn on the basis of wealth"—citing Harper and adding, before a citation of Douglas, that "wealth" (like "race") is one of the "factors which would independently render a classification highly suspect and thereby demand a more exacting judicial scrutiny."

1. *Payment requirements as unconstitutional discriminations.* If Douglas "classifies" in a suspect manner, are all payment requirements under a constitutional cloud? Note the comment (after suggesting that no such broad doctrine is required to justify any court decision as of 1969) that such a view is "endemically troublesome as a matter of principle." Michelman, "Foreword: On Protecting the Poor through the Fourteenth Amendment," 83 Harv.L.Rev. 7, 27 (1969). Consider Michelman's elaboration:

"The trouble is that, unlike a de facto racial classification which usually must seek its justifications in purposes completely distinct from its race-related impacts, a de facto pecuniary classification typically carries a highly persuasive justification inseparable from the very effect which excites antipathy —i.e., the hard choices it forces upon the financially straitened. For the typical form assumed by such a classification is simply the charging of a price, reasonably approximating cost, for some good or service which the complaining person may freely choose to purchase or not to purchase. A de facto pecuniary classification, that is, is usually nothing more or less than the making of a market (e. g., in trial transcripts) or the failure to relieve someone of the vicissitudes of market pricing (e. g., for appellate legal services). But the risk of exposure to markets and their decisions is not normally deemed objectionable, to say the least, in our society. Not only do we not inveigh generally against unequal distribution of income or full-cost pricing for most goods. We usually regard it as both the fairest and most efficient arrangement to require each consumer to pay the full market price of what he consumes, limiting his consumption to what his income permits. Exceptions, of course, exist. The point is precisely that such commodities as a vote, an effective defense to criminal prosecution, perhaps education, conceivably some others, *are* exceptional, and that the exceptions depend on the special qualities of the excepted commodities. It is uninformative at best, and very likely misleading as well, to defend such exceptional holdings through formulas of disparagement (invidious or suspect classification; lines . . . drawn on the basis of wealth; discrimination against the indigent) which apply non-selectively to the pricing practice and refer not at all to any exceptional attributes in the excepted commodities."

Michelman prefers a formulation which avoids treating "the pricing practice rather than nonsatisfaction of a particular want, as chiefly constituting the evil to be curbed." He suggests as an appropriate doctrinal statement regarding payment requirements: "It is no justification for deprivation of a fundamental right (i.e. involuntary nonfulfillment of a just want) that the deprivation results from a general practice of requiring persons to pay for what they get." He adds: "Such a construction forces the inquiry on the crucial variable—the nature and quality of the deprivation—and thereby avoids the distractions, false stirring of hopes, and tunneling of vision which results from a rhetorical emphasis on acts of discrimination that consist of nothing more than charging a price."

2. *Michelman's "minimum protection."* But what wants should qualify for constitutional protection? When is government under an affirmative duty to supply wants? That problem is pursued in the next section, in examining the contours of the most amorphous aspects of the new equal protection. But Michelman's suggestion should be noted briefly here, for he suggests abandoning "equal protection" entirely as a "conceptual strategy"— even the equal protection approach that would limit invalidations to certain economic disparities in matters of "fundamental" concern. Michelman suggests instead a "minimum protection" approach. It would emphasize "severe deprivations" rather than "inequalities." It would identify "instances in which persons have important needs or interests which they are prevented from satisfying because of traits or predicaments not adopted by free and proximate choice"; it would then seek to determine which of these instances are intolerable ones by asking which risks of deprivation would be consensually deemed unacceptable in a "just society."

3. *Economic inequalities and fundamental rights.* Would that complex and sophisticated analysis, developed at 83 Harv.L.Rev. 7 (1969), be preferable to the Court's statements? To elaborations of the criteria for identifying those areas of "fundamental importance" in which inequalities give rise to affirmative state duties? Note the materials at the end of sec. 4, p. 1046. Compare, e. g., a more usual technique of exploring the potential reach of the Harper-Griffin-Douglas suspicions of wealth "discriminations," in Note, "Discriminations Against the Poor under the Fourteenth Amend-

ment," 81 Harv.L.Rev. 162 (1967): "[T]he principles might also be extended to civil litigation,[1] education,[2] medical care, or any area in which there is an important state involvement."

SECTION 4. "FUNDAMENTAL" INTERESTS AND THE NEW EQUAL PROTECTION: AMORPHOUS CATEGORY IN SEARCH OF CONTENT

Introduction. Voting and hearings for the accused—the interests found sufficiently important to warrant strict judicial scrutiny in the preceding cases—are reasonably well defined areas which have received considerable protection traditionally. For what other interests is the new equal protection appropriate? How shall the protected areas be selected—by their "fundamentalness," by the "suspectness" of the classifications, by ad hoc assessment of "importance"? This section contains the major decisions selecting "fundamental" interests for special protection in this still undefined area at the frontiers of the new equal protection. The suggestions in 1942, in Skinner (which follows) have borne considerable fruit in the additions of new fields for special scrutiny in Levy v. Louisiana and Shapiro v. Thompson. After examining these opinions for what guidance

1. On the potential implications of Griffin for civil litigation, consider the opinion by Justice Douglas, joined by Chief Justice Warren, dissenting from the denial of certiorari in Williams v. Shaffer, 385 U.S. 1037 (1967). The case arose under the Georgia summary eviction statute. Justice Douglas described its impact as follows: "If the tenant is not able to furnish the security bond, he is summarily evicted. The effect is that the indigent tenant is deprived of his shelter, and the life of his family is disrupted—all without a hearing—solely because of his poverty." He commented: "It is no answer to say that the Georgia procedure is fairer than the procedures of some States, whereby a tenant can be evicted without any opportunity for a hearing. Though a State may not constitutionally be required to afford a hearing before its process is used to evict a tenant, having provided one it cannot discriminate between rich and poor." See Note, "Poverty and Equal Access to the Courts: The Constitutionality of Summary Dispossess in Georgia," 20 Stan.L.Rev. 766 (1968).

More generally, Justice Douglas noted: "The plight of the poor is being somewhat ameliorated by federal and state programs (particularly the Neighborhood Legal Services under OEO) and by private organizations dedicated to the representation of indigents in civil matters. This Court of course does not sit to cure social ills that beset the country. But when we are faced with a statute that apparently violates the Equal Protection Clause by patently discriminating against the poor and thereby worsening their already sorry plight, we should address ourselves to it." See also Justice Douglas' opinion for the Court invalidating Wisconsin's wage garnishment procedure on the basis of procedural due process requirements rather than the Griffin principle. Sniadach v. Family Finance Corp., 395 U.S. 337 (1969) (chap. 12, p. 911, supra).

2. Note the unsuccessful equal protection challenge to inequalities in the Illinois system of financing public education. McInnis v. Shapiro, 293 F.Supp. 327 (N.D.Ill.1968), appeal dismissed sub. nom. McInnis v. Ogilvie, 394 U.S. 322 (1969) (Justice Douglas dissenting). See generally Coons, Clune and Sugarman, "Educational Opportunity: A Workable Constitutional Test for State Financial Structures," 57 Calif.L.Rev. 305 (1969); Horowitz and Neitring, "Equal Protection Aspects of Inequalities in Public Education and Public Assistance Programs From Place to Place Within a State," 15 U.C.L.A.L.Rev. 787 (1968).

they give regarding the probable and desirable growth of the new equal protection, consider the additional suggestions which conclude this chapter.

SKINNER v. OKLAHOMA

316 U.S. 535, 62 S.Ct. 1110, 86 L.Ed. 1655 (1942).

Certiorari to the Supreme Court of Oklahoma.

Mr. Justice DOUGLAS delivered the opinion of the Court.

This case touches a sensitive and important area of human rights. Oklahoma deprives certain individuals of a right which is basic to the perpetuation of a race—the right to have offspring. Oklahoma has decreed the enforcement of its law against petitioner, overruling his claim that it violated the Fourteenth Amendment. Because that decision raised grave and substantial constitutional questions, we granted the petition for certiorari.

The statute involved is Oklahoma's Habitual Criminal Sterilization Act. That Act defines an "habitual criminal" as a person who, having been convicted two or more times for crimes "amounting to felonies involving moral turpitude," either in an Oklahoma court or in a court of any other State, is thereafter convicted of such a felony in Oklahoma and is sentenced to a term of imprisonment in an Oklahoma penal institution. Machinery is provided for the institution by the Attorney General of a proceeding against such a person in the Oklahoma courts for a judgment that such person shall be rendered sexually sterile. Notice, an opportunity to be heard, and the right to a jury trial are provided. The issues triable in such a proceeding are narrow and confined. If the court or jury finds that the defendant is an "habitual criminal" and that he "may be rendered sexually sterile without detriment to his or her general health," then the court "shall render judgment to the effect that said defendant be rendered sexually sterile" by the operation of vasectomy in case of a male, and of salpingectomy in case of a female. Only one other provision of the Act is material here, and [that] provides that "offenses arising out of the violation of the prohibitory laws, revenue acts, embezzlement, or political offenses, shall not come or be considered within the terms of this Act."

Petitioner was convicted in 1926 of the crime of stealing chickens, and was sentenced to the Oklahoma State Reformatory. In 1929 he was convicted of the crime of robbery with firearms, and was sentenced to the reformatory. In 1934 he was convicted again of robbery with firearms, and was sentenced to the penitentiary. He was confined there in 1935 when the Act was passed. In 1936 the Attorney General instituted proceedings against him. Petitioner in his answer challenged the Act as unconstitutional by reason of the Fourteenth Amendment. A jury trial was had. The court instructed the jury that the crimes of which petitioner had been convicted were felonies involving moral turpitude, and that the only question for the jury was whether the operation of vasectomy could be performed on petitioner without detriment to his general health. The jury found that it could be. A judgment directing that the operation of vasectomy be performed on petitioner was affirmed by the Supreme Court of Oklahoma by a five to four decision. 189 Okla. 235, 115 P.2d 123.

Several objections to the constitutionality of the Act have been pressed upon us. It is urged that the Act cannot be sustained as an exercise of the police power, in view of the state of scientific authorities respecting inheritability of criminal traits. It is argued that due process is lacking because, under this Act, unlike the Act upheld in Buck v. Bell, 274 U.S. 200, [a law providing for sterilization of feeble-minded persons in state institutions] the defendant is given no opportunity to be heard on the issue as to whether he is the probable potential parent of socially undesirable offspring. . . . We pass those points without intimating an opinion on them, for there is a feature of the Act which clearly condemns it. That is, its failure to meet the requirements of the equal protection clause of the Fourteenth Amendment.

We do not stop to point out all of the inequalities in this Act. A few examples will suffice. In Oklahoma, grand larceny is a felony. Larceny is grand larceny when the property taken exceeds $20 in value. Embezzlement is punishable "in the manner prescribed for feloniously stealing property of the value of that embezzled." Hence, he who embezzles property worth more than $20 is guilty of a felony. A clerk who appropriates over $20 from his employer's till and a stranger who steals the same amount are thus both guilty of felonies. If the latter repeats his act and is convicted three times, he may be sterilized. But the clerk is not subject to the pains and penalties of the Act no matter how large his embezzlements nor how frequent his convictions. A person who enters a chicken coop and steals chickens commits a felony; and he may be sterilized if he is thrice convicted. If, however, he is a bailee of the property and fraudulently appropriates it, he is an embezzler. Hence, no matter how habitual his proclivities for embezzlement are and no matter how often his conviction, he may not be sterilized. Thus, the nature of the two crimes is intrinsically the same and they are punishable in the same manner. Furthermore, the line between them follows close distinctions—distinctions comparable to those highly technical ones which shaped the common law as to "trespass" or "taking." . .

It was stated in Buck v. Bell, supra, that the claim that state legislation violates the equal protection clause of the Fourteenth Amendment is "the usual last resort of constitutional arguments." Under our constitutional system the States in determining the reach and scope of particular legislation need not provide "abstract symmetry." They may mark and set apart the classes and types of problems according to the needs and as dictated or suggested by experience. Only recently we reaffirmed the view that the equal protection clause does not prevent the legislature from recognizing "degrees of evil." Thus, if we had here only a question as to a State's classification of crimes, such as embezzlement or larceny, no substantial federal question would be raised. For a State is not constrained in the exercise of its police power to ignore experience which marks a class of offenders or a family of offenses for special treatment. Nor is it prevented by the equal protection clause from confining "its restrictions to those classes of cases where the need is deemed to be clearest."

But the instant legislation runs afoul of the equal protection clause, though we give Oklahoma that large deference which the rule of the foregoing cases requires. We are dealing here with legislation which involves one of the basic civil rights of man. Marriage and procreation are fundamental to the very existence and survival of the race. The power to sterilize, if exercised, may have subtle, far-reaching and devastating effects. In evil or reckless hands it can cause races or types which are inimical to the dominant group to wither and disappear. There is no redemption for the individual whom the law touches. Any experiment which the State conducts is to his irreparable injury. He is forever deprived of a basic liberty. We mention these matters not to reëxamine the scope of the police power of the States. We advert to them merely in emphasis of our view that strict scrutiny of the classification which a State makes in a sterilization law is essential, lest unwittingly, or otherwise, invidious discriminations are made against groups or types of individuals in violation of the constitutional guaranty of just and equal laws. The guaranty of "equal protection of the laws is a pledge of the protection of equal laws." Yick Wo v. Hopkins, 118 U.S. 356, 369. When the law lays an unequal hand on those who have committed intrinsically the same quality of offense and sterilizes one and not the other, it has made as invidious a discrimination as if it had selected a particular race or nationality for oppressive treatment. Sterilization of those who have thrice committed grand larceny, with immunity for those who are embezzlers, is a clear, pointed, unmistakable discrimination. Oklahoma makes no attempt to say that he who commits larceny by trespass or trick or fraud has biologically inheritable traits which he who commits embezzlement lacks. Oklahoma's line between larceny by fraud and embezzlement is determined, as we have noted, "with reference to the time when the fraudulent intent to convert the property to the taker's own use" arises. We have not the slightest basis for inferring that that line has any significance in eugenics, nor that the inheritability of criminal traits follows the neat legal distinctions which the law has marked between those two offenses. In terms of fines and imprisonment, the crimes of larceny and embezzlement rate the same under the Oklahoma code. Only when it comes to sterilization are the pains and penalties of the law different. The equal protection clause would indeed be a formula of empty words if such conspicuously artificial lines could be drawn. In Buck v. Bell, supra, the Virginia statute was upheld though it applied only to feeble-minded persons in institutions of the State. But it was pointed out that "so far as the operations enable those who otherwise must be kept confined to be returned to the world, and thus open the asylum to others, the equality aimed at will be more nearly reached." Here there is no such saving feature. Embezzlers are forever free. Those who steal or take in other ways are not. If such a classification were permitted, the technical common law concept of a "trespass" based on distinctions which are "very largely dependent upon history for explanation" (Holmes, The Common Law, p. 73) could readily become a rule of human genetics. . . .

It is true that the Act has a broad severability clause. But we will not endeavor to determine whether its application would solve the equal protection difficulty. The Supreme Court of Oklahoma sustained the Act without reference to the severability clause. We have therefore a situation where the Act as construed and applied to petitioner is allowed to perpetuate the discrimination which we have found to be fatal. Whether the severability clause would be so applied as to remove this particular constitutional objection is a question which may be more appropriately left for adjudication by the Oklahoma court. That is reëmphasized here by our uncertainty as to what excision, if any, would be made as a matter of

Oklahoma law. It is by no means clear whether, if an excision were made, this particular constitutional difficulty might be solved by enlarging on the one hand or contracting on the other the class of criminals who might be sterilized.

Reversed.

Mr. Chief Justice STONE, concurring:

I concur in the result, but I am not persuaded that we are aided in reaching it by recourse to the equal protection clause.

If Oklahoma may resort generally to the sterilization of criminals on the assumption that their propensities are transmissible to future generations by inheritance, I seriously doubt that the equal protection clause requires it to apply the measure to all criminals in the first instance, or to none.

Moreover, if we must presume that the legislature knows—what science has been unable to ascertain—that the criminal tendencies of any class of habitual offenders are transmissible regardless of the varying mental characteristics of its individuals, I should suppose that we must likewise presume that the legislature, in its wisdom, knows that the criminal tendencies of some classes of offenders are more likely to be transmitted than those of others. And so I think the real question we have to consider is not one of equal protection, but whether the wholesale condemnation of a class to such an invasion of personal liberty, without opportunity to any individual to show that his is not the type of case which would justify resort to it, satisfies the demands of due process.

There are limits to the extent to which the presumption of constitutionality can be pressed, especially where the liberty of the person is concerned (see United States v. Carolene Products Co., 304 U.S. 144, 152, n. 4) and where the presumption is resorted to only to dispense with a procedure which the ordinary dictates of prudence would seem to demand for the protection of the individual from arbitrary action. . . .

Science has found and the law has recognized that there are certain types of mental deficiency associated with delinquency which are inheritable. But the State does not contend—nor can there be any pretense—that either common knowledge or experience, or scientific investigation, has given assurance that the criminal tendencies of any class of habitual offenders are universally or even generally inheritable. In such circumstances, inquiry whether such is the fact in the case of any particular individual cannot rightly be dispensed with. [W]hile the state may protect itself from the demonstrably inheritable tendencies of the individual which are injurious to society, the most elementary notions of due process would seem to require it to take appropriate steps to safeguard the liberty of the individual by affording him, before he is condemned to an irreparable injury in his person, some opportunity to show that he is without such inheritable tendencies.

Mr. Justice JACKSON concurring:

I join the Chief Justice in holding that the hearings provided are too limited in the context of the present Act to afford due process of law. I also agree with the opinion of Mr. Justice Douglas that the scheme of classification set forth in the Act denies equal protection of the law. I disagree with the opinion of each in so far as it rejects or minimizes the grounds taken by the other.

I also think the present plan to sterilize the individual in pursuit of a eugenic plan to eliminate from the race characteristics that are only vaguely identified and which in our present state of knowledge are uncertain as to transmissibility presents other constitutional questions of gravity. This Court has sustained such an experiment with respect to an imbecile, a person with definite and observable characteristics, where the condition had persisted through three generations and afforded grounds for the belief that it was transmissible and would continue to manifest itself in generations to come. Buck v. Bell, 274 U.S. 200.

There are limits to the extent to which a legislatively represented majority may conduct biological experiments at the expense of the dignity and personality and natural powers of a minority—even those who have been guilty of what the majority define as crimes. But this Act falls down before reaching this problem, which I mention only to avoid the implication that such a question may not exist because not discussed. On it I would also reserve judgment.

SKINNER: POTENT SEED

Did the law run "afoul of the equal protection clause, though [as Justice Douglas stated] we give Oklahoma that large deference" which the traditional cases require? Did those cases require "that strict scrutiny of the classification" which Justice Douglas found appropriate later in the same paragraph? What made that "strict scrutiny" appropriate here?

Note Kenneth Karst's admiring comment, in "Invidious Discrimination: Justice Douglas and the Return of the 'Natural-Law-Due-Process Formula,'" 16 U.C.L.A.L.Rev. 716 (1969): "In 1942, for Justice Douglas to get a majority to invert the presumption of constitutionality . . . was an awesome accomplishment." Karst praises the opinion as laying "a *doctrinal* foundation" for "the most significant constitutional development of our time." If Harper, supra, seems an "improvised innovation," it is only because insufficient attention was paid to what Skinner had in effect said: "a classification that discriminates with respect to a right of very great importance is not to be sustained merely because the classification has a rational basis; if the state fails to supply a substantial justification, its discrimination is invidious and unconstitutional."

With cases such as Levy and Shapiro, which follow, "the doctrinal seed planted nearly three decades ago in Skinner has come to full flower. And each new flowering provides seeds for the future." In each of the modern cases, the legislative choice was not "wholly arbitrary"; rather, it lacked "justification, considering the importance of the interests which it harm[ed]." Karst, supra, at 736. What were the important interests harmed in Skinner, Levy, and Shapiro? What kinds of justifications will do when interests of such importance are harmed? What seeds do these flowers provide? Is it possible to say? To guess? Or can the seeds not be classified until they reach full bloom?

Should Skinner have rested on substantive due process rather than equal protection grounds? How would a substantive due process approach differ from the doctrines whose origins Professor Karst finds in Skinner? Was the equal protection rationale in Skinner "fanciful"? Was it an "abdication of the Court's responsibility" not to consider the "biological evidence" that was "overwhelmingly against the reasonableness of the statute"—and thus to fail to help the "thousands of institutional inmates" subject to sterilization laws who "don't get into court very often," who would have been aided by a substantive due process ruling, but who could not benefit from "the vague Skinner formulation"? See Foote, "The Proper Role of the United States Supreme Court in Civil Liberties Cases," 10 Wayne L.Rev. 457 (1964). Compare Karst's response, supra: "[T]here was an egalitarian basis" for Skinner; the exemptions covered "areas of white-collar crime"; the law "was class legislation in the worst sense, discriminating—invidiously—against criminals who were not sophisticated enough to do their stealing in a genteel manner."

LEVY v. LOUISIANA

391 U.S. 68, 88 S.Ct. 1509, 20 L.Ed.2d 436 (1968).

Appeal from the Supreme Court of Louisiana.

Mr. Justice DOUGLAS delivered the opinion of the Court.

Appellant sued on behalf of five illegitimate children to recover, under a Louisiana statute [1] (La.Civ.Code Art. 2315) for two kinds of damages as a result of the wrongful death of their mother: (1) the damages to them for the loss of their mother; and (2) those based on the survival of a cause of action which the mother had at the time of her death for pain and suffering. Appellees are the doctor who treated her and the insurance company.

We assume in the present state of the pleadings that the mother, Louise Levy, gave birth to these five illegitimate children and that they lived with her; that she treated them as a parent would treat any other child; that she worked as a domestic servant to support them, taking them to church every Sunday and enrolling them, at her own expense, in a parochial school. The [state court] dismissed the suit, holding that "child" in Article 2315 means "legitimate child," the denial to illegitimate children of "the right to recover" being "based on morals and general welfare because it discourages bringing children into the world out of wedlock." . . .

We start from the premise that illegitimate children are not "nonpersons." They are humans, live and have their being. They are clearly "persons" within the meaning of the Equal Protection Clause of the Fourteenth Amendment.

1. "Every act whatever of man that causes damage to another obliges him by whose fault it happened to repair it.

"The right to recover damages to property caused by an offense or quasi offense is a property right which, on the death of the obligee, is inherited by his legal, instituted, or irregular heirs, subject to the community rights of the surviving spouse.

"The right to recover all other damages caused by an offense or quasi offense, if the injured person dies, shall survive for a period of one year from the death of the deceased in favor of:

(1) the surviving spouse and child or children of the deceased, or either such spouse or such child or children;
(2) the surviving father and mother of the deceased, or either of them, if he left no spouse or child surviving; and
(3) the surviving brothers and sisters of the deceased, or any of them, if he left no spouse, child, or parent surviving. The survivors in whose favor this right of action survives may also recover the damages which they sustained through the wrongful death of the deceased. . . . " [Footnote by the Court.]

While a State has broad power when it comes to making classifications, it may not draw a line which constitutes an invidious discrimination against a particular class. See [Skinner v. Oklahoma]. Though the test has been variously stated, the end result is whether the line drawn is a rational one. See [Morey v. Doud].

In applying the Equal Protection Clause to social and economic legislation, we give great latitude to the legislature in making classifications. [Williamson v. Lee Optical]. Even so, would a corporation, which is a "person," for certain purposes, within the meaning of the Equal Protection Clause, be required to forego recovery for wrongs done its interests because its incorporators were all bastards? However that might be we have been extremely sensitive when it comes to basic civil rights [Skinner v. Oklahoma; Harper v. Board of Elections] and have not hesitated to strike down an invidious classification even though it had history and tradition on its side. [Brown v. Board of Education]. The rights asserted here involve the intimate, familial relationship between a child and his own mother. When the child's claim of damage for loss of his mother is in issue, why, in terms of "equal protection," should the tortfeasors go free merely because the child is illegitimate? Why should the illegitimate child be denied rights merely because of his birth out of wedlock? He certainly is subject to all the responsibilities of a citizen, including the payment of taxes and conscription under the Selective Service Act. How under our constitutional regime can he be denied correlative rights which other citizens enjoy?

Legitimacy or illegitimacy of birth has no relation to the nature of the wrong allegedly inflicted on the mother by appellees. These children, though illegitimate, were dependent on her; she cared for them and nurtured them; they were indeed hers in the biological and in the spiritual sense; in her death they suffered wrong in the sense that any dependent would.

We conclude that it is invidious to discriminate against them when no action, conduct, or demeanor of theirs [2] is possibly relevant to the harm that was done the mother.

Reversed.

Mr. Justice HARLAN, whom Mr. Justice BLACK and Mr. Justice STEWART join, dissenting [in Levy and in a companion case, Glona*].

2. We can say with Shakespeare: "Why bastard, wherefore base? When my dimensions are as well compact, My mind as generous, and my shape as true, As honest madam's issue? Why brand they us With base? with baseness? bastardy? base, base?" King Lear, Act I, Scene 2. [Footnote by the Court.]

* Glona v. American Guarantee & Liability Ins. Co., 391 U.S. 73 (1968), involved the application of the Louisiana statute to deny recovery to a mother for the wrongful death of her illegitimate son. Justice Douglas' majority opinion concluded that "we see no possible rational basis (Morey v. Doud, 354 U.S. 457, 465–466) for assuming that if the natural mother is allowed recovery for the wrongful death of her illegitimate child, the cause of illegitimacy will be served. It would, indeed, be farfetched to assume that women have illegitimate children so that they can be compensated in damages for their death. . . . To say that the test of equal protection should be the 'legal' rather than the biological relationship is to avoid the issue. For the Equal Protection Clause necessarily limits the authority of a State to draw such 'legal' lines as it chooses."

Note also Justice Douglas' concurrence on equal protection grounds in King v. Smith, 392 U.S. 309 (1968). The Court held invalid Alabama's "substitute father" regulation which denied federally funded AFDC (Aid to Families with Dependent Children) pay-

These decisions can only be classed as constitutional curiosities.

. . . By statute, Louisiana has created both rights in favor of certain classes of persons. The question in these cases is whether the way in which Louisiana has defined the classes of persons who may recover is constitutionally permissible. The Court has reached a negative answer to this question by a process that can only be described as brute force.

One important reason why recovery for wrongful death had everywhere to await statutory delineation is that the interest one person has in the life of another is inherently intractable. Rather than hear offers of proof of love and affection and economic dependence from every person who might think or claim that the bell had tolled for him, the courts stayed their hands pending legislative action. Legislatures, responding to the same diffuseness of interests, generally defined classes of proper plaintiffs by highly arbitrary lines based on family relationships, excluding issues concerning the actual effect of the death on the plaintiff.

Louisiana has followed the traditional pattern. . . . According to this scheme, a grown man may sue for the wrongful death of parents he did not love, even if the death relieves him of a great economic burden or entitles him to a large inheritance. [But] a minor child cared for by neighbors or relatives "as if he were their own son" does not therefore have a right to sue for their death. Perhaps most dramatic, a surviving parent, for example, of a Louisiana deceased may sue if and only if there is no surviving spouse or child; it does not matter who loved or depended on whom, or what the economic situation of any survivor may be, or even whether the spouse or child elects to sue. In short, the whole scheme of the Louisiana wrongful death statute, which is similar in this respect to that of most other States, makes everything the Court says about affection and nurture and dependence altogether irrelevant. The only question in any case is whether the plaintiff falls within the classes of persons to whom the State has accorded a right of action for the death of another.

Louisiana has chosen, as have most other States in one respect or another, to define these classes of proper plaintiffs in terms of their legal rather than their biological relation to the deceased. A man may recover for the death of his wife, whether he loved her or not, but may not recover for the death of his paramour. A child may recover for the death of his adopted parents. An illegitimate may recover for the wrongful death of a parent who has taken a few hours to acknowledge him formally, but not for the death of a person who he claims is his parent but who has not acknowledged him. A parent may recover for the death of an illegitimate child he has acknowledged, but not for the death of a child he may have fathered or borne but whom he did not bother to acknowledge until the possibility of tort recovery arose.

The Court today, for some reason which I am at a loss to understand, rules that the State must base its arbitrary definition of the plaintiff class

ments "to the children of a mother who 'cohabits' in or outside her home with any single or married able-bodied man." Chief Justice Warren's majority opinion found the regulation inconsistent with the Social Security Act and accordingly found it unnec-essary to reach the Fourteenth Amendment challenge. Justice Douglas' concurrence invoked Levy v. Louisiana: "I would say that the immorality of the mother has no rational connection with the need of her children under any welfare program."

on biological rather than legal relationships. Exactly how this makes the Louisiana scheme even marginally more "rational" is not clear, for neither a biological relationship nor legal acknowledgment is indicative of the love or economic dependence that may exist between two persons. It is, frankly, preposterous to suggest that the State has made illegitimates into "nonpersons," or that, by analogy with what Louisiana has done here it might deny illegitimates constitutional rights or the benefits of doing business in corporate form. The rights at issue here stem from the existence of a family relationship, and the State has decided only that it will not recognize the family relationship unless the formalities of marriage, or of the acknowledgment of children by the parent in question, have been complied with.

There is obvious justification for this decision. If it be conceded, as I assume it is, that the State has power to provide that people who choose to live together should go through the formalities of marriage and, in default, that people who bear children should acknowledge them, it is logical to enforce these requirements by declaring that the general class of rights that are dependent upon family relationships shall be accorded only when the formalities as well as the biology of those relationships are present. . . . That suits for wrongful death, actions to determine the heirs of intestates, and the like, must as a constitutional matter deal with every claim of biological paternity or maternity on its merits is an exceedingly odd proposition.

The Equal Protection Clause states a complex and difficult principle. Certain classifications are "inherently suspect," which I take to mean that any reliance upon them in differentiating legal rights requires very strong affirmative justification. The difference between a child who has been formally acknowledged and one who has not is hardly one of these. Other classifications are impermissible because they bear no intelligible proper relation to the consequences that are made to flow from them. This does not mean that any classification this Court thinks could be better drawn is unconstitutional. But even if the power of this Court to improve on the lines that Congress and the States have drawn were very much broader than I consider it to be, I could not understand why a State which bases the right to recover for wrongful death strictly on family relationships could not demand that those relationships be formalized. . . .

SHAPIRO v. THOMPSON

394 U.S. 618, 89 S.Ct. 1322, 22 L.Ed.2d 600 (1969).

Appeal from the United States District Court for the District of Connecticut.*

Mr. Justice BRENNAN delivered the opinion of the Court.

These three appeals were restored to the calendar for reargument. . . . Each is an appeal from a decision of a three-judge District Court holding unconstitutional a State or District of Columbia statutory provision which denies welfare assistance to residents of the State or District who

---

* Together with Washington v. Legrant, on appeal from the United States District Court for the District of Columbia, and Reynolds v. Smith, on appeal from the United States District Court for the Eastern District of Pennsylvania.

have not resided within their jurisdictions for at least one year immediately preceding their applications for such assistance.[1]   We affirm the judgments of the District Courts in the three cases. . . .

[I and II.] . . .

There is no dispute that the effect of the waiting-period requirement in each case is to create two classes of needy resident families indistinguishable from each other except that one is composed of residents who have resided a year or more, and the second of residents who have resided less than a year, in the jurisdiction.   One the basis of this sole difference the first class is granted and the second class is denied welfare aid upon which may depend the ability of the families to obtain the very means to subsist—food, shelter, and other necessities of life.   [A]ppellees' central contention is that the statutory prohibition of benefits to residents of less than a year creates a classification which constitutes an invidious discrimination denying them equal protection of the laws.   We agree.   The interests which appellants assert are promoted by the classification either may not constitutionally be promoted by government or are not compelling governmental interests.

III.

Primarily, appellants justify the waiting-period requirement as a protective device to preserve the fiscal integrity of state public assistance programs.   It is asserted that people who require welfare assistance during their first year of residence in a State are likely to become continuing burdens on state welfare programs.   Therefore, the argument runs, if such people can be deterred from entering the jurisdiction by denying them welfare benefits during the first year, state programs to assist long-time residents will not be impaired by a substantial influx of indigent newcomers. . . .

We do not doubt that the one-year waiting period device is well suited to discourage the influx of poor families in need of assistance.   An indigent who desires to migrate, resettle, find a new job, start a new life will doubtless hesitate if he knows that he must risk making the move without the possibility of falling back on state welfare assistance during his first year of residence, when his need may be most acute.   But the purpose of inhibiting migration by needy persons into the State is constitutionally impermissible.

This Court long ago recognized that the nature of our Federal Union and our constitutional concepts of personal liberty unite to require that all citizens be free to travel throughout the length and breadth of our land uninhibited by statutes, rules, or regulations which unreasonably burden or restrict this movement. . . .

We have no occasion to ascribe the source of this right to travel interstate to a particular constitutional provision.[2]   [See United States v. Guest, 383 U.S. 745 (1966) (see chap. 6, p. 505, supra).]

1. All but one of the appellees herein applied for assistance under the Aid to Families with Dependent Children Program (AFDC) which was established by the Social Security Act of 1935. 49 Stat. 620, as amended, 42 U.S.C. §§ 301–1394.   The program provides partial federal funding of state assistance plans which meet certain spec-

ifications.   One appellee applied for Aid to the Permanently and Totally Disabled which is also jointly funded by the States and the Federal Government.   42 U.S.C. §§ 1351–1355.   [All footnotes to this opinion by the Court.]

2. In Corfield v. Coryell, 6 F.Cas. 546, 552 (No. 3230) (C.C.E.D.Pa.1823), Paul

Thus, the purpose of deterring the in-migration of indigents cannot serve as justification for the classification created by the one-year waiting period, since that purpose is constitutionally impermissible. If a law has "no other purpose . . . than to chill the assertion of constitutional rights by penalizing those who choose to exercise them, then it [is] patently unconstitutional." United States v. Jackson, 390 U.S. 570, 581 (1968).

Alternatively, appellants argue that even if it is impermissible for a State to attempt to deter the entry of all indigents, the challenged classification may be justified as a permissible state attempt to discourage those indigents who would enter the State solely to obtain larger benefits. We observe first that none of the statutes before us is tailored to serve that objective. . . . More fundamentally, a State may no more try to fence out those indigents who seek higher welfare benefits than it may try to fence out indigents generally. Implicit in any such distinction is the notion that indigents who enter a State with the hope of securing higher welfare benefits are somehow less deserving than indigents who do not take this consideration into account. But we do not perceive why a mother who is seeking to make a new life for herself and her children should be regarded as less deserving because she considers, among other factors, the level of a State's public assistance. Surely such a mother is no less deserving than a mother who moves into a particular State in order to take advantage of its better educational facilities.

Appellants argue further that the challenged classification may be sustained as an attempt to distinguish between new and old residents on the basis of the contribution they have made to the community through the payment of taxes. . . . Appellants' reasoning would logically permit the State to bar new residents from schools, parks, and libraries or deprive them of police and fire protection. Indeed it would permit the State to apportion all benefits and services according to the past tax contributions of its citizens. The Equal Protection Clause prohibits such an apportionment of state services.

We recognize that a State has a valid interest in preserving the fiscal integrity of its programs. It may legitimately attempt to limit its expenditures, whether for public assistance, public education, or any other program. But a State may not accomplish such a purpose by invidious distinctions between classes of its citizens. It could not, for example, reduce expenditures for education by barring indigent children from its schools. Similarly, in the cases before us, appellants must do more than show that denying welfare benefits to new residents saves money. The saving of welfare costs cannot be an independent ground for an invidious classification.

v. Virginia, 8 Wall. 168, 180 (1808), and Ward v. Maryland, 12 Wall. 418, 430 (1870), the right to travel interstate was grounded upon the Privileges and Immunities Clause of Art. IV, § 2. See also Slaughter-House Cases, 16 Wall. 36, 79 (1872); Twining v. New Jersey, 211 U.S. 78, 97 (1908). In Edwards v. California, 314 U.S. 160, 181, 183–185 (Douglas and Jackson, JJ., concurring), and Twining v. New Jersey, supra, reliance was placed on the Privileges and Immunities Clause of the Fourteenth Amendment. See also Crandall v. Nevada, 6 Wall. 35 (1868). In Edwards v. California, supra, and Passenger Cases, 7 How. 283 (1849), a Commerce Clause approach was employed.

See also Kent v. Dulles, 357 U.S. 116, 125 (1958); Aptheker v. Rusk, 378 U.S. 500, 505–506 (1964); Zemel v. Rusk, 381 U.S. 1, 14 (1966), where the freedom of Americans to travel outside the country was grounded upon the due process clause of the Fifth Amendment.

In sum, neither deterrence of indigents from migrating to the State nor limitation of welfare benefits to those regarded as contributing to the State is a constitutionally permissible state objective.

IV.

Appellants next advance as justification certain administrative and related governmental objectives allegedly served by the waiting-period requirement. They argue that the requirement (1) facilitates the planning of the welfare budget; (2) provides an objective test of residency; (3) minimizes the opportunity for recipients fraudulently to receive payments from more than one jurisdiction; and (4) encourages early entry of new residents into the labor force.

At the outset, we reject appellants' argument that a mere showing of a rational relationship between the waiting period and these four admittedly permissible state objectives will suffice to justify the classification. See Lindsley v. Natural Carbonic Gas Co., 220 U.S. 61, 78 (1911); Flemming v. Nestor, 363 U.S. 603, 611 (1960); McGowan v. Maryland, 366 U.S. 420, 426 (1961). [In moving], appellees were exercising a constitutional right, and any classification which serves to penalize the exercise of that right, unless shown to be necessary to promote a *compelling* governmental interest, is unconstitutional. Cf. Skinner v. Oklahoma, 316 U.S. 535, 541 (1942); Korematsu v. United States, 323 U.S. 214, 216 (1944); Bates v. Little Rock, 361 U.S. 516, 524 (1960); Sherbert v. Verner, 374 U.S. 398, 406 (1963).

The argument that the waiting-period requirement facilitates budget predictability is wholly unfounded. The records in all three cases are utterly devoid of evidence that either State or the District of Columbia in fact uses the one-year requirement as a means to predict the number of people who will require assistance in the budget year. . . .

The argument that the waiting period serves as an administratively efficient rule of thumb for determining residency similarly will not withstand scrutiny. The residence requirement and the one-year waiting-period requirement are distinct and independent prerequisites for assistance under these three statutes, and the facts relevant to the determination of each are directly examined by the welfare authorities. Before granting an application, the welfare authorities investigate the applicant's employment, housing, and family situation and in the course of the inquiry necessarily learn the facts upon which to determine whether the applicant is a resident.[3]

Similarly, there is no need for a State to use the one-year waiting period as a safeguard against fraudulent receipt of benefits; for less drastic means

3. See, e. g., D.C. Handbook, chapters on Eligibility Payments, Requirements, Resources, and Reinvestigation for an indication of how thorough those investigations are. . . .

The Department of Health, Education, and Welfare has proposed the elimination of individual investigations, except for spot checks, and the substitution of a declaration system, under which the "agency accepts the statements of the applicant for or recipient of assistance, about facts that are within his knowledge and competence . . . as a basis for decisions regarding his eligibility and extent of entitlement." Dept. of HEW, Determination of Eligibility for Public Assistance Programs, 33 Fed.Reg. 17189 (1968). . . . Presumably the statement of an applicant that he intends to remain in the jurisdiction would be accepted under a declaration system.

are available, and are employed, to minimize that hazard. . . . Since double payments can be prevented by a letter or a telephone call, it is unreasonable to accomplish this objective by the blunderbuss method of denying assistance to all indigent newcomers for an entire year.

. . . A state purpose to encourage employment provides no rational basis for imposing a one-year waiting-period restriction on new residents only.

We conclude therefore that appellants in these cases do not use and have no need to use the one-year requirement for the governmental purposes suggested. Thus, even under traditional equal protection tests a classification of welfare applicants according to whether they have lived in the State for one year would seem irrational and unconstitutional.[4] But, of course, the traditional criteria do not apply in these cases. Since the classification here touches on the fundamental right of interstate movement, its constitutionality must be judged by the stricter standard of whether it promotes a *compelling* state interest. Under this standard, the waiting period requirement clearly violates the Equal Protection Clause.[5]

V.

Connecticut and Pennsylvania argue, however, that the constitutional challenge to the waiting period requirements must fail because Congress expressly approved the imposition of the requirement by the States as part of the jointly funded AFDC program.

Section 402(b) of the Social Security Act of 1935, as amended, 42 U.S.C. § 602(b), provides that:

"The Secretary shall approve any [state assistance] plan which fulfills the conditions specified in subsection (a) of this section, except that he shall not approve any plan which imposes as a condition of eligibility for aid to families with dependent children, a residence requirement which denies aid with respect to any child residing in the State (1) who has resided in the State for one year immediately preceding the application for such aid, or (2) who was born within one year immediately preceding the application, if the parent or other relative with whom the child is living has resided in the State for one year immediately preceding the birth."

On its face, the statute does not approve, much less prescribe, a one-year requirement. It merely directs the Secretary of Health, Education, and Welfare not to disapprove plans submitted by the States because they include such a requirement. The suggestion that Congress enacted that directive to encourage state participation in the AFDC program is completely refuted by the legislative history of the section. That history discloses that Congress enacted the directive to curb hardships resulting from lengthy residence re-

4. Under the traditional standard, equal protection is denied only if the classification is "without any reasonable basis," Lindsley v. Natl. Carbonic Gas Co., 220 U.S. 61, 78 (1911); see also Flemming v. Nestor, 363 U.S. 603 (1960).

5. We imply no view of the validity of waiting period or residence require-

ments determining eligibility to vote, eligibility for tuition-free education, to obtain a license to practice a profession, to hunt or fish, and so forth. Such requirements may promote compelling state interests on the one hand, or, on the other, may not be penalties upon the exercise of the constitutional right of interstate travel.

quirements.   Rather than an approval or a prescription of the requirement in state plans, the directive was the means chosen by Congress to deny federal funding to any State which persisted in stipulating excessive residence requirements as a condition of the payment of benefits. . . .

But even if we were to assume, *arguendo,* that Congress did approve the imposition of a one-year waiting period, it is the responsive *state* legislation which infringes constitutional rights.   By itself § 402(b) has absolutely no restrictive effect.   It is therefore not that statute but only the state requirements which pose the constitutional question.

Finally, even if it could be argued that the constitutionality of § 402(b) is somehow at issue here, it follows from what we have said that the provision, insofar as it permits the one-year waiting-period requirement, would be unconstitutional.   Congress may not authorize the States to violate the Equal Protection Clause.   Perhaps Congress could induce wider state participation in school construction if it authorized the use of joint funds for the building of segregated schools.   But could it seriously be contended that Congress would be constitutionally justified in such authorization by the need to secure state cooperation?   Congress is without power to enlist state cooperation in a joint federal-state program by legislation which authorizes the States to violate the Equal Protection Clause.   Katzenbach v. Morgan, 384 U.S. 641, 651, n. [1] [chap. 6, p. 545] (1966). *↑ note Douglas dissent*

VI.

The waiting-period requirement in the District of Columbia Code . . is also unconstitutional even though it was adopted by Congress as an exercise of federal power.   In terms of federal power, the discrimination created by the one-year requirement violates the Due Process Clause of the Fifth Amendment.   "[W]hile the Fifth Amendment contains no equal protection clause, it does forbid discrimination that is 'so unjustifiable as to be violative of due process.' "   Schneider v. Rusk, 377 U.S. 163, 168 (1964); Bolling v. Sharpe, 347 U.S. 497 (1954). . . .

Affirmed.*

Mr. Justice STEWART, concurring.

In joining the opinion of the Court, I add a word in response to the dissent of my Brother Harlan, who I think, has quite misapprehended what the Court's opinion says.   The Court today does *not* "pick out particular human activities, characterize them as 'fundamental,' and give them added protection . . . ."   To the contrary, the Court simply recognizes as it must, an established constitutional right, and gives to that right no less protection than the Constitution itself demands.   "The constitutional right to travel from

---

* Note also the Court's 1970 holding that procedural due process requires that welfare recipients be afforded an evidentiary hearing before the termination of benefits, with a statement in Justice Brennan's majority opinion that public assistance "is not mere charity, but a means to 'promote the general Welfare, and secure the Blessings of Liberty to ourselves and our Posterity.' "   Goldberg v. Kelly, 397 U.S. — (1970) (noted supra, chap. 12, p. 915).   See also an appeal challenging a state welfare regulation placing an absolute maximum on amounts received for aid for dependent children, irrespective of need, argued in December 1969, 38 U. S. Law Week 3019. The Court sustained the regulation in a 5:3 decision in April 1970.   Dandridge v. Williams, 397 U.S. — (1970).

one State to another . . . has been firmly established and repeatedly recognized." United States v. Guest, 383 U.S. 745, 757. . . . It follows [that permissible] purposes offered in support of a law that so clearly impinges upon the constitutional right of interstate travel must be shown to reflect a *compelling* governmental interest. . . . The Court today, therefore, is not "contriving new constitutional principles." It is deciding these cases under the aegis of established constitutional law.

Mr. Chief Justice WARREN, with whom Mr. Justice BLACK joins, dissenting.

In my opinion the issue before us can be simply stated: may Congress, acting under one of its enumerated powers, impose minimal nationwide residence requirements or authorize the States to do so? Since I believe that Congress does have this power and has constitutionally exercised it in these cases, I must dissent.

. . . An examination of the relevant legislative materials compels, in my view, the [conclusion that] Congress intended to authorize state residence requirements of up to one year. . . . Faced with the competing claims of States who feared that abolition of residence requirements would result in an influx of persons seeking higher welfare payments and of organizations who stressed the unfairness of such requirements to transient workers forced by the economic dislocation of the depression to seek work far from their homes, Congress chose a middle course. It required those States seeking federal grants for categorical assistance to reduce their existing residence requirements to what Congress viewed as an acceptable maximum. However, Congress accommodated state fears by allowing the States to retain minimal residence requirements. . . .

. . . Appellees insist that . . . Congress, even under its "plenary" power to control interstate commerce, is constitutionally prohibited from imposing residence requirements. I reach a contrary conclusion for I am convinced that the extent of the burden on interstate travel when compared with the justification for its imposition requires the Court to uphold this exertion of federal power.

Congress, pursuant to its commerce power, has enacted a variety of restrictions upon interstate travel. . . . Although each of these restrictions operates as a limitation upon free interstate movement of persons, their constitutionality appears well settled. . . .

The Court's right-to-travel cases lend little support to the view that congressional action is invalid merely because it burdens the right to travel. . . . [Here], travel itself is not prohibited. Any burden inheres solely in the fact that a potential welfare recipient might take into consideration the loss of welfare benefits for a limited period of time if he changes his residence. Not only is this burden of uncertain degree,[1] but appellees themselves assert there is evidence that few welfare recipients have in fact been deterred by residence requirements. . . .

1. The burden is uncertain because indigents who are disqualified from categorical assistance by residence requirements are not left wholly without assistance. Each of the appellees in these cases found alternative sources of assistance after their disqualification. [Footnote by Chief Justice Warren.]

The insubstantiality of the restriction imposed by residence requirements must then be evaluated in light of the possible congressional reasons for such requirements. Our cases require only that Congress have a rational basis for finding that a chosen regulatory scheme is necessary to the furtherance of interstate commerce. See e. g., Katzenbach v. McClung, 379 U.S. 294 (1964); Wickard v. Filburn, 317 U.S. 111 (1942). Certainly, a congressional finding that residence requirements allowed each State to concentrate its resources upon new and increased programs of rehabilitation ultimately resulting in an enhanced flow of commerce as the economic condition of welfare recipients progressively improved is rational and would justify imposition of residence requirements under the Commerce Clause. [Congress acted] to further its conviction that an impediment to the commercial life of this Nation would be removed by a program of cooperative federalism combining federal contributions with enhanced state benefits. . . . I cannot say that Congress is powerless to decide that residence requirements would promote this permissible goal and therefore must conclude that such requirements cannot be termed arbitrary.

The Court, after interpreting the legislative history in such a manner that the constitutionality of § 402(b) is not at issue, gratuitously adds that § 402(b) is unconstitutional. . . . Assuming that the constitutionality of § 402(b) is properly treated by the Court, the cryptic footnote in Katzenbach v. Morgan, 384 U.S. 641, 651–652, n. [1] [p. 547, above] (1966), does not support its conclusion. Footnote [1] indicates that Congress is without power to undercut the equal-protection guaranty of racial equality in the guise of implementing the Fourteenth Amendment. I do not mean to suggest otherwise. However, I do not understand this footnote to operate as a limitation upon Congress' power to further the flow of interstate commerce by reasonable residence requirements. Although the Court dismisses § 402(b) with the remark that Congress cannot authorize the States to violate equal protection, I believe that the dispositive issue is whether under its commerce power Congress can impose residence requirements.

Nor can I understand the Court's implication in footnote [5] that other state residence requirements such as those employed in determining eligibility to vote do not present constitutional questions. . . . If a State would violate equal protection by denying welfare benefits to those who have recently moved interstate, then it would appear to follow that equal protection would also be denied by depriving those who have recently moved interstate of the fundamental right to vote. There is nothing in the opinion of the Court to explain this dichotomy. . . .

The era is long past when this Court under the rubric of due process has reviewed the wisdom of a congressional decision that interstate commerce will be fostered by the enactment of certain regulations. . . . The Court's decision reveals only the top of the iceberg. Lurking beneath are the multitude of situations in which States have imposed residence requirements including eligibility to vote, to engage in certain professions or occupations or to attend a state-supported university. Although the Court takes pains to avoid acknowledging the ramifications of its decision, its implications cannot be ignored. I dissent.

Mr. Justice HARLAN, dissenting. . . . .

In upholding the equal protection argument, the Court has applied an equal protection doctrine of relatively recent vintage: the rule that statutory classifications which either are based upon certain "suspect" criteria or affect "fundamental rights" will be held to deny equal protection unless justified by a "compelling" governmental interest. [Most of the excerpts from Justice Harlan's opinion printed in the introduction to this chapter, at p. 985, are omitted here.]

The "compelling interest" doctrine, which today is articulated more explicitly than ever before, constitutes an increasingly significant exception to the long-established rule that a statute does not deny equal protection if it is rationally related to a legitimate governmental objective. The "compelling interest" doctrine has two branches. [One branch] requires that classifications based upon "suspect" criteria be supported by a compelling interest . . . . Today the list [of "suspect" criteria] apparently has been further enlarged to include classifications based upon recent interstate movement, and perhaps those based upon the exercise of *any* constitutional right . . . . .

The second branch of the "compelling interest" principle is even more troublesome. For it has been held that a statutory classification is subject to the "compelling interest" test if the result of the classification may be to affect a "fundamental right," regardless of the basis of the classification. This rule was foreshadowed in Skinner v. Oklahoma . . . .[1] It has reappeared today in the Court's cryptic suggestion . . . that the "compelling interest" test is applicable merely because the result of the classification may be to deny the appellees "food, shelter, and other necessities of life," as well as in the Court's statement . . . that "[s]ince the classification here touches on the fundamental right of interstate movement, its constitutionality must be judged by the stricter standard of whether it promotes a *compelling* state interest."

I think this branch of the "compelling interest" doctrine particularly unfortunate and unnecessary. It is unfortunate because it creates an exception which threatens to swallow the standard equal protection rule. Virtually every state statute affects important rights. This Court has repeatedly held, for example, that the traditional equal protection standard is applicable to statutory classifications affecting such fundamental matters as the right to pursue a particular occupation, the right to receive greater or smaller wages or to work more or less hours, and the right to inherit property. Rights such as these are in principle indistinguishable from those involved here, and to extend the "compelling interest" rule to all cases in which such rights are af-

---

1. Analysis is complicated when the statutory classification is grounded upon the exercise of a "fundamental" right. For then the statute may come within the first branch of the "compelling interest" doctrine because exercise of the right is deemed a "suspect" criterion and also within the second because the statute is considered to affect the right by deterring its exercise. Williams v. Rhodes, supra, is such a case insofar as the statutes involved both inhibited exercise of the right of political association and drew distinctions based upon the way the right was exercised. The present case is another instance, insofar as welfare residence statutes both deter interstate movement and distinguish among welfare applicants on the basis of such movement. Consequently, I have not attempted to specify the branch of the doctrine upon which these decisions rest. [Footnote by Justice Harlan.]

fected would go far toward making this Court a "super-legislature." This
branch of the doctrine is also unnecessary. When the right affected is one
assured by the federal Constitution, any infringement can be dealt with under
the Due Process Clause. But when a statute affects only matters not mentioned in the federal Constitution and is not arbitrary or irrational, I must reiterate
that I know of nothing which entitles this Court to pick out particular human
activities, characterize them as "fundamental," and give them added protection under an unusually stringent equal protection test.

.   .   . If the issue is regarded purely as one of equal protection, then
for the reasons just set forth this nonracial classification should be judged
by ordinary equal protection standards. The applicable criteria are familiar
and well-established. [A] legislature might rationally find that the imposition of a welfare residence requirement would aid in the accomplishment of at
least four valid governmental objectives. It might also find that residence
requirements have advantages not shared by other methods of achieving the
same goals. In light of this undeniable relation of residence requirements to
valid legislative aims, it cannot be said that the requirements are "arbitrary"
or "lacking in rational justification." Hence, I can find no objection to these
residence requirements under the Equal Protection Clause .   .   ..

The next issue, which I think requires fuller analysis than that deemed
necessary by the Court under its equal protection rationale, is whether a one-
year welfare residence requirement amounts to an undue burden upon the
right of interstate travel. Four considerations are relevant: *First,* what is
the constitutional source and nature of the right to travel which is relied upon? *Second,* what is the extent of the interference with that right? *Third,*
what governmental interests are served by welfare residence requirements?
Fourth, how should the balance of the competing considerations be struck?

[I conclude] that the right to travel interstate is a "fundamental" right
which, for present purposes, should be regarded as having its source in the
Due Process Clause of the Fifth Amendment. .   .   .

Taking all of [the] competing considerations into account, I believe that
the balance definitely favors constitutionality. In reaching that conclusion,
I do not minimize the importance of the right to travel interstate. However,
the impact of residence conditions upon that right is indirect and apparently
quite insubstantial. On the other hand, the governmental purposes served
by the requirements are legitimate and real, and the residence requirements
are clearly suited to their accomplishment. To abolish residence requirements
might well discourage highly worthwhile experimentation in the welfare
field. The statutes come to us clothed with the authority of Congress and
attended by a correspondingly heavy presumption of constitutionality. Moreover, although the appellees assert that the same objectives could have been
achieved by less restrictive means, this is an area in which the judiciary should
be especially slow to fetter the judgment of Congress and of some 46 states
legislatures in the choice of methods. Residence requirements have advantages, such as administrative simplicity and relative certainty, which are not
shared by the alternative solutions proposed by the appellees. In these circumstances, I cannot find that the burden imposed by residence requirements
upon ability to travel outweighs the governmental interests in their continued
employment. Nor do I believe that the period of residence required in these

cases—one year—is so excessively long as to justify a finding of unconstitutionality on that score.

I conclude with the following observations. Today's decision, it seems to me, reflects to an unusual degree the current notion that this Court possesses a peculiar wisdom all its own whose capacity to lead this Nation out of its present troubles is contained only by the limits of judicial ingenuity in contriving new constitutional principles to meet each problem as it arises. For anyone who, like myself, believes that it is an essential function of this Court to maintain the constitutional divisions between state and federal authority and among the three branches of the Federal Government, today's decision is a step in the wrong direction. This resurgence of the expansive view of "equal protection" carries the seeds of more judicial interference with the state and federal legislative process, much more indeed than does the judicial application of "due process" according to traditional concepts, . . . about which some members of this Court have expressed fears as to its potentialities for setting us judges "at large." I consider it particularly unfortunate that this judicial roadblock to the powers of Congress in this field should occur at the very threshold of the current discussions regarding the "federalizing" of these aspects of welfare relief.

THE OPEN-ENDED NEW EQUAL PROTECTION: CRITERIA AND DIRECTIONS

Introduction. When is the strict scrutiny, high justification burden of the new equal protection appropriate? Levy and Shapiro raise that question with renewed intensity. Do the opinions adequately explain the holdings? Do they contain sufficient standards to guide future development? Can better ones be articulated? Consider, e. g., Karst's three-part formula for determining whether a classification is an unconstitutional "invidious discrimination": (1) does it "discriminate" against "a disadvantaged group"; (2) does that discrimination relate to an interest that is "basic" or "fundamental" or "critical"; if so, (3) is the state's justification " 'compelling' enough to overcome the presumptive invalidity implied in a phrase like 'strict scrutiny.' " Karst, "Invidious Discrimination: Justice Douglas and the Return of the 'Natural-Law-Due-Process Formula,' " 16 U.C.L.A.L.Rev. 716, 739 (1969). Is that where the Court is? Where it should be? Compare that formulation with other suggestions noted below.

1. *"Discrimination."* Is it helpful to speak of "discrimination" when the aim is to explain analytical processes rather than to express conclusions? Compare the earlier notes in this chapter. As Karst recognizes, the issue here is not the "easy case" of racial discrimination "written into law." The new equal protection cases typically involve varieties of de facto "discriminations"—the results of "formally nondiscriminatory" classifications. Karst notes: "Since most legislation has differential effects on various groups, discrimination of this kind can be found in almost anything the legislature does—or fails to do."

2. *"Disadvantaged groups."* Which groups in addition to racial minorities qualify for special protection under this criterion? The poor? Nonresidents? Women (including women bartenders)? Women students? Illegitimate children who are prospective plaintiffs in wrongful death cases?

(Cf. Karst on Levy, at 742: Cases like Levy are "easily explained" if one takes into account "the probability that the legislative classification was a covert form of racial discrimination.") Any group that loses in the political process (cf. the last paragraph of Justice Stone's Carolene Products footnote, which follows at the beginning of the next chapter, at p. 1051)? Karst warns that "looming down that path is the spectre of economic due process, of judges riding to the rescue of Oklahoma's opticians or the Railway Express Agency." Is there a "doctrinal escape" by limiting the "new solicitude" to "minorities that seem permanently 'voiceless and invisible,' " to whom the power structure in the political process "may incline to pay little heed"? [See Judge J. Skelly Wright's discussion of racial minorities and the poor in the D.C. School segregation case, Hobson v. Hansen, 269 F.Supp. 401 (D.D.C. 1967)].

3. *"Fundamental rights."* What rights are sufficiently "basic" to evoke the new careful scrutiny? Voting, clearly. Hearings for criminal defendants, clearly. The right in Levy, whatever it may have been. Interstate travel, according to Shapiro. All other constitutional rights, such as those in the First Amendment, cf. Williams v. Rhodes, p. 1016, supra? Is there need to press equal protection analysis to safeguard those rights, which already have independent constitutional footing? What other rights? Procreation? Education? "Food, shelter, and other necessities of life"? Right to engage in a particular occupation? Liberty of contract? Use of property? Cf. Karst, supra, at 744: "The parallel to the pre-1937 'natural-law-due-process' doctrine is close; the old Court had no trouble in placing any right within the coverage of 'life, liberty or property.' " Note also his conclusion, and compare with the formulations below: "What emerges . . . is an extremely flexible sliding scale for measuring the required degree of intensity of judicial scrutiny . . .. The more the victims of legislative classification appear to be disadvantaged, the less need there is for their interests to be basic." So, too, should there be "close scrutiny" when the right is fundamental, "even when the claimant's assertion that he is disadvantaged is less than persuasive."

4. *The interaction of "suspect" distinctions and "fundamental" rights.* Consider an evaluation of the new equal protection written in 1966, shortly after the Harper case, supra: "The decisions appear to rest on two largely subjective judgments, perhaps coupled with a sense of how fast a change the community desires. One element is the relative invidiousness of the particular differentiation, such as between men of different race, farmer and city-dweller, rich and poor, literate and illiterate, or men and women. The second is the relative importance of the subject with respect to which equality is sought, such as the vote, the defense of criminal prosecutions, or civil litigation. But although one can identify the critical elements, the opinions seem notably unsuccessful in elaborating a rational standard, or even points of reference, by which to judge what differentiations are permitted and when equality is required." Cox, "Foreword—Constitutional Adjudication and the Promotion of Human Rights," 80 Harv.L.Rev. 91, 95 (1966).

Do the post-1966 cases elaborate rational standards more adequately? Do the commentators? Consider the effort in "Developments in the Law—Equal Protection," 82 Harv.L.Rev. 1065, 1120 (1969): "The interaction of these two factors [noted by Cox] can be visualized by imagining two gradients. Along the first of these gradients is a hierarchy of classifications, with those which are most invidious—suspect classifications based on traits such as race—at the top. Along the second, arranged in ascending order of importance, are interests such as employment, education, and voting. When the classification drawn lies at the top of the first gradient, it will be subject to strict review even when the interest it affects ranks law on the second gradient—for example, the denial of a driver's license on the basis of race. As the nature of the classification becomes less invidious (descending on the first gradient) the measure will continue to elicit strict review only as it affects interests progressively more important (ascending on the second gradient). Thus, restrained review might be applied when a state disqualifies indigents by requiring a fee from all persons desiring a driver's license or a university education, whereas strict review is applied when indigents are disqualified from voting through a fee imposed for the exercise of that right."

Consider also Michelman's description of the equal protection analytical process, "On Protecting the Poor Through the Fourteenth Amendment," 83 Harv.L.Rev. 7, 34 (1969): "We are concerned about the degree of special importance (in some sense) which attaches to the unequally served personal interest; we factor this with the degree of invidiousness of the classifying trait. The resultant is a kind of 'prejudice' variable which, if it exceeds a certain critical magnitude, we are to balance against the governmental interest—a procedure crudely described by the statement that in such cases the governmental interest can prevail only if it is 'compelling.' (There are special or limiting cases in which the invidiousness factor is '1'—i.e., neutrality of classifying trait—but in which the unaugmented personal interest factor is itself a prejudice variable weighty enough to call for balancing. [The Reapportionment Cases, chap. 18, infra] seem to be an example. And there are converse limiting cases, notably involving de jure racial segregation [also chap. 18, infra], where the personal interest factor may be '1'—signifying no special importance—but the unaugmented invidiousness factor is of critical magnitude.)"

5. *How far can the Court go?—Institutional limitations as restrictions on the expansion of the new equal protection.* Do inherent limits on judicial capabilities suggest and require limits on the new equal protection? Consider, in contrast with Karst's confident admiration, supra, the reservations indicated in the comments that follow.

a. Sager, "Tight Little Islands: Exclusionary Zoning, Equal Protection, and the Indigent," 21 Stan.L.Rev. 767, 779 (1969): "In Griffin, Douglas, and Harper the Court went beyond the limits of purposeful discriminations against racial minorities. Those cases extended the substantive aspects of equal protection doctrine to the indigent, and they did so in the context of de facto discriminations. They involve, however, cherished aspects of a government's contact with citizens: criminal defense and the franchise. Any move away from race as such, away from purposeful discrimination, and away from criminal defense and the franchise, stretches thin the fabric of judicial restraint. It would not be surprising if the Court were to assimilate a single area at a time into the new equal protection fold, and were to do so rather cautiously."

b. "Developments in the Law—Equal Protection," 82 Harv.L.Rev. 1065, 1192 (1969): "But the suggestion that government has an affirmative duty to raise everyone to a minimum acceptable standard of living has not yet assumed the dignity of a constitutional proposition. Three major reasons for this lack of development may be suggested. The first is the conceptual difficulty of finding support for the proposition in the Constitution. [T]he guarantee of a minimum standard of living appears to be on a completely different level from the guarantee of effectively equal access to the criminal process, to the political process, to education, or even to other state activities. The latter find their sources primarily, if not exclusively, in the state. One seeking income, housing, or a job, on the other hand, is remitted primarily to the private sector for satisfaction of his needs. Extending the equal protection clause from a guarantee of equal participation in fundamental state benefits to a guarantee of similar equality in these areas seems improper precisely because the latter are not benefits we customarily think the state is in the habit of distributing at all. Second, the practical problems in reallocating resources according to an infinite variety of needs, and in establishing acceptable minimum norms would be far greater than those which have already attended judicial efforts to impose precise standards of equality on the states. Finally, state and federal legislatures themselves have taken significant, if as yet small, strides through social security and other welfare measures to provide minimum standards for selected groups of people. . . . The role of the courts thus seems better confined to protecting and broadening the new approach to equality in the areas already established and to assuring adherence to traditional equal protection standards in areas where the legislature takes the lead. . . . The constitutional obligation to enforce the equal protection guarantee rests alike, after all, on the legislative as well as the judicial branch of the government."

c. Cox, "Foreword: Constitutional Adjudication and the Promotion of Human Rights," 80 Harv.L.Rev. 91 (1966): "Once loosed, the idea of Equality is not easily cabined. . . . [T]he cases expanding the concept of equal protection . . . require the state to make changes in the *status quo* [and] impose affirmative obligations upon the states. . . . [A]bility to rationalize a constitutional judgment in terms of principles referable to accepted sources of law is an essential, major element of constitutional adjudication. It is one of the sources of power of the Court— including the power to gain acceptance for the occasional great leaps forward which lack such justification. . . . Out of such a *coup de main* [as Reynolds v. Sims, the reapportionment decision] great legal principles may occasionally be created. As a staple diet, however, political perceptions without roots in objective standards are an inadequate basis for law, and to accept them would give judges unacceptably dangerous powers. Such a course is even self-defeating."

Are the predictions and warnings of these comments borne out by the equal protection decisions since?

Chapter 15

FREEDOM OF EXPRESSION AND THE RISKS OF CRIME, DISORDER, AND REVOLUTION

Introduction. The history of Supreme Court litigation regarding First Amendment freedoms is short in years but heavy in volume. The Court's first major encounter with freedom of speech claims did not come until after World War I; yet in the little more than 50 years since, claimed infringements of freedoms of expression and association have become a staple of Supreme Court business—and a frequent source of controversy.

What are the ingredients and dimensions of the constitutionally protected values? What analyses are helpful, what techniques useful? An extensive and at times bewildering array of phrases, slogans and standards abounds in the cases. What is the meaning and scope of the "clear and present danger" test? What are the alternative judicial approaches and doctrinal tools? Is it meaningful to talk about "preferred positions" of certain freedoms? Of presumptions of unconstitutionality? How significant is the clash between judicial positions of "balancing" and of "absolute" guarantees?

The problems of freedom of expression are too varied and multi-faceted to lend themselves to solution by any single, simple, all-embracing formula. Most cases involve more than one value of constitutional dimensions, and the resolution of value clashes cannot be a mechanical process. But, after a half century of First Amendment litigation, there is special justification for an effort to examine the complex and diffuse materials in an orderly manner. Aiding that effort is the purpose of the next two chapters.

Chapter 15 explores the most pervasive doctrines at the core of First Amendment analysis; chapter 16 tests and elaborates these core concepts in additional settings. To introduce the core ingredients, this chapter focuses on two recurrent contexts: the first is criminal legislation directed at the content of speech critical of national policies (sec. 1); the second is the local regulation of the manner of expression in public places (sec. 2). An initial understanding of the judicial techniques for interpreting the First Amendment can best be obtained in connection with these problems, as the text materials below will repeatedly note.

Section 3 of this chapter reviews the strengths and weaknesses of the basic analyses developed in the opening sections and illustrates their interaction in several "symbolic expression" cases of the late sixties. Chapter 16 continues the critical testing of the core doctrines and introduces a variety of elaborations by examining a series of special problems of free expression.

This grouping of the materials makes possible the exploration of the central ideas through a study of a limited number of materials, gathered in this chapter. More intensive investigation can then be pursued by selecting additional problems in chapter 16.

FIRST AMENDMENT RIGHTS AND JUDICIAL RESPONSI-
BILITY: OF DOUBLE STANDARDS AND
PREFERRED POSITIONS

Most of the recurrent doctrines and slogans characteristic of free speech litigation are best explored in connection with the later materials in these chapters. But one of the problems is so pervasive—and has so often been touched on in earlier chapters—that it warrants mention at the outset. The problem is that of a special judicial responsibility to safeguard First Amendment rights—the problem that underlies the controversies over double standards, presumptive unconstitutionality, and preferred positions.

Should the Court give more careful scrutiny to alleged infringements of personal, noneconomic liberties than to restrictions on property use and related interests? The problem of justifying different levels of scrutiny was raised in chap. 13, on substantive due process and economic regulation (see especially the questions at p. 981); and chap. 14 examined the inchoate modern efforts to explain special protections of some claims via the new equal protection. In the First Amendment setting, Court attention to the double standard problem has been more continuous and rigorous, and judicial articulation of rationales has been less amorphous.

1. *Justice Stone's Carolene Products footnote.* Perhaps the most influential statement of reasons to scrutinize restraints on freedom of expression with special care came in a footnote to an opinion by Justice Stone in 1938 —shortly after the Court crisis of 1937, shortly after decisions such as West Coast Hotel v. Parrish (chap. 13, p. 971, supra) had signaled the Court's new hands-off attitude toward economic regulation. Justice Stone sought to explain why the new reluctance to reexamine legislative judgments should not be applied across the board. United States v. Carolene Products Co., 304 U.S. 144 (1938).

In the text of his opinion, Justice Stone stated that "regulatory legislation affecting ordinary commercial transactions is not to be pronounced unconstitutional unless in the light of the facts made known or generally assumed it is of such a character as to preclude the assumption that it rests upon some rational basis within the knowledge and experience of the legislators." At that point, he added the famous footnote 4:

"There may be narrower scope for operation of the presumption of constitutionality when legislation appears on its face to be within a specific prohibition of the Constitution, such as those of the first ten Amendments, which are deemed equally specific when held to be embraced within the Fourteenth. See Stromberg v. California, 283 U.S. 359, 369–370; Lovell v. Griffin, 303 U.S. 444, 452.

"It is unnecessary to consider now whether legislation which restricts those political processes which can ordinarily be expected to bring about repeal of undesirable legislation, is to be subjected to more exacting judicial scrutiny under the general prohibitions of the Fourteenth Amendment than are most other types of legislation. On restrictions upon the right to vote, see Nixon v. Herndon, 273 U.S. 536; Nixon v. Condon, 286 U.S. 73; on restraints upon the dissemination of information, see Near v. Minnesota, 283 U.S. 697, 713–714, 718–720, 722; Grosjean v. American Press Co., 297 U. S. 233; Lovell v. Griffin, supra; on interferences with political organizations, see Stromberg v. California, supra, 369; Fiske v. Kansas, 274 U.S. 380; Whitney v. California, 274 U.S. 357, 373–378; Herndon v. Lowry, 301 U.S. 242; and see Holmes, J., in Gitlow v. New York, 268 U.S. 652, 673; as to prohibition of peaceable assembly, see De Jonge v. Oregon, 299 U.S. 353, 365.

"Nor need we enquire whether similar considerations enter into the review of statutes directed at particular religious, Pierce v. Society of Sisters, 268 U.S. 510, or national, Meyer v. Nebraska, 262 U.S. 390; Bartels v. Iowa, 262 U.S. 404; Farrington v. Tokushige, 273 U.S. 284, or racial minorities, Nixon v. Herndon, supra; Nixon v. Condon, supra; whether prejudice against discrete and insular minorities may be a special condition, which tends seriously to curtail the operation of those political processes ordinarily to be relied upon to protect minorities, and which may call for a correspondingly more searching judicial inquiry. Compare McCulloch v. Maryland, 4 Wheat. (17 U.S.) 316, 428; South Carolina v. Barnwell Bros., 303 U.S. 177, 184, n. 2, and cases cited."

2. *Some comments on Carolene Products.* Are the suggested distinctions persuasive? Are First Amendment rights more "specific" than the constitutional recognitions of "property" and the contract clause? Is the general rationale of the third paragraph ("minorities") as persuasive as that of the second ("political processes")? To the extent that the minorities are racial or religious ones, the background of the post-Civil War Amendments and the religion clauses of the First provide "specific" bases for judicial intervention. Does that third paragraph support special protection of all other minorities as well? Including economic interests that have lost their battles in the political arena? Why not?

Does reference to "political processes ordinarily to be relied upon to protect minorities" exclude some "minorities" from judicial protection? Is not the majoritarian political processes a generally unreliable protection of minorities? Restrictions of the political process through curtailment of political debate or voting (the second paragraph) is a clear enough concept. Can the same be said of restrictions on the "process"—though all may speak and vote—because the *results* bear harshly on certain minorities? If that is justification for "more searching judicial inquiry," did some of the claims summarily dismissed in the economic regulation cases, chap. 13 supra, deserve more careful scrutiny? Cf. the questions at p. 981, supra.

Compare Judge Learned Hand's comment on Stone and the double standard rationales (from Hand, "Chief Justice Stone's Concept of the Judicial Function," in The Spirit of Liberty (Dilliard ed. 1952), 201, 205): "Even before [Stone became Chief Justice in 1941] it began to seem as though, when 'personal rights' were in issue, something strangely akin to the discredited attitude toward the Bill of Rights of the old apostles of the institution of property, was regaining recognition. . . . It needed little acquaintance with the robust and loyal character of [Chief Justice Stone] to foretell that he would not be content with what to him was an opportunistic reversion. . . . He could not understand how the principle which he had all along supported, could mean that, when concerned with interests other than property, the courts should have a wider latitude for enforcing their own predilections. . . ." Note the remark on this passage in Freund, On Understanding the Supreme Court (1949), 13: "It is not uncommon that memorial addresses provide an even truer insight into the speaker than into the subject; and it is probably safer that the views so pointedly put by Judge Hand be ascribed to himself than to the late Chief Justice." [Recall Justice Black's attack on the double standard due process rationale (though not on the case for special protection of "specific," "absolute" First Amendment rights) in his Griswold v. Connecticut dissent, chap. 11, p. 831, supra.]

3. *Other justifications of the double standard.* Justice Stone's Carolene Products footnote is by no means the only judicial effort to justify special protection of First Amendment rights. Others appear in the cases that follow (see, among the most important, Justice Holmes' dissent in Abrams, p. 1063, Justice Brandeis' concurrence in Whitney, p. 1082, Justice Jackson's opinion in Barnette, p. 1395, and Justice Brennan's opinion in the New York Times case, p. 1063). And some explanations have already surfaced in earlier materials. Recall, for example, Justice Cardozo on "freedom of thought and speech" in his discussion of "absorption" in Palko v. Connecticut, p. 798, supra: "Of that freedom one may say that it is the matrix, the indispensable condition of nearly every other form of freedom. [A] pervasive recognition of that truth can be traced in our history, political and legal."

4. *Justice Frankfurter and the "preferred position" talk.* The debate about the "preferred position" of First Amendment rights, has been a controversial by-product of the double standard debate. Is the "preferred position" debate a meaningful one? A helpful one? Consider the famous review of (and attack on) "preferred position" statements by Justice Frankfurter. Do the passages he quotes demonstrate that use of "preferred position" language is the equivalent of a presumption of unconstitutionality? What does that mean? Is that sound? Is Justice Frankfurter's rejection of "preferred position" the equivalent of Judge Hand's repudiation of *any* double standard? Or does Justice Frankfurter, too, recognize a hierarchy of values, with free speech at or near the apex? Justice Frankfurter said in a concurring opinion in Kovacs v. Cooper, 336 U.S. 77 (1949) (see the Loudspeaker Cases, p. 1149 infra):

". . . My brother Reed speaks of 'the preferred position of freedom of speech' . . .. This is a phrase that has uncritically crept into some recent opinions of this Court. I deem it a mischievous phrase, if it carries the thought, which it may subtly imply, that any law touching communication is infected with presumptive invalidity. . . . I say the phrase is mischievous because it radiates a constitutional doctrine without avowing it. Clarity and candor in these matters, so as to avoid gliding unwittingly into error, make it appropriate to trace the history of the phrase 'preferred position.' The following is a chronological account of the evolution of talk about 'preferred position' except where the thread of derivation is plain enough to be indicated.

"1. Herndon v. Lowry, 301 U.S. 242, 258 [p. 1089 infra]: 'The power of a state to abridge freedom of speech and of assembly is the exception rather than the rule and the penalizing even of utterances of a defined character must find its justification in a reasonable apprehension of danger to organized government. The judgment of the legislature is not unfettered. The limitation upon individual liberty must have appropriate relation to the safety of the state.'

"2. United States v. Carolene Products Co., 304 U.S. 144, 152, n. 4 [supra]. A footnote hardly seems to be an appropriate way of announcing a new constitutional doctrine, and the Carolene footnote did not purport to announce any new doctrine; incidentally, it did not have the concurrence of a majority of the Court. . . .

"(3) Schneider v. State, 308 U.S. 147, 161 [see p. 1138 infra]: 'In every case, therefore, where legislative abridgment of the rights [freedom of speech and of the press] is asserted, the courts should be astute to examine the effect of the challenged legislation. Mere legislative preferences or beliefs respecting matters of public convenience may well support regulation directed at other personal activities, but be insufficient to justify such as diminishes the exercise of rights so vital to the maintenance of democratic institutions. And so, as cases arise, the delicate and difficult task falls upon the courts to weigh the circumstances and to appraise the substantiality of the reasons advanced in support of the regulation of the free enjoyment of the rights.'

"(4) Bridges v. California, 314 U.S. 252, 262–63: 'Moreover, the likelihood, however great, that a substantive evil will result cannot alone justify a restriction upon freedom of speech or the press. The evil itself must be "substantial," Brandeis, J., concurring in Whitney v. California, [p. 1082, infra]; it must be "serious". id. And even the expression of "legislative preferences or beliefs" cannot transform minor matters of public inconvenience or annoyance into substantive evils of sufficient weight to warrant the curtailment of liberty of expression. Schneider v. State. . . .

"What finally emerges from the 'clear and present danger' cases is a working principle that the substantive evil must be extremely serious and the degree of imminence extremely high before utterances can be punished." . . .

"(5) A number of Jehovah's Witnesses cases refer to the freedoms specified by the First Amendment as in a 'preferred position.' The phrase was apparently first used in the dissent of Chief Justice Stone in Jones v. Opelika, 316 U.S. 584, 600, 608. It reappears in Murdock v. Pennsylvania, 319 U.S. 105, 115 [p. 1139 infra] . . .

"(6) West Virginia State Board of Education v. Barnette, 319 U.S. 624, 639 [p. 1394 infra]: 'The test of legislation which collides with the Fourteenth Amendment, because it also collides with the principles of the First, is much more definite than the test when only the Fourteenth is involved. Much of the vagueness of the due process clause disappears when the specific prohibitions of the First become its standard. The right of a State to regulate, for example, a public utility may well include, so far as the due process test is concerned, power to impose all of the restrictions which a legislature may have a "rational basis" for adopting. But freedoms of speech and of press, of assembly, and of worship may not be infringed on such slender grounds. They are susceptible of restriction only to prevent grave and immediate danger to interests which the State may lawfully protect.'

"(7) Thomas v. Collins, 323 U.S. 516, 530 [see p. 1138, infra]: 'For these reasons any attempt to restrict those liberties must be justified by clear public interest, threatened not doubtfully or remotely, but by clear and present danger. The rational connection between the remedy provided and the evil to be curbed, which in other contexts might support legislation against attack on due process grounds, will not suffice. These rights rest on firmer foundation. Accordingly, whatever occasion would restrain orderly discussion and persuasion, at appropriate time and place must have clear support in public danger, actual or impending. Only the gravest abuses, endangering paramount interests, give occasion for permissible limitation.' This is perhaps the strongest language dealing with the constitutional aspect of legislation touching utterance. But it was the opinion of only four members of the Court . . . .

"In short, the claim that any legislation is presumptively unconstitutional which touches the field of the First Amendment and the Fourteenth Amendment, insofar as the latter's concept of 'liberty' contains what is specifically protected by the First, has never commended itself to a majority of this Court.

"Behind the notion sought to be expressed by the formula as to 'the preferred position of freedom of speech' lies a relevant consideration in determining whether an enactment relating to the liberties protected by the Due Process Clause of the Fourteenth Amendment is violative of it. In law also, doctrine is illuminated by history. The ideas now governing the constitutional protection of freedom of speech derive essentially from the opinions of Mr. Justice Holmes.

"The philosophy of his opinions on that subject arose from a deep awareness of the extent to which sociological conclusions are conditioned by time and circumstance. Because of this awareness Mr. Justice Holmes seldom felt justified in opposing his own opinion to economic views which the legislature embodied in law. But since he also realized that the progress of civilization is to a considerable extent the displacement of error which once held sway as official truth by beliefs which in turn have yielded to other beliefs, for him the right to search for truth was of a different order than some transient economic dogma. And without freedom of expression, thought becomes checked and atrophied. Therefore, in considering what interests are so fundamental as to be enshrined in the Due Process Clause, those liberties of the individual which history has attested as the indispensable conditions of an open as against a closed society come to this Court with a momentum for respect lacking when appeal is made to liberties which derive merely from shifting economic arrangements. Accordingly, Mr. Justice Holmes was far more ready to find legislative invasion where free inquiry was involved than in the debatable area of economics. See my Mr. Justice Holmes and the Supreme Court, 58 et seq.

"The objection to summarizing this line of thought by the phrase 'the preferred position of freedom of speech' is that it expresses a complicated process of constitutional adjudication by a deceptive formula. And it was Mr. Justice Holmes who admonished us that 'To rest upon a formula is a slumber that, prolonged, means death.' Collected Legal Papers, 306. Such a formula makes for mechanical jurisprudence. . . . ."

5. *A concluding note on "attitudes" and analyses.* Justice Frankfurter's position on the First Amendment is often represented as one of extreme deference to legislative judgments and of emphatic disavowal of double standards. Yet his Kovacs attack on "preferred position" recognizes that freedom of expression is a liberty that comes to the Court "with a momentum for respect lacking when appeal is made to liberties which derive from shifting economic arrangements." What, then, is the fighting all about? All modern Justices have agreed that the First Amendment is "special" in some

senses; the disputes have been over the implementations of that "special-ness."

Does the criticism of the Frankfurter position rest on the notion that "preferred position" is a useful concept because it suggests an attitude, "a whole manner of approaching" free speech? See McKay, "The Preference for Freedom," 34 N.Y.U.L.Rev. 1184 (1959). But is it fruitful to discuss attitude in general? As with the related "balancing"-"absolutes" contro-versy,* is it not more useful to examine concrete conflicts and disparate judicial techniques? If "preferred position" consists of "a variety of devices" to pro-tect speech—including "the clear and present danger test" and "prohibitions against prior restraint and subsequent punishment," see McKay, supra—is it not more important to examine the varied "devices" in detail, in the con-text of recurrent problems, than to debate moods and attitudes? A more particularistic exploration of those devices and problems is the aim of the two chapters that follow.

SECTION 1. REGULATION OF POLITICAL SPEECH BE-CAUSE OF ITS CONTENT: THE PROBLEM OF SUBVERSIVE ADVOCACY

A. THE WORLD WAR I CASES: CLEAR AND PRESENT DANGER—ORIGINS, WEAKNESSES, ALTERNATIVES

Introduction. The Court's first significant encounter with the problem of articulating the scope of constitutionally protected speech came in a series of cases involving agitation against the war and the draft during World War I. The "clear and present danger" language stems from the first of these cases, Justice Holmes' opinion for the Court in Schenck v. United States.

"Clear and present danger" has been a prominent and controversial ingredient of First Amendment law. When is restriction on speech permis-sible? "Clear and present danger" has been hailed as an answer that avoids extremes yet draws the line on the libertarian side of the spectrum. At one extreme, it can be argued that restriction on speech, at least political speech, is *never* legitimate—that punishment must be limited to illegal action, even if the speech directly "incites" that action. Holmes rejected that "perfect im-munity" for speech. But Holmes also, as one of the strongest defenders of "clear and present danger" emphasized, rejected a far more restrictive, far more widely supported, alternative: that "any tendency in speech to produce bad acts, no matter how remote, would suffice to validate a repressive statute." See Chafee, Book Review, 62 Harv.L.Rev. 891 (1949), Selected Essays

* On the "balancing"-"absolutes" dis-pute, see, e. g., the closing note of this chapter, p. 1208, the excerpts from the Black-Harlan debate in the second Konigsberg case, p. 1308, and generally Bickel, The Least Dangerous Branch (1962); Emerson, "Toward a General Theory of the First Amendment," 72 Yale L.J. 877 (1963); Shapiro, Free-dom of Speech: The Supreme Court and Judicial Review (1966); Frantz, "The First Amendment in the Bal-ance," 71 Yale L.J. 1424 (1962); and Mendelson, ". . . Absolutes in the Balance," 50 Calif.L.Rev. 821 (1962).

1938–62 (1963), 618.   "Clear and present danger" purports to draw the line somewhere in-between, but with a strong leaning toward protection of speech.

But what is the meaning of "clear and present danger"? What are its uses, what its weaknesses? The test has been criticized as too simplistic. It has been charged with being insensitive to legitimate state interests for curtailing speech. It has been criticized from another direction as too flexible, as permitting too much incursion on speech, as a shield too likely to collapse under stress. It has been employed far outside its original context. It has had periods of disfavor as well as of popularity with Justices and commentators. See generally Strong, "Fifty Years of 'Clear and Present Danger': From Schenck to Brandenburg—and Beyond," 1969 S.Ct.Rev. 41. It is less widely invoked today than it once was; yet it remains an important strain at the core of Court efforts to protect expression; and from it later doctrinal variations have grown.

Attention to the origins and meaning of clear and present danger is one of the justifications for beginning this chapter with an examination of the post-World War I cases. The Schenck case gave birth to the language; but Schenck was followed within a week by two other Holmes decisions, Frohwerk and Debs, which purported to follow Schenck, and those opinions are important to an understanding of the original Schenck criterion. Later in the same year came Holmes' dissent in Abrams. Did the Abrams dissent simply apply the Schenck standard, or did it give new meaning to clear and present danger? To pursue the critical examination of the Schenck-Abrams criterion, District Judge Learned Hand's opinion in the Masses case is printed: does Hand's analysis, dealing with the same World War I statute about two years before Schenck, suggest a useful alternative to that of Holmes? Yet doctrinal significance is not the only justification for beginning with these cases: their factual context—of agitation against war and the draft—is obviously of more than historical interest.

[Most of the cases below arose under section 3 of Title I of the 1917 Espionage Act. (The Abrams case involved 1918 amendments to the law.) The 1917 Act created three new offenses: "[1] Whoever, when the United States is at war, shall willfully make or convey false reports or false statements with intent to interfere with the operation or success of the military or naval forces of the United States or to promote the success of its enemies [2] and whoever, when the United States is at war, shall willfully cause or attempt to cause insubordination, disloyalty, mutiny, or refusal of duty, in the military or naval forces of the United States, [3] or shall willfully obstruct the recruiting or enlistment service of the United States, to the injury of the service or of the United States, shall be punished by a fine of not more than $10,000 or imprisonment for not more than twenty years, or both."]

SCHENCK v. UNITED STATES

249 U.S. 47, 39 S.Ct. 247, 63 L.Ed. 470 (1919).

Error to the District Court of the United States for the Eastern District of Pennsylvania.

Mr. Justice HOLMES delivered the opinion of the Court.

This is an indictment in three counts. The first charges a conspiracy to violate the Espionage Act of June 15, 1917, c. 30, § 3, 40 Stat. 217, 219, by causing and attempting to cause insubordination, &c., in the military and naval forces of the United States, and to obstruct the recruiting and enlistment service of the United States, when the United States was at war with the German Empire, to-wit, that the defendants wilfully conspired to have printed and circulated to men who had been called and accepted for military service under the Act of May 18, 1917, a document set forth and alleged to be calculated to cause such insubordination and obstruction. The count alleges overt acts in pursuance of the conspiracy, ending in the distribution of the document set forth. The second count alleges a conspiracy to commit an offence against the United States, to-wit, to use the mails for the transmission of matter declared to be non-mailable by Title XII, § 2 of the Act of June 15, 1917, to-wit, the above mentioned document, with an averment of the same overt acts. The third count charges an unlawful use of the mails for the transmission of the same matter and otherwise as above. The defendants were found guilty on all the counts. They set up the First Amendment to the Constitution forbidding Congress to make any law abridging the freedom of speech, or of the press, and bringing the case here on that ground have argued some other points also . . . ..

The document in question upon its first printed side recited the first section of the Thirteenth Amendment, said that the idea embodied in it was violated by the Conscription Act and that a conscript is little better than a convict. In impassioned language it intimated that conscription was despotism in its worst form and a monstrous wrong against humanity in the interest of Wall Street's chosen few. It said "Do not submit to intimidation," but in form at least confined itself to peaceful measures such as a petition for the repeal of the act. The other and later printed side of the sheet was headed "Assert Your Rights." It stated reasons for alleging that any one violated the Constitution when he refused to recognize "your right to assert your opposition to the draft," and went on "If you do not assert and support your rights, you are helping to deny or disparage rights which it is the solemn duty of all citizens and residents of the United States to retain." It described the arguments on the other side as coming from cunning politicians and a mercenary capitalist press, and even silent consent to the conscription law as helping to support an infamous conspiracy. It denied the power to send our citizens away to foreign shores to shoot up the people of other lands, and added that words could not express the condemnation such cold-blooded ruthlessness deserves, &c., &c., winding up "You must do your share to maintain, support and uphold the rights of the people of this country." Of course the document would not have been sent unless it had been intended to have some effect, and we do not see what effect it could be expected to have upon persons subject to the draft except to influence them to obstruct the carrying of it out. The defendants do not deny that the jury might find against them on this point.

But it is said, suppose that that was the tendency of this circular, it is protected by the First Amendment to the Constitution. Two of the strongest expressions are said to be quoted respectively from well-known public men. It well may be that the prohibition of laws abridging the freedom of speech is not confined to previous restraints, although to prevent them may have been the main purpose, as intimated in Patterson v. Colorado, 205 U.S. 454, 462. We admit that in many places and in ordinary times the defendants in saying all that was said in the circular would have been within their constitutional rights. But the character of every act depends upon the circumstances in which it is done. Aikens v. Wisconsin, 195 U.S. 194, 205, 206. The most stringent protection of free speech would not protect a man in falsely shouting fire in a theatre and causing a panic. It does not even protect a man from an injunction against uttering words that may have all the effect of force. Gompers v. Bucks Stove & Range Co., 221 U.S. 418, 439. The question in every case is whether the words used are used in such circumstances and are of such a nature as to create a clear and present danger that they will bring about the substantive evils that Congress has a right to prevent. It is a question of proximity and degree. When a nation is at war many things that might be said in time of peace are such a hindrance to its effort that their utterance will not be endured so long as men fight, and that no Court could regard them as protected by any constitutional right. It seems to be admitted that if an actual obstruction of the recruiting service were proved, liability for words that produced that effect might be enforced. The statute of 1917 in § 4 punishes conspiracies to obstruct as well as actual obstruction. If the act (speaking, or circulating a paper), its tendency and the intent with which it is done are the same, we perceive no ground for saying that success alone warrants making the act a crime. Goldman v. United States, 245 U.S. 474, 477. Indeed that case might be said to dispose of the present contention if the precedent covers all *media concludendi*. But as the right to free speech was not referred to specially, we have thought fit to add a few words. . . .

Judgments affirmed.

FROHWERK v. UNITED STATES

249 U.S. 204, 39 S.Ct. 249, 63 L.Ed. 561 (1919).

Error to the United States District Court for the Western District of Missouri.

Mr. Justice HOLMES delivered the opinion of the court.

This is an indictment in thirteen counts. The first alleges a conspiracy between the plaintiff in error and one Carl Gleeser, they then being engaged in the preparation and publication of a newspaper, the Missouri Staats Zeitung, to violate the Espionage Act of June 15, 1917 c. 30, § 3, 40 Stat. 217, 219. It alleges as overt acts the preparation and circulation of twelve articles, &c. in the said newspaper at different dates from July 6, 1917, to December 7 of the same year. The other counts allege attempts to cause disloyalty, mutiny and refusal of duty in the military and naval forces of the United States, by the same publications, each count being confined to the publication of a single date. Motion to dismiss and a demurrer on constitutional and other grounds, especially that of the First Amendment as to free speech, were overruled . . . .. Frohwerk was found guilty [and] was sentenced to a fine and to ten years imprisonment on each count, the imprisonment on the later counts to run concurrently with that on the first.

. . . With regard to [the constitutional] argument we think it necessary to add to what has been said in [Schenck] only that the First Amendment while prohibiting legislation against free speech as such cannot have been, and obviously was not, intended to give immunity for every possible use of language. . . . We venture to believe that neither Hamilton nor Madison, nor any other competent person then or later, ever supposed that to make criminal the counselling of a murder within the jurisdiction of Congress would be an unconstitutional interference with free speech.

Whatever might be thought of the other counts on the evidence, if it were before us, we have decided in Schenck v. United States, that a person may be convicted of a conspiracy to obstruct recruiting by words of persuasion. [S]o far as the language of the articles goes there is not much to choose between expressions to be found in them and those before us in Schenck v. United States.

The first begins by declaring it a monumental and inexcusable mistake to send our soldiers to France, says that it comes no doubt from the great trusts, and later that it appears to be outright murder without serving anything practical; speaks of the unconquerable spirit and undiminished strength of the German nation, and characterizes its own discourse as words of warning to the American people. [A]fter deploring "the draft riots in Oklahoma and elsewhere" in language that might be taken to convey an innuendo of a different sort, it is said that the previous talk about legal remedies is all very well for those who are past the draft age and have no boys to be drafted . . . .. Who then, it is asked, will pronounce a verdict of guilty upon him if he stops reasoning and follows the first impulse of nature: self-preservation; and further, whether, while technically he is wrong in his resistance, he is not more sinned against than sinning; and yet again whether the guilt of those who voted the unnatural sacrifice is not greater than the wrong of those who now seek to escape by ill-advised resistance. . . . There is much more to the general effect that we are in the wrong and are giving false and hypocritical reasons for our course, but the foregoing is enough to indicate the kind of matter with which we have to deal.

It may be that all this might be said or written even in time of war in circumstances that would not make it a crime. We do not lose our right to condemn either measures or men because the Country is at war. It does not appear that there was any special effort to reach men who were subject to the draft; and if the evidence should show that the defendant was a poor man, turning out copy for Gleeser, his employer, at less than a day laborer's pay, for Gleeser to use or reject as he saw fit, in a newspaper of small circulation, there would be a natural inclination to test every question of law to be found in the record very thoroughly before upholding the very severe penalty imposed. But we must take the case on the record as it is, and on that record it is impossible to say that it might not have been found that the circulation of the paper was in quarters where a little breath would be enough to kindle a flame and that the fact was known and relied upon by those who sent the paper out. Small compensation would not exonerate the defendant if it were found that he expected the result, even if pay were his chief desire. When we consider that we do not know how strong the Government's evidence may have been we find ourselves unable to say that the articles could not furnish a basis for a conviction upon the first count at least. We pass therefore to the other points that are raised.

It is said that the first count is bad because it does not allege the means by which the conspiracy was to be carried out. But a conspiracy to obstruct recruiting would be criminal even if no means were agreed upon specifically by which to accomplish the intent. It is enough if the parties agreed to set to work for that common purpose. That purpose could be accomplished or aided by persuasion as well as by false statements, and there was no need to allege that false reports were intended to be made or made. It is argued that there is no sufficient allegation of intent, but intent to accomplish an object cannot be alleged more clearly than by stating that parties conspired to accomplish it. . . .

Affirmed.

DEBS v. UNITED STATES

249 U.S. 211, 39 S.Ct. 252, 63 L.Ed. 566 (1919).

Error to the United States District Court for the Northern District of Ohio.

Mr. Justice HOLMES delivered the opinion of the court.

This is an indictment under the Espionage Act of June 15, 1917 . . . It has been cut down to two counts, originally the third and fourth. The former of these alleges that on or about June 16, 1918, at Canton, Ohio, the defendant caused and incited and attempted to cause and incite insubordination, disloyalty, mutiny and refusal of duty in the military and naval forces of the United States and with intent so to do delivered, to an assembly of people, a public speech, set forth. The fourth count alleges that he obstructed and attempted to obstruct the recruiting and enlistment service of the United States and to that end and with that intent delivered the same speech, again set forth. The defendant was found guilty and was sentenced to ten years' imprisonment on each of the two counts, the punishment to run concurrently on both.

The main theme of the speech was socialism, its growth, and a prophecy of its ultimate success. With that we have nothing to do, but if a part or the manifest intent of the more general utterances was to encourage those present to obstruct the recruiting service and if in passages such encouragement was directly given, the immunity of the general theme may not be enough to protect the speech. The speaker began by saying that he had just returned from a visit to the workhouse in the neighborhood where three of their most loyal comrades were paying the penalty for their devotion to the working class— these being Wagenknecht, Baker and Ruthenberg, who had been convicted of aiding and abetting another in failing to register for the draft. Ruthenberg v. United States, 245 U.S. 480. He said that he had to be prudent and might not be able to say all that he thought, thus intimating to his hearers that they might infer that he meant more, but he did say that those persons were paying the penalty for standing erect and for seeking to pave the way to better conditions for all mankind. Later he added further eulogies and said that he was proud of them. . . .

There followed personal experiences and illustrations of the growth of socialism, a glorification of minorities, and a prophecy of the success of the international socialist crusade, with the interjection that "you need to know that you are fit for something better than slavery and cannon fodder." The rest of the discourse had only the indirect though not necessarily ineffective bearing on the offences alleged that is to be found in the usual contrasts between capitalists and laboring men, sneers at the advice to cultivate war gardens, attribution to plutocrats of the high price of coal, &c. . . . The defendant addressed the jury himself, and while contending that his speech did not warrant the charges said "I have been accused of obstructing the war. I admit it. Gentlemen, I abhor war. I would oppose the war if I stood alone." The statement was not necessary to warrant the jury in finding that one purpose of the speech, whether incidental or not does not matter, was to oppose not only war in general but this war, and that the opposition was so expressed that its natural and intended effect would be to obstruct recruiting. If that was intended and if, in all the circumstances, that would be its probable effect, it would not be protected by reason of its being part of a general program and expressions of a general and conscientious belief.

[The chief defense is] that based upon the First Amendment to the Constitution, disposed of in Schenck v. United States . . . .

There was introduced [in evidence] an "Anti-war Proclamation and Program" adopted at St. Louis in April, 1917, coupled with testimony that about an hour before his speech the defendant had stated that he approved of that platform in spirit and in substance. [C]ounsel argued against its admissibility, at some length. This document contained the usual suggestion that capitalism was the cause of the war and that our entrance into it "was instigated by the predatory capitalists in the United States." . . . Its first recommendation was, "continuous, active, and public opposition to the war, through demonstrations, mass petitions, and all other means within our power." Evidence that the defendant accepted this view and this declaration of his duties at the time that he made his speech is evidence that if in that speech he used words tending to obstruct the recruiting service he meant that they should have that effect. The principle is too well established and too manifestly good sense to need citation of the books. We should add that the jury were most carefully instructed that they could not find the defendant guilty for advocacy of any of his opinions unless the words used had as their natural tendency and reasonably probable effect to obstruct the recruiting service, &c., and unless the defendant had the specific intent to do so in his mind.

Without going into further particulars we are of opinion that the verdict on the fourth count, for obstructing and attempting to obstruct the recruiting service of the United States, must be sustained. Therefore it is less important to consider whether that upon the third count, for causing and attempting to cause insubordination, &c., in the military and naval forces, is equally impregnable. The jury were instructed that for the purposes of the statute the persons designated by the Act of May 18, 1917, registered and enrolled under it, and thus subject to be called into the active service, were a part of the military forces of the United States. The Government presents a strong argument from the history of the statutes that the instruction was correct and in accordance with established legislative usage. We see no sufficient reason for differing from the conclusion but think it unnecessary to discuss the question in detail.

Affirmed.

THE ABRAMS CASE AND THE BEGINNING OF THE CLEAR AND PRESENT DANGER DISSENTS

1. *The Abrams case.* In 1918, the Espionage Act was amended to add to the provisions relied on in the Schenck group of cases a new series of offenses, including urging any curtailment of production of materials necessary to the prosecution of the war with intent to hinder its prosecution. The convictions of the defendants in Abrams v. United States, 250 U.S. 616 (1919), rested in part on that amendment; they were found guilty of unlawfully writing and publishing language "intended to incite, provoke and encourage resistance to the United States" during World War I, and of conspiring "to urge, incite and advocate curtailment of production of . . . ordnance and ammunition, necessary . . . to the prosecution of the war." The Court sustained the convictions: it rejected the constitutional attack summarily on the basis of Schenck and found the proof sufficient to sustain the charges.

Justice Clarke's majority opinion noted that it was part of the charge "that the defendants would attempt to accomplish their unlawful purpose by printing, writing and distributing in the City of New York many copies of a leaflet or circular, printed in the English language, and of another printed in the Yiddish language, copies of which, properly identified, were attached to the indictment." He added: "All of the five defendants were born in Russia. They were intelligent, had considerable schooling, and at the time they were arrested they had lived in the United States terms varying from five to ten years, but none of them had applied for naturalization. Four of them testified as witnesses in their own behalf and of these, three frankly avowed that they were 'rebels,' 'revolutionists,' 'anarchists' . . . . It was admitted on the trial that the defendants had united to print and distribute the described circulars and that five thousand of them had been printed and distributed about the 22d day of August, 1918. . . . The circulars were distributed some by throwing them from a window of a building where one of the defendants was employed and others secretly, in New York City." The contents of the circulars are summarized in the dissenting opinion, below.

2. *The Holmes dissent in Abrams.* [The Abrams affirmance provoked one of the most famous Holmes dissents, joined by Brandeis. Justice Holmes stated:]

This indictment is founded wholly upon the publication of two leaflets which I shall describe in a moment. [There were four counts; the majority found sufficient evidence to justify conviction under the third and fourth.] The third count alleges a conspiracy to encourage resistance to the United States in the [war with Germany] and to attempt to effectuate the purpose by publishing the [two] leaflets. The fourth count lays a conspiracy to incite curtailment of production of things necessary to the prosecution of the war and to attempt to accomplish it by publishing the second leaflet.

The first of these leaflets says that the President's cowardly silence about the intervention in Russia reveals the hypocrisy of the plutocratic gang in Washington. It intimates that "German militarism combined with allied capitalism to crush the Russian revolution"—goes on that the tyrants of the world fight each other until they see a common enemy—working class enlightenment, when they combine to crush it; and that now militarism and capitalism; that it is a crime for workers of America, &c., to fight the says that there is only one enemy of the workers of the world and that is capitalism; that it is a crime for workers of America, &c., to fight the the workers' republic of Russia, and ends "Awake! Awake, you Workers of the World! Revolutionists." A note adds "It is absurd to call us pro-German. We hate and despise German militarism more than do you hypocritical tyrants. We have more reasons for denouncing German militarism than has the coward of the White House."

The other leaflet, headed "Workers—Wake Up," with abusive language says that America together with the Allies will march for Russia to help the Czecko-Slovaks in their struggle against the Bolsheviki, and that this time the hypocrites shall not fool the Russian emigrants and friends of Russia in America. It tells the Russian emigrants that they now must spit in the face of the false military propaganda by which their sympathy and help to the prosecution of the war have been called forth and says that with the money they have lent or are going to lend "they will make bullets not only for the Germans but also for the Workers Soviets of Russia," and further, "Workers in the ammunition factories, you are producing bullets, bayonets, cannon, to murder not only the Germans, but also your dearest, best, who are in Russia and are fighting for freedom." It then appeals to the same Russian emigrants at some length not to consent to the "inquisitionary expedition to Russia," and says that the destruction of the Russian revolution is "the politics of the march to Russia." The leaflet winds up by saying "Workers, our reply to this barbaric intervention has to be a general strike!," and after a few words on the spirit of revolution, exhortations not to be afraid, and some usual tall talk ends "Woe unto those who will be in the way of progress. Let solidarity live! The Rebels."

[With regard to the fourth count] it seems too plain to be denied that the suggestion to workers in the ammunition factories that they are producing bullets to murder their dearest, and the further advocacy of a general strike, both in the second leaflet, do urge curtailment of production of things necessary to the prosecution of the war within the meaning of the Act of May 16, 1918, amending § 3 of the earlier Act of 1917. But to make the conduct criminal that statute requires that it should be "with intent by such curtailment to cripple or hinder the United States in the prosecution of the war." It seems to me that no such intent is proved.

I am aware of course that the word intent as vaguely used in ordinary legal discussion means no more than knowledge at the time of the act that the consequences said to be intended will ensue. Even less than that will satisfy the general principle of civil and criminal liability. A man may have to pay damages, may be sent to prison, at common law might be hanged, if at the time of his act he knew facts from which common experience showed that the consequences would follow, whether he individually could foresee them or not. But, when words are used exactly, a deed is not done with intent to produce a consequence unless that consequence is the aim of the deed. It may be obvious, and obvious to the actor, that the consequence will follow, and he may be liable for it even if he regrets it, but he does not do the act with intent to produce it unless the aim to produce it is the proximate motive of the specific act, although there may be some deeper motive behind.

It seems to me that this statute must be taken to use its words in a strict and accurate sense. They would be absurd in any other. A patriot might think that we were wasting money on aeroplanes, or making more cannon of a certain kind than we needed, and might advocate curtailment with success, yet even if it turned out that the curtailment hindered and was thought by other minds to have been obviously likely to hinder the United States in the prosecution of the war, no one would hold such conduct a crime. I admit that my illustration does not answer all that might be said but it is enough to show what I think and to let me pass to a more important aspect of the case. I refer to the First Amendment to the Constitution that Congress shall make no law abridging the freedom of speech.

I never have seen any reason to doubt that the questions of law that alone were before this Court in the cases of Schenck, Frohwerk and Debs, 249 U.S. 47, 204, 211, were rightly decided. I do not doubt for a moment that by the same reasoning that would justify punishing persuasion to murder, the United States constitutionally may punish speech that produces or is intended to produce a clear and imminent danger that it will bring about forthwith certain substantive evils that the United States constitutionally may seek to prevent. The power undoubtedly is greater in time of war than in time of peace because war opens dangers that do not exist at other times.

But as against dangers peculiar to war, as against others, the principle of the right to free speech is always the same. It is only the present danger of immediate evil or an intent to bring it about that warrants Congress in setting a limit to the expression of opinion where private rights are not concerned. Congress certainly cannot forbid all effort to change the mind of the country. Now nobody can suppose that the surreptitious publishing of a silly leaflet by an unknown man, without more, would present any immediate danger that its opinions would hinder the success of the government arms or have any appreciable tendency to do so. Publishing those opinions for the very purpose of obstructing however, might indicate a greater danger and at any rate would have the quality of an attempt. So I assume that the second leaflet if published for the purposes alleged in the fourth count might be punishable. But it seems pretty clear to me that nothing less than that would bring these papers within the scope of this law. An actual intent in the sense that I have explained is necessary to constitute an attempt, where a further act of the same individual is required to complete the substantive crime, for reasons given in Swift & Co. v. United States, 196 U.S. 375, 396. It is necessary where the success of the attempt depends upon others because if that intent is not present the actor's aim may be accomplished without bringing about the evils sought to be checked. An intent to prevent interference with the revolution in Russia might have been satisfied without any hindrance to carrying on the war in which we were engaged.

I do not see how anyone can find the intent required by the statute in any of the defendants' words. The second leaflet is the only one that affords even a foundation for the charge, and there, without invoking the hatred of German militarism expressed in the former one, it is evident from the beginning to the end that the only object of the paper is to help Russia and stop American intervention there against the popular government—not to impede the United States in the war that it was carrying on. To say that two phrases taken literally might import a suggestion of conduct that would have interference with the war as an indirect and probably undesired effect seems to me by no means enough to show an attempt to produce that effect.

I [turn] for a moment to the third count. That charges an intent to provoke resistance to the United States in its war with Germany. Taking the clause in the statute that deals with that in connection with the other elaborate provisions of the act, I think that resistance to the United States means some forcible act of opposition to some proceeding of the United States in pursuance of the war. I think the intent must be the specific intent that I have described and for the reasons that I have given I think that no such intent was proved or existed in fact. I also think that there is no hint at resistance to the United States as I construe the phrase.

In this case sentences of twenty years imprisonment have been imposed for the publishing of two leaflets that I believe the defendants had as much right to publish as the Government has to publish the Constitution of the United States now vainly invoked by them. Even if I am technically wrong and enough can be squeezed from these poor and puny anonymities to turn the color of legal litmus paper; I will add, even if what I think the necessary intent were shown; the most nominal punishment seems to me all that possibly could be inflicted, unless the defendants are to be made to suffer not for what the indictment alleges but for the creed that they avow—a creed that I believe to be the creed of ignorance and immaturity when honestly held, as I see no reason to doubt that it was held here, but which, although made the subject of examination at the trial, no one has a right even to consider in dealing with the charges before the Court.

Persecution for the expression of opinions seems to me perfectly logical. If you have no doubt of your premises or your power and want a certain result with all your heart you naturally express your wishes in law and sweep away all opposition. To allow opposition by speech seems to indicate that you think the speech impotent, as when a man says that he has squared the circle, or that you do not care whole-heartedly for the result, or that you doubt either your power or your premises. But when men have realized that time has upset many fighting faiths, they may come to believe even more than they believe the very foundations of their own conduct that the ultimate good desired is better reached by free trade in ideas—that the best test of truth is the power of the thought to get itself accepted in the competition of the market, and that truth is the only ground upon which their wishes safely can be carried out. That at any rate is the theory of our Constitution. It is an experiment, as all life is an experiment. Every year if not every day we have to wager our salvation upon some prophecy based upon imperfect knowledge. While that experiment is part of our system I think that we should be eternally vigilant against attempts to check the expression of opinions that we loathe and believe to be fraught with death, unless they so imminently threaten immediate interference with the lawful and pressing purposes of the law that an immediate check is required to save the country. I wholly disagree with the argument of the Government that the First Amendment left the common law as to seditious libel in force. History seems to me against the notion. I had conceived that the United States through many years had shown its repentance for the Sedition Act of 1798, by repaying fines that it imposed. Only the emergency that makes it immediately dangerous to leave the correction of evil counsels to time warrants making any exception to the sweeping command, "Congress shall make no law . . . abridging the freedom of speech." Of course I am speaking only of expressions of opinion and exhortations, which were all that were uttered here, but I regret that I cannot put into more impressive words my belief that in their conviction upon this indictment the defendants were deprived of their rights under the Constitution of the United States.

3. *The majority's evaluation of the evidence in Abrams.* Compare with Justice Holmes' evaluation of the circulars in Abrams, the following comments in the majority opinion's review of the evidence. Which estimate seems closer to the approach of Schenck-Frohwerk-Debs: the majority's or the dissent's? Justice Clarke's majority opinion stated:

"It will not do to say, as is now argued, that the only intent of these defendants was to prevent injury to the Russian cause. Men must be held to have intended, and to be accountable for, the effects which their acts were likely to produce. Even if their primary purpose and intent was to aid the cause of the Russian Revolution, the plan of action which they adopted necessarily involved, before it could be realized, defeat of the war program of the United States, for the obvious effect of this appeal, if it should become effective, as they hoped it might, would be to persuade persons of character such as those whom they regarded themselves as addressing, not to aid government loans and not to work in ammunition factories, where their work would produce 'bullets, bayonets, cannon' and other munitions of war, the use of which would cause the 'murder' of Germans and Russians. . . .

"That the interpretation we have put upon these articles, circulated in the greatest port of our land, from which great numbers of soldiers were at the time taking ship daily, and in which great quantities of war supplies of every kind were at the time being manufactured for transportation overseas, is not only the fair interpretation of them, but that it is the meaning which their authors consciously intended should be conveyed by them to others is further shown by the additional writings found in the meeting place of the defendant group and on the person of one of them. One of these circulars is headed: 'Revolutionists! Unite for Action!' . . .

"These excerpts sufficiently show, that while the immediate occasion for this particular outbreak of lawlessness, on the part of the defendant alien anarchists, may have been resentment caused by our Government sending troops into Russia as a strategic operation against the Germans on the eastern battle front, yet the plain purpose of their propaganda was to excite, at the supreme crisis of the war, disaffection, sedition, riots, and, as they hoped, revolution, in this country for the purpose of embarrassing and if possible defeating the military plans of the Government in Europe."

4. *The Schaefer case.* Soon after Abrams, Justice Holmes also joined in dissents from other decisions affirming convictions under the 1917 Act. See Pierce v. United States, 252 U.S. 239 (1920), and Schaefer v. United States, 251 U.S. 466 (1920). In his Schaefer dissent, Justice Brandeis said of the Schenck standard: "This is a rule of reason. Correctly applied, it will preserve the right of free speech both from suppression by tyrannous, well-meaning majorities and from abuse by irresponsible, fanatical minorities. Like many other rules for human conduct, it can be applied only by the exercise of good judgment; and to the exercise of good judgment, calmness is, in times of deep feeling and on subjects which excite passion, as essential as fearlessness and honesty. The question whether in a particular instance the words spoken or written fall within the permissible curtailment of free speech is, under the rule enunciated by this court, one of degree. And because it is a question of degree the field in which the jury may exercise its judgment is, necessarily, a wide one. But its field is not unlimited. . . . In my opinion, no jury acting in calmness could reasonably say that any of the publications set forth in the indictment was of such a character or was made under such circumstances as to create a clear and present danger either that they would obstruct recruiting or that they would promote the success of the enemies of the United States."

CLEAR AND PRESENT DANGER FROM SCHENCK TO ABRAMS—EVOLUTION OR REBIRTH?

1. *Some questions about the Schenck-Frohwerk-Debs approach.* Clear and present danger supposedly assures special attention to the time dimension: speech may not be curtailed until there is an immediate risk of an evil; speech with a remote tendency to cause danger cannot be curtailed. Is that sense conveyed by the language of the Schenck group of cases? By the facts?

a. *Schenck.* What showing was there that the substantive evil had come about, or that the words would "bring about" the evils? Does Schenck clearly reject a "tendency" criterion and replace it with one of "clear and present" immediacy? Note the reference to "the act, . . . its tendency and the intent" at the end of the opinion. What is the relevance of "intent" to immediate risk of harm? "Tendency"? Is the "shouting fire" analogy apt? To political speech? Are truth and falsity relevant? What if the speaker thought there was a fire?

b. *Frohwerk.* Was the Frohwerk "counselling of a murder" reference helpful in delineating the requisite "proximity and degree"? Was the language in Frohwerk indistinguishable from that in Schenck? Frohwerk refers to "language that might be taken to convey an innuendo of a different sort." Is talk of risks of "innuendos" consistent with a sensitive regard for speech? Is talk of the possibility of evidence about "a little breath" that might "kindle a flame"? Does that suggest insistence on showing a high probability of harm? Is that talk more protective of speech than "bad tendency"?

c. *Debs.* Did Holmes demonstrate the "clear and present danger" of Eugene V. Debs' speeches? Did he deprecate the "general theme" unduly? Did he unduly emphasize what "his hearers . . . might infer"? Does the talk of "natural tendency and reasonably probable effect" sound like an immediacy-emphasizing alternative to a "bad tendency" approach?

2. *The impact of Abrams.* Does Abrams give new content to "clear and present danger"? Can it be said that the Schenck phrase was not turned into an effective safeguard of speech until the Abrams dissent? A great admirer of Holmes has suggested about the Schenck-Abrams sequence that the Justice "was biding his time until the Court should have before it a conviction so clearly wrong as to let him speak out his deepest thoughts about the First Amendment." Chafee, Free Speech in the United States (1941), 862. Is that persuasive? *Were* the Abrams convictions more "clearly wrong" than those in the Schenck group of cases? Was the Abrams majority fairly following the Schenck approach? Does the Holmes dissent indicate a change of views since Schenck?

How useful is the approach of the Abrams dissent? It emphasizes immediacy more than the predecessors. Does it concentrate adequately on immediate proximity of speech to danger? Note the comment about a "silly leaflet" that would not present "any immediate danger" *or* "have any appreciable tendency to do so." Is "tendency" enough? Note also the reference to "the present danger of immediate evil" *or* "an intent to bring it about." Is "intent" enough? Are "tendency" or "intent" reliable indicia of immediacy of danger?

Is the Abrams approach applicable only in contexts where the law is mainly directed at an evil other than speech, and where speech is evidence of the risk of that evil? Is it also useful when the legislature proscribes speech directly, as in Gitlow and Whitney, infra? Does Holmes accept the legislative statement of the evil? Must speech cause immediate risk of causing the legislatively determined evil—e. g., interference with recruiting? Or does the Court define the evil? Note the reference to "an immediate check . . . required to save the country," in Holmes' last paragraph. Is Holmes concerned with the gravity of the evil? Do immediacy requirements vary with gravity? What light is cast on these questions by the elaborations of clear and present danger in Gitlow and Whitney? Before turning to those cases, consider the alternative analysis suggested by Judge Learned Hand's Masses opinion, which follows.

LEARNED HAND AND THE MASSES CASE: PREFERABLE TO CLEAR AND PRESENT DANGER?

Introduction. Two years before Schenck, the problem of interpreting the Espionage Act of 1917 arose in a case before Learned Hand, then a District Judge. The Hand opinion plainly reveals considerable solicitude for speech, and it does so without mentioning clear and present danger. Consider the advantages and disadvantages of Hand's approach in the World War I context. How would Schenck, Debs, or Abrams have gone under that standard? Would Hand's approach have avoided some of the difficulties clear and present danger encountered in later years? Has Hand's approach surfaced in substance in some of the later Supreme Court cases—e. g., the Yates and Scales cases under the Smith Act, pp. 1111 and 1113, infra?

MASSES PUBLISHING CO. v. PATTEN

244 Fed. 535 (1917).

United States District Court, Southern District of New York.

LEARNED HAND, District Judge. The plaintiff applies for a preliminary injunction against the postmaster of New York to forbid his refusal to accept its magazine in the mails under the following circumstances: The plaintiff is a publishing company in the city of New York engaged in the production of a monthly revolutionary journal called "The Masses," containing both text and cartoons . . . . In July, 1917, the postmaster of New York, acting upon the direction of the Postmaster General, advised the plaintiff that the August number to which he had had access would be denied the mails under the Espionage Act of June 15, 1917. [T]he defendant, while objecting generally that the whole purport of the number was in violation of the law, since it tended to produce a violation of the law, to encourage the enemies of the United States, and to hamper the government in the conduct of the war, specified four cartoons and four pieces of text as especially falling within sections 1 and 2 of title 12 of the act and by the reference of section 1 as within section 3 of title 1. These sections are quoted in the margin.[1]

. . . . In this case there is no dispute of fact which the plaintiff can successfully challenge except the meaning of the words and pictures in the magazine. As to these the query must be: What is the extreme latitude of the interpretation which must be placed upon them, and whether that extremity certainly falls outside any of the provisions of the act of June 15, 1917. Unless this be true, the decision of the postmaster must stand. It will be necessary, first, to interpret the law, and, next, the words and pictures.

[N]o question arises touching the war powers of Congress. . . . . Here is presented solely the question of how far Congress after much discus-

---

1. Title I. Espionage.

Sec. 3. Whoever, when the United States is at war, shall willfully make or convey false reports or false statements with intent to interfere with the operation or success of the military or naval forces of the United States or to promote the success of its enemies and whoever when the United States is at war, shall willfully cause or attempt to cause insubordination, disloyalty, mutiny, or refusal of duty, in the military or naval forces of the United States, or shall willfully obstruct the recruiting or enlistment service of the United States, to the injury of the service or of the United States, shall be punished by a fine of not more than $10,000 or imprisonment for not more than twenty years, or both.

Title XII. Use of Mails.

Section 1. Every letter, writing, circular, postal card, picture, print, en-graving, photograph, newspaper, pamphlet, book, or other publication, matter or thing, of any kind, in violation of any of the provisions of this act is hereby declared to be nonmailable matter and shall not be conveyed in the mails or delivered from any post office or by any letter carrier: Provided, that nothing in this act shall be so construed as to authorize any person other than an employé of the dead letter office, duly authorized there to, or other person upon a search warrant authorized by law, to open any letter not addressed to himself.

Sec. 2. Every letter, writing, circular, postal card, picture, print, engraving, photograph, newspaper, pamphlet, book, or other publication, matter or thing, of any kind, containing any matter advocating or urging treason, insurrection, or forcible resistance to any law of the United States, is hereby declared to be nonmailable. [Footnote by the Court.]

sion has up to the present time seen fit to exercise a power which may extend to measures not yet even considered, but necessary to the existence of the state as such. . . .

Coming to the act itself, [I] turn directly to section 3 of title 1, which the plaintiff is said to violate. That section contains three provisions. The first is, in substance, that no one shall make any false statements with intent to interfere with the operation or success of the military or naval forces of the United States or to promote the success of its enemies. The defendant says that the cartoons and text of the magazine, constituting, as they certainly do, a virulent attack upon the war . . ., may interfere with the success of the military forces of the United States. That such utterances may have the effect so ascribed to them is unhappily true; . . Dissension within a country is a high source of comfort and assistance to its enemies; the least intimation of it they seize upon with jubilation. . .

All this, however, is beside the question whether such an attack is a willfully false statement. That phrase properly includes only a statement of fact which the utterer knows to be false, and it cannot be maintained that any of these statements are of fact, or that the plaintiff believes them to be false. They are all within the range of opinion and of criticism; they are all certainly believed to be true by the utterer. As such they fall within the scope of that right to criticise either by temperate reasoning, or by immoderate and indecent invective, which is normally the privilege of the individual in countries dependent upon the free expression of opinion as the ultimate source of authority. The argument may be trivial in substance, and violent and perverse in manner, but so long as it is confined to abuse of existing policies or laws, it is impossible to class it as a false statement of facts of the kind here in question. To modify this provision, so clearly intended to prevent the spreading of false rumors which may embarrass the military, into the prohibition of any kind of propaganda, honest or vicious, is to disregard the meaning of the language, established by legal construction and common use, and to raise it into a means of suppressing intemperate and inflammatory public discussion, which was surely not its purpose.

The next phrase relied upon is that which forbids any one from willfully causing insubordination, disloyalty, mutiny, or refusal of duty in the military or naval forces of the United States. The defendant's position is that to arouse discontent and disaffection among the people with the prosecution of the war and with the draft tends to promote a mutinous and insubordinate temper among the troops. This, too, is true; men who become satisfied that they are engaged in an enterprise dictated by the unconscionable selfishness of the rich, and effectuated by a tyrannous disregard for the will of those who must suffer and die, will be more prone to insubordination than those who have faith in the cause and acquiesce in the means. Yet to interpret the word "cause" so broadly would, as before, involve necessarily as a consequence the suppression of all hostile criticism, and of all opinion except what encouraged and supported the existing policies, or which fell within the range of temperate argument. It would contradict the normal assumption of democratic government that the suppression of hostile criticism does not turn upon the justice of its substance or the decency and propriety of its temper. Assuming that the power to repress such opinion may rest in Congress in the throes of a struggle for the very existence of the state, its exercise is so contrary to the use and wont of our people that only the clearest expression of such a power justifies the conclusion that it was intended.

The defendant's position, therefore, in so far as it involves the suppression of the free utterance of abuse and criticism of the existing law, or of the policies of the war, is not, in my judgment, supported by the language of the statute. Yet there has always been a recognized limit to such expressions, incident indeed to the existence of any compulsive power of the state itself. One may not counsel or advise others to violate the law as it stands. Words are not only the keys of persuasion, but the triggers of action, and those which have no purport but to counsel the violation of law cannot by any latitude of interpretation be a part of that public opinion which is the final source of government in a democratic state. The defendant asserts not only that the magazine indirectly through its propaganda leads to a disintegration of loyalty and a disobedience of law, but that in addition it counsels and advises resistance to existing law, especially to the draft. The consideration of this aspect of the case more properly arises under the third phrase of section 3, which forbids any willful obstruction of the recruiting or enlistment service of the United States, but, as the defendant urges that the magazine falls within each phrase, it is as well to take it up now. To counsel or advise a man to an act is to urge upon him either that it is his interest or his duty to do it. While, of course, this may be accomplished as well by indirection as expressly, since words carry the meaning that they impart, the definition is exhaustive, I think, and I shall use it. Political agitation, by the passions it arouses or the convictions it engenders, may in fact stimulate men to the violation of law. Detestation of existing policies is easily transformed into forcible resistance of the authority which puts them in execution, and it would be folly to disregard the causal relation between the two. Yet to assimilate agitation, legitimate as such, with direct incitement to violent resistance, is to disregard the tolerance of all methods of political agitation which in normal times is a safeguard of free government. The distinction is not a scholastic subterfuge, but a hard-bought acquisition in the fight for freedom, and the purpose to disregard it must be evident when the power exists. If one stops short of urging upon others that it is their duty or their interest to resist the law, it seems to me one should not be held to have attempted to cause its violation. If that be not the test, I can see no escape from the conclusion that under this section every political agitation which can be shown to be apt to create a seditious temper is illegal. I am confident that by such language Congress had no such revolutionary purpose in view.

It seems to me, however, quite plain that none of the language and none of the cartoons in this paper can be thought directly to counsel or advise insubordination or mutiny, without a violation of their meaning quite beyond any tolerable understanding. I come, therefore, to the third phrase of the section, which forbids any one from willfully obstructing the recruiting or enlistment service of the United States. I am not prepared to assent to the plaintiff's position that this only refers to acts other than words, nor that the act thus defined must be shown to have been successful. One may obstruct without preventing, and the mere obstruction is an injury to the service; for it throws impediments in its way. Here again, however, since the question is of the expression of opinion, I construe the sentence, so far as it restrains public utterance, as I have construed the other two, and as therefore limited to the direct advocacy of resistance to the recruiting and enlistment service. If so, the inquiry is narrowed to the question whether any of the challenged matter may be said to advocate resistance to the draft, taking the meaning of the words with the utmost latitude which they can bear.

As to the cartoons it seems to me quite clear that they do not fall within such a test. Certainly the nearest is that entitled "Conscription," and the most that can be said of that is that it may breed such animosity to the draft as will promote resistance and strengthen the determination of those disposed to be recalcitrant. There is no intimation that, however hateful the draft may be, one is in duty bound to resist it, certainly none that such resistance is to one's interest. . . .

The text offers more embarrassment. The poem to Emma Goldman and Alexander Berkman, at most, goes no further than to say that they are martyrs in the cause of love among nations. Such a sentiment holds them up to admiration, and hence their conduct to possible emulation. . . . The paragraphs upon conscientious objectors are of the same kind. . . . It is plain enough that the paper has the fullest sympathy for these people, that it admires their courage, and that it presumptively approves their conduct. . . .

Moreover, these passages, it must be remembered, occur in a magazine which attacks with the utmost violence the draft and the war. That such comments have a tendency to arouse emulation in others is clear enough, but that they counsel others to follow these examples is not so plain. Literally at least they do not, and while, as I have said, the words are to be taken, not literally, but according to their full import, the literal meaning is the starting point for interpretation. One may admire and approve the course of a hero without feeling any duty to follow him. There is not the least implied intimation in these words that others are under a duty to follow. The most that can be said is that, if others do follow, they will get the same admiration and the same approval. Now, there is surely an appreciable distance between esteem and emulation; and unless there is here some advocacy of such emulation, I cannot see how the passages can be said to fall within the law. . . .

The question before me is quite the same as what would arise upon a motion to dismiss an indictment at the close of the proof: Could any reasonable man say, not that the indirect result of the language might be to arouse a seditious disposition, for that would not be enough, but that the language directly advocated resistance to the draft? I cannot think that upon such language any verdict would stand. . . . .

SOME FURTHER QUESTIONS ON THE MASSES
APPROACH

Is the Masses standard distinctively different from the clear and present danger test? How does it differ? How would Eugene Debs have fared under the Masses approach? Is Hand more sensitive than Holmes to the risk of sustaining convictions based on the "natural tendency" and "probable effect" of words? Is he more sensitive because he focuses less on the proximity of danger (e. g., of draft obstruction) and more on the speaker and the value of speech—on the protection that must be afforded if widespread critical debate of governmental policy is to be maintained?

Is the shift in focus from proximity of danger to content of speech an assurance of greater protection of speech? Is it an approach courts are more competent to conduct? Does it involve less concern about "circumstances" and variable degrees of dangers? Does it draw on more traditional judicial tools? Are courts better at concentrating on what the defendant said than on how near (and serious) the danger is? More competent to define "counselling" than to assess risks? Or are these simply different ways to state the same question? Does Masses articulate speech values more effectively than Schenck? Than Abrams? Does Masses foreshadow emphasis on articulating the nature of protected debate in a free society, as in the New York Times case, p. 1214, infra? Is the Masses approach usable in situations where the legislature has described prohibited speech, as in Gitlow and Whitney which follow? Does it avoid a judicial second-guessing of the legislative determination of danger?

B. LEGISLATION AGAINST FORBIDDEN ADVOCACY IN THE TWENTIES AND THIRTIES

THE GITLOW AND WHITNEY DISSENTS AND THE INCREASING PROTECTION OF SPEECH

GITLOW v. NEW YORK

268 U.S. 652, 45 S.Ct. 625, 69 L.Ed. 1138 (1925).

Error to the Supreme Court of New York.

Mr. Justice SANFORD delivered the opinion of the Court.

Benjamin Gitlow was indicted . . . , with three others, for the statutory crime of criminal anarchy, New York Penal Law, §§ 160, 161. He was separately tried, convicted, and sentenced to imprisonment. . . .

The contention here is that the statute, by its terms and as applied in this case, is repugnant to the due process clause of the Fourteenth Amendment. Its material provisions are:

"§ 160. *Criminal Anarchy Defined.* Criminal anarchy is the doctrine that organized government should be overthrown by force or violence, or by assassination of the executive head or of any of the executive officials of government, or by any unlawful means. The advocacy of such doctrine either by word of mouth or writing is a felony.

"§ 161. *Advocacy of Criminal Anarchy.* Any person who:

"1. By word of mouth or writing advocates, advises or teaches the duty, necessity or propriety of overthrowing or overturning organized government by force or violence, or by assassination of the executive head or of any of the executive officials of government, or by any unlawful means; or,

"2. Prints, publishes, edits, issues or knowingly circulates, sells, distributes or publicly displays any book, paper, document, or written or printed matter in any form, containing or advocating, advising or teaching the doctrine that organized government should be overthrown by force, violence or any unlawful means . . .

"Is guilty of a felony and punishable" by imprisonment or fine, or both.

The indictment was in two counts. The first charged that the defendant had advocated, advised and taught the duty, necessity and propriety of overthrowing and overturning organized government by force, violence and unlawful means, by certain writings therein set forth entitled "The Left Wing Manifesto"; the second that he had printed, published and knowingly circulated and distributed a certain paper called "The Revolutionary Age," containing the writings set forth in the first count . . . .

The following facts were established on the trial by undisputed evidence and admissions: The defendant is a member of the Left Wing Section of the Socialist Party, a dissenting branch or faction of that party formed in opposition to its dominant policy of "moderate Socialism." Membership in both is open to aliens as well as citizens. The Left Wing Section was organized nationally at a conference in New York City in June, 1919 . . . . The conference elected a National Council, of which the defendant was a member, and left to it the adoption of a "Manifesto." This was published in The Revolutionary Age, the official organ of the Left Wing. The defendant was on the board of managers of the paper and was its business manager. He arranged for the printing of the paper and took to the printer the manuscript of the first issue which contained the Left Wing Manifesto, and also a Communist Program and a Program of the Left Wing that had been adopted by the conference. Sixteen thousand copies were printed, which were delivered at the premises in New York City used as the office of the Revolutionary Age and the headquarters of the Left Wing, and occupied by the defendant and other officials. . . . It was admitted that the defendant signed a card subscribing to the Manifesto and Program of the Left Wing, which all applicants were required to sign before being admitted to membership; that he went to different parts of the State to speak to branches of the Socialist Party about the principles of the Left Wing and advocated their adoption; and that he was responsible for the Manifesto as it appeared, that "he knew of the publication, in a general way and he knew of its publication afterwards, and is responsible for the circulation."

There was no evidence of any effect resulting from the publication and circulation of the Manifesto.

No witnesses were offered in behalf of the defendant. . . . Coupled with a review of the rise of Socialism, [the Manifesto] condemned the dominant "moderate Socialism" for its recognition of the necessity of the democratic parliamentary state . . . and advocated, in plain and unequivocal language, the necessity of accomplishing the "Communist Revolution" by a militant and "revolutionary Socialism," based on "the class struggle" and mobilizing the "power of the proletariat in action," through mass industrial revolts developing into mass political strikes and "revolutionary mass action," for the purpose of conquering and destroying the parliamentary state and establishing in its place, through a "revolutionary dictatorship of the proletariat," the system of Communist Socialism. [R]evolutionary Socialism, it was urged, must use . . . mass industrial revolts to broaden the strike, make it general and militant, and develop it into mass political strikes and revolutionary mass action for the annihilation of the parliamentary state. . . .

The court, among other things, charged the jury, in substance, that they must determine what was the intent, purpose and fair meaning of the Manifesto; . . . that a mere statement or analysis of social and economic facts and historical incidents, in the nature of an essay, accompanied by prophecy as to the future course of events, but with no teaching, advice or advocacy of action, would not constitute the advocacy, advice or teaching of a doctrine for the overthrow of government within the meaning of the statute; that a mere statement that unlawful acts might accomplish such a purpose would be insufficient, unless there was a teaching, advising and advocacy of employing such unlawful acts for the purpose of overthrowing government . . . . .

The defendant's counsel submitted two requests to charge which embodied in substance the statement that to constitute criminal anarchy within the meaning of the statute it was necessary that the language used or published should advocate, teach or advise the duty, necessity or propriety of doing "some definite or immediate act or acts" of force, violence or unlawfulness directed toward the overthrowing of organized government. These were denied further than had been charged. . . .

. . . The sole contention here is, essentially, that as there was no evidence of any concrete result flowing from the publication of the Manifesto or of circumstances showing the likelihood of such result, the statute as construed and applied by the trial court penalizes the mere utterance, as such, of "doctrine" having no quality of incitement, without regard either to the circumstances of its utterance or to the likelihood of unlawful consequences . . . . .

The statute does not penalize the utterance or publication of abstract "doctrine" or academic discussion having no quality of incitement to any concrete action. It is not aimed against mere historical or philosophical essays. It does not restrain the advocacy of changes in the form of government by constitutional and lawful means. What it prohibits is language advocating, advising or teaching the overthrow of organized government by unlawful means. These words imply urging to action. . . .

The Manifesto, plainly, is neither the statement of abstract doctrine nor as suggested by counsel, mere prediction that industrial disturbances and revolutionary mass strikes will result spontaneously in an inevitable process of evolution in the economic system. It advocates and urges in fervent language mass action which shall progressively foment industrial disturbances and through political mass strikes and revolutionary mass action overthrow and destroy organized parliamentary government. It concludes with a call to action in these words: "The proletarian revolution and the Communist reconstruction of society—*the struggle for these*—is now indispensable. . . . The Communist International calls the proletariat of the world to the final struggle!" This is not the expression of philosophical abstractions, the mere prediction of future events; it is the language of direct incitement.

The means advocated for bringing about the destruction of organized parliamentary government, namely, mass industrial revolts usurping the functions of municipal government, political mass strikes directed against the parliamentary state, and revolutionary mass action for its final destruction, necessarily imply the use of force and violence, and in their essential nature are inherently unlawful in a constitutional government of law and order. That the jury were warranted in finding that the Manifesto advocated not merely the abstract doctrine of overthrowing organized government by force, violence and unlawful means, but action to that end is clear.

For present purposes we may and do assume that freedom of speech and press—which are protected by the First Amendment from abridgment by Congress—are among the fundamental personal rights and liberties protected by the Fourteenth Amendment from impairment by the States.

It is a fundamental principle, long established, that the freedom of speech and of the press which is secured by the Constitution, does not confer an absolute right to speak or publish, without responsibility, whatever one may choose, or an unrestricted and unbridled license that gives immunity for every possible use of language and prevents the punishment of those who abuse this freedom. . . .

That a State in the exercise of its police power may punish those who abuse this freedom by utterances inimical to the public welfare, tending to corrupt public morals, incite to crime, or disturb the public peace, is not open to question. . . . .

And, for yet more imperative reasons, a State may punish utterances endangering the foundations of organized government and threatening its overthrow by unlawful means.   These imperil its own existence as a constitutional State.   Freedom of speech and press, said Story, supra [2 Story on the Constitution, 5th Ed., § 1580], does not protect disturbances to the public peace or the attempt to subvert the government.   . . .   In short this freedom does not deprive a State of the primary and essential right of self-preservation; which, so long as human governments endure, they cannot be denied. . . .

By enacting the present statute the State has determined, through its legislative body, that utterances advocating the overthrow of organized government by force, violence and unlawful means, are so inimical to the general welfare and involve such danger of substantive evil that they may be penalized in the exercise of its police power.   That determination must be given great weight.   Every presumption is to be indulged in favor of the validity of the statute.   Mugler v. Kansas, 123 U.S. 623, 661. . . . .   That utterances inciting to the overthrow of organized government by unlawful means, present a sufficient danger of substantive evil to bring their punishment within the range of legislative discretion, is clear.   Such utterances, by their very nature, involve danger to the public peace and to the security of the State.   They threaten breaches of the peace and ultimate revolution.   And the immediate danger is none the less real and substantial, because the effect of a given utterance cannot be accurately foreseen.   The State cannot reasonably be required to measure the danger from every such utterance in the nice balance of a jeweler's scale.   A single revolutionary spark may kindle a fire that, smouldering for a time, may burst into a sweeping and destructive conflagration.   It cannot be said that the State is acting arbitrarily or unreasonably when in the exercise of its judgment as to the measures necessary to protect the public peace and safety, it seeks to extinguish the spark without waiting until it has enkindled the flame or blazed into the conflagration.   It cannot reasonably be required to defer the adoption of measures for its own peace and safety until the revolutionary utterances lead to actual disturbances of the public peace or imminent and immediate danger of its own destruction; but it may, in the exercise of its judgment, suppress the threatened danger in its incipiency. . . .

We cannot hold that the present statute is an arbitrary or unreasonable exercise of the police power of the State unwarrantably infringing the freedom of speech or press; and we must and do sustain its constitutionality.

This being so it may be applied to every utterance—not too trivial to be beneath the notice of the law—which is of such a character and used with such intent and purpose as to bring it within the prohibition of the statute. . . . In other words, when the legislative body has determined generally, in the constitutional exercise of its discretion, that utterances of a certain kind involve such danger of substantive evil that they may be punished, the question whether any specific utterance coming within the prohibited class is likely, in and of itself, to bring about the substantive evil, is not open to consideration. It is sufficient that the statute itself be constitutional and that the use of the language comes within its prohibition.

It is clear that the question in such cases is entirely different from that involved in those cases where the statute merely prohibits certain acts involving the danger of substantive evil, without any reference to language itself, and it is sought to apply its provisions to language used by the defendant for the purpose of bringing about the prohibited results. There, if it be contended that the statute cannot be applied to the language used by the defendant because of its protection by the freedom of speech or press, it must necessarily be found, as an original question, without any previous determination by the legislative body, whether the specific language used involved such likelihood of bringing about the substantive evil as to deprive it of the constitutional protection. In such cases it has been held that the general provisions of the statute may be constitutionally applied to the specific utterance of the defendant if its natural tendency and probable effect was to bring about the substantive evil which the legislative body might prevent. . . . And the general statement in the Schenck case, . . . that the "question in every case is whether the words are used in such circumstances and are of such a nature as to create a clear and present danger that they will bring about the substantive evils,"—upon which great reliance is placed in the defendant's argument—was manifestly intended, as shown by the context, to apply only in cases of this class, and has no application to those like the present, where the legislative body itself has previously determined the danger of substantive evil arising from utterances of a specified character.

. . . It was not necessary, within the meaning of the statute, that the defendant should have advocated "some definite or immediate act or acts" of force, violence or unlawfulness. It was sufficient if such acts were advocated in general terms; and it was not essential that their immediate execution should have been advocated. Nor was it necessary that the language should have been "reasonably and ordinarily calculated to incite certain persons" to acts of force, violence or unlawfulness. The advocacy need not be addressed to specific persons. Thus, the publication and circulation of a newspaper article may be an encouragement or endeavor to persuade to murder, although not addressed to any person in particular. . . .

We need not enter upon a consideration of the English common law of seditious libel or the Federal Sedition Act of 1798, to which reference is made in the defendant's brief. These are so unlike the present statute, that we think the decisions under them cast no helpful light upon the questions here. . . . .

Affirmed.

Mr. Justice HOLMES (dissenting). Mr. Justice BRANDEIS and I are of opinion that this judgment should be reversed. The general principle of free speech, it seems to me, must be taken to be included in the Fourteenth Amendment, in view of the scope that has been given to the word "liberty" as there used, although perhaps it may be accepted with a somewhat larger latitude of interpretation than is allowed to Congress by the sweeping language that governs or ought to govern the laws of the United States. If I am right then I think that the criterion sanctioned by the full Court in Schenck v. United States, 249 U.S. 47, 52, applies. . . . It is true that in my opinion, this criterion was departed from in Abrams v. United States, 250 U.S. 616, but the convictions that I expressed in that case are too deep for it to be possible for me as yet to believe that it and Schaefer v. United States, 251 U.S. 466, have settled the law. If what I think the correct test is applied it is manifest that there was no present danger of an attempt to overthrow the government by force on the part of the admittedly small minority who shared the defendant's views. It is said that this manifesto was more than a theory, that it was an incitement. Every idea is an incitement. It offers itself for belief and if believed it is acted on unless some other belief outweighs it or some failure of energy stifles the movement at its birth. The only difference between the expression of an opinion and an incitement in the narrower sense is the speaker's enthusiasm for the result. Eloquence may set fire to reason. But whatever may be thought of the redundant discourse before us it had no chance of starting a present conflagration. If in the long run the beliefs expressed in proletarian dictatorship are destined to be accepted by the dominant forces of the community, the only meaning of free speech is that they should be given their chance and have their way.

If the publication of this document had been laid as an attempt to induce an uprising against government at once and not at some indefinite time in the future it would have presented a different question. The object would have been one with which the law might deal, subject to the doubt whether there was any danger that the publication could produce any result, or in other words, whether it was not futile and too remote from possible consequences. But the indictment alleges the publication and nothing more.

THE GITLOW PROBLEM AND THE HOLMES DISSENT

Was the majority right in claiming that the question in a case such as Gitlow "is entirely different from cases where the statute merely prohibits certain acts involving the danger of substantive evil, without any reference to language itself, and it is sought to apply its provisions to language used by the defendants for the purpose of bringing about the prohibited result"? Was it accurate to say that the Schenck standard only applied to such cases, "and has no application to those like the present, where the legislative body itself has previously determined the danger of substantive evil arising from utterances of a specified character"? Or *did* the clear and present danger test, as it had been formulated in Schenck, apply—explicitly or implicitly—to the Gitlow (and Whitney, infra) problem?

How does Justice Holmes answer the majority's assertion? Does he answer? What is his view in the Gitlow dissent regarding the weight to be given the legislative judgment? Does he have any view? Is the question of the weight appropriate for the legislative judgment irrelevant here? Compare Justice Holmes concern with legislative judgments in his 14th Amendment dissents in cases such as Lochner, chap. 13, p. 956, supra.

Consider the following comment: "In Gitlow, Holmes was confronted by, and evaded, the difficulty of applying his Schenck remark without modification to this different kind of problem." Rogat, "The Judge as Spectator," 31 U.Chi.L.Rev. 213 (1964). Do you agree? What is "evaded"? Does Brandeis' opinion in Whitney, which follows, adequately confront what Holmes "evaded"? Professor Rogat argues that when the legislature prohibits advocacy of a specific doctrine, the question is no longer "proximity" to a specified act: "Here a court may have to establish . . . the importance (or the legitimacy) of forbidding the completed act." The important question, he argues, may well not be "proximity," but "which 'evils' a legislature may prohibit." What does Whitney say about that question? Would that be the important question if Masses provided the constitutional approach? Would Masses emphasize instead what speech is protected? Is that simply another way of putting the same "important question"? Compare the responses to the problem of prior legislative judgments in Dennis (p. 1097, infra) and subsequent cases.

WHITNEY v. CALIFORNIA

274 U.S. 357, 47 S.Ct. 641, 71 L.Ed. 1045 (1927).

Error to the District Court of Appeal, First Appellate District, Division One, of California.

Mr. Justice SANFORD delivered the opinion of the Court.

By a criminal information filed in the Superior Court of Alameda County, California, the plaintiff in error was charged, in five counts, with violations of the Criminal Syndicalism Act of that State. Statutes 1919, c. 188, p. 281. She was tried, convicted on the first count, and sentenced to imprisonment. . . .

The pertinent provisions of the Criminal Syndicalism Act are:

"Section 1. The term 'criminal syndicalism' as used in this act is hereby defined as any doctrine or precept advocating, teaching or aiding and abetting the commission of crime, sabotage (which word is hereby defined as meaning willful and malicious physical damage or injury to physical property), or unlawful acts of force and violence or unlawful methods of terrorism as a means of accomplishing a change in industrial ownership or control, or effecting any political change.

"Sec. 2. Any person who: . . . 4. Organizes or assists in organizing, or is or knowingly becomes a member of, any organization, society, or group or assemblage of persons organized or assembled to advocate, teach or aid and abet criminal syndicalism; . . .

"Is guilty of a felony and punishable by imprisonment."

The first count of the information, on which the conviction was had, charged that on or about November 28, 1919, in Alameda County, the defendant, in violation of the Criminal Syndicalism Act, "did then and there unlawfully, willfully, wrongfully, deliberately and feloniously organize and assist in organizing, and was, is, and knowingly became a member of an organization, society, group and assemblage of persons organized and assembled to advocate, teach, aid and abet criminal syndicalism." . . .

[In its summary of the facts, the Court stated that Miss Whitney had attended the 1919 national convention of the Socialist Party as a delegate from the Oakland branch. The convention split, and the "radicals"—including Miss Whitney—went to another hall and formed the Communist Labor Party. Later in 1919, she was a branch delegate to a convention called to organize a California unit of the new Party. As a member of that convention's resolutions committee, she supported a resolution endorsing "the value of political action" and urging workers "to cast their votes for the party which represents their immediate and final interest—the C. L. P.—at all elections." The proposed resolution was defeated on the floor of the convention and a more extreme program was adopted. Miss Whitney remained a member of the Party and testified at the trial "that it was not her intention that the Communist Labor Party of California should be an instrument of terrorism or violence."]

1. While it is not denied that the evidence warranted the jury in finding that the defendant became a member of and assisted in organizing the Communist Labor Party of California, and that this was organized to advocate, teach, aid or abet criminal syndicalism as defined by the Act, it is urged that the Act, as here construed and applied, deprived the defendant of her liberty without due process of law . . . . . The argument is, in effect, that the character of the state organization could not be forecast when she attended the convention; that she had no purpose of helping to create an instrument of terrorism and violence; that she "took part in formulating and presenting to the convention a resolution which, if adopted, would have committed the new organization to a legitimate policy of political reform by the use of the ballot"; that it was not until after the majority of the convention turned out to be "contrary-minded, and other less temperate policies prevailed" that the convention could have taken on the character of criminal syndicalism; and that as this was done over her protest, her mere presence in the convention, however violent the opinions expressed therein, could not thereby become a crime. This contention, while advanced in the form of a constitutional objection to the Act, is in effect nothing more than an effort to review the weight of the evidence for the purpose of showing that the defendant did not join and assist in organizing the Communist Labor Party of California with a knowledge of its unlawful character and purpose. This question, which is foreclosed by the verdict of the jury, . . . is one of fact merely which is not open to review in this Court, involving as it does no constitutional question whatever. . . .

2. It is clear that the Syndicalism Act is not repugnant to the due process clause by reason of vagueness and uncertainty of definition. . . .

4. Nor is the Syndicalism Act as applied in this case repugnant to the due process clause as a restraint of the rights of free speech, assembly, and association.

That the freedom of speech which is secured by the Constitution does not confer an absolute right to speak, without responsibility, whatever one may choose . . .; and that a State in the exercise of its police power may punish those who abuse this freedom by utterances inimical to the public welfare, tending to incite to crime, disturb the public peace, or endanger the foundations of organized government and threaten its overthrow by unlawful means, is not open to question. Gitlow v. New York . . .

By enacting the provisions of the Syndicalism Act the State has declared, through its legislative body, that to knowingly be or become a member of or assist in organizing an association to advocate, teach or aid and abet the commission of crimes or unlawful acts of force, violence or terrorism . . . involves such danger to the public peace and the security of the State, that these acts should be penalized in the exercise of its police power. That determination must be given great weight. . . .

The essence of the offense denounced by the Act is the combining with others in an association for the accomplishment of the desired ends through the advocacy and use of criminal and unlawful methods. It partakes of the nature of a criminal conspiracy. . . . That such united and joint action involves even greater danger to the public peace and security than the isolated utterances and acts of individuals, is clear. We cannot hold that, as here applied, the Act is an unreasonable or arbitrary exercise of the police power of the State, unwarrantably infringing any right of free speech, assembly or association, or that those persons are protected from punishment by the due process clause who abuse such rights by joining and furthering an organization thus menacing the peace and welfare of the State. . . .

Affirmed.

Mr. Justice BRANDEIS, concurring. . . .

The felony which the statute created is a crime very unlike the old felony of conspiracy or the old misdemeanor of unlawful assembly. The mere act of assisting in forming a society for teaching syndicalism, of becoming a member of it, or of assembling with others for that purpose is given the dynamic quality of crime. There is guilt although the society may not contemplate immediate promulgation of the doctrine. Thus the accused is to be punished, not for contempt, incitement or conspiracy, but for a step in preparation, which, if it threatens the public order at all, does so only remotely. The novelty in the prohibition introduced is that the statute aims, not at the practice of criminal syndicalism, nor even directly at the preaching of it, but at association with those who propose to preach it.

Despite arguments to the contrary which had seemed to me persuasive, it is settled that the due process clause of the Fourteenth Amendment applies to matters of substantive law as well as to matters of procedure. Thus all fundamental rights comprised within the term liberty are protected by the Federal Constitution from invasion by the States. The right of free speech, the right to teach and the right of assembly are, of course, fundamental rights. See Meyer v. Nebraska, 262 U.S. 390 . . .; Gitlow v. New York, 268 U.S. 652, 666 . . .. These may not be denied or abridged. But, although the rights of free speech and assembly are fundamental, they are not in their nature absolute. Their exercise is subject to restriction, if the particular restriction proposed is required in order to protect the State from destruction or from serious injury, political, economic or moral. That the necessity which is essential to a valid restriction does not exist unless speech would produce, or is intended to produce, a clear and imminent danger of some substantive evil which the State constitutionally may seek to prevent has been settled. See Schenck v. United States, 249 U.S. 47, 52.

It is said to be the function of the legislature to determine whether at a particular time and under the particular circumstances the formation of, or assembly with, a society organized to advocate criminal syndicalism constitutes a clear and present danger of substantive evil; and that by enacting the law here in question the Legislature of California determined that question in the affirmative. Compare Gitlow v. New York . . . . The legislature must obviously decide, in the first instance, whether a danger exists which calls for a particular protective measure. But where a statute is valid only in case certain conditions exist, the enactment of the statute cannot alone establish the facts which are essential to its validity. Prohibitory legislation has repeatedly been held invalid, because unnecessary, where the denial of liberty involved was that of engaging in a particular business. The power of the courts to strike down an offending law is no less when the interests involved are not property rights, but the fundamental personal rights of free speech and assembly.

This Court has not yet fixed the standard by which to determine when a danger shall be deemed clear; how remote the danger may be and yet be deemed present; and what degree of evil shall be deemed sufficiently substantial to justify resort to abridgment of free speech and assembly as the means of protection. To reach sound conclusions on these matters, we must bear in mind why a State is, ordinarily, denied the power to prohibit dissemination of social, economic and political doctrine which a vast majority of its citizens believes to be false and fraught with evil consequence.

Those who won our independence believed that the final end of the State was to make men free to develop their faculties; and that in its government the deliberative forces should prevail over the arbitrary. They valued liberty both as an end and as a means. They believed liberty to be the secret of happiness and courage to be the secret of liberty. They believed that freedom to think as you will and to speak as you think are means indispensable to the discovery and spread of political truth; that without free speech and assembly discussion would be futile; that with them, discussion affords ordinarily adequate protection against the dissemination of noxious doctrine; that the greatest menace to freedom is an inert people; that public discussion is a political duty; and that this should be a fundamental principle of the American government. They recognized the risks to which all human institutions are subject. But they knew that order cannot be secured merely through fear of punishment for its infraction; that it is hazardous to discourage thought, hope and imagination; that fear breeds repression; that repression breeds hate; that hate menaces stable government; that the path of safety lies in the opportunity to discuss freely supposed grievances and proposed remedies; and that the fitting remedy for evil counsels is good ones. Believing in the power of reason as applied through public discussion, they eschewed silence coerced by law—the argument of force in its worst form. Recognizing the occasional tyrannies of governing majorities, they amended the Constitution so that free speech and assembly should be guaranteed.

Fear of serious injury cannot alone justify suppression of free speech and assembly. Men feared witches and burnt women. It is the function of speech to free men from the bondage of irrational fears. To justify suppression of free speech there must be reasonable ground to fear that serious evil will result if free speech is practiced. There must be reasonable ground to believe that the danger apprehended is imminent. There must be reasonable ground to believe that the evil to be prevented is a serious one. Every denunciation of existing law tends in some measure to increase the probability that there will be violation of it. Condonation of a breach enhances the probability. Expressions of approval add to the probability. Propagation of the criminal state of mind by teaching syndicalism increases it. Advocacy of law-breaking heightens it still further. But even advocacy of violation, however reprehensible morally, is not a justification for denying free speech where the advocacy falls short of incitement and there is nothing to indicate that the advocacy would be immediately acted on. The wide difference between advocacy and incitement, between preparation and attempt, between assembling and conspiracy, must be borne in mind. In order to support a finding of clear and present danger it must be shown either that immediate serious violence was to be expected or was advocated, or that the past conduct furnished reason to believe that such advocacy was then contemplated.

Those who won our independence by revolution were not cowards. They did not fear political change. They did not exalt order at the cost of liberty. To courageous, self-reliant men, with confidence in the power of free and fearless reasoning applied through the processes of popular government, no danger flowing from speech can be deemed clear and present, unless the incidence of the evil apprehended is so imminent that it may befall before there is opportunity for full discussion. If there be time to expose through discussion the falsehood and fallacies, to avert the evil by the processes of education, the remedy to be applied is more speech, not enforced silence. Only an emergency can justify repression. Such must be the rule if authority is to be reconciled with freedom. Such, in my opinion, is the command of the Constitution. It is therefore always open to Americans to challenge a law abridging free speech and assembly by showing that there was no emergency justifying it.

Moreover, even imminent danger cannot justify resort to prohibition of these functions essential to effective democracy, unless the evil apprehended is relatively serious. Prohibition of free speech and assembly is a measure so stringent that it would be inappropriate as the means for averting a relatively trivial harm to society. A police measure may be unconstitutional merely because the remedy, although effective as means of protection, is unduly harsh or oppressive. Thus, a state might, in the exercise of its police power, make any trespass upon the land of another a crime, regardless of the results or of the intent or purpose of the trespasser. It might, also, punish an attempt, a conspiracy, or an incitement to commit the trespass. But it is hardly conceivable that this court would hold constitutional a statute which punished as a felony the mere voluntary assembly with a society formed to teach that pedestrians had the moral right to cross uninclosed, unposted, waste lands and to advocate their doing so, even if there was imminent danger that advocacy would lead to a trespass. The fact that speech is likely to result in some violence or in destruction of property is not enough to justify its suppression. There must be the probability of serious injury to the State. Among free men, the deterrents ordinarily to be applied to prevent crime are education and punishment for violations of the law, not abridgment of the rights of free speech and assembly.

[The California] legislative declaration satisfies the requirement of the constitution of the State concerning emergency legislation. . . . But it does not preclude enquiry into the question whether, at the time and under the circumstances, the conditions existed which are essential to validity under the Federal Constitution. As a statute, even if not void on its face, may be challenged because invalid as applied, Dahnke-Walker Milling Co. v. Bondurant, 257 U.S. 282, the result of such an enquiry may depend upon the specific facts of the particular case. Whenever the fundamental rights of free speech and assembly are alleged to have been invaded, it must remain open to a defendant to present the issue whether there actually did exist at the time a clear danger; whether the danger, if any, was imminent; and whether the evil apprehended was one so substantial as to justify the stringent restriction interposed by the legislature. The legislative declaration, like the fact that the statute was passed and was sustained by the highest court of the State, creates merely a rebuttable presumption that these conditions have been satisfied.

Whether in 1919, when Miss Whitney did the things complained of, there was in California such clear and present danger of serious evil, might have been made the important issue in the case. She might have required that the issue be determined either by the court or the jury. She claimed below that the statute as applied to her violated the Federal Constitution; but she did not claim that it was void because there was no clear and present danger of serious evil, nor did she request that the existence of these conditions of a valid measure thus restricting the rights of free speech and assembly be passed upon by the court or a jury. On the other hand, there was evidence on which the court or jury might have found that such danger existed. I am unable to assent to the suggestion in the opinion of the Court that assembling with a political party, formed to advocate the desirability of a proletarian revolution by mass action at some date necessarily far in the future, is not a right within the protection of the Fourteenth Amendment. In the present case, however, there was other testimony which tended to establish the existence of a conspiracy, on the part of members of the International Workers of the World, to commit present serious crimes; and likewise to show that such a conspiracy would be furthered by the activity of the society of which Miss Whitney was a member. Under these circumstances the judgment of the state court cannot be disturbed.

Our power of review in this case is limited not only to the question whether a right guaranteed by the Federal Constitution was denied, Murdock v. City of Memphis, 20 Wall. 590; . . . but to the particular claims duly made below, and denied. . . . We lack here the power occasionally exercised on review of judgments of lower federal courts to correct in criminal

cases vital errors, although the objection was not taken in the trial court.
. . . This is a writ of error to a state court. Because we may not enquire
into the errors now alleged, I concur in affirming the judgment of the state
court.

Mr. Justice HOLMES joins in this opinion.

OTHER CASES OF THE TWENTIES AND THIRTIES: THE GROWING PROTECTION OF SPEECH

Introduction. Most states enacted anti-sedition laws in the immediate
post-World War I years—some patterned on the New York and California
ones in Gitlow and Whitney, some going off in different and often more
extreme directions. See generally Chafee, Free Speech in the United States
(1941). In a number of cases in the 1920's and 1930's, the Court set aside
convictions under such laws.*

Did the protection of speech in the cases that follow rest on the Schenck
standard? On the minority views in Abrams, Gitlow, or Whitney? Or do
these decisions represent new doctrinal developments? Is Herndon in effect
a Court acceptance of the temporal, immediacy ingredient of clear and present
danger—an ingredient not emphasized in the Court decisions in Gitlow and
Whitney? Do these cases begin to articulate the contours of political discussion and agitation required by First Amendment values (at some point short
of "incitement" or "counselling") in much the same manner as Hand had in
the Masses case? Compare the analytical process in Yates and Scales, pp. 1111
and 1113, infra, and in New York Times v. Sullivan, p. 1214, infra: is the effort to define the protected area of debate at the core of the First Amendment
more productive than the immediacy-of-danger preoccupation of the clear and
present danger test? Do the cases which follow speak to the Gitlow or Whitney problem (of legislative judgments regarding the danger of specified
speech) more directly than the Gitlow dissent had? Do the cases which follow provide clear guidance regarding the constitutionality of the post-World
War II Smith Act prosecutions of Communists, in cases such as Dennis, p.
1097, infra?

1. *Fiske v. Kansas.* The Fiske case, 274 U.S. 380 (1927), decided on
the same day as Whitney, held unconstitutional an application of the Kansas
version of the criminal syndicalism law. Fiske was convicted for soliciting
new members for a branch of the IWW (Industrial Workers of the World).
The only trial evidence of IWW doctrine was the preamble to its constitution, containing such statements as: "Between [the working and employing]
classes a struggle must go on until the workers of the World organize as a
class, take possession of the earth, and the machinery of production and abolish
the wage system." Fiske insisted that the preamble taught "peaceful," not

* In addition to the three decisions
considered here (Fiske, DeJonge, and
Herndon v. Lowry), note also Stromberg v. California, 283 U.S. 359 (1931)
(holding unconstitutional a version of
a widely adopted red flag law;
Stromberg is noted with the materials
on symbolic expression, at p. 1189), and
two cases not directly involving "Red
scare," antisubversion concerns: Near
v. Minnesota, 283 U.S. 697 (1931) (invalidating injunctive remedies against
"malicious, scandalous and defamatory" periodicals, see p. 1258, infra)
and Hague v. CIO, 307 U.S. 496 (1939)
(invalidating a licensing requirement
for meetings on public property).

"criminal or unlawful," action, and that he had not advocated criminal syndicalism or sabotage.

In affirming the conviction, the highest state court said: "The language quoted from the I.W.W. preamble need not—in order to sustain the judgment—be held, necessarily and as a matter of law, to advocate, teach or even affirmatively suggest physical violence as a means of accomplishing industrial or political ends. It is open to that interpretation and is capable of use to convey that meaning. . . . The jury were not required to accept the defendant's testimony as a candid and accurate statement. There was room for them to find . . . that the equivocal language of the preamble and of the defendant in explaining it to his prospects was employed to convey and did convey the sinister meaning attributed to it by the state." The United States Supreme Court unanimously reversed, in an opinion by Justice Sanford:

"[T]his Court will review the finding of facts by a State court where a federal right has been denied as the result of a finding shown by the record to be without evidence to support it; or where a conclusion of law as to a Federal right and a finding of fact are so intermingled as to make it necessary, in order to pass upon the Federal question, to analyze the facts. . . .

". . . . No substantial inference can, in our judgment, be drawn from the language of this preamble, that the organization taught, advocated or suggested the duty, necessity, propriety, or expediency of crime, criminal syndicalism, sabotage, or other unlawful acts or methods. . . . And standing alone, as it did in this case, there was nothing which warranted the court or jury in ascribing to this language, either as an inference of law or fact, 'the sinister meaning attributed to it by the state.' In this respect the language of the preamble is essentially different from that of the manifesto involved in Gitlow v. New York . . . . . And it is not as if the preamble were shown to have been followed by further statements or declarations indicating that it was intended to mean, and to be understood as advocating, that the ends outlined therein would be accomplished or brought about by violence or other related unlawful acts or methods. . . .

"The result is that the Syndicalism Act has been applied in this case to sustain the conviction of the defendant, without any charge or evidence that the organization in which he secured members advocated any crime, violence or other unlawful acts or methods as a means of effecting industrial or political changes or revolution. Thus applied the Act is an arbitrary and unreasonable exercise of the police power of the State, unwarrantably infringing the liberty of the defendant in violation of the due process clause of the Fourteenth Amendment."

[Note that Fiske was written by Justice Sanford, the author of the majority opinion in Gitlow. Was Fiske an early example of a double standard—of special protection for personal liberties? Or was it simply one more example of the Lochner-substantive due process approach—of judicial reexamination of legislative value choices (see chap. 13, sec. 3, supra)?]

2. *DeJonge v. Oregon.* Ten years later, the DeJonge case, 299 U.S. 353 (1937), set aside a conviction under Oregon's criminal syndicalism act. The statute defined criminal syndicalism as "the doctrine which advocates crime, physical violence, sabotage, or any unlawful acts or methods as a means

of accomplishing or effecting industrial or political change or revolution." DeJonge was charged with assisting in the conduct of a meeting "which was called under the auspices of the Communist Party, an organization advocating criminal syndicalism." At the trial, he moved for acquittal on the ground "that the meeting was public and orderly and was held for a lawful purpose; that while it was held under the auspices of the Communist Party, neither criminal syndicalism nor any unlawful conduct was taught or advocated at the meeting either by appellant or by others." The motion was overruled. The highest state court affirmed this ruling, holding that there was no charge that criminal syndicalism was advocated at the meeting; rather, the court construed the indictment as simply charging that DeJonge conducted a meeting called by the Party, and that the Party advocated criminal syndicalism. Accordingly, lack of proof of illegal advocacy at the meeting itself was immaterial. The Supreme Court unanimously reversed. Chief Justice Hughes' opinion included the following passages:

"We must take the indictment as thus construed. Conviction upon a charge not made would be sheer denial of due process. It thus appears that, while defendant was a member of the Communist Party, he was not indicted for participating in its organization, or for joining it, or for soliciting members or for distributing its literature. He was not charged with teaching or advocating criminal syndicalism or sabotage or any unlawful acts, either at the meeting or elsewhere. . . . His sole offense . . . was that he had assisted in the conduct of a public meeting, albeit otherwise lawful, which was held under the auspices of the Communist Party.

"The broad reach of the statute as thus applied is plain. While defendant was a member of the Communist Party, that membership was not necessary to conviction on such a charge. A like fate might have attended any speaker, although not a member who 'assisted in the conduct' of the meeting. However innocuous the object of the meeting, however lawful the subjects and tenor of the addresses, however reasonable and timely the discussion, all those assisting in the conduct of the meeting would be subject to imprisonment as felons if the meeting were held by the Communist Party. . . .

"The right of peaceable assembly is a right cognate to those of free speech and free press and is equally fundamental. . . . The First Amendment of the Federal Constitution expressly guarantees that right against abridgment by Congress. But explicit mention there does not argue exclusion elsewhere. For the right is one that cannot be denied without violating those fundamental principles of liberty and justice which lie at the base of all civil and political institutions—principles which the Fourteenth Amendment embodies in the general terms of its due process clause. . . .

"These rights may be abused by using speech or press or assembly in order to incite to violence and crime. . . . But the legislative intervention can find constitutional justification only by dealing with the abuse. The rights themselves must not be curtailed. . . .

"It follows from these considerations that, consistently with the Federal Constitution, peaceable assembly for lawful discussion cannot be made a crime. The holding of meetings for peaceable political action cannot be proscribed. Those who assist in the conduct of such meetings cannot be branded as criminals on that score. The question, if the rights of free speech and peaceable assembly are to be preserved, is not as to the auspices under which the meeting is held but as to its purpose; not as to the relations of the speakers, but whether their utterances transcend the bounds of the freedom of speech which the Constitution protects. If the persons assembling have committed crimes elsewhere, if they have formed or are engaged in a conspiracy against the public peace and order they may be prosecuted for their conspiracy or other violation of valid laws. But it is a different matter when the State, instead of prosecuting them for such offenses, seizes upon mere participation in a peaceable assembly and a lawful public discussion as the basis for a criminal charge.

"We are not called upon to review the findings of the state court as to the objectives of the Communist Party. Notwithstanding those objectives, the defendant still enjoyed his personal right of free speech and to take part in a peaceable assembly having a lawful purpose, although called by that Party. The defendant was none the less entitled to discuss the public issues of the day and thus in a lawful manner, without incitement to violence or crime, to seek redress of alleged grievances. That was of the essence of his guaranteed personal liberty.

"We hold that the Oregon statute as applied to the particular charge as defined by the state court is repugnant to the due process clause of the Fourteenth Amendment."

HERNDON v. LOWRY

301 U.S. 242, 57 S.Ct. 732, 81 L.Ed. 1066 (1937).

Appeal from the Supreme Court of Georgia.

Mr. Justice ROBERTS delivered the opinion of the Court. [Recall the Court's earlier encounter with Herndon's conviction, in Herndon v. Georgia, 295 U.S. 441 (1935) (chap. 2, sec. 3, p. 125, supra). There, the Court had refused to consider the federal objections because of the adequate state grounds barrier. The state courts subsequently considered Herndon's objections on habeas corpus; that action permitted Supreme Court review of the merits in this case.]

The charge was founded on § 56 of the [Georgia] Penal Code, one of four related sections. Section 55 defines insurrection, § 56 defines an attempt to incite insurrection, § 57 prescribes the death penalty for conviction of the offenses described in the two preceding sections unless the jury shall recommend mercy, and § 58 penalizes, by imprisonment, the introduction and circulation of printed matter for the purpose of inciting insurrection, riot, conspiracy, etc. The sections are copied in the margin.[1] . . .

The evidence on which the judgment rests consists of appellant's admissions and certain documents found in his possession. The appellant told the state's officers that some time prior to his arrest he joined the Communist

---

1. "55. Insurrection shall consist in any combined resistance to the lawful authority of the State, with intent to the denial thereof, when the same is manifested or intended to be manifested by acts of violence.

"56. Any attempt, by persuasion or otherwise, to induce others to join in any combined resistance to the lawful authority of the State shall constitute an attempt to incite insurrection. . . ." [Footnote by the Court.]

Party in Kentucky and later came to Atlanta as a paid organizer for the party, his duties being to call meetings, to educate and disseminate information respecting the party, to distribute literature, to secure members, and to work up an organization of the party in Atlanta . . . .

Certain documents in his possession when he was arrested were placed in evidence [including membership blanks. These] indicate more specific aims for which members of the Communist Party are to vote. They are to vote Communist for:

"1. Unemployment and Social Insurance at the expense of the State and employers.

"2. Against Hoover's wage-cutting policy.

"3. Emergency relief for the poor farmers without restrictions by the government and banks; exemption of poor farmers from taxes and from forced collection of rents or debts.

"4. Equal rights for the Negroes and self-determination for the Black Belt.

"5. Against capitalistic terror: against all forms of suppression of the political rights of the workers.

"6. Against imperialist war; for the defense of the Chinese people and of the Soviet Union."

None of these aims is criminal upon its face. As to one, the fourth, the claim is that criminality may be found because of extrinsic facts. [T]he state especially relies upon a booklet entitled "The Communist Position on the Negro Question," on the cover of which appears a map of the United States having a dark belt across certain Southern states and the phrase "Self-Determination for the Black Belt." The booklet affirms that the source of the Communist slogan "Right of Self-Determination of the Negroes in the Black Belt" is a resolution of the Communist International on the Negro question in the United States adopted in 1930, which states that the Communist Party in the United States has been actively attempting to win increasing sympathy among the Negro population, that certain things have been advocated for the benefit of the Negroes in the Northern states, but that in the Southern portion of the United States the Communist slogan must be "The Right of Self-Determination of the Negroes in the Black Belt." . . .

There is no evidence the appellant distributed any writings or printed matter found in the box he carried when arrested, or any other advocating forcible subversion of governmental authority. There is no evidence the appellant advocated, by speech or written word, at meetings or elsewhere, any doctrine or action implying such forcible subversion. . . . Appellant's intent to incite insurrection, if it is to be found, must rest upon his procuring members for the Communist Party and his possession of that party's literature when he was arrested. . . .

To ascertain how the Act is held to apply to the appellant's conduct we turn to the rulings of the state courts in his case. [The Georgia Supreme Court] sustained the conviction by construing the statute thus: "Force must have been contemplated, but, as said above, the statute does not include either its occurrence or its imminence as an ingredient of the particular offense charged. . . . ." The affirmance of conviction upon the trial record necessarily gives § 56 the construction that one who seeks members for or attempts to organize a local unit of a party which has the purposes and objects disclosed by the documents in evidence may be found guilty of an attempt to incite insurrection.

The questions are whether this construction and application of the statute deprives the accused of the right of freedom of speech and of assembly guaranteed by the Fourteenth Amendment, and whether the statute so construed and applied furnishes a reasonably definite and ascertainable standard of guilt.

The appellant, while admitting that the people may protect themselves against abuses of the freedom of speech safeguarded by the Fourteenth Amendment by prohibiting incitement to violence and crime, insists that legislative regulation may not go beyond measures forefending against "clear and present danger" of the use of force against the state. For this position he relies upon our decisions under the Federal Espionage Acts and cognate state legislation. [The Court quoted the clear and present danger language of Schenck.] The legislation under review differs radically from the Espionage Acts in that it does not deal with a wilful attempt to obstruct a described and defined activity of the government.

The State, on the other hand, insists that our decisions uphold state statutes making criminal utterances which have a "dangerous tendency" towards the subversion of government. It relies particularly upon Gitlow v. New York, 268 U.S. 652. There, however, we dealt with a statute which, quite unlike § 56 of the Georgia Criminal Code, denounced as criminal certain acts carefully and adequately described.

It is evident that [Gitlow, permitting the penalizing of "utterances which openly advocate" overthrow by unlawful means,] furnishes no warrant for the appellee's contention that under a law general in its description of the mischief to be remedied and equally general in respect of the intent of the actor, the standard of guilt may be made the "dangerous tendency" of his words.

The power of a state to abridge freedom of speech and of assembly is the exception rather than the rule and the penalizing even of utterances of a defined character must find its justification in a reasonable apprehension of danger to organized government. The judgment of the legislature is not unfettered. The limitation upon individual liberty must have appropriate relation to the safety of the state. Legislation which goes beyond this need violates the principle of the Constitution. . . .

1. The appellant had a constitutional right to address meetings and organize parties unless in so doing he violated some prohibition of a valid statute. The only prohibition he is said to have violated is that of § 56 forbidding incitement or attempted incitement to insurrection by violence. If the evidence fails to show that he did so incite, then, as applied to him, the statute unreasonably limits freedom of speech and freedom of assembly and violates the Fourteenth Amendment. We are of opinion that the requisite proof is lacking. From what has been said above with respect to the evidence offered at the trial it is apparent that the documents found upon the appellant's person were certainly, as to some of the aims stated therein, innocent and consistent with peaceful action for a change in the laws or the constitution. The proof wholly fails to show that the appellant had read these documents;

that he had distributed any of them; that he believed and advocated any or all of the principles and aims set forth in them, or that those he had procured to become members of the party knew or approved of any of these documents.

Thus, the crucial question is not the formal interpretation of the statute by the Supreme Court of Georgia but the application given it. In its application the offense made criminal is that of soliciting members for a political party and conducting meetings of a local unit of that party when one of the doctrines of the party, established by reference to a document not shown to have been exhibited to anyone by the accused, may be said to be ultimate resort to violence at some indefinite future time against organized government. It is to be borne in mind that the legislature of Georgia has not made membership in the Communist Party unlawful by reason of its supposed dangerous tendency even in the remote future. The question is not whether Georgia might, in analogy to what other states have done, so declare.[2] The appellant induced others to become members of the Communist Party. Did he thus incite to insurrection by reason of the fact that they agreed to abide by the tenets of the party, some of them lawful, others, as may be assumed, unlawful, in the absence of proof that he brought the unlawful aims to their notice, that he approved them, or that the fantastic program they envisaged was conceived of by anyone as more than an ultimate ideal? Doubtless circumstantial evidence might affect the answer to the question if appellant had been shown to have said that the Black Belt should be organized at once as a separate state and that that objective was one of his principal aims. But here circumstantial evidence is all to the opposite effect. The only objectives appellant is proved to have urged are those having to do with unemployment and emergency relief which are void of criminality. His membership in the Communist Party and his solicitation of a few members wholly fails to establish an attempt to incite others to insurrection. . . . The same may be said with respect to the other books and pamphlets, some of them of more innocent purport. In these circumstances to make membership in the party and solicitation of members for that party a criminal offense, punishable by death, in the discretion of a jury, is an unwarranted invasion of the right of freedom of speech.

2. The statute, as construed and applied in the appellant's trial, does not furnish a sufficiently ascertainable standard of guilt. The Act does not prohibit incitement to violent interference with any given activity or operation of the state. By force of it, as construed, the judge and jury trying an alleged offender cannot appraise the circumstances and character of the defendant's utterances or activities as begetting a clear and present danger of forcible obstruction of a particular state function. Nor is any specifed conduct or utterance of the accused made an offense.

. . . . If the jury conclude that the defendant should have contemplated that any act or utterance of his in opposition to the established order or advocating a change in that order, might, in the distant future, eventuate in a combination to offer forcible resistance to the State, or as the State says, if the jury believe he should have known that his words would have "a danger-

---

2. See the statutes drawn in question in Gitlow v. New York, 268 U.S. 652, at 654, and in Whitney v. California,   274 U.S. 357, 359. [Footnote by the Court.]

ous tendency" then he may be convicted. To be guilty under the law, as construed, a defendant need not advocate resort to force. He need not teach any particular doctrine to come within its purview. Indeed, he need not be active in the formation of a combination or group if he agitate for a change in the frame of government, however peaceful his own intent. If, by the exercise of prophecy, he can forecast that, as a result of a chain of causation, following his proposed action a group may arise at some future date which will resort to force, he is bound to make the prophesy and abstain, under pain of punishment, possibly of execution. Every person who attacks existing conditions, who agitates for a change in the form of government, must take the risk that if a jury should be of opinion he ought to have foreseen that his utterances might contribute in any measure to some future forcible resistance to the existing government he may be convicted of the offense of inciting insurrection. Proof that the accused in fact believed that his effort would cause a violent assault upon the state would not be necessary to conviction. It would be sufficient if the jury thought he reasonably might foretell that those he persuaded to join the party might, at some time in the indefinite future, resort to forcible resistance of government. The question thus proposed to a jury involves pure speculation as to future trends of thought and action. Within what time might one reasonably expect that an attempted organization of the Communist Party in United States would result in violent action by that party? If a jury returned a special verdict saying twenty years or even fifty years the verdict could not be shown to be wrong. . . .

The statute, as construed and applied, amounts merely to a dragnet which may enmesh anyone who agitates for a change of government if a jury can be persuaded that he ought to have foreseen his words would have some effect in the future conduct of others. . . . So vague and indeterminate are the boundaries thus set to the freedom of speech and assembly that the law necessarily violates the guarantees of liberty embodied in the Fourteenth Amendment. . . .

Reversed.

Mr. Justice VAN DEVANTER, dissenting. . . .

It plainly appears, I think, that the offense defined in the statute, and of which Herndon was convicted, was not that of advocating a change in the state government by lawful means, such as an orderly exertion of the elective franchise or of the power to amend the state constitution, but was that of attempting to induce and incite others to join in combined *forcible* resistance to the lawful authority of the State. . . .

It should not be overlooked that Herndon was a negro member and organizer in the Communist Party and was engaged actively in inducing others, chiefly southern negroes, to become members of the party and participate in effecting its purposes and program. The literature placed in his hands by the party for that purpose was particularly adapted to appeal to negroes in that section, for it pictured their condition as an unhappy one resulting from asserted wrongs on the part of white landlords and employers, and sought by alluring statements of resulting advantages to induce them to join in an effort to carry into effect the measures which the literature proposed. These measures included a revolutionary uprooting of the existing capitalist state, as it was termed; confiscation of the landed property of white landowners and capitalists for the benefit of negroes; establishment in the black belt of an independent State, possibly followed by secession from the United States; organization of mass demonstrations, strikes and tax boycotts in aid of this measure; adoption of a fighting alliance with the revolutionary white proletariat; revolutionary overthrow of capitalism and establishment of Communism through effective physical struggles against the class enemy. Proposing these measures was nothing short of advising a resort to force and violence, for all know that such measures could not be effected otherwise. Not only so, but the literature makes such repelling use of the terms "revolution," "national rebellion," "revolutionary struggle," "revolutionary overthrow," "effective physical struggle," "smash the National Guard," "mass strikes," and "violence," as to leave no doubt that the use of force in an unlawful sense is intended.

The purpose and probable effect of such literature, when under consideration in a prosecution like that against Herndon, are to be tested and determined with appropriate regard to the capacity and circumstances of those who are sought to be influenced. In this instance the literature is largely directed to a people whose past and present circumstances would lead them to give unusual credence to its inflaming and inciting features. . . . That the constitutional guaranty of freedom of speech and assembly does not shield or afford protection for acts of intentional incitement to forcible resistance to the lawful authority of a State is settled by repeated decisions of this Court. . . .

C. THE SMITH ACT PROSECUTIONS

CLEAR AND PRESENT DANGER IN THE FORTIES: WIDENING USE; RISING DISSATISFACTION

Introduction. The post-World War II prosecutions of Communist Party leaders were brought under the Smith Act of 1940, a law quite similar to the New York statute sustained in Gitlow. When the first group of defendants brought their appeals to the Supreme Court, in the 1951 Dennis case, p. 1097, infra, they relied extensively on clear and present danger; and the opinions in Dennis reexamine that standard at length.

The defendants' reliance on the test was understandable: the Court had spoken of it with increasing frequency. But the appearances had often been in contexts far removed from subversive advocacy. For example, an early use in a majority opinion was Schneider v. State, 308 U.S. 147 (1939), involving an ordinance against littering streets. And the most consistent use of the test had been to strike down contempt of court penalties imposed for newspaper comments allegedly interfering with the administration of justice. See, e. g., Craig v. Harney, 331 U.S. 367 (1947) (p. 1276, infra).

Moreover, there had been increasing criticism of the standard itself. Some critics then, and later, thought clear and present danger afforded either too much or too little protection to free speech: the Dennis majority, for example, finds the immediacy emphasis too restrictive on government; the Douglas opinion in Brandenburg v. Ohio, the 1969 decision below (at p. 1123), illustrates the dissatisfaction with the use of the standard to "balance away" liberties.

But much of the criticism dealt less with the scope of protection afforded by the Schenck phrase than with its suitability: it was argued that the standard was used in inappropriate contexts, that it was too simplistic, that in any event it did not deal adequately with the type of problem presented by Gitlow and Dennis.

1. *Clear and present danger and legislative balancing.* For example, as early as 1941—a few months after the Smith Act was enacted, eight years before the Dennis trial—Herbert Wechsler suggested that the Smith Act variety of statute had "little positive merit" as a legislative formula—and that the clear and present danger judicial formula urged as a protection of speech had "little positive content" and "prescribes no rigid limitation on legislative action." Symposium on Civil Liberties, 9 Am.L.Sch.Rev. 881 (1941), Selected Essays 1938–62 (1963), 628. The Smith Act, an "advocacy of violent overthrow" statute, was unresponsive to current dangers: it was "an uncritical acceptance of a formula devised during the days when the Communist manifesto represented the technique of revolution; when revolutionaries operated by declaring rather than disguising their principles." And clear and present danger was of limited utility to courts: what it "can do, and all that it can do, is to require an extended judicial review in the fullest legislative sense of the competing values which the particular situation presents"; but that review "may be limited" by a "deference to legislative judgment, at least where the legislation condemns specific doctrine."

2. *"Clear and present danger" as oversimplification.* Compare an evaluation of clear and present danger near the end of the decade, just before Dennis (an evaluation quoted by Justice Frankfurter in Dennis): "The truth is that the clear-and-present-danger test is an over-simplified judgment unless it takes account also of a number of other factors: the relative seriousness of the danger in comparison with the value of the occasion for speech or political activity; the availability of more moderate controls than those which the state has imposed; and perhaps the specific intent with which the speech or activity is launched. No matter how rapidly we utter the phrase 'clear and present danger,' or how closely we hyphenate the words, they are not a substitute for the weighing of values. They tend to convey a delusion of certitude when what is most certain is the complexity of the strands in the web of freedoms which the judge must disentangle." Freund, On Understanding the Supreme Court (1949), 27.

3. *Clear and present danger and Learned Hand.* Among the critics of clear and present danger was Judge Learned Hand. His "Bill of Rights" lectures in 1958 included a skeptical aside on Holmes' Schenck formulation: "Homer nodded." More generally, those lectures revealed deep skepticism that substantive constitutional guarantees were judicially enforceable at all. Yet as District Judge in Masses, supra, Hand had tried to articulate judicial criteria of his own. And it fell to him on the Circuit Court of Appeals to pass on the Dennis defendants' clear and present danger defense—and reformulate it in words adopted by the majority opinion in the Supreme Court, infra.

Note Judge Hand's puzzled comment on the variety of clear and present danger invocations [in the course of his effort to restate the test in the Dennis case, 183 F.2d 201 (2d Cir. 1950)]: "[Cases such as Gitlow] concerned the validity of statutes which had made it unlawful to stir up opposition to the Government or a state in the discharge of some vital function. There followed several which held that an ordinance or statute might not trench upon freedom of speech in order to promote minor public convenience: e. g., preventing the streets from being littered by broadsides, Schneider v. State, 308 U.S. 147 (1939); requiring a license to solicit contributions for societies, Cantwell v. Connecticut, 310 U.S. 296 (1940); requiring a union leader to register his name and union affiliation with the Secretary of State, Thomas v. Collins, 323 U.S. 516 (1945). The opinions in all these cases [all infra] did however repeat the rubric of Schenck v. United States [clear and present danger], though none of them attempted to define how grave, or how imminent the danger must be, or whether the two factors are mutually interdependent. Moreover, the situation in all was wholly different from that in the preceding decisions. It is one thing to say that the public interest in keeping streets clean, or in keeping a register of union leaders, or in requiring solicitors to take out licenses, will not justify interference with freedom of utterance . . .; but it is quite another matter to say that an organized effort to inculcate the duty of revolution may not be repressed. It does not seem to us therefore that these decisions help towards a solution here."

4. *Clear and present danger and Dennis.* Consider the use of clear and present danger in Dennis, infra, against the background of these criticisms. Does Dennis give inadequate protection to speech? If so, is that because it failed to apply clear and present danger? Or because of problems inherent in clear and present danger? Was a greater emphasis on immediacy in Dennis compelled by the earlier cases? What different approach to speech would have been preferable in Dennis?

5. *Clear and present danger as inadequate protection of Meiklejohn's "public" speech.* While the clarity and applicability of clear and present danger were being questioned during the forties, another—and increasingly influential—challenge attacked it for protecting speech insufficiently. In 1948, philosopher Alexander Meiklejohn took direct issue with Schenck because its standard authorized some suppression of speech that should be wholly immune. The First Amendment, he insisted, "means that certain substantive evils which, in principle, Congress has a right to prevent, must be endured if the only way of avoiding them is by the abridging of that freedom of speech upon which the entire structure of our free institutions rests." Meiklejohn, Free Speech and Its Relation to Self-Government (1948), 48. Meiklejohn would distinguish among varieties of speech: only "public" speech —speech on public issues, speech connected with "self-government"—must be immune from regulation; "private" speech is entitled to less complete protection. Note the criticism in Chafee's Book Review, 62 Harv.L.Rev. 891 (1949), Selected Essays 1938–62 (1963), 618.

Would the Meiklejohn approach have been preferable in Dennis? Has it had greater acceptance in the cases since Dennis? See Brennan, "The Supreme Court and the Meiklejohn Interpretation of the First Amendment," 79 Harv.L.Rev. 1 (1965). In New York Times v. Sullivan, 376 U.S. 254 (1964) (p. 1214, infra)? In Brandenburg v. Ohio, 395 U.S. 444 (1969) (p. 1123, infra)? See generally Strong, "Fifty Years of 'Clear and Present Danger': From Schenck to Brandenburg—and Beyond," 1969 S.Ct.Rev. 41.

DENNIS v. UNITED STATES

341 U.S. 494, 71 S.Ct. 857, 95 L.Ed. 1137 (1951).

Certiorari to the Court of Appeals for the Second Circuit.

Mr. Chief Justice VINSON announced the judgment of the Court and an opinion in which Mr. Justice REED, Mr. Justice BURTON and Mr. Justice MINTON join.

Petitioners were indicted in July, 1948, for violation of the conspiracy provisions of the Smith Act . . . during the period of April, 1945, to July, 1948. . . . A verdict of guilty as to all the petitioners was returned by the jury on October 14, 1949. The Court of Appeals affirmed the convictions. 183 F.2d 201. We granted certiorari, 340 U.S. 863, limited to the following two questions: (1) Whether either § 2 or § 3 of the Smith Act, inherently or as construed and applied in the instant case, violates the First Amendment and other provisions of the Bill of Rights; (2) whether either § 2 or § 3 of the Act inherently or as construed and applied in the instant case, violates the First and Fifth Amendments because of indefiniteness.

Sections 2 and 3 of the Smith Act (see present 18 U.S.C. § 2385), provide as follows:

"Sec. 2.   (a) It shall be unlawful for any person—

"(1) to knowingly or willfully advocate, abet, advise, or teach the duty, necessity, desirability, or propriety of overthrowing or destroying any government in the United States by force or violence, or by the assassination of any officer of such government; . . .

"(3) to organize or help to organize any society, group, or assembly of persons who teach, advocate, or encourage the overthrow or destruction of any government in the United States by force or violence, or to be or become a member of, or affiliate with, any such society, group, or assembly of persons, knowing the purpose thereof. . . .

"Sec. 3. It shall be unlawful for any person to attempt to commit, or to conspire to commit, any of the acts prohibited by . . . this title."

The indictment charged the petitioners with wilfully and knowingly conspiring (1) to organize as the Communist Party of the United States of America a society, group and assembly of persons who teach and advocate the overthrow and destruction of the Government of the United States by force and violence, and (2) knowingly and wilfully to advocate and teach the duty and necessity of overthrowing and destroying the Government of the United States by force and violence. The indictment further alleged that § 2 of the Smith Act proscribes these acts and that any conspiracy to take such action is a violation of § 3 of the Act.

The trial of the case extended over nine months, six of which were devoted to the taking of evidence, resulting in a record of 16,000 pages. Our limited grant of the writ of certiorari has removed from our consideration any question as to the sufficiency of the evidence to support the jury's determination that petitioners are guilty of the offense charged. Whether on this record petitioners did in fact advocate the overthrow of the Government by force and violence is not before us, and we must base any discussion of this point upon the conclusions stated in the opinion of the Court of Appeals, which treated the issue in great detail. [T]he Court of Appeals held that the record supports the following broad conclusions: By virtue of their control over the political apparatus of the Communist Political Association, petitioners were able to transform that organization into the Communist Party; that the policies of the Association were changed from peaceful cooperation with the United States and its economic and political structure to a policy which had existed before the United States and the Soviet Union were fighting a common enemy, namely, a policy which worked for the overthrow of the Government by force and violence; that the Communist Party is a highly disciplined organization, adept at infiltration into strategic positions, use of aliases, and double-meaning language; that the Party is rigidly controlled; that Communists, unlike other political parties, tolerate no dissension from the policy laid down by the guiding forces, but that the approved program is slavishly followed by the members of the Party; that the literature of the Party and the statements and activities of its leaders, petitioners here, advocate, and the general goal of the Party was, during the period in question, to achieve a successful overthrow of the existing order by force and violence. . . .

I.

. . . The structure and purpose of the statute demand the inclusion of intent as an element of the crime. Congress was concerned with those who advocate and organize for the overthrow of the Government. Certainly those who recruit and combine for the purpose of advocating overthrow intend to bring about that overthrow. We hold that the statute requires as an essential element of the crime proof of the intent of those who are charged with its violation to overthrow the Government by force and violence. . . .

II.

The obvious purpose of the statute is to protect existing Government, not from change by peaceable, lawful and constitutional means, but from change by violence, revolution and terrorism. That it is within the *power* of the Congress to protect the Government of the United States from armed rebellion is a proposition which requires little discussion. Whatever theoretical merit there may be to the argument that there is a "right" to rebellion against dictatorial governments is without force where the existing structure of the government provides for peaceful and orderly change. We reject any principle of governmental helplessness in the face of preparation for revolution, which principle, carried to its logical conclusion, must lead to anarchy. No one could conceive that it is not within the power of Congress to prohibit acts intended to overthrow the Government by force and violence. The question with which we are concerned here is not whether Congress has such *power*, but whether the *means* which it has employed conflict with the First and Fifth Amendments to the Constitution.

One of the bases for the contention that the means which Congress has employed are invalid takes the form of an attack on the face of the statute on the grounds that by its terms it prohibits academic discussion of the merits of Marxism-Leninism, that it stifles ideas and is contrary to all concepts of a free speech and a free press. . . .

The very language of the Smith Act negates the interpretation which petitioners would have us impose on that Act. It is directed at advocacy, not discussion. Thus, the trial judge properly charged the jury that they could not convict if they found that petitioners did "no more than pursue peaceful studies and discussions or teaching and advocacy in the realm of ideas." . . . . Congress did not intend to eradicate the free dicussion of political theories, to destroy the traditional rights of Americans to discuss and evaluate ideas without fear of governmental sanction. Rather Congress was concerned with the very kind of activity in which the evidence showed these petitioners engaged.

III.

But although the statute is not directed at the hypothetical cases which petitioners have conjured, its application in this case has resulted in convictions for the teaching and advocacy of the overthrow of the Government by force and violence, which, even though coupled with the intent to accomplish that overthrow, contains an element of speech. For this reason, we must pay special heed to the demands of the First Amendment marking out the boundaries of speech.

[T]he basis of the First Amendment is the hypothesis that speech can rebut speech, propaganda will answer propaganda, free debate of ideas will result in the wisest governmental policies. . . . An analysis of the leading cases in this Court which have involved direct limitations on speech, however, will demonstrate that both the majority of the Court and the dissenters in particular cases have recognized that this is not an unlimited, unqualified right, but that the societal value of speech must, on occasion, be subordinated to other values and considerations. . . .

The rule we deduce from [the World War I Espionage Act cases, sec. 1A, supra] is that where an offense is specified by a statute in nonspeech or nonpress terms, a conviction relying upon speech or press as evidence of violation may be sustained only when the speech or publication created a "clear and present danger" of attempting or accomplishing the prohibited crime, e. g., interference with enlistment. The dissents, ... in emphasizing the value of speech, were addressed to the argument of the sufficiency of the evidence.

Although no case subsequent to Whitney and Gitlow has expressly overruled the majority opinions in those cases, there is little doubt that subsequent opinions have inclined toward the Holmes-Brandeis rationale. [N]either Justice Holmes nor Justice Brandeis ever envisioned that a shorthand phrase should be crystallized into a rigid rule to be applied inflexibly without regard to the circumstances of each case. Speech is not an absolute, above and beyond control by the legislature when its judgment, subject to review here, is that certain kinds of speech are so undesirable as to warrant criminal sanction. Nothing is more certain in modern society than the principle that there are no absolutes, that a name, a phrase, a standard has meaning only when associated with the considerations which gave birth to the nomenclature. . . . . To those who would paralyze our Government in the face of impending threat by encasing it in a semantic straitjacket we must reply that all concepts are relative.

cl. + pr.
danger,
what does
it mean?

In this case we are squarely presented with the application of the "clear and present danger" test, and must decide what that phrase imports. We first note that many of the cases in which this Court has reversed convictions by use of this or similar tests have been based on the fact that the interest which the State was attempting to protect was itself too insubstantial to warrant restriction of speech. . . . Overthrow of the Government by force and violence is certainly a substantial enough interest for the Government to limit speech. Indeed, this is the ultimate value of any society, for if a society cannot protect its very structure from armed internal attack, it must follow that no subordinate value can be protected. If, then, this interest may be protected, the literal problem which is presented is what has been meant by the use of the phrase "clear and present danger" of the utterances bringing about the evil within the power of Congress to punish.

Obviously, the words cannot mean that before the Government may act, it must wait until the *putsch* is about to be executed, the plans have been laid and the signal is awaited. If Government is aware that a group aiming at its overthrow is attempting to indoctrinate its members and to commit them to a course whereby they will strike when the leaders feel the circumstances permit, action by the Government is required. The argument that there is no need for Government to concern itself, for Government is strong, it possesses ample powers to put down a rebellion, it may defeat the revolution with ease, needs no answer. For that is not the question. Certainly an attempt to overthrow the Government by force, even though doomed from the outset because of inadequate numbers or power of the revolutionists, is a sufficient evil for Congress to prevent. The damage which such attempts create both physically and politically to a nation makes it impossible to measure the validity in terms of the probability of success, or the immediacy of a successful attempt. In the instant case the trial judge charged the jury that they could not convict unless they found that petitioners intended to overthrow the Government "as speedily as circumstances would permit." This does not mean, and could not properly mean, that they would not strike until there was certainty of success. What was meant was that the revolutionists would strike when they thought the time was ripe. We must therefore reject the contention that success or probability of success is the criterion.

The situation with which Justices Holmes and Brandeis were concerned in Gitlow was a comparatively isolated event, bearing little relation in their minds to any substantial threat to the safety of the community. . . . They were not confronted with any situation comparable to the instant one— the development of an apparatus designed and dedicated to the overthrow of the Government, in the context of world crisis after crisis.

standard
adopted by ct

Chief Judge Learned Hand, writing for the majority below, interpreted the phrase as follows: "In each case [courts] must ask whether the gravity of the 'evil,' discounted by its improbability, justifies such invasion of free speech as is necessary to avoid the danger." 183 F.2d at 212. We adopt this statement of the rule. As articulated by Chief Judge Hand, it is as succinct and inclusive as any other we might devise at this time. It takes into consideration those factors which we deem relevant, and relates their significances. More we cannot expect from words.

Likewise, we are in accord with the court below, which affirmed the trial court's finding that the requisite danger existed. The mere fact that from the period 1945 to 1948 petitioners' activities did not result in an attempt to overthrow the Government by force and violence is of course no answer to the fact that there was a group that was ready to make the attempt. The formation by petitioners of such a highly organized conspiracy, with rigidly disciplined members subject to call when the leaders, these petitioners, felt that the time had come for action, coupled with the inflammable nature of world conditions, similar uprisings in other countries, and the touch-and-go nature of our relations with countries with whom petitioners were in the very least ideologically attuned, convince us that their convictions were justified on this score. And this analysis disposes of the contention that a conspiracy to advocate, as distinguished from the advocacy itself, cannot be constitutionally restrained, because it comprises only the preparation. It is the existence of the conspiracy which creates the danger. . . . If the ingredients of the reaction are present, we cannot bind the Government to wait until the catalyst is added.

defense's contention

IV.

Although we have concluded that the finding that there was a sufficient danger to warrant the application of the statute was justified on the merits, there remains the problem of whether the trial judge's treatment of the issue was correct. . . .

The first paragraph of the . . . instructions calls for the jury to find the facts essential to establish the substantive crime, violation of §§ 2(a) (1) and 2(a) (3) of the Smith Act, involved in the conspiracy charge. There can be no doubt that if the jury found those facts against the petitioners violation of the Act would be established. The argument that the action of the trial court is erroneous, in declaring as a matter of law that such violation shows sufficient danger to justify the punishment despite the First Amendment, rests on the theory that a jury must decide a question of the application of the First Amendment. We do not agree.

When facts are found that establish the violation of a statute the protection against conviction afforded by the First Amendment is a matter of law. The doctrine that there must be a clear and present danger of a substantive evil that Congress has a right to prevent is a judicial rule to be applied as a matter of law by the courts. The guilt is established by proof of facts. Whether the First Amendment protects the activity which constitutes the violation of the statute must depend upon a judicial determination of the scope of the First Amendment applied to the circumstances of the case. . . .

V.

There remains to be discussed the question of vagueness—whether the statute as we have interpreted it is too vague, not sufficiently advising those who would speak of the limitations upon their activity. [The contention was rejected.]

We hold that §§ 2(a) (1), 2(a) (3) and 3 of the Smith Act, do not inherently, or as construed or applied in the instant case, violate the First Amendment and other provisions of the Bill of Rights, or the First and Fifth Amendments because of indefiniteness. Petitioners intended to overthrow the Government of the United States as speedily as the circumstances would permit. Their conspiracy to organize the Communist Party and to teach and advocate the overthrow of the Government of the United States by force and violence created a "clear and present danger" of an attempt to overthrow the Government by force and violence. They were properly and constitutionally convicted for violation of the Smith Act. The judgments of conviction are

Affirmed.

Mr. Justice CLARK took no part in the consideration or decision of this case.

Mr. Justice FRANKFURTER concurring in affirmance of the judgment.

. . .

Just as there are those who regard as invulnerable every measure for which the claim of national survival is invoked, there are those who find in the Constitution a wholly unfettered right of expression. . . . The historic antecedents of the First Amendment preclude the notion that its purpose was to give unqualified immunity to every expression that touched on matters within the range of political interest. . . . Absolute rules would inevitably lead to absolute exceptions, and such exceptions would eventually corrode the rules. The demands of free speech in a democratic society as well as the interest in national security are better served by candid and informed weighing of the competing interests, within the confines of the judicial process, than by announcing dogmas too inflexible for the non-Euclidian problems to be solved.

But how are competing interests to be assessed? . . . Full responsibility for the choice cannot be given to the courts. Courts are not representative bodies. . . . Their judgment is best informed, and therefore most dependable, within narrow limits. Their essential quality is detachment, founded on independence. History teaches that the independence of the judiciary is jeopardized when courts become embroiled in the passions of the day and assume primary responsibility in choosing between competing political, economic and social pressures.

Primary responsibility for adjusting the interests which compete in the situation before us of necessity belongs to the Congress. . . .

. . . In reviewing statutes which restrict freedoms protected by the First Amendment, we have emphasized the close relation which those freedoms bear to maintenance of a free society. See Kovacs v. Cooper, 336 U.S. 77, 89, 95 (concurring). Some members of the Court—and at times a majority—have done more. They have suggested that our function in reviewing statutes restricting freedom of expression differs sharply from our normal duty in sitting in judgment on legislation. . . . It has been suggested, with the casualness of a footnote, that such legislation is not presumptively valid, see United States v. Carolene Products Co., 304 U.S. 144, 152, n. 4, and it has been weightily reiterated that freedom of speech has a "preferred position" among constitutional safeguards. Kovacs v. Cooper, 336 U.S. 77, 88.

The precise meaning intended to be conveyed by these phrases need not now be pursued. It is enough to note that they have recurred in the Court's opinions, and their cumulative force has, not without justification, engendered belief that there is a constitutional principle, expressed by those attractive but imprecise words, prohibiting restriction upon utterance unless it creates a situation of "imminent" peril against which legislation may guard. It is on this body of the Court's pronouncements that the defendants' argument here is based.

In all fairness, the argument cannot be met by reinterpreting the Court's frequent use of "clear" and "present" to mean an entertainable "probability." In giving this meaning to the phrase "clear and present danger," the Court of Appeals was fastidiously confining the rhetoric of opinions to the exact scope of what was decided by them. We have greater responsibility for having given unconstitutional support, over repeated protests, to uncritical libertarian generalities.

. . . . Unless we are to compromise judicial impartiality and subject these defendants to the risk of an *ad hoc* judgment influenced by the impregnating atmosphere of the times, the constitutionality of their conviction must be determined by principles established in cases decided in more tranquil periods. If those decisions are to be used as a guide and not as an argument, it is important to view them as a whole and to distrust the easy generalizations to which some of them lend themselves.

We have recognized and resolved conflicts between speech and competing interests in six different types of cases. . . . . I must leave to others the ungrateful task of trying to reconcile all these decisions. In some instances we have too readily permitted juries to infer deception from error, or intention from argumentative or critical statements. Abrams v. United States, supra; Schaefer v. United States, supra . . . . . In other instances we weighted the interest in free speech so heavily that we permitted essential conflicting values to be destroyed. Bridges v. California; Craig v. Harney. [Both decisions applied the clear and present danger test to set aside contempt holdings against press interference with the administration of justice. See chap. 16, p. 1276, infra.] Viewed as a whole, however, the decisions express an attitude toward the judicial function and a standard of values which for me are decisive of the case before us.

First.—Free-speech cases are not an exception to the principle that we are not legislators, that direct policy-making is not our province. . . . In Gitlow v. New York, we put our respect for the legislative judgment in terms which, if they were accepted here, would make decision easy. . . . It has not been explicitly overruled. But it would be disingenuous to deny that the dissent in Gitlow has been treated with the respect usually accorded to a decision. . . . . It requires excessive tolerance of the legislative judgment to suppose that the Gitlow publication in the circumstances could justify serious concern.

In contrast, there is ample justification for a legislative judgment that the conspiracy now before us is a substantial threat to national order and security. . . . . Our decision today certainly does not mean that the Smith Act can constitutionally be applied to facts like those in Gitlow v. New York. . . .

Second.—A survey of the relevant decisions indicates that the results which we have reached are on the whole those that would ensue from careful weighing of conflicting interests. The complex issues presented by regulation of speech in public places, by picketing, and by legislation prohibiting advocacy of crime have been resolved by scrutiny of many factors besides the imminence and gravity of the evil threatened. . . .

It is a familiar experience in the law that new situations do not fit neatly into legal conceptions that arose under different circumstances to satisfy different needs. . . . So it is with the attempt to use the direction of thought lying behind the criterion of "clear and present danger" wholly out of the context in which it originated, and to make of it an absolute dogma and definitive measuring rod for the power of Congress to deal with assaults against security through devices other than overt physical attempts.

Bearing in mind that Mr. Justice Holmes regarded questions under the First Amendment as questions of "proximity and degree," Schenck v. United States, 249 U.S. at 52, it would be a distortion, indeed a mockery, of his reasoning to compare the "puny anonymities" . . . to which he was addressing himself in the Abrams case in 1919 or the publication that was "futile and too remote from possible consequences" . . . in the Gitlow case in 1925 with the setting of events in this case in 1950. . . .

Third.—Not every type of speech occupies the same position on the scale of values. There is no substantial public interest in permitting certain kinds of utterances: "the lewd and obscene, the profane, the libelous, and the insulting or 'fighting' words—those which by their very utterance inflict injury or tend to incite an immediate breach of the peace." Chaplinsky v. New Hampshire, 315 U.S. 568, 572 [p. 1154, infra]. On any scale of values which we have hitherto recognized, speech of this sort ranks low.

Throughout our decisions there has recurred a distinction between the statement of an idea which may prompt its hearers to take unlawful action, and advocacy that such action be taken. . . . It is true that there is no divining rod by which we may locate "advocacy." Exposition of ideas readily merges into advocacy. . . . The object of the conspiracy before us is so clear that the chance of error in saying that the defendants conspired to advocate rather than to express ideas is slight. Mr. Justice Douglas quite properly points out that the conspiracy before us is not a conspiracy to overthrow the Government. But it would be equally wrong to treat it as a seminar in political theory.

These general considerations underlie decision of the case before us.

On the one hand is the interest in security. The Communist Party was not designed by these defendants as an ordinary political party. For the circumstances of its organization, its aims and methods, and the relation of the defendants to its organization and aims we are concluded by the jury's verdict. . . .

In finding that the defendants violated the statute, we may not treat as established fact that the Communist Party in this country is of significant size, well-organized, well-disciplined, conditioned to embark on unlawful activity when given the command. But in determining whether application of the statute to the defendants is within the constitutional powers of Congress, we are not limited to the facts found by the jury. We must view such a question in the light of whatever is relevant to a legislative judgment. We may take judicial notice that the Communist doctrines which these defendants have conspired to advocate are in the ascendency in powerful nations who cannot be acquitted of unfriendliness to the institutions of this country. We may take account of evidence brought forward at this trial and elsewhere, much of which has long been common knowledge. In sum, it would amply justify a legislature in concluding that recruitment of additional members for the Party would create a substantial danger to national security. . . .

On the other hand is the interest in free speech. The right to exert all governmental powers in aid of maintaining our institutions and resisting their physical overthrow does not include intolerance of opinions and speech that cannot do harm although opposed and perhaps alien to dominant, traditional opinion. . . . It is better for those who have almost unlimited power of government in their hands to err on the side of freedom. . . .

. . . No matter how clear we may be that the defendants now before us are preparing to overthrow our Government at the propitious moment, it is self-delusion to think that we can punish them for their advocacy without adding to the risks run by loyal citizens who honestly believe in some of the reforms these defendants advance. It is a sobering fact that in sustaining the convictions before us we can hardly escape restriction on the interchange of ideas. . . .

It is not for us to decide how we would adjust the clash of interests which this case presents were the primary responsibility for reconciling it ours. Congress has determined that the danger created by advocacy of overthrow justifies the ensuing restriction on freedom of speech. The determination was made after due deliberation, and the seriousness of the congressional purpose is attested by the volume of legislation passed to effectuate the same ends. . . .

To make validity of legislation depend on judicial reading of events still in the womb of time—a forecast, that is, of the outcome of forces at best appreciated only with knowledge of the topmost secrets of nations—is to charge the judiciary with duties beyond its equipment. . . .

[I]t is relevant to remind that in sustaining the power of Congress in a case like this nothing irrevocable is done. The democratic process at all events is not impaired or restricted. Power and responsibility remain with the people and immediately with their representatives. All the Court says is that Congress was not forbidden by the Constitution to pass this enactment and that a prosecution under it may be brought against a conspiracy such as the one before us. . . .

Mr. Justice JACKSON, concurring.

This prosecution is the latest of never-ending, because never successful, quests for some legal formula that will secure an existing order against revolutionary radicalism. It requires us to reappraise, in the light of our own times and conditions, constitutional doctrines devised under other circumstances to strike a balance between authority and liberty. . . .

The Communist Party . . . does not seek its strength primarily in numbers. Its aim is a relatively small party whose strength is in selected, dedicated, indoctrinated, and rigidly disciplined members. From established policy it tolerates no deviation and no debate. It seeks members that are, or may be, secreted in strategic posts in transportation, communications, industry, government, and especially in labor unions where it can compel employers to accept and retain its members. It also seeks to infiltrate and control organizations of professional and other groups. Through these placements in positions of power it seeks a leverage over society that will make up in power of coercion what it lacks in power of persuasion.

[V]iolence is not with them, as with the anarchists, an end in itself. The Communist Party advocates force only when prudent and profitable. . . . They resort to violence as to truth, not as a principle but as an expedient. Force or violence, as they would resort to it, may never be necessary, because infiltration and deception may be enough. . . .

The United States, fortunately, has experienced Communism only in its preparatory stages and for its pattern of final action must look abroad. . . . But Communist technique in the overturn of a free government was disclosed by the *coup d'etat* in which they seized power in Czechoslovakia. . . .

The foregoing is enough to indicate that, either by accident or design, the Communist stratagem outwits the anti-anarchist pattern of statute aimed against "overthrow by force and violence" if qualified by the doctrine that only "clear and present danger" of accomplishing that result will sustain the prosecution.

The "clear and present danger" test was an innovation by Mr. Justice Holmes in the Schenck case, reiterated and refined by him and Mr. Justice Brandeis in later cases, all arising before the era of World War II revealed the subtlety and efficacy of modernized revolutionary techniques used by totalitarian parties. In those cases, they were faced with convictions under so-called criminal syndicalism statutes aimed at anarchists but which, loosely construed, had been applied to punish socialism, pacifism, and left-wing ideologies, the charges often resting on far-fetched inferences which, if true, would establish only technical or trivial violations. They proposed "clear and present danger" as a test for the sufficiency of evidence in particular cases.

I would save it, unmodified, for application as a "rule of reason" in the kind of case for which it was devised. When the issue is criminality of a hot-headed speech on a street corner, or circulation of a few incendiary pamphlets, or parading by some zealots behind a red flag, or refusal of a handful of school children to salute our flag, it is not beyond the capacity of the judicial process to gather, comprehend, and weigh the necessary materials for decision whether it is a clear and present danger of substantive evil or a harmless letting off of steam. It is not a prophecy, for the danger in such cases has matured by the time of trial or it was never present. The test applies and has meaning where a conviction is sought to be based on a speech or writing which does not directly or explicitly advocate a crime but to which such tendency is sought to be attributed by construction or by implication from external circumstances. The formula in such cases favors freedoms that are vital to our society, and, even if sometimes applied too generously, the consequences cannot be grave. But its recent expansion has extended, in particular to Communists, unprecedented immunities. Unless we are to hold our Government captive in a judge-made verbal trap, we must approach the problem of a well-organized, nation-wide conspiracy, such as I have described, as realistically as our predecessors faced the trivialities that were being prosecuted until they were checked with a rule of reason.

I think reason is lacking for applying that test to this case.

If we must decide that this Act and its application are constitutional only if we are convinced that petitioner's conduct creates a "clear and present danger" of violent overthrow, we must appraise imponderables, including international and national phenomena which baffle the best informed foreign offices and our most experienced politicians. . . . No doctrine can be sound whose application requires us to make a prophecy of that sort in the guise of a legal decision. The judicial process simply is not adequate to a trial of such far-flung issues. The answers given would reflect our own political predilections and nothing more.

The authors of the clear and present danger test never applied it to a case like this, nor would I. If applied as it is proposed here, it means that the Communist plotting is protected during its period of incubation; its preliminary stages of organization and preparation are immune from the law; the Government can move only after imminent action is manifest, when it would, of course, be too late. . . .

What really is under review here is a conviction of conspiracy, after a trial for conspiracy, on an indictment charging conspiracy, brought under a statute outlawing conspiracy. With due respect to my colleagues, they seem to me to discuss anything under the sun except the law of conspiracy. . . .

The Constitution does not make conspiracy a civil right. . . . While I consider criminal conspiracy a dragnet device capable of perversion into an instrument of injustice in the hands of a partisan or complacent judiciary, it has an established place in our system of law, and no reason appears for applying it only to concerted action claimed to disturb interstate commerce and withholding it from those claimed to undermine our whole Government. . . .

. . . The Communist Party realistically is a state within a state, an authoritarian dictatorship within a republic. . . . The law of conspiracy has been the chief means at the Government's disposal to deal with the growing problems created by such organizations. I happen to think it is an awkward and inept remedy, but I find no constitutional authority for taking this weapon from the Government. There is no constitutional right to "gang up" on the Government.

While I think there was power in Congress to enact this statute and that as applied in this case, it cannot be held unconstitutional, I add that I have little faith in the long-range effectiveness of this conviction to stop the rise of the Communist movement. . . . No decision by this Court can forestall revolution whenever the existing government fails to command the respect and loyalty of the people and sufficient distress and discontent is allowed to grow up among the masses. . . . Corruption, ineptitude, inflation, oppressive taxation, militarization, injustice, and loss of leadership capable of intellectual initiative in domestic or foreign affairs are allies on which the Communists count to bring opportunity knocking to their door. Sometimes I think they may be mistaken. But the Communists are not building just for today—the rest of us might profit by their example.

Mr. Justice BLACK, dissenting. . . . .

. . . The indictment is that they conspired to organize the Communist Party and to use speech or newspapers and other publications in the future to teach and advocate the forcible overthrow of the Government. No matter how it is worded, this is a virulent form of prior censorship of speech and press, which I believe the First Amendment forbids. I would hold § 3 of the Smith Act authorizing this prior restraint unconstitutional on its face and as applied.

But let us assume, contrary to all constitutional ideas of fair criminal procedure, that petitioners although not indicted for the crime of actual advocacy, may be punished for it. Even on this radical assumption, the other opinions in this case show that the only way to affirm these convictions is to repudiate directly or indirectly the established "clear and present danger" rule. This the Court does in a way which greatly restricts the protections afforded by the First Amendment. . . .

So long as this Court exercises the power of judicial review of legislation, I cannot agree that the First Amendment permits us to sustain laws suppressing freedom of speech and press on the basis of Congress' or our own notions of mere "reasonableness." Such a doctrine waters down the First Amendment so that it amounts to little more than an admonition to Congress. The Amendment as so construed is not likely to protect any but those "safe" or orthodox views which rarely need its protection. I must also express my objection to the holding because, as Mr. Justice Douglas' dissent shows, it sanctions the determination of a crucial issue of fact by the judge rather than by the jury. . . .

Public opinion being what it now is, few will protest the conviction of these Communist petitioners. There is hope, however, that in calmer times, when present pressures, passions and fears subside, this or some later Court will restore the First Amendment liberties to the high preferred place where they belong in a free society.

Mr. Justice DOUGLAS, dissenting.

If this were a case where those who claimed protection under the First Amendment were teaching the techniques of sabotage, the assassination of the President, the filching of documents from public files, the planting of bombs, the art of street warfare, and the like, I would have no doubts. The freedom to speak is not absolute; the teaching of methods of terror and other seditious conduct should be beyond the pale along with obscenity and immorality. This case was argued as if those were the facts. The argument imported much seditious conduct into the record. That is easy and it has popular appeal, for the activities of Communists in plotting and scheming against the free world are common knowledge. But the fact is that no such evidence was introduced at the trial. There is a statute which makes a seditious conspiracy unlawful. Petitioners, however, were not charged with a "conspiracy to overthrow" the Government. They were charged with a conspiracy to form a party and groups and assemblies of people who teach and advocate the overthrow of our Government by force or violence and with a conspiracy to advocate and teach its overthrow by force and violence. It may well be that indoctrination in the techniques of terror to destroy the Government would be indictable under either statute. But the teaching which is condemned here is of a different character.

So far as the present record is concerned, what petitioners did was to organize people to teach and themselves teach the Marxist-Leninist doctrine contained chiefly in four books: Foundations of Leninism by Stalin (1924), The Communist Manifesto by Marx and Engels (1848), State and Revolution by Lenin (1917), History of the Communist Party of the Soviet Union (B) (1939).

Those books are to Soviet Communism what Mein Kampf was to Nazism. If they are understood, the ugliness of Communism is revealed, its deceit and cunning are exposed, the nature of its activities becomes apparent, and the chances of its success less likely. That is not, of course, the reason why petitioners chose these books for their classrooms. They are fervent Communists to whom these volumes are gospel. They preached the creed with the hope that some day it would be acted upon.

The opinion of the Court does not outlaw these texts nor condemn them to the fire, as the Communists do literature offensive to their creed. But if the books themselves are not outlawed, if they can lawfully remain on library shelves, by what reasoning does their use in a classroom become a crime? . . . The Act, as construed, requires the element of intent— that those who teach the creed believe in it. The crime then depends not on what is taught but on who the teacher is. That is to make freedom of speech turn not on *what is said,* but on the *intent* with which it is said. Once we start down that road we enter territory dangerous to the liberties of every citizen. . . .

There comes a time when even speech loses its constitutional immunity. Speech innocuous one year may at another time fan such destructive flames that it must be halted in the interests of the safety of the Republic. That is the meaning of the clear and present danger test. When conditions are so critical that there will be no time to avoid the evil that the speech threatens, it is time to call a halt. Otherwise, free speech which is the strength of the Nation will be the cause of its destruction.

Yet free speech is the rule, not the exception. The restraint to be constitutional must be based on more than fear, on more than passionate opposition against the speech, on more than a revolted dislike for its contents. There must be some immediate injury to society that is likely if speech is allowed. . . .

I had assumed that the question of the clear and present danger, being so critical an issue in the case, would be a matter for submission to the jury. . . . The Court, I think, errs when it treats the question as one of law.

Yet, whether the question is one for the Court or the jury, there should be evidence of record on the issue. This record, however, contains no evidence whatsoever showing that the acts charged, *viz.*, the teaching of the Soviet theory of revolution with the hope that it will be realized, have created any clear and present danger to the Nation. The Court, however, rules to the contrary. . . .

That ruling is in my view not responsive to the issue in the case. We might as well say that the speech of petitioners is outlawed because Soviet Russia and her Red Army are a threat to world peace.

The nature of Communism as a force on the world scene would, of course, be relevant to the issue of clear and present danger of petitioners' advocacy within the United States. But the primary consideration is the strength and tactical position of petitioners and their converts in this country. On that there is no evidence in the record. If we are to take judicial notice of the threat of Communists within the nation, it should not be difficult to conclude that *as a political party* they are of little consequence. . . . Communism in the world scene is no bogeyman; but Communism as a political faction or party in this country plainly is. Communism has been so thoroughly exposed in this country that it has been crippled as a political force. Free speech has destroyed it as an effective political party. It is inconceivable that those who went up and down this country preaching the doctrine of revolution which petitioners espouse would have any success. . . . .

How it can be said that there is a clear and present danger that this advocacy will succeed is, therefore, a mystery. Some nations less resilient than the United States, where illiteracy is high and where democratic traditions are only budding, might have to take drastic steps and jail these men for merely speaking their creed. But in America they are miserable merchants of unwanted ideas; their wares remain unsold. The fact that their ideas are abhorrent does not make them powerful.

The political impotence of the Communists in this country does not, of course, dispose of the problem. Their numbers; their positions in industry and government; the extent to which they have in fact infiltrated the police, the armed services, transportation, stevedoring, power plants, munitions works, and other critical places—these facts all bear on the likelihood that their advocacy of the Soviet theory of revolution will endanger the Republic. But the record is silent on these facts. If we are to proceed on the basis of judicial notice, it is impossible for me to say that the Communists in this country are so potent or so strategically deployed that they must be suppressed for their speech. I could not so hold unless I were willing to conclude that the activities in recent years of committees of Congress, of the Attorney General, of labor unions, of state legislatures, and of Loyalty Boards were so futile as to leave the country on the edge of grave peril. To believe that petitioners and their following are placed in such critical positions as to endanger the Nation is to believe the incredible. . . . .

This is my view if we are to act on the basis of judicial notice. But the mere statement of the opposing views indicates how important it is that we know the facts before we act. Neither prejudice nor hate nor senseless fear should be the basis of this solemn act. Free speech—the glory of our system of government—should not be sacrificed on anything less than plain and objective proof of danger that the evil advocated is imminent. . . . .

SMITH ACT CASES AFTER DENNIS: DEFINING SPEECH RATHER THAN GUESSING ABOUT DANGERS?

1. *The problems of Dennis and the impact of Yates and Scales.* Recall the questions immediately preceding Dennis (in note 4, p. 1096). Did Dennis ignore clear and present danger? Distort clear and present danger? What did the Holmes standard say about the Dennis problem? What "substantive evil" was relevant? Actual overthrow? Risk of overthrow? Conspiracy to overthrow? Conspiracy to advocate overthrow?

What weight did the legislative judgment deserve? Should it have been weighed in terms of the 1940 circumstances, when the Smith Act became law? 1948? Should the Court have insisted on greater record evidence of the 1948 situation? Should it have ignored the world situation? Did the Court deemphasize the temporal dimension—i. e., the *immediacy* of the risk

—unduly? Did it consider risks more remote than the Abrams dissent would permit? Than the Whitney concurrence? Than Herndon v. Lowry?*

What alternative approaches would have been preferable in Dennis? Consider the subsequent Smith Act cases "clarifying" Dennis—and, in the view of many, assuring greater protection of speech (notes 2 and 3 infra). Does the emphasis in Yates, Scales, and Noto on the distinction between advocacy of abstract doctrine and advocacy of action, and on the need for scrutiny of the evidence, repudiate Dennis? Do these cases shift to an earlier clear and present danger approach? Do they apply the Masses approach—of defining the contours of protected speech and of using traditional judicial techniques of construing statutes and scrutinizing evidence? Do these post-Dennis cases suggest that courts should concentrate on defining protected speech rather than on second-guessing legislatures about the risks of dangerous consequences?

2. *The Yates case.* After Dennis, the Government brought Smith Act cases against a number of Communists who were "lower echelon" rather than "first string" leaders. In Yates v. United States, 354 U.S. 298 (1957), the Court reversed the convictions of fourteen defendants. In "explaining" the requirements of Dennis, the Court made it clear that Smith Act convictions would not be easy to sustain. Justice Harlan wrote the majority opinion. Justices Burton and Black, joined by Justice Douglas, submitted separate opinions. Justice Clark dissented. On an examination of the record, Justice Harlan concluded that the lower courts had given too broad a meaning to the term "organize" in the Smith Act; that the trial court's instructions to the jury gave inadequate guidance on the distinction between advocacy of abstract doctrine and advocacy of action; and that the evidence was insufficient to support conviction. Some excerpts from his opinion follow:

"Petitioners contend that the instructions to the jury were fatally defective in that the trial court refused to charge that, in order to convict, the jury must find that the advocacy which the defendants conspired to promote was of a kind calculated to 'incite' persons to action for the forcible overthrow of the Government. . . . The Government [argues] that the true constitutional dividing line is not between inciting and abstract advocacy of forcible overthrow, but rather between advocacy as such, irrespective of its inciting qualities, and the mere discussion or exposition of violent overthrow as an abstract theory. [The trial court charged:]

" 'Any advocacy or teaching which does not include the urging of force and violence as the means of overthrowing and destroying the Government of the United States is not within the issue of the indictment here and can constitute no basis for any finding against the defendants.

" 'The kind of advocacy and teaching which is charged and upon which your verdict must be reached is not merely a desirability but a necessity that the Government of the United States be overthrown and destroyed by force and violence and not merely a propriety but a duty to overthrow and destroy the Government of the United States by force and violence.'

* For a sampling of the extensive commentary on Dennis, see Richardson, "Freedom of Expression and the Function of the Courts," 65 Harv.L.Rev. 1 (1951), Mendelson, "Clear and Present Danger—From Schenck to Dennis," 52 Colum.L.Rev. 313 (1952), Gorfinkel and Mack, "Dennis v. United States and the Clear and Present Danger Rule," 39 Calif.L.Rev. 475 (1951), and Konefsky, The Legacy of Holmes and Brandeis (1956).

"There can be no doubt from the record that in so instructing the jury the court regarded as immaterial, and intended to withdraw from the jury's consideration, any issue as to the character of the advocacy in terms of its capacity to stir listeners to forcible action. . . . We are thus faced with the question whether the Smith Act prohibits advocacy and teaching of forcible overthrow as an abstract principle, divorced from any effort to instigate action to that end, so long as such advocacy or teaching is engaged in with evil intent. We hold that it does not.

"The distinction between advocacy of abstract doctrine and advocacy directed at promoting unlawful action is one that has been consistently recognized in the opinions of this Court . . .. We need not, however, decide the issue before us in terms of constitutional compulsion, for our first duty is to construe this statute. In doing so we should not assume that Congress chose to disregard a constitutional danger zone so clearly marked, or that it used the words 'advocate' and 'teach' in their ordinary dictionary meanings when they had already been construed as terms of art carrying a special and limited connotation. . . .

"In failing to distinguish between advocacy of forcible overthrow as an abstract doctrine and advocacy of action to that end, the District Court appears to have been led astray by the holding in Dennis that advocacy of violent action to be taken at some future time was enough. It seems to have considered that, since 'inciting' speech is usually thought of as something calculated to induce immediate action, and since Dennis held advocacy of action for future overthrow sufficient, this meant that advocacy, irrespective of its tendency to generate action, is punishable, provided only that it is uttered with a specific intent to accomplish overthrow. In other words, the District Court apparently thought that Dennis obliterated the traditional dividing line between advocacy of abstract doctrine and advocacy of action.

"This misconceives the situation confronting the Court in Dennis and what was held there. Although the jury's verdict, interpreted in light of the trial court's instructions, did not justify the conclusion that the defendants' advocacy was directed at, or created any danger of, immediate overthrow, it did establish that the advocacy was aimed at building up a seditious group and maintaining it in readiness for action at a propitious time. In such circumstances, said Chief Justice Vinson, the Government need not hold its hand 'until the *putsch* is about to be executed, the plans have been laid and the signal is awaited.' . . . The essence of the Dennis holding was that indoctrination of a group in preparation for future violent action, as well as exhortation to immediate action, by advocacy found to be directed to 'action for the accomplishment' of forcible overthrow to violence as 'a rule or principle of action,' and employing 'language of incitement,' . . . is not constitutionally protected when the group is of sufficient size and cohesiveness, is sufficiently oriented towards action, and other circumstances are such as reasonably to justify apprehension that action will occur. This is quite a different thing from the view of the District Court here that mere doctrinal justification of forcible overthrow, if engaged in with the intent to accomplish overthrow, is punishable *per se* under the Smith Act. That sort of advocacy, even though uttered with the hope that it may ultimately lead to violent revolution, is too remote from concrete action to be regarded as the kind of indoctrination preparatory to action which was condemned in Dennis. [Dennis was] not concerned with a conspiracy to engage at some future time in seditious advocacy, but rather with a conspiracy to advocate presently the taking of forcible action in the future. It was action, not advocacy, that was to be postponed until 'circumstances' would 'permit.' . . .

"In light of the foregoing we are unable to regard the District Court's charge upon this aspect of the case as adequate. The jury was never told that the Smith Act does not denounce advocacy in the sense of preaching abstractly the forcible overthrow of the Government. We think that the trial court's statement that the proscribed advocacy must include the 'urging,' 'necessity,' and 'duty' of forcible overthrow, and not merely its 'desirability' and 'propriety,' may not be regarded as a sufficient substitute for charging that the Smith Act reaches only advocacy of action for the overthrow of government by force and violence. The essential distinction is that those to whom the advocacy is addressed must be urged to *do* something, now or in the future, rather than merely to *believe* in something. . . .

"We recognize that distinctions between advocacy or teaching of abstract doctrines, with evil intent, and that which is directed to stirring people to action, are often subtle and difficult to grasp, for in a broad sense, as Mr. Justice Holmes said in his dissenting opinion in Gitlow, 268 U.S., at 673: 'Every idea is an incitement.' But the very subtlety of these distinctions required the most clear and explicit instructions with reference to them, for they concerned an issue which went to the very heart of the charges against these petitioners. The need for precise and understandable instructions on this issue is further emphasized by the equivocal character of the evidence in this record . . .. Instances of speech that could be considered to amount to 'advocacy of action' are so few and far between as to be almost completely overshadowed by the hundreds of instances in the record in which overthrow, if mentioned at all, occurs in the course of doctrinal disputation so remote from action as to be almost wholly lacking in probative value. Vague references to 'revolutionary' or 'militant' action of an unspecified character, which are found in the evidence, might in addition be given too great weight by the jury in the absence of more precise instructions. Particularly in light of this record, we must regard the trial court's charge in this respect as furnishing wholly inadequate guidance to the jury on this central point in the case." [On remand, the indictments were dismissed at the Government's request, because of expected inability to meet the Yates requirements.]

3. *The Scales and Noto cases.* a. In Scales v. United States, 367 U.S. 203 (1961), the Court sustained the membership clause of the Smith Act and clarified the evidentiary requirements of Yates. The challenged clause, as described in Justice Harlan's majority opinion, "makes a felony the acquisition or holding of knowing membership in any organization which advocates the overthrow of the Government of the United States by force or violence." Petitioner was charged with having been a member of the Communist Party "with knowledge of the Party's illegal purpose and a specific intent to accomplish overthrow 'as speedily as circumstances would permit.' " The Court found that the trial judge had properly construed the statute to require "specific intent" and "active" rather than merely "nominal" membership. As so construed, the Court rejected the claim that the statute violated the Fifth Amendment "in that it impermissibly imputes guilt to an individual merely on the basis of his associations and sympathies, rather than because of some

concrete personal involvement in criminal conduct." Moreover, the majority refused to find a First Amendment violation:

"It was settled in Dennis that the advocacy with which we are here concerned is not constitutionally protected speech, and it was further established that a combination to promote such advocacy, albeit under the aegis of what purports to be a political party, is not such association as is protected by the First Amendment. We can discern no reason why membership, when it constitutes a purposeful form of complicity in a group engaging in this same forbidden advocacy, should receive any greater degree of protection from the guarantees of that Amendment.

"If it is said that the mere existence of such an enactment tends to inhibit the exercise of constitutionally protected rights, in that it engenders an unhealthy fear that one may find himself unwittingly embroiled in criminal liability, the answer surely is that the statute provides that a defendant must be proven to have knowledge of the proscribed advocacy before he may be convicted. . . . The clause does not make criminal all association with an organization, which has been shown to engage in illegal advocacy. There must be clear proof that a defendant 'specifically intend[s] to accomplish [the aims of the organization] by resort to violence.' Noto v. United States [infra]. Thus the member for whom the organization is a vehicle for the advancement of legitimate aims and policies does not fall within the ban of the statute: he lacks the requisite specific intent 'to bring about the overthrow of the government as speedily as circumstances would permit.' Such a person may be foolish, deluded, or perhaps merely optimistic, but he is not by this statute made a criminal."

The Court then proceeded to examine the sufficiency of the evidence in considerable detail, "to make sure that substantive constitutional standards have not been thwarted." Justice Harlan stated that the evidentiary question was "controlled in large part by Yates" and explained at some length the Yates criteria for the evaluation of evidence. He noted: "The decision in Yates rested on the view (not articulated in the opinion, though perhaps it should have been) that the Smith Act offenses, involving as they do subtler elements than are present in most other crimes, call for strict standards in assessing the adequacy of the proof needed to make out a case of illegal advocacy." In discussing the "type of evidence . . . needed to permit a jury to find that (a) there was 'advocacy of action' and (b) the Party was responsible for such advocacy," he stated that Yates indicated "at least two patterns of evidence sufficient to show illegal advocacy: (a) the teaching of forceful overthrow, accompanied by directions as to the type of illegal action which must be taken when the time for the revolution is reached; and (b) the teaching of forceful overthrow, accompanied by a contemporary, though legal, course of conduct clearly undertaken for the specific purpose of rendering effective the later illegal activity which is advocated."

b. The Court found these evidentiary criteria satisfied in Scales, but not in a companion case, Noto v. United States, 367 U.S. 290 (1961). In Noto, the Court, in an opinion by Justice Harlan, reversed the conviction under the membership clause because "the evidence of illegal Party advocacy was insufficient." The opinion noted that the evidence of "advocacy of action" was "sparse indeed," was not "broadly based" geographically, and "lacked the compelling quality which in Scales was supplied by the petitioner's utterances and systematic course of conduct as a high Party official." He added: "It need hardly be said that it is upon the particular evidence in a particular record that a particular defendant must be judged, and not upon the evidence in some other record or upon what may be supposed to be the tenets of the Communist Party." In Scales, there were three dissenting opinions: one by Justice Black, one by Justice Douglas, and one by Justice Brennan, joined by Chief Justice Warren and Justice Douglas. In Noto, there were a number of separate concurring opinions.

D. THE COURT AND CONGRESSIONAL ANTI-COMMUNIST LEGISLATION OF THE FIFTIES

Introduction. The federal anti-Communist legislation of the 1950's, unlike the Smith Act of 1940, did not follow the traditional pattern of the Gitlow-Whitney sedition-syndicalism statutes. For example, the 1950 Act, considered in the next case, aims at least in part at registration and disclosure rather than direct "prohibition of speech because of its content." Although most cases on disclosure requirements involving subversion are considered in chap. 16, infra, the laws of the fifties are considered here, to bring together the major federal criminal legislation on Communism and to lay the groundwork for examination of the evolving approaches and most recent encounters with Gitlow-Whitney problems in sec. 1E, p. 1123, infra.

COMMUNIST PARTY OF AMERICA v. SUBVERSIVE ACTIVITIES CONTROL BOARD

367 U.S. 1, 81 S.Ct. 1357, 6 L.Ed.2d 625 (1961).

Certiorari to the Court of Appeals for the District of Columbia Circuit.

Mr. Justice FRANKFURTER delivered the opinion of the Court.

This is a proceeding pursuant to § 14(a) of the Subversive Activities Control Act of 1950 to review an order of the Subversive Activities Control Board requiring the Communist Party of the United States to register as a Communist-action organization under § 7 of the Act. The Court of Appeals for the District of Columbia has affirmed the Board's registration order.
. . . .

The Subversive Activities Control Act is Title I of the Internal Security Act of 1950, 64 Stat. 987, 50 U.S.C. § 781 et seq. . . .

Section 2 of the Act recites legislative findings based upon evidence adduced before various congressional committees. . . . . Finally, in § 2(15), Congress concludes that

"The Communist movement in the United States is an organization numbering thousands of adherents, rigidly and ruthlessly disciplined. . . . The Communist organization in the United States, pursuing its stated objectives, the recent successes of Communist methods in other countries, and the nature and control of the world Communist movement itself, present a clear and present danger to the security of the United States and to the existence of free American institutions, and make it necessary that Congress, in order to provide for the common defense, to preserve the sovereignty of the United States as an independent nation, and to guarantee to each State a republican form of government, enact appropriate legislation recognizing the existence of such worldwide conspiracy and designed to prevent it from accomplishing its purpose in the United States."

Pursuant to these findings, § 7(a) of the Act requires the registration with the Attorney General, on a form prescribed by him by regulations, of all Communist-action organizations. . . . The Party's constitutional attack assails virtually every provision of this extended and intricate regulatory statute. . . . Many of these questions [including self-incrimination] are prematurely raised in this litigation. Merely potential impairment of constitutional rights under a statute does not of itself create a justiciable controversy in which the nature and extent of those rights may be litigated. . . .

A. *"Outlawry" and Attainder.* . . . The Act is not a bill of attainder. It attaches not to specified organizations but to described activities in which an organization may or may not engage. . . .

B. *The Freedoms of Expressions and Association Protected by the First Amendment.* The Communist Party would have us hold that the First Amendment prohibits Congress from requiring the registration and filing of information, including membership lists, by organizations substantially dominated or controlled by the foreign powers controlling the world Communist movement and which operate primarily to advance the objectives of that movement: the overthrow of existing government by any means necessary and the establishment in its place of a Communist totalitarian dictatorship. . . . We cannot find such a prohibition in the First Amendment. So to find would make a travesty of that Amendment and the great ends for the well-being of our democracy that it serves.

No doubt, a governmental regulation which requires registration as a condition upon the exercise of speech may in some circumstances affront the constitutional guarantee of free expression. Thomas v. Collins, 323 U.S. 516. . . . The present statute does not, of course, attach the registration requirement to the incident of speech, but to the incidents of foreign domination and of operation to advance the objectives of the world Communist movement—operation which, the Board has found here, includes extensive, long-continuing organizational, as well as "speech" activity. Thus the Thomas case is applicable here only insofar as it establishes that subjection to registration requirements may be a sufficient restraint upon the exercise of liberties protected by the First Amendment to merit that it be weighed in the constitutional balance.

Similarly, we agree that compulsory disclosure of the names of an organization's members may in certain instances infringe constitutionally protected rights of association. N. A. A. C. P. v. Alabama, 357 U.S. 449; Bates v. Little Rock, 361 U.S. 516; Shelton v. Tucker, 364 U.S. 479 [all infra]. But to say this much is only to recognize one of the points of reference from which analysis must begin. . . . Against the impediments which particular governmental regulation causes to entire freedom of individual action, there must be weighed the value to the public of the ends which the regulation may achieve. [Those cases] hold that where the required making public of an organization's membership lists bears no rational relation to the interest which is asserted by the State to justify disclosure, and where because of community temper publication might prejudice members whose names were revealed, disclosure cannot constitutionally be compelled. . . .

The present case differs from Thomas v. Collins and from N.A.A.C.P., Bates, and Shelton in the magnitude of the public interests which the registration and disclosure provisions are designed to protect and in the pertinence which registration and disclosure bear to the protection of those interests. Congress itself has expressed in § 2 of the Act [supra] both what those interests are and what, in its view, threatens them. . . .

It is not for the courts to re-examine the validity of these legislative findings and reject them. . . . They are the product of extensive investigation by Committees of Congress over more than a decade and a half. Cf. Nebbia v. New York, 291 U.S. 502, 516, 530. We certainly cannot dismiss them as unfounded or irrational imaginings. . . . And if we accept them, as we must, as a not unentertainable appraisal by Congress of the threat which Communist organizations pose . . . , we must recognize that the power of Congress to regulate Communist organizations of this nature is extensive. "Security against foreign danger is one of the primitive objects of civil society," James Madison wrote in The Federalist (No. 41). . . . Means for effective resistance against foreign incursion—whether in the form of organizations which function, in some technical sense, as "agents" of a foreign power, or in the form of organizations which, by complete dedication and obedience to foreign directives, make themselves the instruments of a foreign power—may not be denied to the national legislature. . . .

Of course, congressional power in this sphere, as in all spheres, is limited by the First Amendment. Individual liberties fundamental to American institutions are not to be destroyed under pretext of preserving those institutions, even from the gravest external dangers. But where the problems of accommodating the exigencies of self-preservation and the values of liberty are as complex and intricate as they are in the situation described in the findings of § 2 of the Subversive Activities Control Act—when existing government is menaced by a world-wide integrated movement which employs every combination of possible means, peaceful and violent, domestic and foreign, overt and clandestine, to destroy the government itself—the legislative judgment as to how that threat may best be met consistently with the safeguarding of personal freedom is not to be set aside merely because the judgment of judges would, in the first instance, have chosen other methods. Especially where Congress, in seeking to reconcile competing and urgently demanding values within our social institutions legislates not to prohibit individuals from organizing for the effectuation of ends found to be menacing to the very existence of those institutions, but only to prescribe the conditions under which such organization is permitted, the legislative determination must be respected. . . .

[W]e are not insensitive to the fact that the public opprobrium and obloquy which may attach to an individual listed with the Attorney General as a member of a Communist-action organization is no less considerable than that with which members of the National Association for the Advancement of Colored People were threatened in N.A.A.C.P. and Bates. But while an angry public opinion, and the evils which it may spawn, are relevant considerations . . . , the existence of an ugly public temper does not, as such and without more, incapacitate government to require publicity demanded by rational interests high in the scale of national concern. Where the mask of anonymity which an organization's members wear serves the double purpose of protecting them from popular prejudice and of enabling them to cover over a foreign-directed conspiracy, infiltrate into other groups, and enlist the support of persons who would not, if the truth were revealed, lend their support, see § 2(1), (6), (7), it would be a distortion of the First Amendment to hold that it prohibits Congress from removing the mask.

. . .

It is argued that if Congress may constitutionally enact legislation requiring the Communist Party to register, to list its members, to file financial statements, and to identify its printing presses, Congress may impose similar requirements upon any group which pursues unpopular political objectives or which expresses an unpopular political ideology. Nothing which we decide here remotely carries such an implication. The Subversive Activities Control Act applies only to *foreign-dominated* organizations which work primarily to advance the objectives of a world movement controlled by the government of a *foreign* country. . . . There is no attempt here to impose stifling obligations upon the proponents of a particular political creed as such, or even to check the importation of particular political ideas from abroad for propagation here. . . . The registration requirement of § 7, on its face and as here applied, does not violate the First Amendment.

C. *Self-Incrimination of the Party's Officers.* . . . Officers of the Party, it is argued, are compelled, in the very act of filing a signed registration statement, to admit that they *are* Party Officers—an admission which we have held incriminating. . . . We find that the self-incrimination challenge to § 7(a) and (d), as implemented by the Attorney General's regulations and forms, is also premature at this time. The privilege against self-incrimination is one which normally must be claimed by the individual who seeks to avail himself of its protection. . . . We cannot, on the basis of supposition that privilege will be claimed and not honored, proceed now to adjudicate the constitutionality under the Fifth Amendment of the registration provisions. . . .

Affirmed.

Mr. Chief Justice WARREN, dissenting. . . .

I think it is unwise for the Court to brush aside the non-constitutional errors disclosed by this record. However, since the Court insists upon doing so, I feel constrained to express my views on a dispositive constitutional issue which now confronts us by virtue of the Court's holding on the nonconstitutional questions. I agree with Mr. Justice Brennan that . . . the Act does constitute a violation of the Fifth Amendment.

Mr. Justice BLACK, dissenting. . . .

In my judgment, the Act here under consideration is unconstitutional on at least three grounds in addition to its direct conflict with the self-incrimination provisions of the Fifth Amendment. It is, in the first instance, a classical bill of attainder, [for] it is a legislative act that inflicts pains, penalties and punishments in a number of ways without a judicial trial. . . .

I think also that this outlawry of the Communist Party and imprisonment of its members violates the First Amendment. The question under that Amendment is whether Congress has power to outlaw an association, group or party either on the ground that it advocates a policy of violent overthrow of the existing government at some time in the distant future or on the ground that it is ideologically subservient to some foreign country. In my judgment, neither of these factors justifies an invasion of rights protected by the First Amendment. . . .

Mr. Justice DOUGLAS, dissenting. . . .

The Bill of Rights was designed to give fullest play to the exchange and dissemination of ideas that touch the politics, culture, and other aspects of our life. When an organization is used by a foreign power to make advances here, questions of security are raised beyond the ken of disputation and debate between the people resident here. Espionage, business activities, formation of cells for subversion, as well as the exercise of First Amendment rights, are then used to pry open our society and make intrusion of a foreign power easy. These machinations of a foreign power add additional elements to free speech just as marching up and down adds something to picketing that goes beyond free speech.

These are the reasons why, in my view, the bare requirement that the Communist Party register and disclose the names of its officers and directors is in line with the most exacting adjudications touching First Amendment activities. . . .

My conclusion is that while the Communist Party can be compelled to register, no one acting for it can be compelled to sign a statement that he is an officer or director nor to disclose the names of its officers, directors, or members—unless the required immunity is granted. Why then, one may ask, do we have a registration law? Congress (past or present) is attempting to have its cake and eat it too. In my view Congress can require full disclosure of all the paraphernalia through which a foreign dominated and controlled organization spreads propaganda, engages in agitation, or promotes politics in this country. But the Fifth Amendment bars Congress from requiring full disclosure by one Act and by another Act making the facts admitted or disclosed *under compulsion* the ingredients of a crime. . . .

Mr. Justice BRENNAN, with whom The Chief Justice [WARREN] joins, dissenting in part.

I agree with the Court and with Mr. Justice Douglas that the order requiring that the Party register and disclose its officers and members is not constitutionally invalid as an invasion of the rights of freedom of advocacy and association guaranteed by the First Amendment to Communists as well as to all others. . . .

As to the merits of the Fifth Amendment claim, I believe that officials cannot be compelled to complete, sign and file the registration statement without abridging their privilege against self-incrimination. . . .

THE FATE OF THE LAWS OF THE FIFTIES

1. *Subsequent proceedings under the 1950 Act.* a. As a result of the 1961 decision in the Communist Party v. SACB, supra, the Board order finding the Party to be a "Communist-action organization" became final. Un-

der the Act, the Party was accordingly under a duty to register. Instead, the Party sent a letter to the Attorney General—"signed only with the Party seal"—stating that its officers declined, for fear of self-incrimination, to submit the forms or to authorize anyone to submit them. The Party was convicted for failure to register and sentenced to fines of $120,000. In Communist Party v. United States, 331 F.2d 807 (D.C.Cir.1963), cert. denied, 377 U.S. 968 (1964), the Court of Appeals set aside the conviction. The Court held "that the availability of someone to sign the forms was an element of the offense; that the officers, who should otherwise have signed, were unavailable by reason of their valid claim of the privilege against self-incrimination; that the government had the burden of showing that a volunteer was available; and that its failure to discharge this burden requires reversal of the conviction."

b.   After the Party's failure to register, Albertson v. Subversive Activities Control Board, 332 F.2d 318 (D.C.Cir.1964), sustained a Board order directing two members of the Party to register, under Section 8 of the Act. The Court of Appeals followed the approach of the principal case in finding that most of the constitutional challenges were premature. That decision was unanimously reversed, 382 U.S. 70 (1965). Justice Brennan's opinion held that the Board orders directing the petitioners to register as Party members violated the privilege against self-incrimination. The Court of Appeals, relying on the principal case, had thought the Fifth Amendment objection premature; the Supreme Court found that "the considerations which led the Court in Communist Party to hold that the claims on behalf of unnamed officers were premature are not present in this case." Note also the subsequent decision by that Court of Appeals, in Communist Party v. United States, 384 F.2d 957 (1967), reversing, on Fifth Amendment grounds, convictions of the Party for failing to register as a Communist-action organization and for failing to file a membership statement. (Compare the unsuccessful effort to bypass SACB proceedings in DuBois Clubs v. Clark, 389 U.S. 309 (1967). The Supreme Court's per curiam decision affirmed the lower court's dismissal, for failure to exhaust administrative remedies, of appellants' attack on the Communist-front registration provisions of the Act. Justice Douglas, joined by Justice Black, thought the provisions void on their face and opposed any delay in adjudication.)

2.   *The Communist Control Act of 1954.*   a.   Federal legislation directed at the Communist Party culminated with the 1954 Act, 50 U.S.C. § 841 et seq., a response to a Democratic proposal that membership in the Party be made a crime. That proposal was introduced by Senator Hubert Humphrey—with the statement: "I am tired of reading headlines about being 'soft' toward communism"—and supported by a number of other Democrats (including Senators Lehman, Douglas, Kennedy, and Johnson). See Chase, "The Libertarian Case for Making It a Crime To Be a Communist," 29 Temp.L.Q. 121 (1956). President Eisenhower opposed the proposal on the ground that it would obstruct enforcement of the Smith Act and the 1950 registration law. The 1954 Act was substituted by the Republicans as a compromise. In its "findings," § 841, the Act states that the Party, "although purportedly a political party, is in fact an instrumentality of a conspiracy to overthrow the Government of the United States." The section—which uses some of Justice Jackson's language describing the Party in the Den-

nis case, supra—concludes: "Therefore, the Communist Party should be out-lawed."

The Act proceeds to state, in Section 842, that the Party "or any succes-sors . . . are not entitled to any of the rights, privileges, and immuni-ties attendant upon legal bodies created under . . . the laws of the United States or any subdivision thereof . . . *Provided, however,* That nothing in this section shall be construed as amending the Internal Security Act of 1950. . . ." Section 843 provides that whoever "knowingly and willfully becomes or remains a member" of the Party shall be subject to the 1950 Act as a member of a "Communist-action" organization. Section 844, finally, lists 13 types of evidence a jury "shall consider" in "determining membership or participation" in the Party—including evidence as to whether the accused "(9) Has prepared documents, . . . books, or any other type of publication in behalf of the objectives and purposes of the organiza-tion"; and "(12) Has indicated by word, action, conduct, writing or in any other way a willingness to carry out in any manner and to any degree the plans, designs, objectives, or purposes of the organization." See Note, "The Com-munist Control Act of 1954," 64 Yale L.J. 712 (1955).

b. New York's courts relied on Section 842 of the 1954 Act in uphold-ing the termination of the Party's registration and liability to state taxation as an employer under the New York State Unemployment Insurance Law. In Communist Party v. Catherwood, 367 U.S. 389 (1961), the Supreme Court, in an opinion by Justice Harlan, held that the state courts' reliance on Section 842 had been erroneous. The Court avoided petitioner's numerous constitu-tional contentions because the state's interpretation of the statute, "raising as it does novel Constitutional questions, the answers to which are not neces-sarily controlled by decisions of this Court in connection with other legislation dealing with the Communist Party, must, we think, be rejected." Justice Black concurred in the result.

3. *The 1950 Act and the Aptheker case.* The SACB order that became final as a result of the decision in the principal case also put into effect Sec-tion 6, the passport provision of the 1950 Act. In January 1962, accordingly, the State Department notified Elizabeth Gurley Flynn, the Chairman of the Party, and Herbert Aptheker, the editor of the Party magazine "Political Af-fairs," that "their passports were revoked because the Department . . . believed that their use of the passports would violate § 6." After admin-istrative hearings, Aptheker and Flynn brought court action. The Supreme Court held Section 6 "unconstitutional on its face" because it "too broadly and indiscriminately restricts the right to travel and thereby abridges the liberty guaranteed by the Fifth Amendment." Aptheker v. Secretary of State, 378 U.S. 500 (1964). [In relying on the "right to travel abroad" rather than free speech, Justice Goldberg's majority opinion cited Kent v. Dulles, 357 U.S. 116 (1958) (see chap. 2, p. 160, supra)]. In voiding the provision "on its face," the Court rejected the Government's argument that "surely Section 6 was reasonable as applied to the top-ranking Party leaders involved here": "The clarity and preciseness of the provision in question make it im-possible to narrow its indiscriminately cast and overly broad scope without substantial rewriting."

Justice Goldberg explained that the section "sweeps within its prohibi-tion both knowing and unknowing members" and "renders irrelevant the member's degree of participation in the organization and his commitment to its purpose." He noted that the provision "cannot, as the Government admits, be limited by adopting an interpretation analogous to this Court's interpretation of the so-called 'membership clause' in the Smith Act. In Scales v. United States the Smith Act, which imposes criminal penalties for membership, was interpreted to include only ' "active" members having also a guilty knowledge and intent.' The membership clause in that case, however, explicitly required 'that a defendant must have knowledge of the organization's illegal advocacy.' That requirement was intimately connected with the construction limiting membership to 'active' members. With regard to the Control Act, however, as the Government concedes, 'neither the words nor history of Section 6 suggests limiting its application to "active" members.' "

The Court's conclusion that the section "too broadly" restricted the right to travel has been of special significance in the free speech area: the emphasis on "overbroadness" in Aptheker and other cases has provided an increasingly popular basis for decisions in the Court. See, e. g., the Robel case, in note 4 infra. The "overbreadth" doctrine in general is examined further infra, sec. 1E, p. 1130.

The Aptheker opinion emphasized that it was "important to consider that Congress has within its power 'less drastic' means of achieving the congressional objective of safeguarding our national security." It concluded: "The prohibition against travel is supported only by a tenuous relationship between the bare fact of organizational membership and the activity Congress sought to proscribe. The broad and enveloping prohibition indiscriminately excludes plainly relevant considerations such as the individual's knowledge, activity, commitment, and purposes in and places for travel."

4. *The 1950 Act and the Robel case.* Section 5(a)(1)(D) of the 1950 Act made it a crime for any member of a Communist-action organization "to engage in any employment in any defense facility," if he had knowledge or notice that there was in effect a final order of the SACB requiring such organization to register. That provision was found to be "an unconstitutional abridgment of the right of association protected by the First Amendment" in United States v. Robel, 389 U.S. 258 (1967). Chief Justice Warren's majority opinion noted that it was irrelevant under the statute "that an individual may be a passive or inactive member of a designated organization, that he may be unaware of the organization's unlawful aims, or that he may disagree with those unlawful aims." Moreover, it was irrelevant under the section that an individual subject to it "may occupy a nonsensitive position in a defense facility." He concluded that the provision "contains the fatal defect of overbreadth because it seeks to bar employment both for association which may be proscribed and for association which may not be proscribed consistently with First Amendment rights." See Gunther, "Reflections on Robel . . . ," 20 Stan.L.Rev. 1140 (1968).

E. SUBVERSIVE ADVOCACY AND THE COURT AFTER A HALF CENTURY: OLD PRECEDENTS AND NEW TOOLS

Introduction. This section returns to the statutory and factual context of the Schenck-Gitlow-Whitney era. What do evolving free speech doctrines say about the modern counterparts of those problems? The Brandenburg case is the Warren Court's response to a Whitney-type statute. And the anti-Vietnam protests considered in the materials after Brandenburg involve contemporary variations on the setting of the World War I Espionage Act prosecutions.

What is the role of clear and present danger in the handling of these questions? What of the Masses approach? What of the impact of Dennis and the later Smith Act cases? What newly evolved ingredients of free speech doctrine are now available? In order to explore the last of these questions the final portion of this section samples some additional judicial techniques of free speech protection (those illustrated by the New York Times and Keyishian cases) more fully developed in the next chapter.

BRANDENBURG v. OHIO

395 U.S. 444, 89 S.Ct. 1827, 23 L.Ed.2d 430 (1969).

Appeal from the Supreme Court of Ohio.

PER CURIAM. — *" By the Court — usually written by Chief Justice, but not attributed to anyone person,*

The appellant, a leader of a Ku Klux Klan group, was convicted under the Ohio Criminal Syndicalism statute of "advocat[ing] . . . the duty, necessity, or propriety of crime, sabotage, violence, or unlawful methods of terrorism as a means of accomplishing industrial or political reform" and of "voluntarily assembl[ing] with any society, group or assemblage of persons formed to teach or advocate the doctrines of criminal syndicalism." Ohio Rev.Code ¶ 2923.13. He was fined $1,000 and sentenced to one to 10 years' imprisonment. The appellant challenged the constitutionality of the criminal syndicalism statute under the First and Fourteenth Amendments to the United States Constitution, but the intermediate appellate court of Ohio affirmed his conviction without opinion. The Supreme Court of Ohio dismissed his appeal, *sua sponte*, "for the reason that no substantial constitutional question exists herein." . . . We reverse.

The record shows that a man, identified at trial as the appellant, telephoned an announcer-reporter on the staff of a Cincinnati television station and invited him to come to a Ku Klux Klan "rally" to be held at a farm in Hamilton County. With the cooperation of the organizers, the reporter and a cameraman attended the meeting and filmed the events. Portions of the films were later broadcast on the local station and on a national network.

The prosecution's case rested on the films and on testimony identifying the appellant as the person who communicated with the reporter and who spoke at the rally. The State also introduced into evidence several articles appearing in the film, including a pistol, a rifle, a shotgun, ammunition, a Bible, and a red hood worn by the speaker in the films.

One film showed 12 hooded figures, some of whom carried firearms. They were gathered around a large wooden cross, which they burned. No one was present other than the participants and the newsmen who made the film. Most of the words uttered during the scene were incomprehensible when the film was projected, but scattered phrases could be understood that were derogatory of Negroes and, in one instance, of Jews.[1] Another scene on the same film showed the appellant, in Klan regalia, making a speech. The speech, in full, was as follows:

> "This an organizers' meeting. We have had quite a few members here today which are—we have hundreds, hundreds of members throughout the State of Ohio. I can quote from a newspaper clipping from the Columbus Ohio Dispatch, five weeks ago Sunday morning. The Klan has more members in the State of Ohio than does any other organization. We're not a revengent organization, but if our President, our Congress, our Supreme Court, continues to suppress the white, Caucasian race, it's possible that there might have to be some revengence taken.
>
> "We are marching on Congress July the Fourth, four hundred thousand strong. From there we are dividing into two groups, one group to march on St. Augustine, Florida, the other group to march into Mississippi. Thank you."

The second film showed six hooded figures one of whom, later identified as the appellant, repeated a speech very similar to that recorded on the first film. The reference to the possibility of "revengence" was omitted, and one sentence was added: "Personally, I believe the nigger should be returned to Africa, the Jew returned to Israel." Though some of the figures in the films carried weapons, the speaker did not.

The Ohio Criminal Syndicalism Statute was enacted in 1919. From 1917 to 1920, identical or quite similar laws were adopted by 20 States and two territories. . . . In 1927, this Court sustained the constitutionality of California's Criminal Syndicalism Act, the text of which is quite similar to that of the laws of Ohio. Whitney v. California, 274 U.S. 357 (1927). The Court upheld the statute on the ground that, without more, "advocating" violent means to effect political and economic change involves such danger to the security of the State that the State may outlaw it. Cf. Fiske v. Kansas, 274 U.S. 380 (1927). But Whitney has been thoroughly discredited by later decisions. See Dennis v. United States, 341 U.S. 494, at 507 (1951). These later decisions have fashioned the principle that the constitutional guarantees of free speech and free press do not permit a State to forbid or proscribe advocacy of the use of force or of law violation except where such advocacy is directed to inciting or producing imminent lawless action and is

---

1. The significant portions that could be understood were:

"How far is the nigger going to—yeah."
"This is what we are going to do to the niggers."
"A dirty nigger."
"Send the Jews back to Israel."
"Let's give them back to the dark garden."
"Save America."

"Let's go back to constitutional betterment."
"Bury the niggers."
"We intend to do our part."
"Give us our state rights."
"Freedom for the whites."
"Nigger will have to fight for every inch he gets from now on." [All footnotes to this opinion by the Court.]

likely to incite or produce such action.[2] As we said in Noto v. United States, 367 U.S. 290, 297–298 (1961), "the mere abstract teaching . . . of the moral propriety or even moral necessity for a resort to force and violence, is not the same as preparing a group for violent action and steeling it to such action." See also Herndon v. Lowry, 301 U.S. 242, 259–261 (1937); Bond v. Floyd, 385 U.S. 116, 134 (1966) [which follows]. A statute which fails to draw this distinction impermissibly intrudes upon the freedoms guaranteed by the First and Fourteenth Amendments. It sweeps within its condemnation speech which our Constitution has immunized from governmental control. Cf. Yates v. United States, 354 U.S. 298 (1957); De Jonge v. Oregon, 299 U.S. 353 (1937); Stromberg v. California, 283 U.S. 359 (1931).

Measured by this test, Ohio's Criminal Syndicalism Act cannot be sustained. The Act punishes persons who "advocate or teach the duty, necessity, or propriety" of violence "as a means of accomplishing industrial or political reform"; or who publish or circulate or display any book or paper containing such advocacy; or who "justify" the commission of violent acts "with intent to exemplify, spread or advocate the propriety of the doctrines of criminal syndicalism"; or who "voluntarily assemble" with a group formed "to teach or advocate the doctrines of criminal syndicalism." Neither the indictment nor the trial judge's instructions to the jury in any way refined the statute's bald definition of the crime in terms of mere advocacy not distinguished from incitement to imminent lawless action.[3]

Accordingly, we are here confronted with a statute which, by its own words and as applied, purports to punish mere advocacy and to forbid, on pain of criminal punishment, assembly with others merely to advocate the described type of action.[4] Such a statute falls within the condemnation of the First and Fourteenth Amendments. The contrary teaching of Whitney v. California, supra, cannot be supported, and that decision is therefore overruled.

Reversed.*

2. It was on the theory that the Smith Act, 54 Stat. 670, 18 U.S.C. § 2385, embodied such a principle and that it had been applied only in conformity with it that this Court sustained the Act's constitutionality. Dennis v. United States, 341 U.S. 494 (1951). That this was the basis for Dennis was emphasized in Yates v. United States, 354 U.S. 298, 320–324 (1957), in which the Court overturned convictions for advocacy of the forcible overthrow of the Government under the Smith Act, because the trial judge's instructions had allowed conviction for mere advocacy, unrelated to its tendency to produce forcible action.

3. The first count of the indictment charged that appellant "did unlawfully by word of mouth advocate the necessity, or propriety of crime, violence, or unlawful methods of terrorism as a means of accomplishing political reform. . . ." The second count charged that appellant "did unlawfully voluntarily assemble with a group or assemblage of persons formed to advocate the doctrines of criminal syndicalism. . . ." The trial judge's charge merely followed the language of the indictment. No construction of the statute by the Ohio courts has brought it within constitutionally permissible limits. . . .

4. Statutes affecting the right of assembly, like those touching on freedom of speech, must observe the established distinctions between mere advocacy and incitement to imminent lawless action, for as Chief Justice Hughes wrote in De Jonge v. Oregon, supra, at 364: "The right of peaceable assembly is a right cognate to those of free speech and free press and is equally fundamental." . . .

* During the 1968–69 Term in which Brandenburg was decided—the last Term under Chief Justice Warren—

Mr. Justice BLACK, concurring.

I agree with the views expressed by Mr. Justice Douglas in his concurring opinion in this case that the "clear and present danger" doctrine should have no place in the interpretation of the First Amendment. I join the Court's opinion, which, as I understand it, simply cites Dennis v. United States, 341 U.S. 494 (1951), but does not indicate any agreement on the Court's part with the "clear and present danger" doctrine on which Dennis purported to rely.

Mr. Justice DOUGLAS, concurring.

While I join the opinion of the Court, I desire to enter a *caveat*.

The "clear and present danger" test was adumbrated by Mr. Justice Holmes in a case arising during World War I—a war "declared" by the Congress, not by the Chief Executive. The case was Schenck . . . . [Schenck, Frohwerk, Debs, Abrams, Schaefer, and Pierce, all supra], then, were the World War I cases that put the gloss of "clear and present danger" on the First Amendment. Whether the war power—the greatest leveler of them all —is adequate to sustain that doctrine is debatable. The dissents in Abrams, Schaefer, and Pierce show how easily "clear and present danger" is manipulated to crush what Brandeis called "[t]he fundamental right of free men to strive for better conditions through new legislation and new institutions" by argument and discourse [Pierce] even in time of war. Though I doubt if the "clear and present danger" test is congenial to the First Amendment in time of a declared war, I am certain it is not reconcilable with the First Amendment in days of peace.

The Court quite properly overrules [Whitney], which involved advocacy of ideas which the majority of the Court deemed unsound and dangerous.

Mr. Justice Holmes, though never formally abandoning the "clear and present danger" test, moved closer to the First Amendment ideal when he said in dissent in Gitlow [the passage beginning "Every idea is an incitement," p. 1079, supra]. We have never been faithful to the philosophy of that dissent.

The Court in Herndon v. Lowry overturned a conviction for exercising First Amendments rights to incite insurrection because of lack of evidence of incitement. In Bridges v. California, we approved the "clear and present danger" test in an elaborate dictum that tightened it and confined it to a narrow category. But in Dennis v. United States, we opened wide the door, distorting the "clear and present danger" test beyond recognition. . . .

Out of the "clear and present danger" test came other offspring. Advocacy and teaching of forcible overthrow of government as an abstract principle is immune from prosecution [Yates]. But an "active" member, who has a guilty knowledge and intent of the aim to overthrow the Government by violence [Noto] may be prosecuted. Scales v. United States, 367 U.S.

the Court also heard arguments in appeals from District Court decisions invalidating the California syndicalism law involved in Whitney [Younger v. Harris, 281 F.Supp. 507] and sustaining the New York criminal anarchy law [Samuels v. Mackell, 288 F.Supp. 348—relying on a narrowing construc-

tion of the Gitlow statute in Epton v. New York, 19 N.Y.2d 496, appeal dismissed, 390 U.S. 29 (1968)]. A week after the decision in Brandenburg, the Court set those cases for reargument during the 1969–70 Term—the first of Chief Justice Burger's tenure.

203, 228. And the power to investigate, backed by the powerful sanction of contempt, includes the power to determine which of the two categories fits the particular witness. Barenblatt v. United States, 360 U.S. 109, 130 [chap. 16, p. 1235, infra]. And so the investigator roams at will through all of the beliefs of the witness, ransacking his conscience and his innermost thoughts.

Judge Learned Hand, who wrote for the Court of Appeals in affirming the judgment in Dennis, coined the "not improbable" test, which this Court adopted and which Judge Hand preferred over the "clear and present danger" test. Indeed, in his book, The Bill of Rights 59 (1958), in referring to Holmes' creation of the "clear and present danger" test, he said, "I cannot help thinking that for once Homer nodded."

My own view is quite different. I see no place in the regime of the First Amendment for any "clear and present danger" test whether strict and tight as some would make it or free-wheeling, as the Court in Dennis rephrased it.

When one reads the opinions closely and sees when and how the "clear and present danger" test has been applied, great misgivings are aroused. First, the threats were often loud but always puny and made serious only by judges so wedded to the status quo that critical analysis made them nervous. Second, the test was so twisted and perverted in Dennis as to make the trial of those teachers of Marxism an all-out political trial which was part and parcel of the cold war that has eroded substantial parts of the First Amendment.

Action is often a method of expression and within the protection of the First Amendment. Suppose one tears up his own copy of the Constitution in eloquent protest to a decision of this Court. May he be indicted? Suppose one rips his own Bible to shreds to celebrate his departure from one "faith" and his embrace of atheism. May he be indicted?

Last Term the Court held in United States v. O'Brien, 391 U.S. 367, 382 [p. 1189, infra], that a registrant under Selective Service who burned his draft card in protest of the war in Vietnam could be prosecuted. The First Amendment was tendered as a defense and rejected . . ..

But O'Brien was not prosecuted for not having his draft card available when asked for by a federal agent. He was indicted, tried, and convicted for burning the card. And this Court's affirmance of that conviction was not, with all respect, consistent with the First Amendment.

The act of praying often involves body posture and movement as well as utterances. It is nonetheless protected by the Free Exercise Clause. Picketing, as we have said on numerous occasions, is "free speech plus." [See chap. 16, p. 1295, infra.] That means that it can be regulated when it comes to the "plus" or "action" side of the protest. It can be regulated as to the number of pickets and the place and hours (see Cox v. Louisiana [p. 1165, infra]) because traffic and other community problems would otherwise suffer.

But none of these considerations are implicated in the symbolic protest of the Vietnam war in the burning of a draft card.

One's beliefs have long been thought to be sanctuaries which government could not invade. Barenblatt is one example of the ease with which that sanctuary can be violated. The lines drawn by the Court between the criminal act of being an "active" Communist and the innocent act of being a nominal or inactive Communist mark the difference only between deep and abiding belief and casual or uncertain belief. But I think that all matters of belief are beyond the reach of subpoenas or the probings of investigators. That is why the invasions of privacy made by investigating committees was notoriously unconstitutional. That is the deep-seated fault in the infamous loyalty-security hearings which, since 1947 when President Truman launched them, have processed 20,000,000 men and women. Those hearings were primarily concerned with one's thoughts, ideas, beliefs, and convictions. They were the most blatant violations of the First Amendment we have ever known.

The line between what is permissible and not subject to control and what may be made impermissible and subject to regulation is the line between ideas and overt acts.

The example usually given by those who would punish speech is the case of one who falsely shouts fire in a crowded theatre. This is, however, a classic case where speech is brigaded with action. . . . They are indeed inseparable and a prosecution can be launched for the overt acts actually caused. Apart from rare instances of that kind, speech is, I think, immune from prosecution. Certainly there is no constitutional line between advocacy of abstract ideas as in Yates and advocacy of political action as in Scales. The quality of advocacy turns on the depth of the conviction; and government has no power to invade that sanctuary of belief and conscience.

OPPOSITION TO VIETNAM POLICY AND TO THE DRAFT

Consider the scope given to freedeom of expression (and the criteria applied) in the following modern cases—all war and draft protest counterparts to the milieu of the Espionage Act cases.

1. *Criticism and state legislators' oaths: the Julian Bond case.* In Bond v. Floyd, 385 U.S. 116 (1966), the Court held that the Georgia House of Representatives resolution excluding Julian Bond from membership violated the First Amendment. The State's justification was that Bond could not conscientiously take the required oath to "support the Constitution of this State and of the United States." The House relied on Bond's endorsement of a SNCC statement and his supplementary remarks critical of the draft and of Vietnam policy. Chief Justice Warren's opinion for a unanimous Court, after stating that this was not a case "where a legislator swears to an oath *pro forma* while declaring or manifesting his disagreement with or indifference to the oath," continued:

"[W]e do not quarrel with the State's contention that the oath provisions . . . do not violate the First Amendment. But this requirement does not authorize a majority of state legislators to test the sincerity with which another duly elected legislator can swear to uphold the Constitution. Such a power could be utilized to restrict the right of legislators to dissent from national or state policy or that of a majority of their colleagues under the guise of judging their loyalty to the Constitution. Certainly there can be no question but that the First Amendment protects expressions in opposition to national foreign policy in Vietnam and to the Selective Service system. The

State does not contend otherwise. But it argues that Bond went beyond expressions of opposition, and counseled violations of the Selective Service laws, and that advocating violation of federal law demonstrates a lack of support for the Constitution. The State declines to argue that Bond's statements would violate any law if made by a private citizen, but it does argue that even though such a citizen might be protected by his First Amendment rights, the State may nonetheless apply a stricter standard to its legislators. We do not agree.

"Bond could not have been constitutionally convicted under 50 U.S.C. § 462(a), which punishes any person who 'counsels, aids or abets another to refuse or evade registration.' Bond's statements were at worst unclear on the question of the means to be adopted to avoid the draft. While the SNCC statements said 'We are in sympathy with, and support, the men in this country who are unwilling to respond to a military draft,' this statement alone cannot be interpreted as a call to unlawful refusal to be drafted. Moreover, Bond's supplementary statements tend to resolve the opaqueness in favor of legal alternatives to the draft, and there is no evidence to the contrary. On the day the statement was issued, Bond explained that he endorsed it 'because I like to think of myself as a pacifist and one who opposes that war and any other war and eager and anxious to encourage people not to participate in it for any reason that they choose.' In the same interview, Bond stated categorically that he did not oppose the Vietnam policy because he favored the Communists; that he was a loyal American citizen and supported the Constitution of the United States. He further stated 'I oppose the Viet Cong fighting in Viet Nam as much as I oppose the United States fighting in Viet Nam.' At the hearing before the Special Committee of the Georgia House, when asked his position on persons who burned their draft cards, Bond replied that he admired the courage of persons who 'feel strongly enough about their convictions to take an action like that knowing the consequences that they will face.' When pressed as to whether his admiration was based on the violation of federal law, Bond stated:

'I have never suggested or counseled or advocated that any one other person burn their draft card. In fact, I have mine in my pocket and will produce it if you wish. I do not advocate that people should break laws. What I simply try to say was that I admired the courage of someone who could act on his convictions knowing that he faces pretty stiff consequences.'

"Certainly this clarification does not demonstrate any incitement to violation of law. No useful purpose would be served by discussing the many decisions of this Court which establish that Bond could not have been convicted for these statements consistently with the First Amendment. See, e. g., Wood v. Georgia, 370 U.S. 375 (1962), Yates v. United States, 354 U.S. 298 (1957); Terminiello v. Chicago, 337 U.S. 1 (1949). . . .

"The State attempts to circumvent the protection the First Amendment would afford to these statements if made by a private citizen by arguing that a State is constitutionally justified in exacting a higher standard of *loyalty* from its legislators than from its citizens. [W]hile the State has an interest in requiring its legislators to swear to a belief in constitutional processes of government, surely the oath gives it no interest in limiting its legislators' capacity to discuss their views of local or national policy. The manifest function of the First Amendment in a representative government requires that legislators be given the widest latitude to express their views on issues of policy. . . . Just as erroneous statements must be protected to give freedom of expression the breathing space it needs to survive, so statements criticizing public policy and the implementation of it must be similarly protected. The State argues that . . . the policy of encouraging free debate about governmental operations only applies to the citizen-critic of his government. . . . The interest of the public in hearing all sides of a public issue is hardly advanced by extending more protection to citizen-critics than to legislators. Legislators have an obligation to take positions on controversial political questions so that their constituents can be fully informed by them, and be better able to assess their qualifications for office; also so they may be represented in governmental debates by the person they have elected to represent them."

2. *Counseling draft evasion and the Bond case.* Consider the First Amendment comments in Bond in light of the Spock-Coffin prosecution, see 416 F.2d 165 (1st Cir. 1969); and compare O'Brien, the 1968 draft-card burning case, see note 4, infra, as well as at p. 1189. Compare the Bond opinion with the "counseling" and "admiration" approaches in Hand's Masses opinion (p. 1070, supra) and Holmes' Debs opinion (p. 1061, supra), respectively. Note, moreover, the cases cited by the Court on First Amendment protection: Wood and Terminiello as well as Yates; the first two prominently featured clear and present danger language.

3. *The Watts case.* For a per curiam decision considering anti-draft comments in an unusual context, note the Court's reversal without argument in Watts v. United States, 394 U.S. 705 (1969). Petitioner had been convicted under a 1917 statute making it a felony "knowingly and willfully" to make "any threat to take the life" of the President. Petitioner had said at a public rally (after it had been urged that young people get more education before speaking): "They always holler at us to get an education. And now I have already received my draft classification as 1–A . . . .. I am not going. If they ever make me carry a rifle, the first man I want to get is L.B.J. They are not going to make me kill my black brothers."

The Court had no doubt that the statute was constitutional on its face but added that "a statute such as this one, which makes criminal a form of pure speech, must be interpreted with the commands of the First Amendment clearly in mind. What is a threat must be distinguished from what is constitutionally protected speech." It was important to "interpret the language Congress chose 'against the background of a profound national commitment to the principle that debate on public issues should be uninhibited, robust, and wide-open, and that it may well include vehement, caustic, and sometimes unpleasantly sharp attacks on government and public officials.' New York Times Co. v. Sullivan [376 U.S. 254 (1964), pp. 1131 and 1214, infra.]"

Here, there was not a true "threat," only a "kind of political hyperbole." Language in the political arena, the Court added, "is often vituperative, abusive, and inexact. We agree with petitioner that his only offense was 'a kind of very crude offensive method of stating a political opposition to the President.' Taken in context, and regarding the expressly conditional nature of the statement and the reaction of the listeners [there had been laughter after the statement], we do not see how it could be interpreted otherwise." Justice

Fortas, joined by Justice Harlan, objected to ruling on the merits without hearing oral argument; Justice White dissented without opinion.

4. *Protests through symbols rather than words.* Do the applicable judicial criteria change when anti-war, anti-draft protest is expressed symbolically, through behavior rather than words? How? Is the First Amendment inapplicable because "conduct" rather than "speech" is involved? Is less First Amendment protection appropriate? Issues such as these have repeatedly come before the modern Court. See, e. g., United States v. O'Brien, 391 U.S. 367 (1968) (p. 1189), sustaining a conviction for burning a draft card against a First Amendment symbolic expression defense, and Tinker v. Des Moines Comm. School Dist., 393 U.S. 503 (1969) (p. 1195), protecting the wearing of black armbands by school children as a war protest symbol. See also Street v. New York, 394 U.S. 576 (1969) (p. 1202), setting aside a conviction for words uttered in a flag burning protest.

These "symbolic expression" cases can usefully be considered at this point, for the purpose of investigating further the reach and content of contemporary protection of expression. Consideration of these cases is postponed in these materials, however, to the concluding section of this chapter (sec. 3). Before turning to them, sec. 2 examines those cases in which the state concern purports to be with the manner rather than the content of speech—where the impact of the law on speech is allegedly the indirect consequence of a regulatory concern with "conduct." In the symbolic speech cases, the "conduct"-"speech" and "manner-content" distinctions of the cases in sec. 2 compete with the doctrines developed in the sec. 1 materials for "pure speech" cases. Postponing consideration of that symbolic speech area to the end of this chapter accordingly offers the opportunity to explore the boundaries—and indeed the inherent sense and viability—of these categories and distinctions.

"UNINHIBITED DEBATE ON PUBLIC ISSUES" AND "OVERBROAD" STATUTES: NEW TOOLS TO PROTECT SPEECH?

Introduction. The preceding pages have considered a variety of analytical approaches central to the Court's protection of political speech critical of government. Two further modern doctrinal tools warrant noting here, even though they were developed in contexts not fully explored until later in these materials. Sampling these doctrinal themes at this point is of importance because they provide related, alternative, possibly more effective, and increasingly popular techniques for the protection of freedom of expression.

1. *Debate of public issues and the New York Times case.* Consider the effort to articulate the major thrust of the speech guarantee in New York Times Co. v. Sullivan, 376 U.S. 254 (1964) (chap. 16, p. 1214, infra), a case concerned with the scope of the First Amendment defense in a libel action brought by a public official against a newspaper. Justice Brennan's majority opinion included the following passage: "[W]e consider this case against the background of a profound national commitment to the principle that debate on public issues should be uninhibited, robust, and wide-open, and that it may well include vehement, caustic, and sometimes unpleasantly sharp at-

tacks on government and public officials." In the course of the opinion he noted (as had Justice Holmes' Abrams dissent) the historical roots of those protected values: "the great controversy over the Sedition Act of 1798, 1 Stat. 596, which first crystallized a national awareness of the central meaning of the First Amendment." * He explained: "Although the Sedition Act was never tested in this Court, the attack upon its validity has carried the day in the court of history. . . . These views reflect a broad consensus that the Act, because of the restraint it imposed upon criticism of government and public officials, was inconsistent with the First Amendment. . . . What a State may not constitutionally bring about by means of a criminal statute is likewise beyond the reach of its civil law of libel."

Does this articulation add anything to the preceding cases? Does it suggest greater protection for "public" than "private" speech? Does it reinforce the Masses focus on what is most valued by democratic presuppositions, rather than on "dangers"? Does it stress defining protected speech, rather than assessing risks? Note the use of the New York Times phrase as guidance in statutory interpretation in the Watts case, note 3, p. 1130, supra; compare the Masses and Yates approaches. See Kalven, " 'Uninhibited, Robust, and Wide-Open'—A Note on Free Speech and the Warren Court," 67 Mich.L.Rev. 289 (1968), and Kalven, "The New York Times Case: A Note on the Central Meaning of the First Amendment," 1964 Sup.Ct.Rev. 191.

2. *Overbroadness.* The Warren Court has repeatedly, and in a variety of circumstances, invoked the principle that "a governmental purpose to control or prevent activities constitutionally subject to state regulation may not be achieved by *means which sweep unnecessarily broadly and thereby invade the area of protected freedoms.*" (Emphasis added.) The increasing popularity of that "overbreadth" doctrine may be attributable to its relatively technical appearance: on its face, it does not, like many of the techniques considered earlier, deal explicitly with substantive values such as speech; it purports to be concerned with *means* to legitimate ends, not ultimate quasi-legislative choices. Yet, as applied in the free speech area, it necessarily involves determining what expression is protected by the First Amendment, albeit more obliquely and less explicitly than do other techniques. To strike down an excessively broad means because it impinges on an "area of protected freedom" presupposes, after all, at least an implicit judgment about what the contours of that "area" are. Indeed, the popularity and importance of the doctrine may stem from its usefulness as a technique of deciding speech problems somewhat more indirectly, often more sketchily, than the more open confrontations of ultimate speech issues noted earlier.

The technique will appear in a variety of contexts below. (See especially the comments at p. 1325 of chap. 16.) It has surfaced occasionally earlier. See, e. g., the Aptheker case, p. 1121, supra, invalidating the passport provisions of the 1950 Subversive Activities Control Act.† This section will close

---

* On that historical background, see generally Smith, Freedom's Fetters (1956), Levy, Legacy of Suppression: Freedom of Speech and Press in Early American History (1960), and Levy, "Liberty and the First Amendment," 68 Am.Hist.Rev. 22 (1962).

† See also the Robel case, p. 1122, supra, and note Gunther, "Reflections on

Robel . . .," 20 Stan.L.Rev. 1140 (1968). For another early example of the overbroadness theme, see Shelton v. Tucker, 364 U.S. 479 (1960) (p. 1320, infra), invalidating a law compelling a teacher to list every organization with which he was affiliated over a 5-year period. The Court explained: "[E]ven though the governmental purpose be legitimate and substantial,

with a decision illustrating its operation more fully—Keyishian v. Board of Regents. Keyishian, to be sure, concerns government employee security programs, a subject considered more fully in chap. 16; unlike the earlier case in this section, Keyishian does not involve criminal prohibitions of subversive speech. But Keyishian may appropriately be considered here not simply as a preview of the pervasive overbreadth technique; it bears on the preceding materials in other respects as well. It considers one more context of the regulation of subversion. It illustrates the increasing impact of prohibited advocacy and membership decisions such as Yates and Scales on "regulation" cases. It demonstrates that assumptions about the boundaries of protected speech underlie the judgment that the challenged "means" are unduly broad. And, because of the closeness of the Keyishian subversion context to the preceding materials, it may suggest potential applications of the overbreadth technique to the problems considered earlier. See generally Note, "The First Amendment Overbreadth Doctrine," 83 Harv.L.Rev. 844 (1970).

KEYISHIAN v. BOARD OF REGENTS

385 U.S. 589, 87 S.Ct. 675, 17 L.Ed.2d 629 (1967).

Appeal from the United States District Court for the Western District of New York.

Mr. Justice BRENNAN delivered the opinion of the Court.

Appellants were members of the faculty of the privately owned and operated University of Buffalo, and became state employees when the University was merged in 1962 into the State University of New York . . . . As faculty members of the State University their continued employment was conditioned upon their compliance with a New York plan, formulated partly in statutes and partly in administrative regulations, which the State utilizes to prevent the appointment or retention of "subversive" persons in state employment. . . .

[Each faculty appellant] refused to sign, as regulations then in effect required, [the "Feinberg Certificate"—] a certificate that he was not a Communist, and that if he had ever been a Communist, he had communicated that fact to the President of the State University of New York. Each was notified that his failure to sign the certificate would require his dismissal. . . . Appellants brought this action for declaratory and injunctive relief alleging that the state program violated the Federal Constitution in various respects. A three-judge federal court held that the program was constitutional. . . . We reverse.

We considered some aspects of the constitutionality of the New York plan 15 years ago in Adler v. Board of Education [chap. 2, p. 80]. That litigation arose after New York passed the Feinberg Law which added § 3022 to the Education Law. The Feinberg Law was enacted to implement and en-

that purpose cannot be pursued by means that broadly stifle fundamental personal liberties when the end can be more narrowly achieved. The breadth of legislative abridgment must be viewed in the light of less drastic means for achieving the same basic purpose." (A footnote suggested an analogy to the less-drastic-alternatives rationale of Dean Milk Co. v. Madison, 340 U.S. 349, the commerce clause case in chap. 8, p. 657, supra).

force two earlier statutes. The first was a 1917 law, now § 3021 of the Education Law, under which "the utterance of any treasonable or seditious word or words or the doing of any treasonable or seditious act" is a ground for dismissal from the public school system. The second was a 1939 law which was § 12–a of the Civil Service Law when Adler was decided and, as amended, is now § 105 of that law. This law disqualifies from the Civil Service and from employment in the educational system any person who advocates the overthrow of government by force, violence, or any unlawful means, or publishes material advocating such overthrow or organizes or joins any society or group of persons advocating such doctrine.

The Feinberg Law charged the State Board of Regents with the duty of promulgating rules and regulations providing procedures for the disqualification or removal of persons in the public school system who violate the 1917 law or who are ineligible for appointment to or retention in the public school system under the 1939 law. The Board of Regents was further directed to make a list, after notice and hearing, of "subversive" organizations, defined as organizations which advocate the doctrine of overthrow of government by force, violence, or any unlawful means. Finally, the Board was directed to provide in its rules and regulations that membership in any listed organization should constitute prima facie evidence of disqualification for appointment to or retention in any office or position in the public schools of the State. [The Board thereupon issued implementing regulations.]

Adler was a declaratory judgment suit in which the Court held, in effect, that there was no constitutional infirmity in former § 12–a or in the Feinberg Law on their faces and that they were capable of constitutional application. But the contention urged in this case that both § 3021 and § 105 are unconstitutionally vague was not heard or decided. . . . [T]hat question is now properly before us for decision. Moreover, to the extent that Adler sustained the provision of the Feinberg Law constituting membership in an organization advocating forceful overthrow of government a ground for disqualification, pertinent constitutional doctrines have since rejected the premises upon which that conclusion rested. Adler is therefore not dispositive of the constitutional issues we must decide in this case. . . .

Section 3021 requires removal for "treasonable or seditious" utterances or acts. The 1958 amendment to § 105 of the Civil Service Law, now subsection 3 of that section, added such utterances or acts as a ground for removal under that law also. . . . The difficulty centers upon the meaning of "seditious." Subsection 3 equates the term "seditious" with "criminal anarchy" as defined in the Penal Law. The teacher cannot know the extent, if any, to which a "seditious" utterance must transcend mere statement about abstract doctrine, the extent to which it must be intended to and tend to indoctrinate or incite to action in furtherance of the defined doctrine. The crucial consideration is that no teacher can know just where the line is drawn between "seditious" and nonseditious utterances and acts.

Other provisions of § 105 also have the same defect of vagueness.
. . .

We emphasize once again that " . . . standards of permissible statutory vagueness are strict in the area of free expression. . . ." New York's complicated and intricate scheme plainly violates that standard.
. . . The danger of that chilling effect upon the exercise of vital First

Amendment rights must be guarded against by sensitive tools which clearly inform teachers what is being sanctioned. . . .

The regulatory maze created by New York . . . . has the quality of "extraordinary ambiguity" found to be fatal to the oaths considered in Cramp and Baggett v. Bullitt [p. 1326, infra]. Vagueness of wording is aggravated by prolixity and profusion of statutes, regulations, and administrative machinery, and by manifold cross-references to interrelated enactments and rules. . . .

Appellants have also challenged the constitutionality of the discrete provisions of subsection (1) (c) of § 105 and subsection (2) of the Feinberg Law, which make Communist Party membership, as such, prima facie evidence of disqualification. The provision was added to subsection (1) (c) of § 105 in 1958 after the Board of Regents, following notice and hearing, listed the Communist Party of the United States and the Communist Party of the State of New York as "subversive" organizations. Subsection (2) of the Feinberg Law was, however, before the Court in Adler and its constitutionality was sustained. But constitutional doctrine which has emerged since that decision has rejected its major premise. That premise was that public employment, including academic employment, may be conditioned upon the surrender of constitutional rights which could not be abridged by direct government action. . . . [T]hat theory was expressly rejected in a series of decisions following Adler.

We proceed then to the question of the validity of the provisions of subsection (c) of § 105 and subsection (2) of § 3022, barring employment to members of listed organizations. Here again constitutional doctrine has developed since Adler. Mere knowing membership without a specific intent to further the unlawful aims of an organization is not a constitutionally adequate basis for exclusion from such positions as those held by appellants.

In Elfbrandt v. Russell [p. 1327, infra], we . . . found that "[a]ny lingering doubt that proscription of mere knowing membership, without any showing of 'specific intent,' would run afoul of the Constitution was set at rest by our decision in Aptheker . . .." [M]ere Party membership, even with knowledge of the Party's unlawful goals, cannot suffice to justify criminal punishment, see [Scales, Noto, Yates]; nor may it warrant a finding of moral unfitness justifying disbarment. Schware v. Board of Bar Examiners [p. 1307, infra].

These limitations clearly apply to a provision, like § 105(1) (c), which blankets all state employees regardless of the "sensitivity" of their positions. But even the Feinberg Law provision, applicable primarily to activities of teachers, who have captive audiences of young minds, are subject to these limitations in favor of freedom of expression and association; the stifling effect on the academic mind from curtailing freedom of association in such manner is manifest, and has been documented in recent studies. Elfbrandt and Aptheker state the governing standard: legislation which sanctions membership unaccompanied by specific intent to further the unlawful goals of the organization or which is not active membership violates constitutional limitations.

Measured against this standard, both Civil Service Law § 105(1) (c) and Education Law § 3022(2) sweep overbroadly into association which may not be sanctioned. The presumption of disqualification arising from proof of mere membership may be rebutted, but only by (a) a denial of membership, (b) a denial that the organization advocates the overthrow of government by force, or (c) a denial that the teacher has knowledge of such advocacy. . . . Thus proof of nonactive membership or a showing of the absence of intent to further unlawful aims will not rebut the presumption and defeat dismissal. . . .

Thus § 105(1) (c) and § 3022(2) suffer from impermissible "overbreadth." * . . . They seek to bar employment both for association which legitimately may be sanctioned and for association which may not be sanctioned consistently with First Amendment rights. Where statutes have an overbroad sweep, just as where they are vague, "the hazard of loss or substantial impairment of those precious rights may be critical," . . . since those covered by the statute are bound to limit their behavior to that which is unquestionably safe. As we said in Shelton v. Tucker, . . . "The breadth of legislative abridgment must be viewed in the light of less drastic means for achieving the same basic purpose."

We therefore hold that Civil Service Law § 105(1) (c) and Education Law § 3022(2) are invalid insofar as they sanction mere knowing membership without any showing of specific intent to further the unlawful aims of the Communist Party of the United States or of the State of New York.

Reversed and remanded.

Mr. Justice CLARK, with whom Mr. Justice HARLAN, Mr. Justice STEWART and Mr. Justice WHITE join, dissenting. . . .

It is clear that the Feinberg Law, in which this Court found "no constitutional infirmity" in 1952, has been given its death blow today. Just as the majority here finds that there "can be no doubt of the legitimacy of New York's interest in protecting its education system from subversion" there can also be no doubt that "the be-all and end-all" of New York's effort is here. And regardless of it correctness neither New York nor the several States that have followed the teaching of Adler for some 15 years, can ever put the

---

* See Justice Brennan's emphasis on the distinction between "overbreadth" and "vagueness" in Zwickler v. Koota, 389 U.S. 241 (1967). Zwickler was a challenge to a New York ban on the distribution of anonymous handbills. In explaining why federal court abstention was not appropriate, Justice Brennan's opinion for the Court noted that there was no question here of a construction of the statute that would avoid the federal question: "Appellant's challenge is not that the statute is void for 'vagueness,' that is, that it is a statute 'which either forbids or requires the doing of an act in terms so vague that men of common intelligence must necessarily guess at its meaning and differ as to its application . . . .' Connally v. General Construction Co., 269 U.S. 385, 391. Rather his constitutional attack is that the statute, although lacking nei- ther clarity nor precision, is void for 'overbreadth,' that is, that it offends the constitutional principle that 'a governmental purpose to control or prevent activities constitutionally subject to state regulation may not be achieved by means which sweep unnecessarily broadly and thereby invade the area of protected freedoms.' NAACP v. Alabama, 377 U.S. 288, 307. See Aptheker v. Secretary of State, 378 U.S. 500, 508–509; NAACP v. Button, 371 U.S. 415, 438; Louisiana ex rel. Gremillion v. NAACP, 366 U.S. 293; Shelton v. Tucker, 364 U.S. 479, 488; Schware v. Board of Bar Examiners, 353 U.S. 232, 246; Martin v. City of Struthers, 319 U.S. 141, 146–149; Cantwell v. Connecticut, 310 U.S. 296, 304–307; Schneider v. State, 308 U.S. 147, 161, 165. . . . " [See also the comments in chap. 16, p. 1325, infra.]

pieces together again. No court has ever reached out so far to destroy so much with so little. . . .

The majority says that the Feinberg Law is bad because it has an "overbroad sweep." I regret to say—and I do so with deference—that the majority has by its broadside swept away one of our most precious rights, namely, the right of self-preservation. Our public educational system is the genius of our democracy. The minds of our youth are developed there and the character of that development will determine the future of our land. Indeed, our very existence depends upon it. The issue here is a very narrow one. It is not freedom of speech, freedom of thought, freedom of press, freedom of assembly, or of association, even in the Communist Party. It is simply this: May the State provide that one who, after a hearing with full judicial review, is found to wilfully and deliberately advocate, advise, or teach that our Government should be overthrown by force or violence or other unlawful means; or who wilfully and deliberately prints, publishes, etc., any book or paper that so advocates *and who personally* advocates such doctrine himself; or who wilfully and deliberately becomes a member of an organization that advocates such doctrine, is prima facie disqualified from teaching in its university? My answer, in keeping with all of our cases up until today, is "Yes"! . . .*

SECTION 2. EXPRESSION IN PUBLIC PLACES AND THE MAINTENANCE OF ORDER: REGULATING THE PLACE AND MANNER RATHER THAN THE CONTENT OF SPEECH

A. DOCTRINAL FOUNDATIONS AND RECURRENT QUESTIONS

INTRODUCTION: THE FRANKFURTER SURVEY AND THE CONTOURS OF THE "PUBLIC FORUM"

Introduction. To what extent may cities regulate those who want to march in the streets or ring doorbells or meet in the parks to publicize their views? To what extent does concern with such values as order, quiet, and traffic justify the channeling of expression? Questions of governmental stability raised by subversive speech problems (sec. 1, supra) had been coming to the Court for 20 years before these issues of municipal tranquility spawned massive constitutional litigation. But the problems of the public forum have produced a constant flow of judicial business since the late 1930's, as a variety of minorities, from the Jehovah's Witnesses at the beginning to the civil rights demonstrators more recently, have sought access to streets and parks to change ideas and induce action. To what degree are these recurrent problems distinguishable from those considered in the preceding section?

---

* Note the further consideration of government employee security program problems in chap. 16, sec. 6, infra (including the reexamination of the Keyishian case, at p. 1330).

To what extent are the values and doctrines articulated there useful here? To what extent do these problems require new analyses?

1. *Justice Frankfurter's 1951 review.* [Consider, for an initial over-view, the following suggestions for grouping and handling the range of prob-lems. They are from a survey of the background written by Justice Frank-furter in 1951, after only a little more than a decade of Court experience with these questions. Justice Frankfurter undertook this review in a concurring opinion (in Niemotko v. Maryland, 340 U.S. 268, 273) reexamining the problem of "how to reconcile the interest in allowing free expression of ideas in public places with the protection of the public peace and the primary uses of streets and parks."* Justice Frankfurter stated in Niemotko:]

[The] precise problem presented by the three situations before us [is] how to reconcile the interest in allowing free expression of ideas in public places with the protection of the public peace and of the primary uses of streets and parks. [Past cases primarily] concerned with restrictions upon expression in its divers forms in public places have answered problems varying greatly in content and difficulty.

1.   The easiest cases have been those in which the only interest opposing free communication was that of keeping the streets of the community clean. This could scarcely justify prohibiting the dissemination of information by handbills or censoring their contents. [See Lovell v. Griffin, 303 U.S. 444 (1938), p. 1142 infra, on inadequate licensing standards.] In Schneider v. State, 308 U.S. 147 [1938], three of the four ordinances declared invalid by the Court prohibited the distribution of pamphlets. . . .

2.   In a group of related cases, regulation of solicitation has been the issue.   Here the opposing interest is more substantial—protection of the public from fraud and from criminals who use solicitation as a device to enter homes.   The fourth ordinance considered in Schneider v. State, supra, allowed the chief of police to refuse a permit if he found, in his discretion, that the canvasser was not of good character or was canvassing for a project not free from fraud.   The ordinance was found invalid because the officer who could, in his discretion, make the determinations concerning "good char-acter" and "project not free from fraud" in effect held the power of censor-ship.   In Cantwell v. Connecticut, 310 U.S. 296 [1941, p. 1147, infra], con-viction was, in part, under a State statute requiring a permit for religious solicitation.   The statute was declared invalid because the licensing official could determine what causes were religious, allowing a "censorship of re-ligion." . . . .   In Thomas v. Collins, 323 U.S. 516 [1945], the solicita-tion was in the interest of labor rather than religion.   There a State statute requiring registration of labor organizers was found unconstitutional when invoked to enjoin a speech in a public hall.   The interest of the State in protecting its citizens through the regulation of vocations was deemed in-sufficient to support the statute.

3.   Whether the sale of religious literature by Jehovah's Witnesses can be subjected to nondiscriminatory taxes on solicitation has introduced another opposing interest—the right of the community to raise funds for the support

---

* Justice Frankfurter's opinion was one concurring in the result in three cases (all considered further below): Feiner v. New York, 340 U.S. 315 (p. 1156) and   Kunz v. New York, 340 U.S. 290 (p. 1161), as well as Niemotko v. Mary-land, 340 U.S. 268 (p. 1159).

of the government.   [I]n Murdock v. Pennsylvania, 319 U.S. 105 [1944], the Court held that imposition of the tax upon itinerants was improper.   In Follett v. McCormick, 321 U.S. 573 [1944], the Court went further to hold unconstitutional the imposition of a flat tax on book agents upon a resident who made his living selling religious books.

4.   Martin v. Struthers, 319 U.S. 141 [1943], represents another situation.   An ordinance of the City of Struthers, Ohio, forbade knocking on the door or ringing the doorbell of a residence in order to deliver a handbill. Prevention of crime and assuring privacy in an industrial community where many worked on night shifts, and had to obtain their sleep during the day, were held insufficient to justify the ordinance in the case of handbills distributed on behalf of Jehovah's Witnesses.*

5.   In contrast to these decisions, the Court held in Prince v. Massachusetts, 321 U.S. 158 [1944], that the application to Jehovah's Witnesses of a State statute providing that no boy under 12 or girl under 18 should sell periodicals on the street was constitutional.   Claims of immunity from regulation of religious activities were subordinated to the interest of the State in protecting its children.†

6.   Control of speeches made in streets and parks draws on still different considerations—protection of the public peace and of the primary uses of travel and recreation for which streets and parks exist.   [An attempt to assert] the right of a city to exercise any power over its parks, however arbitrary or discriminatory, was rejected in Hague v. C. I. O. [307 U.S. 147 (1939)].   The ordinance presented in the Hague case required a permit for meetings on public ground, the permit to be refused by the licensing official only "for the purpose of preventing riots, disturbances or disorderly assemblage."   The facts of the case, however, left no doubt that the licensing power had been made an "instrument of arbitrary suppression of free expression of views on national affairs."   And the construction given the ordinance in the State courts gave the licensing officials wide discretion.   The holding of the Hague case was not that a city could not subject the use of its streets and parks to reasonable regulation.   The holding was that the licensing officials could not be given power arbitrarily to suppress free expression, no matter under what cover of law they purported to act.   Cox v. New Hampshire, 312 U.S. 569 [1941], made it clear that the United States Constitution does not deny localities the power to devise a licensing system if the

---

* Compare Breard v. City of Alexandria, 341 U.S. 622 (1951), where the Court sustained a city ordinance prohibiting door-to-door solicitation (in this case for subscriptions to nationally known out-of-State magazines) without the prior consent of the owners of the residences. Appellant's conviction for violation of the ordinance was affirmed by the Supreme Court. The rejection of his commerce clause claim is noted in chap. 8, p. 658, supra. The Court also found "no abridgment of the principles" of the First Amendment.   The constitutionality of the ordinance turns "upon a balancing of the conveniences between some householders' desire for privacy and the publisher's right to distribute publications in the precise way that those soliciting for him think brings the best results." Justice Black, joined by Justice Douglas, dissenting, thought the majority had revitalized the "judicial views which prevailed before this Court embraced the philosophy that the First Amendment gives a preferred status to the liberties it protects."

† On the cases in paragraphs 3, 4, and 5, see also the materials on the "free exercise of religion" guarantee, chap. 17, sec. 2, infra.

exercise of discretion by the licensing officials is appropriately confined [see p. 1143, infra].

(b) Two cases have involved the additional considerations incident to the use of sound trucks. [See the Saia and Kovacs cases, p. 1149, infra.]

(c) On a few occasions the Court has had to pass on a limitation upon speech by a sanction imposed after the event rather than by a licensing statute. In Cantwell v. Connecticut, supra, one of the convictions was for common-law breach of the peace. [See p. 1147, infra.] In Chaplinsky v. New Hampshire, 315 U.S. 568 [1942], a State statute had enacted the common-law doctrine of "fighting words." [See p. 1154, infra.]

7. One other case should be noted, although it involved a conviction for breach of peace in a private building, rather than in a public place. [Terminiello v. Chicago, 337 U.S. 1 (1940), see p. 1155, infra.]

The results in these multifarious cases have been expressed in language looking in two directions. While the Court has emphasized the importance of "free speech," it has recognized that "free speech" is not in itself a touch-stone. The Constitution is not unmindful of other important interests, such as public order, if interference with free expression of ideas is not found to be the overbalancing consideration. More important than the phrasing of the opinions are the questions on which the decisions appear to have turned.

(1) What is the interest deemed to require the regulation of speech? The State cannot of course forbid public proselyting or religious argument merely because public officials disapprove the speaker's views. It must act in patent good faith to maintain the public peace, to assure the availability of the streets for their primary purposes of passenger and vehicular traffic, or for equally indispensable ends of modern community life.

(2) What is the method used to achieve such ends as a consequence of which public speech is constrained or barred? A licensing standard which gives an official authority to censor the content of a speech differs *toto cælo* from one limited by its terms, or by nondiscriminatory practice, to considerations of public safety and the like. Again, a sanction applied after the event assures consideration of the particular circumstances of a situation. The net of control must not be cast too broadly.

(3) What mode of speech is regulated? A sound truck may be found to affect the public peace as normal speech does not. A man who is calling names or using the kind of language which would reasonably stir another to violence does not have the same claim to protection as one whose speech is an appeal to reason.

(4) Where does the speaking which is regulated take place? Not only the general classifications—streets, parks, private buildings—are relevant. The location and size of a park; its customary use for the recreational, esthetic and contemplative needs of a community; the facilities, other than a park or street corner, readily available in a community for airing views, are all pertinent considerations in assessing the limitations the Fourteenth Amendment puts on State power in a particular situation. . . .

2. *Substantive evils, "primary uses," and the "public forum."* a. Are the problems surveyed by Justice Frankfurter susceptible to solution via the clear and present danger formula? That test is mentioned in a number of the opinions—several early ones (e. g., Schneider v. State and Cantwell v. Con-

necticut, among those cited by Justice Frankfurter) as well as a few subsequent ones (e. g., Edwards v. South Carolina, 372 U.S. 299 (1963), p. 1164, infra). But, as suggested earlier, (p. 1079, supra), *proximity* to the "substantive evil" is not the major problem here, is it? Is not the often more difficult issue the assessment of the *gravity* of the evil? If street-littering is the risk, is not the more significant question whether that risk is sufficiently substantial to warrant a ban on leafleting, rather than whether leafleting creates an immediate risk of the littering evil? Is the problem more susceptible to a less-restrictive-alternatives, overbroadness analysis than to a clear and present danger one? To other analyses?

b.   Justice Frankfurter and many of the cases speak of "protection of public peace" and "the primary use of streets and parks" as the interests limiting expression. Does that formulation adequately confront the importance of access to streets and parks if certain views are to be heard? Does "primary use of streets [traffic?] and parks [recreation?]" suggest that use of streets and parks for speech is ordinarily a secondary one, to be subordinated whenever traffic or recreation are really threatened? Does it suggest that a state can bar the use of public places for expression completely, for the purpose of protecting the "primary" uses? But should not free speech values compel traffic and recreation to give way to speech, sometimes? If the dimensions of that "sometimes" are a central issue in this area, do the Court analyses sufficiently promote inquiry into those dimensions?

c.   Is an emphasis different from that of Justice Frankfurter suggested by a comment in one of the early cases cited by him, Hague v. CIO, 307 U.S. 496 (1939): "Wherever the title of streets and parks may rest, they have immemorially been held in trust for the use of the public and, time out of mind, have been used for purposes of assembly, communicating thoughts between citizens, and discussing public questions. Such use of the streets and public places has, from ancient times, been a part of the privileges, immunities, rights and liberties of citizens." * Does that not suggest that "discussing public questions" is also a "primary use" of streets and parks? And does that not suggest delineation of the contours of the "public forum" as a major focus of free speech cases in this area? Does the Frankfurter discussion reflect such a focus? To what extent do the cases that follow?

See generally Kalven, "The Concept of the Public Forum: Cox v. Louisiana," 1965 Sup.Ct.Rev. 1. Professor Kalven suggests that "public places are an important facility for public discussion"; that "only confusion can result from distinguishing sharply between 'speech pure' and 'speech plus'"; and that "what is required is in effect a set of Robert's Rules of Order for the new uses of the public forum." To what extent do the cases in this section adequately recognize the importance of the public forum? How useful are distinctions of "speech pure"-"speech plus"? Of "speech"-"conduct"? Of "manner"-"content"? Is the "Robert's Rules" concept a "happy analogy" because, as Kalven suggests, "concern ought not to be with censorship,

---

* Compare that emphasis with Holmes' Davis v. Massachusetts position, on which the city had relied in Hague to justify a permit scheme for use of public places. Davis v. Massachusetts, 167 U.S. 43 (1897), affirmed a decision in which Justice Holmes had said on the state court: "For the legislature absolutely or conditionally to forbid public speaking on a highway or public park is no more an infringement of rights of a member of the public than for the owner of a private house to forbid it in the house."

or with the content of what is said; what is needed is a phasing or timing of the activity, not a ban on it"? What should be the content of a judicially developed set of "Robert's Rules of Order" for the "uses of the public forum"?

SOME EARLY CASES

What did the early public forum cases contribute to the pursuit of these questions? In addition to the cases noted in the Frankfurter review and related materials above, note the cases which follow: Lovell v. Griffin and Cox v. New Hampshire, early guideposts regarding the impermissible and the permissible in licensing ordinances, and Cantwell v. Connecticut, an early example of the control of street use through a breach of the peace prosecution. Both techniques of control—prior licensing and subsequent punishment—recur in the later materials on the use of public places.

LOVELL v. CITY OF GRIFFIN

303 U.S. 444, 58 S.Ct. 666, 82 L.Ed. 949 (1938).

Appeal from the Court of Appeals of Georgia.

Mr. Chief Justice HUGHES delivered the opinion of the Court.

Appellant, Alma Lovell, was convicted in the Recorder's Court of the City of Griffin, Georgia, of the violation of a city ordinance and was sentenced to imprisonment for fifty days in default of the payment of a fine of fifty dollars. . . . . The ordinance in question is as follows:

"Section 1. That the practice of distributing . . . circulars, handbooks, advertising, or literature of any kind, . . . within the limits of the City of Griffin, without first obtaining written permission from the City Manager of the City of Griffin, ... shall be deemed a nuisance, and punishable as an offense against the City of Griffin.

"Section 2. The Chief of Police of the City of Griffin and the police force of the City of Griffin are hereby required and directed to suppress the same and to abate any nuisance as is described in the first section of this ordinance."

The violation, which is not denied, consisted of the distribution without the required permission of a pamphlet and magazine in the nature of religious tracts, setting forth the gospel of the "Kingdom of Jehovah." Appellant did not apply for a permit, as she regarded herself as sent "by Jehovah to do His work" and that such an application would have been "an act of disobedience to His commandment". [At the trial, appellant claimed that the ordinance abridged "freedom of the press" and "the free exercise of (her) religion."]

The ordinance in its broad sweep prohibits the distribution of "circulars, handbooks, advertising, or literature of any kind." It manifestly applies to pamphlets, magazines and periodicals. The evidence against appellant was that she distributed a certain pamphlet and a magazine called the "Golden Age". Whether in actual administration the ordinance is applied, as apparently it could be, to newspapers does not appear. The City Manager testified that "every one applied to me for a license to distribute literature in this City.

None of these people (including de_endant) secured a permit from me to distribute literature in the City of Griffin." The ordinance is not limited to "literature" that is obscene or offensive to public morals or that advocates unlawful conduct. There is no suggestion that the pamphlet and magazine distributed in the instant case were of that character. The ordinance embraces "literature" in the widest sense.

The ordinance is comprehensive with respect to the method of distribution. It covers every sort of circulation "either by hand or otherwise." There is thus no restriction in its application with respect to time or place. It is not limited to ways which might be regarded as inconsistent with the maintenance of public order or as involving disorderly conduct, the molestation of the inhabitants, or the misuse or littering of the streets. The ordinance prohibits the distribution of literature of any kind at any time, at any place, and in any manner without a permit from the City Manager.

We think that the ordinance is invalid on its face. Whatever the motive which induced its adoption, its character is such that it strikes at the very foundation of the freedom of the press by subjecting it to license and censorship. The struggle for the freedom of the press was primarily directed against the power of the licensor. It was against that power that John Milton directed his assault by his "Appeal for the Liberty of Unlicensed Printing." And the liberty of the press became initially a right to publish "*without* a license what formerly could be published only *with* one." While this freedom from previous restraint upon publication cannot be regarded as exhausting the guaranty of liberty, the prevention of that restraint was a leading purpose in the adoption of the constitutional provision. [Near v. Minnesota, 283 U.S. 697, p. 1258, infra.] . . .

As the ordinance is void on its face, it was not necessary for appellant to seek a permit under it. She was entitled to contest its validity in answer to the charge against her. . . .

Reversed.

There are no standards in the statute for giving or not giving a license, thus making this ordinance bad.

COX v. NEW HAMPSHIRE

312 U.S. 569, 61 S.Ct. 762, 85 L.Ed. 1049 (1941).

Appeal from the Supreme Court of New Hampshire.

Mr. Chief Justice HUGHES delivered the opinion of the Court.

Appellants are five "Jehovah's Witnesses" who, with sixty-three others of the same persuasion, were convicted in the municipal court of Manchester, New Hampshire, for violation of a state statute prohibiting a "parade or procession" upon a public street without a special license.

[A]ppellants raised the questions that the statute was invalid under the Fourteenth Amendment of the Constitution of the United States in that it deprived appellants of their rights of freedom of worship, freedom of speech and press, and freedom of assembly, vested unreasonable and unlimited arbitrary and discriminatory powers in the licensing authority, and was vague and indefinite. These contentions were overruled and the case comes here on appeal.

The statutory prohibition is as follows (New Hampshire, P.L., Chap. 145, § 2): "No theatrical or dramatic representation shall be performed or exhibited, and no parade or procession upon any public street or way, and no open-air public meeting upon any ground abutting thereon, shall be permitted, unless a special license therefor shall first be obtained from the selectmen of the town, or from a licensing committee for cities hereinafter provided for." The provisions for licensing are set forth in the margin.[1]

The facts, which are conceded by the appellants to be established by the evidence, are these: The sixty-eight defendants and twenty other persons met at a hall in the City of Manchester on the evening of Saturday, July 8, 1939, "for the purpose of engaging in an information march." The company was divided into four or five groups, each with about fifteen to twenty persons. Each group then proceeded to a different part of the business district of the city and there "would line up in single-file formation and then proceed to march along the sidewalk, 'single-file,' that is, following one another." Each of the defendants carried a small staff with a sign reading "Religion is a Snare and a Racket" and on the reverse "Serve God and Christ the King." Some of the marchers carried placards bearing the statement "Fascism or Freedom. Hear Judge Rutherford and Face the Facts." The marchers also handed out printed leaflets announcing a meeting to be held at a later time in the hall from which they had started, where a talk on government would be given to the public free of charge. Defendants did not apply for a permit and none was issued.

. . . The recital of facts which prefaced the opinion of the state court thus summarizes the effect of the march: "Manchester had a population of over 75,000 in 1930, and there was testimony that on Saturday nights in an hour's time 26,000 persons passed one of the intersections where the defendants marched. The marchers interfered with the normal sidewalk travel, but no technical breach of the peace occurred. The march was a prearranged affair, and no permit for it was sought, although the defendants understood that under the statute one was required." . . .

The sole charge against appellants was that they were "taking part in a parade or procession" on public streets without a permit as the statute required. They were not prosecuted for distributing leaflets, or for conveying information by placards or otherwise, or for issuing invitations to a public meeting, or for holding a public meeting, or for maintaining or expressing

---

1. New Hampshire, P.L., Chap. 145, §§ 3, 4, and 5 are as follows:

"Section 3: Licensing Board. Any city may create a licensing board to consist of the person who is the active head of the police department, the mayor of such city and one other person who shall be appointed by the city government, which board shall have delegated powers to investigate and decide the question of granting licenses under this chapter, and it may grant revocable blanket licenses to fraternal and other like organizations, to theatres and to undertakers.

"Section 4: Licenses: Fees. Every such special license shall be in writing, and shall specify the day and hour of the permit to perform or exhibit or of

such parade, procession or open-air public meeting. Every licensee shall pay in advance for such license, for the use of the city or town, a sum not more than three hundred dollars for each day such licensee shall perform or exhibit, or such parade, procession or open-air public meeting shall take place; but the fee for a license to exhibit in any hall shall not exceed fifty dollars.

"Section 5: Penalty. If any person shall violate the provisions of the preceding sections he shall be fined not more than five hundred dollars; and it shall be the duty of the selectmen to prosecute for every violation of this chapter." [Footnote by the Court.]

religious beliefs. Their right to do any one of these things apart from engaging in a "parade or procession" upon a public street is not here involved and the question of the validity of a statute addressed to any other sort of conduct than that complained of is not before us.

Civil liberties, as guaranteed by the Constitution, imply the existence of an organized society maintaining public order without which liberty itself would be lost in the excesses of unrestrained abuses. The authority of a municipality to impose regulations in order to assure the safety and convenience of the people in the use of public highways has never been regarded as inconsistent with civil liberties but rather as one of the means of safeguarding the good order upon which they ultimately depend. The control of travel on the streets of cities is the most familiar illustration of this recognition of social need. Where a restriction of the use of highways in that relation is designed to promote the public convenience in the interest of all, it cannot be disregarded by the attempted exercise of some civil right which in other circumstances would be entitled to protection. One would not be justified in ignoring the familiar red traffic light because he thought it his religious duty to disobey the municipal command or sought by that means to direct public attention to an announcement of his opinions. As regulation of the use of the streets for parades and processions is a traditional exercise of control by local government, the question in a particular case is whether that control is exerted so as not to deny or unwarrantedly abridge the right of assembly and the opportunities for the communication of thought and the discussion of public questions immemorially associated with resort to public places. Lovell v. Griffin, 303 U.S. 444, 451; Hague v. Committee for Industrial Organization, 307 U.S. 496, 515, 516; Schneider v. State, 308 U.S. 147, 160; Cantwell v. Connecticut, 310 U.S. 296, 306, 307.

In the instant case, we are aided by the opinion of the Supreme Court of the State, which construed the statute and defined the limitations of the authority conferred for the granting of licenses for parades and processions. The court observed that if the clause of the Act requiring a license "for all open-air public meetings upon land contiguous to a highway" was invalid, that invalidity did not nullify the Act in its application to the other situations described. Recognizing the importance of the civil liberties invoked by appellants, the court thought it significant that the statute prescribed "no measures for controlling or suppressing the publication on the highways of facts and opinions, either by speech or by writing"; that communication "by the distribution of literature or by the display of placards and signs" was in no respect regulated by the statute; that the regulation with respect to parades and processions was applicable only "to organized formations of persons using the highways"; and that "the defendants, separately, or collectively in groups not constituting a parade or procession," were "under no contemplation of the Act." In this light, the court thought that interference with liberty of speech and writing seemed slight; that the distribution of pamphlets and folders by the groups "traveling in unorganized fashion" would have had as large a circulation, and that "signs carried by members of the groups not in marching formation would have been as conspicuous, as published by them while in parade or procession."

It was with this view of the limited objective of the statute that the state court considered and defined the duty of the licensing authority and the rights of the appellants to a license for their parade, with regard only to considerations of time, place and manner so as to conserve the public convenience. The obvious advantage of requiring application for a permit was noted as giving the public authorities notice in advance so as to afford opportunity for proper policing. And the court further observed that, in fixing time and place, the license served "to prevent confusion by overlapping parades or processions, to secure convenient use of the streets by other travelers, and to minimize the risk of disorder." But the court held that the licensing board was not vested with arbitrary power or an unfettered discretion; that its discretion must be exercised with "uniformity of method of treatment upon the facts of each application, free from improper or inappropriate considerations and from unfair discrimination"; that a "systematic, consistent and just order of treatment, with reference to the convenience of public use of the highways, is the statutory mandate." The defendants, said the court, "had a right, under the Act, to a license to march when, where and as they did, if after a required investigation it was found that the convenience of the public in the use of the streets would not thereby be unduly disturbed, upon such conditions or changes in time, place and manner as would avoid disturbance."

If a municipality has authority to control the use of its public streets for parades or processions, as it undoubtedly has, it cannot be denied authority to give consideration, without unfair discrimination, to time, place and manner in relation to the other proper uses of the streets. We find it impossible to say that the limited authority conferred by the licensing provisions of the statute in question as thus construed by the state court contravened any constitutional right.

There remains the question of license fees which, as the court said, had a permissible range from $300 to a nominal amount. The court construed the Act as requiring "a reasonable fixing of the amount of the fee." . . . "The charge," said the court, "for a circus parade or a celebration procession of length, each drawing crowds of observers, would take into account the greater public expense of policing the spectacle, compared with the slight expense of a less expansive and attractive parade or procession, to which the charge would be adjusted." The fee was held to be "not a revenue tax, but one to meet the expense incident to the administration of the Act and to the maintenance of public order in the matter licensed." There is nothing contrary to the Constitution in the charge of a fee limited to the purpose stated. The suggestion that a flat fee should have been charged fails to take account of the difficulty of framing a fair schedule to meet all circumstances, and we perceive no constitutional ground for denying to local governments that flexibility of adjustment of fees which in the light of varying conditions would tend to conserve rather than impair the liberty sought.

There is no evidence that the statute has been administered otherwise than in the fair and non-discriminatory manner which the state court has construed it to require.

The decisions upon which appellants rely are not applicable. In Lovell v. Griffin, supra, the ordinance prohibited the distribution of literature of any kind at any time, at any place, and in any manner without a permit from the city manager, thus striking at the very foundation of the freedom of the press by subjecting it to license and censorship. In Hague v. Committee for

Industrial Organization, supra, the ordinance dealt with the exercise of the right of assembly for the purpose of communicating views; it did not make comfort or convenience in the use of streets the standard of official action but enabled the local official absolutely to refuse a permit on his mere opinion that such refusal would prevent "riots, disturbances or disorderly assemblage." The ordinance thus created, as the record disclosed, an instrument of arbitrary suppression of opinions on public questions. . . .

In Schneider v. State, supra, the ordinance was directed at canvassing and banned unlicensed communication of any views, or the advocacy of any cause, from door to door, subject only to the power of a police officer to determine as a censor what literature might be distributed and who might distribute it. In Cantwell v. Connecticut, supra, the statute dealt with the solicitation of funds for religious causes and authorized an official to determine whether the cause was a religious one and to refuse a permit if he determined it was not, thus establishing a censorship of religion. . . .

The argument as to freedom of worship is also beside the point. No interference with religious worship or the practice of religion in any proper sense is shown, but only the exercise of local control over the use of streets for parades and processions.

Affirmed.*

CANTWELL v. CONNECTICUT

310 U.S. 296, 60 S.Ct. 900, 84 L.Ed. 1213 (1940).

Appeal from and certiorari to the Supreme Court of Errors of Connecticut.

Mr. Justice ROBERTS delivered the opinion of the Court.

Newton Cantwell and his two sons, Jesse and Russell, members of a group know as Jehovah's Witnesses, and claiming to be ordained ministers, were arrested in New Haven, Connecticut, and each was charged by information in five counts, with statutory and common law offenses. [E]ach of them was convicted on the third count, which charged a violation of [a statute] and on the fifth count, which charged commission of the common law offense of inciting a breach of the peace. On appeal to the Supreme Court the conviction of all three on the third count was affirmed. The conviction of Jesse Cantwell, on the fifth count, was also affirmed, but the conviction of Newton and Russell on that count was reversed and a new trial ordered as to them. [The third count charged violation of a statute banning solicitation without a permit. Justice Roberts concluded: "[T]o condition the solicitation of aid for the perpetuation of religious views or systems upon a license, the grant of which rests in the exercise of a determination by state authority

---

* Why could the appellants in Cox not claim that the statute was void on its face because of the vague standards at the time of their march, and that this vagueness could not be cured as to them by the state court's post-conviction narrowing of the statute? Compare the Court's explanation and distinction of this aspect of Cox in Shuttlesworth v. Birmingham, 394 U.S. 147 (1969), p. 1187, infra. Note the Court's frequent reliance on Cox, however, with respect to the state's power to regulate "time, place, or manner" through "properly drawn" licensing statutes. See, e. g., Cox v. Louisiana, 379 U.S. 536 (1965), p. 1165, infra.

as to what is a religious cause, is to lay a forbidden burden upon the exercise of liberty protected by the Constitution."]

We hold that, in the circumstances disclosed the conviction of Jesse Cantwell on the fifth count must [also] be set aside. Decision as to the lawfulness of the conviction demands the weighing of two conflicting interests. The fundamental law declares the interest of the United States that the free exercise of religion be not prohibited and that freedom to communicate information and opinion be not abridged. The State of Connecticut has an obvious interest in the preservation and protection of peace and good order within her borders. We must determine whether the alleged protection of the State's interest, means to which end would, in the absence of limitation by the Federal Constitution, lie wholly within the State's discretion, has been pressed, in this instance, to a point where it has come into fatal collision with the overriding interest protected by the federal compact.

Conviction on the fifth count was not pursuant to a statute evincing a legislative judgment that street discussion of religious affairs, because of its tendency to provoke disorder, should be regulated, or a judgment that the playing of a phonograph on the streets should in the interest of comfort or privacy be limited or prevented. Violation of an Act exhibiting such a legislative judgment and narrowly drawn to prevent the supposed evil, would pose a question differing from what we must here answer. Such a declaration of the State's policy would weigh heavily in any challenge of the law as infringing constitutional limitations. Here however, the judgment is based on a common law concept of the most general and undefined nature. The court below has held that the petitioner's conduct constituted the commission of an offense under the state law, and we accept its decision as binding upon us to that extent.

The offense known as breach of the peace embraces a great variety of conduct destroying or menacing public order and tranquility. It includes not only violent acts but acts and words likely to produce violence in others. No one would have the hardihood to suggest that the principle of freedom of speech sanctions incitement to riot or that religious liberty connotes the privilege to exhort others to physical attack upon those belonging to another sect. When clear and present danger of riot, disorder, interference with traffic upon the public streets, or other immediate threat to public safety, peace, or order appears, the power of the State to prevent or punish is obvious. Equally obvious is it that a State may not unduly suppress free communication of views, religious or other, under the guise of conserving desirable conditions. Here we have a situation analogous to a conviction under a statute sweeping in a great variety of conduct under a general and indefinite characterization, and leaving to the executive and judicial branches too wide a discretion in its application.

Having these considerations in mind, we note that Jesse Cantwell, on April 26, 1938, was upon a public street, where he had a right to be, and where he had a right peacefully to impart his views to others. There is no showing that his deportment was noisy, truculent, overbearing or offensive. . . . . It is not claimed that he intended to insult or affront the hearers by playing the record. It is plain that he wished only to interest them in his propaganda. The sound of the phonograph is not shown to have disturbed residents of the street, to have drawn a crowd, or to have impeded traffic. Thus far he had invaded no right or interest of the public or of the men accosted.

The record played by Cantwell embodies a general attack on all organized religious systems as instruments of Satan and injurious to man; it then singles out the Roman Catholic Church for strictures couched in terms which naturally would offend not only persons of that persuasion, but all others who respect the honestly held religious faith of their fellows. The hearers were in fact highly offended. One of them said he felt like hitting Cantwell and the other that he was tempted to throw Cantwell off the street. The one who testified he felt like hitting Cantwell said, in answer to the question "Did you do anything else or have any other reaction?" "No, sir, because he said he would take the victrola and he went." The other witness testified that he told Cantwell he had better get off the street before something happened to him and that was the end of the matter as Cantwell picked up his books and walked up the street.

Cantwell's conduct, in the view of the court below, considered apart from the effect of his communication upon his hearers, did not amount to a breach of the peace. One may, however, be guilty of the offense if he commit acts or make statements likely to provoke violence and disturbance of good order, even though no such eventuality be intended. Decisions to this effect are many, but examination discloses, that in practically all, the provocative language which was held to amount to a breach of the peace consisted of profane, indecent, or abusive remarks directed to the person of the hearer. Resort to epithets or personal abuse is not in any proper sense communication of information or opinion safeguarded by the Constitution, and its punishment as a criminal act would raise no question under that instrument.

We find in the instant case no assault or threatening of bodily harm, no truculent bearing, no intentional discourtesy, no personal abuse. On the contrary, we find only an effort to persuade a willing listener to buy a book or to contribute money in the interest of what Cantwell, however misguided others may think him, conceived to be true religion. . . .

Although the contents of the record not unnaturally aroused animosity, we think that, in the absence of a statute narrowly drawn to define and punish specific conduct as constituting a clear and present danger to a substantial interest of the State, the petitioner's communication, considered in the light of the constitutional guarantees, raised no such clear and present menace to public peace and order as to render him liable to conviction of the common law offense in question. . . .

Reversed.

B. EVOLVING DOCTRINES: NOISY, ABRASIVE SPEAKERS; SENSITIVE, HOSTILE AUDIENCES

THE LOUDSPEAKER CASES

Introduction. Two decisions in the late 1940's dealing with control of amplified sounds bear not only on the specific loudspeaker question but also suggest evolving approaches to more general problems: the justifications that may support total prohibition of some manifestations of speech; the significance of the city's methods of control as well as the speaker's method of communication; the Justices' varying sensitivity toward a claim that a particular forum is necessary to enable the speaker to reach an audience.

1. *Saia.* In Saia v. New York, 334 U.S. 558 (1948), the Court held "invalid on its face" a Lockport, N. Y., ordinance prohibiting the use of amplification devices without the permission of the police chief. Justice Douglas' opinion for the majority found that the ordinance established an unconstitutional "previous restraint" on free speech with "no standards prescribed for the exercise of" the administrative discretion. He stated:

"Loud-speakers are today indispensable instruments of effective public speech. The sound truck has become an accepted method of political campaigning. It is the way people are reached. Must a candidate for governor or the Congress depend on the whim or caprice of the Chief of Police in order to use his sound truck for campaigning? Must he prove to the satisfaction of that official that his noise will not be annoying to people?

"The present ordinance would be a dangerous weapon if it were allowed to get a hold on our public life. Noise can be regulated by regulating decibels. The hours and place of public discussion can be controlled. But to allow the police to bar the use of loud-speakers because their use can be abused is like barring radio receivers because they too make a noise. The police need not be given the power to deny a man the use of his radio in order to protect a neighbor against sleepless nights. The same is true here.

"Any abuses which loud-speakers create can be controlled by narrowly drawn statutes. When a city allows an official to ban them in his uncontrolled discretion, it sanctions a device for suppression of free communication of ideas. In this case a permit is denied because some persons were said to have found the sound annoying. In the next one a permit may be denied because some people find the ideas annoying. Annoyance at ideas can be cloaked in annoyance at sound. The power of censorship inherent in this type of ordinance reveals its vice."

Justice Frankfurter, joined by Justices Reed and Burton, dissented: "[M]odern devices for amplifying the range and volume of the voice, or its recording, afford easy, too easy, opportunities for aural aggression. If uncontrolled, the result is intrusion into cherished privacy. The refreshment of mere silence, or meditation, or quiet conversation, may be disturbed or precluded by noise beyond one's personal control.

"Municipalities have conscientiously sought to deal with the new problems to which sound equipment has given rise and have devised various methods of control to make city life endurable. . . . Surely there is not a constitutional right to force unwilling people to listen. . . . And so I cannot agree that we must deny the right of a State to control these broadcasting devices so as to safeguard the rights of others not to be assailed by intrusive noise but to be free to put their freedom of mind and attention to uses of their own choice." Justice Jackson also dissented.

2. *Kovacs.* In Kovacs v. Cooper, 336 U.S. 77 (1949), one year after Saia, the Court sustained application of a Trenton, N. J., ordinance designed to regulate loud-speakers. Kovacs was convicted of violating a ban on "any device known as a sound truck, loud speaker or sound amplifier . . .

which emits therefrom loud and raucous noises and is attached to and upon any vehicle operated or standing upon . . . streets or public places."

Justice Reed's opinion announcing the judgment of the Court was joined only by Chief Justice Vinson and Justice Burton. He rejected the claim that "loud and raucous" were unduly vague terms. He continued: "Unrestrained use throughout a municipality of all sound amplifying devices would be intolerable. Absolute prohibition within limits of all sound amplification, even though reasonably regulated in place, time and volume, is undesirable and probably unconstitutional as an unreasonable interference with normal activities." He found that the ordinance, as construed by the state court, "applies only to vehicles with sound amplifiers emitting loud and raucous noises" and proceeded:

"City streets are recognized as a normal place for the exchange of ideas by speech or paper. But this does not mean the freedom is beyond all control. We think it is a permissible exercise of legislative discretion to bar sound trucks with broadcasts of public interest, amplified to a loud and raucous volume, from the public ways of municipalities. On the business streets of cities like Trenton, with its more than 125,000 people, such distractions would be dangerous to traffic at all hours useful for the dissemination of information, and in the residential thoroughfares the quiet and tranquility so desirable for city dwellers would likewise be at the mercy of advocates of particular religious, social or political persuasions. We cannot believe that rights of free speech compel a municipality to allow such mechanical voice amplification on any of its streets.

"The right of free speech is guaranteed every citizen that he may reach the minds of willing listeners and to do so there must be opportunity to win their attention. This is the phase of freedom of speech that is involved here. We do not think the Trenton ordinance abridges that freedom. The preferred position of freedom of speech in a society that cherishes liberty for all does not require legislators to be insensible to claims by citizens to comfort and convenience. To enforce freedom of speech in disregard of the rights of others would be harsh and arbitrary in itself. That more people may be more easily and cheaply reached by sound trucks, perhaps borrowed without cost from some zealous supporter, is not enough to call forth constitutional protection for what those charged with public welfare reasonably think is a nuisance when easy means of publicity are open. . . . There is no restriction upon the communication of ideas or discussion of issues by the human voice, by newspapers, by pamphlets, by dodgers. We think that the need for reasonable protection in the homes or business houses from the distracting noises of vehicles equipped with such sound amplifying devices justifies the ordinance."

Justice Black, joined by Justices Douglas and Rutledge, dissented: "The appellant was neither charged with nor convicted of operating a sound truck that emitted 'loud and raucous noises'. The charge . . . in the police court was that he violated the city ordinance 'in that he did, on South Stockton Street, in said City, play, use and operate a device known as a sound truck.' The record reflects not even a shadow of evidence to prove that the noise was either 'loud or raucous,' unless these words of the ordinance refer to any noise coming from an amplifier, whatever its volume or tone. [The] ordinance here sustained goes beyond a mere prior censorship of all loud speakers with authority in the censor to prohibit some of them. This Trenton ordinance wholly bars the use of all loud speakers mounted upon any vehicle in any of the city's public streets. In my view this repudiation of the prior Saia opinion makes a dangerous and unjustifiable breach in the constitutional barriers designed to insure freedom of expression. . . . The basic premise of the First Amendment is that all present instruments of communication, as well as others that inventive genius may bring into being, shall be free from governmental censorship or prohibition. Laws which hamper the free use of some instruments of communication thereby favor competing channels. [Laws like this] can give an overpowering influence to views of owners of legally favored instruments of communication. [I]t is an obvious fact that public speaking today without sound amplifiers is a wholly inadequate way to reach the people on a large scale. . . .

"A city ordinance that reasonably restricts the volume of sound, or the hours during which an amplifier may be used, does not, in my mind, infringe the constitutionally protected area of free speech. It is because this ordinance does none of these things, but is instead an absolute prohibition of all uses of an amplifier on any of the streets of Trenton at any time that I must dissent." Justice Rutledge submitted a separate dissenting opinion. Justice Murphy also dissented, without opinion.

Justice Jackson concurred on the ground that "operation of mechanical sound-amplifying devices conflicts with quiet enjoyment of home and park and with safe and legitimate use of street and market place, and that it is constitutionally subject to regulation or prohibition by the state or municipal authority. No violation of the Due Process Clause of the Fourteenth Amendment by reason of infringement of free speech arises unless such regulation or prohibition undertakes to censor the contents of the broadcasting. Freedom of speech for Kovacs does not, in my view, include freedom to use sound amplifiers to drown out the natural speech of others.

"I do not agree that, if we sustain regulations or prohibitions of sound trucks, they must therefore be valid if applied to other methods of 'communication of ideas.' The moving picture screen, the radio, the newspaper, the handbill, the sound truck and the street corner orator have differing natures, values, abuses and dangers. Each, in my view, is a law unto itself, and all we are dealing with now is the sound truck.

"But I agree with Mr. Justice Black that this decision is a repudiation of that in Saia . . . . Like him, I am unable to find anything in this record to warrant a distinction because of 'loud and raucous' tones of this machine. The Saia decision struck down a more moderate exercise of the state's police power than the one now sustained. Trenton, as the ordinance reads to me, unconditionally bans all sound trucks from the city streets. Lockport relaxed its prohibition with a proviso to allow their use, even in areas set aside for public recreation, when and where the Chief of Police saw no objection."

In another concurring opinion, Justice Frankfurter said it would be "an unreality" to dispose of this case on the assumption that Saia was rightly decided and reaffirmed his dissenting views in Saia. Most of his opinion was devoted to "observations" on Justice Reed's reference to "the preferred position of freedom of speech." [Some of these comments are printed at the beginning of this chapter, p. 1053, supra].

3. *The noisy speaker's public forum.*   Do Saia and Kovacs make sense if Kovacs is read in accordance with the Jackson and Black views? Is the vice of the administrative censorship risk in a vague licensing ordinance (cf. Lovell v. Griffin, p. 1142, supra) greater than the vice of total silencing of the communication channel?   Was virtually total prohibition of loudspeakers justified because of a legislative judgment that a particular method of communication is obnoxious?   Would a specific ban on all speeches or marches in residential neighborhoods be similarly supportable on grounds of deference to legislative judgment?   A ban on all street demonstrations?   Would it depend on the available alternative communication channels?   On those available to the particular speaker?   Unless at least some inquiry into alternative outlets is made, can there be adequate respect for the public forum concept?   Was there such an inquiry in Kovacs?   Was total prohibition of loudspeakers permissible only because those speakers had other adequate outlets?   Or was it enough that a legislative ordinance had decided that this outlet was too annoying?

4. *The captive audience.*   In his Kovacs opinion, Justice Reed distinguished the loudspeaker problem from other restrictions on expression: "While [the Court] has invalidated an ordinance forbidding a distributor of pamphlets or handbills from summoning householders to their doors to receive the distributor's writings, this was on the ground that the home owner could protect himself from such intrusion by an appropriate sign 'that he is unwilling to be disturbed.'   The Court never intimated that the visitor could insert a foot in the door and insist on a hearing.   Martin v. City of Struthers [319 U.S. 141 (1943)]."   But "the unwilling listener is not like the passerby who may be offered a pamphlet in the street but cannot be made to take it.   In his home or on the street he is practically helpless to escape this interference with his privacy by loud speakers except through the protection of the municipality."   And in dissenting in Saia, Justice Jackson had considered sound truck regulation "not only appropriate," but "a duty of the city."

Can the unwilling listener make a First Amendment claim to protection from "aural aggression"?   See Public Utilities Comm'n v. Pollak, 343 U.S. 451 (1951), where a bus company installed FM radio receivers in its vehicles and broadcast special programs consisting of 90% music, 5% news, and 5% commercial advertising.   The District Public Utilities Commission initiated an investigation.   Pollak and Martin, two protesting passengers, intervened.   The Commission found that the use of the radios was "not inconsistent with public convenience, comfort and, safety."   Did the passengers have any basis for a constitutional challenge?   The Court majority found no First Amendment or Fifth Amendment (privacy) flaw.   Justice Douglas' dissent emphasized the right to be let alone.   Justice Frankfurter refused to participate because "my feelings are so strongly engaged as a victim of the practice in controversy."   See C. L. Black, "He Cannot Choose But Hear: The Plight of the Captive Auditor," 53 Colum.L.Rev. 960 (1953).

PROVOCATIVE SPEECH AND THE HOSTILE AUDIENCE

Introduction. Does hostile audience reaction justify restricting the speaker? Only if the speaker uses extremely provocative words? Even if the audience is very easily provoked, by speeches short of "fighting words"? Does the First Amendment impose an obligation on the government to protect the speaker from the angry crowd? Must government attempt to preserve peace by restraining listeners rather than speakers? Or may government stop the speaker simply by showing that his words provoked disorder (or created an immediate danger of disorder)? Does that legitimate a "heckler's veto"? Must some protection of the provocative speaker be assured lest the public forum be blocked by the "heckler's veto"? How effectively have the cases dealt with this Robert's Rules problem?

Recall the Court's comments on that problem in its disposition of Jesse Cantwell's breach of the peach conviction, p. 1154, supra. Was Cantwell freed because there was not a sufficiently "clear and present danger" of disorder? Would he have been punishable for what he said if a more specific statute had been invoked and disorder had resulted? Or would his speech have been protected by the First Amendment even if it had provoked greater hostility?

The Cantwell opinion suggested that some speech, in any event, might not have been protected—e. g., "personal abuse." A year later, in the much-quoted Chaplinsky case (note 1 below), the Court elaborated that "fighting words" are not entitled to speech protection. But Terminiello (note 2 below) reversed a conviction of a provocative speaker, though without reaching the "fighting words" issue. And the problem of the speaker using words short of the "fighting words" category has recurred in subsequent cases. Feiner (p. 1156 infra) was the Court's 1951 response to the hostile audience question. Demonstrations of the 1960's have produced similar problems, as some of the materials in sec. 1C show. A concurrence in the 1969 Gregory case is included in this section (p. 1159 below) because it illustrates the persistence of this complex issue and because the opinion is an unusually direct confrontation of the problem.

1. *Chaplinsky and "fighting words."* In Chaplinsky v. New Hampshire, 315 U.S. 568 (1942), the Court unanimously upheld the conviction of a Jehovah's Witness who had gotten into a fight on a sidewalk after calling a policeman "a God damned racketeer" and "a damned Fascist." The statute had enacted the common law "fighting words" doctrine: "No person shall address any offensive, derisive or annoying word to any other person who is lawfully in any street or other public place, nor call him by any offensive or derisive name." The state court had interpreted it to ban "words likely to cause an average addressee to fight," "face-to-face words plainly likely" to cause a breach of the peace by the addressee. The Court thought it obvious that Chaplinsky's words were "likely to provoke the average person to retaliation."

In the course of the opinion, Justice Murphy commented "There are certain well-defined and narrowly limited classes of speech, the prevention and punishment of which have never been thought to raise any Constitutional problem. These include the lewd and obscene, the profane, the libelous, and the insulting or 'fighting' words—those which by their very utterance inflict injury or tend to incite an immediate breach of the peace. It has been well observed that such utterances are no essential part of any exposition of ideas and are of such slight social value as a step to truth that any benefit that may be derived from them is clearly outweighed by the social interest in order and morality."

That passage has been widely relied on, even by Justices who profess to support a wide range of speech protection. Does reliance on the passage risk undue interference with speech? Does the approach of categorizing speech into "classes" and placing some outside the First Amendment? In later years, the "obscene," the "profane," and the "libelous"—other unprotected classes mentioned in Chaplinsky—were found to raise substantial First Amendment problems. See chap. 16, infra—e. g., the New York Times case on libel (p. 1214); and compare the "obscenity-is-not-speech" approach of Roth, p. 1227, with later obscenity cases. Should the "classification" approach be abandoned for "fighting words" as well?

Note Justice Brennan's comment in New York Times Co. v. Sullivan, 376 U.S. 254 (1964): "Like 'insurrection,' contempt, advocacy of unlawful acts, breach of the peace, obscenity, solicitation of legal business, and the various other formulae for the repression of expression that have been challenged in this Court, libel can claim no talismanic immunity from constitutional limitations. It must be measured by standards that satisfy the First Amendment." Should "fighting words" have "talismanic immunity"? Or is it better to recognize explicitly that "fighting words" problems have First Amendment dimensions? Would abandonment of the "fighting words" rubric mean protection for all speech, no matter how obviously provocative to the audience?

2. *Terminiello and speech which "invites disputes."* In Terminiello v. Chicago, 337 U.S. 1 (1949), the Court reversed the breach of peace conviction of an abrasive speaker, but on the basis of an improper charge to the jury and without reaching the "hostile words" issue. The speaker viciously denounced various political and racial groups; outside the auditorium, an angry crowd gathered; the speaker then condemned the crowd as "snakes," "slimy scum," etc. After the disturbance, he was convicted under a breach of the peace statute construed by the trial judge to include speech which "stirs the public to anger, invites dispute, brings about a condition of unrest or creates a disturbance." Justice Douglas majority opinion found that standard unconstitutional: "[A] function of free speech under our system of government is to invite dispute. It may indeed best serve its high purpose when it induces a condition of unrest, creates dissatisfaction with conditions as they are, or even stirs people to anger. Speech is often provocative and challenging. It may strike at prejudices and preconceptions and have profound unsettling effects as it presses for acceptance of an idea. That is why freedom of speech, though not absolute [Chaplinsky], is nevertheless protected against censorship or punishment, unless shown likely to produce a clear and present danger of a serious substantive evil that rises far above public inconvenience, annoyance, or unrest."

3. *Feiner, protected words, and restricting environments.* The Feiner case, which follows, elicited more extensive consideration of the problems first encountered in Cantwell, supra. To what extent does the scope of the First Amendment turn on the content of the speech? To what extent on the audi-

ence response? Can the Court delineate the protected area by stating, e. g., that words short of "incitement" are protected, no matter what their actual impact? Or do the boundaries of protection depend on the environment, including the actual response of the audience? Must the state accept responsibility for restraining the sensitive audience, or does the speaker bear the risk of having his provocative words stopped by the hecklers' disorder? Were Feiner's words "incitements" outside the First Amendment? Or were they words made punishable by reason of the audience response?

FEINER v. NEW YORK

340 U.S. 315, 71 S.Ct. 303, 95 L.Ed. 295 (1951).

Certiorari to the Court of Appeals of New York.

Mr. Chief Justice VINSON delivered the opinion of the Court.

Petitioner was convicted of the offense of disorderly conduct, a misdemeanor under the New York penal laws. [Petitioner claims] that the conviction is in violation of his right of free speech under the Fourteenth Amendment.

In the review of state decisions where First Amendment rights are drawn in question, we of course make an examination of the evidence to ascertain independently whether the right has been violated. . . . Our appraisal of the facts is . . . based upon the uncontroverted facts and, where controversy exists, upon that testimony which the trial judge did reasonably conclude to be true.

On the evening of March 8, 1949, petitioner Irving Feiner was addressing an open-air meeting at the corner of South McBride and Harrison Streets in the City of Syracuse. At approximately 6:30 p. m., the police received a telephone complaint concerning the meeting, and two officers were detailed to investigate. [Two policemen] found a crowd of about seventy-five or eighty people, both Negro and white, filling the sidewalk and spreading out into the street. Petitioner, standing on a large wooden box on the sidewalk, was addressing the crowd through a loud-speaker system attached to an automobile. Although the purpose of his speech was to urge his listeners to attend a meeting to be held that night in the Syracuse Hotel, in its course he was making derogatory remarks concerning President Truman, the American Legion, the Mayor of Syracuse, and other local political officials.

The police officers made no effort to interfere with petitioner's speech, but were first concerned with the effect of the crowd on both pedestrian and vehicular traffic. They observed the situation from the opposite side of the street, noting that some pedestrians were forced to walk in the street to avoid the crowd. Since traffic was passing at the time, the officers attempted to get the people listening to petitioner back on the sidewalk. The crowd was restless and there was some pushing, shoving and milling around. . . .

At this time, petitioner was speaking in a "loud, high-pitched voice." He gave the impression that he was endeavoring to arouse the Negro people against the whites, urging that they rise up in arms and fight for equal rights. The statements before such a mixed audience "stirred up a little excitement." Some of the onlookers made remarks to the police about their inability to handle the crowd and at least one threatened violence if the police did not act. There were others who appeared to be favoring petitioner's arguments. Because of the feeling that existed in the crowd both for and against the speaker, the officers finally "stepped in to prevent it from result-ing in a fight." . . . Although the officer . . . twice requested petitioner to stop over the course of several minutes, petitioner not only ignored him but continued talking. During all this time, the crowd was press-ing closer around petitioner and the officer. Finally, the officer told peti-tioner he was under arrest and ordered him to get down from the box, reach-ing up to grab him. Petitioner stepped down . . . . In all, the offi-cer had asked petitioner to get down off the box three times over a space of four or five minutes. Petitioner had been speaking for over a half hour.

. . . The bill of particulars . . . gave in detail the facts upon which the prosecution relied to support the charge of disorderly conduct. Paragraph C is particularly pertinent here: "By ignoring and refusing to heed and obey reasonable police orders issued . . . to regulate and con-trol said crowd and to prevent a breach or breaches of the peace and to prevent injury to pedestrians attempting to use said walk, . . . and prevent in-jury to the public generally."

We are not faced here with blind condonation by a state court of arbitrary police action. Petitioner was accorded a full, fair trial. . . . The exercise of the police officers' proper discretionary power to prevent a breach of the peace was . . . approved by the trial court and later by two courts on review. The courts below . . . found that the officers in making the arrest were motivated solely by a proper concern for the preservation of order and protection of the general welfare, and that there was no evidence which could lend color to a claim that the acts of the police were a cover for suppression of petitioner's views and opinions. Petitioner was thus neither arrested nor convicted for the making or the content of his speech. Rather, it was the reaction which it actually engendered.

The language of Cantwell v. Connecticut, 310 U.S. 296 (1940), is appropriate here. ". . . When clear and present danger of riot, dis-order, interference with traffic upon the public streets, or other immediate threat to public safety, peace, or order, appears, the power of the State to prevent or punish is obvious." The findings of the New York courts as to the condition of the crowd and the refusal of petitioner to obey the police requests, supported as they are by the record of this case, are persuasive that the conviction of petitioner for violation of public peace, order and authority does not exceed the bounds of proper state police action. This Court respects, as it must, the interests of the community in maintaining peace and order on its streets. . . . We cannot say that the preservation of that interest here encroaches on the constitutional rights of this petitioner.

We are well aware that the ordinary murmurings and objections of a hostile audience cannot be allowed to silence a speaker, and are also mindful of the possible danger of giving overzealous police officials complete dis-cretion to break up otherwise lawful public meetings. . . . But we are not faced here with such a situation. It is one thing to say that the police cannot be used as an instrument for the suppression of unpopular views, and another to say that, when as here the speaker passes the bounds of argument or persuasion and undertakes incitement to riot, they are power-less to prevent a breach of the peace.   Nor in this case can we condemn the considered judgment of three New York courts approving the means which the police, faced with a crisis, used in the exercise of their power and duty to preserve peace and order.   The findings of the state courts as to the existing situation and the imminence of greater disorder coupled with peti-tioner's deliberate defiance of the police officers convince us that we should not reverse this conviction in the name of free speech.

Affirmed.

Mr. Justice BLACK, dissenting.

The record before us convinces me that petitioner, a young college student, has been sentenced to the penitentiary for the unpopular views he expressed on matters of public interest while lawfully making a street-corner speech in Syracuse, New York.   Today's decision, however, indicates that we must blind ourselves to this fact because the trial judge fully accepted the testimony of the prosecution witnesses on all important points. . . .

But still more has been lost today.   Even accepting every "finding of fact" below, I think this conviction makes a mockery of the free speech guarantees of the First and Fourteenth Amendments.   The end result of the affirmance here is to approve a simple and readily available technique by which cities and states can with impunity subject all speeches, political or otherwise, on streets or elsewhere, to the supervision and censorship of the local police.   I will have no part or parcel in this holding which I view as a long step toward totalitarian authority. . . .

. . . . As to the existence of a dangerous situation on the street corner, it seems far-fetched to suggest that the "facts" show any imminent threat of riot or uncontrollable disorder.   It is neither unusual nor unexpected that some people at public street meetings mutter, mill about, push, shove, or disagree, even violently, with the speaker. . . . Nor does one isolated threat to assault the speaker forebode disorder.   Especially should the danger be discounted where, as here, the person threatening was a man whose wife and two small children accompanied him and who, so far as the record shows, was never close enough to petitioner to carry out the threat.

Moreover, assuming that the "facts" did indicate a critical situation, I reject the implication of the Court's opinion that the police had no obliga-tion to protect petitioner's constitutional right to talk.   The police of course have power to prevent breaches of the peace.   But if, in the name of pre-serving order, they ever can interfere with a lawful public speaker, they first must make all reasonable efforts to protect him.   Here the policemen did not even pretend to try to protect petitioner.   According to the officers' testimony, the crowd was restless but there is no showing of any attempt to quiet it; pedestrians were forced to walk into the street, but there was no effort to clear a path on the sidewalk; one person threatened to assault petitioner but the officers did nothing to discourage this when even a word might have sufficed.   Their duty was to protect petitioner's right to talk, even to the extent of arresting the man who threatened to interfere.[1]   Instead, they shirked that duty and acted only to suppress the right to speak.

1. In Schneider v. State, 308 U.S. 147, we held that a purpose to prevent lit-tering of the streets was insufficient to justify an ordinance which pro-hibited a person lawfully on the street from handing literature to one willing to receive it. We said at page 162, "There are obvious methods of pre-

Finally, I cannot agree with the Court's statement that petitioner's disregard of the policeman's unexplained request amounted to such "deliberate defiance" as would justify an arrest or conviction for disorderly conduct. On the contrary, I think that the policeman's action was a "deliberate defiance" of ordinary official duty as well as of the constitutional right of free speech. For at least where time allows, courtesy and explanation of commands are basic elements of good official conduct in a democratic society. Here petitioner was "asked" then "told" then "commanded" to stop speaking, but a man making a lawful address is certainly not required to be silent merely because an officer directs it. Petitioner was entitled to know why he should cease doing a lawful act. Not once was he told. I understand that people in authoritarian countries must obey arbitrary orders. I had hoped that there was no such duty in the United States.

In my judgment, today's holding means that as a practical matter, minority speakers can be silenced in any city. Hereafter, despite the First and Fourteenth Amendments, the policeman's club can take heavy toll of a current administration's public critics. Criticism of public officials will be too dangerous for all but the most courageous. This is true regardless of the fact that in two other cases decided this day, Kunz v. New York, 340 U.S. 290 [p. 1169, infra]; Niemotko v. Maryland, 340 U.S. 268,* a majority, in obedience to past decisions of this Court, provides a theoretical safeguard for freedom of speech. For whatever is thought to be guaranteed in Kunz and Niemotko is taken away by what is done here. The three cases read together mean that while previous restraints probably cannot be imposed on an unpopular speaker, the police have discretion to silence him as soon as the customary hostility to his views develops. . . .

Mr. Justice DOUGLAS, with whom Mr. Justice MINTON concurs, dissenting. . . .

A speaker may not, of course, incite a riot . . . . But this record shows no such extremes. It shows an unsympathetic audience and the threat of one man to haul the speaker from the stage. It is against that kind of threat that speakers need police protection. If they do not receive it and instead the police throw their weight on the side of those who would break up the meetings, the police become the new censors of speech. Police cen-

venting littering. Amongst these is the punishment of those who actually throw papers on the streets." In the present case as well, the threat of one person to assault a speaker does not justify suppression of the speech. There are obvious available alternative methods of preserving public order. One of these is to arrest the person who threatens an assault. Cf. Dean Milk Co. v. Madison, 340 U.S. 349 [chap. 8, p. 657, supra] decided today, in which the Court invalidates a municipal health ordinance under the Commerce Clause because of a belief that the city could have accomplished its purposes by reasonably adequate alternatives. The Court certainly should not be less alert to protect freedom of speech than it is to protect freedom of trade. [Footnote by Justice Black.]

* In Niemotko v. Maryland, 340 U.S. 268 (1951), members of Jehovah's Witnesses had been found guilty of disorderly conduct because of their attempt to hold a meeting in a municipal park without a permit. There was no evidence of disorder. Appellants had previously applied for and been refused a permit by officials acting pursuant to a local custom of nonstatutory character under which permits had been granted to other religious and fraternal organizations. In applying for permits, the Witnesses had been questioned as to their religious beliefs rather than matters related to the orderly use of the park. On appeal the convictions were reversed, the Court concluding that use of the park was denied because of dislike for the appellants and their views.

sorship has all the vices of the censorship from city halls which we have repeatedly struck down. . . .

Mr. Justice FRANKFURTER, concurring in the result [in this case, Feiner, as well as in Kunz and Niemotko. Justice Frankfurter's review of the cases, printed at p. 1138 above, came in this opinion.] . . .

. . . It is pertinent . . . to note that all members of the New York Court accepted the finding that Feiner was stopped not because the listeners or police officers disagreed with his views but because these officers were honestly concerned with preventing a breach of the peace. This unanimity is all the more persuasive since three members of the Court had dissented, only three months earlier, in favor of Kunz, a man whose vituperative utterances must have been highly offensive to them. . . .

. . . Where conduct is within the allowable limits of free speech, the police are peace officers for the speaker as well as for his hearers. But the power effectively to preserve order cannot be displaced by giving a speaker complete immunity. Here, there were two police officers present for 20 minutes. They interfered only when they apprehended imminence of violence. It is not a constitutional principle that, in acting to preserve order, the police must proceed against the crowd, whatever its size and temper, and not against the speaker.

It is true that breach-of-peace statutes, like most tools of government, may be misused. . . . But the possibility of misuse is not alone a sufficient reason to deny New York the power here asserted or so limit it by constitutional construction as to deny its practical exercise.

THE GREGORY CASE: STREET DEMONSTRATIONS AND THE UNSOLVED PROBLEM OF THE HOSTILE AUDIENCE

Was the Feiner solution adequate? Are better Robert's Rules possible for that situation? Are they equally applicable to the street demonstration context of later years? Are they equally applicable when the audience is genuinely outraged in the clash of "deep-seated" view on the streets? Though most modern street demonstration cases are noted in sec. 1C, p. 1163, infra, one 1969 decision warrants consideration here, to suggest the unsolved elements (and changing contexts) of the hostile audience problem.

1. *The decision.* In Gregory v. Chicago, 394 U.S. 111 (1969), petitioners had "marched in a peaceful and orderly procession from city hall to the mayor's residence to press their claims for desegregation of the public schools." When "the number of bystanders increased" and "the onlookers became unruly," Chicago police, "to prevent what they regarded as an impending civil disorder," demanded that the demonstrators disperse. When petitioners refused to do so, they were arrested for disorderly conduct.

Chief Justice Warren's very brief opinion justifying the Court's reversal of the convictions asserted that this was "a simple case": as in Edwards v. South Carolina, p. 1164, infra, petitioners' peaceful conduct was activity protected by the First Amendment; as in Thompson v. Louisville, p. 912, supra, the convictions were "totally devoid of evidentiary support" showing that the conduct was disorderly; and the trial judge's charge permitted the jury to convict for acts clearly entitled to First Amendment protection.   Nor could the conviction rest on refusal to follow the dispersal request: petitioners were convicted for the demonstration, "not for a refusal to obey a police officer."

2. *The concurrence.*   Justice Black's concurrence, joined by Justice Douglas, found some lurking complexities in the "simple case."   After reviewing the facts, he noted that "both police and demonstrators made their best efforts faithfully to discharge their responsibilities as officers and citizens, but they were nevertheless unable to restrain these hostile hecklers within decent and orderly bounds."   More generally, he concluded "that when groups with diametrically opposed, deep-seated views are permitted to air their emotional grievances, side by side, on city streets, tranquility and order cannot be maintained even by the joint efforts of the finest and best officers and of those who desire to be the most law-abiding protestors of their grievances."   Here, he emphasized, the disorderly conduct convictions were especially vulnerable because the ordinance was not a narrowly drawn law, but rather "a meat-ax ordinance": the Court had repeatedly warned against the "use of sweeping-dragnet statutes that may, because of vagueness, jeopardize" First Amendment freedoms.   But, he added, the Court had also been careful to assure that "the Constitution does not bar enactment of laws regulating conduct, even though connected with speech, press, assembly, and petition, if such laws specifically bar only the conduct deemed obnoxious and are carefully and narrowly aimed at that forbidden conduct.   The dilemma revealed by this record is a crying example of a need for some such narrowly drawn law."

3. *Some questions, not all rhetorical.*   Is Gregory—either in the Warren or Black emphases—a step forward toward evolution of Robert's Rules for the hostile audience problem?   Is the Black-Douglas concluding reliance on the speech-conduct distinction helpful?   What "specific ban on conduct" would do, in their view?   Would a specific ban on marches in all residential areas be a constitutional "narrowly drawn" law?   A ban on processions during certain hours?   A specific ban on demonstrations near the mayor's residence?   A limit on the number of participants?   What "conduct," in short, may a "narrowly drawn" ordinance "deem obnoxious" ?   Anything, so long as it is "conduct," not pure speech, and so long as it is identified in a "narrowly drawn" statute?   If so, what of streets as a public forum?

PERMIT REQUIREMENTS AND THE KUNZ CASE

The recurrent problem of prior restraints and permit requirements, raised by Lovell v. Griffin and Cox v. New Hampshire, pp. 1142 and 1143, supra, reemerged in one of the cases decided together with Feiner.   Note especially the last paragraph of the Jackson dissent, and consider the parallel to the Saia-Kovacs contrast in the Loudspeaker Cases, p. 1149, supra: Does it make sense to be so suspicious of prior licensing schemes (Saia, Kunz) when the state may penalize the speech by other routes (Kovacs, Feiner)?   Compare the surfacing of permit problems in the street demonstrations context, infra, p. 1163.

Kunz v. New York, 340 U.S. 290 (1951) reversed a conviction for violating a New York City ordinance which prohibited public worship meetings in the street "without first obtaining a permit" from the police commissioner. The ordinance also made it unlawful "to ridicule or denounce any form of religious belief" or to "expound atheism or agnosticism . . . in any street." Kunz, a Baptist minister, was convicted for holding a meeting in 1948 without a permit. He had obtained a permit in 1946, but that was revoked in the same year after an administrative hearing: there had been complaints that Kunz had engaged in "scurrilous attacks on Catholics and Jews," and the revocation was based on "evidence that he had ridiculed and denounced other religious beliefs in his meetings." Kunz's application for permits in 1947 and 1948 were "disapproved," without stated reason. Chief Justice Vinson's majority opinion included the following passages:

"Disapproval of the 1948 permit application by the police commissioner was justified by the New York courts on the ground that a permit had previously been revoked 'for good reasons.' It is noteworthy that there is no mention in the ordinance of reasons for which such a permit application can be refused. This interpretation allows the police commissioner, an administrative official, to exercise discretion in denying subsequent permit applications on the basis of his interpretation, at that time, of what is deemed to be conduct condemned by the ordinance. We have here, then, an ordinance which gives an administrative official discretionary power to control in advance the right of citizens to speak on religious matters on the streets of New York. As such, the ordinance is clearly invalid as a prior restraint on the exercise of First Amendment rights. . . .

"The court below has mistakenly derived support for its conclusion from the evidence . . . that appellant's religious meetings had, in the past, caused some disorder. There are appropriate public remedies to protect the peace and order of the community if appellant's speeches should result in disorder or violence. . . . We do not express any opinion on the propriety of punitive remedies which the New York authorities may utilize. We are here concerned with suppression—not punishment. It is sufficient to say that New York cannot vest restraining control over the right to speak on religious subjects in an administrative official where there are no appropriate standards to guide his action." *

Justices Black and Frankfurter concurred in the result. Justice Jackson submitted a lengthy dissent; it included the following passages: "Essential freedoms are today threatened from without and within. It may become difficult to preserve here what a large part of the world has lost—the right to speak, even temperately, on matters vital to spirit and body. In such a setting, to blanket hateful and hate-stirring attacks on races and faiths under the protections for freedom of speech may be a noble innovation. On the other hand, it may be a quixotic tilt at windmills which belittles

---

* On the eve of the modern demonstration cases which follow, there was general agreement about the vulnerability of vague licensing requirements. The consensus, based on the decisions since Lovell v. Griffin, was stated in Staub v. City of Baxley, 355 U.S. 313 (1958):

An ordinance prohibited the solicitation of membership in dues-paying organizations without a permit from the Mayor and Council of the City. It was held 'invalid on its face'. "It is set-

tled by a long line of recent decisions of this Court that an ordinance which, like this one, makes the peaceful enjoyment of freedoms which the Constitution guarantees contingent upon the uncontrolled will of an official— as by requiring a permit or license which may be granted or withheld in the discretion of such official—is an unconstitutional censorship or prior restraint upon the enjoyment of those freedoms."

great principles of liberty. Only time can tell. But I incline to the latter view and cannot assent to the decision. [The question] is not whether New York could, if it tried, silence Kunz, but whether it must place its streets at his service to hurl insults at the passerby. . . . Of course, people might pass this speaker by as a mental case, and so they might file out of a theatre in good order at the cry of 'fire.' But in both cases there is genuine likelihood that someone will get hurt. . . . We should weigh the value of insulting speech against its potentiality for harm. Is the Court, when declaring Kunz has the *right* he asserts, serving the great end for which the First Amendment stands? . . . It seems hypercritical to strike down local laws on their faces for want of standards when we have no standards. And I do not find it required by existing authority. I think that where speech is outside of constitutional immunity the local community or the State is left a large measure of discretion as to the means for dealing with it. . . .

"[I]f the Court conceives, as Feiner indicates, that upon uttering insulting, provocative or inciting words the policeman on the beat may stop the meeting, then its assurance of free speech in this decision is 'a promise to the ear to be broken to the hope,' if the patrolman on the beat happens to have prejudices of his own. . . . It seems to me that this [permit] procedure better protects freedom of speech than to let everyone speak without leave, but subject to surveillance and to being ordered to stop in the discretion of the police."

C. DEMONSTRATIONS IN THE STREETS AND OTHER PUBLIC PLACES: THE MODERN CONTEXT OF THE PUBLIC FORUM

Introduction. How useful are the analyses developed in the public places cases of the thirties and forties for the solution of the street demonstration problems of the sixties and seventies? Most of the cases surveyed by Justice Frankfurter at the beginning of this section were stimulated by the "robust evangelism" of the Jehovah's Witnesses. During the fifties, as Professor Kalven remarks, "the story of the streets became a bit quaint." But by the sixties, it became clear "that the story is not over": the civil rights movement took to the streets; it was predictable that "the Court's formidable business in the immediate future will require it to confront the issues raised by today's Negro 'evangelism.'" Kalven, "The Concept of a Public Forum," 1965 Sup.Ct.Rev. 1.

The Jehovah's Witnesses' evangelism may have been "robust," but it was largely the proselytizing of the single evangelist, selling magazines, ringing doorbells, speaking at street corners. The modern "evangelism" is one of numbers, of parades in streets and vigils in parks, of protest meetings in front and inside of public buildings. With a greater need than ever for Robert's Rules, how has the Court responded? Are old Rules being clarified and adapted to new circumstances? Are the judicial techniques responsive and adequate to the task? The doctrinal tools developed in the preceding pages interwine in the cases that follow; new techniques emerge; but the problems of principle and practice raised earlier persist as challenges in the examination of the modern cases.

EDWARDS v. SOUTH CAROLINA: "A FAR CRY" FROM FEINER?

1. *The decision.* In Edwards v. South Carolina, 372 U.S. 229 (1963), the Court reversed breach of peace convictions of 187 Negro student demonstrators. Petitioners had walked along the South Carolina State House grounds to protest against racial discrimination. After a large crowd of onlookers gathered, they were ordered to disperse within fifteen minutes; when they did not do so, they were arrested. The Supreme Court, in an opinion by Justice Stewart, held that "South Carolina infringed the petitioners' constitutionally protected rights of free speech, free assembly, and freedom to petition for redress of their grievances." Justice Stewart noted that there had been no violence by the demonstrators or the onlookers; that there was no evidence of "fighting words"; and that the circumstances were "a far cry from the situation" in Feiner v. New York. He noted, too, that the convictions did not arise "from the even-handed application of a precise and narrowly drawn regulatory statute evincing a legislative judgment that certain specific conduct be limited or proscribed. If, for example, the petitioners had been convicted upon evidence that they had violated a law regulating traffic, or had disobeyed a law reasonably limiting the periods during which the State House grounds were open to the public, this would be a different case." He added: "The Fourteenth Amendment does not permit a State to make criminal the peaceful expression of unpopular views."

Justice Clark's dissent viewed the record differently. To him, this "was by no means the passive demonstration which this Court relates. . . . The question . . . seems to me whether a State is constitutionally prohibited from enforcing laws to prevent breach of the peace in a situation where city officials in good faith believe, and the record shows, that disorder and violence are imminent, merely because the activities constituting that breach contain claimed elements of constitutionally protected speech and assembly. To me the answer under our cases is clearly in the negative." The situation in Feiner was "no more dangerous than that found here. . . . It is my belief that anyone conversant with the almost spontaneous combustion in some Southern communities in such a situation will agree that the City Manager's action may well have averted a major catastrophe."

2. *Some questions.* Why was the protest march in Edwards " a far cry" from Feiner? Because here there was "peaceful expression of unpopular views" rather than "incitement to riot," as the Court described Feiner's speech? Were these persuasive descriptions? Have the bounds of provocative speech changed since Feiner? Should the Court have said so? Note the reference to Edwards in the cases that follow.

Does the difference lie in the fact that the onlookers in Edwards in fact remained peaceful and that ample police were at hand? What if there had been some disorder: would the speech still have been protected because most onlookers in most cities would remain peaceful? The demonstrators carried placards with such messages as "Down with segregation," and engaged in "chanting," "stamping feet," and "clapping hands"—conduct that created a "much greater danger of riot and disorder" than in Feiner, given the atmosphere in "some Southern communities," according to the dissent. Would an outbreak of disorder in these circumstances simply show police failure to protect "peaceful" speech? Or would it suggest that the speakers had used "fighting words"? Should the Court have spoken further about the hostile audience problem in Edwards? Did the Court clarify the modern Robert's Rules more effectively two years later in the Cox cases, which follow?

COX v. LOUISIANA

[COX I—No. 24, 1964 Term]

379 U.S. 536, 85 S.Ct. 453, 13 L.Ed.2d 471 (1965).

Appeal from the Supreme Court of Louisiana.

Mr. Justice GOLDBERG delivered the opinion of the Court.

Appellant, the Reverend Mr. B. Elton Cox, the leader of a civil rights demonstration, was arrested and charged with four offenses under Louisiana law—criminal conspiracy, disturbing the peace, obstructing public passages, and picketing before a courthouse. In a consolidated trial before a judge without a jury, and on the same set of facts, he was acquitted of criminal conspiracy but convicted of the other three offenses. He was sentenced to serve four months in jail and pay a $200 fine for disturbing the peace, to serve five months in jail and pay a $500 fine for obstructing public passages, and to serve one year in jail and pay a $5,000 fine for picketing before a courthouse. The sentences were cumulative.

. . . Appellant filed two separate appeals to this Court . . . contending that the three statutes under which he was convicted were unconstitutional on their face and as applied. We noted probable jurisdiction of both appeals, 377 U.S. 921. This case, No. 24, involves the convictions for disturbing the peace and obstructing public passages, and No. 49 [Cox II, which follows] concerns the conviction for picketing before a courthouse.

I.—THE FACTS.

On December 14, 1961, 23 students from Southern University, a Negro college, were arrested in downtown Baton Rouge, Louisiana, for picketing stores that maintained segregated lunch counters. This picketing, urging a boycott of those stores, was part of a general protest movement against racial segregation, directed by the local chapter of the Congress of Racial Equality . . .. The appellant, an ordained Congregational minister, the Reverend Mr. B. Elton Cox, a Field Secretary of CORE, was an advisor to this movement. On the evening of December 14, [he] spoke at a mass meeting at the college. The students resolved to demonstrate the next day in front of the courthouse in protest of segregation and the arrest and imprisonment of the picketers who were being held in the parish jail located on the upper floor of the courthouse building.

The next morning about 2,000 students left the campus, which was located approximately five miles from downtown Baton Rouge. . . . Because [the student leaders were in jail], Cox felt it his duty to take over the demonstration and see that it was carried out as planned. . . .

As Cox, . . . at the head of the group, approached the vicinity of the courthouse, he was stopped . . . and brought to Police Chief

Wingate White . . .. The Chief then inquired as to the purpose of the demonstration. Cox, reading from a prepared paper, oulined his program to White, stating that it would include a singing of the Star Spangled Banner and a "freedom song," recitation of the Lord's Prayer and the Pledge of Allegiance, and a short speech. White testified that he told Cox that "he must confine" the demonstration "to the west side of the street." White added, "This, of course, was not—I didn't mean it in the import that I was giving him any permission to do it, but I was presented with a stiuation that was accomplished, and I had to make a decision." Cox testified that the officals agreed to permit the meeting. . . .

The students were then directed by Cox to the west sidewalk, across the street from the courthouse, 101 feet from its steps. They were lined up on this sidewalk about five deep and spread almost the entire length of the block. The group did not obstruct the street. It was close to noon and, being lunch time, a small crowd of 100 to 300 curious white people . . . gathered on the east sidewalk and courthouse steps, about 100 feet from the demonstrators. Seventy-five to eighty policemen, including city and state patrolmen and members of the Sheriff's staff, as well as members of the fire department and a fire truck were stationed in the street between the two groups. . . .

[The students] sang "God Bless America," pledged allegiance to the flag, prayed briefly, and sang one or two hymns, including "We Shall Overcome." The 23 students, who were locked in jail cells in the courthouse building out of the sight of the demonstrators, responded by themselves singing; this in turn was greeted with cheers and applause by the demonstrators. Appellant gave a speech, described by a State's witness as follows:

"He said that in effect that it was a protest against the illegal arrest of some of their members and that other people were allowed to picket . . . and he said that they were not going to commit any violence, that if anyone spit on them, they would not spit back on the person that did it."

Cox then said:

"All right. It's lunch time. Let's go eat. There are twelve stores we are protesting. A number of these stores have twenty counters; they accept your money from nineteen. They won't accept it from the twentieth counter. This is an act of racial discrimination. These stores are open to the public. You are members of the public. We pay taxes to the Federal Government and you who live here pay taxes to the State."

In apparent reaction to these last remarks, there was what state witnesses described as "muttering" and "grumbling" by the white onlookers.

The Sheriff, deeming, as he testified, Cox's appeal to the students to sit in at the lunch counters to be "inflammatory," then took a power microphone and said, "Now you have been allowed to demonstrate. Up until now your demonstration has been more or less peaceful, but what you are doing now is a direct violation of the law, a disturbance of the peace, and it has got to be broken up immediately." The testimony as to what then happened is disputed. Some of the State's witnesses testified that Cox said, "don't move"; others stated that he made a "gesture of defiance." It is clear from the record, however, that Cox and the demonstrators did not then and there break up the demonstration. . . .

Almost immediately thereafter—within a time estimated variously at two to five minutes—one of the policemen exploded a tear gas shell at the crowd. This was followed by several other shells. The demonstrators quickly dispersed, running back towards the State Capitol and the downtown area. . . . No Negroes participating in the demonstration were arrested on that day. . . . The next day appellant was arrested and charged with the four offenses above described.

II.—The Breach of the Peace Conviction.

Appellant was convicted of violating a Louisiana "disturbing the peace" statute, which provides:

"Whoever with intent to provoke a breach of the peace, or under circumstances such that a breach of the peace may be occasioned thereby . . . crowds or congregates with others . . . in or upon . . . a public street or public highway, or upon a public sidewalk, or any other public place or building . . . and who fails or refuses to disperse and move on, . . . when ordered so to do by any law enforcement officer of any municipality, or parish, in which such act or acts are committed, or by any law enforcement officer of the state of Louisiana, or any other authorized person . . . shall be guilty of disturbing the peace." . . .

It is clear to us that on the facts of this case, which are strikingly similar to those present in Edwards v. South Carolina, 372 U.S. 229, and Fields v. South Carolina, 375 U.S. 44, Louisiana infringed appellant's rights of free speech and free assembly by convicting him under this statute. . . . We hold that Louisiana may not constitutionally punish appellant under this statute for engaging in the type of conduct which this record reveals, and also that the statute as authoritatively interpreted by the Louisiana Supreme Court is unconstitutionally broad in scope.

[O]ur independent examination of the record, which we are required to make, shows no conduct which the State had a right to prohibit as a breach of the peace. . . .

The State argues . . . that while the demonstrators started out to be orderly, the loud cheering and clapping by the students in response to the singing from the jail converted the peaceful assembly into a riotous one. The record, however, does not support this assertion. . . . Our conclusion that the entire meeting from the beginning until its dispersal by tear gas was orderly and not riotous is confirmed by a film of the events taken by a television news photographer, which was offered in evidence as a state exhibit. We have viewed the film, and it reveals that the students, though they undoubtedly cheered and clapped, were well-behaved throughout. . . .

Finally, the State contends that the conviction should be sustained because of fear expressed by some of the state witnesses that "violence was about to erupt" because of the demonstration. It is virtually undisputed, however, that the students themselves were not violent and threatened no violence. The fear of violence seems to have been based upon the reaction of the group of white citizens looking on from across the street. . . . There is no indication, however, that any member of the white group threatened violence. And this small crowd estimated at between 100 and 300 were separated from the students by "seventy-five to eighty" armed policemen . . .. As Inspector Trigg testified, they could have handled the crowd.

This situation, like that in Edwards, is "a far cry from the situation in Feiner v. New York, 340 U.S. 315." . . . Nor is there any evidence here of "fighting words." . . .

There is an additional reason why this conviction cannot be sustained. The statute at issue in this case, as authoritatively interpreted by the Louisiana Supreme Court, is unconstitutionally vague in its overly broad scope. The statutory crime consists of two elements: (1) congregating with others "with intent to provoke a breach of the peace, or under circumstances such that a breach of the peace may be occasioned," and (2) a refusal to move on after having been ordered to do so by a law enforcement officer. While the second part of this offense is narrow and specific, the first element is not. [It] would allow persons to be punished merely for peacefully expressing unpopular views. . . . The Louisiana statute, as interpreted by the Louisiana court, is at least as likely to allow conviction for innocent speech as was the charge of the trial judge in [Terminiello v. Chicago, 337 U.S. 1]. Therefore, as in Terminiello and Edwards the conviction under this statute must be reversed as the statute is unconstitutional in that it sweeps within its broad scope activities that are constitutionally protected free speech and assembly. . . .

III. The Obstructing Public Passages Conviction.

We now turn to the issue of the validity of appellant's conviction for violating the Louisiana statute . . . which provides:

"Obstructing Public Passages

"No person shall wilfully obstruct the free, convenient and normal use of any public sidewalk, street, . . . or other passageway, or the entrance, corridor or passage of any public building, . . . by impeding, hindering, stifling, retarding or restraining traffic or passage thereon or therein.

"Providing however nothing herein contained shall apply to a bona fide legitimate labor organization or to any of its legal activities such as picketing . . .."

Appellant was convicted under this statute . . . for leading the meeting on the sidewalk across the street from the courthouse. . . . In upholding appellant's conviction under this statute, the Louisiana Supreme Court thus construed the statute so as to apply to public assemblies which do not have as their specific purpose the obstruction of traffic. There is no doubt from the record in this case that this far sidewalk was obstructed, and thus, as so construed, appellant violated the statute.

[Appellant's free speech contention] raises an issue with which this Court has dealt in many decisions. . . . From these decisions certain clear principles emerge. The rights of free speech and assembly, while fundamental in our democratic society, still do not mean that everyone with opinions or beliefs to express may address a group at any public place and at any time. The constitutional guarantee of liberty implies the existence of an organized society maintaining public order, without which liberty itself would be lost in the excesses of anarchy. The control of travel on the streets

is a clear example of governmental responsibility to insure this necessary order. A restriction in that relation, designed to promote the public convenience in the interest of all, and not susceptible to abuses of discriminatory
application, cannot be disregarded by the attempted exercise of some civil
right which, in other circumstances, would be entitled to protection. One
would not be justified in ignoring the familiar red light because this was
thought to be a means of social protest. Nor could one, contrary to traffic
regulations, insist upon a street meeting in the middle of Times Square at the
rush hour as a form of freedom of speech or assembly. Governmental authorities have the duty and responsibility to keep their streets open and available for movement. A group of demonstrators could not insist upon the right
to cordon off a street, or entrance to a public or private building, and allow
no one to pass who did not agree to listen to their exhortations. . . .

    We emphatically reject the notion urged by appellant that the First
and Fourteenth Amendments afford the same kind of freedom to those who
would communicate ideas by conduct such as patrolling, marching, and picketing on streets and highways, as these amendments afford to those who
communicate ideas by pure speech. . . . We reaffirm the statement
of the Court in Giboney v. Empire Storage & Ice Co., [336 U.S. 490], that
"it has never been deemed an abridgment of freedom of speech or press
to make a course of conduct illegal merely because the conduct was in part
initiated, evidenced, or carried out by means of language, either spoken, written, or printed."

    We have no occasion in this case to consider the constitutionality of the
uniform, consistent, and nondiscriminatory application of a statute forbidding
all access to streets and other public facilities for parades and meetings.
Although the statute here involved on its face precludes all street assemblies
and parades, it has not been so applied and enforced by the Baton Rouge
authorities. City officials who testified for the State clearly indicated that
certain meetings and parades are permitted in Baton Rouge, even though
they have the effect of obstructing traffic, provided prior approval is obtained. . . . The statute itself provides no standards for the determination of local officials as to which assemblies to permit or which to prohibit.
. . . From all the evidence before us it appears that the authorities
in Baton Rouge permit or prohibit parades or street meetings in their completely uncontrolled discretion.

    The situation is thus the same as if the statute itself expressly provided
that there could only be peaceful parades or demonstrations in the unbridled
discretion of the local officials. The pervasive restraint on freedom of discussion by the practice of the authorities under the statute is not any less
effective than a statute expressly permitting such selective enforcement.
. . .

    This Court has recognized that the lodging of such broad discretion in
a public official allows him to determine which expressions of view will be
permitted and which will not. This thus sanctions a device for the suppression of the communication of ideas and permits the official to act as a
censor. . . . Also inherent in such a system allowing parades or
meetings only with the prior permission of an official is the obvious danger
to the right of a person or group not to be denied equal protection of the
laws. . . . It is clearly unconstitutional to enable a public official
to determine which expressions of view will be permitted and which will

not or to engage in invidious discrimination among persons or groups either by use of a statute providing a system of broad discretionary licensing power or, as in this case, the equivalent of such a system by selective enforcement of an extremely broad prohibitory statute. . . . . It is, of course, undisputed that appropriate, limited discretion, under properly drawn statutes or ordinances, concerning the time, place, duration, or manner of use of the streets for public assemblies may be vested in administrative officials. [Cox v. New Hampshire] . . .

Reversed.

[The separate opinions are printed with Cox II, the next principal case.]

COX v. LOUISIANA

[COX II—No. 49, 1964 Term]

379 U.S. 559, 85 S.Ct. 476, 13 L.Ed.2d 487 (1965).

Appeal from the Supreme Court of Louisiana.

Mr. Justice GOLDBERG delivered the opinion of the Court.

Appellant was convicted of violating a Louisiana statute which provides:

"Whoever, with the intent of interfering with, obstructing, or impeding the administration of justice, or with the intent of influencing any judge, juror, witness, or court officer, in the discharge of his duty pickets or parades in or near a building housing a court of the State of Louisiana . . . . shall be fined not more than five thousand dollars or imprisoned not more than one year, or both." . . .

This charge was based upon the same set of facts as the charges involved and set forth in No. 24 [supra]. Appellant was convicted on this charge also and was sentenced to the maximum penalty under the statute of one year in jail and a $5,000 fine, which penalty was cumulative . . . . .

We shall first consider appellant's contention that this statute must be declared invalid on its face as an unjustified restriction upon freedoms guaranteed by the First and Fourteenth Amendments to the United States Constitution.

This statute was passed by Louisiana in 1950 and was modeled after a bill pertaining to the federal judiciary, which Congress enacted later in 1950, 64 Stat. 1018, 18 U.S.C. § 1507 (1958 ed.). Since that time, Massachusetts and Pennsylvania have passed similar statutes. . . . . The federal statute resulted from the picketing of federal courthouses by partisans of the defendants during trials involving leaders of the Communist Party. [See the Dennis case, p. 1097, supra.]

This statute, unlike the two previously considered, is a precise, narrowly drawn regulatory statute which proscribes certain specific behavior. . . . . It prohibits a particular type of conduct, namely, picketing and parading, in a few specified locations, in or near courthouses.

There can be no question that a State has a legitimate interest in protecting its judicial system from the pressures which picketing near a courthouse might create. Since we are committed to a government of laws and not of men, it is of the utmost importance that the administration of justice be absolutely fair and orderly. This Court has recognized that the unhindered and untrammeled functioning of our courts is part of the very foundation of our constitutional democracy. See Wood v. Georgia, 370 U.S. 375, 383 [p. 1279, infra]. The constitutional safeguards relating to the integrity of the criminal process attend every stage of a criminal proceeding [and] they exclude influence or domination by either a hostile or friendly mob. There is no room at any stage of judicial proceedings for such intervention; mob law is the very antithesis of due process. . . . A State may adopt safeguards necessary and appropriate to assure that the administration of justice at all stages is free from outside control and influence. A narrowly drawn statute such as the one under review is obviously a safeguard both necessary and appropriate to vindicate the State's interest in assuring justice under law.

Nor does such a statute infringe upon the constitutionally protected rights of free speech and free assembly. The conduct which is the subject of this statute—picketing and parading—is subject to regulation even though intertwined with expression and association. The examples are many of the application by this Court of the principle that certain forms of conduct mixed with speech may be regulated or prohibited. . . .

Bridges v. California, 314 U.S. 252, and Pennekamp v. Florida, 328 U.S. 331 [chap. 16, p. 1276, infra] do not hold to the contrary. . . . Here we deal not with the contempt power [but with] a statute narrowly drawn . . . .. We are not concerned here with such a pure form of expression as newspaper comment or a telegram by a citizen to a public official. We deal in this case not with free speech alone, but with expression mixed with particular conduct. . . .

We hold that this statute on its face is a valid law dealing with conduct subject to regulation so as to vindicate important interests of society and that the fact that free speech is intermingled with such conduct does not bring with it constitutional protection.

We now deal with the Louisiana statute as applied to the conduct in this case. The group of 2,000, led by appellant, paraded and demonstrated before the courthouse. Judges and court officers were in attendance to discharge their respective functions. It is undisputed that a major purpose of the demonstration was to protest what the demonstrators considered an "illegal" arrest of 23 students the previous day. . . .

It is, of course, true that most judges will be influenced only by what they see and hear in court. However, judges are human; and the legislature has the right to recognize the danger that some judges, jurors, and other court officials, will be consciously or unconsciously influenced by demonstrations in or near their courtrooms both prior to and at the time of the trial. A State may also properly protect the judicial process from being misjudged in the minds of the public. Suppose demonstrators paraded and picketed for weeks with signs asking that indictments be dismissed, and that a judge completely uninfluenced by these demonstrations, dismissed the indictments. A State may protect against the possibility of a conclusion by the public under these circumstances that the judge's action was in part a product of intimidation and did not flow only from the fair and orderly working of the judicial process. . . .

Appellant invokes the clear and present danger doctrine in support of his argument that the statute cannot constitutionally be applied to the conduct involved here [relying upon Pennekamp and Bridges]. He defines the standard to be applied . . . to be whether the expression of opinion presents a clear and present danger to the administration of justice.

We have already pointed out the important differences between the contempt cases and the present one . . .. Here we deal not with the contempt power but with a narrowly drafted statute and not with speech in its pristine form but with conduct of a totally different character. Even assuming the applicability of a general clear and present danger test, it is one thing to conclude that the mere publication of a newspaper editorial or a telegram to a Secretary of Labor, however critical of a court, presents no clear and present danger to the administration of justice and quite another thing to conclude that crowds, such as this, demonstrating before a courthouse may not be prohibited by a legislative determination based on experience that such conduct inherently threatens the judicial process. We therefore reject the clear and present danger argument of appellant. . . .

There are, however, more substantial constitutional objections arising from appellant's conviction on the particular facts of this case. Appellant was convicted for demonstrating not "in," but "near" the courthouse. It is undisputed that the demonstration took place on the west sidewalk, the far side of the street, exactly 101 feet from the courthouse steps and, judging from the pictures in the record, approximately 125 feet from the courthouse itself. The question is raised as to whether the failure of the statute to define the word "near" renders it unconstitutionally vague. . . . It is clear that there is some lack of specificity in a word such as "near." While this lack of specificity may not render the statute unconstitutionally vague, at least as applied to a demonstration within the sight and hearing of those in the courthouse, it is clear that the statute, with respect to the determination of how near the courthouse a particular demonstration can be, foresees a degree of on-the-spot administrative interpretation by officials charged with responsibility for administering and enforcing it. It is apparent that demonstrators, such as those involved here, would justifiably tend to rely on this administrative interpretation of how "near" the courthouse a particular demonstration might take place. . . . This administrative discretion to construe the term "near" . . . is the type of narrow discretion which this Court has recognized as the proper role of responsible officials in making determinations concerning the time, place, duration, and manner of demonstrations. . . . It is not the type of unbridled discretion which would allow an official to pick and choose among expressions of view the ones he will permit to use the streets and other public facilities, which we have invalidated in the obstruction of public passages statute [Cox I, supra].

The record here clearly shows that the officials present gave permission for the demonstration to take place across the street from the courthouse. In effect, appellant was advised that a demonstration at the place it was held would not be one "near" the courthouse within the terms of the statute. [U]nder all the circumstances of this case, after the public officials acted as they did, to sustain appellant's later conviction for demonstrating where they told him he could "would be to sanction an indefensible sort of entrapment by the State—convicting a citizen for exercising a privilege which the State had clearly told him was available to him." [Raley v. Ohio, 360 U.S. 423]. The Due Process Clause does not permit convictions to be obtained under such circumstances. . . . There remains just one final point: the effect of the Sheriff's order to disperse. The State in effect argues that this order somehow removed the prior grant of permission and reliance on the officials' construction that the demonstration on the far side of the street was not illegal as being "near" the courthouse. This, however, we cannot accept. [I]t is our conclusion from the record that the dispersal order had nothing to do with any time or place limitation, and thus, on this ground alone, it is clear that the dispersal order did not remove the protection accorded appellant by the original grant of permission.

Of course this does not mean that the police cannot call a halt to a meeting which though originally peaceful, becomes violent. Nor does it mean that, under properly drafted and administered statutes and ordinances, the authorities cannot set reasonable time limits for assemblies related to the policies of such laws and then order them dispersed when these time limits are exceeded. . . . We merely hold that, under circumstances such as those present in this case, appellant's conviction cannot be sustained on the basis of the dispersal order.

Nothing we have said here or in No. 24, ante, is to be interpreted as sanctioning riotous conduct in any form or demonstrations, however peaceful their conduct or commendable their motives, which conflict with properly drawn statutes and ordinances designed to promote law and order, protect the community against disorder, regulate traffic, safeguard legitimate interests in private and public property, or protect the administration of justice and other essential governmental functions.

. . . We reaffirm the repeated holdings of this Court that our constitutional command of free speech and assembly is basic and fundamental and encompasses peaceful social protest, so important to the preservation of the freedoms treasured in a democratic society. We also reaffirmed the repeated decisions of this Court that there is no place for violence in a democratic society dedicated to liberty under law, and that the right of peaceful protest does not mean that everyone with opinions or beliefs to express may do so at any time and at any place. There is a proper time and place for even the most peaceful protest and a plain duty and responsibility on the part of all citizens to obey all valid laws and regulations. There is an equally plain requirement for laws and regulations to be drawn so as to give citizens fair warning as to what is illegal; for regulation of conduct that involves freedom of speech and assembly not to be so broad in scope as to stifle First Amendment freedoms, which "need breathing space to survive," NAACP v. Button, 371 U.S. 415, 433; for appropriate limitations on the discretion of public officials where speech and assembly are intertwined with regulated conduct; and for all such laws and regulations to be applied with an equal hand. We believe that all of these requirements can be met in an ordered society dedicated to liberty. . . .

Reversed.

Mr. Justice BLACK, concurring in No. 24 and dissenting in No. 49.

I concur in the Court's judgment reversing appellant Cox's conviction for violation of the Louisiana statutes prohibiting breach of the peace and obstructing public passages, but I do so for reasons which differ somewhat from those stated in the Court's opinion. . . . On the other hand, I have no doubt that . . . the Louisiana statute which protects the administration of justice by forbidding such interferences is constitutional, both as written and as applied. . . .

The First and Fourteenth Amendments, I think, take away from government, state and federal, all power to restrict freedom of speech, press, and assembly *where people have a right to be for such purposes.* This does not mean, however, that these amendments also grant a constitutional right to engage in the conduct of picketing or patrolling, whether on publicly owned streets or on privately owned property. . . . Were the law otherwise, people on the streets, in their homes and anywhere else could be compelled to listen against their will to speakers they did not want to hear. Picketing, though it may be utilized to communicate ideas, is not speech, and therefore is not of itself protected by the First Amendment. . . . However, because Louisiana's breach-of-peace statute is not narrowly drawn to assure non-discriminatory application, I think it is constitutionally invalid under our holding in Edwards v. South Carolina . . . ..

. . . I believe that the First and Fourteenth Amendments require that if the streets of a town are open to some views, they must be open to all. [B]y specifically permitting picketing for the publication of labor union views, Louisiana is attempting to pick and choose among the views it is willing to have discussed on its streets. . . .

I would sustain the conviction [for picketing near a courthouse]. Certainly the most obvious reason for their protest at the courthouse was to influence the judge and other court officials . . . .. The Court attempts to support its holding by its inference that the Chief of Police gave his consent to picketing the courthouse. But quite apart from the fact that a police chief cannot authorize violations of his State's criminal laws, there was strong, emphatic testimony that if any consent was given it was limited to telling Cox and his group to come no closer to the courthouse than they had already come without the consent of any official, city, state, or federal. And there was also testimony that when told to leave appellant Cox defied the order by telling the crowd not to move. I fail to understand how the Court can justify the reversal of this conviction because of a permission which testimony in the record denies was given, which could not have been authoritatively given anyway, and which even if given was soon afterwards revoked. . . .

. . . Those who encourage minority groups to believe that the United States Constitution and federal laws give them a right to patrol and picket in the streets whenever they choose, in order to advance what they think to be a just and noble end, do no service to those minority groups, their cause, or their country. I am confident from this record that this appellant violated the Louisiana statute because of a mistaken belief that he and his followers had a constitutional right to do so, because of what they believed were just grievances. But the history of the past 25 years if it shows nothing else shows that his group's constitutional and statutory rights have to be protected by the courts, which must be kept free from intimidation and coercive pressures of any kind. Government under law as ordained by our Constitution is too precious, too sacred, to be jeopardized by subjecting the courts to intimidatory practices that have been fatal to individual liberty and minority rights wherever such practices have been allowed to poison the streams of justice. I would be wholly unwilling to join in moving this country a single step in that direction.

Mr. Justice CLARK, concurring in No. 24 and dissenting in No. 49.

. . .

[T]he Court excuses Cox's brazen defiance of the statute—the validity of which the Court upholds—on a . . . subtle ground. . . . With due deference, the record will not support this novel theory. . . . [I] join my Brother Black on this facet of the case. I also agree with him that the statute prohibiting obstruction of public passages is invalid under the Equal Protection Clause. And, as will be seen, I arrive at the same conclusion for the same reason on the question regarding the breach of the peace statute. However, I cannot agree that the latter Act is unconstitutionally vague. . . .

Mr. Justice WHITE, with whom Mr. Justice HARLAN joins, concurring in part and dissenting in part.

In No. 49, I agree with the dissent filed by my Brother Black in [the last part] of his opinion. In No. 24, although I do not agree with everything the Court says concerning the breach of peace conviction, particularly its statement concerning the unqualified protection to be extended to Cox's exhortations to engage in sit-ins in restaurants, I agree that the conviction for breach of peace is governed by Edwards v. South Carolina, 372 U.S. 229, and must be reversed.

Regretfully, I also dissent from the reversal of the conviction for obstruction of public passages. The Louisiana statute is not invalidated on its face but only in its application. But this remarkable emasculation of a prohibitory statute is based on only very vague evidence that other meetings and parades have been allowed by the authorities. . . . There is no evidence in the record that other meetings of this magnitude had been allowed on the city streets, had been allowed in the vicinity of the courthouse or had been permitted completely to obstruct the sidewalk and to block access to abutting buildings. . . .

Under the Court's broad, rather uncritical approach it would seem unavoidable that these same demonstrators could have met in the middle of any street during the rush hour or could have extended their meeting at any location hour after hour, day after day, without risking any action under this statute for interfering with the normal use of the streets and sidewalks. I doubt that this bizarre intrusion into local management of public streets is either required or justified by the prior cases in this Court.

Furthermore, even if the obstruction statute, because of prior permission granted to others, could not be applied in this case so as to prevent the demonstration, it does not necessarily follow that the federal license to use the streets is unlimited as to time and circumstance. . . . If the crowd was entitled to obstruct in order to demonstrate as the Court holds, it is nevertheless unnecessary to hold that the demonstration and the obstruction could continue *ad infinitum*. Here the demonstration was permitted to proceed for the period of time that the demonstrators had requested. When they were asked to disband, Cox twice refused. If he could refuse at this point I think he could refuse at any later time as well. But in my view at some point the authorities were entitled to apply the statute and to clear the streets. That point was reached here. To reverse the conviction under these circumstances makes it only rhetoric to talk of local power to control the streets under a properly drawn ordinance.

DEMONSTRATIONS AND COX: ADEQUATE GUIDELINES? ADEQUATE TECHNIQUE FOR DEVELOPING GUIDELINES?

Do the Cox cases make significant progress in developing Robert's Rules? Adequate progress? Are the Rules suggested sound? How should the gaps be filled? Is Professor Kalven persuasive in perceiving "a certain scheme of legal results" from the opinions: (1) at one extreme, it is "clear" that "this kind of use" of public places cannot be summarily suppressed as a breach of the peace, though there is some risk of violence; (2) at the other extreme, all picketing of courthouses can be prohibited; (3) "in the middle" is the "obstructing streets" question—a question the Court "colored with dicta but studiously avoided deciding." Kalven, "The Concept of the Public Forum: Cox v. Louisiana," 1965 Sup.Ct.Rev. 1. Is (1) "clear", after Feiner and Edwards? Is (2) sound? How should (2) be decided?

Was the rejection of clear and present danger regarding (2) sound? Would the clear and present danger test have been relevant here? At least as useful as in the contempt by publication cases distinguished in Cox I? Compare the comments on the contempt cases, chap. 16, p. 1284, infra. What *does* justify the ban on courthouse picketing? Is the "speech"-"conduct" distinction helpful? Kalven comments: "[A]ll speech is necessarily 'speech plus'." He also suggests that the "essential feature" of most civil rights demonstrations in public places is "appeal to public opinion." If that is so, can the Court respond to the communication element by labeling it conduct? If there is justification for restricting these forms of communication, should it not be explicitly stated why this "speech" is controllable, rather than suggesting there is no "speech" at all? Is the Court more sensitive in Brown, which follows? In Adderley, p. 1181 below? In Logan Valley Plaza, p. 1185 below?

Compare the "speech"-"conduct" distinction in the remaining cases in this section, and in the symbolic expression cases in the next section. Does the speech-conduct distinction tend to extend exaggerated protection to the (slim) "pure speech" category—and tend to give inadequate protection to communication outside that category? Does the "conduct" label unduly minimize the speech elements (and exaggerate the permissibility of restrictions)? Does the speech-conduct distinction promote insensitivity to speech ingredients in situations that involve *some* First Amendment elements? Do the draft card burning (O'Brien) and flag burning (Street) cases infra, pp. 1189 and 1202, illustrate that risk? Does the all-or-nothing distinction of two categories artificially separate matters of gradation and degree—and promote inadequate judicial scrutiny of the "conduct" category? And excessive scrutiny in the "speech" category?

BROWN v. LOUISIANA

383 U.S. 131, 86 S.Ct. 719, 15 L.Ed.2d 637 (1966).

Certiorari to the Supreme Court of Louisiana.

Mr. Justice FORTAS announced the judgment of the Court and an opinion in which The Chief Justice [WARREN] and Mr. Justice DOUGLAS join.

This is the fourth time in little more than four years that this Court has reviewed convictions by the Louisiana courts for alleged violations, in a civil rights context, of that State's breach of the peace statute. In the three preceding cases the convictions were reversed. [Garner v. Louisiana, 368 U.S. 157 (1961); Taylor v. Louisiana, 370 U.S. 154 (1962); Cox v. Louisiana, 379 U.S. 536 (1965).] Since the present case was decided under precisely the statute involved in Cox but before our decision in that case was announced, it might well be supposed that, without further ado, we would vacate and remand in light of Cox. But because the incident leading to the present convictions occurred in a public library and might be thought to raise materially different questions, we have heard argument and have considered the case *in extenso.*

The locus of the events was the Audubon Regional Library in the town of Clinton, Louisiana, Parish of East Feliciana. . . . The Audubon Regional Library [has] three branches and two bookmobiles. [Negroes could borrow books, but only from one of the bookmobiles.]

This tidy plan was challenged on Saturday, March 7, 1964, at about 11:30 a.m. Five young Negro males, all residents of East or West Feliciana Parishes, went into the adult reading or service room of the Audubon Regional Library at Clinton. The branch assistant, Mrs. Katie Reeves, was alone in the room. . . . Petitioner Brown requested a book . . .. Mrs. Reeves checked the card catalogue, ascertained that the Branch did not have the book, so advised Mr. Brown, and told him that she would request the book from the State Library, that he would be notified upon its receipt and that "he could either pick it up or it would be mailed to him." . . . Mrs. Reeves testified that she expected that the men would then leave; they did not, and she asked them to leave. They did not. Petitioner Brown sat down and the others stood near him. They said nothing; there was no noise or boisterous talking. . . .

[I]n "10 to 15 minutes" from the time of the arrival of the men at the library, the sheriff and deputies arrived. The sheriff asked the Negroes to leave. They said they would not. The sheriff then arrested them. . . .

On March 25, 1964, Mr. Brown and his four companions were tried and found guilty. . . . The charge was that they had congregated together in the public library of Clinton, Louisiana, "with the intent to provoke a breach of the peace and under circumstances such that a breach of the peace might be occasioned thereby" and had failed and refused "to leave said premises when ordered to do so" by the librarian and by the sheriff.

The Louisiana breach of peace statute under which they were accused reads as follows: "Whoever with intent to provoke a breach of the peace, or under circumstances such that a breach of the peace may be occasioned thereby: (1) crowds or congregates with others . . . in . . . a . . . public place or building . . . and who fails or refuses to disperse and move on, or disperse or move on, when ordered so to do by any law enforcement officer . . . or any other authorized person . . . shall be guilty of disturbing the peace." . . .

We come, then, to the barebones of the problem. Petitioners, five adult Negro men, remained in the library room for a total of ten or fifteen minutes. The first few moments were occupied by a ritualistic request for service and a response. We may assume that the response constituted service, and we need not consider whether it was merely a gambit in the ritual. This ceremony being out of the way, the Negroes proceeded to the business in hand. They sat and stood in the room, quietly, as monuments of protest against the segregation of the library. They were arrested and charged and convicted of breach of the peace under a specific statute.

[T]here is not the slightest evidence which would or could sustain the application of the statute to petitioners. . . . Nor were the circumstances such that a breach of the peace might be "occasioned" by their actions, as the statute alternatively provides. [But the State argues that the issue is "much simpler."] The issue, asserts the State, is simply that petitioners were using the library room "as a place in which to loaf or make a nuisance of themselves." The State argues that the "test"—the permissible civil rights demonstration —was concluded when petitioners entered the library, asked for service and were served. Having satisfied themselves, the argument runs, that they could get service, they should have departed. Instead, they simply sat there, "staring vacantly," and this was "enough to unnerve a woman in the situation Mrs. Reeves was in."

This is a piquant version of the affair, but the matter is hardly to be decided on points. It was not a game. It could not be won so handily by the gesture of service to this particular request. There is no dispute that the library system was segregated, and no possible doubt that these petitioners were there to protest this fact. But even if we were to agree with the State's ingenuous characterization of the events, we would have to reverse. There was no violation of the statute which petitioners are accused of breaching; no disorder, no intent to provoke a breach of the peace and no circumstances indicating that a breach might be occasioned by petitioners' actions. The sole statutory provision invoked by the State contains not a word about occupying the reading room of a public library for more than 15 minutes . . ..

But there is another and sharper answer which is called for. We are here dealing with an aspect of a basic constitutional right—the right under the First and Fourteenth Amendments guaranteeing freedom of speech and of assembly, and freedom to petition the Government for a redress of grievances. . . . As this Court has repeatedly stated, these rights are not confined to verbal expression. They embrace appropriate types of action which certainly include the right in a peaceable and orderly manner to protest by silent and reproachful presence, in a place where the protestant has every right to be, the unconstitutional segregation of public facilities. Accordingly, even if the accused action were within the scope of the statutory instrument, we would be required to assess the constitutional impact of its application, and we would have to hold that the statute cannot constitutionally be applied to punish petitioners' actions in the circumstances of this case. See Edwards v. South Carolina . . . .. The statute was deliberately and purposefully applied solely to terminate the reasonable, orderly, and limited exercise of the right to protest the unconstitutional segregation of a public facility. Interference with this right, so exercised, by state action is intolerable under our Constitution. . . .

It is an unhappy circumstance that the locus of these events was a public library—a place dedicated to quiet, to knowledge, and to beauty. It is a sad commentary that this hallowed place in the Parish of East Feliciana bore the ugly stamp of racism. It is sad, too, that it was a public library which, reasonably enough in the circumstances, was the stage for a confrontation between those discriminated against and the representatives of the offending parishes. Fortunately, the circumstances here were such that no claim can be made that use of the library by others was disturbed by the demonstration. Perhaps the time and method were carefully chosen with this in mind. Were it otherwise, a factor not present in this case would have to be considered. Here, there was no disturbance of others, no disruption of library activities, and no violation of any library regulations.

A State or its instrumentality may, of course, regulate the use of its libraries or other public facilities. But it must do so in a reasonable and non-discriminatory manner, equally applicable to all and administered with equality to all. It may not do so as to some and not as to all. It may not provide certain facilities for whites and others for Negroes. And it may not invoke regulations as to use—whether they are *ad hoc* or general—as a pretext for pursuing those engaged in lawful, constitutionally protected exercise of their fundamental rights. . . .

Reversed.

Mr. Justice BRENNAN, concurring in the judgment. . . .

Since the overbreadth of § 14:103.1 as construed clearly requires the reversal of these convictions, it is wholly unnecessary to reach, let alone rest reversal, as the prevailing opinion seems to do, on the proposition that even a narrowly drawn "statute cannot constitutionally be applied to punish petitioners' actions in the circumstances of this case."

Mr. Justice WHITE, concurring in the result. . . .

[I]t is difficult to believe that if this group had been white its members would have been asked to leave on such short notice, much less asked to leave by the sheriff and arrested, rather than merely escorted from the building, when reluctance to leave was demonstrated. . . . In my view, the behavior of these petitioners and their use of the library building, even though it was for the purposes of a demonstration, did not depart significantly from what normal library use would contemplate. The conclusion that petitioners were making only a normal and authorized use of this public library requires the reversal of their convictions. . . . On this record, it is difficult to avoid the conclusion that petitioners were asked to leave the library because they were Negroes. If they were, their convictions deny them equal protection of the laws.

Mr. Justice BLACK, with whom Mr. Justice CLARK, Mr. Justice HARLAN, and Mr. Justice STEWART join, dissenting. . . .

. . . The case relied on most heavily by the prevailing opinion and my Brother Brennan is [Cox I, supra]. That case, unlike this one, involved picketing and patrolling in the streets, and correspondingly that part of the Louisiana breach of the peace statute which prohibited certain kinds of street activity. The language of the phase of the statute under consideration here, relating to congregating in public buildings and refusing to move on when ordered to do so by an authorized person, was in no way involved or discussed in Cox. The problems of state regulation of the streets on the one hand, and public buildings on the other, are quite obviously separate and distinct. Public buildings such as libraries, schoolhouses, fire departments, courthouses, and executive mansions are maintained to perform certain specific and vital functions. Order and tranquillity of a sort entirely unknown to the public streets are essential to their normal operation. Contrary to the implications in the prevailing opinion it is incomprehensible to me that a State must measure disturbances in its libraries and on the streets with identical standards. . . .

[T]here simply was no racial discrimination practiced in this case. These petitioners . . . asked for a book, perhaps as the prevailing opinion suggests more as a ritualistic ceremonial than anything else. The lady in charge nevertheless hunted for the book, found she did not have it, sent for it, and later obtained it from the state library for petitioners' use. . . .

. . . The only factual question which can possibly arise regarding the application of the statute here is whether under Louisiana law petitioners either intended to breach the peace or created circumstances under which a breach might have been occasioned. . . . A tiny parish branch library, staffed by two women, is not a department store as in Garner v. Louisiana, supra, nor a bus terminal as in Taylor v. Louisiana, supra, nor a public thoroughfare as in Edwards v. South Carolina, supra, and Cox. Short of physical violence, petitioners could not have more completely upset the normal, quiet functioning of the Clinton branch of the Audubon Regional Library. The state courts below thought the disturbance created by petitioners constituted a violation of the statute. So far as the reversal here rests on a holding that the Louisiana statute was not violated, the Court simply substitutes its judgment for that of the Louisiana courts as to what conduct satisfies the requirements of that state statute. . . .

. . . Apparently unsatisfied with or unsure of the "no evidence" ground for reversing the convictions, the prevailing opinion goes on to state that the statute was used unconstitutionally in the circumstances of this case because it was "deliberately and purposefully applied solely to terminate the reasonable, orderly, and limited exercise of the right to protest the unconstitutional segregation of a public facility." First, I am constrained to say that this statement is wholly unsupported by the record in this case. . . . Moreover, the conclusion . . . establishes a completely new constitutional doctrine. In this case this new constitutional principle means that even though these petitioners did not want to use the Louisiana public library for library purposes, they had a constitutional right nevertheless to stay there over the protest of the librarians who had lawful authority to keep the library orderly for the use of people who wanted to use its books, its magazines, and its papers. But the principle espoused also has a far broader meaning. It means that the Constitution, the First and the Fourteenth Amendments, requires the custodians and supervisors of the public libraries in this country to stand helplessly by while protesting groups advocating one cause or another, stage "sit-ins" or "stand-ups" to dramatize their particular views on particular issues. And it should be remembered that if one group can take over libraries for one cause, other groups will assert the right to do so for causes which, while wholly legal, may not be so appealing to this Court. The States are thus paralyzed with reference to control of their libraries for library purposes, and I suppose that inevitably the next step will be to paralyze the schools. Efforts to this effect have already been made all over the country. . . .

[The First Amendment] does not guarantee to any person the right to use someone else's property, even that owned by government and dedicated to other purposes, as a stage to express dissident ideas. The novel constitutional doctrine of the prevailing opinion nevertheless exalts the power of private nongovernmental groups to determine what use shall be made of governmental property over the power of the elected governmental officials of the States and the Nation. . . .

. . . I am deeply troubled with the fear that powerful private groups throughout the Nation will read the Court's action, as I do—that is, as granting them a license to invade the tranquillity and beauty of our libraries whenever they have quarrel with some state policy which may or may not exist. It is an unhappy circumstance in my judgment that the group, which more than any other has needed a government of equal laws and equal justice, is now encouraged to believe that the best way for it to advance its cause, which is a worthy one, is by taking the law into its own hands from place to place and from time to time. Governments like ours were formed to substitute the rule of law for the rule of force. Illustrations may be given where crowds have gathered together peaceably by reason of extraordinarily good discipline reinforced by vigilant officers. "Demonstrations" have taken place without any manifestations of force at the time. But I say once more that the crowd moved by noble ideals today can become the mob ruled by hate and passion and greed and violence tomorrow. If we ever doubted that, we know it now. The peaceful songs of love can become as stirring and provocative as the Marseillaise did in the days when a noble revolution gave way to rule by successive mobs until chaos set in. The holding in this case today makes it more necessary than ever that we stop and look more closely at where we are going. . . .

ADDERLEY v. FLORIDA

385 U.S. 39, 87 S.Ct. 242, 17 L.Ed.2d 149 (1966).

Certiorari to the Florida District Court of Appeals.

Mr. Justice BLACK delivered the opinion of the Court.

Petitioners, Harriett Louise Adderley and 31 other persons, were convicted by a jury in a joint trial in the County Judge's Court of Leon County, Florida, on a charge of "trespass with a malicious and mischievous intent" upon the premises of the county jail contrary to § 821.18 of the Florida statutes set out below.[1] Petitioners, apparently all students of the Florida A. & M. University in Tallahassee, had gone from the school to the jail about a mile away, along with many other students, to "demonstrate" at the jail their protests because of arrests of other protesting students the day before, and perhaps to protest more generally against state and local policies and practices of racial segregation, including segregation of the jail. The county sheriff, legal custodian of the jail and jail grounds, tried to persuade the students to leave the jail grounds. When this did not work, he notified them that they must leave, notified them that they must leave or he would arrest them for trespassing, and notified them further that if they resisted arrest he would arrest them for resisting arrest as well. Some of the students left but others, including petitioners, remained and they were arrested. . . .

Petitioners have insisted from the beginning of these cases that they are controlled and must be reversed because of our prior cases of Edwards v. South Carolina, 372 U.S. 229, and Cox v. Louisiana, 379 U.S. 536, 559. We cannot agree. . . . In Edwards, the demonstrators went to the South Carolina

---

1. "Every trespass upon the property of another, committed wtih a malicious and mischievous intent, the punishment of which is not specially provided for, shall be punished by impris- onment not exceeding three months, or by fine not exceeding one hundred dollars." Fla.Stat. § 821.18, F.S.A. (1965). [Footnote by the Court.]

State Capitol grounds to protest. In this case they went to the jail. Traditionally, state capitol grounds are open to the public. Jails, built for security purposes, are not. The demonstrators at the South Carolina Capitol went in through a public driveway and as they entered they were told by state officials there that they had a right as citizens to go through the State House grounds as long as they were peaceful. Here the demonstrators entered the jail grounds through a driveway used only for jail purposes and without warning to or permission from the sheriff. More importantly, [t]he South Carolina breach-of-the-peace statute was . . . struck down as being so broad and all-embracing as to jeopardize speech, press, assembly and petition . . . .. And it was on this same ground of vagueness that . . . the Louisiana breach-of-the-peace law used to prosecute Cox was invalidated.

The Florida trespass statute under which these petitioners were charged cannot be challenged on this ground. It is aimed at conduct of one limited kind, that is for one person or persons to trespass upon the property of another with a malicious and mischievous intent. There is no lack of notice in this law, nothing to entrap or fool the unwary. . . .

Petitioners here contend that "Petitioners' convictions are based on a total lack of relevant evidence." If true, this would be a denial of due process under Garner v. Louisiana, 368 U.S. 157, and Thompson v. Louisville, 362 U.S. 199. [P]etitioners' summary of facts as well as that of the Circuit Court show an abundance of facts to support the jury's verdict of guilty in these cases.

In summary both these statements show testimony ample to prove this: Disturbed and upset by the arrest of their schoolmates the day before, a large number of Florida A. & M. students assembled on the school grounds and decided to march down to the county jail. Some apparently wanted to get themselves put in jail too, along with the students already there. A group of around 200 marched from the school and arrived at the jail singing and clapping. They went directly to the jail door entrance where they were met by a deputy sheriff, evidently surprised by their arrival. He asked them to move back, claiming they were blocking the entrance to the jail and fearing that they might attempt to enter the jail. They moved back part of the way, where they stood or sat, singing, clapping and dancing on the jail driveway and on an adjacent grassy area upon the jail premises. This particular jail entrance and driveway were not normally used by the public, but by the sheriff's department for transporting prisoners to and from the courts several blocks away and by commercial concerns for servicing the jail. Even after their partial retreat, the demonstrators continued to block vehicular passage over this driveway up to the entrance of the jail. Someone called the sheriff . . . .. He told [two of the leaders] that they were trespassing upon jail property and that he would give them 10 minutes to leave or he would arrest them. . . . After about 10 minutes, the sheriff, in a voice loud enough to be heard by all, told the demonstrators that he was the legal custodian of the jail and its premises, that they were trespassing on county property in violation of the law, that they should all leave forthwith or he would arrest them, and that if they attempted to resist arrest, he would charge them with that as a separate offense. Some of the group then left. Others, including all petitioners, did not leave. Some of them sat down. In a few minutes, . . . the sheriff ordered his deputies to surround those remaining on jail premises and placed them, 107 demonstrators, under arrest. . . .

Under the foregoing testimony the jury was authorized to find that the State had proven every essential element of the crime, as it was defined by the state court. That [leaves] only the question of whether conviction of the state offense, thus defined, unconstitutionally deprived petitioners of their rights to freedom of speech, press, assembly or petition. We hold it does not. The sheriff, as jail custodian, had power, as the state courts have here held, to direct that this large crowd of people get off the grounds. There is not a shred of evidence in this record that this power was exercised . . . . because the sheriff objected to what was being sung or said by the demonstrators or because he disagreed with the objectives of their protest. The record reveals that he objected only to their presence on that part of the jail grounds reserved for jail uses. There is no evidence at all that on any other occasion had similarly large groups of the public been permitted to gather on this portion of the jail grounds for any purpose. Nothing in the Constitution of the United States prevents Florida from even-handed enforcement of its general trespass statute against those refusing to obey the sheriff's order to remove themselves from what amounted to the curtilage of the jailhouse. The State, no less than a private owner of property, has power to preserve the property under its control for the use to which it is lawfully dedicated. For this reason there is no merit to the petitioners' argument that they had a constitutional right to stay on the property, over the jail custodian's objections, because this "area chosen for the peaceful civil rights demonstration was not only 'reasonable' but also particularly appropriate . . .." Such an argument has as its major unarticulated premises the assumption that people who want to propagandize protests or views have a constitutional right to do so whenever and however and wherever they please. That concept of constitutional law was vigorously and forthrightfully rejected in two of the cases petitioners rely on, Cox v. Louisiana . . . .. We reject it again. The United States Constitution does not forbid a State to control the use of its own property for its own lawful nondiscriminatory purpose.

Affirmed.

Mr. Justice DOUGLAS, with whom The Chief Justice [WARREN], Mr. Justice BRENNAN, and Mr. Justice FORTAS concur, dissenting. . . .

[T]he Court errs in treating this case as if it were an ordinary trespass case or an ordinary picketing case.

The jailhouse, like an executive mansion, a legislative chamber, a courthouse, or the statehouse itself, . . . is one of the seats of government whether it be the Tower of London, the Bastille, or a small county jail. And when it houses political prisoners or those whom many think are unjustly held, it is an obvious center for protest. The right to petition for the redress of grievances has an ancient history and is not limited to writing a letter or sending a telegram to a congressman; it is not confined to appearing before the local city council, or writing letters to the President or Governor or Mayor. See NAACP v. Button, 371 U.S. 415, 429–431. Conventional methods of petitioning may be, and often have been, shut off to large groups of our citizens. Legislators may turn deaf ears; formal complaints may be routed endlessly through a bureaucratic maze; courts may let the wheels of justice grind very slowly. Those who do not control television and radio, those who cannot afford to advertise in newspapers or circulate elaborate pamphlets may have only a more limited type of access to public officials. Their methods should not be condemned as tactics of obstruction and harassment as long as the assembly and petition are peaceable, as these were.

There is no question that petitioners had as their purpose a protest against the arrest of Florida A. & M. students for trying to integrate public theatres. . . . The petitioners . . . stated that the group was protesting the arrests, and state and local policies of segregation, including segregation of the jail. . . . The fact that no one gave a formal speech, that no elaborate handbills were distributed, and that the group was not laden with signs would seem to be immaterial. Such methods are not the *sine qua non* of petitioning for the redress of grievances. The group did sing "freedom" songs. And history shows that a song can be a powerful tool of protest. . . . There was no violence; no threats of violence; no attempted jail break; no storming of a prison; no plan or plot to do anything but protest. The evidence is uncontradicted that the petitioners' conduct did not upset the jailhouse routine . . . . There was no shoving, no pushing, no disorder or threat of riot. It is said that some of the group blocked part of the driveway leading to the jail entrance. . . . If there was congestion, the solution was a further request to move to lawns or parking areas, not complete ejection and arrest. . . . Finally the fact that some of the protestants may have felt their cause so just that they were willing to be arrested for making their protest outside the jail seems wholly irrelevant. A petition is nonetheless a petition, though its futility may make martyrdom attractive.

We do violence to the First Amendment when we permit this "petition for redress of grievances" to be turned into a trespass action. It does not help to analogize this problem to the problem of picketing. Picketing is a form of protest usually directed against private interests. . . . The Court forgets that prior to this day our decisions have drastically limited the application of state statutes inhibiting the right to go peacefully on public property to exercise First Amendment rights. . . . When we allow Florida to construe her "malicious trespass" statute to bar a person from going on property knowing it is not his own and to apply that prohibition to public property, we discard Cox and Edwards. Would the case be any different if, as is common, the demonstration took place outside a building which housed both the jail and the legislative body? I think not.

There may be some public places which are so clearly committed to other purposes that their use for the airing of grievances is anomalous. There may be some instances in which assemblies and petitions for redress of grievances are not consistent with other necessary purposes of public property. A noisy meeting may be out of keeping with the serenity of the statehouse or the quiet of the courthouse. No one, for example, would suggest that the Senate gallery is the proper place for a vociferous protest rally. And, in other cases it may be necessary to adjust the right to petition for redress of grievances to the other interests inhering in the uses to which the public property is normally put. . . . But this is quite different than saying that all public places are off-limits to people with grievances. . . . And it is farther yet from saying that the "custodian" of the public property in his discretion can decide when public places shall be used for the communication of ideas, especially the constitutional right to assemble and petition for redress of grievances. . . .

Today a trespass law is used to penalize people for exercising a constitutional right. Tomorrow a disorderly conduct statute, a breach of the peace statute, a vagrancy statute will be put to the same end. It is said that the sheriff did not make the arrests because of the views which petitioners espoused. That excuse is usually given, as we know from the many cases involving arrests of minority groups for breaches of the peace, unlawful assemblies, and parading without a permit.   [S]uch arrests are usually sought to be justified by some legitimate function of government.   Yet by allowing these orderly and civilized protests against injustice to be suppressed, we only increase the forces of frustration which the conditions of second-class citizenship are generating amongst us.*

PUBLIC PLACES, PRIVATE PROPERTY, AND PICKETING: THE LOGAN VALLEY PLAZA CASE

Did the Logan Valley Plaza case contain a more adequate analysis of the public forum problem than Adderley and the prior cases?   Amalgamated Food Employees v. Logan Valley Plaza, 391 U.S. 308 (1968), was a 5:4 decision holding that state trespass law could not be applied to enjoin peaceful union picketing of a supermarket in a private shopping center.†   In the course of the majority opinion, Justice Marshall commented: "It is clear that if the shopping center premises were not privately owned but instead constituted the business area of a municipality, which they to a large extent resemble, petitioners could not be barred from exerting their First Amendment rights there on the sole ground that title to the property was in the municipality.   The essence of [cases such as Lovell v. Griffin, Hague v. CIO, and Schneider v. New Jersey, supra] is that streets, sidewalks, parks, and other similar places are so historically associated with the exercise of First Amendment rights that access to them for the purpose of exercising such rights cannot constitutionally be denied broadly and absolutely.

"The fact that [decisions such as Lovell and Schneider] were concerned with handbilling rather than picketing is immaterial so far as the question is solely one of right of access for the purpose of expression of views.   Handbilling, like picketing, involves conduct other than speech, namely, the physical presence of the person distributing leaflets on municipal property.   If title to municipal property is, standing alone, an insufficient basis for prohibiting all entry onto such property for the purpose of distributing printed matter, it is likewise an insufficient basis for prohibiting all entry for the purpose of carrying an informational placard.   While the patrolling involved in picketing may in some cases constitute an interference with the use of public property greater than that produced by handbilling, it is clear that in other cases the converse may be true. . . .   That the manner in which handbilling, or picketing, is carried out may be regulated does not mean that either can be barred under all circumstances on publicly owned property simply by recourse to traditional concepts of property law concerning the incidents of ownership of real property."

---

* For a subsequent Court encounter with demonstrations, recall Gregory v. Chicago, 394 U.S. 111 (1969), noted at p. 1166, supra, where the Court reversed disorderly conduct convictions of petitioners who "marched in a peaceful and orderly procession from city hall to the mayor's residence to press their claims" for school desegregation.

† The "state action" aspect of the case has been noted earlier (chap. 6, p. 466, supra).   Other First Amendment aspects of labor picketing are considered infra (chap. 16, p. 1299).

Justice Marshall distinguished decisions sustaining restrictions on use of public property—such as Adderley—by noting that, "where property is not ordinarily open to the public, this Court has held that access to it for the purpose of exercising First Amendment rights may be denied altogether. Even where municipal or state property is open to the public generally, the exercise of First Amendment rights may be regulated so as to prevent interference with the use to which the property is ordinarily put by the State. . . . . In addition, the exercise of First Amendment rights may be regulated where such exercise will unduly interfere with the normal use of the public property by other members of the public with an equal right of access to it. Thus it has been held that persons desiring to parade along city streets may be required to secure a permit in order that municipal authorities be able to limit the amount of interference with use of the sidewalks by other members of the public by regulating the time, place, and manner of the parade." [Note also the limits on schoolroom protests imposed by interference with "normal use"; see the Tinker and Barker cases, sec. 3, pp. 1195 and 1201, infra.]

The detailed scope of permissible restrictions was not at issue here, however: "Because the Pennsylvania courts have held that 'picketing and trespassing' can be prohibited absolutely on respondents' premises, we have no occasion to consider the extent to which respondents are entitled to limit the location and manner of the picketing or the number of picketers within the mall in order to prevent interference with either access to the market building or vehicular use of the parcel pickup area and parking lot. Likewise, Adderley furnishes no support for the decision below because it is clear that the public has virtually unrestricted access to the property at issue here. [T]he restraints on picketing and trespassing approved by the Pennsylvania courts here substantially hinder the communication of the idea which petitioners seek to express . . . . The fact that the non-speech aspect of petitioners' activity are also rendered less effective is not particularly compelling in light of the absence of any showing . . . that the patrolling accompanying the picketing sought to be carried on was significantly interfering with the use to which the mall property was being put by both respondents and the general public. [T]he mere fact that speech is accompanied by conduct does not mean that the speech can be suppressed under the guise of prohibiting the conduct. Here it is perfectly clear that a prohibition against trespass on the mall operates to bar all speech within the shopping center to which respondents object. Yet this Court stated many years ago, '[O]ne is not to have the exercise of his liberty of expression in appropriate places abridged on the plea that it may be exercised in some other place.' Schneider v. New Jersey. . . . ."

Justice Black's dissent included the comment: "[O]f course, picketing, that is patrolling, is not free speech and not protected as such." Justice White's dissent stated, in partial reliance on Adderley: "[S]ome public property is available for some uses and not for others; some public property is neither designed nor dedicated for use by pickets or for other communicative activities. [W]hether Logan Valley Plaza is public or private property, it is a place for shopping and not a place for picketing."

COMPLIANCE WITH PERMIT REQUIREMENTS AND INJUNCTIONS IN THE DEMONSTRATIONS CONTEXT

To what extent do the doctrines of the early licensing cases—see Lovell v. Griffin and Cox v. New Hampshire, pp. 1142 and 1143, supra, — govern the modern regulation of meetings and parades through permit requirements and other "prior restraints"? When may the demonstrator ignore the requirement? When can he challenge it only after an attempt to comply with it? The Court considered these questions in connection with two efforts to challenge the Birmingham parade permit ordinance. Both efforts involved the Good Friday civil rights protest march in Birmingham in 1963, led by several Negro ministers including Martin Luther King, Jr. The first effort failed: in Walker v. City of Birmingham, 388 U.S. 307 (1967), the Court held that the demonstrators, who had marched in the face of an ex parte injunction which they had refused to challenge in court, could not defend contempt charges by asserting the unconstitutionality of the ordinance or the injunction. But two years later, in Shuttlesworth v. Birmingham, 394 U.S. 147 (1969), where the charge was parading without a permit rather than disobeying an injunction, the Court held the ordinance unconstitutional.

1. *Walker.* In Walker, a 5:4 decision sustained a state court's refusal to consider constitutional challenges to the injunction and to the ordinance at the contempt hearing: petitioners had openly flouted the injunction because they considered it "raw tyranny"; Alabama had justifiably relied on the general rule that court orders must be obeyed until "reversed for error by orderly review." Justice Stewart concluded: "This Court cannot hold that the petitioners were constitutionally free to ignore all the procedures of the law and carry their battle to the streets." Justice Brennan's dissent, joined by Chief Justice Warren and Justices Douglas and Fortas, insisted that the Court had elevated a "rule of judicial administration above the right of free expression." [Compare the First Amendment limits imposed on ex parte injunctions in a subsequent case in which petitioners obeyed the injunction and then challenged it in court. Carroll v. President & Comm'rs of Princess Anne, 393 U.S. 175 (1968), note 3, infra.]

2. *Shuttlesworth.* In Shuttlesworth, however, one of the petitioners in Walker was permitted to challenge the parade ordinance in attacking his conviction for marching without a permit. The ordinance directed the city commission to issue a permit "unless in its judgment the public welfare, peace, safety, health, decency, good order, morals, or convenience require that it be refused." Justice Stewart's opinion for the Court had "no doubt" that, as written, the ordinance was unconstitutional: it conferred "virtually unbridled and absolute power" and therefore "fell squarely within the ambit of the many decisions of this Court over the last 30 years, holding that a law subjecting the exercise of First Amendment freedoms to the prior restraint of a license, without narrow, objective, and definite standards to guide the licensing authority," is void.

The state countered that the conviction should nevertheless stand because the highest state court here—following the pattern accepted by the Court in Cox v. New Hampshire, p. 1143, supra—had given a narrow construction to the broadly written law in reviewing petitioner's case. The Court conceded that the Alabama judges' "remarkable job of plastic surgery upon the face of the ordinance" had transformed it into one "authorizing no more than the objective and even-handed regulation of traffic." But here, unlike Cox, the narrowing effort came too late. Here, it was difficult to anticipate the subsequent construction: it "would have taken extraordinary clairvoyance for anyone" in 1963 to perceive that the ordinance meant what the highest state court construed it to mean in 1967. Moreover, the city officials had demonstrated in 1963 that they thought "the ordinance meant exactly what it said" on its face: they had given petitioner to understand that "under no circumstances" would he be permitted to demonstrate in Birmingham. In Cox, unlike here, there had been no prior administration different from the state court's subsequent narrowing construction. Justice Black concurred in the result; Justice Harlan submitted a concurring opinion. See generally Blasi, "Prior Restraints on Demonstrations," to appear in 68 Mich.L.Rev. (1970).

3. *Carroll.* Contrast with the impact of the injunction in Walker the restrictions imposed on injunctions in a properly raised challenge, in the Carroll case mentioned at the end of note 1, supra. In Carroll v. President & Comm'rs of Princess Anne, 393 U.S. 175 (1968), the Court found unconstitutional the ex parte procedure followed in issuing a 10-day temporary restraining order against holding a public rally. Petitioners had held a meeting at which they made "aggressively and militantly racist" speeches to a crowd of both whites and Negroes. They announced that they would resume the rally the following night. Before that time, local officials obtained the order restraining petitioners and their "white supremacist" National States Rights Party from holding meetings "which will tend to disturb and endanger the citizens of the County." There was no notice to petitioners prior to the issuance of the order. The rally was cancelled and petitioners (rather than ignoring the injunction as in Walker) challenged the injunction in court.

Justice Fortas' opinion for the Court found no adequate justification for the ex parte nature of the proceedings. In the rare situations where prior restraints were permissible (see Freedman v. Maryland, infra, p. 1267), "the Court has insisted upon careful procedural provisions." "There is a place in our jurisprudence for ex parte issuance, without notice, of temporary restraining orders of short duration; but there is no place within the area of basic freedoms guaranteed by the First Amendment for such orders where no showing is made that it is impossible to serve or to notify the opposing parties and to give them an opportunity to participate." Here, procedural care was even more important than in the obscenity area: "The present case involves a rally and 'political' speech in which the element of timeliness may be important." Moreover, without an adversary hearing, "there is insufficient assurance of the balanced analysis and careful conclusions which are essential in the area of First Amendment adjudication."

SECTION 3. SYMBOLIC EXPRESSION

---

1. *Some introductory questions.* In the three cases of the late sixties that follow, individuals expressed criticism of public policies in part through symbolic behavior rather than words: by burning a draft card; by wearing a black armband in a classroom; by burning the flag. In each case, the critic

claimed immunity from governmental restraint on the ground that the expression, albeit partly non-verbal, was constitutionally protected "speech." The cases appear in this concluding section of the basic First Amendment chapter not only because of the functional importance of the protest methods and contexts. (Two of the symbolic protests stemmed from anti-war views, the third from civil rights concerns.) Even stronger reasons for grouping the decisions here lie in issues of analysis and doctrine.

In these cases, many of the themes developed in the preceding two sections meet and are put to a test; the problems of these cases serve to bring under critical examination the techniques of the earlier cases. How useful, for example, are distinctions between "speech" and "conduct," between "direct" and "indirect" regulations of expression? If threats to First Amendment values warrant a high level of judicial scrutiny, in contrast to the lower level of inquiry appropriate for most areas of social and economic regulation, what are the criteria for invoking that strict as against the "mere rationality," low level degree of scrutiny? Did the cases that follow involve regulations of "speech", or of "speech plus"? Of "direct", or of "indirect" restraints on communication? What degrees of legislative justification should have been required? What degrees were in fact demanded by the Court? What levels of judicial inquiry were appropriate? What levels were in fact applied? (Note also the questions at the end of this chapter, at p. 1208.)

2. *The background.* The perception that "speech" may be nonverbal did not originate in these cases of the sixties. As the opinions reflect, earlier decisions had given First Amendment protection to some varieties of symbolic expression. For example, as early as 1931, in Stromberg v. California, 283 U.S. 359, the Court held unconstitutional a California prohibition on displaying a red flag "as a sign, symbol or emblem of opposition to organized government." Chief Justice Hughes' majority opinion stated that a law "so vague and indefinite as to permit the punishment of the fair use" of "the opportunity for free political discussion" was "repugnant to the guaranty of liberty" in the 14th Amendment.

In the following decade, moreover, West Virginia State Board of Education v. Barnette, 319 U.S. 624 (1943) (p. 1394, infra), held that public school children could not be compelled to salute the flag in violation of their religious scruples. And the prevailing opinion in Brown v. Louisiana, 383 U.S. 131 (1966) (the public library demonstration case, supra, p. 1176), emphasized that First Amendment rights "are not confined to verbal expression" and "embrace appropriate types of action." The constitutional claims in the symbolic expression cases which follow sought to build on these premises.

UNITED STATES v. O'BRIEN

391 U.S. 367, 88 S.Ct. 1673, 20 L.Ed.2d 672 (1968).

Certiorari to the United States Court of Appeals for the First Circuit.

Mr. Chief Justice WARREN delivered the opinion of the Court.

On the morning of March 31, 1966, David Paul O'Brien and three companions burned their Selective Service registration certificates on the steps of the South Boston Courthouse. A sizable crowd, including several agents of the Federal Bureau of Investigation, witnessed the event. Immediately after the burning, members of the crowd began attacking O'Brien and his companions. An FBI agent ushered O'Brien to safety inside the courthouse. After he was advised of his right to counsel and to silence, O'Brien stated to FBI agents that he had burned his registration certificate because of his beliefs, knowing that he was violating federal law. He produced the charred remains of the certificate, which, with his consent, were photographed.

For this act, O'Brien was indicted, tried, convicted, and sentenced in the United States District Court for the District of Massachusetts. He did not contest the fact that he had burned the certificate. He stated in argument to the jury that he burned the certificate publicly to influence others to adopt his antiwar beliefs, as he put it, "so that other people would reevaluate their positions with Selective Service, with the armed forces, and reevaluate their place in the culture of today, to hopefully consider my position."

The indictment upon which he was tried charged that he "willfully and knowingly did mutilate, destroy, and change by burning . . . [his] Registration Certificate (Selective Service System Form No. 2); in violation of Title 50, App., United States Code, Section 462(b)." Section 462(b) is part of the Universal Military Training and Service Act of 1948. Section 462(b)(3), one of six numbered subdivisions of § 462(b), was amended by Congress in 1965, 79 Stat. 586 (adding the words italicized below), so that at the time O'Brien burned his certificate an offense was committed by any person,

"who forges, alters, *knowingly destroys, knowingly mutilates,* or in any manner changes any such certificate . . . . ." (Italics supplied.)

In the District Court, O'Brien argued that the 1965 Amendment prohibiting the knowing destruction or mutilation of certificates was unconstitutional because it was enacted to abridge free speech, and because it served no legitimate legislative purpose. The District Court rejected these arguments [but the Court of Appeals] held the 1965 Amendment unconstitutional as a law abridging freedom of speech. At the time the Amendment was enacted, a regulation of the Selective Service System required registrants to keep their registration certificates in their "personal possession at all times." Wilful violations of regulations promulgated pursuant to the Universal Military Training and Service Act were made criminal by statute. The Court of Appeals, therefore, was of the opinion that conduct punishable under the 1965 Amendment was already punishable under the nonpossession regulation, and consequently that the Amendment served no valid purpose; further, that in light of the prior regulation, the Amendment must have been "directed at public as distinguished from private destruction." On this basis, the court concluded that the 1965 Amendment ran afoul of the First Amendment by singling out persons engaged in protests for special treatment. . . . We hold that the 1965 Amendment is constitutional both as enacted and as applied. . . .

I.

When a male reaches the age of 18, he is required by the Universal Military Training and Service Act to register with a local draft board. He is assigned a Selective Service number, and within five days he is issued a registration certificate (SSS Form No. 2). Subsequently, and based on a questionnaire completed by the registrant, he is assigned a classification denoting his eligibility for induction, and "[a]s soon as practicable" thereafter he is issued a Notice of Classification (SSS Form No. 110). . . . .

Congress demonstrated its concern that [registration and classification] certificates issued by the Selective Service System might be abused well before the 1965 Amendment here challenged. The 1948 Act itself prohibited many different abuses involving "any registration certificate, . . . or any other certificate issued pursuant to or prescribed by the provisions of this title, or rules or regulations promulgated hereunder . . . ." Under §§ 12(b) (1)–(5) of the 1948 Act, it was unlawful (1) to transfer a certificate to aid a person in making false identification; (2) to possess a certificate not duly issued with the intent of using it for false identification; (3) to forge, alter, "or in any manner" change a certificate or any notation validly inscribed thereon; (4) to photograph or make an imitation of a certificate for the purpose of false identification; and (5) to possess a counterfeited or altered certificate. In addition, as previously mentioned, regulations of the Selective Service System required registrants to keep both their registration and classification certificates in their personal possession at all times. . . . And § 12(b) (6) of the Act made knowing violation of any provision of the Act or rules and regulations promulgated pursuant thereto a felony.

By the 1965 Amendment, Congress added to § 12(b) (3) of the 1948 Act the provision here at issue, subjecting to criminal liability not only one who "forges, alters, or in any manner changes" but also one who "knowingly destroys, [or] knowingly mutilates" a certificate. We note at the outset that the 1965 Amendment plainly does not abridge free speech on its face, and we do not understand O'Brien to argue otherwise. Amended § 12(b) (3) on its face deals with conduct having no connection with speech. It prohibits the knowing destruction of certificates issued by the Selective Service System, and there is nothing necessarily expressive about such conduct. The Amendment does not distinguish between public and private destruction, and it does not punish only destruction engaged in for the purpose of expressing views. Compare Stromberg v. California, 283 U.S. 359 (1931). A law prohibiting destruction of Selective Service certificates no more abridges free speech on its face than a motor vehicle law prohibiting the destruction of drivers' licenses, or a tax law prohibiting the destruction of books and records.

O'Brien nonetheless argues that the 1965 Amendment is unconstitutional in its application to him, and is unconstitutional as enacted because what he calls the "purpose" of Congress was "to suppress freedom of speech." We consider these arguments separately.

II.

O'Brien first argues that the 1965 Amendment is unconstitutional as applied to him because his act of burning his registration certificate was protected "symbolic speech" within the First Amendment. His argument is that the freedom of expression which the First Amendment guarantees includes all modes of "communication of ideas by conduct," and that his conduct is within this definition because he did it in "demonstration against the war and against the draft."

We cannot accept the view that an apparently limitless variety of conduct can be labeled "speech" whenever the person engaging in the conduct intends thereby to express an idea. However, even on the assumption that the alleged communicative element in O'Brien's conduct is sufficient to bring into play the First Amendment, it does not necessarily follow that the destruction of a registration certificate is constitutionally protected activity. This Court has held that when "speech" and "nonspeech" elements are combined in the same course of conduct, a sufficiently important governmental interest in regulating the nonspeech element can justify incidental limitations on First Amendment freedoms. To characterize the quality of the governmental interest which must appear, the Court has employed a variety of descriptive terms: compelling; [1] substantial; [2] subordinating; [3] paramount; [4] cogent; [5] strong.[6] Whatever imprecision inheres in these terms, we think it clear that a government regulation is sufficiently justified if it is within the constitutional power of the Government; if it furthers an important or substantial governmental interest; if the governmental interest is unrelated to the suppression of free expression; and if the incidental restriction on alleged First Amendment freedoms is no greater than is essential to the furtherance of that interest. We find that the 1965 Amendment to § 12(b) (3) of the Universal Military Training and Service Act meets all of these requirements, and consequently that O'Brien can be constitutionally convicted for violating it.

The constitutional power of Congress to raise and support armies and to make all laws necessary and proper to that end is broad and sweeping. . . . The power of Congress to classify and conscript manpower for military service is "beyond question." Lichter v. United States, [334 U.S. 742 (1948)]; Selective Draft Law Cases, [245 U.S. 366 (1918)]. Pursuant to this power, Congress may establish a system of registration for individuals liable for training and service, and may require such individuals within reason to cooperate in the registration system. The issuance of certificates indicating the registration and eligibility classification of individuals is a legitimate and substantial administrative aid in the functioning of this system. And legislation to insure the continuing availability of issued certificates serves a legitimate and substantial purpose in the system's administration.

O'Brien's argument to the contrary is necessarily premised upon his unrealistic characterization of Selective Service certificates. He essentially adopts the position that such certificates are so many pieces of paper designed to notify registrants of their registration or classification, to be retained or tossed in the wastebasket according to the convenience or taste of the registrant. Once the registrant has received notification, according to this view, there is no reason for him to retain the certificates. O'Brien notes that most of the information on a registration certificate serves no notification purpose at all; the registrant hardly needs to be told his address and physical characteristics. We agree that the registration certificate contains much information of which the registrant needs no notification. This circumstance, however, does not lead to the conclusion that the certificate serves no purpose, but that, like the classification certificate, it serves purposes in addition to initial notification. Many of

1. NAACP v. Button, 371 U.S. 415, 438 (1963) [infra, p. 1285]; see also Sherbert v. Verner, 374 U.S. 398, 403 (1963) [infra, p. 1387]. [All footnotes by the Court.]

2. NAACP v. Button, 371 U.S. 415, 444 (1963); NAACP v. Alabama ex rel. Patterson, 357 U.S. 449, 464 (1958) [infra, p. 1316].

3. Bates v. Little Rock, 361 U.S. 516, 524 (1960) [infra, p. 1315].

4. Thomas v. Collins, 323 U.S. 516, 530 (1945) [supra, p. 1138]; see also Sherbert v. Verner, 374 U.S. 398, 406 (1963).

5. Bates v. Little Rock, 361 U.S. 516, 524 (1960).

6. Sherbert v. Verner, 374 U.S. 398, 408 (1963).

these purposes would be defeated by the certificates' destruction or mutilation. Among these are:

1. The registration certificate serves as proof that the individual described thereon has registered for the draft. The classification certificate shows the eligibility classification of a named but undescribed individual. Voluntarily displaying the two certificates is an easy and painless way for a young man to dispel a question as to whether he might be delinquent in his Selective Service obligations. Correspondingly, the availability of the certificates for such display relieves the Selective Service System of the administrative burden it would otherwise have in verifying the registration and classification of all suspected delinquents. Further, since both certificates are in the nature of "receipts" attesting that the registrant has done what the law requires, it is in the interest of the just and efficient administration of the system that they be continually available, in the event, for example, of a mix-up in the registrant's file. Additionally, in a time of national crisis, reasonable availability to each registrant of the two small cards assures a rapid and uncomplicated means for determining his fitness for immediate induction, no matter how distant in our mobile society he may be from his local board.

2. The information supplied on the certificates facilitates communication betwen registrants and local boards, simplifying the system and benefiting all concerned. . . .

3. Both certificates carry continual reminders that the registrant must notify his local board of any change of address, and other specified changes in his status. The smooth functioning of the system requires that local boards be continually aware of the status and whereabouts of registrants, and the destruction of certificates deprives the system of a potentially useful notice device.

4. The regulatory scheme involving Selective Service certificates includes clearly valid prohibitions against the alteration, forgery, or similar deceptive misuse of certificates. The destruction or mutilation of certificates obviously increases the difficulty of detecting and tracing abuses such as these. Further, a mutilated certificate might itself be used for deceptive purposes.

The many functions performed by Selective Service certificates establish beyond doubt that Congress has a legitimate and substantial interest in preventing their wanton and unrestrained destruction and assuring their continuing availability by punishing people who knowingly and wilfully destroy or mutilate them. And we are unpersuaded that the pre-existence of the nonpossession regulations in any way negates this interest. In the absence of a question as to multiple punishment, it has never been suggested that there is anything improper in Congress' providing alternative statutory avenues of prosecution to assure the effective protection of one and the same interest. . . .

Equally important, a comparison of the regulations with the 1965 Amendment indicates that they protect overlapping but not identical governmental interests, and that they reach somewhat different classes of wrongdoers. The gravamen of the offense defined by the statute is the deliberate rendering of certificates unavailable for the various purposes which they may serve. Whether registrants keep their certificates in their personal possession at all times, as required by the regulations, is of no particular concern under the 1965 Amendment, as long as they do not mutilate or destroy the certificates so as to render them unavailable. Although as we note below we are not concerned here with the nonpossession regulations, it is not inappropriate to observe that the essential elements of nonpossession are not identical with those of mutilation or destruction. Finally, the 1965 Amendment, like § 12(b) which it amended, is concerned with abuses involving *any* issued Selective Service certificates, not only with the registrant's own certificates. The knowing destruction or mutilation of someone else's certificates would therefore violate the statute but not the nonpossession regulations.

We think it apparent that the continuing availability to each registrant of his Selective Service certificates substantially furthers the smooth and proper functioning of the system that Congress has established to raise armies. We think it also apparent that the Nation has a vital interest in having a system for raising armies that functions with maximum efficiency and is capable of easily and quickly responding to continually changing circumstances. For these reasons, the Government has a substantial interest in assuring the continuing availability of issued Selective Service certificates.

It is equally clear that the 1965 Amendment specifically protects this substantial governmental interest. We perceive no alternative means that would more precisely and narrowly assure the continuing availability of issued Selective Service certificates than a law which prohibits their wilful mutilation or destruction. Compare Sherbert v. Verner, 374 U.S. 398, 407–408 (1963) [p. 1387, infra], and the cases cited therein. The 1965 Amendment prohibits such conduct and does nothing more. In other words, both the governmental interest and the operation of the 1965 Amendment are limited to the noncommunicative aspect of O'Brien's conduct. The governmental interest and the scope of the 1965 Amendment are limited to preventing harm to the smooth and efficient functioning of the Selective Service System. When O'Brien deliberately rendered unavailable his registration certificate, he wilfully frustrated this governmental interest. For this noncommunicative impact of his conduct, and for nothing else, he was convicted.

The case at bar is therefore unlike one where the alleged governmental interest in regulating conduct arises in some measure because the communication allegedly integral to the conduct is itself thought to be harmful. In Stromberg v. California, 283 U.S. 359 (1931) [the "red flag" case, supra], for example, the statute was aimed at suppressing communication [and therefore] could not be sustained as a regulation of noncommunicative conduct. . . .

In conclusion, we find that because of the Government's substantial interest in assuring the continuing availability of issued Selective Service certificates, because amended § 462(b) is an appropriately narrow means of protecting this interest and condemns only the independent noncommunicative impact of conduct within its reach, and because the noncommunicative impact of O'Brien's act of burning his registration certificate frustrated the Government's interest, a sufficient governmental interest has been shown to justify O'Brien's conviction.

III.

O'Brien finally argues that the 1965 Amendment is unconstitutional as enacted because what he calls the "purpose" of Congress was "to suppress freedom of speech." We reject this argument because under settled principles the purpose of Congress, as O'Brien uses that term, is not a basis for declaring this legislation unconstitutional. . . . [See the passages from this opinion noted supra, chap. 5, p. 445.]

We think it not amiss, in passing, to comment upon O'Brien's legislative-purpose argument. . . . It is principally on the basis of the statements by [three] Congressmen that O'Brien makes his congressional "purpose" argument. We note that if we were to examine legislative purpose in the instant case, we would be obliged to consider not only these statements but also the more authoritative reports of the Senate and House Armed Services Committees. . . . While both reports make clear a concern with the "defiant" destruction of so-called "draft cards" and with "open" encouragement to others to destroy their cards, both reports also indicate that this concern stemmed from an apprehension that unrestrained destruction of cards would disrupt the smooth functioning of the Selective Service System. . . .

Reversed.

Mr. Justice HARLAN, concurring.

. . . I wish to make explicit my understanding that [the Court's criteria do] not foreclose consideration of First Amendment claims in those rare instances when an "incidental" restriction upon expression, imposed by a regulation which furthers an "important or substantial" governmental interest and satisfies the Court's other criteria, in practice has the effect of entirely preventing a "speaker" from reaching a significant audience with whom he could not otherwise lawfully communicate. This is not such a case, since O'Brien manifestly could have conveyed his message in many ways other than by burning his draft card.

Mr. Justice DOUGLAS, dissenting.

. . . The underlying and basic problem in this case, is whether conscription is permissible in the absence of a declaration of war. That question has not been briefed nor was it presented in oral argument; but it is, I submit, a question upon which the litigants and the country are entitled to a ruling. . . . [See chap. 7, p. 601, supra.] [This case should be restored] to the calendar for reargument on the question of the constitutionality of a peacetime draft. [Note also Justice Douglas' view that O'Brien's conviction violated the First Amendment—expressed not in this case but in a concurring opinion a year later, in Brandenburg v. Ohio, 395 U.S. 444 (1969), printed supra, at p. 1123.]

TINKER v. DES MOINES SCHOOL DISTRICT

393 U.S. 503, 89 S.Ct. 733, 21 L.Ed.2d 731 (1969).

Certiorari to the United States Court of Appeals for the Eighth Circuit.

Mr. Justice FORTAS delivered the opinion of the Court.

Petitioner John F. Tinker, 15 years old, and petitioner Christopher Eckhardt, 16 years old, attended high schools in Des Moines, Iowa. Petitioner Mary Beth Tinker, John's sister, was a 13-year-old student in junior high school.

In December 1965, a group of adults and students in Des Moines held a meeting at the Eckhardt home. The group determined to publicize their objections to the hostilities in Vietnam and their support for a truce by wearing black armbands during the holiday season and by fasting on December 16 and

New Year's Eve. Petitioners and their parents had previously engaged in similar activities, and they decided to participate in the program.

The principals of the Des Moines schools became aware of the plan to wear armbands. On December 14, 1965, they met and adopted a policy that any student wearing an armband to school would be asked to remove it, and if he refused he would be suspended until he returned without the armband. Petitioners were aware of the regulation that the school authorities adopted.

On December 16, Mary Beth and Christopher wore black armbands to their schools. John Tinker wore his armband the next day. They were all sent home and suspended from school until they would come back without their armbands. They did not return to school until after the planned period for wearing armbands had expired—that is, until after New Year's Day.

[The District Court] upheld the constitutionality of the school authorities' action on the ground that it was reasonable in order to prevent disturbance of school discipline. The court referred to but expressly declined to follow the Fifth Circuit's holding in a similar case that the wearing of symbols like the armbands cannot be prohibited unless it "materially and substantially interfere[s] with the requirements of appropriate discipline in the operation of the school." Burnside v. Byars, 363 F.2d 744, 749 (1966).[1] [The Court of Appeals, en banc, was equally divided and accordingly affirmed without opinion.]

I

The District Court recognized that the wearing of an armband for the purpose of expressing certain views is the type of symbolic act that is within the Free Speech Clause of the First Amendment. See West Virginia v. Barnette, 319 U.S. 624 (1943); Stromberg v. California, 283 U.S. 359 (1931). . . . As we shall discuss, the wearing of armbands in the circumstances of this case was entirely divorced from actually or potentially disruptive conduct by those participating in it. It was closely akin to "pure speech" which, we have repeatedly held, is entitled to comprehensive protection under the First Amendment. Compare Cox v. Louisiana, 379 U.S. 536, 555 (1965); Adderley v. Florida, 385 U.S. 39 (1966).

First Amendment rights, applied in light of the special characteristics of the school environment, are available to teachers and students. It can hardly be argued that either students or teachers shed their constitutional rights to freedom of speech or expression at the schoolhouse gate. This has been the unmistakable holding of this Court for almost 50 years. [See Meyer v. Nebraska, 262 U.S. 390 (1923), where the Court] held that the Due Process Clause of the Fourteenth Amendment prevents States from forbidding the teaching of a foreign language to young students. Statutes to this effect, the Court held, unconstitutionally interfere with the liberty of teacher, student, and parent. . . . On the other hand, the Court has repeatedly emphasized the need for affirming the comprehensive authority of the States and of school officials, consistent with fundamental constitutional safeguards, to pre-

---

1. In Burnside, the Fifth Circuit ordered that high school authorities be enjoined from enforcing a regulation forbidding students to wear "freedom buttons." It is instructive that in Blackwell v. Issaquena County Board of Education, 363 F.2d 749 (1966), the same panel on the same day reached the opposite result on different facts. It declined to enjoin enforcement of such a regulation in another high school where the students wearing freedom buttons harassed students who did not wear them and created much disturbance. [All footnotes by the Court.]

scribe and control conduct in the schools. . . . Our problem lies in the area where students in the exercise of First Amendment rights collide with the rules of the school authorities.

II.

The problem posed by the present case does not relate to regulation of the length of skirts or the type of clothing, to hair style, or deportment. . . . It does not concern aggressive, disruptive action or even group demonstrations. Our problem involves direct, primary First Amendment rights akin to "pure speech."

The school officials banned and sought to punish petitioners for a silent, passive expression of opinion, unaccompanied by any disorder or disturbance on the part of petitioners. There is here no evidence whatever of petitioners' interference, actual or nascent, with the schools' work or of collision with the rights of other students to be secure and to be let alone. . . . There is no indication that the work of the schools or any class was disrupted. Outside the classrooms, a few students made hostile remarks to the children wearing armbands, but there were no threats or acts of violence on school premises.

The District Court concluded that the action of the school authorities was reasonable because it was based upon their fear of a disturbance from the wearing of the armbands. But, in our system, undifferentiated fear or apprehension of disturbance is not enough to overcome the right to freedom of expression. Any departure from absolute regimentation may cause trouble. Any variation from the majority's opinion may inspire fear. Any word spoken, in class, in the lunchroom, or on the campus, that deviates from the views of another person may start an argument or cause a disturbance. But our Constitution says we must take this risk, Terminiello v. Chicago, 337 U.S. 1 (1949); and our history says that it is this sort of hazardous freedom—this kind of openness—that is the basis of our national strength and of the independence and vigor of Americans who grow up and live in this relatively permissive, often disputatious, society.

In order for the State in the person of school officials to justify prohibition of a particular expression of opinion, it must be able to show that its action was caused by something more than a mere desire to avoid the discomfort and unpleasantness that always accompany an unpopular viewpoint. Certainly where there is no finding and no showing that engaging in the forbidden conduct would "materially and substantially interfere with the requirements of appropriate discipline in the operation of the school," the prohibition cannot be sustained. Burnside v. Byars, supra, at 749.

In the present case, the District Court made no such finding, and our independent examination of the record fails to yield evidence that the school authorities had reason to anticipate that the wearing of the armbands would substantially interfere with the work of the school or impinge upon the rights of other students. Even an official memorandum prepared after the suspension that listed the reasons for the ban on wearing the armbands made no reference to the anticipation of such disruption.[2]

2. The only suggestions of fear of disorder in the report are these:

"A former student of one of our high schools was killed in Viet Nam. Some

On the contrary, the action of the school authorities appears to have been based upon an urgent wish to avoid the controversy which might result from the expression, even by the silent symbol of armbands, of opposition to this Nation's part in the conflagration in Vietnam.[3] . . .

It is also relevant that the school authorities did not purport to prohibit the wearing of all symbols of political or controversial significance. The record shows that students in some of the schools wore buttons relating to national political campaigns, and some even wore the Iron Cross, traditionally a symbol of Nazism. The order prohibiting the wearing of armbands did not extend to these. Instead, a particular symbol—black armbands worn to exhibit opposition to this Nation's involvement in Vietnam—was singled out for prohibition. Clearly, the prohibition of expression of one particular opinion, at least without evidence that it is necessary to avoid material and substantial interference with schoolwork or discipline, is not constitutionally permissible.

In our system, state-operated schools may not be enclaves of totalitarianism. School officials do not possess absolute authority over their students. Students in school as well as out of school are "persons" under our Constitution. They are possessed of fundamental rights which the State must respect, just as they themselves must respect their obligations to the State. In our system, students may not be regarded as closed-circuit recipients of only that which the State chooses to communicate. They may not be confined to the expression of those sentiments that are officially approved. In the absence of a specific showing of constitutionally valid reasons to regulate their speech, students are entitled to freedom of expression of their views. [In Meyer v. Nebraska], Mr. Justice McReynolds expressed this Nation's repudiation of the principle that a State might so conduct its schools as to "foster a homogeneous people." . . .

[The] principle of these cases is not confined to the supervised and ordained discussion which takes place in the classroom. The principal use to which the schools are dedicated is to accommodate students during prescribed hours for the purpose of certain types of activities. Among those activities is personal intercommunication among the students.[4] This is not only an inevi-

of his friends are still in school and it was felt that if any kind of a demonstration existed, it might evolve into something which would be difficult to control."

"Students at one of the high schools were heard to say they would wear arm bands of other colors if the black bands prevailed."

Moreover, the testimony of school authorities at trial indicates that it was not fear of disruption that motivated the regulation prohibiting the armbands; the regulation was directed against "the principle of the demonstration" itself. School authorities simply felt that "the schools are no place for demonstrations," and if the students "didn't like the way our elected officials were handling things, it should be handled with the ballot box and not in the halls of our public schools."

3. The District Court found that the school authorities, in prohibiting black armbands, were influenced by the fact that "[t]he Viet Nam war and the involvement of the United States therein has been the subject of a major controversy for some time. When the arm band regulation involved herein was promulgated, debate over the Viet Nam war had become vehement in many localities. A protest march against the war had been recently held in Washington, D. C. A wave of draft card burning incidents protesting the war had swept the country. At that time two highly publicized draft card burning cases were pending in this Court. Both individuals supporting the war and those opposing it were quite vocal in expressing their views." 258 F.Supp., at 972–973.

4. In Hammond v. South Carolina State College, 272 F.Supp. 947 (D.C.S.C.1967),

table part of the process of attending school; it is also an important part of the educational process. A student's rights, therefore, do not embrace merely the classroom hours. When he is in the cafeteria, or on the playing field, or on the campus during the authorized hours, he may express his opinions, even on controversial subjects like the conflict in Vietnam, if he does so without "materially and substantially interfer[ing] with the requirements of appropriate discipline in the operation of the school" and without colliding with the rights of others. Burnside v. Byars, supra, at 749. But conduct by the student, in class or out of it, which for any reason—whether it stems from time, place, or type of behavior—materially disrupts classwork or involves substantial disorder or invasion of the rights of others is, of course, not immunized by the constitutional guarantee of freedom of speech. . . . We properly read [the Constitution] to permit reasonable regulation of speech-connected activities in carefully restricted circumstances. But we do not confine the permissible exercise of First Amendment rights to a telephone booth or the four corners of a pamphlet, or to supervised and ordained discussion in a school classroom.
. . .

[T]he record does not demonstrate any facts which might reasonably have led school authorities to forecast substantial disruption of or material interference with school activities, and no disturbances or disorders on the school premises in fact occurred. . . . In the circumstances, our Constitution does not permit officials of the State to deny their form of expression.
. . .

Reversed and remanded.

Mr. Justice STEWART, concurring.

Although I agree with much of what is said in the Court's opinion, and with its judgment in this case, I cannot share the Court's uncritical assumption that, school discipline aside, the First Amendment rights of children are co-extensive with those of adults. Indeed, I had thought the Court decided otherwise just last Term in Ginsberg v. New York, 390 U.S. 629 [with the obscenity cases, at p. 1250, infra]. . . .

Mr. Justice WHITE, concurring.

While I join the Court's opinion, I deem it appropriate to note . . . that the Court continues to recognize a distinction between communicating by words and communicating by acts or conduct which sufficiently impinges on some valid state interest . . . .

Mr. Justice BLACK, dissenting.

The Court's holding in this case ushers in what I deem to be an entirely new era in which the power to control pupils by the elected "officials of state supported public schools . . ." in the United States is in ultimate effect transferred to the Supreme Court. . . . Assuming that the Court is correct in holding that the conduct of wearing armbands for the purpose of con-

District Judge Hemphill had before him a case involving a meeting on campus of 300 students to express their views on school practices. He pointed out that a school is not like a hospital or a jail enclosure. Cf. Cox v. Louisiana, 379 U.S. 536 (1965); Adderley v. Florida, 385 U.S. 39 (1966). It is a public place, and its dedication to specific uses does not imply that the constitutional rights of persons entitled to be there are to be gauged as if the premises were purely private property. Cf. Edwards v. South Carolina, 372 U.S. 229 (1963); Brown v. Louisiana, 383 U.S. 131 (1966).

veying political ideas is protected by the First Amendment, compare, e. g., Giboney v. Empire Storage & Ice Co., 336 U.S. 490 (1949), the crucial remaining questions are whether students and teachers may use the schools at their whim as a platform for the exercise of free speech—"symbolic" or "pure"—and whether the courts will allocate to themselves the function of deciding how the pupils' school day will be spent. . . . .

. . . . While the absence of obscene remarks or boisterous and loud disorder perhaps justifies the Court's statement that the few armband students did not actually "disrupt" the classwork, I think the record overwhelmingly shows that the armbands did exactly what the elected school officials and principals foresaw they would, that is, took the students' minds off their classwork and diverted them to thoughts about the highly emotional subject of the Vietnam war. And I repeat that if the time has come when pupils of state-supported schools, kindergartens, grammar schools, or high schools, can defy and flout orders of school officials to keep their minds on their own schoolwork, it is the beginning of a new revolutionary era of permissiveness in this country fostered by the judiciary.

. . . . There was at one time a line of cases holding "reasonableness" as the court saw it to be the test of a "due process" violation. [T]he Court today heavily relies [on one that] used this test of reasonableness, Meyer v. Nebraska, 262 U.S. 390 (1923). . . . . This constitutional test of reasonableness prevailed in this Court for a season. It was this test that brought on President Franklin Roosevelt's well-known Court fight. His proposed legislation did not pass, but the fight left the "reasonableness" constitutional test dead on the battlefield. . . . . If the majority of the Court today, by agreeing to the opinion of my Brother Fortas, is resurrecting that old reasonableness-due process test, I think the constitutional change should be plainly, unequivocally, and forthrightly stated for the benefit of the bench and bar. It will be a sad day for the country, I believe, when the present-day Court returns to the McReynolds due process concept. . . . .

[E]ven if the record were silent as to protests against the Vietnam war distracting students from their assigned class work, members of this Court, like all other citizens, know, without being told, that the disputes over the wisdom of the Vietnam war have disrupted and divided this country as few other issues ever have. Of course students, like other people, cannot concentrate on lesser issues when black armbands are being ostentatiously displayed in their presence to call attention to the wounded and dead of the war, some of the wounded and the dead being their friends and neighbors. It was, of course, to distract the attention of other students that some students insisted up to the very point of their own suspension from school that they were determined to sit in school with their symbolic armbands.

. . . . We cannot close our eyes to the fact that some of the country's greatest problems are crimes committed by the youth, too many of school age. School discipline, like parental discipline, is an integral and important part of training our children to be good citizens—to be better citizens. Here a very small number of students have crisply and summarily refused to obey a school order designed to give pupils who want to learn the opportunity to do so. One does not need to be a prophet or the son of a prophet to know that after the Court's holding today some students in Iowa schools and indeed in all schools will be ready, able, and willing to defy their teachers on practically all orders. This is the more unfortunate for the schools since groups of students all over the land are already running loose, conducting break-ins, sit-ins, lie-ins, and smash-ins. . . . It is no answer to say that the particular students here have not yet reached such high points in their demands to attend classes in order to exercise their political pressures. Turned loose with lawsuits for damages and injunctions against their teachers as they are here, it is nothing but wishful thinking to imagine that young, immature students will not soon believe it is their right to control the schools rather than the right of the States that collect the taxes to hire the teachers for the benefit of the pupils. This case, therefore, wholly without constitutional reasons in my judgment, subjects all the public schools in the country to the whims and caprices of their loudest-mouthed, but maybe not their brightest, students. I, for one, am not fully persuaded that school pupils are wise enough, even with this Court's expert help from Washington, to run the 23,390 public school systems in our 50 States. I wish, therefore, wholly to disclaim any purpose on my part to hold that the Federal Constitution compels the teachers, parents, and elected school officials to surrender control of the American public school system to public school students. I dissent.

Mr. Justice HARLAN, dissenting.

I certainly agree that state public school authorities in the discharge of their responsibilities are not wholly exempt from the requirements of the Fourteenth Amendment respecting the freedoms of expression and association. At the same time I am reluctant to believe that there is any disagreement between the majority and myself on the proposition that school officials should be accorded the widest authority in maintaining discipline and good order in their institutions. To translate that proposition into a workable constitutional rule, I would, in cases like this, cast upon those complaining the burden of showing that a particular school measure was motivated by other than legitimate school concerns—for example, a desire to prohibit the expression of an unpopular point of view, while permitting expression of the dominant opinion.

Finding nothing in this record which impugns the good faith of respondents in promulgating the armband regulation, I would affirm the judgment below.

JUSTICE FORTAS ELABORATES ON TINKER

Compare, with Justice Fortas' standard in the majority opinion, his approach in the dissent in Street, which follows. Can his positions be reconciled? See the comments at the end of this chapter, at p. 1208. On the specific Tinker problem of students' free speech, compare Justice Fortas' notation—a few weeks after Tinker—concurring in the denial of certiorari in Barker v. Hardway, 394 U.S. 905 (1969):

"I agree that certiorari should be denied. The petitioners were suspended from college not for expressing their opinions on a matter of substance, but for violent and destructive interference with the rights of others. An adequate hearing was afforded them on the issue of suspension. The petitioners contend that their conduct was protected by the First Amendment, but the findings of the District Court, which were accepted by the Court of Appeals, establish that the petitioners here engaged in an aggressive and violent demonstration, and not in peaceful, nondisruptive expression, such as was involved in

[Tinker]. The petitioners' conduct was therefore clearly not protected by the First and Fourteenth Amendments." *

STREET v. NEW YORK

394 U.S. 576, 89 S.Ct. 1354, 22 L.Ed.2d 572 (1969).

Appeal from the Court of Appeals of New York.

Mr. Justice HARLAN delivered the opinion of the Court.

Appellant Street has been convicted in the New York courts of violating former § 1425, subd. 16, par. d, of the New York Penal Law, which makes it a misdemeanor "publicly [to] mutilate, deface, defile, or defy, trample upon, or cast contempt upon either by words or act [any flag of the United States]." He was given a suspended sentence. We must decide whether, in light of all the circumstances, that conviction denied to him rights of free expression protected by the First Amendment and assured against state infringement by the Fourteenth Amendment. . . .

According to evidence given at trial, the events which led to the conviction were these. Appellant testified that during the afternoon of June 6, 1966, he was listening to the radio in his Brooklyn apartment. He heard a news report that civil rights leader James Meredith had been shot by a sniper in Mississippi. Saying to himself, "They didn't protect him," appellant, himself a Negro, took from his drawer a neatly folded, 48-star American flag which he formerly had displayed on national holidays. Appellant left his apartment and carried the still-folded flag to the nearby intersection of St. James Place and Lafayette Avenue. Appellant stood on the northeast corner of the intersection, lit the flag with a match, and dropped the flag on the pavement when it began to burn.

Soon thereafter, a police officer halted his patrol car and found the burning flag. The officer testified that he then crossed to the northwest corner of the intersection, where he found appellant "talking out loud" to a small group of persons. The officer estimated that there were some 30 persons on the corner near the flag and five to 10 on the corner with appellant. The officer testified that as he approached within 10 or 15 feet of appellant, he heard appellant say, "We don't need no damn flag," and that when he asked appellant whether he had burned the flag appellant replied: "Yes; that is my flag; I burned it. If they let that happen to Meredith we don't need an American flag." Appellant admitted making the latter response, but he denied that he said anything else and asserted that he always had remained on the corner with the flag.

---

* Note also Jones v. Tennessee State Board of Education, 397 U.S. —— (1970), a per curiam dismissal of certiorari after review had been granted to consider a student's claim that he had been suspended from college "solely because of his distribution of leaflets urging a boycott" of registration. The Court explained that it had become clear after oral argument that the suspension was based in part on a finding that the student had lied at his disciplinary hearing: "This fact sufficiently clouds the record to render the case an inappropriate vehicle for this Court's first decision on the extent of First Amendment restrictions upon the power of state universities to expel or indefinitely suspend students for the expression of views alleged to be disruptive of the good order of the campus." Justice Black voted to affirm the judgment sustaining the suspension. Justice Douglas, joined by Justice Brennan, submitted a dissenting opinion discussing procedural due process as well as the First Amendment.

Street argues that his conviction was unconstitutional for three different reasons. *First*, he claims that § 1425, subd. 16, par. d, is overbroad, both on its face and as applied, because the section makes it a crime "publicly [to] defy . . . or cast contempt upon [an American flag] *by words* . . . ." (Emphasis added.) *Second*, he contends that § 1425, subd. 16, par. d, is vague and imprecise because it does not clearly define the conduct which it forbids. *Third*, he asserts that New York may not constitutionally punish one who publicly destroys or damages an American flag as a means of protest, because such an act constitutes expression protected by the Fourteenth Amendment. We deem it unnecessary to consider the latter two arguments, for we hold that § 1425, subd. 16, par. d, was unconstitutionally applied in appellant's case because it permitted him to be punished merely for speaking defiant or contemptuous words about the American flag. . . .

In the face of an information explicitly setting forth appellant's words as an element of his alleged crime, and of appellant's subsequent conviction under a statute making it an offense to speak words of that sort, we find this record insufficient to eliminate the possibility either that appellant's words were the sole basis of his conviction or that appellant was convicted for both his words and his deed.

We come finally to the question whether, in the circumstances of this case, New York may constitutionally inflict criminal punishment upon one who ventures "publicly [to] defy . . . or cast contempt upon [any American flag] by words . . ." . . . .

In these circumstances, we can think of four governmental interests which might conceivably have been furthered by punishing appellant for his words: (1) an interest in deterring appellant from vocally inciting others to commit unlawful acts; (2) an interest in preventing appellant from uttering words so inflammatory that they would provoke others to retaliate physically against him, thereby causing a breach of the peace; (3) an interest in protecting the sensibilities of passers-by who might be shocked by appellant's words about the American flag; and (4) an interest in assuring that appellant, regardless of the impact of his words upon others, showed proper respect for our national emblem.

In the circumstances of this case, we do not believe that any of these interests may constitutionally justify appellant's conviction under § 1425, subd. 16, par. d, for speaking as he did. We begin with the interest in preventing incitement. Appellant's words, taken alone, did not urge anyone to do anything unlawful. They amounted only to somewhat excited public advocacy of the idea that the United States should abandon, at least temporarily, one of its national symbols. It is clear that the Fourteenth Amendment prohibits the States from imposing criminal punishment for public advocacy of peaceful change in our institutions. See, e. g. [Cox I, Edwards v. South Carolina, Terminiello; cf. Yates, all supra]. Even assuming that appellant's words might be found incitive when considered together with his simultaneous burning of the flag, § 1425, subd. 16, par. d, does not purport to punish only those defiant or contemptuous words which amount to incitement, and there is no evidence that the state courts regarded the statute as so limited. Hence, a conviction for words could not be upheld on this basis. . . .

Nor could such a conviction be justified on the second ground mentioned above: the possible tendency of appellant's words to provoke violent retaliation. Though it is conceivable that some listeners might have been moved to retaliate upon hearing appellant's disrespectful words, we cannot say that appellant's remarks were so inherently inflammatory as to come within that small class of "fighting words" which are "likely to provoke the average person to retaliation, and thereby cause a breach of the peace." [Chaplinsky v. New Hampshire.] And even if appellant's words might be found in that category, § 1425, subd. 16, par. d, is not narrowly drawn to punish only words of that character, and there is no indication that it was so interpreted by the state courts. Hence, this case is again distinguishable from Chaplinsky, supra, in which the Court emphasized that the statute was "carefully drawn so as not unduly to impair liberty of expression . . . ."

Again, such a conviction could not be sustained on the ground that appellant's words were likely to shock passers-by. Except perhaps for appellant's incidental use of the word "damn," upon which no emphasis was placed at trial, any shock effect of appellant's speech must be attributed to the content of the ideas expressed. It is firmly settled that under our Constitution the public expression of ideas may not be prohibited merely because the ideas are themselves offensive to some of their hearers. See, e. g., [Cox I, Edwards, Terminiello; cf. Cantwell v. Conn., all supra]. And even if such a conviction might be upheld on the ground of "shock," there is again no indication that the state courts regarded the statute as limited to that purpose.

Finally, such a conviction could not be supported on the theory that by making the above-quoted remarks about the flag appellant failed to show the respect for our national symbol which may properly be demanded of every citizen. In Board of Educ. v. Barnette, 319 U.S. 624 (1943), this Court held that to require unwilling schoolchildren to salute the flag would violate rights of free expression assured by the Fourteenth Amendment. In his opinion for the Court, Mr. Justice Jackson wrote words which are especially apposite here:

> "The case is made difficult not because the principles of its decision are obscure but because the flag involved is our own. Nevertheless, we apply the limitations of the Constitution with no fear that freedom to be intellectually and spiritually diverse or even contrary will disintegrate the social organization. . . . [F]reedom to differ is not limited to things that do not matter much. That would be a mere shadow of freedom. The test of its substance is the right to differ as to things that touch the heart of the existing order.

> "If there is any fixed star in our constitutional constellation, it is that no official, high or petty, can prescribe what shall be orthodox in politics, nationalism, religion, or other matters of opinion or force citizens to confess by word or act their faith therein. If there are any circumstances which permit an exception, they do not now occur to us."

We have no doubt that the constitutionally guaranteed "freedom to be intellectually . . . diverse or even contrary," and the "right to differ as to things that touch the heart of the existing order," encompass the freedom to express publicly one's opinions about our flag, including those opinions which are defiant or contemptuous.

Since appellant could not constitutionally be punished under § 1425, subd. 16, par. d, for his speech, and since we have found that he may have been so punished, his conviction cannot be permitted to stand. In so holding, we reiterate that we have no occasion to pass upon the validity of this conviction insofar as it was sustained by the state courts on the basis that Street could be punished for his burning of the flag, even though the burning was an act of protest. Nor do we perceive any basis for our Brother White's fears that our decision today may be taken to require reversal whenever a defendant is convicted for burning a flag in protest, following a trial at which his words have been introduced to prove some element of that offense. Assuming that such a conviction would otherwise pass constitutional muster, a matter about which we express no view, nothing in this opinion would render the conviction impermissible merely because an element of the crime was proved by the defendant's words rather than in some other way. See United States v. O'Brien, 391 U.S. 367 (1968).

We add that disrespect for our flag is to be deplored no less in these vexed times than in calmer periods of our history. Cf. Halter v. Nebraska, 205 U.S. 34 (1907). Nevertheless, we are unable to sustain a conviction that may have rested on a form of expression, however distasteful, which the Constitution tolerates and protects. . . . .

Mr. Chief Justice WARREN, dissenting. . . .

[A]ppellant was convicted for his act not his words. . . .

I am in complete agreement with the general rule that this Court should not treat broad constitutional questions when narrow ones will suffice to dispose of the litigation. However, where only the broad question is presented, it is our task and our responsibility to confront that question squarely and resolve it. In a time when the American flag has increasingly become an integral part of public protests, the constitutionality of the flag desecration statutes enacted by all of the States and Congress is a matter of the most widespread concern. Both those who seek constitutional shelter for acts of flag desecration perpetrated in the course of a political protest and those who must enforce the law are entitled to know the scope of constitutional protection. The Court's explicit reservation of the constitutionality of flag burning prohibitions encourages others to test in the streets the power of our States and National Government to impose criminal sanctions upon those who would desecrate the flag.

I believe that the States and the Federal Government do have the power to protect the flag from acts of desecration and disgrace. But because the Court has not met the issue, it would serve no purpose to delineate my reasons for this view. However, it is difficult for me to imagine that, had the Court faced this issue, it would have concluded otherwise. Since I am satisfied that the constitutionality of appellant's conduct should be resolved in this case and am convinced that this conduct can be criminally punished, I dissent.

Mr. Justice BLACK, dissenting.

. . . . The entire state court construed the statute as applied to this appellant as making it an offense publicly to burn an American flag in order to protest something that had occurred. In other words the offense which that court sustained was the burning of the flag and not the making of any statements about it. The Court seems to console itself for holding this New York flag-burning law unconstitutional as applied by saying that, as it reads the record, the conviction could have been based on the words spoken by the appellant as he was burning the flag. Those words indicated a desire on appellant's part to degrade and defame the flag. If I could agree with the Court's interpretation of the record as to the possibility of the conviction's resting on these spoken words, I would firmly and automatically agree that the law is unconstitutional. I would not feel constrained, as the Court seems to be, to search my imagination to see if I could think of interests the State may have in suppressing this freedom of speech. I would not balance away the First Amendment mandate that speech not be abridged in any fashion whatsoever. But I accept the unanimous opinion of the New York Court of Appeals that the conviction does not and could not have rested merely on the spoken words but that it rested entirely on the fact that the defendant had publicly burned the American flag—against the law of the State of New York.

It passes my belief that anything in the Federal Constitution bars a State from making the deliberate burning of the American flag an offense. It is immaterial to me that words are spoken in connection with the burning. It is the *burning* of the flag that the State has set its face against. "It rarely has been suggested that the constitutional freedom for speech and press extends its immunity to speech or writing used as an integral part of conduct in violation of a valid criminal statute." Giboney v. Empire Storage & Ice Co., 336 U.S. 490, 498 (1949). In my view this quotation from the Giboney case precisely applies here. The talking that was done took place "as an integral part of conduct in violation of a valid criminal statute" against burning the American flag in public. I would therefore affirm this conviction.

Mr. Justice WHITE, dissenting. . . .

The Court's schema is this: the statute forbids insults to the flag either by act or words; the charge alleged both flag burning and speech; the court rendered a general judgment; since the conviction might logically have been for speech alone or for both words and deeds and since in either event the conviction is invalid, the judgment of the New York courts must be set aside without passing upon the validity of a conviction for burning the flag.[1] I reach precisely the opposite conclusion; before Street's conviction can be either reversed or affirmed, the Court *must* reach and decide the validity of a conviction for flag burning. . . .

The Court is obviously wrong in reversing the judgment below because it believes that Street was unconstitutionally convicted for speaking. Reversal can follow only if the Court reaches the conviction for flag burning and finds that conviction, as well as the assumed conviction for speech, to be violative of the First Amendment.[2] For myself, without the benefit of the majority's thinking if it were to find flag burning protected by the First Amendment, I would sustain such a conviction. I must dissent.

1. The Court's theory is not that of unconstitutional overbreadth; it does not argue that New York may not convict for burning because the entire statute is unconstitutional for permitting convictions for insulting speech as well as for the act of flag burning. [Footnote by Justice White.]

2. Arguably, under today's decision any conviction for flag burning where the defendant's words are critical to proving intent or some other element of the crime would be invalid since the conviction would be based in part on speech. The Court disclaims this result but without explaining why it would not reverse a conviction for burning where words spoken at the time are necessarily used to prove a case and yet reverse burning convictions on precisely the same evidence simply because on that evidence the defendant might also have been convicted for speaking. . . . [Footnote by Justice White.]

Mr. Justice FORTAS, dissenting.

I agree with the dissenting opinion filed by The Chief Justice, but I believe that it is necessary briefly to set forth the reasons why the States and the Federal Government have the power to protect the flag from acts of desecration committed in public.

If the national flag were nothing more than a chattel, subject only to the rules governing the use of private personalty, its use would nevertheless be subject to certain types of state regulation. For example, regulations concerning the use of chattels which are reasonably designed to avoid danger to life or property, or impingement upon the rights of others to the quiet use of their property and of public facilities, would unquestionably be a valid exercise of police power. They would not necessarily be defeated by a claim that they conflicted with the rights of the owner of the regulated property. See, e. g., Village of Euclid v. Ambler Realty Co., 272 U.S. 365 (1926); Berman v. Parker, 348 U.S. 26 (1954). [See chap. 13, supra.]

If a state statute provided that it is a misdemeanor to burn one's shirt or trousers or shoes on the public thoroughfare, it could hardly be asserted that the citizen's constitutional right is violated. If the arsonist asserted that he was burning his shirt or trousers or shoes as a protest against the Government's fiscal policies, for example, it is hardly possible that his claim to First Amendment shelter would prevail against the State's claim of a right to avert danger to the public and to avoid obstruction to traffic as a result of the fire. This is because action, even if clearly for serious protest purposes, is not entitled to the pervasive protection that is given to speech alone. See Cantwell v. Connecticut, 310 U.S. 296, 303–304 (1940). It may be subjected to reasonable regulation that appropriately takes into account the competing interests involved.

The test that is applicable in every case where conduct is restricted or prohibited is whether the regulation or prohibition is reasonable, due account being taken of the paramountcy of First Amendment values. If, as I submit, it is permissible to prohibit the burning of personal property on the public sidewalk, there is no basis for applying a different rule to flag burning. And the fact that the law is violated for purposes of protest does not immunize the violator. United States v. O'Brien, 391 U.S. 367 (1968); see Giboney v. Empire Storage & Ice Co., 336 U.S. 490 (1949).

Beyond this, however, the flag is a special kind of personalty. Its use is traditionally and universally subject to special rules and regulation. As early as 1907, this Court affirmed the constitutionality of a state statute making it a crime to use a representation of the United States flag for purposes of advertising. Halter v. Nebraska, 205 U.S. 34 (1907). Statutes prescribe how the flag may be displayed; how it may lawfully be disposed of; when, how, and for what purposes it may and may not be used. A person may "own" a flag, but ownership is subject to special burdens and responsibilities. A flag may be property, in a sense; but it is property burdened with peculiar obligations and restrictions. Certainly, as Halter v. Nebraska, supra, held, these special conditions are not *per se* arbitrary or beyond governmental power under our Constitution.

One may not justify burning a house, even if it is his own, on the ground, however sincere, that he does so as a protest. One may not justify breaking the windows of a government building on that basis. Protest does not exonerate lawlessness. And the prohibition against flag burning on the public thoroughfare being valid, the misdemeanor is not excused merely because it is an act of flamboyant protest.

O'BRIEN—TINKER—STREET
AS THE CULMINATION OF 50 YEARS OF FREE SPEECH LITIGATION: SOME ANXIOUS THOUGHTS ABOUT UNEVEN RESULTS AND UNSTABLE DOCTRINES

Introduction. These symbolic expression cases of the late sixties warrant attention not only for their own sake but also as a vantage point for assessment of the accomplishments of the Court's first half-century of First Amendment cases—for evaluation of the basic doctrinal developments in the preceding materials and as framework for the critical examination of the special problems in the next chapter. O'Brien-Tinker-Street came near the close of Chief Justice Warren's tenure. The Warren Court, especially during the sixties, had upheld a large number of First Amendment claims, in a variety of contexts; and it had been almost as prolific in its doctrinal innovations as in its libertarian results. Yet this group of cases suggests not only uncertainty of results but also shakiness of doctrinal foundations. The First Amendment claimant prevailed in two of the three cases, to be sure. But in one of the cases—Street—a tortured reading of the legal posture of the case was necessary to assure reversal of the conviction. And, more important, the range and content of the Justices' doctrinal positions left considerable doubt (despite a half century of talk about "absolute" rights, "preferred" positions, and "immediate" risks) that a coherent, comprehensive, consistent framework for First Amendment protection had yet emerged.

1. *Oversimplifications, evasions, and O'Brien.* Was there not reason to expect a fuller evaluation of the speech ingredients of symbolic draft-card burning protests from the Warren Court than the Chief Justice's opinion in O'Brien provided? Were the criteria suggested at the outset of Part II of O'Brien adequate? Or did they sidestep the problem of balancing the restriction on expression against the harm caused by the defendant's behavior? Did the justification for the statute spelled out in the opinion approach the high level of governmental need suggested by the "compelling," "substantial," "strong" adjectives as applied in other contexts? Was the Court's scrutiny of the need for the criminal statute, and of possible alternative means, as intensive as it has been in most other First Amendment cases?

Is there justification for describing the Warren Court's disposition of O'Brien's "by no means frivolous" claim as "astonishingly cavalier"? Is there basis for saying that the Court "chose not to deal with the complexities" of the problem, "made no attempt to discuss, let alone to answer, the difficult and disturbing constitutional questions presented," instead "trivialized the issues and handed down an opinion that has all the deceptive simplicity and superficial force that can usually be achieved by begging the question"? Those are among the critical comments in Alfange, Jr., "Free Speech and Symbolic Conduct: The Draft-Card Burning Case," 1968 Sup.Ct.Rev. 1 (which concludes, it should be noted, that "the result in O'Brien is defensible despite the deficiencies of manifest oversimplification in the Court's opinion").

2. *Question-begging distinctions, Tinker, and Justice Fortas.* May the "question-begging" quality of the O'Brien opinion be a reflection of the weak-

nesses of the doctrinal techniques in vogue, rather than an aberration, or a response to the pressures of de facto war? Does the "speech"-"conduct" distinction, especially, tend to avoid subtle judgments and to evoke overstatements? Compare, for example, Justice Fortas in Tinker with Justice Fortas in Barker v. Hardway (the cert. denied concurrence)—and with Justice Fortas in Street. Does his Tinker opinion convey a sense of greater protection of student behavior than intended because the "akin to 'pure speech' " categorization generates libertarian rhetoric—which promptly requires qualification regarding the "conduct" in Barker? Does the same oversimplified and obscuring "speech"-"conduct" premise in turn give rise to the equally extreme—albeit restrictive rather than libertarian—rhetoric in the Street dissent, which apparently finds a "mere rationality" requirement appropriate via the easy route of an "action"-"speech alone" distinction? How does Justice Fortas' Street dissent give the "due" recognition to the "paramountcy" of First Amendment values that he professes to be necessary? A protest purpose does not "immunize" against law violation, to be sure—but was that the issue?

3. *The excessive aversion to "balancing" and Street.* Is the temptation to "solve" hard cases of "indirect" regulation of expression via the simplistic "speech"-"conduct" distinction attributable to the aversion of many of the Justices to "balancing" talk? And yet do not these cases, more than most, demonstrate the necessity of discriminating, sensitive, articulate balancing for many speech problems?

Justice Fortas and Chief Justice Warren were among those generally identified with the libertarian wing during the closing years of the Warren Court; Justice Harlan, by contrast, was a chief target of those who, like Justice Black, saw in "balancing" a frittering away of First Amendment rights. (For an especially elaborate Harlan-Black "balancing"-"absolutes" clash, see the Konigsberg II excerpts, p. 1308, infra.) Is it not ironic, then, that Justice Harlan should write the majority opinion in Street—with Chief Justice Warren as well as Justices Fortas and Black finding little difficulty in sustaining the conviction? Would Justice Harlan have applied his analysis if he had focused on the flag-burning, and not just the words, in Street—i. e., would he have sought to identify the governmental interests and to determine whether any were sufficiently furthered to justify the conviction? Would a conviction for the act of burning have been sustainable under that approach?

Does not the Street opinion's variety of balancing lay bare the competing values, including the "speech" ingredients, more effectively than alternative techniques? Does "balancing" not encourage more articulate, less simplistic analyses? If so, is the division in Street not only ironic but, more important, a symbol of the weaknesses of "conduct"-"speech" distinctions and "absolutes" emphases as guarantors of First Amendment protections? (Compare the results reached via Justice Black's analyses in these cases.) Or does the uncertain course of these techniques suggest at least that "absolutes," "balancing," "speech"-"conduct" distinctions and their offshoots have not yet proved wholly adequate to the task of supplying principled, intellectually respectable, and pragmatically effective tools for the implementation of First Amendment values? The cases in the next chapter apply old doctrines and evolve new variations. Do those materials suggest the ingredients of more satisfactory analytical tools?

Chapter 16

FREEDOM OF EXPRESSION:
SOME ADDITIONAL PROBLEMS

Introduction. The preceding chapter introduced the most pervasive elements of First Amendment doctrine by exploring two of the most troublesome problems of free speech: criminal penalties directed at speech critical of national policies and local regulation of expression in public places. This chapter pursues the critical testing of the analytical tools developed in those contexts by examining their applications and elaborations in a number of other settings. The division of chapters is not a sharp one: for example, the concern with words which injure reputation or threaten the administration of justice (secs. 1 and 3 below) is foreshadowed in some of the preceding materials; the concern with subversion manifested earlier in the criminal prosecutions under the Smith Act (sec. 1D of chap. 15) continues with the government employees security programs and legislative investigations below (secs. 6 and 7). Nevertheless, the arrangement has justification: chapter 15 traces core doctrines in the context of separable functional problems; the problems of chapter 16 contain additional variables that not only test the preceding analyses but require new doctrinal ingredients.

The materials in the opening sections of this chapter emphasize control of expression because of its content: as with many of the subversive advocacy problems in chap. 15, sec. 1, restriction of libel, obscenity, and contemptuous comments on courts rests on the allegedly harmful or obnoxious nature of the expression itself. To what extent are the earlier analyses—e. g., as to clear and present danger, First Amendment values, legislative judgments—applicable here? Are the problems manageable by placing some kinds of expression—e. g., nonpolitical speech, obscene speech—wholly outside the First Amendment sphere?

In the later sections of this chapter, the state's main concern purports not to be with the content of speech but with other objectives—e. g., legislative access to information, quality of the professions, and fitness of government employees. As with the public places problems in sec. 2 of chap. 15, can these regulations be distinguished as having only "indirect" impact on speech or as concerned with "conduct" rather than "speech"? Do those distinctions justify significantly less judicial scrutiny of state justifications, means, and alternatives than when First Amendment values are "directly" threatened?

SECTION 1. LIBEL

THE BACKGROUND AND THE BEAUHARNAIS CASE

Introduction. In 1942, in Chaplinsky v. New Hampshire, chap. 15, p. 1154, supra, the unanimous Court was able confidently to list libel and obscenity with "fighting words" as examples of expression plainly not entitled to First

Amendment protection. But, as this section and the next indicate, the First Amendment problems of libel and obscenity regulation have absorbed considerable Court attention in recent years. The sustaining of the Illinois criminal libel law in the Beauharnais case in 1952 reflected a more permissive judicial attitude toward libel regulation than toward other laws directed at expression; the New York Times case in the following decade committed the Court to a more intense scrutiny which is manifested in the proliferating libel cases of the sixties. The New York Times emphasis on the importance of debate on public issues has had considerable influence outside the libel area as well, as noted earlier (p. 1131, supra). The purpose of this section is to explore the New York Times approach both for its utility in general First Amendment analysis and its effectiveness in the specific area of libel.

The Beauharnais case. In Beauharnais v. Illinois, 343 U.S. 250 (1952), petitioner was convicted of violating an Illinois statute which made it "unlawful for any person .   .   .   to manufacture, sell, publish, .   .   . or exhibit in any public place in this state any lithograph, moving picture, play .   .   .   which publication or exhibition portrays depravity, criminality, unchastity, or lack of virtue of a class of citizens, of any race, color, creed or religion, [or which] exposes the citizens of any race, color, creed or religion to contempt, derision, or obloquy, or which is productive of breach of the peace or riots." Beauharnais, president of the White Circle League, had organized the circulation of a leaflet calling on Chicago officials "to halt the further encroachment, harassment and invasion of white people, their property, neighborhoods and persons, by the Negro." The leaflet called on Chicago's white people to unite and warned that if "persuasion and the need to prevent the white race from becoming mongrelized by the negro will not unite us, then the aggressions, .   .   .   rapes, robberies, knives, guns and marijuana of the negro, surely will." The trial court refused to give a "clear and present danger" charge requested by petitioner. Moreover, it refused offered evidence on the issue of truth, in accordance with its position that the statute was "a form of criminal libel law." Justice Frankfurter's majority opinion sustaining the conviction included the following passages:

"No one will gainsay that it is libelous falsely to charge another with being a rapist, robber, carrier of knives and guns, user of marijuana. The precise question before us, then, is whether the protection of liberty in the Due Process Clause of the Fourteenth Amendment prevents a State from punishing such libels—as criminal libel has been defined, limited and constitutionally recognized time out of mind—directed at designated collectivities and flagrantly disseminated. .   .   .   We cannot say .   .   .   that the question is concluded by history and practice. But if an utterance directed at an individual may be the object of criminal sanctions, we cannot deny to a State power to punish the same utterance directed at a defined group, unless we can say that this is a wilful and purposeless restriction unrelated to the peace and well-being of the State.

"Illinois did not have to look beyond her own borders or await the tragic experience of the last three decades to conclude that wilful purveyors of falsehood concerning racial and religious groups promote strife and tend powerfully to obstruct the manifold adjustments required for free, ordered life in a metropolitan, polyglot community. From the murder of the abolitionist Lovejoy in 1837 to the Cicero riots of 1951, Illinois has been the scene of exacerbated tension between races, often flaring into violence and destruction. In many of these outbreaks, utterances of the character here in question, so the Illinois legislature could conclude, played a significant part. . . .

"In the face of this history and its frequent obligato of extreme racial and religious propaganda, we would deny experience to say that the Illinois legislature was without reason in seeking ways to curb false or malicious defamation of racial and religious groups, made in public places and by means calculated to have a powerful emotional impact on those to whom it was presented. . . . It is not within our competence to confirm or deny claims of social scientists as to the dependence of the individual on the position of his racial or religious group in the community. It would, however, be arrant dogmatism, quite outside the scope of our authority in passing on the powers of a State, for us to deny that the Illinois Legislature may warrantably believe that a man's job and his educational opportunities and the dignity accorded him may depend as much on the reputation of the racial and religious group to which he willy-nilly belongs, as it does on his own merits. This being so, we are precluded from saying that speech concededly punishable when immediately directed at individuals cannot be outlawed if directed at groups with whose position and esteem in society the affiliated individual may be inextricably involved. . . .

"We are warned that the choice open to the Illinois legislature may be abused. . . . Every power may be abused but the possibility of abuse is a poor reason for denying Illinois the power to adopt measures . . . sanctioned by centuries of Anglo-American law. 'While this Court sits' it retains and exercises authority to nullify action which encroaches on freedom of utterance under the guise of punishing libel. . . .

"Libelous utterances, not being within the area of constitutionally protected speech, it is unnecessary, either for us or for the State courts, to consider the issues behind the phrase 'clear and present danger.' Certainly no one would contend that obscene speech, for example, may be punished only upon a showing of such circumstances. Libel, as we have seen, is in the same class."*

Justice Black, joined by Justice Douglas, dissented: "The Court condones this expansive state censorship by painstakingly analogizing it to the law of criminal libel. As a result of this refined analysis, the Illinois statute emerges labeled a 'group libel law.' This label may make the Court's holding more palatable for those who sustain it, but the sugar-coating does not make the censorship less deadly. However tagged, the Illinois law is not that criminal libel which has been 'defined, limited and constitutionally recognized time out of mind.' For as 'constitutionally recognized' that crime has provided for punishment of false, malicious, scurrilous charges against individuals, not against huge groups. This limited scope of the law of criminal libel is of no small importance. It has confined state punishment of speech and expression to the narrowest of areas involving nothing more than purely private feuds. Every expansion of the law of criminal libel so as to punish discussion of matters of public concern means a corresponding invasion of the area dedicated to free expression by the First Amendment. . . .

"No rationalization on a purely legal level can conceal the fact that state laws like this one present a constant overhanging threat to freedom of speech,

---

* See Riesman, "Democracy and Defamation: Control of Group Libel," 42 Colum.L.Rev. 727 (1942), cited by both majority and minority. See also Tanenhaus, "Group Libel," 35 Cornell L.Q. 261 (1950); Beth, "Group Libel and Free Speech," 39 Minn.L.Rev. 167 (1955).

press and religion. . . . I think the First Amendment, with the Fourteenth, 'absolutely' forbids such laws without any 'ifs' or 'buts' or 'whereases.' Whatever the danger, if any, in such public discussions, it is a danger the Founders deemed outweighed by the danger incident to the stifling of thought and speech."

Justice Reed also dissented, in an opinion joined by Justice Douglas: "These words—'virtue,' 'derision', and 'obloquy'—have neither general or special meanings well enough known to apprise those within their reach as to limitations on speech. . . . Since this judgment may rest upon these vague and undefined words, which permit within their scope the punishment of incidents secured by the guarantee of free speech, the conviction should be reversed."

In a separate dissent, Justice Douglas stated: "My view is that if in any case other public interests are to override the plain command of the First Amendment, the peril of speech must be clear and present, leaving no room for argument, raising no doubts as to the necessity of curbing speech in order to prevent disaster. The First Amendment is couched in absolute terms— freedom of speech shall not be abridged. Speech has therefore a preferred position as contrasted to some other civil rights. For example, privacy, equally sacred to some, is protected by the Fourth Amendment only against unreasonable searches and seizures. There is room for regulation of the ways and means of invading privacy. No such leeway is granted the invasion of the right of free speech guaranteed by the First Amendment."

Still another dissenting opinion was submitted by Justice Jackson: "The assumption of other dissents is that the 'liberty' which the Due Process Clause of the Fourteenth Amendment protects against denial by the States is the literal and identical 'freedom of speech or of the press' which the First Amendment forbids only Congress to abridge. The history of criminal libel in America convinces me that the Fourteenth Amenndment did not 'incorporate' the First, that the powers of Congress and of the States over this subject are not of the same dimensions, and that because Congress probably could not enact this law it does not follow that the States may not. . . .

"This Court has never sustained a federal criminal libel Act. One section of the Sedition Act of 1798 was close to being a 'group libel' Act. While there were convictions under it, no attack on its validity reached this Court. I think today's better opinion regards the enactment as a breach of the First Amendment and certainly Mr. Justice Holmes and Mr. Justice Brandeis thought so. But even in the absence of judicial condemnation, the political disapproval of the Sedition Act was so emphatic and sustained that federal prosecution of the press ceased for a century. . . .

"More than forty State Constitutions, while extending broad protections to speech and press, reserve a responsibility for their abuse and implicitly or explicitly recognize validity of criminal libel laws. . . . Certainly this tolerance of state libel laws by the very authors and partisans of the Fourteenth Amendment shows either that they were not intending to incorporate the First Amendment or that they believed it would not prevent federal libel laws. Adoption of the incorporation theory today would lead to the dilemma of either confining the States as closely as the Congress or giving the Federal Government the latitude appropriate to state governments. The treatment of libel powers corroborates the conclusions against the incorporationist theory reached by the most comprehensive and objective studies of the origin and adoption of the Fourteenth Amendment. . . .

"As the principle by which to judge the constitutionality of this statute, I accept the dissent in Gitlow and the decision in Palko. What restraints upon state power to punish criminal libel are implied by the 'concept of ordered liberty'? . . . If one can claim to announce the judgment of legal history on any subject, it is that criminal libel laws are consistent with the concept of ordered liberty only when applied with safeguards evolved to prevent their invasion of freedom of expression. . . .

"In this case, neither the court nor jury found or were required to find any injury to any person, or group, or to the public peace, nor to find any probability, let alone any clear and present danger, of injury to any of these. Even though no individuals were named or described as targets of this pamphlet, if it resulted in a riot or caused injury to any individual Negro, such as being refused living quarters in a particular section, house or apartment, or being refused employment, certainly there would be no constitutional obstacle to imposing civil or criminal liability for actual results. But in this case no actual violence and no specific injury was charged or proved.

"The leaflet was simply held punishable as criminal libel *per se* irrespective of its actual or probable consequences. . . . The conviction rests on judicial attribution of a likelihood of evil results."

NEW YORK TIMES CO. v. SULLIVAN

376 U.S. 254, 84 S.Ct. 710, 11 L.Ed.2d 686 (1964).

Certiorari to the Supreme Court of Alabama.[*]

Mr. Justice BRENNAN delivered the opinion of the Court.

We are required for the first time in this case to determine the extent to which the constitutional protections for speech and press limit a State's power to award damages in a libel action brought by a public official against critics of his official conduct.

Respondent L. B. Sullivan is one of the three elected Commissioners of the City of Montgomery, Alabama. He testified that he was "Commissioner of Public Affairs and the duties are supervision of the Police Department, Fire Department, Department of Cemetery and Department of Scales." He brought this civil libel action against the four individual petitioners, who are Negroes and Alabama clergymen, and against petitioner the New York Times Company, a New York corporation which publishes the New York Times, a daily newspaper. A jury in the Circuit Court of Montgomery County awarded him damages of $500,000, the full amount claimed, against all the petitioners, and the Supreme Court of Alabama affirmed. . . .

Respondent's complaint alleged that he had been libeled by statements in a full-page advertisement that was carried in the New York Times on March 29, 1960. Entitled "Heed Their Rising Voices," the advertisement began by stating that "As the whole world knows by now, thousands of Southern Negro students are engaged in widespread non-violent demonstrations in positive af-

---

[*] Together with Abernathy v. Sullivan, also on certiorari to the Supreme Court of Alabama.

firmation of the right to live in human dignity as guaranteed by the U. S. Constitution and the Bill of Rights." It went on to charge that "in their efforts to uphold these guarantees, they are being met by an unprecedented wave of terror by those who would deny and negate that document which the whole world looks upon as setting the pattern for modern freedom. . . . ." Succeeding paragraphs purported to illustrate the "wave of terror" by describing certain alleged events. The text concluded with an appeal for funds for three purposes: support of the student movement, "the struggle for the right-to-vote," and the legal defense of Dr. Martin Luther King, Jr., leader of the movement, against a perjury indictment then pending in Montgomery. . . .

Of the 10 paragraphs of text in the advertisement, the third and a portion of the sixth were the basis of respondent's claim of libel. They read as follows:

Third paragraph:

"In Montgomery, Alabama, after students sang 'My Country, 'Tis of Thee' on the State Capitol steps, their leaders were expelled from school, and truckloads of police armed with shotguns and tear-gas ringed the Alabama State College Campus. When the entire student body protested to state authorities by refusing to re-register, their dining hall was padlocked in an attempt to starve them into submission."

Sixth paragraph:

"Again and again the Southern violators have answered Dr. King's peaceful protests with intimidation and violence. They have bombed his home almost killing his wife and child. They have assaulted his person. They have arrested him seven times—for 'speeding,' 'loitering' and similar 'offenses.' And now they have charged him with 'perjury'—a *felony* under which they would imprison him for *ten years*. . . . ."

Although neither of these statements mentions respondent by name, he contended that the word "police" in the third paragraph referred to him as the Montgomery Commissioner who supervised the Police Department, so that he was being accused of "ringing" the campus with police. He further claimed that the paragraph would be read as imputing to the police, and hence to him, the padlocking of the dining hall in order to starve the students into submission. As to the sixth paragraph, he contended that since arrests are ordinarily made by the police, the statement "They have arrested [Dr. King] seven times" would be read as referring to him; he further contended that the "They" who did the arresting would be equated with the "They" who committed the other described acts and with the "Southern violators." . . .

It is uncontroverted that some of the statements contained in the two paragraphs were not accurate descriptions of events which occurred in Montgomery. Although Negro students staged a demonstration on the State Capitol steps, they sang the National Anthem and not "My Country, 'Tis of Thee." Although nine students were expelled by the State Board of Education, this was not for leading the demonstration at the Capitol, but for demanding service at a lunch counter in the Montgomery County Courthouse on another day. Not the entire student body, but most of it, had protested the expulsion, not by refusing to register, but by boycotting classes on a single day; virtually all the students did register for the ensuing semester. The campus dining hall was not padlocked on any occasion, and the only students who may have been barred from eating there were the few who had neither signed a preregistration application nor requested temporary meal tickets. [Other examples of in-accuracies are omitted.]

. . . We reverse the judgment. We hold that the rule of law applied by the Alabama courts is constitutionally deficient for failure to provide the safeguards for freedom of speech and of the press that are required by the First and Fourteenth Amendments in a libel action brought by a public official against critics of his official conduct. We further hold that under the proper safeguards the evidence presented in this case is constitutionally insufficient to support the judgment for respondent.

I.

We may dispose at the outset of two grounds asserted to insulate the judgment of the Alabama courts from constitutional scrutiny. The first is the proposition relied on by the State Supreme Court—that "The Fourteenth Amendment is directed against State action and not private action." That proposition has no application to this case. Although this is a civil lawsuit between private parties, the Alabama courts have applied a state rule of law which petitioners claim to impose invalid restrictions on their constitutional freedoms of speech and press. . . .

The second contention is that the constitutional guarantees of freedom of speech and of the press are inapplicable here, at least so far as the Times is concerned, because the allegedly libelous statements were published as part of a paid, "commercial" advertisement. . . . That the Times was paid for publishing the advertisement is as immaterial in this connection as is the fact that newspapers and books are sold. . . . Any other conclusion would discourage newspapers from carrying "editorial advertisements" of this type, and so might shut off an important outlet for the promulgation of information and ideas by persons who do not themselves have access to publishing facilities—who wish to exercise their freedom of speech even though they are not members of the press. . . . To avoid placing such a handicap upon the freedoms of expression, we hold that if the allegedly libelous statements would otherwise be constitutionally protected from the present judgment, they do not forfeit that protection because they were published in the form of a paid advertisement.

II.

Under Alabama law as applied in this case, a publication is "libelous per se" if the words "tend to injure a person . . . in his reputation" or to "bring [him] into public contempt"; the trial court stated that the standard was met if the words are such as to "injure him in his public office, or impute misconduct to him in his office, or want of official integrity, or want of fidelity to a public trust . . .." The jury must find that the words were published "of and concerning" the plaintiff, but where the plaintiff is a public official his place in the governmental hierarchy is sufficient evidence to support a finding that his reputation has been affected by statements that reflect upon the agency of which he is in charge. Once "libel per se" has been established, the defendant has no defense as to stated facts unless he can persuade the jury that they were true in all their particulars. . . . Unless he can discharge the burden of proving truth, general damages are presumed, and may be awarded without proof of pecuniary injury. A showing of actual malice is apparently a prerequisite to recovery of punitive damages, and the defendant may in any event forestall these by a retraction meeting the statutory requirements. Good motives and belief in truth do not negate an inference of malice, but are relevant only in mitigation of punitive damages if the jury chooses to accord them weight. . . .

The question before us is whether this rule of liability, as applied to an action brought by a public official against critics of his official conduct, abridges the freedom of speech and of the press that is guaranteed by the First and Fourteenth Amendments.

Respondent relies heavily, as did the Alabama courts, on statements of this Court to the effect that the Constitution does not protect libelous publications. Those statements do not foreclose our inquiry here. None of the cases sustained the use of libel laws to impose sanctions upon expression critical of the official conduct of public officials. . . . In Beauharnais v. Illinois, 343 U.S. 250, the Court sustained an Illinois criminal libel statute as applied to a publication held to be both defamatory of a racial group and "liable to cause violence and disorder." But the Court was careful to note that it "retains and exercises authority to nullify action which encroaches on freedom of utterance under the guise of punishing libel" . . . . In deciding the question now, we are compelled by neither precedent nor policy to give any more weight to the epithet "libel" than we have to other "mere labels" of state law. N. A. A. C. P. v. Button, 371 U.S. 415, 429 [p. 1285, infra]. Like "insurrection," contempt, advocacy of unlawful acts, breach of the peace, obscenity, solicitation of legal business, and the various other formulae for the repression of expression that have been challenged in this Court, libel can claim no talismanic immunity from constitutional limitations. It must be measured by standards that satisfy the First Amendment. . . .

[W]e consider this case against the background of a profound national commitment to the principle that debate on public issues should be uninhibited, robust, and wide-open, and that it may well include vehement, caustic, and sometimes unpleasantly sharp attacks on government and public officials. . . . The present advertisement, as an expression of grievance and protest on one of the major public issues of our time, would seem clearly to qualify for the constitutional protection. The question is whether it forfeits that protection by the falsity of some of its factual statements and by its alleged defamation of respondent.

Authoritative interpretations of the First Amendment guarantees have consistently refused to recognize an exception for any test of truth, whether administered by judges, juries, or administrative officials—and especially not one that puts the burden of proving truth on the speaker. Cf. Speiser v. Randall, 357 U.S. 513, 525–526. The constitutional protection does not turn upon "the truth, popularity, or social utility of the ideas and beliefs which are offered." N. A. A. C. P. v. Button, 371 U.S. 415, 445. . . .

Just as factual error affords no warrant for repressing speech that would otherwise be free, the same is true of injury to official reputation. . . . If judges are to be treated as "men of fortitude, able to thrive in a hardy climate," Craig v. Harney, 331 U.S., at 376, surely the same must be true of other government officials, such as elected city commissioners. Criticism of their official conduct does not lose its constitutional protection merely because it is effective criticism and hence diminishes their official reputations.

If neither factual error nor defamatory content suffices to remove the constitutional shield from criticism of official conduct, the combination of the two elements is no less inadequate. This is the lesson to be drawn from the great controversy over the Sedition Act of 1798, 1 Stat. 596, which first crystallized a national awareness of the central meaning of the First Amendment.

. . . . .

Although the Sedition Act was never tested in this Court, the attack upon its validity has carried the day in the court of history. Fines levied in its prosecution were repaid by Act of Congress on the ground that it was unconstitutional. . . . Jefferson, as President, pardoned those who had been convicted and sentenced under the Act and remitted their fines, stating: "I discharged every person under punishment or prosecution under the sedition law, because I considered, and now consider, that law to be a nullity, as absolute and as palpable as if Congress had ordered us to fall down and worship a golden image." Letter to Mrs. Adams, July 22, 1804, 4 Jefferson's Works (Washington ed.), pp. 555, 556. The invalidity of the Act has also been assumed by Justices of this Court. . . . These views reflect a broad consensus that the Act, because of the restraint it imposed upon criticism of government and public officials, was inconsistent with the First Amendment.

. . . . .

What a State may not constitutionally bring about by means of a criminal statute is likewise beyond the reach of its civil law of libel. The fear of damage awards under a rule such as that invoked by the Alabama courts here may be markedly more inhibiting than the fear of prosecution under a criminal statute. . . . The judgment awarded in this case—without the need for any proof of actual pecuniary loss—was one thousand times greater than the maximum fine provided by the Alabama criminal statute, and one hundred times greater than that provided by the Sedition Act. And since there is no double jeopardy limitation applicable to civil lawsuits, this is not the only judgment that may be awarded against petitioners for the same publication. Whether or not a newspaper can survive a succession of such judgments, the pall of fear and timidity imposed upon those who would give voice to public criticism is an atmosphere in which the First Amendment freedoms cannot survive. . . .

The state rule of law is not saved by its allowance of the defense of truth. A defense for erroneous statements honestly made is no less essential here than was the requirement of proof of guilty knowledge which, in Smith v. California, 361 U.S. 147 [p. 1271, infra], we held iindispensable to a valid conviction of a bookseller for possessing obscene writings for sale. . . . Allowance of the defense of truth, with the burden of proving it on the defendant, does not mean that only false speech will be deterred. . . . Under such a rule, would-be critics of official conduct may be deterred from voicing their criticism, even though it is believed to be true and even though it is in fact true, because of doubt whether it can be proved in court or fear of the expense of having to do so. . . . The rule thus dampens the vigor and limits the variety of public debate. It is inconsistent with the First and Fourteenth Amendments.

The constitutional guarantees require, we think, a federal rule that prohibits a public official from recovering damages for a defamatory falsehood relating to his official conduct unless he proves that the statement was made with "actual malice"—that is, with knowledge that it was false or with reckless disregard of whether it was false or not. . . .

Such a privilege for criticism of official conduct is appropriately analogous to the protection accorded a public official when *he* is sued for libel by a private citizen. [Barr v. Matteo, 360 U.S. 564, 575.] It would give public servants an unjustified preference over the public they serve, if critics of official conduct did not have a fair equivalent of the immunity granted to the officials themselves. . . .

III.

We hold today that the Constitution delimits a State's power to award damages for libel in actions brought by public officials against critics of their official conduct. Since this is such an action,[1] the rule requiring proof of actual malice is applicable. While Alabama law apparently requires proof of actual malice for an award of punitive damages, where general damages are concerned malice is "presumed." Such a presumption is inconsistent with the federal rule. . . . Since the trial judge did not instruct the jury to differentiate between general and punitive damages, it may be that the verdict was wholly an award of one or the other. But it is impossible to know, in view of the general verdict returned. Because of this uncertainty, the judgment must be reversed and the case remanded. . . .

Since respondent may seek a new trial, we deem that considerations of effective judicial administration require us to review the evidence in the present record to determine whether it could constitutionally support a judgment for respondent. This Court's duty is not limited to the elaboration of constitutional principles; we must also in proper cases review the evidence to make certain that those principles have been constitutionally applied. . . .

Applying these standards, we consider that the proof presented to show actual malice lacks the convincing clarity which the constitutional standard demands, and hence that it would not constitutionally sustain the judgment for respondent under the proper rule of law. . . .

We also think the evidence was constitutionally defective in another respect: it was incapable of supporting the jury's finding that the allegedly libelous statements were made "of and concerning" respondent. . . .

Reversed and remanded.

---

1. We have no occasion here to determine how far down into the lower ranks of government employees the "public official" designation would extend for purposes of this rule, or otherwise to specify categories of persons who would or would not be included. . . . Nor need we here determine the boundaries of the "official conduct" concept. It is enough for the present case that respondent's position as an elected city commissioner clearly made him a public official, and that the allegations in the advertisement concerned what was allegedly his official conduct as Commissioner in charge of the Police Department. . . . [Footnote by the Court.]

[In Rosenblatt v. Baer, 383 U.S. 75 (1966), Justice Brennan's majority opinion found it unnecessary to draw "precise lines" for determining the content of the "public official" category, but suggested that the designation "applies at the very least to those among the hierarchy of government employees who have, or appear to the public to have, substantial responsibility for or control over the conduct of governmental affairs." He added: "Where a position in government has such apparent importance that the public has an independent interest in the qualifications and performance of the person who holds it, beyond the general public interest in the qualifications and performance of all government employees, both elements we identified in New York Times are present and the New York Times malice standards apply."]

— by becoming an official he waives any
— official acts by an official are important to democracy.

Mr. Justice BLACK, with whom Mr. Justice DOUGLAS joins, (concurring). . . . "Malice," even as defined by the Court, is an elusive, abstract concept, hard to prove and hard to disprove. The requirement that malice be proved provides at best an evanescent protection for the right critically to discuss public affairs and certainly does not measure up to the sturdy safeguard embodied in the First Amendment. Unlike the Court, therefore, I vote to reverse exclusively on the ground that the Times and the individual defendants had an absolute, unconditional constitutional right to publish in the Times advertisement their criticisms of the Montgomery agencies and officials. . . .

Mr. Justice GOLDBERG, with whom Mr. Justice DOUGLAS joins (concurring in the result). . . .

In my view, the First and Fourteenth Amendments to the Constitution afford to the citizen and to the press an absolute, unconditional privilege to criticize official conduct despite the harm which may flow from excesses and abuses. . . .

We must recognize that we are writing upon a clean slate. . . . We should be particularly careful, therefore, adequately to protect the liberties which are embodied in the First and Fourteenth Amendments. It may be urged that deliberately and maliciously false statements have no conceivable value as free speech. That argument, however, is not responsive to the real issue presented by this case, which is whether that freedom of speech which all agree is constitutionally protected can be effectively safeguarded by a rule allowing the imposition of liability upon a jury's evaluation of the speaker's state of mind. If individual citizens may be held liable in damages for strong words, which a jury finds false and maliciously motivated, there can be little doubt that public debate and advocacy will be constrained. And if newspapers, publishing advertisements dealing with public issues, thereby risk liability, there can also be little doubt that the ability of minority groups to secure publication of their views on public affairs and to seek support for their causes will be greatly diminished. . . .

This is not to say that the Constitution protects defamatory statements directed against the private conduct of a public official or private citizen. Freedom of press and of speech insure that government will respond to the will of the people and that changes may be obtained by peaceful means. Purely private defamation has little to do with the political ends of a self-governing society. The imposition of liability for private defamation does not abridge the freedom of public speech.[1] This, of course, cannot be said "where public officials are concerned or where public matters are involved. . . ." Douglas, The Rights of the People (1958), p. 41. . . .

The conclusion that the Constitution affords the citizen and the press an absolute privilege for criticism of official conduct does not leave the public of-

---

1. In most cases, as in the case at bar, there will be little difficulty in distinguishing defamatory speech relating to private conduct from that relating to official conduct. I recognize, of course, that there will be a gray area. The difficulties of applying a public-private standard are, however, certainly, of a different genre from those attending the differentiation between a malicious and nonmalicious state of mind. If the constitutional standard is to be shaped by a concept of malice, the speaker takes the risk not only that the jury will inaccurately determine his state of mind but also that the injury will fail properly to apply constitutional standard set by the elusive concept of malice. . . . [Footnote by Justice Goldberg.]

ficial without defenses against unsubstantiated opinions or deliberate misstatements. . . . The public official certainly has equal if not greater access than most private citizens to media of communication. . . .

APPLICATIONS AND ELABORATIONS OF THE NEW YORK TIMES PRINCIPLES

1. *Garrison v. Louisiana.* The Garrison case, 379 U.S. 64 (1964), held the New York Times principles applicable to a criminal libel prosecution. Appellant, a District Attorney, engaged in a dispute with eight judges of the local criminal court, issued a statement disparaging their judicial conduct. He charged inefficiency, laziness, and obstruction of his efforts to enforce the vice laws. He was convicted under the Louisiana Criminal Defamation Statute. The Supreme Court held that, though criminal libel has a "different history and purpose" than civil libel, "the New York Times rule also limits state power to impose criminal sanctions for criticism of the official conduct of public officials." Passages from Justice Brennan's opinion for the Court follow:

"At common law, truth was no defense to criminal libel. Although the victim of a true but defamatory publication might not have been unjustly damaged in reputation by the libel, the speaker was still punishable since the remedy was designed to avert the possibility that the utterance would provoke an enraged victim to a breach of peace. . . . Changing mores and the virtual disappearance of criminal libel prosecutions lend support to the observation that '. . . under modern conditions, when the rule of law is generally accepted as a substitute for private physical measures, it can hardly be urged that the maintenance of peace requires a criminal prosecution for private defamation.' Emerson, Toward a General Theory of the First Amendment, 72 Yale L.J. 877, 924 (1963). The absence in the Proposed Official Draft of the Model Penal Code of the American Law Institute of any criminal libel statute on the Louisiana pattern reflects this modern consensus. . . .

"The [ALI] Reporters . . . recommended only narrowly drawn statutes designed to reach words tending to cause a breach of the peace . . . or designed to reach speech, such as group vilification, 'especially likely to lead to public disorders,' such as the statute sustained in Beauharnais v. Illinois . . . . But Louisiana's rejection of the clear-and-present-danger standard as irrelevant to the application of its statute, . . . coupled with the absence of any limitation in the statute itself to speech calculated to prevent breaches of the peace, leads us to conclude that the Louisiana statute is not this sort of narrowly drawn statute.

"We next consider whether the historical limitation of the defense of truth in criminal libel to utterances published 'with good motives and for justifiable ends' should be incorporated into the New York Times rule as it applies to criminal libel statutes; in particular, we must ask whether this history permits negating the truth defense, as the Louisiana statute does, on a showing of malice in the sense of ill-will. [W]here the criticism is of public officials and their conduct of public business, the interest in private reputation is overborne by the larger public interest, secured by the Constitution, in the dissemination of truth. . . . Moreover, even where the utterance is false, the great principles of the Constitution . . . preclude attaching adverse consequences to any except the knowing or reckless falsehood. [O]nly those false statements made with the high degree of awareness of their probable falsity demanded by New York Times may be the subject of either civil or criminal sanctions. . . .

"The use of calculated falsehood, however, would put a different cast on the constitutional question. . . . That speech is used as a tool for political ends does not automatically bring it under the protective mantle of the Constitution. For the use of the known lie as a tool is at once at odds with the premises of democratic government and with the orderly manner in which economic, social, or political change is to be effected. . . . Hence the knowingly false statement and the false statement made with reckless disregard of the truth, do not enjoy constitutional protection. . . .

"We find no difficulty in bringing the appellant's statement within the purview of criticism of the official conduct of public officials, entitled to the benefit of the New York Times rule. . . . The New York Times rule is not rendered inapplicable merely because an official's private reputation, as well as his public reputation is harmed. . . . Few personal attributes are more germane to fitness for office than dishonesty, malfeasance, or improper motivation, even though these characteristics may also affect the official's private character. . . .

"Applying the principles of the New York Times case, we hold that the Louisiana statute . . . incorporates constitutionally invalid standards [for] the statute directs punishment for true statements made with actual malice . . .. The statute is also unconstitutional as interpreted to cover false statements against public officials. The New York Times standard forbids the punishment of false statements, unless made with knowledge of their falsity or in reckless disregard of whether they are true or false. But the Louisiana statute punishes false statements without regard to that test if made with ill-will; even if ill-will is not established, a false statement concerning public officials can be punished if not made in the reasonable belief of its truth. . . .

"The reasonable-belief standard applied by the trial judge is not the same as the reckless-disregard-of-truth standard. . . . The test which we laid down in New York Times is not keyed to ordinary care; defeasance of the privilege is conditioned, not on mere negligence, but on reckless disregard for the truth. . . ."

Justice Black, joined by Justice Douglas concurred: "I believe that the First Amendment, made applicable to the States by the Fourteenth, protects every person from having a State or the Federal Government fine, imprison, or assess damages against him when he has been guilty of no conduct, see Giboney v. Empire Storage & Ice Co., 336 U.S. 490, 498 [p. 1296, infra], other than expressing an opinion, even though others may believe that his views are unwholesome, unpatriotic, stupid or dangerous. I believe that the Court is mistaken if it thinks that requiring proof that statements were 'malicious' or 'defamatory' will really create any substantial hurdle to block public officials from punishing those who criticize the way they conduct their office. . . . I would hold now and not wait to hold later . . . that under our Constitution there is absolutely no place in this country for the old, discredited English Star Chamber law of seditious criminal libel."

In a separate concurrence Justice Douglas, joined by Justice Black, stated: "I feel that the gloss which the Court has put on 'the freedom of speech' in the

First Amendment . . . makes that basic guarantee almost unrecognizable. . . . The philosophy of the Sedition Act of 1798 which punished 'false, scandalous and malicious' writings . . . is today allowed to be applied by the States. Yet Irving Brant has shown that seditious libel was 'entirely the creation of the Star Chamber.' * It is disquieting to know that one of its instruments of destruction is abroad in the land today."

   2. *Time, Inc. v. Hill and privacy laws.* In Time, Inc. v. Hill, 385 U.S. 374 (1967), the Court applied the New York Times standard of "knowing or reckless falsehood" to a statutory "right of privacy" action by a private individual against a publisher. Justice Brennan delivered an opinion described as "the opinion of the Court," but the separate opinions revealed that only Justices Stewart and White joined Justice Brennan without reservation. In 1952, appellee and his family "involuntarily became a front-page news story" after being held hostage by escaped convicts. Appellees' suit alleged that a 1955 Life Magazine story had falsely reported that a new play portrayed this experience. The state courts sustained a $30,000 compensatory damages award. The Supreme Court set the judgment aside for a new trial.

   In reviewing the state courts' interpretations of the statute, Justice Brennan noted that "although the New York statute affords 'little protection' to the 'privacy' of a newsworthy person, 'whether he be such by choice or involuntarily,' the statute gives him a right of action when his name, picture, or portrait is the subject of a 'fictitious' report or article." In the state courts, accordingly, appellee "was regarded to be a newsworthy person 'substantially without a right to privacy' insofar as his hostage experience was involved, but to be entitled to his action insofar as that experience was 'fictionalized' and 'exploited for the defendant's commercial benefit.' " Justice Brennan noted that, under state law, "material and substantial falsification" had to be shown in order to establish the essential element of "fictionalization," but added: "However, it is not clear whether proof of knowledge of the falsity or that the article was prepared with reckless disregard for the truth is also required." That uncertainty proved fatal: "We hold that the constitutional protections for speech and press preclude the application of the New York statute to redress false reports of matters of public interest in the absence of proof that the defendant published the report with knowledge of its falsity or in reckless disregard of the truth."

   Justice Black's concurrence joined by Justice Douglas, made it clear that he supported Justice Brennan's opinion only to enable the Court to dispose of the case on the basis of the prevailing New York Times doctrine. That did not mean, he emphasized, that he receded from any of his earlier views "about the much wider press and speech freedoms" granted by the Constitution. Justice Harlan agreed with the reversal because New York had permitted liability upon a "mere showing of substantial falsity." He thought, however, that the majority had imposed too high a standard on remand: "Were the jury on retrial to find negligent rather than, as the Court requires, reckless or knowing 'fictionalization,' I think that federal constitutional requirements would be met." His opinion noted that this was "not 'privacy' litigation in its truest sense," for there was no claim of any intrusion upon appellee's "solitude or private affairs" nor publication of facts "of such limited public interest and so intimate

---

* Brant, "Seditious Libel: Myth and Reality," 39 N.Y.U.L.Rev. 1 (1964). See also Franklin, "The Origins and Constitutionality of Limitations on Truth as a Defense in Tort Law," 16 Stan.L.Rev. 789 (1964).

and potentially embarrassing to an individual" that a state might impose sanctions. He objected to the "sweeping extension" of the New York Times principle, to the granting of "a 'talismanic immunity' to all unintentional errors." The situation here was sufficiently different to justify "a more limited 'breathing space' than that granted in criticism of public officials."

Justice Fortas' dissent, joined by Chief Justice Warren and Justice Clark, insisted that there was no "significant cause" for requiring a new trial. For him, the instructions to the jury adequately complied with the majority's principles: "Perhaps the purpose of the decision here is to indicate that this Court will place insuperable obstacles in the way of recovery by persons who are injured by reckless and heedless assaults, provided they are in print, and even though they are totally divorced from fact." Though he supported "generous construction" of First Amendment freedoms, "I do not believe that whatever is in words, however much of an aggression it may be upon individual rights, is beyond the reach of the law, no matter how heedless of others' rights—how remote from public purpose, how reckless, irresponsible, and untrue it may be. I do not believe that the First Amendment precludes effective protection of the right of privacy—or, for that matter, an effective law of libel."

3. *The Butts and Walker cases.* The question in Curtis Publishing Co. v. Butts and Associated Press v. Walker—decided together, at 388 U.S. 130 (1967)—was the impact of the New York Times decision "on libel actions instituted by persons who are not public officials, but who are 'public figures' and involved in issues in which the public has a justified and important interest." The Justices could not agree on an answer: four of them (Justices Harlan, Clark, Stewart and Fortas) opposed extending the New York Times rule and favored curtailing press immunity in this context; three (Chief Justice Warren and Justices Brennan and White) wished to apply the New York Times standard of liability; two (Justices Black and Douglas) urged a broader press immunity.

Justice Harlan examined the similarities and differences between libel actions by public officials and by other "public figures," "viewed in the light of the principles of liability which are of general applicability in our society"; agreed that "public figures" actions "cannot be left entirely to state libel laws"; but insisted that "the rigorous federal requirements of New York Times are not the only appropriate accommodation of the conflicting interests at stake." He accordingly concluded: "We consider and would hold that a 'public figure' who is not a public official may also recover damages for a defamatory falsehood whose substance makes substantial danger to reputation apparent, on a showing of highly unreasonable conduct constituting an extreme departure from the standards of investigation and reporting ordinarily adhered to by responsible publishers."

Chief Justice Warren found that "unusual and uncertain" standard inadequate either for guidance to a jury or for protection of the First Amendment. He urged that the New York Times standard should apply to all "public figures," not merely "public officials": they should not be able to recover without proof of "actual malice"—i. e., proof that the defamatory statement was made "with knowledge that it was false or with reckless disregard of whether it was false or not." [For a subsequent discussion of "reckless disregard," see St. Amant v. Thompson, 390 U.S. 727 (1968).]

The third position was stated by Justice Black. He commented that "the Court is getting itself in the same quagmire in the field of libel in which it is now helplessly struggling in the field of obscenity [sec. 2, infra]." He suggested that the Justices' "various experimental expedients" all "boil down to a determination of how offensive to this Court a particular libel judgment may be" and reiterated his insistence that New York Times be abandoned in favor of full press immunity "from the harassment of libel judgments."

In the Walker case, these three positions led to a common result: reversal of a libel judgment. (Former General Walker's suit had challenged a report that he had led a violent crowd in opposition to federal enforcement of a court decree ordering the enrollment of James Meredith at the University of Mississippi in 1962.) But, Justice Harlan emphasized in announcing the judgment of the Court, the governing standard on remand was to be the New York Times rule rather than his new "public figures" proposal, since Justices Black and Douglas had joined the New York Times adherents for the purpose of guidance in further proceedings in this case. In the Butts case, on the other hand, one of the New York Times rule supporters—the Chief Justice—joined the Harlan group to produce a 5:4 affirmance of a libel judgment. (Former University of Georgia athletic director Butts had sued because of an article accusing him of conspiring to fix a football game.) Though the trial judge's charge was not in "strict compliance" with the subsequently announced New York Times standard, Chief Justice Warren found justification for not insisting "on the financial and emotional expenses of retrial" here.*

GOVERNMENT REGULATION OF BROADCASTING TO ASSURE A RIGHT TO REPLY: THE RED LION CASE

In most libel cases since New York Times, the governmental interest in shielding reputation is not found sufficient to justify restrictions on the speaker. But may government safeguard individual reputations by requiring a broadcaster to afford reply time to the target of an attack? Does that requirement in turn violate the First Amendment rights of the broadcaster? Those were among the issues presented when the unanimous Court rejected First Amendment challenges to Federal Communications Commission requirements that radio and television stations give reply time to answer personal attacks and political editorials. Red Lion Broadcasting Co. v. FCC (decided together with United States v. RTNDA), 395 U.S. 367 (1969). The FCC's traditional "fairness doctrine" requires stations to present discussion of public issues, and to assure fair coverage for each side. Recent FCC rulings and regulations elaborated the personal attack and political editorials aspects of the fairness doctrine by specifying the circumstances in which free reply time had to be made available. Justice White's opinion found

---

* Note also the successful invocation of the New York Times standard by a teacher dismissed for writing a letter to a newspaper attacking a school board's handling of financing matters. Pickering v. Board of Education, 391 U.S. 563 (1968). Justice Marshall's majority opinion concluded: "In these circumstances . . . the interest of the school administration in limiting teachers' opportunities to contribute to public debate is not significantly greater than its interest in limiting a similar contribution by any member of the general public. [Accordingly,] absent proof of false statements knowingly or recklessly made by him, a teacher's exercise of his right to speak on issues of public importance may not furnish the basis for his dismissal from public employment." There were separate opinions by Justice Douglas, joined by Justice Black, and by Justice White.

that these applications of the fairness doctrine "enhance rather than abridge the freedoms of speech and press." The Court emphasized the "scarcity of broadcast frequencies, the Government's role in allocating those frequencies, and the legitimate claims of those unable without governmental assistance to gain access to those frequencies for expression of their views."

In response to the broadcasters' First Amendment claims, the Court stressed the speech interests of the public: "Where there are substantially more individuals who want to broadcast than there are frequencies to allocate, it is idle to posit an unabridgeable First Amendment right to broadcast comparable to the right of every individual to speak, write, or publish. . . It is the purpose of the First Amendment to preserve an uninhibited marketplace of ideas in which truth will ultimately prevail, rather than to countenance monopolization of that market, whether it be by the Government itself or a private licensee. . . . It is the right of the public to receive suitable access to social, political, esthetic, moral, and other ideas and experiences which is crucial here" and which justified this "enforced sharing of a scarce resource."

The Court commented, moreover: "Although broadcasting is clearly a medium affected by a First Amendment interest, differences in the characteristics of news media justify differences in the First Amendment standards applied to them. Just as the Government may limit the use of sound amplifying equipment potentially so noisy that it drowns out civilized private speech, so may the Government limit the use of broadcast equipment. The right of free speech of a broadcaster, the user of a sound truck, or any other individual does not embrace a right to snuff out the free speech of others. . . There is nothing in the First Amendment which prevents the Government from requiring a licensee to share his frequency with others and to conduct himself as a proxy or fiduciary with obligations to present those views and voices which are representative of his community and which would otherwise, by necessity, be barred from the airwaves."

It would be "a serious matter," to be sure, if the FCC requirements induced self-censorship by licensees and made their coverage of controversial public issues "ineffective." But that was only a speculative possibility. And if licensees "should suddenly prove timorous, the Commission is not powerless to insist that they give adequate and fair attention to public issues. It does not violate the First Amendment to treat licensees given the privilege of using scarce radio frequencies as proxies for the entire community, obligated to give suitable time and attention to matters of great public concern." Rejection of the broadcasters' claim here did not mean that they might not "raise more serious first amendment issues" in other circumstances: here, there was no question, for example, of any FCC "refusal to permit the broadcaster to carry a particular program or to publish his own views," or "of government censorship of a particular program," or "of the official government view dominating public broadcasting."

SECTION 2. OBSCENITY AND IMMORALITY

Introduction. Obscenity, like libel and "fighting words," had been considered expression outside the First Amendment protection in the 1942

Chaplinsky dictum, p. 1154, supra; and the Court's first major encounter with the constitutionality of obscenity control, in the Roth case 15 years later, purported to preserve that assumption. Yet Roth also made clear that, even if obscenity was not "speech," obscenity legislation raised free speech issues. The many decisions and numerous opinions since Roth have revealed this as one of the most controversial and troublesome areas of First Amendment litigation.

Part A of this section considers the 12 years of cases, from Roth to Stanley, that have sought to define obscenity and to explain why it may be prohibited. Most cases say very little about the justification. That silence may be traceable to the "obscenity-is-not-speech" assumption with which Roth began, and the Roth rejection of ordinary First Amendment criteria that involve articulation of state interests. Is it important to confront the justification problem—if only to permit the Court to engage more effectively in its usual preoccupation with the meaning of obscenity? Does Stanley, the 1969 decision, begin to confront that problem more explicitly? Part B of this section turns to the special constitutional problems raised by the methods of obscenity regulation.

A. WHAT IS OBSCENITY? WHAT JUSTIFIES RESTRICTING IT?

ROTH v. UNITED STATES
ALBERTS v. CALIFORNIA

354 U.S. 476, 77 S.Ct. 1304, 1 L.Ed.2d 1498 (1957).

Certiorari to the United States Court of Appeals for the Second Circuit and appeal from the Superior Court of California, Los Angeles County, Appellate Department.

Mr. Justice BRENNAN delivered the opinion of the Court.

Ques. The constitutionality of a criminal obscenity statute is the question in each of these cases. In Roth, the primary constitutional question is whether the federal obscenity statute [1] violates the provision of the First Amendment that "Congress shall make no law . . . . abridging the freedom of speech, or of the press . . . ." In Alberts, the primary constitutional question is

---

1. The federal obscenity statute provided, in pertinent part:
"Every obscene, lewd, lascivious, or filthy book, pamphlet, picture, . . . or other publication of an indecent character; and—
"Every written or printed card, letter, circular, book, pamphlet, advertisement, or notice of any kind giving information, directly or indirectly, where, or how, or from whom, or by what means any of such mentioned matters, articles, or things may be obtained or made, . . . whether sealed or unsealed . . .

"Is declared to be nonmailable matter and shall not be conveyed in the mails or delivered from any post office or by any letter carrier.
"Whoever knowingly deposits for mailing or delivery, anything declared by this section to be nonmailable, or knowingly takes the same from the mails for the purpose of circulating or disposing thereof, or of aiding in the circulation or disposition thereof, shall be fined not more than $5,000 or imprisoned not more than five years, or both. . . ." 18 U.S.C. § 1461. [This and other numbered footnotes are by Justice Brennan.]

whether the obscenity provisions of the California Penal Code [2] invade the freedoms of speech and press as they may be incorporated in the liberty protected from state action by the Due Process Clause of the Fourteenth Amendment.

Constitutional Ques. →

Other constitutional questions are: whether these statutes violate due process, because too vague to support conviction for crime; whether power to punish speech and press offensive to decency and morality is in the States alone, so that the federal obscenity statute violates the Ninth and Tenth Amendments (raised in Roth); and whether Congress, by enacting the federal obscenity statute, under the power delegated by Art. I, § 8, cl. 7, to establish post offices and post roads, pre-empted the regulation of the subject matter (raised in Alberts).

Roth conducted a business in New York in the publication and sale of books, photographs and magazines. He used circulars and advertising matter to solicit sales. He was convicted by a jury in the District Court for the Southern District of New York upon 4 counts of a 26-count indictment charging him with mailing obscene circulars and advertising, and an obscene book, in violation of the federal obscenity statute. . . .

Alberts conducted a mail order business from Los Angeles. He was convicted by the Judge of the Municipal Court of the Beverly Hills Judicial District [of] lewdly keeping for sale obscene and indecent books, and [of] writing, composing and publishing an obscene advertisement of them . . . .

— The dispositive question is whether obscenity is utterance within the area of protected speech and press.[3] Although this is the first time the question has been squarely presented to this Court, either under the First Amendment or under the Fourteenth Amendment, expressions found in numerous opinions indicate that this Court has always assumed that obscenity is not protected by the freedoms of speech and press. . . .

The guaranties of freedom of expression in effect in 10 of the 14 States which by 1792 had ratified the Constitution, gave no absolute protection for every utterance. Thirteen of the 14 States provided for the prosecution of libel, and all of those States made either blasphemy or profanity, or both, statutory crimes. As early as 1712, Massachusetts made it criminal to publish "any filthy, obscene, or profane song, pamphlet, libel or mock sermon" in imitation or mimicking of religious services. . . . Thus, profanity and obscenity were related offenses.

In light of this history, it is apparent that the unconditional phrasing of the First Amendment was not intended to protect every utterance. This phrasing did not prevent this Court from concluding that libelous utterances

---

2. The California Penal Code provides, in pertinent part:
"Every person who wilfully and lewdly, either: . . .
"3. Writes, composes, stereotypes, prints, publishes, sells, distributes, keeps for sale, or exhibits any obscene or indecent writing, paper, or book; or designs, copies, draws, engraves, paints, or otherwise prepares any obscene or indecent picture or print; or molds, cuts, casts, or otherwise makes any obscene or indecent figure; or,

"4. Writes, composes, or publishes any notice or advertisement of any such writing, paper, book, picture, print or figure; . . .
"6. . . . is guilty of a misdemeanor. . . ." West's Cal.Penal Code Ann., 1955, § 311.

3. No issue is presented in either case concerning the obscenity of the material involved.

are not within the area of constitutionally protected speech. Beauharnais v. Illinois, 343 U.S. 250, 266. At the time of the adoption of the First Amendment, obscenity law was not as fully developed as libel law, but there is sufficiently contemporaneous evidence to show that obscenity, too, was outside the protection intended for speech and press. . . .

All ideas having even the slightest redeeming social importance—unorthodox ideas, controversial ideas, even ideas hateful to the prevailing climate of opinion—have the full protection of the guaranties, unless excludable because they encroach upon the limited area of more important interests. But implicit in the history of the First Amendment is the rejection of obscenity as utterly without redeeming social importance. This rejection for that reason is mirrored in the universal judgment that obscenity should be restrained, reflected in the international agreement of over 50 nations, in the obscenity laws of all of the 48 States, and in the 20 obscenity laws enacted by the Congress from 1842 to 1956. This is the same judgment expressed by this Court in Chaplinsky v. New Hampshire, 315 U.S. 568, 571–572:

> ". . . There are certain well-defined and narrowly limited classes of speech, the prevention and punishment of which have never been thought to raise any Constitutional problem. *These include the lewd and obscene . . . . It has been well observed that such utterances are no essential part of any exposition of ideas, and are of such slight social value as a step to truth that any benefit that may be derived from them is clearly outweighed by the social interest in order and morality. . . ."* (Emphasis added.)

We hold that obscenity is not within the area of constitutionally protected speech or press.

It is strenuously urged that these obscenity statutes offend the constitutional guaranties because they punish incitation to impure sexual *thoughts,* not shown to be related to any overt antisocial conduct which is or may be incited in the persons stimulated to such *thoughts.* . . . It is insisted that the constitutional guaranties are violated because convictions may be had without proof either that obscene material will perceptibly create a clear and present danger of antisocial conduct, or will probably induce its recipients to such conduct. But, in light of our holding that obscenity is not protected speech, the complete answer to this argument is in the holding of this Court in Beauharnais v. Illinois, supra, at 266:

> "Libelous utterances not being within the area of constitutionally protected speech, it is unnecessary, either for us or for the State courts, to consider the issues behind the phrase 'clear and present danger.' Certainly no one would contend that obscene speech, for example, may be punished only upon a showing of such circumstances. Libel, as we have seen, is in the same class."

However sex and obscenity are not synonymous. Obscene material is material which deals with sex in a manner appealing to prurient interest.[4]

---

4. I. e., material having a tendency to excite lustful thoughts. Webster's New International Dictionary (Unabridged, 2d ed., 1949) defines *prurient*, in pertinent part, as follows:

". . . Itching; longing; uneasy with desire or longing; of persons, having itching, morbid, or lascivious longings;

of desire, curiosity or propensity, lewd. . . ."

Pruriency is defined, in pertinent part as follows:

". . . Quality of being prurient; lascivious desire or thought. . . ."

The portrayal of sex, e. g., in art, literature and scientific works, is not itself sufficient reason to deny material the constitutional protection of freedom of speech and press.   Sex, a great and mysterious motive force in human life, has indisputably been a subject of absorbing interest to mankind through the ages; it is one of the vital problems of human interest and public concern.

. . . .

The fundamental freedoms of speech and press have contributed greatly to the development and well-being of our free society and are indispensable to its continued growth.   Ceaseless vigilance is the watchword to prevent their erosion by Congress or by the States.   The door barring federal and state intrusion into this area cannot be left ajar; it must be kept tightly closed and opened only the slightest crack necessary to prevent encroachment upon more important interests.   It is therefore vital that the standards for judging obscenity safeguard the protection of freedom of speech and press for material which does not treat sex in a manner appealing to prurient interest.

The early leading standard of obscenity allowed material to be judged merely by the effect of an isolated excerpt upon particularly susceptible persons.   Regina v. Hicklin, [1868] L.R. 3 Q.B. 360.   Some American courts adopted this standard but later decisions have rejected it and substituted this test: whether to the average person, applying contemporary community standards, the dominant theme of the material taken as a whole appeals to prurient interest.   The Hicklin test, judging obscenity by the effect of isolated passages upon the most susceptible persons, might well encompass material legitimately treating with sex, and so it must be rejected as unconstitutionally restrictive of the freedoms of speech and press.   On the other hand, the substituted standard provides safeguards adequate to withstand the charge of constitutional infirmity.

Both trial courts below sufficiently followed the proper standard.   Both courts used the proper definition of obscenity. . . .

It is argued that the statutes do not provide reasonably ascertainable standards of guilt and therefore violate the constitutional requirements of due process.   Winters v. New York, 333 U.S. 507. . . . . The thrust of the argument is that these words are not sufficiently precise because they do not mean the same thing to all people, all the time, everywhere.

Many decisions have recognized that these terms of obscenity statutes are not precise.   This Court, however, has consistently held that lack of precision is not itself offensive to the requirements of due process.   "[T]he Constitution does not require impossible standards"; all that is required is that the language "conveys sufficiently definite warning as to the proscribed conduct when measured by common understanding and practices. . . ." United States v. Petrillo, 332 U.S. 1, 7–8.   These words, applied according to the proper standard for judging obscenity, already discussed, give adequate warning of the conduct proscribed. . . .

We perceive no significant difference between the meaning of obscenity developed in the case law and the definition of the A.L.I. Model Penal Code, § 207.10(2) (Tent.Draft No. 6, 1957), viz.:
". . . . A thing is obscene if, considered as a whole, its predominant appeal is to prurient interest, i. e., a shameful or morbid interest in nudity, sex, or excretion, and if it goes substantially beyond customary limits of candor in description or representation of such matters. . . ." . . . .

In summary, then, we hold that these statutes, applied according to the proper standard for judging obscenity, do not offend constitutional safeguards against convictions based upon protected material, or fail to give men in acting adequate notice of what is prohibited. . . .

[No merit was found in the objections based on the Ninth and Tenth Amendments or on congressional pre-emption of the field.]

Affirmed.*

Mr. Chief Justice WARREN, concurring in the result. . . .

. . . The defendants in both these cases were engaged in the business of purveying textual or photographic matter openly advertised to appeal to the erotic interest of their customers. They were plainly engaged in the commercial exploitation of the morbid and shameful craving for materials with prurient effect. I believe that the State and Federal Governments can constitutionally punish such conduct. That is all that these cases present to us, and that is all we need to decide. . . .

Mr. Justice HARLAN, concurring in the result in [Alberts] and dissenting in [Roth]. . . .

My basic difficulties with the Court's opinion are three-fold. First, the opinion paints with such a broad brush that I fear it may result in a loosening of the tight reins which state and federal courts should hold upon the enforcement of obscenity statutes. Second, the Court fails to discriminate between the different factors which, in my opinion, are involved in the constitutional adjudication of state and federal obscenity cases. Third, relevant distinctions between the two obscenity statutes here involved, and the Court's own definition of "obscenity," are ignored. . . .

[T]he Court finds the "dispositive question" to be "whether obscenity is utterance within the area of protected speech and press," and then holds that "obscenity" is not so protected because it is "utterly without redeeming social importance." This sweeping formula appears to me to beg the very question before us. The Court seems to assume that "obscenity" is a peculiar *genus* of "speech and press," which is as distinct, recognizable, and classifiable as poison ivy is among other plants. On this basis the *constitutional* question before us simply becomes, as the Court says, whether "obscenity," as an abstraction, is protected by the First and Fourteenth Amendments, and the ques-

---

* Note also Butler v. Michigan, 352 U.S. 380 (1957), decided shortly before Roth, involving a Michigan statute which made it a misdemeanor to sell or make available to the public any book containing language "tending to the corruption of the morals of youth." Appellant was convicted for selling such a book to a policeman. "The State insists [said the Court] that, by thus quarantining the general reading public against books not too rugged for grown men and women in order to shield juvenile innocence, it is exercising its power to promote the general welfare. Surely, this is to burn the house to roast the pig." The conviction was reversed: "We have before us legislation not reasonably re-stricted to the evil with which it is said to deal. The incidence of this enactment is to reduce the adult population of Michigan to reading only what is fit for children. It thereby arbitrarily curtails one of those liberties of the individual, now enshrined in the Due Process Clause of the Fourteenth Amendment, that history has attested as the indispensable conditions for the maintenance and progress of a free society." Cf. Ginsberg v. New York, 390 U.S. 629 (1968), p. 1250, infra, sustaining a statute prohibiting sales to minors and defining obscenity on the basis of the appeal of the material to minors, "whether or not it would be obscene to adults."

tion whether a *particular* book may be suppressed becomes a mere matter of classification, of "fact," to be entrusted to a fact-finder and insulated from independent constitutional judgment. But surely the problem cannot be solved in such a generalized fashion. Every communication has an individuality and "value" of its own. The suppression of a particular writing or other tangible form of expression is, therefore, an *individual* matter, and in the nature of things every such suppression raises an individual constitutional problem, in which a reviewing court must determine for *itself* whether the attacked expression is suppressable within constitutional standards. Since those standards do not readily lend themselves to generalized definitions, the constitutional problem in the last analysis becomes one of particularized judgments which appellate courts must make for themselves.

. . . Many juries might find that Joyce's "Ulysses" or Bocaccio's "Decameron" was obscene, and yet the conviction of a defendant for selling either book would raise, for me, the gravest constitutional problems, for no such verdict could convince me, without more, that these books are "utterly without redeeming social importance." In short, I do not understand how the Court can resolve the constitutional problems now before it without making its own independent judgment upon the character of the material upon which these convictions were based. . . .

[T]he Court has not been bothered by the fact that the two cases involve different statutes. In California the book must have a "tendency to deprave or corrupt its readers"; under the federal statute it must tend "to stir sexual impulses and lead to sexually impure thoughts." [1] The two statutes do not seem to me to present the same problems. Yet the Court compounds confusion when it superimposes on these two statutory definitions a third, drawn from the American Law Institute's Model Penal Code, Tentative Draft No. 6: "A thing is obscene if, considered as a whole, its predominant appeal is to prurient interest." The bland assurance that this definition is the same as the ones with which we deal flies in the face of the authors' express rejection of the "deprave and corrupt" and "sexual thoughts" tests:

> "Obscenity [in the Tentative Draft] is defined in terms of material which appeals predominantly to prurient interest in sexual matters and which goes beyond customary freedom of expression in these matters. We reject the prevailing test of tendency to arouse lustful thoughts or desires because it is unrealistically broad for a society that plainly tolerates a great deal of erotic interest in literature, advertising, and art, and because regulation of thought or desire, unconnected with overt misbehavior, raises the most acute constitutional as well as practical difficulties. We likewise reject the common definition of obscene as that which 'tends to corrupt or debase.' If this means anything different from tendency to arouse lustful thought and desire, it suggests that change of character or actual misbehavior follows from contact with obscenity. Evidence of such consequences is lacking. . . . On the

---

1. . . . The two definitions do not seem to me synonymous. Under the federal definition it is enough if the jury finds that the book as a whole leads to certain thoughts. In California, the further inference must be drawn that such thoughts will have a substantive "tendency to deprave or corrupt"—i. e., that the thoughts induced by the material will affect character and action. See American Law Institute, Model Penal Code, Tentative Draft No. 6, § 207.10(2), Comments, p. 10. [Footnote by Justice Harlan.]

other hand, 'appeal to prurient interest' refers to qualities of the material itself: the capacity to attract individuals eager for a forbidden look . . .."

As this passage makes clear, there is a significant distinction between the definitions used in the prosecutions before us, and the American Law Institute formula. If, therefore, the latter is the correct standard, . . . then these convictions should surely be reversed. Instead, the Court merely assimilates the various tests into one indiscriminate potpourri. . . .

What, then, is the purpose of this California statute? Clearly the state legislature has made the judgment that printed words *can* "deprave or corrupt" the reader—that words can incite to antisocial or immoral action. The assumption seems to be that the distribution of certain types of literature will induce criminal or immoral sexual conduct. It is well known, of course, that the validity of this assumption is a matter of dispute among critics, sociologists, psychiatrists, and penologists. There is a large school of thought, particularly in the scientific community, which denies any causal connection between the reading of pornography and immorality, crime, or delinquency. Others disagree. Clearly it is not our function to decide this question. That function belongs to the state legislature. Nothing in the Constitution requires California to accept as truth the most advanced and sophisticated psychiatric opinion. It seems to me clear that it is not irrational, in our present state of knowledge, to consider that pornography can induce a type of sexual conduct which a State may deem obnoxious to the moral fabric of society. In fact the very division of opinion on the subject counsels us to respect the choice made by the State.

Furthermore, even assuming that pornography cannot be deemed ever to cause, in an immediate sense, criminal sexual conduct, other interests within the proper cognizance of the States may be protected by the prohibition placed on such materials. The State can reasonably draw the inference that over a long period of time the indiscriminate dissemination of materials, the essential character of which is to degrade sex, will have an eroding effect on moral standards. And the State has a legitimate interest in protecting the privacy of the home against invasion of unsolicited obscenity.

Above all stands the realization that we deal here with an area where knowledge is small, data are insufficient, and experts are divided. Since the domain of sexual morality is pre-eminently a matter of state concern, this Court should be slow to interfere with state legislation calculated to protect that morality. . . .

What has been said, however, does not dispose of the case. It still remains for us to decide whether the state court's determination that this material should be suppressed is consistent with the Fourteenth Amendment; and that, of course, presents a federal question as to which we, and not the state court, have the ultimate responsibility. And so, in the final analysis, I concur in the judgment because, upon an independent perusal of the material involved, and in light of the considerations discussed above, I cannot say that its suppression would so interfere with the communication of "ideas" in any proper sense of that term that it would offend the Due Process Clause. . .

. . . To me, [the Roth] question is of quite a different order than one where we are dealing with state legislation under the Fourteenth Amendment. . . . I agree with Mr. Justice Jackson that the historical evidence does not bear out the claim that the Fourteenth Amendment "incorporates" the First in any literal sense. [Beauharnais.] But . . . I prefer to rest my views about this case on broader and less abstract grounds. . . .

. . . [T]he interests which obscenity statutes purportedly protect are primarily entrusted to the care, not of the Federal Government, but of the States. Congress has no substantive power over sexual morality. Such powers as the Federal Government has in this field are but incidental to its other powers, here the postal power, and are not of the same nature as those possessed by the States, which bear direct responsibility for the protection of the local moral fabric. . . .

Not only is the federal interest in protecting the Nation against pornography attenuated, but the dangers of federal censorship in this field are far greater than anything the States may do. [I]t seems to me that no overwhelming danger to our freedom to experiment and to gratify our tastes in literature is likely to result from the suppression of a borderline book in one of the States, so long as there is no uniform nation-wide suppression of the book, and so long as other States are free to experiment with the same or bolder books.

. . . But the dangers to free thought and expression are truly great if the Federal Government imposes a blanket ban over the Nation on such a book. The prerogative of the States to differ on their ideas of morality will be destroyed, the ability of States to experiment will be stunted. The fact that the people of one State cannot read some of the works of D. H. Lawrence seems to me, if not wise or desirable, at least acceptable. But that no person in the United States should be allowed to do so seems to me to be intolerable, and violative of both the letter and spirit of the First Amendment.

I judge this case, then, in view of what I think is the attenuated federal interest in this field, in view of the very real danger of a deadening uniformity which can result from nation-wide federal censorship, and in view of the fact that the constitutionality of this conviction must be weighed against the First and not the Fourteenth Amendment. So viewed, I do no think that this conviction can be upheld. . . . I cannot agree that any book which tends to stir sexual impulses and lead to sexually impure thoughts necessarily is "utterly without redeeming social importance." Not only did this charge fail to measure up to the standards which I understand the Court to approve, but as far as I can see, much of the great literature of the world could lead to conviction under such a view of the statute. Moreover, in no event do I think that the limited federal interest in this area can extend to mere "thoughts." The Federal Government has no business, whether under the postal or commerce power, to bar the sale of books because they might lead to any kind of "thoughts."

It is no answer to say, as the Court does, that obscenity is not protected speech. The point is that this statute, as here construed, defines obscenity so widely that it encompasses matters which might very well be protected speech. I do not think that the federal statute can be constitutionally construed to reach other than what the Government has termed as "hard-core" pornography. . . .

Mr. Justice DOUGLAS, with whom Mr. Justice BLACK concurs, dissenting.

When we sustain these convictions, we make the legality of a publication turn on the purity of thought which a book or tract instills in the mind of the reader. I do not think we can approve that standard and be faithful to the command of the First Amendment . . ..

The tests by which these convictions were obtained require only the arousing of sexual thoughts. Yet the arousing of sexual thoughts and desires happens every day in normal life in dozens of ways. Nearly 30 years ago a questionnaire sent to college and normal school women graduates asked what things were most stimulating sexually. Of 409 replies, 9 said "music"; 18 said "pictures"; 29 said "dancing"; 40 said "drama"; 95 said "books"; and 218 said "man." Alpert, Judicial Censorship of Obscene Literature, 52 Harv.L.Rev. 40, 73.

The test of obscenity the Court endorses today gives the censor free range over a vast domain. To allow the State to step in and punish mere speech or publication that the judge or the jury thinks has an *undesirable* impact on thoughts but that is not shown to be a part of unlawful action is drastically to curtail the First Amendment. . . .

The legality of a publication in this country should never be allowed to turn either on the purity of thought which it instills in the mind of the reader or on the degree to which it offends the community conscience. By either test the role of the censor is exalted, and society's values in literary freedom are sacrificed.

The Court today suggests a third standard. It defines obscene material as that "which deals with sex in a manner appealing to prurient interest." Like the standards applied by the trial judges below, that standard does not require any nexus between the literature which is prohibited and action which the legislature can regulate or prohibit. Under the First Amendment, that standard is no more valid than those which the courts below adopted.

I do not think that the problem can be resolved by the Court's statement that "obscenity is not expression protected by the First Amendment." With the exception of Beauharnais v. Illinois, 343 U.S. 250, none of our cases have resolved problems of free speech and free press by placing any form of expression beyond the pale of the absolute prohibition of the First Amendment. . . . I reject too the implication that problems of freedom of speech and of the press are to be resolved by weighing against the values of free expression, the judgment of the Court that a particular form of that expression has "no redeeming social importance." The First Amendment, its prohibition in terms absolute, was designed to preclude courts as well as legislatures from weighing the values of speech against silence. The First Amendment puts free speech in the preferred position. . . .

GROPINGS POST–ROTH: *
THE EVOLVING MEANING OF OBSCENITY, 1957–1966

Roth held that obscenity could be suppressed; it did not specify what expressions could constitutionally be placed into that prohibitable category of "obscenity." In the decade that followed, it became clear—from what the Court did rather than from any reasons the Justices were able to agree on— that the category was quite a narrow one. Indications that the Court would carefully scrutinize application of the constitutional standard of obscenity came in the main from two sources: (1) incidental remarks in cases primarily concerned with the governmental methods used; and (2) a number of per curiam orders simply citing Roth in reversing lower court decisions that had found publications obscene, e. g., One, Incorporated v. Olesen, 355 U.S. 371 (1958), and Sunshine Book Co. v. Summerfield, 355 U.S. 372 (1958). See also Manual Enterprises v. Day, 370 U.S. 478 (1962). In 1964, finally, the Court undertook a major reexamination of the basic Roth issue: the constitutional requirements in defining obscenity. The case was Jacobellis v. Ohio, 378 U.S. 184 (1964), and it produced a large number of separate opinions rather than a majority position.

In Jacobellis, the Court reversed the conviction of a theater manager for possessing and exhibiting an obscene film in violation of Ohio law. The case involved the French film "The Lovers." The opinion announcing the judgment of the Court was written by Justice Brennan, but only Justice Goldberg joined that opinion. The opinion stated: "We have viewed the film . . . and we conclude that it is not obscene within the standards enunciated in Alberts v. California and Roth v. United States, which we reaffirm here." Justice Brennan insisted that "this Court cannot avoid making an independent constitutional judgment on the facts of the case as to whether the material involved is constitutionally protected." Recognizing that the Roth test "is not perfect," he stated that "any substitute would raise equally difficult problems, and we therefore adhere to that standard." Moreover, he rejected the argument that the "contemporary community standards" aspect of the Roth test justified determination of obscenity "by the standards of the particular local community from which the case arises." Rather, "the constitutional status of an allegedly obscene work must be determined on the

---

* Without profound apologies to Professor Magrath (or even to Allan Sherman, or to John Steinbeck admirers). See Magrath, "The Obscenity Cases: Grapes of Roth," 1966 Sup.Ct.Rev. 7, one of the best of the many articles provoked by the Court's difficulties regarding obscenity (and not the only one unable to resist the temptation of puns and other varieties of academic humor). Among the later commentaries, see Krislov, "From Ginzburg to Ginsberg: The Unhurried Children's Hour in Obscenity Litigation," 1968 Sup.Ct.Rev. 153, and Katz, "Privacy and Pornography: Stanley v. Georgia," 1969 Sup.Ct.Rev. 203. Among the most useful earlier pieces, see Kalven, "The Metaphysics of the Law of Ob-

scenity," 1960 Sup.Ct.Rev. 1; Lockhart and McClure, "Censorship of Obscenity: The Developing Constitutional Standards," 45 Minn.L.Rev. 5 (1960); and Henkin, "Morals and the Constitution: The Sin of Obscenity," 63 Colum.L.Rev. 391 (1963).

[I am advised that a footnote to this footnote may be in order, to explain the reference to Allan Sherman in the first sentence. His splendid version of the "Battle Hymn of the Republic" ("The Ballad of Harry Lewis") mentions "the drapes of Roth"; that Roth handled textiles, not obscene books. See "My Son, the Folk Singer," Warner Bros. Record No. W1475 (1962).]

basis of a national standard. It is, after all, a national Constitution we are expounding."

Four other Justices concurred merely in the judgment of reversal. Justice White did not explain his vote. Justice Black's opinion, joined by Justice Douglas, stated that the First Amendment prohibited conviction for exhibiting a motion picture. Justice Stewart's concurrence, after noting that Roth could be read "in a variety of ways", stated that he had concluded that "criminal laws in this area are constitutionally limited to hard-core pornography." He added: "I shall not today attempt further to define the kinds of material I understand to be embraced within that short-hand description; and perhaps I could never succeed in intelligibly doing so. But I know it when I see it, and the motion picture involved in this case is not that."

Three Justices dissented. Chief Justice Warren's dissent, joined by Justice Clark, complained that the decisions since Roth had given inadequate guidance as to obscenity. He stated that the Roth test had not been "proved unsound, and I believe that we should try to live with it—at least until a more satisfactory definition is evolved. . . . There must be a rule of reason in this as in other areas of the law, and we have attempted in the Roth case to provide such a rule." He stated that the Roth reference to "community standards" meant "community standards—not a national standard, as is sometimes argued." With regard to Justice Stewart's suggestion, he said: "But who can define 'hard-core pornography' with any greater clarity than 'obscenity'?" He added: "In my opinion, the use to which various materials are put—not just the words and pictures themselves—must be considered in determining whether or not the materials are obscene." Finally, he argued that the Court should limit review of applications of the Roth standard "to a consideration only of whether there is sufficient evidence in the record upon which a finding of obscenity could be made. . . . This is the only reasonable way I can see to obviate the necessity of this Court's sitting as the Super Censor of all the obscenity purveyed throughout the Nation." Justice Harlan's dissent stated that he would apply the Roth standard to the national government, but would make the test "one of rationality" as to the states.

SEXUAL IMMORALITY—THE KINGSLEY PICTURES CASE

One case during this period—though (and perhaps because of) not dealing directly with "obscenity"—spoke more explicitly about the speech issues raised by state regulations of expression pertaining to sex. Kingsley International Pictures Corp. v. Regents, 360 U.S. 684 (1959) involved a revised version of New York's motion picture licensing law. [Earlier versions had been invalidated because of vague criteria—see Burstyn v. Wilson, 343 U.S. 684 (1959) (p. 1263, infra), and Commercial Films v. Regents, 346 U.S. 587 (1954) (p. 1267 infra).]

The law banned films found "obscene, indecent, immoral, inhuman, sacrilegious, or . . . of such a character that . . . exhibition would tend to corrupt morals and incite to crime." The amendment sought to clarify the references to morality. Under the clarification, the law was applicable if a film, inter alia, "expressly or impliedly presents . . . acts [of sexual immorality] as desirable, acceptable or proper patterns of behavior."

Pursuant to this statute, the state denied a license to the film "Lady Chatterley's Lover" because "its subject matter is adultery presented as being right and desirable for certain people under certain circumstances."

The Supreme Court reversed. Justice Stewart's opinion emphasized that "sexual immorality" under the statute was "entirely different from" concepts like "obscenity" or "pornography," and that New York had not claimed "that the film would itself operate as an incitement to illegal action." He concluded that New York had prevented "the exhibition of a motion picture because that picture advocates an idea—that adultery under certain circumstances may be proper behavior. Yet the First Amendment's basic guarantee is of freedom to advocate ideas. The State, quite simply, has thus struck at the very heart of constitutionally protected liberty." It was no justification that the film "attractively portrays a relationship which is contrary to the moral standards, the religious precepts, and the legal code" of a state's citizenry. The constitutional guarantee, he insisted, "is not confined to the expression of ideas that are conventional or shared by a majority. It protects advocacy of the opinion that adultery may sometimes be proper, no less than advocacy of socialism or the single tax. And in the realm of ideas it protects expression which is eloquent no less than that which is unconvincing."

Justice Frankfurter's concurrence said that he would reverse because the statute "cannot constitutionally be applied" to the specific film in issue: "We cannot escape such instance-by-instance, case-by-case application" of the due process clause. Justice Black's concurrence objected to an appraisal of the particular film, because "this Court is about the most inappropriate Supreme Board of Censors that could be found." Justice Clark concurred in the result because of the vagueness of the statutory standard. Justice Harlan wrote an opinion concurring in the result, joined by Justices Frankfurter and Whittaker. He thought that the state courts had construed the statute as requiring "incitement, not just mere abstract expression of opinion." But he thought the ban was nevertheless invalid as applied, because the film lacked "anything that could properly be deemed obscene or corruptive of the public morals by inciting the commission of adultery." Justice Douglas, joined by Justice Black, concurred on the ground that all "censorship of movies is unconstitutional." [Note the additional motion picture censorship cases in sec. 2B, p. 1257, infra.]

MEMOIRS v. MASSACHUSETTS

383 U.S. 413, 86 S.Ct. 975, 16 L.Ed.2d 1 (1966).

Appeal from the Supreme Judicial Court of Massachusetts.

Mr. Justice BRENNAN announced the judgment of the Court and delivered an opinion in which the Chief Justice [WARREN] and Mr. Justice FORTAS join.

This is an obscenity case in which *Memoirs of a Woman of Pleasure* (commonly known as *Fanny Hill*), written by John Cleland in about 1750, was adjudged obscene in a proceeding that put on trial the book itself, and not its publisher or distributor. The proceeding was a civil equity suit brought by the Attorney General of Massachusetts, pursuant to General Laws of Massachusetts, Chapter 272, §§ 28C–28H, to have the book declared obscene.

Section 28C requires that the petition commencing the suit be "directed against [the] book by name" and that an order to show cause "why said book should not be judicially determined to be obscene" be published in a daily newspaper and sent by registered mail "to all persons interested in the publication." Publication of the order in this case occurred in a Boston daily newspaper, and a copy of the order was sent by registered mail to G. P. Putnam's Sons, alleged to be the publisher and copyright holder of the book.

As authorized by § 28D, G. P. Putnam's Sons intervened in the proceedings in behalf of the book, but it did not claim the right provided by that section to have the issue of obscenity tried by a jury. At the hearing before a justice of the Superior Court, . . . the court received the book in evidence and . . . heard the testimony of experts and accepted other evidence, such as book reviews, in order to assess the literary, cultural, or educational character of the book. This constituted the entire evidence, as neither side availed itself of the opportunity provided by the section to introduce evidence "as to the manner and form of its publication, advertisement, and distribution."[1] The trial justice entered a final decree, which adjudged *Memoirs* obscene and declared that the book "is not entitled to the protection of the First and Fourteenth amendments to the Constitution of the United States against action by the Attorney General or other law enforcement officers pursuant to the provisions of . . . § 28B, or otherwise."[2] The Massachusetts Supreme Judicial Court affirmed the decree. . . . We reverse.[3] . . .

The term "obscene" appearing in the Massachusetts statute has been interpreted by the Supreme Judicial Court to be as expansive as the Constitution permits . . . . Thus the sole question before the state courts was whether *Memoirs* satisfies the test of obscenity established in Roth v. United States, 354 U.S. 476.

1. The record in this case is thus significantly different from the records in Ginzburg v. United States . . . and Mishkin v. New York, . . . also decided today. [Footnote by Justice Brennan. The Ginzburg and Mishkin cases follow this case.]

2. Section 28B makes it a criminal offense, *inter alia*, to import, print, publish, sell, loan, distribute, buy, procure, receive, or possess for the purpose of sale, loan, or distribution, "a book, knowing it to be obscene." Section 28H provides that in any prosecution under § 28B the decree obtained in a proceeding against the book "shall be admissible in evidence" and further that "[i]f prior to the said offense a final decree had been entered against the book, the defendant, if the book be obscene . . . shall be conclusively presumed to have known said book to be obscene . . . ." Thus a declaration of obscenity such as that obtained in this proceeding is likely to result in the total suppression of the book in the Commonwealth.

The constitutionality of § 28H has not been challenged in this appeal. [Footnote by Justice Brennan.]

3. Although the final decree provides no coercive relief but only a declaration of the book's obscenity, our adjudication of the merits of the issue tendered, viz., whether the state courts erred in declaring the book obscene, is not premature. There is no uncertainty as to the content of the material challenged, and the Attorney General's petition commencing this suit states that the book "is being imported, sold, loaned, or distributed in the Commonwealth." The declaration of obscenity is likely to have a serious inhibitory effect on the distribution of the book, and this probable impact is to no small measure derived from possible collateral uses of the declaration in subsequent prosecutions under the Massachusetts criminal obscenity statute. See n. [2], supra. [Footnote by Justice Brennan.]

We defined obscenity in Roth in the following terms: "[W]hether to the average persons, applying contemporary community standards, the dominant theme of the material taken as a whole appeals to prurient interest." 354 U.S., at 489. Under this definition, as elaborated in subsequent cases, three elements must coalesce: it must be established that (a) the dominant theme of the material taken as a whole appeals to a prurient interest in sex; (b) the material is patently offensive because it affronts contemporary community standards relating to the description or representation of sexual matters; and (c) the material is utterly without redeeming social value.

The Supreme Judicial Court purported to apply the Roth definition of obscenity and held all three criteria satisfied. We need not consider the claim that the court erred in concluding that *Memoirs* satisfied the prurient appeal and patent offensiveness criteria; for reversal is required because the court misinterpreted the social value criterion. The court applied the criterion in this passage:

> "It remains to consider whether the book can be said to be 'utterly without social importance.' We are mindful that there was expert testimony, much of which was strained, to the effect that Memoirs is a structural novel with literary merit; that the book displays a skill in characterization and a gift for comedy; that it plays a part in the history of the development of the English novel; and that it contains a moral, namely, that sex with love is superior to sex in a brothel. But the fact that the testimony may indicate this book has some minimal literary value does not mean it is of any social importance. We do not interpret the 'social importance' test as requiring that a book which appeals to prurient interest and is patently offensive must be unqualifiedly worthless before it can be deemed obscene." . . .

The Supreme Judicial Court erred in holding that a book need not be "unqualifiedly worthless before it can be deemed obscene." A book can not be proscribed unless it is found to be *utterly* without redeeming social value. This is so even though the book is found to possess the requisite prurient appeal and to be patently offensive. Each of the three federal constitutional criteria is to be applied independently; the social value of the book can neither be weighed against nor canceled by its prurient appeal or patent offensiveness. Hence, even on the view of the court below that *Memoirs* possessed only a modicum of social value, its judgment must be reversed as being founded on an erroneous interpretation of a federal constitutional standard. . . .

It does not necessarily follow from this reversal that a determination that *Memoirs* is obscene in the constitutional sense would be improper under all circumstances. On the premise, which we have no occasion to assess, that *Memoirs* has the requisite prurient appeal and is patently offensive, but has only a minimum of social value, the circumstances of production, sale, and publicity are relevant in determining whether or not the publication and distribution of the book is constitutionally protected. Evidence that the book was commercially exploited for the sake of prurient appeal, to the exclusion of all other values, might justify the conclusion that the book was utterly without redeeming social importance. It is not that in such a setting the social value test is relaxed so as to dispense with the requirement that a book be *utterly* devoid of social value, but rather that, as we elaborate in Ginzburg v. United States, [infra], where the purveyor's sole emphasis is on the sexually provocative aspects of his publications, a court could accept his evaluation at its face value. In this proceeding, however, the courts were asked to judge the obscenity of *Memoirs* in the abstract, and the declaration of obscenity was neither aided nor limited by a specific set of circumstances of production, sale, and publicity. All possible uses of the book must therefore be considered, and the mere risk that the book might be exploited by panderers because it so pervasively treats sexual matters cannot alter the fact—given the view of the Massachusetts court attributing to *Memoirs* a modicum of literary and historical value—that the book will have redeeming social importance in the hands of those who publish or distribute it on the basis of that value.

Reversed.

Mr. Justice BLACK and Mr. Justice STEWART concur in the reversal for the reasons stated in their respective dissenting opinions in [Ginzburg and Mishkin, infra].

Mr. Justice DOUGLAS, concurring. . . .

. . . I do not believe that the Court should decide this case on so disingenuous a basis as this. I base my vote to reverse on my view that the First Amendment does not permit the censorship of expression not brigaded with illegal action. But even applying the prevailing view of the Roth test, reversal is compelled by this record which makes clear that *Fanny Hill* is not "obscene." . . .

Mr. Justice CLARK, dissenting. . . .

In my view evidence of social importance is relevant to the determination of the ultimate question of obscenity. But social importance does not constitute a separate and distinct constitutional test. Such evidence must be considered together with evidence that the material in question appeals to prurient interest and is patently offensive. Accordingly, we must first turn to the book here under attack. . . .

There can be no doubt that the whole purpose of the book is to arouse the prurient interest. Likewise the repetition of sexual episode after episode and the candor with which they are described renders the book "patently offensive." These facts weigh heavily in any appraisal of the book's claims to "redeeming social importance."

Let us now turn to evidence of the book's alleged social value. While unfortunately the state offered little testimony, the defense called several experts to attest that the book has literary merit and historical value. A careful reading of testimony, however, reveals that it has no substance. . . . So-called "literary obscenity," i. e., the use of erotic fantasies of the hard-core type clothed in an engaging literary style, has no constitutional protection. If a book deals solely with erotic material in a manner calculated to appeal to the prurient interest, it matters not that it may be expressed in beautiful prose. There are obviously dynamic connections between art and sex— the emotional, intellectual, and physical—but where the former is used solely to promote prurient appeal, it cannot claim constitutional immunity. . . . In my view, the book's repeated and unrelieved appeals to the prurient interest of the average person leave it utterly without redeeming social importance. . . .

But this is not all that Massachusetts courts might consider. I believe it can be established that the book "was commercially exploited for the sake of prurient appeal, to the exclusion of all other values" and should therefore be declared obscene under the test of commercial exploitation announced today in Ginzburg and Mishkin. . . .

Mr. Justice HARLAN, dissenting.

The central development that emerges from the aftermath of Roth v. United States, 354 U.S. 476, is that no stable approach to the obscenity problem has yet been devised by this Court. . . . Given this tangled state of affairs, I feel free to adhere to the principles first set forth in my separate opinion in Roth . . ., which I continue to believe represent the soundest constitutional solution to this intractable problem. My premise is that in the area of obscenity the Constitution does not bind the States and the Federal Government in precisely the same fashion. . . .

Mr. Justice WHITE, dissenting. . . .

To say that material within the Roth definition of obscenity is nevertheless not obscene if it has some redeeming social value is to reject one of the basic propositions of the Roth case—that such material is not protected *because* it is inherently and utterly without social value. . . .

In my view, "social importance" is not an independent test of obscenity but is relevant only to determining the predominant prurient interest of the material, a determination which the court or the jury will make based on the material itself and all the evidence in the case, expert or otherwise.

Application of the Roth test, as I understand it, necessarily involves the exercise of judgment by legislatures, courts and juries. But this does not mean that there are no limits to what may be done in the name of Roth. . . . Nor does it mean that if books like *Fanny Hill* are unprotected, their nonprurient appeal is necessarily lost to the world. Literary style, history, teachings about sex, character description (even of a prostitute) or moral lessons need not come wrapped in such packages. The fact that they do impeaches their claims to immunity from legislative censure. . . .

GINZBURG v. UNITED STATES

383 U.S. 463, 86 S.Ct. 942, 16 L.Ed.2d 31 (1966).

Certiorari to the United States Court of Appeals for the Third Circuit.

Mr. Justice BRENNAN delivered the opinion of the Court.

A judge sitting without a jury in the District Court for the Eastern District of Pennsylvania convicted petitioner Ginzburg and three corporations controlled by him upon all 28 counts of an indictment charging violation of the federal obscenity statute, 18 U.S.C. § 1461.* 224 F.Supp. 129. Each count alleged that a resident of the Eastern District received mailed matter, either one of three publications challenged as obscene, or advertising telling how and where the publications might be obtained. The Court of Appeals for the Third Circuit affirmed . . . .. We affirm. Since petitioners do not argue that the trial judge misconceived or failed to apply the standards we first enunciated in Roth v. United States, 354 U.S. 476, the only serious question is whether those standards were correctly applied.[1]

---

* For the text of § 1461, see footnote 1 to Roth, p. 1227, supra.

1. The Government stipulated at trial that the circulars advertising the pub-

In the cases in which this Court has decided obscenity questions since Roth, it has regarded the materials as sufficient in themselves for the determination of the question. In the present case, however, the prosecution charged the offense in the context of the circumstances of production, sale, and publicity and assumed that, standing alone, the publications themselves might not be obscene. We agree that the question of obscenity may include consideration of the setting in which the publications were presented as an aid to determining the question of obscenity, and assume without deciding that the prosecution could not have succeeded otherwise. As in Mishkin v. New York [infra], and as did the courts below, . . . we view the publications against a background of commercial exploitation of erotica solely for the sake of their prurient appeal.[2] The record in that regard amply supports the decision of the trial judge that the mailing of all three publications offended the statute.[3]

The three publications were EROS, a hard-cover magazine of expensive format; Liaison, a bi-weekly newsletter; and *The Housewife's Handbook on Selective Promiscuity* (hereinafter the *Handbook*), a short book. The issue of EROS specified in the indictment, Vol. 1, No. 4, contains 15 articles and photo-essays on the subject of love, sex, and sexual relations. The specified issue of Liaison, Vol. 1, No. 1, contains a prefatory "Letter from the Editors" announcing its dedication to "keeping sex an art and preventing it from becoming a science." The remainder of the issue consists of digests of two articles concerning sex and sexual relations which had earlier appeared in professional journals and a report of an interview with a psychotherapist who favors the broadest license in sexual relationships. As the trial judge noted, "[w]hile the treatment is largely superficial, it is presented entirely without restraint of any kind. According to defendants' own expert, it is entirely without literary merit." . . . The *Handbook* purports to be a sexual autobiography detailing with complete candor the author's sexual experiences from age 3 to age 36. The text includes, and prefatory and concluding sections of the book elaborate, her views on such subjects as sex education of children, laws regulating private consensual adult sexual practices, and the equality of women in sexual relationships. It was claimed at trial that women would find the book valuable, for example as a marriage manual or as an aid to the sex education of their children.

lications were not themselves obscene; therefore the convictions on the counts for mailing the advertising stand only if the mailing of the publications offend the statute. [Footnote by the Court.]

2. Our affirmance of the convictions for mailing EROS and Liaison is based upon their characteristics as a whole, including their editorial formats, and not upon particular articles contained, digested, or excerpted in them. Thus we do not decide whether particular articles, for example, in EROS, although identified by the trial judge as offensive, should be condemned as obscene whatever their setting. Similarly, we accept the Government's concession . . . that the prosecution rested upon the manner in which the

petitioners sold the *Handbook*; thus our affirmance implies no agreement with the trial judge's characterizations of the book outside that setting. [Footnote by the Court.]

3. It is suggested in dissent that petitioners were unaware that the record being established could be used in support of such an approach, and that petitioners should be afforded the opportunity of a new trial. However, the trial transcript clearly reveals that at several points the Government announced its theory that made the mode of distribution relevant to the determination of obscenity, and the trial court admitted evidence, otherwise irrelevant, toward that end. [Footnote by the Court.]

defense

Besides testimony as to the merit of the material, there was abundant evidence to show that each of the accused publications was originated or sold as stock in trade of the sordid business of pandering—"the business of purveying textual or graphic matter openly advertised to appeal to the erotic interest of their customers." [4] EROS early sought mailing privilege from the postmasters of Intercourse and Blue Ball, Pennsylvania. The trial court found the obvious, that these hamlets were chosen only for the value their names would have in furthering petitioners' efforts to sell their publications on the basis of salacious appeal; the facilities of the post offices were inadequate to handle the anticipated volume of mail, and the privileges were denied. Mailing privileges were then obtained from the postmaster of Middlesex, New Jersey. . . .

The "leer of the sensualist" also permeates the advertising for the three publications. The circulars sent for EROS and Liaison stressed the sexual candor of the respective publications, and openly boasted that the publishers would take full advantage of what they regarded as unrestricted license allowed by law in the expression of sex and sexual matters.[5] The advertising for the *Handbook* . . . consisted almost entirely of a reproduction of the introduction of the book, written by one Dr. Albert Ellis. Although he alludes to the book's informational value and its putative therapeutic usefulness, his remarks are preoccupied with the book's sexual imagery. The solicitation was indiscriminate, not limited to those such as physicians or psychiatrists, who might independently discern the book's therapeutic worth. . . .

This evidence, in our view, was relevant in determining the ultimate question of "obscenity" and, in the context of this record, serves to resolve all ambiguity and doubt. The deliberate representation of petitioner's publications as erotically arousing, for example, stimulated the reader to accept them as prurient; he looks for titillation, not for saving intellectual content. Similarly, such representation would tend to force public confrontation with the potentially offensive aspects of the work; the brazenness of such an appeal heightens the offensiveness of the publications to those who are offended by such material. And the circumstances of presentation and dissemination of material are equally relevant to determining whether social importance claimed for material in the courtroom was, in the circumstances, pretense or reality—whether it was the basis upon which it was traded in the market-place or a spurious claim for litigation purposes. Where the purveyor's sole emphasis is on the sexually provocative aspects of his publications, that fact may be decisive in the determination of obscenity. Certainly in a prosecution which, as here, does not necessarily imply suppression of the materials involved, the fact that they originate, or are used as a subject of pandering is relevant to the application of the Roth test.

—— A proposition argued as to EROS, for example, is that the trial judge improperly found the magazine to be obscene as a whole, since he concluded that only four of the 15 articles predominantly appealed to prurient interest

4. Roth v. United States, supra, 354 U.S., at 495–496 (Warren, C. J., concurring). [Footnote by the Court.]

5. Thus, one EROS advertisement claimed "EROS is a child of its times. . . [It] is the result of recent court decisions that have realistically interpreted America's obscenity laws and that have given to this country a new breath of freedom of expression. . . . EROS takes full advantage of this new freedom of expression. It is *the* magazine of sexual candor." . . . [Footnote by the Court.]

and substantially exceeded community standards of candor, while the other articles were admittedly non-offensive. But the trial judge found that "[t]he deliberate and studied arrangement of EROS is editorialized for the purpose of appealing predominantly to prurient interest and to insulate through the inclusion of non-offensive material." . . . However erroneous such a conclusion might be if unsupported by the evidence of pandering, the record here supports it. EROS was created, represented and sold solely as a claimed instrument of the sexual stimulation it would bring. Like the other publications, its pervasive treatment of sex and sexual matters rendered it available to exploitation by those who would make a business of pandering to "the widespread weakness for titillation by pornography."[6] [B]y animating sensual detail to give the publication a salacious cast, petitioners reinforced what is conceded by the Government to be an otherwise debatable conclusion.

A similar analysis applies to the judgment regarding the Handbook. The bulk of the proofs directed to social importance concerned this publication. Before selling publication rights to petitioners, its author had printed it privately; she sent circulars to persons whose names appeared on membership lists of medical and psychiatric associations, asserting its value as an adjunct in therapy. Over 12,000 sales resulted from this solicitation, and a number of witnesses testified that they found the work useful in their professional practice. The Government does not seriously contest the claim that the book has worth in such a controlled, or even neutral, environment. Petitioners, however, did not sell the book to such a limited audience, or focus their claims for it on its supposed therapeutic or educational value; rather, they deliberately emphasized the sexually provocative aspects of the work, in order to catch the salaciously disposed. They proclaimed its obscenity; and we cannot conclude that the court below erred in taking their own evaluation at its face value and declaring the book as a whole obscene despite the other evidence. . . . .

We perceive no threat to First Amendment guarantees in thus holding that in close cases evidence of pandering may be probative with respect to the nature of the material in question and thus satisfy the Roth test.[7] No weight is ascribed to the fact that petitioners have profited from the sale of publications which we have assumed but do not hold cannot themselves be adjudged obscene in the abstract; to sanction consideration of this fact might indeed induce self-censorship, and offend the frequently stated principle that commercial activity, in itself, is no justification for narrowing the protection of expression secured by the First Amendment. Rather, the fact that each of these publications was created or exploited entirely on the basis of its appeal to prurient interests[8] strengthens the conclusion that the transactions

---

6. Schwartz, Morals Offenses and the Model Penal Code, 63 Col.L.Rev. 669, 677 (1963). [Footnote by the Court.]

7. Our conclusion is consistent with the statutory scheme. Although § 1461, in referring to "obscene . . . matter" may appear to deal with the qualities of material in the abstract, it is settled that the mode of distribution may be a significant part in the determination of the obscenity of the material involved. . . . Because the statute creates a criminal remedy, . . . it readily admits such an interpretation . . . .. [Footnote by the Court.]

8. See Valentine v. Chrestensen, 316 U.S. 52, where the Court viewed handbills purporting to contain protected expression as merely commercial advertising. Compare that decision with Jamison v. State of Texas, 318 U.S. 413, and Murdock v. Pennsylvania, 319 U.S. 105 where speech having the

here were sales of illicit merchandise, not sales of constitutionally protected matter. A conviction for mailing obscene publications, but explained in part by the presence of this element, does not necessarily suppress the materials in question, nor chill their proper distribution for a proper use. Nor should it inhibit the enterprise of others seeking through serious endeavor to advance human knowledge or understanding in science, literature, or art. All that will have been determined is that questionable publications are obscene in a context which brands them as obscene as that term is defined in Roth—a use inconsistent with any claim to the shelter of the First Amendment.[9] "The nature of the materials is, of course, relevant as an attribute of the defendant's conduct, but the materials are thus placed in context from which they draw color and character. A wholly different result might be reached in a different setting." Roth v. United States, 354 U.S. at 495 (Warren, C. J., concurring).

It is important to stress that this analysis simply elaborates the test by which the obscenity vel non of the material must be judged. Where an exploitation of interests in titillation by pornography is shown with respect to material lending itself to such exploitation through pervasive treatment or description of sexual matters, such evidence may support the determination that the material is obscene even though in other contexts the material would escape such condemnation. . . .

Affirmed.

Mr. Justice BLACK, dissenting.

Only one stark fact emerges with clarity out of the confusing welter of opinions and thousands of words written in this and two other cases today. That fact is that Ginzburg, petitioner here, is now finally and authoritatively condemned to serve five years in prison for distributing printed matter about sex which neither Ginzburg nor anyone else could possibly have known to be criminal. . . . I think that the criteria declared by a majority of the Court today as guidelines for a court or jury to determine whether Ginzburg or anyone else be punished as a common criminal for publishing or circulating obscene material are so vague and meaningless that they practically leave the fate of a person charged with violating censorship statutes to the unbridled discretion, whim and caprice of the judge or jury which tries him.

. . . .

Mr. Justice DOUGLAS, dissenting.

The use of sex symbols to sell literature today condemned by the Court, engrafts another exception on First Amendment rights that is as unwarranted as the judge-made exception concerning obscenity. This new exception condemns an advertising technique as old as history. The advertisements of our best magazines are chock-full of thighs, ankles, calves, bosoms, eyes, and hair, to draw the potential buyers' attention to lotions,

characteristics of advertising was held to be an integral part of religious discussions and hence protected. Material sold solely to produce sexual arousal, like commercial advertising, does not escape regulation because it has been dressed up as speech, or in other contexts might be recognized as speech. [Footnote by the Court.]

9. One who advertises and sells a work on the basis of its prurient appeal is not threatened by the perhaps inherent residual vagueness of the Roth test . . . ; such behavior is central to the objectives of criminal obscenity laws. . . . [Footnote by the Court.]

tires, food, liquor, clothing, autos, and even insurance policies. The sexy advertisement neither adds to nor detracts from the quality of the merchandise being offered for sale. And I do not see how it adds to or detracts one whit from the legality of the book being distributed. A book should stand on its own, irrespective of the reasons why it was written or the wiles used in selling it. I cannot imagine any promotional effort that would make chapters 7 and 8 of the Song of Solomon any the less or any more worthy of First Amendment protection than does its unostentatious inclusion in the average edition of the Bible. . . . .

Mr. Justice HARLAN, dissenting.

I would reverse the convictions of Ginzburg and his three corporate co-defendants. The federal obscenity statute . . . is concerned with unlawful shipment of "nonmailable" matter . . . and its focus [is] solely on the character of the material in question. . . . I believe that under this statute the Federal Government is constitutionally restricted to banning from the mails only "hardcore pornography" . . . .. While the precise holding of the Court is obscure, I take it that the objective test of Roth, which ultimately focuses on the material in question, is to be supplemented by another test that goes to the question whether the mailer's aim is to "pander" to or "titillate" those to whom he mails questionable matter.

Although it is not clear whether the majority views the panderer test as a statutory gloss or as constitutional doctrine, I read the opinion to be in the latter category. The First Amendment, in the obscenity area, no longer fully protects material on its face nonobscene for such material must now also be examined in the light of the defendant's conduct, attitude, motives. This seems to me a mere euphemism for allowing punishment of a person who mails otherwise constitutionally protected material just because a jury or a judge may not find him or his business agreeable. Were a State to enact a "panderer" statute under its police power, I have little doubt that—subject to clear drafting to avoid attacks on vagueness and equal protection grounds— such a statute would be constitutional. Possibly the same might be true of the Federal Government acting under its postal or commerce powers. What I fear the Court has done today is in effect to write a new statute, but without the sharply focused definitions and standards necessary in such a sensitive area. Casting such a dubious gloss over a straightforward 101-year-old statute . . . is for me an astonishing piece of judicial improvisation.

It seems perfectly clear that the theory on which these convictions are now sustained is quite different from the basis on which the case was tried and decided by the District Court and affirmed by the Court of Appeals. . . . If there is anything to this new pandering dimension to the mailing statute, the Court should return the case for a new trial, for petitioners are at least entitled to a day in court on the question on which their guilt has ultimately come to depend. . . .

. . . Conceivably someone mailing to the public selective portions of a recognized classic with the avowed purpose of titillation would run the risk of conviction for mailing nonmailable matter. Presumably the Post Office under this theory might once again attempt to ban Lady Chatterley's Lover, which a lower court found not bannable in 1960 by an abstract application of Roth. Grove Press, Inc. v. Christenberry, 276 F.2d 433. I would suppose that if the Government could show that Grove Press is pandering to people who are interested in the book's sexual passages and not in D. H.

Lawrence's social theories or literary technique § 1461 could properly be invoked. . . .

Mr. Justice STEWART, dissenting. . . .

Censorship reflects a society's lack of confidence in itself. It is a hallmark of an authoritarian regime. Long ago those who wrote our First Amendment charted a different course. They believed a society can be truly strong only when it is truly free. In the realm of expression they put their faith, for better or for worse, in the enlightened choice of the people, free from the interference of a policeman's intrusive thumb or a judge's heavy hand. So it is that the Constitution protects coarse expression as well as refined, and vulgarity no less than elegance. A book worthless to me may convey something of value to my neighbor. In the free society to which our Constitution has committed us, it is for each to choose for himself.[1]

Because such is the mandate of our Constitution, there is room for only the most restricted view of this Court's decision in Roth v. United States, 354 U.S. 476. . . . It is [hardcore pornography], and that alone, which I think government may constitutionally suppress, whether by criminal or civil sanctions. . . . Jacobellis v. Ohio, 378 U.S. 184, at 197 (concurring opinion). In order to prevent any possible misunderstanding, I have set out in the margin a description, borrowed from the Solicitor General's brief, of the kind of thing to which I have reference.[2] . . .

The Court today appears to concede that the materials Ginzburg mailed were themselves protected by the First Amendment. [And] Ginzburg was not charged with "commercial exploitation"; he was not charged with "pandering"; he was not charged with "titillation." Therefore, to affirm his conviction now on any of those grounds, even if otherwise valid, is to deny him due process of law. Cole v. Arkansas, 333 U.S. 196. But those grounds are *not,* of course, otherwise valid. Neither the statute under which Ginzburg was convicted nor any other federal statute I know of makes "commercial exploitation" or "pandering" or "titillation" a criminal offense. And any criminal law that sought to do so in the terms so elusively defined by the Court would, of course, be unconstitutionally vague and therefore void. . . .

For me, however, there is another aspect of the Court's opinion in this case that is even more regrettable. Today the Court assumes the power

1. Different constitutional questions would arise in a case involving an assault upon individual privacy by publication in a manner so blatant or obtrusive as to make it difficult or impossible for an unwilling individual to avoid exposure to it. . . . Still other considerations might come into play with respect to laws limited in their effect to those deemed insufficiently adult to make an informed choice. No such issues were tendered in this case. [Footnote by Justice Stewart.]

2. ". . . Such materials include photographs, both still and motion picture, with no pretense of artistic value, graphically depicting acts of sexual intercourse, including various acts of sodomy and sadism, and sometimes involving several participants in scenes of orgy-like character. They also include strips of drawings in comic-book format grossly depicting similar activities in an exaggerated fashion. There are, in addition, pamphlets and booklets, sometimes with photographic illustrations, verbally describing such activities in a bizarre manner with no attempt whatsoever to afford portrayals of character or situation and with no pretense to literary value. All of this material . . . cannot conceivably be characterized as embodying communication of ideas or artistic values inviolate under the First Amendment. . . ." [Footnote by Justice Stewart.]

to deny Ralph Ginzburg the protection of the First Amendment because it disapproves of his "sordid business." That is a power the Court does not possess. For the First Amendment protects us all with an even hand. It applies to Ralph Ginzburg with no less completeness and force than to G. P. Putnam's Sons. In upholding and enforcing the Bill of Rights, this Court has no power to pick or to choose. When we lose sight of that fixed star of constitutional adjudication, we lose our way. For then we forsake a government of law and are left with government by Big Brother. . . .

THE MISHKIN CASE

Mishkin v. New York, 383 U.S. 502, was the last of the 1966 (Memoirs-Ginzburg-Mishkin) trilogy of obscenity decisions. The Court sustained appellant's conviction under a New York obscenity statute. As described by the Court, the books involved in the case "portray sexuality in many guises. Some depict relatively normal heterosexual relations, but more depict such deviations as sadomasochism, fetishism, and homosexuality. Many have covers with drawings of scantily clad women being whipped, beaten, tortured, or abused. Many, if not most, are photo-offsets of typewritten books written and illustrated by authors and artists according to detailed instructions given by the appellant. . . .   All the books are cheaply prepared paper-bound 'pulps' with imprinted sales prices that are several thousand percent above costs."

Appellant's major contention was that the material was not obscene under the Roth standard: he insisted that at least some of the books—those "depicting various deviant sexual practices, such as flagellation, fetishism, and lesbianism"—did not satisfy the prurient-appeal requirement because "they do not appeal to a prurient interest of the 'average person' in sex," that instead of stimulating the erotic, they disgust and sicken." Justice Brennan's majority opinion rejected this argument "as being founded on an unrealistic interpretation of the prurient appeal requirement." He explained: "Where the material is designed for and primarily disseminated to a clearly defined deviant sexual group, rather than the public at large, the prurient-appeal requirement of the Roth test is satisfied if the dominant theme of the material taken as a whole appeals to the prurient interest in sex of the members of that group." The Court found the restated prurient-appeal standard easily satisfied here: "Not only was there proof of the books' prurient appeal, . . . but the proof was compelling; in addition appellant's own evaluation of his material confirms such a finding. See Ginzburg . . .." Justice Harlan concurred separately; Justices Black, Douglas, and Stewart dissented.

REDRUP: THE 1967 CLARIFICATION

A paragraph in the per curiam disposition of three obscenity cases in 1967 suggested an emerging consensus regarding the justifications that would sustain control of obscenity. (See also Stanley v. Georgia, p. 1254, infra.) The Court memorandum, 386 U.S. 767 (1967), applied to three cases, Redrup v. New York, Austin v. Kentucky, and Gent v. Arkansas. In none did the Court reach the questions that had been argued.

The cases involved state criminal and civil proceedings relating to paperback books and magazines. In setting the cases for argument, the Court acted on the hypothesis that the materials involved were clearly "obscene in the constitutional sense." After argument, the majority of the Justices "concluded that the hypothesis upon which the Court originally proceeded was invalid." After summarizing the variety of prevailing viewpoints regarding obscenity control, the per curiam opinion stated: "Whichever of these constitutional views is brought to bear upon the cases before us, it is clear that the judgments cannot stand." The Court rested on "a common and controlling fundamental constitutional basis": all of the publications were constitutionally protected "from governmental suppression, whether criminal or civil, *in personam* or *in rem*."

A brief paragraph in the course of the Court's description of the cases was of particular interest: "In none of the cases was there a claim that the statute in question reflected a specific and limited state concern for juveniles. [See the 1968 Ginsberg case, which follows.] See Prince v. Massachusetts, 321 U.S. 158; cf. Butler v. Michigan, 352 U.S. 380. In none was there any suggestion of an assault upon individual privacy by publication in a manner so obtrusive as to make it impossible for an unwilling individual to avoid exposure to it. Cf. Breard v. Alexandria, 341 U.S. 622; Public Utilities Comm'n v. Pollak, 343 U.S. 451. And in none was there evidence of the sort of 'pandering' which the Court found significant in Ginzburg v. United States, 383 U.S. 463." [Justice Harlan's dissent, joined by Justice Clark, insisted that the Court should decide either the argued issues or none at all since, as a result of the Court's own orders setting the cases for argument, "the obscenity *vel non* of these publications was not discussed" by the parties.]*

GINSBERG v. NEW YORK

390 U.S. 629, 88 S.Ct. 1274, 20 L.Ed.2d 195 (1968).

Appeal from the Supreme Court of New York, Appellate Term, Second Department.

Mr. Justice BRENNAN delivered the opinion of the Court.

This case presents the question of the constitutionality on its face of a New York criminal obscenity statute which prohibits the sale to minors under 17 years of age of material defined to be obscene on the basis of its appeal to them whether or not it would be obscene to adults.

Appellant and his wife operate "Sam's Stationery and Luncheonette" in Bellmore, Long Island. They have a lunch counter, and among other things, also sell magazines including some so-called "girlie" magazines.

---

* Note also an early indication of Chief Justice Burger's views on obscenity control, in Cain v. Kentucky, 397 U.S. ——, a March 1970 film case. The majority reversed in a per curiam order simply citing Redrup v. New York. Justice Harlan's dissent, while reiterating his position allowing "greater flexibility" to state than to federal control, nevertheless found that "suppression of this particular film presents a borderline question." Chief Justice Burger's dissent disclosed less doubt: "In my view we should not inflexibly deny to each of the States the power to adopt and enforce its own standards as to obscenity and pornographic materials; States ought to be free to deal with varying conditions and problems in this area. I am unwilling to say that Kentucky is without power to bar public showing of this film . . . ."

Appellant was prosecuted under two informations, each in two counts, which charged that he personally sold a 16-year-old boy two "girlie" magazines on each of two dates in October 1965, in violation of § 484–h of the New York Penal Law. He was tried before a judge . . . and was found guilty on both counts.[1] The judge found (1) that the magazines contained pictures which depicted female "nudity" in a manner defined in subsection 1(b), that is "the showing of . . . female . . . buttocks with less than a full opaque covering, or the showing of the female breast with less than a fully opaque covering of any portion thereof below the top of the nipple . . . ," and (2) that the pictures were "harmful to minors" in that they had, within the meaning of subsection 1(f) " . . . that quality of . . . representation . . . of nudity [which] (i) predominantly appeals to the prurient, shameful or morbid interest of minors, and (ii) is patently offensive to prevailing standards in the adult community as a whole with respect to what is suitable material for minors, and (iii) is utterly without redeeming social importance for minors." He held that both sales to the 16-year-old boy therefore constituted the violation under § 484–h of "knowingly to sell . . . to a minor" under 17 of "(a) any picture . . . which depicts nudity . . . and which is harmful to minors," and "(b) any . . . magazine . . . which contains [such pictures] and which, taken as a whole, is harmful to minors." . . . We affirm. . . .

The "girlie" picture magazines involved in the sales here are not obscene for adults, Redrup v. New York, 386 U.S. 767. But § 484–h does not bar the appellant from stocking the magazines and selling them to persons 17 years of age or older, and therefore the conviction is not invalid under our decision in Butler v. Michigan, 352 U.S. 380.

Obscenity is not within the area of protected speech or press. Roth v. United States, 354 U.S. 476, 485. The three-pronged test of subsection 1(f) for judging the obscenity of material sold to minors under 17 is a variable from the formulation for determining obscenity under Roth stated in the plurality opinion in Memoirs v. Massachusetts, 383 U.S. 413, 418. Appellant's primary attack upon § 484–h is leveled at the power of the State to adapt this Memoirs formulation to define the material's obscenity on the basis of its appeal to minors, and thus exclude material so defined from the area of protected expression. . . .

Appellant's contention [handwritten marginal note]

The New York Court of Appeals "upheld the Legislature's power to employ variable concepts of obscenity"[2] in a case in which the same challenge to state power to enact such a law was also addressed to § 484–h. . . . [Appellant's] contention is the broad proposition that the scope of the con-

1. Appellant makes no attack upon § 484–h as applied. We therefore have no occasion to consider the sufficiency of the evidence, or such issues as burden of proof, whether expert evidence is either required or permissible, or any other questions which might be pertinent to the application of the statute. . . . [Footnote by the Court.]

2. . . . The concept of variable obscenity is developed in Lockhart & McClure, Censorship of Obscenity: The Developing Constitutional Standards,

45 Minn.L.Rev. 5 (1960). At p. 85 the authors state:

"Variable obscenity . . . furnishes a useful analytical tool for dealing with the problem of denying adolescents access to material aimed at a primary audience of sexually mature adults. For variable obscenity focuses attention upon the make-up of primary and peripheral audiences in varying circumstances, and provides a reasonably satisfactory means for delineating the obscene in each circumstance." [Footnote by the Court.]

stitutional freedom of expression secured to a citizen to read or see material concerned with sex cannot be made to depend upon whether the citizen is an adult or a minor. . . . It is enough for the purposes of this case that we inquire whether it was constitutionally impermissible for New York, insofar as § 484–h does so, to accord minors under 17 a more restricted right than that assured to adults to judge and determine for themselves what sex material they may read or see. We conclude that we cannot say that the statute invades the area of freedom of expression constitutionally secured to minors. . . .

[Section] 484–h simply adjusts the definition of obscenity ". . . to social realities by permitting the appeal of this type of material to be assessed in terms of the sexual interest . . . ." of such minors. Mishkin v. New York, 383 U.S. 502, 509 . . . . That the State has power to make that adjustment seems clear, for we have recognized that even where there is an invasion of protected freedoms ". . . the power of the state to control the conduct of children reaches beyond the scope of its authority over adults . . . ." Prince v. Massachusetts, 321 U.S. 158, 170. In Prince we sustained the conviction of the guardian of a nine-year-old girl, both members of the sect of the Jehovah's Witnesses, for violating the Massachusetts Child Labor Law by permitting the girl to sell the sect's religious tracts on the streets of Boston.

The well-being of its children is of course a subject within the State's constitutional power to regulate, and, in our view, two interests justify the limitations in § 484–h upon the availability of sex material to minors under 17, at least if it was rational for the legislature to find that the minors' exposure to such material might be harmful. First of all, constitutional interpretation has consistently recognized that parents' claims to authority in their own households to direct the rearing of their children is basic in the structure of our society. . . . The legislature could properly conclude that parents and others, teachers for example, who have this primary responsibility for children's well-being are entitled to the support of laws designed to aid discharge of that responsibility. . . .

The State also has an independent interest in the well-being of its youth . . . an interest "to protect the welfare of children" and to see that they are "safeguarded from abuses" which might prevent their "growth into free and independent well-developed men and citizens." The only question remaining, therefore, is whether the New York Legislature might rationally conclude, as it has, that exposure to the materials proscribed by § 484–h constitutes such an "abuse."

Section 484–e of the law states a legislative finding that the material condemned by § 484–h is "a basic factor in impairing the ethical and moral development of our youth and a clear and present danger to the people of the state." It is very doubtful that this finding expresses an accepted scientific fact. But obscenity is not protected expression and may be suppressed without a showing of the circumstances which lie behind the phrase "clear and present danger" in its application to protected speech. Roth v. United States, supra, at 486–487. To sustain state power to exclude material defined as obscenity by § 484–h requires only that we be able to say that it was not irrational for the legislature to find that exposure to material condemned by the statute is harmful to minors. In Meyer v. Nebraska, [262 U.S. 390, striking down a statute forbidding children to study German], we were able to say that children's knowledge of the German language "cannot reasonably be regarded as harmful." That cannot be said by us of minors' reading and seeing of sex material. To be sure, there is no lack of "studies" which purport to demonstrate that obscenity is or is not "a basic factor in impairing the ethical and moral development of . . . youth and a clear and present danger to the people of the state." But the growing consensus of commentators is that "[w]hile these studies all agree that a causal link has not been demonstrated, they are equally agreed that a causal link has not been disproved either." We do not demand of legislatures a "scientifically certain criteria of legislation." Noble State Bank v. Haskell, 219 U.S. 104, 110. We therefore cannot say that § 484–h, in defining the obscenity of material on the basis of its appeal to minors under 17, has no rational relation to the objective of safeguarding such minors from harm. . . .*

Affirmed.

Mr. Justice STEWART, concurring in the result. . . .

I think a State may permissibly determine that, at least in some precisely delineated areas, a child—like someone in a captive audience—is not possessed of that full capacity for individual choice which is the presupposition of First Amendment guarantees. . . .

Mr. Justice DOUGLAS, with whom Mr. Justice BLACK concurs, dissenting. . . .

. . . As I read the First Amendment, it was designed to keep the State and the hands of all state officials off the printing presses of America and off the distribution systems for all printed literature. . . .

Mr. Justice FORTAS, dissenting. . . .

. . . The conviction of Ginsberg on the present facts is a serious invasion of freedom. To sustain the conviction without inquiry as to whether

---

* The Court also rejected claims that subsections (f) and (g) were void for vagueness [see the vagueness cases in sec. 2B, infra]. On the same day, however, the Court sustained vagueness challenges to a Dallas ordinance authorizing an administrative board to classify films as "suitable for young persons" or as "not suitable for young persons." Interstate Circuit v. Dallas, 390 U.S. 676 (1968). Among the statutory standards defining "not suitable for young persons" were references to films portraying "sexual promiscuity . . . in such a manner as to be, in the judgment of the Board, likely to incite or encourage delinquency or sexual promiscuity on the part of young persons or to appeal to their prurient interests." Another provision stated: "A film shall be considered 'likely to incite or encourage' crime, delinquency, or sexual promiscuity on the part of young persons, if, in the judgment of the Board, there is a substantial probability that it will create the impression on young persons that such conduct is profitable, desirable, acceptable, respectable, praiseworthy or commonly accepted." The film

"Viva Maria" was classified as "not suitable" under these standards. Justice Marshall's majority opinion emphasized that "sexual promiscuity" was not defined and that the "likely to incite or encourage" definition did not effectively limit administrative discretion. Vagueness, he noted, was no less objectionable "because the regulation of expression is one of classification rather than direct suppression." And the objective of protecting children could not save the ordinance: "The permissible extent of vagueness is not directly proportional to, or a function of, the extent of the power to regulate or control expression with respect to children. . . . The vices —the lack of guidance to those who seek to adjust their conduct and to those who seek to administer the law, as well as the possible practical curtailing of the effectiveness of judicial review—are the same." Justice Harlan's dissent insisted "that the Court has demanded greater precision of language from the City of Dallas than the Court can itself give, or even than can sensibly be expected in this area of the law."

the material is "obscene" and without any evidence of pushing or pandering, in face of this Court's asserted solicitude for First Amendment values, is to give the State a role in the rearing of children which is contrary to our traditions and to our conception of family responsibility. Cf. In re Gault, 387 U.S. 1 (1967) [chap. 12, p. 915, supra]. . . .

Mr. Justice HARLAN, concurring in [Ginsberg], and dissenting in [Interstate Circuit]. . . .

As the Court enters this new area of obscenity law it is well to take stock of where we are at present in this constitutional field. The subject of obscenity has produced a variety of views among the members of the Court unmatched in any other course of constitutional adjudication.[1] The upshot of all this divergence in viewpoint is that anyone who undertakes to examine the Court's decisions since Roth which have held particular material obscene or not obscene would find himself in utter bewilderment. . . .

I believe that no improvement in this chaotic state of affairs is likely to come until it is recognized that this whole problem is primarily one of state concern, and that the Constitution tolerates much wider authority and discretion in the States to control the dissemination of obscene materials than it does in the Federal Government. . . . And in the juvenile field I think that the Constitution is still more tolerant of state policy and its applications.
. . .

STANLEY v. GEORGIA

394 U.S. 557, 89 S.Ct. 1243, 22 L.Ed.2d 542 (1969).

Appeal from the Supreme Court of Georgia.

Mr. Justice MARSHALL delivered the opinion of the Court.

An investigation of appellant's alleged bookmaking activities led to the issuance of a search warrant for appellant's home. Under authority of this warrant, federal and state agents secured entrance. They found very little evidence of bookmaking activity, but while looking through a desk drawer in an upstairs bedroom, one of the federal agents, accompanied by a state officer, found three reels of eight-millimeter film. Using a projector and screen found in an upstairs living room, they viewed the films. The state officer concluded that they were obscene and seized them. [Appellant] was later indicted for "knowingly hav[ing] possession of obscene matter" in violation of Georgia law. Appellant was tried before a jury and convicted. . . .

Appellant argues here, and argued below, that the Georgia obscenity statute, insofar as it punishes mere private possession of obscene matter, violates the First Amendment, as made applicable to the States by the Fourteenth Amendment. For reasons set forth below, we agree that the mere private possession of obscene matter cannot constitutionally be made a crime. . . .

Georgia concedes that the present case appears to be one of "first impression . . . on this exact point," but contends that since "obscenity is not within the area of constitutionally protected speech or press," Roth v.

---

1. In the 13 obscenity cases since Roth in which a signed opinion was written for the Court, there have been a total of 55 separate opinions among the Justices. . . . [Footnote by Justice Harlan.]

United States, 354 U.S. 476, 485 (1957), the States are free, subject to the limits of other provisions of the Constitution . . . ., to deal with it any way deemed necessary, just as they may deal with possession of other things thought to be detrimental to the welfare of their citizens. If the State can protect the body of a citizen, may it not, argues Georgia, protect his mind?

It is true that Roth does declare, seemingly without qualification, that obscenity is not protected by the First Amendment. . . . . However, neither Roth nor any subsequent decision of this Court dealt with the precise problem involved in the present case. . . . . Those cases dealt with the power of the State and Federal Governments to prohibit or regulate certain public actions taken or intended to be taken with respect to obscene matter. . . .

In this context, we do not believe that this case can be decided simply by citing Roth. Roth and its progeny certainly do mean that the First and Fourteenth Amendments recognize a valid governmental interest in dealing with the problem of obscenity. But the assertion of that interest cannot, in every context, be insulated from all constitutional protections. [Roth] cannot foreclose an examination of the constitutional implications of a statute forbidding mere private possession of such material.

[The] right to receive information and ideas, regardless of their social worth, see Winters v. New York, 333 U.S. 507, 510 (1948), is fundamental to our free society. Moreover, in the context of this case—a prosecution for mere possession of printed or filmed matter in the privacy of a person's own home—that right takes on an added dimension. For also fundamental is the right to be free, except in very limited circumstances, from unwanted governmental intrusions into one's privacy. . . .

These are the rights that appellant is asserting in the case before us. He is asserting the right to read or observe what he pleases—the right to satisfy his intellectual and emotional needs in the privacy of his own home. He is asserting the right to be free from state inquiry into the contents of his library. Georgia contends that appellant does not have these rights, that there are certain types of materials that the individual may not read or even possess. Georgia justifies this assertion by arguing that the films in the present case are obscene. But we think that mere categorization of these films as "obscene" is insufficient justification for such a drastic invasion of personal liberties guaranteed by the First and Fourteenth Amendments. Whatever may be the justifications for other statutes regulating obscenity, we do not think they reach into the privacy of one's own home. If the First Amendment means anything, it means that a State has no business telling a man, sitting alone in his own house, what books he may read or what films he may watch. Our whole constitutional heritage rebels at the thought of giving government the power to control men's minds.

And yet, in the face of these traditional notions of individual liberty, Georgia asserts the right to protect the individual's mind from the effects of obscenity. We are not certain that this argument amounts to anything more than the assertion that the State has the right to control the moral content of a person's thoughts.[1] To some, this may be a noble purpose, but it is

---

1. "Communities believe, and act on the belief, that obscenity is immoral, is wrong for the individual, and has no place in a decent society. They believe, too, that adults as well as children are corruptible in morals and character, and that obscenity is a source of corruption that should be eliminated. Obscenity is not suppressed primarily for the protection of

wholly inconsistent with the philosophy of the First Amendment. [Kingsley International Pictures Corp. v. Regents, 360 U.S. 684, 688–689 (1959).] Nor is it relevant that obscenity in general, or the particular films before the Court, are arguably devoid of any ideological content. The line between the transmission of ideas and mere entertainment is much too elusive for this Court to draw, if indeed such a line can be drawn at all. . . . . Whatever the power of the state to control public dissemination of ideas inimical to the public morality, it cannot constitutionally premise legislation on the desirability of controlling a person's private thoughts.

Perhaps recognizing this, Georgia asserts that exposure to obscenity may lead to deviant sexual behavior or crimes of sexual violence. There appears to be little empirical basis for that assertion. But more importantly, if the State is only concerned about literature inducing antisocial conduct, we believe that in the context of private consumption of ideas and information we should adhere to the view that "[a]mong free men, the deterrents ordinarily to be applied to prevent crime are education and punishment for violations of the law . . . ." Whitney v. California, 274 U.S. 357, 378 (1927) (Brandeis, J., concurring). See Emerson, Toward a General Theory of the First Amendment, 72 Yale L. J. 877, 938 (1963). Given the present state of knowledge, the State may no more prohibit mere possession of obscenity on the ground that it may lead to antisocial conduct than it may prohibit possession of chemistry books on the ground that they may lead to the manufacture of homemade spirits.

It is true that in Roth this Court rejected the necessity of proving that exposure to obscene material would create a clear and present danger of antisocial conduct or would probably induce its recipients to such conduct. 354 U.S., at 486–487. But that case dealt with public distribution of obscene materials and such distribution is subject to different objections. For example, there is always the danger that obscene material might fall into the hands of children, see Ginsberg v. New York, supra, or that it might intrude upon the sensibilities or privacy of the general public.[2] See Redrup v. New York, 386 U.S. 767, 769 (1967). No such dangers are present in this case.

Finally, we are faced with the argument that prohibition of possession of obscenity is a necessary incident to statutory schemes prohibiting distribution. That argument is based on alleged difficulties of proving an intent to distribute or in producing evidence of actual distribution. We are not convinced that such difficulties exist, but even if they did we do not think that they would justify infringement of the individual's right to read or observe what he pleases. Because that right is so fundamental to our scheme of individual liberty, its restriction may not be justified by the need to ease the administration of otherwise valid criminal laws.

---

others. Much of it is suppressed for the purity of the community and for the salvation and welfare of the 'consumer.' Obscenity, at bottom, is not crime. Obscenity is sin." Henkin, Morals and the Constitution: The Sin of Obscenity, 63 Col.L.Rev. 391, 395 (1963). [Footnote by the Court.]

2. The Model Penal Code provisions dealing with obscenity are limited to cases of commercial dissemination. Model Penal Code § 251.4 (Prop.Official Draft 1962); see also Model Penal Code § 207.10 and comment 4 (Tent. Draft No. 6, 1957); H. Packer, The Limits of the Criminal Sanction 316–328 (1968); Schwartz, Morals Offenses and the Model Penal Code, 63 Col.L. Rev. 669 (1963). [Footnote by the Court.]

We hold that the First and Fourteenth Amendments prohibit making mere private possession of obscene material a crime.[3] Roth and the cases following that decision are not impaired by today's holding. As we have said, the States retain broad power to regulate obscenity; that power simply does not extend to mere possession by the individual in the privacy of his own home. Accordingly, the judgment of the court below is reversed and the case is remanded for proceedings not inconsistent with this opinion.

It is so ordered.

[Justice Black submitted a brief concurring opinion. Justice Stewart, joined by Justices Brennan and White, concurred in the result because "the films were seized in violation of the Fourth and Fourteenth Amendments." He commented that "the Court today disregards this preliminary issue in its hurry to move on to newer constitutional frontiers."]

B. THE METHODS OF REGULATION: CENSORSHIP AND OTHER CONTROLS

Introduction. Many of the problems of censorship have arisen in the context of obscenity control, but that has by no means been the only context. For example, the Court's first major discussion of prior restraints (Near v. Minnesota, the first case in this section), involved materials thought offensive for reasons other than obscenity; and that was true of the first major motion picture censorship case as well (see Burstyn v. Wilson, which follows Near). These cases form the background, however, for the later obscenity control cases emphasized here. Though obscenity is the major focus here, the cases in this section illustrate a wider phenomenon: the concern with substantive First Amendment values frequently evokes an auxiliary judicial scrutiny of the methods employed by the government; procedural safeguards often have a special bite in the First Amendment context. As the Court put it in Smith v. California, p. 1271, infra: "Our decisions furnish examples of legal devices and doctrines in most applications consistent with the Constitution, which cannot be applied in settings where they have the collateral effect of inhibiting the freedom of expression, by making the individual the more reluctant to exercise it." See generally Monaghan, "First Amendment 'Due Process,'" 83 Harv.L.Rev. 518 (1970). (Recall the problems of prior restraint raised by licensing ordinances in First Amendment contexts considered earlier, e. g., Lovell v. Griffin and Cox v. New Hampshire, chap. 15, pp.

---

3. What we have said in no way infringes upon the power of the State or Federal Government to make possession of other items, such as narcotics, firearms, or stolen goods, a crime. Our holding, in the present case turns upon the Georgia statute's infringement of fundamental liberties protected by the First and Fourteenth Amendments. No First Amendment rights are involved in most statutes making mere possession criminal.

Nor do we mean to express any opinion on statutes making criminal possession of other types of printed, filmed, or recorded materials. See, e. g., 18 U.S.C. § 793(d), which makes criminal the otherwise lawful possession of materials which "the possessor has reason to believe could be used to the injury of the United States or to the advantage of any foreign nation . . ." In such cases, compelling reasons may exist for overriding the right of the individual to possess those materials. [Footnote by the Court.]

1142 and 1143, supra; and note the comments on vagueness and other procedural devices, chap. 12, p. 911, supra.)

NEAR v. MINNESOTA

283 U.S. 697, 51 S.Ct. 625, 75 L.Ed. 1357 (1931).

Appeal from the Supreme Court of Minnesota.

Mr. Chief Justice HUGHES delivered the opinion of the Court.

Chapter 285 of the Session Laws of Minnesota for the year 1925 provides for the abatement, as a public nuisance, of a "malicious, scandalous and defamatory newspaper, magazine or other periodical." Section one of the Act is as follows:

"Section 1. Any person who . . . shall be engaged in the business of regularly or customarily producing, publishing or circulating, having in possession, selling or giving away

"(a) an obscene, lewd and lascivious newspaper, magazine, or other periodical, or

"(b) a malicious, scandalous and defamatory newspaper, magazine or other periodical,
is guilty of a nuisance, and all persons guilty of such nuisance may be enjoined, as hereinafter provided. . . .

"In actions brought under (b) above, there shall be available the defense that the truth was published with good motives and for justifiable ends and in such actions the plaintiff shall not have the right to report (*sic*) to issues or editions of periodicals taking place more than three months before the commencement of the action."

Section two provides that whenever any such nuisance is committed or exists, the County Attorney of any county where any such periodical is published or circulated . . . may maintain an action in the district court of the county in the name of the State to enjoin perpetually the persons committing or maintaining any such nuisance from further committing or maintaining it. . . .

Under this statute, clause (b), the County Attorney of Hennepin County brought this action to enjoin the publication of what was described as a "malicious, scandalous and defamatory newspaper, magazine and periodical," known as "The Saturday Press," published by the defendants in the city of Minneapolis. [T]he articles charged in substance that a Jewish gangster was in control of gambling, bootlegging and racketeering in Minneapolis, and that law enforcing officers and agencies were not energetically performing their duties. Most of the charges were directed against the Chief of Police; he was charged with gross neglect of duty, illicit relations with gangsters, and with participation in graft. The County Attorney was charged with knowing the existing conditions and with failure to take adequate measures to remedy them. The Mayor was accused of inefficiency and dereliction. One member of the grand jury was stated to be in sympathy with the gangsters. A special grand jury and a special prosecutor were demanded to deal with the situation . . . . There is no question but that the articles made serious accusations. . . .

. . . . Judgment was entered [in the lower court] adjudging that "the newspaper, magazine and periodical known as The Saturday Press," as a public nuisance, "be and is hereby abated." The judgment perpetually enjoined the defendants "from producing, editing, publishing, circulating, having in their possession, selling or giving away any publication whatsoever which is a malicious, scandalous or defamatory newspaper, as defined by law," and also "from further conducting said nuisance under the name and title of said The Saturday Press or any other name or title." . . . From the judgment [as affirmed] the defendant Near appeals to this Court.

This statute, for the suppression as a public nuisance of a newspaper or periodical, is unusual, if not unique, and raises questions of grave importance transcending the local interests involved in the particular action. It is no longer open to doubt that the liberty of the press, and of speech, is within the liberty safeguarded by the due process clause of the Fourteenth Amendment from invasion by state action. It was found impossible to conclude that this essential personal liberty of the citizen was left unprotected by the general guaranty of fundamental rights of person and property. . . .

First. The statute is not aimed at the redress of individual or private wrongs. Remedies for libel remain available and unaffected. . . . It is aimed at the distribution of scandalous matter as "detrimental to public morals and to the general welfare," tending "to disturb the peace of the community" and "to provoke assaults and the commission of crime." In order to obtain an injunction to suppress the future publication of the newspaper or periodical, it is not necessary to prove the falsity of the charges that have been made in the publication condemned. In the present action there was no allegation that the matter published was not true. It is alleged, and the statute requires the allegation that the publication was "malicious." But, as in prosecutions for libel, there is no requirement of proof by the State of malice in fact as distinguished from malice inferred from the mere publication of the defamatory matter. The judgment in this case proceeded upon the mere proof of publication. The statute permits the defense, not of the truth alone, but only that the truth was published with good motives and for justifiable ends. It is apparent that under the statute the publication is to be regarded as defamatory if it injures reputation, and that it is scandalous if it circulates charges of reprehensible conduct, whether criminal or otherwise, and the publication is thus deemed to invite public reprobation and to constitute a public scandal. . . .

Second. The statute is directed not simply at the circulation of scandalous and defamatory statements with regard to private citizens, but at the continued publication by newspapers and periodicals of charges against public officers of corruption, malfeasance in office, or serious neglect of duty. . . .

Third. The object of the statute is not punishment, in the ordinary sense, but suppression of the offending newspaper or periodical. The reason for the enactment, as the state court has said, is that prosecutions to enforce penal statutes for libel do not result in "efficient repression or suppression of the evils of scandal." . . .

Fourth. The statute not only operates to suppress the offending newspaper or periodical but to put the publisher under an effective censorship. When a newspaper or periodical is found to be "malicious, scandalous and defamatory," and is suppressed as such, resumption of publication is punishable as a contempt of court by fine or imprisonment. Thus, where a newspaper or periodical has been suppressed because of the circulation of charges against public officers of official misconduct, it would seem to be clear that the renewal of the publication of such charges would constitute a contempt and that the judgment would lay a permanent restraint upon the publisher, to escape which he must satisfy the court as to the character of a new publication. Whether he would be permitted again to publish matter deemed to be derogatory to the same or other public officers would depend upon the court's ruling. . . . .

If we cut through mere details of procedure, the operation and effect of the statute in substance is that public authorities may bring the owner or publisher of a newspaper or periodical before a judge upon a charge of conducting a business of publishing scandalous and defamatory matter—in particular that the matter consists of charges against public officers of official dereliction—and unless the owner or publisher is able and disposed to bring competent evidence to satisfy the judge that the charges are true and are published with good motives and for justifiable ends, his newspaper or periodical is suppressed and further publication is made punishable as a contempt. This is of the essence of censorship.

The question is whether a statute authorizing such proceedings in restraint of publication is consistent with the conception of the liberty of the press as historically conceived and guaranteed. In determining the extent of the constitutional protection, it has been generally, if not universally, considered that it is the chief purpose of the guaranty to prevent previous restraints upon publication. The struggle in England, directed against the legislative power of the licenser, resulted in renunciation of the censorship of the press. The liberty deemed to be established was thus described by Blackstone: "The liberty of the press is indeed essential to the nature of a free state; but this consists in laying no *previous* restraints upon publications, and not in freedom from censure for criminal matter when published. Every freeman has an undoubted right to lay what sentiments he pleases before the public; to forbid this, is to destroy the freedom of the press; but if he publishes what is improper, mischievous or illegal, he must take the consequence of his own temerity." . . . .

The criticism upon Blackstone's statement has not been because immunity from previous restraint upon publication has not been regarded as deserving of special emphasis, but chiefly because that immunity cannot be deemed to exhaust the conception of the liberty guaranteed by state and federal constitutions. . . . .

The objection has also been made that the principle as to immunity from previous restraint is stated too broadly, if every such restraint is deemed to be prohibited. That is undoubtedly true; the protection even as to previous restraint is not absolutely unlimited. But the limitation has been recognized only in exceptional cases . . . . . . No one would question but that a government might prevent actual obstruction to its recruiting service or the publication of the sailing dates of transports or the number and location of troops. On similar grounds, the primary requirements of decency may be enforced against obscene publications. The security of the community life may be protected against incitements to acts of violence and the overthrow by force

of orderly government. . . . These limitations are not applicable here.
. . .

The exceptional nature of its limitations places in a strong light the
general conception that liberty of the press, historically considered and taken
up by the Federal Constitution, has meant, principally although not exclusively, immunity from previous restraints or censorship. The conception of the
liberty of the press in this country had broadened with the exigencies of the
colonial period and with the efforts to secure freedom from oppressive administration. That liberty was especially cherished for the immunity it afforded from previous restraint of the publication of censure of public officers
and charges of official misconduct. . . .

The fact that for approximately one hundred and fifty years there has
been almost an entire absence of attempts to impose previous restraints upon
publications relating to the malfeasance of public officers is significant of the
deep-seated conviction that such restraints would violate constitutional right.
Public officers, whose character and conduct remain open to debate and free
discussion in the press, find their remedies for false accusations in actions under libel laws providing for redress and punishment, and not in proceedings
to restrain the publication of newspapers and periodicals. . . .

The importance of this immunity has not lessened. While reckless assaults upon public men, and efforts to bring obloquy upon those who are
endeavoring faithfully to discharge official duties, exert a baleful influence
and deserve the severest condemnation in public opinion, it cannot be said
that this abuse is greater, and it is believed to be less, than that which characterized the period in which our institutions took shape. Meanwhile, the administration of government has become more complex, the opportunities for
malfeasance and corruption have multiplied, crime has grown to most serious
proportions, and the danger of its protection by unfaithful officials and of the
impairment of the fundamental security of life and property by criminal alliances and official neglect, emphasize the primary need of a vigilant and
courageous press, especially in great cities. The fact that the liberty of the
press may be abused by miscreant purveyors of scandal does not make any
the less necessary the immunity of the press from previous restraint in dealing with official misconduct. Subsequent punishment for such abuses as may
exist is the appropriate remedy, consistent with constitutional privilege.
. . .

The statute in question cannot be justified by reason of the fact that
the publisher is permitted to show, before injunction issues, that the matter
published is true and is published with good motives and for justifiable ends.
. . . The recognition of authority to impose previous restraint upon publication in order to protect the community against the circulation of charges
of misconduct, and especially of official misconduct, necessarily would carry
with it the admission of the authority of the censor against which the constitutional barrier was erected. The preliminary freedom, by virtue of the
very reason for its existence, does not depend, as this Court has said, on
proof of truth. . . .

Equally unavailing is the insistence that the statute is designed to prevent the circulation of scandal which tends to disturb the public peace and
to provoke assaults and the commission of crime. Charges of reprehensible
conduct, and in particular of official malfeasance, unquestionably create a

public scandal, but the theory of the constitutional guaranty is that even a more serious public evil would be caused by authority to prevent publication. . . .

For these reasons we hold the statute, so far as it authorized the proceedings in this action under clause (b) of section one, to be an infringement of the liberty of the press guaranteed by the Fourteenth Amendment. We should add that this decision rests upon the operation and effect of the statute, without regard to the question of the truth of the charges contained in the particular periodical. The fact that the public officers named in this case, and those associated with the charges of official dereliction, may be deemed to be impeccable, cannot affect the conclusion that the statute imposes an unconstitutional restraint upon publication.

Judgment reversed.

Mr. Justice BUTLER, dissenting. . . .

The Minnesota statute does not operate as a *previous* restraint on publication within the proper meaning of that phrase. It does not authorize administrative control in advance such as was formerly exercised by the licensers and censors but prescribes a remedy to be enforced by a suit in equity. In this case there was previous publication made in the course of the business of regularly producing malicious, scandalous and defamatory periodicals. The business and publications unquestionably constitute an abuse of the right of free press. The statute denounces the things done as a nuisance on the ground, as stated by the state supreme court, that they threaten morals, peace and good order. There is no question of the power of the State to denounce such transgressions. The restraint authorized is only in respect of continuing to do what has been duly adjudged to constitute a nuisance. . . . There is nothing in the statute purporting to prohibit publications that have not been adjudged to constitute a nuisance. It is fanciful to suggest similarity between the granting or enforcement of the decree authorized by this statute to prevent *further* publication of malicious, scandalous and defamatory articles and the *previous restraint* upon the press by licensers as referred to by Blackstone and described in the history of the times to which he alludes.

The opinion seems to concede that under clause (a) of the Minnesota law the business of regularly publishing and circulating an obscene periodical may be enjoined as a nuisance. It is difficult to perceive any distinction, having any relation to constitutionality, between clause (a) and clause (b) under which this action was brought. Both nuisances are offensive to morals, order and good government. As that resulting from lewd publications constitutionally may be enjoined it is hard to understand why the one resulting from a regular business of malicious defamation may not.

It is well known, as found by the state supreme court, that existing libel laws are inadequate effectively to suppress evils resulting from the kind of business and publications that are shown in this case. The doctrine that measures such as the one before us are invalid because they operate as previous restraints to infringe freedom of press exposes the peace and good order of every community and the business and private affairs of every individual to the constant and protracted false and malicious assaults of any insolvent publisher who may have purpose and sufficient capacity to contrive and put into effect a scheme or program for oppression, blackmail or extortion. . . .

Mr. Justice VAN DEVANTER, Mr. Justice McREYNOLDS, and Mr. Justice SUTHERLAND concur in this opinion.

Holds: *Films can invoke freedom of speech + press. Also you can't ban a film because it is sacrilegious — too broad*

BURSTYN v. WILSON

343 U.S. 495, 72 S.Ct. 777, 96 L.Ed. 1098 (1952).

Appeal from the Court of Appeals of New York.

Mr. Justice CLARK delivered the opinion of the Court.

The issue here is the constitutionality, under the First and Fourteenth Amendments, of a New York statute which permits the banning of motion picture films on the ground that they are "sacrilegious." That statute . . provides:

"The director of the [motion picture] division [of the education department] shall cause to be promptly examined every motion picture film submitted . . . ., and unless such film or a part thereof is obscene, indecent, immoral, inhuman, sacrilegious, or is of such a character that its exhibition would tend to corrupt morals or incite to crime, shall issue a license therefor. . . . ."

Appellant is a corporation engaged in the business of distributing motion pictures. It owns the exclusive rights to distribute throughout the United States a film produced in Italy entitled "The Miracle." On November 30, 1950, after having examined the picture, the motion picture division . . . issued to appellant a license authorizing exhibition of "The Miracle," with English subtitles, as one part of a trilogy called "Ways of Love." Thereafter, for a period of approximately eight weeks, "Ways of Love" was exhibited publicly in a motion picture theater in New York City . . . .

During this period, the New York State Board of Regents, which by statute is made the head of the education department, received "hundreds of letters, telegrams, post cards, affidavits and other communications" both protesting against and defending the public exhibition of "The Miracle." . . . On February 16, 1951, the Regents, after viewing "The Miracle," determined that it was "sacrilegious" and for that reason ordered the Commissioner of Education to rescind appellant's license to exhibit the picture. The Commissioner did so.

Appellant brought the present action in the New York courts to review the determination of the Regents. Among the claims advanced by appellant were (1) that the statute violates the Fourteenth Amendment as a prior restraint upon freedom of speech and of the press; (2) that it is invalid under the same Amendment as a violation of the guaranty of separate church and state and as a prohibition of the free exercise of religion; and, (3) that the term "sacrilegious" is so vague and indefinite as to offend due process. . . *← appellant's case*

As we view the case, we need consider only appellant's contention that the New York statute is an unconstitutional abridgment of free speech and a free press. [T]he present case is the first to present squarely to us the question whether motion pictures are within the ambit of protection which the First Amendment, through the Fourteenth, secures to any form of "speech" or "the press." *← what court will consider*

It cannot be doubted that motion pictures are a significant medium for the communication of ideas. . . . . The importance of motion pictures as an organ of public opinion is not lessened by the fact that they are designed to entertain as well as to inform. . . . .

defendant's position

It is urged that motion pictures do not fall within the First Amendment's aegis because their production, distribution, and exhibition is a large-scale business conducted for private profit. We cannot agree. That books, newspapers, and magazines are published and sold for profit does not prevent them from being a form of expression whose liberty is safeguarded by the First Amendment. We fail to see why operation for profit should have any different effect in the case of motion pictures.

defen. position →

It is further urged that motion pictures possess a greater capacity for evil, particularly among the youth of a community, than other modes of expression. Even if one were to accept this hypothesis, it does not follow that motion pictures should be disqualified from First Amendment protection. If there be capacity for evil it may be relevant in determining the permissible scope of community control, but it does not authorize substantially unbridled censorship such as we have here. For the foregoing reasons, we conclude that expression by means of motion pictures is included within the free speech and free press guaranty of the First and Fourteenth Amendments. . . .

To hold that liberty of expression by means of motion pictures is guaranteed by the First and Fourteenth Amendments, however, is not the end of our problem. It does not follow that the Constitution requires absolute freedom to exhibit every motion picture of every kind at all times and all places. . . . Nor does it follow that motion pictures are necessarily subject to the precise rules governing any other particular method of expression. Each method tends to present its own peculiar problems. But the basic principles of freedom of speech and the press, like the First Amendment's command, do not vary. Those principles, as they have frequently been enunciated by this Court, make freedom of expression the rule. There is no justification in this case for making an exception to that rule.

The statute involved here does not seek to punish, as a past offense, speech or writing falling within the permissible scope of subsequent punishment. On the contrary, New York requires that permission to communicate ideas be obtained in advance from state officials who judge the content of the words and pictures sought to be communicated. This Court recognized many years ago that such a previous restraint is a form of infringement upon freedom of expression to be especially condemned. Near v. Minnesota, 283 U.S. 697 (1931).

previous restraint is prohibited

New York's highest court says there is "nothing mysterious" about the statutory provision applied in this case: "It is simply this: that no religion, as that word is understood by the ordinary, reasonable person, shall be treated with contempt, mockery, scorn and ridicule . . .." This is far from the kind of narrow exception to freedom of expression which a state may carve out to satisfy the adverse demands of other interests of society. In seeking to apply the broad and all-inclusive definition of "sacrilegious" given by the New York courts, the censor is set adrift upon a boundless sea amid a myriad of conflicting currents of religious views, with no charts but those provided by the most vocal and powerful orthodoxies. New York cannot vest such unlimited restraining control over motion pictures in a censor. . . . Under such a standard the most careful and tolerant censor would find it virtually impossible to avoid favoring one religion over another, and he would be subject to an inevitable tendency to ban the expression of unpopular sentiments sacred to a religious minority. Application of the "sacrilegious" test, in these or other respects, might raise substantial questions under the First Amendment's guaranty of separate church and state with freedom of worship for all. However, from the standpoint of freedom of speech and the press, it is enough to point out that the state has no legitimate interest in protecting any or all religions from views distasteful to them which is sufficient to justify prior restraints upon the expression of those views. It is not the business of *court opinion* government in our nation to suppress real or imagined attacks upon a particular religious doctrine, whether they appear in publications, speeches, or motion pictures.

Since the term "sacrilegious" is the sole standard under attack here, it is not necessary for us to decide, for example, whether a state may censor motion pictures under a clearly drawn statute designed and applied to prevent the showing of obscene films. That is a very different question from the one now before us. We hold only that under the First and Fourteenth Amendments a state may not ban a flim on the basis of a censor's conclusion that it is "sacrilegious."

Reversed.

Mr. Justice REED, concurring in the judgment of the Court.

. . . This film does not seem to me to be of a character that the First Amendment permits a state to exclude from public view.

Mr. Justice FRANKFURTER, whom Mr. Justice JACKSON joins, concurring in the judgment of the Court; Mr. Justice BURTON, having concurred in the opinion of the Court, also joins this opinion. . . .

. . . Prohibition through words that fail to convey what is permitted and what is prohibited for want of appropriate objective standards, offends Due Process in two ways. First, it does not sufficiently apprise those bent on obedience of law of what may reasonably be foreseen to be found illicit by the law-enforcing authority, whether court or jury or administrative agency. Secondly, where licensing is rested, in the first instance, in an administrative agency, the available judicial review is in effect rendered inoperative. On the basis of such a portmanteau word as "sacrilegious," the judiciary has no standards with which to judge the validity of administrative action which necessarily involves, at least in large measure, subjective determinations. Thus, the administrative first step becomes the last step. . . . This principle is especially to be observed when what is so vague seeks to fetter the mind and put within unascertainable bounds the varieties of religious experience.

PRIOR VERSUS SUBSEQUENT RESTRAINT OF OBSCENITY— THE KINGSLEY BOOKS CASE

Kingsley Books v. Brown, 354 U.S. 436 (1957), sustained a special procedure under New York law which, as a supplement to the existing conventional criminal provision dealing with pornography, authorized the legal officer of a municipality to invoke a limited injunctive remedy against the sale and distribution of written and printed matter found after due trial to be obscene, and to obtain an order for the seizure of condemned publications. The statute, § 22–a, required a trial within one day after joinder of issue, and a decision within two days of the end of the trial. Kingsley's books were found obscene, further distribution was enjoined, and destruction of the materials was ordered. The publisher did not challenge the finding of obscenity, but objected to the injunction as a prior restraint. The Supreme Court sustained the procedure. Justice Frankfurter's opinion stated:

"The judicial angle of vision in testing the validity of a statute like § 22–a is 'the operation and effect of the statute in substance.' . . . The phrase 'prior restraint' is not a self-wielding sword. Nor can it serve as a talismanic test. The duty of closer analysis and critical judgment in applying the thought behind the phrase has thus been authoritatively put by one who brings weighty learning to his support of constitutionally protected liberties: 'What is needed,' writes Professor Paul A. Freund, 'is a pragmatic assessment of its operation in the particular circumstances. The generalization that prior restraint is particularly obnoxious in civil liberties cases must yield to more particularistic analysis.' The Supreme Court and Civil Liberties, 4 Vand.L.Rev. 533, 539 [also in Selected Essays 1938–62 (1963), 449].

"Wherein does § 22–a differ in its effective operation from the type of statute upheld in Alberts [decided with the Roth case, supra, p. 1227]? . . . Instead of requiring the bookseller to dread that the offer for sale of a book may, without prior warning, subject him to a criminal prosecution . . ., the civil procedure assures him that such consequences cannot follow unless he ignores a court order specifically directed to him for a prompt and carefully circumscribed determination of the issue of obscenity. Until then, he may keep the book for sale and sell it on his own judgment rather than steer 'nervously among the treacherous shoals.' . . .

"Criminal enforcement and the proceeding under § 22–a interfere with a book's solicitation of the public precisely at the same stage. In each situation the law moves after publication; the book need not in either case have yet passed into the hands of the public. . . . In each case the bookseller is put on notice by the complaint that sale of the publication charged with obscenity in the period before trial may subject him to penal consequences. In the one case he may suffer fine and imprisonment for violation of the criminal statute, in the other, for disobedience of the temporary injunction. The bookseller may of course stand his ground and confidently believe that in any judicial proceeding the book could not be condemned as obscene, but both modes of procedure provide an effective deterrent against distribution prior to adjudication of the book's content—the threat of subsequent penalization. . . . In each case a judge is the conventional trier of fact; in each, a jury may as a matter of discretion be summoned. . . .

"It only remains to say that the difference between Near v. Minnesota, supra, and this case is glaring in fact. The two cases are no less glaringly different when judged by the appropriate criteria of constitutional law. . . . Unlike Near, § 22–a is concerned solely with obscenity and, as authoritatively construed, it studiously withholds restraint upon matters not already published and not yet found to be offensive." Chief Justice Warren and Justices Black, Douglas, and Brennan dissented.

MOTION PICTURE CENSORSHIP, PRIOR RESTRAINT, AND THE TIMES FILM CASE

After the decision in Burstyn v. Wilson, the Court, in a number of per curiam decisions citing Burstyn and Winters v. New York, 333 U.S.

Holds you cannot reject totally prior restraint.

507 (1948), found various restrictions unconstitutional because of the vagueness of the standards. See Gelling v. Texas, 343 U.S. 960 (1952) ("prejudicial to the best interests of the people of the city"); Superior Films v. Department of Education and Commercial Pictures v. Regents, 346 U.S. 587 (1954) ("moral, educational or amusing and harmless character" and "immoral" or "tend to corrupt morals"). After the Court held in Roth, p. 1227, supra, that "obscenity" was a sufficiently specific standard in criminal legislation, film censorship cases produced a variety of reactions from the Justices—most commonly, as in the publications area, a tendency to limit adjudication to the particular film involved. Compare the variety of views in the Kingsley Pictures case, p. 1237, supra. But in Times Film Corp. v. Chicago, 365 U.S. 43 (1961), the Court considered and rejected a "broadside attack" on film censorship.

Times Film involved a Chicago ordinance which required submission of all motion pictures for examination by city officials prior to public exhibition. Petitioner refused to submit his film for examination and sued for issuance of the permit, claiming that the submission requirement was invalid on its face as a prior restraint. Justice Clark's majority opinion pointed out that the validity of the Chicago standards for denying a permit and the content of the film were not before the Court. He stated the sole "justiciable issue" to be "whether the ambit of constitutional protection includes complete and absolute freedom to exhibit, at least once, any and every kind of motion picture." The Court refused to hold "that the public exhibition of motion pictures must be allowed under any circumstances," with the state limited to criminal penalties after exhibition. Justice Clark stated that there was no "absolute privilege against prior restraint" and that the submission requirement was accordingly not "void on its face."

Chief Justice Warren's dissent, joined by Justices Black, Douglas and Brennan, insisted that the Court had stated the question too broadly. He claimed that the issue was whether Chicago could "require all motion picture exhibitors to submit all films" to a city official for licensing and censorship prior to public exhibition. He stated that the decision presented "a real danger of eventual censorship for every form of communication." Justice Douglas also submitted a dissenting opinion, joined by Chief Justice Warren and Justice Black.

FREEDMAN v. MARYLAND

380 U.S. 51, 85 S.Ct. 734, 13 L.Ed.2d 649 (1965).

Appeal from the Court of Appeals of Maryland.

Mr. Justice BRENNAN delivered the opinion of the Court.

Appellant sought to challenge the constitutionality of the Maryland motion picture censorship statute, Md.Ann.Code, 1957, Art. 66A, and exhibited the film "Revenge at Daybreak" at his Baltimore theatre without first submitting the picture to the State Board of Censors as required by § 2 of the statute. The State concedes that the picture does not violate the statutory standards and would have received a license if properly submitted, but the appellant was convicted of a § 2 violation despite his contention that the statute in its entirety unconstitutionally impaired freedom of expression. The Court of Appeals of Maryland affirmed . . . . . We reverse.

I.

In Times Film Corp. v. City of Chicago, 365 U.S. 43, we considered and upheld a requirement of submission of motion pictures in advance of exhibition. The Court of Appeals held, on the authority of that decision, that "the Maryland censorship law must be held to be not void on its face . . . ." This reliance on Times Film was misplaced. The only question tendered for decision in that case was "whether a prior restraint was necessarily unconstitutional *under all circumstances.*" . . .

Freedman's case ← Unlike the petitioner in Times Film, appellant does not argue that § 2 is unconstitutional simply because it may prevent even the first showing of a film whose exhibition may legitimately be the subject of an obscenity prosecution. He presents a question quite distinct from that passed on in Times Film; accepting the rule in Times Film, he argues that § 2 constitutes an invalid prior restraint because, in the context of the remainder of the statute, it presents a danger of unduly suppressing protected expression. He focuses particularly on the procedure for an initial decision by the censorship board, which, without any judicial participation, effectively bars exhibition of any disapproved film, unless and until the exhibitor undertakes a time-consuming appeal to the Maryland courts and succeeds in having the Board's decision reversed. Under the statute, the exhibitor is required to submit the film to the Board for examination, but no time limit is imposed for completion of Board action, § 17. If the film is disapproved, or any elimination ordered, § 19 provides that

> "the person submitting such film . . . will receive immediate notice . . ., and if appealed from, such film . . . will be promptly re-examined, . . . and the same finally approved or disapproved promptly after such re-examination, with the right of appeal from the decision of the Board to the Baltimore City Court . . . . . There shall be a further right of appeal . . . to the Court of Appeals of Maryland . . . ."

Thus there is no statutory provision for judicial participation in the procedure which bars a film, nor even assurance of prompt judicial review. Risk of delay is built into the Maryland procedure, as is borne out by experience; in the only reported case indicating the length of time required to complete an appeal, the initial judicial determination has taken four months and final vindication of the film on appellate review, six months. . . .

In the light of the difference between the issues presented here and in Times Film, the Court of Appeals erred in saying that, since appellant's refusal to submit the film to the Board was a violation only of § 2, "he has restricted himself to an attack on that section alone, and lacks standing to challenge any of the other provisions (or alleged short-comings) of the statute." . . . Appellant has not challenged the submission requirement in a vacuum but in a concrete statutory context. His contention is that § 2 effects an invalid prior restraint because the structure of the other provisions of the statute contributes to the infirmity of § 2; he does not assert that the other provisions are independently invalid. *weakness*

In the area of freedom of expression it is well established that one has standing to challenge a statute on the ground that it delegates overly broad licensing discretion to an administrative office, whether or not his conduct could be proscribed by a properly drawn statute, and whether or not he applied for a license. "One who might have had a license for the asking may . . . call into question the whole scheme of licensing when he is prosecuted for failure to procure it." Thornhill v. State of Alabama, 310 U.S. 88, 97 . . . . Standing is recognized in such cases because of the ". . . danger of tolerating, in the area of First Amendment freedoms, the existence of a penal statute susceptible of sweeping and improper application." NAACP v. Button, 371 U.S. 415, 433 . . . . Although we have no occasion to decide whether the vice of overbroadness infects the Maryland statute, we think that appellant's assertion of a similar danger in the Maryland apparatus of censorship—one always fraught with danger and viewed with suspicion—gives him standing to make that challenge. In substance his argument is that, because the apparatus operates in a statutory context in which judicial review may be too little and too late, the Maryland statute lacks sufficient safeguards for confining the censor's action to judicially determined constitutional limits, and therefore contains the same vice as a statute delegating excessive administrative discretion.

II.

[I]t is as true [of motion pictures] as of other forms of expression that "[a]ny system of prior restraints of expression comes to this Court bearing a heavy presumption against its constitutional validity." Bantam Books, Inc. v. Sullivan, 372 U.S. at 70 . . . . The administration of a censorship system for motion pictures presents peculiar dangers to constitutionally protected speech. Unlike a prosecution for obscenity, a censorship proceeding puts the initial burden on the exhibitor or distributor. Because the censor's business is to censor, there inheres the danger that he may well be less responsive than a court—part of an independent branch of government—to the constitutionally protected interests in free expression.[1] And if it is made unduly onerous, by reason of delay or otherwise, to seek judicial review, the censor's determination may in practice be final.

Applying the settled rule of our cases, we hold that a noncriminal process which requires the prior submission of a film to a censor avoids constitutional infirmity only if it takes place under procedural safeguards designed to obviate the dangers of a censorship system. First, the burden of proving that the film is unprotected expression must rest on the censor. As we said in Speiser v. Randall, 357 U.S. 513, 526, "Where the transcendent value of speech is involved, due process certainly requires . . . that the State bear the burden of persuasion to show that the appellants engaged in criminal speech." Second, while the State may require advance submission of all films, in order to proceed effectively to bar all showings of unprotected films, the requirement cannot be administered in a manner which would lend an effect of finality to the censor's determination whether a film constitutes protected expression. The teaching of our cases is that, because only a judicial determination in an adversary proceeding ensures the necessary sensitivity to freedom of expression, only a procedure requiring a judicial determination suffices to impose a valid final restraint. . . . To this end, the exhibitor must be assured, by statute or authoritative judicial construction, that the

---

1. See Emerson, The Doctrine of Prior Restraint, 20 L. & Contemp.Prob. 648, 656–659 (1955). This is well illustrated by the fact that the Maryland Court of Appeals has reversed the Board's disapproval in every reported case. . . . [Footnote by the Court.]

censor will, within a specified brief period, either issue a license or go to court to restrain showing the film. Any restraint imposed in advance of a final judicial determination on the merits must similarly be limited to preservation of the status quo for the shortest fixed period compatible with sound judicial resolution. Moreover, we are well aware that, even after expiration of a temporary restraint, an administrative refusal to license, signifying the censor's view that the film is unprotected, may have a discouraging effect on the exhibitor. . . . Therefore, the procedure must also assure a prompt final judicial decision, to minimize the deterrent effect of an interim and possibly erroneous denial of a license.

Without these safeguards, it may prove too burdensome to seek review of the censor's determination. Particularly in the case of motion pictures, it may take very little to deter exhibition in a given locality. The exhibitor's stake in any one picture may be insufficient to warrant a protracted and onerous course of litigation. The distributor, on the other hand, may be equally unwilling to accept the burdens and delays of litigation in a particular area when, without such difficulties, he can freely exhibit his film in most of the rest of the country; for we are told that only four States and a handful of municipalities have active censorship laws.[2]

It is readily apparent that the Maryland procedural scheme does not satisfy these criteria. First, once the censor disapproves the film, the exhibitor must assume the burden of instituting judicial proceedings and of persuading the courts that the film is protected expression. Second, once the Board has acted against a film, exhibition is prohibited pending judicial review, however protracted. Under the statute, appellant could have been convicted if he had shown the film after unsuccessfully seeking a license, even though no court had ever ruled on the obscenity of the film. Third, it is abundantly clear that the Maryland statute provides no assurance of prompt judicial determination. We hold, therefore, that appellant's conviction must be reversed. The Maryland scheme fails to provide adequate safeguards against undue inhibition of protected expression, and this renders the § 2 requirement of prior submission of films to the Board an invalid previous restraint.

III.

How or whether Maryland is to incorporate the required procedural safeguards in the statutory scheme is, of course, for the State to decide. But a model is not lacking: . . . . The New York procedure [in Kingsley Books v. Brown, p. 1265, supra] operates without prior submission to a censor, but the chilling effect of a censorship order, even one which requires judicial action for its enforcement, suggests all the more reason for expeditious determination of the question whether a particular film is constitutionally protected. . . . .

The requirement of prior submission to a censor sustained in Times Film is consistent with our recognition that films differ from other forms of expression. Similarly, we think that the nature of the motion picture in-

2. An appendix to the brief *amici curiae* of the American Civil Liberties Union and its Maryland Branch lists New York, Virginia and Kansas as the three States having statutes similar to the Maryland statute, and the cities of Chicago, Detroit, Fort Worth and Providence as having similar ordinances. Twenty-eight of the remaining 39 municipal ordinances and codes are listed as "inactive." [Footnote by the Court.]

dustry may suggest different time limits for a judicial determination. It is common knowledge that films are scheduled well before actual exhibition, and the requirement of advance submission in § 2 recognizes this. One possible scheme would be to allow the exhibitor or distributor to submit his film early enough to ensure an orderly final disposition of the case before the scheduled exhibition date—far enough in advance so that the exhibitor could safely advertise the opening on a normal basis. Failing such a scheme or sufficiently early submission under such a scheme, the statute would have to require adjudication considerably more prompt than has been the case under the Maryland statute. Otherwise, litigation might be unduly expensive and protracted, or the victorious exhibitor might find the most propitious opportunity for exhibition past. We do not mean to lay down rigid time limits or procedures, but to suggest considerations in drafting legislation to accord with local exhibition practices, and in doing so to avoid the potentially chilling effect of the Maryland statute on protected expression.

Reversed.*

Mr. Justice DOUGLAS, whom Mr. Justice BLACK joins, concurring.

On several occasions I have indicated my view that movies are entitled to the same degree and kind of protection under the First Amendment as other forms of expression. . . . [1]

. . . I do not believe any form of censorship—no matter how speedy or prolonged it may be—is permissible. As I see it, a pictorial presentation occupies as preferred a position as any other form of expression. . . . I would put an end to all forms and types of censorship and give full literal meaning to the command of the First Amendment.

SMITH v. CALIFORNIA

361 U.S. 147, 80 S.Ct. 215, 4 L.Ed.2d 205 (1959)

Appeal from the Appellate Department of the Superior Court of California, Los Angeles County.

Mr. Justice BRENNAN delivered the opinion of the Court.

Appellant, the proprietor of a bookstore, was convicted in a California Municipal Court under a Los Angeles city ordinance which makes it unlawful "for any person to have in his possession any obscene or indecent writing, [or] book . . . in any place of business where . . . books . . . are sold or kept for sale." The offense was defined . . . as consisting

---

* Note the relevance of the procedural protections emphasized in Freedman to other First Amendment areas— e. g., hearings on ex parte injunctions, Carroll v. President & Comm'rs of Princess Anne, 393 U.S. 175 (1968) (p. 1188, supra). See generally Monaghan, "First Amendment 'Due Process,'" 83 Harv.L.Rev. 518 (1970).

1. The Court today holds that a system of movie censorship must contain at least three procedural safeguards if it is not to run afoul of the First Amendment: (1) the censor must have the burden of instituting judicial proceedings; (2) any restraint prior to judicial review can be imposed only briefly in order to preserve the status quo; and (3) a prompt judicial determination of obscenity must be assured. Thus the Chicago censorship system, upheld by the narrowest of margins in Times Film Corp. v. City of Chicago, 365 U.S. 43, could not survive under today's standards, for it provided not one of these safeguards, as the dissenters there expressly pointed out. . . . [Footnote by Justice Douglas.]

solely of the possession in the appellant's bookstore, of a certain book found upon judicial investigation to be obscene. The definition included no element of scienter—knowledge by appellant of the contents of the book. . .

California here imposed a strict or absolute criminal responsibility on appellant not to have obscene books in his shop. "The existence of a *mens rea* is the rule of, rather than the exception to, the principles of Anglo-American criminal jurisprudence." Dennis v. United States, 341 U.S. 494, 500. Still, it is doubtless competent for the States to create strict criminal liabilities by defining criminal offenses without any element of scienter . . . . But the question here is as to the validity of this ordinance's elimination of the scienter requirement—an elimination which may tend to work a substantial restriction on freedom of speech. Our decisions furnish examples of legal devices and doctrines in most applications consistent with the Constitution, which cannot be applied in settings where they have the collateral effect of inhibiting the freedom of expression, by making the individual the more reluctant to exercise it. The States generally may regulate the allocation of the burden of proof in their courts, and it is a common procedural device to impose on a taxpayer the burden of proving his entitlement to exemptions from taxation, but where we conceived that this device was being applied in a manner tending to cause even a self-imposed restriction of free expression, we struck down its application. Speiser v. Randall, 357 U.S. 513. See Near v. Minnesota. . . . It has been stated here that the usual doctrines as to the separability of constitutional and unconstitutional applications of statutes may not apply where their effect is to leave standing a statute patently capable of many unconstitutional applications, threatening those who validly exercise their rights of free expression with the expense and inconvenience of criminal prosecution. Thornhill v. Alabama, 310 U.S. 88, 97–98. . . . And this Court has intimated that stricter standards of permissible statutory vagueness may be applied to a statute having a potentially inhibiting effect on speech; a man may the less be required to act at his peril here, because the free dissemination of ideas may be the loser. Winters v. New York, 333 U.S. 507. Very much to the point here, where the question is the elimination of the mental element in an offense, is this Court's holding in Wieman v. Updegraff, 344 U.S. 183 [p. 1301, infra]. There an oath as to past freedom from membership in subversive organizations, exacted by a State as a qualification for public employment, was held to violate the Constitution in that it made no distinction between members who had, and those who had not, known of the organization's character. . . .

These principles guide us to our decision here. We have held that obscene speech and writings are not protected by the constitutional guarantees of freedom of speech and the press. [Roth.] The ordinance here in question, to be sure, only imposes criminal sanctions on a bookseller if there in fact is to be found in his shop an obscene book. But our holding in Roth does not recognize any state power to restrict the dissemination of books which are not obscene; and we think this ordinance's strict liability feature would tend seriously to have that effect, by penalizing booksellers, even though they had not the slightest notice of the character of the books they sold. The appellee and the court below analogize this strict-liability penal ordinance to familiar forms of penal statutes which dispense with any element of knowledge on the part of the person charged, food and drug legislation being a principal example. We find the analogy instructive in our examination of the question before us. The usual rationale for such statutes is that the public interest in the purity of its food is so great as to warrant the imposition of the highest standard of care on distributors—in fact an absolute standard which will not hear the distributor's plea as to the amount of care he has used. Cf. United States v. Balint, 258 U.S. 250, 252–253, 254. His ignorance of the character of the food is irrelevant. There is no specific constitutional inhibition against making the distributors of food the strictest censors of their merchandise, but the constitutional guarantees of the freedom of speech and of the press stand in the way of imposing a similar requirement on the bookseller. By dispensing with any requirement of knowledge of the contents of the book on the part of the seller, the ordinance tends to impose a severe limitation on the public's access to constitutionally-protected matter. For if the bookseller is criminally liable without knowledge of the contents, and the ordinance fulfills its purpose, he will tend to restrict the books he sells to those he has inspected; and thus the State will have imposed a restriction upon the distribution of constitutionally protected as well as obscene literature. . . . If the contents of bookshops and periodical stands were restricted to material of which their proprietors had made an inspection, they might be depleted indeed. The bookseller's limitation in the amount of reading material with which he could familiarize himself, and his timidity in the face of his absolute criminal liability, thus would tend to restrict the public's access to forms of the printed word which the State could not constitutionally suppress directly. The bookseller's self-censorship, compelled by the State, would be a censorship affecting the whole public, hardly less virulent for being privately administered. Through it, the distribution of all books, both obscene and not obscene, would be impeded.

It is argued that unless the scienter requirement is dispensed with, regulation of the distribution of obscene material will be ineffective, as booksellers will falsely disclaim knowledge of their books' contents or falsely deny reason to suspect their obscenity. We might observe that it has been some time now since the law viewed itself as impotent to explore the actual state of a man's mind. . . .

We need not and most definitely do not pass today on what sort of mental element is requisite to a constitutionally permissible prosecution of a bookseller for carrying an obscene book in stock; whether honest mistake as to whether its contents in fact constituted obscenity need be an excuse; whether there might be circumstances under which the State constitutionally might require that a bookseller investigate further, or might put on him the burden of explaining why he did not, and what such circumstances might be. Doubtless any form of criminal obscenity statute applicable to a bookseller will induce some tendency to self-censorship and have some inhibitory effect on the dissemination of material not obscene, but we consider today only one which goes to the extent of eliminating all mental elements from the crime.

. . . The existence of the State's power to prevent the distribution of obscene matter does not mean that there can be no constitutional barrier to any form of practical exercise of that power. Cf. Dean Milk Co. v. City of Madison, 340 U.S. 349. It is plain to us that the ordinance in question, though aimed at obscene matter, has such a tendency to inhibit constitutionally protected expression that it cannot stand under the Constitution.

Reversed.

Mr. Justice BLACK, concurring. . . .

Censorship is the deadly enemy of freedom and progress. The plain language of the Constitution forbids it. I protest against the judiciary giving it a foothold here

Mr. Justice FRANKFURTER, concurring. . . .

The uncertainties pertaining to the scope of scienter requisite for an obscenity prosecution and the speculative proof that the issue is likely to entail, are considerations that reinforce the right of one charged with obscenity— a right implicit in the very nature of the legal concept of obscenity—to enlighten the judgment of the tribunal, be it the jury or as in this case the judge, regarding the prevailing literary and moral community standards and to do so through qualified experts. It is immaterial whether the basis of the exclusion of such testimony is irrelevance, or the incompetence of experts to testify to such matters. The two reasons coalesce, for community standards or the psychological or physiological consequences of questioned literature can as a matter of fact hardly be established except through experts. Therefore, to exclude such expert testimony is in effect to exclude as irrelevant evidence that goes to the very essence of the defense and therefore to the constitutional safeguards of due process. . . .

Mr. Justice DOUGLAS, concurring. . . .

. . . This role of censor in which we find ourselves is not an edifying one. But since by the prevailing school of thought we must perform it, I see no harm, and perhaps some good, in the rule fashioned by the Court which requires a showing of *scienter.* . . .

Mr. Justice HARLAN, concurring in part and dissenting in part.

. . . In my view . . . the *scienter* question involves considerations of a different order depending on whether a state or a federal statute is involved. We have here a state ordinance, and on the meager data before us I would not reach the question whether the absence of a *scienter* element renders the ordinance unconstitutional. I must say, however, that the generalities in the Court's opinion striking down the ordinance leave me unconvinced. . . .

In my opinion this conviction is fatally defective in that the trial judge, as I read the record, turned aside *every* attempt by appellant to introduce evidence bearing on community standards. The exclusionary rulings were not limited to offered expert testimony. This had the effect of depriving appellant of the opportunity to offer any proof of a constitutionally relevant issue. On this ground I would reverse the judgment below, and remand the case for a new trial.

OTHER PROCEDURAL SAFEGUARDS IN STATE CONTROL OF OBSCENE PUBLICATIONS

1. *Searches and seizures.* a. In Marcus v. Search Warrants of Property, 367 U.S. 717 (1961), the Court, in an opinion by Justice Brennan, found that Missouri's use of "the search and seizure power to suppress obscene publications involved abuses inimical to protected expression" because the "procedures as applied in this case lacked the safeguards which due process demands to assure nonobscene material the constitutional protection to which it

is entitled." Acting ex parte, a state judge issued warrants authorizing the seizure of any obscene publications at six places of business. The police seized "approximately 11,000 copies of 280 publications." About two weeks later, a hearing was held at which the owners of the publications appeared. About seven weeks thereafter, the judge ruled that 100 of the publications were obscene and should be held for ultimate burning. The Court emphasized that the warrants were issued "on the strength of the conclusory allegations of a single police officer"; that the officers executing the warrants "made ad hoc decisions on the spot"; and that the officers' task "was simply an impossible one to perform with any realistic expectation that the obscene might be accurately separated from the constitutionally protected." It concluded that "discretion to seize allegedly obscene materials cannot be confided to law enforcement officials without greater safeguards than were here operative." The Court found the state's reliance on the Kingsley Books case [p. 1265, supra] "misplaced," since the Missouri restriction on circulation "was far more thoroughgoing and drastic." Justice Black, joined by Justice Douglas, concurred because "the State has used a general warrant in this case in violation of the prohibitions of the Fourth and Fourteenth Amendments."

b.   A Quantity of Books v. Kansas, 378 U.S. 205 (1964), also involved action under a statute "authorizing the seizure of allegedly obscene books before an adversary determination of their obscenity." Here however, the officers had no discretion as to which books they might seize: the warrant specifically designated the books by their titles. Relying heavily on Marcus, Justice Brennan's plurality opinion—joined by Chief Justice Warren, Justice White, and Justice Goldberg—nevertheless held the procedures "constitutionally insufficient because they did not adequately safeguard against the suppression of nonobscene books." Justice Black, joined by Justice Douglas, voted to reverse without considering "the procedural questions"; he insisted that the Kansas "book-burning" statute was a substantive violation of the First Amendment. Justice Harlan's dissent, joined by Justice Clark, insisted that "the present case is governed by the principles serving to sustain the New York procedure involved in Kingsley Books rather than those which condemned that followed by Missouri in Marcus."

2.   *Blacklists.* In Bantam Books, Inc. v. Sullivan, 372 U.S. 58 (1963), the Court condemned certain activities of the Rhode Island Commission to Encourage Morality in Youth as unconstitutional "informal censorship." The Commission compiled and distributed lists of "objectionable" publications and sought "cooperation" in order to "eliminate the necessity of our recommending prosecution to the Attorney General's department." Justice Brennan's opinion for the Court stated: "It would be naive to credit the State's assertion that these blacklists are in the nature of mere legal advice, when they plainly serve as instruments of regulation independent of the laws against obscenity. . . . Herein lies the vice of the system. The Commission's operation is a form of effective state regulation superimposed upon the State's criminal regulation of obscenity and making such regulation largely unnecessary. In thus obviating the need to employ criminal sanctions, the State has at the same time eliminated the safeguards of the criminal process." Justice Douglas joined the opinion of the Court in a separate opinion; Justices Black and Clark concurred in the result. Justice Harlan's dissent objected to the Court's "opaque pronouncements which leave the Commission in the dark as to the permissible constitutional scope of its future activities."

SECTION 3. INTERFERENCE WITH THE ADMINISTRATION OF JUSTICE

CRAIG v. HARNEY

331 U.S. 367, 67 S.Ct. 1249, 91 L.Ed. 1546 (1947).

Certiorari to the Court of Criminal Appeals of Texas.

Opinion of the Court by Mr. Justice DOUGLAS . . ..

Petitioners were adjudged guilty of constructive criminal contempt by the County Court of Nueces County, Texas, and sentenced to jail for three days. They sought to challenge the legality of their confinement by applying to the Court of Criminal Appeals for a writ of habeas corpus. That court by a divided vote denied the writ and remanded petitioners to the custody of the county sheriff. . . . The case is here on a petition for a writ of certiorari which we granted because of the importance of the problem and because the ruling of the Texas court raised doubts whether it conformed to the principles announced in Bridges v. California, 314 U.S. 252 [1941],[1] and Pennekamp v. Florida, 328 U.S. 331 [1946].[2]

Petitioners are a publisher, an editorial writer, and a news reporter of newspapers published in Corpus Christi, Texas. [In the course of a case in the local courts petitioners were charged with contempt by publication because of certain editorial and news stories in the newspapers with which petitioners were connected.]

The Court of Criminal Appeals, in denying the writ of habeas corpus, stated that the "issue before us" is "whether the publications . . . were reasonably calculated to interfere with the due administration of justice" in the pending case. . . . It concluded that the facts of this case satisfied the "clear and present danger" rule of the Bridges case. . . .

1. In the Bridges case, a newspaper editorially asserted that the trial judge should make an example of several union men then awaiting pronouncement of sentence. Moreover, Harry Bridges, a union official, caused the publication of a telegram to the Secretary of Labor stating that the CIO "does not intend to allow state courts to override the majority vote of members in choosing its officers and representatives and to override the National Labor Relations Board." Contempt citations resting on these publications were affirmed by the California Supreme Court, but the United States Supreme Court (in an opinion by Justice Black) reversed, holding that the 14th Amendment limited the state's power to adjudge contempts for publication. Punishment is permitted only where there is a clear and present danger that justice will be obstructed; the publications in question did not fall within that rule. Justice Frankfurter, joined by Chief Justice Stone and Justices Roberts and Byrnes, dissented: "A trial is not 'a free trade in ideas,' nor is the best test of truth in a courtroom 'the power of the thought to get itself accepted in the competition of the market.'"

2. In the Pennekamp case, a newspaper engaged in an anti-vice crusade published editorials and a cartoon implying that the judges were using legal technicalities to hinder the prosecution of several rape and gambling cases. The newspaper and its associate editor, Pennekamp, were held in contempt and fined by the Florida court. The Supreme Court, as in Bridges, applied the clear and present danger test and reversed: "What is meant by clear and present danger to a fair administration of justice? No definition could give an answer. Certainly this criticism of the judges' inclinations or actions in these pending non-jury proceedings could not directly affect such administration."

Neither [the Bridges and Pennekamp] cases nor the present one raises questions concerning the full reach of the power of the state to protect the administration of justice by its courts. The problem presented is only a narrow, albeit important, phase of that problem—the power of a court promptly and without a jury trial to punish for comment on cases pending before it and awaiting disposition. The history of the power to punish for contempt   .   .   .   and the unequivocal command of the First Amendment serve as constant reminders that freedom of speech and of the press should not be impaired through the exercise of that power, unless there is no doubt that the utterances in question are a serious and imminent threat to the administration of justice.

In a case where it is asserted that a person has been deprived by a state court of a fundamental right secured by the Constitution, an independent examination of the facts by this Court is often required to be made.   .   .   . This is such a case.

We start with the news articles.   .   .   .   They did not reflect good reporting, for they failed to reveal the precise issue before the judge.   .   .   . But it takes more imagination than we possess to find in this rather sketchy and one-sided report of a case any imminent or serious threat to a judge of reasonable fortitude.   .

The only substantial question raised pertains to the editorial. It called the judge's refusal to hear both sides "high handed," a "travesty on justice," and the reason that public opinion was "outraged." It said that his ruling properly "brought down the wrath of public opinion upon his head" since a service man "seems to be getting a raw deal." The fact that there was no appeal from his decision to a "judge who is familiar with proper procedure and able to interpret and weigh motions and arguments by opposing counsel and to make his decisions accordingly" was a "tragedy." It deplored the fact that the judge was a "layman" and not a "competent attorney". It concluded that the "first rule of justice" was to give both sides an opportunity to be heard and when that rule was "repudiated," there was "no way of knowing whether justice was done."   .   .   .

We agree with the court below that the editorial must be appraised in the setting of the news articles which both preceded and followed it. It must also be appraised in light of the community environment which prevailed at that time.   .   .   .   A judge who is part of such a dramatic episode can hardly help but know that his decision is apt to be unpopular. But the law of contempt is not made for the protection of judges who may be sensitive to the winds of public opinion. Judges are supposed to be men of fortitude, able to thrive in a hardy climate. Conceivably a campaign could be so managed and so aimed at the sensibilities of a particular judge and the matter pending before him as to cross the forbidden line. But the episodes we have here do not fall in that category. Nor can we assume that the trial judge was not a man of fortitude.   .   .   .

There is a suggestion that the case is different from Bridges v. California, supra, in that we have here only private litigation, while in the Bridges case labor controversies were involved, some of them being criminal cases. The thought apparently is that the range of permissible comment is greater where the pending case generates a public concern. The nature of the case may, of course, be relevant in determining whether the clear and present danger

test is satisfied.   But, the rule of the Bridges and Pennekamp cases is fashioned
to serve the needs of all litigation, not merely select types of pending cases.

Reversed.

[A concurring opinion by Mr. Justice MURPHY is omitted.]

Mr. Justice FRANKFURTER, with whom The Chief Justice [VINSON]
concurs, dissenting.

Today's decision, in effect though not in terms, holds unconstitutional
a power the possession of which by the States this Court has heretofore deemed
axiomatic.   .   .   .

Mr. Justice JACKSON, dissenting.   .   .   .

The right of the people to have a free press is a vital one, but so is the
right to have a calm and fair trial free from outside pressures and influences.
Every other right, including the right of a free press itself, may depend on
the ability to get a judicial hearing as dispassionate and impartial as the
weakness inherent in men will permit.   I think this publisher passed beyond
the legitimate use of press freedom and infringed the citizen's right to a
calm and impartial trial.   I do not think we can say that it is beyond the power
of the state to exert safeguards against such interference with the course of
trial as we have here.   .   .   .

The fact that [the judge] did not yield to it does not prove that the
attack was not an effective interference with the administration of justice.
The judge was put in a position in which he either must appear to yield his
judgment to public clamor or to defy public sentiment.   The consequence of
attacks may differ with the temperament of the judge.   Some judges may take
fright and yield while others become more set in their course if only to make
clear that they will not be bullied.   This judge was evidently of the latter
type.   He was diverted from the calm consideration of the litigation before
him by what he regarded as a duty to institute a contempt proceeding of his
own against his tormentors.

For this Court to imply that this kind of attack during a pending case
is all right seems to me to compound the wrong.   The press of the country
may rightfully take the decision of this Court to mean indifference toward,
if not approval of, such attacks upon courts during pending cases.   I think
this opinion conveys a wrong impression of the responsibilities of a free press
for the calm and dispassionate administration of justice and that we should
not hesitate to condemn what has been done here.

But even worse is that this Court appears to sponsor the myth that
judges are not as other men are, and that therefore newspaper attacks on
them are negligible because they do not penetrate the judicial armor.   .   .   .

From our sheltered position, fortified by life tenure and other defenses
to judicial independence, it is easy to say that this local judge ought to have
shown more fortitude in the face of criticism.   But he had no such protection.
He was an elective judge, who held office for a short term.   I do not take it
that an ambition of a judge to remain a judge is either unusual or dishonorable.
.   .   .   Of course, the blasts of these little papers in this small community
do not jolt us, but I am not so confident that we would be indifferent if a
news monopoly in our entire jurisdiction should perpetrate this kind of an
attack on us.   .   .   .

WOOD v. GEORGIA

370 U.S. 375, 82 S.Ct. 1364, 8 L.Ed.2d 569 (1962).

Certiorari to the Court of Appeals of Georgia.

Mr. Chief Justice WARREN delivered the opinion of the Court.

We granted certiorari to consider the scope of the constitutional protection to be enjoyed by persons when the publication of their thoughts and opinions is alleged to be in conflict with the fair administration of justice in state courts. The petitioner, an elected sheriff in Bibb County, Georgia, contends that the Georgia courts, in holding him in contempt of court for expressing his personal ideas on a matter that was presently before the grand jury for its consideration, have abridged his liberty of free speech . . . ..

On June 6, 1960, a judge of the Bibb Superior Court issued a charge to a regularly impaneled grand jury, giving it special instructions to conduct an investigation into a political situation which had allegedly arisen in the county. The jury was advised that there appeared to be "an inane and inexplicable pattern of Negro bloc voting" in Bibb County, and that "rumors and accusations" had been made which indicated candidates for public office had paid large sums of money in an effort to gain favor and to obtain the Negro vote. The charge explained that certain Negro leaders, after having met and endorsed a candidate, had switched their support to an opposing candidate who put up a large sum of money. [C]ertain questions were posed to the jury which it was to investigate in inquiring into the charges of election law violations. The instructions were given in the midst of a local political campaign and the judge, in order to publicize the investigation, requested reporters for all local news media to be present in the courtroom when the charge was delivered.

The following day, . . . the petitioner issued to the local press a written statement in which he criticized the judges' action and in which he urged the citizenry to take notice when their highest judicial officers threatened political intimidation and persecution of voters in the county under the guise of law enforcement. This news release, which was published and disseminated to the general public, stated:

> "Whatever the Judges' intention, the action . . . ordering [the grand jury] to investigate 'negro block voting' will be considered one of the most deplorable examples of race agitation to come out of Middle Georgia in recent years.

> "At a time when all thinking people want to preserve the good will and cooperation between the races in Bibb County, this action appears either as a crude attempt at judicial intimidation of negro voters and leaders, or, at best, as agitation for a 'negro vote' issue in local politics.
> . . .

> "Negro people will find little difference in principle between attempted intimidation of their people by judicial summons and inquiry and attempted intimidation by physical demonstration such as used by the K. K. K. . . .

> "It seems incredible that all three of our Superior Court Judges, who themselves hold high political office, are so politically nieve [naive] as to actually believe that the negro voters in Bibb County sell their

votes in any fashion, either to candidates for office or to some negro leaders.

"If anyone in the community [should] be free of racial prejudice, it should be our Judges. It is shocking to find a Judge charging a Grand Jury in the style and language of a race baiting candidate for political office. . . .

"James I. Wood."

The following day, the petitioner delivered to the bailiff of the court, stationed at the entrance to the grand jury room, "An Open Letter to the Bibb County Grand Jury," which was made available to the grand jury at petitioner's request. This letter, implying that the court's charge was false, asserted that in the petitioner's opinion, the Bibb County Democratic Executive Committee was the organization responsible for corruption in the purchasing of votes, and that the grand jury would be well-advised also to investigate that organization.

A month later, on July 7, 1960, the petitioner was cited in two counts of contempt based on the above statements. The citation charged that the language used by the petitioner was designed and calculated to be contemptuous of the court, to ridicule the investigation ordered by the charge, and "to hamper, hinder, interfere with and obstruct" the grand jury in its investigation. . . . An amendment to the citation alleged that the statements "in and of [themselves] created . . . a clear, present and imminent danger to the investigation being conducted . . . and . . . to the proper administration of justice in Bibb Superior Court."

The next day the petitioner issued a further press release in which he repeated substantially the charges he had made in the release on June 7, and in which he asserted that his defense to the contempt citation would be that he had spoken the truth. The contempt citation was thereupon amended by including a third count based on this latter statement. . . .

. . . No witnesses were presented at the hearing and no evidence was introduced to show that the publications resulted in any actual interference or obstruction of the court or the work of the grand jury. The gravamen of the contempt citation, and of the State's case against the petitioner, was that the mere publishing of the news release and defense statement constituted a contempt of court, and in and of itself was a clear and present danger to the administration of justice.

The trial court, without making any findings and without giving any reasons, adjudged petitioner guilty on all counts and imposed concurrent sentences of 20 days and separate fines of $200 on each. On writ of error to the Court of Appeals the convictions on counts one and three were affirmed and the conviction on count two, based on the open letter to the grand jury, was reversed. . . .

We start with the premise that the right of courts to conduct their business in an untrammeled way lies at the foundation of our system of government and that courts necessarily must possess the means of punishing for contempt when conduct tends directly to prevent the discharge of their functions. . . . Here it is asserted that the exercise of the contempt power, to commit a person to jail for an utterance out of the presence of the court, has abridged the accused's liberty of free expression. In this situation the burden upon this Court is to define the limitations upon the contempt power according to the terms of the Federal Constitution. . . . .

What court must decide

It is with these principles [of Bridges, Pennekamp, and Craig v. Harney, supra] in mind that we consider the case before us. . . .

This case differs from Bridges and Pennekamp, first, in that the court below has upheld petitioner's conviction on the basis that his conduct presented a clear and present danger to the proceedings of the court and grand jury, a standard this Court has held to warrant punishment for alleged contemptuous conduct. But state courts may not preclude us from our responsibility to examine "the evidence to see whether it furnishes a rational basis for the characterization put on it" . . . . by the enunciation of a constitutionally acceptable standard in describing the effect of the conduct. The ultimate responsibility to define the limits of state power regarding freedom of speech and expression rests with this Court, . . . and when it is claimed that such liberties have been abridged, we cannot allow a presumption of validity of the exercise of state power to interfere with our close examination of the substantive claim presented.

Despite its conclusion that the petitioner's conduct created a serious evil to the fair administration of justice, the Court of Appeals did not cite or discuss the Bridges, Pennekamp or Harney cases, nor did it display an awareness of the standards enunciated in those cases to support a finding of clear and present danger. It simply adopted as conclusions of law the allegations made in the contempt citation. The court did not indicate in any manner *how* the publications interfered with the grand jury's investigation, or with the administration of justice. [N]o showing was made that the members of the grand jury, upon reading the petitioner's comments in the newspapers, felt unable or unwilling to complete their assigned task because petitioner "interfered" with its completion. There is nothing in the record to indicate that the investigation was not ultimately successful or, if it was not, that the petitioner's conduct was responsible for its failure. . .

Thus we have simply been told, as a matter of law without factual support, that if a State is unable to punish persons for expressing their views on matters of great public importance when those matters are being considered in an investigation by the grand jury, a clear and present danger to the administration of justice will be created. We find no such danger in the record before us. The type of "danger" evidenced by the record is precisely one of the types of activity envisioned by the Founders in presenting the First Amendment for ratification. . . . Men are entitled to speak as they please on matters vital to them; errors in judgment or unsubstantiated opinions may be exposed, of course, but not through punishment for contempt for the expression. Under our system of government, counterargument and education are the weapons available to expose these matters, not abridgment of the rights of free speech and assembly. Cf. Mr. Justice Brandeis, concurring in Whitney v. California, 274 U.S. 357, 378. Hence, in the absence of some other showing of a substantive evil actually designed to impede the course of justice in justification of the exercise of the contempt power to silence the petitioner, his utterances are entitled to be protected.

The respondent attempts to distinguish this case from Bridges by offering, as support for the Georgia court's conclusion that the petitioner's conduct presented a clear and present danger to the administration of justice, the fact that here there was an alleged interference with a grand jury and not an attempt to influence or coerce a judge. In the circumstances of this case, we find this argument unpersuasive.

First, it is important to emphasize that this case does not represent a situation where an individual is on trial; there was no "judicial proceeding pending" in the sense that prejudice might result to one litigant or the other by ill-considered misconduct aimed at influencing the outcome of a trial or a grand jury proceeding. . . . Moreover, we need not pause here to consider the variant factors that would be present in a case involving a petit jury. Neither Bridges, Pennekamp nor Harney involved a trial by jury. . . .

. . . Particularly in matters of local political corruption and investigations is it important that freedom of communication be kept open and that the real issues not become obscured to the grand jury. . . . The necessity to society of an independent and informed grand jury becomes readily apparent in the context of the present case. For here a panel of judges, themselves elected officers and charged under state law with the responsibility of instructing a grand jury to investigate political corruption, have exercised the contempt power to hold in contempt another elected representative of the people for publishing views honestly held and contrary to those contained in the charge. And, an effort by the petitioner to prove the truth of his allegations was rejected, the court holding irrelevant the truth or falsity of the facts and opinions expressed in the publications. . . If the petitioner could be silenced in this manner, the problem to the people in the State of Georgia and indeed in all the States becomes evident.

The administration of the law is not the problem of the judge or prosecuting attorney alone, but necessitates the active cooperation of an enlightened public. Nothing is to be gained by an attitude on the part of the citizenry of civic irresponsibility and apathy in voicing their sentiments on community problems. The petitioner's attack on the charge to the grand jury would have been likely to have an impeding influence on the outcome of the investigation only if the charge was so manifestly unjust that it could not stand inspection. In this sense discussion serves as a corrective force to political, economic and other influences which are inevitably present in matters of grave importance. The charge given to the jury indicated that the motivation for it was founded on rumor, but that the situation had existed for several years. Yet the charge was directed primarily against one group in the community and was given at the height of the highly important Democratic primary, in which, because of their elected positions, both the judges and the petitioner were interested personally . . . .. The First Amendment envisions that persons be given the opportunity to inform the community of both sides of the issue under such circumstances. . . .

Moreover, it is difficult to imagine how the voting problem may be alleviated by an abridgment of talk and comment regarding its solution. . . When the grand jury is performing its investigatory function into a general problem area, without specific regard to indicting a particular individual, society's interest is best served by a thorough and extensive investigation, and a greater degree of disinterestedness and impartiality is assured by allowing free expression of contrary opinion. Consistent suppression of discussion likely to affect pending investigations would mean that some continuing public grievances could never be discussed at all, or at least not at the moment when public discussion is most needed. . . . Thus, in the absence of any showing of an actual interference with the undertakings of the grand jury, this record lacks persuasion in illustrating the serious degree of harm to the administration of law necessary to justify exercise of the contempt power. . . .

Finally, we are told by the respondent that, because the petitioner is sheriff of Bibb County and thereby owes a special duty and responsibility to the court and its judges, his right to freedom of expression must be more severely curtailed than that of an average citizen. Under the circumstances of this case, this argument must be rejected. . . .

The petitioner was an elected official and had the right to enter the field of political controversy, particularly where his political life was at stake. . . . The role that elected officials play in our society makes it all the more imperative that they be allowed freely to express themselves on matters of current public importance.

Our examination of the content of petitioner's statements and the circumstances under which they were published leads us to conclude that they did not present a danger to the administration of justice that should vitiate his freedom to express his opinions in the manner chosen.

The judgment is reversed.

Mr. Justice FRANKFURTER and Mr. Justice WHITE took no part in the decision of this case.

Mr. Justice HARLAN, whom Mr. Justice CLARK joins, dissenting. . .

Accepting as I do for present purposes the Bridges test, this conviction must be upheld if the record supports the inference of clear and present danger. . . . That test is amply met here. . . . Surely the Court cannot mean that attempts to influence judicial proceedings are punishable only if they are successful. Speech creating sufficient danger of an evil which the State may prevent may certainly be punished regardless of whether that evil materializes. See Feiner v. New York, 340 U.S. 315, 320–321. Indeed, the test suggested by the Court is even more stringent than that which it applies in determining whether a conviction should be set aside because of prejudicial "outside" statements reaching a trial jury. In such cases, although the question is whether the rights of the accused have been infringed rather than whether there has been a clear and present danger of their infringement, it is necessary only to show a substantial likelihood that the verdict was affected, and it is no answer that each juror expresses his belief that he remains able to be fair and impartial. Irvin v. Dowd, [366 U.S. 717, chap. 12, p. 901, supra.] The test for punishing attempts to influence a grand or petit jury should be less rather than more stringent.

I cannot agree with the Court that petitioner's statements would have been likely to affect the outcome of the investigation "only if the charge was so manifestly unjust that it could not stand inspection." . . . This is to discredit the persuasiveness of argument, which the Court purports to value so highly. Any expression of opinion on the merits of a pending judicial proceeding is likely to have an impact on deliberations. In this instance that likelihood was increased by two factors which were not present in Bridges, Pennekamp, or Craig . . . . None of those cases involved statements by officers of the court; and all concerned statements whose alleged interference was with the deliberations of a judge rather than a jury. . . . It cannot be assumed with grand jurors, as it has been with judges, . . . that they are all "men of fortitude, able to thrive in a hardy climate." What may not seriously endanger the independent deliberations of a judge may well jeopardize those of a grand or petit jury. . . .

Moreover, the statements themselves were of such a nature as to distinguish this case from Bridges, Pennekamp, and Craig. It cannot be said here, as it was in Bridges, that petitioner's charges of racial bias, hypocrisy, political intimidation, persecution, and political naiveté, and his comparison of the judges with the Ku Klux Klan, "did no more than threaten future adverse criticism which was reasonably to be expected anyway". . . . . The sheriff's remarks were not, as in Pennekamp, . . . general criticisms with respect to rulings already made, but specific attacks directed toward the disposition of the pending investigation. They cannot be characterized, as in Craig, . . . as merely unfair reports of the activities of others; unlike the editorial in that case, . . . petitioner's criticisms went squarely to the merits of the investigation and impugned as well the motives and honesty of those conducting it. I do not understand how it can be denied that a grand juror, reading in the course of this investigation the sheriff's statement, . . . might well be influenced in his deliberations. . . .

Finally, petitioner's case is not saved by the fact that both he and the judges he attacked are elected officials, or by the fact that the statement concerned an issue of some political moment. There was ample opportunity to bring the judges' performance to the voters after the investigation was closed. "Political interest" cannot be used as an excuse for affecting the result of a judicial inquiry. . . . *

CONTEMPT BY PUBLICATION, CLEAR AND PRESENT DANGER, AND THE PROBLEM OF IDENTIFYING THE "SUBSTANTIVE EVILS"

1. *Clear and present danger of what?* In no other area has the Court more consistently invoked clear and present danger language than in this Bridges-Pennekamp-Craig-Wood line of cases. Recall the questions raised about the test earlier (e. g., chap. 15, p. 1094). How useful is emphasis on immediacy of harm in this area? To what extent is the problem that of

* Compare Mills v. Alabama, 384 U.S. 214 (1966), involving a state restriction on publication threatening to interfere with elections rather than judicial proceedings. The Court held that the free press guarantee prohibited a state from making it a crime "for the editor of a daily newspaper to write and publish an editorial *on election day* urging people to vote a certain way on issues submitted to them." Justice Black's majority opinion stated that the case did not involve the State's power "to regulate conduct in and around the polls in order to maintain peace, order and decorum there" and rejected the highest state court's justification of the statute as one protecting "the public from confusive last-minute charges and countercharges and the distribution of propaganda in an effort to influence voters on an election day; when as a practical matter, because of lack of time, such matters cannot be answered or their truth determined until after the election is over."

identifying the "substantive evil," and of assessing its gravity? Is the "evil" that of *any* impact on judicial processes? Is it serious impact, distortion, interruption? Is it the appearance of impact? Which of these are serious or grave enough to justify restricting speech? Compare the approach in these cases with those examining the proof and risk of impact of publicity on fair trial in the context of reviewing criminal convictions. See chap. 12, p. 901, supra. See also the reversal of the criminal libel conviction in Garrison v. Louisiana, 379 U.S. 64 (1964) (sec. 1, p. 1221, supra).

2. *The contrast with Cox II.* Compare these cases, moreover, with Cox v. Louisiana (Cox II, chap. 15, p. 1170, supra) upholding the ban on courthouse picketing. In Cox II, the Court distinguished these contempt cases: "We are not concerned here with such a pure form of expression as a newspaper comment . . .. We deal in this case not with free speech alone but with expression mixed with particular conduct." Is that persuasive? Moreover, the Cox Court insisted that "even assuming" clear and present danger were the applicable test, "mere publication" in these contempt cases was "quite another thing" from demonstrators barred "by a legislative determination based on experience that such conduct inherently threatens the judicial process." Is that persuasive? Recall, moreover, the Cox Court's statements about "evils" the legislature might legitimately consider: the danger that some judges . . . will be consciously or unconsciously influenced by demonstrations"; the risk of "the judicial process . . . being misjudged in the minds of the public" even if the judge were "completely uninfluenced" —the danger, in other words, of "the possibility of a conclusion by the public . . . that the judge's action was in part a product of intimidation." Were there such risks in the contempt cases? Were those dangers "clear and present" there? Is the Court persuasive in distinguishing the contempt situations?

SECTION 4. THE FURNISHING OF LEGAL SERVICES: LAY GROUPS, SOCIAL GOALS, AND THE LAWYER–CLIENT RELATIONSHIP

NAACP v. BUTTON

371 U.S. 415, 83 S.Ct. 328, 9 L.Ed.2d 405 (1963).

Certiorari to the Supreme Court of Appeals of Virginia.

Mr. Justice BRENNAN delivered the opinion of the Court. . . .

There is no substantial dispute as to the facts; the dispute centers about the constitutionality under the Fourteenth Amendment of Chapter 33, as construed and applied by the Virginia Supreme Court of Appeals to include NAACP's activities within the statute's ban against "the improper solicitation of any legal or professional business." . . .

The basic aims and purposes of NAACP are to secure the elimination of all racial barriers which deprive Negro citizens of the privileges and burdens of equal citizenship rights in the United States. . . . For more than 10 years, the Virginia Conference [of **NAACP** branches] has concentrated upon financing litigation aimed at ending racial segregation in the public schools of the Commonwealth.

The Conference ordinarily will finance only cases in which the assisted litigant retains an NAACP staff lawyer to represent him. The Conference maintains a legal staff of 15 attorneys, all of whom are Negroes and members of the NAACP. . . . Each legal staff member must agree to abide by the policies of the NAACP, which . . . limit the kinds of litigation which the NAACP will assist. Thus the NAACP will not underwrite ordinary damages actions, criminal actions in which the defendant raises no question of possible racial discrimination, or suits in which the plaintiff seeks separate but equal rather than fully desegregated public school facilities. . . . The Conference defrays all expenses of litigation in an assisted case . . .. The actual conduct of assisted litigation is under the control of the attorney, although the NAACP continues to be concerned that the outcome of the lawsuit should be consistent with NAACP's policies already described. A client is free at any time to withdraw from an action.

The members of the legal staff of the Virginia Conference and other NAACP or Defense Fund lawyers called in by the staff to assist are drawn into litigation in various ways. One is for an aggrieved Negro to apply directly to the Conference or the legal staff for assistance. . . . In litigation involving public school segregation, the procedure tends to be different. Typically, a local NAACP branch will invite a member of the legal staff to explain to a meeting of parents and children the legal steps necessary to achieve desegregation. The staff member will bring printed forms to the meeting authorizing him, and other NAACP, or Defense Fund attorneys of his designation, to represent the signers in legal proceedings to achieve desegregation. On occasion, blank forms have been signed by litigants, upon the understanding that a member or members of the legal staff, with or without assistance from other NAACP lawyers, or from the Defense Fund, would handle the case. . . . In effect, then, the prospective litigant retains not so much a particular attorney as the "firm" of the NAACP and Defense Fund lawyers . . . .

Statutory regulation of unethical and nonprofessional conduct by attorneys has been in force in Virginia since 1849. These provisions outlaw, *inter alia,* solicitation of legal business in the form of "running" or "capping." Prior to 1956, however, no attempt was made to proscribe under such regulations the activities of the NAACP . . . .. In 1956, however, the legislature amended, by the addition of Chapter 33, the provisions of the Virginia Code forbidding solicitation of legal business by a "runner" or "capper" to include, in the definition of "runner" or "capper," an agent for an individual or organization which retains a lawyer in connection with an action to which it is not a party and in which it has no pecuniary right or liability. The Virginia Supreme Court of Appeals held that the chapter's purpose "was to strengthen, the existing statutes to further control the evils of solicitation of legal business . . . .." . . . The court held that the activities of NAACP, the Virginia Conference, the Defense Fund, and the lawyers furnished by them, fell within, and could constitutionally be proscribed by, the chapter's expanded definition of improper solicitation of legal business, and also violated Canons 35 and 47 of the American Bar Association's Canons of Professional Ethics, which the court had adopted in 1938.[1] . . .

We reverse the judgment of the Virginia Supreme Court of Appeals. We hold that the activities of the NAACP, its affiliates and legal staff shown on this record are modes of expression and association protected by the First and Fourteenth Amendments which Virginia may not prohibit, under its power to regulate the legal profession, as improper solicitation of legal business violative of Chapter 33 and the Canons of Professional Ethics.

A.

We meet at the outset the contention that "solicitation" is wholly outside the area of freedoms protected by the First Amendment. To this contention there are two answers. The first is that a State cannot foreclose the exercise of constitutional rights by mere labels. The second is that abstract discussion is not the only species of communication which the Constitution protects; the First Amendment also protects vigorous advocacy, certainly of lawful ends, against governmental intrusion. . . . In the context of NAACP objectives, litigation is not a technique of resolving private differences; it is a means for achieving the lawful objectives of equality of treatment by all government, federal, state and local, for the members of the Negro community in this country. It is thus a form of political expression. Groups which find themselves unable to achieve their objectives through the ballot frequently turn to the courts. Just as it was true of the opponents of New Deal legislation during the 1930's, for example, no less is it true of the Negro minority today. And under the conditions of modern government, litigation may well be the sole practicable avenue open to a minority to petition for redress of grievances. . . .

The NAACP is not a conventional political party; but the litigation it assists, while serving to vindicate the legal rights of members of the American Negro community, at the same time and perhaps more importantly, makes possible the distinctive contribution of a minority group to the ideas and beliefs of our society. For such a group, association for litigation may be the most effective form of political association.

B.

Our concern is with the impact of enforcement of Chapter 33 upon First Amendment freedoms. . . . We have no doubt that the opinion of the Supreme Court of Appeals in the instant case was intended as a full and authoritative construction of Chapter 33 as applied in a detailed factual context. That construction binds us. . . .

1. . . . . Canon 35 reads in part as follows:

"*Intermediaries.*—The professional services of a lawyer should not be controlled or exploited by any lay agency, personal or corporate, which intervenes, between client and lawyer. A lawyer's responsibilities and qualifications are individual. He should avoid all relations which direct the performance of his duties by or in the interest of such intermediary. A lawyer's relation to his client should be personal, and the responsibility should be directed to the client. Charitable societies rendering aid to the indigent are not deemed such intermediaries."

Canon 47 reads as follows:

"*Aiding the Unauthorized Practice of Law.*—No lawyer shall permit his professional services, or his name, to be used in aid of, or to make possible, the unauthorized practice of law by any lay agency, personal or corporate." [Footnote by the Court.]

But it does not follow that this Court now has only a clear-cut task to decide whether the activities of the petitioner deemed unlawful by the Supreme Court of Appeals are constitutionally privileged. If the line drawn by the decree between the permitted and prohibited activities of the NAACP, its members and lawyers is an ambiguous one, we will not presume that the statute curtails constitutionally protected activity as little as possible. For standards of permissible statutory vagueness are strict in the area of free expression. . . . It makes no difference that the instant case was not a criminal prosecution and not based on a refusal to comply with a licensing requirement. The objectionable quality of vagueness and overbreadth does not depend upon absence of fair notice to a criminally accused or upon unchanneled delegation of legislative powers, but upon the danger of tolerating, in the area of First Amendment freedoms, the existence of a penal statute susceptible of sweeping and improper application. . . .

We read the decree of the Virginia Supreme Court of Appeals in the instant case as proscribing any arrangement by which prospective litigants are advised to seek the assistance of particular attorneys. No narrower reading is plausible. We cannot accept the reading suggested . . . that the Supreme Court of Appeals construed Chapter 33 as proscribing control only of the actual litigation by the NAACP after it is instituted. . . .

We conclude that under Chapter 33, as authoritatively construed by the Supreme Court of Appeals, a person who advises another that his legal rights have been infringed and refers him to a particular attorney or group of attorneys (for example, to the Virginia Conference's legal staff) for assistance has committed a crime, as has the attorney who knowingly renders assistance under such circumstances. There thus inheres in the statute the gravest danger of smothering all discussion looking to the eventual institution of litigation of behalf of the rights of members of an unpopular minority. Lawyers on the legal staff or even mere NAACP members or sympathizers would understandably hesitate, at an NAACP meeting or on any other occasion, to do what the decree purports to allow, namely, acquaint "persons with what they believe to be their legal rights and [advise] them to assert their rights by commencing or further prosecuting a suit . . .." For if the lawyers, members or sympathizers also appeared in or had any connection with any litigation supported with NAACP funds contributed under the provision of the decree by which the NAACP is not prohibited "from contributing money to persons to assist them in commencing or further prosecuting such suits," they plainly would risk (if lawyers) disbarment proceedings and, lawyers and nonlawyers alike, criminal prosecution for the offense of "solicitation," to which the Virginia court gave so broad and uncertain a meaning. It makes no difference whether such prosecutions or proceedings would actually be commenced. It is enough that a vague and broad statute lends itself to selective enforcement against unpopular causes. We cannot close our eyes to the fact that the militant Negro civil rights movement has engendered the intense resentment and opposition of the politically dominant white community of Virginia; litigation assisted by the NAACP has been bitterly fought. In such circumstances, a statute broadly curtailing group activity leading to litigation may easily become a weapon of oppression, however evenhanded its terms appear. Its mere existence could well freeze out of existence all such activity on behalf of the civil rights of Negro citizens. . . .

We hold that Chapter 33 as construed violates the Fourteenth Amendment by unduly inhibiting protected freedoms of expression and association.

In so holding, we reject two further contentions of respondents. The first is that the Virginia Supreme Court of Appeals has guaranteed free expression by expressly confirming petitioner's right to continue its advocacy of civil-rights litigation. But in light of the whole decree of the court, the guarantee is of purely speculative value. As construed by the Court, Chapter 33, at least potentially, prohibits every cooperative activity that would make advocacy of litigation meaningful. If there is an internal tension between proscription and protection in the statute, we cannot assume that, in its subsequent enforcement, ambiguities will be resolved in favor of adequate protection of First Amendment rights. Broad prophylactic rules in the area of free expression are suspect. . . . Precision of regulation must be the touchstone in an area so closely touching our most precious freedoms.

C.

The second contention is that Virginia has a subordinating interest in the regulation of the legal profession, embodied in Chapter 33, which justifies limiting petitioner's First Amendment rights. Specifically, Virginia contends that the NAACP's activities in furtherance of litigation, being "improper solicitation" under the state statute, fall within the traditional purview of state regulation of professional conduct. . . .

However valid may be Virginia's interest in regulating the traditionally illegal practices of barratry, maintenance and champerty, that interest does not justify the prohibition of the NAACP activities disclosed by this record. Malicious intent was of the essence of the common-law offenses of fomenting or stirring up litigation. . . . Even more modern, subtler regulations of unprofessional conduct or interference with professional relations, not involving malice, would not touch the activities at bar; regulations which reflect hostility to stirring up litigation have been aimed chiefly at those who urge recourse to the courts for private gain, serving no public interest.[2] Hostility still exists to stirring up private litigation where it promotes the use of legal machinery to oppress: as, for example, to sow discord in a family; to expose infirmities in land titles, as by hunting up claims of adverse possession; to harass large companies through a multiplicity of small claims; or to oppress debtors as by seeking out unsatisfied judgments. . . .

Objection to the intervention of a lay intermediary, who may control litigation or otherwise interfere with the rendering of legal services in a confidential relationship, also derives from the element of pecuniary gain. Fearful of dangers thought to arise from that element, the courts of several States have sustained regulations aimed at these activities. We intimate no view one way or the other as to the merits of those decisions with respect to the particular arrangements against which they are directed. It is enough that the superficial resemblance in form between those arrangements and that at bar cannot obscure the vital fact that here the entire arrangement employs constitutionally privileged means of expression to secure constitution-

2. . . . But truly nonpecuniary arrangements involving the solicitation of legal business have been frequently upheld. [F]or example, the American Civil Liberties Union has for many years furnished counsel in many cases in many different parts of the country without governmental interference. Although this intervention is mostly in the form of amicus curiae briefs, occasionally counsel employed by the Union appears directly on behalf of the litigant. See Comment, *Private Attorneys-General: Group Action in the Fight for Civil Liberties*, 58 Yale L.J. 574, 576 (1949). . . . [Footnote by the Court.]

ally guaranteed civil rights. There has been no showing of a serious danger here of professionally reprehensible conflicts of interest which rules against solicitation frequently seek to prevent. This is so partly because no monetary stakes are involved, and so there is no danger that the attorney will desert or subvert the paramount interests of his client to enrich himself or an outside sponsor. And the aims and interests of NAACP have not been shown to conflict with those of its members and nonmember Negro litigants . . . .

We conclude that although the petitioner has amply shown that its activities fall within the First Amendment's protections, the State has failed to advance any substantial regulatory interest, in the form of substantive evils flowing from petitioner's activities, which can justify the broad prohibitions which it has imposed. Nothing that this record shows as to the nature and purpose of NAACP activities permits an inference of any injurious intervention in or control of litigation which would constitutionally authorize the application of Chapter 33 to those activities. *A fortiori*, nothing in this record justifies the breadth and vagueness of the Virginia Supreme Court of Appeals' decree.

A final observation is in order. Because our disposition is rested on the First Amendment as absorbed in the Fourteenth, we do not reach the considerations of race or racial discrimination which are the predicate of petitioner's challenge to the statute under the Equal Protection Clause. That the petitioner happens to be engaged in activities of expression and association on behalf of the rights of Negro children to equal opportunity is constitutionally irrelevant to the ground of our decision. The course of our decisions in the First Amendment area makes plain that its protections would apply as fully to those who would arouse our society against the objectives of the petitioner. . . .

Reversed.

Mr. Justice DOUGLAS, concurring.

While I join the opinion of the Court, I add a few words. This Virginia Act is not applied across the boards to all groups that use this method of obtaining and managing litigation but instead reflects a legislative purpose to penalize the N.A.A.C.P. because it promotes desegregation of the races. . . .

Mr. Justice WHITE, concurring in part and dissenting in part. . . .

If we had before us, which we do not, a narrowly drawn statute proscribing only the actual day-to-day management and dictation of the tactics, strategy and conduct of litigation by a lay entity such as the NAACP, the issue would be considerably different, at least for me; for in my opinion neither the practice of law by such an organization nor its management of the litigation of its members or others is constitutionally protected. Both practices are well within the regulatory power of the State. In this regard I agree with my Brother Harlan.

It is not at all clear to me, however, that the opinion of the majority would not also strike down such a narrowly drawn statute. To the extent that it would, I am in disagreement. . . .

Mr. Justice HARLAN, whom Mr. Justice CLARK and Mr. Justice STEWART join, dissenting. . . .

[T]o declare that litigation is a form of conduct that may be associated with political expression does not resolve this case. Neither the First Amendment nor the Fourteenth constitutes an absolute bar to government regulation in the fields of free expression and association. . . .

So here, the question is whether the particular regulation of conduct concerning litigation has a reasonable relation to the furtherance of a proper state interest, and whether that interest outweighs any foreseeable harm to the furtherance of protected freedoms. . . .

The regulation before us has its origins in the long-standing common-law prohibitions of champerty, barratry, and maintenance, the closely related prohibitions in the Canons of Ethics against solicitation and intervention by a lay intermediary, and statutory provisions forbidding the unauthorized practice of law. The Court recognizes this formidable history, but puts it aside in the present case on the grounds that there is here no element of malice or of pecuniary gain, that the interests of the NAACP are not to be regarded as substantially different from those of its members, and that we are said to be dealing here with a matter that transcends mere legal ethics—the securing of federally guaranteed rights. But these distinctions are too facile. They do not account for the full scope of the State's legitimate interest in regulating professional conduct. For although these professional standards may have been born in a desire to curb malice and self-aggrandizement by those who would use clients and the courts for their own pecuniary ends, they have acquired a far broader significance during their long development.

First, with regard to the claimed absence of the pecuniary element . . .. The reference is presumably to the fact that petitioner itself is a non-profit organization not motivated by desire for financial gain but by public interest and to the fact that no monetary stakes are involved in the litigation.

But a State's felt need for regulation of professional conduct may reasonably extend beyond mere "ambulance chasing." . . . Of particular relevance here is a series of nationwide adjudications culminating in 1958 in In re Brotherhood of Railroad Trainmen, 13 Ill.2d 391, 150 N.E.2d 163. . . . The practices of the Brotherhood, similar in so many respects to those engaged in by the petitioner here, have been condemned by every state court which has considered them.* . . .

Underlying this impressive array of relevant precedent is the widely shared conviction that avoidance of improper pecuniary gain is not the only relevant factor in determining standards of professional conduct. Running perhaps even deeper is the desire of the profession, of courts, and of legislatures to prevent any interference with the uniquely personal relationship between lawyer and client and to maintain untrammeled by outside influences the responsibility which the lawyer owes to the courts he serves.

When an attorney is employed by an association or corporation to represent individual litigants, two problems arise, whether or not the association is organized for profit and no matter how unimpeachable its motives. The lawyer becomes subject to the control of a body that is not itself a litigant and that, unlike the lawyers it employs, is not subject to strict professional discipline as an officer of the court. In addition, the lawyer necessarily

---

* But see Brotherhood of Railroad
Trainmen v. Virginia, 377 U.S. 1
(1964), which follows.

finds himself with a divided allegiance—to his employer and to his client—which may prevent full compliance with his basic professional obligations. . . .

Second, it is claimed that the interests of petitioner and its members are sufficiently identical to eliminate any "serious danger" of "professionally reprehensible conflicts of interest." . . .

The NAACP may be no more than the sum of the efforts and views infused in it by its members; but the totality of the separate interests of the members and others whose causes the petitioner champions, even in the field of race relations, may far exceed in scope and variety that body's views of policy, as embodied in litigating strategy and tactics. Thus it may be in the interest of the Association in every case to make a frontal attack on segregation, to press for an immediate breaking down of racial barriers, and to sacrifice minor points that may win a given case for the major points that may win other cases too. But in a particular litigation, it is not impossible that after authorizing action in his behalf, a Negro parent, concerned that a continued frontal attack could result in schools closed for years, might prefer to wait with his fellows a longer time for good-faith efforts by the local school board than is permitted by the centrally determined policy of the NAACP. Or he might see a greater prospect of success through discussions with local school authorities than through the litigation deemed necessary by the Association. The parent, of course, is free to withdraw his authorization, but is his lawyer, retained and paid by petitioner and subject to its directions on matters of policy, able to advise the parent with that undivided allegiance that is the hallmark of the attorney-client relation? I am afraid not. . . .

Third, it is said that the practices involved here must stand on a different footing because the litigation that petitioner supports concerns the vindication of constitutionally guaranteed rights.

But surely state law is still the source of basic regulation of the legal profession, whether an attorney is pressing a federal or a state claim within its borders. . . . The true question is whether the State has taken action which unreasonably obstructs the assertion of federal rights. Here, it cannot be said that the underlying state policy is inevitably inconsistent with federal interests. [T]he state policy is not unrelated to the federal rules of standing. . . . This is a requirement of substance as well as form. It recognizes that, although litigation is not something to be avoided at all costs, it should not be resorted to in undue haste, without any effort at extrajudicial resolution, and that those lacking immediate private need may make unnecessary broad attacks based on inadequate records. . . .

There remains to be considered on this branch of the argument the question whether this particular exercise of state regulatory power bears a sufficient relation to the established and substantial interests of the State to overcome whatever indirect impact this statute may have on rights of free expression and association. . . .

. . . The important function of organizations like petitioner in vindicating constitutional rights is not of course to be minimized, but that function is not, in my opinion, substantially impaired by this statute. [I]t does not, in my view, prevent petitioner from recommending the services of attorneys who are not subject to its directions and control. And since petitioner may contribute to those who need assistance, the prohibition should not significantly discourage anyone with sufficient interest from pressing his claims in litigation or from joining with others similarly situated to press those claims.   .   .   .

The Court's remaining line of reasoning is that Chapter 33 as construed .   .   . must be struck down on the score of vagueness and ambiguity. I think that this "vagueness" concept has no proper place in this case and only serves to obscure rather than illuminate the true questions presented.

The Court's finding of ambiguity rests on the premise that the statute may prohibit *mere* recommendation of "any particular attorney," whether or not a member of the NAACP's legal staff or otherwise subject to the Association's direction and control.   .   .   .

The cardinal difficulty with this argument is that there simply is no real uncertainty in the statute.   .   .   . It is true that the concept of vagueness has been used to give "breathing space" to "First Amendment freedoms," see Amsterdam, Note, The Void-For-Vagueness Doctrine in the Supreme Court, 109 U. of Pa.L.Rev. 67, but it is also true, as that same commentator has well stated, that "vagueness is not an extraneous ploy or a judicial *deus ex machina.*" Id., at 88. There is, in other words, "an actual vagueness component in the vagueness decisions." Ibid. And the test is whether the law in question has established standards of guilt sufficiently ascertainable that men of common intelligence need not guess at its meaning.   .   .   . Laws that have failed to meet this standard are, almost without exception, those which turn on language calling for the exercise of subjective judgment, unaided by objective norms.   .   .   .

Ambiguity in the present statute can be made to appear only at the price of strained reading of the state court's opinion.   .   .   .

THE GROUNDS AND APPLICATIONS OF BUTTON

1. *The cases.* a. A year after Button, the Court relied on it to invalidate a Virginia injunction against the union's alleged solicitation and unauthorized practice of law. Brotherhood of Railroad Trainmen v. Virginia, 377 U.S. 1 (1964). The Brotherhood admitted that it advised its members to obtain legal advice before making settlements of their claims, that it recommended particular attorneys, and that the result of its plan was "to channel legal employment to the particular lawyers approved by the Brotherhood." Justice Black's majority opinion concluded that First and 14th Amendment rights had been violated: "The State can no more keep these workers from using their cooperative plan to advise one another than it could use more direct means to bar them from resorting to the courts to vindicate their legal rights." As in the Button case, "the State again has failed to show any appreciable public interest in preventing the Brotherhood from carrying out its plan to recommend the lawyers it selects to represent injured workers. The Brotherhood's activities fall just as clearly within the protection of the First Amendment. And the Constitution protects the associational rights of the members of the union precisely as it does those of the NAACP."

Justice Clark's dissent, joined by Justice Harlan, claimed that the decision "overthrows state regulation of the legal profession and relegates the practice of law to the level of a commercial enterprise." He insisted that the

Button decision was not applicable: "Personal injury litigation is not a form of political expression, but rather a procedure for the settlement of damage claims. No guaranteed civil right is involved. Here, the question involves solely the regulation of the profession, a power long recognized as belonging peculiarly to the State. . . . Finally, no substantive evil would result from the activity permitted in Button. But here the past history of the union indicates the contrary. . . . Virginia has sought only to halt the gross abuses of channeling and soliciting litigation, as have been going on here for 30 years. The potential for evil in the union's system is enormous and, in my view, will bring disrepute to the legal profession. The system must also work to the disadvantage of the Brotherhood members by directing their claims into the hands of the 16 approved attorneys who are subject to the control of one man, the president of the union. Finally, it will encourage further departures from the high standards set by canons of ethics as well as by state regulatory procedures and will be a green light to other groups who for years have attempted to engage in similar practices."

b. The Button and Trainmen cases in turn provided the basis for setting aside a state order against another variety of alleged unauthorized practice of law by a union. United Mine Workers v. Illinois Bar Ass'n, 389 U.S. 217 (1967). The Union had employed an attorney on a salary basis to assist its members with workmen's compensation claims. Justice Black's majority opinion concluded that the state ban "substantially impairs the associational rights of the mine workers and is not needed to protect the State's interest in high standards of legal ethics." Justice Harlan dissented: "Although I agree with the balancing approach employed by the majority, I find the scales tipped differently."

2. *The grounds.* What was the source of the associational rights in Button? Compare the freedom of association discussion when the Court, several years before Button, protected NAACP membership lists from state inquiries. NAACP v. Alabama, 357 U.S. 449 (1958) (p. 1316, infra). Were those associational rights of the NAACP cases equally applicable in the union cases? Would refusal to apply Button in the subsequent cases have shown Button to be a non-neutral decision (a charge the Court was concerned about in the last paragraph of the Button case)? Would a distinction between "personal injury litigation" and "civil rights litigation" have been non-neutral?

Should the Court have inquired further into state motives in Button? Recall the materials on "purpose"-"motive" inquiries in chap. 5, sec. 6, p. 444, supra. May reluctance to characterize motives in cases such as Button lead the Court to give inadequate weight in other cases to "purer" state concerns regarding professional ethics and conflicts of interest? See generally Kalven, The Negro and the First Amendment (1965), and Symposium, "Group Legal Services in Perspective," 12 U.C.L.A.L.Rev. 279 (1965).

SECTION 5.   LABOR PICKETING

TEAMSTERS UNION v. VOGT, INC.

354 U.S. 284, 77 S.Ct. 1166, 1 L.Ed.2d 1347 (1957).

Certiorari to the Supreme Court of Wisconsin.

Mr. Justice FRANKFURTER delivered the opinion of the Court.

This is one more in the long series of cases in which this Court has been required to consider the limits imposed by the Fourteenth Amendment on the power of a State to enjoin picketing. . . . Respondent owns and operates a gravel pit in Oconomowoc, Wisconsin, where it employs 15 to 20 men. Petitioner unions sought unsuccessfully to induce some of respondent's employees to join the unions and commenced to picket the entrance to respondent's place of business with signs reading, "The men on this job are not 100% affiliated with the A.F.L." "In consequence," drivers of several trucking companies refused to deliver and haul goods to and from respondent's plant, causing substantial damage to respondent. Respondent thereupon sought an injunction to restrain the picketing.

The trial court . . . held that by virtue of Wis.Stat. § 103.535, prohibiting picketing in the absence of a "labor dispute," the petitioners must be enjoined from maintaining any pickets near respondent's place of business, from displaying at any place near respondent's place of business signs indicating that there was a labor dispute between respondent and its employees or between respondent and any of the petitioners, and from inducing others to decline to transport goods to and from respondent's business establishment.

On appeal, the Wisconsin Supreme Court . . . canvassed the whole circumstances surrounding the picketing and held that "One would be credulous, indeed, to believe under the circumstances that the union had no thought of coercing the employer to interfere with its employees in their right to join or refuse to join the defendant union." Such picketing, the court held, was for "an unlawful purpose," since Wis.Stat. § 111.06(2) (b) made it an unfair labor practice for an employee individually or in concert with others to "coerce, intimidate or induce any employer to interfere with any of his employes in the enjoyment of their legal rights. . . . ." Relying on Building Service Employees v. Gazzam, 339 U.S. 532, and Pappas v. Stacey, 151 Me. 36, 116 A.2d 497 [dismissed for lack of a substantial federal question, 350 U.S. 870], the Wisconsin Supreme Court therefore affirmed the granting of the injunction on this different ground. . . .

. . . . It is not too surprising that the response of States—legislative and judicial—to use of the injunction in labor controversies should have given rise to a series of adjudications in this Court relating to the limitations on state action contained in the provisions of the Due Process Clause of the Fourteenth Amendment. It is also not too surprising that examination of these adjudications should disclose an evolving, not a static, course of decision.

. . .

[In 1940], in passing on a restrictive instead of a permissive state statute, the Court made sweeping pronouncements about the right to picket in holding unconstitutional a statute that had been applied to ban all picketing, with "no exceptions based upon either the number of persons engaged in the proscribed activity, the peaceful character of their demeanor, the nature of their dispute with an employer, or the restrained character and the accurateness of the terminology used in notifying the public of the facts of the dispute." Thornhill v. Alabama, 310 U.S. 88, 99. As the statute dealt at large with all picketing, so the Court broadly assimilated peaceful picketing in general to freedom of speech, and as such protected against abridgment by the Fourteenth Amendment.

These principles were applied by the Court in A. F. of L. v. Swing, 312 U.S. 321, to hold unconstitutional an injunction against peaceful picketing, based on a State's common-law policy against picketing when there was no immediate dispute between employer and employee. On the same day, however, the Court upheld a generalized injunction against picketing where there had been violence because "it could justifiably be concluded that the momentum of fear generated by past violence would survive even though future picketing might be wholly peaceful." Milk Wagon Drivers Union v. Meadowmoor Dairies, 312 U.S. 287, 294.

Soon, however, the Court came to realize that the broad pronouncements, but not the specific holding, of Thornhill had to yield "to the impact of facts unforeseen," or at least not sufficiently appreciated. . . . Cases reached the Court in which a State had designed a remedy to meet a specific situation or to accomplish a particular social policy. These cases made manifest that picketing, even though "peaceful," involved more than just communication of ideas and could not be immune from all state regulation. "Picketing by an organized group is more than free speech, since it involves patrol of a particular locality and since the very presence of a picket line may induce action of one kind or another, quite irrespective of the nature of the ideas which are being disseminated." Bakery Drivers Local v. Wohl, 315 U.S. 769, 776 (concurring opinion); see Carpenters Union v. Ritter's Cafe, 315 U.S. 722, 725–728.

These latter two cases required the Court to review a choice made by two States between the competing interests of unions, employers, their employees, and the public at large. . . .

. . . Although the Court in Ritter's Cafe and Wohl did not question the holding of Thornhill, the strong reliance on the particular facts in each case demonstrated a growing awareness that these cases involved not so much questions of free speech as review of the balance struck by a State between picketing that involved more than "publicity" and competing interests of state policy. . . .

The implied reassessments of the broad language of the Thornhill case were finally generalized in a series of cases sustaining injunctions against peaceful picketing, even when arising in the course of a labor controversy, when such picketing was counter to valid state policy in a domain open to state regulation. The decisive reconsideration came in Giboney v. Empire Storage & Ice Co., 336 U.S. 490. A union, seeking to organize peddlers, picketed a wholesale dealer to induce it to refrain from selling to nonunion peddlers. The state courts, finding that such an agreement would constitute a conspiracy in restraint of trade in violation of the state antitrust laws, enjoined the picketing. This Court affirmed unanimously.

"It is contended that the injunction against picketing adjacent to Empire's place of business is an unconstitutional abridgment of free speech because the picketers were attempting peacefully to publicize truthful facts about a labor dispute. . . . But the record here does not permit this publicizing to be treated in isolation. For . . . the sole immediate object of the publicizing adjacent to the premises of Empire, as well as the other activities of the appellants and their allies, was to compel Empire to agree to stop selling ice to nonunion peddlers. Thus all of appellants' activities . . . constituted a single and integrated course of conduct, which was in violation of Missouri's valid law. In this situation, the injunction did no more than enjoin an offense against Missouri law, a felony." Id., at 497–498.

The Court therefore concluded that it was "clear that appellants were doing more than exercising a right of free speech or press. . . . They were exercising their economic power together with that of their allies to compel Empire to abide by union rather than by state regulation of trade." Id., at 503.

The following Term, the Court decided a group of cases applying and elaborating on the theory of Giboney. In Hughes v. Superior Court, 339 U.S. 460, the Court held that the Fourteenth Amendment did not bar use of the injunction to prohibit picketing of a place of business solely to secure compliance with a demand that its employees be hired in percentage to the racial origin of its customers. "We cannot construe the Due Process Clause as precluding California from securing respect for its policy against involuntary employment on racial lines by prohibiting systematic picketing that would subvert such policy." . . .

On the same day, the Court decided Teamsters Union v. Hanke, 339 U.S. 470, holding that a State was not restrained by the Fourteenth Amendment from enjoining picketing of a business, conducted by the owner himself without employees, in order to secure compliance with a demand to become a union shop. . . .

A third case, Building Service Employees v. Gazzam, 339 U.S. 532, was decided the same day. . . . The State, finding that the object of the picketing was in violation of its statutory policy against employer coercion of employees' choice of bargaining representative, enjoined picketing for such purpose. This Court affirmed, rejecting the argument that "the Swing case, supra, is controlling. . . ."

A similar problem was involved in Plumbers Union v. Graham, 345 U.S. 192, where a state court had enjoined, as a violation of its "Right to Work" law, picketing that advertised that nonunion men were being employed on a building job. . . .

This series of cases, then, established a broad field in which a State, in enforcing some public policy, whether of its criminal or its civil law, and whether announced by its legislature or its courts, could constitutionally enjoin peaceful picketing aimed at preventing effectuation of that policy.

In the light of this background, the Maine Supreme Judicial Court in 1955 decided [Pappas v. Stacey]. From the statement, it appeared that three union employees went on strike and picketed a restaurant peacefully "for the sole purpose of seeking to organize other employees of the Plaintiff, ultimately to have the Plaintiff enter into collective bargaining and negotiations with the Union . . .." Maine had a statute providing that workers should have full liberty of self-organization, free from restraint by employers or other persons. The Maine Supreme Judicial Court . . . enjoined the picketing, and an appeal was taken to this Court.

The whole series of cases discussed above allowing, as they did, wide discretion to a State in the formulation of domestic policy, and not involving a curtailment of free speech in its obvious and accepted scope, led this Court, without the need of further argument, to grant appellee's motion to dismiss the appeal in that it no longer presented a substantial federal question. . . .

The Stacey case is this case. . . . As in Stacey, the highest state court drew the inference from the facts that the picketing was to coerce the employer to put pressure on his employees to join the union, in violation of the declared policy of the State. . . . The cases discussed above all hold that, consistent with the Fourteenth Amendment, a State may enjoin such conduct.

Of course, the mere fact that there is "picketing" does not automatically justify its restraint without an investigation into its conduct and purposes. State courts, no more than state legislatures, can enact blanket prohibitions against picketing. . . . The series of cases following Thornhill and Swing demonstrate that the policy of Wisconsin enforced by the prohibition of this picketing is a valid one. In this case, the circumstances set forth in the opinion of the Wisconsin Supreme Court afford a rational basis for the inference it drew concerning the purpose of the picketing. . . .

Affirmed.

Mr. Justice WHITTAKER took no part in the consideration or decision of this case.

Mr. Justice DOUGLAS, with whom The Chief Justice [WARREN] and Mr. Justice BLACK concur, dissenting.

The Court has now come full circle. In [Thornhill v. Alabama] we struck down a state ban on picketing on the ground that "the dissemination of information concerning the facts of a labor dispute must be regarded as within that area of free discussion that is guaranteed by the Constitution." Less than one year later, we held that the First Amendment protected organizational picketing on a factual record which cannot be distinguished from the one now before us. [A.F.L. v. Swing.] Of course, we have always recognized that picketing has aspects which make it more than speech. . . . That difference underlies our decision in [Giboney v. Empire Storage & Ice Co.] There, picketing was an essential part of "a single and integrated course of conduct, which was in violation of Missouri's valid law." . . . We emphasized that "there was clear danger, imminent and immediate, that unless restrained, appellants would succeed in making [the state] policy a dead letter . . . .." Speech there was enjoined because it was an inseparable part of conduct which the State constitutionally could and did regulate.

But where, as here, there is no rioting, no mass picketing, no violence, no disorder, no fisticuffs, no coercion—indeed nothing but speech—the principles announced in Thornhill and Swing should give the advocacy of one side of a dispute First Amendment protection.

The retreat began when, in [Teamsters Union v. Hanke], four members of the Court announced that all picketing could be prohibited if a state court decided that that picketing violated the State's public policy. The retreat became a rout in [Plumbers Union v. Graham]. It was only the "purpose" of the picketing which was relevant. The state court's characterization of the picketers' "purpose" had been made well-nigh conclusive. Considerations of the proximity of picketing to conduct which the State could control or prevent were abandoned . . ..

Today, the Court signs the formal surrender. State courts and state legislatures cannot fashion blanket prohibitions on all picketing. But, for practical purposes, [state] courts and state legislatures are free to decide whether to permit or suppress any particular picket line for any reason other than a blanket policy against all picketing. I would adhere to the principle announced in Thornhill. I would adhere to the result reached in Swing. I would return to the test enunciated in Giboney—that this form of expression can be regulated or prohibited only to the extent that it forms an essential part of a course of conduct which the State can regulate or prohibit. . . .

PICKETING AND THE CONSTITUTION

The declining significance of the First Amendment in the labor picketing area, after the broad statements in Thornhill, is traced in Vogt. That decline was not only attributable to the judicial acceptance of limits on picketing; even more important was the congressional occupation of the field and the growing displacement of state control of picketing because of pre-emption principles. See chap. 8, sec. 2A, supra, and Meltzer, "The Supreme Court, Congress, and State Jurisdiction over Labor Relations," 59 Colum.L.Rev. 6 (1959).

Nevertheless, the picketing cases remain an important source of First Amendment doctrine,* especially for the demonstration problems considered in chap. 15, sec. 2, supra. And the First Amendment continues to play some direct role in labor picketing as well. See, e. g., the material on Amalgamated Food Employees v. Logan Valley Plaza, 391 U.S. 308 (1968) (chap. 15, sec. 2, p. 1185, supra), where the Court set aside, on the basis of the First Amendment, a state injunction resting simply on trespass grounds and banning all peaceful picketing. The majority opinion noted that "we have no occasion to consider the extent to which respondents are entitled to limit the location and manner of the picketing or the number of picketers."

---

* For example, the Giboney case (discussed in Vogt) is frequently cited as a major source of the "speech"-"conduct" or "speech"-"speech plus" distinction—especially by those who, like Justices Black and Douglas, urge absolute protection for "speech" but find permissible the restricting of "conduct" as in Giboney.

SECTION 6. GOVERNMENT DEMANDS FOR INFORMATION AND AFFIRMATION: SECURITY PROGRAMS AND OATH REQUIREMENTS FOR PUBLIC EMPLOYEES AND LICENSEES

Introduction. When may government demand answers from those who work for it or those who (like bar admission applicants, for example) ask for recognition of a special status? To what extent do First Amendment values restrict government with respect to what disclosures or assurances it may seek from employees or licensees? Questions such as these have most commonly arisen in the context of internal security. Criminal legislation against dangerous advocacy, the focus of attention in chap. 15, sec. 1, has not been the only manifestation of the concern with subversion; as the Keyishian case (p. 1133) illustrated, security programs and oath requirements have also been a prolific source of litigation; and they are the major concern of this section.

The problems here are obviously related to those of the Gitlow-Dennis-Scales variety: What critical speech is protected? What associations may be forbidden? But these materials differ in important respects. The criminal provisions considered in chap. 15 were immediately concerned with the content of speech. Here, the state's concern purports to be with issues such as fitness of employees and integrity of lawyers. Inquiries related to beliefs and associations may affect First Amendment interests, to be sure. Are they constitutionally more tolerable because their impact is not "direct," because their effect on free expression is only an indirect consequence of a regulation?

To what extent are questions about beliefs and associations relevant to legitimate governmental concerns regarding public employment and professional qualifications? To what extent may an individual refuse to answer even a "relevant" question, because the effect on his First Amendment rights outweighs the public need to know? How strong must state justifications be to make an answer obligatory? What action may the state take on the basis of the answer? Is the last the same question as the earlier ones: May a state ask a question only if an answer might justify dismissal of an employee for example? Or may the state's right to know be broader than the permissible bases for dismissal?

The materials that follow explore these and related questions. Section 1A concentrates on the Court responses during the fifties, the first decade of frequent encounters with these problems; section 1B traces the sharply changing analyses since. The First Amendment is the dominant limitation, but other guarantees are also involved—especially the Fifth Amendment privilege against self-incrimination and the bill of attainder restrictions (see United States v. Brown, and related materials in chap. 7, on separation of powers, at p. 587, supra). Internal security provides the most common context, but the materials are not restricted to it: relevant developments have involved demands for information about civil rights activities as well. Indeed, the relationship between inquiry cases involving alleged subversives on the one hand and NAACP activities on the other suggests a series of provocative and illuminating comparisons in this section and the next, culminating in the last principal case in this chapter (the Gibson case, p. 1341, which involves a legislative committee's demand for information about NAACP membership in the course of an investigation into Communist infiltration).

A. THE BACKGROUND OF THE FIFTIES

THE GARNER AND WIEMAN CASES: RELEVANT INQUIRIES; SUSPECT METHODS

Introduction. Demands for information and disavowals regarding sub-version are relevant and legitimate so long as the methods of inquiry are clear and limited: that was the usual theme at the beginning of the modern Court's encounters with these problems. The Garner and Wieman cases illustrate that approach of the early fifties.

1. *Garner.* Garner v. Los Angeles Board of Public Works, 341 U.S. 716 (1951), involved a 1941 state legislative amendment of the Los Angeles City Charter which barred from public employment anyone who (1) within the past 5 years had "advised, advocated or taught," or thereafter should "advise, advocate or teach" the "overthrow by force or violence" of the state or national government; or (2) within the past 5 years had, or thereafter should, become a member of or affiliated with an organization engaging in such advocacy. A 1948 city ordinance implemented that legislation by re-quiring employees to take an oath (covering the 5 years prior to 1948) regard-ing the forbidden activities, as well as to execute an affidavit disclosing whether or not he was or had ever been a Communist Party member, and if so, for what period.

The Court sustained both provisions. Justice Clark's majority opinion found the affidavit inquiry relevant: a city may inquire of its employees "as to matters that may prove relevant to their fitness and suitability for the public service. Past conduct may well relate to present fitness; past loyalty may have a reasonable relationship to present and future trust. Both are commonly inquired into in determining fitness for both high and low positions in private industry and are not less relevant in public employment." The Court noted, however, that it was not deciding whether the city could say that disclosure of Party membership by an employee "justifies his discharge"; the category of relevant questions was apparently broader than the category of grounds for discharge.

The oath requirement was also found valid: it had no retroactive effect, given the 1941 and 1948 dates for state and local provisions; the 1948 oath obligation applied only to those engaging in the forbidden advocacy or as-sociation after the 1941 state law: "The provisions operating thus prospective-ly were a reasonable regulation to protect the municipal service by establishing an employment qualification of loyalty." Finally, the oath was found suffi-ciently narrow by being read as limited to *knowing* membership: "We have no reason to suppose that the oath [will be] construed [to apply to members of organizations who were] innocent of its purpose. We assume that scienter is implicit in each clause of the oath."

2. *Wieman.* In Wieman v. Updegraff, 344 U.S. 183 (1952), by contrast, the unanimous Court struck down an Oklahoma loyalty oath re-quiring employees to state that they were not "affiliated directly or indirectly," and for the previous 5 years had "not been a member of," any organization "which has been officially determined by the United States Attorney General or other authorized public agency of the United States to be a communist front or subversive organization." Justice Clark again wrote the opinion. He

noted that the state had construed the oath so that here, unlike Garner, "knowledge is not a factor" and continued: "We are thus brought to the question touched on in Garner [note 1 above], Adler [1] and Gerende: [2] whether the Due Process Clause permits a state, in attempting to bar disloyal individuals from its employ, to exclude persons solely on the basis of organizational membership, regardless of their knowledge concerning the organizations to which they had belonged. For, under the statute before us, the fact of membership alone disqualifies. But membership may be innocent. A state servant may have joined a proscribed organization unaware of its activities and purposes. In recent years, many completely loyal persons have severed organizational ties after learning for the first time of the character of groups to which they had belonged. . . . At the time of affiliation, a group itself may be innocent, only later coming under the influence of those who would turn it toward illegitimate ends. Conversely, an organization formerly subversive and therefore designated as such may have subsequently freed itself from the influences which originally led to its listing.

"There can be no dispute about the consequences visited upon a person excluded from public employment on disloyalty grounds. In the view of the community, the stain is a deep one; indeed, it has become a badge of infamy. . . . Yet under the Oklahoma Act, the fact of association alone determines disloyalty and disqualification; it matters not whether association existed innocently or knowingly. To thus inhibit individual freedom of movement is to stifle the flow of democratic expression and controversy at one of its chief sources. We hold that the distinction observed between the case at bar and Garner, Adler and Gerende is decisive. Indiscriminate classification of innocent with knowing activity must fall as an assertion of arbitrary power. The oath offends due process."

THE CONSEQUENCES OF SILENCE IN THE FACE OF RELEVANT INQUIRIES: DISMISSALS FROM EMPLOYMENT AND DENIALS OF BAR ADMISSION FOR FAILURE TO DISCLOSE

Introduction. In a series of cases in the late fifties, the Court considered constitutional claims by employees and licensees who had refused to answer state questions relating to subversion. Typically, the state insisted that the dismissal or license refusal was based on the failure to answer questions "relevant" to a legitimate state interest (in the sense of cases such as

1. Adler v. Board of Education, 342 U.S. 485 (1952) (see chap. 2, p. 80, supra), sustained the New York Feinberg law directed at subversive teachers; it was overruled in Keyishian v. Board of Regents, 385 U.S. 589 (1967) (chap. 15, p. 1133, supra).

2. Gerende v. Board of Supervisors, 341 U.S. 56 (1951), was a per curiam decision sustaining the Maryland Ober Law requirement that any candidates for public office file an affidavit that he was not a "subversive person." In sustaining it, the Court expressed its understanding that the candidate "need only make oath that he is not a person who is engaged 'in one way or another in the attempt to overthrow the government *by force or violence*,' and that he is not knowingly a member of an organization engaged in such an attempt." Compare Whitehill v. Elkins, 38 U.S. 54 (1967), invalidating a teacher's oath prepared pursuant to the same Law that the teacher was "not engaged in one way or another in the attempt to overthrow the government . . . by force or violence." Justice Douglas' majority opinion, construing the requirement in relation to the Ober Law, found the definition of "subversive person" unconstitutionally vague. For other loyalty oath cases of the sixties, see p. 1326, infra.

Garner, p. 1301, supra). The usual government claim was that its action was a permissible response to the individual's lack of candor vis-à-vis relevant inquiries. The individual, by contrast, insisted that the real basis for the state's action was hostility to dissident political views and suspicious inferences about the claimant's beliefs. The divisions on the Court were often differences about assessments of the record: there was agreement in principle that penalties for political differences would violate First Amendment rights and that inferences of guilt from invocations of the self-incrimination privilege would violate the Fifth; the immediately troublesome issues were problems such as the scope of permissible Court inquiry into "real" state motives and purposes, and the deference appropriate for state judgments in this area. There were other underlying difficulties, to be sure: the contours of relevance; the probable cause a state should show to justify questions in a sensitive area; the nature of beliefs and associations that would permit a state to end employment or deny licenses. But questions of that variety were more obscured in the decisions of the fifties than in the subsequent First Amendment cases (considered in sec. 6B, infra).

Moreover, reliance on the Fifth rather than the First Amendment in many of the refusals to answers added another variable to the early cases; changes in views in the sixties about the "incorporation" of the Fifth into the 14th accordingly affected the bounds of state inquiries (see p. 1313, infra). In Slochower, Lerner, and Beilan (notes 1 to 3), employees were discharged by states after invoking the Fifth Amendment in congressional inquiries of the fifties—during a period when the Fifth was not yet applicable in state inquiries via the 14th (see Malloy v. Hogan, chap. 12, p. 875, supra). In the bar admission cases (Schware and Konigsberg I, pp. 1307 and 1308, infra), the refusals to answer rested directly on First Amendment grounds. The note at p. 1313 considers the impact of the availability since the sixties of a self-incrimination privilege in state inquires.

This section concludes with NAACP v. Alabama, a case of special importance for the evolving approach of the sixties: it involved a civil rights organization rather than concerns about Communist infiltration; it focused on the competing claims of the state and the individual more explicitly than most; and it is a major example of a Court finding of inadequate justification for a state demand for information though the information was "relevant" to a legitimate state concern. As in Shelton v. Tucker in 1960, the first case in sec. 6B, p. 1320, NAACP v. Alabama found the state need for an answer to a relevant question outweighed by the "indirect" impact a duty to answer would have on First Amendment rights.

1. *Slochower: improper inference from Fifth Amendment privilege?* Slochower v. Board of Higher Education, 350 U.S. 551 (1956), held unconstitutional § 903 of the New York City Charter which provided that whenever an employee of the City utilized the privilege against self-incrimination to avoid answering a question relating to his official conduct, "his term or tenure of office or employment shall terminate." Slochower, a tenured faculty member at a city college, claimed the Fifth Amendment to certain questions at a 1952 hearing of a congressional committee investigating subversion in education. He stated that he was not a Communist, that he was willing to testify about his associations since 1941, but claimed the self-incrimination privilege about inquiries dealing with 1940–41. (He had testified about his affiliations during 1940–41 in earlier state inquiries). He

was discharged under § 903, without the usual hearings for tenured faculty members.

The Court concluded in a 5:4 decision that the summary dismissal violated due process. As Justice Clark read the record, application of § 903 "falls squarely within the prohibition of Wieman v. Updegraff [p. 1301, supra]." He explained: "[As applied, § 903] operates to discharge every city employee who invokes the Fifth Amendment. In practical effect the questions asked are taken as confessed and made the basis of the discharge. No consideration is given to such factors as the subject matter of the questions, remoteness of the period to which they are directed, or justification for exercise of the privilege. It matters not whether the plea resulted from mistake, inadvertence or legal advice conscientiously given, whether wisely or unwisely." The section had converted the privilege "into a conclusive presumption of guilt." He noted, moreover: "It is one thing for the city authorities themselves to inquire into Slochower's fitness, but quite another for his discharge to be based entirely on events occurring before a federal committee." He concluded: "The State has broad powers in the selection and discharge of its employees, and it may be that proper inquiry would show Slochower's continued employment to be inconsistent with a real interest of the State. But there has been no such inquiry here."

Justice Reed's dissent, joined by Justices Burton and Minton, insisted that "the city does have reasonable ground to require its employees either to give evidence regarding facts of official conduct within their knowledge or to give up the positions they hold." He emphasized: "Discharges under § 903 do not depend upon any conclusion as to the guilt of the employee . . . .. We disagree with the Court's assumption that § 903 as a practical matter takes the questions asked as confessed. Cities, like other employers, may reasonably conclude that a refusal to furnish appropriate information is enough to justify discharge. Legally authorized bodies have a right to demand that citizens furnish facts pertinent to official inquiries. The duty to respond may be refused for personal protection against prosecution only, but such avoidance of public duty to furnish information can properly be considered to stamp the employee as a person unfit to hold certain official positions. Such a conclusion is reinforced when the claimant for protection has the role of instructor to youth."

Justice Harlan's dissent also disagreed with Justice Clark's view of the record: "[I]t is the exercise of the privilege itself which is the basis for the discharge, quite apart from any inference of guilt." He added: "A requirement that public school teachers shall furnish information as to their past or present membership in the Communist Party is a relevant step in the implementation of a state policy [discharging for "knowing membership"], and a teacher may be discharged for refusing to comply with that requirement. [Garner.] Moreover, I think that a State may justifiably consider that teachers who refuse to answer questions concerning their official conduct are no longer qualified for public school teaching, on the ground that their refusal to answer jeopardizes the confidence that the public should have in its school system."

2. *Lerner and Beilan: discharging employees for "lack of candor"?* Two years later, Justice Harlan wrote one of the majority opinions when the Court, in two 5:4 decisions, sustained discharges of employees who had refused to answer on self-incrimination grounds questions put by local in-

quirers about present subversive associations. Lerner v. Casey, 357 U.S. 468, and Beilan v. Board of Education, 357 U.S. 399 (1958). Lerner was a New York City subway conductor dismissed on the stated ground that "reasonable grounds exist for belief that because of his doubtful trust and reliability" he was a "security risk" under state law. Beilan involved a Philadelphia school teacher dismissed for "incompetency" based on refusal to answer school officials' questions.

a.   As Justice Harlan's majority opinion in Lerner read the record, Lerner "had been discharged neither because of any inference of Communist Party membership which was drawn from the exercise of the Fifth Amendment privilege, nor because of the assertion of that constitutional protection, but rather because of the doubt created as to his 'reliability' by his refusal to answer a relevant question put by his employer, a doubt which the court held justifiable quite independently of appellant's reasons for his silence. In effect, administrative action was interpreted to rest solely on the refusal to respond. It was this lack of candor which provided the evidence of appellant's doubtful trust and reliability which under the New York statutory scheme constituted him a security risk."

Justice Harlan added: "We think it scarcely debatable that had there been no claim of Fifth Amendment privilege, New York would have been constitutionally entitled to conclude from appellant's refusal to answer what must be conceded to have been a question relevant to the purposes of the statute and his employment, cf. [Garner], that he was of doubtful trust and reliability. Such a conclusion is not 'so strained as not to have a reasonable relation to the circumstances of life as we know them.' Tot v. United States, 319 U.S. 463, 468 [see chap. 12, p. 912, supra]. The fact that New York has chosen to base its dismissal of employees whom it finds to be of doubtful trust and reliability on the ground that they are in effect 'security risks' hardly requires a different determination. . . . Neither the New York statute nor courts purported to equate this ground for dismissal with 'disloyalty.'

"The issue then reduces to the narrow question whether the conclusion which could otherwise be reached from appellant's refusal to answer is constitutionally barred because his refusal was accompanied by the assertion of a Fifth Amendment privilege. We think it does not. The federal privilege against self-incrimination was not available to appellant through the Fourteenth Amendment in this state investigation." [Note the impact of the "incorporation" of the Fifth Amendment, p. 1313, infra.]

b.   In Beilan, similarly, the majority opinion by Justice Burton emphasized that the Board based dismissal of the teacher upon "refusal to answer any inquiry about his relevant activities—not upon those activities themselves. It took care to charge petitioner with incompetency, and not with disloyalty. It found him insubordinate and lacking in frankness and candor—it made no finding as to his loyalty." He stated further: "By engaging in teaching in the public schools, petitioner did not give up his right to freedom of belief, speech or association. He did, however, undertake obligations of frankness, candor and cooperation in answering inquiries made of him by his employing Board examining into his fitness to serve it as a public school teacher."

Justice Douglas' dissent, joined by Justice Black, concluded: "[W]e have here only a bare refusal to testify; and the Court holds that sufficient to show these employees are unfit to hold their public posts. That makes qualification for public office turn solely on a matter of belief—a notion very much at war with the Bill of Rights." Earlier, he noted: "I would allow no inference of wrongdoing to flow from the invocation of any constitutional right. If it be said that we deal not with guilt or innocence but with frankness, the answer is the same. There are areas where government may not probe. [G]overnment has no business penalizing a citizen merely for his beliefs or associations. [I]n N.A.A.C.P. v. Alabama, decided this day [see p. 1316, infra], [we protected against] governmental probing into political activities and associations of one dissident group of people. We should do the same here."

Separate dissents by Chief Justice Warren and Justice Brennan emphasized that Beilan had lost his job more than 13 months after his refusal to answer the school authorities' questions—and only 5 days after a refusal before a congressional committee. Justice Brennan insisted that Beilan was "actually" discharged because of the latter refusal. More generally, he argued that Lerner and Beilan each had been "branded a disloyal American" and that the record was "wholly devoid of [evidence] to support the ultimate finding of disloyalty. Cf. Tot v. United States [at chap. 12, p. 912, supra; see also Schware v. Board of Bar Examiners, note 4, infra]."

3. *Other government employee security problems, state and federal.* a. *State.* Justice Clark, who had written Slochower, note 1 supra, also wrote the majority opinion in Nelson v. County of Los Angeles, 362 U.S. 1 (1960), a 5:3 decision sustaining a dismissal of an employee for silence. Nelson involved a temporary County employee who had refused, on First and Fifth Amendment grounds, to answer questions about present Communist membership before a congressional committee after having been ordered to do so by the County. He was discharged for "insubordination."

Justice Clark, writing for the majority, found his opinion in Slochower distinguishable because "the test here, rather than being the invocation of any constitutional privilege, is the failure of the employee to answer. California has not predicated discharge on any 'built-in' inference of guilt in its statute, but solely on employees' insubordination for failure to give information which we have held that the State has a legitimate interest in securing." He accordingly found the case controlled by Beilan and Lerner. Justice Black, joined by Justice Douglas, dissented: "I would hold that no State can put any kind of penalty on any person for claiming a privilege authorized by the Federal Constitution." Justice Brennan, joined by Justice Douglas, also dissented, because he believed "this case to be governed squarely by Slochower."

b. *Federal.* During the fifties, there were several constitutional challenges to federal loyalty-security programs as well, but the Court usually avoided the constitutional issues in the federal program cases by holding that the administrators had violated the applicable regulations and statutes. See, e. g., Peters v. Hobby, 349 U.S. 331 (1955); Service v. Dulles, 354 U.S. 363 (1957); and Vitarelli v. Seaton, 359 U.S. 535 (1959). Compare Bailey v. Richardson, 182 F.2d 46 (D.C.Cir.1950), affirmed by an equally divided Court, 341 U.S. 918 (1951), and Joint Anti-Fascist Refugee Committee v. McGrath, 341 U.S. 123 (1951). Note also, on the applicability of due process criteria regarding federal security hearings, Greene v. McElroy, 360 U.S. 474 (1959), chap. 12, p. 907, supra; and for a rejection of a constitutional challenge to dismissal without a hearing, Cafeteria Workers v. McElroy, 367 U.S. 886 (1961). On the pervasiveness of loyalty-security programs during this period, see generally Brown, Loyalty and Security (1958), and Gellhorn, Individual Freedom and Governmental Restraints (1956).

4. *The 1957 bar admission cases—Schware and Konigsberg I.* a. Schware v. Board of Bar Examiners, 353 U.S. 232 (1957), was one of two decisions in 1957 in which the Court found inadequate support for state refusals to admit applicants to the bar: the state's inferences regarding present moral character were found irrational on the basis of the records adduced and accordingly violated due process.

The New Mexico Board had refused to let Schware take the bar examination because, "taking into consideration the use of aliases by the applicant, his former connection with subversive organizations, and his record of arrests, he has failed to satisfy the Board as to the requisite moral character for admission to the bar of New Mexico." All of these grounds of the 1953 Board decision were based on matters that had occurred during several years up to 1940. Upon his request, the applicant was given a formal hearing, at which he offered evidence of his excellent moral character since 1940, and he took the stand himself.

Justice Black noted for the Court: "We need not enter into a discussion whether the practice of law is a 'right' or 'privilege'. Regardless of how the states grant of permission to engage in this occupation is characterized, it is sufficient to say that a person cannot be prevented from practicing except for valid reasons. Certainly the practice of law is not a matter of the State's grace." And here the reasons were insufficient: in light of Schware's "forceful showing of good moral character, the evidence upon which the State relies—the arrests for offenses for which petitioner was neither tried nor convicted, the use of an assumed name many years ago, and membership in the Communist Party during the 1930's—cannot be said to raise substantial doubts about his present good moral character." In the absence of evidence which "rationally justifies a finding that Schware was morally unfit to practice law," denial of the opportunity to qualify deprived petitioner of due process of law. Justice Frankfurter, joined by Justices Clark and Harlan, delivered a concurring opinion, concluding that the state court's holding "that Communist affiliation for six to seven years up to 1940 . . . in and of itself made the petitioner 'a person of questionable character' is so dogmatic an inference as to be wholly unwarranted." *

b. Were the grounds relied on in Schware appropriate for the disposition of Konigsberg I, the companion case? In Konigsberg v. State Bar, 353 U.S. 252 (1957), petitioner, who had satisfactorily passed the bar examination and who had appeared at hearings before the Committee of Bar Examiners, was denied admission to the California bar because he "failed to demonstrate that he was a person of good moral character" and because he "failed

---

* Compare a bar admission case a decade earlier, In re Summers, 325 U.S. 561 (1945)—a 5:4 decision sustaining a state refusal to admit to the bar a conscientious objector, on the ground that he could not take the required oath to support the state constitution. Note also Barsky v. Board of Regents, 347 U.S. 442 (1954), sustaining the license suspension of a physician who had been convicted for failure to produce in a congressional inquiry certain financial records of the Joint Anti-Fascist Refugee Committee. Justices Black, Frankfurter and Douglas delivered dissenting opinions emphasizing that the conduct constituting the crime had no bearing on the appellant's competency to practice medicine.

to show that he did not advocate the overthrow of the Government of the United States or the State by force, violence, or other unconstitutional means." At the hearings, petitioner refused, on First Amendment grounds, to answer questions about his political associations and beliefs; but the denial of admission was not based on such refusal. Petitioner offered evidence as to his good moral character and in disproof of his advocacy of violent overthrow of Government. Upon an examination of the record, the Supreme Court concluded that the evidence did not rationally support the grounds for denial of admission. Justice Frankfurter dissented on jurisdictional grounds. Justice Harlan, joined by Justice Clark, after joining the views of Justice Frankfurter, dissented on the merits: "The Court decides the case as if the issue were whether the record contains evidence demonstrating . . . that Konigsberg had a bad moral character. I do not think this is the issue. The question before us, it seems to me, is whether it violates the Fourteenth Amendment for a state bar committee to decline to certify for admission to the bar an applicant who obstructs a proper investigation into his qualifications by deliberately, and without constitutional justification, refusing to answer questions relevant to his fitness under valid standards, and who is therefore deemed by the State, under its law, to have failed to carry his burden of proof to establish that he is qualified." The subsequent proceedings on Konigsberg's application came before the Court in Konigsberg II (which follows).

"ABSOLUTES," "BALANCING," AND THE SECOND KONIGSBERG CASE

In the state proceedings after Konigsberg I (note 4b, supra), the petitioner was once again denied admission to the bar; but this time, the state clearly relied on his refusal to answer, and the Supreme Court (as in the employee cases, notes 2 and 3, supra), sustained that ban on bar admission in a 5:4 decision. Konigsberg v. State Bar of California, 366 U.S. 36 (1961). As Justice Harlan's majority opinion described the second round of Committee hearings, "Konigsberg introduced further evidence as to his good moral character (none of which was rebutted), reiterated unequivocally his disbelief in violent overthrow, and stated that he had never knowingly been a member of any organization which advocated such action. He persisted, however, in his refusals to answer any questions relating to his membership in the Communist Party. The Committee again declined to certify him, this time on the ground that his refusals to answer had obstructed a full investigation into his qualifications."

Justice Harlan emphasized that the 14th Amendment does not forbid a State from denying admission to a bar applicant so long as he refuses to provide unprivileged answers to questions having a substantial relevance to his qualifications. He dismissed as "untenable" the claim "that the questions as to Communist Party membership were made irrelevant . . . by the fact that bare, innocent membership is not a ground of disqualification . . .." The Bar Committee's response was quoted as the "entirely correct" answer to that contention: "You see, by failing to answer the initial question there certainly is no basis and no opportunity for us to investigate with respect to the other matters to which the initial question might very well be considered preliminary." [Compare Keyishian v. Board of Regents, 385 U.S. 589 (1967), chap. 15, p. 1133, supra.]

The rejection of Konigsberg's final claim—that "he was privileged not to respond to questions dealing with Communist Party membership because they unconstitutionally impinged upon rights of free speech and association protected by the Fourteenth Amendment"—evoked an extensive debate between Justice Harlan and Justice Black on "absolutes" and "balancing." (See also their clash in a congressional investigation case two years earlier, Barenblatt v. United States, p. 1335, infra.) Justice Harlan insisted:

"[W]e reject the view that freedom of speech and association . . . are absolutes, not only in the undoubted sense that where the constitutional protection exists it must prevail, but also in the sense that the scope of that protection must be gathered solely from a literal reading of the First Amendment.[1] Throughout its history this Court has consistently recognized at least two ways in which constitutionally protected freedom of speech is narrower than an unlimited license to talk. On the one hand certain forms of speech, or speech in certain contexts, have been considered outside the scope of constitutional protection.[2] . . . On the other hand, general regulatory statutes, not intended to control the content of speech but incidentally limiting its unfettered exercise, have not been regarded as the type of law the First or Fourteenth Amendments forbade Congress or the States to pass, when they have been found justified by subordinating valid governmental interests, a prerequisite to constitutionality which has necessarily involved a weighing of the governmental interest involved. . . . It is in the latter class of cases that this Court has always placed rules compelling disclosure of prior association as an incident of the informed exercise of a valid governmental function. . . . Whenever, in such a context, these constitutional protections are asserted against the exercise of valid governmental powers a reconciliation must be effected, and that perforce requires an appropriate weighing of the respective interests involved. . . . With more particular reference to the present context of a state decision as to character qualifications, it is difficult, indeed, to imagine a view of the constitutional protections of speech and association which would automatically and without consideration of the extent of the deterrence of speech and association and of the importance of the state function, exclude all reference to prior speech or association on such issues as character, purpose, credibility, or intent.

"As regards the questioning of public employees relative to Communist Party membership it has already been held that the interest in not

1. "That view, which of course cannot be reconciled with the law relating to libel, slander, misrepresentation, obscenity, perjury, false advertising, solicitation of crime, complicity by encouragement, conspiracy, and the like, is said to be compelled by the fact that the commands of the First Amendment are stated in unqualified terms. . . . But as Mr. Justice Holmes once said: 'The provisions of the Constitution are not mathematical formulas having their essence in their form; they are organic living institutions transplanted from English soil. Their significance is vital not formal; it is to be gathered not simply by taking the words and a dictionary, but by considering their origin and the line of their growth.' Gompers v. United States, 233 U.S. 604, 610. In this connection also compare the equally unqualified command of the Second Amendment . . . ." [Footnote by the Court.]

2. "That the First Amendment immunity for speech, press and assembly has to be reconciled with valid but conflicting governmental interests was clear to Holmes, J. (. . . Abrams v. United States, 250 U.S. 616, 627); to Brandeis, J. (. . . Whitney v. People of State of California, 274 U.S. 357, 373); and to Hughes, C. J. (. . . Near v. State of Minnesota ex rel. Olson, 283 U.S. 697, 716)." [Footnote by the Court]

subjecting speech and association to the deterrence of subsequent disclosure is outweighed by the State's interest in ascertaining the fitness of the employee for the post he holds, and hence that such questioning does not infringe constitutional protections. [See notes 2 and 3, supra.] With respect to this same question of Communist Party membership, we regard the State's interest in having lawyers who are devoted to the law in its broadest sense, including not only its substantive provisions, but also its procedures for orderly change, as clearly sufficient to outweigh the minimal effect upon free association occasioned by compulsory disclosure in the circumstances here presented.

"There is here no likelihood that deterrence of association may result from foreseeable private action, see NAACP v. Alabama [infra, p. 1316], for bar committee interrogations such as this are conducted in private. . . . Nor is there the possibility that the State may be afforded the opportunity for imposing undetectable arbitrary consequences upon protected association, see Shelton v. Tucker [infra, p. 1320], for a bar applicant's exclusion by reason of Communist Party membership is subject to judicial review, including ultimate review by this Court, should it appear that such exclusion has rested on substantive or procedural factors that do not comport with the Federal Constitution. . . . In these circumstances it is difficult indeed to perceive any solid basis for a claim of unconstitutional intrusion into rights assured by the Fourteenth Amendment."

Justice Black's dissent, joined by Chief Justice Warren and Justice Douglas insisted that the record showed, "beyond any shadow of a doubt, that the reason Konigsberg has been rejected is because the Committee suspects that he was at one time a member of the Communist Party. . . . The majority avoids the otherwise unavoidable necessity of reversing the judgment below on that ground by simply refusing to look beyond the reason given by the Committee to justify Konigsberg's rejection." He proceeded to attack "balancing" as follows:

"The Court attempts to justify its refusal to apply the plain mandate of the First Amendment in part by reference to the so-called 'clear and present danger test' forcefully used by Mr. Justice Holmes and Mr. Justice Brandeis, not to narrow but to broaden the then prevailing interpretation of First Amendment freedoms. I think very little can be found in anything they ever said that would provide support for the 'balancing test' presently in use.

. . . .

"I recognize, of course, that the 'clear and present danger test,' though itself a great advance toward individual liberty over some previous notions of the protections afforded by the First Amendment, does not go as far as my own views as to the protection that should be accorded these freedoms. [I] fear that the creation of 'tests' by which speech is left unprotected under certain circumstances is a standing invitation to abridge it. After the 'clear and present danger test' was diluted and weakened by being recast in terms of this 'balancing' formula [in Dennis, supra, p. 1097], there seems to me to be much room to doubt that Justices Holmes and Brandeis would even have recognized their test. And the reliance upon that weakened 'test' by the majority here, without even so much as an attempt to find either a 'clear' or a 'present' danger, is only another persuasive reason for rejecting all such 'tests' and enforcing the First Amendment according to its terms.

"The Court suggests that a 'literal reading of the First Amendment' would be totally unreasonable because it would invalidate many widely accepted laws. I do not know to what extent this is true. I do not believe, for example, that it would invalidate laws resting upon the premise that where speech is an integral part of unlawful conduct that is going on at the time, the speech can be used to illustrate, emphasize and establish the unlawful conduct.[1] On the other hand, it certainly would invalidate all laws that abridge the right of the people to discuss matters of religious or public interest, in the broadest meaning of those terms, for it is clear that a desire to protect this right was the primary purpose of the First Amendment. Some people have argued, with much force, that the freedoms guaranteed by the First Amendment are limited to somewhat broad areas like those. But I believe this Nation's security and tranquility can best be served by giving the First Amendment the same broad construction that all Bill of Rights guarantees deserve. . . . .

"Whatever may be the wisdom, however, of an approach that would reject exceptions to the plain language of the First Amendment based upon such things as 'libel,' 'obscenity' or 'fighting words,' such is not the issue in this case. [T]he only issue presently before us is whether speech that must be well within the protection of the Amendment should be given complete protection or whether it is entitled only to such protection as is consistent in the minds of a majority of this Court with whatever interest the Government may be asserting to justify its abridgement. The Court, by stating unequivocally that there are no 'absolutes' under the First Amendment, necessarily takes the position that even speech that is admittedly protected by the First Amendment is subject to the 'balancing test' and that therefore no kind of speech is to be protected if the Government can assert an interest of sufficient weight to induce this Court to uphold its abridgement. In my judgment, such a sweeping denial of the existence of any inalienable right to speak undermines the very foundation upon which the First Amendment, the Bill of Rights, and, indeed, our entire structure of government rests. . . .

"[There is a] difference between the sort of 'balancing' that the majority has been doing and the sort of 'balancing' that was intended when that concept was first accepted as a method for insuring the complete protection of First Amendment freedoms even against purely incidental or inadvertent consequences. The term came into use chiefly as a result of the cases in which the power of municipalities to keep their streets open for normal traffic was attacked by groups wishing to use those streets for religious or political purposes. When those cases came before this Court, we did not treat the issue posed by them as one primarily involving First Amendment rights.

. . .

"But those cases never intimated that we would uphold as constitutional an ordinance which purported to rest upon the power of a city to regulate traffic but which was aimed at speech or attempted to regulate the content of speech. . . . Those cases have only begun to take on that meaning by being relied upon, again and again as they are here, to justify the ap-

---

1. "Roth v. United States, 354 U.S. 476, 514 (dissenting opinion). See also National Labor Relations Board v. Virginia Electric & Power Co., 314 U.S. 469; Giboney v. Empire Storage & Ice Co., 336 U.S. 490." [Footnote by Justice Black.]

plication of the 'balancing test' to governmental action that is aimed at speech and depends for its application upon the content of speech. . . .

"The Court seeks to bring this case under the authority of the street-regulation cases and defend its use of the 'balancing test' on the ground that California is attempting only to exercise its permissible power to regulate its Bar and that any effect its action may have upon speech is purely 'incidental.' But I cannot agree that the questions asked Konigsberg with regard to his suspected membership in the Communist Party had nothing more than an 'incidental' effect upon his freedom of speech and association. . . . I think the conclusion is inescapable that this case presents the question of the constitutionality of action by the State of California designed to control the content of speech. As such, it is a 'direct,' and not an 'incidental' abridgment of speech. . . .

"But even if I thought the majority was correct in its view that 'balancing' is proper in this case, I could not agree with its decision. The interest of the Committee in satisfying its curiosity with respect to Konigsberg's 'possible' membership in the Communist Party two decades ago has been inflated out of all proportion to its real value—the vast interest of the public in maintaining unabridged the basic freedoms of speech, press and assembly has been paid little if anything more than lip service—and important constitutional rights have once again been 'balanced' away. This of course, is an ever-present danger of the 'balancing test' for the application of such a test is necessarily tied to the emphasis particular judges give to competing societal values." *

Justice Brennan, joined by Chief Justice Warren, dissented because the Committee had not come forward "with evidence to show that Konigsberg unlawfully advocated the overthrow of the government. Under our decision in Speiser v. Randall, 357 U.S. 513 [1958], the Fourteenth Amendment therefore protects Konigsberg from being denied admission to the Bar for his refusal to answer the questions." Justice Harlan's majority opinion disposing of that argument included the following comments: "[Speiser] held unconstitutional a state procedural rule that in order to obtain an exemption a taxpayer must bear the burden of proof, including both the burdens of establishing a prima facie case and of ultimate persuasion, that he did not advocate the violent overthrow of government. . . . It would be a sufficient answer to any suggestion of the applicability of that holding to the present proceeding to observe that Speiser was explicitly limited so as not to reach cases where, as here, there is no showing of an intent to penalize political beliefs. . . . But there are also additional factors making the rationale of Speiser inapplicable to the case before us. There is no unequivocal indication that California in this proceeding has placed upon petitioner the burden of proof of nonadvocacy of violent overthrow, as dis-

---

* Note the comments on the "balancing" —"absolutes" controversy, supra, especially in the introductory materials to chap. 15, at p. 1056; note also the references to some of the literature on that controversy, at p. 1056, note * .

For elaboration of Justice Black's views on "absolutes," literal reading, and "balancing," see his lecture, "The Bill of Rights," 35 N.Y.U.L.Rev. 865 (1960).

Compare his opinion, on the Contract Clause, in El Paso v. Simmons, 379 U.S. 497 (1965), chap. 11, supra; and see Cahn, "Mr. Justice Black and First Amendment 'Absolutes': A Public Interview," 37 N.Y.U.L.Rev. 549 (1962). For subsequent elaborations of Justice Black's position, see his dissent in Griswold v. Connecticut, chap. 11, p. 824, supra, and his lectures, A Constitutional Faith (1968).

tinguished from its other requirement of 'good moral character.' All it has presently required is an applicant's cooperation with the Committee's search for evidence of forbidden advocacy. Petitioner has been denied admission to the California bar for obstructing the Committee in the performance of its necessary functions of examination and cross-examination, a ruling which indeed presupposes that the burden of producing substantial evidence on the issue of advocacy was not upon petitioner but upon the Committee." *

PUBLIC DEMANDS FOR INFORMATION: THE IMPACT OF THE EXPANDED SELF-INCRIMINATION PRIVILEGE

In the foregoing cases of the fifties, one of the assumptions supporting the Court's views regarding the permissible scope of state inquiries affecting public employees and the bar was that the federal self-incrimination privilege did not apply to the states. In 1964, in Malloy v. Hogan (chap. 12, p. 875, supra), the Court found the privilege applicable via the 14th Amendment. To what extent does that "incorporation" of the Fifth Amendment affect the constitutionally acceptable scope of inquiries—quite apart from modern evolutions in First Amendment doctrine to be considered in sec. 6B below?

1. *Spevack.* In Spevack v. Klein, 385 U.S. 511 (1967), a lawyer had relied on the self-incrimination privilege in refusing to testify and to produce financial records at a state judicial inquiry into allegations of professional misconduct. The state courts ordered him disbarred, relying in part on a 1961 Supreme Court holding—in Cohen v. Hurley, 366 U.S. 117—that no federal self-incrimination privilege was available in state disbarment proceedings. The Supreme Court reversed, holding that Cohen v. Hurley must be overruled in view of the 1964 ruling in Malloy v. Hogan. Justice Douglas'

---

* In a companion case to Konigsberg II, In re Anastaplo, 366 U.S. 82 (1961), the Court upheld Illinois' refusal to admit petitioner to the bar, largely on the authority of Konigsberg. Justice Harlan again delivered the majority opinion. He described the proceedings before the Committee on Character and Fitness as "a wide-ranging exchange . . . in which the Committee sought to explore Anastaplo's ability conscientiously to swear support of the Federal and State Constitutions, . . . and Anastaplo undertook to expound and defend, on historical and ideological premises, his abstract belief in the 'right of revolution,' and to resist, on grounds of asserted constitutional right and scruple, Committee questions which he deemed improper." He stated that the Konigsberg case was not distinguishable merely because in that case "there was some, though weak, independent evidence that the applicant had once been connected with the Communist Party, while here there was no such evidence as to Anastaplo." The State's interrogation is justified even though it "arises merely from a good faith belief in the need for exploratory or testing questioning of the applicants." The Court also found that there had been "adequate warning as to the consequences of his refusal to answer" and that the exclusion from the bar was not "arbitrary or discriminatory" in the circumstances of this case. On the latter point, the Court noted that "there is nothing in the record which would justify our holding that the State has invoked its exclusionary refusal-to-answer rule as a mask for its disapproval of petitioner's notions on the right to overthrow tyrannical government." Justice Black again wrote a dissenting opinion, joined by Chief Justice Warren and Justices Douglas and Brennan. The dissent saw the case as "a striking illustration of the destruction that can be inflicted upon individual liberty when this Court fails to enforce the First Amendment to the full extent of its express and unequivocal terms." Justice Brennan, joined by Chief Justice Warren, again added that the judgment should be reversed on the authority of Speiser v. Randall.

plurality opinion, joined by Chief Justice Warren and Justices Black and Brennan, concluded "that the Self-Incrimination Clause . . . extends its protection to lawyers as well as to other individuals, and that it should not be watered down by imposing the dishonor of disbarment and the deprivation of a livelihood as a price for asserting it." He insisted that the state may impose no sanction which makes assertion of the Fifth Amendment privilege "costly."

Justice Fortas' concurring opinion agreed with the overruling of Cohen v. Hurley but added: "I would distinguish between a lawyer's right to remain silent and that of a public employee who is asked questions specifically, directly, and narrowly relating to the performance of his official duties as distinguished from his beliefs or other matters that are not within the scope of the specific duties which he undertook faithfully to perform as part of his employment by the State. . . . But a lawyer is not an employee of the State. . . . The special responsibilities that he assumes as licensee of the State and officer of the court do not carry with them a diminution, however limited, of his Fifth Amendment rights." Justice Harlan's dissent, joined by Justices Clark and Stewart, insisted that this application of the privilege "serves only to hamper appropriate protection of other fundamental public values." To Justice Harlan, cases like Beilan and Lerner, when read with Slochower, "make plain that so long as state authorities do not derive any imputation of guilt from a claim of the privilege, they may in the course of a bona fide assessment of an employee's fitness for public employment require that the employee disclose information reasonably related to his fitness, and may order his discharge if he declines. Identical principles have been applied by his Court to applicants for admission to the bar." Justice White also dissented.

2. *Garrity.* In a companion case to Spevack, Garrity v. New Jersey, 386 U.S. 493 (1967), the appellants were policemen who had answered questions in a state investigation after having been warned that refusals to answer would subject them to removal from office. Their answers were used in a subsequent prosecution for conspiracy to obstruct the administration of the traffic laws. The Supreme Court's 5:4 decision held that their statements were "coerced" and accordingly reversed their convictions. Justice Douglas' majority opinion stated that the state could not "use the threat of discharge to secure incriminatory evidence against an employee" and that "policemen, like teachers and lawyers, are not relegated to a watered-down version of constitutional rights. There are rights of constitutional stature whose exercise a State may not condition by the exaction of a price." He concluded that the constitutional ban on coerced confessions "prohibits use in subsequent criminal proceedings of confessions obtained under threat of removal from office." Justices White and Harlan, joined by Justices Clark and Stewart, dissented.

3. *Gardner v. Broderick.* Spevack and Garrity left in doubt the question whether public employees could be discharged for refusal to testify at hearings on official misconduct. In Gardner v. Broderick, 392 U.S. 273 (1968), the Court made it clear that they could under certain conditions, even though it found appellant's dismissal unconstitutional. Appellant, a policeman, was dismissed because of his failure to sign a "waiver of immunity" from prosecution after being called before a grand jury investigating police misconduct in connection with unlawful gambling operations. Justice Fortas' opinion

emphasized that appellant was "discharged from office not for failure to answer relevant questions about his official duties, but for refusal to waive a constitutional right." If he had "refused to answer questions specifically, directly, and narrowly relating to the performance of his official duties, without being required to waive his immunity with respect to the use of his answers or the fruits thereof in a criminal prosecution of himself, Garrity v. New Jersey," Justice Fortas elaborated, "the privilege against self-incrimination would not have been a bar to his dismissal." A policeman, in short, is under a greater duty to respond to inquiries than a lawyer. In reaching that conclusion, Justice Fortas adopted for the Court the distinction he had urged in his concurrence in Spevack: The policeman is "directly, immediately, and entirely responsible to the city or State which is his employer. He owes his entire loyalty to it. . . . Unlike the lawyer who is directly responsible to his client, the policeman is either responsible to the State or to no one." Justice Black concurred in the result. [See also the companion case, Uniformed Sanitation Men Ass'n v. Comm'r of Sanitation, 392 U.S. 280 (1968). Justice Harlan, joined by Justice Stewart, concurred in the result in both cases under the compulsion of Spevack and Garrity. He took comfort, however, in being able to find in these opinions "a procedural formula whereby, for example, public officials may now be discharged and lawyers disciplined for refusing to divulge to appropriate authority information pertinent to the faithful performance of their offices. I add only that this is a welcome breakthrough in what Spevack and Garrity might otherwise have been thought to portend."]

THE EMERGENCE OF THE MODERN APPROACH: JUSTIFICATIONS FOR STATE INQUIRIES AND THE NAACP MEMBERSHIP LISTS

During the late fifties, while most First Amendment defenses to public demands for information were proving unsuccessful (e. g., Lerner v. Casey, p. 1304, supra, and Barenblatt v. United States, p. 1335, infra), the Court blocked a state effort to obtain access to NAACP membership lists in NAACP v. Alabama, 357 U.S. 449 (1958), which follows. The Court's critical scrutiny of the asserted state justification for the inquiry and its sensitivity to collateral impacts of disclosure on First Amendment areas foreshadowed the broader constitutional restrictions evolved in the cases of the sixties.

NAACP v. Alabama was followed by a similar ruling in a similar context: Bates v. Little Rock, 361 U.S. 516 (1960), again protected NAACP membership lists. In Bates, as an aid in the collection of a license tax on any "trade, business, profession, vocation or calling," the city required all organizations to submit certain information, including the names of persons contributing money. Petitioner, custodian of records of a local branch of the organization, was convicted for failing to give this information. The Supreme Court, in an opinion by Justice Stewart, reversed. It found sufficient evidence that the disclosure of the lists "would work a significant interference with the freedom of association" of the members and concluded that there was a "complete failure" in the record "to demonstrate a controlling justification" for such interference. Justice Stewart noted that no plausible claim could be made that the NAACP was subject to the license tax. [See also the NAACP membership list context of a major case of the sixties curtailing legislative investigations, Gibson v. Florida Legislative Investigation Committee, 372 U.S. 539 (1963) (sec. 7, p. 1341, infra).]

In NAACP v. Alabama and in Bates, the Court found the state's claim that it was seeking relevant information weak indeed. In Shelton v. Tucker, 364 U.S. 479 (1960), with NAACP activity once again providing the background, the relevance of the inquiry into teachers' associations could not be denied. Nevertheless, the Court blocked the questioning. Building on the membership list cases, the Court found relevance an inadequate justification for an inquiry so broad. The Shelton case, with which Sec. 6B on the sixties begins (p. 1320, infra), together with the NAACP v. Alabama decision, with which this section 6A on the fifties ends, form a bridge between the judicial emphases of the two decades. Shelton, moreover, symbolizes the greater judicial scrutiny of public inquiries and marks the emergence of doctrines (e. g., overbreadth, see pp. 1132, supra, and 1325, infra) increasingly prominent in the later cases.

NAACP v. ALABAMA

357 U.S. 449, 78 S.Ct. 1163, 2 L.Ed.2d 1488 (1958).

Certiorari to the Supreme Court of Alabama.

Mr. Justice HARLAN delivered the opinion of the Court.

We review from the standpoint of its validity under the Federal Constitution a judgment of civil contempt entered against petitioner, the National Association for the Advancement of Colored People, in the courts of Alabama. The question presented is whether Alabama, consistently with the Due Process Clause of the Fourteenth Amendment, can compel petitioner to reveal to the State's Attorney General the names and addresses of all its Alabama members and agents, without regard to their positions or functions in the Association. The judgment of contempt was based upon petitioner's refusal to comply fully with a court order requiring in part the production of membership lists. . . .

Alabama has a statute similar to those of many other States which requires foreign corporations, except as exempted, to qualify before doing business by filing the corporate charter with the Secretary of State and designating a place of business and an agent to receive service of process. The statute imposes a fine on a corporation transacting intrastate business before qualifying and provides for criminal prosecution of officers of such a corporation. . . . The National Association for the Advancement of Colored People is a nonprofit membership corporation organized under the laws of New York. [I]t operates through chartered affiliates which are independent unincorporated associations, with membership therein equivalent to membership in petitioner. The first Alabama affiliates were chartered in 1918. Since that time the aims of the Association have been advanced through activities of its affiliates, and in 1951 the Association itself opened a regional office in Alabama, at which it employed two supervisory persons and one clerical worker. The Association has never complied with the qualification statute, from which it considered itself exempt.

In 1956 the Attorney General of Alabama brought an equity suit in the State Circuit Court, Montgomery County, to enjoin the Association from conducting further activities within, and to oust it from, the State. . . .

On the day the complaint was filed, the Circuit Court issued *ex parte* an order restraining the Association, *pendente lite,* from engaging in further activities within the State and forbidding it to take any steps to qualify itself to do business therein.

Petitioner demurred [and] contended that its activities did not subject it to the qualification requirements of the statute and that in any event what the State sought to accomplish by its suit would violate rights to freedom of speech and assembly . . .. Before the date set for a hearing on this motion, the State moved for the production of a large number of the Association's records and papers, including . . . records containing the names and addresses of all Alabama "members" and "agents" of the Association. It alleged that all such documents were necessary for adequate preparation for the hearing, in view of petitioner's denial of the conduct of intrastate business within the meaning of the qualification statute. Over petitioner's objections, the court ordered the production of a substantial part of the requested records, including the membership lists, and postponed the hearing on the restraining order to a date later than the time ordered for production.

Thereafter petitioner filed its answer to the bill in equity. It admitted its Alabama activities substantially as alleged in the complaint and that it had not qualified to do business in the State. Although still disclaiming the statute's application to it, petitioner offered to qualify if the bar from qualification made part of the restraining order were lifted, and it submitted with the answer an executed set of the forms required by the statute. However petitioner did not comply with the production order, and for this failure was adjudged in civil contempt and fined $10,000. The contempt judgment provided that the fine would be subject to reduction or remission if compliance were forthcoming within five days but otherwise would be increased to $100,000.

At the end of the five-day period petitioner produced substantially all the data called for by the production order except its membership lists, as to which it contended that Alabama could not constitutionally compel disclosure. [T]he Circuit Court made a further order adjudging petitioner in continuing contempt and increasing the fine already imposed to $100,000. Under Alabama law, . . . the effect of the contempt adjudication was to foreclose petitioner from obtaining a hearing on the merits of the underlying ouster action, or from taking any steps to dissolve the temporary restraining order which had been issued *ex parte,* until it purged itself of contempt. . . .

[The Court rejected two contentions by respondent: (1) that the Court had no jurisdiction because the judgment below could be supported on an independent and adequate state ground, and (2) that the Association had no standing to assert the constitutional rights of its members. See the discussion of this case and the subsequent proceedings in chap. 2, pp. 122 and 123, supra.]

We thus reach petitioner's claim that the production order in the state litigation trespasses upon fundamental freedoms protected by the Due Process Clause of the Fourteenth Amendment. . . .

Effective advocacy of both public and private points of view, particularly controversial ones, is undeniably enhanced by group association, as this

Court has more than once recognized by remarking upon the close nexus between the freedoms of speech and assembly. . . . It is beyond debate that freedom to engage in association for the advancement of beliefs and ideas is an inseparable aspect of the "liberty" assured by the Due Process Clause of the Fourteenth Amendment, which embraces freedom of speech. . . . Of course, it is immaterial whether the beliefs sought to be advanced by association pertain to political, economic, religious or cultural matters, and state action which may have the effect of curtailing the freedom to associate is subject to the closest scrutiny.

The fact that Alabama, so far as is relevant to the validity of the contempt judgment presently under review, has taken no direct action . . . to restrict the right of petitioner's members to associate freely, does not end inquiry into the effect of the production order. . . . In the domain of these indispensable liberties, whether of speech, press, or association, the decisions of this Court recognize that abridgment of such rights, even though unintended, may inevitably follow from varied forms of governmental action. [R]ecognition of possible unconstitutional intimidation of the free exercise of the right to advocate underlay this Court's narrow construction of the authority of a congressional committee investigating lobbying and of an Act regulating lobbying, although in neither case was there an effort to suppress speech. United States v. Rumely, 345 U.S. 41, 46–47; United States v. Harriss, 347 U.S. 612, 625–626.* . . .

It is hardly a novel perception that compelled disclosure of affiliation with groups engaged in advocacy may constitute as effective a restraint on freedom of association as the forms of governmental action in the cases above were thought likely to produce upon the particular constitutional rights there involved. This Court has recognized the vital relationship between freedom to associate and privacy in one's associations. . . . Inviolability of privacy in group association may in many circumstances be indispensable to preservation of freedom of association, particularly where a group espouses dissident beliefs. . . .

---

* United States v. Rumely, 345 U.S. 41 (1953), set aside a contempt conviction arising out of a lobbying investigation. United States v. Harriss, 347 U.S. 612 (1954), involved the Federal Regulation of Lobbying Act. It requires certain designated reports to Congress by every person receiving contributions or expending money for the purpose of influencing the passage or defeat of legislation by Congress, and it also requires every person to register with Congress and make certain disclosures who engages for pay to attempt to influence the passage or defeat of legislation by Congress. As construed, the Act was sustained against First Amendment objections. The evil which the Lobbying Act was designed to help prevent is that "the voice of the people may all too easily be drowned out by the voice of special interest groups seeking favored treatment while masquerading as proponents of the public weal." To that end Congress has sought, not to prohibit these pressures, but to provide for a "modicum of information from those who for hire attempt to influence legislation or who collect or spend funds for that purpose. It acted in the same spirit and for a similar purpose in passing the Federal Corrupt Practices Act—to maintain the integrity of a basic governmental process." Justice Douglas, with whom Justice Black concurred, delivered a dissenting opinion: "Since the Act touches on the exercise of First Amendment rights, and is not narrowly drawn to meet precise evils, its vagueness has some of the evils of a continuous and effective restraint." Justice Jackson also dissented: "I think we should point out the defects and limitations which condemn this Act so clearly that the Court cannot sustain it as written, and leave its rewriting to Congress."

We think that the production order, in the respects here drawn in question, must be regarded as entailing the likelihood of a substantial restraint upon the exercise by petitioner's members of their right to freedom of association. Petitioner has made an uncontroverted showing that on past occasions revelation of the identity of its rank-and-file members has exposed these members to economic reprisal, loss of employment, threat of physical coercion, and other manifestations of public hostility. Under these circumstances, we think it apparent that compelled disclosure of petitioner's Alabama membership is likely to affect adversely the ability of petitioner and its members to pursue their collective effort to foster beliefs which they admittedly have the right to advocate, in that it may induce members to withdraw from the Association and dissuade others from joining it because of fear of exposure of their beliefs shown through their associations and of the consequences of this exposure.

It is not sufficient to answer, as the State does here, that whatever repressive effect compulsory disclosure of names of petitioner's members may have upon participation by Alabama citizens in petitioner's activities follows not from *state* action but from *private* community pressures. The crucial factor is the interplay of governmental and private action, for it is only after the initial exertion of state power represented by the production order that private action takes hold.

We turn to the final question whether Alabama has demonstrated an interest in obtaining the disclosures it seeks from petitioner which is sufficient to justify the deterrent effect which we have concluded these disclosures may well have on the free exercise by petitioner's members of their constitutionally protected right of association. . . . Such a ". . . subordinating interest of the State must be compelling," Sweezy v. New Hampshire, 354 U.S. 234, 265 (concurring opinion) [p. 1333, infra].

It is important to bear in mind that petitioner asserts no right to absolute immunity from state investigation, and no right to disregard Alabama's laws. As shown by its substantial compliance with the production order, petitioner does not deny Alabama's right to obtain from it such information as the State desires concerning the purposes of the Association and its activities within the State. . . . It has urged the rights solely of its ordinary rank-and-file members. This is therefore not analogous to a case involving the interest of a State in protecting its citizens in their dealings with paid solicitors or agents of foreign corporations by requiring identification. See [Cantwell v. Connecticut].

Whether there was "justification" in this instance turns solely on the substantiality of Alabama's interest in obtaining the membership lists. The exclusive purpose [claimed by the state] was to determine whether petitioner was conducting intrastate business in violation of the Alabama foreign corporation registration statute, and the membership lists were expected to help resolve this question. . . . Without intimating the slightest view upon the merits of these issues, we are unable to perceive that the disclosure of the names of petitioner's rank-and-file members has a substantial bearing on . . . them. As matters stand in the state court, petitioner (1) has admitted its presence and conduct of activities in Alabama since 1918; (2) has offered to comply in all respects with the state qualification statute, although preserving its contention that the statute does not apply to it; and (3) has apparently complied satisfactorily with the production order, except for the membership lists. [W]hatever interest the State may have in obtaining names of ordinary members has not been shown to be sufficient to overcome petitioner's constitutional objections to the production order.

From what has already been said, we think it apparent that Bryant v. Zimmerman, 278 U.S. 63, cannot be relied on in support of the State's position, for that case involved markedly different considerations in terms of the interest of the State in obtaining disclosure. There, this Court upheld, as applied to a member of a local chapter of the Ku Klux Klan, a New York statute requiring any unincorporated association which demanded an oath as a condition to membership to file with state officials copies of its ". . . constitution, by-laws, rules, regulations and oath of membership, together with a roster of its membership and a list of its officers for the current year." In its opinion, the Court took care to emphasize the nature of the organization which New York sought to regulate. The decision was based on the particular character of the Klan's activities, involving acts of unlawful intimidation and violence, which the Court assumed was before the state legislature when it enacted the statute, and of which the Court itself took judicial notice. Furthermore, the situation before us is significantly different from that in Bryant, because the organization there had made no effort to comply with any of the requirements of New York's statute but rather had refused to furnish the State with *any* information as to its local activities.

We hold that the immunity from state scrutiny of membership lists which the Association claims on behalf of its members is here so related to the right of the members to pursue their lawful private interest privately and to associate freely with others in so doing as to come within the protection of the Fourteenth Amendment. And we conclude that Alabama has fallen short of showing a controlling justification for the deterrent effect on the free enjoyment of the right to associate which disclosure of membership lists is likely to have. Accordingly, the judgment of civil contempt and the $100,000 fine which resulted from petitioner's refusal to comply with the production order in this respect must fall. . . .

Reversed.*

B. THE CHANGES SINCE THE SIXTIES

SHELTON v. TUCKER †

364 U.S. 479, 81 S.Ct. 247, 5 L.Ed.2d 231 (1960).

Appeal from the United States District Court for the Eastern District of Arkansas.

---

* Claims to freedom from coerced association were argued but not reached by a majority of the Court in several cases challenging union shop and integrated bar arrangements. See, e. g., International Association of Machinists v. Street, 367 U.S. 740 (1961) (claim that dues under union shop agreement were used to support political causes with which members disagreed), and Lathrop v. Donohue, 367 U.S. 820 (1961) (attack on dues requirements under integrated bar system). See also Railway Employes' Department v. Hanson, 351 U.S. 225 (1956), and Brotherhood of Railway Clerks v. Allen, 373 U.S. 113 (1963).

† Together with Carr v. Young, on certiorari to the Supreme Court of Arkansas.

Mr. Justice STEWART delivered the opinion of the Court.

An Arkansas statute compels every teacher, as a condition of employment in a State supported school or college, to file annually an affidavit listing without limitation every organization to which he has belonged or regularly contributed within the preceding five years. At issue in these two cases is the validity of that statute under the Fourteenth Amendment to the Constitution. . . .

The plaintiffs in the Federal District Court (appellants here) were B. T. Shelton, a teacher employed in the Little Rock Public School System, suing for himself and others similarly situated, together with the Arkansas Teachers Association and its Executive Secretary, suing for the benefit of members of the Association. Shelton had been employed in the Little Rock Special School District for twenty-five years. In the spring of 1959 he was notified that, before he could be employed for the 1959–1960 school year, he must file the affidavit required by Act 10, listing all his organizational connections over the previous five years. He declined to file the affidavit, and his contract for the ensuing school year was not renewed. At the trial the evidence showed that he was not a member of the Communist Party or of any organization advocating the overthrow of the Government by force, and that he was a member of the National Association for the Advancement of Colored People. The court upheld Act 10, finding the information it required was "relevant," and relying on several decisions of this Court. . . . [1]

The plaintiffs in the State court proceedings (petitioners here) were Max Carr, an associate professor at the University of Arkansas, and Ernest T. Gephardt, a teacher at Central High School in Little Rock, each suing for himself and others similarly situated. Each refused to execute and file the affidavit required by Act 10. Carr executed an affirmation in which he listed his membership in professional organizations, denied ever having been a member of any subversive organization, and offered to answer any questions which the University authorities might constitutionally ask touching upon his qualifications as a teacher. Gephardt filed an affidavit stating that he had never belonged to a subversive organization, disclosing his membership in the Arkansas Education Association and the American Legion, and also offering to answer any questions which the school authorities might constitutionally ask touching upon his qualifications as a teacher. Both were advised that their failure to comply with the requirements of Act 10 would make impossible their re-employment as teachers for the following school year. . . .

I.

It is urged here, as it was unsuccessfully urged throughout the proceedings in both the Federal and State courts, that Act 10 deprives teachers in Arkansas of their rights to personal, associational, and academic liberty, protected by the Due Process Clause of the Fourteenth Amendment from invasion by state action. In considering this contention, we deal with two basic postulates.

1. In the same proceeding the court held constitutionally invalid an Arkansas statute (Acts 1959, Act 115) making it unlawful for any member of the National Association for the Advancement of Colored People to be employed by the State of Arkansas or any of its subdivisions. 174 F.Supp. 351. [Footnote by the Court.]

First. There can be no doubt of the right of a state to investigate the competence and fitness of those whom it hires to teach in its schools, as this Court before now has had occasion to recognize. . . .

This controversy is thus not of a pattern with such cases as N.A.A.C.P. v. Alabama, 357 U.S. 449, and Bates v. Little Rock, 361 U.S. 516. In those cases the Court held that there was no substantially relevant correlation between the governmental interest asserted and the state's effort to compel disclosure of the membership lists involved. Here, by contrast, there can be no question of the relevance of a state's inquiry into the fitness and competence of its teachers.[2]

Second. It is not disputed that to compel a teacher to disclose his every associational tie is to impair that teacher's right of free association, a right closely allied to freedom of speech and a right which, like free speech, lies at the foundation of a free society. DeJonge v. Oregon, 299 U.S. 353, 364; Bates v. Little Rock, supra, 361 U.S. at pages 522–523. Such interference with personal freedom is conspicuously accented when the teacher serves at the absolute will of those to whom the disclosure must be made— those who any year can terminate the teacher's employment without bringing charges, without notice, without a hearing, without affording an opportunity to explain.

The statute does not provide that the information it requires be kept confidential. Each school board is left free to deal with the information as it wishes. The record contains evidence to indicate that fear of public disclosure is neither theoretical nor groundless.[3] Even if there were no disclosure to the general public, the pressure upon a teacher to avoid any ties which might displease those who control his professional destiny would be constant and heavy. Public exposure, bringing with it the possibility of public pressures upon school boards to discharge teachers who belong to unpopular or minority organizations, would simply operate to widen and aggravate the impairment of constitutional liberty.

The vigilant protection of constitutional freedoms is nowhere more vital than in the community of American schools. . . .

II.

The question to be decided here is not whether the State of Arkansas can ask certain of its teachers about all their organizational relationships. It is not whether the State can ask all of its teachers about certain of their associational ties. It is not whether teachers can be asked how many organizations they belong to, or how much time they spend in organizational ac-

2. The declared purpose of Act 10 is "to provide assistance in the administration and financing of the public schools . . . ." The declared justification for the emergency clause is "to assist in the solution" of problems raised by "the decisions of the United States Supreme Court in the school segregation cases." . . . But neither the breadth and generality of the declared purpose nor the possible irrelevance of the emergency provision detract from the existence of an actual relevant state interest in the inquiry. [Footnote by the Court.]

3. In the state court proceedings a witness who was a member of the Capital Citizens Council testified that his group intended to gain access to some of the Act 10 affidavits with a view to eliminating from the school system persons who supported organizations unpopular with the group. Among such organizations he named the American Civil Liberties Union, the Urban League, the American Association of University Professors, and the Women's Emergency Committee to Open Our Schools. [Footnote by the Court.]

tivity. The question is whether the State can ask every one of its teachers to disclose every single organization with which he has been associated over a five-year period. The scope of the inquiry required by Act 10 is completely unlimited. . . . The statute requires a teacher . . . to list, without number, every conceivable kind of associational tie—social, professional, political, avocational, or religious. Many such relationships could have no possible bearing upon the teacher's occupational competence or fitness.

In a series of decisions this Court has held that, even though the governmental purpose be legitimate and substantial, that purpose cannot be pursued by means that broadly stifle fundamental personal liberties when the end can be more narrowly achieved.[4] The breadth of legislative abridgment must be viewed in the light of less drastic means for achieving the same basic purpose. . . . As recently as last Term we held invalid an ordinance prohibiting the distribution of handbills because the breadth of its application went far beyond what was necessary to achieve a legitimate governmental purpose. Talley v. California, 362 U.S. 60.* . . .

The unlimited and indiscriminate sweep of the statute now before us brings it within the ban of our prior cases. The statute's comprehensive interference with associational freedom goes far beyond what might be justified in the exercise of the State's legitimate inquiry into the fitness and competency of its teachers. The judgments in both cases must be reversed.

It is so ordered.

Mr. Justice FRANKFURTER, dissenting. . . .

Where state assertions of authority are attacked as impermissibly restrictive upon thought, expression, or association, the existence vel non of other possible less restrictive means of achieving the object which the State seeks is, of course, a constitutionally relevant consideration. This is not because some novel, particular rule of law obtains in cases of this kind. Whenever the reasonableness and fairness of a measure are at issue . . . the availability or unavailability of alternative methods of proceeding is germane. Thus, a State may not prohibit the distribution of literature on

---

4. In other areas, involving different constitutional issues, more administrative leeway has been thought allowable in the interest of increased efficiency in accomplishing a clearly constitutional central purpose. See Purity Extract & Tonic Co. v. Lynch, 226 U.S. 192 . . . . But cf. Dean Milk Co. v. Madison, 340 U.S. 349.

*Talley involved a Los Angeles ordinance which prohibited the distribution of any handbill "in any place under any circumstances" unless the handbill had printed on it the name and address of the person who prepared, distributed or sponsored it. The ordinance was held "void on its face." The Court noted that the identification requirement itself "would tend to restrict freedom to distribute information and thereby freedom of expression," and added: "We have recently had occasion to hold in two cases that there are times and circumstances

when States may not compel members of groups engaged in the dissemination of ideas to be publicly identified. Bates v. City of Little Rock, 361 U.S. 516; NAACP v. Alabama, 357 U.S. 449, 462. The reason for those holdings was that identification and fear of reprisal might deter perfectly peaceful discussions of public matters of importance. This broad Los Angeles ordinance is subject to the same infirmity. We hold that it, like the Griffin, Georgia, ordinance [see Lovell v. Griffith, p. 1142, supra], is void on its face." The Court rejected the argument that the ordinance was a justifiable "way to identify those responsible for fraud, false advertising, and libel," stating that "the ordinance is in no manner so limited." Justice Clark, joined by Justices Frankfurter and Whittaker, dissented: "I stand second to none in supporting Talley's right of free speech—but not his freedom of anonymity."

its cities' streets as a means of preventing littering, when the same end might be achieved with only slightly greater inconvenience by applying the sanctions of the penal law not to the pamphleteer who distributes the paper but to the recipient who crumples it and throws it away. . . . But the consideration of feasible alternative modes of regulation in these cases did not imply that the Court might substitute its own choice among alternatives for that of a state legislature, or that the States were to be restricted to the "narrowest" workable means of accomplishing an end. . . . Consideration of alternatives may focus the precise exercise of state legislative authority which is tested in this Court by the standard of reasonableness, but it does not alter or displace that standard. The issue remains whether, in light of the particular kind of restriction upon individual liberty which a regulation entails, it is reasonable for a legislature to choose that form of regulation rather than others less restrictive. To that determination, the range of judgment easily open to a legislature in considering the relative degrees of efficiency of alternative means in achieving the end its seeks is pertinent.

In the present case the Court strikes down an Arkansas statute requiring that teachers disclose to school officials all of their organizational relationships, on the ground that "many such relationships could have no possible bearing upon the teacher's occupational competence or fitness." Granted that a given teacher's membership in the First Street Congregation is, standing alone, of little relevance to what may rightly be expected of a teacher, is that membership equally irrelevant when it is discovered that the teacher is in fact a member of the First Street Congregation *and* the Second Street Congregation *and* the Third Street Congregation *and* the 4–H Club *and* the 3–H Club *and* half a dozen other groups? Presumably, a teacher may have so many divers associations, so many divers commitments, that they consume his time and energy and interest at the expense of his work or even of his professional dedication. Unlike wholly individual interests, organizational connections—because they involve obligations undertaken with relation to other persons—may become inescapably demanding and distracting. Surely, a school board is entitled to inquire whether any of its teachers has placed himself, or is placing himself, in a condition where his work may suffer. Of course, the State might ask: "To how many organizations do you belong? " or "How much time do you expend at organizational activity? " But the answer to such questions could reasonably be regarded by a state legislature as insufficient, both because the veracity of the answer is more difficult to test, in cases where doubts as to veracity may arise, than in the case of the answers required by the Arkansas statute, and because an estimate of time presently spent in organizational activity reveals nothing as to the quality and nature of that activity, upon the basis of which, necessarily, judgment or prophesy of the extent of future involvement must be based. A teacher's answers to the questions which Arkansas asks, moreover, may serve the purpose of making known to school authorities persons who come into contact with the teacher in all of the phases of his activity in the community, and who can be questioned, if need be, concerning the teacher's conduct in matters which this Court can certainly not now say are lacking in any pertinence to professional fitness. It is difficult to understand how these particular ends could be achieved by asking "certain of [the State's] teachers about all their organizational relationships," or "all of its teachers about certain of their associational ties," or all of its teachers how many associations currently involve them or during how many hours; and difficult, therefore, to appreciate why the Court deems unreasonable and forbids what Arkansas does ask. . . .

I am authorized to say that Mr. Justice CLARK, Mr. Justice HARLAN and Mr. Justice WHITTAKER agree with this opinion.

Mr. Justice HARLAN, whom Mr. Justice FRANKFURTER, Mr. Justice CLARK and Mr. Justice WHITTAKER join, dissenting. . . .

I do not mean to say that alternatives such as an enquiry limited to the names of organizations of whose character the State is presently aware, or to a class of organizations defined by their purposes, would not be more consonant with a decent respect for the privacy of the teacher, nor that such alternatives would be utterly unworkable. I do see, however, that these alternatives suffer from deficiencies so obvious where a State is bent upon discovering everything which would be relevant to its proper purposes, that I cannot say that it must, as a matter of constitutional compulsion, adopt some such means instead of those which have been chosen here. . . .

ALTERNATIVE MEANS AND OVERBROADNESS: A FURTHER COMMENT, PROMPTED BY SHELTON v. TUCKER

When the Court finds the state interest legitimate, yet the means chosen too broad, is it under an obligation to explain what narrower means to achieve the state's objective were available? The Court's footnote 4 suggests the Dean Milk Case as an analogy. See chap. 8, p. 657, supra. But in setting aside the city "health" ordinance on commerce grounds there, the Court did suggest narrower available alternatives. Yet in the increasing resort to the Shelton v. Tucker approach, the Court tends to be silent about alternatives. See, e. g., United States v. Robel, 389 U.S. 258 (1967) (p. 1122, supra); see Gunther, "Reflections on Robel . . . ," 20 Stan.L.Rev. 1140 (1968).

When the Court does *not* spell out alternatives, is it really using the Dean Milk technique as a facade? Should the Court say simply that state justifications are outweighed by the burdens imposed on First Amendment rights? Is overbroadness talk more palatable to the Court because it gives the appearance of leaving alternatives open to the legislature—of intervening in legislative choices more marginally than outright "balancing" would?

Is a decision that fails to spell out in what respect a means is too broad, as in Shelton, a decision that "lacks intellectual coherence"? See Bickel, The Least Dangerous Branch (1962). Would spelling out of alternatives as the Court did in Dean Milk subject the Court to charges of "legislating" without adequate knowledge—as Justice Black's dissent in Dean Milk charged? Is it too much to expect the Court to say more about alternatives than it did in Shelton, even if the degree of detail offered in Dean Milk is not required? Do the later overbroadness cases—e. g., Keyishian—do better in achieving a happy medium? See p. 1133, supra.

LOYALTY OATHS AND EMPLOYEE SECURITY
PROGRAMS IN THE SIXTIES

Recall the loyalty oath cases of the early fifties considered above—e. g. Wieman v. Updegraff, p. 1301. Did the Court's encounters with similar problems in the early sixties, in Cramp and Baggett, infra, depart sharply from the earlier analyses? Do Cramp and Baggett explain the invalidation of a loyalty oath statute in Elfbrandt v. Russell, which follows? Or were the obscurities of Elfbrandt explainable as an implicit repudiation of the approaches of the fifties, including Lerner and Beilan? See Israel, "Elfbrandt v. Russell: The Demise of the Oath?" 1966 Sup.Ct.Rev. 193.

Did Keyishian, a year after Elfbrandt, provide retroactive explanation of Elfbrandt and make explicit the new directions? Is Keyishian sound? In his critique of Elfbrandt, Professor Israel commented: "[O]pinions relying upon the 'overbroadness' rule often provide no more indication of the Court's analysis than a conclusionary statement that a particular aspect of the statutory infringement on speech was overly broad as it applied to the particular interest that the state advanced in that case. The majority opinion in Elfbrandt fits this pattern and, indeed, is more delinquent, since the Court failed in large part even to identify the state interest against which the legislation was balanced." Is that comment justified? Is it less applicable to Keyishian?

1. *Cramp.* Cramp v. Board of Public Instruction, 368 U.S. 278 (1961), involved a Florida statute requiring each public employee to swear that he had never lent his "aid, support, advice, counsel or influence to the Communist Party." Failure to execute the oath resulted in immediate discharge. The Florida Supreme Court ruled that "the element of scienter was implicit in . . . the statute." The United States Supreme Court nevertheless sustained a teacher's challenge to the law. Justice Stewart's opinion emphasized that the "extraordinary ambiguity of the statutory language" was "completely lacking in . . . terms susceptible of objective measurement" and noted that the "vice of unconstitutional vagueness is further aggravated where, as here, the statute in question operates to inhibit the exercise of individual freedoms affirmatively protected by the Constitution."

2. *Baggett.* In Baggett v. Bullitt, 377 U.S. 360 (1964), the Court, relying in part on the Cramp decision, invalidated two loyalty oath requirements imposed by the State of Washington. One required teachers to swear, for example, that they "will by precept and example promote respect for the flag and the institutions of the United States of America and the State of Washington"; the other required all state employees to swear that they were not members of a "subversive organization." In an opinion by Justice White, the Court held the requirements "invalid on their face because their language is unduly vague, uncertain and broad." Justice Clark, joined by Justice Harlan, dissented. As to the first oath, he argued that the state courts should be given an opportunity to construe it. As to the second, he claimed that Cramp was "not apposite"; that the Washington statute was "much more clear than the Smith Act"; that the Gerende decision (p. 1302, supra) was in effect being overruled; and that the majority's interpretation of the Washington oath "is to build up a whimsical and farcical straw man which is not only grim but Grimm." See also Whitehill v. Elkins, 389 U.S. 54 (1967), holding the Maryland teachers' oath unconstitutionally vague (as noted at p. 1302, supra).

ELFBRANDT v. RUSSELL

384 U.S. 11, 86 S.Ct. 1238, 16 L.Ed.2d 321 (1966).

Certiorari to the Supreme Court of Arizona.

Mr. Justice DOUGLAS delivered the opinion of the Court.

This case . . . involves questions concerning the constitutionality of an Arizona Act requiring an oath from state employees . . . . The oath reads in conventional fashion as follows:

> "I, (type or print name) do solemnly swear (or affirm) that I will support the Constitution of the United States and the Constitution and laws of the state of Arizona; that I will bear true faith and allegiance to the same, and defend them against all enemies whatever, and that I will faithfully and impartially discharge the duties of the office of (name of office) according to the best of my ability, so help me God (or so I do affirm)."

The Legislature put a gloss on the oath by subjecting to a prosecution for perjury and for discharge from public office anyone who took the oath and who "knowingly and wilfully becomes or remains a member of the communist party of the United States or its successors or any of its subordinate organizations" or "any other organization" having for "one of its purposes" the overthrow of the government of Arizona or any of its political subdivisions where the employee had knowledge of the unlawful purpose. Petitioner, a teacher and a Quaker, decided she could not in good conscience take the oath, not knowing what it meant and not having any chance to get a hearing at which its precise scope and meaning could be determined. This suit for declaratory relief followed. . . .

We recognized in Scales v. United States [p. 1113, supra] that "quasi-political parties or other groups . . . may embrace both legal and illegal aims." We noted that a "blanket prohibition of association with a group having both legal and illegal aims" would pose "a real danger that legitimate political expression or association would be impaired." The statute with which we dealt in Scales, the so-called "membership clause" of the Smith Act (18 U.S.C. § 2385), was found not to suffer from this constitutional infirmity because as the Court construed it, the statute reached only "active" membership . . . with the "specific intent" of assisting in achieving the unlawful ends of the organization . . . .

Any lingering doubt that proscription of mere knowing membership, without any showing of "specific intent," would run afoul of the Constitution was set at rest by our decision in Aptheker v. Secretary of State, [p. 1121, supra]. We dealt there with a statute which provided that no member of a Communist organization ordered by the Subversive Activities Control Board to register shall apply for or use a passport. We concluded that the statute would not permit a narrow reading of the sort we gave § 2385 in Scales. . . . The statute, as we read it, covered membership which was not accompanied by a specific intent to further the unlawful aims of the organization, and we held it unconstitutional.

The oath and accompanying statutory gloss challenged here suffer from an identical constitutional infirmity. One who subscribes to this Arizona oath and who is, or thereafter becomes, a knowing member of an organization which has as "one of its purposes" the violent overthrow of the government, is subject to immediate discharge and criminal penalties. Nothing in the oath, the statutory gloss, or the construction of the oath and statutes given by the Arizona Supreme Court, purports to exclude association by one who does not subscribe to the organization's unlawful ends. Here as in Baggett v. Bullitt, supra, the "hazard of being prosecuted for knowing but guiltless behavior" . . . is a reality. People often label as "communist" ideas which they oppose; and they make up our juries. "[P]rosecutors too are human." Cramp v. Board of Public Instruction, 368 U.S. 278, 287. Would a teacher be safe and secure in going to a Pugwash Conference? Would it be legal to join a seminar group predominantly Communist and therefore subject to control by those who are said to believe in the overthrow of the government by force and violence? Juries might convict though the teacher did not subscribe to the wrongful aims of the organization. And there is apparently no machinery provided for getting clearance in advance.

Those who join an organization but do not share its unlawful purposes and who do not participate in its unlawful activities surely pose no threat, either as citizens or as public employees. Laws such as this which are not restricted in scope to those who join with the "specific intent" to further illegal action impose, in effect, a conclusive presumption that the member shares the unlawful aims of the organization. See Aptheker v. Secretary of State, supra. The unconstitutionality of this Act follows *a fortiori* from Speiser v. Randall, 357 U.S. 513, where we held that a State may not even place on an applicant for a tax exemption the burden of proving that he has not engaged in criminal advocacy.

This Act threatens the cherished freedom of association protected by the First Amendment, made applicable to the States through the Fourteenth Amendment. . . . And as a committee of the Arizona Legislature which urged adoption of this law itself recognized, public employees of character and integrity may well forgo their calling rather than risk prosecution for perjury or compromise their commitment to intellectual and political freedom . . . . A statute touching those protected rights must be "narrowly drawn to define and punish specific conduct as constituting a clear and present danger to a substantial interest of the State." Cantwell v. Connecticut, 310 U.S. 296, 311. Legitimate legislative goals "cannot be pursued by means that broadly stifle fundamental personal liberties when the end can be more narrowly achieved." Shelton v. Tucker, 364 U.S. 479, 488. . . . A law which applies to membership without the "specific intent" to further the illegal aims of the organization infringes unnecessarily on protected freedoms. It rests on the doctrine of "guilt by association" which has no place here. . . . Such a law cannot stand.

    Reversed.

    Mr. Justice WHITE, with whom Mr. Justice CLARK, Mr. Justice HARLAN and Mr. Justice STEWART concur, dissenting.

    According to unequivocal prior holdings of this Court, a state is entitled to condition public employment upon its employees abstaining from knowing membership in the Communist Party and other organizations advocating the violent overthrow of the government which employs them; the state is constitutionally authorized to inquire into such affiliations and it may discharge those who refuse to affirm or deny them. Gerende v. Board of Supervisors of Elections, 341 U.S. 56; Garner v. Board of Public Works, 341 U.S. 716; Adler v. Board of Education, 342 U.S. 485; Beilan v. Board of Education, 357 U.S. 399; Lerner v. Casey, 357 U.S. 468; Nelson v. County of Los Angeles, 362 U.S. 1; see also Wieman v. Updegraff, 344 U.S. 183; Slochower v. Board of Education, 350 U.S. 551. The Court does not mention or purport to overrule these cases; nor does it expressly hold that a state must retain, even in its most sensitive positions, those who lend such support as knowing membership entails to those organizations, such as the Communist Party, whose purposes include the violent destruction of democratic government.

Under existing constitutional law, then, Arizona is free to require its teachers to refrain from knowing membership in the designated organizations and to bar from employment all knowing members as well as those who refuse to establish their qualifications to teach by executing the oath prescribed by the statute. Arizona need not retain those employees on the governor's staff, in the Phoenix police department or in its schools who insist on holding membership in and lending their name and influence to those organizations aiming at violent overthrow. Adler v. Board of Education, 342 U.S. 485.

It would seem, therefore, that the Court's judgment is aimed at the criminal provisions of the Arizona law which expose an employee to a perjury prosecution if he swears falsely about membership when he signs the oath or if he later becomes a knowing member while remaining in public employment. But the State is entitled to condition employment on the absence of knowing membership; and if an employee obtains employment by falsifying his present qualifications, there is no sound constitutional reason for denying the State the power to treat such false swearing as perjury. . . . By the same token, since knowing membership in specified organizations is a valid disqualification, Arizona cannot sensibly be forbidden to make it a crime for a person, while a state employee, to join an organization knowing of its dedication to the forceful overthrow of his employer and knowing that membership disqualifies him for state employment. The crime provided by the Arizona law is not just the act of becoming a member of an organization but it is that membership plus concurrent public employment. If a State may disqualify for knowing membership and impose criminal penalties for falsifying employment applications, it is likewise within its powers to move criminally against the employee who knowingly engages in disqualifying acts during his employment. If a government may remove from office, 5 U.S.C. § 118(i) (1964 ed.), United Public Workers of America v. Mitchell, 330 U.S. 75, and criminally punish, 18 U.S.C. § 607 (1964 ed.), its employees who engage in certain political activities, it is unsound to hold that it may not, on pain of criminal penalties, prevent its employees from affiliating with the Communist Party or other organizations prepared to employ violent means to overthrow constitutional government. Our Constitution does not require this kind of protection for the secret proselyting of government employees into the Communist Party, an organization which has been found to be controlled by a foreign power and to be dedicated to the overthrow of the government by any illegal means necessary to achieve this end. Communist Party of the United States v. Subversive Activities Control Board, 367 U.S. 1.

KEYISHIAN v. BOARD OF REGENTS

385 U.S. 589, 87 S.Ct. 675, 17 L.Ed.2d 629 (1967).

[This case is printed in chap. 15, sec. 1, at p. 1133, supra.]

SECTION 7. GOVERNMENT DEMANDS FOR INFORMATION: LEGISLATIVE INVESTIGATIONS

BACKGROUND AND EARLY CASES

Extensive Supreme Court litigation regarding the permissible scope of legislative investigations is a fairly recent phenomenon. But legislative committees have long conducted investigations. Congress authorized an investigation of a military disaster as early as 1792, for example. For an excellent study, see Taylor, Grand Inquest—The Story of Congressional Investigations (1955). In the early years, congressional inquiries dealt mainly with the conduct of the executive department. By the 1820's, however, committees began to summon witnesses to aid in considering proposed legislation.

Congress has the power to impose punishment on non-members for the contempt of its authority. See Anderson v. Dunn, 6 Wheat. 204 (1821), a case involving an attempted bribe of a Congressman. But imprisonment for contempt by one of the Houses cannot extend beyond the adjournment date. Accordingly, since 1857, Congress has provided criminal penalties for refusals to answer pertinent questions. See 2 U.S.C. § 192.

Kilbourn v. Thompson, 103 U.S. 168 (1881), was the first important Supreme Court decision on congressional investigations. The Court set aside the conviction of a recalcitrant witness at an inquiry into Jay Cooke's financial operations. Justice Miller condemned investigations that were "judicial" in nature and stated that Congress cannot constitutionally inquire "into the private affairs of individuals" if the investigation "could result in no valid legislation on the subject to which the inquiry referred." Compare Woodrow Wilson's famous statement, in Congressional Government (1885), 303: "The informing function of Congress should be preferred even to its legislative function." But see Justice Douglas' opinion in Russell v. United States, 369 U.S. 749, 778 (1962): "Wilson was speaking not of a congressional inquiry roaming at large, but of one that inquired into and discussed the functions and operations of government."

In the 1920's, attempts to punish recalcitrant witnesses fared better than in Kilbourn. In McGrain v. Daugherty, 273 U.S. 135 (1927), the Court, in a case arising out of an investigation of Attorney General Daugherty's conduct of the Justice Department, stated that "the power of inquiry" is "an essential and appropriate auxiliary to the legislative function." And, in order to obtain information needed to exercise the legislative function, Congress may "compel a private individual to appear before it or one of its committees." Two years later, in Sinclair v. United States, 279 U.S. 263 (1929), the Court reemphasized that it no longer subscribed to the Kilbourn attitude of hostility to congressional inquiries. In Sinclair, the witness in an investigation of federal oil leases refused to answer on the grounds that the questions related to his private affairs and that judicial proceedings were pending. After conceding that "Congress is without authority to compel disclosures for the purpose of aiding the prosecution of pending suits," the Court insisted that the autority "to require pertinent disclosures in aid of its own constitutional power is not abridged because the information sought to be elicited may also be of use in such suits."

LEGISLATIVE INVESTIGATIONS IN THE FIFTIES

Introduction. Claims that congressional investigators were unconstitutionally engaging in "exposure for exposure's sake" and were violating First Amendment rights were made in cases involving inquiries into subversion that came to the Court in the early fifties. Typically, however, these challenges were joined with Fifth Amendment objections, and the Court was able to dispose of the cases on the basis of broad interpretations of the protection against self-incrimination, without reaching other constitutional issues. See, e. g., Quinn v. United States, 349 U.S. 155 (1955) (chap. 12, p. 872, supra). Two years later, in the Watkins case, no Fifth Amendment claim was raised, and the Court addressed itself to other constitutional issues—albeit mainly in dictum. At the same time, state inquiries came under scrutiny, in Sweezy v. New Hampshire. In examining the congressional and state investigating cases of the fifties and sixties below, note the parallels to the evolution of attitudes considered in sec. 6, supra, as well as in sec. 1 of chap. 15. To what extent do legislative inquiries raise distinctive questions?

1. *Watkins.* The petitioner in Watkins v. United States, 354 U.S. 178 (1957), was a labor union official who had been called as a witness before the House Un-American Activities Committee. He testified freely about his own political activities, stating that he had never been a Communist Party member but that he had "cooperated" with the Party. Moreover, he was willing to identify Party members he had known, provided that he thought "they still were members." He refused to answer, however, when asked to tell whether he knew a number of persons to have been members of the Party: "I am not going to plead the fifth amendment, but I refuse to answer certain questions that I believe are outside the proper scope of your committee's activities"; he would not testify about persons "who to my best knowledge and belief have long since removed themselves from the Communist movement." He was convicted of "contempt of Congress," for refusing to answer questions "pertinent to the questions under inquiry," 2 U.S.C. § 192.

The Supreme Court reversed. The specific basis for the holding was that Watkins was not "accorded a fair opportunity to determine whether he was within his rights in refusing to answer, and his conviction is necessarily invalid under the Due Process Clause of the Fifth Amendment." Chief Justice Warren's opinion for the Court stated that a defendant under 2 U.S. C. § 192 must be accorded "every right which is guaranteed to defendants in all other criminal cases," including the right to have "knowledge of the subject to which the interrogation is deemed pertinent," "with the same degree of explicitness and clarity that the Due Process Clause requires in the expression of any element of a criminal offense." The "vice of vagueness" must be avoided. The Court, after exhausting the several possible indicia of the question at issue, remained "unenlightened as to the subject to which the questions asked petitioner were pertinent."

Before reaching that due process basis for the reversal, Chief Justice Warren spoke at length about "basic premises" regarding the history and constitutional status of legislative investigations. The opinion included the following passages: "The power of the Congress to conduct investigations is inherent in the legislative process. . . . But, broad as is this power of inquiry, it is not unlimited. There is no general authority to expose the private affairs of individuals without justification in terms of the functions of the Congress. . . . Nor is the Congress a law enforcement or trial agency. These are functions of the executive and judicial departments of government. No inquiry is an end in itself; it must be related to, and in furtherance of, a legitimate task of the Congress. Investigations conducted solely for the personal aggrandizement of the investigators or to 'punish' those investigated are indefensible. [Compare the bill of attainder materials in the separation of powers chapter, chap. 7, p. 576, supra.]

"It is unquestionably the duty of all citizens to cooperate with the Congress in its efforts to obtain the facts needed for intelligent legislative action. . . . This, of course, assumes that the constitutional rights of witnesses will be respected by the Congress as they are in a court of justice. . . . We have no doubt that there is no congressional power to expose for the sake of exposure. The public is, of course, entitled to be informed concerning the workings of its government. That cannot be inflated into a general power to expose where the predominant result can only be an invasion of the private rights of individuals. But a solution to our problem is not to be found in testing the motives of committee members for this purpose. Such is not our function. Their motives alone would not vitiate an investigation which had been instituted by a House of Congress if that assembly's legislative purpose is being served. . . .

"It is the responsibility of the Congress, in the first instance, to insure that compulsory process is used only in furtherance of a legislative purpose. That requires that the instructions to an investigating committee spell out that group's jurisdiction and purpose with sufficient particularity. . . . An excessively broad charter, like that of the House Un-American Activities Committee, places the courts in an untenable position if they are to strike a balance between the public need for a particular interrogation and the right of citizens to carry on their affairs free from unnecessary governmental interference. It is impossible in such a situation to ascertain whether any legislative purpose justifies the disclosures sought and, if so, the importance of that information to the Congress in furtherance of its legislative function."

In a concurring opinion, Justice Frankfurter gave his understanding of the Court's holding: "[B]y making the federal judiciary the affirmative agency for enforcing the authority that underlies the congressional power to punish for contempt, Congress necessarily brings into play the specific provisions of the Constitution relating to the prosecution of offenses and those implied restrictions under which courts function. [T]he actual scope of the inquiry that the Committee was authorized to conduct and the relevance of the questions to that inquiry must be shown to have been luminous at the time when asked and not left, at best, in cloudiness. The circumstances of this case were wanting in these essentials." Justice Clark dissented, objecting to the "mischievous curbing of the informing function of Congress" and finding the Court's requirements for the operation of legislative inquiries "both unnecessary and unworkable."

2. *Sweezy.* Sweezy v. New Hampshire, 354 U.S. 234 (1957)—decided on the same day as Watkins—was the first of several Court encounters with state rather than congressional investigations; and the first of several coming from New Hampshire. The Court held that a New Hampshire contempt conviction for refusal to answer violated the due process clause of the 14th Amendment. Chief Justice Warren's opinion announcing the judgment of the Court was joined only by Justices Black, Douglas, and Brennan. Justice Frankfurter, joined by Justice Harlan, delivered an opinion concurring in the result. Justice Clark, joined by Justice Burton, dissented.

The New Hampshire legislature had authorized the state Attorney General to act as a one-man investigation committee into subversive activities. Petitioner refused to answer questions about the Progressive Party and about a lecture he had delivered at the University of New Hampshire. He insisted that the questions "were not pertinent to the matter under inquiry" and that they "infringed upon an area protected by the First Amendment." At the request of the Attorney General, a lower state court then put the questions to the petitioner. When he persisted in his refusal, he was jailed for contempt.

Chief Justice Warren's opinion, as in Watkins, concluded with a relatively narrow holding after some broad introductory observations: "We do not now conceive of any circumstance wherein a state interest would justify infringement of rights in these fields. But we do not need to reach such fundamental questions of state power to decide this case." Although the highest state court had held that the questions were authorized by the legislature, Chief Justice Warren found that "it cannot be stated authoritatively that the legislature asked the Attorney General to gather the kind of facts comprised in the subjects upon which petitioner was interrogated." He concluded:

"[I]f the Attorney General's interrogation of petitioner were in fact wholly unrelated to the object of the legislature in authorizing the inquiry, the Due Process Clause would preclude the endangering of constitutional liberties. We believe that an equivalent situation is presented in this case. The lack of any indications that the legislature wanted the information the Attorney General attempted to elicit from petitioner must be treated as the absence of authority. It follows that the use of the contempt power, notwithstanding the interference with constitutional rights, was not in accordance with the due process requirements of the Fourteenth Amendment."

Justice Frankfurter's concurrence, joined by Justice Harlan, rested on grounds of substantive due process. He emphasized that, for him, this was "a very different case from Watkins v. United States": "[W]e cannot concern ourselves with the fact that New Hampshire chose to make its Attorney General in effect a standing committee of its legislature . . . . The case must be judged as though the whole body of the legislature had demanded the information of petitioner. It would make the deepest inroads upon our federal system for this Court now to hold that it can determine the appropriate distribution of powers and their delegation within the forty-eight States. [W]hether the Attorney General of New Hampshire acted within the scope of the authority given him by the state legislature is a matter for the decision of the courts of that State, as it is for the federal courts to determine whether an agency to which Congress has delegated power has acted within the confines of its mandate."

He concluded on the basis of broad "balancing" [recall the reliance on this opinion in NAACP v. Alabama, p. 1316, supra]: "When weighed against the grave harm resulting from governmental intrusion into the intellectual life of a university, [the] justification for compelling a witness to discuss the contents of his lecture appears grossly inadequate. Particularly is this so where the witness has sworn that neither in the lecture nor at any other time did he ever advocate overthrowing the Government by force and violence. [T]he inviolability of privacy belonging to a citizen's political loyalties has so overwhelming an importance to the well-being of our kind of society that it cannot be constitutionally encroached upon on the basis of so meagre a countervailing interest of the State as may be argumentatively found in the remote, shadowy threat to the security of New Hampshire allegedly presented in the origins and contributing elements of the Progressive Party and in petitioner's relations to these." *

3. *Uphaus.*   Sweezy, note 2, was the state companion decision to Watkins, the congressional inquiry case of 1957, note 1. Uphaus v. Wyman, 360 U.S. 72 (1959), was the state case decided on the same day as the congressional Barenblatt case, which follows. Like Sweezy, Uphaus arose out of an investigation by the New Hampshire Attorney General, acting as a one-man legislative investigating committee. Appellant, Executive Director of World Followship, Inc., was held in contempt for refusal to produce a list of the guests at his organization's summer camp during 1954 and 1955. Justice Clark's majority opinion affirmed the civil contempt order and rejected the 14th Amendment claim:

"[T]he Attorney General had valid reason to believe that the speakers and guests at World Fellowship might be subversive persons within the meaning of the New Hampshire Act. . . . Although the evidence as to the nexus between World Fellowship and subversive activities may not be conclusive, we believe it sufficiently relevant to support the Attorney General's action. . . . The record reveals that appellant had participated in 'Communist front' activities and that '[n]ot less than nineteen speakers invited by Uphaus to talk at World Fellowship had either been members of the Communist Party or had connections or affiliations with it or with one or more of the organizations cited as subversive or Communist controlled in the United States Attorney General's list.' . . . Certainly the investigatory power of the State need not be constricted until sufficient evidence of subversion is gathered to justify the institution of criminal proceedings.

". . . We recognize, of course, that compliance with the subpoena will result in exposing the fact that the persons therein named were guests at World Fellowship. But so long as a committee must report to its legislative parent, exposure—in the sense of disclosure—is an inescapable incident of an investigation into the presence of subversive persons within a State. And the

---

* The decisions in Watkins and Sweezy —together with several others of the same year bearing on subversion, e. g., Yates v. United States, 354 U.S. 298 (1957) (p. 1111, supra), and Konigsberg v. State Bar, 353 U.S. 252 (1957) (p. 1307, supra)—provoked considerable criticism, and were frequently mentioned in congressional debates on the 1958 proposals to curtail the Court's appellate jurisdiction. See chap. 1, p. ——, supra. Compare Barenblatt and Uphaus, the federal and state investigation cases of 1959, which follow. Is there basis for the claim that the 1959 decisions were inconsistent with— and marked a retreat from—the 1957 cases? Cf. Murphy, Congress and the Court—A Case Study in the American Political Process (1962), and Pritchett, Congress Versus the Supreme Court, 1957–1960 (1961).

governmental interest in self-preservation is sufficiently compelling to subordinate the interest in associational privacy of persons who, at least to the extent of the guest registration statute, made public at the inception the association they now wish to keep private. . . . "

Justice Brennan, joined by Chief Justice Warren, Justice Black, and Justice Douglas, dissented: "I do not agree that a showing of any requisite legislative purpose or other state interest that constitutionally can subordinate appellant's rights is to be found in this record. Exposure purely for the sake of exposure is not such a valid subordinating purpose. . . . This record, I think, not only fails to reveal any interest of the State sufficient to subordinate appellant's constitutionally protected rights, but affirmatively shows that the investigatory objective was the impermissible one of exposure for exposure's sake.

"The investigation, as revealed by the report, was overwhelmingly and predominantly a roving, self-contained investigation of individual and group behavior, and behavior in a constitutionally protected area. Its whole approach was to name names, disclose information about those named, and observe that 'facts are facts.' . . . The report discloses an investigation in which the processes of law-making and law-evaluating were submerged entirely in exposure of individual behavior—in adjudication, of a sort, however much disclaimed, through the exposure process. . . .

"The Court describes the inquiry we must make in this matter as a balancing of interests. I think I have indicated that there has been no valid legislative interest of the State actually defined and shown in the investigation as it operated, so that there is really nothing against which the appellant's rights of association and expression can be balanced. But if some proper legislative end of the inquiry can be surmised, through what must be a process of speculation, I think it is patent that there is really no subordinating interest in it demonstrated on the part of the State. . . . Here we must demand some initial showing by the State sufficient to counterbalance the interest in privacy as it relates to freedom of speech and assembly. On any basis that has practical meaning, New Hampshire has not made such a showing here. . . ." In a separate notation, Justices Black and Douglas stated that they joined Justice Brennan's dissent "because he makes clear to them that New Hampshire's legislative program . . . violates Art. I, § 10 of the Constitution which provides that 'No State shall . . . pass any Bill of Attainder.' "

BARENBLATT v. UNITED STATES

360 U.S. 109, 79 S.Ct. 1081, 3 L.Ed.2d 1115 (1959).

Certiorari to the Court of Appeals for the District of Columbia.

Mr. Justice HARLAN delivered the opinion of the Court.

Once more the Court is required to resolve the conflicting constitutional claims of congressional power and of an individual's right to resist its exercise. . . . . The scope of the power of inquiry . . . is as penetrating and far-reaching as the potential power to enact and appropriate under the Constitution.

Broad as it is, the power is not, however, without limitations. Since Congress may only investigate into those areas in which it may potentially legislate or appropriate, it cannot inquire into matters which are within the exclusive province of one or the other branch of the Government. Lacking the judicial power given to the Judiciary, it cannot inquire into matters that are exclusively the concern of the Judiciary. Neither can it supplant the Executive in what exclusively belongs to the Executive. And the Congress, in common with all branches of the Government, must exercise its powers subject to the limitations placed by the Constitution on governmental action, more particularly in the context of this case the relevant limitations of the Bill of Rights.

". . . . In the present case congressional efforts to learn the extent of a nationwide, indeed worldwide, problem have brought one of its investigating committees into the field of education. Of course, broadly viewed, inquiries cannot be made into the teaching that is pursued in any of our educational institutions. . . . But this does not mean that the Congress is precluded from interrogating a witness merely because he is a teacher. An educational institution is not a constitutional sanctuary from inquiry into matters that may otherwise be within the constitutional legislative domain merely for the reason that inquiry is made of someone within its walls. . . . .

"We here review petitioner's conviction under 2 U.S.C. § 192 for contempt of Congress, arising from his refusal to answer certain questions put to him by a Subcommittee of the House Committee on Un-American Activities during the course of an inquiry concerning alleged Communist infiltration into the field of education. . . . .

"Pursuant to a subpoena, and accompanied by counsel, petitioner on June 28, 1954, appeared as a witness before this congressional Subcommittee. After answering a few preliminary questions and testifying that he had been a graduate student and teaching fellow at the University of Michigan from 1947 to 1950 and an instructor in psychology at Vassar College from 1950 to shortly before his appearance before the Subcommittee, petitioner objected generally to the right of the Subcommittee to inquire into his "political" and "religious" beliefs or any "other personal and private affairs" or "associational activities," upon grounds set forth in a previously prepared memorandum which he was allowed to file with the Subcommittee. Thereafter petitioner specifically declined to answer each of the following five questions:

"Are you now a member of the Communist Party? (Count One.)

"Have you ever been a member of the Communist Party? (Count Two.)

"Now, you have stated that you knew Francis Crowley. Did you know Francis Crowley as a member of the Communist Party? (Count Three.)

"Were you ever a member of the Haldane Club of the Communist Party while at the University of Michigan? (Count Four.)

"Were you a member while a student of the University of Michigan Council of Arts, Sciences, and Professions?" (Count Five.)

In each instance the grounds of refusal were those set forth in the prepared statement. Petitioner expressly disclaimed reliance upon "the Fifth Amendment."

"Following receipt of the Subcommittee's report of these occurrences the House duly certified the matter to the District of Columbia United States Attorney for contempt proceedings. An indictment in five Counts, each embracing one of petitioner's several refusals to answer, ensued. With the consent of both sides the case was tried to the court without a jury, and upon conviction under all Counts a general sentence of six months' imprisonment and a fine of $250 was imposed.

Since this sentence was less than the maximum punishment authorized by the statute for conviction under any one Count, the judgment below must be upheld if the conviction upon any of the Counts is sustainable. . . . As we conceive the ultimate issue in this case to be whether petitioner could properly be convicted of contempt for refusing to answer questions relating to his participation in or knowledge of alleged Communist Party activities at educational institutions in this country, we find it unnecessary to consider the validity of his conviction under the Third and Fifth Counts, the only one involving questions which on their face do not directly relate to such participation or knowledge. . . .

CONSTITUTIONAL CONTENTIONS. . . .

The Court's past cases establish sure guides to decision. Undeniably, the First Amendment in some circumstances protects an individual from being compelled to disclose his associational relationships. However, the protections of the First Amendment, unlike a proper claim of the privilege against self-incrimination under the Fifth Amendment, do not afford a witness the right to resist inquiry in all circumstances. Where First Amendment rights are asserted to bar governmental interrogation resolution of the issue always involves a balancing by the courts of the competing private and public interests at stake in the particular circumstances shown. . . .

The first question is whether this investigation was related to a valid legislative purpose. . . .

That Congress has wide power to legislate in the field of Communist activity in this Country, and to conduct appropriate investigations in aid thereof, is hardly debatable. The existence of such power has never been questioned by this Court, and it is sufficient to say, without particularization, that Congress has enacted or considered in this field a wide range of legislative measures, not a few of which have stemmed from recommendations of the very Committee whose actions have been drawn in question here. In the last analysis this power rests on the right of self-preservation, "the ultimate value of any society," Dennis v. United States, 341 U.S. 494, 509. Justification for its exercise in turn rests on the long and widely accepted view that the tenets of the Communist Party include the ultimate overthrow of the Government of the United States by force and violence, a view which has been given final expression by the Congress.

On these premises, this Court in its constitutional adjudications has consistently refused to view the Communist Party as an ordinary political party, and has upheld federal legislation aimed at the Communist problem which in a different context would certainly have raised constitutional issues of the gravest character. See, e. g., Carlson v. Landon, 342 U.S. 524; Galvan v. Press, 347 U.S. 522. . . . To suggest that because the Communist Party may also sponsor peaceable political reforms the constitutional issues before us should now be judged as if that Party were just an ordinary political party from the standpoint of national security, is to ask this Court to blind itself to world affairs which have determined the whole course of our national policy since the close of World War II, affairs to which Judge Learned Hand gave vivid expression in his opinion in United States v. Dennis, 183 F.2d 201, 213, and to the vast burdens which these conditions have entailed for the entire Nation.

We think that investigatory power in this domain is not to be denied Congress solely because the field of education is involved. . . . Indeed we do not understand petitioner here to suggest that Congress in no circumstances may inquire into Communist activity in the field of education. Rather, his position is in effect that this particular investigation was aimed not at the revolutionary aspects but at the theoretical classroom discussion of communism.

In our opinion this position rests on a too constricted view of the nature of the investigatory process, and is not supported by a fair assessment of the record before us. An investigation of advocacy of or preparation for overthrow certainly embraces the right to identify a witness as a member of the Communist Party . . . and to inquire into the various manifestations of the Party's tenets. The strict requirements of a prosecution under the Smith Act, see Dennis v. United States, supra, and Yates v. United States, 354 U.S. 298, are not the measure of the permissible scope of a congressional investigation into "overthrow," for of necessity the investigatory process must proceed step by step. Nor can it fairly be concluded that this investigation was directed at controlling what is being taught at our universities rather than at overthrow. The statement of the Subcommittee Chairman at the opening of the investigation evinces no such intention, and so far as this record reveals nothing thereafter transpired which would justify our holding that the thrust of the investigation later changed. . . .

Nor can we accept the further contention that this investigation should not be deemed to have been in furtherance of a legislative purpose because the true objective of the Committee and of the Congress was purely "exposure." So long as Congress acts in pursuance of its constitutional power, the judiciary lacks authority to intervene on the basis of the motives which spurred the exercise of that power. . . . Having scrutinized this record we cannot say that the unanimous panel of the Court of Appeals which first considered this case was wrong in concluding that "the primary purposes of the inquiry were in aid of legislative processes." 240 F.2d at 881. . . .

Finally, the record is barren of other factors which in themselves might sometimes lead to the conclusion that the individual interests at stake were not subordinate to those of the state. There is no indication in this record that the Subcommittee was attempting to pillory witnesses. Nor did petitioner's appearance as a witness follow from indiscriminate dragnet procedures, lacking in probable cause for belief that he possessed information which might be helpful to the Subcommittee. And the relevancy of the questions put to him by the Subcommittee is not open to doubt.

We conclude that the balance between the individual and the governmental interests here at stake must be struck in favor of the latter, and that therefore the provisions of the First Amendment have not been offended. . . .

Affirmed.

Mr. Justice BLACK, with whom The Chief Justice [WARREN] and Mr. Justice DOUGLAS concur, dissenting. . . .

. . . The Court today affirms, and thereby sanctions the use of the contempt power to enforce questioning by congressional committees in the realm of speech and association. I cannot agree with this disposition of the case for I believe that the resolution establishing the House Un-American Activities Committee and the questions that Committee asked Barenblatt violate the Constitution in several respects. (1) Rule XI creating the Committee authorizes such a sweeping, unlimited, all-inclusive and undiscriminating compulsory examination of witnesses in the field of speech, press, petition and assembly that it violates the procedural requirements of the Due Process Clause of the Fifth Amendment. (2) Compelling an answer to the questions asked Barenblatt abridges freedom of speech and association in contravention of the First Amendment. (3) The Committee proceedings were part of a legislative program to stigmatize and punish by public identification and exposure all witnesses considered by the Committee to be guilty of Communist affiliations, as well as all witnesses who refused to answer Committee questions on constitutional grounds; the Committee was thus improperly seeking to try, convict, and punish suspects, a task which the Constitution expressly denies to Congress and grants exclusively to the courts, to be exercised by them only after indictment and in full compliance with all the safeguards provided by the Bill of Rights. . . . .

. . . . I do not agree that laws directly abridging First Amendment freedoms can be justified by a congressional or judicial balancing process. There are, of course, cases suggesting that a law which primarily regulates conduct but which might also indirectly affect speech can be upheld if the effect on speech is minor in relation to the need for control of the conduct. With these cases I agree. Typical of them are Cantwell v. Connecticut, 310 U.S. 296 and Schneider v. Irvington, 308 U.S. 147. Both of these involved the right of a city to control its streets. [Recall the "balancing" - "absolutes" debate between Justices Black and Harlan in Konigsberg II, supra, at 1308.]

But even assuming what I cannot assume, that some balancing is proper in this case, I feel that the Court after stating the test ignores it completely. At most it balances the right of the Government to preserve itself, against Barenblatt's right to refrain from revealing Communist affiliations. Such a balance, however, mistakes the factors to be weighed. In the first place, it completely leaves out the real interest in Barenblatt's silence, the interest of the people as a whole in being able to join organizations, advocate causes and make political "mistakes" without later being subjected to governmental penalties for having dared to think for themselves. It is this right, the right to err politically, which keeps us strong as a Nation. . . . .

Finally, I think Barenblatt's conviction violates the Constitution because the chief aim, purpose and practice of the House Un-American Activities Committee, as disclosed by its many reports, is to try witnesses and punish them because they are or have been Communists or because they refuse to admit or deny Communist affiliations. The punishment imposed is generally punishment by humiliation and public shame. . . . It seems to me that the proof that the Un-American Activities Committee is here undertaking a purely judicial function is overwhelming. . . .

Mr. Justice BRENNAN, dissenting.

I would reverse this conviction. It is sufficient that I state my complete agreement with my Brother Black that no purpose for the investigation of Barenblatt is revealed by the record except exposure purely for the sake of exposure. This is not a purpose to which Barenblatt's rights under the First

Amendment can validly be subordinated.   An investigation in which the processes of law-making and law-evaluating are submerged entirely in exposure of
individual behavior—in adjudication, of a sort, through the exposure process
—is outside the constitutional pale of congressional inquiry.

LEGISLATIVE INVESTIGATIONS—FROM BARENBLATT TO GIBSON

In a number of congressional investigation cases soon after Barenblatt, the
Court adhered to its broadly permissive constitutional principles yet repeatedly
found narrow grounds to reverse contempt convictions.   Four years later, in
Gibson, a state investigation involving information about the NAACP, the
Court reexamined the constitutional framework.   Did Gibson indicate a significant shift from Barenblatt?   Compare the contrast between the fifties and
sixties in sec. 6 of this chapter and in sec. 1 of chap. 15.

Thus, in companion cases decided in the term after Barenblatt, Wilkinson
v. United States, 365 U.S. 399 (1961), and Braden v. United States, 365 U.S.
431 (1961), the Supreme Court affirmed convictions for refusal to answer
congressional committee inquiries largely on the authority of—and with the
same division as in—Barenblatt.   Justice Stewart delivered the majority
opinion in each case.   A few months later, however, Deutch v. United States,
367 U.S. 456 (1961), reversed a contempt conviction, on statutory grounds.
The division was again five to four, and Justice Stewart again wrote for the
majority.

The conviction of Deutch was reversed because "the Government at the
trial failed to carry its burden of proving the pertinence of the questions."
Justice Stewart's majority opinion distinguished two quite different issues regarding "pertinency" which may be involved in contempt prosecutions: (1)
the due process requirement that pertinency "must be brought home to the
witness at the time the questions are put to him"—an objection here waived by
failure to object on pertinency grounds at the hearing; and (2) the prosecution's duty at the trial to prove that the committee questions were in fact "pertinent to the question under inquiry," an element of the offense under 2 U.S.C.
§ 192.   Justices Harlan, Frankfurter, Whittaker, and Clark dissented.

A new basis for challenging contempt of Congress convictions was sanctioned by the decision in six companion cases in the following year, reported as
Russell v. United States, 369 U.S. 749 (1962).   The convictions were reversed
because in each case "the indictment returned by the grand jury failed to identify the subject under congressional subcommittee inquiry at the time the witness was interrogated.   The indictments were practically identical in this respect, stating only that the questions to which answers were refused 'were pertinent to the question then under inquiry' by the subcommittee."   Justice Stewart's opinion for the court concluded that the "vice of these indictments
.   .   .   is that they failed to satisfy the first essential criteria by which
the sufficiency of an indictment is to be tested, i. e., that they failed to
sufficiently apprise the defendant 'of what he must be prepared to meet.' "

Justice Clark's dissent noted that "the Court has now upset 10 convictions
under § 192" since the Watkins decision.   "This continued frustration of the
Congress .   .   .   indicates to me that the time may have come for
Congress to revert to 'its original practice of utilizing the coercive sanction of

contempt proceedings at the bar of the House [affected].' " Justice Harlan also dissented in a sequel to Russell, Gojack v. United States, 384 U.S. 702 (1966).

GIBSON v. FLORIDA LEGISLATIVE INVESTIGATION COMMITTEE

372 U.S. 539, 83 S.Ct. 889, 9 L.Ed.2d 929 (1963).

Certiorari to the Supreme Court of Florida.

Mr. Justice GOLDBERG delivered the opinion of the Court.

This case is the culmination of protracted litigation involving legislative investigating committees of the State of Florida and the Miami branch of the National Association for the Advancement of Colored People. . . .

The petitioner, then president of the Miami branch of the N. A. A. C. P., was ordered to appear before the respondent Committee on November 4, 1959, and . . . to bring with him records of the association which were in his possession or custody and which pertained to the identity of members of, and contributors to, the Miami and state N. A. A. C. P. organizations. Prior to interrogation of any witnesses the Committee chairman . . . stated that the inquiry would be directed to Communists and Communist activities, including infiltration of Communists into organizations operating in the described fields [including race relations].

The petitioner told the Committee that he had not brought [the] records with him to the hearing and announced that he would not produce them for the purpose of answering questions concerning membership in the N. A. A. C. P. He did, however, volunteer to answer such questions on the basis of his own personal knowledge; when given the names and shown photographs of 14 persons previously identified as Communists or members of Communist front or affiliated organizations, the petitioner said that he could associate none of them with the N. A. A. C. P.

The petitioner's refusal to produce his organization's membership lists was based on the ground that to bring the lists to the hearing and to utilize them as the basis of his testimony would interfere with the free exercise of Fourteenth Amendment associational rights of members and prospective members of the N. A. A. C. P.

In accordance with Florida procedure, the petitioner was brought before a state court and, after a hearing, was adjudged in contempt, and sentenced to six months' imprisonment and fined $1,200, or, in default in payment thereof, sentenced to an additional six months' imprisonment. . . .

I. . . .

This Court has repeatedly held that rights of association are within the ambit of the constitutional protections afforded by the First and Fourteenth Amendments. . . . At the same time, however, this Court's prior holdings demonstrate that there can be no question that the State has power adequately to inform itself—through legislative investigation, if it so desires—in order to act and protect its legitimate and vital interests. . . . It is no less obvious, however, that the legislative power to investigate, broad as it may be, is not without limit. . . . When, as in this case, the claim is made that particular legislative inquiries and demands infringe substantially upon First and Fourteenth Amendment associational rights of individuals, the courts are called upon to, and must, determine the permissibility of the challenged actions . . .. The interests here at stake are of significant magnitude, and neither their resolution nor impact is limited, to, or dependent upon, the particular parties here involved. . . .

II.

Significantly, the parties are in substantial agreement as to the proper test to be applied to reconcile the competing claims of government and individual and to determine the propriety of the Committee's demands. As declared by the respondent Committee in its brief to this Court, "Basically, this case hinges entirely on the question of whether the evidence before the Committee [was] sufficient to show probable cause or nexus between the N. A. A. C. P. Miami Branch, and Communist activities." We understand this to mean—regardless of the label applied, be it "nexus," "foundation," or whatever—that it is an essential prerequisite to the validity of an investigation which intrudes into the area of constitutionally protected rights . . . that the State convincingly show a substantial relation between the information sought and a subject of overriding and compelling state interest. Absent such a relation between the N. A. A. C. P. and conduct in which the State may have a compelling regulatory concern, the Committee has not "demonstrated so cogent an interest in obtaining and making public" the membership information sought to be obtained as to "justify the substantial abridgment of associational freedom which such disclosures will effect." Bates v. Little Rock, 361 U.S., at 524 . . .

Applying these principles to the facts of this case, the respondent Committee contends that the prior decisions of this Court . . . compel a result here upholding the legislative right of inquiry. In Barenblatt, Wilkinson, and Braden, however, it was a refusal to answer a question or questions concerning the witness' *own* past or present membership *in the Communist Party* which supported his conviction. It is apparent that the necessary preponderating governmental interest and, in fact, the very result in those cases were founded on the holding that the Communist Party is not an ordinary or legitimate political party, as known in this country, and that because of its particular nature, membership therein is *itself* a permissible subject of regulation and legislative scrutiny. Assuming the correctness of the premises on which those cases were decided, no further demonstration of compelling governmental interest was deemed necessary . . . ..

Here, however, it is not alleged Communists who are the witnesses before the Committee and it is not discovery of their membership in that party which is the object of the challenged inquiries. Rather, it is the N. A. A. C. P. itself which is the subject of the investigation, and it is its local president [who was] held in contempt . . . .. There is no suggestion that the Miami branch of the N. A. A. C. P. or the national organization with which it is affiliated was, or is, itself a subversive organization. Nor is there any indication that the activities or policies of the N. A. A. C. P. were either Communist dominated or influenced. In fact, this very record indicates that the association was and is against communism and has voluntarily taken steps to keep Communists from being members. . . . .

Thus, unlike the situation in Barenblatt, Wilkinson and Braden, supra, the Committee was not here seeking from the petitioner . . . any information as to whether he, himself, or even other persons were members of the Communist Party [or other] subversive groups; instead, the entire thrust of the demands on the petitioner was that he disclose whether other persons were members of the N. A. A. C. P., itself a concededly legitimate and non-subversive organization. Compelling such an organization, engaged in the exercise of First and Fourteenth Amendment rights, to disclose its membership presents, under our cases, a question wholly different from compelling the Communist Party to disclose its own membership. Moreover, even to say, as in Barenblatt, . . . that it is permissible to inquire into the subject of Communist infiltration of educational or other organizations does not mean that it is permissible to demand or require from such other groups disclosure of their membership by inquiry into their records when such disclosure will seriously inhibit or impair the exercise of constitutional rights and has not itself been demonstrated to bear a crucial relation to a proper governmental interest or to be essential to fulfillment of a proper governmental purpose. The prior holdings that governmental interest in controlling subversion and the particular character of the Communist Party and its objectives outweigh the right of individual Communists to conceal party membership or affiliations by no means require the wholly different conclusion that other groups—concededly legitimate—automatically forfeit their rights to privacy of association simply because the general subject matter of the legislative inquiry is Communist subversion or infiltration. The fact that governmental interest was deemed compelling in Barenblatt, Wilkinson, and Braden and held to support the inquiries there made into membership in the Communist Party does not resolve the issues here, where the challenged questions go to membership in an admittedly lawful organization.

Respondent's reliance on Uphaus v. Wyman, supra, as controlling is similarly misplaced. . . . In Uphaus this Court found that there was demonstrated a sufficient connection between subversive activity—held there to be a proper subject of governmental concern—and the World Fellowship, itself, to justify discovery of the guest list; no semblance of such a nexus between the N. A. A. C. P. and subversive *activities* has been shown here. . . . Finally, in Uphaus, the State was investigating whether subversive persons were within its boundaries and whether their presence constituted a threat to the State. No such purpose or need is evident here. The Florida Committee is not seeking to identify subversives by questioning the petitioner; apparently it is satisfied that it already knows who they are.

III.

In the absence of directly determinative authority, we turn, then, to consideration of the facts now before us. [W]e rest our result on the fact that the record in this case is insufficient to show a substantial connection between the Miami branch of the N. A. A. C. P. and Communist *activities* which the respondent Committee itself concedes is an essential prerequisite to demonstrating the immediate, substantial, and subordinating state interest necessary to sustain its right of inquiry into the membership lists of the association. . . . .

This summary of the evidence discloses the utter failure to demonstrate the existence of any substantial relationship between the N. A. A. C. P. and subversive or Communist activities. In essence, there is here merely indirect, less than unequivocal, and mostly hearsay testimony that in years past some 14 people who were asserted to be, or to have been, Communists or members of Communist front or "affiliated organizations" attended occasional meetings of the Miami branch of the N. A. A. C. P. "and/or" were members of that branch, which had a total membership of about 1,000.

On the other hand, there was no claim made at the hearings, or since, that the N. A. A. C. P. or its Miami branch was engaged in any subversive activities or that its legitimate activities have been dominated or influenced by Communists. . . . The respondent Committee has laid no adequate foundation for its direct demands upon the officers and records of a wholly legitimate organization for disclosure of its membership . . . .. The strong associational interest in maintaining the privacy of membership lists of groups engaged in the constitutionally protected free trade in ideas and beliefs may not be substantially infringed upon such a slender showing as here made by the respondent. While, of course, all legitimate organizations are the beneficiaries of these protections, they are all the more essential here, where the challenged privacy is that of persons espousing beliefs already unpopular with their neighbors and the deterrent and "chilling" effect on the free exercise of constitutionally enshrined rights of free speech, expression, and association is consequently the more immediate and substantial. . . .

Of course, a legislative investigation—as any investigation—must proceed "step by step," Barenblatt v. United States, supra, 360 U.S., at 130, but step by step or in totality an adequate foundation for inquiry must be laid. . . . No such foundation has been laid here. . . .

Nothing we say here impairs or denies the existence of the underlying legislative right to investigate or legislate with respect to subversive activities by Communists or anyone else; our decision today deals only with the manner in which such power may be exercised and we hold simply that groups which themselves are neither engaged in subversive or other illegal or improper activities nor demonstrated to have any substantial connections with such activities are to be protected in their rights of free and private association. . . .

To permit legislative inquiry to proceed on less than an adequate foundation would be to sanction unjustified and unwarranted intrusions into the very heart of the constitutional privilege to be secure in associations in legitimate organizations engaged in the exercise of First and Fourteenth Amendment rights; to impose a lesser standard than we here do would be inconsistent with the maintenance of those essential conditions basic to the preservation of our democracy. . . .

Reversed.

Mr. Justice BLACK, concurring.

. . . I would reverse here on the ground that there has been a direct abridgment of the right of association . . .. But, since the Court assumes for purposes of this case that there was no direct abridgment of First Amendment freedoms, I concur in the Court's opinion . . ..

Mr. Justice DOUGLAS, concurring. . . .

In my view, government is not only powerless to legislate with respect to membership in a lawful organization; it is also precluded from probing the intimacies of spiritual and intellectual relationships in the myriad of such societies and groups that exist in this country, regardless of the legislative purpose sought to be served. . . .

Mr. Justice HARLAN, whom Mr. Justice CLARK, Mr. Justice STEWART, and Mr. Justice WHITE, join dissenting. . . .

The Court's reasoning is difficult to grasp. I read its opinion as basically proceeding on the premise that the governmental interest in investigating Communist infiltration into admittedly nonsubversive organizations as distinguished from investigating organizations themselves suspected of subversive activities, is not sufficient to overcome the countervailing right to freedom of association. . . . On this basis "nexus" is seemingly found lacking because it was never claimed that the N. A. A. C. P. Miami Branch had itself engaged in subversive activity, . . . and because none of the Committee's evidence relating to any of the 52 alleged Communist Party members was sufficient to attribute such activity to the local branch or to show that it was dominated, influenced, or used "by Communists." . . .

But, until today, I had never supposed that any of our decisions relating to state or federal power to investigate in the field of Communist subversion could possibly be taken as suggesting any difference in the degree of governmental investigatory interest as between Communist infiltration *of* organizations and Communist activity *by* organizations. See, e. g., Barenblatt v. United States, 360 U.S. 109 (infiltration into education); Wilkinson v. United States, 365 U.S. 399, and Braden v. United States, 365 U.S. 431 (infiltration into basic industries); Russell v. United States, 369 U.S. 749, 773 (infiltration of newspaper business). . . .

Given the unsoundness of the basic premise underlying the Court's holding as to the absence of "nexus," this decision surely falls of its own weight. For unless "nexus" requires an investigating agency to prove in advance the very things it is trying to find out, I do not understand how it can be said that the information preliminarily developed by the Committee's investigator was not sufficient to satisfy, under any reasonable test, the requirement of "nexus."

Apart from this, the issue of "nexus" is surely laid at rest by the N. A. A. C. P.'s own "Anti-Communism" resolution, first adopted in 1950, which petitioner had voluntarily furnished the Committee before the curtain came down on his examination. . . . It hardly meets the point at issue to suggest . . . that the resolution only serves to show that the Miami Branch was in fact free of any Communist influences—unless self-investigation is deemed constitutionally to block official inquiry.

I also find it difficult to see how this case really presents any serious question as to interference with freedom of association. Given the willingness of the petitioner to testify from recollection as to individual memberships in the local branch of the N. A. A. C. P., the germaneness of the membership records to the subject matter of the Committee's investigation, and the limited purpose for which their use was sought—as an aid to refreshing the witness' recollection, involving their divulgence only to the petitioner himself . . . .—this case of course bears no resemblance whatever to NAACP v. Alabama, 357 U.S. 449, or Bates v. Little Rock, 361 U.S. 516. In both of those cases the State had sought general divulgence of local N. A. A. C. P. membership lists without any showing of a justifying state interest. In effect what we are asked to hold here is that the petitioner had a constitutional right to give only partial or inaccurate testimony, and that indeed seems to me the true effect of the Court's holding today. . . .

Mr. Justice WHITE, dissenting.

In my view, the opinion of the Court represents a serious limitation upon the Court's previous cases dealing with . . . the right of the legislature to investigate the Communist Party and its activities. Although one of the classic and recurring activities of the Communist Party is the infiltration and subversion of other organizations, either openly or in a clandestine manner, the Court holds that even where a legislature has evidence that a legitimate organization is under assault and even though that organization is itself sounding open and public alarm, an investigating committee is nevertheless forbidden to compel the organization or its members to reveal the fact, or not, of membership in that organization of named Communists assigned to the infiltrating task.

While the Court purports to be saving such a case for later consideration, it is difficult for me to understand how under today's decision a Communist in the process of performing his assigned job could be required to divulge not only his membership in the Communist Party but his membership or activities in the target organization as well. The Court fails to articulate why the State's interest is any the more compelling or the associational rights any the less endangered when a known Communist is asked whether he belongs to a protected association than here when the organization is asked to confirm or deny that membership. As I read the Court's opinion the exposed Communist might well, in the name of the associational freedom of the legitimate organization and of its members including himself, successfully shield his activities from legislative inquiry. Thus to me the decision today represents a marked departure from the principles of Barenblatt v. United States, 360 U.S. 109, and like cases.

On the other hand, should a legislature obtain ostensibly reliable information about the penetration of Communists into a particular organization, information which in the course of things would be placed on public record like the testimony here, there could no longer be a weighty interest on the part of that organization to refuse to verify that information or to brand it as false. This is particularly true here where an officer of the association is willing to identify persons from memory and where the organization itself has called upon its own members to root out Communists who are bent upon using the association to serve the goals of the Communist Party. Unbending resistance to answering, one way or the other, a legislative committee's limited inquiries in the face of already public information to the same effect reduces the association's interest in secrecy to sterile doctrine. I would have thought that the freedom of association which is and should be entitled to constitutional protection would be promoted, not hindered, by disclosure which permits members of an organization to know with whom they are associating and affords them the opportunity to make an intelligent choice as to whether certain of their associates who are Communists should be allowed to continue their membership. In these circumstances, I cannot join the Court in attaching great weight to the organization's interest in concealing the presence of infiltrating Communists, if such be the case.

The net effect of the Court's decision is, of course, to insulate from effective legislative inquiry and preventive legislation the time-proven skills of the

Communist Party in subverting and eventually controlling legitimate organizations. Until such a group, chosen as an object of Communist Party action, has been effectively reduced to vassalage, legislative bodies may seek no information from the organization under attack by duty-bound Communists. When the job has been done and the legislative committee can prove it, it then has the hollow privilege of recording another victory for the Communist Party, which both Congress and this Court have found to be an organization under the direction of a foreign power, dedicated to the overthrow of the Government if necessary by force and violence. I respectfully dissent.

THE DeGREGORY CASE:
NEW HAMPSHIRE INVESTIGATIONS REVISITED

DeGregory v. New Hampshire Attorney General, 383 U.S. 825 (1966), like Sweezy and Uphaus, arose out of a New Hampshire subversive activities investigation. Appellant was jailed for contempt for refusal to answer, in 1964, questions relating to Communist activities prior to 1957. The Supreme Court, applying the principles of Gibson and asserting distinctions from Uphaus, reversed in a 6:3 decision. Justice Douglas stated for the majority:

"The substantiality of appellant's First Amendment claim can best be seen by considering what he was asked to do. Appellant had already testified that he had not been involved with the Communist Party since 1957 and that he had no knowledge of Communist activities during that period. The Attorney General further sought to have him disclose information relating to his political associations of an earlier day, the meetings he attended, and the views expressed and ideas advocated at any such gatherings. Indeed, the Attorney General here relied entirely upon a 1955 Report on Subversive Activities in New Hampshire to justify renewed investigation of appellant. The Report connects appellant with the Communist Party only until 1953, over 10 years prior to the investigation giving rise to the present contempt.

"On the basis of our prior cases, appellant had every reason to anticipate that the details of his political associations to which he might testify would be reported in a pamphlet purporting to describe the nature of subversion in New Hampshire. (See Uphaus v. Wyman, 360 U.S. 72, 88–95, Brennan, J., dissenting.) Admittedly, 'exposure—in the sense of disclosure—is an inescapable incident of an investigation into the presence of subversive persons within a State.' Uphaus v. Wyman, supra, at 81. But whatever justification may have supported such exposure in Uphaus is absent here; the staleness of both the basis for the investigation and its subject matter makes indefensible such exposure of one's associational and political past . . . . .

"There is no showing of 'overriding and compelling state interest' (Gibson v. Florida Legislative Comm., 372 U.S. 539, 546) that would warrant intrusion into the realm of political and associational privacy protected by the First Amendment. The information being sought was historical, not current. Lawmaking at the investigatory stage may properly probe historic events for any light that may be thrown on present conditions and problems. But the First Amendment prevents the Government from using the power to investigate enforced by the contempt power to probe at will and without relation to existing need. Watkins v. United States, 354 U.S., at 197–200. The present record is devoid of any evidence that there is any Communist movement in

New Hampshire. The 1955 Report deals primarily with 'world-wide communism' and the Federal Government. There is no showing whatsoever of present danger of sedition against the State itself, the only area to which the authority of the State extends. There is thus absent that 'nexus' between petitioner and subversive activities in New Hampshire which the Court found to exist in Uphaus v. Wyman, supra, at 79. New Hampshire's interest on this record is too remote and conjectural to override the guarantee of the First Amendment that a person can speak or not, as he chooses, free of all governmental compulsion.''

Justice Harlan, joined by Justices Stewart and White, dissented: "New Hampshire in my view should be free to investigate the existence or nonexistence of Communist Party subversion, or any other legitimate subject of concern to the State, without first being asked to produce evidence of the very type to be sought in the course of the inquiry. Then, given that the subject of investigation in this case is a permissible one, the appellant seems to me a witness who could properly be called to testify about it; I cannot say as a constitutional matter that inquiry into the current operations of the local Communist Party could not be advanced by knowledge of its operations a decade ago.''

Chapter 17

THE CONSTITUTION AND RELIGION:
"ESTABLISHMENT" AND "FREE EXERCISE"

Introduction. The First Amendment (and its "incorporation" into the 14th) bars any law "respecting an establishment of religion, or prohibiting the free exercise thereof." Section 1 of this chapter focuses on the "establishment" clause, section 2 on "free exercise." But this organization of the materials, which reflects the separate treatment typical in the cases, should not obscure the fact that in many contexts both clauses are relevant: the provisions protect overlapping values, yet they may exert conflicting pressures; articulating criteria that will accommodate both provisions is accordingly a recurrent challenge.

One context and two characteristic problems mark the establishment materials in section 1. The context is schools. The problems involve two methods by which the separation between church and state may be breached: (1) the rendering of governmental aid to religious organizations [e. g., the aid to parochial school students challenged in Everson in 1947 and Allen in 1968, pp. 1350 and 1373 below]; and (2) the intrusion of religious matters into governmental activities [as in the challenges to public school cooperation with religious instruction in Zorach (in 1952, at p. 1358), to school prayers in Engel (in 1962, at p. 1363), and to Bible reading in Schempp (in 1963, at p. 1367)].

In most "free exercise" problems, in section 2, religious scruples are raised as defenses to applications of general state regulations. May the Orthodox Jew refuse to observe a Sunday Closing Law, as in Braunfeld v. Brown (in 1961, at p. 1381)? May the Seventh Day Adventist claim unemployment compensation though she is unavailable for work on Saturdays, as in Sherbert v. Verner (in 1963, at p. 1387)? In situations such as these, the religious objector in effect claims an exemption from general statutes. Does the free exercise clause compel the exemption? That problem illustrates the tension between free exercise and establishment: if the state *must* grant a religious exemption because of "free exercise," is it not granting a preference to religion in violation of the separation assured by "establishment"? Even if the state is not compelled to exempt, may it, without running afoul of "establishment," give special treatment because of an individual's religious scruples (as in the conscientious objector exemption in the draft law—see, e. g., the Seeger case, p. 1396, infra)?

Consider the Court's controversial struggles to articulate criteria for the religion clauses in the light of these questions. Are the problems susceptible to a simple, embracive principle? Was the "wall of separation" statement in Everson the wrong principle? Is "neutrality" a better one? Or is the search for all-encompassing generalities futile? Does the range of religion problems with constitutional dimensions require more numerous, complex, discriminating criteria? *

---

* These problems have generated much controversy and an extraordinary amount of writing off the Court as well as on. See generally, e. g., Kur- land, "Of Church and State and the Supreme Court," 29 U.Chi.L.Rev. 1 (1961), Selected Essays 1938–62 (1963), 699 [see also Religion and the Law

SECTION 1. "ESTABLISHMENT": THE SEPARATION OF CHURCH AND STATE

A. FINANCIAL AID TO RELIGION: THE BACKGROUND

EVERSON v. BOARD OF EDUCATION

330 U.S. 1, 67 S.Ct. 504, 91 L.Ed. 711 (1947).

Appeal from the Court of Errors and Appeals of New Jersey.

Mr. Justice BLACK delivered the opinion of the Court.

A New Jersey statute authorizes its local school districts to make rules and contracts for the transportation of children to and from schools. The appellee, a township board of education, acting pursuant to this statute, authorized reimbursement to parents of money expended by them for the bus transportation of their children on regular busses operated by the public transportation system. Part of this money was for the payment of transportation of some children in the community to Catholic parochial schools. These church schools give their students, in addition to secular education, regular religious instruction conforming to the religious tenets and modes of worship of the Catholic Faith. The superintendent of these schools is a Catholic priest.

The appellant, in his capacity as a district taxpayer, filed suit in a state court challenging the right of the Board to reimburse parents of parochial school students. . . . The New Jersey Court of Errors and Appeals [held] that neither the statute nor the resolution passed pursuant to it was in conflict with the State constitution or the provisions of the Federal Constitution in issue. . . . The only contention here is that the state statute and the resolution, insofar as they authorized reimbursement to parents of children attending parochial schools, violate the Federal Constitution in these two respects, which to some extent overlap. *First.* They authorize the State to take by taxation the private property of some and bestow it upon others, to be used for their own private purposes. This, it is alleged, violates the due process clause of the Fourteenth Amendment. *Second.* The statute and the resolution forced inhabitants to pay taxes to help support and maintain schools which are dedicated to, and which regularly teach, the Catholic Faith. This is alleged to be a use of state power to support church schools contrary to the prohibition of the First Amendment which the Fourteenth Amendment made applicable to the states. . . .

First. . . . It is much too late to argue that legislation intended to facilitate the opportunity of children to get a secular education serves no public purpose. Cochran v. Louisiana State Board of Education, 281 U.S.

(1962)]; Howe, "The Constitutional Question," in The Churches and the Public (1960), Selected Essays 1938–62 (1963), 780; Pfeffer, Church, State and Freedom (1953); Oaks (ed.), The Wall Between Church and State (1963); Kauper, Religion and the Constitution (1964); Schwarz, "No Im-

position of Religion: The Establishment Clause Value," 77 Yale L.J. 692 (1968); and Giannella, "Religious Liberty, Nonestablishment, and Doctrinal Development," 80 Harv.L.Rev. 1381 (1967) and 81 Harv.L.Rev. 513 (1968).

370.[1] . . . The same thing is no less true of legislation to reimburse needy parents, or all parents, for payment of the fares of their children so that they can ride in public busses to and from schools rather than run the risk of traffic and other hazards incident to walking or "hitchhiking." . . .

Second. The New Jersey statute is challenged as a "law respecting an establishment of religion." The First Amendment, as made applicable to the states by the Fourteenth, . . . commands that a state "shall make no law respecting an establishment of religion, or prohibiting the free exercise thereof." . . . Whether this New Jersey law is one respecting an "establishment of religion" requires an understanding of the meaning of that language, particularly with respect to the imposition of taxes. . . .

A large proportion of the early settlers of this country came here from Europe to escape the bondage of laws which compelled them to support and attend government-favored churches. The centuries immediately before and contemporaneous with the colonization of America had been filled with turmoil, civil strife, and persecutions, generated in large part by established sects determined to maintain their absolute political and religious supremacy. . . . In efforts to force loyalty to whatever religious group happened to be on top and in league with the government of a particular time and place, men and women had been fined, cast in jail, cruelly tortured, and killed. Among the offenses for which these punishments had been inflicted were such things as speaking disrespectfully of the views of ministers of government-established churches, non-attendance at those churches, expressions of non-belief in their doctrines, and failure to pay taxes and tithes to support them.

These practices of the old world were transplanted to and began to thrive in the soil of the new America. The very charters granted by the English Crown to the individuals and companies designated to make the laws which would control the destinies of the colonials authorized these individuals and companies to erect religious establishments which all, whether believers or nonbelievers, would be required to support and attend. An exercise of this authority was accompanied by a repetition of many of the old-world practices and persecutions. . . . And all of these dissenters were compelled to pay tithes and taxes to support government-sponsored churches whose ministers preached inflammatory sermons designed to strengthen and consolidate the established faith by generating a burning hatred against dissenters.

These practices became so commonplace as to shock the freedom-loving colonials into a feeling of abhorrence. The imposition of taxes to pay ministers' salaries and to build and maintain churches and church property aroused their indignation. It was these feelings which found expression in the First Amendment. . . . Virginia, where the established church had achieved a dominant influence in political affairs and where many excesses attracted wide public attention, provided a great stimulus and able leadership for the movement. The people there, as elsewhere, reached the conviction that individual religious liberty could be achieved best under a government which was stripped of all power to tax, to support, or otherwise to assist any or all religions, or to interfere with the beliefs of any religious individual or group.

---

1. In the Cochran case, in 1930, the Court sustained the expenditure of state funds for the purchase of books for children attending private and parochial schools, against a challenge that no "public purpose" was involved. The Court said of the legislation: "Its interest is education, broadly; its method, comprehensive." There was no federal "establishment" challenge in the case.

The movement toward this end reached its dramatic climax in Virginia in 1785–86 when the Virginia legislative body was about to renew Virginia's tax levy for the support of the established church.   Thomas Jefferson and James Madison led the fight against this tax.   Madison wrote his great Memorial and Remonstrance against the law.   In it, he eloquently argued that a true religion did not need the support of law; that no person, either believer or non-believer, should be taxed to support a religious institution of any kind; that the best interest of a society required that the minds of men always be wholly free; and that cruel persecutions were the inevitable result of government-established religions.   Madison's Remonstrance received strong support throughout Virginia, and the Assembly postponed consideration of the proposed tax measure until its next session.   When the proposal came up for consideration at that session, it not only died in committee, but the Assembly enacted the famous "Virginia Bill for Religious Liberty" originally written by Thomas Jefferson.   The preamble to that Bill stated among other things that

> "Almighty God hath created the mind free; that all attempts to influence it by temporal punishments or burthens, or by civil incapacitations, tend only to beget habits of hypocrisy and meanness   .   .   ., that to compel a man to furnish contributions of money for the propagation of opinions which he disbelieves, is sinful and tyrannical;   .   .   .   ."

And the statute itself enacted

> "That no man shall be compelled to frequent or support any religious worship, place, or ministry whatsoever, nor shall be enforced, restrained, molested, or burthened in his body or goods, nor shall otherwise suffer on account of his religious opinions or belief   .   .   .."

This Court has previously recognized that the provisions of the First Amendment, in the drafting and adoption of which Madison and Jefferson played such leading roles, had the same objective and were intended to provide the same protection against governmental intrusion on religious liberty as the Virginia statute.   .   .   .

The meaning and scope of the First Amendment, preventing establishment of religion or prohibiting the free exercise thereof,   .   .   .   have been several times elaborated by the decisions of this Court prior to the application of the First Amendment to the states by the Fourteenth.   The broad meaning given the Amendment by these earlier cases has been accepted by this Court in its decisions concerning an individual's religious freedom rendered since the Fourteenth Amendment was interpreted to make the prohibitions of the First applicable to state action abridging religious freedom.   There is every reason to give the same application and broad interpretation to the "establishment of religion" clause.   The interrelation of these complementary clauses was well summarized in [Watson v. Jones, 13 Wall. 679]: "The structure of our government has, for the preservation of civil liberty, rescued the temporal institutions from religious interference.   On the other hand, it has secured religious liberty from the invasions of the civil authority."

The "establishment of religion" clause of the First Amendment means at least this: Neither a state nor the Federal Government can set up a church. Neither can pass laws which aid one religion, aid all religions, or prefer one religion over another.   Neither can force nor influence a person to go to or to remain away from church against his will or force him to profess a belief or disbelief in any religion. No person can be punished for entertaining or professing religious beliefs or disbeliefs, for church attendance or nonattendance. No tax in any amount, large or small, can be levied to support any religious activities or institutions, whatever they may be called, or whatever form they may adopt to teach or practice religion. Neither a state nor the Federal Government can, openly or secretly, participate in the affairs of any religious organizations or groups and *vice versa.* In the words of Jefferson, the clause against establishment of religion by law was intended to erect "a wall of separation between church and State." . . .

We must consider the New Jersey statute in accordance with the foregoing limitations imposed by the First Amendment. But we must not strike that state statute down if it is within the State's constitutional power even though it approaches the verge of that power. . . . New Jersey cannot consistently with the "establishment of religion" clause of the First Amendment contribute tax-raised funds to the support of an institution which teaches the tenets and faith of any church. On the other hand, other language of the amendment commands that New Jersey cannot hamper its citizens in the free exercise of their own religion. Consequently, it cannot exclude individual Catholics, Lutherans, Mohammedans, Baptists, Jews, Methodists, Non-believers, Presbyterians, or the members of any other faith, *because of their faith, or lack of it,* from receiving the benefits of public welfare legislation. While we do not mean to intimate that a state could not provide transportation only to children attending public schools, we must be careful, in protecting the citizens of New Jersey against state-established churches, to be sure that we do not inadvertently prohibit New Jersey from extending its general state law benefits to all its citizens without regard to their religious belief.

Measured by these standards, we cannot say that the First Amendment prohibits New Jersey from spending tax-raised funds to pay the bus fares of parochial school pupils as a part of a general program under which it pays the fares of pupils attending public and other schools. It is undoubtedly true that children are helped to get to church schools. There is even a possibility that some of the children might not be sent to the church schools if the parents were compelled to pay their children's bus fares out of their own pockets when transportation to a public school would have been paid for by the State. The same possibility exists where the state requires a local transit company to provide reduced fares to school children including those attending parochial schools . . .. Moreover, state-paid policemen, detailed to protect children going to and from church schools from the very real hazards of traffic, would serve much the same purpose and accomplish much the same result as state provisions intended to guarantee free transportation of a kind which the state deems to be best for the school children's welfare. And parents might refuse to risk their children to the serious danger of traffic accidents going to and from parochial schools, the approaches to which were not protected by policemen. Similarly, parents might be reluctant to permit their children to attend schools which the state had cut off from such general government services as ordinary police and fire protection, connections for sewage disposal, public highways and sidewalks. Of course, cutting off church schools from these services, so separate and so indisputably marked off from the religious function, would make it far more difficult for the schools to operate. But such is obviously not the purpose of the First Amendment. That Amendment requires the state to be a neutral in its relations with groups of religious believers and non-believers; it does not require the state to be their adversary. State power is no more to be used so as to handicap religions than it is to favor them.

This Court has said that parents may, in the discharge of their duty under state compulsory education laws, send their children to a religious rather than a public school if the school meets the secular educational requirements which the state has power to impose. See Pierce v. Society of Sisters, 268 U.S. 510. It appears that these parochial schools meet New Jersey's requirements. The State contributes no money to the schools. It does not support them. Its legislation, as applied, does no more than provide a general program to help parents get their children, regardless of their religion, safely and expeditiously to and from accredited schools.

The First Amendment has erected a wall between church and state. That wall must be kept high and impregnable. We could not approve the slightest breach. New Jersey has not breached it here.

Affirmed.

Mr. Justice JACKSON (joined by Mr. Justice FRANKFURTER), dissenting. . . .

. . . The Court's opinion marshals every argument in favor of state aid and puts the case in its most favorable light, but much of its reasoning confirms my conclusions that there are no good grounds upon which to support the present legislation. In fact, the undertones of the opinion, advocating complete and uncompromising separation of Church from State, seem utterly discordant with its conclusion yielding support to their commingling in educational matters. The case which irresistibly comes to mind as the most fitting precedent is that of Julia who, according to Byron's reports, "whispering 'I will ne'er consent,'—consented." . . .

Mr. Justice RUTLEDGE, with whom Mr. Justice FRANKFURTER, Mr. Justice JACKSON and Mr. Justice BURTON agree, dissenting. [After an extensive historical study, he continued:]

Compulsory attendance upon religious exercises went out early in the process of separating church and state, together with forced observance of religious forms and ceremonies. Test oaths and religious qualification for office followed later. These things none devoted to our great tradition of religious liberty would think of bringing back. Hence today, apart from efforts to inject religious training or exercises and sectarian issues into the public schools, the only serious surviving threat to maintaining that complete and permanent separation of religion and civil power which the First Amendment commands is through use of the taxing power to support religion, religious establishments, or establishments having a religious foundation whatever their form or special religious function.

Does New Jersey's action furnish support for religion by use of the taxing power? Certainly it does, if the test remains undiluted as Jefferson and Madison made it, that money taken by taxation from one is not to be used or given to support another's religious training or belief, or indeed one's own. Today as then the furnishing of "contributions of money for the propagation of opinions which he disbelieves" is the forbidden exaction; and the prohibition is absolute for whatever measure brings that consequence and whatever amount may be sought or given to that end.

The funds used here were raised by taxation. The Court does not dispute, nor could it, that their use does in fact give aid and encouragement to religious instruction. It only concludes that this aid is not "support" in law. But Madison and Jefferson were concerned with aid and support in fact, not as a legal conclusion "entangled in precedents." . . . Here parents pay money to send their children to parochial schools and funds raised by taxation are used to reimburse them. This not only helps the children to get to school and the parents to send them. It aids them in a substantial way to get the very thing which they are sent to the particular school to secure, namely, religious training and teaching. . . .

[I]t cannot be said that the cost of transportation is no part of the cost of education or of the religious instruction given. That it is a substantial and a necessary element is shown most plainly by the continuing and increasing demand for the state to assume it. Nor is there pretense that it relates only to the secular instruction given in religious schools or that any attempt is or could be made toward allocating proportional shares as between the secular and the religious instruction. It is precisely because the instruction is religious and relates to a particular faith, whether one or another, that parents send their children to religious schools under the Pierce doctrine. And the very purpose of the state's contribution is to defray the cost of conveying the pupil to the place where he will receive not simply secular, but also and primarily religious, teaching and guidance. . . . [T]ransportation where it is needed is as essential to education as any other element. Its cost is as much a part of the total expense, except at times in amount, as the cost of textbooks, of school lunches, of athletic equipment, of writing and other materials; indeed of all other items composing the total burden. . . .

But we are told that the New Jersey statute is valid in its present application because the appropriation is for a public, not a private purpose, namely, the promotion of education, and the majority accept this idea in the conclusion that all we have here is "public welfare legislation." If that is true and the Amendment's force can be thus destroyed, what has been said becomes all the more pertinent. For then there could be no possible objection to more extensive support of religious education by New Jersey. . . .

It is not because religious teaching does not promote the public or the individual's welfare, but because neither is furthered when the state promotes religious education, that the Constitution forbids it to do so. Both legislatures and courts are bound by that distinction. In failure to observe it lies the fallacy of the "public function"-"social legislation" argument, a fallacy facilitated by easy transference of the argument's basing from due process unrelated to any religious aspect to the First Amendment. . . . Legislatures are free to make, and courts to sustain, appropriations only when it can be found that in fact they do not aid, promote, encourage or sustain religious teaching or observances, be the amount large or small. No such finding has been or could be made in this case. The Amendment has removed this form of promoting the public welfare from legislative and judicial competence to make a public function. It is exclusively a private affair. . . .

No one conscious of religious values can be unsympathetic toward the burden which our constitutional separation puts on parents who desire religious instruction mixed with secular for their children. They pay taxes for others' children's education, at the same time the added cost of instruction for their own. Nor can one happily see benefits denied to children which others receive, because in conscience they or their parents for them desire a different kind of training others do not demand.

But if those feelings should prevail, there would be an end to our historic constitutional policy and command. No more unjust or discriminatory in fact is it to deny attendants at religious schools the cost of their transportation than it is to deny them tuitions, sustenance for their teachers, or any other educational expense which others receive at public cost. Hardship in fact there is which none can blink. But, for assuring to those who undergo it the greater, the most comprehensive freedom, it is one written by design and firm intent into our basic law. . . .

[I]t is only by observing the prohibition rigidly that the state can maintain its neutrality and avoid partisanship in the dissensions inevitable when sect opposes sect over demands for public moneys to further religious education, teaching or training in any form or degree, directly or indirectly. Like St. Paul's freedom, religious liberty with a great price must be bought. And for those who exercise it most fully, by insisting upon religious education for their children mixed with secular, by the terms of our Constitution the price is greater than for others. . . .

Nor is the case comparable to one of furnishing fire or police protection, or access to public highways. These things are matters of common right, part of the general need for safety.[1] Certainly the fire department must not stand idly by while the church burns. Nor is this reason why the state should pay the expense of transportation or other items of the cost of religious education.

Two great drives are constantly in motion to abridge, in the name of education, the complete division of religion and civil authority which our forefathers made. One is to introduce religious education and observances into the public schools. The other, to obtain public funds for the aid and support of various private religious schools. . . . In my opinion both avenues were closed by the Constitution. Neither should be opened by this Court. The matter is not one of quantity, to be measured by the amount of money expended. Now as in Madison's day it is one of principle, to keep separate the separate spheres as the First Amendment drew them; to prevent the first experiment upon our liberties; and to keep the question from becoming entangled in corrosive precedents. We should not be less strict to keep strong and untarnished the one side of the shield of religious freedom than we have been of the other.

EVERSON, THE "WALL OF SEPARATION," AND FINANCIAL AID TO RELIGIOUS ACTIVITIES

1. *Establishment and the states.* Justice Black in Everson assumed that the applicability of the establishment clause to the states followed from the earlier "incorporation" of the free exercise guarantee into the 14th. Did that conclusion warrant further explanation? For example, does the 14th Amend-

1. The protections are of a nature which does not require appropriations specially made from the public treasury and earmarked, as is New Jersey's here, particularly for religious institutions or uses. The First Amendment does not exclude religious property or activities from protection against disorder or the ordinary accidental incidents of community life. It forbids support, not protection from interference or destruction. . . . [Footnote by Justice Rutledge.]

ment present any textual barrier to "incorporation" of the establishment clause? Note Justice Brennan's comment in his concurring opinion in Abington School District v. Schempp, 374 U.S. 203 (1963) (p. 1369, infra): "It has . . . been suggested that the 'liberty' guaranteed by the Fourteenth Amendment logically cannot absorb the Establishment Clause because that clause is not one of the provisions of the Bill of Rights which in terms protects a 'freedom' of the individual. See Corwin, A Constitution of Powers in a Secular State (1951), 113–116. The fallacy in this contention, I think, is that it underestimates the role of the Establishment Clause as a coguarantor, with the Free Exercise Clause, of religious liberty. The Framers did not entrust the liberty of religious beliefs to either clause alone."

Note also Justice Brennan's response in Schempp to other objections to "incorporating" the establishment clause: "It has been suggested, with some support in history, that absorption of the First Amendment's ban against congressional legislation 'respecting an establishment of religion' is conceptually impossible because the Framers meant the Establishment Clause also to foreclose any attempt by Congress to disestablish the existing official state churches. [But] it is clear on the record of history that the last of the formal state establishments was dissolved more than three decades before the Fourteenth Amendment was ratified, and thus the problem of protecting official state churches from federal encroachments could hardly have been any concern of those who framed the post-Civil War Amendments. [The 14th Amendment] created a panoply of new federal rights for the protection of citizens of the various States. And among those rights was freedom from such state governmental involvement in the affairs of religion as the Establishment Clause had originally foreclosed on the part of Congress.

"[It has also been contended] that absorption of the Establishment Clause is precluded by the absence of any intention on the part of the Framers of the Fourteenth Amendment to circumscribe the residual powers of the States to aid religious activities and institutions in ways which fell short of formal establishments. That argument relies in part upon the express terms of the abortive Blaine Amendment—proposed several years after the adoption of the Fourteenth Amendment—which would have added to the First Amendment a provision that '[n]o state shall make any law respecting an establishment of religion. . . .' Such a restriction would have been superfluous, it is said, if the Fourteenth Amendment had already made the Establishment Clause binding upon the States. The argument proves too much, for the Fourteenth Amendment's protection of the free exercise of religion can hardly be questioned; yet the Blaine Amendment would also have added an explicit protection against state laws abridging that liberty." *

2. *Financial aid.* The Court's attention to financial assistance involving religious groups is long-standing, but it did not become intense and controversial until recently. The first Supreme Court decision on the establishment clause, for example, sustained a federal appropriation for the construction of a public ward to be administered as part of a hospital under the control of Sisters

---

* Note that many state constitutions contain prohibitions of aid to religious groups. Some of these provisions have been interpreted to bar practices sustained against federal establishment clause attacks. For example, compare with the Everson holding the state constitutional prohibition of transportation for parochial school students in Visser v. Nooksack Valley School Dist., 33 Wash.2d 669, 207 P.2d 198 (1949). See generally Antieau, Carroll and Burke, Religion under the State Constitutions (1965).

of the Roman Catholic Church. Bradfield v. Roberts, 175 U.S. 291 (1899). But the constitutional problem became far more pressing after Everson and with the increasing demands for federal spending. On the range of potential sources of controversy in direct and indirect supports, see the list of "aids" in footnote 1 to Justice Douglas' opinion in Engel v. Vitale, at p. 1363, infra.

Proposals for federal financial aid to education provoked the most widespread constitutional debate. Court statements in Everson and in subsequent establishment cases not directly involving financing, infra, were frequently mentioned in that debate, but for years the Justices did not speak directly to the issues. See, e. g., the contrasting interpretations of Court decisions in the 1961 memoranda on the constitutionality of federal aid to parochial schools, by the Department of HEW and the National Catholic Welfare Conference, reprinted in 50 Geo.L.J. 349, 396 (1961).

The enactment of the broad-ranging federal aid to education law in 1965 raised anew the problems of the permissible scope of assistance to parochial schools under Everson and its progeny. The Court assured that it would play a central role with the Flast v. Cohen holding, 392 U.S. 83 (1968) (chap. 2, p. 93, supra), that federal taxpayers had standing to raise establishment challenges to spending. And, in a case involving a state textbook aid program, the Court in 1968 reexamined the implications of Everson in light of the cases of the intervening two decades. Board of Education v. Allen, 392 U.S. 236 (p. 1373, infra). Problems of financial aid will accordingly be pursued further in connection with the Allen decision and the related materials printed at the end of this section.

B. INTRUSION OF RELIGION INTO GOVERNMENTAL ACTIVITIES

ZORACH v. CLAUSON

343 U.S. 306, 72 S.Ct. 679, 96 L.Ed. 954 (1952).

Appeal from the Court of Appeals of New York.

Mr. Justice DOUGLAS delivered the opinion of the Court.

New York City has a program which permits its public schools to release students during the school day so that they may leave the school buildings and school grounds and go to religious centers for religious instruction or devotional exercises. A student is released on written request of his parents. Those not released stay in the classrooms. The churches make weekly reports to the schools, sending a list of children who have been released from public school but who have not reported for religious instruction.

This "released time" program involves neither religious instruction in public school classrooms nor the expenditure of public funds. All costs, including the application blanks, are paid by the religious organizations. The case is therefore unlike McCollum v. Board of Education, 333 U.S. 203 [1948], which involved a "released time" program from Illinois. In that case the classrooms were turned over to religious instructors. We accordingly held that the program violated the First Amendment which (by reason of the Fourteenth Amendment) prohibits the states from establishing religion or prohibiting its free exercise.

Appellants, who are taxpayers and residents of New York City and whose children attend its public schools, challenge the present law, contending it is in essence not different from the one involved in the McCollum case. Their argument, stated elaborately in various ways, reduces itself to this: the weight and influence of the school is put behind a program for religious instruction; public school teachers police it, keeping tab on students who are released; the classroom activities come to a halt while the students who are released for religious instruction are on leave; the school is a crutch on which the churches are leaning for support in their religious training; without the cooperation of the schools this "released time" program, like the one in the McCollum case, would be futile and ineffective. The New York Court of Appeals sustained the law against this claim of unconstitutionality. . . .

The briefs and arguments are replete with data bearing on the merits of this type of "released time" program. They largely concern the wisdom of the system . . . . Those matters are of no concern here, since our problem reduces itself to whether New York by this system has either prohibited the "free exercise" of religion or has made a law "respecting an establishment of religion" within the meaning of the First Amendment.

It takes obtuse reasoning to inject any issue of the "free exercise" of religion into the present case. No one is forced to go to the religious classroom and no religious exercise or instruction is brought to the classrooms of the public schools. A student need not take religious instruction. He is left to his own desires as to the manner or time of his religious devotions, if any.

There is a suggestion that the system involves the use of coercion to get public school students into religious classrooms. There is no evidence in the record before us that supports that conclusion.[1] The present record indeed tells us that the school authorities are neutral in this regard and do no more than release students whose parents so request. If in fact coercion were used, if it were established that any one or more teachers were using their office to persuade or force students to take the religious instruction, a wholly different case would be presented.[2] Hence we put aside that claim of coercion both as respects the "free exercise" of religion and "an establishment of religion" within the meaning of the First Amendment.

Moreover, apart from that claim of coercion, we do not see how New York by this type of "released time" program has made a law respecting an establishment of religion within the meaning of the First Amendment. There is much talk of the separation of Church and State in the history of the Bill of

1. Nor is there any indication that the public schools enforce attendance at religious schools by punishing absentees from the released time programs for truancy. [Footnote by the Court.]

2. Appellants contend that they should have been allowed to prove that the system is in fact administered in a coercive manner. The New York Court of Appeals declined to grant a trial on this issue, noting, inter alia, that appellants had not properly raised their claim in the manner required by state practice. . . . This independent state ground for decision precludes appellants from raising the issue of maladministration in this proceeding. . . .

The only allegation in the complaint that bears on the issue is that the operation of the program "has resulted and inevitably results in the exercise of pressure and coercion upon parents and children to secure attendance by the children for religious instruction." . . . Since the allegation did not implicate the school authorities in the use of coercion, there is no basis for holding that the New York Court of Appeals under the guise of local practice defeated a federal right . . . . [Footnote by the Court.]

Rights and in the decisions clustering around the First Amendment.
. . . There cannot be the slightest doubt that the First Amendment
reflects the philosophy that Church and State should be separated. And so far
as interference with the "free exercise" of religion and an "establishment" of
religion are concerned, the separation must be complete and unequivocal. The
First Amendment within the scope of its coverage permits no exception; the
prohibition is absolute. The First Amendment, however, does not say that in
every and all respects there shall be a separation of Church and State. Rather,
it studiously defines the manner, the specific ways, in which there shall be no
concert or union or dependency one on the other. That is the common sense
of the matter. Otherwise the state and religion would be aliens to each other
—hostile, suspicious, and even unfriendly. Churches could not be required to
pay even property taxes. Municipalities would not be permitted to render police or fire protection to religious groups. Policemen who helped parishioners
into their places of worship would violate the Constitution. Prayers in our
legislative halls; the appeals to the Almighty in the messages of the Chief Executive; the proclamations making Thanksgiving Day a holiday; "so help me
God" in our courtroom oaths—these and all other references to the Almighty
that run through our laws, our public rituals, our ceremonies would be flouting
the First Amendment. A fastidious atheist or agnostic could even object to the
supplication with which the Court opens each session: "God save the United
States and this Honorable Court."

We would have to press the concept of separation of Church and State to
these extremes to condemn the present law on constitutional grounds. The
nullification of this law would have wide and profound effects. A Catholic
student applies to his teacher for permission to leave the school during hours
on a Holy Day of Obligation to attend a mass. A Jewish student asks his
teacher for permission to be excused for Yom Kippur. A Protestant wants the
afternoon off for a family baptismal ceremony. In each case the teacher requires parental consent in writing. In each case the teacher, in order to make
sure the student is not a truant, goes further and requires a report from the
priest, the rabbi, or the minister. The teacher in other words cooperates in a
religious program to the extent of making it possible for her students to participate in it. Whether she does it occasionally for a few students, regularly for
one, or pursuant to a systematized program designed to further the religious
needs of all the students does not alter the character of the act.

We are a religious people whose institutions presuppose a Supreme
Being. We guarantee the freedom to worship as one chooses. We make
room for as wide a variety of beliefs and creeds as the spiritual needs of man
deem necessary. We sponsor an attitude on the part of government that shows
no partiality to any one group and that lets each flourish according to the zeal
of its adherents and the appeal of its dogma. When the state encourages religious instruction or cooperates with religious authorities by adjusting the
schedule of public events to sectarian needs, it follows the best of our traditions. For it then respects the religious nature of our people and accommo-
dates the public service to their spiritual needs. To hold that it may not would
be to find in the Constitution a requirement that the government show a cal-
lous indifference to religious groups. That would be preferring those who believe in no religion over those who do believe. Government may not finance
religious groups nor undertake religious instruction nor blend secular and sectarian education nor use secular institutions to force one or some religion on

any person. But we find no constitutional requirement which makes it necessary for government to be hostile to religion and to throw its weight against efforts to widen the effective scope of religious influence. The government must be neutral when it comes to competition between sects. It may not thrust any sect on any person. It may not make a religious observance compulsory. It may not coerce anyone to attend church, to observe a religious holiday, or to take religious instruction. But it can close its doors or suspend its operations as to those who want to repair to their religious sanctuary for worship or instruction. No more than that is undertaken here. . . .

In the McCollum case the classrooms were used for religious instruction and the force of the public school was used to promote that instruction. Here, as we have said, the public schools do no more than accommodate their schedules to a program of outside religious instruction. We follow the McCollum case. But we cannot expand it to cover the present released time program unless separation of Church and State means that public institutions can make no adjustments of their schedules to accommodate the religious needs of the people. We cannot read into the Bill of Rights such a philosophy of hostility to religion.

Affirmed.

Mr. Justice BLACK, dissenting. . . .

I see no significant difference between the invalid Illinois system and that of New York here sustained. Except for the use of the school buildings in Illinois, there is no difference between the systems which I consider even worthy of mention. In the New York program, as in that of Illinois, the school authorities release some of the children on the condition that they attend the religious classes, get reports on whether they attend, and hold the other children in the school building until the religious hour is over. . . .

I am aware that our McCollum decision on separation of church and state has been subjected to a most searching examination throughout the country. Probably few opinions from this Court in recent years have attracted more attention or stirred wider debate. . . . In dissenting today, I mean to do more than give routine approval to our McCollum decision. I mean also to reaffirm my faith in the fundamental philosophy expressed in McCollum and Everson v. Board of Education, 330 U.S. 1. . . .

. . . In considering whether a state has entered this forbidden field the question is not whether it has entered too far but whether it has entered at all. New York is manipulating its compulsory education laws to help religious sects get pupils. This is not separation but combination of Church and State. . . .

Mr. Justice FRANKFURTER, dissenting.

By way of emphasizing my agreement with Mr. Justice Jackson's dissent, I add a few words.

. . . Of course a State may provide that the classes in its schools shall be dismissed, for any reason, or no reason, on fixed days, or for special occasions. The essence of this case is that the school system did not "close its doors" and did not "suspend its operations." There is all the difference in the world between letting the children out of school and letting some of them out of school into religious classes. If every one is free to make what use he will of time wholly unconnected from schooling required by law—those who wish sectarian instruction devoting it to that purpose, those who have ethical instruction at home, to that, those who study music, to that—then of course there is no conflict with the Fourteenth Amendment.

The pith of the case is that formalized religious instruction is substituted for other school activity which those who do not participate in the released-time program are compelled to attend. The school system is very much in operation during this kind of released time. If its doors are closed, they are closed upon those students who do not attend the religious instruction in order to keep them within the school. That is the very thing which raises the constitutional issue. It is not met by disregarding it. Failure to discuss this issue does not take it out of the case.

Again, the Court relies upon the absence from the record of evidence of coercion in the operation of the system. . . . [T]he Court disregards the fact that as the case comes to us, there could be no proof of coercion, for the petitioners were not allowed to make proof of it. . . .

Mr. Justice JACKSON, dissenting.

This released time program is founded upon a use of the State's power of coercion, which, for me, determines its unconstitutionality. Stripped to its essentials, the plan has two stages, first, that the State compel each student to yield a large part of his time for public secular education and, second, that some of it be "released" to him on condition that he devote it to sectarian religious purposes.

No one suggests that the Constitution would permit the State directly to require this "released" time to be spent "under the control of a duly constituted religious body." This program accomplishes that forbidden result by indirection. If public education were taking so much of the pupils' time as to injure the public or the student's welfare by encroaching upon their religious opportunity, simply shortening everyone's school day would facilitate voluntary and optional attendance at Church classes. But that suggestion is rejected upon the ground that if they are made free many students will not go to the Church. Hence, they must be deprived of freedom for this period, with Church attendance put to them as one of the two permissible ways of using it.
. . .

The greater effectiveness of this system over voluntary attendance after school hours is due to the truant officer who, if the youngster fails to go to the Church school, dogs him back to the public schoolroom. Here schooling is more or less suspended during the "released time" so the nonreligious attendants will not forge ahead of the churchgoing absentees. But it serves as a temporary jail for a pupil who will not go to Church. It takes more subtlety of mind than I possess to deny that this is governmental constraint in support of religion. It is as unconstitutional, in my view, when exerted by indirection as when exercised forthrightly.

As one whose children, as a matter of free choice, have been sent to privately supported Church schools, I may challenge the Court's suggestion that opposition to this plan can only be antireligious, atheistic, or agnostic. My evangelistic brethren confuse an objection to compulsion with an objection to religion. It is possible to hold a faith with enough confidence to believe that what should be rendered to God does not need to be decided and collected by Caesar.

.   .   .   The same epithetical jurisprudence used by the Court today to beat down those who oppose pressuring children into some religion can devise as good epithets tomorrow against those who object to pressuring them into a favored religion.   .   .   .   We start down a rough road when we begin to mix compulsory public education with compulsory godliness.

A number of Justices just short of a majority of the majority that promulgates today's passionate dialectics joined in answering them in McCollum v. Board of Education, 333 U.S. 203.   The distinction attempted between that case and this is trivial, almost to the point of cynicism, magnifying its nonessential details and disparaging compulsion which was the underlying reason for invalidity.   A reading of the Court's opinion in that case along with its opinion in this case will show such difference of overtones and undertones as to make clear that the McCollum case has passed like a storm in a teacup.   The wall which the Court was professing to erect between Church and State has become even more warped and twisted than I expected.   Today's judgment will be more interesting to students of psychology and of the judicial processes than to students of constitutional law.

ENGEL v. VITALE

370 U.S. 421, 82 S.Ct. 1261, 8 L.Ed.2d 601 (1962).

Certiorari to the Court of Appeals of New York.

Mr. Justice BLACK delivered the opinion of the Court.

The respondent Board of Education of Union Free School District No. 9, New Hyde Park, New York,   .   .   .   directed the School District's principal to cause the following prayer to be said aloud by each class in the presence of a teacher at the beginning of each school day:

"Almighty God, we acknowledge our dependence upon Thee, and we beg Thy blessings upon us, our parents, our teachers and our country."
This daily procedure was adopted on the recommendation of the State Board of Regents   .   .   .   These state officials composed the prayer which they recommended and published as a part of their "Statement on Moral and Spiritual Training in the Schools," saying: "We believe that this Statement will be subscribed to by all men and women of good will, and we call upon all of them to aid in giving life to our program."   .   .   .

We think that by using its public school system to encourage recitation of the Regents' prayer, the State of New York has adopted a practice wholly inconsistent with the Establishment Clause.   There can, of course, be no doubt that New York's program of daily classroom invocation of God's blessings as prescribed in the Regents' prayer is a religious activity.   It is a solemn avowal of divine faith and supplication for the blessings of the Almighty. .   .   .   .

[W]e think that the constitutional prohibition against laws respecting an establishment of religion must at least mean that in this country it is no part of the business of government to compose official prayers for any group of the American people to recite as a part of a religious program carried on by government.

It is a matter of history that this very practice of establishing governmentally composed prayers for religious services was one of the reasons which caused many of our early colonists to leave England and seek religious freedom in America. . . .

It is an unfortunate fact of history that when some of the very groups which had most strenuously opposed the established Church of England found themselves sufficiently in control of colonial governments in this country to write their own prayers into law, they passed laws making their own religion the official religion of their respective colonies. . . .

By the time of the adoption of the Constitution, our history shows that there was a widespread awareness among many Americans of the dangers of a union of Church and State. These people knew, some of them from bitter personal experience, that one of the greatest dangers to the freedom of the individual to worship in his own way lay in the Government's placing its official stamp of approval upon one particular kind of prayer or one particular form of religious services. . . . Our Founders were no more willing to let the content of their prayers and their privilege of praying whenever they pleased be influenced by the ballot box than they were to let these vital matters of personal conscience depend upon the succession of monarchs. The First Amendment was added to the Constitution to stand as a guarantee that neither the power nor the prestige of the Federal Government would be used to control, support or influence the kinds of prayer the American people can say . . . .. Under that Amendment's prohibition against governmental establishment of religion, as reinforced by the provisions of the Fourteenth Amendment, government in this country, be it state or federal, is without power to prescribe by law any particular form of prayer which is to be used as an official prayer in carrying on any program of governmentally sponsored religious activity.

. . . Neither the fact that the prayer may be denominationally neutral, nor the fact that its observance on the part of the students is voluntary, can serve to free it from the limitations of the Establishment Clause, as it might from the Free Exercise Clause, of the First Amendment, both of which are operative against the States by virtue of the Fourteenth Amendment. Although these two clauses may in certain instances overlap, they forbid two quite different kinds of governmental encroachment upon religious freedom. The Establishment Clause, unlike the Free Exercise Clause, does not depend upon any showing of direct governmental compulsion and is violated by the enactment of laws which establish an official religion whether those laws operate directly to coerce nonobserving individuals or not. This is not to say, of course, that laws officially prescribing a particular form of religious worship do not involve coercion of such individuals. When the power, prestige and financial support of government is placed behind a particular religious belief, the indirect coercive pressure upon religious minorities to conform to the prevailing officially approved religion is plain. But the purposes underlying the Establishment Clause go much further than that. Its first and most immediate purpose rested on the belief that a union of government and religion tends to destroy government and to degrade religion. . . . Another purpose of the Establishment Clause rested upon an awareness of the historical fact that governmentally established religions and religious persecutions go hand in hand. . . . The New York laws officially prescribing the Regents' prayer are inconsistent with both the purposes of the Establishment Clause and with the Establishment Clause itself.

It has been argued that to apply the Constitution in such a way as to prohibit state laws respecting an establishment of religious services in public schools is to indicate a hostility toward religion or toward prayer. Nothing, of course, could be more wrong. The history of man is inseparable from the history of religion. [The men] who led the fight for adoption of our Constitution and also for our Bill of Rights . . . knew that the First Amendment, which tried to put an end to governmental control of religion and of prayer, was not written to destroy either. . . . It is neither sacrilegious nor antireligious to say that each separate government in this country should stay out of the business of writing or sanctioning official prayers and leave that purely religious function to the people themselves and to those the people choose to look to for religious guidance.* . . .

Reversed and remanded.

Mr. Justice FRANKFURTER took no part in the decision of this case. Mr. Justice WHITE took no part in the consideration or decision of this case.

Mr. Justice DOUGLAS, concurring.

. . . The point for decision is whether the Government can constitutionally finance a religious exercise. Our system at the federal and state levels is presently honeycombed with such financing.[1] Nevertheless, I think it is an unconstitutional undertaking whatever form it takes. . . .

Plainly, our Bill of Rights would not permit a State or the Federal Government to adopt an official prayer and penalize anyone who would not utter it. This, however, is not that case, for there is no element of compulsion or coercion in New York's regulation. . . .

* There is of course nothing in the decision reached here that is inconsistent with the fact that school children and others are officially encouraged to express love for our country by reciting historical documents such as the Declaration of Independence which contain references to the Deity or by singing officially espoused anthems which include the composer's professions of faith in a Supreme Being, or with the fact that there are many manifestations in our public life of belief in God. Such patriotic or ceremonial occasions bear no true resemblance to the unquestioned religious exercise that the State of New York has sponsored in this instance. [Footnote by the Court.]

1. "There are many 'aids' to religion in this country at all levels of government. To mention but a few at the federal level, one might begin by observing that the very First Congress which wrote the First Amendment provided for chaplains in both Houses and in the armed services. There is compulsory chapel at the service academies, and religious services are held in federal hospitals and prisons. The President issues religious proclamations. The Bible is used for the administration of oaths. N. Y. A. and

W. P. A. funds were available to parochial schools during the depression. Veterans receiving money under the 'G. I.' Bill of 1944 could attend denominational schools, to which payments were made directly by the government. During World War II, federal money was contributed to denominational schools for the training of nurses. The benefits of the National School Lunch Act are available to students in private as well as public schools. The Hospital Survey and Construction Act of 1946 specifically made money available to non-public hospitals. The slogan 'In God We Trust' is used by the Treasury Department, and Congress recently added God to the pledge of allegiance. There is Bible-reading in the schools of the District of Columbia, and religious instruction is given in the District's National Training School for Boys. Religious organizations are exempt from the federal income tax and are granted postal privileges. Up to defined limits . . . contributions to religious organizations are deductible for federal income tax purposes. . . . This list of federal 'aids' could easily be expanded, and of course there is a long list in each state." Fellman, The Limits of Freedom (1959), pp. 40–41. [Footnote by Justice Douglas.]

. . . I cannot say that to authorize this prayer is to establish a religion in the strictly historic meaning of those words. A religion is not established in the usual sense merely by letting those who choose to do so say the prayer that the public school teacher leads. Yet once government finances a religious exercise it inserts a divisive influence into our communities. . . .

"We are a religious people whose institutions presuppose a Supreme Being." Zorach v. Clauson, 343 U.S. 306, 313. . . . The First Amendment leaves the Government in a position not of hostility to religion but of neutrality. . . .

My problem today would be uncomplicated but for [the Everson case, which] seems in retrospect to be out of line with the First Amendment. Its result is appealing, as it allows aid to be given to needy children. Yet by the same token, public funds could be used to satisfy other needs of children in parochial schools—lunches, books, and tuition being obvious examples. Mr. Justice Rutledge stated in dissent what I think is durable First Amendment philosophy. . . .

Mr. Justice STEWART, dissenting. . . .

. . . I cannot see how an "official religion" is established by letting those who want to say a prayer say it. On the contrary, I think that to deny the wish of these school children to join in reciting this prayer is to deny them the opportunity of sharing in the spiritual heritage of our Nation.

. . . I think that the Court's task, in this as in all areas of constitutional adjudication, is not responsibly aided by the uncritical invocation of metaphors like the "wall of separation," a phrase nowhere to be found in the Constitution. . . .

At the opening of each day's Session of this Court we stand, while one of our officials invokes the protection of God. Since the days of John Marshall our Crier has said, "God save the United States and this Honorable Court." Both the Senate and the House of Representatives open their daily Sessions with prayer. Each of our Presidents, from George Washington to John F. Kennedy, has upon assuming his Office asked the protection and help of God. . . .

Countless similar examples could be listed, but there is no need to belabor the obvious.[2] It was all summed up by this Court just ten years ago in a single sentence: "We are a religious people whose institutions presuppose a Supreme Being." Zorach v. Clauson, 343 U.S. 306, 313.[*]

2. I am at a loss to understand the Court's unsupported *ipse dixit* that these official expressions of religious faith in and reliance upon a Supreme Being "bear no true resemblance to the unquestioned religious exercise that the State of New York has sponsored in this instance." . . . I can hardly think that the Court means to say that the First Amendment imposes a lesser restriction upon the Federal Government than does the Fourteenth Amendment upon the States. Or is the Court suggesting that the Constitution permits judges and Congressmen and Presidents to join in prayer, but prohibits school children from doing so? [Footnote by Justice Stewart.]

* Compare, with the use of the Zorach v. Clauson language in the opinions of Justices Stewart and Douglas, the 1961 case of Torcaso v. Watkins, 367 U.S. 488: Appellant had been denied a commission as notary public for his refusal to comply with a state constitutional provision requiring a declaration of belief in God. The Court, in an opinion by Justice Black, concluded: "This Maryland religious test for public office unconstitutionally in-

I do not believe that this Court, or the Congress, or the President has by the actions and practices I have mentioned established an "official religion" in violation of the Constitution. And I do not believe the State of New York has done so in this case. What each has done has been to recognize and to follow the deeply entrenched and highly cherished spiritual traditions of our Nation.

. . . .

THE BIBLE READING CASES AND THE SEARCH FOR NEW FORMULATIONS: "NEUTRALITY," "PURPOSE," "PRIMARY EFFECT," AND THE BRENNAN CONCURRENCE

One year after Engel v. Vitale, the Justices extended its principles beyond state-composed prayers—and in the process tried their hands at reformulating establishment criteria. In Abington School District v. Schempp and Murray v. Curlett, 374 U.S. 203 (1963), the Court held that the establishment clause prohibits state laws and practices "requiring the selection and reading at the opening of the school day of verses from the Holy Bible and the recitation of the Lord's Prayer by the students in unison."

In the Schempp case a Pennsylvania law provided: "At least ten verses from the Holy Bible shall be read, without comment, at the opening of each public school on each school day. Any child shall be excused from such Bible reading, or attending such Bible reading, upon the written request of his parent or guardian." The Schempp family, members of the Unitarian Church, attacked high school opening exercises involving the recitation of the Lord's Prayer as well as the reading of the Bible verses. In Murray, Mrs. Murray and her son, "both professed atheists," challenged a Baltimore school rule adopted pursuant to Maryland law providing for the holding of opening exercises consisting primarily of the "reading, without comment, of a chapter in the Holy Bible and/or the use of the Lord's Prayer." That rule also permitted children to be excused at the request of a parent.

1. *The majority standard.* Justice Clark's opinion for the Court reaffirmed two "basic conclusions of the Court": first, that the First Amendment's religion provisions have "been made wholly applicable to the states by the Fourteenth Amendment"; second, that "this Court has rejected unequivocally the contention that the establishment clause forbids only governmental preference of one religion over another." Though these principles had not been questioned in these cases, Justice Clark noted, "others continue to question their history, logic and efficacy. Such contentions . . . seem entirely untenable and of value only as academic exercises." After reviewing deci-

---

vades the appellant's freedom of belief and religion and therefore cannot be enforced against him." The Maryland Court of Appeals had thought that the Zorach case had "in part repudiated" statements in Everson and McCollum concerning complete separation between the state and religion. Justice Black answered: "Nothing decided or written in Zorach lends support to the idea that the Court there intended to open up the way for government, state or federal, to restore the historically and constitutionally discredited policy of probing religious beliefs by test oaths or limiting public offices to persons who have, or perhaps more properly, profess to have a belief in some particular kind of religious concept." Justices Frankfurter and Harlan concurred in the result. The Court did not reach the contention that the "no religious test" provision of Article VI applies to state as well as federal offices.

sions from Cantwell to Engel v. Vitale, he concluded that both the establishment clause and the free exercise clause require "neutrality." He explained:

"The wholesome 'neutrality' of which this Court's cases speak thus stems from a recognition of the teachings of history that powerful sects or groups might bring about a fusion of governmental and religious functions or a concert or dependency of one upon the other to the end that official support of the State or Federal Government would be placed behind the tenets of one or of all orthodoxies. This the Establishment Clause prohibits. And a further reason for neutrality is found in the Free Exercise Clause, which recognizes the value of religious training, teaching and observance and, more particularly, the right of every person to freely choose his own course with reference thereto, free of any compulsion from the state. This the Free Exercise Clause guarantees. Thus, as we have seen, the two clauses may overlap. As we have indicated, the Establishment Clause has been directly considered by this Court eight times in the past score of years and, with only one Justice dissenting on the point, it has consistently held that the clause withdrew all legislative power respecting religious belief or the expression thereof. The test may be stated as follows: *what are the purpose and the primary effect of the enactment?* If either is the advancement or inhibition of religion then the enactment exceeds the scope of legislative power as circumscribed by the Constitution. That is to say that to withstand the strictures of the Establishment Clause *there must be a secular legislative purpose and a primary effect that neither advances nor inhibits religion.* Everson v. Board of Education, supra; McGowan v. Maryland, [which follows]. The Free Exercise Clause, likewise considered many times here, withdraws from legislative power, state and federal, the exertion of any restraint on the free exercise of religion. Its purpose is to secure religious liberty in the individual by prohibiting any invasions thereof by civil authority. Hence it is necessary in a free exercise case for one to show the coercive effect of the enactment as it operates against him in the practice of his religion. The distinction between the two clauses is apparent—a violation of the Free Exercise Clause is predicated on coercion while the Establishment Clause violation need not be so attended." [Emphasis added.]

The Court concluded: "Nothing we have said here indicates that . . . study of the Bible or of religion, when presented objectively as part of a secular program of education, may not be effected consistent with the First Amendment. But the exercises here do not fall into those categories. They are religious exercises, required by the States in violation of the command of the First Amendment that the Government maintain strict neutrality, neither aiding nor opposing religion."

Three additional opinions concurred in the opinion and judgment of the Court. Justice Douglas saw two different violations of the establishment clause. The challenged practices were unconstitutional, he insisted, not only because they constituted state-conducted religious exercises in violation of the required "neutrality" but also because of "the additional reason that public funds, though small in amount, are being used to promote a religious exercise." Justice Goldberg's separate opinion, joined by Justice Harlan, spoke of the "unavoidable accommodations necessary" to achieve the "fullest realization of true religious liberty." He concluded: "The practices here involved do not fall within any sensible or acceptable concept of compelled or permitted accommodation and involve the state so significantly and directly in the realm of the sectarian as to give rise to those very divisive influences and inhibitions of freedom which both religion clauses of the First Amendment preclude."

2. *The Brennan concurrence.* Justice Brennan's concurrence was far the most extensive. The invalidation of the practices here, he stated, was compelled by the ruling in Engel v. Vitale, for "it is constitutionally irrelevant that the State has not composed the material for the inspirational exercises presently involved." He then proceeded to explore at length the history and interpretations of the religion provisions to explain his conclusion that "not every involvement of religion in public life is unconstitutional." His discussion of "the line we must draw between the permissible and the impermissible" is of particular interest:

"What the Framers meant to foreclose, and what our decisions under the Establishment Clause have forbidden, are those involvements of religious with secular institutions which (a) serve the essentially religious activities of religious institutions; (b) employ the organs of government for essentially religious purposes; or (c) use essentially religious means to serve governmental ends, where secular means would suffice.   .   .   .   On the other hand, there may be myriad forms of involvements of government with religion which do not import such dangers and therefore should not in my judgment be deemed to violate the Establishment Clause.   .   .   .

"   .   .   .   I think a brief survey of certain of these forms of accommodation will reveal that the First Amendment commands not official hostility toward religion, but only a strict neutrality in matters of religion. Moreover, it may serve to suggest that the scope of our holding today is to be measured by the special circumstances under which these cases have arisen, and by the particular dangers to church and state which religious exercises in the public schools present.   .   .   .

"A.   *The Conflict Between Establishment and Free Exercise.*—There are certain practices, conceivably violative of the Establishment Clause, the striking down of which might seriously interfere with certain religious liberties also protected by the First Amendment.   .   .   .

"   .   .   .   In my view, government cannot sponsor religious exercises in the public schools without jeopardizing   .   .   .   neutrality. On the other hand, hostility, not neutrality, would characterize the refusal to provide chaplains and places of worship for prisoners and soldiers cut off by the State from all civilian opportunities for public communion, the withholding of draft exemptions for ministers and conscientious objectors, or the denial of the temporary use of an empty public building to a congregation whose place of worship has been destroyed by fire or flood. I do not say that government *must* provide chaplains or draft exemptions, or that the Court should intercede if it fails to do so.

"B.   *Establishment and Exercises in Legislative Bodies.*—The saying of invocational prayers in legislative chambers, state or federal, and the appointment of legislative chaplains, might well represent no involvements of the kind prohibited by the Establishment Clause. Legislators, federal and state, are mature adults.   .   .   .

"C.   *Non-Devotional Use of the Bible In the Public Schools.*—The holding of the Court today plainly does not foreclose teaching *about* the Holy Scriptures   .   .   .   .

"D. *Uniform Tax Exemptions Incidentally Available to Religious Institutions.*—Nothing we hold today questions the propriety of certain tax deductions or exemptions which incidentally benefit churches and religious institutions, along with many secular charities and nonprofit organizations. If religious institutions benefit, it is in spite of rather than because of their religious character. For religious institutions simply share benefits which government makes generally available to educational, charitable, and eleemosynary groups. There is no indication that taxing authorities have used such benefits in any way to subsidize worship or foster belief in God. And as among religious beneficiaries, the tax exemption or reduction can be truly nondiscriminatory, available on equal terms to small as well as large religious bodies, to popular and unpopular sects, and to those organizations which reject as well as those which accept a belief in God. . . .

"E. *Religious Considerations in Public Welfare Programs.*—Since government may not support or directly aid religious *activities* . . . ., there might be some doubt whether non-discriminatory programs of governmental aid may constitutionally include *individuals* who become eligible wholly or partially for religious reasons. . . . Such a construction would, it seems to me, require government to impose religious discriminations and disabilities, thereby jeopardizing the free exercise of religion, in order to avoid what is thought to constitute an establishment.

" . . . The Framers were not concerned with the effects of certain incidental aids to individual worshipers which come about as byproducts of general and non-discriminatory welfare programs. . . .

"F. *Activities Which, Though Religious in Origin, Have Ceased to Have Religious Meaning.*— . . . As we said in McGowan [the Sunday Closing Law case which follows] . . . ., 'the Establishment clause does not ban federal or state regulation of conduct whose reason or effect merely happens to coincide or harmonize with the tenets of some or all religions.' This rationale suggests that the use of the motto 'In God We Trust' on currency, on documents and public buildings and the like may not offend the clause. . . .

"This general principle might also serve to insulate the various patriotic exercises and activities used in the public schools and elsewhere which, whatever may have been their origins, no longer have a religious purpose or meaning. The reference to divinity in the revised pledge of allegiance, for example, may merely recognize the historical fact that our Nation was believed to have been founded 'under God.' Thus reciting the pledge may be no more of a religious exercise than the reading aloud of Lincoln's Gettysburg Address, which contains an allusion to the same historical fact."

3. *The Stewart dissent.* Justice Stewart dissented. He insisted that the cases should be remanded for additional evidence. He emphasized that there was no evidence "as to whether there would exist any coercion of any kind upon a student who did not want to participate," and he urged that school authorities be given an opportunity to demonstrate that they could "administer a system of religious exercises during school hours . . . in such a way as completely to free from any kind of official coercion those who do not affirmatively want to participate." He remarked that it was "a fallacious oversimplification" to regard the religion clauses "as establishing a single constitutional standard of 'separation of church and state,' which can be mechanically

applied in every case." He insisted that "religion and government must necessarily interact in countless ways" and that "there are areas in which a doctrinaire reading of the Establishment Clause leads to irreconcilable conflict with the Free Exercise Clause." He added: "I cannot agree with what seems to me the insensitive definition of the Establishment Clause contained in the Court's opinion, nor with the different but, I think, equally mechanistic definitions contained in the separate opinions which have been filed." *

SOME OTHER ASPECTS OF SEPARATION

1. *The Sunday Closing Cases.* In reformulating establishment criteria in the Bible Reading cases, the Court relied in part on McGowan v. Maryland, 366 U.S. 420 (1961). McGowan was one of the few establishment controversies in the Court that did not involve schools. It was one of four 1961 companion cases in which the Court rejected claims that Sunday Closing Laws were "laws respecting an establishment of religion or prohibiting the free exercise thereof." In two of the cases, Two Guys from Harrison-Allentown v. McGinley, 366 U.S. 582, as well as McGowan, the Court held that the establishment claim was the only religion issue which appellants could raise. In the McGowan case, the Court pointed out that "appellants allege only economic injury to themselves; they do not allege any infringement of their own religious freedoms due to Sunday closing."

Chief Justice Warren wrote the opinions for the Court in these cases. He noted in McGowan that there is "no dispute that the original laws which dealt with Sunday labor were motivated by religious forces." He concluded, however: "In light of the evolution of our Sunday Closing Laws through the centuries, and of their more or less recent emphasis upon secular considerations, it is not difficult to discern that as presently written and administered, most of them, at least, are of a secular rather than of a religious character, and that presently they bear no relationship to establishment of religion as those words are used in the Constitution of the United States. . . . The present purpose and effect of most of them is to provide a uniform day of rest for all citizens; the fact that this day is Sunday, a day of particular significance for the dominant Christian sects, does not bar the State from achieving its secular goals. . . . Sunday is a day apart from all others. The cause is irrelevant; the fact exists." [Recall also the rejection of the equal protection claims in McGowan, chap. 14, p. 988, supra.]

Braunfeld v. Brown, 366 U.S. 599, was the major case raising the free exercise contention as well. That case appears below, sec. 2, p. 1381. Gallagher

---

* As a result of criticism of the Bible Reading Cases, a large number of constitutional amendments were proposed. The House Judiciary Committee held hearings on the proposals in the spring of 1964. The most widely discussed suggestion was the proposed Becker Amendment:

"Section 1. Nothing in this Constitution shall be deemed to prohibit the offering, reading from, or listening to prayers or biblical scriptures if participation therein is on a voluntary basis, in any governmental or public school, institution, or place.

"Section 2. Nothing in this Constitution shall be deemed to prohibit making reference to belief in, reliance upon, or invoking the aid of God or a Supreme Being in any governmental or public document, proceeding, activity, ceremony, school, institution, or place, or upon any coinage, currency, or obligation of the United States.

"Section 3. Nothing in this article shall constitute an establishment of religion." (H.J.Res. 693, 88th Cong., 1st Sess.)

v. Crown Kosher Market, 366 U.S. 617, involved a "similar, although not as grave," challenge. Justice Frankfurter submitted an extensive separate opinion, joined by Justice Harlan. He substantially agreed with Chief Justice Warren in all four cases. Justice Douglas dissented in all of the cases on establishment and free exercise grounds. The views of Justices Brennan and Stewart, dissenting only on the free exercise issue, appear in Braunfeld, below.

2. *The "Monkey Law" Case.* Arkansas' version of the Tennessee "anti-evolution" law which gained national notoriety in the Scopes trial in 1927 was found to be in conflict with the establishment clause mandate of "governmental neutrality" in Epperson v. Arkansas, 393 U.S. 97 (1968). The Arkansas statute prohibited teachers in state schools from teaching "the theory or doctrine that mankind ascended or descended from a lower order of animals." The highest state court had expressed "no opinion" on "whether the Act prohibits any explanation of the theory of evolution or merely prohibits teaching that the theory is true." On either interpretation, Justice Fortas' majority opinion concluded, the law could not stand: "The overriding fact is that Arkansas' law selects from the body of knowledge a particular segment which it proscribes for the sole reason that it is deemed to conflict with a particular religious doctrine; that is, with a particular interpretation of the Book of Genesis by a particular religious group."

The Court found it unnecessary to rely on broad academic freedom principles because of the availability of the "narrower terms" of the First Amendment's religion provisions. "The State's undoubted right to prescribe the curriculum for its public schools" did not include the right to bar "the teaching of a scientific theory or doctrine where that prohibition is based upon reasons that violate the First Amendment." Here, clearly, "fundamentalist sectarian conviction was and is the law's reason for existence." This plainly was not the required religious neutrality: "Arkansas did not seek to excise from the curricula of its schools and universities all discussion of the origin of man. The law's effort was confined to an attempt to blot out a particular theory because of its supposed conflict with the biblical account, literally read."

In separate opinions, Justices Black and Stewart explained that they concurred solely on the ground of vagueness. Justice Black criticized the majority for reaching out to "troublesome" First Amendment questions. He noted, for example, that "a state law prohibiting all teaching of human development or biology is constitutionally quite different from a law that compels a teacher to teach as true only one theory of a given doctrine" and he stated that he was not ready to hold "that a person hired to teach schoolchildren takes with him into the classroom a constitutional right to teach sociological, economic, political, or religious subjects that the school's managers do not want discussed." He questioned, moreover, whether the majority's view achieved "religious neutrality": If some considered evolution anti-religious, was the state constitutionally bound to permit teaching of anti-religious doctrine? Did the Court's holding infringe "the religious freedom of those who consider evolution an anti-religious doctrine?"

3. *Internal church disputes.* Civil courts have traditionally been reluctant to intervene in disputes arising from church schisms. See, e. g., Kreshik v. St. Nicholas Cathedral, 363 U.S. 190 (1960) (relying on free exercise grounds). The Supreme Court reaffirmed that tradition in Presbyterian Church v. Mary Eliz. Blue Hull Memorial Presbyterian Church, 393 U.S. 440 (1969). The Georgia courts had decided a church property dispute in favor

INDIANA STATE
UNIVERSITY
— BOOK STORE —
Register No. 6

E	03.90	NB
E	13.00	UB
E	06.70	UB
E	01.30	UB
E	04.95	NB
E	05.50	NB
E	35.35	TL
E	00.71	SL TX
E	36.06	TL
E	40.00	AM TD
E	03.94	CG

LAST AMOUNT
IS YOUR CHANGE!
— THANK YOU —

of local dissident churches that had withdrawn from the general church pursuant to state law providing that the property rights at issue turned on "a civil court jury decision as to whether the general church abandoned or departed from the tenets of faith and practice it held at the time the local churches affiliated with it." The Court held that Georgia could not constitutionally apply this "departure-from-doctrine" element of its law. Justice Brennan's opinion for the Court emphasized that state law required civil courts "to determine matters at the very core of a religion—the interpretation of particular church doctrines and the importance of those doctrines to religion." "Marginal judicial involvement" in church disputes was not prohibited. "Neutral principles of law, developed for use in all property disputes," could be applied to church property without violating the free exercise or establishment guarantees. But the First Amendment "commands civil courts to decide church property disputes without resolving underlying controversies over religious doctrine."

C. FINANCIAL AID TO RELIGION: THE CONTEMPORARY DIMENSIONS

BOARD OF EDUCATION v. ALLEN

302 U.S. 236, 88 S.Ct. 1923, 20 L.Ed.2d 1060 (1968).

Appeal from the New York Court of Appeals.

Mr. Justice WHITE delivered the opinion of the Court.

A law of the State of New York requires local public school authorities to lend textbooks free of charge to all students in grades seven through 12; students attending private schools are included. This case presents the question whether this statute is a "law respecting an establishment of religion, or prohibiting the free exercise thereof," and so in conflict with the First and Fourteenth Amendments to the Constitution, because it authorizes the loan of textbooks to students attending parochial schools. We hold that the law is not in violation of the Constitution.

Until 1965, § 701 of the Education Law of the State of New York authorized public school boards to designate textbooks for use in the public schools, to purchase such books with public funds, and to rent or sell the books to public school students. In 1965 the Legislature amended § 701, basing the amendments on findings that the "public welfare and safety require that the state and local communities give assistance to educational programs which are important to our national defense and the general welfare of the state." Beginning with the 1966–1967 school year, local school boards were required to purchase textbooks and lend them without charge "to all children residing in such district who are enrolled in grades seven to twelve of a public or private school which complies with the compulsory education law." The books now loaned are "text-books which are designated for use in any public, elementary or secondary schools of the state or are approved by any boards of education," and which—according to a 1966 amendment—"a pupil is required to use as a text for a semester or more in a particular class in the school he legally attends."

Appellant Board of Education of Central School District No. 1 in Rensselaer and Columbia Counties brought suit in the New York courts against appellee James Allen. The complaint alleged that § 701 violated both the State and Federal Constitutions; that if appellants, in reliance on their interpretation of the Constitution, failed to lend books to parochial school students within their counties appellee Allen would remove appellants from office; and that to prevent this, appellants were complying with the law and submitting to their constituents a school budget including funds for books to be lent to parochial school pupils. Appellants therefore sought a declaration that § 701 was invalid, an order barring appellee Allen from removing appellants from office for failing to comply with it, and another order restraining him from apportioning state funds to school districts for the purchase of textbooks to be lent to parochial students. . . .[1]

Everson v. Board of Education, 330 U.S. 1 (1947), is the case decided by this Court that is most nearly in point for today's problem. . . . As with public provision of police and fire protection, sewage facilities, and streets and sidewalks, payment of bus fares was of some value to the religious school, but was nevertheless not such support of a religious institution as to be a prohibited establishment of religion within the meaning of the First Amendment.

Everson and later cases have shown that the line between state neutrality to religion and state support of religion is not easy to locate. . . . Based on Everson, Zorach, McGowan, and other cases, Abington School District v. Schempp, 374 U. S. 203 (1963), fashioned a test subscribed to by eight Justices for distinguishing between forbidden involvements of the State with religion and those contacts which the Establishment Clause permits:

> "The test may be stated as follows: what are the purpose and the primary effect of the enactment? If either is the advancement or inhibition of religion then the enactment exceeds the scope of legislative power as circumscribed by the Constitution. That is to say that to withstand the strictures of the Establishment Clause there must be a secular legislative purpose and a primary effect that neither advances nor inhibits religion. Everson v. Board of Education. . . ." 374 U. S., at 222.

This test is not easy to apply, but the citation of Everson by the Schempp Court to support its general standard made clear how the Schempp rule would be applied to the facts of Everson. The statute upheld in Everson would be considered a law having "a secular legislative purpose and a primary effect that neither advances nor inhibits religion." We reach the same result with respect to the New York law requiring school books to be loaned free of charge to all students in specified grades. The express purpose of § 701 was stated by the New York Legislature to be furtherance of the educational opportunities available to the young. Appellants have shown us nothing about the necessary effects of the statute that is contrary to its stated purpose. The law merely makes available to all children the benefits of a general program to lend school

---

1. Appellees do not challenge the standing of appellants to press their claim in this Court. Appellants have taken an oath to support the United States Constitution. Believing § 701 to be unconstitutional, they are in the position of having to choose between violating their oath and taking a step— refusal to comply with § 701—that would be likely to bring their expulsion from office and also a reduction in state funds for their school districts. There can be no doubt that appellants thus have a "personal stake in the outcome" of this litigation. Baker v. Carr, 369 U.S. 186, 204 (1962). [Footnote by the Court.]

books free of charge. Books are furnished at the request of the pupil and ownership remains, at least technically, in the State. Thus no funds or books are furnished to parochial schools, and the financial benefit is to parents and children, not to schools.[2] Perhaps free books make it more likely that some children choose to attend a sectarian school, but that was true of the state-paid bus fares in Everson and does not alone demonstrate an unconstitutional degree of support for a religious institution.

Of course books are different from buses. Most bus rides have no inherent religious significance, while religious books are common. However, the language of § 701 does not authorize the loan of religious books, and the State claims no right to distribute religious literature. Although the books loaned are those required by the parochial school for use in specific courses, each book loaned must be approved by the public school authorities; only secular books may receive approval. The law was construed by the Court of Appeals of New York as "merely making available secular textbooks at the request of the individual student," and the record contains no suggestion that religious books have been loaned. Absent evidence, we cannot assume that school authorities, who constantly face the same problem in selecting textbooks for use in the public schools, are unable to distinguish between secular and religious books or that they will not honestly discharge their duties under the law. In judging the validity of the statute on this record we must proceed on the assumption that books loaned to students are books that are not unsuitable for use in the public schools because of religious content.

The major reason offered by appellants for distinguishing free textbooks from free bus fares is that books, but not buses, are critical to the teaching process, and in a sectarian school that process is employed to teach religion. However this Court has long recognized that religious schools pursue two goals, religious instruction and secular education. In the leading case of Pierce v. Society of Sisters, 268 U.S. 510 (1925), the Court held that although it would not question Oregon's power to compel school attendance or require that the attendance be at an institution meeting State-imposed requirements as to quality and nature of curriculum, Oregon had not shown that its interest in secular education required that all children attend publicly operated schools.

2. While the record and the state court opinions in this case contained no information about how the books are in fact transferred from the Boards of Education to individual students, both parties suggested in their briefs and on oral argument before this Court that New York permits private schools to submit to boards of education summaries of the requests for textbooks filed by individual students, and also permits private schools to store on their premises the textbooks being loaned by the Board of Education to the students. This interpretation of the State's administrative procedure is supported by an "Opinion of Counsel" made available by the Board of Regents and the State Department of Education to local school superintendents. For purposes of this case we consider the New York statute to permit these procedures. So construing the statute, we find it in conformity with the Constitution, for the books are furnished for the use of individual students and at their request.

It should be noted that the record contains no evidence that any of the private schools in appellants' districts previously provided textbooks for their students. There is some evidence that at least some of the schools did not: intervenor defendants asserted that they had previously purchased all their children's textbooks. And see statement of then Commissioner of Education Keppel: "Nonpublic schools rarely provide free textbooks." Hearings on Elementary and Secondary Education Act of 1965 before General Subcommittee on Education of House Committee on Education and Labor, 89th Cong., 1st Sess., Pt. 1, 93 (1965). [Footnote by the Court.]

A premise of this holding was the view that the State's interest in education would be served sufficiently by reliance on the secular teaching that accompanied religious training in the schools maintained by the Society of Sisters. Since Pierce, a substantial body of case law has confirmed the power of the States to insist that attendance at private schools, if it is to satisfy state compulsory-attendance laws, be at institutions which provide minimum hours of instruction, employ teachers of specified training, and cover prescribed subjects of instruction.[3] . . . These cases were a sensible corollary of Pierce v. Society of Sisters: if the State must satisfy its interest in secular education through the instrument of private schools, it has a proper interest in the manner in which those schools perform their secular educational function. Another corollary was Cochran v. Louisiana State Board of Education, 281 U. S. 370 (1930) [see footnote 1 to the Everson case, p. 1351, supra]. . . .

Underlying these cases, and underlying also the legislative judgments that have preceded the court decisions, has been a recognition that private education has played and is playing a significant and valuable role in raising national levels of knowledge, competence, and experience. Americans care about the quality of the secular education available to their children. They have considered high quality education to be an indispensable ingredient for achieving the kind of nation, and the kind of citizenry, that they have desired to create. Considering this attitude, the continued willingness to rely on private school systems, including parochial systems, strongly suggests that a wide segment of informed opinion, legislative and otherwise, has found that those schools do an acceptable job of providing secular education to their students.[4] This judgment is further evidence that parochial schools are performing, in addition to their sectarian function, the task of secular education.

Against this background of judgment and experience, unchallenged in the meager record before us in this case, we cannot agree with appellants either that all teaching in a sectarian school is religious or that the processes of secular and religious training are so intertwined that secular textbooks furnished to students by the public are in fact instrumental in the teaching of religion. This case comes to us after summary judgment entered on the pleadings. Nothing in this record supports the proposition that all textbooks, whether they deal with mathematics, physics, foreign languages, history, or literature, are used by the parochial schools to teach religion. No evidence has been offered about particular schools, particular courses, particular teachers, or particular books. We are unable to hold, based solely on judicial notice, that this statute results in unconstitutional involvement of the State with religious instruction or that § 701, for this or the other reasons urged, is a law respecting the establishment of religion within the meaning of the First Amendment.

3. . . . New York State regulates private schools extensively, especially as to attendance and curriculum. New York Education Law §§ 3201–3229 (1953). Regents examinations are given to private school students. Id., § 209. The basic requirement is that the instruction given in private schools satisfying the compulsory attendance law be "at least substantially equivalent to the instruction given to minors of like age and attainments at the public schools of the city or district where the minor resides." . . . [Footnote by the Court.]

4. In 1965–1966 in New York State, over 900,000 students, or 22.2% of total state enrollment, attended nonpublic schools. University of State of New York, Education Statistics Estimates 1966–67, Table I (1966). The comparable statistic for the Nation was at least 10%. United States Bureau of the Census, Statistical Abstract of the United States: 1967, at 111 (1967). [Footnote by the Court.]

Appellants also contend that § 701 offends the Free Exercise Clause of the First Amendment. However, "it is necessary in a free exercise case for one to show the coercive effect of the enactment as it operates against him in the practice of his religion," Abington School District v. Schempp, 374 U.S. 203, 223 (1963), and appellants have not contended that the New York law in any way coerces them as individuals in the practice of their religion.

Affirmed.

Mr. Justice HARLAN, concurring.

Although I join the opinion and judgment of the Court, I wish to emphasize certain of the principles which I believe to be central to the determination of this case, and which I think are implicit in the Court's decision.

The attitude of government toward religion must, as this Court has frequently observed, be one of neutrality. Neutrality is, however, a coat of many colors. . . . I would hold that where the contested governmental activity is calculated to achieve nonreligious purposes otherwise within the competence of the State, and where the activity does not involve the State "so significantly and directly in the realm of the sectarian as to give rise to . . . divisive influences and inhibitions of freedom" [Schempp], it is not forbidden by the religious clauses of the First Amendment.

In my opinion, § 701 of the Education Law of New York does not employ religion as its standard for action or inaction, and is not otherwise inconsistent with these principles.

Mr. Justice BLACK, dissenting.

. . . I believe the New York law held valid is a flat, flagrant, open violation of the First and Fourteenth Amendments which together forbid Congress or state legislatures to enact any law "respecting an establishment of religion." . . .

The Everson and McCollum cases plainly interpret the First and Fourteenth Amendments as protecting the taxpayers of a State from being compelled to pay taxes to their government to support the agencies of private religious organizations the taxpayers oppose. To authorize a State to tax its residents for such church purposes is to put the State squarely in the religious activities of certain religious groups that happen to be strong enough politically to write their own religious preferences and prejudices into the laws. This links state and churches together in controlling the lives and destinies of our citizenship—a citizenship composed of people of myriad religious faiths, some of them bitterly hostile to and completely intolerant of the others. It was to escape laws precisely like this that a large part of the Nation's early immigrants fled to this country. . . .

It is true, of course, that the New York law does not as yet formally adopt or establish a state religion. But it takes a great stride in that direction and coming events cast their shadows before them. The same powerful sectarian religious propagandists who have succeeded in securing passage of the present law to help religious schools carry on their sectarian religious purposes can and doubtless will continue their propaganda, looking toward complete domination and supremacy of their particular brand of religion. And it nearly always is by insidious approaches that the citadels of liberty are most successfully attacked.

I know of no prior opinion of this Court upon which the majority here can rightfully rely to support its holding this New York law constitutional. In saying this, I am not unmindful of the fact that the New York Court of Appeals purported to follow [Everson], an opinion written by me. [The law in Everson] was treated in the same way as a general law paying the streetcar fare *of all school children*, or a law providing midday lunches for all children or all school children, or a law to provide police protection for children going to and from school, or general laws to provide police and fire protection for buildings, including, of course, churches and church school buildings as well as others.

[U]pholding a State's power to pay bus or streetcar fares for school children cannot provide support for the validity of a state law using tax-raised funds to buy school books for a religious school. The First Amendment's bar to establishment of religion must preclude a State from using funds levied from all of its citizens to purchase books for use by sectarian schools, which, although "secular," realistically will in some way inevitably tend to propagate the religious views of the favored sect. Books are the most essential tool of education since they contain the resources of knowledge which the educational process is designed to exploit. In this sense it is not difficult to distinguish books, which are the heart of any school, from bus fares, which provide a convenient and helpful general public transportation service. With respect to the former, state financial support actively and directly assists the teaching and propagation of sectarian religious viewpoints in clear conflict with the First Amendment's establishment bar; with respect to the latter, the State merely provides a general and nondiscriminatory transportation service in no way related to substantive religious views and beliefs.

. . . It requires no prophet to foresee that on the argument used to support this law others could be upheld providing for state or federal government funds to buy property on which to erect religious school buildings or to erect the buildings themselves, to pay the salaries of the religious school teachers, and finally to have the sectarian religious groups cease to rely on voluntary contributions of members of their sects while waiting for the Government to pick up all the bills for the religious schools. Arguments made in favor of this New York law point squarely in this direction, namely, that the fact that government has not heretofore aided religious schools with tax-raised funds amounts to a discrimination against those schools and against religion. And that there are already efforts to have government supply the money to erect buildings for sectarian religious schools is shown by a recent Act of Congress which apparently allows for precisely that. See Higher Education Facilities Act of 1963, 77 Stat. 363, 20 U.S.C. § 701 et seq.

I still subscribe to the belief that tax-raised funds cannot constitutionally be used to support religious schools, buy their school books, erect their buildings, pay their teachers, or pay any other of their maintenance expenses, even to the extent of one penny. The First Amendment's prohibition against governmental establishment of religion was written on the assumption that state aid to religion and religious schools generates discord, disharmony, hatred, and strife among our people, and that any government that supplies such aids is to that extent a tyranny. And I still believe that the only way to protect minority religious groups from majority groups in this country is to keep the wall of separation between church and state high and impregnable as the First and Fourteenth Amendments provide. The Court's affirmance here bodes nothing but evil to religious peace in this country.

Mr. Justice DOUGLAS, dissenting. . . . . . .

The statute on its face empowers each parochial school to determine for itself which textbooks will be eligible for loans to its students, for the Act provides that the only text which the State may provide is "a book which a pupil is required to use as a text for a semester or more in a particular class in the school he legally attends." New York Education Law § 701, subd. 2. This initial and crucial selection is undoubtedly made by the parochial school's principal or its individual instructors, who are, in the case of Roman Catholic schools, normally priests or nuns.

The next step under the Act is an "individual request" for an eligible textbook (§ 701, subd. 3), but the State Education Department has ruled that a pupil may make his request to the local public board of education through a "private school official." Local boards have accordingly provided for those requests to be made by the individual or "by groups or classes." And forms for textbook requisitions to be filled out by the head of the private school are provided.

The role of the local public school board is to decide whether to veto the selection made by the parochial school. This is done by determining first whether the text has been or should be "approved" for use in public schools and second whether the text is "secular," "non-religious," or "non-sectarian." The local boards apparently have broad discretion in exercising this veto power.

Thus the statutory system provides that the parochial school will ask for the books that it wants. Can there be the slightest doubt that the head of the parochial school will select the book or books that best promote its sectarian creed?

If the board of education supinely submits by approving and supplying the sectarian or sectarian-oriented textbooks, the struggle to keep church and state separate has been lost. If the board resists, then the battle line between church and state will have been drawn and the contest will be on to keep the school board independent or to put it under church domination and control.

Whatever may be said of Everson, there is nothing ideological about a bus. There is nothing ideological about a school lunch, or a public nurse, or a scholarship. The constitutionality of such public aid to students in parochial schools turns on considerations not present in this textbook case. The textbook goes to the very heart of education in a parochial school. It is the chief, although not solitary, instrumentality for propagating a particular religious creed or faith. How can we possibly approve such state aid to a religion?

. . . .

Even where the treatment given to a particular topic in a school textbook is not blatantly sectarian, it will necessarily have certain shadings that will lead a parochial school to prefer one text over another. . . . .

[H]owever the case be viewed—whether sectarian groups win control of school boards or do not gain such control—the principle of separation of church and state, inherent in the Establishment Clause of the First Amendment, is violated by what we today approve. . . . .

Mr. Justice FORTAS, dissenting.

The majority opinion of the Court upholds the New York statute by ignoring a vital aspect of it. Public funds are used to buy, for students in sectarian schools, textbooks which are selected and prescribed by the sectarian schools themselves. As my Brother Douglas points out, despite the transparent camouflage that the books are furnished to students, the reality is that they are selected and their use is prescribed by the sectarian authorities. . . .

. . . This is not a "general" program. It is a specific program to use state funds to buy books prescribed by sectarian schools which, in New York, are primarily Catholic, Jewish, and Lutheran sponsored schools. It could be called a "general" program only if the school books made available to all children were precisely the same—the books selected for and used in the public schools. . . . This program, in its unconstitutional features, is hand-tailored to satisfy the specific needs of sectarian schools. Children attending such schools are given *special* books—books selected by the sectarian authorities. How can this be other than the use of public money to aid those sectarian establishments? . . .

This case is not within the principle of Everson v. Board of Education, 330 U.S. 1 (1947). Apart from the differences between textbooks and bus rides, the present statute does not call for extending to children attending sectarian schools the same service or facility extended to children in public schools. This statute calls for furnishing special, separate, and particular books, specially, separately, and particularly chosen by religious sects or their representatives for use in their sectarian schools. This is the infirmity, in my opinion. This is the feature that makes it impossible, in my view, to reach any conclusion other than that this statute is an unconstitutional use of public funds to support an establishment of religion. . . .

MODERN CHALLENGES TO FINANCIAL AIDS

1. *Federal spending and the 1965 Act.* The eligibility of schools operated by religious groups for federal financial aid under the Elementary and Secondary Education Act of 1965 intensified a long-standing constitutional controversy, as noted supra, p. 1358. And the Court's lowering of the standing barrier to permit federal taxpayers to challenge spending programs on establishment grounds, in Flast v. Cohen, 392 U.S. 83 (1968) (chap. 2, p. 93, supra), assures the Court's participation in that controversy. The Court described the complaint found justiciable in Flast as emphasizing "that federal funds appropriated under the Act were being used to finance instruction in reading, arithmetic, and other subjects in religious schools, and to purchase textbooks and other materials for use in such schools."

Is that complaint likely to succeed under the criteria of the Allen case? Under those of earlier cases? The 1965 Act (20 U.S.C. §§ 241 et seq., 821 et seq.) bars spending "for religious worship or instruction," but private as well as public schools are eligible for participation in several of the programs. See, e. g., the special services for "educationally deprived children" in Title I, and the Title II grants for "library resources" for the "use of children and teachers in public and private" schools (though title to the materials must be "only in a public agency"). May buses and books be constitutionally distinguished from salaries and buildings? See, e. g., Note, "The Elementary and Secondary Education Act of 1965 and the First Amendment," 41 Ind.L.J. 302 (1966). Grants to schools from grants to students? Loans from grants? The HEW memorandum, noted at p. 1358, supra, and printed at 50 Geo.L.J. 351 (1961), suggested as relevant criteria the closeness of the benefits to the "religious aspects" of the institution aided, the economic significance of the benefits, and "what alternative means are available to accomplish the legislative objective without resulting in the religious benefits ordinarily proscribed." Are these the appropriate criteria? Are they applied in Allen? In the prior cases? Note the response to the HEW suggestions in the National Catholic Welfare Conference paper noted above and printed at 50 Geo.L.J. 397 (1961). Would exclusion of religious schools from the federal financial program violate the free exercise guarantee? Under Everson? Under Allen? Under Sherbert v. Verner, sec. 2, p. 1387, infra? Compare Drinan, Federal Aid to Education (1962) and Religion, the Courts, and Public Policy (1963), with Freund, "Public Aid to Parochial Schools," 82 Harv.L.Rev. 1680 (1969).

2. *Tax exemptions.* Benefits to religious organizations under tax laws were among the subjects that received special attention because of the "wall of separation" language in Everson. See, e. g., the Note on tax exemptions for church property, 49 Colum.L.Rev. 968 (1949). But that issue was only occasionally mentioned in Court dicta in the Supreme Court (see, e. g., paragraph D of Justice Brennan's Schempp concurrence, p. 1369, supra), and the Court twice dismissed appeals raising tax exemption issues "for want of a substantial federal question." See General Finance Corp. v. Archetto, 369 U.S. 423 (1962) (a Rhode Island personal property tax case), and Heisey v. County of Alameda, 352 U.S. 921 (1956) (California real property tax).

In 1969, however, the Court noted probable jurisdiction of a state taxpayer's appeal challenging exemptions from state and local taxes of real property used exclusively for religious purposes. Walz v. Tax Comm'n of the City of New York, 395 U.S. 957 (1969). The highest state court had rejected the challenge, noting that courts "have long and consistently held that the exemption of such real property from taxation does not violate the Constitution of the United States." See 298 N.Y.S.2d 711, 712 (1969).

Can tax exemptions be distinguished from grants? Do exemptions violate the establishment clause? See Bittker, "Churches, Taxes and the Constitution," 78 Yale L.J. 1285 (1969). Are tax exemptions supportable on free exercise grounds, in view of cases such as Follett v. McCormick, 321 U.S. 573 (1944) (see note 1 to Braunfeld, the next case, at p. 1384) (license tax on sellers cannot be applied to Jehovah's Witnesses spreading religious doctrine through house-to-house sales of pamphlets)? In light of Sherbert v. Verner, p. 1387, infra, are property tax exemptions for religious organizations mandatory if charitable organizations are exempt? See sec. 2, which follows.

SECTION 2. THE "FREE EXERCISE" OF RELIGION

BRAUNFELD v. BROWN
366 U.S. 599, 81 S.Ct. 1144, 6 L.Ed.2d 563 (1961).

Appeal from the District Court for the Eastern District of Pennsylvania.

Mr. Chief Justice WARREN anounced the judgment of the Court and an opinion in which Mr. Justice BLACK, Mr. Justice CLARK, and Mr. Justice WHITTAKER concur.

This case concerns the constitutional validity of the application to appellants of the Pennsylvania criminal statute . . . . which proscribes the Sunday retail sale of certain enumerated commodities. [T]he only question for consideration is whether the statute interferes with the free exercise of appellants' religion.

Appellants are merchants in Philadelphia who engage in the retail sale of clothing and home furnishings within the proscription of the statute in issue. Each of the appellants is a member of the Orthodox Jewish faith, which requires the closing of their places of business and a total abstention from all manner of work from nightfall each Friday until nightfall each Saturday. [They allege] that appellants had previously kept their places of business open on Sunday; that each of appellants had done a substantial amount of business on Sunday, compensating somewhat for their closing on Saturday; that Sunday closing will result in impairing the ability of all appellants to earn a livelihood and will render appellant Braunfeld unable to continue in his business, thereby losing his capital investment . . . . .

Appellants contend that the enforcement against them of the Pennsylvania statute will prohibit the free exercise of their religion because, due to the statute's compulsion to close on Sunday, appellants will suffer substantial economic loss, to the benefit of their non-Sabbatarian competitors, if appellants also continue their Sabbath observance by closing their businesses on Saturday; that this result will either compel appellants to give up their Sabbath observance, a basic tenet of the Orthodox Jewish faith, or will put appellants at a serious economic disadvantage if they continue to adhere to their Sabbath. Appellants also assert that the statute will operate so as to hinder the orthodox Jewish faith in gaining new adherents. And the corollary to these arguments is that if the free exercise of appellants' religion is impeded, that religion is being subjected to discriminatory treatment by the State. . . . .

Certain aspects of religious exercise cannot, in any way, be restricted or burdened by either federal or state legislation. Compulsion by law of the acceptance of any creed or the practice of any form of worship is strictly forbidden. The freedom to hold religious beliefs and opinions is absolute. Cantwell v. Connecticut, 310 U.S. 296, 303; Reynolds v. United States, 98 U.S. 145, 166. Thus, in West Virginia State Board of Education v. Barnette, 319 U.S. 624, this Court held that state action compelling school children to salute the flag, on pain of expulsion from public school, was contrary to the First and Fourteenth Amendments when applied to those students whose religious beliefs forbade saluting a flag. But this is not the case at bar; the statute before us does not make criminal the holding of any religious belief or opinion, nor does it force anyone to embrace any religious belief or to say or believe anything in conflict with his religious tenets.

However, the freedom to act, even when the action is in accord with one's religious convictions, is not totally free from legislative restrictions. [Cantwell v. Connecticut.] As pointed out in [Reynolds v. United States], legislative power over mere opinion is forbidden but it may reach people's actions when they are found to be in violation of important social duties or subversive of good order, even when the actions are demanded by one's religion. [I]n the Barnette case, the Court was careful to point out that "The freedom asserted by these appellees does not bring them into collision with rights asserted by any other individual. It is such conflicts which most frequently require intervention of the State to determine where the rights of one end and those of another begin. [It is] to be noted that the compulsory flag salute and pledge requires *affirmation of a belief* and an *attitude of mind.*"

Thus, in Reynolds v. United States, this Court upheld the polygamy conviction of a member of the Mormon faith despite the fact that an accepted doctrine of his church then imposed upon its male members the *duty* to practice polygamy. And, in Prince v. Massachusetts, 321 U.S. 158, this Court upheld a statute making it a crime for a girl under eighteen years of age to sell any newspapers, periodicals or merchandise in public places despite the fact that a child of the Jehovah's Witnesses faith believed that it was her religious *duty* to perform this work.

It is to be noted that, in the two cases just mentioned, the religious practices themselves conflicted with the public interest. In such cases, to make accommodation between the religious action and an exercise of state authority is a particularly delicate task because resolution in favor of the State results in the choice to the individual of either abandoning his religious principle or facing criminal prosecution.

But, again, this is not the case before us because the statute at bar does not make unlawful any religious practices of appellants; the Sunday law simply regulates a secular activity and, as applied to appellants, operates so as to make the practice of their religious beliefs more expensive. Furthermore, the law's effect does not inconvenience all members of the Orthodox Jewish faith but only those who believe it necessary to work on Sunday. And even these are not faced with as serious a choice as forsaking their religious practices or subjecting themselves to criminal prosecution. Fully recognizing that the alternatives open to appellants and others similarly situated—retaining their present occupations and incurring economic disadvantage or engaging in some other commercial activity which does not call for either Saturday or Sunday labor—may well result in some financial sacrifice in order to observe their religious beliefs, still the option is wholly different than when the legislation attempts to make a religious practice itself unlawful.

To strike down, without the most critical scrutiny, legislation which imposes only an indirect burden on the exercise of religion, i. e., legislation which does not make unlawful the religious practice itself, would radically restrict the operating latitude of the legislature. Statutes which tax income and limit the amount which may be deducted for religious contributions impose an indirect economic burden on the observance of the religion of the citizen whose religion requires him to donate a greater amount to his church; statutes which require the courts to be closed on Saturday and Sunday impose a similar indirect burden on the observance of the religion of the trial lawyer whose religion requires him to rest on a weekday. The list of legislation of this nature is nearly limitless.

Needless to say, when entering the area of religious freedom, we must be fully cognizant of the particular protection that the Constitution has accorded it. Abhorrence of religious persecution and intolerance is a basic part of our heritage. But we are a cosmopolitan nation made up of people of almost every conceivable religious preference. These denominations number almost three hundred. . . . Consequently, it cannot be expected, much less required, that legislators enact no law regulating conduct that may in some way result in an economic disadvantage to some religious sects and not to others because of the special practices of the various religions. We do not believe that such an effect is an absolute test for determining whether the legislation violates the freedom of religion protected by the First Amendment.

Of course, to hold unassailable all legislation regulating conduct which imposes solely an indirect burden on the observance of religion would be a gross oversimplification. If the purpose or effect of a law is to impede the observance of one or all religions or is to discriminate invidiously between religions, that law is constitutionally invalid even though the burden may be characterized as being only indirect. But if the State regulates conduct by enacting a general law within its power, the purpose and effect of which is to advance the State's secular goals, the statute is valid despite its indirect burden on religious observance unless the State may accomplish its purpose by means which do not impose such a burden. See [Cantwell v. Connecticut].[1]

As we pointed out in [McGowan v. Maryland], we cannot find a State without power to provide a weekly respite from all labor and, at the same time, to set one day of the week apart from the others as a day of rest, repose, recreation and tranquillity . . . . Also, in McGowan, we examined several suggested alternative means by which it was argued that the State might accomplish its secular goals without even remotely or incidentally affecting religious freedom. We found there that a State might well find that those alternatives would not accomplish bringing about a general day of rest.

. . . .

However, appellants advance yet another means at the State's disposal which they would find unobjectionable. They contend that the State should cut an exception from the Sunday labor proscription for those people who, because of religious conviction, observe a day of rest other than Sunday. By such regulation, appellants contend, the economic disadvantages imposed by the present system would be removed and the State's interest in having all people rest one day would be satisfied.

A number of States provide such an exemption, and this may well be the wiser solution to the problem. But our concern is not with the wisdom of legislation but with its constitutional limitation. Thus, reason and experience teach that to permit the exemption might well undermine the State's goal of providing a day that, as best possible, eliminates the atmosphere of commercial noise and activity. Although not dispositive of the issue, enforcement problems would be more difficult since there would be two or more days to police rather than one and it would be more difficult to observe whether violations were occurring.

Additional problems might also be presented by a regulation of this sort. To allow only people who rest on a day other than Sunday to keep their businesses open on that day might well provide these people with an economic

1. Thus in cases like Murdock v. Pennsylvania, 319 U.S. 105, and Follett v. McCormick, 321 U.S. 573, this Court struck down municipal ordinances which, in application, required religious colporteurs to pay a license tax as a condition to the pursuit of their activities because the State's interest, the obtaining of revenue, could be easily satisfied by imposing this tax on nonreligious sources. [Footnote by the Court.]

advantage over their competitors who must remain closed on that day . . . .
With this competitive advantage existing, there could well be the temptation
for some, in order to keep their businesses open on Sunday, to assert that they
have religious convictions which compel them to close their businesses on
what had formerly been their least profitable day. This might make necessary a state-conducted inquiry into the sincerity of the individual's religious
beliefs, a practice which a State might believe would itself run afoul of the
spirit of constitutionally protected religious guarantees. Finally, in order to
keep the disruption of the day at a minimum, exempted employers would
probably have to hire employees who themselves qualified for the exemption
because of their own religious beliefs, a practice which a State might feel to
be opposed to its general policy prohibiting religious discrimination in hiring.
For all of these reasons, we cannot say that the Pennsylvania statute before us
is invalid, either on its face or as applied.

. . . Mr. Justice FRANKFURTER and Mr. Justice HARLAN have
rejected appellant's claim under the Free Exercise Clause in a separate opinion.

Affirmed.

Mr. Justice BRENNAN [dissenting].

[T]he issue in this case . . . is whether a State may put an individual to a choice between his business and his religion. The Court today
holds that it may. But I dissent, believing that such a law prohibits the free
exercise of religion.

The first question to be resolved [is] the appropriate standard of constitutional adjudication in cases in which a statute is assertedly in conflict with
the First Amendment . . .. The Court in such cases is not confined to
the narrow inquiry whether the challenged law is rationally related to some
legitimate legislative end. Nor is the case decided by a finding that the State's
interest is substantial and important, as well as rationally justifiable. . . .
The honored place of religious freedom in our constitutional hierarchy,
. . . foreshadowed by a prescient footnote in United States v. Carolene
Products Co., 304 U.S. 144, 152, n. 4 (1938), must now be taken to be
settled. Or at least so it appeared until today. For in this case the Court
seems to say, without so much as a deferential nod towards that high place
which we have accorded religious freedom in the past, that any substantial
state interest will justify encroachments on religious practice, at least if those
encroachments are cloaked in the guise of some non-religious public purpose.

Admittedly, these laws do not compel overt affirmation of a repugnant
belief, as in Barnette, nor do they prohibit outright any of appellants' religious practices, as did the federal law upheld in Reynolds v. United States,
98 U.S. 145 (1878), cited by the Court. That is, the laws do not say that
appellants must work on Saturday. But their effect is that appellants may not
simultaneously practice their religion and their trade, without being hampered
by a substantial competitive disadvantage. Their effect is that no one may
at one and the same time be an Orthodox Jew and compete effectively with
his Sunday-observing fellow tradesmen. This clog upon the exercise of religion, this state-imposed burden on Orthodox Judaism, has exactly the same
economic effect as a tax levied upon the sale of religious literature. And yet,
such a tax, when applied in the form of an excise or license fee, was held invalid in Follet v. Town of McCormick, supra. All this the Court, as I read
its opinion, concedes.

What, then, is the compelling state interest which impels the Commonwealth of Pennsylvania to impede appellants' freedom of worship? What overbalancing need is so weighty in the constitutional scale that it justifies this substantial, though indirect, limitation of appellants' freedom? It is not the desire to stamp out a practice deeply abhorred by society, such as polygamy, as in Reynolds, for the custom of resting one day a week is universally honored, as the Court has amply shown. Nor is it the State's traditional protection of children, as in Prince v. Massachusetts, 321 U.S. 158 (1944), for appellants are reasoning and fully autonomous adults. It is not even the interest in seeing that everyone rests one day a week, for appellants' religion requires that they take such a rest. It is the mere convenience of having everyone rest on the same day. It is to defend this interest that the Court holds that a State need not follow the alternative route of granting an exemption for those who in good faith observe a day of rest other than Sunday.

It is true, I suppose, that the granting of such an exemption would make Sundays a little noisier, and the task of police and prosecutor a little more difficult. It is also true that a majority—21—of the 34 States which have general Sunday regulations have exemptions of this kind. We are not told that those States are significantly noisier, or that their police are significantly more burdened, than Pennsylvania's. Even England, not under the compulsion of a written constitution, but simply influenced by considerations of fairness, has such an exemption for some activities. The Court conjures up several difficulties with such a system which seem to me more fanciful than real. Non-Sunday observers might get an unfair advantage, it is said. A similar contention against the draft exemption for conscientious objectors (another example of the exemption technique) was rejected with the observation that "its unsoundness is too apparent to require" discussion. Selective Draft Law Cases, 245 U.S. 366, 390 (1918). However widespread the complaint, it is legally baseless, and the State's reliance upon it cannot withstand a First Amendment claim. . . . . .

In fine, the Court, in my view, has exalted administrative convenience to a constitutional level high enough to justify making one religion economically disadvantageous. The Court would justify this result on the ground that the effect on religion, though substantial, is indirect. The Court forgets, I think, a warning uttered during the congressional discussion of the First Amendment itself: ". . . the rights of conscience are, in their nature, of peculiar delicacy, and will little bear the gentlest touch of governmental hand."

I would . . . . remand for a trial of appellants' allegations . . . . ..

Mr. Justice STEWART, dissenting.

I agree with substantially all that Mr. Justice Brennan has written. Pennsylvania has passed a law which compels an Orthodox Jew to choose between his religious faith and his economic survival. That is a cruel choice. It is a choice which I think no State can constitutionally demand. For me this is not something that can be swept under the rug and forgotten in the interest of enforced Sunday togetherness. I think the impact of this law upon these appellants grossly violates their constitutional right to the free exercise of their religion.

SHERBERT v. VERNER

374 U.S. 398, 83 S.Ct. 1790, 10 L.Ed.2d 965 (1963).

Appeal from the Supreme Court of South Carolina.

Mr. Justice BRENNAN delivered the opinion of the Court.

Appellant, a member of the Seventh-day Adventist Church was discharged by her South Carolina employer because she would not work on Saturday, the Sabbath Day of her faith. When she was unable to obtain other employment because from conscientious scruples she would not take Saturday work,[1] she filed a claim for unemployment compensation benefits under the South Carolina Unemployment Compensation Act. That law provides that, to be eligible for benefits, a claimant must be "able to work and is available for work"; and, further, that a claimant is ineligible for benefits "[i]f . . . he has failed, without good cause . . . to accept available suitable work when offered him by the employment office or the employer . . . .." The appellee Employment Security Commission . . . found that appellant's restriction upon her availability for Saturday work brought her within the provision disqualifying for benefits insured workers who fail, without good cause, to accept "suitable work when offered . . . .." The State Supreme Court held . . . that appellant's ineligibility infringed no constitutional liberties . . . .[2] We reverse the judgment . . . .

[If] the decision of the South Carolina Supreme Court is to withstand appellant's constitutional challenge, it must be either because her disqualification as a beneficiary represents no infringement by the State of her constitutional rights of free exercise; or because any incidental burden on the free exercise of appellant's religion may be justified by a "compelling state interest in the regulation of a subject within the State's constitutional power to regulate . . . .." NAACP v. Button, 371 U.S. 415, 438.

We turn first to the question whether the disqualification for benefits imposes any burden on the free exercise of appellant's religion. We think it is clear that it does. In a sense the consequences of such a disqualification to religious principles and practices may be only an indirect result of welfare legislation within the State's general competence to enact; it is true that no

---

1. After her discharge, appellant sought employment with three other mills in the Spartanburg area, but found no suitable five-day work available at any of the mills. In filing her claim with the Commission, she expressed a willingness to accept employment at other mills, or even in another industry, so long as Saturday work was not required. The record indicates that of the 150 or more Seventh-day Adventists in the Spartanburg area, only appellant and one other have been unable to find suitable non-Saturday employment. [Footnote by the Court.]

2. It has been suggested that appellant is not within the class entitled to benefits under the South Carolina statute because her unemployment did not result from discharge or layoff due to lack of work. It is true that unavailability for work for some personal reasons not having to do with matters of conscience or religion has been held to be a basis of disqualification for benefits. . . . But appellant claims that the Free Exercise Clause prevents the State from basing the denial of benefits upon the "personal reason" she gives for not working on Saturday. Where the consequence of disqualification so directly affects First Amendment rights, surely we should not conclude that every "personal reason" is a basis for disqualification in the absence of explicit language to that effect in the statute or decisions of the South Carolina Supreme Court. . . . [Footnote by the Court.]

criminal sanctions directly compel appellant to work a six-day week. But this is only the beginning, not the end of our inquiry. . . . Here not only is it apparent that appellant's declared ineligibility for benefits derives solely from the practice of her religion, but the pressure upon her to forego that practice is unmistakable. The ruling forces her to choose between following the precepts of her religion and forfeiting benefits, on the one hand, and abandoning one of the precepts of her religion in order to accept work, on the other hand. Governmental imposition of such a choice puts the same kind of burden upon the free exercise of religion as would a fine imposed against appellant for her Saturday worship. . . .

Significantly South Carolina expressly saves the Sunday worshipper from having to make the kind of choice which we here hold infringes the Sabbatarian's religious liberty. When in times of "national emergency" the textile plants are authorized by the State Commissioner of Labor to operate on Sunday, "no employee shall be required to work on Sunday . . . who is conscientiously opposed to Sunday work; and if any employee should refuse to work on Sunday on account of conscientious . . . objections he or she shall not jeopardize his or her seniority by such refusal or be discriminated against in any other manner." S.C. Code, § 64–4. No question of the disqualification of a Sunday worshipper for benefits is likely to arise, since we cannot suppose that an employer will discharge him in violation of this statute. The unconstitutionality of the disqualification of the Sabbatarian is thus compounded by the religious discrimination which South Carolina's general statutory scheme necessarily effects.

We must next consider whether some compelling state interest enforced in the eligibility provisions of the South Carolina statute justifies the substantial infringement of appellant's First Amendment right. It is basic that no showing merely of a rational relationship to some colorable state interest would suffice; in this highly sensitive constitutional area, "[o]nly the gravest abuses, endangering paramount interest, give occasion for permissible limitation," Thomas v. Collins, 323 U.S. 516, 530. No such abuse or danger has been advanced in the present case. The appellees suggest no more than a possibility that the filing of fraudulent claims by unscrupulous claimants feigning religious objections to Saturday work might not only dilute the unemployment compensation fund but also hinder the scheduling by employers of necessary Saturday work. But that possibility is not apposite here because no such objection appears to have been made before the South Carolina Supreme Court, and we are unwilling to assess the importance of an asserted state interest without the views of the state court. Nor, if the contention had been made below, would the record appear to sustain it; there is no proof whatever to warrant such fears of malingering or deceit as those which the respondents now advance. Even if consideration of such evidence is not foreclosed by the prohibition against judicial inquiry into the truth or falsity of religious beliefs, United States v. Ballard, 322 U.S. 78,—a question as to which we intimate no view since it is not before us—it is highly doubtful whether such evidence would be sufficient to warrant a substantial infringement of religious liberties. For even if the possibility of spurious claims did threaten to dilute the fund and disrupt the scheduling of work, it would plainly be incumbent upon the appellees to demonstrate that no alternative forms of regulation would combat such abuses without infringing First Amendment rights. . . .

In these respects, then, the state interest asserted in the present case is wholly dissimilar to the interests which were found to justify the less direct burden upon religious practices in Braunfeld v. Brown, supra. [That statute was] saved by a countervailing factor which finds no equivalent in the instant case—a strong state interest in providing one uniform day of rest for all workers. That secular objective could be achieved, the Court found, only by declaring Sunday to be that day of rest. . . . In the present case no such justifications underlie the determination of the state court that appellant's religion makes her ineligible to receive benefits. . . .

In holding as we do, plainly we are not fostering the "establishment" of the Seventh-day Adventist religion in South Carolina, for the extension of unemployment benefits to Sabbatarians in common with Sunday worshippers reflects nothing more than the governmental obligation of neutrality in the face of religious differences, and does not represent that involvement of religious with secular institutions which it is the object of the Establishment Clause to forestall. . . . Nor do we, by our decision today, declare the existence of a constitutional right to unemployment benefits on the part of all persons whose religious convictions are the cause of their unemployment. This is not a case in which an employee's religious convictions serve to make him a nonproductive member of society. . . . Our holding today is only that South Carolina may not constitutionally apply the eligibility provisions so as to constrain a worker to abandon his religious convictions respecting the day of rest. This holding but reaffirms a principle that we announced a decade and a half ago, namely that no State may "exclude individual Catholics, Lutherans, Mohammedans, Baptists, Jews, Methodists, Non-believers, Presbyterians, or the members of any other faith, *because of their faith, or lack of it,* from receiving the benefits of public welfare legislation." Everson v. Board of Education, 330 U.S. 1, 16. . . .

Reversed and remanded.

Mr. Justice DOUGLAS, concurring. . . .

This case is resolvable not in terms of what an individual can demand of government, but solely in terms of what government may not do to an individual in violation of his religious scruples. The fact that government cannot exact from me a surrender of one iota of my religious scruples does not, of course, mean that I can demand of government a sum of money, the better to exercise them. . . .

Those considerations, however, are not relevant here. If appellant is otherwise qualified for unemployment benefits, payments will be made to her not as a Seventh-day Adventist, but as an unemployed worker. Conceivably these payments will indirectly benefit her church, but no more so than does the salary of any public employee. Thus, this case does not involve the problems of direct or indirect state assistance to a religious organization—matters relevant to the Establishment Clause, not in issue here.

Mr. Justice STEWART, concurring in the result.

Although fully agreeing with the result which the Court reaches in this case, I cannot join the Court's opinion. This case presents a double-barreled dilemma, which in all candor I think the Court's opinion has not succeeded in papering over. The dilemma ought to be resolved. . . .

I am convinced that no liberty is more essential to the continued vitality of the free society which our Constitution guarantees than is the religious liberty protected by the Free Exercise Clause . . . . And I regret that on occasion, and specifically in Braunfeld v. Brown, supra, the Court has shown what has seemed to me a distressing insensitivity to the appropriate demands of this constitutional guarantee. By contrast I think that the Court's approach to the Establishment Clause has on occasion, and specifically in Engel, Schempp and Murray, been not only insensitive, but positively wooden, and that the Court has accorded to the Establishment Clause a meaning which neither the words, the history, nor the intention of the authors of that specific constitutional provision even remotely suggests.

But my views as to the correctness of the Court's decisions in these cases are beside the point here. The point is that the decisions are on the books. And the result is that there are many situations where legitimate claims under the Free Exercise Clause will run into head-on collision with the Court's insensitive and sterile construction of the Establishment Clause. The controversy now before us is clearly such a case.

Because the appellant refuses to accept available jobs which would require her to work on Saturdays, South Carolina has declined to pay unemployment compensation benefits to her. Her refusal to work on Saturdays is based on the tenets of her religious faith. The Court says that South Carolina cannot under these circumstances declare her to be not "available for work" within the meaning of its statute because to do so would violate her constitutional right to the free exercise of her religion.

Yet what this Court has said about the Establishment Clause must inevitably lead to a diametrically opposite result. If the appellant's refusal to work on Saturdays were based on indolence, or on a compulsive desire to watch the Saturday television programs, no one would say that South Carolina could not hold that she was not "available for work" within the meaning of its statute. That being so, the Establishment Clause as construed by this Court not only *permits* but affirmatively *requires* South Carolina equally to deny the appellant's claim for unemployment compensation when her refusal to work on Saturdays is based upon her religious creed.

To require South Carolina to so administer its laws as to pay public money to the appellant under the circumstances of this case is thus clearly to require the State to violate the Establishment Clause as construed by this Court. This poses no problem for me, because I think the Court's mechanistic concept of the Establishment Clause is historically unsound and constitutionally wrong. I think the process of constitutional decision in the area of the relationships between government and religion demands considerably more than the invocation of broad-brushed rhetoric . . . .. And I think that the guarantee of religious liberty embodied in the Free Exercise Clause affirmatively requires government to create an atmosphere of hospitality and accommodation to individual belief or disbelief.

South Carolina would deny unemployment benefits to a mother unavailable for work on Saturdays because she was unable to get a babysitter. Thus, we do not have before us a situation where a State provides unemployment compensation generally, and singles out for disqualification only those persons who are unavailable for work on religious grounds. This is not, in short, a scheme which operates so as to discriminate against religion as such. But the Court nevertheless holds that the State must prefer a religious over a secular ground for being unavailable for work . . . . .

Yet in cases decided under the Establishment Clause the Court has decreed otherwise. It has decreed that government must blind itself to the differing religious beliefs and traditions of the people. With all respect, I think it is the Court's duty to face up to the dilemma posed by the conflict between the Free Exercise Clause of the Constitution and the Establishment Clause as interpreted by the Court. It is a duty, I submit, which we owe to the people, the States, and the Nation, and a duty which we owe to ourselves. For so long as the resounding but fallacious fundamentalist rhetoric of some of our Establishment Clause opinions remains on our books, to be disregarded at will as in the present case, or to be undiscriminatingly invoked as in the Schempp case .   .   . , so long will the possibility of consistent and perceptive decision in this most difficult and delicate area of constitutional law be impeded and impaired. And so long, I fear, will the guarantee of true religious freedom in our pluralistic society be uncertain and insecure. . . .

My second difference with the Court's opinion is that I cannot agree that today's decision can stand consistently with Braunfeld v. Brown, supra. The Court says that there was a "less direct burden upon religious practices" in that case than in this. With all respect, I think the Court is mistaken, simply as a matter of fact.   .   .   .

The impact upon the appellant's religious freedom in the present case is considerably less onerous [than in Braunfeld]. We deal here not with a criminal statute, but with the particularized administration of South Carolina's Unemployment Compensation Act. Even upon the unlikely assumption that the appellant could not find suitable non-Saturday employment, the appellant at the worst would be denied a maximum of 22 weeks of compensation payments. I agree with the Court that the possibility of that denial is enough to infringe upon the appellant's constitutional right to the free exercise of her religion. But it is clear to me that in order to reach this conclusion the Court must explicitly reject the reasoning of Braunfeld v. Brown. I think the Braunfeld case was wrongly decided and should be overruled, and accordingly I concur in the result reached by the Court in the case before us.

Mr. Justice HARLAN, whom Mr. Justice WHITE joins, dissenting.

Today's decision is disturbing both in its rejection of existing precedent and in its implications for the future.   .   .   . [T]he purpose of the legislature was to tide people over, and to avoid social and economic chaos, during periods when *work was unavailable*. But at the same time there was clearly no intent to provide relief for those who for purely personal reasons were or became *unavailable for work*.   .   .   .

The South Carolina Supreme Court has uniformly applied this law in conformity with its clearly expressed purpose. It has consistently held that one is not "available for work" if his unemployment has resulted not from the inability of industry to provide a job but rather from personal circumstances, no matter how compelling. The reference to "involuntary unemployment" in the legislative statement of policy, whatever a sociologist, philosopher, or theologian might say, has been interpreted not to embrace such personal circumstances.   .   .   .

In the present case all that the state court has done is to apply these accepted principles. Since virtually all of the mills in the Spartanburg area were operating on a six-day week, the appellant was "unavailable for work," and thus ineligible for benefits, when personal considerations prevented her from accepting employment on a full-time basis in the industry and locality in which she had worked. The fact that these personal considerations sprang from her religious convictions was wholly without relevance to the state court's application of the law. Thus in no proper sense can it be said that the State discriminated against the appellant on the basis of her religious beliefs or that she was denied benefits *because* she was a Seventh-day Adventist. She was denied benefits just as any other claimant would be denied benefits who was not "available for work" for personal reasons.[1]

With this background, this Court's decision comes into clearer focus. What the Court is holding is that if the State chooses to condition unemployment compensation on the applicant's availability for work, it is constitutionally compelled to *carve out an exception*—and to provide benefits—for those whose unavailability is due to their religious convictions.[2] Such a holding has particular significance in two respects.

First, despite the Court's protestations to the contrary, the decision necessarily overrules Braunfeld v. Brown . . . . Clearly, any differences between this case and Braunfeld cut against the present appellant.[3]

Second, the implications of the present decision are far more troublesome than its apparently narrow dimensions would indicate at first glance. The meaning of today's holding, as already noted, is that the State must furnish unemployment benefits to one who is unavailable for work if the unavailability stems from the exercise of religious convictions. The State, in other words, must *single out* for financial assistance those whose behavior is religiously motivated, even though it denies such assistance to others whose identical behavior (in this case, inability to work on Saturdays) is not religiously motivated.

1. I am completely at a loss to understand note [2] of the Court's opinion. Certainly the Court is not basing today's decision on the unsupported supposition that *some* day, the South Carolina Supreme Court may conclude that there is *some* personal reason for unemployment that may not disqualify a claimant for relief. In any event, I submit it is perfectly clear that South Carolina would not compensate persons who became unemployed for *any* personal reason, as distinguished from layoffs or lack of work, since the State Supreme Court's decisions make it plain that such persons would not be regarded as "available for work" within the manifest meaning of the eligibility requirements. . . . [Footnote by Justice Harlan.]

2. The Court does suggest, in a rather startling disclaimer, that its holding is limited in applicability to those whose religious convictions do not make them "nonproductive" members of society, noting that most of the Seventh-day Adventists in the Spartanburg area are employed. But surely this disclaimer cannot be taken seriously, for the Court cannot mean that the case would have come out differently if none of the Seventh-day Adventists in Spartanburg had been gainfully employed, or if the appellant's religion had prevented her from working on Tuesdays instead of Saturdays. Nor can the Court be suggesting that it will make a value judgment in each case as to whether a particular individual's religious convictions prevent him from being "productive." I can think of no more inappropriate function for this Court to perform. [Footnote by Justice Harlan.]

3. The Court's reliance on South Carolina Code § 64–4, to support its conclusion with respect to free exercise, is misplaced. Section 64–4, which is not a part of the Unemployment Compensation Law, is an extremely narrow provision that becomes operative only during periods of national emergency and thus has no bearing in the circumstances of the present case. And plainly under our decisions in the "Sunday law" cases, appellant can derive no support for her position from the State's general statutory provisions setting aside Sunday as a uniform day of rest. [Footnote by Justice Harlan.]

It has been suggested that such singling out of religious conduct for special treatment may violate the constitutional limitations on state action. See Kurland, Of Church and State and The Supreme Court, 29 U. of Chi. L.Rev. 1 . . . .. My own view, however, is that at least under the circumstances of this case it would be a permissible accommodation of religion for the State, if it *chose* to do so, to create an exception to its eligibility requirements for persons like the appellant. The constitutional obligation of "neutrality," see [Schempp], is not so narrow a channel that the slightest deviation from an absolutely straight course leads to condemnation. There are too many instances in which no such course can be charted, too many areas in which the pervasive activities of the State justify some special provision for religion to prevent it from being submerged by an all-embracing secularism. The State violates its obligation of neutrality when, for example, it mandates a daily religious exercise in its public schools, with all the attendant pressures on the school children that such an exercise entails. . . . But there is, I believe, enough flexibility in the Constitution to permit a legislative judgment accommodating an unemployment compensation law to the exercise of religious beliefs such as appellant's.

For very much the same reasons, however, I cannot subscribe to the conclusion that the State is constitutionally *compelled* to carve out an exception to its general rule of eligibility in the present case. Those situations in which the Constitution may require special treatment on account of religion are, in my view, few and far between, and this view is amply supported by the course of constitutional litigation in this area. . . . Such compulsion in the present case is particularly inappropriate in light of the indirect, remote, and insubstantial effect of the decision below on the exercise of appellant's religion and in light of the direct financial assistance to religion that today's decision requires. . . .

SOME PROBLEMS OF FREE EXERCISE

1. *The criteria of Braunfeld and Sherbert.* Are Braunfeld and Sherbert reconcilable? On the basis of the criteria in the prevailing opinions? On the basis of other criteria? Are Braunfeld and Sherbert—and the other free exercise problems mentioned in the opinions and these notes—usefully analyzed in terms of "direct" and "indirect" burdens? In terms of the strength of the state justification for the restriction? In terms of the availability of alternative, less restrictive means to achieve the state objective? In terms of the "purpose" and "effect" of the restriction? In terms of "belief" and "action"?

2. *Free exercise and establishment.* Does Sherbert suggest a "double-barreled dilemma," as Justice Stewart insists? How should it be resolved? Does Sherbert rule out one widely discussed, simple, "neutrality" solution for reconciling free exercise and establishment? [Note Justice Harlan's comment in Sherbert on Professor Kurland's "neutrality" thesis. Kurland had suggested reading the clauses "as stating a single precept: that government cannot utilize religion for action or inaction because these clauses, read together as they should be, prohibit classification in terms of religion either to confer a benefit or to impose a burden."]

If pure neutrality of that sort is inappropriate, is Justice Harlan's suggestion the preferable one—that government may, but need not, carve out an exception in the face of religious scruples? If that variety of accommodation with (special treatment of?) religion, rather than pure neutrality, is permissible, are some of the establishment decisions (e. g., the Bible Reading Cases) wrong? If Sherbert requires even more "accommodation" than Justice Harlan suggests, did additional establishment decisions take the "wall of separation" metaphor too literally?

3. *The "belief"-"action" distinction in Cantwell.* Chief Justice Warren's examination of past decisions in Braunfeld relied on the "belief"-"action" distinction set forth in a much-cited passage in Cantwell v. Connecticut, 310 U.S. 296 (1940) (one of the Jehovah's Witnesses proselytizing cases, see chap. 16, p. 1147, supra). Is that distinction helpful? Justice Roberts stated: "The constitutional inhibition of legislation on the subject of religion has a double aspect. On the one hand, it forestalls compulsion by law of the acceptance of any creed or the practice of any form of worship. Freedom of conscience and freedom to adhere to such religious organization or form of worship as the individual may choose cannot be restricted by law. On the other hand, it safeguards the free exercise of the chosen form of religion. Thus the Amendment embraces two concepts,— freedom to believe and freedom to act. The first is absolute but, in the nature of things, the second cannot be. Conduct remains subject to regulation for the protection of society. The freedom to act must have appropriate definition to preserve the enforcement of that protection. In every case the power to regulate must be so exercised as not, in attaining a permissible end, unduly to infringe the protected freedom. No one would contest the proposition that a State may not, by statute, wholly deny the right to preach or to disseminate religious views. . . . It is equally clear that a State may by general and non-discriminatory legislation regulate the times, the places, and the manner of soliciting upon its streets, and of holding meetings thereon; and may in other respects safeguard the peace, good order and comfort of the community, without unconstitutionally invading the liberties protected by the Fourteenth Amendment."

4. *The flag salute cases.* Chief Justice Warren in Braunfeld also considers Barnette, the 1943 flag salute case. That was the second major Court encounter with the flag salute issue, and it overruled a decision reached only a few years earlier which had sustained a requirement that public school children salute the flag. In both Minersville School Dist. v. Gobitis, 310 U.S. 586 (1940) and West Virginia State Board of Education v. Barnette, 319 U.S. 624 (1943), the regulations were attacked by Jehovah's Witnesses, who insisted that the salutes were "forbidden by command of Scripture." The opinions in both cases considered at length the Court's responsibility in protecting individual liberties.

a. In Gobitis, Justice Frankfurter's majority opinion concluded: "The mere possession of religious convictions which contradict the relevant concerns of a political society does not relieve the citizen from the discharge of political responsibilities. . . . It is not our province to choose among competing considerations in the subtle process of securing effective loyalty . . ., while respecting at the same time individual idiosyncracies . . . . So to hold would in effect make us the school board for the country. . . . Except where the trangression of . . . liberty is too plain for argument, personal freedom is best maintained—so long as the remedial channels of the democratic process remain open and unobstructed—

when it is ingrained in a people's habits. [T]o the legislature no less than the courts is committed the guardianship of deeply cherished liberties." Justice Stone dissented: "This seems to me no less than the surrender of the constitutional protection of the liberty of small minorities to the popular will." He insisted on "careful scrutiny" of efforts "to secure conformity of belief . . . by a compulsory affirmation of the desired belief."

b. In Barnette, Justice Jackson's majority opinion overruled Gobitis: "The very purpose of the Bill of Rights was to withdraw certain subjects from the vicissitudes of political controversy, to place them beyond the reach of majorities . . . . Much of the vagueness of the due process clause disappears when the specific prohibitions of the First become its standard. [First Amendment rights] are susceptible of restriction only to prevent grave and immediate danger to interests which the state may lawfully protect. . . . Nor does our duty . . . depend upon our possession of marked competence in the field where the invasion of rights occurs. [W]e act in these matters not by authority of our competence but by force of our commissions. . . . If there is any fixed star in our constitutional constellation, it is that no official, high or petty, can prescribe what shall be orthodox in politics, nationalism or other matters of opinion or force citizens to confess by word or act their faith therein." Justices Roberts and Reed announced their adherence to Gobitis. Justice Black, joined by Justice Douglas, submitted a "statement of reasons for our change of view" since Gobitis. Justice Murphy also concurred.

Justice Frankfurter's dissenting opinion began: "One who belongs to the most vilified and persecuted minority in history is not likely to be insensible to the freedoms guaranteed by our Constitution. Were my purely personal attitude relevant I should wholeheartedly associate myself with the general libertarian views in the Court's opinion, representing as they do the thought and action of a lifetime. But as judges we are neither Jew nor Gentile, neither Catholic nor agnostic. We owe equal attachment to the Constitution and are equally bound by our judicial obligations whether we derive our citizenship from the earliest or the latest immigrants to these shores. As a member of this Court I am not justified in writing my private notions of policy into the Constitution, no matter how deeply I may cherish them or how mischievous I may deem their disregard." He concluded: "Of course patriotism cannot be enforced by the flag salute. But neither can the liberal spirit be enforced by judicial invalidation of illiberal legislation. . . . The tendency of focusing attention on constitutionality is to make constitutionality synonymous with wisdom, to regard a law as all right if it is constitutional. Such an attitude is a great enemy of liberalism." [Recall the later decision on symbolic speech in the classroom, Tinker v. Des Moines School District, 393 U.S. 503 (1969) (chap. 15, p. 1195, supra).]

5. *State regulation and religious scruples.* Note, in addition to the cases discussed in Braunfeld and Sherbert [e. g., Barnette (flag salute), Reynolds (Mormon polygamy), and Prince (child labor)], these additional examples of free exercise conflicts with state power (and consider the suggested criteria in the light of these decisions): In re Jenison, 375 U.S. 14 (1963) (remanding for reconsideration in light of Sherbert a conviction of a woman who had refused jury duty for religious reasons); Jacobson v. Massachusetts, 197 U.S. 11 (1905) (compulsory vaccination); Memorial Hospital v. Anderson, 42 N.J. 421, cert. den., 377 U.S. 958 (1964), and Application

of Georgetown College, 331 F.2d 1000 (D.C.Cir.), cert. den., 377 U.S. 978 (1964) (compulsory blood transfusion); People v. Woody, 61 Cal.2d 716 (1964) (ban on the drug peyote unconstitutional as applied to use in bona fide religious practices), see Comment, 17 Stan.L.Rev. 494 (1965); and compare Lawson v. Commonwealth, 164 S.W.2d 972 (Ky.1942) (use of poisonous snakes in religious ceremonies).

Is it important to distinguish in these cases between action affecting others and noncooperation affecting primarily the individual claiming exemption because of religious scruples? See generally Fernandez, "The Free Exercise of Religion," 36 So.Cal.L.Rev. 546 (1963), Giannella, "Religious Liberty, Nonestablishment, and Doctrinal Development: Part I. The Religious Liberty Guarantee," 80 Harv.L.Rev. 1381 (1967), and Clark, "Guidelines for the Free Exercise Clause," 83 Harv.L.Rev. 327 (1969). The Fernandez article suggests that the free exercise clause should generally assure no more than "equality of treatment," with special protection only for acts of "worship." Is that solution barred by Sherbert? Note also the materials on religious scruples and military service, which follow.

MILITARY SERVICE, THE CONSCIENTIOUS OBJECTOR, AND RELIGION

1. *The background.* The traditional view was that a congressional grant of exemption from military service to those opposed to war on religious grounds did not violate the establishment clause, but that the exemption was not constitutionally compelled by the free exercise clause. Do the recent interpretations of the clauses cast doubt on this view? The World War I version of the conscientious objector exemption was sustained in the Selective Draft Law Cases, 245 U.S. 366 (1918), where the Court summarily rejected free exercise and establishment clause objections. And in Hamilton v. Regents of Univ. of Calif., 293 U.S. 245 (1934), a requirement that all male students take military science courses was sustained against a claim that it violated the religious beliefs of a conscientious objector.

2. *The Seeger decision.* Section 6(j) of the Universal Military Training and Service Act, 50 U.S.C.A. App. § 456(j), exempts from combatant military service those persons who are conscientiously opposed to participation in war in any form by reason of their "religious training and beliefs." The quoted phrase is defined as a "belief in a relation to a Supreme Being involving duties superior to those arising from any human relation, but [not including] essentially political, sociological, or philosophical views or a merely personal moral code." The section was attacked under the establishment, free exercise, and due process clauses, on the grounds that it did not exempt nonreligious conscientious objectors and that it discriminated among different forms of religious expression.

In three cases decided as United States v. Seeger, 380 U.S. 163 (1965), the Court did not reach these constitutional claims; rather, Justice Clark's opinion interpreted Section 6(j) to entitle all of the petitioners to exemption: "We have concluded that Congress, in using the expression 'Supreme Being' rather than the designation 'God,' was merely clarifying the meaning of religious training and belief so as to embrace all religions and to exclude essentially political, sociological, or philosophical views. We believe that under this construction, the test of belief 'in a relation to a Supreme Being' is whether a given belief that is sincere and meaningful occupies a place in the life of its possessor parallel to that filled by the orthodox belief in God of one who clearly qualifies for the exemption. Where such beliefs have parallel positions in the lives of their respective holders we cannot say that one is 'in a relation to a Supreme Being' and the other is not. To hold otherwise would not only fly in the face of Congress' entire action in the past; it would ignore the historic position of our country on this issue since its founding. . . . Moreover, we believe this construction embraces the ever-broadening understanding [of God] of the modern religious community." [1]

In a concurring opinion, Justice Douglas discussed "the idea of God" in Hinduism and Buddhism to illustrate the "fluidity and evanescent scope of the concept." He stated, moreover, that he "would have difficulties" if he "read the statute differently" from the Court: "For then those who embraced one religious faith rather than another would be subject to penalties; and that kind of discrimination, as we held in Sherbert v. Verner [supra] . . ., would violate the Free Exercise Clause . . .. It would also result in a denial of equal protection by preferring some religions over others—an invidious discrimination that would run afoul of the Due Process Clause of the Fifth Amendment."

3. *The Sisson case.* The District Court ruled that Sisson, a selective conscientious objector, could not "constitutionally be subjected to military orders which may require him to kill in the Vietnam conflict"; the Supreme Court heard argument on the Government's appeal from that ruling in February 1970. United States v. Sisson, 297 F.Supp. 902 (D.Mass.1969). After a jury had found Sisson guilty of refusing to submit to induction, Chief Judge Wyzanski sustained two contentions by the defendant: a "broad," primarily "free exercise" claim "that no statute can require combat service of a conscientious objector whose principles are either religious or akin thereto"; and a "narrower," "establishment" assertion "that the 1967 draft act invalidly discriminates in favor of certain types of religious objectors to the prejudice of Sisson."

---

1. In discussing the application of this standard, the Court emphasized "that in resolving these exemption problems one deals with the beliefs of different individuals who will articulate them in a multitude of ways. In such an intensely personal area, of course, the claim of the registrant that his belief is an essential part of a religious faith must be given great weight. . . . The validity of what he believes cannot be questioned. Some theologians, and indeed some examiners, might be tempted to question the existence of the registrant's 'Supreme Being' or the truth of his concepts. But these are inquiries foreclosed to Government. As Mr. Justice Douglas stated in United States v. Ballard, 322 U.S. 78, 86 (1944) [a mail fraud prosecution for soliciting money for the "I Am" movement]: 'Men may believe what they cannot prove. They may not be put to the proof of their religious doctrines or beliefs. Religious experiences which are real as life to some may be incomprehensible to others.' Local boards and courts in this sense are not free to reject beliefs because they consider them 'incomprehensible.' Their task is to decide whether the beliefs professed by a registrant are sincerely held and whether they are, in his own scheme of things, religious. But we hasten to emphasize that while the 'truth' of a belief is not open to question, there remains the significant question whether it is 'truly held.' This is the threshold question of sincerity which must be resolved in every case." See Rabin, "When is a Religious Belief Religious . . .," 51 Corn.L.Q. 231 (1966), and White, "Processing Conscientious Objector Claims: A Constitutional Inquiry," 56 Calif.L.Rev. 652 (1968).

In examining the free exercise contention, Chief Judge Wyzanski applied the Sherbert v. Verner "balancing" approach: he explained that his "chief reason for reaching this conclusion after examining the competing interests [was] the magnitude of Sisson's interest in not killing in the Vietnam conflict as against the want of magnitude in the country's present need for him to be so employed." Earlier, he noted that he assumed "that in time of declared war or in the defense of the homeland against invasion, all persons may be conscripted even for combat service."

In finding Sisson to be "religious" for purposes of the free exercise clause, the trial judge relied on the broad reading given "religion" in the statute in Seeger, note 2, supra; nevertheless, Sisson's belief was found not to be "religious" under the 1967 draft law's exemption provision.* That narrow reading of the statutory exemption in turn provided some of the basis for sustaining the establishment claim: "In short, in the draft act Congress unconstitutionally discriminated against atheists, agnostics, and men, like Sisson, who, whether they be religious or not, are motivated in their objection to the draft by profound moral beliefs which constitute the central convictions of their beings."

Would the decision be sustainable on Fifth Amendment liberty-due process grounds if it were found that Sisson's beliefs were not religious for free exercise purposes? On other grounds?† (Chief Judge Wyzanski referred to the Fifth Amendment in a passing remark.) Is the establishment aspect of the holding a stronger basis than the free exercise ground? (The trial judge spoke at length about the latter, only briefly about the "narrower" establishment issue.) Should the trial court have given alternative reasons? Chief Judge Wyzanski stated: "The Supreme Court may not address itself to the broad issue just decided. Being a court of last resort, it, unlike an inferior court, can confidently rest its judgment on a narrow issue. Indeed Seeger foreshadows exactly that process." Why is an inferior court "unlike" the Supreme Court in this respect?

On the constitutional claims not reached in Seeger and discussed in Sisson, see generally Mansfield, "Conscientious Objection—1964 Term," 1965 Religion and the Public Order 3; Macgill, "Selective Conscientious Objection: Divine Will and Legislative Grace," 54 Va.L.Rev. 1355 (1968); Note, "The Conscientious Objector and the First Amendment: There But for the Grace of God," 34 U.Chi.L.Rev. 79 (1966); and Note, "Religious Conscientious Objection," 21 Stan.L.Rev. 1734 (1969).

---

* A 1967 amendment to the draft provision involved in Seeger, supra, deleted the statutory language requiring a "belief in a relation to a Supreme Being" in order to have a conscientious objection qualify as one based on "religious training and belief." For a suggestion of two possible reasons—"neither is at all convincing"—for the court's unexplained ruling that Sisson's belief did not qualify under the current statutory definition of religion, see Recent Case, 83 Harv.L.Rev. 453–55, n. 11 (1969).

† See Redlich and Feinberg, "Individual Conscience and the Selective Conscientious Objector: The Right Not to Kill," 44 N.Y.U.L.Rev. 875 (1969), rejecting the use of the religion clauses as the bases for such a right, but finding adequate grounds for it in the 13th, Ninth, Fifth and First Amendments. (The First Amendment contribution is a "right of conscience" "emanating" from the specific rights in that Amendment, by analogy to the Griswold v. Connecticut "penumbras" and "emanations," see p. 824, supra. Note the reference to Professor Redlich's article urging reliance on the Ninth Amendment to attack Connecticut's birth control law, quoted in a footnote to Justice Black's dissent in Griswold, at p. 834.)

Chapter 18

TWO PROBLEMS OF EQUAL PROTECTION:
RACE AND REAPPORTIONMENT

Scope Note. The basic materials on the evolution of equal protection principles (chap. 14) deferred detailed consideration of two strands in that development. This chapter examines those strands—the long-standing and continuous concern with racial discrimination and the recent but intensive preoccupation with legislative apportionment. The central themes were touched on in chap. 14: the "suspect" nature of racial classifications, and the "fundamental interest" in voting. Each of those themes has generated special problems of doctrine and implementation. These ramifications are the concern of this chapter.

SECTION 1. RACE

Introduction. Racial discrimination was a major target of the 14th Amendment; racial classifications are "suspect": these are among the few clear and continuously voiced themes in equal protection doctrine, and they have been echoed repeatedly in the preceding pages. They were prominent not only in the materials on the changing ingredients of equal protection (chap. 14); they were central as well in the examination of congressional power under the post-Civil War Amendments (chap. 6), and in the Court's recital of the background of the 14th Amendment in the Slaughter-House Cases (chap. 11, p. 787).

But perception of those themes does not answer all troublesome questions. What is necessary to demonstrate unconstitutional discrimination? Must there be purposeful racial bias, expressed in formal statements of state policy? May bias be inferred from the administration of law? May discrimination be de facto as well as de jure? Is there a constitutional claim in the absence of hostile purpose that places the victim at a disadvantage because of race?

When, if ever, may racial criteria be relied on in state action? Are all racial classifications forbidden—must government be truly "colorblind"? Are racial classifications always highly "suspect"? Are they never permissible unless the state can advance a strong justification? What justifications will do? Are racial criteria acceptable if their purpose is benign rather than hostile? Is segregation unconstitutional per se, even if facilities are equal? Does constitutionality depend on who imposes the separation? Questions such as these are raised by the materials that follow.

A. RACIAL DISCRIMINATION

1. *Strauder: Discrimination on the face of the law.* Seven years after the Slaughter-House Cases had emphasized the racial concerns central

to the adoption of the 14th Amendment, the Court recalled and applied that background in Strauder v. West Virginia, 100 U.S. 303 (1880). Strauder had sought to remove his state prosecution for murder to a federal court on the ground that "by virtue of the laws of the State of West Virginia no colored man was eligible to be a member of the grand jury or to serve on a petit jury in the State." Justice Strong's majority opinion agreed that removal should have been granted. He noted that the question was not whether a Negro had a right to a jury "composed in whole or in part of persons of his own race or color" but whether in selecting the jury, all persons of his race or color may be excluded by law solely because of their race or color." Justice Strong continued:

"This [Fourteenth Amendment] is one of a series of constitutional provisions having a common purpose; namely, securing to a race recently emancipated, a race that through many generations had been held in slavery, all the civil rights that the superior race enjoy. It was designed to assure to the colored race the enjoyment of all the civil rights that under the law are enjoyed by white persons, and to give to that race the protection of the general government, in that enjoyment, whenever it should be denied by the States. . . .

"What is this [equal protection clause] but declaring that the law in the States shall be the same for the black as for the white; that all persons, whether colored or white, shall stand equal before the laws of the States, and, in regard to the colored race, for whose protection the amendment was primarily designed, that no discrimination shall be made against them by law because of their color? The words of the amendment, it is true, are prohibitory, but they contain a necessary implication of a positive immunity, or right, most valuable to the colored race,—the right to exemption from unfriendly legislation against them distinctively as colored,—exemption from legal discriminations, implying inferiority in civil society, lessening the security of their enjoyment of the rights which others enjoy, and discriminations which are steps towards reducing them to the condition of a subject race.

"That the West Virginia statute respecting juries—the statute that controlled the selection of the grand and petit jury in the case of the plaintiff in error—is such a discrimination ought not to be doubted. Nor would it be if the persons excluded by it were white men. If in those States where the colored people constitute a majority of the entire population a law should be enacted excluding all white men from jury service, . . . we apprehend no one would be heard to claim that it would not be a denial to white men of the equal protection of the laws. Nor if a law should be passed excluding all naturalized Celtic Irishmen, would there be any doubt of its inconsistency with the spirit of the amendment. The very fact that colored people are singled out and expressly denied by a statute all right to participate in the administration of the law, as jurors, because of their color, though they are citizens, and may be in other respects fully qualified, is practically a brand upon them, affixed by the law, an assertion of their inferiority, and a stimulant to that race prejudice which is an impediment to securing to individuals of the race that equal justice which the law aims to secure to all others."

2. *Yick Wo: Discrimination in the administration of law.* a. Yick Wo v. Hopkins, 118 U.S. 356 (1886), involved a San Francisco ordinance which prohibited operating a laundry without the permission of city officials,

except in a brick or stone building. Chinese aliens who had operated laundries for many years were denied permission and convicted under the ordinance. It was admitted that about 310 out of 320 laundries were in wooden buildings, that about 240 were operated by Chinese, that about 150 Chinese had been arrested under the ordinance, and that about 80 non-Chinese operating "under similar conditions are left unmolested."

The Court found unconstitutional discrimination: "In the present cases, we are not obliged to reason from the probable to the actual and pass upon the validity of the ordinances complained of, as tried merely by the opportunities which their terms afford, of unequal and unjust discrimination in their administration. For the cases present the ordinances in actual operation, and the facts shown establish an administration directed so exclusively against a particular class of persons as to warrant and require the conclusion that whatever may have been the intent of the ordinances as adopted, they are applied by the public authorities charged with their administration, and thus representing the State itself, with a mind so unequal and oppressive as to amount to a practical denial by the State of that equal protection of the laws which is secured to the petitioners, as to all other persons, by the broad and benign provisions of the Fourteenth Amendment to the Constitution of the United States. Though the law itself be fair on its face and impartial in appearance, yet, if it is applied and administered by public authority with an evil eye and an unequal hand, so as practically to make unjust and illegal discriminations between persons in similar circumstances, material to their rights, the denial of equal justice is still within the prohibition of the Constitution. . . .

"The present cases, as shown by the facts disclosed in the record, are within this class. It appears that both petitioners have complied with every requisite, deemed by the law or by the public officers charged with its administration necessary for the protection of neighboring property from fire, or as a precaution against injury to the public health. No reason whatever, except the will of the supervisors, is assigned why they should not be permitted to carry on, in the accustomed manner, their harmless and useful occupation, on which they depend for a livelihood. And while this consent of the supervisors is withheld from them and from two hundred others who have also petitioned, all of whom happened to be Chinese subjects, eighty others, not Chinese subjects, are permitted to carry on the same business under similar conditions. The fact of this discrimination is admitted. No reason for it is shown, and the conclusion cannot be resisted, that no reason for it exists except hostility to the race and nationality to which the petitioners belong, and which in the eye of the law is not justified."

b.   The difficult problems of proving discrimination from administration have repeatedly arisen in the context of jury selection. See the materials in chap. 12, p. 903, supra. On the possibility of asserting in defense that individual differences in application were not deliberate discriminations, see Snowden v. Hughes, 321 U.S. 1 (1944), stating that "unequal application" of statutes fair on their face is not a violation of equal protection "unless there is shown an element of intentional or purposeful discrimination." What if patterns of selective law enforcement rather than individual inequalities are shown? What justifications are allowable? See Note, "The Right to Nondiscriminatory Enforcement of State Penal Laws," 61 Colum.L.Rev. 1103 (1961), and note Oyler v. Boles, 368 U.S. 448 (1962), where the Court rejected a challenge to sentencing under a habitual criminal statute based on failure to prosecute other habitual offenders. Justice Clark stated that the allegations did not state whether the failure to prosecute was due to a deliberate policy or to lack of knowledge. If there was lack of knowledge, there would clearly be no equal protection violation, Justice Clark stated. He added: "Moreover, the conscious exercise of some selectivity in enforcement is not in itself a federal constitutional violation. Even though the statistics in this case might imply a policy of selective enforcement, it was not stated that the selection was deliberately based upon an unjustifiable standard such as race, religion, or other arbitrary classification. Therefore grounds supporting a finding of a denial of equal protection were not alleged."

KOREMATSU v. UNITED STATES

323 U.S. 214, 65 S.Ct. 193, 89 L.Ed. 194 (1944).

Certiorari to the Circuit Court of Appeals for the Ninth Circuit.

Mr. Justice BLACK delivered the opinion of the Court.

The petitioner, an American citizen of Japanese descent, was convicted in a federal district court for remaining in San Leandro, California, a "Military Area," contrary to Civilian Exclusion Order No. 34 of the Commanding General of the Western Command, U. S. Army, which directed that after May 9, 1942, all persons of Japanese ancestry should be excluded from that area. No question was raised as to petitioner's loyalty to the United States. . . .

It should be noted, to begin with, that all legal restrictions which curtail the civil rights of a single racial group are immediately suspect. That is not to say that all such restrictions are unconstitutional. It is to say that courts must subject them to the most rigid scrutiny. Pressing public necessity may sometimes justify the existence of such restrictions; racial antagonism never can.

In the instant case prosecution of the petitioner was begun by information charging violation of an Act of Congress, of March 21, 1942, 56 Stat. 173, which provides that

". . . whoever shall enter, remain in, leave, or commit any act in any military area or military zone prescribed, under the authority of an Executive order of the President, by the Secretary of War, or by any military commander designated by the Secretary of War, contrary to the restrictions applicable to any such area or zone . . . shall, if it appears that he knew or should have known of the existence and extent of the restrictions . . . and that his act was in violation thereof, be guilty of a misdemeanor . . ."

Exclusion Order No. 34, which the petitioner knowingly and admittedly violated was one of a number of military orders and proclamations, all of which were substantially based upon Executive Order No. 9066, 7 Fed.Reg. 1407. That order, issued after we were at war with Japan, declared that "the successful prosecution of the war requires every possible protection against espionage and against sabotage to national-defense material, national-defense premises, and national-defense utilities. . . ."

One of the series of orders and proclamations, a curfew order, which like the exclusion order here was promulgated pursuant to Executive Order 9066, subjected all persons of Japanese ancestry in prescribed West Coast military areas to remain in their residences from 8 p. m. to 6 a. m. [In] Hirabayashi v. United States, 320 U.S. 81, we sustained a conviction obtained for violation of the curfew order. . . . We upheld the curfew order as an exercise of the power of the government to take steps necessary to prevent espionage and sabotage in an area threatened by Japanese attack.

In the light of the principles we announced in the Hirabayashi case, we are unable to conclude that it was beyond the war power of Congress and the Executive to exclude those of Japanese ancestry from the West Coast war area at the time they did. [E]xclusion from a threatened area, no less than curfew, has a definite and close relationship to the prevention of espionage and sabotage. The military authorities, charged with the primary responsibility of defending our shores, concluded that curfew provided inadequate protection and ordered exclusion. They did so . . . . in accordance with Congressional authority to the military . . . . .

In this case the petitioner challenges the assumptions upon which we rested our conclusions in the Hirabayashi case. He also urges that by May 1942, when Order No. 34 was promulgated, all danger of Japanese invasion of the West Coast had disappeared. After careful consideration of these contentions we are compelled to reject them.

Here, as in [Hirabayashi], "we cannot reject as unfounded the judgment of the military authorities and of Congress that there were disloyal members of that population, whose number of strength could not be precisely and quickly ascertained. We cannot say that the war-making branches of the Government did not have ground for believing that in a critical hour such persons could not readily be isolated and separately dealt with, and constituted a menace to the national defense and safety, which demanded that prompt and adequate measures be taken to guard against it."

Like curfew, exclusion of those of Japanese origin was deemed necessary because of the presence of an unascertained number of disloyal members of the group, most of whom we have no doubt were loyal to this country. It was because we could not reject the finding of the military authorities that it was impossible to bring about an immediate segregation of the disloyal from the loyal that we sustained the validity of the curfew order as applying to the whole group. In the instant case, temporary exclusion of the entire group was rested by the military on the same ground. The judgment that exclusion of the whole group was for the same reason a military imperative answers the contention that the exclusion was in the nature of group punishment based on antagonism to those of Japanese origin. That there were members of the group who retained loyalties to Japan has been confirmed by investigations made subsequent to the exclusion. Approximately five thousand American citizens of Japanese ancestry refused to swear unqualified allegiance to the United States and to renounce allegiance to the Japanese Emperor, and several thousand evacuees requested repatriation to Japan.

We uphold the exclusion order as of the time it was made and when the petitioner violated it. . . . . In doing so, we are not unmindful of the hardships imposed by it upon a large group of American citizens. . . . But hardships are part of war, and war is an aggregation of hardships. All citizens alike, both in and out of uniform, feel the impact of war in greater or lesser measure. Citizenship has its responsibilities as well as its privileges, and in time of war the burden is always heavier. Compulsory exclusion of large groups of citizens from their homes, except under circumstances of direst emergency and peril, is inconsistent with our basic governmental institutions. But when under conditions of modern warfare our shores are threatened by hostile forces, the power to protect must be commensurate with the threatened danger. . . .

We are . . . being asked to pass at this time upon the whole subsequent detention program in both assembly and relocation centers, although the only issues framed at the trial related to petitioner's remaining in the prohibited area in violation of the exclusion order. Had petitioner here left the prohibited area and gone to an assembly center we cannot say either as a matter of fact or law, that his presence in that center would have resulted in his detention in a relocation center. Some who did report to the assembly center were not sent to relocation centers, but were released upon condition that they remain outside the prohibited zone until the military orders were modified or lifted. This illustrates that they pose different problems and may be governed by different principles. The lawfulness of one does not necessarily determine the lawfulness of the others. . . . *

Since the petitioner has not been convicted of failing to report or to remain in an assembly or relocation center, we cannot in this case determine the validity of those separate provisions of the order. . . . It will be time enough to decide the serious constitutional issues which petitioner seeks to raise when an assembly or relocation order is applied or is certain to be applied to him, and we have its terms before us. . . .

It is said that we are dealing here with the case of imprisonment of a citizen in a concentration camp solely because of his ancestry, without evidence or inquiry concerning his loyalty and good disposition towards the United States. Our task would be simple, our duty clear, were this a case involving the imprisonment of a loyal citizen in a concentration camp because of racial prejudice. Regardless of the true nature of the assembly and relocation centers—and we deem it unjustifiable to call them concentration camps with all the ugly connotations that term implies—we are dealing specifically with nothing but an exclusion order. To cast this case into outlines of racial prejudice, without reference to the real military dangers which were presented, merely confuses the issue. Korematsu was not excluded from the Military Area because of hostility to him or his race. He was excluded because we are at war with the Japanese Empire, because the properly constituted military authorities feared an invasion of our West Coast and felt constrained to take proper security measures, because they decided that the military urgency of the situation demanded that all citizens of Japanese ancestry be segregated from the West Coast temporarily, and finally, because Congress, reposing its confidence in this time of war in our

---

* Ex parte Endo, 323 U.S. 283 (1944), decided on the same day as Korematsu, involved the validity of continued detention under the relocation program. The War Relocation Authority gave "leave" from the relocation centers only under certain conditions. The Court held petitioner entitled to release, finding "no authority" in the statutes and regulations "to subject citizens who are concededly loyal" to this "leave procedure." Though the Court did not reach the constitutional challenges, it relied on the analogy of interpreting statutes to give them a "greater chance of surviving the test of constitutionality."

On these cases and on the evacuation program generally, see, e. g., Rostow, "The Japanese American Cases—A Disaster," 54 Yale L.J. 489 (1945); Dembitz, "Racial Discrimination and the Military Judgment," 45 Colum.L. Rev. 175 (1945); and Grodzins, Americans Betrayed: Politics and the Japanese Evacuation (1949).

military leaders—as inevitably it must—determined that they should have the power to do just this. There was evidence of disloyalty on the part of some, the military authorities considered that the need for action was great, and time was short. We cannot—by availing ourselves of the calm perspective of hindsight—now say that at that time these actions were unjustified.

Affirmed.

[A concurring opinion by Justice FRANKFURTER and a dissent by Justice ROBERTS are omitted.]

Mr. Justice MURPHY, dissenting.

This exclusion of "all persons of Japanese ancestry, both alien and non-alien," from the Pacific Coast area on a plea of military necessity in the absence of martial law ought not to be approved. Such exclusion goes over "the very brink of constitutional power" and falls into the ugly abyss of racism.

In dealing with matters relating to the prosecution and progress of a war, we must accord great respect and consideration to the judgments of the military authorities who are on the scene and who have full knowledge of the military facts. . . . At the same time, however, it is essential that there be definite limits to military discretion, especially where martial law has not been declared. Individuals must not be left impoverished of their constitutional rights on a plea of military necessity that has neither substance nor support. Thus, like other claims conflicting with the asserted constitutional rights of the individual, the military claim must subject itself to the judicial process of having its reasonableness determined and its conflicts with other interests reconciled. . . .

The judicial test of whether the Government, on a plea of military necessity, can validly deprive an individual of any of his constitutional rights is whether the deprivation is reasonably related to a public danger that is so "immediate, imminent, and impending" as not to admit of delay and not to permit the intervention of ordinary constitutional processes to alleviate the danger. . . . Civilian Exclusion Order No. 34, banishing from a prescribed area of the Pacific Coast "all persons of Japanese ancestry, both alien and non-alien," clearly does not meet that test. Being an obvious racial discrimination, the order deprives all those within its scope of the equal protection of the laws as guaranteed by the Fifth Amendment. It further deprives these individuals of their constitutional rights to live and work where they will, to establish a home where they choose and to move about freely. In excommunicating them without benefit of hearings, this order also deprives them of all their constitutional rights to procedural due process. Yet no reasonable relation to an "immediate, imminent, and impending" public danger is evident to support this racial restriction which is one of the most sweeping and complete deprivations of constitutional rights in the history of this nation in the absence of martial law.

It must be conceded that the military and naval situation in the spring of 1942 was such as to generate a very real fear of invasion of the Pacific Coast, accompanied by fears of sabotage and espionage in that area. . . . In adjudging the military action taken in light of the then apparent dangers, . . . it is necessary only that the action have some reasonable relation to the removal of the dangers of invasion, sabotage and espionage. But the exclusion, either temporarily or permanently, of all persons with

Japanese blood in their veins has no such reasonable relation. And that relation is lacking because the exclusion order necessarily must rely for its reasonableness upon the assumption that *all* persons of Japanese ancestry may have a dangerous tendency to commit sabotage and espionage and to aid our Japanese enemy in other ways. It is difficult to believe that reason, logic or experience could be marshalled in support of such an assumption.

That this forced exclusion was the result in good measure of this erroneous assumption of racial guilt rather than bona fide military necessity is evidenced by the Commanding General's Final Report on the evacuation from the Pacific Coast area. In it he refers to all individuals of Japanese descent as "subversive," as belonging to "an enemy race" whose "racial strains are undiluted," and as constituting "over 112,000 potential enemies . . . at large today" along the Pacific Coast. In support of this blanket condemnation of all persons of Japanese descent, however, no reliable evidence is cited to show that such individuals were generally disloyal, or had generally so conducted themselves in this area as to constitute a special menace to defense installations or war industries, or had otherwise by their behavior furnished reasonable ground for their exclusion as a group.

Justification for the exclusion is sought, instead, mainly upon questionable racial and sociological grounds not charged or proved . . . . The reasons appear . . . to be largely an accumulation of much of the misinformation, half-truths and insinuations that for years have been directed against Japanese Americans by people with racial and economic prejudices—the same people who have been among the foremost advocates of the evacuation. A military judgment based upon such racial and sociological considerations is not entitled to the great weight ordinarily given the judgments based upon strictly military considerations. . . .

. . . No one denies, of course, that there were some disloyal persons of Japanese descent on the Pacific Coast who did all in their power to aid their ancestral land. . . . But to infer that examples of individual disloyalty prove group disloyalty and justify discriminatory action against the entire group is to deny that under our system of law individual guilt is the sole basis for deprivation of rights. . . .

[T]here was no adequate proof that the Federal Bureau of Investigation and the military and naval intelligence services did not have the espionage and sabotage situation well in hand . . . . Nor is there any denial of the fact that not one person of Japanese ancestry was accused or convicted of espionage or sabotage after Pearl Harbor while they were still free,[1] a fact which is some evidence of the loyalty of the vast majority of these individuals and of the effectiveness of the established methods of combating these evils. It seems incredible that under these circumstances it would have been impossible to hold loyalty hearings for the mere 112,000 persons involved—or at least for the 70,000 American citizens—especially when a large part of this number represented children and elderly men and women.[2] . . .

1. The Final Report, p. 34, makes the amazing statement that as of February 14, 1942, "The very fact that no sabotage has taken place to date is a disturbing and confirming indication that such action will be taken." Apparently, in the minds of the military leaders, there was no way that the Japa- nese Americans could escape the suspicion of sabotage. [Footnote by Justice Murphy.]

2. During a period of six months, the 112 alien tribunals or hearing boards set up by the British Government shortly after the outbreak of the pres-

I dissent, therefore, from this legalization of racism. Racial discrimination in any form and in any degree has no justifiable part whatever in our democratic way of life. . . . All residents of this nation are kin in some way by blood or culture to a foreign land. Yet they are primarily and necessarily a part of the new and distinct civilization of the United States. They must accordingly be treated at all times as the heirs of the American experiment and as entitled to all the rights and freedoms guaranteed by the Constitution.

Mr. Justice JACKSON, dissenting. . . .

[T]he series of military orders which made this conduct a crime . . . were so drawn that the only way Korematsu could avoid violation was to give himself up to the military authority. . . . A citizen's presence in the locality, however, was made a crime only if his parents were of Japanese birth. Had Korematsu been one of four—the others being, say, a German alien enemy, an Italian enemy, and a citizen of American-born ancestors, convicted of treason but out on parole—only Korematsu's presence would have violated the order. The difference between their innocence and his crime would result, not from anything he did, said, or thought, different than they, but only in that he was born of different racial stock.

. . .

[T]he "law" which this prisoner is convicted of disregarding is not found in an act of Congress, but in a military order. Neither the Act of Congress nor the Executive Order of the President, nor both together, would afford a basis for this conviction. It rests on the orders of General DeWitt. And it is said that if the military commander had reasonable military grounds for promulgating the orders, they are constitutional and become law, and the Court is required to enforce them. There are several reasons why I cannot subscribe to this doctrine.

It would be impracticable and dangerous idealism to expect or insist that each specific military command in an area of probable operations will conform to conventional tests of constitutionality. When an area is so beset that it must be put under military control at all, the paramount consideration is that its measures be successful, rather than legal. . . . Defense measures will not, and often should not, be held within the limits that bind civil authority in peace. No court can require such a commander in such circumstances to act as a reasonable man; he may be unreasonably cautious and exacting. Perhaps he should be. . . . He issues orders, and they may have a certain authority as military commands, although they may be very bad as constitutional law.

But if we cannot confine military expedients by the Constitution, neither would I distort the Constitution to approve all that the military may deem expedient. That is what the Court appears to be doing, whether consciously or not. I cannot say, from any evidence before me, that the orders of General DeWitt were not reasonably expedient military precautions, nor could I say that they were. But even if they were permissible military procedures, I deny that it follows that they are constitutional. If, as the Court holds,

ent war summoned and examined approximately 74,000 German and Austrian aliens. These tribunals determined whether each individual enemy alien was a real enemy of the Allies or only a "friendly enemy." About 64,000 were freed from internment and from any special restrictions, and only 2,000 were interned. [Footnote by Justice Murphy.]

it does follow, then we may as well say that any military order will be constitutional and have done with it. . . .

Much is said of the danger to liberty from the Army program for deporting and detaining these citizens of Japanese extraction. But a judicial construction of the due process clause that will sustain this order is a far more subtle blow to liberty than the promulgation of the order itself. A military order, however unconstitutional, is not apt to last longer than the military emergency. . . . But once a judicial opinion rationalizes such an order to show that it conforms to the Constitution, or rather rationalizes the Constitution to show that the Constitution sanctions such an order, the Court for all time has validated the principle of racial discrimination in criminal procedure and of transplanting American citizens. The principle then lies about like a loaded weapon ready for the hand of any authority that can bring forward a plausible claim of an urgent need. . . . A military commander may overstep the bounds of constitutionality, and it is an incident. But if we review and approve, that passing incident becomes the doctrine of the Constitution. There it has a generative power of its own, and all that it creates will be in its own image. . . .

I should hold that a civil court cannot be made to enforce an order which violates constitutional limitations even if it is a reasonable exercise of military authority. The courts can exercise only the judicial power, can apply only law, and must abide by the Constitution, or they cease to be civil courts and become instruments of military policy.

. . . I would not lead people to rely on this Court for a review that seems to me wholly delusive. The military reasonableness of these orders can only be determined by military superiors. If the people ever let command of the war power fall into irresponsible and unscrupulous hands, the courts wield no power equal to its restraint. The chief restraint upon those who command the physical forces of the country, in the future as in the past, must be their responsibility to the political judgments of their contemporaries and to the moral judgments of history.

My duties as a justice as I see them do not require me to make a military judgment as to whether General DeWitt's evacuation and detention program was a reasonable military necessity. I do not suggest that the courts should have attempted to interfere with the Army in carrying out its task. But I do not think they may be asked to execute a military expedient that has no place in law under the Constitution. I would reverse the judgment and discharge the prisoner.

TAKAHASHI v. FISH AND GAME COMMISSION

334 U.S. 410, 68 S.Ct. 1138, 92 L.Ed. 1478 (1948).

Certiorari to the Supreme Court of California.

Mr. Justice BLACK delivered the opinion of the Court.

The respondent, Torao Takahashi, born in Japan, came to this country and became a resident of California in 1907. Federal laws, based on distinctions of "color and race," . . . have permitted Japanese and certain other non-white racial groups to enter and reside in the country, but have made them ineligible for United States citizenship. The question presented is whether California can, consistently with the Federal Constitution and laws passed pursuant to it, use this federally created racial ineligibility for citizenship as a basis for barring Takahashi from earning his living as a commercial fisherman in the ocean waters off the coast of California.

Prior to 1943 California issued commercial fishing licenses to all qualified persons without regard to alienage or ineligibility to citizenship. From 1915 to 1942 Takahashi, under annual commercial fishing licenses issued by the State, fished in ocean waters off the California coast . . . and brought his fresh fish ashore for sale. In 1942, while this country was at war with Japan, Takahashi and other California residents of Japanese ancestry were evacuated from the State under military orders. . . . In 1943, during the period of war and evacuation, an amendment to the California Fish and Game Code was adopted prohibiting issuance of a license to any "alien Japanese." . . . In 1945, the state code was again amended by striking the 1943 provision for fear that it might be "declared unconstitutional" because directed only "against alien Japanese"; the new amendment banned issuance of licenses to any "person ineligible to citizenship," which classification included Japanese. . . . Because of this state provision barring issuance of commercial fishing licenses to persons ineligible for citizenship under federal law, Takahashi, who met all other state requirements, was denied a license by the California Fish and Game Commission upon his return to California in 1945. . . . .

We may well begin our consideration of the principles to be applied in this case by a summary of this Court's holding in Truax v. Raich, 239 U.S. 33 [1915], not deemed controlling by the majority of the California Supreme Court . . . . . That case involved an attack upon an Arizona law which required all . . . . employers of more than five workers to hire not less than eighty (80) per cent qualified electors or native-born citizens of the United States. Raich, an alien who worked as a cook in a restaurant which had more than five employees, was about to lose his job solely because of the state law's coercive effect on the restaurant owner. This Court, in upholding Raich's contention that the Arizona law was invalid, declared that Raich, having been lawfully admitted into the country under federal law, had a federal privilege to enter and abide in "any State in the Union" and thereafter under the Fourteenth Amendment to enjoy the equal protection of the laws of the state in which he abided; that this privilege to enter in and abide in any state carried with it the "right to work for a living in the common occupations of the community" . . . . .

Had the Truax decision said nothing further . . . ., its reasoning, if followed, would seem to require invalidation of this California code provision barring aliens from the occupation of fishing as inconsistent with federal law . . . . . However, the Court there went on to note that it had on occasion sustained state legislation that did not apply alike to citizens and non-citizens, the ground for the distinction being that such laws were necessary to protect special interests either of the state or of its citizens as such. The Truax opinion pointed out that the Arizona law, aimed as it was against employment of aliens in *all* vocations, failed to show a "special public interest with respect to any particular business . . . that could possibly be deemed to support the enactment." The Court noted that it had previously upheld various state laws which restricted the privilege of planting oysters in the tidewater rivers of a state to citizens of that state, and which denied to aliens within a state the privilege of possessing a rifle and of shooting game within that state . . . . .

California now urges, and the State Supreme Court held, that the California fishing provision here challenged falls within the rationale of the "special public interest" cases distinguished in the Truax opinion, and thus that the state's ban upon commercial fishing by aliens ineligible to citizenship is valid. . . .

First. The state's contention that its law was passed solely as a fish conservation measure is vigorously denied. The petitioner argues that it was the outgrowth of racial antagonism directed solely against the Japanese, and that for this reason alone it cannot stand. . . . We find it unnecessary to resolve this controversy concerning the motives that prompted enactment of the legislation. . . .

Second. It does not follow, as California seems to argue, that because the United States regulates immigration and naturalization in part on the basis of race and color classifications, a state can adopt one or more of the same classifications to prevent lawfully admitted aliens within its borders from earning a living in the same way that other state inhabitants earn their living. The Federal Government has broad constitutional powers in determining what aliens shall be admitted to the United States, the period they may remain, regulation of their conduct before naturalization, and the terms and conditions of their naturalization. See Hines v. Davidowitz, 312 U.S. 52, 66. Under the Constitution the states are granted no such powers; they can neither add to nor take from the conditions lawfully imposed by Congress upon admission, naturalization and residence of aliens in the United States or the several states. State laws which impose discriminatory burdens upon the entrance or residence of aliens lawfully within the United States conflict with this constitutionally derived federal power to regulate immigration, and have accordingly been held invalid. . . . The Fourteenth Amendment and the laws adopted under its authority . . . embody a general policy that all persons lawfully in this country shall abide "in any state" on an equality of legal privileges with all citizens under non-discriminatory laws. [T]he power of a state to apply its laws exclusively to its alien inhabitants as a class is confined within narrow limits.

Third. We are unable to find that the "special public interest" on which California relies provides support for this state ban on Takahashi's commercial fishing. . . . California's claim of "special public interest" is that its citizens are the collective owners of fish swimming in the three-mile belt. . . . To whatever extent the fish in the three-mile belt off California may be "capable of ownership" by California, we think that "ownership" is inadequate to justify California in excluding any or all aliens who are lawful residents of the State from making a living by fishing in the ocean off its shores while permitting all others to do so.

This leaves for consideration the argument that this law should be upheld on authority of those cases which have sustained state laws barring aliens ineligible to citizenship from land ownership. Assuming the continued validity of those cases, we think they could not in any event be controlling here. They rested solely upon the power of states to control the devolution and ownership of land within their borders, a power long exercised and supported on reasons peculiar to real property. They cannot be extended to cover this case.

Reversed.

[A concurring opinion by Justice MURPHY, joined by Justice RUT-LEDGE, is omitted.]

Mr. Justice REED, dissenting.

. . . As fishing rights have been treated traditionally as a natural resource, in the absence of federal regulation, California as a sovereign state has power to regulate the taking and handling of fish in the waters bordering its shores. It is, I think, one of the natural resources of the state that may be preserved from exploitation by aliens. The ground for this power in the absence of any exercise of federal authority is California's authority over its fisheries.

The right to fish is analogous to the right to own land, a privilege which a state may deny to aliens as to land within its borders. Terrace v. Thompson, 263 U.S. 197. It is closely akin to the right to hunt, a privilege from which a state may bar aliens, if reasonably deemed advantageous to its citizens. A state's power has even been held to extend to the exclusion of aliens from the operation of pool and billiard halls when a city deemed them not as well qualified as citizens for the conduct of a business thought to have harmful tendencies. Clarke v. Deckebach, 274 U.S. 392.

The Federal Government has not pursued a policy of equal treatment of aliens and citizens. Citizens have rights superior to those of aliens in the ownership of land and in exploiting natural resources. Perhaps Congress as a matter of immigration policy may require that states open every door of opportunity in America to all resident aliens, but until Congress so determines as to fisheries, I do not feel that the judicial arm of the Government should require the states to admit all aliens to this privilege. . . .

Mr. Justice JACKSON joins in this dissent.

OTHER DISCRIMINATIONS AGAINST ORIENTAL ALIENS

In addition to the decisions described in the principal case, see Oyama v. California, 332 U.S. 633 (1948), decided shortly before Takahashi. There the Court considered the constitutionality of the California Alien Land Laws which effected an escheat of agricultural lands acquired by aliens ineligible for citizenship and provided for a prima facie presumption that conveyances of title where the consideration was paid by the ineligible alien were not gifts but were for the benefit of the alien. Title had been acquired by an ineligible alien in the name of his minor son, and the state courts declared the lands escheated to the state. The petitioner urged that the Act discriminated against the citizen-son and the alien-father. The Court held the presumption invalid as applied since the normal presumption under California law was that a gift to a child was intended by such a transfer. The changed presumption where the father was an alien unreasonably deprived the child of the equal protection of the laws. Justice Black, joined by Justice Douglas, wrote a separate concurrence urging that the statute violated the alien's right to equal protection of the laws and conflicted with federal laws and treaties governing the rights of aliens. Justice Murphy, joined by Justice Rutledge, also concurred in a separate opinion on the ground that the statute was in fact nothing more than racial discrimination. Justice Reed and Justice Burton dissented in one opinion, and Justice Jackson in another, stating that the presumption was a reasonable means of effectuating the purpose of the statute. See also Fujii v. California, 38 Cal.2d 718, 242 P.2d 617 (1952) (see chap. 5, p. 399, supra), where the California Supreme Court held the California Alien Land Law invalid as a denial of equal protection.

LOVING v. VIRGINIA

388 U.S. 1, 87 S.Ct. 1817, 18 L.Ed.2d 1010 (1967).

Appeal from the Supreme Court of Appeals of Virginia.

Mr. Chief Justice WARREN delivered the opinion of the Court.

This case presents a constitutional question never addressed by this Court: whether a statutory scheme adopted by the State of Virginia to prevent marriages between persons solely on the basis of racial classifications violates the Equal Protection and Due Process Clauses of the Fourteenth Amendment. For reasons which seem to us to reflect the central meaning of those constitutional commands, we conclude that these statutes cannot stand consistently with the Fourteenth Amendment.

In June 1958, two residents of Virginia, Mildred Jeter, a Negro woman, and Richard Loving, a white man, were married in the District of Columbia pursuant to its laws. Shortly after their marriage, the Lovings returned to Virginia. [They were indicted for] violating Virginia's ban on interracial marriages . . ., pleaded guilty [and] were sentenced to one year in jail; however, the trial judge suspended the sentence for a period of 25 years on the condition that the Lovings leave the State and not return to Virginia together for 25 years. . . . After their convictions, the Lovings took up residence in the District of Columbia. On November 6, 1963, they filed a motion in the state trial court to vacate the judgment and set aside the sentence on the ground that the statutes which they had violated were repugnant to the Fourteenth Amendment. [The trial court denied that motion and the highest state court, after modifying the sentence, "affirmed the convictions."]

Virginia is now one of 16 States which prohibit and punish marriages on the basis of racial classifications.[1] Penalties for miscegenation arose as an incident to slavery and have been common in Virginia since the colonial period. The present statutory scheme dates from the adoption of the Racial Integrity Act of 1924, passed during the period of extreme nativism which followed the end of the First World War.

I.

In upholding the constitutionality of these provisions in the decision below, the Supreme Court of Appeals of Virginia referred to its 1955 decision

---

[1] . . . Over the past 15 years, 14 States have repealed laws outlawing interracial marriages: Arizona, California, Colorado, Idaho, Indiana, Maryland, Montana, Nebraska, Nevada, North Dakota, Oregon, South Dakota, Utah, and Wyoming. The first state court to recognize that miscegenation statutes violate the Equal Protection Clause was the Supreme Court of California. Perez v. Sharp, 32 Cal.2d 711, 198 P.2d 17 (1948). [Footnote by the Court.]

in Naim v. Naim, 197 Va. 80, 87 S.E.2d 749 [see chap. 2, p. 149, supra, on the Supreme Court's dismissal of the Naim appeal], as stating the reasons supporting the validity of these laws. In Naim, the state court concluded that the State's legitimate purposes were "to preserve the racial integrity of its citizens," and to prevent "the corruption of blood," "a mongrel breed of citizens," and "the obliteration of racial pride," obviously an endorsement of the doctrine of White Supremacy. The court also reasoned that marriage has traditionally been subject to state regulation without federal intervention . . .

[T]he State does not contend in its argument before this Court that its powers to regulate marriage are unlimited notwithstanding the commands of the Fourteenth Amendment. Nor could it do so in light of Meyer v. Nebraska, 262 U.S. 390 (1923), and Skinner v. Oklahoma, 316 U.S. 535 (1942). Instead, the State argues that the meaning of the Equal Protection Clause, as illuminated by the statements of the Framers, is only that state penal laws containing an interracial element as part of the definition of the offense must apply equally to whites and Negroes in the sense that members of each race are punished to the same degree. Thus, the State contends that, because its miscegenation statutes punish equally both the white and the Negro participants in an interracial marriage, these statutes, despite their reliance on racial classifications, do not constitute an invidious discrimination based upon race. The second argument advanced by the State assumes the validity of its equal application theory. The argument is that, if the Equal Protection Clause does not outlaw miscegenation statutes because of their reliance on racial classifications, the question of constitutionality would thus become whether there was any rational basis for a State to treat interracial marriages differently from other marriages. On this question, the State argues, the scientific evidence is substantially in doubt and, consequently, this Court should defer to the wisdom of the state legislature in adopting its policy of discouraging interracial marriages.

Because we reject the notion that the mere "equal application" of a statute containing racial classifications is enough to remove the classifications from the Fourteenth Amendment's proscription of all invidious racial discriminations, we do not accept the State's contention that these statutes should be upheld if there is any possible basis for concluding that they serve a rational purpose. The mere fact of equal application does not mean that our analysis of these statutes should follow the approach we have taken in cases involving no racial discrimination where the Equal Protection Clause has been arrayed against a statute discriminating between the kinds of advertising which may be displayed on trucks in New York City, Railway Express Agency, Inc. v. New York, 336 U.S. 106 (1949), or an exemption in Ohio's ad valorem tax for merchandise owned by a nonresident in a storage warehouse, Allied Stores of Ohio, Inc. v. Bowers, 358 U.S. 522 (1959). In these cases, involving distinctions not drawn according to race, the Court has merely asked whether there is any rational foundation for the discriminations, and has deferred to the wisdom of the state legislatures. In the case at bar, however, we deal with statutes containing racial classifications, and the fact of equal application does not immunize the statute from the very heavy burden of justification which the Fourteenth Amendment has traditionally required of state statutes drawn according to race.

The State argues that statements in the Thirty-ninth Congress about the time of the passage of the Fourteenth Amendment indicate that the Framers did not intend the Amendment to make unconstitutional state miscegenation laws. . . . As for the various statements directly concerning the Fourteenth Amendment, we have said in connection with a related problem, that although these historical sources "cast some light" they are not sufficient to resolve the problem; "[a]t best, they are inconclusive. . . ." Brown v. Board of Education, 347 U.S. 483, 489 (1954). We have rejected the proposition that the debates in the Thirty-ninth Congress or in the state legislatures which ratified the Fourteenth Amendment supported the theory advanced by the State, that the requirement of equal protection of the laws is satisfied by penal laws defining offenses based on racial classifications so long as white and Negro participants in the offense were similarly punished. McLaughlin v. Florida, 379 U.S. 184 (1964).

The State finds support for its "equal application" theory in the decision of the Court in Pace v. Alabama, 106 U.S. 583 (1883). In that case, the Court upheld a conviction under an Alabama statute forbidding adultery or fornication between a white person and a Negro which imposed a greater penalty than that of a statute proscribing similar conduct by members of the same race. The Court reasoned that the statute could not be said to discriminate against Negroes because the punishment for each participant in the offense was the same. However, as recently as the 1964 Term, in rejecting the reasoning of that case, we stated "Pace represents a limited view of the Equal Protection Clause which has not withstood analysis in the subsequent decisions of this Court." McLaughlin v. Florida.[2] As we there demonstrated, the Equal Protection Clause requires the consideration of whether the classifications drawn by any statute constitute an arbitrary and invidious discrimination. The clear and central purpose of the Fourteenth Amendment was to eliminate all official state sources of invidious racial discrimination in the States. Slaughter-House Cases, 16 Wall. 36, 71 (1873); Strauder v. West Virginia,

---

2. McLaughlin v. Florida, 379 U.S. 184 (1964), invalidated a criminal statute prohibiting cohabitation by interracial unmarried couples. Justice White's majority opinion emphasized: "Judicial inquiry under [equal protection], does not end with a showing of equal application among the members of the class defined by the legislation. The courts must reach and determine the question whether the classifications drawn in a statute are reasonable in light of its purpose . . . . We deal here with a racial classification. . . . Our inquiry, therefore, is whether there clearly appears in the relevant materials some overriding statutory purpose requiring the proscription of the specified conduct when engaged in by a white person and a Negro, but not otherwise. Without such justification the racial classification [here] is reduced to an invidious discrimination forbidden by the Equal Protection Clause."

Justice Stewart's concurrence, joined by Justice Douglas, stated: "[T]he Court

implies that a criminal law of the kind here involved might be constitutionally valid if a State could show 'some overriding statutory purpose.' This is an implication in which I cannot join, because I cannot conceive of a valid legislative purpose under our Constitution for a state law which makes the color of a person's skin the test of whether his conduct is a criminal offense. . . . There might be limited room under the Equal Protection Clause for a civil law requiring the keeping of racially segregated public records for statistical or other valid public purposes. Cf. Tancil v. Woolls, 379 U.S. 19 [p. 1416, infra]. But we deal here with a criminal law which imposes criminal punishment. And I think it is simply not possible for a state law to be valid under our Constitution which makes the criminality of an act depend upon the race of the actor. Discrimination of that kind is invidious per se."

100 U.S. 303, 307–308 (1880); . . . Burton v. Wilmington Parking Authority, 365 U.S. 715 (1961).

There can be no question but that Virginia's miscegenation statutes rest solely upon distinctions drawn according to race. The statutes proscribe generally accepted conduct if engaged in by members of different races. Over the years, this Court has consistently repudiated "[d]istinctions between citizens solely because of their ancestry" as being "odious to a free people whose institutions are founded upon the doctrine of equality." Hirabayashi v. United States, 320 U.S. 81, 100 (1943). At the very least, the Equal Protection Clause demands that racial classifications, especially suspect in criminal statutes, be subjected to the "most rigid scrutiny," Korematsu v. United States, 323 U.S. 214, 216 (1944), and, if they are ever to be upheld, they must be shown to be necessary to the accomplishment of some permissible state objective, independent of the racial discrimination which it was the object of the Fourteenth Amendment to eliminate. Indeed, two members of this Court have already stated that they "cannot conceive of a valid legislative purpose . . . which makes the color of a person's skin the test of whether his conduct is a criminal offense." McLaughlin v. Florida (Stewart, J., joined by Douglas, J., concurring).

There is patently no legitimate overriding purpose independent of invidious racial discrimination which justifies this classification. The fact that Virginia prohibits only interracial marriages involving white persons demonstrates that the racial classifications must stand on their own justification, as measures designed to maintain White Supremacy.[3] We have consistently denied the constitutionality of measures which restrict the rights of citizens on account of race. There can be no doubt that restricting the freedom to marry solely because of racial classifications violates the central meaning of the Equal Protection Clause.

II.

These statutes also deprive the Lovings of liberty without due process of law in violation of the Due Process Clause of the Fourteenth Amendment. The freedom to marry has long been recognized as one of the vital personal rights essential to the orderly pursuit of happiness by free men.

Marriage is one of the "basic civil rights of man," fundamental to our very existence and survival. [Skinner v. Oklahoma.] To deny this fundamental freedom on so unsupportable a basis as the racial classifications embodied in these statutes, classifications so directly subversive of the principle of equality at the heart of the Fourteenth Amendment, is surely to deprive all the State's citizens of liberty without due process of law. The Fourteenth Amendment requires that the freedom of choice to marry not be restricted by

---

3. Appellants point out that the State's concern in these statutes, as expressed in the words of the 1924 Act's title, "An Act to Preserve Racial Integrity," extends only to the integrity of the white race. While Virgina prohibits whites from marrying any nonwhite (subject to the exception for the descendants of Pocahontas), Negroes, Orientals, and any other racial class may intermarry without statutory interference. Appellants contend that this distinction renders Virginia's miscegenation statutes arbitrary and unreasonable even assuming the constitutional validity of an official purpose to preserve "racial integrity." We need not reach this contention because we find the racial classifications in these statutes repugnant to the Fourteenth Amendment, even assuming an even-handed state purpose to protect the "integrity" of all races. [Footnote by the Court.]

invidious racial discriminations. Under our Constitution, the freedom to marry, or not marry, a person of another race resides with the individual and cannot be infringed by the State.

Reversed.

Mr. Justice STEWART, concurring.

I have previously expressed the belief that "it is simply not possible for a state law to be valid under our Constitution which makes the criminality of an act depend upon the race of the actor." McLaughlin v. Florida, 379 U.S. 184, 198 (concurring opinion). Because I adhere to that belief, I concur in the judgment of the Court.

COLORBLINDNESS, RACE CONSCIOUSNESS, AND BENIGN PURPOSES: WHEN ARE RACIAL CRITERIA JUSTIFIABLE?

Introduction. "Our Constitution is color-blind," insisted the first Justice Harlan's dissent in Plessy v. Ferguson (p. 1420 infra). Over the years, some Justices have found in equal protection a per se rule invalidating all governmental distinctions between individuals because of their race. And some commentators have suggested that such a total ban is the most persuasive justification for a number of Court decisions—e. g., the invalidations of racial segregation in public facilities generally (p. 1426, infra) after the 1954 decision in the school segregation case. But, as the preceding cases illustrate, the Court has not stated so comprehensive a prohibition; rather, racial classifications are "suspect," must be subjected to "the most rigid scrutiny," and bear a "very heavy burden of justification."

Consider, in light of the foregoing cases and the materials which follow, when racial criteria are and should be constitutionally permissible. What justification is strong enough? Is "rigid scrutiny" required when the aim or effect is to *help* the minority race? Is benign purpose a "justification" for racial classifications? What if the purpose is unclear? What if members of the minority group disagree about the purpose and effect of a "benign" program?

1. *Official records.* In per curiam orders in Tancil v. Woolls and Virginia Board of Elections v. Hamm, 379 U.S. 19 (1964), the Court affirmed decisions (a) invalidating Virginia laws requiring separated lists of whites and Negroes in voting, tax and property records, but (b) sustaining a Virginia law requiring that every divorce decree indicate the race of the husband and wife. The District Judge stated that "the designation of race . . . may in certain records serve a useful purpose"—for example, "for identification or statistical use." He found no such purpose in the separate records law: it served "no other purpose than to classify and distinguish official records on the basis of race." The divorce law requirement, on the other hand, aided "vital statistics."

2. *Identification of political candidates.* Anderson v. Martin, 375 U.S. 399 (1964), invalidated a statute requiring that every candidate's race appear on the ballot. The Court concluded that the law placed the "power of the State behind a racial classification that induces racial prejudice at the polls." What if it were argued that racial designations helped elect more

minority candidates—that, while making most voters more race-conscious and inducing majority race voters to reject minority candidates, it induced minority voters to vote and elect some candidates of their own race? Would that argument satisfy the "very heavy burden of justification"?

3. *Racial classifications and lawmaking processes: Hunter v. Erickson.* Hunter v. Erickson, 393 U.S. 385 (1969), invalidated an Akron City Charter amendment adopted by popular vote after the City Council had enacted a fair housing ordinance. The Charter amendment provided that any Council ordinance regulating real property transactions "on the basis of race, color, religion, national origin or ancestry must first be approved by a majority of the electors voting on the question at a regular or general election before said ordinance shall be effective." Justice White's majority opinion emphasized the amendment's impact in creating a special obstacle to minorities seeking favorable legislation as well as the suspect and inadequately justified racial classification on the face of the provision, "treating racial housing matters differently from other racial and housing matters."

In exploring the impact of the amendment, the Court noted that popular referendum approval of City Council ordinances was mandatory in only a few cases under the new Akron scheme. Most City Council measures were not followed by referenda: under the general provisions for a popular vote, a referendum ensued only if 10% of the electors so requested. But ordinances subject to the amendment, including those seeking to ban racial bias, had *always* to run the gauntlet of a referendum. "It is true that the section draws no distinctions among racial and religious groups. Negroes and whites, Jews and Catholics are all subject to the same requirements if there is housing discrimination against them which they wish to end." Nevertheless, the amendment "disadvantages those who would benefit from laws barring racial, religious, or ancestral discriminations as against those who would bar other discriminations or who would otherwise regulate the real estate market in their favor. The automatic referendum system does not reach housing discrimination on sexual or political grounds, or against those with children or dogs, nor does it affect tenants seeking more heat or better maintenance from landlords, nor those seeking rent control, urban renewal, public housing, or new building codes. Moreover, although the law on its face treats Negro and white, Jew and gentile in an identical manner, the reality is that the law's impact falls on the minority. The majority needs no protection against discrimination and if it did, a referendum might be bothersome but no more than that. Like the law requiring specification of candidates' race on the ballot" [see note 2, supra], the amendment "places special burdens on racial minorities within the governmental process."

The Court was "unimpressed" with the city's effort to justify the suspect racial classification. "The amendment was unnecessary either to implement a decision to go slowly" in the race relations area, "or to allow the people of Akron to participate in that decision," in view of the "perfectly reasonable" general referendum provisions. And "though Akron might have proceeded by majority vote at town meeting on all its municipal legislation, it has instead chosen a more complex system. Having done so, the State may no more disadvantage any particular group by making it more difficult to enact legislation in its behalf than it may dilute any person's vote or give any group a smaller representation than another of comparable size."

In a concurring opinion, Justice Harlan, joined by Justice Stewart, stressed that the charter amendment did not attempt to allocate governmental power on the basis of any general, neutral principle. The 10% referendum provision, by contrast, was valid, even though it might "occasionally operate to disadvantage Negro political interests. If a governmental institution is to be fair, one group cannot always be expected to win. If the Council's Fair Housing legislation were defeated at a referendum, Negroes would undoubtedly lose an important political battle, but they would not thereby be denied Equal Protection." But here, the amendment was "discriminatory on its face" by making it more difficult for certain minorities to achieve legislation, and the city had failed to sustain the "far heavier burden of justification" required for such a provision. Justice Black dissented.

4. *Public security as justification.* To what extent may arguments emphasizing national emergencies or local order justify racial ingredients in regulatory controls? Recall the Korematsu case, supra, and note Lee v. Washington, 390 U.S. 333 (1968), a per curiam approval of a federal court order holding unconstitutional Alabama statutes requiring racial segregation in prisons and jails and establishing a schedule for desegregation. The one paragraph affirmance noted Alabama's argument "that the specific orders directing desegregation of prisons and jails make no allowance for the necessities of prison security and discipline" and commented that "we do not so read" the District Court order, "which when read as a whole we find unexceptionable." A separate concurring paragraph, by Justices Black, Harlan, and Stewart, elaborated: "[W]e wish to make explicit [that] prison authorities have the right, acting in good faith and in particularized circumstances, to take into account racial tensions in maintaining security, discipline, and good order in prisons and jails. We are unwilling to assume that state or local prison authorities might mistakenly regard such an explicit pronouncement as evincing any dilution of this Court's firm commitment to the Fourteenth Amendment's prohibition of racial discrimination."

5. *Race consciousness and benign purposes.* May the state single out racial minorities for special treatment? Is "strict scrutiny" appropriate when the aim is to extend special help on racial lines in such areas as public welfare, employment, public housing, and education? Or is "mere rationality" enough?

Colorblindness has never been required when a state is under a duty to eliminate past de jure discriminations. (See the school desegregation materials, infra, p. 1429.) Are racial criteria "suspect" but "justified" when a state voluntarily moves to end de facto school segregation? Do preferential employment programs stand on a different footing? Benign quotas to promote integrated housing (note 7, infra)? See generally Kaplan, "Equal Justice in an Unequal World: Equality for the Negro—The Problem of Special Treatment," 61 Nw.U.L.Rev. 363 (1966); "Developments in the Law—Equal Protection," 82 Harv.L.Rev. 1065 (1969).

For decisions rejecting attacks on "color conscious" school integration programs, see Balaban v. Rubin, 14 N.Y.2d 193, cert. denied, 379 U.S. 881 (1964); School Comm. v. Board of Educ., 352 Mass. 693 (1967), appeal dismissed, 389 U.S. 572 (1968); and Tometz v. Board of Educ., 39 Ill.2d 593, 237 N.E.2d 498 (1968). Some of these cases apply a permissive, "mere rationality" standard. Is there adequate reason to abandon the "suspect" criteria degree of scrutiny in these cases? Because race is "relevant" here? Because the aim is to "help"? Should "relevance" and "helpfulness" go to the issue of whether justification is adequate rather than reducing the high justification requirement to a "reasonableness" one? Should courts ask whether nonracial alternatives exist?

Is a more permissive, reasonableness standard for benign uses of racial criteria supported by Katzenbach v. Morgan, 384 U.S. 1966 (chap. 6, p.545, supra), and McDonald v. Board of Election Commissioners, 394 U.S. 802 (1969) (chap. 14, p. 1015, supra)? Both of those cases involved nonracial voting issues; both applied permissive rather than strict review standards because the laws "extended" rather than "denied" rights, because "remedial" rather than "restrictive" measures were involved. Are those distinctions persuasive? Are they applicable to racial classifications?

6. *When is a racial classification "benign"?* Is judicial permissiveness toward benign programs (against a background of ordinarily strict scrutiny for racial criteria) questionable because of the ambiguity of the "benign" characterization and of the difficulties in assessing whether the challenged government action truly is "benign"? Can courts view integration programs that are clearly pro-integration in purpose and effect as "benign" even if some segments of the "benefited" minority group assert that separation is needed at least temporarily to develop the group's cohesiveness, power and pride? See "Developments in the Law," supra, at 1114, suggesting that evaluating the benefits of integration as against separatism is not a problem "susceptible of objective judicial resolution" and is "precisely the sort of judgment that should be left to the political process wherever possible," but warning about the "manifest possibilities of abuse": "A state program permitting or encouraging racial separatism could also be used to create a system of segregation." That comment accordingly seeks a middle course between permissive and strict review, emphasizing scrutiny to determine the actual "predominant purpose": the classification would be permissible if "truly benign"—i. e., is used in a program "designed to achieve an equal position in society for all races." Would that approach help with the judicial problems created, e. g., by the "divisions of opinion within the black community itself"? Do the segregation cases which follow commit the Court to adhering to integration as the only legitimate goal, and to opposing separateness as an ideal, whether it is called "separatism" or "segregation"?

7. *Benign quotas.* What if the doubts about the benign quality of a program arise not because of doubts regarding general benefit to the minority but because of harm to specific members of the group? That problem has been discussed most commonly in connection with quota and "tipping point" programs designed to promote integrated housing: e. g., may racial exclusion of a Negro from a housing project be justified on the ground that the exclusion is pursuant to a quota designed to provide integrated housing for Negroes generally? Cf. Hughes v. Superior Court, 339 U.S. 460 (1950) (permitting enforcement of state policy against picketing to induce employment of workers in proportion to racial origin of customers). Do the harsh impacts of such quotas, precluding individuals solely because of race, and the risks of abuse of quota systems, compel their rejection? Should they be permitted if, after strict scrutiny, the Court is satisfied that no adequate alternative means exist? See generally Bittker, "The Case of the Checker-Board Ordinance: An Experiment in Race Relations," 71 Yale L.J. 1387 (1962), and Navasky, "The Benevolent Housing Quota," 6 Howard L.J. 30 (1960).

B. RACIAL SEGREGATION

THE "SEPARATE BUT EQUAL" DOCTRINE

1. *Plessy v. Ferguson.* In Plessy v. Ferguson, 163 U.S. 537 (1896), the Court sustained a Louisiana statute of 1890 requiring "equal but separate accommodations" for white and Negro railway passengers. Justice Brown stated: "The object of the [14th] Amendment was undoubtedly to enforce the absolute equality of the two races before the law, but in the nature of things it could not have been intended to abolish distinctions based upon color, or to enforce social, as distinguished from political equality, or a commingling of the two races upon terms unsatisfactory to either. Laws permitting, and even requiring, their separation in places where they are liable to be brought into contact do not necessarily imply the inferiority of either race to the other, and have been generally, if not universally, recognized as within the competency of the state legislatures in the exercise of their police power. The most common instance of this is connected with the establishment of separate schools for white and colored children, which has been held to be a valid exercise of the legislative power even by courts of States where the political rights of the colored race have been longest and most earnestly enforced. [T]he case reduces itself to the question whether the statute of Louisiana is a reasonable regulation, and with respect to this there must necessarily be a large discretion on the part of the legislature. In determining the question of reasonableness it is at liberty to act with reference to the established usages, customs and traditions of the people, and with a view to the promotion of their comfort, and the preservation of the public peace and good order. Gauged by this standard, we cannot say that [the law] is unreasonable, or more obnoxious to the Fourteenth Amendment than the acts of Congress requiring separate schools for colored children in the District of Columbia, the constitutionality of which does not seem to have been questioned, or the corresponding acts of state legislatures.

"We consider the underlying fallacy of the plaintiff's argument to consist in the assumption that the enforced separation of the two races stamps the colored race with a badge of inferiority. If this be so, it is not by reason of anything found in the act, but solely because the colored race chooses to put that construction upon it. . . . The argument also assumes that social prejudices may be overcome by legislation, and that equal rights cannot be secured to the negro except by an enforced commingling of the two races. We cannot accept this proposition. If the two races are to meet upon terms of social equality, it must be the result of natural affinities, a mutual appreciation of each other's merits and a voluntary consent of individuals. . . . Legislation is powerless to eradicate racial instincts or to abolish distinctions based upon physical differences, and the attempt to do so can only result in accentuating the difficulties of the present situation. If the civil and political rights of both races be equal one cannot be inferior to the other civilly or politically. If one race be inferior to the other socially, the Constitution of the United States cannot put them upon the same plane." *

---

* See also Gong Lum v. Rice, 275 U.S. 78 (1927), involving the power of the state to classify children of "a Chinese   citizen of the United States" as among the colored races and exclude them from public schools maintained for

Mr. Justice Harlan dissented: "It was said in argument that the statute of Louisiana does not discriminate against either race, but prescribes a rule applicable alike to white and colored citizens. But this argument does not meet the difficulty. Every one knows that [it] had its origin in the purpose, not so much to exclude white persons from railroad cars occupied by blacks, as to exclude colored people from coaches occupied by or assigned to white persons. . . . The thing to accomplish was, under the guise of giving equal accommodation for whites and blacks, to compel the latter to keep to themselves while travelling in railroad passenger coaches. No one would be so wanting in candor as to assert the contrary. The fundamental objection, therefore, to the statute is that it interferes with the personal freedom of citizens. . . .

"The white race deems itself to be the dominant race in this country. And so it is, in prestige, in achievements, in education, in wealth and in power. So, I doubt not, it will continue to be for all time, if it remains true to its great heritage and holds fast to the principles of constitutional liberty. But in view of the Constitution, in the eye of the law, there is in this country no superior, dominant, ruling class of citizens. There is no caste here. Our Constitution is color-blind, and neither knows nor tolerates classes among citizens. . . . It is, therefore, to be regretted that this high tribunal, the final expositor of the fundamental law of the land, has reached the conclusion that it is competent for a State to regulate the enjoyment by citizens of their civil rights solely upon the basis of race. In my opinion, the judgment this day rendered will, in time, prove to be quite as pernicious as the decision made by this tribunal in the Dred Scott case. . . . Sixty millions of whites are in no danger from the presence here of eight millions of blacks. The destinies of the two races, in this country, are indissolubly linked together, and the interests of both require that the common government of all shall not permit the seeds of race hate to be planted under the sanction of law. What can more certainly arouse race hate, what more certainly create and perpetuate a feeling of distrust between these races, than state enactments, which, in fact, proceed on the ground that colored citizens are so inferior and degraded that they cannot be allowed to sit in public coaches occupied by white citizens? That, as all will admit, is the real meaning of such legislation as was enacted in Louisiana.

"The arbitrary separation of citizens, on the basis of race, while they are on a public highway, is a badge of servitude wholly inconsistent with the civil freedom and the equality before the law established by the Constitution. It cannot be justified upon any legal grounds. . . . The thin disguise of 'equal' accommodations for passengers in railroad coaches will not mislead anyone, nor atone for the wrong this day done."

white children. Were this a new question, the Court stated, it would call for very full argument and consideration, but "it is the same question which has been many times decided to be within the constitutional power of the state legislature to settle without intervention of the federal courts under the Federal Constitution." After citing, inter alia, Plessy v. Ferguson, the Court added: "Most of the cases arose, it is true, over the establishment of separate schools as between white pupils and black pupils, but we cannot think that the question is any different . . . ." The state power was sustained. Note also Cumming v. County Board of Education, 175 U.S. 528 (1899), mentioned together with Gong Lum in the next principal case.

2. *The Gaines case.* Gaines, a Negro, was refused admission to the University of Missouri School of Law because of his race. He unsuccessfully sought mandamus in the state courts to obtain admission. The State's defense was that a Negro law school was planned and that, pending its establishment, Missouri would pay petitioner's tuition in an out-of-state school. The Supreme Court reversed. Missouri ex rel. Gaines v. Canada, 305 U.S. 337 (1937). Chief Justice Hughes concluded that the State must furnish petitioner "within its borders facilities for legal education substantially equal to those which the State there offered for persons of the white race, whether or not other negroes sought the same opportunity." Justices McReynolds and Butler dissented. [The Gaines case was the first of the "modern" school segregation cases. Subsequent decisions dealing with segregated facilities in graduate education are described in the Court's opinion in the next principal case.]

BROWN v. BOARD OF EDUCATION
347 U.S. 483, 74 S.Ct. 686, 98 L.Ed. 873 (1954).

Appeal from the United States District Court for the District of Kansas.

Mr. Chief Justice WARREN delivered the opinion of the Court.

These cases come to us from the States of Kansas, South Carolina, Virginia, and Delaware. They are premised on different facts and different local conditions, but a common legal question justifies their consideration together in this consolidated opinion.

In each of the cases, minors of the Negro race, through their legal representatives, seek the aid of the courts in obtaining admission to the public schools of their community on a nonsegregated basis. In each instance, they had been denied admission to schools attended by white children under laws requiring or permitting segregation according to race. This segregation was alleged to deprive the plaintiffs of the equal protection of the laws under the Fourteenth Amendment. In each of the cases [the court below relied on] the so-called "separate but equal" doctrine announced by this Court in Plessy v. Ferguson, 163 U.S. 537. Under that doctrine, equality of treatment is accorded when the races are provided substantially equal facilities, even though these facilities be separate. . . .

The plaintiffs contend that segregated public schools are not "equal" and cannot be made "equal," and that hence they are deprived of the equal protection of the laws. Because of the obvious importance of the question presented, the Court took jurisdiction. Argument was heard in the 1952 Term, and reargument was heard this Term on certain questions propounded by the Court.

Reargument was largely devoted to the circumstances surrounding the adoption of the Fourteenth Amendment in 1868. It covered exhaustively consideration of the Amendment in Congress, ratification by the states, then existing practices in racial segregation, and the views of proponents and opponents of the Amendment. This discussion and our own investigation convince us that, although these sources cast some light, it is not enough to resolve the problem with which we are faced. At best, they are inconclusive. The most avid proponents of the post-war Amendments undoubtedly intended them to remove all legal distinctions among "all persons born or naturalized in the United States." Their opponents, just as certainly, were antagonistic to both the letter and the spirit of the Amendments and wished them to have the most limited effect. What others in Congress and the state legislatures had in mind cannot be determined with any degree of certainty.

An additional reason for the inconclusive nature of the Amendment's history, with respect to segregated schools, is the status of public education at that time. In the South, the movement toward free common schools, supported by general taxation, had not yet taken hold. Education of white children was largely in the hands of private groups. Education of Negroes was almost nonexistent, and practically all of the race were illiterate. In fact, any education of Negroes was forbidden by law in some states. Today, in contrast, many Negroes have achieved outstanding success in the arts and sciences as well as in the business and professional world. It is true that public education had already advanced further in the North, but the effect of the Amendment on Northern States was generally ignored in the congressional debates. Even in the North, the conditions of public education did not approximate those existing today. The curriculum was usually rudimentary; ungraded schools were common in rural areas; the school term was but three months a year in many states; and compulsory school attendance was virtually unknown. As a consequence, it is not surprising that there should be so little in the history of the Fourteenth Amendment relating to its intended effect on public education.

In the first cases in this Court construing the Fourteenth Amendment, decided shortly after its adoption, the Court interpreted it as proscribing all state-imposed discriminations against the Negro race.[1] The doctrine of "separate but equal" did not make its appearance in this Court until 1896 in the case of Plessy v. Ferguson, supra, involving not education but transportation.[2] American courts have since labored with the doctrine for over half a century. In this Court, there have been six cases involving the "separate but equal" doctrine in the field of public education. In Cumming v. County Board of Education, 175 U.S. 528, and Gong Lum v. Rice, 275 U.S. 78, the validity of the doctrine itself was not challenged.[3] In more recent cases, all on the graduate school level, inequality was found in that specific benefits enjoyed by white students were denied to Negro students of the same educational qualifications.

1. Slaughter-House Cases, 16 Wall. 36, 67–72 (1873); Strauder v. West Virginia, 100 U.S. 303, 307–308 (1880) . . . . . See also Virginia v. Rives, 100 U.S. 313, 318 (1880); Ex parte Virginia, 100 U.S. 339, 344–345 (1880). [All footnotes by the Court.]

2. The doctrine apparently originated in Roberts v. City of Boston, 59 Mass. 198, 206 (1849), upholding school segregation against attack as being violative of a state constitutional guarantee of equality. Segregation in Boston public schools was eliminated in 1855. Mass. Acts 1855, c. 256. But elsewhere in the North segregation in public education has persisted until recent years. It is apparent that such segregation has long been a nationwide problem, not merely one of sectional concern. [Footnote by the Court.]

3. In the Cumming case, Negro taxpayers sought an injunction requiring the defendant school board to discontinue the operation of a high school for white children until the board resumed operation of a high school for Negro children. Similarly, in the Gong Lum case, the plaintiff, a child of Chinese descent, contended only that state authorities had misapplied the doctrine by classifying him with Negro children and requiring him to attend a Negro school. [Footnote by the Court.]

Missouri ex rel. Gaines v. Canada, 305 U.S. 337; Sipuel v. Oklahoma, 332 U.S. 631; Sweatt v. Painter, 339 U.S. 629; McLaurin v. Oklahoma State Regents, 339 U.S. 637. In none of these cases was it necessary to reexamine the doctrine to grant relief to the Negro plaintiff. And in Sweatt v. Painter, supra, the Court expressly reserved decision on the question whether Plessy v. Ferguson should be held inapplicable to public education.

In the instant cases, that question is directly presented. Here, unlike Sweatt v. Painter, there are findings below that the Negro and white schools involved have been equalized or are being equalized, with respect to buildings, curricula, qualifications and salaries of teachers, and other "tangible" factors. Our decision, therefore, cannot turn on merely a comparison of these tangible factors in the Negro and white schools involved in each of the cases. We must look instead to the effect of segregation itself on public education.

In approaching this problem, we cannot turn the clock back to 1868 when the Amendment was adopted, or even to 1896 when Plessy v. Ferguson was written. We must consider public education in the light of its full development and its present place in American life throughout the Nation. Only in this way can it be determined if segregation in public schools deprives these plaintiffs of the equal protection of the laws.

Today, education is perhaps the most important function of state and local governments. Compulsory school attendance laws and the great expenditures for education both demonstrate our recognition of the importance of education to our democratic society. It is required in the performance of our most basic public responsibilities, even service in the armed forces. It is the very foundation of good citizenship. Today it is a principal instrument in awakening the child to cultural values, in preparing him for later professional training, and in helping him to adjust normally to his environment. In these days, it is doubtful that any child may reasonably be expected to succeed in life if he is denied the opportunity of an education. Such an opportunity, where the state has undertaken to provide it, is a right which must be made available to all on equal terms.

We come then to the question presented: Does segregation of children in public schools solely on the basis of race, even though the physical facilities and other "tangible" factors may be equal, deprive the children of the minority group of equal educational opportunities? We believe that it does.

In Sweatt v. Painter, supra, in finding that a segregated law school for Negroes could not provide them equal educational opportunities, this Court relied in large part on "those qualities which are incapable of objective measurement but which make for greatness in a law school." In McLaurin v. Oklahoma State Regents, supra, the Court in requiring that a Negro admitted to a white graduate school be treated like all other students, again resorted to intangible considerations: ".   .   . his ability to study, to engage in discussions and exchange views with other students, and, in general, to learn his profession." Such considerations apply with added force to children in grade and high schools. To separate them from others of similar age and qualifications solely because of their race generates a feeling of inferiority as to their status in the community that may affect their hearts and minds in a way unlikely ever to be undone. The effect of this separation on their educational opportunities was well stated by a finding in the Kansas case by a court which nevertheless felt compelled to rule against the Negro plaintiffs:

"Segregation of white and colored children in public schools has a detrimental effect upon the colored children. The impact is greater when it has the sanction of the law; for the policy of separating the races is usually interpreted as denoting the inferiority of the Negro group. A sense of inferiority affects the motivation of a child to learn. Segregation with the sanction of law, therefore, has a tendency to retard the educational and mental development of Negro children and to deprive them of some of the benefits they would receive in a racially integrated school system." Whatever may have been the extent of psychological knowledge at the time of Plessy v. Ferguson, this finding is amply supported by modern authority.[4] Any language in Plessy v. Ferguson contrary to this finding is rejected.

We conclude that in the field of public education the doctrine of "separate but equal" has no place. Separate educational facilities are inherently unequal. Therefore, we hold that the plaintiffs and others similarly situated for whom the actions have been brought are, by reason of the segregation complained of, deprived of the equal protection of the laws guaranteed by the Fourteenth Amendment. This disposition makes unnecessary any discussion whether such segregation also violates the Due Process Clause of the Fourteenth Amendment.

Because these are class actions, because of the wide applicability of this decision, and because of the great variety of local conditions, the formulation of decrees in these cases presents problems of considerable complexity. On reargument, the consideration of appropriate relief was necessarily subordinated to the primary question—the constitutionality of segregation in public education. We have now announced that such segregation is a denial of the equal protection of the laws. In order that we may have the full assistance of the parties in formulating decrees, the cases will be restored to the docket, and the parties are requested to present further argument on Questions 4 and 5 previously propounded by the Court for the reargument of this Term. [The questions appear in the footnote to the second Brown case, infra.] The Attorney General of the United States is again invited to participate. The Attorneys General of the states requiring or permitting segregation in public education will also be permitted to appear as *amici curiae* upon request to do so by September 15, 1954, and submission of briefs by October 1, 1954.

It is so ordered.*

---

4. K. B. Clark, Effect of Prejudice and Discrimination on Personality Development (Midcentury White House Conference on Children and Youth) (1950); Witmer and Kotinsky, Personality in the Making (1952), c. VI; Deutscher and Chein, The Psychological Effects of Enforced Segregation: A Survey of Social Science Opinion, 26 J.Psychol. 259 (1948); Chein, What are the Psychological Effects of Segregation Under Conditions of Equal Facilities?, 3 Int.J.Opinion and Attitude Res. 229 (1949); Brameld, Educational Costs, in Discrimination and National Welfare (McIver, ed., 1949), 44–48; Frazier,

The Negro in the United States (1949), 674–681. And see generally Myrdal, An American Dilemma (1944).

* For a sampling of the extensive commentary on this opinion, see the articles reprinted in Selected Essays 1938–62 (1963), 463, 819, 844: Wechsler, "Toward Neutral Principles of Constitutional Law," 73 Harv.L.Rev. 1 (1959); Pollak, "Racial Discrimination and Judicial Integrity: A Reply to Professor Wechsler," 108 U.Pa.L. Rev. 1 (1959); C. L. Black, Jr., "The Lawfulness of the Segregation Decisions," 69 Yale L.J. 421 (1960). See

BOLLING v. SHARPE, 347 U.S. 497 (1954): In this case, decided on the same day as Brown, the Court held that racial segregation in the District of Columbia public schools violated the due process clause of the Fifth Amendment. Chief Justice Warren's opinion stated: "The Fifth Amendment . . . . does not contain an equal protection clause . . . .. But the concepts of equal protection and due process, both stemming from our American ideal of fairness, are not mutually exclusive. The 'equal protection of the laws' is a more explicit safeguard of prohibited unfairness than 'due process of law,' and, therefore, we do not imply that the two are always interchangeable phrases. But, as this Court has recognized, discrimination may be so unjustifiable as to be violative of due process. Classifications based solely upon race must be scrutinized with particular care, since they are contrary to our traditions and hence constitutionally suspect. . . .

"Although the Court has not assumed to define 'liberty' with any great precision, that term is not confined to mere freedom from bodily restraint. Liberty under law extends to the full range of conduct which the individual is free to pursue, and it cannot be restricted except for a proper governmental objective. Segregation in public education is not reasonably related to any proper governmental objective, and thus it imposes on Negro children of the District of Columbia a burden that constitutes an arbitrary deprivation of their liberty in violation of the Due Process Clause. In view of our decision that the Constitution prohibits the states from maintaining racially segregated public schools, it would be unthinkable that the same Constitution would impose a lesser duty on the Federal Government."

SEGREGATION AFTER BROWN

1. *Legally compelled segregation in other public facilities.* After the 1954 decision in Brown v. Board of Education, the Court found segregation unconstitutional in other public facilities as well. Despite the emphasis on the school context in Brown, the results in the later cases were reached in curt per curiam orders simply citing Brown. See, e. g., Mayor and City Council of Baltimore v. Dawson, 350 U.S. 877 (1955) (beaches); Gayle v. Browder, 352 U.S. 903 (1956) (buses); Holmes v. City of Atlanta, 350 U.S. 879 (1955) (golf courses); New Orleans City Park Imp. Ass'n v. Detiege, 358 U.S. 54 (1958) (parks). Cf. Turner v. City of Memphis, 369 U.S. 350 (1962). In Johnson v. Virginia, 373 U.S. 61, 62 (1963), petitioner had been convicted of contempt for refusal to comply with a state judge's order to move to a section of a courtroom reserved for Negroes. In reversing, the Supreme Court said: "Such a conviction cannot stand, for it is no longer open to question that a State may not constitutionally require segregation of public facilities." See also Lee v. Washington, 390 U.S. 333 (1968), prohibiting segregated prison facilities, noted at p. 1418, supra; and recall the comments on "separatism" for "benign" purposes, p. 1418, supra.

also Bickel, "The Original Understanding and the Segregation Decision," 69 Harv.L.Rev. 1 (1955), Selected Essays 1938–62 (1963), 853.

For comments on the social science evidence in Brown, see Cahn, "Jurispru-

dence," 30 N.Y.U.L.Rev. 150 (1955); Clark, "The Desegregation Cases," 5 Vill.L.Rev. 224 (1959); and Stell v. Chatham Bd. of Ed., 220 F.Supp. 667 (S.D.Ga.1963).

2. *The Brown rationale and de facto segregation.* Can Brown support a claim that de facto—as well as legally compelled—segregation in public schools is unconstitutional? Does its rationale contain support for imposing an affirmative duty on school officials to achieve racial balance where schools are segregated because of residential patterns not compelled by law? [Compare the question of duty to take affirmative steps to undo the effects of prior official discrimination, p. 1433 infra; and recall the problems, at p. 1418, supra, regarding the permissibility of using "suspect" racial criteria in voluntary efforts to overcome de facto segregation through programs such as building placement and busing.] See generally Fiss, "Racial Imbalance in the Public Schools: The Constitutional Concepts," 78 Harv.L.Rev. 564 (1965), and Kaplan, "Segregation Litigation and the Schools," 58 Nw.U.L.Rev. 1, 157 (1963). Note the unsuccessful efforts to challenge de facto segregation in Bell v. School City of Gary, 324 F.2d 209 (7th Cir. 1963), cert. denied, 377 U.S. 924 (1964), and Deal v. Cincinnati Board of Education 369 F.2d 55 (6th Cir.), cert. denied, 389 U.S. 847 (1967). Compare the extensive discussion of de facto segregation by Judge J. Skelly Wright in the District of Columbia school segregation case, Hobson v. Hansen, 269 F.Supp. 401 (D.D.C.1967), aff'd sub nom. Smuck v. Hobson, 408 F.2d 175 (D.C.Cir. 1969).

Note, moreover, the efforts to apply pressure to end de facto segregation in the North through executive and legislative action—partly in response to growing demands by the Court (see p. 1429, infra) that the South take immediate affirmative action to undo the impacts of past de jure segregation. See, e. g., the Senate debate on an amendment to a school aid bill (by Senator Stennis of Mississippi) which would state a policy of cutting off federal aid to segregated school districts "shall be applied uniformly in all regions of the United States . . . without regard to the origin or cause of such segregation." Senator Ribicoff of Connecticut, after criticizing the "monumental hypocrisy" of the North, supported the effort to treat de facto and de jure segregation alike; other Northern liberals countered with a proposal for a study of the impact of federal policies on equal educational opportunity and on segregation, "whatever the origin or cause of such segregation." See, e. g., the New York Times, Feb. 10 and 12, 1970, and 116 Cong.Rec. § 1461 (Feb. 9, 1970). The Senate adopted the Stennis amendment on February 18, 1970. The amendment was dropped from the bill as finally enacted by Congress on April 7, 1970. Note President Nixon's 8000-word statement on desegregation, designed to "reduce the prevailing confusion" (see the New York Times, March 25, 1970). It said of "the prevailing trend of judicial opinion": "There is a fundamental distinction between so-called 'de jure' and 'de facto' segregation: De jure segregation arises by law or by the deliberate act of school officials and is unconstitutional; de facto segregation results from residential housing patterns and does not violate the Constitution." Compare Bickel, "Desegregation—Where Do We Go from Here?" The New Republic, Feb. 7, 1970, p. 20, urging a "prudent judgment" to "distinguish between the requirements of disestablishment and plans that cannot work, or can work only, if at all, in special areas that inevitably feel victimized." [See generally Bickel, The Supreme Court and the Idea of Progress (1970).] Note also the materials on disestablishment of de jure segregation, p. 1429, infra.

BROWN v. BOARD OF EDUCATION

[IMPLEMENTATION DECISION]

349 U.S. 294, 75 S.Ct. 753, 99 L.Ed. 1083 (1955).

Mr. Chief Justice WARREN delivered the opinion of the Court.

These cases were decided on May 17, 1954. The opinions of that date, declaring the fundamental principle that racial discrimination in public education is unconstitutional, are incorporated herein by reference. All provisions of federal, state, or local law requiring or permitting such discrimination must yield to this principle. There remains for consideration the manner in which relief is to be accorded.

Because these cases arose under different local conditions and their disposition will involve a variety of local problems, we requested further argument on the question of relief.[1] In view of the nationwide importance of the decision, we invited the Attorney General of the United States and the Attorneys General of all states requiring or permitting racial discrimination in public education to present their views on that question. The parties, the United States, and the States of Florida, North Carolina, Arkansas, Oklahoma, Maryland, and Texas filed briefs and participated in the oral argument.

These presentations were informative and helpful to the Court in its consideration of the complexities arising from the transition to a system of public education freed of racial discrimination. The presentations also demonstrated that substantial steps to eliminate racial discrimination in public schools have already been taken, not only in some of the communities in which these cases arose, but in some of the states appearing as *amici curiae*, and in other states as well. Substantial progress has been made in the District of Columbia and in the communities in Kansas and Delaware involved in this litigation. The defendants in the cases coming to us from South Carolina and Virginia are awaiting the decision of this Court concerning relief.

Full implementation of these constitutional principles may require solution of varied local school problems. School authorities have the primary responsibility for elucidating, assessing, and solving these problems; courts will have to consider whether the action of school authorities constitutes good faith

---

1. Further argument was requested on the following questions, . . . previously propounded by the Court:

"4. Assuming it is decided that segregation in public schools violates the Fourteenth Amendment

"(a) would a decree necessarily follow providing that, within the limits set by normal geographic school districting, Negro children should forthwith be admitted to schools of their choice, or

"(b) may this Court, in the exercise of its equity powers, permit an effective gradual adjustment to be brought about from existing segregated systems to a system not based on color distinctions?

"5. On the assumption on which questions 4(a) and (b) are based, and assuming further that this Court will exercise its equity powers to the end described in question 4(b),

"(a) should this Court formulate detailed decrees in these cases;

"(b) if so, what specific issues should the decrees reach;

"(c) should this Court appoint a special master to hear evidence with a view to recommending specific terms for such decrees;

"(d) should this Court remand to the courts of first instance with directions to frame decrees in these cases, and if so what general directions should the decrees of this Court include and what procedures should the courts of first instance follow in arriving at the specific terms of more detailed decrees?" [Footnote by the Court.]

implementation of the governing constitutional principles. Because of their proximity to local conditions and the possible need for further hearings, the courts which originally heard these cases can best perform this judicial appraisal. Accordingly, we believe it appropriate to remand the cases to those courts.

In fashioning and effectuating the decrees, the courts will be guided by equitable principles. Traditionally, equity has been characterized by a practical flexibility in shaping its remedies and by a facility for adjusting and reconciling public and private needs. These cases call for the exercise of these traditional attributes of equity power. At stake is the personal interest of the plaintiffs in admission to public schools as soon as practicable on a nondiscriminatory basis. To effectuate this interest may call for elimination of a variety of obstacles in making the transition to school systems operated in accordance with the constitutional principles set forth in our May 17, 1954, decision. Courts of equity may properly take into account the public interest in the elimination of such obstacles in a systematic and effective manner. But it should go without saying that the vitality of these constitutional principles cannot be allowed to yield simply because of disagreement with them.

While giving weight to these public and private considerations, the courts will require that the defendants make a prompt and reasonable start toward full compliance with our May 17, 1954, ruling. Once such a start has been made, the courts may find that additional time is necessary to carry out the ruling in an effective manner. The burden rests upon the defendants to establish that such time is necessary in the public interest and is consistent with good faith compliance at the earliest practicable date. To that end, the courts may consider problems related to administration, arising from the physical condition of the school plant, the school transportation system, personnel, revision of school districts and attendance areas into compact units to achieve a system of determining admission to the public schools on a nonracial basis, and revision of local laws and regulations which may be necessary in solving the foregoing problems. They will also consider the adequacy of any plans the defendants may propose to meet these problems and to effectuate a transition to a racially nondiscriminatory school system. During this period of transition, the courts will retain jurisdiction of these cases.

The judgments below . . . are accordingly . . . remanded [to the lower courts] to take such proceedings and enter such orders and decrees consistent with this opinion as are necessary and proper to admit to public schools on a racially nondiscriminatory basis with all deliberate speed the parties to these cases. . . .

THE IMPLEMENTATION OF SCHOOL DESEGREGATION—FROM TERMINATING DUAL SCHOOL SYSTEMS "WITH ALL DELIBERATE SPEED" TO OPERATING UNITARY SYSTEMS "AT ONCE"

Introduction. After its promulgation of general guidelines in Brown II in 1955, the Court maintained silence about implementation for several years. Enforcement of the desegregation requirement was left largely to lower court litigation—and to the political arena. In 1958, the Court broke its silence firmly but briefly: in Cooper v. Aaron, 358 U.S. 1 (see chap. 1, p. 30, supra), all of the Justices signed an opinion reaffirming the Brown principles in the face of the official resistance in Little Rock, Arkansas. It was not until the early sixties, however, that the Court began to consider the details of desegregation plans.

During the late sixties (after the doctrine of the Brown decision had been adopted by the other branches of the national government through the Civil Rights Act of 1964) Court rulings on implementation came with greater frequency, specificity, and urgency—culminating in insistence at the end of the decade on effective desegregation "now." From Brown through the sixties, all Court holdings on desegregation were unanimous. Early in 1970, a dissent was noted for the first time: in the last case in this section, Chief Justice Burger and Justice Stewart opposed the summary reversal of a unanimous Fifth Circuit decision which had granted a one-semester delay for student desegregation.*

1. *School closing: the Prince Edward County case.* Prince Edward County, Virginia, was one of the communities involved in the cases decided together with Brown v. Board of Education. The attempts of the County to avoid implementation came before the Court in 1964, Griffin v. County School Board of Prince Edward County, 377 U.S. 218. Since 1959, the County had avoided desegregation "by a combination of closed public schools and state and county grants to white children" to attend private schools. The Court, in an opinion by Justice Black, held that this system violated the equal protection clause. Though Prince Edward County was the only county without public schools in Virginia, "there is no rule that counties, as counties, must be treated alike." But in this case, "public schools were closed and private schools operated in their place with state and county assistance, for one reason, and one reason only: to insure . . . that white and colored children in Prince Edward County would not, under any circumstances, go to the same school. Whatever nonracial grounds might support a State's allowing a county to abandon public schools, the object must be a constitutional one, and grounds of race and opposition to desegregation do not qualify as constitutional." In remanding, the Court urged "quick and effective" relief. Justice Black noted that the District Court "may if necessary to prevent further racial discrimination, require the Supervisors to exercise the power that is theirs to levy taxes to raise funds adequate to reopen, operate, and maintain without racial discrimination a public school system in Prince Edward County like that operated in other counties in Virginia."

2. *Unacceptable transfer plans and the rising impatience with delay (1963): Goss and Watson.* a. *Goss.* The first Supreme Court opinion to address itself to the details of a school desegregation plan was Goss v. Board

---

* For an early examination of evasion and delaying devices, see Leflar and Davis, "Segregation in the Public Schools—1953," 67 Harv.L.Rev. 377 (1954), Selected Essays 1938–62 (1963), 897. For a survey of the experience in the lower courts in the years immediately after Brown, see McKay, "With All Deliberate Speed," 31 N.Y. U.L.Rev. 991 (1956) and 43 Va.L.Rev. 1205 (1957), and Note, "Implementa-

tion of Desegregation by the Lower Courts," 71 Harv.L.Rev. 486 (1958). For a review of the problems in the years before the Court rendered the picture, see Bickel, "A Decade of School Desegregation," 64 Colum.L. Rev. 193 (1964). For a subsequent evaluation by that observer, see The Supreme Court and the Idea of Progress (1970).

of Education, 373 U.S. 683 (1963). The case involved transfer provisions under which "a student, upon request, would be permitted, solely on the basis of his own race and the racial composition of the school to which he has been assigned by virtue of rezoning, to transfer from such school, where he would be in the racial minority, back to his former segregated school where his race would be in the majority." A unanimous Court, in an opinion by Justice Clark, held that the "transfer plans being based solely on racial factors which, under their terms, inevitably lead towards segregation of the students by race," were unconstitutional under the standards of the second Brown decision. "Classifications based on race for purposes of transfers between public schools, as here, violate the Equal Protection Clause of the Fourteenth Amendment. As the Court said in Steele v. Louisville & Nashville R. Co., 323 U.S. 192, 203 (1944), racial classifications are 'obviously irrelevant and invidious.'" The Court commented moreover: "Now, eight years after [Brown II] and over nine years after the first Brown decision, the context in which we must interpret and apply this language [of the Brown II decree] to plans for desegregation has been significantly altered. Compare Watson v. City of Memphis [which follows]."

b. *Watson.* In the Watson case, 373 U.S. 526, decided one week before Goss, the Court held unanimously that Memphis could not rely on the second Brown decision to justify delay in full desegregation of its municipal recreational facilities. Justice Goldberg stated: "Given the extended time which has elapsed, it is far from clear that the mandate of the second Brown decision requiring that desegregation proceed with 'all deliberate speed' would today be fully satisfied by types of plans or programs for desegregation of public educational facilities which eight years ago might have been deemed sufficient. Brown never contemplated that the concept of 'deliberate speed' would countenance indefinite delay in elimination of racial barriers in schools let alone other public facilities not involving the same physical problems or comparable conditions."

3. *The insistence on plans that promise "realistically to work" now," freedom of choice, and the Green case (1968).* Southern "freedom of choice" plans came under critical scrutiny in companion cases in 1968 and evoked particularly urgent demands for compliance from the Court. Green v. County School Board, 391 U.S. 430; Raney v. Board of Education, 391 U.S. 443. Both school districts had adopted the plans in 1965, to remain eligible for federal financial aid. In both cases, after three years of operation, no white child had chosen to attend a former Negro school and about 85% of the Negro children remained in all-Negro schools. Under these circumstances, the unanimous Court found the plans to be inadequate compliance with the desegregation requirement of the second Brown decision.

Justice Brennan's opinion in the major case, Green, considered that scheme as essentially "a dual system, part 'white' and part 'Negro,'" and proceeded to review the evolution of implementation requirements since Brown II: "It was such dual systems that 14 years ago Brown I held unconstitutional and a year later Brown II held must be abolished; school boards operating such school systems were *required* by Brown II 'to effectuate a transition to a racially nondiscriminatory school system.' . . . It is of course true that for the time immediately after Brown II the concern was with making the initial break in a long-established pattern of excluding Negro children from schools attended by white children. The principal focus was on obtaining for those Negro children courageous enough to break with tradition a place in the 'white' schools. Cooper v. Aaron, 358 U.S. 1. Under Brown II that immediate goal was only the first step, however. The transition to a unitary, nonracial system of public education was and is the ultimate end to be brought about; it was because of the 'complexities arising from the transition to a system of public education freed of racial discrimination' that we provided for 'all deliberate speed' in the implementation of the principles of Brown I. . . .

"It is against this background that 13 years after Brown II commanded the abolition of dual systems we must measure the effectiveness of respondent School Board's 'freedom-of-choice' plan to achieve that end. The School Board contends that it has fully discharged its obligation by adopting a plan by which every student, regardless of race, may 'freely' choose the school he will attend. The Board attempts to cast the issue in its broadest form by arguing that its 'freedom-of-choice' plan may be faulted only by reading the Fourteenth Amendment as universally requiring 'compulsory integration,' a reading it insists the wording of the Amendment will not support. But that argument ignores the thrust of Brown II. In the light of the command of that case, what is involved here is the question whether the Board has achieved the 'racially nondiscriminatory school system' Brown II held must be effectuated in order to remedy the established unconstitutional deficiencies of its segregated system. In the context of the state-imposed segregated pattern of long standing, the fact that in 1965 the Board opened the doors of the former 'white' school to Negro children and of the 'Negro' school to white children merely begins, not ends, our inquiry whether the Board has taken steps adequate to abolish its dual, segregated system. Brown II was a call for dismantling of well-entrenched dual systems tempered by an awareness that complex and multifaceted problems would arise which would require time and flexibility for their successful resolution. School boards such as the respondent then operating state-compelled dual systems were nevertheless clearly charged with the affirmative duty to take whatever steps might be necessary to convert to a unitary system in which racial discrimination would be eliminated root and branch. The constitutional rights of Negro school children articulated in Brown I permit no less than this; and it was to this end that Brown II commanded school boards to bend their efforts.*

"In determining whether respondent School Board met that command by adopting its 'freedom-of-choice' plan, it is relevant that this first step did not come until some 11 years after Brown I was decided and 10 years after Brown II directed the making of a 'prompt and reasonable start.' This deliberate perpetuation of the unconstitutional dual system can only have compounded the harm of such a system. Such delays are no longer tolerable. . . . Moreover, a plan that at this late date fails to provide meaningful assurance of prompt and effective disestablishment of a dual system is also intolerable. . . . The burden on a school board today is to come forward with a plan that promises realistically to work, and promises realistically to work *now*."

The Court refused to rule out all resort to "freedom of choice," however, although the experience to date suggested "its ineffectiveness as a tool of

---

* " 'We bear in mind that the court has not merely the power but the duty to render a decree which will so far as possible eliminate the discriminatory effects of the past as well as bar like discrimination in the future.' Louisiana v. United States, 380 U.S. 145, 154 [see chap. 6, p. 531, supra] . . ." [Footnote by the Court.]

desegregation." But "if there are reasonable available other ways, such for illustration as zoning, promising speedier and more effective conversion to a unitary, nonracial school system, 'freedom of choice' must be held unacceptable." The school authorities in Green, accordingly, were directed to "fashion steps which promise realistically to convert promptly to a system without a 'white' school and a 'Negro' school, but just schools." [Note also another companion case, Monroe v. Board of Commissioners, 391 U.S. 450 (1968), applying the Green principles to hold inadequate a variant of "freedom of choice," a "free transfer" plan. The Court found that the "free transfer" provision as applied in this zoned school area "patently operates as a device to allow resegregation of the races to the extent desegregation would be achieved by geographically drawn zones." Justice Brennan concluded: "We do not hold that 'free transfer' can have no place in a desegregation plan. But like 'freedom of choice' if it cannot be shown that such a plan will further rather than delay conversion to a unitary, non-racial, nondiscriminatory school system, it must be held unacceptable."]

4. *Affirmative integration duties as remedies for past official discrimination.* In per curiam rulings in 1965, in Bradley v. School Board of Richmond, 382 U.S. 103, and Rogers v. Paul, 382 U.S. 198, the Court emphasized that "[d]elays in desegregating public school systems are no longer tolerable" and insisted, moreover, on lower court hearings on claims that desegregation plans were inadequate because of allocation of faculty on an alleged racial basis. See also United States v. Montgomery County Board of Education, 395 U.S. 225 (1969), affirming an order designed to bring about racial desegregation of faculties in an Alabama school system. The District Court required the school board to move (according to a specific schedule) toward a goal under which "in each school the ratio of white to Negro faculty members is substantially the same as it is throughout the system." Justice Black's opinion noted that the Government had not argued "for precisely equal ratios in every single school under all circumstances," had not claimed "that racially balanced faculties are constitutionally or legally required," and had recognized that the trial court's order "is designed as a remedy for past racial assignment." (Recall the problems of voluntary preferential hiring plans, benign quotas, and racial classifications considered above, at p. 1418.)

On the growing emphasis on affirmative obligations to overcome past de jure segregation, see also the extensive discussion of the "duty to desegregate"-"duty to integrate" distinction in United States v. Jefferson County Board of Educ., 372 F.2d 836 (1966), aff'd en banc, 380 F.2d 385 (5th Cir.), cert. denied, 389 U.S. 840 (1967). That case considers as well the relationship between standards applicable to districts desegregating under judicial supervision and those desegregating under the typically more demanding executive guidelines formulated by HEW during the sixties pursuant to Title VI of the 1964 Civil Rights Act. See generally Dunn, "Title VI, the Guidelines, and School Desegregation in the South," 53 Va.L.Rev. 42 (1967).

The increasing pressure by HEW and the lower courts to overcome sham compliance produced a variety of specific remedial requirements: e. g., percentage figures to assure racial balance, rezoning, pairing of schools by grades, some busing. Those affirmative obligations, and the Court's demands for "immediate" compliance (see notes 6 and 7), provoked renewed Southern resistance and demands that de facto segregation in the North and the dismantling of de jure segregation in the South be treated identically. (See p. 1427, supra).

Consider the evaluation and comment in Bickel, "Desegregation—Where Do We Go From Here?," The New Republic, Feb. 7, 1970, p. 20: "[I]t is true both that the school desegregation effort has been a considerable success, and that it has not worked. . . . What is the use of a process of racial integration in the schools that very often produces, in absolute numbers, more black and white children attending segregated schools than before the process was put into motion? The credible disestablishment of a legally enforced system of segregation is essential, but it ought to be possible to achieve it without driving school systems past the tipping point of resegregation. . . . [S]ubstantial, concrete changes vindicating the principle of the Brown case were attainable in the South without at the same time producing the absurd result of resegregation." See also Bickel, The Supreme Court and the Idea of Progress (1970). Compare the Court's 1970 stance, note 7, infra.

5. *Ending dual school systems "at once": the Alexander case (1969).* At the end of August 1969, the Court of Appeals for the Fifth Circuit granted a request (supported by the executive branch of the Federal Government) to delay that court's earlier mandate for desegregation in certain Mississippi school districts. At the beginning of its 1969–70 Term, the Supreme Court unanimously set aside the Fifth Circuit's permission to delay. The brief per curiam opinion noted the "paramount importance" of the question, "involving as it does, the denial of fundamental rights to many thousands of school children who are presently attending Mississippi school under segregated conditions contrary to the applicable decisions of this Court." The Court concluded that, "[a]gainst this background," the Fifth Circuit "should have denied all motions for additional time because continued operation of segregated schools under a standard of allowing 'all deliberate speed' for desegregation is no longer constitutionally permissible. Under explicit holdings of this Court the obligation of every school district is to terminate dual school systems at once and to operate now and hereafter only unitary schools." The Court ordered that, on remand, the school districts be directed "that they begin immediately to operate as unitary school systems." Alexander v. Holmes County Bd. of Educ., 396 U.S. 19 (1969).

6. *What is "at once"? The Justices disagree about the Alexander requirements (1970).* Interpretation of the call for an immediate end to dual school systems in districts before the courts produced the first divisions on the Court in an implementation case soon after the Alexander decision. Carter v. West Feliciana Parish School Board, 396 U.S. 290 (1970) (38 U.S. Law Week 3265). In Carter, the District Court in July 1969 had rejected plans prepared by HEW calling for "terminal desegregation" of several Louisiana School Districts during the 1969–70 school year. In October 1969, the Supreme Court decided Alexander (note 5 supra). In December 1969, the Fifth Circuit unanimously reversed the District Court's order and directed complete faculty desegregation and adoption of plans for conversion to unitary systems by February 1, 1970, but authorized a delay in pupil desegregation until September 1970. Petitioners immediately asked the Supreme Court to direct adoption of the original HEW proposal calling for student assignments by February, 1970. (See Justice Black's order of Dec. 13, 1969, grant-

ing a temporary injunction pending Supreme Court review, 396 U.S. 226 (1969).)

On January 14, 1970, a divided Court summarily granted petitioners' request. The per curiam order stated simply that "insofar as the Court of Appeals authorized deferral of student desegregation beyond February 1, 1970, that court misconstrued our holding in Alexander"; but there were several separate opinions. Chief Justice Burger and Justice Stewart stated: "We would not peremptorily reverse the judgments." Since the Court of Appeals had required "total desegregation for the upcoming school year, we are not prepared summarily to set aside its judgments. That court is far more familiar than we with the various situations of these several school districts, some large, some small, some rural and some metropolitan, and has exhibited responsibility and fidelity to the objectives of our holdings in school desegregation cases. To say peremptorily that the Court of Appeals erred in its application of the Alexander doctrine to these cases, and to direct summary reversal without argument and without opportunity for exploration of the varying problems of individual school districts, seems unsound to us." *

Justice Harlan, joined by Justice White, joined the Court's order with a concurring opinion which in turn provoked a statement of disagreement from the four other justices. Justice Harlan agreed that the Fifth Circuit's order did not fulfill the Alexander requirements but added: "[I]n fairness to the Court of Appeals and to the parties, and with a view of giving further guidance to litigants in future cases of this kind, I consider that something more is due to be said respecting the intended effect of the Alexander decision. Since the Court has not seen fit to do so, I am constrained to set forth at least my own understanding of the procedure to be followed in these cases.

"The intent of Alexander, as I see it, was that the burden in actions of this type should be shifted from plaintiffs, seeking redress for a denial of constitutional rights, to defendant school boards. What this means is that upon a prima facie showing of noncompliance with this Court's holding in Green v. New Kent County School Board, 391 U.S. 430 (1968), sufficient to demonstrate a likelihood of success at trial, plaintiffs may apply for immediate relief that will at once extirpate any lingering vestiges of a constitutionally prohibited dual school system.

"Such relief, I believe it was intended, should consist of an order providing measures for achieving disestablishment of segregated school systems, and should, if appropriate, include provisions for pupil and teacher reassignments, rezoning, or any other steps necessary to accomplish the desegregation of the public school system as required by Green. Graduated implementation

---

* Note also Chief Justice Burger's opinion concurring in the result, in a summary disposition of a March 1970 desegregation case, Northcross v. Board of Ed. of Memphis, Tenn., 397 U.S. —— (1970). The Chief Justice stated that, were it not for the fact that the Court would be limited to seven justices in the case, he would have voted to hear argument: "the time has come to clear up what seems to be a confusion, genuine or simulated, concerning this Court's prior mandates." He explained: "These school cases present widely varying factors: some records reveal plans for desegregating schools, others have none or only partial plans; some records reflect rezoning of school districts, others do not; some use traditional bus transportation such as began with consolidated schools where such transportation was imperative, others use school bus transportation for a different purpose and unrelated to the availability of a school as to which such transportation is not required."

of the relief is no longer constitutionally permissible. Such relief shall become effective immediately after the courts, acting with dispatch, have formulated and approved an order that will achieve complete disestablishment of all aspects of a segregated public school system.

"It was contemplated, I think, that in determining the character of such relief the courts may consider submissions of the parties or any recommendations of the Department of Health, Education, and Welfare that may exist or may request proposals from the Department of Health, Education, and Welfare. If Department recommendations are already available the school districts are to bear the burden of demonstrating beyond question, after a hearing, the unworkability of the proposals, and if such proposals are found unworkable, the courts shall devise measures to provide the required relief. It would suffice that such measures will tend to accomplish the goals set forth in Green, and if they are less than educationally perfect, proposals for amendments may thereafter be made. Such proposals for amendments are in no way to suspend the relief granted in accordance with the requirements of Alexander.

"Alexander makes clear that any order so approved should thereafter be implemented in the minimum time necessary for accomplishing whatever physical steps are necessary to permit transfers of students and personnel or other changes that may be necessary to effectuate the required relief. Were [Courts of Appeals orders implementing Alexander] to be taken as a yardstick, this would lead to the conclusion that in no event should the time from the finding of noncompliance with the requirements of the Green case to the time of the actual operative effect of the relief, including the time for judicial approval and review, exceed a period of approximately eight weeks. This, I think, is indeed the 'maximum' timetable established by the Court today for cases of this kind."

That elaboration was not acceptable to the other Justices. Justices Black, Douglas, Brennan, and Marshall "express[ed] their disagreement" with Justice Harlan's position: "They believe that those views retreat from our ['at once'] holding in [Alexander]."

SECTION 2. LEGISLATIVE REAPPORTIONMENT

BAKER v. CARR

369 U.S. 186, 82 S.Ct. 691, 7 L.Ed.2d 663 (1962).

[This case appears at chap. 2, p. 177, supra.]

FROM BAKER v. CARR TO REYNOLDS v. SIMS

1. *Gray v. Sanders.* a. In Gray v. Sanders, 372 U.S. 368 (1963), the Court invalidated the use of the Georgia county unit system in primary elections for statewide offices. (Cf. South v. Peters, chap. 2, p. 176, supra.) The Court purported not to reach most of the questions left open by Baker v. Carr. The majority opinion by Justice Douglas viewed the Gray case as "only

a voting case" and emphasized that the case had nothing to do "with the composition of the state or federal legislature."

The Georgia system gave every qualified voter one vote in a statewide election. In counting the votes, however, the state used the county unit system "which in end result weights the rural vote more heavily than the urban vote and weights some small rural counties heavier than other larger rural counties." The plaintiff was a voter in Fulton County. At the time the action was filed, Fulton County, with 14.11 percent of the total Georgia population, had 1.46 percent of the total unit votes; Echols, the smallest county, had .05 percent of the population and was entitled to .48 percent of the total units. Justice Douglas stated the applicable equal protection requirement as follows: "Once the geographical unit for which a representative is to be chosen is designated, all who participate in the election are to have an equal vote . . . . The concept of 'we the people' under the Constitution visualizes no preferred class of voters but equality among those who meet the basic qualifications." Elsewhere in the opinion, Justice Douglas stated: "The conception of political equality from the Declaration of Independence, to Lincoln's Gettysburg address, to the Fifteenth, Seventeenth, and Nineteenth Amendments can mean only one thing—one person, one vote." Justice Stewart, joined by Justice Clark, concurred: "We do not deal here with 'the basic ground rules implementing Baker v. Carr.' . . . Within a given constituency, there can be room for but a single constitutional rule—one voter, one vote."

Justice Harlan was the only dissenter. He insisted that the Court "can no longer escape the necessity of coming to grips with the thorny problems it so studiously strove to avoid in Baker v. Carr." On the merits, he thought the Court's holding "surely flies in the face of history." He insisted that the electoral college pattern was relevant: "One need not close his eyes to the circumstance that the Electoral College was born in compromise . . . in order to agree with the court below that 'it could hardly be said that such a system used in a state among its counties . . . could be termed invidious'."

b. Note the Court's rejection of an effort to rely on Gray, in Fortson v. Morris, 385 U.S. 231 (1966). The Georgia Constitution provides that, if no candidate for Governor receives a majority of popular votes, the majority of the Georgia General Assembly shall elect the Governor from the two persons having the highest number of votes at the general election. A three-judge District Court held this provision unconstitutional, in reliance on Gray v. Sanders. The Supreme Court disagreed, in a 5:4 decision. Justice Black's majority opinion stated that Gray had not "either expressly or impliedly decided that a State cannot, if it wishes, permit its legislative body to elect its Governor." He saw in the state scheme two separable methods of selection: a preferred one, by the majority of the people; an alternative one, by the Assembly. He concluded: "A method which would be valid if initially employed is equally valid when employed as an alternative."

Justice Douglas, joined by Chief Justice Warren and Justices Brennan and Fortas, dissented, insisting that "the legislative choice is only a part of the popular election machinery." He concluded: "If the legislature is used to determine the outcome of a general election, the votes cast in that election would be weighted, contrary to the principle of 'one person, one vote.' " There was an additional dissenting opinion by Justice Fortas, joined by Chief

Justice Warren and Justice Douglas. He stated: "The integrity of the vote is undermined and destroyed by any scheme which can result in the selection of a person as Governor who receives the lesser number of popular votes." Moreover, he objected to the majority's "off-hand" announcement "that a State may today, as some States did long ago, provide that its Governor shall be selected by its legislature in total disregard of the voters. . . . Much water has gone under the bridge since the late 1700's and the early 1800's."

2. *Wesberry v. Sanders.* In Wesberry v. Sanders, 376 U.S. 1 (1964), Fulton County voters challenged Georgia's congressional districting statute as unconstitutional. (Cf. Colegrove v. Green, chap. 2, p. 175, supra.) The three-judge district court dismissed the complaint. The Supreme Court reversed. Justice Black stated that the dismissal could "no more be justified on the ground of 'want of equity' than on the ground of 'non-justiciability.' " On the merits, the Court held—without reaching 14th Amendment claims— "that, construed in its historical context, the command of Art. I, § 2, that Representatives be chosen 'by the People of the several States' means that as nearly as is practicable one man's vote in a congressional election is to be worth as much as another's." In a separate opinion, Justice Clark stated: "I would examine the Georgia congressional districts against the requirements of the Equal Protection Clause of the Fourteenth Amendment." In a long dissent, Justice Harlan found the Court opinion "unsound logically on its face and demonstrably unsound historically." [For elaborations of the "as nearly equal as practicable" standard of Wesberry, see Kirkpatrick v. Preisler, 394 U.S. 526 (1969), and Wells v. Rockefeller, 394 U.S. 542 (1969), noted below, p. 1450.]

REYNOLDS v. SIMS

377 U.S. 533, 84 S.Ct. 1362, 12 L.Ed.2d 506 (1964).

Appeal from the District Court for the Middle District of Alabama.

[Note: On June 15, 1964, the Supreme Court held that the legislatures of six states—Alabama, Colorado, Delaware, Maryland, New York and Virginia—had been unconstitutionally apportioned. Chief Justice Warren wrote all of the opinions for the Court. The major Court opinion answering some of the questions left open in Baker v. Carr came in the Alabama case, Reynolds v. Sims. It is printed below, together with a dissent by Justice Harlan, applicable to all six cases, and a dissent by Justice Stewart, joined by Justice Clark, applicable to the Colorado and New York cases.*

[One week after these decisions, the Court, in per curiam orders, found apportionments in nine additional states unconstitutional, again by majorities ranging from 6:3 to 8:1.]

Mr. Chief Justice WARREN delivered the opinion of the Court.

Involved in these cases are an appeal and two cross-appeals from a decision of the Federal District Court for the Middle District of Alabama

---

* The Colorado case was Lucas v. Forty-Fourth General Assembly, 377 U.S. 713 (see the footnotes, infra); the New York case was WMCA, Inc. v. Lomenzo, 377 U.S. 633. The others: Maryland Committee for Fair Representation v. Tawes, 377 U.S. 656; Davis v. Mann, 377 U.S. 678 (Virginia); and Roman v. Sincock, 377 U.S. 695 (Delaware). The nine decisions handed down one week later are reported beginning at 378 U.S. 553.

holding invalid, under the Equal Protection Clause of the Federal Constitution, the existing and two legislatively proposed plans for the apportionment of seats in the two houses of the Alabama Legislature, and ordering into effect a temporary reapportionment plan comprised of parts of the proposed but judicially disapproved measures. . . .

. . . The spate of similar cases filed and decided by lower courts since our decision in [Baker v. Carr] amply shows that the problem of state legislative malapportionment is one that is perceived to exist in a large number of the States.[1] . . . We intimated no view [in Baker] as to the proper constitutional standards for evaluating the validity of a state legislative apportionment scheme. . . .

[Gray v. Sanders and Wesberry v. Sanders, both supra] are of course not dispositive of or directly controlling on our decision in these cases involving state legislative apportionment controversies. Admittedly, those decisions . . . were based on different constitutional considerations and were addressed to rather distinct problems. But neither are they wholly inapposite. Gray, though not determinative here since involving the weighting of votes in statewide elections, established the basic principle of equality among voters within a State, and held that voters cannot be classified, constitutionally, on the basis of where they live, at least with respect to voting in statewide elections. And our decision in Wesberry was of course grounded on that language of the Constitution which prescribes that members of the Federal House of Representatives are to be chosen "by the People," while attacks on state legislative apportionment schemes . . . are principally based on the Equal Protection Clause of the Fourteenth Amendment. Nevertheless, Wesberry clearly established that the fundamental principle of representative government in this country is one of equal representation for equal numbers of people, without regard to race, sex, economic status, or place of residence within a State. Our problem, then, is to ascertain, in the instant cases, whether there are any constitutionally cognizable principles which would justify departures from the basic standard of equality among voters in the apportionment of seats in state legislatures. . . .

Legislators represent people, not trees or acres. Legislators are elected by voters, not farms or cities or economic interests. As long as ours is a representative form of government, and our legislatures are those instruments of government elected directly by and directly representative of the people, the right to elect legislators in a free and unimpaired fashion is a bedrock of our political system. It could hardly be gainsaid that a constitutional claim had been asserted by an allegation that certain otherwise qualified voters had been entirely prohibited from voting for members of their state legislature. . . . And it is inconceivable that a state law to the effect that, in counting votes for legislators, the votes of citizens in one part of the State would be multiplied by two, five, or 10, while the votes of persons in another area would be counted only at face value, could be constitutionally sustainable. Of course, the effect of state legislative districting schemes which give the same number of representatives to unequal numbers of constituents is identical. Overweighting and overvaluation of the votes of those

1. Litigation challenging the constitutionality of state legislative apportionment schemes had been instituted in at least 34 States prior to end of 1962—within nine months of our decision in Baker v. Carr. . . . [Footnote by the Court.]

living here has the certain effect of dilution and undervaluation of the votes of those living there. The resulting discrimination against those individual voters living in disfavored areas is easily demonstrable mathematically. Their right to vote is simply not the same right to vote as that of those living in a favored part of the State. Two, five, or 10 of them must vote before the effect of their voting is equivalent to that of their favored neighbor. Weighting the votes of citizens differently, by any method or means, merely because of where they happen to reside, hardly seems justifiable. . . . .

. . . . Full and effective participation by all citizens in state government requires . . . that each citizen has an equally effective voice in the election of members of his state legislature. Modern and viable state government needs, and the Constitution demands, no less.

Logically, in a society ostensibly grounded on representative government, it would seem reasonable that a majority of the people of a State could elect a majority of that State's legislators. To conclude differently, and to sanction minority control of state legislative bodies, would appear to deny majority rights in a way that far surpasses any possible denial of minority rights that might otherwise be thought to result. Since legislatures are responsible for enacting laws by which all citizens are to be governed, they should be bodies which are collectively responsive to the popular will. And the concept of equal protection has been traditionally viewed as requiring the uniform treatment of persons standing in the same relation to the governmental action questioned or challenged. With respect to the allocation of legislative representation, all voters, as citizens of a State, stand in the same relation regardless of where they live. Any suggested criteria for the differentiation of citizens are insufficient to justify any discrimination, as to the weight of their votes, unless relevant to the permissible purposes of legislative apportionment. Since the achieving of fair and effective representation for all citizens is concededly the basic aim of legislative apportionment, we conclude that the Equal Protection Clause guarantees the opportunity for equal participation by all voters in the election of state legislators. Diluting the weight of votes because of place of residence impairs basic constitutional rights under the Fourteenth Amendment just as much as invidious discriminations based upon factors such as race . . . or economic status, [Griffin v. Illinois; Douglas v. California, chap. 14, p. 1021, supra]. Our constitutional system amply provides for the protection of minorities by means other than giving them majority control of state legislatures. And the democratic ideals of equality and majority rule, which have served this Nation so well in the past, are hardly of any less significance for the present and the future.

We are told that the matter of apportioning representation in a state legislature is a complex and many-faceted one. We are advised that States can rationally consider factors other than population in apportioning legislative representation. We are admonished not to restrict the power of the States to impose differing views as to political philosophy on their citizens. We are cautioned about the dangers of entering into political thickets and mathematical quagmires. Our answer is this: a denial of constitutionally protected rights demands judicial protection; our oath and our office require no less of us. . . . To the extent that a citizen's right to vote is debased, he is that much less a citizen. The fact that an individual lives here or there is not a legitimate reason for overweighting or diluting the efficacy of his vote. The complexions of societies and civilizations change, often with amazing rapidity. . . . . But the basic principle of representative government remains, and must remain, unchanged—the weight of a citizen's vote cannot be made to depend on where he lives. Population is, of necessity, the starting point for consideration and the controlling criterion for judgment in legislative apportionment controversies. A citizen, a qualified voter, is no more nor no less so because he lives in the city or on the farm. This is the clear and strong command of our Constitution's Equal Protection Clause. This is an essential part of the concept of a government of laws and not men. This is at the heart of Lincoln's vision of "government of the people, by the people, [and] for the people." The Equal Protection Clause demands no less than substantially equal state legislative representation for all citizens, of all places as well as of all races. . . .

We hold that, as a basic constitutional standard, the Equal Protection Clause requires that the seats in both houses of a bicameral state legislature must be apportioned on a population basis. Simply stated, an individual's right to vote for state legislators is unconstitutionally impaired when its weight is in a substantial fashion diluted when compared with votes of citizens living in other parts of the State. . . .

Since neither of the houses of the Alabama Legislature, under any of the three plans considered by the District Court, was apportioned on a population basis, we would be justified in proceeding no further. However, one of the proposed plans, that contained in the so-called 67-Senator Amendment, at least superficially resembles the scheme of legislative representation followed in the Federal Congress. . . .

[We] find the federal analogy inapposite and irrelevant to state legislative districting schemes. Attempted reliance on the federal analogy appears often to be little more than an after-the-fact rationalization offered in defense of maladjusted state apportionment arrangements. . . .

The system of representation in the two Houses of the Federal Congress is one ingrained in our Constitution, as part of the law of the land. It is one conceived out of compromise and concession indispensable to the establishment of our federal republic. Arising from unique historical circumstances, it is based on the consideration that in establishing our type of federalism a group of formerly independent States bound themselves together under one national government. . . .

Political subdivisions of States—counties, cities, or whatever—never were and never have been considered as sovereign entities. Rather, they have been traditionally regarded as subordinate governmental instrumentalities created by the State to assist in the carrying out of state governmental functions. . . .

Thus, we conclude that the plan contained in the 67-Senator Amendment for apportioning seats in the Alabama Legislature cannot be sustained by recourse to the so-called federal analogy. Nor can any other inequitable state legislative apportionment scheme be justified on such an asserted basis. This does not necessarily mean that such a plan is irrational or involves something other than a "republican form of government." We conclude simply that such a plan is impermissible for the States under the Equal Protection Clause, since perforce resulting, in virtually every case, in submergence of the equal-population principle in at least one house of a state legislature.

Since we find the so-called federal analogy inapposite to a consideration of the constitutional validity of state legislative apportionment schemes, we necessarily hold that the Equal Protection Clause requires both houses of a state legislature to be apportioned on a population basis. The right of a citizen to equal representation and to have his vote weighted equally with those of all other citizens in the election of members of one house of a bicameral state legislature would amount to little if States could effectively submerge the equal-population principle in the apportionment of seats in the other house. If such a scheme were permissible, an individual citizen's ability to exercise an effective voice in the only instrument of state government directly representative of the people might be almost as effectively thwarted as if neither house were apportioned on a population basis. . . . In summary, we can perceive no constitutional difference, with respect to the geographical distribution of state legislative representation, between the two houses of a bicameral state legislature.

We do not believe that the concept of bicameralism is rendered anachronistic and meaningless when the predominant basis of representation in the two state legislative bodies is required to be the same—population. A prime reason for bicameralism, modernly considered, is to insure mature and deliberate consideration of, and to prevent precipitate action on, proposed legislative measures. Simply because the controlling criterion for apportioning representation is required to be the same in both houses does not mean that there will be no differences in the composition and complexion of the two bodies. Different constituencies can be represented in the two houses. One body could be composed of single-member districts while the other could have at least some multimember districts. The length of terms of the legislators in the separate bodies could differ. The numerical size of the two bodies could be made to differ, even significantly, and the geographical size of districts from which legislators are elected could also be made to differ. . . .

By holding that as a federal constitutional requisite both houses of a state legislature must be apportioned on a population basis, we mean that the Equal Protection Clause requires that a State make an honest and good faith effort to construct districts, in both houses of its legislature, as nearly of equal population as is practicable. We realize that it is a practical impossibility to arrange legislative districts so that each one has an identical number of residents, or citizens, or voters. Mathematical exactness or precision is hardly a workable constitutional requirement.

. . . Lower courts can and assuredly will work out more concrete and specific standards for evaluating state legislative apportionment schemes in the context of actual litigation. For the present, we deem it expedient not to attempt to spell out any precise constitutional tests. . . . Thus, we proceed to state here only a few rather general considerations which appear to us to be relevant.

A State may legitimately desire to maintain the integrity of various political subdivisions, insofar as possible, and provide for compact districts of contiguous territory in designing a legislative apportionment scheme. Valid considerations may underlie such aims. Indiscriminate districting, without any regard for political subdivision or natural or historical boundary lines, may be little more than an open invitation to partisan gerrymandering. Single-member districts may be the rule in one State, while another State might desire to achieve some flexibility by creating multimember or floterial districts. Whatever the means of accomplishment, the overriding objective must be substantial equality of population among the various districts   .   .   .   .

   .   .   .   So long as the divergences from a strict population standard are based on legitimate considerations incident to the effectuation of a rational state policy, some deviations from the equal-population principle are constitutionally permissible with respect to the apportionment of seats in either or both of the two houses of a bicameral state legislature. But neither history alone, nor economic or other sorts of group interests, are permissible factors in attempting to justify disparities from population-based representation. Citizens, not history or economic interests, cast votes. Considerations of area alone provide an insufficient justification for deviations from the equal-population principle. Again, people, not land or trees or pastures, vote. Modern developments and improvements in transportation and communications make rather hollow, in the mid-1960's, most claims that deviations from population-based representation can validly be based solely on geographical considerations. Arguments for allowing such deviations in order to insure effective representation for sparsely settled areas and to prevent legislative districts from becoming so large that the availability of access of citizens to their representatives is impaired are today, for the most part, unconvincing.

   A consideration that appears to be of more substance in justifying some deviations from population-based representation in state legislatures is that of insuring some voice to political subdivisions, as political subdivisions. .   .   .   In many States much of the legislature's activity involves the enactment of so-called local legislation, directed only to the concerns of particular political subdivisions. And a State may legitimately desire to construct districts along political subdivision lines to deter the possibilities of gerrymandering.   .   .   .   But if, even as a result of a clearly rational state policy of according some legislative representation to political subdivisions, population is submerged as the controlling consideration   .   .   ., then the right of all of the State's citizens to cast an effective and adequately weighted vote would be unconstitutionally impaired.

   That the Equal Protection Clause requires that both houses of a state legislature be apportioned on a population basis does not mean that States cannot adopt some reasonable plan for periodic revision of their apportionment schemes.   .   .   .   While we do not intend to indicate that decennial reapportionment is a constitutional requisite, compliance with such an approach would clearly meet the minimal requirements for maintaining a reasonably current scheme of legislative representation. And we do not mean to intimate that more frequent reapportionment would not be constitutionally permissible or practicably desirable. But if reapportionment were accomplished with less frequency, it would assuredly be constitutionally suspect. .   .   .

   We do not consider here the difficult question of the proper remedial devices which federal courts should utilize in state legislative apportionment cases. Remedial technique in this new and developing area of the law will probably often differ with the circumstances of the challenged apportionment and a variety of local conditions. It is enough to say now that, once a State's legislative apportionment scheme has been found to be unconstitutional, it would be the unusual case in which a court would be justified in not taking appropriate action to insure that no further elections are conducted under the invalid plan. However, under certain circumstances, such as where an impending election is imminent and a State's election machinery is already in progress, equitable considerations might justify a court in withholding the granting of immediately effective relief in a legislative apportionment case, even though the existing apportionment scheme was found invalid.

. . .

We find . . . that the action taken by the District Court in this case, in ordering into effect a reapportionment of both houses of the Alabama Legislature for purposes of the 1962 primary and general elections, by using the best parts of the two proposed plans which it had found, as a whole, to be invalid, was an appropriate and well-considered exercise of judicial power. . . . Since the District Court evinced its realization that its ordered reapportionment could not be sustained as the basis for conducting the 1966 election of Alabama legislators, and avowedly intends to take some further action should the reapportioned Alabama Legislature fail to enact a constitutionally valid, permanent apportionment scheme in the interim, we affirm the judgment below and remand the cases for further proceedings consistent with the views stated in this opinion.

It is so ordered.

Mr. Justice HARLAN, dissenting.

In these cases the Court holds that seats in the legislatures of six States are apportioned in ways that violate the Federal Constitution. Under the Court's ruling it is bound to follow that the legislatures in all but a few of the other 44 States will meet the same fate. These decisions . . . have the effect of placing basic aspects of state political systems under the pervasive overlordship of the federal judiciary. Once again, I must register my protest.

. . . Whatever may be thought of this holding as a piece of political ideology—and even on that score the political history and practices of this country from its earliest beginnings leave wide room for debate . . . —I think it demonstrable that the Fourteenth Amendment does not impose this political tenet on the States or authorize this Court to do so.

The Court's constitutional discussion . . . is remarkable . . . for its failure to address itself at all to the Fourteenth Amendment as a whole or to the legislative history of the Amendment pertinent to the matter at hand. Stripped of aphorisms, the Court's argument boils down to the assertion that petitioners' right to vote has been invidiously "debased" or "diluted" by systems of apportionment which entitle them to vote for fewer legislators than other voters, an assertion which is tied to the Equal Protection Clause only by the constitutionally frail tautology that "equal" means "equal." . . .

. . . It is meaningless to speak of constitutional "development" when both the language and history of the controlling provisions of the Constitution are wholly ignored. Since it can, I think, be shown beyond doubt that state legislative apportionments, as such, are wholly free of constitutional limitations, save such as may be imposed by the Republican Form of Government Clause (Const., Art. IV, § 4), the Court's action now bringing them within the purview of the Fourteenth Amendment amounts to nothing less than an exercise of the amending power by this Court. . . .

. . . Whatever one might take to be the application to these cases of the Equal Protection Clause if it stood alone, I am unable to understand the Court's utter disregard of the second section which expressly recognizes the States' power to deny "or in any way" abridge the right of their inhabitants to vote for "the members of the [State] Legislature," and its express provision of a remedy for such denial or abridgment. The comprehensive scope of the second section and its particular reference to the state legislatures precludes the suggestion that the first section was intended to have the result reached by the Court today. . . .

The history of the adoption of the Fourteenth Amendment provides conclusive evidence that neither those who proposed nor those who ratified the Amendment believed that the Equal Protection Clause limited the power of the States to apportion their legislatures as they saw fit. Moreover, the history demonstrates that the intention to leave this power undisturbed was deliberate and was widely believed to be essential to the adoption of the Amendment. . . . .

. . . In my judgment, today's decisions are refuted by the language of the Amendment which they construe and by the inference fairly to be drawn from subsequently enacted Amendments. They are unequivocally refuted by history and by consistent theory and practice from the time of the adoption of the Fourteenth Amendment until today.

Generalities cannot obscure the cold truth that cases of this type are not amenable to the development of judicial standards. No set of standards can guide a court which has to decide how many legislative districts a State shall have, or what the shape of the districts shall be, or where to draw a particular district line. No judicially manageable standard can determine whether a State should have single-member districts or multimember districts or some combination of both. No such standard can control the balance between keeping up with population shifts and having stable districts. In all these respects, the courts will be called upon to make particular decisions with respect to which a principle of equally populated districts will be of no assistance whatsoever. Quite obviously, there are limitless possibilities for districting consistent with such a principle. Nor can these problems be avoided by judicial reliance on legislative judgments so far as possible. Reshaping or combining one or two districts, or modifying just a few district lines, is no less a matter of choosing among many possible solutions, with varying political consequences, than reapportionment broadside.[1]

Although the Court . . . provides only generalities in elaboration of its main thesis, its opinion nevertheless fully demonstrates how far removed these problems are from fields of judicial competence. Recognizing that "indiscriminate districting" is an invitation to "partisan gerrymandering," . . . the Court nevertheless excludes virtually every basis for the formation of electoral districts other than "indiscriminate districting." In one or another of today's opinions, the Court declares it unconstitutional for a State to give effective consideration to any of the following in establishing legislative districts:

(1) history;

(2) "economic or other sorts of group interests";

(3) area;

1. It is not mere fancy to suppose that in order to avoid problems of this sort, the Court may one day be tempted to hold that all state legislators must be elected in statewide elections. [Footnote by Justice Harlan.]

    (4) geographical considerations;

    (5) a desire "to insure effective representation for sparsely settled areas";

    (6) "availability of access of citizens to their representatives";

    (7) theories of bicameralism (except those approved by the Court);

    (8) occupation;

    (9) "an attempt to balance urban and rural power";

    (10) the preference of a majority of voters in the State.*

So far as presently appears, the *only* factor which a State may consider, apart from numbers, is political subdivisions. But even "a clearly rational state policy" recognizing this factor is unconstitutional if "population is submerged as the controlling consideration . . . ."

    I know of no principle of logic or practical or theoretical politics, still less any constitutional principle, which establishes all or any of these exclusions. . . . So far as the Court says anything at all on this score, it says only that "legislators represent people, not trees or acres," . . . . All this may be conceded. But it is surely equally obvious, and, in the context of elections, more meaningful to note that people are not ciphers and that legislators can represent their electors only by speaking for their interests —economic, social, political—many of which do reflect the place where the electors live. The Court does not establish, or indeed even attempt to make a case for the proposition that conflicting interests within a State can only be adjusted by disregarding them when voters are grouped for purposes of representation.

    With these cases the Court approaches the end of the third round set in motion by the complaint filed in Baker v. Carr. What is done today deepens my conviction that judicial entry into this realm is profoundly ill-advised and constitutionally impermissible. . . .

    [N]o thinking person can fail to recognize that the aftermath of these cases, however desirable it may be thought in itself, will have been achieved at the cost of a radical alteration in the relationship between the States and the Federal Government, more particularly the Federal Judiciary. Only one who has an overbearing impatience with the federal system and its political processes will believe that that cost was not too high or was inevitable.

    Finally, these decisions give support to a current mistaken view of the Constitution and the constitutional function of this Court. This view, in a nutshell, is that every major social ill in this country can find its cure in some constitutional "principle," and that this Court should "take the lead" in promoting reform when other branches of government fail to act. The Constitution is not a panacea for every blot upon the public welfare, nor should

---

* Chief Justice Warren's opinion in one of the companion cases, from Colorado (Lucas v. General Assembly, 377 U.S. 713), noted that it differed "from the others decided this date in that the initiative device provides a practicable political remedy to obtain relief against alleged legislative malapportionment." He found "no significance in the fact," except as "an interim remedial procedure justifying a court in staying its hand temporarily." He added: "A citizen's constitutional right can hardly be infringed simply because a majority of the people choose to do so." In the Lucas case, moreover, the invalidated plan had been adopted in a popular vote in 1962. The Court stated: "Manifestly, the fact that an apportionment plan is adopted in a popular referendum is insufficient to sustain its constitutionality . . . ."

this Court, ordained as a judicial body, be thought of as a general haven for reform movements. . . . This Court, limited in function in accordance with that premise, does not serve its high purpose when it exceeds its authority, even to satisfy justified impatience with the slow workings of the political process. For when, in the name of constitutional interpretation, the Court *adds* something to the Constitution that was deliberately excluded from it, the Court in reality substitutes its view of what should be so for the amending process.

I dissent in each of these cases, believing that in none of them have the plaintiffs stated a cause of action. To the extent that Baker v. Carr, expressly or by implication, went beyond a discussion of jurisdictional doctrines independent of the substantive issues involved here, it should be limited to what it in fact was: an experiment in venturesome constitutionalism. . . .

Mr. Justice STEWART, whom Mr. Justice CLARK joins, dissenting. . . .

To put the matter plainly, there is nothing in all the history of this Court's decisions which supports this constitutional rule. The Court's draconian pronouncement, which makes unconstitutional the legislatures of most of the 50 States, finds no support in the words of the Constitution, in any prior decision of this Court, or in the 175-year political history of our Federal Union. With all respect, I am convinced these decisions mark a long step backward into that unhappy era when a majority of the members of this Court were thought by many to have convinced themselves and each other that the demands of the Constitution were to be measured not by what it says, but by their own notions of wise political theory. . . .

I.

What the Court has done is to convert a particular political philosophy into a constitutional rule, binding upon each of the 50 States, . . . without regard and without respect for the many individualized and differentiated characteristics of each State, characteristics stemming from each State's distinct history, distinct geography, distinct distribution of population, and distinct political heritage. My own understanding of the various theories of representative government is that no one theory has ever commanded unanimous assent among political scientists, historians, or others who have considered the problem. But even if it were thought that the rule announced today by the Court is, as a matter of political theory, the most desirable general rule which can be devised . . . , I could not join in the fabrication of a constitutional mandate which imports and forever freezes one theory of political thought into our Constitution, and forever denies to every State any opportunity for enlightened and progressive innovation in the design of its democratic institutions . . . .

Representative government is a process of accommodating group interests through democratic institutional arrangements. Its function is to channel the numerous opinions, interests, and abilities of the people of a State into the making of the State's public policy. Appropriate legislative apportionment, therefore, should ideally be designed to insure effective representation in the State's legislature, in cooperation with other organs for political power, of the various groups and interests making up the electorate. In practice, of course, this ideal is approximated in the particular apportionment system of any State by a realistic accommodation of the diverse and often conflicting political forces operating within the State.

I do not pretend to any specialized knowledge of the myriad of individual characteristics of the several States, beyond the records in the cases before us today. But I do know enough to be aware that a system of legislative apportionment which might be best for South Dakota, might be unwise for Hawaii with its many islands, or Michigan with its Northern Peninsula. I do know enough to realize that Montana with its vast distances is not Rhode Island with its heavy concentrations of people. I do know enough to be aware of the great variations among the several States in their historic manner of distributing legislative power . . . . . The Court today declines to give any recognition to these considerations and countless others, tangible and intangible, in holding unconstitutional the particular systems of legislative apportionment which these States have chosen. Instead, the Court says that the requirements of the Equal Protection Clause can be met in any State only by the uncritical, simplistic, and heavy-handed application of sixth-grade arithmetic.

But legislators do not represent faceless numbers. They represent people, or, more accurately, a majority of the voters in their districts—people with identifiable needs and interests which require legislative representation, and which can often be related to the geographical areas in which these people live. The very fact of geographic districting, the constitutional validity of which the Court does not question, carries with it an acceptance of the idea of legislative representation of regional needs and interests. Yet if geographical residence is irrelevant, as the Court suggests, and the goal is solely that of equally "weighted" votes, I do not understand why the Court's constitutional rule does not require the abolition of districts and the holding of all elections at large.[1]

The fact is, of course, that population factors must often to some degree be subordinated in devising a legislative apportionment plan which is to achieve the important goal of ensuring a fair, effective, and balanced representation of the regional, social, and economic interests within a State. . . . What constitutes a rational plan reasonably designed to achieve this objective will vary from State to State, since each State is unique, in terms of topography, geography, demography, history, heterogeneity and concentration of population, variety of social and economic interests, and in the operation and interrelation of its political institutions. But so long as a State's apportionment plan reasonably achieves, in the light of the State's own characteristics, effective and balanced representation of all substantial interests, without sacrificing the principle of effective majority rule, that plan cannot be considered irrational.

---

1. Even with legislative districts of exactly equal voter population, 26% of the electorate (a bare majority of the voters in a bare majority of the districts) can, as a matter of the kind of theoretical mathematics embraced by the Court, elect a majority of the legislature under our simple majority electoral system. Thus, the Court's constitutional rule permits minority rule.

Students of the mechanics of voting systems tell us that if all that matters is that votes count equally, the best vote-counting electoral system is proportional representation in statewide elections. . . . It is just because electoral systems are intended to serve functions other than satisfying mathematical theories, however, that the system of proportional representation has not been widely adopted. . . . [Footnote by Justice Stewart.]

II.

This brings me to what I consider to be the proper constitutional standards to be applied in these cases. Quite simply, I think the cases should be decided by application of accepted principles of constitutional adjudication under the Equal Protection Clause. . . .

. . . I think that the Equal Protection Clause demands but two basic attributes of any plan of state legislative apportionment. First, it demands that, in the light of the State's own characteristics and needs, the plan must be a rational one. Secondly, it demands that the plan must be such as not to permit the systematic frustration of the will of a majority of the electorate of the State. I think it is apparent that any plan of legislative apportionment which could be shown to reflect no policy, but simply arbitrary and capricious action or inaction, and that any plan which could be shown systematically to prevent ultimate effective majority rule, would be invalid under accepted Equal Protection Clause standards. But, beyond this, I think there is nothing in the Federal Constitution to prevent a State from choosing any electoral legislative structure it thinks best suited to the interests, temper, and customs of its people. In the light of these standards, I turn to the Colorado and New York plans of legislative apportionment. . . .

In the allocation of representation in their State Legislatures, Colorado and New York have adopted completely rational plans which reflect an informed response to their particularized characteristics and needs. The plans are quite different, just as Colorado and New York are quite different. But each State, while clearly ensuring that in its legislative councils the will of the majority of the electorate shall rule, has sought to provide that no identifiable minority shall be completely silenced or engulfed. . . . *

"ONE MAN–ONE VOTE" APPLIED: SOME ELABORATIONS OF THE REAPPORTIONMENT PRINCIPLES *

1. *Burns v. Richardson.* Burns v. Richardson, 384 U.S. 73 (1966), rejected several objections to an interim Hawaii legislative apportionment. The Court found that multi-member rather than single-member districts were

---

* The congressional debates on proposals to delay implementation of this decision, in the fall of 1964, have already been noted, chap. 1, p. 55, supra. The subsequent sessions had before them a number of proposals for constitutional amendments on apportionment. The most widely supported proposal would permit one house of a state legislature to be apportioned on a basis other than population, if a majority of the state's voters approved the plan. See the footnote to Justice Harlan's opinion, supra, on the Colorado plan invalidated in Lucas v. General Assembly, 377 U.S. 713 (1964). An effort to promote such a proposal through the alternative, "Convention" method of initiating constitutional amendments attracted widespread support: by the spring of 1969, legislatures in 33 states—one short of the necessary two-thirds—were reported to have approved "Applications" to Congress for a call of a Constitutional Convention. See Bonfield, "The Dirksen Amendment and the Article V Convention Process," 66 Mich.L.Rev. 949 (1968).

* For evaluations of Reynolds v. Sims and its progeny, see generally McKay, "Reapportionment: Success Story of the Warren Court," 67 Mich.L.Rev. 223 (1968); Dixon, Democratic Representation: Reapportionment in Law and Politics (1968); and Bickel, The Supreme Court and the Idea of Progress (1970).

permissible, absent a showing that they were "designed to or would operate to minimize or cancel out the voting strength of racial or political elements of the voting population." Compare Fortson v. Dorsey, 379 U.S. 433 (1965). Moreover, the Court permitted the use of registered voters figures as the apportionment base, since that base "produced a distribution of legislators not substantially different from that which would have resulted from the use of a permissible population base"—in this case, "state citizen population."

2. *Swann v. Adams.* Swann v. Adams, 385 U.S. 440 (1967), invalidated a Florida legislative reapportionment plan under which, for example, house districts ranged from 18.28% over-represented to 15.27% under-represented and the ratio between the largest and the smallest district was 1.41:1. Justice White's majority opinion rested on "the failure of the State to present or the District Court to articulate acceptable reasons for the variations among the populations of the various legislative districts." Reynolds v. Sims did not require "mathematical exactness" and "de minimis deviations" were unavoidable, "but variations of 30% among senate districts and 40% among house districts can hardly be deemed de minimis and none of our cases suggests that differences of this magnitude will be approved without a satisfactory explanation grounded on acceptable state policy." Justice Harlan, joined by Justice Stewart, dissented.

3. *Kirkpatrick and Wells.* The Court moved closer to an absolute mathematical equality standard in companion cases developing the Wesberry v. Sanders congressional districting requirement (p. 1438, supra) "that as nearly as is practicable, one man's vote in a congressional election is to be worth as much as another's." Kirkpatrick v. Preisler, 394 U.S. 526 (1969); Wells v. Rockefeller, 394 U.S. 542 (1969). In Kirkpatrick, the Court rejected a Missouri plan which "varied from this ideal [of "absolute population equality"] within a range of 12,260 [2.83%] below it to 13,542 [3.13%] above it." Justice Brennan's majority opinion rejected the argument that these variances were acceptable because they were de minimis: no fixed numercial or percentage population variance could be considered de minimis because the "as nearly as practicable standard" requires that "the State make a good-faith effort to achieve precise mathematical equality." Accordingly, each variation required justification. And here, none of the offered justifications would do. Most were flatly unacceptable as a matter of law: the desire "to avoid fragmenting areas with distinct economic and social interests"; the need to reflect "practical political problems" of "legislative compromise"; the attempt to preserve existing political subdivision boundaries. The remaining justifications—regard for geographical compactness, projected population shifts, and disproportionate distribution of nonvoters—were unacceptable on the record here. Justice Fortas' concurrence stated that the Court had rejected "seriatim, every type of justification that has been—possibly, every one that could be—advanced" and insisted that "the majority's pursuit of precision is a search for a will-o'-the-wisp."

In Wells, the Court rejected a New York congressional redistricting plan designed "to keep regions with distinct interests intact." The plan treated "seven sections of the State as homogeneous regions and to divide each region ["sub-state"] into congressional districts of virtually identical population." The statute was attacked under the equal-population principle and as "a systematic and intentional partisan gerrymander." The Court did not reach the gerrymander claim since the Kirkpatrick analysis made New York's justification for population inequality unacceptable: "Equality of population among districts in a sub-state is not a justification for inequality among all the districts in the State."

Justice Harlan (joined by Justice Stewart) and Justice White dissented in opinions applicable to both cases. Justice Harlan objected to requiring "that mathematics be a substitute for common sense in the art of statecraft" and warned "that the rule of absolute equality is perfectly compatible with 'gerrymandering' of the worst sort." Justice White noted that "the Court invokes Reynolds today and in no way distinguishes federal from state districting"; warned that the Court's groping "for a clean-cut, *per se* rule" would be unsuccessful because "quibbling disputes" about mathematical variations would continue; and regretted that the decision, by inviting legislatures to "ignore political boundaries and compact districts," downgraded "a restraint on a far greater potential threat to equality of representation, the gerrymander."

4. *Moore v. Ogilvie.* In Moore v. Ogilvie, 394 U.S. 814 (1969), the Court held that its voter equality principles applied to requirements regarding geographical distribution of signatures on nominating petitions for candidates of new parties: it relied on "our recent apportionment cases" in overruling the 1948 decision in MacDougall v. Green, p. 176, supra. The Illinois requirement of 25,000 signatures on nominating petitions for independent candidates for president included the proviso that they must be "signatures of 200 qualified voters from each of at least 50 counties." Justice Douglas' majority opinion held that the law "discriminates against the residents of the populous counties of the State in favor of rural sections."

The claim that the proviso was "designed to require statewide support for launching a new political party rather than support from a few localities" could not justify it: "This law applies a rigid, arbitrary formula to sparsely settled counties and populous counties alike, contrary to the constitutional theme of equality among citizens in the exercise of their political rights. The idea that one group can be granted greater voting strength than another is hostile to the one man-one vote basis of our representative government." Justice Stewart's dissent, joined by Justice Harlan, objected to "the Court's casual extension of the 'one voter-one vote' slogan" to a case involving neither "voters" nor "votes." Moreover, any reliance on Williams v. Rhodes (noted in chap. 14, p. 1016 and, surprisingly, not mentioned by Justice Douglas) "would be misplaced": the geographical distribution requirement for new parties was not "a burden at all comparable to that involved in Williams v. Rhodes."

REAPPORTIONMENT AND LOCAL GOVERNMENT

a. *Avery.* In Avery v. Midland County, 390 U.S. 474 (1968), the Court addressed itself to the much litigated question of whether the Reynolds v. Sims principles apply to local government—and answered in the affirmative. Justice White's majority opinion held "that the Constitution permits no substantial variation from equal population in drawing districts for units of local government having general governmental powers over the entire geographic area served by the body." He noted that the "responsible and responsive operation" of local government "is today of increasing importance to the quality of life of more and more of our citizens." Whether state power was exercised through legislatures or through local elected officials, the equal protection clause required assurance "that those qualified to vote have the right to an equally effective voice in the election process." But the Court insisted that the Constitution "does not require that a uniform straitjacket bind citizens in devising mechanisms of local government." For example, Justice White left open the possibility that deviations from "one man-one vote" might be permissible in special purpose units of government: agencies "assigned the performance of functions affecting definable groups of constituents more than other constituents" might raise the question "whether such bodies may be apportioned in ways which give greater influence to the citizens most affected by the organizations' functions." And in a concluding passage, the Court pointed to two 1967 decisions as evidence of its sensitivity to "the greatly varying problems" of local government:

"Last Term, for example, the Court upheld a procedure for choosing a school board that placed the selection with school boards of component districts even though the component boards had equal votes and served unequal populations. Sailors v. Board of Education, 387 U.S. 105 (1967). The Court rested on the administrative nature of the area school board's functions and the essentially appointive form of the scheme employed. In Dusch v. Davis, 387 U.S. 112 (1967), the Court permitted Virginia Beach to choose its legislative body by a scheme that included at-large voting for candidates, some of whom had to be residents of particular districts, even though the residence districts varied widely in population. . . . Our decision today is only that the Constitution imposes one ground rule . . . : a requirement that units with general governmental powers over an entire geographic area not be apportioned among single-member districts of substantially unequal population."

Justices Harlan, Fortas, and Stewart wrote separate dissents. Each contended that certiorari should have been dismissed as improvidently granted. On the merits, Justice Harlan thought the extension of Reynolds v. Sims to 80,000 units of local government "both unjustifiable and ill-advised." He commented that the "practical necessities" which some had pointed to as justifications for Reynolds v. Sims were "not present here." Moreover, there were "convincing functional reasons why the Reynolds rule should not apply to local governmental units at all"—especially the need for structural flexibility at the local level in view of the wide range of functions performed by local units. Justice Fortas also emphasized the "complex and involved" nature of the problem and found "powerful reasons why, while insisting upon reasonable regard for the population-suffrage ratio, we should reject a rigid, theoretical, and authoritarian approach to the problems of local government." He insisted that the county government problems were like those arising from special purpose units: both units characteristically "affect different citizens residing within their geographical jurisdictions in drastically different ways." The majority's characterization of the county government here—the Midland County Commissioners Court—as a unit with "general governmental powers" was "not so except in the most superficial sense": in substance, "its primary focus" was "in nonurban areas and upon the nonurban people." The Midland County structure was unacceptable, to be sure: the County had been divided into four districts for purposes of representation on the Commissioners Court; the City of Midland located in the County constituted one district, with over 67,000 people; the rural area was divided into three districts, with less than 1,000 people each. Yet "neither tax im·pact nor the relatively few services rendered within the City of Midland should compel the State to vest practically all voting power in the city residents to the virtual denial of a voice to those who are dependent on the county government for roads, welfare, and other essential services." The majority's solution "merely errs in the opposite direction" from rural over-representation: "Texas should have a chance to devise a scheme which, within wide tolerance, eliminates the gross under-representation of the city, but at the same time provides an adequate, effective voice for the nonurban, as well as the urban, areas and peoples."

b. *Hadley*. A divided Court extended the principles of Avery in February 1970 in a case involving the election of trustees of a junior college district, Hadley v. Junior College Dist. of Metro. Kansas City, Mo., 397 U.S. —— (1970). Justice Black's majority opinion found the "one man-one vote" requirement applicable even though the trustees' powers were not as broad as those of the commissioners in Avery. He stated the "general rule" as follows: "[W]henever a state or local government decides to select persons by popular election to perform governmental functions, the Equal Protection Clause of the Fourteenth Amendment requires that each qualified voter must be given an equal opportunity to participate in that election, and when members of an elected body are chosen from separate districts, each district must be established on a basis which will insure, as far as is practicable, that equal numbers of voters can vote for proportionally equal numbers of officials. It is of course possible that there might be some case in which a State elects certain functionaries whose duties are so far removed from normal governmental activities and so disproportionately affect different groups that a popular election in compliance with [Reynolds v. Sims] might not be required . . .." Justice Black rejected several suggested limitations on the scope of the equal voting power requirement. The "purpose of a particular election" could not be determinative: "We cannot readily perceive judicially manageable standards" to draw distinctions on that basis. And to distinguish between elections for "legislative" and for "administrative" officials "would leave courts with an equally unmanageable principle."

Justice Harlan's dissent, joined by Chief Justice Burger and Justice Stewart, stated that neither Reynolds v. Sims nor Avery justified this ruling which "forebodes, if indeed [it] does not decide, that ["one man-one vote"] is to be applied to every elective public body, no matter what its nature." He insisted that Avery, which involved an agency with "general governmental powers," should not be extended to bar "flexibility in the design of local governmental units that serve specialized functions and must meet particular local conditions." Chief Justice Burger also submitted a separate dissent. See generally "Symposium: One Man-One Vote and Local Government," 36 Geo.Wash.L.Rev. 689 (1968).

APPENDIX

TABLE OF JUSTICES OF THE SUPREME COURT
OF THE UNITED STATES [1]

Two sets of dates are given for each Justice, indicating his entire life as well as his years on the Supreme Court; but only the term of office is indicated for a President. Those Presidents who made no appointments to the Supreme Court are not included in the table. They are Presidents William H. Harrison (Mar.–Apr. 1841), Zachary Taylor (1849–50), and Andrew Johnson (1865–1869)

The symbol * and the figure (1) designate the Chief Justices. The other figures trace lines of succession in filling vacancies among the Associate Justices. For example, by following the figure (2) it can be seen that Justice Rutledge was succeeded by Justice Thomas Johnson, he by Justice Paterson, he in turn by Justice Livingston, etc.

Appointed by President Washington, Federalist from Virginia
(1789–1797)

*(1) Jay, John (1745–1829) Fed. from N.Y. (1789–1795) Resigned.

(2) Rutledge, John (1739–1800) Fed. from S.C. (1789–1791) Resigned without ever sitting.

(3) Cushing, William (1732–1810) Fed. from Mass. (1789–1810) Died.

(4) Wilson, James (1724–1798) Fed. from Pa. (1789–1798) Died.

(5) Blair, John (1732–1800) Fed. from Va. (1789–1796) Resigned.

(6) Iredell, James (1750–1799) Fed. from N.C. (1790–1799) Died.

(2) Johnson, Thomas (1732–1819) Fed. from Md. (1791–1793) Resigned.

(2) Paterson, William (1745–1806) Fed. from N.J. (1793–1806) Died.

*(1) Rutledge, John (1739–1800) Fed. from S.C. (1795) Unconfirmed recess appointment.

(5) Chase, Samuel (1741–1811) Fed. from Md. (1796–1811) Died.

*(1) Ellsworth, Oliver (1745–1807) Fed. from Conn. (1796–1800) Resigned.

Appointed by President John Adams, Federalist from Massachusetts
(1797–1801)

(4) Washington, Bushrod (1762–1829) Fed. from Pa. (1798–1829) Died.

(6) Moore, Alfred (1755–1810) Fed. from N.C. (1799–1804) Resigned.

*(1) Marshall, John (1755–1835) Fed. from Va. (1801–1835) Died.

[1] This table was originally prepared by Professor Margaret Spahr, Hunter College of the City University of New York.

Appointed by President Jefferson, Republican from Virginia
(1801–1809)

(6) Johnson, William (1771–1834) Rep. from S.C. (1804–1834) Died.

(2) Livingston, [Henry] Brockholst (1757–1823) Rep. from N.Y. (1806–1823) Died.

(7) Todd, Thomas (1765–1826) Rep. from Ky. (1807–1826) Died.

Appointed by President Madison, Republican from Virginia
(1809–1817)

(5) Duvall, Gabriel (1752–1844) Rep. from Md. (1811–1835) Resigned.

(3) Story, Joseph (1779–1845) Rep. from Mass. (1811–1845) Died.

Appointed by President Monroe, Republican from Virginia
(1817–1825)

(2) Thompson, Smith (1768–1843) Rep. from N.Y. (1823–1843) Died.

Appointed by President John Quincy Adams, Republican from Massachusetts
(1825–1829)

(7) Trimble, Robert (1777–1828) Rep. from Ky. (1826–1828) Died.

Appointed by President Jackson, Democrat from Tennessee
(1829–1837)

(7) McLean, John (1785–1861) Dem. (later Rep.) from Ohio (1829–1861) Died.

(4) Baldwin, Henry (1780–1844) Dem. from Pa. (1830–1844) Died.

(6) Wayne, James M. (1790–1867) Dem. from Ga. (1835–1867) Died.

*(1) Taney, Roger B. (1777–1864) Dem. from Md. (1836–1864) Died.

(5) Barbour, Philip P. (1783–1841) Dem. from Va. (1836–1841) Died.

Appointed by President Van Buren, Democrat from New York
(1837–1841)

(8) Catron, John (1778–1865) Dem. from Tenn. (1837–1865) Died.

(9) McKinley, John (1780–1852) Dem. from Ky. (1837–1852) Died.

(5) Daniel, Peter V. (1784–1860) Dem. from Va. (1841–1860) Died

Appointment by President Tyler, Whig from Virginia
(1841–1845)

(2) Nelson, Samuel (1792–1873) Dem. from N.Y. (1845–1872) Resigned.

Appointed by President Polk, Democrat from Tennessee
(1845–1849)

(3) Woodbury, Levi (1789–1851) Dem. from N.H. (1845–1851) Died.

(4) Grier, Robert C. (1794–1870) Dem. from Pa. (1846–1870) Resigned.

Appointed by President Fillmore, Whig from New York
(1850–1853)

(3) Curtis, Benjamin R. (1809–1874) Whig from Mass. (1851–1857) Resigned.

Appointed by President Pierce, Democrat from New Hampshire
(1853–1857)

(9) Campbell, John A. (1811–1889) Dem. from Ala. (1853–1861) Resigned.

Appointed by President Buchanan, Democrat from Pennsylvania
(1857–1861)

(3) Clifford, Nathan (1803–1881) Dem. from Me. (1858–1881) Died.

Appointed by President Lincoln, Republican from Illinois
(1861–1865)

(7) Swayne, Noah H. (1804–1884) Rep. from Ohio (1862–1881) Resigned.

(5) Miller, Samuel F. (1816–1890) Rep. from Iowa (1862–1890) Died.

(9) Davis, David (1815–1886) Rep. (later Dem.) from Ill. (1862–1877) Resigned.

(10) Field, Stephen J. (1816–1899) Dem. from Cal. (1863–1897) Resigned.

*(1) Chase, Salmon P. (1808–1873) Rep. from Ohio (1864–1873) Died.

Appointed by President Grant, Republican from Illinois
(1869–1877)

(4) Strong, William (1808–1895) Rep. from Pa. (1870–1880) Resigned.

(6) Bradley, Joseph P. (1803–1892) Rep. from N.J. (1870–1892) Died.

(2) Hunt, Ward (1810–1886) Rep. from N.Y. (1872–1882) Resigned.

*(1) Waite, Morrison (1816–1888) Rep. from Ohio (1874–1888) Died.

Appointed by President Hayes, Republican from Ohio
(1877–1881)

(9) Harlan, John Marshall (1833–1911) Rep. from Ky. (1877–1911) Died.

(4) Woods, William B. (1824–1887) Rep. from Ga. (1880–1887) Died.

Appointed by President Garfield, Republican from Ohio
(Mar.–Sept. 1881)

(7) Matthews, Stanley (1824–1889) Rep. from Ohio (1881–1889) Died.

Appointed by President Arthur, Republican from New York
(1881–1885)

(3) Gray, Horace (1828–1902) Rep. from Mass. (1881–1902) Died.

(2) Blatchford, Samuel (1820–1893) Rep. from N.Y. (1882–1893) Died.

Appointed by President Cleveland, Democrat from New York
(1885–1889)

(4) Lamar, Lucius Q. C. (1825–1893) Dem. from Miss. (1888–1893) Died.

*(1) Fuller, Melville W. (1833–1910) Dem. from Ill. (1888–1910) Died.

Appointed by President Harrison, Republican from Indiana
(1889–1893)

(7) Brewer, David J. (1837–1910) Rep. from Kansas (1889–1910) Died.

(5) Brown, Henry B. (1836–1913) Rep. from Mich. (1890–1906) Resigned.

(6) Shiras, George (1832–1924) Rep. from Pa. (1892–1903) Resigned.

(4) Jackson, Howell E. (1832–1895) Dem. from Tenn. (1893–1895) Died.

Appointed by President Cleveland, Democrat from New York
(1893–1897)

(2) White, Edward D. (1845–1921) Dem. from La. (1894–1910) Promoted to chief justiceship.

(4) Peckham, Rufus W. (1838–1909) Dem. from N.Y. (1895–1909) Died.

Appointed by President McKinley, Republican from Ohio
(1897–1901)

(10) or (8)
     McKenna, Joseph (1843–1926) Rep. from Cal. (1898–1925) Resigned.

Appointed by President Theodore Roosevelt, Republican from New York
(1901–1909)

(3) Holmes, Oliver Wendell (1841–1935) Rep. from Mass. (1902–1932) Resigned.

(6) Day, William R. (1849–1923) Rep. from Ohio (1903–1922) Resigned.

(5) Moody, William H. (1853–1917) Rep. from Mass. (1906–1910) Resigned.

Appointed by President Taft, Republican from Ohio
(1909–1913)

(4) Lurton, Horace H. (1844–1914) Dem. from Tenn. (1909–1914) Died.

(7) Hughes, Charles E. (1862–1948) Rep. from N.Y. (1910–1916) Resigned.

*(1) White, Edward D. (1845–1921) Promoted from associate justiceship. (1910–1921) Died.

(2) Van Devanter, Willis (1859–1941) Rep. from Wyo. (1910–1937) Retired.

(5) Lamar, Joseph R. (1857–1916) Dem. from Ga. (1910–1916) Died.

(9) Pitney, Mahlon (1858–1924) Rep. from N.J. (1912–1922) Retired.

Appointed by President Wilson, Democrat from New Jersey
(1913–1921)

(4) McReynolds, James C. (1862–1946) Dem. from Tenn. (1914–1941) Retired.

(5) Brandeis, Louis D. (1856–1941) Dem. from Mass. (1916–1939) Retired.

(7) Clarke, John H. (1857–1945) Dem. from Ohio (1916–1922) Resigned.

Appointed by President Harding, Republican from Ohio
(1921–1923)

*(1) Taft, William H. (1857–1930) Rep. from Conn. (1921–1930) Resigned.

(7) Sutherland, George (1862–1942) Rep. from Utah (1922–1938) Retired.

(6) Butler, Pierce (1866–1939) Dem. from Minn. (1922–1939) Died.

(9) Sanford, Edward T. (1865–1930) Rep. from Tenn. (1923–1930) Died.

Appointed by President Coolidge, Republican from Massachusetts
(1923–1929)

(8) Stone, Harlan F. (1872–1946) Rep. from N.Y. (1925–1941) Promoted to chief justiceship.

Appointed by President Hoover, Republican from California
(1929–1933)

*(1) Hughes, Charles E. (1862–1948) Rep. from N.Y. (1930–1941)
      Retired.
 (9) Roberts, Owen J. (1875–1955) Rep. from Pa. (1930–1945) Re-
      signed.
 (3) Cardozo, Benjamin N. (1870–1938) Dem. from N.Y. (1932–
      1938) Died.

Appointed by President Franklin D. Roosevelt, Democrat from New York
(1933–1945)

 (2) Black, Hugo L. (1886–   ) Dem. from Ala. (1937–   ).
 (7) Reed, Stanley F. (1884–   ) Dem. from Ky. (1938–1957) Re-
      tired.
 (3) Frankfurter, Felix (1882–1965) Ind. from Mass. (1939–1962)
      Retired.
 (5) Douglas, William O. (1898–   ) Dem. from Conn. (1939–
).
 (6) Murphy, Frank (1893–1949) Dem. from Mich. (1940–1949)
      Died.
 (4) Byrnes, James F. (1879–   ) Dem. from S.C. (1941–1942)
      Resigned.
*(1) Stone, Harlan F. (1872–1946) Promoted from associate justice-
      ship (1941–1946) Died.
 (8) Jackson, Robert H. (1892–1954) Dem. from N.Y. (1941–1954)
      Died.
 (4) Rutledge, Wiley B. (1894–1949) Dem. from Ia. (1943–1949)
      Died.

Appointed by President Truman, Democrat from Missouri
(1945–1953)

 (9) Burton, Harold H. (1888–1964) Rep. from Ohio (1945–1958)
      Retired.
*(1) Vinson, Fred M. (1890–1953) Dem. from Kentucky (1946–
      1953) Died.
 (6) Clark, Tom C. (1899–   ) Dem. from Texas (1949–1967)
      Retired.
 (4) Minton, Sherman (1890–1965) Dem. from Indiana (1949–1956)
      Retired.

Appointed by President Eisenhower, Republican from New York
(1953–1961)

*(1) Warren, Earl (1891–   ) Rep. from Cal. (1953–1969) Retired.
 (8) Harlan, John Marshall (1899–   ) Rep. from New York (1955–
).
 (4) Brennan, William J., Jr., (1906–   ) Dem. from New Jersey
      (1956–   ).
 (7) Whittaker, Charles E. (1901–   ) Rep. from Missouri (1957–
      1962) Retired.
 (9) Stewart, Potter (1915–   ) Rep. from Ohio (1958–   ).

Appointed by President Kennedy, Democrat from Massachusetts
(1961–1963)

(7) White, Byron R. (1917–   ) Dem. from Colorado (1962–   ).
(3) Goldberg, Arthur J. (1908–   ) Dem. from Illinois (1962–1965) Resigned.

Appointed by President Lyndon B. Johnson, Democrat from Texas
(1963–1969)

(3) Fortas, Abe (1910–   ) Dem. from Tenn. (1965–1969) Resigned.
(6) Marshall, Thurgood (1908–   ) Dem. from N.Y. (1967–   ).

Appointed by President Nixon, Republican from California
(1969–   )

*(1) Burger, Warren E. (1907–   ) Rep. from Virginia (1969–   ).
(3) [The nominations of Judges Haynsworth and Carswell for this vacancy failed in the Senate: Judge Haynsworth's on November 21, 1969, by a 55:45 vote; Judge Carswell's on April 8, 1970, by a vote of 51:45. On April 14, 1970, Judge Harry A. Blackmun was nominated to fill the vacancy. On May 12, 1970, the Senate confirmed Judge Blackmun's nomination by a 94:0 vote.]

INDEX

END OF VOLUME